THE STATESMAN'S YEAR-BOOK

1992–93

Man hat behauptet, die Welt werde durch Zahlen regiert: das aber weiss ich, dass die Zahlen uns belehren, ob sie gut oder schlecht regiert werde.   GOETHE

Editors

COMPARATIVE
STATISTICAL
TABLES

Part II: Countries of the World A–Z

CONTENTS

Part I: International Organizations

CONVERSION OF UNITS

To convert from	To	Multiply by
acre	hectare	0·4047
barrel (oil)	cu. metre	0·159
bushel (imperial)	litre	36·37
bushel (US)	litre	35·24
carat	gramme	0·2
cu. foot	cu. metre	0·028317
cu. metre	cu. foot	35·315
foot	metre	0·3048
gigawatt-hour	kilowatt-hour	1,000,000
hectare	acre	2·471
hundredweight (long)	kilogramme	50·802
hundredweight (short)	kilogramme	45·359
inch	millimetre	25·4
kilogramme	pound	2·2046
kilometre	mile (statute)	0·62137
megawatt	kilowatt	1,000
metre	foot	3·2808
mile (nautical)	kilometre	1·852
mile (statute)	kilometre	1·6093
millimetre	inch	0·03937
ounce (troy)	gramme	31·103
pound	kilogramme	0·45359
register ton	cu. metre	2·832
sq. kilometre	sq. mile	0·3861
sq. mile	sq. kilometre	2·590
per sq. mile	per sq. kilometre	0·3861
ton (long)	tonne (metric)	1·016
ton (short)	tonne (metric)	0·9072

ABBREVIATIONS

Abbreviations of the names of organizations also appear in the index.

The three-letter groups in parentheses after the names of currencies are the codes of the International Standardization Organization (ISO).

ACP	African Caribbean Pacific
Adm.	Admiral
b.	born
bbls.	barrels
bd	board
Brig.	Brigadier
bu.	bushel
Cdr	Commander
CFA	Communauté Financière Africaine
CFP	Communauté Financière Pacifique
c.i.f.	cost, insurance, freight
C.-in-C.	Commander-in-Chief
CIS	Commonwealth of Independent States
cu.	cubic
CUP	Cambridge University Press
cwt	hundredweight
D.	Democratic Party
DWT	dead weight tonnes
ECOWAS	Economic Community of West African States
EEA	European Economic Area
EEZ	Economic Exclusion Zone
EMS	European Monetary System
ERM	Exchange Rate Mechanism
f.o.b.	free on board
ft	foot/feet
G7 Group	Canada, France, Germany, Italy, Japan, UK, USA
GDP	gross domestic product
Gen.	General
GNP	gross national product
GRT	gross registered tonnes
ha	hectare(s)
ind	independent(s)
K	kindergarten
kg	kilogramme(s)
kl	kilolitre(s)
km	kilometre(s)
kw	kilowatt
kwh	kilowatt hours
lb(s)	pound(s) (weight)
Lieut.	Lieutenant

ABBREVIATIONS—*contd.*

m.	million
Maj.	Major
mw	megawatt
NRT	net registered tonnes
OUP	Oxford University Press
oz.	ounce(s)
PAYE	Pay-As-You-Earn
R.	Republican Party
SADCC	South African Development Co-ordination Council
SDR	Special Drawing Rights
sq.	square
SSI	Supplemental Security Income
TAFE	technical and further education
TBVC	Transkei, Bophuthatswana, Venda, Ciskei
TV	television
Univ.	University
vfd	value for duty

PREFACE

The past year has again been rich in national and international development, particularly, of course, the dramatic demise of the Soviet Union. Nineteen new names have been added to the tally of the 'Countries of the World' for this edition of THE STATESMAN'S YEAR-BOOK. The Baltic states have regained their independence; following the dissolution of the USSR eleven former Soviet republics are now grouped in a new type of union, the Commonwealth of Independent States, whose functions are largely residual and sometimes mutually disputed; two former US dependencies in the Pacific have achieved nationhood; and Croatia and Slovenia have seceded from Yugoslavia in the midst of inter-ethnic civil war. The nation-making is by no means at an end: Bosnia-Herzegovina has now gained, and Macedonia is seeking, international recognition, and there are separatist rumblings from Slovakia to Somalia. And perhaps one might stretch a point to mention the 'new South African nation' (in the words of its President), following its referendum in favour of racial equality.

Alongside these centrifugal tendencies there have also been trends towards integration: the EC and EFTA have established a common European Economic Area, and several common markets have been initiated or boosted in different regions of the world.

It has been possible to include details of the United Kingdom government elected in April 1992, but the reader is reminded of the existence of the Addenda for other developments which occurred as this edition was going to press.

The editor would like to express his warm thanks to his colleagues who have so ably supported him in what has been a very busy year, and to all those correspondents throughout the world whose kind contributions add so much to the authority and topicality of the YEAR-BOOK.

The previous editor, Dr John Paxton, has thoroughly revised THE STATESMAN'S YEAR-BOOK WORLD GAZETTEER for its fourth edition, and this is available for those seeking further details about towns and regions.

THE STATESMAN'S YEAR-BOOK OFFICE,   B.H.
THE MACMILLAN PRESS LTD,
LITTLE ESSEX STREET,
LONDON WC2R 3LF

WEIGHTS AND MEASURES

On 1 Jan. 1960 following an agreement between the standards laboratories of Great Britain, Canada, Australia, New Zealand, South Africa and the USA, an international yard and an international pound (avoirdupois) came into existence. 1 yard = 91·44 centimetres; 1 lb. = 453·59237 grammes.

The abbreviation 'm.' signifies 'million(s)' and tonnes implies metric tons.

LENGTH		DRY MEASURE	
Centimetre	0·394 inch	Litre	0·91 quart
Metre	1·094 yards	Hectolitre	2·75 bushels
Kilometre	0·621 mile		
		WEIGHT—AVOIRDUPOIS	
LIQUID MEASURE			
		Gramme	15·42 grains
Litre	1·75 pints	Kilogramme	2·205 pounds
Hectolitre	22 gallons	Quintal (=	
		100 kg)	220·46 pounds
		Tonne (=	0·984 long ton
		1,000 kg)	1·102 short tons
SURFACE MEASURE			
		WEIGHT—TROY	
Square metre	10·76 sq. feet	Gramme	15·43 grains
Hectare	2·47 acres	Kilogramme	32·15 ounces
Square kilometre	0·386 sq. mile		2·68 pounds

BRITISH WEIGHTS AND MEASURES

LENGTH		WEIGHT	
1 foot	0·305 metre	1 ounce (=	
1 yard	0·914 metre	437·2 grains)	28·350 grammes
1 mile (=		1 lb. (= 7,000	
1,760 yds)	1·609 kilometres	grains)	453·6 grammes
		1 cwt. (= 112	
		lb.)	50·802 kilo-
			grammes
		1 long ton (=	
		2,240 lb.)	1·016 tonnes
		1 short ton (=	
		2,000 lb.)	0·907 tonne
SURFACE MEASURE		**LIQUID MEASURE**	
1 sq. foot	9·290 sq. decimetres		
1 sq. yard	0·836 sq. metre	1 pint	0·568 litre
1 acre	0·405 hectare	1 gallon	4·546 litres
1 sq. mile	2·590 sq. kilometres	1 quarter	2·909 hectolitres

First Published in 1864
129th edition 1992

For information, write:
ST. MARTIN'S PRESS, INC.
175 Fifth Avenue, New York, N.Y. 10010

Typeset in Great Britain by
A. J. LATHAM LIMITED
Dunstable, Bedfordshire

Printed in Great Britain by
RICHARD CLAY (THE CHAUCER PRESS) LTD
Bungay, Suffolk

Library of Congress Catalog Card No. 4–3776

ISBN 0–312–07975–3

This edition published in the United States of America in 1992

THE
STATESMAN'S
YEAR-BOOK

STATISTICAL AND HISTORICAL ANNUAL

OF THE STATES OF THE WORLD

FOR THE YEAR

1992–1993

EDITED BY

BRIAN HUNTER

ST. MARTIN'S PRESS
NEW YORK

WHEAT[2]

Countries	Area (1,000 ha)					Production (1,000 tonnes)				
	Average 1979-81	1987	1988	1989	1990	Average 1979-81	1987	1988	1989	1990
Afghanistan	2,127	2,300	1,619*	1,619	1,619*	2,521	2,800	1,925*	1,925*	1,925*
Argentina	5,245	4,875	4,544	5,348	5,800*	8,060	9,000*	8,360	10,100*	10,800
Australia[1]	11,440	9,005	8,903	8,936	9,851	14,468	12,287	14,266	14,256	15,712
Bulgaria[1]	986	1,085	1,182	1,138	1,163	3,881	4,149	4,743	5,425	5,095
Canada	11,386	13,474	12,987	13,627	14,050	20,430	25,950	15,996	24,578	31,798
Chile[1]	513	677	577	540	583	882	1,874	1,734	1,766	1,718
China[1]	28,930	28,799	29,786	29,842	30,201*	59,196	87,775	85,433	91,810	96,004*
Czechoslovakia	1,121	1,212	1,239	1,239	1,237	4,482	6,154	6,547	6,356	6,707
Egypt[1]	577	577	597	644	819*	1,844	2,721	2,838	3,182	4,267
France	4,473	4,932	4,825	5,012	5,143	22,362	27,415	29,677	31,817	33,363
Germany, Fed. Rep. of	1,642	1,671	1,743	1,671	1,671	8,177	9,932	11,922	11,032	11,053
Greece	1,022	886	895	888	899*	2,770	2,213	2,498	2,030	1,580
Hungary[1]	1,187	1,315	1,281	1,242	1,221	4,800	5,748	7,026	6,540	6,159
India	22,364	23,131	23,063	24,109	23,457	34,550	44,323	46,169	54,110	49,652
Iran	5,824	6,725	6,147	5,788	6,500*	6,215	7,960	7,265	5,525	7,000
Iraq	1,215	859	1,041	587	975*	854	722	929	491	805*
Italy[1]	3,373	3,087	2,876	2,773	2,773	8,989	9,381	7,952	7,413	8,109
Japan[1]	188	271	282	284	260	571	864	1,021	985	952
Mexico	723	988	912	1,145	933	2,754	4,415	3,665	4,374	3,899
Morocco	1,673	2,288	2,316	2,630	2,719	1,500	2,427	4,019	3,927	3,711
Pakistan[1]	6,865	7,706	7,308	7,730	7,845	10,760	12,016	12,675	14,419	14,315
Poland[1]	1,525	2,133	2,179	2,195	2,281	4,189	7,942	7,582	8,462	9,026
Romania[1]	2,154	2,400	2,375	2,319	2,230	5,471	9,672	8,572	7,880*	7,320*
S. Africa, Republic of	1,770	1,927	1,985	1,831	1,701	1,966	3,135	3,539	2,026	1,794
Spain	2,628	2,221	2,339	2,317	2,006	4,510	5,791	6,514	5,468	4,760
Turkey	9,208	9,331	9,388	9,227	2,435*	17,058	18,932	20,523	16,221	20,000
USSR[1,3]	59,463	46,684	48,058	47,676	48,214	89,859	83,312	84,445	92,307*	108,000*
UK	1,434	1,992	1,886	2,083	2,013	8,116	11,941	11,720	14,030	13,900
USA	28,898	22,646	21,525	25,167	28,066	66,229	57,357	49,320	55,429	74,534
Yugoslavia	1,475	1,498	1,507	1,479	1,485*	4,624	5,345	6,300	5,599	6,359*
World total	234,968	221,609	218,085	225,796	231,548	443,139	517,152	506,909	541,765	595,149

* Unofficial figures.   [1] Sown area.   [2] Includes spelt.   [3] Does not include spelt.

RYE

Countries	Area (1,000 ha)					Production (1,000 tonnes)				
	Average 1979–81	1987	1988	1989	1990	Average 1979–81	1987	1988	1989	1990
Argentina	199	96	55	75	50	169	88	41	71	48
Austria	105	85	88	91	87	327	309	356	381	375
Belgium [3]	12	5*	4	2*	2	43	20	16	12*	12
Bulgaria [1]	21	32	32	25	24	29	49	61	52	48
Canada	362	313	257	501	541	638	493	268	873	939
China	733	650	650*	650*	650*	1,167	1,000	1,000*	1,000*	1,000*
Czechoslovakia	171	142	143	175	171	534	496	534	708	736
Denmark	59	136*	80	101	111	221	513	366	487	585
Finland	44	38	26	69	81	88	74	49	196	244
France	121	82	79	74	67	368	299	276	262	248
German Demo. Rep.	671	655	607	624	644*	1,848	2,283	1,785	2,103	2,056*
Germany, Fed. Rep. of	532	412	378	382	413	1,980	1,599	1,579	1,797	1,945
Hungary [1,2]	72	94	97	97	92	117	186	255	257	226
Netherlands	10	6	7	7	9	39	25	33	33	36
Poland [1]	2,970	2,647	2,325	2,275	2,314	6,166	6,817	5,501	6,216	6,044
Portugal	166	128	121	127	102	128	108	77	106	77
Romania [1]	33	37	40*	40*	40*	38	55	60*	55*	59*
Spain	219	222	221	223	207	239	318	357	332	274
Sweden	58	40	34	68	71	197	137	128	319	340
Turkey	439	240	179	180	190*	558	380	280	191	250
USSR [1]	7,557	9,725	10,115	10,745	10,371	9,309	18,082	18,546	20,057	21,000*
USA [1]	295	276	241	196	151	474	503	373	347	257*
Yugoslavia	56	41	40	37	37*	78	69	76	75	72*
World total	15,042	16,272	15,948	16,562	16,562	24,925	34,145	32,175	36,111	37,007

* Unofficial figures. ¹ Sown area. ² Fields crops and other crops. ³ Includes Luxembourg.

BARLEY

Countries	Area (1,000 ha)					Production (1,000 tonnes)				
	Average 1979–81	1987	1988	1989	1990	Average 1979–81	1987	1988	1989	1990
Australia [1]	2,539	2,346	2,231	2,368	2,496	3,278	3,417	3,306	4,096	3,968
Austria	370	291	292*	292	288	1,288	1,179	1,366	1,422	1,437
Belgium [3]	173	139	138	122	109	844	736	803	693	625*
Bulgaria [1]	425	295	345	360	360	1,439	1,091	1,313	1,572	1,345
Canada	4,631	5,005	4,151	4,858	4,571	11,199	13,957	10,212	11,672	13,521
China	1,295	990	980*	960*	960*	3,133	2,800	3,000*	3,200*	3,100*
Czechoslovakia	972	834	793	751	745	3,524	3,551	3,411	3,550	4,071
Denmark	1,580	943	1,154	997	895	6,250	4,292	5,419	4,959	5,030
Finland	579	583	682	517	486	1,421	1,306	1,612	1,630	1,720
France	2,670	1,992	1,916	1,830	1,549	10,997	10,489	10,086	9,810	10,067
German Demo. Rep.	959	891	874	895	889*	3,592	4,198	3,798	4,683	4,878*
Germany, Fed. Rep. of	2,011	1,850	1,836	1,746	1,693	8,566	8,571	9,587	9,716	9,195
Greece	344	241	240	245	230	838	573	605	660	400
Hungary [1,2]	265	208	264	283	297	848	794	1,183	1,340	1,359
India	1,802	1,225	1,143	1,081	991	2,020	1,669	1,577	1,722	1,469
Iran	1,336	2,200	2,383	2,510	2,500*	1,397	2,500	3,394	2,750	2,700
Ireland	349	276	266	263	236	1,603	1,599	1,562	1,474	1,337
Italy	324	445	450	471	467	914	1,710	1,562	1,644	1,703
Japan [1]	120	105	114	113	107	392	353	399	371	346
Korea, South [1]	386	204	195	179	159*	1,059	516	561*	516	416*
Morocco	2,190	2,314	2,499	2,399	2,415	1,712	1,543	3,454	2,999	2,138
Poland [1]	1,362	1,286	1,250	1,175	1,174	3,563	4,335	3,804	3,909	4,217
Romania [1]	833	560	764	768	749	2,360	3,231	3,202	3,436	2,680
Spain	3,520	4,401	4,257	4,312	4,359	6,571	9,836	12,070	9,394	9,415
Sweden	678	545	476	476	461	2,323	1,907	1,879	1,870	2,052
Syria	1,220	1,570	2,540	859	1,600*	1,129	576	2,836	271	846*
Turkey	2,846	3,298	3,300	2,800	3,445*	5,480	6,900	7,500	4,500	7,200
USSR [1]	33,456	30,654	30,000	27,611	26,116	46,540	58,409	47,000	52,000	57,000
UK	2,333	1,831	1,878	1,652	1,515	10,058	9,226	8,710	8,070	7,900
USA	3,214	4,070	3,090	3,364	3,035	8,838	11,529	6,314	8,800	9,119
World total	80,880	78,088	75,527	72,741	71,493	156,479	181,699	167,319	167,817	180,437

* Unofficial figures.   [1] Sown area.   [2] Field crops and other crops.   [3] Including Luxembourg.

OATS

Countries	Area (1,000 ha) Average 1979–81	1987	1988	1989	1990	Production (1,000 tonnes) Average 1979–81	1987	1988	1989	1990
Argentina	353	476	446	445	470*	431	718	620	668	670*
Australia	1,201	1,275	1,332	1,136	1,159	1,386	1,698	1,867	1,838	1,645
Austria	93	69	69	67	66*	298	246	273	249	262*
Belgium [2]	39	22	22	20	16*	171	65	108	63*	60*
Canada	1,501	1,263	1,371	1,708	1,489	2,993	2,995	2,993	3,546	3,507
Chile	84	56	61	69	78	151	128	157	165	205
China	400	400	400*	400*	400*	600	600	600*	600*	600*
Czechoslovakia	132	108	102	103	93	418	406	366	330	421
Denmark	40	23	41	27	20	166	95	192	115	109
Finland	444	368	388	446	453	1,183	813*	857	1,444	1,662
France	525	281	273	266	222	1,850	1,122	1,074	1,025	875
German Demo. Rep.	154	149	148	143	140*	571	637	507	476	580
Germany, Fed.Rep.of	700	459	474	419	339	2,777	2,008	2,039	1,534	1,536
Ireland	25	20	20	19	23	98	106	113	99	136
Italy	223	177	171	169	158	433	361	382	296	307
Netherlands	20	9	13	8	3*	106	47	60	32	16
Norway	108	115	126	132	126	424	466	374	423	404
Poland [1]	1,082	856	850	803	747	2,387	2,429	2,222	2,186	2,119
Spain	453	353	346	359	349	527	502	537	507	524
Sweden	461	397	425	411	358	1,635	1,440	1,330	1,455	1,614
Turkey	199	178	149	140	150*	350	325	276	216	260
USSR [1]	12,160	11,790	10,946	10,751	10,691	14,372	18,495	15,287	16,828*	18,800*
UK	142	99	120	119	107	587	451	545	525	535
USA	3,743	2,802	2,239	2,785	2,404	7,234	5,429	3,158	5,423	5,184
Yugoslavia	199	140	135	144	140*	296	232	253	279	260*
World total	25,653	23,489	22,219	22,833	21,841	42,521	43,223	37,404	42,197	43,665

* Unofficial figures.   [1] Sown area.   [2] Including Luxembourg.

MAIZE

Countries	Area (1,000 ha)					Production (1,000 tonnes)				
	Average 1979–81	1987	1988	1989	1990	Average 1979–81	1987	1988	1989	1990
Argentina	2,895	2,900	2,438	1,520	1,626*	9,333	9,250	9,200	4,260	5,049*
Austria	190	207	201	194	189*	1,338	1,685	1,700	1,491	1,400*
Brazil	11,430	13,499	13,182	12,919	11,395	19,265	26,787	24,748	26,590	21,298
Bulgaria	605	497	490	563	424	2,626	1,858	1,557	2,265	1,241
Canada	1,039	999	981	1,003	1,040	5,901	7,015	5,369	6,379	7,033
China	19,986	20,291	19,774	20,435	21,087*	60,720	80,127	77,672	79,258	87,345*
Egypt	800	761	823	830*	830*	3,159	3,367	4,088	4,400*	4,400*
France	1,774	1,743	1,970	1,920	1,549	9,641	12,470	14,120	12,926	8,996
Greece	157	262	245	200	194	1,165	2,156	2,251	1,740	1,700
Hungary	1,270	1,170	1,145	1,106	1,100	7,022	7,234	6,256	4,560	4,500
India	5,887	5,542	5,897	5,900	5,900	6,486	5,629	8,229	9,409	9,500
Indonesia	2,761	2,626	3,406	2,944	3,169	4,035	5,155	6,652	6,193	6,741
Italy	956	768	842	804	768	6,590	5,764	6,289	6,360	5,864
Kenya	1,273	1,600*	1,451	1,554	1,500*	1,714	2,250*	2,761	2,925	2,700*
Malawi	1,077	1,153	1,212	1,271	1,343	1,275	1,225	1,427	1,510	1,343
Mexico	6,836	6,788	6,506	6,468	7,439	11,866	11,575	10,600	10,945	14,762
Nigeria	443	700	1,556*	1,600*	1,600*	599	1,202	2,080	2,132	1,832
Philippines	3,267	3,683	3,745	3,689	3,820	3,174	4,278	4,428	4,522	4,854
Portugal	333	262	255	257	261	486	655	658	666	643
Romania	3,309	2,894	2,583	2,738	2,470	11,823	18,378	7,182	6,857	6,810
South Africa	4,900	4,014*	3,657*	3,778*	3,475*	11,322	7,372	7,253	12,061	9,442
Spain	450	542	556	528	477	2,227	3,557	3,577	3,228	3,051
Tanzania	1,350	1,650*	1,850*	1,980*	1,651*	1,762	2,359	2,339	3,125	2,445
Thailand	1,412	1,357	1,786	1,710	1,713	3,103	2,781	4,675	4,393	3,675
Turkey	583	570	498	509	500*	1,263	2,400	2,000	2,000	2,000
USSR ¹	3,063	4,573	4,431	4,120	4,414	9,076	14,808	16,030	15,305	16,000*
USA	29,661	23,960	23,573	27,094	27,094	192,084	179,638	125,194	191,156	201,509
Yugoslavia	2,250	2,218	2,260	2,300*	2,300*	9,736	8,863	7,700	9,415	6,270*
Zimbabwe	1,097	1,211	1,300	1,150	1,150	1,829	931	2,253	1,927	1,993
World total	126,346	125,983	127,378	129,664	129,116	423,724	458,028	400,263	470,646	475,429

* Unofficial figures.   ¹ For dry grain only.

RICE (Paddy)

Countries	Area (1,000 ha)					Production (1,000 tonnes)				
	Average 1979–81	1987	1988	1989	1990	Average 1979–81	1987	1988	1989	1990
Bangladesh	10,310	10,322	9,807	10,554	10,600*	20,125	23,120	23,097	27,961	28,140*
Brazil	5,932	6,000	5,959	5,254	3,944	8,533	10,425	11,809	11,030	7,425
Burma	4,684	4,641	4,527	4,732	4,797	12,637	13,722	13,168	13,807	13,965
Cambodia	1,186	1,546	1,801*	1,800*	1,800*	1,160	1,855	2,400	2,500*	2,400*
China	34,323	32,694	32,459	33,176*	32,890*	145,665	176,958	171,416	182,461*	188,403*
Colombia	428	385	349	356	521	1,831	1,865	1,775	2,102	2,117
Egypt	416	412	352	413	445*	2,376	2,279	2,132	2,679	2,800*
India	40,091	38,319	41,736	41,117	41,800*	74,557	84,538	106,369	111,147	112,500*
Indonesia	9,063	9,923	10,138	10,531	10,301	29,570	40,078	41,676	44,726	44,490
Iran	433	510	465	506	450*	1,448	1,920	1,419	1,852	1,400
Italy	176	190	198	206	213	989	1,064	1,093	1,246	1,282
Japan	2,384	2,146	2,110	2,097	2,074*	13,320	13,284	12,419	12,934	13,124*
Korea, North	635	875	670*	670*	670*	4,733	6,200	5,400*	5,500*	5,500*
Korea, South	1,230	1,262	1,260	1,257	1,244*	6,780	7,596	8,260	8,192*	7,786*
Madagascar	1,182	1,214	1,111	1,146	1,150*	2,055	2,296	2,149	2,380*	2,400*
Malaysia	658	641	666	647	628*	2,053	1,697	1,783	1,744	1,650*
Mexico	153	155	126	186	100	528	591	456	637	378
Nepal	1,275	1,423	1,450	1,433	1,431*	2,361	2,982	3,283	3,390	3,300*
Nigeria	517	730*	871	870*	900*	1,027	1,450*	2,000	2,000*	1,900*
Pakistan	1,981	1,963	2,042	2,107	2,127*	4,884	4,861	4,800	4,830	4,713
Philippines	3,513	3,256	3,393	3,497	3,319	7,893	8,540	8,971	9,459	9,319
Sri Lanka	819	679	816	690	735*	2,093	2,128	2,477	2,063	2,200*
Thailand	8,986	9,083	9,906	9,983	9,700*	16,967	18,042	21,263	20,177	19,000*
USSR	637	657	671	656	610	2,558	2,683	2,866	2,560	2,473
USA	1,345	944	1,174	1,087	1,138	6,968	5,879	7,253	7,007	7,027
Vietnam	5,579	5,594	5,726	5,884	5,900*	11,812	15,103	17,000	18,990*	18,400*
World total	143,676	141,497	145,881	148,390	145,776	396,196	464,514	490,609	517,565	518,508

* Unofficial figures.

MILLET

Countries	Area (1,000 ha)					Production (1,000 tonnes)				
	Average 1979–81	1987	1988	1989	1990	Average 1979–81	1987	1988	1989	1990
Argentina	203	59	55	45	55*	245	80	91	50	91*
Australia	26	42	39	26	34	26	39	50	23	30*
Burkina Faso	803	1,168	1,277	1,278	1,150	390	632	817	649	597*
Cameroon	130	465	40*	40*	40*	98	400	60	52*	50*
Chad	360	950	460	400*	350*	182	518*	367*	179*	172*
China	3,981	2,689	2,514	2,397	2,601	5,790	4,539	4,413	3,754	4,401*
Ethiopia	226	230	230*	200*	220*	203	180	180*	155*	160*
Ghana	182	220	228	244	124	117	121*	139	180	75
India	17,845	13,886	17,106	15,855*	17,000*	9,189	6,775	11,353	10,514*	11,500*
Kenya	80	60	110	96*	100*	84	60	72	60*	62*
Korea, North	62	50*	50*	50*	50*	66	60*	60*	60*	60*
Korea, South	3	2	2	3	3*	4	3	2	3	3*
Mali	643	1,540	1,196	1,083	900*	461	1,207*	1,000	842	695*
Nepal	122	165	183	193	200*	121	150	183	225	240*
Niger	3,011	3,000	3,526	3,385	3,100*	1,311	1,020	1,766	1,335	1,133
Nigeria	2,836	3,874	3,900*	3,400*	4,000*	2,420	3,905	4,117	4,594	4,000*
Pakistan	509	293	510	512	520*	255	135	201	204	210*
Senegal	932	1,074	893	953	865	555	801	485	639*	514*
Sudan	1,094	1,091*	2,320	1,559*	1,150*	458	153*	495	162	112*
Tanzania	450	290*	274	300	178*	360	291*	280	300	200*
Togo	121	128	119	126	70*	44	71	56	97	50*
Uganda	297	295	371*	380*	400*	473	471	578	600*	620*
USSR	2,794	2,763	2,615	2,765	2,903	1,759	3,926	3,171	4,108	3,647
Zimbabwe [1]	353	310	374*	296	233	153	81	278*	142	143
World total	38,124	36,284	39,613	37,409	37,565	25,563	27,679	31,232	29,662	29,817

* Unofficial figures.   [1] On farms and estates.

SORGHUM

Countries	Area (1,000 ha)					Production (1,000 tonnes)				
	Average 1979–81	1987	1988	1989	1990	Average 1979–81	1987	1988	1989	1990
Argentina	1,866	1,005	956	597	688*	5,641	3,040	3,200	1,360	2,016*
Australia	548	818	745	645	406	1,084	1,419	1,677	1,283	933
Burkina Faso	1,051	1,176	1,295	1,362	1,250*	620	848	1,009	991	917*
China	2,828	1,884	1,806	1,654	1,900*	7,034	5,531	5,714	4,535	5,310*
Colombia	220	259	266	239	273	488	704	707	695	777
Ethiopia [1]	1,048	900	800*	850*	870*	1,419	950	964*	974*	1,000*
France	75	36	43	70	66	332	209	234	300	271
India	16,361	15,648	14,599	14,948	15,300*	11,380	11,847	10,170	12,915	12,500*
Mexico	1,491	1,853	1,800	1,524	1,830	4,991	6,296	4,807	5,754	6,230
Niger	822	1,100	1,470	1,200*	1,300*	347	360	560	421	415
Nigeria	3,050	4,200	4,247	4,954	6,000*	3,341	5,182	4,948	4,831	4,000*
South Africa	377	314	313	281	285*	540	467	483	466	400*
Sudan	3,163	3,360	5,883	3,801	2,925*	2,361	1,300	4,425	1,536	1,502*
Thailand	220	160	174	178	186	237	192	215	231	230
Uganda	175	185	233	235*	238*	312	286	344	347*	350*
USA	5,273	4,291	3,659	4,493	3,674	19,157	18,778	14,648	15,632	14,516
Venezuela	227	350*	392	289	190*	365	777	820	595	376*
Yemen	631	566	584	585	570*	616	450	542	547	500*
World total	45,548	42,684	46,083	44,695	44,352	65,651	62,843	61,861	59,911	58,190

* Unofficial figures.   [1] Includes teff.

CENTRIFUGAL RAW SUGAR
(in 1,000 tonnes)

Countries	Average 1979–81	1985	1986	1987	1988	1989	1990
Argentina	1,584	1,174	1,120*	1,063	1,132	1,018	1,367*
Australia [1]	3,243	3,379	3,371	3,440	3,679	3,797	3,570
Barbados [2]	113	100	111	83	80	67*	70*
Brazil	7,991	8,274*	8,649*	8,458*	8,582*	7,793*	7,900*
Canada	112	54	122	147*	129	104*	110*
China	3,809	6,347*	6,340*	5,219*	5,966*	6,226*	6,430*
Colombia	1,192	1,367	1,297	1,390	1,364	1,492	1,695
Cuba	7,510	8,101*	7,467	7,232	8,119*	7,579*	8,050*
Czechoslovakia	808	939*	862	818	614	703	676
Dominican Rep.	1,142	921	895	866	777	733	620*
Egypt	666	887*	959	1,007	1,011*	975*	975*
France	4,720	4,324	3,734*	3,973*	4,372	4,198*	4,595*
Fiji [1]	446	341	502	401	363	461	479
German Demo. Rep.	675	798*	790*	760*	507*	665*	883*
Germany, Fed. Rep. of	3,261	3,454	3,479	2,963*	3,004	3,337	3,396*
Guyana	291	265	249	234*	170	167	130*
India [3]	5,380	6,650	7,051	8,533	9,456	9,051	11,946*
Indonesia [4]	1,286	1,767	2,013	2,073	1,864	1,817	2,180*
Italy	1,956	1,352*	1,868*	1,867*	1,607	1,879*	1,584*
Jamaica	247	225	206	189*	222	200	209
Mauritius	615	684	707	694	634	568	624
Mexico	2,796	3,489*	4,031*	3,986*	3,852*	3,698*	3,406*
Pakistan [3]	738	1,430	1,210	1,364	1,936	2,008*	2,017*
Peru	571	757*	599	560*	571	594	603
Philippines	2,289	1,718	1,447	1,337	1,335	1,645*	1,740*
Poland	1,530	1,811	1,891	1,823	1,825	1,865	2,170*
Puerto Rico	158	98	87	87	93	83	62
South Africa	2,011	2,280	2,248*	2,235*	2,469*	2,293*	2,230*
Spain	934	976	1,111	1,108	1,291*	1,038*	1,042*
Sweden	350	346	386	275	360	360	429*
Thailand	1,534	2,572	2,586	2,637	2,704	4,022	3,641
Trinidad	125	81	92	85	91	97	118
Turkey	1,178	1,398*	1,414*	1,784*	1,414*	1,378*	1,793
USSR	7,017	8,260*	8,700*	9,565*	8,913*	9,506*	9,130
UK	1,215	1,317	1,433	1,335*	1,417	1,334	1,358
USA	5,342	5,473	6,075	6,651	6,264	5,972	5,888
World total	88,631	99,283	101,273	101,781	103,528	105,050	109,717

[1] 94° net titre.
[2] Includes the sugar equivalent of fancy molasses.
[3] Includes sugar (raw value) refined from gur.
[4] Tel quel.
* Unofficial figures.

WORLD ESTIMATED CRUDE OIL PRODUCTION [1]

(in 1,000 tonnes)

	1960	1970	1990	1991
Africa				
Algeria*	8,630	47,253	56,673	58,454
Angola	70	5,066	23,553	24,588
Congo	—	—	7,578	7,409
Côte d'Ivoire	—	—	215	161
Egypt	—	—	43,805	45,264
Gabon*	850	5,460	13,754	14,982
Libya*	—	159,201	65,990	73,567
Nigeria*	880	53,420	90,736	96,352
Tunisia	—	4,151	4,491	5,192
Zaïre	—	—	1,411	1,477
Caribbean Area				
Colombia	8,100	11,071	22,151	21,059
Cuba	—	—	736	817
Trinidad	6,075	7,225	7,794	7,638
Venezuela*	148,690	193,209	110,550	122,438
Far East				
Australia	—	8,292	26,840	25,263
Brunei	4,690	6,916	6,554	7,329
Burma	530	750	781	658
China	5,000	20,000	137,599	138,592
India	440	6,809	33,309	32,684
Indonesia*	20,560	42,102	70,104	78,859
Japan	510	750	534	686
Malaysia	—	—	28,584	30,911
New Zealand	—	—	1,726	1,890
Pakistan	360	486	2,925	3,359
Thailand	—	—	1,816	1,970
Vietnam	—	—	2,482	3,901
Middle East				
Abu Dhabi*	—	33,288	79,301	95,117
Bahrain	2,250	3,834	2,084	2,096
Dubai*	—	—	20,901	20,901
Iran*	52,065	191,663	157,084	166,024
Iraq*	47,480	76,600	100,681	14,876
Kuwait*	81,860	137,397 [2]	58,729 [2]	9,567 [2]
Oman	—	—	32,848	34,857
Qatar*	8,210	17,257	19,125	19,085
Saudi Arabia*	61,090	176,851 [2]	321,928 [2]	409,839 [2]
Sharjah*	—	—	1,802	1,922
Syria	—	4,350	20,292	24,638
Turkey	350	3,461	3,773	4,925
Yemen	—	—	9,931	9,932

[1] Excluding small scale production in Afghanistan, Bangladesh and Mongolia; including other small producers not specified here.
[2] Figures for Saudi Arabia and Kuwait include shares of production from the Neutral Zone, all allocated to Saudi Arabia from Aug. 1990 to Jan. 1991.
*Member of OPEC.

WORLD ESTIMATED CRUDE OIL PRODUCTION

(contd.)

(in 1,000 tonnes)

	1960	1970	1990	1991
North America				
Canada	27,480	69,954	92,239	92,212
USA	384,080	533,677	414,500	418,870
Latin America				
Argentina	9,160	19,969	24,959	24,745
Bolivia	990	1,128	973	1,033
Brazil	390	8,009	32,144	31,886
Chile		1,620	980	940
Ecuador*	2,680	191	14,482	14,843
Mexico	14,125	21,877	147,697	155,406
Peru	450	3,450	6,897	6,198
USSR and Eastern Europe				
Albania	600	1,199	1,986	1,639
Bulgaria	200	334	322	248
Czechoslovakia	140	203	125	133
Hungary	1,215	1,937	1,974	1,800
Poland	195	424	126	148
Romania	11,500	13,377	7,930	6,911
USSR	148,000	352,667	569,309	515,416
Yugoslavia	1,040	2,854	3,143	2,770
Western Europe				
Austria	2,440	2,798	1,151	1,281
Denmark	—	—	5,995	6,801
France	2,260	2,308	3,023	2,930
Germany, Fed. Rep. of	5,560	7,536	3,595	3,450
Italy	1,990	1,408	4,788	4,413
Netherlands	1,920	1,919	3,976	3,772
Norway	—	49,500	81,782	92,944
Spain	—	156	795	1,045
UK	90	84	91,645	91,453
World total	1,090,080	2,336,153	3,153,730	3,148,913

*Member of OPEC.

MARITIME LIMITS (IN MILES)

State	Territorial Sea	Jurisdiction over fisheries (measured from the baseline of the territorial sea)
Albania	12 (1976)	—
Algeria	12 (1963)	—
Angola	20 (1975)	200 (1975)
Antigua and Barbuda	12 (1982)	200 (1982) [1]
Argentina	200 (1967)	—
Australia	12 (1990)	200 (1979)
Bahamas	12 (1991)	200 (1977)
Bahrain	3	
Bangladesh	12 (1974)	200 (1974) [1]
Barbados	12 (1977)	200 (1979) [1]
Belgium	12 (1987)	up to median line (1978)
Belize	3 (1878)	—
Benin	200 (1976)	—
Brazil	12 (1988)	200 (1988)
Brunei Darussalam	12 (1983)	200 (1983) (or median line)
Bulgaria	12 (1951)	200 (1987) [1]
Burma	12 (1968)	200 (1977) [1]
Cambodia	12(1969)	200 (1979) [1]
Cameroon	50 (1974)	—
Canada	12 (1970)	200 (1977)
Cape Verde	12 (1977)	200 (1977) [1]
Chile	12 (1986)	200 (1986) [1]
China	12 (1958)	—
Colombia	12 (1978)	200 (1978) [1]
Comoros	12 (1976)	200 (1982) [1]
Congo	200 (1977)	—
Costa Rica	12 (1982)	200 (1975) [1]
Côte d'Ivoire	12 (1977)	200 (1977) [1]
Cuba	12 (1977)	200 (1977) [1]
Cyprus	12 (1964)	—
Denmark (including Faroe Islands and Greenland)	3 (1966)	200 (1977)
Djibouti	12 (1979)	200 (1979) [1]
Dominica	12 (1981)	200 (1981) [1]
Dominican Republic	6 (1967)	200 (1977) [1]
Ecuador	200 (1966)	—
Egypt	12 (1958)	—
El Salvador	200 (1983)	—
Equatorial Guinea	12 (1984)	200 (1984) [1]
Ethiopia	12 (1953)	—
Fiji	12 (1977)	200 (1981) [1]
Finland	4 (1956)	12 (1975) (or agreed boundary)
France	12 (1971)	200 (1977) [1] (except Mediterranean)
Gabon	12 (1986)	200 (1986) [1]
Gambia	12 (1969)	200 (1978)
Germany	3 [2]	200 (1977)
Ghana	12 (1986)	200 (1986) [1]
Greece	6 (1936)	—
Grenada	12 (1978) [3]	200 (1978) [1]
Guatemala	12 (1976)	200 (1976) [1]
Guinea	12 (1980)	200 (1980) [1]
Guinea-Bissau	12 (1978)	200 (1978) [1]

[1] Economic Exclusion Zone. [2] In the Baltic Sea; off the former GDR, 12 miles; in the German Bight, at least 12 miles; area defined by coordinates. [3] 10 miles for aviation purposes.

MARITIME LIMITS (IN MILES)—contd.

State	Territorial Sea	Jurisdiction over fisheries (measured from the baseline of the territorial sea)
Guyana	12 (1977)	200 (1977)
Haiti	12 (1972)	200 (1977) [1]
Honduras	12 (1965)	200 (1951) [1]
Iceland	12 (1979)	200 (1979) [1]
India	12 (1967)	200 (1977) [1]
Indonesia	12 (1957) [2]	200 (1980) [1,7]
Iran	12 (1959)	[8]
Iraq	12 (1958)	—
Ireland	12 (1988)	200 (1977)
Israel	12 (1990)	—
Italy	12 (1974)	—
Jamaica	12 (1971)	—
Japan	12 (1977)	200 (1977)
Jordan	3 (1943)	—
Kenya	12 (1971)	200 (1979) [1]
Kiribati	12 (1983)	200 (1983) [1]
Korea (North)	12 (1967)	200 (1977) [1]
Korea (South)	12 (1978)	12
Kuwait	12 (1967)	—
Lebanon	12 (1983)	—
Liberia	200 (1976)	—
Libya	12 (1959)	—
Madagascar	12 (1985)	200 (1985) [1]
Malaysia	12 (1969)	200 (1984) [1]
Maldive, Republic of	12 (1975)	(1976) [1,3]
Malta	12 (1978)	25 (1978)
Mauritania	12 (1988)	200 (1988) [1]
Mauritius	12 (1977)	200 (1977) [1]
Mexico	12 (1972)	200 (1976) [1]
Monaco	12 (1973)	(1985) [9]
Morocco	12 (1973) [4]	200 (1981) [1,4]
Mozambique	12 (1976)	200 (1976) [1]
Namibia	12 (1990)	200 (1990)
Nauru	12 (1971)	200 (1978)
Netherlands	12 (1985)	200 (1977)
New Zealand	12 (1977)	200 (1978) [1]
Nicaragua	(1979) [5]	200 (1979) [5]
Nigeria	30 (1971)	200 (1978) [1]
Norway	4 (1812)	200 (1977) [1]
Oman	12 (1977)	200 (1981) [1]
Pakistan	12 (1976)	200 (1976) [1]
Panama	200 (1967)	
Papua New Guinea	12 (1977)	200 (1978) (offshore waters)
Peru	(1947) [5]	200 (1947) [5]
Philippines	[6]	200 (1978) [1]

[1] Economic Exclusion Zone.

[2] The territorial sea of Indonesia is measured by straight lines surrounding the archipelago.

[3] Territorial limits and economic zone defined by geographical co-ordinates.

[4] Limits with opposite or adjacent states to be fixed by agreement, failing which median line principle to apply.

[5] Sovereignty and jurisdiction over the sea, its soil and subsoil up to 200 miles.

[6] The territorial sea of the Philippines is determined by straight base-lines joining appropriate points of the outermost islands forming the Philippine archipelago in accordance with Treaties of 1898, 1900 and 1930 (1961).

[7] 200 mile exclusive fisheries zone established 1985.

[8] Outer limits of the superjacent waters of the continental shelf. 50-mile fishing zone in the Sea of Oman (1973).

[9] Half way to Corsica.

MARITIME LIMITS (IN MILES)—*contd.*

State	Territorial Sea	Jurisdiction over fisheries (measured from the baseline of the territorial sea)
Poland	12 (1978)	to be determined by international agreement (1978)
Portugal	12 (1977)	200 (1977) [2]
Qatar	12	[1]
Romania	12 (1956)	200 (1986) [2]
Russia [9]	12 (1982)	200 (1982) [2]
St Kitts and Nevis	12 (1984)	200 (1984) [2]
St Lucia	12 (1984)	200 (1984) [2]
St Vincent and the Grenadines	12 (1983)	200 (1983) [2]
São Tomé and Principe	12 (1978)	200 (1978) [2]
Saudi Arabia	12 (1958)	[6]
Senegal	12 (1985)	200 (1985) [2]
Seychelles	12 (1977)	200 (1977) [2]
Sierra Leone	200 (1971)	—
Singapore	3 (1878)	—
Solomon Islands	12 (1978)	200 (1986)
Somalia	200 (1972)	—
South Africa	12 (1977)	200 (1977)
Spain	12 (1977)	200 (1978) [2] (except Mediterranean)
Sri Lanka	12 (1977)	200 (1977) [2]
Sudan	12 (1987)	—
Suriname	12 (1978)	200 (1978) [2]
Sweden	12 (1980)	up to equidistance line with neighbouring states
Syria	35 (1981)	—
Tanzania	12 (1989)	200 (1989) [1]
Thailand	12 (1966)	200 (1980) [2]
Togo	30 (1977)	200 (1977) [2]
Tonga	12 (1978) [3]	200 (1978)
Trinidad and Tobago	12 (1969)	200 (1986) [2]
Tunisia	12 (1973)	—
Turkey	[7]	to be determined by international agreements
Tuvalu	12 (1984)	200 (1984) [2]
Ukraine [9]	12 (1982)	200 (1984) [2]
United Arab Emirates	3 [4]	[5]
UK	12 (1987)	200 (1977)
USA	12 (1988)	200 (1983) [2]
Uruguay	200 (1969)	—
Vanuatu	12 (1978–82)	200 (1978–82) [2]
Venezuela	12 (1956)	200 (1978) [2]
Vietnam	12 (1977)	200 (1977) [2]
Western Samoa	12 (1971)	200 (1980) [2]
Yemen [8]	—	—
Yugoslavia	12 (1979)	—
Zaïre	12 (1974)	—

[1] Limited by agreement by the outer limits of the superjacent waters of the continental shelf or by a median line (1974).
[2] Economic Exclusion Zone.
[3] 1978 legislation not yet in force.
[4] Sharjah, 12 miles.
[5] Limits to be defined by agreement, failing which median line to apply (1980).
[6] Outer limits of the superjacent waters of the continental shelf.
[7] 6 Aegean (1964), 12 Black Sea and Mediterranean.
[8] Situation under review following unification.
[9] Limits as determined for the former USSR.

The table above is reproduced from a survey prepared by the FAO.

Further Reading

Attard, D. J., *The Exclusive Economic Zone in International Law*. Oxford, 1987

Booth, K., *Law, Force and Diplomacy at Sea*. London, 1985

Buzan, B., *Seabed Politics*. New York, 1976

Churchill, R. R. and Lowe, A. V., *The Law of the Sea*. Manchester, 1988

Janis, M. W., *Sea Power and the Law of the Sea*. Lexington, 1977

Luard, E., *The Control of the Sea-Bed*. London, 1974

Moore, G., *Coastal State Requirements for Foreign Fishing. FAO Legislative Study No. 21*. 3rd revision, Rome, 1988

Sangar, C., *Ordering the Oceans: The Making of the Law of the Sea*. Univ. of Toronto Press, 1987

UN. *Law of the Sea: a Select Bibliography*. 1991

CHRONOLOGY

1991
April   1   *Chile* Assassination of Senator Jaime Guzmán Errázuriz, the founder and leader of right-wing Independent Democratic Union.

2   *Canada* Rita Johnson sworn in as Premier of British Columbia, first Canadian woman provincial premier.
USSR Major retail price rises introduced as part of move towards market economy.

3   *Persian Gulf* UN Security Council votes in favour of Resolution 687, fixing the terms of a definitive ceasefire with Iraq.

4   *Mali* Appointment of new government under Prime Minister Soumana Sacko after overthrow by military of President Moussa Traore on 26 March.

5   *Iraq/UN* Adoption by UN Security Council of Resolution 688 condemning oppression of Iraqi civilian population, including Kurds.
Italy Prime Minister Giulio Andreotti asked to form a new government, his seventh.
Russia Extraordinary session of Congress of People's Deputies supports Boris Yeltsin's proposal of direct elections for an executive presidency.
South Africa Ultimatum issued by African National congress demanding government action to end violence in black townships.

7   *Albania* In second round of parliamentary elections, the Workers' Party gains overall majority.

8   *Brazil* Preliminary agreement on interest arrears signed with creditor banks.
EC Extraordinary meeting of heads of state to discuss Middle East backed UK Prime Minister John Major's plan for the creation of 'safe havens' for Kurds in northern Iraq.

9   *South Korea* Opposition parties merged as New Democratic Union under leadership of Kim Dae Jung.
Georgia Supreme Soviet makes formal declaration of state independence.
Zaïre President Mobutu agrees to holding of national conference in face of mounting political tensions.

12   *South Africa* Publication by African National Congress of document containing principles for post-apartheid constitution, with an independent judiciary and a bill of rights.

15   *EC* Meeting of foreign ministers agrees to lift most of remaining economic sanctions on South Africa.
Presentation by Luxembourg of draft treaty document focusing on political union.
USA House of Representatives rejects presidential budget for fiscal year 1992 and adopts alternative.

18   *Poland* Additional IMF financing programme announced to support government's economic reforms.
South Africa President F. W. de Klerk announces all-party peace summit.

20   *Iceland* General election leads to formation of centre-right coalition under David Oddsson of the Independence Party.

CHRONOLOGY—*contd.*

1991

April	20	*Kuwait* New cabinet appointed under Crown Prince Shaikh Saad al Abdullah as Salim as Sabah.
	21	*Canada* Major Cabinet reshuffle with aim of addressing issues of national unity and economy.
	23	*Czechoslovakia* Vladimír Mečiar dismissed as head of Slovak government. *USSR* President Mikhail Gorbachev signs pact with presidents of 9 out of 15 union republics aimed at achieving stable relations between central and republican governments.
	24	*Hungary* National Assembly approves bill for compensating former landowners expropriated under communist regime. *Iraq* Announcement by Patriotic Union of Kurdistan leader Jalal Talabani that Iraqi President Saddam Hussein had agreed in principle to grant some autonomy to Kurds.
	24–25	*Guatemala* Peace talks between government and guerrilla umbrella group Guatemalan National Revolutionary Unity. *USSR* Attempt to remove President Gorbachev from post as party General Secretary defeated at closed session of CPSU Central Committee.
	26	*Mexico* Commercial accord signed with EC.
	29–30	*Bangladesh* Cyclone kills nearly 139,000.
	30	*Lesotho* Overthrow of Maj.-Gen. Lekhanya, in power since 1986, by military. *Northern Ireland* Start of all-party talks on future of province.
May	1	*Angola* Ceasefire and peace agreement initialled by government and the National Union for the Total Independence of Angola (UNITA). *Cambodia* Implementation of ceasefire in attempt to activate UN peace plan.
	2	*Lesotho* Col. Ramaema sworn in as chairman of ruling military council.
	3	*Albania* New government formed under existing Prime Minister Fatos Nano. *Thailand* Martial law, imposed after Feb. coup, lifted.
	7	*Iraq* Resumption of talks between government and Kurdish leaders on Kurdish autonomy.
	8	*Iraq* Withdrawal of remaining US troops from southern Iraq.
	9	*Yugoslavia* Federal army given wide powers in Croatia following clashes in predominantly Serb-inhabited areas.
	12	*Nepal* Nepali congress overall winner in first multi-party general election since 1959.
	15	*Yugoslavia* Serbia refuses to endorse Croat Štipe Mesić as head of collective state Presidency under system of annual rotation.
	15–16	*Yemen* New constitution approved in referendum.
	16	*France* Edith Cresson replaces Michel Rocard as prime minister. *Germany* Resignation of Bundesbank president Pöhl.
	18	*Somalia* The Somali National Movement proclaimed an independent state in the north-east, the 'Somaliland Republic'.

CHRONOLOGY—*contd.*

1991
May 20 *Iraq* UN Security Council adopts Resolution 692 establishing compensation fund to pay Gulf War damages to be financed by Iraqi oil exports.

21 *Czechoslovakia* Legislation approved for restitution of former landowners dispossessed after Communist takeover.
Ethiopia President Mengistu driven out by insurgent groups.
India Assassination of Rajiv Gandhi, leader of Congress (I) Party and former prime minister; general election postponed.

22 *Lebanon* Treaty of co-operation signed with Syria.

24 *GATT* El Salvador becomes 102nd contracting party to General Agreement on Trade and Tariffs.

24–25 *Ethiopia* 14,000 Ethiopian Jews airlifted to Israel.
South Africa All-party conference called by President F. W. de Klerk to combat black township violence boycotted by African National Congress.

25 *Suriname* Multiracial coalition New Front for Democracy wins parliamentary elections.

26 *Georgia* Zviad Gamsakhurdia wins presidential election in republic of Georgia.
Czechoslovakia Final withdrawal of Soviet forces, ahead of schedule.

27 *Afghanistan* President Najibullah and mujaheddin announce ceasefire to allow implementation of UN peace plan.

28 *Ethiopia* Meles Zenawi, leader of Ethiopian People's Revolutionary Democratic Front, announces transitional government.

28–29 *NATO* Endorsement of new defence structure based on mobile multinational units.

29 *Romania* Extensive cabinet reshuffle by Prime Minister Petre Român.
Croatia Croatia announces sovereignty.

June 1 *Chile* Manuel Rodríguez's Patriotic Front, major left-wing guerrilla group, abandons armed struggle.

2 *Switzerland* Referendum rejects by 54% to 46% financial reforms to bring fiscal system more in line with rest of western Europe.

3 *Australia* Prime Minister Bob Hawke re-elected leader of Australian Labour Party.

3–5 *OAU* 27th assembly of heads of state sign treaty for African Economic Community.

5 *Algeria* President Chadli announces state of siege; Prime Minister Mouloud Hamrouche replaced by Sid Ahmed Ghozali.
South Africa House of Assembly passes Repeal of Discriminatory Land Measures Act.

6 *Mongolia* Publication of new draft constitution.

7 *Congo* National conference names André Milango prime minister.
Gabon Resignation of Prime Minister Casimir Oye Mba's second government; he is subsequently reappointed on 18th.

9 *Jordan* National charter for pluralism adopted by multi-party congress.

CHRONOLOGY—*contd.*

1991

June   9–10   *Italy* Majority of 96% in referendum approves package of reforms to voting procedure for parliamentary elections.

          12   *Albania* New 'governemnt of national stability' takes office in preparation for general election.
Togo President Eyadéma agrees to holding of national conference.
Russia Boris Yeltsin elected President of Russia. Leningrad votes by 55% to 43% to change name back to St Petersburg.

      12–15   *India* Congress Party returned to power in remaining rounds of general election, although losing its traditional support base in the north.

          13   *USSR* President Gorbachev invited to meet leaders of G7 Group in July to discuss Soviet economic reform.

          17   *Northern Ireland* Delayed all-party talks on future of province begin.
Poland/Germany Signature of treaty of co-operation.
Turkey New administration under former Foreign Minister Mesut Yilmaz.
South Africa House of Assembly repeals Population Registration Act of 1950, legal foundation of apartheid.

          18   *Peru* Emergency legislative powers granted to President Alberto Fujimori to combat guerrilla and drug-related terrorism.

          19   *Hungary* and *Czechoslovakia* Last Soviet troops leave.

      19–20   *CSCE* Albania admitted as 35th member.

          20   *Germany* Deputies vote for gradual transfer of seat of government from Bonn to Berlin.

          23   *India* Prime Minister Narasimha Rao, leader of Congress Party, forms government.

      24–26   *Cambodia* Supreme National Council, meeting in Thailand under presidency of Prince Norodom Sihanouk, gains tentative all-party agreement for permanent ceasefire.

      24–27   *Vietnam* Seventh congress of ruling Communist Party held.

          25   *Croatia* and *Slovenia* Unilateral declaration of independence.

          26   *Hungary* National Assembly approves bill compensating former landowners expropriated by Communist regime.
Kuwait Martial law lifted.

          28   *Comecon* Official dissolution.

          28   *Poland* Attempt by President Lech Wałęsa to block legislation establishing procedures for first democratic general election overridden by parliament.

      28–29   *EC* Interim meeting of heads of state and government to discuss progress on economic, monetary and political union.

July   1   *EC* Sweden applies for membership.
USSR Formation of Democratic Reform Movement announced by nine prominent political figures.
Warsaw Pact Formal dissolution.

        1–5   *Ethiopia* Conference for peace and democracy elects Council of Republic, which appoints government.

CHRONOLOGY—*contd.*

1991
July

2	*North Korea* Application submitted to join UN.
2–7	*South Africa* Nelson Mandela elected President of African National Congress at first national conference inside South Africa for 32 years.
3	*Northern Ireland* All-party talks end without agreement.
4–5	*Somalia* United Somali Congress endorses interim President Ali Mahdi Mohammed for further two years.
5	*Colombia* New constitution into effect, replacing one dating from 1886.
7	*Jordan* Martial law provisions in force since 1967 largely ended.
8	*Togo* National conference to determine future political structure opens.
9	*Kuwait* Inauguration of 75-member interim National Council.
10	*South Africa/USA* Repeal by USA of 1986 anti-apartheid Act.
11	*China* Urgent appeal for international aid following two months of rain and worst floods since 1954.
12	*Bulgaria* New constitution providing for parliamentary form of government and direct presidential elections into effect. *Mauritania* Referendum on new constitution approves by 97% multi-party system with elected executive president.
15–17	*G7 Group* 17th annual summit dominated by question of Western assistance to Soviet Union.
16–18	*Central America* 10th regional Central American summit signs protocol to treaty creating Central American Parliament.
18	*Pakistan* National Assembly overwhelmingly approves bill amending constitution and granting government special powers to combat terrorism. *Yugoslavia* Meeting of collective state Presidency agrees to withdraw all troops from Slovenia.
18–19	*Latin America* First Ibero-American summit held in Mexico.
19	*Angola* Fernando José França Van-Dúnem appointed first president since suspension of post in 1977.
19–21	*Nicaragua* First congress of Sandinista Liberation Front after 12 years in power.
22	*Yugoslavia* Talks on future of Yugoslav federation call in EC observers.
23	*USSR* Announcement of intention to apply for membership of IMF and World Bank.
26	*Nepal* Ruling Nepali Congress wins majority in elections to newly formed National Council.
28	*Madagascar* President Ratsiraka dismisses government and announces referendum on new constitution before end of 1991.
29	*Mali* National conference on future political system opens. *Niger* National conference opens in preparation for first multi-party elections, scheduled for 1992.
30	*Afghanistan* Mujaheddin leaders provisionally accept UN peace plan.

CHRONOLOGY—*contd.*

1991
July   30   *New Zealand* Controversial budget curtailing proportion of population eligible to use welfare state.

        30–31   *USA/USSR* Third summit of Presidents Bush and Gorbachev leads to signing of Strategic Arms Reduction Treaty (START), committing both to reducing nuclear weapons by 30%.

Aug.   1   *Zambia* New Constitution Act passed providing for multi-party democracy.

        4   *Israel* Conditional attendance at Middle East peace conference agreed by Cabinet.

        4–9   *Islamic Conference Organisation* 20th session supports sanctions against Iraq and endorses Middle East peace conference.

        5   *South Korea* Formal application for UN membership.

        6   *Bangladesh* MPs vote unanimously in favour of restoration of parliamentary democracy after 16 years presidential rule.

        7   *Zaïre* Opening of national conference.

        8   *Czechoslovakia* Privatization of industry begins with 50 of largest businesses put up for sale on international market.
            Lebanon Release of British hostage John McCarthy.

        9   *Niger* National conference suspends constitution and strips President Ali Saibon of his executive power.
            Vietnam Premier Du Muoi succeeded by First Vice-Premier Vo Van Kiet.

        10   *Ethiopia* Transitional government appointed under Prime Minister Tamirat Layne.

        13–15   *Laos* Supreme People's Assembly endorses new constitution providing for elected executive president.

        14   *Hong Kong* Vietnam breaks off talks on Hong Kong's 62,000 Vietnamese boat people.
            Romania Law signed privatizing all state enterprises except utilities.

        15   *Iraq* UN condemns Iraq for failing to disclose full details of weapons programme.

        19   *USSR* Announcement of coup replacing President Gorbachev with Vice-President Genadii Yanaev.

        20–21   *Yugoslavia* Presidency and leaders of six republics agree measures to keep federation functioning in light of continuing civil war.

        21   *USSR* Gorbachev reinstated as president.

        22   *Indonesia* Launch of new pro-democracy Forum for the Purification of the People's Sovereignty.
            Yugoslavia Ultimatum from President Tudjman of Croatia that federal army will be declared occupying force unless withdrawn by 31 Aug.

        24   *USSR* Resignation of President Gorbachev as General Secretary of Communist Party after most republics declared independence from Soviet Union.

        27   *Philippines* Formal signature of agreement on future of US bases in Philippines.

CHRONOLOGY—*contd.*

1991
Aug.   27   *Yugoslavia* EC proposals for monitored ceasefire accepted by Croatia but not Serbia.

        28   *Togo* National conference elects Koukou Koffigoh prime minister of transitional government.

Sept.   2–6   *USSR* Congress of People's Deputies calls for signing of treaty on union of sovereign states.

        3   *Sierra Leone* Formal announcement of constitutional changes creating multi-party democracy following late Aug. referendum.

        4   *Nigeria* Decree promulgated creating 9 new states and renaming 3 others.

        6   *Baltic States* State Council of Soviet Union votes to recognize as independent republics Estonia, Latvia and Lithuania.
              Vanuatu Prime Minister Walter Lini replaced by Donald Kalpokac.
              Western Sahara Ceasefire after 16 years of civil war.
              Zaïre IMF suspends Zaïre's eligibility for credit.

        7   *Suriname* Ronald Venetiaan, candidate of coalition New Front for Democracy and Development, elected president.
              Yugoslavia Peace conference proposed by EC foreign ministers meets in The Hague.

        8   *Argentina* Ruling Justicialist Party successful in second stage of mid-term elections.
              Yugoslavia Referendum in Macedonia in favour of independence within a union of sovereign Yugoslav states.

        10   *Baltic States* Estonia, Latvia and Lithuania admitted to Conference on Security and Co-operation in Europe.
              Niger National conference votes to dissolve government and replace army Chief of Staff, Col. Toumba Boubacar.

        11   *Cuba* Announcement of withdrawal of Soviet troops.

        12   *Peru* IMF approves debt agreements ending Peru's isolation from international financial community.
              Yugoslavia EC peace monitors admit failure of peace mission.

        13   *Afghanistan* US-Soviet agreement announced halting arms supplies to all parties.

        14   *Poland* Bill to give Solidarity-dominated government right to rule by decree until elections defeated by parliament.
              South Africa Multilateral peace accord drafted by government, African National Congress and Inkatha formally signed.

        15   *Hong Kong* Liberal Democratic candidates win sweeping victory in first direct elections to Hong Kong parliament.
              Mauritius Ruling coalition government of Prime Minister Sir Anerood Jugnauth wins overwhelming majority in general election.
              Sweden Ruling Social Democrat Party narrowly defeated in general election after 40 years in power.

        16   *Philippines* Senate votes not to ratify naval base treaty agreed with US.

        17   *Czechoslovakia* Resignation of Deputy Prime Minister Václav Valeš.

CHRONOLOGY—*contd.*

1991
Sept. 17 *UN* Estonia, Latvia and Lithuania; North and South Korea; Federated States of Micronesia and Marshall Islands elected new members.

19 *Bangladesh* New cabinet sworn in by acting president, Chief Justice Shehabuddin Ahmed.
Kuwait Defence pact signed with USA.
Yugoslavia At third session of Hague peace conference Serbia rejects suggested despatch of peacekeeping force to Yugoslavia.

20 *Senegal* National Assembly adopts constitutional law making electoral changes.

23 *Sierra Leone* President Joseph Momoh names new 18-member Cabinet.

24 *Canada* Constitutional reform package presented by Progressive Conservative Party government of Prime Minister Brian Mulroney.
Lebanon British hostage Jackie Mann released following release of 51 Arab prisoners by Israeli-backed south Lebanon Army.
Zaïre French and Belgian troops sent to Kinshasa.

25 *El Salvador* Accord offering permanent ceasefire between President Cristiani and leaders of Marti National Liberation Front guerrillas.
Yugoslavia UN Security council calls for complete arms embargo and immediate cessation of hostilities.

26 *Romania* Prime Minister Petre Român resigns.

28–29 *Zaïre* President Mobutu appoints Etienne Tshisekedi prime minister of crisis government.

30 *Haiti* Father Jean-Bertrand Aristide, first democratically elected president, deposed in military coup.

Oct. 1 *Czechoslovakia* Ten-year friendship treaty with France followed by one with USSR (3 Oct.) and Germany (10 Oct).
Papua New Guinea Resignation of Governor-General Sir Vincent Serei Eri.
Somalia 72-member new Cabinet appointed by Prime Minister Umar Arteh Ghalib.

2 *Philippines* Compromise formula announced for closure of US base at Subic Bay.

3 *Sweden* Coalition government formed under Carl Bildt, leader of conservative Moderate Party.
Yugoslavia Remaining members of collective state Presidency, representing Serbia and Montenegro, vote to assume powers of Yugoslav Assembly.

5–6 *Central Europe* Czechoslovakia, Hungary and Poland adopt Kraków Declaration for union with united Europe and integration with NATO.

6 *Portugal* Ruling Social Democratic Party returned to power in legislative elections.

8 *Bangladesh* Abdur Rahman Biswas elected president.
Montserrat Newly formed National Progressive Party under Reuben Meade wins overall majority in general election.

CHRONOLOGY—contd.

1991
Oct.   11   *Cameroon* President Paul Biya announces Feb. 1992 elections.
              Iraq UN Security Council adopts Resolution 715 aimed at
              eliminating Iraq's weapons arsenal.
              USSR Abolition of KGB security forces.

        12   *Swaziland* Prime Minister Obed Dlamini announces major cabinet
              reshuffle.

        13   *Algeria* Postponed general elections announced for December.
              Bulgaria Coalition Union of Democratic Forces wins narrow vic-
              tory in general election.

        16   *Romania* New reforming government of Prime Minister Teodor
              Stolojan approved by National Assembly.

     17–18   *NATO* Agreement to reduce ground-launched and air-delivered
              nuclear arsenal in Europe by 80% following US arms reduction
              announcement in Sept.

 17 and 24   *Canada* Landslide victories in provincial elections in British
              Columbia and Saskatchewan for opposition New Democratic
              Party.

        18   *Yugoslavia* Hague peace conference proposal of free association
              of sovereign states accepted by five of six republics.

        20   *Switzerland* 4 largest parties retain control in elections to
              Nationalrat (lower house).

        21   *Hong Kong* Agreement between UK and Vietnam announced for
              forcible repatriation from Hong Kong of Vietnamese 'boat
              people'.
              Turkey Prime Minister Mesut Yilmaz resigns after inconclusive
              general election but remains as head of caretaker government.
              USSR First session of new Supreme Soviet discusses draft union
              treaty.
              Zaire President Mobutu dismisses new Prime Minister Etienne
              Tshisekedi.

        22   *EC/EFTA* Agreement on creation of common European Economic
              Area from Jan. 1993.

        23   *Cambodia* Peace agreement signed in Paris, ending 13 years of
              civil war.
              Latin America G3 (Colombia, Mexico, Venezuela) meeting joined
              by Cuban President Fidel Castro to discuss Cuba's political iso-
              lation and economic crisis.

     25–27   *South Africa* African National Congress and Pan-African Con-
              gress combine to form Patriotic Front for negotiating with gov-
              ernment.

        27   *Argentina* Gains for ruling Justicialist Party in third round of elec-
              tions.
              Central America Roberto Carpio Nicolle, former Vice-President
              of Guatemala, elected president of Central American Parliament.
              Colombia Ruling Liberal Party wins majority in first elections to
              be held under new constitution.
              Japan Prime Minister Toshiki Kaifu defeated by former Finance
              Minister Kiichi Miyazawa in contest for leadership of ruling
              Liberal Democratic Party.
              Poland Free multi-party elections produce fractured National
              Assembly.

CHRONOLOGY—*contd.*

1991

Oct.   29   *Haiti* USA imposes strict economic sanctions in protest at military coup of 30 Sept.

        29–31   *Liberia* Peace agreement reached at summit of Economic Community of West African States (ECOWAS).

        30   *Middle East* First session of peace conference in Madrid attended by delegations from Israel, Syria, Lebanon, Egypt and Jordan/ Palestine.

Nov.   1   *Madagascar* Transitional administration agreed leaving nominal power only to President Didier Ratsirak.

                Russia Russian Congress of People's Deputies agrees to grant Russian President Boris Yeltsin special powers for radical economic reform.

                Zambia President Kenneth Kaunda overwhelmingly defeated by Frederick Chiluba's Movement for Multi-Party Democracy in first free elections for nearly 20 years.

    4   *Yugoslavia* Serbia's ruling Socialist Party rejects EC plan for association of Yugoslav republics.

                Zaïre Last Belgian peace-keeping forces leave country.

    5   *Japan* Kiichi Miyazawa forms government.

    6   *Kuwait* Last oil well fire started during Gulf War capped.

    7   *Turkey* President Turgut Özal invites centre-right True Path leader Suleyman Demirel to form government.

    8   *Bulgaria* Filip Dimitrov, leader of Democratic Union, forms minority government.

                Russia President Boris Yeltsin declares state of emergency and curfew in rebel autonomous republic of Chechen-Ingush.

                Yugoslavia EC announces immediate economic sanctions in response to continuing civil war.

                Zambia New government of President Frederick Chiluba ends 27-year state of emergency as part of new constitution adopted in preparation for return to multi-party rule.

    10   *China/Vietnam* Announcement of peace accord.

                Haiti Arrival of mission organised by Organization of American States in attempt to restore democratic rule.

                Mozambique Partial accord on ending civil war signed by government and Mozambique National Resistance (RENAMO).

    11   *Afghanistan* First direct talks between mujaheddin leaders and USSR.

                Angola First multi-party elections timetabled for Sept. 1992.

                Russia Parliament votes to overturn state of emergency in Chechen-Ingush.

                Yugoslavia Bosnian Serbs vote in referendum to join new Serbian-dominated federation.

    13   *Cameroon* Truce between government and opposition parties aimed at ending political unrest.

                Poland President Lech Wałęsa's proposal of Democratic Union leader Bronisław Geremek as new prime minister fails to gain support.

Nov.   14   *Cambodia* Return from exile of Prince Norodom Sihanouk to lead Supreme National Council under UN-inspired peace plan.

                El Salvador Marti National Liberation Front guerrillas announce unilateral ceasefire.

CHRONOLOGY—*contd.*

1991

Nov. 14 *Peru* Government of Alberto Fujimori introduces tough anti-terrorist measures.

USSR President Mikhail Gorbachev and leaders of republics reach agreement in principle on new union treaty.

Yugoslavia Federal national army begins new offensive in eastern Croatia.

16 *India* Prime Minister Narasimha Rao and ruling Congress Party gain majority of seats in by-elections.

17 *Jordan* Resignation of Prime Minister Taher al-Masri.

18 *Lebanon* Release of hostages Terry Waite and Thomas Sutherland.

Somalia Overthrow of interim President Ali Mahdi Mohammed by General Mohamed Farah Aideed.

Yugoslavia Fall of Croatian town of Vukovar to federal army.

19 *Turkey* Suleyman Demirel forms coalition government.

21 *G7 Group/USSR* Financial accord signed deferring repayments on Soviet foreign debts.

UN Egyptian Deputy Prime Minister Boutros Boutros Ghali elected Secretary-General of UN to succeed Javier Perez de Cuéllar on 1 Jan. 1992.

South Africa Announcement by government, African National Congress and Inkatha Freedom Party of full negotiations on equal political rights.

22 *EC* Poland, Hungary and Czechoslovakia sign association accords with EC.

23 *Zaïre* National conference on democracy signs power-sharing accord.

24 *Belgium* General election.

25 *Guyana* President Desmond Hoyte announces indefinite postponement of general elections due on 16th Dec.

Poland First democratic Sejm (lower house of parliament) for 50 years opened by President Lech Wałesa.

Zaire President Mobutu appoints opposition leader Nguza Karl I Bond prime minister under new power-sharing agreement.

27 *Togo* Transitional government bans party led by President Gnassingbe Eyadéma.

USSR Soviet parliament refuses additional credits for central state budget.

Dec. 3 *Ukraine* Vote of 9:1 in favour of independence from USSR.

4 *Lebanon* Last US hostage Terry Anderson relased.

Middle East Second round of peace talks begin in Washington without Israel.

Paraguay Ruling Colorado Party gains overall majority in constituent assembly elections.

Seychelles President Albert René announces adoption of multiparty political system.

6 *CSCE* Estonia, Latvia and Lithuania sign charter.

Poland Jan Olszewski approved by parliament as prime minister.

Yugoslavia Historic Croatian port of Dubrovnik heavily bombarded by federal army.

CHRONOLOGY—*contd.*

1991
Dec.   8   *Middle East* Israel representatives arrive in Washington for peace talks.
             CIS Leaders of Russia, Ukraine and Belorussia announce dissolution of USSR and formation of a Commonwealth of Independent States.

       10   *EC* Maastricht summit agrees timetable on economic and social union; UK retains right to remain outside single currency and common social policy.

       11   *Albania* Vilson Ahmeti appointed prime minister.

       12   *North* and *South Korea* Terms of draft non-aggression pact for Korean peninsula agreed.

       13   *Argentina/Brazil* Agreement signed to prevent development of nuclear weaponry.
             Romania New multi-party constitution into effect.

       15   *Burma* Nobel Peace Prize winner Aung San Suu Kyu expelled from National League of Democracy.
             Nigeria National Republican Convention victorious in transitional state governorship elections.

       16   *UN* Majority vote to overturn 1975 resolution equating Zionism with racism.

       17   *Trinidad and Tobago* Opposition People's National Movement wins parliamentary election.

       18   *Middle East* Second round of peace talks in Washington end in deadlock.

       19   *Australia* Prime Minister Bob Hawke replaced by Paul Keating.
             South Africa Opening of Convention for a Democratic South Africa (Codesa).

       21   *Taiwan* Ruling Kuomintang party wins National Assembly elections.
             CIS Remaining republics of the former USSR except Georgia join Russia, Belorussia and the Ukraine in the Commonwealth of Independent States.
             Yugoslavia Bosnia and Herzegovina to seek recognition as separate state; Bosnian Serbs proclaim republic in protest.

       23   *CIS* Mikhail Gorbachev resigns as Soviet president.
             Poland Parliament approves coalition cabinet proposed by Prime Minister Jan Olszewski.

       26   *Algeria* Islamic Salvation Front wins first round of free elections.

       30   *CIS* EC recognizes former Soviet republics joining CIS.
             El Salvador Formal peace agreement ends civil war.

1992
Jan.   1   *North* and *South Korea* Pact agreed banning nuclear weapons from Korean peninsula.
             Yugoslavia Serbia and Croatia consent to UN plan to send peacekeeping forces to Yugoslavia.

Jan.   2   *CIS* Most price controls lifted in Russia, Ukraine and many other CIS republics.
             Kenya Formation of opposition Democratic Party under former Health Minister Mwai Kibaki.

CHRONOLOGY—*contd.*

1992
Jan.   3   *Israel* 12 Palestinians ordered to be deported from occupied territories.

6   *Georgia* Two-week siege of government buildings in capital Tbilisi by rebel forces ends with flight of President Zviad Gamsakhurdia.

7   *Philippines* Imelda Marcos announces presidential candidacy in May elections.

8   *Bangladesh* Talks with Burma on frontier tension end in stalemate.
France Laurent Fabius replaces Pierre Mauroy as Socialist Party leader.

11   *Algeria* Sudden resignation of President Chadli Benjedid.

12   *Algeria* High Security Council formed in response to presidential resignation cancels second round of electoral poll due on 16 Jan.
CIS Russia and Ukraine agree to divide Black Sea fleet originally claimed by Russia.

13   *Bulgaria* Inconclusive presidential elections forces second round vote.
Middle East Resumption of peace talks in Washington sees breaking of procedural deadlock between Israelis, Palestinians and Jordanians.

15   *Israel* Tehiya and Moledet parties quit government of Prime Minister Yitzhak Shamir, ending parliamentary majority.
Croatia and *Slovenia* EC recognises Croatia and Slovenia as independent republics.

16   *Georgia* Ousted Georgian President Zviad Gamsakhurdia declares war on rebels.

20   *Congo* Attempted military coup against interim Prime Minister André Milongo.

23   *Estonia* Resignation of Prime Minister Edgar Savisaar's government.

25   *Mauritania* Military ruler Col. Maaouiya Ould Sidi Ahmed Taya wins disputed democratic elections.

26   *South Africa* EC lifts economic sanctions.

28   *Middle East* First session of third round of peace talks in Moscow boycotted by Palestinians.

30   *Ireland* Resignation of Prime Minister Charles Haughey.

Feb.   1   *El Salvador* UN-negotiated truce comes into effect, ending 12 years of civil war.

2   *Italy* President Francesco Cossiga dissolves parliament and announces general elections for 5th April.
Yugoslavia Serbs accept UN peace plan, permitting deployment of UN peace-keeping troops in Croatia.

4   *Iraq* Talks with UN aimed at resuming oil exports called off by Baghdad.
Israel Knesset votes to dissolve itself and calls election for 23 June.
Venezuela Attempted military coup against President Carlos Andres Pérez's democratically-elected government crushed.

CHRONOLOGY—*contd.*

CHRONOLOGY—contd.

ADDENDA

UN. In Feb. 1992 San Marino, Armenia, Azerbaijan, Moldavia, Kazakhstan, Kirghizia, Tajikistan, Turkmenistan and Uzbekistan became members.

EBRD. All the republics of the former USSR except Georgia became members in March 1992. Lending restrictions were dropped.

NATO. The retirement in June of Supreme Allied Commander Europe Gen. Galvin was announced in April.

AFGHANISTAN. As mujahideen insurgents closed in on Kabul President Najibullah stepped down on 16 April.

ALBANIA. At the elections for the 140-member National Assembly held in March, the Democratic Party (DP) gained 92 seats, the Socialist Party 38, the Social Democratic Party 7, Omonia 2 and the Republican Party 1. Sali Berisha (b. 1945; DP) was elected President by the Assembly on 9 April. An 18-member government was formed including Alexander Meksi (b. 1939; DP; *Prime Minister*), Alfred Sarreqi (*Foreign Affairs*), Baskim Kopliku (*Interior*) and Genc Rulli (*Economy and Finance*).

AUSTRIA. In April Viktor Klima became Minister for Public Economy and Transport, Dr Michael Ausserwinkler Minister for Health, Sport and Consumer Protection and Brigitte Ederer Secretary of State for Europe and Integration.

AZERBAIJAN. Hasan Hasanov was dismissed as Prime Minister in April.

BERMUDA. In April Lord Waddington was appointed governor.

BOSNIA-HERZEGOVINA. The country was recognized as an independent state by the EC and USA in April 1992.

BRAZIL. The President appointed a new cabinet in April including Celso Lafer (*Foreign Affairs*), Marcilio Marques Moreira (*Economy*), João Mello (*Labour and Federal Administration*), Pratini de Moraes (*Mines and Energy*), Alfonso Camargo (*Transport and Communications*), Antônio Cabrera (*Agriculture*), Jorge Bornhausen (*Minister-in-Chief of the Government Secretariat*) and Angelo Calmon de Sá (*Chief of the Secretariat for Regional development*).

BURMA. Gen. Than Shwe became Chairman of the Law and Order Restoration Council and Prime Minister in April.

BURUNDI. A new government was sworn in on 4 April. Adrien Sibomana remained Prime Minister.

CAMBODIA. Chea Sim replaced Heng Samrin as head of state in April.

CAMEROON. Simon Achidi Achu (Cameroon People's Democratic Movement) was appointed Prime Minister on 9 April.

ESTONIA. Jaan Manitski (b. 1942) became Foreign Minister in April.

FINLAND. Jorma Huuhtanen (Cen) became Minister of Social Affairs and Health in April.

THE GAMBIA. Sir Dawda Kairaba Jawala (b. 1929) was re-elected President by 58·4% of votes cast on 29 April. Turn-out was 55·8%. At the elections for the National Assembly on the same day, the People's Progressive Party won 25 seats, the National Convention Party 6 and the People's Party of The Gambia 2.

GERMANY. Volker Rühe (b. 1943; CDU) became Defence Minister in April, Klaus Kinkiel (b. 1937; ind) Foreign Minister and Sabine Leutheusser-Schnarrenberger (FDP) Justice Minister in May; Economy Minister Jürgen Mölleman (FDP) became Deputy Chancellor.

GHANA. A new constitution was approved at a referendum on 28 April. Turn-out was some 50%.

GREECE. The Prime Minister took over the Foreign Ministry from Antonis Samaras on 13 April.

INDIA. Madhavsinh Solanki resigned as Foreign Minister on 31 March.

IRAN. Elections to the Majlis were held on 10 April.

ITALY. At the general election on 5 and 6 April turn-out was 86·4%. In the *Chamber of Deputies* the Christian Democrats won 206 seats with 29·7% of votes cast (234 seats with 34·3% in 1987), the Democratic Party of the Left (formerly Communists) 107 with 16·1%, the Refounded Communists 35 with 5·6% (the former Communist Party won 177 with 26·6% in 1987), the Socialists 92 with 13·6% (94 with 14·3%), the Northern League 55 with 8·7% (1 with 0·5%), the Italian Social Movement 34 with 5·4% (35 with 5·9%), the Republicans 27 with 4·4% (21 with 3·7%), the Liberals 17 with 2·8% (11 with 2·1%), Greens 16 with 2·8% (13 with 2·5%), the Social Democrats 16 with 2·7% (17 with 3%), La Rete 12 with 1·9%, others 13 with 6·3%. In the *Senate* the Christian Democrats won 107 seats (125 in 1987), the Democratic Party of the Left 64, the Refounded Communists 20 (the former Communists won 101 in 1987), the Socialists 49 (36), the Northern League 25 (1), the Italian Social Movement 16 (16), the Republicans 10, Greens 4 (1), the Liberals 4 (3), the Social Democrats 3 (5), others 13. President Cossiga resigned on 26 April.

SOUTH KOREA. At the National Assembly elections of 24 March 1,047 candidates stood. Turn-out was 71·9%. The Democratic Liberal party gained 149 seats with 38·5% of votes cast, the Democratic Party 97 with 29·2%, the Unification National Party 31 with 17·3%, the Party for New Political Reform 1 and independents 21.

MALI. Government and insurgents concluded a National Pact on 11 April agreeing to a special administration for the Tuareg north. On 29 April Alpha Oumar Konaré won the second round of presidential elections against one opponent with 69·56% of votes cast. Turn-out was 20·87%.

MAURITANIA. At the elections of March 1992 the Democratic and Socialist Republican Party (PRDS) of Ould Taya won 67 seats, the Rally for Democracy and Unity (RDU) 1, the Mauritanian Renewal Party (PMR) 1 and independents 10. Turn-out was 38·86%. The government formed in April includes Sidi Mohamed Ould Boubacar *(Prime Minister)*, Col. Ahmed Ould Minnih *(Defence)*, Hasni Ould Didi *(Interior)* and Mohamed Ould Amar *(Equipment)*.

NIGER. The Prime Minister dissolved the government on 23 March.

PERU. On 6 April the President suspended the constitution and dissolved Congress. The cabinet resigned, and was replaced by a new cabinet of 12 members led by Oscar de La Puente with one new minister, Absalon Vasquez *(Agriculture)*.

PORTUGAL. Portugal joined the European Exchange Rate Mechanism in April.

RUSSIA. On 31 March the Russian Federation government concluded a treaty with all the 20 republics within it, except the Checheno-Ingush Republic and Tatarstan, defining their mutual responsibilities.

RWANDA. Dismas Nsengiyaremye (Democratic Republican Movement) became Prime Minister on 3 April, and formed a transitional government on 16 April including Faustin Munyazesa (*Interior*) and James Gasana (*Defence*).

SÃO TOMÉ E PRINCIPE. Daniel Daio was dismissed as Prime Minister in April.

SLOVENIA. Janez Drnovsek (Liberal Democrat) became Prime Minister in April.

THAILAND. A new government was appointed on 17 April, including Montri Pongpanit (*Deputy Prime Minister*), Narong Wongwan (*Deputy Prime Minister*), Suthee Singhasaneh (*Finance*), Pongpol Idireksan (*Foreign Affairs*) and Air Marshal Anant Kalitha *(Interior)*. Prime Minister Gen. Suchinda Kraprayoon is also Minister of Defence.

VIETNAM. The National Assembly approved a new constitution on 15 April.

YUGOSLAVIA. On 27 April Serbia and Montenegro announced the formation of a new federal Yugoslavia as legal successor to the former republic.

ZAÏRE. The national conference resumed its activities on 6 April and on 15 April declared itself sovereign.

PART I

INTERNATIONAL ORGANIZATIONS

THE UNITED NATIONS (UN)

The United Nations is an association of states which have pledged themselves, through signing the Charter, to maintain international peace and security and to co-operate in establishing political, economic and social conditions under which this task can be securely achieved. Nothing contained in the Charter authorizes the organization to intervene in matters which are essentially within the domestic jurisdiction of any state.

The United Nations Charter originated from proposals agreed upon at discussions held at Dumbarton Oaks (Washington, D.C.) between the USSR, US and UK from 21 Aug. to 28 Sept., and between US, UK and China from 29 Sept. to 7 Oct. 1944. These proposals were laid before the United Nations Conference on International Organization, held at San Francisco from 25 April to 26 June 1945, and (after amendments had been made to the original proposals) the Charter of the United Nations was signed on 26 June 1945 by the delegates of 50 countries. Ratification of all the signatures had been received by 31 Dec. 1945. (For the complete text of the Charter *see* THE STATESMAN'S YEAR-BOOK, 1946, pp. xxi–xxxii.)

The United Nations formally came into existence on 24 Oct. 1945, with the deposit of the requisite number of ratifications of the Charter with the US Department of State. The official languages of the United Nations are Arabic, Chinese, English, French, Russian and Spanish.

The headquarters of the United Nations is in New York City, USA.

Flag: UN emblem in white centred on a light blue ground.

Membership. Membership is open to all peace-loving states whose admission will be effected by the General Assembly upon recommendation of the Security Council. The table on pp. 7–8 shows the 166 member states.

The Principal Organs of the United Nations are: 1. The General Assembly. 2. The Security Council. 3. The Economic and Social Council. 4. The Trusteeship Council. 5. The International Court of Justice. 6. The Secretariat.

1. **The General Assembly** consists of all the members of the United Nations. Each member has only 1 vote. The General Assembly meets regularly once a year, commencing on the third Tuesday in Sept.; the session normally lasts until mid-December and is resumed for some weeks in the new year if this is required. Special sessions may be convoked by the Secretary-General if requested by the Security Council, by a majority of the members of the United Nations or by 1 member concurred with by the majority of the members. The Assembly also meets in emergency special session. The General Assembly elects its President for each session.

The first regular session was held in London from 10 Jan. to 14 Feb. and in New York from 23 Oct. to 16 Dec. 1946.

Special sessions have been held on Palestine (1947, 1948), Tunisia (1961), Financial Situation of UN (1963), South West Africa, Peace-Keeping, Postponement of Outer Space Conference (1967), Raw Materials and Development (1974), New International Economic Order (1975), Peace-keeping force in the Lebanon, Namibia, Disarmament (1978, 1982), Economic Issues (1980); Emergency Special sessions were held on Suez, Hungary (1956), Lebanon-Jordan-United Arab Republic dispute (1958), Congo (1960), Middle East (1967), Afghanistan, Palestine (1980, resumed 1982), Namibia (1981), Economic Situation in Africa (1986), Namibia (1986) and Third Special Session on Disarmament (1988).

The work of the General Assembly is divided between 7 Main Committees, on which every member state is represented. These are: First committee (disarmament and related international security matters); special political committee; second committee (economic and financial matters); third committee (social, humanitarian and cultural matters); fourth committee (decolonisation matters); fifth committee (administrative and budgetary matters); sixth committee (legal matters).

In addition there is a General Committee charged with the task of co-ordinating the proceedings of the Assembly and its Committees; and a Credentials Committee which verifies the credentials of the delegates. The General Committee consists of 29 members, comprising the President of the General Assembly, its 17 Vice-Presidents and the Chairmen of the 7 Main Committees. The Credentials Committee consists of 9 members, elected at the beginning of each session of the General Assembly. The Assembly has 2 standing committees—an Advisory Committee on Administrative and Budgetary Questions, and a Committee on Contributions. The General Assembly establishes subsidiary and *ad hoc* bodies when necessary to deal with specific matters. These include: Special Committee on Peace-keeping Operations (33 members), Commission on Human Rights (43 members), Committee on the peaceful uses of outer space (53 members), Conciliation Commission for Palestine (3 members), Conference on Disarmament (40 members), International Law Commission (34 members), Scientific Committee on the effects of atomic radiation (20 members), Special Committee on the implementation of the declaration on the granting of independence to colonial countries and peoples (24 members), Special Committee on the policies of Apartheid of the Government of the Republic of South Africa (18 members) and UN Commission on International Trade Law (36 members).

The General Assembly may discuss any matters within the scope of the Charter, and, with the exception of any situation or dispute on the agenda of the Security Council, may make recommendations on any such questions or matters. For decisions on important questions a two-thirds majority is required, on other questions a simple majority of members present and voting. In addition, the Assembly at its fifth session, in 1950, decided that if the Security Council, because of lack of unanimity of the permanent members, fails to exercise its primary responsibility for the maintenance of international peace and security in any case where there appears to be a threat to the peace, breach of the peace or act of aggression, the General Assembly shall consider the matter immediately with a view to making appropriate recommendations to members for collective measures, including in the case of a breach of the peace or act of aggression the use of armed force when necessary, to maintain or restore international peace and security.

The General Assembly receives and considers reports from the other organs of the United Nations, including the Security Council. The Secretary-General makes an annual report to it on the work of the Organization.

2. **The Security Council** consists of 15 members, each of which has 1 vote. There are 5 permanent and 10 non-permanent members elected for a 2-year term by a two-thirds majority of the General Assembly.

Retiring members are not eligible for immediate re-election. Any other member of the United Nations may be invited to participate without vote in the discussion of questions specially affecting its interests.

The Security Council bears the primary responsibility for the maintenance of peace and security. Decisions on procedural questions are made by an affirmative vote of 9 members. On all other matters the affirmative vote of 9 members must include the concurring votes of all permanent members (in practice, however, an abstention by a permanent member is not considered a veto), subject to the provision that when the Security Council is considering methods for the peaceful settlement of a dispute, parties to the dispute abstain from voting.

For the maintenance of international peace and security the Security Council can, in accordance with special agreements to be concluded, call on armed forces, assistance and facilities of the member states. It is assisted by a Military Staff Committee consisting of the Chiefs of Staff of the permanent members of the Security Council or their representatives.

The Presidency of the Security Council is held for 1 month in rotation by the member states in the English alphabetical order of their names.

The Security Council functions continuously. Its members are permanently represented at the seat of the organization, but it may meet at any place that will best facilitate its work.

The Council has 2 standing committees of Experts and on the Admission of New Members. In addition, from time to time, it establishes *ad hoc* committees and commissions such as the Truce Supervision Organization in Palestine.

Permanent Members: China, France, Russia, UK, USA. Russia took over the seat of the former USSR in Dec. 1991.

Non-Permanent Members: Cape Verde, Hungary, Japan, Morocco, Venezuela (until 31 Dec. 1993); Austria, Belgium, Ecuador, India and Zimbabwe (until 31 Dec. 1992).

3. **The Economic and Social Council** is responsible under the General Assembly for carrying out the functions of the United Nations with regard to international economic, social, cultural, educational, health and related matters.

By Nov. 1977, 15 'specialized' inter-governmental agencies working in these fields had been brought into relationship with the United Nations. The Economic and Social Council may also make arrangements for consultation with international non-governmental organizations and, after consultation with the member concerned, with national organizations; by 1983 over 600 non-governmental organizations had been granted consultative status.

The Economic and Social Council consists of 54 Member States elected by a two-thirds majority of the General Assembly for a 3-year term. Retiring members are eligible for immediate re-election. Each member has 1 vote. Decisions are made by a majority of the members present and voting.

The Council nominally holds 2 sessions a year, and special sessions may be held if required. The President is elected for 1 year and is eligible for immediate re-election.

The Economic and Social Council has the following commissions:

Regional Economic Commissions: ECE (Economic Commission for Europe. Geneva); ESCAP (Economic and Social Commission for Asia and the Pacific. Bangkok); ECLAC (Economic Commission for Latin America and the Caribbean. Santiago, Chile); ECA (Economic Commission for Africa. Addis Ababa). ESCWA (Economic Commission for Western Asia. Baghdad). These Commissions have been established to enable the nations of the major regions of the world to co-operate on common problems and also to produce economic information.

Six functional commissions, including: (1) a Statistical Commission with sub-commission on Statistical Sampling. (2) Commission on Human Rights; with sub-commission on Prevention of Discrimination and Protection of Minorities; (3) Social Development Commission; (4) Commission on the Status of Women; (5) Commission on Narcotic Drugs; (6) Population Commission.

The Economic and Social Council has the following standing committees: The Committee on Non-Governmental Organizations, the Committee for Programme and Co-ordination, the Committee on Natural Resources, the Committee on Negotiations with Intergovernmental Agencies, the Commission on Transnational Corporations and the Commission on Human Settlements.

Other special bodies are the International Narcotics Control Board, the Interim Co-ordinating Committee for International Commodity Arrangements and the Administrative Committee on Co-ordination to ensure (1) the most effective implementation of the agreements entered into between the United Nations and the specialized agencies and (2) co-ordination of activities.

Membership: Algeria, Bahrain, Bulgaria, Burkina Faso, Canada, China, Ecuador, Finland, Iran, Jamaica, Mexico, Pakistan, Romania, Russia, Rwanda, Sweden, UK, Zaïre (until 31 Dec. 1992). Argentina, Austria, Botswana, Chile, France, Germany, Guinea, Japan, Malaysia, Morocco, Peru, Somalia, Spain, Syria, Togo, Trinidad and Tobago, Turkey, Yugoslavia (until 31 Dec. 1993); Angola, Australia, Bangladesh, Belgium, Belorussia, Benin, Brazil, Colombia, Ethiopia, India, Italy, Kuwait, Madagascar, Philippines, Poland, Suriname, Swaziland, USA (until 31 Dec. 1994).

4. The Trusteeship Council. The Charter provides for an international trusteeship system to safeguard the interests of the inhabitants of territories which are not yet fully self-governing and which may be placed thereunder by individual trusteeship agreements. These are called trust territories.

All of the original 11 trust territories except one, the Republic of Belau (Palau), administered by the USA, have become independent or joined independent countries. The Trusteeship Council consists of the 1 member administering trust territories: USA; the permanent members of the Security Council that are not administering trust territories: China, France, Russia and UK. Decisions of the Council are made by a majority of the members present and voting, each member having 1 vote. The Council holds one regular session each year, and special sessions if required.

5. The International Court of Justice was created by an international treaty, the Statute of the Court, which forms an integral part of the United Nations Charter. All members of the United Nations are *ipso facto* parties to the Statute of the Court.

The Court is composed of independent judges, elected regardless of their nationality, who possess the qualifications required in their countries for appointment to the highest judicial offices, or are jurisconsults of recognized competence in international law. There are 15 judges, no 2 of whom may be nationals of the same state. They are elected by the Security Council and the General Assembly of the United Nations sitting independently. Candidates are chosen from a list of persons nominated by the national groups in the Permanent Court of Arbitration established by the Hague Conventions of 1899 and 1907. In the case of members of the United Nations not represented in the Permanent Court of Arbitration, candidates are nominated by national groups appointed for the purpose by their governments. The judges are elected for a 9-year term and are eligible for immediate re-election. When engaged on business of the Court, they enjoy diplomatic privileges and immunities.

The Court elects its own *President* and *Vice-President* for 3 years and remains permanently in session, except for judicial vacations. The full court of 15 judges normally sits, but a quorum of 9 judges is sufficient to constitute the Court. It may form chambers of 3 or more judges for dealing with a particular case or particular categories of cases. Sir Robert Jennings (UK) and Shigeru Oda (Japan) are, respectively, President and Vice-President of the Court until 1994.

Competence and Jurisdiction. Only states may be parties in cases before the Court, which is open to the states parties to its Statute. The conditions under which the Court will be open to other states are laid down by the Security Council. The Court exercises its jurisdiction in all cases which the parties refer to it and in all matters provided for in the Charter, or in treaties and conventions in force. Disputes concerning the jurisdiction of the Court are settled by the Court's own decision.

The Court may apply in its decision: *(a)* international conventions; *(b)* international custom; *(c)* the general principles of law recognized by civilized nations; and *(d)* as subsidiary means for the determination of the rules of law, judicial decisions and the teachings of highly qualified publicists. If the parties agree, the Court may decide a case *ex aequo et bono*. The Court may also give advisory opinions on legal questions to the General Assembly, the Security Council, certain other organs of the UN and a number of international organizations.

Procedure. The official languages of the Court are French and English. All questions are decided by a majority of the judges present. If the votes are equal, the President has a casting vote. The judgment is final and without appeal, but a revision may be applied for within 10 years from the date of the judgment on the ground of a new decisive factor. No court fees are paid by parties to the Statute.

Judges. The judges of the Court, elected by the Security Council and the General Assembly, are as follows: (1) To serve until 5 Feb. 1994: Prince Bola Ajibola (Nigeria), Manfred Lachs (Poland), Jens Evensen (Norway), Shigeru Oda (Japan), Ni Zhengyu (China). (2) To serve until 5 Feb. 1997: Roberto Ago (Italy), Mohamed Shahabuddeen (Guyana), Stephen Schwebel (USA), Mohammed Bedjaoui

(Algeria), Nikolai K. Tarasov (USSR). (3) To serve until 5 Feb. 2000: Sir Robert Jennings (UK), Gilbert Guillaume (France), Andrés Aguilar Mawdsley (Venezuela), Christopher G. Weeramantry (Sri Lanka), Raymond Ranjeva (Madagascar).

If there is no judge on the bench of the nationality of a party to a case, that party has the right to choose a person to sit as judge for that case. Such judges take part in the decision on terms of complete equality with their colleagues.

The Court has its seat at The Hague, but may sit elsewhere whenever it considers this desirable. The expenses of the Court are borne by the UN.

Registrar: Eduardo Valencia-Ospina (Colombia).

6. **The Secretariat** is composed of the Secretary-General, who is the chief administrative officer of the organization, and an international staff appointed by him under regulations established by the General Assembly. However, the Secretary-General, the High Commissioner for Refugees and the Managing Director of the Fund are appointed by the General Assembly. The first Secretary-General was Trygve Lie (Norway), 1946–53; the second, Dag Hammarskjöld (Sweden), 1953–61; the third, U. Thant (Burma), 1961–71; the fourth, Kurt Waldheim (Austria), 1972–81; the fifth, Javier Pérez de Cuéllar (Peru), 1982–91.

The Secretary-General acts as chief administrative officer in all meetings of the General Assembly, the Security Council, the Economic and Social Council and the Trusteeship Council.

The financial year coincides with the calendar year; accountancy is in US$. Budget for 1988–89, $1,400m.

Secretary-General: Boutros Boutros Ghali (Egypt; b. 1922) appointed 1 Jan. 1992 for a 5-year term.

The Secretary-General is assisted by Under-Secretaries-General and Assistant Secretaries-General.

MEMBER STATES OF THE UN

The 166 member states as at Feb. 1992, with percentage scale of contribution:

Afghanistan	0·01	1946	Cape Verde	0·01	1975
Albania	0·01	1955	Central African Rep.	0·01	1960
Algeria	0·14	1962	Chad	0·01	1960
Angola	0·01	1976	Chile [1]	0·07	1945
Antigua and Barbuda	0·01	1981	China [1]	0·79	1945
Argentina [1]	0·62	1945	Colombia [1]	0·13	1945
Australia [1]	1·66	1945	Comoros	0·01	1975
Austria	0·74	1955	Congo	0·01	1960
Bahamas	0·01	1973	Costa Rica [1]	0·02	1945
Bahrain	0·02	1971	Côte d'Ivoire	0·02	1960
Bangladesh	0·02	1974	Cuba [1]	0·09	1945
Barbados	0·01	1966	Cyprus	0·02	1960
Belgium [1]	1·18	1945	Czechoslovakia [1]	0·70	1945
Belize	0·01	1981	Denmark [1]	0·72	1945
Belorussia [1]	0·34	1945	Djibouti	0·01	1977
Benin	0·01	1960	Dominica	0·01	1978
Bhutan	0·01	1971	Dominican Republic [1]	0·03	1945
Bolivia [1]	0·01	1945	Ecuador [1]	0·03	1945
Botswana	0·01	1966	Egypt [1]	0·07	1945
Brazil [1]	1·40	1945	El Salvador [1]	0·01	1945
Brunei Darussalam	0·04	1984	Equatorial Guinea	0·01	1968
Bulgaria	0·16	1955	Estonia [3]	···	1991
Burkina Faso	0·01	1960	Ethiopia [1]	0·01	1945
Burma	0·01	1948	Fiji	0·01	1970
Burundi	0·01	1962	Finland	0·50	1955
Cambodia	0·01	1955	France [1]	6·37	1945
Cameroon	0·01	1960	Gabon	0·03	1960
Canada [1]	3·06	1945	Gambia	0·01	1965

Germany	9·59	1973	Norway [1]		0·54	1945
Ghana	0·01	1957	Oman		0·02	1971
Greece [1]	0·44	1945	Pakistan		0·06	1947
Grenada	0·01	1974	Panama [1]		0·02	1945
Guatemala [1]	0·02	1945	Papua New Guinea		0·01	1975
Guinea	0·01	1958	Paraguay [1]		0·02	1945
Guinea-Bissau	0·01	1974	Peru [1]		0·07	1945
Guyana	0·01	1966	Philippines [1]		0·10	1945
Haiti [1]	0·01	1945	Poland [1]		0·64	1945
Honduras [1]	0·01	1945	Portugal		0·18	1955
Hungary	0·22	1955	Qatar		0·04	1971
Iceland	0·03	1946	Romania		0·19	1955
India [1]	0·35	1945	Russia [1,2]		10·20	1945
Indonesia	0·14	1950	Rwanda		0·01	1962
Iran [1]	0·63	1945	St Kitts and Nevis		0·01	1983
Iraq [1]	0·12	1945	St Lucia		0·01	1979
Ireland	0·18	1955	St Vincent and the			
Israel	0·22	1949	Grenadines		0·01	1980
Italy	3·79	1955	Samoa, Western		0·01	1976
Jamaica	0·02	1962	São Tomé and Principe		0·01	1975
Japan	10·84	1956	Saudi Arabia [1]		0·97	1945
Jordan	0·01	1955	Senegal		0·01	1960
Kenya	0·01	1963	Seychelles		0·01	1976
Korea (North) [3]	...	1991	Sierra Leone		0·01	1961
Korea (South) [3]	...	1991	Singapore		0·10	1965
Kuwait	0·29	1963	Solomon Islands		0·01	1978
Laos People's Dem. Rep.	0·01	1955	Somalia		0·01	1960
Latvia	...	1991	South Africa [1]		0·44	1945
Lebanon [1]	0·01	1945	Spain		2·03	1955
Lesotho	0·01	1966	Sri Lanka		0·01	1955
Liberia [1]	0·01	1945	Sudan		0·01	1956
Libyan Arab Jamahiriya	0·26	1955	Suriname		0·01	1975
Liechtenstein	0·01	1990	Swaziland		0·01	1968
Lithuania [3]	...	1991	Sweden		1·25	1946
Luxembourg [1]	0·05	1945	Syrian Arab Rep.[1]		0·04	1945
Madagascar	0·01	1960	Tanzania		0·01	1961
Malawi	0·01	1964	Thailand		0·09	1946
Malaysia	0·10	1957	Togo		0·01	1960
Maldives	0·01	1965	Trinidad and Tobago		0·04	1962
Mali	0·01	1960	Tunisia		0·03	1956
Malta	0·01	1964	Turkey [1]		0·34	1945
Marshall Islands [3]	...	1991	Uganda		0·01	1962
Mauritania	0·01	1961	Ukraine [1]		1·28	1945
Mauritius	0·01	1968	United Arab Emirates		0·18	1971
Mexico [1]	0·89	1945	UK [1]		4·86	1945
Micronesia [3]	...	1991	USA [1]		25·00	1945
Mongolia	0·01	1961	Uruguay [1]		0·04	1945
Morocco	0·05	1956	Vanuatu		0·01	1981
Mozambique	0·01	1975	Venezuela [1]		0·60	1945
Nepal	0·01	1955	Vietnam		0·01	1977
Netherlands [1]	1·74	1945	Yemen		0·02	1947
New Zealand [1]	0·24	1945	Yugoslavia [1]		0·46	1945
Nicaragua [1]	0·01	1945	Zaïre		0·01	1960
Niger	0·01	1960	Zambia		0·01	1964
Nigeria	0·19	1960	Zimbabwe		0·02	1980

[1] Original member.   [2] As USSR, 1945–1991.   [3] Contribution to be determined.

Further Reading

Yearbook of the United Nations. New York, 1947 ff. Annual
United Nations Chronicle. Quarterly
Monthly Bulletin of Statistics
General Assembly: Official-Records: Resolutions
Reports of the Secretary-General of the United Nations on the Work of the Organization. 1946 ff.
Documents of the United Nations Conference on International Organization, San Francisco, 1945. 16 vols.

Charter of the United Nations and Statute of the International Court of Justice. Text in English, French, Chinese, Russian and Spanish.
Repertory of Practice of UN's Organs. 5 vols. New York, 1955
Official Records of the Security Council, the Economic and Social Council, Trusteeship Council and the Disarmament Commission
Demographic Yearbook, 1948 ff. New York, 1969
Everyone's United Nations. New York. 10th ed., 1986
Statistical Yearbook. New York, 1947 ff.
Yearbook of International Statistics. New York, 1950 ff.
World Economic Survey. New York, 1947 ff.
Economic Survey of Asia and the Far East. New York, 1946 ff.
Economic Survey of Latin America. New York, 1948 ff.
Economic Survey of Europe. New York, 1948 ff.
Economic Survey of Africa. New York, 1960 ff.
Forsythe, D., *United Nations Peacemaking: The Conciliation Commission for Palestine.* Johns Hopkins Univ. Press, 1973
Humana, C., *World Human Rights Guide.* 2nd ed. London, 1986
Lie, T., *In the Cause of Peace.* London, 1954
Luard, E., *A History of the United Nations.* Vol. 1. London, 1982
Osmanczyk, E., *Encyclopaedia of the United Nations.* London, 1985
Peterson, M. J., *The General Assembly in World Politics.* Winchester, Mass, 1986
Thant, U., *Towards World Peace.* New York, 1964
Walters, F. P., *A History of the League of Nations.* 2 vols. London, 1952
Williams, D., *The Specialised Agencies of the United Nations.* London, 1987

United Nations Information Centre. 20 Buckingham Gate, London SW1E 6LB

UNITED NATIONS SYSTEM

The bulk of the work of the UN, measured in terms of money and personnel, is aimed at achieving the pledge made in Article 55 of the Charter to 'promote higher standards of living, full employment and conditions of economic and social progress and development'.

In addition to the 18 independent specialized agencies, there are some 14 major United Nations programmes and funds devoted to achieving economic and social progress in the developing countries.

Total contributions to the funds and programmes of the UN and specialized agencies for development activities amounted to $1,100m. (not including contributions to the World Bank group) in 1987. The highest total contributions in 1989 went to the UN Development Programme (UNDP – $1,200m.) the UN Children's Fund (UNICEF – $290m.) and the UN Fund for Population Activities (UNFPA – $167m.). The World Food Programme, which provides food aid to support development projects and emergency relief operations, provided aid worth $900m. in 1983, making it the largest single source of development assistance in the UN system, apart from the World Bank.

The *United Nations Development Programme* (UNDP) is the world's largest agency for multilateral technical and pre-investment co-operation. It is the funding source for most of the technical assistance provided by the United Nations system, and UNDP is active in 152 countries and territories and in virtually every economic and social sector. UNDP assistance is provided only at the request of Governments and in response to their priority needs, integrated into over-all national and regional plans.

There were (1988) 5,900 UNDP-supported projects currently in operation at the national, regional, inter-regional and global levels, all aimed at helping developing countries make better use of their assets, improve living standards and expand productivity. The volume of such work was $1,200m. in 1988.

UNICEF, established in 1946 to deliver post-war relief to children, now concentrates its assistance on development activities aimed at improving the quality of life for children and mothers in developing countries. During 1991, UNICEF was working in over 110 countries with a child population of some 1,300m., concentrating on basic services for children and maternal health care, nutrition, water supply and sanitation and education. *The State of the World's Children Report*, published annually by UNICEF, has helped to spread acceptance by local and national leaders of a strategy for child health and nutrition which UNICEF estimates could save the lives of 7m. children. UNICEF has focused on popularising four primary health care techniques which are low in cost and produce results in a relatively short time. These include: Oral rehydration therapy to fight the effects of diarrhoeal infections, which kill some 4m. children each year; expanded immunization against the 6 most common childhood diseases; child growth monitoring, and promotion of breast-feeding. The World Health Organization and UNICEF work closely together, providing training, equipment and the services of health care professionals. UNICEF is the world's largest supplier of vaccines and the 'cold chain' equipment needed to deliver them, as well as oral rehydration salts.

Executive Director: James P. Grant (USA).

The UN Population Fund (UNFPA) carries out programmes in over 130 countries and territories. The Fund's aims are to build up capacity to respond to needs in population and family planning; to promote awareness of population problems in both developed and developing countries and possible strategies to deal with them; to assist developing countries at their request in dealing with population problems. More than 25% of international population assistance to developing countries is channeled through UNFPA.

Executive Director: Dr Nafis Sadik (Philippines).

An International Conference on Population was convened by the United Nations in 1984 in Mexico City to review the World Population Plan of Action adopted by the 1974 population conference, and make recommendations for its future implementation.

Humanitarian relief to refugees and victims of natural and man-made disasters is also an important function of the UN system. Among the organizations involved in such relief activities are the Office of the UN Disaster Relief Co-ordinator (UNDRO), the Office of the UN High Commissioner for Refugees (UNHCR) and the UN Relief and Works Agency for Palestine Refugees in the Near East (UNRWA).

UNRWA was created by the General Assembly in 1949 as a temporary, non-political agency to provide relief to the nearly 750,000 people who became refugees as a result of the disturbances during and after the creation of the State of Israel in the former British Mandate territory of Palestine. 'Palestine refugees', as defined by UNRWA's mandate, are persons or descendants of persons whose normal residence was Palestine for at least 2 years prior to the 1948 conflict and who, as a result of the conflict, lost their homes and means of livelihood. UNRWA has also been called upon to assist persons displaced as a result of renewed hostilities in the Middle East in 1967. The situation of Palestine refugees in south Lebanon was of special concern to the Agency in 1984 which has carried out an emergency relief programme in that area for Palestine refugees affected in the aftermath of the Israeli invasion of Lebanon in 1982.

Over 2m. refugees are registered with the Agency which provides education, health care, supplementary feeding and relief services. Education and basic health care account for over 80% of the Agency's budget, which is financed by voluntary contributions from Governments. In 1986 its operating budget amounted to $230m., while cash contributions were expected to total only $194m.

Commissioner-General: Giorgio Giacomelli.

The *Office of the United Nations High Commissioner for Refugees* (UNHCR) was established by the UN General Assembly with effect from 1 Jan. 1951, originally for three years. Since 1954, its mandate has been renewed for successive five-year periods.

The work of UNHCR is of a purely humanitarian and non-political character. The main functions of the Office are to provide international protection for refugees and to seek permanent solutions to their problems through voluntary repatriation, local integration into the country of first asylum or resettlement in other countries.

UNHCR may also be called upon to provide emergency relief and on-going material assistance where necessary.

UNHCR concerns itself with refugees who have been determined to come within its mandate under the Statute, and with persons in analogous circumstances whom it assists under the terms of the 'good offices' resolutions adopted by the General Assembly.

The High Commissioner is elected by the General Assembly and follows policy directives given by the General Assembly or the Economic and Social Council, mainly through the Geneva-based Executive Committee of the High Commissioner's Programme.

International protection is the primary function of UNHCR. Its main objective is to promote and safeguard the rights and interests of refugees. In so doing UNHCR devotes special attention to promoting a generous policy of asylum on the part of Governments and seeks to improve the status of refugees in their country of residence. It also helps them to cease being refugees through the acquisition of the nationality of their country of residence when voluntary repatriation is not possible. UNHCR pursues its objectives in the field of protection by encouraging the conclusion of intergovernmental legal instruments in favour of refugees, by supervising the implementation of their provisions and by encouraging Governments to adopt legislation and administrative procedures for the benefit of refugees.

UNHCR also provides material assistance to refugees, largely in camps and settlements, and seeks to promote their self-sufficiency leading to the attainment of durable solutions for their plight. Since 1951 UNHCR has assisted and found solutions for an estimated 30 million refugees and displaced persons. In Oct. 1991 there were estimated to be some 17m. refugees.

In 1989 a number of major movements occurred in Africa and there were repatriations from the Sudan to Ethiopia and Uganda and of Ethiopians from Somalia and Djibouti. Afghans, estimated at 3m. in Pakistan and 2m. in Iran, remained the largest single refugee population in the world. An international Conference on Indo-Chinese refugees which took place in June 1984 adopted a comprehensive Plan of Action (CPA) which presents a package of inter-related measures covering such aspects of the problem as clandestine departures, regular departure programmes, reception of new arrivals, determination of the status of asylum-seekers and resettlement. The objective is to rechannel, to the extent possible, departures through legal means, while limiting entitlement to resettlement to recognized and *bona fide* refugees and encouraging voluntary return to countries of origin of rejected cases.

In Oct. 1991 the *Executive Committee* of the High Commissioner's Programme had 44 members. The 1990 budget was US$345m. for general programmes in 1990. Member countries' contributions are voluntary. Inability to collect the full revenue projected for 1990 led to a closure of 19 of the 100 regional bureaux.

The UNHCR was awarded the Nobel Peace Prize in 1955 and 1981.

Headquarters: Palais des Nations, 1211, Geneva 10, Switzerland.
UK Office: 36 Westminster Palace Gardens, London, SW1P 1RR.

High Commissioner: Sadako Ogata (till Dec. 1993).

UN funds and programmes participating in the 1984 pledging conference for development activities:
UN Development Programme; Special Measures Fund for the Least Developed Countries; UN Development Programme Energy Account; UN Capital Development Fund; UN Special Fund for Land-Locked Developing Countries; UN Revolving Fund for National Resources Exploration; Special Voluntary Fund for the UN Volunteers; UN Financing System for Science and Technology for Development; UN Trust Fund for Sudano-Sahelian Activities; UN Children's Fund; UN Fund for Population Activities; UN Industrial Development Fund; UN Trust Fund for African Development Activities; Voluntary Fund for the UN Decade for Women; UN Trust Fund for the International Research and Training Institute for the Advancement of Women; UN Centre for Human Settlements (Habitat): UN Habitat and Human Settlements Foundation; UN Trust Fund for the Transport and

Communications Decade in Africa; Trust Fund for the UN Centre on Transnational Corporations; UN Institute for Training and Research; UN Fund for Drug Abuse Control; UN Trust Fund for Social Defence; UN Development Programme Study Programme; Fund of the UN Environment Programme.

SPECIALIZED AGENCIES OF THE UN

INTERNATIONAL ATOMIC ENERGY AGENCY (IAEA)

Origin. The International Atomic Energy Agency came into existence on 29 July 1957. Its statute had been approved on 26 Oct. 1956, at an international conference held at UN Headquarters, New York. A relationship agreement links it with the United Nations. The IAEA had 112 member states in 1990.

Functions. (1) To accelerate and enlarge the contribution of atomic energy to peace, health and prosperity throughout the world, and (2) to ensure that assistance provided by it or at its request or under its supervision or control is not used in such a way as to further any military purpose. In addition, under the terms of the Non-Proliferation Treaty, the Treaty of Tlatelolco and the Treaty of Rarotonga, to verify states' obligation to prevent diversion of nuclear energy from peaceful uses to nuclear weapons or other nuclear explosive devices.

The IAEA gives advice and technical assistance to developing countries on nuclear power development, on nuclear safety, on radioactive waste management, on legal aspects of the use of atomic energy, and on prospecting for and exploiting nuclear raw materials; in addition it promotes the use of radiation and isotopes in agriculture, industry, medicine and hydrology through expert services, training courses and fellowships, grants of equipment and supplies, research contracts, scientific meetings and publications. During 1989, a total of 1,135 projects were operational of which 165 were completed and 106 training courses were held. These activities involved 2,144 expert assignments while 1,975 persons received training abroad. The IAEA has research laboratories in Austria and Monaco. At Trieste, the International Centre for Theoretical Physics was established in 1964 which is now operated jointly by UNESCO and IAEA.

In Dec. 1989, a total of 172 safeguards agreements were in force with 101 states. Safeguards are the technical means applied by the IAEA to verify that nuclear equipment or materials are used exclusively for peaceful purposes. IAEA safeguards cover more than 95% of the civilian nuclear installations outside the 5 nuclear-weapon states (China, France, UK, USA and USSR). All nuclear-weapon states have opened all (UK, USA, USSR) or some (China, France) of their civilian nuclear plants to IAEA safeguards inspection. Installations in non-nuclear-weapon states under safeguards or containing safeguarded material at 31 Dec. 1989 were 183 power reactors, 173 research reactors and critical assemblies, 8 conversion plants, 43 fuel fabrication plants, 5 reprocessing plants, 7 enrichment plants, and 405 other installations.

Organization. The Statute provides for an annual General Conference, a Board of Governors of 35 members and a Secretariat headed by a Director-General.

Headquarters: Vienna International Centre, PO Box 100, A-1400 Vienna, Austria.
Director-General: Hans Blix (Sweden).

INTERNATIONAL LABOUR ORGANISATION (ILO)

Origin. The ILO, established in 1919 as an autonomous part of the League of Nations, is an intergovernmental agency with a tripartite structure, in which representatives of governments, employers and workers participate. It seeks through international action to improve labour conditions, raise living standards and promote productive employment. In 1946 the ILO was recognized by the United

Nations as a specialized agency. In 1969 it was awarded the Nobel Peace Prize. In 1992 it numbered 151 members.

Functions. One of the ILO's principal functions is the formulation of international standards in the form of International Labour Conventions and Recommendations. Member countries are required to submit Conventions to their competent national authorities with a view to ratification. If a country ratifies a Convention it agrees to bring its laws into line with its terms and to report periodically how these regulations are being applied. More than 5,500 ratifications of 172 Conventions had been deposited by mid-1991. Machinery is available to ascertain whether Conventions thus ratified are effectively applied.

Recommendations do not require ratification, but member states are obliged to consider them with a view to giving effect to their provisions by legislation or other action. By the end of 1990 the International Labour Conference had adopted 179 recommendations.

Organization. The ILO consists of the International Labour Conference, the Governing Body and the International Labour Office.

The Conference is the supreme deliberative organ of the ILO; it meets annually at Geneva. National delegations are composed of 2 government delegates, 1 employers' delegate and 1 workers' delegate.

The Governing Body, elected by the Conference, is the executive council. It is composed of 28 government members, 14 workers' members and 14 employers' members.

Ten governments hold permanent seats on the Governing Body because of their industrial importance, namely, Brazil, China, Germany, France, India, Italy, Japan, USA, USSR and UK. The remaining 18 government seats were, at the end of 1991, held by Australia, Bangladesh, Belgium, Belorussia, Bulgaria, Cameroon, Canada, Costa Rica, Lesotho, Madagascar, Mexico, Morocco, Nigeria, Philippines, Togo, United Arab Emirates, Uruguay and Venezuela.

The Office serves as secretariat, operational headquarters, research centre and publishing house.

The ILO budget for 1992–93 amounted to US$405·7m.

Activities. In addition to its research and advisory activities, the ILO extends technical co-operation to governments under its regular budget and under the UN Development Programme and Funds-in-Trust in the fields of employment promotion, human resources development (including vocational and management training), development of social institutions, small-scale industries, rural development, social security, industrial safety and hygiene, productivity, etc. Technical co-operation also includes expert missions and a fellowship programme. Over $152m. was spent on technical co-operation in 1990. Projects were in progress in some 115 countries and about 900 experts involved.

Major emphasis is being given to the ILO's World Employment Programme, launched in 1969 with the purpose of stimulating national and international efforts to increase the volume of productive employment, and so to counter the problem of rising unemployment in developing countries. A World Employment Conference in 1976 linked employment generation to the satisfaction of over-all basic human needs. Employment strategy missions have provided policy guidance to numerous developing countries while practical assistance continues through regional teams of specialists in Africa, Asia and Latin America, backed by an intensive programme of world-wide research. The Programme is currently focusing on action—in which the major financial institutions are involved—to mitigate the social consequences of economic structural adjustment.

The International Labour Conference (Geneva, June 1991) adopted a Convention concerning night work and the use of chemicals at work, began a 2-year process of setting new standards relating to working conditions in hotels and restaurants, and began a 2-year process of setting new standards on the protection of workers' claims in the event of the insolvency of their employer.

In 1960 the ILO established in Geneva the International Institute for Labour Studies. The Institute specializes in advanced education and research on social and labour policy. It brings together for group study experienced persons from all parts of the world—government administrators, trade-union officials, industrial experts, management, university and other specialists.

The International Training Centre of the ILO, in Turin, was set up to try out and lead the training programmes implemented by the ILO as part of its technical co-operation activities. Member States and the United Nations system also call on its resources and experience to assist their own programmes.

Headquarters: International Labour Office, CH-1211 Geneva 22, Switzerland.
Director-General: Michel Hansenne (Belgium).
Chairman of the Governing Body: Yvon Chotard (France).
London Branch Office: Vincent House, Vincent Square, London, SW1P 2NB.

The ILO has regional offices in Abidjan (for Africa), Bangkok (for Asia and the Pacific), Lima (for Latin America and the Caribbean) and Geneva (for Arab States).

Further Reading

Publications: Regular periodicals in English, French and Spanish include the *International Labour Review, Labour Law Documents, Bulletin of Labour Statistics, Year Book of Labour Statistics, Official Bulletin* and *Labour Education.* The *Social and Labour Bulletin* are issued in English and French.

New volumes published in 1991 included: *International Standard Classification of Occupations: ISCO-88; Towards social adjustment: Labour market issues in structural adjustment; In search of flexibility: The new Soviet labour market; Gender and population in the adjustment of African economies: Planning for change; Conditions of Work Digest: Child labour; Working together: Labour-management co-operation in training and in technological and other changes; The unfinished story: Turkish labour migration to Western Europe; Training for older people; Prevention of major industrial accidents; Building for tomorrow: International experience in construction industry development; Teachers in developing countries;* and *Unemployment and labour market flexibility: Austria.*

FOOD AND AGRICULTURE ORGANIZATION OF THE UNITED NATIONS (FAO)

Origin. The International on Food and Agriculture in May 1943, at Hot Springs, Virginia, set up an Interim Commission in Washington in July 1943 which planned the Organization on 16 Oct. 1945. The Constitution was signed in Quebec City. The Headquarters, initially in Washington, D.C. moved to Rome in 1951.

Aims and Activities. In 1992 160 countries were members. In 1991 the EEC became a member as a 'regional economic integration organization'. Puerto Rico has associate membership. The aims of FAO are to raise levels of nutrition and standards of living; to improve the production and distribution of all food and agricultural products from farms, forests and fisheries; to improve the living conditions of rural populations; and, by these means, to eliminate hunger.

In carrying out these aims, FAO promotes investment in agriculture, better soil and water management, improved yields of crops and livestock, agricultural research, and the transfer of technology to developing countries. FAO promotes the conservation of natural resources and the rational use of fertilizers and pesticides. The Organization combats animal diseases, promotes the development of marine and inland fisheries, and encourages the sustainable management of forest resources. Technical assistance is provided in all these fields and others such as nutrition, agricultural engineering, agrarian reform, development communications, remote sensing for climate and vegetation, and the prevention of post-harvest food losses.

Special FAO programmes help countries prepare for, and provide relief in the event of, emergency food situations, in particular through the setting up of food reserves. Since the early 1980s, Africa has needed special emphasis and FAO continues to channel considerable resources and efforts there. In 1990 it launched an international scheme for Conservation and Rehabilitation of African Lands to promote national policies in agriculture and rural development that stress food security, popular participation and environmental protection through the sustainable use of land and water resources. The Global Information and Early Warning System provides current information on the world food situation and identifies countries threatened by shortages to guide potential donors.

The Organization also has a major rôle in the collection, analysis and dissemination of information on agricultural production, including commodities.

FAO sponsors the World Food Programme (WFP) with the UN; WFP uses food commodities, cash and services contributed by member States of the UN to back programmes of social and economic development, as well as for relief in emergency situations.

Finance and Administration. The FAO Conference, composed of all member states, meets every other year to determine the policy and approve the budget and work programme of FAO. The Council, consisting of 49 member nations elected by the Conference, serves as FAO's governing body between Sessions of the Conference. The proposed working budget for the 1992-93 biennium is US$645·6m., representing zero growth from the previous biennium. The working budget of FAO's Regular Programme, financed by contributions from member governments, covers the cost of the Organization's secretariat, its Technical Cooperation Programme (TCP) and part of the costs of several special programmes.

The technical assistance programme, however, is funded from extra-budgetary sources. The single largest contributor is the United Nations Development Programme (UNDP), which in 1991 accounted for US$176m., or 43% of field project expenditures. Increasingly important are the trust funds that come mainly from donor countries and international financing institutions, totalling US$194·89m., or 45·8% of technical assistance funds. FAO's contribution under its TCP was some US$35·9m., or 9%. FAO's total field programme expenditure for 1991 was an estimated US$406·7m. An estimated 42% of the expenditure was in Africa, 22% in Asia and the Pacific, 16% in the Near East, 7% in Latin America and the Caribbean, 2% in Europe, and 11% on interregional or global projects.

Headquarters: Via delle Terme di Caracalla, 00100 Rome, Italy.
Director-General: Dr Edouard Saouma (Lebanon).

Further Reading

FAO publications include: Ceres (bi-monthly) 1968 ff; *Unasylva* (quarterly) 1947 ff; FAO in ··· (annual) 1971 ff; *The State of Food and Agriculture* (annual), 1947 ff.; *Animal Health Yearbook* (annual), 1957 ff.; *Production Yearbook* (annual), 1947 ff.; *Trade Yearbook* (annual), 1947 ff.; *FAO Commodity Review* (annual), 1961 ff.; *Yearbook of Forest Products Statistics* (annual), 1947 ff.; *Yearbook of Fishery Statistics* (in two volumes). *FAO Fertilizer Yearbook, FAO Plant Protection Bulletin* (quarterly).

UNITED NATIONS EDUCATIONAL, SCIENTIFIC AND CULTURAL ORGANIZATION (UNESCO)

Origin. A Conference for the establishment of an Educational, Scientific and Cultural Organization of the United Nations was convened by the Government of the UK in association with the Government of France, and met in London, 1–16 Nov. 1945. UNESCO came into being on 4 Nov. 1946.

Functions. The purpose of UNESCO is to contribute to peace and security by promoting collaboration among the nations through education, science and culture in order to further universal respect for justice, for the rule of law and for the human rights and fundamental freedoms which are affirmed for the peoples of the world, without distinction of race, sex, language or religion, by the Charter of the United Nations.

Activities. The education programme has four main objectives: The extension of education; the improvement of education; and life-long education for living in a world community.

To train teachers specialized in the techniques of fundamental education UNESCO is helping to establish regional and national training centres. A centre for Latin America was opened in Mexico in 1951, one for the Arab States was set up in Egypt in 1953. UNESCO seeks to promote the progressive application of the right to free and compulsory education for all and to improve the quality of education everywhere.

In the natural sciences, UNESCO seeks to promote international scientific co-operation, such as the International Hydrological Programme which began in 1966. It encourages scientific research designed to improve the living conditions of mankind. Science co-operation offices have been set up in Montevideo, Cairo, New Delhi, Nairobi and Jakarta.

In the field of communication, UNESCO endeavours, by disseminating information, carrying out research and providing advice, to increase the scope and quality of press, film and radio services throughout the world.

In the cultural field, UNESCO assists member states in studying and preserving both the physical and the non-physical heritage of each society.

In the social sciences UNESCO helps in the development of research and teaching facilities and focuses on questions concerning Peace, Human Rights, Philosophy, Youth and Development Studies.

Organization. The organs of UNESCO are a General Conference (composed of representatives from each member state), an Executive Board (consisting of 51 government representatives elected by the General Conference) and a Secretariat. The 26th general conference in Oct.–Nov. 1991 amended its constitution by consensus, making the members of the Executive Board direct representatives of their countries. UNESCO had 164 members in 1991.

National commissions act as liaison groups between UNESCO and the educational, scientific and cultural life of their own countries.

Budget for 1988–89: $350,386,000.

Headquarters: UNESCO House, 7 Place de Fontenoy, Paris.
Director-General: Federico Mayor (Spain).

Further Reading

Periodicals. Museum (quarterly, English and French); *International Social Science Journal* (quarterly, English and French); *Impact of Science on Society* (quarterly, English and French); *Unesco Courier* (monthly, English, French and Spanish); *Prospects* (quarterly, English, French and Spanish); *Copyright Bulletin* (twice-yearly, English and French); *Unesco News* (English and French); *Nature and Resources* (quarterly, English, French and Spanish).

Hajnal, P. I., *Guide to UNESCO.* London and New York, 1983

WORLD HEALTH ORGANIZATION (WHO)

Origin. An International Conference, convened by the UN Economic and Social Council, to consider a single health organization resulted in the adoption on 22 July 1946 of the constitution of the World Health Organization. This constitution came into force on 7 April 1948.

Structure. The principal organs of WHO are the World Health Assembly, the Executive Board and the Secretariat. Each of the 170 member states has the right to be represented at the Assembly, which meets annually usually in Geneva, Switzerland. The 31-member Executive Board is composed of technically qualified health experts designated by as many member states elected by the Assembly. The Secretariat consists of technical and administrative staff headed by a Director-General. Health activities in member countries are carried out through regional organizations which have been established in Africa (regional office, Brazzaville), South-East Asia (New Delhi), Europe (Copenhagen), Eastern Mediterranean (Alexandria) and Western Pacific (Manila). The Pan American Sanitary Bureau in Washington serves as the Regional Office of WHO for the Americas.

Functions. WHO's objective, as stated in the first article of the Constitution is 'the attainment by all peoples of the highest possible level of health'. As the directing and co-ordinating authority on international health it establishes and maintains collaboration with the UN, specialized agencies, government health administrations, professional and other groups concerned with health. The Constitution also directs WHO to assist governments to strengthen their health services, to stimulate and advance work to eradicate diseases, to promote maternal and child health, mental health, medical research and the prevention of accidents; to improve standards of teaching and training in the health professions, and of nutrition, housing, sanitation, working conditions and other aspects of environment health. The Organization also is empowered to propose conventions, agreements and regulations and make recommendations about international health matters; to revise the international nomenclature of diseases, causes of death and public health practices; to develop, establish and promote international standards concerning foods, biological, pharmaceutical and similar substances.

Methods of work. Co-operation in country projects is undertaken only on the request of the government concerned, through the 6 regional offices of the Organization. Worldwide technical services are made available by headquarters. Expert committees whose members are chosen from the 54 advisory panels of experts meet to advise the Director-General on a given subject. Scientific groups and consultative meetings are called for similar purposes. To further the education of health personnel of all categories, seminars, technical conferences and training courses are organized and advisors, consultants and lecturers are provided. WHO awards fellowships for study to nationals of member countries.

Activities. The main thrust of WHO's activities in recent years has been towards promoting national, regional and global strategies for the attainment of the main social target of the Member States for the coming years: 'Health for All by the Year 2000', or the attainment by all citizens of the world of a level of health that will permit them to lead a socially and economically productive life.

Almost all countries indicated a high level of political commitment to this goal, and guiding principles for formulating corresponding strategies and plans of action were prepared.

The 43rd World Health Assembly which met in May 1991 approved a programme budget of US$734,936,000 for the biennium 1992-93. The Assembly adopted numerous resolutions, including calls for the elimination of leprosy as a public health problem by the year 2000, and urged stepped-up efforts against tuberculosis, acute respiratory infections, dracunculiasis and cholera. It also called for the intensified development of new children's vaccines, greater emergency relief efforts, improvements for the health of refugees, alleviation of the urban crisis, and more support for women, health and development.

Children's Summit. The Director-General and the Executive Director of UNICEF urged delegates to work swiftly to maintain the momentum for improving the health for children and their mothers generated by the World Summit for Children, held in New York on 30 September 1990. The Assembly recognized that the Summit goals and Plan for Action are in accord with the global policy and strategy of health for all by the year 2000, based on the primary health care approach, and reflect the international health priorities and goals adopted by Assemblies of recent years.

The Urban Crisis. The Assembly noted that, from 1950 to 1990, the world's urban population almost tripled, from 734 million to 2,390 million, or from 19% to 45% of the total population of the planet, and the increase is continuing. Most of the urban population increase was in cities of developing countries, whose urban population increased fivefold, from 286 million in 1950 to 1,515 million in 1990. Annual urban population growth rates of 3% or more have been common in developing countries and may continue over the next 20 years. Such growth exceeds the capacity of a city and exposes urban dwellers to the hazards of poverty, unemployment, inadequate housing, poor sanitation, pollution, disease vectors, poor transport, as well as psychological and social stress.

Acute Respiratory Infections. Acute respiratory infections are causing high morbidity and mortality in children, particularly in developing countries. Progress made in the development of the WHO programme for the control of these diseases, which focuses on the prevention of pneumonia, was noted with satisfaction by the Assembly, which requested the Director-General to intensify support to clinical, sociocultural, disease-prevention and health systems research on acute respiratory infections, with a view to developing and applying appropriate methods of prevention, diagnosis and treatment of pneumonia in children, including essential antibiotics at an affordable cost.

Tuberculosis. The Assembly expressed concern that 3m. tuberculosis deaths and 8m. new cases continue to occur in the world annually. It also recognized that in some countries the disease is rapidly increasing owing to AIDS. It urged Member States to give high priority to tuberculosis control as an integral part of primary health care, particularly in the light of the HIV pandemic, and requested the Director-General to intensify collaboration with countries on treatment, case-finding and research, in order to attain a global target of cure of 85% sputum-positive patients under treatment, and detection of 70% of cases, by the year 2000.

Leprosy. The Assembly noted that over the past 5 years multi-drug therapy and case-finding in the majority of countries where the disease is endemic has reduced prevalence. It urged Member States in which leprosy is endemic to give high priority to leprosy control. It also requested the Director-General to strengthen support to Member States so as to achieve the global elimination of the disease by the year 2000.

Cholera. Considering the cholera epidemic in parts of Latin America and other regions, the Assembly called on Member States and multilateral organizations to consider health and environmental issues as an integral part of development policies and plans, and to allocate resources and to undertake action accordingly, including health education and public information, in order to prevent risks of epidemics or diminish them, giving due attention to the situation and needs of the population groups most at risk. It also urged Member States not to apply to countries affected restrictions that cannot be justified, in particular as regards importation of products from these countries.

Children's Vaccines. The Assembly noted the accomplishments of the WHO/UNDP programme for vaccine development during its first 6 years of existence, and endorsed its objectives and targets. These include: Improved access to immunization and concentration on developing better vaccines that would require only one or two doses, be given earlier in life, and be combined in novel ways. It advocated the acceleration of the development of new vaccines against bacterial meningitis, acute respiratory infections, diarrhoeal diseases, viral hepatitis, dengue, tuberculosis and other communicable diseases.

Smoking. WHO estimates that the annual number of deaths in the world attributable to smoking will be about 3m. in the 1990s. The Assembly expressed deep concern over the dangers to the health, and the violation of the right to health of non-smokers, caused by enforced and passive smoking, i.e. involuntary exposure to tobacco smoke in enclosed public places and transports. The Assembly noted that establishing a smoke-free environment in many public conveyances is technically difficult, especially trains and aircraft. Thus, the Assembly urged all Member States to adopt appropriate measures for effective protection from involuntary exposure to tobacco smoke in public transport, to ban smoking in public conveyances where protection against involuntary exposure cannot be ensured, and to promote educational activities necessary to inform people of the importance of protecting themselves and their families, especially children, against passive smoking.

Human Organ Transplantation. The Assembly endorsed WHO's Guiding Principles on Human Organ Transplantation, and requested the Director-General to disseminate them as widely as possible and to review the principles from time to time in the light of national experience.

Eradication of Dracunculiasis. Noting with satisfaction progress made by affected countries in eliminating dracunculiasis, the Assembly declared its commitment to the goal of eradicating dracunculiasis by the end of 1995, this being technically feasible given appropriate political, social and economic support. It called upon all Member States still affected to determine the full extent of the disease and elaborate plans of actions, and urged the Director-General immediately to initiate country-by-country certification of elimination, so that the certification process can be completed by the end of the 1990s.

Water and Environmental Sanitation. Concerned that 1,200m. people in the developing countries still lack adequate and safe water, and that 1,800m. are without appropriate sanitation, the Assembly urged Member States to reaffirm the priority accorded to safe water and environmental sanitation programmes, as essential to disease prevention and in particular water-borne diseases. The Assembly requested the Director-General to promote innovative and cost-effective approaches in technology and finance for the provision of safe water and sanitation and asked the Organization to co-operate with all other relevant organizations of the UN in this action.

Women, Health and Development. The United Nations Decade for Women (1976–1985) emphasized the crucial role of women in health and development and recognized that effective socio-economic development cannot be realized without improvements in the health, economic and social status of women. Recognizing the urgency of promoting women's health and development worldwide, the Assembly called on countries to accelerate the implementation of measures in this area, notably through improved female literacy, promotion of family planning and safe motherhood and women's income-generating opportunities. The resolution requests WHO to intensify its advocacy rule in this area, in particular by ensuring that the objectives of women's health and development are integrated in all WHO programmes and that indicators that are sensitive to changes in women's health are developed.

Health Conditions of the Arab Population in the Occupied Arab Territories, including Palestine. The Assembly adopted a resolution asserting WHO's responsibility to promote for the Palestinian people the enjoyment of the highest attainable standard of health as one of the fundamental rights of every human being. The Assembly requested that the Director-General pursue the implementation of special technical assistance to improve the health conditions of the Palestinian people, in co-operation with all concerned WHO members and observers referred to in Health Assembly resolutions related to this item, taking into consideration a comprehensive health plan for Palestinian people.

Health Situation of Displaced Persons in Iraq and Neighbouring Countries (Kuwait and the Iraq/Turkey and Iraq/Iran border areas). Expressing its grave concern about the risks to the health of the refugees and displaced people who move towards and across international frontiers, the Assembly recognized the need to create conditions conducive to the early and safe return of Iraqi displaced people to their homes. Consequently, it urged WHO, in full co-operation with other agencies taking part in the coordinated UN humanitarian relief effort in the region, to alleviate the heavy burden placed on countries neighbouring Iraq by improving the delivery of health care to refugees and displaced people, including preventive and hygienic measures.

Emergency Relief Operations. Deploring the succession of natural and man-made disasters that have occurred in various regions, including the severe cyclone and tornadoes which struck Bangladesh in April and May, and the risk of outbreaks of epidemic diseases among stricken populations, the Assembly also recognized the limited capabilities of affected countries to cope with such emergencies. Consequently, it urged international and regional institutions to afford greater priority to assistance aimed at mitigating the health effects of natural and man-made disasters and requested the Director-General to strengthen WHO's ability to respond to the health needs of victims, working with the different agencies of the UN, non-governmental organizations and other parties. The resolution also requested that the Director-General assist countries to reinforce their capabilities for emergency preparedness.

International Programme to mitigate the health effects of the Chernobyl Accident. The Assembly endorsed an international programme involving a long-term collaborative effort of the USSR and other interested Member States, and organized under the auspices of WHO with the collaboration of other relevant international organizations. The programme intends to mitigate the health consequences of accidents, conduct research on the health effects of exposure to radiation, and develop guidelines for dealing with radiation emergencies in the future.

World Health Days. World Health Day 1991, 7 April 1991, was devoted to the theme of disaster preparedness. The theme for 1992 is cardiovascular diseases.

Headquarters: 1211 Geneva 27, Switzerland.
Director-General: Dr Hiroshi Nakajima (Japan).

Further Reading

Basic Documents. 38th ed., 1990 (Arabic, Chinese, English, French, Russian, Spanish)
Handbook of Resolutions and Decisions. Vol. I, 1973, Vol. II, 1985 and Vol. III, 2nd ed., 1990 (Arabic, Chinese, English, French, Russian, Spanish)
World Health Forum (from 1980, quarterly; Arabic, Chinese, English, French, Italian, Russian and Spanish)
Bulletin of WHO (quarterly, 1947–51; 6 issues a year from 1978; bilingual English/French, Arabic, Russian; selection in Chinese)
International Digest of Health Legislation (quarterly, from 1948; English and French)
World Health, the Magazine of WHO. 1957 ff. (6 issues a year; English, French, German, Portuguese, Russian and Spanish; and 4 issues a year. Arabic and Persian)
Environmental Health Criteria, 1976 ff.
Health and Safety Guides, 1987 ff.
WHO Technical Report Series, 1950 ff. (Arabic, Chinese, English, French, Russian, Spanish)
WHO AIDS series, 1988 ff. (Arabic, Chinese, English, French, Russian, Spanish)
Public Health Papers, 1959 ff. (Arabic, Chinese, English, French, Russian, Spanish)
World Health Statistics Annual (from 1952; English, French and Russian)
World Health Statistics Quarterly (monthly, 1947–76 then quarterly; bilingual English/ French)
Weekly Epidemiological Record (from 1926; bilingual English/French)
WHO Drug Information (from 1987, quarterly; English and French)
Publications of the WHO, 1948–89; Catalogue of New Books, 1986–1990.—New Books, 1991
World Directories:
Medical Schools, 1988; Schools of Public Health and Postgraduate Training Programmes in Public Health (1985); Schools for Medical Assistants, 1973 (1976); *Auxiliary Sanitarians 1973* (1978); *Dental Auxiliaries 1973* (1977); *Medical Lab. Technicians and Assistants, 1973* (1977)
The International Pharmacopoeia. 3rd. ed., 3 vols, 1979, 1981, 1988 (English, French and Spanish)
International Statistical Classification of Diseases and Related Health Problems. 10th rev. (1992; English, French, Russian, Spanish)
IARC Monographs on the Evaluation of Carcinogenic Risk of Chemicals to Humans. 1967 ff. (English)
Report on the World Health Situation. 1959 ff. (Arabic, Chinese, English, French, Russian, Spanish); Seventh report (1987)
The Work of WHO, 1990–91: Biennial Report of the Director-General (1992) (Arabic, Chinese, English, French, Russian, Spanish)
International Health Regulations (1969). 3rd annotated ed., 1983 (Arabic, Chinese, English, French, Russian, Spanish)

INTERNATIONAL MONETARY FUND (IMF)

The International Monetary Fund was established on 27 Dec. 1945 as an independent international organization and began operations on 1 March 1947; its relationship with the UN is defined in an agreement of mutual co-operation which came into force on 15 Nov. 1947. The first amendment to the Fund's articles creating the special drawing right (SDR; ISO code, XDR) took effect on 28 July 1969 and the second amendment took effect on 1 April 1978.

The capital resources of the Fund comprise SDRs and currencies that the members pay under quotas calculated for them when they join the Fund. Members' quotas in the Fund, in 1991, amounted to SDR 91,102·6m. and are closely related to (*i*) subscription to the Fund, (*ii*) their drawing rights on the Fund under both regular and special facilities, (*iii*) their voting power, and (*iv*) their share of any allocations of SDRs. Every Fund member is required to subscribe to the Fund an amount equal to its quota. An amount not exceeding 25% of the quota has to be paid in reserve assets, the balance in the member's own currency. In June 1990 the Board of Governors adopted a resolution for a 50% increase in total IMF quotas. Once the requisite number of members notify their consent to increases in their quota, the ranking of top subscribers will be: 1st, the USA; joint 2nd, Germany and Japan; joint 4th, France and the UK.

The Fund is authorized under its Articles of Agreement to supplement its resources by borrowing. In Jan. 1962, a 4-year agreement was concluded with 10 industrial members (Belgium, Canada, France, Federal Republic of Germany, Italy, Japan, Netherlands, Sweden, UK, USA) who undertook to lend the Fund up to $6,000m. in their own currencies, if this should be needed to forestall or cope with an impairment of the international monetary system. Switzerland subsequently joined the group. These arrangements, known as the General Arrangements to Borrow (GAB), have been extended several times and the most recent 5-year renewal was to end in Dec. 1993. In early 1983 agreement was reached to increase the credit arrangements under the GAB to SDR 17,000m.; to permit use of GAB resources in transactions with Fund members that are not GAB participants; to authorize Swiss participation; and to permit borrowing arrangements with non-participating members to be associated with the GAB. Saudi Arabia and the Fund have entered into such an arrangement under which the Fund will be able to borrow up to SDR 1,500m. to assist in financing purchases by any member for the same purpose and under the same circumstances as in the GAB. The changes became effective by 26 Dec. 1983. The Fund has also borrowed from member countries and official institutions for 2 oil facilities, a supplementary financing facility and to finance enlarged access by members.

Purposes: To promote international monetary co-operation, the expansion of international trade and exchange rate stability; to assist in the removal of exchange restrictions and the establishment of a multilateral system of payments; and to alleviate any serious disequilibrium in members' international balance of payments by making the financial resources of the Fund available to them, usually subject to conditions to ensure the revolving nature of Fund resources.

Activities. Each member of the Fund undertakes a broad obligation to collaborate with the Fund and other members to ensure orderly exchange arrangements and to promote a system of stable exchange rates. In addition, members are subject to certain obligations relating to domestic and external policies that can affect the balance of payments and the exchange rate. The Fund makes its resources available, under proper safeguards, to its members to meet short-term or medium-term payments difficulties. The first allocation of special drawing rights was made on 1 Jan. 1970 with five SDR allocations since then. SDRs in existence now total SDR 21,400m. To further enhance its balance of payments assistance to its members the Fund established a compensatory financing facility on 27 Feb. 1963, temporary oil facilities in 1974 and 1975, a trust fund in 1976, and an extended facility for medium-term assistance to members with special balance of payments problems on 13 Sept. 1974 with additional financing now provided through a policy of enlarged access. In March 1986, it established the structural adjustment facility to provide assistance to low-income countries. In Dec. 1987, the Fund established the enhanced structural adjustment facility to provide further assistance to low-income countries facing high levels of indebtedness. In Aug. 1988, the compensatory and contingency financing facility was established, succeeding the compensatory financing facility; the new facility provides broader protection to members pursuing Fund-supported adjustment programmes.

The Committee on Reform of the International Monetary System and Related Issues, generally known as the Committee of Twenty, held its first session at the 1972 annual meeting, with the mandate to advise and report to the Board of Governors on all aspects of the international monetary system, including proposals for any amendments of the Articles of Agreement. The Committee of Twenty disbanded after submitting its final report in 1974. An Interim Committee of the Board of Governors on the International Monetary System and a Joint Ministerial Committee of the Boards of Governors of the World Bank and the Fund on the Transfer of Real Resources to Developing Countries (Development Committee) were established and held their initial meetings in Jan. 1975 and since then have met on a semi-annual basis. Details of the reform of the international monetary system were incorporated in the second amendment of the Fund's Articles of Agreement, effective April 1978. In order to oversee the compliance of members with their obligations under the Articles of Agreement, the Fund is required to exercise firm surveillance over their exchange rate policies.

Organization. The highest authority in the Fund is exercised by the Board of Governors on which each member government is represented. Normally the Governors meet once a year, although the Governors may take votes by mail or other means between annual meetings. The Board of Governors has delegated many of its powers to the executive directors in Washington, of whom there are 22, of which 6 are appointed by individual members and the other 16 elected by groups of countries. Each appointed director has voting power proportionate to the quota of the government he represents, while each elected director casts all the votes of the countries which elected him. The 6 appointed executive directors represent the US, UK, France, Germany, Japan and Saudi Arabia.

The managing director is selected by the executive directors; he presides as chairman at their meetings, but may not vote except in case of a tie. His term is for 5 years, but may be extended or terminated at the discretion of the executive directors. He is responsible for the ordinary business of the Fund, under general control of the executive directors, and supervises a staff of about 1,900.

There were 156 members of the IMF in 1991; the USSR became an associate member in 1991.

Headquarters: 700 19th St. NW, Washington, D.C., 20431. Offices in Paris and Geneva.

Managing Director: Michel Camdessus (France).

Further Reading

Publications. Summary Proceedings of Annual Meetings of the Board of Governors.— Annual Report of the Executive Board.—Selected Decisions of the International Monetary Fund and Selected Documents.—International Financial Statistics (monthly).—*IMF Survey* (bi-weekly).—*Balance of Payments Statistics.* Washington, monthly.—*IMF Staff Papers* (four times a year). Washington, from Feb. 1950.—*IMF Occasional Papers.—IMF Pamphlets.— Annual Report on Exchange Arrangements and Exchange Restrictions.* Washington, 1950 ff.—*Finance and Development.* Washington, from June 1964 (quarterly).—*Direction of Trade Statistics.* Washington (quarterly). *IMF World Economic and Financial Surveys.* Washington. *Government Finance Statistics Yearbook. The International Monetary Fund, 1945–65: Twenty Years of International Monetary Co-operation.* 3 vols. Washington, 1969.—de Vries, M. G., *The International Monetary Fund, 1966–1971: The System Under Stress.* 2 vols. Washington D.C. 1976.—*The International Monetary Fund 1972–1978: Co-operation on Trial.* 3 vols. Washington D.C., 1985

Salda, A. C. M., *The International Monetary Fund.* New Brunswick (NJ), 1992

INTERNATIONAL BANK FOR RECONSTRUCTION AND DEVELOPMENT (IBRD)

Conceived at the Bretton Woods Conference, July 1944, the 'World Bank' began operations in June 1946. Its purpose is to provide funds and technical assistance to facilitate economic development in its porer member countries.

The Bank obtains its funds from the following sources: Capital paid in by member countries; sales of its own securities; sales of parts of its loans; repayments; and net earnings. The subscribed capital of the Bank amounted to $139,120m. at 30 June 1991. On 27 April 1988, the Board of Governors adopted a resolution that increased the authorized capital stock of the Bank to $174,700m. This represented an increase of approximately $74,800m. The resolution provides that the paid-in portion of the shares authorized to be subscribed under it will be 3%. Outstanding medium- and long-term borrowings had reached $84,708m. by 30 June 1991. The Bank is self-supporting. Its net earnings for year ending 30 June 1991 amounted to $1,004m.

By 30 June 1991 the Bank had made 3,302 loans totalling $203,054m. in 108 of its 155 member countries. Lending was for the following purposes: Agriculture and rural development, $38,025m.; Development Finance Companies, $20,592m.; education, $8,170m.; energy, $43,382m.; industry (including tourism), $15,450m.; non-project, $17,074m.; population, health and nutrition, $2,349m.; public-sector management, $1,616m.; small-scale enterprises, $4,692m.; telecommunications, $3,459m.; transportation, $29,401m.; urban development, $8,928m.; water supply and sewerage, $9,184m., and technical assistance, $733m. In order to eliminate wasteful overlapping of development assistance and to ensure that the funds available are used to the best possible effect, the Bank has organized consortia or consultative groups of aidgiving nations for the following countries: Bangladesh, Bolivia, Burma, Colombia, Côte d'Ivoire, Egypt, El Salvador, Ethiopia, Ghana, Guinea, Guinea-Bissau, Honduras, India, Kenya, Korea, Madagascar, Malawi, Mauritania, Mauritius, Morocco, Mozambique, Nepal, Nicaragua, Nigeria, Pakistan, Papua New Guinea, Peru, the Philippines, Senegal, Somalia, Sri Lanka, Sudan, Tanzania, Thailand, Togo, Tunisia, Uganda, Zaïre, Zambia and the Caribbean Group for Co-operation in Economic Development. The Bank furnishes a wide variety of technical assistance. It acts as executing agency for a number of pre-investment surveys financed by the UN Development Programme. Resident missions have been established in 43 developing member countries as well as 4 regional offices for East and West Africa, Thailand, and Europe and the Commonwealth of Independent States, primarily to assist in the preparation of projects. The Bank maintains a staff college, the Economic Development Institute in Washington, D.C., for senior officials of the member countries.

Headquarters: 1818 H St., NW, Washington, D.C., 20433, USA. *European office:* 66 avenue d'Iéna, 75116 Paris, France. *London office:* New Zealand House, Haymarket, SW1Y 4TE, England. *Tokyo office:* Kokusai Building, 1–1, Marunouchi 3-chome, Chiyoda-ku, Tokyo 100, Japan.
President: Lewis Preston (USA).

Further Reading

Publications. Annual Reports. 1946 ff.—*Summary Proceedings of Annual Meetings.* 1947 ff.—*The World Bank & International Finance Company.* 1986.—*The World Bank Atlas.* 1967 ff.—*Catalog of Publications,* 1986 ff.—*World Development Report.* 1978 ff.
Wilson, C. R., *The World Bank Group: A Guide to Information Sources.* New York, 1991

INTERNATIONAL DEVELOPMENT ASSOCIATION (IDA)

A lending agency which came into existence on 24 Sept. 1960. Administered by the World Bank, IDA is open to all members of the Bank.

IDA concentrates its assistance on those countries with an annual *per capita* gross national product of less than $580 (1989 rate). Its resources consist mostly of subscriptions, general replenishments from its more industrialized and developed members, special contributions, and transfers from the net earnings of the Bank. IDA credits are made to Governments only. It had committed $64,515m. for 2,108 development projects in 84 countries, by 30 June 1991.

INTERNATIONAL FINANCE CORPORATION (IFC)

The Corporation, an affiliate of the World Bank, was established in July 1956. Paid-in capital at 30 June 1991 was $1,100m., subscribed by 143 member countries. In addition, it has accumulated earnings of $958m. IFC supplements the activities of the World Bank by encouraging the growth of productive private enterprises in developing member countries. Chiefly, IFC makes investments in the form of subscriptions to the share capital of privately owned companies, or long-term loans, or both. The Corporation will help finance new ventures and assist established enterprises to expand, improve or diversify. It also provides a variety of advisory services to public and private sector clients.

During 1990–91, the IFC approved US$2,800m. in financing for projects in 46 countries.

President: Lewis Preston (USA).
Executive Vice-President: Sir William Ryrie (UK).

Publications. Annual Reports. 1956 ff.—*What IFC Does.* 1988,—*How to Work with IFC,* 1988

INTERNATIONAL CIVIL AVIATION ORGANIZATION (ICAO)

Origin. The Convention providing for the establishment of the International Civil Aviation Organization was drawn up by the International Civil Aviation Conference held in Chicago from 1 Nov. to 7 Dec. 1944. A Provisional International Civil Aviation Organization (PICAO) operated for 20 months until the formal establishment of ICAO on 4 April 1947.

The Convention on International Civil Aviation superseded the provisions of the Paris Convention of 1919, which established the International Commission for Air Navigation (ICAN), and the Pan American Convention on Air Navigation drawn up at Havana in 1928.

Functions. It assists international civil aviation by establishing technical standards for safety and efficiency of air navigation and promoting simpler procedures at borders; develops regional plans for ground facilities and services needed for international flying; disseminates air-transport statistics and prepares studies on aviation economics; fosters the development of air law conventions. As an administrative arm of the UN Development Programme it provides technical assistance to states in developing civil aviation programmes.

Organization. The principal organs of ICAO are an Assembly, consisting of all members of the Organization, and a Council, which is composed of 33 states elected by the Assembly, for 3 years, and meets in virtually continuous session. In electing these states, the Assembly must give adequate representation to: (1) states of major importance in air transport; (2) states which make the largest contribution to the provision of facilities for the international civil air navigation; (3) those states not otherwise included whose election will ensure that all major geographical areas of the world are represented. The main subsidiary bodies are: The Air Navigation Commission, composed of 15 members appointed by the Council; Air Transport Committee, open to council members; and the Legal Committee, on which all members of ICAO may be represented. There are 164 members. Budget for 1992: US$43,917,000.

Headquarters: 1000 Sherbroke St. West, Montreal, Quebec, Canada H3A 2R2.
President: Dr Assad Kotaite (Lebanon).
Secretary-General: Dr Philippe Rochat (Switzerland).

Annual Report of the Council. (English, French, Russian, Spanish)
ICAO Journal (Monthly in English, French, Spanish; quarterly in Russian)

UNIVERSAL POSTAL UNION (UPU)

Origin. The UPU was established on 1 July 1875, when the Universal Postal Convention adopted by the Postal Congress of Berne on 9 Oct. 1874 came into force. The UPU was known at first as the General Postal Union, its name being changed at the Congress of Paris in 1878. In 1991 there were 168 member countries.

Functions. The aim of the UPU is to assure the organization and perfection of the various postal services and to promote, in this field, the development of international collaboration. To this end, the members of UPU are united in a single postal territory for the reciprocal exchange of correspondence.

Organization. The UPU is composed of a Universal Postal Congress which usually meets every 5 years, a permanent Executive Council consisting of 40 members, a consultative Committee, which consists of 35 members elected on a geographical basis by each Congress, and an International Bureau, which functions as the permanent secretariat.

A specialized agency of the UN since 1948, the Union is governed by the Constitution of the UPU adopted at the 1964 Vienna Congress, and amended by the 1969

(Tokyo), 1974 (Lausanne), 1984 (Hamburg) and 1989 (Washington) Additional Protocols.

Budget for 1990: US$18m.

Headquarters: Weltpoststrasse 4, 3000, Berne 15, Switzerland.
Director-General: Adwaldo Cardoso Botto de Barros (Brazil).

Further Reading

Acts of the Universal Postal Union: revised at Hamburg in 1984 and annotated by the International Bureau. vols 1–4.—*The Postal Union* (quarterly, Arabic, Chinese, English, French, German, Spanish, Russian).—*The UPU: Its Foundation and Development.* Bern, 1959.

INTERNATIONAL TELECOMMUNICATION UNION (ITU)

Origin. In 1932, at Madrid, the Union decided to merge the Telegraph Convention adopted in 1865 and the Radiotelegraph Convention adopted in 1906 into a single International Telecommunication Convention within annex, the Telephone, Telegraph and Radio Regulations. It also decided to change its name to International Telecommunication Union to better reflect all its new responsibilities. The ITU has been governed since 1 Jan. 1984 by the International Telecommunication Convention adopted in Nairobi in 1982. A constitution and convention were adopted at Nice in 1989. This will come into force after 55 members have ratified it.

Functions. (1) to maintain and extend international co-operation for the improvement and rational use of telecommunications of all kinds, as well as to promote and to offer technical assistance to developing countries in the field of telecommunications; (2) to promote the development of technical facilities and their most efficient operation with a view to improving the efficiency of telecommunication services, increasing their usefulness and making them, so far as possible, generally available to the public; (3) to harmonize the actions of nations in the attainment of those ends.

Organization. The ITU consists of the Plenipotentiary Conference, Administrative Conferences, the Administrative Council of 43 members, and of 5 permanent organs (the General Secretariat, the International Frequency Registration Board, and 2 international consultative committees, one for radio and one for telephone and telegraph and the Telecommunications Development Bureau).

Budget for 1989: Sw.Frs.132,087,000.
166 countries were members in 1991.

Headquarters: Place des Nations, CH-1211 Geneva 20, Switzerland.
Secretary-General: Dr Pekka Tarjanne (Finland).

Further Reading

International Telecommunication Union. *Annual Report.—The International Telecommunication Union Activities: an Executive Summary.* (Annual).—*The International Telecommunication Union: its Aims, Structure and Functioning.* 1990.

WORLD METEOROLOGICAL ORGANIZATION (WMO)

Origin. A Conference of Directors of the International Meteorological Organization (set up in 1873), meeting in Washington in 1947, adopted a Convention creating the World Meteorological Organization. The WMO Convention became effective on 23 March 1950, and WMO was formally established on 19 March 1951, when the first session of its Congress was convened in Paris. An agreement to bring WMO into relationship with the United Nations was approved by this Congress and came into force on 21 Dec. 1951 with its approval by the General Assembly of the United Nations.

Functions. (1) To facilitate world-wide co-operation in the establishment of networks of stations for the making of meteorological observations as well as hydrological or other geophysical observations related to meteorology, and to promote the establishment and maintenance of meteorological centres charged with the provision of meteorological and related services; (2) to promote the establishment and maintenance of systems for the rapid exchange of meteorological and related information; (3) to promote standardization of meteorological and related observations and to ensure the uniform publication of observations and statistics; (4) to further the application of meteorology to aviation, shipping, water problems, agriculture and other human activities; (5) to promote activities in operational hydrology and to further close co-operation between meteorological and hydrological services; and (6) to encourage research and training in meteorology and, as appropriate, to assist in co-ordinating the international aspects of such research and training.

Organization. WMO is an inter-governmental organization of 155 member states and 5 member territories responsible for the operation of their own meteorological services. Constituent bodies of WMO are the World Meteorological Congress which meets every 4 years, the executive council composed of 36 members elected in their personal capacity and including the President and 3 Vice-Presidents of the Organization, 6 regional associations of members and 8 technical commissions established by the Congress. A permanent secretariat is maintained in Geneva.
Budget for 1992–93: Sw.Frs.236·1m.

Headquarters: Case postale No. 2300, CH-1211, Geneva 2, Switzerland.
Secretary-General: G. O. P. Obasi (Nigeria).

Publications. WMO Bulletin. 1952 ff.—*Meteorological Services of the World.* 1985. *—Publications of the World Meteorological Organization, 1951–1986.*

INTERNATIONAL MARITIME ORGANIZATION (IMO)

Origin. The International Maritime Organization, until 1982 known as Inter-Governmental Maritime Consultative Organization (IMCO), was established as a specialized agency of the UN by a convention drawn up at the UN Maritime Conference held at Geneva in Feb./March 1948. The Convention became effective on 17 March 1958 when it had been ratified by 21 countries, including 7 with at least 1m. gross tons of shipping each. The International Maritime Organization started operations in Jan. 1959.

Functions. To facilitate co-operation among governments on technical matters affecting merchant shipping, especially concerning safety at sea; to prevent and control marine pollution caused by ships; to facilitate international maritime traffic. The International Maritime Organization is responsible for convening international maritime conferences and for drafting international maritime conventions. It also provides technical assistance to countries wishing to develop their maritime activities.

Organization. The International Maritime Organization had 135 members (and 2 associate members) in 1991. The Assembly, composed of all member states, normally meets every 2 years. The Council of 32 member states acts as governing body between Assembly sessions. The Maritime Safety Committee deals with all technical questions relating to maritime safety. It has established several sub-committees to deal with specific problems and like the Marine Environment Protection Committee, Legal Committee, Facilitation Committee and Committee on Technical Co-operation is open to all International Maritime Organization members. The Secretariat is composed of international civil servants.
  The International Maritime Organization is depositary authority for the International Convention for the Safety of Life at Sea, 1960, and the Regulations for Preventing Collisions at Sea, 1948 and 1960; the International Convention for the Prevention of Pollution of the Sea by Oil, 1954, as amended in 1962 and 1969; the Convention on Facilitation of International Maritime Traffic, 1965; the International Convention on Load Lines, 1966; the International Convention on Tonnage Measurement of Ships, 1969; the International Convention relating to Intervention on the High Seas in cases of Oil Pollution Casualties, 1969; the International Convention on Civil Liability for Oil Pollution Damage, 1969; Convention on International Compensation Fund for Oil Pollution Damage, 1971; Special Trade Passenger Ships Agreement, 1971; Convention on International Regulations for Preventing Collisions at Sea, 1972; the International Convention for Safe Containers, 1972; the International Convention on Prevention of Pollution from Ships,

1973 as modified by the Protocol of 1978; the International Convention for the Safety of Life at Sea, 1974; Athens Convention relating to the Carriage of Passengers and their Luggage by Sea, 1974; Convention on the International Maritime Satellite Organization, 1976; Convention on Limitation of Maritime Claims, 1976; Torremolinos International Convention for the Safety of Fishing Vessels, 1977; International Convention on Standards of Training, Certification and Watchkeeping for Seafarers, 1978; International Convention on Maritime Search and Rescue, 1979; International Convention on Sabotage, 1979; Convention for the Suppression of Unlawful Acts Against the Safety of Maritime Navigation, 1988; International Convention on Salvage, 1989; International Convention on Oil Pollution Preparedness, Response and Co-operation, 1990.

Headquarters: 4 Albert Embankment, London SE1 7SR.
Secretary-General: William O'Neil (Canada).
IMO News

GENERAL AGREEMENT ON TARIFFS AND TRADE (GATT)

Origin. The General Agreement on Tariffs and Trade was negotiated in 1947 and entered into force on 1 Jan. 1948. Its 23 original signatories were members of a Preparatory Committee appointed by the UN Economic and Social Council to draft the charter for a proposed International Trade Organization. Since this charter was never ratified, the General Agreement, intended as an interim arrangement, has instead remained as the only international instrument laying down trade rules accepted by countries responsible for nearly 90% of the world's trade. In Dec. 1991 there were 103 contracting parties and a further 29 countries applying GATT rules on a *de facto* basis.

Functions. GATT functions both as a multilateral treaty that lays down a common code of conduct in international trade and trade relations and as a forum for negotiation and consultation to overcome trade problems and reduce trade barriers. Key provisions of the Agreement guarantee most-favoured-nation treatment (exceptions being granted to customs unions and free trade areas, and for certain preferences in favour of developing countries); require that protection be given to domestic industry only through tariffs (apart from specified exceptions); provide for negotiations to reduce tariffs (which are then 'bound' against subsequent increase) and other trade distortions; and lay down principles (particularly in Part IV of the Agreement, added in 1965) to assist the trade of developing countries. The Agreement also provides for consultation on, and settlement of, disputes, for 'waivers' (the grant of authorization, when warranted, to derogate from specific GATT obligations) and for emergency action in defined circumstances.

7 'rounds' of multilateral trade negotiations have been completed in GATT, the last of which, the Tokyo Round, was completed in 1979.

Ninety-nine countries participated in the Tokyo Round. In Nov. 1979, the negotiations were concluded with agreements covering: An improved legal framework for the conduct of world trade (which includes recognition of tariff and nontariff treatment in favour of and among developing countries as a permanent legal feature of the world trading system); non-tariff measures (subsidies and countervailing duties; technical barriers to trade; government procurement; customs valuation; import licensing procedures; and a revision of the 1967 GATT anti-dumping code); bovine meat; dairy products; tropical products; and an agreement on free trade in civil aircraft. The agreements contain provisions for special and more favourable treatment for developing countries.

Participating countries also agreed to reduce tariffs on thousands of industrial and agricultural products, for the most part over a period of 7 years ending on 1 Jan. 1987. As a result of these concessions, industrialized countries reduced the average level of their import duties on manufactures by about 34%, a cut comparable to that achieved in the Kennedy Round.

The agreements providing an improved framework for the conduct of world trade took effect in Nov. 1979. The other agreements took effect on 1 Jan. 1980, except for those covering government procurement and customs valuation, which took effect on 1 Jan. 1981, and the concessions on tropical products which began as early as 1977. Committees were established to supervise implementation of each of the Tokyo Round agreements.

On 20 Sept. 1986, agreement was reached to launch the Uruguay Round of multi-lateral trade negotiations. In Dec. 1991 there were 108 states participating in the negotiations.

The Declaration is divided into two sections. The first covers negotiations on trade in goods. Its objectives are to bring about further liberalization and expansion of world trade; to strengthen the role of GATT and improve the multilateral trading system; to increase the responsiveness of GATT to the evolving international economic environment; and to encourage co-operation in strengthening the inter-relationship between trade and other economic policies affecting growth and development.

In the area of trade in goods, Ministers committed themselves to a 'standstill' on new trade measures inconsistent with their GATT obligations and to a 'rollback' programme aimed at phasing out existing inconsistent measures. Negotiations are being undertaken in the following areas: Tariffs, non-tariff measures, tropical products, natural resource-based products, textiles and clothing, agriculture, subsidies, safeguards, trade-related aspects of intellectual property rights, including trade in counterfeit goods, and trade-related investment measures. Participants are review-ing certain GATT Articles, attempting to improve and strengthen the dispute settle-ment procedure, and negotiating to improve, clarify or expand the agreements reached during the Tokyo Round. One part of the negotiation is devoted to the func-tioning of the GATT system itself. The second part of the Declaration covers a negotiation on trade in services.

The first three years of the Uruguay Round were marked by intensive activity, both in Geneva, where the negotiations take place, and in the capitals of the partici-pating countries. During this time the groups responsible for the negotiations held around 300 formal meetings and around 1,500 negotiating proposals and working papers were tabled.

In Dec. 1988, ministers met in Montreal for the Mid-term Review meeting of the Trade Negotiations Committee. Agreements on the future conduct of the Round were reached in 11 of the 15 negotiating areas. At the same time, ministers were able to agree a package of concessions on tropical products covering trade worth around US$20,000m.; a series of measures to streamline the disputes settlement system and a new trade policy review mechanism under which the trade policies of individual GATT contracting countries are subject to regular assessment. Each of these was implemented provisionally in 1989. In April 1989, a Trade Negotiations Committee meeting in Geneva succeeded in securing Mid-term agreements on the remaining 4 negotiating areas: Agriculture (covering both short-term commitments and long-term objectives), safeguards, textiles and clothing and intellectual prop-erty. Meetings of the Round held in Dec. 1990, in Brussels, were unable to reach agreement owing to differences over the EC's Common Agricultural Policy. Talks were resumed in Feb. 1991.

To assist the trade of developing countries, GATT established in 1964 the *Inter-national Trade Centre* (since 1968 operated jointly with the UN, the latter acting through the UN Conference on Trade and Development) to provide information and training on export markets and marketing techniques. Other GATT action in favour of developing countries includes training courses on trade policy questions, organi-zation of seminars and briefings, and technical assistance to delegations in the form of data and background documentation.

Budget for 1992: Sw. Frs. 85,973,327.

Headquarters: Centre William Rappard, 154 rue de Lausanne, 1211 Geneva 21, Switzerland.

Director-General: Arthur Dunkel (Switzerland).

Further Reading

Publications. Basic Instruments and Selected Documents. 4 vols. and 34 supplements 1952–87.—*International Trade* [i.e., annual review], 1952 ff. Annually from 1953.—*Review of*

Development in the Trading System. Semi-annually from 1987.—*GATT, What It Is, What It Does.*—*GATT Activities*, 1960 ff. Annually from 1972.—*GATT Focus*. From Feb. 1981 (10 issues a year).—*News of the Uruguay Round*. Monthly from March 1987.—*GATT Studies in International Trade*. 1971 ff. (irregular series).—*The Tokyo Round of Multilateral Trade Negotiations*. Report of the Director-General, 2 vols., 1979.—*Textile and Clothing in the World Economy*, 1984.—*The World Markets for Dairy Products*. Annually from 1981.—*The International Markets for Meat*. Annually from 1981.—*Trade in Natural Resource Products: Aluminium* (1987), *Lead* (1987), *Zinc* (1988), *Nickel* (1990).

Hudec, R. E., *The GATT Legal System and World Trade Diplomacy*. New York, 1975
Long, O., *Law and its Limitations in the GATT Multilateral Trade System*. Dordrecht, 1985

WORLD INTELLECTUAL PROPERTY ORGANIZATION (WIPO)

Origin. The Convention establishing WIPO was signed at Stockholm in 1967 by 51 countries, and entered into force in April 1970. In Dec. 1974 WIPO became a specialized agency of the UN. *Inter alia* it took over the functions of the United International Bureaux for the Protection of Intellectual Property, also known as BIRPI (the French acronym of that name), which were established in 1893 to administer the affairs of the two principal international intellectual property treaties – the Paris Convention for the Protection of Industrial Property of 1883 and the Berne Convention for the Protection of Literary and Artistic Works of 1886.

Functions. WIPO is responsible for the promotion of the protection of intellectual property throughout the world. Intellectual property comprises two main branches: Industrial property (chiefly in inventions, trademarks and industrial designs) and copyright and neighbouring rights (chiefly in literary, musical, artistic, photographic and audiovisual works). WIPO administers various international treaties, of which the most important are the Paris Convention for the Protection of Industrial Property and the Berne Convention for the Protection of Literary and Artistic Works. WIPO carries out a substantial programme of activities to promote creative intellectual activity, protection of intellectual property, international co-operation and the transfer of technology, especially to and among developing countries.

Membership of WIPO is open to any State which is a member of at least one of the Unions created by the Paris Convention and the Berne Convention and to other States which are members of the organizations of the United Nations system, are party to the Statute of the International Court of Justice, or are invited to join by the General Assembly of WIPO. Membership of the Unions is open to any State. The number of member states was 127 in 1991; in addition, 9 States are party to treaties administered by WIPO but have not yet become members of WIPO.

Organization. The bodies of WIPO are: The *General Assembly* consisting of all member states of WIPO which are members of any of the Unions. Among its other functions, the General Assembly appoints and gives instructions to the Director General, reviews and approves his reports and adopts the biennial budget of expenses common to the Unions. The *Conference,* consisting of all States members of WIPO whether or not they are members of any of the Unions. Among its functions, the Conference adopts its biennial budget and establishes the biennial programme of legal-technical assistance. The *Co-ordination Committee,* consisting of the States members of WIPO which are members of the Executive Committees of the Paris or Berne Unions.

In addition, the Paris and Berne Unions have Assemblies and Executive Committees, with functions similar to those of the WIPO bodies in respect of the biennial budgets and programmes of the Unions.

The *WIPO Permanent Committees for Development Co-operation Related to Industrial Property* and *Related to Copyright and Neighbouring Rights* plan and review activities in the said fields; the *WIPO Permanent Committee on Industrial Property Information* is responsible for intergovernmental co-operation in industrial property documentation and information matters such as the standardization and exchange of patent documents.

The budget for 1990–91 was Sw. Fr. 155,399m.

WIPO has an international staff of 400. Its working languages are Arabic, English, French, Russian and Spanish.

Headquarters: 34, chemin des Colombettes, 1211 Geneva 20, Switzerland.
Director-General: Dr Arpad Bogsch (USA).

Further Reading

Periodicals. Industrial Property (monthly, in English and French; quarterly, in Spanish).—*Copyright* (monthly, in English and French; quarterly, in Spanish).—*Les Marques internationales* (monthly, in French).—*International Designs Bulletin* (monthly, in English and French)—*Newsletter* (irregular, in Arabic, English, French, Portuguese, Russian and Spanish)—*PCT Gazette* (fortnightly, in English and French)—*Les appellations d'origine* (irregular)—*Intellectual Property in Asia and the Pacific* (quarterly). *Collection of Industrial Property and Copyright Laws and Treaties.*

INTERNATIONAL FUND FOR AGRICULTURAL DEVELOPMENT (IFAD)

The establishment of IFAD was one of the major actions proposed by the 1974 World Food Conference. The agreement for IFAD entered into force on 30 Nov. 1977, and the agency began its operations the following month. By the end of 1991 the Fund had invested US$3·4m. in financing 313 projects in 94 developing countries. IFAD's purpose is to mobilise additional funds for agricultural and rural development in developing countries through projects and programmes directly benefiting the poorest rural populations while preserving their natural resource base. In line with the Fund's focus on the rural poor, its resources are being made available mainly in highly concessional loans as well as grants.

Organization. The highest body is the Governing Council, on which all 145 member countries are represented. Operations are overseen by an 18-member Executive Board (with 17 alternate members), which is responsible to the Governing Council. The President of IFAD is chair of the Executive Board.

President: Idriss Jazairy (Algeria).
Headquarters: 107 Via del Serafico, Rome, 00142, Italy.

THE COMMONWEALTH

The Commonwealth is a free association of sovereign independent states, numbering 50 at the beginning of 1992. There is no charter, treaty or constitution; the association is expressed in co-operation, consultation and mutual assistance for which the Commonwealth Secretariat is the central co-ordinating body.

The Commonwealth was first defined by the Imperial Conference of 1926 as a group of 'autonomous Communities within the British Empire, equal in status, in no way subordinate one to another in any aspect of their domestic or external affairs, though united by a common allegiance to the Crown, and freely associated as members of the British Commonwealth of Nations'. The basis of the association changed from one owing allegiance to a common Crown, and the modern Commonwealth was born in 1949 when the member countries accepted India's intention of becoming a republic at the same time continuing 'her full membership of the Commonwealth of Nations and her acceptance of the King as the symbol of the free association of its independent member nations and as such the Head of the Commonwealth'. There were (1992) 16 Queen's realms, 29 republics, and 5 indigenous monarchies in the Commonwealth. All acknowledge the Queen symbolically as Head of the Commonwealth.

The Queen's legal title rests on the statute of 12 and 13 Will. III, c. 3, by which the succession to the Crown of Great Britain and Ireland was settled on the Princess Sophia of Hanover and the 'heirs of her body being Protestants'. By proclamation of 17 July 1917 the royal family became known as the House and Family of Windsor. On 8 Feb. 1960 the Queen issued a declaration varying her confirmatory declaration of 9 April 1952 to the effect that while the Queen and her children should continue to be known as the House of Windsor, her descendants, other than descendants entitled to the style of Royal Highness and the title of Prince or Princess, and female descendants who marry and their descendants should bear the name of Mountbatten-Windsor. The Royal Style and Titles of Queen Elizabeth are: In *Antigua and Barbuda* 'Elizabeth the Second, by the Grace of God, Queen of Antigua and Barbuda and of Her other Realms and Territories, Head of the Commonwealth'. In *Australia*: 'Elizabeth the Second, by the Grace of God Queen of Australia and Her other Realms and Territories, Head of the Commonwealth'. In the *Bahamas*: 'Elizabeth the Second, by the Grace of God, Queen of the Commonwealth of the Bahamas and of Her other Realms and Territories, Head of the Commonwealth'. In *Barbados*: 'Elizabeth the Second, by the Grace of God, Queen of Barbados and of Her other Realms and Territories, Head of the Commonwealth'. In *Belize*: 'Elizabeth the Second, by the Grace of God, Queen of Belize and of Her Other Realms and Territories, Head of the Commonwealth'. In *Canada*: 'Elizabeth the Second, by the Grace of God of the United Kingdom, Canada and Her other Realms and Territories Queen, Head of the Commonwealth, Defender of the Faith'. In *Grenada*: 'Elizabeth the Second, by the Grace of God, Queen of the United Kingdom of Great Britain and Northern Ireland and of Grenada and Her other Realms and Territories, Head of the Commonwealth'. In *Jamaica*: 'Elizabeth the Second, by the Grace of God of Jamaica and of Her other Realms and Territories Queen, Head of the Commonwealth'. In *New Zealand*: 'Elizabeth the Second, by the Grace of God Queen of New Zealand and Her Other Realms and Territories, Head of the Commonwealth, Defender of the Faith'. In *Papua New Guinea*: 'Elizabeth the Second, Queen of Papua New Guinea and Her other Realms and Territories, Head of the Commonwealth'. In *Saint Christopher and Nevis:* 'Elizabeth the Second, by the Grace of God, Queen of Saint Christopher and Nevis and Her other Realms and Territories, Head of the Commonwealth'. In *Saint Lucia*: 'Elizabeth the Second, by the Grace of God, Queen of Saint Lucia and of Her other Realms and Territories, Head of Commonwealth'. In *Saint Vincent and the Grenadines*: 'Elizabeth the Second, by the Grace of God, Queen of Saint Vincent and the Grenadines and of Her other Realms and Territories, Head of the Commonwealth'. In *Solomon Islands*: 'Elizabeth the Second by the Grace of God Queen of Solomon Islands and of Her other Realms and Territories, Head of the Commonwealth'. In *Tuvalu*: 'Elizabeth the Second by the Grace of God Queen of Tuvalu and of Her other Realms and Territories, Head of the Commonwealth'. In the *United Kingdom*: 'Elizabeth the Second, by the Grace of God of the United Kingdom of Great Britain and Northern Ireland and of Her other Realms and Territories Queen, Head of the Commonwealth, Defender of the Faith'.

A number of territories, formerly under British jurisdiction or mandate did not join the Commonwealth: Egypt, Iraq, Transjordan, Burma, Palestine, Sudan, British Somaliland, South Cameroons, and Aden. 3 countries, Ireland in 1948, the Republic of South Africa in 1961 and Pakistan in 1972, have left the Commonwealth. Fiji's membership lapsed with the emergence of its Republic in 1987. Pakistan was re-admitted to the Commonwealth on 1 Oct. 1989.

Nauru and Tuvalu are special members, with the right to participate in all functional Commonwealth meetings and activities but not to attend meetings of Commonwealth Heads of Government.

Member States. The following are the member countries, with their dates of independence, and, where appropriate, the date on which they became republics: *United Kingdom*; *Canada* 1 July 1867[1]; *Australia* 1 Jan. 1901[1]; *New Zealand* 26 Sept. 1907[1]; *India* 15 Aug. 1947 (Republic on 26 Jan. 1950); *Sri Lanka* 4 Feb. 1948 (Republic on 22 May 1972); *Ghana* 6 March 1957 (Republic on 1 July 1960); *Malaysia* 31 Aug. 1957 as Federation of Malaya, 16 Sept. 1963 as Federation of Malaysia; *Cyprus* 16 Aug. 1960 (Republic on independence; joined Commonwealth on 13 March 1961); *Nigeria* 1 Oct. 1960 (Republic on 1 Oct. 1963); *Sierra Leone* 27 April 1961 (Republic on 19 April 1971); *Tanzania*–Tanganyika 9 Dec. 1961 (Republic on 9 Dec. 1962), Zanzibar 10 Dec. 1963 (Republic on 12 Jan. 1964), United Republic of Tanganyika and Zanzibar 26 April 1964; renamed United Republic of Tanzania

29 Oct. 1964; *Western Samoa* 1 Jan. 1962 (joined Commonwealth on 28 Aug. 1970); *Jamaica* 6 Aug. 1962; *Trinidad and Tobago* 31 Aug. 1962 (Republic on 1 Aug. 1976); *Uganda* 9 Oct. 1962 (Republic 8 Sept. 1967, second republic 25 Jan. 1971); *Kenya* 12 Dec. 1963 (Republic on 12 Dec. 1964); *Malawi* 6 July 1964 (Republic on 6 July 1966); *Malta* 21 Sept. 1964 (Republic on 13 Dec. 1974); *Zambia* 24 Oct. 1964 (Republic on independence); *The Gambia* 18 Feb. 1965 (Republic on 24 April 1970); *Maldives* 26 July 1965 (Republic on independence, joined Commonwealth on 9 July 1982); *Singapore* 16 Sept. 1963 as a state in the Federation of Malaysia, 9 Aug. 1965 as an independent state and republic not part of Malaysia; *Guyana* 26 May 1966 (Republic on 23 Feb. 1970); *Botswana* 30 Sept. 1966 (Republic on independence); *Lesotho* 4 Oct. 1966; *Barbados* 30 Nov. 1966; *Nauru* [2] 31 Jan. 1968 (Republic on independence); *Mauritius* 12 March 1968 (Republic on 12 March 1992); *Swaziland* 6 Sept. 1968; *Tonga* [3] 4 June 1970; *Bangladesh* seceded from Pakistan as Republic 16 Dec. 1971, recognized by United Kingdom 4 Feb. 1972 (joined Commonwealth on 18 April 1972); *Bahamas* 10 July 1973; *Grenada* 7 Feb. 1974; *Papua New Guinea* 16 Sept. 1975; *Seychelles* 29 June 1976 (Republic on independence); *Solomon Islands* 7 July 1978; *Tuvalu* 1 Oct. 1978; *Dominica* 3 Nov. 1978 (Republic on independence); *Saint Lucia* 22 Feb. 1979; *Kiribati* 12 July 1979 (Republic on independence); *Saint Vincent and the Grenadines* 27 Oct. 1979; *Zimbabwe* 18 April 1980 (Republic on independence); *Vanuatu* 30 July 1980 (Republic on independence); *Belize* 21 Sept. 1981; *Antigua* and *Barbuda* 1 Nov. 1981; *Saint Christopher and Nevis* 19 Sept. 1983; *Brunei* [2] 1 Jan 1984; *Pakistan* 15 Aug. 1947 (Republic on 23 March 1956); left Commonwealth 30 Jan. 1972, re-admitted 1 Oct. 1989; *Namibia* 21 March 1990 (Republic on independence).

[1] These are the effective dates of independence, given legal effect by the Statute of Westminster 1931.

[2] Nauru had been first a Mandate, then a Trust territory.

[3] Brunei and Tonga had been sovereign states in treaty relationship with the UK, whereby the UK was responsible for the conduct of external affairs and had a consultative responsibility for defence.

Dependent Territories and Associated States. There are 15 British dependent territories, 7 Australian external territories, 2 New Zealand dependent territories and 2 New Zealand associated states. A dependent territory is a territory belonging by settlement, conquest or annexation to the British, Australian or New Zealand Crown.

United Kingdom dependent territories administered through the Foreign and Commonwealth Office comprise, in the Far East: Hong Kong; in the Indian Ocean: British Indian Ocean Territory; in the Mediterranean: Gibraltar; in the Atlantic Ocean: Bermuda, Falkland Islands, South Georgia and the South Sandwich Islands, British Antarctic Territory, St Helena, St Helena Dependencies (Ascension and Tristan da Cunha); in the Caribbean: Montserrat, British Virgin Islands, Cayman Islands, Turks and Caicos Islands, Anguilla; in the Western Pacific: Pitcairn Group of Islands. The Australian external territories are: Coral Sea Islands Territory, Cocos (Keeling) Islands, Christmas Island, Heard Island and McDonald Islands, Norfolk Island, Australian Antarctic Territory and the Territory of Ashmore and Cartier Islands. The New Zealand dependent territories are: Tokelau and Ross Dependency. The New Zealand associated states are: Cook Islands and Niue.

While constitutional responsibility to Parliament for the government of the British dependent territories rests with the Secretary of State for Foreign and Commonwealth Affairs, the administration of the territories is carried out by the Governments of the territories themselves.

British Government Department. With effect from 17 Oct. 1968, the Secretary of State for Foreign and Commonwealth Affairs is responsible for the conduct of relations with members of the Commonwealth as well as with foreign countries, and for the administration of British dependent territories.

Commonwealth Secretariat. The Commonwealth Secretariat is an international body at the service of all 50 member countries. It provides the central organization for joint consultation and co-operation in many fields. It was established in 1965 by Commonwealth Heads of Government and has observer status at the UN General Assembly.

The Secretariat disseminates information on matters of common concern, organizes and services meetings and conferences, co-ordinates many Commonwealth activities, and provides expert technical assistance for economic and social development through the multilateral Commonwealth Fund for Technical Cooperation. The Secretariat is organized in divisions and sections which correspond to its main areas of operation: International affairs, economic affairs, food production and rural development, youth, education, information, applied studies in government, science and technology, law and health. Within this structure the Secretariat organizes the biennial meetings of Commonwealth Heads of Government, annual meetings of Finance Ministers of member countries, and regular meetings of Ministers of Education, Law, Health, and others as appropriate.

To emphasize the multilateral nature of the association, meetings are held in different cities and regions within the Commonwealth. Heads of Government decided that the Secretariat should work from London as it has the widest range of communications of any Commonwealth city, as well as the largest assembly of diplomatic missions.

The Commonwealth Secretary-General, who has access to Heads of Government, is the head of the Secretariat which is staffed by officers from member countries and financed by contributions from member governments.

Commonwealth Day is observed throughout the Commonwealth on the second Monday in March.

Flag: Royal blue with the emblem of a globe surrounded by 50 rays, all in gold.

Headquarters: Marlborough House, Pall Mall, London, SW1Y 5HX.
Secretary-General: Emeka Anyaoku (Nigeria).

Further Reading

The Commonwealth Year-Book, HMSO, Annual
The Cambridge History of the British Empire. 8 vols. CUP, 1929 ff.
Austin, D., *The Commonwealth and Britain.* London, 1988
Chadwick, J., *The Unofficial Commonwealth.* London, 1982
Dale, W., *The Modern Commonwealth.* London, 1983
Garner, J., *The Commonwealth Office, 1925–1968.* London, 1978
Hall, H. D., *Commonwealth: A History of the British Commonwealth.* London and New York, 1971
Judd, D. and Slinn, P., *The Evolution of the Modern Commonwealth.* London, 1982
Keeton, G. W. (ed.) *The British Commonwealth: Its Laws and Constitutions.* 9 vols. London, 1951 ff.
Mansergh, N., *The Commonwealth Experience.* 2 vols. London, 1982
McIntyre, W. D., *The Significance of the Commonwealth, 1965–90.* London, 1991
Maxwell, W. H. and L. F., *A Legal Bibliography of the British Commonwealth of Nations.* 2nd ed. London, 1956
Moore, R. J., *Making the New Commonwealth.* Oxford, 1987
Papadopoulos, A. N., *Multilateral Diplomacy within the Commonwealth: A Decade of Expansion.* The Hague, 1982
Smith, A. and Sanger, C., *Stitches in Time: The Commonwealth in World Politics.* New York, 1983

WORLD COUNCIL OF CHURCHES

The World Council of Churches was formally constituted on 23 Aug. 1948, at Amsterdam, by an assembly representing 147 churches from 44 countries. By 1991 the member churches numbered over 300, from more than 100 countries.

The basis of membership (1975) states: 'The World Council of Churches is a fellowship of Churches which confess the Lord Jesus Christ as God and Saviour according to the Scriptures and therefore seek to fulfil together their common calling to the glory of the one God, Father, Son and Holy Spirit.' Membership is open to Churches which express their agreement with this basis and satisfy such criteria as the Assembly or Central Committee may prescribe. Today 320 Churches of Protestant, Anglican, Orthodox, Old Catholic and Pentecostal confessions belong to this fellowship.

The World Council was founded by the coming together of several diverse Christian movements. These included the overseas mission groups gathered from 1921 in the International Missionary Council, the Faith and Order Movement founded by American Episcopal Bishop Charles Brent, and the Life and Work Movement led by Swedish Lutheran Archbishop Nathan Söderblom.

On 13 May 1938 at Utrecht a provisional committee was appointed to prepare for the formation of a World Council of Churches. It was under the chairmanship of William Temple, then Archbishop of York.

Assembly. The governing body of the World Council, consisting of delegates specially appointed by the member Churches. It meets every 7 or 8 years to frame policy and to consider some main theme. The Assembly has no legislative powers and depends for the implementation of its decisions upon the action of the member Churches. Assemblies have been held in Amsterdam (1948), Evanston (1954), New Delhi (1961), Uppsala (1968), Nairobi (1975), Vancouver (1983) and Canberra (1991). In between assemblies, a 150-member Central Committee meets annually to carry out the assembly mandate, with a smaller 22-member Executive Committee meeting twice a year.

Presidents: Prof. Anne-Marie Aagaard (Denmark), Bishop Vinton Anderson (USA), Bishop Leslie Boseto (Solomon Islands), Ms Priyanka Mendis (Sri Lanka), His Beatitude Parthenios of Alexandria (Egypt), Rev. Dr Eunice Santana (Puerto Rico), His Holiness Pope Shenouda (Egypt), Dr Aaron Tolen (Cameroon).

WCC programmes are organized from headquarters in Geneva, Switzerland, by a staff of 290 and a range of supervisory committees drawn from member churches. The 4 programme units are:

(i) Unity and Renewal – bringing together the concern for the Search for visible Unity, the Search for inclusive Community; Renewal through Worship and Spirituality; Ecumenical Formation and Theological Education including the work of the Ecumenical Institute Bossey; theological reflection and inter-faith dialogue; reflection on justice, peace and the integrity of creation.

(ii) Mission, Education and Witness – focusing on unity in Mission, Mission to challenge unjust structures, Gospel and Culture, Evangelism, Healing and Transformation; Education for all God's people; Education in Mission; the theological significance of religions.

(iii) Justice, Peace and Creation – is the base for concerns relating to Justice, Peace and the integrity of Creation (JPIC) as a conciliar process; for theological, ethical, socio-economic and ecological analysis; economic justice; Peace Ministries and Conflict Resolution; Human Rights; issues of Indigenous Peoples and land rights; continuing emphasis on combating Racism; the Churches' response to International Affairs; concerns and perspectives of Women; concerns and perspectives of Youth; Education for justice, peace and creation; Communication as power.

(iv) Sharing and Service – is concerned with the service of human need, solidarity by sharing of resources, comprehensive diakonia, development of human resources; new models for sharing and service; biblical and theological analysis in partnership with those concerned with mission and diakonia.

The General Secretariat includes Offices for Church and Ecumenical Relations, Inter-religious Relations, Programme Co-ordination, together with the Department of Communication and the Office of Management and Finance.

Since 1975 the WCC has held several major world conferences on such diverse themes as 'Faith, Science and the Future', 'Your Kingdom Come', 'Family Power and Social Change', 'Strategies for Churches Combating Racism in the 1980's', 'The Community of Women and Men in the Church', 'Giving an Account of the Hope that is in Us', 'Called to be Neighbours', 'Your Will be Done—Mission in

Christ's Way' and 'Justice, Peace and the Integrity of Creation'—World Convocation 1990.

Officers of the Central and Executive Committees: *Moderator:* Archbishop Aram Keshishian (Lebanon). *Vice-moderators:* Ephorus Dr S. A. E. Nababan (Indonesia), Pastor Nélida Ritchie (Argentina). *General Secretary:* The Rev. Dr Emilio Castro.

Office: PO Box 2100, 150 route de Ferney, 1211 Geneva 2, Switzerland.

Further Reading

Official Reports: The First [. . . *etc.*] *Assembly* (London, 1948, 1955, 1962, Geneva, 1968, 1975, 1983, 1991)
Dictionary of the Ecumenical Movement. Geneva, 1991
Directory of Christian Councils. 1985
Handbook of Member Churches of the WCC. Geneva, 1985
The Ecumenical Review. Quarterly
Nairobi to Vancouver, 1975–1983. Geneva, 1983
One World. 10 a year.
Vancouver to Canberra, 1983–1990. Geneva, 1990
Official Reports of the Faith and Order Conferences at Lausanne 1927, Edinburgh 1937, Lund 1952, Montreal 1963; Meeting of Faith and Order Commission, Louvain 1972, Accra 1974, Bangalore 1978, Lima 1982, Stavanger 1985, Budapest, 1989
Reports of Conferences of WCC Commission on World Mission and Evangelism, Mexico City 1963, Bangkok 1973, Melbourne 1980, San Antonio 1990
Minutes of the WCC Central Committee. Geneva, 1949 to date
Potter, P., *Life in all its Fullness.* Geneva, 1981
Van Elderen, M., *And So Set Up Signs.* Geneva, 1988.—*Introducing the World Council of Churches.* Geneva, 1990
Vermaat, J. A. A., *The World Council of Churches and Politics.* New York, 1989
Visser 't Hooft, W. A., *The Genesis and Formation of the World Council of Churches.* Geneva, 1982

BANK FOR INTERNATIONAL SETTLEMENTS

Founded in 1930,the BIS is the 'central banks' bank'. Its assets are owned by 29 central banks, and in 1991 it held US$70,00m. on behalf of 80 central banks.

In 1988 it defined standard minimum levels of capital adequacy for banks: in 1990 a capital-to-asset ratio of 7·25%, rising to 8% in 1992.

Headquarters: Basel.
Chairman: Bengt Dennis.

INTERNATIONAL TRADE UNIONISM

There are three main international trade union confederations *(i)* the International Confederation of Free Trade Unions (ICFTU) which has in membership most of the national trade union confederations in the Western industrialized countries, unions in Czechoslovakia and Poland and national organizations in Asia, Africa, and Latin America; *(ii)* the World Federation of Trade Unions (WFTU) which until 1989 drew its support mainly from Eastern Europe, but which now has one affiliated organization in Poland and one in the USSR, an affiliate in France and affiliates in Cuba and other developing countries; and *(iii)* the World Confederation of Labour (WCL) which has affiliates in Western Europe, Latin America and a small number of African and Asian countries. In addition, national trade unions are frequently members of international trade union federations, set up to protect the interests of working people in particular industries or trades, which are associated with the international confederations. The International Trade Secretariats (ITS) are associated with the ICFTU; Trade Union Internationals (TUI) with the WFTU; and the International Trade Federations (ITF) with the WCL.

History. The international trade union structure between 1945 and 1989 was shaped mainly by political factors. In 1945 the WFTU was set up with world-wide membership. Attempts by trade unions in Eastern Europe to turn the WFTU into an organization voicing unquestioning support for the policies of the USSR led most of the affiliates of the Western European countries to break away from the WFTU and to form the ICFTU in 1949.

EUROPEAN TRADE UNION CONFEDERATION. In Feb. 1973 the European Trade Union Confederation was formed by trade unionists in 15 Western European countries to deal with questions of interest to European working people arising inside and outside the EC. All the founding organizations were ICFTU affiliates but subsequently they accepted into membership European WCL affiliates, the Irish Congress of Trade Unions and the Italian Communist and Socialist trade union centre (CGIL) and other national organizations. The ETUC Congress meets every 3 years and the Executive Committee 5 times a year. The membership was (June 1990) about 45m. from 39 centres in 21 countries.

   General Secretary: Mathias Hinterscheid.
   Headquarters: Rue Montagne aux Herbes Potagères 37, 1000 Brussels.

INTERNATIONAL   CONFEDERATION   OF   FREE   TRADE UNIONS. The first congress of ICFTU was held in London in Dec. 1949. The constitution as amended provides for co-operation with the United Nations and the International Labour Organization and for regional organizations to promote free trade unionism, especially in less-developed countries.

Organization. The Congress meets every 4 years. It elects the Executive Board of 37 members nominated on an area basis for a 4-year period; 1 seat is reserved for a woman nominated by the Women's Committee; the Board meets at least twice a year. Various committees cover policy *vis-à-vis* such problems as those connected with nuclear energy and also the administration of the International Solidarity Fund. There are joint ICFTU–ITS committees for co-ordinating activities.

   Headquarters: 37–41, rue Montagne aux Herbes Potagères, Brussels 1000, Belgium.

   General Secretary: John Vanderveken.

   Regional organizations exist in America, office in Mexico City; Asia, office in New Delhi; and Africa, office in Sierre Leone.

Membership. The ICFTU had in Dec. 1991 151 affiliated organizations in 108 countries, which together represent about 110m. workers. The largest organizations were the American Federation of Labor and Congress of Industrial Organizations (13·7m.), the British Trades Union Congress (8·5m.), the Japanese Confederation of Labour, Rengo (8m.), the German Deutscher Gewerkschaftsbund (7·1m.), the Confederazione Generale Italiana di Lavoro (5m.), the Confederazione Italiana Sindacati Lavoratori (3·1m.), the Swedish Landsorganisationen (2·1m.), the Indian National Trade Union Congress (4·7m.), the Argentinian Confederacion General de Trabajo (6m.), the Czechoslovak CSKOS (6m.) and the Indian Hind Mazdoor Sabha (2·6m.).

   Publications (in 4 languages). *Free Labour World* (fortnightly).

THE WORLD FEDERATION OF TRADE UNIONS. The WFTU formally came into existence on 3 Oct. 1945, representing trade-union organizations in more than 50 countries of the world, both Communist and non-Communist, excluding Federal Republic of Germany and Japan, as well as a number of lesser and colonial territories. Representation from the USA was limited to the Congress of Industrial Organizations, as the American Federation of Labor declined to participate.

   In Jan. 1949 the British, USA and Netherlands trade unions withdrew from WFTU, which had come under complete Communist control; and by June 1951 all non-Communist trade-unions, and the Yugoslav Federation, had left WFTU.

Organization. The Congress meets every 4 years. In between, the General Council, of 134 members (including deputies), is the governing body, meeting (in theory) at least once a year. The Bureau controls the activities of WFTU between meetings of the General Council; it consists of the President, the General Secretary and members from different continents, the total number being decided at each Congress. The Bureau is elected by the General Council. Regional bureaux were instituted in 1990 as a move towards decentralization.

President: I. Zakaria (Sudan).
General Secretary: Aleksandr Zharikov (USSR).

Membership. With the collapse of many Communist-type trade union organizations membership became very fluid after 1990. 105 organizations in 83 countries with a total membership of some 200m. were members in 1991, including the former official unions of the USSR and Poland, and the French Confederation of Labour (CGT).

The headquarters was in Prague, but in Aug. 1991 the Czechoslovak government requested it to move.

Publications. World Trade Union Movement (monthly, in 9 languages); *Trade Union Press* (fortnightly, in 6 languages).

WORLD CONFEDERATION OF LABOUR. The first congress of the International Federation of Christian Trade Unions (IFCTU), as the WCL was then called, met in 1920; but a large proportion of its 3·4m. members were in Italy and Germany, where affiliated unions were suppressed by the Fascist and Nazi régimes, and in 1940 IFCTU went out of existence. It was reconstituted in 1945, and declined to merge with WFTU and, later, with ICFTU. The policy of IFCTU was based on the papal encyclicals *Rerum novarum* (1891) and *Quadragesimo anno* (1931), but in 1968, when the Federation became the WCL, it was broadened to include other concepts. The WCL now has Protestant, Buddhist and Moslem member confederations as well as its mainly Roman Catholic members.

Organization. The WCL is organized on a federative basis which leaves wide discretion to its autonomous constituent unions. Its governing body is the Congress, which meets every 4 years. The Congress appoints (or re-appoints) the Secretary-General at each 4-yearly meeting. The General Council which meets at least once a year, is composed of the members of the Confederal Board (at least 22 members, elected by the Congress) and representatives of national confederations, international trade federations, and trade union organizations where there is no confederation affiliated to the WCL. The Confederal Board is responsible for the general leadership of the WCL, in accordance with the decisions and directives of the Council and Congress. Headquarters: 71 rue Joseph II, Brussels 1040, Belgium.

Secretary-General: Carlos Luís Custer.

There are regional organizations in Latin America (office in Caracas), Africa (office in Banjul, Gambia) and Asia (office in Manila) There is also a liaison centre in Montreal.

Membership. A total membership of 11m. in about 90 countries is claimed. The biggest group is the Confederation of Christian Trade Unions of Belgium (1·2m.).

Publication. Labour Press and Information (11 each year, in 5 languages).

ORGANISATION FOR ECONOMIC CO-OPERATION AND DEVELOPMENT (OECD)

History and Membership. On 30 Sept. 1961 the Organisation for European Economic Co-operation (OEEC), after a history of 13 years (*see* THE STATESMAN'S YEAR-BOOK, 1961, p. 32), was replaced by the Organisation for Economic Co-operation and Development. The change of title marks the Organisation's altered status and functions: With the accession of Canada and USA as full members it ceased to be a purely European body; while at the same time it added development aid to the list of its other activities. The member countries are now Australia, Austria, Belgium, Canada, Denmark, Finland, France, Germany, Greece, Iceland, Ireland, Italy, Japan, Luxembourg, the Netherlands, New Zealand, Norway, Portugal, Spain, Sweden, Switzerland, Turkey, UK and USA. Yugoslavia participates in the Organisation's activities with a special status. The Commission of the European Communities generally takes part in OECD's work.

Objectives. To promote economic and social welfare throughout the OECD area by assisting its member governments in the formulation of policies designed to this end and by co-ordinating these policies; and to stimulate and harmonize its members' efforts in favour of developing countries.

Organs. The supreme body of the Organisation is the Council composed of one representative for each member country. It meets either at Heads of Delegations level (about twice a month) under the Chairmanship of the Secretary-General, or at Ministerial level (usually once a year) under the Chairmanship of a Minister of a country elected annually to assume these functions. Decisions and Recommendations are adopted by mutual agreement of all members of the Council.

The Council is assisted by an Executive Committee composed of 14 members of the Council designated annually by the latter. The major part of the Organisation's work is, however, prepared and carried out in numerous specialized committees, working parties and sub-groups, of which there exist over 200. Thus, the Organisation comprises Committees for Economic Policy; Economic and Development Review; Development Assistance (DAC); Commodities; Trade; Capital Movements and Invisible Transactions; Financial Markets; Fiscal Affairs; Competition Law and Policy; Consumer Policy; Maritime Transport; International Investment and Multinational Enterprises; Tourism; Energy Policy; Industry; Steel; Scientific and Technological Policy; Information, Computer and Communications Policy; Road Transport Research; Education; Manpower and Social Affairs; Environment; Urban Affairs; Control of Chemicals; Agriculture; Fisheries, etc.

In 1990 the Centre for Co-operation with European Economics in Transition (CCEET) was established to act as OECD's point of contact for Central and East European countries seeking guidance in moving towards a market economy.

Four autonomous or semi-autonomous bodies also belong to the Organisation: The International Energy Agency (IEA); the Nuclear Energy Agency (NEA); the Development Centre and the Centre for Educational Research and Innovation (CERI). Each one of these bodies has its own governing committee.

The Council, the committees and the other bodies are serviced by an international Secretariat headed by the Secretary-General of the Organisation.

All member countries have established permanent Delegations to OECD, each headed by an Ambassador.

Chairman of the Council (ministerial): A minister from the country elected (annually) to assume this function.
Chairman of the Council (official level): The Secretary-General.
Secretary-General: Jean-Claude Paye (France).
Deputy Secretaries-General: Robert A. Cornell (USA), Pierre Vinde (Sweden), Makoto Taniguchi (Japan).
Executive Director of the International Energy Agency: Helga Steeg (Federal Republic of Germany).
Headquarters: 2, rue André Pascal, 75775 Paris Cedex 16, France.

Further Reading

OECD publishes numerous reports and statistical papers. Regular features include:
Activities of OECD. Annual.—*News from OECD.* Monthly.—*Main Economic Indicators.* Monthly.—*The OECD Observer.* Bi-monthly.—*The OECD Economic Outlook.* Semi-annual.—*OEEC/OECD Economic Surveys of Member Countries.—OECD Employment Outlook.* Annual.—*Geographical Distribution of Financial Flows to Developing Countries.*

Annual.—*Development Co-operation Report.* Annual.—*Tourism Policy and International Tourism in OECD Member Countries.—Maritime Transport.* Annual.—*Energy Policies and Programmes of the IEA Member Countries.*

NORTH ATLANTIC TREATY ORGANIZATION (NATO)

Western perceptions of the political situation in Europe following World War II gave rise, in 1947, to 2 major US initiatives – the Truman Doctrine and the Marshall Plan. These policies were designed to increase the ability of Western European countries to resist outside pressure and to assist them in bringing about their economic recovery. By 1948, on the initiative of the Foreign Secretary of the UK Ernest Bevin, 5 Western European nations had also entered into a treaty of mutual assistance in which they pledged themselves to come to each other's aid in the event of armed aggression against them (Brussels Treaty, 17 March 1948). The idea of a single mutual defence system involving North America as well as the European signatories of the Brussels Treaty was put forward by the Canadian Secretary of State for External Affairs in April 1948. It led, via the Vandenberg Resolution which enabled the US constitutionally to participate, to the creation of the Atlantic Alliance.

On 4 April 1949 the foreign ministers of Belgium, Canada, Denmark, France, Iceland, Italy, Luxembourg, the Netherlands, Norway, Portugal, the UK and the USA met in Washington and signed a treaty, the main clauses of which read as follows:

Article 1. The parties undertake, as set forth in the Charter of the United Nations, to settle any international disputes in which they may be involved by peaceful means in such a manner that international peace and security and justice are not endangered, and to refrain in their international relations from the threat or use of force in any manner inconsistent with the purposes of the United Nations.

Article 2. The parties will contribute toward the further development of peaceful and friendly international relations by strengthening their free institutions, by bringing about a better understanding of the principles upon which these institutions are founded, and by promoting conditions of stability and well-being. They will seek to eliminate conflict in their international economic policies and will encourage economic collaboration between any or all of them.

Article 3. In order more effectively to achieve the objectives of this treaty, the parties, separately and jointly by means of continuous and effective self-help and mutual aid, will maintain and develop their individual and collective capacity to resist armed attack.

Article 4. The parties will consult together whenever, in the opinion of any of them, the territorial integrity, political independence or security of any of the parties is threatened.

Article 5. The parties agree that an armed attack against one or more of them in Europe or North America shall be considered an attack against them all and consequently they agree that, if such an armed attack occurs, each of them, in exercise of the right of individual or collective self-defence recognized by article 51 of the Charter of the United Nations, will assist the party or parties so attacked by taking forthwith, individually and in concert with the other parties, such action as it deems necessary, including the use of armed force, to restore and maintain the security of the North Atlantic area. Any such armed attack and all measures taken as a result thereof shall immediately be reported to the Security Council. Such measures shall be terminated when the Security Council has taken the measures necessary to restore and maintain international peace and security.

Article 6. For the purpose of Article 5 an armed attack on one or more of the parties is deemed to include an armed attack *(i)* on the territory of any of the parties in Europe or North America, on the Algerian Departments of France, on the territory of Turkey or on the islands under the jurisdiction of any of the parties in the North Atlantic area north of the Tropic of Cancer; *(ii)* on the forces, vessels or aircraft of any of the parties, when in or over these territories or any other area in Europe in which occupation forces of any of the parties were stationed on the date when the treaty entered into force or the Mediterranean Sea or the North Atlantic area north of the Tropic of Cancer.

Article 8. Each party declares that none of the international engagements now in force between it and any other of the parties or any third state is in conflict with the provisions of this treaty, and undertakes not to enter into any international engagement in conflict with this treaty.

Article 10. The parties may, by unanimous agreement, invite any other European state in a position to further the principles of this treaty and to contribute to the security of the North Atlantic area to accede to this treaty. Any state so invited may become a party to the treaty by depositing its instrument of accession with the government of the United States of America. The government of the United States of America will inform each of the parties of the deposit of each such instrument of accession.

Article 12. After the treaty has been in force for 10 years, or at any time thereafter, the parties shall, if any of them so requests, consult together for the purpose of reviewing the treaty, having regard for the factors then affecting peace and security in the North Atlantic area, including the development of universal as well as regional arrangements under the Charter of the United Nations for the maintenance of international peace and security.

Article 13. After the treaty has been in force for 20 years, any party may cease to be a party one year after its notice of denunciation has been given to the government of the United States of America, which will inform the governments of the other parties of the deposit of each notice of denunciation.

The treaty came into force on 24 Aug. 1949. Greece and Turkey were admitted as parties to the treaty in 1952, the Federal Republic of Germany in 1955 and Spain in 1982. Since 1990 the USSR has had diplomatic representation at NATO. Hungary gained associate membership in Jan. 1991.

In their London Declaration of June 1990 the member states noted that Europe had 'entered a new, promising era' and 'as a consequence, this Alliance can and will adapt'; it was resolved to 'remain a defensive alliance' but to 'enhance the political component', and to propose to Warsaw Pact members a 'joint declaration in which we solemnly state that we are no longer adversaries'. It was further proposed that the Conference on Security and Co-operation in Europe (CSCE) should be instititutionalized. At their Rome summit in Nov. 1991 members agreed a strategy document which drops all references to the USSR as the main threat and identifies the disintegration of Moscow's centralized authority, and instability throughout East Europe, as the new danger.

NATO is an organization of sovereign states equal in status. Decisions taken are expressions of the collective will of member governments arrived at by common consent.

The *North Atlantic Council* is composed of representatives of the 16 member countries. At Ministerial Meetings of the Council, member nations are represented by Ministers of Foreign Affairs. These meetings are held twice a year. The Council also meets on occasion at the level of Heads of State and Government. In permanent session, at the level of Ambassadors, the Council meets at least once a week.

The *Defence Planning Committee* is composed of representatives of all member countries except France. Like the Council, it meets both in permanent session at the level of Ambassadors and twice a year at Ministerial level. At Ministerial Meetings member nations are represented by Defence Ministers.

The Council and Defence Planning Committee are chaired by the Secretary General of NATO at whatever level they meet. Opening sessions of Ministerial Meetings of the Council are presided over by the President, an honorary position held annually by the Foreign Minister of one of the member nations.

Nuclear matters are discussed by the *Nuclear Planning Group* in which 15 countries now participate. It meets regularly at the level of Permanent Representatives (Ambassadors) and twice a year at the level of Ministers of Defence.

The Permanent Representatives of member countries are supported by the National Delegations located at NATO Headquarters. The Delegations are composed of advisors and officials qualified to represent their countries on the various committees created by the Council. The Committees are supported by the International Staff responsible to the Secretary General.

In Dec. 1991 the *North Atlantic Co-operation Council* was set up for regular consultation with the CIS countries and East Europe.

Headquarters: 1110 Brussels, Belgium.
Secretary-General: Manfred Wörner (Germany).

Flag: Dark blue with a white compass rose of 4 points in the centre.

The *Military Committee* is responsible for making recommendations to the Council and the Defence Planning Committee on military matters and for supplying guidance to the Allied Commanders. Composed of the Chiefs-of-Staff of all member countries except France and Iceland (which has no military forces), the Committee is assisted by an International Military Staff. It meets at Chiefs-of-Staff level at least twice a year but remains in permanent session at the level of national military representatives. Liaison between the Military Committee and the French High Command is effected through the French Mission to the Military Committee. The chairman of the Military Committee is elected by the Chiefs-of-Staff for a period of 2–3 years.

The area covered by the North Atlantic Treaty is divided among three commands: The Atlantic Ocean Command, the European Command and the Channel Command. Defence plans for the North American area are developed by the Canada–US Regional Planning Group. Changes being introduced in 1992 to adapt to post-Cold War requirements will reduce the 3 major commands to 2 (Europe and Atlantic) and set up 3 subordinate commands within the former for the southern, central and north-west regions.

The *Allied Command Europe* (ACE) covers the area extending from the North Cape to the Mediterranean and from the Atlantic to the eastern border of Turkey. Responsibilities relating to the defence of Portugal and the UK are included but these come within the purview of more than one NATO Command. The European area, which is subdivided into a number of subordinate commands, is under the Supreme Allied Commander Europe (SACEUR) whose Headquarters, near Mons in Belgium, are known as SHAPE (Supreme Headquarters Allied Powers Europe).

SACEUR has also under his orders the ACE Mobile Force, composed of both land and air force units from different member countries, which can be ready for action at very short notice in any threatened area.

Under the Supreme Allied Commander Atlantic (SACLANT) the *Atlantic Command* extends from the North Pole to the Tropic of Cancer and from the coastal waters of North America to those of Europe and Africa, but excludes the Channel and the British Isles. SACLANT, who would have the primary task in wartime of ensuring the security of the sea lanes in the whole Atlantic area, is an operational rather than an administrative commander. Under his direct command is the Standing Naval Force Atlantic (STANAVFORLANT) which is a permanent international squadron of ships drawn from NATO navies which normally operate in the Atlantic. SACLANT headquarters are in Norfolk (USA).

The *Channel Command* covers the English Channel and the southern North Sea. Under the Allied Commander-in-Chief Channel (CINCHAN) its mission is to control and protect merchant shipping in the area, co-operating with SACEUR in the air defence of the Channel. The forces earmarked to the Command in emergency are predominantly naval but include maritime air forces. CINCHAN also has under his command the NATO Standing Naval Force Channel (STANAVFORCHAN) which is a permanent force comprizing mine counter-measure ships of different NATO countries. CINCHAN headquarters are at Northwood (UK).

The *Canada–US Regional Planning Group*, which covers the North American area, develops and recommends to the Military Committee plans for the defence of this area. It meets alternately in Washington and Ottawa.

Further Reading

The NATO Information Service publishes documentation, reference material and information brochures including: *The NATO Handbook; NATO: Facts and Figures; The NATO Review* (periodical).—*The Alliance's Strategic Concept.* 1991.—*Change and Continuity in the North Atlantic Alliance.* 1991.—*The Prague Conference on the Future of European Security.* 1991.—*The Rome Declaration.* 1991.

Cook, D., *The Forging of an Alliance.* London, 1989
De Staercke, A., *Nato's Anxious Birth: The Prophetic Vision of the 1940's.* London, 1985
Henderson, N., *The Birth of NATO.* London, 1982
Smith, J. (ed.) *The Origins of NATO.* Exeter Univ. Press, 1990

WESTERN EUROPEAN UNION

On 17 March 1948 a 50-year treaty 'for collaboration in economic, social and cultural matters and for collective self-defence' was signed in Brussels by the Foreign Ministers of the UK, France, the Netherlands, Belgium and Luxembourg. (*See* THE STATESMAN'S YEAR-BOOK, 1954, pp. 32 f.)

On 20 Dec. 1950 the functions of the Western Union defence organization were transferred to the North Atlantic Treaty command, but it was decided that the reorganization of the military machinery should not affect the right of the Western Union Defence Ministers and the Chiefs of Staff to meet as they please to consider matters of mutual concern to the Brussels Treaty powers.

After the breakdown of the European Defence Community on 30 Aug. 1954 a conference was held in London from 28 Sept. to 3 Oct. 1954, attended by Belgium, Canada, France, the Federal Republic of Germany, Italy, Luxembourg, the Netherlands, the UK and the USA, at which it was decided to invite the Federal Republic of Germany and Italy to accede to the Brussels Treaty, to end the occupation of Western Germany and to invite the latter to accede to the North Atlantic Treaty; the Federal Republic agreed that it would voluntarily limit its arms production, and provision was made for the setting up of an agency to control the armaments of the 7 Brussels Treaty powers; the UK undertook not to withdraw from the Continent her 4 divisions and the Tactical Air Force assigned to the Supreme Allied Commander against the wishes of a majority, *i.e.*, 4 of the Brussels Treaty powers, except in the event of an acute overseas emergency.

At a Conference of Ministers held in Paris from 20 to 23 Oct. 1954 these decisions were embodied in 4 Protocols modifying the Brussels Treaty which were signed in Paris on 23 Oct. 1954 and came into force on 6 May 1955.

At a meeting of the Foreign and Defence Ministers of WEU members held in Rome on 26–27 Oct. 1984, the Council adopted the 'Rome Declaration' and a document on institutional reform. Member Governments support the reactivation of the Organization as a means of strengthening the European contribution to the North Atlantic Alliance and improving defence co-operation among the countries of Western Europe.

Since the 1984 reforms, the WEU *Council of Ministers* (Foreign and Defence) meets twice a year in the capital of the presiding country. The presidency rotates annually. The *Permanent Council*, which consists of the member states' ambassadors to the UK and an official of the UK Foreign and Commonwealth Office, meets regularly at the seat of the Secretariat-General. The WEU *Assembly* in Paris comprises 108 parliamentarians of the member states and meets twice a year.

On 14 Nov. 1988, Spain and Portugal became members.

In Feb. 1992 the member nations were: Belgium, France, Germany, Italy, Luxembourg, the Netherlands, Portugal, Spain and the UK.

Secretariat-General: 9 Grosvenor Place, London, SW1X 7HL.
Secretary-General: Willem van Eekelen.

COUNCIL OF EUROPE

In 1948 the 'Congress of Europe', bringing together at The Hague nearly 1,000 influential Europeans from 26 countries, called for the creation of a united Europe, including a European Assembly. This proposal, examined first by the Ministerial Council of the Brussels Treaty Organization, then by a conference of ambassadors, was at the origin of the Council of Europe, which is, with its 26 member States, the widest organization bringing together all European democracies. The Statute of the Council was signed at London on 5 May 1949 and came into force 2 months later. The founder members were Belgium, Denmark, France, Ireland, Italy, Luxembourg, the Netherlands, Norway, Sweden and the UK. Turkey and Greece joined in 1949, Iceland in 1950, the Federal Republic of Germany in 1951 (having been an associate since 1950), Austria in 1956, Cyprus in 1961, Switzerland in 1963, Malta in 1965, Portugal in 1976, Spain in 1977, Liechtenstein in 1978, San Marino in 1988, Finland in 1989, Hungary in 1990 and Czechoslovakia and Poland in 1991.

Membership is limited to European States which 'accept the principles of the rule of law and of the enjoyment by all persons within [their] jurisdiction of human rights and fundamental freedoms'. The Statute provides for both withdrawal (Art. 7) and suspension (Arts. 8 and 9). Greece withdrew from the Council in Dec. 1969 and rejoined in Nov. 1974.

Structure. Under the Statute two organs were set up: An inter-governmental *Committee of [Foreign] Ministers* with powers of decision and of recommendation to governments, and an inter-parliamentary deliberative body, the *Parliamentary Assembly* (referred to in the Statute as the *Consultative Assembly*)—both of which are served by the Secretariat. In addition, a number of committees of experts have been established. On municipal matters the Committee of Ministers receives recommendations from the Standing Conference of Local and Regional Authorities of Europe.

The Committee of Ministers meets usually twice a year, their deputies for several days each month.

The Parliamentary Assembly normally consists of 204 parliamentarians elected or appointed by their national parliaments (Austria 6, Belgium 7, Cyprus 3, Czechoslovakia 8, Denmark 5, Finland 5, France 18, Federal Republic of Germany 18, Greece 7, Hungary 7, Iceland 3, Ireland 4, Italy 18, Liechtenstein 2, Luxembourg 3, Malta 3, Netherlands 7, Norway 5, Poland 12, Portugal 7, San Marino 2, Spain 12, Sweden 6, Switzerland 6, Turkey 12, UK 18); it meets 3 times a year for approximately a week. The work of the Assembly is prepared by parliamentary committees. Since June 1989 representatives of a number of central and East European countries have been permitted to attend as non-voting members ('special guests').

The *Joint Committee* acts as an organ of co-ordination and liaison between representatives of the Committee of Ministers and members of the Parliamentary Assembly and gives members an opportunity to exchange views on matters of important European interest.

The European Convention on Human Rights, signed in 1950, set up special machinery to guarantee internationally fundamental rights and freedoms. The *European Commission of Human Rights* investigates alleged violations of the Convention submitted to it either by States or, in most cases, by individuals. Its findings can then be examined by the *European Court on Human Rights* (set up in 1959), whose obligatory jurisdiction has been recognized by 23 States, or by the Committee of Ministers, empowered to take binding decisions by two-thirds majority vote.

The Social Development Fund, formerly the Resettlement Fund was created in 1956. The main purpose of the Fund is to give financial aid, particularly in the spheres of housing, vocational training, regional planning and development. Since 1956 the Fund has granted loans totalling ECU 7,000m.

In 1970 the Council set up a European Youth Centre at Strasbourg, where young people can discuss their own approach to international co-operation. More recently, a European Youth Foundation was created, and which provides money to subsidize activities by European Youth Organizations in their own countries.

Aims and Achievements. Art. 1 of the Statute states that the Council's aim is 'to achieve a greater unity between its members for the purpose of safeguarding and realising the ideals and principles which are their common heritage and facilitating their economic and social progress'; 'this aim shall be pursued. . . by discussion of questions of common concern and by agreements and common action'. The only limitation is provided by Art. 1 *(d)*, which excludes 'matters relating to national defence'.

Although without legislative powers, the Assembly acts as the power-house of the Council, initiating European action in key areas by making recommendations to the Committee of Ministers. As the widest parliamentary forum in Western Europe, the Assembly also acts as the conscience of the area by voicing its opinions on important current issues. These are embodied in resolutions. The Ministers' rôle is to translate the Assembly's recommendations into action, particularly as regards lowering the barriers between the European countries, harmonizing their legislation or introducing where possible common European laws, abolishing discrimination on grounds of nationality and undertaking certain tasks on a joint European basis.

The main areas of the Council's activity are: Human rights, the media, social and socio-economic questions, education, culture and sport, youth, public health, heritage and environment, local and regional government, and legal co-operation.

Some 142 Conventions and Agreements have been concluded covering such matters as social security, cultural affairs, conservation of European wild life and natural habitats, protection of archaeological heritage, extradition, medical treatment, equivalence of degrees and diplomas, the protection of television broadcasts, adoption of children and transportation of animals. Treaties in the legal field include the adoption of the European Convention on the Suppression of Terrorism, the European Convention on the Legal Status of Migrant Workers and the Transfer of Sentenced Persons. The Committee of Ministers adopted a European Convention for the protection of individuals with regard to the automatic processing of personal data (1981), a Convention on the compensation of victims of violent crimes (1983), a Convention on spectator violence and misbehaviour at sport events and in particular at football matches (1985), the European Charter of Local Government (1985), and a Convention for the Prevention of Torture and Inhuman or Degrading Treatment or Punishment (1987). The European Social Charter of 1961 sets out the social and economic rights which all member governments agree to guarantee to their citizens.

The official languages are English and French.

Chairman of the Committee of Ministers: (held in rotation).
President of the Parliamentary Assembly: Anders Björck (Sweden).
President of the European Court on Human Rights: Rolv Ryssdal (Norway).
President of the European Commission of Human Rights: Carl Aage Nørgaard (Denmark).
Secretary-General: Catherine Lalumière.
Headquarters: Palais de l'Europe, 67006, Strasbourg, Cedex, France.
Flag: Blue with a ring of 12 gold stars in the centre.

Further Reading

The Information Department, Council of Europe, BP 431, R6-67006 Strasbourg-Cedex.
European Yearbook. The Hague, from 1955
Forum. Strasbourg, from 1978, 4 times a year
Yearbook on the Convention on Human Rights. Strasbourg, from 1958
Cook, C. and Paxton, J., *European Political Facts, 1918–90.* London, 1992

EUROPEAN COMMUNITIES

In May 1950 Belgium, France, the Federal Republic of Germany, Italy, Luxembourg and the Netherlands started negotiations with the aim of ensuring continual peace by a merging of their essential interests. The negotiations culminated in the signing in 1951 of the Treaty of Paris creating the European Coal and Steel Community (ECSC). Two more communities with the aims of gradually integrating the economies of the 6 nations and of moving towards closer political unity, the European Economic Community (EEC) and the European Atomic Energy Community (EAEC or Euratom) were created in 1957 by the signing of the Treaties of Rome.

On 30 June 1970 membership negotiations began between the Six and the UK, Denmark, Ireland and Norway. On 22 Jan. 1972 those 4 countries signed a Treaty of Accession, although this was rejected by Norway in a referendum in Nov. 1972. On 1 Jan. 1973 the UK, Denmark and Ireland became full members. Greece joined the Community on 1 Jan. 1981; Spain and Portugal on 1 Jan. 1986, although Community legislation will only apply to them entirely after a transitional period. In Dec. 1985 the Treaties were amended again by the Single European Act of Luxembourg. Further amendments were agreed at the Maastricht Summit of Dec. 1991, whereby moves to a common currency were agreed subject to specific conditions including an 'opt-out' clause for the UK, and the social dimension was recognized in a protocol not applicable to the UK allowing the other member states to use EC institutions for this purpose. Turkey applied for membership in April 1987, but is unlikely to be accepted in the near future. The territory of the former German Democratic Republic entered into full membership on re-unification with Federal Germany in Oct. 1990. Malta formally applied for membership in July 1990, Cyprus and Sweden in July 1991 and Finland in March 1992. The membership of Austria has been put in question by its commitment under the 1955 State Treaty to permanent neutrality, but it made a formal application early in 1990. Associate membership agreements were initialled with Czechoslovakia, Hungary and Poland in 1991.

Greenland exercised its autonomy under the Danish Crown to secede in 1985.

The institutional arrangements of the Communities provide an independent executive with powers of proposal (the Commission), various consultative bodies, and a decision-making body drawn from the Governments (the Council). Until 1967 the 3 Communities were completely distinct, although they shared some nondecision-making bodies: From that date the executives were merged in the European Commission, and the decision-taking bodies in the Council. The institutions and organs of the Communities are as follows:

The *Commission* consists of 17 members appointed by the member states to serve for 4 years. The Commission acts independently of any country in the interests of the Community as a whole, with as its mandate the implementation and guardianship of the Treaties. In this it has the right of initiative (putting proposals to the Council for action); and execution (once the Council has decided); and can take the other institutions or individual countries before the Court of Justice (see below) should any of these renege upon its responsibilities. The Commission operates through 23 Directorates-General.

Flag: Blue with a ring of 12 gold stars.
President: Jacques Delors (b. 1925).
Address: 200 rue de la Loi, 1049, Brussels, Belgium.

The *Council of Ministers* consists of foreign ministers from the 12 national governments and represents the national as opposed to the Community interests. It is the body which takes decisions under the Treaties. Since the adoption of the Single Act of Luxembourg, an increasing number of its decisions are taken by majority vote, though some areas (e.g. taxation) are still reserved to unanimity. Specialist Councils (e.g. the *Agriculture Council*) meet to discuss matters related to individual policies. The Single Act also formalizes the meetings of Heads of State and Government in the *European Council*, which meets 3 times a year; and of Foreign Ministers in *Political Co-operation*, to discuss co-operation outside the framework of the Treaties. The Presidency of the Council is held for a 6-month term in the following order: Belgium, Denmark, Federal Republic of Germany, Greece, Spain, France, Ireland, Italy, Luxembourg, Netherlands, Portugal, UK.

Address: 170 rue de la Loi, 1048, Brussels.

The *European Parliament* consists of 518 members, directly elected from all Member States. France, Germany, Italy and the UK return 81 members each (Germany having also 18 observers from the former German Democratic Republic). Spain 60, the Netherlands 25, Belgium, Greece and Portugal 24, Denmark 16, Ireland 15 and Luxembourg 6. Party representation in Parliament is as follows: Socialists, 180; European People's Party (Christian Democratic Group), 121; Liberal Democratic and Reform Group 49; European Democrats (formerly European Conservatives), 34; Greens, 29; European United Left, 28; European Democratic Alliance, 22; the European Right, 17; the 'Rainbow' group (a group of mixed tendencies), 14; Left Unity, 14; Independents, 10. The Parliament has a right to be consulted on a wide range of legislative proposals, and forms one arm of the Community's Budgetary Authority. Since the Single Act it has an increased role in legislation, through the 'concertation' procedure, under which it can reject certain Council drafts in a second reading procedure. Elections were held in June 1989 for a 5-year mandate.

President: Egon Klepsch.
Address: Centre européen du Kirchberg, Luxembourg.

European Parliament. *Members of the European Parliament, 3rd Electoral Period, 1989–94.* 1991

Lodge, J. (ed.) *The 1989 Election of the European Parliament.* London, 1990

The *Economic and Social Committee* has an advisory role and consists of 189 representatives, employers, trade unions, consumers, etc. The *Consultative Committee*, of 96 members, performs a similar role for the ECSC.

President: François Staedelin.
Address: 2, rue Ravenstein, 1000 Brussels.

The *European Court of Justice* is composed of 13 judges and 6 advocates-general, is responsible for the adjudication of disputes arising out of the application of the treaties, and its findings are enforceable in all member countries. A Court of First Instance was created in 1989.

President: Ole Due.
Address: Palais de la Cour de Justice, Kirchberg, Luxembourg.

The *Court of Auditors* was established by a Treaty signed on 22 July 1975 which took effect on 1 June 1977. It consists of 12 members, and replaced the former *Audit Board.* It audits all income and current and past expenditure of the European Communities.

President: Aldo Angioi.
Address: 29 rue Aldringen, Luxembourg.
Annual Report of the Court of Auditors, from 1977

The *European Investment Bank* (EIB) was created by the EEC Treaty to which its statute is annexed. Its governing body is the Board of Governors consisting of ministers designated by member states. Its main task is to contribute to the balanced development of the common market in the interest of the Community by financing projects: Developing less-developed regions; for modernizing or converting undertakings; or developing new activities.

President: Günter Bröder.
Address: 100 boulevard Konrad Adenauer, Plateau du Kirchberg, Luxembourg.
Annual Report of the European Investment Bank

Community Law. Provisions of the Treaties and secondary legislation may be either directly applicable in Member States or only applicable after Member States have enacted their own implementing legislation. Secondary legislation consists of: Regulations, which are of general application and binding in their entirety and directly applicable in all member states; directives which are binding upon each Member State as to the result to be achieved within a given time, but leave the national authority the choice of form and method of achieving this result; decisions, which are binding in their entirety on their addressees. In addition the Council and Commission can issue recommendations and opinions, which have no binding force.

The Community's Legislative Process starts with a proposal from the Commission (either at the suggestion of its services or in pursuit of its declared political aims) to the Council. The Council generally seeks the views of the European Parliament on the proposal, and the Parliament adopts a formal Opinion, after consideration of the matter by its specialist Committees. The Council may also (and in some cases is obliged to) consult the Economic and Social Committee, which similarly delivers an opinion. When these opinions have been received, the Council will decide. Most decisions are taken on a majority basis, but will take account of reserves expressed by individual member states. The text eventually approved may differ substantially from the original Commission proposal.

Community Finances. Revenue for financial years in ECU1m.:

	1989	1990	1991
Own resources	41,881	42,160	53,237
Surpluses	1,162	3,645	1,371
Miscellaneous Community taxes, levies and dues	226,293	248,633	265,515
Administrative operation of the institutions	69,970	32,720	40,269
Total	45,900	46,928	55,556

Expenditure for 1991 was ECU55,556m.

The resources of the Community (the levies and duties mentioned above, and up to a 1·4% VAT charge) have been surrendered to it by Treaty. The Budget is made by the Council and the Parliament acting jointly as the Budgetary Authority. The Parliament has control, within a certain margin, of non-obligatory expenditure (*i.e.*, expenditure where the amount to be spent is not set out in the legislation concerned), and can also reject the Budget. Otherwise, the Council decides. ECSC operations are partly funded by a turnover levy (1988: 0·31%) on the coal and steel industries of the Community, partly from the general budget. The ECSC operating budget for 1988 was ECU432m.

THE EUROPEAN COAL AND STEEL COMMUNITY. The ECSC was the first of the 3 Communities, coming into existence on 10 Aug. 1952 following the signature of the Treaty of Paris on 18 April 1951. Its aim was to contribute towards economic expansion, growth of employment and a rising standard of living in Member States, through common action in the coal and steel sector, in a Community open to other nations. Since 1957 it has had the same membership as the other Communities.

THE EUROPEAN ECONOMIC COMMUNITY (EEC) or COMMON MARKET

Based on the Treaty of Rome of 25 March 1957 the EEC came into being on 1 Jan. 1958 with the same original members as the ECSC. The Treaty guarantees certain rights to the citizens of all Member States (*e.g.*, the outlawing of economic discrimination by nationality, and equal pay for equal work as between men and women) and sets out certain other areas where secondary legislation is to fill in the details. The most important policy areas are as follows:

Freedom of movement for persons, goods and capital. Under the Treaty individuals or companies from one Member State may establish themselves in another country (for the purposes of economic activity) or sell goods or services there on the same basis as nationals of that country. With a few exceptions, restrictions on the movement of capital have also been ended. Under the Single Act the Member States bound themselves to achieve the suppression of all barriers to free movement of persons, goods and services by 31 Dec. 1992.

Customs Union and External Trade Relations. Goods or Services originating in one Member State have free circulation within the EEC, which implies common arrangements for trade with the rest of the world. Member States can no longer make bilateral trade agreements with third countries: This power has been ceded to the Community. The Customs Union was achieved in July 1968, with the abolition of internal customs tariffs (or equivalents) and quantitative restrictions, and the establishment of the Common External Tariff. Denmark, Ireland and the UK adopted these from July 1977; Greece from Jan. 1986.

In Oct. 1991 a treaty forming the European Economic Area (EEA) was approved by the member states of the EC and EFTA. For details *see* p. 49. Association agreements which could lead to accession or customs union have been made with Cyprus, Malta and Turkey; and commercial, industrial, technical and financial aid agreements with Algeria, Egypt, Israel, Jordan, Lebanon, Morocco, Syria, Tunisia and Yugoslavia. In 1976 Canada signed a framework agreement for co-operation in industrial trade, science and natural resources. Co-operation agreements also exist with a number of Latin American countries and groupings (e.g. the Andean Group) and with Arab and Asian countries; and an economic and commercial agreement has been signed with ASEAN.

In the *Development Aid* sector, the Community has an agreement (the Lomé Convention, originally signed in 1975 but renewed and enlarged in 1979 and 1984) with some 60 African, Caribbean and Pacific countries which removes customs duties without reciprocal arrangements for most of their imports to the Community, and under which ECU8,760m. of aid was granted between 1986–90. An economic and commercial agreement has also been signed with ASEAN.

The Common Agricultural Policy (CAP). The objectives set out in the Treaty are to increase agricultural productivity, to ensure a fair standard of living for the agricultural community, to stabilise markets, to assure supplies, and to ensure reasonable consumer prices. In Dec. 1960 the Council laid down the fundamental principles on which the CAP is based: A single market, which calls for common prices, stable currency parities and the harmonising of health and veterinary legislation; Community preference, which protects the single Community market from imports; common financing, through the European Agricultural Guidance and Guarantee Fund (EAGGF), which seeks to improve agriculture through its Guidance section, and to stabilise markets against world price fluctuations through market intervention, with levies and refunds on exports. At present common market organizations cover over 95% of EEC agricultural production. Greece is bringing its agricultural prices into line with the Community over a period of up to 7 years.

Following the disappearance of stable currency parities, artificial currency levels have been applied in the CAP. This factor, together with over-production due to high producer prices, means that the CAP consumes about two-thirds of the Communities' budget. In Jan. 1991 the European Commission began discussion of plans to reform the CAP. These 'MacSharry Proposals' may form the basis of a final agreement in the context of the reform of GATT and trade liberalization generally.

The European Monetary System (EMS). Founded in March 1979 to control inflation, protect European trade from international disturbances and ultimately promote convergence between the European economies. The *Exchange Rate Mechanism (ERM)* is run by the finance ministries and central banks of the EC countries on a day-to-day basis; monthly reviews are carried out by the EC Monetary Committee (finance ministries) and the EC Committee of Central Bankers. All EC countries are members of EMS, but only Belgium, Denmark, France, Germany, Italy, Luxembourg, the Netherlands, Spain and the UK are in the ERM. Members are obliged to restrict the fluctuations in the value of their currencies to a variation 'band', usually of 2·25% (though this may be widened to 6% on a country's initial joining) higher or lower than a central rate established by comparing all the currencies in the ERM and the European Currency Unit, the ECU (XEU). If a currency reaches its top or bottom limits, central banks are obliged to buy or sell currency on the foreign exchanges. Further stabilization measures would involve adjustment of national interest rates, central bank borrowing from other central banks or withdrawal of reserves from the European Monetary Co-operation Fund. The adjustment of last resort is reor devaluation.

Dod's European Companion. Hurst Green, East Sussex, 1990

Competition. The Competition (anti-trust) law of the Community is based on 2 principles: That businesses should not seek to nullify the creation of the common market by the erection of artificial national (or other) barriers to the free movement of goods; and against the abuse of dominant positions in any market. These two principles have led among other things to the outlawing of prohibitions on exports to other Member States, of price-fixing agreements and of refusal to supply; and to the refusal by the Commission to allow mergers or take-overs by dominant undertakings in specific cases. Increasingly heavy fines are imposed on offenders.

THE EUROPEAN ATOMIC ENERGY COMMUNITY (EURATOM)

Like the EEC, Euratom came into being on 1 Jan. 1958 following a Treaty signed in Rome on 25 March 1957, and it had the same Member States as the EEC. Its task is to promote common efforts between its members in the development of nuclear energy for peaceful purposes, and for this purpose it has monopoly powers of acquisition of fissile materials for civil purposes. It is in no way concerned with military uses of nuclear power.

The execution of the Treaty now rests with the European Commission, which is advised by the Scientific and Technical Committee (28 members). Major decisions rest with the Council. Euratom has 1 substantial research institute of its own, at Ispra, in Italy; it does other work in co-operation with research institutes in the Member States, or in joint and international undertakings.

A common market for nuclear materials and equipment came into force, and external tariffs were suspended, in Jan. 1959.

European Community Delegation to the US: 2111 M Street NW (Suite 707), Washington DC 20037.
Head of Delegation: Andreas van Agt.
US Delegation to the European Community: 40 Boulevard du Régent, 1000 Brussels.
Head of Delegation: Thomas M. T. Niles.
European Community Delegation to the United Nations: 1 Dag Hammarskjöld Plaza, 245 East 47th Street, New York NY 10017.
Head of Delegation: Eamonn Gallagher.

Further Reading

Official Journal of the European Communities.—General Report on the Activities of the European Communities (annual, from 1967).—*The Agricultural Situation in the Community.* (annual).—*The Social Situation in the Community.* (annual).—*Report on Competition Policy in the European Community.* (annual).—*Basic Statistics of the Community* (annual).— *Bulletin of the European Community* (monthly).—*Register of Current Community Legal Instruments.* 1983
Europe (monthly), obtainable from the Information Office of the European Commission, 8 Storey's Gate, London, SW1P 3AT
The Arthur Andersen European Community Sourcebook. Chicago, 1991
Cox, A. and Furlong, P., *A Modern Companion to the European Community: a Guide to Key Facts, Institutions and Terms.* Aldershot, 1992
Hitiris, T., *European Community Economics: a Modern Introduction.* London, 1991
Kirschner, E. J., *Decision-Making in the European Community: the Council Presidency and European Integration.* Manchester Univ. Press, 1992
Lodge, J., *The European Community: Bibliographical Excursions.* London, 1983
Morris, B. and Boehm, K., *The European Community: A Practical Directory and Guide for Business, Industry and Trade.* London, 2nd ed. 1986
Nugent, N., *The Government and Politics of the European Community.* 2nd ed. London, 1991
Paxton, J., *A Dictionary of the European Communities.* 2nd ed. London, 1982.—*European Communities.* [Bibliography]. New Brunswick (NJ), 1992
Twitchett, C. C., *Harmonisation in the EEC.* London, 1981
Walsh, A. E. and Paxton, J., *Competition Policy.* London, 1975
Williams, A. M., *The European Community: the Contradictions of Integration.* Oxford, 1991

EUROPEAN FREE TRADE ASSOCIATION (EFTA)

The European Free Trade Association has 7 member countries: Austria, Finland (an associate member from 1961–1985), Iceland, Liechtenstein, Norway, Sweden and Switzerland. The Stockholm Convention establishing the Association entered into force on 3 May 1960 and Finland became associated on 27 March 1961. Founder members were Austria, Denmark, Norway, Portugal, Sweden, Switzerland and the UK. The UK and Denmark left EFTA on 31 Dec. 1972 to join the EEC as did Portugal on 31 Dec. 1985.

The first objective of EFTA was to establish free trade in industrial goods among its members. This was achieved in 1966. Its second objective was the creation of a single market in Western Europe. This goal was partially achieved in 1972 and 1973 when the EFTA countries signed free trade agreements with the EC covering trade in industrial products.

EFTA-EC co-operation continued to grow and in 1984, at a meeting marking the final abolition of remaining tariffs on industrial products, EFTA and EC ministers set out their objectives for increased co-operation.

This process was carried a step further in 1989 when exploratory talks began on the free movement of goods, services, capital and labour throughout the 19-country area. The talks also covered increased co-operation in other fields such as education, the environment, social policy, and research and development. Formal negotiations on the establishment of a European Economic Area (EEA), encompassing all the EFTA and EC countries, began in 1990. EFTA and EC ministers aimed at concluding these negotiations in 1991, so that the EEA treaty could come into force at the same time as the single market of the EC – on the 1st of January 1993.

The EEA treaty was approved by all members of the EC and EFTA on 22 Oct. 1991. It must be approved by the European Paliament and ratified by the parliament of every EC and EFTA country. An EEA Council of Ministers is to be set up, but EFTA members will not be able to vote on EC legislation. The treaty is to be reviewed every 2 years, starting in 1993.

Its main provisions are: Free movement of products within the EEA from 1993 (special arrangements to cover food, energy, coal and steel); EFTA to assume EC rules on company law, consumer protection, education, the environment, research and development and social policy; EFTA to adopt EC competition rules on anti-trust matters, abuse of a dominant position, public procurement, mergers and state aid; an independent joint court to deal with disputes; individuals to be free to live, work and offer services throughout the EEA, with mutual recognition of profession qualifications; capital movements to be free with some restrictions on investments; EFTA countries to maintain their own domestic agricultural policies if they wish.

In addition to its other activities, EFTA has formal ties with several states. In 1990 the Association adopted declarations outlining co-operation with Czechoslovakia, Hungary and Poland. A similar declaration had already been signed with Yugoslavia in 1983. The main purpose of these declarations is to assist economic reform, and to that end EFTA in 1990 and 1991 began negotiating free trade agreements with these countries. EFTA also signed a free trade agreement with Turkey in 1991 and began to explore the possibility of similar agreements with Israel and the Gulf Co-operation Council.

The operation of the EFTA Convention is the responsibility of the EFTA Council which meets regularly at the level of ministers or ambassadors. The Council is assisted by a Secretariat and a number of standing committees. Each EFTA country holds the chairmanship of the Council for 6 months.

Flag: White with the letters EFTA in black in the centre, within a ring of the flags of the member countries.

Secretary-General: Georg Reisch (Austria).
Headquarters: 9–11 rue de Varembé, 1211 Geneva 20, Switzerland.
Brussels Office: 118 rue d'Arlon, B-1040, Brussels.

Convention Establishing the European Free Trade Association
EFTA Bulletin (Quarterly)
EFTA news. (10 a year)
The European Free Trade Association

CONFERENCE ON SECURITY AND CO-OPERATION IN EUROPE (CSCE)

Initiatives from both NATO and the Warsaw Pact culminated in the first summit CSCE of heads of state and government in Helsinki on 30 July–1 Aug. 1975, which adopted a 'Final Act' laying down 10 principles concerning human rights, self-determination and the inter-relations of the participant states. Conferences followed in Belgrade (1977–78), Madrid (1980–83), Stockholm (1984–86) and Vienna (1986–89). At the Paris summit of 19–21 Nov. 1990 the members of NATO and the Warsaw Pact signed a Treaty on the Reduction of Conventional Forces in Europe (CFE) and a declaration that they are 'no longer adversaries' and do not intend to 'use force against the territorial integrity or political independence of any state'. All the 34 participants adopted the Confidence and Security-Building Measures (CSBMs), which pertain to the exchange of military information, verification of military installations, objection to unusual military activities etc., and signed the Charter of Paris.

The signatories of the Charter comprised the USA, Canada and all the sovereign states of Europe (except Albania, which had observer status), viz., Austria,

Belgium, Bulgaria, Cyprus, Czechoslovakia, Denmark, Finland, France, Germany, Greece, Hungary, Iceland, Ireland, Italy, Liechtenstein, Luxembourg, Malta, Monaco, the Netherlands, Norway, Poland, Portugal, Romania, San Marino, Spain, Sweden, Switzerland, Turkey, USSR (now Russia), UK, Vatican and Yugoslavia.

The Charter sets out principles of human rights, democracy and the rule of law to which all the signatories undertake to adhere, lays down the bases for east-west co-operation and other future action, and institutionalizes the CSCE, establishing a *Secretariat* in Prague, a *Conflict Prevention Centre* in Vienna and an *Election Observation Office* in Warsaw. In April 1991 the 34 member states voted to create a parliamentary 'Assembly of Europe' made up of 245 representatives from national parliaments and meeting at the Council of Europe Assembly in Strasbourg. It will have a consultative role, proposing and recommending measures.

Albania was admitted in Sept. and Estonia, Latvia and Lithuania in Oct. 1991, and the other 10 CIS republics in Jan. 1992 bringing the membership to 48.

Further Reading

Freeman, J., *Security and the CSCE Process: the Stockholm Conference and Beyond.* London, 1991

THE WARSAW PACT

The unified military command of this Soviet-dominated alliance (for details *see* THE STATESMAN'S YEAR-BOOK, 1991–92, p. 49) was dissolved in March, and the residual political organization in July, 1991.

COUNCIL FOR MUTUAL ECONOMIC ASSISTANCE (COMECON; CMEA)

For details *see* THE STATESMAN'S YEAR-BOOK, 1991–92, p. 50. The 9 member states signed a protocol on 28 June 1991 providing for this organization's dissolution within 90 days, and it was formally dissolved on 26 Sept.

Further Reading

Brine, J., *COMECON: The Rise and Fall of an International Socialist Organization.* [Bibliography] New Brunswick (NJ), 1992

EUROPEAN BANK FOR RECONSTRUCTION AND DEVELOPMENT (EBRD, BERD)

History and Membership. A treaty to establish the EBRD was signed May 1990; it was inaugurated on 15 April 1991. It had 41 original members: the European Commission, the European Investment Bank, all the EEC countries and all the countries of East Europe except Albania. Albania became a member in Oct. 1991, bringing membership to 42.

Its founding capital was of ecu 10m., of which the USA contributed 10%, the UK, France, Germany, Italy, Japan 8·5% each, and the USSR 6%.

Objectives. It was set up to lend funds at market rates to East European companies and countries 'which are committed to, and applying, the principles of multi-party democracy and market economics'. The USSR will be eligible for lending, but for an initial 3-year period only up to the amount of its capital, and for private projects.

A policy statement of May 1991 says that initial emphasis will be place on pro-grammes to support the creation and strengthening of infrastructure; privatization, reform of the financial sector, including development of capital markets and privatization of commercial banks; development of productive competitive private sectors of small and medium-sized enterprises in industry, agriculture and services; restructuring industrial sectors to put them on a competitive basis; encouraging foreign investment and cleaning up the environment.

There is a 23-member board of directors which is involved in day-to-day management.

Headquarters: 175, Broadgate, London EC2.

President: Jacques Attali.
General Secretary: Bart le Blanc.

COLOMBO PLAN

History: Founded in 1950 to promote the development of newly independent Asian member countries, the Colombo Plan has grown from its modest beginning as a group of seven Commonwealth nations into an international organization of 26 countries.

Originally the Plan was conceived for a period of six years. Its life has since been extended from time to time, generally at five-year intervals. The Consultative Committee, the Plan's highest deliberative body, at its meeting in Jakarta in 1980, gave the Plan an indefinite span of life; its need and relevance will henceforth be examined only if considered necessary.

The Plan is multilateral in approach but bilateral in operation: Multilateral in that it takes cognizance of the problems of development of member countries in the Asia and Pacific region and endeavours to deal with them in a co-ordinated way; bilateral because negotiations for assistance are made direct between a donor and a recipient country.

Aims: The aims of the Colombo Plan are: *(a)* to promote interest in and support for the economic and social development in Asia and the Pacific; *(b)* to keep under review economic and social progress in the region and help accelerate development through co-operative effort; and *(c)* to facilitate development assistance to and within the region.

Member Countries: Afghanistan, Australia, Bangladesh, Bhutan, Burma, Cambodia, Canada, Fiji, India, Indonesia, Iran, Japan, South Korea, Laos, Malaysia, Maldives, Nepal, New Zealand, Pakistan, Papua New Guinea, Philippines, Singapore, Sri Lanka, Thailand, UK and USA.

Development Assistance: Colombo Plan aid covers all fields of socio-economic development and amounted to US$6,841·3m. in 1989. It takes three principal forms:

(i)   *Capital Aid* including grants and loans for national projects mainly from the six developed member countries of the Plan.
      The total amount of capital aid and technical co-operation assistance provided by the developed donors under the plan in 1989 was as follows:

	US$1m.
Japan	4,286·0
USA	1,335·1
Australia	504·1
UK	410·3
Canada	277·8
New Zealand	8·0
Total	6,841·3

(ii) *Technical Co-operation:* Assistance is provided in the form of services of experts and volunteers, fellowships, and equipment for training and research. During 1988, 35,002 students and trainees received training, 8,226 experts and 1,615 volunteers were sent out. Total disbursements on technical co-operation by the developed member countries in 1988 amounted to $1,020·7m.

(iii) Technical Co-operation Among Developing Countries (TCDC): The promotion of TCDC is a major objective of the Plan. Under TCDC programmes in 1988, 2,356 students and trainees received training and 69 experts were sent out. TCDC expenditures during 1986 amounted to $9·8m.

Structure: There are four organs which give focus to the Plan:

Consultative Committee: The Committee is the highest deliberative body of the Plan and consists of Ministers of member Governments who meet once in two years. The Ministerial meeting is preceded by a meeting of senior officials who are directly concerned with the operation of the Plan in various countries.

Colombo Plan Council: The Council is also a deliberative body which meets several times a year in Colombo, where most member countries have resident diplomatic missions, to review the economic and social development of the Asia-Pacific region and promote co-operation among member countries.

Colombo Plan Bureau: Its functions include servicing the meetings of the Colombo Plan Council and the Consultative Committee, carrying out research, and dissemination of statistical and other information relating to activities under the Plan. Since 1973 the Bureau has been operating a Drug Advisory Programme to assist national and regional efforts to eliminate the causes and ameliorate the effects of drug abuse.

Colombo Plan Staff College: The Colombo Plan Staff College for Technician Education, established in 1975, transferred from Singapore to the Philippines in 1987. The College helps member countries in developing their systems of technician education, mainly through training courses, seminars and consultancies. It is separately financed by most Colombo Plan member countries and functions under the guidance of its own Governing Board consisting of the heads of member countries' diplomatic missions resident in the Philippines.

Flag: Dark blue with a central white disc containing the Colombo Plan logo in black.

Headquarters: Colombo Plan Bureau, 12 Melbourne Avenue, PO Box 596, Colombo 4, Sri Lanka.

The Colombo Plan (Cmd. 8080). HMSO, 1950; reprinted 1952.—*Annual Report.* HMSO 1952 to 1971 followed by Colombo Plan Bureau, Sri Lanka, 1971–86
Reports of the Council for Technical Co-operation. HMSO annually until 1966–67 followed by the Colombo Plan Bureau, Sri Lanka, 1967–68 to date

ASSOCIATION OF SOUTH EAST ASIAN NATIONS (ASEAN)

History and Membership. The Association of South East Asian Nations is a regional organization formed by the governments of Indonesia, Malaysia, the Philippines, Singapore and Thailand through the Bangkok Declaration which was signed by the Foreign Ministers of ASEAN countries on 8 Aug. 1967. Brunei joined in 1984.

Objectives. The main objectives are to accelerate economic growth, social progress and cultural development, to promote active collaboration and mutual assistance in matters of common interest, to ensure the stability of the South East Asian region and to maintain close co-operation with existing international and regional organizations with similar aims. Principal projects concern economic co-operation and development, with the intensification of intra-ASEAN trade and trade between the region and the rest of the world; joint research and technological programmes; co-operation in transportation and communications; promotion of tourism and South East Asian studies; including cultural, scientific, educational and administrative exchanges.

Organs. The highest authority in ASEAN are the Heads of Government of the Member Countries who meet as and when necessary to give directions to ASEAN.

The highest policy-making body is the Meeting of Foreign Ministers, commonly known as the Annual Ministerial Meeting, which convenes in each of the ASEAN member countries on a rotational basis in alphabetical order. The Standing Committee, comprising the Foreign Minister of the country hosting the Ministerial Meeting in that particular year and the accredited ambassadors of the other member countries, carries out the work of the Association in between the Ministerial Meetings and handles the routine matters to ensure continuity and to make decisions based on the guidelines or policies set by the Ministerial Meetings and submit for the consideration of the Foreign Ministers all reports and recommendations of the various ASEAN committees. There are five economic committees under the ASEAN Economic Ministers and three non-economic committees that recommend and draw up programmes for ASEAN co-operation. These committees are responsible for the operation and implementation of ASEAN projects in their respective fields. Each ASEAN capital has an ASEAN National Secretariat. The central secretariat for ASEAN is located in Jakarta, Indonesia, and is headed by the Secretary General, a post that revolves among the member states in alphabetical order every 3 years. Bureau directors and other officers of the ASEAN Secretariat remain in office for 3 years.

The *Asean Free Trade Area (AFTA)* was set up by all the member states in Oct. 1991 with the aim of creating a common market in 15 years, with a common tariff regime for manufactured goods (Common Effective Preferential Tariff) as a first step.

Secretary-General: Roderick Yong (Brunei Darussalam).

Further Reading

Broinowski, A., *Understanding ASEAN*. London, 1982;—(ed.) *ASEAN into the 1990s*. London, 1990
Wawn, B., *The Economies of the ASEAN Countries*. London, 1982

ORGANIZATION OF AMERICAN STATES (OAS)

On 14 April 1890 representatives of the American republics, meeting in Washington at the First International Conference of American States, established an 'International Union of American Republics' and, as its central office, a 'Commercial Bureau of American Republics', which later became the Pan American Union. This international organization's object was to foster mutual understanding and co-operation among the nations of the western hemisphere. Since that time, successive inter-American conferences have greatly broadened the scope of work of the organization.

This led to the adoption on 30 April 1948 by the Ninth International Conference of American States, at Bogotá, Colombia, of the Charter of the Organization of American States. This co-ordinated the work of all the former independent official entities in the inter-American system and defined their mutual relationships.

The Charter of 1948 subsequently was amended by the Protocol of Buenos Aires (1967) and the Protocol of Cartagena de Indias (1985). The purposes of the OAS are to strengthen the peace and security of the continent; promote and consolidate representative democracy, with due respect for the principle of non-intervention; prevent possible causes of difficulties and ensure the pacific settlement of disputes among member states; provide for common action in the event of aggression; seek the solution of political, juridical and economic problems; promote by co-operative action economic, social and cultural development; and achieve an effective limitation of conventional weapons in order to devote maximum resources to economic and social development. Within the framework of the UN, the OAS is a regional organization.

Membership is on a basis of absolute equality. Each country has one vote and there is no veto power. The member countries were (1992): Antigua and Barbuda, Argentina, Bahamas, Barbados, Belize, Bolivia, Brazil, Canada, Chile, Colombia, Costa Rica, Cuba, Commonwealth of Dominica, Dominican Republic, Ecuador, El Salvador, Grenada, Guatemala, Guyana, Haiti, Honduras, Jamaica, Mexico, Nicaragua, Panama, Paraguay, Peru, St Kitts and Nevis, St Lucia, St Vincent and the Grenadines, Suriname, Trinidad and Tobago, USA, Uruguay, Venezuela.

With the emergence of democratically-elected governments throughout the continent, the OAS has been increasingly concerned with the preservation, protection and promotion of democracy. At its 21st Regular Session (Santiago, Chile, June 1991) the OAS General Assembly adopted *The Santiago Commitment to Democracy and the Renewal of the Inter-American System,* as well as a resolution on representative democracy. The latter calls for collective action in the event of a 'sudden or irregular interruption of the democratic political institutional process or of the legitimate exercise of power by the democratically-elected government in any of the Organization's member states'.

The OAS also carries out programmes to promote the economic and social development of its member states. Specialized training is provided for Latin American and Caribbean citizens each year in development-related fields, and development projects are executed each year in response to requests from member governments.

Under the amended Charter, the OAS accomplishes its purposes by means of:

(a) The *General Assembly,* which meets annually.

(b) The *Meeting of Consultation of Ministers of Foreign Affairs,* held to consider problems of an urgent nature and of common interest.

(c) The Councils: The *Permanent Council,* which meets on a permanent basis at OAS headquarters amd carries out decisions of the General Assembly, assists the member states in the peaceful settlement of disputes, acts as the Preparatory Committee of that Assembly, submits recommendations with regard to the functioning of the Organization, and considers the reports to the Assembly of the other organs; the *Inter-American Economic and Social Council* and the *Inter-American Council for Education, Science and Culture,* both of which promote and co-ordinate the Organization's activities in their respective spheres of competence and render the governments such specialized services as they may request. Each of the Councils is composed of a representative from each member state, appointed by the government of that state.

(d) The *Inter-American Juridical Committee* which acts as an advisory body to the OAS on juridical matters and promotes the development and codification of international law. Eleven jurists, elected for 4-year terms by the General Assembly, represent all the American States.

(e) The *Inter-American Commission on Human Rights* which oversees the observance and protection of human rights. 7 members elected for 4-year terms by the General Assembly represent all the OAS member states.

(f) The *General Secretariat* is the central and permanent organ of the OAS.

(g) The *Specialized Conferences,* meeting to deal with special technical matters or to develop specific aspects of inter-American co-operation.

(h) The *Specialized Organizations,* inter-governmental organizations established by multilateral agreements to discharge specific functions in their respective fields of action, such as women's affairs, agriculture, child welfare, Indian affairs, geography and history, and health.

Secretary General: João Clemente Baena Soares (Brazil).
Assistant Secretary General: Christopher Thomas (Trinidad and Tobago).

The Secretary General and the Assistant Secretary General are elected by the General Assembly for 5-year terms. The General Assembly approves the annual budget for the Organization, which is financed by quotas contributed by the member governments.

General Secretariat: Washington, D.C., 20006, USA.
Flag: Light blue with the OAS seal in colour in the centre.

Further Reading

Publications of the OAS General Secretariat include:

Charter of the Organization of American States. 1948.—*As Amended by the Protocol of Buenos Aires in 1967 and the Protocol of Cartagena de Indias in 1985*
Americas. Illustrated bi-monthly, from 1949 (Spanish and English editions)
The OAS and the Evolution of the Inter-American System. 1991
Inter-American Review of Bibliography. Quarterly, from 1951
Annual Report of the Secretary-General
Status of Inter-American Treaties and Conventions. Annual

Publications on Latin America (*see also* the bibliographical notes appended to each country):

Revenue, Expenditure and Public Debts of the Latin American Republics. Division of Financial Information, US Department of Commerce. Annual
Boundaries of the Latin American Republics: An Annotated List of Documents, 1493–1943. Department of State, Office of the Geographer. Washington, 1944
Burgin, M. (ed.) *Handbook of Latin American Studies.* Gainesville, Fla., 1935 ff.
Hirschman, A. O., *Latin American Issues:* [11] *Essays and Comments.* New York, 1961
Plaza, G., *The Organization of American States: Instrument for Hemispheric Development.* Washington, 1969.—*Latin America Today and Tomorrow.* Washington, 1971
Steward, J. H. (ed.) *Handbook of the South American Indian.* 7 vols. Washington, 1946–59
Thomas, A. V. W. and A. J., *The Organization of American States.* Southern Methodist Univ. Press, 1963

LATIN AMERICAN ECONOMIC GROUPINGS

Latin American Integration Association (LAIA) /*Asociación Latinoamericana de Integración* (ALADI). The Association took over from the Latin American Free Trade Area (LAFTA) on 1 Jan. 1981 which was created in 1960 to further trade be tween the member states and promote regional integration. Members: Argentina, Bolivia, Brazil, Chile, Colombia, Ecuador, Mexico, Paraguay, Peru, Uruguay and Venezuela.

Headquarters: Cebollati 1461, Casilla 577, Montevideo, Uruguay.

Síntesis ALADI (monthly, Spanish)
Newsletter (six issues a year, Spanish)

Central American Common Market (CACM) /*Mercado Común Centroamericano.* In Dec. 1960 El Salvador, Guatemala, Honduras and Nicaragua concluded the General Treaty of Central American Economic Integration *(Tratado General de Integración Económica Centroamericana)* under the auspices of the Organization of Central American States (ODECA) in Managua. Costa Rica acceded in 1962. Members: Costa Rica, El Salvador, Guatemala, Honduras and Nicaragua.

Headquarters: 4a Avda 10–25, Zona 14, Apdo 1237, Guatemala City, Guatemala.
Carta Informativa (monthly)
Anuario Estadística Centroamericano de Comercio Exterior (annual)

The Andean Group *(Grupo Andino).* On 26 May 1969 an agreement was signed by Bolivia, Chile, Colombia, Ecuador and Peru creating the Andean Group. Venezuela was initially actively involved but did not sign the agreement until 1973. Chile withdrew from the Group in 1977. Members: Bolivia, Colombia, Ecuador, Peru and Venezuela. The Act of Caracas signed at the Group's 5th meeting in May 1991 established a free trade zone between member states to come into effect on 1 Jan. 1992 as the first step towards the creation of a common market in 1995.

The Group's *Presidential Council* is composed of the presidents of the member states.

Headquarters: Avda Paseo de la Republica 3895, Casilla 18–1177, Lima 27, Peru.

Latin American Economic System/*Sistema Económico Latinoamericano* (SELA). SELA was created by 25 Latin American and Caribbean countries (Suriname joined in 1979) meeting in Panama, 17 Oct. 1975. The System provides member countries with permanent institutional machinery for joint consultation, coordination, co-operation and promotion in economic and social matters at both intraregional and extraregional levels.

Headquarters: Apdo 17035, El Conde, Caracas 1010, Venezuela.

Latin American Association of Development Financing Institutions/Asociación Latinoamericana de Instituciones Financieros de Desarrollo (ALIDE). Founded in 1968 to promote co-operation among regional development financing organizations.

Headquarters: Paseo de la Republica 3211, POB 3988, Lima, Peru.

Latin American Banking Federation/Federación Latinoamericana de Bancos (FELABAN). Established to co-ordinate efforts towards a wider and accelerated economic development in Latin American countries.

Headquarters: Apdo Aereo 091959, Bogotá, DE8, Colombia.

Organization of the Cooperatives of America/Organización de las Cooperativas de América. Founded in 1963 to improve social, economic, cultural and moral conditions through the co-operative system.

Headquarters: POB 13568–24163, Calle 97A no. 11–31, Oficina 201, Bogotá, Colombia.
Cooperativa America (six times a year, Spanish)

Southern Cone Common Market (Mercosur)
Founded in March 1991 by the Treaty of Asunción between Argentina, Brazil, Paraguay and Uruguay which commits the signatories to the progressive reduction of tariffs culminating in the formation of a common market of 1 Jan. 1995. The member states' foreign ministers form a council responsible for political questions, the chairmanship of which rotates every 6 months. The permanent executive body is the 'group' of member states, which takes decisions by consensus. There is an arbitration tribunal whose decisions are binding on member countries.

Further Reading

British Bulletin of Publications on Latin America, the Caribbean, Portugal and Spain. London, from June 1949 (half-yearly)
South America, Central America and the Caribbean, 1988. London, 1987
The Latin America and Caribbean Review, 1989. Saffron Walden, 1988
Angarita, C. and Coffey, P., *Europe and the Andean Countries: A Comparison of Economic Policies and Institutions.* London, 1988
Box, B., (ed.) *1990 South American Handbook.* Bath (annual)
Bulmer-Thomas, V., *The Political Economy of Central America since 1920.* CUP, 1987.
——*Britain and Latin America: A Changing Relationship,* 1989
Duran, E., *European Interests in Latin America.* London, 1985
Ferguson, J. and Pearce, J., *The Thatcher Years: Britain and Latin America.* London, 1988
Inter-American Development Bank, *Economic and Social Progress in Latin America: Economic Integration.* Washington, 1984

CARIBBEAN COMMUNITY
(CARICOM)

Establishment and Functions. The Treaty establishing the Caribbean Community, including the Caribbean Common Market, and the Agreement establishing the Common External Tariff for the Caribbean Common Market, was signed by the Prime Ministers of Barbados, Guyana, Jamaica and Trinidad and Tobago at Chaguaramas, Trinidad, on 4 July 1973, and entered into force on 1 Aug. 1973. Six less developed countries of CARIFTA signed the Treaty of Chaguaramas on 17 April 1974. They were Belize, Dominica, Grenada, Saint Lucia, St Vincent and Montserrat, and the Treaty came into effect for those countries on 1 May 1974. Antigua acceded to membership on 4 July 1974 and on 26 July the Associated State of St

Kitts–Nevis–Anguilla signed the Treaty of Chaguaramas in Kingston, Jamaica, and became a member of the Caribbean Community, Bahamas became a member of the Community but not of the Common Market on 4 July 1983.

The Caribbean Community has 3 areas of activity: *(i)* economic co-operation through the Caribbean Common Market; *(ii)* co-ordination of foreign policy; *(iii)* functional co-operation in areas such as health, education and culture, youth and sports, science and technology, and tax administration.

The Caribbean Common Market provides for the establishment of a Common External Tariff, a common protective policy and the progressive co-ordination of external trade policies; the adoption of a scheme for the harmonization of fiscal incentives to industry; double taxation arrangements among member countries; the co-ordination of economic policies and development planning; and a special regime for the less developed countries of the community.

In 1990 a target date of 1994 for the creation of a common market was agreed. A common tariff on imports from third countries was applied by some member countries from the beginning of 1991; other members implemented it by Feb. 1992.

Membership: Antigua and Barbuda, Bahamas, Barbados, Belize, Dominica, Grenada, Guyana, Jamaica, Montserrat, St Kitts and Nevis, St Lucia, St Vincent and the Grenadines, Trinidad and Tobago, Turks and Caicos Islands and the British Virgin Islands.

Structure: The *Conference of Heads of Government* is the principal organ of the Community, and its primary responsibility is to determine the policy of the Community. It is the final authority of the Community and the Common Market, and for the conclusion of treaties and relationships between the Community and international organizations and States. It is responsible for financial arrangements for meeting the expenses of the Community.

The *Common Market Council* is the principal organ of the Common Market and consists of a Minister of Government designated by each member state. Decisions in both the Conference and the Council are in the main taken on the basis of unanimity.

The *Secretariat*, successor to the Commonwealth Caribbean Regional Secretariat, is the principal administrative organ of the Community and of the Common Market. The Secretary-General is appointed by the Conference on the recommendation of the Council for a term not exceeding 5 years and may be reappointed. The Secretary-General shall act in that capacity in all meetings of the Conference, the Council, and of the institutions of the Community.

Institutions of the Community, established by the Heads of Government Conference, are: Conference of Ministers responsible for Health; Standing Committees of Ministers responsible for Education, Tourism, Labour, Foreign Affairs, Finance, Agriculture, Energy, Mines and Natural Resources, Industry, Science and Technology, Transport and Legal Affairs, respectively.

Associate Institutions: Caribbean Development Bank; Caribbean Examinations Council; Council of Legal Education; University of the West Indies; University of Guyana; Caribbean Meteorological Organization; West Indies Shipping Corporation.

Flag: Divided horizontally light blue over dark blue; in the centre a white disc bearing the linked letters CC in light blue and dark blue respectively.

Chairman: Kennedy Simmonds (St Kitts and Nevis).

Secretary-General: Edwin Carrington.

Deputy Secretary-General: Frank Abdulah.

Headquarters: Bank of Guyana Building, PO Box 10827, Georgetown, Guyana.

The language of the Community is English.

Further Reading

CARICOM Bibliography. Georgetown, CARICOM Secretariat, annual
CARICOM Perspective. (3 times a year). Georgetown, CARICOM Secretariat

CARICOM Secretary-General's Report. Georgetown, annual *Treaty Establishing the Caribbean Community.* Georgetown, CARICOM Secretariat, 1982

Parry, J. H., *et. al. A Short History of the West Indies.* Rev. ed. London, 1987

SOUTH PACIFIC FORUM

The South Pacific Forum held its first meeting of Heads of Government in New Zealand in 1971. Membership (and year of adhesion): Australia (1971), Cook Islands (1971), the Federated States of Micronesia (1987), Fiji (1971), Kiribati (1979), Nauru (1971), New Zealand (1971), Niue (1975), Papua New Guinea (1974), the Republic of the Marshall Islands (1987), Solomon Islands (1978), Tonga (1971), Tuvalu (1978), Vanuatu (1980) and Western Samoa (1971).

The South Pacific Bureau for Economic Co-operation was established by the Agreement of 17 April 1973; a Memorandum of Understanding of 16 June 1977 established the Pacific Forum Line. The South Pacific Regional Trade and Economic Co-operation Agreement was signed on 14 July 1980.

In 1985 the Forum adopted a treaty for a nuclear-free zone in the South Pacific, and in 1987 a treaty on fisheries with the USA; and in 1978, 1986 and 1989 conventions on fishery and protection of marine resources.

THE LEAGUE OF ARAB STATES

Origin. The formation of the League of Arab States in 1945 was largely inspired by the Arab awakening of the 19th century. This movement sought to re-create and reintegrate the Arab community which, though for 400 years a part of the Ottoman Empire, had preserved its identity as a separate national group held together by memories of a common past, a common religion and a common language, as well as by the consciousness of being part of a common cultural heritage. The leaders of the Arab movement in the 19th century and of the Arab revolt against Turkey in the First World War sought to achieve these aims through secession from the Ottoman Empire into a united and independent Arab state comprising all the Arab countries in Asia. However the 1919 peace settlement divided the Arab world in Asia (with the exception of Saudi Arabia and the Yemen) into British and French spheres of influence and established in them a number of separate states and administrations (Syria, Lebanon, Iraq, Jordan and Palestine) under temporary mandatory control.

By 1943, however, 7 of these countries had substantially achieved their independence. An Arab conference therefore met in Alexandria in the autumn of 1944; it formulated the 'Alexandria Protocol', which delineated the outlines of the Arab League. It was found that neither a unitary state nor a federation could be achieved, but only a league of sovereign states. A covenant, establishing such a league, was signed in Cairo on 22 March 1945 by the representatives of Egypt, Iraq, Saudi Arabia, Syria, Lebanon, Jordan and Yemen. There were (1992) 21 members of the League: Algeria, Bahrain, Djibouti, Egypt, Iraq, Jordan, Kuwait, Lebanon, Libya, Mauritania, Morocco, Oman, the Palestine Liberation Organization, Qatar, Saudi Arabia, Somalia, Sudan, Syria, Tunisia, United Arab Emirates and Yemen.

In the Charter's Special Annex on Palestine, the signatories considered the special circumstances of Palestine and decided that until the country can effectively exercise its independence, the Council of the League should take charge in the selection of an Arab representative from Palestine to take part in its work.

Egypt's membership of the League was suspended in March 1979 and the secretariat moved from Cairo to Tunis. This action was taken in response to the signing of a bilateral peace treaty between Egypt and Israel. Egypt was readmitted in May 1989 and the secretariat again moved to Cairo.

Organization. The machinery of the League consists of a Council, a number of Special Committees and a Permanent Secretariat. On the Council each state has one vote. The Council may meet in any of the Arab capitals. Its functions include mediation in any dispute between any of the League states or a League state and a country outside the League. The Council has a Political Committee consisting of the Foreign Ministers of the Arab states. There are also 22 specialized agencies.

The Permanent Secretariat of the League, under a Secretary-General (who enjoys, along with his senior colleagues, full diplomatic status), has its seat in Cairo.

The League considers itself a regional organization within the framework of the United Nations at which its secretary-general is an observer.

Secretary-General: Esmat Abdel Meguid (Egypt; b. 1923; elected for a 5-year term May 1991).

Flag: Dark green with the seal of the Arab League in white in the centre.

Arab Common Market. The Arab Common Market came into operation on 1 Jan. 1965. The agreement, reached on 13 Aug. 1964 and open to all the Arab League states, has been signed by Iraq, Jordan, Syria and Egypt. The agreement provides for the abolition of customs duties on agricultural products and natural resources within 5 years, by reducing tariffs at an annual rate of 20%. Customs duties on industrial products are to be reduced by 10% annually. The agreement also provides for the free movement of capital and labour between member countries, the establishment of common external tariffs, the co-ordination of economical development and the framing of a common foreign economic policy.

Further Reading

Clements, F. A., *Arab Regional Organizations.* [Bibliography] New Brunswick (NJ), 1992
Gomaa, A. M., *The Foundation of the League of Arab States.* London, 1977

GULF CO-OPERATION COUNCIL

Members in 1992 were Bahrain, Kuwait, Oman, Qatar, Saudi Arabia and the United Arab Emirates.

In March 1991 the 6 member states together with Egypt and Syria established an armed regional peace-keeping force by the Declaration of Damascus, which also envisages political and economic co-operation. In April 1991 members created an aid fund to promote development in Arab countries which had helped liberate Kuwait in 1991.

ORGANIZATION OF THE PETROLEUM EXPORTING COUNTRIES (OPEC)

Aims. The Organization was founded in Baghdad, Iraq, in 1960 with the following founder members, Iran, Iraq, Kuwait, Saudi Arabia and Venezuela. The principal aims are unifying the petroleum policies of member countries and determining the best means for safeguarding their interests, individually and collectively; to devise ways and means of ensuring the stabilization of prices in international oil markets with a view to eliminating harmful and unnecessary fluctuations; and to secure a steady income for the producing countries, an efficient, economic and regular supply of petroleum to consuming nations, and a fair return on their capital to those investing in the petroleum industry.

Membership (1991). Algeria, Ecuador, Gabon, Indonesia, Iran, Iraq, Kuwait, Libya, Nigeria, Qatar, Saudi Arabia, United Arab Emirates and Venezuela. Membership is open to any other country having substantial net exports of crude petroleum, which has fundamentally similar interests to those of member countries.

OPEC Fund for International Development: The Fund was established in 1976 to provide financial aid to developing countries, other than OPEC members, on advantageous terms.

Secretary-General: Dr Subroto.
Deputy Secretary-General: Dr Ramzi Salman.

Headquarters: Obere Donaustrasse 93, A–1020 Vienna, Austria.

Flag: Light blue with the Opec logo in white in the centre.

Further Reading

OPEC publications include: *Annual Statistical Bulletin. Annual Report. OPEC Bulletin* (monthly). *OPEC Review* (quarterly).
Ahrari, M. E., *Opec: The Failing Giant.* Univ. Press of Kentucky, 1986
Al-Chalabi, F., *OPEC and the International Oil Industry: A Changing Structure.* OUP, 1980
El Mallakh, R., *OPEC: Twenty Years and Beyond.* London, 1982
Griffin, J. and Teece, D. J., *OPEC Behaviour and World Oil Prices.* London and Boston, 1982
Skeet, *OPEC: Twenty-five years of Prices and Policies.* CUP, 1988

ORGANIZATION OF AFRICAN UNITY

On 25 May 1963 the heads of state or government of 32 African countries, at a conference in Addis Ababa, signed a charter establishing an 'Organization of African Unity'. It had 51 members in 1991.

In June 1991 the heads of state of member countries signed a treaty to create an Africa-wide economic community by 2000.

Its chief objects are the furtherance of African unity and solidarity; the coordination of the political, economic, cultural, health, scientific and defence policies and the elimination of colonialism in Africa.

The organs of the Organization are: (1) the assembly of the heads of state and government; (2) the council of ministers; (3) the general secretariat; (4) a commission of mediation, conciliation and arbitration. Arabic, French, Portuguese and English are recognized as working languages.

Chairman: Gen. Ibrahim Babangida (Nigeria).
Secretary-General: Salim Ahmed Salim.
Headquarters: Addis Ababa.
Flag: Horizontally green, white, green, with the white fimbriated yellow, and the seal of the OAU in the centre.

DANUBE COMMISSION

The Danube Commission was constituted in 1949 based on the Convention regarding the regime of navigation on the Danube, which was signed in Belgrade on 18 Aug. 1948. The Belgrade Convention reaffirmed that navigation on the Danube from Ulm to the Black Sea, with access to the sea through the Sulina arm and the Sulina Canal, is equally free and open to the nationals, merchant shipping and merchandise of all states as to harbour and navigation fees as well as conditions of merchant navigation.

The Danube Commission is composed of representatives from the countries on the Danube (1 for each of these countries), namely, Austria, Bulgaria, Hungary, Romania, Czechoslovakia, the Ukraine, USSR and Yugoslavia. Since 1957, representatives of the Ministry of Transport from the Federal Republic of Germany have attended the meetings of the Commission with consultative status.

The functions of the Danube Commission are to check that the provisions of the Convention are carried out, to establish a uniform buoying system on all the Danube's navigable waterways and to establish the basic regulations for navigation on the river. The Commission co-ordinates the regulations for river, customs and sanitation control as well as the hydrometeorological service and collects statistical data concerning navigation on the Danube.

The Danube Commission enjoys legal status. It has its own seal and flag. The members of the Commission and elected officers enjoy diplomatic immunity. The Commission's official buildings, archives and documents are inviolable. French and Russian are the official languages of the Commission.

Since 1954 the headquarters of the Commission have been in Budapest.

Flag: Blue, with a red strip fimbriated white along the bottom edge, and the initials of the Commission within a wreath in the canton—Latin letters on obverse Cyrillic on reverse.

Further Reading

Danube Commission's publications include: Compilation of Agreements on Danube Navigation; Basic Regulations of Navigation; Recommendations relating to the establishment of the dimensions of the channel and hydrotechnical and other works (1969; 1975; 1979; 1988 Editions); Recommendations on the Prevention of Water Pollution by Navigation; Recommendations on the Use of Radiocommunications on the Danube; Plan of basic works aiming at obtaining the dimensions of the channel and hydrotechnical and other works recommended on the Danube for the period 1980–1990 (1984 ed.); Danubian Bridges; Danubian Ships; Danube Maintenance; Danube Profile; Mileage Charts; Pilots' Charts; Sailing Direction; Hydrological Yearbooks; Hydrological Manuals; Statistical Yearbooks; Statistical Manuals; Recommendations on unified rules for sanitary, veterinary, plant protection and customs control; Rules of Procedure and other organization documents of the Danube Commission; Proceedings of Sessions; General Information on the Danube Commission and on its activity (with the text of the Convention regarding the regime of navigation on the Danube in annex).

ANTARCTIC TREATY

Antarctica is an island continent some 15·5m. sq. km in area which lies almost entirely within the Antarctic Circle. Its surface is composed of an ice sheet over rock, and it is uninhabited except for research and other workers in the course of duty. It is in general ownerless; for countries with territorial claims, *see* Argentina (p. 93), Australian Antarctic Territory (p. 125), British Antarctic Territory (p. 238), Chile (p. 349), French Southern and Antarctic Territories (p. 582), the Ross dependency, New Zealand (p. 1019) and Queen Maud Land, Norway (p. 1050).

12 countries which had maintained research stations in Antarctica during International Geophysical Year, 1957–58, (Argentina, Australia, Belgium, Chile, France, Japan, New Zealand, Norway, South Africa, the USSR, the UK and the USA) signed the Antarctic Treaty (Washington Treaty) on 1 Dec. 1959. Austria, Brazil, Bulgaria, Canada, China, Colombia, Cuba, Czechoslovakia, Denmark, Ecuador, Finland, Germany, Greece, Hungary, India, Italy, South Korea, North Korea, the Netherlands, Papua New Guinea, Peru, Poland, Romania, Spain, Sweden, Switzerland and Uruguay have subsequently acceded to the Treaty. The Treaty reserves the Antarctic area south of 60° S. lat. for peaceful purposes, provides for international co-operation in scientific investigation and research, and preserves, for the duration of the Treaty, the *status quo* with regard to territorial sovereignty, rights and claims. The Treaty entered into force on 23 June 1961. The 39 nations party to the Treaty (26 full voting signatories and 13 adherents) meet biennially. Decisions taken by the signatories of the 1959 Washington Treaty must be unanimous.

An agreement reached in Madrid in April 1991 and signed by all 39 parties in Oct. imposes a ban on mineral exploitation in Antarctica for 50 years, at the end of which any one of the 26 voting parties may request a review conference. After this the ban may be lifted by agreement of three quarters of the nations then voting, which must include the present 26. The agreement demilitarizes the continent, establishes the right to scientific research for all countries and creates a procedure for monitoring the environment.

Further Reading

Jørgensen-Dahl, A. and Østreng, W., *The Antarctic Treaty System in World Politics*. London, 1991

PART II

COUNTRIES OF THE WORLD
A—Z

AFGHANISTAN

Capital: Kabul
Population: 16·56m. (1990)
GNP per capita: US$250 (1985)

Jamhuria Afghanistan

(Republic of Afghanistan)

HISTORY. A military coup on 17 July 1973 led by Mohammad Daoud overthrew King Zahir Shah and set up a Republic. President Daoud was killed in a military coup in April 1978 which led to the establishment of a pro-Soviet government of the People's Democratic Party of Afghanistan (PDPA).

In Dec. 1979 Soviet troops invaded Afghanistan and Hafizullah Amin was deposed and replaced by Babrak Karmal, the pretext being the Treaty of Friendship signed in Dec. 1978 between the USSR and Afghanistan. In May 1986 Karmal was replaced as General Secretary of the PDPA by Dr Sayid Mohammed Najibullah who was elected President in Sept. 1987 by the Revolutionary Council. In 1988 there were some 115,000 Soviet troops in Afghanistan but under the Geneva accords signed in April 1988 all were withdrawn by 15 Feb. 1989. After talks in Nov. 1991 with Afghan opposition movements ('mujahideen') the Soviet government agreed to transfer its support from the Najibullah regime to an 'Islamic Interim Government' which would hold power for 2 years while preparing for elections. The USSR denounced its decision to invade Afghanistan in 1978, and agreed to cease arms supplies after 1 Jan. 1992 and to withdraw its military advisers. Under the 'negative symmetry' agreement the USA also stopped arms supplies from 1 Jan.

A 150-member negotiating body representing the government, insurgents, Pakistan, Iran and Saudi Arabia was scheduled to meet in April 1992 to set up a commission to recommend an interim government and hold elections.

AREA AND POPULATION. Afghanistan is bounded in the north by Turkmenistan, Uzbekistan and Tajikistan, east and south by Pakistan and west by Iran.

The area is 251,773 sq. miles (652,090 sq. km). Population according to the last (1979) census was 15,551,358, of which some 2·5m. were nomadic tribes. Estimate (1990, excluding nomads) 16·56m. (21% urban). Population density, 25 per sq. km. Approximately 3m. Afghans have sought refuge in Pakistan, over 1m. in Iran and several hundred thousand have been killed since 1979. Infant mortality rates, averaged over 1985–90, were 172 per 1,000 live births; annual growth rate, 2·6%; expectation of life, 41·5 years. The population of Kabul is over 2m. There are no current reliable population figures for other cities and major towns.

Census (1979), Kabul 913,164; Kandahar, 178,409; Herat, 140,323; Mazar-i-Sharif, 103,372; Jalalabad, 53,915; Kunduz, 53,251; Baghlan, 39,228; Maimana, 38,251; Pul-i-Khumri, 31,101; Ghazni, 30,425; Charikar, 22,424; Shiberghan, 18,955; Gardez, 9,550; Faizabad, 9,098; Qala-i-nau, 5,340; Uiback, 4,938; Meterlam, 3,987; Cheghcheran, 2,974.

The main ethnic group are the Pathans. Other ethnic groups include Tajiks, Hazaras, Turkmens and Uzbeks.

CLIMATE. The climate is arid, with a big annual range of temperature and very little rain, apart from the period Jan. to April. Winters are very cold, with considerable snowfall, which may last the year round on mountain summits. Kabul. Jan. 27°F (–2·8°C), July 76°F (24·4°C). Annual rainfall 13" (338 mm).

CONSTITUTION AND GOVERNMENT. A new Constitution was approved in Nov. 1987. The PDPA remains the leading political force in the country. It is governed by a Central Committee (112 full members and 63 alternate members), which elects a Political Bureau, currently of 14 full, and 4 alternate, members to decide policy. At that time, the name of the country was changed from the Democratic Republic of Afghanistan to the Republic of Afghanistan.

65

A State of Emergency was declared on 19 Feb. 1989 following the withdrawal of Soviet forces and a Military Council headed by President Najibullah (b. 1947) was announced. On 20 Feb. the Prime Minister Dr Mohammed Hasan Sharq resigned when the 20-man Supreme Military Council for the Defence of the Homeland took over full control of economic, political and military policy. The state of emergency was lifted in May 1990.

The *Loya Jirga* (Grand Assembly) was convened on 21 May 1989 following elections on 17 May.

In May 1990 Fazal Haq Khaliqyar (PDPA) was appointed *Prime Minister* and Sultan Ali Keshtmand *Vice-President.*

In June 1990 the PDPA adopted new rules and renamed itself the Fatherland Party. An Executive Committee of 15 and a Central Committee of 14 replaced the Politburo and former Central Committee.

National flag: Three equal horizontal stripes of red, black and green, with the national arms in the canton.

National anthem: Tar so chi da zmaka asman ('As long as the earth and heavens exist; words by Addul Rauf Benawa, tune by Abdul Ghafoor Bereshna and Abdul Jalil Zaland.)

The official languages are Pushtu and Dari (Persian).

Local Government: There are 31 provinces each administered by an appointed governor.

DEFENCE. Conscription is currently for a period of 2 years, followed soon after by another period of 2 years for non-graduates.

Army. The Army is organized in 3 armoured brigades and 16 infantry divisions, 5 special guard brigades, 1 mechanized infantry brigade, 1 artillery brigade and 5 commando brigades. Equipment includes 500 T-54/-55 and 300 T-62 main battle tanks. Strength was (1992) about 50,000, mainly conscripts, but most units of the Army are well below strength, largely as a result of desertions.

Air Force. The Air Force, which is Soviet-equipped, has about 180 combat aircraft and 5,000 officers and men. Nominal strength comprises 3 squadrons of Su-7 and Su-20 attack aircraft, 4 squadrons of MiG-21 interceptors (about 60 aircraft), 3 squadrons of MiG-17s and 2 squadrons of MiG-23s, a helicopter attack force of at least 50 Mi-24s, a transport wing with 12 An-12s, 25 twin-turboprop An-26s and An-32s, about 10 piston-engined An-2s, 50 Mi-8/17 and 10 Mi-4 helicopters and 2 turboprop Il-18s, and Yak-18, Aero L-29 and L-39 and MiG-15UTI trainers. The main fighter station is Bagram, with facilities for the largest jet transports and bombers. There is a fighter-bomber station at Shindand, a training station at Mazar-i-Sharif and an air academy at Sherpur. Most transport aircraft are based at Kabul. Large numbers of SA-2 and SA-3 surface-to-air missiles are operational.

Police and Militia. In addition to the Army and Air Force there are a number of paramilitary units, including a 50,000-strong gendarmerie, secret police and 'Defence of the Revolution' forces.

INTERNATIONAL RELATIONS

Membership. Afghanistan is a member of the UN and Colombo Plan.

ECONOMY

Policy. A 5-year plan was adopted in 1986 to cover 1986–1991. Emphasis is on reconstruction of agriculture and irrigation systems as well as exploitation of natural gas resources.

Budget. In 1983–84 the budget envisaged expenditure of Afs. 49,941m. and revenue of Afs. 34,120m.

Currency. The unit of currency is the *afghani* (AFA) of 100 *puls.* Rates of exchange were fixed, March 1992: Afs. 99·25 = £1; Afs. 56·37 = US$1; unofficial rates are: Afs. 345 = £1; Afs. 225 = US$1. Inflation was 56·8% in 1989.

Banking and Finance. The Afghan State Bank *(Da Afghanistan Bank)* is the largest of the 3 main banks and also undertakes the functions of a central bank, holding the exclusive right of note issue. Total assets of the 3 main banks were: Da Afghanistan Bank (1981), Afs. 22,839m.; Pashtany Tejaraty Bank (1981), Afs. 6,997m.; Bank-i-Milli (1981), Afs. 3,087m. Foreign banks have been permitted to operate since May 1990.

Weights and Measures. Weights and measures used in Kabul are: Weights: 1 *khurd* = 0·244 lb.; 1 *pao* = 0·974 lb.; 1 *charak* = 3·896 lb.; 1 *sere* = 16 lb.; 1 *kharwár* = 1,280 lb. or 16 maunds of 80 lb. each. Long measure: 1 yard or *gaz* = 40 in. The metric system is in increasingly common use. Square measures: 1 *jaríb* = 60 x 60 kábuli yd or ¹/₂ acre; 1 *kulbá* = 40 jaríbs (area in which 2¹/₂ kharwárs of seed can be sown); 1 jaríb yd = 29 in. Local weights and measures are in use in the provinces.

ENERGY AND NATURAL RESOURCES

Electricity. Hydro-electric plants have been constructed at Sarobi, Nangarhar, Naghlu, Mahipar, Pul-i-Khumri and Kandahar. Production (1986) 1,390m. kwh. Supply 220 volts; 50 Hz.

Natural gas. Production (1985) 2,400m. cu. metres. Natural gas is found in northern Afghanistan around Shiberghan and Sar-i-Pol; over 2,000m. cu. metres, about 95% of production, is piped to the USSR annually.

Minerals. Mineral resources are scattered and little developed. Coal is mined at Karkar in Pul-i-Khumri, Ishpushta near Doshi, north of Kabul and Dar-i-Suf south of Mazar (total production, 1983–84, 145,300 tonnes). Rich, but as yet unexploited, deposits of iron ore exist in the Hajigak hills about 100 miles west of Kabul; beryllium has been found in the Kunar valley and barite in Bamian province. Other deposits include gold; silver (now unexploited, in the Panjshir valley); lapis lazuli (in the Panjshir valley and Badakhshan); asbestos; mica; sulphur (near Maimana); chrome (in the Logar valley and near Herat); and copper (in the north).

Agriculture. Although the greater part of Afghanistan is more or less mountainous and a good deal of the country is too dry and rocky for successful cultivation, there are many fertile plains and valleys, which, with the assistance of irrigation from small rivers or wells, yield very satisfactory crops of fruit, vegetables and cereals. In 1988 there were 38·05m. ha of agricultural land, of which 8m. ha were cultivable. 9·07m. persons depended on agriculture in 1990. Before 1979 Afghanistan was virtually self-supporting in foodstuffs but in 1989 it was estimated that 33% of the land had been destroyed by war. The castor-oil plant, madder and the asafœtida plant abound.

Fruit forms a staple food (with bread) of many people throughout the year, both in the fresh and preserved state, and in the latter condition is exported in great quantities. The fat-tailed sheep furnish the principal meat diet, and the grease of the tail is a substitute for butter. Wool and skins provide material for warm apparel and one of the more important articles of export. Persian lambskins (Karakuls) are one of the chief exports.

Production, 1990, in 1,000 tonnes: Wheat, 1,925; barley, 250; maize, 800; rice, 430.

Livestock (1988): Cattle, 1·65m.; horses, 0·4m.; donkeys, 1·3m.; sheep, 13·5m.; goats 2·15m.; chickens, 7m.

INDUSTRY. At Kabul there are factories for the manufacture of cotton and woollen textiles, leather, boots, marble-ware, furniture, glass, bicycles, prefabricated houses and plastics. A large machine shop has been constructed and equipped by the USSR, with a capability of manufacturing motor spares. There is a wool factory and there are several cotton-ginning plants; a small cotton factory at Jabal-us-Seraj and a larger one at Pul-i-Khumri; a cotton-seed oil extraction plant at Lashkargah; a cotton textile factory at Gulbahar, and a cotton plant at Balkh.

An ordnance factory manufactures arms and ammunition, boots and clothing, etc. for the Army. There is a beet sugar plant at Baghlan and a fruit-canning factory in Kandahar.

Industries include cement, coalmining, cotton textiles, small vehicle assembly plants, fruit canning, carpet making, leather tanning, footwear manufacture, sugar manufacture, preparation of hides and skins, and building. Most of these are relatively small and, with the exception of hides and skins, carpets and fruits, do not meet domestic requirements.

Labour. The economically active population was 4·91m. in 1990, of whom 54·8% worked in agriculture.

FOREIGN ECONOMIC RELATIONS. Foreign debt was US$4,850m. in 1985. Trade has been supervised by the Ministries of Commerce and Finance and the Da Afghanistan Bank, but it was announced in May 1990 that trade was to be deregulated. The Government monopoly controls the import of petrol and oil, sugar, cigarettes and tobacco, motor vehicles and consignment goods from bilateral trading countries. The principal surface routes for imports to Afghanistan are via the former Soviet rail system and the border posts at Torghundi and Hairatan; and from Karachi via the border post at Torkham.

Commerce. In 1988 imports totalled US$1,558m. and exports US$558m. Main export commodities in 1985 were karakul skins (US$13·5m.), raw cotton (US$12·5m.), dried fruit and nuts (US$141m.), fresh fruit (US$53·3m.) and natural gas (US$302·4m.). Main items imported in 1985 were petroleum products (US$164m.), textiles (US$122·5m.). The USSR supplied 58·1% of imports in 1988 and received 49·1% of exports.

Total trade between Afghanistan and UK (in £1,000 sterling, British Department of Trade returns):

	1988	1989	1990	1991
Imports to UK	11,501	4,813	9,194	5,207
Exports and re-exports from UK	12,109	5,376	7,815	6,956

Tourism. Owing to internal political instability there has been negligible tourism since 1979.

COMMUNICATIONS

Roads. There were in 1986 22,000 km of roads. The Americans asphalted the Kandahar–Chaman and Kabul–Torkham roads. The Russians constructed a road and tunnel through the Salang pass (over 11,000 ft) which was opened in Sept. 1964 and cut 120 miles off the old road from Kabul to the north; they continued this road to Kunduz and Sherkhan Bandar (Qizil Qala) on the Oxus. In addition, the Americans in 1966 completed the road between Kabul and Kandahar and the Russians constructed a concrete road between Kandahar and Herat. In 1968 the Americans completed an asphalt road from Herat to the Iranian frontier at Islam Qala. With Soviet assistance a metalled road from Pul-i-Khumri to Mazar-i-Sharif was completed in 1969 and Mazar-i-Sharif to Shiberghan in 1971. A Soviet-built road and rail bridge across the Oxus (Amu Darya) River was opened in May 1982. There are about 90,000 cars and commercial vehicles registered in Kabul. All roads, particularly outside the towns, are in a very poor state of repair as a result of the war.

Railways. There are no railways in the country, but the Oxus bridge opened in 1982, brought Soviet Railways' track into the country. A 200 km line of 1,520 mm gauge has been authorized from Termez to Pul-i-Khumri.

Civil Aviation. There is an international airport at Kabul (Khwaja Rawash Airport) and 18 domestic airports. The national carrier is Ariana Afghan Airlines; Air India and the former Soviet airline Aeroflot also operate services. There are direct flights from Kabul to Amritsar, Bandar Abbas (Iran), Delhi, Dubai, Moscow, Prague and Tashkent.

Shipping. There are practically no navigable rivers, and timber is the only article of commerce conveyed by water, floated down the Kunar and Kabul rivers from

Chitral on rafts. A port has been built at Qizil Qala on the Oxus; barge traffic is increasing on the Oxus. Three river ports on the Amu Darya have been built at Sherkhan Bandar, Tashguzar and Hairatan, linked by road to Kabul.

Telecommunications. Telephones, installed in most of the large towns, numbered 31,200 in 1978. There is telegraphic communication between all the larger towns and with other parts of the world. Radio and TV Afghanistan is government-controlled. In 1990 there were 1·4m. radio receivers and about 100,000 television receivers (colour by PAL and SECAM).

Newspapers. In 1983 there were 3 daily newspapers with a circulation of 67,000.

JUSTICE, RELIGION, EDUCATION AND WELFARE

Justice. A Supreme Court was established in June 1978. If no provision exists in the Constitution or in the general laws of the State, the courts follow the Hanafi jurisprudence of Islamic law.

Religion. The predominant religion is Islam. In 1989 there were 10·97m. Sunni Moslems and 2·22m. Shiites.

Education. Some 25% of the population were estimated to be literate in 1990. There are elementary schools throughout the country, but secondary schools exist only in Kabul and provincial capitals. Both elementary and secondary education are free. In 1985 there were 580,000 pupils (16,000 teachers) in primary education and 105,000 pupils (5,700 teachers) in secondary education. There are 3 teacher-training institutions in Kabul and 11 elsewhere; UNESCO is supporting an expansion programme. Technical, art, commercial and medical schools exist for higher education. Kabul University was founded in 1932 and has 9 faculties (medicine, science, agriculture, engineering, law and political science, letters, economics, theology, pharmacology). The University of Nangarhar in Jalalabad was founded in 1963. A Polytechnic in Kabul was completed in 1968. In 1982 there were 13,115 students in higher education, 4,427 in teacher-training schools and 1,230 in technical schools.

Health. In 1982 there were 1,215 doctors and 6,875 hospital beds. Two-thirds of the doctors and half the beds were in Kabul.

DIPLOMATIC REPRESENTATIVES

Of Afghanistan in Great Britain (31 Prince's Gate, London, SW7 1QQ)
Chargé d'Affaires: Taza Khan Wial.

Of Great Britain in Afghanistan (Karte Parwan, Kabul)
Staff temporarily withdrawn.

Of Afghanistan in the USA (2341 Wyoming Ave., NW, Washington, D.C., 20008)
Chargé d'Affaires: Abdul Ghafoor Jawshan.

Of the USA in Afghanistan (Wazir Akbar Khan Mina, Kabul)
Ambassador: Vacant.

Of Afghanistan to the United Nations
Ambassador: Khodaidad Basharmal.

Further Reading

Amin, S. H., *Law, Reform and Revolution in Afghanistan*. London, 1991
Arney, G., *Afghanistan*. London, 1990
Ghaus, A. S., *The Fall of Afghanistan: An Insider's Account*. Oxford, 1988
Giradet, E. R., *Afghanistan: The Soviet War*. London, 1985
Hammond, T. T., *Red Star over Afghanistan*. Boulder and London, 1984
Hanifi, M. J., *Historical and Cultural Dictionary of Afghanistan*. Metuchen, 1976
Hyman, A., *Afghanistan under Soviet Domination, 1964–1991*. 3rd ed. London, 1992
Jones, S., *Afghanistan*. [Bibliography]. Oxford and Santa Barbara, 1991
Roy, O., *Islam and Resistance in Afghanistan*. 2nd ed. CUP, 1990
Sykes, P. M., *A History of Afghanistan*. 2 vols. New York, 1975

ALBANIA

Capital: Tirana
Population: 3·2m. (1989)
GNP per capita: US$930 (1986)

Republika e Shqipërisë

HISTORY. For the history of Albania before the Second World War *see* THE STATESMAN'S YEAR-BOOK 1985–86, p. 66.

For the Second World War and the establishment of the Communist regime *see* THE STATESMAN'S YEAR-BOOK 1991–92, p. 68.

Beginning in July 1990 there were several demonstrations against the government often led by students. In Dec. the Communist Party dismissed 5 members of its Politburo and the People's Assembly adopted a decree legalizing opposition parties. A Communist government was elected in March 1991, but following a general strike organized by independent trade unions demanding higher wages and the protection of living standards it resigned in June. A successor government was itself repalced by a non-party government in Dec. 1991 led by Vilson Ahmeti.

AREA AND POPULATION. Albania is bounded in the north and east by Yugoslavia, south by Greece and west by the Adriatic. The area of the country is 28,748 sq. km (11,101 sq. miles). By the peace treaty Italy restored the island of Sazan (Saseno) to Albania. At the census of 1982 the population was, 2,786,100. The population in 1988 was 3,138,100 (1,522,000 female; 1,111,440 urban). Population in 1989, 3·2m. (34% urban in 1987; density 109·2 per sq. km). The capital is Tirana (population in 1,000 in 1990, 21); other large towns are Durrës (Durazzo) (72), Shkodër (Scutari) (71), Elbasan (70), Vlorë (Vlonë, Valona) (61), Korçë (Koritza) (57), Fier (37), Berat (37), Lushnjë (24), Kavajë (23) and Gjirokastër (Argyrocastro) (21).

Ethnic minorities (mainly Greeks) numbered some 300,000 in 1990.

Vital statistics, 1988: Marriages, 28,174; births, 80,241; deaths, 17,027; divorces, 2,597. Rates (per 1,000, 1988): Births, 25·5; deaths, 5·4; marriages, 9; divorces, 0·8; natural increase, 20·1 per thousand. Life expectancy in 1988 was 69·4 years, males; 74·9, females. In 1988 33% of the population were under 15. 20,000 persons emigrated legally in 1990.

The country is administratively divided into 26 districts (*rreth*) (*see* map in THE STATESMAN'S YEAR-BOOK, 1962. N.B. The district of Ersekë has been renamed Kolonjë), 66 towns, 306 town boroughs, 537 village unions and 2,844 villages.

Districts	Area (sq. km)	Population (in 1,000) (1988)	Districts	Area (sq. km)	Population (in 1,000) (1988)
Berat	1,027	173·7	Lushnjë	712	132·2
Dibrë	1,568	148·2	Mat	1,028	75·9
Durrës	848	242·5	Mirditë	867	49·7
Elbasan	1,481	238·6	Permet	929	39·4
Fier	1,175	239·7	Pogradec	725	70·5
Gjirokastër	1,137	65·5	Pukë	1,034	48·2
Gramsh	695	43·8	Sarandë	1,097	86·6
Kolonjë	805	24·6	Shkodër	2,528	233·0
Korçë	2,181	213·2	Skrapar	775	45·8
Krujë	607	105·3	Tepelenë	817	49·1
Kukës	1,330	99·4	Tirana	1,238	363·1
Lezhë	479	61·6	Tropojë	1,043	44·2
Librazhd	1,013	70·8	Vlorë	1,609	174·0

Districts are named after their capitals; exceptions: Tropojë, capital—Bajram Curri; Mat—Burrel; Mirditë—Rrëshen; Skrapar—Çorovodë; Dibrë—Peshkopi; Kolonjë—Ersekë.

The Albanian language is divided into two dialects—Gheg, north of the river Shkumbi, and Tosk in the south. Many places therefore have two forms of name:

Vlonë (Gheg), Vlorë (Tosk), etc., and many are known also by an Italian name, *e.g.*, Valona. Since 1945 the official language has been based on Tosk.

CLIMATE. Mediterranean-type, with rainfall mainly in winter, but thunderstorms are frequent and severe in the great heat of the plains in summer. Winters in the highlands can be severe, with much snow. Tirana. Jan. 44°F (6·8°C), July 75°F (23·9°C). Annual rainfall 54" (1,353 mm). Shkodër. Jan. 39°F (3·9°C), July 77°F (25°C). Annual rainfall 57" (1,425 mm).

CONSTITUTION AND GOVERNMENT. The Communist political structure derived from constitutions of 1946 and 1976. The supreme legislative body is the single-chamber National Assembly of 140 deputies. Election to the National Assembly is by universal suffrage at 18 years and above every 4 years.

A law of Nov. 1990 permitted independent candidates to stand in secret-ballot elections. In Dec. an opposition Democratic Party was allowed to form.

Effective rule was exercised by the Albanian Labour (*i.e.*, Communist) Party (founded 8 Nov. 1941) between 1945 and 1990, during which period it enjoyed a monopoly of political power. Its governing body was its Politburo. In June 1991 the party was renamed the Socialist Party.

At the elections of March 1992 the Democratic Party, led by Dr Sali Berisha, gained 68% of votes cast and the Socialist Party, 22%.

Titular Head of State, Chairman of the Presidium of the People's Assembly: Ramiz Alia (b. 1926), elected Nov. 1982, re-elected 30 April 1991 against a Communist opponent by 68% of votes cast.

An interim non-party 19-member government was formed in Dec. 1991 and held office until the elections of March 1992.

Local government is carried out by People's Councils at village, village union, town borough, town and district level. Councillors are elected for 3 years. Elections were held in May 1989; turn-out was 99·99%.

National flag: Red, with a black double-headed eagle and a red, gold-edged 5-pointed star above it. *Mercantile flag:* Red, black, red (horizontal) with a red yellow-edged star in the centre.

National anthem: Rreth Flamurit te per bashkuar (The flag that united us in the struggle).

DEFENCE. The Constitution precludes the stationing of foreign troops in Albania. Conscription is for 2 years. Military ranks were re-introduced in 1991. The defence budget was cut by 20%.

Army. The Army consists of 1 tank brigade, 4 infantry brigades, 1 engineer, and 3 artillery regiments. Equipment includes 190 T-34 and T-54 main battle tanks. Strength (1992) 35,000 (including 20,000 conscripts) and reserves number 150,000. The former paramilitary internal security force (Sigurimi) was abolished in 1991. Frontier guards number 7,000.

Navy. The combatant navy includes 2 submarines, 2 offshore patrol craft, 29 hydrofoil torpedo boats, 6 inshore patrol craft and 1 fleet minesweeper. Auxiliaries include 1 tanker and about 10 service craft. Navy personnel in 1991 totalled 2,000 officers and ratings, including 400 coastal defence guards. Service for ratings is 3 years. There are naval bases at Durrës and Vlorë.

Air Force. The Air Force, controlled by the Army, had (1992) about 11,000 officers and men (1,400 conscripts), and in 1991 operated 95 combat aircraft, of which about 80 had been received before relations with China were broken. The force included 20 Chinese-built F-7s and 30 F-6s, and 3 ground attack squadrons of F-2s and F-4s. Transport and training types include 3 Il-14s, 10 An-2s, Mi-4 helicopters, Yak-18s and MiG-15UTIs. Serviceability is reported to be reported to be low because of a shortage of operating funds.

INTERNATIONAL RELATIONS

Membership. Albania is a member of the UN. In 1990 Albania applied for observer status in the CSCE and agreed to sign the Non-Proliferation of Nuclear Weapons Treaty.

ECONOMY

Policy. For the first seven 5-year plans *see* THE STATESMAN'S YEAR-BOOK, 1989–90. Cautious moves towards 'economic logic', a recognition of market forces were made in 1989. Prices of consumer staples and fares rose in Nov. 1991 after subsidies were removed.

Budget. Budget figures for 1989: Revenue, 9,550m. leks; expenditure, 9,500m. leks. Revenue in 1988 (in 1m. leks): Centralized state income, 3,880; from enterprises, 2,850; social insurance, 889. Expenditure: Economy, 4,211; social 2,725; defence, 955 (998 in 1986); administration, 155.

Currency. The monetary unit is the *lek* (ALL) of 100 *qintars*. It replaced the gold franc *(franc ar)* in July 1947. In Aug. 1965 a new *lek* was introduced: 10 old *leks* = 1 new *lek*. There are 5, 10, 20 and 50 *qintar* coins and a 1 *lek* coin; notes are for 1, 3, 5, 10, 25, 50 and 100 *leks*. In Sept. 1991 the lek was pegged to the ecu at a rate of 30 leks = 1 ecu. Inflation was 25% in mid-1991. Exchange rates, March 1992: US$1 = 49·96 *leks*; £1 = 87·70.

Banking and Finance. The Albanian State Bank was founded in 1925 with Italian aid. Its *Director General* is Niko Gjyzari. In 1988 savings deposits amounted to 1,478m. leks. The ecu is used as a basis for foreign exchange deals.

Weights and Measures. The metric system is in force.

ENERGY AND NATURAL RESOURCES

Electricity. Albania is rich in hydro-electric potential. Electric power production in 1988 was 3,984m. kwh. 2,000m. kwh. were exported in 1984 to Yugoslavia, Bulgaria, Romania and Greece.

Oil. Oil reserves are some 20m. tonnes. Output in 1991: Crude, 1·63m. tonnes; refined (1973), 1,596,000 tonnes. Refining capacity in 1970 was over 1m. tonnes. Oil is produced chiefly at Qytet Stalin which a pipeline connects to the port of Vlorë. Natural gas is extracted. Reserves: 8,000m. cu. metres; 1985 production, 420m. cu. metres.

Minerals. The mineral wealth of Albania is considerable and includes lignite, oil, chrome and ferro-nickel ores, but it is only recently being developed. Production (in 1,000 tonnes), (1988): Lignite, 2,184; chromium ore, 1,109; copper ore, 1,087; iron-nickel ore, 1,067.

Agriculture. The country for the greater part is rugged, wild and mountainous, the exceptions being along the Adriatic littoral and the Korçë (Koritza) Basin, which are fertile. In 1988 the cultivated area was 714,200 ha, of which 589,800 ha were sown to crops, 59,600 ha were orchards, 44,500 ha olive groves and 20,300 ha vineyards. There were 403,000 ha of pasture. 58·2% of arable land was irrigated.

Land is held by the State (largely forests and non-agricultural), state farms (50 in 1982 averaging 3,000 ha of arable land) and co-operatives (460 in 1989 covering 528,700 ha).

A law of Aug. 1991 privatized co-operatives' land. Families are receiving allocations according to their size made by village committees. Emigrants are eligible to receive land. Land may not be sold for 3 years. In 1988 there were 21,033 tractors (in 15HP units).

Production (in 1,000 tonnes) (and sown area in 1,000 ha) of the main crops in 1988: Wheat, 589 (199); sugar-beet, 360 (7·4); maize, 306 (72·1); potatoes, 137 (12·9); fruit, 216; grapes, 88; oats, 30; sorghum, 38; seed cotton, 14 (14·5); barley, 40; sunflower seeds, 27 (25·6); wine, 25; rice, 11 (3·2); tobacco, 29 (32).

Livestock, 1988: Cattle, 696,000 (including 284,000 milch cows); sheep,

1,525,000; goats, 1,076,000; pigs, 197,000; horses and mules, 176,000; poultry, 5m; beehives, 82,000.

Forestry. Forests covered 1,046,150 ha in 1988, mainly oak, elm, pine and birch. Some 40,000 ha per annum are afforested or improved. In 1988 171,000 cubic metres of sawn timber were produced.

Fisheries. The catch in 1988 was 4,000 tonnes.

INDUSTRY. Industry was completely nationalized under the Communist regime, but since July 1990 individuals have been permitted to own craft businesses. Output is small, and the principal industries are agricultural product processing, textiles, oil products and cement. Chemical and engineering industries are being built up. In 1988 (in 1,000 tonnes): Blister copper, 15; copper cable, 11·6; carbonic ferro-chrome, 38·7; coke, 291; rolled steel, 96; phosphate fertilizer, 165; ammonium nitrate, 96; urea, 77; sulphuric acid, 81; caustic soda, 31; soda ash, 22; cement, 746; machinery (in 1m. lek) 496; 16,500 TV sets; 25,000 radio sets; 5·4m. pairs of footwear.

Labour. In 1988 the workforce was 811,000 (46·8% women), of whom 51·7% worked in agriculture, 22·9% in industry, 7% in building, 4·8% in trade, 4·5% in education and culture, 2·9% in transport and communications and 2·9% in the health service.

Minimum wages (450 leks per month in 1990) may not fall below one-third of maximum. Hours of labour: 8-hour day, 6-day week and 12 days yearly paid holiday. Retirement age is 60 for men and 55 for women. Wage increases of up to 20% were introduced in Oct. 1990. Average monthly wage, 1990: 570 leks.

Trade Unions. Independent trade unions became legal in Feb. 1991. The leader of the Independent Trade Union Federation is Valer Xheka.

FOREIGN ECONOMIC RELATIONS. Yugoslavia is Albania's main trading partner. Trade links with China were reestablished in 1983. Foreign investment was legalized in Nov. 1990.

Commerce. Exports in 1988 totalled 2,709m. leks; imports, 3,218m. leks. In 1988 exports included 39·8% minerals, 16·1% plant and animal products, 8·7% processed foodstuffs, 7·3% electricity; imports: 28·5% machinery, 25·2% fuels and minerals, 14% plant and animal raw materials, 13·1% chemical products.

Share of export market in 1988: Czechoslovakia, 10%; Romania, 9·7%; Bulgaria, 9·4%; German Democratic Republic, 8·2%; Poland, 7·5%; Yugoslavia, 7·1%; Italy, 6·3%; Hungary, 5·9%; Austria, 5·4%; China, 5·1%.

Total trade between Albania and UK (British Department of Trade returns, in £1,000 sterling):

	1988	1989	1990	1991
Imports to UK	2,764	605	413	274
Exports and re-exports from UK	1,126	1,957	4,542	3,179

Tourism. The right of Albanian citizens to apply for a passport was announced in May 1990. 30,000 foreign tourists visted in 1990.

COMMUNICATIONS

Roads. There were, in 1981, 21,000 km of roads suitable for motor traffic. The mountain districts of the north are still often inaccessible for wheeled vehicles. Motor vehicles in 1970: Cars, 3,500; lorries and buses, 11,000. Road traffic carried 77·29m. passengers in 1988; goods carried, 76·98m. tonnes. Private ownership of motor vehicles became legal in Feb. 1991.

Railways. Total length, in 1988 was 417 km. They comprise the lines from Durrës to Tirana, Vlorë, Ballsh, Korcë, Shkodër and across the Yugoslav border to Titograd. In 1990 the Milot-Klos line was completed. 10·97m. passengers and 7·66m. tonnes of freight were carried in 1988.

Civil Aviation. Tirana (Rinas Airport) is serviced by Alitalia, Malév, Olympic, Swissair and Tarom airlines, and there are scheduled flights to Athens, Bari, Bucharest, Budapest, Ioannina, Rome and Zurich. In 1990 Albania opened its air space to foreign commercial aircraft. A small national carrier, Adalbanair, was set up in Oct. 1990 and plans flights to Italy and Greece. It is 50% state-owned.

Shipping. In 1986 there were 20 ships totalling 56,133 GRT. The main ports are the Enver Hoxha Port of Durrës, Vlorë, Sarandë and Shëngjin. There is a ferry service from Trieste to Durrës. 1·1m. tonnes of freight were carried in 1988 (769,000 tonnes overseas).

Telecommunications. Number of post and telegraph offices (1988), 635; telephones (1990), 6,000. The government-controlled Radiotelevisione Shqiptar broadcasts a national radio programme and a second radio programme from 14 stations. There are also regional programmes and an external service. There are 9 TV stations (colour by PAL). In 1991 there were 525,000 radio and 246,220 TV receivers.

Cinemas and Theatres. In 1988 there were 106 cinemas with an attendance of 3·03m. and 28 theatres with an attendance of 1·84m. 14 full-length films were produced in 1980.

Newspapers and Books. In 1988 there were 42 newspapers with an annual circulation of 62·4m. and 74 periodicals. 1,018 book titles were published in 1981. There were 45 public libraries in 1988.

JUSTICE, RELIGION, EDUCATION AND WELFARE

Justice is administered by People's Courts. Minor crimes are tried by tribunals. Judges of the Supreme Court are elected by the People's Assembly for 4-year terms. The Office of the Procurator-General oversees the administration of justice. In 1983 an Investigator's Office was set up, separate from the Ministry of the Interior and answerable to the People's Assembly. A Ministry of Justice was re-established in 1990 and a Bar Council set up. In May 1990 capital offences were reduced from 34 to 11 and the death penalty abolished for women.

Religion. Albania is constitutionally an atheist state but in 1990 the ban on religious propaganda was lifted. In 1967 the Government closed all mosques and churches; they were permitted to re-open in 1990. For details of the situation before 1967 *see* THE STATESMAN'S YEAR-BOOK, 1969–70. The population had been 70% Moslem, 20% Orthodox and 10% Roman Catholic. There were 32 Roman Catholic priests in 1990.

Education. Primary education is free and compulsory in 8-year schools from 7 to 15 years. Secondary education is available in 12-year (general), technical-professional or lower vocational schools. There were, in 1988, 3,251 nursery schools with 121,000 pupils and 5,299 teachers, 1,691 primary schools with 547,000 pupils (5,000 part-time) and 27,862 teachers, 485 secondary schools with 194,000 pupils (63,000 part-time) and 9,004 teachers (including 442 vocational secondary schools with 135,000 pupils and 7,221 teachers), and 8 tertiary institutions, with 25,000 students (5,000 part-time) and 1,659 lecturers. There were 19,953 (10,143 female) full-time students and 5,248 (2,524 female) part-time students in higher education in 1988, including 13,329 at the University of Tirana. An Albanian Academy was founded in 1972. Schools suffered serious material damage and losses during 1990–91. In 1991–92 there were some 2,500 schools with 0·8m. pupils and 50,000 teachers. Since 1991 there have been 4 universities (Tirana; Tirana Polytechnical; Tirana Agricultural, and the Luigj Gurakuqi University in Shkodër) and 5 other institutes of higher education.

Welfare. 981m. leks were expended on pensions in 1988.

Health. Medical services are free, though medicines are charged for. In 1988 there were 158 hospitals with 12,350 beds. There were 5,497 doctors and dentists. In 1988 there were 3,210 out-patient clinics and 630 maternity homes.

DIPLOMATIC REPRESENTATIVE

Diplomatic relations between Great Britain and Albania were resumed in May 1991. Diplomatic relations were resumed between the USA and Albania in March 1991.

Of Albania to the United Nations
Ambassador: Vacant.

Further Reading

Vjetari Statistikor i R.P.S. të Shqipërisë/Statistical Yearbook of P.S.R. of Albania, 1989 [In English and Albanian]. Tirana, 1989
Bland, W. B., *Albania.* [Bibliography] Oxford and Santa Barbara, 1988
Halliday, J., (ed.) *The Artful Albanian: The Memoirs of Enver Hoxha.* London, 1986
Hetzer, A. and Roman, V. S. *Albania: A Bibliographic Research Survey.* Munich, 1983
Logoreci, A., *The Albanians: Europe's Forgotten Survivors.* London, 1977
Marmullaku, R., *Albania and the Albanians.* London, 1975
Pollo, S. and Arben, P., *The History of Albania.* London, 1981
Prifti, P. R., *Socialist Albania since 1944.* Cambridge, Mass., 1978
Sjoberg, O., *Rural Change and Development in Albania.* Boulder (Colo.), 1992

ALGERIA

Capital: Algiers
Population: 25·36m. (1990)
GNP per capita: US$2,170 (1989)

Jumhuriya al-Jazairiya
ad-Dimuqratiya ash-Shabiya

(People's Democratic Republic
of Algeria)

HISTORY. For post-colonial history *see* THE STATESMAN'S YEAR-BOOK, 1991–92, p. 76. France declared Algeria independent on 3 July 1962; the Republic was declared on 25 Sept. 1962.

The Government was overthrown by a junta of army officers which, on 19 June 1965, established a Revolutionary Council under Col. Houari Boumédienne.

After the first round of elections was decisively won by the Islamic Salvation Front (FIS) on 26 Dec. 1991 the President resigned on 11 Jan. 1992 and his functions were assumed by a High Committee of State. The second round of elections was cancelled. A new government led by Sid Ahmed Ghozali was formed in Feb. In March 1992 a state of emergency was proclaimed for 12 months and the FIS was dissolved by court order.

AREA AND POPULATION. Algeria is bounded west by Morocco and Western Sahara, south-west by Mauritania and Mali, south-east by Niger, east by Libya and Tunisia, and north by the Mediterranean Sea. It has an area of 2,381,741 sq. km (919,595 sq. miles). Population (census 1987) 22,971,558; estimate (1990) 25·36m. (44·3% urban). Population density (1988), 10 per sq. km. Annual growth rate (averaged over 1985–90), 3·1%; infant mortality, 74 per 1,000; expectation of life, 62·5 years. Some 2m. Algerians live abroad.

In 1987, 49% lived in urban areas and 46% were under 15 years of age. 83% speak Arabic, 17% Berber; French is widely spoken. A law of Dec. 1990 makes Arabic the sole official language.

The populations (1987 Census) of the 48 *wilayat* were as follows:

Adrar	216,931	Mila	511,047
Ain Defla	536,205	Mostaganem	504,124
Ain Témouchent	271,454	M'Sila	605,578
Annaba (Bône)	453,951	Naâma	112,858
Batna	757,059	Ouahran (Oran)	916,578
al-Bayadh	155,494	Ouargla	286,696
Béchar	183,896	al-Oued	379,512
Béjaia (Bougie)	697,669	Oum al-Bouaghi	402,683
Biskra	429,217	Qacentina (Constantine)	662,330
Bordj Bou Arreridj	429,009	Relizane	545,061
Bouira	525,460	Saida	235,240
al-Boulaida (Blida)	704,462	Setif	997,482
Boumerdes	646,870	Sidi bel-Abbès	444,047
Cheliff (Orléansville)	679,717	Skikda	619,094
Djelfa	490,240	Souk Ahras	298,236
Guelma	353,329	Tamanrasset	94,219
Ghardaia	215,955	at-Tarf	276,836
Illizi	19,698	Tébessa	409,317
al-Jaza'ir (Algiers)	1,687,579	Tiaret	574,786
Jijel	471,319	Tindouf	16,339[1]
Khenchela	243,733	Tipaza	615,140
Laghouat	215,183	Tissemsilt	227,542
Mascara	562,806	Tizi-Ouzou	931,501
Médéa	650,623	Tlemcen	707,453

[1] Excluding Saharawi refugees (170,000 in 1988) in camps.

The capital is Algiers (1987 population, 1,507,000). Other major towns (with 1983 populations): Oran, 663,504; Constantine, 448,578; Annaba, 348,322; Blida, 191,314; Sétif, 186,978; Sidi-Bel-Abbès, 186,978; Tlemcen, 146,089; Skikda,141,159; Bejaia, 124,122; Batna, 122,788; al Asnam, 118,996; Tizi-Ouzou, 100,749; Médéa, 84,292.

CLIMATE. Coastal areas have a warm temperate climate, with most rain in winter, which is mild, while summers are hot and dry. Inland, conditions become more arid beyond the Atlas Mountains. Algiers. Jan. 54°F (12·2°C), July 76°F (24·4°C). Annual rainfall 30" (762 mm). Biskra. Jan. 52°F (11·1°C), July 93°F (33·9°C). Annual rainfall 6" (158 mm). Oran. Jan. 54°F (12·2°C), July 76°F (24·4°C). Annual rainfall 15" (376 mm).

CONSTITUTION AND GOVERNMENT. A Constitution was approved by referendum in Feb. 1989. There was a turnout of 83% and 92% of the voters approved of the constitutional reforms which included the beginning of the separation of the National Liberation Front (FLN) from the State in that the Prime Minister is to be responsible to the National Assembly rather than the FLN, the legalization of opposition parties and the omission of references to socialism.

The President of the Republic is Head of State, Head of the Armed Forces, and Head of Government. He is elected by universal suffrage for 5-year terms (renewable).

Past president: Bendjedid Chadli (sworn in 9 Feb. 1979, re-elected in 1984 and 1989; resigned 11 Jan. 1992).

A Constitutional Council functions as an electoral supervisory body.

The President appoints a Prime Minister and other Ministers, and presides over meetings of the Council of Ministers.

Legislative power is held by the National People's Assembly, whose 295 members are elected for a 5-year term by universal suffrage. Beginning in 1989 the political system was being liberalized. Proportional representation was adopted in March 1990. Elections due in June 1991 were postponed to 26 Dec. with a second round on 15 Jan. 1992. The electorate was 13·5m.; 5,712 candidates stood. At the first round 231 seats were decided out of the 430 in the National Assembly. Turnout was 58·5%. The Islamic Salvation Front (FIS) won 188 seats, the Socialist Forces Front (FFS – a Berber party) 25 and the FLN 15.

Before the second round the President resigned and his functions were assumed by a High Committee of State consisting of:

Mohamed Boudiaf (b. 1920; Chairman), Maj.-Gen. Khaled Nezzar, Ali Khafi, Tedjini Haddam and Ali Haroun.

The Committee is assisted by a National Consultative Council.

A 28-member government was formed on 22 Feb. 1992 including:

Prime Minister, Minister of the Economy: Sid Ahmed Ghozali (b. 1937).

Defence: Maj.-Gen. Khaled Nezzar. *Interior and Local Collectives:* Larbi Belkheir. *Foreign:* Lakhdar Brahimi. *Culture and Communication:* Aboubakr Belkaid. *Energy:* Nordine Ait-Laoussine. *Transport and Communications:* Hachemi Nait-Djoudi (FFS). *Professional Training and Labour:* Said Guechi (FIS). *Religious Affairs:* Sassi Lamouri. *Treasury:* Ahmed Ben Bitour.

National flag: Vertically green and white, a red crescent and star over all in centre.

National anthem: Qassaman bin nazilat Il-mahiqat ('We swear by the lightning that destroys'; words by Mufoli Zakaria, tune by Mohamed Fawzi.

Local government: There are 48 provincial councils and 1,539 local authorities. At elections in June 1990 turn-out was 65%. The Islamic Salvation Front (FIS) gained control of 32 provincial and 853 local councils, the FLN of 14 and 487.

DEFENCE. Conscription is for a period of 6 months at the age of 19.

Army. The Army had a strength of 107,000 (70,000 conscripts) in 1992, organized in 3 armoured, 8 mechanized and 9 motorized brigades; 31 infantry, 4 paratroop, 5 artillery, 5 air defence and 4 engineer battalions; and 12 companies of desert troops. Equipment includes 113 T-34, 390 T-54/-55, 300 T-62 and 100 T-72 main battle tanks.

Navy. The Naval combatant force, largely supplied from the USSR, consists of 4 diesel-powered patrol submarines, 3 frigates, 3 missile-armed corvettes, 11 fast missile craft, 6 other patrol craft, 1 ocean minesweeper, 2 tank landing ships, and 1 tank landing craft. There are some 10 auxiliaries. An associated coastguard operates 20 fast cutters. Naval personnel in 1991 totalled 6,500. There are naval bases at Algiers, Annaba and Mers el Kebir.

Air Force. Five MiG-15 jet-fighters were delivered in 1962 as the nucleus of an Algerian Air Force. Since then many more aircraft of Soviet design have followed, and the Air Force currently has about 250 combat aircraft and 12,000 personnel. Training and technical assistance have been given by Egypt and the Soviet Union. There are 8 squadrons of MiG-21s, 3 squadrons of MiG-23 variable-geometry interceptors and fighter-bombers, 3 squadrons of Su-7 and Su-20 variable-geometry attack aircraft, 2 squadrons with MiG-25 fighter and reconnaissance aircraft, more than 30 Mi-24 assault helicopters and gunships, 17 C-130H Hercules, 3 F.27, 4 Il-76 and 5 An-12 transports, an Il-18 and a variety of smaller transports, a wing of 4 Mi-6, 30 Mi-8, about 30 Mi-4, 5 Puma, 6 Alouette III and 6 Hughes 269 helicopters, and training units equipped with CM.170 Magister armed jet counter-insurgency/trainers (20), 8 Beech Queen Air twin-engine/instrument trainers, MiG-15UTIs and MiG-17s, and two-seat versions of operational types. Surface-to-air missile units have Soviet-built 'Guidelines', 'Goas', 'Gainfuls' and 'Gaskins'.

INTERNATIONAL RELATIONS

Membership. Algeria is a member of UN, OAU, the Arab League and OPEC.

ECONOMY

Policy. The fourth development plan (1985–89) envisaged expenditure of DA 550,000m. primarily on housing, agriculture and water resources.

Budget. Administrative expenditure for 1988 was DA 63,000m.

Currency. The unit of currency is the *Algerian dinar* (DZD) of 100 *centimes*. There are in circulation banknotes of DA 5, 10, 50 and 100 and coins of 1, 2, 5, 20 and 50 centimes and DA 1, 5 and 10. Inflation was 9·2% in 1989. DA 120,000m. was in circulation in 1989. The dinar was devalued 22% in Sept. 1991. In March 1992, £1 = 38·81 DA; US$1 = 22·11 DA.

Banking and Finance. The Central Bank and bank of issue is the Banque Centrale d'Algérie. The *Governor* is Abderrahmane Hadj Nacer. Other banks operating in Algeria are Banque National d'Algérie, Crédit Populaire d'Algérie, Banque Extérieure d'Algérie, Caisse Algérienne de Développement, Banque Algérienne de Développement, Banque de l'Agriculture et du Développement. Bank deposits were DA 130,000m. in 1989.

Weights and Measures. The metric system is in use.

ENERGY AND NATURAL RESOURCES

Electricity. Production (1986) 12,410m. kwh. Supply 127 and 220 volts; 50 Hz.

Oil. In 1960 about 200 wells were productive. Natural gas was discovered at Djebel Berga in 1954 and at Hassi-R'Mel in 1956. Oil pipelines from Edjéle to Skirra (Tunisia) and from Hassi Messaoud to Béjaia, and a gas pipeline from Hassi Messaoud via Hassi-R'Mel to Mostaganem–Oran–Algiers, have been completed. A law of Nov. 1991 permits foreign companies to acquire up to 49% of known oil and gas reserves. Oil production in 1991, 58·45m. tonnes.

Gas. Production of natural gas in 1985 was 50,000m. cu. metres. Proven reserves are 3,700,000m. cu. metres.

Minerals. Algeria possesses deposits of iron, zinc, lead, mercury, silver, copper and antimony. Kaolin, marble and onyx, salt and coal are also found. Mineral output in 1985 (1,000 tonnes): Iron ore, 3,370; copper, 0·9; lead, 3·6; phosphates (1988), 1,207; barite, 100; clay, 58; sulphur, 10; zinc, 10; coal, 8.

Agriculture. The greater part of Algeria is of limited value for agricultural purposes. In the northern portion the mountains are generally better adapted to grazing and forestry than agriculture. There were an estimated 7·07m. ha of arable land in 1989, 0·54m. ha of permanent crops and 31·18m. ha of permanent pasture. 0·37m. ha were irrigated. In 1987 the government sold back to the private sector land which had been nationalized on the declaration of independence in 1962; a further 0·5m. ha, expropriated in 1973, were returned to some 30,000 small landowners in 1990. In 1990 5·95m. persons were dependant upon agriculture, the agricultural workforce being 1·39m. There were 98,000 tractors and 9,400 combine harvesters in 1989.

The chief crops in 1990 were (in 1,000 tonnes): Wheat, 750; barley, 700; dates, 212; potatoes, 1,107; oranges, 177; mandarins and tangerines, 95; watermelons, 356; wine, 100; tomatoes, 537; olives, 179; onions, 210; oats, 40.

Livestock (in 1,000), 1990: 195 horses, 430 mules and asses, 1,427 cattle, 13,350 sheep, 3,699 goats and 135 camels.

Forestry. Forests cover 4·7m. ha or 2% of the land area. The greater part of the state forests are brushwood, but there are large areas with cork-oak trees, Aleppo pine, evergreen oak and cedar. The dwarf-palm is grown on the plains, alfa on the table-land. Timber is cut for firewood and for industrial purposes and for bark for tanning. Considerable portions of the forest area are also leased for tillage, or for pasturage for cattle and sheep.

Fisheries. There are extensive fisheries for sardines, anchovies, sprats, tunny fish, etc., and also shellfish. Fish taken in 1986 amounted to 70,000 tonnes.

INDUSTRY. In 1981, 10·5m. tonnes of petroleum products were refined. Production of cement (1981) 4·45m. tonnes, crude steel (1989) 880,000 tonnes.

Labour. In 1990 the economically active population was estimated at 5·71m. In 1985 41% of the active population worked in services, 32·1% in industry and 26·9% in agriculture. The minimum wage was raised by 40% in Nov. 1991, to reach DA 3,000 per month on 1 Jan. 1992 and DA 3,500 on 1 July 1992. Unemployment was 22% in 1989.

Trade Unions. The General Union of Algerian Workers (leader, Abdelhak Benhammouda) had in 1982 about 1m. members in 8 affiliated groups, while the National Union of Algerian Peasants had 700,000. The Islamic Federation of Trade Unions was formed in July 1990.

FOREIGN ECONOMIC RELATIONS. In Feb. 1990 Algeria signed a treaty of economic co-operation with the other countries of the Maghreb: Libya, Mauritania, Morocco and Tunisia.

Foreign debt was US$25,300m. in 1990.

Foreign investors are permitted to hold 100% of the equity of companies,and to repatriate all profits.

Commerce. Foreign trade was as follows (in US$1m.):

	1986	1987	1988	1990
Imports	9,234	7,029	7,396	10,500
Exports	7,831	8,186	8,164	13,200

Main trade partners in 1990, with percentages of total trade: France (exports, 13·5%; imports, 24·7%); Italy (20·3%; 14·5%); USA (18·8%; 9·3%); Federal Germany (7·4%; 9·5%). In 1988 oil and gas made up 94·7% of exports.

Total trade between Algeria and UK (British Department of Trade returns, in £1,000 sterling):

	1988	1989	1990	1991
Imports to UK	159,748	177,546	259,959	194,874
Exports and re-exports from UK	86,615	74,368	73,831	55,685

Tourism. In 1989, there were 851,181 foreign visitors.

COMMUNICATIONS

Roads. There were in 1986, 78,410 km of national highway including 45,070 km of concrete or bituminous roads. The mountainous regions are accessible only with difficulty. Motor vehicles in 1980 included 472,483 passenger cars and 283,966 commercial vehicles.

Railways. In 1988 there were 3,836 km of which 2,698 km is of 1,435mm gauge (299 km electrified) and 1,138 km of 1,055mm gauge railway open for traffic. In 1989 the railways carried 12·06m. tonnes of freight and 52·5m. passengers.

Civil Aviation. There are 5 international airports as well as another 65 airfields controlled by government and 135 owned by petroleum companies. Air Algeria serves the main Algerian cities, and an international network. Algeria is also served by Swissair, Royal Air Maroc and United Arab Airline. In 1980 the airports handled 2·84m. passengers and 22,479 tonnes of freight. In May 1990 the Maghreb countries (Algeria, Libya, Mauritania, Morocco and Tunisia) agreed to merge their national airlines into Air Maghreb.

Shipping. In 1982, 69·4m. tonnes of goods were handled at Algerian ports.

A state shipping line, Compagnie Nationale Algérienne de Navigation, was formed in Jan. 1964.

Telecommunications. There were, in 1980, 1,534 post offices; number of telephones (1985), 769,000. The state-controlled Radiodiffusion-Télévision Algérienne broadcasts home services in Arabic, Kabyle (Berber) and French from 27 radio stations and an external service. There are 18 TV transmitting stations (colour by PAL). In 1991 there were 5·5m. radio and 1·6m. TV receivers.

Cinemas. In 1985 there were 216 cinemas with 110,000 seats. 21,000 attendances were recorded.

Newspapers (1989). There were 6 daily newspapers, with a combined circulation of 1m.

JUSTICE, RELIGION, EDUCATION AND WELFARE

Justice. There are appeal courts at Algiers, Constantine and Oran; and in the *arrondissements* are 17 courts of first instance. There are also commercial courts and justices of the peace with extensive powers. Criminal justice is organized as in France. The Supreme Court is at the same time Council of State and High Court of Appeal.

Religion. Virtually the whole population are Sunni Moslems. There are about 150,000 Christians, mainly Roman Catholic.

Education. Literacy was some 54% in 1987. In 1987 there were 11,692 state primary schools with (in 1988–89) 140,000 teachers and 3,911,000 pupils. In 1988–89 there were 1,900 secondary schools with 85,000 teachers and 1,955,000 pupils; and 71 technical and teacher-training colleges with 2,528 teachers. In 1988–89 there were 181,000 students and 18,000 teachers in tertiary education.

There are universities at Algiers, Oran, Constantine, Annaba, Sétif and Boumerdes. There are also Universities of Science and Technology at Algiers and Oran and university centres at Tlemcen, Tizi-Ouzou, Batna, Tiaret, Constantine, Mostaganem, Sidi-Bel-Abbés and Boulaida.

Health. There were in 1986, 49,280 hospital beds; there were 15,361 doctors. There were also 1,422 dispensaries and consulting rooms, 747 health centres and 175 specializing centres for tuberculosis, venereal disease and trachoma in 1980.

DIPLOMATIC REPRESENTATIVES

Of Algeria in Great Britain (54 Holland Park, London, W11 3RS)
Ambassador: Ali Lakhdari.

Of Great Britain in Algeria (Résidence Cassiopée, 7 Chemin des Glycines, Algiers)
Ambassador: C. C. R. Battiscombe, CMG.

Of Algeria in the USA (2118 Kalorama Rd., NW, Washington, D.C., 20008)
Ambassador: Abderrahmane Bensid.

Of the USA in Algeria (4 Chemin Cheich Bachir Ibrahimi, Algiers)
Ambassador: Christopher W. S. Ross.

Of Algeria to the United Nations
Ambassador: Dr Messaoud Ait Chaalal.

Further Reading

Service de Statistique Générale. *Statistique Générale de l'Algérie, Documents statistiques sur le commerce de l'Algérie* (from 1902). Annual.

Ageron, C.-R., *of Modern Algeria: a History from 1830 to the Present.* London, 1991
Bennoune, M., *The Making of Contempory Algeria, 1830–1987.* CUP, 1988
Horne, A., *A Savage War of Peace: Algeria 1954–1962.* London, 1977
Knapp, W., *North West Africa: A Political and Economic Survey.* OUP, 1977
Lawless, R. I., *Algeria.* [Bibliography] Oxford and Santa Barbara, 1981

National statistical office: Service de Statistique Générale.

ANDORRA

Capital: Andorra-la-Vella
Population: 53,435 (1990)

Principat d'Andorra

HISTORY. The political status of Andorra was regulated by the *Paréage* of 1278 which placed Andorra under the joint suzerainty of the Comte de Foix and of the Bishop of Urgel. The rights vested in the house of Foix passed by marriage to that of Bearn and, on the accession of Henri IV, to the French crown.

AREA AND POPULATION. The co-principality of Andorra is situated in the eastern Pyrenees on the French–Spanish border. The country consists of gorges, narrow valleys and defiles, surrounded by high mountain peaks varying between 1,880 and 3,000 metres. Its maximum length is 30 km and its width 20 km; it has an area of 453 sq. km (175 sq. miles) and a population (census, 1986) of 46,976 (65% urban); estimate (1990) 53,435, scattered in 7 parishes (*parròquia*). The chief towns (1986) are Andorra-la-Vella, the capital (15,639) and its suburb Escaldes-Engordany (11,955).

Catalan is the official language and was spoken by 30% of the population in 1986 but 59% spoke Spanish and 6% French.

CLIMATE. Escaldes-Engordany. Jan. 36°F (2·3°C), July 67°F (19·3°C). Annual rainfall 32" (808 mm).

CONSTITUTION AND GOVERNMENT. Sovereignty is exercised jointly by the President of the French Republic and the Bishop of Urgel. The co-princes are represented in Andorra by the *'Viguier français'* and the *'Viguier Episcopal'*. Each co-prince has set up a Permanent Delegation for Andorran affairs; the Prefect of the Eastern Pyrenees is the French Permanent Delegate.

The valleys pay every second year a due of 960 francs to France and 460 pesetas to the bishop.

The *General Council of the Valleys* is an elected assembly which submits motions and proposals to the Permanent Delegations. Its 28 members are elected for 4 years; half of the council is renewed every 2 years. The Council nominates as its Chairman a First Syndic from among its members and a Second Syndic from outside. In 1982 an *Executive Council* was appointed and legislative and executive powers were separated.

Elections to the General Council were held in Dec. 1989. Electorate, 7,185 (most residents are classified as 'foreign' and ineligible to vote). Turn-out was 80%.

The General Council of the Valleys was dissolved on 26 Jan. 1992.
Elections were scheduled for 5 April 1992.

National flag: Three vertical strips of blue, yellow, red, with the arms of Andorra in the centre.

National anthem. El Gran Carlemany, mon pare ('Great Charlemagne, my father'; words by Enric Marfany, tune by D.J. Benlloch i Vivò.

INTERNATIONAL RELATIONS. Andorra's foreign affairs are conducted by France.

ECONOMY

Budget. In 1986 the budget balanced at 6,655m. pesetas.

Currency. French and Spanish currency are both in use.

ENERGY AND NATURAL RESOURCES

Electricity. Production (1986) 140m. kwh. Andorra imported another 200m. kwh from Spain.

Agriculture. In 1990 there were some 1,000 ha of arable land, 10,000 ha of forests and 25,000 ha of pasture. Tobacco is a principal crop.

Livestock (1982): 9,000 sheep, 1,115 cattle, 217 horses.

INDUSTRY

Labour. 20% of the workforce is employed in agriculture, the rest in tourism, commerce, services and light industry.

FOREIGN ECONOMIC RELATIONS. Andorra is a member of the EEC Customs Union for industrial goods, and a third country for agricultural produce. There is a free economic zone.

Commerce. In 1986, imports amounted to 74,313m. pesetas (42% from Spain and 27% from France) and exports to 2,325m. pesetas (54% to France and 33% to Spain).

Total trade between Andorra and UK (British Department of Trade returns, in £1,000 sterling):

	1989	1990	1991
Imports to UK	236	9	36
Exports and re-exports from UK	10,493	15,763	14,188

Tourism. Tourism is the main industry.

COMMUNICATIONS

Roads. There are 220 km of roads (120 km paved). A good road connects the Spanish and French frontiers by way of Sant Julia, Andorra-la-Vella, Escaldes-Engordany, Encamp, Canillo and Soldeu: it crosses the Col d'Envalira (2,400 metres). Another road connects Andorra-la-Vella with La Massana and Ordino. Motor vehicles (1983) 24,789.

Civil Aviation. The nearest airports are at Barcelona, Perpignan and Toulouse.

Telecommunications. Number of telephones (1982) 17,719. Servei de Telecomunicacions d'Andorra relays French and Spanish programmes. Number of receivers (1991), radio, 10,000; TV, 4,000.

JUSTICE, RELIGION, EDUCATION AND WELFARE

Justice. Judicial power is exercised in civil matters in the first instance, according to the plaintiff's choice, by either the *Bayle Français* or the *Bayle Episcopal*, who are nominated by the respective co-princes. The judge of appeal is nominated alternately for 5 years by each co-prince; the third instance *(Tercera Sala)* is either the supreme court of Andorra at Perpignan or the supreme court of the Bishop at Urgel.

Criminal justice is administered by the *Corts* consisting of the 2 Viguiers, the judge of appeal, 2 *rahonadors* elected by the general council of the valleys, a general attorney and an attorney nominated for 5 years alternatively by each of the co-princes. The accused may be assisted by a barrister.

Religion. The prevailing religious denomination is Roman Catholic.

Education. Schooling is compulsory to age 16. In 1986–87 there were 1,866 pupils at infant schools, 3,458 at primary schools, 3,271 at secondary schools, 230 at technical schools and 46 at special schools.

Health. In 1988 there were 112 doctors and 113 hospital beds.

Further Reading

Corts Peyret, J., *Geografía e Historia de Andorra*. Barcelona, 1945
Llobet, S., *El medio y la vida en Andorra*. Barcelona, 1947
Riberaygua-Argelich, B., *Les Valls d'Andorra*. Barcelona, 1946

ANGOLA

Capital: Luanda
Population: 10·02m. (1990)
GNP per capita: US$620 (1989)

República Popular de Angola

HISTORY. The first Europeans to arrive in Angola were the Portuguese in 1482, and the first settlers arrived there in 1491. Luanda was founded in 1575. Apart from a brief period of Dutch occupation from 1641 to 1648, Angola remained a Portuguese colony until 11 June 1951, when it became an Overseas Province of Portugal. On 11 Nov. 1975 Angola became fully independent as the People's Republic of Angola. The People's Liberation Movement of Angola (MPLA) and the National Union for the Total Independence of Angola (UNITA) committed themselves to putting their rival claims to power to a popular vote, but the agreement broke down in battles which left MPLA in control of the capital and the other factions banished to the countryside. After talks in Lisbon which began in 1990 a peace agreement between the government and the insurgent National Union for the Total Independence of Angola (UNITA) was signed on 31 May 1991. The agreement provides for a political-military mission backed by US, Soviet and Portuguese experts to supervise the ceasefire under UN monitoring.

AREA AND POPULATION. Angola is bounded by Congo on the north, Zaïre on the north and north-east, Zambia on the east, Namibia on the south and the Atlantic ocean on the west. The area is 1,246,700 sq. km (481,351 sq. miles) including the 7,107 sq. km province of Cabinda, an enclave of territory separated by 30 km of Zaïre. The population at census, 1970, was 5,646,166, of whom 14% urban. Expectation of life was 49 years in 1989. Estimate (1990) 10,015,000, including (in 1988) 114,000 in Cabinda. Urban population (1986) 30% of whom 38% speak Umbundu, 27% Kimbundu, 13% Lunda and 11% Kikongo. Portuguese remains the official language.

The most important towns (with 1970 populations) are Luanda, the capital (480,613; 1988, 1·2m.), Huambo (61,885), Lobito (59,258), Benguela (40,996), Lubango (31,674; 1984, 105,000), Malange (31,559) and Namibe (formerly Moçâmedes, 23,145; 1981, 100,000).

CLIMATE. The climate is tropical, with low rainfall in the west but increasing inland. Temperatures are constant over the year and most rain falls in March and April. Luanda. Jan. 78°F (25·6°C), July 69°F (20·6°C). Annual rainfall 13" (323 mm). Lobito. Jan. 77°F (25°C), July 68°F (20°C). Annual rainfall 14" (353 mm).

CONSTITUTION AND GOVERNMENT. Under the Constitution adopted at independence, the sole legal party is the MPLA. In Dec. 1990, however, MPLA announced that the Constitution would be revised to permit opposition parties by March 1991. Under the May 1991 agreement between the government and UNITA multi-party elections were scheduled for 1992. The supreme organ of state is the unicameral National People's Assembly, whose members were first elected in Aug. 1980 for a 3-year term. There is an executive President elected for renewable terms of 5 years, who appoints a Council of Ministers to assist him. The post of prime minsiter abolished in 1977, was re-established in July 1991.

Substantial parts of the country are, however, under the control of the anti-government forces of UNITA.

The Council of Ministers in Nov. 1991 included:

President: José Eduardo dos Santos (re-elected 9 Dec. 1985).
Prime Minister and Minister of Planning: Fernando França Van-Dúnem.
Defence: Col.-Gen. Pedro Maria Tonha (Pedalé). *External Relations:* Lieut.-Col.

Pedro de Castro Van-Dúnem. *Education:* Augusto Lopes Teixeira (Tutu). *Health:* Flavio Joào Fernandes. *Finance:* Aguinaldo Jaime. *Foreign Trade:* Domingo das Chagas Simoes Rangel. *Internal Trade:* Joaquim Guerreiro Dias. *Industry:* Henrique de Carvalho dos Santos (Onambwe). *Transport and Communications:* Carlos António Fernandes. *Labour and Social Security:* Diogo Jorge de Jesus. *Agriculture:* Fernando Faustino Muteka. *Interior:* Francisco Magalhaes Paiva. *Construction:* Joào Henriques Garcia. *Fisheries:* José Ramos da Cruz. *Territorial Administration:* Lopo do Nascimento.

Flag: Horizontally red over black, with a star and an arc of cogwheel crossed by a machete, all yellow over all in the centre.

Local government: Angola is divided into 18 provinces divided into 139 districts – (Cabinda, Zaïre, Uíge, Luanda, Cuanza Norte, Cuanza Sul, Malange, Lunda Norte, Lunda Sul, Benguela, Huambo, Bié, Moxico, Cuando-Cubango, Namibe, Huíla, Cunene and Bengo) each under a Provincial Commissioner, appointed by the President and an elected legislative of from 55 to 85 members.

DEFENCE. Conscription is for a period of 2 years. The last Cuban forces left in May 1991. The armed forces are being restructured with British and French assistance and will total about 50,000, following the merger of government and UNITA forces agreed in May 1991. The previous status of government forces was:

Army. The Army had 70 brigades, each with infantry, tank, armoured personnel carriers, artillery and anti-aircraft units; and 10 SAM batteries. Total strength (1990) 91,500. Equipment included Soviet 100 T-34, 300 T-54/55 and more than 100 T-62 and PT-76 tanks.

Navy. 20 Portuguese naval craft were transferred on independence in 1975 of which most have been discarded, and 9 vessels were acquired from the Soviet Navy in 1977-79. There are 6 fast missile boats, 4 fast torpedo boats, 7 inshore patrol boats, 2 mine-hunters, 3 landing ships and 9 landing craft, together with 10 auxiliary vessels. Naval personnel in 1991 totalled about 1,500.

Air Force. The Angolan People's Air Force (FAPA) was formed in 1976. The combat force had been expanded since 1983 with Soviet assistance. It included (1991) 50 MiG-21, 30 MiG-23 and 40 Su-22 fighters, plus 25 Mi-24 and 12 Gazelle armed helicopters. (The MiG-17 is being withdrawn from service.) There are 10 An-2, 15 An-26, 12 Islander, 4 Turbo-Porter, 8 Aviocar and 2 F.27 transports, 2 Embraer EMB-111 maritime surveillance aircraft, 4 PC-9, 15 PC-7 and 3 MiG-15UTI trainers, and 40 Mi-8/17, 6 Dauphin, 2 Lama and 40 Alouette III helicopters. Personnel (1991) 3,000.

INTERNATIONAL RELATIONS

Membership. Angola is a member of the UN, OAU and is an ACP state of the EEC.

ECONOMY

Policy. Reforms are in train to introduce a market economy and restore private property.

Budget. The 1986 budget included 90,400m. kwanza for capital and current expenditure and revenue at 78,500m. kwanza.

Currency. The unit of currency is the *kwanza* (AOK) of 100 *lwei*. Coins are of 50 *lwei*, 1, 2, 5, 10 and 20 *kwanza*; notes are of 20, 50, 100, 500 and 1,000 *kwanza*. The *kwanza* was devalued 50% in 1991. In March 1992, £1 = 320·55 *kwanza*; US$1 = 182·60 *kwanza*.

Banking and Finance. All banking was nationalized in 1975. The *Banco Nacional de Angola* is the central bank and bank of issue, while the *Banco Popular de Angola* handles all commercial activities throughout the country.

Weights and Measures. The metric system is in force.

ENERGY AND NATURAL RESOURCES

Electricity. Production (1986) totalled 851m. kwh, mainly hydro-electricity. In Nov. 1984 an agreement was signed with Brazil and USSR to construct a hydro-electric plant at Kapanda on the river Kwanza, 250 miles south of Luanda.

Oil. Total production (1991) 24·59m. tonnes.

Minerals. Production of diamonds during 1985 totalled 625,000 carats. Production (1985) of salt, 10,000 tonnes. There has been no production of iron ore since 1975, but the mines at Kassinga were restarted in 1985. Phosphate mining commenced in the north in 1981. Manganese and copper deposits exist.

Agriculture. In 1989 there were 3·05m. ha of arable land, 0·55m. ha of permanent crops and 29m. ha of permanent pasture. In 1990 6·99m. persons depended upon agriculture, of whom 2·85m. were economically active. The principal cash crops (with 1990 production, in 1,000 tonnes): Sugarcane (330), coffee (180), bananas (280), palm oil (40), palm kernels (12), seed cotton (33); others include tobacco, citrus fruit and sisal. Food crops comprise cassava (1,920), maize (180), sweet potatoes (170) and dry beans (40).

Livestock (1990): 3·1m. cattle, 275,000 sheep, 985,000 goats, 493,000 pigs.

Forestry. In 1990 there were 52·95m. ha of forests. Mahogany and other hardwoods are exported, chiefly from the tropical rain forests of the north, especially Cabinda. Production (1986) 10m. cu. metres.

Fisheries. Total catch (1984) 70,700 tonnes.

INDUSTRY. In 1985, 10,000 tonnes of steel were produced and 350,000 tonnes of cement.

Labour. The economically active population was 4·09m. in 1990, of whom 69·8% worked in agriculture.

FOREIGN ECONOMIC RELATIONS. In 1991 foreign debt was some US$7,000m., of which at least half was to the USSR.

Commerce. Imports and exports for 4 calendar years in 1m. Kwanza.

	1982	1983	1984 [1]	1985 [1]
Imports	25,946	20,197	19,448	41,240
Exports	48,736	54,508	60,112	59,280

[1] Provisional.

The chief imports are textiles, transport equipment, foodstuffs, pig-iron and steel; chief exports are crude oil, coffee, diamonds, sisal, fish, maize, palm-oil. In 1983, crude petroleum represented 85% of exports, petroleum products, 5·6%, coffee 3·9% and diamonds 5·6%. In 1985 Portugal provided 13% of imports, France 12%, the USA 11%, and Brazil 11%, while 45% of exports went to the USA, 14% to Spain and 11% (all diamonds) to the Bahamas.

Total trade between Angola and UK (British Department of Trade returns, in £1,000 sterling):

	1988	1989	1990	1991
Imports to UK	10,036	1,286	5,142	65,078
Exports and re-exports from UK	20,154	24,785	29,284	34,812

COMMUNICATIONS

Roads. There were, in 1986, 73,830 km of roads, and in 1984, 56,625 cars and 29,000 commercial vehicles.

Railways. The length of railways open for traffic in 1987 was 2,952 km comprising 2,798 km of 1,067 mm gauge and 154 km of 600 mm gauge. The Benguela Railway runs from Lobito to the Zaïre border at Dilolo where it connects with the National Railways of Zaïre. Other lines link Luanda with Malange; Gunza with Gabela; and Namibe with Menongue. In 1986 Angola's railways carried 4·1m. passengers and 2·5m. tonnes of freight.

Civil Aviation. Luanda Fourth Februrary airport had international air links to Lisbon, Rome, Paris, Moscow, Budapest, Brazzaville, Saõ Tomé, Lusaka, Maputo, Sal (Cape Verde Islands), Havana, Kinshasa, Libreville, Berlin, Tripoli, Lagos, Algiers, Niamey, Sofia, Malta, Rio de Janeiro and São Paulo, but most were inoperative during the civil war.

Shipping. In 1975, 2·85m. tonnes were discharged and 16m. tonnes loaded in Angolan ports. In 1986 there were 100 merchant vessels (over 100 GRT) totalling 127,000 GRT.

Telecommunications. Angola is connected by cable with east, west and south African telegraph systems. There were, in 1973, 1,808 km of telegraph lines, 77 telephone stations (with 40,000 instruments in 1982), 162 telegraph stations and 31 wireless stations.

Rádio Nacional de Angola is the largest of the 18 stations operating on medium-and short-waves. *Rádio Nacional* transmits 3 programmes as well as operating 2 regional stations. Number of radio receivers (1988) 1·2m. and television receivers 200,000.

The government-controlled Rádio Nacional de Angola broadcasts 3 programmes and an international service. There are also regional stations. Televisão Popular de Angola transmits from 7 stations (colour by PAL). In 1991 there were 0·45m. radio and 50,000 TV receivers.

Cinemas. There were, in 1972, 47 cinemas with seating capacity of 35,142.

Newspaper. The national daily newspaper is *Jornal de Angola*, with a circulation of 41,000 in 1988.

JUSTICE, RELIGION, EDUCATION AND WELFARE

Justice. The Supreme Court and Court of Appeal are in Luanda.

Religion. Article 7 of the Constitution of the People's Republic of Angola states that: 'The People's Republic of Angola is a secular state, where there is a complete separation of religious institutions from the state'. All religions will be respected.

In 1988 there were 8·45m. Christians, the remainder following traditional animist religion.

Education. In 1983 there were 2·4m. pupils in primary schools, 153,000 in secondary schools and 4,746 students in higher education. The *Universidade de Angola* (founded 1963) at Luanda with faculties at Huambo and Lubango, had 3,500 students in 1982.

Health. In 1980 there were 436 doctors and 20,700 hospital beds and in 1973, 87 pharmacists, 284 midwives and 3,115 nursing personnel.

DIPLOMATIC REPRESENTATIVES

Of Angola in Great Britain (98 Park Lane, London, W1)
Ambassador: José Primo.

Of Great Britain in Angola (Rua Diogo Cão, 4, Luanda)
Ambassador: J. G. Flynn.

Of Angola to the United Nations
Ambassador: Alfonso Van Dúnem-Mbinda.

Further Reading

Anuário Estatistico de Angola. Luanda, from 1897
Bhagavan, M. R., *Angola's Political Economy 1975–1985.* Uppsala, 1986
James, W. M., *Political History of the War in Angola.* New York, 1991
Somerville, K., *Angola: Politics, Economics and Society.* London and Boulder, 1986

ANGUILLA

Capital: The Valley
Population: 7,019 (1989)

HISTORY. Anguilla was probably given its name by the Spaniards because of its eel-like shape. After British settlements in the 17th century, the territory was administered as part of the Leeward Islands. From 1825 it became more closely associated with St Kitts and ultimately incorporated in the colony of St Kitts-Nevis-Anguilla. Opposition to this association grew and finally in 1967 the island seceded unilaterally. Following direct intervention by the UK in 1969 Anguilla became *de facto* a separate dependency of Britain; and this was formalized on 19 Dec. 1980 under the Anguilla Act 1980. A new Constitution came into effect in April 1982.

AREA AND POPULATION. Anguilla is the most northerly of the Leeward Islands, some 70 miles (112 km) to the north-west of St Kitts and 5 miles (8 km) to the north of St Martin/St Maarten. The territory also comprises the island of Sombrero and several other off-shore islets or cays. The total area of the territory is about 60 sq. miles (155 sq. km). Census population (1984) was 6,987. Estimate, 1989, 7,019. The capital is The Valley.

CONSTITUTION AND GOVERNMENT. A set of new amendments to the constitution came into effect in May 1990, providing for a Deputy Governor, a Parliamentary secretary and an Opposition Leader, among other provisions. The House of Assembly consists of a Speaker, Deputy Speaker, 7 elected members, 2 nominated members and 2 *ex-officio* members: the Deputy Governor and the Attorney General.

Executive power is vested in the Governor who is appointed by HM The Queen. Apart from his special responsibilities (External Affairs, Defence, Internal Security, including the Police, and the Public Service) and his reserve powers in respect of legislation, the Governor discharges his executive powers on the advice of an Executive Council comprising a Chief Minister, 3 Ministers and 2 *ex-officio* members: the Deputy Governor and Attorney-General. A Secretary to the Executive Council is to be appointed.

Governor: B. G. J. Canty.
Chief Minister: Emile Gumbs.

National flag. British Blue Ensign with the shield of Anguilla in the fly.

ECONOMY

Budget. In 1990, the budget was: Expenditure EC$32,122,292; revenue EC$34,715,425. Anguilla finances its recurrent budget and a small part of its capital budget but for the most part aid for capital projects comes from UK and other donors.

Currency. The currency is the Eastern Caribbean *dollar*.

ENERGY AND NATURAL RESOURCES

Electricity. Production (1990) 5m. kwh.

Agriculture. Because of low rainfall agriculture potential is limited. Main crops are pigeon peas, corn and sweet potatoes. Livestock consists of sheep, goats, cattle and poultry.

Fisheries. Fishing is a thriving industry with exports to neighbouring islands.

FOREIGN ECONOMIC RELATIONS

Commerce. Total trade between Anguilla and UK (British Department of Trade returns, in £1,000 sterling):

	1988	*1989*	*1990*	*1991*
Imports to UK	68	1,402	122	197
Exports and re-exports from UK	1,372	1,952	1,853	2,687

Tourism. There are a few hotels of international standing and others are under construction. There are also several locally-owned hotels, guest houses and apartments. In 1990 there were 90,506 tourists, of which 59,325 were day visitors.

COMMUNICATIONS

Roads. There are about 43 miles of tarred roads and 25 miles of secondary roads. In 1991 there were 2,450 passenger cars and 733 commercial vehicles.

Civil Aviation. Wallblake is the airport for The Valley. Anguilla is served by American Airlines, Air Coastal Transport Services, Leeward Islands Air Transport and Windward Islands Airways International. There are direct flights to Guadeloupe, the Netherlands Antilles, Puerto Rico, St Kitts and Nevis and the British and US Virgin Islands. LIAT operates a weekly connecting flight to the UK.

Shipping. The main seaports are Road Bay and Blowing Point, the latter serving passenger and cargo traffic to and from St Martin.

Telecommunications. There is a modern internal telephone service with (1990–91) 2,810 exchange lines; and international telegraph, telex, fax and telephone services, all operated by Cable & Wireless. In 1991 there were 2,500 radio receivers.

Newspapers. In 1990 there was 1 monthly and 1 quarterly periodical.

RELIGION, EDUCATION AND WELFARE

Religion. There were in 1990 Anglicans, Roman Catholics, Methodists, Seventh Day Adventists, Church of God and Baptists.

Education. There are 6 government primary schools with (1991) 1,360 pupils and 1 comprehensive school with (1991) 772 pupils. Tertiary education is provided at regional universities and similar institutions.

Health. There is a 24-bed cottage hospital, clinics and a modern dental clinic. A new 36-bed hospital has been constructed. There were (1991) 5 government-employed doctors and 3 private doctors.

Further Reading

Petty, C. L., *Anguilla: Where there's a Will, there's a Way*. Anguilla, 1984

ANTIGUA AND BARBUDA

Capital: St John's
Population: 85,000 (1990)
GNP per capita: US$2,800 (1988)

HISTORY. Antigua was discovered by Colombus in 1493 and named by him after a church in Seville (Spain). It was first colonized by English settlers in 1632; nearby Barbuda was colonized in 1661 from Antigua. Formed part of the Leeward Islands Federation from 1871 until 30 June 1956, when Antigua became a separate Crown Colony, which was part of the West Indies Federation from 3 Jan. 1958 until 31 May 1962. It became an Associated State of the UK on 27 Feb. 1967 and obtained independence on 1 Nov. 1981.

AREA AND POPULATION. Antigua and Barbuda comprises 3 islands of the Lesser Antilles situated in the Eastern Caribbean with a total land area of 442 sq. km (171 sq. miles); it consists of Antigua (280 sq. km), Barbuda, 40 km to the north (161 sq. km) and uninhabited Redonda, 40 km to the southwest (1 sq. km).

The population at the Census of 7 April 1970 was 65,525. In 1990 the estimated population was 85,000 of whom 31·8% were urban. 1,500 lived in Barbuda in 1986. Expectation of life was 73 years in 1989. The chief towns are St John's, the capital on Antigua (30,000 inhabitants in 1982) and Codrington, the only settlement on Barbuda.

CLIMATE. A tropical climate, but drier than most West Indies islands. The hot season is from May to Nov., when rainfall is greater. Mean annual rainfall is 40" (1,000 mm).

CONSTITUTION AND GOVERNMENT. H.M. Queen Elizabeth, as Head of State, is represented by a Governor-General appointed by her on the advice of the Prime Minister. There is a bicameral legislature, comprising a 17-member Senate appointed by the Governor-General and a 17-member House of Representatives elected by universal suffrage for a 5-year term. The Governor-General appoints a Prime Minister and, on the latter's advice, other members of the Cabinet.

Governor-General: Sir Wilfred Ebenezer Jacobs, GCMG, GCVO, OBE, QC.

Prime Minister and Finance: Right Hon. Vere C. Bird, Sen., PC (b. 1910).
Deputy Prime Minister, Foreign Affairs, Economic Development, Tourism and Energy: Lester Bryant Bird. *Finance:* John E. St Luce. *Attorney-General and Minister of Legal Affairs:* Keith B. Ford. *Public Utilities and Aviation:* Robin Yearwood. *Agriculture, Fisheries, Lands and Housing:* Hillroy Humphries. *Home Affairs:* Christopher Manasseh O'Mard. *Education, Culture and Youth Affairs:* Reuben H. Harris. *Labour and Health:* Adolphus Eleazer Freeland. *Trade, Industry and Commerce:* Hugh Marshall. *Public Works and Communications:* Eustace Cochrane. *Ministers without Portfolio:* Donald Christian, Donald Shepherd, Hugh Marshall, Henderson Simon, Molwyn Joseph.

At the general elections held on 17 April 1984, the ruling Antigua Labour Party won all 16 seats on Antigua and there was one independent (representing Barbuda).

Flag: Red, with a triangle based on the top edge, divided horizontally black, blue, white, with a rising sun in gold on the black portion.

DEFENCE. The defence force has a strength of about 700. A coastguard service has been formed.

INTERNATIONAL RELATIONS

Membership. Antigua and Barbuda is a member of UN, the Commonwealth, CARICOM and is an ACP state of the EEC.

ECONOMY

Budget. The budget for 1988 envisaged revenue at EC$217m. and expenditure of EC$231·7m.

Currency. The unit of currency is the *Eastern Caribbean dollar* (XCD). In March 1992, £1 = EC$4·74; US$1 = EC$2·70.

Banking. Barclays Bank International, Royal Bank of Canada, Canadian Imperial Bank of Commerce, the Virgin Islands National Bank, the Antilles International Trust Co. and the Bank of Nova Scotia have branches at St John's. There is also the Antigua Co-operative Bank and a government savings bank.

ENERGY AND NATURAL RESOURCES

Electricity. Production (1986) 63·8m. kwh.

Agriculture. Cotton and fruits are the main crops. Production (1988) of fruits, 9,000 tonnes.

Livestock (1990): Cattle, 18,000; pigs, 4,000; sheep, 13,000; goats, 13,000.

Fisheries. Catch (1983) 1,013 tonnes.

INDUSTRY. An oil refinery was opened in 1982. Manufactures include toilet tissue, stoves, refrigerators, blenders, fans, garments and rum (molasses imported from Guyana).

Labour. In 1985 the workforce numbered 32,254, and there was 21% unemployment.

FOREIGN ECONOMIC RELATIONS

Commerce. Imports in 1990 amounted to US$340m. and exports to US$28m. The main trading partners were the USA, the UK and Canada.

Total trade between Antigua and Barbuda and UK (British Department of Trade returns, in £1,000 sterling):

	1988	1989	1990	1991
Imports to UK	10,845	3,447	2,931	5,765
Exports and re-exports from UK	20,755	23,954	17,980	19,687

Tourism. There were 149,000 tourists (excluding cruise passengers) in 1986.

COMMUNICATIONS

Roads. There are 600 miles of roads (150 miles main road). In 1985 there were 10,000 passenger cars and 15,000 commercial vehicles.

Civil Aviation. V. C. Bird international airport is near St John's. Antigua is served by Air Canada, American Airlines, British Airways, British West Indies International, Leeward Islands Air Transport and Lufthansa. There are direct scheduled flights to Barbados, Dominica, Frankfurt, Grenada, Guadeloupe, Jamaica, Martinique, Miami, Montserrat, the Netherlands Antilles, New York, Orlando, Puerto Rico, St Kitts and Nevis, St Lucia, St Vincent, Toronto, Trinidad, the UK, the British and US Virgin Islands and Washington DC. A domestic flight links Antigua and Barbuda Airport.

Shipping. The main harbour is the St John's deep water harbour. There are 2 tugs for the berthing of ships and all modern and efficient general cargo handling equipment. The harbour can also accommodate 3 large cruise ships simultaneously.

Telecommunications. In 1983 there were 10,470 telephones. The government-controlled Antigua and Barbuda Broadcasting Service broadcasts a radio and TV programme (colour by NTSC). There is a commercial radio and a commercial TV station, a religious radio station and relay stations. In 1991 there were estimated to be 35,000 radio and 28,000 TV receivers.

RELIGION, EDUCATION AND WELFARE

Religion. The vast majority of the population are Christian, preponderantly Anglican.

Education. In 1985 there were 10,551 pupils and 436 teachers in 48 primary schools, and 5,106 pupils and 304 teachers in (1983) 16 secondary schools.

Health. There is a general hospital (Holberton) with 215 beds, a mental hospital with 200 beds, a geriatric unit with 150 beds, 4 health centres and 16 dispensaries.

DIPLOMATIC REPRESENTATIVES

Of Antigua and Barbuda in Great Britain (15 Thayer St., London, W1M 5LD)
High Commissioner: James A. E. Thomas.

Of Great Britain in Antigua and Barbuda (38 St Mary's St., St John's)
High Commissioner: E. T. Davies, CMG (resides in Bridgetown).

Of Antigua and Barbuda in the USA (3400 International Dr., NW, Washington, D.C., 20008)
Ambassador: (Vacant).

Of the USA in Antigua and Barbuda (FPO Miami 34054, St. Johns)
Ambassador: (Vacant)

Of Antigua and Barbuda to the United Nations
Ambassador: Lionel Alexander Hurst.

Further Reading

Dyde, B., *Antigua and Barbuda: The Heart of the Caribbean.* London, 1986

ARGENTINA

República Argentina

Capital: Buenos Aires
Population: 32·69m. (1990)
GNP per capita: US$2,160 (1989)

HISTORY. In 1515 Juan Díaz de Solis discovered the Río de La Plata. In 1534 Pedro de Mendoza was sent by the King of Spain to take charge of the 'Gobernación y Capitanía de las tierras del Rio de La Plata', and in Feb. 1536 he founded the city of the 'Puerto de Santa María del Buen Aire'. In 1810 the population rose against Spanish rule, and in 1816 Argentina proclaimed its independence. Civil wars and anarchy followed until, in 1853, stable government was established.

Military leaders supported by the Navy and Air Force staged a *coup d'état* on 24 March 1976, and The Junta of Commanders in Chief deposed Isobel Perón and her Government elected in 1972. The Commander in Chief of the Army, Lieut-Gen. Videla, was appointed President. The previous Constitution remained in force in so far as it was consistent with the statutes and objectives of the Junta. Return to civilian rule took place on 10 Dec. 1983. For details of earlier history and Constitutions *see* THE STATESMAN'S YEAR-BOOK, 1982–83 and 1985–86.

AREA AND POPULATION. The Argentine Republic is bounded in the north by Bolivia, in the north-east by Paraguay, in the east by Brazil, Uruguay and the Atlantic Ocean and the west by Chile. The republic consists of 22 provinces, 1 federal district and the National Territories of Tierra del Fuego, the Antarctic and the South Atlantic Islands (census of 1980) as follows:

Provinces	Area: Sq. km. 1960	Population Estimate 1989	Capital	Population census, 1980 (1,000)
Litoral				
Federal Capital	200	2,900,794	Buenos Aires	2,908
Buenos Aires	307,571	12,604,018	La Plata	455
Corrientes	88,199	748,834	Corrientes	180
Entre Ríos	78,781	1,005,885	Paraná	160
Chaco	99,633	824,447	Resistencia	218
Santa Fé	133,007	2,765,678	Santa Fé	287
Formosa	72,066	354,512	Formosa	95
Misiones	29,801	723,839	Posadas	140
Norte				
Jujuy	53,219	502,694	San Salvador de Jujuy	124
Salta	154,775	822,378	Salta	260
Santiago del Estero	135,254	641,273	Santiago del Estero	148
Tucumán	22,524	1,134,309	San Miguel de Tucumán	393
Centro				
Córdoba	168,766	2,748,006	Córdoba	969
La Pampa	143,440	237,386	Santa Rosa	52
San Luis	76,748	246,087	San Luis	71
Andina				
Catamarca	100,967	232,523	Catamarca	78
La Rioja	89,680	191,468	La Rioja	67
Mendoza	148,827	1,387,914	Mendoza	118
San Juan	89,651	528,838	San Juan	118
Neuquén	94,078	326,313	Neuquén	90
Patagonia				
Chubut	224,686	327,780	Rawson	13
Rio Negro	203,013	466,713	Viedma	24
Santa Cruz	243,943	147,928	Rio Gallegos	43
Tierra del Fuego	21,263	27,358	Ushuaia	11

The total area is 2,780,092 sq. km excluding the claimed 'Antarctic Sector' and the population at the 1980 Census was 27,947,446; estimate (1990) 32,686,000. In 1980, 95% spoke the national language, Spanish, while 3% spoke Italian, 1% Guaraní and 1% other languages. In 1983, 83% lived in urban areas and 17% rural, while 98% were white and 2% mestizo (mixed). Expectation of life in 1989 was 71 years.

The official census including the 'Antarctic Sector', and stated to comprise the 'Malvinas' (Falklands), South Orcadas (Orkneys), South Georgias, South Sandwich Islands and the 'sovereign territories of Argentina in the Antarctic': population 3,300.

The principal metropolitan areas (1980 Census) are Buenos Aires (9,927,404), Córdoba (982,018), Rosario (954,606), Mendoza (596,796), La Plata (560,341), San Miguel de Tucumán (496,914), Mar del Plata (407,024), and San Juan (290,479). The suburbs of Buenos Aires, outside the Federal District, include San Justo (946,715), Morón (596,769), Lomas de Zamora (508,620), General Sarmiento (499,648), Lanus (465,891), Quilmes (441,780), General San Martín (384,306), Caseros (340,343), Almirante Brown (332,548), Avellaneda (330,654), Vicente López (289,815), San Isidro (287,048), Merlo (282,828), Tigre (205,926), Berazategui (200,926), and Esteban Echeverría (187,969).

Other large cities (1980 Census) are Rosario (875,664), Mar del Plata (407,024), Bahía Blanca (220,765), Guaymallén (157,334), Godoy Cruz (141,553), Rio Cuarto (110,254), Comodoro Rivadavia (98,985), San Nicolás (96,313) and Concordia (93,618).

In April 1990 the National Congress declared that the Falklands and other British-held islands in the South Atlantic were part of a new province of Tierra del Fuego.

CLIMATE. The climate is warm temperate over the pampas, where rainfall occurs at all seasons, but diminishes towards the west. In the north and west, the climate is more arid, with high summer temperatures, while in the extreme south conditions are also dry, but much cooler. Buenos Aires. Jan. 74°F (23·3°C), July 50°F (10°C). Annual rainfall 37" (950 mm). Bahía Blanca. Jan. 74°F (23·3°C), July 48°F (8·9°C). Annual rainfall 21" (523 mm). Mendoza. Jan. 75°F (23·9°C), July 47°F (8·3°C). Annual rainfall 8" (190 mm). Rosario. Jan. 76°F (24·4°C), July 51°F (10·6°C). Annual rainfall 35" (869 mm). San Juan. Jan. 78°F (25·6°C), July 50°F (10°C). Annual rainfall 4" (89 mm). San Miguel de Tucumán. Jan. 79°F (26·1°C), July 56°F (13·3°C). Annual rainfall 38" (970 mm). Ushuaia. Jan. 50°F (10°C), July 34°F (1·1°C). Annual rainfall 19" (475 mm).

CONSTITUTION AND GOVERNMENT. Presidential, congressional and municipal elections took place on 30 Oct. 1983 and a return to civilian rule took place on 10 Dec. 1983. With the return to constitutional rule the Constitution of 1853 (as amended up to 1898) is again in effect. The President and Vice-President are elected by a 600-member electoral college (directly elected by popular vote) for 6-year terms; both must be Roman Catholics of Argentine birth. The President may not run for 2 terms. The President is Commander-in-Chief of the Armed Services, and appoints to all civil and judicial offices.

The following is a list of Presidents from 1973 onwards:

Gen. Juan Domingo Perón. 12 Oct. 1973–1 July 1974.

Maria Estela (Isabel) Martinez Perón. 1 July 1974 (a.i. from 29 June 1974)–23 March 1976. (Deposed.)

Gen. Jorge Rafael Videla. 29 March 1976–29 March 1981.

Gen. Roberto Viola, 29 March–22 Dec. 1981.

Gen. Leopoldo Fortunato Galtieri, 22 Dec. 1981–17 June 1982.

Gen. Reynaldo Benito Antonio Bignone, 1 July 1982–10 Dec. 1983.

Dr Raúl Alfonsín, 10 Dec. 1983–30 June 1989.

The National Congress consists of a Senate and a House of Deputies: The Senate comprises 46 members, 2 nominated by each provincial legislature and 2 from the Federal District for 9 years (one-third retiring every 3 years). The House of Deputies comprises 254 members directly elected by universal suffrage (at age 18). Elections for half the 254 seats were held Aug.–Dec. 1991.

In the presidential elections held on 14 May 1989 Carlos Saúl Menem (b. 1930) of the Justicialist ('Peronist') Party won the support of 310 electors in the 600-member electoral college.

President of the Republic: Carlos Saúl Menem (sworn in 8 July 1989).

The Cabinet in Jan. 1992 was composed as follows:
Defence: Antonio Erman González. *Economy:* Domingo Cavallo. *Education:* Antonio Francisco Salonia. *Foreign Relations:* Guido José Maria di Tella. *Interior:* José Luís Manzano. *Labour and Social Security:* Rodolfo Diaz. *Public Health and Social Action:* Avelino Porto. *Secretary-General of the Presidency:* Alberto Kohan. *Justice:* Raúl Granillo Ocampo.

National flag: Three horizontal stripes of light blue, white and light blue, with the gold Sun of May in the centre.

National anthem: Oid, mortales, el grito sagrado Libertad ('Hear, mortals, the sacred cry of Liberty'; words by V. López y Planes, 1813; tune by J. Blas Parera).

Provincial and Local Government. 23 provincial gubernatorial were held Aug.–Dec. 1991. Peronists won 14 governorships, the Radical Civil Union 4 and the Union of the Democratic Centre, 3.

DEFENCE. Conscription is up to 14 months.

Army. There are 5 military regions. The Army is organized in 3 corps HQ, 2 armoured brigades, 2 mechanized infantry brigades, 2 mountain infantry brigades, 2 infantry brigades, 1 jungle brigade and 1 airborne brigade. Equipment in 1991 included 250 100 M-4 Sherman and 150 TAM main battle tanks and 60 AMX-13 light tanks.

In 1991 the Army was 45,000 strong, of whom 10,000 were conscripts.

The trained reserve numbers about 250,000, of whom 200,000 belong to the National Guard and 50,000 to the Territorial Guard.

Navy. The flagship of the Armada Republica Argentina is the light aircraft carrier *Veinticinco de Mayo* displacing 20,200 tonnes full load, and embarking an air group of 4 Super-Etendard, 3 S-2 Tracker and 4 S-61D Sea King aircraft. She is currently undergoing a major refit including re-engining.

Other combatant forces include 4 German-built diesel submarines, 4 modern German-built destroyers, 2 British-built guided missile destroyers (Type 42), 4 German-designed and 3 French-built frigates, 2 old training frigates, 2 fast torpedo craft, 9 patrol ships, 4 coastal minesweepers, 2 minehunters and 1 tank landing ship. Auxiliaries include 1 survey ship, 2 training ships, 3 transports, 1 icebreaker and numerous harbour and service craft.

The new construction programme includes 2 diesel submarines (both building – but slowly) and 2 small frigates.

The Naval Aviation Service has some 40 combat aircraft and 10 helicopters with (1991) 2,000 personnel, in 5 wings. Aircraft include 11 Super-Etendard strike aircraft, 15 EMB-326 and 5 EMB-339A light jet armed trainers, 1 Lockheed Electra maritime surveillance aircraft and 6 S-2E carrier-adapted Tracker anti-submarine aircraft, as well as varied training, transport and general purpose aircraft. There is a squadron of S-61 anti-submarine helicopters and 6 Alouettes. A variable mix of Super Etendards, Skyhawks and Trackers plus Sea King and Alouette helicopters will operate from the aircraft carrier if her refit is completed.

Main bases are at Buenos Aires, Puerto Belgrano (HQ and Dockyard), Mar del Plata, Ushuaia and Puerto Deseado.

The active personnel of the navy in 1991 comprised 25,000, 3,000 of whom were conscripts, and including 5,000 marines.

The Prefectura Naval Argentina (PNA) for Coast Guard and rescue duties operates 5 new 910-tonne corvettes with helicopter and hangar, an ex-whaler of 700 tonnes, and 23 patrol vessels.

Air Force. The Air Force is organized into Air Operations, Air Regions, Materiel and Personnel Commands. Air Operations Command, responsible for all operational flying, is made up of air brigades, each with 1 to 4 squadrons, usually operating from a single base. No. I Air Brigade is a military air transport service, with responsibility also for LADE (state airline) operations into areas of Argentina not served by civilian companies. Its equipment includes 6 C-130E/H Hercules and 10 F.27 Friendship/Troopship turboprop transports, 2 KC-130H Hercules tanker/transports, 4 twin-turbofan F.28 Fellowship freighters, 7 Twin Otters, 15 Guarani IIs, the Presidential Boeing 707-320B and 707-320C, 4 more 707s, 2 VIP Fellowships, and many older or smaller types. No. II Air Brigade has 4 Canberra twin-jet bombers and 2 Canberra trainers; a photographic squadron with Guarani IIs and Learjets. No. III Air Brigade has 2 squadrons of IA 58 Pucara twin-turboprop COIN aircraft. No. IV Air Brigade comprises 2 ground attack squadrons equipped with about 30 Paris light jet combat and liaison aircraft, now being replaced by IA 63 Pampas, and one squadron with Mirage IIIs. No. V Air Brigade comprises 2 squadrons with a total of about 15 A-4P Skyhawk strike aircraft. No. VI Air Brigade has 30 Dagger (Israeli-built Mirage III) fighters, equipping 2 squadrons, and 1 squadron with 15 Mirage IIIE fighter-bombers and 4 Mirage IIID trainers. No. VII Air Brigade has 2 helicopter squadrons with 12 armed Hughes 500M, 6 Bell 212, 4 Bell UH-1 and 2 Chinook helicopters. No. X Air Brigade has 1 squadron of Mirage IIIC/5 fighters. There is a flying school at Córdoba, equipped with turboprop-powered Embraer Tucanos and Paris jets. There were (1991) about 13,000 personnel (3,000 conscripts) and about 150 combat aircraft.

INTERNATIONAL RELATIONS

Membership. Argentina is a member of the UN, OAS, Mercosur and LAIA.

ECONOMY

Policy. In 1990, to reduce the public deficit (US$5,000m. in 1989), the government introduced a programme privatizing some 40 public enterprises. An economic plan entering into force 1 April 1991 guaranteed the convertibility of the currency, lowered interest rates and opened the economy to foreign imports. Agricultural export taxes were abolished in March 1991.

Budget. The financial year commences on 1 Jan. Budget receipts in 1988 were 151,208m. australes and expenditure, 156,029m. australes.

Currency. The monetary unit is the *peso* which replaced the austral on 1 Jan. 1992 at a rate of 1 peso = 10,000 australs. (In 1983 the austral replaced the peso argentino at 1 to 10,000; the peso argentino replaced the peso ley in 1970 at 1 to 1,000). Inflation was 84% in 1991 (1,344% in 1990). 22,000m. australs were in circulation in 1989. In March 1992, US$1 = 0·99 *pesos*; £1 = 1·74 *pesos*.

Banking and Finance. In 1988 there were 36 government banks, 109 private banks and 33 foreign banks. Bank deposits totalled 489,000m. australs in 1989. The *Governor* of the Central Bank is Roque Fernández. Convertibility regulations of April 1991 require the Central Bank to back the entire currency in circulation with its foreign currency reserves.

There is a stock exchange at Buenos Aires.

Weights and Measures. Since 1 Jan. 1887 the use of the metric system has been compulsory.

ENERGY AND NATURAL RESOURCES

Electricity. Electric power production (1988) was 48,965m. kwh (6,000m. kwh nuclear). Supply 220 volts; 50 Hz.

Oil. Crude oil production (1991) 24·74m. tonnes. The oil industry was deregulated in Jan. 1991.

Gas. Natural gas production (1983) 13,500,000m. cu. metres. New offshore fields were reported in 1988.

Minerals. Argentina produced 505,000 tonnes of washed coal in 1988. Iron ore (654,800 tonnes in 1988), gold (31,000 troy oz. in 1988), silver (83,000 tonnes in 1989), tungsten, beryllium, clay, marble, lead (25,000 tonnes in 1989), barites, zinc (32,000 tonnes in 1989), borate (245,000 tonnes in 1988), bentonite and granite are produced. Primary aluminium production was 162,000 tonnes in 1989.

Agriculture. In 1989 there were 26m. ha of arable land, 9·75m. ha of permanent crops and 142·3m. ha of permanent pasture. 3·35m. persons depended on agriculture in 1990, of whom 1,197,000 were economically active.

Livestock (1990): Cattle 50,582,000; sheep, 28,571,000; pigs, 4·4m.; horses, 3m. Wool production, 1988, was 138,000 tonnes; butter, 1989, 37,000 tonnes; beef, 1990, 2·65m. tonnes.

Production (in 1,000 tonnes) in 1990: Wheat, 10,800; sugar cane, 16,000; potatoes, 2,500; tobacco, 68.

Cotton, vine, citrus fruit, olives, rice, soya, and yerba maté (Paraguayan tea) are also cultivated.

Sunflower seed (production, 1990, 3,850,000 tonnes), first grown by Russian immigrants in 1900, now furnishes the country's most popular edible oil. There are more than 10m. olive trees. Argentina is the world's largest source of tannin.

Forestry. In 1989 woodland covered 22% of the land area (59·5m. ha).

Fisheries. Fish landings in 1986 amounted to 420,300 tonnes.

INDUSTRY. Production (1988 in tonnes) Paper, 761,393; iron and steel (1989), 3·27m.; crude steel (1989), 3·86m.; sulphuric acid, 258,024; cement, 6,024,000; non-ferrous metals (1989), 164,000; synthetic rubber (1989), 48,000; cotton yarn (1989), 80,000; cotton fabric (1989), 80,000; raw sugar (1989), 1,017,000. Motor vehicles produced totalled 131,253; television receivers, 454,429; washing machines (1989), 128,000; TV sets (1989), 290,000.

Labour. The economically active population was 11·55m. in 1990, of whom 10·4% worked in agriculture.

FOREIGN ECONOMIC RELATIONS. In April 1990 Argentina signed a treaty of trade and co-operation with the EEC. In Dec. 1990 Argentina and the UK signed a treaty protecting investments.

Commerce. Import values include charges for carriage, insurance and freight; export values are on a f.o.b. basis. Real values of foreign trade (in US$1m.):

	1986	1987	1988
Imports	4,724	5,818	5,322
Exports	6,852	6,360	9,135

Total trade between Argentina and UK (British Department of Trade returns, in £1,000 sterling):

	1987	1988	1989	1990	1991
Imports to UK	64,595	66,281	98,490	144,205	135,512
Exports and re-exports from UK	10,267	12,991	13,585	35,953	69,671

Argentina's meat exports are calculated in terms of actual weight; not 'carcase weight', as is the international practice.

Tourism. In 1988, 2,119,140 tourists visited Argentina.

COMMUNICATIONS

Roads. In 1983 there were 220,093 km of national and provincial highways. The 4 main roads constituting Argentina's portion of the Pan-American Highway were opened in 1942. In 1986 there were 3,898,000 private cars, 60,000 buses, 1,375,000 lorries and 760,000 motor cycles.

Railways. The system based on the 1949 amalgamation of 18 government, British and French-owned railways, comprised 7 railways with a total route-km in 1989 of 34,509 km (210 km electrified) on metre, 1,435 mm and 1,676 mm gauges. In 1989 railways carried 8,274m. tonne-km and 10,651m. passenger-km. In 1991 privatization of several parts of these railways was completed, including Buenos Aires suburban lines and the network of export grain routes on the Rosario-Bahía Blanca axis.

The metro and light rail network in Buenos Aires extends to 44 km.

Civil Aviation. 85% of the former state-owned airline, Aerolineas, was privatized in July 1990. There were (1986) 10 international airports and 54 other airports.

Shipping. Tonnage of the merchant fleet, 1990, was 1,890,000 GRT, of which 568,000 GRT were tankers.

Telecommunications. The nationalized telephone service Entel was privatized in Nov. 1990. Instruments numbered 3,250,000 in 1984. There were (1984) 122 radio stations and 4 television channels in Buenos Aires. In 1986 there were 6m. radio receivers and 5·9m. television receivers.

There are state-owned, provincial, municipal and private radio stations overseen by the Secretaria de Comunicaciones, the Comité Federal de Radiodifusión, the Servicio Oficial de Radiodifusión (which also operates an external service and a station in Antarctica) and the Asociación de Teleradiodifusoras Argentinas. In 1991 there were 21,582,456 radio and 7,165,000 TV (colour by PAL) receivers.

Newspapers and Books. Daily newspapers numbered 218 in 1986 with a circulation of 2·63m. 4,836 book titles were published in 1987.

JUSTICE, RELIGION, EDUCATION AND WELFARE

Justice. Justice is administered by federal and provincial courts. The former deal only with cases of a national character, or in which different provinces or inhabitants of different provinces are parties. The chief federal court is the Supreme Court, with 5 judges at Buenos Aires. Other federal courts are the appeal courts, at Buenos Aires, Bahía Blanca, La Plata, Córdoba, Mendoza, Tucumán and Resistencia. Each province has its own judicial system, with a Supreme Court (generally so designated) and several minor chambers. Trial by jury is established by the Constitution for criminal cases, but never practised, except occasionally in the provinces of Buenos Aires and Córdoba.

The death penalty was re-introduced in 1976 for the killing of government, military police and judicial officials, and for participation in terrorist activities.

The police force is centralized under the Federal Security Council.

Religion. The Roman Catholic religion is supported by the State and membership was 30·15m. in 1989. There are several Protestant denominations with a total congregation (1983) of 500,000. The Jewish congregation numbered 350,000 in 1992.

Education. In 1988–89 the primary schools had 252,000 teachers and 4,999,000 pupils; secondary schools had 262,000 teachers and 1,862,000 pupils, and tertiary schools had 70,000 teachers and 959,000 pupils.

There are National Universities at Buenos Aires (2), Córdoba (2), La Plata, Tucumán, Santa Fé (Litoral), Rosario, Corrientes (Nordeste), Mendoza (Cuyo), Bahía Blanca (Sur), Catamarca, Tandil, Neuquén (Comahue), San Salvador de Jujuy, Salta, Santa Rosa (La Pampa), Mar del Plata, Comodoro Rivadavia (Patagonia), Río Cuarto, Entre Ríos, Resistencia, San Juan and Santiago del Estero. There are also private universities in Buenos Aires (6), Mendoza (3), Córdoba, Comodoro Rivadavia, La Plata, Morón, Tucumán, Salta, Santa Fé and Santiago del Estero.

Health. Free medical attention is obtainable from public hospitals. Many trade unions provide medical, dental and maternity services for their members and dependants.

DIPLOMATIC REPRESENTATIVES

Of Argentina in Great Britain (53, Hans Place, London, SW1X 0LA)
Ambassador: Mario Cámpora.

Of Great Britain in Argentina (Dr Luis Agote 2412/52, 1425 Buenos Aires)
Ambassador: The Hon. Humphrey Maud, CMG.

Of Argentina in the USA (1600 New Hampshire Ave., NW, Washington, D.C., 20009)
Ambassador: Carlos Ortiz de Rosas.

Of the USA in Argentina (4300 Colombia, 1425, Buenos Aires)
Ambassador: Terence A. Todman.

Of Argentina to the United Nations
Ambassador: Dr Jorge Vazquez.

Further Reading

Boletín del comercio exterio Argentino y estadisticas económicas retrospectivas. Annual
Anuario de comercio exterior de la República Argentina. Annual
Economic Review, Banco de la Nación. Buenos Aires
Sintesis Estadistica Mensual. Dirección General de Estadistica. Buenos Aires, 1947 ff.
Boletín Internacional de Bibliografia Argentina. Ministry of Foreign Relations. Buenos Aires. Monthly
Geografia de la República Argentina. Ed. by the Sociedad Argentina de Estudios Geográficos. 7 vols. Buenos Aires. 1945–53
Biggins, A., *Argentina.* [Bibliography]. Oxford and Santa Barbara, 1990
Crawley, E., *A House Divided: Argentina 1880–1980.* London, 1984
Ferns, H. S., *Britain and Argentina in the 19th Century.* OUP, 1960.—*The Argentine Republic 1516–1971.* Newton Abbot, 1973
Graham-Yooll, A., *The Forgotten Colony: A History of the English-Speaking Communities in Argentina.* London, 1981
Lewis, P., *The Crisis of Argentine Capitalism.* North Carolina Univ. Press, 1990
Rock, D., *Argentina 1516–1982.* London, 1986
Shumway, N., *The Invention of Argentina.* California Univ. Press, 1991
Simpson, J. and Bennett, J., *The Disappeared: Voices from a Secret War.* London, 1985
Wynia, G. W., *Argentina.* Hoddesdon, 1986

AUSTRALIA

Capital: Canberra
Population: 17·2m. (1990)
GNP per capita: US$14,440 (1989)

Commonwealth
of Australia

HISTORY. On 1 Jan. 1901 the former British colonies of New South Wales, Victoria, Queensland, South Australia, Western Australia and Tasmania were federated under the name of the 'Commonwealth of Australia', the designation of 'colonies' being at the same time changed into that of 'states'—except in the case of Northern Territory, which was transferred from South Australia to the Commonwealth as a 'territory' on 1 Jan. 1911.

In 1911 the Commonwealth acquired from the State of New South Wales the Canberra site for the Australian capital.

External under the administration of Australia comprise the Ashmore and Cartier Islands, Australian Antarctic Territory, Christmas Island, the Cocos (Keeling) Islands, the Coral Sea Islands, the Heard and McDonald Islands and Norfolk Island. For these *see* pp. 125–29.

AREA AND POPULATION. Australia, including Tasmania but excluding external territories, covers a land area of 7,682,300 sq. km, extending from Cape York (10° 41' S) in the north some 3,680 km to Tasmania (43° 39' S), and from Cape Byron (153° 39' E) in the east some 4,000 km west to Western Australia (113° 9' E). Growth in Census population has been:

1901	3,774,310	1947	7,579,358	1971	12,755,638
1911	4,455,005	1954	8,986,530	1976	13,915,500
1921	5,435,734	1961	10,508,186	1981	15,053,600
1933	6,629,839	1966	11,599,498	1986	15,763,000

A census was held in Aug. 1991.

Area and resident population (estimate), 30 Dec. 1990, 17,210,800 (8,618,400 females), divided as follows:

States and Territories	Area (sq. km)	Total	Per sq. km
New South Wales (NSW)	801,600	5,862,200	7·3
Victoria (Vic.)	227,600	4,406,600	19·4
Queensland (Qld.)	1,727,200	2,938,500	1·7
South Australia (SA)	984,000	1,447,900	1·5
Western Australia (WA)	2,525,500	1,649,900	0·7
Tasmania (Tas.)	67,800	458,600	6·8
Northern Territory (NT)	1,346,200	158,400	0·1
Australian Capital Territory (ACT)	2,400	288,700	120·3
Total	7,682,300	17,210,800	2·2

Rate of population increase (per 1,000) in 1990: 7·9 (natural), 15 (with migration). 85·4% of the population was urban in 1986. Resident population (estimate) in State capitals and other major cities (statistical districts), 31 Dec. 1990:

Capitals	State	Population	Statistical district	State	Population
Canberra [1]	ACT	310,000	Darwin	NT	73,300
Sydney	NSW	3,656,900	Newcastle	NSW	428,800
Melbourne	Vic.	3,080,800	Wollongong	NSW	238,200
Brisbane	Qld.	1,301,700	Gold Coast [2]	Qld.	265,600
Adelaide	SA	1,049,900	Geelong	Vic.	151,400
Perth	WA	1,193,100	Townsville	Qld.	114,100
Hobart	Tas.	183,600			

[1] Includes Queanbeyan.   [2] Includes part of Tweed Shire (in NSW).

100

At 30 June 1990 the age-group distribution was: Under 15, 3,741,699; 15-64, 11,436,918; 65 and over, 1,907,580. Life expectancy in 1989 was 73·3 (males), 79·6 (females).

Australians born overseas (30 June 1990), 3·85m., of whom 1·2m. came from the UK and Ireland; 1·16m. from continental Europe; 814,295 from Asia and 288,900 from New Zealand.

Aboriginals have been included in population statistics only since 1967. At the 1986 census they numbered 227,645.

Vital statistics for 1990:

States and Territories	Marriages	Divorces	Births	Deaths	Infant deaths
New South Wales	41,455	12,414	90,928	43,608	714
Victoria	30,121	10,406	67,166	30,988	523
Queensland	19,677	8,509	44,549	19,372	357
South Australia	9,609	4,066	20,014	10,988	168
Western Australia	10,613	3,845	25,237	9,418	211
Tasmania	3,024	1,170	7,005	3,625	64
Northern Territory	716	421	3,538	788	46
ACT	1,730	1,804	4,856	1,245	43
Total	116,945	42,635	262,746	120,032	2,126
Rate [1]	6·8	2·5	15·4	7·0	8·1 [2]

[1] Resident (estimate). [2] Per 1,000 live births registered.

Overseas arrivals and departures:

	1989	1990
Arrivals	4,231,000	4,558,300
of whom long-term	238,050	234,050
(including settlers)	(131,060)	(121,560)
Departures	4,130,300	4,470,100
of whom long-term	120,040	137,470
(including former settlers and other residents)	(24,830)	(30,370)

There were 121,560 immigrants in 1990. The 1991–92 quota for settlers was 111,000. The Migration Act of Dec. 1989 sought to curb illegal entry and ensure that annual immigrant intakes were met but not exceeded. Provisions for temporary visitors to become permanent were restricted.

CLIMATE. Over most of the continent, four seasons may be recognised. Spring is from Sept. to Nov., Summer from Dec. to Feb., Autumn from March to May and Winter from June to Aug., but because of its great size there are climates that range from tropical monsoon to cool temperate, with large areas of desert as well. In Northern Australia there are only two seasons, the wet one lasting from Nov. to March, but rainfall amounts diminish markedly from the coast to the interior. Central and southern Queensland are subtropical, north and central New South Wales are warm temperate, as are parts of Victoria, Western Australia and Tasmania, where most rain falls in winter. Canberra. Jan. 68°F (20°C), July 42°F (5·6°C). Annual rainfall 23" (629 mm). Adelaide. Jan. 73°F (22·8°C), July 52°F (11·1°C). Annual rainfall 21" (528 mm). Brisbane. Jan. 77°F (25°C), July 58°F (14·4°C). Annual rainfall 45" (1,153 mm). Darwin. Jan. 83°F (28·3°C), July 77°F (25°C). Annual rainfall 59" (1,536 mm). Hobart. Jan. 62°F (16·7°C), July 46°F (7·8°C). Annual rainfall 24" (629 mm). Melbourne. Jan. 67°F (19·4°C), July 49°F (9·4°C). Annual rainfall 26" (659 mm). Perth. Jan. 74°F (23·3°C), July 55°F (12·8°C). Annual rainfall 35" (873 mm). Sydney. Jan. 71°F (21·7°C), July 53°F (11·7°C). Annual rainfall 47" (1,215 mm).

CONSTITUTION AND GOVERNMENT. *Federal Government:* Under the Constitution legislative power is vested in a Federal Parliament, consisting of the Queen, represented by a Governor-General, a Senate and a House of Representatives. Under the terms of the constitution there must be a session of parliament at least once a year.

The *Senate* comprises 76 Senators (12 for each State voting as one electorate and as from Aug. 1974, 2 Senators respectively for the Australian Capital Territory and the Northern Territory). Senators representing the States are chosen for 6 years. The terms of Senators representing the Territories expire at the close of the day next preceding the polling day for the general elections of the House of Representatives. In general, the Senate is renewed to the extent of one-half every 3 years, but in case of disagreement with the House of Representatives, it, together with the House of Representatives, may be dissolved, and an entirely new Senate elected. The *House of Representatives* consists, as nearly as practicable, of twice as many Members as there are Senators, the numbers chosen in the several States being in proportion to population as shown by the latest statistics, but not less than 5 for any original State. Elections to the Senate are on the single transferable vote system; voters list candidates in order of preference. A candidate must reach a quota to be elected, otherwise the lowest-placed candidate drops out and his or her votes are transferred to other candidates. Elections to the House of Representatives are on the alternative vote system; voters list candidates in order of preference, and if no one candidate wins an overall majority, the lowest-placed drops out and his or her votes are transferred. The numerical size of the House after the election in 1990 was 148, including the Members for Northern Territory and the Australian Capital Territory. The Northern Territory has been represented by 1 Member in the House of Representatives since 1922, and the Australian Capital Territory by 1 Member since 1949 and 2 Members since May 1974. The Member for the Australian Capital Territory was given full voting rights as from the Parliament elected in Nov. 1966. The Member for the Northern Territory was given full voting rights in 1968. The House of Representatives continues for 3 years from the date of its first meeting, unless sooner dissolved. The annual salary of both Senators and Representatives is $A58,300, with increments for holders of office.

Every Senator or Member of the House of Representatives must be a subject of the Queen, be of full age, possess electoral qualifications and have resided for 3 years within Australia. The franchise for both Houses is the same and is based on universal (males and females aged 18 years) suffrage. Compulsory voting was introduced in 1925. If a Member of a State Parliament wishes to be a candidate in a federal election, he must first resign his State seat.

Executive power is vested in the *Governor-General* advised by an Executive Council. The Governor-General presides over the Council, and its members hold office at his pleasure. All Ministers of State, who are members of the party or parties commanding a majority in the lower House, are members of the Executive Council under summons. A record of proceedings of meetings is kept by the Secretary to the Council. At Executive Council meetings the decisions of the Cabinet are (where necessary) given legal form, appointments made, resignations accepted, proclamations, regulations and the like made.

The policy of a ministry is, in practice, determined by the Ministers of State meeting without the Governor-General under the chairmanship of the Prime Minister. This group is known as the *Cabinet*. There are 11 Standing Committees of the Cabinet comprising varying numbers of Cabinet and non-Cabinet Ministers. In Labour Governments all Ministers have been members of Cabinet. In Liberal and National Country Party Governments, only the senior ministers. Cabinet meetings are private and deliberative and records of meetings are not made public. The Cabinet does not form part of the legal mechanisms of Government; the decisions it takes have, in themselves, no legal effect. The Cabinet substantially controls, in ordinary circumstances, not only the general legislative programme of Parliament but the whole course of Parliamentary proceedings. In effect, though not in form, the Cabinet, by reason of the fact that all Ministers are members of the Executive Council, is also the dominant element in the executive government of the country.

The legislative powers of the Federal Parliament embrace trade and commerce, shipping, etc.; taxation, finance, banking, currency, bills of exchange, bankruptcy, insurance; defence; external affairs, naturalization and aliens, quarantine, immigration and emigration; the people of any race for whom it is deemed necessary to make special laws; postal, telegraph and like services; census and statistics; weights and measures; astronomical and meteorological observations; copyrights; railways; conciliation and arbitration in disputes extending beyond the limits of any one

State; social services; marriage, divorce etc.; service and execution of the civil and criminal process; recognition of the laws, Acts and records, and judicial proceedings of the States. The Senate may not originate or amend money bills; and disagreement with the House of Representatives may result in dissolution and, in the last resort, a joint sitting of the two Houses. No religion may be established by the Commonwealth. The Federal Parliament has limited and enumerated powers, the several State parliaments retaining the residuary power of government over their respective territories. If a State law is inconsistent with a Commonwealth law, the latter prevails.

The Constitution also provides for the admission or creation of new States. Proposed laws for the alteration of the Constitution must be submitted to the electors, and they can be enacted only if approved by a majority of the States and by a majority of all the electors voting.

The Australia Acts 1986 removed residual powers of the British government to intervene in the government of Australia or the individual states.

The 36th Parliament was elected on 24 March 1990.

House of Representatives (1991): Australian Labor Party, 78 seats; Liberal Party, 55; National Party, 14; independent, 1.

Senate (1991): Australian Labor Party, 32; Liberal Party, 30; Australian Democratic Party, 7; National Party, 4; independent, 2.

Governor-General: Sir William George Hayden.

The following is a list of former Governors-General of the Commonwealth:

Earl of Hopetoun	1901–02	HRH the Duke of Gloucester	1945–47
Lord Tennyson	1902–04	Sir William McKell	1947–53
Lord Northcote	1904–08	Viscount Slim	1953–60
Earl of Dudley	1908–11	Viscount Dunrossil	1960–61
Lord Denman	1911–14	Viscount De L'Isle	1961–65
Viscount Novar	1914–20	Lord Casey	1965–69
Lord Forster	1920–25	Sir Paul Hasluck	1969–74
Lord Stonehaven	1925–31	Sir John Kerr	1974–77
Sir Isaac Isaacs	1931–36	Sir Zelman Cowen	1977–82
Earl Gowrie	1936–45	Sir Ninian Stephen	1982–89

National flag: The British Blue Ensign with a large star of 7 points beneath the Union Flag, and in the fly 5 stars of the Southern Cross, all in white.

National Anthem: 'Advance Australia Fair' (adopted 19 April 1984). The 'Royal Anthem' (i.e. 'God Save the Queen') is used in the presence of the British Royal Family.

A new Labour cabinet was formed on 27 Dec. 1991 composed as follows:

Prime Minister: Paul Keating (b. 1945).
Treasurer: John Dawkins.
Industry, Technology and Commerce: John Button.
Foreign Affairs and Trade: Gareth Evans.
Finance: Ralph Willis.
Employment, Education and Training: Kim Beazley.
Attorney General: Michael Duffy.
Transport and Communications: Graham Richardson.
Primary Industries and Energy: Simon Crean.
Community Services and Health, Deputy Prime Minister: Brian Howe.
Social Security: Neal Blewett.
Defence: Robert Ray.
Immigration, Local Government and Ethnic Affairs: Gerry Hand.
Arts, Sport, the Environment, Tourism and Territories: Alan Griffiths.
Industrial Relations: Peter Cook.
Administrative Services: Nick Bolkus.
Science: Ross Free.
Aviation and Shipping: Bob Collins.

The leader of the Liberal Party is John Hewson; of the National Party, Tim Fischer.

State Government: In each of the 6 States (New South Wales, Victoria, Queensland, South Australia, Western Australia, Tasmania) there is a State government whose constitution, powers and laws continue, subject to changes embodied in the Australian Constitution and subsequent alterations and agreements, as they were before federation. The system of government is basically the same as that described above for the Commonwealth—*i.e.*, the Sovereign, her representative (in this case a Governor), an upper and lower house of Parliament (except in Queensland, where the upper house was abolished in 1922), a cabinet led by the Premier and an Executive Council. Among the more important functions of the State governments are those relating to education, health, hospitals and charities, law, order and public safety, business undertakings such as railways and tramways, and public utilities such as water supply and sewerage. In the domains of education, hospitals, justice, the police, penal establishments, and railway and tramway operation, State government activity predominates. Care of the public health and recreative activities are shared with local government authorities and the Federal Government, social services other than those referred to above are now primarily the concern of the Federal Government, and the operation of public utilities is shared with local and semi-government authorities.

Administration of Territories. Since 1911, responsibility for administration and development of the Australian Capital Territory (ACT) has been vested in Federal Ministers and Departments. The ACT became self-governing on 11 May 1989.

The ACT House of Assembly has been accorded the forms of a legislature, but continues to perform an advisory function for the Minister for the Capital Territory.

On 1 July 1978 the Northern Territory of Australia became a self-governing Territory with expenditure responsibilities and revenue-raising powers broadly approximating those of a State.

Local Government. The system of municipal government is broadly the same throughout Australia, although local government legislation is a State matter.

Each State is sub-divided into areas known variously as municipalities, cities, boroughs, towns, shires or district councils, totalling about 900. Within these areas the management of road, street and bridge construction, health, sanitary and garbage services, water supply and sewerage, and electric light and gas undertakings, hospitals, fire brigades, tramways and omnibus services and harbours is generally part of the functions of elected aldermen and councillors. State governments may also be responsible for some services.

In some instances, *e.g.*, in New South Wales, a number of local government authorities combine to conduct a public undertaking such as the supply of water or electricity. State taxation revenue was $A20,069m. in 1989–90; local, $A4,055.

DEFENCE. The Minister for Defence has responsibility under legislation for the control and administration of the Defence Force. The Chief of Defence Force Staff is vested with command of the Defence Force. He is the principal military adviser to the Minister. The Secretary, Department of Defence is the Permanent Head of the Department. He is the principal civilian adviser to the Minister and has statutory responsibility for financial administration of the Defence outlay. The Chief of Defence Force Staff and the Secretary are jointly responsible for the administration of the Defence Force except with respect to matters falling within the command of the Defence Force or any other matter specified by the Minister.

The Chief of Naval Staff, the Chief of the General Staff and the Chief of the Air Staff command the Navy, Army and Air Force respectively. They have delegated authority from the Chief of Defence Force Staff and the Secretary to administer matters relating to their particular Service.

The structure of Defence is characterized by 3 organizational types: *(i)* A Central Office comprising 5 groups of functional orientated Divisions: Strategic Policy and Force Development; Supply and Support; Manpower and Financial Services; Management and Infrastructure Services; and, Defence Science and Technology; *(ii)* the

3 Armed Services of the Defence Force, each having a Service Office element in addition to the command structure; and *(iii)* a small number of outrider organizations concerned with such specialist fields as intelligence and natural disasters.

Defence Support. The Department of Defence Support purchases goods and services for defence purposes; provides technical expertise and other assistance to the defence industry; involves Australian industry in defence equipment to the maximum practical extent; administers the Australian Offsets Program so as to stimulate technological advancement and broaden the capabilities of strategic industries; within overall defence policies helps the capacity, efficiency and capability of Australian industry to design and export defence materiel; manages the Government's munitions and aircraft factories, and dockyards; markets defence and allied products and services to help maintain strategic industries.

In 1989–90 the Department employed 3,873 civilians.

Army. Overall organization and financial control of the Australian Army is vested in the Chief of General Staff. A functional command structure, Land Command, Logistic Command, and Training Command, with Headquarters in 5 military districts, was introduced in 1973.

The strength of the Army was 30,300, including 8,500 women, in 1992. The Command troops consist of 1 regiment each of Air Defence, engineering, aviation and special forces; the 1 infantry division is composed of 1 mechanized and 2 infantry brigades, 3 artillery regiments, and 1 regiment each of reconnaissance, armoured personnel carriers, engineering and aviation. Equipment included 103 Leopard 1A3 main battle tanks. The Army Aviation Corps has 22 GAF N22-B Missionmaster and 14 Turbo-Porter transports, and 125 helicopters, including over 40 taken over from the Air Force in 1990.

The effective strength of the Army Reserve in 1992 was 26,000.

Staff and command training is carried out at the Command and Staff College, Queenscliff, Victoria, and the Land Warfare Centre, Canungra, Queensland.

In Jan. 1986 the Australian Defence Force Academy, Canberra, accepted its first officer cadets for the 3 Services. Cadets will study at the academy for degrees in arts, science and engineering. During semester breaks they will carry out military training with their particular Services.

At the end of 3 years at the academy, army officer cadets will undertake a year of military training at the Royal Military College, Duntroon. This will culminate with commissioning as a lieutenant.

From 1986 the Royal Military College have taken officer cadets for commissioning.

Navy. The Chief of Naval Staff is assisted by the Deputy Chief of Naval Staff and Assistant Chiefs for Personnel, Operational Requirements and Plans, Material and Logistics. The command, operation and administration of the Fleet is now vested in the Maritime Commander, Australia headquartered at Sydney.

Combatants include 6 UK-built Oxley class diesel submarines, 3 US-built guided missile destroyers, 4 US- and 1 Australian-built guided missile frigates, commissioned 1980-90 and 3 older frigates, 6 mine countermeasure vessels, 1 tank landing ship, 5 tank landing craft and 18 inshore patrol craft. Major auxiliaries include 2 fleet replenishment tankers, 1 training ship, 2 survey ships, and there are some 80 minor auxiliaries and service craft.

New procurement includes 6 replacement submarines of Swedish design, with construction of the first 2 under way, 1 guided-missile frigate and 8 German-designed frigates, construction of which started in 1991.

The Fleet Air Arm operates a shore-based anti-submarine helicopter squadron of 7 Sea Kings and 16 S-70B Seahawk helicopters for the guided missile frigates. There are additionally 2 transport aircraft and 9 transport and utility helicopters.

The fleet main base is at Sydney, with subsidiary bases at Garden Island, Cairns and Darwin.

The all-volunteer Navy was (1991) 15,700 strong including 900 Fleet Air Arm.

Air Force. Command of the Royal Australian Air Force (RAAF) is vested in the Chief of the Air Staff (CAS) assisted by the Deputy Chief of the Air Staff, Chief of

Air Force Operations and Plans, Chief of Air Force Materiel, Chief of Air Force Personnel, Chief of Air Force Technical Services, Director-General Supply—Air Force and Assistant Secretary Resources Planning.

The CAS administers and controls RAAF units through two commands: Operational Command and Support Command. Operational Command is responsible to the CAS for the command of operational units and the conduct of their operations within Australia and overseas. Support Command is responsible to the CAS for training of personnel, and the supply and maintenance of service equipment.

Flying establishment comprises 16 squadrons, of which 2 are equipped with 24 F-111 strike/reconnaissance aircraft. Of the others, 3 are equipped with missile-armed F-18 Hornet interceptors and 2 with Orion maritime reconnaissance aircraft. There are 6 transport squadrons, 2 with Hercules turboprop transports, 2 with Caribou STOL transports, 1 with Boeing 707 tanker and transport aircraft, and 1 with Falcon 900 VIP transports. All helicopters have either been transferred to the Army or retired. Training aircraft include piston-engined Airtrainers, built in New Zealand, Pilatus PC-9 turboprop-powered basic trainers, Aermacchi MB 326H jets for pilot training, and HS 748 aircraft for navigator training. A training unit has F-18 Hornets for crew conversion.

Training for commissioned rank is carried out at the RAAF Academy and Officers' Training School, both located at Point Cook, Victoria. Other major training activities which lead to commissioned rank include basic aircrew training and technical and commercial cadet schemes. Basic ground training to tradesman level is conducted at RAAF technical training schools. Higher command and staff training is, in the main, carried out at the RAAF Staff College, Fairbairn, ACT.

Personnel (1991) 22,300, including 3,500 women. There is also an Australian Air Force Reserve.

INTERNATIONAL RELATIONS

Membership. Australia is a member of the UN, the Commonwealth, GATT, OECD, Colombo Plan, the South Pacific Forum and the South Pacific Bureau for Economic Co-operation.

ECONOMY

Policy. Since 1942 the Federal Government alone has levied taxes on incomes. In return for vacating this field of taxation, the State Governments are reimbursed by grants from the Federal Government out of revenue received. Payments to the States represent about one-third of Federal Government outlays, and in turn the payments State Governments receive from the Federal Government account for nearly half of their revenues.

The Financial Agreement of 1927 established the Australian Loan Council which represents the Federal and six State Governments, and co-ordinates domestic and overseas borrowings by these governments, including annual borrowing programmes. The Federal Government acts as a central borrowing agency in raising loans to finance the major part of those programmes. The Loan Council in 1984 agreed upon arrangements for the co-ordination of borrowings by semi-government and local authorities and government-owned companies.

Reforms were initiated at a special Premiers' Conference in Oct. 1990 to form a partnership between the Commonwealth, States, Territories and local government with a view to improving national efficiency, international competitiveness and enhancing delivery and quality of government services. In July 1991 the premiers agreed a programme of inter-state standardization and integration in such areas as the railway system, electricity grid, product control and professional qualifications.

Budget. In 1929, under a financial agreement between the Federal Government and States, approved by a referendum, the Federal Government took over all State debts existing on 30 June 1927 and agreed to pay $A15·17m. a year for 58 years towards the interest charges thereon, and to make substantial contributions towards a sinking fund on State debt. The Sinking Fund arrangements were revised under an amendment to the agreement in 1976.

Outlays and revenues of the Commonwealth Government for years ending 30 June (in $A1m.):

	1989–90	1990–91
Total outlays	86,951	95,019
including		
Defence	8,476	9,066
Education	6,566	7,459
Health	11,924	12,958
Social security		
and welfare	26,329	30,542
Housing	1,296	1,079
Culture and		
recreation	1,064	1,197
Economic services	5,356	6,668
Public services	5,621	6,347
Payments to States,		
NT and local government	14,117	13,793
Public debt interest	7,271	6,073
Other	−1,068	−162
Total revenue	94,987	96,914
including		
Customs duty	4,011	3,366
Excise duty	9,094	9,482
Sales tax	10,132	9,365
PAYE income tax	40,213	39,752
Other individual tax	8,072	9,058
Prescribed payments	1,734	1,358
Company tax	12,926	14,166
Superannuation	376	1,053
Withholding	957	1,193
Fringe benefits tax	1,168	1,262
Bank accounts		
debit tax	378	229
Other	1,439	1,957

Foreign currency reserves were $A24,047m. in 1991.
Gross foreign debt at 30 June 1990 was $A36,073m.
The Consumer Price Index rose by 7·5% over the year to Sept. 1990.

Australian National Accounts. Australian Bureau of Statistics. 1953–54 to date
Public Authority Finance: Commonwealth Government Finance, Australia. Australian Bureau
of Statistics, 1962–63 to date
Public Authority Finance: State and Local Government Finance, Australia. Australian Bureau
of Statistics, 1971–72 to date
National Income and Expenditure. Australian Bureau of Statistics. Canberra, 1946 to date
Treasury Information Bulletin (and Supplements). Canberra Treasury Dept., 1956 to date
(quarterly)
Hagger, A. J., *A Guide to Australian Economic and Social Statistics.* Sydney, 1983

Currency. On 14 Feb. 1966 Australia adopted a system of decimal currency. The currency unit, the *Australian dollar* (AUD) is divided into 100 *cents*. Notes are issued in denominations of $A1, 2, 5, 10, 20, 50 and 100. Coins are issued in denominations of 1, 2, 5, 10, 20 and 50 cents and $A1. Gold bullion legal tender coins weighing 1 kg (the 'Australian Nugget'), 10 oz. and 2 oz. with respective face values of $A10,000, $A2,500 and $A500 were introduced in March 1991.

The underlying inflation rate for the year ending June 1991 was 3·4%.

Money in circulation in May 1991, $A12,193m. In March 1992, US$1 = 1·33 *dollars*; £1 = 2·33 *dollars*.

Banking and Finance. The banking system comprises:

(*a*) The Reserve Bank of Australia is the central bank and bank of issue. The *Governor* is Bernie Fraser. Its Rural Credits Department provides short-term credit for the marketing of primary produce. Its assets were $A28,129m. in June 1991 and its liabilities $A26,129m., of which notes on issue, $14,621m.; deposits by trading banks, $2,541m.; deposits by Commonwealth Government, $1,164m.; assets $28,129m. of which gold and foreign exchange (including IMF Special Drawing Rights), $24,308m., treasury notes $116m., other Commonwealth Government securities $2,844m. Its functions and responsibilities derive from the Reserve Bank Act 1959, the Banking Act 1959, and the Financial Corporations Act 1974. For the history of the Reserve Bank *see* THE STATESMAN'S YEAR-BOOK 1986–87, p. 104.

(b) Four major trading banks: (i) The Commonwealth Bank of Australia; (ii) 3 private trading banks: The Australia and New Zealand Banking Group Ltd, West-pac Banking Corporation and the National Commercial Banking Corporation of Australia Ltd.

(c) Other trading banks: (i) 3 State Government banks—The State Bank of New South Wales, The State Bank of South Australia, and the Rural and Industries Bank of Western Australia; (ii) one joint stock bank—The Bank of Queensland Ltd, formerly The Brisbane Permanent Building and Banking Co. Ltd, which has specialized business in one district only; (iii) The Australian Bank Ltd; (iv) branches of 17 overseas banks—the restrictions on foreign banks operating in Australia, and on foreign investment in the merchant banks, were lifted in 1984–85.

(d) The Commonwealth Development Bank of Australia commenced operations on 14 Jan. 1960. Its function is to provide finance for primary production and small business.

(e) The Australian Resources Development Bank Ltd opened on 29 March 1968, to assist Australian enterprises in developing Australia's natural resources, through direct loans and equity investment or by re-financing loans made by trading banks. The bank is jointly owned by the 4 major Australian trading banks.

(f) The Primary Industry Bank of Australia Ltd commenced operations on 22 Sept. 1978. The equity capital of the bank consists of eight shares. Seven shares are held by the Australian Government and the major trading banks while the eighth share is held equally by the 4 State banks. The main objective of the bank is to facilitate the provision of loans to primary producers on longer terms than are otherwise generally available. The role of the bank is restricted to re-financing loans made by banks and other financial institutions.

(g) Savings banks, with total deposits of $86,855m. at 30 May 1991 ($79,724m. in 1990). In 1990 16 savings banks were operating in Australia. These comprise subsidiaries of the four major trading banks; four State-owned banks, six private banks, one trustee bank and one overseas bank. At 30 June 1990 these savings banks had 6,572 branches and 8,072 agencies.

In March 1991 there were 51 building societies. Assets were $A22,429m. in June 1990. Building societies are permitted to have up to 50% of their assets in non-home loans. 3 major societies collapsed in June 1990.

There is an Australian Stock Exchange (ASX).

Weights and Measures. Conversion to the metric system is in progress.

ENERGY AND NATURAL RESOURCES

Electricity. Electricity supply is the responsibility of the State governments. Production 1990–91, 155,755m. kwh (17,879m. hydro-electric in 1990–91). Supply 240 and 250 volts; 50 Hz.

Oil and gas. The main fields are Gippsland (Vic.) and Carnarvon (WA). Crude oil production was 28,663m. litres in 1990-91; natural gas, 20,742,000m. litres.

Minerals. Australia is a leading producer of bauxite (41% of world production in 1990) and diamonds (36·2%). Coal is Australia's major source of energy. Reserves are large (1990 estimate: 51,100m. tonnes) and easily worked. The main fields are in New South Wales and Queensland. Production in 1990-91 was 201·6m. tonnes. Brown coal (lignite) reserves are mainly in Victoria and were estimated at 41,700m. tonnes in 1990. Production, 1990-91: 49·97m. tonnes.

Production of other major minerals in 1990-91 (1,000 tonnes): Bauxite, 41,751; copper ore and concentrate, 1,089; iron ore and concentrate, 110,000; manganese ore and concentrate, 1,573; tungsten, 691; nickel ore, 1,124; uranium, 4,389; gold bullion, 256,362 kg.

Agriculture. In 1989 there were 127,547 farms. Farms in 1989 covered 467m. ha. 332m. ha were grazing or fallow, 17·53m. ha sown to crops, of which the most important are wheat (13·94m. tonnes from 8·83m. ha in 1989); sugar cane (27·15m. from 394,000 ha); barley (3·24m. from 2·19m. ha); oats (1·84m. from 1·3m. ha) and rice (748,000 from 97,000 ha). Vineyards (59,335 ha) produced 439m. litres of wine from 531,951 tonnes of grapes in 1989-90; grapes in 1989, 562,942 tonnes.

Gross value of agricultural production in 1989-90, $A23,509m., including (in $A1m.): Crops, 9,961; livestock slaughtering, 5,719; wool, 5,742; other livestock products, 2,068. Wool taxes were raised in 1990 in order to combat price falls caused by over-production.

In 1989 74,005 farms had cattle and 63,138 sheep. A cull of some 10·5m. sheep was carried out between Dec. 1990 and April 1991 because of declining wool prices.

Livestock (in 1,000) at 31 March 1991:

	NSW	Vic.	Qld	SA	WA	Tas.	NT	ACT	Australia
Cattle	5,787	3,447	9,899	997	1,660	582	1,380	12	23,765
Sheep	60,779	25,935	17,288	17,482	36,141	5,082	1	113	162,774
Pigs	718	414	575	390	276	40	3	—	2,417
Poultry	24,379	11,935	7,579	4,121	4,677	799	215	219	53,903

Livestock products (in 1,000 tonnes) for the year ending 30 June 1991: Beef, 1,693; veal, 37; lamb and mutton, 674; pigmeat, 310; poultry meat, 388; milk, 6,402m. litres, 185,910 sheep were shorn, producing 846,524 tonnes of wool.

Forestry. The Federal Government is responsible for forestry at the national level. Each State is responsible for the management of publicly-owned forests. Total forest area was 40·97m. ha in 1989, of which 30·09m. ha were publicly-owned. The major part of wood supplies derives from coniferous plantations, of which there were 913,556 ha in 1989. Timber production was 3·17m. cubic metres in 1989-90.

INDUSTRY. Statistics of manufacturing industries, 1988–89: Number of firms, 31,161; persons employed, 1,068,400; salaries paid, $A25,558m.; turnover, $A150,351m. (excludes small single-establishment enterprises employing fewer than 4 persons).

Manufacturing by sector as at June 1989:

	No. of firms	Persons employed	Salaries in $A1m.	Turnover in $A1m.
Food, beverages and tobacco	3,738	176,300	4,040	30,913
Textiles	706	32,100	743	4,049
Clothing and footwear	2,344	74,700	1,339	5,350
Wood, wood products and furniture	4,838	83,600	1,648	7,855
Paper, paper products, printing and publishing	3,382	110,600	2,838	13,150
Chemical, petroleum and coal products	938	52,600	1,564	13,596
Non-metallic mineral products	1,484	42,600	1,141	7,210
Basic metal products	603	72,000	2,252	19,299
Fabricated metal products	4,784	105,100	2,378	11,504
Transport equipment	1,591	116,100	2,793	14,426
Other machinery equipment	4,133	137,500	3,328	15,083
Miscellaneous manufacturing	2,620	65,100	1,472	7,917

Manufactured products in 1990-91 included: Beer, 1,791m. litres; bricks, 1,636m.; cement, 5·7m. tonnes; carpets, 39·3m. square metres; confectionery, 157,023 tonnes; electric motors, 2·3m.; washing machines, 305,553; refrigerators, 338,701; TV sets, 153,974; cars, 310,660; caravans, 3,252; pig iron, 5·6m. tonnes; crude steel, 6·22m. tonnes; sulphuric acid, 0·92m. tonnes; superphosphates, 1·49m. tonnes; tobacco, 24,838 tonnes; woollen wove, 7m. square metres; woollen yarn, 17,106 tonnes; scoured wool, 96,531 tonnes.

Labour. In May 1991 the total workforce (persons aged 15 and over) numbered (in 1,000s) 8,551, of whom there were employed: 7,739, including women, 3,243 (of whom married, 1,992). In 1991 the labour force included 346,500 employers, 6,551,800 wage and salary earners and 766,200 self-employed. The majority of wage and salary earners have had their minimum wages and conditions of work prescribed in awards by the Industrial Relations Commission, which in April 1991 awarded a 2·5% rise, making the minimum weekly wage about $A442, but in Oct. 1991 the Commission decided to allow direct employer-employee wage bargaining, provided agreements reached are endorsed by the Commission. In some States, some conditions of work (*e.g.*, weekly hours of work, leave) are set down in State legislation. Average weekly wage, Aug. 1989: A$423 (women, A$326). Average working week, 1989: 36·1 hours (males 40·7; females 29·5). 4 weeks annual leave is standard.

Employees in all States are covered by workers' compensation legislation and by certain industrial award provisions relating to work injuries.

During 1989 industrial disputes involving stoppages of work of 10 working days or more accounted for 1,202,200 working days lost. In these disputes 709,600 workers were involved.

The following table shows the distribution of employed persons by industry in 1989, by sex and average weekly hours worked:

| Industry | Numbers (in 1,000) | | Hours worked | |
	Persons	(Females)	Per person	(Females)
Agriculture, forestry, fishing and hunting	406·2	(115·0)	40·5	(26·8)
Mining	105·4	(11·3)	41·5	(35·1)
Manufacturing	1,236·0	(340·7)	38·8	(33·4)
Food, beverages and tobacco	–	–	37·8	(31·1)
Metal products	–	–	40·0	(32·4)
Other manufacturing	–	–	38·8	(34·0)
Electricity, Gas and Water	113·4	(10·4)	36·0	(31·6)
Construction	601·4	(75·4)	38·3	(20·6)
Wholesale and retail trade	1,606·9	(735·4)	34·9	(27·7)
Transport and storage	407·5	(82·4)	39·1	(31·9)
Communication	139·8	(38·3)	35·2	(31·6)
Finance, property and business services	875·2	(424·0)	37·1	(31·8)
Public administration and defence	324·0	(126·7)	34·0	(30·7)
Community services	1,356·9	(880·4)	32·8	(29·2)
Recreation, personal and other services	554·7	(315·7)	32·9	(28·3)
Totals	7,727·6	(3,155·7)	36·1	(29·5)

In May 1989 1,729,600 wage and salary earners worked in the public sector and 4,422,800 in the private sector.

The following table shows the distribution of employed persons in 1989 according to the *Australian Standard Classification of Occupations*:

| | Employed persons (in 1,000) | |
Occupation	Persons	(Females)
Managers and administrators	821·2	(189·8)
Professionals	960·6	(375·1)
Para-professionals	453·8	(202·3)
Tradespersons	1,239·7	(124·3)
Clerks	1,317·9	(1,011·6)
Salespersons and personnel service	1,128·9	(729·1)
Plant and machine operators, and drivers	604·4	(102·7)
Labourers and related workers	1,201·1	(420·8)
	7,727·6	(3,155·7)

In July 1991 801,800 persons (10·3% of the labour force) were unemployed, (including 313,600 females of whom 81,500 persons were seeking part-time work. In Aug. 1989, 108,200 persons had been unemployed for more than one year. In Nov. 1989 there were 62,700 job vacancies. In the year ended June 1990 725,000 unemployment beneficiaries received a total of $A3,068m., 116,000 sickness beneficiaries received a total of $A611m. and 170,000 special beneficiaries received a total of $A214·8m.

Trade Unions. In June 1989 there were 299 trade unions with 3,410,300 members (1,219,300 females). About 54% of wage and salary earners (44% females) were estimated to be members of unions. In 1989 there were 38 unions with fewer than

100 members and 11 unions with 80,000 or more members. Many of the larger trade unions are affiliated with central labour organizations, the oldest and by far the largest being the Australian Council of Trade Unions formed in 1927. In an agreement of Nov. 1990 the government agreed to increase tax cuts in exchange for wage restraint, and in Oct. 1991 unions agreed to limit wage demands to 5% increases until June 1992.

Labour Statistics 1989. Australian Bureau of Statistics. Canberra, 1991

FOREIGN ECONOMIC RELATIONS. In 1990 Australia and New Zealand completed a Closer Economic Relations agreement (initiated in 1983) which establishes free trade in goods. External debt was $A103,500m. in Dec. 1990.

Commerce. Merchandise imports and exports for years ending 30 June, in $A1m.:

	Imports	Exports
1988–89	47,073	43,409
1989–90	50,991	47,815
1990–91	49,250	51,793

The Australian customs tariff provides for preferences to goods produced in and shipped from certain countries as a result of reciprocal trade agreements. These include UK, New Zealand, Canada and Ireland.

Exports and imports, 1989-90 (in $A1m.):

	Exports	Imports
Live animals	198·4	139·1
Meat and preparations	2,914·4	21·7
Dairy goods and eggs	731·0	105·6
Fish, shellfish and their preparations	681·5	425·2
Cereals and preparations	3,525·8	93·7
Vegetables and fruit	527·9	415·3
Sugar and honey	1,119·5	51·1
Coffee, tea, cocoa, spices and their manufacturers	69·6	331·4
Animal feed (excl. unmilled cereal)	260·6	69·4
Miscellaneous edible products	97·7	246·2
Beverages	224·1	304·2
Tobacco and manufactures	17·7	92·0
Raw hides and skins	574·1	12·4
Oil seeds and fruit	50·6	26·7
Crude rubber (incl. synthetic and reclaimed)	8·0	93·3
Cork and wood	394·3	517·8
Pulp and waste paper	24·6	243·0
Textile fibres (not wool tops)	4,800·2	149·4
Crude fertilizers, minerals (not coal, petroleum, gems)	221·8	230·0
Metal ores and scrap	7,332·9	146·0
Crude animal and vegetable materials	144·0	120·2
Coal, coke and briquettes	5,807·2	18·2
Petroleum and products	2,008·6	2,505·2
Gas, natural and manufactured	489·4	16·4
Animal oils and fats	109·2	1·7
Fixed vegetable oils and fats	2·4	110·0
Processed oils and fats, waxes thereof	10·4	12·3
Organic chemicals	85·6	1,071·8
Inorganic chemicals	157·1	767·4
Dyeing, colouring and tanning materials	259·0	232·7
Medicinal and pharmaceutical products	265·6	819·9
Essential oils, perfume and cleansing preparations	85·5	330·8
Manufactured fertilizers	11·2	252·3
Plastics in primary forms	136·7	649·4
Plastics in non-primary forms	64·2	483·7
Chemical materials and products	176·6	626·4

	Exports	Imports
Leather and manufactures, dressed furskins	167·3	136·6
Rubber manufactures	67·1	750·1
Cork and wood manufactures (not furniture)	21·7	226·7
Paper, board and pulp	161·4	1,297·4
Textile yarn, fabrics and products	176·5	1,954·5
Non-metallic mineral goods	467·0	1,068·8
Iron and steel	746·1	1,038·5
Non-ferrous metals	3,923·3	395·9
Metal manufactures	365·7	1,349·8
Power generators	418·3	1,383·8
Special machinery, industrial	422·9	2,755·8
Metalworking machinery	62·7	392·2
General machinery and parts, industrial	376·7	2,976·0
Office machines and data-processing equipment	566·4	3,557·0
Telecommunications and sound equipment	237·1	1,805·5
Electrical machinery and parts	363·5	2,718·0
Road vehicles (inc. air-cushion vehicles)	546·2	5,061·9
Other transport equipment	602·3	2,800·7
Sanitary, plumbing, heating and lighting fittings, pre-fabricated buildings	30·8	144·6
Furniture and parts	40·8	337·3
Travel goods, handbags etc.	5·3	210·0
Clothing and accessories	109·4	907·6
Footwear	24·8	338·9
Professional, scientific and controlling instruments	252·3	1,143·7
Photographic and optical goods, watches and clocks	231·7	783·3
Miscellaneous manufactured articles	662·4	3,015·0
Other commodities and transactions	186·9	607·1
Gold and other coin	275·4	35·1
Non-monetary gold	2,838·5	284·2
Confidential items	1,093·0	123·3
Total trade	49,131·6	51,331·7

Trade by country in 1989–90:

	Exports		Imports	
	$A1m.	%	$A1m.	%
ASEAN	4,976	10·1	2,965	5·8
Indonesia	1,032	2·1	441	0·6
Malaysia	919	1·9	658	1·3
Singapore	1,957	4·0	1,213	2·4
Other	1,068	2·2	653	1·3
Canada	727	1·5	1,228	2·4
China	1,192	2·4	1,241	2·4
EEC	6,848	13·9	11,318	22·0
France	874	1·8	1,166	2·3
Germany, Federal Republic of	1,225	2·5	3,426	6·7
Italy	1,043	2·1	1,635	3·2
Netherlands	1,057	2·2	520	1·0
UK	1,734	3·5	3,356	6·5
Other	915	1·7	1,215	2·4
Hong Kong	1,323	2·7	847	1·7
Japan	12,811	26·1	9,872	19·2
Korea, South	2,676	5·5	1,254	2·4
New Zealand	2,600	5·3	2,174	4·2

	Exports		Imports	
	$Alm.	%	$Alm.	%
Papua New Guinea	840	1·7	235	0·5
Saudi Arabia	293	0·6	676	1·3
Switzerland	738	1·5	567	1·1
Taiwan	1,828	3·7	1,946	3·8
USA	5,345	10·9	12,373	24·1
USSR	675	1·4	37	0·1
Other countries	6,259	12·7	4,599	9·0
	49,131	100·0	51,332	100·0

Total trade between UK and Australia (British Department of Trade returns, in £1,000 sterling):

	1987	1988	1989	1990	1991
Imports to UK	673,837	745,570	864,965	1,039,080	870,823
Exports and re-exports from UK	1,223,613	1,377,997	1,711,241	1,645,620	1,356,127

Tourism. During 1989, 2·1m. overseas visitors arrived in Australia intending to stay for less than 12 months; tourists spent $A4,094m.

COMMUNICATIONS

Roads. In 1988 there were 38,219 km of state highways and freeways and 107,753 km of main roads.

At 30 June 1989, 7,442,200 cars, 2,047,300 vans, trucks and buses and 316,600 motor cycles were registered. New registrations, 1988-89, include 447,911 cars, 121,310 vans, trucks and buses and 19,076 motor cycles.

494·48m. passenger journeys were made by bus in 1988-89.

In 1990 there were 20,048 road accidents in which 2,330 persons were killed.

Railways. There are six government-owned railway systems. Statistics for the year ended 30 June 1989:

System	Route length in km [4]	Passenger journeys, 1,000	Goods carried, (1,000 tonnes)	Gross earnings, ($Alm.)
State:				
New South Wales	7,755	249,296	50,188	1,114·1
Victoria	5,186	99,325	9,950	...
Queensland	10,094	50,943	80,508	1,107·1
South Australia [3]	125	7,023	...	17·6
Western Australia	5,553	9,719	24,294	306·2
Australian National [1, 2]	7,050	350	13,821	315·5
	35,763	416,656	178,761	...

[1] The Australian National Railways operates services of the former Commonwealth Railways, the non-metropolitan South Australian Railways and the Tasmanian Railways.
[2] Excludes Adelaide metropolitan rail passenger services and the Tasmanian Region.
[3] The South Australian State Transport Authority operates services in the Adelaide metropolitan area.
[4] Inter-system traffic is included in the total for each system over which it passes.

The State railway gauges are: New South Wales, 1,435 mm; Victoria, 1,600 mm (325 km 1,435 mm); Queensland, 1,067 mm (111 km 1,435 mm); South Australia, 1,600 mm for 2,533 km, 1,824 km 1,435 mm and the rest 1,067 mm; West Australia, 137 km, 1,435 mm and the rest 1,067 mm, and Tasmania, 1,067 mm. Of the Australian National Railways, the gauge of the Trans-Australian and Australian Capital Territory is 1,435 mm, and for the Central Australia 1,067 mm for 869 km and 1,435 mm for 350 km. Under various Commonwealth–State standardization agreements, all the State capitals are now linked by 1,435 mm gauge track. The Central Australia railway extends as far north as Alice Springs (now standard gauge on new alignment from Tarcoola to Alice Springs).

There are also private industrial and tourist railways.

Civil Aviation. With effect from 1 July 1988 the Civil Aviation Authority has been responsible for aviation safety under the Civil Aviation Act, 1988.

In 1990 Australia had air service agreements with 28 countries, and 38 international airlines were operating scheduled services. Qantas Airways, Australia's international airline, operated 30 Boeing 747s and 12 Boeing 767s. All shares in Qantas are owned by the Commonwealth Government. In 1988-89 7·92m. passengers and 324,344 tonnes of freight were flown on international flights. The major international airports are Adelaide, Brisbane, Darwin, Melbourne, Perth, Sydney and Townsville.

Internal airlines carried 9·9m. passengers and 99,400 tonnes of freight in 1988-89. Domestic airlines were deregulated in Oct. 1990.

At 30 June 1990 there were 428 licensed aerodromes (42 owned by the Commonwealth Government) and (in 1988) 9 helicopter pads.

Shipping. The chief ports are Sydney, Newcastle, Port Kembla (NSW); Melbourne, Geelong, Westernport (Vic.); Hay Point, Gladstone, Brisbane (Qld.); Port Hedland, Dampier, Port Walcott, Fremantle (WA). As at 30 June 1989 the Australian merchant marine (vessels of 150 tonnes gross and over) consisted of 43 coastal vessels of 967,351 tonnes gross and 33 overseas vessels of 1,454,645 tonnes gross.

Arrivals and departures of vessels engaged in overseas trade:

	Arrivals			*Departures*		
			Cargo discharged			Cargo loaded
	No of port visits	DWT (1,000 tonnes)	(1,000 tonnes gross)	No. of port visits	DWT (1,000 tonnes)	(1,000 tonnes gross)
1988-89	12,153	465,978	36,603	12,029	458,595	267,230
1989-90	15,195	354,831	32,295	15,107	520,159	282,620

42·89m. tonnes of cargo were carried by coastal shipping in 1988-89.

Telecommunications. Postal services are operated by Australia Post, established by the Postal Services Act, 1975. Revenue was $A1,811·2m. in 1989, expenditure $A1,765·3m. There were 4,432 post offices and other agencies in 1989. 3,916m. postal items were handled.

Telecommunications are operated by Telecom Australia under the Telecommunications Act, 1975. Revenue was $A7,976·8m. in 1989, expenditure $A7,003·7m. There were 7,419,982 telephones. Services to other countries are operated by the Overseas Telecommunications Commission Australia (OTC), established by the Overseas Telecommmunications Act, 1946.

Australia's National Satellite System is owned and operated by AUSSAT Pty Ltd under the Satellite Communications Act, 1984. 75% of its shares are owned by the Commonwealth Government and the rest by Telecom Australia; 3 satellites are in orbit covering the entire continent.

Broadcasting is regulated by the Broadcasting Act, 1942 and the Broadcasting Ownership and Control Acts, 1987. Foreign ownership of commercial radio and TV companies is restricted to 20%. The National Broadcasting Service is provided by the Australian Broadcasting Corporation (ABC), which at 30 June 1991 operated 109 MW, 250 FM and 6 high-frequency radio stations. In addition, 140 MW commercial stations and 46 public stations were operating. The short-wave international service Radio Australia broadcasts in English, Bahasa Malay, Cantonese, Chinese, French, Japanese, Thai, Tok Pisin and Vietnamese.

The National Television Service is provided by the ABC (colour by PAL). In addition, 47 commercial companies were operating.

In 1991 there were estimated to be 29·1m. radios and 8·3m. TV sets in use.

Cinemas. In 1990 there were 851 cinemas.

Newspapers (1990). There were 4 national newspapers (average daily circulation 248,567), 18 metropolitan daily newspapers and 121 suburban newspapers with a weekly combined circulation of some 5m.

JUSTICE, RELIGION, EDUCATION AND WELFARE

Justice. The judicial power of the Commonwealth of Australia is vested in the High Court of Australia (the Federal Supreme Court), in the Federal courts created by the

Federal Parliament (the Federal Court of Australia and the Family Court of Australia) and in the State courts invested by Parliament with Federal jurisdiction.

High Court. The High Court consists of a Chief Justice and 6 other Justices, appointed by the Governor-General in Council. The Constitution confers on the High Court original jurisdiction, *inter alia*, in all matters arising under treaties or affecting consuls or other foreign representatives, matters between the States of the Commonwealth, matters to which the Commonwealth is a party and matters between residents of different States. Federal Parliament may make laws conferring original jurisdiction on the High Court, *inter alia*, in matters arising under the Constitution or under any laws made by the Parliament. It has in fact conferred jurisdiction on the High Court in matters arising under the Constitution and in matters arising under certain laws made by Parliament.

The High Court may hear and determine appeals from its own Justices exercising original jurisdiction, from any other Federal Court, from a Court exercising Federal jurisdiction and from the Supreme Courts of the States. It also has jurisdiction to hear and determine appeals from the Supreme Courts of the Territories. The right of appeal from the High Court to the Privy Council was abolished in 1986.

Other Federal Courts. Since 1924, 4 other Federal courts have been created to exercise special Federal jurisdiction, *i.e.* the Federal Court of Australia, the Family Court of Australia, the Australian Industrial Court and the Federal Court of Bankruptcy. The Federal Court of Australia was created by the Federal Court of Australia Act 1976 and began to exercise jurisdiction on 1 Feb. 1977. It exercises such original jurisdiction as is invested in it by laws made by the Federal Parliament including jurisdiction formerly exercised by the Australian Industrial Court and the Federal Court of Bankruptcy, and in some matters previously invested in either the High Court or State and Territory Supreme Courts. The Federal Court also acts as a court of appeal from State and Territory courts in relation to Federal matters. Appeal from the Federal Court to the High Court will be by way of special leave only. The State Supreme Courts have also been invested with Federal jurisdiction in bankruptcy.

State Courts. The general Federal jurisdiction of the State courts extends, subject to certain restrictions and exceptions, to all matters in which the High Court has jurisdiction or in which jurisdiction may be conferred upon it.

Industrial Tribunals. The chief federal industrial tribunal is the Australian Conciliation and Arbitration Commission, constituted by presidential members (with the status of judges) and commissioners. The Commission's functions include settling industrial disputes, making awards, determining the standard hours of work and wage fixation. Questions of law, the judicial interpretation of awards and imposition of penalties in relation to industrial matters, are dealt with by the Industrial Division of the Federal Court.

Australian Digest of Reported Decisions of the Australian Courts and of Australian Appeals to the Privy Council. 2nd ed. Sydney, Law Book Co. 1963—Supplements 1964 ff.

Baalman, J., *Outline of Law in Australia.* 4th ed. Sydney, 1979

Bates, N., *Introduction to Legal Studies.* 4th ed. Melbourne, 1984

Cowen, Z., *Federal Jurisdiction in Australia.* 2nd ed. Melbourne, 1978

Fleming, J. G., *The Law of Torts.* 7th ed. Sydney, 1987

Gunn, J. A. L., *Australian Income Tax Law and Practice.* 10th ed. by F. C. Bock and E. F. Mannix, Sydney, 1971–73, and *Butterworth's Taxation Service* to date

Hotop, S. D., *Principles of Australian Administrative Law.* 6th ed. Sydney, 1985

Howard, C., *Criminal Law.* 5th ed. Sydney, 1990

Mills, C. P. and Sorrell, G. H., *Federal Industrial Law. (Nolan and Cohen.)* 5th ed. Sydney, 1975

O'Connell, D. P. (ed.) *International Law in Australia.* Sydney, 1966

Paterson, W. E. and Ednie, H. H., *Australian Company Law.* 2nd ed. Sydney, 1976, and *Butterworth's Company Service* to date

Sawer, G., *The Australian and the Law.* Melbourne, 1976

Twyford, J., *The Layman and the Law in Australia.* 2nd ed. Sydney, 1980

Wynes, A., *Legislative, Executive and Judicial Powers in Australia.* 5th ed. Sydney, 1976

Yorston, R. K. *et al., Australian Mercantile Law.* 18th ed. Sydney, 1990

Religion. Under the Constitution the Commonwealth cannot make any law to establish any religion, to impose any religious observance or to prohibit the free exercise of any religion. The following percentages refer to those religions with the largest number of adherents at the census of 1986. The census question on religious adherence was not obligatory, however.

Christian, 73% of population; Catholic, 26%; Anglican, 23·9%; Uniting, 7·6%; Presbyterian, 3·6%; Orthodox, 2·7%; Baptist, 1·3%; Lutheran, 1·3%; Church of Christ, 0·6%; Religion other than Christian 2·%, No religion 12·7%, No statement 12·3%.

The Anglican Church ordained 10 women priests in March 1992.

Education. The Governments of the Australian States and the Northern Territory have the major responsibility for education, including the administration and substantial funding of primary, secondary, and technical and further education. In most States, a single Education Department is responsible for these three levels, but in New South Wales and South Australia there is a separate department responsible solely for technical and further education and in Victoria, a Technical and Further Education Board. Furthermore, in New South Wales an Education Commission advises the Minister on primary, secondary and post-secondary education.

The Australian Government is responsible for education in Norfolk Island, Christmas Island and the Cocos (Keeling) Islands. It also provides supplementary finance to the States and is responsible for the total funding of universities and colleges of advanced education. It has special responsibilities for student assistance, education programmes for Aboriginal people and children from non-English-speaking backgrounds, and for international relations in education.

The Australian Constitution empowers the Federal Government to make grants to the States and to place conditions upon such grants. The National Board of Employment, Education and Training (NBEET) was established in 1988 to advise the Federal Government on the financial needs of educational institutions. It is assisted by 4 councils: The Schools Council, the Higher Education Council, the Employment and Skills Formation Council and the Australian Research Council.

The Commonwealth has been working with the states to develop a national perspective for schools and a common curriculum. The Curriculum Corporation has been established under the auspices of the Australian Education Council.

School attendance is compulsory between the ages of 6 and 15 years (16 years in Tasmania), at either a government school or a recognized non-government educational institution. Many children attend pre-schools for a year before entering school (usually in sessions of 2-3 hours, for 2-5 days per week). Government schools are usually co-educational and comprehensive. Non-government schools have been traditionally single-sex, particularly in secondary schools, but there is a trend towards co-education. Tuition is free at government schools, but fees are normally charged at non-government schools.

Primary and secondary schools at July 1990:

	Schools		Teachers [1]		Pupils [2]	
	Govern-	Non- govern-	Govern- ment	Non- govern- ment	Govern- ment	Non- govern- ment
States and Territories	ment	ment	schools	schools	schools	schools
New South Wales	2,181	850	45,620	17,691	743,186	287,437
Victoria	2,038	715	39,950	16,508	526,576	257,786
Queensland	1,310	397	24,439	7,678	391,249	130,057
South Australia	706	185	13,604	3,682	184,868	57,867
Western Australia	760	244	13,636	4,376	215,311	69,575
Tasmania	250	66	4,546	1,208	65,349	19,030
Northern Territory	147	24	1,986	391	26,256	6,071
ACT	98	36	2,698	1,203	40,552	20,487
Australia	7,490	2,517	146,477	52,737	2,193,347	848,310

[1] Full-time teachers plus the full-time equivalent of part-time teaching.
[2] Full-time pupils only.

In post-secondary education, tuition fees were abolished in 1974 and student allowances are provided for full-time students subject to a means test. Universities are autonomous institutions. From 1 Jan. 1989 the university and college of advanced education sectors were merged by the Federal Government. The resulting institutions are self-governing, though funded by the Federal Government. A private university sector is developing. The major part of technical and further education is provided in government-administered technical and further education institutions (TAFE). These had 1,505,417 students in 1989.

There were 32 universities in 1990. They were, with numbers of academic staff (and students): Sydney, 1,767 (24,143); New South Wales (including the Australian Defence Force Academy), 1,152 (18,860); New England, 490 (11,056); Newcastle, 335 (10,292); Macquarie, 565 (10,157); Wollongong, 392 (6,990); Melbourne, 2,177 (20,692); Monash, 1,551 (14,060); La Trobe, 1,132 (11,524); Deakin, 364 (5,346); Queensland, 1,177 (17,959); James Cook, 317 (4,633); Griffith, 414 (7,632); Adelaide, 636 (8,660); Flinders, 345 (5,516); Western Australian, 642 (9,617); Murdoch, 474 (4,717); Tasmania, 375 (4,918); Australian National, 697 (6,238); Charles Sturt, 473 (8,939); Sydney University of Technology, 630 (14,083); Western Sydney, 693 (10,630); Queensland University of Technology, 408 (8,817); University College of Central Queensland, 184 (4,081); University College of Southern Queensland, 9 (7,002); Curtin University of Technology, 543 (12,663); Northern Territory, 56 (1,885); Canberra, 307 (5,734).

The Victoria University of Technology was founded in 1990, and also a Catholic University under the sponsorship of La Trobe. A private university in Queensland, the Bond University, was founded in 1989 with 800 students.

Teacher education usually takes place in colleges of advanced education, though a substantial number of secondary teachers and a few primary teachers receive their pre-service education in a university.

The Australian Government provides assistance for students. The Secondary Allowances Scheme aims to help parents with a limited income to keep their children at school for the final 2 years of secondary education. The Assistance for Isolated Children Scheme provides special support to families whose children are isolated from schooling or are handicapped. The Adult Secondary Education Assistance Scheme provides assistance for mature-age students undertaking a full-time one-year matriculation level programme or a two-year programme if studies beyond the tenth year in the Australian secondary school system have not previously been undertaken. The Tertiary Education Assistance Scheme is a means-tested scheme to assist students enrolled for full-time study in approved courses at post-secondary institutions. Allowances are also available for post-graduate study and overseas study. Aboriginal students are eligible for assistance under the Aboriginal Secondary Grants Scheme and the Aboriginal Study Grants Scheme. The States also offer various schemes of assistance, principally at the primary and secondary levels.

National bodies with a co-ordinating, planning or funding rôle include: the Australian Education Council, comprising the Federal and State Ministers of Education, the Conference of Directors-General of Education and an advisory body, the National Aboriginal Education Committee.

Total expenditure on education (public and private sectors) in 1987–88 was estimated at $A14,673m.

Health. In 1990 there were an average 5 hospital beds per 1,000 population. There were 1,072 hospitals (general). The Royal Flying Doctor Service serves remote areas.

Social Security and Welfare. All Commonwealth Government social security pensions, benefits and allowances are financed from the Commonwealth Government's general revenue. In addition, assistance is provided for welfare services.

Expenditure on main programmes, 1990–91, $A29,561m.

The following summarizes the conditions of the major benefits.

Age and invalid pensions—age pensions are payable to men 65 years of age or more and women 60 years of age or more who have lived in Australia for a specified period and, unless permanently blind, also satisfy an income test. Persons over 16 years of age who are permanently blind or permanently incapacitated for work to the extent of at least 85% may receive an invalid pension. Invalid pension is paid subject to a residence qualification, income and assets test, unless the person is permanently blind. Additional amounts are paid to pensioners with dependent children. Supplementary assistance may be paid to a pensioner paying rent or private lodging subject to an income test. Remote area allowance is payable to pensioners living in certain remote areas, except for those aged 70 or more receiving the special rate of age pension. Supplementary assistance, additional pension for children, mother's/guardian's allowance and remote area allowance are not taxable.

In 1989-90 1,340,468 age pensioners received a total of $A8,182m., and 316,713 invalid pensioners received $A2,681m.

Wife's pension—payable to the wife of an age or invalid pensioner if she is not eligible for a pension in her own right. The maximum rate and the income test are identical to those for age and invalid pensioners.

Carer's pension—payable to a person who is providing constant care and attention at home for a severely disabled age or invalid pensioner living in the same house, where the carer is not eligible for pension in his own right. The maximum rate and the income test are identical to those for age and invalid pensions.

Sole parent pensions—sole parents who have custody, care and control of any dependent children may, if they satisfy a residence requirement and an income test, receive sole parent pensions. Mother's/guardian's allowance, additional pension for each dependent child, supplementary assistance and remote area allowance are also payable.

In 1989-90 248,886 beneficiaries received a total of $A2,334m.

Sheltered employment allowance—is payable to disabled persons under age—pension age engaged in approved sheltered employment who are qualified to receive invalid pension. The rates of payment and allowances and income test are the same as invalid pension.

Rehabilitation allowance—persons undertaking a rehabilitation programme with the Commonwealth Rehabilitation Service who are eligible for a social security pension or benefit are eligible to receive a non taxable rehabilitation allowance during treatment or training and for up to 6 months thereafter. The allowance is equivalent to the invalid pension and is subject to the same income test.

Family Allowance—is paid subject to an income test to assist families with children under 16 years or dependent full-time students aged 16 years to under 25 years. It is not subject to income tax.

In 1989-90 1,890,859 families comprising 3,672,525 children received a total of $A1,810m.

Family income supplement—payable subject to an income test to families with one or more children eligible for family allowances so long as they are not in receipt of any Commonwealth pension, benefit or allowance which provides additional payment for dependent children; this is not taxable.

In 1989-90 178,247 families received a total $A513·3m.

Child disability allowance—payable to parents or guardians of severely physically or mentally handicapped children in the family home and needing constant care and attention. The allowance is free of an income test but is subject to a residence qualification similar to that for family allowance.

In 1989-90 40,222 allowances totalling $A61·7m. were paid.

Double orphan's pension—the guardian of a child under 16 years of age or of a full-time student under 25, both of whose parents are dead, or one of whose parents is dead and the whereabouts of the other parent unknown, and for refugee children where both parents are outside Australia or in prison, may receive double orphan's pension. The payment is not subject to an income test nor is it taxable.

Unemployment and sickness benefits—are paid, subject to an income test, to persons between the ages of 18 and 16 respectively and age pension age who are unemployed, able and willing to work and making efforts to obtain work, or temporarily unable to work because of sickness or injury. The 1990 Budget abolished the existing indefinite benefits of $A105 per week in favour of a 'job search allowance' of $A57 per week for up to one year. To be granted benefit a person must have resided in Australia for at least 12 months preceding his or her claim or intend to remain in Australia permanently. For unemployment benefit purposes unemployment must not be due to industrial action by that person or by members of a union to which that person is a member. Special benefits may be granted to persons not qualified above. For numbers of beneficiaries and amounts paid *see* **Labour** p. 109.

Service Pensions are paid by the Department of Veterans' Affairs, similar to the age and invalid pensions provided by the Department of Social Security. Male Veterans who have reached the age of 60 years or are permanently unemployable, and who served in a theatre of war, are eligible subject to an income test. Female Veterans who served abroad and who have reached the age of 55 or are permanently unemployable, are also eligible. Wives of service pensioners are also eligible provided that they do not receive a pension from the Department of Social Security. *Disability pension* is a compensatory payment in respect of incapacity attributable to war service. It is paid at a rate commensurate with the degree of incapacity and is free of any income test. A separate allowance may be paid to dependents. In 1989-90 386,348 persons received $A2,164m. of service pensions and 354,082 received $A1,220m. of disability pensions.

In addition to cash benefits, welfare services are provided either directly or through State and Local government authorities and voluntary agencies, for people with special needs.

Medicare. On 1 Feb. 1984 the Commonwealth Government introduced a universal health scheme known as Medicare. This covers: Automatic entitlement under a single public health fund to medical and optometrical benefits of 85% of the Medical Benefits Schedule fee, with a maximum patient payment for any service where the Schedule fee is charged; access without direct charge to public hospital accommodation and to inpatient and outpatient treatment by doctors appointed by the hospital; the restoration of funds for community health to approximately the same real level as 1975; a reduction in charges for private treatment in shared wards of public hospitals, and increases in the daily bed subsidy payable to private hospitals.

The Medicare programme is financed in part by a 1·25% levy on taxable incomes, with low income cut-off points, which were $A11,745 p.a. for a single person in 1990 and $A19,045 p.a. for a family with a $A2,100 reduction for each child. The Commonwealth Government subsidises registered health insurance organizations by contributing to the Health Benefits, and makes an annual contribution to the Reinsurance Trust Fund of $A20m. for payments of benefits to patients with hospital treatment in excess of 35 days.

Medicare benefits are available to all persons ordinarily resident in Australia. Visitors from UK, New Zealand and Malta have immediate access to necessary medical treatment, as do all visitors staying more than 6 months.

Medical Benefits. The Health Insurance Act provides for a Medical Benefits Schedule which lists medical services and the Schedule (standard) fee applicable in each State in respect of each medical service. Schedule fees are set and updated by an independent fees tribunal appointed by the Government. The fees so determined are to apply for Medicare benefits purposes.

Home and Community Care Program was introduced in 1985 to provide support services to enable aged and disabled persons to live at home. It is jointly funded by the Commonwealth and State or Territory Governments. Commonwealth funding was $A242m. in 1989-90.

DIPLOMATIC REPRESENTATIVES

Of Australia in Great Britain (Australia House, Strand, London, WC2B 4LA)
High Commissioner: Richard Smith.

Of Great Britain in Australia (Commonwealth Ave., Canberra)
High Commissioner: Sir Brian Barder, KCMG.

Of Australia in the USA (1601 Massachusetts Ave., NW, Washington, D.C., 20036)
Ambassador: Michael John Cork.

Of the USA in Australia (Moonah Pl., Canberra)
Ambassador: Melvin F. Sembler.

Of Australia to the United Nations
Ambassador: Dr Peter Stephen Wilenski, AO.

Further Reading

Official Publications

Australian Bureau of Statistics. *Year Book Australia.—Pocket Year Book Australia.—Monthly Summary of Statistics.* ABS also publish numerous specialized statistical digests, for which *see* their annual *Catalogue of Publications.*
Department of Foreign Affairs. *Annual Report.—Australian Foreign Affairs Record.— Australian Treaty List.—Consular and Trade Representatives.—Diplomatic List.*
Reserve Bank of Australia. *Bulletin.* Sydney, monthly

Coxon, H., *Australian Official Publications.* Oxford, 1981

Non-Official Publications

Australian Encyclopædia. 12 vols. Sydney, 1983
Australian Quarterly: A Quarterly Review of Australian Affairs. Sydney, 1929 to date
Blainey, G., *The Tyranny of Distance: How Distance Shaped Australia's History.* Melbourne, 1982
Caves, P. E. and Krause, L. B., *The Australian Economy: A View from the North.* Sydney, 1984
Clark, M., *A Short History of Australia.* Melbourne, 1981
Deery, S. and Plowman, D., *Australian Industrial Relations.* Sydney, 1985
Emy, H. and Hughes, O., *Australian Politics: Realities in Conflict.* Sydney, 1991
Gilbert, A. D. and Inglis, K. S. (eds.) *Australians: A Historical Library.* 5 vols. CUP, 1988
Grey, J., *A Military History of Australia.* CUP, 1991
Hancock, K. (ed.) *Australian Society.* Cambridge Univ. Press, 1990
Hocking, B. (ed.) *Australia towards 2000* London, 1990
Howard, C., *Australia's Constitution.* Melbourne, 1985
Hurst, J., *Hawke P. M.* Sydney, 1983
Kepars, I., *Australia.* [Bibliography] Oxford and Santa Barbara, 1984
Lucy, R., *The Australian Form of Government.* Melbourne, 1985
Moore, D. and Hall, R., *Australia: Image of a Nation.* London, 1983
Oxford History of Australia. vol 5: 1942–88. OUP, 1990
Serle, P., *Dictionary of Australian Biography.* 2 vols. Sydney, 1949
Solomon, D., *Australia's Government and Parliament.* Melbourne, 1981
Who's Who in Australia. Melbourne, 1906 to date
Williams, D. B. (ed.), *Agriculture in the Australian Economy.* 3rd ed. Sydney Univ. Press and OUP, 1991

National library: The National Library, Canberra, ACT.
National statistical office: Australian Bureau of Statistics (ABS), Belconnen, ACT. The statistical services of the states are integrated with the Bureau.

AUSTRALIAN TERRITORIES

AUSTRALIAN CAPITAL TERRITORY

HISTORY. The area, now the Australian Capital Territory (ACT), was first visited by Europeans in 1820 and settlement commenced in 1824. Until its selection as the seat of government it was a quiet pastoral and agricultural community.

AREA AND POPULATION. The area is 2,432 sq. km (including Jervis Bay area). The population (estimate) at 30 June 1990 was 284,300. Previous census population:

	Males	Females	Total		Males	Females	Total
1911	992	722	1,714	1966	49,991	46,041	96,032
1921	1,567	1,005	2,572	1971	73,589	70,474	144,063
1933	4,805	4,142	8,947	1976	100,103	95,519	197,622
1947	9,092	7,813	16,905	1981	110,415	111,194	221,609
1954	16,229	14,086	30,315	1986	132,100	132,300	264,400
1961	30,858	27,970	58,828				

(Figures before 1961 exclude particulars of full-blood Aborigines.)

CONSTITUTION AND GOVERNMENT. The Constitution of Australia provided (Sec. 125) that the seat of government should be selected by parliament and that it should be within New South Wales, distance not less than 160 km from Sydney. The present area was surrendered by New South Wales and accepted by the Australian Government from 1 Jan. 1911. In 1915 an additional 73 sq. km at Jervis Bay was transferred from New South Wales to serve as a port. In 1911 an international competition was held for the city plan. The plan chosen was that of W. Burley Griffin, of Chicago. Construction, delayed by the First World War, began in 1923 and on 9 May 1927 Parliament was opened and Canberra became the seat of government. Most Australian Government departments now have their headquarters in Canberra.

The general administration lies with the ACT Administration, responsible to the Federal Minister for the Arts, Sport, Environment, Tourism and Territories. The Administration provides all municipal and Territorial services except police and courts (responsibility of the Federal Attorney-General).

The Australian Capital Territory Representation (House of Representatives) Act, 1973, provided for the representation of residents of the Territory by 2 elected members in the House of Representatives. The Senate (Representation of Territories) Act 1973 provided for the election of 2 Senators from the Territory. Elections took place on 1 Dec. 1984. The ACT became self-governing on 11 May 1989.

FINANCE. In 1987–88 the ACT was given its own budget. It is treated equitably with the States regarding local revenue raising, expenditure and assistance by the Commonwealth government.

PRODUCTION. Outside Canberra the Territory is mainly reserved for forestry and nature conservation (Namadgi National Park is 94,000 ha). A considerable amount of reafforestation (mostly pine) has been undertaken, the total area of coniferous plantations at 30 June 1988 being 16,194 ha. Farming is mainly in grazing: Livestock (1990), 11,574 cattle, 113,188 sheep, and 218,704 poultry.

EDUCATION. In July 1990 there were 98 government schools comprising 65 primary schools, 25 secondary schools and colleges, 1 combined primary/secondary school and 4 special schools. Non-government schools numbered 36 of which there were 22 primary schools, 6 secondary schools and 8 schools with both primary and secondary enrolments. Students enrolled full-time in government schools in 1990 numbered 22,275 and 18,277 in primary and secondary school levels respectively. Enrolments at non-government schools comprised 10,221 primary school students and 10,266 secondary school students. Pre-school education was provided at 78 centres with a total enrolment of 4,165. There is an Institute of Technical and Further Education. There are 5 higher education institutions: the Australian National University (7,176 students in 1990); the University of Canberra (formerly the Canberra College of Advanced Education, 7,809); the Australian Defence Force Academy (1,228); the Canberra Institute of Arts (581); and the Signadou College of Education (357).

Further Reading

Australian Capital Territory Statistical Summary. Australian Bureau of Statistics. From 1960
Wigmore, L., *Canberra: A History of Australia's National Capital.* 2nd ed. Canberra, 1971

NORTHERN TERRITORY

HISTORY. The Northern Territory, after forming part of New South Wales, was annexed on 6 July 1863 to South Australia and in 1901 entered the Commonwealth as a corporate part of South Australia. The Commonwealth Constitution Act of 1900 made provision for the surrender to the Commonwealth of any territory by any state, and under this provision an agreement was entered into on 7 Dec. 1907 for the transfer of the Northern Territory to the Commonwealth, and it formally passed under the control of the Commonwealth Government on 1 Jan. 1911. For details of Constitutional development until 1978 *see* THE STATESMAN'S YEAR-BOOK 1980–81 pp. 123–24. The Commonwealth Government retained responsibility until Self-Government was granted on 1 July 1978.

AREA AND POPULATION. The Northern Territory is bounded by the 26th parallel of S. lat. and 129° and 138° E. long. Its total area is 1,346, 200 sq. km. The coastline is about 6,200 km in length, and the Territory includes adjacent islands between 129° and 138° E. long. The greater part of the interior consists of a tableland rising gradually from the coast to a height of about 700 metres. On this tableland there are large areas of excellent pasturage. The southern part of the Territory is generally sandy and has a small rainfall, but water may be obtained by means of sub-artesian bores.

The population of the Territory in June 1990 was 157,304. The capital, seat of Government and principal port is Darwin, on the north coast; population 73,300 in June 1990. Other main centres include Katherine (7,500), 330 km south of Darwin; Alice Springs (24,000), in Central Australia; Tennant Creek (3,000), a rich mining centre 500 km north of Alice Springs; Nhulunbuy (3,400), a bauxite mining centre on the Gove Peninsula in eastern Arnhem Land; and Jabiru, a model town built to serve the rich Uranium Province in eastern Arnhem Land with a planned population of 6,000 (actual, 1986, 1,410). Palmerston is a Darwin satellite town (1990, 7,900); Yulara (1,158) is a resort village serving Uluru National Park and Ayers Rock. There also are a number of large self-contained Aboriginal communities. Aboriginals were 34,739 at the 1986 Census. On 31 July 1984, 26,692,400 ha were designated Aboriginal Land under the Aboriginal Land Rights (N.T.) Act 1976.

Vital statistics for 1989: Births, 3,379; deaths, 787; marriages, 778.

CONSTITUTION AND GOVERNMENT. The Northern Territory (Self-Government) Act 1978 established the Northern Territory as a body politic as from 1 July 1978, with Ministers having control over and responsibility for Territory finances and the administration of the functions of government as specified by the Federal Government. Regulations have been made conferring executive authority for the bulk of administrative functions. At 31 Dec. 1979 the only important powers retained by the Commonwealth related to rights in respect of Aboriginal land, some significant National Parks and the mining of uranium and other substances prescribed in the Atomic Energy Act. Proposed laws passed by the Legislative Assembly require the assent of the Administrator, who may assent, withhold assent, return them with recommended amendments or reserve them for the Governor-General's pleasure. The Governor-General may disallow any law assented to by the Administrator within 6 months of the Administrator's assent.

The Northern Territory has federal representation, electing 1 member to the House of Representatives and 2 members to the Senate.

The Legislative Assembly has 25 members, directly elected for a period of 4 years. The Chief Minister, Deputy Chief Minister and Speaker are elected by, and from, the members. The *Administrator* (J. H. Muirhead, AC, QC) appoints Ministers on the advice of the Leader of the majority party.

The Legislative Assembly, elected in 1990, in Feb. 1991 comprised: Country Liberal Party, 14; Australian Labor Party, 9; Independents, 2.

The Country Liberal Party Cabinet was as follows in Sept. 1991:

Chief Minister, Police, Fire and Emergency Services: Marshall Perron.
Deputy Chief Minister, Treasurer, Mines and Energy: Barry Coulter. *Attorney-*

General, Health and Community Services: Daryl Manzie. *Industries and Development:* Steve Hatton. *Education and the Arts, Employment and Training:* Shane Stone. *Transport and Works:* Fred Finch. *Primary Industry and Fisheries, Conservation, Correctional Services:* Mike Reed. *Tourism, Sport, Recreation, Ethnic Affairs and Local Government:* Roger Vale. *Lands and Housing:* Max Ortmann.

Local Government: Local government was established in Darwin in 1957 and later in 5 regional centres. These are each managed by a mayor and a municipal council elected at intervals of not more than 4 years by universal adult franchise. Provision has been made for a limited form of local government for smaller communities.

FINANCE. Budgets in $A1m.:

	1987–88	1988–89	1989–90	1990–91
Revenue	1,506·5	1,666·9	1,756·6	1,861·0
Expenditure	1,506·2	1,666·8	1,749·1	1,861·0

The revenue in 1990–91 comprised $A1,038·3m. in grants and allowances to the Northern Territory from the Commonwealth, as established by agreement at the time of self-government, together with $A948m. raised by the Northern Territory which included $A162·1m. through state-like taxes.

Expenditure during 1990–91 included $A294m. for education; $A189m. for housing and community amenities; $A203m. for health; $A124m. for public order and safety; $A225m. for energy.

ENERGY AND NATURAL RESOURCES

Oil and Gas. Significant oil and gas reserves have been discovered offshore in the Joseph Bonaparte Gulf and Timor Sea areas and onshore in the Amadeus Basin. In July 1990 offshore production was some 80,000 bbls a day. Total value of oil and gas production in 1990 was $A222m. Natural gas is piped from the Amadeus Basin to Darwin.

Minerals. The most important natural resources are minerals, and mining is the largest industry. Uranium, gold, manganese, bauxite, lead, silver, zinc and copper production dominated the minerals sector in 1988–89. Gross value of output, $A1,231m. in 1990.

The Northern Territory has large reserves of uranium. It has the world's largest manganese mine at Groote Eyland, and the world's largest known deposit of lead, silver and zinc at McArthur River. Bauxite is mined at Gove, and alumina is produced and exported to Europe, the USA, Canada, the USSR and China. The Territory is Australia's third largest producer of gold and has major deposits of platinum and palladium.

Agriculture. Cattle and buffalo production constitute the largest farming industry in the Northern Territory. Value of live cattle exports, 1989-90, $A15·5m.; total value of beef cattle industry, 1989-90, $A118m. Total value of the buffalo industry in 1989–90 was $A8·2m.

The USA is the largest importer of Territory beef, followed by Taiwan and the EEC.

There are 239 pastoral stations in the Northern Territory which produce cattle for Australian and overseas markets. They vary from smalls tations of 270 sq. km. to huge properties like Wave Hill Station which runs cattle over 12,359 sq. km.

Other animal industries contribute approximately $A12m. per annum. This sector consists of dairying, poultry and pig production, as well as crocodile farming for hides and meat. The horticultural industry is valued at $A20m. per annum and is increasing in importance. The main commodities in value are mangoes, rock melons and grapes. Some 800 ha are under sesame and mung beans, and cattle feeds including sorghum, rice and maize.

Fisheries. The total value of fish products landed in 1989-90 was $A28·2m. Of this, prawns contributed $A21m. and barramundi $A1·8m. Mud crabs, threadfin salmon, shark, mackerel, mother of pearl, bay lobster and molluscs made up most of the remainder. An expanding aquaculture industry produces crayfish, prawns, giant clams and beta carotene extraction.

INDUSTRY. In 1988–89 there were 158 manufacturing establishments (with 4 or more persons employed). Turnover was $A542m. 3,280 persons were employed in these factories. The labour force totalled 82,100 in 1990. In 1989, 71 trade unions had 19,300 members.

Tourism. In 1990-91, 821,000 people travelled to the Territory and tourism generated approximately $A430m. to the economy.

National Parks and Reserves. There are 98 areas totalling more than 4,325,076 ha set aside as National Parks or Conservation Reserves, and many other areas are managed by the Conservation Commission.

COMMUNICATIONS

Roads. There were (in 1990) 5,701 km of sealed road and 5,940 km of gravel and crushed stone road within the Northern Territory. They include three major inter-state links: The Stuart Highway from Darwin to Adelaide (1,486 km), the Barkly Highway, Tennant Creek to the Queensland border (636 km), and the Victoria Highway, Katherine to the Western Australian border (468 km). In addition to this there are 4,605 km of formed roads and 4,144 km of unformed roads or tracks, totalling approximately 20,390 km of roads. In 1989–90 74,600 motor vehicles were registered.

Railways. In 1980 Alice Springs was linked to the Trans-continental network by a standard (1,435 mm) gauge railway to Tarcoola (831 km). Direct services from Sydney started in 1984. The standard gauge railway is to be extended to Darwin, providing Australia with its first north-south rail link.

Aviation. There are daily flights from Darwin to Alice Springs with connexions to all Australian capital cities by 2 major domestic carriers, Australian Airlines and Ansett Airlines. Darwin is a first port of call for international aircraft flying in from Asia and a departure point for flights to such places as Singapore, Bali, Brunei and Timor.

Shipping. Regular freight shipping services connect Darwin with Western Australia, the eastern States and overseas. Passenger vessels also call at Darwin at irregular intervals.

The Port of Darwin is 997 km in extent; it is equipped to handle bulk, container and roll-on-roll-off traffic. There is a cyclone shelter for fishing vessels.

The ports of Melville Bay (Gove) and Milner Bay (Groote Eylandt) are connected with Darwin, the eastern States and overseas by regular shipping freight services.

The inland and coastal communities around the coast are provided with regular freight barge services from Darwin. Some of these communities also receive a barge freight-transhipment service out of a Brisbane vessel which calls at Melville and Milner Bays.

Telecommunications. Darwin's radio services include four ABC stations, one commercial station and a public station. In 1991 a second commercial FM station was established.

Darwin has one commercial and one ABC television service.

Alice Springs radio services include three ABC stations, one commercial and two public stations. It has one commercial and one ABC television service.

The rest of the Northern Territory is serviced through the AUSSAT satellite which provides one commercial and one ABC television station. The ABC provides two radio services to all other major regional centres.

EDUCATION AND WELFARE

Education. Education is compulsory from the age of 6-15 years. There were (1989) about 32,000 pre-school, primary and secondary students enrolled in about 165

Government and non-Government schools. The proportion of migrant and Aboriginal students in the Territory is high with the latter comprising about 30% of total school enrolments. Schools range from single classrooms and transportable units catering for the needs of small Aboriginal communities and pastoral properties to urban high schools and secondary colleges (years 11–12) catering for over 1,000 pupils. Bilingual programmes operate in some Aboriginal communities where traditional Aboriginal culture prevails. Secondary education extends from school years 8 to 12. The Northern Territory University was founded in 1989 by amalgamating the existing University College of the Northern Territory and the Darwin Institute of Technology, with the technical and further education courses hitherto offered by the latter to be conducted by an Institute of Technical and Further Education within the new University. The Alice Springs College of TAFE, the Katherine Rural College, the Northern Territory Open College and Batchelor College (a tertiary institution providing courses for Aboriginal people) offer a wide range of specialized courses.

Health. In 1990 there were 6 hospitals (5 public and 1 private). Community health services are provided from urban and rural Health Centres including mobile units. Remote communities are served by the Aerial Medical Service and by resident Aboriginal health workers.

Further Reading

The Northern Territory: Annual Report. Dept. of Territories, Canberra, from 1911. Dept. of the Interior, Canberra, from 1966–67. Dept. of Northern Territory, from 1972
Australian Territories, Dept. of Territories, Canberra, 1960 to 1973. Dept. of Special Minister of State, Canberra, 1973–75. Department of Administrative Services, 1976
Northern Territory Statistical Summary. Australian Bureau of Statistics, Canberra, from 1960
Donovan, P. F., *A Land Full of Possibilities: A History of South Australia's Northern Territory 1863–1911.* 1981.—*At the Other End of Australia: The Commonwealth and the Northern Territory 1911–1978.* Univ. of Queensland Press, 1984
Heatley, A., *The Government of the Northern Territory.* Univ. of Queensland Press, 1979.—*Almost Australians: the Politics of Northern Territory Self-Government.* Australian National Univ. Press, 1990
Mills, C. M., *A Bibliography of the Northern Territory.* Canberra, 1977
Powell, A., *Far Country: A Short History of the Northern Territory.* Melbourne Univ. Press, 1982

AUSTRALIAN EXTERNAL TERRITORIES

AUSTRALIAN ANTARCTIC TERRITORY. An Imperial Order in Council of 7 Feb. 1933 placed under Australian authority all the islands and territories other than Adélie Land situated south of 60° S. lat. and lying between 160° E. long. and 45° E. long. The Order came into force with a Proclamation issued by the Governor-General on 24 Aug. 1936 after the passage of the Australian Antarctic Territory Acceptance Act 1933. The boundaries of Adélie Land were definitively fixed by a French Decree of 1 April 1938 as the islands and territories south of 60° S. lat. lying between 136° E. long. and 142° E. long. The Australian Antarctic Territory Act 1954 declared that the laws in force in the Australian Capital Territory are, so far as they are applicable and are not inconsistent with any ordinance made under the Act, in force in the Australian Antarctic Territory.

The area of the territory is estimated at 6,119,818 sq. km (2,362,875 sq. miles).

On 13 Feb. 1954 the Australian National Antarctic Research Expeditions (ANARE) established a station on MacRobertson Land at lat. 67° 37' S. and long. 62° 52' E. The station was named Mawson in honour of the late Sir Douglas Mawson. Meteorological and other scientific research is conducted at Mawson, which is the centre for coastal and inland survey expeditions.

A second Australian scientific research station was established on the coast of Princess Elizabeth Land on 13 Jan. 1957 at lat. 68° 34' S. and long. 77° 58' E. The station was named Davis in honour of Capt. John King Davis, Mawson's second-in-command on 2 expeditions. The station was temporarily closed down in Jan. 1965 and re-opened in Feb. 1969.

In Feb. 1959 the Australian Government accepted from the US Government custody of Wilkes Station, which was established by the US on 16 Jan. 1957 on the Budd Coast of Wilkes Land, at lat. 66° 15′ S. and long. 110° 32′ E. The station was named in honour of Lieut. Charles Wilkes, who commanded the 1838–40 US expedition to the area, and was closed in Feb. 1969. Operations were then transferred to the new station, Casey. Construction commenced on Casey station in Jan. 1965 and was continued, mainly during summer visits, until Feb. 1969, when it was opened. The station, specially designed to withstand blizzard winds and prevent inundation by snow, is situated 2·4 km south of Wilkes at lat. 66° 17′ S. and long. 110° 32′ E. The Antarctic Division has also operated a station, since March 1948, at Macquarie Island, about 1,360 km south-east of Hobart. Macquarie Island is part of the State of Tasmania.

COCOS (KEELING) ISLANDS. The Cocos (Keeling) Islands are 2 separate atolls comprising some 27 small coral islands with a total area of about 14·2 sq. km, and are situated in the Indian Ocean at 12° 05′ S. lat. and 96° 53′ E. long. They lie 2,768 km north-west of Perth and 3,685 km west of Darwin, while Colombo is 2,255 km to the north-west of the group.

The main islands in this Australian Territory are West Island (the largest, about 10 km from north to south) on which is an airport and an animal quarantine station, and most of the European community; Home Island, occupied by the Cocos Malay community; Direction, South and Horsburgh Islands, and North Keeling Island, 24 km to the north of the group.

Although the islands were discovered in 1609 by Capt. William Keeling of the East India Company, they remained uninhabited until 1826, when the first settlement was established on the main atoll by an Englishman, Alexander Hare, with a group of followers, predominantly of Malay origin. Hare left the islands in 1831, by which time a second settlement had been formed on the main atoll by John Clunies-Ross, a Scottish seaman and adventurer, who began commercial development of the islands' coconut palms.

In 1857 the islands were annexed to the Crown; in 1878 responsibility was transferred from the Colonial Office to the Government of Ceylon, and in 1886 to the Government of the Straits Settlement. By indenture in 1886 Queen Victoria granted all land in the islands to George Clunies-Ross and his heirs in perpetuity (with certain rights reserved to the Crown). In 1903 the islands were incorporated in the Settlement of Singapore and in 1942–46 temporarily placed under the Governor of Ceylon. In 1946 a Resident Administrator, responsible to the Governor of Singapore, was appointed.

On 23 Nov. 1955 the Cocos Islands were placed under the authority of the Australian Government as the Territory of Cocos (Keeling) Islands. An Administrator, appointed by the Governor-General, is the Government's representative in the Territory and is responsible to the Minister for Territories and Local Government. The Cocos (Keeling) Islands Council, established as the elected body of the Cocos Malay community in July 1979, advises the Administrator on all issues affecting the Territory.

In 1978 the Australian Government purchased the Clunies-Ross family's entire interests in the islands, except for the family residence. A Cocos Malay co-operative was established to take over the running of the Clunies-Ross copra plantation and to engage in other business with the Commonwealth in the Territory, including construction projects.

The population of the Territory at 30 June 1990 was 603, distributed between Home Island (413) and West Island (190).

The islands are low-lying, flat and thickly covered by coconut palms, and surround a lagoon in which ships drawing up to 7 metres may be anchored, but which is extremely difficult for navigation.

An equable and pleasant climate, affected for much of the year by the south-east trade winds. Temperatures range over the year from 68° F (20° C) to 88° F (31·1° C) and rainfall averages 80" (2,000 mm) a year.

The Cocos (Keeling) Islands Act 1955 is the basis of the Territory's administrative, legislative and judicial systems. Under section 8 of this Act, those laws which were in force in the Territory immediately before the transfer continued in force there.

Roads. There are 15 km of roads.

Telecommunications. In 1986 there were 150 radio receivers and in 1991 200 telephones.

Religion. About 75% are Moslems and 25% Christians.

Education. In 1991 there were 2 primary schools (on Home Island and West Island) with 125 pupils and 8 teachers and a secondary school (on West Island) with 25 pupils and 7 staff.

Health. In 1991 there was a doctor and 4 nursing personnel, with 4 beds in clinics.

Administrator: W. Young.

CHRISTMAS ISLAND is an isolated peak in the Indian Ocean, lat. 10° 25' 22" S., long. 105° 39' 59" E. It lies 360 km S., 8° E. of Java Head, and 417 km N. 79° E. from Cocos Islands, 1,310 km from Singapore and 2,623 km from Fremantle. Area about 135 sq. km. The climate is tropical with temperatures varying little over the year at 27° C. The wet season lasts from Nov. to April with an annual total of about 2,673 mm. The island was formally annexed by the UK on 6 June 1888, placed under the administration of the Governor of the Straits Settlements in 1889, and incorporated with the Settlement of Singapore in 1900. Sovereignty was transferred to the Australian Government on 1 Oct. 1958. The population (Census, 1981) was 2,871; estimate (1991) 1,770 of whom 60% were of Chinese, 15% of Malay and 25% of Australian/European origin.

The legislative, judicial and administrative systems are regulated by the Christmas Island Act, 1958–73. They are the responsibility of the Commonwealth Government and operated by an Administrator. The laws of Singapore which were in force before the transfer have been continued but can be amended, repealed or substituted by ordinances made by the Governor-General. The first Island Assembly was elected in Sept. 1985.

Extraction and export of rock phosphate dust was the island's only industry until 1987. In Dec. 1948 Australia and New Zealand bought the lease rights of the Christmas Island Phosphate Co. and set up the Christmas Island Phosphate Commission (CIPC), which conducted the mining operation until mid-1981. The Phosphate Mining Co. of Christmas Island Ltd (PMCI) acted as managing agents for the CIPC until the Commission was wound up and then mined in its own right. The Commonwealth Government appointed liquidators on 11 Nov. 1987, with a view to ending all mining, but in 1989 invited tenders to operate the phosphate mine, with a closing date in May 1990. The Government is also encouraging the private sector development of tourism.

Electricity. Production (1991) 10·1m. kwh.

Roads. There are 100 km of roads (25 km sealed), 600 passenger cars and 300 commercial vehicles.

Civil Aviation. There are weekly flights to Perth (Western Australia) and fortnightly to Singapore.

Shipping. In 1991, 40,000 tonnes of cargo were loaded and 45,600 tonnes discharged at the port. 2,000 cu. metres of general cargo were also discharged.

Telecommunications. There is one post office (1991) and (1986) 2,500 radio receivers.

Religion. About 35% are Buddhists, 25% Muslims and 20% Christians.

Education. In 1991 there were 325 pupils in the Christmas Island Area School (pre-school to 10th year) and 60 students in a technical school.

Health. In 1991 there were 2 doctors, a pharmacist and a hospital with 20 beds.

Administrator: T. F. Paterson.

NORFOLK ISLAND. 29° 02' S. lat. 167° 57' E. long., area 3,455 hectares, population, (June 1986), 1,977. The island was formerly part of the colony of New South Wales and then of Van Diemen's Land. It was a penal colony 1788–1814 and 1825–55. In 1856 it received all 194 descendants of the *Bounty* mutineers from Pitcairn Island. It has been a distinct settlement since 1856, under the jurisdiction of the state of New South Wales; and finally by the passage of the Norfolk Island Act 1913, it was accepted as a Territory of the Australian Government. The Norfolk Island Act 1957 is the basis of the Territory's legislative, administrative and judicial systems. An Administrator, appointed by the Governor-General and responsible to the Minister for Territories and Local Government, is the senior government representative in the Territory.

The Norfolk Island Act 1979 gives Norfolk Island responsible legislative and executive government to enable it to run its own affairs to the greatest practicable extent. Wide powers are exercised by the Norfolk Island Legislative Assembly of 9 elected members, and by an Executive Council, comprising the executive members of the Legislative Assembly who have ministerial-type responsibilities. The seat of administration is Kingston, the only major settlement. The Act preserves the Commonwealth's responsibility for Norfolk Island as a Territory under its authority, indicating Parliament's intention that consideration would be given to an extension of the powers of the Legislative Assembly and the political and administrative institutions of Norfolk Island within 5 years. Some powers were transferred in 1985 and further transfers are being considered.

The Territory Administration is financed from local revenue which for 1988–89 totalled $A5,249,000; expenditure, $A5,121,000.

Public revenue is derived mainly from tourism, the sale of postage stamps, customs duties, liquor sales and company registration and licence fees. Residents are not liable for income tax on earnings within the Territory, nor are death and personal stamp duties levied.

In 1989–90, 23,201 visitors travelled to Norfolk. Descendants of the *Bounty* mutineer families constitute the 'original' settlers and are known locally as 'Islanders', while later settlers, mostly from Australia, New Zealand and UK, are identified as 'mainlanders'. Over the years the Islanders have preserved their own lifestyle and customs, and their language remains a mixture of West Country English, Gaelic and Tahitian. The resident population at 30 June 1986 was 1,977.

Roads. There are 80 km of roads (53 km paved), 1,802 passenger cars and 90 commercial vehicles.

Telecommunications. There is one post office and (1984) 1,090 telephones, 400 television and (1987) 1,500 radio receivers.

Newspapers. There is one weekly with a circulation of 1,200.

JUSTICE, RELIGION, EDUCATION AND WELFARE

Justice. The island's Supreme Court sits as required and a Court of Petty Sessions exercises both civil and criminal juristiction.

Religion. 40% of the population are Anglicans.

Education. A school is run by the New South Wales Department of Education covering pre-school to 10th year. It had 322 pupils at 30 June 1990.

Health. In 1985 there were 2 doctors, a pharmacist and a hospital with 20 beds.

Administrator: Commodore J. A. Matthew, CVO, MBE.
Chief Minister: David E. Buffett.

HEARD AND McDONALD ISLANDS. These islands, about 2,500 miles south-west of Fremantle, were transferred from UK to Australian control as from 26 Dec. 1947. Heard Island is about 43 km long and 21 km wide; Shag Island is about 8 km north of Heard. The total area is 412 sq. km (159 sq. miles). The McDonald Islands are 42 km to the west of Heard.

TERRITORY OF ASHMORE AND CARTIER ISLANDS. By Imperial Order in Council of 23 July 1931, Ashmore Islands (known as Middle, East and West Islands) and Cartier Island, situated in the Indian Ocean, some 320 km off the north-west coast of Australia (area, 5 sq. km), were placed under the authority of the Commonwealth.

Under the Ashmore and Cartier Islands Acceptance Act, 1933, the islands were accepted by the Commonwealth under the name of the Territory of Ashmore and Cartier Islands, and the effective date was proclaimed by the Governor-General to be 10 May 1934. It was the intention that the Territory should be administered by the State of Western Australia, but owing to administrative difficulties the Territory was annexed to and deemed to form part of the Northern Territory of Australia (by amendment to the Act in 1938) with relevant laws of the Northern Territory, applying to the Territory of Ashmore and Cartier Islands. Responsibility for the administration of Ashmore and Cartier Islands rests with the Minister for the Arts, Sport, the Environment, Tourism and Territories.

On 16 Aug. 1983 a national nature reserve was declared over Ashmore Reef and the area so declared is now known as Ashmore Reef National Nature Reserve.

The islands are uninhabited but Indonesian fishing boats, which have traditionally plied the area, fish within the Territory and land to collect water in accordance with an agreement between the governments of Australia and Indonesia.

Periodic visits are made to the islands by ships of the Royal Australian Navy, and aircraft of the Royal Australian Air Force make aerial surveys of the islands and neighbouring waters.

TERRITORY OF CORAL SEA ISLANDS. The Coral Sea Islands became a Territory of the Commonwealth of Australia under the Coral Sea Islands Act 1969. It comprises scattered reefs and islands over a sea area of about 1m. sq. km. The Territory is uninhabited apart from a manned meteorological station on Willis Island.

Further Reading

Australian Department of Arts, Sport, the Environment, Tourism and Territories. *Christmas Island: Annual Report.—Cocos (Keeling) Islands: Annual Report.—Norfolk Island: Annual Report.*

NEW SOUTH WALES

HISTORY. New South Wales became a British possession in 1770; the first settlement was established at Port Jackson in 1788; a partially elective Council was established in 1843, and an elective Parliament and responsible government in 1856. New South Wales federated with the other Australian states to form the Commonwealth of Australia in 1901.

AREA AND POPULATION. New South Wales is situated between the 29th and 38th parallels of S. lat. and 141st and 154th meridians of E. long., and comprises 309,433 sq. miles (801,428 sq. km), inclusive of Lord Howe Island, 6 sq. miles (17 sq. km), but exclusive of the Australian Capital Territory (911 sq. miles, 2,359 sq. km) and 28 sq. miles (73 sq. km) at Jervis Bay.

Lord Howe Island, 31° 33' 4" S., 159° 4' 26" E., which is part of New South Wales, is situated about 702 km north-east of Sydney; area, 1,654 ha, of which only about 120 ha are arable; resident population, estimate (30 June 1989), 320. The Island, which was discovered in 1788, is of volcanic origin. Mount Gower, the highest point, reaches a height of 866 metres.

The Lord Howe Island Board manages the affairs of the Island and supervises the Kentia palm-seed industry.

Census population of New South Wales (including full-blood Aboriginals from 1966):

	Males	Females	Persons	Population per sq. km	Average annual increase % since previous census
1901	710,264	645,091	1,355,355	2	1·86
1911	857,698	789,036	1,646,734	2	1·97
1921	1,071,501	1,028,870	2,100,371	3	2·46
1933	1,318,471	1,282,376	2,600,847	3	1·76
1947	1,492,211	1,492,627	2,984,838	4	0·99
1954	1,720,860	1,702,669	3,423,529	4	1·98
1961	1,972,909	1,944,104	3,917,013	5	1·94
1966	2,126,652	2,111,249	4,237,901	5	1·58
1971	2,307,210	2,293,970	4,601,180	6	1·66
1976	2,380,172	2,396,931	4,777,103	6	0·75
1981	2,548,984	2,577,233	5,126,217	6	1·42
1986	2,684,570	2,717,311	5,401,881	7	1·05

At 30 June 1990 the estimated resident population was 5,827,400 (2,924,600 females); population density, 7·3 per sq.km.

The state is divided into 12 *Statistical Divisions*. The population of these (in 1,000) in 1990 was: Sydney, 3,656·9; Hunter, 513·2; Illawarra, 338; Richmond-Tweed, 174·8; Mid-North Coast, 233·9; Northern, 183·8; North Western, 113·3; Central West, 166·8; South Eastern, 166·5; Murrumbidgee, 144·6; Murray, 109·4; Far West, 26. Population of the Statistical Subdivisions Newcastle (within Hunter) and Wollongong (within Illawarra) was 428·8 and 238·2 respectively.

Vital statistics for calendar years:

	Live births	Marriages	Divorces	Deaths
1987	86,093	40,650	12,044	42,189
1988	84,647	40,812	11,880	44,676
1989	85,790	41,300	12,743	45,060

The annual rates per 1,000 of mean estimated resident population in 1989 were: Births, 14·9; deaths, 7·8; marriages, 7·2; natural increase, 9·5; infant mortality, 8·7.

CONSTITUTION AND GOVERNMENT. Within the State there are three levels of government: The Commonwealth Government, with authority derived from a written constitution; the State Government with residual powers; the local government authorities with powers based upon a State Act of Parliament, operating within incorporated areas extending over almost 90% of the State.

The Constitution of New South Wales is drawn from several diverse sources; certain Imperial statutes such as the Commonwealth of Australia Constitution Act (1900); the Australian States Constitution Act (1907); an element of inherited English law; amendments to the Commonwealth of Australia Constitution Act; the (State) Constitution Act; the Australia Acts of 1986; the Constitution (Amendment) Act 1987 and certain other State Statutes; numerous legal decisions; and a large amount of English and local convention.

The Parliament of New South Wales may legislate for the peace, welfare and good government of the State in all matters not specifically reserved to the Commonwealth Government.

The State Legislature consists of the Sovereign, represented by the Governor, and two Houses of Parliament, the Legislative Council (upper house) and the Legislative Assembly (lower house).

Australian citizens aged 18 and over, and other British subjects who were enrolled prior to 25 Jan. 1984, men and women aged 18 years and over, are entitled to the franchise. Voting is compulsory. The optional preferential method of voting is used for both houses.

The Legislative Council has 42 members elected for a term of office equivalent to three terms of the Legislative Assembly, with 15 members retiring at the same time as the Legislative Assembly elections. The whole State constitutes a single electoral district. In Oct. 1991, the Council consisted of the following parties: Australian Labor Party (ALP), 18; Liberal Party of Australia (Lib), 13; National Party (NP), 7; Call to Australia Group (CTA), 2; Australian Democrats (AD), 2.

The President of the Legislative Council has an annual salary (1988) of $A77,985; the Leader of the Opposition members, the Chairman of Committees and the Deputy Leader of the Government members (if not a Minister), $A58,771 each; the Deputy Leader of the Opposition members and Government and Opposition Whips, $A54,388 each. The President is paid an annual expense allowance of $A12,977; the Leader of the Opposition members, the Chairman of Committees, the Deputy Leader of the Government members (if not a Minister) and the Deputy Leader of the Opposition members (when a leader of a party), $7,133 each; the Deputy Leader of the Opposition members (when not a leader of a party) and Government and Opposition Whips, $A2,861 each. Other members who are not Ministers receive an annual salary of $A48,750. All members receive an annual electoral allowance of $A16,180.

The Legislative Assembly has 99 members elected in single seat electoral districts for a maximum period of 4 years. The Legislative Assembly, elected on 25 May 1991, consisted in Jan. 1992 of the following parties: Lib/NP coalition, 47; ALP, 47; Independents, 5.

The Speaker of the Legislative Assembly and the Leader of the Opposition members receive a salary of (1988) $A77,985 each; the Chairman of Committees and Deputy Leader of the Opposition members, $A58,771 each; Government and Opposition Whips, $A55,383 each. The Speaker and the Leader of the Opposition members also receive an expense allowance of $A12,977 each; the Chairman of Committees and Deputy Leader of the Opposition members, $A7,133 each; Government and Opposition Whips, and Deputy Leader of the National Party, $A3,367 each. Members who are not Ministers receive an annual salary of $A48,750. All members receive an annual electoral allowance ranging from $A16,180 to $A31,359 according to the location of their constituencies.

Executive power is vested in the Governor, who is appointed by the Crown, and an Executive Council consisting of members of the Cabinet. Ministers receive the following annual salaries (1988): Premier, $A96,946; Deputy Premier, $A87,585; the Leader of the Government members in the Legislative Council, $A88,537; Deputy Leader of Government members in the Legislative Council, $A84,477; other Ministers, $A82,869. Ministers also receive an expense allowance (Premier, $A27,777; Deputy Premier, $A13,888; other Ministers, $A12,977 each). Ministers also receive an electoral allowance ranging from $A16,180 to $A27,221 to members of the Legislative Assembly, according to the location of their electorate; and $A16,180 to each member of the Legislative Council.

Governor: Rear-Adm. Peter Sinclair, AO.
The New South Wales Ministry, in Oct. 1991, was as follows:

Premier, Treasurer and Minister for Ethnic Affairs: The Hon. N. F. Greiner, MP.
Deputy Prime Minister, Minister for State Development and Minister for Public Works: The Hon. W. T. J. Murray, MP. *Minister for Health and Minister for the Arts:* The Hon. P. E. J. Collins, MP. *Minister for Agriculture and Rural Affairs:* The Hon. I. M. Armstrong, OBE, MP. *Attorney-General:* The Hon. J. R. A. Dowd, MP. *Minister for Housing:* The Hon. J. J. Schipp, MP. *Minister for the Environment and Assistant Minister for Transport:* The Hon. T. J. Moore, MP. *Chief Secretary and Minister for Tourism:* The Hon. G. B. West, MP. *Minister for Police and Emergency Services and Vice-President of the Executive Council:* The Hon. E. P. Pickering, MLC. *Minister for Sport, Recreation and Racing:* The Hon. R. B. R. Smith, MLC. *Minister for Family and Community Services:* The Hon. Virginia Chadwick, MLC. *Minister for Education and Youth Affairs:* The Hon. T. A. Metherell, MP. *Minister for Transport:* The Hon. B. G. Baird, MP. *Minister for Administrative Services and Assistant Minister for Transport:* The Hon. Matthew Singleton, MP. *Minister for Business and Consumer Affairs:* The Hon. G. B. P.

Peacocke, MP. *Minister for Mineral Resources and Minister for Energy:* The Hon. N. E. W. Pickard, MP. *Minister for Industrial Relations and Employment and Minister Assisting the Premier:* The Hon. J. J. Fahey, MP. *Minister for Natural Resources:* The Hon. I. R. Causley, MP. *Minister for Local Government and Minister for Planning:* The Hon. D. A. Hay, MP. *Minister for Corrective Services:* The Hon. M. R. Yabsley, MP.

Agent-General in London: Norman Brunsdon (66 Strand, WC2N 5LZ).

Local Government. A system of local government extends over most of the State, including the whole of the Eastern and Central land divisions and almost three-quarters of the sparsely populated Western division. At 26 Sept. 1988 there were 65 municipalities, and 110 corporate bodies called shires. A number of the municipalities and shires have combined to form 41 county councils, which administer electricity or water supply undertakings or render other services of common benefit.

ECONOMY

Budget. State Consolidated Fund: Statement of receipts and expenditure (in $A1m.) for financial years ending 30 June:

	1984–85	1985–86	1986–87	1987–88
Receipts: Recurrent	7,348	8,220	10,657	12,379
Capital	654	659	1,508	1,384
Total Receipts	8,002	8,879	12,165	13,763
Expenditure: Recurrent	7,511	8,305	10,634	11,871
Capital	491	573	1,531	1,592
Revenue Equalization	...	...	...	...
Total Expenditure	8,002	8,879	12,165	13,519
Surplus/deficit	—	—	—	245

State Government receipts (in $A1m.) for 1987–88 included receipts from loan raisings, 114; Commonwealth general revenue grant, 4,269; and state taxation, 5,423. Expenditure included capital works and services, 1,592; education, 2,646; health, 3,137; and public debt charges, 750.

Public Debt. The long term debt of the State has three components. Debt outstanding at 30 June 1988 (in $A1m.) for each of these components was:

Debt of statutory bodies under State Government guarantee	18,142·1
Loan liability to the Commonwealth under the 1927 Financial Agreement	5,962·7
Loan liability to the Commonwealth outside the Financial Agreement	3,178·0
Total debt	27,282·8

Since 1983, access to the capital markets for borrowings has been principally through the New South Wales Treasury Corporation which acts as the central borrowing authority of the State.

Banking and Finance. There were 27 trading banks operating at 30 June 1988. The trading bank business is transacted chiefly by the Commonwealth Bank of Australia, the State Bank of New South Wales (government banks) and 3 private banks. At 30 June 1988 27 banks operated 1,960 branches and 293 agencies.

The weekly average amount of deposits held by the 27 banks was $A38,644m. in June 1989, consisting of $A29,100m. fixed and $A9,544m. current. Bank advances, overdrafts, bills discounted, etc., amounted to $A36,267m. A statement of other assets and liabilities of the banks in New South Wales is of little significance, as banking business is conducted on an Australia-wide basis.

Savings bank deposits at the end of June 1988 amounted to $A20,155·9m., representing $A3,548 per head of population.

ENERGY AND NATURAL RESOURCES

Electricity. At 30 June 1989 the total nominal capacity of the Electricity Commission of New South Wales system was 11,950 mw.

Minerals. New South Wales contains extensive mineral deposits. The most important minerals mined are: Coal (which accounted for 66% of the value of the State's mineral production in 1987–88); silver–lead–zinc (13%); construction materials (sand, gravel, stone, etc., 10%); and mineral sands (rutile, zircon, etc., 1%). At 30 June 1988, there were 440 mining establishments. Average employment in mining, 1986–87, was 26,005 persons. During 1987–88, wages and salaries paid were $A938m., and value added was $A2,086m. Mine production of coal and metallic minerals (gross content) is shown below:

	1984–85	1985–86	1986–87	1987–88
Antimony (tonnes)	1,409	1,264	1,202	1,146
Cadmium (tonnes)	1,735	1,216	1,113	952
Coal (1,000 tonnes)	70,034	64,082	73,312	63,945
Cobalt (tonnes)	66	55	55	74
Copper (tonnes)	23,038	26,733	32,400	31,378
Gold (kg)	1,464	1,015	2,227	5,224
Lead (tonnes)	251,595	233,270	206,139	223,953
Manganese (tonnes)	...	3,897	3,858	3,413
Silver (kg)	355,827	367,751	408,829	428,123
Sulphur (tonnes)	248,681	253,800	264,631	293,008
Tin (tonnes)	1,306	1,280	249	3
Titanium dioxide (tonnes)	41,283	47,240	58,066	59,961
Zinc (tonnes)	385,075	355,443	362,180	373,520
Zircon (tonnes)	47,113	53,607	50,234	49,885

The value of output in mining and quarrying in 1987–88 was $A3,222m.

Agriculture. In 1988–89 GDP at factor cost for agriculture, forestry, hunting and fishing was $A3,665m. Farm income was $A1,205m. At 31 March 1989 there were 37,809 establishments with agricultural activity. Area under cultivation (in ha) during 3 years (ended 31 March) and the principal crops (in tonnes) produced were as follows (Data relates to farms whose estimated value of agricultural operations was $A20,000 or more at the census):

	1986	1987	1988	1989
Area under cultivation	5,925,308	5,325,305	4,908,459	4,837,838

	1987		1988		1989	
Principal crops	Sown area	Production	Sown area	Production	Sown area	Production
Wheat {Grain	3,098,826	4,855,244	2,463,707	3,996,913	2,309,463	4,105,301
Wheat {Hay	19,237	55,456	20,128	57,915	....	....
Barley {Grain	408,315	613,646	464,746	744,000	412,668	....
Barley {Hay	1,801	4,574	....	8,000	....	....
Oats {Grain	482,257	635,185	525,798	707,000	547,961	....
Oats {Hay	39,066	111,344	43,305	120,391	....	....
Grain Sorghum	188,062	391,582	174,669	...	151,474	....
Potatoes	6,225	121,573	6,440	119,875	6,346	110,126
Lucerne (hay)	71,710	341,859	77,208	369,823	....	....
Rice	92,281	589,074	101,825	721,000	94,187	....
Cotton (raw and seed)	125,026	676,428	163,631	757,419	140,836	....
Oilseeds	149,760	156,452	109,258	115,392	103,020	....

In 1989, 15,438 ha of sugar-cane were cut for crushing. The total area under grapes was 12,433 (including 797 not bearing) ha; the production of table grapes was 9,319 tonnes; of wine grapes, 139,940 tonnes; for drying, 40,721 tonnes (fresh weight).

In 1989, there were 4,399 ha of banana plantations; production, 89,243 tonnes. There were 4·14m. citrus fruit trees; production, 198,400 tonnes.

At 31 March 1989 there were 59·11m. sheep and lambs, 5·4m. cattle and 0·86m. pigs. The production of shorn and crutched wool in 1987–88 was 251,610 tonnes (greasy). In the year ended 30 June 1990 production of butter was 1,110 tonnes; cheese, 14,055 tonnes, and pig meat, 100,878 tonnes.

Forestry. The estimated area of Crown and private lands is 15m. ha. The total area of State forests amounts to 3·2m. ha, and 223,000 ha have been set apart as timber reserves.

In 1986–87, 3,466,000 cu. metres of timber (excluding firewood) were produced, including 1,214,000 cu. metres of forest hardwoood and 1,323,000 cu. metres of pulpwoods.

INDUSTRY AND TRADE

Industry. A wide range of manufacturing is undertaken in the Sydney area, and there are large iron and steel works near the coalfields at Newcastle and Port Kembla.

Manufacturing establishments' operations, 1988–89:

Industry	No. of establishments [1]	Persons employed (1,000) [2]	Wages and salaries [3] ($A1m.)	Turnover ($A1m.)
Food, beverages and tobacco	1,160	52,485	1,257·9	9,035·1
Textiles	307	8,444	187·2	1,178·4
Clothing and footwear	1,078	22,730	391·1	1,761·9
Wood, wood products and furniture	2,197	26,786	529·2	2,590·7
Paper, paper products, printing and publishing	1,835	41,185	1,065·7	5,050·9
Chemical, petroleum and coal products	465	24,251	713·3	5,770·0
Non-metallic mineral products	625	13,846	380·5	2,441·6
Basic metal products	236	33,448	1,073·9	8,176·4
Fabricated metal products	2,471	38,652	873·4	4,280·2
Transport equipment	657	28,077	693·8	2,641·2
Other machinery and equipment	2,192	57,397	1,409·1	6,305·1
Miscellaneous manufacturing	1,406	23,135	529·8	2,907·6
Total manufacturing	14,692	370,436	9,105·0	52,139·2

[1] Operating at 30 June 1989. Excludes single-establishment manufacturing enterprises with less than 4 persons employed.
[2] Persons employed at 30 June 1989, including working proprietors.
[3] Excludes drawings of working proprietors.

Some of the principal articles manufactured in 1988–89 were:

Article	Quantity	Article	Quantity
Flour (1,000 tonnes)	552	Ready mixed concrete (1,000 cu. metres)	5,177
Footwear (1,000 pairs)	6,492	Clay bricks (1m.) [1]	786
Raw steel (1,000 tonnes)	5,259	Electricity (1m. kwh.) [1]	51,813

[1] Includes the Australian Capital Territory.

Value of building jobs, 1988–89:

Commenced	Under construction	Completed
$A10,499m.	$A11,580	$A7,984

Value of building work, 1988–89; private sector, $A8,116m.; public sector, $A1,344m.

Labour. In Aug. 1990 2,600,900 persons (61·3% of the population over 15) were employed out of a total workforce of 2,779,100. 178,200 persons were unemployed. 251,500 persons were employed in manufacturing, 241,000 in trade, 157,600 in finance, 147,700 in community service, 82,400 in transport and 78,500 in building.

Industrial tribunals are authorized to fix minimum rates of wages and other conditions of employment. Their awards may be enforced by law, as may be industrial agreements between employers and organizations of employees, when registered.

The principal State arbitration and conciliation tribunal is the Industrial Commission of New South Wales. The Commission is empowered to exercise all the powers conferred on subsidiary tribunals, and has in addition authority to determine any widely defined 'industrial matter', to adjudicate in case of illegal strikes and lockouts, to investigate union ballots when irregularities are alleged and to hear appeals from subsidiary tribunals. Subsidiary tribunals are Conciliation Committees for various industries, each having an equal number representing employers and employees and a Conciliation Commissioner as chairman.

Trade Unions. Registration of trade unions is effected under the New South Wales Trade Union Act 1881, which follows substantially the Trade Union Acts of 1871 and 1876 of England. Registration confers a quasi-corporate existence with power to hold property, to sue and be sued, etc., and the various classes of employees covered by the union are required to be prescribed by the constitution of the union. For the purpose of bringing an industry under the review of the State industrial tribunals, or participating in proceedings relating to disputes before Commonwealth tribunals, employees and employers must be registered as industrial unions, under State or Commonwealth industrial legislation respectively. At 30 June 1990, there were 163 trade unions with a total membership of 1,263,500. 57% of employees were members of trade unions.

Commerce. External commerce, exclusive of inter-state trade, is included in the statement of the commerce of Australia. Overseas commerce of New South Wales in $A1m. for years ending 30 June:

	Imports	Exports		Imports	Exports
1984–85	12,478·4	6,674·0	1987–88	18,087·4	10,582·1
1985–86	15,129·9	7,363·2	1988–89	20,873·9	10,903·7
1986–87	16,055·9	8,364·2	1989–90	23,383·2	12,279·3

The major commodities exported in 1989–90 (in $A1m.) were coal, coke and briquettes (2,362), sheep's and lamb's wool (1,309·6) and aluminium (759·3). Principal imports were computers (1,667·3), road vehicles (1,569·3) and electrical equipment (1,227·3).

Principal destinations of exports in 1989–90 (in $A1m.) were Japan (3,612·6), Republic of Korea (952·2), USA (787·4), New Zealand (745·8) and Taiwan (585). Major sources of supply were USA (6,667·1), Japan (4,119·1), UK (1,653·2), Federal Republic of Germany (1,392·8), New Zealand (1,024·9), Taiwan (921·6).

Tourism. In the year ended 30 June 1990, 976,000 overseas visitors arrived for short term visits. At 30 June 1990 there were 1,691 hotels providing 49,913 rooms, and 821 caravan parks.

COMMUNICATIONS

Roads. In 1987 there were some 205,000 km of public roads of all sorts. The Roads and Traffic Authority of New South Wales is responsible for the administration and upkeep of major roads. In 1989 there were 38,988 km of roads under its control, including 10,397 km of state highways, 25,124 km of main roads and 292 km of secondary roads.

The number of registered motor vehicles (excluding tractors and trailers) at 30 June 1990 was 3,217,700, including 2,410,600 cars and station wagons, 196,300 utilities, 239,500 panel vans, 222,300 trucks, 59,300 buses and 89,700 motor cycles. There were 800 fatalities in road accidents in 1990.

Railways. At 30 June 1990, 9,917 km of government railway were open (618 km electrified). The revenue (including supplements) in 1987–88 was $A2,065m.; the expenditure from revenue, $A2,065m. In 1989–90 251m. passengers were carried and 53·2m. tonnes of freight. Also open for traffic are 325 km of Victorian Government railways which extend over the border; 68 km of private railways (mainly in mining districts) and 53 km of Commonwealth Government-owned track.

Civil Aviation. Sydney is the major airport in New South Wales and Australia's principal international air terminal. During the year ended 31 Dec. 1987 scheduled aircraft movements at Sydney totalled 114,632. Passengers totalled 7,006,689 on domestic services and 3,462,604 on international services. Freight handled on domestic and international services was 61,232 tonnes and 153,337 tonnes respectively.

Shipping. The main ports are at Sydney, Newcastle, Port Kembla and Port Botany. Arrivals of vessels engaged in overseas trade in the ports of New South Wales in

1989 totalled 3,953 (84·78m. GRT). The number of overseas vessels which entered in 1989 was 1,602.

JUSTICE, RELIGION, EDUCATION AND WELFARE

Justice. Legal processes may be conducted in Local Courts presided over by magistrates or in higher courts (District Court or Supreme Court) presided over by judges. There is also an appellate jurisdiction. Persons charged with the more serious crimes must be tried before a higher court.

Children's Courts have been established with the object of removing children as far as possible from the atmosphere of a public court. There are also a number of tribunals exercising special jurisdiction, *e.g.*, the Industrial Commission and the Compensation Court.

At 30 June 1990 there were 5,646 persons in prison.

Religion. There is no established church in New South Wales, and freedom of worship is accorded to all.

The following table shows the statistics of the religious denominations in New South Wales at the census in 1986, and of ministers of religion registered for the celebration of marriages in 1987:

Denomination	Ministers	Adherents	Denomination	Ministers	Adherents
Catholic	1,701	1,529,176	Other Christian	1,496	288,865
Anglican	1,008	1,519,806	Muslim	11	57,551
Uniting Church	603	327,360	Jewish	29	28,236
Presbyterian	228	227,663	Other Non-Christian	38	57,079
Orthodox	66	165,659	Others	...	1,101,409 [1]
Baptist	443	67,187			
Lutheran	38	31,890	Total	5,661	5,401,881

[1] Comprises 539,467 'no religion' and 561,942 'religion not stated' or 'inadequately described' (this is not a compulsory question in the census schedule).

Education. The State Government maintains a system of free primary and secondary education, and attendance at school is compulsory from 6 to 15 years of age. Non-government schools are subject to government inspection.

In 1990 there were 2,181 government schools with 743,186 students and 45,620 teachers, including (in 1989) 1,659 primary (434,098 students and 21,593 teachers), 381 secondary and 62 combined primary and secondary (310,765 students and 23,345 teachers), and 98 special schools (4,400 students and 875 teachers); and 858 non-government schools, with 284,330 students and 17,281 teachers, including 542 primary (148,819 students and 7,129 teachers), 152 secondary and 132 combined primary and secondary (134,662 students and 9,983 teachers), and 32 special schools (849 students and 169 teachers). In 1990 there were 850 non-government schools with 287,437 students and 17,691 teachers.

There were 150,606 students in higher education in 1990.

The University of Sydney, founded in 1850, had 18,236 students in 1988. There are 7 colleges providing residential facilities at the university. The University of New England at Armidale, previously affiliated with the University of Sydney, was incorporated in 1954, and in 1988 had 9,427 students.

The University of New South Wales was established in 1949. Enrolments in 1988 numbered 18,706. There are 7 colleges providing residential facilities at the university. The University of Newcastle, previously affiliated with the University of New South Wales, was granted autonomy from 1965, and in 1988 had 6,375 students. The University of Wollongong, also previously associated with the University of New South Wales, became autonomous in 1975, and in 1988 had 7,964 students. Macquarie University in Sydney, established in 1964, had 11,194 students in 1988.

Colleges of advanced education were merged with universities in 1990.

Post-school technical and further education is provided at State technical and further education colleges. Enrolments in 1988 totalled 474,051 (87% being part-time).

State Government expenditure (including capital expenditure and federal grants) on education in 1985–86 was $A3,787m.

Social Welfare. The Commonwealth Government makes provision for social bene-fits, such as age and invalid pensions, widows' pensions, supporting parents' benefits, family allowances, and unemployment, sickness and special benefits.

The number of age and invalid pensions (including wives' and carers' pensions) current in New South Wales on 30 June 1990 was: Age, 477,430 (carers, 9,385); invalid, 105,369 (carers, 30,584). Expenditure for the year ended 30 June 1990 was $A2,947m. for age pensions and $A895m. for invalid pensions.

In addition there were 29,081 widows' pensions current at 30 June 1990. Expen-diture on widows' pensions totalled $A205m. Sole parents' benefits 88,756; expen-diture was $A841m.

Under the Family Allowance scheme, which commenced in 1976, 650,557 allow-ances to families and approved institutions for children under 16 years and full-time students under 18 years (under 25 in special circumstances) in 1990 amounting to $A627m.

142,849 unemployment, 35,802 sickness and 11,308 special benefits were paid in 1989–90 totalling $A1,500m.

Direct State Government social welfare services are limited, for the most part, to the assistance of persons not eligible for Commonwealth Government pensions or benefits and the provision of certain forms of assistance not available from the Commonwealth Government. The State also subsidizes many approved services for needy persons.

Health. At 30 June 1990 there were 20,175 medical practitioners, 3,658 dentists and 70,299 nurses. In 1990 there were 210 public hospitals with 26,786 beds and 91 private hospitals with 5,943 beds.

Further Reading

Statistical Information: The NSW Government Statistician's Office was established in 1886, and in 1957 was integrated with the Commonwealth Bureau of Census and Statistics (now called the Australian Bureau of Statistics). *Deputy Commonwealth Statistician:* John Wilson. Its principal publications are:

New South Wales Year Book (1886/87–1900/01 under the title *Wealth and Progress of New South Wales*). Annual
Regional Statistics: latest issue, 1991
New South Wales Pocket Year Book. Published since 1913; latest issue, 1991
Monthly Summary of Statistics. Published since May 1931
New South Wales in Brief. 1991

New South Wales Dept. of Business and Consumer Affairs, *New South Wales Business Hand-book.* Sydney, 1987
New South Wales Department of Environment and Planning, *Sydney Into Its Third Century: Metropolitan Strategy for the Sydney Region.* Sydney, 1988
New South Wales Government Information Service, *New South Wales Government Directory.* 5th ed. Sydney, 1987

State Library: The State Library of NSW, Macquarie St., Sydney. *State Librarian:* Alison Crook, BA (Hons), MBA, Dip Lib, Dip Ed, ALAA, AAIM.

QUEENSLAND

AREA AND POPULATION. Queensland comprises the whole northeastern portion of the Australian continent, including the adjacent islands in the Pacific Ocean and in the Gulf of Carpentaria. Estimated area 1,727,000 sq. km.

The increase in the population as shown by the censuses since 1901 has been as follows:

Year	Males	Females	Total	Numerical	Rate per annum %
		Census counts		*Intercensal increase*	
1901	277,003	221,126	498,129	—	—
1911	329,506	276,307	605,813	107,684	1·98
1921	398,969	357,003	755,972	150,159	2·24
1933	497,217	450,317	947,534	191,562	1·86
1947	567,471	538,944	1,106,415	158,881	1·11

Year	Males	Census counts Females	Total	Intercensal increase Numerical	Rate per annum %
	1954	676,252	642,007	1,318,259	211,844 2·53
1961	774,579	744,249	1,518,828	200,569	2·04
1966	849,390 [1]	824,934 [1]	1,674,324 [1]	144,857	1·84
1971	921,665 [1]	905,400 [1]	1,827,065 [1]	152,741 [1]	1·76 [1]
1976	1,024,611 [1]	1,012,586 [1]	2,037,197 [1]	210,132 [1]	2·20 [1]
1981	1,153,404 [1]	1,141,719 [1]	2,295,123 [1]	257,926 [1]	2·41 [1]
1986	1,295,630 [1]	1,291,685 [1]	2,587,315 [1]	292,192 [1]	2·43 [1]

[1] Including Aboriginals.

Since the 1981 census, official population estimates are according to place of usual residence and are referred to as estimated resident population. Estimated resident population at 30 June 1990, 2,906,838 (1,448,227 females).

Statistics on birthplaces from the 1986 census are as follows: Australia, 2,162,995 (83·6%); UK and Ireland, 158,949 (6·1%); other countries, 229,760 (8·9%); at sea and not stated, 35,611 (1·4%).

Vital statistics (including Aboriginals) for calendar years:

	Total births	Marriages	Divorces	Deaths
1987	39,365	18,265	6,918	18,861
1988	40,561	18,850	7,690	18,803
1989	42,071	19,088	7,123	18,803

The annual rates per 1,000 population in 1989 were: Marriages, 6·7; divorces, 2·52; births, 14·8; deaths, 7·2. The infant death rate was 8·5 per 1,000 births.

Brisbane, the capital, had at 30 June 1988 (estimate) a resident population of 1,240,286 (Statistical Division). The resident populations of the other major centres (Statistical Districts) at the same date were: Gold Coast-Tweed, 207,966; Townsville, 109,699; Sunshine Coast, 95,683; Toowoomba, 79,934; Cairns, 76,475; Rockhampton, 61,124; Mackay, 50,301; Bundaberg, 43,837 and Gladstone, 30,623. Other cities included Mount Isa, 24,104; Maryborough, 22,986; Hervey Bay, 21,151.

CONSTITUTION AND GOVERNMENT. Queensland, formerly a portion of New South Wales, was formed into a separate colony in 1859, and responsible government was conferred. The power of making laws and imposing taxes is vested in a Parliament of one House—the Legislative Assembly, which comprises 89 members, returned from 4 electoral zones for 3 years, elected for single-member constituencies at compulsory ballot. Members are entitled to $A54,500 per annum, with individual electorate allowances for travelling, postage, etc., of from $A21,525 to $A43,884.

At the general election of 1 Nov. 1986 there were 1,563,294 persons registered as qualified to vote under the Elections Act 1983. This Act provides franchise for all males and females, 18 years of age and over, qualified by 6 months' residence in Australia and 3 months in the electoral district.

At the elections to the Legislative Assembly of 2 Dec. 1989 the Australian Labor Party won 51 seats, the National Party, 29 and the Liberals, 3. (Previous Assembly: National, 49; Labor, 30; Liberal, 10).

Governor of Queensland: Sir Walter Benjamin Campbell, QC (assumed office 22 July 1985).

The Executive Council of Ministers in Nov. 1991 consisted of:

Premier, Minister for Economic and Trade Development and Minister for the Arts: Wayne Goss

Deputy Premier, Minister for Housing and Local Government: Tom Burns. *Police and Emergency Services:* Terry Mackenroth. *Treasurer and Minister for Regional Development:* Keith De Lacy. *Tourism, Sport and Racing:* Robert Gibbs. *Transport and Minister Assisting the Premier on Economic and Trade Development:* David Hamill. *Employment, Training and Industrial Relations:* Neville Warburton. *Resource Industries:* Kenneth Vaughan. *Primary Industries:* Ed Casey. *Health:* Kenneth McElligott. *Education:* Paul Braddy. *Environment and Heritage:* Pat

Comben. *Attorney-General:* Deane Wells. *Family Services and Aboriginal and Islander Affairs:* Anne Warner. *Justice and Corrective Services:* Glen Milliner. *Administrative Services:* Ronald McLean. *Manufacturing and Commerce:* Geoffrey Smith. *Land Management:* Bill Eaton.

Ministers have a salary of $A88,229, the Premier receives $A111,524, the Deputy Premier, $A95,941, and the Leader of the Opposition, $A79,666.

Agent-General in London: Hon. D. T. McVeigh (392–3 Strand, WC2R 0LZ).

Local Government. Provision is made for local government by the subdivision of the State into cities, towns and shires. These are under the management of aldermen or councillors, who are elected by all persons 18 years and over. Local Authorities are charged with the control of all matters of a parochial nature, such as sewerage, cleansing and sanitary services, health services, domestic water supplies, and roads and bridges within their allotted areas. In addition to Government grants and subsidies, Local Authority revenue is derived from general rates, paid by landowners on the unimproved capital value of land, and by charging for some specific services.

For the year ended 30 June 1988, the receipts and expenditure (including loans) for the 134 Local Authorities were $A2,047·6m. and $A2,018·6m. respectively and their rateable values amounted to $A27,601·2m.

ECONOMY

Budget. Revenue and expenditure of the Consolidated Revenue Fund of Queensland during 5 years ending 30 June (in $A1,000):

	1985–86	1986–87	1987–88	1988–89	1989–90
Revenue	5,190,941	5,649,027	6,308,439	7,164,200	7,847,900
Expenditure	5,190,727	5,648,701	6,270,305	9,265,700	7,836,800

Total receipts of the state authorities in 1988–89 were $A8,657·5m., of which taxation amounted to $A2,465·4m. and Commonwealth payments $A3,476·7m. for current purposes and $A549·9m. for capital purposes. Expenditure from these funds included: Education, $A2,191·1m.; fuel and energy, $A330·1m.; transport and communications, $A929·3m.; health, $A1,239·9m.

Debt. The public debt of the State at 30 June 1989 was $A2,420·3m.

Banking and Finance. The major national trading and savings banks dominate banking operations. The privately-owned Bank of Queensland and several licensed foreign banks also provide trading and savings bank facilities. In June 1989 the average of weekly deposits held in trading banks amounted to $A10,197m. while the average of advances owing to the banks was $A9,321m. The total depositors' balances held in savings banks at 30 June 1989 was $A9,687m.

ENERGY AND NATURAL RESOURCES

Electricity. Installed capacity in 1989–90 was 5,098 mw. Output, 25·36m. mwh to 1·16m. consumers. Some 3% of production is hydro-electric.

Minerals. Principal minerals produced during 1989–90 (in 1,000 tonnes): Copper, 196; coal, 74,931; lead, 208; zinc, 250; bauxite, 10,094; mineral sands concentrates, 397; silver, 537; gold, 30·2; liquid petroleum, 1,685,000 kilolitres. Value of output, at the mine, was $A5,366m. The chief mines are at Mount Isa (copper, silver, lead, zinc), Weipa (bauxite), Kidston, Mount Leyshon, Mount Morgan, Red Dame, Pajingo and Cracow (gold), Moreton and Bowen Basin (coal), Greenvale (nickel), Cooper-Eromanga Basin (petroleum) and North Stradbroke Island (mineral sands).

Land Settlement. At 30 June 1990, of the 172·7m. ha of the State, 121·3m. ha was Crown leasehold, 19·4m. ha was in process of freeholding and 32m. ha was roads, reserves, freehold, mining tenures and vacant land.

In the western portion of the State water is comparatively easily found by sinking artesian bores. At 30 June 1988, 3,700 such bores had been drilled, of which 2,595 were flowing.

Agriculture. Livestock on farms and stations at 31 March 1990 numbered 9·49m. cattle, 16·67m. sheep and 599,828 pigs. The wool production (greasy) was, in 1989–90, 72·84m. kg. The total area under crops during 1989–90 was 2·64m. ha.

| | Area (ha) | | Production (tonnes) | |
Crop	1987–88	1989–90	1987–88	1989–90
Sugar-cane, crushed	291,169	307,391	23,199,753	25,552,263
Wheat	646,140	894,335	718,395	1,419,957
Maize	36,930	34,218	124,209	114,594
Sorghum	565,174	237,598	1,213,117	577,646
Barley	169,427	179,422	244,173	320,706
Oats	19,486	15,404	13,566	14,318
Potatoes	6,617	6,224	120,048	121,909
Pumpkins	3,538	4,003	33,071	39,648
Tomatoes	3,424	4,091	81,411	100,151
Peanuts	31,137	18,061	35,651	17,856
Tobacco	2,816	2,777	7,105	6,958
Apples [1]	2,669	2,411	33,640	32,431
Grapes [2]	982	964	4,190	4,223
Citrus [1]	1,546	1,714	46,651	47,338
Bananas [2]	3,505	3,802	79,183	106,750
Pineapples [2]	3,764	3,978	146,463	141,584
Green fodder [3]	582,100	485,925	...	...
Hay	62,722	44,942	258,026	232,453
Cotton (raw)	80,918	64,786	72,099	70,207

[1] Area of trees 6 years and over.　　[2] Bearing area only.
[3] Excluding lucerne and other pastures.

The gross value of agricultural commodity production (in $A1m.) during 1989–90, amounted to 4,780·7, which included crops, livestock disposals, (1,670·7); livestock products, (747·9).

Forestry. A considerable area consists of natural forest, eucalyptus, pine and cabinet woods being the timbers mostly in evidence; a large quantity of ornamental woods is utilized by cabinet makers. The amount of timber processed in 1989–90 was 1,529,057 cu. metres.

INDUSTRY AND TRADE

Industry. In 1988–89, there were 4,841 establishments, with 4 or more workers, employing 133,743 persons, and producing goods and services worth $A20,091m. The manufacturing establishments contributing most to the overall production were those predominantly engaged in the processing of food, beverages and tobacco.

Labour. In 1990 the labour force (civilian population aged over 15 years) numbered 1,443,900 (599,400 females), of whom 112,600 (47,900 females) were unemployed. 796,800 persons were not in the labour force.

Trade Unions. Unions both of employees and employers must be registered with the State or Australian Commission. There were 66 trade unions in 1989 with 380,857 members.

Commerce. The overseas commerce of Queensland is included in the statement of the commerce of Australia.

Total value of direct overseas imports and exports (in $A1,000) f.o.b. port of shipment for both imports and exports:

	1984–85	1985–86	1986–87	1987–88	1988–89	1989–90
Imports	2,315,492	2,649,953	2,503,854	2,844,208	3,788,296	4,394,340
Exports	6,602,936 [1]	7,737,046 [1]	7,928,406 [1]	8,289,659 [1]	9,083,994 [1]	10,901,410 [1]

[1] State of origin.

In 1989–90 interstate exports totalled $A4,080·3m. and imports $A9,018·4m. The chief exports overseas are minerals including alumina, coal, meat (preserved or frozen), sugar, wool, cereal grains, copper and lead, and manufactured goods. Principal overseas imports are machinery, motor vehicles, mineral fuels (including lubricants, etc.), chemicals and manufactured goods classified by material. Chief sources of imports in 1989–90 were Japan ($A960·5m.), USA ($A905·7m.), UK ($A209·9m.). Exports went chiefly to Japan ($A3,896·9m.), USA ($A1,009·6m.), UK ($A478·2m.).

Tourism. In 1990 there were 283 hotels, 828 motels and 281 caravan parks.

COMMUNICATIONS

Roads. At 30 June 1989 there were 154,195 km of roads. Of these 56,652 km were surfaced with sealed pavement.

At 30 June 1990 motor vehicles registered (in 1,000) totalled 1,751·9, comprising 1,272·1 cars and station wagons, 415·3 commercial vehicles and 64·6 motor cycles. There were 428 fatalities in road accidents in 1989.

Railways. Practically all the railways are owned by the State Government. Total length of line at 30 June 1991 was 10,015 km, of which 2,460 km were electrified. In 1990–91 passengers and 83m. tonnes of goods and livestock were carried.

Civil Aviation. Queensland is well served with a network of air services, with overseas and interstate connexions. Subsidiary companies provide planes for taxi and charter work, and the Flying Doctor Service operates throughout western Queensland.

Shipping. In 1988–89, cargo discharged was 3·53m. GWT and cargo loaded was 72·78m. GWT.

Telecommunications. At 30 June 1988, 113 broadcasting and 98 television and translator stations were in operation throughout Queensland.

JUSTICE, RELIGION, EDUCATION AND WELFARE

Justice. Justice is administered by Higher Courts (Supreme and District), Magistrates' Courts and Children's Courts. The Supreme Court comprises a Chief Justice, a senior puisne judge, 18 puisne judges and 2 masters; the District Courts, 24 district court judges of whom 1 is chairman. Stipendiary magistrates preside over the Magistrates' and Children's Courts, except in the smaller centres, where justices of the peace officiate. A parole board may recommend prisoners for release.

The total number of appearances resulting in conviction as the most serious outcome in the Higher Courts in 1989–90 was 3,032; summary convictions in Magistrates' Courts and proven offences in Children's Courts totalled 169,444. There were, at 30 June 1990, 5 prisons, 2 prison farms conducted on the honour system and 1 prison for criminally-insane patients, with 2,367 male and 115 female prisoners. The total police force was 5,882 at 30 June 1990.

Religion. There is no State Church. Membership, census 1986: Anglican, 640,867; Catholic, 628,906; Uniting Church, 255,287; Presbyterian, 120,239; Lutheran, 56,910; Baptist, 39,099; other Christian, 211,316; Buddhist, 5,769; Muslim, 3,731; Hebrew, 2,631; all others (including not stated and no religion), 622,560.

Education. Education in Queensland ranges from pre-school level through to tertiary level. In addition, child care, kindergarten and adult education facilities are available. Education is compulsory between the ages of 6 and 15 years and is provided free in government schools. Expenditure on education by State and local government authorities for 1986–87 was $A1,954·6m.

At July 1990, pre-school education and child care was provided at 1,466 centres with 5,226 teaching and other staff and 85,072 children.

Primary and secondary education comprises 12 years of full-time formal schooling and is provided by both the government and non-government sectors. At July 1990, the State administered 1,310 schools with 247,554 primary students and 143,695 secondary students. In 1988–89, 65 special schools provided educational programmes for 3,543 children. State education programmes were provided by 12,982 primary, 10,465 secondary and 810 special school teachers. There were 401 private schools in July 1989 with 66,481 primary students and 63,576 secondary students. Educational programmes at schools were provided by 7,367 teachers in 1988–89.

In 1988–89 there were 126,123 students following vocational and preparatory courses and 76,857 adult education courses at institutes of technical and advanced education (TAFE). Universities and other higher education institutes had 38,962 full-time students in 1988–89.

Social Welfare. Welfare institutions providing shelter and social care for the aged, the handicapped, and children, are maintained or assisted by the State. A child health service is provided throughout the State. Age, invalid, widows', disability and war service pensions, family allowances, and unemployment and sickness benefits are paid by the Federal Government. Age pensioners in the State at 30 June 1990 numbered 213,485; invalid pensioners, 64,730; disability pensioners, 67,188; and service pensioners, 75,097 (including dependants).

There were 58,996 widows' pensions current at 30 June 1990, and at the same date family allowances were being paid for 659,129 children in families under 16 years and eligible students aged 16 to 24 years. Since 1988 the number of children in institutions is not available.

Health. In 1989 there were 188 hospitals with 15,955 beds, 3 psychiatric institutions and 76 nursing homes.

Further Reading

Statistical Information: The Statistical Office (313 Adelaide St., Brisbane) was set up in 1859. *Deputy Commonwealth Statistician:* J. K. Cornish. *A Queensland Official Year Book* was issued in 1901, the annual *ABC of Queensland Statistics* from 1905 to 1936 with exception of 1918 and 1922. Present publications include: *Queensland Year Book.* Annual, from 1937 (omitting 1942, 1943, 1944, 1987, 1991).—*Queensland Pocket Year Book.* Annual from 1950.—*Monthly Summary of Statistics, Queensland.* From Jan. 1961
Australian Sugar Year Book. Brisbane, from 1941
Endean, R., *Australia's Great Barrier Reef.* Brisbane, 1982
Johnston, W. R., *A Bibliography of Queensland History.* Brisbane, 1981.—*The Call of the Land: A History of Queensland to the Present Day.* Brisbane, 1982
Johnston, W. R. and Zerner, M., *Guide to the History of Queensland.* Brisbane, 1985
Queensland State Public Relations Bureau, *Queensland Resources Atlas,* Brisbane, 1980
Queensland Department of Commercial and Industrial Development, *Resources and Industry of Far North Queensland,* Brisbane, 1980

State Library: The State Library of Queensland, Queensland Cultural Centre, South Bank, South Brisbane. *State Librarian:* D. H. Stephens.

SOUTH AUSTRALIA

AREA AND POPULATION. The total area of South Australia is 380,070 sq. miles (984,377 sq. km). The settled part is divided into counties and hundreds. There are 49 counties proclaimed, covering 23m. ha, of which 19m. ha are occupied. Outside this area there are extensive pastoral districts, covering 76m. ha, 49m. of which are under pastoral leases.

Census population (exclusive of full-blood Aboriginals before 1966):

	Males	Females	Total		Males	Females	Total
1901	180,485	177,861	358,346	1966	550,196	544,788	1,094,984
1911	207,358	201,200	408,558	1971	586,051	587,656	1,173,707
1921	248,267	246,893	495,160	1976	620,162	624,594	1,244,756
1933	290,962	289,987	580,949	1981	635,696	649,337	1,285,033
1947	320,031	326,042	646,073	1986	665,960	679,985	1,345,945
1961	490,225	479,115	969,340				

The number of Aboriginals and Torres Strait Islanders (as reported on Census schedules) in the State at the Census of 30 June 1986 was 14,291.

Vital statistics for calendar years:

	Live Births	Marriages	Divorces	Deaths
1987	19,235	9,695	4,050	10,565
1988	19,155	10,128	4,031	10,690
1989	19,610	9,776	3,740	11,348
1990	19,863	9,609	4,066	10,938

The infant mortality rate in 1990 was 8·41 per 1,000 live births.

The Adelaide Statistical Division had 1,049,873 inhabitants at 30 June 1990 in 22 cities and 8 municipalities and other districts. Cities outside this area (with populations at 30 June 1990) are Whyalla (26,478), Mount Gambier (22,405), Port Augusta (15,694), Port Pirie (15,114) and Port Lincoln (12,828).

CONSTITUTION AND GOVERNMENT. South Australia was formed into a British province by letters patent of Feb. 1836, and a partially elective Legislative Council was established in 1851. The present Constitution bears date 24 Oct. 1856. It vests the legislative power in an elected Parliament, consisting of a Legislative Council and a House of Assembly. The former is composed of 22 members. Every 4 years half the members retire, and the resulting vacancies are filled at a general election on the basis of proportional representation with the State as one multi-member electorate. The qualifications of an elector are, to be an Australian citizen, or a British subject who on 25 Jan. 1984 was enrolled on a Commonwealth electoral roll and/or at some time between 26 Oct. 1983 and 25 Jan. 1984 inclusive was enrolled on an electoral roll for a South Australian Assembly district or a Commonwealth electoral roll in any State. The person must be of at least 18 years of age and have lived continuously in Australia for at least 6 months, in South Australia for at least 3 months and in the sub-division for which he is enrolled at least 1 month. War service may substitute for residential qualifications in some cases. By the Constitution Act Amendment Act, 1894, the franchise was extended to women, who voted for the first time at the general election of 25 April 1896. The qualifications for election as a member of both Houses are the same as for an elector. Certain persons are ineligible for election to either House.

The House of Assembly consists of 47 members elected for 4 years, representing single electorates. Election of members of both Houses takes place by preferential secret ballot. Voting is compulsory for those on the Electoral Roll.

The House of Assembly, elected on 25 Nov. 1989, consists of the following members: Liberal Party of Australia, 22; Australian Labor Party, 22; Independent Labor, 2; National Party 1. The Legislative Council consists of 10 Liberal Party of Australia, 10 Labor and 2 Australian Democrat members.

Each member of Parliament receives $A65,387 per annum with allowances of $A14,816–45,245 according to location of electorate, a free pass over government railways and superannuation rights. Electors enrolled (Aug. 1991) numbered 968,339.

The executive power is vested in a Governor appointed by the Crown and an Executive Council, consisting of the Governor and the Ministers of the Crown. The Governor has the power to dissolve the House of Assembly but not the Legislative Council unless that Chamber has twice consecutively with an election intervening defeated the same or substantially the same Bill passed in the House of Assembly by an absolute majority.

Governor: Dame Hon. Roma Mitchell, AC, DBE.

The South Australian Labor Ministry in Nov. 1991 was as follows:

Premier, Treasurer and Minister of State Development: John Charles Bannon, MP.

Deputy Premier, Minister of Health, Minister of Family and Community Services and Minister for the Aged: Donald Jack Hopgood, MP. *Attorney-General, Minister of Crime Prevention and Minister of Corporate Affairs:* Christopher John Sumner, MLC. *Minister of Industry, Trade and Technology, Minister of Agriculture, Minister of Fisheries and Minister of Ethnic Affairs:* Lynn Maurice Ferguson Arnold, MP. *Minister of Education and Minister of Children's Services:* Gregory John Crafter, MP. *Minister of Transport, Minister of Correctional Services and Minister of*

Finance: Frank Trevor Blevins, MP. *Minister of Tourism, Minister of Consumer Affairs and Minister of Small Business:* Barbara Jean Wiese, MLC. *Minister of Housing and Construction, Minister of Public Works and Minister of Recreation and Sport:* Milton Kym Mayes, MP. *Minister of Environment and Planning, Minister of Water Resources and Minister of Lands:* Susan Mary Lenehan, MP. *Minister of Emergency Services, Minister of Mines and Energy and Minister of Forests:* John Heinz Cornelis Klunder, MP. *Minister of Labour, Minister of Occupational Health and Safety and Minister of Marine:* Robert John Gregory, MP. *Minister for the Arts and Cultural Heritage, Minister of Local Government Relations and Minister of State Services:* Judith Anne Winstanley Levy, MLC. *Minister of Employment and Further Education, Minister of Youth Affairs, Minister of Aboriginal Affairs and Minister Assisting the Minister of Ethnic Affairs:* Michael David Rann, MP.

Ministers are jointly and individually responsible to the legislature for all their official acts, as in the UK.

———————

Agent-General in London: G. Walls (50 Strand, WC2N 5LW).

Local Government. The closely settled part of the State (mainly near the sea-coast and the River Murray) is incorporated into local government areas, and sub-divided into district councils (rural areas only), municipal corporations (mainly metropolitan, but including larger country towns) and cities (more densely populated areas with a qualification of 15,000 residents in the Adelaide metropolitan area, and 10,000 in the country). The main functions of councils are the construction and maintenance of roads and bridges, sport and recreational facilities and garbage collection and disposal.

The number and area of the sub-divisions, together with expenditure (in $A1,000) for the year ended 30 June 1990, were:

	No.	Area (1,000 ha)	Roads and bridges	Recreation and culture	All other	Total expenditure
Adelaide statistical division	30	189·3	67,333	83,755	264,516	415,604
Other municipal corporations and district councils	91	15,227·0	56,192	21,420	120,659	198,271
Total	121	15,416·3	123,525	105,175	385,175	613,875

ECONOMY

Budget. Recurrent revenue and expenditure (in $A1,000) for years ended 30 June:

	1986	1987	1988	1989	1990	1991
Revenue	2,966,345	3,217,176	4,225,669	4,123,056	4,554,600	4,594,232
Expenditure	2,955,350	3,214,926	4,215,265	4,206,418	4,483,600	4,710,426

Banking. In June 1991 the average weekly balance of deposits held by all banks was $A12,709m. The average weekly balance of loans, advances and bills discounted was $A15,853m.

NATURAL RESOURCES

Minerals. The value of minerals produced in 1989–90 was $A1,215·1m. The principal minerals produced are opals, natural gas, iron ore, copper, uranium, crude oil, condensates, liquid petroleum gas and sub-bituminous coal.

Agriculture. Of the total area of South Australia (984,377 sq. km), 261,172 sq. km were alienated, 488,931 sq. km were held under lease and 234,274 sq. km were unoccupied. Area used for agricultural purposes, at 31 March 1990, was 574,796 sq. km.

Soil Conservation. Under the direction of special officers in the Department of Agriculture, determined efforts are made to deal with the problems of erosion and soil conservation. Included in the programme are the planting of cereal rye, perennial rye and other grasses to check sand drifts; contour-furrowing and contour banking; contour planting with vines and fruit trees and several water-diversion schemes.

Irrigation. For the year ended 31 March 1990, 98,907 ha were under irrigated culture, being used as follows: Vineyards, 18,151; orchards, 13,410; vegetables, 7,395, and other crops and pasture, 59,951. Most of these areas are along the river Murray.

Gross value of agricultural production (in $A1,000), 1989–90: Crops, 1,442,421; livestock slaughtering, 401,159; livestock products, 723,348. Total gross value, 2,455,927; local value (*i.e.* less marketing costs), 2,302,019.

	1988–89		1989–90	
Chief crops	Ha	Tonnes	Ha	Tonnes
Wheat	1,520,012	1,361,138	1,556,643	2,607,195
Barley	836,641	1,032,927	899,501	1,724,472
Oats	155,513	131,426	172,015	249,918
Hay	195,026	528,913	248,374	809,991
Vines	...	259,127,000 [1]	...	244,993,000 [1]

[1] Litres of wine.

Fruit culture is extensively carried on, and in 1989–90, 268,180 tonnes of fresh fruit were produced. Other products, in addition to all kinds of root crops and vegetables, are grass seeds and oil seeds. Livestock, March 1990: 969,087 cattle, 18,363,417 sheep and 437,249 pigs. In 1989–90, 134,260 tonnes of wool and 357m. litres of milk were produced.

INDUSTRY AND TRADE

Industry. The turnover for manufacturing industries for 1988–89 was $A13,066m.

Industry sub-division	Establish-ments (No.)	Persons employed (No.)	Wages and salaries ($A1m.)	Turnover ($A1m.)
Food, beverages and tobacco	381	16,307	348	2,471
Textiles	48	2,493	55	378
Clothing and footwear	106	4,152	73	273
Wood, wood products and furniture	394	7,977	152	725
Paper, paper products, printing and publishing	239	7,841	197	831
Chemical, petroleum and coal products	50	2,333	62	514
Non-metallic mineral products	126	3,890	96	549
Basic metal products	48	7,675	218	1,440
Fabricated metal products	419	8,883	181	853
Transport equipment	148	18,752	444	2,884
Other machinery and equipment	372	15,344	331	1,409
Miscellaneous manufacturing	211	7,308	154	740
Total	2,542	102,955	2,312	13,066

Practically all forms of secondary industry are to be found, the most important being, motor vehicle manufacture, saw-milling and the manufacture of household appliances, basic iron and steel, meat and meat products, and wine and brandy.

Labour. Two systems of industrial arbitration and conciliation for the adjustment of industrial relations between employers and employees are in operation—the State system, which operates when industrial disputes are confined to the territorial limits of the State, and the Federal system, which applies when disputes involve other parts of Australia as well as South Australia.

The industrial tribunals are authorized to fix minimum rates of wages and other conditions of employment, and their awards may be enforced by law. Industrial agreements between employers and organizations of employees, when registered, may be enforced in the same manner as awards. In March 1989 the minimum wage under State awards was $A204.10.

Commerce. The commerce of South Australia, exclusive of inter-state trade, is comprised in the statement of the commerce of Australia given under the heading of the Commonwealth, *see* pp. 109–11.

Overseas imports and exports in $A1m. (year ending 30 June):

	1986–87	1987–88	1988–89	1989–90	1990–91
Imports	1,503·4	1,804·6	1,861·4	2,049·9	2,194·2
Exports	2,044·2	2,263·3	2,446·8	2,841·3	2,953·3

Principal exports in 1989–90 were (in $A1m.): Wheat, 310·5; petroleum and petroleum products, 291·8; meat and meat preparations, 231·7; wool, 227·8; barley, 200·5; copper, 122·6.

Principal imports in 1989–90 were (in $A1m.): Machinery, 511·3; petroleum and petroleum products, 425·3; transport equipment, 389·8.

In 1990–91 the leading suppliers of imports were (in $A1m.): Japan (498·6), USA (343·3), Saudi Arabia (243·0), Germany (155·4), Indonesia (139·4), UK (99·5); main exports went to Japan (438·2), USA (322·0), Singapore (202·3), New Zealand (190·9), UK, (179·4), Iran (149·1).

Tourism. In June 1991 there were 374 hotels and motels with 10,445 rooms; 204 caravan parks had a total of 23,775 sites.

COMMUNICATIONS

Roads. At 30 June 1991, of the roads customarily used by the public, there were 2,460 km of national roads, 9,817 km of arterial roads and 82,630 km of local roads, totalling 94,907 km. Lengths of road classified by surface were as follows: Sealed, 23,347 km; unsealed, 70,560 km. Costs of construction and maintenance are shared by the State and Commonwealth governments and by the councils of the local areas. Motor vehicles registered at 30 June 1990 included 574,617 cars, 122,807 station wagons, 153,714 commercial vehicles and 29,629 cycles. In 1990 there were 224 fatalities in road accidents.

Railways. At 30 June 1991, Australian National Railways operated 4,904 km of railway in country areas. The State Transport Authority operated 124 km of railway in the metropolitan area of Adelaide. All public freight and non-metropolitan passenger services are operated by Australian National.

Civil Aviation. For the year ended 30 June 1990 there were 2,049,188 passengers and 15,826 tonnes of freight handled by 42,958 aircraft movements at Adelaide, South Australia's principal airport (including Adelaide International). On 30 June 1990 there were 5 government and 30 licensed aerodromes.

Shipping. There are several good harbours, of which Port Adelaide is the principal one. In 1990, 928 vessels conducting overseas trade entered South Australia with 1,880,000 import tonnes of cargo and left with 6,532,000 export tonnes.

Telecommunications. At 30 June 1990, there were 517 post offices. Telephone services totalled 707,176 on 30 June 1990. There were 55 radio and 31 television stations at 30 June 1990.

JUSTICE, RELIGION, EDUCATION AND WELFARE

Justice. There is a Supreme Court, which incorporates admiralty, civil, criminal, land and valuation, and testamentary jurisdiction; district criminal courts, which have jurisdiction in many indictable offences; local courts and courts of summary jurisdiction. Circuit courts are held at several places. In the year ended 31 Dec. 1989, 1,385 criminal charges were heard in higher courts, with 999 outcomes being guilty as charged. During the year 1990-91 there were 1,653 sequestrations and schemes under the Bankruptcy Act. There were 2,936 prisoners received under sentence in 1989-90.

Religion. At the Census of 1986 the religious distribution of the population (as reported on Census schedules) was as follows: Catholic, 267,137; Anglican, 242,722; Uniting Church, 176,980; Lutheran, 64,851; Orthodox, 37,149; Baptist, 21,415; Presbyterian, 18,566; other Christians, 108,048; non-Christian, 13,843; indefinite, 5,458; no religion, 227,564; not stated, 162,212.

Education. Education is secular and is compulsory for children 6–15 years of age.

Primary and secondary education at government schools is free. In 1990 there were 891 schools operating, including 185 non-government and 706 government schools, comprising 635 primary, 108 primary and secondary, 119 secondary schools and 29 special schools. There were 184,868 full-time students attending government schools and 57,867 non-government. The Department of Technical and Further Education is responsible for technical, adult and vocational education. In 1990 there were 19 colleges of technical and further education, among the facilities are an adult migrant education service, a further education, a centre for performing arts and schools of music, maritime and external studies. Tertiary education, including teacher education, is provided by the 3 universities. In 1990 there were 420 pre-school centres with an enrolment of 24,170 pre-school children.

Social Welfare. Age, invalidity, war, unemployment, etc., pensions are paid by the Commonwealth Government. The number of pensioners in South Australia at 30 June 1990 was: Disability and service, 71,158; age, 138,705; invalid, 32,861; unemployment, 41,210. There are schemes for family allowances, widows, supporting parents and sickness and hospital and pharmaceutical benefits.

Further Reading

Statistical Information: The State branch of the Australian Bureau of Statistics is at 41 Currie St., Adelaide (GPO Box 2272). *Deputy Commonwealth Statistician:* R. J. Rogers. Although the first printed statistical publication was the *Statistics of South Australia, 1854* with the title altered to *Statistical Register* in 1859, there is a written volume for each year back to 1838. These contain simple records of trade, demography, production, etc. and were prepared only for the use of the Colonial Office; one copy was retained in the State.

The publications of the State branch include the *South Australian Year Book*, the *Pocket Year Book of South Australia* and a *Monthly Summary of Statistics, South Australia*, a quarterly bulletin of building activity, a quarterly bulletin of tourist accommodation and approximately 40 special bulletins issued each year as particulars of various sections of statistics become available.

South Australia: Premier's Department, Adelaide, 1980
Douglas, J., *South Australia from Space.* Adelaide, 1980
Finlayson, H. H., *The Red Centre: Man and Beast in the Heart of Australia.* 2nd ed. Sydney, 1952
Gibbs, R. M., *A History of South Australia: From Colonial Days to the Present.* Adelaide, 1984
Whitelock, D., *Adelaide, 1836–1976: A History of Difference.* Univ. of Queensland Press, 1977

State Library: The State Library of S.A., North Terrace, Adelaide. *State Librarian:* E. M. Miller, MA (Hons), Dip. NZLS, ANZLA, ALAA.

TASMANIA

HISTORY. Abel Janzoon Tasman discovered Van Diemen's Land (Tasmania) on 24 Nov. 1642. The island became a British settlement in 1803 as a dependency of New South Wales; in 1825 its connexion with New South Wales was terminated; in 1851 a partially elective Legislative Council was established, and in 1856 responsible government came into operation. On 1 Jan. 1901 Tasmania was federated with the other Australian states into the Commonwealth of Australia.

AREA AND POPULATION. Tasmania is an island separated from the mainland by the Bass Strait with an area (including islands) of 68,331 sq. km, or 6·83m. hectares, of which 6,441,000 hectares form the area of the main island. The population at 10 consecutive censuses was:

	Population	Increase % per annum		Population	Increase % per annum
1921	213,780	1·12	1966	371,436	1·18
1933	227,599	0·52	1971	398,100 [1]	0·99
1947	257,078	0·87	1976	412,300 [1]	0·70 [2]
1954	308,752	2·65	1981	427,200 [1]	0·72 [2]
1961	350,340	1·82	1986	436,353	...

[1] Resident population.   [2] Not comparable with previous censuses.

At the census of 30 June 1986, 5·32% were born in the UK and Ireland, 2·68% in other European countries and 88·61% in Australia. The last full-blooded Tasmanian Aboriginal died in 1876.

Vital statistics for calendar years:

	Marriages	Divorces	Births	Deaths
1988	3,035	1,220	6,745	3,519
1989	3,111	1,269	6,788	3,676
1990	3,026	1,170	7,005	3,625

The largest cities and towns (with populations at the 1986 Census) are Hobart (175,082), Launceston (88,486), Devonport (1981, 21,424) and Burnie (20,585).

CONSTITUTION AND GOVERNMENT. Parliament consists of the Governor, the Legislative Council and the House of Assembly. The Council has 19 members, elected by adults with 6 months' residence. Members sit for 6 years, 3 retiring annually and 4 every sixth year. There is no power to dissolve the Council. Vacancies are filled by by-elections. The House of Assembly has 35 members; the maximum term for the House of Assembly is 4 years. Members of both Houses are paid a basic salary of $A46,829 (Oct. 1991), plus an electorate allowance, according to the division represented. The annual allowance payable is calculated as a percentage of basic salary. The amounts vary from $A5,151 (11%) to $A16,390 (35%). Women received the right to vote in 1903. Proportional representation was adopted in 1907, the method now being the single transferable vote in 7-member constituencies. Casual vacancies in the House of Assembly are determined by a transfer of the preference of the vacating member's ballot papers to consenting candidates who were unsuccessful at the last general election.

A Minister must have a seat in one of the two Houses; all present Ministers are members of the House of Assembly.

In addition to the salary paid to Ministers as members of either House, the following allowances are payable: Premier, in conjunction with a ministerial office, $A47,160; Deputy Premier, in conjunction with a ministerial office, $A32,069; other Ministers, $A26,410. The Leader of the Opposition in the House of Assembly receives an allowance of $A26,410. The holders of some other offices receive allowances ranging from $A2,264 to $A12,576.

An election in May 1989 resulted in a 'hung parliament' with 17 Liberals, 13 Labor and 5 Independents. The most likely result was predicted to be a minority Liberal government, however, the final outcome was a Labor Party Government in an alliance with the 5 Independents.

The Legislative Council is predominantly independent without formal party allegiance; 1 member is Labor-endorsed.

Governor: Gen. Sir Phillip Bennett, AC, KBE, DSO.

The Labor Party Cabinet was composed as follows in Oct. 1991:

Premier, Minister for Finance, Treasurer, Minister for State Development: M. W. Field.

Deputy Premier, Justice and Attorney-General, Environment and Planning: P. J. Patmore. *Employment, Industrial Relations and Training, Education and the Arts, Minister Assisting Premier on Youth Affairs:* M. A. Aird. *Administrative Services, Consumer Affairs, Construction and Minister Assisting Premier on Status of Women:* F. M. Bladel. *Tourism, Sport and Recreation, Parks, Wildlife and Heritage:* H. N. Holgate. *Community Services, Roads and Transport:* J. L. Jackson. *Primary Industry, Forests:* D. E. Llewellyn. *Resources and Energy, Police and Emergency Services:* M. W. Weldon. *Health, Minister Assisting the Premier on Aboriginal Affairs and on Multicultural Affairs:* J. C. White.

Local Government. For the purposes of local government, the State is divided into 46 municipal areas comprising the cities of Hobart, Launceston, Glenorchy and Devonport and 42 municipalities. The number of municipalities was reduced from

45 in May 1985 because of the amalgamation of 2 municipalities with the City of Launceston. The cities and municipalities are managed by elected aldermen and councillors, respectively, with reference to local matters such as sanitation and health services, domestic water supplies and roads and bridges within each particular area. The chief source of revenue is rates (based on assessed annual value) levied on owners of property.

Tasmanian Islands. Three inhabited Tasmanian islands (Bruny, King and Flinders) are organized as municipalities. Nearly 1,360 km south-east lies Macquarie Island (230 sq. km), part of the State, and used only as an Australian research base and meteorological station.

ECONOMY

Budget. The revenue is derived chiefly from taxation (pay-roll, motor, lottery and land tax, business franchises and stamp duties), and from grants and reimbursements from the Commonwealth Government. Customs, excise, sales and income tax are levied by the Commonwealth Government, which makes grants to Tasmania for both revenue and capital purposes. Commonwealth payments to Tasmania in 1990–91 totalled $A982·9m. These included General Revenue Funds, $A521·9m.; Specific Purpose Payments, $A433·4m. and Capital Funds, $A27·5m.

Specific Purpose Grants are mainly used to provide essential services such as hospitals, housing, roads and educational services, while General Purpose Revenue Funds have been paid since 1942 to compensate the State for the loss of income tax to the federal government.

Consolidated Revenue Fund receipts and expenditure, in $A1,000, for financial years ending 30 June:

	1985–86	1986–87	1987–88	1988–89	1989–90	1990–91
Revenue	1,024,697	1,107,870	1,201,397	1,259,754	1,674,955	1,665,020
Expenditure	1,036,954	1,106,608	1,201,175	1,258,945	1,684,849	1,671,808

The public debt at current exchange rates amounted to $A1,809m. at 30 June 1991.

In 1990–91 State taxation revenue amounted to $A456m., of which pay-roll tax provided $A144·8m.; motor tax, $A20·3m.; stamp duties, $A88·7m.; business franchises, $A77·6m.; and lottery tax, $A21m.

Banking. Trading bank activity in Tasmania is divided between 3 private banks and the Commonwealth Trading Bank. For the month of Dec. 1988 liabilities represented by depositors' balances averaged $A749m. and assets represented by advances, $A929m. The 6 savings banks operating in Tasmania are the Commonwealth Savings Bank, 2 trustee savings banks and 3 private savings banks operated by trading banks. At 31 Dec. 1988 total savings bank deposits were $A1,761m.

ENERGY AND NATURAL RESOURCES

Electricity. Tasmania has good supplies of hydro-electric power because of assured rainfall and high level water storages (natural and artificial). The Hydro-Electric Commission, Tasmania's sole commercial supplier of electricity, has been surveying water power resources of the State for many years and it is estimated that about 3m. kw. can be economically developed. With the addition of the Reece Dam, 2,315,000 kw. of generating plant was in commission in 1990–91. In 1990–91 the peak loading was 1,445,000 kw. The Pieman River Power Development, comprising 3 stations, was completed in 1987. The Gordon River Power Development Stage 2 (the Gordon-below-Franklin scheme) was halted by a High Court decision.

Minerals. The assayed content of principal metallic minerals contained in locally produced concentrates for 1988–89 was (in tonnes): Zinc, 107,439; iron pellets, 1,556,000; copper, 22,257; lead, 42,915; tin, 6,820; gold, 1,926 kg; silver, 110,950 kg. Coal production, 356,282 tonnes.

Primary Industries. The estimated gross value of recorded production from agriculture in 1989–90 was (in $A1m.): Livestock products, 261; livestock slaughterings and other disposals, 144·2; crops, 222·2; total gross value, 627·4. Estimated gross value of fisheries was $A117·1m. in 1988-89.

Agriculture. From 1986–87 the scope of the Census includes only those establishments undertaking agricultural activity and having an EVAO (Estimated Value of Agricultural Operations) of $A20,000 or more. The scope of previous Censuses was establishments undertaking agricultural activity having an EVAO of $A2,500 or more.

The area occupied by the 3,699 holdings in 1989–90 totalled 1,933,375 ha, of which 938,655 were devoted to crops and sown pasture. The following table shows the area and production, in tonnes, of the principal crops:

| | 1987–88 | | 1988–89 | | 1989–90 | |
	Ha	Production	Ha	Production	Ha	Production
Wheat	1,179	3,815	771	2,199	792	2,687
Barley	8,024	21,549	7,820	22,022	7,983	19,320
Oats	9,560	15,552	10,233	17,925	7,568	12,824
Green peas	6,211	28,552	6,329	29,585	6,535	30,486
Potatoes	6,380	248,303	6,001	256,849	6,852	297,488
Hay	41,162	163,434	56,752	272,893	50,700	241,013
Hops (bearing) (dry)	821	1,563	809	1,752	765	1,489

Livestock at 31 March 1990: Sheep, 5·3m.; cattle, 569,000; pigs, 42,200.

Wool produced during 1989–90 was 27,065 tonnes, valued at $A163·4m. In 1989–90 butter production was 5,051 tonnes; cheese, 18,172 tonnes.

Forestry. Indigenous forests cover a considerable part of the State, and the sawmilling and woodchipping industries are very important. Production of sawn timber in 1990–91 was 287,100 cu. metres. 735,900 cu. metres of logs were used for milling in 1990–91 and a further 3,516,200 cu. metres were used for chipping, grinding or flaking. Newsprint and paper are produced from native hardwoods, principally eucalypts.

INDUSTRY AND TRADE

Industry. The most important manufactures for export are refined metals, newsprint and other paper manufactures, pigments, woollen goods, fruit pulp, confectionery, butter, cheese, preserved and dried vegetables, sawn timber, and processed fish products. The electrolytic-zinc works at Risdon near Hobart treat large quantities of local and imported ore, and produce zinc, sulphuric acid, superphosphate, sulphate of ammonia, cadmium and other by-products. At George Town, large-scale plants produce refined aluminium and manganese alloys. During 1990–91, 3,559,100 tonnes (green weight) of woodchips were produced. In 1988–89 the average employment in manufacturing establishments employing 4 or more persons was 27,532; wages and salaries (excluding proprietors' drawings), $A652·2m.; turnover, $A3,860·9m.; and number operating at 30 June 1989, 962.

Labour. The Commonwealth Industrial Court (judicial powers) and Commonwealth Conciliation and Arbitration Commission (arbitral powers) have jurisdiction over federal unions, *i.e.*, with interstate membership. Most Tasmanian employees are covered by federal awards.

State Industrial Boards, established for the various trades by resolution of Parliament or proclamation of the Governor, cover most of the remaining employees. Each Board consists of a Chairman appointed by the Governor with equal representation of employers and employees. The Boards have authority over minimum rates for wages or piecework, number of working hours for which the wage is payable, conditions of apprenticeship, annual leave and adjustment of wage and piecework rates. Industrial Boards follow to a large extent the wage rates fixed by the Conciliation and Arbitration Commission.

Commerce. In 1989–90 exports totalled $A1,474,335,000 to overseas countries. The principal countries of destination (with values in $A1m.) for overseas exports were: Japan, 491·4; USA, 188·7; Malaysia, 104·5; Taiwan, 84·2; Germany, 65·3; UK, 56·7; and Indonesia, 52·1. In 1989–90 imports totalled $A352,915,000 from overseas countries. The principal countries of origin (with values in $A1m.) for overseas imports were: USA, 73·8; Japan, 40·5; Canada, 39; New Zealand, 32·9; Singapore, 28·9; and China, 7·1.

The main commodities by value (with values in $A1m.) exported to overseas countries during 1989–90 were: Non-ferrous metals (mainly copper, lead, tin and tungsten), 341; metalliferous ores and metal scrap, 316; fish, crustaceans and molluscs, 103; iron and steel, 53; and meat and meat preparations, 44. Other main exports, for which details are not available for separate publication were woodchips, newsprint, printing and writing papers, refined aluminium, ferro-alloys and chocolate confectionery. The main imports from overseas countries in 1989–90 (with values in $A1m.) were: Pulp and waste paper, 49; road vehicles, 48; coffee, tea, cocoa and spices, 25; petroleum products, 23.

Tourism. In 1988, 681,500 passengers arrived in Tasmania by sea and air from interstate and New Zealand of whom 406,000 or just over 59% were visitors.

COMMUNICATIONS

Roads. The total road length at 30 June 1988 was 22,984 km, consisting of a classified road system of 3,178 km maintained by the State Department of Main Roads, and the remainder maintained by local government authorities, the Forestry Commission and the Hydro-Electric Commission. Motor vehicles registered at 30 June 1990 comprised 220,400 cars and station wagons, 67,600 other vehicles and 6,400 motor cycles.

Railways. There is an 813-km network of 1,067-mm gauge lines linking Hobart and Launceston with coastal and country areas, part of Australian National Railways. A private railway of 132 km, operated by the Emu Bay Railway Co. Ltd, connects Burnie with the mining settlements on the west coast.

Civil Aviation. Regular daily passenger and freight services connect the south, north and north-west of the State with the mainland of Australia. In 1988 there was a total of 31,809 scheduled aircraft movements at Tasmanian airports; a total of 1·13m. passengers and 39,153 tonnes of freight, including mail, was carried.

Shipping. In 1987–88 there were, 1,736 ship visits to Tasmania with 11,066,913 mass tonnes of cargo carried through Tasmanian ports.

JUSTICE, RELIGION, EDUCATION AND WELFARE

Justice. The Supreme Court of Tasmania, with civil, criminal, ecclesiastical, admiralty and matrimonial jurisdiction, established by Royal Charter on 13 Oct. 1823, is a superior court of record, with both original and appellate jurisdiction, and consists of a Chief Justice and 6 puisne judges. There are also inferior civil courts with limited jurisdiction, licensing courts, mining courts, courts of petty sessions and coroners' courts.

During 1990, 24,851 offences were finalized in the lower courts, 1,709 in the higher courts and 4,030 in the children's courts. The total police force at Oct. 1991 was 978. There is 1 prison, with 653 imprisonments in 1989-90.

Religion. There is no State Church. At the census of 1986 the following numbers of adherents of the principal religions were recorded:

Anglican Church	154,748	Other religions	33,625
Roman Catholic	80,479	No religion	47,852
Methodist } Uniting Church	36,724	Not stated	61,742
Presbyterian	12,084	Total	435,346
Baptist	8,092		

Education. Education is controlled by the State and is free, secular and compulsory between the ages of 6 and 16. At 1 July 1990 government schools had a total enrolment of 65,349 pupils, including 27,468 at secondary level; private schools had a total enrolment of 19,030 pupils, including 8,709 at secondary level.

Technical and further education is conducted at technical and community colleges in the major centres throughout the state. In 1987 there were 20,523 students enrolled in the Division of Technical and Further Education and 25,004 students in the Division of Adult Education.

Tertiary education is offered at the University of Tasmania in Hobart, the Tasmanian State Institute of Technology and the Australian Maritime College, in Launceston. The University (established 1890) had (1990) 4,232 full-time and 1,549 part-time students, and 375 full-time teachers. There were 2,619 full-time and 1,159 part-time students enrolled in advanced education courses in 1990.

Social Welfare. The number of pensioners in Tasmania on 30 June 1990 was: Age (including wife and carer pensioners), 38,839; invalid, 9,461; war (service), 16,775; widows, 2,902.

Further Reading

Statistical Information: The State Government Statistical Office (175 Collins St., Hobart), established in 1877, became in 1924 the Tasmanian Office of the Australian Bureau of Statistics, but continues to serve State statistical needs as required.

 Deputy Commonwealth Statistician and Government Statistician of Tasmania: Stuart Jackson.

 Main publications: *Annual Statistical Bulletins (e.g., Demography, Courts, Agricultural Industry, Finance, Manufacturing Establishments* etc.).—*Tasmanian Pocket Year Book.* Annual (from 1913).—*Tasmanian Year Book.* Annual (from 1967).—*Monthly Summary of Statistics* (from July 1945).

Tasmanian Development Authority, *Tasmanian Manufacturers Directory.* Hobart, 1985
Angus, M., *The World of Olegas Truchanas.* Hobart, 1975
Green, F. C. (ed.) *A Century of Responsible Government.* Hobart, 1956
Phillips, D., *Making more Adequate Provisions: State Education in Tasmania 1839–1985.* Hobart, 1985
Robson, L., *A History of Tasmania. Volume 1: Van Diemen's Land from the Earliest Times to 1855.* Melbourne, 1983
Townsley, W. A., *The Government of Tasmania.* Brisbane, 1976

State Library: The State Library of Tasmania, Hobart.

VICTORIA

AREA AND POPULATION. The State has an area of 227,600 sq. km, and a resident population (estimate) of 4,379,800 at 31 Dec. 1990. Density, 19 per sq. km.

The population is estimated within 13 'Statistical Local Areas' or 'Statistical Divisions' as follows (with 1989 population in 1,000): Melbourne (3,044); Barwon (221·5); South Western (103·9); Central Highlands (135·6); Wimmera (53·8); Northern Mallee (77·3); Loddon-Campaspe (174·4); Goulburn (149·8); North Eastern (89·4); East Gippsland (65·6); Central Gippsland (150·4); East Central (56·4).

The census count (exclusive of full-blood aboriginals prior to 1971) was:

Date of census enumeration	Males	Population Females	Total	On previous census Numerical increase	Increase %
5 April 1891	598,222	541,866	1,140,088	278,522	32·33
31 March 1901	603,720	597,350	1,201,070	60,982	5·35
3 April 1911	655,591	659,960	1,315,551	114,481	9·53
4 April 1921	754,724	776,556	1,531,280	215,729	16·40
30 June 1933	903,244	917,017	1,820,261	288,981	18·87
30 June 1947	1,013,867	1,040,834	2,054,701	234,440	12·88
30 June 1954	1,231,099	1,221,242	2,452,341	397,640	19·35
30 June 1961	1,474,395	1,455,718	2,930,113	477,772	19·48
30 June 1966	1,614,240	1,605,977	3,220,217	290,104	9·90
30 June 1971	1,750,061	1,752,290	3,502,351	282,134	8·76
30 June 1976	1,814,783	1,832,192	3,646,975	144,624	4·13
30 June 1981	1,901,411	1,931,032	3,832,443	185,468	5·09
30 June 1986	1,991,469	2,028,009	4,019,478	187,035	4·88

The count for the Melbourne Statistical Division (S.D.) on 30 June 1986 was 2,942,600. The count for the Geelong S.D. was 139,792; Ballarat S.D., 75,210;

Bendigo S.D., 62,380; Shepparton-Mooroopna S.D., 37,086; and the Victorian component of Albury-Wodonga S.D., 35,183. Other urban centres: Warrnambool, 22,706; Traralgon, 19,233; Morwell, 16,387; Wangaratta, 16,598; Mildura, 18,382; Sale, 13,559; Horsham, 12,174; Colac, 9,532; Hamilton, 9,969; Bairnsdale, 10,328; Portland, 10,934; Swan Hill, 8,831; Ararat, 8,015; Benalla, 8,490; Maryborough, 7,705; Castlemaine, 6,603.

Vital statistics for calendar years:

	Births	Marriages	Divorces	Deaths
1987	61,507	29,682	9,626	31,549
1988	62,134	30,687	10,250	30,726
1989	64,002	30,624	10,253	32,357

The annual rates per 1,000 of the mean resident population (estimate) in 1989 were: Marriages, 7·1; births, 14·8; deaths, 7·5; divorces, 2·4. Expectation of life: Males, 73·6 years; females, 79·7.

CONSTITUTION AND GOVERNMENT. Victoria, formerly a portion of New South Wales, was, in 1851, proclaimed a separate colony, with a partially elective Legislative Council. In 1856 responsible government was conferred, the legislative power being vested in a parliament of two Houses, the Legislative Council and the Legislative Assembly. At present the Council consists of 44 members who are elected for 2 terms of the Assembly, one-half retiring at each election. The Assembly consists of 88 members, elected for 4 years from the date of its first meeting unless sooner dissolved by the Governor. Members and electors of both Houses must be aged 18 years and Australian citizens or those British subjects previously enrolled as electors, according to the Constitution Act 1975. No property qualification is required, but judges, members of the Commonwealth Parliament, undischarged bankrupts and persons convicted of an offence which is punishable by life imprisonment, may not be members of either House. Single voting (one elector one vote) and compulsory preferential voting apply to Council and Assembly elections. Enrolment for Council and Assembly electors is compulsory. The Council may not initiate or amend money bills, but may suggest amendments in such bills other than amendments which would increase any charge. A bill shall not become law unless passed by both Houses.

The Legislative Assembly, elected on 1 Oct. 1988, is composed as follows: Labor Party, 46; Liberal Party, 33; National Party, 9.

Governor: Dr J. Davis McCaughey, AC.

In the exercise of the executive power the Governor is advised by a Cabinet of responsible Ministers. Section 50 of the Constitution Act 1975 provides that the number of Ministers shall not at any one time exceed 18, of whom not more than 6 may sit in the Legislative Council and not more than 13 may sit in the Legislative Assembly.

Private members of both Houses receive the base salary of $A65,887. Members holding certain offices and responsible Ministers receive additional salary and, in some cases, an expense allowance. The additional salary and the allowance are provided for as a proportion of the base salary and are as follows: Prime Minister, 100% of base salary as additional salary and 42% of base salary as expense allowance; Deputy Prime Minister, 85% and 21%; Ministers and Leader of the Opposition, 75% and 18%; President of the Council and Speaker of the Assembly, 75% and 11%. Members, including the Premier, Ministers and office-holders receive electorate allowances and travelling allowances. Some members who reside outside the metropolitan area also receive an allowance to establish a second residence in Melbourne.

The Cabinet was as follows in Nov. 1991:

Prime Minister, Minister for Ethnic Affairs, Minister for Women's Affairs: Joan Kirner.

Deputy Prime Minister, Attorney-General: Jim Kennan. *Minister for Conservation and the Environment, Minister for Tourism:* Steve Crabb. *Health:* C. Hogg. *Minister for Local Government, Minister for the Aged:* M. Lyster. *Minister for Planning and Urban Growth, Minister for the Arts:* A. McCutcheon. *Minister for Consumer Affairs, Minister for Prices, Minister for Aboriginal Affairs:* B. Mier. *Minister for Labour, Minister for Youth Affairs:* N. Pope. *Housing and Construction:* B. Pullen. *Treasurer:* Tom Roper. *Agriculture and Rural Affairs:* B. Rome. *Minister for Police and Emergency Services, Minister for Corrections:* M. Sandon. *Community Services:* K. Setches. *Transport:* P. Spyker. *Sport and Recreation:* N. Trezise. *Property and Services:* R. Walsh. *Industry and Economic Planning:* David White.

Agent-General in London: Ian Haig (Victoria House, Melbourne Place, Strand, London, WC28 4LG).

Local Government. With the exception of Yallourn Works area (26·9 sq. km) and the unincorporated areas—French Island (154 sq. km), Lady Julia Percy Island (1·3 sq. km), the Bass Strait Islands and part of Gippsland Lakes (312·8 sq. km) and Tower Hill Lake Reserve (5 sq. km), the State is divided into 210 municipal districts, namely 68 cities, 1 rural city, 5 towns, 6 boroughs and 130 shires. The constitution of cities, towns, boroughs and shires is based on statutory requirements concerning population, rate revenue and net annual value of rateable property.

ECONOMY

Budget. State and local government outlays and receipts (excluding financial enterprises e.g. government savings banks, insurance offices, etc.) for 1988–89 (in $A1m.):

State: Current outlays, 12,763·5; capital outlays, 2,802·3. Revenue, 13,079·4. State expenditure included (with expenditure on new fixed assets): Education, 3,137·8 (228·4); health, 2,266·4 (189·3); general services, 737·6 (7·1); public order and safety, 664 (144·8). Revenue included: Property taxes, 1,685·2; payroll taxes, 1,403·8; taxes on financial transactions, 1,418·9; taxes on goods and services, 893·5.

Local: Outlays, 2,142, including roads, 476·7; recreation and culture, 373·7; administration, 363·6; amenities, 274·3; welfare, 204·3. Revenue, 2,422·2, including rates, 1,059·7; other charges, 243; state government grants, 412·8.

Banking and Finance. The State Bank of Victoria, the largest bank in the State, provides domestic and international services for business and personal customers and is the largest supplier of housing finance in Victoria. In 1990 it ran into debt and was acquired by the Commonwealth from the Victorian government in Sept. 1990.

There are 4 major trading banks in Victoria (Commonwealth Bank of Australia, Australia and New Zealand Banking Group Ltd, Westpac Banking Corporation and National Australia Bank) with a total of 1,218 branches and 168 agencies between them at 30 June 1987. There are 4 other trading banks. Private savings banks had 1,102 branches and 246 agencies at 30 June 1987. On 30 June 1986 there were 8·8m. operative accounts (excluding school bank accounts) in savings banks in Victoria. The total credit due to depositors at 30 June 1987 amounted to $A19,670m., made up of State Savings Bank, $A9,197·4m.; Commonwealth Savings Bank, $A2,862·1m.; private savings banks, $A7,610·6m.

The weekly average of deposits and advances of trading banks operating in Victoria during June 1987 were as follows: Deposits, not bearing interest, $A3,874m.; deposits, bearing interest, $A9,791m.; total deposits, $A13,665m.; loans, advances, and bills discounted, $A15,427m. The weekly average of debits to customers' accounts (excluding debits to Federal and State Government accounts at City branches in State capitals) for the same period totalled $A26,514m.

There were 19 building societies in 1989.

ENERGY AND NATURAL RESOURCES

Electricity. Electricity is supplied by the State Electricity Commission of Victoria either directly or through 11 metropolitan councils which buy in bulk and distribute electricity through their own systems.

Electricity production in 1989–90 was 37,804,000 kwh.

About 75% of the power generated for the state system is supplied by 4 brown-coal fired generating stations. There are 2 other thermal stations and 3 hydro-electric stations in north east Victoria. Victoria is also entitled to approximately 30% of the output of the Snowy Mountains hydro-electric scheme and half the output of the Hume hydro-electric station, both of which are in New South Wales.

Oil and Natural Gas. Crude oil in commercially recoverable quantities was first discovered in 1967 in 2 large fields offshore in East Gippsland in Bass Strait between 65 and 80 km from land. These fields, with 10 other fields since discovered, have been assessed as containing initial recoverable reserves of more than 2,930m. bbls of treated crude oil. Estimated reserves of crude oil (1989) 148m. cu. metres; gas, 167m. cu. metres.

In 1987-88 Gippsland Basin produced 84% of Australia's crude oil and 39% of its natural gas. Production of crude oil (1989), 113,383,000 bbls.

Natural gas was discovered offshore in East Gippsland in 1965. The initial recoverable reserves of treated gas are 220,400m. cu. metres. Reserves are sufficient for at least 30 years. Natural gas is distributed to residential and industrial consumers through a network of 20,289 km of mains.

Liquefied petroleum gas is produced after extraction of the propane and butane fractions from the untreated oil and gas.

Brown Coal. Major deposits of brown coal are located in the Central Gippsland region and comprise approximately 94% of the total resources in Victoria. The resource is estimated to be 202,000 megatonnes, of which about 31,000 megatonnes are regarded as readily accessible reserves. It is young and soft with a water content of 60% to 70%. In the La Trobe Valley section of the region, the thick brown coal seams underlie an area from 10 to 30 km wide extending over approximately 70 kilometres from Yallourn in the west to the south of Sale in the east. It can be won continuously in large quantities and at low cost by specialized mechanical plant.

The primary use of these reserves is to fuel electricity generating stations. Production of brown coal in 1988-89 was 43,663,000 tonnes, value \$A357,774,000.

Minerals. Production (in tonnes) and value, 1988–89: Gold, 2·5, \$33,435,000; kaolin, 117,000, \$A13,402,000; gypsum, 241,000, \$A2,276,000; bauxite, 6,211, \$A102,000; clays, 1,991,000, \$A7,256,000; limestone, 2,684,000, \$A23,183,000.

Land Settlement. Of the total area of Victoria (22·76m. ha), 13,973,915 ha on 30 June 1984 were either alienated or in process of alienation. The remainder (8,786,085) constituted Crown land as follows: Perpetual leases, grazing and other leases and licences, 2,160,352; reservations including forest and timber reserves, water, catchment and drainage purposes, national parks, wildlife reserves, water frontages and other reserves, plus unoccupied and unreserved including areas set aside for roads, 6,625,733.

Agriculture. In 1988-89 the total area of land utilized for agricultural activity was 13,096,000 ha, and the gross value of agricultural commodities produced was \$A5,039·7m. There were 32,035 agricultural establishments. The following table shows the area under the principal crops and the produce of each for 3 seasons (in 1,000 units) [1]:

	Total crop area	Wheat		Oats		Barley		Potatoes		Hay	
Season	Ha	Ha	Tonnes	Ha	Tonnes	Ha	Tonnes	Ha	Tonnes	Ha	Tonnes
1986–87	2,340	1,364	2,795	215	356	265	444	13	364	483	1,932
1987–88	2,001	1,026	1,882	216	325	366	529	14	398	379	1,458
1988–89	1,990	931	1,691	189	276	350	544	13	368	485	1,863

[1] Excluding establishments with an estimated value of agricultural operations less than \$A20,000.

In 1988–89 there were 18,857 ha of vineyards with 17,590 ha of bearing vines, yielding 104,275 tonnes of grapes for wine-making and 221,921 tonnes for drying or table use. Other produce (in tonnes), 1988-89: Nuts, 1,575; pears, 119,012;

apples, 99,554; oranges, 57,412; kiwi fruit, 1,656; strawberries, 1,621; tobacco (dry), 4,089.

Livestock (in 1,000), 1988-89: Beef cattle, 2,071; dairy cattle, 1,438; sheep, 28,067; pigs, 423.

Animal products (in tonnes), 1988-89: Wool clip, 132,493; poultry, 97·4; mutton, 63,000; lamb, 114,000; milk, 3,792m. litres; eggs, 48·57m. dozens; honey, 2,886.

INDUSTRY AND TRADE

Industry. At 30 June 1989 there were 9,771 manufacturing establishments employing 4 or more persons. Selected articles manufactured (in tonnes): Butter, 91,423; cheese, 103,216; white flour, 266,842; cotton yarn, 8,605; wool yarn, 14,896; cotton cloth, 16,992,000 sq. metres; wool cloth, 2,679,000 sq. metres; 223,000 cars and station wagons; plastic and synthetic resins, 673,000 tonnes; 439m. clay bricks; ready mixed concrete, 4,256,000 cu. metres.

Labour. In Aug. 1990 there were 2,073,100 employed persons (64·4% of the civilian population aged 15 years and over): Agriculture, forestry, fishing and hunting, 96,900; mining, 6,000; manufacturing, 392,800; electricity, gas and water, 28,600; construction, 149,900; wholesale and retail trade, 428,400; transport and storage, 87,800; communication, 41,000; finance, property and business services, 239,500; public administration and defence, 84,100; community services, 349,200; recreation, personal and other services, 130,200. There were 138,800 unemployed persons in Aug. 1990 (6·3% of the labour force).

Trade Unions. There were 160 trade unions with a total membership of 931,200 operating in Victoria in June 1989.

Commerce. The commerce of Victoria, exclusive of inter-state trade, is included in the statement of the commerce of Australia, *see* pp. 111–13.

The total value of the overseas imports and exports of Victoria, including bullion and specie but excluding inter-state trade, was as follows (in $A1m.):

	1984–85	1985–86	1986–87	1987–88	1988–89	1989–90
Imports	10,501	12,409	13,473	14,015	15,968	16,782
Exports [1]	6,452	6,806	7,398	9,051	8,519	8,514

[1] Includes re-exports.

The chief exports in 1989–90 (in $A1m.) were: Textile fibres and their wastes, 1,321; non-ferrous metals, 1,070; dairy products and birds' eggs, 613; petroleum, petroleum products and related materials, 512; hides, skins, and fur skins (raw), 230; power generating machinery and equipment, 222; road vehicles, 229. Exports in 1989–90 went mainly to Japan ($A1,415m.), USA ($A824m.) and New Zealand ($A720m.).

The chief imports in 1989–90 (in $A1m.) were: Road vehicles, 1,842; general industrial machinery, equipment and machine parts, 1,220; textile yarns, fabrics, made-up articles and related products, 963. Imports in 1989–90 came mainly from the USA ($A3,567m.), Japan ($A3,307m.) and the Federal Republic of Germany ($A1,498m.).

COMMUNICATIONS

Roads. In 1987–88 there were 160,398 km of roads open for general traffic, consisting of 7,537 km of state highways and freeways, 14,793 km of main roads, 1,848 km of tourist and forest roads and 136,220 km of other roads and streets. The number of registered motor vehicles (other than tractors) at 30 June 1989 was 2,585,200. There were 546 fatalities in road accidents in 1990.

Railways. All the railways are the property of the State and are under the management of the Public Transport Corporation, responsible to the Victorian Government.

At 30 June 1991, 5,047 km of government railway were open. 10·2m. tonnes of freight and 6m. passengers (non-urban) were carried. Melbourne's suburban railways carried 94m. passengers. Melbourne's tramway and light rail network extends to 228 km.

Civil Aviation. There were (1988) 70,047 domestic and 13,864 international aircraft movements at Essendon and Melbourne airports. Passengers totalled (1988) 6,033,785 on domestic flights and 1,525,368 on international flights. Freight handled (1988) 96,883 tonnes on domestic flights and 82,297 tonnes on international flights.

Telecommunications. In 1990 there were 2·9m. telephones. In 1989 there were 55 broadcasting stations and 18 television stations.

JUSTICE, RELIGION, EDUCATION AND WELFARE

Justice. There is a Supreme Court with a Chief Justice and 21 puisne judges. There are a county court, magistrates' courts, a court of licensing, and a bankruptcy court, etc.

Major crime during 1988–89: 314,755 offences were reported to the police; 96,219 offences were cleared and 54,677 people were proceeded against.

At 30 June 1990 there were 13 prisons and 2,101 prisoners in custody.

Religion. There is no State Church, and no State assistance has been given to religion since 1875. At the 1986 census the following were the enumerated numbers of each of the principal religions: Catholic,[1] 1,104,044; Church of England, 715,414; Uniting, 280,262 (including Methodist); Orthodox, 177,565; Presbyterian, 138,000; Protestant (undefined), 87,557; other Christian, 90,756; Moslem, 37,965; Hebrew, 32,387; no religion, 557,939; no reply, 574,712; other groups, 222,877.

[1] So described on individual census schedules.

Education. On 12 July 1989 there were 2,059 government schools with 527,700 pupils and 40,737 full-time teaching staff plus full-time equivalents of part-time teaching staff: 270,695 pupils were in primary schools, 228,021 in secondary schools and 4,911 attended special schools. There were at 12 July 1989, 719 non-government schools, excluding commercial colleges, with 16,400 teaching staff and 257,407 pupils.

In 1989 there were 14 colleges of advanced education; 3 other institutions of higher education with 2,670 students; and 4 universities: Deakin (founded 1974), with 8,262 students, Latrobe (1964), with 13,491, Melbourne (1853), with 21,819 and Monash (1958), with 14,847.

Health. At 30 June 1990 there were 282 approved hospitals with 21,257 beds, of which 128 with 6,366 beds were private.

Social Services. Victoria was the first State of Australia to make a statutory provision for the payment of Age Pensions. The Act providing for the payment of such pensions came into operation on 18 Jan. 1901, and continued until 1 July 1909, when the Australian Invalid and Old Age Pension Act came into force. The Social Services Consolidation Act, which came into operation on 1 July 1947, repealed the various legislative enactments relating to age (previously old-age) and invalid pensions, maternity allowances, child endowment, and unemployment, and sickness benefits and while following in general the Acts repealed, considerably liberalized many of their provisions: it has since been amended. On 30 June 1989 there were 344,523 age and 77,263 invalid pensioners. The amount paid in pensions, including payments to wives and spouse carers of age and invalid pensioners, during 1987–88 was $A2,343,434,000.

Under the Australian Unemployment and Sickness Benefit Act 1944, there were 63,992 unemployment, 16,299 sickness, 50,778 sole parent's and 5,419 special benefits granted during 1988-89. The amount paid in benefits totalled $A708,333,000 during 1987-88. Unemployment benefits amounted to $A529·5m. in 1988-89.

The number of widows' pensions in force at 30 June 1989 was 20,790. The total amount paid during 1987-88 was $A255,417,000.

The number of family allowances in force in 1987-88 was 966,737. In addition, endowment was being paid in respect of 1,249 children who were being maintained in approved institutions. The total amount paid in family allowances and endowment in 1987-88 was $A345,688,000. In 1988-89, sole parent's benefits were paid to 50,770 beneficiaries, $A11·74m. were paid to 8,640 recipients of child disability allowance and $A85·54m. in family income supplement to 35,310 families with 88,834 children.

Further Reading

Australian Bureau of Statistics Victorian Office. *Victorian Year Book–Summary of Statistics (annual).*

Historical Records of Victoria. Victorian Government Printing Office, Melbourne (From 1981)
Victoria: The First Century. Official History of Victoria. Melbourne, 1934
Victorian Municipal Directory. Melbourne, (From 1866)
Broome, R., *The Victorians: Arriving.* New South Wales, 1984
Christie, M. F., *Aborigines in Colonial Victoria, 1835–86.* Sydney Univ. Press, 1979
Dingle, T., *The Victorians: Settling.* New South Wales, 1984
Grant, J. and Serle, G., *The Melbourne Scene 1803–1956.* Melbourne Univ. Press, 1956
Pratt, A., *The Centenary History of Victoria.* Melbourne, 1934
Priestley, S., *The Victorians: Making Their Mark.* Melbourne, 1984

State library: The State Library of Victoria, 328 Swanston St., Melbourne, 3000. *State statistical ofice:* Victorian Office, Australian Bureau of Statistics, 525 Collins Street, Melbourne 3000.

WESTERN AUSTRALIA

HISTORY. In 1791 Vancouver, in the *Discovery*, took formal possession of the country about King George Sound. In 1826 the Government of New South Wales sent 20 convicts and a detachment of soldiers to King George Sound and formed a settlement then called Frederickstown. In 1827 Captain (afterwards Sir) James Stirling surveyed the coast from King George Sound to the Swan River, and in May 1829 Captain (afterwards Sir) Charles Fremantle took possession of the territory. In June 1829 Captain Stirling, newly appointed Lieut.-Governor, founded the colony now known as the State of Western Australia. On 1 Jan. 1901 Western Australia became one of the 6 federated States within the Commonwealth of Australia.

AREA AND POPULATION. Western Australia lies between 113° 09' and 129° E. long. and 13° 44' and 35° 08' S. lat.; its area is 2,525,500 sq. km.
The population at each census from 1947 was as follows [1]:

	Males	Females	Total		Males	Females	Total
1947	258,076	244,404	502,480	1971	539,332	514,502	1,053,834
1954	330,358	309,413	639,771	1976	599,959	578,383	1,178,342
1961	375,452	361,177	736,629	1981	659,249	642,807	1,300,056
1966	432,569	415,531	848,100	1986	736,131	722,888	1,459,019

[1] 1961 and earlier exclude persons of predominantly Aboriginal descent; from 1966 figures refer to total population (*i.e.*, including Aborigines). Figures from 1971 are based on estimated resident population.

The population count at the 1986 census was 1,406,929 (707,569 males and 699,360 females). Of these 1,020,362 were born in Australia. Married persons numbered 617,382 (308,974 males and 308,408 females); widowers, 10,787; widows, 49,776; divorced, 23,505 males and 28,268 females; never married, 348,343 males and 294,771 females. The number of males under 21 was 247,826 and of females 235,620. Estimated resident population at 30 June 1990 was 1,633,800.

Perth, the capital, had an estimated resident population of 1,158,387 at June 1989. Of this, the area administered by the City of Perth had a population of 82,413 while the population in the area for which the City of Fremantle is responsible (which includes the chief port of the State) was 23,981.

Principal local government areas outside the metropolitan area, with population at 30 June 1989 (estimate): Bunbury, 26,398; Geraldton, 20,968; Mandurah, 23,107; Roebourne, 16,537; Port Hedland, 13,820; Albany, 14,958; Busselton, 13,422; Kalgoorlie-Boulder, 26,813.

Vital statistics for calendar years [1]:

	Births	Ex-nuptial births	Marriages	Divorces	Deaths
1987	23,332	4,623	10,150	4,044	8,880
1988	25,143	5,314	10,578	3,964	9,532
1989	24,693	5,377	10,739	4,089	9,543

[1] Figures are on State of usual residence basis.

CONSTITUTION AND GOVERNMENT. In 1870 partially representative government was instituted, and in 1890 the administration was vested in the Governor, a Legislative Council and a Legislative Assembly. The Legislative Council was, in the first instance, nominated by the Governor, but it was provided that in the event of the population of the colony reaching 60,000, it should be elective. In 1893 this limit of population being reached, the Colonial Parliament amended the Constitution accordingly.

The Legislative Council consists of 34 members, 2, representing each of the 17 electoral regions. Each member is elected for a term of 4 years.

There are 57 members of the Legislative Assembly, each member representing one of the 57 electoral districts of the State. Members are elected for the duration of the Parliament, normally 4 years. The qualifications applying to candidates and electors are identical for the Legislative Council and the Legislative Assembly. A candidate must have resided in Western Australia for a minimum of 12 months, be at least 18 years of age and free from legal incapacity, be an Australian citizen, and be enrolled, or qualified for enrolment, as an elector. A judge of the Supreme Court, the Sheriff of Western Australia, an undischarged bankrupt or a debtor against whose estate there is a subsisting order in bankruptcy may not be elected to Parliament. No person may hold office as a member of the Legislative Assembly and the Legislative Council at the same time. An elector must be at least 18 years of age, be an Australian citizen free from legal incapacity, must have resided in the Commonwealth of Australia for 6 and in Western Australia for 3 months continuously and in the electoral district for which he or she claims enrolment for a continuous period of 1 month immediately preceding the date of his or her claim. Enrolment is compulsory for all qualified persons except Aboriginal natives of Australia, who are entitled but not required to enrol. Voting at elections is on the preferential system and is compulsory for all enrolled persons.

Ordinary members of the legislature are paid a salary of $A64,150 a year with an additional electorate allowance, ranging from $A16,431 to $A29,819 a year according to location of the electorate. All members of Parliament also receive a basic postage and lettergram allowance of $A4,310 a year.

In addition to the basic Member's salary, electorate and postage allowances, the Premier receives a salary and expense of office allowances of $A80,376. On the same basis the Deputy Premier receives $A50,288; the Leader of the Government in the Legislative Council $A44,000; and other Ministers $A37,010.

The Legislative Assembly representation as at Sept 1991 was: Australian Labor Party, 28; Liberal Party, 19; National Party of Australia, 6; Independent, 4. The Legislative Council was 16 Australian Labor Party, 14 Liberal Party, 3 National Party of Australia; Independent, 1.

Governor: His Excellency the Hon Sir Francis Burt, AC, KCMG, QC.
Lieut-Governor: The Honourable David Kingsley Malcolm.
The Australian Labor Party Cabinet was at Nov. 1991:

Premier, Treasurer, The Family, Women's Interests: Hon. Carmen Mary Lawrence, MLA.
Deputy Premier, State Development, Trade, Goldfields: Hon. Ian Frederick Taylor, MLA. *Attorney General, Corrective Services, Leader of the Government in the Legislative Council:* Hon. Joseph Max Berinson, MLC. *Education, Employment and Training, the Arts, Deputy Leader of the Government in the Legislative Council:* Hon. Elsie Kay Hallahan, MLC. *Transport, Racing and Gaming, Tourism:* Hon. Pamela Anne Beggs, MLA. *Environment, Leader of the House in the Legislative Assembly:* Hon. Robert John Pearce, MLA. *Health:* Hon. Keith James Wilson,

MLA. *Transport, Racing and Gaming, Tourism:* Hon. Pamela Anne Beggs, MLA. *Agriculture, Water Resources, North-West:* Hon. Ernest Francis Bridge, MLA. *Mines, Fisheries, Mid-West, Minister assisting the Minister for State Development:* Hon. Gordon Leslie Hill, MLA. *Police, Emergency Services, Sport and Recreation:* Hon. Graham John Edwards, MLC. *Productivity and Labour Relations, Consumer Affairs:* Hon. Yvonne Daphne Henderson, MLA. *Lands, Planning, Justice, Local Government, South-West:* Hon. David Lawrence Smith, MLA. *Fuel and Energy, Microeconomic Reform, Parliamentary and Electoral Reform, Minister assisting the Treasurer:* Hon. Geoffrey Ian Gallop, MLA. *Aboriginal Affairs, Multicultural and Ethnic Affairs, Seniors, Minister Assisting the Minister for Women's Interests:* Judyth Watson, MLA. *Community Services, Disability Services:* Hon Eric Stephen Ripper, MLA. *Housing, Construction, Services Heritage:* Hon. James Andrew McGinty, MLA. *Parliamentary Secretary of the Cabinet:* William Ian Thomas, MLA.

Agent-General in London: D. Fischer (Western Australia House, 115 Strand, WC2R 0AJ).

Local Government. The only unincorporated area in mainland Western Australia is King's Park, a public reserve of about 403 ha. in Perth. Including the lord-mayoralty of Perth there were 19 cities, 10 towns and 99 shires at 30 June 1990. The executive body in each of these districts is normally an elective council, presided over by a mayor (city and town) or a president (shire), but in certain circumstances it may be a commissioner appointed by the Governor. Their functions include road construction and repair, the provision of parks and recreation grounds, the administration of building controls and local services such as health and library services. Finance is derived largely from rates levied on property owners as well as charges for services and government grants (mainly for road construction).

ECONOMY

Budget. Revenue and expenditure (in $A), as reported in the Consolidated Revenue Fund, in years ended 30 June:

	1989	1990	1991	1992[1]
Revenue	4,270,268,532	4,838,556,662	4,940,799,000	5,225,000,000
Expenditure	4,269,990,881	4,838,256,430	4,940,799,000	5,225,000,000

[1] Estimates.

Main items of revenue in 1989–90: Railways ($A275,101,375), taxation ($A1,300,918,315), lands, timber and mining ($A427,841,917), from Federal funds ($A1,962,993,167). Western Australia had a net public debt of $A1,538,099,306 on 30 June 1989, the charge for that year being $A194,305,932.

Banking and Finance. There are 20 trading banks including the Commonwealth Trading Bank and the Rural and Industries Bank of Western Australia. In Dec. 1989, the average of customers' balances was $A6,604m.

At 31 Dec. 1989, the 8 savings banks held deposits of $A5,845m.

In 1989 building society assets totalled $A1,983·2m.

ENERGY AND NATURAL RESOURCES

Minerals. The mining industry has been for many years of considerable significance in the Western Australian economy. Until the mid-1960s the major mineral produced was gold. It was then replaced by iron ore in terms of value, and has at various times fallen behind nickel concentrates, bauxite, oil, mineral sands and salt. In the latter half of the 1980s it enjoyed a resurgence and in 1987-88 exceeded iron ore in value terms.

The total ex-mine value of minerals from mining and quarrying in the State in 1987–88 was $A5,935·5m. Principal minerals produced in 1987–88 were: Iron ore, 98·0m. tonnes, value $A1,669·8m.; bauxite, 21·0m. tonnes; gold bullion, 106·8m. grammes, value $A1,839·5m.; nickel concentrates, 389,000 tonnes; tin concentrates,

434 tonnes; black coal, 3·7m. tonnes; crude oil, 3,100m.; natural gas, 3,887,000m. kilolitres; salt, 5·5m. tonnes, value $A107·2m.; diamonds, 30·2m. carats, value $A248·2m.; mineral sands concentrates valued at $A196·9m. (1986–87).

Agriculture.

	1987–88		1988–89	
	Area	Production	Area	Production
Crop	1,000 ha	1,000 tonnes	1,000 ha	1,000 tonnes
Wheat	3,312	3,882	3,297	5,225
Oats	373	502	389	618
Barley	461	617	383	552
Hay	243	778	248	873
Potatoes	2	72	2	78
Cauliflower	1	14	1	18

	1987–88		1988–89	
	No. Trees	Production	No. Trees	Production
Crop	(1,000)	Tonnes	(1,000)	Tonnes
Apples	702	40,196	667	46,695
Pears	132	6,604	143	6,974
Oranges	179	5,217	198	5,087

Irrigation has been established by the Government along the south-western coastal plain and in the north of the State. Reservoirs with an aggregate capacity of 6,207m. cu. metres provided irrigation water for 20,402 ha in 6 districts during 1985–86.

Livestock at 31 March 1989 included 1,702,000 cattle, 37,090,000 sheep and 285,000 pigs.

The wool clip in 1988–89 was 203,173 tonnes.

Forestry. The area of State forests and timber reserves at 30 June 1989 was 1,892,266 ha; 1988–89 production of sawn timber was 335,191 cu. metres, principally Jarrah and Karri hardwoods.

Fisheries. The catch of fish, crustaceans and molluscs in Western Australia in 1988–89 totalled 35,392 tonnes for a gross value of $A242·4m. Of this, rock lobsters, with a total catch of 11,776 tonnes accounted for $A177·9m.

Value of Agricultural Commodities Produced. The estimated gross values of Western Australian agricultural commodities during 1988–89 were: Crops and pastures, $A1,799·7m.; livestock slaughterings and other disposals, $A424·9m.; livestock products, $A1,495·0m.

INDUSTRY AND TRADE

Industry. Heavy industry is concentrated in the South-West of the state, and is largely tied to export-orientated mineral processing, especially alumina and nickel. Other significant manufacturing industries include meat and seafood processing, production of timber and wood products, metal fabrication and production of industrial and mining machinery. The North West Shelf development has stimulated recent growth in industries involved in providing materials and equipment during the construction phase, as well as in new and existing industries using gas in processing.

The following table shows manufacturing industry statistics for 1988–89 [1]:

Industry sub-division	Number of establishments operating at 30 June	Persons employed [2] 1,000	Wages and salaries $Am.	Turnover $Am.
Food, beverages and tobacco	364	12·1	274	2,217
Textiles	41	1·3	23	117
Clothing and footwear	69	1·8	30	80
Wood, wood products and furniture	451	9·0	182	847
Paper, paper products, printing and publishing	255	7·9	161	684
Chemical, petroleum and coal products	75	3·2	94	826

Industry sub-division	Number of establishments operating at 30 June	Persons employed [2] 1,000	Wages and salaries $Am.	Turnover $Am.
Non-metallic mineral products	144	5·1	130	804
Basic metal products	43	5·7	193	2,194
Fabricated metal products	466	9·9	230	1,138
Transport equipment	179	5·0	116	402
Other machinery and equipment	378	8·5	206	835
Miscellaneous manufacturing	186	3·2	70	434
Total	2,651	72·7	1,710	10,579

[1] Excludes single establishment enterprises with less than 4 persons employed.
[2] At 30 June. Includes working proprietors.

Labour. The labour force was 762,600 employed and 62,600 unemployed in June 1990.

A Court of Arbitration was established in 1901 and was replaced in 1964 by the Western Australian Industrial Appeal Court and The Western Australian Industrial Commission, authorities constituted in terms of the *Industrial Arbitration Act 1912*. These authorities continue to operate under the provisions of the *Industrial Relations Act 1979* which was proclaimed on 1 March 1980.

The Western Australian Industrial Appeal Court consists of 3 Judges, one of whom is the Presiding Judge. The members are nominated by the Chief Justice of Western Australia. An appeal lies to the Court from decisions of the President of the Western Australian Industrial Commission, the Full Bench or the Commission in Court Session but only on the ground that the decision is erroneous in law or is in excess of jurisdiction.

The Western Australian Industrial Commission consists of a President, a Chief Industrial Commissioner, a Senior Commissioner, and 'such number of other Commissioners as may, from time to time, be necessary'. There were 8 'other Commissioners' at Oct. 1989. A person shall not be appointed as President unless he is qualified to be a Judge, and on appointment he is entitled to the status of a Puisne Judge. The President or a Commissioner sitting or acting alone constitutes the Commission and may exercise the appropriate powers of the Commission.

The Commission can inquire into any industrial matter and make an award, order or declaration relating to such matter. The Commission may also make inquiries where industrial action has occurred or is likely to occur.

The Commission in Court Session is constituted by not less than 3 Commissioners sitting or acting together, and may make General Orders, hear matters referred by the Commission, and hear appeals from decisions of Boards of Reference.

The Full Bench is constituted by not less than 3 members of the Commission, 1 of whom is the President, and may hear matters referred by the Commission on questions of law, and appeals from decisions of the Commission and Industrial Magistrates.

The following table shows details of the number of industrial awards, unions and members registered with the Western Australian Industrial Commission.

At 30 June	1985	1987	1988	1989	1990
Awards in force	608	592	610	628	610
Employee organizations:					
Number	72	69	70	69	72
Membership	176,769	189,770	186,608	187,206	174,312
Employer organizations:					
Number	15	15	15	16	15
Membership	3,561	2,690	2,825	2,817	2,180

Commerce. Foreign commerce is comprised in the statement of the commerce of Australia.

The total value of imports and exports, including interstate trade, but excluding interstate value of horses, in 5 years (30 June) is, in $A1m., as follows:

	1984–85	1985–86	1986–87	1987–88	1988–89
Imports	6,446·5	6,984·9	7,878·2	8,621·5	10,012·5
Exports [1]	7,535·8	8,149·6	8,721·4	9,300·3	10,633·7

[1] Including ships' stores.

Selected overseas exports (in $A million) for 1989–90: Iron ore and concentrates, 2,246; wheat, 1,001; wool, 769; petroleum and petroleum products, 601; gold bullion, 325; live sheep and lambs, 62; beef and veal, 103; salt, 120; mutton and lamb, 57; barley, 64; prawns, 29; hides and skins (including fur skins), 39; whole rock lobsters, 109; fruit and nuts (fresh or dried), 10; oats, 18.

Selected overseas imports (in $A million) for 1989–90: Petroleum and petroleum products, 672; machinery, 942; transport equipment, 704; iron and steel, 94; chemicals, 277; food, 99; crude fertilizer, 35; rubber manufactures, 103.

The chief countries exporting to Western Australia in 1989–90 were (in $A million): Japan, 798; USA, 639; United Arab Emirates, 370; UK, 259; Federal Republic of Germany, 219; Canada, 173; Singapore, 145.

Western Australia's exports in 1989–90 (in $A million) went chiefly to: Japan, 2,695; USA, 1,684; China, 495; Republic of Korea, 494; Singapore, 454 Indonesia, 345; Taiwan, 271.

Tourism. In 1989 there were 182,800 overseas visitors.

COMMUNICATIONS

Roads. At 30 June 1988 there were 122,380 km of prepared and formed roads in Western Australia comprising 41,585 km of bituminous surface, 40,635 km other constructed surfaces and 40,159 km formed but not metalled or otherwise prepared. In addition, there are 19,539 km of roads unprepared except for clearing which are used for general traffic.

New motor vehicles registered during the year ended 30 June 1990 were 59,338.

In 1989 there were 242 fatalities in road accidents.

Railways. At 30 June 1990 the State had 5,553 km of State government railway and 731 km of Federal line, the latter being the western portion of the Trans-Australian line (Kalgoorlie–Port Pirie), which links the State railway system to those of the other States of the Commonwealth. At 30 June 1989, mining companies operated 1,198 km of private railways for the transport of ore to ports on the north-west coast. In 1989–90 state railways carried 25m. tonnes and 0·5m. passengers. Perth suburban lines (63 km electrified), controlled by a separate authority, carried 5·9m. passengers.

Civil Aviation. An extensive system of regular air services operates for passengers, freight and mail. During the year ended 31 Dec. 1988, Perth Airport handled 22,062 aircraft movements and 2,185,227 passengers on domestic and international services.

Shipping. In 1988–89, the number of overseas direct vessels through the major ports was: Port of Fremantle, 1,123 entered, 1,122 cleared; Port Hedland, 367 entered, 357 cleared; other ports, 1,183 entered, 1,210 cleared. The gross weight (in tonnes) of overseas cargo through those ports was: Port of Fremantle, 29,902,254 discharged, 29,303,629 loaded; Port Hedland, 38,260,602 discharged, 36,020,485 loaded; other ports, 86,438 313 discharged, 87,438,808 loaded.

Telecommunications. Postal, telephone and telegraph facilities are afforded at 397 offices. Telephone services connected totalled 676,800 at 30 June 1989.

There were 96 radio broadcasting and 96 television stations, including translator stations, in operation at 30 June 1988.

JUSTICE, RELIGION, EDUCATION AND WELFARE

Justice. In Western Australia justice is administered by a Supreme Court, consisting of a Chief Justice, 11 puisne judges and 3 masters; a District Court comprising a chief judge and 14 other judges; a Magistrates Court, a Chief Stipendiary Magistrate, 36 Stipendiary Magistrates and Justices of the Peace, as at 30 June 1990. All courts exercise both civil and criminal jurisdiction except Justices of the Peace who deal with summary criminal matters only. Juvenile offenders are dealt with by the Children's Court. Overall responsibility for the Children's Court is vested in a President, who has the status of a District Court Judge. A children's court may be constituted by a judge, a magistrate or 2 lay members. Each has different sentencing powers. For certain offences involving first offenders under the age of 16 years who have pleaded guilty, such cases may be dealt with by the Children's (suspended Proceedings) Panel which comprises a representative from the Department for Community Services and one from the Police Department. The Family Court also forms part of the justice system and comprises a Chief Judge, 4 other judges, 7 magistrates/registrars and exercises both State and Federal jurisdictions.

Offences against law	1984–85	1985–86	1986–87	1987–88
Charges	115,739 [1]	...	211,966	...
Lower Court convictions [2]	105,025 [1]	...	190,372	...
Higher Court convictions	3,369	4,142	3,912	5,239

[1] Excludes Perth and East Perth Lower Courts.
[2] Includes convictions for traffic offences: 43,851 in 1984–85; 87,140 in 1986–87. In addition, small fines were imposed for minor traffic offences as follows: 1984, 373,662; 1985, 416,774; 1986, 401,415; 1987, 533,012; 1988, 525,581; 1989, 516,362.

Persons in prison at 30 June 1989 numbered 1,494 males and 92 females.

Religion. There is no State Church, and freedom of worship is accorded to all. At the census, 30 June 1986, the principal denominations were: Anglican, 371,302; Catholic, 347,695; Uniting, 82,876; Presbyterian, 31,641; Baptist, 16,869; Orthodox, 16,722; other Christian, 110,922; Buddhist, 7,178; all other, including not stated and no religion, 421,724.

Education. School attendance is compulsory from the age of 6 until the end of the year in which the child attains 15 years. A non-compulsory year of education is available to children from the beginning of the year in which they reach 5 years of age, at pre-primary centres attached to most government primary schools or at community-based and privately owned pre-school centres, and at some non-government schools. Children may be enrolled during their fourth year where vacancies exist. In 1990 there were 761 government primary and secondary schools providing free education to 217,441 students and 249 non-government primary and secondary schools providing education, for which fees are charged, to 69,547 students.

Technical and Further Education (TAFE) is offered by the Department of TAFE, a sub-department of the Ministry of Education, and by three independent regional colleges. The latter also provide higher education facilities. Additionally, higher education is available through a multi-campus college of advanced education and three universities.

Tertiary education:	Teaching Staff [1]	Students Enrolled
University of Western Australia [2]	703	10,423
Murdoch University [3]	276	6,014
Curtin University of Technology [3]	799	15,615
Western Australian College of Advanced Education [2]	683	14,108

[1] Full-time staff and part-time staff on the basis of equivalent full-time staff.
[2] March 1989.   [3] April 1989.

State Government expenditure from consolidated revenue on education during the year ended 30 June 1990, amounted to $A1,064,679,000.

Social Welfare. At 30 June 1989 there were 89 acute public hospitals, 20 acute private hospitals, 5 public nursing homes, 100 private nursing homes and 7 permanent/ extended care units attached to public hospitals.

The Health Department of Western Australia Psychiatric Services comprised 4 approved psychiatric hospitals, 7 outpatient clinics for adults, 1 rehabilitation unit, 5 psychiatric extended care units, 2 other residential units, 1 halfway-house, 2 specialist units, 2 full-time country clinics, 4 sessional country clinics, 4 occupational day clinics and 1 rehabilitation hostel. Specifically for children are: 3 outpatient clinics and 4 in-patient clinics. The Authority for the Intellectually Handicapped comprised 20 hostels and 27 group homes.

The Department for Community Services is responsible for the provision of welfare and community services throughout the State. There were 10 directorates in the Department on 30 June 1990. Six were regionally based, 3 in the Perth metropolitan area and 3 were in the country. These are concerned with direct service delivery, which is provided through 22 divisional and 33 district offices. The remaining 4 directorates provide central support and administrative functions.

Direct services provided to the community include emergency financial assistance, family and substitute care, and counselling and psychological services. The Department supervises children's Day Care Centres. There is a 24-hour emergency welfare service provided through the Crisis Care Unit. Specialist units work in the areas of child abuse, adoptions, youth activities and Family Court counselling.

The Department provides residential facilities for the temporary accommodation, care and training of children, is responsible for young offenders recommended for detention or remand by a Court and also supervises young offenders subject to non-custodial court orders.

Age, invalid, widows', disability and service pensions, and unemployment benefits are paid by the Federal Government. The number of pensioners in Western Australia at 30 June 1989 was: Age, 104,816; invalid, 29,706; widows, 6,901; disability, 30,761; service, 36,246; and sole parents, 23,357. There were 31,697 recipients of unemployment benefits at 30 June 1989.

During 1989–90 the department provided emergency assistance in 69,250 cases. This assistance, valued at $A4,690,000, was in the form of cash, vouchers to purchase goods and services, and payment on behalf of individuals.

Further Reading

Statistical Information: The State Government Statistician's Office was established in 1897 and now functions as the Western Australian Office of the Australian Bureau of Statistics (Merlin Centre, 30 Terrace Road, Perth). *Deputy Commonwealth Statistician and Government Statistician:* B. N. Pink. Its principal publications are: *Western Australian Year Book* (new series, from 1957). *Western Australia: Facts and Figures* (from 1989). *Monthly Summary of Statistics* (from 1958)

Battye, J. S., *Western Australia: A History from its Discovery to the Inauguration of the Commonwealth.* Oxford, 1924.—*The Cyclopedia of Western Australia.* Adelaide, Vol. 1 (1912), Vol. 2 (1913)

Crowley, F. K., *Australia's Western Third: A History of Western Australia from the First Settlements to Modern Times.* (Rev. ed.). Melbourne, 1970

Kimberly, W. B., *History of Western Australia: A Narrative of Her Past.* Melbourne, 1897

Stannage, C. T. (ed.) *A New History of Western Australia.* Perth, 1980

Stephenson, G. and Hepburn, J. A., *Plan for the Metropolitan Region: Perth and Fremantle.* Perth, 1955

State Library: Alexander Library Building, Perth. *State Librarian:* Lynn Allen, BA (Hon.), MA, PhD, ALAA, AIMM.

AUSTRIA

Republik Österreich

Capital: Vienna
Population: 7·8m. (1991)
GNP per capita: US$20,231 (1990)

HISTORY. Following the break-up of the Austro–Hungarian Empire, the Republic of Austria was proclaimed on 12 Nov. 1918. On 12 March 1938 Austria was forcibly absorbed in the German Reich as *Ostmark* until it was liberated by the Allied armies in 1945. On 27 April 1945 a provisional government was set up and was recognized by the Allies on 20 Oct. 1945. Austria recovered its full independence by the Austrian State Treaty, signed on 15 May 1955.

AREA AND POPULATION. Austria is a land-locked country bounded in the north by Germany and Czechoslovakia, east by Hungary, south by Yugoslavia and Italy, and west by Switzerland and Liechtenstein. It has an area of 83,857 sq. km (32,377 sq. miles) and its population at recent censuses has been as follows:

1923	6,534,481	1951	6,933,905	1971	7,491,526
1934	6,760,233	1961	7,073,807	1981	7,555,338

Preliminary population figures at the 1991 census, 7,812,100. In 1981, 65% were urban and 96% were German-speaking, with linguistic minorities of Slovenes (19,000), Croats (26,000), Hungarians (16,000) and Czechs (7,000). The areas, populations and capitals of the 9 federal states are as follows:

Federal States	Area sq. km	Population [1] (1991)	State capitals
Vienna (Wien)	415	1,533,176	Vienna
Lower Austria (Niederösterreich)	19,172	1,480,927	St Pölten
Burgenland	3,966	273,541	Eisenstadt
Upper Austria (Oberösterreich)	11,980	1,340,076	Linz
Salzburg	7,154	483,880	Salzburg
Styria (Steiermark)	16,387	1,184,593	Graz
Carinthia (Kärnten)	9,533	552,421	Klagenfurt
Tirol	12,647	630,358	Innsbruck
Vorarlberg	2,601	333,128	Bregenz

[1] Preliminary results.

Vital statistics for calendar years:

	Live births	Still births	Deaths [1]	Marriages	Divorces
1987	86,503	289	84,907	76,205	14,639
1988	88,052	325	83,263	35,361	14,924
1989	88,759	347	83,407	42,523	15,489
1990	90,454	325	82,952	45,212	16,282

[1] Excluding still births.

The populations of the principal towns (excluding Vienna), according to the census (preliminary results) of 15 May 1991 were as follows:

Graz	232,155	Dornbirn	40,881	Klosterneu-		Mödling	20,607
Linz	202,855	Steyr	39,542	burg	24,591	Lustenau	18,579
Salzburg	143,971	Wiener		Baden	23,998	Hallein	17,338
Innsbruck	114,996	Neustadt	35,268	Kapfenburg	23,486	Braunau	
Klagenfurt	89,502	Leoben	28,504	Krems a.d.D.	22,829	am Inn	16,457
Villach	55,165	Wolfsberg	28,105	Traun	22,268	Ternitz	15,526
Wels	53,042	Bregent	27,236	Amstetten	22,109	Bruck an	
St Pölten	49,805	Feldkirch	26,743	Leonding	21,355	der Mur	14,155

CLIMATE. Climate ranges from cool temperate to mountain type according to situation. Winters are cold, with considerable snowfall, but summers are very warm. The wettest months are May to August.

Vienna, Jan. 28°F (–2°C), July 67°F (19·5°C). Annual rainfall 25·6" (640 mm).
Graz, Jan. 28°F (–2°C), July 67°F (19·5°C). Annual rainfall 34" (849 mm).
Innsbruck, Jan. 27°F (–2·7°C), July 66°F (18·8°C). Annual rainfall 34·7" (868 mm).
Salzburg, Jan. 28°F (–2·0°C), July 65°F (18·3°C). Annual rainfall 50·6" (1,266 mm).

CONSTITUTION AND GOVERNMENT. Austria recovered its sovereignty and independence on 27 July 1955 by the coming into force of the Austrian State Treaty between the UK, the USA, the USSR and France on the one part and the Republic of Austria on the other part (signed on 15 May).

The Constitution of 1 Oct. 1920 was restored on 27 April 1945. Austria is a democratic federal republic comprising 9 states *(Länder)*, with a federal President *(Bundespräsident)* directly elected for not more than 2 successive 6-year terms, and a bicameral National Assembly which comprises a National Council and a Federal Council.

The National Council *(Nationalrat)* comprises 183 members directly elected for a 4-year term by proportional representation on a national basis. At the General Elections of 7 Oct. 1990 the electorate was 5·6m. and turn-out was 86·14%. The Socialist Party (in June 1991 renamed Social-Democratic Party, SPÖ) won 80 seats (with 42·8% of the vote), the People's Party (ÖVP), 60 seats (32·06%), the Freedom Party (FPÖ), 33 seats (16·63%) and the Greens (VGÖ), 10 seats (4·78%). The Federal Council *(Bundesrat)* has 63 members appointed by the 9 states for the duration of the individual State Assemblies' terms; in 1991 the ÖVP held 29 seats, the SPÖ 30 and the FPÖ 5.

The head of government is a Federal Chancellor, who is appointed by the President from the party winning the most seats in National Council elections. The Chancellor nominates a Vice-Chancellor and other Ministers for the President to appoint to a Council of Ministers which the Chancellor leads.

Federal President: Dr Kurt Waldheim (elected 8 June 1986; took office 8 July).
Presidential elections were due in April 1992.

The coalition government was formed on 17 Dec. 1990 by the SPÖ and ÖVP and was composed in Nov. 1991, as follows:

Chancellor: Dr Franz Vranitzky. (SPÖ)
Vice Chancellor: Dr Erhard Busek (ÖVP). *Foreign Affairs:* Dr Alois Mock (ÖVP). *Economic Affairs:* Dr Wolfgang Schüssel (ÖVP). *Employment and Social Affairs:* Josef Hesoun (SPÖ). *Finance:* Ferdinand Lacina. *Federalism and Administrative Reform:* Jurgen Weiss. *Health, Sport and Consumer Protection:* Harald Ettl (SPÖ). *Interior:* Dr Franz Löschnak (SPÖ). *Justice:* Dr Nikolaus Michalek (Ind). *National Defence:* Dr Werner Fasslabend (ÖVP). *Agriculture and Forestry:* Dr Franz Fischler (ÖVP). *Environment, Youth and Family:* Ruth Feldgrill-Zankel (ÖVP). *Education and Arts:* Dr Rudolf Scholten (SPÖ). *Public Economy and Transport:* Dr Rudolf Streicher (SPÖ). *Science and Research:* Dr Erhard Busek (ÖVP). *Women's Affairs:* Johanna Dohnal (SPÖ). *Secretaries of State:* Dr Peter Jankowitsch (SPÖ; *Europe and Integration*); Dr Peter Kostelka (SPÖ; *Civil Service*); Dr Johannes Ditz (ÖVP; *Finance*); Dr Maria Fekter (ÖVP; *Construction and Tourism*).

National flag: Three horizontal stripes of red, white, red.
National anthem: Land der Berge, Land am Strome ('Land of mountains, land on the river'; words by Paula Preradović; tune attributed to Mozart).

The official language is German.

State and local government. Each state *(Land)* has its assembly. At the elections of Oct. 1991 in Styria the ÖVP gained 26 seats, the SPÖ 21 and the FPÖ 9. In Upper Austria the ÖVP gained 26 seats, the SPÖ 19 and the FPÖ 11. In Vienna in Nov. 1991 the SPÖ gained 52 seats, the FPÖ 23, the ÖVP 18 and the Green Alternative 7.

Every community has a Council, which chooses one of its members to be head of the Community (burgomaster) and a committee for the administration and execution of its resolutions.

DEFENCE. Conscription is for a 6-month period, with liability for 60 days reservist refresher training spread over 15 years.

Army. The Army consists of an alert force *(Bereitschaftstruppe)*, mainly the 1st Armoured Division organized in 3 armoured infantry brigades; 1 air-missile and mountain battalion; field units with 3 artillery, 2 anti-aircraft, 1 anti-tank and 2 engineering battalions; and territorial troops, comprising 26 regiments and security companies. Strength was (1992) 38,000 (20,000 conscripts).

Army Aviation. *(Heeresfliegerkräfte):* The Division comprises 10 squadrons with about 4,500 personnel and about 200 aircraft, organized in three Aviation Regiments each of which including air defence battalions. PC-7 Turbo-trainers are also in service. Some 24 Draken interceptors equip 2 squadrons of a surveillance wing responsible for defence of Austrian airspace and a fighter-bomber wing of two squadrons operates SAAB 105s. Helicopters equip six squadrons for transport/support, communications, observation, search and rescue duties. Types in service include 24 Alouette III, 12 OH-58 Kiowas and 42 Agusta-Bell AB.204, AB.206 and AB.212s. Fixed-wing transports comprise two Skyvans, 12 Turbo-Porters and a government-owned BAe 146.

INTERNATIONAL RELATIONS. Following the peace treaty signed with France, the USSR, the UK and the USA in May 1955, the National Assembly adopted a statute of permanent neutrality in Oct. 1955.

Membership. Austria is a member of UN, OECD and EFTA. With Czechoslovakia, Hungary, Italy and Yugoslavia, Austria was an inaugural member of the Pentagonale meeting on economic and political co-operation in July 1990. Poland adhered in May 1991 and the group was renamed 'Hexagonal'.

Austria has applied for EC membership.

ECONOMY

Policy. In 1991 some 50% of production derived from the state-owned or state-protected sector, but there is a partial privatization programme in anticipation of EC membership.

Budget. The budget for calendar years provided revenue and expenditure (ordinary and extraordinary) as follows (in 1m. schilling):

	1985	1986	1987	1988	1989	1990 [1]
Revenue	372,895	391,675	409,556	451,343	477,958	501,859
Expenditure	464,673	498,390	514,461	517,824	540,664	564,736

[1] Estimates.

External debt. The budgetary external debt was (1990) 135,359m. schilling.

Currency. The unit of currency is the *schilling* (ATS) of 100 *groschen*. The schilling is linked to the German Mark at DM1 = 7 schillings. All restrictions on foreign currency transactions were abolished by Nov. 1991. The rate of exchange in March 1992, £1 = 20·27 *schilling*, US$1 = 11·54 *schilling*.

Banking and Finance. The National Bank of Austria, opened on 2 Jan. 1923, was taken over by the German Reichsbank on 17 March 1938. It was re-established on 3 July 1945. Its *President* is Maria Schaumayer. In Dec. 1990 foreign exchange amounted to 92,231m. and note circulation to 119,264m. schilling. Bank accounts are anonymous for Austrians, but foreign depositors of all but small amounts must declare their identity. There were 65 foreign banks operating in 1991.

Principal banks with total assets (in 1m. schilling 1990): Creditanstalt-Bankverein, 459,209; Girozentrale und Bank der Österreichischen Sparkassen (the central institution for savings banks), 308,490; Zentralsparkasse und Kommerzialbank, 254,563; Österreichische Nationalbank, 241,351; Österreichische Länderbank, 227,673; Österreichische Kontrollbank, 215,692; Bank für Arbeit und Wirtschaft, 192,210; Bank der Österreichische Postsparkasse, 183,045; Raiffeisen Zentralbank Österreich, 180,575; Die Erste Österreichische Spar-Casse-Bank, 160,744;

Österreichische Volksbanken, 63,370; Bank für Oberösterreich und Salzburg (Oberbank), 57,125; Raiffeisen Bausparkasse, 47,831; Österreichische Investitions-kredit, 47,610; Österreichische Credit-Institut, 41,059. The state has a 51% stake in Creditanstalt-Landverein, Zentralsparkasse und Kommerzialbank and Öster-reichische Länderbank were merged in Oct. 1991. The state retains a 26% stake in the former and a 25% stake in the latter.

There is a stock exchange in Vienna.

Weights and Measures. The metric system is in force.

ENERGY AND NATURAL RESOURCES

Electricity. In 1990 there were 8 nationalised electricity supply companies. Electric energy produced (1m. kwh.): 1990, 50,410. Supply 220 volts; 50 Hz.

Oil. The commercial production of petroleum began in the early 1930s. Production of crude oil (in tonnes): 1990, 1,148,593.

Gas. Production of natural gas (in 1,000 cu. metres): 1989, 148,593.

Minerals. The mineral production (in tonnes) was as follows:

	1989	1990		1989	1990
Lignite	2,065,815	2,477,710	Pig-iron	3,822,549	...
Iron ore	2,410,000	2,300,000	Raw steel	4,717,596	291,448
Lead and zinc ore [1]	274,748	276,077	Rolled steel	3,731,810	718,905
Raw magnesite [1]	1,204,942	1,179,162	Gypsum	805,654	752,542

[1] Including recovery from slag.

Austria is one of the world's largest sources of high-grade graphite. Production (in tonnes): 1990, 22,705.

Agriculture. In 1990 the total area cultivated amounted to 3,500,298 ha (estimate). The chief products (area in hectares, yield in tonnes) were as follows:

	1988		1989		1990	
	Area	Yield	Area	Yield	Area	Yield
Wheat	291,938	1,559,993	278,068	1,362,951	278,226	1,404,468
Rye	87,889	355,888	91,019	381,188	93,041	396,355
Barley	292,384	1,366,424	291,876	1,421,645	292,424	1,520,554
Oats	69,145	273,067	67,150	249,063	61,956	244,197
Potatoes	33,115	1,001,044	32,395	845,466	31,760	793,537

Farmers are subsidized through the price mechanism.

Livestock (1990): Cattle, 2,583,914; pigs, 3,687,981; sheep, 308,312; goats, 37,343; horses, 49,270; poultry, 13,139,152.

Forestry. Forested area in 1988, 3·2m. ha (46% of the land area) of which 75% coniferous. Felled timber, in cu. metres: 1989, 13,822; 1990, 15,710,585.

INDUSTRY. On 26 July 1946 the Austrian parliament passed a government bill, nationalizing some 70 industrial concerns. As from 17 Sept. 1946 ownership of the 3 largest commercial banks, most oil-producing and refining companies and the principal firms in the following industries devolved upon the Austrian state: River navigation; coal extraction; non-ferrous mining and refining; iron-ore mining; pig-iron and steel production; manufacture of iron and steel products, including structural material, machinery, railroad equipment and repairs, and shipbuilding; electrical machinery and appliances. Six companies supplying electric power were nationalized in accordance with a law of 26 March 1947.

Production of refined sugar was 422,877 tonnes in 1989.

In 1990, 9,080 industrial establishments (including 1,985 sawmills) employed 555,287 persons, producing a value of 774,467m. schillings (excluding value added tax).

Labour. In June 1991 there were 3·00m. employed persons; the unemployment rate was 4·7%. There were 55,888 job vacancies.

The number of foreigners who may be employed in Austria is limited to 10% of the potential workforce.

FOREIGN ECONOMIC RELATIONS

Commerce. Imports and exports are as follows (excluding coined gold):

	Imports			Exports		
	1988	1989	1990	1988	1989	1990
Quantity (1,000 tonnes)	40,974	41,829	43,713	20,038	20,980	22,259
Value (1m. sch.)	451,442	514,680	556,234	383,213	429,310	466,067

The total trade between Austria and UK (British Department of Trade returns, in £1,000 sterling):

	1987	1988	1989	1990	1991
Imports to UK	781,986	824,616	933,971	957,789	916,265
Exports and re-exports from UK	463,187	509,991	598,099	705,850	766,735

Tourism. Tourism is an important industry. In 1990, 19,406 hotels and boarding-houses had a total of 650,559 beds available; 19,011,397 foreigners visited Austria; of these 935,475 came from the UK and 885,337 from the USA. Revenue was 133,600m. schillings.

COMMUNICATIONS

Roads. On 31 Dec. 1990 federal roads had a total length of 11,828 km, 1,447 km autobahn; provincial roads, 26,000 km. On 31 Dec. 1990 there were registered 4,239,784 motor vehicles, including 2,991,284 passenger cars, 252,504 lorries, 386,438 tractors and 339,775 trailers.

Railways. The major railways are nationalized. Length of route in 1991, 5,782 km, of which 3,231 km were electrified. There are also 19 private railways with a total length of 567 km. Passengers in 1990 numbered 168·4m., and 62·6m. tonnes of freight were carried.

Civil Aviation. Austrian Airlines is being privatized. In April 1990 the state's stake was reduced to 51·9%. Austria has 6 airports in Vienna (Schwechat), Linz, Salzburg, Graz, Klagenfurt and Innsbruck. In 1990, 125,094 commercial aircraft and 7,375,069 passengers arrived and departed at Austrian airports; 65,277 tonnes of freight, 14,518 tonnes of transit freight and 6,950 tonnes of mail were handled.

Shipping. Austria has no sea frontiers, but the Danube is an important waterway. Goods traffic (in tonnes): 9,145,423 in 1989; 8,140,289 in 1990. Ore and metal, coal and coke and iron ore comprise in bulk more than two-thirds of these cargoes. The Danube Steamship Co. (DDSG) is the main Austrian shipping company.

Telecommunications. All postal, telegraph and telephone services are run by the State. In 1990 there were 3,223,161 telephone main connections.

The 'Österreichische Rundfunk' transmits 2 national and 9 regional programmes. In the local area of Vienna there is an additional special service in English and French; there is also a 24 hour foreign service (short wave). Broadcasting is financed by licence payments and advertisements. There were 4·7m. registered listeners in Dec. 1990. 2 TV programmes are transmitted, (colour by PAL) with 2·68m. licences in Dec. 1990.

Cinemas (1990). There were 390 cinemas.

Newspapers (1990). There were 25 daily newspapers (7 of them in Vienna) and a circulation of 2·7m. of all Austrian daily newspapers.

JUSTICE, RELIGION, EDUCATION AND WELFARE

Justice. The Supreme Court of Justice *(Oberster Gerichtshof)* in Vienna is the highest court in the land. Besides there are 4 higher provincial courts *(Oberlandesgerichte)*, 21 provincial and district courts *(Landes- und Kreisgerichte)* and 206 local courts *(Bezirksgerichte)* (1990).

Religion. In 1981 there were 6,372,645 Roman Catholics (84·3%), 423,162 Protestants (5·6%), 228,475 others (3%), 452,039 without religious allegiance (6%) and 79,017 (1%) unknown. The Roman Catholic Church has 2 archbishoprics and 7 bishoprics. There were (1988) 60,000 Moslems in Austria.

Education (1989–90). There were in Austria 5,087 elementary and special schools with 68,442 teachers and 646,961 pupils. Of all kinds of secondary schools there were 1,505 with 485,483 pupils.

There were also 114 commercial academies with 36,570 students and 4,666 teachers. There were 275 schools of technical and industrial training (including schools of hotel management and catering) with 6,604 teachers and 66,850 pupils; 55 higher schools of women's professions (secondary level) with 14,343 pupils; 9 training colleges of social workers with 807 pupils. 120 trade schools had 13,228 pupils.

Austria has 12 universities and 6 colleges of arts maintained by the State: Universities at Vienna (3,231 teachers, 64,628 students), Graz (1,206 teachers, 23,098 students), Innsbruck (1,528 teachers, 20,259 students) and Salzburg (523 teachers, 10,036 students). There are also technical universities at Vienna (1,288 teachers, 18,323 students) and Graz (645 teachers, 9,741 students), a mining university at Leoben (151 teachers, 1,914 students), an agricultural university at Vienna (357 teachers, 5,774 students), a veterinary university at Vienna (172 teachers, 2,517 students), a commercial university at Vienna (297 teachers, 19,115 students), a university for social and economic sciences at Linz (404 teachers, 9,825 students) and a university for educational science at Klagenfurt (156 teachers, 3,078 students). There is an academy of fine arts at Vienna (159 teachers, 514 students), a college of applied arts at Vienna (265 teachers, 1,011 students), 3 colleges of music and dramatic art at Vienna (590 teachers, 2,120 students), 'Mozarteum' Salzburg (352 teachers, 1,358 students) and Graz (325 teachers, 1,205 students); the college for industrial design at Linz (124 teachers, 451 students).

Health and Welfare. In 1989 there were 24,895 doctors, 332 hospitals and 81,619 hospital beds. Maternity leave is for 2 years, and applies to mothers or fathers.

DIPLOMATIC REPRESENTATIVES

Of Austria in Great Britain (18 Belgrave Mews West, London, SW1X 8HU)
Ambassador: Dr Walter F. Magrutsch (accredited 11 Feb. 1988).

Of Great Britain in Austria (Jaurèsgasse 12, 1030 Vienna)
Ambassador: Terence Wood.

Of Austria in the USA (2343 Massachusetts Ave., NW, Washington, D.C., 20008)
Ambassador: Dr Friedrich Hoess (accredited 21 Dec. 1988).

Of the USA in Austria (Boltzmanngasse, 16, A-1091 Vienna)
Ambassador: Roy M. Huffington.

Of Austria to the United Nations
Ambassador: Dr Peter Hohenfellner (accredited 24 Feb. 1988).

Further Reading

Statistical Information: The Austrian Central Statistical Office was founded in 1829. *Address:* Hintere Zollamtsstrasze 2b, 1033 Vienna. *President:* Mag. Erich Bader.

Main publications:
  Statistisches Handbuch für die Republik Österreich. New Series from 1950. Annually
  Statistische Nachrichten. Monthly
  Beiträge zur österreichischen Statistik (1,025 vols.)
  Statistik in Österreich 1918–1938. [Bibliography] Vienna, 1985
  Veröffentlichungen des Österr. Statist. Zentralamtes 1945-1985. [Bibliography] Vienna, *von der Direction der Administrativenstatistik zum Österreichischen Statistischen Zentralamt 1840–1990.* Vienna, 1990

Bobek, H. (ed.) *Atlas der Republik Österreich.* 3 vols. Vienna, 1961 ff.
Fitzmaurice, J., *Austrian Politics and Society Today: in Defence of Austria.* London, 1990
Salt, D., *Austria.* [Bibliography] Oxford and Santa Barbara, 1986
Sotriffer, K., *Greater Austria: 100 Years of Intellectual and Social Life from 1800 to the Present Time.* Vienna, 1982
Sully, M. A., *A Contemporary History of Austria.* London, 1990

National library: Österreichische Nationalbibliothek, Josefsplatz, 1015 Vienna. *Director General:* Dr Magda Strebl.

BAHAMAS

Capital: Nassau
Population: 255,000 (1990)
GNP per capita: US$11,370 (1989)

Commonwealth of The Bahamas

HISTORY. The Bahamas were discovered by Columbus in 1492 but the Spanish did not make a permanent settlement. British settlers arrived in the 17th century and it was occupied by Britain, except for a short period in the 18th century, until it gained independence. Internal self-government with cabinet responsibility was introduced on 7 Jan. 1964 and full independence achieved on 10 July 1973.

AREA AND POPULATION. The Commonwealth of The Bahamas consists of 700 islands and more than 1,000 cays off the south-east coast of Florida. They are the surface protuberances of two oceanic banks, the Little Bahama Bank and the Great Bahama Bank. Land area, 5,353 sq. miles (13,864 sq. km).

The areas and populations of the major islands are as follows:

	Sq. km	1990		Sq. km	1990
Grand Bahama	1,373	41,035	Exuma Islands	290	3,539
Abaco	1,681	10,061	San Salvador	163	539
Bimini Islands	23	1,638	Rum Cay	78	
Berry Islands	31	634	Long Island	448	3,107
New Providence	207	171,542	Ragged Island	23	89
Andros	5,957	8,155	Crooked Island	238	423
Eleuthera, Harbour Island			Acklins Island	389	428
and Spanish Wells	518	9,300	Mayguana	110	308
Cat Islands	388	1,678	Inagua Islands	1,671	985

The capital is Nassau on New Providence Island (135,437 inhabitants in 1980) and the only other large town is Freeport (24,423) on Grand Bahama. About 13% of the population were (1980) of British extraction, the rest being of African and mixed descent.

Vital statistics, 1987: Births, 4,018; deaths, 1,212 (excluding still-births); marriages, 1,830. Expectation of life was 68 years in 1989.

CLIMATE. Winters are mild and summers pleasantly warm. Most rain falls in May, June, Sept. and Oct., and thunderstorms are frequent in summer. Rainfall amounts vary over the islands from 30" (750 mm) to 60" (1,500 mm). Nassau. Jan. 71°F (21·7°C), July 81°F (27·2°C). Annual rainfall 47" (1,179 mm).

CONSTITUTION AND GOVERNMENT. The Commonwealth of The Bahamas is a free and democratic sovereign state. Executive power rests with Her Majesty the Queen, who appoints a Governor-General to represent her, advised by a Cabinet whom he appoints. There is a bicameral legislature. The Senate comprises 16 members all appointed by the Governor-General, 9 on the advice of the Prime Minister, 4 on the advice of the Leader of the Opposition, and 3 after consultation with both of them. The House of Assembly consists of 49 members elected from single-member constituencies for a maximum term of 5 years. At the general election of 19 June 1987, the Progressive Liberal Party obtained 31 seats, the Free National Movement 16 seats and 2 independents.

Governor-General: Sir Henry Taylor.

The Cabinet in Nov. 1991 was composed as follows:

Prime Minister, Tourism: Rt. Hon. Sir Lynden O. Pindling, KCMG.
Deputy Prime Minister, Foreign Affairs and Public Personnel: Sir Clement T. Maynard. *Finance:* Paul L. Adderley. *National Security:* Darrell E. Rolle. *Employ-*

ment and Immigration: Alfred T. Maycock. *Works and Lands:* Philip M. Bethel. *Ministry of Youth, Sports and Community Affairs:* Dr Norman R. Gay. *Minister of Housing and National Insurance:* George W. Mackey. *Health:* E. Charles Carter. *Education:* Dr Bernard J. Nottage. *Transport:* Peter J. Bethell. *Attorney-General:* Sean G. A. McWeeny. *Agriculture, Trade and Industry:* Perry G. Christie. *Local Government:* Leo Marvin Pinder. *Consumer Affairs:* Vincent A. Peet.

National flag: Three horizontal stripes of aquamarine, gold, aquamarine, with a black triangle on the hoist.

National anthem: March on, Bahamaland (words and tune by T. Gibson).

DEFENCE. The Royal Bahamian Defence Force is a maritime force tasked with naval patrols and protection duties in the extensive waters of the archipelago. Equipment comprises 3 fast patrol craft, 15 smaller patrol craft and high speed craft for shallow water duty and 1 transport. There are 3 Jetstream Commander and 2 Cessna twin-engined light reconnaissance aircraft. Personnel in 1991 numbered 750, and the base is at Coral Harbour on New Providence Island.

INTERNATIONAL RELATIONS

Membership. The Commonwealth of The Bahamas is a member of the UN, OAS, the Commonwealth, CARICOM and is an ACP state of the EEC.

ECONOMY

Budget (in B$):

	1987	1988	1989	1990
Revenue	468,849,335	472,123,389	555,279,397	581,489,340
Expenditure	478,199,453	514,941,790	564,214,210	583,080,745

The main sources of revenue were customs duties and receipts from fees, post office and public utilities.

Currency. The unit of currency is the *Bahamian dollar* (BSD) of 100 *cents.* Notes: B$0.50, 1, 3, 5, 10, 20, 50, 100; coins: 1, 5, 10, 15, 25, 50 cents, $1, 2, 5. American currency is generally accepted. In March 1992, £1 = B$1.76; US$1 = B$1.00.

Banking and Finance. The Central Bank of The Bahamas was established in June 1974. Its Governor is James Smith. At June 1989, it had assets of B$244·36m. and capital and reserves of B$55·76m. On 31 Dec. 1989 there were 391 institutions licensed to carry on banking and/or trust business under the Banks and Trust Companies Regulation Act. Of these, 274 were public institutions, 18 of which were designated by the Exchange Control Department as authorized agents or dealers; 116 were Eurocurrency branches of banks based abroad; 106 were subsidiaries of banks or other institutions based outside The Bahamas; and 34 were Bahamian-based or trust companies. There were 18 designated institutions by the Exchange Control Department as authorized dealers and agents. The Bahamas Development Bank was established in 1974 and began operations in Jan. 1978. At June 1989 it had total assets of B$20·3m. and paid-up capital of B$7·25m.

The Post Office Savings Bank, 31 Dec. 1984, had deposits of B$2·7m.

Weights and Measures. The UK (Imperial) system is in force.

ENERGY AND NATURAL RESOURCES

Electricity. Electricity is provided primarily by The Bahamas Electricity Corporation in conjunction with a few private franchises in the Family Islands. As at 31 Dec. 1987, total generated capacity was 306·1 mw; total units generated for the year ending 30 Sept. 1989, 730 mwh. Supply 110/220 volts; 60 Hz.

Agriculture. In 1988 agricultural production was B$28·83m. (1973, B$17·5m.). Chicken and poultry production was estimated at 15·2m. lb in 1988, (16·9m. lb in 1987). Egg production (1988) declined to 3·6m. dozen. Production of sheep, goats and pigs in 1988: 129 sheep, 165 goats and 2,236 pigs were slaughtered. Beef production increased, with 27 beef cattle slaughtered.

Total agricultural production was valued at B$28·8m. in 1988. Production, 1988 (in 1,000 tonnes): Sugar-cane, 240; vegetables, 27; fruit, 14.

The quantity of meat derived from livestock in 1988 was: Mutton, 4,441 lb; goat meat, 6,559 lb; beef, 13,000 lb; pork, 158,770 lb.

Livestock (1988): Cattle, 5,000; sheep, 40,000; goats, 19,000; pigs, 20,000; poultry, 1m.

Fisheries. In 1988 the total catch was valued at B$33·3m.

INDUSTRY. 2 industrial sites, one in New Providence and the other in Grand Bahama, have been developed as part of an industrialization programme. Industries include garment manufacturing, ice, furniture, purified water, plastic containers, perfumes, industrial gases, jewellery, alcoholic beverages, pharmaceuticals, aragonite mining and solar salt production.

Trade Unions. In 1986 there were 36 unions, the largest being The Bahamas Hotel Catering and Allied Workers' Union (5,000 members).

FOREIGN ECONOMIC RELATIONS

Commerce. In 1988 imports (excluding bullion and specie) were valued at B$2,243,258,474, and exports at B$691,859,246.

The principal exports in 1988 were chemicals (B$339,887,053), mineral fuels, lubricants and related materials (B$278,533,075), food and live animals (B$29,878,396) and beverages and tobacco (B$23,837,184). Exports of spiny lobster and snappers in 1988 were B$26,954,490 (B$24·6m. in 1987) and of rum, B$23,456,387. Exports in 1988 were mainly to the USA (B$1,701,667,649).

The principal imports in 1988 were mineral fuels, lubricants and related materials (B$1,261,840,604), machinery and transport equipment (B$216,895,718) and manufactured goods (B$204,129,808). Imports of fish in 1987 were B$4,971,284. Imports in 1988 were mainly from the USA (B$896,833,048).

Total trade in £1,000 sterling, between Bahamas and UK (British Department of Trade returns):

	1987	1988	1989	1990	1991
Imports to UK	15,943	24,781	17,681	15,053	37,142
Exports and re-exports from UK	27,063	20,708	22,543	22,917	19,631

Tourism. Tourism is the most important industry. In 1989 there were 3,398,258 foreign arrivals, and tourist spending came to B$1,200m.

COMMUNICATIONS

Roads. There are 245 miles of paved roads in New Providence, and approximately 885 miles in Grand Bahama and the Family Islands. In 1987, 74,062 motor vehicles were registered. There are no railroads.

Civil Aviation. There are international airports at Nassau and Freeport (Grand Bahama Island). Scheduled flights are operated by Air Canada (Montreal and Toronto to Nassau); Bahamasair (Nassau to Miami, Newark, Orlando and Tampa); Delta Airlines (Nassau to Dallas, Fort Lauderdale, Atlanta, Boston and New York); Eastern Airlines (Nassau to Miami, Freeport to Miami); British Airways (London to Nassau); Midway Airlines (Nassau to Fort Lauderdale and Chicago); Pan-Am (Nassau to New York and Freeport to Miami); Aero Coach (Freeport to Fort Lauderdale and West Palm Beach); Carnival Airlines (Nassau to Miami and Fort Lauderdale). There are 58 airstrips on the various Family Islands. During 1986, 1,343,324 passengers landed at Nassau from 61,431 aircraft arrivals. At Freeport in 1986, 618,555 passengers landed from 33,157 aircraft arrivals.

Shipping. In 1987, 2,279 cruise liners cleared Nassau carrying 1,540,000 passengers. In 1984, 542 cargo vessels discharged 757,737 tons of cargo at Nassau. There are indirect cargo services with UK and Canada via the USA and passenger services with the USA only.

Telecommunications. In 1985 there were 127 post offices. New Providence and most of the other major islands have automatic telephone systems in operation, interconnected by an extensive multi-channel radio network, while local distribution within the islands is by overhead and underground cables. The total number of telephones in use at 31 Dec. 1987 was 119,061. International telecommunications service is provided by a submarine cable system to Florida, USA, and an INTELSAT Standard 'A' Earth Station. International operator assisted and direct dialling telephone services are available to all major countries. There is an automatic Telex system and a packet switching system for data transmission, and land mobile and marine telephone services. The Broadcasting Corporation of The Bahamas is a commercial company which operates radio broadcasting stations at Nassau and Freeport and runs Bahamas Television. In 1991 there were 50,000 television and 0·2m. radio receivers. TV colour is by NTSC.

Cinemas (1990). There is 1 cinema.

Newspapers (1988). There are 2 daily and 1 weekly newspapers in Nassau.

JUSTICE, RELIGION, EDUCATION AND WELFARE

Justice (1986). 32,878 cases (traffic, 11,334; criminal, 17,970; civil, 2,178; domestic, 1,396) were dealt with in the magistrates' court, and civil, 1,561; divorce, 516; criminal, 200 in the Supreme Court. The strength of the police force (1988) was 1,665 officers and other ranks.

Religion. Over 94% of the population is Christian, with 26% being Roman Catholic, 21% Anglican and 48% other Protestants.

Education. Education is under the jurisdiction of the Ministry of Education and Culture. In 1988–89 there were 226 schools, and of these, 185 are fully maintained by Government and 41 are independent schools. Total school enrolment, 59,961. There are 35 government-owned schools in New Providence and 150 on the Family Islands. 26 independent schools are located on New Providence and 15 on the Family Islands. 268 students attended 5 special schools, 3 on New Providence and 2 on Grand Bahama. Free education is available in ministry schools in New Providence and the Family Islands. Courses lead to The Bahamas Junior Certificate and the General Certificate of Secondary Education (GCSE). Independent schools provide education at primary, secondary and higher levels.

The 4 institutions offering higher education are: The Government-sponsored College of The Bahamas, established in 1974; the University of the West Indies (regional), affiliated with The Bahamas since 1960; the Bahamas Hotel Training College, sponsored by the Ministry of Education and the hotel industry; and the Industrial Training Programme established to provide basic skills. Several schools of continuing education offer secretarial and academic courses. The Government-operated Princess Margaret Hospital offers a nursing course at two levels.

Health. In 1988 there was a government general hospital (454 beds) and a psychiatric/geriatric care centre (457 beds) in Nassau, and a hospital in Freeport (74 beds). The Family Islands, comprising 20 health districts, had 13 health centres, 38 main clinics and 52 satellite clinics. There was 1 private hospital (24 beds) in Nassau.

DIPLOMATIC REPRESENTATIVES

Of The Bahamas in Great Britain (10 Chesterfield St., London, W1X 8AH)
High Commissioner: Dr Patricia Rodgers.

Of Great Britain in The Bahamas (Bitco Bldg., East St., Nassau)
High Commissioner: M. E. J. Gore, CBE.

Of The Bahamas in the USA (2220 Massachusetts Ave., NW, Washington, D.C., 20008)
Ambassador: Margaret MacDonald, CVO, CBE.

Of the USA in The Bahamas (Mosmar Bldg., Queen St., Nassau)
Ambassador: Chic Hecht.

Of The Bahamas to the United Nations
Ambassador: James B. Moultrie.

Further Reading

Bahamas Handbook and Businessman's Annual (Annual)
Albury, P., *The Story of The Bahamas*. London, 1975.—*Paradise Island Story*. London, 1984
Barrett, P. J. H., *Grand Bahama*. London, 1982
Boultbee, P. G., *Bahamas*. [Bibliography] Oxford and Santa Barbara, 1989
Craton, M. A., *A History of The Bahamas*. London, 1962
Hughes, C. A., *Race and Politics in The Bahamas*. Univ. of Queensland Press, 1981
Hunte, G., *The Bahamas*. London, 1975
Stevenson, C. St. J., *The Bahamas Reference Annual*. Annual

Library: Nassau Public Library.

BAHRAIN

Capital: Manama
Population: 486,000 (1990)
GNP per capita: US$6,610 (1987)

Dawlat al Bahrayn

(State of Bahrain)

HISTORY. Treaties with Britain of 1882 and 1892 were replaced by a treaty of friendship which was signed on 15 Aug. 1971. Under the earlier treaties Britain had been responsible for Bahrain's defence and foreign relations. On the same day the State of Bahrain declared its independence.

AREA AND POPULATION. The State of Bahrain forms an archipelago of about 33 small islands in the Arabian Gulf, between the Qatar peninsula and the mainland of Saudi Arabia. The total area is about 265·5 sq. miles (687·75 sq. km). Bahrain ('Two Seas'), is 30 miles long and 10 miles wide (578 sq. km). It is connected by a causeway nearly 1·5 miles long, carrying a motor road, with the second largest island, Muharraq, 4 miles long and 1 mile wide, to the north-east, and by a causeway with Sitra, an island 3 miles long and 1 mile wide, to the east. In Nov. 1986 a causeway linking Bahrain with Saudi Arabia was officially opened. Other islands are Umm Al-Nassan, 3 miles by 2 miles, and Jidda, 1 mile by 0·5 mile, both to the west; Nabih Saleh, to the east; the Hawar group of 16 small islands off Qatar, to the south-east, and several islets, some uninhabited. From Sitra oil pipelines and a causeway carrying a road extend out to sea for 3 miles to a deep-water anchorage. The islands are low-lying, the highest ground being a hill in the centre of Bahrain, 450 ft. (122·4 metres) high.

The population in 1981 (census) was 350,798. Estimate (1990) 486,000, including some 155,000 resident foreigners. The population is 83% urban. The majority of the people are Arabs. Expectation of life was 71 years in 1990, infant mortality was 14 per 1,000 live births; annual growth rate (1985–90), 3·7 per 1,000.

Arabic is the official language. English is widely used in business.

Manama, the capital of the state and the commercial centre, is situated at the northern end of the largest island and extends for 1·5 miles along the shore. It had a population, 1988, of 151,500 (1981 census, 108,684). Other towns are Muharraq, 1988, 78,000 (46,061); Jidhafs, 48,000 (7,232); Rifa'a, 28,150 (22,408); Isa Town (21,275) and Hidd (7,111).

CLIMATE. The climate is pleasantly warm between Dec. and March but from June to Sept. the conditions are very hot and humid. The period June to Nov. is virtually rainless. Bahrain. Jan. 66°F (19°C), July 97°F (36°C). Annual rainfall 5·2" (130 mm).

CONSTITUTION AND GOVERNMENT. A Constitution was ratified in June 1973 providing for a National Assembly of 30 members, popularly elected for a 4-year term, together with all members of the Cabinet (appointed by the Amir). Elections took place in Dec. 1973, but in Aug. 1975 the Amir dissolved the Assembly and has since ruled through the Cabinet alone.

Reigning Amir: The ruling family is the Al Khalifa, an Arab dynasty, who have been in power since 1782. The present Amir, HH Shaikh Isa bin Sulman Al-Khalifa (born 1933) succeeded on 2 Nov. 1961. *Crown Prince:* Shaikh Hamad bin Isa Al-Khalifa.

In 1991 the cabinet was composed as follows:

Prime Minister: Shaikh Khalifa bin Sulman Al-Khalifa (b. 1935).

Defence: Shaikh Khalifa bin Ahmed Al-Khalifa. *Transport:* Ibrahim Mohammed Hassan Homaidan. *Housing:* Shaikh Khalid bin Abdulla Al-Khalifa. *Information:* Tariq Abdulrahman Almoayed. *Education:* Dr Ali Fakhro. *Health:* Jawad Salim Al-Arrayed. *Justice and Islamic Affairs:* Shaikh Abdullah bin Khalid Al-Khalifa. *Labour and Social Affairs:* Shaikh Khalifa bin Sulman bin Mohammed Al-Khalifa. *Works, Power and Water:* Majid Jawad Al Jishi. *Interior:* Shaikh Mohammed bin Khalifa Al-Khalifa. *Foreign Affairs:* Shaikh Mohammed bin Mubarak Al-Khalifa. *Finance and National Economy:* Ibrahim Abdul-Karim. *Development and Industry:* Yousuf Ahmed Al-Shirawi. *Commerce and Agriculture:* Habib Ahmed Kassim. *Acting Minister of State for Cabinet Affairs:* Yousuf Ahmed Al-Shirawi. *Minister of State for Legal Affairs:* Dr Hussain Al Baharna.

National flag: Red, with white serrated vertical strip on hoist.
The *national anthem* has no words.

DEFENCE. An agreement with the USA of Oct. 1991 gives port facilities to the US Navy and provides for mutual manoeuvres.

Army. The Army consists of 1 brigade, 2 infantry and 1 tank battalion, 1 special forces battalion, 1 armoured car squadron, 2 artillery and 2 mortar batteries with a personnel strength of 6,000 (1992). Equipment includes 81 M-60A3 main battle tanks, 8 Saladin armoured cars, 22 AML-90 and 8 Ferret scout cars. There is a paramilitary police force of 6,000.

Navy. The Naval force consists of 2 West German-built missile corvettes with helicopter facilities, 4 fast missile craft and 7 fast patrol craft. Personnel in 1991 numbered 1,000. There is also a Coast Guard of 250 with 6 coastal patrol craft and 4 other vessels.

Air Force. An independent Air Force was created in 1985 as the successor to the Air Wing of the Army (Bahrain Defence Force). 1 fighter squadron operates 12 F-5E/F Tiger IIs, while a second unit has 16 F-16s. 3 MBB BO 105 helicopters are also in use as well as an S-70 VIP helicopter. Police and security forces both also operate helicopters. Personnel (1991) 450.

INTERNATIONAL RELATIONS

Membership. Bahrain is a member of UN, the Arab League, the Gulf Co-operation Council and OAPEC.

ECONOMY

Budget. The revenue of the State is derived from oil royalties and from customs duties, which are 10% *ad valorem* for luxury goods and 5% for essential goods. The exceptions are motor vehicles (20%); tobacco (30%); alcoholic beverages (100%); fresh fruit and vegetables (7%). Total revenues in 1988, BD 490m. (of which oil BD 252m.) and expenditure BD 365m.

On 2 Jan. 1958 Manama was declared a free transit port and the former 2% transit duty was abolished, but storage charges are levied.

Currency. The unit of currency is the *Bahraini dinar* (BHD), divided into 1,000 *fils*. The Bahrain currency board issues notes of 20, 10, 5 and 1 *dinars*, and 500 *fils*, and coins of 100, 50, 25, 10, 5 and 1 *fils*. Inflation was 0·9% in 1990. £1 = BD 0·66 in March 1992; US$1 = BD 0·38.

Banking and Finance. The Bahrain Monetary Agency has central banking powers. Since Nov. 1984 it has been responsible for licensing and monitoring the activities of money changers. There were (1988) 20 full commercial banks (including Bahrain Islamic Bank), 6 of which are locally incorporated and the rest branches of foreign banks. Total assets at 31 Dec. 1988, BD 2,184·9m. Two types of offshore banking units were operating in 1988: 15 locally incorporated banks (including 4 Islamic) with headquarters in Bahrain, and 50 branches of foreign banks. Total assets at 31 Dec. 1988 US$68,100m. There are 15 investment banks (3 Islamic), with assets of US$1,750m. in Dec. 1985. The state-owned Housing Bank provides financing for construction, development of real estate and reclamation of land.

Weights and Measures. The metric system of weights and measures is officially in use.

ENERGY AND NATURAL RESOURCES

Electricity. Production (1988) 2,996·1m. kwh. Supply 230 volts; 50 Hz.

Oil. In 1931 oil was discovered. Operations were conducted by the Bahrain Petroleum Co., registered in Canada but owned by US interests, under a concession granted by the Shaikh. Production of crude oil in 1991 was 2·10m. tonnes. A large oil refinery on Bahrain Island, besides treating crude oil produced locally, also processes oil from Saudi Arabia transported by pipeline.

In 1975 the Bahrain Government assumed a direct 60% interest in the Bahrain oilfield and related crude oil facilities of BAPCO.

Bahrain's proven oil reserves in 1988 were 150m. bbls.

Gas. There is an abundant supply of natural gas with known reserves of 7·1m. cu. ft. in 1987. Production, 1987, 252,431m. cu. ft. Bahrain's gas reserves are 100% government-owned.

Water. Water is obtained from artesian wells and desalination plants and there is a piped supply to Manama, Muharraq, Isa Town, Rifa'a and most villages. In 1987 total water production was about 60m. gallons per day; daily consumption 59·7m. gallons by Aug. 1987. A further desalination plant with a capacity of 10m. gallons per day was due on stream in 1988.

Agriculture. The 6-year agricultural plan, commissioned in 1982, aimed to increase food production from 6–16% of total domestic requirements and to improve conservation of natural water and irrigation techniques.

There are about 900 farms and small holdings (average 2·5 ha) operated by about 2,500 farmers who produce a wide variety of fruits (49,000 tonnes in 1988) and vegetables (12,000 tonnes in 1988). The major crop is alfalfa for animal fodder. 46,000 tonnes of dates were produced in 1990.

Livestock (1990): Cattle, 6,000; camels, 1,000; sheep, 8,000; goats, 16,000; poultry 1m.

Fisheries. The government operates a fleet of 2 large and 5 smaller trawlers. In 1987 total landings weighed 7,841·5 tonnes.

INDUSTRY. Bahrain is being developed as a major manufacturing state, the first important enterprise being the Aluminium Bahrain (ALBA), a company whose original shareholders included the Bahrain Government and British, Swedish, Federal German and US interests. In 1975, the government acquired a majority shareholding in the enterprise. The aluminium smelter operation is the largest non-oil industry in the Gulf; output, 1989, 187,000 tonnes. Ancillary industries developed around aluminium smelting include the production of aluminium powder. A plant producing aluminium alloys went on stream in 1987. The Gulf Aluminium Rolling Mill Company (GARMCO), a joint venture between Bahrain, Saudi Arabia, Kuwait, Iraq, Oman and Qatar, was inaugurated in Feb. 1986. The Arab Shipbuilding and Repair Yard (ASRY), commissioned in 1977, is now in service. The dry dock can handle up to 50 tankers (500,000 DWT each) annually. A US$207m. iron ore pelletizing plant was inaugurated in Dec. 1984 (output, 1985, 680,000 tonnes) and a US$400m. petrochemical complex started operations in 1985.

In addition to the traditional minor industries such as boat-building, weaving, pottery, etc., other modern industries have developed, which include electronics assembly and the production of building materials, furniture, syringes and other medical items, matches, asbestos pipes and plastics, foodstuffs and textiles.

The pearling industry for which Bahrain used to be famous has considerably declined.

Labour. Total work force in the private sector (estimate 1987) 85,979, of which 25·2% Bahraini. The non-national workforce (1987) was 79,550.

FOREIGN ECONOMIC RELATIONS. Totally foreign-owned companies have been permitted to register since 1991.

Commerce. In 1989 total imports were US$2,886 and total exports were US$2,869. In 1988 refined petroleum accounted for almost 78% of exports; crude oil accounted for 41·9% of merchandise imports.

The major non-oil imports in 1988 were machinery and transport, BD198·1m.; classified manufactured goods, including Alumina, BD111·5m.; chemicals, BD64·5m.; food and live animals, BD81·2m., and miscellaneous manufactured articles, BD78·2m. The chief sources of supply (in BD1,000) were UK (116,115); USA (62,566); Japan (58,850); Federal Republic of Germany (35,573), and Australia (33,615).

The chief non-oil exports in 1988 were classified manufactured goods, including aluminium, BD135·5m., and machinery and transport, BD31m. The main markets (in BD1m.) were Saudi Arabia (42·9); Japan (27·7); United Arab Emirates (26·3); USA (14·4), and Kuwait (11·3).

Import of arms and ammunition and telecommunication equipment is subject to special permission; the sale of alcoholic liquor is restricted and the import of cultured pearls is forbidden.

Total trade between Bahrain and UK (British Department of Trade returns, in £1,000 sterling):

	1987	1988	1989	1990	1991
Imports to UK	60,687	75,786	61,018	48,459	39,120
Exports and re-exports from UK	125,189	138,150	138,529	127,309	147,494

Tourism. More than 165,000 tourists from the Gulf area arrived in 1985.

COMMUNICATIONS

Roads. The 25 km causeway links Bahrain with Saudi Arabia. In 1987 there were 112,520 registered vehicles.

Civil Aviation. The airport, situated at Muharraq, can take the largest aircraft and is considered one of the most modern and efficient in the Middle East, used by 2,486,582 arriving and 2,512,882 departing passengers in 1987. British Airways, Gulf Air, Middle East Airlines, Pakistan International Airways, Qantas, Kuwait Airways, Air India International, Singapore Airlines, UTA, Saudi Arabian Airlines, KLM, Air Lanka, Cathay Pacific Airways, Iraqi Airways, Korean Airways, Philippine Airlines, Thai Airways International, Trans-Mediterranean Airways, Egyptair, Alia, Cyprus Airways, Ethiopia Airlines and Sudan Airways also operate to and from Bahrain. Bahrain International Airport is the Arabian Gulf's main air communication centre.

Shipping. Bahrain's traditional position as the entrepôt of the Southern Gulf has been supplemented by the development of Mina Sulman—the new modern harbour—as a free transit and industrial area. Local and international companies have developed industries in this area, which is also used as a storage centre for firms selling elsewhere in the Gulf. The facilities offered by Mina Sulman include engineering and ship repairing yards; the Basrec slipway is probably the largest between Rotterdam and Hong Kong.

Telecommunications. There were, at Dec. 1987, 120,000 telephones. Radio Bahrain is government controlled, Bahrain Television part-commercial. In 1991 there were 0·25m. radio and 185,952 TV receivers (colour by PAL).

Cinemas. There were 6 cinemas in 1987.

Newspapers. In 1988 there were several Arabic newspapers, and 1 English language daily newspaper, published in Manama.

JUSTICE, RELIGION, EDUCATION AND WELFARE

Justice. Criminal law is codified, based on English jurisprudence.

Religion. Islam is the State religion. In 1981 85% of the population were Moslem (60% Shi'ite in 1990) and 7·3% Christian. There are also Jewish, Bahai, Hindu and Parsee minorities.

Education. Government schools provide free education from primary to technical college level. There were, in 1987, 143 schools for boys and girls with 4,967 teachers and 88,132 pupils. In 1984, 5 boys' general and commercial schools had 2,177 pupils; 3 boys' industrial schools at secondary level, had 1,306 pupils. In addition there were 7 private schools. The Men's Teacher Training College (established 1966) and the Women's Teacher Training College (established 1967) give 2-year courses. In 1987, 1,665 Bahrainis were in higher education abroad. The Gulf Technical College opened in Bahrain in Sept. 1968 and Bahrain University in 1978. In 1987, 6,922 adult education centres were open throughout Bahrain. Literacy was claimed to be 77·4% of the adult population in 1990.

Health. There is a free medical service for all residents of Bahrain. In 1987, there were 4 government hospitals and 19 health centres, an American mission hospital, an oil company hospital, a military hospital and an international hospital.

Social Security. In Oct. 1976, pensions, sickness and industrial injury benefits, unemployment, maternity and family allowances were established.

DIPLOMATIC REPRESENTATIVES

Of Bahrain in Great Britain (98 Gloucester Rd., London, SW7 4AU)
Ambassador: Karim Ebrahim Al-Shakar.

Of Great Britain in Bahrain (21 Government Ave., P.O. Box 114, Manama, 306)
Ambassador: vacant.

Of Bahrain in the USA (3502 International Dr., NW, Washington D.C., 20008)
Ambassador: Ghazi Mohammed Al-Gosaibi.

Of the USA in Bahrain (Road No. 3119, P.O. Box 26431, Manama)
Ambassador: Charles W. Hostler.

Of Bahrain to the United Nations
Ambassador: Muhammad Abdul Ghaffar.

Further Reading

Bahrain Business Directory. Manama (annual)
Statistical and General Information: Ministry of Information, PO Box 253, Manama
Statistical Abstract. Central Statistics Organisation (annual)

Lawson, F. H., *Bahrain: The Modernization of Autocracy*. Boulder, 1989
Rumaihi, M. G., *Bahrain: Social and Political Change since the First World War*. New York and London, 1976
Unwin, P. T. H., *Bahrain*. [Bibliography]. London and Santa Barbara, 1984

BANGLADESH

Capital: Dhaka
Population: 108m. (1991)
GNP per capita: US$180 (1989)

Gana Prajatantri Bangladesh

(People's Republic of Bangladesh)

HISTORY. The state was formerly the Eastern Province of Pakistan. In Dec. 1970 Sheikh Mujibur Rahman's Awami League Party gained 167 seats out of 300 at the Pakistan general election and immediately made known their wish for greater independence for the then Eastern Province. Martial law was imposed following disturbances in Dhaka, and civil war developed in March 1971. The war ended in Dec. 1971 and Bangladesh was proclaimed an independent state.

For developments between Jan. 1975 and March 1982, *see* THE STATESMAN'S YEAR-BOOK, 1986–87, pp. 186–187.

On 23 March 1982 there was a bloodless military coup, by which Lieut.-Gen. Hossain Mohammad Ershad became chief martial law administrator. President Sattar was deposed. The Constitution was suspended and parliament ceased to function. Assanuddin Chowdhury was sworn in as civilian president on 27 March. Lieut.-Gen. Ershad assumed the presidency on 11 Dec. 1983. He was re-elected on 15 Oct. 1986.

Martial law ended on 10 Nov. 1986. The Constitution (Seventh Amendment) Act restored the constitution but protected the legality of President Ershad's decrees under martial law.

Following popular unrest President Ershad declared a state of emergency on 27 Nov. 1990, but was forced to resign on 4 Dec. and arrested on 12 Dec.

AREA AND POPULATION. Bangladesh is bounded west and north by India, east by India and Burma and south by the Bay of Bengal. The area is 55,598 sq. miles (143,998 sq. km). At the 1981 census the population was enumerated as 87,120,000. An adjustment for under-enumeration produced a revised figure of 89,912,000 (46·3m. male, 14·09m. urban). Preliminary results of the 1991 census, 108m. In 1987 the birth-rate was 33·3 per 1,000 population; death-rate, 11·85; marriage rate, 11·6; infant mortality, 111 per 1,000 live births. Growth rate was 2·5% in 1990. Life expectancy, 1989, 51 years. The capital is Dhaka (population, 1987, 4·77m. The other major cities are Chittagong (1·84m.), Khulna (860,000) and Rajshahi (430,000). The country is administratively divided into 4 divisions, subdivided into 21 regions of 64 districts:

		Area (sq. km)	Population 1981			Area (sq. km)	Population 1981
Dinajpur	(3 districts)	6,566	3,198,000	Kushtia	(3)	3,440	2,292,000
Rangpur	(5)	9,593	6,510,000	Jessore	(4)	6,573	4,020,000
Bogra	(2)	3,888	2,728,000	Khulna	(3)	12,168	4,329,000
Rajshahi	(4)	9,456	5,270,000	Barisal	(4)	7,299	4,667,000
Pabna	(2)	4,732	3,424,000	Patuakhali	(2)	4,095	1,843,000
Rajshahi division		*34,238*	*21,132,000*	Khulna division		*33,575*	*17,151,000*
Tangail	(1)	3,403	2,444,000	Sylhet	(4)	12,718	5,656,000
Mymensingh	(3)	9,668	6,568,000	Comilla	(3)	6,599	6,881,000
Jamalpur	(2)	3,349	2,452,000	Noakhali	(3)	5,460	3,816,000
Dhaka	(6)	7,470	10,014,000	Chittagong	(2)	7,457	5,491,000
Faridpur	(5)	6,882	4,764,000	Chittagong Hill Tracts	(2)	8,679	580,000
Dhaka division		*30,772*	*26,242,000*	Bandarban	(1)	4,501	171,000
				Chittagong division		*45,414*	*22,595,000*

The official language is Bangla (Bengali). English is also in use for official, legal and commercial purposes.

CLIMATE. A tropical monsoon climate with heat, extreme humidity and heavy rainfall in the monsoon season, from June to Oct. The short winter season (Nov.-Feb.) is mild and dry. Rainfall varies between 50" (1,250 mm) in the west to 100" (2,500 mm) in the south-east and up to 200" (5,000 mm) in the north-east. Dhaka. Jan. 66°F (19°C), July 84°F (28·9°C). Annual rainfall 81" (2,025 mm). Chittagong. Jan. 66°F (19°C), July 81°F (27·2°C). Annual rainfall 108" (2,831 mm).

CONSTITUTION AND GOVERNMENT. Bangladesh is a unitary republic. The Constitution came into force on 16 Dec. 1972 and provides for a parliamentary democracy.

The head of state is the *President*, directly elected by parliament every five years. He appoints a *Vice-President*.

There is a *Council of Ministers* to assist and advise the President. The President appoints the Prime Minister from among the members of Parliament who appears to him to command the support of a majority of members; he also appoints the other ministers.

Parliament has one chamber of 300 members directly elected every 5 years by citizens over 18. There are 30 seats reserved for women members elected by Parliament.

At the elections of Feb. 1991 the Bangladesh National Party (BNP) won 140 seats, the Awami League 95, the Jatiya Party (led by Hossain Ershad) 35 and Jamit-e-Islami 18. A referendum of Sept. 1991 was in favour of abandoning the executive presidential system and opted for a parliamentary system. Turn-out was low. Abdur Rahman Biswas (b. 1926; BNP) was elected president by 172 votes to 92 against a single opponent.

Prime Minister: Khaleda Zia (b. 1944; BNP; sworn in 19 Sept. 1991).

National flag: Bottle green with a red disc in the centre.

National anthem: Amar Sonar Bangla, ami tomay bhalobashi (My golden Bengal, I love you). Words by Rabindranath Tagore.

Local government: Elections were held in March 1990. In Nov. 1991 the government dismissed all 460 elected mayors and dissolved opposition-controlled local councils.

DEFENCE. The supreme command of defence services is vested in the President.

Army. There are 6 infantry divisional headquarters, with 14 infantry brigades, and 2 armoured and 6 artillery regiments, and 6 engineer battalions. Strength (1991) 93,000, with an additional 55,000 paramilitary volunteers, including an armed police reserve and the Bangladesh Rifles (border guard). Equipment includes 30 Soviet T-54 and 20 Chinese Type-59 tanks.

Navy. Naval bases are at Chittagong, Kaptai, Khulna and Dhaka. The fleet comprises 2 new Chinese-built missile-armed frigates, 3 ex-British frigates, 8 Chinese-built fast missile craft, 4 Chinese-built fast torpedo boats, 2 ex-Yugoslav 200-tonne patrol craft, 8 ex-Chinese 155-tonne fast gunboats, 8 other patrol craft, 5 locally built 70-tonne river gunboats, 1 oiler, 1 repair vessel and 12 auxiliaries. The manpower of the Navy in 1991 was 7,500.

Air Force. Deliveries, from the USSR and China successively, comprised 6 MiG-21 and 16 F-17M interceptors and about 20 J-6 (MiG-19) fighter-bombers; 1 An-24 and 3 An-26 turboprop transports; over 30 Mi-8, Bell 212, Bell 206L and Alouette III helicopters; 20 Chinese CJ-6 piston-engined primary trainers, FT-2 (MiG-15UTI) jet advanced trainers, 15 Magister armed jet trainers and some light aircraft. Pakistan supplied about 40 surplus J-6s in 1990, but most were written off, along with other aircraft, during serious floods in the spring of 1991. Personnel strength, (1991) 6,000.

INTERNATIONAL RELATIONS

Membership. Bangladesh is a member of the Commonwealth, the Asian Development Bank, the Organisation for South Asian Regional Co-operation, the UN and all its related agencies, the Colombo Plan and the Islamic Conference.

External Debt. Estimated debt, June 1985, US$6,000m. Most of this was in loans from the Western aid group through the World Bank.

Treaties. Bangladesh signed an economic and technical co-operation agreement with China on 4 Jan. 1977. The amended constitution of 1977 states that Bangladesh seeks fraternal relations with Moslem countries based on Islamic solidarity.

ECONOMY

Planning. The third 5-year development plan, 1985–90, envisaged an annual growth rate of 5·4%, and an industrial growth rate of 10·1% annually; of industrial development funds, 55% is for the private sector. Agriculture received 30% of total plan expenditure, and the plan aimed at self-sufficiency in food by 1990.

Budget. The fiscal year ends 30 June. In 1986-87 total Government receipts were Tk.92,764m., of which Tk.45,594m. were revenue receipts, and total expenditure was Tk.82,301m., divided into Tk.40,218m. revenue expenditure and Tk.42,083m. development expenditure. In 1987-88 revenue receipts were Tk.49,150m., revenue expenditure Tk.45,693m. and development expenditure Tk.42,083m. Revenue receipts included (in Tk.1m.) 40,731 from taxation (33,310 indirect). Expenditures: Education, 9,254; administration, 9,107; defence, 7,695; debt servicing, 5,179; justice, 3,992.

Currency. The unit of currency is the *taka* (BDT) of 100 *paisas,* which was floated in 1976. There are 1, 5, 10, 25, 50 and 100 paisa coins and 1, 2, 5, 10, 20, 50, 100 and 500 taka notes. Money supply, 1988: Tk.50,477m. (of which Tk.24,150m. were in circulation). Foreign exchange reserves: Tk.26,963m. (Tk.66·45 = £1 and Tk.37·85 = US$1 in March 1992).

Banking and Finance. Bangladesh Bank is the central bank. There are 4 nationalized commercial banks, 9 private commercial banks, 3 specialized banks and 7 foreign commercial banks. In May 1988 the Bangladesh Bank had Tk.19,971m. deposits; Tk.25,886m. foreign liabilities, Tk.52,709m. assets. The scheduled banks had Tk.131,764m. deposits, Tk.32,210m. assets and Tk.24,313m. borrowings from the Bangladesh Bank. Post office savings deposits were Tk.1,070m. in 1987.

Weights and Measures. The metric system was introduced from July 1982, but imperial measures are still in use. Weight is in the *seer* (1 *seer* = 2 lb.); the *maund* (1 *maund* = 40 *seers*) and the ton.

ENERGY AND NATURAL RESOURCES

Electricity. Electric power is generated and distributed by the Bangladesh Power Development Board and the Rural Electrification Board. Installed capacity, June 1987, 1,757 mw.; electricity generated, 1986–87, 5,288·01m. kwh.; consumption, 3,479·38m. kwh. Supply 220 volts; 50 Hz.

Oil. Supplies have been located in the Bay of Bengal. Drilling is in progress.

Gas. There are 14 natural gas fields with recoverable reserves of 12,610,000m. cu. ft. Production, 1987–88, 147,454m. cu. ft. Consumption, 140,600 cu. ft.

Water. India and Bangladesh are working towards agreement on sharing the water of the river Ganges. The flow will be monitored daily at the Farakka barrage and two other points.

Minerals. The principal minerals are lignite, limestone, china clay and glass sand. Production, 1986–87: Limestone, 44,660m. tons (value Tk.13·34m.); china clay, 12,272m. tons (Tk.17·2m.).

Agriculture. At the 1983-84 census of agriculture there were 10·05m. farm holdings (7·07m. under 2·5 acres; 2·48m. of 2·5 to 7·5 acres; 496,000 over 7·5 acres.

28·3% of households had no cultivable land. In 1990 79·22m. persons depended upon agriculture, of whom 23·19m. were economically active. Agriculture contributed 41% of GDP in 1987–88. The cultivable area was 22·84m. acres in 1987, of which 21·88m. acres were cropped (26·2m. under rice, 1·4m. wheat and 1·9m. jute). About 2·74m. ha (1989) is irrigated.

Bangladesh is a major producer of jute. Production, 1990, 849,000 tonnes.

Rice is the most important food crop; production in 1990, 28·14m. tonnes. Other crops (1,000 tonnes): Sugar cane, 6,900; wheat, 890; tobacco, 45; pulses, 505; tea, 45; potatoes, 100.

Fertilizers used (1986–87), 1·32m. tonnes, of which 915m. tonnes was urea.

Livestock in 1988 (1,000): Poultry, 89,000; cattle, 23,357; goats, 11,200; sheep, 1,160; buffalo, 1,800. Livestock products in 1988 (tonnes): Beef and veal, 137,000; cow and buffalo milk, 750,000; goats' milk, 224,000; eggs, 110,000.

Forestry. The area under forests in 1989 was 1·95m. ha. Output of timber, 1986-87, was 12·76m. cu. ft.

Fisheries. Being bounded on the south by the Bay of Bengal and having numerous inland waterways, Bangladesh is a major producer of fish and products. In 1987-88 there were 497,000 sea- and 752,000 inland-fishermen, with 1,249 mechanized boats, including 52 trawlers, and 3,317 motor boats. Inland catch was 610,000 tonnes, sea, 227,000 tonnes.

INDUSTRY. Industry contributed 8·9% of GDP in 1987-88. The principal industries are jute and cotton textiles, tea, paper, newsprint, cement, chemical fertilizers and light engineering. In 1986-87 there were 4,386 factories (including 881 textile, 801 food and 564 chemical). New government policy in 1982 aimed to restore public-sector jute and textile mills to private ownership and encourage the private sector. Arms and ammunition, atomic energy, forestry, air transport, communications and electrical industries would remain in the public sector.

Production, 1987–88: Jute goods, 529,000 tonnes; cotton yarn, 103m. lb.; cotton cloth, 68m. yards; cement, 310,000 tonnes; sugar, 175,000 tonnes; vegetable products, 6,337 tonnes; fertilizer, 729,000 tonnes, newsprint, 49,000 tonnes; bicycles 19,749; 8,039 motor cycles; 121,000 radios.

Labour. In 1985–86, the labour force was 27·7m. (3·2m. female), of whom 27·4m. (3·1m.) were employed (2·8m. children between 10 and 14 years were also employed). 57·6% worked in agriculture and fishery, 11·5% in trade and 7·1% in production and transport. Average daily industrial wage, 1987-88: Skilled, Tk.49; unskilled, Tk.31. In 1989 there were 12 industrial stoppages involving 59,700 employees; 83,770 working days were lost.

FOREIGN ECONOMIC RELATIONS

Commerce. The main exports are jute and jute goods, tea, hides and skins, newsprint, fish and garments, and the main imports are machinery, transport equipment, manufactured goods, minerals, fuels and lubricants. In 1989 exports were valued at US$1,305m., and imports at US$3,524m.

Main sources of imports in 1987-88: Japan (mainly machinery and vehicles), Tk.10,098m.; USA (foodstuffs), Tk.8,161m.; Singapore (petroleum), Tk.6,327m.; Hong Kong, Tk.4,271m.; UK, 4,197m. Main export markets: USA, Tk.12,045m.; Italy, Tk.3,677m.; UK, Tk.2,433m. Federal Germany, Tk.2,306m.

Total trade between Bangladesh and UK (British Department of Trade returns, in £1,000 sterling):

	1988	1989	1990	1991
Imports to UK	50,249	52,527	72,515	80,568
Exports and re-exports from UK	64,018	78,270	70,534	39,086

Foreign investment is encouraged and legally protected. The Board of Investment must approve joint ventures if the foreign participation exceeds 49%. There is a duty-free Export Processing Zone at Chittagong.

Tourism. In 1989 there were 28,064 foreign visitors. Foreign exchange earnings in 1987, Tk.192·4m.

COMMUNICATIONS

Roads. In 1986 there were 4,039 miles of roads with cement, concrete or bitumen surfaces. In 1987 there were 8,827 buses, 16,375 lorries and 27,120 private cars.

Railways. In 1990 there were 2,745 km of railways, comprising 923 km of 1,676 mm gauge and 1,822 km of metre gauge. They carried 2·4m. tonnes of freight and 55·4m. passengers.

Civil Aviation. There are international airports at Dhaka (Zia), Chittagong and Sylhet, and 7 domestic airports. Bangladesh Biman (Bangladesh Airways) had 11 aircraft in 1988 and has domestic flights from Zia International Airport and services to Calcutta, Kathmandu, Bombay, Dubai, Abu Dhabi, Jeddah, Bangkok, Singapore, London, Doha, Kuwait, Amsterdam, Rome, Karachi, Kuala Lumpur, Bahrain, Tripoli, Athens and Muscat. In 1987 Zia handled 1·18m. passengers out of a total of 1·6m. Freight and mail handled, Zia, 32,413 tons; total, 34,376: Aircraft movements, Zia, 29,393; total, 55,051.

Shipping. There are sea ports at Chittagong and Mongla, and inland ports at Dhaka, Chandpur, Barisal, Khulna and five other towns. There are 5,000 miles of navigable channels. The three principle navigable rivers, the Padma, Brahmaputra and Meghna serve areas where railways cannot be economically constructed. The Bangladesh Shipping Corporation owned 21 ships in 1987. There are also 881 private cargo and 1,506 passenger vessels. In 1986–87 the port of Chittagong handled 5·8m. tons of imports and 402,000 tons of exports; total, all ports 7·4m. tons of imports and 1·1m. tons of exports. Vessels entered (all ports) 1,792 and cleared, 1,770. The Bangladesh Inland Water Transport Corporation had 430 vessels in 1988.

Telecommunications. There were 7,810 post offices and 187,650 telephones in 1988. International communications are by the Indian Ocean Intelsat IV satellite.

The government-controlled Radio Bangladesh and part-commercial Bangladesh Television transmit a home service and an external service radio programmes and a TV programme (colour by PAL). In 1991 there were 4·5m. radio and 0·35m. TV receivers.

Cinema. In 1987 there were 681 cinemas with 363,000 seats. 75 full-length films were made.

Newspapers and Books. In 1987 there were 49 daily newspapers in Bangla with a circulation of 736,000 and 10 in English with a circualtion of 112,000. There were 171 other periodicals (15 in English) with a circulation of 737,000. Most papers are published in Dhaka. The Government has set up a paper *(Dainik Barta-at Rajshahi)* to stimulate a regional press. There is a Press Institute. In 1987 1,022 book titles were published (90 in English).

JUSTICE, RELIGION, EDUCATION AND WELFARE

Justice. The Supreme Court comprises an Appellate and a High court Division, the latter having control over all subordinate courts. There are benches at Comilla, Rangpur, Jessore, Barisal, Chittagong and Sylhet, and courts at District level. The Chief Justice and other judges of the High Court are appointed by the President and must retire at 62 years.

Religion. Islam is the State Religion. In 1989 the population was 86·7% Moslem and 12·1% Hindu.

Education. About 29·2% of the population over 15 was literate in 1989 (male 39·7%, female 18%). The Government has taken over school administration. The compulsory primary education scheme has been replaced by model primary education.

In 1987–88 there were 44,502 primary schools (6,864 private), with 11·08m. pupils (4·83m. female) and 186,597 teachers (33,575 female); 10,157 secondary schools (9,895 private), with 2·81m. pupils (927,000 female) and 116,835 teachers (11,432 female); 812 colleges of further education (630 private), with 792,000 students (183,000 female) and 17,215 teachers (2,268 female); and 77 technical colleges with 17,360 students (996 female) and 1,307 teachers (46 female). There is an Islamic University (891 students and 19 teachers in 1987-88) and universities at Dhaka (16,622 and 973), Rajshahi (11,755 and 469), Chittagong (6,025 and 420) and Jahingirnagar (2,660 and 181). There are also universities of agriculture (4,573 and 379) and engineering (3,758 and 349). There were 10 teacher-training colleges in 1987-88, with 3,624 students (1,040 female) and 160 teachers (47 female), and 53 primary training institutes with 6,893 students (4,122 female) and 532 teachers (106 female).

Health. In 1987 there were 608 state and 267 private hospitals with a total of 33,038 beds. There were 16,929 doctors. State expenditure on health, Tk.3,540m. There are 10 medical schools.

DIPLOMATIC REPRESENTATIVES

Of Bangladesh in Great Britain (28 Queen's Gate, London, SW7)
High Commissioner: (Vacant).
(There are also Assistant High Commissioners in Birmingham and Manchester)

Of Great Britain in Bangladesh (Abu Bakr Hse., Gulshan, Dhaka 12)
High Commissioner: C. H. Imray, CMG.

Of Bangladesh in the USA (2201 Wisconsin Ave., NW, Washington, D.C., 20007)
Ambassador: A. H. S. Ataul Karim.

Of the USA in Bangladesh (Madani Ave., Baridhara, Dhaka 1212)
Ambassador: William B. Millam.

Of Bangladesh to the United Nations
Ambassador: Humayun Kabir.

Further Reading

Official statistics are issued by the Bangladesh Bureau of Statistics (Director-General A. M. A. Rahim). Publications include: *Statistical Yearbook of Bangladesh.* 1976; 1979 to date. *Statistical Pocket Book of Bangladesh.* 1980 to date.

Bangladesh Planning Commission, *The First Five Year Plan—The Second Five Year Plan.*
Abdullah, T. and Zeidenstein, S., *Village Women of Bangladesh: Prospects for Change.* Oxford, 1981
Baxter, C., *Bangladesh: A New Nation in an Old Setting.* Boulder, 1986
Chowdhury, R., *The Genesis of Bangladesh.* London, 1972
Dutt, K., *Bangladesh Economy: An Analytical Study.* New Delhi, 1973
Franda, M., *Bangladesh: The First Decade.* New Delhi, 1982
Hartmann, B. and Boyce, J., *A Quiet Violence: View from a Bangladesh Village.* London, 1983
Kamal, K. A., *Sheikh Mujibur Rahman.* 2nd ed. Dhaka, 1970
Khan, A. R., *The Economy of Bangladesh.* London, 1972
de Lucia, R. J. and Jacoby, H. D., *Energy Planning for Developing Countries: A Study of Bangladesh.* John Hopkins Univ. Press, 1982
de Vylder, S., *Agriculture in Chains. Bangladesh: A Case Study in Contradictions and Constraints.* London, 1982
O'Donnell, C. P., *Bangladesh: Biography of a Muslim Nation.* Boulder, 1986
Rahman, M., *Bangladesh Today: An Indictment and a Lament.* London, 1978

BARBADOS

Capital: Bridgetown
Population: 257,082 (1990)
GNP per capita: US$6,370 (1989)

HISTORY. Barbados was occupied by the British in 1627 and during its colonial history never changed hands. Full internal self-government was attained in 1961. Barbados became an independent sovereign state within the Commonwealth on 30 Nov. 1966.

AREA AND POPULATION. Barbados lies to the east of the Windward Islands. Area 166 sq. miles (430 sq. km). In 1980 the census population was 248,983, and in 1990 (provisional) 257,082 (44·2% urban in 1980). Bridgetown is the principal city: Population, 6,720 in 1990.

Growth rate (1985–90), 6 per 1,000; infant mortality, (1990), 13 per 1,000; expectation of life, 1989, 75 years.

CLIMATE. An equable climate in winter, but the wet season, from June to Nov., is more humid. Rainfall varies from 50" (1,250 mm) on the coast to 75" (1,875 mm) in the higher interior. Bridgetown. Jan. 76°F (24·4°C), July 80°F (26·7°C). Annual rainfall 51" (1,275 mm).

CONSTITUTION AND GOVERNMENT. The Legislature consists of the Governor-General, a Senate and a House of Assembly. The Senate comprises 21 members appointed by the Governor-General, 12 being appointed on the advice of the Prime Minister, 2 on the advice of the leader of the opposition and 7 in the Governor-General's discretion. The House of Assembly comprises 28 members elected every 5 years. In 1963 the voting age was reduced to 18.

The Privy Council is appointed by the Governor-General after consultation with the Prime Minister. It consists of 12 members and the Governor-General as chairman. It advises the Governor-General in the exercise of the royal prerogative of mercy and in the exercise of his disciplinary powers over members of the public and police services.

In the general election of Jan. 1991 the Democratic Labour Party gained 18 seats and the Barbados Labour Party 10 seats. Turn-out was 62%.

Governor-General: Dame Nita Barrow, GCMG.

The Cabinet, in Jan. 1992, was composed as follows:

Prime Minister, Minister of Finance and Economic Affairs and Minister of the Civil Service: Erskine Sandiford.
Deputy Prime Minister, International Transport, Transport and Works, Immigration and Telecommunications, Leader of the House of Assembly: Philip Greaves.
Attorney-General, Foreign Affairs: Maurice A. King, QC. *Labour, Consumer Affairs and the Environment:* Warwick O. Franklyn. *Agriculture, Food and Fisheries, Leader of the Senate:* L. V. Harcourt Lewis. *Health:* Brandford Taitt. *Housing and Lands:* E. Evelyn Greaves. *Tourism and Sport:* Wesley Hall. *Trade, Industry and Commerce:* Dr Carl Clarke. *Education:* Cyril Walker. *Justice and Public Safety:* Keith Simmons. *Community Development and Culture:* David J. H. Thompson. There was one Minister of State.

National flag: Three vertical strips of blue, gold, blue, with a black trident in the centre.

National anthem. In plenty and in time of need (words by Irvine Burgie; tune by V. R. Edwards).

INTERNATIONAL RELATIONS

Membership. Barbados is a member of UN, OAS, CARICOM, the Commonwealth and an ACP state of the EEC.

ECONOMY

Budget. The budget for 1990–91 envisaged capital expenditure of BD$231·6 and current expenditure of BD$1,050·5m.

Currency. The unit of currency is the *Barbados dollar* (BBD) of 100 *cents*. Inflation was 3·1% in 1990. In March 1992, £1 = BD$3.53; US$1 = BD$2.00.

Banking and Finance. Barclays Bank International, the Royal Bank of Canada, Canadian Imperial Bank of Commerce, the Bank of Nova Scotia, Caribbean Commercial Bank, The Barbados National Bank, have offices.

Barbados is headquarters for the Caribbean Development Bank. The Barbados Development Bank opened on 15 April 1969 and Barbados became a member of the Inter-American Development Bank on 19 March 1969.

There is a stock exchange which participates in the regional Caribbean exchange.

NATURAL RESOURCES

Electricity. Production (1990) 512m. kwh. Supply 150 volts; 50 Hz.

Oil. Crude oil production (1991) 63,000 tonnes and reserves (1990), 3·1m. bbls.

Gas. Output of gas (1990) 32·9m. cu. metres and reserves 209·3m. cu. metres.

Agriculture. Of the total area of 106,240 acres, about 55,000 acres are arable land. The land is intensely cultivated. In 1990, 10,500 ha were under sugar-cane cultivation. Cotton was successfully replanted in 1983, but production declined for the third consecutive year when the 1990 harvest yielded 42,700 kg of lint and 49,400 kg of seed cotton. The agricultural sector accounted for 8·5% (provisional) of GDP in 1990 (1946, 45%; 1967, 24%). In 1991, 6·2% of the total labour force were employed in agriculture. In 1990, 69,300 tonnes of sugar were produced. There are 3 sugar factories and 2 rum refineries in production. In 1990, about 1,230 ha were planted with vegetables and root crops, of which 59% were sweet potatoes, yams and carrots. Production, 1990 (in 1,000 kg): Sweet potatoes, 2,646; yams, 1,755; carrots, 1,447·2; onions, 794·5; tomatoes, 334·8; cucumbers, 350·4; cabbages, 330·4; melons, 117·6; okra, 115; beets, 78·4; eddoes, 248·2; cassava, 162. Meat and dairy products, 1990: Pork, 1·45m. kg; mutton, 45,800 kg; beef, 880,200 kg; veal, 26,100 kg; milk, 14·2m. kg;, eggs, 1·6m. kg.

Livestock (1988): Cattle, 18,000; sheep, 56,000; goats, 33,000; pigs, 49,000; poultry, 1m.

Fisheries. There are about 755 (1990) powered boats and many men and women are employed during the flying-fish season. Large numbers of these boats are laid up from July to Oct. The fish catch landed in 1990 was 2,966 tonnes.

INDUSTRY. Industrial establishments operating in 1987 numbered approximately 330 and ranged from the manufacture of processed food to small specialized products such as garment manufacturing, furniture and household appliances, electrical components, plastic products and electronic parts.

FOREIGN ECONOMIC RELATIONS

Commerce. Total trade for calendar years in BD$1,000:

	1984	1985	1986	1987	1988
Domestic Imports [1]	1,324,623	1,221,595	1,181,075	1,035,891	1,170,316
Domestic Exports [1]	583,667	496,471	420,614	214,511	242,738

[1] Exclusive of bullion and specie.

In 1988 the principal imports (BD$1m.) were: Machinery and transport equipment, 275·7; manufactured goods, 360·5; food and live animals, 181·9; lubricants, mineral fuels, etc., 110·5; chemicals, 125·9; crude minerals, 36·2; beverages and tobacco, 29; animal and vegetable oils and fats, 12·9. In 1988 the principal domestic exports (BD$1m.) were: Sugar, 57·7; electronic components, 42·8; clothing, 30·4.

Total trade between Barbados and UK (British Department of Trade returns, in £1,000 sterling):

	1987	1988	1989	1990	1991
Imports from UK	23,320	19,487	22,304	24,294	13,316
Exports and re-exports to UK	33,067	32,061	38,136	35,811	33,454

Tourism. In 1990, 432,092 tourists visited Barbados spending BD$987m. The industry employs over 10,000 people.

COMMUNICATIONS

Roads. There are 1,035 miles of road open to traffic, of which 855 miles are all-weather roads. In Dec. 1990 there were 38,832 private cars, 3,089 hired cars and taxis, 447 buses including minibuses and 5,821 other vehicles including motor-cycles.

Civil Aviation. There is an international airport at Seawell, Christ Church, Barbados, served by British Airways, BWIA, Leeward Islands Air Transport, PANAM, American Airlines, Wardair, Air Martinique Cruziero (SC), Air Canada, Caribbean Airways, Cubana Airlines and Venezuelan Airlines.

Shipping. A deep-water harbour opened in 1961 at Bridgetown provides 8 berths for ships 500–600 ft in length, including one specially designed for bulk sugar loading. The number of merchant vessels entering in 1990 was 1,791 of 10,992,000 net tons.

Telecommunications. There is a general post office in Bridgetown and 16 branches on the island. In 1990 there were 86,306 telephones in service. The Caribbean Broadcasting Corporation is a part-government, part-commercial TV and radio service. There are 2 other commercial services (one for rediffusion). In 1991 there were 200,000 radios and 68,400 television sets (colour by NTSC).

Cinemas. There were (1990) 3 cinemas and 1 drive-in cinema for 600 cars.

Newspapers. In 1987 there were 2 daily newspapers with a total circulation of 41,000.

JUSTICE, RELIGION, EDUCATION AND WELFARE

Justice. Justice is administered by the Supreme Court and by magistrates' courts. All have both civil and criminal jurisdiction. There is a Chief Justice and 3 puisne judges of the Supreme Court and 8 magistrates.

Religion. At the 1980 census count, 39·7% of the population were Anglicans, 7·6% Pentecostalists, 7·1% Methodists, 4·4% Roman Catholics, 3·5% Seventh Day Adventists, 17·5% other religions and 20·2% no stated religion.

Education. In 1988–89 children in 96 government primary schools numbered 28,113; in 21 secondary schools, 21,172; in 5 vocational centres, 834; in 15 assisted private approved secondary schools, 4,013. There are 22 independent primary schools with (1988–89) 1,925 pupils and a number of independent schools for which no accurate figures are available. Education is free in all government-owned and maintained institutions from primary to university level.

The University of the West Indies in Barbados was opened in Sept. 1963 and Cave Hill campus in 1967, which in 1988–89 had 1,865 students. In 1988–89, 105 students attended Erdiston College, 2,102 the Barbados Community College for higher education and 1,544 the Samuel Jackman Prescod Polytechnic.

Health. In 1986 there were 2,054 hospital beds and 243 doctors.

DIPLOMATIC REPRESENTATIVES

Of Barbados in Great Britain (1 Great Russell St., London, WC1B 3NH)
High Commissioner: Sir William Douglas, KCMG.

Of Great Britain in Barbados (Lower Collymore Rock, Bridgetown)
High Commissioner: E. T. Davies, CMG.

Of Barbados in the USA (2144 Wyoming Ave., NW, Washington, D.C. 20008)
Ambassador: Rudy Webster.

Of the USA in Barbados (PO Box 302, Bridgetown)
Ambassador: G. Philip Hughes.

Of Barbados to the United Nations
Ambassador: E. Besley Maycock.

Further Reading

Beckles, H., *A History of Barbados: from Amerindian Settlement to Nation-State*. Cambridge Univ. Press, 1990
Dann, G., *The Quality of Life in Barbados*. London, 1984
Hoyos, F. A., *Barbados: A History from the Amerindians to Independence*. 2nd ed. London, 1992.—*Tom Adams: A Biography*. London, 1988
Potter, R. B. and Dann, G. M. S., *Barbados* [Bibliography]. Oxford and Santa Barbara, 1987
Warren, A. and Frazer, H., *The Barbados Carolina Connection*. London, 1989
Worrell, D., *The Economy of Barbados 1946–1980*. Bridgetown, 1982

National library: The Barbados Public Library, Bridgetown.
National statistical office: Barbados Statistical Service, Fairchild Street, Bridgetown.

BELGIUM

Capital: Brussels
Population: 9·98m. (1991)
GNP per capita: US$16,390 (1989)

Royaume de Belgique—
Koninkrijk België

(Kingdom of Belgium)

HISTORY. The kingdom of Belgium formed itself into an independent state in 1830, having from 1815 been part of the Netherlands. The secession was decreed on 4 Oct. 1830 by a provisional government, established in consequence of a revolution which broke out at Brussels, on 25 Aug. 1830. A National Congress elected Prince Leopold of Saxe-Coburg King of the Belgians on 4 June 1831; he ascended the throne 21 July 1831. The Treaty of London, 19 April 1839, established peace between King Leopold I and the King of the Netherlands.

AREA AND POPULATION. Belgium is bounded in the north by the Netherlands, north-west by the North Sea, west and south by France, east by Germany and Luxembourg. Belgium has an area of 30,518 sq. km (11,778 sq. miles). The Belgian exclave of Baarle-Hertog in the Netherlands has an area of 7 sq. km, and a population (1 Jan. 1991) of 1,102 males and 1,035 females.

Dutch (Flemish) is spoken by the Flemish section of the population in the north, French by the Wallon south. The linguistic frontier bisects Brussels, which is bilingual. Some German is spoken in the east.

Percentage of the population in the language communities was on 1 Jan. 1991: Flemish, 57·8; French, 32; bilingual, 9·6; German, 0·7. Each language has official status in its own community. (*See* map in THE STATESMAN'S YEAR-BOOK, 1967–68). Bracketed names below contain French or Dutch alternatives.

Census	Population	Increase % per annum	Census	Population	Increase % per annum
1900	6,693,548	1·03	1961	9,189,741	0·52
1910	7,423,784	1·09	1970	9,650,944	0·55
1920	7,405,569	0·06	1981	9,848,647	0·18
1930	8,092,004	0·84	1991	9,978,681	0·10
1947	8,512,195	0·36			

Provinces	Provincial capitals	Area (ha)	Estimated population (1 Jan.) 1989	1990	1991
Antwerp	Antwerp	286,726	1,592,437	1,597,310	1,604,566
Brabant	Brussels	335,811	2,240,926	2,243,026	2,252,613
Flanders { West	Bruges (Brugge)	313,439	1,099,384	1,102,501	1,106,529
Flanders { East	Ghent	298,167	1,329,830	1,331,608	1,335,694
Hainaut	Mons (Bergen)	378,669	1,278,255	1,278,039	1,280,336
Liège (Luik)	Liège	386,213	997,364	998,213	1,000,696
Limbourg	Hasselt	242,231	740,974	745,034	950,082
Luxembourg	Arlon	444,114	229,587	230,827	232,740
Namur (Namen)	Namur	366,501	418,855	421,224	423,719
Total		3,051,871	9,927,612	9,947,782	9,986,975

In 1991 there were 5,106,290 females. On 1 Jan. 1991 there were 904,528 resident foreigners.

Vital statistics:

	Births	Deaths	Marriages	Divorces	Immigration	Emigration
1985	114,283	112,691	57,630	18,530	47,042	54,021
1988	118,764	104,551	59,075	20,809	54,048	54,621
1989	120,550	107,332	63,511	20,256	446,426	435,798
1990	123,554	104,545	64,658	20,311	453,490	433,807

The most populous towns, with estimated population on 1 Jan. 1991:

Brussels and suburbs [1]	960,324	St Niklaas (St Nicolas)	68,213
Antwerp and suburbs [2]	467,875	Tournai (Doornik)	67,700
Ghent	230,446	Hasselt	66,559
Charleroi	206,928	Genk	61,376
Liège (Luik)	195,201	Seraing	60,887
Brugge (Bruges)	117,100	Verviers	53,681
Namur (Namen)	103,935	Mouscron (Moeskroen)	53,649
Mons (Bergen)	92,158	Roeselare (Roulers)	52,825
Leuven (Louvain)	85,462	Turnhout	37,897
La Louvière	76,592	Herstal	36,563
Aalst (Alost)	76,364	Lokeren	34,945
Kortrijk (Courtrai)	76,121	Vilvoorde (Vilvorde)	32,953
Mechelen (Malines)	75,352	Lier (Lierre)	31,181
Ostend	68,534		

[1] The suburbs comprise 18 communes: Anderlecht, Etterbeek, Forest, Ixelles, Jette, Koekelberg, Molenbeek St Jean, St Gilles, St Josse-ten-Noode, Schaerbeek, Uccle, Woluwe-St Lambert, Auderghem, Watermael-Boitsfort, Woluwe-St Pierre, Berchem Ste Agathe, Evere and Ganshoren.

[2] Including Berchem, Borgerhout, Deurne, Hoboken, Merksem and Wilrijk.

CLIMATE. Cool temperate climate, influenced by the sea, giving mild winters and cool summers. Brussels. Jan. 36°F (2·2°C), July 64°F (17·8°C). Annual rainfall 33" (825 mm). Ostend. Jan. 38°F (3·3°C), July 62°F (16·7°C). Annual rainfall 31" (775 mm).

KING. Baudouin, born 7 Sept. 1930, succeeded his father, Leopold III, on 17 July 1951, when he took the oath on the constitution before the two Chambers: Married on 15 Dec. 1960 to Fabiola de Mora y Aragón, daughter of the Conde de Mora and Marqués de Casa Riera.

The King receives a tax-free sum from the civil list voted by parliament each year. In 1991 this was 200m. francs.

The royal succession is in direct male line in the order of primogeniture. By marriage without the King's consent, however, the right of succession is forfeited, but may be restored by the King with the consent of the two Chambers. A constitutional amendment of June 1991 permits women to accede to the throne.

Brother and Sister of the King. (1) Josephine Charlotte, Princess of Belgium, born 11 Oct. 1927; married to Prince Jean of Luxembourg, 9 April 1953; (2) Albert, Prince of Liège, born 6 June 1934; married to Paola Ruffo di Calabria, 2 July 1959; *offspring:* Prince Philippe, born 15 April 1960; Princess Astrid, born 5 June 1962; married to Archduke Lorenz of Austria, 22 Sept. 1984; Prince Laurent, born 19 Oct. 1963. *Half-brother and half-sisters of the King.* Prince Alexandre, born 18 July 1942; Princess Marie Christine, born 6 Feb. 1951; Princess Maria-Esmeralda, born 30 Sept. 1956.

Aunt of the King. Princess Marie-José, born 4 Aug. 1906, married to Prince Umberto (King Umberto II of Italy in 1946) on 8 Jan. 1930.

BELGIAN SOVEREIGNS

Leopold I	1831–65	Leopold III	1934–44, 1950–51
Leopold II	1865–1909	Regency	1944–50
Albert	1909–34	Baudouin	1951–

CONSTITUTION AND GOVERNMENT. According to the constitution of 1831, Belgium is a constitutional, representative and hereditary monarchy. The legislative power is vested in the King, the *Senate* and the *Chamber of Representatives.* No act of the King can have effect unless countersigned by one of his Ministers, who thus becomes responsible for it. The King convokes, prorogues and dissolves the Chambers.

National flag: Three vertical strips of black, yellow, red.

National anthem: Après des siècles d'esclavage ('After centuries of slavery'; La Brabançonne; words by Jenneval, 1830; tune by F. van Campenhout). A Flemish version 'O Vaderland, oedel land der Belgen' (Oh Fatherland, noble land of the Belgians) replaced a specifically Flemish anthem in 1951.

Those sections of the Belgian Constitution which regulate the organization of the legislative power were revised in Oct. 1921. For both Senate and Chamber all elections are held on the principle of universal suffrage. Voting is by proportional representation and is obligatory. Voters choose between party lists of candidates in multi-party constituencies.

The Senate consists of members elected for 4 years, partly directly and partly indirectly. The number elected directly is equal to half the number of members of the Chamber of Representatives. The constituent body is similar to that which elects deputies to the Chamber; the minimum age of electors is 18 years.

Senators are elected indirectly by the provincial councils, on the basis of 1 for 200,000 inhabitants. Every addition of 125,000 inhabitants gives the right to 1 senator more. Each provincial council elects at least 3 senators. There are at present 51 provincial senators. No one, during 2 years preceding the election, must have been a member of the council appointing him. Senators are elected by the Senate itself in the proportion of half the preceding category. The senators belonging to these two latter categories are also elected by the method of proportional representation. All senators must be at least 40 years of age. They receive about 2m. francs per annum. Sons of the King, or failing these, Belgian princes of the reigning branch of the royal family, are by right senators at the age of 18, but have no voice in the deliberations till the age of 25 years; this prerogative is hardly ever used.

The members of the Chamber of Representatives are elected by the electoral body. Their number, at present 212 (law of 3 April 1965), is proportional to the population, and cannot exceed one for every 40,000 inhabitants. They sit for 4 years. Deputies must be not less than 21 years of age, and resident in Belgium.

Each deputy has an annual allowance of about 2m. francs.

The Senate and Chamber meet annually in October and must sit for at least 40 days; but the King has the power of convoking extraordinary sessions and of dissolving them either simultaneously or separately. In the latter case a new election must take place within 40 days and a meeting of the chambers within 2 months.

An adjournment cannot be made for a period exceeding 1 month without the consent of the Chambers.

Constitutional legislation of Dec. 1970, July 1971, July 1974 and Aug. 1980 has led to the establishment of 3 regions with considerable autonomy: **Brussels**; **Flanders** (Dutch-speaking, seat of government at Ghent); and **Wallonia** (French-speaking, seat of government at Namur), all with Regional Councils and the two latter with Community Councils). Some 40% of public revenues go directly to the regions and communities. The regions are responsible for territorial matters: planning, infrastructure, roads, regional development, water, energy and the municipalities. The language communities run welfare services, culture (including broadcasting) and education. The 186-member *Flemish Council* is drawn from the national parliament and has a cabinet of 11.

Elections were held on 24 Nov. 1991. The electorate was 7,144,884; turn-out was 6,592,441. Flemish Christian Social Party (CVP) won 39 (43 in 1987) seats with 16·7% of votes cast, Francophone Socialist Party (FS) 35 (40) with 13·6%, Flemish Socialist Party (SP) 28 (32) with 12%, Liberal Flemish Freedom and Progress Party (PVV) 26 (25) with 11·9%, Francophone Liberal Reform Party (PRL) 20 (23) with 8·2%, Francophone Christian Social Party (PSC) 18 (19) with 7·8%, Vlaams Blok 12 (2) with 6·6%, Volksunie 10 (16) with 5·9%, Francophone Ecology Party 10 (3) with 5·1%, Flemish Ecology Party 7 (6) with 4·9%, Van Rossem List 3 (nil) with 3·2%, Francophone Democratic Front 3 (3) with 1·5%, National Front 1 (1) with 1·1%.

A 4-party coalition government was formed in March 1992:

Prime Minister: Jean-Luc Dehaene (CVP).

Deputy Prime Ministers: Guy Coëme, (PS) (*Communications and Public Enterprises*); Willy Claes, (SP) (*Foreign Affairs*); Melchior Wathelet, (PSC) (*Justice and Economic Affairs*). 14 *Cabinet Ministers: Finance:* Philippe Maystadt

(PSC). *Foreign Trade and European Affairs:* Robert Urbain (PS). *Social Affairs:* Philippe Moureaux (PS). *National Defence:* Leo Delcroix (CVP). *Interior and Civil Service:* Louis Tobback (SP). *Pensions:* Freddy Wyllockx (PS). *Employment and Work, with responsibility for Equality of the Sexes:* Miet Smet (CVP). *Agriculture:* André Bourgeois (CVP). *Science Policy:* Jean-Maurice Dehousse (PS). *Social Integration:* Laurette Onkelinx (PS). *Budget:* Mieke Offeciers-Van De Wiele (CVP).

There are Secretaries of State and Regional Ministers.

Local Government. There are 9 provinces and 589 communes. They have a large measure of autonomous government. All Belgians over 18 years of age, who are recorded in the registers of population of the commune have the right to vote in the communal elections. Proportional representation is applied to the communal elections, and communal councils are renewed every 6 years. In each commune there is a college composed of the burgomaster as the president and a certain number of aldermen.

DEFENCE. According to the Law of 30 April 1962, the Belgian Armed Forces are recruited by annual calls to the colours and by voluntary enlistments.

Military service is 10 months for conscripts serving in the Federal Republic of Germany and 12 months for those serving in Belgium, 13 months for voluntary reserve officers and 15 for the paracommando regiment. Duration of military obligation varies between 8 and 15 years for soldiers called for compulsory service.

The Medical Service has a strength of 4,000 personnel. Beside the medical units and detachments in the Armed Forces, the medical service manages 6 military hospitals and a central pharmacy.

Army. The Army comprises as major units 1 armoured and 3 mechanized brigades, 1 armoured reconnaissance brigade and 1 paracommando regiment. There are also 2 motorized, 1 missile, 6 engineer, 4 artillery, 1 bridging and 1 equipment battalions. Total strength (1991) 55,100. *Gendarmerie,* 15,400.

Equipment includes 320 LEOPARD Main Battle Tanks, 136 SCORPION Light Tanks, 153 SCIMITAR Armoured Fighting Vehicles, 1,452 Armoured Personnel Carriers and 80 JPK 90mm Self-Propelled Anti-Tank Guns; Artillery Battalions are equipped with 155mm and 203mm Self-Propelled Howitzers, LANCE Surface-to-Surface Missiles, HAWK Surface-to-Air Missiles and GEPARD Armoured Vehicles with 35mm Anti-Aircraft Guns.

Other equipment in use: MILAN Anti-Tank Guided Weapon, STRIKER Armoured Fighting Vehicle with SWINGFIRE Anti-Tank Guided Weapon, Islander aircraft, Alouette II helicopters, Epervier Remotely Piloted Vehicle. Delivery of 46 A-109 anti-armour and observation helicopters is scheduled in 1992–93.

Navy. The naval forces, based mainly at Ostend, include 4 frigates, 6 ocean minehunters, 2 command and logistic support ships, 10 coastal tripartite minehunters, 2 coastal minesweepers, 4 inshore minesweepers, 1 research ship, 1 ammunition transport, 6 tugs and 2 service craft. Naval personnel in 1991 totalled 4,400 officers and ratings.

The naval air arm comprises 4 Alouette SA-318 general utility helicopters.

Air Force. The Air Force has a strength of (1991) 17,400 personnel and more than 230 aircraft in 12 operational squadrons and support units. There are 5 flying wings. The all-weather fighter wing consists of 2 squadrons of F-16s. One fighter-bomber wing has 2 squadrons of F-16s. Another fighter-bomber wing operates 2 squadrons of F-16s. The fourth wing operates 1 squadron of Mirage 5 tactical reconnaissance fighter. The transport wing consists of 1 squadron equipped with 12 C-130H Hercules turboprop transports, and 1 squadron flying 2 Boeing 727s, 3 HS 748 twin-turboprop transports, 5 Swearingen Merlin III light turboprop transports and 2 light twin-jet Falcons. Other types in service include Sea King Mk 48 search and rescue helicopters, SIAI-Marchetti SF.260M and Alpha Jet training aircraft. Two surface-to-air missile squadrons, stationed in Germany, are equipped with Nike Hercules missiles.

INTERNATIONAL RELATIONS

Membership. Belgium is a member of the UN, EC, Benelux Economic Union, Council of Europe, NATO, OECD and WEU. The Schengen Accord of June 1990 abolished border controls between Belgium, France, Germany, Luxembourg and the Netherlands. Italy, Portugal and Spain have now also acceded.

ECONOMY

Budget. Revenue and expenditure for both national and community and regional sectors (in 1,000m. francs):

	1985	1986	1987	1988	1989	1990
Receipts						
Current	1,487·6	1,509·6	1,567·0	1,608·8	1,635·5	1,729·8
Capital [1]	436·2	250·4	393·4	504·6	426·0	455·2
Total	1,923·8	1,760·0	1,954·4	2,113·4	2,061·5	2,185·0
Expenditure						
Current [2]	1,902·2	1,945·6	1,916·2	1,951·0	2,014·5	2,014·8
Capital	212·0	213·0	194·2	194·0	171·8	124·7
Total	2,114·0	2,158·6	2,110·4	2,145·0	2,186·3	2,139·5

[1] Including bond issues.   [2] Including debt discharges.

On 31 Dec. 1990 the public debt consisted of (in 1,000m. francs): Internal debt consolidated, 4,167·3; short and middle terms, 1,846·4; at sight, 99·2.

Currency. The unit of currency is the *Belgian franc* (BEF) of 100 *centimes*.

In May 1990 the Belgian franc was pegged to operate within a very narrow band against the German Deutschmark within the European Monetary System. Note circulation 31 Dec. 1990, 431,978m. francs.

In March 1992 £1 = BFr59·40; US$1 = BFr33·84.

Banking and Finance. The bank of issue is the National Bank (*Governor*, Alfons Verplaetse), instituted in 1850. The Governor is appointed for 5 years. It is the cashier of the State, and is authorized to carry on the usual banking operations. Its articles of association were modified in 1948 to strengthen public control.

Savings banks: The General Savings and Superannuation Bank (*Caisse Générale d'Epargne et de Retraite*), a state institution under the authority of the Minister of Finance, consists of a unit (the Caisse d'Epargne) which performs the whole range of banking activities and a further unit which embodies the funds engaged in social security and insurance activities. It co-operates with the postal service, obviating the need of a postal-savings system. The savings deposits and savings bonds of the Caisse d'Epargne amounted to BFr1,065,774m. on 31 Dec. 1990. The Banking and Finance Commission supervises the financial situation and the activities of the Caisse d'Epargne, and also of the private savings banks, whose liabilities expressed in savings accounts and bonds amounted to BFr1,373,341m. on 31 Dec. 1990.

There is a stock exchange in Brussels. Stock exchange reforms of Jan. 1991 provided for the formation of stockbroking firms into limited companies (which may be owned by banks or insurance companies), and set new strict rules on capital adequacy. The Banking and Finance Commission (formerly the Banking Commission) was renamed and given wider powers.

Weights and Measures. The metric system is in force.

ENERGY AND NATURAL RESOURCES

Electricity. The production of electricity amounted to 67,162m. kwh. in 1990. In 1990 66% of electricity was nuclear-produced. Supply 127 and 220 volts; 50 Hz.

Gas. Production of gas (in 1m. cu. metres): 675 in 1980; 690 in 1981; 594 in 1982; 623 in 1983; 717 in 1984; 716 in 1985; 636 in 1986; 674 in 1987; 689 in 1988.

Minerals. Output (in tonnes) for 4 calendar years:

	1987	1988	1989	1990
Coal	4,356,455	2,487,217	1,892,600	1,035,832
Coke	5,226,272	5,548,724	5,458,820	5,421,351
Cast iron	8,242,366	9,146,905	8,862,655	9,415,851
Wrought steel	9,786,422	11,220,497	10,952,815	10,419,201
Finished steel	7,415,200	8,771,198	8,599,877	9,127,256

Agriculture. There were, in 1990, 1,357,366 ha under cultivation, of which 334,555 were under cereals, 296,097 vegetables, 127,647 industrial plants, 153,569 root crops and 633,126 pastures and meadows.

Chief crops	Area in ha			Produce in tonnes		
	1988	1989	1990	1988	1989	1990
Wheat	186,258	202,784	205,050	1,251,782	1,402,100	1,266,265
Barley	120,292	107,725	92,506	737,760	646,986	532,350
Oats	15,728	12,737	8,842	54,892	44,708	34,040
Rye	3,365	3,133	2,954	14,299	12,531	12,612
Potatoes	41,104	41,529	48,271	1,613,659	1,442,703	1,664,948
Beet (sugar)	109,316	105,800	107,837	6,108,603	6,061,292	6,418,459
Beet (fodder)	12,332	11,939	11,587	1,163,938	1,114,052	1,049,279
Tobacco	415	439	444	1,461	1,623	1,493

In 1990 there were 21,141 horses, 3,248,780 cattle, 192,133 sheep, 8,174 goats and 6,700,422 pigs.

Forestry. In 1990 forest covered 609,744 ha.

Fisheries. Fish landed, 1990: 30,186 tonnes valued at 2,966m. francs. The fishing fleet had a total tonnage of 25,498 gross tons.

INDUSTRY. Output in 1990 of sugar factories and refineries, 1,022,677 tonnes; 8 distilleries, 24,681 hectolitres of alcohol; 126 breweries, 14·14m. hectolitres of beer; margarine factories, 188,816 tonnes.

Six trusts control the greater part of Belgian industry: The Société Générale (founded in 1822) owns about 40% of coal, 50% of steel, 65% of non-ferrous metals and 35% of electricity; Brufina-Confinindus operates in steel, coal, electricity and heavy engineering; the Groupe Solvay rules the chemical industry; the Groupe Copée has interests in steel and coal; Empain controls tramways and electrical equipment; the Banque Lambert owns petroleum firms and their accessories.

FOREIGN ECONOMIC RELATIONS. In 1922 an economic union was formed by Belgium and Luxembourg, and the customs frontier between them was abolished. On 1 Jan. 1948 a customs union came into force between Belgium and Luxembourg on the one hand and The Netherlands on the other known as the *Benelux Economic Union*. A full economic union of the three countries came into operation on 1 Nov. 1960.

Benelux information is supplied by the Secretariat General of the Benelux Economic Union, Rue de la Régence, 39, 1000 Brussels. It publishes *Benelux. Bulletin Trimestriel de Statistique; Statistisch Kwartaalbericht* (1955 ff.).

External debt was 1,131,100m. francs in 1990.

Commerce. Trade by selected countries (in 1,000 Belgian francs):

	Imports from			Exports to		
	1988	1989	1990	1988	1989	1990
France	522,017,828	578,373,841	635,542,707	675,428,913	806,793,789	797,713,381
USA	144,308,070	183,330,015	179,284,559	168,334,379	189,790,287	170,255,394
UK	258,982,640	305,974,772	331,371,530	315,503,055	370,201,871	342,128,965
Netherlands	602,058,448	684,611,051	704,092,022	496,597,430	540,130,963	536,944,790
German Dem. Rep.	7,275,266	8,088,530	5,260,059	5,637,680	5,430,082	4,371,480
Germany, Fed. Rep.	829,074,083	912,174,054	711,027,513	657,665,780	744,629,445	598,718,675

	Imports from			*Exports to*		
	1988	1989	1990	1988	1989	1990
Argentina	9,621,813	11,694,046	9,835,544	2,725,186	1,815,384	1,373,614
Italy	144,480,019	164,069,857	180,809,311	210,426,308	250,994,947	258,281,927
Switzerland	61,273,525	63,132,618	65,621,842	77,240,373	89,455,894	81,314,471
Zaïre	31,286,766	34,107,648	28,265,925	11,312,419	12,652,442	11,172,097
Denmark	20,849,828	22,720,109	24,771,387	32,096,727	35,025,811	35,279,436
USSR	45,927,319	46,522,015	47,080,785	19,324,636	21,225,586	14,987,697
India	19,415,820	27,921,187	23,747,151	50,780,290	63,958,221	49,024,270
South Africa	20,687,750	28,837,005	22,085,069	13,541,472	15,185,749	12,913,341
Canada	23,241,765	25,810,237	22,263,171	17,205,073	19,037,636	17,143,914
Brazil	19,045,975	22,818,768	21,847,887	4,148,598	6,089,295	5,034,233
Australia	14,487,917	17,740,232	13,558,023	9,610,003	13,311,949	11,248,366

Imports and exports for 6 calendar years (in 1,000 Belgian francs):

	Imports	*Exports*		*Imports*	*Exports*
1985	3,317,811,996	3,167,691,043	1988	3,386,496,188	3,381,088,190
1986	3,065,238,630	3,070,326,871	1989	3,883,879,983	3,943,071,108
1987	3,110,090,284	3,100,148,807	1990	4,002,058,505	3,942,852,100

The total trade between Belgium-Luxembourg and the UK was as follows (British Department of Trade returns, in £1,000 sterling):

	1987	1988	1989	1990	1991
Imports to UK	4,362,463	4,956,037	5,700,534	5,732,427	5,472,663
Exports and re-exports from UK	3,857,717	4,251,961	4,872,641	5,648,625	5,870,876

Principal Belgian-Luxembourg exports to UK in 1990[1] (tonnes; francs): Textiles (174,230; 30,511m.); metals (801,914; 30,637m.); chemical and pharmaceutical products (622,056; 29,659m.); precious stones and manufactures thereof (439; 43,515m.).

Principal Belgian-Luxembourg imports from the UK in 1990[1] (tonnes; francs): Machinery and electrical apparatus (135,882; 67,828m.); vehicles, chiefly motor cars, and aircraft (149,497; 34,713m.); textiles (54,189; 12,648m.); precious stones (104; 92,730m.); base metals and manufactures thereof (426,980; 16,165m.).

[1] Provisional.

Tourism. In 1990 receipts totalled 123·6m. francs.

COMMUNICATIONS

Roads. Length of roads, 1990: Motorways,1,631 km; other state roads, 12,885 km; provincial roads, 1,360 km. The number of motor vehicles registered on 1 Aug. 1991 was 4,730,774, including 3,970,317 passenger cars, 15,378 buses, 360,472 lorries, 38,416 non-agricultural tractors, 154,434 agricultural tractors, 148,627 motor cycles and 43,130 special vehicles.

Railways. The main Belgian lines were a State enterprise from their inception in 1834. In 1926 the *Société Nationale des Chemins de Fer Belges (SNCB)* was formed to take over the railways. The State is sole holder of the ordinary shares of SNCB, which carry the majority vote at General Meetings. The length of railway operated in 1991 was 3,479 km, (electrified, 2,293 km). Revenue (1990), 72,523m. francs; expenditure, 71,612m. francs. In 1990, 67·3m. tonnes of freight and 142·3m. passengers were carried.

The regional transport undertakings Vlaamse Vervoermaatschappij and Société Régionale Wallonne de Transport operate electrified light railways around Charleroi (97 km) and from De Panne to Knokke (68 km). There is also a metro and tramway in Brussels (165 km), and tramways in Antwerp (180 km) and Ghent (29 km).

Civil Aviation. The national Belgian airline SABENA (*Société anonyme belge d'exploitation de la navigation aérienne*) was set up in 1923. Its capital is 750m. francs. It was announced in Nov. 1990 that it was to be partially privatized, the state retaining a 25% stake. SABENA operates routes to Europe, North and South

America, North, Central and South Africa and to the Near, Middle and Far East. In 1990 its airfleet comprised 30 aircraft. In 1989 SABENA flew 72m. km, carrying 2,811,792 passengers and 662 tonne/km of freight.

Shipping. [1] On 1 Jan. 1991 the merchant fleet was composed of 70 vessels of 1,919,570 tons. There were 38 shipping companies.

[1] Belgian shipping returns are given in the official 'Moorsom tons', which may be converted into net tons by deducting 19·85% from the Moorsom total.

The navigation at the port of Antwerp in 1990: Number of vessels entered, 15,749; tonnage, 138,220,267. Number of vessels cleared, 15,979; tonnage, 139,735,786.

The total length of navigable waterways was 1,569·3 km in 1990.

Telecommunications. On 31 Dec. 1989 there were 1,832 post offices. The gross revenue of the post office in 1990 was 38,251m. francs.

In 1989 there were 5,138,282 telephones. In 1990 there were 3,912,629 telephone subscribers, 44,501 mobile telephone subscribers and 17,720 telex subscribers. There were 35,883 data transmission lines.

Broadcasting is organized according to the language communities. BRTN, RTBF and BRF are public institutions transmitting in Dutch, French and German respectively. BRTN has 6 radio and 2 TV services: Radio 1 (documentary and drama), Radio 2 (news and entertainment), Radio 3 (cultural), Studio Brussels (youth emphasis), World Service, Night Radio, TV-1 and TV-2. It transmits from 10 radio and 7 TV stations. RTBF has 4 radio and 2 TV services: Radio 1 (documentary), Radio 2 (news and entertainment), Radio 3 (cultural), Radio 21 (youth emphasis), RTBF1 (TV) and Télé 21. It transmits from 12 radio and 7 TV stations. BRF transmits a radio programme from 3 stations. TV colour is by PAL. There are also 3 commercial networks: VTM (Dutch; cable only), RTL-TV1 (French; 1 station) and Canal Plus (French; 3 stations). Number of receivers (1990), radio, 2,252,116; TV, 3,296,076 (including 2,898,954 colour).

Cinemas (1990). There were 441 cinemas, with a seating capacity of 106,443.

Newspapers (1989). There are 35 daily newspapers (some of them only regional or local editions of larger dailies), of which 19 are in French, 15 in Dutch and 1 in German.

JUSTICE, RELIGION, EDUCATION AND WELFARE

Justice. Judges are appointed for life. There is a court of cassation, 5 courts of appeal, and assize courts for political and criminal cases. There are 27 judicial districts, each with a court of first instance. In each of the 222 cantons is a justice and judge of the peace. There are, besides, various special tribunals. There is trial by jury in assize courts. The death penalty, which had been in abeyance for 45 years, was formally abolished in 1991.

Religion. Of the inhabitants professing a religion the majority are Roman Catholic, but no inquiry as to the profession of faith is now made at the censuses. There are, however, statistics concerning the clergy, and according to these there were in 1991: Roman Catholic higher clergy, 155; inferior clergy, 4,416; Protestant pastors, 85; Anglican Church, 8 chaplains; Jews (rabbis and ministers), 25; Greek Orthodox priests, 30. The State does not interfere in any way with the internal affairs of any church. There is full religious liberty, and part of the income of the ministers of all denominations is paid by the State. There are 8 Roman Catholic dioceses subdivided into 260 deaneries.

The Protestant (Evangelical) Church is under a synod. There is also a Central Jewish Consistory, a Central Committee of the Anglican Church and a Free Protestant Church.

Education. Following the constitutional reform of 1988, education is the responsibility of the Flemish and Wallon communities, who in 1990 received respectively BFr165,000m. and BFr135,000m.

Elementary Education. There were 4,577 (1989–90) primary schools, with 952,024 pupils and 4,125 (1989–90) infant schools, with 371,838 pupils.

Secondary Education. 2,069 (1989–90) middle schools had a total of 71,710 pupils in the general classes and 111,278 in the technical classes in the traditional system and 626,185 pupils in the new system.

Normal Schools. Under the French and German linguistic systems there were 22 (1989–90) schools for training secondary teachers (2,825 students); 25 for training elementary teachers (3,010 students); 16 technical normal schools with 743 students and 17 normal infant schools with 2,111 pupils.

Higher Education (1989–90). Higher education is given in state universities: Ghent (12,532 students), Liège (10,424), Mons (2,212), the Polytechnic Faculty in Mons (1,000), the Antwerp State University Centre (2,006), the Gembloux Faculty of Agronomical Sciences (900), the Royal Military School in Brussels (926) and in the private universities: Catholic University of Louvain (40,790), the Free University of Brussels (23,079), University Institution Antwerp (1,945), St Ignatius Antwerp (3,656), Our Lady of Peace in Namur (4,187), Catholic University Faculty in Mons (1,401), St Louis in Brussels (1,208), St Aloysius in Brussels (910), the Limbourg University Centre (757) and the Protestant Faculty of Theology in Brussels (144). The total number of students in university colleges, faculties and institutes was 108,480.

There are 5 royal academies of fine arts and 5 royal conservatoires at Brussels, Liège, Ghent, Antwerp and Mons.

Health. In 1990 there were 33,442 physicians (including 458 dentists), 6,592 other dentists and 12,014 pharmacists. Hospital beds numbered 50,354 on 1 Jan. 1989.

Social Security. Social security is based on the law of Dec. 1944. It applies to all workers subject to an employment contract, and is administered by the Central National Office of Social Security (ONSS), which collects from employers and employees all contributions referring to family allowances, health insurance, old age insurance, holidays and unemployment. These sums are distributed by the Central Office to the various institutions concerned with these benefits. Insurance against unemployment is organized through a common fund, which also undertakes to retrain the unemployed for another employment while providing for their families. Since 1944 further laws have increased allowances, made fresh provisions for housing (1945), injuries while working, professional illnesses, etc. (1948).

Apart from private charity, the poor are assisted by the communes through the agency of the *Centre Public d'Aide Sociale* in French-speaking parts of the country and *Openbaar Centrum voor Maatschappelijk Welzijn* in Dutch-speaking areas. Provisions of a national character have been made for looking after war orphans and men disabled in the war. Certain other establishments, either state or provincial, provide for the needs of the deaf-mutes and the blind, and of children who are placed under the control of the courts. Provision is also made for repressing begging and providing shelter for the homeless.

DIPLOMATIC REPRESENTATIVES

Of Belgium in Great Britain (103 Eaton Sq., London, SW1W 9AB)
Ambassador: Herman Dehennin.

Of Great Britain in Belgium (Britannia Hse., rue Joseph II 28, 1040 Brussels)
Ambassador: Robert James O'Neill, CMG.

Of Belgium in the USA (3330 Garfield St., NW, Washington, D.C., 20008)
Ambassador: J. Cassiers.

Of the USA in Belgium (Blvd. du Régent 27, 1000 Brussels)
Ambassador: Maynard W. Glitman.

Of Belgium to the United Nations
Ambassador: M. Paul Noterdaeme.

Further Reading

The Institut National de Statistique. *Statistiques du commerce extérieur* (monthly). *Bulletin de Statistique*. Bi-monthly. *Annuaire Statistique de la Belgique* (from 1870).—*Annuaire statistiquede poche* (from 1965). *Statistiques Agricoles*. Irregular.

Annuaire administratif et judiciaire de Belgique. Annual. Brussels
Ministère des Affaires Economiques. *L'économie belge*. Annual (from 1947)
Guide des Ministères: Revue de l'Administration Belge. Brussels, Annual
Hermans, T. J. *et al*. (eds.) *The Flemish Movement: a Documentary History*. London, 1992
Riley, R. C., *Belgium*. [Bibliography] Oxford and Santa Barbara, 1989

National statistical office: Institut National de Statistique, Rue de Louvain 44, 1000 Brussels.

BELIZE

Capital: Belmopan
Population: 193,000 (1990)
GNP per capita: US$1,600 (1989)

HISTORY. The early settlement of the territory was probably effected by British woodcutters about 1638; from that date to 1798, in spite of armed opposition from the Spaniards, settlers held their own and prospered. In 1780 the Home Government appointed a superintendent, and in 1862 the settlement was declared a colony, subordinate to Jamaica. It became an independent colony in 1884. Self-government was attained in 1964. Independence was achieved on 21 Sept. 1981.

AREA AND POPULATION. Belize is bounded in the north by Mexico, west and south by Guatemala and east by the Caribbean. Fringing the coast there are 3 atolls and some 400 islets (cays) in the world's second longest barrier reef (140 miles). Area, 22,963 sq. km. There are 6 districts:

	Sq. km	Population census, 1980		Sq. km	Population census, 1980
Corozal	1,860	22,902	Cayo	5,338	22,337
Belize	4,204	50,801	Stann Creek	2,176	14,181
Orange Walk	4,737	22,870	Toledo	4,649	11,762

Total population (census, 1980) 145,353. Estimate (1990) 193,000. In 1989 the birth rate per 1,000 was 37·2 and the death rate 4·2; infantile mortality 19·4 per 1,000 births and there were 1,138 marriages. Life expectancy was 67 years.

English is the official language. Spanish is spoken by 31·6% of the population. The main ethnic groups are Creole (African descent), Mestizo (Spanish-Maya) and Garifuna (Caribs).

Main city, Belize City; population, census 1980, 39,771. Estimate (1989) 43,621. Following the severe hurricane which struck the territory on 31 Oct. 1961 the then capital Belmopan was moved to a new site 50 miles inland; construction began in Jan. 1967 and it became the seat of government on 3 Aug. 1970 (population, 1989, 5,276). *See* map in the 1978–79 edition of THE STATESMAN'S YEAR-BOOK.

CLIMATE. A tropical climate with high rainfall and small annual range of temperature. The driest months are Feb. and March. Belize. Jan. 74°F (23·3°C), July 81°F (27·2°C). Annual rainfall 76" (1,890 mm). –

CONSTITUTION AND GOVERNMENT. Having achieved self-government in Jan. 1964 delays occurred in achieving independence because of the outstanding territorial claim by Guatemala. Attempts to reach agreement on the claim finally failed prior to independence being granted, but guarantees were given by Britain that a military force would remain.

The Constitution, which came into force on 21 Sept. 1981, provided for a National Assembly, with a 5-year term, comprising a 28-member House of Representatives elected by universal adult suffrage, and a Senate consisting of 8 members appointed by the Governor-General on the advice of the Prime Minister, 2 on the advice of the Leader of the Opposition and 1 on the advice of the Belize Advisory Council.

At the general election in Sept. 1989 the People's United Party (PUP) won 15 seats in the House of Representatives and the United Democratic Party (UDP) 13.

Governor-General: Dame Elmira Minita Gordon, GCMG, GCVO.
The cabinet in Oct. 1991 was composed as follows:
Prime Minister and Minister of Finance, Trade, Commerce, Home Affairs and Defence: The Rt Hon. George Cadle Price.
Deputy Prime Minister and Minister of Natural Resources: Florencio Marin. *Foreign Affairs, Economic Development and Education:* Said Musa. *Industry, Hous-*

ing and Co-operatives: Leopoldo Briceño. *Works:* Samuel Waight. *Health and Urban Development:* Dr Theodore Aranda. *Attorney-General and Minister of Tourism and the Environment:* Glenn Godfrey. *Social Services and Community Development:* Remijio Montejo. *Agriculture and Fisheries:* Michael Espat. *Labour, Public Service and Local Government:* Valdemar Castillo. *Energy and Communications:* Carlos Diaz.

There are 5 Ministers of State.

National flag: Blue with red band along the top and bottom edges. In the centre a white disc containing the coat of arms surrounded by a green garland.

Local Government. At elections to 7 municipalities in March 1991 the electorate was 23,215 and 19,527 votes were cast. The PUP gained control of 5 town boards and the UDP of 2.

DEFENCE. In June 1990 Belize assumed full responsibility for the Belize Defence Force, which consists of 1 infantry battalion, with 4 active and 3 reserve companies. The Air Wing operates two twin-engined BN-2B Defenders for maritime patrol and transport duties. There is also a Maritime wing of the Belize Defence Force. It operates 2 armed Wasp patrol vessels and a number of smaller vessels utilized for anti-smuggling and coast guard duties. Naval personnel (1991) 50. British Army Forces in Belize number about 1,500, including a detachment of the Royal Air Force which deploys Harrier V/STOL ground attack/reconnaissance aircraft and Puma and Gazelle helicopters. Personnel (1992) 660.

INTERNATIONAL RELATIONS. While not giving up its territorial claims, Guatemala recognised Belize's independence in Sept. 1991. In return Guatemala is to make some use of Belizean ports, and Belize reduced its maritime zones to 3 miles.

Membership. Belize is a member of the UN, the Commonwealth, OAS, CARICOM and is an ACP state of the EEC.

ECONOMY

Budget. The budget for 1991–92 envisaged expenditure (in $B1m.) of 307·4 (260 in 1990–91), made up of 175·4 for recurrent expenditure, 73·1 for capital expenditure financed from abroad and 58·9 for capital expenditure financed from domestic sources. Of the recurrent expenditure, salaries accounted for 90·1, goods and services for 33·8, debt-servicing for 29·9, transfer payments for 13·3 and pensions for 8·3. Of total expenditure 127·5 was devoted to economic services (which included 15·7 to administration, 27·3 to agriculture, 9·8 to industry and 37·5 to roads and waterways), 50·8 to education, 35·4 to general services, 22·2 to health, 11·9 to welfare, 10·8 to defence and 10·1 to housing.

Currency. The unit of currency is the *Belize dollar* (BZD) of 100 *cents*. There are notes of $B100, 20, 10, 5 and 1, and coins of 1-, 5-, 10-, 25- and 50-cent and $B1. Money supply was $B380·2m. in 1991. In March 1992, £1 = $B3·51 and US$1 = $B2·00.

Banking. A Central Bank was established in 1981. There were (1987) 4 commercial banks with a total of 14 branches: Belize Bank, Barclays Bank PLC, Bank of Nova Scotia and the locally incorporated Atlantic Bank. The Development Finance Corporation provides long-term credit for development of agriculture and industry. There were (1985) 7 government savings banks and 17 insurance companies, and (1989) 40 registered credit unions. Amendments to the Banking Ordinance permit offshore banking.

ENERGY AND NATURAL RESOURCES

Electricity. Production (1988) 90·5m. kwh. Supply 110 and 220 volts; 60 Hz. A rural electrification unit was set up in 1991.

Oil. Several oil companies were (1990) exploring for oil both off-shore and on-shore. Oil was discovered in the north in 1981 but not in commercial quantities.

Agriculture. In 1986 agriculture provided 65% of total foreign exchange earnings and employed 30% of the total labour force. The main agricultural export is sugar, followed by citrus fruit, chiefly grapefruit and oranges processed into oil, squash and concentrates. Citrus production, 1989, 1,447,834 boxes of oranges, 889,092 boxes of grapefruit. Sugar-cane production in 1989 was 867,267 tonnes. Bananas are the third export crop; production, 1989, 1,440,099 boxes. [Ed. note: Box of grapefruit, 80 lb., oranges, 90 lb., bananas, 42 lb.]. Cacao is becoming increasingly important as an export crop. Mangoes are also grown commercially; production, 1989, 200 tonnes. Main cultivated food crops (with production, 1989) are maize (51,104,859 lb), rice (11,115,000 lb) and red kidney beans (9,279,925 lb). Belize is self-sufficient in fresh beef and pork, poultry and eggs. A dairy plant (daily milk processing capacity 400 gallons) began operations in 1986. Beekeeping co-operatives produced 206,216 lb of honey in 1989.

Livestock (1988): Cattle, 54,025; sheep, 2,585; pigs, 16,417; poultry, 2·5m.

Forestry. 1m. ha, 44% of the total land area, were under forests in 1988, which include mahogany, cedar, Santa Maria, pine and rosewood, and many secondary hardwoods of known or probable market value, as well as woods suitable for pulp production. Exports of forest produce in 1989 amounted to $B4·7m.

Fisheries. There were (1988) 8 registered fishing co-operatives. Food and game fish are plentiful, and domestic consumption is heavy. Main export markets for scale fish are in the USA, Mexico and Jamaica. Fish products exported in 1989 to the USA were valued at $B12.8m. Turtles—Hawksbill, Loggerhead and Green—are plentiful but as yet are not exported. There were 747 fishing vessels in 1988.

INDUSTRY. In 1989 production of the major commodities was: Sugar, 90,934 tonnes; molasses, 28,440 tonnes; cigarettes, 97·1m.; beer, 740,000 gallons; batteries, 8,835; wheat flour, 21·5m. lb.; rum 15,000 proof gallons; fertilizer, 8,954 tonnes; garments, 3,492,000; citrus concentrates, 3,029,000 gallons; soft drinks, 881,000 cases.

Labour. The labour market alternates between full employment, often accompanied by local shortages in the citrus and sugar-cane harvesting (Jan.–July), and under-employment during the wet season (Aug.–Dec.), aggravated by the seasonal nature of the major industries.

Trade Unions. There are 14 accredited unions with an estimated membership of 8,200.

FOREIGN ECONOMIC RELATIONS

Commerce. In 1989 total imports amounted to $B431·4m. Total exports, $B248·1m. The principal domestic exports were timber ($B4·7m.), 78,750 long tons of sugar ($B68·1m.), fish products ($B38·9m.), garments, 1988 ($B37·3m.), 56·6m. lbs of bananas, 1·85m. gallons of citrus products ($B57·6m.), molasses ($B1·3m.) and honey ($B200,000).

Total trade between Belize and UK (British Department of Trade returns, in £1,000 sterling):

	1987	1988	1989	1990	1991
Imports to UK	22,757	22,461	24,272	22,734	20,849
Exports and re-exports from UK	7,543	12,064	11,842	12,439	14,574

Tourism. Tourists totalled 216,187 in 1989 spending US$35m.

COMMUNICATIONS

Roads. There are four major highways and all principal towns and villages are linked by road to Belmopan and Belize City. In 1988, there were 14,014 licensed vehicles.

Civil Aviation. The Philip Goldson International Airport is 14 km from Belize

City. In 1989, 5 airlines maintained international services to and from the USA, Central America and Mexico. In 1988, 765,430 passengers arrived and departed on international flights. Domestic air services provide connections to all main towns and 3 of the main offshore islands.

Shipping. The main port is Belize City, with a modern deep water port able to handle containerized shipping. During 1989, 276 port calls were made by cargo vessels carrying 304,960 short tons of cargo. The second largest port, Commerce Bight just south of Dangriga, can accommodate vessels up to 23 ft draft.

Telecommunications. Number of telephones (1990), 15,917 (8,628 in Belize City). Belize Telecommunications Ltd has instituted a country-wide fully automatic telephone dialling facility. There are 7 main post offices and 61 sub-post offices.

In Aug. 1990, the Belize Broadcasting Network became the Broadcasting Corporation of Belize (BCB). The BCB broadcasts daily. Proportion of programmes; 70% in English: 25% in Spanish and 5% in the Maya, Mopan, Maya Ketchi and Garifuna dialects. In 1989 there were 12 television stations. There are satellite links with Bermuda, the USA and the UK, and radio links with Central America.

Cinemas (1988). There were 5 cinemas with seating capacity of 5,000.

Newspapers. There were 4 weekly newspapers and 2 monthly magazines in 1990.

JUSTICE, RELIGION, EDUCATION AND WELFARE

Justice. Each of the 6 judicial districts has summary jurisdiction courts (criminal) and district courts (civil), both of which are presided over by magistrates. There is a Supreme Court, a Court of Appeal and a Family Court was established in May 1989 to deal with domestic and juvenile cases. There is a Director of Public Prosecutions, a Chief Justice and 2 Puisne Judges.

Religion. In 1986 about 62% of the population was Roman Catholic and 28% Protestant, including Anglican, Methodist, Seventh Day Adventist, Mennonite, Nazarene, Jehovah's Witness, Pentecostal and Baptist. There was a small group of Bahai.

Education. State education is managed by the main religious groups, Roman Catholic and Anglican. It is compulsory for children between 6-14 years and primary education is free. In 1989, 228 primary schools had a total enrolment of 44,000 pupils with 1,861 teachers; 31 secondary schools, 8,814 pupils with, in 1988, 576 teachers; (1987) 8 other technical schools, 932 students with 69 teachers. The Belize Teachers' College offers courses for primary and secondary school teachers. The 2-year course leads to a teachers' diploma. The University College of Belize opened in 1986. There is 1 government-maintained special school for handicapped children. The University of the West Indies maintains an extra-mural department in Belize City.

93% literacy was claimed in 1991.

Health. In 1990 there were 7 government hospitals (1 in Belmopan, 1 in Belize City and 1 in each of the other 5 districts) and an infirmary for geriatric and chronically ill patients, with 94 doctors and 525 hospital beds. Medical services in rural areas are provided by health care centres and mobile clinics.

DIPLOMATIC REPRESENTATIVES

Of Belize in Great Britain (200 Sutherland Ave., London, W9 1RX)
High Commissioner: Robert Leslie.

Of Great Britain in Belize (P.O. Box 91, Belmopan)
High Commissioner: David MacKilligin.

Of Belize in the USA (3400 International Dr., NW, Washington, D.C., 20008)
Ambassador: James Hyde.

Of the USA in Belize (Gabourel Lane and Hutson St., Belize City)
Ambassador: Eugene L. Scassa.

Of Belize to the United Nations
Ambassador: Carl Lindberg B. Rogers.

Further Reading

Abstract of Statistics 1981. Government Printer, Belize City, 1982
Belize Today. Government Printer, monthly
Bianchi, W. J., *Belize: The Controversy Between Guatemala and Great Britain.* New York, 1959
Dobson, D., *A History of Belize.* Belize, 1973
Fernandez, J., *Belize: Case Study for Democracy in Central America.* Aldershot, 1989
Grant, C. H., *The Making of Modern Belize.* CUP, 1976
Setzekorn, W. D., *Formerly British Honduras: A Profile of the New Nation of Belize.* Ohio Univ. Press, 1981
Woodward, R. L., Jr, *Belize.* [Bibliography] Oxford and Santa Barbara, 1980

BENIN

Capital: Porto-Novo
Population: 4·76m. (1990)
GNP per capita: US$380 (1989)

République du Bénin

HISTORY. The territory of the present State was occupied by France in 1892 and was constituted a division of French West Africa in 1904 under the name of Dahomey. It became an independent republic within the French Community on 4 Dec. 1958, and acquired full independence on 1 Aug. 1960.

In the sixth coup since independence, Maj. Mathieu (now Ahmed) Kerekou came to power on 26 Oct. 1972 and proclaimed a Marxist–Leninist state, whose name was altered from Dahomey to Benin on 1 Dec. 1975.

In Dec. 1989 the leadership abandoned Marxism-Leninism and called a national conference in Feb. 1990 to steer the country towards pluralist democracy.

AREA AND POPULATION. Benin is bounded east by Nigeria, north by Niger and Burkina Faso, west by Togo and south by the Gulf of Guinea. The area is 112,622 sq. km, and the population, census 1979, 3,338,240. Estimate (1990) 4,758,000.

Vital statistics, 1985–90: Growth rate, 3·2%; infant mortality, 110 per 1,000; expectation of life, 1989, 51 years.

The seat of government is Porto-Novo (208,258 inhabitants in 1982); the chief port and business centre is Cotonou (487,020 in 1982); other important towns (1982) are Parakou (65,945), Natitingou (50,800, 1979), Abomey (54,418), Kandi (53,000) and Ouidah. On 1 Jan. 1988 there were 3,033 refugees in Benin, primarily from Chad.

The areas, populations and capitals of the 6 provinces are as follows:

Province	Sq. km	Census 1979	Estimate 1987	Capital
Atakora	31,200	479,604	622,000	Natitingou
Borgou	51,000	490,669	630,000	Parakou
Zou	18,700	570,433	731,000	Abomey
Mono	3,800	477,378	610,000	Lokossa
Atlantique	3,200	686,258	909,000	Cotonou
Ouémé	4,700	626,868	806,000	Porto-Novo

French is the official language, while 47% of the people speak Fon, 12% Adja, 10% Bariba, 9% Yoruba, 6% Fulani, 5% Somba and 5% Aizo.

CLIMATE. In coastal parts there is an equatorial climate, with a long rainy season from March to July and a short rainy season in Oct. and Nov. The dry season increases in length from the coast, with inland areas having rain only between May and Sept. Porto Novo. Jan. 82°F (27·8°C), July 78°F (25·6°C). Annual rainfall 52" (1,300 mm). Cotonou. Jan. 81°F (27·2°C), July 77°F (25°C). Annual rainfall 53" (1,325 mm).

CONSTITUTION AND GOVERNMENT. The Benin Party of Popular Revolution (PRPB) held a monopoly of power from 1977 to 1989.

In Feb. 1990 a 'National Conference of the Vital Elements (*Vives forces*') of the Nation proclaimed its sovereignty and appointed Nicéphore Soglo *Prime Minister* of a provisional government. At a referendum in Dec. 1990 93·2% of votes cast were in favour of the new constitution, which has introduced a presidential regime. At the elections of Feb. 1991 24 of the 34 legal parties fielded candidates and 17 gained seats.

At the presidential elections of March 1991 Nicéphor Soglo defeated the incumbent president, Brig.-Gen. Ahmed Kerekou, by gaining 67·7% of votes cast. He was sworn in as *President* on 4 April.

The *Speaker* of the National Assembly is Adrien Houngbedji (Democratic Renewal Party).

National flag: Horizontally yellow over red with a green vertical strip in the hoist.

National anthem: L'Aube Nouvelle (New Dawn; words and tune by Gilbert Dagnon).

Local Government. The 6 provinces are divided into 84 districts. In Nov. 1990 elections were held for mayors and district chiefs.

DEFENCE. There is selective conscription for 18 months.

Army. The Army consists of 3 infantry, 1 para-commando and 1 engineer battalions, 1 armoured reconnaissance squadron and 1 artillery battery. Strength (1991) 3,800, with an additional 2,000-strong paramilitary gendarmerie.

Navy. A naval force was formed in 1979 with 2 Soviet torpedo craft and 4 inshore patrol craft now unserviceable. A new French inshore patrol craft was delivered in 1987, and there is 1 tug. Personnel in 1991 numbered 200, and the force is based at Cotonou.

Air Force. The Air Force had a strength of (1991) about 350 officers and men, 2 twin-turboprop An-26 and 2 C-47 transports, 1 Cessna Skymaster, 1 Aero Commander 500, 2 Broussard communications aircraft and 1 Alouette and 2 Ecureuil helicopters.

INTERNATIONAL RELATIONS

Membership. Benin is a member of the UN, OAU and is an ACP state of EEC.

ECONOMY

Policy. A 10-year development plan (1981–90) envisaged an expenditure of 958,800m. francs CFA.

Budget. In 1987 revenue, 51,929m. francs CFA and expenditure, 53,737m. francs CFA.

Currency. The monetary unit is the *franc CFA* (XOF), with a parity value of 50 *francs CFA* to 1 French *franc*. There are coins of 1, 2, 5, 10, 25, 50 and 100 *francs CFA*, and banknotes of 50, 100, 500, 1,000, 5,000 and 10,000 *francs CFA*. In March 1992, £1 = 489·62 *francs CFA*; US$1 = 278·90 *francs CFA*.

Banking and Finance. The *Banque Centrale des Etats de l'Afrique de l'Ouest* is the bank of issue and the central bank. The *Banque Commerciale du Bénin*, in Cotonou, conducts all government business.

ENERGY AND NATURAL RESOURCES

Electricity. *Société Béninoise d'Electricité et d'Eau*, produced 172m. kwh in 1985 from generating plants at Cotonou, Porto-Novo and Parakou. Major development of hydro-electric resources along the Mono river are being conducted jointly with Togo. Supply 220 volts; 50 Hz.

Oil. The Semé oilfield, located 10 miles offshore, was discovered in 1968. Production commenced in 1982 and was 141,000 tonnes in 1991.

Agriculture. In 1990 2·84m. persons depended on agriculture, of whom 1·34m. were economically active. In 1989 1·41m. ha were arable, 0·45m. ha permanent cropland and 0·44m. permanent pasture. The chief products, 1990 (in 1,000 tonnes) were: Cassava, 827; yams, 992; maize, 407; sorghum, 110; groundnuts, 79; dry beans, 50; rice, 10; and sweet potatoes, 24, while cash crops were palm kernels, 25, palm oil, 40; cotton seed, 118; and coffee, 6.

Livestock (1990 in 1,000): Cattle (951), sheep (921), goats (1,028), pigs (714), poultry (25,000).

Forestry. There were (1989) 3·52m ha of forest, mainly in the north. Roundwood production in 1986 was 4·5m. cu. metres.

Fisheries. Total catch in 1986 was 23,500 tonnes (68% from inland and lagoon waters).

INDUSTRY. Industrial plants are few, limited mainly to palm-oil processing and brewing. There is a sugar complex at Savé, a cement plant at Onigbolo and textile mills at Cotonou and Parakou. Production (1985) included 51,000 tonnes of sugar, 37,000 tonnes of palm oil and 318,000 tonnes of cement.

Labour. The economically active population numbered 1·34m. in 1990. In 1973 the small trade unions were amalgamated to form a single body, now named the *Union Nationale des Syndicats des Travailleurs du Bénin*.

FOREIGN ECONOMIC RELATIONS. Foreign debt was US$1,005m. in 1988.

Commerce. Imports in 1983, US$113m.; exports, US$78m. The main exports are palm oil and kernels, cocoa, cotton and sugar. In 1984, 32% of exports were to Spain, 21% to Federal Republic of Germany and 16% to France, which provided the largest share (23%) of imports.

Total trade between Benin and UK (British Department of Trade returns, in £1,000 sterling):

	1987	1988	1989	1990	1991
Imports to UK	2,930	2,450	356	1,197	589
Exports and re-exports from UK	7,207	8,169	7,294	6,130	10,716

Tourism. There were 72,000 foreign tourists in 1985.

COMMUNICATIONS

Roads. There were 7,445 km of roads in 1985, 2,740 passenger cars and 567 goods vehicles.

Railways. There are 579 km of metre-gauge railway. One line connects Cotonou with Parakou (438 km) and is being extended to Dosso (in Niger); the second runs from Cotonou *via* Porto-Novo to Pobé (107 km); and the third from Cotonou *via* Ouidah to Segboroué on the Togo frontier (34 km), continuing to Lomé. In 1988 1·5m. passengers and 184m. tonne-km of freight were carried.

Civil Aviation. In 1981, 80,400 passengers and 9,763 tonnes of freight passed through Cotonou airport.There are other airports at Abomey, Natitingou, Kandi and Parakou.

Shipping. In 1983, 736,000 tonnes were unloaded and 64,400 tonnes loaded at the port of Cotonou. There were (1986) 15 vessels of 4,887 GRT registered in Benin.

Telecommunications. There were, in 1985, 8,650 telephones. Telegraph lines connect Cotonou with Togo, Niger and Senegal. The government-controlled Office de Radiodiffusion et Télévision du Bénin broadcasts a radio programme from Cotonou and a regional programme from Parakou, and a TV service (colour by SECAM) from Cotonou. In 1991 there were 326,920 radio and 16,346 TV sets.

Cinemas. In 1976 there were 4 cinemas with a seating capacity of 4,400.

Newspapers. In 1990 there were 31 daily newspapers.

JUSTICE, RELIGION, EDUCATION AND WELFARE

Justice. The Supreme Court is at Cotonou. There are Magistrates Courts in Cotonou, Porto-Novo, Natitingou, Abomey, Kandi, Ouidah and Parakou, and a *tribunal de conciliation* in each district.

Religion. 61% of the population follow traditional animist beliefs, about 22% are Christian, mainly Roman Catholic, and 15% Moslem.

Education. There were, in 1988, 471,016 pupils in 2,850 primary schools and 97,000 in 184 secondary schools. The University of Benin (Cotonou) had 6,302 students in 1983. Adult literacy (1980) 28%.

Health. In 1982 there were 6 hospitals, 31 health centres, 186 dispensaries and 65 maternity clinics with (1978, combined) 4,968 beds, and in 1979 there were 204 doctors, 13 dentists, 55 pharmacists and 1,294 midwives.

DIPLOMATIC REPRESENTATIVES

Of Benin in Great Britain
Ambassador: (Vacant) (resides in Paris).

Of Great Britain in Benin
Ambassador: A. C. D. S. MacRae, CMG (resides in Lagos).

Of Benin in the USA (2737 Cathedral Ave., NW, Washington, D.C., 20008)
Ambassador: Candide Ahouansou.

Of the USA in Benin (Rue Caporal Anani Bernard, Cotonou)
Ambassador: Harriet W. Isom.

Of Benin to the United Nations
Ambassador: René Valéry Mongbe.

BERMUDA

Capital: Hamilton
Population: 59,588 (1990)
GNP per capita: US$25,000 (1991)

HISTORY. The Spaniards visited the islands in 1515, but, according to a 17th-century French cartographer, they were discovered in 1503 by Juan Bermudez, after whom they were named. No settlement was made, and they were uninhabited until a party of colonists under Sir George Somers was wrecked there in 1609. A company was formed for the 'Plantation of the Somers' Islands', as they were called at first, and in 1684 the Crown took over the government.

AREA AND POPULATION. Bermuda consists of a group of some 150 small islands (about 20 inhabited), situated in the western Atlantic (32° 18' N. lat., 64° 46' W. long.); the nearest point of the mainland, about 570 miles distant, is Cape Hatteras, N.C., and 690 miles from New York.

The area is 20·59 sq. miles (53·3 sq. km), of which 2·3 sq. miles were leased in 1941 for 99 years to the US Government for naval and air bases. The civil population (i.e., excluding British and American military, naval and air force personnel) in 1980 (Census) was 54,893. Estimate (1990) 59,588.

Chief town, Hamilton; population, about 3,000.

In 1990 there were 912 live births, 884 marriages and 462 deaths. In 1988 the infantile mortality rate was 3·2 per 1,000 live births.

CLIMATE. A pleasantly warm and humid climate, with up to 60" (1,500 mm) of rain, spread evenly throughout the year. Hamilton. Jan. 63°F (17·2°C), July 79°F (26·1°C). Annual rainfall 58" (1,463 mm).

CONSTITUTION AND GOVERNMENT. Bermuda is a colony with representative government. Under the constitution of 8 June 1968 the Governor, appointed by the Crown, is normally bound to accept the advice of the Cabinet in matters other than external affairs, defence, internal security and the police, for which he retains special responsibility. The Cabinet is appointed from among members of the bicameral legislature, on the recommendation of the Premier. The Senate, of whom one or two members may serve on Cabinet, consists of 11 members. As a result of a Constitutional Conference held in Feb. 1979, it was decided that 5 Senators would be appointed by the Governor on the recommendation of the Premier, 3 by the Governor on the recommendation of the Opposition Leader and 3 by the Governor in his own discretion. The 40 members of the House of Assembly are elected 2 from each of 20 constituencies under full universal, adult suffrage. A general election was held in Feb. 1989. The United Bermuda Party won 23 seats, the Progressive Labour Party 15, and others, 2.

Governor: Sir Desmond Langley, KCVO, MBE.
Premier: Sir John W. D. Swan, KBE.
Flag: The British Red Ensign with the badge of the Colony in the fly.

DEFENCE. The Bermuda Regiment had 713 men and women in 1991.

ECONOMY

Budget. Revenue and expenditure in BD$1m. for years ending 31 March:

	1987–88	1988–89	1989–90	1990–91	1991–92
Revenue	251,550	297,639	307,439	342,000	361,600
Expenditure	220,172	245,542	274,738	306,081	322,536

Expenditure in BD$1,000 (excluding capital items) was earmarked as follows:

	1987–88	1988–89	1989–90	1990–91	1991–92
Education	30,063	32,775	35,814	39,495	41,459
Health and Social Services	565,783	801,500	59,803	70,109	74,723
Public Works	25,713	27,226	32,974	33,174	32,773
Police	18,589	20,572	22,817	25,614	25,427
Tourism	22,316	25,508	26,596	27,569	28,831
Marine and Ports Services	6,809	7,246	7,815	8,731	8,482
Public Transportation	3,932	5,318	5,298	6,207	5,925
Agriculture and Fisheries	6,747	7,647	7,753	9,228	9,258
Post Office	6,724	6,828	7,259	8,242	8,150

The estimated chief sources of revenue in 1991–92 were: Customs duties, $130m.; employment tax, $29m.; land tax, $19m.; hospital levy, $48m.; vehicle licenses, $11m.; stamp duties, $13m.; passenger taxes, $14m. Public debt, as at 31 March 1989, was nil.

Currency. Decimal currency based on a *Bermuda dollar* (BMD) of 100 *cents* was introduced 6 Feb. 1970. The Bermuda Monetary Authority issues notes in denominations of BD$100, 50, 20, 10, 5 and 2, and coins in values of BD$5, 1, 50c, 25c, 10c, 5c and 1c. In March 1992 £1 = BD$1.76 and US$1 = BD$1.00.

Banking and Finance. There are 3 banks, the Bank of Bermuda, Ltd, the Bank of N. T. Butterfield and Son, Ltd, and the Bermuda Commercial Bank, Ltd, with correspondent banks and representatives in either New York, London, Canada or Hong Kong.

There is a stock exchange.

Weights and Measures. Metric, except that US and Imperial (British) measures are used in certain fields.

ENERGY AND NATURAL RESOURCES

Electricity. Production (1990) 429m. kwh. Supply 115 volts; 60 Hz.

Agriculture. The chief products are fresh vegetables, bananas and citrus fruit. In 1990, 838 acres were being used for agricultural produce, pasture, forage and fallow. 6,554 persons were employed in agriculture, fishing and quarrying.

In 1990, total value of agricultural products was BD$10,616,923.

INDUSTRY

Trade Unions. Legislation providing for trade unions was enacted in Oct. 1946, and there are 9 trade unions with a total membership (1990) of 8,791.

FOREIGN ECONOMIC RELATIONS. Foreign firms conducting business overseas only are not subject to a 60% Bermuda ownership requirement. In 1989 270 international firms had a physical presence in Bermuda.

Commerce. The visible adverse balance of trade is more than compensated for by invisible exports, including tourism and off-shore insurance business.

Imports and exports in BD$:

	1987	1988	1989
Imports	419,939,867	488,285,238	534,409,715
Exports	29,218,856	30,815,235	50,398,458

Imports in 1988 from USA, $303m.; UK, $48m.; Canada, $31m; Japan, $29m.

In 1989 the principal imports were food, drink and tobacco ($98·052m.); electric equipment ($50m.); clothing ($37m.), transport equipment ($37m.). The bulk of exports comprise sales of fuel to aircraft and ships, and re-exports of pharmaceuticals.

Total trade between Bermuda and UK, in £1,000 sterling (British Department of Trade returns):

	1987	1988	1989	1990	1991
Imports to UK	1,208	6,767	4,517	12,849	3,559
Exports and re-exports from UK	25,383	24,995	27,122	28,114	16,205

Tourism. In 1990, 426,049 tourists visited Bermuda.

COMMUNICATIONS

Roads. In 1948 the railway service was discontinued and a government-operated bus service introduced.

Between 1908 and Aug. 1946 the use of motor vehicles, with the exception of ambulances, fire engines and other essential services, was prohibited. In 1990, out of 47,785 registered vehicles, 19,112 were private cars.

Civil Aviation. Bermuda is served on a regularly scheduled basis by Air Canada, British Airways, American Airlines, Delta Airlines, Eastern Airlines, Pan American World Airways, Continental and Piedmont. Bermuda is connected by direct flights to Toronto, Canada; New York, Newark, Baltimore, Boston, Raleigh Durham, Tampa, Philadelphia and Atlanta in the USA; and London. The Caribbean is reached through scheduled connexions in the USA and Europe is reached through Gatwick.

Shipping. In 1990, there were 121 visits by cruise ships, 272 visits by cargo ships and 22 visits by oil and gas tankers.

Telecommunications (1990). There are 15 post offices. The Bermuda Telephone Company is privately owned. There is International Direct Dialling to over 140 countries. Cable and Wireless Ltd provide external communications including telephone, telex, packet-switching, facsimile and electronic mail in conjunction with the Bermuda Telephone Company, and an International Database Access Service. Radio and television broadcasting is commercial.

Newspapers (1991). There is 1 daily newspaper with a circulation of about 18,000 and 3 weeklies with a total circulation of 27,500.

JUSTICE, EDUCATION AND WELFARE

Justice. There are 3 magistrates' courts, 3 Supreme Courts and a court of appeal. The police had a strength of 476 men and women in 1989.

Education. Education is compulsory between the ages of 5 and 16, and government assistance is given by the payment of grants, and, where necessary, of school fees. In 1988, there were 18 primary schools, 14 secondary schools (of which 5 are private, including 2 denominational schools and one run by the US Armed Forces in Bermuda), 4 special schools at the primary and secondary levels for handicapped persons aged 14–21, and 11 pre–schools. There were 650 full-time students attending the Bermuda College in 1990. Extra-mural courses are available from Queen's University in Canada and the University of Maryland in the USA.

Health. In 1990 there were 2 hospitals, 59 doctors, 27 dentists, 548 nurses and 36 pharmacists.

Further Reading

Report of the Manpower Survey 1989. Hamilton, 1989
Bermuda Report, Second Edition 1985–88. Hamilton, 1988
Hayward, S. J., Holt-Gomez, V. and Sterrer, W., *Bermuda's Delicate Balance: People and the Environment.* Hamilton, 1981
Warwick, J. B., (ed.) *Who's Who in Bermuda 1980–81.* Hamilton, 1982
Wilkinson, H. C., *Bermuda from Sail to Steam.* OUP, 1973
Zuill, W. S., *The Story of Bermuda and Her People.* 2nd ed. London, 1992

National library: The Bermuda Library, Hamilton. *Head Librarian:* Cyril O. Packwood.

BHUTAN

Druk-yul

(Kingdom of Bhutan)

Capital: Thimphu
Population: 0·6m. (1990)
GNP per capita: US$470 (1989)

HISTORY. In 1774 the East India Company concluded a treaty with the ruler of Bhutan. Under a treaty signed in Nov. 1865 the Bhutan Government was granted an annual subsidy. By an amending treaty concluded in Jan. 1910 the British Government undertook to exercise no interference in the internal affairs of Bhutan, and the Bhutan Government agreed to be guided by the advice of the British Government in regard to its external relations.

The Government of India concluded a fresh treaty with Bhutan on 8 Aug. 1949. Under this treaty the Government of Bhutan continues to be guided by the Government of India in regard to its external relations, and the Government of India have undertaken not to interfere in the internal administration of Bhutan. The subsidy paid to Bhutan has been increased to Rs 500,000, and the Government of India agreed to retrocede to Bhutan an area of about 32 sq. miles in the territory known as Dewangiri, which was annexed in 1865.

AREA AND POPULATION. Bhutan is situated in the eastern Himalayas, bounded in the north by China and on all other sides by India. Extreme length from east to west 190 miles: extreme breadth 90 miles. Area about 18,000 sq. miles (46,500 sq. km); population estimated at approximately 600,000 (1991). A Nepali minority makes up 30%-35% of the population, mainly in the south. Life expectancy (1985) was 48 years. The capital is at Thimphu (1991, 27,000 population).

CLIMATE. The climate is largely controlled by altitude. The mountainous north is cold, with perpetual snow on the summits, but the centre has a more moderate climate, though winters are cold, with rainfall under 40" (1,000 mm). In the south, the climate is humid sub-tropical and rainfall approaches 200" (5,000 mm).

KING. Jigme Singye Wangchuck, succeeded his father Jigme Dorji Wangchuck who died 21 July 1972.

In 1907 the Tongsa Penlop (the governor of the province of Tongsa in central Bhutan), Sir Ugyen Wangchuk, GCIE, KCSI, was elected as the first hereditary Maharaja of Bhutan. The Bhutanese title is Druk Gyalpo, and his successor is now addressed as King of Bhutan.

CONSTITUTION AND GOVERNMENT. From Oct. 1969 the absolute monarchy was changed to a form of 'democratic monarchy'. The National Assembly (*Tshogdu*) was reinstituted in 1953. It has 150 members and meets once a year. Two-thirds are representatives of the people and are elected for a 3-year term. All Bhutanese over 25 years may be candidates. 12 monastic representatives are elected by the central and regional ecclesiastical bodies, while the remaining members are nominated by the King, and include members of the Council of Ministers (the Cabinet) and the Royal Advisory Council.

The official languages are Dzongkha, English and Nepali.

National flag: Diagonally yellow over orange, over all in the centre a white dragon.
Local government: There are 18 districts, each under a district officer (*dzongda*) responsible to the Royal Civil Service Commission through the Home Ministry.

DEFENCE

Army. There was (1992) an Army of 5,500 men. 3 to 5 weeks militia training was introduced in 1989 for senior students and government officials, and 3 months training for the general population in 1990.

INTERNATIONAL RELATIONS

Membership. Bhutan is a member of the UN.

ECONOMY

Policy. The revised 6th development plan (1987–92) allows for expenditure of Nu9,559m. Forest and mineral wealth is to be exploited and educational and medical facilities extended.

Budget. The preliminary budget for 1991–92 envisaged expenditure of Nu1,960m. and internal revenue of Nu1,194m.

Currency. Paper currency known as the *Ngultrum* was introduced in the early 1970s. Cupronickel and bronze currency coinage is known as *Chetrum* (100 *Chetrum* = 1 *Ngultrum*). Indian currency is also legal tender. In March 1992, £1 = Nu45·95; US$1 = Nu26·17.

Banking and Finance. The Bank of Bhutan was established in 1968. The headquarters are at Phuntsholing with 26 branches throughout the country. The Royal Monetary Authority, Thimphu, was founded in 1982 to act as Bhutan's central bank. Deposits (Dec. 1990) Nu1,132m.

ENERGY AND NATURAL RESOURCES

Electricity. Installed capacity at June 1991 was 1,132 mw (of which 347 mw were hydro-electric) with maximum generation of 1,556m. units. Production (1990) 1,950m. kwh, and 28 towns and 221 villages had electricity.

Minerals. Large deposits of limestone, marble, dolomite, slate, graphite, lead, copper, coal, talc, gypsum, beryl, mica, pyrites and tufa have been found. Most mining activity (principally limestone, coal, slate and dolomite) is small-scale.

Agriculture. The area under cultivation in 1988 was some 0·13m. ha. The chief products (1990 production in 1,000 tonnes) are rice (43), millet (7), wheat (5), barley (4), maize (40), potatoes (31), oranges (58), apples (5), handloom cloth, timber, cardamom and yaks.

Livestock (1990, in 1,000): Cattle, 422; pigs, 73; sheep, 54; goats, 37; horses, 27; yaks (1988), 36.

Forestry. In 1989, 2·61m. ha were forested.

INDUSTRY. In 1986 there were 349 manufacturing and mining firms (14 government-owned). 249 were in the food industry, mostly with fewer than 10 employees. There are a cement plant, a tea-chest ply veneer factory, a resin and turpentine factory, a salt iodization plant and 3 distilleries.

FOREIGN ECONOMIC RELATIONS. The cumulative outstanding convertible currency debt at 30 June 1991 was some US$75·82m. (about 32% of GNP), together with a rupee debt of some Rs1,000m. To the same date, debt service payments totalled US$4·4m.

Financial support is received from India, the UN and other international aid organizations.

Commerce. Trade with India dominates but oranges and apples, timber, cardamom and liquor are also exported to the Middle East, Singapore and Europe.

Total trade between Bhutan and UK (British Department of Trade returns, in £1,000 sterling):

	1988	1989	1990	1991
Imports to UK	175	328	111	231
Exports and re-exports from UK	12,464	363	778	565

Tourism. Tourism is the largest source of foreign exchange (1990, US$1·93m. gross). In 1990, 1,540 tourists visited Bhutan (1,480 in 1989).

COMMUNICATIONS

Roads. In 1990 there were about 2,336 km of roads and 7,664 registered vehicles, including 5,660 private cars, jeeps or scooters, and 1,504 heavy vehicles.

Civil Aviation. In 1991 Druk-Air made 1 flight weekly between Paro and Calcutta, 2 weekly flights to Delhi via Kathmandu and 2 weekly services to Bangkok via Dhaka using a 78-seater BAe-146.

Telecommunications. A modern postal system was introduced in 1962. In 1989 there were 2 general post offices, 55 post offices and 28 branch post offices. In 1989 there were 754 km of telephone lines, 13 automatic exchanges and 2,105 telephones.

An international microwave link connects Thimphu to the Calcutta and Delhi satellite connexions. A telecommunications link between Thimphu and London by Intelsat-satellite was inaugurated in 1990. Thimphu and Phuntsholing are connected by telex to Delhi.

In 1989 there were 44 radio stations for internal administrative communications, and 13 hydro-met stations, with an estimated 15,000 radio receivers. Bhutan Broadcasting Service, Thimphu, broadcasts a daily programme in English, Sharchopkha, Dzongkha and Nepali.

Cinemas. There are 2 in Thimpu and 4 others.

Newspapers. The only weekly newspaper, *Kuensel*, began publication in Aug. 1986 to replace the government weekly bulletin. It is published in English, Dzongkha and Nepali. Total circulation (1991) about 12,000.

JUSTICE, RELIGION, EDUCATION AND WELFARE

Justice. The High Court consists of 8 judges (2 elected by the National Assembly for 5-year terms) appointed by the King. There is a Magistrate's Court in each district, under a *Thrimpon*, from which appeal is to the High Court at Thimphu.

Religion. In 1991 there were some 1,500 monks in the Central Monastic Body (Thimphu and Punakha) and 2,120 in the District Monk Bodies. The monks are headed by an elected Je Khenpo (Head Abbot). The majority of the people are Mahayana Buddhists of the Drukpa subsect of the Kagyud School which was first introduced from Tibet during the 12th century. Hindus of Nepalese origin represent approximately 30-35% of the population.

Education. In April 1991 there were 5,576 pupils and 149 teachers in community schools, 34,807 pupils and 1,453 teachers in primary schools, 10,029 pupils and 552 teachers in junior high and high schools and 1,693 pupils and 184 teachers in technical, vocational and tertiary-level schools. Many students receive higher technical training in India, as well as under the UN Development Programme, the Colombo Plan, etc., in Australia, Germany, New Zealand, Japan, Singapore, the USA and the UK. In Oct. 1990 140 students were receiving university education in India.

Health. There were (1989) 26 hospitals (1 indigenous), 46 dispensaries, 69 basic health units, 6 indigenous dispensaries, 5 leprosy hospitals, 1 mobile hospital, 1 health school and 15 malaria eradication centres. In 1989 beds totalled 944; there were 157 doctors and 671 paramedics.

DIPLOMATIC REPRESENTATIVE

Of Bhutan to the United Nations
Ambassador: Ugyen Tshering.

Further Reading

Bhutan, Himalayan Kingdom. Bhutan Government, Thimphu, 1979
Aris, M., *Bhutan: The Early History of an Himalayan Kingdom.* Warminster, 1979
Chakravarti, B., *A Cultural History of Bhutan.* 2nd rev. ed., 2 vols. Chitteranjan, 1981
Collister, P., *Bhutan and the British.* London, 1987
Das, N., *The Dragon Country.* New Delhi, 1973
Dogra, R. C., *Bhutan:* [Bibliography]. Oxford and Santa Barbara, 1991
Edmunds, T. O., *Bhutan: Land of the Thunder Dragon.* London, 1988
Hickman, K., *Dreams of the Peaceful Dragon: a Journey through Bhutan.* London, 1987
Mehra, G. N., *Bhutan: Land of the Peaceful Dragon.* Rev. ed. New Delhi, 1985

Misra, H. N., *Bhutan: Problems and Policies*. New Delhi, 1988
Rahul, R., *Royal Bhutan*. New Delhi, 1983
Ronaldshay, the Earl of, *Lands of the Thunderbolt*. 2nd ed. London, 1931
Rose, L. E., *The Politics of Bhutan*. Cornell Univ. Press, 1977
Rustomji, N., *Bhutan: The Dragon Kingdom in Crisis*. OUP, 1978
Sinha, A. C., *Bhutan: Ethnic Identity and National Dilemma*. Delhi, 1991
Strydonck, G. van, *et al, Bhutan: a Kingdom of the Eastern Himalayas*. Geneva and London, 1984
Verma, R., *India's Role in the Emergence of Contemporary Bhutan*. Delhi, 1988

BOLIVIA

República de Bolivia

Capital: Sucre
Seat of Government: La Paz
Population: 6·41m. (1989)
GNP per capita: US$600 (1989)

HISTORY. Until 1884, when Bolivia was defeated by Chile, she had a strip bordering on the Pacific which contains extensive nitrate beds and at that time the port of Cobija (which no longer exists). She lost this area to Chile; but in Sept. 1953 Chile declared Arica a free port and, although it is no longer a free port for Bolivian imports, Bolivia still has certain privileges.

AREA AND POPULATION. Bolivia is a landlocked state bounded north and east by Brazil, south by Paraguay and Argentina and west by Chile and Peru, with an area of some 424,165 sq. miles (1,098,581 sq. km).

Population estimate, 1989: 6·41m. Area and population of the departments (capitals in brackets) at the 1982 census and in 1988:

Departments	Area (sq. km)	Census 1982	Estimated population, 1988 (in 1,000)	Per sq. km 1988
La Paz (La Paz)	133,985	1,913,184	1,926·2	14·3
Cochabamba (Cochabamba)	55,631	908,674	982·0	17·6
Potosí (Potosí)	118,218	823,485	667·8	5·6
Santa Cruz (Santa Cruz)	370,621	942,986	1,110·1	2·9
Chuquisaca (Sucre)	51,524	435,406	442·6	8·5
Tarija (Tarija)	37,623	246,691	246·6	6·5
Oruro (Oruro)	53,588	385,121	388·3	7·2
Beni (Trinidad)	213,564	217,700	215·4	1·0
Pando (Cobija)	63,827	42,594	41·0	0·6
Total	1,098,581	5,915,841	6,405·1	5·8

Population (1988 estimate, in 1,000) of the principal towns: La Paz, 669·4; Santa Cruz, 529·2; Cochabamba, 403·6; El Alto, 307·4; Oruro, 176·7; Sucre, 105·8; Tarija, 66·9.

Spanish is the official and commercial language. The Amerindian languages Aymara and Quechua are spoken exclusively by 22% and 5·2% of the population respectively.

CLIMATE. The very varied geography of Bolivia produces several different climates. The two most significant are the low-lying areas in the Amazon Basin, which are very warm and damp throughout the year, with heavy rainfall from Nov. to March, and the alti-plano, which is generally dry between May and Nov. with abundant sunshine, but the nights are cold in June and July, while the months from Dec. to March are the wettest. La Paz. Jan. 53°F (11·7°C), July 47°F (8·3°C). Annual rainfall 23" (574 mm). Sucre. Jan. 55°F (13°C), July 49°F (9·4°C). Annual rainfall 27" (675 mm).

CONSTITUTION AND GOVERNMENT. The Republic of Bolivia was proclaimed on 6 Aug. 1825; its first constitution was adopted on 19 Nov. 1826.
Presidents since 1966 and the date on which they took office:

Gen. René Barrientos Ortuño (Constitutional President killed in air accident), 6 Aug. 1966–27 April 1969.
Dr Luis Adolfo Siles Salinas (deposed), 27 April 1969–26 Sept. 1969.
Gen. Alfredo Ovando Candia, 26 Sept. 1969–6 Oct. 1970.

Gen. Juan José Torres, 7 Oct. 1970–21 Aug. 1971.
Gen. Hugo Banzer Suarez, 21 Aug. 1971–21 July 1978.
Gen. Juan Pereda Asbun, 21 July 1978–24 Nov. 1978.

Gen. David Padilla Arancibia, 24 Nov. 1978–8 Aug. 1979.
Dr Walter Guevara Arze (deposed), 8 Aug. 1979–1 Nov. 1979.
Dr Lydia Gueiler Tejada (deposed), 16 Nov. 1979–17 July 1980.
Maj.-Gen. Luis García Meza Tejada (resigned), 18 July 1980–4 Aug. 1981.
Military Junta, 4 Aug. 1981–4 Sept. 1981.

Gen. Celso Torrelio Villa, (resigned), 4 Sept. 1981–19 July 1982.
Brig.-Gen. Guido Vildoso Calderón, 21 July 1982–10 Oct. 1982.
Dr Hernan Siles Zuazo, 10 Oct. 1982–6 Aug. 1985.
Dr Victor Paz Esstensoro, 6 Aug. 1985–6 Aug. 1989

The President and Vice-President are elected by universal suffrage for a 4-year term. The President appoints the members of his Cabinet. There is a bicameral legislature; the Senate comprises 27 members, 3 from each department, and the Chamber of Deputies 130 members, all elected for 4 years.

The Cabinet was composed as follows in Nov. 1991:

President: Jaime Paz Zamora (sworn in 6 Aug. 1989).

Foreign Affairs and Worship: Carlos Iturralde Ballivían. *Interior, Migration and Justice:* Carlos Saavedra Bruno. *Defence:* Héctor Ormachea Peñaranda. *Finance:* Miguel Angel Sabalo. *Planning and Coordination:* Enrique Garcia Rodriquez. *Industry, Commerce and Tourism:* Guido Céspedes Argandoña. *Mining and Metallurgy:* Walter Soriano Lea Plaza. *Energy and Hydrocarbons:* Angel Zanil Claros. *Agriculture and Peasant Affairs:* Mauro Bertero Gutiérrez. *Labour and Labour Development:* Oscar Zamora Medinacelli. *Education and Culture:* Mariano Bapista Gumucio. *Housing and Urban Affairs:* Elena Velasco de Urresti. *Transport and Communications:* Willy Vargas Vacaflor. *Without Portfolio:* Guillermo Fortún Suárez.

National flag: Three horizontal stripes of red, yellow, and green.

National anthem: Bolivianos, el hado propicio ('Bolivians, the propitious fate'; words by I. de Sanjinés; tune by B. Vincenti).

Local Government: The republic is divided into 9 departments, established in Jan. 1826, with 108 provinces administered by sub-prefects, and 1,713 cantons administered by corregidores. The supreme authority in each department is vested in a prefect appointed by the President.

DEFENCE. Bolivia is divided into 6 military regions; regional HQ are located at La Paz, Sucre, Tarija, Potosí, Trinidad and Cobija. There is selective conscription for 12 months at the age of 18 years.

Army. The Army consists of 8 cavalry groups, 1 motorized infantry regiment, 22 infantry, 1 artillery, 1 armoured, 1 airborne and 6 engineer battalions. Equipment, 36 Kuerassier SK105 light tanks and 24 EE-9 Cascavel armoured cars. There are 1 King Air 200 and 2 Aviocar transports. Strength (1992) 23,000 (15,000 conscripts).

Navy. A small force exists for river and lake patrol duties, comprising 10 patrol craft operating on Lake Titicaca, and in the 6,000-mile Beni and Bolivia-Paraguay river systems, and also a Cessna 402 transport and 1 Cessma 206 for patrol duties. 1 ocean-going transport for use to and from Bolivian free zones in Argentina and Uruguay and 2 17-tonne hospital craft on Lake Titicaca complete the inventory.

Personnel in 1991 totalled 4,000, including 1,200 marines. Most training of officers and petty officers is carried out in Argentina while junior ratings are almost entirely re-trained soldiers.

Air Force. The Air Force, established in 1923, has 3 combat-capable Groups, 2 equipped with T-33 armed jet trainers, and one with armed PC-7s and Hughes 500 helicopters, for counter-insurgency operations. A search and rescue helicopter Group has 15 Brazilian-assembled Lamas and 6 UH-1 Iroquois. Other types in service include Brazilian T-23 Uirapuru and American T-41 primary trainers and Italian SF-260 basic trainers, 1 Electra 4-turbo-prop transport, 6 Fokker F.27 and 2 Israeli-built Arava twin-turboprop light transports, 2 Convair transports, 3 Learjet VIP aircraft, 7 C-130/L-900 Hercules, 6 C-47s, 15 Turbo-Porters and some single-

and twin-engined light aircraft, some confiscated from drug smugglers. Personnel strength (1991) about 4,000 (2,000 conscripts).

INTERNATIONAL RELATIONS

Membership. Bolivia is a member of the UN, OAS, GATT, LAIA, the Andean Group and the Amazon Pact.

ECONOMY

Budget. Expenditure in 1984 was envisaged at 6,891,200m. *pesos bolivianos.*

Currency. On 1 Jan. 1987 the *boliviano* ($b. equal to 1m. *pesos*) was introduced. Inflation was 20% in 1991. Exchange rates were $b.3·49 = US$1 and $b.6·61 = £1 in March 1991.

Banking and Finance. In 1990 the principal banks were Banco Central de Bolivia, Banco del Estado, Banco de Santa Cruz de la Sierra, Banco Agricola de Bolivia, Banco Boliviano Americano, Banco Hipotecario Nacional, Banco Mercantil, Banco Minero de Bolivia, Banco Nacional de Bolivia, Banco de Cochabamba, Banco de la Paz, Banco de Inversión Boliviano, Banco Ganadero de Beni, Banco Industrial, Banco Real, Banco de la Nacion Argentina, Banco Popular del Peru, Banco Industrial S.A., First National City Bank, Banco del Progreso Nacional and Bank of America.

A stock exchange opened in La Paz in 1989.

Weights and Measures. The metric system of weights and measures is used by the administration and prescribed by law, but the old Spanish system is also employed.

ENERGY AND NATURAL RESOURCES

Electricity. Electric power production is expanding. Installed capacity was estimated at 490,000 kw. in 1985. Estimated production from all sources (1986), 2,080m. kwh. Supply 110 volts in La Paz but 220 volts in most other cities; 60 Hz.

Oil and Gas. There are petroleum and natural gas deposits in the Santa Cruz-Camiri areas. A pipeline for crude oil connects Caranda (Santa Cruz) with the Pacific coast at Arica (Chile) and a natural gas pipeline to Argentina was inaugurated in May 1972. All production, refining and internal distribution is now in the hands of *Yacimientos Petroliferos Fiscales Bolivianos* (the State Petroleum Organization). Total production of crude oil in 1991 was estimated at 1·03m. tonnes. Production of natural gas in 1981 was estimated at 175,478m. cu. ft.

Minerals. Mining is the most important industry, accounting for about 70% of the foreign-exchange earnings. A mining code of April 1991 gives tax incentives to foreign investors and opens border areas to mining. In 1990 zinc was the main mineral produced, followed by tin, silver and gold. Tin mines are at altitudes of from 12,000 to 18,000 ft; transport is costly. The tin is extracted by shaft-mining, frequently very deep; the ore yields only 0·7% or less of tin and is very refractory; tin is exported in concentrates for refining. Smelting capacity was increased in 1980 and it is planned to smelt all the ores from the State Mining Co. but complex ores still have to be exported for smelting. Tin production in 1984 was 17,875 tonnes.

Alluvial gold deposits in the Alto Beni region are being exploited. Production (1987) 2·7 tonnes.

Agriculture. The extensive and still largely undeveloped region east of the Andes comprises about three-quarters of the entire area of the country, and since the agrarian reform of 1953 sugar-cane, rice and cotton have been grown in this *Oriente* in increasing abundance, reaching self-sufficiency in all these products. Output in 1,000 tonnes in 1990 was: Sugar cane, 2,100; rice, 207; coffee, 25; maize, 261; potatoes, 534; wheat, 61. Coca is the largest crop. In 1990 Bolivia received US$18m. of US aid for destroying coca (the source of cocaine). Some 60,000 coca farmers received US$2,000 for every ha destroyed.

Livestock: In 1990 there were 5·95m. head of cattle, mostly in the Santa Cruz and

Beni departments; horses, 320,000; asses, 630,000; pigs, 2·22m.; sheep, 12·5m.; goats, 2·4m.; poultry, 16m.

Forestry. Forests cover 55·8m. ha (51% of the land area). Tropical forests with woods ranging from the 'iron tree' to the light *palo de balsa* are beginning to be exploited.

INDUSTRY. There are few industrial establishments.

FOREIGN ECONOMIC RELATIONS. Bolivia relies on imports for the supply of many consumer goods. However an investment law passed in 1971 provides incentives and protection for new foreign investment, and for reinvestment in various fields including manufacturing industry, mining, agriculture, construction and tourism. A mining code of April 1991 gives tax incentives to foreign investors.

Commerce. The value of imports and exports in US$1,000 has been as follows:

	1984	1985	1986	1987	1988	1989
Imports	713,800	551,900	711,500	776,000	595,000	615,000
Exports	609,500	672,500	637,500	569,600	597,000	817,000

Mineral exports made up 44% of all exports in 1990, totalling US$401·25m. in value (including US$51·5m. for gold).

Imports (in US$1m.), by country, 1989: USA, 86; Brazil, 63·4; Argentina, 40·9; Federal Germany, 21·7; Chile, 21·5; Peru, 9·1; UK, 5·6; Belgium, 2·9; Switzerland, 2·9; France, 2·4.

Total exports, 1984, of all minerals, in concentrates, ingots or solder, were valued at US$363·9m.

Bolivia having no seaport, imports and exports pass chiefly through the ports of Arica and Antofagasta in Chile, Mollendo-Matarani in Peru, through La Quiaca on the Bolivian-Argentine border and through river-ports on the rivers flowing into the Amazon.

Total trade between Bolivia and UK (British Department of Trade returns in £1,000 sterling):

	1987	1988	1989	1990	1991
Imports to UK	14,799	13,224	17,666	12,387	9,303
Exports and re-exports from UK	3,658	6,029	6,148	6,234	5,787

Tourism. There were 133,000 visitors in 1986.

COMMUNICATIONS

Roads. A highway, in poor condition, 497 km long, runs from Cochabamba to the lowland farming region of Santa Cruz. La Paz and Oruro are also connected by a metalled road. Of other main highways (unmetalled) there is one from La Paz through Guaqui into Peru, another from La Paz, via Oruro, Potosí, Tarija and Bermejo, into Argentina, with branches to Cochabamba, Sucre and Camiri, passable throughout the year except at the height of the rainy season, and others from Villazón to Villa Montes via Tarija, passable during the dry season. The total length of the road system is 41,000 km (1984). Motor vehicles in use in 1984, 168,600, including 43,677 cars.

Railways. In 1964 Bolivian National Railways (ENFE) was formed by the amalgamation of the Bolivian Government Railways, Bolivian Railway Co. and the Bolivian section of the Antofagasta (Chili) & Bolivia Railway. The Guaqui-La Paz Railway, formerly operated by Peru, became part of ENFE in 1973 and the privately-owned Marchacamarca Uncia mineral line was taken over in 1987. Access to the Pacific is by 3 routes: To Antofagasta and Arica in Chile, and to Mollendo in Peru via Guaqui, the Lake Titicaca train ferry to Puno (Peru), then rail to the coast. Construction began in 1978 of a 150-km line linking Puno with Desaguadero on the Bolivian border which would by-pass the train ferry, though gauge difference would still prevent through running to Peru. Current network totals 3,642 km of metre gauge, comprising unconnected Eastern (1,386 km) and Western (2,257 km) systems. In 1990 the railways carried 1·1m. passengers and 1·1m. tonnes of freight.

Civil Aviation. The 2 international airports are El Alto ($8\frac{1}{2}$ miles from La Paz) and Viru Viru (10 miles from Santa Cruz). The national airline is Lloyd Aéreo Boliviano. The airline runs regular services between La Paz and Lima, São Paulo, Buenos Aires, Miami, Caracas, Salta and Arica as well as many internal services. Eastern Airways runs regular flights between La Paz, Buenos Aires, Santiago and Asunción linking Bolivia to the USA. Lufthansa links Bolivia with Europe. Other airlines serving Bolivia are Aerolineas Argentinas, Cruzeiro, Aero Peru and Lan Chile.

Shipping. Traffic on Lake Titicaca between Guaqui and Puno is carried on by the steamers of the Peruvian Corporation. About 12,000 miles of rivers, in 4 main systems (Beni, Pilcomayo, Titicaca-Desaguadero, Mamoré), are open to navigation by light-draught vessels.

Telecommunications. There were, in 1978, 458 post offices, of these, 205 provided telegraph and telephone services together with a further 245 offices for telegraph and telephone service only. There is telephone service in the cities of La Paz, Cochabamba, Oruro, Sucre, Potosí, Santa Cruz, Tarija, Camiri, Tupiza, Villazon, Riberalta and Trinidad with (1983), 204,747 telephones. There were (1987) about 85 radio stations, the majority of which are local and commercial. There is a commercial government television service. There are 4 private television stations and 1 University station (educational channel) in La Paz. In 1991 there were 4m. radio and 0·4m. TV (colour by NTSC) receivers. The broadcasting authority is the Asociación Boliviana de Radiodifusoras.

Cinemas. In 1989 there were 30 cinemas in La Paz and 50 in other cities.

Newspapers. There were (1984) 7 daily newspapers in La Paz, 2 in Oruro, and 1 in Cochabamba. Several other towns have regular newspapers devoted to local news, but most of them appear only a few times a week. 4 daily newspapers are produced in Santa Cruz.

JUSTICE, RELIGION, EDUCATION AND WELFARE

Justice. Justice is administered by the Supreme Court, superior district courts (of 5 or 7 judges) and courts of local justice. The Supreme Court, with headquarters at Sucre, is divided into two sections, civil and criminal, of 5 justices each, with the Chief Justice presiding over both. Members of the Supreme Court are chosen on a two-thirds vote of Congress.

Religion. The Roman Catholic is the recognized religion of the state; the free exercise of other forms of worship is permitted. The Catholic Church is under a cardinal (in Sucre), an archbishop (in La Paz), 6 bishops (Cochabamba, Santa Cruz, Oruro, Potosí, Riberalta and Tarija) and vicars apostolic (titular bishops resident in Cueva, Trinidad, San Ignacio de Velasco, Riberalta and Rurrenabaque). It had 6·65m. adherents in 1989.

Education. Primary instruction is free and obligatory between the ages of 6 and 14 years. In 1986 there were 1·4m. pupils and 51,000 teachers in 9,093 primary and elementary schools, and 225,000 pupils, 10,400 teachers in 2,300 secondary schools.

At Sucre, Oruro, Potosí, Cochabamba, Santa Cruz, Tarija, Trinidad and La Paz are universities; La Paz is the most important of them while the San Francisco Xavier University at Sucre is one of the oldest in America, founded in 1624.

Health. In 1972 there were 2,143 doctors.

DIPLOMATIC REPRESENTATIVES

Of Bolivia in Great Britain (106 Eaton Sq., London, SW1W 9AD)
Ambassador: Gary Prado.

Of Great Britain in Bolivia (Avenida Arce 2732–2754, La Paz)
Ambassador: R. M. Jackson, CVO.

Of Bolivia in the USA (3014 Massachusetts Ave, NW, Washington, D.C., 20008)
Ambassador: Jorge Crespo Velasco.

Of the USA in Bolivia (Banco Popular Del Peru Bldg, La Paz)
Ambassador: Robert S. Gelbard.

Of Bolivia to the United Nations
Ambassador: Hugo Navajas-Mogro.

Further Reading

Anuario Geográfico y Estadístico de la República de Bolivia
Anuario del Comercia Exterior de Bolivia
Boletín Mensual de Información Estadistica
Dunkerley, J., *Rebellion in the Veins: Political Struggle in Bolivia 1952–1982.* London, 1984
Fifer, J. V., *Bolivia: Land, Location and Politics Since 1825.* CUP, 1972
Guillermo, L., *A History of the Bolivian Labour Movement 1848–1971.* CUP, 1977
Klein, H., *Bolivia: The Evolution of a Multi-Ethnic Society.* OUP, 1982
Yeager, G. M., *Bolivia.* [Bibliography] Oxford and Santa Barbara, 1988

BOTSWANA

Capital: Gaborone
Population: 1·35m. (1991)
GNP per capita: US$1,050 (1988)

Republic of Botswana

HISTORY. In 1885 the territory was declared to be within the British sphere; in 1889 it was included in the sphere of the British South Africa Company, but was never administered by the company; in 1890 a Resident Commissioner was appointed, and in 1895, on the annexation of the Crown Colony of British Bechuanaland to the Cape of Good Hope, the British Government was in favour of transferring the Protectorate to the BSA Company, but the three major chiefs of the Bakwena, the Bangwaketse and the Bamangwato went to England to protest against this proposal, and agreement was reached that their country should remain a British Protectorate if they ceded a strip of land on the eastern side of the country for railway construction. This railway was built in 1896–97.

On 30 Sept. 1966 the Bechuanaland Protectorate became an independent and sovereign member of the Commonwealth under the name of the Republic of Botswana.

AREA AND POPULATION. Botswana is bounded west and north by Namibia, north-east by Zambia and Zimbabwe and east and south by South Africa. 70-80% of the country, in the centre, west and south-west, is desert. The north-west has lush vegetation and forest; land in the east and north-east is broken by rocky hills. The area is 581,730 sq. km. Population estimate, 1991, 1,347,000 (census, 1981, 941,027). Life expectancy in 1990: Males, 52·7 years; females, 59·3. Population growth rate, 1990, was 3·4%.

The country is divided into 9 districts: Central, North East, North West, Ghanzi, Kgalagadi, Kweneng, Kgatleng, South East and Southern.

The main business centres (with estimated population, 1989) are Gaborone (138,471 in 1991), Mahalapye (104,450), Serowe (95,041), Tutume (86,405), Bobonong (55,060), Francistown (52,725), Selebi-Phikwe (49,542), Boteti (32,711), Lobatse (26,841), Palapye (16,959), Jwaneng (13,895), Tlokweng (11,760), Orapa (8,894).

The official language is English; the national language is Setswana.

CLIMATE. In winter, days are warm and nights cold, with occasional frosts. Summer heat is tempered by prevailing north-east winds. Rainfall comes mainly in summer, from Oct. to April, while the rest of the year is almost completely dry with very high sunshine amounts. Gaborone. Jan. 79°F (26·1°C), July 55°F (12·8°C). Annual rainfall varies from 650 mm in the north to 250 mm in the south-east. The country is prone to droughts..

CONSTITUTION AND GOVERNMENT. The Constitution adopted on 30 Sept. 1966 provides for a republican form of government headed by the President with 3 main organs: The Legislature, the Executive and the Judiciary.

The executive rests with the President of the Republic who is responsible to the National Assembly. The President is elected for 5-year terms at the general elections.

The National Assembly consists of 40 members, 34 elected by universal suffrage, 4 elected by the Assembly, the Speaker and the Attorney-General (who does not vote). Elections are held every 5 years. Voting is on the first-past-the-post system. The general election, held in Oct. 1989, returned 31 members of the Botswana Democratic Party and 3 Botswana National Front.

The President is an *ex-officio* member of the Assembly. If the President is already a member of the National Assembly, a by-election will be held in that constituency.

There is also a House of Chiefs to advise the Government. It consists of the Chiefs of the 8 tribes who were autonomous during the days of the British protectorate, and 4 members elected by and from among the sub-chiefs in 4 districts.

The first President of Botswana, who was re-elected 3 times, was Sir Seretse Khama, KBE, who died 13 July 1980.

President of the Republic: Dr Quett Ketumile Joni Masire, KCMG (b.1925; re-elected 1989).

In Nov. 1991 the Cabinet was as follows:

Vice President and Minister of Local Government, Lands and Housing: P. S. Mmusi. *Presidential Affairs and Public Administration:* Lieut.-Gen. Mompati Merafhe. *External Affairs:* Gaositwe K. T. Chiepe. *Health:* Kebatlamang P. Morake. *Works, Transport and Communications:* C. J. Butale. *Commerce and Industry:* Ponatshego Kedikilwe. *Mineral Resources and Water Affairs:* Archie M. Mogwe. *Education:* Ray Molombo. *Finance and Development Planning:* Festus Mogae. *Labour and Home Affairs:* Patrick Balopi.

National flag: Light blue with a horizontal black stripe, edged white, across the centre.

National anthem: Fatshe la Rona (Blessed noble land; words and tune by K. T. Motsete).

Local Government. Local government is carried out by 9 district councils, 1 city and 5 town councils. Revenue is obtained mainly from sales taxes, from rates in the towns and from central government subventions in the districts.

DEFENCE

Army. A defence force has been created for border control and comprises 5 infantry, 1 armoured car, 1 reconnaissance and 1 engineer companies. Personnel (includes Air Force) in 1992, 4,500.

Air Force. Equipment includes 6 BAC Strikemaster light strike aircraft, 5 Britten-Norman Defender armed light transports for border patrol, counter-insurgency and casualty evacuation duties, 7 PC-7 basic trainers, 2 CN-235 turboprop-powered medium transports, 2 Skyvan turboprop passenger/cargo transports, 2 Ecureuil and 5 Bell 412 helicopters and 2 Cessna 152 light aircraft. Personnel numbers are included with the Army.

INTERNATIONAL RELATIONS

Membership. Botswana is a member of the UN, OAU, Southern African Development Co-ordination Conference, the Non-Aligned Movement, the Commonwealth and is an ACP state of the EEC.

ECONOMY

Policy. The Seventh National Development Plan is running from 1991 to 1997. It aimed to diversify the economy and create jobs.

Budget. The 1989–90 budget envisaged expenditure of P2,164m., revenue was envisaged at P1,032m.

Currency. The unit of currency is the *pula* (BWP) of 100 *thebe*. Inflation was 12% in 1990. Foreign exchange reserves were P6,500m. in 1991. P3·76 = £1 sterling and P2·14 = US$1 in March 1992.

Banking and Finance. There were 3 commercial banks in 1990 (Barclays, Standard Chartered and Bank of Credit and Commerce) with 34 branches and sub-branches, and 44 agencies. The Bank of Botswana, established in 1976, is the central bank. The National Development Bank, founded in 1964, has 6 regional offices and agricultural, industrial and commercial development divisions. The Botswana Co-operative Bank is banker to co-operatives and thrift and loan societies. The government-owned Post Office Savings Bank operates throughout the country.

Total assets and liabilities of the 3 commercial banks at 31 March 1989, P897m. and of the Bank of Botswana, P4,785·1m.

There is a share market.

Weights and Measures. The metric system is in use.

ENERGY AND NATURAL RESOURCES

Electricity. The coal-fired power station at Morupule supplies all major cities. Production (1986) 533m. kwh. Supply 220 volts; 50 Hz.

Water. Surface water resources are about 18,000m. cu. metres a year. Nearly all flows into northern districts from Angola through the Okavango and Kwando river systems. The Zambezi, also in the north, provides irrigation in Chobe District. In the south-east, there are dams to exploit the ephemeral flow of the tributaries of the Limpopo. 80% of the land has no surface water, and must be served by some 6,000 boreholes.

Minerals. An important part of government revenue comes from the diamond mines at Orapa and Jwaneng and the nickel–copper complex at Selebi-Phikwe. An open-pit coalmine has been developed at Morupule. Coal reserves are estimated at 17,000m. tonnes. There is also salt and soda ash. Mineral production 1988: Diamonds, 15,229,000 carats; copper–nickel, 43,238 tonnes (value P81,374,000); coal, 612,713 tonnes (P11,300,000).

Agriculture. 80% of the population is rural, 71% of all land is 'tribal', protected and allocated to prevent over-grazing, maintain small farmers and foster commercial ranching. Cattle-rearing is the chief industry after diamond-mining, and the country is more a pastoral than an agricultural one, crops depending entirely upon the rainfall. In 1990, 128,000 ha were sown to sorghum. In 1991 the number of cattle was 2·9m. 80% were owned by traditional farmers, about half owning fewer than 20 head. In 1990 there were: goats, 2·09m.; sheep, 301,000; poultry, 2m.; pigs, 16,000.

Production (1990, in 1,000 tonnes): Maize, 8; sorghum, 43; millet, 2; roots and tubers, 7; pulses, 14; seed cotton, 3; vegetables, 16; fruit, 11.

Forestry. There are forest nurseries and plantations. Concessions have been granted to harvest 7,500 cu. metres in Kasane and Chobe Forest Reserves and up to 2,500 cu. metres in the Masame area.

Conservation. About 17% of land is set aside for wildlife preservation. In 1986 there were 4 national parks, 6 game reserves, 3 game sanctuaries and 40 controlled hunting areas for photographic and game viewing safaris and recreational (safari) and subsistence hunting.

INDUSTRY. Textiles, foodstuffs and soap are manufactured. Rural technology is being developed and traditional crafts encouraged.

Labour. 1987 there were 80,449 Botswana nationals employed in the mines of South Africa. The estimated total number of paid employees in all sectors in Botswana in Sept. 1987 was 150,200.

FOREIGN ECONOMIC RELATIONS. Botswana is a member of the South African customs union with Lesotho, South Africa and Swaziland. There are no foreign exchange restrictions.

Commerce. In 1987 imports totalled P1,572,456 and in 1990 exports P3,262,000. Of imports, 79·6% came from the South African customs area, 7·7% from other African countries. Exports are mainly diamonds (to Switzerland), copper–nickel matte (to USA), beef and beef products (to EEC).

Imports (1987 in P1,000) included vehicles and transport equipment, 242,785; food, beverages and tobacco, 253,422; machinery and electrical equipment, 260,370: Exports were mainly diamonds, 2,252,453. Imports in 1987 were mainly from the South African customs area (P1,250,954,000) and exports mainly to Europe (P2,412,152,000).

Total trade between Botswana and UK (British Department of Trade returns, in £1,000 sterling):

	1987	1988	1989	1990	1991
Imports to UK	11,836	6,942	13,135	18,854	22,552
Exports and re-exports from UK	10,275	26,763	34,582	24,777	35,233

Tourism. There were 432,323 foreign visitors in 1987. Tourist earnings were P60m. in 1988.

COMMUNICATIONS

Roads. In 1992 some 2,000 km of road were bitumen-surfaced out of a total of 15,000km. In 1988 there were 46,560 registered motor vehicles including 14,199 cars, 16,350 light delivery vans and 6,895 lorries.

Railways. The main line from Mafikeng in Bophuthatswana to Bulawayo in Zimbabwe traverses Botswana. With 3 branches the total was (1991) 888 km. These lines, formerly operated by National Railways of Zimbabwe, were taken over by the new Botswana Railways organization in 1987. In 1989–90 railways carried 0·4m. passengers and 2·3m. tonnes of freight.

Civil Aviation. The Seretse Khama International Airport at Gaborone opened in 1984. There are 6 domestic airports. Regular international flights are flown by Air Botswana, Air Zimbabwe, Royal Swazi Air, Zambian Airways, Comair, UTA, Air Tanzania, Kenya Airways, South African Airways and British Airways. Direct services are operated to the UK, Kenya, Lesotho, Namibia, Swaziland, Tanzania, Zambia and Zimbabwe. In 1988, 77,250 passengers arrived by air, 65,519 departed and 4,056 were in transit.

Telecommunications. In 1986 there were 66 post offices and 72 agencies. There were 12,511 telephones installed in 1987. The government-controlled Radio Botswana broadcasts daily in English and Setswana. There were 160,000 radio sets in 1991.

Newspapers. In 1987 there was 1 daily newspaper, the bilingual (Setswana-English) *Daily News*, which is published by the Department of Information and Broadcasting; circulation, 36,000. There are 4 other privately-owned weeklies and 2 periodicals.

JUSTICE, RELIGION, EDUCATION AND WELFARE

Justice. Law is based on the Roman-Dutch law of the former Cape Colony, but judges and magistrates are also qualified in English common law. The Court of Appeal was established in 1954. It has jurisdiction in respect of criminal and civil appeals emanating from the High Court and in all criminal and civil cases and proceedings. Magistrates' courts and traditional courts are in each of the 10 administrative districts. There is a national police force, 2,359 in 1985 and local customary law enforcement officers.

Religion. Freedom of worship is guaranteed under the Constitution. About 50% of the population is Christian. Christian denominations include the United Congregational Church of Southern Africa, the Catholic Church, Anglican, Lutheran, Dutch Reformed, Seventh Day Adventist, Assemblies of God, Methodist and Quaker groups. Non-Christian religions include Bahais, Moslems and Hindus.

Education. Basic free education, introduced in 1986, consists of 7 years of primary and 2 years of junior secondary schooling. 83% of eligible children were in schools in 1990. In 1988 enrolment in primary schools was 259,152 with (1987) 7,704 teachers, and in secondary schools 40,000 with (1987) 1,682 teachers. In 1987 there were 1,316 students with 78 teachers in teacher training colleges and 2,261 students with 328 instructors in vocational and technical training. There is a Polytechnic and an Auto Trades Training School. Throughout the country, 'Brigades' (community-managed private bodies) provide lower level vocational training. The Department of Non-Formal Education offers secondary level correspondence courses and is the executing agency for the National Literacy Programme. The University of Botswana (became autonomous in 1982) had 2,298 full-time students and 250 academic staff in 1989-90.

In 1990, 70% literacy was claimed.

Health (1990). There were 14 general hospitals, a mental hospital, 7 health centres, 81 clinics and 246 health posts. There were also 438 stops for mobile health teams. In 1986 there were 156 registered medical practitioners, 14 dentists, and 1,530 nurses. The health facilities are the concern of central and local government, medical missions, mining companies and voluntary organizations.

DIPLOMATIC REPRESENTATIVES

Of Botswana in Great Britain (6 Stratford Pl., London, W1N 9AE)
High Commissioner: Margaret Nasha.

Of Great Britain in Botswana (Private Bag 0023, Gaborone)
High Commissioner: (Vacant).

Of Botswana in the USA (4301 Connecticut Ave., NW, Washington, D.C., 20008)
Ambassador: Kingsele Sebele.

Of the USA in Botswana (PO Box 90, Gaborone)
Ambassador: David Passage.

Of Botswana to the United Nations
Ambassador: Legwaila Joseph Legwaila.

Further Reading

Central Statistics Office. *Statistical Bulletin* (Quarterly). Ministry of Information and Broadcasting. *Botswana Handbook.* – *Kutlwano* (monthly). – *The Botswana Daily News.* – *Facts on Botswana.* – *Botswana in Brief* – *Botswana Up To Date.*
Botswana '86: An Official Handbook. Department of Information and Broadcasting, Gaborone, 1986
Statistical Bulletins. Quarterly. Central Statistical Office, Gaborone
Report on the Population Census, 1981. Government Printer, Gaborone, 1982
Campbell, A. C., *The Guide to Botswana.* Gaborone, 1980
Colclough, C. and McCarthy, S., *The Political Economy of Botswana.* OUP, 1980
Harvey, C., (ed.) *Papers on the Economy of Botswana.* London and Nairobi, 1981
Parson, J., *Botswana: Liberal Democracy and Labour Reserve in Southern Africa.* Aldershot, 1984

National statistical office: Central Statistics Office, Private Bag 0024, Gaborone.

BRAZIL

Capital: Brasília, (Federal District)
Population: 155·6m. (1990)
GNP per capita: US$2,550 (1989)

República Federativa do Brasil

HISTORY. Brazil was discovered on 22 April 1500 by the Portuguese Admiral Pedro Alvares Cabral, and thus became a Portuguese settlement; in 1815 the colony was declared 'a kingdom', and it was proclaimed an independent Empire in 1822. The monarchy was overthrown in 1889 and a republic declared. Following a coup in 1964 the armed forces retained overall control until civilian government was restored on 15 March 1985.

AREA AND POPULATION. Brazil is bounded east by the Atlantic and on its northern, western and southern borders by all the South American countries except Chile and Ecuador. The area is 8,511,996 sq. km (3,286,485 sq. miles) including 55,457 sq. km of inland water. Population as at 1 Sept. 1980 (census) and 1 July 1990 (estimate):

Federal Unit and Capital	Area (sq. km)	Census 1980	Estimate 1990
North	3,851,560	5,880,268	10,581,561
Rondônia (Pôrto Velho)	238,379	491,069	1,125,118
Acre (Rio Branco)	153,698	301,303	434,708
Amazonas (Manaus)	1,567,954	1,430,089	2,213,966
Roraima (Boa Vista)	225,017	79,159	135,956
Pará (Belém)	1,246,833	3,403,391	5,391,864
Amapá (Macapá)	142,359	175,257	267,576
Tocantins (Palmas)	277,322	–	1,012,373
North-east	1,556,001 [1]	34,812,356	44,429,181
Maranhão (São Luís)	329,556	3,996,404	5,274,797
Piaui (Teresina)	251,273	2,139,021	2,799,919
Ceará (Fortaleza)	145,694	5,288,253	6,666,651
Rio Grande do Norte (Natal)	53,167	1,898,172	2,451,076
Paraíba (João Pessoa)	53,958	2,770,176	3,420,340
Pernambuco (Recife)	101,023	6,141,993	7,603,176
Alagoas (Maceió)	29,107	1,982,591	2,522,197
Sergipe (Aracajú)	21,863	1,140,121	1,516,064
Bahia (Salvador)	566,979	9,454,346	12,174,961
South-east:	924,266	51,734,125	67,067,873
Minas Gerais (Belo Horizonte)	586,624	13,378,553	16,854,745
Espírito Santo (Vitória)	45,733	2,023,340	2,635,307
Rio de Janeiro (Rio de Janeiro)	43,653	11,291,520	14,061,694
São Paulo (São Paulo)	248,256	25,040,712	33,516,127
South	575,316	19,031,162	23,393,001
Parana (Curitiba)	199,324	7,629,392	9,341,569
Santa Catarina (Florianópolis)	95,318	3,627,933	4,601,500
Rio Grande do Sul (Pôrto Alegre)	280,674	7,773,837	9,449,932
Central West	1,604,852	7,544,795	10,091,301
Mato Grosso (Cuiabá)	901,421	1,138,691	2,118,197
Mato Grosso do Sul (Campo Grande)	357,472	1,369,567	1,881,211
Goiás (Goiânia)	340,166	3,859,602	4,288,415
Distrito Federal (Brasília)	5,794	1,176,935	1,803,478
Total	8,511,996	119,002,706	155,562,917

[1] Including litigious areas between states of Piauí and Ceará (3,382 sq. km).

Population (1990) 155,562,917; density, 18 per sq. km. The 1980 census showed 59,123,361 males and 59,879,345 females. The urban population comprised 74·4% in 1989. Life expectancy was 66 years in 1989.

The official language is Portuguese.

Population of principal cities (1990 estimate):

São Paulo	11,128,848	Duque de Caxias	739,699	São José dos	
Rio de Janeiro	6,042,411	Santo André	690,830	Campos	430,326
Belo Horizonte	2,415,908	Osasco	671,011	Ribeirão Preto	426,966
Salvador	2,050,133	São Bernardo do		Aracaju	418,671
Fortaleza	1,824,991	Campo	655,403	Feira de Santana	409,941
Brasília	1,803,478	São Luis	641,983	Olinda	389,244
Nova Iguaçu	1,511,915	Natal	600,214	Juiz de Fora	388,310
Curitiba	1,398,599	Teresina	556,364	Diadema	382,319
Porto Alegre	1,386,828	Maceió	548,015	Londrina	378,903
Recife	1,375,404	São João de Meriti	508,221	Uberlândia	377,026
Belém	1,203,151	Jaboatão	491,774	Campos dos	
Manaus	1,113,676	Santos	486,810	Goytacazes	368,224
Goiânia	1,064,567	Niterói	479,834	Sorocaba	366,557
Campinas	960,801	Contagem	478,522	Joinville	358,094
Guarulhos	836,359	João Pessoa	459,954	Jundiaí	350,882
São Gonçalo	825,338	Campo Grande	459,554		

The principal metropolitan areas (estimate, 1990) were São Paulo (17,112,712), Rio de Janeiro (11,205,567), Belo Horizonte (3,615,234), Porto Alegre (2,906,472), Recife (2,814,795), Salvador (2,424,878), Fortaleza (2,119,774), Curitiba (1,966,426) and Belém (1,418,061).

CLIMATE. Because of its latitude, the climate is predominantly tropical, but factors such as altitude, prevailing winds and distance from the sea cause certain variations, though temperatures are not notably extreme. In tropical parts, winters are dry and summers wet, while in Amazonia conditions are constantly warm and humid. The N.E. sertao is hot and arid, with frequent droughts. In the south and east, spring and autumn are sunny and warm, summers are hot, but winters can be cold when polar air-masses impinge. Brasilia. Jan. 72°F (22·3°C), July 68°F (19·8°C). Annual rainfall 63" (1,603 mm). Belém. Jan. 78°F (25·8°C), July 80°F (26·4°C). Annual rainfall 102" (2,315 mm). Manaus. Jan. 79°F (26·1°C), July 80°F (26·7°C). Annual rainfall 110" (2,842 mm). Recife. Jan. 80°F (26·6°C), July 77°F (24·8°C). Annual rainfall 94" (2,474 mm). Rio de Janeiro. Jan. 83°F (28·5°C), July 67°F (19·6°C). Annual rainfall 67" (1,758 mm). São Paulo. Jan. 75°F (24°C), July 57°F (13·7°C). Annual rainfall 71" (1,800 mm). Salvador. Jan. 80°F (26·5°C), July 74°F (23·5°C). Annual rainfall 90" (2,315 mm). Porto Alegre. Jan. 75°F (23·9°C), July 62°F (16·7°C). Annual rainfall 67" (1,775 mm).

CONSTITUTION AND GOVERNMENT. The present Constitution came into force on 5 Oct. 1988, the eighth since independence from the Portuguese in 1822. *President* and *Vice-President* are elected for a 5-year term and are not immediately re-eligible. To be elected candidates must secure 51% of the votes, otherwise a second round of voting is held to elect the President between the two most voted candidates. Voting is compulsory for men and women between the ages of 18 and 70 and optional for illiterates, persons from 16 to 18 years old and persons over 70.

Congress consists of a 91-member *Senate* (3 Senators per state) and a 503-member *Chamber of Deputies*. The Senate is two-thirds directly elected (50% of these elected for 8 years in rotation) and one-third indirectly elected. The Chamber of Deputies is elected by universal franchise for 4 years. The two Chambers of Congress are to become a constituent body in 1993. There is a *Council of the Republic* which is convened only in national emergencies. Elections were held in Oct. 1990 for the governors of the 27 states, territories and federal district, 27 senators (one-third of the Senate), 503 federal deputies and 1,049 state deputies. Some 70,000 candidates from 22 parties stood. The electorate was 84m.

Voting is voluntary from 16 and compulsory for men and women between the ages of 18 and 65 and optional for persons over 65. Enlisted men (who numbered 339,849 at the 1980 census) may not vote. The Constitutional Amendment number 25 of 15 May 1985 granted illiterate persons (until then disenfranchised) the right to vote and also provided for the direct election of the President.

Former Presidents since 1961 have been as follows:

João Belchior Marques Goulart, 7 Sept. 1961–31 March 1964 (deposed).

Marshal Humberto de Alencar Castello Branco, 15 April 1964–15 March 1967.

Gen. Arthur da Costa e Silva, 15 March 1967–31 Aug. 1969 (resigned).

Gen. Emilio Garrastazu Medici, 30 Oct. 1969–15 March 1974.

Gen. Ernesto Geisel, 15 March 1974–15 March 1979.

Gen. João Baptista de Oliveira Figueiredo, 15 March 1979–21 March 1985.

José Sarney, 21 March 1985–15 March 1990.

President of the Republic: Fernando Collor de Mello (b. 1949), assumed office 15 March 1990; *Vice-President:* Itamar Franco.

In March 1992 the government included the following ministers: *Foreign Relations*, José Francisco Resek; *Economy*, Marcilio Marques Moreira; *Infrastructure*, João Eduardo Cerdeira de Santana; *Labour*, Reinold Stefanis; *Social Security*, Ricardo Fiuza; *Environment and Education*, José Goldemberg; *Agriculture*, Antônio Cabrera; *Navy*, Adm. Mario Flores; *Armed Forces*, Gen. Carlos Ribeiro Gomes; *Air Force*, Brig. Sócrates da Costa Monteiro; *Justice*, Jarbas Passarinho.

National flag: Green, with yellow lozenge on which is placed a blue sphere, containing 23 white stars and crossed with a band bearing the motto *Ordem e Progresso*.

National anthem: Ouviram do Ipiranga... ('They hear the river Ipiranga' words by J. O. Duque Estrada; tune by F. M. da Silva).

Local Government. Brazil consists of 26 states and 1 federal district. Each state has its distinct administrative, legislative and judicial authorities, its own constitution and laws, which must, however, agree with the constitutional principles of the Union. Taxes on interstate commerce, levied by individual states, are prohibited. The governors and members of the legislatures are elected for 4-year terms, but magistrates are appointed and are not removable from office save by judicial sentence. The country is sub-divided into 4,491 *municípios*, each under an elected mayor *(prefeito)* and municipal council, and then further sub-divided into *distritos*. The Federal District is the national capital, inaugurated in 1960; it is divided into 13 administrative Regions, the first Region being Brasília. Gubernatorial elections were held for all 27 states etc. in Oct.–Nov. 1990.

DEFENCE. Conscription is for 12 months.

Army. There are 7 military commands and 12 military regions. The Army consists of 8 divisions, 1 armoured cavalry, 3 armoured infantry, 4 mechanized cavalry, 12 motor infantry, 1 mountain, 2 jungle, 1 frontier, 2 airborne and 2 coast and air defence brigades, 3 cavalry guard regiments, 28 artillery and 2 engineer groups. Equipment includes 520 light tanks. Strength (1992) 196,000 (126,500 conscripts). A helicopter brigade is being formed with an initial strength of 52 Dauphin and Ecureuil helicopters.

There are para-military state militias under Army control and considered an Army reserve, totalling about 243,000 personnel.

Navy. The principal ship of the Brazilian Navy is the 20,200 tonne Light Aircraft Carrier *Minas Gerais*, formerly the British *Vengeance*, completed in 1945, purchased in 1956, and capable of operating an air group of 8 S-2E Tracker anti-submarine aircraft, and 8 ASH-3H anti-submarine Sea King helicopters. She is currently non-operational.

There are also 5 diesel submarines (1 built in Germany, 3 British Oberon-class and 1 old ex-US), 11 frigates including 4 ex-US Garcia class leased in 1989 for 5 years, 6 built to two variants of a British design in the 1970s, and the first of a class of 4 locally designed and built. The fleet still includes 2 old ex-US Gearing class destroyers, but these are decommissioning following acquisition of the Garcias. There are also 6 inshore minesweepers and a patrol force of 9 tug/trawler types, 6 ex-US inshore craft, 2 locally built and a number for work on the rivers. Major auxiliaries include 1 oiler, 1 repair ship, 4 transports, 4 survey and rescue, 1 training frigate and 5 tugs. There are some 70 minor auxiliaries. Amphibious forces consist of 2 recently-acquired ex-US landing ships (Dock) and 1 tank landing ship. A further 2 diesel submarines and 3 small frigates are being built, and there is a long term project to build a nuclear-powered submarine.

Fleet Air Arm personnel only fly helicopters, the 11 S-2E Tracker anti-submarine aircraft held for carrier operations and the 21 shore-based maritime patrol EMB-111 being operated by the Air Force. Naval aircraft include 3 ASH-3 Sea King for carrier service, 7 Lynx, and 20 Esquilo for embarkation in the smaller ships. Utility and search-and-rescue duties are performed by 16 Bell 206B Sea Ranger, and 4 Super Puma helicopters. Naval bases are at Rio de Janeiro, Aratu (Bahia), Belém, Natal, Rio Grande do Sul and Salvador, with river bases at Ladario and Manaus.

Active personnel in 1991 totalled 50,000, including 15,000 Marines and 700 Naval Aviation.

Air Force. The Air Force is organized in 6 zones, centred on Belém, Recife, Rio de Janeiro, São Paulo, Porto Alegre and Brasília. The 1a ALADA (air defence wing) has 16 Mirage IIIE fighters and 5 Mirage IIID trainers, integrated with Roland mobile short-range surface-to-air missile systems deployed by the Army, and a radar/communications/computer network. Two fighter groups have 3 squadrons of F-5E Tiger II supersonic fighter-bombers and two-seat F-5Bs; 4 others operate AT-26 (Aermacchi MB 326G) Xavante light jet attack/trainers, licence-built by Embraer in Brazil. The AM-X fighter-bomber, jointly developed by Italy and Brazil, is now entering service in a new group; it is planned to buy 94 AM-Xs. Counter-insurgency squadrons are also equipped with Neiva Regente lightplanes, Universal armed piston-engined trainers, Super Puma transports and UH-1D/H Iroquois and armed Ecureuil helicopters for liaison and observation. 2 air-sea rescue units are equipped with Bandeirantes. Equipment of transport units includes 1 squadron of C-130E/H Hercules transports; 1 squadron of Boeing 707 and KC-130H Hercules tanker/transports; 1 group made up of a squadron of HS 748 and a second squadron of Bandeirante turboprop transports; 2 troop-carrier groups with DHC-5 Buffaloes; 1 group with Bandeirantes; 1 group with UH-1 Iroquois and Super Puma helicopters; and 7 independent squadrons with Bandeirantes and Buffaloes. Light aircraft for liaison duties include 30 Embraer U-7s (licence-built Piper Senecas) and 9 Cessna Caravans. The VIP transport group has 2 Boeing 737s, 11 HS 125 twin-jet light transports, several Embraer Brasilias, 6 Embraer Xingu (VU-9) twin-turboprop pressurized transports and Ecureuil and JetRanger helicopters. Training is performed primarily on locally-built T-25 Universal and turboprop T-27 Tucano (EMB-312) basic trainers, and AT-26 Xavante armed jet basic trainers.

Personnel strength (1992) 50,700, with more than 600 aircraft of all types.

INTERNATIONAL RELATIONS

Membership. Brazil is a member of the UN, OAS, SELA, LAIA and Mercosur.

ECONOMY

Policy. In 1991 a National Reconstruction Plan was introduced to promote growth and investment and reduce the role of the state. State monopolies in ports, communications and fuels were abolished and agricultural and industrial subsidies ended. In order to contain inflation, private savings were frozen until late 1991.

Budget. In 1988 the budget balanced at 4,667,963,808,000m. cruzeiros.

Internal federal debt, Dec. 1989 was Cr$1,366,877m. Internal states and municipalities (main securities outstanding), Dec. 1989, Cr$119,627m.

Currency. The *cruzeiro* (BRC) is the monetary unit which was introduced in

March 1990 at parity with the former *cruzado*. The cruzeiro was devalued by 17% in Sept. 1991. The exchange rate in March 1992 was US$1 = Cr$2,869·20; £1 = Cr$996·25.

Banking and Finance. The Bank of Brazil (founded in 1853 and reorganized in 1906) is a state-owned commercial bank; it had 2,547 branches in 1989 throughout the republic. On 31 Dec. 1987 deposits were Cr$837,912,257,000.

On 31 Dec. 1964 the Banco Central do Brasil (*President*, Francisco Gros) was founded as the national bank of issue; assets (1985) Cr$639,424m.

There are 9 stock exchanges of which Rio de Janeiro and São Paulo are the most important, Rio de Janeiro and the remaining 7 are linked in the National Electronic Trading System (Senn).

Weights and Measures. The metric system has been compulsory since 1872.

ENERGY AND NATURAL RESOURCES

Electricity. Brazil's hydro-electric potential capacity for electric power production was estimated at 106,500 mw per year in Dec. 1989, one of the largest in the world, of which 34% belongs to the Amazon hydro-electric basin. Installed capacity (1989) 56,972 mw of which 49,643 mw hydro-electric. Production (1989) 243,034m. kwh (227,670m. kwh hydro-electric). Supply 110, 127 and 220 volts; 60 Hz.

Oil. There are 13 oil refineries, of which 11 are state owned. Crude oil production (1991) 31·87m. tonnes; (1988) 28·92m. tonnes of which 67% was from the continental shelf. Promising results have been obtained with the exploration of that area.

The country imported substantial amounts of oil in 1990: 28,245,531 tonnes (value f.o.b. US$4,354m.). Imports came mainly from Saudi Arabia and Iraq.

Gas. Production (1989) 6,091,120 cu. metres of which 64% was from the continental shelf.

Minerals. Brazil is the only source of high-grade quartz crystal in commercial quantities; output, 1988, 247,465 tonnes raw, 51,253 tonnes processed. It is a major producer of chrome ore (reserves of 15·0m. tonnes; output, 1988, 779,258 tonnes); other minerals are mica (124 tonnes in 1988); zirconium, 560,005; beryllium 3; graphite 730,851; titanium ore 3,383,406 tonnes, and magnesite 890,565 tonnes. Along the coasts of the states of Rio de Janeiro, Espírito Santo and Bahia are found monazite sands containing thorium; output, 1988, 3,194 tonnes; reserves are estimated at 48,000 tonnes. Manganese ores of high content are important (reserves in 1988 were estimated at 86·0m. tonnes); output, 1988, 2,603,360 tonnes. Output of bauxite, 1988, 10,925,089 tonnes; mineral salt (1988), 1,050,118; tungsten ore, 268,631, unrough, 1,212; lead, 280,258; asbestos, 3,544,916; coal (1988), 20,984,357. Primary aluminium production in 1989 was 888,000 tonnes. Deposits of coal exist in Rio Grande do Sul, Santa Catarina and Paraná. Total reserves were estimated at 5,190·2m. tonnes in 1988.

Iron is found chiefly in Minas Gerais, notably the Cauê Peak at Itabira. The Government is now opening up what is believed to be one of the richest iron-ore deposits in the world, situated in Carajás, in the northern state of Para, with estimated reserves of 35,000m. tonnes, representing the largest concentration of high-grade (66%) iron ore in the world. Total output of iron ore, 1988, mainly from the Cia. Vale do Rio Doce mine at Itabira, was 200,616,550 tonnes.

Production of tin ore (cassiterite, processed) was 56,029 tonnes in 1988. Output of barytes, 970,989 tonnes. Output of phosphate rock, 28·1m. tonnes in 1987.

Gold is chiefly from Pará (16,697 kg in 1988), Mato Grosso (7,185 kg) and Minas Gerais (14,504 kg); total production (1988), 55,529 kg processed. Silver output (processed in 1988) 84 kg. Diamond output in 1988 was 544,588 carats (77,992 carats from Minas Gerais, 368,028 carats from Mato Grosso).

Agriculture. In 1985, 23,273,517 people were employed in agriculture, and there were 5·83m. farms. Production (in tonnes):

	1989	1990 [1]		1989	1990 [1]
Bananas			Grapes	716,550	786,217
(1,000 bunches)	550,475	550,190	Coconut	681,044	709,345
Beans	2,310,576	2,233,139	(1,000 fruits)		
Cassava	23,668,473	24,284,704	Coffee	3,059,685	2,926,184
Castor beans	128,586	147,659	Cotton	1,860,517	1,812,803
Oranges			Jute	8,328	3,650
(1,000 fruits)	89,016,188	87,531,484	Maize	26,572,592	21,339,439
Potatoes	2,132,286	2,219,097	Soya	24,071,360	19,887,642
Rice	11,044,453	7,418,527	Sugar-cane	252,642,623	262,604,613
Sisal	220,956	185,083	Wheat	5,552,841	3,093,780
Tomatoes	2,177,467	2,255,552	Cocoa	392,610	359,625

[1] Preliminary.

Harvested coffee area, 1990, 2,905,818 ha, principally in the states of São Paulo, Paraná, Espírito Santo and Minas Gerais. Harvested cocoa area, 1990, 664,369 ha. Bahia furnished 83% of the output in 1990. Two crops a year are grown. Harvested castor-bean area, 1990, 286,259 ha. Tobacco output was 444,314 tonnes in 1990, grown chiefly in Rio Grande do Sul and Santa Catarina.

In March 1990 the Government abolished the Brazilian Coffee Institute and the privileges (support prices, regulated foreign exchange rates) previously accorded the coffee trade. Minimum support prices for beans, maize and rice were raised in 1990. In Nov. 1990 the Government ended its monopoly of wheat distribution, though retaining control of imports.

Rubber is produced chiefly in the states of Acre, Amazonas, Rondônia and Pará. Output, 1989, 30,657 tonnes (natural). Brazilian consumption of rubber in 1988, was 125,325 tonnes. Plantations of tung trees were established in 1930; output, 1989, 3,807 tonnes. Soyabean production was estimated at 14·5m. tonnes (from 9·5m. ha) in 1991.

Livestock (in 1,000): 1989, 144,154 cattle, 33,015 swine, 20,041 sheep, 11,669 goats, 6,098 horses, 1,322 asses and 2,009 mules. In 1990, 13,375,000 cattle, 10,993,000 swine, 818,000 sheep and lambs, 693,000 goats and 962,260,000 poultry were slaughtered for meat.

Forestry. Roundwood production (1987) 93,679,451 cu. metres.

Fisheries. The fishing industry had a 1988 catch of 798,638 tonnes.

INDUSTRY. The value of production was Cr$1,132,812,000 in 1985.

The National Iron and Steel Co. at Volta Redonda, State of Rio de Janeiro, furnishes a substantial part of Brazil's steel. Total output, 1990: Pig-iron, 21,260,900 tonnes; crude steel, 20,569,000 tonnes.

Cement output, 1990, was 25,741,000 tonnes. Output of paper, 1989, was 4,867,036 tonnes. Production (1990) of rubber tyres for motor vehicles, 29·16m. units; motor vehicles, 914,535.

Labour. The work force in 1989 numbered 62,513,176, of whom 14,034,883 were in agriculture and 14,368,258 (including the construction industry) worked in industry.

Trade Unions. The main union is the United Workers' Centre (CUT).

FOREIGN ECONOMIC RELATIONS. In 1990 Brazil repealed most of its protectionist legislation. Since June 1991 direct foreign investment on equal terms with domestic has been permitted. In June 1991 the government permitted an annual US$100m. of foreign debt to be converted into funds for environmental protection.

Foreign debt (including states and municipalities) on 30 Sept. 1990 amounted to US$97,731·4m.

Commerce. Imports and exports for calendar years in US$1m.:

	1987	1988	1989	1990
Imports	15,050,827	14,605,254	18,263,238	20,661,361
Exports	26,223,925	33,789,365	34,382,620	31,391,426

Principal imports in 1990 were (in US$1m.): Crude oil, 4,354; oil products, 380; mechanical machinery, 3,210; electrical machinery, 1,997; fuels and lubricants, 5,363; transport equipment, 756; chemical products, 1,691; iron and steel, 710; nonferrous metals, 412.

Principal exports in 1990 were (in US$1m.): Coffee, 2,359; soybean bran, 1,610; iron ore, 2,407; soya, 910; orange juice, 1,468; footwear, 1,184; cocoa beans, 127; pig iron, 417.

Of exports (in US$1m.) in 1988, USA took 8,715; Japan, 2,274; Netherlands, 2,585; Germany (Fed. Rep.), 1,424; Italy, 1,378; France, 850; Argentina, 975; UK, 1,065; China, 718. Of 1989 imports, USA furnished 3,349; Germany (Fed. Rep.), 1,530; Iraq, 1,358; Japan, 1,058; Saudi Arabia, 1,090; Argentina, 739.

Total trade between Brazil and UK (according to British Department of Trade returns, in £1,000 sterling):

	1988	1989	1990	1991
Imports to UK	742,145	817,545	719,849	765,102
Exports and re-exports from UK	304,735	338,634	328,234	339,442

Tourism. In 1988, 1,742,939 tourists visited Brazil. 353,405 were Argentinian, 237,280 US citizens, 212,467 Uruguayan, 121,573 Paraguayan, 95,054 German, 89,800 Italian, 63,034 French, 29,291 Bolivian, 65,624 Spanish, 39,127 Chilean, 41,091 UK citizens, 42,423 Swiss, 32,162 Portuguese, 38,612 Japanese.

COMMUNICATIONS

Roads. There were (1989) 1,663,987 km of highways of which 1,496,131 km were in operation. In 1988 there were 12,682,199 motor vehicles, including 10,274,419 passenger cars, 2,283,384 commercial vehicles and an estimated 124,396 buses and minibuses. A total of 914,684 motor vehicles were produced in 1990.

Railways. Public railways are operated by two administrations, the Federal Railways (RFFSA) formed in 1957 and São Paulo Railways (FEPASA) formed in 1971, which is confined to the state of São Paulo. RFFSA had a route-length of 22,007 km (84 km electrified) in 1990 and FEPASA 4,929 km (1,112 km electrified). An RFFSA subsidiary CBTU (the Brazilian Urban Train Company) runs passenger services in the principal cities. Principal gauges are metre (23,267 km) and 1,600 mm (3,330 km). Traffic moved by RFFSA in 1990 amounted to 75·2m. tonnes of freight and 507m. passengers. FEPASA carried 18·3m. tonnes and 118m. passengers.

There are several important independent freight railways, including the Vitoria à Minas (798 km in 1987), the Carajas (opened 1985, 1,153 km in 1987) and the Amapa (194 km). There are metros in São Paulo (37 km), Rio de Janeiro (19 km), Belo Horizonte (14 km) and Pôrto Alegre (28 km). There is a light rail line in Campinas (6 km).

Civil Aviation. There were 34 companies (30 foreign) operating in 1985. The 4 Brazilian companies cover the whole territory and in 1989 they carried 17,978,000 passengers (15,312,000 in domestic traffic). Their commercial fleet consisted of 248 aircraft on 31 Dec. 1984. There were 243 taxiplane companies on 31 Dec. 1985. The 4 airlines are Viação Aérea Rio Grande do Sul (VARIG), Cruzeiro do Sul, Trans Brasil and VASP. In 1986 there were 126 airports with scheduled flights.

Shipping. Inland waterways, mostly rivers, are open to navigation over some 43,000 km. Santos and Rio de Janeiro are the 2 leading ports; there are 19 other large ports. During 1988, 41,112 vessels entered and cleared the Brazilian ports. 320m. tonnes of cargo were loaded and unloaded in 1990. Port services were deregulated and privatized in 1991. Brazilian shipping, 1984 amounted to 1,636 vessels of 10,001,356 DWT. Petrobrás, the government oil monopoly, took over the government tanker fleet of 26 vessels in 1958; total tanker fleet in 1984 was 70 vessels of 5,090,494 DWT (private and government-owned).

Telecommunications. Of the telegraph system of the country, about half, including all interstate lines, is under control of the Government. There were 12,687 post and telegraph offices in 1988. There were 14,059,524 telephones in 1989 (São Paulo,

5,145,748; Rio de Janeiro, 1,666,491; Federal District, 410,493). In 1986 there were 2,073 radio and (in 1991) 119 television stations (colour by PAL). In 1991 there were 60m. radio and 36m. television receivers.

Cinemas (1987). Cinemas numbered 1,344.

Newspapers (1985). There were 322 daily newspapers with a total yearly circulation of 1,699m. Foreigners and corporations (except political parties) are not allowed to own or control newspapers or wireless stations.

JUSTICE, RELIGION, EDUCATION AND WELFARE

Justice. There is a Supreme Federal Court of Justice at Brasília composed of 11 judges, and a Supreme Court of Justice; all judges are appointed by the President with the approval of the Senate. There are also Regional Federal Courts, Labour Courts, Electoral Courts and Military Courts. Each state organizes its own courts and judicial system in accordance with the federal Constitution.

Religion. At the 1980 census Roman Catholics numbered 105,861,113 (89% of the total), Protestants, 7,885,846 (6·6%) and Spiritualists, 1,538,230.

There are numerous sects, some evangelical and some African derived (such as *Candomble*).

Roman Catholic estimates in 1991 suggest that 90% were baptised Roman Catholic but only 35% were regular attenders.

In 1991 there were 338 bishops and some 14,000 priests. In 1992 there were 0·2m. Jews.

Education. Elementary education is compulsory. In 1989 there were 76,058,259 persons aged 15 years or over who could read and write; this was 78% of that age group (78·09% among men; 78·04% among women).

In 1984 there were 37,348 pre-primary schools with 2,493,381 pupils and 107,338 teachers. In 1988 there were 201,541 primary schools, with 26,821,134 pupils and 1,119,907 teachers; 10,174 secondary schools, with 3,339,930 pupils and 229,183 teachers; and 871 higher education institutions, with 1,921,878 pupils and 138,016 teachers. This tertiary level comprises 83 universities and 788 other institutions.

Of the 83 universities, 19 are in the state of São Paulo, 11 in Rio Grande do Sul and 9 in Rio de Janeiro. There are also foundations in Niterói, Belo Horizonte, João Pessoa, Salvador, Pôrto Alegre, Recife, Manaus, Curitiba, Fortaleza and Natal. There are federal, state and private universities; the largest state university is that of São Paulo (founded 1934), and there are 2 Municipal universities.

The private universities include 11 Catholic universities in Rio de Janeiro, São Paulo, Pôrto Alegre, Campinas, Recife, Belo Horizonte, Goiânia, Curitiba, Pelotas, Salvador and Petrópolis.

Health. In 1987 there were 32,450 hospitals and clinics (12,276 private) of which 7,062 were for in-patients (5,359 private). In 1987 there were 206,382 doctors, 28,772 dentists, 6,094 pharmacists and 29,082 nurses.

DIPLOMATIC REPRESENTATIVES

Of Brazil in Great Britain (32 Green St., London, W1Y 4AT)
Ambassador: Paulo Tarso Flecha de Lima.

Of Great Britain in Brazil (Setor de Embaixadas Sul, Av. das Nações, Lote 08.70.408, Brasília, D.F.)
Ambassador: M. J. Newington, CMG.

Of Brazil in the USA (3006 Massachusetts Ave., NW, Washington, D.C., 20008)
Ambassador: Rubens Recúpero.

Of the USA in Brazil (Av. das Nações, Lote 03, Brasília, D.F.)
Ambassador: Richard Melton.

Of Brazil to the United Nations
Ambassadors: Luís Augusto de Araujo Castro *and* Ronaldo Mota Sardenberg.

Further Reading

Anuário do Transporte Aéreo. Ministério da Aeronáutica, DAC. Rio de Janeiro, 1986
Anuário Estatístico do Brasil. Vol. 49. Fundação Instituto Brasileiro de Geografia e Estatística, Rio de Janeiro, 1990
Anuário Estatístico do Transporte Aquaviário. 1987
Anuário Mineral Brasileiro. Departamento Nacional da Produção Mineral. Brasília, 1988
Boletim do Banco Central do Brasil. Banco Central do Brasil. Brasília. Monthly
Constituicão da Republica Federativa do Brazil. 1988
Indicadores – IBGE. Monthly
Estatísticas da Saúde – 1987 IBGE
Bruneau, T. C., *The Church in Brazil: The Politics of Religion*. Univ. of Texas Press, 1982
Bryant, S. V., *Brazil* [Bibliography] Oxford and Santa Barbara, 1985
Burns, E. B., *A History of Brazil*. 2nd ed. Columbia Univ. Press, 1980
Falk, P. S. and Fleischer, D. V., *Brazil's Economic and Political Future*. Boulder, 1988
Font, M. A., *Coffee, Contention and Change in the Making of Modern Brazil*. Oxford, 1990
Guirmaraes, R. P., *Politics and Environment in Brazil: ecopolitics of development in the third world*. USA L. Riener, 1991
Hanbury-Tenison, R., *A Question of Survival for the Indians of Brazil*. London, 1973
Lees, F. A. *et al.* (eds.), *Banking and Financial Deepening in Brazil*. London, 1990
McDonough, P., *Power and Ideology in Brazil*. Princeton Univ. Press, 1981
Mainwaring, S., *The Catholic Church and Politics in Brazil, 1916–86*. Stanford Univ. Press, 1986
Micallef, J., (ed.) *Brazil: Country with a Future*. London, 1982
Moraes, R. Borba de., *Bibliographia Brasiliana (1504–1900)*. 2 vols. 1958
Trebat, T. J., *Brazil's State-Owned Enterprises*. CUP, 1983
Tyler, W. G., *The Brazilian Industrial Economy*. Aldershot, 1981
Young, J. M., *Brazil: Emerging World Power*. Malabar, 1982

National Library: Biblioteca Nacional Avenida Rio Branco 219–39, Rio de Janeiro, RJ.

BRITISH ANTARCTIC TERRITORY

HISTORY. The British Antarctic Territory was established on 3 March 1962, as a consequence of the entry into force of the Antarctic Treaty (*see* p. 60), to separate those areas of the then Falkland Islands Dependencies which lay within the Treaty area from those which did not (i.e. South Georgia and the South Sandwich Islands see p. 1207).

AREA AND POPULATION. The territory encompasses the lands and islands within the area south of 60°S latitude lying between 20°W and 80°W longitude (approximately due south of the Falkland Islands and the Dependencies). It covers an area of some 660,000 sq. miles, and its principal components are the South Orkney and South Shetland Islands, the Antarctic Peninsula (Palmer Land and Graham Land) the Filchner and Ronne Ice Shelves and Coats Land.

The British Antarctic Territory has no indigenous or permanently resident population. There is however an itinerant population of scientists and logistics staff of about 300, manning a number of research stations.

The territory was administered by a High Commissioner resident in Port Stanley, Falkland Islands until 1989 and thereafter by the Foreign and Commonwealth Office in London. Designated personnel of the scientific stations of the British Antarctic Survey are appointed to exercise certain legal and administrative functions.

Commissioner: M. S. Baker-Bates (non-resident).
Administrator: Dr. J. A. Heap (non-resident).

Fox, R., *Antarctica and the South Atlantic*. London, 1985
Parsons, A., *Antarctica: The Next Decade*. CUP, 1987

BRITISH INDIAN OCEAN TERRITORY

HISTORY. This territory was established by an Order in Council on 8 Nov. 1965, consisting then of the Chagos Archipelago (formerly administered from Mauritius) and the islands of Aldabra, Desroches and Farquhar (all formerly administered from Seychelles). The latter islands became part of Seychelles when that country achieved independence on 29 June 1976.

AREA AND POPULATION. The group, with a total land area of 23 sq. miles (60 sq. km) comprises 5 coral atolls (Diego Garcia, Peros Banhos, Salomon, Eagle and Egmont) of which the largest and southern-most, Diego Garcia, covers 17 sq. miles (44 sq. km) and lies 450 miles (724 km) south of the Maldives. The British Indian Ocean Territory was established to meet UK and US defence requirements in the Indian Ocean. In accordance with the terms of Exchanges of Notes between the UK and US governments in 1966 and 1976, a US Navy support facility has been established on Diego Garcia. There is no permanent population in the British Indian Ocean Territory.

Commissioner: T. G. Harris (non-resident).
Administrator: R. G. Wells (non-resident).
Commissioner's Representative: Cdr P. A. W. Paine, RN.
Flag: Blue and white wavy stripes with the Union Flag in the canton and a crowned palm-tree in the fly.

BRUNEI

Capital: Bandar Seri Begawan
Population: 256,500 (1991)
GNP per capita: US$14,120 (1987)

Negara Brunei Darussalam

(State of Brunei Darussalam)

HISTORY. The Sultanate of Brunei was a powerful state in the early 16th century, with authority over the whole of the island of Borneo and some parts of the Sulu Islands and the Philippines. At the end of the 16th century its power had begun to decline and various cessions were made to Great Britain, the Rajah of Sarawak and the British North Borneo Company in the 19th century to combat piracy and anarchy. By the middle of the 19th century the State had been reduced to its present limits. In 1847 the Sultan of Brunei entered into a treaty with Great Britain for the furtherance of commercial relations and the suppression of piracy, and in 1888, by a further treaty, the State was placed under the protection of Great Britain. As a result of negotiations in June 1978, the Sultan and the British Government signed a new treaty on 7 Jan. 1979 under which Brunei became a fully sovereign and independent State on 31 Dec. 1983.

AREA AND POPULATION. Brunei, on the coast of Borneo, is bounded in the north-west by the South China Sea and on all other sides by Sarawak territory, which splits the State into two separate parts, with the smaller portion forming Temburong district. Area, about 2,226 sq. miles (5,765 sq. km), with a coastline of about 100 miles. Population (1981 census) was 192,832; estimate (1991) 256,500 (132,400 males and 124,100 females). Population density, 44 per sq. km. The 4 districts are Brunei/Muara (147,300 in 1988), Belait (56,000), Tutong (28,500), Temburong (about 9,000). The capital is Bandar Seri Begawan (census, 1981) 49,902, 9 miles from the mouth of Brunei River; other large towns are Seria (23,415 in 1988) and Kuala Belait (19,335). 50% of the population speak Malay and 26% Chinese.

Vital statistics rates, 1990: Birth per 1,000, 26·8; death, 3·1; natural increase, 23·7 (annual rate 3%); infant mortality per 1,000 live births, 8·4. There were 1,618 marriages in 1990. Life expectancy in 1986: Males, 67·5 years; females, 71·4.

CLIMATE. The climate is tropical marine, hot and moist, but nights are cool. Humidity is high and rainfall heavy, varying from 100" (2,500 mm) on the coast to 200" (5,000 mm) inland. There is no dry season. Bandar Seri Begawan. Jan. 80°F (26·7°C), July 82°F (27·8°C). Annual rainfall 131" (3,275 mm).

RULER. The Sultan and Yang Di Pertuan of Brunei Darussalam is HM Paduka Seri Baginda Sultan Haji Hassanal Bolkiah Mu'izzadin Waddaulah. He succeeded on 5 Oct. 1967 at his father's abdication and was crowned on 1 Aug. 1968.

CONSTITUTION AND GOVERNMENT. On 29 Sept. 1959 the Sultan promulgated a Constitution, but parts of it have been in abeyance since Dec. 1962. At independence, the Privy Council, Council of Ministers, and the posts of Chief Minister and State Secretary were abolished. There is no legislature (the 33-member Legislative Council was dissolved in Feb. 1984) and supreme political powers are vested in the Sultan.

The Council of Ministers was composed as follows in Dec. 1991:

Prime Minister, Minister of Defence: HM The Sultan and Yang Di Pertuan of Brunei Darussalam.

Foreign Affairs: Prince Haji Mohammad Bolkiah. *Finance:* Prince Haji Jefri Bolkiah. *Special Adviser to HM The Sultan and Yang Di Pertuan of Brunei Darussalam in the Prime Minister's Department, Home Affairs:* Pehin Dato Haji Isa. *Education:* Pehin Dato Haji Abdul Aziz. *Law:* Pengiran Haji Bahrin. *Industry and Primary Resources:* Pehin Dato Haji Abdul Rahman. *Religious Affairs:* Pehin

Dato Dr Haji Mohammad Zain. *Development:* Pengiran Dato Dr Haji Ismail. *Culture, Youth and Sports:* Pehin Dato Haji Hussain. *Health:* Dato Dr Haji Johar. *Communications:* Dato Haji Zakaria.

The official language is Malay, but English may be used for other purposes. The Chinese community mainly use the Hokkien dialect.

National flag: Yellow, with 2 diagonal strips of white over black with the national arms in red placed over all in the centre.

National anthem: 'Ya Allah, lanjutkan lah usia' (O God, long live His Majesty; words by P. Rahim, tune by I. Sagap).

DEFENCE

Army. The armed forces are known as the Task Force and contain the naval and air elements. Strength (1991) 3,400. Military units include 2 infantry battalions, 1 armoured reconnaissance squadron, 1 engineer squadron and 1 surface-to-air missile battalion. Equipment includes 16 Scorpion light tanks, 24 Sankey AT-104 armoured personnel carriers and 12 Rapier missiles.

Navy. The Royal Brunei Armed Forces Flotilla comprises 3 fast missile-armed attack craft of 200 tonnes and 3 coastal patrol boats. There are also 2 landing craft, 2 utility craft and 3 small patrol boats. The River Division operates 24 fast assault boats. Personnel in 1991 numbered 550.

2 coastal patrol craft operate with 7 smaller boats for the Marine Police.

Air Wing. The Air Wing of the Royal Brunei Armed Forces was formed in 1965. Current equipment includes 6 MBB BO 105, 2 Bell 206B JetRanger, 1 Bell 214, 2 Sikorsky S-70 and 11 Bell 212 helicopters, and 2 SF.260M piston-engined trainers. Personnel (1991), 300.

Police. The Royal Brunei Police numbers 1,750 officers and men (1991). In addition, there are 500 additional police officers mostly employed on static guard duties.

INTERNATIONAL RELATIONS

Membership. Brunei is a member of the UN, the Commonwealth and ASEAN.

ECONOMY

Policy. A fifth Five-Year National Development Plan (1986–90) aimed to further improve the economic, social and cultural life of the people.

Budget. The budget for 1990 envisaged expenditure of B\$2,790·5m. and revenue of B\$2,796·4m. Taxes and duties made up 57·8% of revenue.

Currency. The unit of currency is the *Brunei dollar* (BRD) of 100 *cents*, with a par value of 0·290 299 gramme of gold. B\$404·1m. were in circulation in 1990. In March 1992, £1 = B\$2·89; US\$1 = B\$1·64.

Banking and Finance. In 1988 there were 7 banks (1 incorporated in Brunei) with a total of 28 branches. Savings deposits totalled B\$1,042·5m. in 1990, fixed time deposits B\$1,092·8m. Total assets of banks in 1990 were B\$5,284·1m.

ENERGY AND NATURAL RESOURCES

Electricity. Electric power production (1990) was 1,420m. kwh. Installed capacity, was 404,000 kw, consumption, 1,382m. kwh. Supply 240 volts; 50 Hz.

Oil. The Seria oilfield, discovered in 1929, has passed its peak production. The high level of crude oil production is maintained through the increase of offshore oilfields production, which exceeds onshore oilfields production. There were 564 producing wells at 31 Dec. 1988. Production was 7·33m. tonnes in 1991. The crude oil is exported directly, and only a small amount is refined at Seria for domestic uses.

Gas. Natural gas is produced (8,544m. cu. metres in 1988) at one of the largest liquefied natural gas plants in the world and is exported to Japan.

Agriculture. The main crops produced in 1989 were, rice (1,600 tonnes), vegetables (1,600 tonnes), arable crops (1,200 tonnes) and fruits (3,900 tonnes).

Production, 1988 (in tonnes): Buffalo meat, 212; beef, 57; goat meat, 4·8; pork, 3,193; broilers, 3,750; and 59m. eggs.

Livestock in 1990: Cattle, 1,600; buffaloes, 5,200; pigs, 32,500; goats, 3,200; chickens, 1·42m.

Forestry. Most of the interior is under forest, containing large potential supplies of serviceable timber. In 1990 production of round timber was 101,600 cu. metres; sawn timber, 67,200 cu. metres.

Fisheries. The 1990 catch totalled 1,865 tonnes, including 1,273 tonnes of marine fish.

INDUSTRY. Brunei depends primarily on its oil industry. Other minor products are rubber, pepper, sawn timber, gravel and animal hides. Local industries include boat-building, cloth weaving and the manufacture of brass- and silverware.

FOREIGN ECONOMIC RELATIONS

Commerce. In 1990 imports c.i.f. totalled B$1,847·8m.; exports f.o.b. B$4,316·5m. In 1990 crude oil exports totalled B$2,336·1m., liquefied natural gas, B$1,605·4m. In 1986 Singapore supplied 24% of imports, the USA 15·2% and Japan 20%. Japan took 68% of all exports.

Total trade between Brunei and UK (British Department of Trade returns, in £1,000 sterling):

	1987	1988	1989	1990	1991
Imports to UK	34,144	142,461	186,110	158,516	147,665
Exports and re-exports from UK	204,129	171,556	264,371	224,562	215,222

Tourism. There were 366,100 visitor arrivals in 1990 (7,800 tourists). 1,581 males and 1,657 females made the pilgrimage to Mecca.

COMMUNICATIONS

Roads. There were (1990) 2,248 km of road, of which 1,107 km have a permanent surface. The main road connects Bandar Seri Begawan with Kuala Belait and Seria. In 1990 there were 107,799 private cars, 11,823 goods vehicles and 3,998 motor cycles. There were 47 fatalities in 3,058 road accidents in 1990.

Civil Aviation. Brunei International Airport serves 400,000 passengers annually. Royal Brunei Airlines (RBA) and Singapore Airlines provide daily services linking Brunei and Singapore. RBA also operates services to Bangkok, Manila, Kuala Lumpur, Kuching, Kota Kinabalu, Hong Kong, Darwin, Jakarta, Taipei and Dubai (*via* Singapore). Cathay Pacific Airways also operates to Brunei and on to Western Australia from Hong Kong. British Airways provides a weekly service between Brunei and UK. Malaysian Airlines System has air connections from neighbouring regions. In 1990 243·7m. passengers and 8,816 tonnes of freight were carried.

Shipping. Regular shipping services operate from Singapore, Hong Kong, and from ports in Sarawak and Sabah to Bandar Seri Begawan. Private companies operate a passenger ferry service between Bandar Seri Begawan and Labuan daily. 162 seagoing vessels were licensed in 1990.

Telecommunications. There are 15 post offices (1990) and a telephone network (53,300 telephones in 1990) linking the main centres. Radio Television Brunei, operates on medium- and shortwaves in Malay, English, Chinese and Nepali. Number of receivers (1990): Radio 98,000 and television 67,000.

Newspapers. In 1990 there was a local newspaper with a circulation of 96,200.

JUSTICE, RELIGION, EDUCATION AND WELFARE

Justice. The Supreme Court comprises a High Court and a Court of Appeal and the Magistrates' Courts. The High Court receives appeals from subordinate courts in the districts and is itself a court of first instance for criminal and civil cases. Appeal from the High Court is to a Court of Appeal. The Judicial Committee of the Privy Council in London is the final court of appeal. Shariah Courts deal with Islamic law. 13,700 crimes were reported in 1990.

Religion. The official religion is Islam. In 1986, 66% of the population were Moslem (mostly Malays), 12% Buddhists and 9% Christian.

Education. The government provides free education to all citizens from pre-school up to the highest level at local and overseas universities and institutions. In 1989–90 there were 181 kindergartens and schools, with 8,664 children in kindergartens, 40,611 in primary and 19,761 in secondary schools and 2,912 teachers in kindergarten and primary schools and 1,713 in secondary schools. There were 5 technical and vocational colleges with 1,287 students and 295 teachers and a teacher training college with 278 students and 31 teachers.

In 1989–90 the University of Brunei Darussalam (founded 1985) had 900 students and 169 teachers, and an institute of advanced education 210 students and 45 teachers.

Health. Medical and health services are free to citizens and those in government service and their dependants. Citizens are sent overseas at government expense for medical care not available in Brunei. Flying medical services are provided to remote areas. In 1990 there were 8 hospitals with 893 beds; there were 171 doctors, 30 dentists, 8 pharmacists, 173 midwives and 870 nursing personnel.

DIPLOMATIC REPRESENTATIVES

Of Brunei in Great Britain (49 Cromwell Rd, London, SW7 2ED)
High Commissioner: Pengiran Haji Mustapha.

Of Great Britain in Brunei (Hong Kong Bank Chambers, Bandar Seri Begawan 2085)
High Commissioner: Adrian Sindall.

Of Brunei in the USA (2600 Virginia Ave., NW, Washington, D.C., 20037)
Ambassador: D. H. Mohammad Kassim.

Of the USA in Brunei (Teck Guan Plaza, Bandar Seri Begawan 2085)
Ambassador: Christopher H. Phillips.

Of Brunei to the United Nations
Ambassador: Dato Paduka Haji Jaya Bin Abdul Latif.

Further Reading

Krausse, S. C. E. and G. H., *Brunei*. [Bibliography] Oxford and Santa Barbara, 1988

BULGARIA

Republika Bulgaria

Capital: Sofia
Population: 8·99m. (1991)
GNP per capita: US$2,320 (1989)

HISTORY. The Bulgarian state was founded in 681, but fell under Turkish rule in 1396. By the Treaty of Berlin (1878), the Principality of Bulgaria and the Autonomous Province of Eastern Rumelia, both under Turkish suzerainty, were constituted. In 1885 Rumelia was reunited with Bulgaria. On 5 Oct. 1908 Bulgaria declared her independence of Turkey.

In 1941 Bulgaria signed the Three Power Pact and the Anti-Comintern Pact. After a referendum which abolished the monarchy (for details *see* THE STATESMAN'S YEAR-BOOK, 1986–87) the Fatherland Front government asked for an armistice, which was signed on 28 Oct. 1944 by the USSR, the UK and the USA. A People's Republic was proclaimed on 15 Sept. 1946. The peace treaty was signed in Paris on 10 Feb. 1947. It restored the frontiers as on 1 Jan. 1941.

Following demonstrations in Sofia in Nov. 1989 which were occasioned by the Helsinki Agreement ecological conference, but broadened into demands for political reform, Todor Zhivkov was replaced as Communist Party leader and head of state by the foreign minister Petŭr Mladenov. In Dec. the National Assembly approved 21 measures of constitutional reform, including the abolition of the Communist Party's sole right to govern. The government resigned in Feb. 1990 but was succeeded by the Communist government of Andrei Lukanov as opposition parties declined to join a coalition. President Mladenov resigned in July 1990 following allegations that he brutally suppressed a demonstration in Dec. 1989. Following demonstrations and a general strike Lukanov's government resigned in Nov. 1990 and was replaced by a caretaker government.

AREA AND POPULATION. The area of Bulgaria is 110,994 sq. km (42,855 sq. miles) and is bounded in the north by Romania, east by the Black Sea, south by Turkey and Greece and west by Yugoslavia.

The country is divided into 9 regions (*oblast*) formed from amalgamations of 28 former provinces in 1987 (for these *see* THE STATESMAN'S YEAR-BOOK 1989-90, p. 243). Area and population in 1990:

Region	Area (sq. km)	Pop. (1,000)	Region	Area (sq. km)	Pop. (1,000)
Burgas	14,657	875·3	Razgrad	10,842	848·7
Khaskovo	13,892	1,054·4	Sofia (city)	1,331	1,221·4
Lovech	15,150	1,053·9	Sofia (region)	18,979	1,013·9
Mikhailovgrad	10,607	658·3	Varna	11,929	987·0
Plovdiv	13,628	1,279·4			

The capital, Sofia, has regional status. The population at the census of Dec. 1985 was 8,942,976 (females, 4,515,936). Population on 1 Jan. 1991 was 8,988,888 (6,097,000 urban; 4,556,558 female). Population density 81 per sq. km.

Ethnic minorities are not identified officially, but there are some 1·2m. Moslem Turks. Attempts forcibly to Bulgarianize these led to an exodus of some 300,000 of them into Turkey in 1989. There are also some 300,000 Moslem 'Pomaks' of Bulgarian origin. Both groups were granted linguistic and religious freedom in Dec. 1989. There are also about 0·7m. Gipsies.

Population of principal towns (1989): Sofia, 1,141,537; Plovdiv, 374,004; Varna, 311,123; Ruse, 192,659; Burgas, 203,093; Stara Zagora, 162,754; Pleven, 137,964; Shumen, 109,761; Tolbukhin, 114,377; Sliven, 111,632; Pernik, 98,650; Yambol, 98,651; Khaskovo, 95,036; Gabrovo, 80,480; Pazardzhik, 85,609; Vratsa, 84,043.

Vital statistics, 1989: Live births, 112,289; deaths, 106,902; marriages (1990), 59,874; divorces, 12,636. Rates per 1,000 population, 1990: Birth, 11·7; death, 12·1; infant deaths, 14·8; growth –0·4. Abortions, 1987: 134,097.

Expectation of life in 1989 was 71·4 years (males, 68·33; females, 74·7).

CLIMATE. The southern parts have a Mediterranean climate, with winters mild and moist and summers hot and dry, but further north the conditions become more continental, with a larger range of temperature and greater amounts of rainfall in summer and early autumn. Sofia. Jan. 28°F (–2·2°C), July 69°F (20·6°C). Annual rainfall 25·4" (635 mm).

CONSTITUTION AND GOVERNMENT. The 'Tŭrnovo' Constitution of 1879 was replaced by the 'Dimitrov' Constitution in 1947. This was in turn replaced by a new constitution on 18 May 1971. For an account of the political structure of the Communist régime see THE STATESMAN'S YEAR-BOOK, 1990-91, p. 244. A new constitution was adopted, again at Tŭrnovo, in July 1991.

The *President* of the Republic is directly elected for not more than 2 5-year terms. Candidates for the presidency must be at least 40 years old and have lived for the last 5 years in Bulgaria.

Presidential elections were held in 2 rounds on 12 and 19 Jan. 1992. There were 23 candidates at the first round; turn-out was 73%. 44% of votes cast were for Zhelyu Zhelev (b. 1936; UDF). At the second round against 1 opponent Zhelyu Zhelev was elected with 58·85% of votes cast. Turn-out was 76%.

The National Assembly has 240 seats. At the elections of Oct. 1991 the Union of Democratic Forces (UDF) won 110 seats with 34·38% of votes cast, the Socialist Party (formerly Communist) 106 with 33·11% and the Movement for Rights and Liberties (Turkish) 24 with 7·56%. There was a 4% threshold.

A 14-member government was formed in Nov. 1991, including:

Prime Minister: Filip Dimitrov (b. 1955; UDF).

Defence: Dimitŭr Ludzhiev. *Finance.* Ivan Kostov. *Industry, Commerce and Technology:* Ivan Pushkarov. *Foreign:* Stoyan Ganev.

National flag: Three horizontal stripes of white, green, red, with the national emblem in the canton.

National anthem: An arrangement of Mila Rodino (Dear Fatherland), a popular patriotic song, was declared the national anthem in 1964.

Local Government. People's Councils for the 9 regions and 273 districts within them are elected for 30 months. In addition to their civic functions they supervise the management of publicly owned enterprises. The Councils' executive organs are Permanent Committees. Elections were held for mayors and councillors at the same time as the National Assembly elections on 13 Oct. 1991.

DEFENCE. Conscription was reduced from 18 to 12 months in 1992.

Army. There are 3 military districts based on Sofia, Plovdiv and Sliven. In 1991 the Army had a strength of 75,000, including 49,000 conscripts, and is organized in 8 motor rifle divisions and 4 tank brigades. Equipment includes 670 T-34, 1,145 T-55 and 334 T-72 main battle tanks. There are 12 regiments of border guards numbering 12,000.

Navy. The reducing number of Navy combatants, all ex-Soviet, comprise 1 operational and 2 reserve 'Romeo' class diesel submarines, 2 'Riga' and 1 Konl class small frigates, 2 'Poti', 2 'Tarantul' and 1 'Pank' class corvettes, 6 'Osa' class missile craft, 7 patrol vessels, 4 torpedo craft, 5 coastal minesweepers and 28 inshore minesweepers. There are 2 medium landing ships and 21 craft. Major auxiliaries include 2 oilers, 2 research ships, an electronic intelligence gatherer, 2 training ships and 2 tugs. There are some 20 minor auxiliaries and service craft. There are 2 regiments of coastal artillery including some missile-armed, and some 8 shore-based Ka-25 and Mi-14 helicopters. The naval headquarters is at Varna, and there are bases at Atiya, Burgas and Sozopol. Personnel in 1991 totalled 10,000 of whom half were conscripts.

Air Force. The Air Force has about 250 Soviet-built combat aircraft and (1991) 22,000 personnel (16,000 conscripts). There are 3 regiments of MiG-21/23/29 interceptors; 2 regiments of fighter/ground attack MiG-23s and Su-22/25s; 1 reconnaissance squadron of MiG-21s; some Mi-24 helicopter gunships; a total of about 35 Tu-134, L-410, An-2 and An-24/26 transport aircraft; a total of about 60 Mi-4, Mi-2, Ka-26, and Mi-8 helicopters; and L-29 Delfin, L-39 Albatros, MiG-15UTI and Zlin 42 trainers. Soviet-built 'Guideline', 'Goa' and 'Ganef' surface-to-air missiles have also been supplied to Bulgaria.

INTERNATIONAL RELATIONS

Membership. Bulgaria is a member of the UN, CSCE and IMF.

ECONOMY

Policy. For planning until 1990 *see* THE STATESMAN'S YEAR-BOOK, 1990-91, p. 245. Legislation of Nov. 1990 broke up large monopolies as a preparation for privatization by granting firms political and financial independence. In Feb. 1991 anti-inflationary measures were introduced, and some consumer prices rose 250%.

Budget. The revenue and expenditure of Bulgaria for calendar years were as follows (in 1m. leva):

	1977	1980	1981	1982	1983	1984	1985	1986	1987
Revenue	9,498	13,187	15,385	15,824	16,812	17,754	18,097	19,506	20,672
Expenditure	9,477	13,167	15,370	15,809	16,663	17,392	18,087	19,491	20,662

Of the 1984 revenue 92% came from the national economy. 1983 expenditure was: National economy, 8,630m. leva; education, 2,945m.; social security, 2,846m.

Currency. The unit of currency is the *lev* (BGL) of 100 *stotinki*. Notes are issued for 1, 2, 5, 10 and 20 *leva* and coins for 1, 2, 5, 10, 20, 50 *stotinki* and 1, 2 and 5 *leva*. In March 1992, £1 = 32·24 leva; US$1 = 18·37 leva.

Banking and Finance. Under a 1987 reform the National Bank (*Governor*, Todor Vŭlchev) remains the central bank and is responsible for issuing currency. The Foreign Trade Bank (founded 1964) and the State Savings Bank also remain, the latter now serving local enterprises as well as the public. In 1990, 10·66m. depositors had savings totalling 16,817m. leva. Five commercial banks serving various specific industrial sectors, and three more broadly-based (the Economic Bank, the Agricultural Bank and the Bank for Economic Initiative) have been set up. The first private bank opened in Aug. 1990.

Weights and Measures. The metric system is in general use. On 1 April 1916 the Gregorian calendar came into force.

ENERGY AND NATURAL RESOURCES

Electricity. Bulgaria has little oil, gas or high-grade coal and energy policy is based on the exploitation of its low-grade coal and hydro-electric resources, which produce 20% of the electricity supply. Supply 220 volts; 50 Hz. In 1989 there were 135 power stations with a potential of 11·1m. kw. (thermal, (46) 6·5m. kw.; hydroelectric, (88) 2m. kw.; nuclear, (1) 2·26m. kw.). Output, 1990, 42,130m. kwh. The single nuclear plant at Kozlodui supplies 25% of output, but 2 of its 4 reactors were shut down in July 1991 for safety reasons.

Oil. Oil is extracted in the Balchik district on the Black Sea, in an area 100 km north of Varna and at Dolni Dubnik near Pleven. There are refineries at Burgas (annual capacity 5m. tonnes) and Dolni Dubnik (7m. tonnes). Crude oil production (1991) was 248,000 tonnes; gas, 13·57m. cu. metres.

Minerals. Production in 1990: Manganese ore, 9,900 tonnes; iron ore, 321,000 tonnes; lignite, 27·83m. tonnes; brown coal, 3·7m. tonnes. 92 tonnes of salt were extracted in 1987.

Agriculture. In 1990 agricultural land covered 6,159,000 ha, of which 4,642,700 ha were arable. The sown area was 3,769,400 ha; there were 286,800 ha of meadows and 1,516,300 ha of commons and pastures.

Collective and state farms had been incorporated into 'agricultural-industrial complexes'. There were 285 of these in 1987.

A law of Feb. 1991 provides for the redistribution of collectivized land to its former owners up to 30 ha. Landless peasants receive state land or compensation in lieu. Foreigners and Bulgarians resident abroad may not acquire such land. It may be rented out, but not sold for 3 years.

Production in 1990 (in 1,000 tonnes): Wheat, 5,095; maize, 1,214; barley, 1,345; sugar beet, 576; sunflower seed, 365; seed cotton, 8; tobacco, 52; tomatoes, 792; potatoes, 427; grapes, 708; rose oil, 911 kg. Other products (in 1,000 tonnes) in 1990: Meat, 909; wool, 28; honey, 10·4; 2,471m. eggs; 2,387m. litres of milk.

Livestock (1991, in 1,000s): 1,457 cattle, including 609 milch cows, 7,927 sheep, 4,201 pigs, 27,998 poultry and 596 beehives.

In 1990 a Federation of Independent Agricultural Trade Unions was formed.

Forestry. Forest area, 1990, was 3,871,000 ha (1·34m. ha coniferous, 2·54m. ha broad-leaved). 46,000 ha were afforested in 1990 and 8·86m. cu. metres of timber were cut.

Fisheries. Catch, 1990: 66,800 tonnes. There is a 200-mile economic exclusion zone.

INDUSTRY. In 1991 there were 3,491 registered firms, of which 3,155 were manufacturers and 336 services. Firms by ownership: State, 900; municipal, 768; co-operative; 23; social organizations, 123; associations, 315; foreign and joint ventures, 204; agricultural collectives, 1,158.

In 1990 there were produced (in 1,000 tonnes): Pig iron and ferro-alloys, 1,159; steel, 2,180; rolled steel, 2,156; artificial fertilizers, 958; sulphuric acid, 522; plastics, 256; cement, 4,700; paper, 272; cotton yarn, 68; woollen yarn, 28. 25,400 cars were made; 98,700 bicycles; 214,200 TV sets; 38,000 radios.

Labour. There is a 42½-hour 5-day working week. The average wage (excluding peasantry) was 4,200 leva per annum in 1990; minimum wage was 1,980 leva. Population of working age (males 16–59; females 16–54), 1991, 5·02m. (2·7m. males). The labour force (excluding peasantry) in 1990 was 3,819,015, of whom 2,757,387 (45·5% women) were manual labourers. 1,456,450 worked in industry, 312,370 in building and 672,251 in agriculture and forestry. There were 402,065 registered unemployed in Dec. 1991.

Trade Unions. An independent white-collar trade union movement, Podkrepa, was formed in 1989. It claimed 100,000 members in July 1990. The former official Central Council of Trade Unions reconstituted itself in 1990 as the Executive Committee of Independent Trade Unions.

FOREIGN ECONOMIC RELATIONS. Legislation in force as of Feb. 1992 abolished restrictions imposed in 1990 on the repatriation of profits and allows foreigners to own and set up companies in Bulgaria. Joint Western-Bulgarian industrial ventures have been permitted since 1980. There were 366 early in 1991. Western share participation may exceed 50%. In April 1991 the Club of Paris creditor governments agreed to reschedule Bulgaria's US$1,800m. debt over 10 years with a 6-year period of grace.

A trade-pact was signed with the EEC in May 1990.

The USA granted most-favoured-nation status in Nov. 1991.

Commerce. Foreign trade (in 1m. foreign exchange leva):

	1985	1989	1990
Imports	14,067	12,796	10,160
Exports	13,739	13,673	10,496

Proportion of major exports in 1990: Production machinery, 58%; foods, 12%; industrial consumer goods, 11%.

Main export markets in 1990 (% of total exports): USSR, 64; Czechoslovakia, 4·4; Germany, 4·2; Libya, 4; Romania, 3·9. Main import suppliers: USSR, 56·5; Germany, 10·4; Poland, 5; Czechoslovakia, 4·6.

Total trade between Bulgaria and UK (British Department of Trade returns, in £1,000 sterling):

	1987	1988	1989	1990	1991
Imports to UK	24,249	28,068	34,272	32,787	36,786
Exports and re-exports from UK	88,761	82,156	86,209	45,022	35,547

Tourism. Since 1988 5-year passports have been issued instead of ad hoc exeats. Exit visas were abolished in Jan. 1991. Bulgaria received 10·33m. foreign visitors in 1990 and 2·39m. Bulgarians made visits abroad.

COMMUNICATIONS

Roads. In 1989 there were 33,766 km of hard-surfaced roads, including 266 km of motorways and 2,935 km of main roads. 2,181m. passengers and 267m. tonnes of freight were carried in 1990.

Railways. In 1990 there were 4,299 km of standard gauge railway, including 2,609 km electrified. 102m. passengers and 63m. tonnes of freight were carried.

Civil Aviation. BALKAN (Bulgarian Airlines) operated 152,900 km of routes (2,700 km domestic) in 1990 and ran internal flights from Sofia (airport: Vrazhdebna) and international flights to Algiers, Amsterdam, Athens, Baghdad, Bratislava, Belgrade, Benghazi, Berlin, Brussels, Bucharest, Budapest, Cairo, Casablanca, Copenhagen, Damascus, Dresden, Frankfurt, Istanbul, London, Madrid, Moscow, Nicosia, Paris, Prague, Rome, Stockholm, Syktyvkar, Tunis, Vienna, Warsaw and Zurich. There are also flights from Burgas to Leningrad and Kiev, and from Varna to Leningrad, Kuwait, Athens and Stockholm. In 1990 BALKAN had 48 aircraft, all Soviet. In 1990 BALKAN carried 2·19m. passengers and 25,000 tonnes of freight.

Shipping. Ports, shipping and shipbuilding are controlled by the Bulgarian United Shipping and Shipbuilding Corporation. In 1982 it had 194 ocean-going vessels with a loading capacity of 1·6m. DWT. Burgas is a fishing and oil-port open to tankers of 20,000 tons. Varna is the other important port. There is a rail ferry between Varna and Ilitchovsk (USSR). In 1990 there were 254,000 km of sea passenger route. 240,000 passengers and 2,469,300 tonnes of cargo were carried. There were 45,000 km of inland waterways in 1990. 26,000 passengers and 2·63m. tonnes of freight were carried.

Pipeline. Pipelines conveyed 13·76m. tonnes in 1990.

Telecommunications. In 1990 there were 4,164 post and telecommunications offices, 2,634,900 telephones (1,722,700 private), 85 radio transmitters and 44 television transmitters. 2 TV programmes and 3 radio programmes on medium- and short-waves. A service for tourists is broadcast via the Varna II transmitter on 774 kHz. Bulgaria receives transmissions from the French satellite channel TV5. Colour programmes by SECAM system. Radio receiving sets licensed in 1989, 1,994,212; television, 1,662,558.

Cinemas and Theatres (1990). There were 75 theatres (attendance, 3·7m.) and 2,174 cinemas (attendance, 47·69m.). 520 films were made in 1989 (46 full-length).

Newspapers and Books. In 1990 there were 541 newspapers with an annual circulation of 900,456 and 967 other periodicals. 4,589 book titles were published in 1990.

JUSTICE, RELIGION, EDUCATION AND WELFARE

Justice. A law of Nov. 1982 provides for the election (and recall) of all judges by the National Assembly. There are a Supreme Court, 28 provincial courts (including Sofia), 105 regional courts and 'Comrades' Courts' for minor offences. Jurors are elected at the local government elections.

The maximum term of imprisonment is 20 years. 'Exceptionally dangerous crimes' carry the death penalty. In 1985 harsh penalties were imposed for terrorist acts and drug smuggling following incidences of both.

The Prosecutor General who is elected by the National Assembly for 5 years and subordinate to it alone, exercises supreme control over the observance of the law by all government bodies, officials and citizens. He appoints and discharges all Prosecutors of every grade.

In 1990 there were 11,631 crimes (156 murders) and 11,968 convictions (1,624 females; 990 under 17).

Religion. 'The traditional church of the Bulgarian people' (as it is officially described), is that of the Eastern Orthodox Church. It was disestablished under the 1947 Constitution. In 1953 the Bulgarian Patriarchate was revived. The Patriarch Maksim (enthroned 1971) was dismissed in 1992 for collaborating with the former Communist government. The seat of the Patriarch is at Sofia. There are 11 dioceses, each under a Metropolitan, 10 bishops, 2,600 parishes, 1,700 priests, 400 monks and nuns, 3,700 churches and chapels, one seminary and one theological college.

The Constitution provides for freedom of conscience and belief but forbids propaganda against the Government. The State provides 17% of Church funds.

Churches may not maintain schools or colleges, except theological seminaries, or organize youth movements.

In 1990 there were some 70,000 Roman Catholics with 53 priests, in 2 bishoprics. In 1987 there were 10,000 Uniates with 20 priests. In 1984 there were 5 Protestant groups: Pentecostals (10,000 members, 120 churches, 30 pastors); Baptists (1,000 members, 20 churches); Methodists; Congregationalists; Adventists. There were estimated to be about 700,000 practising Moslems in 1984 under a Chief Mufti elected by 7 regional muftis. There were about 1,000 mosques in 1987.

Education. Education is free, and compulsory for children between the ages of 7 and 16. Complete literacy is claimed. The gradual introduction of unified secondary polytechnical schools offering compulsory education for all children from the ages of 7 to 17 was begun in 1973–74.

Educational statistics: In 1989–90 there were 4,562 kindergartens (317,559 children, 28,312 teachers). In 1990–91 there were 3,458 unified secondary polytechnical schools with 72,310 teachers and 1,110,733 pupils; 126 special needs schools with 2,341 teachers and 14,696 pupils; 4 vocational technical schools with 64 teachers and 2,631 pupils; 236 secondary vocational technical schools with 6,602 teachers and 113,139 pupils; 257 technical colleges and schools of art with 10,865 teachers and 125,728 students; 46 post-secondary institutions with 2,947 teachers and 31,943 students; 38 institutes of higher education, with 20,716 teachers and 151,510 students. There are 3 state universities: the Kliment Ohrid University in Sofia (founded 1888) had 1,502 teachers and 15,501 students (in 1987–88); the Kirill i Metodii University in Veliko Túrnovo (founded 1971) had 417 teachers and 5,042 students and the Paisi Hilendarski University in Plovdiv (founded 1961) had 487 teachers and 5,117 students. An independent university for law, management and political science was founded in Burgas in 1990 with 500 full-time and 150 part-time students.

The Academy of Sciences was founded in 1869.

Social Welfare. Retirement and disablement pensions and temporary sick pay are calculated as a percentage of previous wages (respectively 55–80%, 35–100%, 69–90%) and according to the nature of the employment.

Monthly family allowances for children under 16: 15 leva for 1 child, 60 leva for 2 children and 115 leva for 3 children.

In 1990 the average monthly pension was 140 leva. Pension disbursements totalled 3,932·2m. leva.

All medical services are free. Private medical services were authorized in Jan. 1991. In 1990 there were 256 hospitals with 88,027 beds. There were 28,490 doctors and 6,115 dentists.

DIPLOMATIC REPRESENTATIVES

Of Bulgaria in Great Britain (186 Queen's Gate, London, SW7 5HL)
Ambassador: Ivan Stancioff.

Of Great Britain in Bulgaria (Blvd. Marshal Tolbukhin 65–67, Sofia)
Ambassador: Richard Thomas, CMG.

Of Bulgaria in the USA (1621 22nd St., NW, Washington, D.C., 20008)
Ambassador: Ognyan Pishev.

Of the USA in Bulgaria (1 Stamboliski Blvd., Sofia)
Ambassador: Kenneth Hill.

Of Bulgaria to the United Nations
Ambassador: Svetlomir Baev.

Further Reading

Kratka Bŭlgarska Entsiklopediia (Short Bulgarian Encyclopaedia), 5 vols. Sofia, 1963–69
Statistical Reference Book: PR of Bulgaria. Sofia, annual from 1988
Statisticheski Godishnik (Statistical Yearbook). Sofia from 1956
Crampton, R. J., *A Short History of Modern Bulgaria.* CUP, 1987.—*Bulgaria.* [Bibliography] Oxford and Santa Barbara, 1989
Lampe, J. R., *The Bulgarian Economy in the Twentieth Century.* London, 1986

BURKINA FASO

Capital: Ouagadougou
Population: 8·76m. (1990)
GNP per capita: US$310 (1989)

République Démocratique
Populaire de Burkina Faso

HISTORY. A separate colony of Upper Volta was in 1919 carved out of the colony of Upper Senegal and Niger, which had been established in 1904. In 1932 it was abolished and most of its territory transferred to Ivory Coast, with small parts added to French Sudan and Niger, but it was re-constituted with its former borders on 4 Sept. 1947. Upper Volta became an autonomous republic within the French Community on 11 Dec. 1958 and reached full independence on 5 Aug. 1960.

On 3 Jan. 1966 the government of Maurice Yameogo was overthrown by a military coupled by Lieut-Col. Sangoulé Lamizana, who assumed the Presidency. In a further coup on 25 Nov. 1980, President Lamizana was overthrown and a military regime assumed power. Further coups took place on 7 Nov. 1982, 4 Aug. 1983 and 15 Oct. 1987 and 18 Sept. 1989. The name of the country was changed to Burkina Faso in 1984.

AREA AND POPULATION. Burkina Faso is bounded north and west by Mali, east by Niger, south by Benin, Togo, Ghana and the Côte d'Ivoire. The republic covers an area of 274,122 sq. km; population (census, 1985) 7,967,019 (3,846,518 males). Estimate (1990) 8·76m. (8·8% urban). Vital statistics (1985–90): rate, 2·7%; infant mortality, 138 per 1,000 live births; expectation of life, 47·2 years. The largest cities (1985 census) are Ouagadougou, the capital (442,223), Bobo-Dioulasso (231,162), Koudougou (51,670), Ouahigouya (38,604), Banfora (35,204), Kaya (25,799), Fada N'Gourma and Tenkodogo.

The areas and populations of the 30 provinces were:

Province	Sq. km	Census 1985	Province	Sq. km	Census 1985
Bam	4,017	164,263	Nahouri	3,843	105,273
Bazéga	5,313	306,976	Namentenga	7,755	198,798
Bougouriba	7,087	221,522	Oubritenga	4,693	303,229
Boulgou	9,033	403,358	Oudalan	10,046	105,715
Boulkiemde	4,138	363,594	Passoré	4,078	225,115
Comoé	18,393	250,510	Poni	10,361	234,501
Ganzourgou	4,087	196,006	Sanguie	5,165	218,289
Gnagna	8,600	229,249	Sanmatenga	9,213	368,365
Gourma	26,613	294,123	Sèno	13,473	230,043
Houet	16,472	585,031	Sissili	13,736	246,844
Kadiogo	1,169	459,138	Soum	13,350	190,464
Kénédougou	8,307	139,722	Sourou	9,487	267,770
Kossi	13,177	330,413	Tapoa	14,780	159,121
Kouritenga	1,627	197,027	Yatenga	12,292	537,205
Mouhoun	10,442	289,213	Zoundwéogo	3,453	155,142

The principal ethnic groups are the Mossi (48%), Fulani (10%), Lobi-Dagari (7%), Mandé (7%), Bobo (7%), Sénoufo (6%), Gourounsi (5%), Bissa (5%), Gourmantché (5%). French is the official language.

CLIMATE. A tropical climate with a wet season from May to Nov. and a dry season from Dec. to April. Rainfall decreases from south to north. Ouagadougou. Jan. 76°F (24·4°C), July 83°F (28·3°C). Annual rainfall 36" (894 mm).

CONSTITUTION AND GOVERNMENT. At a referendum in June 1991 a new constitution was approved, and the president dissolved the government. At the presidential elections of 1 Dec. 1991 Blaise Compaoré was the sole candidate, and was elected by 86·4% of votes cast. The electorate was 3·5m.; turn-out was 27·3%.

Head of State and Government: Capt. Blaise Compaoré.

The *Assembly of the People* has 77 members elected by universal suffrage. The *Chamber of Representatives* is a consultative body, comprising representatives of social, religious, professional and political organizations.

National flag: Horizontally red over green with a yellow star over all in the centre.

Local government: The country is divided into 30 provinces and 250 districts.

DEFENCE. There are 6 military regions. All forces form part of the Army.

Army. The Army consists of 5 infantry companies, 1 airborne company and tank, artillery and engineer support units. Equipment includes 83 armoured cars. Strength (1992), 7,000 with a further 1,750 men in paramilitary forces.

Air Force. Creation of a small air arm to support the land forces began, with French assistance, in 1964. Combat equipment includes 3 MiG-21 fighters and 1 MiG-21U trainer and 10 SF.260W Warrior light strike aircraft. Other equipment comprises 2 HS.748 twin-turboprop freighters, 1 C-47, 2 twin-turboprop Nord 262s, an Aero Commander 500, 2 Broussard and 1 Reims/Cessna Super Skymaster for transport and liaison duties, 1 Cessna 172 trainer, and 2 Dauphin and 1 Alouette III helicopters. Personnel total (1991) 200.

INTERNATIONAL RELATIONS

Membership. Burkina Faso is a member of the UN, OAU and is an ACP state of the EEC.

ECONOMY

Policy. The second 5-year plan (1991–96) was scaled down by 50% in 1991. It is proposed to privatize and restructure the banking and industrial sectors.

Budget. Government revenue in 1988 was 90,295m. francs CFA and expenditure 96,285m. francs CFA.

Currency. The unit of currency is the *franc CFA* (XOF) with a parity rate of 50 *francs* CFA to 1 French *franc*. In March 1992, £1 = 489·63 *francs*; US$1 = 278·90 *francs*.

Banking. The *Banque Centrale des Etats de l'Afrique de l'Ouest* is the bank of issue. The main commercial bank is the *Banque Internationale du Burkina*. In Dec. 1982 it had deposits of 32,046m. francs CFA.

ENERGY AND NATURAL RESOURCES

Electricity. Production of electricity (1986) was 159m. kwh.

Minerals. There are deposits of manganese near Tambao in the north, but exploitation is limited by existing transport facilities. Magnetite, bauxite, zinc, lead, nickel and phosphates have been found in the same area. Gold was discovered in 1987 at Assakan, near the Malian border.

Agriculture. In 1989 there were 3·55m. ha of arable land and 10m. ha of permanent pasture. 16,000 ha were irrigated. 7·59m. persons depended on agriculture, of whom 4m. were economically active. Production (1989, in 1,000 tonnes): Sorghum, 991; millet, 649; sugar-cane, 340; maize, 257; groundnuts, 131; rice, 42; seed cotton, 179; sesame, 11. Rice and groundnuts are of increasing importance.

Livestock (1990, in 1,000): Cattle, 2,900; sheep, 3,150; goats, 5,700; pigs, 496; asses, 450; horses, 70.

Forestry. In 1989, 6·66m. ha were forested, chiefly in the deep river valleys of the Mouhoun (Black Volta), Nakambe, (White Volta) and Nazinon (Red Volta). Production (1986), 6·93m. cu. metres.

Fisheries. River fishing produced 7,000 tonnes in 1986.

INDUSTRY. In 1982 gross manufacturing (including energy) was 68,146,600 francs CFA, of which textiles (3,666,600 francs CFA) and metal products (2,795,100 francs CFA).

Labour. In 1990 the labour force was 4,744,000. In 1991 a 3-year wage-freeze was imposed.

Trade Unions. The trade union federation is the *Confédération syndicale burkinabe*.

FOREIGN ECONOMIC RELATIONS

Commerce. In 1988 imports totalled US$489m. and exports US$142m. The major exports were cotton and karite nuts. In 1983 France provided 28%, the Côte d'Ivoire 24% and USA 9% of imports, while the Côte d'Ivoire took 9%, France 12%, Taiwan 27%, China 11% and UK 8% of exports.

Total trade between Burkina Faso and UK (British Department of Trade returns, in £1,000 sterling):

	1988	1989	1990	1991
Imports to UK	546	954	967	235
Exports and re-exports from UK	3,732	4,647	6,557	6,472

Tourism. There were 68,304 tourists in 1987 spending 2,300m. francs CFA.

COMMUNICATIONS

Roads. The road system comprises 13,134 km, of which 4,396 km are national, 1,744 km departmental, 2,364 km regional and 1,940 km unclassified roads. In 1982 there were 33,769 vehicles, comprising 16,463 private cars, 419 buses, 14,852 commercial vehicles, 411 special vehicles and 1,123 tractors.

Railway. An independent Burkina Faso railway organization was established in 1988 to run the portion in Burkina (622 km of metre-gauge) of the former Abidjan-Niger Railway. It carried 0·7m. passengers and 0·4m. tonnes of freight in 1990. An extension was under construction (1990) from the terminus at Ouagadougou to Kaya (107 km).

Civil Aviation. Ouagadougou and Bobo-Dioulasso are regularly served by UTA and Air Afrique and in 1982 dealt with 120,684 passengers and 6,778 tonnes of freight. Air Burkina operates all internal flights to 47 domestic airports.

Telecommunications. There were, in 1982, some 42 post offices and (1984) 14,000 telephones. Radio and television services (colour by SECAM) are provided by the state-controlled Radiodiffusion-Télévision Burkina. Radio Bobo is a regional service and there is a commercial radio station. In 1991 there were estimated to be 0·2m. radio and 41,500 television receivers.

Cinemas. In 1982 there were 12 cinemas with 14,000 seats.

Newspapers. Four daily newspapers were published in Ouagadougou in 1986.

JUSTICE, RELIGION, EDUCATION AND WELFARE

Justice. There is a Supreme Court in Ouagadougou and Courts of Appeal at Ouagadougou and Bobo-Dioulasso. Revolutionary People's Tribunals have replaced the former lower courts.

Religion. In 1989 there were 3·75m. Moslems and 1·06m. Christians (mainly Roman Catholic). Many of the remaining population follow traditional animist religions.

Education. There were (in 1986) 351,807 pupils and 6,091 teachers in 1,758 primary schools, 48,875 pupils and 1,514 teachers in 107 secondary schools, 4,808 students with 421 teachers in 18 technical schools and 347 students in a teacher-training establishment. The Université d'Ouagadougou had 3,869 students and 325 teaching staff in 1986.

Health (1980). There were 5 hospitals, 254 dispensaries, 11 medical centres, 65 regional clinics and 167 mobile clinics with a total of 4,587 beds. There were 119 doctors, 14 surgeons, 52 pharmacists, 163 health assistants, 229 midwives and 1,345 nursing personnel.

A 10-year health programme started in 1979, providing for 7,000 village health centres, 515 district health centres, regional and sub-regional medical centres, 10 departmental hospitals, 2 national hospitals and a university centre of health sciences in Ouagadougou.

DIPLOMATIC REPRESENTATIVES

Of Burkina Faso in Great Britain
Ambassador: Salifou Rigobert Kongo (resides in Brussels).

Of Great Britain in Burkina Faso
Ambassador: Margaret Rothwell (resides in Abidjan).

Of Burkina Faso in the USA (2340 Massachusetts Ave., NW, Washington, D.C., 20008)
Ambassador: Paul-Désiré Kabore.

Of the USA in Burkina Faso (PO Box 35, Ouagadougou)
Ambassador: Edward P. Brynn.

Of Burkina Faso to the United Nations
Ambassador: Gaëtan Rimwanguiya Ouedraogo.

Further Reading

MacFarlane, D. M., *Historical Dictionary of Upper Volta*. Metuchen, 1978
Nnaji, B. O., *Blaise Compaore: Architect of the Burkina Faso Revolution*. Lagos, 1991

BURMA

Capital: Rangoon (Yangon)
Population: 40·78m. (1991)
GNP per capita: US$200 (1986)

Myanmar Naingngandaw

(Union of Myanmar)

HISTORY. A treaty establishing Burma's independence from the UK was signed in London on 17 Oct. 1947. For the history of Burma's connexion with Great Britain *see* THE STATESMAN'S YEAR-BOOK, 1950, p. 836. The Union of Burma came formally into existence on 4 Jan. 1948 and became the Socialist Republic of the Union of Burma in 1974. On 19 June 1989 the military government changed the official name of the country in English to the Union of Myanmar.

AREA AND POPULATION. Burma is bounded east by China, Laos and Thailand, west by the Indian ocean, Bangladesh and India. The total area of the Union is 261,228 sq. miles (676,577 sq. km). The population in 1983 (census) was 35,313,905. Estimate (1991) 40·78m. (20·57m. female). Growth rate in 1991, 1·88%. Birth rate (1990 estimate), 28·4 per 1,000; death rate, 8·8 per 1,000; infant deaths, 47 per 1,000 live births; still births, 10·8 per 1,000 live births. Expectation of life was 61 years in 1989.

The leading towns are: Rangoon (Yangon), the capital (1983), 2,458,712; other towns, Mandalay, 532,985; Moulmein, 219,991; Pegu, 150,447; Bassein, 144,092; Sittwe (Akyab), 107,907; Taunggye, 107,607; Monywa, 106,873.

The population of the 7 States and 7 Divisions at the 1983 census (provisional): Kachin State, 903,982; Kayah State, 168,355; Karen State, 1,057,505; Chin State, 368,985; Sagaing Division, 3,855,991; Tenasserim Division, 917,628; Pegu Division, 3,800,240; Magwe Division, 3,241,103; Mandalay Division, 4,580,923; Mon State, 1,682,041; Rakhine State, 2,045,891; Rangoon Division, 3,973,782; Shan State, 3,718,706; Irrawaddy Division, 4,991,057.

CLIMATE. The climate is equatorial in coastal areas, changing to tropical monsoon over most of the interior, but humid temperate in the extreme north, where there is a more significant range of temperature and a dry season lasting from Nov. to April. In coastal parts, the dry season is shorter. Very heavy rains occur in the monsoon months May to Sept. Rangoon. Jan. 77°F (25°C), July 80°F (26·7°C). Annual rainfall 104" (2,616 mm). Akyab. Jan. 70°F (21·1°C), July 81°F (27·2°C). Annual rainfall 206" (5,154 mm). Mandalay. Jan. 68°F (20°C), July 85°F (29·4°C). Annual rainfall 33" (828 mm).

CONSTITUTION AND GOVERNMENT. On 18 Sept. 1988, the Armed Forces, under Chief of Defence Staff Gen. Saw Maung, seized power and set up a State Law and Order Restoration Council, with Gen. Saw Maung as Chairman.

In March 1992 the government comprised 19 generals and the civilian Minister of Foreign Affairs (U Ohn Gyaw), and included:

Prime Minister: Gen. Saw Maung.

Planning and Finance, Trade: Brig.-Gen. D. O. Abel. *Energy and Mines:* Vice-Adm. Maung Maung Khin. *Transport and Communications, Social Welfare and Labour:* Lieut.-Gen. Tin Tun. *Construction, Co-operatives:* Lieut.-Gen. Aung Ye Kyaw. *Home and Religious Affairs, Information and Culture:* Maj.-Gen. Phone Myint. *Health, Education:* Col. Pe Thein. *Industry:* Maj.-Gen. Sein Aung. *Defence:* Gen. Than Shwe.

In elections in May 1990 the opposition National League for Democracy (NLD), led by Aung San Suu Kyi (b. 1945), won 392 of the 485 People's Assembly seats contested with some 60% of the valid vote. Turn-out was 72%, but 12·4% of ballots cast were declared invalid. The ruling State Law and Order Restoration Council at first said it would hand over power after the People's Assembly had agreed on a new constitution, but in July 1990 it stipulated that any such constitution must conform to guidelines which it would itself prescribe.

In May 1991 48 members of the NLD were given prison sentences on charges of treason. In July, opposition members of the People's Assembly were unseated for alleged offences ranging from treason to illicit foreign exchange dealing. Such members, and unsuccessful candidates in the May 1990 elections, are forbidden to stand in future elections. Aung San Suu Kyi was awarded the Nobel Peace Prize in 1991. She was expelled from the NLD in Dec. 1991 on the grounds that it had links with rebel and foreign organizations.

National flag: Red with a blue canton bearing 2 ears of rice within a cog-wheel and a ring of 14 stars, all in white.

Language: The official language is Burmese; the use of English is permitted.

Local government: Burma is divided into 7 states and 7 administrative divisions; these are sub-divided into 314 townships and thence into villages and wards.

DEFENCE

Army. The strength of the Army (1992) was 259,000. The Army is organized into 10 regional commands comprising 9 light infantry divisions. Combat units comprise 2 armoured, 223 independent infantry and 5 artillery battalions, and 1 anti-aircraft battery. Equipment includes 26 Comet main battle tanks, 40 Humber armoured cars, 30 locally-manufactured Mazda and 45 Ferret scout cars. In addition, there are 2 paramilitary units: People's Police Force (50,000) and People's Militia (35,000).

Navy. The fleet includes 2 old escort patrol vessels (ex-USA PCE and MSF types), 2 small indigenously built coastal patrol craft, 44 patrol craft, and 5 river gunboats. Auxiliaries include 1 patrol craft support ship, 1 survey ship and 13 small landing craft. Personnel in 1991 totalled 12,000 including 800 naval infantry.

The Fishery Protection Service (under the Pearl and Fishery Department) operates 3 coastal and 9 inshore patrol craft.

Air Force. The Air Force is intended primarily for internal security duties. Its combat force comprises about 20 G-4 Super Galeb supplied in 1990 by Yugoslavia, supplemented by 15 SIAI-Marchetti SF.260W light piston-engined attack/trainers. Other training aircraft include 20 turboprop Pilatus PC-7s and PC-9s. Transport and second-line units are equipped with 4 FH-227, 7 Turbo-Porter, 1 Citation and 6 Cessna 180 aircraft, 12 Polish-built W-3 Sokol, 12 Bell UH-1, and 10 Alouette III helicopters. China has agreed to supply 36 F-7 (MiG-21) and J-6 (MiG-19) combat aircraft. Personnel (1991) 9,000.

INTERNATIONAL RELATIONS

Membership. Burma is a member of the UN and Colombo Plan.

ECONOMY

Policy. The Development Plan, 1986–90, envisaged a total investment of K.14,000m. There are now annual plans with targets. Liberalization measures to promote a market economy were introduced in 1990.

Budget. Estimates for 1990–91: Revenue, K.35,570m.; expenditure, K.51,990m.

State budget estimates are classified into 3 parts, *viz.* State Administrative Organizations, State Economic Enterprises and Town and City Development Committees.

Currency. The unit of currency is the *kyat* (BUK) of 100 *pyas*. There are notes of *kyat* 200, 90, 45, 15, 10, 5 and 1, and coins of *kyat* 1 and *pyas* 50, 25, 10, 5 and 1. In 1990 K.27,510m. were in circulation.

In March 1992, £1 = K.10·76 and US$1 = K.6·13.

Banking and Finance. A Central Bank was established in July 1990. Other banks include the Myanmar Economic Bank, the Myanmar Foreign Trade Bank, the

Myanmar Investment and Commercial Bank and the Myanmar Agricultural and Rural Development Bank. The state insurance company is the Myanmar Insurance Corporation. Deposits in savings banks were K.10,685m. in 1990.

Weights and Measures. The metric system is in use alongside traditional measures. A *viss* = 3·6lb.

ENERGY AND NATURAL RESOURCES

Electricity. In 1990–91 the total installed capacity of the Electric Power Enterprise was 1,091,000 kw, of which 259,000 was hydro-electricity, 92,000 thermal, 357,000 natural gas and 100,000 diesel. Production was 2,478m. kwh. Supply 220 volts; 50 Hz.

Oil. Production (1991) of crude oil was 658,000 tonnes; natural gas (1990–91), 35,650m. cu. feet.

Minerals. Production in 1990–91 (in tonnes): Zinc concentrates, 4,500; nickel speiss, 80; antimonial lead, 150; refined lead, 2,750; tin concentrates, 326; tungsten concentrates, 30; tin, tungsten and scheelite mixed, 1,300. Refined silver, 220,000 fine oz.; gold, 25,200 troy oz; refined tin metal, 250; copper concentrates, 31,500; steel billets, 15,000.

Agriculture. In 1990-91 4·39m. peasant families cultivated 24·26m. acres. Liberalization measures of 1990 permit farmers to grow crops of their choice. The cultivated area in 1990-91 was 25·1m. acres. 2·5m. acres were irrigated. Production (1990–91) in 1,000 tonnes: Paddy, 13,961; sugar-cane, 1,998; maize, 186; jute, 29; cotton, 64; wheat, 138; butter beans, 51; soya beans, 29; rubber, 15.

Livestock (1990–91): Cattle, 9·3m.; buffaloes, 2·1m.; pigs, 2·2m.; sheep and goats, 1·3m.; poultry, 26·4m.

Net output of agriculture for 1990–91 was valued at K.21,942m.

Forestry. Forest area in 1990-91 was 80·14m. acres (25·37m. acres reserved). Teak extracted in 1990–91, 415,000 cu. tons; hardwood, 1,884,000 cu. tons.

Fisheries. In 1990–91 sea fishing produced 367m. *viss* and freshwater fisheries 88·5m. *viss*.

INDUSTRY. Of the 35,729 industrial enterprises in 1990-91, 1,765 were state-owned, 629 were co-operatives and 33,335 were private. Production (1990–91) in 1,000 tonnes: Cement, 420; fertilizers, 286·8; sugar, 24·99; paper, 15·41; cotton yarn, 10·76. 1,200 motor cars, 300 tractors and 8,240 bicycles were produced. In 1990–91 manufacturing output was valued at K.4,644m.

Labour. The population of working age (15 to 59) in 1991 was 23·47m. Economically active persons in 1990–91: 15·74m., of whom 66% were employed in agriculture, 9% in trade, 7% in manufacturing and 4% in administration.

FOREIGN ECONOMIC RELATIONS. In Aug. 1991 the USA imposed trade sanctions in response to alleged civil rights violations. Foreign debt was some US$4,200m. in 1990, of which US$2,000m. was owed to Japan. A law of 1989 permitted joint ventures, with foreign companies or individuals able to hold 100% of the shares.

Commerce. Imports and exports were controlled by the government trading organizations but since 1990 in line with market-oriented measures firms have been able to participate directly in trade.

Imports and exports (K.1m.) for 1990–91: Imports 7,181·2 and exports 3,523·2.

Total trade between Burma and UK (British Department of Trade returns, in £1,000 sterling):

	1987	1988	1989	1990	1991
Imports to UK	3,826	4,427	3,484	4,582	2,771
Exports and re-exports from UK	24,715	11,68	12,217	15,951	8,294

Tourism. There were 8,968 tourists in 1989 (41,904 in 1987), bringing a revenue of K.40·46m.

COMMUNICATIONS

Roads. There were 14,533 miles of road in 1987–88, of which 2,452 miles were union highway. In 1990–91 91·71m. passengers and 0·87m. tonnes of freight were carried by road.

Railways. In 1990 there were 4,621 km of route on metre gauge. In 1990–91 Myanma Railways carried 2·13m. tonnes of freight and 55·14m. passengers.

Civil Aviation. Myanma Airways maintains international services only to Bangkok and Singapore. There were, in 1991, 37 civil airfields. In 1990–91 368,000 passengers were carried on domestic, and 38,000 on international, flights.

Shipping. There are 60 miles of navigable canals. The Irrawaddy is navigable up to Myitkyina, 900 miles from the sea, and its tributary, the Chindwin, is navigable for 390 miles. The Irrawaddy delta has nearly 2,000 miles of navigable water. The Salween, the Attaran and the G'yne provide about 250 miles of navigable waters around Moulmein. In 1990–91 21·93m. passengers and 2·47m. tonnes of freight were carried on inland waterways and 45,000 passengers and 656,000 tonnes of freight coastally and overseas.

Telecommunications. In 1990–91 there were 1,124 post offices, 73,545 telephones, 328 telegraph offices, 144 telexes and 11 fax machines. The government runs a TV and a radio station. In 1991 there were 3·2m. radio and 1m. television receivers.

Newspapers. 1 newspaper is published, by the government, in Burmese and English versions.

JUSTICE, RELIGION, EDUCATION AND WELFARE

Justice. The highest judicial authority is the Chief Judge, appointed by the State Law and Order Restoration Council.

Religion. Religious freedom is allowed. At the 1983 census, 68% of the population was Buddhist.

Education. The medium of instruction in all schools is Burmese; English is taught as a compulsory second language from kindergarten level.

Education is free in primary, middle and vocational schools; fees are charged in senior secondary schools and universities. In 1990–91 there were 36,499 primary schools with 198,909 teachers and 5,423,537 pupils; 2,062 middle schools with 49,122 teachers and 930,207 pupils and 858 high schools with 18,381 teachers and 331,849 pupils.

In higher education in 1990–91 there was 1 Academy for Development of National Group with 80 teachers and 827 students, 14 teacher training schools with 271 teachers and 2,810 students, 4 teacher training institutes with 185 teachers and 1,923 students, 14 technical high schools with 411 teachers and 5,538 students, 10 technical institutes, with 520 teachers and 6,493 students, 9 agricultural high schools with 92 teachers and 380 students, 7 agricultural institutes with 161 teachers and 695 students, 35 vocational schools with 266 teachers and 4,235 students, 3 universities with 3,369 teachers and 78,062 students, 11 degree colleges with 651 teachers and 12,964 students and 3 colleges with 568 teachers and 3,510 students.

There were also institutes of medicine, dentistry, veterinary science, economics, technology, agriculture, education, foreign languages and computer science, with a combined teaching staff of 721 and student body of 15,130. Universities were closed from 1988 to 1991.

Health. In 1990–91 there were 12,427 doctors and 633 hospitals with 26,294 beds.

DIPLOMATIC REPRESENTATIVES

Of Burma in Great Britain (19A Charles St., London, W1X 8ER)
Ambassador: (Vacant).

Of Great Britain in Burma (80 Strand Rd., Rangoon)
Ambassador: Julian D. N. Hartland-Swann.

Of Burma in the USA (2300 S. St., NW, Washington, D.C., 20008)
Ambassador: (Vacant).

Of the USA in Burma (581 Merchant St., Rangoon)
Chargé d'affaires: (Vacant).

Of Burma to the United Nations
Ambassador: Kyaw Min.

Further Reading

Union of Myanmar, Ministry of Planning and Finance. *Review of the Financial, Economic and Social Conditions for 1991–92.* 1991
Herbert, P., *Burma* [bibliography]. Santa Barbara and Oxford, 1991
Lintner, B., *Outrage: Burma's Struggle for Democracy.* 2nd ed. London, 1990
O'Brien, H., *Forgotten Land: a Rediscovery of Burma.* London, 1991
Silverstein, J., *Burma: Military Rule and the Politics of Stagnation.* Cornell Univ. Press, 1978.
   —*Burmese Politics: The Dilemma of National Unity.* Rutgers Univ. Press, 1980
Smith, M., *Burma: Insurgency and the Politics of Insurgency.* London, 1991
Steinberg, D. I., *Burma.* Boulder, 1982
Suu Kyi, Aung San, *Freedom from Fear and Other Writings.* London, 1991
Taylor, R. H., *The State in Burma.* London, 1988

BURUNDI

Republika y'Uburundi

Capital: Bujumbura
Population: 5·46m. (1990)
GNP per capita: US$220 (1989)

HISTORY. Tradition recounts the establishment of a Tutsi kingdom under successive Mwamis as early as the 16th century. German military occupation in 1890 incorporated the territory into German East Africa. From 1919 Burundi formed part of Ruanda-Urundi administered by the Belgians, first as a League of Nations mandate and then as a UN trust territory. Internal self-government was granted on 1 Jan. 1962, followed by independence on 1 July 1962.

On 8 July 1966 Prince Charles Ndizeye deposed his father Mwami Mwambutsa IV, suspended the constitution and made Capt. Michel Micombero Prime Minister. On 1 Sept. Prince Charles was enthroned as Mwami Ntare V. On 28 Nov., while the Mwami was attending a Head of States Conference in Kinshasa (Congo), Micombero declared Burundi a republic with himself as president.

On 31 March 1972 Prince Charles returned to Burundi from Uganda and was placed under house arrest. On 29 April 1972 President Micombero dissolved the Council of Ministers and took full power; that night heavy fighting broke out between rebels from both Burundi and neighbouring countries, and the ruling Tutsi, apparently with the intention of destroying the Tutsi hegemony. Prince Charles was killed during the fighting and it was estimated that up to 120,000 were killed. On 14 July 1972 President Micombero reinstated a Government with a Prime Minister. On 1 Nov. 1976 President Micombero was deposed by the Army. as was President Bagaza on 3 Sept. 1987. Pierre Buyoya assumed the presidency on 1 Oct. 1987.

AREA AND POPULATION. Burundi is bounded north by Rwanda, east and south by Tanzania and west by Zaïre, and has an area of 27,834 sq. km (10,759 sq. miles).

The population at the census in 1986 was 4,782,406; estimate (1990) 5·46m. 5·5% of the population is urban; life expectancy was 49 years in 1989. There are three ethnic groups—Hutu (Bantu, forming over 83% of the total): Tutsi (Nilotic, less than 15%); Twa (pygmoids, less than 1%). There are some 3,500 Europeans and 1,500 Asians. In 1988 some 270,000 Tutsi refugees were living in Burundi, the majority from Rwanda.

Bujumbura, the capital, had (1986 census) 272,600 inhabitants. Gitega (95,300) was formerly the royal residence.

The local language is Kirundi, a Bantu language. French is also an official language. Kiswahili is spoken in the commercial centres.

CLIMATE. An equatorial climate, modified by altitude. The eastern plateau is generally cool, the easternmost savanna several degrees hotter. The wet seasons are from March to May and Sept. to Dec. Bujumbura. Jan. 73°F (22·8°C), July 73°F (22·8°C). Annual rainfall 33" (825 mm).

CONSTITUTION AND GOVERNMENT. The Constitution of 21 Nov. 1981 provided for a one-party state. It was suspended following the coup of Sept. 1987. A new government was set up under Pierre Buyoya as President, only candidate as leader of the sole party, the Party of Unity and National Progress (UPRONA).

In Jan. 1991 UPRONA unanimously adopted a charter of national unity which was submitted to a referendum in March 1992 proposing a new constitution which would legalize parties not based on ethnic group, region or religion, and provide for presidential elections by direct universal suffrage. 89% of votes cast were in favour.

President of the Republic, Minister of Defence: Major Pierre Buyoya (assumed office 1 Oct. 1987).

In Jan. 1992 the government included:

Prime Minister: Adrien Sibomana.
Foreign Affairs and Co-operation: Cyprien Mbonimpa. *Finance:* Gerard Niyibigira.

National flag: White diagonal cross dividing triangles of red and green, in the centre a white disc bearing 3 red green-bordered 6-pointed stars.
National anthem; Uburundi Bwacu (Dear Burundi; words by a committee; tune by M. Barengayabo).

Local Government: There are 15 provinces, each under a military governor, and sub-divided into 114 districts and then into communes.

DEFENCE. The national armed forces total (1992), 7,200 (there are also about 1,500 in paramilitary units) and include a small naval flotilla and air force flight of 3 SF 260, 3 Cessna 150 and 1 DO27 liaison aircraft, 4 Alouette III and 2 armed Gazelle helicopters. The Army comprises 2 infantry battalions, 1 parachute battalion, 1 commando battalion and 1 armoured-car company.

INTERNATIONAL RELATIONS

Membership. Burundi is a member of the UN and OAU and is an ACP state of EEC.

ECONOMY

Policy. The 5th, 5-year economic and social development plan, 1988-92 envisages investment of 159,000 Burundi francs.

Budget. The 1989 budget envisaged receipts of 28,679m. Burundi francs and expenditure at 34,790m. Burundi francs.

Currency. The unit of currency is the *Burundi franc* (BIF) of 100 *centimes.* There are coins of 1, 5 and 10 francs and bank notes of 10, 20, 50, 100, 500, 1,000 and 5,000 francs. 9,868m. francs were in circulation in 1989. The exchange rate was 347·25 francs = £1 and 197·81 francs = US$1 in March 1992.

Banking and Finance. The Bank of the Republic of Burundi is the central bank and 4 commercial banks have headquarters in Bujumbura. Bank deposits totalled 10,680m. Burundi francs in 1989.

Weights and Measures. The metric system operates.

ENERGY AND NATURAL RESOURCES

Electricity. Electricity production was (1986) 44m. kwh. The majority of the electricity is supplied by Zaïre. Supply 220 volts; 50 Hz.

Minerals. Mineral ores such as bastnasite and cassenite were formerly mined but output is now insignificant. Gold is mined on a small scale. Deposits of nickel (280m. tonnes) and vanadium remain to be exploited.

Agriculture. The main economic activity and 85% of employment is subsistence agriculture. Beans, cassava, maize, sweet potatoes, groundnuts, peas, sorghum and bananas are grown according to the climate and the region.
The main cash crop is coffee, of which about 95% is arabica. It accounts for 90% of exports and taxes and levies on coffee constitute a major source of revenue. A coffee board (OCIBU) manages the grading and export of the crop. Production (1990) 35,000 tonnes. The main food crops (production 1990, in 1,000 tonnes) are cassava (670), yams (4), bananas (1,608), dry beans (149), maize (190), sorghum (88), groundnuts (87) and peas (27). Other cash crops are cotton (5) and tea (5).
Cattle play an important traditional role, and there were about 450,000 head in 1990. There were (1990) some 848,000 goats, 420,000 sheep and 88,000 pigs.

Forestry. Forests covered an estimated 66,000 ha in 1989. Production (1985) 3·6m. cu. metres. For most of the population wood is the main form of energy.

Fisheries. There is a small commercial fishing industry on Lake Tanganyika. The catch in 1985 totalled 14,900 tonnes.

INDUSTRY. Industrial development is rudimentary. In Bujumbura there are plants for the processing of coffee and by-products of cotton, a brewery, cement works, a textile factory, a soap factory, a shoe factory and small metal workshops.

FOREIGN ECONOMIC RELATIONS. With Rwanda and Zaïre, Burundi forms part of the Economic Community of the Great Lakes.

Commerce. The total value of exports in 1989 was US$78m., and of imports, US$187m. Main exports are coffee and tea. Main imports, petrol products, food, vehicles and textiles. In 1984, 34% of exports were to the Federal Republic of Germany, while Belgium supplied 15% and France 14% of imports.

Total trade between Burundi and the UK (British Department of Trade returns, in £1,000 sterling):

	1987	1988	1989	1990	1991
Imports to UK	1,330	1,807	1,974	541	2,341
Exports and re-exports from UK	2,867	2,922	2,738	2,804	3,817

Tourism. Tourism is developing and there were 66,000 visitors in 1986.

COMMUNICATIONS

Roads. There is a road network of 5,144 km connecting with Rwanda, Zaïre and Tanzania. In 1984 there were 7,533 cars and 4,364 commercial vehicles.

Civil Aviation. In 1984, 38,141 passengers arrived or departed through Bujumbura International airport, and there are local airports at Gitega, Nyanza-Lac, Kiofi and Nyakagunda.

Shipping. There are lake services from Bujumbura to Kigoma (Tanzania) and Kalémie (Zaïre). The main route for exports and imports is *via* Kigoma, and thence by rail to Dar es Salaam.

Telecommunications. In 1983 there were 38 post offices and 6,033 telephones. Broadcasting is provided by the state-controlled Radiodiffusion et Télévision du Burundi. In 1991 there were estimated to be 0·03m. radio and 4,500 TV (colour by SECAM) receivers.

Cinemas. In 1980 there were 7 cinemas with 2,000 seats.

Newspapers. There was (1984) one daily newspaper *(Le Renouveau)* with a circulation of 20,000.

JUSTICE, RELIGION, EDUCATION AND WELFARE

Justice. There is a Supreme Court, an appeal court and a *tribunal de première instance* at Bujumbura and provincial tribunals in each provincial capital.

Religion. In 1989 there were 4·14m. Roman Catholics with an archbishop and 3 bishops. About 3% of the population are Pentecostal, 1% Anglican and 1% Moslem, while the balance follow traditional tribal beliefs.

Education. In 1984 there were 387,710 pupils in 1,023 primary schools, 13,037 in 62 secondary schools, 12,902 in 47 technical schools and 2,783 students in higher education.

Health. In 1983 there were 216 doctors, 6 dentists, 24 pharmacists, 1,126 nursing personnel and 33 hospitals with 5,709 beds.

DIPLOMATIC REPRESENTATIVES

Of Burundi in Great Britain
Ambassador: Vacant (resides in Brussels).

Of Great Britain in Burundi
Ambassador: Roger Westbrook, CMG (resides in Kinshasa).

Of Burundi in the USA (2233 Wisconsin Ave., NW, Washington, D.C., 20007)
Ambassador: Julien Kavakure.

Of the USA in Burundi (PO Box 1720, Ave. du Zaïre, Bujumbura)
Ambassador: Cynthia S. Perry.

Of Burundi to the United Nations
Ambassador: Benoît Seburyamo.

Further Reading

Lemarchand, R., *Rwanda and Burundi*. London, 1970
Weinstein, W., *Historical Dictionary of Burundi*. Metuchen, 1976

CAMBODIA

Capital: Phnom Penh
Population: 8·3m. (1990)

Roat Kampuchea

(State of Cambodia)

HISTORY. The recorded history of Cambodia starts at the beginning of the Christian era with the Kingdom of Fou-Nan, whose territories at one time included parts of Thailand, Malaya, Cochin-China and Laos. The religious, cultural and administrative inspirations of this state came from India. The Kingdom was absorbed at the end of the 6th century by the Khmers, under whose monarchs was built, between the 9th and 13th centuries, the splendid complex of shrines and temples at Angkor. Attacked on either side by the Vietnamese and the Thai from the 15th century on, Cambodia was saved from annihilation by the establishment of a French protectorate in 1863. Thailand eventually recognized the protectorate and renounced all claims to suzerainty in exchange for Cambodia's north-western provinces of Battambang and Siem Reap, which were, however, returned under a Franco-Thai convention of 1907, confirmed in the Franco-Thai treaty of 1937. In 1904 the province of Stung Treng, formerly administered as part of Laos, was attached to Cambodia. For history to 1969 *see* THE STATESMAN'S YEAR-BOOK, 1973–74, p. 1112.

Prince Sihanouk was deposed in March 1970 and on 9 Oct. 1970 the Kingdom of Cambodia became the Khmer Republic. From 1970 hostilities extended throughout most of the country involving North and South Vietnamese and US forces as well as Republican and anti-Republican Khmer troops. During 1973 direct American and North Vietnamese participation in the fighting came to an end, leaving a civil war situation between the forces of the Khmer Republic supported by American arms and economic aid and the forces of the United National Cambodian Front including 'Khmer Rouge' communists supported by North Vietnam and China. The Khmer Rouge captured Phnom Penh in April 1975, and instituted a harsh and highly regimented régime, cutting the country off from normal contact with the world and expelling all foreigners. All towns were forcibly evacuated and the population set to work in the fields.

The régime had difficulties with the Vietnamese from 1975 and this escalated into full-scale fighting in 1977–78. On 7 Jan. 1979, Phnom Penh was captured by the Vietnamese, and the Khmer Rouge government under Pol Pot was ousted. The Vietnam-backed Kampuchean National United Front for National Salvation (KNUFNS) proclaimed a People's Republic on 8 Jan. 1979.

In June 1982 the Khmer Rouge (who claim to have abandoned their Communist ideology and to have disbanded their Communist Party) entered into a coalition with Son Sann's Khmer People's National Liberation Front and Prince Sihanouk's group. This 'Coalition Government of Democratic Kampuchea' occupied Cambodia's seat at the UN.

In 1988 there were unofficial talks in Jakarta between the 4 Cambodian factions with the aim of obtaining a settlement of the political situation. From 30 July-30 Aug. 1989 an international conference, held in Paris, aiming to solve the political problems of Cambodia, was unsuccessful. The last Vietnamese forces withdrew in Sept. 1989. In Mid-1990 the Khmer Rouge still had about 25,000 resistance fighters.

In Aug. 1990 the UN Security Council agreed to set up a Supreme National Council (SNC) in Cambodia, and to place the foreign, defence, interior, finance and information ministries under UN control until elections could be held. The SNC was at first to consist of six members from the Government, and two from each group in the guerilla coalition: the Khmer Rouge, the Khmer People's National Liberation Front and Prince Norodom Sihanouk's group. The first meeting of the SNC in Sept. was unable to agree on a chairman.

On 15 Oct. 1990 the UN General Assembly adopted the Security Council resolution by consensus. On 26 Nov. Indonesia and the 5 permanent members of the Security Council agreed a plan for a ceasefire and elections under UN supervision.

In May 1991 a month's ceasefire was maintained by the 4 factions, and talks resumed in June in Jakarta, with France and Indonesia as the co-chairs of the Paris International Conference on Cambodia, and a UN representative. No agreement was reached. Talks resumed in Bangkok later in June and an unconditional and unlimited ceasefire was agreed by all 4 factions. Following further talks in Beijing Sihanouk was made chairman of the SNC. On 23 Oct. the 4 factions and 19 countries signed an agreement in Paris instituting a ceasefire in Cambodia to be monitored by UN troops. On 31 Oct. the UN Security Council unanimously agreed to establish a UN Transitional Authority in Cambodia (UNTAC), and on 28 Feb. 1992 the Security Council voted to send a force of 22,000 soldiers, police and officials to disarm the factions and organize elections.

On 20 Nov. 1991 Prince Sihanouk was recognized as head of state as before the coup of 18 March 1970.

AREA AND POPULATION. Cambodia is bounded in the north by Laos and Thailand, west by Thailand, east by Vietnam and south by the Gulf of Thailand. It has an area of about 181,035 sq. km (69,898 sq. miles).

The total population was 5,756,141 (census, 1981) of whom 93% were Khmer, 4% Vietnamese and 3% Chinese. Estimate (1990), 8·3m.

The capital, Phnom Penh is located at the junction of the Mekong and Tonle Sap rivers. Populations of major towns have fluctuated greatly since 1970 by flows of refugees from rural areas and from one town to another. Phnom Penh formerly had a population of at least 2·5m. but a 1990 estimate puts it at 800,000. Other cities are Kompong Cham and Battambang. Khmer is the official language.

CLIMATE. A tropical climate, with high temperatures all the year. Phnom Penh. Jan. 78°F (25·6°C), July 84°F (28·9°C). Annual rainfall 52" (1,308 mm).

CONSTITUTION AND GOVERNMENT. The Kampuchean National United Front for National Salvation (KNUFNS) on 8 Jan. 1979 proclaimed a People's Republic of Kampuchea, and established a People's Revolutionary Council to administer the country. A 117-member National Assembly was elected on 1 May 1981 for a 5-year term, which was extended by its own decision in Feb. 1986; in June 1981 it ratified a new Constitution under which it appointed a 7-member Council of State and a 16-member Council of Ministers, replacing the Revolutionary Council. A new Constitution of 1989 renamed the country the State of Cambodia. Real power lay with the Cambodian People's Party (formerly Kampuchean People's Revolutionary Party) (Communists), whose President is Chea Sim.

President of the Council of State: Heng Samrin.

Prime Minister: Hun Sen (b. 1950). *Deputy Prime Minister:* Say Chum; *Deputy Prime Minister and Foreign Minister:* Hor Nam Hong; *Minister of Agriculture:* Nguon Nhel. *Speaker of the National Assembly:* Chea Sim.

National flag: Divided red over blue with a depiction of the temple of Angkor Vat in yellow over all in the centre.

DEFENCE

Army. Strength (1991) 55,500 including 6 infantry divisions and some 50 supporting units. Equipment reported includes 60 T-54/-55 main battle tanks and 10 PT-76 light tanks. There are also provincial (22,500) and district (32,500) forces, and paramilitary local forces of some 50,000.

Navy. The navy is believed to include 2 ex-Soviet hydrofoil torpedo craft, 8 inshore patrol craft and a miscellany of riverine and support craft. Naval personnel in 1991 did not exceed 1,000.

Air Force. Aviation operations were resumed in 1988 under the aegis of the Army, equipment includes a newly-formed fighter squadron with MiG-21s and a small number of Mil Mi-8/17 transport helicopters and Mi-24 gunships. At least 2 An-24 and 2 Yak-40 transports are in use.

ECONOMY

Policy. Reforms of 1989 permit a much greater role for the private sector.

Currency. Under the Khmer Rouge money was abolished, but in 1980 the use of money was restored by the People's Republic of Kampuchea. The unit of currency is the *riel* (KHR) of 100 *sen*. There are banknotes of 5, 50 and 100 *riel*. The riel was devalued three times in 1990. In March 1992, £1 = 1,315·50 *riel*; US$1 = 749·36 *riel*.

Banking. In 1964 all bank functions were taken over by the Government bank.

ENERGY AND NATURAL RESOURCES

Electricity. Production (1986) 142m. kwh. Supply 120 and 220 volts; 50 Hz.

Minerals. A phosphate factory, jointly controlled by the State and private interests, was set up in 1966 near a deposit of an estimated 350,000 tons. Another deposit of about the same size is earmarked for exploitation. High-grade iron-ore deposits (possibly as much as 2·5m. tons) exist in Northern Cambodia, but are not exploited commercially because of transportation difficulties. Some small-scale gold panning (6,687 troy oz. in 1963) and gem (mainly zircon) mining is carried out at Pailin where there is potential for considerable expansion.

Agriculture. The overwhelming majority of the population is normally engaged in agriculture, fishing or forestry. Some 8m. ha of the total land area are cultivable. In 1980, 1·5m. ha were cultivated. Before the spread of war the high productivity provided for a low, but well-fed standard of living for the peasant farmers, the majority of whom owned the land they worked before agriculture was collectivised. A relatively small proportion of the food production entered the cash economy. The war and unwise pricing policies have led to a disastrous reduction in production to a stage in which the country had become a net importer of rice. Private ownership of land was restored by the 1989 Constitution.

A crop of about 2m. tonnes of paddy was produced in 1988. Rubber production in 1988 amounted to 25,000 tonnes. Production of other crops (1988 in tonnes): Maize, 100,000; dry beans, 36,000; soybeans, 2,000.

Livestock (1988): Cattle, 1·95m.; buffaloes, 700,000; sheep, 1,000; pigs, 1·5m.; horses, 15,000; poultry, 10m.

Forestry. Some 8m. ha of the land area are covered by potentially valuable forests, 3·8m. ha of which are reserved by the Government to be awarded to concessionaires, and are not at present worked to an appreciable extent. The remainder is available for exploitation by the local residents, and as a result some areas are over-exploited and conservation is not practised. There are substantial reserves of pitch pine. Roundwood production (1982), 5·1m. cu. metres.

Fisheries. There are very large freshwater fish resources. Production in 1982 was 84,700 tonnes.

INDUSTRY. Some development of industry had taken place before the spread of open warfare in 1970, but little was in operation in 1990 except rubber processing, sea-food processing, jute sack making and cigarette manufacture. In the private sector there are about 3,200 manufacturing enterprises, producing a wide range of goods; most of them are small family concerns.

FOREIGN ECONOMIC RELATIONS. Foreign investment has been encouraged since 1989.

Commerce. Principal imports by order of value (1972) were petroleum products, metals and machinery (including vehicles), general foodstuffs and chemicals.

The only recorded export in 1972 was 7,328 tonnes of rubber. Much of the country's trade is with Hong Kong and Singapore.

Total trade between Cambodia and UK (British Department of Trade returns, in £1,000 sterling):

	1987	1988	1989	1990	1991
Imports to UK	268	55	219	56	29
Exports and re-exports from UK	435	322	530	478	409

COMMUNICATIONS

Roads. There were, in 1981, 2,670 km of asphalt roads (including the 'Khmer-American Friendship Highway' from outside Phnom Penh to close to Kompong Som, built under the US aid programme and opened in July 1959), and 10,680 km of unsurfaced roads.

Railways. A line of 385 km (metre gauge) links Phnom Penh to Poipet (Thai frontier). In 1988 0·9m. passengers and 0·2m. tonnes of freight were carried. Work was completed during 1969 on a line Phnom Penh-Kompong Som *via* Takeo and Kampot. Total length, 649 km but by 1973 only a short stretch between Battambang and the Thai border remained in operation, the remainder having been closed by military action. Irregular passenger and freight trains were running over all the network in 1988.

Civil Aviation. Pochentong airport is 10 km from Phnom Penh. Air Kampuchea has three aircraft. There are regular services to Hanoi and Vientiane (weekly), Ho Chi Minh City (twice weekly) and Moscow (three a month) by Air Kampuchea, Air Vietnam, Air Lao and Aeroflot.

Shipping. The port of Phnom Penh can be reached by the Mekong (through Vietnam) by ships of between 3,000 and 4,000 tons. In 1970, 97 ocean-going vessels imported 51,300 tons of cargo at Phnom Penh and exported 86,400 tons.

A new ocean port has been built under the French aid programme at Kompong Som (formerly Sihanoukville) on the Gulf of Siam and is being increasingly used by long-distance shipping.

Telecommunications. There are telephone exchanges in all the main towns; number of telephones in 1981, 7,315. There is an International Telex network in Phnom Penh and direct telephone and telegraphic links with Singapore. Broadcasting is provided by the state-owned Voice of the People of Cambodia and Democratic Cambodia TV (colour by SECAM). In 1991 there were 48,605 TV sets and an estimated 0·8m. radio sets.

Newspapers. In 1984 there were 16 daily newspapers.

RELIGION, EDUCATION AND WELFARE

Religion. The majority of the population practises Theravada Buddhism. The Constitution of 1989 reinstated Buddhism as the state religion. There are small Roman Catholic and Moslem minorities.

Education. In 1984 there were 1,504,840 pupils in primary schools, 147,730 in secondary schools and 7,334 in vocational establishments. Phnom Penh University reopened in 1988.

Health. In 1984 there were 200 doctors, 130 pharmacists and 146 hospitals and clinics with 16,200 beds.

DIPLOMATIC REPRESENTATIVES

The UK and USA restored diplomatic relations in Nov. 1991.

Of Great Britain in Cambodia
Counsellor: David Burns.

Of the USA in Cambodia
Chargé d'affaires: Charles Twining.

Of Cambodia to the United Nations
Ambassador: Thiounn Prasith.

Further Reading

Ablin, D. A. and Hood, M., (eds.) *The Cambodian Agony.* London and New York, 1987
Chandler, D. P., *The Tragedy of Cambodian History: Power, War and Revolution since 1945.*
   Yale Univ. Press, 1992
Etcheson, C., *The Rise and Demise of Democratic Kampuchea.* London, 1984
Kiljunen, K., (ed.) *Kampuchea: Decade of the Genocide.* London, 1984
Vickery, M., *Cambodia: 1975–1982.* London, 1984

CAMEROON

Capital: Yaoundé
Population: 11·54m. (1990)
GNP per capita: US$1,010 (1989)

République du Cameroun—Republic of Cameroon

HISTORY. The former German colony of Kamerun was occupied by French and British troops in 1916. The greater portion of the territory (422,673 sq. km) was in 1919 placed under French administration, excluding the territory ceded to Germany in 1911, which reverted to French Equatorial Africa. The portion under French trusteeship was granted full internal autonomy on 1 Jan. 1959 and complete independence was proclaimed on 1 Jan. 1960.

The portion assigned to British trusteeship consisted of 2 parts where separate plebiscites were held in Feb. 1961. The northern part decided in favour of joining Nigeria, while the southern part decided to join the Cameroon Republic. This was implemented on 1 Oct. 1961 with the formation of a Federal Republic of Cameroon. As a result of a national referendum, Cameroon became a unitary republic on 2 June 1972. In Jan. 1984 the country was renamed the Republic of Cameroon.

AREA AND POPULATION. Cameroon is bounded west by the Gulf of Guinea, north-west by Nigeria and east by Chad, with Lake Chad at its northern tip, and the Central African Republic, and south by Congo, Gabon and Equatorial Guinea. The total area is 475,442 sq. km. Population (1976 census) 7,663,246 (28·5% urban). Estimate (1990) 11,540,000; density, 24·3 per sq. km. Population growth rate (1985–90): 2·6%; infant mortality, 94 per 1,000 live births; expectation of life, 51 years.

The areas, populations and chief towns of the 10 provinces were:

Province	Sq. km	Census 1976	Chief town	Estimate 1981
Adamaoua	63,691	359,227	Ngaoundéré	47,508
Centre	68,926	1,176,206	Yaoundé	775,729 [1]
Est	109,011	366,235	Bertoua	18,254
Extrême-Nord	34,246	1,394,958	Maroua	106,242 [2]
Littoral	20,239	935,166	Douala	1,211,387 [1]
Nord (Bénoué)	65,576	479,072	Garoua	102,057 [2]
Nord-Ouest	17,810	980,531	Bamenda	58,697
Ouest	13,872	1,035,597	Bafoussam	99,404 [2]
Sud	47,110	315,739	Ebolowa	22,222
Sud-Ouest	24,471	620,515	Buéa	29,953

[1] 1988.　　[2] 1987.

Other large towns (1981): Nkongsamba (86,870), Kumba (53,823), Foumban (41,358), Limbe (32,917), Edéa (31,016), Mbalmayo (26,934) and Dschang (21,705).

The population is composed of Sudanic-speaking people in the north (Fulani, Sao and others) and Bantu-speaking groups, mainly Bamileke, Beti, Bulu, Tikar, Bassa, Duala, in the rest of the country. The official languages are French and English.

CLIMATE. An equatorial climate, with high temperatures and plentiful rain, especially from March to June and Sept. to Nov. Further inland, rain occurs at all seasons. Yaoundé. Jan. 76°F (24·4°C), July 73°F (22·8°C). Annual rainfall 62" (1,555 mm). Douala. Jan. 79°F (26·1°C), July 75°F (23·9°C). Annual rainfall 160" (4,026 mm).

CONSTITUTION AND GOVERNMENT. The 1972 Constitution, subsequently amended, provides for a President as head of state and government and commander of the armed forces. He is directly elected for a 5-year term, and there is a Council of Ministers whose members must not be members of parliament.

The National Assembly, elected by universal adult suffrage for 5 years, consists of 180 representatives. After 1966 the sole legal party was the Cameroon People's Democratic Movement (RDPC), but in Dec. 1990 the National Assembly legalized opposition parties. At the elections of March 1992 751 candidates from 32 parties stood. Turn-out was 60·58%. The RDPC won 89 seats, the National Union for Democracy and Progress 65, the Cameroon People's Union 20, and the Democratic Movement for the Defence of the Republic 6.

The Council of Ministers in Oct. 1991 comprised:

President: Paul Biya (assumed office 6 Nov. 1982, re-elected April 1988).

Prime Minister and Minister of Finance: Sadou Hayatou (b. 1941).

Minister-Delegate at the Presidency, Defence: Michel Meva'a M'Eboutou. *Territorial Administration:* Ibrahim Mbomo Njoya. *Social and Women's Affairs:* Aissatou Yaou. *Agriculture:* John Niba Ngu. *Special Duties at the Presidency:* Ogork Ebot Ntui. *Industrial and Commercial Development:* Joseph Tsanga Abanda. *National Education:* Joseph Mbui. *Livestock, Fisheries and Animal Industries:* Dr Hamadjoda Adjoudji. *Higher Education, Computer Services and Scientific Research:* Abdoulaye Babale. *Public Service and State Control:* Joseph Owona. *Information and Culture:* Henri Bandolo. *Youth and Sports:* Dr Joseph Fofe. *Justice, Keeper of the Seals:* Adolphe Moudiki. *Water Resources and Energy:* Francis Nkwain. *Plan and Regional Development:* Elisabeth Tankeu. *Posts and Telecommunications:* Oumarou Sanda. *External Relations:* Jacques-Roger Booh Booh. *Public Health:* Joseph Mbede. *Public Works and Transport:* Claude Tchepanou. *Labour and Social Welfare:* Jean Baptiste Bokam. *Town Planning and Housing:* Ferdinand Leopold Oyono. *Tourism:* Benjamin Itoue.

There were 7 Secretaries of State.

The *Speaker* of the National Assembly is Lawrence Fonka Shang.

National flag: Three vertical strips of green, red, yellow, with a gold star in the centre.

National anthem: O Cameroon, Thou Cradle of our Fathers.

Local Government: The 10 provinces are each administered by a governor appointed by the President. They are sub-divided into 49 *départements* (each under a *préfet*) and then into *arrondissements* (each under a *sous-préfet*).

DEFENCE

Army. There are 3 military regions. The Army consists of a Presidential Guard, 3 infantry companies, 5 infantry battalions, 1 armoured car, 1 para-commando, 1 engineer, 1 artillery and 1 anti-aircraft batteries. Equipment includes 8 Ferret scout cars. Total strength (1991) 6,600; there are an additional 4,000 paramilitary troops.

Navy. The Navy, all French-built, operates 1 missile craft and 1 inshore patrol vessel. There are 7 landing craft and 32 boats and service craft. Personnel in 1991 numbered 800.

The marine wing of the Gendarmerie operates 1 coastal and 12 inshore patrol craft.

Air Force. The Air Force has 3 C-130H Hercules turboprop transports, 4 Buffalo and 1 Caribou STOL transports, 3 C-47s for transport and communications duties, 3 Broussard liaison aircraft, 10 Magister armed jet basic trainers, 5 Alpha Jet close support/trainers, and 5 Alouette and 3 Bell 206 helicopters. Some of 4 Gazelle light helicopters are armed with anti-tank missiles. A small VIP transport fleet, maintained in civil markings, comprises 1 Boeing 727 jet aircraft, 1 Gulfstream III and 3 Aerospatiale helicopters. Radar-equipped Dornier 128-6 twin-turboprop aircraft serve for offshore patrol. Personnel (1991), 300.

INTERNATIONAL RELATIONS

Membership. Cameroon is a member of the UN, OAU, the Non-Aligned Movement and is an ACP state of the EEC.

ECONOMY

Policy. The Sixth 5-year Development Plan (from 1 July 1986 to 30 June 1991) gives priority to rural development and food self-sufficiency.

Budget. The budget for 1990 balanced at 600,000m. francs CFA.

Currency. The unit of currency is the *franc CFA* (XAF), with a parity rate of 50 *francs CFA* to 1 French *franc*. In March 1992, £1 = 489·63 *francs CFA*; US$1 = 278·91 *francs CFA*.

Banking and Finance. The Banque des Etats de l'Afrique Centrale is the sole bank of issue. The commercial banks are Banque Internationale pour l'Afrique Occidentale, Société Camerounaise de Banque, Société Générale de Banque au Cameroun, Banque International pour le Commerce et l'Industrie du Cameroun, Cameroon Bank, Banque Camerounaise de Développement, Bank of Credit and Commerce Cameroon, Paribas Cameroun, Boston Bank Cameroon Ltd, Chase Bank Cameroon Ltd and Bank of America Cameroon. Most of the banks operate in all the large cities and towns throughout the Republic.

ENERGY AND NATURAL RESOURCES

Electricity. There are 3 hydro-electric power stations at Edéa on the Sanaga river with a capacity of 180,000 kw. Total production (1986) 4,200m. kwh. Supply 127 and 220 volts; 50 Hz.

Oil. Production (estimate, 1991) mainly from Kole oilfield was 7·93m. tonnes.

Minerals. There are considerable deposits of bauxite and kyanite around Ngaoundéré. Further deposits of bauxite and cassiterite remain to be exploited in the Adamaoua plateau.

Agriculture. The main food crops (with 1990 production in 1,000 tonnes): Cassava, 1,583; millet, 50; maize, 350; plantains, 1,600; yams, 234; groundnuts, 87; bananas, 70. Cash crops include palm oil, 108; palm kernels, 50; cocoa, 115; coffee, 100; rubber, 38; cotton lint, 47; raw sugar, 81.

Livestock (1990): 4·7m. cattle, 3·5m. sheep, 3·5m. goats, 3·6m. pigs.

Forestry. Forests cover 24·65m. ha, ranging from tropical rain forests in the south (producing hardwoods such as mahogany, ebony and sapele) to semi-deciduous forests in the centre and wooded savannah in the north. Production in 1986 amounted to 12·2m. cu. metres.

Fisheries. In 1986 the total catch was 84,000 tonnes.

INDUSTRY. There is a major aluminium smelting complex at Edéa; aluminium production in 1989 amounted to 87,000 tonnes. Production of cement totalled 227,000 tonnes in 1980. There are also factories producing shoes, beer, soap, oil and food products, cigarettes. Agro-industrial production (1984–85, in tonnes): Rubber, 17,679; palm-oil, 76,954; sugar, 73,717; oil palm, 14,849; tea, 2,279.

Labour. In 1990 the work-force numbered 4,351,000 of whom 61% were occupied in agriculture.

Trade Unions. The principal trade union federation is the *Organisation des syndicats des travailleurs camerounais* (OSTC) established on 7 Dec. 1985 to replace the former body, the UNTC.

FOREIGN ECONOMIC RELATIONS

Commerce. Imports and exports in 1m. francs CFA were as follows:

	1984–85	1985–86	1986–87
Imports	482,297	513,898	558,265
Exports	822,041	816,912	508,200

In 1984–85, exports (in 1m. francs CFA) went mainly to the Netherlands (136,057), France (127,966), Italy (58,333), Federal Republic of Germany (35,089),

USA (30,098) and Spain (25,517), while imports were mainly from France (193,176), USA (51,687), Japan (36,354), Federal Republic of Germany (31,220) and Italy (26,610); the main exports were crude oils (123,398), coffee and by-products (111,201) and cocoa and by-products (105,858).

Total trade between Cameroon and UK (British Department of Trade returns, in £1,000 sterling):

	1987	1988	1989	1990	1991
Imports to UK	14,201	16,180	11,362	8,241	6,135
Exports and re-exports from UK	28,057	20,472	24,838	20,652	23,813

Tourism. There were an estimated 115,203 foreign visitors in 1987.

COMMUNICATIONS

Roads. In 1986 there were 66,910 km of roads, of which 2,922 km were tarmac. In 1984–85 there were 73,963 passenger cars and 43,165 commercial vehicles.

Railways. Cameroon Railways, *Regifercam* (1,104 km in 1990) link Douala with Nkongsamba and Ngaoundéré, with branches M'Banga–Kumba and Makak–M'Balmayo. In 1989–90 railways carried 2·5m. passengers and 1·4m. tonnes of freight.

Civil Aviation. Douala is the main international airport; other airports are at Yaoundé and Garoua. Camair, the national airline, serves 7 domestic airports.

Shipping. The merchant-marine consisted (1986) of 48 vessels (over 100 GRT) of 76,433 GRT. The major port of Douala handled (1984) 3m. tonnes of imports and 1m. tonnes of exports and in 1984–85, 671 cargo ships and 2,582 other ships entered the port. Timber is exported mainly through the south-west ports of Kribi and Campo. Other ports are Bota, Tiko, Limbe and Garoua.

Telecommunications. There were (1975) 150 post offices supplemented by a mobile postal service; telephones (1984), 47,200. The state-controlled Cameroon Radio Television provides home, national, provincial and urban radio programmes and a TV service (colour by PAL). In 1991 there were about 2m. radio and 5,000 TV receivers.

Cinemas. There were (1987) 69 cinemas and 163 mobile cinemas with a capacity of 41,000 seats.

Newspapers. There was (1984) 1 daily newspaper with a circulation of 20,000. It was announced in Dec. 1990 that press censorship would be lifted.

JUSTICE, RELIGION, EDUCATION AND WELFARE

Justice. The Supreme Court sits at Yaoundé, as does the High Court of Justice (consisting of 9 titular judges and 6 surrogates all appointed by the National Assembly). There are magistrates' courts situated in the provinces.

Religion. In 1989 there were 3·99m. Roman Catholics, 2·51m. Moslems and 2·01m. Protestants. Some of the population follow traditional animist religions.

Education (1986–87). There were 1,795,254 pupils and 35,728 teachers in primary schools, 291,842 pupils and 9,017 teachers in general secondary schools and 90,666 pupils and 3,714 teachers in technical secondary schools. In 1984–85 there were 13,753 students and 572 teaching staff at higher education institutions of the University of Yaoundé. 59% literacy was claimed in 1987.

Health. In 1981 there were 1,003 hospitals and health centres with 24,541 beds; there were also (1982) 604 doctors and 17 dentists, 96 pharmacists, 399 midwives and 1,086 nursing personnel.

DIPLOMATIC REPRESENTATIVES

Of Cameroon in Great Britain (84 Holland Pk., London, W11 3SB)
Ambassador: Dr Gibering Bol-Alima.

Of Great Britain in Cameroon (Ave. Winston Churchill, BP 547, Yaoundé)
Ambassador: William Quantrill.

Of Cameroon in the USA (2349 Massachusetts Ave., NW, Washington, D.C., 20008)
Ambassador: Vincent Paul-Thomas Pondi.

Of the USA in Cameroon (Rue Nachtigal, BP 817, Yaoundé)
Ambassador: Frances D. Cook.

Of Cameroon to the United Nations
Ambassador: M. Pascal Biloa Tang.

Further Reading

Statistical Information: The Service de la Statistique Générale, at Douala, set up in 1945, publishes a monthly bulletin (from Nov. 1950)

DeLancey, M. W., *Cameroon: Dependence and Independence*. London, 1989
DeLancey, M. W. and Schraeder, P. J., *Cameroon*. [Bibliography] Oxford and Santa Barbara, 1986
Ndongko, W. A., *Planning for Economic Development in a Federal State: The Case of Cameroon, 1960–71*. New York, 1975
Rubin, N., *Cameroon*. New York, 1972

CANADA

Capital: Ottawa
Population: 27m. (1991)
GNP per capita: US$16,760 (1988)

HISTORY. The territories which now constitute Canada came under British power at various times by settlement, conquest or cession. Nova Scotia was occupied in 1628 by settlement at Port Royal, was ceded back to France in 1632 and was finally ceded by France in 1713 to England, by the Treaty of Utrecht; the Hudson's Bay Company's charter, conferring rights over all the territory draining into Hudson Bay, was granted in 1670; Canada, with all its dependencies, including New Brunswick and Prince Edward Island, was formally ceded to Great Britain by France in 1763; Vancouver Island was acknowledged to be British by the Oregon Boundary Treaty of 1846, and British Columbia was established as a separate colony in 1858. As originally constituted, Canada was composed of Upper and Lower Canada (now Ontario and Quebec), Nova Scotia and New Brunswick. They were united under an Act of the Imperial Parliament, 'The British North America Act, 1867', which came into operation on 1 July 1867 by royal proclamation. The Act provided that the constitution of Canada should be 'similar in principle to that of the United Kingdom'; that the executive authority shall be vested in the Sovereign, and carried on in his name by a Governor-General and Privy Council; and that the legislative power shall be exercised by a Parliament of two Houses, called the 'Senate' and the 'House of Commons'.

On 30 June 1931 the British House of Commons approved the enactment of the Statute of Westminster freeing the Provinces as well as the Dominion from the operation of the Colonial Laws Validity Act, and thus removing what legal limitations existed as regards Canada's legislative autonomy. A joint address of the Senate and the House of Commons was sent to the Governor-General for transmission to London on 10 July 1931. The statute received the royal assent on 12 Dec. 1931.

Provision was made in the British North America Act for the admission of British Columbia, Prince Edward Island, Newfoundland, Rupert's Land and Northwest Territory into the Union. In 1869 Rupert's Land, or the Northwest Territories, was purchased from the Hudson's Bay Company. On 15 July 1870, Rupert's Land and the Northwest Territory were annexed to Canada and named the Northwest Territories, Canada having agreed to pay the Hudson's Bay Company in cash and land for its relinquishing of claims to the territory. By the same action the Province of Manitoba was created from a small portion of this territory and they were admitted into the Confederation on 15 July 1870. On 20 July 1871 the province of British Columbia was admitted, and Prince Edward Island on 1 July 1873. The provinces of Alberta and Saskatchewan were formed from the provisional districts of Alberta, Athabaska, Assiniboia and Saskatchewan and originally parts of the Northwest Territories and admitted on 1 Sept. 1905. Newfoundland formally joined Canada as its tenth province on 31 March 1949.

In Feb. 1931 Norway formally recognized the Canadian title to the Sverdrup group of Arctic islands. Canada thus holds sovereignty in the whole Arctic sector north of the Canadian mainland.

In Nov. 1981 the Canadian government agreed on the provisions of an amended constitution, to the end that it should replace the British North America Act and that its future amendment should be the prerogative of Canada. These proposals were adopted by the Parliament of Canada and were enacted by the UK Parliament as the Canada Act of 1982.

The enactment of the Canada Act was the final act of the UK Parliament in Canadian constitutional development. The Act gave to Canada the power to amend the Constitution according to procedures determined by the Constitutional Act 1982, which was proclaimed in force by the Queen on 17 April 1982. The Constitution Act 1982 added to the Canadian Constitution a charter of Rights and Freedoms, and provisions which recognize the nation's multi-cultural heritage, affirm the existing rights of native peoples, confirm the principle of equalization of benefits among the provinces, and strengthen provincial ownership of natural resources.

AREA AND POPULATION. Canada is bounded north-west by the Beaufort Sea, north by the Arctic Ocean, north-east by Baffin Bay, east by the Davis Strait, Labrador Sea and Atlantic Ocean, south by the USA and west by the Pacific Ocean and USA (Alaska). Population of the area now included in Canada:

1851	2,436,297	1901	5,371,315	1951 [1]	14,009,429
1861	3,229,633	1911	7,206,643	1961	18,238,247
1871	3,689,257	1921	8,787,949	1971	21,568,311
1881	4,324,810	1931	10,376,786	1981	24,343,181
1891	4,833,239	1941	11,506,655		

[1] From 1951 figures include Newfoundland.

Population (census), 3 June 1986, was 25,354,064. Estimate (June 1991) 27m. There was a census on 4 June 1991.

Areas of the provinces, etc. (in sq. km) and population at recent censuses:

Province	Land area	Fresh water area	Total land and fresh water area	Popula- tion, 1976	Popula- tion, 1981	Popula- tion, 1986 [1]
Newfoundland	371,690	34,030	405,720	557,725	567,681	568,349
Prince Edward Island	5,660	—	5,660	118,229	122,506	126,646
Nova Scotia	52,840	2,650	55,490	828,571	847,442	873,199
New Brunswick	72,090	1,350	73,440	677,250	696,403	710,442
Quebec	1,356,790	183,890	1,540,680	6,234,445	6,438,403	6,540,276
Ontario	891,190	177,390	1,068,580	8,264,465	8,625,107	9,113,515
Manitoba	548,360	101,590	649,950	1,021,506	1,026,241	1,071,232
Saskatchewan	570,700	81,630	652,330	921,323	968,313	1,010,198
Alberta	644,390	16,800	661,190	1,838,037	2,237,724	2,375,278
British Columbia	929,730	18,070	947,800	2,466,608	2,744,467	2,889,207
Yukon	478,970	4,480	483,450	21,836	23,153	23,504
Northwest Territories	3,293,020	133,300	3,426,320	42,609	45,471	52,238
Total	9,215,430	755,180	9,970,610	22,992,604	24,343,181	25,354,064

[1] Including estimates of incompletely enumerated Indian reserves and Indian settlements.

Of the total population in 1986, 21,113,855 were Canadian born, 3,908,150 foreign born, 282,025 of the latter being USA born and 2,435,100 European born.

The population (1986) born outside Canada in the provinces was in the following ratio (%): Newfoundland, 1·6; Prince Edward Island, 3·5; Nova Scotia, 4·7; New Brunswick, 3·8; Quebec, 8·3; Ontario, 23·1; Manitoba, 13·6; Saskatchewan, 7·2; Alberta, 15·6; British Columbia, 22·1; Yukon, 11·5; Northwest Territories, 5·4.

In 1986, figures for the population, according to ethnic origin, were [1]:

Single origins	18,035,665	Portuguese	199,595
Austrian	24,900	Romanian	18,745
Belgian	28,395	Russian	32,080
British	6,332,725	Scandinavian	171,715
Czech and Slovak	55,535	Spanish	57,125
Chinese	360,320	Swiss	19,130
Dutch (Netherlands)	351,765	Ukrainian	420,210
Finnish	40,565	Other single origins	99,025
French [2]	6,093,160		
German	896,720	Multiple origins	6,986,345
Greek	143,780	British and French	1,139,345
Hungarian	97,850	British and Other	2,262,525
Italian	709,590	French and Other	325,655
Japanese	40,245	Other multiple origins	616,000
Polish	222,260		

[1] Data on ethnic origins for the 1986 Census excludes the population on incompletely enumerated Indian reserves and settlements. For Canada there were 136 such reserves and settlements and the total population was estimated to be about 45,000 in 1986.

[2] Includes the single origins of French, Acadian, French Canadian and Québécois.

In April 1990 62·1% of the population gave their mother tongue as English, 25·1% as French, 16·2% stated themselves bilingual.

The total aboriginal population single origins numbered 373,265 in 1986 and the Inuit population was 27,290 in 1986. In 1991 there were some 466,000.

Populations of Census Metropolitan Areas (CMA) and Cities (proper), 1986 census:

	CMA	City proper		CMA	City proper
Toronto	3,427,168	612,289	Halifax	295,990	113,577
Montreal	2,921,357	1,015,420	Victoria	255,547	66,303
Vancouver	1,380,729	431,147	Windsor	253,988	193,111
Ottawa-Hull	819,263	—	Oshawa	203,543	123,651
Ottawa	—	300,763	Saskatoon	200,665	177,641
Hull	—	58,722	Regina	186,521	175,064
Edmonton	785,465	573,982	St John's	161,901	96,216
Calgary	671,326	636,104	Chicoutimi-		
Winnipeg	623,304	594,551	Jonquière	158,468	—
Quebec	603,267	164,580	Chicoutimi	—	61,083
Hamilton	557,029	306,728	Jonquière	—	58,467
St Catharines-			Sudbury	148,877	88,717
Niagara	343,258	—	Sherbrooke	129,960	74,438
St Catharines	—	123,455	Trois Rivières	128,888	50,122
Niagara Falls	—	72,107	Thunder Bay	122,217	112,272
London	342,302	269,140	Saint John	121,265	76,381
Kitchener	311,195	150,604			

The total 'urban' population of Canada in 1986 was 19,352,085, against 20,496,000 in 1990.

While the registration of births, marriages and deaths is under provincial control, the statistics are compiled on a uniform system by Statistics Canada.

The following table gives the results for the year 1989:

Province	Live births Number	Marriages Number	Deaths Number
Newfoundland	7,310	3,420	3,660
Prince Edward Island	1,970	1,020	1,190
Nova Scotia	12,290	6,660	7,510
New Brunswick	9,730	4,820	5,570
Quebec	91,200	31,820	48,740
Ontario	135,960	76,520	70,360
Manitoba	17,140	7,820	9,120
Saskatchewan	17,120	6,360	8,000
Alberta	43,780	18,940	13,910
British Columbia	42,590	24,100	22,760
Yukon Territory	510	210	120
N.W. Territories	1,440	240	210
	381,040	181,930	191,150

Source: Statistics Canada

Immigrant arrivals by country of last permanent residence:

Country	1988	1989	1990 [1]
UK	9,172	8,419	7,959
France	2,589	2,883	2,538
Germany	1,696	2,025	1,617
Netherlands	821	824	617
Greece	579	771	528
Italy	860	1,036	906
Portugal	6,467	5,415	7,906
Other Europe	17,728	30,715	29,328
Asia	81,136	93,202	110,665
Australia	745	626	680
USA	6,537	6,927	5,960
Caribbean	9,439	10,902	11,628
All other	24,160	28,227	31,834
Total	161,929	191,971	212,166

[1] Preliminary.

Source: Employment and Immigration Canada

CLIMATE. The climate ranges from polar conditions in the north to cool temperate in the south, but with considerable differences between east coast, west coast and the interior, affecting temperatures, rainfall amounts and seasonal distribution. Winters are very severe over much of the country, but summers can be very hot inland. *See* individual provinces for climatic details.

CONSTITUTION AND GOVERNMENT. Parliament consists of the Senate and the House of Commons. The members of the *Senate* are appointed until age 75 by summons of the Governor-General under the Great Seal of Canada. Members appointed before 2 June 1965 may remain in office for life. The Senate consists of 104 senators, namely, 24 from Ontario, 24 from Quebec, 10 from Nova Scotia, 10 from New Brunswick, 4 from Prince Edward Island, 6 from Manitoba, 6 from British Columbia, 6 from Alberta, 6 from Saskatchewan, 6 from Newfoundland, 1 from the Yukon Territory and 1 from the Northwest Territories. Each senator must be at least 30 years of age, be a subject of the Queen, reside in the province for which he or she is appointed and have a total net worth of at least $4,000. The *House of Commons* is elected by universal secret suffrage, for 5 years, unless sooner dissolved. From 1867 to the election of 1945, representation was based on Quebec having 65 seats and the other provinces the same proportion of 65 which their population had to the population of Quebec. In the General Election of 1949 readjustments were based on the population of all the provinces taken as a whole. Generally speaking, this format for representation has prevailed in all subsequent elections with readjustments made after each decennial census. Under the Constitution Act, 1986 (Representation), effective March 1986, the formula contained in section 51 of the Constitution Act, 1867 dealing with the number of seats in the House of Commons and their distribution throughout the country, was changed.

On 27 June 1991 a 12-member commission, the Citizen's Forum on Canada's Future, started sounding public opinion on the Constitutional future of Canada.

Indians have representation in the *Assembly of First Nations* (Chief, Ovide Mercredi).

The thirty-fourth Parliament, elected in Nov. 1988, comprises 295 members and the provincial and territorial representation are: Ontario, 99; Quebec, 75; Nova Scotia, 11; New Brunswick, 10; Manitoba, 14; British Columbia, 32; Prince Edward Island, 4; Saskatchewan 14; Alberta, 26; Newfoundland, 7; Yukon, 1; Northwest Territories, 2.

State of the parties in the Senate (Aug. 1991): Progressive Conservatives, 53; Liberals, 48; Independent, 1; Independent Liberal, 1; Reform Party, 1; Vacant, 0; total 107.

State of the parties in the House of Commons (Aug. 1991): Progressive Conservatives, 159; Liberals, 81; New Democratic Party, 44; Reform Party, 1; Independent, 10; Vacant, 0; total, 295.

The following is a list of Governors-General of Canada:

Viscount Monck	1867–1868	Viscount Willington	1926–1931
Lord Lisgar	1868–1872	Earl of Bessborough	1931–1935
Earl of Dufferin	1872–1878	Lord Tweedsmuir	1935–1940
Marquess of Lorne	1878–1883	Earl of Athlone	1940–1946
Marquess of Lansdowne	1883–1888	Field-Marshal Viscount	
Lord Stanley of Preston	1888–1893	Alexander of Tunis	1946–1952
Earl of Aberdeen	1893–1898	Vincent Massey	1952–1959
Earl of Minto	1898–1904	Georges Philias Vanier	1959–1967
Earl Grey	1904–1911	Roland Michener	1967–1974
HRH the Duke of Connaught	1911–1916	Jules Léger	1974–1979
Duke of Devonshire	1916–1921	Edward Schreyer	1979–1984
Viscount Byng of Vimy	1921–1926	Jeanne Sauvé	1984–1989

Governor-General: Hon. Ramon Hnatyshyn.

National flag: Vertically red, white, red with the white of double width and bearing a stylized red maple leaf.

The office and appointment of the Governor-General are regulated by letters patent, signed by the King on 8 Sept. 1947, which came into force on 1 Oct. 1947. In 1977 the Queen approved the transfer to the Governor-General of functions discharged by the Sovereign. He is assisted in his functions, under the provisions of the Act of 1867, by a Privy Council composed of Cabinet Ministers.

The following is the list of the Conservative Cabinet in Aug. 1991, in order of precedence, which attaches generally rather to the person than to the office:

Prime Minister: The Rt. Hon. Martin Brian Mulroney.

President of the Queen's Privy Council for Canada and Minister Responsible for Constitutional Affairs: The Rt. Hon. Charles Joseph Clark.

Minister of Fisheries and Oceans and Minister for the Atlantic Canada Opportunities Agency: The Hon. John Carnell Crosbie.

Deputy Prime Minister and Minister of Finance: The Hon. Donald Frank Mazankowski.

Minister of Public Works: The Hon. Elmer MacIntosh Mackay.

Minister of Energy, Mines and Resources: The Hon. Arthur Jacob Epp.

Secretary of State of Canada: The Hon. Robert R. de Cotret.

Minister of Communications: The Hon. Henry Perrin Beatty.

Minister of Industry, Science and Technology and Minister for International Trade: The Hon. Michael Holcombe Wilson.

Minister of State and Leader of the Government in the House of Commons: The Hon. Harvie Andre.

Minister of National Revenue: The Hon. Otto John Jelinek.

Minister of Indian Affairs and Northern Development: The Hon. Thomas Edward Siddon.

Minister of Western Economic Diversification and Minister of State (Grains and Oilseeds): The Hon. Charles James Mayer.

Minister of Agriculture: The Hon. William Hunter McKnight.

Minister of National Health and Welfare: The Hon. Benoit Bouchard.

Minister of National Defence: The Hon. Marcel Masse.

Secretary of State for External Affairs: The Hon. Barbara Jean McDougall.

Minister of Veterans Affairs: The Hon. Gerald Stairs Merrithew.

Minister of State (Employment and Immigration) and Minister of State (Seniors): The Hon. Monique Vézina.

Minister of Forestry: The Hon. Frank Oberle.

Leader of the Government in the Senate: The Hon. Lowell Murray.

Minister of Supply and Services: The Hon. Paul Wyatt Dick.

Minister of State (Fitness and Amateur Sport) and Minister of State (Youth) and Deputy Leader of the Government in the House of Commons: The Hon. Pierre H. Cadieux.

Minister of the Environment: The Hon. Jean J. Charest.

Minister of State (Small Businesses and Tourism): The Hon. Thomas Hockin.

Minister for External Relations and Minister of State (Indian Affairs and Northern Development): The Hon. Monique Landry.

Minister of Employment and Immigration: The Hon. Bernard Valcourt.

Minister of Multiculturalism and Citizenship: The Hon. Gerry Weiner.

Solicitor General of Canada: The Hon. Douglas Grinslade Lewis.

Minister of Consumer and Corporate Affairs and Minister of State (Agriculture): The Hon. Pierre Blais.

Minister of State (Finance and Privatization): The Hon. John Horton McDermid.

Minister of State (Transport): The Hon. Shirley Martin.

Associate Minister of National Defence and Minister Responsible for the Status of Women: The Hon. Mary Collins.

Minister for Science: The Hon. William Charles Winegard.

Minister of Justice and Attorney-General of Canada: The Hon. Kim Campbell.

Minister of Transport: The Hon. Jean Corbeil.

President of the Treasury Board and Minister of State (Finance): The Hon. Gilles Loiselle.

Minister of Labour: The Hon. Marcel Danis.

Minister of State (Environment): The Hon. Pauline Browes.

The salary of a member of the House of Commons (Jan. 1991) is $64,400 with a tax-free allowance ranging from $21,300 to $28,200. The salary of a senator is

$64,400 with a tax-free allowance of $10,100. The salary and allowances of the Prime Minister total $161,300, that of the Speaker of the House of Commons is $138,800; of the Speaker of the Senate is $109,500; of the Opposition Leader is $136,800 and of the National Democratic Party Leader is $120,100.

An Act to provide retiring allowances, on a contributory basis, to members of the House of Commons was given the Royal Assent on 4 July 1952. Subsequent amendments provide allowances for surviving spouses and for former Prime Ministers or their surviving spouses.

Guide to Federal Programs and Services 1991. 11th ed. Supply and Services Canada, Ottawa
A consolidation of the *The Constitution Acts 1867 to 1982*. Department of Justice Canada. Ottawa, 1989
Bureaucracy in Canadian Government: Selected Readings. 2nd edition, edited by W. D. K. Kernaghan, Toronto, 1973
Laskin's Canadian Constitutional Law. 5th ed., Vol. 2, Neil Finkelstein. Toronto: Carswell, 1986
Federalism and the Charter: Leading Constitutional decisions. Edited and with an introduction by Peter H. Russell, 5th edition. Carleton Univ. Press, Ottawa, 1989

The Canadian Parliamentary Guide. Annual. Ottawa
Report of the Royal Commission on Dominion–Provincial Relations, Canada 1867–1939. 3 vols. Ottawa, 1940
Bayehsky, A. F., *Canada's Constitution Act 1982 and Amendments: a Documentary History*. 2 vols. Toronto, 1989
Bejermi, J., *Canadian Parliamentary Handbook*. Ottawa, 1991
Byers, R. B. (ed.) *Canada Challenged: The Viability of Confederation*. Toronto, 1979
Cheffins, R. I. and Johnson, P. A., *The Revised Canadian Constitution, Politics as law*. Toronto, 1986
Fox, P. W., and White, G., *Politics Canada*. 7th ed. Toronto, 1991
Franks, C. E. S., *The Parliament of Canada*. Univ. of Toronto Press, 1987
Hogg, P. W., *Constitutional Law of Canada*. 2nd ed. Toronto, 1985
Kennedy, W. F. M., *Statutes, Treaties and Documents of the Canadian Constitution, 1713–1929*. 2nd ed. Toronto, 1939
Morton, W. L., *The Kingdom of Canada; A General History From Earliest Times*. Toronto, 1969

DEFENCE. The Department of National Defence was created by the National Defence Act, 1922, which established one civil Department of Government in place of the previous Departments of Militia and Defence, Naval Service and the Air Board. The Department now operates under authority of RSC 1970, c.N1-4. The Minister of National Defence has the control and management of the Canadian Forces and all matters relating to national defence establishments and works for the defence of Canada. He is the Minister responsible for presenting before the Cabinet matters of major defence policy for which Cabinet direction is required. He is also responsible for the emergency measures organization known since 1 July 1986 as 'Emergency Preparedness Canada'.

In Dec. 1976, the Minister of National Defence was named as minister responsible for all aspects of air Search and Rescue (SAR) in the areas of Canadian SAR responsibility, and for the overall co-ordination of marine Search and Rescue including provision of air resources for marine SAR within Canadian territorial waters and in designated oceanic areas off the Pacific and Atlantic Coasts in accordance with agreements made with the United States Coast Guard. A group from Transport Canada, the Department of National Defence and the Department of Fisheries and Oceans was set up at the same time, as a co-ordinating body.

Since September 1985 the Minister has shared his responsibilities with an Associate Minister of National Defence.

The Canadian Forces (CF) are the military element of the Canadian government and are part of the Department of National Defence (DND). Government policy concerning the CF takes into account national and foreign policy. The roles of the CF are developed within this framework. They are:
- the protection of Canada and Canadian national interests at home and abroad; this includes the provision of aid of the civil power and national development;
- the defence of North America in co-operation with the United States' military forces;

- the fulfillment of such North Atlantic Treaty Organization (NATO) commitments to security as may be agreed upon; the performance of such international peacekeeping roles as Canada may from time to time assume.

Personnel and Budget

The 1990-91 Department of National Defence Main Estimate of $12,000m. represents 8·1% over the 1989–90 actual expenditures.

The strength of the Regular Force for 1991 was approximately 87,000.

Command Structure. The missions and roles of the CF are undertaken by functional and regional commands. Commands and major organizations report directly to National Defence Headquarters (NDHQ) in Ottawa, Ontario from headquarters situated as follows:

- Mobile Command, St Hubert, Quebec;
- Maritime Command, Halifax, Nova Scotia;
- Air Command, Winnipeg, Manitoba;
- Canadian Forces Training System, Trenton, Ontario;
- Canadian Forces Communication Command, Ottawa, Ontario;
- Canadian Forces Europe, Lahr, Germany; and
- Northern Region, Yellowknife, NWT.

1. *Mobile Command.* Mobile Command (FMC) maintains combat ready land forces to meet Canada's defence commitments.

Defence of North America

Mobile Command is prepared to undertake defence of North America operations in conjunction with the forces of the United States. Under the Canada-United States Basic Defence Agreement, a number of mutual defence treaties exist. One that directly concerns Mobile Command is Canada-United States Land Operations (CANUS LANDOP). It is designed to provide the co-ordination of the land defence of Canada, Alaska, and the continental United States. Under this plan, Mobile Command is responsible for co-ordinating the land defence of Canada by both Canadian and US forces, if required, and must be prepared to assist US forces in the defence of Alaska and the United States. Both this and the National Security task force involves Mobile Command in maintaining a presence in the Canadian North through surveillance and patrols and numerous exercises.

NATO Commitment

Mobile Command is assigned several NATO tasks. It has an infantry battalion group committed to the Allied Command. Europe Mobile Force (Land) to deter aggression in northern Norway. In addition, the battalion group is also assigned to the NATO Composite Force, which is a force designed to deter aggression in northern Norway and to reinforce Norwegian defences. These roles are filled by 1st Battalion, Princess Patricia's Canadian Light Infantry in Calgary, with augmentation from other elements of the command.

The 1st Canadian Division, with headquarters in Kingston, Ontario, is tasked with the defence of the Central Region of Europe. The division's role is to deploy to Europe as the main reserve formation for the Commander Central Arm group, an expansion of the earlier role of 4 Canadian Mechanized Brigade.

International Peacekeeping or Stability Operations

Mobile Command is committed to providing forces for international peacekeeping or stability operations. In 1990–91, its UN involvement included commitments in Cyprus, on the Golan Heights and in Namibia, Iran-Iraq, Afghanistan, El Salvador, Angola, and Iraq-Kuwait. Non-UN commitments included the Multi-National Peacekeeping Force (MFO) in the Sinai and a group of engineers in Pakistan teaching Afghan refugees mine recognition.

Budget and Personnel

In 1990–91, the FMC budget was approximately $399m. for operations and maintenance costs, cadets, the militia and support to visiting forces. This excluded salaries. Expenditures in support of British, German and US Army units training on FMC bases were recovered from the nations concerned.

Personnel included approximately 18,900 Regular Force, 23,300 Militia and 6,500 civilians.

2. *Maritime Command*. The Maritime Command (MARCOM) role is to maintain combat-ready general purpose maritime forces to meet Canada's defence commitments. This role is fulfilled using MARCOM resources and designated Air Command aircraft under MARCOM control.

Maritime Command comprises operational maritime forces, headquarters and supporting units located primarily on the east and west coasts of Canada, but also extending as far north as Iqaluit, Northwest Territories and as far south as Bermuda.

Operational forces include 18 destroyers, 3 submarines, 2 mine counter-measures vessels, 3 operational support ships, 12 patrol vessels/training ships, 2 research vessels, 14 tugboats, 1 small tanker, 5 gate vessels, 14 Reserve tenders and 70 auxiliary/yard craft. The first of the new Canadian Patrol Frigates, *HMCS Halifax* was delivered on 28 June 1991. Two more frigates are scheduled for delivery in 1992.

Protection of Canada and National Interests

Maritime Command conducts military surveillance of Canadian territorial waters on both coasts. Surveillance patrols in support of Canadian national interests are conducted in the 370 km economic zone by surface and air units. Fisheries patrols are conducted on both coasts.

Operations and Training

The air, surface and sub-surface resources of MARCOM maintain a high level of combat readiness through operations, tactical research, joint exercises and planned maintenance. Training is conducted on both coasts through exercises run by the destroyer squadrons. Advanced training, designed to maintain combat readiness and evaluate new tactics, is accomplished through Maritime co-ordinated exercises. During 1990, MARCOM activities included multi-threat training in national, multinational and NATO exercises.

NATO Exercises

Canada is continuously represented in NATO's Standing Naval Force Atlantic (STANAVFORLANT) by a destroyer. This multi-national squadron provides a highly visible demonstration of NATO solidarity. The squadron visits ports throughout Europe, the Mediterranean and the east coast of North America, strengthening ties with NATO's member countries. On the east coast destroyers participate in the NATO Squadron and are involved in a number of exercises on both sides of the Atlantic. West coast ships conduct national exercises on a regular basis.

Personnel and Budget

MARCOM's budget for fiscal year 1990 was $253·3m. for operations and maintenance, naval reserve, cadets and miscellaneous. Personnel included 10,317 Regular Force personnel, 4,212 Naval Reserve personnel and 7,150 civilians.

3. *Air Command*. Air Command's five functional groups provide combat-ready air forces to meet Canada's defence commitments.

Functional Organization

Air Command is divided into five functional air groups. The Commander, Air Command, delegates operational control to the commanders of the air groups over their assigned resources. The Commander retains responsibility for flight safety, as well as air doctrine and standards relating to flying operations throughout the Canadian Forces, including units located outside Canada. The air groups are:

(*a*) Fighter Group (North Bay, Ontario) maintains the sovereignty of Canada's airspace, supports Mobile and Maritime Command training and operations, and fulfills Canada's commitments to NATO and NORAD.
(*b*) Air Transport Group (Trenton, Ontario) provides airlift resources and Search and Rescue (SAR) forces for the CF.
(*c*) Maritime Air Group (MAG) (Halifax, Nova Scotia) provides operationally ready air forces to MARCOM in areas including anti-submarine warfare, surveillance, sovereignty, fisheries and pollution monitoring.
(*d*) 10 Tactical Air Group (St Hubert, Quebec) provides combat-ready tactical avia-

tion forces for operational employment in support of Mobile Command operations, training and other defence commitments.

(e) Air Reserve Group (Winnipeg, Manitoba) provides support to Air Command by provision of reserve operational units and individual augmentees. On 1 Aug. 1990, 14 Training Group was disbanded. The position of Commander, 14 Training Group was absorbed into Air Command as the Chief of Staff, Personnel and Training. The resulting reorganization saw the amalgamation of 14 Training Group personnel with Air Command personnel, Reserve and Civilian Personnel divisions.

Personnel and Budget

Air Command consists of 19,114 Regular Force members, 1,472 Air Reserves and 5,741 civilians for a total of 26,327 members. The operations and maintenance budget for 1990–91 was $475·8m. including aviation fuel and operations and maintenance, travel reserve and cadet costs.

4. *Canadian Forces Training System*. The role of Canadian Forces Training System (CFTS) is to plan, organize, conduct and control the training of service personnel whose trade is required by more than one command. As such, CFTS is a joint formation manned by personnel from FMC, MARCOM and Air Command. The commander of CFTS exercises command over 20 schools located on five CFTS bases and two schools located on bases assigned to other commands.

Training

Canadian Forces Training System plans, controls and conducts all basic recruit and officer training as well as occupational training for 18 of 36 officer classifications and 53 of 100 non-commissioned member trades that are common to more than one operational command. Additionally, CFTS conducts specialty and advanced training for most members of the Canadian Forces. This role was expanded in 1989, when CFTS assumed command of the Canadian Forces Management Development School.

Personnel and Budget

In 1990 CFTS included more than 4,600 military personnel, of whom almost 1,600 were instructors. CFTS employed 3,627 civilian personnel. The CFTS budget is $126·1m., which included operations and maintenance, dependent education, cadets, travel and base utilities.

5. *Canadian Forces Communication Command (CFCC)*. Canadian Forces Communication Command (CFCC) provides strategic communication services, including communications research message handling and data transfer, telephone systems and high frequency radio direction-finding services for the CF. To effect these services CFCC operates and maintains several data networks and voice communications systems.

It is implicit in the provision of strategic communications for the CF and emergency government that the organization be capable of extending services to the various military and civil headquarters during a national emergency. As well, it must supply reliable strategic communications from Canada to CF combat elements anywhere in the world. To these ends, Communication Command personnel exercise their equipment and procedures regularly.

Personnel and Budget

The Canadian Forces Communication Command's (CFCC) 6,150 personnel includes a regular force contingent of 3,500 members, a Communication Reserve of 2,100 and a civilian force of approximately 550.

The 1990 command budget was $117·9m. which includes operations and maintenance, reserves, telecommunication services, travel and civilian pay.

6. *Canadian Forces Europe (CFE)*. Throughout 1990 Canadian Forces Europe (CFE) continued to provide, maintain and support European-based, combat-ready land and air forces to Supreme Allied Commander Europe in accordance with Canada's NATO commitment. European-based forces consist of 4 Canadian Mechanized Brigade, 1 Canadian Air Division, 4th Air Defence Regiment and national

command units supported by Canadian Forces Bases Lahr and Baden-Soellinger in Germany. These forces all completed challenging and realistic training programmes to maintain their operational readiness at the highest possible level.

Personnel and Budget
During 1990 service personnel at CFE numbered 8,000. There were approximately 4,400 civilian employees and a total of about 20,000 Canadian military and civilian personnel and their dependents.

During the fiscal year 1989–90, CFE was allocated an operations and maintenance budget of $271m., which includes civilian salaries, transport, rations and building rentals.

7. *Northern Region Headquarters.* Situated in Yellowknife, NWT, the Northern Region Headquarters (NRHQ) was formed on 15 May 1970 to assist in maintaining Canadian sovereignty and support ongoing Canadian Forces activities in the north.

Training
During 1990, NRHQ continued to provide planning advice and liaison support to territorial governments and military units for exercises 'north of 60'.

Regional organization. A regional structure is superimposed over the functional organization to most effectively respond to support requirements within Canada. This was accomplished by dividing Canada into six geographic regions and appointing the senior commander in each region as the region commander. Thus the following interrelationship of functional command/region/geographical area exists: *Maritime Command* – Atlantic Region (Newfoundland, New Brunswick, Nova Scotia and Prince Edward Island); *Mobile Command* – Eastern Region (Quebec); *Training System* – Central Region (Ontario); *Air Command* – Prairie Region (Manitoba, Saskatchewan, and Alberta); *Maritime Forces Pacific* – Pacific Region (British Columbia); and *Northern Region Headquarters* – Northern Region (Yukon and Northwest Territories). In 1989, a move was made to transfer the operational responsibilities from the regions to Mobile Command. Central Region operations was the first affected; others will be transferred in the future. Operational responsibilities include vital points defence, aid of the civil power, explosive ordinance disposal and many others. Responsibilities remaining with the regions include medical, dental, support to cadets, civilian personnel administration, etc.

The *Reserve Force* consists of 27,500 officers and non-commissioned members who are enrolled for other than continuing full-time military service. The subcomponents of the Reserve Force are the Primary Reserve, the Supplementary Ready Reserve, the Supplementary Holding Reserve, the Cadet Instructors List and the Canadian Rangers.

The elements of the Primary Reserve are the Naval Reserve, Militia, Air Reserve and Communication Reserve. Funded personnel levels for these four elements are 4,212; 20,105; 1,472 and 1,712, respectively. Officers and non-commissioned members of the Primary Reserve undergo part-time training at local armouries or collective training at central locations, often during the summer months.

The Supplementary Ready Reserve consists of former Regular and Reserve Force officers and non-commissioned members who are militarily fit and current, and prepared to report for duty when required in an emergency. The Supplementary Holding Reserve includes former members required to report for such duty only when the entire Supplementary Reserve was put on active service.

The Cadet Instructors List consists of commissioned officers whose primary duty is the supervision, administration and training of cadets. There are about 6,000 CIL members.

The Canadian Rangers consists of officers and non-commissioned members who volunteer to hold then selves in readiness for service but are not required to undergo annual training. Their role is to provide a military force in sparsely settled, northern coastal and isolated areas of Canada. There are currently (1991) over 1,800 members of the Canadian Rangers.

Source: Department of National Defence

Royal Canadian Mounted Police. The Royal Canadian Mounted Police is a civil force maintained by the federal government. It was established in 1873, as the North-West Mounted Police for service in what was then the North-West Territories and, in recognition of its services, was granted the use of the prefix 'Royal' by King Edward VII in 1904. Its sphere of operations was expanded in 1918 to include all of Canada west of Thunder Bay. In 1920 the force absorbed the Dominion Police, its headquarters was transferred from Regina to Ottawa, and its title was changed to Royal Canadian Mounted Police. The force is responsible to the Solicitor-General of Canada and is controlled and managed by a Commissioner who holds the rank and status of a Deputy Minister. The Commissioner is empowered under the Royal Canadian Mounted Police Act to appoint members to be peace officers in all provinces and territories of Canada.

The responsibilities of the Royal Canadian Mounted Police are national in scope. The administration of justice within the provinces, including the enforcement of the Criminal Code of Canada, is part of the power and duty delegated to the provincial governments.

All provinces except Ontario and Quebec have entered into contracts with the Royal Canadian Mounted Police to enforce criminal and provincial laws under the direction of the respective Attorneys-General. In addition, in these 8 provinces the Force is under agreement to provide police services to 191 municipalities, thereby assuming the enforcement responsibility of municipal as well as criminal and provincial laws within these communities. The Royal Canadian Mounted Police is also responsible for all police work in the Yukon and Northwest Territories enforcing federal law and territorial ordinances. The 13 Divisions, alphabetically designated, make up the strength of the Force across Canada; they comprise 52 sub-divisions which include 723 detachments. Headquarters Division, as well as the Office of the Commissioner, is located in Ottawa. The Force maintains liaison officers in 18 countries and represents Canada in the International Criminal Police Organization (Interpol) which has its headquarters in Lyons, France.

Thorough training is emphasized for members of the Force. Recruits receive 6 months of basic training at the Royal Canadian Mounted Police Academy in Regina. This is followed by a further 6 months of supervised on-the-job training. The RCMP also operates the Canadian Police College at which its members and selected representatives of other Canadian and foreign police forces may study the latest advances in the fields of crime prevention and detection.

Many of these advances have been incorporated into the operation of the Force. A modern communications system links the widespread divisional headquarters with the administrative centre at Ottawa and a network of fixed and mobile radio units operates within the provinces. Assisting the criminal investigation work of the Force is the Directorate of Identification Services; its services, together with those of divisional and sub-divisional units, and of 8 Crime Detection Laboratories, are available to police forces throughout Canada. The Canadian Police Information Centre at RCMP Headquarters, a national computer network, is staffed and operated by the Force. Law Enforcement agencies throughout Canada have access via remote terminals to information on stolen vehicles, licences and wanted persons.

In Oct. 1991, the Force had a total strength of 21,586 including regular members, special constables, civilian members and public service employees. It maintained 7,120 motor vehicles, 87 police service dogs and 156 horses.

The Force has 13 divisions actively engaged in law enforcement, 1 Headquarters Division and 1 training division. Maritime services are divisional responsibilities and the Force currently has 394 boats at various points across Canada. The Air Directorate has stations throughout the country and maintains a fleet of 21 fixed-wing aircraft and 8 helicopters.

Source: Publishing Unit, RCMP Headquarters

INTERNATIONAL RELATIONS

Membership. Canada is a member of the UN, the Commonwealth, OAS, OECD, NATO and Colombo Plan.

ECONOMY

Budget. Budgetary revenue and expenditure of the Government of Canada for years ended 31 March (in $1m.):

	1986–87	1987–88	1988–89	1989–90	1990–91
Revenue	85,784	97,452	104,067	113,707	119,353
Expenditure	116,389	125,535	133,018	142,703	149,971

Main items of revenue in 1990–91 (estimates in $1m.):

Unemployment contributions	12,707	Other tax revenue	279
Income tax, personal	57,601	Other non-tax revenue	2,718
Income tax, corporate	11,726	Customs import duties	4,001
Goods and services tax	2,574	Non-resident tax	1,372
Sales and excise taxes	19,568	Return on investments	6,807

Main estimates of expenditure in 1990–91 (in $1m.): Old age security benefits, guaranteed income supplements and spouses' benefits, 17,131; unemployment benefit, 14,665; family allowances, 2,736; medical care, 6,033; Canada Assistance Plan, 5,788; education support, 1,862; defence, 12,122; official development assistance, 2,519; public debt charges, 42,537.

On 31 March 1991 the net public debt was $388,579m. (preliminary).

On 1 Jan. 1991 a 7% Goods and Services Tax (GST) was introduced, superseding a 13·5% manufacturers' sales tax.

Sources: Finance Canada and Statistics Canada

Currency. The unit of currency is the *Canadian dollar* (CAD) of 100 *cents*. There are coins of 1, 5, 10, 25, 50 cents and $1, and notes of $2, $5, $10, $20, $50, $100 and $1,000. The $1 note was withdrawn in 1989. The monetary standard is gold of 900 millesimal fineness (23·33 grains of pure gold equal to 1 gold dollar). The Currency Act provides for gold coins in the denominations of $5, $10 and $20, which are legal tender. The British and US gold coins are also legal tender, at the par rate of exchange. The legal equivalent of the British sovereign is 4.86^{2/3}$.

Since 1935 the Bank of Canada has the sole right to issue paper money for circulation in Canada. Restrictions introduced by the 1944 revisions of the Bank Act cancelled the right of chartered banks to issue or re-issue notes after 1 Jan. 1945; and in Jan. 1950 the chartered banks' liability for such of their notes as then remained outstanding was transferred to the Bank of Canada in return for payment of a like sum to the Bank of Canada. On 31 May 1970 the Canadian dollar which was stabilized at 92·50 US cents was allowed to fluctuate. Inflation was an annualized 5·6% in 1991. The value of the US$ in Canadian funds was $1·18 and £1 sterling = Canadian $2·07 in March 1992.

The Ottawa Mint was established in 1908 as a branch of the Royal Mint, in pursuance of the Ottawa Mint Act, 1901. In Dec. 1931 control of the Mint was passed over to the Canadian Government, and since that time it has operated as the Royal Canadian Mint. The Mint issues nickel, bronze and cupronickel coins for circulation in Canada. In 1967, in celebration of Canada's Centennial of Confederation, a $20 gold piece was minted, the first gold coin struck since 1919. In 1935, on the occasion of His Majesty's Silver Jubilee, the Royal Canadian Mint issued the first Canadian silver dollar. Commemorative dollars were also issued in 1939 on the occasion of the visit of King George VI and Queen Elizabeth to Canada; in 1949, when Newfoundland became the tenth Province of Canada; in 1958, the one-hundredth anniversary of the establishment of the Colony of British Columbia; in 1964, the centennial of the Charlottetown and Quebec Conferences which paved the way to confederation. The silver dollar bearing the design of the canoe manned by an Indian and a Voyageur has been issued in the years 1935–38, 1945–48, 1950–57, 1959–63, 1965 and 1966. In 1968, the coin bore the same design but its composition changed from silver to nickel. This composition remained for all the following years. The design was used again in 1969, 1972, 1975–87. For centennial year the Canada goose replaced the usual canoe design on the silver dollar. Because of a world-wide shortage of silver, the Government, in Aug. 1967, authorized the Mint to change the metal content of the 25-cent and 10-cent coins. Commencing in Sept. 1968, 10-cent, 25-cent, 50-cent and $1 coins were minted in pure nickel. Gold refining is one of the principal activities of the Mint. On average the Mint refines about 70% of Canada's total gold production. In 1990 the Mint refined over 4·39m. troy ounces of gold. Coins produced (1990): 1,396m. Gold bullion sold (1990): 1,013,200 oz.

Source: Bank of Canada

Banking and Finance. Commercial banks in Canada are known as chartered banks and are incorporated under the terms of the Bank Act, which imposes strict conditions as to capital, returns to the Federal government, types of lending operations and other matters. In July 1991 there were 66 chartered banks (7 Schedule I banks which have widely held ownership and 59 Schedule II banks) incorporated under the provisions of the Bank Act. The banks had 7,400 branches serving more than 1,700 communities in all provinces in Canada, in addition to branches in other countries. The banks employed over 181,000 people across the country. The Bank Act is subject to revision by Parliament every 10 years. Bank charters expire every 10 years and are renewed at each decennial revision of the Bank Act. The chartered banks make detailed monthly and yearly returns to the Minister of Finance and are subject to periodic inspection by the Superintendent of Financial Institutions, an official appointed by the Government.

The Bank of Canada Act, effective from 3 July 1934, provided for the establishment of a central bank for the Dominion. This bank commenced operations on 11 March 1935 with a paid-up capital of $5m. By reason of certain changes introduced into the composition of stockholders of the bank (for which *see* THE STATESMAN'S YEAR-BOOK, 1944 pp. 322–23), the Minister of Finance on behalf of Canada is the sole registered owner of the capital stock of the bank. The revised Bank Act, which came into force on 1 Dec. 1980, requires chartered banks to maintain a statutory primary reserve of 10% on demand deposits, 3% on foreign-currency deposits and 2% on notice deposits, with an additional 1% on the portion of notice deposits exceeding $500m. This reserve is required to be maintained in the form of notes and deposits with the Bank of Canada. A secondary reserve of 4% in the form of treasury bills, government bonds, etc., is also required. All gold held in Canada by the chartered banks was transferred to the Bank of Canada along with the gold held by the Government as reserve against Dominion notes outstanding at the time of the commencement of operations of the Bank of Canada. The liability of the Dominion notes outstanding at the commencement of business of the Bank of Canada was assumed by the bank. The *Governor* of the Bank of Canada is John Crow.

Source: Canadian Bankers' Association

Weights and Measures. The legal weights and measures are in transition from the Imperial to the International system of units. The Metric Commission, established in June 1971, co-ordinates Canada's conversion to the metric system.

ENERGY AND NATURAL RESOURCES

Electricity. Electricity generation in 1990 was 467,619,100 mwh., of which 431,013,400 mwh. was to meet domestic demand. Of the total, 62·9% was from hydro generation, 22·4% from thermal generation and 14·7% nuclear. Supply 115 volts; 60 Hz.

Oil and Natural Gas. Production of marketable crude oil and equivalent, 1990, 89,608,000 cu. metres; natural gas, 1990, 98,334,000 cu. metres, and natural gas by-products 23,317,000 cu. metres.

Minerals. Alberta accounted for 46·8% of the value of mineral products in 1990. Total value of minerals produced in 1990 (preliminary) was $41,305m. Principal minerals produced in 1990 (preliminary):

	Quantity (1,000)	Value ($1m.)
Metallic		
Copper (kg)	779,566	2,495
Nickel (kg)	196,606	2,024
Zinc (kg)	1,285,439	2,477
Iron ore (tonnes)	36,443	1,312
Gold (grammes)	164,991	2,378
Lead (kg)	224,000	268
Silver (kg)	1,400	255
Uranium 'U' (kg)	9,458	868
Others	...	701
Total metallic	...	12,778
Non-metallic		
Asbestos (tonnes)	665	256
Potash (K_2O) (tonnes)	7,015	907
Salt (tonnes)	11,097	240
Sulphur, elemental (tonnes)	5,802	364
Others	...	618
Total non-metallic	...	2,385
Fuels		
Crude oil (cu. metres)	89,608	13,832
Natural gas (1,000 cu. metres)	98,334	5,598
Natural gas by-products (cu. metres)	23,317	2,209
Coal (tonnes)	68,450	1,871
Total fuels	...	23,510
Structural material		
Cement (tonnes)	11,252	865
Sand and gravel (tonnes)	250,070	794
Stone (tonnes)	112,005	651
Others	...	323
Total structural materials	...	2,633

Value (in $1m.) of mineral production by provinces:

Provinces	1989	1990[1]	Provinces	1989	1990[1]
Newfoundland	896	862	Saskatchewan	3,011	3,230
Pr. Ed. Island	2	3	Alberta	16,456	19,339
Nova Scotia	441	452	British Columbia	4,123	4,108
New Brunswick	864	886	Yukon Territory	534	541
Quebec	2,856	2,968	N.W. Territories	1,149	1,168
Ontario	7,257	6,420			
Manitoba	1,668	1,330	Total	39,257	41,307

[1] Preliminary.

Source: Statistics Canada

Agriculture. According to the census of 1986 the total land area is 2,278·6m. acres of which 167·6m. acres are agricultural land.

Grain growing, dairy farming, fruit farming, ranching and fur farming are all carried on successfully. Total farm cash receipts (1989) $22,415·6m.

The following table shows the value of farm cash receipts for 1990, for selected agricultural commodities, in $1,000:

Wheat	3,069,040	Tobacco	280,241
Oats and barley	728,056	Cattle and calves	3,974,415
Canola	783,935	Hogs	2,032,750
Potatoes	413,711	Sheep and lambs	32,525
Vegetables	735,498	Dairy products	3,135,467
Fruit	322,276	Poultry and eggs	1,676,105

Number of occupied farms (census of 1986) was 293,089; average farm size, 571·8 acres.

Field Crops. The estimated acreage and production of the principal field crops, by provinces, in 1990 were:

Provinces	Wheat		Tame hay		Oats	
	1,000 acres	1,000 bushels	1,000 acres	1,000 tons	1,000 acres	1,000 bushels
Newfoundland	—	—	13	26	—	—
Prince Edward Island	10	467	139	320	20	1,240
Nova Scotia	6	280	170	480	20	1,100
New Brunswick	8	380	176	460	30	1,650
Quebec	135	6,240	2,560	8,070	240	17,180
Ontario	830	52,000	2,550	8,200	220	13,700
Manitoba	5,560	221,000	1,750	3,600	390	24,000
Saskatchewan	20,880	653,500	2,100	3,000	800	45,500
Alberta	8,010	263,000	4,650	10,500	1,200	75,000
British Columbia	125	5,000	865	2,400	85	5,500
Total, Canada	35,564	1,201,867	14,973	37,056	3,005	184,870

Provinces	Barley		Rye		Corn for Grain	
	1,000 acres	1,000 bushels	1,000 acres	1,000 bushels	1,000 acres	1,000 bushels
Prince Edward Island	78	3,950	—	—	—	—
Nova Scotia	18	850	—	—	4	250
New Brunswick	32	1,800	—	—	—	—
Quebec	385	24,110	—	—	699	75,740
Ontario	445	26,700	50	1,700	1,770	199,000
Manitoba	1,550	92,500	170	5,800	80	6,100
Saskatchewan	3,550	179,000	670	17,000	—	—
Alberta	5,650	317,000	170	3,800	7	650
British Columbia	115	5,650	9	350	—	—
Total, Canada	11,823	651,560	1,069	28,650	2,560	281,740

Provinces	Canola		Mixed grains		Soybeans	
	1,000 acres	1,000 bushels	1,000 acres	1,000 bushels	1,000 acres	1,000 bushels
Prince Edward Island	—	—	42	2,580	—	—
Nova Scotia	—	—	—	—	—	—
New Brunswick	—	—	—	—	—	—
Quebec	—	—	73	4,409	45	1,874
Ontario	50	1,900	470	29,800	1,170	45,600
Manitoba	890	20,800	80	3,800	—	—
Saskatchewan	2,800	64,000	80	3,300	—	—
Alberta	2,550	56,500	300	15,000	—	—
British Columbia	90	1,500	10	580	—	—
Total, Canada	6,380	144,700	1,055	59,469	1,215	47,474

Livestock. In parts of Saskatchewan and Alberta stockraising is still carried on as a primary industry, but the livestock industry of the country at large is mainly a subsidiary of mixed farming. The following table shows the numbers of livestock (in 1,000) by provinces in July 1991:

Provinces	Milk cows	Other cattle and calves	Sheep and lambs	Pigs
Newfoundland	4·7	4·2	7·5	17·5
Prince Edward Island	19·5	75·5	5·5	100·0
Nova Scotia	32·7	96·6	35·0	134·0
New Brunswick	26·3	79·7	10·0	79·0
Quebec	536·0	832·0	123·8	2,994·0
Ontario	430·0	1,780·0	209·1	3,112·0
Manitoba	63·0	1,037·0	23·8	1,245·0
Saskatchewan	50·0	2,150·0	59·0	828·0
Alberta	123·0	4,280·0	247·3	1,702·0
British Columbia	74·0	675·0	59·3	229·0
Total	1,359·2	11,009·0	780·3	10,440·5

Net production of farm eggs in 1990, 471·8m. doz. ($482·7m.). Wool production in 1990, 1,439 tonnes.

Dairying. In 1988 [1], the dairy products industry (which includes fluid milk industries and other dairy products industries) reported 364 for the number of establishments. The number of production workers for the same period was 15,149. Production, 1990: Butter, 99,884 tonnes; cheddar cheese, 112,983 tonnes [2]; concentrated whole milk products, 45,794 tonnes; concentrated milk by-products, 92,853 tonnes.

[1] The number of establishments/employees are based on the 1980 Standard Industrial Classification.
[2] Includes cheddar used to make processed cheese.

Fruit Farming. The value of fruit production (excluding apples) in 1990 was (in $1,000): Ontario, 86,555; British Columbia, 62,072; Quebec, 32,576; New Brunswick, 6,477; Newfoundland, 2,437; Prince Edward Island, 1,932; Nova Scotia, 15,584. Total apple production in Canada in 1989 was 536,720 tonnes, value $107,903,000; in 1990, 539,722 tonnes.

Tobacco. Commercial production of tobacco is confined to Ontario, Quebec and the Maritime provinces. Farm cash receipts for 1990 totalled $280·2m.

Forestry. As of 1986, the total area of land covered by forests is estimated at about 453·3m. ha, of which 243·7m. ha are classed as productive forest land.

The values of shipments from forestry-related industries in 1988 were: Logging, $8,061·9m; sawmill and planing mill products, $9,139·4m.; shingle and shale, $227m.; veneer and plywood, $1,050·9m.; pulp and paper, $19,850·4m.; paper and allied products, $25,661·1m.

Fur Trade. In 1989–90, 2,580,809 pelts valued at $52,338,611, were taken (3,023,197 pelts in 1988–89). In wild-life pelt production marten led in total value; in fur farm production, mink. The value of mink pelts from fur farms in 1990 was $23,974,287 ($25,774,364 in 1989). There were, in 1990, 764 fur farms reporting fox and 366 mink.

Source: Statistics Canada

Fisheries. During 1990, landings in commercial fisheries reached 1,589,423 tonnes. The landed value was $1,433m. and the estimated market value was $3,092m. The landed value of principal fish in 1990 was (in $1,000): Salmon, 226,617; cod, 245,504; lobster, 226,496; herring, 111,683; scallops, 86,701; freshwater fish, 82,000; halibut, 30,419.

Canadian Mines Handbook. Annual. Toronto, from 1931
Canadian Fisheries Highlights. Dept. of Fisheries and Oceans

Source: Department of Fisheries and Oceans

INDUSTRY. Principal statistics by major industry groups, 1988:

Industry	Production workers	Wages ($1,000)	Cost of materials ($1,000)	Value of shipments ($1,000)
Food industries	143,502	3,354,759	24,673,634	37,159,464
Beverage industries	17,392	552,599	2,442,408	5,865,415
Tobacco products	3,024	117,000	716,268	1,778,643
Rubber products	19,402	540,193	1,296,827	2,694,724
Plastic products	41,191	861,212	3,314,124	5,893,127
Leather and allied industries	17,767	285,732	687,186	1,293,255
Primary textile industries	19,225	451,793	1,651,245	3,173,285
Textile products	30,872	559,740	1,879,910	3,411,008
Clothing industries	102,988	1,571,197	3,343,536	6,656,698
Wood industries	106,992	2,850,576	8,826,951	15,322,237
Furniture and fixtures	54,372	1,079,912	2,261,283	4,619,738
Paper and allied industries	90,976	3,184,039	11,470,623	25,661,082
Printing, publishing and allied industries	83,347	2,353,975	4,843,165	12,525,710

Industry	Production workers	Wages ($1,000)	Cost of materials ($1,000)	Value of shipments ($1,000)
Primary metal industries	83,926	3,069,233	11,697,708	22,715,441
Metal fabricating industries	141,228	3,489,977	9,338,905	17,946,337
Machinery industries	69,593	1,747,097	5,049,620	10,012,347
Transport equipment industries	182,229	5,781,464	35,887,438	51,718,059
Electrical and electronic products	103,779	2,625,049	9,332,311	18,191,653
Non-metallic mineral products	45,974	1,309,458	3,076,719	7,803,552
Refined petroleum and coal prods.	6,837	318,581	11,323,383	14,273,753
Chemical and chemical prods.	50,733	1,566,816	10,454,080	22,628,022
Other manufacturing	57,983	1,182,618	2,937,551	6,092,331
All industries	1,473,332	38,853,020	166,504,875	297,435,881

Source: Statistics Canada

Labour. In 1988 (annual average) the industrial distribution of the employed was estimated as follows (in 1,000): Community, business and personal services, 4,062; manufacturing, 2,104; trade, 2,168; transport, communication and other utilities, 904; construction, 726; public administration, 815; finance, insurance and real estate, 728; agriculture, 444; non-agriculture, 11,801; other primary industries, 294; total employed, 12,245; unemployed, 1,030. Unemployment was 8·3% in Aug. 1990 (1·14m.).

Certain specific minimum standards in regard to working conditions are set by law, for the most part by provincial labour legislation. Minimum wages, maximum hours of work or an overtime rate of pay after a specified number of hours, minimum weekly rest periods, annual vacations with pay, statutory holidays, maternity protection and parental leave and notice of termination of employment are established for the majority of workers. The average weekly wage in April 1991 was $535·06.

Trade Unions. Union returns filed for 1988 in compliance with the Corporations and Returns Act (1983), show 494 labour organizations reporting on 15,176 local union branches. Union membership in 1988 was 3·78m. 53% of the membership belonged to national unions, with 58% of the membership affiliated to the Canadian Labour Congress.

It is generally established by legislation, both federal and provincial, that a trade union to which the majority of employees in a unit suitable for collective bargaining belong, is given certain rights and duties. An employer is required to meet and negotiate with such a trade union to determine wage-rates and other working conditions of his employees. The employer, the trade union and the employees affected are bound by the resulting agreement. If an impasse is reached in negotiation conciliation services provided by the appropriate government board are available. Generally, work stoppages do not take place until an established conciliation or mediation procedure has been carried out and are prohibited while an agreement is in effect.

Freedom of association is a civil right, and under common law workers are at liberty to join unions and participate in their activities. This right has also been guaranteed by statutes which make it an offence to interfere with freedom of association.

Source: Department of Labour

FOREIGN ECONOMIC RELATIONS. Canada is one of the signatories of the General Agreement on Tariffs and Trade (GATT) and an active participant in the subsequent GATT negotiations. On 1 Jan. 1989, the Canada-US Free Trade Agreement came into effect. The Agreement, which provides for the phased removal of tariffs and other barriers, is consistent with Canada's obligation to its trading partners.

Commerce. Imports and exports (in $1m.) for calendar years:

	Imports	Exports		Imports	Exports
1960	5,843	5,256	1987	116,238	125,086
1970	13,952	16,820	1988	131,171	134,852
1980	69,273	76,158	1989	135,191	134,843
1985	104,355	116,145	1990	136,224	141,474

Exports by countries in 1990 (in $1m.):

Commonwealth countries

Australia	902	Guatemala	28
Bahamas	50	Guinea	6
Bangladesh	85	Haiti	15
Barbados	35	Honduras	10
Belize	3	Hungary	8
Bermuda	26	Iceland	9
Cyprus	12	Indonesia	310
Ghana	18	Iran	360
Guyana	10	Iraq	197
Hong Kong	685	Ireland	139
India	321	Israel	144
Jamaica	110	Italy	1,188
Kenya	56	Japan	8,230
Malawi	2	Jordan	5
Malaysia	256	Korea, South	1,554
Malta	4	Kuwait	38
New Zealand	158	Lebanon	8
Nigeria	30	Liberia	1
Pakistan	93	Libya	53
Singapore	406	Luxembourg	3
Sri Lanka	17	Mexico	608
Tanzania	21	Morocco	234
Trinidad and Tobago	63	Mozambique	26
Uganda	3	Netherlands	1,641
UK	3,536	Netherlands Antilles	21
Zambia	10	Nicaragua	11
Zimbabwe	22	Norway	555
		Panama	16
		Peru	58
Non-Commonwealth countries		Philippines	206
Algeria	291	Poland	34
Angola	25	Portugal	180
Argentina	48	Puerto Rico	–
Austria	158	Qatar	4
Bahrain	2	Romania	24
Belgium	1,249	St Pierre and Miquelon	39
Bolivia	5	Saudi Arabia	278
Brazil	502	Senegal	12
Cameroon	31	Somalia	3
Chile	200	South Africa	179
China	1,655	Spain	387
Colombia	213	Sudan	7
Costa Rica	27	Sweden	327
Côte d'Ivoire	10	Switzerland	1,054
Cuba	176	Syria	8
Czechoslovakia	16	Taiwan	798
Denmark	138	Thailand	505
Dominican Republic	57	Togo	2
Ecuador	37	Tunisia	53
Egypt	75	Turkey	158
El Salvador	16	USSR	1,125
Ethiopia	21	United Arab Emirates	30
Fiji	2	USA	111,380
Finland	146	US Virgin Islands	–
France	1,304	Uruguay	20
Gabon	5	Venezuela	274
German Democratic Rep.	22	Vietnam	7
Germany, Fed. Rep. of	2,322	Yemen (South)	6
Greece	97	Yugoslavia	59
Greenland	3	Zaïre	11

Imports by countries in 1990 (in $1m.):

Commonwealth countries		Germany	3,859
Australia	766	Greece	71
Bahamas	29	Guatemala	37
Bangladesh	36	Guinea	14
Barbados	15	Haiti	14
Belize	10	Honduras	13
Bermuda	2	Hungary	45
Ghana	5	Iceland	257
Guyana	24	Indonesia	202
Hong Kong	1,058	Iran	20
India	226	Iraq	112
Jamaica	157	Ireland	257
Kenya	13	Israel	124
Malaysia	380	Italy	1,954
Malta	3	Japan	9,523
Mauritius	7	Korea, South	2,254
New Zealand	213	Lebanon	3
Nigeria	597	Liberia	3
Pakistan	95	Libya	–
Sierra Leone	5	Luxembourg	27
Singapore	552	Mexico	1,748
Sri Lanka	42	Morocco	39
Trinidad and Tobago	24	Netherlands	720
Uganda	5	Netherlands Antilles	14
UK	4,841	Nicaragua	63
Zimbabwe	21	Norway	1,683
		Panama	4
Non-Commonwealth countries		Peru	128
Algeria	62	Philippines	202
Angola	56	Poland	78
Argentina	139	Portugal	171
Austria	406	Puerto Rico	–
Bahrain	9	Romania	87
Belgium	539	Saudi Arabia	708
Bolivia	22	South Africa	141
Brazil	798	Spain	496
Chile	180	Sweden	899
China	1,393	Switzerland	648
Colombia	132	Taiwan	2,109
Costa Rica	57	Thailand	406
Côte d'Ivoire	21	Togo	35
Cuba	130	Turkey	84
Czechoslovakia	70	USSR	193
Denmark	249	United Arab Emirates	58
Dominican Republic	39	USA	87,894
Ecuador	147	US Virgin Islands	–
Egypt	9	Uruguay	45
El Salvador	18	Venezuela	577
Ethiopia	5	Vietnam	15
Fiji	11	Yugoslavia	93
Finland	360	Zaïre	9
France	2,448		

Categories of imports in 1990, estimate (in $1,000):

Live animals	113,370	Fabricated materials, inedible	26,527,485
Food, feed, beverages and tobacco	7,989,390	End products, inedible	89,358,074
		Special transactions	2,963,041
Crude materials, inedible	9,272,759		

Categories of exports (Canadian produce) in 1990, estimate (in $1,000):

Live animals	887,612	Fabricated materials, inedible	47,559,982
Food, feed, beverages and tobacco	10,684,183	End products, inedible	61,187,883
		Special transactions	1,575,925
Crude materials, inedible	19,578,578		

Crude oil exports were 35,031,890 cu. metres in 1990; imports, 32,190,765 cu. metres. Natural gas exports were 47,372m. cu. metres in 1990.

Export of fishery products in 1989 were valued at $2,409m.

Total trade of Canada with UK (British Department of Trade returns, in £1,000 sterling):

	1988	1989	1990	1991
Imports to UK	2,038,245	2,174,334	2,259,099	1,992,549
Exports and re-exports from UK	2,038,433	2,165,731	1,901,939	1,701,051

Tourism. The number of visitors to Canada in 1989 was 37,981,925 (1990, 37,990,470). In 1989, 34,705,087 came from the USA (1990, 34,734,079).

Source: Statistics Canada

COMMUNICATIONS

Roads. The total length of federal and provincial territorial roads and highways at the end of March 1987 was 291,463 km. Expenditures by these two levels of government on roads and highways during the fiscal year 1985–86 amounted to approximately $5,347·7m.

In general highways are controlled and maintained by the provinces who also have the responsiblity of providing assistance to their municipalities and townships. Federal expenditures are directed largely to the maintenance of national park highways, Indian Reserve roads and designated provincial/territorial highway construction in projects. The Alaska Highway is part of the Canadian highway system. For the Trans-Canada Highway *see* map in THE STATESMAN'S YEAR-BOOK, 1962.

In 1988 intercity and rural bus services carried 18m. passengers 156m. km, earning $332·8m.

Registered motor vehicles totalled 16,715,529 in 1989; they included 12,811,318 passenger cars and taxis, 3,395,874 trucks and buses and 348,125 motor cycles.

There were 4,210 fatalities in road accidents in 1990.

Railways. The total length of track in 1989 was 89,104 km, including: Mainline track, 38,922 km; branch line, 27,420 km and industrial and siding track, 24,692 km.

Canada has 2 great trans-continental systems: The Canadian National Railway system (CN), a government-owned body which operates 47,243 km (1989) of track, and the Canadian Pacific Railway (CP), a joint-stock corporation operating 31,720 km (1989). From 1 April 1978, a government-funded organization known as Via Rail took over passenger services formerly operated by CP and CN; 6m. passengers were carried in 1989.

There are metros in Montreal, Toronto and Vancouver, and tram/light rail systems in Calgary, Edmonton and Toronto. In 1989 urban transit systems carried 1,527m. passengers for an operating revenue of $2,626m.

Selected statistics for 1989: Passenger revenue $317·5m.; freight revenue, $6,084m.; total railway operating revenues, $7,446·6m.; total operating expenses, $7,080·3m.

Civil Aviation. Civil aviation is under the jurisdiction of the federal government. The technical and administrative aspects are supervised by Transport Canada, while the economic functions are assigned to the National Transportation Agency.

In 1990 Canadian airports handled 43,991,350 revenue passengers on major scheduled services and 721,987·2 tonnes of cargo. Operating revenue for commercial air carriers (1990) was $8,231·9m.; operating expenditure, $8,228·1m.

The 2 major airlines are Air Canada (privatized in July 1989) and Canadian Airlines International. Air Canada had 114 aircraft and Canadian Airlines International 87 on 15 July 1991.

Shipping. Total vessel arrivals and departures at Canadian ports in domestic shipping was 56,801 in 1989, totalling a cumulative GRT of 224,433,364. A total of 58,297 vessel movements in international shipping at Canadian ports in 1989 loaded and unloaded 236m. tonnes of cargo, totalling a GRT of 592,231,671.

The major canals in Canada are those of the St Lawrence–Great Lakes waterway with their 7 locks, providing navigation for vessels of 26-ft draught from Montreal to Lake Ontario; the Welland Canal by-passing the Niagara River between Lake Ontario and Lake Erie with its 8 locks; and the Sault Ste Marie Canal and lock between Lake Huron and Lake Superior. These 16 locks overcome a drop of 582 ft from the head of the lakes to Montreal. The St Lawrence Seaway was opened to navigation on 1 April 1959 (*see* map in THE STATESMAN'S YEAR-BOOK, 1957). In 1990, traffic on the Montreal–Lake Ontario Section of the Seaway numbered 2,768 transits carrying 36·7m. cargo tonnes; on the Welland Canal Section, 3,577 transits with 39·4m. cargo tonnes. Value of capital assets was $523,811,000 and investments, $36,911,000 at 31 March 1991.

Source: Statistics Canada

Coast Guard. The Canadian Coast Guard (formed in 1962) is responsible to the Minister of Transport. In 1990 it comprised 8 heavy icebreakers; 9 medium icebreakers; 1 light icebreaker/navigational aid tender; 7 ice-strengthened/navigational aid tenders; 16 navigational aid tenders; 1 hydrographic survey and sounding vessel; 73 search and rescue vessels; 4 hovercraft; 35 helicopters and 1 fixed-wing aircraft (DC-3).

Source: Canadian Coast Guard

Telecommunications. At the end of the fiscal year 1990–91 Canada Post Corporation's retail network consisted of 17,231 points of sale. During fiscal year 1990–91, 9,657m. pieces of mail were processed. Total revenue (1990–91) was $3,785m.; total expenditure, $3,771m.

There were 15m. telephone access lines reported by major telephone companies in 1990.

There were 837 originating stations operating at 31 March 1991, of which 377 were AM radio stations, 333 FM radio stations and 127 television stations.

Sources: Statistics Canada, Canada Post Corporation, Canadian Radio-Television Telecommunication Commission

Cinemas. (1989). There were 650 cinemas and 123 drive-in theatres.

Newspapers. In 1989 there were 96 dailies in English (total circulation, 5·3m.) and 11 in French (1m.).

Source: Communications Canada

JUSTICE, RELIGION, EDUCATION AND WELFARE

Justice. There is a Supreme Court in Ottawa, having general appellate jurisdiction in civil and criminal cases throughout Canada. The Exchequer Court (established in 1875) was replaced by the Federal Court in 1971. This has a Trial Division, consisting of the Associate Chief Justice and 9 other judges, and an Appeal Division, consisting of the Chief Justice and 3 other judges. Its seat is in Ottawa, but each Division may sit in any place in Canada. Decisions of the Trial Division may be appealed to the Appeal Division, those of the latter to the Supreme Court. There is a Superior Court in each province and county courts, with limited jurisdiction, in most of the provinces, all the judges in these courts being appointed by the Governor-General. Police, magistrates and justices of the peace are appointed by the provincial governments.

For the year ended 31 Dec. 1990, 2,635,610 Criminal Code Offences were reported and 440,724 adults were charged.

Source: Statistics Canada

Religion. The *Yearbook of American and Canadian Churches*, published by the National Council of the Churches of Christ in the USA, New York, presents the latest figures available (1989) from official statisticians of church bodies:

Religious body	Inclusive membership	Number of churches	Number of clergy
Anglican Church of Canada	817,020	1,765	3,250
Canadian Baptist Federation	133,032	1,135	1,325
Evangelical Lutheran Church	205,846	655	849
Pentecostal Assemblies of Canada	192,706	962	1,399
Presbyterian Church	217,664	1,022	1,194
Roman Catholic Church	11,375,914	5,922	11,302
Ukrainian Greek Orthodox (1988)	120,000	258	91
United Church of Canada (1990)	2,013,258	4,112	3,669

Membership of other denominations: Mormons (1987), 118,000; Jewish (1981), 296,425; Jehovah's Witnesses (1989), 97,808; Lutheran Church – Canada (1988), 90,944; Salvation Army (1988), 88,899.

Education. Under the Constitution the various provincial legislatures have powers over education. These are subject to certain qualifications respecting the rights of denominational and minority language schools. Newfoundland and Quebec legislations provide for Roman Catholic and Protestant school boards. School Acts in Ontario, Saskatchewan and Alberta provide tax support for both public and separate schools. School board revenues derive from local taxation on real property and government grants from general provincial revenue.

Statistics for 1991–92 (estimates) of all elementary and secondary schools, public, federal and private:

Province	Schools	Teachers	Pupils
Newfoundland	522	7,900	124,150
Prince Edward Island	71	1,360	24,570
Nova Scotia	529	10,230	167,930
New Brunswick	460	8,060	141,850
Quebec	2,917	63,860	1,143,800
Ontario	5,346	122,240	2,059,200
Manitoba	850	13,080	220,200
Saskatchewan	979	11,380	211,300
Alberta	1,730	27,650	523,900
British Columbia	1,986	30,850	593,200
Yukon	26	330	5,450
Northwest Territories	77	870	14,750
National Defence (overseas)	8	250	3,500
Total	15,501	298,060	5,233,800

Source: Statistics Canada

Enrolment for Indian and Inuit children, 1990-91: Federal schools, 8,052; band operated schools, 40,513; provincial schools, 41,501; private schools, 1,952.

In 1990–91, 532,132 full-time regular students (graduates and undergraduates) were enrolled in universities. In 1990-91 109,814 received first degrees of which 18,424 were in education; 13,880 in humanities; 7,846 in engineering and applied sciences; 3,580 in fine and applied arts; 42,410 in social sciences; 7,207 in agriculture/biological sciences; 7,599 in health professions; 6,290 in mathematics/physical sciences; and 2,778 were unclassified.

Health. Constitutional responsibility for health care services rests with the ten provinces and two territories of Canada. Accordingly, Canada's national health insurance system consists of an interlocking set of provincial and territorial hospital and medical insurance plans conforming to certain national standards rather than a single national programme. These national standards, which are set out in the Canada Health Act, include: Provision of a comprehensive range of hospital and medical benefits; universal population coverage; access to necessary services on uniform terms and conditions; portability of benefits; and public administration of provincial and territorial insurance plans.

Provinces and territories satisfying these national standards are eligible for federal financial transfer payments according to the provisions of the Federal-Provincial Fiscal Arrangements and Federal Post-Secondary Education and Health Contributions Act. Under this Act, the provinces and territories are entitled to receive equal-per-capita federal health contributions escalated annually by the three-year average increase in nominal Gross National Product. Federal restraint has frozen this escalator through 1994–95. These federal contributions, estimated at $13,123m. in 1991–92, are paid in the form of a combination of tax point and cash transfers. Over and above these health transfers, the federal government also provides financial support for such provincial and territorial extended health care service programmes as nursing home care, certain home care services, ambulatory health care services and adult residential care services. These supplementary equal-per-capita cash payments are estimated at $1,388m. in 1991–92. The contributors for hospital and medical insurance and for extended health care services will continue to increase with population increases during the restraint period.

The national health insurance programmes were introduced in stages. The Hospital Insurance and Diagnostic Services Act was passed in 1958, providing prepaid coverage to all Canadians for in-patient and, at the option of each province and territory, out-patient hospital services. The Medical Care Act was introduced in 1968 to extend universal coverage to all medically equipped services provided by medical practitioners. The Canada Health Act, which took effect 1 April 1984, consolidated the original federal health insurance legislation and clarified the national standards provinces and territories are required to meet in order to qualify for full federal health contributions.

The approach taken by Canada is one of state-sponsored health insurance. Accordingly, the advent of insurance programmes produced little change in the ownership of hospitals, almost all of which are owned by non-government non-profit corporations, or in the rights and privileges of private medical practice. Patients are free to choose their own general practitioner. Except for 3·8% of the population whose care is provided for under other legislation (such as serving members of the Canadian Armed Forces and inmates of federal penitentiaries), all residents are eligible, regardless of whether they are in the work force. Benefits are available without upper limit so long as they are medically necessary, provided any registration obligations are met. Benefits are also portable during any temporary absence from Canada anywhere in the world—subject to any limitation a province or territory may impose upon treatment electively sought outside the particular province or territory without prior approval and available on a substantially similar basis within the province or territory.

In addition to the benefits qualifying for federal contributions, provinces and territories provide additional benefits at their own discretion. All provinces and territories provide benefits covering a variety of services (*e.g.*, optometric care, drug benefits). Most fund their portion of health costs out of general provincial and territorial revenues. Two provinces levy health premiums which meet part of the provincial costs and 5 provinces levy health and specific taxes. There are no co-charges for medically necessary short-term hospital care or medical care. Most provinces and territories have charges for long-term chronic hospital care geared, approximately, to the room and board portion of this OAS–GIS payment mentioned under Social Welfare. In 1989, total health expenditures were about $56·1m., representing 8·9% of GNP. Public sector spending accounts for about 75% of total national health expenditure.

Social Welfare. The social security system provides financial benefits and social services to individuals and their families through a variety of programmes administered by federal, provincial and municipal governments, and voluntary organizations. Federally, the Department of Health and Welfare Canada is responsible for research into the areas of health and social issues, provision of grants and contributions for various social services, improvement and construction of health facilities, the administration of several of Canada's income security programmes and the development and promotion of measures designed to improve the health and well-being of Canadians. These programmes are: The Family Allowances programme, introduced in 1945 and amended in 1973; the Old Age Security programme, introduced in 1952 and to which were added the Guaranteed Income Supplement in 1967 and the Spouse's Allowance in 1975; and the Canada Pension Plan and Canada Assistance Plan which came into being in 1966.

The 1973 Family Allowances Act provides for the payment of a monthly Family Allowance ($33.93 in 1991) in respect of a dependent child under the age of 18 who is a resident of Canada and is wholly or substantially maintained by a parent or guardian. At least one parent must be a Canadian citizen, or admitted to Canada as a permanent resident under the Immigration Act, or admitted to Canada for a period of not less than 1 year, if during that time his or her income is subject to Canadian income tax. Benefits are also paid under prescribed circumstances to Canadian citizens living abroad. Eligibility for Family Allowances (FA) is a precondition for receipt of the refundable Child Tax Credit discussed below. A Special Allowance ($50.61 monthly in 1991) is paid on behalf of a child under the age of 18 who is maintained by a welfare agency, a government department or an institution. In some cases, payment is made directly to a foster parent.

The Family Allowances Act specifies that a provincial government may request the federal government to vary the allowance rates payable within the province by age and/or family size subject to the fulfillment of stipulated conditions. Only the provinces of Alberta and Quebec have exercised this option. During the month of Aug. 1991, over 3·7m. Canadian families (including 6·8m. eligible children) received Family Allowances; the Special Allowance was paid on behalf of 31,000 of these children. The total bill for FA and Special Allowances for 1991–92 was $2,784m.

The Old Age Security (OAS) pension is payable to persons 65 years of age and over who satisfy the residence requirements stipulated in the Old Age Security Act. The amount payable, whether full or partial, is also governed by stipulated conditions, as is the payment of an OAS pension to a recipient who absents himself from Canada. OAS pensioners with little or no income apart from OAS may, upon application, receive a full or partial supplement known as the Guaranteed Income Supplement (GIS). Entitlement is normally based on the pensioner's income in the preceding year, calculated in accordance with the Income Tax Act. The spouse of an OAS pensioner, aged 60 to 64, meeting the same residence requirements as those stipulated for OAS, may be eligible for a full or partial Spouse's Allowance (SPA). SPA is payable, on application, depending on the annual combined income of the couple (not including the pensioner spouse's basic OAS pension or GIS). In 1979, the SPA programme was expanded to include a spouse, who is eligible for SPA in the month the pensioner spouse dies, until the age of 65 or until remarriage (Extended Spouse's Allowance). Since Sept. 1985, SPA has also been available to low income widow(er)s aged 60–64 regardless of the age of their spouse at death. For the fourth quarter of 1991, the basic OAS pension was $373.32 monthly; the maximum Guaranteed Income Supplement was $443.65 monthly for a single pensioner or a married pensioner whose spouse was not receiving a pension or a Spouse's Allowance, and $288.97 monthly for each spouse of a married couple where both were pensioners. The maximum Spouse's Allowance for the same quarter was $662.29 monthly (equal to the basic pension plus the maximum GIS married rate), and $731.17 for widow(er)s. Total OAS/GIS/SPA benefit expenditures for 1991–92 were $18,291m.; in Aug. 1991, over 3m. Canadians received benefits through these programmes.

The Canada Pension Plan (CPP) is designed to provide workers with a basic level of income protection in the event of retirement, disability or death. Benefits may be payable to a contributor, a surviving spouse or an eligible child. As of 1 Jan. 1987, payment of actuarially adjusted retirement benefits may begin as early as age 60 or as late as age 70. Benefits are determined by the contributor's earnings and contributions made to the Plan. Contribution is compulsory for most employed and self-employed Canadians 18 to 65 years of age. The Canada Pension Plan does not operate in Quebec, which has exercised its constitutional prerogative to establish a similar plan, the Quebec Pension Plan (QPP), to operate in lieu of CPP; there is reciprocity between the two to ensure coverage for all adult Canadians in the labour force. In 1991, the maximum retirement pension payable under CPP and QPP was $604.86, the maximum disability pension was $743.64, and the maximum surviving spouse's pension was $362.92 (for survivors 65 years of age and over). For survivors under 65 years of age CPP pays a reduced flat rate while QPP pays varied rates depending on the age of the survivor. In 1991 both CPP and QPP were funded by equal contributions of 2·3% of pensionable earnings from the employer and 2·3% from the employee (self-employed persons contribute the full 4·6%), in addition to the interest on the investment of excess funds. In 1991, the range of yearly pensionable earnings was from $3,000 to $30,500; a person who earned and contributed at less than the maximum level receives monthly benefits at rates lower than the maximum allowable under CPP/QPP. In Oct. 1991, over 3·4m. Canadians received Canada or Quebec Pension Plan benefits. Total expenditures in 1991–92 for CPP were about $12,096m.

Social security programme agreements co-ordinate the operation of the Old Age Security programme and the Canada Pension Plan with the comparable programmes of another country in order to accomplish four basic objectives: To remove restrictions, based on nationality, which may otherwise prevent Canadians from receiving benefits under the legislation of the other country; to ease or eliminate restrictions on the payment of social security benefits abroad; to eliminate situations in which a worker may have to contribute to the social security programmes of both countries for the same work; to assist migrants in qualifying for benefits based on the periods they have lived or worked in each country. Such agreements are in force with Italy, France, Portugal, the USA, Greece, Jamaica, Barbados, Belgium, Denmark, Norway, Sweden, Austria, St Lucia, Spain, Australia, Dominica, Luxembourg, the Netherlands, Germany, Finland, Iceland and Cyprus. In addition, agreements have been signed with Malta and Ireland.

Ismael, J. S., (ed.) *Canadian Welfare State: Evolution and Transition*. Univ. of Alberta Press, 1987

Source: Health and Welfare Canada

DIPLOMATIC REPRESENTATIVES

Of Canada in Great Britain (Macdonald House., Grosvenor Sq., London, W1X 0AB)
High Commissioner: Fredrik S. Eaton.

Of Great Britain in Canada (80 Elgin St., Ottawa, K1P 5K7)
High Commissioner: Nicholas Payne.

Of Canada in the USA (501 Pennsylvania Ave., NW, Washington, D.C., 20001)
Ambassador: Derek H. Burney.

Of the USA in Canada (100 Wellington St., Ottawa, K1P 5TI)
Ambassador: Edward N. Ney.

Of Canada to the United Nations
Ambassador: Louise Frechette.

Further Reading

Statistical Information: Statistics Canada, Ottawa, has been the official central statistical organization for Canada since 1918. The Agency, which reports to Parliament through the Minister responsible for the Department of Regional Industrial Expansion, serves as the statistical agency for federal government departments; co-ordinates the statistics of the provincial governments along national lines; and channels all Canadian statistical data to internal organizations. *Chief Statistician of Canada:* Dr I. P. Fellegi.

Publications of Statistics Canada are classified as periodical (issued more frequently than once a year), annual, biennial and occasional publications. The occasional publications frequently supplement the annual reports and usually contain historical information. A complete list is contained in the Statistics Canada catalogue 1990, available at a nominal cost. Reference publications include:

The Canada Year Book. Biennial, from 1905
Canada: A Portrait. Biennial, from 1980
Canadian Economic Observer. Monthly, with annual historical supplements, from 1988
Thirteenth Decennial Census of Canada, 1991. Ottawa
Atlas and Gazetteer of Canada. Dept. of Energy, Mines and Resources. Ottawa, 1969
Cambridge History of the British Empire. Vol. VI. Canada and Newfoundland. Cambridge, 1930

Canadian Almanac and Directory. Toronto. Annual

Canadian Annual Review. Annual, from 1960

Canadian Dictionary: French–English. Toronto, 1970

Canadian Encyclopedia. 2nd ed. 4 vols. Edmonton, 1988

Canadiana; A List of Publications of Canadian Interest. National Library, Ottawa. Monthly, with annual cumulation. 1951 ff.

Cook, R., *French-Canadian Nationalism; An Anthology*. Toronto, 1970.—*The Maple Leaf Forever; Essays on Nationalism and Politics in Canada*. Toronto, 1971

Creighton, D. G., *Canada's First Century*. Toronto, 1970.—*Towards the Discovery of Canada*. Toronto, 1974

Dawson, R. M. and Dawson, W. F. *Democratic Government in Canada*. 5th ed. Toronto Univ. Press, 1989

Dewitt, D. B. and Kirton, J. J., *Canada as a Principal Power: A Study in Foreign Policy*. Toronto, 1983

Dictionnaire Bélisle de la langue française au Canada; dictionnaire Oxford. 1970

Dictionnaire canadien; français–anglais–français. Toronto, 1962

Encyclopedia Canadiana. 10 vols. Rev. ed. Ottawa, 1967

Granatstein, J. L., *Twentieth Century Canada*. Toronto, 1983

Hardy, W. G., *From Sea to Sea; Canada, 1850–1920: The Road to Nationhood*. Toronto, 1960

Harris, R. C., (ed.) *Historical Atlas of Canada*. Vol 1. Univ. of Toronto, 1987

Hillicker, J., *Canada's Department of External Affairs*. Kingston (Ont.), 1990

Hockin, T. A., *Government in Canada*. London, 1976

Ingles, E., *Canada*. [Bibliography] Oxford and Santa Barbara, 1990

Jackson, R. J., *Politics in Canada: Culture, Institutions, Behaviour and Public Policy*. 2nd ed. Scarborough, Ont., 1990

Kerr, D. G. G., *Historical Atlas of Canada*. Toronto, 1960

Leacy, F. H., (ed.) *Historical Statistics of Canada*. Government Printer, Ottawa, 1983

Longille, P., *Changing the Guard: Canada's Defence in a World in Transition*. Toronto Univ. Press, 1991

McCann, L. D., (ed.) *Heartland and Hinterland: A Geography of Canada*. Scarborough, Ontario, 1982

Mallory, J. R., *The Structure of Canadian Government*. Toronto, 1971

Moir, J. and Saunders, R., *Northern Destiny: A History of Canada*. Toronto, 1970

Nurgitz, N. and Segal, H., *No Small Measure: The Progressive Conservatives and the Constitution*. Ottawa, 1983

Smith, D. L., (ed.) *History of Canada: An Annotated Bibliography*. Oxford and Santa Barbara, 1983

White, W. L., *Introduction to Canadian Politics and Government*. 5th ed. Toronto, 1990

National Library: The National Library of Canada, Ottawa, Ontario. *Librarian:* Marianne Scott.

CANADIAN PROVINCES

The 10 provinces have each a separate parliament and administration, with a Lieut.-Governor, appointed by the Governor-General in Council at the head of the executive. They have full powers to regulate their own local affairs and dispose of their revenues, provided only they do not interfere with the action and policy of the central administration. Among the subjects assigned exclusively to the provincial legislatures are: The amendment of the provincial constitution, except as regards the office of the Lieut.-Governor; property and civil rights; direct taxation for revenue purposes; borrowing; management and sale of Crown lands; provincial hospitals, reformatories, etc.; shop, saloon, tavern, auctioneer and other licences for local or provincial purposes; local works and undertakings, except lines of ships, railways, canals, telegraphs, etc., extending beyond the province or connecting with other provinces, and excepting also such works as the Dominion Parliament declares are for the general good; marriages, administration of justice within the province; education.

Local Government. Under the terms of the British North America Act the provinces are given full powers over local government. All local government institutions are, therefore, supervised by the provinces, and are incorporated and function under provincial acts.

The acts under which municipalities operate vary from province to province. A municipal corporation is usually administered by an elected council headed by a mayor or reeve, whose powers to administer affairs and to raise funds by taxation and other methods are set forth in provincial laws, as is the scope of its obligations to, and on behalf of, the citizens. Similarly, the types of municipal corporations, their official designations and the requirements for their incorporation vary between provinces. The following table sets out the classifications as at 1 Jan. 1988.

Type and size of group	Nfld.	PEI	NS	NB	Que.	Ont.	Man.
Type:							
Regional municipalities	—	—	—	—	98	39	—
Metropolitan and regional municipalities [1]	—	—	—	—	3	12	—
Counties and regional districts	—	—	—	—	95	27	—
Unitary municipalities	170	86	66	114	1,500	792	184
Cities [2]	3	1	3	6	65	50	5
Towns	167	8	39	25	193	145	35
Villages	—	—	—	83	233	119	39
Rural municipalities [3]	—	77	24	—	1,009	478	105
Quasi-municipalities [4]	143	—	—	—	—	8	17
Total	313	86	66	114	1,598	839	201
Population size group (1986 census):							
Unitary municipalities—							
Over 100,000	—	—	2	—	4	18	1
50,000 to 99,999	1	—	1	2	16	14	—
10,000 to 49,999	4	1	18	4	80	81	4
Under 10,000	165	85	45	108	1,400	679	179
Total	170	86	66	114	1,500	792	184

Type and size of group	Sask.	Alta.	BC	YT	NWT	Canada
Type:						
Regional municipalities	—	—	28	—	—	165
Metropolitan and regional municipalities [1]	—	—	—	—	—	15
Counties and regional districts	—	—	28	—	—	150
Unitary municipalities	821	345	144	8	8	4,238
Cities [2]	12	15	37	2	1	200
Towns	146	108	12	2	5	885
Villages	364	172	48	4	2	1,064
Rural municipalities [3]:	299	50	47	—	—	2,089
Quasi-municipalities [4]	14	19	—	—	30	231
Total	835	364	172	8	38	4,634
Population size group (1986 census):						
Unitary municipalities—						
Over 100,000	2	2	4	—	—	33
50,000 to 99,999	—	—	10	—	—	44
10,000 to 49,999	7	18	29	1	1	248
Under 10,000	812	325	101	7	7	3,913
Total	821	345	144	8	8	4,238

[1] Includes urban communities in Quebec; and Metropolitan Toronto, regional municipalities and the district municipality of Muskoka in Ontario. [2] Includes the borough of East York. [3] Includes municipalities in Nova Scotia; parishes, townships, united townships and municipalities without designation in Quebec; townships in Ontario; rural municipalities in Manitoba and Saskatchewan; municipal districts and counties in Alberta; and districts in British Columbia. [4] Includes local government communities and the metropolitan area in Newfoundland; improvement districts in Ontario and Alberta; local government districts in Manitoba; and hamlets in the Northwest Territories.

ALBERTA

HISTORY. The southern half of the province of Alberta was part of Rupert's land which was granted by royal charter in 1670 to the Hudson's Bay Company. The intervention by the North West Company in the fur trade after 1783 led to the establishment of trading posts. In 1869 Rupert's land was transferred from the Hudson's Bay Company (which had absorbed its rival in 1821) to the new Dominion, and in the following year this land was combined with the former Crown land of the North Western Territories to form the Northwest Territories.

In 1882 'Alberta' first appeared as a provisional 'district', consisting of the southern half of the present province. In 1905 the Athabasca district to the north was added when provincial status was granted to Alberta.

Four parties have held office: The Liberals 1905–21; the United Farmers 1921–35; Social Credit 1935–71, and Progressive Conservative since Sept. 1971.

AREA AND POPULATION. The area of the province is 661,185 sq. km; 644,389 sq. km being land area and 16,796 sq. km water area. The population (estimate 1 July 1991) was 2,525,200; the urban population (1986), centres of 1,000 or over, was 1,877,758 and the rural 488,067. Population (30 June 1990) of the 16 cities (*see below under* Local Government for definition): Calgary, 692,885; Edmonton, 605,538; Lethbridge, 60,614; Red Deer, 56,922; Medicine Hat, 42,929; St Albert, 40,707; Fort McMurray, 33,698; Grande Prairie, 27,558; Leduc, 13,566; Camrose, 12,968; Spruce Grove, 12,403; Fort Saskatchewan, 11,753; Airdrie, 11,904; Lloydminster (Alberta portion), 10,201; Wetaskiwin, 10,203; Drumheller, 6,366.

Vital statistics, *see* p. 275.

CLIMATE. A continental climate: Long, cold winters and mild summers. Rainfall amounts are greatest between May and Sept. Edmonton. Jan. 5°F (–15°C), July 63°F (17°C). Annual rainfall 13·6" (345·6 mm).

CONSTITUTION AND GOVERNMENT. The constitution of Alberta is contained in the British North America Act of 1867, and amending Acts; also in the Alberta Act of 1905, passed by the Parliament of the Dominion of Canada, which created the province out of the then Northwest Territories. All the provisions of the British North America Act, except those with respect to school lands and the public domain, were made to apply to Alberta as they apply to the older provinces of Canada. On 1 Oct. 1930 the natural resources were transferred from the Dominion to provincial government control. The province is represented by 6 members in the Senate and 26 in the House of Commons of Canada.

The executive is vested nominally in the Lieut.-Governor, who is appointed by the federal government, but actually in the Executive Council or the Cabinet of the legislature. Legislative power is vested in the Assembly in the name of the Queen.

Members of the Legislative Assembly are elected by the universal vote of adults over the age of 18 years.

There are 83 members in the legislature (elected 20 March 1989): 59 Progressive Conservative, 16 New Democratic Party, 8 Liberal.

Lieut.-Governor: Hon. Gordon Towers (sworn in 11 March 1991).
Flag: Blue with the shield of the province in the centre.
The members of the Ministry were as follows in Oct. 1991:

Premier, President of Executive Council: Hon. D. R. Getty.
Deputy Premier and Minister of Federal and Intergovernmental Affairs: Hon. J. Horsman. *Transportation and Utilities:* Hon. J. A. Adair. *Consumer and Corporate Affairs:* Hon. D. Anderson. *Health:* Hon. N. Betkowski. *Education:* Hon. J. Dinning. *Economic Development and Trade:* Hon. J. Elzinga. *Forestry, Lands and Wildlife:* Hon. E. L. Fjordbotten. *Solicitor General:* Hon. D. Fowler. *Advanced Education:* Hon. J. Gogo. *Agriculture:* Hon. E. Isley. *Provincial Treasurer:* Hon. A. D. Johnston. *Environment:* Hon. R. Klein. *Public Works, Supply and Services:* Hon. K. Kowalski. *Culture and Multiculturalism:* Hon. D. Main. *Labour:* Hon. E. McCoy. *Family and Social Services:* Hon. J. Oldring. *Energy:* Hon. R. Orman. *Attorney-General:* Hon. K. Rostad. *Tourism:* Hon. D. Sparrow. *Municipal Affairs:* Hon. R. Speaker. *Technology, Research and Telecommunications:* Hon. F. Stewart. *Occupa-

tional Health and Safety: Hon. P. Trynchy. *Career Development and Employment:* Hon. N. Weiss. *Recreation and Parks:* Hon. S. West.

Local Government. The local government units are City, Town, New Town, Village, Summer Village, County, Municipal District and Improvement District.

There are 16 cities (*see* Area and Population, above). These cities operate under the Municipal Government Act. The governing body consists of a mayor and a council of from 6 to 20 members. A city can be incorporated by order of the Lieut.-Governor-in-Council. A population of 10,000 is required for incorporation.

There are no limits of area specified in the statutes for any of the different local government units. The population requirement for a Town as specified in the Municipal Government Act is 1,000 people, and the area at incorporation is that of the original village.

A Village must contain 75 separate and occupied dwellings. The Municipal Government Act requires each dwelling to have been occupied continuously for a period of at least 6 months. A Summer Village must contain 50 separate dwellings.

A rural county area is an area incorporated through an order of the Lieut.-Governor-in-Council under the provisions of the County Act. One board of councillors deal with both municipal and school affairs.

A rural Municipal District is an area which has been incorporated under the Municipal Government Act. In Municipal Districts separate boards control municipal and school affairs.

Areas not incorporated as counties or Municipal Districts are termed Improvement Districts or Special Areas. Sparsely populated, such districts are administered and taxed by the Department of Municipal Affairs of the provincial government. There are no requirements as to the minimum number of residents of a County or Municipal District.

FINANCE. The budgetary revenue and expenditure (in $1m.) for years ending 31 March were as follows:

	1987–88	1988–89	1989–90	1990–91 [1]	1991–92 [2]
Revenue	9,466	9,106	9,720	11,896	12,618
Expenditure	10,399	10,889	12,044	12,982	12,585

[1] Forecast. [2] Estimates.

Personal income *per capita* (1989), $21,099.

ENERGY AND NATURAL RESOURCES

Oil. In 1990, 72,841,000 cu. metres of crude oil were produced with gross sales value of $11,394m. Alberta produced 82% of Canada's crude petroleum output in 1988.

Oil sands underlie some 60,000 sq. km of Alberta, the 4 major deposits being: The Athabasca, Cold Lake, Peace River and Buffalo Head Hills deposits. Some 7% (3,250 sq. km) of the Athabasca deposit can be exploited through open-pit mining. The rest of the Athabasca, and all the deposits in the other areas, are deeper reserves which must be developed through in situ techniques. These reserves reach depths of 760 metres.

Two oil sands mining plants in the Fort McMurray area produced 11·7m. cu. metres of synthetic crude oil in 1988.

Gas. Natural gas is found in abundance in numerous localities. In 1990, 81,652m. cu. metres valued at $4,716·5m. were produced. Production of natural gas by-products was 22,486,000 cu. metres, valued at $2,120m.

Minerals. Coal reserves are estimated at 2,600,000m. tonnes, of which 800,000m. tonnes are recoverable. Production (1990) 30·28m. tonnes valued at $485·8m.

Value of total mineral production increased from $16,455·8m. in 1989 to $19,338·7m. in 1990.

Agriculture. Total area of farms (1986) 51,040,463 acres; improved land, 31,891,516; (under crops, 22,641,092; improved pasture, 3,402,183; summer fallow, 5,255,965; other improved land, 592,276); unimproved land, 19,148,947; (unimproved pasture, 16,057,185; woodland, 713,699; other unimproved land, 2,378,063). Number of farms (1986) 57,777.

For particulars of agricultural production and livestock *see* pp. 000–00. Farm cash receipts in 1990 totalled $4,221·1m., of which crops contributed $1,604·8m., livestock and products, $2,298·1m., and direct payments, $318·2m.

Forestry. Forest land in 1990 covered some 202,000 sq. km. In 1989–90 8,827,849 cu. metres were cut from land managed by the Crown.

Fisheries. The largest catch in commercial fishing is whitefish. Perch, tullibee, walley, pike and lake trout are also caught in smaller quantities. In 1984 a provincial fish marketing policy was implemented and a new commercial fishery licensing system was implemented in 1987. Commercial fish production in 1989–90 was 2,217 tonnes, value $2·2m.

INDUSTRY. The leading manufacturing industries are food and beverages, petroleum refining, metal fabricating, wood industries, primary metal, chemical and chemical products and non-metallic mineral products industries. There were in 1987 2,590 manufacturing establishments, in which were employed 78,220 persons, who earned in salaries and wages $2,278,685,000.

Manufacturing shipments had a total value of $18,952m. in 1990. Chief among these shipments were: Food and beverages, $4,516·8m.; chemicals and chemical products, $3,259m.; refined petroleum and coal products, $3,607m.; primary metals, $872·4m.; fabricated metal products, $1,036·8m.; wood, $930m.; printing, publishing and allied products, $770·8m.; machinery, $705·7m.; paper and allied products, $702·3m.; non-metal mineral products, $663m.; other, $258·7m.

Total retail sales (1990) $19,878m.

Tourism is important and in 1991 contributed an estimated $2,730m. to the economy.

COMMUNICATIONS

Roads. In 1991 there were 154,864 km of roads and highways, including 110,500 km gravelled and 22,568 km paved.

At 31 March 1991 there were 1,921,020 motor vehicles registered, including 1,468,324 passenger cars.

Railways. In 1991 the length of main railway lines was 10,340 km. There are rail local transit networks in Edmonton (11·2 km) and Calgary (29·2 km).

Telecommunications. The telephone system is owned and operated by the Telus Corporation (in which the Alberta Government holds 44% of the shares), except in the city of Edmonton (owned and operated by the City Council). There were 1,431,280 telephone subscriber lines in service in April 1991.

JUSTICE AND EDUCATION

Justice. The Supreme Judicial authority of the province is the Court of Appeal. Judges of the Court of Appeal and Court of Queen's Bench are appointed by the Federal Government and hold office until retirement at the age of 75. There are courts of lesser jurisdiction in both civil and criminal matters. The Court of Queen's Bench has full jurisdiction over civil proceedings. A Provincial Court which has jurisdiction in civil matters up to $2,000 is presided over by provincially appointed judges. Youth Courts have power to try boys and girls 12–17 years old inclusive for offences against the Young Offenders Act.

The jurisdiction of all criminal courts in Alberta is enacted in the provisions of the Criminal Code. The system of procedure in civil and criminal cases conforms as nearly as possible to the English system.

Education. Schools of all grades are included under the term of public school (including those in the separate school system which are publicly supported). The same board of trustees controls the schools from kindergarten to university entrance. In 1990–91 there were 468,718 pupils enrolled in grades 1-12, including private schools and special education programmes. The University of Alberta (in Edmonton), organized in 1907, had, in 1989–90, 24,678 full-time students; the University of Calgary, formerly part of the University of Alberta and autonomous from April 1966, had 18,025 and the University of Lethbridge, organized in 1966, had 3,548. The Athabasca University had in 1988–89, 10,936 part-time students. Banff Centre for Continuing Education had in 1988–89, 1,130 part-time students. The full-time enrolment at Alberta's 11 public colleges totalled 19,861 students in 1988–89.

Further Reading

Statistical Information: The Alberta Bureau of Statistics (Dept. of Treasury, Edmonton), which was established in 1939, collects, compiles and distributes information relative to Alberta. Among its publications are: *Alberta Statistical Review* (Quarterly).—*Alberta Economic Accounts* (Annual).—*Alberta Facts* (Annual).—*Population Projections, Alberta* (Occasional).—*Alberta Population Growth* (Quarterly).
Dept. of Economic Development and Trade, *Alberta Industry and Resources Database*. Edmonton, (Biannual)

MacGregor, J. G., *A History of Alberta*. 2nd ed. Edmonton, 1981
Masson, J., *Alberta's Local Governments and their Politics*. Univ. of Alberta Press, 1985
Richards, J., *Prairie Capitalism: Power and Influence in the New West*. Toronto, 1979
Wiebe, Rudy., *Alberta, a Celebration*. Edmonton, 1979

BRITISH COLUMBIA

HISTORY. Vancouver Island was organized as a colony in 1849; the mainland as far as the watershed of the Rocky Mountains was organized as a colony following a gold rush on the Fraser River in 1859. The two were united as the colony of British Columbia in 1866; this became a Canadian Province in 1871.

AREA AND POPULATION. British Columbia has an area of 952,263 sq. km. The capital is Victoria. The province is bordered westerly by the Pacific ocean and Alaska Panhandle, northerly by the Yukon and Northwest Territories, easterly by the Province of Alberta and southerly by the USA along the 49th parallel. A chain of islands, the largest of which are Vancouver Island and the Queen Charlotte Islands, affords protection to the mainland coast.

The 1986 census population was 2,889,207; estimate (1991) 3,131,700.

The principal cities and their 1990 estimated populations are as follows: Metropolitan Vancouver, 1,535,301; Metropolitan Victoria, 280,364; Kelowna, 70,716; Prince George, 65,144; Kamloops, 63,110; Matsqui, 62,966; Nanaimo, 55,643; Chilliwack, 48,173; Penticton, 25,963; Vernon, 21,139; Campbell River, 19,901; Prince Rupert, 16,022; Cranbrook, 15,159; Fort St. John, 12,894.

Vital statistics, *see* p. 275.

CLIMATE. The climate is cool temperate, but mountain influences affect temperatures and rainfall very considerably. Driest months occur in summer. Vancouver. Jan. 36°F (2·2°C), July 64°F (17·8°C). Annual rainfall 58" (1,458 mm).

CONSTITUTION AND GOVERNMENT. British Columbia (then known as New Caledonia) originally formed part of the Hudson's Bay Company's concession. In 1849 Vancouver Island and in 1858 British Columbia were constituted Crown Colonies; in 1866 the two colonies amalgamated. The British North America Act of 1867 provided for eventual admission into Canadian Confederation, and on 20 July 1871 British Columbia became the sixth province of the Dominion.

British Columbia has a unicameral legislature of 69 elected members. Government policy is determined by the Executive Council responsible to the Legislature.

The Lieut.-Governor is appointed by the Governor-General of Canada, usually for a term of 5 years, and is the head of the executive government of the province.

Lieut.-Governor: The Hon. David See-Chai Lam.

Flag: A banner of the arms, *i.e.,* blue and white wavy stripes charged with a setting sun in gold, across the top of a Union Flag with a gold coronet in the centre.

The Legislative Assembly is elected for a maximum term of 5 years. There are 75 electoral districts. Every Canadian citizen 19 years and over, having resided a minimum of 6 months in the province, duly registered, is entitled to vote. The province is represented in the Federal Parliament by 32 members in the House of Commons, and 6 Senators.

At the Legislative Assembly elections of Oct. 1991 the New Democratic Party (NDP) gained 41% of votes cast and 51 seats, the Liberal Party gained 17 seats and Social Credit 7.

The 19-member NDP Executive Council included in Jan. 1992:

Premier and President of the Executive Council: Mike Harcourt (b. 1943).

Deputy Premier and Minister of Education: Anita Hagen. *Finance and Corporate Relations:* Glen Clark. *Labour and Consumer Affairs, Social Services and Housing:* Moe Sihota. *Advanced Education, Training and Technology:* Dr Tom Perry. *Attorney General and Solicitor General:* Colin Gabelmann.

Agent-General in London: Garde Gardom (British Columbia House, 1 Regent St., London, SW1Y 4NS).

Local Government. Vancouver City was incorporated by statute and operates under the provisions of the Vancouver Charter of 1953 and amendments. This is the only incorporated area in British Columbia not operating under the provisions of the Municipal Act. Under this Act municipalities are divided into the following classes: *(a)* a village with a population between 500 and 2,500, governed by a council consisting of a mayor and 4 aldermen; *(b)* a town with a population between 2,500 and 5,000, governed by a council consisting of a mayor and 4 aldermen; *(c)* a city where the population exceeds 5,000 governed by a council consisting of a mayor and 6 or 8 aldermen depending on population; *(d)* a district where the area exceeds 810 hectares and the average density is less than 5 persons per hectare, governed by a council consisting of a mayor and 6 or 8 aldermen depending on population; *(e)* an Indian government district.

There are 3 other forms of local government: There are 8 Development Regions each represented in Cabinet by a Minister of State; the regional district covering a number of areas both incorporated and unincorporated, governed by a board of directors; and the improvement district governed by a board of 3 trustees.

Revenue for municipal services is derived mainly from real-property taxation, although additional revenue is derived from licence fees, business taxes, fines, public utility projects and grants-in-aid from the provincial government.

ECONOMY

Budget. Current provincial revenue and expenditure, including all capital expenditures, in Canadian $1m. for fiscal years ending 31 March:

	1988–89	1989–90	1990–91 [1]	1991–92 [2]
Revenue	11,618·1	13,487·0	15,308·0	16,150·0
Expenditure	11,939·1	13,350·4	15,293·0	16,545·0

[1] Forecast   [2] Estimate

The main sources of current revenue are the income taxes, contributions from the federal government, and privileges, licences and natural resources taxes and royalties.

The main items of expenditure in 1991–92 (estimate) are as follows: Health, $5,486m.; education, $4,482m.; social services, $1,908m.; transportation, $1,271m.;

natural resources and economic development, $1,160m.; protection of persons and property, $724m.; debt servicing, $615m.

Banking. On 31 Oct. 1990, Canadian chartered banks maintained 819 branches and had total assets of $42·400m. in British Columbia; credit unions at 114 locations had total assets of $9·378m. Several foreign banks have Canadian head offices in Vancouver and several others have branches.

ENERGY AND NATURAL RESOURCES

Electricity. Generation in 1990 totalled 60,662m. kwh. of which a net 6,689m. kwh. were exported. Available within the province was 57,206m. kwh. (with imports 3,233m. kwh.).

Minerals. Copper, coal, natural gas, crude oil, gold and silver are the most important minerals produced. The 1990 total of mineral production was estimated at $3,963m. Total value of mineral fuels produced in 1990 was estimated at: Coal, $1,059m.; oil and gas, $914m.

Agriculture. Only 2·4m. ha or 4% of the total land area is arable or potentially arable. Farm cash receipts, in 1990, were $1,186m. of which livestock and products $761m., crops, $362m.

Forestry. About 46% of British Columbia's land is productive forest land, with 43·3m. hectares bearing commercial forest. Over 94% of the forest area is owned or administered by the provincial government. The total cut from forests in 1990 was 78·3m. cu. metres. Output of forest-based products, 1990: Lumber, 33,515,000 cu. metres; plywood, 1·64m. cu. metres; pulp, 6·61m. tonnes; paper and paperboard, 1,231,000 tonnes; newsprint, 1,754,000 tonnes.

Fisheries. In 1990, the total landed value of the catch was $544m., wholesale value $1,030m.

INDUSTRY AND TRADE

Industry. The selling value of factory shipments from all manufacturing industries reached an estimated $24,538m. in 1990.

Labour. The labour force averaged 1,601,000 persons in 1990 with 1,469,000 employed, of which 538,000 were in service industries, 281,000 in trade, 172,000 in manufacturing, 128,000 in transportation, communication and other utilities, 90,000 in finance, insurance and real estate, 82,000 in public administration, 106,000 in construction, 27,000 in agriculture, 23,000 in forestry, 16,000 in mining and 7,000 in fishing and trapping.

Commerce. Exports of British Columbia origin during 1990 totalled $16,648m. in value, while imports amounted to $14,299m. USA is the largest market for products exported through British Columbia customs ports ($6,980m. in 1990) followed by Japan ($4,636m.).

The leading exports were: Lumber, $3,792m.; pulp, $3,081m.; coal, $1,548m.; paper and newsprint, $1,491m.

Tourism. In 1990, 23·4m. tourists spent $5,183m.

COMMUNICATIONS

Roads. In 1990 there were 42,105·1 km of provincial roads and rights of way in the province, of which 20,554 km were paved. In 1990, 1,430,850 passenger cars and 498,725 commercial vehicles were licensed.

Railways. The province is served by two transcontinental railways, the Canadian Pacific Railway and the Canadian National Railway. Passenger service is provided by VIA Rail, a Crown Corporation. British Columbia is also served by the publicly owned British Columbia Railway, the Railway Freight Service of the B.C. Hydro and Power Authority, the Northern Alberta Railways Company and the Burlington

Northern Inc. The combined route-mileage of mainline track operated by the CPR, CNR and BCR totals 7,500 km. The system also includes CPR and CNR wagon ferry connections to Vancouver Island, between Prince Rupert and Alaska, and interchanges with American railways at southern border points. A metro line was opened in Vancouver in 1986.

Aviation. International airports are located at Vancouver and Victoria. Daily interprovincial and intraprovincial flights serve all main population centres. Small public and private airstrips are located throughout the province. Total passenger arrivals and departures on scheduled services (1989) 9,651,000.

Shipping. The major ports are Vancouver, New Westminster, Victoria, Nanaimo and Prince Rupert. The volume of domestic cargo handled through the port of Vancouver during 1990 was 7·3m. tonnes; international cargo, 59·1m. tonnes.

The British Columbia Ferries connect Vancouver Island with the mainland and also provide service to other coastal points; in 1990, 16·2m. passengers and 6·3m. vehicles were carried. Service by other ferry systems is also provided between Vancouver Island and the USA. The Alaska State Ferries connect Prince Rupert with centres in Alaska.

Telecommunications. The British Columbia Telephone Company had (1990) approximately 1·8m. telephones in service. In March 1990 there were 91 radio and 10 television stations originating in British Columbia. In addition there were 259 rebroadcasting stations in the province.

JUSTICE, EDUCATION AND WELFARE

Justice. The judicial system is composed of the Court of Appeal, the Supreme Court, County Courts, and various Provincial Courts, including Magistrates' Courts and Small Claims Courts. The federal courts include the Supreme Court of Canada and the Federal Court of Canada.

Education. Education, free up to Grade XII levels, is financed jointly from municipal and provincial government revenues. Attendance is compulsory from the age of 7 to 15. There were 522,706 pupils enrolled in 1,585 public schools from kindergarten to Grade XII in Sept. 1990.

The universities had a full-time enrolment of approximately 40,432 for 1990–91. They include University of British Columbia, Vancouver; University of Victoria, Victoria and Simon Fraser University, Burnaby. The regional colleges are Camosun College, Victoria; Capilano College, North Vancouver; Cariboo College, Kamloops; College of New Caledonia, Prince George; Douglas College, New Westminster; East Kootenay Community College, Cranbrook; Fraser Valley College, Chilliwack/Abbotsford; Kwantlen College, Surrey; Malaspina College, Nanaimo; North Island College, Comox; Northern Lights College, Dawson Creek/Fort St John; Northwest Community College, Terrace/Prince Rupert; Okanagan College, Kelowna with branches at Salmon Arm and Vernon; Selkirk College, Castlegar; Vancouver Community College, Vancouver.

There are also the British Columbia Institute of Technology, Burnaby; Emily Carr College of Art and Design, Vancouver; Justice Institute of British Columbia, Vancouver; Open Learning Institute, Richmond; Pacific Marine Training Institute, North Vancouver; Pacific Vocational Institute, Burnaby/Maple Ridge/ Richmond. A televised distance education and special programmes through KNOW, the Knowledge Network of the West is provided.

Health. The Government operates a hospital insurance scheme giving universal coverage after a qualifying period of 3 months' residence in the province. The province has come under a national medicare scheme which is partially subsidized by the provincial government and partially by the federal government.

Further Reading

Statistical Information: Planning and Statistics Division (Ministry of Finance and Corporate Relations, Parliament Buildings, Victoria, B.C., V8V 1X4), collects, compiles and distributes information relative to the Province.

Publications include *Manufacturers' Directory; External Trade Report* (annual); *British Columbia Economic Accounts* (annual); *British Columbia Population Forecast* (annual).

Ministry of Finance, *British Columbia Economic and Statistical Review.* Victoria, B.C. (annual)

Barman, J., *The West beyond the West: a History of British Columbia.* Toronto Univ. Press, 1991

Morley, J. T., *The Reins of Power: Governing British Columbia.* Vancouver, 1983

MANITOBA

HISTORY. The Hudson's Bay Company formed a colony on the Red River in 1812, which was part of territory annexed to Canada in 1870. The Metis colonists (part-Indian, mostly French-speaking, Catholic) objected to the arrangements for the purchase of the Company territory by Canada and the province of Manitoba was created to accommodate them. It was extended northwards and westwards in 1881 and to Hudson Bay in 1912.

AREA AND POPULATION. The area of the province is 250,946 sq. miles (649,947 sq. km), of which 211,721 sq. miles are land and 39,225 sq. miles water. From north to south it is 1,225 km and at the widest point it is 793 km.

In 1990 the population was 1,089,900. Population (Estimate 1990): Winnipeg, the capital, 647,100; other principal cities: Brandon, 39,366; Thompson, 14,379; Portage la Prairie, 13,522; Flin Flon, 7,708.

Vital statistics, *see* p. 275.

CLIMATE. The climate is cold continental, with very severe winters but pleasantly warm summers. Rainfall amounts are greatest in the months May to Sept. Winnipeg. Jan. −3°F (−19·3°C), July 67°F (19·6°C). Annual rainfall 21" (539 mm).

CONSTITUTION AND GOVERNMENT. Manitoba was known as the Red River Settlement before its entry into the Dominion in 1870. The provincial government is administered by a *Lieut.-Governor* assisted by an *Executive Council* (Cabinet) which is appointed from and responsible to a *Legislative Assembly* of 57 members elected for 5 years. Women were enfranchised in 1916. The Electoral Division Act, 1955, created 57 single-member constituencies and abolished the transferable vote. There are 28 rural electoral divisions, and 29 urban electoral divisions. The province is represented by 6 members in the Senate and 14 in the House of Commons of Canada.

Lieut.-Governor: Dr George Johnson (sworn in 12 Dec. 1986).
Flag: The British Red Ensign with the shield of the province in the fly.

Elections to the Legislative Assembly were held on 11 Sept. 1990: the Progressive Conservative Party gained 30 seats (with 42% of votes cast), the New Democratic Party, 20 (29%) and the Liberal Party, 7 (28%).

The members of the Progressive Conservative Ministry (sworn in as of Feb. 1991) were:

President of the Executive Council, Minister of Federal-Provincial Relations: Gary Albert Filmon.
Deputy-Premier, Minister of Northern and Native Affairs, Minister of Rural Development: James E. Downey. *Health:* Donald W. Orchard. *Highways and Transportation:* Albert Driedger. *Finance:* Clayton S. Manness. *Family Services:* Harold Gilleshammer. *Natural Resources:* Harry Enns. *Environment:* Glen Cummings. *Justice:* James McCrae. *Consumer and Corporate Affairs:* Linda McIntosh. *Industry, Trade and Tourism:* Eric Stefanson. *Agriculture:* Glen Findlay. *Education and Training:* Leonard Derkach. *Urban Affairs, Housing:* James A. Ernst. *Culture, Heritage and Recreation:* Bonnie Mitchelson. *Energy and Mines:* Harold Neufeld. *Labour:* Darren Praznik.

Local Government. Rural Manitoba is organized into rural municipalities which vary widely in size. Some have only 4 townships (a township is 6 sq. miles), while the largest has 22 townships. The province has 105 rural municipalities, as well as 35 incorporated towns, 39 incorporated villages and 5 incorporated cities.

On 1 Jan. 1972, the cities and towns comprising the metropolitan area of Winnipeg were amalgamated to form the City of Winnipeg. A mayor and council are elected to a central government, but councillors also sit on 'community committees' which represent the areas or wards they serve. These committees are advised by non-elected residents of the area on provision of municipal services within the community committee jurisdiction. Taxing powers and overall budgeting rest with the central council. The mayor is elected at the same time as the councillors in a city-wide vote. Revisions to the City of Winnipeg Act came into effect with the municipal elections held in Oct. 1977.

Since Jan. 1945, 17 Local Government Districts have been formed in the less densely populated areas of the province. They are administered by a provincially appointed person, who acts on the advice of locally elected councils.

In the extreme north, many communities have locally elected councils, while others are administered directly by the Department of Northern Affairs. This department provides most of the funding in all these northern settlements.

FINANCE. Provincial revenue and expenditure (current account) for fiscal years ending 31 March (in Canadian $):

	1987–88	*1988–89*	*1989–90*	*1990–91*	*1991–92* [1]
Revenue	3,772,600,000	4,678,670,300	4,658,000,000	4,798,000,000	4,917,000,000
Expenditure	4,187,900,000	4,766,060,500	4,802,000,000	5,081,000,000	5,241,000,000

[1] Budgeted.

ENERGY AND NATURAL RESOURCES

Electricity. The total generating capacity of Manitoba's power stations is 4·4m. kw. The Manitoba Hydro system, owned by the province, provides most of this power, while the city-owned Winnipeg Hydro provides about 190,000 kw. The systems have about 562,000 customers and consumption was 14·3m. kwh. in 1991.

Oil. Crude oil production in 1990 was valued at $114·8m. for the 738,000 cu. metres produced.

Minerals. Total value of minerals in 1990 was about $1,300m. Principal minerals mined are nickel, zinc, copper, and small quantities of gold and silver. Manitoba has the world's largest deposits of caesium ore.

Agriculture. Rich farmland is the main primary resource, although the area of Manitoba in farms is only about 14% of the total land area. In 1990 the total value of agricultural production in Manitoba was $2,400m., with $1,600m. from crops, $818m. from livestock and from the sale of other products.

Forestry. About 51% of the land area is wooded, of which 334,460 sq. km is productive forest land. Total sales of wood-using industries (1990, estimate) $500m.

Fur Trade. Value of fur production to the trapper was $5m. in 1986; later information is not available.

Fisheries. From 57,000 sq. km of rivers and lakes fisheries production was about $18·1m. in 1989–90. Whitefish, sauger, pickerel and pike are the principal varieties of fish caught.

INDUSTRY AND TRADE

Industry. Manufacturing, the largest industry in the province, encompasses almost every major industrial activity in Canada. Estimated shipments in 1991 totalled $7,200m. Manufacturing employed about 54,000 persons. Due to the agricultural base of the province, the food and beverage group of industries is by far the largest, valued at $1,766m. in 1990. The next largest segments are transportation equipment, $817m., primary metals, $742m. and machinery, $512m.

Trade. Products grown and manufactured in Manitoba find ready markets in other parts of Canada, in the USA, particularly the upper midwest region, and in other countries. Export shipments to foreign countries from Manitoba in 1990 were valued at $2,900m. Of total exports, $1·1m. were raw materials and $1·8m. processed and manufactured products.

Tourism. In 1989, non-Manitoban tourists numbered 2·6m. All tourists including Manitobans contributed $999m. to the economy.

COMMUNICATIONS

Roads. Highways and provincial roads totalled 19,721 km in 1991.

Railways. At 30 June 1988 the province had 6,600 km of track, not including industrial track, yards and sidings.

Aviation. A total of 108 licensed commercial air carriers operate from bases in Manitoba, as well as 5 regularly scheduled major national and international airlines.

Telecommunications. The Manitoba Telephone System provided network access to over 601,000 customers (1991).

EDUCATION. Education is controlled through locally elected school divisions. There are about 197,000 children (1991–92) enrolled in the province's elementary and secondary schools. Manitoba has 4 universities with an enrolment of about 37,000 during the 1991–92 year; the University of Manitoba, founded in 1877, in Winnipeg, the University of Winnipeg, and Brandon University. Expenditure (estimate) on education in the 1990–91 fiscal year was $935m.

Three community colleges, in Brandon, The Pas and Winnipeg, offer 2-year diploma courses in a number of fields, as well as specialized training in many trades. They also give a large number and variety of shorter courses, both at their campuses and in many communities throughout the province.

Further Reading

General Information: Inquiries may be addressed to the Information Services Branch, Room 29, Legislative Building, Winnipeg, R3C OV8.

The Department of Agriculture publishes: *Year Book of Manitoba Agriculture*
Information Services Branch publishes: *Manitoba Facts*
Manitoba Statistical Review. Manitoba Bureau of Statistics, Quarterly
Twelfth Census of Canada: Manitoba. Statistics Canada, 1981
Jackson, J. A., *The Centennial History of Manitoba*. Toronto, 1970
Morton, W. L., *Manitoba: A History*. Univ. of Toronto Press, 1967

NEW BRUNSWICK

HISTORY. Touched by Jacques Cartier in 1534, New Brunswick was first explored by Samuel de Champlain in 1604. It was ceded by the French in the Treaty of Utrecht in 1713 and became a permanent British possession in 1763. It was separated from Nova Scotia and became a province in June 1784, as a result of the great influx of United Empire Loyalists. Responsible government came into being in 1848, and consisted of an executive council, a legislative council (later abolished) and a House of Assembly.

AREA AND POPULATION. The area of the province is 28,354 sq. miles (73,440 sq. km), of which 27,633 sq. miles (71,569 sq. km) are land area. The population (census 1986) was 710,422. Estimate (1991) 726,800. Of the individuals identifying a single ethnic origin (at the 1986 census), 46·9% were British and 33·3% French. Other significant ethnic groups were German, Dutch and Scandinavian. Among those who provided a multiple response 9·9% were of British and French descent and 4·3% British and other. In 1986 there were 9,375 Native People or Native People and other. Census 1986 population of urban centres: Saint John, 76,381; Moncton, 55,468; Fredericton (capital), 44,352; Bathurst, 14,683; Edmundston, 11,497; Campbellton, 9,073.

Vital statistics, *see* p. 275.

CLIMATE. A cool temperate climate, with rain at all seasons but temperatures modified by the influence of the Gulf Stream. Saint John. Jan. 18°F (−7·8°C), July 62°F (16·7°C). Annual rainfall 57" (1,444·4 mm).

CONSTITUTION AND GOVERNMENT. The government is vested in a Lieut.-Governor and a Legislative Assembly of 58 members each of whom is individually elected to represent the voters in one constituency or riding. A simultaneous translation system is used in the Assembly. Any Canadian subject of full age and 6 months' residence is entitled to vote. As a result of the provincial election held on 23 Sept. 1991, the Legislative Assembly consists of 46 Liberals, 8 from the Confederation of Regions Party, 3 Progressive Conservatives and 1 from the New Democratic Party. The Liberals won 47% of votes cast. The province has 10 members in the Canadian Senate and 10 members in the federal House of Commons.

Lieut.-Governor: Hon. Gilbert Finn (appointed Aug. 1987).

Flag: A banner of the Arms, *i.e.,* yellow charged with a black heraldic ship on wavy lines of blue and white; across the top a red band with a gold lion.

The members of the Liberal government are as follows (Oct. 1991):

Premier: Hon. Francis J. McKenna.
Intergovernmental Affairs, Justice, Attorney General: Hon. Edmond Blanchard. *Finance and Board of Management:* Hon. Allan Maher. *Supply and Services:* Hon. Laureen Jarett. *Transportation:* Hon. Sheldon Lee. *Natural Resources and Energy:* Hon. Alan Graham. *Agriculture:* Hon. Gerald Clavette. *Health and Community Services:* Hon. Russell King, MD. *Income Assistance:* Hon. Ann Breault. *Advanced Education and Labour:* Hon. Vaughn Blaney. *Education:* Hon. Paul Duffie. *Municipal Affairs and Housing:* Hon. Marcelle Mersereau. *Environment:* Hon. Jane Barry. *Economic Development and Tourism:* Hon. Denis Losier. *Fisheries and Aquaculture:* Hon. Camille Theriault. *Chairman of NB Brunswick Power:* Hon. Raymond Frenette. *Solicitor General:* Hon. Bruce Smith.

Local Government. Under the reforms introduced in 1967 the province has assumed complete administrative and financial responsibility for education, health, welfare and administration of justice. Local government is now restricted to provision of services of a strictly local nature. Under the new municipal structure, units include existing and new cities, towns and villages. Counties have disappeared as municipal units. Areas with limited populations have become local service districts. The former local improvement districts have become towns, villages or local service districts depending on their size.

FINANCE. The ordinary budget (in Canadian $1m.) is shown as follows (financial years ended 31 March):

	1987	1988	1989	1990
Gross revenue	2,770·0	3,024·9	3,322·7	3,583·3
Gross expenditure	2,891·0	3,131·7	3,253·9	3,470·8

Funded debt and capital loans outstanding (exclusive of Treasury Bills) as of 31 March 1990 was $4,331m. Sinking funds held by the province at 31 March 1990, $1,393m. The ordinary budget excludes capital spending.

ENERGY AND NATURAL RESOURCES

Electricity. Hydro-electric, thermal and nuclear generating stations of the NB Power had an installed capacity of 3,221,976 kw. at 31 March 1991, consisting of

14 generating stations. The Mactaquac hydroelectric development near Fredericton, has a name plate capacity of 653,400 kw. The largest thermal generating station, Coleson Cove, near Saint John, has over 1m. kw. of installed capacity. Atlantic Canada's first nuclear generating station, a 630,000 kw. plant on a promontory in the Bay of Fundy, near Saint John, went into operation in 1983. New Brunswick is electrically inter-connected with utilities in neighbouring provinces of Quebec, Nova Scotia and Prince Edward Island, as well as the New England States of the USA. Electricity exports accounted for 29·3% of revenue in 1990–91. Total revenue amounted to $908·5m.

Minerals. In 1990, approximately 18 different metals, minerals and commodities were produced. These included lead, zinc, copper, cadmium, bismuth, gold, silver, antimony, potash, salt, limestone, oil, gas, coal, sand, gravel, clay, peat and marl. The total value of minerals produced in 1990 reached $886·1m. The largest contributors to mineral production are zinc, silver, lead and peat accounting for over 65% of total value in 1990. In Canada in 1990, New Brunswick ranked first in the production of bismuth, second in lead and antimony, third in zinc, fourth in silver and fifth in the production of copper. Antimony is mined at Lake George and production resumed at the Durham Resources mine near Fredericton in 1985. Peat, rapidly becoming a major industry, is produced from 18 operations in the north. Two potash mines are in operation in the Sussex area, including the Potacan Mining Company where production commenced in 1985. Oil and natural gas continue to be produced in the Stoney Creek and Hillsborough areas. Gordex Minerals produced its first gold in 1986 using the heap leach process. Coal is strip-mined at Grand Lake, producing some 550,000 tonnes annually. Not all of the province's minerals have been explored sufficiently and research continues. A new 5-year, $10m. Canada-New Brunswick Cooperation Agreement on Minerals was signed in Sept. 1990. Federal and Provincial agencies are co-operating on field, laboratory and other projects.

Agriculture. The total area under crops is estimated at 129,475 ha. Farms numbered 3,554 and averaged 115 ha each (census 1986). Potatoes account for 28·4% of total farm cash income. Mixed farming is common throughout the province. Dairy farming is centred around the larger urban areas, and is located mainly along the Saint John River Valley and in the south-eastern sections of the province. Income from dairy operations provides 21·4% of farm cash income. New Brunswick is self-sufficient in fluid milk and supplies a processing industry. For particulars of agricultural production and livestock, *see under* CANADA, pp. 000–00. Farm cash receipts in 1990 were $276m.

Forestry. New Brunswick contains some 63,000 sq. km of productive forest lands. The value of manufacturing shipments for the wood related industries in 1990 was $2,213·6m., representing 36% of total shipments in the province. The paper and allied industry group is the largest component of the industry contributing 74·2% of forestry output. Wood industries employ about 13,000 people for all aspects of the forest industry, including harvesting, processing and transportation. Practically all forest products are exported from the province's numerous ports and harbours near which many of the mills are located or sent by road or rail to the USA.

Fisheries. Commercial fishing is one of the most important primary industries of the province, employing 7,764. Nearly 50 commercial species of fish and shellfish are landed, including scallop, shrimp, crab, herring and cod. Landings in 1990 (153,046 tonnes) amounted to $99·5m. In 1991 there were 163 fish processing plants employing nearly 7,700 people in peak periods. In 1990 molluscs and crustaceans ranked first with a value of $70·7m., 71% of the total landed value; pelagic fish second, 17·8%, and groundfish third, 10·9%. Exports (1990) $245·7m., mainly to the USA and Japan.

INDUSTRY. In 1991 there were 1,642 manufacturing and processing establishments, employing about 45,600 persons. New Brunswick's location, with deepwater harbours open throughout the year and container facilities at Saint John, makes it ideal for exporting. Industries include food and beverages, paper and allied industries, timber products. About 20% of the industrial labour force work in Saint John.

TOURISM. Tourism is one of the leading contributors to the economy. In 1990, expenditures of non-resident and resident travellers were approximately $612m.

COMMUNICATIONS

Roads. There are about 1,541·9 km of arterial highways and 2,381·7 km of collector roads, all of which are hard-surfaced. 12,279·9 km of local roads provide access to most areas in the province. The main highway system, including 596·4 km of the Trans-Canada Highway, links the province with the principal roads in Quebec, Nova Scotia, and Prince Edward Island, as well as the Interstate Highway System in the eastern seaboard states of the USA. Passenger vehicles, 31 March 1989, numbered 309,307; commercial vehicles, 129,814; motor cycles, 9,901.

Railways. New Brunswick is served by main lines of both Canadian Pacific and Canadian National railways.

Telecommunications. In 1990 the New Brunswick Telephone Co. Ltd had 546,106 telephones in service. The province is served by 25 radio stations. Eighteen are privately owned and 4 owned by the Canadian Broadcasting Corporation and 3 are university stations. Eight stations broadcast in the French language, 2 are bilingual and the CBC International Service broadcasts in several languages from its station at Sackville. The province is served by 7 television stations, 2 of which broadcast in French.

Newspapers. New Brunswick had (1990) 4 daily newspapers, 1 in French, and 24 weekly newspapers, 6 in French or bilingual.

EDUCATION. Public education is free and non-sectarian. There are 4 universities. The University of New Brunswick at Fredericton (founded 13 Dec. 1785 by the Loyalists, elevated to university status in 1823, reorganized as the University of New Brunswick in 1859) had 7,114 full-time students at the Fredericton campus and 1,383 full-time students at the Saint John campus (1990–91); Mount Allison University at Sackville had 1,854 full-time students; the Université de Moncton at Moncton, 3,940 full-time students, with 316 and 573 full-time students respectively at its satellite campuses at Shippegan and Edmundston; St Thomas University at Fredericton, 1,496 full-time students. During the period 1 July 1990 to 30 June 1991, there were 17,940 students enrolled full-time at 10 Community College campuses and at various campus training centres.

There were, in Sept. 1990, 132,843 students and 7,968 full-time (equivalent) teachers in the province's 421 schools. There are 42 school boards.

Further Reading

Industrial Information: Dept. of Economic Development and Tourism, Fredericton. *Economic Information:* Dept. of Finance and Board of Management, New Brunswick Statistics Agency, Fredericton. *General Information:* Communications New Brunswick, Fredericton.

Directory of Products and Manufacturers. Department of Commerce and Development; Annual
Thompson, C., *New Brunswick Inside Out.* Ottawa, 1977
Trueman, S., *The Fascinating World of New Brunswick.* Fredericton, 1973

NEWFOUNDLAND AND LABRADOR

HISTORY. Archaeological finds at L'Anse-au-Meadow in northern Newfoundland show that the Vikings had established a colony there at about A.D. 1000. This site is the only known Viking colony in North America. Newfoundland was discovered by John Cabot 24 June 1497, and was soon frequented in the summer months by the Portuguese, Spanish and French for its fisheries. It was formally occupied in Aug. 1583 by Sir Humphrey Gilbert on behalf of the English Crown, but various attempts to colonize the island remained unsuccessful. Although British sovereignty was recognized in 1713 by the Treaty of Utrecht, disputes over fishing rights with the French were not finally settled till 1904. By the Anglo-French Convention of 1904, France renounced her exclusive fishing rights along part of the coast, granted under the Treaty of Utrecht, but retained sovereignty of the offshore islands of St Pierre and Miquelon.

AREA AND POPULATION. Area, 143,501 sq. miles (371,690 sq. km) of which freshwater, 13,139 sq. miles (34,030 sq. km). In March 1927 the Privy Council decided the boundary between Canada and Newfoundland in Labrador. This area, now part of the Province of Newfoundland and Labrador, is 102,699 sq. miles. The coastline is extremely irregular. Bays, fiords and inlets are numerous and there are many good harbours with deep water close to shore. The coast is rugged with bold rocky cliffs from 200 to 400 ft high; in the Bay of Islands some of the islands rise 500 ft, with the adjacent shore 1,000 ft above tide level. The interior is a plateau of moderate elevation and the chief relief features trend north-east and south-west. Long Range, the most notable of these, begins at Cape Ray and extends north-east for 200 miles, the highest peak reaching 2,673 ft. Approximately one-third of the area is covered by water. Grand Lake, the largest body of water, has an area of about 200 sq. miles. The principal rivers flow towards the north-east. On the borders of the lakes and water-courses good land is generally found, particularly in the valleys of the Terra Nova River, the Gander River, the Exploits River and the Humber River, which are also heavily timbered.

Census population, 1986, was 568,349.

The capital of Newfoundland is the City of St John's (161,901, metropolitan area). The other cities are Corner Brook (22,719), Mt Pearl (20,293); important towns are Labrador City (8,664), Gander (10,207), Conception Bay South (15,531), Stephenville (7,994), Grand Falls (9,121), Happy Valley–Goose Bay (7,248), Marystown (6,660), Channel-Port aux Basques (5,901), Windsor (5,545), Carbonear (5,337), Bonavista (4,605), Wabana (4,057), Wabush (2,637).

Vital statistics, *see* p. 275.

CLIMATE. The cool temperate climate is marked by heavy precipitation, distributed evenly over the year, a cool summer and frequent fogs in spring. St. John's. Jan. 25°F (–4°C), July 60°F (15·5°C). Annual rainfall 54" (1,367 mm).

CONSTITUTION AND GOVERNMENT. Until 1832 Newfoundland was ruled by the Governor under instructions of the Colonial Office. In that year a Legislature was brought into existence, but the Governor and his Executive Council were not responsible to it. Under the constitution of 1855, which lasted until its suspension in 1934, the government was administered by the Governor appointed by the Crown with an Executive Council responsible to the House of Assembly of 27 elected members and a Legislative Council of 24 members nominated for life by the Governor in Council. Women were enfranchised in 1925. At the Imperial Conference of 1917 Newfoundland was constituted as a Dominion.

In 1933 the financial situation had become so critical that the Government of Newfoundland asked the Government of the UK to appoint a Royal Commission to investigate conditions. On the strength of their recommendations, the parliamentary form of government was suspended and Government by Commission was inaugurated on 16 Feb. 1934.

A National Convention, elected in 1946, made, in 1948, recommendations to H.M. Government in Great Britain as to the possible forms of future government to be submitted to the people at a national referendum. Two referenda were held. In the first referendum (June 1948) the three forms of government submitted to the people were: Commission of government for 5 years, confederation with Canada and responsible government as it existed in 1933. No one form of government received a clear majority of the votes polled, and commission of government, receiving the fewest votes, was eliminated. In the second referendum (July 1948) confederation with Canada received 78,408 and responsible government 71,464 votes.

In the Canadian Senate on 18 Feb. 1949 Royal assent was given to the terms of union of Newfoundland and Labrador with Canada, and on 23 March 1949, in the House of Lords, London, Royal assent was given to an amendment to the British North America Act made necessary by the inclusion of Newfoundland and Labrador as the tenth Province of Canada.

Under the terms of union of Newfoundland and Labrador with Canada, which was signed at Ottawa on 11 Dec. 1948, the constitution of the Legislature of Newfoundland and Labrador as it existed immediately prior to 16 Feb. 1934 shall, subject to the terms of the British North America Acts, 1867 to 1946, continue as the constitution of the Legislature of the Province of Newfoundland and Labrador until altered under the authority of the said Acts.

The franchise was in 1965 extended to all male and female residents who have attained the age of 19 years and are otherwise qualified as electors.

The House of Assembly (Amendment) Act, 1979, established 52 electoral districts and 52 members of the Legislature.

In Oct. 1991 there were 34 Liberals, 17 Progressive-Conservatives and 1 New Democrat.

The province is represented by 6 members in the Senate and by 7 members in the House of Commons of Canada.

Lieut.-Governor: Hon. Frederick William Russell (assumed office 5 Nov. 1991).

Flag: White, in the hoist 4 solid blue triangles; in the fly 2 red triangles voided white, and between them a yellow tongue bordered in red.

The Liberal Executive Council was, in Nov. 1991, composed as follows:

Premier: Clyde Kirby Wells.

President of Executive Council and President of Treasury Board: Richard Winston Baker. *Fisheries:* Walter Carmichael Carter. *Employment and Labour Relations:* Roger Dale Grimes. *Health:* Christopher Robert Decker. *Justice:* Paul David Dicks. *Social Services:* William Patrick Hogan. *Forestry and Agriculture:* Graham Ralph Flight. *Development:* Charles Joseph Furey. *Mines and Energy:* Dr Rex Vincent Gibbons. *Works, Services and Transportation:* David Samuel Gilbert. *Municipal and Provincial Affairs:* Eric Augustus Gullage. *Environment and Lands:* Patricia Anne Cowan. *Finance:* Dr Hubert William Kitchen. *Education:* Dr Philip John Warren. *Speaker of the House of Assembly:* Thomas Lush.

Agent-General in London: H. Watson Jamer (60 Trafalgar Sq., WC2).

FINANCE. Budget[1] in Canadian $1,000 for fiscal years ended 31 March:

	1986–87	1987–88	1988–89	1989–90	1990–91 [2]	1991–92 [3]
Gross revenue	2,233,339	2,424,887	2,600,429	2,844,163	2,878,506	3,042,251
Gross expenditure	2,260,845	2,456,146	2,601,221	2,766,308	2,995,724	3,096,041

Capital account:

	1988–89	1989–90	1990–91 [2]	1991–92 [3]
Gross revenue	63,968,000	87,139,000	97,552,000	176,652,000
Gross expenditure	289,101,000	339,852,000	357,324,000	417,969,000

[1] Current amount only.   [2] Revised estimates.   [3] Estimates.

Public debenture debt as at 31 March 1991 (preliminary) was $4,729m.; sinking fund, $1,447·2m.

ENERGY AND NATURAL RESOURCES

Electricity. The electrical energy requirements of the province are met mainly by hydro-electric power, with petroleum fuels being utilized to provide the balance.

The total amount of energy generated in the province in 1989 was 34,940,125 mwh., of which 94% was derived from hydro-electric facilities. The greater part of the energy produced in 1989 came from Churchill Falls, of which 24,370,591 mwh. was sold to Hydro-Quebec under the terms of a long-term contract. Energy consumed in the province during 1989 totalled 10,569,534 mwh., with 8,447,338 mwh., or 80%, coming from hydro-electric facilities.

At Dec. 1989 total electrical generating capacity in the province was 7,465 mw., with hydro-electric plants accounting for 6,656 mw., or 89%. It is estimated that potential additional hydro-electric generating capacity of up to 4·5m. kw. can be developed at various sites in Labrador.

Oil. Since 1965, 140 wells have been drilled on the Continental Margin of the Province. In 1990 offshore exploration expenditures were $36m. (preliminary).

By 31 Dec. 1985 there had been 20 significant hydrocarbon discoveries off Newfoundland and delineation drilling had been initiated or was ongoing at 6: Terra Nova, Ben Nevis, Whiterose, North Ben Nevis and Mara. In 1986 only the Hibernia discovery had commercial capability and the Canada-Newfoundland Offshore Petroleum Board approved Mobil Oil Canada's development plan for the Hibernia Project, with production starting in the early 1990's. In Sept. 1990 the governments of Canada and Newfoundland and a development consortium signed an agreement to start developing the Hibernia discovery from Oct. 1990.

In 1979, a discovery of oil was made on the Hibernia geological structure located 164 nautical miles east of Cape Spear. The discovery well, Hibernia H-15, tested medium gravity, sweet crude from several intervals with a reported total producing capability in excess of 20,000 bbls of oil per day.

Minerals. The mineral resources are vast but only partially documented. Large deposits of iron ore, with an ore reserve of over 5,000m. tons at Labrador City, Wabush City and in the Knob Lake area are supplying approximately half of Canada's production. Other large deposits of iron ore are known to exist in the Julienne Lake area.

There are a variety of other minerals being produced in the province in more limited amounts.

Uranium deposits in the Kaipokak Bay area near Makkovik in Labrador are presently being studied by Brinex. The Central Mineral Belt, which extends from the Smallwood Reservoir to the Atlantic coast near Makkovik, holds uranium, copper, beryllium and molybdenite potential.

In 1986 a gold mine was being developed at Hope Brook on the south coast east of Port aux Basques. Full production from an underground operation using conventional carbon-in-pulp gold processing was planned to start in late 1988. The gold mine closed temporarily in May 1991 for environmental reasons.

Production in 1990 (preliminary): Iron ore, 19,955,000 tonnes ($695,824,000); zinc, 21,498,000 kg ($41,426,000); asbestos, 66,000 tonnes ($26,377,000); sand and gravel, 4,093,000m. tonnes ($17,445,000); stone, 1,116,000 tonnes ($5,951,000); peat, 2,000 tonnes ($96,000).

Agriculture. The estimated value of agricultural products sold, including livestock, 1990, was $57·8m.

Forestry. The forestry economy in the province is mainly dependent on the operation of 3 newsprint mills. In 1990 the gross value of newsprint exported from these 3 mills totalled $483·8m. Lumber mills and saw-log operations produced 48m. flat board metres in 1989–90.

Fisheries. The principal fish landings are cod, flounder, redfish, Queen crabs, lobster, salmon and herring. In 1990 (preliminary) a yearly average of some 8,200 persons were employed by the fish-processing industry and there were 27,904 licensed full-, part-time and casual fishermen engaged in harvesting operations. 250 processing operations were licensed in 1990. The production of fresh and frozen fish products was $630m. (estimate) in 1990.

The total catch in 1990 (preliminary) was 491,575 tonnes valued at $251,383,000, which comprised: Cod, 239,407 tonnes ($130,415,000); flounders and soles, 51,708

($19,515,000); herring, 25,738 tonnes ($3,249,000); redfish, 25,150 ($6,932,000); lobster, 2,752 ($12,011,000); salmon, 544 ($2,403,000); capelin, 88,972 ($16,084,000); crab, 11,024 ($13,151,000); other, 46,282 ($48,540,000).

INDUSTRY. The total value of manufacturing shipments in 1990 was $1,494m. This consists largely of first-stage processing of primary resource products with two of the largest components being paper and fish products.

TRADE UNIONS. There were 540 unions in 1989 representing 80,429 members of international and national unions and government employee associations.

COMMUNICATIONS

Roads. In 1989 there were 8,088 km, of which 5,887 were paved.

Railways. In 1989 the Quebec North Shore and Labrador Railway operated 576 km of standard-gauge main railway track. The route runs from Sept-Iles, Quebec, to Shefferville, Quebec, with a branch at Ross Bay Junction to Wabush, Labrador.

Aviation. The province is linked to the rest of Canada by regular air services provided by Air Canada, Canadian International Airways, Quebecair and a number of smaller air carriers.

Shipping. At 31 Dec. 1990 there were 1,632 ships on register in Newfoundland. In 1989 Marine Atlantic provided a freight and passenger service all year round to the south of the island and during the ice-free season as far north as Nain. There is a year-round ferry from Port-aux-Basques to North Sydney, Nova Scotia, and seasonal ferries connect Argentia with North Sydney, and Lewisporte with Goosebay, Labrador.

Post. There were 466 post offices in 1989. Telephone access lines numbered 221,198 in 1988 (170,335 private). There were 2,935 public pay phones.

EDUCATION. The number of schools in 1990–91 was 538. The enrolment was 127,618; full-time teachers numbered 8,180. The Memorial University, offering courses in arts, science, engineering, education, nursing and medicine, had 17,635 full- and part-time students in 1991 (calendar year). Total expenditure for education by the Government in 1991–92 (estimate) was $779·2m.

Further Reading

Blackburn, R. H. (ed.) *Encyclopaedia of Canada: Newfoundland Supplement*. Toronto, 1949
Horwood, H., *Newfoundland*. Toronto, 1969
Loture, R. de, *Histoire de la grande pêche de Terre-Neuve*. Paris, 1949
Mercer, G. A., *The Province of Newfoundland and Labrador: Geographical Aspects*. Ottawa, 1970
Perlin, A. B., *The Story of Newfoundland, 1497–1959*. St John's, 1959
Tanner, V., *Outlines of Geography. Life and Customs of Newfoundland–Labrador*. 2 vols. Helsinki, 1944, and Toronto, 1947
Taylor, T. G., *Newfoundland: A Study of Settlement*. Toronto, 1946

NOVA SCOTIA

HISTORY. The first permanent settlement was made by the French early in the 17th century, and the province was called Acadia until finally ceded to the British by the Treaty of Utrecht in 1713.

AREA AND POPULATION. The area of the province is 21,425 sq. miles (55,000 sq. km), of which 20,401 sq. miles are land area, 1,024 sq. miles water area. The population (census 1986) was 873,199; (estimate 1991) 899,600.

Population of the principal cities and towns (census 1986): Halifax, 113,577; Dartmouth 65,243; Sydney, 27,754; Glace Bay, 20,467; Truro, 12,124; New

Glasgow, 10,022; Amherst, 9,671; New Waterford, 8,326; Sydney Mines, 8,063; Bedford, 8,010; North Sydney, 7,472; Yarmouth, 7,617.

Vital statistics, *see* p. 275.

CLIMATE. A cool temperate climate, with rainfall occurring evenly over the year. The Gulf Stream moderates the temperatures in winter so that ports remain ice-free. Halifax. Jan. 23°F (–5°C), July 64°F (17·8°C). Annual rainfall 56" (1,412 mm).

CONSTITUTION AND GOVERNMENT. Under the British North America Act of 1867 the legislature of Nova Scotia may exclusively make laws in relation to local matters, including direct taxation within the province, education and the administration of justice. The legislature of Nova Scotia consists of a Lieut.-Governor, appointed and paid by the federal government, and holding office for 5 years, and a House of Assembly of 52 members, chosen by popular vote at least every 5 years. The province is represented in the Canadian Senate by 11 members, and in the House of Commons by 11.

The franchise and eligibility to the legislature are granted to every person, male or female, if of age (19 years), a British subject or Canadian citizen, and a resident in the province for 1 year and 2 months before the date of the writ of election in the county or electoral district of which the polling district forms part, and if not by law otherwise disqualified. State of parties in Sept. 1991: 26 Progressive Conservatives, 22 Liberals, 3 New Democrats, 1 independent.

Lieut.-Governor: Lloyd Crouse.

Flag: A banner of the Arms, *i.e.*, white with a blue diagonal cross, bearing in the centre the royal shield of Scotland.

The members of the Progressive Conservative Ministry were as follows in Sept. 1991:

Premier, President of the Executive Council, Minister of Intergovernmental Affairs, Minister responsible for Sydney Steel Corporation: Hon. Donald Cameron.

Deputy Premier, Deputy President of the Executive Council, Minister of Industry, Trade and Technology, Chairman of the Policy Board, Minister responsible for the Administration of the Nova Scotia Research Foundation Corporation Act, for the Nova Scotia business Capital Corporation Act, for Small Business Development Corporation, for Voluntary Planning Act, for Youth: Hon. Tom McInnis. *Tourism and Culture, Minister responsible for the Heritage Property Act:* Hon. Terry Donahoe. *Transport and Communications:* Hon. Kenneth Streatch. *Finance, Chairman of the Management Board, Minister in charge of the Lottery Act, Minister responsible for the Civil Service Act:* Hon. Greg Kerr. *Attorney-General, Solicitor-General, Provincial Secretary, Minister for the Administration of the Human Rights Act, Minister in charge of the Regulations Act:* Hon. Joel Matheson, QC. *Education, Advanced Education and Job Training:* Hon. Ron Giffin. *Labour:* Hon. Leroy Legere. *Environment, responsible for the Emergency Measures Organization Act:* Hon. John Leefe. *Health and Fitness, Registrar General, Minister in charge of the Administration of the Drug Dependency Act:* Hon. George C. Moody. *Community Services, Minister responsible for reporting on Disabled Persons, responsible for the Administration of the Advisory Council on the Status of Women Act:* Hon. Marie Dechman. *Municipal Affairs:* Hon. Brian Young. *Minister of Fisheries, Minister responsible for Acadian Affairs, responsible for Aboriginal Affairs:* Hon. Guy LeBlanc. *Consumer Affairs, Minister in charge of the Residential Tenancies Act, responsible for the Housing Development Act:* Hon. Don McInnes. *Agriculture and Marketing:* Hon. George Archibald. *Lands and Forests, responsible for Tidal Power Corporation:* Hon. Charles MacNeil. *Minister of Government Services, responsible for the Sport and Recreation Commission, for the Administration of the Liquor Control Act, for the Communications and Information Act:* Hon. Neil LeBlanc.

Representative in the UK: Ray Vandry, (14 Pall Mall, London, SW1Y 5LU).

Representative in the USA: Wendell Sandford, (4 Copley Place, Boston, Mass. 02116).

Local Government. The main divisions of the province for governmental purposes are the 3 cities, the 39 towns and the 24 rural municipalities, each governed by a council and a mayor or warden. The cities have independent charters, and the various towns take their powers from and are limited by The Towns Act, and the various municipalities take their powers from and are limited by The Municipal Act as revised in 1967. The majority of municipalities comprise 1 county, but 6 counties are divided into 2 municipalities each. In no case do the boundaries of any municipality overlap county lines. The 18 counties as such have no administrative functions.

Any city (of which there are 3) or incorporated town (of which there are 39) that lies within the boundaries of a municipality is excluded from any jurisdiction by the municipal council and has its own government.

FINANCE. Revenue is derived from provincial sources, payments from the federal government under the Federal-Provincial Fiscal Arrangements and Established Programs Financing Act. Recoveries consist generally of amounts received under various federal cost-shared programmes. Main sources of provincial revenues include income and sales taxes.

Revenue, expenditure and debt (in Canadian $1m.) for fiscal years ending 31 March:

	1988	1989	1990	1991 [1]	1992 [2]
Budgetary Transactions					
Current Expenditure	3,283·6	3,526·6	3,773·9	4,057·4	4,254·4
Current Revenues and Recoveries	3,164·5	3,465·5	3,712·1	3,895·5	4,062·6
Operating Deficit (Surplus)	119·1	61·1	61·8	162·1	191·8
Sinking Fund Instalments and Serial Retirements	86·5	90·9	100·8	99·9	108·0
Net Capital Expenditures	219·3	297·9	335·9	254·4	263·1
Net Budgetary Transactions	421·1	449·9	498·5	500·1	562·9
Non-Budgetary Transactions					
Capital Expenditures	2·5	2·7	3·2	1·0	3·0
Net Increase (Decrease) in Advances and Investments	(18·8)	7·7	(1·8)	38·9	36·8
Net Other Transactions	12·8	4·6	(21·7)	(22·1)	(2·8)
Non-Budgetary Transactions	(29·1)	15·0	20·3	17·8	37·0
	(392·0)	464·9	478·2	517·9	599·9

[1] Forecast. [2] Estimate.

Banking. All major Canadian banks are represented with numerous branch locations throughout the Province. In March 1991 total deposits with chartered banks in Nova Scotia totalled $5,103m.

NATURAL RESOURCES

Minerals. Principal minerals in 1990 were: Coal, 3·4m. tonnes, valued at $199·2m.; gypsum, 6·2m. tonnes, valued at $54·2m.; sand and gravel, 6m. tonnes, valued at $18·9m. Total value of mineral production in 1990 was about $452·3m.

Agriculture. Dairying, poultry and egg production, livestock and fruit growing are the most important branches. Farm cash receipts for 1990 were estimated at $315·7m., with an additional $3·8m. going to persons on farms as income in kind.

Cash receipts from sale of dairy products were $86·9m., with total milk and cream sales of 177,602,000 litres.

The production of poultry meat in 1990 was 23,810 tonnes, of which 20,456 tonnes were chickens and fowls and 3,354 tonnes were turkeys. Egg production was 19·4m. dozen.

The main 1990 fruit crops were apples, 62,868 tonnes; blueberries, 12,773 tonnes; and strawberries, 2,155 tonnes.

Forestry. The estimated forest area of Nova Scotia is 15,555 sq. miles (40,298 sq. km), of which about 25% is owned by the province. The principal trees are spruce, balsam fir, hemlock, pine, larch, birch, oak, maple, poplar and ash. 3,905,217 cu. metres of round forest products were produced in 1989.

Fisheries. The fisheries of the province in 1990 had a landed value of $426m. of sea fish including scallop fishery, $71·7m., and lobster fishery, $119·7m. In 1988 there were 7,364 employees in the fish processing industry; the value of shipment of goods was $1,066·6m.

INDUSTRY. The number of manufacturing establishments was 816 in 1988; the number of employees was 39,928; wages and salaries, $985·7m. The value of shipments in 1990, was $6,015m., and the leading industries were food, paper and allied industries and transportation equipment.

TRADE UNIONS. Total union membership in 1990 was 109,623 belonging to 99 unions comprised of 662 individual locals. The largest union membership was in the service sector followed by public administration and defence.

COMMUNICATIONS

Roads. In 1990 there were 25,975 km of highways; paved included 128 km freeway, 2,667 km arterial, 4,916 km collector and 5,454 km local. 12,770 km of highway are unpaved.

Railways. The province is covered with a network of 705 km of mainline track. In 1990 it carried 20·6m. tonnes of freight.

Civil Aviation. There is direct air service to all major Canadian points and international scheduled service to Boston, New York, Bermuda, London, Glasgow and Amsterdam. There are winter charter services to Florida and the Caribbean.

Shipping. Ferry services connect Nova Scotia with Newfoundland, Prince Edward Island, New Brunswick and Maine. Direct service by container vessels is provided from the Port of Halifax to ports in the USA (east and west coast), Europe, Asia, Australia/New Zealand and the Caribbean.

JUSTICE AND EDUCATION

Justice. The Supreme Court (Trial Division and Appeal Division) is the superior court of Nova Scotia and has original and appellate jurisdiction in all civil and criminal matters unless they have been specifically assigned to another court by Statute. An appeal from the Supreme Court, Appeal Division, is to the Supreme Court of Canada. The other courts in the Province are the Provincial Court, which hears criminal matters only, the Small Claims Court, which has limited monetary jurisdiction, Probate Court, County Court, which has jurisdiction in criminal matters as well as original jurisdiction over actions not exceeding $50,000, and Family Court. Young offenders are tried in the Family Court or the Provincial Court.

For the year ending 31 March 1990 there were 3,509 adult admissions to provincial custody; of these, 1,993 were sentenced.

Education. Public education in Nova Scotia is free, compulsory and undenominational through elementary and high school. Attendance is compulsory to the age of 16. In addition to 495 public schools there are the Atlantic Provinces Resource Centres for the Hearing Handicapped and for the Visually Impaired; the Shelburne Youth Centre for young offenders and the Nova Scotia Residential Centre for delinquent children; and the Nova Scotia Youth Training Centre for mentally handicapped children. The province has 19 universities, colleges and technical institutions, of which the largest is Dalhousie University in Halifax. The Nova Scotia Agricultural College and the Nova Scotia Teachers' College are located at Truro. The Technical University of Nova Scotia at Halifax grants degrees in engineering and architecture.

The Department of Vocational and Technical Training administers 2 institutes of technology, a nautical institute and 14 other facilities under the system of Community colleges. It also provides in-school training for the Department of Labour Apprenticeship programme.

The Nova Scotia government offers financial support and organizational assistance to local school boards for provision of weekend and evening courses in academic and avocational subjects, and citizenship for new Canadians. It also provides local authorities with specialist support services to assist them in providing community workshops and it operates a correspondence study service for children and adults.

Total estimated expenditure on all levels of education for the year 1991-92 was $1,489·7m., of which 70% was borne by the provincial government. In 1991–92, classrooms operated in 529 elementary-secondary schools, with 10,230 teachers and 167,930 pupils.

Further Reading

Nova Scotia Fact Book. N.S. Department of Industry, Trade and Technology, Halifax, 1991
Nova Scotia Resource Atlas. N.S. Department of Industry, Trade and Technology, Halifax, 1986
Nova Scotia Statistical Review. N. S. Department of Industry, Trade and Technology, Halifax, 1991
Nova Scotia Facts at a Glance. N. S. Department of Industry, Trade and Technology, Halifax, 1991

Atlantic Provinces Economic Council. *The Atlantic Vision, 1990.* Halifax, 1979
Beck, M., *The Evolution of Municipal Government in Nova Scotia, 1749–1973.* 1973
McCreath, P. and Leefe, J., *History of Early Nova Scotia.* Halifax, 1982
Vaison, R., *Nova Scotia Past and Present: A Bibliography and Guide.* Halifax, 1976

ONTARIO

HISTORY. The French explorer Samuel de Champlain explored the Ottawa River from 1613. The area was governed by the French, first under a joint stock company and then as a royal province, from 1627 and was ceded to Great Britain in 1763. A constitutional act of 1791 created there the province of Upper Canada, largely to accommodate loyalists of English descent who had immigrated after the United States war of independence. Upper Canada entered the Confederation as Ontario in 1867.

AREA AND POPULATION. The area is 412,582 sq. miles (1,068,630 sq. km), of which some 344,100 sq. miles (891,200 sq. km) are land area and some 64,490 sq. miles (189,196 sq. km) are lakes and fresh water rivers. The province extends 1,050 miles (1,690 km) from east to west and 1,075 miles (1,730 km) from north to south. It is bounded on the north by the Hudson and James Bays, on the east by Quebec, on the west by Manitoba, and on the south by the USA.

Estimated population in 1991 was 9,906,400. Population of the principal cities (1986 census): Hamilton, 306,728 (city), 594,600 (metropolitan area); Kitchener, 150,604 (city), 346,000 (metropolitan area); London, 276,000 (city; 1985 estimate); Ottawa (federal capital), 300,763 (city), 863,900 (metropolitan area); Sudbury, 88,717 (city), 149,200 (metropolitan area); Toronto (provincial capital), 612,289 (city), 2,147,600 (metropolitan area); Windsor, 193,111 (city), 260,700 (metropolitan area).

There are some 0·5m. French speakers, and 0·17m.–0·2m. native Indians. An agreement with the Ontario government of Aug. 1991 recognized Indians' right to self-government.

Vital statistics, see p. 275.

CLIMATE. A temperate continental climate, but conditions are quite severe in winter, though proximity to the Great Lakes has a moderating influence on temperatures. Ottawa. Jan. 12°F (−11·1°C), July 69°F (20·6°C). Annual rainfall 35" (871 mm). Toronto. Jan. 23°F (−5°C), July 69°F (20·6°C). Annual rainfall 33" (815 mm).

CONSTITUTION AND GOVERNMENT. The provincial government is administered by a *Lieut.-Governor*, a cabinet and a single-chamber 130-member *Legislative Assembly* elected by a general franchise for a period of 5 years. The minimum voting age is 18 years.

At the elections of Sept. 1990 to the *Legislative Assembly*, the New Democratic Party won 74 seats, the Liberal Party, 36, and the Progressive Conservative Party, 20. The parties' standing in Aug. 1991 was New Democrats, 73 seats; Liberals, 36; Progressive Conservatives, 20 and 1 independent.

Lieut.-Governor: Right Hon. Hal Jackman (b. 1932; appointed Dec. 1991).
Flag: The British Red Ensign with the shield of Ontario in the fly.

The members of the Executive Council in Nov. 1991 were as follows:

Premier, President of the Council and Minister of Intergovernmental Affairs: Hon. Bob Rae.
Deputy Premier, Treasurer and Minister of Economics: Hon. Floyd Laughren. *Agriculture and Food:* Hon. Elmer Buchanan. *Attorney-General:* Hon. Howard Hampton. *Citizenship:* Hon. Elaine Ziemba. *Colleges and Universities:* Hon. Richard Allen. *Community and Social Services:* Hon. Marion Boyd. *Consumer and Commercial Relations:* Hon. Marilyn Churley. *Correctional Services and Solicitor General:* Hon. Allan Pilkey. *Culture and Communications:* Hon. Karen Haslam. *Education:* Hon. Tony Silipo. *Energy:* Hon. Will Ferguson. *Environment:* Hon. Ruth Grier. *Financial Institutions:* Hon. Brian Charlton. *Transportation and Francophone Affairs:* Hon. Gilles Pouliot. *Government Services:* Hon. Fred Wilson. *Health:* Hon. Frances Lankin. *Housing:* Hon. Evelyn Gigantes. *Industry, Trade and Technology:* Hon. Norm Jamison. *Labour:* Hon. Bob MacKenzie. *Municipal Affairs:* Hon. David Cooke. *Native Affairs, Natural Resources:* Hon. Bud Wildman. *Northern Development and Mines:* Hon. Shelley Martel. *Revenue:* Hon. Shelly Wark-Martyn. *Tourism and Recreation:* Hon. Peter North. *Ministers Without Portfolio:* Hon. Shirley Coppen, Hon. Anne Swarbrick (*Responsible for Women's Issues*). The *Speaker* is the Hon. David Warner.
Leader of the Opposition: Murray Elston.

Local Government. Local government in Ontario is divided into two branches, one covering municipal institutions and the other education.

The present municipal system dates from The Municipal Corporations Act enacted by The Province of Canada in 1849. It has been considerably modified in recent years with the creation of the Municipality of Metropolitan Toronto in 1954 and the launching of the Government of Ontario's local government restructuring programme in 1968. Generally, there are two levels of municipal government in Ontario. The upper level consists of 27 counties plus 12 restructured regional municipalities. The local level comprises more than 800 cities, towns and townships. Cities in the traditional county system function independently of the county in which they lie, as do 4 towns which have been separated for municipal purposes. There are no separated municipal units in regional governments.

Ontario's local municipalities are governed by councils elected by popular vote.

A city council usually consists of a mayor, aldermen and, sometimes, an executive committee known as a board of control.

Councils of towns, villages and townships usually consist of a mayor, reeve, deputy reeve, councillors and, in the case of the newer regional municipalities, one or more regional councillors who represent the area municipalities on the regional council.

County and regional government councils are federated assemblies.

A county council consists of the reeves and deputy reeves of the towns, villages and townships. The head of the county council is the warden, who is elected by the council from among its own members.

A regional council consists of the heads of council of the local municipalities, as well as a varying number of regional councillors, who are elected on the basis of representation, either directly or indirectly. The head of the regional council is the chairman who is elected by council but who, unlike a county warden, need not have been a council member.

No municipality in Ontario may incur long-term debts without the sanction of the tribunal created by the Provincial Legislature and known as the Ontario Municipal Board. Debenture obligations incurred by municipalities for utility undertakings (water-works and electric light and power systems) are discharged ordinarily out of revenues derived from the sale of utility services and do not fall upon the ratepayers.

Municipal councils have no jurisdiction for education beyond the collection of taxes for school purposes. Responsibility for providing, operating and maintaining school facilities, and for the supply of teachers, rests with local education authorities known as Boards of Education or School Boards. These Boards are now generally organized on a county or regional basis. Apart from some of the larger cities, local municipal school boards no longer exist.

Municipal institutions come under the jurisdiction of the Provincial Ministry of Intergovernmental Affairs. One of the principal functions of the Ministry is to advise and assist municipalities on such matters as accounting, reporting, auditing, budgeting and planning. Educational support and guidance at the provincial level is the responsibility of the Ministry of Education, which deals with the training of teachers and the formulation of curriculum. (At the university and community college level, education support services are provided by the Ministry of Colleges and Universities.)

There are considerable areas in the northernmost parts of Ontario where as yet there is little or no settlement of population. In such areas no municipal organization exists, and control for all purposes over such areas remains in the hands of the Provincial Government.

FINANCE. Provincial revenue and expenditure (in Canadian $1,000) for years ending 31 March:

	1987–88	1988–89	1989–90	1990–91
Gross revenue	32,453	37,256	41,692	43,470
Gross expenditure	32,319	35,467	38,210	43,315

Gross revenue and expenditure figures include all non-budgetary transactions, *i.e.*, the lending and investment activity of the Government to Crown corporations, agencies and municipalities as well as the repayment of these loans or recovery of investments. Transactions on behalf of Ontario Hydro are excluded.

Personal income per capita, 1990-91, was $25,264.

ENERGY AND NATURAL RESOURCES

Electricity (1990). Ontario Hydro recorded for the calendar year an installed generating capacity of 31,150m. kw. and a net energy output generated and purchased of 137,321. kwh.

Minerals (1990). The total value of shipments from mines was $6,420m. Important commodities (in $1m.) were: Nickel, 1,316; copper, 887; uranium, 635; gold, 1,148; zinc, 541. The mining industry employed about 24,000 people in 1990.

Agriculture. In 1990, 3·5m. ha were under field crops with total farm receipts of $5,554m.

Forestry. According to the most recent inventory (1988) the total area of productive forest is 39·9m. ha, comprising: Softwoods, 26·3m.; hardwoods, 13·6m. The growing stock equals 5,102m. cu. metres. The estimated value of shipments by the forest products industry (including logging) was (1988) $10,220m.

INDUSTRY AND TRADE

Industry. Ontario is Canada's most highly industrialized province. In 1990 about 73% of value added in commodity-producing industries was accounted for by manufacturing.

In 1990, the labour force was 5,268,000. Total labour income was $148,679m. The 1990 Gross Provincial Product (GPP) was $277,397m.

The leading manufacturing industries are motor vehicles and parts, iron and steel, meat and meat preparations, dairy products, paper and paperboard, chemical products, petroleum and coal products, machinery and equipment, metal stamping and pressing and communications equipment.

Trade. In 1990 Ontario was responsible for 50% ($74,400m.) of Canada's exports.

COMMUNICATIONS

Roads. There were, in 1989, 156,390·3 km of roads. Motor licences (on the road) numbered (1990) 7,552,822, of which 4,756,855 were passenger cars, 1,089,127 commercial vehicles, 29,502 buses, 1,143,883 trailers, 120,411 motor cycles and 328,343 snow vehicles.

Railways. The provincially-owned Ontario Northland Railway has about 550 miles of track and the Algoma Central Railway 325 miles. The Canadian National and Canadian Pacific Railways operate a total of about 9,500 miles in Ontario. There is a metro and tramway network in Toronto.

Post (1991). Telephone service is provided by 30 independent systems and Bell Canada. There are some 12m. telephones.

EDUCATION. There is a complete provincial system of elementary and secondary schools as well as private schools. In 1990 publicly financed elementary and secondary schools had a total enrolment of 1,935,751 pupils.

There are 16 universities (Brock, Carleton, Guelph, Lakehead, Laurentian, McMaster, Ottawa, Queen's, Toronto, Trent, Waterloo, Western Ontario, Windsor, York, Wilfred Laurier and Dominicain) and 2 institutes of equivalent status (Ryerson Polytechnic, Ontario College of Art) with a total enrolment in 1990-91 of 194,915. All receive grants from the Ontario government. There are also 23 publicly-owned Colleges of Applied Arts and Technology (CAATS).

Expenditure by the Ontario government on education for 1989-90 was $8,297.

Further Reading

Statistical Information: Annual publications of the Ontario Ministry of Treasury and Economics include: *Ontario Statistics; Ontario Budget; Public Accounts; Financial Report.*
Guillet, E. C., *Pioneer Days in Upper Canada.* Toronto, 1933
McDonald, D. C. (ed.) *The Government and Politics of Ontario.* 2nd ed. Toronto, 1980
Middleton, J. E., *The Province of Ontario: A History 1615–1927.* Toronto, 1927, 4 vols.
Schull, J., *Ontario since 1867.* Toronto, 1978

PRINCE EDWARD ISLAND

HISTORY. After 10 millennia of Amerindian settlement, the first recorded European visit was by Jacques Cartier in 1534, who named it Isle St-Jean. In 1719 it was settled by the French, but was taken from them by the English in 1758, annexed to Nova Scotia in 1763, and constituted a separate colony in 1769. Named Prince Edward Island in honour of Prince Edward, Duke of Kent, in 1799, it joined the Canadian Confederation on 1 July 1873.

AREA AND POPULATION. The province lies in the Gulf of St Lawrence, and is separated from the mainland of New Brunswick and Nova Scotia by Northumberland Strait. The area of the island is 2,185 sq. miles (5,660 sq. km). Total population (census, 1986), 126,646; (estimate, 1990), 130,400. Population of the principal cities: Charlottetown (capital), 15,776; Summerside, 8,020.

Vital statistics, *see* p. 275.

CLIMATE. The cool temperate climate is affected in winter by the freezing of the St. Lawrence, which reduces winter temperatures. Charlottetown. Jan. 19°F (−7·2°C), July 67°F (19·4°C). Annual rainfall 43" (1,077 mm).

CONSTITUTION AND GOVERNMENT. The provincial government is administered by a Lieut.-Governor-in-Council (Cabinet) and a Legislative Assembly of 32 members who are elected for up to 5 years. In June 1989, parties in the Legislative Assembly were: Liberals, 30; Progressive Conservatives, 2.

Lieut.-Governor: Marion L. Reid (sworn in 16 Aug. 1990).

The Executive Council was composed as follows in Feb. 1991:

Premier, President of the Executive Council, Minister of Justice and Attorney-General: Hon. Joseph A. Ghiz, QC.

Finance and Environment: Hon. Gilbert R. Clements. *Community and Cultural Affairs and Fisheries and Aquaculture:* Hon. J. G. Leonce Bernard. *Industry:* Hon. Robert J. Morrissey. *Health and Social Services:* Hon. Wayne D. Cheverie, QC. *Transportation and Public Works:* Hon. Gordon MacInnis. *Agriculture:* Hon. Keith Milligan. *Education:* Hon. Paul Connolly. *Energy and Forestry:* Hon. Barry Hicken. *Tourism and Parks:* Hon. Nancy Guptill. *Labour:* Hon. Roberta Hubley.

Flag: A banner of the arms, *i.e.,* a white field bearing 3 small trees and a larger tree on a compartment, all green, and at the top a red band with a golden lion; on 3 sides a border of red and white rectangles.

Local Government. The Municipalities Act, 1983, provides for the incorporation of Towns and Communities. The City of Charlottetown and the town of Summerside are incorporated under private Acts of the Legislature.

FINANCE. Revenue and expenditure (in Canadian $) for 5 financial years ending 31 March:

	1987–88	1988–89	1989–90	1990–91	1991-92
Revenue	533,231,248	646,674,829	656,622,400	684,881,400	720,329,500
Expenditure	546,010,988	653,317,478	654,338,000	678,679,000	725,092,600

ENERGY AND NATURAL RESOURCES

Electricity. Electric power is supplied to 100% of the population. In 1990, total supply of electric energy was 752,456 mwh; net generation, 80,768 mwh. An undersea cable links the island with New Brunswick and the Maritime Power Grid. Electricity received from other provinces in 1990 totalled 671,688 mwh. In 1990, 89·3% of power requirements were supplied through this system.

Agriculture. Total area of farms occupied approximately 673,000 acres in 1989 out of the total land area of 1,399,040 acres. Farm cash receipts in 1990 were $247·6m. with cash receipts from potatoes accounting for 46·1% of the total. Cash receipts from dairy products, cattle and hogs followed in importance. For particulars of agricultural production and livestock, *see* pp. 000–00.

Forestry. Forested lands cover 278,000 ha. During 1990, 100,000 cords of round-wood were burnt for heating, and 22m. board feet of timber, worth some $7m., were sawn.

Fisheries. The catch in 1990 had a landed value of $66·8m. Lobsters and shellfish accounted for 78·7% of the total. Value of groundfish landings accounted for 9·7%; ocean and estuarial, 6·4%; Irish moss, 5·1%.

INDUSTRY AND TRADE

Industry. Value of manufacturing shipments for all industries in 1990 was $457·6m.

Labour. Per capita personal income rose from $14,615 in 1988 to $15,300 in 1989. The average weekly wage (industrial aggregate) rose from $400·68 in 1989 to $419·67 in 1990. The labour force averaged 65,000 in 1990, while employment averaged 55,000.

In 1990, provincial GDP in constant prices for manufacturing was $112·1m.; construction, $119·6m. In 1990 the total value of retail trade was $796m.

Tourism. The value of the tourist industry was estimated at $84·1m. in 1990 with 229,874 tourist parties.

COMMUNICATIONS

Roads. At the end of 1990 there were 5,296 km of road, including 3,784 km of paved highway. A bus service operates 3 times daily to the mainland.

Railways. Rail service closed on 31 Dec. 1989.

Civil Aviation. (1991). Air Canada provides daily jet service between Charlottetown and Toronto. Air Nova and Air Atlantic provide turbo-prop service between Charlottetown and other centres, including Toronto, to connect with Air Canada and Canadian Airlines International flights at Halifax.

Shipping. Modern car ferries link the Island to New Brunswick and Nova Scotia. Service is provided year round to New Brunswick on schedules which vary from 14 to 20 return crossings daily, with ice-breaking ferries maintaining the service during the winter months. Ferry service is operated to Nova Scotia from late April to mid-Dec. on schedules ranging from 9 to 19 return crossings daily. A third ferry service, to the Magdalen Islands (Quebec), operates from 1 April to 31 Jan. There is also a substantial water movement of certain commodities.

Telecommunications. In 1989 there were 91,495 telephones.

EDUCATION (1990–91). Under the regional school boards there were 70 public schools, 1,470 teaching positions and 24,504 students. There is one undergraduate university (2,317 full-time students), and a veterinary college (200 students), both in Charlottetown. Holland College provides training for employment at semi-professional levels in business, applied arts and technology, with approximately 950 students registering each year in post-secondary programmes within the college. The college is also responsible for the operation of the vocational high school and vocational trade programmes and adult night classes.

Annual expenditure on education exceeded $151m. in the 1990-91 government fiscal year.

Further Reading

Baldwin, D. O., *Abegweit: Land of the Red Soil*. Charlottetown, 1985
Bolger, F. W. P., *Canada's Smallest Province*. Charlottetown, 1973
Clark, A. H., *Three Centuries and the Island*. Toronto, 1959
Hocking, A., *Prince Edward Island*. Toronto, 1978
MacKinnon, F., *The Government of Prince Edward Island*. Toronto, 1951

QUEBEC—QUÉBEC

HISTORY. Quebec was formerly known as New France or Canada from 1534 to 1763; as the province of Quebec from 1763 to 1790; as Lower Canada from 1791 to 1846; as Canada East from 1846 to 1867, and when, by the union of the four original provinces, the Confederation of the Dominion of Canada was formed, it again became known as the province of Quebec (Québec).

The Quebec Act, passed by the British Parliament in 1774, guaranteed to the people of the newly conquered French territory in North America security in their religion and language, their customs and tenures, under their own civil laws.

In the referendum held 20 May 1980, 59·5% voted against and 40·5% for 'separatism'.

AREA AND POPULATION. The area of Quebec (as amended by the Labrador Boundary Award) is 1,667,926 sq. km (594,860 sq. miles), of which 1,315,134 sq. km is land area and 352,792 sq. km water. Of this extent, 911,106 sq. km represent the Territory of Ungava, annexed in 1912 under the Quebec Boundaries Extension Act. The population (census 1986) was 6,532,461. Estimate (1990) 6,762,200.

Principal cities (estimate, 1990): Quebec (capital), 168,600; Montreal, 1,030,900; Laval, 313,500; Sherbrooke, 77,618; Verdun, 61,200; Hull, 60,900; Trois-Rivières, 51,800.

Vital statistics, see p. 275.

CLIMATE. Cool temperate in the south, but conditions are more extreme towards the north. Winters are severe and snowfall considerable, but summer temperatures are quite warm. Rain occurs at all seasons. Quebec. Jan. 10°F (−12·2°C), July 66°F (18·9°C). Annual rainfall 40" (1,008 mm). Montreal. Jan. 11°F (−11·7°C), July 67°F (19·4°C). Annual rainfall 30" (776 mm).

CONSTITUTION AND GOVERNMENT. There is a Legislative Assembly consisting of 125 members, elected in 125 electoral districts for 4 years. At the provincial general elections held Sept. 1989, Liberals won 92 seats, *Parti Québecois*, 29 and *Parti Egalité*, 4.

Lieut.-Governor: The Hon. Martial Asselin.
Flag: The Fleurdelysé flag, blue with a white cross, and in each quarter a white fleur-de-lis.

Members of the Executive Council as in Sept. 1991, included:

Prime Minister: Robert Bourassa.
Deputy Prime Minister and Energy and Resources: Lise Bacon. *Finance:* Gérard D. Lévesque. *Education:* Michel Pagé. *Justice:* Gil Rémillard. *Communications:* Lawrence Cannon. *Cultural Affairs:* Liza Frulla-Hébert. *International Affairs:* John Claccia. *Autochthonous Affairs:* Christos Sirros. *Transport:* Sam Elkas. *Public Security:* Claude Ryan.

General-delegate in London: Harold Mailhot (59 Pall Mall, London SW1Y 5JH).
General-delegate in New York: Léo Paré (17 West 50th St., Rockefeller Center, New York 10020).
General-delegate in Paris: Marcel Bergeron (66 Pergolèse, Paris 75116).

ECONOMY

Budget. Ordinary revenue and expenditure (in Canadian $1,000) for fiscal years ending 31 March:

	1985–86	1986–87	1987–88	1988–89	1989-90
Revenue	24,080,778	25,646,247	28,363,891	29,967,892	31,073,900
Expenditure	27,222,178	28,465,454	30,738,141	31,578,118	32,733,300

The total net debt at 31 March 1990 was $33,486,135,000.

ENERGY AND NATURAL RESOURCES

Electricity. Water power is one of the most important natural resources of the province of Quebec. Its turbine installation represents about 40% of the aggregate of Canada. At the end of 1989 the installed generating capacity was 33,481 mw. Production, 1990, was 135,458 gwh.

Minerals (1990). The estimated value of the mineral production (metal mines only) was $2,920,159,000. Chief minerals: Iron ore, (confidential); copper, $301,462,000; gold, $567,778,000; zinc, $196,317,000.

The second major iron-ore development in northern Quebec is, like the one at

Knob Lake which gave birth to Schefferville, based on the Quebec–Labrador Trough which extends from Lac Jeannine to the northern tip of Ungava peninsula. The port of Sept-Iles and the railway connecting it with Schefferville allow easy shipment to the furnaces and steel mills of Canada, the USA and Europe.

Non-metallic minerals produced include: Asbestos ($177,135,000; about 69·2% of Canadian production), titane-dioxide (confidential), industrial lime, dolomite and brucite, quartz and pyrite. Among the building materials produced were: Stone, $240,316,000; cement, $165,547,000; sand and gravel, $71,394,000; lime, (confidential).

Agriculture. In 1990 the total area (estimate) of the principal field crops was 2,056,800 ha. The yield of the principal crops was (1990 in 1,000 tonnes):

Crops	Yield	Crops	Yield
Tame hay	7,000	Fodder corn	1,770
Oats for grain	315	Maize for grain	1,800
Potatoes	382	Barley	530
Mixed grains	90	Buckwheat	13

The farm cash receipts from farming operations estimated in 1990 amounted to $3,725,465,000. The principal items being: Livestock and products, $2,584,202,000; crops, $685,712,000; dairy supplements payments, $124,368,000, forest and maple products, $96,314,000.

Forestry. Forests cover an area of 912,123 sq. km. About 734,316 sq. km are classified as productive forests, of which 664,209 sq. km are provincial forest land and 66,866 sq. km are privately owned. Quebec leads the Canadian provinces in pulp and paper production, having nearly half of the Canadian estimated total.

In 1989 production of lumber was softwood and hardwood, 10,596,000 cu. metres; pulp and paper, 7,655,000 tonnes.

Fisheries. The principal fish are cod, herring, red fish, lobster and salmon. Total catch of sea fish, 1990, 72,885 tonnes, valued at $71,554,000.

INDUSTRY AND TRADE

Industry. In 1989 there were 11,365 industrial establishments in the province; employees, 523,348; salaries and wages, $15,086,402,000; cost of materials, $45,371,769,000; value of shipments, $82,262,634,000. Among the leading industries are petroleum refining, pulp and paper mills, smelting and refining, dairy products, slaughtering and meat processing, motor vehicle manufacturing, women's clothing, saw-mills and planing mills, iron and steel mills, commercial printing.

Commerce. In 1990 the value of Canadian exports through Quebec custom ports was $22,926,740,000; value of imports, $26,406,998,000.

COMMUNICATIONS

Roads. In 1990 there were 61,043 km of roads and 3,964,739 registered motor vehicles.

Railways. There were (1990) 7,000 km of railway. There is a metro system in Montreal (64 km).

Civil Aviation. In 1990 Quebec had 2 international airports, Dorval (Montreal) with landing runway of 8·4 km and Mirabel (Montreal) with 7·3 km.

Post and Broadcasting. Telephones numbered 3,674,778 in 1989 and there were 34 television and 117 radio stations.

Newspapers (1989). There were 10 French- and 2 English-language daily newspapers.

EDUCATION. The province has 7 universities: 3 English-language universities, McGill (Montreal) founded in 1821, Bishop (Lennoxville) founded in 1845 and the Concordia University (Montreal) granted a charter in 1975; 4 French-language uni-

versities: Laval (Quebec) founded in 1852, Montreal University, opened in 1876 as a branch of Laval and became independent in 1920, Sherbrooke University founded in 1954 and University of Quebec founded in 1968.

In 1989–90 there were 121,872 full-time university students and 122,726 part-time students.

In 1989–90, in pre-kindergartens, there were 7,009 pupils; in kindergartens, 88,200; primary schools, 586,353; in secondary schools, 459,738; in colleges (post-secondary, non-university), 231,154; and in classes for children with special needs, 147,597. The school boards had a total of 59,049 teachers.

Expenditure of the Departments of Education for 1989–90, $8,013,049,000 net. This included $1,330,493,000 for universities, $5,054,902,000 for public primary and secondary schools, $264,333,000 for private primary and secondary schools and $1,101,926,000 for colleges.

Further Reading

Statistical Information: The Quebec Bureau of Statistics was established in 1912. The Bureau, which reports to the Finance Dept. since March 1983, collects, compiles and distributes statistical information relative to Quebec. *Director:* Luc Bessette.

A statistical information list is available on request. Among the most important publications are: *Le Québec Statistique, Statistiques* (quarterly), *Comptes économiques du Québec* (annual), *Situation démographique* (annual), *Commerce international du Québec* (annual), *Investissements privés et publics* (annual).

Hamelin, J., *Histoire du Québec.* St-Hyacinthe, 1978
Jacobs, J., *The Question of Separatism: Quebec and the Struggle for Sovereignty.* London, 1981
McWhinney, E., *Quebec and the Constitution.* Univ. of Toronto Press, 1979
Ouellet, F., *Histoire de la Chambre de Commerce de Québec, 1809–1959.* Québec, 1959
Trofimenkoff, S. M., *Action Française.* Univ. of Toronto Press, 1975
Wade, F. M., *The French Canadians, 1760–1967.* Toronto, 1968.—*Canadian Dualism: Studies of French–English Relations.* Quebec–Toronto, 1960

SASKATCHEWAN

HISTORY. Saskatchewan derives its name from its major river system, which the Cree Indians called 'Kis-is-ska-tche-wan', meaning 'swift flowing'. It officially became a province when it joined the Confederation on 1 Sept. 1905.

In 1670 King Charles II granted to Prince Rupert and his friends a charter covering exclusive trading rights in 'all the land drained by streams finding their outlet in the Hudson Bay'. This included what is now Saskatchewan. The trading company was first known as The Governor and Company of Adventurers of England; later as the Hudson's Bay Company. In 1869 the Northwest Territories was formed, and this included Saskatchewan. In 1882 the District of Saskatchewan was formed. By 1885 the North-West Mounted Police had been inaugurated, with headquarters in Regina (now the capital), and the Canadian Pacific Railway's transcontinental line had been completed, bringing a stream of immigrants to southern Saskatchewan. The Hudson's Bay Company surrendered its claim to territory in return for cash and land around the existing trading posts. Legislative government was introduced.

AREA AND POPULATION. Saskatchewan is bounded on the west by Alberta, on the east by Manitoba, on the north by the Northwest Territories and on the south by the USA. The area of the province is 251,700 sq. miles (570,113 sq. km), of which 220,182 sq. miles is land area and 31,518 sq. miles is water. The population, 1986 census, was 1,010,198. Population of cities, 1986 census: Regina (capital), 175,064; Saskatoon, 177,641; Moose Jaw, 35,073; Prince Albert, 33,686; Yorkton, 15,574; Swift Current, 15,666; North Battleford, 14,876; Estevan, 10,161; Weyburn, 10,153; Lloydminster, 7,155; Melfort, 6,078; Melville, 5,123.

Vital statistics, see p. 275.

CLIMATE. A cold continental climate, with severe winters and warm summers. Rainfall amounts are greatest from May to Aug. Regina. Jan. 0°F (–17·8°C), July 65°F (18·3°C). Annual rainfall 15" (373 mm).

CONSTITUTION AND GOVERNMENT. The provincial government is vested in a Lieut.-Governor, an Executive Council and a *Legislative Assembly*, elected for 5 years by universal suffrage. At the elections of Oct. 1991 the New Democratic Party gained 50% of votes cast and 51 seats, the Progressive Conservative Party 14 seats and the Liberal Party 1 seat.

Lieut.-Governor: Hon. Sylvia O. Fedoruk.

Flag: Green over gold, with the shield of the province in the canton, and a green and red prairie lily in the fly.

The New Democratic Party Ministry in Oct. 1991 was composed as follows:

Premier: Roy Romanow (b. 1939).

Deputy Premier, Minister of Finance: Hon. Ed Tchorzewski. *Economic Diversification and Trade, Government House Leader:* Hon. Dwain Lingenfelter. *Health, Minister Responsible for the Status of Women:* Hon. Louise Simard. *Education, The Family:* Hon. Carol Teichrob. *Agriculture and Food, Highways and Transportation:* Hon. Berny Wiens. *Community Services, Environment and Public Safety:* Hon. Carol Carson. *Justice, Attorney General, Provincial Secretary, Human Resources, Labour and Employment:* Hon. Bob Mitchell. *Social Services, Minister Responsible for Seniors:* Hon. Janice MacKinnon. *Energy and Mines:* Hon. John Penner. *Rural Development, Parks and Renewable Resources:* Hon. Darrel Cunningham.

Agent-General in London: Paul Rousseau, 21 Pall Mall, SW1Y 5LP.

Local Government. The organization of a city requires a minimum population of 5,000 persons; that of a town, 500; that of a village, 100 people. No requirements as to population exist for the rural municipality.

Cities, towns, villages and rural municipalities are governed by elected councils, which consist of a mayor and 6–20 aldermen in a city; a mayor and 6 councillors in a town; a mayor and 2 other members in a village; a reeve and a councillor for each division in a rural municipality (usually 6).

FINANCE. Budget and net assets (years ending 31 March) in Canadian $1,000:

	1988–89	*1989–90*	*1990–91*	*1991-92*[1]
Budgetary revenue	3,607,683	4,083,400	4,283,465	4,554,200
Budgetary expenditure	3,935,896	4,309,460	4,646,610	4,819,266

[1] Estimates

ENERGY AND NATURAL RESOURCES. Agriculture used to dominate the history and economics of Saskatchewan, but the 'prairie province' is now a rapidly developing mining and manufacturing area. It is a major supplier of oil, has the world's largest deposits of potash and the net value of its non-agricultural production accounted for (1990 estimate) 92·5% of the provincial economy.

Electricity. The Saskatchewan Power Corporation generated 13,589m. kwh. in 1990.

Minerals. 1989 mineral sales were valued at $3,343,844,995, including (in $1m.): Petroleum, 1,608·7; natural gas, 381; coal and others, 127·7; gold, 42·9; copper, 1; zinc, 0·4; potash, 794·8; salt, 20·2; uranium, 343·7; sodium sulphate, 23·7.

Agriculture. Saskatchewan produces about two-thirds of Canada's wheat. Wheat production in 1990 (in 1,000 tonnes), was 13,989 from 16·2m. acres; oats, 879 from 1m. acres; barley, 3,832 from 3·5m. acres; rye, 513 from 660,000 acres; rapeseed, 1,273 from 3·2m. acres; flax, 254 from 0·77m. acres. Livestock (1 July 1990): Cattle and calves, 2·2m.; swine, 0·8m.; sheep and lambs, 56,000. Poultry in 1990: Chickens, 11·95m.; turkeys 0·72m. Cash income from the sale of farm products in 1990 was $3,996m. At the June 1986 census there were 63,431 farms in the province, each being a holding of 1 acre or more with sales of agricultural products during the previous 12 months of $250 or more.

The South Saskatchewan River irrigation project, whose main feature is the Gardiner Dam, was completed in 1967. It will ultimately provide for an area of 200,000 to 500,000 acres of irrigated cultivation in Central Saskatchewan. As of 1990, 219,767 acres were irrigated. Total irrigated land in the province, 313,904 acres.

Forestry. Half of Saskatchewan's area is forested, but only 115,000 sq. km are of commercial value at present. Forest products valued at $223m. were produced in 1990. The province's first pulp-mill, at Prince Albert, went into production in 1968; its daily capacity is 1,000 tons of high-grade kraft pulp.

Fur Production. In 1989-90 (and 1988–89) wild fur production was estimated at $1,330,870 ($1,810,746). Ranch-raised fur production amounted to $56,980 ($98,220).

Fisheries. The lakeside value of the 1988–89 commercial fish catch of 3·2m. kg was $3·2m.

INDUSTRY. In 1987 Saskatchewan had 810 manufacturing establishments, employing 19,772 persons. Manufacturing contributed $1,315m., construction $896m. to the total gross domestic product at factor cost of $19,169m. in 1990.

TOURISM. An estimated 1·8m. out-of-province tourists spent $202m. in 1990.

COMMUNICATIONS

Roads. In 1990 there were 25,355 km of provincial highways and 180,000 km of municipal roads (including prairie trails). Motor vehicles registered totalled (1989) 715,000. Bus services are provided by 2 major lines.

Railways. There were (1990) 11,233 km of main railway track.

Civil Aviation. Saskatchewan had 2 major airports, 176 airports and landing strips in 1991.

Telecommunications. There were (1990) 598 post offices (excluding sub-post offices), 85 TV and re-broadcasting stations and 52 AM and FM radio stations. There were 562,179 telephone network access services to the Saskatchewan Telecommunications system in 1990.

EDUCATION. The University of Saskatchewan was established at Saskatoon on 3 April 1907. In 1990–91 it had 14,445 full-time students, 3,589 part-time students and 1,082 full-time staff. The University of Regina was established 1 July 1974; in 1990–91 it had 7,221 full-time and 4,151 part-time students and 386 full-time staff.

The Saskatchewan education system in 1990–91 consisted of 111 school divisions and 4 comprehensive school boards, of which 22 are Roman Catholic separate school divisions, serving 139,222 elementary pupils, 54,557 high-school students and 2,387 students enrolled in special classes. In addition, the Saskatchewan Institute of Applied Science and Technology, established 1 Jan. 1988, had 15,630 full-time and 29,841 part-time students in 1990-91. In addition there are 10 regional colleges with an enrolment of approximately 29,470 students in the 1990–91 school year.

Further Reading

Tourist and industrial publications, descriptive of the Government's programme, are obtainable from the Department of Industry and Commerce; other government publications from Government Information Services (Legislative Building, Regina).
Saskatchewan Economic Review. Executive Council, Regina. Annual
Archer, J. H., *Saskatchewan: A History*. Saskatoon, 1980
Arora, V., *The Saskatchewan Bibliography*. Regina, 1980
Richards, J. S. and Fung, K. I. (eds.) *Atlas of Saskatchewan*. Univ. of Saskatchewan, 1969

THE NORTHWEST TERRITORIES

HISTORY. The Territory was developed by the Hudson's Bay Company and the North West Company (of Montreal) from the 17th century. The Canadian Government bought out the Hudson's Bay Company in 1869 and the Territory was annexed to Canada in 1870. The Arctic Islands lying north of the Canadian mainland were annexed to Canada in 1880 by Queen Victoria.

A plebiscite was scheduled for March 1992 on hiving off the eastern half of the Northwest Territories to form an Inuit territory, Nunavut.

AREA AND POPULATION. The total area of the Territories is 1,304,903 sq. miles (3,376,698 sq. km), divided into 5 administrative regions: Fort Smith, Inuvik, Kitikmeot, Keewatin and Baffin. The population in June 1990 was 53,801, 39% of whom were Inuit (Eskimo), 17% Dene (Indian) and 1% Metis. The capital is Yellowknife, population (1990); 13,698. Other main centres (with population in 1990): Iqaluit (3,016), Hay River (2,891), Inuvik (2,790), Fort Smith (2,487), Rankin Inlet (1,425), Rae-Edzo (1,422) and Arviat (1,299).

CLIMATE. Conditions range from cold continental to polar, with long hard winters and short cool summers. Precipitation is low. Yellowknife. Jan. mean high –24·7°C, low –33°C; July mean high 20·7°C, low 11·8°C. Annual rainfall 26·7 cm.

CONSTITUTION AND GOVERNMENT. The Northwest Territories comprises all that portion of Canada lying north of the 60th parallel of N. lat. except those portions within the Yukon Territory and the Provinces of Quebec and Newfoundland: It also includes the islands in Hudson Bay, James Bay and Ungava Bay except those within the Provinces of Manitoba, Ontario and Quebec.

The Northwest Territories is governed by a Government Leader, with a 7-member cabinet and a Legislative Assembly. The Assembly is composed of 24 members elected for a 4-year term of office. A Commissioner of the Northwest Territories acts as a lieutenant-governor and is the federal government's senior representative in the Territorial government. The seat of government was transferred from Ottawa to Yellowknife when it was named Territorial capital on 18 Jan. 1967.

Government Leader: Nellie Cournoyea.
Commissioner: Daniel L. Norris.
Flag: Vertically, blue, white, blue, with the white of double width and bearing the shield of the Territory.

Legislative powers are exercised by the Executive Council on such matters as taxation within the Territories in order to raise revenue, maintenance of justice, licences, solemnization of marriages, education, public health, property, civil rights and generally all matters of a local nature.

The Territorial Government has assumed most of the responsibility for the administration of the Northwest Territories but political control of Crown lands and nonrenewable resources still rests with the Federal Government. On 6 Sept. 1988, the Federal and Territorial Governments signed an agreement for the transfer of management responsibilities for oil and gas resources, located on- and off-shore, in the Northwest Territories to the Territorial Government. In a Territory-wide plebiscite in April 1982, a majority of residents voted in favour of dividing the Northwest Territories into two jurisdictions, east and west. An east-west boundary line has been arbitrarily drawn to be voted on at the plebiscite of March 1992. A Western Arctic Constitutional Committee has been set up.

ENERGY AND NATURAL RESOURCES

Oil and Gas. As of Nov. 1991, 8 licences for oil and gas exploration were held for 663,415 ha, 18 production licences were held for 17,922 ha and 18 significant discovery licences were retained on 699,107 ha.

Crude oil is produced at Norman Wells and piped to Alberta. In 1986, oil production was 117,520 cu. metres.

Minerals. Mineral production in 1990 was valued at $881m. 6% of Canada's total. The Northwest Territories yielded 17% of lead, 25% of zinc, 9% of gold, 17% of cadmium and 2% of silver produced in Canada in 1990.

Trapping and Game. The 35,602 pelts, furs and hides sold by 1,551 Northwest Territories hunters and trappers in the 1990–91 season were valued at $1·8m. The pelts of highest value are those of the marten, mink, polar bear and lynx. There are some 1·5m. barren-ground caribou, 85,000 muskox and 12,500 polar bears. There are 2 protected herds of wood bison.

Forestry. The principal trees are white and black spruce, jack-pine, tamarack, balsam poplar, aspen and birch. In 1989–90, 45,876 cu. metres of timber, valued at $2·2m., was produced.

Fisheries. Commercial fishing, principally on Great Slave Lake, in 1990–91 produced 1·5m. kg of fish valued at $2m., principally trout, arctic char and whitefish.

CO-OPERATIVES. There are 39 active co-operatives, including 2 housing co-operatives and one central organization to service local co-operatives, in the Northwest Territories. They are active in handicrafts, furs, fisheries, retail stores, hotels and print shops. Total revenue in 1991 was about $41m.

COMMUNICATIONS

Roads. The Mackenzie Route connects Grimshaw, Alberta, with Hay River, Pine Point, Fort Smith, Fort Providence, Rae-Edzo and Yellowknife. The Mackenzie Highway extension to Fort Simpson and a road between Pine Point and Fort Resolution have both been opened.

Highway service to Inuvik in the Mackenzie Delta was opened in spring 1980, extending north from Dawson, Yukon as the Dempster Highway. The Liard Highway connecting the communities of the Liard River valley to British Columbia opened in 1984.

Railways. There is one small railway system in the north which runs from Hay River, on the south shore of Great Slave Lake, 435 miles south to Grimshaw, Alberta, where it connects with the Canadian National Railways, but it is not in use.

Civil Aviation (1991). 9 certified airports are operated by the federal Department of Transport and there are 33 certified and 9 uncertified airports operated by the Government of the Northwest Territories. Numerous certified and uncertified airports are operated privately in support of military operations, mining and resource exploration, and tourism. There are also privately-owned float plane bases. Major communities receive daily jet service to southern points. Most smaller communities are served by scheduled jet-prop air service several times weekly.

Shipping. A direct inland-water transportation route for about 1,700 miles is provided by the Mackenzie River and its tributaries, the Athabasca and Slave rivers. Subsidiary routes on Lake Athabasca, Great Slave Lake and Great Bear Lake total more than 800 miles.

Telecommunications (1991). There were 60 post offices. The CBC northern service operated radio stations at Yellowknife, Inuvik, Frobisher Bay and Rankin Inlet. Virtually all communities of 150 or over were receiving television via satellite. Telephone service is provided by common carriers to nearly all communities in the Northwest Territories. Those few communities without service have high frequency or very high frequency radios for emergency use.

EDUCATION AND WELFARE

Education. In 1990-91 there were 11 divisional boards of education. Two other regions were working towards divisional board status, which provides for more local and regional control of education. There were also three independent boards of education operating in Yellowknife: A separate school board, a public school board and a board of secondary education.

In 1990-91 there were 78 schools operating, with 1,008 teachers for 14,940 enrolled students. Residences in regional larger communities provide accommodation for students from smaller communities that cannot provide all education services up to grade 12. There is a full range of courses available in the school system: Academic, French immersion, native language and culture, commercial, technical and occupational training. Post-secondary programmes include the 6-campus Arctic College, which offers a variety of certificate and diploma programmes, along with a first-year general arts university programme. Financial assistance (from the territorial government) is available to qualifying students for post-secondary studies.

Health. In April 1988 responsibility for health services was transferred to the territorial government by the Government of Canada. In 1989 the Department of Health, Government of the Northwest Territories, was responsible for six hospitals (Yellowknife, Hay River, Inuvik, Churchill, Winnepeg, Montreal), six public health centres (Yellowknife, Hay River, Inuvik, Rae, Fort Simpson, Fort Smith) and six satellite health centres.

Welfare. Welfare services are provided by professional social workers. Facilities included (1991) for children: 11 group homes, 1 residential treatment centre, 3 secure custody facilities for young offenders, 2 open custody young offender centres and 7 homes for the aged.

Further Reading

Annual Report of the Government of the Northwest Territories
Government Activities in the North, 1983–84. Indian and Northern Affairs, Canada
NWT Data Book 90/91. Yellowknife, 1991
Dawson, C. A., *The New North-West.* Toronto, 1947
MacKay, D., *The Honorable Company.* Toronto, 1949
Zaslow, M., *The Opening of the Canadian North 1870–1914.* Toronto, 1971

YUKON TERRITORY

HISTORY. Formerly part of the Northwest Territories, the Yukon was joined to the Dominion as a separate territory on 13 June 1898.

AREA AND POPULATION. The Yukon is situated in the extreme northwestern section of Canada and comprises 483,450 sq. km. of which 4,480 fresh water. The census population in 1981 was 23,153; 1991 (estimate), 29,886. Principal centres are Whitehorse (capital), 21,112; Watson Lake, 1,624; Dawson City, 1,786; Faro, 1,565; Haines Junction, 628.

Vital statistics, *see* p. 275.

CLIMATE. A cold climate in winter with moderate temperatures in summer provide a considerable annual range of temperature and moderate rainfall. Whitehorse. Jan. 5°F (–20°C), July 56°F (14·1°C). Annual rainfall 10" (261 mm). Dawson City. Jan. –22°F (–30°C), July 57°F (15·6°C). Annual rainfall 13" (306·1 mm).

CONSTITUTION AND GOVERNMENT. The Yukon Territory was constituted a separate territory in June 1898. It is governed by a 5-member Executive Council (Cabinet) appointed from the majority party in the 16-member elected Legislative Assembly. The members are elected for a 4-year term. The seat of government is at Whitehorse. A federally appointed Commissioner has the final signing authority for all legislation passed by the Assembly.

Commissioner: Ken McKinnon (appointed 27 March 1986)

Flag: Vertically green, white, blue, in the proportions 2 : 3 : 2, charged in the centre with the arms of the Territory.

The legislative authority of the Assembly includes direct taxation, education, property and civil rights, territorial civil service, municipalities and generally all matters of local or private nature. All other major administration including federal Crown lands, and natural resources is federally controlled. Discussions are continuing between the federal and territorial governments on the transfer of certain federal programmes to the Yukon government. A formula financing agreement allows the Yukon government to determine how it will spend funds transferred from the federal government.

ECONOMY

Activities. GDP grew at a rate of 1% in 1990, reaching an estimated $890m. Territorial government expenditures were just over $382m. The main sectors of the economy are mining and tourism. Renewable resource industries' production was estimated at $10m. in 1989, a reduction of $5m. over 1988 owing to a weak fur market, closure of a lumber mill and a smaller salmon harvest. Processing of renewable resources is an important source of economic diversification. In the manufacturing sector, manufacturers' shipments were valued at $15–20m. in 1989.

Finance. The Territorial Government's revenue and expenditure (in $1,000) for years ended 31 March was:

	1987–88	1988–89	1989–90	1990–91
Revenue	293,300	305,800	330,500	336,600
Expenditure	316,203	316,150	350,400	330,400

ENERGY AND NATURAL RESOURCES

Electricity. Hydro generated power is supplied through plants at Whitehorse Rapids, Aishihik and Mayo. Diesel-generated power is supplied to several other communities (Dawson City, Watson Lake, Old Crow, Teslin). Current capacity is 78 mw hydro and 44 mw diesel-generated power.

Oil. Dome Petroleum, Gulf, Esso Resources, Petro Canada and Shell had been exploring (1986) extensively for oil in the Beaufort Sea but falling world oil prices resulted in much of this exploration being curtailed after 1987.

Minerals. Mining remains the main industry. Lead, zinc, silver and gold are the chief minerals. Production figures for year ending 31 Dec. 1990 (provisional) in tonnes were: Lead, 106,489; zinc, 179,128; silver, 84; gold, 5. The value of mining production sales in 1987 was $136·8m.; in 1988, $151·5m.

Agriculture. There are areas where the climate is suitable for the production of forage crops (occupying the largest acreage and used as feed for the estimated 2,500 horses), early maturing varieties of cereals and grains and vegetables. In 1984 cereal crop and forage fertility trials were initiated and the Yukon New Crop Development Project began in 1985. In 1991 there were 200 full-time and part-time farmers. The total improved area is 8,500 acres and the estimated value of agricultural products (farm gate not retail) $3·2m.

Forestry. The forests are part of the great Boreal forest region of Canada which stretches from the east coast of Canada into Alaska and north well above the Arctic Circle. Vast areas are covered by coniferous stands in the southern portion of Yukon with white spruce and lodgepole pine forming pure stands on wet sites and in northern aspects. Deciduous species form pure stands or occur mixed with conifers throughout forest areas.

The value of forest production in 1989 was approximately $3m.

Fisheries. Commercial fishing concentrates on chinook salmon, chum salmon, lake trout and whitefish. The value of all fisheries sectors was between $3m. and $4m. in 1988.

Game and Furs. The country abounds with big game, such as moose, goat, caribou, mountain sheep and bear (grizzly and black). The fur trapping industry is considered vital to rural and remote residents and especially native people wishing to maintain a traditional lifestyle. In 1990–91, 9,112 pelts were taken for a market value of $429,360. Marten was the most valuable fur and made up 65% of the total harvest bringing in $279,357 in revenues.

TOURISM. In 1990 tourists spent an estimated $75m. Some 231,706 tourists visited in 1990.

COMMUNICATIONS

Roads. The Alaska Highway and its side roads connect Yukon's main communities with Alaska and the provinces and with adjacent mining centres. Interior roads connect the mining communities of Elsa (silver–lead), Faro (lead–zinc–silver) and Dawson City (gold) and mineral exploration properties (lead–zinc and tungsten) north of Ross River. The 727 km Dempster Highway north of Dawson City connects with Inuvik, on the Arctic coast; this highway, the first public road to be built to the Arctic ocean, was opened in Aug. 1979. The Carcross–Skagway road was opened in May 1979, providing a new access to the Pacific Ocean. There are 4,910 km of roads in the Territory, of which about 250 km are paved. The other major roads, including the Alaska Highway, have received a new surface treatment which resembles pavement and the rest are all-weather gravel of which 700 km are accessible during the summer months only.

Railways. The 176-km White Pass and Yukon Railway connected Whitehorse with year-round ocean shipping at Skagway, Alaska, but was closed in 1982. A modified passenger service was restarted in 1988 to take cruise ship tourists from Skagway to the White Pass summit and back. There are no plans to run the service all the way to Whitehorse.

Aviation. In 1991 one commercial airline provided regular daily service between Whitehorse, Watson Lake, Edmonton and Vancouver. A second airline provided a summer service from Whitehorse to Vancouver in 1991. Regularly scheduled air services extend from Whitehorse to interior communities of Faro, Mayo, Dawson City, Old Crow, Ross River and Watson Lake as well as to Yellowknife in the Northwest Territories and to Juneau and Fairbanks in Alaska, with connecting service to Anchorage and other points in Alaska, and Seattle (USA). There are several commercial operations offering charter services.

Shipping. The majority of goods are shipped into the Territory by truck over the Alaska and Stewart–Cassiar Highways. Some goods are shipped by barge to Skagway and Haines, Alaska, and then trucked to Whitehorse, for distribution throughout the Territory. The majority of goods are transported by road within the Territory, while a modest amount is shipped by air. Although navigable, the rivers are no longer used for shipping.

Telecommunications. There are 3 radio stations in Whitehorse and 12 low-power relay radio transmitters operated by CBC, as well as 3 operated by the Yukon Govenrment. CHON-FM, operated by Northern Native Broadcasting Yukon offers 12 hours of programming, 7 days a week, and is transmitted to virtually all Yukon communities by satellite. Dawson City has its own community run radio station, CFYT, which provides 15 hours of local programming 7 days a week. There are also 16 basic and 11 extended pay-cable TV channels in Whitehorse, and private cable operations in Faro and Watson Lake. CBC and TVNC television is provided by satellite and relayed to all communities. All telephone and telecommunications are provided by Northwestel, a subsidiary of Bell Canada Enterprises. Microwave stations, satellite ground stations and radio-telephone facilities provide most of the telephone transmissions services to the communities.

Newspapers. In 1991 there were 2 newspapers, 1 published 5 days a week and 1 twice a week, in Whitehorse, and monthly papers in Faro and Dawson City. *Dann Zha*, a publication for native people, is a monthly. Other publications include a monthly newspaper aimed at the francophone population, a quarterly produced by a women's organization in Whitehorse, and a private monthly magazine which is distributed free.

EDUCATION AND WELFARE

Education. The Yukon Department of Education owns and operates the Territory's 26 schools, both public and separate, from kindergarten to grade 12. There are also 2 private schools. In 1991 there were 387 teachers and 5,485 pupils. A separate francophone school opened in Sept. 1988. French immersion is offered from kindergarten to grade 11. Yukon College provides post-secondary training at 3 campuses at Whitehorse and 11 in communities throughout the territory. In Oct. 1990 some 800 full-time students were enrolled, and about 2,500 part-time. The Yukon government provides financial assistance to students whether they study at the College or outside the territory. Financial assistance is available to students of aboriginal descent from the federal Department of Indian Affairs and Northern Development.

Health. The health care system provides all residents with the care demanded by illness or accident. The federal government operates 1 general hospital at Whitehorse, 2 cottage hospitals, 3 nursing stations, with a total of 160 beds, 8 health centres, 3 health units and 2 health stations. The territorial government also operates a medical travel programme to send patients to Edmonton or Vancouver for specialized treatment not available in the Territory.

Further Reading

Annual Report of the Government of the Yukon.
Yukon Executive Council, *Statistical Review.*
Berton, P., *Klondike.* (Rev. ed.) Toronto, 1987
Coates, K. and Morrison, W., *Land of the Midnight Sun: A History of the Yukon.* Edmonton, 1988
Coults, R., *Yukon Places and Names.* Sidney, 1980
McClelland, C., *Part of the Land, Part of the Water.* Vancouver, 1987
Minter, R., *White Pass: Gateway to the Klondike.* Toronto, 1987

There is a Yukon Archive at Yukon College, Whitehorse.

CAPE VERDE

Capital: Praia
Population: 369,000 (1990)
GNP per capita: US$760 (1989)

República de Cabo Verde

HISTORY. The Cape Verde Islands were discovered in 1460 by Diogo Gomes, the first settlers arriving in 1462. In 1587 its administration was unified under a Portuguese governor. The colony became an Overseas Province on 11 June 1951.

On 30 Dec. 1974 Portugal transferred power to a transitional government headed by the Portuguese High Commissioner. Full independence was granted on 5 July 1975.

AREA AND POPULATION. Cape Verde is situated in the Atlantic Ocean 620 km WNW of Senegal and consists of 10 islands and 5 islets. Praia is the capital. The islands are divided into 2 groups, named Barlavento (windward) and Sotavento (leeward). The total area is 4,033 sq. km (1,557 sq. miles). The population (census, 1980) was 295,703. Estimate (1990) 369,000, 28·7% urban; density, 91·9 per sq. km. About 600,000 Cape Verdeans live abroad.

The areas and populations (1980, census) of the islands are:

	Sq. km	Population		Sq. km	Population
Santo Antão	779	43,321	Maio	269	4,098
São Vicente [1]	227	41,594	São Tiago	991	145,957
São Nicolau	388	13,572	Fogo	476	30,978
Sal	216	5,826	Brava	67	6,985
Boa Vista	620	3,372			
			Sotavento	1,803	188,018
Barlavento	2,230	107,685			
			Total	4,033	295,703

[1] Includes Santa Luzia which is uninhabited.

The main towns (1980 census) are Praia, the capital (37,676) on São Tiago; and Mindelo (36,746) on São Vicente. 70% of the inhabitants are of mixed origins, and another 28% are black. Crioulo serves as the common language of the islands, although the official language is Portuguese.

Annual growth rate, 1985-90, 2·6%; infant mortality, 1990, 40·5 per 1,000 live births; life expectancy, 1990, 66·9 years.

CLIMATE. The climate is arid, with a cool dry season from Dec. to June and warm dry conditions for the rest of the year. Rainfall is sparse, rarely exceeding 5" (127 mm) in the northern islands or 12" (304 mm) in the southern ones. There are periodic severe droughts. Praia. Jan. 72°F (22·2°C), July 77°F (25°C). Annual rainfall 10" (250 mm).

CONSTITUTION AND GOVERNMENT. The Constitution adopted on 12 Feb. 1981 removed all reference to possible future union with Guinea-Bissau, and the *Partido Africano da Independencia de Cabo Verde* (PAICV), founded 20 Jan. 1981, became the sole legal party. The legislature consisted of a unicameral People's National Assembly of 83 members elected for 5 years by universal suffrage; it elects the President, who appoints and leads a Council of Ministers. Elections were held on 7 Dec. 1985.

In Sept. 1990 the People's National Assembly abolished the PAICV's sole right to rule.

Past President: Arístides Maria Pereira (assumed office 5 July 1975; re-elected 1981 and 1986).

Multi-party elections for a new National Assembly of 79 members were held in Jan. 1991. The electorate was 165,000. The Movement for Democracy (MPD) gained some 68% of votes cast and obtained 56 seats; the PAICV won 23 seats.

Presidential elections took place on 17 Feb. 1991. Antonio Mascarenhas Monteiro (b. 1943) was elected by 72% of votes cast, defeating the incumbent President Pereira.

Prime Minister: Carlos Veiga (MPD; b. 1949).

National flag: Horizontally yellow over green, with a vertical red strip in the hoist charged slightly above the centre with a black star surrounded by a wreath of maize, and beneath this a yellow clam shell.

Local government: There are 2 districts (Barlavento and Sotavento) sub-divided into 14 *conçelhos.* Barlavento comprises: Ribeira Grande, Paúl, Porto Novo (these 3 covering Santo Antão island), São Vicente (including Santa Luzia), São Nicolau, Sal, Boa Vista. Sotavento comprises: Maio, Praia, Santa Catarina, Tarrafal, Santa Cruz (these 4 covering São Tiago island), Fogo and Brava.

DEFENCE

Army. The Popular Militia is composed of 4 infantry companies and had a strength of 1,000 in 1991.

Navy. There are 5 fast patrol craft and 1 small hydrographic survey vessel. Personnel (1991), 200.

Air Force. An embryo air force operates two survivors of three An-26 twin-turboprop transports and has (1991) under 100 personnel.

INTERNATIONAL RELATIONS

Membership. Cape Verde is a member of the UN, OAU and an ACP state of the EEC.

ECONOMY

Budget. In 1984, the budget included revenue of 1,630m. escudos and expenditure, 2,134·5m.

Currency. The unit of currency is the *Cape Verde escudo* (CVE) of 100 *centavos.* There are coins of 20 and 50 *centavos* and of 1, $2\frac{1}{2}$, 10, 20 and 50 *escudos,* and banknotes of 100, 500 and 1,000 *escudos.* In March 1992, 122·76 *Escudo* = £1 and 69·92 *Escudo* = US$1.

Banking and Finance. The Banco de Cabo Verde is the bank of issue and commercial bank, with branches at Praia, Mindelo and Espargos airport (Sal).

ENERGY AND NATURAL RESOURCES

Electricity. Production in 1986 amounted to 18m. kwh; capacity (1986), 14,000 kw.

Minerals. Salt is obtained on the islands of Sal, Boa Vista and Maio. Volcanic rock (pozzolana) is mined for export.

Agriculture. Mostly confined to irrigated inland valleys, the chief crops (production, 1990, in 1,000 tonnes) are: Coconuts, 10; sugar-cane, 13; bananas, 5; potatoes, 4; cassava, 4; sweet potatoes, 8; maize, 16; beans, groundnuts and coffee. Bananas and coffee are mainly for export.

Livestock (1990): 110,000 goats, 19,000 cattle, 86,000 pigs and 6,000 asses.

Fisheries. The catch in 1985 was 10,200 tonnes, of which tuna comprised 46%. About 200 tonnes of lobsters are caught annually.

FOREIGN ECONOMIC RELATIONS

Commerce. Imports in 1985 totalled 7,445m. escudos of which 27% came from Portugal, 22% from the Netherlands; exports in 1985 totalled 462m. escudos

Caboverdianos, of which 31% went to Algeria, 30% to Portugal, 14% to Italy. In 1983, expatriated earnings from Cape Verdeans abroad totalled 2,800m. escudos. Exports: Fish, salt and bananas.

Total trade of Cape Verde with UK (British Department of Trade returns, in £1,000 sterling):

	1987	1988	1989	1990	1991
Imports to UK	301	132	178	336	193
Exports and re-exports from UK	1,208	1,812	2,301	1,537	1,908

COMMUNICATIONS

Roads. There were 2,250 km of roads (660 km paved) in 1984 and there were 3,000 private cars and 750 commercial vehicles.

Civil Aviation. Amilcar Cabral International Airport, at Espargos on Sal, is a major refuelling point on flights to Africa and Latin America. Transportes Aéros de Cabo Verde provides regular services to smaller airports on most of the other islands.

Shipping. The main ports are Mindelo and Praia. In 1982 the ports handled 371,812 tonnes of imports and 146,822 tonnes of exports. In 1986, the merchant marine comprised 25 vessels of 14,095 GRT.

Telecommunications. There are 2 radio stations, at Praia and Mindelo; both are government-owned. There were (1991) 50,000 radio receivers and (1984) 2,384 telephones.

JUSTICE, RELIGION, EDUCATION AND WELFARE

Justice. There is a network of People's Tribunals, with a Supreme Court in Praia.

Religion. In 1982, over 98% of the population were Roman Catholic.

Education. In 1987 there were 49,703 pupils and 1,464 teachers at 347 primary schools, 10,304 pupils and 321 teachers at 16 preparatory schools, 5,026 pupils and 170 teachers at 4 secondary schools, and 531 students and 52 teachers at a technical school. There were 211 students and 53 teachers in 3 teacher-training colleges and about 500 students were at foreign universities.

In 1981, 49% of the adult population were literate.

Health. In 1980 there were 21 hospitals and dispensaries with 632 beds; there were also 51 doctors, 3 dentists, 7 pharmacists, 9 midwives and 184 nursing personnel.

DIPLOMATIC REPRESENTATIVES

Of Cape Verde in Great Britain
Ambassador: (Vacant; resides in The Hague).

Of Great Britain in Cape Verde
Ambassador: R. C. Beetham, LVO (resides in Dakar).

Of Cape Verde in the USA (3415 Massachusetts Ave., NW, Washington, D.C., 20007)
Ambassador: Jorge Dos Santos.

Of the USA in Cape Verde (Rua Hojl Ya Yenna 81, Praia)
Ambassador: Francis T. McNamara.

Of Cape Verde to the United Nations
Ambassador: José Luis Jesús.

Further Reading

Annuario Estatistico de Cabo Verde. Praia. Annual
Carreira, A., *The People of the Cape Verde Islands*. London, 1982
Foy, C., *Cape Verde: Politics, Economics and Society*. London, 1988
Shaw, C., *Cape Verde Islands:* [Bibliography]. Oxford and Santa Barbara, 1990

CAYMAN ISLANDS

Capital: George Town
Population: 25,355 (1990)
GNP per capita: US$18,000 (1990)

HISTORY. The islands were discovered by Columbus on 10 May 1503 and (with Jamaica) were recognized as British possessions by the Treaty of Madrid in 1670. Grand Cayman was settled in 1734 and the other islands in 1833. They became a separate Crown Colony on 4 July 1959, administered by the same governor as Jamaica until the latter's independence on 6 Aug. 1962 when they received their own Administrator (From 1972 a governor).

AREA AND POPULATION. Cayman Islands consist of Grand Cayman, Little Cayman and Cayman Brac. Situated in the Caribbean Sea, about 200 miles NW of Jamaica. Area, 100 sq. miles (260 sq. km). Census population of 1989, 25,355 (13,202 Caymanians by birth). Estimate, 1990, 27,980 of which 18,440 (66%) were Caymanians. The spoken language is English. The chief town is George Town, census (1989) 12,921. Vital statistics (1990): Births, 490; marriages, 274; deaths, 109.

The areas and populations of the islands are:

	Sq. km	Census 1979	Census 1989
Grand Cayman	197	15,000	23,881
Cayman Brac	36	1,607	1,441
Little Cayman	26	70	33

CLIMATE. The climate is tropical maritime, with a cool season from Nov. to March and temperatures some 10°F warmer for the remaining months. Rainfall averages 56" (1,400 mm) a year at George Town. Hurricanes may be experienced between July and Nov.

CONSTITUTION AND GOVERNMENT. A new Constitution came into force in Aug. 1972. The Legislative Assembly consists of the Speaker, 3 official members, and 12 elected members.

The Executive Council consists of the Governor (as Chairman), the 3 official members and 4 elected members elected by the elected members of the Legislative Assembly.

Governor: A. J. Scott, CVO, CBE.

Flag: British Blue Ensign with the arms of the Colony on a white disc in the fly.

ECONOMY

Budget. Estimated revenue 1991, CI$110·2m.; expenditure, CI$109·7m. Public debt (31 Dec. 1990), CI$10·9m.; total reserves, CI$12m.

Currency. The unit of currency is the *Cayman Island dollar* (KYD), divided into 100 *cents*. In March 1992, £1 = 1·46 CI$; US$1 = 0·83.

Banking and Finance. 546 commercial banks and trust companies held licences at 31 Dec. 1990, which permit the holders to offer services to the public, over 30 domestically. Barclays Bank PLC has offices at George Town and Cayman Brac. Financial services are the Islands' chief industry.

INDUSTRY

Electricity. Production (1990) 205·86m. kwh.

Industry. At 31 Dec. 1990, 22,260 companies were registered in the islands.

FOREIGN ECONOMIC RELATIONS

Commerce. Exports, 1990 (f.o.b.), totalled CI$3·1m. Imports, (c.i.f.), CI$239·7m.; principally foodstuffs, manufactured items, textiles, building materials, automobiles and petroleum products.

Total trade between Cayman Islands and UK (British Department of Trade returns, in £1,000 sterling):

	1988	1989	1990	1991
Imports to UK	9,858	8,693	2,262	1,736
Exports and re-exports from UK	5,051	5,174	13,394	6,081

Tourism. Tourism is the chief industry, after financial services, and there were (1990) 3,220 beds in hotels and 2,908 in apartments, guesthouses and cottages. There were 614,870 visitors in 1990, including 253,158 by air.

COMMUNICATIONS

Roads. There were (1990) about 150 miles of road and 14,136 motor vehicles.

Civil Aviation. Cayman Airways provides regular services between Grand Cayman and Miami, Houston, Tampa, Atlanta, New York and Jamaica. Pan American, American and Northwest Airlines provide a daily service between Miami and Grand Cayman. CAL provides a regular inter-island service. Air Jamaica also provides services between Grand Cayman and Jamaica.

Shipping. Motor vessels ply regularly between the Cayman Islands, Jamaica, Costa Rica and Florida. Shipping registered at George Town, 506 vessels (June 1991).

Telecommunications. There were 19,394 telephones in 1990 and there are 2 radio broadcasting stations in the islands, with (1990) an estimated 30,000 receivers. A local commercial TV company began transmission in 1990.

Newspapers. The *Caymanian Compass* is published 5 days a week and *The New Caymanian*, weekly.

JUSTICE, RELIGION, EDUCATION AND WELFARE

Justice. There is a Grand Court, sitting 6 times a year for criminal sessions at George Town under a Chief Justice and 2 puisne judges. There are 2 Magistrates presiding over the Summary Court.

Religion. There are Anglican, Roman Catholic, Presbyterian and other Christian communities represented in the islands.

Education. In 1990 there were 10 government primary schools with 1,421 pupils, 6 private elementary schools with 751 pupils and 3 private secondary schools with 392 pupils. Post-primary education at the government high schools and the government middle school was attended by 1,952 pupils. There is also a private institution for tertiary education; a government school for special educational needs; a government-operated community college offering technical, vocational and business studies, as well as adult, educational and recreational courses; and a centre for training of handicapped persons.

Health. In 1990 there was a fully-equipped general hospital in George Town with 23 doctors, a dental clinic, 4 district clinics and a hospital in Cayman Brac.

Further Reading

Annual Report, 1990. Cayman Islands Government, 1991
Statistical Abstract of the Cayman Islands, 1990. Cayman Islands Government Statistics Unit, 1991

CENTRAL AFRICAN REPUBLIC

Capital: Bangui
Population: 3·04m. (1990)
GNP per capita: US$390 (1989)

République Centrafricaine

HISTORY. Central African Republic became independent on 13 Aug. 1960, after having been one of the 4 territories of French Equatorial Africa (under the name of Ubangi Shari) and from 1 Dec. 1958 a member state of the French Community. A new Constitution was adopted in 1976 and it provided for the country to be a parliamentary democracy and to be known as the Central African Empire. President Bokassa became Emperor Bokassa I. The Emperor was overthrown in a coup on 20–21 Sept. 1979 and the empire was abolished. On 15 March 1981 David Dacko was re-elected President but Army Chief General André Kolingba took power in a bloodless coup on 1 Sept. 1981 at the head of a Military Committee for National Recovery (CMRN), which held supreme power until 21 Sept. 1985 when President Kolingba dissolved it and initiated a return towards constitutional rule.

AREA AND POPULATION. The Central African Republic is bounded north by Chad, east by Sudan, south by Zaïre and Congo, and west by Cameroon. The area covers 622,436 sq. km (240,324 sq. miles); its population in 1975 (census), 2,054,610 and estimate in 1990 was 3·04m. of which 46·7% was urban. The capital is Bangui (596,776 inhabitants in 1988).

The areas, populations and capitals of the prefectures are as follows:

Prefecture	Sq. km	Estimate 1988	Capital	Estimate 1988
Bangui [1]	67	596,776	Bangui	596,776
Ombella-M'poko	31,835	137,469	Boali	...
Lobaye	19,235	174,134	M'baiki	29,495
Sangha [2]	19,412	62,977	Nola	...
Haute-Sangha	30,203	253,717	Berbérati	45,432
Nana-Mambere	26,600	213,630	Bouar	49,166
Ouham-Pende	32,100	258,166	Bozoum	22,600
Ouham	50,250	292,132	Bossangoa	41,877
Gribingui [2]	19,996	92,558	Kaga-Bandoro	19,774
Bamingui-Bangoran	58,200	31,082	Ndele	...
Vakaga	46,500	25,629	Birao	...
Kemo-Gribingui	17,204	84,884	Sibut	22,214
Ouaka	49,900	235,277	Bambari	52,092
Basse-Kotto	17,604	199,830	Mobaye	...
Haute-Kotto	86,650	57,583	Bria	24,620
M'bomou	61,150	143,971	Bangassou	36,254
Haut-M'bomou	55,530	39,560	Obo	...

[1] Autonomous commune.   [2] Economic prefecture.

Expectation of life in 1989 was 51 years.
French is the official language.

CLIMATE. A tropical climate with little variation in temperature. The wet months are May, June, Oct. and Nov. Bangui. Jan. 80°F (26·5°C), July 77°F (25°C). Annual rainfall 61" (1,525 mm). Ndele. Jan. 83°F (28·3°C), July 77°F (25°C). Annual rainfall 57" (1,417 mm).

CONSTITUTION AND GOVERNMENT. Under the Constitution adopted by a national referendum on 21 Nov. 1986, the sole legal political party was the *Rassemblement Démocratique Centrafricaine (RDC).* Legislative elections for the 52-member National Assembly were held on 31 July 1987. The President is elected by popular vote for a term of 6 years, and appoints and leads a Council of Ministers.

In July 1991 the National Assembly approved a constitutional revision to permit multi-party democracy.

The Council of Ministers in Jan. 1992 was composed as follows:

President of the Republic and of the RDC, Minister of Defence. Gen. André Kolingba (assumed office 1 Sept. 1981, re-elected 21 Nov. 1986).

Prime Minister: Edouard Frank.

Foreign Affairs: Michel Gbezera-Bria. *Interior, Territorial Administration:* Christophe Grelombe. *Economy, Finance, Planning and International Co-operation:* Dieudonné Wazoua. *National and Higher Education:* Jean Louis Psimhis. *Transport and Civil Aviation:* Pierre Gonifei-Ngaibounanou. *Civil Service, Labour, Social Security and Professional Training:* Daniel Sehoulia. *Justice, Keeper of the Seals:* Thomas Mapouka. *Public Health and Social Affairs:* Jean Willybiro-Sako. *Rural Development:* Théodore Bagayambo. *Energy and Mines, Geology and Hydrology:* Michel Salle. *Tourism, Water Resources, Forestry, Hunting and Fishing:* Raymond Mbitikon. *Trade and Industry, Small and Medium-sized Enterprises:* Thimothée Marboua. *Posts and Telecommunications:* Hugues Dobozendji. *Public Works and Territorial Planning:* Jacques Kithe. *Information, Arts and Culture:* Jean Bengue. *Parliamentary Relations, Secretary to Council of Ministers:* Edouard Franck.

There are also 5 Secretaries of State.

National flag: Four horizontal stripes of blue, white, green, yellow; over all in the centre a vertical red strip, and in the canton a yellow star.

National anthem: La Renaissance (Rebirth; words by B. Boganda; tune by H. Pepper).

Local Government: Central African Republic is divided into 14 prefectures (subdivided into 50 sub-prefectures); 2 'economic prefectures' and the autonomous commune of Bangui (the capital).

DEFENCE. Selective national service for a 2-year period is in force. There are some 2,700 personnel in the para-military gendarmerie. Some 1,200 French military personnel were stationed in 1992.

Army. The Army consisted (1991) of about 3,500 personnel, comprising a Republican Guard, a territorial defence and combined arms regiments. Equipment includes 4 T-55 tanks, 39 armoured personnel carriers and 10 Ferret scout cars.

Navy. The naval wing of the army has 9 river patrol craft and (1991) about 80 personnel.

Air Force. The Air Force has 2 Rallye Guerrier armed light aircraft, 1 DC-4 and 2 C-47 transports, 2 Reims-Cessna 337, 6 Aermacchi AL.60 and 5 Broussard liaison aircraft, 1 Alouette and 1 Ecureuil helicopters. It also maintains and operates the government's Caravelle and Falcon 20 twin-jet VIP aircraft. Personnel strength (1991) about 300.

INTERNATIONAL RELATIONS

Membership. Central African Republic is a member of the UN, OAU and an ACP state of the EEC.

ECONOMY

Policy. The new recovery plan (1983–86) provided for expenditure of 31,300m. francs CFA for development of agriculture, transport and infrastructure.

Budget. The budget for 1987 provided for expenditure of 56,610m. francs CFA, and for revenue of 46,230m. francs CFA.

Currency. The unit of currency is the *franc CFA* with a parity of 50 *francs CFA* to 1 French *franc*. There are coins of 1, 2, 5, 10, 25, 50, 100 and 500 *francs CFA*, and banknotes of 100, 500, 1,000, 5,000 and 10,000 *francs CFA*. In March 1992, £1 = 489·63 *francs CFA*; US$1 = 278·91 *francs CFA*.

Banking. The *Banque des Etats de l'Afrique Centrale* is the bank of issue.

ENERGY AND NATURAL RESOURCES

Electricity. Production in 1987 totalled 92m. kwh. Supply 220 volts; 50 Hz.

Minerals. In 1986 258,701 carats of gem diamonds, 98,678 carats of industrial diamonds and (1987) 224 kg of gold were mined. There are significant regions of uranium in the Bakouma area.

Agriculture. Over 86% of the working population is occupied in subsistence agriculture. The main crops (production 1990, in 1,000 tonnes) are cassava, 560; groundnuts, 100; bananas, 87; plantains, 67; millet, 15; maize, 73; seed cotton, 26; coffee, 27; rice, 15.

Livestock (1990, in 1,000): Cattle, 2,595; goats, 1,250; sheep, 133; pigs, 413.

Forestry. There are 35·8m. ha of forest, representing 58% of the land area. The extensive hardwood forests, particularly in the south-west, provide mahogany, obeche and limba for export. Production (1985) 3·42m. cu. metres.

Fisheries. Catch (1983) 13,000 tonnes.

INDUSTRY. The small industrial sector includes factories producing cotton fabrics, footwear, beer and radios.

FOREIGN ECONOMIC RELATIONS

Commerce. Imports and exports in 1m. francs CFA:

	1984	1985	1986	1987
Imports	77,700	90,370	96,677	...
Exports	50,057	58,720	44,960	39,180

In 1983, France took 30% of exports and provided 46% of imports. Of all exports, coffee comprised 29% (by value), diamonds 24%, timber 19% and cotton 13%.

Total trade of Central African Republic with UK (British Department of Trade returns, in £1,000 sterling):

	1988	1989	1990	1991
Imports to UK	195	418	58	37
Exports and re-exports from UK	733	1,630	1,669	502

Tourism. There were about 4,000 visitors in 1986.

COMMUNICATIONS

Roads. In 1986 there were 20,286 km of roads, of which 442 km bitumenized and (1984) 46,982 vehicles in use.

Civil Aviation. There are international airports at Mpoko, near Bangui, and Berbérati. Air Centrafrique operates extensive internal services to several airstrips.

Shipping. Timber and barges are taken to Brazzaville (Congo).

Telecommunications. There were 3,323 telephones in 1986. Broadcasting is provided by the state-controlled Radiodiffusion-Télévision Centrafricaine. There were 0·54m. radio sets in 1991.

Cinemas. In 1987 there were 5 cinemas.

Newspapers. In 1984 there was one daily newspaper.

JUSTICE, RELIGION, EDUCATION AND WELFARE

Justice. The Criminal Court and Supreme Court are situated in Bangui. There are 16 high courts throughout the country.

Religion. In 1989 there were 1·39m. Protestants and 0·93m. Roman Catholics. Traditional animist beliefs are still current.

Education. The University of Bangui was founded in 1970 and had 1,489 students in 1980. In 1986-87 there were 274,179 pupils at primary schools and 44,804 at secondary schools; technical schools (1984-85) had 2,514 students, while (1982) 327 were at the 2 teacher-training establishments.

Health. In 1984 there were 104 hospitals and health centres with 3,774 beds; there were also 112 doctors, 6 dentists, 16 pharmacists, 168 midwives and 710 nursing personnel.

DIPLOMATIC REPRESENTATIVES

Of Central African Republic in Great Britain
Ambassador: (Vacant; resides in Paris).

Of Great Britain in Central African Republic
Ambassador: William Quantrill (resides in Yaoundé).

Of Central African Republic in the USA (1618 22nd St., NW, Washington, D.C. 20008)
Ambassador: Jean-Pierre Sohahong-Kombet.

Of the USA in Central African Republic (Ave. President Dacko, Bangui)
Ambassador: Daniel H. Simpson.

Of Central African Republic to the United Nations
Ambassador: Jean-Pierre Sohahong-Kombet.

Further Reading

Kalck, H. P., *Historical Dictionary of the Central African Republic*. Metuchen, 1980

CHAD

Capital: N'djaména
Population: 5·54m. (1990)
GNP per capita: US$190 (1989)

République du Tchad

HISTORY. France proclaimed a protectorate over Chad on 5 Sept. 1900, and in July 1908 the territory was incorporated into French Equatorial Africa. It became a separate colony March 1920, and in 1946 one of the four constituent territories of French Equatorial Africa. On 28 Nov. 1958 Chad became an autonomous republic within the French Community and achieved full independence on 11 Aug. 1960, although the northern prefecture of Borkou-Ennedi-Tibesti remained under French military administration until 1965.

Conflicts between the central government and secessionist groups, particularly in the Moslem north and centre of Chad, began in 1965 and flared into a prolonged and confused civil war that continued under different protagonists, with occasional pauses during attempts at reconciliation. On 7 June 1982 the *Forces Armées du Nord* (FAN) led by Hissène Habré gained control of the country. In June 1983 the Libyan-backed forces of former President Goukouni Oueddei re-occupied Bourkou-Ennedi-Tibesti, but by April 1987 most of the rebels rallied to the government side, which then forced the Libyans back into the Aozou Strip, a 114,000 sq. km region in the extreme north of Chad occupied by Libyan forces since 1973. A ceasefire took effect on 11 Sept. 1987. There was an attempted coup on 1 April 1989.

Rebel forces of the Popular Salvation Movement led by Idriss Deby entered Chad from Sudan in Nov. 1990 and, meeting little resistance, overcame the government forces of President Hissène Habré, who took refuge in Cameroon. On 4 Dec. 1990 Deby declared himself President.

AREA AND POPULATION. Chad is bounded west by Cameroon, Nigeria and Niger, north by Libya, east by Sudan and south by the Central African Republic. Area, 1,284,000 sq. km; its population in 1990 was estimated at 5,540,000 (32% urban; census 1975, 4,029,917). The capital is N'djaména with 594,700 inhabitants in 1988, other large towns being Sarh (113,400), Moundou (102,800), Abéché (83,000), Bongor (35,600) and Doba (34,000).

The areas, populations and chief towns of the 14 prefectures were:

Préfecture	sq. km	Population Estimate 1988	Capital
Borkou-Ennedi-Tibesti	600,350	109,000	Faya (Largeau)
Biltine	46,850	216,000	Biltine
Ouaddaï	76,240	422,000	Abéché
Batha	88,800	431,000	Ati
Kanem	114,520	245,000	Mao
Lac	22,320	165,000	Bol
Chari-Baguirmi	82,910	844,000	N'djaména
Guéra	58,950	254,000	Mongo
Salamat	63,000	131,000	Am Timan
Moyen-Chari	45,180	646,000	Sarh
Logone Oriental	28,035	377,000	Doba
Logone Occidental	8,695	365,000	Moundou
Tandjilé	18,045	371,000	Laï
Mayo-Kabbi	30,105	852,000	Bongor

The official languages are French and Arabic, but more than 100 different languages and dialects are spoken. The largest ethnic group is the Sara of southern Chad.

CLIMATE. A tropical climate, with adequate rainfall in the south, though Nov. to April are virtually rainless months. Further north, desert conditions prevail. N'djaména. Jan. 75°F (23·9°C), July 82°F (27·8°C). Annual rainfall 30" (744 mm).

CONSTITUTION AND GOVERNMENT. After overthrowing the regime

346

of Hissène Habré (*see* THE STATESMAN'S YEAR-BOOK, 1991-92, pp. 345-46), Idriss Deby proclaimed himself *President* and was sworn in on 4 March 1991.

A National Salvation Council and a State Council have been set up. In March 1991 the National Salvation Council introduced a national charter to be in force for 30 months. This provides for a 31-member consultative Provisional Republican Council. A law of Oct. 1991 permits the formation of political parties provided they are not based on regionalism, tribalism or intolerance. A national conference and parliamentary elections were scheduled for May 1992.

In Jan. 1992 the Republican Council included:
Prime Minister: Jean Alingué Bawoyeu.
Foreign Minister: Soungi Ahmat. *Defence:* Nadjita Beassoumoul. *Planning and Co-operation:* Ibn Oumar Mahatmah Saleh. *Economy and Finance:* Mansse Nguealbaye. *Information:* Mahamat Saleh Ahmat. *Transport:* Col. Abbas Koti. *Interior:* Ahmat Hassaballah Soubiane.

National flag: Three vertical strips of blue, yellow, red.
National anthem: La Tchadienne (words by Father Gidrol; tune by Father Villard).
Local Government: The 14 *préfectures* are divided into 53 *sous-préfectures*.

DEFENCE

Army. The Army includes 3 infantry and 1 armoured battalions with 2 artillery batteries. Equipment includes 63 armoured fighting vehicles. In 1991 the strength was over 17,000 and there was a paramilitary force of 5,700.

Air Force. The Air Force has 3 C-130 Hercules, 1 VIP Caravelle, 1 C-54, 2 Aviocar and 6 C-47 transports, 4 Reims-Cessna F337 light aircraft, 2 Turbo-Porters, 2 Broussard communications aircraft, 2 Gazelle helicopters, 2 armed PC-7 aircraft and 2 SF.260W Warrior trainers. Personnel (1991) about 200.

INTERNATIONAL RELATIONS

Membership. Chad is a member of the UN, OAU and is an ACP state of the EEC.

ECONOMY

Budget. The budget for 1990 envisaged expenditure of 39,705m. francs CFA and revenue, 33,400m. francs CFA.

Currency. The unit of currency is the *franc CFA* with a parity value of 50 *francs CFA* to 1 French *franc*. In March 1992, £1 = 489·63 *francs*; US$1 = 278·91 *francs*.

Banking. The *Banque des Etats de l'Afrique Centrale* is the bank of issue, and the principal commercial banks are the *Banque de Développement du Tchad* and the *Banque Tchadienne de Crédit et de Dépôts*.

ENERGY AND NATURAL RESOURCES

Electricity. Production (1989) amounted to 80m. kwh. Supply 220 volts; 50 Hz.

Oil. The oilfield in Kanem préfecture has been linked by pipeline to a new refinery at Laï (in Tandjilé) but production has remained minimal.

Minerals. Salt (about 4,000 tonnes per annum) is mined around Lake Chad, and deposits of uranium, gold and bauxite are to be exploited.

Agriculture. Cotton growing (in the south) and animal husbandry (in the central zone) are the most important industries. Production (1990, in 1,000 tonnes) was: Millet, 172; sugar-cane, 290; yams, 240; seed cotton, 142; groundnuts, 80; cassava, 330; rice, 60; dry beans, 42; sweet potatoes, 46; mangoes, 7; dates, 32; maize, 31; cotton lint, 55; cotton seed, 100.

Livestock: Cattle (1990), 4,299,205; sheep (1988), 2·25m.; goats, 2·25m.; chickens, 4m.

Fisheries. Fish production from Lake Chad and the Chari and Logone rivers, was estimated at 110,000 tonnes in 1986.

INDUSTRY. Cotton ginning is the principal activity, undertaken in 51 mills. Sugar refineries produced 37,309 tonnes in 1989. A textile factory produced 10·3m.

metres of woven fabric in 1989, a brewery 114,700 hectolitres of beer and a cigarette factory 186m. cigarettes. There are also rice and flour mills and other factories involved in food processing or light industry.

FOREIGN ECONOMIC RELATIONS

Commerce. Trade (in 1m. francs CFA):

	1988	1989	1990
Imports	68,029	75,103	77,743
Exports	42,901	46,571	51,502

The main trading partners are France and Nigeria. Cotton formed 91% of exports in 1983.

Total trade with UK (British Department of Trade returns, in £1,000 sterling):

	1987	1988	1989	1990	1991
Imports to UK	1,101	1,764	822	369	1,477
Exports and re-exports from UK	1,006	639	3,462	1,567	1,789

COMMUNICATIONS

Roads. In 1983 there were 40,000 km of roads, of which only 400 km are surfaced. In 1985 there were 3,000 private cars and 4,000 lorries and buses.

Civil Aviation. There is an international airport at N'djaména, from which UTA and Air Afrique run 4 flights per week to Paris; there are also flights to Bangui and Kinshasa. Air Tchad operates internal services to 12 secondary airports.

Telecommunications. In 1978 there were 3,850 telephones. The state-controlled Radiodiffusion Nationale Tchadienne broadcasts a national and 2 regional services (Moundou and Sarh). There were estimated to be 1·25m. radio sets in 1991. Television is being developed (colour by SECAM) by the state-controlled Télé-Tchad.

JUSTICE, RELIGION, EDUCATION AND WELFARE

Justice. There are criminal courts and magistrates courts in N'djaména, Moundou, Sarh and Abéché, with a Court of Appeal situated in N'djaména.

Religion. The northern and central parts of the country are predominantly Moslem. In 1989 there were 2·24m. Moslems and 1·83m. Christians. Traditional animist beliefs are still current.

Education. In 1987 there were 300,000 pupils in primary schools, 42,000 in secondary schools, and 4,000 in technical schools and teacher-training establishments. The University of Chad (founded 1971) at N'djaména had (1984) 1,643 students and 141 teaching staff.

Health. There were 33 hospitals with 3,353 beds in 1977 and in 1978 90 doctors, 4 dentists, 9 pharmacists, 98 midwives and 993 nursing personnel.

DIPLOMATIC REPRESENTATIVES

Of Chad in Great Britain
Ambassador: (Vacant; resides in Brussels).

Of Great Britain in Chad
Ambassdor: William Quantrill (resides in Yaoundé).

Of Chad in the USA (2002 R. St., NW, Washington, D.C., 20009)
Ambassador: Mahamat Ali Adoum.

Of the USA in Chad (Ave., Felix Eboue, N'djaména)
Ambassador: Richard W. Bogosian.

Of Chad to the United Nations
Ambassador: Mahamat Ali Adoum.

Further Reading

Kelley, M. P., *Conditions of the State's Survival.* Oxford, 1986
Thompson, V. and Adloff, R., *Conflict in Chad.* London and Berkeley, 1981

CHILE

Capital: Santiago
Population: 13·7m. (1991)
GNP per capita: US$1,770 (1989)

República de Chile

HISTORY. The Republic of Chile threw off allegiance to the crown of Spain, constituting a national government on 18 Sept. 1810, finally freeing itself from Spanish rule in 1818.

The Marxist coalition government of President Salvador Allende Gossens was ousted on 11 Sept. 1973 by the armed services, which formed a government headed by a junta of the four Commanders-in-Chief. Gen. Augusto Pinochet Ugarte, Commander-in-Chief of the Army, took over the presidency. President Allende committed suicide on the day of the coup.

The new government assumed wide-ranging powers. A constitution of 1981 provided for an eventual return to democracy. Gen. Pinochet was rejected as president in a plebiscite in 1988. Patricio Aylwyn Azócar was elected president in Dec. 1989.

AREA AND POPULATION. Chile is bounded in the north by Peru, east by Bolivia and Argentina, and south and west by the Pacific ocean.

Chile has an area of 736,905 sq. km (284,520 sq. miles) excluding the claimed Antarctic territory. Many islands to the west and south belong to Chile: The Islas Juan Fernández (179 sq. km with 516 inhabitants in 1982) lie about 600 km west of Valparaíso, and the volcanic Isla de Pascua (Easter Island or Rapa Nui, 118 sq. km with 1,867 inhabitants in 1982), discovered in 1722, lies about 3,000 km WNW of Valparaíso. Small uninhabited dependencies include Sala y Gomez (400 km east of Easter Is.), San Ambrosio and San Félix (1,000 km northwest of Valparaíso, and 20 km apart) and Islas Diego Ramírez (100 km SW of Cape Horn).

In 1940 Chile declared, and in each subsequent year has reaffirmed, its ownership of the sector of the Antarctic lying between 53° and 90° W. long.; and asserted that the British claim to the sector between the meridians 20° and 80° W. long. overlapped the Chilean by 27°. Seven Chilean bases exist in Antarctica. A law promulgated 21 July 1955 put the Intendente (*now* Gobernador) of the Province (*now* Region) of Magallanes in charge of the 'Chilean Antarctic Territory' which has an area of 1,269,723 sq. km. and a population (1982) of 1,368.

The total population at the census in 1982 was 11,275,440. Estimate (1991) 13,700,000; 85·9% urban. Density, 17·4 per sq. km.

The areas of the 13 regions and their populations (census, 1982) were as follows:

Region	Sq. km	Census 1982	Capital	Estimate 1987
Tarapacá	58,786	273,427	Iquique	132,948
Antofagasta	125,253	341,203	Antofagasta	204,577
Atacama	74,705	183,071	Copiapó	70,241 [1]
Coquimbo	40,656	419,178	La Serena	106,617
Aconcagua	16,396	1,204,693	Valparaíso	278,762
Metropolitan	15,549	4,294,938	Santiago	4,858,342
Liberador	16,456	584,989	Rancagua	172,489
Maule	30,518	723,224	Talca	164,482
Bíobío	36,939	1,516,552	Concepción	294,375
Araucanía	31,946	692,924	Temuco	217,789
Los Lagos	67,247	843,430	Puerto Montt	113,488
Aisén	108,997	65,478	Coihaique	31,167 [1]
Magallanes	132,034	132,333	Punta Arenas	111,724

[1] Census, 1982

Vital statistics (1984): Birth rate 21·2 per 1,000 population; death rate, 6·3; marriage rate, 7 (1982); infant mortality, 1990, 19·5 per 1,000 live births; growth rate, 1985-90, 17 per 1,000 population. Life expectancy (1990) 71·8 years.

Over 92% of the population is mixed or *mestizo*; only about 2% are European im-

349

migrants and their descendants, while the remainder are indigenous Amerindians of the Araucanian, Fuegian and Chango groups. Language and culture remain of European origin, with the 675,000 Araucanian-speaking (mainly Mapuche) Indians the only sizeable minority.

Other large towns (estimate, 1987) are: Viña del Mar (297,294), Talcahuano (231,356), Arica (169,774), San Bernardo (168,534), Puente Alto (165,534), Chillán (148,805), Los Angeles (126,122), Osorno (122,462), Valdívia (117,205), Calama (109,645), Coquimbo (105,252) and Quilpué (103,004).

CLIMATE. With its enormous range of latitude and the influence of the Andean Cordillera, the climate of Chile is very complex, ranging from extreme aridity in the north, through a Mediterranean climate in Central Chile, where winters are wet and summers dry, to a cool temperate zone in the south, with rain at all seasons. In the extreme south, conditions are very wet and stormy. Santiago. Jan. 67°F (19·5°C), July 46°F (8°C). Annual rainfall 15" (375 mm). Antofagasta. Jan. 69°F (20·6°C), July 57°F (14°C). Annual rainfall 0·5" (12·7 mm). Valparaíso. Jan. 64°F (17·8°C), July 53°F (11·7°C). Annual rainfall 20" (505 mm).

CONSTITUTION AND GOVERNMENT. The Government of President Pinochet had assumed wide-ranging powers but the 'state of siege' ended in March 1978. A new Constitution was approved by 67·5% of the voters on 11 Sept. 1980 and came into force on 11 March 1981. It provided for a return to democracy after a minimum period of 8 years. Gen. Pinochet would remain in office during this period after which the Government would nominate a single candidate for President.

A plebiscite was held on 5 Oct. 1988 with President Pinochet as the candidate to be approved or rejected by the people, to continue for 8 more years. Votes against 54·6%, votes in favour 43·31%.

The following is a list of the presidents since 1946:

Gabriel González Videla, 3 Nov. 1946–3 Nov. 1952.
Carlos Ibáñez del Campo, 3 Nov. 1952–3 Nov. 1958.
Jorge Alessandri Rodriguez, 3 Nov. 1958–3 Nov. 1964.
Eduardo Frei Montalva, 3 Nov. 1964–3 Nov. 1970.
Salvador Allende Gossens, 3 Nov. 1970–11 Sept. 1973 (deposed).
Gen. Augusto Pinochet, 17 Dec. 1974-11 March 1990.

President of the Republic: At the presidential elections of 14 Dec. 1989 Patricio Aylwyn Azócar obtained 55·2% of the vote. He assumed office on 11 March 1990.

In Dec. 1991 the Cabinet comprised:
Foreign Affairs: Enrique Silva Cimma. *Agriculture:* Juan Agustin Figueroa. *Interior:* Enrique Krauss. *Justice:* Francisco Cumplido. *Defence:* Patricio Rojas. *Finance:* Alejandro Foxley. *Labour:* Rene Cortázar. *Health:* Jorge Jiménez. *Mining:* Juan Hamilton. *National Planning:* Sergio Molina. *Presidential Secretary:* Edgardo Boeninger. *General Secretary of the Government:* Enrique Correa. *Economy:* Carlos Ominami. *Education:* Ricardo Lagos. *Transportation:* Germán Correa. *National Property:* Luis Alvarado. *Energy:* Jaime Toha. *Public Works:* Carlos Hurtado. *Corporation for Promotion of Production:* Rene Abeliuk. *Housing:* Alberto Etchegaray.

National flag: Two horizontal bands, white, red, with a white star on blue square in top sixth next to staff.

National anthem: Dulce patria, recibe los votos ('Sweet Fatherland, receive the vows'; words by E. Lillo, 1847; tune by Ramón Carnicer, 1828).

Local Government. For the purposes of local government the Military Junta in pursuance of its policy of administrative decentralization divided the republic into 13 regions (12 and Greater Santiago). Each region is presided over by an intendent, while the provinces (51) included in it are in charge of a governor who represents the central government. The provinces are divided into municipalities under a mayor. All these officials are appointed by the President. The first elections to be held since 1970 were scheduled for June 1992.

DEFENCE. Military service is for a period of 2 years at the age of 19.

Army. The Army is organized in 6 divisions, each with infantry, armoured cavalry, artillery, mountain and engineer regiments; and 1 helicopter-borne ranger unit. Equipment includes 60 M-4A3, 150 M-51 and 21 AMX-30 tanks and 157 light tanks. The service operates 24 transport and 16 training aircraft and 45 helicopters. Strength (1991) 54,000 (27,000 conscripts) with 80,000 reserves.

Navy. The principal ships of the Chilean Navy are the 1937-vintage ex-US cruiser *O'Higgins*, of 13,700 tonnes, armed with 9 152mm guns and 8 127mm. She carries one light helicopter. There are also 4 ex-British 'County'-class guided missile armed destroyers renamed *Capitan Prat, Almirante Cochrane, Almirante Latorre,* and *Blanco Encalada,* purchased on their disposal from the Royal Navy between 1982 and 1987. *Cochrane* and *Blanco Encalada* have had the Sea Slug launcher removed and replaced with an extended helicopter hangar and flight deck to operate 2 Super-Puma helicopters.

There are also 2 small modern West German-built diesel submarines, 2 British Oberon class submarines, other British-built destroyers, 3 British Leander class frigates, 4 fast missile craft, 4 torpedo boats, 2 offshore patrol vessels and 20 coastal craft. There are 3 French-built medium landing ships. Major auxiliaries include 2 tankers, 1 submarine support vessel, 1 survey ship, 2 transports, and 1 Antarctic patrol ship. There are 11 service craft and numerous boats.

The Naval Air Service numbering 500 personnel operates 4 squadrons: 8 maritime patrol aircraft, 9 transports utility aircraft, 4 anti-submarine helicopters and 10 training aircraft.

Naval personnel in 1991 totalled 25,000 all ranks (3,000 conscripts) including 5,200 marines.

A separate Coast Guard numbering 1,600 personnel operates 15 patrol craft and a helicopter.

Air Force. Strength (1991) is 12,800 personnel (800 conscripts), with (1991) over 100 first-line and 150 second-line aircraft, divided among 12 groups, each comprising 1 squadron, within 4 combat and support wings. Groups 1 and 12 have twin-jet A-37Bs, from a total of 34 acquired for light strike/reconnaissance duties. Group 2 is equipped for photo-reconnaissance with 2 Canberras. Group 4 has 13 Mirage 50 fighters. Group 5 has 14 Twin Otters for light transport and survey duties. Group 7 has 12 F-5E Tiger II fighter-bombers and 2 F-5F trainers. Groups 8 and 9 are also fighter-bomber units, with a total of 30 Hunter F.71s, ex-RAF FGA.9s, and T.72s. Group 10 is a transport wing, with 2 C-130H Hercules, 4 Boeing 707s, 3 Douglas piston-engined transports and various helicopters. An aerial survey unit has 2 Learjets and 3 Beech twin-engined aircraft. Training aircraft include piston-engined Piper Dakota and T-35 Pillan basic trainers and licence-built CASA C-101BB Aviojets. CASA C-101CC Aviojet light strike aircraft were being delivered in 1991.

INTERNATIONAL RELATIONS

Membership. Chile is a member of the UN, OAS and LAIA.

ECONOMY

Budget. In 1987 revenue was US$8,469·8m. and expenditure, US$8,421·6m.

Currency. The unit of currency is the *Chilean peso* (CLP) of 100 *centavos*. It was revalued by 5% in Jan. 1992. Inflation was 18·7% in 1991.

On 31 Dec. 1987 notes and coins in circulation were 161,337m. pesos.

In March 1992 there were 611·25 *pesos* = £1 and 348·19 *pesos* = US$1.

Banking and Finance. There is a Central Bank and a State Bank. The Central Bank was made independent of government control in March 1990.

In 1988 24 foreign banks and in 1991 15 domestic banks were operating.

In 1988 deposits in foreign currency totalled US$866·9m. and deposits in local currency, 1,745,545m. pesos.

There is a stock exchange in Santiago.

Weights and Measures. The metric system has been legally established since 1865, but the old Spanish weights and measures are still in use to some extent.

ENERGY AND NATURAL RESOURCES

Electricity. In 1987 production of electricity was 14,821m. kwh, of which 80% hydro-electric. Supply 220 volts; 50 Hz.

Oil. Petroleum was discovered in 1945 in the southern area of Magallanes. Production (1991) 940,000 tonnes.

Gas. Production (1987) 4,352·6m. cu. metres.

Minerals. The wealth of the country consists chiefly in its minerals, especially in the northern provinces of Atacama and Tarapacá.

Copper is the most important source of foreign exchange (about 41% of exports in 1987) and government revenues (almost 40%). The copper industry's output in 1989 was 1,609,000 tonnes. In March 1991 the Escondida copper mine opened with an annual production of 0·32m. fine tonnes.

Nitrate of soda is found in the Atacama deserts. Production was 870,000 tonnes in 1985. Iodine is a by-product: 1985 production totalled 2,760 tonnes. The use of solar evaporation as a means of reducing costs has developed the production of potassium salts as an additional by-product.

High-grade deposits of iron ore estimated at over 1,000m. tonnes exist in the provinces of Atacama and Coquimbo. Production in 1987 was 6,690,168 tonnes, as well as 3,684,590 tonnes processed into pellet form.

Coal reserves exceed 2,000m. tons, much of it low in thermal value. Net 1987 production was 1,736,152 tonnes. Lignite production in 1988 was 37,000 tonnes.

Other minerals include molybdenum (16,941 tonnes, pure, 1987), zinc (19,618 tonnes, 1987), manganese (44,000 tonnes, 1989), silver (536,000 tonnes, 1989), gold (0·64m. troy oz., 1988) and lead (829 tonnes, 1987).

Agriculture. Total area of land available for agricultural use in 1986 was 29m. ha, of which 12% was sown crops, 38% grassland and 15% forested.

Some principal crops were as follows:

Crop	Area harvested, 1,000 ha 1988	Production, 1,000 tonnes 1988	Crop	Area harvested, 1,000 ha 1988	Production, 1,000 tonnes 1988
Wheat	577	1,874	Potatoes	62	727
Oats	61	127	Dry beans	77	81
Barley	24	48	Lentils	39	25
Maize	90	617	Green peas	7	24
Rice	39	147	Sugar-beet	47	2,650

In 1987 fruit plantations had expanded to 119,600 ha with 9 types of fruit, mainly apples and table grapes. Production, 1988 (in 1,000 tonnes): Apples, 592; grapes, 440; pears, 80; peaches and nectarines, 78; plums, 72; oranges, 70; lemons and limes, 50. Exports in the season ended May 1988 totalled 90m. cases valued at US$527m.

Production of animal products in 1987 was (in 1,000 tonnes): Cattle, 174·6; sheep, 14·5; pork, 88·3; poultry, 89·5. Eggs, 1,790m.; milk, 1,100m. litres.

Livestock (1990, in 1,000): Cattle, 3,250; horses, 520; asses, 28; sheep, 6,650; goats, 600; pigs, 1,450; poultry, 29,000.

Forestry. In 1987, there were 1,150,000 ha of cultivated forests from Maule to Magallanes, the most important species being the pine (*pinus radiata*) which covers almost 930,000 ha. Eucalyptus and poplar cover some 92,000 ha. Native species of importance amounted to 9·4m. ha in 1983.

Production during 1988 amounted to about 2·7m. cu. metres of sawn timber. Exports of forestry products in 1987 were valued at US$587m.

Fisheries. Chile has 4,200 km of coastline and exclusive fishing rights to 1·6 m. sq. km. There are 220 species of edible fish. Catch of fish and shellfish in 1987 was 4·9m. tonnes; shellfish, 167,000 tonnes. Exports of seafood in 1987 were US$654·3m., of which fishmeal accounted for US$375m. The industry employs 70,000 (1·5% of the working population).

INDUSTRY. Output in 1989 (in 1,000 tonnes): Iron and steel, 679; crude steel, 813; refined copper, 1,071; cotton fabric, 75; sugar, 445; magarine (1988), 31. Cellulose and wood-pulp are two industries which are rapidly developing; in 1987, 673,100 tonnes of cellulose were produced. Cement (1,872,000 tonnes in 1988) and fishmeal (469,400 tonnes in 1987) are also important.

Labour. In Dec. 1987 the total workforce numbered 4·01m., of which 837,000 were employed in agriculture, 208,000 in construction, 607,000 in manufacturing industries, 690,000 in trade, 81,000 in mining and 253,000 in transport and communications. A methanol plant with production capacity of 750,000 tonnes a year began operations in 1988 in Punta Arenas. There were 249,000 persons registered unemployed in 1989 (87,000 females).

Trade Unions. Trade unions began in the middle 1880s.

FOREIGN ECONOMIC RELATIONS. In Sept. 1991 Chile and Mexico signed the free trade Treaty of Santiago envisaging annual tariff reductions of 10% from Jan. 1992.

Commerce. Import tariffs were cut from 15% to 11% in June 1991.
Imports and exports in US$1m.:

	1985	1986	1987	1988	1989	1990
Imports	2,955	3,099	3,967	4,731	6,535	7,880
Exports	3,743	4,199	5,046	5,102	6,954	8,579

In 1987 imports (in US$1m.) from USA, were valued at 773; Venezuela, 144; Brazil, 380; Japan, 387; Federal Republic of Germany, 335; Argentina, 159; Spain, 117; France, 129; UK, 128; Italy, 96.

In 1987 the principal imports were (in US$1m.): Fuels, 460; chemicals, 740; industrial equipment, 718; transport equipment, 260; tools, 38, live animals, 4; foodstuffs, 40. The principal exports in 1987 were (in US$1m.): Copper, 2,100; paper and pulp, 365; gold, 165; fresh fruit, 527; fish meal, 375; nitrate, 99.

Total trade between Chile and UK (British Department of Trade returns, in £1,000 sterling):

	1988	1989	1990	1991
Imports to UK	179,628	193,280	222,469	177,876
Exports and re-exports from UK	80,901	96,003	128,056	108,640

Tourism. Some 560,000 tourists visited Chile in 1987.

COMMUNICATIONS

Roads. In 1986 there were in Chile 78,025 km of highways. There were in 1987 (estimate), 660,000 private cars, 256,000 goods vehicles, 22,000 buses and 36,000 motor cycles.

Railways. The total length of state railway lines was (1990) 4,302 km, including 1,849 km electrified, of broad- and metre-gauge. In 1990 the State Railways carried 5m. tonnes and 8·8m. passengers, including freight traffic on the Northern Railway (1,429 km of metre-gauge) which was taken over by a mixed corporation in 1989. Further electrification is in progress between Concepción and Puerto Montt (600 km). There is a metro in Santiago (27·3 km). The Antofagasta (Chili) and Bolivia Railway (728 km, metre-gauge) links the port of Antofagasta with Bolivia and Argentina and carried 1·6m. tonnes in 1990.

Civil Aviation. There are 7 international airports, 16 domestic airports and about 300 landing grounds. Chile is served by 19 commercial air companies (2 Chilean). In 1986, 999,000 passengers were carried.

Shipping. The mercantile marine has consisted since 1982 of 60 ships of over 100 tons (825,076 DWT) but most of the fleet operates under flags of convenience. Valparaíso is the chief port. The free ports of Magallanes, Chiloé and Aysén serve the southern provinces.

Telecommunications. There are 1,486 post offices and agencies. In 1983 there were 608,200 (Santiago, 360,053) telephones in use.

In 1991 there were 163 radio stations grouped in the Asociación de Radiodifusores de Chile. The state-controlled Televisión Nacional de Chile transmits from 23 stations (colour by NTSC). In 1991 there were 4·25m. radio and 416,000 TV sets.

Cinemas (1986). Cinemas numbered 170; 60 of them are in Santiago.

Newspapers (1986). There were 65 daily newspapers and 100 magazines.

JUSTICE, RELIGION, EDUCATION AND WELFARE

Justice. There are a High Court of Justice in the capital, 12 courts of appeal distributed over the republic, tribunals of first instance in the departmental capitals and second-class judges in the sub-delegations.

Religion. In 1989 there were 10·46m. Roman Catholics with 1 cardinal-archbishop, 5 archbishops, 22 bishops and 2 vicars apostolic. There were 0·13m. Jews in 1991.

Education. Education is in 3 stages: Basic (6–14 years), Middle (15–18) and University (19–23). In 1988-89 there were 2,005,000 pupils and 69,000 teachers in the basic schools, 736,000 pupils and 42,000 teachers in the middle schools and 224,000 students and 15,000 teachers in higher education, including universities.

University education is provided in the state university, University of Chile (founded in 1842), the Catholic University at Santiago (1888), the University of Concepción (1919), the Catholic University at Valparaíso (1928), the Universidad Técnica Federico Santa María at Valparaíso (1930), the Universidad Técnica del Estado (1952), Universidad Austral, Valdivia (1954) and Universidad del Norte, Antofagasta (1957).

Health. In 1982 there were 5,416 doctors, 1,644 dentists, 201 pharmacists, 1,930 midwives and 25,889 nursing personnel. 205 hospitals, 296 health centres and 888 emergency posts.

DIPLOMATIC REPRESENTATIVES

Of Chile in Great Britain (12 Devonshire St., London, W1N 2FS)
Ambassador: German Riesco.

Of Great Britain in Chile (La Concepción 177, Casilla 72-D, Santiago)
Ambassador: Richard Neilson, CMG, LVO.

Of Chile in the USA (1732 Massachusetts Ave., NW, Washington, D.C., 20036)
Ambassador: Patricio Silva.

Of the USA in Chile (Agustinas 1343, Santiago)
Ambassador: Charles A. Gillespie Jr.

Of Chile to the United Nations
Ambassador: Juan Somavia.

Further Reading

Statistical Information: The Instituto Nacional de Estadística (Santiago), was founded 17 Sept. 1847. *Director General:* Alvaro Vial Donoso. Principal publications: *Anuario Estadística* and the bi-monthly *Estadística Chilena.*
Other sources are: *Geografía Económica,* by the Corporación de Fomento de la Production, and *Boletín Mensual,* by the Banco Central de Chile.

Blakemore, H., *Chile.* [Bibliography] Oxford and Santa Barbara, 1988
Davis, N., *The Last Two Years of Salvador Allende.* London, 1985
Falcoff, M., *et al Chile: Prospects for Democracy.* New York, 1988
Garretón, M. A., *The Chilean Political Process.* London and Boston, 1989
Heyerdahl, T., *Easter Island: The Mystery Solved.* New York and London, 1989
Horne, A., *Small Earthquake in Chile. A Visit to Allende's South America.* London, 1972
Smith, B. H., *Church and Politics in Chile: Challenges to Modern Catholicism.* Princeton Univ. Press, 1983

CHINA

Capital: Beijing (Peking)
Population: 1,114m. (1990)
GNP per capita: US$360 (1989)

Zhonghua Renmin
Gonghe Guo

(People's Republic of China)

HISTORY. In the course of 1949 the Communists obtained full control of the mainland of China, and in 1950 also over most islands off the coast (but not Taiwan, *see* p. 367).

On 1 Oct. 1949 Mao Zedong (Tse-tung) proclaimed the establishment of the People's Republic of China. In mid-1966 Mao launched the 'Great Proletarian Cultural Revolution', which lasted until April 1969. For details of the factional disputes which followed *see* THE STATESMAN'S YEAR-BOOK for 1989-90, p. 358. In April 1976 Hua Guofeng became Prime Minister and also, on the death of Mao on 9 Sept., Party Chairman (later General Secretary). Hua was replaced as Prime Minister by Zhao Ziyang in Sept. 1980 and as Party General Secretary by Hu Yaobang in June 1981. Hu was himself forced to resign following student demonstrations in Jan. 1987. Most prominent leader during this period was sometime Party Leader Deng Xiaoping, who resigned from the Politburo in Nov. 1987 and from the chairmanship of the Military Commissions in Nov.1989.

The funeral of Hu Yaobang on 15 April 1989 sparked off mass student demonstrations which escalated into a popular 'pro-democracy' movement in Beijing, Shanghai and other provincial centres demanding reforms. Despite Government appeals to disperse the demonstrations gathered strength during the summit visit of the Soviet President Gorbachev (15-17 May) and culminated in a sit-in in Tiananmen Square, Beijing. This was confronted by army units, at first peacefully. However, on 4 June troops opened fire on the demonstrators and tanks were sent in to disperse them. The official casualty figures are: 'over 200' demonstrators and 'dozens' of soldiers killed, and some 9,000 injured.

A hard-line faction assumed control in the Party Politburo which replaced Zhao Ziyang by Jiang Zemin as General Secretary. Martial law was imposed from May 1989 to Jan. 1990, and several prominent demonstrators were executed.

The visit of President Gorbachev marked the culmination of a process of gradual normalization of Sino-Soviet relations. It was announced that 'both sides favoured a reasonable settlement of the boundary question', and an agreement on the eastern section of the Sino-Soviet border was signed in May 1991.

AREA AND POPULATION. China is bounded in the north by Russia and Mongolia, east by Korea, the Yellow Sea and the East China Sea, with Hong Kong and Macao as enclaves on the south-east coast; south by Vietnam, Laos, Burma, India, Bhutan and Nepal; west by India, Pakistan, Afghanistan, Tajikistan, Kirghizia and Kazakhstan. The capital is Beijing (Peking).

The total area (including Taiwan) is estimated at 9,572,900 sq. km (3,696,100 sq. miles). 51·7% of the population was urban in 1989.

At the 1990 census the population was 1,133,682,501 (51·6% male). Ethnic minorities numbered some 91m. There are 55 ethnic minorities; those numbering more than 3m. were: Zhuang, Hui, Uighur, Yi, Miao, Manchu, Tibetan and Mongolian.

1979 regulations restricting married couples to a single child, a policy enforced by compulsory abortions and economic sanctions, have been widely ignored, and it was admitted in 1988 that the population target of 1,200m. by 2000 would have to be revised to 1,270m. Since 1988 peasant couples have been permitted a second child after 4 years if the first born is a girl, a measure to combat infanticide.

Vital statistics, 1989: Birth rate (per 1,000), 20·83; death rate, 6·5; growth rate,

14·33. Population density, 113 per sq. km. in 1987. There were 9,351,912 marriages and 752,396 divorces in 1989. Expectation of life was 70 in 1989.

Estimates of persons of Chinese race outside China, Taiwan and Hong Kong in 1980 varied from 15m. to 20m. Since 1982 China has permitted the emigration of a limited number of persons to Hong Kong.

A number of widely divergent varieties of Chinese are spoken. The official 'Modern Standard Chinese' is based on the dialect of North China. The ideographic writing system of 'characters' is uniform throughout the country, and has undergone systematic simplification. In 1958 a phonetic alphabet (*Pinyin*) was devised to transcribe the characters, and in 1979 this was officially adopted for use in all texts in the Roman alphabet. The previous transcription scheme (Wade) is still used in Taiwan.

China is administratively divided into 22 provinces, 5 autonomous regions (originally entirely or largely inhabited by ethnic minorities, though in some regions now outnumbered by Han immigrants) and 3 government-controlled municipalities. These are in turn divided into 151 prefectures, 447 cities (of which 185 are at prefecture level and the remainder at county level), 1,919 counties and 648 urban districts. (For earlier administrative divisions *see* THE STATESMAN'S YEAR-BOOK 1986–87).

Government-controlled municipalities	Area (in 1,000 sq. km)	Population in 1987 (in 1,000s)	Density per sq. km	Capital
Beijing	17·8	9,750	580	—
Tianjin	4·0	8,190	725	—
Shanghai	5·8	12,320	1,987	—
Provinces				
Hebei	202·7	56,170	299	Shijiazhuang
Shanxi	157·1	26,550	170	Taiyuan
Liaoning	151·0	37,260	256	Shenyang
Jilin	187·0	23,150	124	Changchun
Heilongjiang	463·6	33,320	71	Harbin
Jiangsu	102·2	62,130	611	Nanjing
Zhejiang	101·8	40,700	400	Hangzhou
Anhui	139·9	52,170	374	Hefei
Fujian	123·1	27,490	227	Fuzhou
Jiangxi	164·8	35,090	211	Nanchang
Shandong	153·3	77,760	507	Jinan
Henan	167·0	78,080	468	Zhengzhou
Hubei	187·5	49,890	266	Wuhan
Hunan	210·5	56,960	271	Changsha
Guangdong	231·4	63,640	299	Guangzhou
Hainan	...	2,098	...	...
Sichuan	569·0	103,200	182	Chengdu
Guizhou	174·0	30,080	171	Guiyang
Yunnan	436·2	34,560	88	Kunming
Shaanxi	195·8	30,430	148	Xian
Gansu	530·0	20,710	46	Lanzhou
Qinghai	721·0	4,120	6	Xining
Autonomous regions				
Inner Mongolia	450·0	20,290	17	Hohhot
Guangxi	220·4	39,460	167	Nanning
Tibet [1]	1,221·6	2,030	2	Lhasa
Ningxia	170.0	4,240	64	Yinchuan
Xinjiang	1,646·8	13,840	9	Urumqi

[1] See also paragraph on Tibet below.

Population of largest cities in 1990: Shanghai, 7·78m.; Beijing (Peking), 6·92m.; Tianjin, 5·7m.; Shenyang, 4·5m.; Wuhan, 3·71m.; Guangzhou (Canton), 3·54m.; Harbin, 2·8m.; Chongqing, 2·96m.; Chengdu, 2·78m.; Zibo, 2·43m.; Xian, 2·71m.; Nanjing, 2·47m.; Taiyuan, 1·9m.; Changchun, 2·07m.; Dalian, 2·37m.; Zhengzhou, 1·66m.; Kunming, 1·5m.; Jinan, 2·29m.; Tangshan, 1·49m.; Guiyang, 1·49m.; Lanzhou, 1·48m.; Fushun, 1·33m.; Qiqihar, 1·37m.; Anshan, 1·37m.; Hangzhou, 1·33m.; Qingdao, 2·04m.; Fuzhou, 1·27m.; Changsha, 1·30m.; Shijiazhuang, 1·3m.;

Nanchang, 1·33m.; Jilin, 1·25m.; Baotou, 1·18m.; Huainan, 1·17m.; Luoyang, 1·16m.; Urumqi, 1·11m.; Ningbo, 1·07m.; Datong, 1·09m.; Handan, 1·09m.; Nanning, 1·05m.

Tibet. For events before and after the revolt of 1959 *see* THE STATESMAN'S YEAR-BOOK, 1964–65 (under TIBET), and 1988–89. On 9 Sept. 1965 Tibet became an Autonomous Region. 301 delegates were elected to the first People's Congress, of whom 226 were Tibetans. The Chief of Government is Gyaincain Norbu. The senior spiritual leader, the Dalai Lama, is in exile. He was awarded the Nobel Peace Prize in 1989. The Banqen Lama died in Jan. 1989. In 1991 the Tibetan population of Tibet was 2·09m., Han 31,000. Birth rate (per 1,000), 1989, 24·17; death rate, 7·94; growth rate, 16·23. Population of the capital, Lhasa, in 1987 was 130,000. Expectation of life was 65 years in 1990. 2m. Tibetans live outside Tibet, in China, and in India and Nepal. Chinese efforts to modernize Tibet include irrigation, road-building and the establishment of light industry: in 1985 296 small and medium-sized factories and mines were producing electric power, coal, building materials, lumber, textiles, chemicals and animal products.

In 1979, 1·6m. were engaged in agriculture, including 0·5m. nomadic herdsmen. By 1984, a large measure of autonomy for the peasantry had been re-introduced: Compulsory deliveries and some taxes were abolished and private ownership of livestock and 30-year disposition of land were granted. There were 23m. cattle in 1984. In 1975 Tibet became self-sufficient in grain. There are now 21,600 km of highways, and air routes link Lhasa with Chengdu, Xian and Kathmandu. Six more were opened in 1987. 30,000 tourists visited Tibet in 1986.

The borders were opened for trade with neighbouring countries in 1980. In July 1988 Tibetan was reinstated as a 'major official language', competence in which is required of all administrative officials.

Since 1980 178 monasteries and 743 shrines have been renovated and reopened. There were some 15,000 monks and nuns in 1987. In 1984 a Buddhist seminary in Lhasa opened with 200 students. Circulation of the Tibetan-language *Xizang Daily* now totals 38,000. In 1988 there were 2,437 primary schools, 67 secondary schools, 14 technical schools and 3 higher education institutes. The total number of students was 166,000. A university was established in 1985. In 1987 there were 7,048 medical personnel (of whom 59% were Tibetan) and 957 medical institutions, with a total of 4,738 beds.

Since 1987 there have been several anti-Chinese demonstrations in which a number of people have been killed. Martial law, declared on 8 March 1989, was lifted in April 1990.

Batchelor, S., *The Tibet Guide*. London, 1987
The Dalai Lama, *My Land and My People* (ed. D. Howarth). London, 1962:-*Freedom in Exile*. London, 1990.
Grunfeld, A. T., *The Making of Modern Tibet*. London, 1987
Jäschke, H. A., *A Tibetan–English Dictionary*. London, 1934
Levenson, C. B., *The Dalai Lama: A Biography*. London, 1988
Pinfold, J., *Tibet: [Bibliography]*. Oxford and Santa Barbara, 1991
Shakabpa, T. W. D., *Tibet: A Political History*. New York, 1984
Sharabati, D., *Tibet and its History*. London, 1986

CLIMATE. Most of China has a temperate climate but, with such a large country, extending far inland and embracing a wide range of latitude as well as containing large areas at high altitude, many parts experience extremes of climate, especially in winter. Most rain falls during the summer, from May to Sept., though amounts decrease inland. Peking (Beijing). Jan. 24°F (−4·4°C), July 79°F (26°C). Annual rainfall 24·9" (623 mm). Chongqing. Jan. 45°F (7·2°C), July 84°F (28·9°C). Annual rainfall 43·7" (1,092 mm). Shanghai. Jan. 39°F (3·9°C), July 82°F (27·8°C). Annual rainfall 45·4" (1,135 mm). Tianjin. Jan. 24°F (−4·4°C), July 81°F (27·2°C). Annual rainfall 21·5" (533·4 mm).

CONSTITUTION AND GOVERNMENT. On 21 Sept. 1949 the 'Chinese People's Political Consultative Conference' met in Peking, convened by the Chinese Communist Party. The Conference adopted a 'Common Programme' of 60 articles and the 'Organic Law of the Central People's Government' (31 articles). Both became the basis of the Constitution adopted on 20 Sept. 1954 by the 1st National People's Congress, the supreme legislative body. The Consultative Conference continued to exist after 1954 as an advisory body. In 1988 it had 2,083 members.

New Constitutions were adopted in 1975 and 1978 (for details *see* THE STATESMAN'S YEAR-BOOK 1986-87).

A further Constitution was adopted in 1982. It defines 'socialist modernisation' as China's basic task and restores the post of State President (*i.e.* Head of State). Constitutional amendments of 1988 legalized private companies and sanction the renting out of 'land-use' rights.

The *National People's Congress* can amend the Constitution, elects and has power to remove from office the highest State dignitaries, decides on the national economic plan, etc. The Congress elects a *Standing Committee* (which supervises the State Council) and the *State President* for a 5-year term: Yang Shangkun was elected in April 1988. *Vice-President:* Wang Zhen.

Congress is elected for a 5-year term and meets once a year for 2 or 3 weeks. When not in session, its business is carried on by its *Standing Committee*. It is composed of deputies elected on a constituency basis by direct secret ballot. Any voter, and certain organizations, may nominate candidates. Nominations may exceed seats by 50-100%. 2,978 deputies were elected to the 7th Congress in March-April 1988.

In Jan. 1992 the government included: *Prime Minister:* Li Peng. *Chairman of the Commission for Economic Restructure:* Chen Jinhua. *Deputy Prime Ministers:* Tian Jiyun, Yao Yilin, Wu Xueqian, Zhu Rongji, Zou Jiahua. Other ministers included: Qian Qichen *(Foreign Affairs)*, Zheng Tuobin *(Foreign Trade)*, Li Lanqing *(Foreign Economic Relations)*, Liu Zhongyi *(Agriculture)*, Qin Jiwei *(Defence)*, Wang Bingqian *(Finance)*, Zou Jiahua *(Chairman, State Planning Commission)* and Tao Siju *(Public Security)*.

State emblem: 5 stars above Peking's Gate of Heavenly Peace, surrounded by a border of ears of grain entwined with drapings, which form a knot in the centre of a cogwheel at the base; the colours are red and gold.

National flag: Red with a large star and 4 smaller stars all in yellow in the canton.

National anthem: 'March of the Volunteers' composed 1935 by Tien Han. (Replacing the 1978 version).

De facto power is in the hands of the Communist Party of China, which had 48m. members in 1989. A purge of members was instituted following the events of June 1989. There are 8 other parties, all members of the Chinese People's Political Consultative Conference. The members of the Politburo in March 1991 (the first 6 constituting its Standing Committee) were Jiang Zemin (*General Secretary*; b. 1926), Li Peng, Qiao Shi, Song Ping, Li Ruihuan, Yao Yilin, Wan Li, Tian Jiyun, Li Tieying, Li Ximing, Yang Rudai, Yang Shangkun, Wu Xueqian, Qin Jiwei, Hu Qili; candidate member, Ding Guangen. Deng Xiaoping has no formal post but is officially still a member of the 'second-generation leadership.'

Local Government. There are 4 administrative levels: (1) Provinces, Autonomous Regions and the municipalities directly administered by the Government; (2) prefectures and autonomous prefectures (*zhou*); (3) counties, autonomous counties and municipalities; (4) towns. Local government organs ('congresses') exist at provincial, county and township levels and in national minority autonomous prefectures, but not in ordinary prefectures which are just agencies of the provincial government. Up to county level congresses are elected directly. Elections take place every 3 years. Any person proposed by 10 electors may stand after political vetting. There are quotas for party members and women. Multiple candidacies are permitted at local elections.

DEFENCE. In Nov. 1989 Jiang Zemin took over from Deng Xiaoping as chairman of the State and Party's Military Commissions. China is divided into 7 military regions. The military commander also commands the air, naval and civilian militia forces assigned to each region.

Conscription is compulsory but for organizational reasons selective: Only some 10% of potential recruits are called up. Service is 3 years with the Army and 4 years with the Air Force and Navy.

A Defence University to train senior officers in modern warfare was established in 1985.

Army. The Army (PLA: 'People's Liberation Army') is divided into main and local forces. Main forces, administered by the 7 military regions in which they are stationed but commanded by the Ministry of Defence, are available for operation anywhere and are better equipped. Local forces concentrate on the defence of their own regions. There are 24 Integrated Group Armies comprising 80 infantry, 10 armoured and 6 artillery divisions; and 50 engineer regiments. Equipment includes some 8,000 T-54, 6,000 T-59 and 200 T-69 main battle tanks. Land-based missile forces consisted of (1991 estimate): 8 intercontinental and 60 intermediate range. Total strength in 1991 was 2·3m. including 1·08m. conscripts.

There is a para-military force of 12m., including 750,000 People's Armed Police.

Navy. The warship construction programme remains slow, with emphasis on foreign sales. Despite technical backwardness, the naval arm of the People's Liberation Army remains an important factor in the balance of power in the eastern hemisphere.

Strength comprises 1 nuclear-powered ballistic missile armed submarine, 4 nuclear-propelled fleet submarines, 1 diesel-powered cruise missile submarine and some 85 old patrol submarines (of which probably no more than 35 are operational). Surface combatant forces include 19 destroyers, 37 frigates, some 215 missile craft and 160 torpedo craft. There is a mixed coastal and inshore patrol force of some 500 vessels and 50 riverine craft. The mine warfare force consists of 35 ex-Soviet offshore minesweepers, some 12 inshore, and about 60 unmanned drones. There are 61 landing ships of various types and some 400 craft. Major auxiliaries number over 100, including 3 underway replenishment oilers and 1 fleet stores ship, and there are several hundred minor auxiliaries, yard craft and service vessels.

The land-based naval air force of almost 900 combat aircraft, primarily for defensive and anti-submarine service, is organized into 3 bomber and 6 fighter divisions. The force includes some 30 H-6 bombers and 130 H-5 torpedo bombers, about 100 Q-5 fighter/ground attack aircraft and 600 fighters including J-5 (MiG-17), J-6 (MiG-19), and J-7 (MiG-21) types. Maritime patrol tasks are performed by 15 Be-6 flying boats, and anti-submarine operations by 50 Z-5, and 12 Super Frelon helicopters from shore and about 10 Z-9 afloat. There are also about 60 communications, research, training and transport aircraft.

Main naval bases are at Qingdao (North Sea Fleet), Shanghai (East Sea Fleet), and Zhanjiang (South Sea Fleet).

Active personnel continue to reduce slowly as tasks are handed over to the militia; in 1991 there were some 240,000, including 25,000 in the naval air force, 27,000 coastal defence troops and 6,000 marines.

Air Force. In 1984 the Air Force was estimated at 4,500 front-line aircraft, organized in over 100 regiments of jet-fighters and about 12 regiments of tactical bombers, plus reconnaissance, transport and helicopter units. Each regiment is made up of 3 or 4 squadrons (each 12 aircraft), and 3 regiments form a division.

Equipment includes about 500 J-7 (MiG-21), 2,000 J-6 (MiG-19) and 600 J-4 and J-5 (MiG-17) interceptors and fighter-bombers, with about 500 H-5 (Il-28) jet-bombers, about 120 H-6 Chinese-built copies of the Soviet Tu-16 twin-jet strategic bomber, plus 500 Q-5 twin-jet fighter-bombers, evolved from the MiG-19. In service in small numbers is a locally-developed fighter designated J-8 (known in the west as 'Finback'). Transport aircraft include about 500 Y-5 (An-2), Y-8 (An-12), Y-12, An-24/26, Li-2, Il-14 and three-turbofan Trident fixed-wing types, plus 300 Z-5 (Mi-4) and Z-6 (Mi-8) helicopters. The MiG fighters and Antonov transports have been manufactured in China, initially under licence, and other types have been assembled there, including several hundred JJ-5 (2-seat MiG-17) trainers. Small quantities of Western aircraft have been procured in the past few years, including 24 Black Hawk and 6 Super Puma transport helicopters, 8 Gazelle armed helicopters and 5 Challenger VIP transports. The USSR supplied a small number of Su-27 interceptors in 1991. Total strength (1991) 470,000 (160,000 conscripts), including 220,000 in air defence organization.

Joffe, E., *The Chinese Army after Mao*. London, 1987

INTERNATIONAL RELATIONS

Membership. The People's Republic of China is a member of UN (and its Security Council), the IMF, the Asian Development Bank, and is an observer at GATT.

ECONOMY

Policy. For planning history 1953–73 *see* THE STATESMAN'S YEAR-BOOK, 1973–74, p. 817.

A programme for fundamental reform of the urban economy was introduced in 1985. State planning was reduced in scope and enterprises gained a degree of freedom in deciding their production and marketing a portion of it. Wages were varied according to work performed, and prices adjusted to reflect market conditions. However, the end of 1988 saw a return to more central economic planning as a response to declining production, inflation, a foreign trade imbalance and unequal regional development. Further measures of state control were introduced in Dec. 1989. 'Key enterprises' (metals, coal, timber) were to be completely government managed, and other firms not meeting production quotas have their supplies reduced. A national economic plan published in Jan. 1990 aimed to reduce inflation, balance state revenue and expenditure and reduce internal debt. Public sector industry received preferential treatment in terms of subsidies and credit terms.

An eighth 5-year plan covers 1991–95; there is also a 10-year plan to 2000.

Staple foods underwent large price increases in April 1991 as government subsidies were reduced, though prices remain below cost.

Budget. 1988 revenue was 262,800m. yuan; expenditure, 270,660m. yuan. Preliminary figures for 1989: Revenue, 291,920m. yuan; expenditure, 301,460m. yuan.

Sources of revenue, 1989 (in million yuan): Tax receipts, 255,710; subsidies for enterprise losses, 52,140; construction funds, 20,500; foreign loans, 16,500. Expenditure: Capital construction, 62,790; education, science and health, 51,380; subsidies, 40,960; defence, 24,550; administration, 22,660; agriculture, 17,390; technical renovation of enterprises, 15,580; urban maintenance, 10,300; debt service, 9,560.

Currency. The currency is called Renminbi (*i.e.,* People's Currency). The unit of currency is the *yuan* (CNY) which is divided into 10 *jiao*, the *jiao,* into 10 *fen*. Notes are issued for 1, 2 and 5 *jiao* and 1, 2, 5 and 10 *yuan* and coins for 1, 2 and 5 *fen*. In Nov. 1990 the *yuan* was devalued by 9·57%. Inflation was 5·3% in Nov. 1990. China's foreign exchange reserves in March 1988 were US\$17,100m. Gold reserves in 1991 were 12·67m. troy oz. of gold. The official rate of exchange in March 1992 was £1 = 9·58 *yuan*; US\$1 = 5·46 *yuan*.

Banking and Finance. A re-organization of the banking system in 1983 resulted in the People's Bank assuming the role of a Central Bank (*Director:* Li Guixian). Its former commercial role has been taken over by the Industrial and Commercial Bank. There are 5 other banks; the Agricultural Bank, the Bank of China, the People's Construction Bank, the Jiaotong Bank and the People's Insurance Company. The Bank of China is responsible for foreign banking operations. It has branches in London, New York, Singapore, Luxembourg, Macao and Hong Kong, and agencies in Tokyo and Paris.

Savings bank deposits were 514,690m. yuan in 1989.

There are stock exchanges in the Shenzhen special economic zone and in Shanghai. A securities trading system linking 6 cities (Securities Automated Quotations System) was inaugurated in 1990 for trading in government bonds.

Weights and Measures. The metric system is in general use alongside traditional units of measurement, for which *see* THE STATESMAN'S YEAR-BOOK, 1975–76, p. 826 and 1954, pp. 877–88.

ENERGY AND NATURAL RESOURCES

Electricity. Sources of energy in 1988: Coal 73·1%; oil, 20·4%; hydroelectric power, 4·5%; gas, 2%. Hydroelectric potential is 676m. kw. Generating is not centralized; local units range between 30 and 60 mw of output. Output in 1990: 615,000m. kwh. Supply 220 volts; 50 Hz. There is a nuclear energy plant at Shanghai. Plans to build further nuclear power plants have been abandoned.

Oil. There are on-shore fields at Daqing, Shengli, Dagang and Karamai, and 10 provinces south of the Yangtze River have been opened for exploration in co-operation with foreign companies. Crude oil production was 138·59m. tonnes in 1991.

Gas. Natural gas is available from fields near Canton and Shanghai and in Sichuan province. Production was 15,050m. cu. metres in 1989, but is only used locally.

Minerals. *Coal.* Most provinces contain coal, and there are 70 major production centres, of which the largest are in Hebei, Shanxi, Shandong, Jilin and Anhui. Coal reserves are estimated at 901,453m. tonnes. Coal production was 1,090m. tonnes in 1990.

Iron. Iron ore deposits are estimated at 49,790m. tonnes and are abundant in the anthracite field of Shanxi, in Hebei and in Shandong and are found in conjunction with coal and worked in the north-east.

Tin. Tin ore is plentiful in Yunnan, where the tin-mining industry has long existed. Tin production was 40,000 tonnes in 1989.

Tungsten. China is a major producer of wolfram (tungsten ore). Mining of wolfram is carried on in Hunan, Guangdong and Yunnan.

Production of other minerals in 1989 (in 1,000 tonnes): Aluminium, 770; copper, 540; nickel, 30; lead, 270; zinc, 430. Other minerals produced: Barite, bismuth, gold, graphite, gypsum, mercury, molybdenum, silver. Reserves (in tonnes) of phosphate ore 15,032m.; sylvite, 272·47m.; salt, 275,579m.

Agriculture. China remains essentially an agricultural country. 95·66m. ha were cultivated in 1990. Intensive agriculture and horticulture have been practised for millennia. Present-day policy aims to avert the traditional threats from floods and droughts by soil conservancy, afforestation, irrigation and drainage projects, and to increase the 'high stable yields' areas by introducing fertilizers, pesticides and improved crops. 44·9m. ha were irrigated in 1989.

Since 1979 agricultural communes have shed the administrative functions which they had in the Maoist period to become 'rural economic associations', whose members manage them jointly and share the costs and benefits. There were 470,600 associations in 1989, with 4,339,500 members. There were also 232,800 agricultural township and village enterprises, engaging 95,454,600 persons. There were 2,312 state farms in 1989 with 4·68m. workers, and 180m. peasant households. Net *per capita* annual peasant income, 1989: 658 yuan.

In 1989 there were 848,220 large and medium-sized tractors and 36,582 combine harvesters.

Agricultural production (in 1m. tonnes), 1989: Rice, 180·13; wheat, 90·81; maize, 78·93; soybeans, 10·23; tubers, 27·30; tea, 0·54; cotton, 3·79; oilseed crops, 12·95; sugar-cane, 48·8; fruit, 18·32. The gross value of agricultural output in 1989 was 653,500m. yuan.

Livestock, 1989 (in 1,000): Horses, 10,294; cattle, 100,725; goats, 98,130; pigs, 52,810; sheep, 113,510. Meat production in 1989 was 23·26m. tonnes; milk, 4·36m. tonnes; eggs, 7·2m. tonnes.

Forestry. Forest area in 1990 was 124·65. ha, including 2·6m. ha of timber forest. Timber reserves were 102,600m. cu. metres in 1985. The chief forested areas are in Heilongjiang, Sichuan and Yunnan. Timber output in 1988 was 63m. cu. metres.

Fisheries. Total catch, 1989: 11·52m. tonnes, of which 4·91m. tonnes were fresh-water produce.

INDUSTRY. 'Cottage' industries persist into the late 20th century. Modern industrial development began with the manufacture of cotton textiles, and the establishment of silk filatures, steel plants, flour-mills and match factories. In 1989 there were 7,980,700 industrial enterprises, of which 12,300 were classified as 'large or medium', 102,300 were state-owned, 1,747,000 were collectives and 6,124,200 were individually owned. 2,520,200 enterprises were engaged in heavy industry. A law of 1988 ended direct state control of firms and provided for the possibility of bankruptcy. Expanding sectors of manufacture are: Steel, chemicals, cement, agricultural implements, plastics and lorries.

Output of major products, 1989 (in tonnes): Cotton yarn, 4·78m.; paper, 13·3m.; sugar, 5·01m.; salt, 28·29m.; plastics, 2·06m.; aluminium ware, 82,200; steel, 61·59m.; rolled steel, 48·59m.; cement, 210·29m.; sulphuric acid, 11·53m.; chemical fertilizers, 18·03m.; pig-iron, 58·2m.; cotton cloth, 18,923m. metres; woollen fabrics, 250m. metres; bicycles, 36·77m.; TV sets, 27·67m.; tape recorders, 24·18m.; cameras, 2·45m.; washing machines, 8·25m.; refrigerators, 6·71m.; motor vehicles, 583,500; large tractors, 39,800; locomotives, 680.

The gross value of industrial output in 1989 was 2,201,700m. yuan.

Labour. Workforce (excluding peasantry), 1990: 553·29m. (36·9% female), including 323m. rural workers, 96m. industrial workers, 29m. workers in service trades and commerce, 24m. in building and 14m. in transport and telecommunications. 19m. worked in private businesses in 1989. At the 1990 census there was a floating population of 21m. internal migrants who tour the country seeking seasonal employment. There were 3·78m. unemployed in 1989. Average annual non-agricultural wage in 1989: 1,935 yuan. There is a 6-day 48-hour working week. Minimum working age was fixed at 16 in 1991.

Trade Unions. The All-China Federation of Trade Unions is headed by Zhu Houze.

FOREIGN ECONOMIC RELATIONS. In 1991 there were six Special Economic Zones at Shanghai and in the provinces of Guangdong and Fujian, in which concessions are made to foreign businessmen. The Pudong New Area in Shanghai is designated a special development area. Since 1979 joint ventures with foreign firms have been permitted. By 1987 4,040 equity joint ventures, 4,864 contractual joint ventures and 176 wholly-owned foreign subsidiaries had been launched. About 80% of the investment was from Hong Kong. A law of April 1991 reduced taxation on joint ventures to 33%. There is no maximum limit on the foreign share of the holdings; the minimum limit is 25%. Contracts between Chinese and foreign firms are only legally valid if in writing and approved by the appropriate higher authority. IMF loans of US$780m. were suspended after the events of June 1989.

In May 1989 the UK and China signed a 6-year trade agreement worth US$3,000m.

In 1988 Japan and China signed an investment protection treaty, putting Japanese firms in China on the same footing as local firms.

In 1978 a most-favoured-nation agreement was signed with the EEC, and in 1980 the EEC extended preferential tariffs to China. In Oct. 1990 the EEC lifted sanctions imposed after the events of June 1989.

In Feb. 1991 China and India resumed cross-border trade, which had ceased in 1962.

In May 1991 the US president extended most-favoured-nation status to China for a further year.

Commerce. Trade in 1989: Imports, US$59,140m.; exports, US$52,540m.

Major exports in 1989 (in 1,000 tonnes): Crude oil, 24,390; grain, 6,560; tea, 205; raw silk, 11·3; tungsten ore, 30·9; coal, 15,340; cotton cloth, 2,338m. metres. Imports: Wheat, 14,800; rolled steel, 9,480; motor vehicles, 85,773 units; chemical fertilizers, 13,930.

Exports to (and imports from) major trade partners in 1989 (in US$1m.): Hong Kong, 21,916 (12,541); Japan, 8,362 (10,534); USA, 4,391 (7,863); German Federal Republic, 1,609 (3,379); USSR, 1,849 (2,147); Singapore, 1,693 (1,492). Customs duties with Taiwan were abolished in 1980.

Total trade between China and UK (British Department of Trade returns, in £1,000 sterling):

	1987	1988	1989	1990	1991
Imports to UK	391,766	443,698	530,720	583,425	706,585
Exports and re-exports from UK	416,012	411,563	417,911	465,585	321,935

China agreed to settle by 1990 British claims for assets totalling £23·4m. confiscated by the present Chinese Government when it took power in 1949.

Tourism. 31·69m. tourists visited in 1988, including 29·77m. Hong Kong, Taiwan and Macao Chinese, and 79,300 other overseas Chinese. Total visitors dropped to 24·5m. (22·97m., 68,000) in 1989 after the suppression of demonstrations in June. Income from tourists in 1989 was US$1,860m. (US$2,247m. in 1988). Restrictions on Chinese wishing to travel abroad were eased in Feb. 1986.

COMMUNICATIONS

Roads. The total road length was 1,014,300 km in 1989. Highways are well graded and 85% are hard-surfaced. In 1989 there were 3·46m. lorries and 1·46m. passenger vehicles. 0·53m. lorries and 0·2m. passenger vehicles were privately owned. The use of bicycles is very widespread.

In 1989, 7,337·81m. tonnes of freight and 6,445·08m. persons were transported by road.

Railways. In 1989 there were 53,200 km of railway including 6,400 km electrified. Gauge is standard except for some 600 mm track in Yunnan.

The principal railways are:

(1) The great north–south trunk lines: (a) Beijing–Canton Railway (over 2,300 km), via Zhengzhou–Wuhan–Zhuzhou–Hengyang. (b) Tianjin–Shanghai Railway (1,500 km), via Pukow and Nanjing. (c) Baoji–Chongqing Railway, via Chengdu (1,174 km). Chongqing with the east–west route from Hengyang to the Vietnam border, and to Kunming, connecting there with the Yunnan Railway to the Vietnam border. Two further lines connect Baoji.

(2) Great east–west trunk lines: (a) Longhai Railway; Lianyungkang–Xuzhou–Zhengzhou (on the Beijing–Canton line) –Xian–Baoji–Tianshui–Lanzhou (1,500 km). (b) Lanzhou–Xinjiang Railway: Lanzhou–Yumen–Hami–Turfan–Urumqi (1,800 km); (c) Shanghai–Youyiguan (Vietnam border) via Hangzhou, Nanchang, Hengyang (on the Beijing–Canton line), Guilin, Liuzhou and Nanning. (d) Beijing–Lanzhou via Xining (from which a branch connects with the lines through Mongolia to the Trans–Siberian Railway), Dadong (from which a branch serves the province of Shanxi), Baotou and Yinchuan (Ningxia). (e) Zhuzhou–Guiyang (632 km). (f) Xiangfan–Chongqing.

Branches link coastal areas (e.g., Fujian province) and the smaller inland centres with the main parts of the system. Surveys have been made for a new 500-km railway, linking the trunk line with the oilfield of Karamai in Xinjiang.

(3) The Manchurian system: (a) Chinese Eastern (Changchun) Railway (2,370 km), from Manzhouli on the Soviet border through northern Inner Mongolia and Manchuria via Qiqihar, Harbin and Mudanjiang to the Soviet border near Vladivostok. (b) South Manchuria Railway (705 km, 1,120 km with branches), Changchun–Shenyang–Luda. (c) Beijing–Shenyang Railway, with branches in Manchuria (854 km, 1,350 km with branches).

The Beijing–Lanzhou line connects through a branch with the Trans–Siberian Railway in the USSR. A line from Xinjiang across the border to Soviet Kazakhstan was due for completion in 1991.

A high-speed 147-km line is being constructed between Guangzhou (Canton) and the Shenzen Special Economic Zone and is scheduled for completion in 1994.

In 1989 the railways carried 1,514·89 tonnes of freight and 1,138·05m. passengers.

Civil Aviation. The Civil Aviation Administration of China is the administrative body for 5 airlines: Air China (based on Beijing); Eastern Airways (Shanghai); Southern Airways (Canton); South-Western Airways (Chengdu) and the Capital Helicopter Company. There were 410 civil aircraft in 1988, including 7 Boeing 747s, 21 737s, 10 707s and 5 Airbus A310s, and 81 Soviet aircraft. There are services to Sharjah, Vancouver, Toronto, Rome, Stockholm, Nagasaki, Pyongyang, Hanoi, Rangoon, Singapore, Bangkok, Karachi, Tokyo, Moscow, Ulan Bator, Teheran, Addis Ababa, Bucharest, Belgrade, Zürich, Paris, Frankfurt, Manila, New York, San Francisco, London, Sydney and Hong Kong. Route lengths in 1989, 471,900 km, of which 166,400 km were international. British Airways have a direct flight London-Beijing. Japan Airlines have a route from Tokyo to Beijing (*via* Osaka and Shanghai), Air France Paris to Beijing (*via* Athens and Karachi), Pakistan Airlines Karachi to Beijing, Aeroflot Moscow to Beijing, Ethiopian Airlines Addis Ababa to Shanghai, Tarom Bucharest to Beijing, Swissair Geneva to Beijing and Shanghai, Iran Air Paris to Beijing and PANAM Beijing *via* Tokyo. Singapore Airlines Singapore to Beijing and Thai Airways Bangkok to Beijing.

In 1989 CAAC carried 12·83m. passengers and 0·3m. tonnes of freight.

Shipping. In 1980 the ocean-going merchant fleet consisted of 431 vessels with a total DWT of 7·92m.

Cargo handled by the major ports in 1989 (in tonnes): Shanghai, 146m.; Qinhuangdao, 66m.; Dalian, 51m.; Guangzhou (Canton), 47m.; Qingdao, 31m.; Ningbo, 23m. In 1989 90·29. tonnes of freight were carried.

Inland waterways totalled 109,000 km in 1989. 784·66m. tonnes of freight and 317·78m. passengers were carried.

Pipeline. There were 15,100 km of pipeline in 1989 which carried a load of 156·41m. tonnes.

Telecommunications. There were 53,100 post offices in 1989. There were 10m. telephones and some 10,000 fax machines in 1990. The use of *Pinyin* transcription of place names has been requested for mail to addresses in China (*e.g.*, 'Beijing' *not* 'Peking').

The Central People's Broadcasting Station provides 2 central programmes, regional services, special services, a Taiwan service and external services. China Central Television (colour by PAL) transmits 3 programmes from Beijing, a programme from Shanghai, and an English-language programme. There are 29 regional programmes transmitted from 361 local stations. In 1991 there were 121,211,690 radio and 126m. TV receivers.

Cinemas and Theatres. There were 12,325 cinemas, 152,300 film projection units and 3,455 theatres in 1989. 136 feature films were made in 1989.

Newspapers and books. In 1989 there were 852 newspapers with a circulation of 15,620m. and 6,078 periodicals. The Party newspaper is *Renmin Ribao* (People's Daily). 74, 968 book titles were produced in 58,645m. copies in 1989. There were 2,512 public libraries in 1989.

JUSTICE, RELIGION, EDUCATION AND WELFARE

Justice. Six new codes of law (including criminal and electoral) came into force in 1980, to regularize the legal unorthodoxy of previous years. There is no provision for *habeas corpus*. An anti-crime campaign was launched in Aug. 1983 which, it was claimed in 1985, had cut the crime rate sharply; by 1986 624,000 sentences of death or long-term imprisonment had been imposed. The death penalty has been extended from treason and murder to include rape, embezzlement, smuggling, drug-dealing, bribery and robbery with violence. Courts will no longer be subject to the intervention of other state bodies, and their decisions will be reversible only by higher courts. 'People's courts' are divided into some 30 higher, 200 intermediate and 2,000 basic-level courts, and headed by the Supreme People's Court. The latter tries cases, hears appeals and supervises the people's courts.

People's courts are composed of a president, vice-presidents, judges and 'people's assessors' who are the equivalent of jurors. 'People's conciliation committees' are charged with settling minor disputes.

There are also special military courts.

Procuratorial powers and functions are exercised by the Supreme People's Procuracy and local procuracies.

Religion. Confucianism, Buddhism and Taoism have long been practised. Confucianism has no ecclesiastical organization and appears rather as a philosophy of ethics and government. Taoism—of Chinese origin—copied Buddhist ceremonial soon after the arrival of Buddhism two millennia ago. Buddhism in return adopted many Taoist beliefs and practices. It is no longer possible to estimate the number of adherents to these faiths. A more tolerant attitude towards religion had emerged by 1979, and the Government's Bureau of Religious Affairs was reactivated.

Ceremonies of reverence to ancestors have been observed by the whole population regardless of philosophical or religious beliefs.

Moslems are found in every province of China, being most numerous in the Ningxia–Hui Autonomous Region, Yunnan, Shaanxi, Gansu, Hebei, Honan, Shandong, Sichuan, Xinjiang and Shanxi. They totalled 14m. in 1986.

Roman Catholicism has had a footing in China for more than 3 centuries. In 1992 there were about 3·5m. Catholics who are members of the Patriotic Catholic Association, which declared its independence of Rome in 1958. In 1979 there were about 1,000 priests. In 1977 there were 78 bishops and 4 apostolic administrators, not all of whom were permitted to undertake religious activity. This figure included 46 'democratically elected' bishops not recognized by the Vatican. A bishop of Beijing was consecrated in 1979 without the consent of the Vatican and 2 auxiliary bishops of Shanghai in 1984. Archbishop Gong Pinmei, arrested in 1955, was freed in 1988. Protestants are members of the All-China Conference of Protestant Churches. 2 Protestant bishops were installed in 1988, the first for 30 years.

Education. In 1988 220m. people (70% women) were illiterate. In 1989 97% of school-age children attended school. In 1989 there were 172,634 kindergartens with 18·5m. children and 709,000 teachers. An educational reform of 1985 is phasing in compulsory 9-year education consisting of six years of primary schooling and three years of secondary schooling, to replace a previous 5-year system. In 1989 there were 777,244 primary schools with 5·54m. teachers and 123·7m. pupils, and 102,732 secondary schools, with 3·42m. teachers and 50·54m. pupils. There were 1,079 institutes of higher education, with 397,365 teachers and 2·08m. students.

University entry is dependent upon entrance examinations and students are funded by competitive scholarships. Following student demonstrations in Jan. 1987 political education courses and periods of labour service were restored to university curricula, and political criteria of selection re-applied. In 1989 the number of university places was cut by 30,000 to 610,000, and a compulsory year of military service inserted before student enrolment. First degree courses usually last 4 years. A further year of labour is obligatory before proceeding to postgraduate studies. In 1988 there were 149,000 full-time postgraduate and 670,000 undergraduate students.

There is an Academy of Sciences with provincial branches. An Academy of Social Sciences was established in 1977.

Among the universities are the following: People's University of China, Peking (founded 1912 by Dr Sun Yat-sen; reorganized 1950; about 3,000 students); Peking University, Peking (1898, enlarged 1945; about 10,000 students); Xiamen University, Fujian (1921 and 1937); Fudan University, Shanghai (1905); Inner Mongolia University, Hohhot; Lanzhou University, Lanzhou (Gansu Prov.); Nankai University, Tianjin (1919); Nanjing University, Nanjing (1888 and 1928); Jilin University, Changchun (Jilin Prov.); North-West University, Xian (Shanxi Prov.); Shandong University, Qingdao (1926); Sun Yat-sen University, Canton (founded 1924 by Dr Sun Yat-sen); Sichuan University, Chengdu (1931); Qinghua University, Peking, Wuhan University, Wuhan (Hubei Prov.; 1905 and 1928); Yunnan University, Kunming. In 1987 some 36,000 students were studying abroad, but in 1988 the number was reduced to 3,000 a year (600 only to USA).

Chen, T. H., *Chinese Education since 1949*. Oxford, 1981
Heyhoe, R., (ed.) *Contemporary Chinese Education*. London, 1984

Health. Medical treatment is free only for certain groups of employees, but where costs are incurred they are partly borne by the patient's employing organization. In 1989 there were 1·72m. doctors, of whom 0·37m. practised Chinese medicine, and 0·92m. nurses. About 10% of doctors are in private practice.

In 1989 there were 61,929 hospitals (including 348 mental hospitals) with 2·87m. beds.

DIPLOMATIC REPRESENTATIVES

Of China in Great Britain (49 Portland Pl., London, W1N 3AH)
Ambassador: Ma Yuzhen.

Of Great Britain in China (Guang Hua Lu 11, Jian Guo Men Wai, Beijing)
Ambassador: Sir Robin McLaren, KCMG.

Of China in the USA (2300 Connecticut Ave., NW, Washington, D.C., 20008)
Ambassador: Zhu Qizhen.

Of the USA in China (Xiu Shui Bei Jie 3, Beijing)
Ambassador: James R. Lilley.

Of China to the United Nations
Ambassador: Li Daoyu.

Further Reading

Beijing Review. Beijing, weekly
China Daily [European ed.]. London, from 1986
China Directory [in Pinyin and Chinese]. Tokyo, annual
The China Quarterly. London, from 1960
China Reconstructs. Beijing, monthly
China's Foreign Trade. Bimonthly. Beijing, from 1966
People's Republic of China Yearbook. Beijing, from 1983
China Statistical Yearbook, 1990. Beijing and the Univ. of Illinois, 1990
The Population Atlas of China. OUP, 1988
Barnett, A. D., *The Making of Foreign Policy in China*. London, 1985
Barnett, A. D. and Clough, R., (eds.) *Modernizing China: Post-Mao Reform and Development*. Boulder, 1986
Bartke, W. (ed.) *Who's Who in the People's Republic of China*. 2nd ed. New York, 1986
Bartke, W. and Schier, P., *China's New Party Leadership: Biographies and Analysis*. London, 1985
Blecher, M., *China: Politics, Economics and Sociology*. London, 1986
Bonavia, D., *The Chinese*. New York, 1980.—*The Chinese: A Portrait*. London, 1981
Boorman, H. L. and Howard, R. C., (eds.) *Biographical Dictionary of Republican China*. 5 vols. Columbia Univ. Press, 1967–79
Brown, D. G., *Partnership with China: Sino-foreign Joint Ventures in Historical Perspective*. Boulder, 1985
Bullard, M., *China's Political-Military Evolution*. Boulder, 1985
The Cambridge History of China. 14 vols. CUP, 1978 ff.
Chang, D. W., *China under Deng Xiao-ping: Political and Economic Reforms*. London, 1989
Cheng, P., *China*. [Bibliography] Oxford and Santa Barbara, 1983
Chow, G. C., *The Chinese Economy*. New York, 1985
Chu, G. C. and Hsu, F. L., (eds.) *China's New Social Fabric*. London, 1983
Cotterell, A., *China: A Concise Cultural History*. London, 1989
Deng Xiaoping, *Speeches and Writings*. 2nd ed. Oxford, 1987
Dietrich, C., *People's China: A Brief History*. OUP, 1986
Domes, J., *The Government and Politics of the PRC*. Boulder, 1985
Fairbank, J. K., *The Great Chinese Revolution 1800–1985*. London, 1987
Fathers, M. and Higgins, A., *Tiananmen: The Rape of Peking*. London and New York, 1989
Glassman, R. M., *China in Transition: Communism, Capitalism and Democracy*. New York, 1991
Goodman, D., *Deng Xiaoping*. London, 1990. —and Segal, G., (eds.) *China in the 90s: Crisis Management and Beyond*. Oxford, 1991
Gray, J., *Rebellions and Revolutions: China from the 1800s to the 1980s*. CUP, 1990

Grummit, K., *China Economic Handbook*. London, 1986
Guide to China's Foreign Economic Relations and Trade. Hong Kong, 1984
Harding, H. (ed.) *China's Foreign Relations in the 1980's*. Yale Univ. Press, 1984.—*China's Second Revolution*. Washington, 1987
Hinton, H. C. (ed.) *The People's Republic of China 1949–1979*. 5 vols. Wilmington, 1980
Hook, B. (ed.) *The Cambridge Encyclopaedia of China*. 2nd ed. CUP, 1991
Hsieh, C. M., *Atlas of China*. New York, 1973
Kaplan, F. M. (ed.) *Encyclopedia of China Today*. 3rd ed. London, 1982
Klein, D. W. and Clark, A. B., *Biographic Dictionary of Chinese Communism, 1921–1965*. Harvard Univ. Press, 1971
Lardy, N. R., *Agriculture in China's Modern Economic Development*. CUP, 1983
Leeming, F., *Rural China Today*. London, 1985
Lichtenstein, P. M., *China at the Brink: the Political Economy of Reform and Retrenchment in the Post-Mao Era*. New York, 1991
Lippit, V. D., *The Economic Development of China*. Armonk, 1987
Loewe, M. *The Pride that was China*. London, 1990
Mabbett, I., *Modern China: The Mirage of Modernity*. New York, 1985
McCormick, B. L., *Political Reform in Post-Mao China: Democracy and Bureaucracy in a Leninist State*. California Univ. Press, 1990
Mackerras, C. and Yorke, A., *The Cambridge Handbook of Contemporary China*. CUP, 1991
Mancall, M., *China at the Center: 300 Years of Foreign Policy*. New York, 1984
Marshall, M., *Organizations and Growth in Rural China*. London, 1985
Maxwell, N. and McFarlane, B. (eds.) *China's Changed Road to Development*. Oxford, 1984
Moise, E. E., *Modern China: A History*. London, 1986
Moser, L. J., *The Chinese Mosaic: the Peoples and Provinces of China*. Boulder, Colo., 1985
Nathan, A. J., *Chinese Democracy*. London, 1986:-*China's Crisis: Dilemmas of Reform and Prospects for Democracy*. Columbia Univ. Press, 1990
Pan, L., *The New Chinese Revolution*. London, 1987
Pannell, C. W. and Laurence, J. C., *China: the Geography of Development and Modernization*. London, 1983
Pearson, M. M., *Joint Ventures in the People's Republic of China: the Control of Foreign Direct Investment under Socialism*. Princeton Univ. Press, 1991
Riskin, C., *China's Political Economy: The Quest for Development since 1949*. OUP, 1987
Rodzinski, W., *A History of China*. Oxford, 1981–84
Schram, S. R. (ed.) *The Scope of State Power in China*. London, 1985
Segal, G., *Defending China*. OUP, 1985
Segal, G. and Tow, W. T. (eds.) *Chinese Defence Policy*. London, 1984
Song, J., *et al, Population Control in China*. New York, 1985
Spence, J. D., *The Search for Modern China*. London, 1990
The Times Atlas of China. London, 1974
White, G., (ed.) *The Chinese State in the Era of Economic Reform: the Road to Crisis*. London, 1991
Wong, K. and Chu, D. (eds.) *Modernization in China: The Case of the Shenzhen Special Economic Zone*. OUP, 1986
Young, G. (ed.) *China: Dilemmas of Modernisation*. London, 1985

TAIWAN [1]

'Republic of China'

Capital: Taipei
Population: 20·4m. (1991)
GNP per capita: US$8,609 (1991)

HISTORY. The island of Taiwan (Formosa) was ceded to Japan by China by the Treaty of Shimonoseki on 8 May 1895. After the Second World War the island was surrendered to Gen. Chiang Kai-shek in Sept. 1945 and was placed under Chinese administration on 25 Oct. 1945. USA broke off diplomatic relations with Taiwan on 1 Jan. 1979 on establishing diplomatic relations with the Peking Government. Relations between the USA and Taiwan are maintained through the American Institute on Taiwan and the Co-ordination Council for North American Affairs in the USA, set up in 1979 and accorded diplomatic status in Oct. 1980.

[1] See note on transcription of names p. 356.

AREA AND POPULATION. Taiwan lies between the East and South China Seas about 100 miles from the coast of Fujian. The total area of Taiwan Island, the Penghu Archipelago and the Kinma area is 13,969 sq. miles (36,179 sq. km). Population (1991), 20·4m., of whom some 2m. are mainland Chinese who came with the Nationalist Government. There are also 338,151 aboriginals. Population density: 565 per sq. km.

In 1990, birth rate was 1·65%; death rate, 0·52%; rate of growth, 1·25% per annum (2000 target: 0·72% per annum). Life expectancy, 1990: Males, 71 years; females, 76·7 years.

Taiwan is divided into two special municipalities (Taipei, the capital, population 2·72m. in 1990 and Kaohsiung, population 1·39m. in 1990), 5 municipalities (Taichung, Keelung, Tainan, Chiayi and Hsinchu) and 16 counties (*hsien*): Changhwa, Chiayi, Hsinchu, Hualien, Ilan, Kaohsiung, Miaoli, Nantou, Penghu, Pingtung, Taichung, Tainan, Taipei, Taitung, Taoyuan, Yunlin. The seat of the provincial government is at Chunghsing New Village.

CLIMATE. A tropical climate with hot, humid conditions and heavy rainfall in the summer months but cooler from Nov. to March when rainfall amounts are not so great. Typhoons may be experienced. Taipei. Jan. 59°F (15·3°C), July 83°F (29·2°C). Annual rainfall 100" (2,500 mm).

CONSTITUTION AND GOVERNMENT. Taiwan remained in the hands of the remnants of the Nationalist Government when mainland China became Communist. On 1 March 1950, Chiang Kai-shek resumed the presidency of the 'Republic of China'. He died 5 April 1975. His son Chiang Ching-kuo was president from March 1978 to his death in Jan. 1988. He was succeeded by Lee Teng-hui, who on 21 March 1990 was re-elected unopposed as *President* for a 6-year term by the National Assembly by 641 votes to 47. The *Vice-President* is Li Yuan-zu.

A *National Assembly* was elected on the Mainland in 1947. A dwindling number of mainland delegates retained their seats until a new Assembly was established in 1991. (For details of the previous system *see* THE STATESMAN'S YEAR-BOOK, 1991–92, p. 368).

At the elections of Dec. 1991 for the new 325-member National Assembly all deputies were elected anew in Taiwan. The electorate was 13m.; turn-out was 70%. The Kuomintang (KMT) gained 71% of votes cast and 254 seats; the Democratic Progressive Party gained 23% of votes cast.

The cabinet included the following in Sept. 1991:

Prime Minister: Hau Pei-tsun (b. 1919).

Vice-Premier: Shih Chi-yang. *Foreign Minister:* Frederick F. Chien. *Minister of National Defence:* Chen Li-an. *Minister of the Interior:* Wu Poh-hsiung. *Minister of Finance:* Wang Chien-hsien. *Minister of Education:* Mao Kao-wen. *Minister of Economic Affairs:* Vincent C. Siew. *Minister of Transportation and Communications:* Eugene Y. H. Chien. *Chairman, Mongolian and Tibetan Affairs Commission:* Wu Hua-peng. *Chairman, Overseas Chinese Affairs Commission:* Tseng Kwang-shun. The *Governor of Taiwan Province* was Lien Chan.

National flag: Red with a blue first quarter bearing the state emblem, a 12-pointed white sun in a blue sky, in white.

National anthem: 'San Min Chu I', words by Dr Sun Yat-sen; tune by Cheng Mao-yun.

Local Government. At the Dec.1989 elections for 21 county executives and city mayors, the DPP won 6 posts with 40% of the vote. At the local authority elections of 1990 the KMT won 60% of the vote, the DPP, 30%.

DEFENCE

Army. The Army, which was formed on the forces which escaped to Taiwan under Chiang Kai-shek at the end of the civil war in 1949, numbered about 270,000 in 1992. It was reorganized, re-equipped and trained by the USA and in 1992 consisted of 20 infantry divisions, 2 mechanized infantry divisions, 1 airborne brigade,

5 independent armoured brigades, 22 field artillery and 5 surface-to-air missile battalions. The aviation element comprises 6 squadrons with about 80 helicopters. There is a conscription system for 2 years and reserve liability to age 30. Equipment includes 309 M-48A5 and 150 M-48H main battle tanks and 275 M-24 and 675 M-41 light tanks.

Navy. The Taiwan navy consists principally of former US Navy ships over 40 years old and well overdue for replacement. A major programme of renewal has been initiated with new submarines, frigates and support ships on order. Current fleet strength is 2 new Netherlands-built diesel submarines, 24 ex-US 1940s destroyers, 9 frigates, 3 corvettes (ex-fleet minesweepers), 52 fast missile craft, 38 other patrol craft and 8 coastal minesweepers. The amphibious force includes 1 amphibious flagship, 1 dock landing ship, 20 landing ships and about 260 amphibious craft. Auxiliary craft include 4 support tankers, 2 repair and salvage ships, 7 tugs and 3 survey ships.

Main bases are at Tsoying, Makung and Keelung.

Active personnel in 1991 totalled 30,000 in the Navy and 30,000 in the Marine Corps. There are over 60,000 naval and marine reservists.

The Naval Air Command operates 12 small anti-submarine helicopters from the destroyers and 12 S-70 Seahawk helicopters based ashore.

The Customs service operates 12 cutters.

Air Force. The Nationalist Air Force is equipped mainly with aircraft of US design, including F-5E fighters built in Taiwan. It has 11 front-line squadrons of F-5E/F Tiger IIs, 3 of F-104G Starfighters, 1 of locally-built AT-3 twin-jet light strike aircraft and 1 tactical reconnaissance squadron of RF-104G Starfighters. The 6 transport squadrons are equipped with a VIP Boeing 720, 4 Boeing 727s, 11 Beech 1900s, 20 C-47s, about 40 C-119Gs and 12 C-130H Hercules. There is a naval co-operation squadron with S-2A/E Trackers. Search and rescue units operate S-70 and Iroquois helicopters, and there are other helicopter and large training elements, some equipped with AT-3 twin-jet trainers designed and built in Taiwan and others with US-supplied T-34Cs. Total strength in 1991: 70,000 personnel.

INTERNATIONAL RELATIONS. By a treaty of 1 Dec. 1954 the USA was pledged to protect Taiwan, but this treaty lapsed 1 year after the USA established diplomatic relations with the People's Republic of China on 1 Jan. 1979. In April 1979 the Taiwan Relations Act was passed by the US Congress to maintain commercial, cultural and other relations between USA and Taiwan.

The People's Republic took over the China seat in the UN from the Nationalists on 25 Oct. 1971.

In April 1991 Taiwan ended its formal state of war with the People's Republic.

ECONOMY

Policy. There have been a series of development plans. The 6-year National Development Plan has the goals of raising national income, developing the industrial base, promoting balanced regional development and raising the quality of life at a cost of NT$8,236,000m. Funding is being raised by new taxes, privatization of state-owned companies and government bonds.

Budget. There are 2 budgets, the national together with a special defence budget (partly secret) and the provincial (*i.e.*, for Taiwan proper). For the fiscal year July 1991–June 1992 the national budget is scheduled for NT$1,223,578m. Expenditure planned: 18·8% on defence; 18·8% on economic development; 18·9% on social security; 21·4% on education, science and culture. Foreign exchange reserves were US$67,397m. in April 1991.

Currency. The unit of currency is the *New Taiwan dollar* (TWD), of 100 *cents*. There are coins of NT$ 1, 5 and 10 and notes of NT$ 50, 100, 500 and 1,000. Mainland currency has been legal tender since 1992. Gold reserves were 13·6m. oz. July 1990. Exchange rates (March 1992): £1 = NT$44·08; US$1 = NT$25·11.

Banking and Finance. The Central Bank of China (reactivated in 1961) regulates the money supply, manages foreign exchange and issues currency. *Governor:* Samuel Shieh.

The Bank of Taiwan is the largest commercial bank and the fiscal agent of the Government. In June 1991 there were 39 domestic commercial banks (including 15 new banks) and 35 local branches of foreign banks. Most banks had been state-controlled until June 1991, when 15 new private-sector commercial banks were licensed.

There were also 74 credit co-operatives, 310 agricultural credit unions, 8 trust and investment companies and 35 insurance companies.

There is a stock exchange in Taipei.

ENERGY AND NATURAL RESOURCES

Electricity. Output of electricity in 1990 was 82,349m. kwh.; total generating capacity was 16·9m. kw. There are 3 nuclear power-stations (capacities 1m., 1m. and 0·6m. kw.) and a fourth is envisaged. Supply 110 volts; 60 Hz.

Minerals. There are reserves of coal (171m. tonnes), gold (1·1m. tonnes), copper (4·7m. tonnes), oil (0·5m. kl.) and natural gas (14·85m. cu. metres). In 1990, coal production was 0·5m. tonnes; refined oil, 2·4m. kl.; natural gas, 1,129m. cu. metres. Crude oil production (1990) 182,384 kl.

Agriculture. The cultivated area was 890,090 ha in 1990, of which 476,997 ha were paddy fields. Production in 1,000 tonnes, in 1990: Rice, 1,807; tea, 22; bananas, 201; pineapples, 235; sugar-cane, 5,581; sweet potatoes, 200; soybeans, 8; peanuts, 65.

Livestock (1990): Cattle, 154,238; pigs, 8,565,250; goats, 172,593.

Forestry. Forest area, 1990: 1,864,970 ha; forest reserves, 326,489,961 cu. metres; timber production, 139,796 cu. metres.

Fisheries. The fleet comprised 6,091 vessels over 20 GRT in 1990; the catch was 1,455,495 tonnes in 1990.

INDUSTRY. Output (in tonnes) in 1990 (and 1989): Steel bars, 5·1m. (4·3m.); pig-iron, 59,570 (29,904); shipbuilding, 1,211,607 (1,201,549); sugar, 479,083 (500,511); cement, 18·5m. (18m.); fertilizers, 1·42m. (1·36m.); paper, 911,452 (879,844); cotton fabrics, 729m. metres (786m.).

Labour. In 1990 the labour force was 8·42m., of whom 1·06m. worked in agriculture, forestry and fisheries, 3·33m. in industry (including 2·6m. in manufacturing and 682,000 in building), 1·63m. in commerce, 459,000 in transport and communications, and 1·75m. in other services. 141,000 were registered unemployed in 1990.

FOREIGN ECONOMIC RELATIONS

Commerce. Foreign trade affairs are handled by the China External Trade Development Council (founded 1970), which operates branches in 20 countries mostly under the name of Far East Trade Service. Principal exports: Textiles, electronic products, agricultural products, metal goods, plastic products. Principal imports: Oil, chemicals, machinery, electronic products. Total trade, in US$1m.:

	1985	1986	1987	1988	1989	1990
Imports	20,102	24,165	34,957	49,656	52,249	54,716
Exports	30,723	39,789	53,538	60,585	66,201	67,214

The USA, Japan and Hong Kong are Taiwan's major trade partners followed by Germany, UK and Canada. A mounting trade surplus has caused friction with the USA and a sharp appreciation of the Taiwan dollar. Economic liberalization measures are being undertaken to improve the position.

Principal exports in 1990, in US$1,000m. (and percentage of total exports): Machinery and electrical equipment, 23·13 (34·4%); textiles, 10·28 (15·3%); metal and metalware, 5·22 (7·8%); footwear, headwear and umbrellas, 4·12 (6·1%); plastic and rubber goods, 4·43 (6·6%); toys, games, sports equipment, 2·91 (4·3%);

vehicles and aircraft, 3·45 (5·1%); animals and products, 1·65 (2·5%); precision instruments, 1·72 (2·6%); leather and fur goods, 1·32 (2%).

Total trade between Taiwan and UK (British Department of Trade returns, in £1,000 sterling):

	1987	1988	1989	1990	1991
Imports to UK	1,006,880	1,150,392	1,351,695	1,211,968	1,271,990
Exports and re-exports from UK	292,275	355,786	407,432	430,643	519,821

Tourism. In 1990 1,934,084 tourists visited Taiwan, and 2,942,316 Taiwanese made visits abroad. The ban on Taiwanese travel to Communist China was lifted in 1987.

COMMUNICATIONS

Roads. In 1990 there were 19,997·8 km of roads (16,984 km surfaced). 11,465,251 motor vehicles were registered including 2,328,439 passenger cars, 21,357 buses, 632,512 trucks and 8,460,138 motor cycles. 1,620m. passengers and 246m. tonnes of freight were transported (including urban buses).

Railways. Total route length in 1990 was 2,469·5 km (1,067 mm to 762 mm gauge), of which a large proportion is owned by the Taiwan Sugar Corporation and other concerns. The state network consisted of 1,072 km. Freight traffic amounted to 28·1m. tonnes and passenger traffic to 132·4m.

Civil Aviation. There are 2 international airports: Chiang Kai-shek at Taoyuan near Taipei, and Kaohsiung which operates daily flights to Hong Kong. There are 9 domestic airlines, including China Airlines (CAL), which also operates international services to Bangkok, Hong Kong, Jakarta, Kuala Lumpur, Manila, Seoul, Singapore, Amsterdam, Saudi Arabia, Japan and USA. In 1990, 18·72m. passengers and 662,134 tonnes of freight were flown.

Shipping. The merchant marine in 1990 comprised 5 passenger ships, 80 container ships, 43 bulk carriers, 16 tankers and 110 mixed service ships, with a total DWT of 9·2m.

There are 4 international ports: Kaohsiung, Keelung, Hwalien and Taichung. The first two are container centres. Suao port is an auxiliary port to Keelung.

Telecommunications. In 1990 there were 12,700 post offices. In 1990 there were 6,300,755 telephone subscribers and 8,431,966 stations for telephone service.The Broadcasting Corporation of China is a private enterprise under government contract. It broadcasts on 3 networks and on news, music and popular networks. The Central Broadcasting System broadcasts to mainland China. There are 2 external services. There are 3 commercial TV services and an educational service (colour by NTSC). In 1991 there were 13·6m. radio and 6·66m. TV sets.

Cinemas (1991). Cinemas numbered 438.

Newspapers and Books. There were 139 daily papers and 4,021 periodicals in 1990. 38,003 book titles were published in 1989.

RELIGION, EDUCATION AND WELFARE

Religion. There were 2·74m. Taoists in 1990 with 8,044 temples and 28,278 priests, 4·86m. Buddhists with 4,020 temples and 9,130 priests, 427,000 Protestants and 0·29m. Catholics.

Education. Since 1968 there has been compulsory education for 9 years (6–15) with free tuition. In that year the curriculum was modernized to give more emphasis to science while retaining the traditional basis of Confucian ethics. Since 1983 school-leavers aged 15-18 receive part-time vocational education. There were, in 1990–91, 2,487 primary schools with 82,583 teachers and 2,354,113 pupils; 1,086 secondary schools with 84,260 teachers and 1,818,301 students; 121 schools of higher education, including 46 universities and colleges, with 27,579 full-time teachers and 576,623 students.

Health. In 1990 there were 91,153 medical personnel, including 19,921 doctors, 5,449 dentists and 2,372 doctors of Chinese medicine. There were 95 public hospitals with 35,768 beds and 732 private hospitals with 47,965 beds.

Further Reading

Statistical Yearbook of the Republic of China. Taipei, annual
Republic of China Yearbook. Taipei, annual
Republic of China: A Reference Book. Taipei, annual
Taiwan Statistical Data Book. Taipei, annual
Annual Review of Government Administration, Republic of China. Taipei, annual
Gälli, A., *Taiwan ROC: A Chinese Challenge to the World*. London, 1987
Gold, T. B., *State and Society in the Taiwan Miracle*. Armonk, 1986
Lee, S.-Y., *Money and Finance in the Economic Development of Taiwan*. London, 1990
Lee, W.-C., *Taiwan:* [Bibliography]. Oxford and Santa Barbara, 1990
Liu, A. P. L., *Phoenix and the Lame Lion: Modernization in Taiwan and Mainland China, 1950–1980*. Stanford, 1987
Long, S., *Taiwan: China's Last Frontier*. London, 1991
Simon, D. F. S., *Taiwan, Technology Transfer, and Transnationalism*. Boulder, 1983

National library: National Central Library, Taipei (established 1986).

COLOMBIA

República de Colombia

Capital: Bogotá
Population: 33m. (1990)
GNP per capita: US$1,280 (1989)

HISTORY. The Vice-royalty of New Granada gained its independence of Spain in 1819, and was officially constituted 17 Dec. 1819, together with the present territories of Panama, Venezuela and Ecuador, as the state of 'Greater Colombia', which continued for about 12 years. It then split up into Venezuela, Ecuador and the republic of New Granada in 1830. The constitution of 22 May 1858 changed New Granada into a confederation of 8 states, under the name of Confederación Granadina. Under the constitution of 8 May 1863 the country was renamed 'Estados Unidos de Colombia', which were 9 in number. The revolution of 1885 led the National Council of Bogotá, composed of 2 delegates from each state, to promulgate the constitution of 5 Aug. 1886, forming the Republic of Colombia, which abolished the sovereignty of the states, converting them into departments, with governors appointed by the President of the Republic, though they retained some of their old rights, such as the management of their own finances.

AREA AND POPULATION. Colombia is bounded north by the Caribbean sea, north-west by Panama, west by the Pacific ocean, south-west by Ecuador and Peru, north-east by Venezuela and south-east by Brazil. The estimated area is 1,141,748 sq. km (440,829 sq. miles). It has a coastline of about 2,900 km, of which 1,600 km are on the Caribbean sea and 1,300 km on the Pacific ocean. Population census, (1985) 29,481,852; estimate (1990) 32,978,172. Bogotá, the capital, (census, 1985) 4,185,174; estimate (1990) 4,819,696.

The following table gives the officially adjusted figures for the 1985 census of population.

Departments	Area (sq. km)	Population census 1985	Capital	Population census 1985
Antioquia	63,612	4,067,664	Medellín	1,480,382
Atlántico	3,388	1,478,213	Barranquilla	927,233
Bolívar	25,978	1,288,985	Cartagena	563,949
Boyacá	23,189	1,209,739	Tunja	94,451
Caldas	7,888	883,024	Manizales	308,784
Caquetá	88,965	264,507	Florencia	87,342
Cauca	29,308	857,731	Popayán	164,809
César	22,905	699,428	Valledupar	223,637
Chocó	46,530	313,567	Quibdó	93,806
Córdoba	25,020	1,013,247	Montería	242,515
Cundinamarca [1]	22,478	1,512,928	Bogotá	4,227,706
La Guajira	20,848	299,995	Riohacha	85,621
Huila	19,890	693,713	Neiva	199,567
La Magdalena	23,188	890,934	Santa Marta	233,632
Meta	85,635	474,046	Villavicencio	191,001
Nariño	33,268	1,085,173	Pasto	136,646
Norte de Santander	21,658	913,491	Cúcuta	388,397
Quindío	1,845	392,208	Armenia	195,453
Risaralda	4,140	652,872	Pereira	300,224
Santander	30,537	1,511,392	Bucaramanga	377,585
Sucre	10,917	561,649	Sincelejo	141,012
Tolima	23,562	1,142,220	Ibagué	314,934
Valle	22,140	3,027,247	Cali	1,429,026

[1] Excluding Bogotá.

New Departments [1]	Area (sq. km)	Population census 1985	Capital	Population census 1985
Arauca	23,818	89,972	Arauca	26,736
Casanare	44,460	147,472	Yopal	29,707
Putumayo	24,885	174,219	Mocoa	27,153
San Andrés	243	35,818	San Andrés	32,142
Providencia	44	. . .	. . .	. . .

New Departments [2]	Area (sq. km)	Population census 1985	Capital	Population census 1985
Amazonas	109,665	39,937	Leticia	24,092
Guainía	72,238	12,345	Puerto Inírida	12,345
Guaviare	42,327	47,073	San José del Guaviare	41,476
Vaupés	54,135	26,178	Mitú	18,007
Vichada	100,242	18,702	Puerto Carreño	10,758

[1] Created 5 July 1991; formerly *Intendencias.*   [2] Created 5 July 1991; formerly *Comisarías.*

Estimated population, 1990: 32,978,172 (females, 16,607,452). Deaths, 1987: 145,218 (infantile, 15,218).

The Amerindian population was 268,359 (131,192 females) in 1985.

The official language is Spanish.

CLIMATE. The climate includes equatorial and tropical conditions, according to situation and altitude. In tropical areas, the wettest months are March to May and Oct. to Nov. Bogotá. Jan. 58°F (14·4°C), July 57°F (13·9°C). Annual rainfall 42" (1,052 mm). Baranquilla. Jan. 80°F (26·7°C), July 82°F (27·8°C). Annual rainfall 32" (799 mm). Cali. Jan. 75°F (23·9°C), July 75°F (23·9°C). Annual rainfall 37" (915 mm). Medellin. Jan. 71°F (21·7°C), July 72°F (22·2°C). Annual rainfall 64" (1,606 mm).

CONSTITUTION AND GOVERNMENT. Simultaneously with the presidential elections of May 1990, a referendum was held in which 7m. votes were cast for the establishment of a special assembly to draft a new constitution. Elections were held on 9 Dec. 1990 for this 74-member 'Constitutional Assembly' which operated from Feb. to July 1991. The electorate was 14·2m.; turn-out was 3·7m. The Liberals gained 24 seats, M-19 (a former guerilla organization), 19. The Assembly produced a new constitution of 397 articles which came into force on 5 July 1991. It stresses the state's obligation to protect human rights, and establishes constitutional rights to health care, social security and leisure. Indians are allotted 2 Senate seats. Congress may dismiss ministers, and representatives may be recalled by their electors.

The legislative power rests with a *Congress* of 2 houses, the *Senate*, of 102 members, and the *House of Representatives*, of 161 members, both elected for 4 years. Congress meets annually at Bogotá on 20 July. Women were given the vote on 25 Aug. 1954.

The President is elected by direct vote of the people for a term of 4 years, and is not eligible for re-election until 4 years afterwards. A vice-presidency was instituted in July 1991.

A National Economic Council, functioning since May 1935, went through several transformations, becoming in 1954 a Directorate of Planning.

National Flag: Three horizontal stripes of yellow, blue, red with the yellow of double width.

National anthem: Oh! Gloria inmarcesible ('Oh Glory unfading!'; words by R. Núñez; tune by O. Síndici).

The following is a list of presidents since 1953:

Gen. Gustavo Rojas Pinilla, 13 June 1953– 10 May 1957.

Military Junta, Maj.-Gen. Gabriel París and 4 others, 10 May 1957–7 Aug. 1958.

Dr Alberto Lleras Camargo (Lib.), 7 Aug. 1958–7 Aug. 1962.

Dr Guillermo León Valencia (Cons.), 7 Aug. 1962–7 Aug. 1966.

Dr Carlos Lleras Restrepo (Lib.), 7 Aug. 1966–7 Aug. 1970.

Dr Misael Pastrana Borrero (Cons.), 7 Aug 1970–7 Aug. 1974.

Dr Alfonso López Michelsen (Cons./Lib.), 7 Aug. 1974–7 Aug. 1978.

Dr Julio Cesar Turbay Ayala (Lib.), 7 Aug. 1978–7 Aug. 1982.

Dr Belisario Betancur Cuartas (Cons.), 7 Aug. 1982–7 Aug. 1986.

Dr Virgilio Barco Vargas (Lib.), 7 Aug. 1986–7 Aug. 1990.

President: At the presidential elections of May 1990 César Gaviria Trujillo was elected by 47% of the vote (turn-out was 45%). He took office on 7 Aug. 1990.

Congressional elections were held on 27 Oct. 1991. The electorate was 16m. Following the elections the President appointed a Cabinet of 9 Liberals, 4 Conservatives and a former member of M-19:

Defence: Rafael Pardo Rueda (Lib). *Finance:* Rudolf Hommes. *Agriculture:* Alfonso López Caballero(Lib). *Economic Development:* Jorge Ospina Sardi. *Labour and Social Security:* Francisco Posada de la Peña. *Health:* Camilo González Posso. *Mines and Energy:* Juan Camilo Restrepo. *Education:* Carlos Holmes Trujillo. *Communications:* Mauricio Vargas Linares. *Public Works and Transport:* Juan Felipe Gaviria. *Government:* Humberto de la Calle Lombana. *Justice:* Fernando Carillo. *Foreign Trade:* Juan Manuel Santos (Lib). *Foreign Affairs:* Nohemi Sanin Posada (Con).

Local government: The country is divided into 32 departments and the Capital District of Bogotá (in full, 'Santa Fé de Bogotá'). The governor of each department is elected by universal suffrage, and each has also a directly-elected legislature. The departments are subdivided into municipalities. The mayors of these, and the Special District of Bogotá, are elected by direct vote for a 2-year term.

DEFENCE. Selective conscription at 18 years varies from 1 to 2 years of service.

Army. The Army consists of 15 infantry brigades, 2 counter-insurgency brigades, 1 training brigade, Presidential Guard and a mechanized group. Equipment includes 12 M-3A1 light tanks. Personnel (1991) 115,000 men (conscripts, 38,000); reserves 100,000. Number of national police (1991) 80,000.

Navy. Colombia has 2 German-built 1,200-ton diesel powered submarines completed in 1975, 2 Italian-built midget submarines, 4 small German-built missile-armed frigates with helicopter decks and 9 fast patrol craft. There are 3 river gunboats and 11 riverine patrol craft. Auxiliaries include 2 surveying vessels, 1 small transport, 1 training ship, 5 service craft and 10 tugs. Personnel in 1991 totalled 6,000. There are also 5 battalions of marines numbering 6,000. An air arm was formed in 1984 which operates 6 light reconnaissance aircraft and 4 BO-105 helicopters for ship-borne anti-submarine and rescue duties.

Air Force. Formed in 1922, the Air Force has been independent of the Army and Navy since 1943, when its reorganization began with US assistance. In 1991 it had over 300 aircraft, including 2 fighter-bomber squadrons, one with Mirage 5s and one with Kfirs. 2 squadrons of A-37B jets for counter-insurgency duties; a transport group equipped with 5 C-130, 12 C-47s, 3 C-54s, 4 DC-6s and a small number of Arava and Turbo-Porter light transports; a presidential F-28 Fellowship jet transport; 1 Boeing 707, UH-1B/H utility helicopters; and a reconnaissance unit with Iroquois, Lama, Hughes OH-6A, 300C and TH-55 helicopters. 8 more C-47s, 11 Aviocars, 2 C-54s, 1 F-28 and 4 HS.748 transports are flown by the Air Force operated airline SATENA. There are several dozen light transports, confiscated from drug-smugglers, in use. Thirty Cessna T-41D primary trainer/light transports were delivered in 1968 and were followed by 10 T-37C jet advanced trainers to supplement piston-engined T-34s. Total strength (1991) 7,000 personnel (1,900 conscripts).

INTERNATIONAL RELATIONS

Membership. Colombia is a member of the UN, OAS, the Andean Group and LAIA.

ECONOMY

Policy. The 1986–90 Development Plan gave priority to the eradication of poverty.

Budget. Revenue and expenditure of central government in 1990: Revenue, 2,998,290m. pesos; expenditure, 2,827,756m. pesos.

Currency. The unit of currency is the *Colombian peso* of 100 *centavos*. There are coins of 50 centavos and 1, 2, 5, 10, 20 and 50 pesos, and notes of 100, 200, 500, 1,000, 2,000 and 5,000 pesos. Money in circulation, May 1991: 773,691m. pesos.

Inflation was 32·4% in 1990. The government target for 1991 was 22%. Exchange rate, March 1992: 1,095·70 *pesos* = £1 sterling; 624·15 *pesos* = US$1.

Banking and Finance. On 23 July 1923 the Bank of the Republic was inaugurated as a semi-official central bank, with the exclusive privilege of issuing bank-notes in Colombia; its charter, in 1951, was extended to 1973. Its note issues must be covered by a reserve in gold of foreign exchange of 25% of their value. Its international reserves in Jan. 1991 were 2,453,944m. pesos. Total assets (Jan. 1991) 3,351,570m.

There are 25 commercial banks, of which 16 are private or mixed, and 8 official. There is also an Agricultural, Industrial and Mining Credit Institute, a Central Mortgage Bank and a Social Savings Bank with total assets of 3,483,559 pesos as of June 1988. Bank deposits totalled 1,446,686 pesos in May 1991.

There are stock exchanges in Bogotá, Medellín and Cali.

Weights and Measures. The metric system was introduced in 1857, but in ordinary commerce Spanish weights and measures are generally used; according to new definitions by the Ministry of Development, *e.g., botella* (750 grammes), *galón* (5 *botellas*), *vara* (70 cm), *arroba* (25 lb., of 500 grammes; 4 *arrobas* = 1 quintal).

ENERGY AND NATURAL RESOURCES

Electricity. Capacity of electric power (1989) was 8·85m. kw. Electric power produced in 1987, 29,650m. kwh. Supply 110, 120 and 150 volts; 60 Hz.

Oil. Production in 1991 was 21·06m. tonnes.

Minerals. Colombia is rich in minerals; gold is found chiefly in Antioquia and moderately in Cauca, Caldas, Tolima, Nariño and Chocó; output in 1990, 943,697 troy oz.

Other minerals are silver (211,920 troy oz. in 1990), copper, lead, mercury, manganese, emeralds (of which Colombia accounts for about half of world production) and platinum; production of platinum, 1990, 42,297 troy oz. The chief emerald mines are those of Muzo and Chivor.

The Government holds the monopoly, which is leased to the Banco de la República, for extracting salts from the outstanding Zipaquirá mines (several hundred feet in depth and several hundred square miles in area) and for evaporating many sea salt pans; salt production in 1990 was 99,309 tonnes of land salt and 267,748 tonnes of sea salt. Coal reserves were estimated at 20,963m. tonnes in 1986; production (1990, provisional) 20·5m. tonnes. Iron ore production was 301,754 tonnes in 1990.

Agriculture. Very little of the country is under cultivation, but much of the soil is fertile and is coming into use as roads improve. The range of climate and crops is extraordinary; the agricultural colleges have different courses for 'cold-climate farming' and 'warm-climate farming'. In 1990 there were 2,461,960 ha under temporary cultivation and 1,340,010 under permanent.

Coffee area harvested (1988) 1m. ha; production (1990) 11,066,000 60 kg. sacks. Crops are grown by smallholders, and are picked all the year round. Production (1990, in 1,000 tonnes): Potatoes, 2,797·6; rice, 2,100·5; maize, 1,187·8; sorghum, 757·8.

The rubber tree grows wild but is also cultivated. Fibres are being exploited, notably the 'fique' fibre, which furnishes all the country's requirements for sacks and cordage; output (1990 estimate) 23,460 tonnes.

Livestock (1988): 24,307,000 cattle, 2,586,000 pigs, 2,652,000 sheep, 152·4m. poultry.

Fisheries. Total catch (1987) 83,569 tonnes.

INDUSTRY. Production (1990): Steel ingots, 164,382 tonnes; cement, 3,080,103 tonnes; motor cars, 17,855; industrial vehicles, 3,515; sugar, 1,592,735 tonnes. In 1987 there were 6,927 manufacturing establishments.

Labour. In 1987 477,170 persons were employed in manufacturing (145,644 women).

FOREIGN ECONOMIC RELATIONS. Import tariffs were reduced in 1990 and 1991, and restrictions on movements of capital were lifted. Foreign debt was US$16,601m. in March 1991.

Commerce. Imports (c.i.f. values) and exports (f.o.b. values) (excluding export tax) for calendar years (in US$1m.):

	1985	1986	1987	1988	1989
Imports	4,131	3,852	4,228	5,005	5,010
Exports	3,552	5,108	5,024	5,026	5,739

Important articles of export in 1989 (in US$1m.) were coffee (1,524), bananas (260), flowers (105), clothing and textiles (148), crude oil (1,045), bituminous (447), fuel oil (304), precious stones and gems (102). The chief imports are machinery, vehicles, tractors, metals and manufactures, rubber, chemical products, wheat, fertilizers and wool.

Imports in 1990 (in US$1m.) from USA were valued at 1,979·3; Japan, 496·2; Federal Republic of Germany, 477·1; Brazil, 186·8; Venezuela, 321·4. Exports in 1990 (in US$1m.) to USA, 3,005; Federal Germany, 570·6; Japan, 259; Netherlands, 293·2; Venezuela, 203·7.

Total trade between Colombia and UK (British Department of Trade returns, in £1,000 sterling):

	1987	1988	1989	1990	1991
Imports to UK	65,331	61,835	71,658	82,507	110,122
Exports and re-exports from UK	61,385	53,132	63,525	60,469	56,426

Tourism. Foreign visitors totalled 828,903 in 1988.

COMMUNICATIONS

Roads. Owing to the mountainous character of the country, the construction of arterial roads and railways is costly and difficult. Total length of highways, about 75,000 km in 1983. Of the 2,300-mile Simón Bolívar highway, which runs from Caracas in Venezuela to Guayaquil in Ecuador, the Colombian portion is complete. Buenaventura and Cali are linked by a highway (Carreterra al Mar). Motor vehicles in 1989 numbered 1,433,956, of which 231,306 were passenger cars and 272,882 lorries. In 1988 4,917m. passengers were carried by road transport.

Railways. The National Railways (2,532 km of route, 914 mm gauge) went into liquidation in 1990 prior to takeover of services and obligations by 3 new public companies in 1992. In 1990 railways carried 1·1m. passengers and 1m. tonnes of freight.

Civil Aviation. There are 670 landing grounds of all kinds. In 1990 1,114,000 passengers and 132,482 tonnes of freight were carried on international flights, and 5,235,000 passengers and 79,470 tonnes of freight on domestic flights.

Shipping. Vessels entering Colombian ports in 1989 unloaded 5,581,000 tonnes of imports and loaded 17,893,000 tonnes of exports.

The Magdelena River is subject to drought, and navigation is always impeded during the dry season, but it is an important artery of passenger and goods traffic. The river is navigable for 900 miles; steamers ascend to La Dorada, 592 miles from Barranquilla. 1,124,537 passengers, 149,852 head of cattle and 3,040 tonnes of freight were carried by inland waterways in 1988.

Telecommunications. The length of telephone lines in service in 1989 was 943,076 km (Bogotá), nationally, 1,976,618 km.; instruments in use, 1 Jan. 1984, 2,547,222. The cable company is government owned. There are 5 radio companies overseen by the Dirección General de Radiocomunicaciones. Instituto Nacional de Radio y Televisión transmits on 3 networks (colour by NTSC) and rents air time to 26 commercial companies. In 1991 there were 33,253,000 radio and 5·5m. TV sets.

Cinemas (1987). There were 657 cinemas, of which 64 were in Bogotá.

Newspapers (1984). There were 31 daily newspapers, with daily circulation totalling 1·5m.

JUSTICE, RELIGION, EDUCATION AND WELFARE

Justice. The July 1991 constitution introduced the offices of public prosecutor and public defence. There is no extradition of Colombians for trial in other countries. The Supreme Court, at Bogotá, of 20 members, is divided into 3 chambers—civil cassation (6), criminal cassation (8), labour cassation (6). Each of the 61 judicial districts has a superior court with various sub-dependent tribunals of lower juridical grade. 257,511 crimes were reported in 1988.

Religion. The religion is Roman Catholic, with the Cardinal Archbishop of Bogotá as Primate of Colombia, the Cardinal Archbishop of Cartagena and 8 other archbishops in Manizales, Medellín, Nueva Pamplona, Popayán, Cali, Bucaramanga, Ibagué, Barranquilla, Santa Fé de Antioquia and Tunja. There are also 44 bishops, 8 apostolic vicars, 5 apostolic prefects and 2 prelates. In 1990 there were 1,546 parishes and 4,020 priests. Other forms of religion are permitted so long as their exercise is 'not contrary to Christian morals or the law.'

Education. Primary education is free but not compulsory, and facilities are limited. Schools are both state and privately controlled. In 1988 there were 7,759 preprimary schools with 14,918 teachers and 340,244 pupils, 37,948 primary schools with 136,549 teachers and 4,044,220 pupils and 6,134 secondary schools with 99,392 teachers and 2,076,455 pupils. There were 235 higher education establishments with 457,680 students.

In 1987 there were 60 institutes of higher education with 79,743 students, 42 technological institutes with 29,729 students and 60 institutes for professional training with 28,891 students.

There are 73 universities including the National University in Bogotá (founded 1886). In 1988 there were 319,319 students.

Health. In 1988 there were 926 hospitals and clinics. There were also 861 health centres.

DIPLOMATIC REPRESENTATIVES

Of Colombia in Great Britain (3 Hans Cres., London, SW1X 0LR)
Ambassador: Dr Virgilio Barco Vargas.

Of Great Britain in Colombia (Calle 98, No. 9–03 Piso 4, Bogotá)
Ambassador: K. Elliott Hedley Morris, CMG.

Of Colombia in the USA (2118 Leroy Pl., NW, Washington, D.C., 20008)
Ambassador: Dr Jaime García Parra.

Of the USA in Colombia (Calle 38, 8-61, Bogotá)
Ambassador: M. D. Busby.

Of Colombia to the United Nations
Ambassador: Dr Fernando Cepeda.

Further Reading

Anuario de Comercio Exterior de Colombia. Departamento Administrativo Nacional de Estadística (DANE)
Anuario de Industria Manufactura. DANE
Anuario Estadístico Bogotá D. E. Bogotá
Boletín Mensual de Estadística. DANE, monthly
Colombia Estadística. DANE, annual
Economía y Estadística. DANE, occasional
Estadística del Sector Agropecuario. Ministerio de Agricultura, annual
Informe Financiero del Contralor General. Annual
Informe del Gerente de la Caja de Crédito Agrario, Industrial y Minero. Annual
Memorias (13) de los Ministros al Congreso Nacional. Annual
Braun, H., *The Assassination of Gaitán: Public Life and Urban Violence in Colombia.* Univ. of Wisconsin Press, 1985
Hartlyn, J., *The Politics of Coalition Rule in Colombia.* CUP, 1988
Thorp, R., *Economic Management and Economic Development in Peru and Colombia.* London, 1991

COMMONWEALTH OF INDEPENDENT STATES (CIS)

Administrative centre: Minsk
Population: 276·65m. (1991)

Sodruzhestvo Nezavisimykh Gosudarstv [1]

For the former **UNION OF SOVIET SOCIALIST REPUBLICS (USSR)** *as a sovereign state see* THE STATESMAN'S YEAR-BOOK, 1991–92, pp. 1226–91.

STATUS. The Commonwealth of Independent States is not a state but a community of independent states which has proclaimed itself the successor to the Union of Soviet Socialist Republics in some aspects of international law and affairs. The member states are the founders, Russia, the Ukraine and Belorussia, and 8 subsequent adherents: Armenia, Azerbaijan, Moldavia and the Central Asian republics of Kazakhstan, Kirghizia, Tajikistan, Turkmenistan and Uzbekistan. As of Feb. 1992, Georgia had not joined.

HISTORY. For the 1917 revolution in the Russian Empire *see* THE STATESMAN'S YEAR-BOOK, 1990–91, p. 1223.

On 25 Jan. 1918 the third All-Russian Congress of Soviets proclaimed Russia a Republic of Soviets (i.e. councils) of Workers', Soldiers' and Peasants' Deputies; and on 10 July 1918 the fifth Congress adopted a Constitution for the Russian Soviet Federal Socialist Republic (RSFSR). In the course of the ensuing civil war Soviet Republics were set up in the Ukraine, Belorussia and Transcaucasia. These first entered into treaty relations with the RSFSR and then, on 30 Dec. 1922, joined with it to form the Union of Soviet Socialist Republics (USSR).

Extended negotiations in the USSR in 1990 and 1991, under the direction of President Gorbachev, sought to establish a 'renewed federation' or, subsequently, to conclude a new union treaty that would embrace all the 15 constituent republics of the USSR at that date. According to a referendum conducted in March 1991, the first of its kind in Soviet history, 76% of the population (on an 80% turnout) wished to maintain the USSR as a 'renewed federation of equal sovereign republics in which the human rights and freedoms of any nationality would be fully guaranteed'. In Sept. 1991 the three Baltic republics – Estonia, Latvia and Lithuania – were nonetheless recognised as independent states by the USSR State Council, and subsequently by the international community. Most of the remaining republics reached agreement on the broad outlines of a new 'union of sovereign states' in Nov. 1991, which would have retained a directly elected President and an all-union legislature, but which would have limited central authority to those powers specifically delegated to it by the members of the union.

A referendum in the Ukraine in Dec. 1991, however, showed overwhelming support for full independence, and following this the three Slav republics (Russia and Belorussia as well as the Ukraine) concluded an agreement in Minsk on 8 Dec. 1991 establishing a Commonwealth of Independent States with its headquarters in Minsk. The new Commonwealth was not a state, but would nonetheless provide for unitary control over strategic armed forces including nuclear arms, a single currency and a 'single economic space'. The USSR, as a subject of international law and a geopolitical reality, was declared no longer in existence, and each of the three republics individually renounced the 1922 treaty through which the USSR had been established.

[1] Russian title.

379

The Commonwealth declared itself open to other former Soviet republics, as well as to states elsewhere that shared its objectives, and on 21 Dec. 1991 in Alma-Ata a further declaration was signed by representatives of the 3 original members and of 8 other republics: Armenia, Azerbaijan, Kazakhstan, Kirghizia, Moldavia, Tajikistan, Turkmenistan and Uzbekistan. The declaration committed those who signed it to recognize the independence and sovereignty of other members, to respect human rights including those of national minorities, and to the observance of existing boundaries. Relations among the members of the Commonwealth are to be conducted on an equal, multilateral basis, but it was agreed to endorse the principle of unitary control of strategic nuclear arms and the concept of a 'single economic space'. Each member of the Commonwealth is entitled, at the same time, to seek to achieve a non-nuclear and/or neutral status. The USSR as such was held to have 'ended its existence', but the members of the Commonwealth pledged themselves to discharge the obligations that arose from the international treaties and agreements to which the USSR had been a party. In a separate agreement the heads of member states agreed that Russia should take up the seat at the United Nations formerly occupied by the USSR, and a framework of inter-state and inter-government consultation was established. Following these developments Mikhail Gorbachev resigned as USSR President on 25 Dec. 1991, his offices in the Kremlin were occupied by representatives of the Russian government, and on 26 Dec. the USSR Supreme Soviet voted a formal end to the treaty of union that had been signed in 1922 and dissolved itself.

AREA AND POPULATION. The area of the USSR in April 1991 was 22·4m. sq. km (8·65m. sq. miles). The census population on 15 Jan. 1970 was 241·7m. (111·4m. males, 130·3m. females; 136m. urban, 105·7m. rural). The census population on 12 Jan. 1989 was 286·7m. (135·5m. males, 151·2m. females, 188·8m. urban, 97·9m. rural). The increase of 25·2m. in urban population between 1979 and 1989 was due to natural increase (14·6m.) and migration from rural areas and the urbanization of large rural centres (10·6m.). Consequently, despite a natural increase in rural areas, there was a net decrease of 0·9m. over this period.

In 1989 49% of the total population were in paid employment, 30·1% were dependants or engaged in individual cultivation, 17·6% were pensioners or others maintained by the state, and 2·4% were in receipt of educational or other stipends.

The areas (in 1,000 sq. km) and population (in 1m., in Jan. 1990) of the constituent republics were as follows (capitals in brackets):

Constituent Republics	Area	Popu-lation	Constituent Republics	Area	Popu-lation
RSFSR (Moscow)	17,075	148·0	Georgia (Tbilisi)	70	5·5
Ukraine (Kiev)	604	51·8	Moldavia (Kishinev)	34	4·4
Uzbekistan (Tashkent)	447	20·3	Tajikistan (Dushanbe)	143	5·3
Kazakhstan (Alma-Ata)	2,717	16·7	Kirghizia Bishkek	199	4·4
Belorussia (Minsk)	208	10·3	Armenia (Yerevan)	30	3·3
Azerbaijan (Baku)	87	7·1	Turkmenistan (Ashkhabad)	488	3·6

Nationalities. The most numerous nationalities at the 1989 census were: 145·2m. Russians, 44·2m. Ukrainians, 16·7m. Uzbeks, 10m. Belorussians, 8·1m. Kazakhs, 6·8m. Azerbaijanians, 6·6m. Tatars, 4·6m. Armenians, 4m. Georgians, 3·4m. Moldavians, 4·2m. Tajiks, 3m. Lithuanians, 2·7m. Turkmenians, 2·5m. Kirghiz, 2m. Germans, 1·8m. Chuvashes, 1·5m. Latvians, 1·5m. Bashkirs, 1·4m. Jews, 1·2m. Mordovians, 1·1m. Poles, 1m. Estonians. The great majority (in each case 71-99%) indicated the language of their nationality as their native tongue; exceptions were the Mordovians (67%), Germans (49%), Poles (31%) and Jews (11%).

The following tables show the growth of the population:

1897 (Russian Empire)	126,900,000	1959 (census)	208,826,650
1913 (Russian Empire)	170,900,000	1970 (census)	241,720,134
1913 (present frontiers)	159,153,000	1979 (census)	262,436,227
1939 (census)	170,557,093	1989 (census)	286,717,000

The following was the population on 1 Jan. 1990 of the larger towns (in 1,000):

Alma-Ata	1,147	Krasnodar	627	Rostov-on-Don	1,025
Astrakhan	510	Krasnoyarsk	922	Ryazan	522
Baku	1,780	Krivoi Rog	717	Samara	1,258
Barnaul	603	Lugansk	501	Saratov	909
Bishkek	625	Lvov	798	St Petersburg	5,035
Chelyabinsk	1,148	Mariupol	520	Tashkent	2,094
Dnepropetrovsk	1,187	Minsk	1,613	Togliatti	642
Donetsk	1,117	Moscow	9,000	Tomsk	506
Dushanbe	602	Naberezhnye Chelny	507	Tula	543
Gomel	506	Nikolaev	508	Ufa	1,094
Irkutsk	635	Nizhni Novgorod	1,443	Ulyanovsk	638
Izhevsk	642	Novokuznetsk	601	Vladivostok	643
Karaganda	613	Novosibirsk	1,443	Volgograd	1,005
Kazan	1,103	Odessa	1,106	Voronezh	895
Kemerovo	521	Omsk	1,159	Yaroslavl	636
Khabarovsk	608	Orenburg	552	Yekaterinburg	1,372
Kharkov	1,618	Penza	548	Yerevan	1,202
Kiev	2,616	Perm	1,094	Zaporozhye	891
Kishinev	676				

Vital statistics rates in the USSR, 1989: Births, 17·6 per 1,000; deaths, 10 per 1,000. Infantile mortality per 1,000 births, 22·7. Life expectancy: Males, 64·6 years; females, 74.

Narodnoe khozyaistvo SSSR. Moscow, annual
Demograficheskii ezhegodnik SSSR. Moscow, annual
Sovetskii Soyuz. Geograficheskoe opisanie, 22 vols. Moscow, 1966–72
Cole, J. P., *Geography of the Soviet Union.* London, 1984
Howe, G. Melvyn, *The Soviet Union: a Geographical Survey* (2nd ed.). London, 1983
Symons, L., (ed.) *The Soviet Union: a Systematic Geography.* London, 1983
Wixman, R., *The Peoples of Russia and the USSR.* London, 1984

CLIMATE. The CIS comprises several different climatic regions, ranging from polar conditions in the north, through sub-arctic and humid continental, to subtropical and semi-arid conditions in the south. Rainfall amounts are greatest in areas bordering the Baltic, Black Sea, Caspian Sea and eastern coasts of Asiatic Russia. In most cases, there is a summer maximum.

Moscow. Jan. 15°F (–9·4°C), July 65°F (18·3°C). Annual rainfall 25·2" (630 mm). Arkhangelsk. Jan. 5°F (–15°C), July 57°F (13·9°C). Annual rainfall 20·1" (503 mm). Kiev. Jan. 21°F (–6·1°C), July 68°F (20°C). Annual rainfall 22" (554 mm). St Petersburg. Jan. 17°F (–8·3°C), July 64°F (17·8°C). Annual rainfall 19·5" (488 mm). Vladivostok. Jan. 6°F (–14·4°C), July 65°F (18·3°C). Annual rainfall 24" (599 mm).

CONSTITUTION. The CIS, according to its founders, is not a state or a suprastate organization, and it has been decided that its common affairs should be regulated on a multilateral, inter-state basis rather than by central institutions. The 'supreme organ' of the CIS, according to the agreement concluded in Alma-Ata on 21 Dec. 1991, is a *Council of Heads of States*; associated with its work is a *Council of Heads of Government.* The CIS provides a framework for military and foreign policy and economic co-ordination, but it has no common citizenship, no president and no parliament elected by the commonwealth as a whole. Of the original 15 constituent republics of the USSR, Estonia, Latvia and Lithuania did not participate in the CIS founding negotiations, and Georgia was represented only by observers.

DEFENCE. The founding treaties of the CIS provided for the unitary command of strategic forces, including nuclear arms. However, the allegiance of conventional forces stationed throughout the republics became a matter of some contention.

Since 1989 it was declared Soviet policy to reduce the size of the armed forces, to take part in international arms control negotiations and to adopt a more defensive operational stance. The Warsaw Pact was wound up, and Soviet troops were withdrawn from most countries abroad. Conscription is for 2 years.

Total strength of the armed forces was about 3·4m. in 1992, with a probable 55m. reserves and a further 570,000 Committee of State Security (KGB) and Interior Ministry troops (MVD).

Estimated budgetary expense on defence for 1991: 96,562m. rubles.

Army. The Army is thought to consist of 32 tank, 100 motor rifle, 7 airborne and 13 artillery divisions; 10 air assault brigades; and various independent tank, artillery, missile and engineer units. Equipment includes some 10,600 T-54/-55, 8,500 T-62, 4,900 T-64A/-B, 9,000 T-72/L/-M and 5,400 T-80 main battle tanks, and 1,000 PT-76 light tanks. Strength (1992), 1·4m. (1m. conscripts).

There are 5 operational rocket armies deploying 1,388 intercontinental ballistic missiles (SS-11,-13,-17,-18,-19-24,-25). Personnel number 164,000.

Navy. The navy of the former Soviet Union has probably been less affected by the dissolution of the Union than the other services. Nonetheless, there are already and will doubtless be more problems to solve. Russia has inherited the great majority of the fleet, and it may be assumed that command and control of these will remain securely in Moscow-based hands. The two most powerful of the fleets, the Northern and Pacific, are both wholly based upon and supported from Russian territory. These fleets count the entirety of the ballistic missile submarine force, all nuclear-powered submarines, all operational aircraft carriers and the majority of the major surface warships including the 3 Kirov class battle-cruisers. In addition, the new aircraft carrier *Admiral Kuznetsov*, which had been carrying out trials in the Black Sea since 1989, sailed to the Northern Fleet in Dec. 1991. In practice, since of the non-Baltic republics of the former union only Georgia, the Ukraine and Russia are not landlocked, any claim for the acquisition of a share of the former Soviet Navy by the remainder is of no consequence.

The Baltic fleet (HQ Kaliningrad) with bases on both Russian territory and in the Baltic Republics will face major re-organization and negotiations regarding re-deployment of ships and reallocation of assets from bases in the Baltic Republics, particuarly Riga in Latvia. However, it is the future of the Black Sea fleet, the great majority of which is based in Sevastopol in the Crimea, and which has been claimed by Ukraine, over which the major questions hang. At the end of 1991, this fleet comprised two large helicopter-carrying cruisers, 3 other cruisers, 45 destroyers and frigates and about 25 diesel-powered submarines, together with over 200 minor vessels. Complications in the resolution of the dispute arise not only from the somewhat ambivalent national status of the Crimea, but from the absence of major naval bases on Russia's extensive Black Sea coastline, and from the fact that the majority of the fleet personnel are Russians.

It would appear likely that in due course, both Baltic and Black Sea fleets, will be divided, with deep sea combatant elements coming under Russian command for possible eventual assignment to any coalition or Commonwealth force structure which may emerge, whilst coastal patrol vessels are transferred to the other littoral republics for tasks arising from their new sovereignty.

However the fleets are divided, economic conditions will continue to reduce Naval new construction; and the future programme must be seen as in some doubt. The loss of major warship building yards in the Ukraine and lesser facilities in the Baltics will have an impact on the Fleet's continued modernization. However, its overall combat capability has for the present been maintained. The scrapping of older ships, and particularly submarines, continues apace, and may be expected to continue for several years. In fact, the numbers of ships in operational service is rather less than listed below: reports indicate that numerous ships and particularly submarines are held in non-operational status awaiting their turn at the scrapyard.

It is probable that the Russian Navy will inherit the wartime roles of the former Soviet Navy, which were defensive in strategic terms. The safe deployment and protection of the strategic missile-firing submarines will remain the first priority; the defence of the Russian (and possibly Commonwealth) homelands, in particular against the threat of sudden attack the second; whilst interdiction of enemy shipping and protection of own shipping will take an increasingly lower priority.

There would appear no need for major changes in the peacetime command and control arrangements of the Russian Navy save in the higher political sense; the strategic missile submarines will continue under command of the Strategic Nuclear Force commander whilst the remainder come under the Main Naval Staff in Moscow, through the Commanders of the fleets. Some changes are likely in the putative wartime command arrangements, following the dissolution of the former

Soviet Theatres of Military Operations and Military Districts. The levels and activity of the detached squadrons in the Mediterranean and Indian Ocean have continued to decline through the past year in response both to economic pressures and reducing military relevance.

The overall strength of the Soviet Navy at the end of the indicated year was as follows:-

Category	1986	1987	1988	1989	1990	1991
Strategic Submarines	77	76	75	64	61	59
Nuclear Attack Submarines	118	127	127	130	104	100
Diesel Submarines	145	140	136	133	86	80
Aircraft Carriers	4	4	4	5	5	5
Cruisers	42	43	44	44	40	38
Destroyers	57	59	54	45	32	29
Frigates	167	168	166	171	148	146

In the tables and listings which follow, it should be noted that, in the west, Soviet ship classes and weapons are generally known by their official NATO nicknames. These may be recognized as follows: Surface ships are given names with an initial letter 'K' *e.g. Kynda, Kresta*, and submarines by letters from the phonetic alphabet, *e.g. Alfa, Kilo*. Surface-to-air missiles are numbered in the SA-N- series, and given nicknames beginning with an initial 'G', *e.g. Goa*, surface-to-surface missiles are numbered SS-N-3 etc., and have nicknames commencing with 'S', fighter aircraft 'F', bombers 'B', and all helicopters 'H'. This practice is slowly being discarded as more information on Soviet ship classes and weapon names becomes known in the west.

The Soviet force of Strategic Submarines is constituted as follows:-

Class	No.	Tonnage (in 1,000)	Speed	Missiles	Other Weapons
Typhoon	6	27·00	27	20 SS-N-20	Torpedoes
Delta-IV	7	12·35	24	16 SS-N-23	Torpedoes
Delta-III	14	11·90	24	16 SS-N-18	Torpedoes
Delta-II	4	11·50	24	16 SS-N-8	Torpedoes
Delta-I	18	11·00	25	12 SS-N-8	Torpedoes
Yankee-I	10	9·75	26	16 SS-N-6	Torpedoes

This wide range of submarine demonstrates the Soviet preference for making small, incremental changes in operational capability. Only with the Typhoon class, completed between 1982 and 1989, and the largest submarine ever built, was this approach dropped. The SS-N-20 'Sturgeon' missile carried by the Typhoon carries 6 warheads to a maximum range of 4,500 nautical miles, while the SS-N-23 'Skiff' in the other currently-building class, the 'Delta-IV', carries 10 warheads over the same range. The other older missiles carry one to 3 warheads over ranges varying between 1,300 and 4,000 nautical miles.

The attack submarine fleet, now reduced to about 180, again comprises a wide range of classes. From the enormous 16,250-tonne 'Oscar' nuclear-powered missile submarine to the small diesel 'Whiskey' of 1,370 tonnes, there are over 20 classes of submarine in service with the navy. The difficulties in training personnel to operate, and the technical and logistic complications supporting such a diverse mix are self-evident. The inventory of anti-ship missile-firing submarines comprises 8 'Oscar', built 1982-91, 24 SS-N-19 'Shipwreck' missiles; 6 'Charlie-II', built 1973-80, 8 SS-N-9; 9 'Charlie-I', 1967-72, 8 SS-N-7 'Starbright'; and 22 'Echo-II', 1961-67, 8 SS-N-3 'Shaddock' or SS-N-12 'Sandbox'. The former are all nuclear-propelled, and there are additionally 14 diesel-powered 'Juliet' class built between 1961 and 1968 carrying 4 SS-N-3. Finally, there are 2 former strategic 'Yankee'-class submarines converted to fire the SS-N-21 'Sampson' land-attack cruise missile, which has a range of 1,600 nautical miles. The list of torpedo-firing boats is equally impressive. The types currently building are the Akula, nuclear-powered and of 8,100 tonnes, of which there are 7, the 'Sierra', nuclear-powered, 7,700 tonnes now numbering 3, and the 'Victor-III', nuclear-powered, 6,400 tonnes, the total of which is now 25. The diesel-powered 'Kilo' class, of which the Navy operates 18, is now building at a reduced rate of 2 per year, 1 of which will be for export. In addition to these classes there are a further 24 nuclear-powered and 38 diesel submarines on the active list. The disposal of a number of old diesel and the first generation of nuclear-powered boats continued through 1991.

Modern Soviet surface warships were assigned categories rather different from western ships. Ships which, in the west, would be called 'Aircraft Carriers' are termed 'Large Aircraft-Carrying Cruisers' by the Navy partly because they usually carry significant ship weaponry as well as aircraft, but also to exempt them from the prohibition on the movement of Aircraft Carriers through the Turkish Straits imposed by the Montreux Convention. Ships of cruiser size (7,500-8,000 tonnes full load and upwards) are divided into two categories; those optimized for anti-submarine warfare (ASW) and those for anti-surface ship operations. Ships of cruiser size in the former category are classified as 'Large Anti-Submarine Ships' while the missile-armed anti-surface warfare ships are classified 'Rocket Cruisers'. The tables following listing the principal surface ships of the Soviet Navy use the most appropriate western classifications:-

Aircraft Carriers

Completed	Name	Tonnage (in 1,000)	Speed	Aircraft	Other Armament
1989	Adm. Kuznetsov (formerly Tbilisi)	65·0	30	See below	Anti-Ship Missiles Anti-Air missiles.
1987	Adm. Gorshkov (formerly Baku)	37·7	32	13 Yak-38 V/STOL 16 Ka-25/27 hel	12 anti-ship missiles 4 SA-N-6 SAM launchers
Kiev Class					
1982	Novorossiisk	37·7	32	13 Yak-38 V/STOL	8 anti-ship missiles.
1978	Minsk	37·7	32	16 Ka-25/27 hel	4 SA-N-3 SAM launchers
1976	Kiev	37·7	32		1 twin ASW missile.

Cruisers

Completed	Name	Tonnage (in 1,000)	Speed	Main Armament	Aircraft
Kirov Class					
1988	Kalinin			20 SS-N-19 anti-ship missiles, 12 X 8 SA-N-6 SAM, 2 SS-N-14 ASW missiles (*Kirov*) 2 100-mm guns (*Kirov*), 1 X 2 130-mm gun (*Frunze, Kalinin*)	2 Ka-27 Helix, 1 Ka-25 Hormone helicopters.
1984	Frunze	28·4	33		
1980	Kirov				
Moskva Class (Helicopter Cruisers).					
1968	Leningrad	16·50	31	1 X 2 ASW missile launcher.	14 Ka-25
1967	Moskva			2 X 2 SA-N-3 SAM launchers.	ASW helos.
Slava Class.					
1988	Chervona Ukraina			16 SS-N-12 anti-ship missiles	
1986	Marshal Ustinov	12·70	34	8 X 8 SA-N-6 Grumble SAM.	1 Ka-27 Helix
1983	Slava			8 533mm Torpedo tubes	helicopter
Nikolayev (or 'Kara') Class.					
1979	Tallin				
1978	Tashkent				
1977	Petropavlovsk			8 SS-N-14 Silex ASW missiles	1 Ka-25
1976	Azov	9·85	34	2 X 2 SA-N-3 SAM	Hormone ASW
1975	Kerch			10 X 533mm Torpedo tubes	helicopter
1974	Ochakov				
1973	Nikolayev				
Kronstadt ('Kresta II') Class.					
1977	Adm. Yumashev				
1976	Vasily Chapayev				
1975	Mar. Timoshenko				
1974	Adm. Isachenkov			8 SS-N-14 ASW missiles	1 Ka-25
1973	Adm. Oktyabrsky	7·83	35	2 X 2 SA-N-3 Goblet SAM	Hormone ASW
1973	Mar. Voroshilov			10 533mm Torpedo tubes	helicopter
1972	Adm. Makarov				

Com-				
pleted	Name	Tonnage (in 1,000)	Speed	Main Armament	Aircraft

Kronshtadt ('Kresta II') Class (continued).

1971	Adm. Nakhimov	
1970	Adm. Isakov	
1969	Khronshtadt	

Admiral Zozulya ('Kresta I') Class.

1968	V-Adm. Drozd	anti-ship missiles	1 Ka-25 Hormone helicopter
1967	Adm. Zozulya	10 533mm Torpedo tubes	

Udaloy Class

1991	Ship No. 12			
1990	Adm. Kharlamov			
1988	Adm. Vinograd			
1988	Adm. Levchenko			
1986	Simferopol			
1985	Mar. Shaposhnikov			8 SS-N-14 Silex ASW missiles, 2 X 100mm guns, 8 X 533mm Torpedo tubes	2 X Ka-27 Helix ASW helicopters.
1985	Adm. Tributs			
1984	Adm. Spiridonov	8·60	30	
1983	Adm. Zakharov			
1983	Mar. Vasilevsky			
1981	V-Adm. Kulakov			
1980	Udaloy			

Trials of the new aircraft carrier *Adm. Kuznetsov* (formerly the *Tbilisi*) commenced in late 1989 and are likely to continue following the deployment of the Northern Fleet. This ship appears to be a unique hybrid between the conventional aircraft carrier equipped with catapults and arrester gear and vertical/short take-off and landing carriers without flight deck machinery. In flight trials she launches aircraft over a ski-jump bow, and recovers them into arrester wires. It remains to be seen how effective this method is in terms of aircraft weapon and fuel loads at launch, and it will be some time before the ship is fully operational. Aircraft used for the initial trials in Nov. 1989 were the Su-27 'Flanker', the MiG-29 'Fulcrum' and the Su-25 'Frogfoot' and it is now believed she will carry about 25 fixed-wing aircraft and about 20 helicopters. These aircraft are potentially much more effective than the Yak-38 'Forger' deployed in the earlier carriers.

The 'Kara', 'Kresta II' and Udaloy classes tabled above are classified as 'Large anti-submarine warfare ships'. The Kirov, Slava and 'Kresta I' cruiser classes above, and the 'Kynda' guided missile destroyers below are classified as 'Rocket Cruisers'. The Kirov class, of which a fourth unit are fitting out, are the largest combatant warships, apart from aircraft carriers, to be built for any navy since the Second World War. The ships have an unusual and ingenious machinery arrangement. The main propulsion outfit comprises 2 nuclear reactors for long-range cruising, boosted by oil-fired superheat boilers for high-speed work.

Among the smaller ships the most impressive are the 14 Sovremenny class guided missile destroyers, of 7,900 tonnes, armed with 8 SS-N-22 'Sunburn' anti-ship missiles, 1 twin SA-N-7 'Gadfly' surface-to-air missile launcher, 4 130mm guns and a helicopter. Also in the anti-surface category are the 4 Grozny (or 'Kynda') class of 5,650 tonnes, with 8 SS-N-3 'Shaddock' anti-ship missiles, and the 3 remaining 'modified Kashin' class. There are a further 10 'Kashin', and 1 other destroyer, 33 large frigates including the first of a new class, the Neustrashimy, and 113 smaller frigates. A considerable additional number of frigates and above are maintained in inactive reserve, but are unlikely to merit deactivation in a crisis. A formidable coastal defence force is headed by 75 missile corvettes, 80 fast missile craft, 30 hydrofoil fast torpedo craft and numerous patrol classes totalling 195 hulls. Mine warfare constituted an important element of Soviet naval strategy; large stocks (some hundreds of thousands) of modern mines are held, and all submarines and many surface ship classes are provided with mine-laying equipment. There are additionally 3 specific minelayers, 65 offshore, 120 coastal and 140 inshore mine countermeasure vessels.

Amphibious capability is provided by 3 large dock landing ships of the Ivan

Rogov class, 24 Ropucha and 14 Alligator class tank landing ships, 36 medium landing ships, as well as some 140 minor craft including about 85 special purpose amphibious surface-effect vessels. Total amphibious lift available to the former Soviet authorities is some 17,000 men, 750 main battle tank equivalents but operating facilities for only 10 helicopters.

Amphibious landing forces are found from the Naval Infantry, 17,000 strong, units of which are assigned to all fleets. Organized into a single division, 7,000 strong, plus 3 independent brigades, the force is equipped to relatively light scales. Principal equipment includes 230 main battle tanks, 150 amphibious light tanks, 90 artillery pieces and over 1,000 armoured personnel carriers. A separate force of almost 30,000 Coastal Defence troops man artillery and missile batteries positioned to defend the main naval bases and ports, together with 4 Motor Rifle Divisions numbering over 20,000 men transferred from the Army to the Coastal Defence Commands, thus evading controls imposed by the Conventional Armed Forces in Europe Treaty.

The operational reach of the Navy is limited by its poor capability for afloat support. A first class multi-purpose underway replenishment ship, the *Berezina*, was completed in 1977, but remains the sole example of her class. There are an additional 6 dual-purpose stores and fuel replenishment ships, 4 purpose-built tankers, and 10 tankers converted from a commercial design with limited underway replenishment capability. Second line support is provided by 14 tankers, and about 260 maintenance and logistic ships, 67 electronic intelligence gatherers, 76 other special-purpose auxiliaries, and 250 survey, research and space support ships.

The principal Baltic warship building yards are in and near St Petersburg (in Russia). Black Sea yards are at Nikolayev, Kerch and Sevastopol (all in the Ukraine), and further building takes place at Severodvinsk in the North Sea Fleet region and at Komsomolsk-on-Amur in the Far East. The shipbuilding programme is believed to include further 'Delta-IV' strategic submarines, and attack submarines of the Akula, 'Victor-III' and 'Kilo' classes. There is a further aircraft carrier similar to the *Admiral Kuznetsov* fitting out, and a third, rather larger unit on the building ways, together with the last of 4 Slava class at Nikolayev. A fourth heavy cruiser of the Kirov class is nearing completion at St Petersburg. The replacement of coastal force units built in the 1950s and early 1960s continues at a steady pace.

Shore-based naval aviation forms a major element of all Fleets, and the numbers reported in 1990 have been increased due to new releases of information under the Conventional Armed Forces in Europe Treaty, and transfers from the Air Force. However, the future of those elements based outside Russia must be in some doubt. In addition to the aircraft held on inventory for seaborne service, there are some 350 bombers, 200 maritime patrol, 550 fighter/ground attack aircraft plus helicopters. Main bomber types held are 160 Tu-26 'Backfire' and 190 Tu-16 'Badger', all of which are armed principally with stand-off anti-ship missiles. Maritime reconnaissance and anti-submarine tasks fall predominantly to the force of 100 Tu-95 and Tu-142 'Bear' with 150 miscellaneous shorter range aircraft tasked to anti-submarine operations, electronic countermeasures, intelligence gathering and tankers. The helicopter inventory amounts to some 300, principally anti-submarine, 25 combat assault, and 15 mine countermeasures. There are over 400 training and transport aircraft.

The total personnel in 1991 numbered 430,000, of whom 250,000 were conscripts who serve 3 years if in seagoing categories, and 2 years if shore-based. Of the total, some 16,000 serve in the strategic submarine force, 68,000 in naval aviation, 15,000 marines or naval infantry, and 30,000 in coastal defence.

Coastguard, customs and border patrol duties are performed by the substantial maritime element of the KGB. Some 20,000 strong, this force operates some 6 large helicopter-carrying frigates of a modified naval Krivak class, 12 small frigates, 8 offshore, 40 coastal and 150 inshore patrol craft divided among all the former Soviet coastal areas.

Air Force. The Air Force (excluding the strategic bomber force and Voyska PVO air defence force) was believed to have a personnel strength, in 1992, of 420,000 (290,000 conscripts). To supplement long-range rocket missiles (estimated at 1,398 emplaced ICBM, 600 MRBM/IRBM), the strategic bomber force has still about 125 Tupolev Tu-95 ('Bear')[1] 4-turboprop bombers, 200 twin-jet Tupolev Tu-16 ('Badger'), and 135 supersonic Tupolev Tu-22 ('Blinder') bombers, ECM and reconnaissance aircraft, and at least 220 Tupolev ('Backfire') swing-wing bombers. All types are used also by the Naval Air Force for long-range maritime reconnaissance; the Tu-16, Tu-95, Tu-22 and 'Backfire' can carry air-to-surface guided self-propelled cruise missiles and all 5 types have provision for flight refuelling. The Tu-16 ('Badger') and Il-78 ('Midas') are used as refuelling tankers. A new swing-wing strategic Tupolev bomber ('Blackjack'), larger and faster than the American B-1, is entering service.

The tactical air forces, under local army command in the field, have an estimated total of 6,000 ground attack, air combat, ECM and reconnaissance aircraft, including 2,600 MiG-23/27 ('Flogger') and 800 two-seat Sukhoi Su-24 ('Fencer') supersonic swing-wing aircraft, 300 twin-jet Yakovlev Yak-28 ('Brewer') reconnaissance aircraft, 1,000 swing-wing Su-17 and Su-22 ('Fitter-C/D/G/H/J'), and 600 MiG-21 ('Fishbed') fighter-bombers, 100 MiG-25 ('Foxbat') reconnaissance aircraft and 250 Su-25 ('Frogfoot') twin-engined ground attack aircraft supported by 60 MiG-21 and 170 MiG-25 ('Foxbat') reconnaissance aircraft, and over 3,500 helicopters, including very large Mi-26 ('Halo') transports and over 1,000 heavily-armed Mi-24 ('Hind') assault helicopters, in gunship/transport versions. Electronic warfare duties are performed by a variety of aircraft, including Su-24s and Mi-8 and Mi-17 helicopters. The Voyska PVO defence forces, organized as a separate service, have a total of 1,300 jet interceptors. A high proportion of the squadrons are equipped with MiG-23 ('Flogger'), Su-15 ('Flagon'), MiG-25 ('Foxbat') and improved MiG-31 ('Foxhound') all-weather interceptors, armed with air-to-air missiles plus the MiG-29 ('Fulcrum') and Su-27 ('Flanker') new-generation aircraft of which 500 are already in service. Early warning and fighter-control duties are performed by about 10 radar-carrying adaptations of the Tu-114 turboprop transport, redesignated Tu-126 ('Moss'), which are being replaced by a more effective radar-equipped AWACS version ('Mainstay') of the Il-76 transport. Very large numbers of surface-to-air guided missiles are operational, on some 10,000 launchers, including the new high-performance SA-10 (low-altitude) and SA-12 (high-altitude) with capability against cruise and submarine-launched missiles respectively, the older 'Guild', 'Guideline', 'Goa', 'Gainful' and 'Ganef', the long-range 'Gammon' and the 'Galosh' which is deployed around Moscow on 32 launchers and has anti-missile capability.

Air Force transport squadrons have 75 An-12 ('Cub') 4-turboprop transports and 100 An-24s ('Coke') and An-26s ('Curl'), with 50 An-22s ('Cock'), and 500 Il-76 ('Candid') heavy four-jet freighters. The very large four-jet An-124 ('Condor') is entering service to replace the An-22. Training aircraft include the piston-engined Yak-18 primary trainer and its Yak-52 successor, the Czech-built L-29 Delfin and L-39 jet basic trainers, MiG-15UTI advanced trainers and versions of operational types such as MiG-21, MiG-23, MiG-25, MiG-29, Su-7, Su-15, Su-17, Su-27 and Tu-22.

[1] Soviet aircraft and missiles were usually referred to by invented English names; *see* p. 383.

Naval Air Force. With 1,100 fixed-wing aircraft and helicopters, the Soviet Navy has the world's second largest naval air arm. Under the control of the various naval commands, *i.e.*, Baltic, Black Sea and Pacific, the Naval Air Arm has an estimated 220 Tu-16 ('Badger') twin-jet bombers, and 160 'Backfire' swing-wing bombers, able to carry air-to-surface missiles, 40 supersonic twin-jet Tu-22 ('Blinder') maritime reconnaissance aircraft, about 70 Su-17 ('Fitter') shore-based fighters, and 90 Beriev M-12 ('Mail') maritime patrol amphibians. For reconnaissance, anti-submarine and electronic warfare there are about 100 Tu-95 and Tu-142 ('Bear') 4-engined bombers, 90 Tu-16s, and a few Tu-22s, plus a small number of Il-20s ('Coot-A') and 60 Il-38s ('May'). The Tu-142 also has an important targeting rôle for ships fitted with anti-shipping missile launchers. Over 250 anti-submarine and missile targeting/guidance helicopters, notably the Ka-27 ('Helix') and Ka-25 ('Hormone'), are carried in naval vessels, including 4 aircraft carriers (which also operate Yak-36 ('Forger') vertical take-off attack/reconnaissance aircraft) and 2 helicopter carriers. Several hundred transport, flight refuelling tanker ('Badger'), utility and training fixed-wing aircraft and 100 Mi-14 ('Haze') shore-based ASW helicopters are also under Navy control.

Berman, H. J. and Kerner, M. (ed.) *Soviet Military Law and Administration.* 2 vols. Harvard Univ. Press, 1955

Moynahan, B., *The Claws of the Bear: A History of the Soviet Armed Forces from 1917 to the Present.* London, 1989

Scott, H. F. and Scott, W. F., *The Armed Forces of the USSR.* 2nd ed. Boulder, 1981

Smith, M. J., *The Soviet Navy, 1941–1978: A Guide to Sources in English.* Oxford and Santa Barbara, 1981

Suvorov, V., *The Liberators: The Soviet Army.* London, 1981

Watson, B. W., *Red Navy at Sea.* Boulder, 1982

CURRENCY. Though republics have announced the introduction of their own currencies, the use of the Soviet ruble persisted into 1992. The unit of Soviet currency was the *ruble* (SUR) of 100 *kopeks.*

The currency in circulation is: (1) State Bank notes in denominations of 10, 25, 50 and 100 *rubles;* (2) Treasury notes in denominations of 1, 3 and 5 *rubles;* (3) cupronickel coins in denominations of 10, 15, 20 and 50 *kopeks* and 1 *ruble*; (4) cuprozinc coins in denominations of 1, 2, 3 and 5 *kopeks.*

In Aug. 1990 it became legal for Soviet citizens to hold hard currency. In Jan. 1991 foreign currency exchanges were set up in major cities under the aegis of the State Bank.

In July 1991 the State Bank announced that its gold reserves were 374 tonnes (12m. troy oz.)

The State Bank freed the tourist exchange rate on 20 Dec. 1991. Official exchange rates, March 1992: £1 = 1·01 rubles; US$1 = 0·57 rubles.

Weights and Measures. The metric system is in use. The Gregorian Calendar was adopted as from 14 Feb. 1918.

COMMUNICATIONS

Roads. The total length of motor roads in 1990 was 868,300 km. Road freights by lorry amounted to 27,873m. tonnes in 1988. Passengers carried were 50,496m. in 1989. In 1987, 24,100 inter-urban bus routes had a total length of 3,642,000 km. There were 63,362 fatal road accidents in 1990.

Railways. All railways were state property. The length of railways in Jan. 1990 was 147,400 km, of which 51,700 km was electrified. In 1986, 47% of all domestic tonne-km of freight and 37% of all passenger-km of traffic went by rail. In 1989 railways carried 4,017m. tonnes of freight (representing 3,851,700 tonne-km) and carried 4,323m. passengers (representing 410,700m. passenger-km).

The Baikal-Amur main line to the east, sited well to the north of the existing Trans-Siberian route to the Pacific ports of Nakhodka and Vladivostok, runs from Lena to Komsomolsk-on-Amur, 3,145 km distant. The Trans-Siberian line is only partially electrified and not double-track throughout.

Underground railways have been built in Moscow, St Petersburg, Kiev, Tbilisi, Kharkov, Tashkent, Baku, Nizhni Novgorod, Minsk, Yerevan, Novosibirsk and Kuibyshev. Others are under construction at Omsk, Dnepropetrovsk and Yekaterinburg.

Civil Aviation. In 1990 length of internal airlines was approximately 915,100 km; 3·2m. tonnes of freight were carried. Some 132m. passengers were carried in 1989. Central Asian and Arctic routes sometimes provide the only means of communication. Vladivostok opened to civil aviation in 1991.

Direct air services are maintained throughout the year between Moscow and the capitals of all the constituent republics as well as London, New York, Montreal, Tokyo, Delhi, Rangoon, Belgrade, Peking, Pyongyang, Ulan Bator, Kabul, Tirana, Paris, Warsaw, Prague, Budapest, Bucharest, Sofia, Vienna, Berlin, Helsinki, Stockholm, Copenhagen, Jakarta, and Dakar. Soviet air services reached 87 countries in 1981, and 20 foreign lines have regular services to the USSR, including British Airways, KLM, SAS, Air France, SABENA, Air India, PANAM. In 1990 the number of aircraft possessed by Aeroflot was still a state secret, but there were estimated to be 1,900 passenger jets. The first Soviet airbus, the 350-seater IL-86, began flights on civil aviation routes in 1981. The 120-seater YAK-42 will gradually replace the TU-134 and AN-24 on major shorter routes.

MacDonald, H., *Aeroflot: Soviet Air Transport Since 1923.* London, 1975

Shipping. In 1977 the Soviet mercantile marine comprised 7,000 self-propelled vessels, of which 80% were built between 1957 and 1966. By May 1977 the gross cargo capacity was (including fishing vessels) 20·8m. registered tonnes (16m. tonnes dead-weight).

Freights carried on domestic waterways were in 1989, 694m. tonnes; 127m. passengers were carried. The Soviet share in world marine tonnage was 2% in 1960 and 6% in 1977. Deep-sea ports are under construction at Vostochny (Far East) and Grigorevsky (Black Sea) with new deep-sea wharves at Ventspils (Latvia), Murmansk and Archangel (for Arctic traffic). Archangel is kept open by icebreakers all the year round from 1979. Foreign freights in 1977 totalled 14% of all Soviet seaborne trade.

The North Sea route affords convenient communication between the European USSR and the Far East along the Soviet coast, for the produce of the basins of the Ob, Yenissei, Lena and Kolyma rivers.

The length of navigable rivers and canals in exploitation was (1989) 122,500 km, of which the length of floatable rivers is 81,000 km. There are several thousand miles of canals and other artificial waterways; among them the Baltic and White Sea Canal (235 km), the Moscow-Volga Canal (130 km). Goods turnover on inland waterways was 239,591m. in 1989.

The Volga-Don Shipping Canal was opened for traffic in 1952. The Volga-Don waterway from Volgograd to Rostov is 540 km long, of which the Volga-Don canal comprises 101 km. The canal has transformed the section of the river from Kalach, where the Don is joined by the Volga-Don canal, to Rostov into a deep-water highway suitable for big Volga shipping. The canal links the White, Baltic, Caspian, Azov and Black Seas into a single water transport system. In Oct. 1964 the 2,430-km Baltic-Volga waterway, linking Klaipeda on the Baltic to Kakhovka at the mouth of the Dnieper and suitable for 5,000-tonne vessels, was begun. Reconstruction of the 18th-century Mariinsky canal system in north-west Russia was completed, providing a through waterway from Leningrad to Rybinsk (on the Upper Volga).

There is a train ferry between Ilichovsk and Varna in Bulgaria.

Telecommunications. In Jan. 1990 the number of post, telegraph and telephone offices was 91,000 and of general telephones 40·1m.

The Television and Radio Broadcasting Corporation produces 3 programmes in Moscow, broadcasting throughout the Union. In addition the regional radio stations produce 1, 2 or 3 programmes for the republics as well as local programmes for a town or region. All the republics have their own radio and TV networks. The foreign service from Moscow is beamed to all parts of the world, in 64 languages. Several republics have their own foreign services. English is broadcast from Moscow, Kiev, Tashkent and Yerevan. There are 120 TV centres, several of them producing more than 1 programme. In Moscow there are 4 programmes. Colour programmes are broadcast by the SECAM system. A nationwide system of space telecommunications, consisting of satellites and ground stations, takes TV broadcasts to distant parts of the country. In 1991 an independent Russian radio and television service began to operate on a national and international basis.

Under the terms of the Law on the Press and Other Media, adopted in June 1990, publishing and broadcasting are free of censorship other than in respect of state secrets, calls for the violent overthrow of the state and social system, war propaganda, the incitement of racial, national or religious hostility and pornography. Individuals as well as public bodies have the right to establish a media outlet, which must then be registered. Legal penalties are prescribed in the event of 'abuse of freedom of speech', the 'dissemination of information that does not correspond to reality' and the defamation of individuals or organizations.

Number of receivers, Jan. 1990: Radio, 84·8m. (1960, 28m); television, 92·4m. (1960, 5m.).

Cinemas and Theatres (Jan. 1990). There were 147,800 cinemas to which 3,205m. visits were made annually. In Jan. 1990 there were 713 theatres, to which 104·4m. visits were made.

Newspapers. In 1989, 8,811 newspapers with a total daily circulation of 230·5m. copies were published in 57 languages of the USSR. Under legislation of Aug. 1991 censorship is limited to the protection of official secrets.

JUSTICE. Since Dec. 1991 there has been no single system of justice, but the legal systems of CIS member states remain largely based on Soviet norms. The basis of the judicial system was the same throughout the Soviet Union, but the constituent republics had the right to introduce modifications and to make their own rules for the application of the codes of laws. Supreme Courts of the CIS member states and Autonomous Republics and of the Autonomous Regions and Areas are elected by the Supreme Soviets of these republics, and Territorial, Regional and City Courts by the respective immediately superior Soviets, each for a term of 10 years. At the lowest level are the People's Courts, which are elected directly by immediately superior soviets of people's deputies and by the population.

Court proceedings are conducted in the local language with full interpreting facilities as required. All cases are heard in public, unless otherwise provided for by law, and the accused is guaranteed the right of defence.

Laws establishing common principles of legislation in various fields are adopted by the Supreme Soviet and are then enacted in more specific form and implemented by subordinate levels of state and judicial authority.

The Law Courts are divided into People's Courts and higher courts. The People's Courts consist of the People's Judge and 2 Assessors, and their function is to examine, as the first instance, most of the civil and criminal cases, except the more important ones, some of which are tried at the Regional Court, and those of the highest importance at the Supreme Court. The Regional Courts supervise the activities of the People's Courts and also act as Courts of Appeal from the decisions of the People's Court. Special chambers of the higher courts deal with offences committed in the Army and the public transport services.

Judges are elected for 10-year terms by panels of their colleagues. They are assisted by assessors, who serve on a rota basis and are elected directly by the citizens of each constituency for a 5-year term. In 1990 a contempt of court law was passed, and the option of trial by jury for serious offences introduced.

The People's Assessors are called upon for duty for 2 weeks in a year. The People's Assessors for the Regional Court must have had at least 2 years' experience in public or trade-union work. The list of Assessors for the Supreme Court is drawn up by the Supreme Soviet of the republic.

The Labour Session of the People's Court supervises the regulations relating to the working conditions and the protection of labour and gives decisions on conflicts arising between managements and employees, or the violation of regulations.

Disputes between State institutions must be referred to an arbitration commission. Disputes between State institutions and foreign business firms may be referred by agreement to a Foreign Trade Arbitration Commission of the relevant Chamber of Commerce.

The *Procurator-General* of the USSR was appointed for 5 years by the USSR Congress of People's Deputies. All procurators of the CIS member states, autonomous republics and autonomous regions are appointed for a term of 5 years. The procurators supervise the correct application of the law by all state organs, and have special responsibility for the observance of the law in places of detention.

Capital punishment was abolished on 26 May 1947, but was restored on 12 Jan. 1950 for treason, espionage and sabotage, on 7 May 1954 for certain categories of murder, in Dec. 1958 for terrorism and banditry, on 7 May 1961 for embezzlement of public property, counterfeiting and attack on prison warders and, in particular circumstances, for attacks on the police and public order volunteers and for rape (15

Feb. 1962) and for accepting bribes (20 Feb. 1962). The sentence was carried out by a single shot to the head. There were 770 executions in 1985; 526 in 1986; 344 in 1987; 271 in 1988; 276 in 1989. 'Especially dangerous crimes against the state' including treason and espionage were dealt with by the Committee of State Security (KGB), whose status was defined in a law on state security adopted in May 1991. In Oct. 1991 the KGB was replaced by 3 separate services: the Central Intelligence Service, the Inter-Republican Security Service and the Committee for the Defence of the USSR State Border. After Dec. 1991 these services were almost entirely devolved to the CIS member states.

Following prolonged discussion, the 'Fundamentals of Criminal Law of the USSR and republics' was adopted in July 1991. Under these provisions, citizens are equal before the law and may be sentenced only by a properly constituted court. Punishment may take the following forms: Fine; exclusion from certain posts or activities; corrective work; limitation of liberty; arrest; imprisonment. The death penalty may be applied in 'exceptional' circumstances. Particular forms of punishment apply to military servicemen and juveniles, and in certain cases compulsory medical treatment may be prescribed. More detailed republican criminal codes are to be adopted on the basis of these Fundamentals.

Butler, W. E., *The Soviet Legal System. Selected Contemporary Legislation and Documents.* New York, 1978.—*Soviet Law.* 2nd ed. London, 1988
Feldbrugge, F. J. M. (ed.) *Encyclopedia of Soviet Law.* 2nd ed. Dordrecht, 1985
Hazard, J., Butler, W. E. and Maggs, P., *The Soviet Legal System.* 3rd ed. New York, 1977
Simons, W. B. (ed.) *The Soviet Codes of Law.* Alphen aan den Rijn, 1980

THE FORMER SOVIET UNION. The Union of Soviet Socialist Republics (USSR) was formed by the union of the Russian Soviet Federal Socialist Republic (RSFSR), the Ukrainian Soviet Socialist Republic (Ukrainian SSR), the Belorussian SSR and the Transcaucasian SSR; the Treaty of Union was adopted by the first Soviet Congress of the USSR on 30 Dec. 1922. In Oct. 1924 the Uzbek and Turkmen Autonomous SSRs and in Dec. 1929 the Tajik Autonomous SSR were declared constituent republics of the USSR.

On 5 Dec. 1936 a new constitution was adopted. The Transcaucasian Republic was split into the Armenian SSR, the Azerbaijan SSR and the Georgian SSR, each of which became constituent republics of the USSR. The Kazakh SSR and the Kirghiz SSR, previously autonomous republics within the RSFSR, also became constituent republics.

In Sept. 1939 Soviet troops occupied Poland to the 'Curzon line', which in 1919 had been drawn on ethnographical grounds as the eastern frontier of Poland, and incorporated it into the Ukrainian and Belorussian SSRs. In Feb. 1951 some districts of the Drogobych Region of the Ukraine and the Lublin Voivodship of Poland were exchanged.

On 31 March 1940 territory ceded by Finland was joined to that of the Autonomous SSR of Karelia to form the Karelo-Finnish SSR, which was admitted into the Union as the 12th Union Republic, but downgraded to the status of an Autonomous Republic within the RSFSR in 1956.

On 2 Aug. 1940 the Moldavian SSR was constituted as the 13th Union Republic. It comprised the former Moldavian Autonomous SSR and Bessarabia (44,290 sq. km, ceded by Romania on 28 June 1940), except for the districts of Khotin, Akerman and Ismail, which, together with Northern Bukovina (10,440 sq. km), were incorporated in the Ukrainian SSR. The Soviet-Romanian frontier thus constituted was confirmed by the peace treaty with Romania, signed on 10 Feb. 1947. On 29 June 1945 Ruthenia (Sub-Carpathian Russia, 12,742 sq. km) was by treaty with Czechoslovakia incorporated into the Ukrainian SSR.

On 3, 5 and 6 Aug. 1940 Lithuania, Latvia and Estonia were incorporated in the USSR as the 14th, 15th and 16th Union Republics respectively.

After the defeat of Germany in 1945 it was agreed by the UK, the USA and the USSR (by the Potsdam declaration) that part of East Prussia should be embodied in the USSR. The area (11,655 sq. km), which includes the town of Königsberg (renamed Kaliningrad) was joined to the RSFSR in April 1946.

By the peace treaty with Finland, signed on 10 Feb. 1947, the province of

Petsamo (Pechenga), ceded to Finland on 14 Oct. 1920 and 12 March 1946, was returned to the USSR. On 19 Sept. 1955 the USSR renounced its treaty rights to the naval base of Porkkala-Udd.

In 1945, after the defeat of Japan, the southern half of Sakhalin (36,000 sq. km) and the Kurile Islands (10,200 sq. km) were, by agreement with the Allies, incorporated in the USSR. This is still a matter of contention with Japan.

According to its 1977 Constitution, valid from 1977 to 1991, the USSR was a socialist state of the whole people, the political units of which were the Soviets (Councils) of People's Deputies. All central and local authority was vested in these Soviets. The economic foundation of the USSR was the socialist system of economy and the socialist ownership of the means of production. There were two forms of socialist property: (1) state property (property of the whole people); (2) co-operative and collective farm (*kolkhoz*) property (property of individual collective farms and property of co-operative associations). The land, mineral deposits, waters, forests, mills, factories, mines, railways, water and air transport, banks, means of communication, state farms (*sovkhozy*), as well as municipal enterprises and the principal dwelling-house properties in the cities and industrial localities, were state property, but the land occupied by collective farmers was secured to them in perpetuity so long as they used it in accordance with the laws of the country. The members of the *kolkhozy* were permitted to have small plots of land attached to their dwellings for their own use. Peasants unwilling to enter a kolkhoz were allowed to retain their individual farms, but not allowed to employ hired labour. The right of personal property of citizens in their income from work and in their savings, in their dwellings and domestic and personal effects, as well as the right of inheritance of such property, were protected by law. The constitution recognized the right of all citizens to work, rest, leisure, education, health protection, housing, maintenance in old age, sickness or incapacity, without distinction of sex, race or nationality, and laid down that any direct or indirect restriction of the rights of, or conversely, the establishment of direct or indirect privileges for, citizens on account of their race, or nationality, as well as the advocacy of racial or national exclusiveness, or hatred or contempt, was punishable by law. The franchise was enjoyed by all citizens of the USSR who had reached the age of 18, irrespective of sex, with the exception of the legally certified insane or incompetent or those serving terms of imprisonment. Candidates for election as a People's Deputy of the USSR were required to be 21 years of age; for sub-national levels of government the minimum age for candidates was 18. A member of any Soviet could be recalled by a majority of electors (a law on the procedure for this was adopted in June 1991).

The USSR until Sept. 1991 consisted of 15 Union Republics, each inhabited by a major nationality which gave its name to the republic. These were divided into 120 territories and regions, and these again into 3,217 districts, 2,200 towns, 603 urban districts and 4,042 urban settlements (1 Jan. 1990). Within the districts there were 43,095 rural Soviets (usually each including a number of villages). The territories and regions also included a number of smaller nationalities, forming their own self-governing units: 20 Autonomous Soviet Socialist Republics, 8 Autonomous Regions and 10 Autonomous Areas.

The structures of government that prevailed until Dec. 1991 included a 2250-member USSR Congress of Peoples's Deputies, meeting at least annually, which in turn elected a 542-member working Supreme Soviet. The President, an office established in Mar. 1990, was elected by a national popular ballot (Mikhail Gorbachev, in the first instance, was elected exceptionally by the Congress of People's Deputies). The President nominated the Prime Minister and a Cabinet of Ministers (for a more detailed account of these arrangements see THE STATESMAN'S YEAR-BOOK, 1990-91, pp. 1228–31).

Under the terms of agreements concluded in Dec. 1991 (*see above*) the USSR was superseded by a Commonwealth of Independent States whose founding members were Russia, the Ukraine and Belorussia, joined later by Armenia, Azerbaijan, Kazakhstan, Kirghizia, Moldavia, Tajikistan, Turkmenistan and Uzbekistan.

The former Soviet government with its ministerial structure has in practice been taken over, with some reduction in numbers and changes of function, by the government of the Russian Federation.

Communist Party of the Soviet Union (CPSU). The CPSU, politically dominant since 1917 and the 'leading force' of Soviet society under the 1977 Constitution, was deprived of its guaranteed leading role by constitutional amendment in March 1990 and in Aug. 1991, following the unsuccessful coup, its activities throughout the USSR were officially suspended. For its organization and activity up to 1990 *see* THE STATESMAN'S YEAR-BOOK, 1990–91, pp. 1231–32.

Economic Policy. For planning till 1990, *see* THE STATESMAN'S YEAR-BOOK, 1991–92, p. 1239.

In 1990 national income produced decreased by 4% (1981–85 average increase, 3·2%), gross industrial production fell by 1·2% (1981–85 average increase, 3·6%) and agricultural production fell by 2·3% (1981–85 average increase, 2·7%).

Private small businesses were made legal in Aug. 1990, and a State Property Fund was set up to oversee the transformation of large state enterprises into joint-stock companies. The Supreme Soviet adopted a law 'preventing and restricting' monopolistic activity in July 1991.

In Oct. 1990 the Supreme Soviet voted by 333 to 12 with 34 abstentions for a programme to reduce state control over the economy and cut government expenditure. A law on the fundamentals of entrepreneurship was adopted in April 1991, and a further law on denationalization and privatization in July 1991. This latter provided for the denationalization (transformation of state enterprises into joint stock companies with all or most shares held by the state) and privatization (sale of such shares to the public) of state property. Workers in denationalized enterprises were allowed to block its sale and had priority in receiving shares. A State Property Fund responsible to the Supreme Soviet and Cabinet of Ministers administered the sales and fixed prices. Union republics fixed their own privatization laws.

Armenia, Belorussia, Kazakhstan, Kirghizia, Russia, Tajikistan, Turkmenistan and Uzbekistan signed a treaty forming an economic community in Oct. 1991; Moldavia and the Ukraine acceded to it in Nov. Members are 'independent states who are or were subjects of the USSR seeking to effect radical economic reforms and considering the common nature of their problems realising the advantages of economic integration.' Members are to conduct co-ordinated policies in transport, energy, monetary and banking systems, finances, taxation and prices, customs rules and tariffs and foreign economic relations. Members recognise that 'private ownership, free enterprise and competition form the basis for economic recovery.' Members are to allow free movement of labour, goods and services. Members 'realise the need to preserve the ruble as common currency,' though they may introduce national currencies if harmonized. The community is to set up a banking union including the central banks of its members, and establish an inter-state bank of issue. The community is the legal successor to all foreign economic commitments of the USSR, and is to set up a bank to succeed Vneshekonombank to handle foreign debt.

Narodnoe khozyaistvo SSSR. Moscow, annual
Resheniya partii i pravitel'stva po khozyaistvennym voprosam. Vol. 1ff. Moscow, 1967ff
Istoriya sotsialisticheskoi ekonomiki SSSR. 7 vols. Moscow, 1976–80
Aslund, A., *Gorbachev's Struggle for Economic Reform.* 2nd ed. London, 1991
Nove, A., *An Economic History of the USSR.* 2nd ed., Harmondsworth, 1989.—*The Soviet Economic System.* 3rd ed., London, 1986
US Congress, Joint Economic Committee, *Gorbachev's Economic Plans.* 2 vols. Washington D.C., 1987

Budget. Revenue and expenditure in 1m. rubles for calendar years:

	1985	1988	1989	1990
Revenue	390,603	378,900	401,900	452,000
Expenditure	386,469	459,500	482,600	510,100

Budgetary spending in 1989 on the economy was 201,500m. rubles, on sociocultural purposes and science 149,300m., on defence 75,200m. and on administration 2·9m.; the budgetary deficit was 80,700m. rubles (in 1985, 13·9m.).

Social insurance expenditure from the state budget accounted for 61,109m. rubles in 1989 (35,296m. in 1980). Of this 45,487m. rubles were allocated to pensions and 13,023m. to other forms of income support.

National income produced was assessed at 656,800m. rubles in 1989 (462,200m. in 1980); GNP in current prices was 924,000m. rubles in 1989 (619,000m. in 1980).

Capital investment (1989) was 228,500m. rubles, including 200,800m. by state and co-operative enterprises, 18,100m. by collective farms and 4,300m. by individuals (on housing). A 5% sales tax was introduced by presidential decree to take effect from 1 Jan. 1990; 70% of the revenue went to the constituent republics.

Banking and Finance. The State Bank *(Gosbank)* began operations on 16 Nov. 1921. Since 1991 its functions have passed to banks under the control of CIS member states. The State Bank itself was taken under the control of the Russian Supreme Soviet in Nov. 1991.

Deposits in 75,300 savings banks were over 337,800m. rubles to the credit of 208m. depositors at 1 Jan. 1990.

Electricity. There were (1983) 57 fuel-burning power stations of over 1m. kw. capacity, and these accounted for over 80% of the country's electricity.

Hydro-electric stations have been constructed on major rivers. Among them are the Bratsk (4·5m. kw.), Ust-Ilimsk, Central Siberia (3·6m. kw.), Krasnoyarsk (6m. kw.) and a 1·26m. kw. station on the River Pechora (Far North).

Total installed capacity was 341m. kw. in 1989. Industry consumed about 70% of the total electricity. Over 35,000 small rural power stations have been closed in recent years owing to supply from State stations becoming available, but there are still many operating in the countryside. 800 towns and urban settlements were heated by central thermal plants.

There were 14 nuclear power stations in 1991. These had a capacity of 37·4m. kw. in 1989 and produced 213,000m. kwh. of electricity.

Total electricity output in 1989 was 1,722,000m. kwh.

An integrated power grid was in operation, covering over 900 power stations, which were handled by a central control panel in Moscow through (in 1989) 1,024,800 km. of cable of 35 kw. or greater capacity. A unified power grid with all the Communist countries of eastern Europe was built up between 1962 and 1967. Supply 127 and 220 volts; 50 Hz.

Oil. In the 1930s practically all Soviet oil came from the Caucasian fields, of which the Baku fields yielded 75-80% and the Grozny and Maikop fields between them 15%. After that the distribution considerably changed. The Ural-Volga area, the 'Second Baku', had 4 large centres in operation, at Samarska Luka, Tuimazy (Bashkiria), Ishimbaev (Bashkiria) and Perm, producing nearly 100m. tonnes annually.

A large new oilfield was developed in the Trans-Volga area of the Saratov region. The Tyumen (West Siberian) complex accounted for over 50% of the USSR's oil output. In 1991 the USSR extracted 515·4m. tonnes of oil.

At the end of 1981 there were 70,800 km of pipeline, through which (in 1981) were conveyed 637·7m. tonnes of oil.

The 'Friendship' pipeline of 5,327 km from the oilfields at Samarska Luka to Poland and Germany (northern branch) and to Czechoslovakia and Hungary (southern branch) had an annual throughput of 50m. tonnes.

In 1989 the USSR exported 184·4m. tonnes of crude oil and oil products.

Meyerhoff, A. A., *The Oil and Gas Potential of the Soviet Far East*. Beaconsfield, 1981

Gas. A natural-gas pipeline from Gazli, near Khiva, to Voskresensk, near Moscow (2,750 km), with a planned capacity of 100m. cu. metres per day, began operating in Oct. 1967. It was later extended to Czechoslovakia, where a 1,000 km extension, for transmission of Soviet gas to Austria, Italy and Germany, is under construction and another to Bulgaria. Another natural-gas pipeline, over 3,000 km from Medvezhye (Tyumen Region) to Moscow, began operating in Oct. 1974. A second pipeline from this region, linking the Urengoi deposit with Petrovsky in the Central European area of the USSR, became operational in 1980. A gas pipeline starting from Orenburg (Urals) across the Ukraine via Kremenchug and Vinnitsa to Czechoslovakia (2,750 km), supplied Czechoslovakia, Poland, Bulgaria and

Hungary with 14,000m. cu. metres annually and Romania with 1,500m. There was a unified gas-grid exceeding 124,000 km.

In 1988, 796,000m. cu. metres of gas were produced. Proven reserves were some 40,000,000m. cu. metres.

Minerals. The country is rich in minerals. There are major reserves of coal, oil, iron ore, gold, apatite, manganese, potassium salts and phosphates. Copper, zinc, lead, tungsten, antimony, silver, baryte, magnesium, bauxite, graphite, asbestos, chromite, molybdenum, cadmium and uranium are also found.

Coal production was 740m. tonnes in 1989. 236m. tonnes of iron ore were produced in 1990.

Agriculture. The Soviet Union, up to about 1928 predominantly agricultural in character, was transformed into an industrial-agricultural country. Of GDP in 1988, industry accounted for 34%, services 20%, agriculture 18%, trade 12%, construction for 10% and transport and communications 6%. Of the total state land fund of 2,227·6m. ha, agricultural land in use in 1990 amounted to 1,055m., state forests and state reserves to 1,098m. ha. 19% of all gainfully employed in 1989 were engaged in agriculture and forestry (1913, 75%; 1940, 54%).

The total area under cultivation (including single-owner peasant farms, state farms and collective farms) was (in the same territory) 118·2m. ha in 1913, 150·6m. in 1940, 146·3m. in 1950, 203m. in 1960, 206·7m. in 1970, 217·3 in 1980, and 209·8m. in 1990.

Collective farms in 1990 possessed 101·2m. ha of cultivated land, of which 60·9m. were under crops of various kinds; state farms and other state agricultural undertakings possessed 120·7m. ha, of which 65·5m. were under crops; personal subsidiary holdings (private plots and allotments) accounted for 4·5m. ha.

State procurements (after consumption by farms) were, in 1m. tonnes, for the present area of the USSR:

	1950	1960	1970	1989		1950	1960	1970	1989
Grain	32·3	46·7	73·3	59·0	Meat[2] and fats	1·3	4·8	8·1	23·3
Raw Cotton[1]	3·5	4·3	6·9	8·6	Milk and milk				
Sugar-beet	19·7	52·2	71·4	91·9	products	11·4	29·1	48·0	78·1
Potatoes	14·0	13·7	18·1	14·6	Sunflower seed	1·1	2·3	4·6	5·6
Other vegetables	4·3	8·0	13·8	19·0	Eggs (1,000m.)	3·5	10·5	22·1	55·8

[1] Seed-cotton unginned. [2] Slaughter weight.

After 1954 grain crops were measured in 'barn crop' (*i.e.*, net quantities delivered to barns) and not in 'gross harvest' or 'biological yield' (*i.e.*, calculated as growing crops) as previously. Average annual crops (in 1m. tonnes): 1909–13, 72·5; 1946–50, 64·8; 1951–55, 88·5; 1956–60, 121·5; 1961–65, 130·3; 1966–70, 167·5; 1971–75, 181·6; 1976–80, 205; 1981–85, 180·3; 1989, 211.

Other produce (in 1m. tonnes) in 1989: Milk, 108·5; sugar-beet, 97·4; potatoes, 72·2; vegetables, 28·7; meat (slaughter weight), 20·1; raw cotton, 8·6; sunflower seed, 7·1; wool, 0·5; eggs, 84,854m.

In 1990 there were 27,900 collective farms employing 11·8m. collective farmers. Total value of output, 82,100m. rubles. In 1985 they produced 89% of all sugar-beet, cotton 66%, milk 37%, meat 30%, potatoes 21%, other vegetables 24%, eggs 7%, sunflower seeds 74%, wool 30%. In Nov. 1969 the Third Congress of collective farmers adopted a new model constitution, considerably enlarging the planning powers of collective farms and making payments to their members a priority.

In 1990 there were 23,303 state farms employing 11·2m. workers (9·2m. engaged in agriculture) and producing an output valued at 80,900m. rubles.

Investments in agriculture in 1989 were 38,400m. rubles (including 25,300m. by the state and 13,100m. by collective farms). Total agricultural output in 1989 was valued at 225,100m. rubles (in 1983 prices).

In 1986 the total of irrigated land was 20·2m. ha. The total of land drained was 14·9m. ha in 1986. In 1986, 2,615m. rubles were spent on conservation measures (1,798m. on water resources and 263m. on the atmosphere).

In 1981, 84m. tonnes of mineral fertilizers were used. On 1 Jan. 1990 there were 2·7m. tractors, 689,000 grain combine harvesters and 1·1m. motorized ploughs.

An All-Union Academy of Agricultural Sciences, founded in 1929, has regional branches in Siberia and Central Asia and 310 research institutes.

Livestock (1 Jan. 1991), in 1m. head: Cattle, 116·2 (including 41·4 milch cows); pigs, 76·8; sheep and goats, 141·7. After 1957 the enumeration of livestock was made on 1 Jan. instead of 1 Oct., *i.e.*, after the winter sales and slaughter for the market. Percentage of farm production in 1985:

	Grain	Cotton	Sugar-beet	Pota-toes	Other vegetables	Meat	Milk	Eggs	Wool
State	48	35	12	18	46	42	32	66	44
Collective	51	65	88	22	25	30	39	6	30
Private [1]	1	0	0	60	29	28	29	28	26

[1] *i.e.*, household plots of collective farmers.

Forestry. Of the 814·3m. ha of forest land in 1988, 795·3m. ha was administered and worked by the State; the remainder was granted for use to the peasantry free of charge.

The largest forest areas were 515m. ha in the Asiatic part of USSR, 51·4m. along the northern seaboard, 25·4m. in the Urals and 17·95m. in the north-west.

Re-afforestation was carried out on 2·2m. ha of state land in 1989.

Fisheries. The fishing catch including whaling (in 1,000 tonnes): 1985, 12,400. There were 422 fishing co-operatives in 1985 with a total output valued at 772m. rubles.

Industry. Under the Communist regime, the organization of industry was based on state ownership and control, administered by a separate ministry for each large industry.

Under the successive 5-year plans, large-scale modern industrial works were constructed, namely: 1st, over 1,500; 2nd, 4,500; 3rd (up to June 1941), 3,000; wartime, 3,500 (apart from reconstruction of destroyed plants); 4th, 6,200; 5th, 3,200; 6th, 2,700; 7th (1959–65), 5,470; 8th (1966–70), 1,870; 9th (1971–75), 2,000; 10th (1976–80), 1,200.

Output of some heavy industries was as follows:

Industry	1950	1960	1970	1980	1990
Pig-iron (1m. tonnes)	19·2	46·8	85·9	107·3	114·0 [2]
Oil (1m. tonnes)	37·9	148·0	353·0	603·2	570·0
Electric power (1,000m. kwh.)	91·2	292·0	740·9	1,295·0	1,728·0
Coal (1m. tonnes)	261·1	509·6	624·1	716·4	703·0
Steel (1m. tonnes)	27·3	65·3	115·9	147·9	154·0
Rolled steel (finished, 1m. tonnes)	18·0	43·7	80·6	102·9	112·0
Steam and gas turbines (1,000 kw.)	2,381·0	9,200·0	16,191·0	20,300·0	21,100·0 [2]
Steel pipe (1m. tonnes)	2·0	5·8	12·4	18·2	19·5
Chemical fibres (1m. tonnes)	0·0	0·2	0·6	1·2	1·5
Mineral fertilizer (1m. tonnes)	1·3	3·3	13·1	24·8	31·7
Automobiles (1,000)	64·6	138·8	344·2	1,327·0	2,119·0
Tractors (1m. h.p.)	5·5	11·4	29·4	47·0	51·6 [2]
Sulphuric acid (1m. tonnes)	2·1	5·4	12·1	23·0	27·3
Excavators (no.)	3,540·0	12,290·0	30,800·0	42,000·0	37,700·0
Timber (commercial, 1m.cu. metres) [1]	161·0	261·5	298·5	277·7	305·3 [2]
Cement (1m. tonnes)	10·2	45·5	95·2	125·0	137·0

[1] Excluding collective farm production.   [2] Production in 1988.

About 93% of Soviet pig-iron and 87% of steel was produced in automatic furnaces.

Output in some consumer industries was as follows:

Industry	1950	1960	1970	1980	1990
Cotton fabrics (1m. linear metres)	3,899	6,387	7,482	8,063	
Woollen fabrics (1m. linear metres)	156	342	496	564	12,700
Sil\: fabrics (1m. linear metres)	130	810	1,241	1,632	
Leather footwear (1m. pairs)	203	419	679	744	820
Clocks and watches (1m.)	8	26	40	67	...
Radio receivers (1m.)	1	4	8	9	9
Television sets (1m.)	–	2	7	8	11

Industry	1950	1960	1970	1980	1990
Refrigerators (1,000)	1	530	4,140	5,925	6,500
Paper (1,000 tonnes)	1,193	2,334	4,185	5,288	6,200
Meat (slaughter weight, 1m. tonnes)	5	9	12	15	20
Butter (1,000 tonnes)	336	737	963	1,278	1,700
Granulated sugar (1,000 tonnes)	2,523	6,360	10,221	10,127	12,200
Canned foods (1m. tins)	1,113	4,864	10,678	15,268	20,400

Labour. Industrial and clerical workers engaged (1989) in the whole national economy were 115·4m., 51% of them women; a further 11·6m. were engaged in collective-farm agriculture. The 7-hour day (6 hours for miners underground and other heavy trades) was generally in operation by the end of 1960. The average working week after 1970 was 39 hours and in industry 39·6 hours. The 5-day week (without reduction of total working hours) was introduced in 1967.

New 'Fundamentals of Labour Legislation', intended to codify and extend labour laws adopted in the last 40 years, were adopted by the Supreme Soviet in July 1970. They laid down, *inter alia,* the right of trade unions to participate in and supervise management and planning, fixing of working conditions and wages, etc. Legislation of Oct. 1989, revised in May 1991, established a procedure for the conduct and resolution of strikes and other disputes. Further legislation, effective from July 1991, provided for unemployment and for the social support of the unemployed. Pensioners in Jan. 1990 numbered 59·7m., including 44·3m. old age. Average monthly wages in the state sector were 240·4 rubles in 1989.

Trade Unions. Trade unions were organized on an industrial basis, all workers, whether white- or blue-collar, in every branch of a given industry being eligible for membership of the same union. Collective farmers could join trade unions.

After 1933 trade unions, centralized in the All-Union Congress of Trade Unions, carried out the functions of the former Labour Commissariat, controlling and supervising the application of labour laws, introducing new labour laws for approval by the Government and administering social insurance and factory inspection. Social insurance was non-contributory. The Congress met at irregular intervals. The 19th Congress, in 1990, reorganized itself on a federal basis as the General Confederation of Trade Unions of the USSR.

In 1987 there were 31 unions. Contributions ranged from 0·5% to 6% of wages. There were 173 regional and Republican Trades Councils. Membership (1990) was 142m. The right to strike eventually became legal, and unions were permitted to work outside the structure of the GCTU. Since the late 1980s a widely supported independent union and workers' movement developed. An independent coal-miners' union was formed in Oct. 1990.

In May 1991 the GCTU came to an agreement with the government envisaging wage indexation, an official minimum wage, wage reform and an agricultural unemployment programme, in return for which unions would refrain from striking.

Foreign Economic Relations. The legal basis for joint ventures with foreign partners was a Council of Ministers Decree of 13 Jan. 1987 with some subsequent additional regulations. Joint ventures benefitted from an initial 2-year tax exemption after the first profits were made; thereafter tax was 30%. Either partner could own up to 99% of the equity. On 1 Jan. 1990, 1,274 joint enterprises had been registered, of which 307 had begun operations.

100% foreign investment ownership with repatriation of profits became legal in Oct. 1990, and in July 1991 new basic principles of foreign investment provided a more comprehensive legal framework.

A Union-Republican Foreign Currency Committee, comprising representatives of the External Economic Commission and the heads of government of the constituent republics was established in Nov. 1990 to centralize the management of foreign currency earnings, and enforce a monopoly of goods of state importance, including oil and gas, gold, precious stones and high technology items.

In Oct. 1991 the constituent republics agreed to share responsibility for the USSR's foreign debt, which stood at about US$60,000m. at that date.

A treaty opening the way to most-favoured-nation status was signed with the USA in April 1991.

Commerce. Foreign trade was organized as a state monopoly. Importation and exportation of goods were effected under licences issued by the Ministry for Foreign Economic Relations and its respective departments in pursuance of a plan annually sanctioned by the Government. The right of purchasing goods for importation, and that of selling Soviet exports abroad, was vested in trade delegations and representatives of the appropriate state corporations in foreign countries.

There were 29 state import and export organizations, including chartering and tourist corporations (one, Vostokintorg, dealing with Mongolia, Sinkiang and Afghanistan). The Central Union of Consumers' Societies (Tsentrosoyuz) was also authorized to conduct foreign trade operations.

Foreign trade in 1990 was conducted with 145 foreign countries (in 1950, 45), and had by 1986 increased 45 times by value since 1950. Exports in 1989 were valued at 68,742m. rubles (37,958m. to the communist countries), and imports at 72,137m. rubles (40,588m. from the communist countries).

Soviet imports of machinery and equipment, between 1940 and 1987, rose from 32·4 to 40·9%, ores and concentrates fell from 26·6 to 8%, foodstuffs rose from 14·9 to 15·8% and manufactured consumer goods rose from 1·4 to 12·8% by value; exports of fuel and electricity increased from 13·2 to 42·1% and of machinery and equipment from 2 to 16·2% by value over the same period.

Main items of exports in 1989:

Crude oil (1m. tonnes)	127·0	Gas (1m. cu. metres)	101,000·0
Iron ore (1m. tonnes)	29·3	Tractors (1,000)	51·3
Rolled metal (1m. tonnes)	9·3	Motor cars (1,000)	365·0
Paper (1,000 tonnes)	668·0	Clocks and watches (1m.)	15·7
Cotton cloth (1,000 tonnes)	791·0	Grain (1m. tonnes)	1·3

Total trade between the USSR and UK (British Department of Trade returns, in £1,000 sterling):

	1988	1989	1990	1991
Imports to UK	732,115	833,369	917,619	901,833
Exports and re-exports from UK	511,653	681,599	606,013	354,705

Tourism. The number of hotels available to tourists was 948 in 1989, with a total accommodation of 453,000; the number of tourist bases, for the hire of equipment and shorter stays, was 8,052, with a total accommodation of 806,000. In 1988 these facilities were used by 32·7m. and 4·2m. tourists respectively. A total of 54m. citizens in 1988 made use of all forms of tourist accommodation, including sanatoria and boarding houses. In 1988 a further 218m. citizens took part in tourist excursions.

Visitors to the USSR from foreign countries were catered for by 'Intourist' and its offices abroad. After losing its monopoly Intourist accounted for 38% of tourist business in 1991. In 1989 the USSR had 7·8m. foreign visitors, of whom 2·7m. were on tourist visits and 8m. Soviet citizens made tourist, business or other visits abroad.

Religion. After the communist revolution the Orthodox Church was disestablished in Feb. 1918 and its property nationalized. All religions were placed on an equal footing. Article 52 of the 1977 Soviet Constitution read as follows: 'Citizens of the USSR are guaranteed freedom of conscience, that is, the right to profess or not to profess any religion, and to conduct religious worship or atheistic propaganda. Incitement of hostility or hatred on religious grounds is prohibited. In the USSR the church is separated from the state, and school from the church.'

About two-thirds of all the churches were closed after 1917, but some 20,000 churches and 18 religious seminaries were reported to be in operation in 1986. The income of religious communities was not subject to taxation. Religious instruction in classes for persons under 18 is forbidden. The state supplied paper and printing facilities to all denominations for producing the Bible, the Koran, prayer books, missals, etc, although in very limited quantities. A freedom of conscience law, adopted in 1990, considerably extended these rights.

Relations between the religious communities of all creeds and the Government was maintained through a Council for Religious Affairs.

O religii i tserkvi: sbornik vazhneishikh vyskazivanii klassikov Marksizma-Leninizma, doku-mentov KPSS i sovetskogo gosudarstva. 2nd ed., Moscow, 1981

Curtiss, J. S., *The Russian Church and the Soviet State, 1917–50.* New York, 1953

Ellis, J., *The Russian Orthodox Church: A Contempory History.* London, 1986

Kochan, L., (ed.) *Jews in Soviet Russia since 1917.* 3rd ed., Oxford, 1977

Lane, C., *Christian Religion in the Soviet Union.* London, 1978

Education. Under the Soviet system education was free and compulsory from 7 to 16/17. There were 2 types of general schools, with an 8-year or a 10-year curriculum; the minimum schoolleaving age was 17. Pupils who left an 8-year school continued their education at either a 10-year school or a vocational training school. A 10-year school pupil could also transfer to vocational school after the 8th year.

In 1989–90 there were 135,000 primary and secondary schools. Pupils in general educational schools numbered 44·6m. (4·9m. of them in the tenth and eleventh forms) and the teachers 3m. Those at vocational and specialized technical secondary schools numbered 9·8m.

At the end of 1940 labour reserve schools (both vocational and industrial) were organized, admitting applicants from 14 to 17 years of age. From 1959 onwards these and other technical schools were reorganized as town and rural vocational and technical schools, at which pupils stayed for a year longer than at general schools, combining completion of general secondary education with vocational training. From 1940 to 1977 inclusive they trained 35m. skilled workers. In 1978, 2·3m. graduated from such schools, including 628,000 for agriculture; 600,000 agricultural mechanics were trained in state and collective farms. Over 4,300 vocational training schools existed in 1981, training 2·17m. boys and girls, all of whom received a full secondary education. In 1990, 17·2m. children of from 3 to 7 years of age attended kindergartens; this represented 57% of all children of the corresponding age.

In 1989–90 there were 4,539 technical colleges with 4·2m. students, and 904 universities, institutes and other places of higher education, with 5·2m. students (including 1·7m. taking correspondence or evening courses).

On 1 Jan. 1989 there were 1·5m. scientific workers in 5,111 places of higher education, research institutes and Academies of Sciences. There are 33,000 foreign students from 130 countries.

The Academy of Sciences of the USSR had 909 members and corresponding members. Total learned institutions under the USSR Academy of Sciences number 244, with 62,363 scientific staff. In Dec. 1991 it became the Russian Academy of Sciences, subordinate to the Russian government. Each Union Republic (other than the RSFSR) had its own Academy of Sciences, with scientific staff numbering 49,988. There are also Siberian, Far Eastern and other branches of the USSR Academy. On 1 Jan. 1989 there were 97,569 post-graduate students in Academy and other higher educational institutions, 52% studying on a part-time basis.

The Academy of Pedagogical Sciences had 14 research institutes with 1,664 staff.

In 1989-90 over 101m. people were studying at schools, colleges and training or correspondence courses. 143 per 1,000 of the employed population had a higher education (1939, 13; 1970, 65).

Grant, N., *Soviet Education.* 4th ed., Harmondsworth, 1979

Matthews, M., *Education in the Soviet Union.* London, 1982

Health and Social Security. All health services were free of charge although payment was required for medicines; but private practice existed. The health service was administered by the Ministry of Health of the USSR, which supervised the work of the Health Ministries of the Union Republics and the Autonomous Republics. Its functions have now passed to the governments of the CIS member states.

In 1944 an Academy of Medical Sciences was formed; in 1989 it had 328 members and corresponding members working in 64 research institutes in which 7,835 staff were employed.

In Jan. 1990 there were 23,700 civil hospitals with 3·8m. beds. There were 3·4m. medical staff and 1,278,000 doctors (including dentists) in the health service. All confinements in towns and 75% in the country were in hospital.

There were 42,810 outpatients' clinics, apart from the 29,200 women's consultation centres and children's clinics.

Social insurance was administered by the trade unions, through social insurance councils elected in places of work and social insurance sub-committees of factory committees: About 5m. volunteers were engaged in this work. 52·5m. people went to holiday sanatoria or rest homes in 1987.

Total number of holiday sanatoria providing toning-up treatment at resorts in 1989 was 2,323, with accommodation for 609,000; in addition, there were 3,517 overnight sanatoria at large plants for treatment of mild disorders without absence from work, accommodating 306,000. There were also 1,186 trade union-managed holiday hotels with a capacity of 372,000, holidays being partly or wholly at trade unions' expense. In 1987, 52m. citizens were systematically engaged in physical culture and sport; there were 3,799 stadiums seating 1,500 or more, 2,295 swimming pools and 80,000 sports halls.

State expenditure (in 1m. rubles) on health services and physical education: 1940, 0·9; 1970, 9,300; 1980, 14,800; 1989, 24,600.

Between 1950 and 1980 62,766,000 apartments (in towns) and houses (in rural areas) were built. In 1989, 2·1m. apartments and houses were built. Rents in the USSR were not increased between 1928 and 1988, and accounted for about 3% of the expenditure of an average worker's family. By the end of 1989, 77% of all urban housing had a gas supply installed, 93% had running water, 90% had central heating and 86% had bathrooms. 60% of total housing space was publicly and 40% was privately owned.

Further Reading

Narodnoe Khozyaistvo SSSR (National Economy of the USSR). Statistical Yearbook. Moscow
Pravda (Truth). Daily paper reflecting the Communist viewpoint
Pravitelstvennyi Vestnik. Weekly publication of the Soviet government
Sovetskaya Torgovlya. Monthly publication of the Ministry of Trade of the USSR
Trud. The daily organ of the General Confederation of Trade Unions
Professionalnye Soyuzy. A trade union fortnightly. Moscow
Svobodnaya Mysl. A fortnightly journal of socialist theory
Bolshaya Sovetskaya Entsiklopedia. 65 vols. Moscow, 1926–47; 2nd ed., 51 vols. Moscow, 1949–58; 3rd ed., Moscow, 1959–78; annual supplement (*Ezhegodnik*)
Soviet Studies. Glasgow, six issues annually.
The Current Digest of the Soviet Press. Published by Joint Committee on Slavic Studies. Columbus, Ohio, weekly.
Bialer, S., *The Soviet Paradox: External Expansion, Internal Decline*. London, 1987
Bourdeaux, M., *Gorbachev, Glasnost and the Gospel*. London, 1991
Brown, A. (ed.) *The Soviet Union: a Biographical Dictionary*. London, 1990
Cambridge Encyclopedia of Russia and the Soviet Union. CUP, 1982
Carr, E. H., *A History of Soviet Russia*. 14 vols. London, 1951–78
Clarke, R. A. and Matko, D. J. I., (eds.) *Soviet Economic Facts 1917–80*. London, 1983
Cracraft, J., *The Soviet Union Today*. Chicago, 2nd ed. 1988
Degras, J. (compiler), *Soviet Documents on Foreign Policy, 1917–41*. 3 vols. London, 1948–52
Dyker, D. A., *Restructuring the Soviet Economy*. London, 1991.
Gorbachev, M., *Perestroika*. English ed. London, 1987.—*The August Coup*. London, 1991
Heisbourg, F. (ed.) *The Strategic Implications of Change in the Soviet Union*. London, 1990
Hill, R. J., *The Soviet Union: Politics, Economics and Society*. 2nd ed. London, 1989
Hosking, G., *A History of the Soviet Union*. 2nd ed. London, 1990.—*The Awakening of the Soviet Union*. 2nd ed. London, 1991
Hough, J. F. and Fainsod, M., *How the Soviet Union is Governed*. Rev. ed. Harvard Univ. Press, 1979
Hutchings, R., *The Soviet Budget*. London, 1983
Jensen, R. G. et al (eds.) *Soviet Natural Resources in the World Economy*. Univ. of Chicago Press, 1983
Jones, D. L., *Books in English in the Soviet Union 1917–73: A Bibliography*. London and New York, 1975
McCauley, A., *The Soviet Union since 1917*. London, 1981.—(ed.) *Gorbachev and Perestroika*. London, 1990
Nahaylo, B. and Swoboda, V., *Soviet Disunion: a History of the Nationalities Problem in the USSR*. London, 1990
Nove, A., *An Economic History of the USSR*. 2nd ed., London, 1989
Novosti Press Agency. *USSR: the Decisive Years – Five Years of Stagnation, Five Years of Perestroika*. Moscow, 1992

Pockney, B. P., *Soviet Statistics since 1945*. New York, 1991
Rahr, A., *A Biographical Directory of 100 Leading Soviet Officials*. Boulder (Colo.), 1991
Schmidt-Häuer, C., *Gorbachov: The Path to Power*. London, 1986
Shaw, W. and Pryce, D., (eds.) *Encyclopedia of the USSR*. London, 1990
Sixsmith, M., *Moscow Coup: the Death of the Soviet System*. New York, 1991
Slusser, R. M. and Triska, J. F., *A Calendar of Soviet Treaties, 1917–57*. Stanford Univ. Press, 1959—and Ginsburgs, G., *A Calendar of Soviet Treaties, 1958–1973*, Alphen aan den Rijn, 1981
Staar, R. F., *The Foreign Policies of the Soviet Union*. Stanford Univ. Press, 1991
Tauris Soviet Directory, The. London, 1989
Thompson, A., *Russia/USSR*. [Bibliography] Oxford and Santa Barbara, 1979
Urban, M. E., *More Power to the Soviets: the Democratic Revolution in the USSR*. Aldershot, 1990.
Walker, M., *The Waking Giant: Gorbachev's Russia*. New York, 1987
White, S., *Gorbachev and After*. CUP, 1991.—*et al* (eds.) *Developments in Soviet Politics*. 2nd ed. London, 1992

MEMBER STATES

RUSSIA

Capital: Moscow
Population: 148.04m. (1990)

Rossiiskaya Federatsiya

AREA AND POPULATION. Russia occupies 17,075,000 sq. km (over 76% of the total area of the former USSR) stretching from the Far North to the Black Sea in the south and from the Far East to Kaliningrad in the west. Its 1989 census population was 147,021,869, of whom 81·5% were Russians, 3·8% Tatars, 3% Ukrainians, 1·2% Chuvash, 0·9% Bashkir, 0·8% Belorussians, and 0·7% Mordovians. Chechens, Germans, Udmurts, Mari, Kazakhs, Avars, Jews and Armenians all numbered 0·5m. or more. The 2 principal cities are Moscow, the capital, with a population (Jan. 1990) of 9m. (without suburbs, 8,801,000) and St Petersburg (formerly Leningrad), the former capital, 5,035,000 (without suburbs, 4,468,000). Among other important cities are Nizhni Novgorod (formerly Gorky), Rostov-on-Don, Volgograd, Yekaterinburg (formerly Sverdlovsk), Novosibirsk, Chelyabinsk, Kazan, Omsk and Samara (formerly Kuibyshev). Population, Jan. 1990, 148,041,000.

The Russian Federation consists of:

(1) *Territories (krai):* Altai, Khabarovsk, Krasnodar, Krasnoyarsk, Primorye, Stavropol.

(2) *Regions (oblast):* Amur, Arkhangel, Astrakhan, Belgorod, Bryansk, Chelyabinsk, Chita, Irkutsk, Ivanovo, Kaluga, Kaliningrad, Kamchatka, Kemerovo, Kirov, Kostroma, Kuibyshev, Kurgan, Kursk, Leningrad, Lipetsk, Magadan, Moscow, Murmansk, Nizhni Novgorod, Novgorod, Novosibirsk, Omsk, Orel, Orenburg, Penza, Perm, Pskov, Rostov, Ryazan, Sakhalin, Saratov, Smolensk, Sverdlovsk, Tambov, Tomsk, Tula, Tver, Tyumen, Ulyanovsk, Vladimir, Volgograd, Vologda, Voronezh, Yaroslavl.

(3) *Autonomous Republics:* Bashkir, Buryat, Chechen-Ingush, Chuvash, Dagestan, Kabardin-Balkar, Kalmyk, Karelian, Komi, Mari, Mordovian, North Ossetia, Tatar, Tuva, Udmurt, Yakut.

Subordinate to and within Territories and Regions are the following:

(4) *Autonomous Regions (avtonomnaya oblast):* Adygei, Gorno-Altai, Jewish, Karachayevo-Cherkess, Khakass.

(5) *Autonomous Areas (avtonomny okrug):* Agin-Buryat, Chukot, Evenki, Khanty-Mansi, Komi-Permyak, Koryak, Nenets, Taimyr (Dolgano-Nenets), Ust-Ordyn-Buryat, Yamalo-Nenets.

CONSTITUTION AND GOVERNMENT. The former Soviet government with its ministerial structure has in practice been taken over, with some reduction in numbers and changes of function.

The Russian Soviet Federative Socialist Republic (RSFSR) adopted a constitution in April 1978. In June 1990, pending the promulgation of a new constitution, it adopted a declaration of republican sovereignty by 544 votes to 271. It became a founding member of the CIS in Dec. 1991, and adopted the name 'Russian Federation'.

There is a 13-member Constitutional Court.

The *President* of the Russian Federation is elected by all citizens over 18 for one or two 5-year terms. Candidates must be Russian citizens between 35 and 65 years of age, and be nominated by parties, trade unions or social organizations with the support of 100,000 electors and one-fifth of the Congress of People's Deputies. A 50% turn-out is required to validate the election.

Boris Yeltsin became Russia's first-ever elected President at the elections of 12 June 1991, gaining 57·3% of the votes cast against 6 opponents. Turnout was 74%. Aleksandr Rutskoi became Vice-President at the same time.

President: Boris Yeltsin (sworn in 10 July 1991).

Vice-President: Aleksandr Rutskoi.

In Nov. 1991 the President assumed the duties of *Prime Minister*, and in March 1992 became the head of a new Ministry of *Defence*. The other members of the government in March 1992 were:

State Secretary and First Deputy Prime Minister, Gennadii Burbulis. *Deputy Prime Minister for Economic Policy, Minister of Economics and Finance,* Yegor Gaidar. *Deputy Prime Minister for Social Policy, Minister for Labour and Employment,* Aleksandr Shokhin. *Trade and Resources,* Stanislav Anisimov. *Communications,* Vladimir Bulgak. *Chairman of the Russian State Committee on the Social Defence of Citizens and the Rehabilitation of Territories affected by Radiation,* Semen Voloshchuk. *Culture:* Evgenii Sidorov. *Health,* Andrei Vorob'ev. *Geology and Use of Nature,* Viktor Danilov-Danil'yants. *Education,* Eduard Dneprov. *Internal Affairs,* Andrei Dunaev. *Transport,* Vitalii Yefimov. *Chairman of the KGB,* Viktor Ivanenko. *Foreign Affairs,* Andrei Kozyrev. *Fuel and Energy,* Vladimir Lopukhin. *Social Security,* Ella Pamfilova. *Publishing and Mass Information,* Mikhail Poltoranin. *Science and Technology Policy,* Boris Saltykov. *Industry,* Aleksandr Titkin. *Justice,* Nikolai Fedorov. *Agriculture,* Viktor Khlystun. *Chairman of the Russian State Committee on the Management of State Property,* Anatolii Chubais. *Foreign Economic Relations,* Petr Aven. *Relations with CIS Republics,* Vladimir Mashits. *Speaker of the Supreme Soviet,* Ruslan Khasbulatov.

On 4 March 1990 elections were held for a 1,068-seat Congress of People's Deputies, which elected a two-chamber parliament, the Supreme Soviet, from amongst its members.

A law of Nov. 1991 extended citizenship to all who lived in Russia at the time of its adoption and to those in other republics who requested it.

National Flag: 3 horizontal stripes of white, blue and red.

Local Government: Elections to local authorities were held on 4 March 1990.

INTERNATIONAL RELATIONS. By Dec. 1991 Russia's independence had been recognized by more than 100 foreign states.

Membership. Russia is a member of the UN (Security Council).

ECONOMY

Policy. A law of 31 Oct. 1990 places Russian economic resources under Russian control. In Aug. 1991 all-union enterprises operating in the republic were placed under the control of the Russian government. In Oct. 1991 the President announced an economic programme whose aim was the establishment of a 'healthy mixed economy with a powerful private sector'. As part of this programme the prices of most commodities were freed on 2 Jan. 1992.

Privatization is overseen by the State Committee on the Management of State Property, and began with small and medium-sized enterprises. Enterprises in oil, gas and pharmaceuticals, or employing more than 10,000 workers, or with assets over 200m. rubles on 1 Jan. 1992 require government permission to be privatized. Employees are alloted preference shares amounting to 25% of an enterprise's stock.

Budget. Revenue and expenditure balanced as follows (in 1m. rubles): 1988, 110,102; 1989 (plan), 126,471. These figures, and those for the other 14 Union Republics, included grants from the Union Budget. Since June 1990 the Government has been able to raise money from enterprises only by taxing profits. Prices are fixed only for monopolies; other firms may sell for whatever price they can obtain. In 1991-92 budgets were set every 3 months. The budget for the first quarter of 1992 was fixed at 258,000m rubles.

Banking and Finance. There is a Central Bank and bank of issue (*governor*, Georgi Matyukhin), In Jan. 1992 it took over the assets of the former Soviet foreign trade bank Vneshekonombank.

ENERGY AND NATURAL RESOURCES

Minerals. Russia contains great mineral resources: Iron ore in the Urals, the Kerch Peninsula and Siberia; coal in the Kuznets Basin, Eastern Siberia, Urals and the sub-Moscow Basin; oil in the Urals, Azov-Black Sea area, Bashkiria, and West Siberia. It also has abundant deposits of gold, platinum, copper, zinc, lead, tin and rare metals.

Agriculture. In Dec. 1990 the Supreme Soviet voted to allow plots for the growing of agricultural products to be privately owned. They may only be resold back to the state, and only after 10 years. A presidential decree of Dec. 1991 authorized the private ownership of land on a general basis. Collective and state farms who wish to start private farming must be allotted land and equipment within a month of their application. Collective and state farms are required to reorganize themselves into co-operatives or share companies.

INDUSTRY

Labour. Legislation of June 1990 renders the previously mandatory election of managers optional, and creates councils of employees empowered to reject or approve state plans. In 1992 the minimum wage was 550 rubles a month. Unemployment benefit is 90% of the minimum wage. Annual paid leave is 24 working days. The workforce was 71.3m. in 1989.

FOREIGN ECONOMIC RELATIONS. In Nov. 1990 Russia concluded an agreement with the Ukraine to co-operate on defence and external policy, to co-ordinate pricing and exchange representatives. A similar agreement was concluded with Belorussia in Dec. 1990.

Enterprises may engage in foreign trade without special registration. Licenced banks may open hard-currency accounts for all citizens.

COMMUNICATIONS

Railways. Length of railways on 1 Jan. 1990 was 87,090 km, hard-surface motor roads, 624,000 km.

Shipping. In 1989, 220,848m. tonne-km of freight was carried on inland waterways. Kaliningrad was opened to shipping in May 1991.

Newspapers. In 1989 there were 4,772 newspapers, 4,471 of them in Russian. Daily circulation of Russian-language newspapers, 159·4m., other languages, 2·7m.

JUSTICE, RELIGION, EDUCATION AND WELFARE

Justice. In Oct. 1991 the Supreme Soviet adopted a law rehabilitating the victims of political repression during the Stalin period.

Religion. The Russian Orthodox Church, represented by the Patriarchate of

Moscow, had, in 1991, an estimated 35-40m. adherents, 6,000 clergy and 6,500 churches in 11,940 parishes. There were 31 convents and 25 monasteries. There are still many Old Believers, whose schism from the Orthodox Church dates from the 17th century. The Russian Church is headed by the Patriarch of Moscow and All Russia (Metropolitan Aleksei II (b. 1929) of St Petersburg and Novgorod, elected June 1990), assisted by the Holy Synod, which has 7 members–the Patriarch himself and the Metropolitans of Krutitsy and Kolomna (Moscow), St Petersburg and Kiev *ex officio*, and 3 bishops alternating for 6 months in order of seniority from the 3 regions forming the Moscow Patriarchate. The Patriarchate of Moscow maintains jurisdiction over a few parishes of Russian Orthodox abroad, in Tehran, Jerusalem, Germany, France (1 archbishop), the UK and in North and South America (2 bishops). There are Jewish communities in Moscow and St Petersburg.

Education. In 1989–90 there were 20·4m. pupils in 69,400 primary and secondary schools; 2,861,000 students in 512 higher educational establishments (including correspondence students) and 2,338,300 students in 2,595 technical colleges of all kinds (including correspondence students); 69% of eligible children were attending preschool institutions. There were, on 1 Jan. 1989, 1,032,100 scientific staff in 3,036 learned and scientific institutions. An independent university for the study of the humanities opened in Moscow in 1991.

In 1957 a Siberian branch of the Academy of Sciences was organized, in charge of all scientific research institutions from the Urals to the Pacific. There are also Far Eastern and Urals divisions. Pre-dating the foundation of a Russian Academy of Sciences, St Petersburg and Urals branches were founded in 1990 and 1991 respectively. The Soviet became the Russian Academy of Sciences in Dec. 1991.

Health. Doctors in 1989 numbered 697,700, and hospital beds 2m. There were 12,697 medical institutions. A transition from state-financed to insurance-based health care is to be effected by 1993.

DIPLOMATIC REPRESENTATIVES

Of Russia in Great Britain (13 Kensington Palace Gdns., London W8 4QX)
Ambassador: Boris Pankin.

Of Great Britain in Russia (Naberezhnaya Morisa Toreza 14, Moscow 72)
Ambassador: Sir Rodric Braithwaite, KCMG.

Of Russia in the USA (1125 16th St., NW, Washington, D.C., 20036)
Ambassador: Vladimir Lukin.

Of the USA in Russia (Ulitsa Chaikovskogo 19, Moscow)
Ambassador: Robert Strauss.

Of Russia to the United Nations
Ambassador: B. Lozinskii.

Further Reading

Rossiiskaya Gazeta. Daily of the Supreme Soviet
Cambridge Encyclopedia of Russia and the Soviet Union. CUP, 1982
Dukes, P., *A History of Russia: Medieval, Modern, Contemporary.* 2nd ed. London, 1990
Pares, B., *A History of Russia.* London, 1962
Paxton, J., *Companion to Russian History.* London and New York, 1984
Riasanovsky, N. V., *A History of Russia.* 4th ed. OUP, 1984
Roxburgh, A., *The Second Russian Revolution: the Struggle for Power in the Kremlin.* London, 1991
Smith, H., *The New Russians.* London, 1990
Treadgold, D. W., *Twentieth Century Russia.* 6th ed. Boston, 1987
Vernadsky, G., *A History of Russia.* 5th ed. Yale Univ. Press, 1961

BASHKIR AUTONOMOUS REPUBLIC

Area 143,600 sq. km (55,430 sq. miles), population (Jan. 1990) 3,964,000. Capital, Ufa. Bashkiria was annexed to Russia in 1557. It was constituted as an Autonomous

Soviet Republic on 23 March 1919. A declaration of republican sovereignty was adopted in 1990, and a declaration of independence in 1991. Population, census 1979, included 24·3% Bashkirians, 40·3% Russians, 24·5% Tatars, and 3·2% Chuvashes.

280 deputies were elected to the republican Supreme Soviet on 24 Feb. 1985, 108 of them women.

In 1988–89 there were 552,000 pupils in 3,164 schools. There is a state university and a branch of the USSR Academy of Sciences with 8 learned institutions (511 research workers). There were 67,200 students in 71 technical colleges and 51,600 in 9 higher educational establishments.

In Jan. 1989 there were 13,992 doctors and 53,500 hospital beds.

There are chemical, coal, steel, electrical engineering, timber and paper industries. There were 629 collective farms and 159 state farms in 1980. Crop area was 4,587,000 ha. Bashkiria is a major oil producer.

BURYAT AUTONOMOUS REPUBLIC

Area is 351,300 sq. km (135,650 sq. miles). The Buryat Republic, situated to the south of the Yakut Republic, adopted the Soviet system 1 March 1920. This area was penetrated by the Russians in the 17th century and finally annexed from China by the treaties of Nerchinsk (1689) and Kyakhta (1727). The population (Jan. 1990) was 1,049,000. Capital, Ulan-Ude (1989 census population, 353,000). The name of the republic was changed from 'Buryat-Mongol' on 7 July 1958. The population (1979 census) includes 23% Buryats and 72% Russians.

170 deputies were elected to the republican Supreme Soviet on 24 Feb. 1985, 60 of them women.

The main industries are coal, timber, building materials, fisheries, sheep and cattle farming. In 1980 there were 105 state and 61 collective farms. Crop area was 827,100 ha. Gold, molybdenum and wolfram are mined.

In 1988–89 there were 574 schools with 179,000 pupils, 21 technical colleges with 17,000 students and 4 higher educational institutions with 20,700 students. A branch of the Siberian Department of the Academy of Sciences had 4 learned institutions with 281 research workers.

In 1989 there were 4,017 doctors and 14,400 hospital beds.

CHECHENO-INGUSH AUTONOMOUS REPUBLIC

Area, 19,300 sq. km (7,350 sq. miles); population (Jan. 1990), 1,290,000. Capital, Grozny (1989 census population, 401,000). After 70 years of almost continuous fighting, the Chechens and Ingushes were conquered by Russia in the late 1850s. In 1918 each nationality separately established its 'National Soviet' within the Terek Autonomous Republic, and in 1920 (after the Civil War) were constituted areas within the Mountain Republic. The Chechens separated out as an Autonomous Region on 30 Nov. 1922 and the Ingushes on 7 July 1924. In Jan. 1934 the two regions were united, and on 5 Dec. 1936 constituted as an Autonomous Republic. This was dissolved in 1944 and the population was deported en masse, allegedly for collaboration with the German occupation forces. It was reconstituted on 9 Jan. 1957: 232,000 Chechens and Ingushes returned to their homes in the next 2 years. The population (1979 census) included 52·9% Chechens, 11·7% Ingushes, and 29·1% Russians.

175 deputies were elected to the republican Supreme Soviet on 24 Feb. 1985, 78 of them women. In 1991 the Supreme Soviet declared the area of republican rather than autonomous republican, status. In Nov. 1991 it declared its independence of Russia. Following disturbances a state of emergency was briefly imposed by Russian presidential decree.

The republic has one of the major Soviet oilfields, and a number of engineering works, chemical factories, building materials works and food canneries. There is timber, woodworking and furniture industry. In 1984 there were 122 state and 39 collective farms. Crop area was 453,900 ha.

There were, in 1988–89, 535 schools with 252,000 pupils, 12 technical colleges with 13,000 students and 3 places of higher education with 14,800 students.

In 1989 there were 3,676 doctors and 13,500 hospital beds.

CHUVASH AUTONOMOUS REPUBLIC

Area, 18,300 sq. km (7,064 sq. miles); population (Jan. 1990), 1,340,000. Capital, Cheboksary (1989 census population, 420,000). The territory was annexed by Russia in the middle of the 16th century. On 24 June 1920 it was constituted as an Autonomous Region, and on 21 April 1925 as an Autonomous Republic. The population (1979 census) includes Chuvashes (68·4%), Russians (26%), Tatars (2·9%) and Mordovians (1·6%).

200 deputies were elected to the republican Supreme Soviet on 24 Feb. 1985, 79 of them women.

The timber industry antedates the Soviet period. Other industries today include railway repair works, electrical and other engineering industries, building materials, chemicals, textiles and food industries; timber felling and haulage are largely mechanized. In 1985 there were 179 collective farms and 104 state farms. Grain crops account for nearly two-thirds of all sowings and fodder crops for nearly a quarter. Fruit and wine-growing are a developing branch of agriculture. Crop area was 732,400 ha.

In 1988–89 there were 208,000 pupils at 687 schools, 23,200 students at 24 technical colleges and 18,200 students at 3 higher educational establishments.

In 1988 there were 4,672 doctors and 18,500 hospital beds.

DAGESTAN AUTONOMOUS REPUBLIC

Area, 50,300 sq. km (19,416 sq. miles); population (Jan. 1990), 1,823,000. Capital, Makhachkala (1989 census population, 315,000). Over 30 nationalities inhabit this republic apart from Russians (11·6% at 1979 census); the most numerous are the Avartsy (25·7%), Dargintsy (15·2%), Lezginy (11·6%), Kumyki (12·4%), Laki (5·1%), Tabasarany (4·4%) and Azerbaijanis (4%). Annexed from Persia in 1723, Dagestan was constituted an Autonomous Republic on 20 Jan. 1921.

210 deputies were elected to the republican Supreme Soviet on 24 Feb. 1985, 84 of them women. In 1991 the Supreme Soviet declared the area of republican, rather than autonomous republican, status.

There are engineering, oil, chemical, woodworking, textile, food and other light industries. Agriculture is varied, ranging from wheat to grapes, with sheep farming and cattle breeding; in 1983 there were 249 collective farms and 262 state farms. Crop area was 427,800 ha. A chain of power stations is under construction in the Sulak River (total capacity 2·5m. kw.).

In 1988–89 there were 1,510 schools with 391,000 pupils, 23,000 students at 28 technical colleges and 5 higher education establishments with 26,000 students; and a branch of the USSR Academy of Sciences with 4 learned institutions (373 research workers). In 1989 there were 7,539 doctors and 22,700 hospital beds.

KABARDINO-BALKAR AUTONOMOUS REPUBLIC

Area, 12,500 sq. km (4,825 sq. miles); population (Jan. 1990) 768,000. Capital, Nalchik (1989 census population, 235,000). Kabarda was annexed to Russia in

1557. The republic was constituted on 5 Dec. 1936. Population (1979 census) includes Kabardinians (45·6%), Balkars (9%), Russians (35·1%).

160 deputies were elected to the republican Supreme Soviet on 24 Feb. 1985, 69 of them women.

Main industries are ore-mining, timber, engineering, coal, food processing, timber and light industries, building materials. Grain, livestock breeding, dairy farming and wine-growing are the principal branches of agriculture. There were, in 1983, 59 state and 66 collective farms.

In 1988–89 there were 239 schools with 123,000 pupils, 8,900 students in 10 technical colleges and 10,700 students at 2 higher educational establishments. In 1989 there were 3,573 doctors and 9,300 hospital beds.

KALMYK REPUBLIC

Area, 75,900 sq. km (29,300 sq. miles); population (Jan. 1990), 325,000. Capital, Elista (85,000). The population (1979 census) includes 41·5% Kalmyks, 42·6% Russians, 6·6% Kazakhs, Chechens and Dagestanis.

The Kalmyks migrated from western China to Russia (Nogai Steppe) in the early 17th century. The territory was constituted an Autonomous Region on 4 Nov. 1920, and an Autonomous Republic on 22 Oct. 1935; this was dissolved in 1943. On 9 Jan. 1957 it was reconstituted as an Autonomous Region and on 29 July 1958 as an Autonomous Republic once more. In Oct. 1990 the republic was renamed the Kalmyk Soviet Socialist Republic.

130 deputies were elected to the republican Supreme Soviet on 24 Feb. 1985, 54 of them women.

Main industries are fishing, canning and building materials. Cattle breeding and irrigated farming (mainly fodder crops) are the principal branches of agriculture. In 1983 there were 79 state and 23 collective farms. Crop area was 859,000 ha.

In 1988–89 there were 53,000 pupils in 245 schools, 6,000 students in 7 technical colleges and 5,000 in higher education. There were 1,372 doctors and 5,000 hospital beds in 1989.

KARELIAN AUTONOMOUS REPUBLIC

HISTORY. Karelia (formerly Olonets Province) became part of the RSFSR after 1917. In June 1920 a Karelian Labour Commune was formed and in July 1923 this was transformed into the Karelian Autonomous Soviet Socialist Republic (one of the autonomous republics of the RSFSR). On 31 March 1940, after the Soviet–Finnish war, practically all the territory (with the exception of a small section in the neighbourhood of the Leningrad area) which had been ceded by Finland to the USSR was added to Karelia and the Karelian Autonomous Republic was transformed into the Karelo-Finnish Soviet Socialist Republic as the 12th republic of the USSR. In 1946, however, the southern part of the republic, including its whole seaboard and the towns of Viipuri (Vyborg) and Keksholm, was attached to the RSFSR, reverting in 1956 to autonomous republican status within the RSFSR. In Nov. 1991 it declared itself the 'Republic of Karelia'.

AREA AND POPULATION. The Karelian Autonomous Republic, capital Petrozavodsk (1989 census population, 270,000), covers an area of 172,400 sq. km, with a population of 796,000 (Jan. 1990). Karelians represent 11·1% of the population, Russians, 71·3%, Belorussians 8·1%, Ukrainians 3·2%, Finns 2·7% (1979 census).

150 deputies were elected to the republican Supreme Soviet on 24 Feb. 1985, 57 of them women.

NATURAL RESOURCES. Karelia is chiefly noted for its wealth of timber, some 70% of its territory being forest land. It is also rich in other natural resources, having large deposits of diabase, spar, quartz, marble, granite, zinc, lead, silver, copper, molybdenum, tin, baryta, iron ore, etc. Karelia takes first place in the USSR for the production of mica. It has 43,643 lakes, which, as well as its rivers, are rich in fish.

Agriculture. There were 9 collective farms and 59 state farms in 1983. The crop area was 78,900 ha (over 85% under fodder crops).

INDUSTRY. The republic has timber mills, paper-cellulose works, mica, chemical plants, power stations and furniture factories. Output, 1986: Timber, 11·1m. cu. metres; paper, 1·3m. tonnes; cellulose, 826,000 tonnes; electricity, 3,634m. kwh.; iron ore, 9·5m. tonnes.

The opening of the White Sea–Baltic Canal influenced economic development. New refrigerating plants, cellulose factories and timber mills began working in 1970.

COMMUNICATIONS. A railway between Petrozavodsk and Suoyarvi connects the capital and the Murmansk Railway with the main railway line Sortavala–Vyborg. A railway line was also laid between Kandalaksha and Kuolayarvi. Length of track, 1,600 km.

EDUCATION. In 1988–89 there were 112,000 pupils in 319 schools. There were 9,800 students in 2 places of higher education and 14,300 in 16 technical colleges.

HEALTH. In 1989 there were 4,020 doctors, and 12,200 hospital beds.

KOMI REPUBLIC

Area, 415,900 sq. km (160,540 sq. miles); population (Jan. 1990), 1,265,000. Capital, Syktyvkar (1989 census population, 233,000). Annexed by the princes of Moscow in the 14th century, the territory was constituted as an Autonomous Region on 22 Aug. 1921 and as an Autonomous Republic on 5 Dec. 1936. The population (1979 census) included Komi (25·3%), Russians (56·7%), Ukrainians and Belorussians (10·7%).

180 deputies were elected to the republican Supreme Soviet on 24 Feb. 1985, 59 of them women.

A declaration of sovereignty was adopted by the republican parliament in Sept. 1990, and the designation 'Autonomous' dropped from the republic's official name.

There are coal, oil, timber, gas, asphalt and building materials industries, and light industry is expanding. Livestock breeding (including dairy farming) is the main branch of agriculture. There were 56 state farms in 1983. Crop area, 92,000 ha.

In 1988–89 there were 192,000 pupils in 564 schools, 11,400 students in 3 higher educational establishments, 16,800 students in 19 technical colleges; and a branch of the Academy of Sciences with 4 learned institutions (297 research workers).

In 1989 there were 5,048 doctors and 17,700 hospital beds.

MARI REPUBLIC

Area, 23,200 sq. km (8,955 sq. miles); population (Jan. 1990), 754,000. Capital, Yoshkar-Ola (1989 census population, 242,000). The Mari people were annexed to Russia, with other peoples of the Kazan Tatar Khanate, when the latter was overthrown in 1552. On 4 Nov. 1920 the territory was constituted as an Autonomous Region, and on 5 Dec. 1936 as an Autonomous Republic. The republic renamed itself the Mari Soviet Socialist Republic in Oct. 1990. In Dec. 1991 V. Zotin was elected the first president. The population (1979 census) included Mari (43·5%), Tatars (5·8%), Chuvashes (1·1%), Russians (47·5%).

150 deputies were elected to the republican Supreme Soviet on 24 Feb. 1985, 60 of them women.

There are over 300 factories. The main industries are metalworking, timber, paper, woodworking and food processing. In 1983 there were 89 collective farms and 82 state farms. Over 69% of cultivated land is grain, but flax, potatoes, fruit and vegetables are also expanding branches of agriculture, as is also livestock farming. 638,000 ha were under crops.

Estimated reserves of the Pechora coalfield are 260,000m. tonnes.

In 1988–89 there were 431 schools with 109,000 pupils; 13 technical colleges and 3 higher education establishments had 10,300 and 15,300 students respectively.

In 1989 there were 2,552 doctors and 10,400 hospital beds.

MORDOVIAN AUTONOMOUS REPUBLIC

Area, 26,200 sq. km (10,110 sq. miles); population (Jan. 1990), 964,000. Capital, Saransk (1989 census population, 312,000). By the 13th century the Mordovian tribes had been subjugated by the Russian princes of Ryazan and Nizhni-Novgorod. In 1928 the territory was constituted as a Mordovian Area within the Middle-Volga Territory, on 10 Jan. 1930 as an Autonomous Region and on 20 Dec. 1934 as an Autonomous Republic. The population (1979 census) included Mordovians (34·2%), Russians (59·7%), Tatars (4·6%)

175 deputies were elected to the republican Supreme Soviet on 24 Feb. 1985, 74 of them women.

The republic has a wide range of industries: Electrical, timber, cable, building materials, furniture, textile, leather and other light industries. Agriculture is devoted chiefly to grain, sugar-beet, sheep and dairy farming. In 1983 there were 78 state and 273 collective farms.

In 1988–89 there were 129,000 pupils in 839 schools, 15,600 students in 21 technical colleges and 20,500 attending 2 higher educational institutions. In 1989 there were 3,788 doctors and 14,500 hospital beds.

NORTH OSSETIAN AUTONOMOUS REPUBLIC

Area, 8,000 sq. km (3,088 sq. miles); population (Jan. 1990), 638,000. Capital, Ordzhonikidze (formerly Vladikavkaz; 1989 census population, 300,000). The Ossetians were annexed to Russia after the latter's treaty of Kuchuk-Kainardji with Turkey, and in 1784 the key fortress of Vladikavkaz was founded on their territory (given the name of Terek region in 1861). On 4 March 1918 the latter was proclaimed an Autonomous Soviet Republic, and on 20 Jan. 1921 this territory with others was set up as the Mountain Autonomous Republic, with North Ossetia as the Ossetian (Vladikavkaz) Area within it. On 7 July 1924 the latter was constituted as an Autonomous Region and on 5 Dec. 1936 as an Autonomous Republic. The population (1979 census) comprised Ossetians (50·5%), Russians (33·9%), Ingushi and other Caucasian nationalities (8·1%).

150 deputies were elected to the republican Supreme Soviet on 24 Feb. 1985, 68 of them women.

The main industries are non-ferrous metals (mining and metallurgy), maize-processing, timber and woodworking, textiles, building materials, distilleries and food processing. There is also a varied agriculture. In 1983 there were 38 state and 45 collective farms.

There were in 1988–89, 98,000 children in 209 schools, 12,800 students in 13 technical colleges and 17,900 students in 4 higher educational establishments (pedagogical, agriculture, medical and mining-metallurgical institutes). In 1989 there were 4,292 doctors and 8,100 hospital beds.

TATAR REPUBLIC
(REPUBLIC OF TATARSTAN)

Area, 68,000 sq. km (26,250 sq. miles); population (Jan. 1990), 3,658,000. Capital, Kazan. From the 10th to the 13th centuries this was the territory of the Volga-Kama Bulgar State; conquered by the Mongols, it became the seat of the Kazan (Tatar) Khans when the Mongol Empire broke up in the 15th century, and in 1552 was conquered again by Russia. On 27 May 1920 it was constituted as an Autonomous Republic. The population (1979 census) included Tatars (47·7%), Chuvashes, Mordovians and Udmurts (5·9%), Russians (44%).

In Aug. 1990 the Supreme Soviet adopted a declaration of sovereignty and renamed the republic the Tatar Soviet Socialist Republic, or the Republic of Tatarstan. In Oct. 1991, a declaration of state independence was adopted. At a referendum in March 1992 61·4% of votes cast were in favour of increased autonomy. The republic's *President* is M. Shaimiev.

The republic has engineering, oil and chemical, timber, building materials, textiles, clothing and food industries. In 1983, 557 collective and 250 state farms served a total area under crops of 3·4m. ha.

In 1988–89 there were 2,300 schools with 500,000 pupils, 61 technical colleges with 58,900 students and 13 higher educational establishments with 67,500 students (including a state university). There is a branch of the USSR Academy of Sciences with 5 learned institutions (512 research workers).

Doctors in 1989 numbered 13,979 and hospital beds 47,200.

TUVA AUTONOMOUS REPUBLIC

Area, 170,500 sq. km (65,810 sq. miles); population (Jan. 1990), 314,000. Capital, Kyzyl (80,000). Tuva was incorporated in the USSR as an autonomous region on 13 Oct. 1944 and elevated to an Autonomous Republic on 10 Oct. 1961. It is situated to the north-west of Mongolia, between 50° and 53°N. lat. and between 90° and 100°E. long. It is bounded to the east, west and north by Siberia, and to the south by Mongolia. The Tuvans are a Turkic people, formerly ruled by hereditary or elective tribal chiefs. (For the earlier history of the former Tannu-Tuva Republic, *see* THE STATESMAN'S YEAR-BOOK, 1946, p. 798.) The population (1979 census) included Tuvans (60·5%) and Russians (36·2%). Tuva renamed itself the 'Republic of Tuva' in Oct. 1991.

130 deputies were elected to the republican Supreme Soviet on 24 Feb. 1985, 53 of them women.

Tuva is well-watered and hydro-electric resources are important. The Tuvans are mainly herdsmen and cattle farmers and there is much good pastoral land, but, in 1983, 371,000 ha were under crops. There are deposits of gold, cobalt and asbestos. The main exports are hair, hides and wool. There are 60 state farms. There are mining, woodworking, garment, leather, food and other industries.

In 1988–89 there were 155 schools with 66,000 pupils; 6 technical colleges with 3,900 students, and 1 higher education institution with 2,800 students.

In 1989 there were 1,125 doctors and 5,500 hospital beds.

UDMURT AUTONOMOUS REPUBLIC

Area, 42,100 sq. km (16,250 sq. miles); population (Jan. 1990), 1,619,000. Capital, Izhevsk. The Udmurts (formerly known as 'Votyaks') were annexed by the Russians in the 15th and 16th centuries. On 4 Nov. 1920 the Votyak Autonomous Region was constituted (the name was changed to Udmurt in 1932), and on 28 Dec. 1934 was raised to the status of an Autonomous Republic. The population (1979 census) included Udmurts (32·2%), Tatars (6·6%), Russians (58·3%).

200 deputies were elected to the republican Supreme Soviet on 24 Feb. 1985, 79 of them women.

Heavy industry includes the manufacture of locomotives, machine tools and other engineering products, timber and building materials. There are also light industries: Clothing, leather, furniture and food.

There were 96 state and 244 collective farms in 1983; crop area 1·4m. ha.

In 1988–89 there were 855 schools with 237,000 pupils; there were 22,600 students at 29 technical colleges and 23,700 at 5 higher educational institutions.

In 1989 there were 6,994 doctors and 21,100 hospital beds.

YAKUT AUTONOMOUS REPUBLIC

The area is 3,103,200 sq. km (1,197,760 sq. miles); population (Jan. 1990), 1,099,000. Capital, Yakutsk (187,000). The Yakuts were subjugated by the Russians in the 17th century. The territory was constituted an Autonomous Republic on 27 April 1922. The population (1979 census) included Yakuts (36·9%), other northern peoples (2·2%), Russians (50·4%).

205 deputies were elected to the republican Supreme Soviet on 24 Feb. 1985, 92 of them women. The *President* (elected in 1991) is Mikhail Nikolaev.

The principal industries are mining (gold, tin, mica, coal) and livestock-breeding. The Soviet Soyuz-Zoloto Trust and a number of individual prospectors are working the fields. Silver- and lead-bearing ores and coal are worked; large diamond fields have been opened up. Timber and food industries are developing. There was 1 collective farm in 1985 and 88 state farms, with an area under crops of 107,100 ha. Trapping and breeding of fur-bearing animals (sable, squirrel, silver fox, etc.) are an important source of income. A severe climate and lack of railways are serious obstacles to the economic development of the republic. There are, however, 10,000 km of roads and internal air lines totalling 10,000 km including an air service between Irkutsk and Yakutsk.

In 1988–89 there were 194,000 pupils in 653 secondary schools, 10,300 students at 18 technical colleges and 7,900 attending 2 higher education institutions.

In 1989 there were 4,814 doctors and 16,400 hospital beds.

ADYGEI AUTONOMOUS REGION

Part of Krasnodar Territory. Area, 7,600 sq. km (2,934 sq. miles); population (Jan. 1990), 436,000. Capital, Maikop (149,000). Established 27 July 1922; granted republican status in 1991.

President: Aslan Dzharimov.

Chief industries are timber, woodworking, food processing and there is some engineering. Cattle breeding predominates in agriculture. There were 38 collective and 33 state farms in 1983.

In 1988–89 there were 164 schools with 59,000 pupils, 6 technical colleges with 7,000 students and a pedagogical institute with 5,200 students. In 1989 there were 1,422 doctors and 5,900 hospital beds.

GORNO-ALTAI AUTONOMOUS REGION

Part of Altai Territory. Area, 92,600 sq. km (35,740 sq. miles); population (Jan. 1990), 194,000. Capital, Gorno-Altaisk (39,000). Established 1 June 1922 as Oirot Autonomous Region; renamed 7 Jan. 1948; granted republican status in 1991.

Chief industries are gold, mercury and brown-coal mining, timber, chemicals and dairying. Cattle breeding predominates; pasturages and hay meadows cover over 1m. ha, but 142,000 ha are under crops. There were 20 collective and 37 state farms in 1983.

In 1988–89 there were 34,000 school pupils in 193 schools; 5 technical colleges had 4,300 students and 2,600 students were attending a pedagogical institute. There were 2,800 hospital beds and 735 doctors.

JEWISH AUTONOMOUS REGION

Part of Khabarovsk Territory. Area, 36,000 sq. km (13,895 sq. miles); population (Jan. 1990), 218,000 (1979 census, Russians, 84·1%; Ukrainians, 6·3%; Jews, 5·4%). Capital, Birobijan (82,000). Established as Jewish National District in 1928, became an Autonomous Region 7 May 1934. In Oct. 1991 the region declared itself an Autonomous Republic

Chief industries are non-ferrous metallurgy, building materials, timber, engineering, textiles, paper and food processing. There were 161,000 ha under cultivation in 1983; main crops are wheat, soya, oats, barley. There were 36 state farms and 2 collective farms in 1983.

In 1988–89 there were 35,000 pupils in 110 schools; students in 6 technical colleges numbered 5,400. There is a Yiddish national theatre, a Yiddish newspaper and a Yiddish broadcasting service. Doctors numbered 820 and hospital beds 3,100 in 1989.

KARACHAEVO-CHERKESS REPUBLIC

Part of Stavropol Territory. Area, 14,100 sq. km (5,442 sq. miles); population (Jan. 1990), 422,000. Capital, Cherkessk (113,000). A Karachai Autonomous Region was established on 26 April 1926 (out of a previously united Karachaevo-Cherkess Autonomous Region created in 1922), and dissolved in 1943. A Cherkess Autonomous Region was established on 30 April 1928. The present Autonomous Region was re-established on 9 Jan. 1957. The Region declared itself a Soviet Socialist Republic in Dec. 1990.

There are ore-mining, engineering, chemical and woodworking industries. The Kuban-Kalaussi irrigation scheme irrigates 200,000 ha. Livestock breeding and grain growing predominate in agriculture; crop area in 1983 was 196,000 ha. There were 15 collective farms and 37 state farms in 1983.

In 1988–89 there were 67,000 pupils in 178 secondary schools, 6 technical colleges with 5,400 students and 1 institute with 4,100 students. In 1989 there were 1,381 doctors and 4,700 hospital beds.

KHAKASS AUTONOMOUS REGION

Part of Krasnoyarsk Territory. Area, 61,900 sq. km (23,855 sq. miles); population (Jan. 1990), 573,000. Capital, Abakan (154,000). Established 20 Oct. 1930; granted republican status in 1991.

There are coal- and ore-mining, timber and woodworking industries. The region is linked by rail with the Trans-Siberian line.

In 1985, 1·8m. ha were under crops. Livestock breeding, dairy and vegetable farming are developed. There are 56 state farms.

In 1988–89 there were 89,000 pupils in 266 secondary schools, 7,900 students in 7 technical colleges and 6,100 students at a higher educational institution. In 1989 there were 1,913 doctors and 8,300 hospital beds.

AUTONOMOUS AREAS

Agin-Buryat Situated in Chita region (Eastern Siberia); area, 19,000 sq. km, population (1990), 77,000. Capital, Aginskoe. Formed 1937, its economy is basically pastoral.

Chukot Situated in Magadan region (Far East), its area of 737,700 sq. km in the far northeast. Population (1990), 156,000. Capital, Anadyr. Formed 1930. Population chiefly Russian, also Chukchi, Koryak, Yakut, Even. Minerals are extracted in the north, including gold, tin, mercury and tungsten.

Evenki Situated in Krasnoyarsk territory (Eastern Siberia); area, 767,600 sq. km, population (1990) 25,000, chiefly Evenks. Capital, Tura.

Khanty-Mansi Situated in Tyumen region (Western Siberia); area, 523,100 sq. km, population (1990) 1,301,000, chiefly Russians but also Khants and Mansi. Capital, Khanti-Mansiisk. Formed 1930.

Komi-Permyak Situated in Perm region (Northern Russia); area, 32,900 sq. km, population (1990) 160,000, chiefly Komi-Permyaks. Formed 1925. Capital, Kudymkar. Forestry is the main occupation.

Koryak Situated in Kamchatka region (Far East); area, 301,500 sq. km, population (1990) 39,000. Capital, Palana. Formed 1930.

Nenets Situated in Archangel region (Northern Russia); area, 176,700 sq. km, population (1990) 55,000. Capital, Naryan-Mar.

Taimyr Situated in Krasnoyarsk territory, this most northerly part of Siberia comprises the Taimyr peninsula and the Arctic islands of Severnaya Zemlya. Area, 862,100 sq. km, population (1990) 55,000, excluding the mining city of Norilsk which is separately administered. Capital, Dudinka.

Ust-Ordyn-Buryat Situated in Irkutsk region (Eastern Siberia); area, 22,400 sq. km, population (1990) 137,000. Capital, Ust-Ordynsk. Formed 1937.

Yamalo-Nenets Situated in Tyumen region (Western Siberia); area, 750,300 sq. km, population (1990) 495,000. Capital, Salekhard. Formed 1930.

Further Reading

Armstrong, T., *Russian Settlement in the North*. CUP, 1965
Kolarz, W., *The Peoples of the Soviet Far East*. London, 1954
Wood, A., (ed.) *Siberia: Problems and Prospects for Regional Development*. London, 1987
Istoriya Sibiri s drevneishikh vremen do nashikh dnei. 5 vols., Leningrad, 1968–69

UKRAINE

Capital: Kiev
Population: 51·84m. (1990)

Ukraina

HISTORY. The Ukrainian Soviet Socialist Republic was proclaimed on 25 Dec. 1917 and was finally established in Dec. 1919. In Dec. 1920 it concluded a military and economic alliance with the RSFSR and on 30 Dec. 1922 formed, together with the other Soviet Socialist Republics, the Union of Soviet Socialist Republics. On 1 Nov. 1939 Western Ukraine (about 88,000 sq. km) was incorporated in the Ukrainian SSR. On 2 Aug. 1940 Northern Bukovina (about 6,000 sq. km) ceded to the USSR by Romania 28 June 1940, and the Khotin, Akkerman and Izmail provinces of Bessarabia were included in the Ukrainian SSR, and on 29 June 1945 Ruthenia (Sub-Carpathian Russia), about 7,000 sq. km, was also incorporated. From the new territories 2 new regions were formed, Chernovits and Izmail.

On 5 Dec. 1991 the Supreme Soviet unanimously repudiated the 1922 Treaty of Union and declared Ukraine's independence. Ukraine was one of the founder members of the CIS in Dec. 1991.

AREA AND POPULATION. The Ukraine is in the south-west of the former USSR; it has a Black Sea coast and western frontiers with Romania, Hungary, Poland and Czechoslovakia. It is bounded in the north by Belorussia and otherwise by Russia. In 1938 the Ukrainian SSR covered an area of 445,000 sq. km (171,770 sq. miles); the Ukraine now covers 603,700 sq. km (231,990 sq. miles).

Population, Jan. 1990, 51,839,000 (the 1989 census population was 51,452,034 of whom 72·7% were Ukrainians, 22·1% Russians, 1% Jews, 0·92% Belorussians).

The principal towns are the capital Kiev, Kharkov, Donetsk, Odessa, Dnepropetrovsk, Lvov, Zaporozhye and Krivoi Rog.

The Ukraine consists of the following regions: Cherkassy, Chernigov, Chernovtsy, Crimea (transferred from the RSFSR on 19 Feb. 1954, and elevated to the status of Autonomous Republic in 1991), Dnepropetrovsk, Donetsk, Ivan Franko, Khmelnitsky (formerly Kamenets-Podolsk), Kharkov, Kherson, Kiev, Kirovograd, Lugansk, Lvov, Nikolayev, Odessa, Poltava, Rovno, Sumy, Ternopol, Vinnitsa, Volhynia, Zakarpatskaya (Transcarpathia), Zaporozhye, Zhitomir.

CONSTITUTION AND GOVERNMENT. A new Constitution, based on that of the USSR, was adopted in April 1978. The 450-member Supreme Soviet was elected on 4 March 1990, Communists gaining 239 seats. In July 1990 it adopted a declaration of republican sovereignty by 355 votes to 4, and in Aug. 1991, following the unsuccessful coup, it declared Ukraine an independent democratic republic. In a referendum on 1 Dec. 1991 90·3% of votes cast were in favour. Turn-out was 83·7%. At a simultaneous presidential election Leonid Kravchuk gained 61·6% of votes cast against 2 opponents.

The former Council of Ministers was reconstituted as a 33-member cabinet in May 1991.

Chairman, Supreme Soviet: Leonid Kravchuk (b. 1934).
Prime Minister: Vitold Fokin (Communist).
Foreign Minister: V. A. Kravtsev.

National flag: Blue over yellow horizontally.

Local Government: Elections were held on 4 March 1990.

INTERNATIONAL RELATIONS. In Nov. 1990 the Ukraine concluded an agreement with Russia to co-operate on defence, external policy and price co-ordination, and to exchange representatives.

Membership. The Ukraine is a member of the UN.

ECONOMY

Policy. Subsidies were removed and prices allowed to find their market level in Jan. 1992.

Budget. Budget estimates (in 1m. rubles), 1988, 33,164; 1989 (plan), 36,885.

Currency. It is intended to replace the ruble with a Ukrainian unit of currency, the *hryvna*, and as an interim measure coupons were issued as legal tender in Jan. 1992.

Banking and Finance. A National Bank was founded in March 1991.

ENERGY AND NATURAL RESOURCES

Electricity. During the first 5-year plan (1929–32) the Dnieper power-station was built; destroyed during the War, it was restored during the fourth plan (1946–50). Another large hydro-electric station at Kakhovka began operations during the fifth plan (1951–55). Power output was 295,000m. kwh. in 1989.

Oil and Gas. Oil and natural gas output was 5·4m. tonnes in 1988.

Minerals. Coal in the Donets field (25,900 sq. km stretching from Donetsk to Rostov), estimated to contain 60% of the bituminous and anthracite coal reserves of the USSR, yielded, in 1988, 192m. tonnes—about 25% of the USSR production. Large seams have been found near Novo-Moskovsk (Dnepropetrovsk region), Kharkov, Lugansk (beyond the Don) and on the left bank of the Dnieper.

The Ukraine also contains rich deposits of salt and various important chemicals.

In Northern Bukovina there are deposits of gypsum, oil, alabaster and brown coal.

Agriculture. The Ukraine contains some of the richest land in the former USSR. It raises wheat, buckwheat, beet, sunflower, cotton, flax, tobacco, soya, hops, the rubber plant kok-sagyz, fruit and vegetables, and in 1989 produced 23% by value of the USSR's total agricultural output. The area under cultivation was 27m. ha in 1939 before the new territories were added, and 48·6m. ha in 1990.

Output (in 1m. tonnes) in 1989: Grain, 51·2; sugar-beet, 51·9; vegetables, 7·4; sunflower seed, 2·9; potatoes, 19·3; meat and fats, 4·4; milk, 24·4; 17,393m. eggs.

On 1 Jan. 1990 there were 25·2m. cattle, 20m. pigs, 9m. sheep and goats. In 1949 silver-fox breeding farms were started.

On 1 Jan. 1987 there were 2,466 state farms and 7,452 collective farms.

Irrigation networks supplied 1·82m. ha of land; 2·2m. ha were drained.

Tractors numbered 431,300 at 1 Jan. 1989 and combine harvesters, 115,300.

INDUSTRY. Combining coal from the Donets field with the iron-ore from the mines in Krivoi Rog has made possible the development of a large ferrous metallurgical industry. Output of steel was 54·8m. tonnes in 1989, and of rolled ferrous metals 47·2m. tonnes. Manganese is obtained at Nikopol; output in 1987, 7·2m. tons. Output of finished rolled metal products, 40m. tonnes in 1988; of steel pipe, 7·11m.

There are chemical and machine-construction industries producing one-fifth of the total output of machinery and chemicals of the former USSR. Output in 1989: Paper, 353,000 tonnes; timber, 9·1m. cu. metres; cement, 23·4m. tonnes; sulphuric acid (1987), 4·2m. tonnes; caustic soda (1987), 489,000 tonnes; TV sets, 3·1m.; refrigerators, 753,000; washing machines, 533,000; vacuum cleaners, 904,000.

Output in 1988 of cardboard, 567,000 tonnes; of mineral fertilizers (recalculated base), 5·6m. tonnes.

Consumer goods and food industries are important. In 1989 consumer goods output was valued at 77,000m. rubles, 18% of the USSR total. Output in 1989 of fabrics, 1,250 sq. metres; knitwear, 354·7m. items; hosiery, 428·2m. pairs; footwear, 193·7m. pairs; butter, 441,000 tonnes; granulated sugar, 7m. tonnes; preserves, 4,891m. standard jars.

Labour. There were 20·3m. industrial and office workers in 1989.

COMMUNICATIONS

Roads. In 1990 there were 227,000 km of hard-surfaced motor roads.

Railways. Total length was 22,730 km in 1990.

Inland Waterways. 11,848 tonne-km of freight were carried in 1989.

Civil Aviation. The national carrier, Avialinie, operates with 17 ex-Polish Soviet-built aircraft. Airlines connect Kiev, Lvov, Chernovtsy and Odessa with Crimean and Caucasian spas, Kiev with Tbilisi, Odessa with Riga and Donetsk.

Newspapers (1989). Out of 1,763 newspapers, 1,241 were in Ukrainian. Daily circulation of Ukrainian-language newspapers, 15·9m., other languages, 8·2m.

JUSTICE, RELIGION, EDUCATION AND WELFARE

Religion. The main churches are the Orthodox and Roman Catholic. The Uniate (Greek Catholic) Church, which practises the Orthodox rite but acknowledges the Pope of Rome, was banned in 1946 but re-legalized in 1991. Its head, Myroslav Lubachivsky (b. 1914) was made a patriarch by the Roman Catholic Pope in April 1991. The hierarchy was restored by the Pope's confirmation of 10 bishops in Jan. 1991. There is also an Autocephalous Orthodox Church of Ukraine (*Patriarch*, Mstislav; b.1898). There are also some 70,000 Reformed Protestants in the Transcarpathian region and a Jewish community in Kiev. There are Roman Catholics in Western Ukraine.

Education. In 1989–90 the number of pupils in 21,700 primary and secondary schools was 7·1m.; 147 higher educational establishments had 888,800 students, and 738 technical colleges 776,600 students; 61% of eligible children were attending pre-school institutions.

An independent university, the reconstituted Mohyla Academy, opened in Kiev in Oct. 1991.

The Ukrainian Academy of Sciences was established in 1919; in 1989 it had 78 institutions with 17,256 scientific staff. There is an academy of building and architecture. Total scientific staff in all institutions was 219,300 in 1989.

Health. Doctors numbered 226,200 in 1989, and hospital beds, 694,800.

DIPLOMATIC REPRESENTATIVES

Of the Ukraine to the United Nations
Ambassador: Gennadi I. Udovenko.

Further Reading

Kubiojovyc, V. (ed.) *Encyclopedia of Ukraine,* 4 vols. Toronto, 1984ff
Magoci, P. R. and Matthews, G. J., *Ukraine: A Historical Atlas.* Univ. of Toronto Press, 1985
Marples, D., *Ukraine under Perestroika: Ecology, Economics and the Workers' Revolt.* London, 1991
Solchanyk, R., (ed.) *Ukraine: from Chernobyl to Sovereignty.* London, 1991
Subtelny, O., *Ukraine: A History.* Toronto, 1989

BELORUSSIA (WHITE RUSSIA)

Capital: Minsk
Population: 10·26m. (1990)

Respublika Belarus

HISTORY. The Belorussian Soviet Socialist Republic was set up on 1 Jan. 1919.

On 25 Aug. 1991, following the unsuccessful coup, the Supreme Soviet adopted a declaration of independence, and the republic was renamed the 'Republic of Belarus' in Sept. In Dec. it became a founder member of the CIS.

AREA AND POPULATION. Belorussia is situated along the Western Dvina and Dnieper. It is bounded in the west by Poland, north by Latvia and Lithuania, east by Russia and south by the Ukraine. The area is 207,600 sq. km (80,134 sq. miles). The capital is Minsk. Other important towns are Gomel, Vitebsk, Mogilev, Bobruisk, Grodno and Brest. On 2 Nov. 1939 western Belorussia was incorporated with an area of over 108,000 sq. km and a population of 4·8m. The population (Jan. 1990) was 10,259,000; the 1989 census population was 10,151,806, of whom 77·9% were Belorussians, 13·2% Russians, 4·12% Poles, 2·9% Ukrainians and 1·1% Jews.

Belorussia comprises the following regions: Brest, Gomel, Grodno, Mogilev, Minsk, Vitebsk.

CONSTITUTION AND GOVERNMENT. A new Constitution was adopted in April 1978. The Supreme Soviet elected on 4 March 1990 consists of 360 seats, 50 of which are filled by public organizations. In July 1990 it adopted a declaration of republican sovereignty by 230 votes to nil with 120 abstentions.

Chairman, Supreme Soviet: Stanislav Shushkevich (b. 1934; elected Sept. 1991).
Chairman, Council of Ministers: Vyacheslav Kebich.
Foreign Minister: A. E. Gurinovich. *Defence:* Petr Chaus.

National Flag: 3 horizontal stripes of white, red and white.

Local Government. Elections were held on 4 March 1990.

ECONOMY

Policy. Subsidies were removed and prices allowed to find their market level in Jan. 1992.

Budget. Budget estimates (in 1m. rubles), 1988, 8,893; 1989 (plan), 11,022.

ENERGY AND NATURAL RESOURCES

Electricity. Output was 38,500 kwh. in 1989.

Minerals. Particular attention has been paid to the development of the peat industry with a view to making Belorussia as far as possible self-supporting in fuel. In 1988 2·3m. tonnes of peat briquettes were produced. There are rich deposits of rock salt.

Agriculture. Belorussia is hilly, with a general slope towards the south. It contains large tracts of marsh land, particularly to the south-west, and valuable forest land wooded with oak, elm, maple and white beech. There are over 6,500 peat deposits.

Agriculturally, it may be divided into 3 main sections—Northern: Growing flax, fodder, grasses and breeding cattle for meat and dairy produce; Central: Potato growing and pig breeding; Southern: Good natural pasture land, hemp cultivation and cattle breeding for meat and dairy produce. The area under cultivation was 12·4m. ha in 1990. There were 7·2m. cattle, 5·2m. pigs and 0·5m. sheep and goats on 1 Jan. 1990.

Output of main agricultural products (in 1m. tonnes) in 1989: Grain, 7·4; meat, 1·2; milk, 7·4; eggs, 3,651m.; potatoes, 11·1; vegetables, 0·9; sugarbeet, 1·8.

On 1 Jan. 1987 there were 1,675 collective farms and 913 state farms. Since 1991 individuals may own land and pass it to their heirs, but not sell it. About 2·5m. ha of marsh land have been drained for agricultural use, 828,200 of these for crops. This reclaimed land is rich and yields good harvests of grain, fodder, potatoes, kok-sagyz and other crops. In Jan. 1989 there were 127,300 tractors and 34,300 grain combine harvesters.

INDUSTRY. There are food-processing, chemical, textile, artificial silk, flax-spinning, motor vehicle, leather, machine-tool and agricultural machinery industries.

In 1989 output was as follows: Rolled ferrous metals, 0·7m. tonnes; steel, 1·1m. tonnes; timber, 6·8m. cu.metres; paper, 203,000 tonnes; cement, 2·3m. tonnes; fabrics, 512m. sq. metres; knitwear, 154·2m. items; hosiery, 174·4m. pairs; footwear, 44·8m. pairs; butter, 158,000 tonnes; granulated sugar, 354,000 tonnes; preserves, 790m. jars.

Labour. The number of workers and office employees in 1989 was 4,311,000.

COMMUNICATIONS

Roads. In 1990 there were 92,200 km of motor roads (60,900 km hard-surfaced).

Railways. In 1990 there were 5,590 km of railways.

Inland Waterways. In 1990 2,084 tonne-km of freight was carried on inland waterways.

Newspapers (1989). Of 220 newspapers published 131 were in Belorussian. Daily circulation of Belorussian-language newspapers, 1·8m., other languages, 3·6m.

JUSTICE, RELIGION, EDUCATION AND WELFARE

Religion. There is a Roman Catholic archdiocese of Minsk and Mogilev, and 5 dioceses embracing 455 parishes.

Education. In 1989–90 there were 189,400 students in 33 places of higher education and 147,100 students in 145 technical colleges. There were (Jan. 1990) 44,100 scientific personnel in 178 institutions, and 639,100 specialists with a higher education employed in the national economy. The Belorussian Academy of Sciences controlled 32 learned institutions with 5,923 scientific staff. The number of children in 5,600 primary and secondary schools was 1·5m. in 1989–90. 73% of eligible children attended pre-school institutions in Jan. 1990.

Health. In 1989 there were 41,400 doctors and 138,300 hospital beds.

DIPLOMATIC REPRESENTATIVES

Of Belorussia to the United Nations
Ambassador: Gennadi N. Buravkin.

Further Reading

Belaruskaya Sovietskaya Entsyklapediya. Minsk, 1960–76
Lubachko, I. S., *Belorussia under Soviet Rule, 1917–57.* Lexington, 1972
Vakar, N. P., *Belorussia.* Harvard Univ. Press, 1956.—*A Bibliographical Guide to Belorussia.* Harvard Univ. Press, 1956

ARMENIA

Capital: Yerevan
Population: 3·29m. (1990)

Haikakan Hanrapetoutioun

(Republic of Armenia)

HISTORY. On 29 Nov. 1920 Armenia was proclaimed a Soviet Socialist Republic. The Armenian Soviet Government, with the Russian Soviet Government, was a party to the Treaty of Kars (March 1921), which confirmed the Turkish possession of the former Government of Kars and of the Surmali District of the Government of Yerevan. From 1922 to 1936 it formed part of the Transcaucasian Soviet Federal Socialist Republic. In 1936 Armenia was proclaimed a constituent republic of the USSR. In Dec. 1991 it became a member of the CIS.

AREA AND POPULATION. Armenia covers an area of 29,800 sq. km (11,490 sq. miles). It is bounded in the north by Georgia, in the east by Azerbaijan and in the south and west by Turkey and Iran. It is a very mountainous country with but little forest land, has many turbulent rivers and a highly fertile soil, but is subject to drought. In Jan. 1990 the population was 3,293,000. The 1989 census population was 3,304,776, of whom Armenians accounted for 93·3%, Azerbaijanis 2·6%, Kurds 1·7% and Russians, 1·6%. The capital is Yerevan. Other large towns are Kumairi (formerly Leninakan) (120,000) and Kirovakan (159,000).

CONSTITUTION AND GOVERNMENT. A new Constitution was adopted in April 1978. The Supreme Soviet has 259 seats. Elections took place on 20 May 1990. The Supreme Soviet adopted a declaration of sovereignty in Aug. 1990, voted to unite Armenia with Nagorno-Karabakh and renamed Armenia the 'Republic of Armenia'. A popular vote in Sept. 1991 resulted in a 99% majority support for a fully independent status.

At elections to the district, urban and rural Soviets (21 June 1987), of 27,776 deputies returned 13,758 (49·5%) were women, 15,681 (56·5%) non-Party and 19,149 (68·9%) industrial workers and collective farmers.

In Aug. 1990 the Supreme Soviet elected Levon Ter-Petrosyan (b. 1945; leader, Armenian National Movement) its Chairman by 140 votes to 80. On 16 Oct. 1991

Ter-Petrosyan was elected the republic's first President in a popular ballot by 83% of votes cast against 5 opponents. Turn-out was 73%.

The *Prime Minister*, elected in Nov. 1991, is G. G. Arutyunyan.

Defence: Vazgen Sarkisyan. *Foreign:* Raffi Hovannisyan.

National flag: 3 horizontal stripes of red, blue and orange.

ECONOMY

Budget. Budget estimates (in 1m. rubles), 1988, 2,243; 1989 (plan), 2,460.

ENERGY AND NATURAL RESOURCES

Electricity. Output of electricity in 1989 was 12,100m. kwh. A chain ('cascade') of 8 hydro-electric stations on the river Razdan, as it falls about 3,300 ft from the mountain lake Sevan to its junction with the Arax, has been completed.

Minerals. Armenia contains large deposits of copper, zinc, aluminium, molybdenum and other metals. It is also rich in marble, granite, cement and other building materials. The mining of these minerals is becoming more and more important.

Agriculture. The chief agricultural area is the valley of the Arax and the area round Yerevan. Here there are considerable cotton plantations as well as orchards and vineyards. Sub-tropical plants, such as almonds and figs, are also grown. Olive groves and pomegranate plantations occupy large areas; experiments are being made to naturalize cork oak. In the mountainous areas the chief pursuit is livestock raising. Land under cultivation in Nov. 1986, 2·3m. ha.

Output of main agricultural products (in 1,000 tonnes) in 1989: Grain, 200; potatoes, 266; vegetables, 485; sugar-beet, 117; fruit, 170; grapes, 119; meat, 105; milk, 491; eggs, 561m.; wool, 3·3.

Area of irrigated land in 1982 was 284,000 ha.

There were, on 1 Jan. 1987, 280 collective farms, and these together with the 513 state farms tilled 99·9% of the total cultivated area. Livestock in Jan. 1990 included 0·7m. cattle, 0·3m. pigs and 1·3m. sheep and goats. There were 13,400 tractors and 1,900 grain and cotton combines in Jan. 1989.

INDUSTRY. Among the chief industries are the chemical, producing chiefly synthetic rubber and fertilizers, and the extraction and processing of building materials such as cement, pumice-stone, tuffs, marble, volcanic basalt and fire-proof clay, ginning- and textile-mills, carpet weaving, food, including wine-making, fruit, meat-canning and creameries. Machine-tool and electrical engineering works have also been established. Among the industrial centres are Yerevan, Kumairi, Alaverdi, Kafan, Kirovakan, Daval, Megri and Oktemberyan.

In 1989 output included 3,300 tonnes of steel, 6,000 cu. metres of timber, 11,000 tonnes of paper, 1·6m. tonnes of cement, 63·4m. sq. metres of fabrics, 90·7m. items of knitwear, 48·6m. pairs of hosiery, 17·9m. pairs of footwear, 700 tonnes of butter, 8,000 tonnes of vegetable oil and 413m. standard jars of preserves.

Labour. There were 1,304,000 employees in the state sector in 1989.

COMMUNICATIONS

Roads. There were 10,200 km (9,500 km with hard surface) of motor roads in 1990.

Railways. Total length was 820 km in 1990.

Newspapers (1989). Out of 85 newspapers 79 appeared in Armenian. Daily circulation of Armenian-language newspapers, 1·5m.; other languages, 103,000.

JUSTICE, RELIGION, EDUCATION AND WELFARE

Religion. The Christian church of Armenia has a Catholicos (patriarch) whose seat is at Etchmiadzin, and who is head of all the Armenian (Gregorian) communities throughout the world. There is an Armenian Orthodox Academy and a seminary.

Education. In 1989–90 there were 600,000 pupils in 1,400 primary and secondary schools; 69 technical colleges with 46,900 students; 13 higher educational institutions with 65,300 students (including correspondence students). Yerevan houses the Armenian Academy of Sciences, 43 scientific institutes, a medical institute and other technical colleges, and a state university. In Jan. 1989, 33 learned institutions with 3,330 scientific staff were under the Academy of Sciences; scientific workers in 101 institutions totalled 21,800.

In Jan. 1990, 35% of eligible children attended pre-school institutions.

Health. In 1989 there were 14,200 doctors and 29,900 hospital beds.

Further Reading

Kurkjian, V., *A History of Armenia*. New York, 1958
Lang, D.M., *Armenia: Cradle of Civilization*. London, 1978.—*The Armenians. A People in Exile*. London, 1981
Walker, C. J., *Armenia*. 2nd ed. London, 1990

AZERBAIJAN

Capital: Baku
Population: 7·13m. (1990)

Azarbaijchan Respublikasy

HISTORY. The 'Mussavat' (Nationalist) party, which dominated the National Council or Constituent Assembly of the Tatars, declared the independence of Azerbaijan on 28 May 1918, with a capital, first at Ganja (Elizavetpol) and later at Baku. On 28 April 1920 Azerbaijan was proclaimed a Soviet Socialist Republic. From 1922, with Georgia and Armenia it formed the Transcaucasian Soviet Federal Socialist Republic. In 1936 it assumed the status of one of the Union Republics of the USSR. In 1990 it adopted a declaration of republican sovereignty, and in Aug. 1991 declared itself formally independent; this was approved by 99·6% of votes at a referendum of Jan. 1992. It joined the CIS in Dec. 1991.

AREA AND POPULATION. Azerbaijan covers an area of 86,600 sq. km (33,430 sq. miles) and has a population (Jan. 1990) of 7,131,000. Its capital is Baku. Other important towns are Ganja (formerly Kirovabad) and Sumgait.

Azerbaijan includes the Nakhichevan Autonomous Republic and the largely Armenian-inhabited Nagorno-Karabakh Autonomous Region, which was declared abolished in 1991. Situated in the eastern area of Transcaucasia, it is bounded in the west by Armenia, in the north by Georgia and the Russian Federation (Dagestan), in the east by the Caspian sea and in the south by Iran. Its climate is inclined to drought.

The 1989 census population was 7,021,178, of whom 82·7% were Azerbaijanis, 5·6% Russians, 5·6% Armenians and 2·4% Lezgins.

CONSTITUTION AND GOVERNMENT. Elections were held to the 350 seats in the Supreme Soviet in Sept. 1990. A new Constitution was adopted in April 1978. At presidential elections held on 8 Sept. 1991, 83·7% of votes cast were for Ayaz Mutalibov, but following public demonstrations he resigned on 6 March 1992.

President: Vacant.

Chairman, Council of Ministers (Prime Minister): Hasan Hasanov.

Deputy Prime Minister and Governor of Nagorno-Karabakh: Mamedov Salam Musa-ogly. *Foreign:* Hussain Sadykhov.

National flag: 3 horizontal stripes of blue, red and green, with a white crescent and 8-pointed star in the centre of the red stripe.

ECONOMY

Budget. (in 1m. rubles). Budget estimates, 1988, 3,361; 1989 (plan), 3,808.

ENERGY AND NATURAL RESOURCES

Electricity. Output was 23,300m. kwh. in 1989.

Oil. The most important industry is the oil industry, especially in the Baku region. The largest producing area lies along the western shore of the Caspian Sea, north and south of Baku, where the largest refineries are located. Other wells lie west of Baku, and some have been drilled in the Caspian itself, off the Apsheron Peninsula. Baku is connected by a double pipeline with Batum on the Black Sea. All the oil-fields have been electrified and are connected with Baku.

Minerals. The republic is rich in natural resources: Iron, aluminium, copper, lead, zinc, precious metals, sulphur pyrites, limestone and salt.

Agriculture. The chief agricultural products are grain, cotton, rice, grapes, fruit, vegetables, tobacco and silk. The Mexican rubber plant *grayule* has been acclimatized. A new kind of high-yielding winter wheat has been produced for use in mountainous parts of the republic. Area under cultivation, 6·7m. ha.

Livestock on 1 Jan. 1990: Cattle, 1·9m.; pigs, 0·2m.; sheep and goats, 5·5m.

Output of main agricultural products (in 1m. tonnes) in 1989: Grain, 0·8; cotton, 0·6; grapes, 1·1; vegetables, 0·9; potatoes, 0·2; tea, 0·03; meat, 0·2; milk, 1·1; eggs, 1,056m.; wool, 10,400 tonnes.

Azerbaijan has become an important cotton-growing and sub-tropical base. About 70% of cultivated land is irrigated. On the irrigated land crops of Egyptian and Sea-Island cotton are obtained. Here, too, rice and lucerne are cultivated, and in the mountain valleys there are also orchards, vineyards and silk cultures.

In the south along the coast of the Caspian, where the climate is more moist, there are tea plantations, and citrus fruits and other sub-tropical plants are grown.

There were on 1 Jan. 1989, 608 collective farms, 808 state farms, 39,300 tractors and 4,600 grain combine harvesters.

INDUSTRY. Iron and steel and aluminium works have been built at Sumgait.

Azerbaijan has also copper, chemical, cement and building material, food, timber, salt, textiles and fishing industries. In 1989, 0·82m. tonnes of steel were produced, 0·7m. tonnes of rolled ferrous metals, 4,000 cu. metres of timber, 1·1m. tonnes of cement, 170m. square metres of fabrics, 41·8m. items of knitwear, 43m. pairs of hosiery, 17·1m. pairs of leather footwear, 5,000 tonnes of butter and 729m. standard jars of conserves.

Ganja, Nukha, Stepanakert, Nakhichevan and Lenkoran are also important industrial centres.

Synthetic rubber works (Sumgait), tyre works and a worsted combine (Baku) and a large textile combine (Mingechaur) have been built.

Labour. The number of workers and office employees in 1989 was 2,058,000.

COMMUNICATIONS

Roads. There were 30,400 km of motor roads (28,600 km hard-surfaced) in 1990.

Railways. Total length was 2,040 km in 1990.

Civil Aviation. There is an international airport at Baku. The national carrier is Azerbaijani Airlines.

Newspapers (1989). There were 158 newspapers, 133 in the Azerbaijani language (circulation 3·3m.), other languages, (circulation 469,000).

JUSTICE, RELIGION, EDUCATION AND WELFARE

Religion. The population is predominantly Shia Moslem.

Education. In 1989–90 there were 1·4m. pupils in 4,300 primary and secondary schools and 21% of eligible children attended pre-school institutions. There were 78 technical colleges with 61,200 students, 16 higher educational institutions, including a state university at Baku, with 99,700 students (including correspondence students). The Azerbaijan Academy of Sciences, founded in 1945, has 30 research institutions with 4,296 research workers. There were 22,700 research workers in the republic as a whole in Jan. 1989.

Health. In 1989 there were 27,800 doctors and 71,100 hospital beds.

NAKHICHEVAN AUTONOMOUS REPUBLIC

Area, 5,500 sq. km (2,120 sq. miles), population (Jan. 1990), 300,000. Capital, Nakhichevan (37,000). This territory, on the borders of Turkey and Iran, forms part of Azerbaijan although separated from it by the territory of Armenia. Its population, mainly Azerbaijanis, had a chequered history for 1,500 years under the ancient Persians, Arabs, Seljuk Turks, Mongols, Ottoman Turks and modern Persians before being annexed by Russia in 1828. On 9 Feb. 1924 it was constituted as an Autonomous Republic within Azerbaijan. Its Supreme Soviet, elected 24 Feb. 1985, has 110 members including 52 women.

The republic has silk, clothing, cotton, canning, meat-packing and other factories. Nearly 70% of the people are engaged in agriculture, of which the main branches are cotton and tobacco growing. Fruit and grapes are also produced in increasing quantity. There are 35 collective and 37 state farms. Crop area 37,400 ha.

In 1984–85 there were 219 primary and secondary schools with 66,000 pupils, and 2,100 were studying in higher educational institutions.

In Jan. 1983 there were 599 doctors and 2,500 hospital beds.

NAGORNO-KARABAKH AUTONOMOUS REGION

Area, 4,400 sq. km (1,700 sq. miles); population (Jan. 1990), 192,000. Capital, Stepanakert (33,000). Populated by Armenians (75·9%) and Azerbaijanis (23%), a separate khanate in the 18th century, it was established on 7 July 1923 as an Autonomous Region within Azerbaijan.

Main industries are silk, wine, dairying and building materials. Crop area is 67,200 ha; cotton, grapes and winter wheat are grown. There are 33 collective and 38 state farms.

In 1984–85 34,000 pupils were studying in primary and secondary schools, 2,400 in colleges and 2,100 in higher educational institutions. In Jan. 1983 there were 523 doctors and 1,800 hospital beds.

Following extensive public demonstrations in Armenia and Azerbaijan as well as Nagorno-Karabakh itself, the area was placed under a 'special form of administration' subordinate to the USSR government in 1989. In Sept. 1991 the regional Soviet and the Shaumyan district Soviet jointly declared a Nagorno-Karabakh republic, which declared itself independent with a 99·9% popular vote in Dec. 1991. The autonomous status of the region was meanwhile abolished by the Azerbaijan Supreme Soviet in Nov. 1991, and the capital renamed Khankendi. A presidential decree of Jan. 1992 placed the region under direct rule. Azeri-Armenian fighting for possession of the region continued into 1992.

Further Reading

Baddeley, J. F., *The Rugged Flanks of Caucasus*. 2 vols. Oxford, 1941

MOLDAVIA

Capital: Kishinev
Population: 4·36m. (1990)

Republica Moldovenească

HISTORY. The Moldavian Soviet Socialist Republic (in 1990 renamed Moldova), capital Kishinev, was formed by the union of part of the former Moldavian Autonomous Soviet Socialist Republic (organized 12 Oct. 1924), formerly included in the Ukrainian Soviet Socialist Republic, and the areas of Bessarabia (ceded by Romania to the USSR, 28 June 1940) with a mainly Moldavian population. As from 2 Aug. 1940 the MSSR included the following regions of the former Moldavian Autonomous Soviet Socialist Republic: Grigoriopol, Dubossarsk, Kamensk, Rybnits, Slobodzeisk and Tiraspol, and the following districts of Bessarabia: Beltsk, Bendery, Kagulsk, Kishinev, Orgeev and Sorok. The republic, however, is divided not into regions but into 36 rural districts, 21 towns and 45 urban settlements.

In Dec. 1991 it became a member of the CIS.

AREA AND POPULATION. Moldavia is bounded in the east and south by the Ukraine and on the west by Romania. The area is 33,700 sq. km (13,000 sq. miles). In Jan. 1990 the population was 4,362,000. The 1989 census population was 4,335,360, of whom Moldavians accounted for 64·5%., Ukrainians 13·9%, Russians 13%, Gagauzi 3·5%, Bulgarians 2% and Jews 1·5%. Apart from Kishinev, larger towns are Tiraspol (182,000), Beltsy (159,000) and Bendery (130,000). The Moldavian language (i.e., Romanian) was written in Cyrillic prior to the restoration of the Roman alphabet in 1989.

CONSTITUTION AND GOVERNMENT. A new Constitution was adopted in April 1978. Elections to the 380 seats in the Supreme Soviet were held on 25 Feb. 1990. A declaration of republican sovereignty was adopted in June 1990 and in Aug. 1991 the republic declared itself independent.

In Dec. 1991 Mircea Snegur (the only candidate) was elected president with 98·2% of votes cast.

President of the Republic: Mircea Snegur.
Chairman of the Supreme Soviet: A. Moseanu
Chairman, Council of Ministers: Tudor Muravschi.

National flag: 3 vertical stripes of blue, yellow and red, with the national arms in the centre.

Local Government. Elections to the district, urban and rural Soviets were held on 25 Feb. 1990.

ECONOMY

Budget. Budget estimates (in 1m. rubles), 1988, 3,000; 1989 (plan), 3,396.

Currency. It is planned to issue a national unit of currency, the *leu*, in 1992.

Agriculture. On 1 Jan. 1989 there were 368 collective farms and 473 state farms. All ploughing and sowing is mechanized. Livestock included (1 Jan. 1990) 1·1m. cattle, 2m. pigs and 1·3m. sheep and goats. There were 50,300 tractors and 4,700 combine harvesters in Jan. 1989. Land under cultivation (Nov. 1990) 2·9m. ha.

Output of main agricultural products (in 1,000 tonnes) in 1989: Grain, 3,300; sugar-beet, 3,612; vegetables, 1,203; fruit, 1,176; grapes, 1,037; meat, 356; milk, 1,548; eggs, 1,154m.

Moldavia has an equable climate and very fertile soil. It contained nearly one quarter of the vineyards of the former USSR.

Fisheries. The south is rich in fish: Sturgeon, mackerel and brill.

INDUSTRY. There are canning plants, wine-making plants, woodworking and metallurgical factories, a factory of ferro-concrete building materials, and footwear and textile plants. Production in 1989 included 685,000 tonnes of steel, 0·7m. tonnes of rolled ferrous metals, 63,000 cu. metres of timber, 2·3m. tonnes of cement, 224m. sq. metres of fabrics, 23·2m. pairs footwear, 67·9m. items knitwear, 41·1m. pairs of hosiery, 29,000 tonnes of butter, 446,000 tonnes of granulated sugar and 1,748m. standard jars of preserves. Food industries include processing of dairy produce. Electricity generated (1989) 17,000m. kwh.

There are lignite, phosphorites, gypsum and valuable building materials.

In 1989 there were 1,491,000 employees in the state sector.

COMMUNICATIONS

Roads. There were 20,100 km of motor roads (14,000 km with hard surface) in 1990.

Railways. Total length in 1990 was 1,150 km.

Inland Waterways. 260 tonne-km of freight were carried in 1990.

Newspapers (1989). There were 200 newspapers, 85 in Moldavian. Daily circulation of Moldavian-language newspapers, 1,143,000; other languages, 1,261,000.

JUSTICE, RELIGION, EDUCATION AND WELFARE

Education. In 1989–90 there were 700,000 pupils in 1,600 primary, secondary and special schools, 52,100 students in 51 technical colleges and 55,500 students in 9 higher educational institutions including the state university. A Moldavian Academy of Sciences was established in 1961; it had 17 research institutions and a scientific staff of 1,264 in Jan. 1989. In all, there are 68 learned institutions with 10,200 scientific staff. In Jan. 1990, 73% of eligible children attended pre-school institutions.

Health. In 1989 there were 17,500 doctors and 55,300 hospital beds.

Further Reading

Zlatova, Y. and Kotelnikov, V., *Across Moldavia* (English ed.). Moscow, 1959
Istoriya Moldavskoi SSR. 2nd ed. 2 vols. Kishinev, 1965–68

CENTRAL ASIA

Soviet Central Asia (a geographical term) embraced Kazakhstan, Uzbekistan, Turkmenistan, Tajikistan and Kirghizia.

Turkestan (by which name part of this territory was then known) was conquered by the Russians in the 1860s. In 1866 Tashkent was occupied and in 1868 Samarkand, and subsequently further territory was conquered and united with Russian Turkestan. In the 1870s Bokhara was subjugated, the emir, by the agreement of 1873, recognizing the suzerainty of Russia. In the same year Khiva became a vassal state to Russia. Until 1917 Russian Central Asia was divided politically into the Khanate of Khiva, the Emirate of Bokhara and the Governor-Generalship of Turkestan.

In the summer of 1919 the authority of the Soviet Government became definitely established in these regions. The Khan of Khiva was deposed in Feb. 1920, and a People's Soviet Republic was set up, the medieval name of Khorezm being revived. In Aug. 1920 the Emir of Bokhara was deposed, and a similar regime was set up in Bokhara. The former Governor-Generalship of Turkestan was constituted an Autonomous Soviet Socialist Republic within the RSFSR on 11 April 1921.

In the autumn of 1924 the Soviets of the Turkestan, Bokhara and Khiva Republics decided to redistribute the territories of these republics on a nationality basis; at the same time Bokhara and Khiva became Socialist Republics. The redistribution was completed in May 1925, when the new states of Uzbekistan, Turkmenistan and

Tajikistan were accepted into the USSR as Union Republics. The remaining districts of Turkestan populated by Kazakhs were united with Kazakhstan which was established as an ASSR in 1925 and became a Union Republic in 1936. Kirghizia, until then part of the RSFSR, was established as a Union Republic in 1936.

Further Reading

Akiner, S., *The Islamic Peoples of the Soviet Union*. Rev. ed. London, 1986
Bennigsen, A. and Broxup, M., *The Islamic Threat to the Soviet State*. London, 1983
Nove, A. and Newth, J. A., *The Soviet Middle East*. London, 1967
Rwykin, M., *Moscow's Muslim Challenge*. New York, 1982
Wheeler, G., *The Modern History of Soviet Central Asia*. London, 1964.—*The Peoples of Soviet Central Asia*. London, 1966

KAZAKHSTAN

Capital: Alma-Ata
Population: 16·69m. (1990)

Kazak Respublikasy

HISTORY. On 26 Aug. 1920 Uralsk, Turgai, Akmolinsk and Semipalatinsk provinces formed the Kirgiz (in 1925 renamed Kazakh) Autonomous Soviet Socialist Republic within the RSFSR. It was made a constituent republic of the USSR on 5 Dec. 1936. To this republic were added the parts of the former Governorship of Turkestan inhabited by a majority of Kazakhs. It consists of the following regions: Aktyubinsk, Alma-Ata, Chimkent, Dzhambul, Dzhezkazgan, East Kazakhstan, Guryev, Karaganda, Kokchetav, Kustanai, Kzyl-Orda, Mangyshlak, North Kazakhstan, Pavlodar, Semipalatinsk, Taldy-Kurgan, Tselinograd, Turgai, Uralsk.

It became a member of the CIS in Dec. 1991.

AREA AND POPULATION. Kazakhstan is bounded in the west by the Caspian Sea and Russia, in the north by Russia, in the east by China and in the south by Uzbekistan and Kirghizia. The area of the republic is 2,717,300 sq. km (1,049,155 sq. miles). Population (Jan. 1990) 16,691,000, of whom 57% live in urban areas. The 1989 census population was 16,464,464, of whom Kazakhs accounted for 39·7%, Russians 37·8%, Germans 5·8%, Ukrainians 5·4%, Uzbeks and Tatars 2% each. The republic's ethnic composition reflects its industrialization since 1941 and the opening of virgin lands since 1945. The population includes over 100 nationalities.

The capital is Alma-Ata, formerly Verny (1,151,000); other large towns are Karaganda, Semipalatinsk, Chimkent and Petropavlovsk. In all there are 82 towns, 197 urban settlements and 221 rural districts.

CONSTITUTION AND GOVERNMENT. The Supreme Soviet elected in 1985 consisted of 510 deputies. New elections were held on 25 March 1990. A declaration of state sovereignty was adopted in Oct. 1990, and a declaration of independence on 16 Dec. 1991.

At the presidential elections of 2 Dec. 1991 Nursultan Nazarbaev (the sole candidate) was elected with 99% of votes cast. Turn-out was 88%.

President: Nursultan Nazarbaev (b. 1940).
Chairman, Supreme Soviet: S. Abdildin.
Chairman, Council of Ministers (i.e. Prime Minister): S. Tereshchenko.

Local Government. Elections were held in Dec. 1989. Local government was directly subordinated to the President in Jan. 1992.

ECONOMY

Budget. The budget (in 1m. rubles) balanced as follows: 1988, 12,697; 1989 (plan), 14,254.

ENERGY AND NATURAL RESOURCES

Electricity. Output in 1989 was 89,700m. kwh.

Mining. Kazakhstan is extremely rich in mineral resources. Coal and tungsten in Karaganda (in the centre), oil along the river Emba (in the west), copper, lead and zinc—Kazakhstan contains about one-half of the total deposits of these three metals contained in the former USSR—Iceland spar (in the south), nickel and chromium in the Kustanai and Semipalatinsk regions, molybdenum and other minerals.

In 1943 big deposits of manganese were found in Eastern Kazakhstan; coal seams were also discovered there. In South Kazakhstan copper and bauxite deposits have been found.

Agriculture. Kazakh agriculture has changed from primarily nomad cattle breeding to production of grain, cotton and other industrial crops. In Nov. 1990 221m. ha were under cultivation—over 20% of the total cultivated area of the former USSR. 2,047,000 ha of land have an irrigation network.

The 'Ukrainka' winter wheat has been transformed into a spring wheat suitable for cultivation in Kazakhstan. Tobacco, rubber plants and mustard are also cultivated. Kazakhstan has rich orchards and vineyards, which accounted for 95,000 ha of cultivated land in 1985. Between 1954 and 1959, over 23m. ha of virgin and long fallow land were opened up, 544 new state grain farms being organized for the purpose. State purchases of grain were 5·9m. in 1989.

Kazakhstan is noted for its livestock, particularly its sheep, from which excellent quality wool is obtained. Livestock on 1 Jan. 1990 included 9·8m. cattle, 36·2m. sheep and goats and 3·3m. pigs.

There were, on 1 Jan. 1988, 388 collective farms and 2,140 state farms with 222,300 tractors and 100,900 grain combine harvesters. There were 5,293 rural power stations of 307,800 kwh. capacity.

Output of main agricultural products (in 1m. tonnes) in 1989: Grain, 18·8; sugar-beet, 1·2; potatoes, 1·8; vegetables, 1·3; fruit, 0·1; grapes, 48,000 tonnes; meat, 1·6; milk, 5·6; eggs, 4,253m.; wool, 0·1.

INDUSTRY. Coal, oil, non-ferrous metallurgy, heavy engineering and chemical industries brought Kazakhstan to the third place among the industrial republics of the former USSR. Production (1m. tonnes) in 1989 included steel, 6·8; rolled ferrous metals, 5·1; timber, 1·9m. cu. metres; paper, 3,000 tonnes; cement, 8·7; fabrics, 330m. sq. metres; knitwear, 122·9m. items; hosiery, 82·6m. pairs; footwear, 35·2m. pairs; butter, 83,000 tonnes; granulated sugar, 377,000 tonnes; preserves, 448m. standard jars. The Leninogorsk and Chimkent lead plants, the Balkhash, Irtysh and Karaskpai copper-smelting works and others supply the country with non-ferrous metals. A meat-packing plant has been built in Semipalatinsk, a fish cannery in Guryev, a chemical plant in Aktyubinsk, a tractor works at Pavlodar, and a superphosphate plant in Dzhambul. The oil industry in Emba and Aktyubinsk yields high-quality aviation oil.

Among enterprises are a large textile combine at Kustanai, hosiery factories at Djezkazgan, Leninogorsk and Aktyubinsk, a sugar factory at Aksu, meat canneries at Djetygar and Kzyl-Orda.

Labour. There were, in 1989, 6,501,000 employees in the state sector.

COMMUNICATIONS

Roads. In Jan. 1990 there were 164,900 km of motor roads (99,000 km hard surface).

Railways. In Jan. 1990 the total length of railways in operation was 14,460 km. Over 600 km of narrow-gauge line and 700 km of broad-gauge line were built in the virgin lands area in 1951-57.

Inland Waterways. In 1989, 3,857m. tonne-km of freight was carried on inland waterways.

Newspapers (1989). Of 443 newspapers, 160 were in the Kazakh language. Daily circulation of Kazakh-language newspapers, 2m.; other languages, 4·6m.

JUSTICE, RELIGION, EDUCATION AND WELFARE

Religion. There were some 170 mosques in 1991. An Islamic Institute opened in 1991 to train imams. A Roman Catholic diocese was established in 1991.

Education. In 1989–90 there were 3·2m. pupils at 8,600 elementary and secondary schools; 244 technical colleges with 255,400 students, 55 higher educational institutions with 285,600 students, and 207 research institutes with 41,300 scientific personnel. The Kazakh Academy of Sciences, founded in 1945, had, in 1989, 31 institutions, the scientific staff of which numbered 4,465. There were 41,400 scientific workers in 1989. 52% of eligible children were attending pre-school institutions in Jan. 1990.

Health. In 1989 there were 68,000 doctors and 225,400 hospital beds.

Further Reading

Istoriya Kazakhskoi SSR. 2 vols. Alma-Ata, 1957–59
Olcott, M. B., *The Kazakhs.* Stanford, 1987

KIRGHIZIA

Kyrgyz Respublikasy

Capital: Bishkek
Population: 4·37m. (1990)

HISTORY. After the establishment of the Soviet regime in Russia, Kirghizia became part of Soviet Turkestan, which itself became an Autonomous Soviet Socialist Republic within the RSFSR in April 1921. In 1924, when Central Asia was reorganized territorially on a national basis, Kirghizia was separated from Turkestan and formed into an autonomous region within the RSFSR. On 1 Feb. 1926 the Government of the RSFSR transformed Kirghizia into an Autonomous Soviet Socialist Republic within the RSFSR, and finally in Dec. 1936 Kirghizia was proclaimed one of the constituent Soviet Socialist Republics of the USSR. The republic adopted a declaration of sovereignty in 1990 and then in Sept. 1991 it declared itself an independent, sovereign and democratic state.

It became a member of the CIS in Dec. 1991.

AREA AND POPULATION. The territory of Kirghizia covers 198,500 sq. km (76,640 sq. miles), and its population in Jan. 1990 was 4,367,000. The republic comprises 6 regions: Djalal-Abad, Issyk-Kul, Naryn, Osh, Talas and Chu. There are 18 towns, 31 urban settlements and 40 rural districts. Its capital is Bishkek (formerly Frunze). Other large towns are Osh (213,000), Przhevalsk (56,000), Kyzyl-Kiya and Tokmak.

Kirghizia is situated on the Tien-Shan mountains and bordered on the east by China, on the west by Kazakhstan and Uzbekistan, on the north by Kazakhstan and in the south by Tajikistan. The Kirghiz are of Turkic origin and form 52·4% (of the 1989 census population of 4,257,755; the rest include Russians (21·5%), Uzbeks (12·9%), Ukrainians (2·5%), Germans, (2·4%) and Tatars (1·6%).

CONSTITUTION AND GOVERNMENT. The Supreme Soviet elected in 1985 consisted of 350 deputies. New elections were held on 25 Feb. 1990. A new Constitution was adopted in April 1978.

In Oct. 1991 Askar Akaev was elected President with 95% of votes cast.

President of the Republic: Askar Akaev.
Chairman, Council of Ministers: T. Chyngyshev.
Foreign Minister: Murat Imanaliev.
Local Government. Elections were held on 25 Feb. 1990.

ECONOMY

Budget. Budget estimates (in 1m. rubles), 1988, 2,388; 1989 (plan), 2,692.

ENERGY AND NATURAL RESOURCES

Electricity. Output was 15,100m. kwh. in 1989.

Agriculture. Kirghizia is famed for its livestock breeding. On 1 Jan. 1990 there were 1·2m. cattle, 411,000 pigs, 10·5m. sheep and goats. Yaks are bred as meat and dairy cattle, and graze on high altitudes unsuitable for other cattle. Crossed with domestic cattle, hybrids are produced much heavier than ordinary Kirghiz cattle and giving twice the yield of milk. The Kirghizian horse is famed for its endurance, but it is of small stature; it has in recent years been crossed with Don, Arab and other breeds.

On 1 Jan. 1986 there were 176 collective and 290 state farms. Area under cultivation (Nov. 1990), 16·1m. ha. There were 28,000 tractors and 4,200 grain combine harvesters in 1989.

Kirghizia raises wheat sufficient for its own use and other grains and fodder, particularly lucerne; also sugar-beet, hemp, kenaf, kendyr, tobacco, medicinal plants and rice. Sericulture, fruit, grapes and vegetables and bee-keeping are major branches of Kirghiz agriculture. Agriculture is highly mechanized; nearly all the area under crops is worked by tractors. In 1983 irrigation networks in collective and state farms covered 974,000 ha; practically all were in use. A canal in the western Tien-Shan ranges and a reservoir in the Urto-Tokoi mountains are being constructed.

Output of main agricultural products (in 1,000 tonnes) in 1989: Grain, 1,600; cotton, 74; potatoes, 324; vegetables, 585; fruit, 82; grapes, 33; meat, 241; milk, 1,202; eggs, 704m.; wool, 38·6.

INDUSTRY. Kirghizia contains over 500 large modern industrial enterprises including sugar refineries, tanneries, cotton and wool-cleansing works, flour-mills, a tobacco factory, food, timber, textile, engineering, metallurgical, oil and mining enterprises.

Production in 1989 included steel, 3,200 tonnes; timber, 7,000 cu. metres; cement, 1·4m. tonnes; fabrics, 150m. sq. metres; knitwear, 20·5m. items; hosiery, 32·9m. pairs; footwear, 11·9m. pairs; butter, 14,000 tonnes; granulated sugar, 415,000 tonnes; preserves, 161m. standard jars.

Hydro-electric power stations are being built in the Central Tien-Shans and the cotton-growing districts in the Osh Region, the Chui valley and on the shore of Lake Issyk-Kul.

Labour. There were, in 1989, 1,249,000 employees in the state sector.

COMMUNICATIONS

Roads. Most of the traffic is by road; there were 28,400 km of motor roads (22,400 km hard surface) in 1990. A road tunnel through the Tien-Shan mountains at an altitude of 9,600 ft, connecting Bishkek and Osh, is being constructed.

Railways. In the north a railway runs from Lugovaya through Bishkek to Rybachi on Lake Issyk-Kul. Towns in the southern valleys are linked by short lines with the Ursatyevskaya–Andizhan railway in Uzbekistan. Total length of railway (Jan. 1990) is 370 km.

Civil Aviation. Airlines link Bishkek with Moscow and Tashkent.

Inland Waterways. Total length was 600 km in 1990.

Newspapers (1989). Of 122 newspapers with a daily 1·6m. circulation, 41 with 819,000 circulation are in the Kirghiz language.

JUSTICE, RELIGION, EDUCATION AND WELFARE

Education. Kirghizia had 1,800 primary and secondary schools with 900,000 pupils in 1989–90; 31% of eligible children were attending pre-school institutions. There were also 9 higher educational institutions with 59,300 students, 48 technical and teachers' training colleges with 46,000 students, as well as music and art schools. The Kirghiz Academy of Sciences was established in 1954. In 1989 there were 18 research institutes, with 1,560 scientific staff, operating under its auspices; altogether there were 10,100 scientific staff in 1989. A university was opened in 1951. In 1940 a new alphabet, based on Cyrillic, was introduced.

Health. In 1989 there were 15,800 doctors and 51,700 hospital beds.

Further Reading

Istoriya Kirgizskoi SSR. 5 vols. Frunze, 1984 ff.

TAJIKISTAN

Capital: Dushanbe
Population: 5·25m. (1990)

Respublika i Tojikiston

HISTORY. The Tajik Soviet Socialist Republic was formed from those regions of Bokhara and Turkestan where the population consisted mainly of Tajiks. It was admitted as a constituent republic of the Soviet Union on 5 Dec. 1929. In Aug. 1990 the Tajik Supreme Soviet adopted a declaration of republican sovereignty, and in Dec. 1991 the republic became a member of the CIS.

AREA AND POPULATION. Tajikistan is situated between 39° 40' and 36° 40' N. lat. and 67° 20' and 75° E. long., north of the Oxus (Amu-Darya). On the west and north it is bordered by Uzbekistan and Kirghizia; on the east by Chinese Turkestan and on the south by Afghanistan. It includes three regions (Khudzand, Kurgan-Tyube and Kulyab) and 43 rural districts, 18 towns and 49 urban settlements, together with the Gorno-Badakhshan Autonomous Region. Its highest mountains are 7,495 metres and 7,127 metres high. Even the lowest valleys in the Pamirs are not below 3,500 metres above sea-level. The huge mountain glaciers are the source of many rapid rivers—the tributaries of the Amu-Darya, which flows from east to west along the southern border. About 62·3% of the 1989 census population of 5,092,603 are Tajiks. They speak an Iranian language, akin to Persian, and they are considered to be the descendants of the original Aryan population of Turkestan. Of the rest, 23·5% are Uzbeks living in the north-west of the republic; Russians number 7·6% (1989 census).

The area of the territory is 143,100 sq. km (55,240 sq. miles). Population (Jan. 1990), 5,248,000. The capital is Dushanbe. Other large towns are Khudzand (formerly Leninabad), Kurgan-Tyube and Kulyab.

CONSTITUTION AND GOVERNMENT. A new Constitution was adopted in April 1978. Elections to the 230-member Supreme Soviet were held on 25 Feb. 1990. At elections in Nov. 1991 Rakhmon Nabiev was elected President with 56·9% of votes cast.

President: Rakhmon Nabiev.

Chairman of the Supreme Soviet: S. Kenzhaev.
Chairman, Council of Ministers: I. Kh. Khaeev.
Foreign Minister: Lakim Kaujumov.
Local and Regional Government. Elections to the district, urban and rural Soviets and the regional Soviet of Gorno-Badakhshan were held in Dec. 1989.

ECONOMY

Budget. Budget estimates (in 1m. rubles), 1988, 2,109; 1989 (plan), 2,375.

ENERGY AND NATURAL RESOURCES

Electricity. There are 80 big electrical stations. The hydro-electric Varzob station began to operate in 1954, that at Kairak-Kum on the Syr Darya River was completed in 1957 and 2 more at Murgab in 1964. Output in 1989 was 15,300m. kwh.

Minerals. There are rich deposits of brown coal, lead, zinc and oil (in the north of the republic), rare elements, such as uranium, radium, arsenic and bismuth. Asbestos, mica, corundum and emery, lapis lazuli, potassium salts, sulphur and other minerals have been found in other parts of the republic.

Agriculture. The occupations of the population are mainly farming, horticulture and cattle breeding. Area under cultivation in Nov. 1990 was 9·6m. ha. There are 43,000 km of irrigation canals; the irrigation networks cover about 634,000 ha of land.

Tajikistan grows many varieties of fruit, including apricots, figs, olives, pomegranates, a local variety of lemons and oranges, and in the south sugar-cane has been grown. Even on the highest mountain plateaux of the Pamirs, 'the roof of the world', the biological station of Tajikistan (3,860 metres above sea-level) has succeeded in raising crops of 60 varieties of barley, 10 varieties of oats, 4 of wheat, as well as vegetables. Eucalyptus and geranium are grown for the perfumery industry. Jute, rice and millet are also grown.

Tajikistan contains rich pasture lands, and cattle breeding is a very important branch of its agriculture. Livestock on 1 Jan. 1990: 1·4m. cattle, 3·4m. sheep and goats and 212,200 pigs.

The Gissar sheep is famous in the south for its meat and fat; the Karakul sheep is widely bred for its wool.

There were 157 collective farms and 299 state farms in 1989, with 34,100 tractors and 1,600 cotton and grain combine harvesters.

Output of main agricultural products (in 1,000 tonnes) in 1989: Grain, 381; cotton, 921; potatoes, 217; vegetables, 567; fruit, 193; grapes, 174; meat, 113; milk, 580; eggs, 619m.; wool, 5·6.

INDUSTRY. The original small-scale handicraft industries have been replaced by big industrial enterprises, including mining, engineering, food, textile, clothing and silk factories.

Industrial output in 1989 included 4,700 tonnes of steel, 187,000 cu. metres of sawn timber, 1·1m. tonnes of cement, 217m. sq. metres of fabrics, 16·2m. items of knitwear, 44·6m. pairs of hosiery, 10·8m. pairs of footwear, 6,000 tonnes of butter and 374m. standard jars of preserves.

Labour. In 1989 there were 1,161,000 employees in the state sector.

COMMUNICATIONS

Roads. In Jan. 1990 there were 28,500 km of motor roads. Of these, 17,700 km are hard surface, including the Osh–Khorog (700 km), Yasui–Bazar–Charm (107 km) and Dushanbe–Khorog in the Pamirs (557 km) roads.

Railways. A railway line between Termez and Dushanbe (258 km) connects the republic with the railway system of the USSR. The mountainous nature of the republic makes ordinary railway construction difficult; accordingly 345 km of narrow gauge railways have been constructed (Kurgan–Tyube–Piandzh and Dushanbe–

Kurgan–Tyube, connecting Dushanbe with the cotton-growing Vakhsh valley are particularly important). Length of railways, 1990, 480 km.

Civil Aviation. Dushanbe is connected by air with Moscow, Tashkent, Baku and the regional and district centres of the republic.

Shipping. A steamship line on the Amu-Darya runs between Termez, Sarava and Jilikulam on the river Vakhsh (200 km).

Newspapers (1989). There were 74 newspapers, 63 in Tajik. Daily circulation of Tajik-language newspapers, 1,208,000; in all languages, 1,598,000.

JUSTICE, RELIGION, EDUCATION AND WELFARE

Religion. The Tajiks are predominantly Sunni Moslems.

Education. In 1989–90 there were 3,100 primary and secondary schools with 1·3m. pupils, 10 higher educational institutions with 65,600 students and 42 technical colleges with 41,700 students; the Tajik State University had 12,467 students. In Jan. 1990, 16% of eligible children were attending pre-school institutions. In 1951 an Academy of Sciences was established; it has 16 institutions, the scientific staff of which numbers 1,499; there are 61 research institutions in all, with 9,100 scientific personnel in Jan. 1989. The Pamir research station is the highest altitude meteorological observatory in the world.

In 1940 a new alphabet based on Cyrillic was introduced.

Health. There are 325 hospitals as well as maternity homes, clinics and special institutes to combat tropical diseases. There were 14,900 doctors in 1989 and 54,900 hospital beds.

GORNO-BADAKHSHAN AUTONOMOUS REGION

Comprising the Pamir massif along the borders of Afghanistan and China, the region was set up on 2 Jan. 1925. Area, 63,700 sq. km (24,590 sq. miles); population (Jan. 1989), 161,000 (83% Tajiks, 11% Kirghiz). Capital, Khorog (14,800). The inhabitants are predominantly Ismaili Moslems.

Mining industries are developed (gold, rock-crystal, mica, coal, salt). Wheat, fruit and fodder crops are grown and cattle and sheep are bred in the western parts. In 1987 there were 74,700 cattle, 343,300 sheep and goats. Total area under cultivation, 18,400 ha.

In 1986 3,494 pupils completed secondary education.

Further Reading

Academy of Science of Tajikistan, *Istoriya Tadzhikskogo Naroda*. 3 vols. Moscow,   1963–65

TURKMENISTAN

Capital: Ashkhabad
Population: 3·62m. (1990)

Turkmenostan Respublikasy

HISTORY. The Turkmen Soviet Socialist Republic was formed on 27 Oct. 1924 and covers the territory of the former Trans-Caspian Region of Turkestan, the Charjiui vilayet of Bokhara and a part of Khiva situated on the right bank of the Oxus. In May 1925 the Turkmen Republic entered the Soviet Union as one of its constituent republics. In Aug. 1990 the Turkmen Supreme Soviet unanimously adopted a declaration of sovereignty.

In Oct. 1991, following 94·1% support in a referendum, it adopted a declaration of independence. It became a member of the CIS in Dec. 1991.

AREA AND POPULATION. Turkmenistan is bounded on the north by the Autonomous Kara-Kalpak Republic, a constituent of Uzbekistan, by Iran and Afghánistán on the south, by the Uzbek Republic on the east and the Caspian Sea on the west. The principal Turkmen tribes are the Tekkés of Merv and the Tekkés of the Attok, the Ersaris, Yomuds and Goklans. All speak closely related varieties of a Turkic language (of the south-western group); many are Sunni Moslems.

The country passed under Russian control in 1881, after the fall of the Turkoman stronghold of Gök Tépé. According to the 1989 census 72% of the republic's 3,522,717 population were Turkmenians, most of whom were nomads before the First World War. Russians, living mostly in urban areas, accounted for 9·5% of the republic's population; 9% were Uzbeks and 2·5% Kazakhs.

The area of Turkmenistan is 488,100 sq. km (186,400 sq. miles), and its population in Jan. 1990 was 3,622,000.

There are 5 regions: Chardzhou, Mary, Ashkhabad, Tashauz and Krasnovodsk, comprising 42 rural districts, 15 towns and 74 urban settlements.

The capital is Ashkhabad (Poltoratsk; 1990 population, 411,000); other large towns are Chardzhou, Mary (Merv), Nebit-Dag and Krasnovodsk.

CONSTITUTION AND GOVERNMENT. A new Constitution was adopted in April 1978. Elections to the Supreme Soviet were held on 7 Jan. 1990.

President of the Republic: Satarmurad Niyazov (elected Oct. 1990).

It was announced in Nov. 1991 that governmental functions would be discharged by the president.

Local Government. Elections to regional, district, urban and rural Soviets were held on 7 Jan. 1990.

ECONOMY

Budget. Budget estimates (in 1m. rubles), 1988, 1,683; 1989 (plan), 1,934.

ENERGY AND NATURAL RESOURCES

Electricity. Output was 14,500m. kwh. in 1989.

Minerals. Turkmenistan is rich in minerals, such as ozocerite, oil, coal, sulphur and salt. In the Kara-Kum Desert deposits of magnesium, minerals and coal have been discovered, as well as some 50 new saltmines. Here a new oil town, Nebit-Dag, has sprung up.

Agriculture. The main occupation of the people is agriculture, based on irrigation. Turkmenistan produces cotton, wool, Astrakhan fur, etc. It is also famous for its carpets, and produces a special breed of Turkoman horses and the famous Karakul sheep.

There were 350 collective farms and 134 state farms in 1989, with 43,800 tractors and 1,600 grain combines. There were 608 rural power stations.

A considerable area is under Egyptian cotton, and from it has been evolved an original Soviet long-fibred cotton.

The main grain grown is maize. Sericulture, fruit and vegetable growing are also important; dates, olives, figs, sesame and other southern plants are grown. 35·8m. ha were under cultivation in Nov. 1990.

Between 1958 and 1970 the Kara-Kum Canal was extended to 860 km. In 1971 the fourth section, to reach the Caspian, was begun to reach 1,000 km. By 1982 over 1,011,000 ha had been irrigated.

Livestock on 1 Jan. 1990: Cattle, 774,300; pigs, 243,300; sheep and goats, 5·4m.

Output of main agricultural products (in 1,000 tonnes) in 1989: Grain, 435; cotton, 1,382; vegetables, 414; fruit, 42; grapes, 124; meat, 103; milk, 423; eggs, 328m.; wool, 15·5.

Fisheries. There is fishing in the Caspian Sea.

INDUSTRY. Industry is being developed, and there are now chemical, tailoring, textile, light, food, agricultural implements, cement and other factories, oil refineries, as well as ore-mining.

On the Kara-Bogaz bay a sulphate industry has been developed. Industrial output in 1989 included steel, 2,100 tonnes; sawn timber, 67,000 cu. metres; cement, 1·1m. tonnes; fabrics, 53·6m. sq. metres; knitwear, 11·1m. items; hosiery, 19·9m. pairs; footwear, 4·8m. pairs; butter, 4,000 tonnes; preserves, 80m. standard jars.

Labour. In 1989 there were 854,000 employees in the state sector.

COMMUNICATIONS

Roads. Length of motor roads in Jan. 1990, 22,600 km (17,800 km hard surface). Motor communication exists between Ashkhabad and Meshed (Iran).

Railways. Length of railways, 2,120 km. The line Chardzhou–Kungrad crosses the Chardzhou and Tashauz regions of Turkmenia and runs across Uzbekistan. Another line connects Chardzhou and Urgench.

Civil Aviation. Airlines connect Leninsk and Tashauz, and Ashkhabad and remote areas in the west, north and east.

Inland Waterways. Waterways extended over 1,300 km in 1990.

Newspapers (1989). Of 66 newspapers, 49 were in the Turkmen language. Daily circulation of Turkmen-language newspapers, 877,000; in all languages, 1,141,000.

JUSTICE, RELIGION, EDUCATION AND WELFARE

Education. In 1989–90 there were 1,800 primary and secondary schools with 800,000 pupils, 9 higher educational institutions with 42,000 students, 38 technical colleges with 35,000 students, and 11 music and art schools. The Turkmen Academy of Sciences, founded in 1951, directs the work of 15 learned institutions with a staff of 1,114 scientific staff; there were 58 research institutions in all, with 5,700 research workers, in Jan. 1989.

In Jan. 1990, 33% of eligible children were attending pre-school institutions.

Health. In 1989 there were 12,800 doctors and 39,900 hospital beds.

Further Reading

Istoriya Turkmenskoi SSR. 2 vols. Ashkhabad, 1957

UZBEKISTAN

Capital: Tashkent
Population: 20·32m. (1990)

Ozbekiston Respublikasy

HISTORY. In Oct. 1917 the Tashkent Soviet assumed authority, and in the following years established its power throughout Turkestan. The semi-independent Khanates of Khiva and Bokhara were first (1920) transformed into People's Republics, then (1923–24) into Soviet Socialist Republics and finally merged in the Uzbek SSR and other republics.

The Uzbek Soviet Socialist Republic was formed on 27 Oct. 1924 from lands formerly included in Turkestan. It includes a large part of the Samarkand region, the southern part of the Syr Darya, Western Ferghana, the western plains of Bukhara, the Kara-Kalpak ASSR and the Uzbek regions of Khorezm. In May 1925 Uzbekistan, by the decision of the Congress of Soviets of the USSR, was accepted as one of the constituent republics of the Soviet Union.

On 20 June 1990 the Uzbek Supreme Soviet adopted a declaration of sovereignty, and in Aug. 1991, following the unsuccessful coup, it declared itself independent as the 'Republic of Uzbekistan', which was confirmed by referendum in Dec. In Dec. 1991 it became a member of the CIS.

AREA AND POPULATION. Uzbekistan is bordered on the north by the Kazakhstan, on the east by Kirghizia and Tajikistan, on the south by Afghanistan and on the west by Turkmenistan. The Uzbeks, who form 71·4% of the republic's 1989 census population of 19,810,077, were the ruling race in Central Asia until the arrival of the Russians during the third quarter of the 19th century. The several native states over which Uzbek dynasties formerly ruled were founded in the 15th century upon the ruins of Tamerlane's empire. The Uzbek speak Jagatai Turkish, which is related to Osmanli and Azerbaijan Turkish. In the 1989 census Russians numbered 8·4%, Tajiks, 4·7%, Kazakhs 4·1%, Tatars 2·4%, Karakalpaks 2·1% and Crimean Tatars 1%.

The area of Uzbekistan is 447,400 sq. km (172,741 sq. miles). The population in Jan. 1990 was 20,322,000 (41% urban). The country comprises the following regions: Andizhan, Bukhara, Dzhizak, Ferghana, Kashkadar, Khorezm, Namangan, Navoi, Samarkand, Surkhan-Darya, Syr-Darya, Tashkent and the Karakalpak Autonomous Republic. The capital of the Republic is Tashkent; other large towns are Samarkand, Andizhan and Namangan. There are 124 towns, 97 urban settlements and 155 rural districts.

On 19 Sept. 1963 the Supreme Soviet of the USSR confirmed decisions of the Supreme Soviets of Kazakhstan and Uzbekistan, transferring over 40,000 sq. km from the former to the latter to ensure more efficient use of the 'Hungry Steppe'.

CONSTITUTION AND GOVERNMENT. Elections to the 500-member Supreme Soviet were held on 18 Feb. 1990. Presidential elections were held on 29 Dec. 1991. Islam Karimov was elected against a single opponent with over 80% of the vote.

President of the Republic: Islam Karimov.
Chairman, Supreme Soviet: Shavkat Yuldeshev.
Prime Minister: Abdukhashim Mutalov.

Local Government: Elections to the regional, district, urban and rural Soviets were held on 18 Feb. 1990.

ECONOMY

Budget. Budget estimates (in 1m. rubles), 1988, 9,012; 1989 (plan), 10,029.

ENERGY AND NATURAL RESOURCES

Electricity. Output was 55,900m. kwh. in 1989.

Gas. Two natural-gas pipelines (Djaikak–Tashkent, Ferghana–Kokand) and a third from Bokhara to the Urals are operating. Natural gas output (1988) was 39,900m. cubic metres.

Minerals. Of its mineral resources, in addition to oil and coal, copper and building materials and ozocerite deposits are now also exploited. Gold is being worked at Muruntalt, Chadak and Kochbulak.

Agriculture. Uzbekistan is a land of intensive farming, based on artificial irrigation. It is the chief cotton-growing area in the USSR. About 3·7m. ha of collective and state farmland have irrigation networks, totalling over 150,000 km in length, and all are in full use.

In 1939 the Ferghana Canal (270 km) was built. During 1940, among the irrigation canals completed were: The North Ferghana Canal (165 km), and Andreyev South Ferghana Canal (108 km) and the first section of the Tashkent Canal (63 km). A canal from the Amu-Darya to Bokhara across the Kzyl-Kum and Ust-Urt deserts (180 km) was completed in 1965. A 200-km canal joining the river Zeravshan with the Kashka Darya at the village of Paruz was completed in Aug. 1955; it is part of the Iski–Angara Canal. The first section (93 km) of a canal irrigating the southern 'Hungry Steppe' was opened in 1960; 500,000 ha of this desert were under cultivation in 1967.

Agriculture flourishes, particularly in the well-watered, warm, rich oases areas, such as the Ferghana valley, Zeravshan, Tashkent and Khorezm, where cotton, fruit, silk and rice are cultivated. In the higher-lying plains grain is grown; the wide desert and semi-desert area of Western Uzbekistan is mainly given to pasture land and the breeding of the Karakul sheep; there is a Karakul institute at Samarkand.

Orchards occupied 206,000 ha and the vineyards 133,000 ha in 1985. The Central Asian Branch of the Scientific Research Institute of Viticulture in Tashkent has produced new frost resistant grapes by crossing the wild Amur grape with Central Asian and European types. In 1989 there were 856 collective farms and 1,085 state farms, with 179,500 tractors and 19,200 cotton picking and grain combines. Ploughing, cotton-sowing and cultivation are completely mechanized; cotton picking over 46%.

Uzbekistan provided 62% of the total cotton, 50% of the total rice and 60% of the total lucerne grown in the former USSR. The area under cultivation was 33·2m. ha in 1990.

Livestock on 1 Jan. 1989: 4·2m. cattle, 8·8m. sheep and goats and 708,300 pigs.

Output of main agricultural products (in 1,000 tonnes) in 1989: Grain, 1,500; cotton, 5,292; potatoes, 325; vegetables, 2,585; fruit, 543; grapes, 416; meat, 478; milk, 2,929; eggs, 2,429m.; wool, 24·4.

Forestry. Afforestation over an area of 50,000 ha has been carried out to protect the Bokhara and Karakul oases from the advancing Kzyl-Kum sands and to stop the sand-drifts in a number of districts of Central Ferghana.

INDUSTRY. There are over 1,600 factories and mills. Output in 1989 included steel, 1·1m. tonnes; rolled ferrous metals, 0·9m. tonnes; sawn timber, 563,000 cu. metres; paper, 26,000 tonnes; cement, 6·2m. tonnes; fabrics, 762m. sq. metres; knitwear, 110m. items; hosiery, 113·7m. pairs; footwear, 44·2m.pairs; butter, 16,000 tonnes; preserves, 1,163m. standard jars.

Labour. In 1989 there were 5,061,000 employees in the state sector.

COMMUNICATIONS

Roads. The Great Uzbek Highway was completed in April 1941. Total length of motor roads in Jan. 1990 was 73,100 km (hard surface, 62,600 km).

Railways. The total length of railway in Jan. 1990 was 3,460 km. Branches lead to Karshe-Kitab, Kerki-Termez, Jalal-Abad, Namangan, Andijan and other centres. In 1947–55 a line was built from Chardzhou to Kungrad.

Inland Waterways. Total length in 1990 was 1,100 km.

Newspapers (1989). There were 185 newspapers in the Uzbek language out of a total of 279. Daily circulation of Uzbek-language newspapers, 4·9m.; in all languages, 6·6m.

JUSTICE, RELIGION, EDUCATION AND WELFARE

Religion. The Uzbeks are predominantly Sunni Moslems.

Educatiion. In 1989–90 there were 8,300 elementary and secondary schools with 4·7m. pupils, 44 higher educational establishments with 331,600 students and 244 technical colleges with 277,300 students. Uzbekistan has an Academy of Sciences, founded in 1943, with 37 institutions and 4,297 academic staff; there were 188 research institutes with a scientific staff of 40,200 in Jan. 1989. There are universities and medical schools in Tashkent and Samarkand. In Jan. 1990, 37% of eligible children were attending pre-school institutions.

The Uzbek Arabic script was in 1929 replaced by the Latin alphabet which in 1940 was superseded by one based on the Cyrillic alphabet.

Health. In 1989 there were 72,400 doctors and 249,000 hospital beds.

Further Reading

Istoriya Uzbekskoi SSR. 4 vols. Tashkent, 1967–68

KARAKALPAK AUTONOMOUS REPUBLIC (KARAKALPAKSTAN)

Area, 164,900 sq. km (63,920 sq. miles); population (Jan. 1989), 1,214,000. Capital, Nukus (1989 census population, 169,000). The Karakalpaks are first mentioned in written records in the 16th century as tributary to Bokhara, and later to the Kazakh Khanate. In the second half of the 19th century, as a result of the Russian conquest of Central Asia, they came under Russian rule. On 11 May 1925 the territory was constituted within the then Kazakh Autonomous Republic (of the Russian Federation) as an Autonomous Region. On 20 March 1932 it became an Autonomous Republic within the Russian Federation, and on 5 Dec. 1936 it became part of the Uzbek SSR. Census (1979) Karakalpaks were 31·1% of population, Uzbeks, 31·5% and Kazakhs, 26·9%.

185 deputies were elected to its Supreme Soviet on 24 Feb. 1985, of whom 69 were women and 118 Communists.

Its manufactures are in the field of light industry—bricks, leather goods, furniture, canning, wine. In Jan. 1987 cattle numbered 348,600 and sheep and goats, 523,900. There were 38 collective and 124 state farms. The total cultivated area in 1985 was 350,400 ha.

In 1986–87 there were 286,800 pupils at schools, 21,400 at technical colleges, and 6,200 at Nukus University. There is a branch of the Uzbek Academy of Sciences with 190 scientific staff.

There were 2,600 doctors and 12,800 hospital beds.

GEORGIA

Capital: Tbilisi
Population: 5·46m. (1990)

Sakartvelos Respublika

(Republic of Georgia)

STATUS. As of March 1992 Georgia had not joined the CIS.

HISTORY. The independence of the Georgian Social Democratic Republic was declared at Tbilisi on 26 May 1918 by the National Council, elected by the National Assembly of Georgia on 22 Nov. 1917. The independence of Georgia was recognized by the USSR on 7 May 1920. On 12 Feb. 1921 a rising broke out in Mingrelia, Abkhazia and Adjaria, and Soviet troops invaded the country, which, on 25 Feb. 1921, was proclaimed the Georgian Soviet Socialist Republic. On 15 Dec.

1922 Georgia was merged with Armenia and Azerbaijan to form the Trancaucasian Soviet Federal Socialist Republic. In 1936 the Georgian Soviet Socialist Republic became one of the constituent republics of the USSR. Following nationalist successes at elections in Oct. 1990, the Supreme Soviet resolved in Nov. 1990 to begin a transition to full independence and in April 1991, following a 98·9% popular vote in favour, unanimously declared the republic an independent state based on the treaty of independence of May 1918.

Following an armed insurrection the president elected in May 1991, Zviad Gamsakhurdia, was deposed on 6 Jan. 1992 and a military council took control, led by Tengiz Sigua.

AREA AND POPULATION. Georgia is bounded west by the Black Sea and south by Turkey, Armenia and Azerbaijan. It occupies the whole of the western part of Transcaucasia and covers an area of 69,700 sq. km (26,900 sq. miles). Its population on 1 Jan. 1990 was 5,456,000. The capital is Tbilisi. Other important towns are Kutaisi (235,000), Rustavi (159,000), Batumi (136,000), Sukhumi (121,000), Poti (54,000), Gori (59,000).

Protected from the north by the Caucasian mountains and receiving in the west the warm, moist winds from the Black Sea into which most of its rivers flow, Georgia is outstanding for its fine, warm climate and its natural wealth, variety and beauty. It has the highest snow-capped peaks of the Caucasian mountains. Georgia contains valuable sulphur and other medicinal springs. Georgians, an ancient people, accounted for 70·1% of the 1989 census population of 5,400,841; others included 8·1% Armenians, 6·3% Russians, 5·7% Azerbaijanis, 3% Ossetians, 1·9% Greeks, 1·8% Abkhazians and 1% Ukrainians. Georgia includes the Abkhazian ASSR, the Adjarian ASSR and the South Ossetian Autonomous Region. The latter was abolished by the Georgian Supreme Soviet on 11 Dec. 1990.

CONSTITUTION AND GOVERNMENT. The Supreme Soviet consists of 250 deputies. At the elections of Nov. 1990 the 7-party coalition Round Table-Free Georgia won 155 seats with 62% of the votes cast. In elections to the Presidency in May 1991 Zviad Gamsakhurdia secured 86·5% of the poll on an 83·4% turnout. After his deposition, Eduard Shevardnadze became Chairman of the State Council.

National flag: Dark red, with a canton divided black over white.

Local Government. Local administration was reorganized in Jan. 1991 into prefectures headed by prefects who report to the central government. Prefects may serve a maximum of two 4-year terms. Villages are administered by councils.

ECONOMY

Budget. (in 1m. rubles). Budget estimates, 1988, 3,360; 1989 (plan), 4,067.

ENERGY AND NATURAL RESOURCES

Electricity. Georgia's fast flowing rivers form an abundant source of energy. The hydro-electric station at Tbilisi has an installed capacity of 1m. kw. Power output in 1989 was 15,800m. kwh.

Minerals. The most important mining industry is the exploitation of the manganese deposits, the richest of which lie in the Chiatura region. Manganese deposits are calculated at 250m. tonnes, distributed over an area of 140 sq. km. The most important coal seams are at Tkvarcheli (deposits estimated at 250m. tonnes) and Tkibuli (deposits of 80m. tonnes). Other important minerals are baryta, the best in the USSR, fire-resisting and other clays, diatomite shale, oil, agate, marble, cement, alabaster, iron and other ores, building stone, arsenic, molybdenum, tungsten and mercury. In 1941 a goldfield was discovered. Output of coal in 1988 was 1·4m. tonnes.

Agriculture. There are 3 main agricultural areas: (1) The moist subtropical area along the Black Sea Coast, where are cultivated tea, citrus fruits (lemons, oranges, mandarins, etc.), the tung tree (which yields special industrial oils), eucalyptus, bamboo, high-quality tobacco; (2) Imeretia (the Kutais region) where the chief cultures are grapes and silk, and (3) Kakhetia, along the Alazani (a tributary of the Kura river), famed for its orchards and wines. Land under cultivation was 4·6m. ha in 1986.

Output of main agricultural products (in 1,000 tonnes) in 1989: Grain, 500; tea leaf, 496; citrus fruit, 94; sugar-beet, 39; potatoes, 332; vegetables, 515; grapes, 514; meat, 179; milk, 712; eggs, 861m.; wool, 6·4.

On 1 Jan. 1986 there were 719 collective farms working over 66% of all agricultural land, 594 state farms working nearly 34% of such land. In the Colchis area 115,000 ha of extremely rich land have been reclaimed. There are 389,000 ha of irrigated land, and 151,400 ha of marsh land have been drained. Tractors numbered 25,900 on 1 Jan. 1989; grain combines, 1,600.

Livestock on 1 Jan. 1990: Cattle, 1·4m.; pigs, 1m.; sheep and goats, 1·8m.

Forestry. Georgia is rich in forest lands where fine varieties of timber are grown. Area covered by forests, 2·4m. ha.

INDUSTRY. The Transcaucasian Metallurgical Plant is at Rustavi (near Tbilisi) and there is a motor works at Kutaisi. There are factories for processing tea, creameries and breweries. There are also textile and silk industries.

In 1989, 1·4m. tonnes of steel were produced, 1·2m. tonnes of rolled ferrous metals, 304,000 cu. metres of timber, 28,000 tonnes of paper, 1·5m. tonnes of cement, 123m. sq. metres of fabrics, 56·2m. items of knitwear, 31·9m. pairs of hosiery, 16·5m. pairs of footwear, 1,000 tonnes of butter, 32,000 tonnes of granulated sugar, and 727m. jars of preserves.

Labour. There were 2,161,000 workers and office employees in 1989.

COMMUNICATIONS

Roads. There were 35,100 km of motor roads in 1990 (31,200 km hard-surfaced).

Railways. Total Length was 1,570 km in 1990.

Newspapers (1989). Out of 149 newspapers, 128 were in Georgian. Daily circulation of Georgian-language newspapers, 3·2m., other languages, 576,000.

JUSTICE, RELIGION, EDUCATION AND WELFARE

Religion. The Georgian Orthodox Church has its own organization under Catholicos (patriarch) Ilya who is resident in Tbilisi and who directs the church's seminary in Mtskheta.

Education. In 1989–90 there were 900,000 pupils in 3,700 primary and secondary schools, 44,100 in 88 technical colleges and 93,100 students in 19 higher educational institutions. Tbilisi University has 16,300 students. In towns, 11 years' education is usual. In Abastuman there is an astro-physical observatory. In 1936 a branch of the Academy of Sciences of the USSR was formed in Tbilisi, and in Feb. 1941 a Georgian Academy of Sciences was opened, which in Jan. 1988 had 42 institutions with scientific staff totalling 6,107. There were in all 194 research institutions with 29,000 scientific staff.

In Jan. 1990, 44% of eligible children were attending pre-school institutions.

Health. There were 31,700 doctors and 59,500 hospital beds in 1989.

ABKHAZIAN AUTONOMOUS REPUBLIC

Area, 8,600 sq. km (3,320 sq. miles); population (Jan. 1990), 538,000. Capital Sukhumi (1989 census population, 121,000). This area, the ancient Colchis, included Greek colonies from the 6th century B.C. onwards. From the 2nd century B.C.

onwards, it was a prey to many invaders—Romans, Byzantines, Arabs, Ottoman Turks—before accepting a Russian protectorate in 1810. However, from the 4th century A.D. a West Georgian kingdom was established by the Lazi princes in the territory (known to the Romans as 'Lazica') and by the 8th century the prevailing language was Georgian and the name Abkhazia. In March 1921 a congress of local Soviets proclaimed it a Soviet Republic, and its status as an Autonomous Republic, within Georgia, was confirmed on 17 April 1930.

Population (1979 census) Abkhazians, 17·1%, Georgians, 43·9% and Russians, 16·4%.

140 deputies were elected to the republican Supreme Soviet on 24 Feb. 1985, 57 of them women.

The Abkhazian coast (along the Black Sea) possesses a famous chain of health resorts—Gagra, Sukhumi, Akhali-Antoni, Gulripsha and Gudauta—sheltered by thickly forested mountains.

The republic has coal, electric power, building materials and light industries. In 1985 there were 89 collective farms and 56 state farms; main crops are tobacco, tea, grapes, oranges, tangerines and lemons. Crop area 43,900 ha.

Livestock, 1 Jan. 1987: 147,300 cattle, 127,900 pigs, 28,800 sheep and goats.

In 1986–87 about 100,000 pupils were engaged in study at all levels. A university has been opened in Sukhumi.

In Jan. 1985 there were 2,300 doctors and 6,000 hospital beds.

ADJARIAN AUTONOMOUS REPUBLIC

Area, 3,000 sq. km (1,160 sq. miles); population (Jan. 1990), 382,000. Capital, Batumi (1989 census population, 136,000). After a history similar to that of Abkhazia, it fell under Turkish rule in the 17th century, and was annexed to Russia (rejoining Georgia) after the Berlin Treaty of 1878. On 16 July 1921 the territory was constituted as an Autonomous Republic within the Georgian SSR.

Population (1979 census) Georgians, 80·1%, Russians, 9·8% and Armenians 4·6%.

110 deputies were elected to the republican Supreme Soviet on 24 Feb. 1985, 45 of them women.

The republic specializes in sub-tropical agricultural products. These include tea, mandarines and lemons, grapes, bamboo, eucalyptus, etc. Livestock (Jan. 1987): 133,400 cattle, 6,300 pigs, 11,600 sheep and goats. In 1980 there were 69 collective farms and 21 state farms.

There are shipyards at Batumi, modern oil-refining plant (the pipeline from the Baku oilfields ends at Batumi), food-processing and canning factories, clothing, building materials, drug factories, etc.

Health resorts are Kobuleti, Tsikhisdziri, Batumi on the coast and Beshumi in the hills. The sub-tropical climate and flora, and the combination of mountains and sea, make this republic (like Abkhazia) a favourite holiday area.

In 1986–87 79,800 pupils were engaged in study at all levels and 1,000 graduated from colleges.

In Jan. 1985 there were 1,430 doctors and 3,900 hospital beds.

SOUTH OSSETIAN AUTONOMOUS REGION

This area was populated by Ossetians from across the Caucasus (North Ossetia), driven out by the Mongols in the 13th century. The region was set up within the Georgian SSR on 20 April 1922. It was abolished as a separate entity by the Georgian Supreme Soviet on 11 Dec. 1990. Area, 3,900 sq. km (1,505 sq. miles); population (Jan. 1990), 99,000 (1979 census, Ossetians, 66·4% and Georgians, 28·8%). Capital, Tskhinvali (34,000).

Main industries are mining, timber, electrical engineering and building materials. Crop area, chiefly grains, was 21,600 ha in 1985; other pursuits are sheepfarming (128,500 sheep and goats on 1 Jan. 1987) and vine-growing. There were 14 collective farms and 18 state farms.

In 1986–87 there were 18,543 pupils in elementary and secondary schools; there were 1,967 graduates from higher educational institutions and 837 from colleges.

In Jan. 1987 there were 511 doctors and 1,400 hospital beds.

Further Reading

Lang, D. M., *A Modern History of Georgia*. London, 1962. — *The Georgians*. London, 1966
Suny, R. G., *The Making of the Georgian Nation*. London, 1989
Istoriya Gruzii. 3 vols. Tbilisi, 1962–73

COMOROS

Capital: Moroni
Population: 503,000 (1990)
GNP per capita: US$460 (1989)

République Fédérale Islamique des Comores

HISTORY. The 3 islands forming the present state became French protectorates at the end of the 19th century, and were proclaimed colonies on 25 July 1912. With neighbouring Mayotte they were administratively attached to Madagascar from 1914 until 1947, when the 4 islands became a French Overseas Territory, achieving internal self-government in Dec. 1961.

In referenda held on each island on 22 Dec. 1974, the 3 western islands voted overwhelmingly for independence, while Mayotte voted to remain French. The Comoran Chamber of Deputies unilaterally declared the islands' independence on 6 July 1975, but Mayotte remained a French dependency.

The first government of Ahmed Abdallah was overthrown on 3 Aug. 1975 by a coup led by Ali Soilih (who assumed the Presidency on 2 Jan. 1976), but Ahmed Abdallah regained the Presidency after a second coup ousted Ali Soilih in May 1978. In Nov. 1989 President Abdallah was assassinated.

AREA AND POPULATION. The Comoros consists of 3 islands in the Indian ocean between the African mainland and Madagascar with a total area of 1,862 sq. km (719 sq. miles). Population (estimate, 1990) 503,000.

	Area sq. km	Population census 1980	Chief town	Population census 1980
Njazídja (Grande Comore)	1,148	192,177	Moroni	20,112
Mwali (Mohéli)	290	17,194	Fomboni	5,663
Nzwani (Anjouan)	424	137,621	Mutsamudu	12,518
	1,862	346,992		

The indigenous population are a mixture of Malagasy, African, Malay and Arab peoples; the vast majority speak Comoran, an Arabised dialect of Swahili, but a small proportion speak Makua (a Bantu language), French or Arabic. In 1990, 27·1% of the population were urban.

CLIMATE. There is a tropical climate, affected by Indian monsoon winds from the north, which gives a wet season from Nov. to April. Moroni. Jan. 81°F (27·2°C), July 75°F (23·9°C). Annual rainfall, 113" (2,825 mm).

CONSTITUTION AND GOVERNMENT. Under the new Constitution approved by referendum on 1 Oct. 1978 (amended 1983), the Comoros are a Federal Islamic Republic. Mayotte has the right to join when it so chooses.

The *President* is Head of State, directly elected for a 6-year term (renewable once). He appoints Ministers to form the Council of Government, on which each island's Governor has a non-voting seat. There is a 42-member unicameral Federal Assembly, directly elected for 5 years. Each of the 3 islands is administered by a Governor (nominated by the President), up to 4 Commissioners whom he appoints to assist him, and a *Legislative Council* directly elected for 5 years.

At the presidential elections of March 1990 Said Mohamed Djohar gained 55% of votes cast, against one opponent. In Aug. 1991 he was impeached by the High Court and removed from office.

President: Ibrahim Ahmed Halidi, *ad interim* since Aug. 1991.

In Jan. 1992 a 12-member Government of Reconciliation was formed with representatives of 12 political parties, including:

Prime Minister: Mohamed Taki Abdoulkarim.

Foreign: Said Hassan Said Hachim. *Finance:* Mohamed Said Abdullah Mchangama.

National flag: Green with a crescent and 4 stars all in white in the centre, tilted towards the lower fly.

DEFENCE

Army. The army had a strength of about 700 in 1988.

Navy. An ex-British landing craft built in 1945 was transferred from France in 1976 and another vessel, with ramps, was purchased in 1981. Two small patrol boats were supplied by Japan in 1982. Personnel in 1991 numbered about 200.

Air Arm. In 1990 only 1 Cessna 402B communications aircraft and an Ecureuil helicopter were in operation.

INTERNATIONAL RELATIONS

Membership. Comoros is a member of the UN and an ACP state of EEC.

ECONOMY

Budget. In 1986, current revenue amounted to 5,816m. Comorian francs and current expenditure to 10,380m. Comorian francs; the separate capital budget totalled 17,400m. Comorian francs revenue against 17,400m. Comorian francs expenditure.

Currency. The unit of currency is the *Comorian franc* (KMF). There are banknotes of 500, 1,000, and 5,000 *Comorian francs*. In March 1992, £1 = CF489·63; US$1 = CF278·91.

Banking. The Institut d'émission des Comores was established as the new bank of issue in 1975. The chief commercial banks are the Banque des Comores, established in 1974 by the separation of the former Comoran section of the Banque de Madagascar et des Comores and the Banque de Développement des Comores.

Weights and Measures. The metric system is in force.

ENERGY AND NATURAL RESOURCES

Electricity. Production (1986) 5m. kwh.

Agriculture. The chief product was formerly sugar-cane, but now vanilla, copra, maize and other food crops, cloves and essential oils (citronella, ylang, lemon-grass) are the most important products. Production (1990 in 1,000 tonnes): Cassava, 45; coconuts, 50; bananas, 50; sweet potatoes, 16; rice, 15; maize, 4 and copra, 4.
    Livestock (1990): Cattle, 47,000; sheep, 13,000; goats, 120,000; asses, 4,000.

Forestry. Njazídja has a fine forest and produces timber for building.

Fisheries. In 1983 the catch was (estimate) 4,000 tonnes.

FOREIGN ECONOMIC RELATIONS

Commerce. Imports in 1985 amounted to 16,481m. Comorian francs, exports to 7,048m. Comorian francs. France provided 41% of imports and took 66% of exports. The main exports (1985) were vanilla (67% of value), cloves (20%), ylang-ylang (9%), essences, copra and coffee.
    Trade between Comoros and UK (British Department of Trade returns, in £1,000 sterling):

	1987	1988	1989	1990	1991
Imports to UK	91	33	60	54	228
Exports and re-exports from UK	527	333	419	236	796

Tourism. In 1986 there were about 5,000 visitors.

COMMUNICATIONS

Roads. In 1983 there were 750 km of classified roads, of which 262 km were tarmac. There were 3,600 passenger cars and about 2,000 commercial vehicles.

Civil Aviation. There is an international airport at Hahaya (on Njazídja). Air Comores have twice-weekly flights to Antananarivo, Dar es Salaam and Mombasa. Air France and Air Madagascar also have twice-weekly flights to Antananarivo. Air Comores has daily internal flights between Moroni and Nzwani, and 5 per week between Moroni and Mwali.

Shipping. In 1982, vessels entering Comoran ports (excluding internal traffic) discharged 39,000 tonnes and loaded 15,000 tonnes.

Telecommunications. There were 496 telephones in 1983. The state-controlled Radio Comoro broadcasts in French and Comorian. Number of radios (1990), 50,000.

JUSTICE, RELIGION, EDUCATION AND WELFARE

Justice. French and Moslem law is in a new consolidated code.The Supreme Court comprises 7 members, 2 each appointed by the President and the Federal Assembly, and 1 by each island's Legislative Council.

Religion. Islam is the official religion, and over 99% of the population are Sunni Moslems; there are about 1,300 Christians.

Education. In 1981 there were 59,709 pupils and 1,292 teachers in 236 primary schools; 32 secondary schools had 13,528 pupils and 432 teachers, 2 technical schools held 151 students with 9 teachers, and a teacher-training college had 119 students and 8 teachers.

Health. In 1978 there were 20 doctors, 1 dentist, 2 pharmacists, 35 midwives and 124 nursing personnel. In 1980 there were 17 hospitals and clinics with 763 beds.

DIPLOMATIC REPRESENTATIVES

Of Great Britain in the Comoros
Ambassador: Dennis Amy, OBE (resides in Antananarivo).

Of the Comoros in the USA
Ambassador: Amini Al Moumin.

Of the USA in the Comoros
Ambassador: Kenneth N. Peltier (resides in Antananarivo).

Of the Comoros to the United Nations
Ambassador: Amini Ali Moumin.

Further Reading

Newitt, N., *The Comoro Islands.* London, 1985

CONGO

Capital: Brazzaville
Population: 2·26m. (1990)
GNP per capita: US$930 (1989)

République du Congo

HISTORY. First occupied by France in 1882, the Congo became (as 'Middle Congo') a territory of French Equatorial Africa from 1910–58, when it became a member state of the French Community. It became an independent Republic on 15 Aug. 1960.

The first President, Fulbert Youlou, was deposed on 15 Aug. 1963 by a *coup* led by Alphonse Massemba-Débat, who became President on 19 Dec. Following a second *coup* in Aug. 1968, the Army took power under the leadership of Major Marien Ngouabi, whose colleague, Major Alfred Raoul, was appointed President from 3 Sept. until 1 Jan. 1969, when Ngouabi himself became President.

The country's present name was established on 3 Jan. 1970, when a Marxist-Leninist state was introduced. Ngouabi was assassinated on 18 March 1977, and succeeded by Col. Joachim Yhombi-Opango, who in turn was replaced on 5 Feb. 1979 by Col. Denis Sassou-Nguesso.

AREA AND POPULATION. The Congo is bounded by Cameroon and the Central African Republic in the north, Zaïre to the east and south, Angola and the Atlantic Ocean to the south-west and Gabon to the west, and covers 341,821 sq. km. At the census of 1984 the population was 1,909,248, including the towns of Brazzaville, the capital (585,812), Pointe-Noire, the main port and oil centre (294,203), Nkayi (formerly Jacob) (35,540) and Loubomo (formerly Dolisie) (49,134). Over 51% were urban.

Estimated population in 1990, 2,264,300 (Brazzaville, 760,300; Pointe-Noire, 387,774; Loubomo, 62,073; Nkayi, 40,019; Mossendjo, 15,570; Ouesso, 14,587).

Area, estimated population and capitals of the regions in 1990 were:

Region	Sq. km	1990	Capital	Region	Sq. km	1990	Capital
Kouilou	13,650	83,156	Pointe-Noire	Capital District	65	760,300	Brazzaville
Niari	25,918	120,057	Loubomo	Plateaux	38,400	114,629	Djambala
Lékoumou	20,950	71,248	Sibiti	Cuvette	71,248	144,427	Owando
Bouenza	12,258	165,967	N'kayi	Sangha	55,796	34,851	Ouesso
Pool	33,955	188,285	Kinkala	Likouala	66,044	61,358	Impfondo

In 1984, 45% spoke Kongo dialects, chiefly in the south and south-west; 20% were Teke (in the south-east); 15% Sanka and 16% Ubangi chiefly inhabit the north. There are also about 12,000 pygmies and 12,000 Europeans (mainly French). French is the official language, but 2 local *patois*, Monokutuba (west of Brazzaville) and Lingala (north of Brazzaville), serve as lingua francas.

CLIMATE. An equatorial climate, with moderate rainfall and a small range of temperature. There is a long dry season from May to Oct. in the S.W. plateaux, but the Congo Basin in the N.E. is more humid, with rainfall approaching 100" (2,500 mm). Brazzaville. Jan. 78°F (25·6°C), July 73°F (22·8°C). Annual rainfall 59" (1,473 mm).

CONSTITUTION AND GOVERNMENT. From Feb. to June 1991 a national conference was held consisting of representatives of 67 political parties, 134 associations and 30 specialists. This abolished the constitution of July 1979 (for details *see* THE STATESMAN'S YEAR-BOOK, 1991–92, pp, 381–82), dissolved the National Assembly, Constitutional Council and Economic Council, and adopted a basic law to regulate a period of transition. It established a presidency of the republic with newly-defined powers, a 153-member Supreme Council of the Republic and a prime ministership. At a referendum in March 1992 proposing multi-party democracy 96·32% of votes were in favour. Turn-out was 70·93%. Parliamentary elections were scheduled for April and presidential elections for June 1992.

President: Gen. Denis Sassou-Nguesso.
Chairman of the Supreme Council: Ernest Kombo.
In Jan. 1992 the government consisted of:
Prime Minister: André Milongo (b. 1935).

Economy, Finance and Planning: Edouard Ebouka Babackas. *Interior and Decentralization:* Alexis Gabou. *Foreign Affairs and Co-operation:* Jean Blaise Kololo. *Justice, Keeper of the Seal, Administrative Reform:* Jean Martin Mbemba. *Communications, Government Spokesperson:* Guy Menga. *Industry and Tourism:* Herbert Kakoula Kadi. *Labour, Social Security and Human Resources:* François Guimbi. *Commerce and Small Business:* Clément Mierassa. *Transport and Civil Aviation:* Jacques Okoko. *Agriculture and Stock-breeding:* Célestin Nkoua. *Public Works, Building and Town Planning:* Ndemba Ntelo. *Health:* Paul Ndouna. *Forestry, Fishery and Environment:* Marcel Boula. *Education:* Anaclet Tsomambet. *Culture and the Arts:* Antoine Letembet Ambilly. *Youth and Sport:* Jean Pierre Berri. *Social Affairs:* Fouty Soungou.

National flag: Diagonal stripes of green, yellow and red.
National anthem: La Congolaise (words and tune by Jean Royer and others).

Local Government: The country is administratively divided into 9 prefectures, subdivided into 47 sub-prefectures, 30 administrative control posts and 6 communes: Brazzaville, Dolisie, Mossendjo, Nkayi, Ouesso and Pointe-Noire.

DEFENCE

Army. The Army consists of 2 infantry battalion groups, 2 armoured and 1 infantry battalion, an artillery group, 1 engineering, and 1 paracommando battalion. Equipment includes 25 T-54/-55 and 15 T-59 tanks. Total personnel (1992) 10,000.

Navy. The combatant flotilla includes 3 modern Spanish-built, 6 ex-Soviet and 3 ex-Chinese inshore patrol craft. There are also 2 French-built tugs and some boats. Personnel in 1991 totalled about 500.

Air Force. The Air Force had (1991) about 500 personnel, 2 MiG-21 and 6 MiG-17 jet fighters, 6 Antonov An-24/26 turboprop transports, 2 C-47, 2 Nord 262, and 1 Noratlas piston-engined transports, 3 Broussard communications aircraft, 4 L-39 jet trainers and 2 Alouette II and 2 Alouette III light helicopters.

INTERNATIONAL RELATIONS

Membership. Congo is a member of the UN, OAU and is an ACP state of the EEC.

ECONOMY

Budget. The 1988 Budget provided for revenue of 251,800m. francs CFA (over 50% from overseas funding) and expenditure of 283,976m. francs CFA, of which 252,800m. were for administration and 31,976m. for investment.

Currency. The unit of currency is the *franc CFA* (BEAC) with a parity value of 50 *francs CFA* to 1 French franc. There are coins of 1, 2, 5, 10, 25, 50, 100 and 500 *francs CFA*, and banknotes of 100, 500, 1,000, 5,000 and 10,000 *francs* CFA. In March 1992, £1 = 489·63 *francs;* US$1 = 278·91 *francs.*

Banking and Finance. The *Banque des États de l'Afrique Centrale* is the bank of issue. There are 4 commercial banks situated in Brazzaville, including the *Banque Commerciale Congolaise* and the *Union Congolaise de Banques.*

ENERGY AND NATURAL RESOURCES

Electricity. Total production in 1990 was 503·99m. kwh (500·73m. kwh. hydro-electric). Supply 220 volts; 50 Hz.

Oil. Oil reserves are estimated at 500–1,000m. tonnes. Output in 1991 was 7,409,000 tonnes from the 26 offshore oil platforms operated by Elf Congo and Agip Congo. There is a refinery at Pointe-Noire.

Minerals. Lead, copper, zinc and gold are the main minerals. 800 kg of gold were mined in 1989. There are reserves of phosphates, bauxite and iron.

Agriculture. Production (1989, in tonnes): Cassava, 667,198; bananas, 31,860; plantains, 61,597; yams, 11,460; maize, 20,608; groundnuts, 39,021; coffee, 1,843; cocoa, 1,994; rice, 1,083.

Livestock (1989, in 1,000): Cattle, 56; pigs, 48; sheep, 101; goats, 400; poultry, 878.

Forestry. Equatorial forests cover 21m. ha from which (in 1989) 809,000 cu. metres of timber were produced, mainly okoumé from the south and sapele from the north.

Fisheries. In 1986 the catch amounted to 30,000 tonnes.

INDUSTRY. There is a growing manufacturing sector, located mainly in the 4 major towns, producing processed foods, textiles, cement, metal goods and chemicals. Production: Printed cloth (1990), 8·79m. metres; cement (1989), 121,000 tonnes; shoes (1989), 14,670 pairs; corrugated iron sheets (1990), 1·68m. tonnes; household goods (1990), 186 tonnes; nails (1990), 377 tonnes.

Trade Unions. In 1964 the existing unions merged into one national body, the *Confédération Syndicale Congolaise*.

FOREIGN ECONOMIC RELATIONS

Commerce. Imports in 1989 (in 1m. francs CFA) totalled 160,967m. francs CFA (mainly machinery, 63,985) and exports 290,275m. (mainly oil products, 238,879). Exports to the USA in 1989, 113,356; to France, 49,.952; to Spain, 11,999.

Total trade between the Congo and UK (British Department of Trade returns, in £1,000 sterling):

	1987	1988	1989	1990	1991
Imports to UK	1,930	2,016	3,442	2,563	2,407
Exports and re-exports from UK	19,219	8,521	5,258	9,211	9,190

Tourism. There were 39,000 tourists in 1986.

COMMUNICATIONS

Roads. In 1986 there were 8,410 km of all-weather roads, of which 1,218 km were bitumenized. In 1982 there were 30,500 cars and 18,600 commercial vehicles. 4,237 cars were registered in 1988.

Railways. A railway (610 km, 1,067 mm gauge) and a telegraph line connect Brazzaville with Pointe-Noire via Loubomo and Bilinga and a 285 km branch links Mont-Belo with Mbinda on the Gabon border. In 1989 railways carried 434m. passenger-km and 1,037m. tonne-km of freight.

Civil Aviation. The principal airports are at Brazzaville (Maya Maya) and Pointe-Noire (A. A. Neto). In addition there are 24 airfields served by the national airline, Lina-Congo and other companies.

Shipping. The main port is Pointe-Noire, which handled 10·2m. tonnes of freight in 1988. There were (1985) 21 vessels of 8,458 GWT registered. There are hydrofoil connexions from Brazzaville to Kinshasa (30 km across the River Congo).

Telecommunications. Telephones (1983) numbered 18,093. In 1985 there were 99,000 radios and 5,000 TV sets in use.

Newspapers. In 1986 there were 3 daily newspapers with a combined circulation of 24,000.

JUSTICE, RELIGION, EDUCATION AND WELFARE

Justice. The Supreme Court, Court of Appeal and a criminal court are situated in Brazzaville, with a network of *tribunaux de grande instance* and *tribunaux d'instance* in the regions.

Religion. In 1989 there were 1·21m. Roman Catholics and 0·5m. Protestants. There are some Moslems and traditional animist beliefs are still practised.

Education. In 1985 there were 475,805 pupils and 7,745 teachers in 1,558 primary schools, 197,491 pupils and 4,773 teachers in secondary schools, 25,142 students with 1,549 teachers in technical schools and teacher-training establishments. The Université Marien-Ngouabi (founded 1972) in Brazzaville had 9,385 students and 565 teaching staff in 1985. Adult literacy (1980) 56%.

Health. There were (1978) 274 doctors, 2 dentists, 28 pharmacists, 413 midwives, 1,915 nursing personnel and 473 hospitals and dispensaries with 6,876 beds.

DIPLOMATIC REPRESENTATIVES

Of the Congo in Great Britain
Ambassador: Jean-Marie Ewengue (resides in Paris).

Of Great Britain in the Congo
Ambassador: Roger Westbrook, CMG (resides in Kinshasa).

Of the Congo in the USA (4891 Colorado Ave., NW, Washington D.C., 20011)
Ambassador: Roger Issombo.

Of the USA in the Congo (PO Box 1015, Brazzaville)
Ambassador: James D. Phillips.

Of the Congo to the United Nations
Ambassador: Dr Martin Adouki.

Further Reading

Thompson, V. and Adloff, R., *Historical Dictionary of the People's Republic of the Congo*. 2nd ed. Metuchen, 1984

COSTA RICA

Capital: San José
Population: 2·91m. (1990)
GNP per capita: US$1,790 (1989)

República de Costa Rica

HISTORY. Part of the Spanish Viceroyalty of New Spain from 1540, Costa Rica (the 'Rich Coast') formed part of Central America when the latter acquired independence on 15 Sept. 1821. Central America seceded to Mexico on 5 Jan. 1822 until 1 July 1823, when it became an independent confederation as the United Provinces of Central America. The province of Guanacaste was acquired from Nicaragua in 1825. Costa Rica left the confederation and achieved full independence in 1838. The first Constitution was promulgated on 7 Dec. 1871.

AREA AND POPULATION. Costa Rica is bounded north by Nicaragua, east by the Caribbean, southeast by Panama, and south and west by the Pacific. The area is estimated at 51,100 sq. km (19,730 sq. miles). The population at the census of 1 June 1984 was 2,416,809. Estimate (1990) 2,914,000.

The area and census of population for 1 June 1984 was as follows:

Province	Area (sq. km)	Population	Capital	Population
San José	4,959·63	1,055,611	San José	284,550
Alajuela	9,753·23	512,886	Alajuela	42,047
Cartago	3,124·67	324,299	Cartago	28,588
Heredia	2,656·27	233,185	Heredia	25,812
Guanacaste	10,140·71	232.414	Liberia	27,637[1]
Puntarenas	11,276·97	321,920	Puntarenas	35,603[1]
Limón	9,188·52	206,675	Limón	64,406[1]

[1] District

In 1988, 44% lived in urban areas, and 36% were aged under 15; population density 56·5 per sq. km.

Vital statistics for calendar years:

	Marriages	Births	Deaths
1987	21,743	80,326	10,687
1988	22,918	81,376	10,944

The population is mainly of Spanish and mixed descent. There are some 15,000 West Indians, mostly in Limón province. The indigenous Amerindian population is dwindling and is now estimated at 1,200. There were (1988) some 23,100 refugees (19,000 from Nicaragua).

Spanish is the official language.

CLIMATE. The climate is tropical, with a small range of temperature and abundant rains. The dry season is from Dec. to April. San José. Jan. 66°F (18·9°C), July 69°F (20·6°C). Annual rainfall 72" (1,793 mm).

CONSTITUTION AND GOVERNMENT. The Constitution was promulgated in Nov. 1949. It forbids the establishment or maintenance of an army. The legislative power is normally vested in a single chamber called the Legislative Assembly, which since 1962 consists of 57 deputies, 1 for every 49,000 inhabitants, elected for 4 years. The President and 2 Vice-Presidents are elected for 4 years; the candidate receiving the largest vote, provided it is over 40% of the total, is declared elected, but a second ballot is required if no candidate gets 40% of the total. Suffrage is universal, there being no exemption for reasons of economic status, race or sex. The vote is direct by secret ballot for all nationals of 18 years or over. Elections are normally held on the first Sunday in February. Voting for President, Deputies and Municipal Councillors is secret and compulsory for all men under 70 years of age. Independent non-party candidates are barred from the ballot.

Presidential elections took place on 4 Feb. 1990 and Rafael Angel Calderón of the Social Christian Unity Party defeated Dr Carlos Manuel Castillo of the ruling National Liberation Party by a 3% margin.

President: Rafael Angel Calderón (b. 1949; assumed office 8 May 1990).

The powers of the President are limited by the constitution, which leaves him the power to appoint and remove at will members of his cabinet. All other public appointments are made jointly in the names of the President and of the minister in charge of the department concerned.

National flag: Five unequal stripes of blue, white, red, white, blue, with the national arms on a white disc near the hoist.

National anthem: Noble patria, tu hermosa bandera ('Noble fatherland, thy beautiful banner'; words by J. M. Zeledón, 1903; tune by M. M. Gutiérrez, 1851).

DEFENCE

Army. The Army was abolished in 1948, and replaced by a Civil Guard 4,600 strong in 1992.

Navy. The para-military Civil Guard flotilla includes 1 fast patrol craft and 5 small coastguard cutters. Personnel (1991), 150 officers and men.

Air Wing. The Civil Guard operates a small air wing equipped with 15 light planes and helicopters.

INTERNATIONAL RELATIONS

Membership. Costa Rica is a member of the UN, CACM and OAS.

ECONOMY

Policy. An austerity programme was introduced in June 1990, including an increase in income tax, rises in public utility prices and a devaluation of the currency.

Budget. The 1985 Budget provided for revenue of 41,101·6m. colones and expenditure of 43,135·5m. colones.

Currency. The unit of currency is the *Costa Rican colón* (CRC) of 100 *céntimos.* The official rate is used for all imports on an essential list and by the Government and autonomous institutions and a free rate is used for all other transactions. The currency was devalued in June 1990. 22,000m. colons were in circulation in 1989. The official rate in March 1992 was ₡138·48 = US$1; 243·10 = £1.

The currency is chiefly notes. The Central Bank issue notes for 5, 10, 20, 50, 100, 500 and 1,000 colones. Silver coins of 1 colon, 50 centimos and 25 centimos were in 1935 replaced by coins (2 and 1 colones and 50 and 25 centimos) made up of 3 parts copper and 1 part nickel, and given the same value as the subsidiary silver currency. There are copper coins (and chromium stainless steel coins) of 10 and 5 centimos.

Banking and Finance. The Central Bank was established in 1950 for the organization and direction of the national monetary system and of dealings in foreign exchange, the promotion of facilities for credit and the supervision of all banking operations in the country. The bank has a board of 7 directors appointed by the Government, including *ex officio* the Minister of Finance and the Planning Office Director. The *Governor* is Jorge Guaradia.

The National Insurance Institute *(Instituto Nacional de Seguros)* is a Government organization, created in 1924, which has a monopoly of new insurance business.

Weights and Measures. The metric system is legally established; but in the country districts the following old Spanish weights and measures are found: *libra =*

1·014 lb. avoirdupois; *arroba* = 25·35 lb. avoirdupois; *quintal* = 101·40 lb. avoirdupois, and *fanega* = 11 Imperial bushels.

ENERGY AND NATURAL RESOURCES

Electricity. Electricity, derived from water power in the highlands, is increasingly used as motive power. Output, 1986, was 2,770m. kwh. Supply 120 volts; 60 Hz.

Minerals. Gold output is about 3,000 troy oz. per year. Salt production from sea water is about 10,000 tonnes annually. Haematite ore was discovered on the Nicoya Peninsula late in 1960 and sulphur near San Carlos in 1966.

Agriculture. Agriculture is the principal industry; 729,000 persons depended upon it in 1990, of whom 251,000 were economically active. The cultivated area is about 1m. acres; grass lands cover 1·8m. acres. The principal agricultural products are coffee, bananas, sugar and cattle. 25,000 ha were planted with bananas in 1991.

Coffee production in 1990 (in tonnes) was 138,000; sugar-cane, 2·4m.; bananas, 1·53m.; cocoa, 4,000; maize, 72,000; tobacco, 2,000; rice, 207,000; potatoes, 41,000.

In 1990 cattle numbered 1·76m. and pigs 224,000.

Forestry. In 1988 there were 1·6m. ha of woodlands. There are extensive tracts of public lands that have never been cleared on which can be found quantities of rosewood, cedar, mahogany and other cabinet woods.

Fisheries. Total catch (1986) 21,000 tonnes.

INDUSTRY. The main manufactured goods are foodstuffs, textiles, fertilizers, pharmaceuticals, furniture, cement, tyres, canning, clothing, plastic goods, plywood and electrical equipment.

Trade Unions. As Costa Rica is still essentially an agricultural country, the organization of labour has made progress only in the larger centres of population, and even there it is not a strong movement. There are two main trade unions, *Rerum Novarum* (anti-Communist) and *Confederación General de Trabajadores Costarricenses* (Communist).

FOREIGN ECONOMIC RELATIONS

Commerce. The value of imports into and exports from Costa Rica in 5 years was as follows in US$:

	1982	1983	1984	1985	1986
Imports	867,000,000	987,826,445	1,093,739,311	1,098,178,489	1,147,500,000
Exports	870,800,000	559,951,375	1,006,389,617	1,084,100,000	1,106,000,000

The values (in US$1m.) of the principal imports in 1984 were: Machinery, including transport equipment, 219·6; manufactures, 317·5; chemicals, 250·1; fuel and mineral oils, 166·7; foodstuffs, 9.

Chief exports (in US$1m.) in 1984 were: Manufactured goods and other products, 450·6; coffee, 267·8 (mostly to Federal Republic of Germany, USA, UK and Italy); bananas, 251 (to USA); sugar, 35·5; cocoa, 1·5.

Total trade between Costa Rica and UK (British Department of Trade returns in £1,000 sterling):

	1987	1988	1989	1990	1991
Imports to UK	16,752	16,902	24,113	17,468	21,823
Exports and re-exports from UK	14,407	11,390	12,780	14,556	11,312

Tourism. There was a total of 261,000 tourists in 1986.

COMMUNICATIONS

Roads. In 1987 there were about 35,000 km of all-weather motor roads open. On the Costa Rica section of the Inter-American Highway it is possible to motor to Panama during the dry season. The Pan-American Highway into Nicaragua is metalled for most of the way and there is now a good highway open almost to Puntarenas. Motor vehicles, 1985, numbered 186,046.

Railways. The nationalized railway system *(Incofer)*, totalling 828·5 km (128 km electrified) of 1,067 mm gauge, connects San José with Limón, the Atlantic port, and San José with Puntarenas, the Pacific port. Total railway traffic in 1988 was 1m. tonnes of freight and 1·3m. passengers.

Civil Aviation. There were 92 airports (59 private) in service in 1984. Passenger movement in and out of Costa Rica is almost entirely by air *via* the local company, LACSA, PANAM and TACA. Passengers carried, 1984, 1,014,559. LACSA links San José by daily services with all the more important towns.

Shipping. In 1981, 1,221 ships entered and cleared the ports of the republic (Puerto Limón, Puntarenas and Golfito).

Telecommunications. There were 281,042 telephones in 1983.
The Government has 202 telegraph offices and 88 official telephone stations. In 1991 there were 255,000 radio and 611,000 television receivers (colour by NTSC).

Cinemas (1979). Cinemas numbered 106, with seating capacity of 105,000.

Newspapers (1984). There were 4 daily newspapers all published in San José.

JUSTICE, RELIGION, EDUCATION AND WELFARE

Justice. Justice is administered by the Supreme Court, 5 appeal courts divided into 5 chambers; the Court of Cassation, the Higher and Lower Criminal Courts, and the Higher and Lower Civil Courts. There are also subordinate courts in the separate provinces and local justices throughout the republic. Capital punishment may not be inflicted.

Religion. Roman Catholicism is the religion of the State, which contributes to its maintenance, controls the Church Patronage and insists on lay instruction in history, economics and similar subjects; there is entire religious liberty under the constitution, but religious appeals are forbidden in current political discussions. The Archbishop of Costa Rica has 4 bishops at Alajuela, Limón, San Isidro el General and Tilarán.
Protestants number about 40,000.

Education. Costa Rica has a very low illiteracy rate. Elementary instruction is compulsory and free; secondary education (since 1949) is also free. Elementary schools are provided and maintained by local school councils, while the national government pays the teachers, besides making subventions in aid of local funds. In 1986 there were 3,107 public primary schools with 13,500 teachers and administrative staff and 380,000 enrolled pupils; there were 241 public and private secondary schools with 8,926 teachers and 141,691 pupils. The University of Costa Rica, founded in San José in 1843, had (1980) 2,337 professors in 13 faculties and 38,629 students.

Health. In 1982 there were 1,929 doctors and 39 hospitals with 7,706 beds. In 1979 there were 239 dentists.

DIPLOMATIC REPRESENTATIVES

Of Costa Rica in Great Britain (19A Cavendish Sq., London, W1M 9AI)
Ambassador: Luís Rafael Tinoco.

Of Great Britain in Costa Rica (Edificio Centro Colón, Apartado 815, San José)
Ambassador and Consul-General: William Marsden, CMG.

Of Costa Rica in the USA (1825 Connecticut Ave., NW Washington D.C., 20009)
Ambassador: Gonzalo Facio.

Of the USA in Costa Rica (Pavas, San José)
Chargé d'affaires: Robert O. Homme.

Of Costa Rica to the United Nations
Ambassador: Cristián Tattenbach.

Further Reading

Statistical Information: Official statistics are issued by the Director General de Estadística (Ministerio de Industria y Comercio, San José) as they become available. The compilation of statistics was started in 1861.

Ameringer, C. D., *Democracy in Costa Rica.* New York, 1982
Biesanz, R., *(et al), The Costa Ricans.* Hemel Hempstead, 1982
Bird, L., *Costa Rica: Unarmed Democracy.* London, 1984
Creedman, T. S. *Historical Dictionary of Costa Rica.* 2nd ed. Metuchen (N.J.), 1991
Fernandez Guardia, L., *Historia de Costa Rica.* 2nd ed., 2 vols. San José, 1941
Seligson, M. A., *Peasants of Costa Rica and the Development of Agrarian Capitalism.* Univ. of
    Wisconsin Press, 1980
Stansifer, C., *Costa Rica.* 2nd ed. [Bibliography] Oxford and Santa Barbara, 1991

CÔTE D'IVOIRE

Capital: Abidjan
Population: 12·10m. (1990)
GNP per capita: US$790 (1989)

République de la
Côte d'Ivoire

(Republic of the Ivory Coast)

HISTORY. France obtained rights on the coast in 1842, but did not actively and continuously occupy the territory till 1882. On 10 Jan. 1889 Ivory Coast was declared a French protectorate, and it became a colony on 10 March 1893; in 1904 it became a territory of French West Africa. On 1 Jan. 1933 most of the territory of Upper Volta was added to the Ivory Coast, but on 1 Jan. 1948 this area was returned to the re-constituted Upper Volta, now Burkina Faso. The Ivory Coast became an autonomous republic within the French Community on 4 Dec. 1958 and achieved full independence on 7 Aug. 1960. From 1 Jan. 1986 the French version of the name of the country became the only correct title.

AREA AND POPULATION. Côte d'Ivoire is bounded west by Liberia and Guinea, north by Mali and Burkina Faso, east by Ghana, and south by the Gulf of Guinea. It has an area of 322,463 sq. km and a population at the 1975 census of 6,702,866 (of whom 31·8% were urban). Estimate (1990) 12,100,000 (45·6% urban).

The areas and populations of the 34 departments were:

Department	Sq. km	Census 1975	Department	Sq. km	Census 1975
Abengourou	6,900	177,692	Ferkéssédougou	17,728	90,423
Abidjan	14,200	1,389,141	Gagnoa	4,500	174,018
Aboisso	6,250	148,823	Guiglo	14,150	137,672
Adzopé	5,230	162,837	Issia	3,590	104,081
Agboville	3,850	141,970	Katiola	9,420	77,875
Biankouma	4,950	75,711	Korhogo	12,500	276,816
Bondoukou	16,530	296,551	Lakota	2,730	76,105
Bongouanou	5,570	216,907	Man	7,050	278,659
Bouaflé	5,670	164,817	Mankono	10,660	82,358
Bouaké	23,800	808,048	Odienné	20,600	124,010
Bouna	21,470	84,290	Oumé	2,400	85,486
Boundiali	7,895	96,449	Sassandra	17,530	116,644
Dabakala	9,670	56,230	Séguéla	11,240	75,181
Daloa	11,610	265,529	Soubré	8,270	75,350
Danané	4,600	170,249	Tingréla	2,200	35,829
Dimbokro	8,530	258,116	Touba	8,720	77,786
Divo	7,920	202,511	Zuénoula	2,830	98,792

The principal cities (populations, census 1975) are the capital, Abidjan (951,216; estimate 1982, 1·85m.), Bouaké (175,264), Daloa (60,837), Man (50,288), Korhogo (45,250) and Gagnoa (42,362). The new capital will be at Yamoussoukro (120,000 in 1984).

The principal ethnic groups are the Akan-speaking peoples of the south-east (Baule, 12% and Anyi, 11%) and the Bete (20%) and Kru of the south-west; in the north-east are Voltaic groups including Senufo (14%), while Malinké (7%) and other Mandé peoples inhabit the north-west.

French is the official language and there were (1985) about 50,000 French residents.

CLIMATE. A tropical climate, affected by distance from the sea. In coastal areas, there are wet seasons from May to July and in Oct. and Nov., but in central areas the periods are March to May and July to Nov. In the north, there is one wet season from June to Oct. Abidjan. Jan. 81°F (27·2°C), July 75°F (23·9°C). Annual rainfall 84" (2,100 mm). Bouaké. Jan. 81°F (27·2°C), July 77°F (25°C). Annual rainfall 48" (1,200 mm).

CONSTITUTION AND GOVERNMENT. The 1960 Constitution was amended in 1971, 1975, 1980, 1985 and 1986. The sole legal Party has been the Democratic Party of Côte d'Ivoire, but opposition parties were legalized in May 1990. There is a 175-member *National Assembly* elected by universal suffrage for a 5-year term. The President is also directly elected for a 5-year term (renewable). He appoints and leads a Council of Ministers who assist him. At the elections of Oct. 1990 Félix Houphouët-Boigny (b. 1905) was elected president for a seventh 5-year term by 81·68% of the votes cast, against one opponent.

In Nov. 1990 the National Assembly voted that its Speaker should become president in the event of the latter's incapacity, and created the post of prime minister to be appointed by the president.

At the National Assembly elections of Nov. 1990 490 candidates stood. The electorate was 4·7m.; turn-out was 60%. The Democratic Party won 163 seats; the Ivorian Popular Front, 9; the Workers' Party, 1; independents, 2.

A new government was formed in Nov. 1990 of 20 ministers including:
Prime Minister: Alassane Ouattara (b. 1952).
Minister of the Economy and Finance: Daniel Duncan. *Raw Materials:* Guy Gauze. *Foreign:* Amara Essy.
The *Speaker* is Henri Konan Bedie.

National flag: Three vertical strips of orange, white, green.
National anthem: L'Abidjanaise (words by M. Ekra and others, tune by P. M Pango).

Local government: There are 34 departments, each under an appointed Prefect and an elected Conseil-Général, sub-divided into 163 sub-prefectures. At the elections of Dec. 1990 turn-out was low. The Democratic Party won 123 out of 132 authorities; the Ivorian Popular Front, 6; independents, 3.

DEFENCE

Army. The Army consisted in 1990 of 1 armoured battalion, 3 infantry battalions and support units. Equipment includes 5 AMX-13 light tanks and 7 ERC-90 armoured cars. Total strength (1991), 5,500. Paramilitary forces, 7,800.

Navy. Offshore, riverine and coastal patrol squadrons include 2 fast missile craft, 2 patrol vessels, 1 riverine defence craft, 1 light transport and 2 minor landing craft. Personnel in 1991 totalled 700 and the force is based at Locodjo (Abidjan).

Air Force. The Air Force, formed in 1962, has 4 Alpha Jet advanced trainers, with combat potential, 1 turbofan Fokker 100, 1 Super-King Air, 1 Cessna 421, 1 Gulfstream transport, 2 Reims-Cessna 150s, 5 Beech F-33Cs and 3 SA330 Puma, 3 Dauphin 2, 1 Alouette III and 3 Gazelle helicopters. Personnel (1991) 900.

INTERNATIONAL RELATIONS

Membership. Côte d'Ivoire is a member of the UN, OAU and is an ACP state of the EEC.

ECONOMY

Policy. Austerity measures were introduced in May 1990.

Budget. The budget for 1988 totalled 493,500m. francs CFA and for recurrent expenditure and 143,600m. francs CFA for investment. Capital expenditure 145,879 francs CFA.

Currency. The currency is the *franc CFA* with a parity rate of 50 *francs CFA* to 1

French *franc*. In March 1992, £1 sterling = 489·63 francs CFA; US$1 = 278·91 francs CFA.

Banking and Finance. The *Banque Centrale des Etats de l'Afrique de l'Ouest* is the bank of issue. Numerous foreign and domestic banks have offices in Abidjan, and *Société Générale de Banque, Société Ivoirienne de Banque, Banque Internationale pour le Commerce et l'Industrie de la Côte d'Ivoire* and *Banque Internationale pour l'Afrique Occidentale* maintain wide branch networks throughout the country.

ENERGY AND NATURAL RESOURCES

Electricity. The electricity industry was privatized in 1990. Production in 1985 amounted to 2,162m. kwh mostly from new hydroelectric projects at Kassou and Taabo on the Bandama river, Buyo on the Sassandra river, and from 2 older dams on the Bia river. Supply 220 volts; 50 Hz.

Oil. Petroleum has been produced (offshore) since Oct. 1977. Production (1991) 161,000 tonnes.

Minerals. Diamond extraction was 700,000 carats in 1985. There are iron ore deposits at Bangolo and gold-mining began in Jan. 1990, reserves are estimated at 4,500 kg.

Agriculture. The main crops (production, 1990 in 1,000 tonnes) are coffee (219), cocoa (720), bananas (97), pineapples (136), palm oil (214), palm kernels (37), seed cotton (134), rubber (2), yams (2,528), cassava (1,393), plantains (1,086), rice (687), maize (484), millet (44), sugar-cane (1,550) and groundnuts (134).
   Livestock, 1990: 1·05m. cattle, 1·13m. sheep, 0·89m. goats and 0·36m. pigs.

Forestry. Equatorial rain forests, especially in the south, cover 3m. ha and produce over 30 commercially valuable species including teak, mahogany and ebony. Production in 1986 was 11·9m. cu. metres.

Fisheries. The catch in 1986 amounted to 97,200.

INDUSTRY. Industrialization has developed rapidly since independence, particularly food processing, textiles and sawmills. Several factories produce palm-oil, fruit preserves and fruit juice.

Trade Unions. The main trade union is the *Union Générale des Travailleurs de Côte d'Ivoire*, with over 100,000 members.

FOREIGN ECONOMIC RELATIONS. External debt was US$15,000m. in 1990.

Commerce. Trade for calendar years in 1m. francs CFA:

	1981	1982	1983	1984	1985
Imports	681,464	718,593	714,828	658,569	772,987
Exports	689,298	747,452	796,774	1,184,347	1,318,059

In 1985 exports of coffee furnished 21% of exports, cocoa 30%, timber 7% and petroleum products, 9%. Of the total 17% went to France, 17% to the Netherlands, 12% to the USA and 9% to Italy. Of the imports, France supplied 32% and Nigeria, 11%.
   Total trade between the Côte d'Ivoire and UK (British Department of Trade returns, in £1,000 sterling):

	1987	1988	1989	1990	1991
Imports to UK	90,246	64,041	65,943	69,849	45,630
Exports and re-exports from UK	26,834	31,172	29,434	26,941	24,131

Tourism. In 1986 there were 187,000 foreign tourists.

COMMUNICATIONS

Roads. In 1984 roads totalled 53,736 km (including 128 km of motorway) and there were 182,956 private cars and 43,001 commercial vehicles.

Railways. From Abidjan a metre-gauge railway runs to Léraba on the border with Burkina Faso (655 km), and thence through Burkina Faso to Ouagadougou. Operation of the railway as a single entity ended in 1986, and in 1988 separate organizations were established in each country. In 1986–87 the railways carried 1·6m. passengers and 684,000 tonnes of freight.

Civil Aviation. The international airport is at Abidjan-Port-Buet. In 1981 it handled 870,000 passengers and 33,000 tonnes of freight and mail. Air Ivoire provides regular domestic services to 10 regional airports and 15 landing strips.

Shipping. The main ports are Abidjan and San Pedro. In 1981 Abidjan port handled 5·8m. tonnes and San Pedro 1·5m. tonnes. In 1986 the merchant marine comprised 61 vessels of 141,674 tons gross.

Telecommunications. There were 87,700 telephones in 1984 and 1,800 telex machines. The government-controlled Radiodiffusion Télévision Ivoirienne is responsible for broadcasting. In 1991 there were 810,000 television (colour by SECAM) and 1·5m. radio receivers.

Newspapers. In 1984 there was 1 daily newspaper, *Fraternité-Matin*.

JUSTICE, RELIGION, EDUCATION AND WELFARE

Justice. There are 28 courts of first instance and 3 assize courts in Abidjan, Bouaké and Daloa, 2 courts of appeal in Abidjan and Bouaké, and a supreme court in Abidjan.

Religion. In 1989 there were 2·4m. Moslems (mainly in the north) and 2·4m. Christians (chiefly Roman Catholics in the south). Traditional animist beliefs are also practised.

Education. There were, in 1984, 1,179,456 pupils in primary schools, 245,342 pupils in secondary schools and (1979) 22,437 in technical schools. The *Université Nationale de Côte d'Ivoire,* at Abidjan (founded 1964), had 12,755 students in 1984.

Health. In 1978 there were 9,962 hospital beds, 429 doctors, 36 dentists, 615 midwives, 3,052 nurses and 76 pharmacists.

DIPLOMATIC REPRESENTATIVES

Of the Côte d'Ivoire in Great Britain (2 Upper Belgrave St., London, SW1X 8BJ)
Ambassador: Gervais Attoungbré.

Of Great Britain in the Côte d'Ivoire (Immeuble 'Les Harmonies', Blvd. Carde, Abidjan)
Ambassador: Margaret Rothwell, CMG.

Of the Côte d'Ivoire in the USA (2424 Massachusetts Ave., NW, Washington, D.C., 20008)
Ambassador: Charles Gomis.

Of the USA in the Côte d'Ivoire (5 Rue Jesse Owens, Abidjan)
Ambassador: Kenneth L. Brown.

Of the Côte d'Ivoire to the United Nations
Ambassador: Jean-Jacques Bechio.

Further Reading

Statistical Information: Service de la Statistique, Abidjan. It publishes *Bulletin Statistique Mensuel and Inventoire Économique de la Côte d'Ivoire.*

Sugar, H., *Ivory Coast.* [Bibliography] Oxford and Santa Barbara, 1990
Zartman, I. W. and Delgado, C., *The Political Economy of Ivory Coast.* New York, 1984
Zolberg, A. R., *One-Party Government in the Ivory Coast.* Rev. ed. Princeton Univ. Press, 1974

CROATIA

Capital: Zagreb
Population: 4·69m. (1990)

Republika Hrvatska

HISTORY. The Croats migrated to their present territory in the 6th century and were converted to Roman Catholicism. Croatia was united with Hungary by a personal union of thrones in 1091 and remained under Hungarian administration until the end of the first world war. On 1 Dec. 1918 Croatia became a part of the new Kingdom of Serbs, Croats and Slovenes, which was renamed Yugoslavia in 1929.

During the second world war an independent fascist (Ustaša) state was set up under the aegis of the German occupiers. During the Communist period Croatia became one of the 6 'Socialist Republics' constituting the Yugoslav federation. (*See* THE STATESMAN'S YEAR-BOOK, 1991–92, p. 1607).

In Feb. 1991 parliament ruled that henceforth Croatian law would take precedence over federal. At a referendum on 19 May 1991 turn-out was 82·97% of the electorate of 3·6m. 94·17% of votes cast were in favour of Croatia becoming an independent sovereign state with the option of joining a future Yugoslav confederation as opposed to remaining in the existing Yugoslav federation. The Krajina, and other predominantly Serbian areas of Croatia, proclaimed the desire for union with Serbia and seized power by force of arms. Croatian forces and Serb insurgents backed by federal forces ostensibly of law and order became embroiled in a conflict throughout 1991 until the arrival of a UN peace-keeping mission at the beginning of 1992.

Croatia was recognized as an independent state by Germany on 23 Dec. 1991, and was granted EC recognition on 15 Jan. 1992.

AREA AND POPULATION. Croatia is bounded in the north by Slovenia and Hungary and in the east by Serbia. It has an extensive Adriatic coastline well provided with ports, and includes the historical areas of Dalmatia, Istria and Slavonia which no longer have administrative status. The capital is Zagreb. Its area is 56,538 sq. km. Population at the 1981 census was 4,601,469 (2,374,579 females), of whom the predominating ethnic groups were Croats (3,454,661) and Serbs (531,502). Population density per sq. km, 1981: 81·4. Population, 1990, 4,685,000.

At the beginning of 1991 there were some 0·6m. resident Serbs. A law of Dec. 1991 guaranteed the autonomy of Serbs in areas where they are in a majority after the establishment of a permanent peace.

Vital statistics:

	Live births	Marriages	Deaths	Growth rate per 1,000
1987	59,209	31,395	53,080	1.3
1988	58,525	29,719	52,686	1.2
1989	57,003	29,399	53,073	0.8

Rates, 1989: Birth, 12·2 per 1,000 population; death, 11·3. Infant mortality, 11·3 per 1,000 live births.

CONSTITUTION AND GOVERNMENT. There is a 3-chamber parliament (*Sabor*) of 365 members. Elections were held in April and May 1990. The electorate was 3·5m.; turn-out was 70%. The Croat Democratic Union (CDU) gained 205 seats, the Party of Democratic Change (formerly Communist), 75. In May 1990 Franjo Tudjman was elected President of Croatia by the Sabor.

A new constitution was adopted on 21 Dec. 1990, proclaiming Croatia's right to secede from federal Yugoslavia.

President: Franjo Tudjman (b. 1922; CDU).

In Feb. 1992 the government included:

Prime Minister: Franjo Greguric. *Deputy Prime Minister:* Jurica Pavelić. *Defence:* Gojko Susak. *Foreign:* Zvonimir Separovic.

National flag: 3 horizontal stripes of red, white and blue with the arms over all in the centre.

DEFENCE. The Croatian National Guard was formed in April 1991.

ECONOMY

Currency. On 23 Dec. 1991 Croatia introduced the *Croatian dinar,* at parity with the Yugoslav dinar and the Slovenian tolar.

Banking and Finance. Total savings deposits in 1990 were 6,692m. dinars.

ENERGY AND NATURAL RESOURCES

Electricity. Output was 8,601m. kwh. in 1989 (4,586m. kwh. hydro-electric). A nuclear power station is planned (the federal Yugoslav ban on such plants being declared no longer applicable).

Oil and Gas. 2·3m. tonnes of crude oil were produced in 1989, and 2,177m. cu. metres of natural gas.

Minerals. Production, 1989 (in 1,000 tonnes): Coal, 160; brown coal and lignite, 37; bauxite, 365; iron ore, 653; china clay, 318.

Agriculture. In 1989 agricultural land totalled 3·22m. ha (1·48m. ha arable, 1·16m. ha pasture, 73,000 ha vineyards). The cultivated area was 2·02m. ha. Yields (in 1,000 tonnes, 1990): Wheat, 1,602; maize, 1,948; potatoes, 596; plums, 30.

Livestock, 1990 (in 1,000): Cattle, 829 (milch cows, 492); sheep, 751; pigs, 1,573; poultry, 17,102. Animal products, 1989: Meat, 312,000 tonnes; honey, 814 tonnes; milk, 947m. litres; eggs, 1,043,000.

Forestry. Forests covered 2,013,000 ha in 1990. 4·16m. cu. metres of timber were cut in 1989.

Fisheries. The total catch was 50,806 tonnes in 1989, of which 9,886 tonnes were freshwater fish.

INDUSTRY. Production, 1989 (in 1,000 tonnes): Steel, 602; coke, 767; nitrogenous fertilizers, 1,466; plastics, 354; cement, 2,819; sugar, 209; cotton fabric, 58m. sq. metres; tractors, 8,168.

Labour. The population of working age (15–59) in 1989 was 3,049,000. The non-agricultural workforce was 1,618,204 (653,000 females; 1,566,710 in the public sector). There were 139,878 registered unemployed.

FOREIGN ECONOMIC RELATIONS

Commerce. Exports in 1989 were worth 8,550m. federal dinars; imports, 12,324m. federal dinars.

The main exports are machinery and transport equipment, chemicals and foodstuffs.

Tourism. 61,849,000 tourist nights were spent in 1989.

COMMUNICATIONS

Roads. In 1989 there were 827,572 passenger cars (795,053 private), 6,276 buses, 47,463 goods vehicles and 22,730 motorcyles. 168m. passengers and 30m. tonnes of freight were carried by public transport.

There were 13,888 traffic accidents in 1989 in which 1,321 persons were killed.

Telecommunications. In 1989 there were 981,976 telephones, 25 radio stations and 1 TV centre.

Cinemas. There were 293 cinemas with a total of 102,000 seats in 1990. 6 feature films were made in 1989.

Newspapers and Books. In 1989 there were 8 daily and 602 other newspapers, and 404 periodicals. 3,427 book titles were published in a total of 350,809 copies.

JUSTICE, RELIGION, EDUCATION AND WELFARE

Religion. Croatia is traditionally Roman Catholic. The province of Zagreb has 4 suffragan sees. There are also independent Old Catholic churches with a Synodial Council in Zagreb.

Education. In 1989 89,729 children attended pre-school institutions. In 1989 there were 2,647 primary schools with 514,437 pupils and 27,698 teachers; 227 secondary schools with 200,175 pupils and 12,900 teachers; 65 special-need schools with 4,502 pupils and 756 teachers; 60 tertiary institutions with 69,021 students and 6,132 teachers; 51 university faculties with 65,514 students and 5,760 teachers; 3 art schools with 691 students and 133 teachers; and 6 other institutes of higher education with 2,816 students and 239 teachers.

Social security. The health insurance scheme covered 1,732,000 persons in 1990, and there were 262,000 age, 164,000 disability and 167,000 veterans pensions issued.

Health. In 1989 there were 12,091 doctors and dentists, 1,886 pharmacists and 35,697 hospital beds.

CUBA

Capital: Havana
Population: 10·58m. (1989)

República de Cuba

HISTORY. Cuba, except for the brief British occupancy in 1762–63, remained a Spanish possession from its discovery by Columbus in 1492 until 10 Dec. 1898, when the sovereignty was relinquished under the terms of the Treaty of Paris, which ended the struggle of the Cubans against Spanish rule. Cuba thus became an independent republic, but the United States stipulated under the 'Platt Amendment' (abrogated by Roosevelt in 1934) that Cuba must enter into no treaty relations with a foreign power, which might endanger its independence.

The revolutionary movement against the Batista dictatorship, led by Dr Fidel Castro Ruíz, started on 26 July 1953 (now a national holiday). It achieved power on 1 Jan. 1959 when Batista fled the country.

An invasion force of émigrés and adventurers landed in Cuba on 17 April 1961; the main body was defeated at the Bay of Pigs (Matanzas province) and mopped up by 20 April.

The US Navy blockaded Cuba from 22 Oct. to 22 Nov. 1962.

AREA AND POPULATION. The island of Cuba forms the largest and most westerly of the Greater Antilles group and lies 135 miles south of the tip of Florida, USA. The Republic of Cuba has an area of 110,860 sq. km, and comprises the island of Cuba, (104,945 sq. km.); the Isle of Youth (Isla de la Juventud, formerly the Isle of Pines; 2,200 sq. km.), and some 1,600 small isles ('cays'; 3,715 sq. km.). Census (1981) 9,723,605; estimate, 1989, 10,577,000 (in 1988 there were 5,270,800 males and 5,197,800 females).

The area, population and density of population of the 14 provinces and the special Municipality of the Isle of Youth were as follows (1989 estimate):

	Area sq. km	Population		Area sq. km.	Population
Pinar del Río	10,860	681,500	Camagüey	14,134	727,700
La Habana	5,671	633,400	Las Tunas	6,373	481,500
Ciudad de La Habana	727	2,068,600	Holguín	9,105	927,700
Matanzas	11,669	599,500	Granma	8,452	777,300
Cienfuegos	4,149	356,700	Santiago de Cuba	6,343	974,100
Villa Clara	8,069	788,800	Guantánamo	6,366	487,900
Sancti Spíritus	6,737	422,300			
Ciego de Avila	6,485	355,500	Isla de la Juventud	2,199	70,900

The chief cities (1986, estimate) were Havana, the capital (2,014,800), Santiago de Cuba (358,800), Camagüey (260,800), Holguín (194,700), Santa Clara (178,300), Guantánamo (174,400), Cienfuegos (109,300), Matanzas (105,400), Bayamo (105,300), Pinar del Río (100,900), Las Tunas (91,400), Ciego de Avila (80,500) and Sancti Spíritus (75,600).

Infant mortality (1989) 11·1 per 1,000 live births.

CLIMATE. Situated in the sub-tropical zone, Cuba has a generally rainy climate, affected by the Gulf Stream and the N.E. Trades, though winters are comparatively dry after the heaviest rains in Sept. and Oct. Hurricanes are liable to occur between June and Nov. Havana. Jan. 72°F (22·2°C), July 82°F (27·8°C). Annual rainfall 48" (1,224 mm).

CONSTITUTION AND GOVERNMENT. The previous Constitution was suspended in Jan. 1959. The first socialist Constitution came into force on 24 Feb. 1976.

Since 1940 the following have been Presidents of the Republic:

	Took office		Took office
Gen. Fulgencio Batista y Zaldívar	10 Oct. 1940	Gen. Fulgencio Batista y Zaldívar	10 March 1952
Dr Ramón Grau San Martín	10 Oct. 1944	Dr Manuel Urratia Lleo	2 Jan. 1959
Dr Carlos Prío Socarrás	10 Oct. 1948	Osvaldo Dórticos Torrado	17 July 1959

460

Legislative power is vested in the National Assembly of People's Power, consisting of 499 deputies elected for a 5-year term by the Municipal Assemblies; elections were held in 1976, 1981 and 1986. The National Assembly elects a 31-member Council of State as its permanent organ. The Council of State's President, who is head of state and of government, nominates and leads a Council of Ministers approved by the National Assembly. A law of Dec. 1991 instituted direct parliamentary elections.

President: Dr Fidel Castro Ruíz became President of the Council of State on 3 Dec. 1976. He is also President of the Council of Ministers, First Secretary of the Cuban Communist Party and C.-in-C. of the Revolutionary Armed Forces.

First Vice-President of the Council of State and of the Council of Ministers, Minister of the Revolutionary Armed Forces: Raúl Castro Ruíz. *Foreign Affairs:* Isidoro Octavio Malmierca Peoli. *Interior:* Gen. Abelardo Colome. *Justice:* Juan Escalona Reguera. *Foreign Trade:* Ricardo Cabrisas Ruíz.

The *Speaker* of the National Assembly is Gen. Juan Escalona.

The Council of Ministers also includes 10 other Vice-Presidents, the Presidents of 10 State Planning Committees and 17 other Ministers.

Dr Castro on 2 Dec. 1961 proclaimed 'a Marxist–Leninist programme adapted to the precise objective conditions existing in our country'. The provisional *Organizaciones Revolucionarias Integradas* (ORI) were established as an intermediate stage towards a single (communist) party, and gave way to the *Partido Unido de la Revolución Socialista* (PURS). This brought together the *Partido Socialista Popular, Movimiento de 26 Julio* and (Students') *Directorio Revolucionario.* The PURS in turn became (3 Oct. 1965) the *Partido Comunista de Cuba.*

The Congress of the PCC elects a Central Committee of 225 members, which in turn appoints a Political Bureau comprising 25 members.

National flag: 3 blue, 2 white stripes (horizontal); a white 5-pointed star in a red triangle at the hoist.

National anthem: Al combate corred bayameses ('Run, Bayamans, to the combat'; words and tune by P. Figueredo, 1868).

Local Government. The country is divided into 14 provinces, the special Municipality (the Isle of Youth) and 169 municipalities. Local Government is the responsibility of the organizations of Peoples' Power. Elections were held in 1976, 1979, 1981, 1984 and 1987 for delegates to the Municipal Assemblies by universal suffrage for $2\frac{1}{2}$ year terms; the Municipal Assemblies then elected the Provincial Assemblies for similar terms.

DEFENCE. On 13 Nov. 1963 conscription was introduced for all men between the ages of 16 and 45, later raised to 50 (2 years); women of the 17–35 age groups may volunteer (for 2 years). Soviet troops withdrew in 1991.

Army. The strength was 145,000 (60,000 conscripts) in 1991. Reserves are estimated at 135,000. The Army is organized in 4 corps, 1 armoured division, 13 mechanized infantry divisions, 9 infantry divisions, 1 independent armoured brigade, 8 independent infantry brigades, 1 airborne brigade, 1 surface-to-air missile brigade and 1 anti-aircraft regiment. Equipment includes 900 T-54/-55, 300 T-62 and 500 T-34 main battle tanks and 60 PT-76 light tanks. Para-military forces total 19,000 and the Territorial Militia, 1·3m. including reservists, all armed.

Navy. Naval combatants, all ex-Soviet, include 3 'Foxtrot' class diesel submarines, 3 'Koni' class frigates, 18 fast missile craft, 9 patrol hydrofoils, 1 coastal and 3 inshore patrol craft, 4 coastal minehunters and 10 inshore minesweepers. There are 2 medium landing ships and 6 craft. The major auxiliaries include 1 tanker, 1 electronic intelligence gatherer, 1 tug, 1 survey ship and 1 training ship. Some 20 minor auxiliaries and service craft complete the total.

Personnel in 1991 totalled 13,500 (8,500 conscripts) including about 500 marines. Main bases are at Cienfuegos, Havana and Mariel. The USA still occupies the Guantánamo naval base, but the Cuban Government refuses to accept the nominal rent of US$5,000 per annum.

There is a coastal defence force equipped with artillery and some anti-ship missiles. A separate coast guard division of the Frontier Guards numbering 4,000 operates about 30 inshore patrol craft.

Air Force. The Air Force has been extensively re-equipped with aircraft supplied by USSR and in 1991 had a strength of some 22,000 officers and men (11,000 conscripts) and 300 combat aircraft. About 12 interceptor and 4 ground-attack squadrons fly MiG-29, MiG-23, MiG-21 and MiG-17 jet fighters. There is a squadron of An-26 twin-turboprop transports, some An-24 twin-turboprop transports, piston-engined Il-14s, and about 100 Mi-24 armed helicopters, Mi-8 (some armed), Mi-17, Mi-2 and Mi-4 helicopters, Zlin 326 piston-engined trainers and L-39, MiG-15UTI, MiG-21U, MiG-23U and MiG-29U jet trainers. An-2M biplanes are operated by the Air Force, mainly on agricultural and liaison duties. Soviet-built surface-to-air ('Guideline', 'Goa' and 'Gainful') and coastal defence ('Samlet') missiles are in service.

INTERNATIONAL RELATIONS

Membership. Cuba is a member of the UN, SELA and the Non-Aligned Movement.

ECONOMY

Policy. The economy is still centrally planned. Food was rationed in Nov. 1990.

Budget. Revenue in 1989 11,900m. pesos and expenditure, 13,500m. pesos.

Currency. The unit of currency is the *Cuban peso* (CUP) of 100 *centavos*, which is not convertible although an official exchange rate is announced daily reflecting any changes in the strength of the US$. In March 1992 £1 = 1·33 *pesos*; US$1 = 0·76 *pesos*.
Copper-nickel coins of 1 *peso* and 20, 5, 2 and 1 *centavo* are issued. Notes are for 100, 50, 20, 10, 5, 3 and 1 *peso*.

Banking and Finance. The central bank was created in 1948 (with capital of US$10m.) and began operating on 27 April 1950.
On 14 Oct. 1960 all banks were nationalized. All banking is now carried out by the National Bank of Cuba through its 250 agencies, or via the Banco Financiero.
All insurance business was nationalized in Jan. 1964. A National Savings Bank was established in 1983.

Weights and Measures. The metric system of weights and measures is legally compulsory, but the American and old Spanish systems are much used. The sugar industry uses the Spanish long ton (1·03 tonnes) and short ton (0·92 tonne). Cuba sugar sack = 329·59 lb. or 149·49 kg. Land is measured in *caballerías* (of 13·4 ha or 33 acres).

ENERGY AND NATURAL RESOURCES

Electricity. Production in 1989 was 15,237m. kwh. Supply 115 and 120 volts; 60 Hz.

Oil. Crude oil production (1991) 817,000 tonnes.

Minerals. Iron ore abounds, with deposits estimated at 3,500m. tonnes. Output of copper concentrate (1989) was 2,800 tonnes; refractory chrome (1987), 52,400 tonnes. Other minerals are nickel (1991, 40,000 tonnes) and cobalt (1989, 46,500 tonnes), silica and barytes. Gold and silver are also worked. Salt output from the solar evaporation of sea water was 114,900 tonnes in 1989.

Agriculture. In May 1959 all land over 30 *caballerías* was nationalized and has since been turned into state farms. In Oct. 1963 private holdings were reduced to a maximum of 5 *caballerías*.
In Sept. 1984 there were 1,472 co-operatives comprising 70,000 *caballerías* of land. The total cultivated land (1982) included state-owned, 3,398,200 ha, and in the private sector, 475,400 ha.

The most important product is sugar and its by-products. The 1989-90 crop was estimated at 8·04m. tonnes. Tobacco, coffee, cotton, maize, rice, potatoes and citrus fruit are grown.

Production of other important crops in 1989 was (in tonnes): Tobacco, 42,900; rice, 532,400; coffee, 22,500; maize (1988), 95,000.

Tobacco is grown mainly in the Vuelta–Abajo district, near Pinar del Río. Coffee is grown chiefly in the province of Oriente.

A fast-growing fibre, *kenaf*, originally from India, soft in texture, is replacing jute for sacking (production, 1986, 13,468 tonnes); the tobacco industry uses *majagua*, another local fibre, while a third fibre, *yarey*, from palms is also used. Rice cultivation is highly mechanized and the sown area produces two crops a year.

In 1987 citrus fruit production was 885,510 tonnes. In 1989 production of pineapples was 20,600 tonnes, tomatoes 244,400 tonnes and potatoes, 281,400 tonnes.

In 1989 the livestock included 1,292,000 pigs; 665,300 horses; 853,100 sheep and goats; 4·98m. head of cattle (in 1988).

Forestry. Cuba has 2·7m ha of forests representing 25% of the land area. These forests contain valuable cabinet woods, such as mahogany and cedar, besides dyewoods, fibres, gums, resins and oils. Cedar is used locally for cigar-boxes, and mahogany is exported. Cedars, mahogany, *majagua*, teca, etc., are also raised. In 1989 182·4m. saplings were planted, which included eucalyptus, pine, majagua, mahogany, cedar and casuarina.

Fisheries. Fishing is the third most important export industry, after sugar and nickel. Catch (1989) 191,889 tonnes.

INDUSTRY. Production in 1989 was: Textiles, 218·6m. sq. metres (cotton fabrics 182·6m. sq. metres); cement (1989), 3,800m. tonnes; wheat flour, 398,000 tonnes; fuel oil (1989), 4,152,800 tonnes; diesel oil (1989), 1,178,500 tonnes; processed crude oil, 7,916,000 tonnes; steel, 314,200 tonnes; steel bars, 367,100 tonnes; nickel and cobalt, 46,500 tonnes; copper, 2,759,100 tonnes; 314,700 tyres; 231,200 inner tubes; leather shoes, 11·00m. pairs; paint (1989), 121,000 hectolitres; soft drinks (1989), 2,396,500 hectolitres; 308,500m. cigars; 16,519,700m. cigarettes; fertilizers, 898,600 tonnes; 2,345 buses; 172,700 radios; 70,500 TVs; 9,100 refrigerators; sulphuric acid, 381,500 tonnes; fine salt, 114,900 tonnes.

Labour. In 1989 the monthly average salary was 188 pesos.

Trade Unions. The Workers' Central Union of Cuba, to which 23 unions are affiliated, had 2m. members in 1978.

FOREIGN ECONOMIC RELATIONS. In 1989 Cuba's hard currency reserves were US$100m. Foreign debt was US$6,200m.

Commerce. Imports and exports (including bullion and specie) for calendar years (in 1m. pesos):

	1985	1986	1987	1988	1989
Imports	7,983	7,569	7,612	4,549	7,580
Exports	7,209	6,702	5,401	5,518	5,519

The principal exports are sugar, minerals, tobacco, citrus fruit and fish. In 1988 exports included (in tonnes): Sugar, 6·9m.; fish, 23,700; citrus fruits, 536,000; alcoholic beverages (excluding wine), 92,500 hectolitres and 69·4m. cigars.

In 1988 imports included (in tonnes): Wheat flour, 18,600; steel sections, 696,400; coke, 66,000; urea, 257,000; medicines, 48·2m. pesos; sawn wood, 477,100 cu. metres; tractors, 8,889; buses, 460; dump trucks, 1,390.

In 1985 the USSR provided 67% of imports (by value) and took 75% of exports. The loss of this covertly subsidized market has caused economic hardship since 1990. In 1984 sugar formed 75% of all exports.

Total trade between Cuba and UK (British Department of Trade returns, in £1,000 sterling):

	1987	1988	1989	1990	1991
Imports to UK	12,776	28,489	34,388	30,294	17,860
Exports and re-exports from UK	41,510	31,162	53,255	37,568	28,413

Tourism. In 1989 there were 514,500 visitors. Revenue amounted to 4,230·8m. pesos. The age at which Cubans may obtain exit visas was lowered to 20 years in Aug. 1991.

COMMUNICATIONS

Roads. In 1986 there were 16,740 km of paved highways open to traffic, traversing the island for 760 miles from Pinar del Río to Santiago. In 1983 there were 49,841 hire cars (including coaches and buses).

Railways. There were (1986) 4,881 km of public railway (mainly 1,435 mm gauge) of which 152 km is electrified. In 1987 it carried 2,189m. passenger-km and 13·2m. tonnes of freight. In addition, the large sugar estates have 7,773 km of lines on 1,435, 914 and 760 mm gauges.

Civil Aviation. The state airline CUBANA operates all internal services, and from Havana to Mexico City, Madrid, Moscow and East Berlin, Montreal, Prague, Paris and Brussels, and also to Lima, Panama, Kingston, Bridgetown, Port of Spain, Georgetown and Managua. The other regular foreign services are Mexican, Spanish, Soviet, Czech, East German and Canadian.

Shipping. The coastline is over 3,500 miles long and has many fine harbours. The merchant marine, in 1989, consisted of 117 sea-going vessels of 1,400,000 DWT.

Telecommunications. The national telephone system (1989) had 311,100 lines in use. There are 3,545 miles of public and 8,902 miles of private telegraph wires.

Broadcasting is the responsibility of the state-controlled Instituto Cubano de Radio y Televisión. There are 5 national radio networks, provincial and local stations and an external service. There are 2 TV channels (colour by NTSC). In 1991 there were 3·5m. radio and 2·1m. TV sets.

Cinemas and Theatres. In 1987 there were 535 (35mm) and 905 (16mm) cinemas. In 1989, 99 films were made, there were 44·8m. cinema attendances; there were 49 theatres and 1,387,700 attendances.

Newspapers. Since Oct. 1990 *Granma* has been the only national daily newspaper due, it was stated, to shortage of paper.

JUSTICE, RELIGION, EDUCATION AND WELFARE

Justice. There is a Supreme Court in Havana and 7 regional courts of appeal. The provinces are divided into judicial districts, with courts for civil and criminal actions, with municipal courts for minor offences. The civil code guarantees aliens the same property and personal rights as are enjoyed by nationals.

The 1959 Agrarian Reform Law and the Urban Reform Law passed on 14 Oct. 1960 have placed certain restrictions on both. Revolutionary Summary Tribunals have wide powers.

Religion. There were 4·17m. Roman Catholics in 1989. There is a bishop of the American Episcopal Church in Havana; there are congregations of Methodists in Havana and in the provinces as well as Baptists and other denominations.

Education. Education is compulsory (between the ages of 6 and 14) and free, and now available everywhere. In 1964 illiteracy was officially declared to have been completely eliminated.

In 1987–88 the universities had 262,225 students and 22,492 teaching staff. In 1989 there were 899,900 pupils and 73,200 teachers at 9,522 primary schools, 800,300 pupils and 77,800 teachers at 1,540 intermediate schools and in 1988 there were 164,891 students at adult primary schools.

In 1989 there were 18,000 foreign pupils from over 30 developing countries attending international secondary/pre-university schools free of charge, including 7 Angolan schools (3,581 pupils) and 4 Mozambiquan schools (2,231 pupils), and about 30,000 foreign students attending polytechnics, teacher training colleges and universities at an annual cost of US$40m. Cuba sends teachers abroad to more than 40 countries.

Health. There were (1989) 34,752 doctors, 6,482 dentists, 58,589 nursing personnel and 264 hospitals with 74,407 beds. The 1989 health and education budget was 2,906·2m. pesos.

Free medical services are provided by the state polyclinics, though a few doctors still have private practices. All serious tropical diseases are effectively kept under control, and virtually all children under the age of 15 have been vaccinated against poliomyelitis.

DIPLOMATIC REPRESENTATIVES

Of Cuba in Great Britain (167 High Holborn, London, WC1)
Ambassador: María de los Angeles Florez.

Of Great Britain in Cuba (Edificio Bolivar, Carcel 101–103, Havana)
Ambassador: Leycester Coltman.

Of Cuba to the United Nations
Ambassador: Ricardo Alarcón de Quesada.

The USA broke off diplomatic relations with Cuba on 3 Jan. 1961 but in 1977 Interest Sections were opened, officially attached to the Swiss Embassy in Havana and to the Czech Embassy in Washington respectively.

Further Reading

Anuario azucarero de Cuba. Havana, from 1937
Anuario Estadístico de a República de Cuba. Havana
Boletín Oficial, Ministerio de Comercio. Monthly
Estadística General: Commercio Exterior. Quarterly and Annual.—*Movimiento de Población.* Monthly and Annual. Havana
Brundenius, C., *Revolutionary Cuba: The Challenge of Economic Growth with Equity.* Oxford, 1984
Domínguez, J. I., *Cuba: Order and Revolution.* Harvard Univ. Press, 1978
Gravette, A. G., *Cuba: Official Guide.* London, 1988
Guerra y Sánchez, R. and others, *Historia de la Nación Cubana.* 10 vols. Havana, 1952
MacEwan, A., *Revolution and Economic Development in Cuba.* London, 1981
Mesa-Lago, C., *The Economy of Socialist Cuba: A Two-Decade Appraisal.* Univ. of New Mexico Press, 1981
O'Connor, J., *The Origins of Socialism in Cuba.* London, Cornell Univ. Press, 1970
Ritter, A. R. M., *The Economic Development of Revolutionary Cuba: Strategy and Performance.* New York, 1974
Ruttin, P., *Capitalism and Socialism in Cuba: a Study of Dependency, Development and Underdevelopment.* London, 1990
Thomas, H., *The Cuban Revolution: 25 Years Later.* Epping, 1984
Zimbalist, A. and Brundenius, C., *The Cuban Economy: Measurement and Analysis of Socialist Performance.* Johns Hopkins Univ. Press, 1990

CYPRUS

Kypriaki Dimokratia—
Kibris Çumhuriyeti

(Republic of Cyprus)

Capital: Nicosia
Population: 702,100 (1990)
GNP per capita government controlled area: US$9,790 (1990)

HISTORY. For the history of Cyprus to 1974 *see* THE STATESMAN'S YEAR-BOOK, 1990–91, p. 400.

On 15 July 1974 a coup was staged by supporters of the Greek ruling junta for the overthrow of President Makarios. The President left the island and the coup was short-lived. The Speaker of the House of Representatives acted as President until the return of President Makarios on Dec. 7 1974.

Turkey invaded the island on 20 July 1974, eventually occupying the northern part of Cyprus. As a result 200,000 Greek Cypriots fled to live as refugees in the south. The UN General Assembly unanimously adopted resolutions calling for the withdrawal of all foreign troops from Cyprus and the return of refugees to their homes, but without result.

On 13 Feb. 1975 at a special meeting of the executive council and legislative assembly of the Autonomous Turkish Cypriot Administration a Turkish Cypriot Federated State was proclaimed. Rauf Denktash was appointed President and he declared that the state would not seek international recognition. The proclamation was denounced by President Makarios and the Greek Prime Minister but welcomed by the Turkish Prime Minister. On 15 Nov. 1983 the Turkish state unilaterally proclaimed itself the 'Turkish Republic of Northern Cyprus'. In Nov. 1983 and May 1984 the UN Security Council declared all secessionist actions illegal. UN-inspired talks on a possible federal state failed in Jan. 1985. On 15 Sept. 1988 the first meeting between President Vassiliou and Rauf Denktash took place following a UN initiative in Aug. to restart substantive talks. A further initiative by the UN Secretary-General was made in July 1989, without success.

AREA AND POPULATION. The island lies in the eastern Mediterranean, about 50 miles off the south coast of Turkey and (at the nearest points) 65 miles off the coast of Syria. Area 3,572 sq. miles (9,251 sq. km); greatest length from east to west about 150 miles, and greatest breadth from north to south about 60 miles. The Turkish occupied area is 3,335 sq. km (about 33% of the total area). Population by ethnic group:

Ethnic group	1946	1960	1973	1989	1990
Greek Orthodox	361,199	441,656	498,511	556,400	562,100
Turkish Moslem	80,548	104,942	116,000	129,600	130,900
Others	8,367	26,968	17,267	9,000	9,100
Total	450,114	573,566	631,778	695,000	702,100

Population estimate (June 1990) 702,100, of which 80% are Greek Cypriot (Armenian, Maronite and Latin minorities included), 19% Turkish Cypriot and 1% other, mainly British. Principal towns with populations (Dec. 1990 estimate): Nicosia (the capital), 171,000 (Government controlled area); Limassol, 135,400; Larnaca, 62,600; Paphos, 28,800.

As a result of the Turkish invasion and the occupation of part of Cyprus, 200,000 Greek Cypriots were displaced and forced to find refuge in the south of the island. The urban centres of Famagusta, Kyrenia and Morphou were completely evacuated. See p. 471 for details of the 'Turkish Republic of Northern Cyprus'.

Vital statistics. The birth rate per 1,000 population in 1990 was 19; death rate, 8·5; infantile mortality per 1,000 live births, 11.

Greek and Turkish are official languages. English is widely spoken.

CLIMATE. The climate is Mediterranean, with very hot, dry summers and variable winters. Maximum temperatures may reach 112°F (44·5°C) in July and Aug., but minimum figures may fall to 22°F (−5·5°C) in the mountains in winter when snow is experienced. Rainfall is generally between 10" and 27" (250 and 675 mm) and occurs mainly in the winter months, but it may reach 48" (1,200 mm) in the Troodos mountains. Nicosia. Jan. 50°F (10·0°C), July 83°F (28·3°C). Annual rainfall 15" (371 mm).

CONSTITUTION AND GOVERNMENT. Under the 1960 Constitution executive power is vested in a President elected for a 5-year term by universal suffrage and exercised through a Council of Ministers appointed by him. The *House of Representatives* exercises legislative power. It is elected by universal suffrage for 5-year terms, and consists of 80 members, of whom 56 are elected by the Greek and 24 by the Turkish community. Voting is by preferential vote in a proportional representation system with reallocation of votes at national level. As from Dec. 1963 the Turkish members have ceased to attend.

Former Presidents: Archbishop Makarios, 1959–77; Spyros Kyprianou, 1977–88. In 1988 George Vassiliou was installed as President following elections held on 14 Feb.

The Speaker of the House of Representatives is Alexis Galunos.

Flag: White with a copper-coloured outline of the island with 2 green olive-branches beneath.

At the elections of May 1991 the electorate was 0·4m. The Democratic Rally won 20 seats with 35·8% of votes cast, the Akel Party (Communists) 18 with 30·6% and the Democratic Party 11 with 19·5%.

The Council of Ministers in Nov. 1991 was as follows:

Foreign Affairs: George Iacovou. *Interior:* Christodoulos Veniamin. *Defence:* Andreas Aloneftis. *Agriculture and Natural Resources:* Andreas Gavrielides. *Commerce and Industry:* Takis Nemitsas. *Health:* Panikos Papageorghiou. *Communications and Works:* Pavlos Savvides. *Finance:* George Syrimis. *Education:* Christoforos Christofides. *Labour and Social Insurance:* Iacovos Aristedou. *Justice:* Nicos Papaioannou.

DEFENCE

National Guard. Total strength (1992) 10,000 organized in 1 armoured brigade, 7 artillery, 13 infantry and 1 commando battalions. Equipment includes 40 AMX-30B-2 main battle tanks and a twin-engined Maritime Islander light transport, 2 PC-9 trainers and 4 armed Gazelle helicopters. There is also a para-military force of 3,700 armed police. Conscription is for 26 months.

There are 2 British bases (Army and Royal Air Force) and some 4,000 personnel.

The Turkish-Cypriot Security Force: 35,000 Turkish mainland troops, 4,000 Turkish Cypriots, and some T-34 tanks are stationed in occupied Cyprus (*see* p. 471). Conscription is for 2 years.

INTERNATIONAL RELATIONS

Membership. Cyprus is a member of the UN, Commonwealth, Council of Europe and the Non-Aligned Movement.

ECONOMY

Policy. There is a Central Planning Commission, headed by the President of the Republic and including the Council of Ministers. Its administrative arm is the Planning Bureau.

Budget. Revenue and expenditure for calendar years (in £C1m.):

	1985	1986	1987	1988	1989	1990
Expenditure	448	491	535	600	664	769
Revenue	390	427	462	536	633	710

Main sources of ordinary revenue in 1990 (in £C1m.) were: Import duties, 111 (including 25 temporary refugee levy on imports); excise duties, 82; income tax, 136; rents, royalties and interest, 25; sales of goods and services, 28; other duties and taxes, 68; social security contributions, 109.

Main divisions of ordinary expenditure in 1990 (in £C1m.): Wages and salaries, 224; pensions and gratuities, 28; commodity subsidies, 34; expenditures on goods and services, 48; public debt charges, 104; social insurance benefits, 108.

Development expenditure for 1990 (in £C1m.) included 15 for water development, 6 for agriculture, forests and fisheries, 6 for rural development, 27 for roads and 2 for airports. (An independent Ports Authority with its own funds was set up in 1977.)

The outstanding long-term public debt as at 31 Dec. 1990 was £C675m. Outstanding foreign loans public and private as at 31 Dec. 1990 totalled £C71m. Foreign debt (1990) public and private, £C714m.

Currency. The *Cyprus pound* (CYP) is divided into 100 *cents*. Notes of the following denominations are in circulation: £C10, £C5, 50 cents. Coins in circulation: 20, 5, 2, 1 cent and ½ cent. Inflation was 4·5% in 1990. Rate of exchange, March 1992: £1 = £C0·81; US$1 = £C0·46.

Banking and Finance. There is a Central and Issuing Bank exercising monetary functions, and the Cyprus Development Bank Ltd established by the Government as a major source of loan funds for industrial development. Commercial banks operating in Cyprus are: Bank of Cyprus Ltd, Turkish Bank Ltd, Cyprus Popular Bank Ltd, Barclays Bank International, National Bank of Greece, Hellenic Bank Ltd, Arab Bank Ltd and Turkiye Is Bankasi. There are 2 central co-operative banks (Co-operative Central Bank Ltd and the Cyprus Turkish Co-operative Central Bank) and 3 specialized financial institutions (Mortgage Bank of Cyprus Ltd, Lombard Natwest Banking Ltd and Housing Finance Corporation). Eighteen offshore banking units were in operation in 1990.

The Central Bank of Cyprus, established in 1963, is responsible for the issue of currency, the regulation of money supply and credit, administration of the exchange control law and the foreign-exchange reserves of the republic. The Bank also acts as a banker of the banks operating in Cyprus and of the Government and acts as supervisor of the banking system.

At the end of Dec. 1990 total deposits in banks were £C1,922m. The country's foreign exchange reserves at the end of Dec. 1990 were £C947·4m.

Weights and Measures. The metric (SI) system was introduced in 1986 and is now widely applied.

ENERGY AND NATURAL RESOURCES

Electricity. Production (1990) 1,975m. kwh. Supply 240 volts; 50 Hz.

Water Resources. In 1990 £C21m. was spent on water dams, water supplies, hydrological research and geophysical surveys. Existing dams had (1990) a capacity of 297m. cu. metres as against 6m. cu. metres before independence.

Minerals. The principal minerals extracted in 1989 were (in tonnes): Flotation pyrites, 57,455; copper concentrates, 1,752; copper precipitates, 1,080. Mining is a declining industry.

Agriculture. Chief agricultural products in 1990 (1,000 tonnes): Grapes, 160; potatoes, 185; milk, 144; cereals (wheat and barley), 110; citrus fruit, 202; meat, 65; carobs, 10; fresh fruit, 29; olives, 11; other vegetables, 118; eggs, 13m. dozen.

Of the island's 2·3m. acres, approximately 1m. are cultivated. About 13% (1990) of the economically active population are engaged in agriculture.

Livestock in 1990 (in 1,000): Cattle, 54; sheep, 330; goats, 210; pigs, 280; poultry, 3,100.

Forestry. By Dec. 1982, the reforesting of burnt areas in the Paphos Forest was completed and an area of 7,492 ha (56,000 donums) was reforested. Reforestation work in other bare areas of state forests was carried out in an area of 6,464 ha (42,318 donums). Total forest area, 1,345 sq. km.

In 1990 the chief forest products were timber, 47,400 cu. metres valued at £C940,000; charcoal, £C1m.; figures relate to the area of Cyprus not occupied by Turkey.

Fisheries. Catch (1990) 2,729 tonnes.

INDUSTRY AND TRADE. The most important industries (in £C1m.) in 1990 were: Food, beverages and tobacco, 262·6; textiles, wearing apparel and leather, 221·4; chemicals and chemical petroleum, rubber and plastic products, 139·5; metal products, machinery and equipment, 123·4; wood and wood products including furniture, 78·9. Manufacturing industry in 1990 contributed about £C362·2m. at current market prices to the GDP and gave employment to 48,930 of the economically active population.

The highest increases in output in 1990 were contributed by textiles and wearing apparel, food, beverages and tobacco, and non-metallic mineral products.

Labour. Unemployment was 1·8% at the end of 1990.

Trade Unions. About 80% of the workforce is organized and the majority of workers belong either to the Pancyprian Federation of Labour or the Cyprus Workers Confederation.

FOREIGN ECONOMIC RELATIONS. Equity capital for foreign investors must come from abroad, and the terms of foreign loans need approval by the Central Bank. Profits may be freely repatriated.

Commerce. Trade figures for calendar years were (in £C1,000):

	1986	1987	1988	1989	1990
Imports	659,073	711,419	866,765	1,130,298	1,174,538
Exports [1]	260,158	297,992	330,861	393,049	435,599

[1] Including re-exports and ships' stores.

Chief civil imports, 1990 (in £C1m.):

Live animals and animal products	22·2	Machinery, electrical equipment, sound and television recorders	203·1
Vegetable products	46·1		
Prepared foodstuffs, beverages and tobacco	91·5	Vehicles, aircraft, vessels and equipment	156·6
Mineral products	126·3	Optical, photographic, medical, musical and other instruments, clocks and watches	29·7
Products of chemical or allied industries	73·5		
Plastics and rubber and articles thereof	46·7	Raw hides and skins, leather and articles, travel goods	13·3
Pulp, waste paper and paperboard and articles thereof	48·0	Wood and articles, charcoal, cork and articles, basketware, etc.	20·4
Textiles and textile articles	120·4	Pearls, precious stones and metals, semi-precious stones and articles	20·0
Footwear, headgear, umbrellas, prepared feathers, etc.	7·0		
Articles of stone, plaster, cement, etc., ceramic and glass products	26·9		

Chief domestic exports, 1990 (in £C1,000):

Grapes	5,276	Paper products	4,938
Citrus fruit	21,864	Cement	8,249
Potatoes	28,985	Clothing	70,320
Wine	7,742	Footwear	13,967
Fruit, preserved and juices	11,282	Medicinal and pharmaceutical products	8,548
Cigarettes	8,321		

In 1990 the EEC countries supplied 53·6% of the imports; Arab countries, 5·2%; others, 41·2%. Of the exports (1990), 28% went to Arab countries and 47·4% to EEC countries.

Total trade between Cyprus and UK (British Department of Trade returns, in £1,000 sterling):

	1987	1988	1989	1990	1991
Imports to UK	118,250	121,828	145,047	154,065	141,138
Exports and re-exports from UK	141,129	159,788	173,092	204,857	209,877

Tourism. Foreign visitors (1990), 1,675,856 (1,561,479 tourists and 114,377 excursionists). Tourist revenue amounted to some £C573m. in 1990.

COMMUNICATIONS

Roads. In 1990 the total length of roads in the Government-controlled area was 9,833 km, of which 5,240 km were bituminous and 4,594 km were earth or gravel roads. The asphalted roads maintained by the Ministry of Communications and Works (Public Works Department) by the end of 1990 totalled 1,978 km, of which 260 km were within the municipal areas. Roads improved or constructed and asphalted in 1990 totalled 175 km. On 31 Dec. 1990, there were 353,605 motor vehicles including 2,743 buses, 80,547 goods vehicles, 64,456 motorcycles, and 9,562 tractors etc.

The area controlled by the Government of the Republic and that occupied by Turkey are now served by separate transport systems, and there are no services linking the two areas.

Civil Aviation. Nicosia airport has been closed since Aug. 1974. In 1990, 32 international airlines operated scheduled services between Cyprus and Europe, Africa and the Middle East, and another 30 airlines operated non-scheduled services. During 1990, 3,737,394 persons travelled and 26,774 tonnes of commercial air-freight was handled through Larnaca and Paphos international airports.

Shipping. The 3 main ports are Limassol, Larnaca and Paphos. In 1990, 5,638 ships of 14,964,140 net tons entered Cyprus ports carrying 7,170,183 tonnes of cargo from, to, and via Cyprus. Ships under Cyprus registry at the end of 1990, numbered 2,075 of 19,742,532 GRT. Famagusta has been closed to international traffic since Aug. 1974.

Telecommunications. In 1990 there were 56 post offices and 722 postal agencies. In 1990 there were 245,570 telephone instruments and 245,384 lines (43·4% per 100 population).

Cyprus Broadcasting Corporation broadcasts mainly in Greek, but also in Turkish, English, and Armenian on medium-waves. The corporation also broadcasts on one TV channel (colour by SECAM). A law of June 1990 permits the operation of commercial radio and TV stations. There are also 2 foreign broadcasting stations. In 1991 there were 0·2m. radio and 234,000 TV sets.

Cinemas (1990). In the government-controlled area there were 6 cinemas.

Newspapers (1990). There were 10 Greek, 8 Turkish and 1 English daily newspapers and 3 Greek, 3 Turkish weeklies and 1 English weekly.

JUSTICE, RELIGION, EDUCATION AND WELFARE

Justice. The administration of justice is exercised by a separate and independent judiciary. There is a Supreme Court, Assize Courts and District Courts.

The Supreme Court is composed of 13 judges one of whom is the President of the Court (in 1990, Andreas Nicolas Loizou). There is a continuing Assize Court that holds sessions in every district according to the cases committed for trial before it. The Assize Courts have unlimited criminal jurisdiction and may order the payment of compensation up to £C3,000. The District Courts exercise original civil and criminal jurisdiction, the extent of which varies with the composition of the Bench.

There is a Supreme Council of Judicature, consisting of the President and Judges of the Supreme Court, entrusted with the appointment, promotion, transfers, termination of appointment and disciplinary control over all judicial officers, other than the Judges of the Supreme Court.

The Attorney-General (in 1991, Michalakis Triantafyllides) is head of the independent Law Office and legal advisor to the President and his Ministers.

Religion. *See* Area and Population, p. 466.

Education. Until 31 March 1965 each community managed its own schooling through its respective Communal Chamber. Intercommunal education had been placed under the Minister of the Interior, assisted by a Board of Education for Intercommunal Schools, of which the Minister was the Chairman. In 1965 the Greek Communal Chamber was dissolved and a Ministry of Education was established to take its place. Intercommunal education has been placed under this Ministry.

Greek-Cypriot Education. Elementary education is compulsory and is provided free in 6 grades to children between $5^1/_2$ and $11^1/_2$ years of age. There are also schools for the deaf and blind, and 9 schools for handicapped children. In 1989–90 the Ministry ran 198 kindergartens for children in the age group $2^1/_2$-5; there were 342 privately run pre-primary schools. There were 378 primary schools with 60,841 pupils and 2,824 teachers in 1989–90.

Secondary education is also free and attendance for the first cycle is compulsory. The secondary school is 6 years, 3 years at the gymnasium followed by 3 years at the *lykeion* (lyceum). In 1978–79 the lyceums of optional subjects were introduced, in which students can choose one of the 5 main fields of specialization: Classical, science, economics, commercial/secretarial and foreign languages. There are also 3-year technical schools which provide technical and vocational education for industry. In 1989–90 there were 108 secondary schools with 3,526 teachers and 43,219 pupils.

Post-secondary education is provided at the Pedagogical Academy, which organizes 3-year courses for the training of pre-primary and primary school teachers, and at the Higher Technical Institute, which provides 3–4-year courses for technicians in civil, electrical, mechanical and marine engineering. There is also a 2-year Forestry College (administered by the Ministry of Agriculture), a Hotel and Catering Institute, the Mediterranean Institute of Management (Ministry of Labour and Social Insurance) and a 1–3-year Nurses' School (Ministry of Health). Adult education is conducted through youth centres in rural areas, foreign language institutes in the towns and private institutions offering courses in business administration and secretarial work.

In 1988–89, 9,410 students were studying in universities abroad, mainly in Greece, the USA, UK, Federal Republic of Germany and Italy.

English and French are compulsory subjects in secondary schools. Illiteracy is largely confined to older people.

Social Security. The administration of the social-security services in Cyprus is in the hands of the Ministry of Labour and Social Insurance, with the Ministry of Health providing medical services through public clinics and hospitals on a means test, except medical treatment for employment accidents, which is given free to all insured employees and financed by the Social Insurance Scheme.

DIPLOMATIC REPRESENTATIVES

Of Cyprus in Great Britain (93 Park St., London, W1Y 4ET)
High Commissioner: Angelos M. Angelides.

Of Great Britain in Cyprus (Alexander Pallis St., Nicosia)
High Commissioner: D. J. M. Dain, CMG.

Of Cyprus in the USA (2211 R. St., NW, Washington, D.C., 20008)
Ambassador: Michael Sherifis.

Of the USA in Cyprus (Therissos St., Nicosia)
Ambassador: Robert E. Lamb

Of Cyprus to the United Nations
Ambassador: Andreas Mavrommatis.

'TURKISH REPUBLIC OF NORTHERN CYPRUS'

HISTORY. *See* p. 466.

AREA AND POPULATION. The Turkish Republic of Northern Cyprus occupies 3,355 sq. km (about 33% of the island of Cyprus) and its population in

1991, was approximately 175,000. Population of principal towns (1985): Nicosia, 37,400; Famagusta, 19,428; Kyrenia, 6,902; Morphou, 10,179; Lefka, 3,785. Ethnic groups: Turks, 158,225; Greeks, 733; Maronites, 368; Others, 961. Passport formalities with Turkey were abolished in July 1990.

CONSTITUTION AND GOVERNMENT. The Turkish Republic of Northern Cyprus was proclaimed on 15 Nov. 1983. Rauf Denktash was re-elected President in April 1990 by 68·6% of the vote. A 50-seat Legislative Assembly was elected in Oct. 1991. The National Unity Party won 45 seats, the New Dawn Party, 2, the Free Democratic Party, 2, and the Social Democratic Party, 1. The Council of Ministers comprised in Nov. 1991 of:

Prime Minister: Derviş Eroğlu.

Foreign Affairs and Defence: Kenan Atakol. *Economy and Finance:* Nazif Borman. *Interior, Rural Affairs and Environment:* Serder Denktas. *Education and Culture:* Esber Serakinci. *Agriculture and Forests:* Ilkay Kamil. *Communications, Works and Tourism:* Mehmet Bayram. *Trade and Industry:* Atay A. Rasit. *Health and Social Welfare:* Ertugrul Hasipoglu. *Housing:* Erkan Enekci.

The Speaker of the Leglislative Assembly is Hakki Atun.

Flag: White with horizontal bars of red set near the top and bottom; between these a crescent and star in red.

Budget. Revenue (in 1m. Turkish lira) in 1991 was 674,764; expenditure, 1,013,030.

Currency. The Turkish lira is used throughout Northern Cyprus.

Banking. 17 Turkish banks are operating in the Turkish-occupied area. No control is exercised by the Central Bank of Cyprus.

Agriculture. Agriculture accounted for 11·8% of GNP in 1990.

Foreign Economic Relations. Exports earned US$65·5m. in 1990. Imports cost US$381·5m. Customs barriers with Turkey were abolished in July 1990.

Tourism. There were over 376,000 tourists in 1990, including 60,000 from Europe. Tourist earnings totalled US$130m.

Aviation. A new international airport was constructed in 1975 at Ercan. Flights operate to Europe, the Middle East and the Gulf via Istanbul and Ankara. There is another international airport at Geçitkale.

Telecommunications. The local radio, Radio Bayrak (BRTK) broadcasts in several languages including Greek, Arabic, English and French. BRT Television broadcasts for an average of 3¹/₂ hours a day.

Newspapers. In 1990 there were 8 daily, and 6 weekly newspapers.

Education. In 1991 there were 19,184 pupils and 936 teachers in primary schools, 16,856 pupils and 937 teachers in secondary schools, 5,852 students and 381 teachers in technical schools, and 1,905 students with 98 teaching staff in higher education. There are 4 universities.

Health. In 1989 there were over 300 doctors, 3 state hospitals and 4 clinics.

Further Reading

Statistical Information: Statistics and Research Department, Nicosia.
North Cyprus Almanack, London, 1987
Denktash, R., *The Cyprus Triangle.* London, 1982
Ertekün, N. M., *The Cyprus Dispute.* Nicosia North, 1984
Genç, A. F., *Cyprus Report: 1974 Diary.* Nicosia, 1978
Georghallides, G. S., *A Political and Administrative History of Cyprus 1918–1926.* Nicosia, 1979
Halil, K., *The Rape of Cyprus.* London, 1982
Hill, Sir George F., *A History of Cyprus.* 4 vols. Cambridge, 1940–52
Hitchins, C., *Cyprus.* London, 1984

Hunt, D., *Footprints in Cyprus*. London, 1982

Ioannides, C. P., *In Turkey's Image: the Transformation of Occupied Cyprus into a Turkish Province*. New Rochelle (N.Y.), 1991

Kitromilides, P. M. and Evriviades, M. L., *Cyprus,* [Bibliography]. Oxford and Santa Barbara, 1982

Kyle, K., *Cyprus*. London, 1984

Loizos, P., *The Heart Grows Bitter: A Chronicle of Cypriot War Refugees*. CUP, 1982

Mayes, S., *Makarios*. London, 1981

Necatigil, Z. M., *Our Republic in Perspective*. Nicosia, 1985

Reddaway, J., *Burdened With Cyprus*. London, 1986

St John-Jones, L. W., *The Population of Cyprus*. London, 1983

CZECHOSLOVAKIA

Capital: Prague
Population: 15·65m. (1990)
GNP per capita: US$8,700 (1985)

Česká a Slovenská
Federativní Republika

(Czech and Slovak
Federative Republic)

HISTORY. The Czechoslovak State came into existence on 28 Oct. 1918, when the Czech *Národní Výbor* (National Committee) took over the government of the Czech lands upon the dissolution of Austria–Hungary. Two days later the Slovak National Council manifested its desire to unite politically with the Czechs. On 14 Nov. 1918 the first Czechoslovak National Assembly declared the Czechoslovak State to be a republic with T. G. Masaryk as President (1918–35).

The Treaty of St Germain-en-Laye (1919) recognized the Czechoslovak Republic, consisting of the Czech lands (Bohemia, Moravia, part of Silesia) and Slovakia. To these lands were added as a trust the autonomous province of Subcarpathian Ruthenia.

This territory was broken up for the benefit of Germany, Poland and Hungary by the Munich agreement (29 Sept. 1938) between UK, France, Germany and Italy.

In March 1939 the German-sponsored Slovak government proclaimed Slovakia independent, and Germany incorporated the Czech lands into the Reich as the 'Protectorate of Bohemia and Moravia'. A government-in-exile, headed by Dr Beneš, was set up in London in July 1940.

Liberation by the Soviet Army and US Forces was completed by May 1945.

Territories taken by Germans, Poles and Hungarians were restored to Czechoslovak sovereignty. Subcarpathian Ruthenia was transferred to the USSR.

Elections were held in May 1946, at which the Communist Party obtained about 38% of the votes.

A coalition government under a Communist Prime Minister, Klement Gottwald, remained in power until 20 Feb. 1948, when 12 of the non-Communist ministers resigned in protest against infiltration of Communists into the police.

In Feb. a predominantly Communist government was formed by Gottwald. In May elections resulted in an 89% majority for the government and President Beneš resigned.

In 1968 pressure for liberalization culminated in the overthrow of the Stalinist leader, Antonín Novotný, and his associates. The Communist Party introduced an 'Action Programme' of far-reaching reforms.

Soviet pressure to abandon this programme was exerted between May and Aug. 1968, and finally, Warsaw Pact forces occupied Czechoslovakia on 21 Aug. The Czechoslovak government was compelled to accept a policy of 'normalization' (*i.e.*, abandonment of most reforms) and the stationing of Soviet forces.

Mass demonstrations demanding political reform began in Nov. 1989. After the authorities' use of violence to break up a demonstration on 17 Nov., the Communist Party leader, Miloš Jakeš, and the entire Politburo resigned. On 30 Nov. the Federal Assembly abolished the Communist Party's sole right to govern, and a new Government was formed on 3 Dec. The protest movement, focussed on the recently-established Civic Forum, in which prominent Charter 77 dissidents were active, continued to grow, and on 10 Dec. another Government was formed. Gustáv Husák resigned as President of the Republic, and was replaced by Václav Havel on the unanimous vote of 323 members of the Federal Assembly on 29 Dec.

In Dec. 1989 the Communist Party denounced the Warsaw Pact invasion of 1968 as 'unjustified and incorrect'.

AREA AND POPULATION. Czechoslovakia is bounded in the west by Germany, north by Poland, east by the USSR and south by Hungary and Austria. At the census of 11 Nov. 1980 the population was 15,283,095 (4,991,168 in Slovakia; 7·9m. females). Population in 1990, 15,690,633 (Slovakia, 5,287,000; females 8m.). There are 12 administrative regions *(Kraj)*, one of which is the capital, Prague (Praha) and one the capital of Slovakia, Bratislava.

Region	Chief city	Area in sq. km	Population 1990
Czech			
Prague	—	496	1,214,772
Středočeský	Prague (Praha)	10,994	1,118,232
Jihočeský	České Budějovice	11,345	699,564
Západočeský	Plzeň (Pilsen)	10,875	869,461
Severočeský	Ustí nad Labem	7,819	1,190,442
Východočeský	Hradec Králove	11,240	1,239,726
Jihomoravský	Brno	15,028	2,058,156
Severomoravský	Ostrava	11,067	1,972,200
Slovak			
Bratislava	—	368	440,421
Západoslovenský	Bratislava	14,492	1,727,800
Středoslovenský	Banská Bystrica	17,982	1,615,438
Východoslovenský	Košice	16,193	1,503,421

The area of Czechoslovakia is 127,899 sq. km (Slovakia, 49,035 sq. km). Population density in 1990: 122 per sq. km (131 in the Czech Republic; 108 in Slovakia). Growth rate in 1988, 2·4 per 1,000. Expectation of life in 1989 was 71.

Ethnic minorities have equal political and cultural rights. In 1988 there were (in 1,000): Czechs, 9,808; Slovaks, 4,984; Hungarians, 599; Poles, 73; Germans, 53; Ukrainians, 48; Russians, 7. There were about 0·7m. gipsies in 1991. An estimated 3·4m. Czechs and Slovaks lived abroad in 1991 (2·78m. in the USA and Canada).

The official languages are Czech in the Czech lands and Slovak in Slovakia; minority languages may be used for official business if its speakers make up at least 20% of the population.

The population of the principal towns in 1990 (in 1,000):

Prague (Praha)	1,215	Liberec	104	Zlín	87
Bratislava	440	Hradec Králové	101	Banská Bystrica	87
Brno	391	České Budějovice	99	Kladno	73
Ostrava	331	Žilina	97	Trnava	73
Košice	236	Pardubice	96	Most	71
Plzeň	175	Havířov	92	Karviná	70
Olomouc	107	Nitra	91	Frýdek-Místek	66
Ustí nad Labem	106	Prešov	89	Martin	66

Vital statistics for calendar years:

	Live births	Marriages	Divorces	Deaths
1987	214,927	122,168	39,522	179,224
1988	215,909	118,951	38,922	178,169
1989	208,552	117,801	39,680	181,628

Infant mortality in 1989 (per 1,000 live births), 4·6. There were 23,802 abortions in 1988.

CLIMATE. A humid continental climate, with warm summers and cold winters. Precipitation is generally greater in summer, with thunderstorms. Autumn, with dry, clear weather and spring, which is damp, are each of short duration. Prague. Jan. 29·5°F (−1·5°C), July 67°F (19·4°C). Annual rainfall 19·3" (483mm). Brno. Jan. 31°F (−0·6°C), July 67°F (19·4°C). Annual rainfall 21" (525mm).

CONSTITUTION AND GOVERNMENT. For details of previous constitutions, *see* THE STATESMAN'S YEAR-BOOK, 1990–91, pp. 408–9. A Bill of Fundamental Rights and Liberties was adopted by parliament in Jan. 1991 as a first step in drafting a new constitution.

Czechoslovakia is a federal republic consisting of two nations of equal rights: The Czech Republic (the Czech lands, previously Bohemia, Moravia and part of Silesia), and the Slovak Republic (Slovakia). A law of 12 Dec. 1990 defines the respective competences of the Czech and Slovak Republics and devolves most of former federal administrative and economic authority to them. Religious and ethnic affairs remain a federal responsibility. Each Republic is governed by a National Council (the Czech with 200 deputies, the Slovak with 150), which delegates to an overall Federal Assembly responsibility for constitutional and foreign affairs, defence and important economic decisions. The Federal Assembly has two chambers which have equal status, and usually meet in joint session: the Chamber of the People which has 101 Czech and 49 Slovak delegates, and the Chamber of the Nations, which has 75 Czech and 75 Slovak delegates. Both Chambers are elected by direct universal suffrage by proportional representation. A party must gain 5% of the vote to enter any chamber (7% for 4-party, 10% for 5 (or more)-party coalitions). Minimum age of voters is 18; of deputies, 21 years.

A *Constitutional Court* was established in 1992 consisting of 12 judges appointed by the federal President. It rules on the constitutionality of proposed laws and disputes between federal and republican bodies.

Elections were held in June 1990. Turn-out was 95% of the 11,247,000 electorate. 22 parties took part. Percentages of vote gained for the Chamber of the People (and Nations): Civic Forum, together with its Slovak ally, Public Against Violence, 46·6% (46·9%); Communist Party, 13·6% (13·7%); Christian Democratic Union, 12% (11·3%); Moravian-Silesian Society, 5·4% (6·2%); Slovak Nationalist Party, 3·5% (3·6%); Coexistence, 2·8% (2·7%).

Seats gained in the Chamber of the People (and Nations): Civic Forum, together with Public Against Violence, 87 (83); Communist Party, 23 (24); Christian Democratic Union, 20 (20); Moravian-Silesian Society, 9 (7); Slovak Nationalist Party, 6 (7); Coexistence, 5 (7). The next elections were scheduled for June 1992.

President of the Republic: Václav Havel, elected on 5 July 1990 for a two-year period by the Federal Assembly by 234 votes to 50. *Speaker of the Federal Assembly:* Alexander Dubček (b. 1921).

In Feb. 1992 the Government consisted of: *Chancellor:* Karel Schwarzenberg; *Commandant of the Military Office:* Lt.-Gen. Ladislav Tomeček; *Chairman of the Council of Consultants:* Milan Šimečka; *Prime Minister:* Marián Čalfa (b. 1946); *Deputy Prime Ministers (in charge of),* Jiří Dienstbier *(Foreign Affairs),* Jozef Mikloško *(Human Rights, Religion and Culture),* Pavel Rychetský *(Legislation); Cabinet Ministers: Economic Control,* Květoslava Kořínková; *Defence,* Luboš Dobrovský; *Economic Affairs,* Vladimír Dlouhý; *Environment,* Josef Vavroušek; *Finance,* Václav Klaus; *Interior,* Ján Langoš; *Labour and Social Affairs,* Petr Miller; *Strategic Planning,* Pavel Hoffman; *Transport,* Jiří Nezval; *Telecommunications,* Theodor Petřík; *Federal Bureau for Economic Competition:* Imřich Flasík.

The Chairman of the Czech National Council is Dagmar Burešová; of the Slovak, František Mikloško. The Czech Prime Minister is Peter Pithart; the Slovak, Ján Čarnogurský.

Local government. At elections in Nov. 1990 turn-out was 75% in the Czech Republic and 63·75% in Slovakia. In the Czech Republic Civic Forum gained 35·6% of the vote, and the Communist Party, 17·2%. In Slovakia the Christian Democratic Movement gained 28·4% of the vote, Public Against Violence, 20·4%. The former National Committees have been replaced by district bureaux with the power to raise local taxes and with responsibility for roads, schools, utilities and public health.

National flag: White and red (horizontal), with a blue triangle of full depth at the hoist, point to the fly.

National anthem: Kde domov můj ('Where is my homeland'; Czech anthem, words by J. K. Tyl); combined with, Nad Tatru sa blýska ('Over Tatra it lightens'; Slovak anthem, words by J. Matuška).

DEFENCE. Conscription is for 12 months.
All Soviet forces had withdrawn by 1991.

Army. The Army had a strength (1991) of 87,300 (69,000 conscripts). It consists of 3 tank, 5 motor rifle and 2 artillery divisions; 2 anti-tank regiments, 1 *Scud*, 4 engineer and 1 airborne brigades. Equipment includes 373 T-34, 1,927 T-55 and 900 T-72 main battle tanks. There are also 3 paramilitary forces: Federal Border Police (9,000), a National Security Corps of 9,000 run by the Ministry of the Interior and 3,200 armed civil defence troops.

Air Force. The Air Force is organized as a tactical force, under overall army command, and had a strength of some 44,800 personnel (18,000 conscripts) and 297 combat aircraft in 1991. Three interceptor regiments (each 3 squadrons of 14 aircraft) are equipped with MiG-29, MiG-23 and MiG-21 jets. There are 4 regiments of Su-22, Su-25, MiG-23 and MiG-21 ground attack aircraft, as well as Mi-24 gunship helicopters. Su-22s and modified L-39 Albatros jet trainers are used for tactical reconnaissance. Transport units have a total of 60 Let L-410, An-24/26, Il-14 and Tu-134 aircraft and about 100 Mil Mi-2 (some armed), Mi-4, Mi-8 and Mi-17 helicopters. Training units are equipped with 2-seat MiG-29s, MiG-23s and MiG-21s and Czech-built aircraft, including L-29 and L-39 Albatros jet advanced trainers and Zlin primary trainers. Surface-to-air ('Guideline', 'Goa', 'Ganef', 'Gainful' and 'Gaskin') missile units are operational.

INTERNATIONAL RELATIONS. In 1974 the German Federal Republic and Czechoslovakia annulled the Munich agreement of 1938. A good neighbours treaty was signed on 27 Feb. 1992.

In Oct. 1991 Czechoslovakia concluded a treaty of friendship with the USSR.

Membership. Czechoslovakia is a member of the UN, CSCE, Council of Europe and IMF, an associate member of the EC and with Austria, Hungary, Italy and Yugoslavia was an inaugural member of the 'Pentagonale' meeting on economic and political co-operation in July 1990. Poland adhered in May 1991, and the group was renamed 'Hexagonal'.

ECONOMY

Policy. For planning under the Communist régime *see* THE STATESMAN'S YEAR-BOOK, 1990–91, p. 410. The Government is pursuing a programme of reallocation of ownership of enterprises. Federal Government will retain control of defence, telecommunications, transport and mining; light and service industries will devolve to the Czech and Slovak Republics, and local public services to municipal control. Small businesses are being privatized first. Sales of some 100,000 small businesses began in Dec. 1990. Subsequently large firms will be de-nationalized and ownership transferred to companies through the National Assets Foundation. Citizens' shares in companies will be mediated through a voucher system. A law of Feb. 1991 restores property confiscated by the Communist regime.

Budget. Budgets for calendar years (in Kčs. 1m.):

	1983	1984	1985	1986	1987	1988	1989
Revenue	324,127	343,805	359,692	368,696	383,732	404,045	415,432
Expenditure	323,890	342,192	358,028	365,949	382,151	401,199	414,946

Main items of the 1989 budget were (in Kčs. 1,000m.): Revenue: From the economy, 308; direct taxes, 2. Expenditure: National economy, 86; health and social services, 111; defence, 4; administration, 4.

Currency. The monetary unit is the *koruna* (CSK) or crown of 100 *haler*. Notes in circulation: Kčs. 10, 20, 50, 100, 500, 1,000. Coin: 5, 10, 20, 50 *halers*, and Kčs. 1, 2, 5. Gold reserves were US$1,832m. in 1987. The crown became fully internally convertible in 1990. It was devalued by 75% in Dec. 1989 and again by 35·3% in Oct. 1990. A single exchange rate for the crown was set in Dec. 1990 and it became convertible on 1 Jan. 1991. Official rates of exchange (March 1992): £1 = Kčs. 50·78; US$1 = Kčs. 28·92.

Banking and Finance. For previous banking history *see* THE STATESMAN'S YEAR-BOOK, 1990–91, p. 410. The central bank and bank of issue is the State Bank (*Governor*, Ján Vit). The Governorship alternates between a Czech and a Slovak.

Decentralization of the banking system began in 1991, and private banks began to operate alongside the 4 main banks (the Investment, Commercial, Foreign Trade and Agrarian Banks) and the 2 savings banks. Under legislation of Dec. 1991 the state retains 40–50% of the equity in these. Foreign investors may acquire up to 25% of major banks' assets (100% of small banks), but no single investor may acquire more than 10%. There were 20·4m. savings accounts totalling 277,668m. Kčs in 1989.

Weights and Measures. The metric system is in force.

ENERGY AND NATURAL RESOURCES

Electricity. Production of electricity in 1989: 89,200m. kwh. In 1990 there were two nuclear power stations, producing 28% of all electricity. Two more were under construction. Supply 120 and 220 volts; 50 Hz.

Oil. Production (1991 estimate) 133,000 tonnes.

Minerals. Czechoslovakia is not rich in minerals. There are hard and soft coal reserves (chief coalfields: Most, Chomutov, Kladno, Ostrava and Sokolov). There is also uranium, glass sand and salt, and small quantities of iron ore, graphite, copper and lead. Gold deposits were found near Prague in 1985. Production in 1989 (in 1,000 tonnes): Coal, 25,070; lignite and brown coal, 94,263.

Agriculture. In 1989 there were 6·8m. ha of agricultural land (4·7m. ha arable, 0·8m. meadow, 0·8m. pasture), of which 4·3m. were held by collective farms, 2m. by state farms and 64,000 as private plots (maximum size 1 ha).

A law of May 1991 returns land seized by the Communist regime to its original owners, to a maximum of 150 ha of arable to a single owner. There are some 3·5m. potential claimants; claims expired on 31 Dec. 1992.

In 1989 there were 1,660 collective farms with 1,000,962 members and 245 state farms with 158,610 employees. Crop production in 1989 (in 1,000 tonnes): Sugarbeet, 6,389; wheat, 6,356; potatoes, 3,167; barley, 3,550; maize, 1,000; rye, 708.

Livestock. In 1989: Cattle, 5·13m. (including 1·8m. milch cows); pigs, 7·5m.; sheep, 1m.; poultry, 49m. In 1989 production of meat was 1,881,257 tonnes (live weight); milk, 6,888m. litres; 5,628m. eggs. In 1989 there were 140,202 tractors. 36,650 ha were irrigated in 1989.

Forestry. Forest area in 1990 was 4,615,021 ha (50% spruce, 16% beech and pine, 7% oak) representing 37% of the land area. The area reafforested in 1989 was 15,356 ha. The timber yield was 17·9m. cu. metres in 1989.

Fisheries. Total catch was 21·57m. tonnes in 1989.

INDUSTRY. Industrialization was well developed before the Communist régime, under which all industry was nationalized. There were 588 state industrial enterprises in 1989.

Output in 1989 (in 1,000 tonnes): Pig-iron, 9,911; crude steel, 15,465; coke, 10,147; rolled-steel products, 11,395; cement, 10,888; paper, 1,027; sulphuric acid, 1,142; nitrogenous fertilizers, 604; phosphate fertilizers, 296; plastics, 1,186; synthetic fibres (1988), 204; sugar, 878; beer, 2,277m. litres; cars, 188,611 (no.).

Textile production (in 1m. metres) in 1989: Cotton, 582; linen, 107; woollen, 59; shoes, 119·1m. pairs.

Labour. There were 8,974,408 persons of employable age in 1989 (*i.e.*, males, 15–59; females 15–54), of whom 7·5m. (46% women) were employed: 5·8m. in production (industry, 2·9m.; agriculture, 0·81m.; building, 0·7m.); and 2m. in services. Unemployment was 5·1% in Sept. 1991.

A 5-day 42-hour week with 4 weeks annual holiday is standard. Average monthly wage in 1989: Kčs. 3,300.

Trade Unions. The former offical trade union organization ROH dissolved itself in March 1990. The Czechoslovak Confederation of Trade Unions (Chairman, Igor Pleskot), evolved from strike committees set up in 1989. It claimed 6m. members in 1990.

FOREIGN ECONOMIC RELATIONS. A trade pact was signed with the EEC in May 1990. External debt was some US$8,000m. in 1990. Foreign currency reserves were US$4,832m. in 1987. Foreign companies are permitted 100% ownership, full repatriation of profits and currency convertibility. In June 1991 50 enterprises were designated for partial or total foreign investment. By March 1991 there were 1,318 joint ventures.

Commerce. Total trade (in Kčs. 1m.) for calendar years (Figures up to 1988 are at the then official exchange rate. Figures from 1988 are at the current convertible rate. Both rates are given for 1988 for purposes of comparison):

	1985	1986	1987	1988 [1]	1988 [2]	1989
Imports	120,323	125,449	127,259	129,134	209,554	214,702
Exports	119,818	121,777	125,875	132,781	213,887	217,530

[1] Former official rate   [2] Convertible

Value (in 1m. Kčs.) of exports (and imports) to major trading partners in 1989: USSR, 66,439, (63,792); Federal Germany, 17,964 (19,931); Poland, 18,438 (18,485); German Democratic Republic, 14,257 (16,797); Austria, 9,938 (11,830); Hungary, 8,641 (10,294); Yugoslavia, 7,095 (7,170); China, 5,546 (5,902).

Total trade between Czechoslovakia and UK for calendar years (British Department of Trade returns, in £1,000 sterling):

	1987	1988	1989	1990	1991
Imports to UK	141,472	148,248	156,649	135,988	131,141
Exports and re-exports from UK	114,101	130,420	131,418	133,158	129,378

Tourism. In 1989, 2·59m. tourists visited Czechoslovakia (1·3m. from the West) and 5·97m. Czechoslovak tourists made visits abroad (0·36m. to the West). Visa-free travel to the West has been permited since Dec. 1989.

COMMUNICATIONS

Roads. In 1989 there were 73,640 km of first-class roads (including 527 km of motorways). In 1989 there were 3,122,307 motor cars (2,931,131 private). In 1989 state road transport carried 2,320m. passengers and 329m. tonnes of freight. In 1989 there were 110,653 accidents with 1,397 fatalities.

Railways. In 1990 the length of railway routes was 13,111 km. Of this, 3,909 km were electrified. In 1990, 19,335m. passenger-km and 59,490m. tonne-km of freight were carried. There is a metro (40 km) and tram/light rail system (496 km) in Prague, and tram/light rail networks in Bratislava, Brno, Košice, Liberec, Most, Olomouc, Ostrava, Plzeň and Teplice-Trečianské.

Civil Aviation. Air transport is run by ČSA (Czechoslovak Airlines), which had 32 aircraft in 1990. The main airports are: Prague (Ruzynė), Brno (Cernovice), Bratislava (Vajnory), Olomouc (Holice), Košice (Barca). In 1989, 1·5m. passengers and 29,000 tonnes of freight were flown. There are 6 internal and 53 international flights from Prague. British Airways operates air traffic London–Prague, Air France Paris–Prague–Bucharest.

Shipping. In 1989 Czechoslovak Maritime Shipping had 20 freighters totalling 393,919 DWT, based on Szczecin. In 1989, 1·97m. tonnes of cargo were carried.

There are 475 km of inland waterways. Freight transport totalled 13·52m. tonnes in 1989. 425,000 passengers were carried in 1989.

Czechoslovak Danube Shipping operate 5 ships totalling 244,000 DWT in the Mediterranean from Bratislava, and Czechoslovak Elbe-Oder Shipping had a fleet of 284,500 DWT in 1985.

Pipeline. There are oil and gas pipelines from the USSR, shared by Austria, Germany and Italy.

Telecommunications. There were 5,132 post offices in 1989. Number of telephones in 1990, 4,131,679. *Ceskoslovenský Rozhlas*, the governmental radio station, broadcasts on 2 networks; 1 from Prague with 3 programmes in Czech and Slovak and 1 from Bratislava with 2 programmes in Slovak and additional broadcasts in Hungarian and Ukrainian. *Ceskoslovenská Televise* broadcast 2 television programmes. (colour by SECAM). In 1989, 4·22m. people held radio and 4·66m. TV licences. Independent radio and TV stations and news agencies have been permitted since 1991.

Cinemas and Theatres (1989). There were 2,796 cinemas and 88 theatres. 39 full-length films were made.

Newspapers and Books (1989). There were 30 daily newspapers, including 12 in Slovak, and 1,056 other periodicals. 6,893 book titles were published in 105·7m. copies. There were 8,398 public libraries.

JUSTICE, RELIGION, EDUCATION AND WELFARE

Justice. The post-Communist judicial system was established by a law of July 1991. This provides for a unified system of 4 types of court: civil, criminal, commercial and administrative. Commercial courts arbitrate in disputes arising from business activities. Administrative courts examine the legality of the decisions of state institutions when appealed by citizens. In addition, there are military courts which operate under the jurisdiction of the Ministry of Defence. There is a Federal Supreme Court, and a hierarchy of courts under the Czech and Slovak Ministries of Justice at republic, region and district level. District courts are courts of first instance. Cases are usually decided by senates comprising a judge and 2 associate judges, though occasionally by a single judge. (Associate judges are citizens in good standing over the age of 25 who are elected for 4-year terms). Regional courts are courts of first instance in more serious cases and also courts of appeal for district courts. Cases are usually decided by a senate of 2 judges and 3 associate judges, although again occasionally by a single judge. The Federal Court and the Supreme Courts of the 2 republics interpret law as a guide to other courts and function also as courts of appeal. Decisions are made by senates of 3 judges (5 if the Federal Court is considering an appeal). The judges of the Federal Supreme Court are nominated by the President of Czechoslovakia; other judges are appointed by the Czech and Slovak National Councils.

The police force numbered 53,000 in 1991.

Religion. A law of July 1991 provides the basis for church-state relations and guarantees the religious and civic rights of citizens and churches. Churches must register to become legal entities but operate independently of the state. In 1991 18 churches were registered in the Czech Republic and 13 in Slovakia. State aid to churches was 559m. Kčs in 1991 (150m. Kčs in 1990).

At a census in March 1991, church membership was: Roman Catholic, 2,217,921 (1,179,201 in Slovakia); Evangelical Church of the Czech Brethren, 182,693; Hussites, 173,232; Uniates, 188,397; Orthodox, 53,613.

Miloslav Vlk (b. 1932) was installed as archbishop of Prague and primate of Czechoslovakia in 1991. There are 13 dioceses. 3 bishops were consecrated in 1988, the first since 1973. There were 2 seminaries and 6 theological faculties in 1989.

The national Czech church, created in 1918, took the name 'Hussite' in 1972. In 1991 it had a patriarch, 5 bishops, 300 pastors (40% women) and some 0·8m. adherents. In 1991 there were also some 0·5m. adherents of a dozen Protestant churches the largest being the Evangelical, which units Calvinists and Lutherans and numbered about 0·2m. In 1981 there were 15,000 Jews (mainly in Prague, where there is a synagogue and, since 1984, a rabbi). In 1986 there were 150,000 Orthodox with 100 congregations in 4 dioceses. The Uniate Church was suppressed in 1950 but maintained a clandestine existence.

Education. In 1989–90 there were 11,380 kindergartens for children from 3 to 6 years, with 50,519 teachers and 634,349 pupils. Education is free and compulsory for 10 years. Children of 6 to 14 years attend primary school (grades 1 to 9). Selection then takes place for secondary schools (4 years), vocational secondary schools (4 years) or apprentice centres (2-4 years). University entrance is mainly from secondary schools. In 1989–90 there were 6,206 primary schools with 1,961,742 pupils and 98,038 teachers, 351 secondary schools with 153,179 pupils and 10,769 teachers and 563 secondary vocational schools with 274,298 students and 18,630 teachers. In higher education in 1989–90, there were 138,656 (62,251 women) full-time students, and 20,317 teachers. There are 36 institutions of higher education, with 112 faculties. These include 5 universities—the Charles University in Prague (founded 1348); the Masaryk (formerly Purkyně) University in Brno (1919); the Comenius University in Bratislava (1919); the Palacký University in Olomouc (1573); the Šafárik University in Košice (1959); and 12 technical universities or institutes.

Welfare. Medical care is free. In 1989 Kčs. 33,366m. were spent on health insurance benefits. There were, in 1989, 230 hospitals with a total of 123,867 beds, and 57,940 doctors and dentists. Family allowances (Kčs. per month): 1 child, 200; 2 children, 650; 3, 1,210. Old age pensions averaging 67% of salary are paid at the age of 60 (men), 53–57 (women).

DIPLOMATIC REPRESENTATIVES

Of Czechoslovakia in Great Britain (25 Kensington Palace Gdns., London, W8 4QY)
Ambassador: Karel Duda.

Of Great Britain in Czechoslovakia (Thunovská 14, 11800 Prague 1)
Ambassador: A. D. Brighty, CMG, CVO.

Of Czechoslovakia in the USA (3900 Linnean Ave., NW, Washington, D.C., 20008)
Ambassador: Rita Klimová.

Of the USA in Czechoslovakia (Tržiste 15–12548 Praha, Prague)
Ambassador: Eduard Kukan.

Of Czechoslovakia to the United Nations
Ambassador: Rita Klimová.

Further Reading

The Constitution of the Czechoslovak Socialist Republic. Prague, 1960
Statistická ročenka CSSR [Statistical Yearbook]. Prague, annual since 1958
Historická statistická ročenka CSSR. Prague, 1985
Czechoslovak Foreign Trade. Prague, monthly
Batt, J., *Economic Reform and Political Change in Eastern Europe: A Comparison of the Czechoslovak and Hungarian Experiences.* Basingstoke, 1988
Bradley, J. F. N. *Politics in Czechoslovakia, 1945–1971.* Lanham, 1981
Havel, V., *Disturbing the Peace.* London, 1990.—*Living in Truth: Twenty-Two Essays.* London, 1990
Hermann, A. H., *A History of the Czechs.* London, 1975
Hejzlar, Z. and Kusin, V. V., *Czechoslovakia, 1968–1969.* New York, 1975
Kalvoda, J., *The Genesis of Czechoslovakia.* New York, 1986
Kaplan, K., *The Communist Party in Power: A Profile of Party Politics in Czechoslovakia.* Boulder, 1987
Korbel, J., *Twentieth-Century Czechoslovakia: The Meanings of its History.* Columbia Univ. Press, 1977
Krejčí, J., *Czechoslovakia at the Crossroads of History.* London, 1990
Krystufek, Z., *The Soviet Régime in Czechoslovakia.* Columbia Univ. Press, 1981
Leff, C. S., *National Conflict in Czechoslovakia: The Making and Remaking of a State, 1918–1987.* Princeton, 1988
Mamatey, V. S. and Luža, R. (eds.) *A History of the Czechoslovak Republic 1918–1948.* Princeton Univ. Press, 1973
Short, D., *Czechoslovakia.* [Bibliography] Oxford and Santa Barbara, 1986
Simmons, M., *The Reluctant President: a Political Life of Vaclav Havel.* London, 1992
Stone, N. and Strouhal, E., (eds.) *Czechoslovakia: Crossroads and Crises, 1918-88.* London, 1989
Wallace, W. V., *Czechoslovakia.* London, 1977

DENMARK

Capital: Copenhagen
Population: 5·15m. (1991)
GNP per capita: US$20,510 (1989)

Kongeriget Danmark

(Kingdom of Denmark)

HISTORY. First organized as a unified state in the 10th century, Denmark acquired approximately its present boundaries in 1815, having ceded Norway to Sweden and its north German territory to Prussia. Denmark became a constitutional monarchy in 1849.

AREA AND POPULATION. According to the census held on 9 Nov. 1970 the area of Denmark proper was 43,075 sq. km (16,631 sq. miles) and the population 4,937,579. Population, Jan. 1991: 5,146,469.

Administrative divisions		Area (sq. km) 1990	Population 1970	Population 1991	Population 1991 per sq. km.
København (Copenhagen)	(city)	88	622,773	464,773	5,866·5
Frederiksberg	(borough)	9	101,874	85,817	9,785·3
Københavns	(county)	526	615,343	601,671	1,485·0
Frederiksborg	,,	1,347	259,442	342,864	254·5
Roskilde	,,	891	153,199	218,611	245·3
Vestsjælland	,,	2,984	259,057	284,233	95·2
Storstrøm	,,	3,398	252,363	257,085	75·7
Bornholm	,,	588	47,239	45,690	77·7
Fyn	,,	3,486	432,699	461,244	132·3
Sønderjylland	,,	3,938	238,062	250,816	63·7
Ribe	,,	3,131	197,843	219,173	70·0
Vejle	,,	2,997	306,263	331,263	110·5
Ringkøbing	,,	4,853	241,327	267,708	55·2
Aarhus	,,	4,561	533,190	600,777	131·7
Viborg	,,	4,123	220,734	229,618	55·7
Nordjylland	,,	6,173	456,171	485,126	78·6
Total		43,093	4,937,579	5,146,469	119·4

The population is almost entirely Scandinavian; in Jan. 1990, of the inhabitants of Denmark proper, 95·7% were born in Denmark, including Faroe Islands and Greenland.

On 1 Jan. 1991 the population of the capital, Copenhagen (comprising Copenhagen, Frederiksberg and Gentofte municipalities), was 616,286 (including suburbs, 1,336,855); Aarhus, 264,136; Odense, 177,639; Aalborg, 155,664; Esbjerg, 81,616; Randers, 60,970; Kolding, 57,586; Heming, 56,961; Helsingør, 56,632; Horsens, 55,088.

Vital statistics for calendar years:

	Living births	Still births	Marriages	Divorces	Deaths	Emigration	Immigration
1985	53,749	240	29,322	14,385	58,378	26,715	36,214
1986	55,312	242	30,773	14,490	58,100	27,928	38,932
1987	56,221	288	31,132	14,381	58,136	30,123	36,296
1988	58,904	292	32,080	14,717	59,034	34,544	35,051
1989	61,351	314	30,894	15,152	59,397	34,949	38,391

Single-parent births: 1985, 43%; 1986, 43·9%; 1987, 44·5%; 1988, 44·7%; 1989, 46·1%.

CLIMATE. The climate is much modified by marine influences, and the effect of the Gulf Stream, to give winters that may be both cold or mild and often cloudy.

Summers may be warm and sunny or chilly and rainy. In general, the east is drier than the west. Long periods of calm weather are exceptional and windy conditions are common. Copenhagen. Jan. 33°F (0·5°C), July 63°F (17°C). Annual rainfall 650 mm. Esbjerg. Jan. 33°F (0·5°C), July 61°F (16°C). Annual rainfall 800 mm. 10% of rainfall precipitates as snow.

REIGNING QUEEN. Margrethe II, born 16 April 1940; married 10 June 1967 to Prince Henrik, born Count de Monpezat; *offspring:* Crown Prince Frederik, born 26 May 1968; Prince Joachim, born 7 June 1969. She succeeded to the throne on the death of her father, King Frederik IX, on 14 Jan. 1972.

Mother of the Queen: Queen Ingrid, born Princess of Sweden, 28 March 1910.
Sisters of the Queen: Princess Benedikte, born 29 April 1944 (married 3 Feb. 1968 to Prince Richard of Sayn-Wittgenstein-Berleburg); Princess Anne-Marie, born 30 Aug. 1946 (married 18 Sept. 1964 to King Constantine of Greece).

The crown of Denmark was elective from the earliest times. In 1448 after the death of the last male descendant of Swein Estridsen the Danish Diet elected to the throne Christian I, Count of Oldenburg, in whose family the royal dignity remained for more than 4 centuries, although the crown was not rendered hereditary by right till 1660. The direct male line of the house of Oldenburg became extinct with King Frederik VII on 15 Nov. 1863. In view of the death of the king, without direct heirs, the Great Powers signed a treaty at London on 8 May 1852, by the terms of which the succession to the crown of Denmark was made over to Prince Christian of Schleswig-Holstein-Sonderburg-Glücksburg, and to the direct male descendants of his union with the Princess Louise of Hesse-Cassel, niece of King Christian VIII of Denmark. In accordance with this treaty, a law concerning the succession to the Danish crown was adopted by the Diet, and obtained the royal sanction 31 July 1853. Linked to the constitution of 5 June 1953, a new law of succession, dated 27 March 1953, has come into force, which restricts the right of succession to the descendants of King Christian X and Queen Alexandrine, and admits the sovereign's daughters to the line of succession, ranking after the sovereign's sons.

The Queen receives a tax-free annual sum of 35m. kroner from the state.
Subjoined is a list of the kings of Denmark, with the dates of their accession, from the time of election of Christian I of Oldenburg:

House of Oldenburg

Christian I	1448	Christian IV	1588	Frederik V	1746
Hans	1481	Frederik III	1648	Christian VII	1766
Christian II	1513	Christian V	1670	Frederik VI	1808
Frederik I	1523	Frederik IV	1699	Christian VIII	1839
Christian III	1534	Christian VI	1730	Frederik VII	1848
Frederik II	1559				

House of Schleswig-Holstein-Sonderburg-Glücksburg

Christian IX	1863	Christian X	1912	Margrethe II	1972
Frederik VIII	1906	Frederik IX	1947		

CONSTITUTION AND GOVERNMENT. The present constitution of Denmark is founded upon the 'Grundlov' (charter) of 5 June 1953.

The legislative power lies with the Queen and the *Folketing* (Diet) jointly. The executive power is vested in the Queen, who exercises her authority through the ministers. The judicial power is with the courts. The Queen must be a member of the Evangelical-Lutheran Church, the official Church of the State. The Queen cannot assume major international obligations without the consent of the *Folketing*. The *Folketing* consists of one chamber. All men and women of Danish nationality of more than 18 years of age and permanently resident in Denmark possess the franchise and are eligible for election to the *Folketing*, which is at present composed of 179 members; 135 members are elected by the method of proportional representation in 17 constituencies. In order to attain an equal representation of the different parties, 40 *tillægsmandater* (additional seats) are divided among such parties which have not obtained sufficient returns at the constituency elections. Two members are elected for the Faroe Islands and 2 for Greenland. The term of the legislature is 4 years, but a general election may be called at any time.

The *Folketing* must meet every year on the first Tuesday in October. Besides its legislative functions, it appoints every 6 years judges who, together with the ordinary members of the Supreme Court *(Højesteret)*, form the *Rigsret*, a tribunal which can alone try parliamentary impeachments. The ministers have free access to the House, but can vote only if they are members.

Folketing: At the elections of 12 Dec. 1990 Social Democrats won 69 seats (with 37·4% of votes cast), Conservatives (C) 30 (16%), Liberals (L) 29 (15·8%), Socialist People's Party 15 (8·3%), Progress Party 12 (6·4%), Centre Democrats 9 (5·1%), Radical Liberals 7 (3·5%), Christian People's Party 4 (2·3%). 2 members were elected for the Faroe Islands and 2 for Greenland.

A coalition government of Conservatives and Liberals was formed on 17 Dec. 1990:

Prime Minister: Poul Schlüter (C).
Foreign Affairs: Uffe Ellemann-Jensen (L). *Finance:* Henning Dyremose (C). *Economic and Fiscal Affairs:* Anders Fogh Rasmussen (L). *Justice:* Hans Engell (L). *Environment:* Per Stig Møller (C). *Education and Research:* Bertel Haarder (L). *Social Affairs:* Else Winther Andersen (L). *Ecclesiastical Affairs and Communications:* Torben Rechendorff (C). *Energy:* Jens Bilgrav Nielsen. *Labour:* Knud Erik Kirkegaard (C). *Fisheries:* Kent Kirk (C). *Industry and Energy:* Anne Birgitte Lundhoff (C). *Culture:* Grethe Rostbøll (C). *Health:* Ester Larsen (L). *Agriculture:* Laurits Tørnœs (L). *Defence:* Knud Enggaard (L). *Housing:* Svend Erik Hovmand (L). *Interior and Nordic Affairs:* Thor Pedersen (L). *Transport:* Kaj Ikast (C).

The ministers are individually and collectively responsible for their acts, and if impeached and found guilty, cannot be pardoned without the consent of the *Folketing*.

In 1948 a separate legislature *(Lagting)* and executive *(Landsstyre)* were established for the Faroe Islands, to deal with specified local matters and in 1979 a separate legislature *(Landsting)* and executive *(Landsstyre)* were established for Greenland, also to deal with specified local matters.

National flag: Red with white Scandinavian cross (Dannebrog).
National anthem: Kong Kristian stod ved højen mast ('King Christian stood by the lofty mast'; words by J. Ewald, 1778; tune by J. E. Hartmann, 1780).

Local Government. For administrative purposes Denmark is divided into 275 municipalities *(kommuner)*; each of them has a district council of between 7 and 31 members, headed by an elected mayor. The city of Copenhagen forms a district by itself and is governed by a city council of 55 members, elected every 4 years, and an executive *(magistraten)*, consisting of the chief burgomaster *(overborgmesteren)* and 6 burgomasters, appointed by the city council for 4 years. There are 14 counties *(amtskommuner)*, each of which is administered by a county council *(amstråd)* of between 13 and 31 members, headed by an elected mayor. All councils are elected directly by universal suffrage and proportional representation for 4-year terms.

The counties and Copenhagen are superintended by the Ministry of Interior Affairs. The municipalities are superintended by 14 local supervision committees, headed by a state county prefect *(statsamtmand)* who is a civil servant appointed by the Queen.

DEFENCE. Military defence is organized in accordance with the Defence Act of May 1982 as amended in April 1990, and the overall organization of the Danish Armed Forces comprises the Defence Command, the Army, the Navy, the Air Force and interservice authorities and institutions. To this should be added the Home Guard, which is an indispensable part of Danish military defence. The Home Guard is based on the Home Guard Act of May 1982.

In accordance with the Defence Act the Chief of Defence has full command of the three services: The Army, the Navy and the Air Force. The Chief of Defence, and the Defence Staff constitute the Defence Command.

The Constitution of 1849 declared it the duty of every fit man to contribute to the national defence, and this provision is still in force. According to the Personnel Act of May 1982, the military personnel comprises officers, n.c.o.s and privates. Private personnel are provided by enlistment and by recruiting of volunteers. Selection of conscripts takes place at the age of 18–19 years, and the conscripts are normally called up for service $\frac{1}{2}$–$1\frac{1}{2}$ years later. Afterwards conscripts may be recalled for refresher training or musters. The initial training period for conscripts is between 4 and 12 months.

Army. The Army comprises field army formations and the local defence forces. The field army formations are organized in a covering force and in reserve units. The covering force numbers about 17,000 men and comprises a standing force (regulars and conscripts with more than six months' service), and a supplementary force consisting of men newly released from service. The standing force is organized in standing brigade units, headquarters units and support units. The brigade units are organized in 5 mechanized infantry brigades. The field army is equipped with 353 battle tanks and about 316 armoured combat vehicles as well as artillery including 76 self-propelled howitzers. The Army has 12 Fennec anti-armour and 14 Hughes 500 observation helicopters for observation and liaison and 12 attack helicopters. The local defence units consist of about 18,000 men organized in 9 infantry battalions and some artillery battalions. The men of the latest annual service groups form the troops of the line, while those of the previous years form the local defence, the reserve and the reserve for the Home Guard. There are 55,000 Army reservists.

Navy. The Navy, in 1992, 7,000 strong (including 2,000 civilians and 794 conscripts) is supported by 5,900 reservists. The fleet includes 5 small submarines, 3 corvettes, 5 offshore patrol vessels with Lynx helicopters, 5 coastal patrol craft, 10 fast missile craft, 4 ocean minelayers, 2 coastal minelayers and 3 coastal minesweepers. Major auxiliaries include 2 tankers, and the Royal Yacht; and there are some 21 minor auxiliaries. The Naval Air Arm comprises 9 Lynx helicopters, and the Home Guard operates 37 inshore patrol craft.

Coastal Defence forces man 2 permanent fortresses armed with 150mm guns.

Additional forces of a para-military nature include 4 icebreakers maintained by the navy at the main base at Frederikshavn.

Air Force. The operational units of the Air Force, in 1992, comprise 8 surface-to-air missile squadrons and 5 flying squadrons.

The air defence force consists of the 8 Hawk surface-to-air missile squadrons and 4 all-weather air-defence squadrons with a total of 63 F-16s. All squadrons have an air-defence and a fighter-bomber rôle.

The fighter bomber force comprises 1 squadron with a total of 16 F 35 Drakens, which has a secondary reconnaissance role.

In addition the Air Force has a number of supplementary units, including 1 transport squadron (C-130 Hercules and Gulfstream III), 1 helicopter rescue squadron (S-61As), and a control and warning system. Supporter aircraft are used for initial training; pilots then go to the USA.

Total strength of the Air Force is about 9,200, and the mobilization force about 10,000 men.

Home Guard. The overall Home Guard organization comprises the Home Guard Command, the Army Home Guard, the Naval Home Guard, the Air Force Home Guard and the Service Corps.

The personnel of the Home Guard is recruited on a voluntary basis. The personnel establishment of the Home Guard is at present about 69,700 persons (54,800 in the Army Home Guard, 4,000 in the Navy Home Guard, 8,800 in the Air Force Home Guard and 2,000 in the Service Corps.).

INTERNATIONAL RELATIONS

Membership. Denmark is a member of the UN, NATO, OECD and the European Communities.

ECONOMY

Budget. The budget *(Finanslovforslag)* must be laid before the Parliament *(Folketing)* not later than 4 months before the beginning of a new fiscal year.

The following shows the actual revenue and expenditure as shown in central government accounts for the calendar years 1989 and 1990, the approved budget figures for 1991 and the budget for 1992 (in 1,000 kroner):

	1989	1990	1991	1992
Revenue	208,441,215	209,221,641	282,608,200	295,719,500
Expenditure	227,138,309	232,387,220	312,095,100	326,226,200

Receipts and expenditures of special government funds and expenditures on public works are included.

The 1992 budget envisaged revenue of 133,250m. kroner from income and property taxes and 135,959m. from consumer taxes.

The central government debt on 31 Dec. 1990 amounted to 483,938m. kroner.

Currency. The monetary unit is the *Danish krone* (DKK) of 100 *øre*.

There are notes of 1,000, 500, 100 and 50 kroner, and coins of 20, 10, 5 and 1 krone and 50 and 25 øre. In March 1992, £1 = 11·17 *kroner*; US$1 = 6·36 *kroner*.

Banking and Finance. On 31 Dec. 1990 the accounts of the National Bank *(Governor,* Erik Hoffmeyer, b. 1925) balanced at 132,357m. kroner. The assets included official net foreign reserves of 63,319m. kroner. The liabilities included notes and coin of 26,983m. kroner. On 31 Dec. 1990 there were 189 commercial banks and savings banks, with deposits of 528,521m. kroner. On 31 Dec. 1990 the money supply was 427,260m. kroner.

There is a stock exchange in Copenhagen.

Weights and Measures. The metric system has been obligatory since 1912.

ENERGY AND NATURAL RESOURCES

Electricity. Production (1990), 23,095m. kwh. Supply 220 volts; Hz 50.

Oil. Production (1991) 6·8m. tonnes.

Agriculture. Land ownership is widely distributed. In June 1990 there were 79,338 holdings with at least 5 ha of agricultural area (or at least a production equivalent to that from 5 ha of barley). There were 14,408 small holdings (with less than 10 ha), 48,917 medium-sized holdings (10–50 ha) and 16,014 holdings with more than 50 ha.

There were 23,639 agricultural workers in 1990.

In 1989 the cultivated area was (in 1,000 ha): Grain, 1,562; peas and beans, 123; root crops, 208; other crops, 329; green fodder and grass, 550; fallow, 5; total cultivated area, 2,774.

Chief crops	Area (1,000 ha)			Production (in 1,000 tonnes)		
	1988	1989	1990	1988	1989	1990
Wheat	308	444	533	2,080	2,224	3,953
Rye	80	100	109	366	487	545
Barley	1,154	988	1,101	5,419	4,959	4,987
Oats [1]	44	30	24	202	125	121
Potatoes	33	34	40	1,246	1,238	1,483
Other root crops	178	124	168	10,391	10,217	10,360

[1] Including mixed grain.

Livestock, 1990: Horses, 38,000; cattle, 2,239,000; pigs, 9,497,000; poultry, 15,498,000.

Production (in 1,000 tonnes) in 1990: Milk, 4,742; butter, 93; cheese, 295; beef, 219; pork and bacon, 1,260; eggs, 82.

In 1989 tractors numbered 165,908 and combine harvesters, 33,863.

Fisheries. The total value of the fish caught was (in 1m. kroner): 1950, 156; 1955, 252; 1960, 376; 1965, 650; 1970, 854; 1975, 1,442; 1980, 2,888; 1985, 3,542; 1986, 3,576; 1987, 3,510; 1988, 3,476; 1989, 3,625; 1990, 3,439 (preliminary).

INDUSTRY. The principal industries are meat and dairy produce, ship-building, furniture-making, the bio-scientific industries, pharmaceuticals and medical equipment. The following table sets forth the gross factor income (in 1m. kroner) by industrial origin in 3 calendar years:

	1988		1989		1990	
	Current Prices	1980 Prices	Current Prices	1980 Prices	Current Prices	1980 Prices
Agriculture, fur-farming, forestry, etc.	25,914	21,285	29,820	22,931	29,200	23,996
Fishing	2,211	1,318	2,106	1,544	2,060	1,613
Total	28,126	22,603	31,926	23,935	31,260	25,609
Mining and quarrying	4,681	10,372	6,308	11,564	7,395	12,085
Manufacturing	118,765	70,212	122,382	71,078	128,524	72,150
Electricity, gas and water	9,914	6,335	12,021	6,733	13,218	6,819
Construction	44,289	25,304	45,055	24,836	44,552	23,346
Total	177,649	112,223	185,766	114,211	193,689	114,400
Wholesale and retail trade	82,958	53,603	87,509	54,802	91,398	57,421
Restaurants and hotels	8,331	4,202	9,483	4,221	10,090	4,185
Transport and storage	40,618	26,266	43,608	26,746	45,130	28,626
Communication	10,653	6,406	12,425	6,552	14,364	7,392
Financing and insurance	21,124	13,476	25,748	15,492	26,627	15,439
Dwellings	55,014	29,869	60,889	30,768	66,463	31,607
Business services	37,333	21,478	40,859	22,440	45,700	23,217
Market services of education, health	7,478	4,276	7,822	4,294	7,910	4,248
Recreational and cultural services	5,933	3,709	7,083	4,232	7,382	4,082
Household services, incl. auto repair	19,141	9,591	20,959	9,689	23,824	10,384
Total	288,584	172,876	316,385	179,237	338,888	186,600
Other producers, excl. government	4,299	2,477	4,704	2,610	4,969	2,541
Producers of government services	142,819	84,068	147,905	83,590	152,895	83,479
Total	147,117	86,546	152,609	86,200	157,864	86,020
Imputed bank service charges	−21,215	−13,468	−25,794	−15,579	−27,263	−15,676
Gross domestic product at factor cost	620,261	380,779	660,891	388,005	694,438	396,953
Plus indirect taxes	139,484 ⎱	64,302	139,478 ⎱	62,203	141,753 ⎱	62,554
Less subsidies	24,226 ⎰		24,354 ⎰		25,743 ⎰	
Gross domestic product at market prices	735,520	445,081	776,015	450,207	810,448	459,507

Some 38,705 manufacturing enterprises registered for value-added tax in 1989. In the following table 'number of wage-earners' refers to 7,200 establishments with 6 employees or more (1989), while 'gross-output' and 'value-added' cover 3,298 enterprises with 20 employees or more (1989).

Branch of industry	Number of wage-earners (1,000)	Gross output in factor values (1m. kroner)	Value added in factor values (1m. kroner)
Mining and quarrying	0·9	815	630
Food products	49·1	95,310	25,130
Beverages	4·6	7,541	4,517

Branch of industry	Number of wage-earners (1,000)	Gross output in factor values (1m. kroner)	Value added in factor values (1m. kroner)
Tobacco	1·4	2,577	1,633
Textiles	10·2	8,695	3,929
Wearing apparel	006·6	003,192	001,596
Leather and products	0·5	409	162
Footwear	0·8	1,056	347
Wood products	8·4	6,413	2,888
Furniture and fixtures	12·0	7,199	3,714
Paper and products	7·1	8,364	3,878
Printing, publishing	14·9	14,529	9,538
Industrial chemicals	12·4	29,221	15,466
Other chemical products, petroleum refineries, petroleum coal products and rubber	2·9	11,440	3,156
Plastic products	7·5	6,613	3,554
Pottery, china, glass and products	3·3	1,778	1,075
Non-metal products	9·1	9,869	5,897
Iron, steel and non-ferrous metals	4·5	4,891	2,138
Metal products	27·7	21,676	10,281
Machinery	40·4	33,779	17,685
Electrical machinery	15·1	15,126	7,798
Transport equipment	16·4	13,950	6,113
Controlling equipment	6·8	6,528	4,015
Other industries	4·5	4,829	2,841
Total manufacturing	267·1	315,799	138,522

Labour. In 1990, 6% of the working population lived on agriculture, forestry and fishery, 21% on industries and handicrafts, 7% on construction, 15% on commerce, etc., 7% on transport and communication, and 45% on administration, professional services, etc.

FOREIGN ECONOMIC RELATIONS

Commerce. The following table shows the value, in 1,000 kroner, of special trade imports and exports (including trade with the Faroe Islands and Greenland) for calendar years:

	1986	1987	1988	1989	1990 [1]
Imports	184,732,811	174,066,090	174,428,775	195,327,934	195,393,955
Exports	171,790,740	175,302,411	182,414,968	205,508,044	215,611,036

[1] Preliminary.

Imports and exports (in 1m. kroner) for calendar years:

Leading commodities	(1989) (Imports)	(Exports)	1990 [1] Imports	Exports
Live animals, meat, etc.	1,478	21,344	1,624	20,831
Dairy products, eggs	936	7,788	707	8,001
Fish and fish preparations	6,218	11,659	6,756	12,621
Cereals and cereal preparations	1,271	4,696	1,255	5,246
Sugar and sugar preparations	638	1,547	692	1,641
Coffee, tea, cocoa, etc.	1,782	512	1,339	497
Feeding stuff for animals	4,404	2,065	3,648	1,603
Wood, lumber and cork	2,887	698	3,069	655
Textiles, fibres, yarns, fabrics, etc.	5,587	3,382	5,492	3,685
Fuels, lubricants, etc.	13,068	5,625	12,674	6,246
Pharmaceutical products	2,963	7,179	3,053	7,671
Fertilizers, etc.	1,360	683	2,884	492
Metals, manufactures of metals	16,788	10,623	16,107	10,796
Machinery, electrical, equipment, etc.	40,826	37,733	42,738	39,475
Transport equipment	18,123	9,604	18,952	12,280

Distribution of Danish foreign trade (in 1,000 kroner) according to countries of origin and destination, for calendar years:

		Imports			Exports	
Countries	1988	1989	1990 [1]	1988	1989	1990 [1]
Belgium	5,933,826	6,331,778	6,441,717	3,671,209	4,111,488	4,548,716
Finland	5,435,364	5,675,399	5,940,923	4,545,625	5,620,741	5,615,578
France	8,642,431	9,720,301	10,419,551	10,426,090	12,387,238	12,952,384
Germany						
(Fed. Rep.)	39,907,494	43,389,516	43,788,003	31,934,335	35,945,720	42,375,285
Norway	7,798,472	8,576,945	9,204,920	12,412,741	11,698,581	12,266,724
Sweden	21,377,630	23,604,816	22,592,735	20,958,329	25,061,370	27,591,207
Switzerland	3,802,755	3,931,259	3,949,100	4,170,381	4,465,446	4,300,367
UK	12,320,004	13,564,993	14,886,054	21,746,325	24,912,259	23,125,631
USA	10,471,953	13,468,312	12,152,306	10,670,988	11,481,942	10,891,661

[1] Provisional.

Total trade between Denmark (without the Faroe Islands) and UK (British Department of Trade returns, in £1,000 sterling):

	1987	1988	1989	1990	1991
Imports to UK	1,873,495	2,028,089	2,229,340	2,278,569	2,226,706
Exports and re-exports from UK	1,231,097	1,170,853	1,209,220	1,413,713	1,408,549

Tourism. In 1990, foreigners visiting Denmark spent some 20,554m. kroner. In 1990 foreigners spent 5·43m. nights in hotels and 3·44m. nights at camping sites.

COMMUNICATIONS

Roads. Denmark proper had (1 Jan. 1990), 601 km of motorways, 3,968 km of other state roads, 7,037 km of provincial roads and 59,168 km of commercial roads. Motor vehicles registered at 31 Dec. 1988 comprised 1,581,344 passenger cars, 293,543 lorries, 11,784 taxicabs (including 5,256 for private hire), 8,093 buses and 42,450 cycles.

Railways. In 1990 there were 2,344 km of State railways (145 km electrified), which carried 4,885m. passenger-km and 1,730m. tonne-km. There were also 494 km of private railways.

Civil Aviation. On 1 Oct. 1950 the 3 Scandinavian airlines, Det Danske Luftfartsselskab, ABA and DNL, combined in the Scandinavian Airlines System (SAS). In 1990 SAS flew 188m. km and carried 14,930,633 passengers.

SAS inaugurated its transpolar routes Copenhagen–Los Angeles on 15 Nov. 1954 and Copenhagen–Tokyo on 25 Feb. 1957, and its trans-Asian express route Copenhagen–Bangkok–Singapore via Tashkent on 4 Nov. 1967.

Shipping. On 31 Dec. 1990 the merchant fleet consisted of 928 vessels (above 20 GRT) of 5,148,134 GRT.

In 1990, 41m. tonnes of cargo were unloaded and 24m. tonnes were loaded in Danish ports; traffic by passenger ships and ferries is not included.

Telecommunications. There were, in 1989, 1,266 post offices. On 31 Dec. 1989 the length of telephone circuits of private companies was 18,152,000 km. On 31 Dec. 1989 there were 4,398,000 telephones. Postal revenues, 1989, 13,458m. kroner; expenditure, 10,987m. kroner.

Danmarks Radio is the government broadcasting station and is financed by licence fees. Television is broadcast by *Danmarks Radio* and *TV2* with colour programmes by PAL system. Number of receivers (1990): TV, 1·96m., including 1·8m. colour sets; radio, 2·04m.

Cinemas. In 1990 there were 347 auditoria with a seating capacity of 57,130.

Newspapers. In 1990 there were 47 daily newspapers with a combined circulation of 1·81m. on weekdays.

JUSTICE, RELIGION, EDUCATION AND WELFARE

Justice. The lowest courts of justice are organized in 82 tribunals *(underretter)*, where minor cases are dealt with by a single judge. The tribunals at Copenhagen have 33 judges and Aarhus 12; the other tribunals have 1 to 9. Cases of greater consequence are dealt with by the superior courts *(Landsretterne)*; these courts are also courts of appeal for the above-named minor cases. Of superior courts there are two: *Østre Landsret* in Copenhagen with 45 judges, *Vestre Landret* in Viborg with 22 judges. From these an appeal lies to the Supreme Court *(Højesteret)* in Copenhagen, composed of 15 judges. Judges under 65 years of age can be removed only by judicial sentence.

In 1990, 15,761 men and 2,095 women were convicted of violations of the criminal code, fines not included. In 1990, the daily average population in penal institutions was 3,267 men and 158 women, of whom 784 men and 46 women were on remand.

Religion. At the Reformation in 1536 the Danish Church ceased to exist as a legally independent unit, a part of the Roman Catholic Church, and became instead a Lutheran Church under the direction of the State. Since that time the State has, in one form or another, continued to exercise supreme authority in the affairs of the Church, and has regulated these by the passing of laws, by royal decree, or other appropriate means. The great majority of Danish citizens (about 90%) belongs to the National Church. Administratively, Denmark is divided into 10 dioceses each with a Bishop who, within the framework of the law, is the supreme diocesan authority in ecclesiastical affairs. The Bishop together with the Chief Administrative Officer of the county make up the diocesan governing body, responsible for all matters of ecclesiastical local finance and general administration. Bishops are appointed by the Crown after an election at which the clergy and parish council members of the diocese have had the opportunity of voting for the candidates nominated. Each diocese is divided into a number of deaneries (107 in the whole country) each with its Dean and Deanery Committee, who have certain financial powers. Local government at parish level (there are about 2,100 parishes in all) is in the hands of Parish Councils, who are elected for a 4-year period of office.

Since the Constitution of 1849 complete religious toleration is extended to every sect, and no civil disabilities attach to Dissenters.

Education. Education has been compulsory since 1814. The *folkeskole* (public primary and lower secondary school) comprises a pre-school class *(børnehaveklasse)*, a 9-year basic school corresponding to the period of compulsory education and a 1-year voluntary tenth form. Compulsory education may be fulfilled either through attending the *folkeskole* or private schools or through home-instruction, on the condition that the instruction given is comparable to that given in the *folkeskole*. The *folkeskole* is mainly a municipal school and no fees are paid. In the year 1989–90, 2,155 primary and lower secondary schools had 630,149 pupils and employed 61,100 teachers. 19% of the total number of schools were private schools and they were attended by 10·5% of the total number of pupils. The 9-year basic school is in practice not streamed. However, a certain differentiation may take place in the eighth and ninth forms.

On completion of the eighth and ninth forms the pupils may sit for the leaving examination of the *folkeskole (folkeskolens afgangsprøve)*. On completion of the tenth form the pupils may sit for either the leaving examination of the *folkeskole (folkeskolens afgangsprøve)* or the advanced leaving examination of the *folkeskole (folkeskolens udvidede afgangsprøve)*.

For 14–18 year olds there is an alternative of completing compulsory education at continuation schools, with the same leaving examinations as in the *folkeskole*. In the year 1989–90 there were 218 continuation schools with 16,345 pupils.

Under certain conditions the pupils may continue school either in the 3-year gymnasium (upper secondary school) or 2-year *studenterkursus* (adult upper secondary school) ending with *studentereksamen* (upper secondary school leaving examination) or in the 2-year higher preparatory examination course ending with the *højere forberedelseseksamen*. There were (1989–90) 156 of these upper secondary schools with 73,329 pupils.

Vocational education and training consists of apprenticeship training, *lærlingeuddannelse*; vocational education, *EFG-uddannelse*, consisting of a 1-year basic course, *EFG-basisar*, followed by a second part, *EFG-2.del*, and courses preparing for a vocation, leading to a diploma.

Vocational education and training cover courses in commerce and trade, iron and metal industry, chemical industry, construction industry, graphic industry, service trades, food industry, agriculture, horticulture, forestry and fishery, transport and communication, and health related auxiliary programmes.

In 1989–90 70,559 students were enrolled within trade and commerce, of whom 5,450 were in apprenticeship training and 41,898 in vocational education. 84,969 students were enrolled within technical education, of whom 29,013 were in apprenticeship training and 41,632 in vocational education. 23,211 students were admitted to the diploma courses within the field of trade and commerce, and 12,823 students were admitted to the technical diploma courses.

Tertiary education comprises all education after the 12th year of education, no matter whether the 3 years after the 9th form of the *folkeskole* have been spent on a course preparing for continued studies *(studentereksamen* or *højere forberedelseseksamen)*, or a course preparing for a vocation *(lærlingeuddannelse, EFG-uddannelse*, etc.). Tertiary education can be divided into 2 main groups, short courses of further education and long courses of higher education. There was a total of 27,641 students at short courses of further education.

There were 25 teacher-training colleges with 6,481 students and 20 colleges for training of teachers for kindergartens and leisure-time activities with 4,960 students.

Degree-courses in engineering: The Technical University of Denmark had 5,615 students. The Engineering Academy had 2,316 students and 9 engineering colleges had 7,944 students.

Universities: The University of Copenhagen (founded 1479) 24,251 students. The University of Aarhus (founded in 1928) 12,622 students. The University of Odense (founded in 1964) 6,762 students. Roskilde University Centre (founded in 1972) 3,289 students. Aalborg University Centre (founded in 1974) 6,750 students.

Other types of post-secondary education: The Royal Veterinary and Agricultural University had 2,819 students. The two dental colleges had 618 students. The Danish School of Pharmacy had 928 students. The 11 colleges of economics, business administration and modern languages had 27,184 students. The 2 schools of architecture had 1,651 students. Five academies of music had 847 students. Two schools of librarianship had 622 students. The Royal Danish School of Educational Studies had 2,560 students. The 5 schools of social work had 847 students. The Danish School of Journalism had 793 students. Ten colleges of physical therapy had 1,386 students. Two schools of Midwifery Education had 107 students. Two colleges of home economics had 371 students. The School of Visual Arts had 180 students. Two schools of nursing had 414 students. Three military academies had 360 students.

Among adult education the most well-known are *Folkeskolehøjskoler*, folk high schools. Adult education in general programmes, single subjects (since 1978) and courses for semi-skilled workers and for skilled workers is organized by counties.

Andreseén, A., *The Danish Folk High School To-day*. Copenhagen, 1981
Struve, K., *Schools and Education in Denmark*. Copenhagen, 1981
Thorsen, L., *Public Libraries in Denmark*. English and French eds., Copenhagen, 1972

Social Security. The main body of Danish social welfare legislation is consolidated in 7 acts concerning (1) public health security, (2) sick-day benefits, (3) social pensions (for early retirement and old age), (4) employment injuries insurance, (5) employment services and unemployment insurance, (6) social assistance including assistance to handicapped, rehabilitation, child and juvenile guidance, day-care institutions, care of the aged and sick, and (7) family allowances.

Public health security, covering the entire population, provides free medical care, substantial subsidies for certain essential medicines together with some dental care and a funeral allowance. Hospitals are primarily municipal and the hospital treatment is normally free. All employed workers are granted daily sickness allowances, others can have limited daily sickness allowances. Daily cash benefits are granted in the case of temporary incapacity for work because of illness, injury or child-birth to all persons who earn an income derived from personal work. The benefit is paid at the rate of 90% of the average weekly earnings. There was a maximum rate of 2,506 kroner a week in 1991.

Social pensions cover the entire population. Entitlement to old-age pensions at the full rates is subject to the condition that the beneficiary has been ordinarily resident in Denmark for a number of years (40). For a shorter period of residence, the benefits are reduced proportionally. The basic amount of the old-age pension in July 1991 was 114,144 kroner a year to married couples and 57,072 to single persons. Various supplementary allowances, depending on age and income, may be payable with the basic amount. Persons aged 55–66 may, depending on health and income, apply for an early-retirement pension. Persons over 67 years of age are entitled to the basic amount. The pensions to a married couple are calculated and paid to the husband and the wife separately. Early retirement pension to a disabled person is payable, having regard to the degree of disability, at a rate of up to 106,632 kroner to a single person. Early-retirement pensions may be subject to income regulation. The same applies to the basic amount of the old age pension to persons aged 67–69.

Employment injuries insurance provides for disablement or survivors' pensions and compensations. The scheme covers practically all employees.

Employment services are provided by regional public employment agencies. The insurance against unemployment provides daily allowances. The unemployment insurance funds had in Dec. 1990 a membership of 2,066,659.

The *Social Assistance Act* applies to the field of social legislation which rules the individually granted benefits in contrast to the other fields of social legislation which apply to fixed benefits.

Total social expenditure, including hospital and health services, statutory pensions, etc, amounted in the financial year 1989 to 219,770m. kroner.

Bibliography of Foreign Language Literature on Industrial Relations and Social Services in Denmark. Ministries of Labour and Social Affairs, Copenhagen, 1975
Social Conditions in Denmark. Vols. 1–8. Ministries of Labour and Social Affairs, Copenhagen
Marcussen, E., *Social Welfare in Denmark.* 4th ed. Copenhagen, 1980

THE FAROE ISLANDS
Føroyar/Færøerne

HISTORY. A Norwegian province to the peace treaty of 14 January 1814, the islands have been represented by 2 members in the Danish parliament since 1851, and in 1852 they obtained an elected assembly of their own, called *løgting*, which in 1948 secured a certain degree of home-rule within the Danish realm. The islands are not included in the EEC, but left EFTA together with Denmark on 31 Dec. 1972.

AREA AND POPULATION. The archipelago is situated due north of Scotland, 300 km from the Shetland Islands, 675 km from Norway and 450 km from Iceland, with a total land area of 1,399 sq. km (540 sq. miles). There are 17 inhabited islands (the main ones being Stremoy, Eysturoy, Vágoy, Suðuroy, Sandoy and Borðoy) and numerous islets, all mountainous and of volcanic origin. The census population in 1977 was 41,969; estimate (31 Dec. 1988) 47,663. The capital is Tórshavn (14,547 inhabitants on 31 Dec. 1988) on Stremoy. The inhabitants speak Faroese (føroyskt), a Scandinavian language which since 1948 has been the official language of the islands along with Danish.

CONSTITUTION AND GOVERNMENT. The parliament *(løgting)*, comprises 32 members elected by proportional representation by universal suffrage at age 18. The *løgting* elected in Nov. 1990 includes 10 Social Democratic Party, 7

People's Party, 6 Unionist Party, 4 Republican Party. Parliament elects a government *(Landsstýri)* of at least 3 members which administers the home rule. Denmark is represented in the *løgting* by the chief administrator *(ríkisumboðsmaður)*.
Chief Minister (Lømaður): Jøgvan Sundstein.

Local government is vested in the 50 *kommunur*, which have 29 or more inhabitants and income taxes of their own.

Flag: White with a red blue-edged Scandinavian cross.

ECONOMY

Budget. The 1988 Budget balanced at 3,151m. kr.

Currency. Since 1940 the currency has been the Faroese *krøna* (kr.) which remains freely interchangeable with the Danish krone.

ENERGY AND NATURAL RESOURCES

Electricity. There are 5 hydro-electric stations at Vestmanna on Stremoy and one at Eiði on Eysturoy. Total production (1988) 215·6m. kwh, of which hydro-electric 60·2m. kwh.

Agriculture. Only 2% of the surface is cultivated. The chief use is for grazing, the traditional mainstay of the economy. A small amount of potatoes is grown for home consumption. Livestock (1988): Sheep, 55,503; cattle, 2,176.

Fisheries. Deep sea fishing now forms the most important sector of the economy, primarily in the 200-mile exclusive zone but also off Greenland, Iceland, Svalbard and Newfoundland and in the Barents Sea. Total catch (1988) 357,000 tonnes, primarily cod, blue whiting, coalfish, prawns, mackerel and herring.

COMMERCE. The main industry is fishery. Exports, mainly fresh, frozen, filleted and salted fish, amounted to 2,345m. kr. in 1988; imports to 3,221m. kr. In 1988 Denmark supplied 39·6% of imports, Norway 21·1%, UK 8·2%, Sweden 6·3% and Federal Republic of Germany 5·8%; exports were mainly to Denmark (18·6%), UK (11·5%), Federal Republic of Germany (5·7%), USA (9·1%) and Norway (8%).

Total trade with UK (British Department of Trade returns, in £1,000 sterling):

	1987	1988	1989	1990	1991
Imports to UK	19,239	23,141	31,042	34,396	32,515
Exports and re-exports from UK	7,165	4,445	6,353	7,882	7,330

COMMUNICATIONS

Roads. In 1988 there were 433 km of roads, 14,232 passenger cars and 3,445 commercial vehicles.

Aviation. The airport is on Vágoy, from which there are regular services to Copenhagen and Reykjavík.

Shipping. The chief port is Tórshavn, with smaller ports at Klaksvik, Vestmanna, Skálafjørður, Tvøroyri, Vágur and Fuglafjørður.

Post and Broadcasting. In 1988 there were 20,816 telephones. *Utvarp Føroya* broadcasts from Tórshavn about 40 hours a week on 4 transmitters. In 1988 there were 17,000 radio and 11,000 television receivers.

RELIGION, EDUCATION AND WELFARE

Religion. About 80% are Evangelical Lutherans and 20% are Plymouth Brethren or belong to small communities of Roman Catholics, Pentecostal, Adventists, Jehovah Witnesses and Bahai.

Education. In 1988–89 there were 5,440 primary and 2,979 secondary school pupils with 601 teachers.

Health. In 1988 there were 87 doctors, 39 dentists, 10 pharmacists, 17 midwives and 344 nursing personnel. In 1989 there were 3 hospitals with 369 beds.

Further Reading

Årbog for Færøerne.
Faroes in Figures. Thorshavn, annual, from 1956
Rutherford, G. K., (ed.) *The Physical Environment of the Færoe Islands.* The Hague, 1982
West, J. F., *Faroe.* London, 1973
Wylie, J., *The Faroe Islands: Interpretations of History.* Lexington, 1987

GREENLAND
Grønland/Kalaallit Nunaat

HISTORY. A Danish possession since 1380, Greenland became on 5 June 1953 an integral part of the Danish kingdom. Following a referendum in Jan. 1979, home rule was introduced from 1 May 1979, and full internal self-government was attained in Jan. 1981 after a transitional period.

AREA AND POPULATION. Area 2,186,000 sq. km (844,000 sq. miles), made up of 1,802,400 sq. km of ice cap and 383,600 sq. km of ice-free land. The population, 1 Jan. 1990, numbered 55,558; West Greenland, 50,217; East Greenland, 3,443; North Greenland (Thule), 843, and 1,052 not belonging to any specific municipality. Of the total, 9,416 were born outside Greenland. The capital is Nuuk (Godthåb), with a population in 1990 of 12,217.

CONSTITUTION. At the introduction of home rule, the council *(Landsråd)* was replaced by a 27-member parliament *(Landsting).* At the elections of March 1991 the *Siumut* gained 11 seats with 37% of votes cast, the *Atassut,* 8 seats, the *Inuit Ataqatigiit,* 5 seats. The *Prime Minister* is Lars-Emil Johansen. There is a 5-member administration, the *Landsstyre.* Denmark is represented by an appointed commissioner. There are 18 local government divisions.

ECONOMY

Budget. The Budget for 1989 balanced at 5,037m. kroner.

Currency. The Danish kroner remains the legal currency.

ENERGY AND NATURAL RESOURCES

Electricity. Production (1989) 161·3m. kwh.

Fisheries. In 1989 the catch totalled 214,200 tonnes.

INDUSTRY. Until the beginning of this century, the hunting of land and sea mammals, especially seals, was the main occupation of the population; now fishing is most important. Fish-processing industries, construction and trade are also important occupations.

Production of lead and zinc concentrates was in 1989 about 35,500 tonnes and 130,500 tonnes respectively. The mine is now worked out.

A hydro-electric power station is under construction 40 miles south of Nuuk.

COMMERCE. Imports (c.i.f. Greenland) (in 1m. kroner): 1987, 3,471; 1988, 3,495; 1989, 2,879 (provisional). Exports (f.o.b. Greenland) (in 1m. kroner): 1987, 2,370; 1988, 2,630; 1989, 2,930 (provisional). Trade is mainly with Denmark.

Total trade with UK (British Department of Trade returns, in £1,000 sterling):

	1987	1988	1989	1990	1991
Imports to UK	838	1,430	3,793	10,322	5,039
Exports and re-exports from UK	735	1,151	1,487	2,256	635

COMMUNICATIONS

Roads. There were (1970) 150 km of roads, of which 60 km were paved.

Aviation. There is an international airport at Søndre Srømfjord, and 12 local airports with scheduled services.

Telecommunications. Greenland Radio (Kalaallit Nunaata Radioa) broadcasts in Greenlandic and Danish. Several towns have local television stations. In 1989 there were 16,561 telephones, (1984) 10,000 television sets and (1984) 13,500 radio sets.

JUSTICE, RELIGION, EDUCATION AND WELFARE

Justice. The High Court in Nuuk comprises one professional judge and 2 lay magistrates, while there are 18 district courts under lay assessors.

Religion. About 98% of the population are Evangelical Lutherans.

Education. There were (1988–89) 8,967 pupils in primary comprehensive schools, of whom 7,459 were in the course of compulsory education (9 years). On 1 Sept. 1988, 2,297 students were enrolled in vocational training.

Health. The medical service is free to all inhabitants. There is a central hospital in Nuuk and 16 smaller district hospitals. In 1989 there were 78 doctors and 444 hospital beds.

Further Reading

The Danish Prime Minister's Office, Greenland Section, has published a yearbook since 1989, *Grønland/Kalaallit Nunaat.*
Statistiske Efterretninger (Statistical News), from 1983 special series: *Færøerne og Grønland* (Faroe Islands and Greenland)
Gad, F., *A History of Greenland.* 2 vols. London, 1970–1973
Hertling, K. (ed.) *Greenland Past and Present.* Copenhagen, 1970
Miller, K. E., *Greenland* [Bibliography]. Oxford and Santa Barbara, 1991

Greenland National Library, P.O. Box 1011, DK-3900, Nuuk

DIPLOMATIC REPRESENTATIVES

Of Denmark in Great Britain (55 Sloane St., London, SW1X 9SR)
Ambassador: Rudolph Thorning-Petersen.

Of Great Britain in Denmark (36–40 Kastelsvej, DK-2100, Copenhagen)
Ambassador: N. C. R. Williams, CMG.

Of Denmark in the USA (3200 Whitehaven St., NW, Washington, D.C., 20008-3683)
Ambassador: Peter Pedersen Dyvig.

Of the USA in Denmark (Dag Hammarskjolds Alle 24, Copenhagen)
Ambassador: Keith L. Brown.

Of Denmark to the United Nations
Ambassador: Bent Haakonsen.

Further Reading

Statistical Information: Danmarks Statistik (Sejrøgade 11, 2100 Copenhagen Ø.) was founded in 1849 and reorganized in 1966 as an independent institution; it is administratively placed under the Minister of Economic Affairs. *Chief:* Hans E. Zeuthen. Its main publications are: *Statistisk Årbog* (Statistical Yearbook). From 1896; *Statistiske Efterretninger* (Statistical News). *Statistiske Månedsoversigt* Monthly Review of Statistics), *Statistisk tiårsoversigt* (Statistical Ten-Year Review).

Ministry of Foreign Affairs. *Facts about Denmark.*
Bibliografi over Danmarks Offentlige Publikationer. Institut for International Udveksling, Copenhagen. Annual
Dania polyglotta. Annual Bibliography of Books ... in Foreign Languages Printed in Denmark. State Library, Copenhagen. Annual

Kongelig Dansk Hof og Statskalender. Copenhagen. Annual
Danstrup, J., *History of Denmark*. 2nd ed. Copenhagen, 1949
Johansen, H. C., *The Danish Economy in the Twentieth Century*. London, 1987
Miller, K. E., *Denmark*. [Bibliography] Oxford and Santa Barbara, 1987.—*Denmark: a Troubled Welfare State*. Boulder (Colo.), 1991

National library: Det kongelige Bibliotek, P.O.B. 2149, DK-1016 Copenhagen K. *Director:* Erland Kolding Nielsen.

DJIBOUTI

Capital: Djibouti
Population: 510,000 (1989)
GNP per capita: US$475 (1986)

Jumhouriyya Djibouti

(Republic of Djibouti)

HISTORY. At a referendum held on 19 March 1967, 60% of the electorate voted for continued association with France rather than independence and the new statute for the territory came into being on 5 July 1967. France affirmed that the Territory of the Afars and the Issas was destined for independence but no date was fixed. Legislative elections were held on 8 May and independence as the Republic of Djibouti was achieved on 27 June 1977.

AREA AND POPULATION. Djibouti is bounded north-east by the Gulf of Aden, south-east by Somalia and all other sides by Ethiopia.

Djibouti has an area of 23,200 sq. km (8,958 sq. miles). The population was estimated in 1989 at 510,000, of whom 47% were Somali (Issa), 37% Afar, 8% European (mainly French) and 6% Arab. Births in 1989, 9,920; infant mortality, 114 per 1,000 live births. Expectation of life, 48 years. There are also refugees from Ethiopia. There are 5 administrative districts (areas in sq. km): Ali-Sabieh (2,600); Dikhil (7,800); Djibouti (600); Obock (5,700); Tadjoura (7,300). The capital is Djibouti (1988 population, 0·29m.).

CLIMATE. Conditions are hot throughout the year, with very little rain. Djibouti. Jan. 78°F (25·6°C), July 96°F (35·6°C). Annual rainfall 5" (130 mm).

CONSTITUTION AND GOVERNMENT. Under an organic law approved by the Constituent Assembly on 10 Feb. 1981, the President is directly elected for a 6-year term (renewable once) and the Constituent Assembly became a 65-member Chamber of Deputies, with a 5-year term. In Oct. 1981, the Assembly declared Djibouti a one-Party state, the ruling Party being the *Rassemblement Populaire pour le Progrès.* Elections for the Chamber of Deputies were held 21 May 1982, when 26 Somali, 23 Afar and 16 Arab members were elected. A 14-member constitutional commission was set up in Jan. 1992.

President: Hassan Gouled Aptidon (elected 1977 and re-elected 1981 and 1987).
The Council of Ministers in Feb. 1992 was composed as follows:
Prime Minister, Planning and Land Development: Barkat Gourad Hamadou.
Interior, Posts and Telecommunications: Khaireh Alleleh Hared. *Justice and Islamic Affairs:* Ougoureh Hassan Ibrahim. *Foreign Affairs and Co-operation:* Ali Mahamade. *Defence:* Ismail Ali Youssouf. *Commerce:* Moussa Bourale Roble. *Finance:* Vacant. *Industry:* Salem Abdou. *Labour:* Ahmed Ibrahim Ardi. *Education:* Suleiman Farah Lodon. *Agriculture:* Muhammad Moussa Chehem. *Public Works:* Ahmed Aden Youssouf. *Health:* Ougoure Hassan Ibrahim. *Ports:* Bourhan Ali Warki. *Youth:* Omar Chirdon Abass.

National flag: Horizontally blue over green, with a white triangle based on the hoist charged with a red star.

DEFENCE. France maintains a naval base and 3,800 troops under an agreement renewed in Feb. 1991.

Army. The Army comprises 1 infantry battalion, 1 armoured squadron, 1 support battalion, 1 border commando battalion and 1 parachute company. Equipment includes 45 armoured cars. The strength of the Army (of which the Navy and Air

Force form part) was (1992) 2,600 men. There is also a paramilitary gendarmerie of some 600 men.

Navy. A coastal patrol is maintained consisting of 8 inshore patrol craft. Personnel (1991) 90.

Air Force. There is a small air force, all equipment via French aid. There are 2 CASA Aviocar and 2 Noratlas transports, 1 Falcon 50 VIP aircraft, 1 Cessna 206 for liaison, 1 Rallye trainer, and 5 helicopters (Alouette II and Ecureuil). Personnel (1992) 80.

INTERNATIONAL RELATIONS

Membership. Djibouti is a member of the UN, OAU, the Arab League and is an ACP state of the EEC.

ECONOMY

Budget. Revenue for 1988 was 25,516m. Djibouti francs and expenditure 23,516m.

Currency. The currency is the *Djibouti franc* (DJB). 8,197m. Djibouti francs were in circulation in 1990. In March 1992, £1 = 311 *Djibouti francs*; US$1 = 177·16 *Djibouti francs*.

Banking. The Banque Nationale de Djibouti is the bank of issue. There are 6 commercial banks.

ENERGY AND NATURAL RESOURCES

Electricity. Production (1989) 187·85m. kwh. Installed capacity, 80,100 kw.

Minerals. Minerals supposed to exist are gypsum, mica, amethyst and sulphur.

Agriculture. Agricultural land was 674 ha in 1989, of which 407 ha were exploited, mainly by market gardening. Tomato production (1989) 750 tonnes. Livestock (1989): 92,900 cattle. FAO estimates for 1990: 416,000 sheep, 502,000 goats, 59,000 camels.

Fisheries. The catch in 1989 was 389·28 tonnes.

INDUSTRY

Labour. In 1986 there were 2,134 persons employed in construction and 1,235 in manufacturing. A 40-hour working week is standard. In 1989 there was a minimum monthly wage of 15,850 Djibouti francs.

FOREIGN ECONOMIC RELATIONS

Commerce. The main economic activity is the operation of the port. The chief imports are cotton goods, sugar, cement, flour, fuel oil and vehicles; the chief exports are hides, cattle and coffee (transit from Ethiopia). In 1989 France supplied 27·9% of imports; Ethiopia, 12·6%. Trade in 1m. Djibouti francs:

	1985	1986	1987	1988	1989
Imports	35,670	33,106	36,487	35,640	35,054
Exports	2,488	3,628	4,976	4,111	4,459

Total trade between Djibouti and UK (British Department of Trade returns, in £1,000 sterling):

	1987	1988	1989	1990	1991
Imports to UK	175	169	489	174	119
Exports and re-exports from UK	12,501	8,479	10,555	14,962	21,889

Tourism. 40,762 visitors spent 76,189 nights in 1989.

COMMUNICATIONS

Roads. There were (1989) 3,067 km of roads, of which 412 km were hard-surfaced. In 1987 there were 11,799 passenger cars and 1,501 commercial vehicles.

Railway. For the line Djibouti–Addis Ababa, of which 106 km lies within Djibouti *see* p. 533. Traffic carried is mainly in transit to and from Ethiopia.

Civil Aviation. Air Djibouti provides services to Addis Ababa, Nairobi, Jidda and the Gulf. Other airlines serving Djibouti international airport (Ambouli) are Ethiopian Airlines, Air France, Air Tanzania and Yemen Airways Corporation. In 1989, 63,904 passengers and 7,137 tonnes of freight arrived at Ambouli, and 65,610 passengers and 1,102 tonnes of freight departed.

Shipping. Djibouti is a free port and container terminal. 950 ships berthed in 1989, (including 177 warships) totalling 3·87m. NRT. 3,211 passengers embarked or disembarked, and 0·88m. tonnes of cargo were handled. In 1981 the merchant marine comprised 8 vessels of 3,185 GRT.

Telecommunications. Number of telephones (1989), 5,100. The state-run *Radio-diffusion-Télévision de Djibouti* broadcasts on medium- and short-waves in French, Somali, Afar and Arabic. There is a television transmitter in Djibouti, broadcasting for 36 hours a week. Number of receivers (1990): Radio, 30,000; TV, 14,000 (colour by SECAM).

JUSTICE, RELIGION, EDUCATION AND WELFARE

Justice. There is a Court of First Instance and a Court of Appeal in the capital. The judicial system is based on Islamic law.

Religion. The vast majority of the population is Moslem, with about 24,000 Roman Catholics.

Education. In 1989–90 there were 57 state primary schools (and 9 private) with 27,884 (2,895) pupils and 641 (66) teachers, 10 (6) secondary schools, with 6,892 (946) pupils and 307 teachers. There was an *école normale* with 112 pupils and 12 teachers. Professional education is all in private hands. In 1989–90 there were 11 institutions and 1,074 students.

Health. In 1989 there were 9 hospitals, 4 medical centres and 11 dispensaries all with 1,383 beds, 91 doctors, 10 dentists and 14 pharmacists.

DIPLOMATIC REPRESENTATIVES

Of Djibouti in Great Britain
Ambassador: Ahmd Omar Farah (resides in Paris).

Of Great Britain in Djibouti
Ambassador: M. A. Marshall, CMG (resides in Sana'a).

Of the USA in Djibouti (Plateau du Serpent Blvd., Djibouti)
Ambassador: Robert S. Barrett IV.

Of Djibouti to the United Nations and in the USA
Ambassador: Roble Olhaye.

Further Reading

Direction Nationale de la Statistique. *Annuaire Statistique de Djibouti*
Schraeder, P. J., *Djibouti*. [Bibliography] Oxford and Santa Barbara, 1990
Thompson, V. and Adloff, R., *Djibouti and the Horn of Africa*. Stanford Univ. Press, 1967

National statistical office: Direction Nationale de la Statistique, Ministère du Commerce, des Transports et du Tourisme, BP 1846, Djibouti

DOMINICA

Capital: Roseau
Population: 108,812 (1991)
GNP per capita: US$1,650 (1988)

Commonwealth of Dominica

HISTORY. Dominica was discovered by Columbus. It was a British possession from 1805, a member of the Federation of the West Indies 1958–62, an Associated State of the UK, 1967–78 and became an independent republic as the Commonwealth of Dominica on 3 Nov. 1978.

AREA AND POPULATION. Dominica is an island in the Windward group of the West Indies situated between Martinique and Guadeloupe. It has an area of 751 sq. km (290 sq. miles) and a population at the 1981 Census of 74,851; estimate (1991) 108,812. The chief town, Roseau, had 8,279 inhabitants in 1981.

The population is mainly of African and mixed origins, with small white and Asian minorities. There is a Carib settlement of about 500, almost entirely of mixed blood.

CLIMATE. A tropical climate, with pleasant conditions between Dec. and March, but there is a rainy season from June to Oct., when hurricanes may occur. Rainfall is heavy, with coastal areas having 70" (1,750 mm) but the mountains may have up to 2250" (6,250 mm). Roseau. Jan. 76°F (24·2°C), July 81°F (27·2°C). Annual rainfall 78" (1,956 mm).

CONSTITUTION AND GOVERNMENT. The House of Assembly has 21 elected and 9 nominated members. The Speaker is elected from among the members of the House or from outside. The Cabinet is presided over by the Prime Minister and consists of 6 other Ministers including the Attorney-General (official member). Elections were held in May 1990. The Dominica Freedom Party won 11 seats, the United Dominica Labour Party 6 seats and the Dominica Labour Party, 4.

President: Sir Clarence Seignoret GCB, OBE.
The Cabinet in Jan. 1992 was composed as follows:
Prime Minister and Minister of Finance, and Economic Affairs: Mary Eugenia Charles (b. 1919).
Minister for Legal Affairs, Information and Public Relations: Jenner Armour. *External Affairs and Organization of Eastern Caribbean States' Unity:* Brian Alleyne. *Trade, Industry and Tourism:* Charles Maynard. *Education and Sports:* Rupert Sorhaindo. *Community Development and Social Affairs:* Henry George. *Health and Social Security:* Allan Guye. *Labour and Immigration:* Heskeith Alexander. *Communications, Works and Housing:* Alleyne Carbon. *Agriculture:* Maynard Joseph. *Without Portfolio:* Dermott Southwell.

National flag: Green with a cross over all of yellow, black, and white pieces, and in the centre a red disc charged with a Sisserou parrot in natural colours facing the hoist within a ring of 10 green yellow-bordered stars.

INTERNATIONAL RELATIONS

Membership. Dominica is a member of the UN, OAS, CARICOM, the Commonwealth and is an ACP state of the EEC.

ECONOMY

Budget. In 1988-89 revenue, EC$105·9m. and expenditure, EC$101·4m.

Currency. The French *franc,* the £ sterling and the *East Caribbean dollar* are legal tender. In March 1992, EC$2·70 = US$1 and EC$4·74 = £1.

Banking and Finance. Savings bank (Dec. 1982), 2,862 depositors, with $593,659 deposits. There are branches of Barclays Bank International and Royal Bank of

Canada in Roseau, and branches of Barclays and National Commercial and Development Bank at Portsmouth. The National Commercial and Development Bank was opened in 1977 and Banque Française Commerciale opened in 1979.

ENERGY AND NATURAL RESOURCES

Electricity. Production (1987) 16m. kwh.

Agriculture. Production (1988): Bananas, 66,000 tonnes; coconuts, 14,000; beef (1987) 439; pork (1987) 420. Livestock (1988): Cattle, 9,000; pigs, 5,000; sheep, 9,000; goats, 10,000; poultry (1986), 115,000.

FOREIGN ECONOMIC RELATIONS

Commerce (1987). Imports, EC$179,215,824; exports and re-exports, EC$129,590,586. Chief products: Bananas, soap, fruit juices, essential oils, coconuts, vegetables, fruit and fruit preparations, and alcoholic drinks.

Total trade between Dominica and UK (British Department of Trade returns, in £1,000 sterling):

	1988	1989	1990	1991
Imports to UK	32,423	23,709	23,483	25,221
Exports and re-exports from UK	8,416	8,727	9,707	11,573

Tourism. Tourists (1987) totalled 41,200.

COMMUNICATIONS

Roads. In 1988 there were 470 miles of road and 280 miles of track. Vehicles totalled (Oct. 1988) 6,933.

Telecommunications. Telephone lines, 210 route miles; number of telephones, 7,700 (Oct. 1988). Radio broadcasting is provided by the part government-controlled, part-commercial Dominica Broadcasting Corporation. There are 2 religious radio networks and a commercial TV channel (colour by NTSC). In 1991 there were 40,000 radio and 5,200 TV sets.

Cinemas. In 1987 there was 1 cinema with a seating capacity of 1,000.

JUSTICE, RELIGION, EDUCATION AND WELFARE

Justice. There are 12 magistrates' courts. There is also a supreme court which dealt with 60 criminal and 307 civil cases in 1987–88. The police force consists of 10 officers and 431 other ranks.

Religion. 80% of the population is Roman Catholic.

Education. In 1987–88 there were 65 primary schools with 15,262 pupils and 10 secondary schools with 3,251 pupils, and 2 colleges of higher education.

Health. In Sept. 1988 there were 3 hospitals with 245 beds, 31 doctors, 4 dentists, 10 pharmacists, 273 nursing personnel, 7 health centres and 44 health clinics.

DIPLOMATIC REPRESENTATIVES

Of Dominica in Great Britain and to the United Nations
High Commissioner: Franklin A. Baron (resides in Roseau).

Of Great Britain in Dominica
High Commissioner: E. T. Davies, CMG (resides in Bridgetown).

Of Dominica in the USA
Ambassador: Edward Watty.

Of the USA in Dominica
Ambassador: C. Philip Hughes.

Further Reading

Myers, R. A., *Dominica*. [Bibliography] Oxford and Santa Barbara, 1987

DOMINICAN REPUBLIC

Capital: Santo Domingo
Population: 7·2m. (1990)
GNP per capita: US$790 (1989)

República Dominicana

HISTORY. On 5 Dec. 1492 Columbus discovered the island of Santo Domingo, which he called La Española; for a time it was called Hispaniola. The city of Santo Domingo, founded by his brother, Bartholomew, in 1496, is the oldest city in the Americas. The western third of the island—now the Republic of Haiti—was later occupied and colonized by the French, to whom the Spanish colony of Santo Domingo was also ceded in 1795. In 1808 the Dominican population, under the command of Gen. Juan Sánchez Ramirez, routed an important French military force commanded by Gen. Ferrand, at the famous battle of Palo Hincado. This battle was the beginning of the end for French rule in Santo Domingo and culminated in the successful siege of the capital. Eventually, with the aid of a British naval squadron, the French were forced to capitulate and the colony returned again to Spanish rule, from which it declared its independence in 1821. It was invaded and held by the Haitians from 1822 to 1844, when they were expelled, and the Dominican Republic was founded and a constitution adopted. Independence day 27 Feb. 1844. Great Britain, in 1850, was the first country to recognize the Dominican Republic. The country was occupied by American Marines from 1916 until 1924. In 1936 the name of the capital city was changed from Santo Domingo to Ciudad Trujillo; and back again in 1961.

AREA AND POPULATION. The Dominican Republic occupies the eastern portion (about two-thirds) of the island of Hispaniola, Quisqueya or Santo Domingo, the western division forming the Republic of Haiti.

Area is 48,442 sq. km (18,700 sq. miles) with 870 miles of coastline, 193 miles of frontier line with Haiti (marked out in 1936).

The populations of the 26 provinces and National District at the 1981 census, and the 3 new provinces with estimates for 1987, were:

La Altagracia	100,112	Pedernales	17,006
Azua	142,770	Peravia	168,123
Bahoruco	78,636	Puerto Plata	206,757
Barahona	137,160	La Romana	109,769
Dajabón	57,709	Salcedo	99,191
Districto Nacional	1,550,739	Samaná	65,699
Duarte	235,544	Sánchez Ramírez	126,567
Espaillat	164,017	San Cristóbal	446,132
La Estrelleta	65,384	San Juan	239,957
Hato Mayor	76,023 [1]	San Pedro de Macorís	152,890
Independencia	38,768	Santiago	550,372
María Trinidad Sánchez	112,629	Santiago Rodríguez	55,411
Monseñor Nouel	121,906 [1]	El Seibo	157,866
Monte Cristi	83,407	Valverde	100,319
Monte Plata	170,758 [1]	La Vega	385,043

[1] Estimate, 1987.

Census (1981) 5,647,977. Estimate (1990) 7,176,000.

Population of the principal municipalities (Census 1981): Santo Domingo, the capital, 1,313,172; Santiago de los Caballeros, 278,638; La Romana, 91,571; San Pedro de Macoris, 78,562; San Francisco de Macoris, 64,906; La Vega, 52,432; San Juan de la Managuana, 49,764; Barahona, 49,334; Puerto Plata, 45,348.

The population is partly of Spanish descent, but is mainly composed of a mixed race of European and African blood.

CLIMATE. A tropical maritime climate with most rain falling in the summer months. The rainy season extends from May to Nov. and amounts are greatest in the north and east. Hurricanes may occur from June to Nov. Santo Domingo. Jan. 75°F (23·9°C), July 81°F (27·2°C). Annual rainfall 56" (1,400 mm).

CONSTITUTION AND GOVERNMENT. A new Constitution was promulgated on 28 Nov. 1966.

The President is elected for 4 years, by direct vote. In case of death, resignation or disability, he is succeeded by the Vice-president. There are 12 secretaries of state, a judicial adviser with secretary-of-state rank and 2 ministers without portfolio in charge of departments. Citizens are entitled to vote at the age of 18, or less when married.

At the general elections held in May 1986, 56 seats were won by the *Partido Reformista Social Cristiano*, 48 by the *Partido Revolucionario Dominicano*, and 16 seats by the *Partido de la Liberación Dominicana*.

At the presidential elections of May 1990 Joaquín Balaguer (b. 1907; Social Christian Reform Party) was elected for a second term by 678,568 votes to 653,423.

There is a bicameral legislature, comprising a 27-member Senate and a 120-member Chamber of Deputies, both elected for 4-year terms at the same date as the President.

President: Dr Joaquín Balaguer (elected May 1990).
Foreign Affairs: Joaquín Ricardo García.

National flag: Blue, red; quartered by a white cross.
National anthem: Quisqueyanos valientes, alcemos ('Valient Quisqueyans, Let us raise our voices'; words by E. Prud'homme, tune by J. Reyes, 1883).

Local Government: The republic consists of a National District (containing the capital, Santo Domingo, and surrounding areas) and 29 provinces, divided into 97 municipalities.

DEFENCE

Army. The Army has a strength (1991) of about 15,000. It is organized in 4 infantry brigades, 1 artillery, 1 engineer and 1 armoured battalions and a Presidential Guard. There were (1991) 14 light tanks and 20 armoured cars.

Navy. The Navy largely comprises former US vessels. The combatant force consists of 1 frigate (built 1944) acting as the flagship, 3 offshore and 14 inshore patrol craft. There is 1 utility landing craft and support is provided by 1 small oiler, 1 ocean tug, and some 12 harbour and service craft. Personnel in 1991 totalled 4,000, based at Santo Domingo and Calderas.

Air Force. The Air Force, with HQ at San Isidoro, has 1 combat squadron with 8 Cessna A-37s; 1 squadron with a total of about 12 Bell 205A-1, OH-6A and Alouette II/III helicopters; 1 transport squadron with 3 C-47s, 5 Cessma 337s and some smaller communications aircraft; a Presidential Dauphin 2 helicopter; and an assortment of trainers, including 10 T-34B Mentors, 6 Cessna T-41s and 2 T-6 Texans. Personnel strength was (1991) 4,200.

INTERNATIONAL RELATIONS

Membership. The Dominican Republic is a member of the UN and OAS and an ACP member of the EEC.

ECONOMY

Budget. Expenditure (1986) RD$2,251m. and revenue RD$2,113m. In 1985 external debt was RD$3,551m.

Currency. The unit of currency is the *Dominica peso* (DOP) of 100 *centavos.*

There are silver coins for 50, 25 and 10 centavos, a copper-nickel 5-centavo piece and a copper 1-centavo piece.

The exchange rate regime was liberalized in 1991 and the 4 rates unified. In March 1992, £1 = RD$22·31; US$1 = RD$12·71.

Banking. There are 5 foreign banks—the Royal Bank of Canada with 12 branches, the Bank of Nova Scotia with 11 branches, the Citibank with 6 branches, the Chase Manhattan Bank with 7 branches and the Bank of America with 4 branches. An agricultural and mortgage bank, with paid-up capital of RD$500,000, was established in 1945; in 1950 its capital was increased to RD$5m. In 1947 the Central Bank of the Dominican Republic was established. (*Governor*, Luis Toral). A Banco Popular Dominicano, with an authorized capital of RD$5m., opened in 1964.

Weights and Measures. The metric system was nominally adopted on 1 Aug. 1913, but English and Spanish units have remained in common use in ordinary commercial transactions; on 17 Sept. 1954 a more drastic law requiring the decimal metric system was passed.

ENERGY AND NATURAL RESOURCES

Electricity. In 1986, 3,800m. kwh. of electricity was generated. There was a severe shortagae in 1990. Supply 110 and 220 volts; 60 Hz.

Minerals. Bauxite output in 1982 was 152,250 tonnes. Silver and platinum have been found, and near Neiba there are several hills of rock salt. Ferronickel production (1986) 58,000 tonnes. Production of gold (1986) 285,458 troy oz.; silver, 1,356,000.

Agriculture. Agriculture and its processing industries are the chief source of wealth, sugar cultivation being the principal industry. Of the total area (1984) meadows and pastures, 43%; permanant cultivation, 30%; forestry 13%.
 Livestock in 1990: 2,240,000 cattle, 431,000 pigs, 114,000 sheep.
 Production, 1990 (in 1,000 tonnes): Sugar-cane, 7,000; cocoa, 59; coffee, 41; bananas, 395; rice, 369; tobacco, 14. There are useful crops of yucca and beans for local consumption. Scientific growing of bananas (1988: 391,000 tonnes) and of leaf tobacco (1988: 30,000 tonnes) is progressing.

Fisheries. The total catch (1986) was 17,200 tonnes.

INDUSTRY. Important products are sugar (89,100 of refined sugar in 1985), cement (960,000 tonnes in 1981). Value of textile manufactures (1983), RD$30·4m.; tobacco products, RD$63·5m.

FOREIGN ECONOMIC RELATIONS. Foreign debt was some US$4,500m. in 1990.

Commerce. Total imports and exports in RD$1m. (equal to US$1m.):

	1985	1986	1987	1988	1989
Imports	1,285	1,432	1,782	1,848	2,241
Exports	739	718	720	892	911

The principal exports are sugar, cofee and ferronickel.
 Total trade between the Dominican Republic and UK (British Department of Trade returns, in £1,000 sterling):

	1987	1988	1989	1990	1991
Imports to UK	8,637	8,523	11,223	17,440	22,076
Exports and re-exports from UK	23,887	17,235	25,519	19,668	19,773

Tourism. 1·32m. tourists visited in 1991.

COMMUNICATIONS

Roads. Total length of roads (1985) 17,120 km. There were 102,000 cars and 61,000 commercial vehicles in 1984.

Railways. Some 142 km of the Dominican Government Railway remains in use between La Vega and the port of Sánchez. Twelve lines, including the Central Romana Railway, exist to serve the sugar industry, totalling 1,600 km.

Civil Aviation. The country is reached from the American continent and the Caribbean islands by 8 international airlines and in 1987 there were 4 airports. Two local aviation companies provide interior services and connect Santo Domingo with San Juan in Puerto Rico, Curaçao, Aruba and Miami.

Shipping. Santo Domingo is the leading port; Puerto Plata ranks next. In 1971, vessels of 9,833,000 tons entered the ports to discharge 3,009,000 tonnes of cargo, and vessels of 5,276,000 tons cleared the ports having loaded 1,986,000 tonnes.

Telecommunications. Number of telephone instruments (1983), 175,054, of which 138,169 in Santo Domingo. The telegraph has a total length of about 500 km, privately owned; they have been leased to All-America Cables, Inc., which also controls submarine cables connecting, in the north, Puerto Plata with Puerto Rico and New York, and in the south, Santo Domingo with Puerto Rico, Cuba and Curaçao.

There were (1989) more than 90 broadcasting stations in Santo Domingo and other towns; this includes the 2 government stations. There are 4 television stations. In 1991 there were 1·15m. radio and 728,000 television receivers.

Newspapers (1985). There were 9 daily newspapers with a circulation of 208,000.

JUSTICE, RELIGION, EDUCATION AND WELFARE

Justice. The judicial power resides in the Supreme Court of Justice, the courts of appeal, the courts of first instance, the communal courts and other tribunals created by special laws, such as the land courts. The Supreme Court consists of a president and 8 judges chosen by the Senate, and the procurator-general, appointed by the executive; it supervises the lower courts. Each province forms a judicial district, as does the *Distrito Nacional*, and each has its own procurator fiscal and court of first instance; these districts are subdivided, in all, into 72 municipalities and 18 municipal districts, each with one or more local justices. The death penalty was abolished in 1924.

Religion. The religion of the state is Roman Catholic; there were 6·45m. adherents in 1989.

Education. Primary instruction (5,956 schools) is free and obligatory for children between 7 and 14 years of age; there are also secondary, normal, vocational and special schools, all of which are either wholly maintained by the State or state-aided; in 1985, primary schools had 28,000 teachers and 1,220,000 pupils and there were 11,754 teachers and 438,922 pupils in secondary schools.

The University of Santo Domingo (founded 1538) and 5 other universities had 88,000 students in 1985–86.

Health. There were, in 1980, 2,142 doctors and 8,953 hospital beds.

DIPLOMATIC REPRESENTATIVES

Of Dominican Republic in Great Britain
Ambassador: (Vacant).

Of Great Britain in the Dominican Republic
Ambassador: Giles Fitzherbert, CMG (resides in Caracas).

Of the Dominican Republic in the USA (1715 22nd St., NW, Washington, D.C., 20008)
Ambassador: Carlos A. Morales.

Of the USA in the Dominican Republic (Calle Cesar Nicolas Penson, Santo Domingo)
Ambassador: Paul D. Taylor.

Of the Dominican Republic to the United Nations
Ambassador: Hector Alcántara.

Further Reading

Anuario estadístico de la República Dominicana, 1944–45. Ciudad Trujillo. 1949. This has been succeeded by separate annual reports covering foreign trade, vital statistics, banking, insurance, housing and communications.

Official Guide to the Dominican Republic, 79–80. Tourist Information Center, Santo Domingo, 1980

Atkins, G. P., *Arms and Politics in the Dominican Republic*. London, 1981

Bell, I., *The Dominican Republic*. London, 1980

Black, J. K., *The Dominican Republic: Politics and Development in an Unsovereign State*. London, 1986

Diederich, B., *Trujillo: The Death of the Goat*. London, 1978

Schoenhals, K., *Dominican Republic: [Bibliography]*. London and Santa Barbara, 1990

Wiarda, H. J. and Kryzanek, M. J., *The Dominican Republic: A Caribbean Crucible*. Boulder, 1982

ECUADOR

República del Ecuador

Capital: Quito
Population: 9·62m. (1990)
GNP per capita: US$1,040 (1989)

HISTORY. The Spaniards under Francisco Pizarro founded a colony after their victory at Cajamarca (16 Nov. 1532). Their rule was first challenged by the rising of 10 Aug. 1809. Marshal Sucre defeated the Spaniards at Pichincha in 1822, and in 1822 Bolívar persuaded the new republic to join the federation of Gran Colombia. The Presidency of Quito became the Republic of Ecuador by amicable secession 13 May 1830.

AREA AND POPULATION. Ecuador is bounded on the north by Colombia, on the east and south by Peru, on the west by the Pacific ocean. The frontier with Peru has long been a source of dispute between the two countries. The latest delimitation of it was in the treaty of Rio, 29 Jan. 1942, when, after being invaded by Peru, Ecuador lost over half her Amazonian territories. Ecuador unilaterally denounced this treaty in Sept. 1961. *See* map in THE STATESMAN'S YEAR-BOOK, 1942. Fighting between Peru and Ecuador began again in Jan. 1981 over this border issue but a ceasefire was agreed in early Feb. Following a confrontation of soldiers in Aug. 1991 the foreign ministers of both countries signed a pact creating a security zone, and took their cases to the UN in Oct. 1991.

No definite figure of the area of the country can yet be given, as a portion of the frontier has not been delimited. One estimate of the area of Ecuador is 270,670 sq. km, excluding the litigation zone between Peru and Ecuador, which is 190,807 sq. km, but including the Galápagos Archipelago (7,844 sq. km), situated in the Pacific ocean about 960 km west of Ecuador and comprising 15 islands.

Mainland Ecuador has 3 zones: the *Sierra* or uplands of the Andes, consisting of high mountain ridges with valleys, with 4·42m. inhabitants (51·2% urban) and farming land; the *Costa*, the coastal plain between the Andes and the Pacific, with 4·74m. and permanent plantations; and the *Amazon* (formerly Oriente), the upper Amazon basin on the east and the site of the main oilfields, consisting of tropical jungles threaded by large rivers (0·38m.). The population is an amalgam of European, Amerindian and African origins. The official language is Spanish. Quechua is also spoken, and various tribes have languages of their own.

Census population in 1990, 9,622,608 [1].

The population was distributed by provinces as follows:

Province	Sq. km	Population	Capital	Population
Azuay	8,092	506,546	Cuenca	332,117
Bolívar	4,142	170,593	Guaranda	77,361
Cañar	3,481	189,109	Azogues	68,557
Carchi	3,744	141,992	Tulcán	70,314
Chimborazo	6,056	360,600	Riobamba	160,433
Cotopaxi	5,198	283,286	Latacunga	128,947
El Oro	5,908	415,073	Machala	159,063
Esmeraldas	15,162	307,190	Esmeraldas	172,649
Guayas	21,382	2,463,423	Guayaquil	1,531,229
Imbabura	4,976	273,261	Ibarra	117,221
Loja	11,472 [2]	389,682	Loja	145,281
Los Ríos	6,370	530,844	Babahoyo	106,326
Manabí	18,105	1,026,066	Portoviejo	201,326
Pichincha	16,587	1,734,942	Quito	1,387,887
Sucumbíos	...	77,450	Nueva Loja	42,613
Tungurahua	3,110	366,523	Ambato	229,188
Napo	52,318 [2]	102,623	Tena	34,817
Pastaza	30,269 [2]	40,714	Puyo	34,807
Morona-Santiago	26,418 [2]	95,685	Macas	37,860
Zamora-Chinchipe	18,394 [2]	66,729	Zamora	28,652
Galápagos	7,994	9,749	San Cristóbal	3,585

[1] Preliminary figures. [2] Excluding Peru-Ecuador litigation zone.

507

Vital statistics for calendar years: Births, (1985) 209,974; deaths, (1985) 51,134. Expectation of life in 1989 was 66 years.

CLIMATE. The climate varies from equatorial, through warm temperate to mountain conditions, according to altitude which affects temperatures and rainfall. In coastal areas, the dry season is from May to Dec., but only from June to Sept. in mountainous parts, where temperatures may be 20°F colder than on the coast. Quito Jan. 59°F (15°C), July 58°F (14·4°C). Annual rainfall 44" (1,115 mm). Guayaquil. Jan. 79°F (26·1°C), July 75°F (23·9°C). Annual rainfall 39" (986 mm).

CONSTITUTION AND GOVERNMENT. A new Constitution came into force on 10 Aug. 1979. It provides for an executive President and a Vice-President to be directly elected for a non-renewable 4-year term by universal suffrage, with a further 'run-off' ballot being held between the two leading candidates where no-one has secured an absolute majority of the votes cast. The President appoints and leads a Council of Ministers.

Legislative power is vested in a unicameral 71-member National Congress, also directly elected for a 4-year term, 12 members on a national basis and 59 on a provincial basis. Voting is obligatory for all literate citizens of 18 years and over. Congressional elections were held in June 1990 for 60 seats.

The following is a list of the presidents and provisional executives since 1948:

Galo Plaza Lasso, 1 Sept. 1948–31 Aug. 1952.
Dr José María Velasco Ibarra, 1 Sept. 1952–31 Aug. 1956.
Dr Camilo Ponce Enríquez, 1 Sept. 1956–31 Aug. 1960.
Dr José María Velasco Ibarra, 1 Sept. 1960–8 Nov. 1961 (withdrew).
Dr Carlos Julio Arosemena Monroy, 8 Nov. 1961–11 July 1963 (deposed).
Military Junta, 11 July 1963–31 March 1966.
Clemente Yerovi Indaburu, 31 March–16 Nov. 1966 (interim).
Dr Otto Arosemena Gómez, 17 Nov. 1966–1 Sept. 1968.
Dr José María Velasco Ibarra, 1 Sept. 1968–15 Feb. 1972 (deposed).
Gen. Guillermo Rodriguez Lara, 16 Feb. 1972–11 Jan. 1976 (resigned).
Adm. Alfredo Poveda Burbano, 11 Jan. 1976–10 Aug. 1979.
Jaime Roldós Aguilera, 10 Aug. 1979–24 May 1981.
Osvaldo Hurtado Larrea, 24 May 1981–10 Aug. 1984.
León Febres Codero Rivadeneira, 10 Aug. 1984–10 Aug. 1988.

President: Rodrigo Borja Cevallos (elected 9 May 1988; installed 10 Aug. 1988). Presidential elections were scheduled for May 1992.

The Cabinet in Feb. 1992 was composed as follows:
Government and Justice: César Verduga. *Defence:* Gen. Jorge Félix. *Education and Culture:* Rául Vallejo Corral. *Agriculture and Livestock:* Alfredo Saltos Guale. *Public Works and Communications:* Raúl Carrasco. *Finance and Public Credit:* Pablo Better. *Foreign Affairs:* Diego Cordóvez. *Industry, Commerce, Integration and Fishing:* Juan Falconí Puig. *Public Health:* Plutarco Naranjo. *Social Welfare:* Raúl Baco Carbo. *Secretary General for Administration:* Gonzalo Ortiz Crespo. *Energy:* Donald Castillo. *Labour and Human Resources:* Roberto Gómez.

National flag: Three horizontal stripes of yellow, blue, red, with the yellow of double width, and in the centre over all the national arms.

National anthem: Indignados tus hijos del yugo ('Indignant thy sons of the yoke'; words by J. L. Mera; music by A. Neumann, 1866).

Local Government. The country is divided administratively into 21 provinces. The provinces are administered by governors, appointed by the Government; their subdivisions, or cantons, by political chiefs and elected cantonal councillors; and the parishes by political lieutenants. The Galápagos Archipelago is administered by the Ministry of Defence. The 21 provinces are made up of 115 cantons, 212 urban parishes and 715 rural parishes. Elections for 50 provincial and 528 municipal councillors were held in June 1990.

DEFENCE. Military service is selective, with a 1-year period of conscription. The country is divided into 4 military zones, with headquarters at Quito, Guayaquil, Cuenca and Pastaza.

Army. The Army consists of 1 infantry division, 1 armoured, 4 infantry and 3 'jungle' brigades. Strength (1992) 50,000, with about 100,000 reservists. Equipment includes 45 American M-3 and 108 French AMX-13 light tanks. The aviation element has about 50 transport and communications aircraft, including over 30 helicopters.

Navy. Navy combatant forces include 2 German-built diesel submarines; 2 ex-UK Leander class frigates, 6 Italian-built missile corvettes (with helicopter deck), 6 fast missile craft and 6 inshore patrol craft. Amphibious capability is 1 landing ship and 6 small craft. Auxiliaries consist of 1 small tanker, 1 survey ship, 2 tugs and a training ship as well as some 8 harbour and service vessels. The Maritime Air Force has 15 aircraft, including 1 CN-235 transport, 4 Cessna light aircraft, 3 T-34C trainers, 5 Bell 206 and 5 Jet Ranger helicopters. Naval personnel in 1991 totalled 4,800 officers and men including some 1,500 marines.

There are 5 inshore Coast Guard cutters and some 12 boats.

Air Force. The Air Force, formed with Italian assistance in 1920, was reorganized and re-equipped with US aircraft after Ecuador signed the Rio Pact of Mutual Defence in 1947 but latest equipment acquired from Europe and Brazil. 1992 strength of about 3,000 personnel and 70 combat aircraft includes a strike squadron equipped with 9 single-seat and 2 two-seat Jaguars; an interceptor squadron of 14 single-seat and 1 two-seat Mirage F.1; an interceptor squadron with 11 Kfirs; 3 counter-insurgency units equipped with 11 Cessna A-37B, 25 T-33 and 12 Strikemaster light jet attack and training aircraft, 1 squadron with 2 C-130, 2 Buffalo and 4 HS 748 turboprop transports; Alouette III, AS 332 Super Puma, SA 330 Puma, Bell 47, Bell 212, UH-1 Iroquois and SA 315B Lama helicopters; and Cessna 150, T-34C-1 and T-41A/D trainers. 1 F.28 and 4 Boeing 727 transports are operated by the military airline TAME.

INTERNATIONAL RELATIONS

Membership. Ecuador is a member of the UN, OAS, the Andean Group and LAIA.

ECONOMY

Budget. Estimated revenue in 1988 was 812,000m. sucres and expenditure, 804,000m. sucres.

Net international reserves, 31 July 1991, were US$573m.

Currency. The monetary unit is the *sucre* (ECS), divided into 100 *centavos*. In circulation are coins of 1, 5, 10, 20 and 50 *sucres*. The currency consists mainly of the notes of the Central Bank in denominations of 100, 500, 1,000 and 5,000 sucres. In March 1992, US$1 = 1,301·97; £1 = 2,285·60.

Banking and Finance. The Central Bank of Ecuador, at Quito, with a capital and reserves of 5,987m. sucres at 30 April 1991, is modelled after the Federal Reserve Banks of US: through branches opened in 16 towns it now deals in mortgage bonds. All commercial banks must be affiliated to the Central Bank. American and European banks include the Bank of London and Canada with branches in Quito and Guayaquil.

Weights and Measures. The metric system is the legal standard but the Spanish measures are in general use. The quintal is equivalent to 101·4 lb.

ENERGY AND NATURAL RESOURCES

Electricity. In 1989, total capacity of hydro-electric and thermal plants was 1,814,700 kw. In 1989 production was 5,443·7m. kwh. Supply 110, 120 and 220 volts; 60 Hz.

Oil. Production of crude oil in 1991 was 14·8m. tonnes. In 1988 management of oil companies was taken over by the government.

Gas. In 1990, natural gas production was 32,243,700m. cu. feet.

Minerals. Production (1983): Silver, 3,137·6 troy oz; gold, 607·6 troy oz; copper, 7,900 kg; zinc, 14,820 kg. The country also has some iron, uranium, lead, coal, cobalt, manganese and titanium.

Agriculture. There are 2 agricultural zones: The coast and lower river valleys (*Costa*), where tropical farming is carried on; and the Andean highlands (*Sierra*) with a temperate climate, adapted to grazing, dairying and the production of cereals, vegetables and flowers.

In 1989, some 3,284,000 persons depended for their living upon agriculture, of whom 993,000 were economically active.

50,000 ha of rich virgin land in the Santo Domingo de los Colorados area has been set aside for settlement by smallholders.

The staple export products are bananas, cacao and coffee. Main crops, in 1,000 tonnes, in 1988: Rice, 420; potatoes, 301; maize, 387; barley, 41; in 1990: Cocoa, 68·5; bananas, 2,201 and coffee, 88·6.

Livestock, 1990 (in 1,000): Cattle, 4,170; sheep, 1,329; pigs, 2,092; goats, 298; poultry, 59,926.

Forestry. Excepting the two agricultural zones and a few arid spots on the Pacific coast, Ecuador is a vast forest. In 1988 11·8m. ha, 43% of the land area, was forested, but much of the forest is not commercially accessible.

Fisheries. In 1990 fish and fish product exports were valued at US$392·2m.

INDUSTRY. Production in 1987: Sugar, 3,000 tonnes; cement 2·87m. tonnes.

FOREIGN ECONOMIC RELATIONS

Commerce. Imports and exports for calendar years, in US$1m.:

	1986	1987	1988	1989	1990
Imports (f.o.b.)	1,631	1,888	1,517	2,354	2,714
Exports (f.o.b.)	2,186	1,928	2,193	1,693	1,711

Of the total exports (1988): petroleum, US$875m.; bananas, US$298m.; cocoa, US$298m.; coffee, US$152m. Ecuador is a major exporter of shrimps.

Total trade between Ecuador and UK (British Department of Trade returns, in £1,000 sterling):

	1987	1988	1989	1990	1991
Imports to UK	14,002	13,120	19,319	19,572	16,264
Exports and re-exports from UK	37,934	50,417	29,410	30,155	45,213

Tourism. There were 670,000 visitors in 1986, spending US$173m.

COMMUNICATIONS

Roads. In 1985, there were 36,187 km of roads. A trunk highway through the coastal plain is under construction which will link Machala in the extreme south-west with Esmeraldas in the north-west and with Quito and the northern section of the Pan-American Highway. In 1984, there were 314,360 cars and 32,379 commercial vehicles.

Railways. A 1,067 mm gauge line runs from San Lorenzo through Quito to Guayaquil and Cuenca, total 971 km. 1·6m. passengers were carried in 1987.

Civil Aviation. There are 2 international airports. The following international lines operate: Air France, Avianca, Eastern, Ecuatoriana de Aviación, KLM, Lufthansa, Pan-Am, Iberia, LAN Chile, Aerovías Peruanas, Aereolinas Argentinas, Air Panama and Varig. They connect Quito with North and Central America, other countries in South America and Europe. All the leading towns are connected by an almost daily service.

Shipping. Ecuador has 3 major seaports, of which Guayaquil is the chief, and 6 minor ones. The merchant navy comprises 39,964 tons of seagoing and 21,232 tons of river craft.

There is river communication, improved by dredging, throughout the principal agricultural districts on the low ground to the west of the Cordillera by the rivers Guayas, Daule and Vinces (navigable for 200 miles by river steamers in the rainy season).

Telecommunications. In 1985 there were 339,040 telephones. In 1991 there were 3m. radios and 0·78m. TV receivers (colour by NTSC).

Newspapers (1984). There were 22 daily newspapers with an aggregate daily circulation of 526,000; 7 papers in Quito and Guayaquil have the bulk of the circulation.

JUSTICE, RELIGION, EDUCATION AND WELFARE

Justice. The Supreme Court in Quito, consisting of a President and 15 Justices, comprises 5 chambers each of 3 Justices. There is a Superior Court in each province, comprising chambers (as appointed by the Supreme Court) of 3 magistrates each. There are numerous lower and special courts. Capital punishment and all forms of torture are prohibited by the constitution.

Religion. The state recognizes no religion and grants freedom of worship to all. In 1984, 92% of the population were Roman Catholics.

Education. In 1989–90 (estimate), there were 114,182 pre-primary pupils with 5,476 teachers. Primary education is free and obligatory. Private schools, both primary and secondary, are under some state supervision. In 1986 there were 14,190 primary schools and 2,207 secondary schools. In 1989–90 (estimate): Primary stage; 1,843,519 pupils and 60,634 teachers; secondary stage; 792,297 pupils and 58,861 teachers. There were (1989) 21 universities and polytechnics.

Health. In 1984 there were 11,000 doctors and 337 hospitals with 15,455 beds. In 1979 there were 795 dentists and 505 pharmacists.

DIPLOMATIC REPRESENTATIVES

Of Ecuador in Great Britain (3 Hans Cres., London, SW1X 0LS)
Ambassador: Dr José Antonio Correa (accredited 7 Feb. 1989).

Of Great Britain in Ecuador (Calle Gonzalez Suarez 111, Quito)
Ambassador: F. B. Wheeler, CMG.

Of Ecuador in the USA (2535 15th St., NW, Washington, D.C., 20009)
Ambassador: Jaime Moncayo García.

Of the USA in Ecuador (Avenida 12 de Octubre y Avenida Patria, Quito)
Ambassador: Paul C. Lambert.

Of Ecuador to the United Nations
Ambassador: Dr José Ayala Lasso.

Further Reading

Boletín General de Estadistica. Tri-monthly
Corkill, D., *Ecuador.* [Bibliography] Oxford and Santa Barbara, 1989
Cueva, A., *The Process of Political Domination in Ecuador.* London, 1982
Martz, J. D., *Ecuador: Conflicting Political Culture and the Quest for Progress.* Boston, 1972.—*Politics and Petroleum in Ecuador.* New Brunswick, 1987
Middleton, A., *Class, Power and the Distribution of Credit in Ecuador.* Glasgow, 1981

EGYPT

Capital: Cairo
Population: 56m. (1991)
GNP per capita: US$630 (1989)

Jumhuriyat
Misr al-Arabiya

(Arab Republic of Egypt)

HISTORY. Part of the Ottoman Empire from 1517 until Dec. 1914 when it became a British protectorate, Egypt became an independent monarchy on 28 Feb. 1922. Following a revolution on 23 July 1952, a Republic was proclaimed on 18 June 1953. Egypt merged with Syria on 22 Feb. 1958 to form the United Arab Republic, retaining that name when Syria broke away from the union on 28 Sept. 1961, finally re-adopting the name of Egypt on 2 Sept. 1971.

AREA AND POPULATION. Egypt is bounded east by Israel, the Gulf of Aqaba and the Red Sea, south by Sudan, west by Libya and north by the Mediterranean. The total area is 1,002,000 sq. km (386,900 sq. miles), but the cultivated and settled area, that is, the Nile valley, delta and oases, covers only about 35,580 sq. km.

At the 1986 census the population was 48,205,049 (23,549,752 female). Population estimate, 1991, 56m.; Greater Cairo, 13·3m.

The area, population (1986 Census) and capitals of the governorates are:

Governorate	Sq. km	1986 census	1989 estimate	Capital
Alexandria	2,679·36	2,917,327	3,098	Alexandria
Aswan	678·50	320,070	861	Aswan
Asyut	1,553·00	618,362	2,390	Asyut
Behera	10,129·49	766,260	3,503	Damanhur
Beni Suef	1,321·65	362,231	1,545	Beni Suef
Cairo	214·20	6,052,836	6,339	Cairo
Dakahlia	3,470·90	916,395	3,734	Mansura
Damietta	589·17	187,053	789	Damietta
Fayum	1,827·15	358,713	1,669	Fayum
Gharbia	1,942·21	939,631	3,044	Tanta
Giza	1,058·20	2,126,364	4,101	Giza
Ismaillia	1,441·59	265,899	601	Ismaillia
Kafr El Sheikh	3,437·12	411,121	1,920	Kafr El Sheikh
Kalyubia	1,001·09	1,099,420	2,765	Benha
Matruh	212,112·00	82,437	176	Matruh
Menia	2,261·72	549,393	2,842	Menia
Menuofia	1,532·13	447,703	2,385	Shibin El Kom
New Valley	376,505·00	50,443	122	El Kharijah
Port Said	72·01	399,793	442	Port Said
Qena	1,850·70	524,365	2,424	Qena
Red Sea	203,685·00	74,010	103	El Gurdakah
Sharkia	4,179·55	721,760	3,667	Zagazig
North Sinai	33,140·00	105,581	188	Af Tur
South Sinai	25,574·00	12,910	32	Al Arish
Suez	17,840·42	326,820	372	Suez
Suhag	1,547·21	536,539	2,623	Suhag

The principal towns, with their (estimate) 1986 populations, were:

Cairo	6,325,000	Asyût	291,300	Sani Suwayf	162,500
Alexandria	2,893,000	Zagâziq	274,400	Uqsur (Luxor)	147,900
Gaza	1,670,800	Suez	265,000	Qinâ	141,700
Shubrâ al-Khayma	533,300	Kafr ad-Dawwar	240,000	Sawhâj	141,500
Mahalla al-Kubrâ	385,300	Ismâiliya	236,300	Shibin al-Kawm	135,900
Port Said	382,000	Fayyûm	227,300	Dumyât	121,200
Tantâ	373,500	Damanhûr	225,900	Banhâ	120,200
Mansûra	357,800	Minyâ	203,300	Kafr ash-Shaykh	104,200
Hulwan	352,300	Aswân	195,700		

Vital statistics: Marriages, 1989, 0·46m. (rate per 1,000, 8·9); divorces, 79,000 (1.5); births, 1988, 1·99m. (37·5); deaths, 0·46m. (8·6). Growth rate, 1988, 28·9 per 1,000. (It is government policy to reduce this to 21 per 1,000). In 1991 the average family size was 4·3. 40% of the population was under 40 years. Expectation of life was 63 years in 1989.

The official language is Arabic, although French and English are widely spoken.

CLIMATE. The climate is mainly dry, but there are winter rains along the Mediterranean coast. Elsewhere, rainfall is very low and erratic in its distribution. Winter temperatures are everywhere comfortable, but summer temperatures are very high, especially in the south. Cairo. Jan. 56°F (13·3°C), July 83°F (28·3°C). Annual rainfall 1·2" (28 mm). Alexandria. Jan. 58°F (14·4°C), July 79°F (26·1°C). Annual rainfall 7" (178 mm). Aswân. Jan. 62°F (16·7°C), July 92°F (33·3°C). Annual rainfall trace. Giza. Jan. 55°F (12·8°C), July 78°F (25·6°C). Annual rainfall 16" (389 mm). Ismailia. Jan. 56°F (13·3°C), July 84°F (28·9°C). Annual rainfall 1·5" (37 mm). Luxor. Jan. 59°F (15°C), July 86°F (30°C). Annual rainfall trace. Port Said. Jan. 58°F (14·4°C), July 78°F (27·2°C). Annual rainfall 3" (76 mm).

CONSTITUTION AND GOVERNMENT. The Constitution was approved by referendum on 11 Sept. 1971. It defines Egypt as 'an Arab Republic with a democratic, socialist system' and the Egyptian people as 'part of the Arab nation' with Islam as the state religion.

The *President* of the Republic is nominated by the People's Assembly and confirmed by plebiscite for a 6-year term. He is the supreme commander of the armed forces and presides over the defence council.

Presidents since the establishment of the Republic have been:

Gen. Mohamed Neguib, 18 June 1953–14 Nov. 1954 (deposed).

Col. Gamal Abdel Nasser, 14 Nov. 1954–28 Sept. 1970 (died).

Col. Muhammad Anwar Sadat, 28 Sept. 1970–6 Oct. 1981 (assassinated).

Lieut.-Gen. Muhammad Hosni Mubarak, 7 Oct. 1981–.

The *People's Assembly* is a unicameral legislature consisting of 454 members directly elected for a 5-year term; the President of the Republic may appoint up to 10 additional members. Following a ruling in June 1990 by the Constitutional High Court that proportional representation was unconstitutional general elections were held in 2 rounds in Nov. and Dec. 1990. 2,681 candidates stood, but the New Wafd Party and Socialist Labour Party abstained. The National Democratic Party (NDP) won 270 seats, the Progressive Unionist Rally 6; the remainder went to independents, more than 80 of whom were NPD members.

The President may appoint one or more Vice-Presidents, and appoints a Prime Minister and a Council of Ministers, whom he may remove as he wishes.

A 210-member consultative body, the Shura Council, was established in 1980. Two-thirds of its members are elected and one-third appointed by the President.

President of the Republic: Hosni Mubarak, sworn in for second 6-year term Oct. 1987.

The Council of Ministers in Feb. 1992 included:

Prime Minister: Dr Atef Mohamed Naguib Sidki.

Deputy Prime Minister: Dr Kamal El Ganzouri. *Defence and Military Production:* Lieut.-Gen. Mohammed Hussein Tantawi. *Economy and Foreign Trade:* Youssri Mustafa. *Finance:* Mohammed Ahmed al Razaz. *Foreign Affairs:* Amr Moussa. *Interior:* Mohammed Abdul-Halim Moussa. *Industry:* Mohammed Abdel Wahab. *Oil and Mineral Wealth:* Dr Hamdi Al Banbi. *Electricity:* Maher Abaza. *Tourism:* Dr Fouad Sultan. *Religious Affairs:* Mohammed Mahjoub.

National flag: Three horizontal stripes of red, white, black, with the national emblem in the centre in gold.

DEFENCE. Conscription is for 3 years, between the ages of 20 and 35. Graduates serve for 1 year.

Army. The Army comprises 4 armoured and 8 mechanized infantry divisions; 1 Republican Guard, 1 independent armoured, 3 independent infantry, 4 independent mechanized, 2 airmobile, 1 parachute, 14 artillery and 2 heavy mortar brigades; 7 commando groups; and 2 surface-to-surface missile regiments. Strength (1991) 320,000 (180,000 conscripts) and about 500,000 reservists. Equipment includes 1,040 T-54/-55, 600 T-62 and 1,550 M-60 tanks.

Navy. 4 of the current submarine force of 8 old ex-Soviet and ex-Chinese 'Romeo' class submarines are to be modernized. Major surface combatants include 1 old destroyer, 2 Spanish-built and 2 Chinese-built missile armed frigates. There are also 21 missile craft of mixed British, Soviet and Chinese origin and 18 coastal and in-shore patrol craft. A small shore-based naval aviation branch operates 5 Sea King and 12 Gazelle helicopters. Mine warfare forces include 7 coastal and 2 inshore minesweepers. 3 ex-Soviet medium landing ships provide amphibious lift supported by 11 minor landing craft. There are 6 major auxiliaries and some 14 minor service vessels. There are naval bases at Alexandria, Port Said, Mersa Matruh, Port Tewfik, Hurghada and Safaqa. Naval personnel in 1991 totalled 20,000 with reserves of 14,000. An associated para-military coastguard about 2,000 strong operates 32 in-shore cutters and numerous boats.

Air Force. Until 1979, the Air Force was equipped largely with aircraft of USSR design, but subsequent re-equipment involves aircraft bought in the West, as well as some supplied by China. Strength (1991) is about 30,000 personnel (10,000 con-scripts) and 495 combat aircraft, of which the interceptors are operated by an independent Air Defence Command, in conjunction with many 'Guideline', 'Goa', 'Gainful', Hawk and Crotale missile batteries. There are about 8 Tu-16 twin-jet strategic bombers, some equipped to carry 'Kelt' air-to-surface missiles. Other interceptor/ground attack fighter divisions are equipped with 75 F-16 Fighting Fal-cons (with 40 more now being delivered), 50 Mirage 5s, 32 F-4E Phantoms, 20 Mirage 2000s, 80 F-6s (Chinese-built MiG-19s), 15 Alpha Jets, more than 120 MiG-21s, and 60 F-7s (Chinese-built MiG-21s). Airborne early warning capability is provided by 4 E-2C Hawkeyes. Transport units have 22 C-130H Hercules turbo-prop heavy freighters, 12 An-12s, 9 twin-turboprop Buffaloes, 6 Beech 1900s, and up to 175 Gazelle, Mi-4, Mi-6, Mi-8, Sea King/Commando and Agusta-built CH-47C helicopters; some Commando helicopters and 2 EC-130H Hercules are equipped for electronic warfare duties. Training units are equipped with Gomhouria piston-engined trainers, Embraer Tucanos, Czech-built L-29 Delfin and L-39 Alba-tros and French-designed Alpha Jet jet trainers, two-seat versions of the MiG-15, MiG-17s, two-seat FT-6s, Mirage 5s, MiG-21Us and UH-12E helicopters. Main aircrew training centre is the Air Force Academy at Bilbeis.

INTERNATIONAL RELATIONS

Membership. Egypt is a member of the UN, OAU, Arab League and OAPEC.

ECONOMY

Policy. A 5-year development plan runs 1987/88–1991–92 and envisages invest-ments totalling £E46,500m.

Budget. Ordinary revenue and expenditure for fiscal years ending 30 June, in £E1m.:

	1985–86	1986–87	1987–88
Revenue	15,010	14,451	17,910
Expenditure	19,910	20,246	23,060

Currency. The monetary unit is the *Egyptian pound* (EGP) of 100 *piastres* of 10 *millièmes*. Coins in circulation are 20, 10, 5, 2 piastres (silver); 2, 1 piastre, 5 mil-lièmes, 1 millième (bronze). The Treasury issues 5- and 10-piastre currency notes, the Central Bank bank-notes of 25 and 50 piastres, £E1, 5, 10, 20, and 100. In Feb. 1991 the official exchange rate was abolished, leaving a free rate, and a rate set by a panel of bankers.

In March 1992, £1 sterling = £E5·81; US$1 = £E3·31.

Banking and Finance. On 18 Aug. 1960 a Central Bank of Egypt was established by decree. It manages the note issue, the Government's banking operations and the control of commercial banks. At the same date the National Bank founded in 1898 ceased to be the central bank and became a purely commercial bank. The *Governor* of the Central Bank is Mohammed Salaheddin Hamid. In 1986 there were 27 commercial banks, 33 business and investment banks (joint ventures and 22 foreign currency branches) and 4 specialized banks. There were also 29 representative offices of foreign banks.

In 1991 4 major public sector commercial banks accounted for some 65% of all banking assets: the National Bank of Egypt, the Banque Misr, the Bank of Alexandria and the Banque du Caïre. From the fiscal year beginning 1 July 1991 banks' assets have been reclassified according to Bank of International Settlements guidelines into internationally-recognized categories.

There are stock exchanges in Cairo and Alexandria.

Weights and Measures. In 1951 the metric system was made official with the exception of the feddân and its subdivisions.

Capacity. Kadah = 1/96th ardeb = 3·36 pints. *Rob* = 4 kadahs = 1·815 gallons. *Keila* = 8 kadahs = 3·63 gallons. *Ardeb* = 96 kadahs = 43·555 gallons, or 5·44439 bu., or 198 cu. decimetres.

Weights. Rotl = 144 dirhems = 0·9905 lb. *Oke* = 400 dirhems = 2·75137 lb. *Qantar* or 100 rotls or 36 okes = 99·0493 lb. 1 *Qantar* of unginned cotton = 315 lb. 1 *Qantar* of ginned cotton = 99·05 lb. The approximate weight of the ardeb is as follows: Wheat, 150 kg; beans, 155 kg; barley, 120 kg; maize, 140 kg; cotton seed, 121 kg.

Surface. Feddan, the unit of measure for land = 4,200·8 sq. metres = 7,468·148 sq. pics = 1·03805 acres. 1 sq. pic = 6·0547 sq. ft = 0·5625 sq. metre.

ENERGY AND NATURAL RESOURCES

Electricity. Electricity generated in 1988–89 was 39,600m. kwh. Installed capacity was 10,838mw. in 1991. Supply 220 volts; 50 Hz.

Oil. Oil was discovered in 1909, but production remained low and often insufficient to meet domestic requirements. Policy is controlled by the Egyptian General Petroleum Corporation (EGPC), a state-owned corporation answerable to the Minister of Petroleum. EGPC is whole or part-owner of the various production and refining companies and controls supplies to the domestic marketing companies. Production 1991, was 45·26m. tonnes of crude oil.

Gas. The first gas field, at Abu Madi in the Nile delta, became operational in 1974. 2 other fields are at Abu Gharadeq in the Western Desert and Abu Qir near Alexandria. Output was 5·5m. tonnes in 1988–89.

Water. The Aswan High Dam, completed in 1970, allows for a perennial irrigation system.

Minerals. Production (1988–89, in tonnes): Phosphate, 1·35m.; iron ore, 2·56m.; salt, 1·16m.; kaolin, 0·12m.; quartz, 19,000; asbestos and fermacolite, 0·58m. Mining for uranium ore began near Aswan in May 1991.

Agriculture. The cultivated area in 1989 at 11·77m. feddans. 5·27m. feddans were under winter crops, 4·98m. under summer crops, 0·86m. under Nile crops and 0·66m. under orchards.

Irrigation occupies a predominant place in the economic development of the country. An intricate irrigation system now reaches most cultivated areas but only about 6·5% of the total land area is arable. The 'vertical' development policy calls for improved methods, better drainage and the introduction of stiff penalties for encroachment of farmland. Under the first phase of the 'horizontal' expansion programme, which aims to add 2·8m. feddans to the arable area over 20 years, 24,000 feddans are being added near Alexandria. Between 1971 and 1989 0·7m. feddan of desert was reclaimed.

In 1989 there were 5,298 agricultural co-operatives. 0·71m. feddan of land had been distributed by 1990 to 0·35m. families under an agrarian reform programme. In 1991 35% of the workforce worked in agriculture. In 1990 agriculture produced 17% of GDP and 40% of domestic food requirements. Cotton, sugar-cane and rice are subject to government price controls and procurement quotas.

Output (in 1,000 tonnes), 1989: Barley, 138; beans, 460; beet, 685; chickpeas, 13; clover seed, 43; cotton seed, 498; ginned cotton, 296; raw cotton, 820; fenugreek, 26; garlic, 93; lentils, 14; linen seed, 28; linen, 113; lupine, 7; maize, 4,529; millet, 585; onion, 445; peanuts, 34; potatoes, 1,657; rice, 2,679; sesame, 12; soybeans, 91; sugar-cane, 11,213; strawberries, 25,909; wheat, 3,182.

Livestock (1989): 3·39m. cattle, 2·5m. buffaloes, 4·03m. sheep, 4·14m. goats, 0·19m. camels and 94,000 pigs. There were 33·91m. chickens (egg production 3,801m.) and 1·67m. beehives.

Forestry. In 1986 total removal of roundwood was 2·06m. cu. metres of which 2m. was fuel wood.

Fisheries. The catch of the Egyptian sea, Nile and lake fisheries in 1986 amounted to 138,800 tonnes.

INDUSTRY. Almost all large-scale enterprises are in the public sector and these account for about two-thirds of total output. The private sector, dominated by food processing and textiles, consists of about 150,000 small and medium businesses, most employing less than 50 workers. A car industry is being established.

Production in 1988–89 (in 1,000 tonnes) included: Refined sugar, 408; tobacco, 14·43; cotton yarn, 249; cotton textiles, 776; synthetic textiles, 75; jute yarn, 26; sulphuric acid, 60; paper, 195; fertilizers, 9,328; steel billets and sections, 334. 13,134 cars, 1,475 lorries, 3,132 tractors, 477,000 refrigerators, 212,000 washing machines, 72,000 bicycles, 43,000 radio and 194,000 TV sets were produced.

FOREIGN ECONOMIC RELATIONS. In May 1991 the Paris Club of Western creditor governments agreed to halve Egypt's US$20,200m. debt; and in July the World Bank offered US$4,000m. in aid over 2 years to help restrict the public sector and decentralize the economy.

Commerce. Imports and exports (in £E1,000):

	1985	1986	1987	1988	1989
Imports	6,973,061	8,051,432	11,357,837	16,308,572	16,623,623
Exports	2,599,941	2,053,959	3,046,010	3,994,436	5,734,726

Export of principal commodities (in £E1m.) in 1989: Crude oil, 1,212·82; raw cotton, 594·16; cotton yarn, 990·22; cotton fabrics, 176·54; clothing, 169·8; refined petroleum, 286·69; aluminium bars, etc., 513·26; oranges, 154·54; potatoes, 58·23. Imports: Wheat, 1,307·69; maize, 423·67; dairy products, 358·97; chemicals, 593·8; iron bars, 396·41; motor car parts, 278·29; motor cars, 169·92; lorries and vans, 53·72; cement, 49·93.

Foreign trade by area (in £E1m.) in 1989: Western Europe, imports 7,248·37, exports 2,448·84; Eastern Europe, 2,542·33, 1,235·13; North America, 3,005·89, 298·57; Arab countries, 358·77, 576·5.

Total trade between Egypt and UK (British Department of Trade returns, in £1,000 sterling):

	1987	1988	1989	1990	1991
Imports to UK	127,261	163,038	212,727	145,323	186,408
Exports and re-exports from UK	342,195	289,309	296,272	298,262	282,928

Tourism. In 1989–90 22·1m. tourist nights were spent (9·65m. from Arab countries, 7·88m. from Europe, 1·27m. from the USA). Visitors totalled 2·5m. (42·6% from Europe, 38% from Arab countries, 8% from the USA). There were 99,500 hotel beds in 1989. The Gulf War, 1990–91, caused a decline in tourist nights to 16·5m. Tourist income was US$2,500m. in 1989–90 and US$1,000m. in 1990–91.

COMMUNICATIONS

Roads. In 1990 there were 30,105 km of highways and 22,690 km of desert roads.

Railways. In 1988 there were 4,548 km of state railways (1,435 mm gauge), of which 42 km were electrified. 44·9m. passengers and 9·4m. tonnes of freight were carried. An underground rail system was opened in Cairo in 1987.

Civil Aviation. There is an international airport at Cairo. There are 95 airfields (77 unusable). The national airline Egyptair operates scheduled flights connecting Cairo with Athens, Rome, Frankfurt, Zürich, London, Khartoum, Tokyo, Bombay, Aden, Jeddah, Doha, Dharan, Kuwait, Beirut, Baghdad, Tripoli, Benghazi, Algiers, Entebbe, Nairobi, Dar-es-Salaam, Kano, Lagos, Accra, Abidjan, Damascus, Amman, Manilla, Paris, Munich, Copenhagen, Nicosia, Karachi, Aleppo, Bahrain, Abu Dhabi, Dubai, Sharjah, Sanaa and Vienna. In addition, Egyptair operates scheduled flights on a widespread domestic network connecting Cairo with Port Said, Mersa Matruh, Asyût, Luxor, Aswan. In 1982, 62,000 tonnes of cargo were carried.

Shipping. Vessels arriving at major ports in 1988 and cargo unloaded (in tons): Alexandria, 3,152, 19·2m.; Port Said, 642, 2·18m.; Suez, 744, 0·7m.

Suez Canal. The Suez Canal was opened for navigation on 17 Nov. 1869. By the convention of Constantinople of 29 Oct. 1888 the canal is open to vessels of all nations and is free from blockade, except in time of war, but the United Arab Republic did not allow Israeli ships to use the canal until May 1979. It is 173 km long (excluding 11 km of approach channels to the harbours), connecting the Mediterranean with the Red Sea. It is being deepened from 17 to 22 metres and widened from 365 to 415 metres to permit the passage of oil-tankers of 250,000 tonnes.

During the war with Israel in June 1967 the Canal was blocked. The canal was cleared and re-opened to shipping on 5 June 1975. In 1989 17,628 vessels (net tonnage, 373m. tons; cargo, 266m. tons; passengers, 7,000) went through the canal. Toll revenue in 1991 was US$1,770m.

Telecommunications. There were, in 1988–89, 1,958 postal agencies, 1,990 mobile offices, 2,367 government and 2,601 private post offices. Number of telephones in 1984, 600,000. Number of radio licences in 1991, 14m. and 3·5m. TV licences. Colour is by SECAM.

The internal telecommunications system is owned and operated by the Telecommunications Organization. Government landlines connect with those of the Gaza sector and the Sudan.

Newspapers. In 1984 there were 11 dailies published in Cairo and 6 in Alexandria.

JUSTICE, RELIGION, EDUCATION AND WELFARE

Justice. The National Courts in 1981 were as follows: Court of Cassation with a bench of 5 judges which constitutes the highest court of appeal in both criminal and civil cases; Courts of Appeal with 3 judges situated in Cairo and 4 other cities; Assize Courts with 3 judges which deal with all cases of serious crime; Central Tribunals with 3 judges which deal with ordinary civil and commercial cases; Summary Tribunals presided over by a single judge which hear civil disputes in matters up to the value of £E3,250, and criminal offences punishable by a fine or imprisonment of up to 3 years.

Religion. In 1986 about 90% of the population were Moslems, mostly of the Sunni sect, and about 7% Coptic Christians, the remainder being Roman Catholics, Protestants or Greek Orthodox, with a small number of Jews.

There are in Egypt large numbers of native Christians connected with the various Oriental Churches; of these, the largest and most influential are the Copts, who adopted Christianity in the 1st century. Their head is the Coptic Patriarch. There are 25 metropolitans and bishops in Egypt; 4 metropolitans for Ethiopia, Jerusalem, Khartoum and Omdurman, and 12 bishops in Ethiopia. Priests must be married before ordination, but celibacy is imposed on monks and high dignitaries. The Copts use the Diocletian (or Martyrs') calendar, which begins in A.D. 284.

Education. Primary education (6 years) was made free in 1944, secondary and technical education in 1950. Compulsory education is provided in primary schools (6 years).

In 1989–90 there were 14,574 primary schools with 6,955,455 pupils, 4,299 preparatory schools with 2,383,336 pupils, 2,259 secondary schools with 1,484,424 pupils and 124 training colleges with 83,536 students.

El Azhar institutes educate students who intend enrolling at El Azhar University. In 1988–89 in the El Azhar system there were 1,147 primary schools with 388,261 pupils, 689 preparatory schools with 153,172 pupils and 368 secondary schools with 81,626 pupils.

In 1988–89 there were 68,458 students in commerce institutes (35,085 women) and 36,902 in technical institutes (6,980 women).

In 1988–89 there were 12 universities: Cairo, Ain Shams, Alexandria, Asyut, El Azhar, Tanta, El Mansoura, El Zagazig, Helwan, Suez Canal, El Menia and El Menufia. There were 587,033 students (198,202 women).

Health. In 1989 there were 904 hospitals (including 348 general) with 101,865 beds.

DIPLOMATIC REPRESENTATIVES

Of Egypt in Great Britain (26 South St., London, W1Y 8EL)
Ambassador: Mohamed I. Shaker.

Of Great Britain in Egypt (Ahmed Ragheb St., Garden City, Cairo)
Ambassador: Sir James Adams, KCMG.

Of Egypt in the USA (2310 Decatur Pl., NW, Washington, D.C., 20008)
Ambassador: Abdel Raouf El-Ridy.

Of the USA in Egypt (Lazougi St., Garden City, Cairo)
Ambassador: Frank G. Wisner.

Of Egypt to the United Nations
Ambassador: Nabil A. Elaraby.

Further Reading

Aliboni, R., *(et al) Egypt's Economic Potential*. London, 1984
Ansari, H., *Egypt: The Stalled Society*. New York, 1986
Hart, V., *Modern Egypt*. Cairo, 1984
Hopwood, D., *Egypt: Politics and Society 1945–1981*. London, 1982
Kepel, G., *Muslim Extremism in Egypt*. Univ. of California Press, 1986
McDermott, A., *Egypt: From Nasser to Mubarak*. London, 1988
Makar, R. N., *Egypt*. [Bibliography] Oxford and Santa Barbara, 1988
Vatikiotis, P. J., *History of Modern Egypt: from Muhammad Ali to Mubarak*. London, 1991
Waterbury, J., *The Egypt of Nasser and Sadat*. Princeton Univ. Press, 1983

EL SALVADOR

Capital: San Salvador
Population: 5·38m. (1991)
GNP per capita: US$1,040 (1989)

República de El Salvador

HISTORY. In 1839 the Central American Federation, which had comprised the states of Guatemala, El Salvador, Honduras, Nicaragua and Costa Rica, was dissolved, and El Salvador declared itself formally an independent republic in 1841.

Throughout the 1980s the Farabundo Marti National Liberation Front (FMLN) waged guerilla war against the government.

Talks between the government and the FMLN in April 1991 led to constitutional reforms in May envisaging the establishment of civilian control over the armed forces and a reduction in their size. In May the UN Security Council decided to send a mission to observe the government-FMLN negotiations, in the first place for one year. An agreement reached in Sept. 1991 permits the FMLN to participate in a newly-created police force under civilian authority. On 16 Jan. 1992 the government and the FMLN signed a peace agreement. A permanent ceasefire began on 1 Feb., and the FMLN agreed to demobilize by 31 Oct.

AREA AND POPULATION. The area (including 247 sq. km of inland lakes) is 21,041 sq. km with population estimate (1991) 5,376,000 (44·4% urban). Population density, 255·5 per sq. km. Vital statistics 1990, (rates per 1,000 population): Birth, 36·3; death, 8·5; infant mortality (per 1,000 births), 59. Expectation of life was 66 years in 1990.

The republic is divided into 14 departments, each under an appointed governor. Areas (in sq. km) and populations in 1985:

Department	Area	Population	Chief town	Population
Ahuachapán	1,240	257,900	Ahuachapán	71,846
Cabañas	1,140	173,300	Sensuntepeque	50,448 [3]
Chalatenango	2,017	226,800	Chalatenango	28,675 [3]
Cuscatlán	756	204,100	Cojutepeque	31,108 [2]
La Libertad	1,653	535,287 [1]	Nueva San Salvador	52,226 [2]
La Paz	1,224	260,100	Zacatecoluca	81,035
La Unión	2,074	328,200	La Unión	27,186 [2]
Morazán	1,447	200,600	San Francisco	13,015 [3]
San Miguel	2,077	419,287 [1]	San Miguel	161,156
San Salvador	886	1,417,953 [1]	San Salvador	972,810
San Vicente	1,184	209,900	San Vicente	65,462
Santa Ana	2,023	476,853 [1]	Santa Ana	208,322
Sonsonate	1,226	397,552 [1]	Sonsonate	47,489 [2]
Usulatán	2,130	391,167 [1]	Usulután	69,355

[1] 1990.   [2] 1984.   [3] 1980.

CLIMATE. Despite its proximity to the equator, the climate is warm rather than hot and nights are cool inland. Light rains occur in the dry season from Nov. to April while the rest of the year has heavy rains, especially on the coastal plain. San Salvador. Jan. 71°F (21·7°C), July 75°F (23·9°C). Annual rainfall 71" (1,775 mm). San Miguel. Jan. 77°F (25°C), July 83°F (28·3°C). Annual rainfall 68" (1,700 mm).

CONSTITUTION AND GOVERNMENT. A new Constitution was enacted in Dec. 1983. The Executive Power is vested in a *President* elected for a non-renewable term of 5 years, with Ministers and Under-Secretaries appointed by him. The Legislative power is an Assembly of 84 members elected by universal suffrage and proportional representation for a term of 3 years. The judicial power is vested in a Supreme Court, of a President and 9 magistrates elected by the Legislative Assembly for renewable terms of 3 years; and subordinate courts.

At the March 1991 elections turn-out was 50%. The Alianza Republicana Nacionalista (ARENA) won 44·3% of votes cast and 39 seats, the Christian Democratic

Party 28% and 26 seats, the Party of National Conciliation, 9% and 9 seats and Democratic Convergence 12·2% and 8 seats.

President: Alfredo Felix Cristiani Burkard (sworn in 1 June 1989).

In June 1990 the Cabinet was composed as follows:

Foreign Affairs: José Manuel Pacas Castro. *Planning and Co-ordination of Economic and Social Development:* Mirna Liévano de Márquez. *Interior:* Col. Juan Antonio Martinez Varela. *Justice:* Dr Réné Hernández Valiente. *Finance:* Rafael Alvarado Cano. *Economics:* Arturo Zablah. *Education:* Dr Cecilia Gallardo de Cono. *Defence and Public Safety:* Col. René Emilio Ponce. *Labour and Social Security:* Mauricio González Dubón. *Public Health and Social Welfare:* Dr Lisandro Vásquez Sosa. *Agriculture and Livestock:* Antonio Cabrales. *Works:* Mauricio Stubig.

The *Speaker* is Roberto Angulo.

National flag: Blue, white, blue (horizontal): the white stripe charged with the arms of the republic.

National anthem: Saludemos la patria orgullosos ('We proudly salute the Fatherland'; words by J. J. Cañas, tune by J. Aberle).

DEFENCE. There is selective national service for 2 years.

Army. The Army comprises 6 infantry brigades, 1 mechanized cavalry regiment, 1 artillery brigade, 1 engineer, 1 anti-aircraft, 1 parachute and 5 rapid-action battalions. Equipment includes 5 M-3A1 light tanks and 5 AML-90 armoured cars. Strength was (1992) 40,000. There are also National Guard, National Police and Treasury Police, paramilitary units, numbering (1992) about 12,000 and an armed territorial civil defence force of up to 24,000.

Navy. A small coastguard force based largely at Acajutla, with 500 (1991) personnel, operates 6 inshore patrol craft, 3 landing craft and numerous boats. There were also (1991) 700 marines.

Air Force. The Air Force underwent a major re-equipment programme in 1974–75, with most aircraft coming from Israel and US aid for transport units, but lost 18 aircraft in a guerrilla attack in Jan. 1982. Counter-insurgency equipment includes 8 A-37B and 6 Magister attack aircraft, 12 Rallye armed trainers, 6 armed C-47 transports and 4 Hughes 500MD helicopters. Other aircraft are 6 C-47, 3 Arava, 1 DC-6 and 2 C-123 transports, 6 Cessna O-2 patrol aircraft, plus 3 Lamas, 3 Alouette III and 45 UH-1H helicopters. Training types include about 15 piston-engined T-41Cs, T-6s and T-34s. Strength totalled about 2,400 personnel in 1992.

INTERNATIONAL RELATIONS

Membership. El Salvador is a member of the UN, CACM, SELA and OAS.

ECONOMY

Policy. An economic liberalization programme aims at raising exports, foreign investment and domestic savings.

Budget. Revenue and expenditure for fiscal years ending 31 Dec., in ₡1,000:

	1985	1986	1987	1988	1989
Revenue	2,391,010	3,508,159	3,232,628	3,175,573	3,330,237
Expenditure	2,276,052	3,481,152	3,397,276	3,428,129	3,900,221

Currency. The monetary unit is the *colón* (SVC) of 100 *centavos*. The *colón* (₡) is issued in denominations of 1, 2, 5, 10, 25 and 100 *colones*; 25 and 50 *centavos* and 1 *colón* (silver); 1, 2, 5 and 10 *centavos* (copper–nickel and copper–zinc); 1 centavo (nickel). In March 1992, £1 = ₡14·09; US$1 = ₡8·03.

Banking and Finance. It is planned to privatize banks and financial institutions. Individual private holdings may not exceed 5% of the total equity. There are 10 native commercial banks, including the Banco Salvadoreño (paid-up capital, ₡6m.).

The Citibank Bank of America and the Bank of Santander and Panama S.A. are the only foreign institutions. The Central Reserve Bank of El Salvador, formed in 1934 from the Banco Agricola Comercial, was nationalized on 20 April 1961.

Weights and Measures. On 1 Jan. 1886 the metric system was made obligatory. But other units are still commonly in use, of which the principal are as follows: *Libra* = 1·014 lb. av.; *quintal* = 101·4 lb. av.; *arroba* = 25·35 lb. av.; *fanega* = 1·5745 bushels.

ENERGY AND NATURAL RESOURCES

Electricity. Installed capacity in 1988 was 500 mw (233 mw hydroelectric, 172 mw thermal, 95 mw geothermal). Production in 1989, 1,979m. kwh. Supply 120 and 240 volts; 60 Hz.

Oil. Production of petroleum derivatives during 1988 totalled ₡1,076,639,000.

Minerals. Production (in tonnes), 1987: Salt, 3,100; limestone, 1·45m.; gypsum, 4,500.

Agriculture. In 1988 0·61m. ha was pasture, 0·57m. ha arable and 0·17m. ha permanent cropland. In 1985, 40% of the working population was engaged in farming.

Production (1989, in 1,000 tonnes): Coffee, 156·4; seed cotton, 12; maize, 582; dry beans, 47; rice, 63; sorghum, 156; sugar-cane, 3,000.

Livestock (1989, 1,000): 1,162 cattle (including 236 milch cows), 450 pigs, 5 sheep, 15 goats. Animal products, 1989 (in 1,000 tonnes): Beef, 23; pork, 14; poultry, 28; milk, 283; eggs, 25.

Forestry. Forest area was 104,000 ha in 1988. In the national forests are found dye woods, mahogany, cedar and walnut. Balsam trees also abound: El Salvador is a major source of this medicinal gum. 4·32m. cu. metres of timber were cut in 1989, mainly for fuel.

Fisheries. In 1989 there were 24 fishing vessels with a tonnage of 3,514 GRD. Total catch 1987, 18,000 tonnes.

INDUSTRY. 1988 production (in 1,000 tonnes) included: Petroleum, 136; fuel oil, 208; paper and products, 16.

Labour. In 1990 the workforce was 2·16m. (0·54m. female).

FOREIGN ECONOMIC RELATIONS. External debt amounted to US$1,826m. in 1989.

Commerce. Imports (including parcels post) and exports in calendar years in ₡1,000:

	1985	1986	1987	1988	1989
Imports	2,403,444	4,284,000	4,970,335	5,034,860	6,448,700
Exports	1,697,420	2,524,700	2,954,705	2,982,095	2,784,100

An estimated 162,000 tonnes of coffee were exported in 1990 (96,000 tonnes in 1989).

In 1988 the USA took ₡904,433,000 of exports and furnished ₡1,417,720,000 of imports. The chief imports in 1988 were manufactured goods (28%), chemical and pharmaceutical products (18·1%), non-edible crude materials, mainly crude oil (8%), electric machinery, tools and appliances and transport equipment (25·6%). The other Central American Republics, Germany, Japan, Canada, Mexico, Spain, France and the Netherlands are also important trading partners.

Total trade between El Salvador and UK (British Department of Trade returns, in £1,000 sterling):

	1987	1988	1989	1990	1991
Imports to UK	1,890	2,961	2,133	1,261	4,063
Exports and re-exports from UK	9,595	8,186	9,594	10,415	14,545

Tourism. There were 134,000 visitors in 1988 (127,000 tourists).

COMMUNICATIONS

Roads. In 1989 there were 15,120 km of national roads, including 1,770 km of main paved roads, 3,507 km of main asphalted roads and 9,843 km of other roads. Vehicles registered, 1987: Cars, 138,000; buses, 7,000 and goods vehicles, 17,000.

Railways. All railways (602 km) came under the control of National Railways of El Salvador *(Fenadesal)* in 1975. Lines run from Acajutla to San Salvador; Cutuco to San Salvador; between San Salvador and Santa Ana, San Miguel and Sonsonate; there is also a link to the Guatemalan system. Total railway traffic in 1989 was 216,000 tonnes of freight and 345,000 passengers.

Civil Aviation. The international airport at Cuscatlán, 40 km from San Salvador, opened in 1979. In 1989, 220,800 passengers arrived and 227,700 departed.

Shipping. The principal ports are La Unión, La Libertad and Acajutla, all on the Pacific. The merchant fleet numbered 14 vessels in 1989 with a total tonnage of 3,819 GRT.

Telecommunications. The telephone and telegraph systems are government-owned; the radio-telephone systems are partly private, partly government-owned. In 1989 there were 94,691 telephones. Broadcasting is under the control of the Administración Nacional de Telecomunicaciones. There were (1992) 3 commercial television channels and 1 educational channel sponsored by the Ministry of Education. In 1991 there were 1,935,000 radio receivers and 425,000 television sets (colour by NTSC).

Cinemas (1976). Cinemas numbered 65.

Newspapers (1990). There are 5 daily newspapers in San Salvador and 1 in Santa Ana.

JUSTICE, RELIGION, EDUCATION AND WELFARE

Justice. Justice is administered by the Supreme Court of Justice, courts of first and second instance, and minor tribunals. Magistrates of the Supreme Court and courts of second instance are elected by the Legislative Assembly for a renewable 3-year term.

Religion. About 90% of the population is Roman Catholic. Under the 1962 Constitution churches are exempted from the property tax; the Catholic Church is recognized as a legal person, and other churches are entitled to secure similar recognition. There is an archbishop in San Salvador and bishops at Santa Ana, San Miguel, San Vicente, Santiago de María, Usulután, Sonsonate and Zacatecoluca. There are about 200,000 Protestants.

Education. Education is run by the state and is free and compulsory.

In 1986 there were 72,500 pupils in nursery schools, 1,140,000 in primary and secondary schools and 73,500 students receiving higher education.

Social Welfare. The Social Security Institute now administers the sickness, old age and death insurance, covering industrial workers and employees earning up to ₡700 a month. Employees in other private institutions with salaries over this amount are included but are excluded from the medical and hospital benefits.

Health. In 1986 there were 5,548 hospital beds. In 1985 there were 1,649 doctors.

DIPLOMATIC REPRESENTATIVES

Of El Salvador in Great Britain (5 Great James St., London, WC1N 3DA)
Ambassador: Dr Mauricio Rosales-Rivera.

Of Great Britain in El Salvador (Paseo General Escalón 4828, POB 1591, San Salvador)
Ambassador and Consul General: M. H. Connor.

Of El Salvador in the USA (2308 California St., NW, Washington, DC., 20008)
Ambassador: Dr Miguel Angel Salaverria.

Of the USA in El Salvador (25 Ave. Norte, Colonia Dueñas, San Salvador)
Ambassador: Vacant.

Of El Salvador to the United Nations
Ambassador: Dr Ricardo G. Castaneda-Cornejo.

Further Reading

Armstrong, R. and Shenk, J., *El Salvador: The Face of Revolution*. London, 1982
Baloyra, E. A., *El Salvador in Transition*. Univ. of North Carolina Press, 1982
Bevan, J., *El Salvador. Education and Repression*. London, 1981
Browning, D., *El Salvador: Landscape and Society*. OUP, 1971
Devire, F. J., *El Salvador: Embassy under Attack*. New York, 1981
Didion, J., *Salvador*. London, 1983
Erdozain, P., *Archbishop Romero: Martyr of El Salvador*. Guildford, 1981
Kufeld, A., *El Salvador*. NY, 1991
Montgomery, T.S., *Revolution in El Salvador: Origins and Evolution*. Boulder, 1982
North, L., *Bitter Grounds: Roots of Revolt in El Salvador*. London, 1981
Schmidt, S. W., *El Salvador: America's Next Vietnam*. Salisbury (N.C.), 1983
Woodward, R. L., *El Salvador*. [Bibliography] Oxford and Santa Barbara, 1988

National statistical office: Dirección General de Estadística y Censos, Calle Arce, San Salvador.

EQUATORIAL GUINEA

Capital: Malabo
Population: 417,000 (1990)
GNP per capita: US$430 (1989)

República de Guinea Ecuatorial

HISTORY. Equatorial Guinea was a Spanish colony (Territorios Españoles del Golfo de Guinea) until 1 April 1960, the territory was then divided into two Spanish provinces with a status comparable to the metropolitan provinces until 20 Dec. 1963, when they were re-joined as an autonomous Equatorial Region. It became an independent Republic on 12 Oct. 1968 as a federation of the two provinces, and a unitary state was established on 4 Aug. 1973. The first President, Francisco Macías Nguema, was declared President-for-Life on 14 July 1972, but was overthrown by a military coup on 3 Aug. 1979. A Supreme Military Council then created was the sole political body until constitutional rule was resumed on 12 Oct. 1982.

AREA AND POPULATION. The mainland part of Equatorial Guinea is bounded north by Cameroon, east and south by Gabon, and west by the Gulf of Guinea in which lie the islands of Bioko (formerly Macías Nguema, formerly Fernando Póo) and Annobón (called Pagalu from 1973 to 1979). The total area is 28,051 sq. km (10,831 sq. miles) and the population at the 1983 census was 300,000. Estimate (1990) 417,000. Another 110,000 are estimated to remain in exile abroad.

The 7 provinces are grouped into 2 regions, Continental (C), chief town Bata and Insular (I), chief town Malabo, with areas and populations as follows:

	Sq. km	Census 1983	Chief town
Annobón (I)	17	2,006	San Antonio de Palea
Bioko Norte (I)	776	46,221	Malabo
Bioko Sur (I)	1,241	10,969	Luba
Centro Sur (C)	9,931	52,393	Evinayong
Kié-Ntem (C)	3,943	70,202	Ebebiyin
Litoral (C)	6,665 [1]	66,370	Bata
Wele-Nzas (C)	5,478	51,839	Mongomo

[1] Including the adjacent islets of Corisco, Elobey Grande and Elobey Chico (17 sq. km).

In 1986 the largest towns were Bata (17,000) and the capital Malabo (10,000).

The main ethnic group on the mainland is the Fang; there are several minority groups along the coast and adjacent islets. On Bioko the indigenous inhabitants (Bubis) constitute 60% of the population there, the balance being mainly Fang and coast people; the formerly numerous immigrant workers from Nigeria and Cameroon have mostly been repatriated. On Annobón the indigenous inhabitants are the descendents of Portuguese slaves and still speak a Portuguese patois. The official language is Spanish.

CLIMATE. The climate is equatorial, with alternate wet and dry seasons. In Río Muni, the wet season lasts from Dec. to Feb.

CONSTITUTION AND GOVERNMENT. A new Constitution was approved in Aug. 1982 by 95% of the votes cast in a plebiscite. It provides for an 11-member Council of State, and for a 41-member House of Representatives of the People, the latter being directly elected on 28 Aug. 1983 for a 5-year term and re-elected on 10 July 1988. The President appoints and leads a Council of Ministers.

On 12 Oct. 1987 a single new political party was formed as the *Partido Democrático de Guinea Ecuatorial.*

524

A referendum on 17 Nov. 1991 approved the institution of multi-party demo-cracy, and a law to this effect was passed in Jan. 1992. The electorate is restricted to citizens who have resided in Equatorial Guinea for at least 10 years.

President of the Supreme Military Council, Defence: Brig.-Gen. Teodoro Obiang Nguema Mbasogo.

Prime Minister: Cristino Seriche Bioko.

Foreign Affairs: Marcelino Nguema Ongueme. *Economy and Finance:* Antonio Fernando Nve. *Justice and Religion:* Angel Ndong Micha.

National flag: Three horizontal stripes of green, white, red; a blue triangle based on the hoist; in the centre the national arms.

DEFENCE

Army. The Army consists of 3 infantry battalions with (1991) 1,100 personnel. There is also a paramilitary force of some 2,000.

Navy. A small force, numbering 100 in 1991, and based at Malabo, operates 4 in-shore patrol craft.

INTERNATIONAL RELATIONS

Membership. Equatorial Guinea is a member of the UN, OAU and is an ACP state of the EEC.

ECONOMY

Budget. The 1988 budget envisaged income at 7,147m. francs CFA and expendi-ture at 7,894m. francs CFA.

Currency. On 2 Jan. 1985 the country joined the franc zone and the *ekuele* was re-placed by the *franc CFA* with a parity value of 50 *francs* CFA to 1 French franc. There are coins of 1, 2, 5, 10, 25, 50, 100 and 500 *francs* CFA, and banknotes of 100, 500, 1,000, 5,000 and 10,000 *francs* CFA. In March 1992, £1 = 489.63 *francs* CFA; US$1 = 278.91 *francs* CFA.

Banking. The *Banque des Etats de l'Afrique Centrale* became the bank of issue in Jan. 1985. There are 2 commercial banks.

ENERGY AND NATURAL RESOURCES

Electricity. Production (1986) 17m. kwh.

Agriculture. The chief products are cocoa (74,000 ha in 1988) and coffee (19,000 ha). Production (in 1,000 tonnes in 1988): Cocoa, 17; coffee 7; palm oil, 5; palm kernels, 3; bananas, 20; cassava, 56; sweet potatoes, 37. Plantations in the hinter-land have been abandoned by their Spanish owners and except for cocoa, commer-cial agriculture is under serious difficulties.

Livestock (1988): Cattle, 5,000; sheep, 35,000; goats, 8,000; pigs, 5,000.

Forestry. In 1988, 1·3m. ha, 46% of the land area was forested. Production: 1981, 465,000 cu. metres.

Fisheries. Catch (1986) 4,400 tonnes.

INDUSTRY. Bioko has very few industries. The mainland has no industry except lumbering. Post-independence political conditions were not conducive to private investment.

Labour. The average monthly wage was 14,000 francs CFA in 1992.

FOREIGN ECONOMIC RELATIONS

Commerce. In 1981 imports amounted to 7,982m. Bikuele (of which 80% came from Spain) and exports to 2,502m. Bikuele (of which Spain took 87%). Cocoa amounted to 71% of all exports and timber to 24%.

Total trade between Equatorial Guinea and UK (British Department of Trade returns, in £1,000 sterling):

	1987	1988	1989	1990	1991
Imports to UK	...	...	2	10	33
Exports and re-exports from UK	1,572	1,029	640	1,159	1,967

COMMUNICATIONS

Roads. Length (1982) 2,760 km of which 330 km surfaced.

Civil Aviation. There are international airports at Malabo and Bata. The line Madrid– Malabo–Bata is subsidized by Spain. Links with Douala (from Malabo) and Libreville (Gabon) exist.

Shipping. Malabo is the main port. The other ports are Luba, formerly San Carlos (bananas, cocoa) in Bioko and Bata, Evinayong and Mbini (wood) on the mainland. A new harbour in Bata has been completed. In 1981 47,731 tonnes were unloaded and 50,843 loaded.

Telecommunications. In Feb. 1989 the radio stations began broadcasting in French in addition to Spanish. Estimated number of telephones (1969), 1,451. In 1985 there were 100,000 radio and 2,200 TV receivers.

JUSTICE, RELIGION, EDUCATION AND WELFARE

Justice. The Constitution guarantees an independent judiciary. The Supreme Tribunal is the highest court of appeal and is located at Malabo. There are Courts of First Instance and Courts of Appeal at Malabo and Bata.

Religion. The population of Equatorial Guinea is nominally Roman Catholic with influential Protestant groups in Malabo and the mainland.

Education. There were in 1981 about 40,110 pupils and 647 teachers in 511 primary schools and 3,013 pupils and 288 teachers in 14 secondary schools.

DIPLOMATIC REPRESENTATIVES

Of Equatorial Guinea in Great Britain
Ambassador: (Vacant; resides in Paris).

Of Great Britain in Equatorial Guinea
Ambassador and Consul-General: W. E. Quantrill (resides in Yaoundé).

Of the USA in Equatorial Guinea (Calle de Los Ministros, Malabo)
Ambassador: William Mithoefer Jr.

Of Equatorial Guinea to the USA and the United Nations
Ambassador: Dámaso-Obiang Ndong.

Further Reading

Fegley, R., *Equatorial Guinea:* [Bibliography]. Oxford and Santa Barbara, 1991
Liniger-Goumaz, M., *La Guinée équatoriale un pays méconnu.* Paris, 1980.—*Connaître la Guinée Equatoriale.* Paris, 1986.—*Guinea Ecuatorial: Bibliografía General.* vols 1-7. Geneva, 1974-91
Pélissier, R., *Les Territoires espagnols d'Afrique.* Paris, 1963.—*Los territorios españoles de Africa.* Madrid, 1964.—*Etudes Hispano-Guinéennes.* Orgeval, 1969

ESTONIA

Capital: Tallinn
Population: 1·58m. (1990)

Eesti Vabariik

(Republic of Estonia)

HISTORY. The early Estonians did not create state units and were subjected to Viking incursions. In 1346 the Danes relinquished Estonia to German rule, and it became part of the Holy Roman Empire and then a Swedish possession in the mid 17th century. On Sweden's defeat by Peter the Great, Estonia passed to the Russian Empire in 1721.

The workers' and soldiers' Soviets in Estonia took over power on 8 Nov. 1917, were overthrown by the German occupying forces in March 1918, and were restored to power as the Germans withdrew in Nov. 1918, establishing the 'Estland Labour Commune'. It was overthrown with the assistance of British naval forces in May 1919, and a democratic republic proclaimed. In March 1934 this regime was, in turn, overthrown by a coup.

The secret protocol of the Soviet-German agreement of 23 Aug. 1939 assigned Estonia to the Soviet sphere of interest. An ultimatum (16 June 1940) led to the formation of a government acceptable to the USSR. On 21 July the Estonian parliament proclaimed the establishment of an Estonian Soviet Socialist Republic and applied to join the USSR; on 6 Aug. the Supreme Soviet of the USSR accepted the application. The incorporation was accorded *de facto* recognition by the UK, but not by the USA, which continued to recognize an Estonian consul-general in New York.

On 30 March 1990 the Estonian Supreme Soviet proclaimed that the Soviet occupation of Estonia on 17 June 1940 had not disrupted the continuity of the former republic, and adopted, by 73 votes to nil with 3 abstentions, a declaration calling for the eventual re-establishment of full sovereignty. At a referendum in March 1991 77·8% of votes cast were in favour of independence. While an attempted coup was taking place in the USSR parliament declared independence on 20 Aug. 1991. A fully independent status was conceded by the USSR State Council on 6 Sept. 1991 and Estonia was subsequently admitted into the UN and other international bodies.

AREA AND POPULATION. Estonia is bounded west and north by the Baltic, east by the RSFSR and south by Latvia. Area, 45,100 sq. km (17,413 sq. miles); population, 1,583,000 (Jan. 1990). The 1989 census population was 1,565,662, of whom Estonians accounted for 61·5% Russians 30·3%, Ukrainians 3·1%, Belorussians 1·8% and Finns 1·1%. In June 1990 the Supreme Soviet established entry quotas for 'foreign citizens'. The capital is Tallinn (505,000). Other large towns are Tartu, Narva, Kohtla-Järve and Pärnu. There are 15 districts, 33 towns and 26 urban settlements.

CLIMATE. Because of its maritime location Estonia has a moderate climate, with cool summers and mild winters. Rainfall is heavy, 500–700 mm per year, and evaporation low.

CONSTITUTION AND GOVERNMENT. The Supreme Soviet, elected on 18 March 1990, consists of 105 deputies. In May 1990 it renamed the republic the 'Republic of Estonia', and restored the pre-1940 flag and national anthem. Alongside the Supreme Soviet, a Congress of Estonia elected by ethnic Estonians has been set up.

527

The *Chairman of the Supreme Soviet* (i.e. President of the Republic) is Arnold Rüütel (b. 1928).

In Feb. 1992 the government consisted of:

Prime Minister: Tiit Vähi (b. 1947).

State Chancellery: Uno Veering. *Construction:* Olari Taal. *Education:* Rein Loik. *Justice:* Märt Rask. *Trade:* Aleksander Sikkal. *Environment:* Tõnis Kaasik. *Culture:* Märt Kubo. *Economy:* Heido Vitsur. *Finance:* Rein Miller. *Interior:* Robert Närska. *Health:* Andres Kork. *Transport and Communications:* Enn Sarap. *Labour:* Arvo Kuddo. *Industry and Energy:* Aksel Treimann. *Foreign Affairs:* Lenart Meri. *Speaker:* Ülo Nugis.

National flag: 3 horizontal stripes of blue, black and white.

National anthem: Mu isamaa, mu õnn ja rõõm (My native land, my pride and joy; words by J. V. Jannsen, tune by F. Pacius).

INTERNATIONAL RELATIONS

Membership. Estonia is a member of the UN.

ECONOMY

Budget. Budget estimates (in 1m. rubles), 1988, 1,797; 1989 (plan), 2,035.

Currency. It is planned to replace the Soviet ruble with an Estonian unit of currency, the *kroon*.

Banking and Finance. A central bank, the Bank of Estonia, was re-established in 1990. (*Governor:* Siim Kallas). There are 10 commercial banks.

Weights and Measures. The metric system is in use.

ENERGY AND NATURAL RESOURCES

Electricity. Output, 1989, was 17,600m. kwh. Some power stations are fuelled by peat.

Oil and Gas. There are rich oil-shale deposits estimated at 3,700m. tonnes. Shale output was 23·3m. in 1988. A factory for the production of gas from shale and a 208 km-pipeline from Kohtla-Järve supplies shale gas to Tallium and exports to St Petersburg.

Minerals. There are extensive peat deposits. Phosphorites and super-phosphates are found and refined.

Agriculture. Farming is concentrated on milk and meat production. Area under cultivation was 2·6m. ha in Nov. 1986. There were 142 agricultural and 8 fishery collectives and 152 state farms in 1990 using 20,500 tractors and 3,300 grain combines. Large state and collective farms are being converted into shareholding enterprises. The remainder are being divided into small private holdings for collective farm workers or former owners. There were some 4,000 such new holdings in 1991.

On 1 Jan. 1990 there were 823,000 head of cattle, 138,100 sheep and goats, and 1·1m. pigs.

Output of main agricultural products (in 1,000 tonnes) in 1989: Grain, 591; potatoes, 864; vegetables, 144; meat, 229; milk, 1,277; eggs, 600m.

966,700 ha of marsh had been reclaimed by 1977.

Forestry. Some 22% of the land is covered by forests which provide material for sawmills, furniture, match and pulp industries, as well as wood fuel. Since 1945, 80,000 ha have been afforested.

INDUSTRY. Estonian factories are now turning out agricultural and peat-digging machines, complex control and measuring instruments.

Output in 1989 included steel, 11,100 tonnes; timber, 2m. cu. metres; paper, 92,000 tonnes; cement, 1·1m. tonnes; fabrics, 235m. sq. metres; hosiery, 17m. pairs; footwear, 7·1m. pairs; knitwear, 23·6m. items; butter, 31,000 tonnes; preserves, 355m. standard jars.

In 1990 there were some 5,600 enterprises of which 51% were state-owned, 32% co-operatives, 5% joint stock companies and 1·4% joint ventures.

Labour. In 1989 there were 675,000 employees in the state sector.

FOREIGN ECONOMIC RELATIONS. On 12 April 1990 Estonia, Latvia and Lithuania concluded a Baltic Economic Co-operation Agreement.

Joint ventures are permitted, but non-Estonians may not own more than 50% of the equity without government permission. New ventures enjoy a 2-year tax exemption. In Feb. 1991 there were 246 joint ventures from 27 countries.

COMMUNICATIONS

Roads. In 1990 there were 30,200 km of motor roads (29,100 km hard-surfaced).

Railways. Length of railways in Jan. 1990 was 1,030 km.

Civil Aviation. There is an international airport at Tallinn. There are services to Frankfurt, Moscow, Riga and St Petersburg, and domestic flights to the Estonian islands. The national carrier is Estonian Air.

Shipping. There are 20 ports, but Tallinn handles four-fifths of sea-going transport.

Newspapers (1989). There were 111 newspapers, 75 of them in Estonian. Daily circulation of Estonian-language newspapers, 2,048,000; other languages, 508,000.

JUSTICE, RELIGION, EDUCATION AND WELFARE

Justice. There is a Supreme Court, a Public Prosecutor and a State Arbitration Tribunal.

Religion. There are about 0·35m. Lutherans and a Methodist Church.

Education. Estonia retained an 11-year school curriculum, when it was reduced to 10 years elsewhere in the USSR. In 1989–90 pupils in 600 primary, secondary and special schools numbered 200,000. There were 26,300 students in 6 higher educational establishments, including Tartu (Dorpat) University, founded in 1632, and 19,900 students in 36 technical colleges.

The Estonian Academy of Sciences, founded in 1946, had 24 institutions with 1,312 scientific staff in Jan. 1989; in all, 7,100 scientific staff were working in 72 institutions.

In Jan. 1990 60% of eligible children attended pre-school institutions.

Health. In 1989 there were 7,600 doctors and 19,200 hospital beds.

DIPLOMATIC REPRESENTATIVES

Of Estonia in Great Britain (18 Chepstow Villas, London W11 2RB)
Chargé d'affaires: Eerik Kross.

Of Great Britain in Estonia
Ambassador: Brian Low.

Of Estonia in the USA (9 Rockefeller Plaza, New York) and to the United Nations
Ambassador: Ernst Jaakson.

Further Reading

Küng, A., *A Dream of Freedom.* Cardiff, 1980
Misiuras, R.-J. and Taagepera, R., *The Baltic States: Years of Dependence 1940–1980.* Farnborough, 1983
Parming, T. and Jarvesro, E., (eds.) *A Case Study of a Soviet Republic.* Boulder, 1978
Raun, T. U., *Estonia and the Estonians.* Stanford, 1987

ETHIOPIA

Capital: Addis Ababa
Population: 45m. (1991)
GNP per capita: US$120 (1989)

Ityopia

HISTORY. The empire of Ethiopia had its origin in the centuries before and after the birth of Christ, at Aksum in the north, as a result of Semitic immigration from South Arabia. The immigrants imposed their language and culture on a basic Hamitic stock. Ethiopia's subsequent history is one of sporadic expansion southwards and eastwards. Modern Ethiopia dates from the reign of the Emperor Theodore (1855–68).

Menelik II (1889–1913) defeated the Italians in 1896 and thereby safeguarded the empire's independence in the scramble for Africa. By successful campaigns in neighbouring kingdoms within Ethiopia (Jimma, Kaffa, Harar, etc.) he united the country under his rule.

In 1936 Ethiopia was conquered by the Italians, who were in turn defeated by the Allied forces in 1941 when the Emperor returned.

The former Italian colony of Eritrea was in accordance with a resolution of the General Assembly of the UN, dated 2 Dec. 1950, handed over to Ethiopia on 15 Sept. 1952. Eritrea thereby became an autonomous unit within the federation of Ethiopia and Eritrea.

This federation became a unitary state on 14 Nov. 1962 when Eritrea was fully integrated with Ethiopia. The Federation gave rise to an Eritrean secessionist movement which has since pursued a campaign of military resistance. The government engaged in preliminary peace talks with the rebels in Sept. 1989 and former president Carter of the USA also acted as mediator. Fierce fighting commenced in Tigre in late 1989.

A provisional military government assumed power on 12 Sept. 1974, deposed the Emperor and executed 60 former military and civilian leaders.

In Feb. 1977 Lieut.-Col. Mengistu Haile Mariam became Chairman of the Provisional Military Administrative Council, and in Sept. 1987 he was elected President of the newly-inaugurated People's Democratic Republic.

Following ever-increasing territorial gains by the insurgent Ethiopian People's Revolutionary Democratic Front (EPRDF, dominated by the Tigrean People's Liberation Front, but also grouping the Ethiopian People's Democratic Movement, the Oromo People's Democratic Organization and the Ethiopian Democratic Officers' Revoluionary Movement) and Eritrean People's Liberation Front (EPLF), Mengistu Haile Mariam stepped down as president and fled the country. Lieut.-Gen. Tesfaye Gebre Gidan took over as temporary head of state. Peace talks in London between the government and the insurgents at the end of May 1991 were ended when the EPRDF occupied Addis Ababa with US approval. The EPLF announced that it would form a provisional government pending a UN-supervised referendum on self-determination in 1993.

For the war with Somalia *see* THE STATESMAN'S YEAR-BOOK, 1989-90, p.462.

AREA AND POPULATION. Ethiopia is bounded north-east by the Red Sea, east by Djibouti and Somalia, south by Kenya and west by Sudan. It has a total area of 1,221,900 sq. km (471,800 sq. miles). The first census was carried out in 1984: Population (preliminary) 42,019,418. Estimate (1991), 45m. Growth rate was 2·9% in 1989; expectation of life, 40·9 years. There were 265,000 refugees in Ethiopia in Jan. 1988.

The dominant race of Ethiopia, the Amhara, inhabit the central Ethiopian highlands. To the north of them are the Tigreans, akin to the Amhara but speaking a different, though related, language. Both these races are of mixed Hamitic and Semitic origin, and further mixed by intermarriage with Oromo (Galla) and other races. The Oromos comprise about 40% of the entire population, and are a pastoral and agricultural people of Hamitic origin. Somalis, another Hamitic race, inhabit the southeast of Ethiopia, in particular the Ogaden desert region. The closely related Afar people stretch northwards from the former Wollo region into Eritrea.

Region	Area (sq. km)	Population May 1984	Chief town	Population May 1984
Addis Ababa	218	1,412,575	—	—
Arussi	23,500	1,662,233	Assela	36,720
Bale	124,600	1,006,491	Goba	22,963
Eritrea	117,600	2,614,700	Asmara	275,385
Gemu Gofa	39,500	1,248,034	Arba Minch	23,030
Gojjam	61,600	3,244,882	Debre Markos	39,808
Gondar (Begemdir)	74,200	2,905,362	Gondar	68,958
Hararge	259,700	4,151,706	Harar	62,160
Illubabor	47,400	963,327	Mattu	12,491
Kefa	54,600	2,450,369	Jimma	60,992
Shoa	85,200	8,090,565	—	—
Sidamo	117,300	3,790,579	Awassa	36,169
Tigre	65,900	2,409,700	Mekele	61,583
Wollega	71,200	2,369,677	Lekemti	28,824
Wollo	79,400	3,609,918	Dessie	68,848

The above-mentioned regions were replaced by 14 new ones in Dec. 1991: Afar, Agau North, Agau South, Amhara, Beni Shangul, Eritrea, Gambela, Gurage Kembatahadiya, Kaffa, Omo, Oromo, Sidama, Somali and Tigre.

The population of the capital, Addis Ababa, was estimated at 1·7m. in 1990. Other large towns (population, May 1984): Dire Dawa, in Hararge, 98,104; Nazret, in Shoa, 76,284; Bahr Dar, 54,800; Debre Zeit, 51,143.

The official language is Amharic.

CLIMATE. The wide range of latitude produces many climatic variations between the high, temperate plateaus and the hot, humid lowlands. The main rainy season lasts from June to Aug., with light rains from Feb. to April, but the country is very vulnerable to drought. Addis Ababa. Jan. 59°F (15°C), July 59°F (15°C). Annual rainfall 50" (1,237 mm). Harar. Jan. 65°F (18·3°C), July 64°F (17·8°C). Annual rainfall 35" (897 mm). Massawa. Jan. 78°F (25·6°C), July 94°F (34·4°C). Annual rainfall 8" (193 mm).

CONSTITUTION AND GOVERNMENT. The People's Democratic Republic of Ethiopia was inaugurated on 10 Sept. 1987 at the first meeting of the newly elected National Assembly. A new Constitution, on a Marxist model, was approved on 1 Feb. 1987 in a referendum. On 14 June 1987 Ethiopia held its first parliamentary election when 813 members belonging to the single political party the Workers' Party of Ethiopia were elected to the new civilian legislature.

An interim EPRDF government led by Meles Zenawi (b. 1955) took over after the flight of President Mengistu. Elections are scheduled for 1993. In July 1991 a conference of 24 political groups called to appoint a transitional government agreed a democratic charter guaranteeing freedom of expression and association and the right to self-determination for ethnic groups. An 87-member Council of Representatives was formed which unanimously elected Meles *President* for 2 years. Tamerat Layne was named *Prime Minister*, and he formed a government of 17 ministers in Aug., including:

Foreign Affairs: Seyoum Mesfin.

National flag: Three horizontal stripes of green, yellow and red.
National anthem: Ityopia, Ityopia Kidemi (tune by Daniel Yohannes, 1975).

Local Government. In Dec. 1991 the Council of Representatives decreed the establishment of 14 new administrative regions, each with its own assembly.

DEFENCE

Army. Following the overthrow of President Mengistu's government organized armed forces ceased to exist. The strengths of the EPRDF and the EPLF are estimated at 65,000 and 60,00 repectively. Former army equipment is now in their hands. It included 300 main battle tanks.

Navy. The Navy, following the insurgent successes of early 1991 and the fall of Dergue has probably ceased to function as an organized force. It consists nominally of 2 small frigates, 4 fast missile craft, 6 fast torpedo craft and 6 patrol craft. There are also 2 medium landing ships and 6 craft, 1 transport and a training ship.

The main base and training establishments were at Massawa, and there were other bases at Assab, and in the Dahlak Islands. Most of the remaining vessels are reported to have fled to the Yemen and possibly Saudi Arabia.

Personnel strength at the time of the fall of Massawa was believed to be about 2,000.

Air Force. The status of the Air Force since the overthrow of President Mengistu is uncertain. At least 2 dozen aircraft were flown to neighbouring countries at that time. Prior to Mengistu's departure, the Air Force was operating some 280 aircraft and had 4,500 personnel. There were fighter, transport, trainer, reconnaissance and air rescue units at Debre Zeyit and fighter units only at Asmara, Gode, Dire Dawa and Deke airfields. US-supplied fighters, reconnaissance aircraft and trainers received in the 1960s and 1970s had been withdrawn from use. About 100 MiG-23, MiG-21 and MiG-17 fighters were in use, backed up by 20 transport aircraft and 100 helicopters of various Soviet and French types. About 50 aircraft served for training.

INTERNATIONAL RELATIONS

Membership. Ethiopia is a member of the UN, OAU and is an ACP state of the EEC.

ECONOMY

Policy. The economy is centrally planned and organized. GDP growth 1974–85 averaged 1·2%.

Budget. Revenue for 1985–86 was EB4,356m. and expenditure EB4,392m.
Of the estimated revenue in 1985–86, EB1,620m. came from taxes.

Currency. The *Ethiopian birr* (ETB), of 100 *cents*, is the unit of currency; it is based on 5·52 grains of fine gold. It consists of notes of EB1, 2, 10, 50 and 100 denominations, and bronze 1-, 5-, 10-, 25- and 50-cent coins. In March 1992 *birr* 3·60 = £1 sterling; *birr* 2·05 = US$1.

Banking and Finance. The State Bank is the National Bank of Ethiopia. The Investment Bank of Ethiopia, was established in 1963 with a capital of EB10m., of which the Government held the majority of shares. In Sept. 1965 it became the Ethiopian Investment Corporation, which is a substantial shareholder in a number of industrial and other ventures. There is also the Agricultural and Industrial Development Bank, SC.

On 1 Jan. 1975 the Government nationalized all banks, mortgage and insurance companies.

Weights and Measures. The metric system of weights and measures is officially in use. Traditional weights and measures vary considerably in the various provinces: the principal ones are: *Frasilla* = approximately 37½ lb.; *gasha*, the principal unit of land measure, which is normally about 100 acres but can vary between 80 and 300 acres, depending on the quality of the land.

ENERGY AND NATURAL RESOURCES

Electricity. Production in 1986 totalled 722m. kwh. Supply 220 volts; 50 Hz. Over 92% of energy supply is from firewood, charcoal, dung and crop residues. The main power source is hydro-electricity although imported fuel supplies 22% of public power systems.

Oil. A Soviet built state-owned oil refinery at Assab came on stream in 1967 with a capacity of 750,000 tonnes of crude per annum.

Minerals. Ethiopia has little proved mineral wealth. Salt is produced mainly in Eritrea, while a placer goldmine is worked by the Government of Adola in the south. Gold production, in 1985–86, was 923 kg. A new mine was under development at Lega Dembi in 1989. Small quantities of other minerals are produced including platinum.

Agriculture. In 1990 farmers were permitted to vote on the dissolution of co-operatives. Land remains the property of the state, but individuals are granted rights of usage which can be passed to their children, and produce may be sold on the open market instead of compulsorily to the state Agriculture Marketing Corporation at low fixed prices.

Coffee is by far the most important source of rural income. Teff (*Eragrastis abyssinica*) is the principal food grain, followed by barley, wheat, maize and durra. Cane sugar is an important crop.

Production (1988 in 1,000 tonnes): Maize, 1,650; sorghum, 1,100; barley, 1,050; pulses, 987.

Livestock (1989): 27m. cattle, 26m. sheep, 17m. goats; smaller numbers of donkeys, horses, mules and camels. Hides and skins and butter (ghee) are important for home consumption and export. Sheep, cattle and chickens are the main providers of meat. In 1989 85% of the population were engaged in agriculture, producing 43% of GDP.

Forestry. In 1988 forests covered 27·4m. ha, representing 25% of the land area. Sawnwood production (1983) 45,000 cu. metres.

Fisheries. Catch (1986) 4,100 tonnes.

INDUSTRY. Industrial output is controlled by the State and most public industrial enterprizes are controlled by the Ministry of Industry. Most individual activity is centred around Addis Ababa and Asmara, although Asmara has been severely hit by the civil war in Eritrea.

FOREIGN ECONOMIC RELATIONS

Commerce. Imports and exports (in EB1m.) for 4 years:

	1983	1984	1985	1986
Imports	1,810	1,601	1,734	1,822
Exports	863	866	689	702

Coffee exports accounted for 90% of foreign earnings in 1989.

Total trade between Ethiopia and UK (British Department of Trade returns, in £1,000 sterling):

	1987	1988	1989	1990	1991
Imports to UK	12,875	8,451	12,772	19,465	14,660
Exports and re-exports from UK	46,146	47,661	44,148	41,403	29,773

Tourism. There were 59,000 tourists in 1986. This figure has substantially decreased due to the civil war and general unrest.

COMMUNICATIONS

Roads. There were (1989) 3,508 km of ashphalt roads and 9,687 km of rural and gravel roads.

Motor vehicles (1984): Cars, 41,300; lorries and trucks, 8,800; buses, 3,041.

Railways. The former Franco-Ethiopian Railway Co. (782 km, metre-gauge) became the Ethiopian-Djibouti Railway Corp. in 1981, when the remaining France-owned shares were bought out. In 1990 the railway carried 126m. tonne-km of freight and 277m. passenger-km.

Civil Aviation. Ethiopian Air Lines, formed in 1946, carried 470,000 passengers in 1988, using Boeing 767s on its long-haul flights. There are international airports at Addis Ababa, Dire Dawa and Asmara.

Shipping. A state shipping line was established in 1964. The ports unloaded 1·75m. tonnes in 1982 and loaded 547,000.

Telecommunications. The postal system serves 301 offices, mainly by air-mail. All the main centres are connected with Addis Ababa by telephone or radio telegraph. International telephone services are available at certain hours to most countries in Europe, North America and India. Number of telephones (1986), 162,000.

The Ethiopian Broadcasting Service makes sound broadcasts on the medium and short waves in English, Amharic and in the vernacular languages spoken within the country. There were about 45,000 television sets and 2m. radio receivers in 1986.

Cinemas (1974). There were 31 cinemas, with seating capacity of about 25,600.

Newspapers. There were (1991) 4 government-controlled daily newspapers with a combined circulation of about 60,000.

JUSTICE, RELIGION, EDUCATION AND WELFARE

Justice. The legal system is said to be based on the Justinian Code. A new penal code came into force in 1958 and Special Penal Law in 1974. Codes of criminal procedure, civil, commercial and maritime codes have since been promulgated.

The extra-territorial rights formerly enjoyed by foreigners have been abolished, but any person accused in an Ethiopian court has the right to have his case transferred to the High Court, provided he asks for this before any evidence has been taken in the court of first instance.

Provincial and district courts have been established, and High Court judges visit the provincial courts on circuit. The Supreme Court at Addis Ababa is presided over by the Chief Justice.

Religion. About 45% of the population are Moslem and 40% Christian, mainly belonging to the Ethiopian Orthodox Church. Amhara, Tigreans and some Oromos are Christian. Somalis, Afars and some Oromos are Moslems.

Education. Primary education commences at 7 years and continues with optional secondary education at 13 years. In the academic year 1988–89 there were more than 2·5m. pupils in primary schools and in secondary schools there were 500,000 students. Higher education is co-ordinated under the National University, chartered in 1961; in 1979–80, there were 14,562 students. The University College, the Engineering, Building and Theological Colleges are in Addis Ababa, the Agricultural College in Harar and the Public Health College in Gondar.

Adult literacy was 62·5% in 1990.

Health. In 1987 there were about 90 hospitals with 11,000 beds.

DIPLOMATIC REPRESENTATIVES

Of Ethiopia in Great Britain (17 Prince's Gate, London, SW7 1PZ)
Ambassador: (Vacant).

Of Great Britain in Ethiopia (Fikre Mariam Abatechan St., Addis Ababa)
Ambassador: M. J. C. Glaze, CMG.

Of Ethiopia in the USA (2134 Kalorama Rd., NW, Washington D.C., 20008)
Chargé d'Affaires: Girma Amare.

Of the USA in Ethiopia (Entoto St., Addis Ababa)
Chargé d'Affaires: James R. Cheek.

Of Ethiopia to the United Nations
Ambassador: (Vacant).

Further Reading

Alemneh Dejene. *Environment, Famine and Politics in Ethiopia: a View from the Village.* Boulder (Colo.), 1991
Clapham, C., *Transformation and Continuity in Revolutionary Ethiopia.* CUP, 1988
Hancock, G., *Ethiopia: The Challenge of Hunger.* London, 1985
Keller, E. J. *Revolutionary Ethiopia: From Empire to People's Republic.* Indiana Univ. Press, 1989
Monro-Hay, S. and Pankhurst, R., *Ethiopia:* [Bibliography]. Oxford and Santa Barbara, 1991
Schwab, P., *Ethiopia: Politics, Economics and Society.* Boulder, 1985.

FALKLAND ISLANDS

Capital: Stanley
Population: 2,121 (1991)

HISTORY. France established a settlement in 1764 and Britain a second settlement in 1765. In 1770 Spain bought out the French and drove off the British. This action on the part of Spain brought that country and Britain to the verge of war. The Spanish restored the settlement to the British in 1771, but the settlement was withdrawn on economic grounds in 1774. In 1806 Spanish rule was overthrown in Argentina, and the Argentine claimed to succeed Spain in the French and British settlements in 1820. The British objected and reclaimed their settlement in 1832 as a Crown Colony.

On 2 April 1982 Argentine forces invaded the Falkland Islands and the Governor was expelled. At a meeting of the UN Security Council, held on 3 April, the voting was 10 to 1 in favour of the resolution calling for Argentina to withdraw. Britain regained possession on 14–15 June after Argentina surrendered.

In April 1990 Argentina's Congress declared the Falkland and other British-held South Atlantic islands part of the new Argentine province of Tierra del Fuego.

AREA AND POPULATION. The Crown Colony is situated in the South Atlantic Ocean about 480 miles north-east of Cape Horn. The numerous islands cover 4,700 sq. miles. The main East Falkland Island, 2,610 sq. miles; the West Falkland, 2,090 sq. miles, including the adjacent small islands. The open country is called 'The Camp'.

The population of the Falkland Islands at census 1991 was 2,121. The only town is Stanley, in East Falkland, with a population of 1,557. The population of the Falkland Islands is nearly all of British descent, with about 67% born in the islands. A garrison of British servicemen was stationed in East Falkland in 1991, but is not included in the population figures.

CLIMATE. A cool temperate climate, much affected by strong winds, particularly in spring. Stanley. Jan. 49°F (9·4°C), July 35°F (1·7°C). Annual rainfall 27" (681 mm).

CONSTITUTION AND GOVERNMENT. A new Constitution came into force on 3 Oct. 1985. This incorporated a chapter protecting fundamental human rights and in the preamble recalled the provisions on the right of self-determination contained in international covenants.

Executive power is vested in the Governor who must consult the Executive Council except on urgent or trivial matters. He must consult the Commander British Forces on matters relating to defence and internal security (except police).

There is a Legislative Council consisting of 8 elected members and 2 *ex officio* members, the Chief Executive and Financial Secretary. Only elected members have a vote. The Commander British Forces has a right to attend and take part in its proceedings but has no vote. The Attorney General also has a similar right to take part in proceedings with the consent of the person presiding. The Governor presides over sittings. He also presides over sittings of the Executive Council which consists of 3 elected members (elected by and from the elected members of Legislative Council) and the Chief Executive and Financial Secretary (*ex officio*). The Commander British Forces and Attorney General have a right to attend but may not vote.

Offices in the Public Service are constituted by the Governor and he makes appointments and is responsible for discipline. The Constitution allows for the establishment of a public service commission.

Governor: William Fullerton, CMG.
Chief Executive: R. Sampson.
Financial Secretary: D. F. Howatt.
Attorney General: David Lang, QC.

Senior Assistant Secretary: P. T. King.
Flag: British Blue Ensign with arms of Colony on a white disc in the fly.

DEFENCE. Since 1982 the Islands have been defended by a large garrison of British servicemen. The Commander British Forces is responsible for all military matters in the Islands. He liaises with the Governor on civilian and political matters, and advises him on matters of defence and internal security, except police. In addition there is a local volunteer defence force.

ECONOMY

Policy. The Falkland Islands Development Corporation was established by statute in June 1983 with the aim of encouraging economic development. It commenced operations in 1984, and has since provided assistance to 206 projects. In 1991 87% of these were still trading. The variety of projects assisted are wide-ranging and include a spinning mill dairy, hydroponic market garden, tourist lodges, agricultural supply co-operatives, and research into seabird populations and their diets.

Budget. Revenue and expenditure (in £ sterling) for fiscal years ending 30 June:

	1986–87	1987–88	1988–89	1989–90	1990–91 [1]	1991–92 [1]
Revenue	19,646,310	32,692,000	42,115,250	44,060,260	41,940,000	40,270,000
Expenditure	12,212,805	24,042,000	82,608,380	35,911,730	45,967,000	39,145,000

[1] Estimate

Revenue from licences to fish illex squid is a major component, amounting to some £30m. in 1990.

Currency. The unit of currency is the *Falkland Islands pound* (FKP) of 100 *pence*, at parity with £1 sterling.

Banking. The Standard Chartered Bank provides a full range of banking facilities.

Oil. The UK government authorized exploration for oil in Nov. 1991 in the 200-mile economic exclusion zone except where it overlapped Argentina's zone in the west.

Agriculture. The economy was formerly based solely on agriculture, principally sheep farming. Following a programme of sub-division, much of the land is divided into family size units. There were 89 farms in 1991, 79 of which were family units. During 1991 the Falklands Islands Co. sold its agricultural holdings to the Falkland Island government. Less than 5% of the total land area is owned outside the islands. Wool is the principal product; output was 2,591 tonnes in 1990. In 1990 there were 739,899 sheep, 5,464 cattle and 1,717 horses in the islands.

Fisheries. Since the establishment of a 150-mile interim conservation and management zone around the Islands in 1986 and the consequent introduction, on 1 Feb. 1987, of a licensing regime for vessels fishing within the zone, income from the associated fishing activities is now the largest source of revenue. Licenses raised £23·7m. in 1991.

On 26 Dec. 1990 the UK and Argentina agreed to enforce a ban on fishing in a further 50-mile semi-circular area to the east of this zone. In Dec. 1991 the 2 countries agreed to extend the ban to the end of 1992. A UK-Argentine South Atlantic Fisheries Commission was set up in 1990; it meets at least twice a year. Some 0·2m. tonnes of illex squid are caught annually.

TRADE. Total trade between the Falkland Islands and UK (British Department of Trade returns, in £1,000 sterling):

	1988	1989	1990	1991
Imports to UK	4,209	5,375	4,817	3,379
Exports and re-exports from UK	9,037	10,200	11,309	16,039

COMMUNICATIONS

Roads. There are 27 km of made-up roads in and around Stanley and another 54 km of all-weather road between Stanley and Mount Pleasant Airport. Other settlements outside Stanley are linked by tracks, which are passable, with high axle clearing four-wheel drive vehicles in all but the worst weather. A rural all-weather road to Port Louis was completed in early 1991 and construction of a further one to the Northern areas of East Falkland was continuing. The Government is also providing assistance to farms which wish to improve tracks and bridges to their immediate area.

Civil Aviation. Air communication is currently via Ascension Island. An airport, completed in 1986, is sited at Mount Pleasant on East Falkland. RAF Tristar aircraft operate a twice-weekly service between the Falklands and the UK. Internal air links are provided by the government-operated air service, which carries passengers, mail, freight and medical patients between the settlements and Stanley on non-scheduled flights in Islander aircraft. A Chilean airline runs a fortnightly service to Punta Arenas. In 1991 Argentina and the UK agreed to a regular service by a Uruguayan airline to Buenos Aires.

Shipping. A charter vessel calls 4 or 5 times a year to/from the UK. There is occasional direct communication with South Georgia, the South Sandwich Islands and British Antarctic Territory by research ships and the ice-patrol vessel HMS *Endurance*. Vessels of the Royal Fleet Auxiliary run regularly to South Georgia. Sea links with Chile and Uruguay began in 1989.

Telecommunications. Number of telephones (Sept. 1991) 1,180. International direct dialling is available, as are international telex and facsimile links. Cable and Wireless plc signed a contract with the Falkland Islands Government in Sept. 1988 for the complete replacement of the telecommunications network with a modern system. There is a government-operated broadcasting station at Stanley and television broadcasts began in 1988.

JUSTICE, EDUCATION AND WELFARE

Justice. There is a Supreme Court, and a Court of Appeal sits in the United Kingdom; appeals may go from that court to the judicial committee of the Privy Council. Judges have security of tenure and may only be removed for inability or misbehaviour on the advice of the judicial committee of the Privy Council. The senior resident judicial officer is the Senior Magistrate. There is an Attorney General and a Senior Crown Counsel. In 1991 there were 2 firms of legal practitioners.

Education. Education is compulsory between the ages of 5 and 15 years. In 1991 there were 342 children receiving education in the Colony. Almost 75% attended schools in Stanley, the others were taught in settlement schools or by itinerant teachers. Estimated expenditure on education and training from own funds 1991-92 £1,804,160.

Health. The Government Medical Department is responsible for all medical services to civilians. Estimated expenditure (1991-92) £1,901,390. The Chief Medical Officer advises the Government on policy, and is chairman of the Board of Health responsible for public health. Medical services for the Islands are run from a temporary hospital; a new hospital and some sheltered accommodation was completed in March 1987. Services include all primary care for Stanley and the flying doctor service for outlying farm settlements.

WILD LIFE. The Falkland Islands are noted for their outstanding wild life, including penguin and seal. Four Nature Reserves have been declared and 18 Wild Animal and Bird Sanctuaries gazetted. The brown trout introduced between 1947 and 1952 can now be found in nearly all the rivers and there are good runs of sea-trout during spring and autumn.

Further Reading

Falkland Islands: The Facts. HMSO, London, 1982
Falkland Islands Journal. Stanley, from 1967
Falkland Islands Review [Franks Report] Cmnd. 8787. HMSO, London, 1983
Falklands/Malvinas, Whose Crisis? Latin American Bureau, London, 1982

Calvert, P., *The Falklands Crisis: The Rights and the Wrongs*. London, 1982
Hanrahan, B. and Fox, R., *'I counted them all out and I counted them all back'*. London, 1982
Hastings, M. and Jenkins, S., *The Battle for the Falklands*. London, 1983
Hoffmann, F. L. and Hoffmann, O. M., *Sovereignty in Dispute*. London, 1984
Shackleton, E., *Falkland Islands Economic Study 1982*. HMSO, London, 1982
Smith, W. S. (ed.) *Towards Resolution? The Falklands/Malvinas Dispute*. London, 1991
Strange, I. J., *The Falkland Islands*. 3rd ed. Newton Abbot, 1983.—*The Falkland Islands and their Natural History*. Newton Abbot, 1987

FIJI

Republic of Fiji

Capital: Suva
Population: 747,000 (1991)
GNP per capita: US$1,640 (1989)

HISTORY. The first European discovery of the Fiji Islands was by the Dutch navigator Abel Tasman in 1643, and they were recorded in detail by Capt. Bligh after the mutiny of the *Bounty* (1789). In the 19th century the search for sandalwood, in which enormous profits were made, brought many ships. The influence of the deserters, shipwrecked sailors and missionaries who settled on the islands disrupted the pattern of life of the indigenous Fijians and gave rise to inter-tribal wars until Fiji was ceded to Britain on 10 Oct. 1874. Fiji became an independent state within the Commonwealth on 10 Oct. 1970. Following the electoral defeat of the Fijian-dominated National Alliance Party by an Indian-supported coalition in April 1987, Brig. Sitiveni Rabuka seized power after two coups, and declared Fiji a republic in Oct.; membership of the Commonwealth lapsed.

AREA AND POPULATION. Fiji comprises about 332 islands and islets (about 110 inhabited) lying between 15° and 22° S. lat. and 174° E. and 177° W. long. The largest is Viti Levu, area 10,429 sq. km (4,027 sq. miles), next is Vanua Levu, area 5,556 sq. km (2,145 sq. miles). The island of Rotuma (47 sq. km, 18 sq. miles), about 12° 30' S. lat., 178° E. long., was added to the colony in 1881. Total area, 7,078 sq. miles (18,333 sq. km).

A population census is taken every 10 years. Total population (census, Aug. 1986), 715,375; average annual increase about 2%. The 1989 estimated total population of 727,104 consisted of the following: 351,966 (48·4%) Fijians; 337,557 (46·4%) Indians (whose ancestors had been introduced as field workers by the British); 37,581 (5·2%) were of other races.

Suva, the capital, is on the south coast of Viti Levu; population (census, 1986), 71,608. Suva was proclaimed a city on 2 Oct. 1953. Lautoka had 28,728 in 1986.

Vital statistics, 1987: Crude birth rate per 1,000 population, Fijian, 30·7, Indian, 25·6; crude death rate per 1,000 population, Fijian, 5·4, Indian, 5·2. Average life expectancy (1989) 68 years.

CLIMATE. A tropical climate, but oceanic influences prevent undue extremes of heat or humidity. The S.E. Trades blow from May to Nov., during which time nights are cool and rainfall amounts least. Suva. Jan. 80°F (26·7°C), July 73°F (22·8°C). Annual rainfall 117" (2,974 mm).

CONSTITUTION AND GOVERNMENT. On 25 July 1990 a new constitution was promulgated giving 'indigenous Fijians' the right to hold the prime ministership and a guaranteed 37 seats in the 70-seat House of Representatives. Fijian citizens of Indian descent have 27 seats, other races 5, and the Polynesian island of Rotuma, 1. The Upper House has 24 seats for Fijians, 9 for other races and 1 for Rotuma.

President: Ratu Sir Penaia Ganilau, GCMG, KCVO, KBE, DSO.
Prime Minister and Minister for Foreign Affairs: Ratu Sir Kamisese Mara, GCMG, KBE.
Deputy Prime Minister and Minister of Home Affairs: Maj.-Gen. Sitiveni Rabuka (b. 1948).
Attorney-General and Justice: Sailosi Kepa. *Finance and Economic Planning:* Josevata Kamikamica. *Education, Youth and Sport:* Filipe Bole. *Primary Industries and Co-operatives:* Viliame Gonelevu. *Health:* Dr Apenisa Kurisaqila. *Indian Affairs:* Irene Jai Narayan. *Fijian Affairs and Rural Development:* Col. Vatiliai Navunisaravi. *Tourism, Civil Aviation and Energy:* David Pickering. *Women and Social Welfare:* Adi Finau Tabakaucoro. *Forests:* Ratu Sir Josaia Tavaiqia. *Lands and Mineral Resources:* Ratu William Toganivalu. *Infrastructure and Public*

Utilities: Apisai Tora. *Housing and Urban Development:* Tomasi Vakatora. *Employment and Industrial Relations:* Taniela Veitata. *Trade and Commerce:* Berenado Vunibobo. *Information, Broadcasting, Television and Telecommunications:* Ratu Inoke Kubuabola.

National flag: Light blue with the Union Flag in the canton and the shield of Fiji in the fly.

National anthem: Blessing grant, oh God of Nations, on the isles of Fiji (words by M. Prescott).

Local Government. Fiji is divided into 14 provinces, each with its own council under which 188 Tikina Councils have been established. The number of Tikina Councils within a province varies from 4 to 22. Tikina Councils have wide powers to make by-laws and levy rates to raise revenue. 50% of the rates collected is credited to the Provincial Council treasury for the running of the Council and 50% is used for the financing of the Tikina and village projects.

DEFENCE. The Fiji Military Forces are for the defence of Fiji, maintenance of law and order and provision of forces to international peace-keeping agencies overseas. The forces have 2 overseas battalions (in Egypt and Lebanon) and 2 battalions and an engineer company at home. Total active strength (1991), 4,700 (reserves, 5,000).

Navy. A naval division of the armed forces was formed in 1974 to perform miscellaneous offshore duties. Present strength is 3 ex-US coastal patrol craft (1 with a helicopter deck) 4 Israeli-built fast inshore patrol craft and 2 inshore craft. There is also 1 naval-manned survey ship. Naval personnel in 1991 numbered 400. The naval base is in Suva.

INTERNATIONAL RELATIONS

Membership. Fiji is a member of the UN, the Colombo Plan, the South Pacific Forum and is an ACP state of the EEC.

ECONOMY

Budget. The financial year corresponds with the calendar year. All figures are in $1m. Fijian.

	1985	1986	1987	1988	1989
Revenue	349·9	348·1	341·2	389·7	390·0
Expenditure	349·3	370·9	393·9	434·6	539·0

Currency. The unit of currency is the *Fiji dollar* (FJD) of 100 *cents*. In March 1992, £1 = $F2·62; US$ = $F1·49.

Banking and Finance. The National Bank of Fiji had, in 1985, deposits amounting to $F62·3m. due to 241,375 accounts. The headquarters are at Suva, and there are 11 branches, 35 postal agencies and 9 private agencies throughout Fiji. The Westpac Banking Corporation has 9 branches, 2 sub-branches and 18 agencies; the Bank of New Zealand has 8 branches, and 18 agencies; the Australia and New Zealand Bank has 9 branches and 7 agencies and the Bank of Baroda has 8 branches and 3 agencies in Fiji.

ENERGY AND NATURAL RESOURCES

Electricity. Production (1986) 220m. kwh. Supply 240 volts; 50 Hz.

Agriculture. Some 600,000 acres of land are in agricultural use. Sugar-cane is the principal cash crop (production, 1990, 3·9m. tonnes); one quarter of the population depend on it directly for their livelihood. Copra, Fiji's second major cash crop (output, 1990, 170,000 tonnes), provides coconut oil and other products for export. Ginger is the third major export crop replacing bananas which has declined through disease and hurricane. Rice production was 32,000 tonnes in 1990. Tobacco and cocoa are also cultivated. There is a small, but fast developing, livestock industry.

Livestock (1990, in 1,000): Cattle, 160; horses, 43; goats, 75; pigs, 12; poultry, 3,000.

Forestry. In 1987 there were 1·2m. ha of forests and woodland; 65% of the land area. Fiji supplies the bulk of its own timber requirements. A comprehensive pine scheme has been implemented.

Fisheries. Catch (1985) 15,900 tonnes. Exports (1986) F$20m.

INDUSTRY. Major industries include 4 large sugar-mills, the goldmines (2,647 kg in 1987) and 2 mills which process copra into coconut oil and coconut meal. There is a great variety of light industries.

Trade Unions. In 1987 there were 46 trade unions operating with about 45,000 members.

FOREIGN ECONOMIC RELATIONS

Commerce. Exports in 1989, US$386m. (including re-exports). Imports, US$633m. Chief exports, 1989: Sugar, 36%, gold, 13%, clothing, 9% and canned fish, 7%.

Total trade between Fiji and UK (British Department of Trade returns, in £1,000 sterling):

	1987	1988	1989	1990	1991
Imports to UK	53,062	65,273	69,558	61,863	81,540
Exports and re-exports from UK	7,381	6,358	10,221	8,168	6,258

Tourism. In 1988, there were 208,155 visitors. Earnings (1988) $F180·6m. There were some 0·25m. visitors in 1989.

COMMUNICATIONS

Roads. Total road mileage is 2,996, of which 376 are sealed (paved), 2,534 are gravelled and 86 are unimproved. In 1987, there were 70,206 vehicles including 29,262 private cars, 23,029 goods vehicles, 1,289 buses, 4,499 tractors, 2,236 taxis and 2,882 rental and hire cars and others.

Railway. Fiji Sugar Cane Corporation runs 600 mm gauge railways at four of its mills on Viti Levu and Vanua Levu, totalling 595 km.

Civil Aviation. Fiji provides an essential staging point for long-haul trunk-route aircraft operating between North America, Australia and New Zealand. Under the South Pacific Air Transport Council, which comprises the UK, Australia, New Zealand and Fiji, the international airport at Nadi has been developed and administered. Eighteen other airports are in use for domestic services. In 1985, 257,646 passengers arrived at airports.

Shipping. The 3 ports of entry are Suva, Lautoka and Leuuka. In 1985, 1,313 vessels called at Suva, 780 at Lautoka and 1,004 at Leuuka. Local shipping provides services to scattered outer islands of the group.

Telecommunications. There were (1988) 50 post offices and 185 postal agencies. Overseas telephone and telegram services are available through the Commonwealth cable to most countries except those in the South Pacific, which are served by direct radio circuits. The automatic telex network operates through New Zealand into the international telex system. There were 60,017 telephones in 1987. The Fiji Broadcasting Commission is an independent statutory body, half commercial and half cultural. There is another commercial network. There were 0·45m. radio sets in 1991. In 1983 there were 400,000 radio receivers.

Newspapers. In 1988 there were 2 daily newspapers (circulation 40,000).

JUSTICE, RELIGION, EDUCATION AND WELFARE

Justice. An independent Judiciary is guaranteed under the Constitution of Fiji. The Constitution allows for a High Court of Fiji which has unlimited original jurisdiction to hear and determine any civil or criminal proceedings under any law.

The High Court also has jurisdiction to hear and determine constitutional and electoral questions including the membership of members of the House of Representatives.

The Chief Justice of Fiji is appointed by the President acting after consultation with the Prime Minister.

The Fiji Court of Appeal of which the Chief Justice is *ex officio* President is formed by three specially appointed Justices of Appeal. The Justices of Appeal are appointed by the President acting after consultation with the Judicial and Legal Services Commission. Generally any person convicted of any offence has a right of appeal from the High Court to the Fiji Court of Appeal. The final appellant court is the Supreme Court. Most matters coming before the Superior Courts originate in Magistrates' Courts.

Police. The Royal Fiji Police Force had (1987) a total strength of 1,561.

Religion. The 1986 census showed: Christians, 378,452; Hindus, 273,088; Sikhs, 4,674; Moslems, 56,001; Confucians, 82.

Education (1987). School attendance is not compulsory in Fiji. There were 815 schools scattered over 56 islands, staffed by 7,082 teachers, of whom about 99·3% were trained. There were also 236 pre-schools. The 674 primary and 141 secondary schools had 180,514 pupils. The technical and vocational schools had 4,039 students and the teachers' college 205. There were 3 teacher-training colleges, 1 medical and 2 agricultural schools.

The University of the South Pacific (USP) opened in Feb. 1968 at Laucala Bay in Suva. In 1987 there were about 2,344 students enrolled in courses on campus and about 4,085 enrolments in extension services. The University has an operating budget of $F12·13m. a year provided by the 11 countries it serves.

Total government expenditure on education in 1987 (including USP) was $F76,184,852.

Health. In 1987 there were 25 hospitals with 1,721 beds, 271 doctors, 48 dentists and 1,543 nurses.

DIPLOMATIC REPRESENTATIVES

Of Fiji in Great Britain (34 Hyde Park Gate, London, SW7 5DN)
Ambassador: Brig.-Gen. Ratu Epeli Nailatikau, LVO, OBE.

Of Great Britain in Fiji (47 Gladstone Rd., Suva)
Ambassador: A. B. Peter Smart, CMG.

Of Fiji in the USA (2233 Wisconsin Ave., NW, Washington, D.C., 20007)
Chargé d'affaires: Ratu Finau Mara.

Of the USA in Fiji (31 Loftus St., Suva)
Ambassador: Evelyn I. H. Teegen.

Of Fiji to the United Nations
Ambassador: Ratu Manasa Seniloli.

Further Reading

Statistical Information: A Bureau of Statistics was set up in 1950 (Government Buildings, Suva).
Trade Report. Annual (from 1887 [covering 1883–86]). Bureau of Statistics, Suva.
Journal of the Fiji Legislative Council. Annual
Fiji Today. Suva, Annual
Fiji Facts and Figures. Suva, 1986
Report of Commission of Inquiry Into Natural Resources and Population Trends in Fiji. Suva, Government Press, 1960
Ali, A., *Plantations to Politics, studies on Fiji Indians.* Suva, 1980
Bain, K., *Fiji at the Crossroads.* London, 1989
Lal, V., *Fiji: Coups in Paradise.* London, 1991
Ravuvu, A., *The Façade of Democracy: Fijian Struggles for Political Control.* Suva, 1991
Scarr, D., *Fiji, A Short History.* Sydney, 1984
Wright, R., *On Fiji Islands.* London, 1987

FINLAND

Suomen Tasavalta— Republiken Finland

Capital: Helsinki
Population: 4·97m. (1989)
GNP per capita: US$23,196 (1989)

HISTORY. Since the Middle Ages Finland was a part of the realm of Sweden. In the 18th century parts of south-eastern Finland were conquered by Russia, and the rest of the country was ceded to Russia by the peace treaty of Hamina in 1809. Finland became an autonomous grand-duchy which retained its previous laws and institutions under its Grand Duke, the Emperor of Russia. After the Russian revolution Finland declared itself independent on 6 Dec. 1917. The Civil War began in Jan. 1918 between the 'whites' and 'reds', the latter being supported by Russian bolshevik troops. The defeat of the red guards in May 1918 consequently meant freeing the country from Russian troops. A peace treaty with Soviet Russia was signed in 1920.

On 30 Nov. 1939 Soviet troops invaded Finland, after Finland had rejected territorial concessions demanded by the USSR. These, however, had to be made in the peace treaty of 12 March 1940, amounting to 32,806 sq. km and including the Carelian Isthmus, Viipuri and the shores of Lake Ladoga.

When the German attack on the USSR was launched in June 1941 Finland again became involved in the war against the USSR. On 19 Sept. 1944 an armistice was signed in Moscow. Finland agreed to cede to Russia the Petsamo area in addition to cessions made in 1940 (total 42,934 sq. km) and to lease to Russia for 50 years the Porkkala headland to be used as a military base. Further, Finland undertook to pay 300m. gold dollars in reparations within 6 years (later extended to 8 years). The peace treaty was signed in Paris on 10 Feb. 1947. The payment of reparations was completed on 19 Sept. 1952. The military base of Porkkala was returned to Finland on 26 Jan. 1956.

AREA AND POPULATION. Finland is bounded north-west and north by Norway, east by the USSR, south by the Baltic Sea and west by the Gulf of Bothnia and Sweden. The area and the population of Finland on 31 Dec. 1990 (Swedish names in brackets):

Province	Area (sq. km) [1]	Population [2]	Population per sq. km [2]
Uusimaa (Nyland)	9,898	1,248,041	126·1
Turku-Pori (Åbo-Björneborg)	22,839	728,157	31·9
Ahvenanmaa (Åland)	1,527	24,604	16·1
Häme (Tavastehus)	16,341	681,588	41·7
Kymi (Kymmene)	10,783	335,159	31·1
Mikkeli (St Michel)	16,342	208,223	12·7
Pohjois-Karjala (Norra Karelen)	17,782	176,836	9·9
Kuopio	16,509	256,781	15·6
Keski-Suomi (Mellersta Finland)	16,230	252,825	15·6
Vaasa (Vasa)	26,416	445,685	16·9
Oulu (Uleåborg)	56,868	439,905	7·7
Lappi (Lappland)	93,057	200,674	2·2
Total	304,623	4,998,478	16·4

[1] Excluding inland water area which totals 33,522 sq. km.   [2] Resident population.

The growth of the population, which was 421,500 in 1750, has been:

End of year	Urban	Rural	Total	Percentage urban
1800	46,600	786,100	832,700	5·6
1900	333,300	2,322,600	2,655,900	12·5
1950	1,302,400	2,727,400	4,029,800	32·3
1960	1,707,000	2,739,200	4,446,200	38·4
1970	2,340,300	2,258,000	4,598,300	50·9
1980	2,865,100	1,922,700	4,787,800	59·8
1990	3,079,800	1,918,700	4,998,500	61·6

The population on 31 Dec. 1990 by language primarily spoken: Finnish, 4,675,223; Swedish, 296,738; other languages, 26,517; Lappish, 1,734.

The principal towns with resident census population, 31 Dec. 1990, are (Swedish names in brackets):

Helsinki (Helsingfors)—capital	492,400	Imatra	33,566
Espoo	172,629	Rovaniemi	33,500
Tampere (Tammerfors)	172,560	Mikkeli (St Michel)	31,876
Turku (Åbo)	159,180	Kouvola	31,740
Vantaa (Vanda)	154,933	Järvenpää	31,525
Oulu (Uleåborg)	101,379	Rauma (Raumo)	29,755
Lahti	93,151	Savonlinna (Nyslott)	28,559
Kuopio	80,613	Seinäjoki	27,765
Pori (Björneborg)	76,357	Kerava	27,597
Jyväskylä	66,526	Nokia	26,063
Kotka	56,634	Kemi	25,374
Lappeenranta (Villmanstrand)	54,941	Riihimäki	25,000
Vaasa (Vasa)	53,429	Varkaus	24,576
Joensuu	47,554	Iisalmi	23,979
Hämeenlinna (Tavastehus)	43,417	Tornio	22,879
Hyvinkää (Hyvinge)	40,194	Valkeakoski	21,660
Kajaani	36,428	Kuusankoski	21,788
Kokkola (Karleby)	34,635		

Vital statistics in calendar years:

	Living births	Of which illegitimate	Still-born	Marriages	Deaths (exclusive of still-born)	Emigration
1982	66,106	9,007	263	30,459	43,408	7,403
1983	66,076	9,386	268	29,474	45,388	6,822
1984	65,076	9,825	260	28,550	45,098	7,467
1985	62,796	10,292	241	25,751	48,198	7,739
1986	60,632	10,931	193	25,820	47,135	8,269
1987	59,827	13,046	305	26,259	47,949	8,475
1988	63,313	...	332	25,993	49,063	8,557
1989	63,348	...	284	24,569	49,110	7,374
1990	65,639	...	...	24,150	50,125	7,405

In 1990 the rate per 1,000 was: Births, 12·8 (1988); marriages, 4.9; deaths, 9·9 (1988), and infantile deaths (per 1,000 live births, 1988), 6·1.

Population Census 1985. 5 vols. Helsinki, 1988
Population. Annual. Helsinki

CLIMATE. The climate is severe in winter, which lasts about 6 months, but mean temperatures in south and south-west are less harsh, 21°F (−6°C). In the north, mean temperatures may fall to 8·5°F (−13°C). Snow covers the ground for three months in the south and for over six months in the far north. Summers are short but quite warm, with occasional very hot days. Precipitation is light throughout the country, with one third falling as snow, the remainder mainly as convectional rain in summer and autumn. Helsinki (Helsingfors). Jan. 21°F (−6°C), July 62°F (16·5°C). Annual rainfall 24·7″ (618 mm).

CONSTITUTION AND GOVERNMENT. Finland is a republic according to the Constitution of 17 July 1919.

Parliament consists of one chamber of 200 members chosen by direct and proportional election in which all Finnish citizens (men or women) who are 18 years have the vote. The country is divided into 15 electoral districts with a representation proportional to their population. Every citizen over the age of 18 is eligible for Parliament, which is elected for 4 years, but can be dissolved sooner by the President.

The President is elected for 6 years by direct popular vote. In case no candidate wins an absolute majority, a second round is held between the 2 most successful candidates.

President of Finland: Dr Mauno Koivisto (elected 1982, re-elected 1988).

At the 19 March 1991 elections for the 200-member parliament, the electorate was 3·8m.; turn-out was 72%; 17 parties contested. The Centre Party (Cen) won 55 seats with 24·8% of votes cast (40 seats in 1987); Social Democratic Party, 48 with 22·1% (56); National Coalition Party (NCP; Conservative), 10 with 19·3% (53); Left Wing Alliance, 19 with 10·1% (20); Swedish Party (SPP), 12 (including 1 for coalition of Åland) with 5·5% (13); Greens, 10 with 6·8% (4); Finnish Christian League (FCL), 8 with 3·1% (5); Rural Party, 7 with 4·8% (9); Liberal Party 1.

The Council of State (Cabinet) was composed as follows in Feb. 1992:

Prime Minister: Esko Aho (b. 1954; Cen).

Foreign Affairs: Paavo Väyrynen (Cen), *Foreign Trade:* Pertti Salolainen (NCP), *Justice:* Hannele Pokka (Cen), *Interior:* Mauri Pekkarinen (Cen), *Defence:* Elisabeth Rehn (SPP), *Finance:* Iiro Viinanen (NCP), *Education:* Riitta Uosukainen (NCP), *Agriculture and Forestry:* Martti Pura (Cen), *Transport and Communication:* Ole Norrback (SPP), *Trade and Industry:* Kauko Juhantalo (Cen), *Social Affairs and Health:* Eeva Kuuskoski (Cen), *Labour:* Ilkka Kanerva (NCP), *Culture:* Tytti Isohookana-Asunmaa (Cen), *Environment:* Sirpa Pietikäinen (NCP), *Housing:* Pirjo Rusanen (NCP), *Development and Cooperation:* Toimi Kankaanniemi (FCL).

National flag: White with a blue Scandinavian cross.

National anthem: Maamme; Swedish: Vårt land ('Our Land'; words by J. L. Runeberg, 1843; tune by F. Pacius, 1848).

Finnish and Swedish are the official languages.

Local Government. For administrative purposes Finland is divided into 12 provinces (*lääni,* Sw.: *län*). The administration of each province is entrusted to a governor (*maaherra,* Sw.: *landshövding*) appointed by the President. He directs the activities of the provincial office (*lääninhallitus,* Sw.: *länsstyrelse*) and of local sheriffs (*nimismies,* Sw.: *länsman*). In 1989 the number of sheriff districts was 224.

The unit of local government is the commune. Main fields of communal activities are local planning, roads and harbours, sanitary services, education, health services and social aid. The communes raise taxes independent from state taxation. Two different kinds of communes are distinguished: Urban communes (*kaupunki,* Sw.: *stad*) and rural communes. In 1991 there were altogether 460 communes of which 94 were urban and 366 rural. In all communes communal councils are elected for terms of 4 years; all inhabitants (men and women) of the commune who have reached their 18th year are entitled to vote and eligible. The executive power is in each commune vested in a board which consists of members elected by the council and one or a few chief officials of the commune. Several communes often form an association for the administration of some common institution, *e.g.,* a hospital or a vocational school.

The autonomous county *(landskap)* of Åland has a county council *(lagting)* of one chamber, elected according to rule corresponding to those for parliamentary elections. In addition to its provincial governor it has a county board with executive power in matters within the field of the autonomy of the county.

Constitution Act and Parliament Act of Finland. Helsinki, 1978

DEFENCE. The period of military training is 240, 285 or 330 days and refresher training obligation 40 to 100 days between conscript service and age 50 (officers and NCOs age 60). Total strength of trained and equipped reserves is about 700,000.

Army. The country is divided into 7 military areas. The Army consisted in 1991 of 1 armoured brigade, 8 infantry brigades, 4 independent infantry battalions, 1 artillery regiment, 2 coastal artillery regiments, 3 independent coastal artillery battalions, 4 anti-aircraft regiments, and 2 engineering battalions, making a total strength, in 1992, of 27,800 (22,300 conscripts).

Navy. The Navy is divided into 4 functional squadrons. About 50% of the combatant units are kept manned, with the others in short-notice reserve and re-activated on a regular basis. The inventory comprises 2 anti-submarine corvettes, 10 missile craft (of which 6 are indigenous Helsinki class), 11 inshore patrol craft, 2 minelayers, and 6 inshore minesweepers. There are 14 landing craft of various types and some 30 minor auxiliaries and tenders.

Naval bases exist at Upinniemi (near Helsinki) and Turku. Total personnel strength (1991) was 2,000 of whom 1,300 are conscripts, and there are about 12,000 reserves.

The maritime section of the frontier guard operates 15 patrol craft and some 30 boats.

The National Board of Navigation has 9 civil-manned icebreakers.

Air Force. The Air Force has 3 fighter squadrons, 1 transport squadron, an air academy, a technical school, a signal school and a depot. The fighter squadrons have 70 MiG-21bis and Saab J35 Draken S and F aircraft, including two-seat trainer models. Other equipment includes 28 Valmet Vinka piston-engined primary trainers of Finnish design and 46 Hawk MK.51 advanced jet trainers, 3 Fokker F.27 Friendship transport aircraft, 3 Gates Learjet 35 transport aircraft, Piper Arrow liaison aircraft, Piper Chieftain utility transports, and 7 Mi-8 and 2 Hughes 500 Ds helicopters. Personnel (1992), 1,800 (600 conscripts) officers and men.

INTERNATIONAL RELATIONS. Finland's role in international relations has been one of neutrality.

Membership. Finland is a member of UN, the Nordic Council, OECD, EFTA and the Council of Europe, and applied for EC membership in March 1992.

Treaties. A Treaty of friendship, co-operation and mutual assistance between Finland and the USSR was concluded in Moscow on 6 April 1948 for 10 years, extended on 19 Sept. 1955 to cover a period of 20 years, extended on 19 July 1970 for a further period of 20 years and extended again on 6 June 1983 for a further period of 20 years.

ECONOMY

Budget. Actual revenue and expenditure for the calendar years 1985–90, the ordinary budget for 1991 and the proposed budget for 1992 in 1m. marks:

	1985	1986	1987	1988	1989	1990	1991	1992
Revenue	96,408	96,769	108,650	119,551	134,828	138,739	158,522	170,175
Expenditure	95,803	95,172	106,988	117,275	129,459	140,893	158,517	170,173

Of the total revenue, 1990, 33% derived from sales tax, 30% from income and property tax, 12% from excise duties, 11% from other taxes and similar revenue, 2% from loans (net) and 11% from miscellaneous sources. Of the total expenditure, 1990: 19% went to education and culture, 7% to transport, 3% to communities and housing policy, 4% to promotion of industry, 17% to other expenditures; 1989 18% went to social security, 8% to agriculture and forestry, 10% to general administration, public order and safety and 5% to defence.

At the end of Dec. 1990 the foreign loans totalled 24,793m. marks. The internal loans amounted to 32,245m. marks. The cash surplus was 1,880m. marks. The total public debt was 57,038m. marks.

Currency. The unit of currency is the *markka* (FIM) or mark of 100 *pennis*. There are coins of 1, 5, 10, 20 and 50 pennis and 1 and 5 marks, and notes of 10, 50, 100, 500 and 1,000 marks. Exchange rate in March 1992: 7·87 marks = £1; 4·48 marks = US$1. The markka was pegged to the Ecu in June 1991 with a 3% margin of fluctuation. It was devalued by 12·3% in Nov. 1991.

Banking and Finance. The central bank is the Bank of Finland (founded in 1811), owned by the State and under the guarantee and supervision of Parliament. Its *Governor* is Rolf Kullberg. It is the only bank of issue, and the limit of its right to issue notes is fixed equal to the value of its assets of gold and foreign holdings plus 500m. marks. Notes in circulation at the end of 1987 amounted to 9,117m. marks.

At the end of 1989 the deposits in banking institutions totalled 306,699m. marks and the loans granted by them 243,800m. marks. The most important groups of banking institutions in 1990 were:

	Number of institutions	Number of offices	Deposits (1m. marks)	Loans (1m. marks)
Commercial banks	10	1,020	110,063	134,339
Savings banks	178	1,307	71,225	79,993
Co-operative banks	361	1,198	61,166	69,871

The 5 largest banks are Kansallis-Osake-Pannki, Union Bank of Finland, Skopbank, Okobank and the state-owned Postipannki.

There is a stock exchange in Helsinki.

Weights and Measures. The metric system is legal.

ENERGY AND NATURAL RESOURCES

Electricity. Electricity production was (in 1m. kwh.) 53,066 in 1988; 53,391 in 1989, of which 24·3% was hydro-electric; 53,435 in 1990 (preliminary). Supply 220 volts; 50 Hz. In 1991 there were 4 nuclear power stations.

Minerals. Notable of the mines are Pyhäsalmi and Vihanti (zinc), Enonkoski (nickel) and Kemi (chromium). In 1990 (preliminary) the metal content (in tonnes) of the output of copper concentrates was 15,985, of zinc concentrates 51,705, of nickel concentrates 9,986 and of lead concentrates 1,659.

Agriculture. The cultivated area covers only 9% of the land and of the economically active population 9% were employed in agriculture and forestry in 1989. The arable area was divided in 1990 into 199,385 farms, and the distribution of this area by the size of the farms was: Less than 5 ha cultivated, 69,015 farms; 5–20 ha, 90,451 farms; 20–50 ha, 35,108 farms; 50–100 ha, 4,311 farms; over 100 ha, 500 farms.

The principal crops (area in 1,000 ha, yield in tonnes) were in 1990:

Crop	Area	Yield	Crop	Area	Yield
Rye	81	244,200	Oats	453	1,661,800
Barley	486	1,729,200	Potatoes	41	991,400
Wheat	180	627,200	Hay	286	1,206,500

The total area under cultivation in 1991 was 2,049,800 ha, including (in 1,000 ha): Rye, 10; barley, 540; wheat, 118; oats, 343; potatoes, 36; hay, 232. Production of dairy butter in 1989 was 63,900 tonnes, and of cheese, 90,500 tonnes.

Livestock (1991): Horses, 15,600 (1990); cattle, 1,309,900; pigs, 1,344,300; poultry, 5,187,900; reindeer (1989), 407,000.

Forestry. The total forest land amounts to 30–31m. ha. The productive forest land covers 19·73m. ha.

In 1989 there were exported: Round timber, 584m. cu. metres; sawn wood, 4,472m. cu. metres; plywood and veneers, 537m. cu. metres.

INDUSTRY. The following data cover establishments with a total personnel of 5 or more in 1990 [1]:

Industry	Establishments [2]	Personnel [3]	Value of production Gross (1m. marks)	Value added (1m. marks)
Mining and quarrying	150	4,043	2,891	1,532
Metal ore mining	7	1,196	968	501
Other mining	143	2,845	1,913	1,032
Manufacturing	6,225	430,890	282,781	102,309
Manufacture of food, beverages and tobacco	858	52,960	50,205	12,840
Textile, wearing apparel and leather industries	635	30,793	8,277	3,583
Manufacture of textiles	229	10,908	3,550	1,508
Manufacture of wearing apparel, except footwear	296	15,389	3,450	1,573
Manufacture of wood and wood products, incl. furniture	940	40,905	21,263	7,995

[2] Preliminary. [2] 1989. [3] Working proprietors, salaried employees and wage earners.

Industry	Establish- ments [2]	Person- nel [3]	Value of production	
			Gross (1m. marks)	Value added (1m. marks)
Manufacture of paper and paper prod., printing, publishing	833	82,267	62,360	22,222
Manufacture of paper and paper products	150	44,234	44,417	14,247
Printing, publishing, etc.	683	38,159	18,174	8,060
Manufacture of chemicals and chemical, petroleum, coal, rubber and plastic products	441	37,391	35,811	12,598
Manufacture of industrial chemicals	154	13,617	13,463	4,927
Manufacture of other chemical products	90	10,259	5,951	2,672
Petroleum refineries	4	3,115	11,092	2,576
Manufacture of non-metallic mineral products	416	19,966	10,079	4,818
Basic metal industries	72	16,921	19,721	4,686
Iron and steel basic industries	48	12,564	12,278	3,272
Non-ferrous metal basic industries	24	4,355	7,444	1,414
Manufacture of fabricated metal products, machinery, etc.	1,932	145,456	74,104	32,970
Manufacture of fabricated metal products, excl. machinery	744	32,204	14,822	6,755
Manufacture of machinery, except electrical	631	51,400	27,499	12,655
Manufacture of electrical machinery, apparatus, etc.	221	28,508	14,491	6,867
Manufacture of transport equipment	243	27,791	14,812	5,393
Other manufacturing industries	98	3,680	1,286	689
Electricity, gas and water	520	26,524	31,975	11,342
All industry	6,895	461,457	317,647	115,183

[2] 1989.   [3] Working proprietors, salaried employees and wage earners.

GDP (at market prices) *per capita* (1990) 105,251 marks.

Trade Unions. Under a 2-year agreement between trade unions and employers wages were frozen in 1992 but will rise in 1993 if inflation exceeds 5·4%.

FOREIGN ECONOMIC RELATIONS

Commerce. Imports and exports for calendar years, in 1m. marks:

	1986	1987	1988	1989	1990
Imports	77,602	86,696	88,229	105,519	105,519
Exports	82,579	87,564	90,854	99,782	101,327

The trade with some principal import and export countries was (in 1,000 marks):

Country	Imports		Exports	
	1989	1990	1989	1990
Australia	378,112	281,991	1,206,870	922,253
Austria	1,294,584	1,401,060	1,174,735	1,116,769
Belgium–Luxembourg	2,931,881	2,838,557	1,946,555	2,247,155
Brazil	632,235	607,608	368,140	333,982
Canada	919,228	809,911	1,359,087	1,123,601
China	688,372	741,118	337,582	589,231
Colombia	329,334	307,977	78,156	63,638
Czechoslovakia	515,067	543,326	353,608	313,389
Denmark	3,289,709	3,368,817	3,257,060	5,538,295
France	4,417,460	4,426,914	5,453,347	6,236,527
German Dem. Rep.	530,372	389,388	534,176	435,711
Germany (Fed. Rep.)	18,233,665	17,508,131	10,784,550	12,567,559
Greece	299,580	375,591	639,661	590,939
Hungary	422,531	394,242	314,086	239,966
Iran	10,619	220,789	238,564	463,465
Iraq	93	12	90,921	120,006
Ireland	503,401	522,109	542,006	578,612
Israel	162,691	183,635	323,581	297,550
Italy	4,900,237	4,765,908	2,989,072	3,227,341

| | Imports | | Exports | |
Country	1989	1990	1989	1990
Japan	7,695,320	6,628,360	2,033,231	1,445,155
Netherlands	3,416,063	3,276,388	3,961,202	4,347,329
Norway	2,456,563	3,511,919	2,919,976	3,066,506
Poland	1,065,181	1,018,711	306,014	367,749
Portugal	884,052	1,199,526	506,483	809,993
Saudi Arabia	377,995	322,513	285,832	322,232
Spain	1,129,257	1,159,522	1,830,757	2,210,204
Sweden	14,314,190	13,407,323	14,313,992	14,456,019
Switzerland	1,829,138	1,804,263	1,680,398	1,806,034
USSR	12,152,159	10,201,995	14,495,880	12,883,723
UK	6,897,931	7,822,537	11,957,969	10,724,091
USA	6,669,113	6,973,936	6,387,682	5,898,160

Principal imports 1990 (in 1m. marks): Machinery, apparatus and appliances, 39,802; mineral fuels, lubricants, etc., 12,055; chemicals, 11,081; food and live animals, 4,277; road vehicles, 9,980; crude materials, inedible, except fuels, 5,407; textile yarn, fabrics, etc., 1,371; iron and steel, 3,642.

Principal exports in 1990 (in 1m. marks): Paper and paper-board, 27,029; machinery and transport equipment, 31,264; wood shaped or simply worked, 4,712; wood pulp, 3,889; ships, 811; clothing, 1,884; veneers, plywood, etc., and other wood manufactures, 2,554; food and live animals, 2,196; road vehicles, 3,285.

Timber exports in 1989 (in 1m. cu. metres): Round timber, 584; sawn wood, 4,472; plywood and veneers, 537.

Total trade between Finland and UK (British Department of Trade returns, in £1,000 sterling):

	1987	1988	1989	1990	1991
Imports to UK	1,539,011	1,813,549	1,893,163	1,775,766	1,522,337
Exports and re-exports from UK	797,236	824,951	925,784	1,041,739	847,671

Tourism. In 1989 the total revenue from tourism was 4,484m. marks and the total expenditure 8,958m. marks.

COMMUNICATIONS

Roads. In Jan. 1991 there were 77,671 km of public roads, of which 46,318 km were paved. At the end of 1990 there were 2,217,729 registered cars, 54,269 lorries, 207,226 vans and pick-ups, 9,287 buses and coaches and 20,621 special automobiles.

Railways. On 31 Dec. 1990 the total length of the line operated was 5,846 km (1,663 km electrified), of which all was owned by the State. The gauge is 1,524 mm. In 1990 46m. passengers and 34·6m. tonnes of freight were carried. The total revenue in 1989 was 3,361m. marks and the total expenditure 4,386m. marks. There is a metro (16 km) and tram/light rail network (68 km) in Helsinki.

Civil Aviation. The scheduled traffic of Finnish airlines covered 61m. km in 1990. The number of passengers was 4·5m. and the number of passenger-km 4,859,000. The air transport of freight and mail amounted to 143m. tonne-km.

Shipping. The total registered mercantile marine on 31 Dec. 1990 was 451 vessels of 1,094,000 gross tons. In 1990 the total number of vessels arriving in Finland from abroad was 19,905 and the goods discharged amounted to 34·8m. tonnes. The goods loaded for export from Finland ports amounted to 24·0m. tonnes.

The lakes, rivers and canals are navigable for about 6,160 km. Timber floating is important, and there are about 9,460 km of floatable inland waterways. In 1990 bundle floating was about 3·7m. tonnes and free floating 1m. tonnes.

On 27 Aug. 1963 the USSR leased to Finland the Russian part of the canal connecting Lake Saimaa with the Gulf of Finland. After extensive rebuilding the canal was opened for traffic in 1968. The Saimaa Canal and deepwater channels on Lake Saimaa (770 km) can be used by vessels with dimensions not larger than as follows: Length 82 metres, width 11·8 metres, draught 4·2 metres and height of mast 24·5 metres.

Telecommunications. In 1990 there were 2,251 post offices and 255 telecommunications offices. The number of telephone subscriber lines (1990), 2·67m. The net sales of Post Finland in 1990 were 4,484m. marks and of Telecom Finland, 4,983m.marks.

On 31 Dec. 1990 the number of television licences was 1,893,514, of which licences for colour television, 1,775,227. *Oy Yleisradio AB* broadcasts 4 programmes (1 in Swedish), covering the whole country on long-, medium- and short-waves, and on FM. Four TV programmes (1 commercial) are broadcast.

Cinemas. In Dec. 1989 there were 344 cinema halls with a seating capacity of 67,000.

Newspapers. In 1990 the number of newspapers published more often than 3 times a week was 66, of which 9 were in Swedish.

JUSTICE, RELIGION, EDUCATION AND WELFARE

Justice. The lowest courts of justice are the municipal courts in towns and district courts in the country. Municipal courts are held by the burgomaster and at least 2 members of court, district court by judge and 5 jurors, the judge alone deciding, unless the jurors unanimously differ from him, when their decision prevails. From these courts an appeal lies to the courts of appeal *(Hovioikeus)* in Turku, Vaasa, Kuopio, Helsinki, Kouvola and Rovaniemi. The Supreme Court *(Korkein oikeus)* sits in Helsinki. Appeals from the decisions of administrative authorities are in the final instance decided by the Supreme Administrative Court *(Korkein hallintooikeus)*, also in Helsinki. Judges can be removed only by judicial sentence.

Two functionaries, the *Oikeuskansleri* or Chancellor of Justice, and the *Oikeusasiamies* (ombudsman), or Solicitor-General, exercise control over the administration of justice. The former acts also as counsel and public prosecutor for the Government; while the latter, who is appointed by the Parliament, exerts a general control over all courts of law and public administration.

At the end of 1990 the prison population numbered 3,322 men and 105 women; the preliminary number of convictions in 1987 was 365,312, of which 340,962 were for minor offences with maximum penalty of fines and 24,220 with penalty of imprisonment. 10,255 of the prison sentences were unconditional.

Religion. Liberty of conscience is guaranteed to members of all religions. National churches are the Lutheran National Church and the Greek Orthodox Church of Finland. The Lutheran Church is divided into 8 bishoprics (Turku being the archiepiscopal see), 79 provostships and 598 parishes. The Greek Orthodox Church is divided into 3 bishoprics (Kuopio being the archiepiscopal see) and 27 parishes, in addition to which there are a monastery and a convent.

Percentage of the total population at the end of 1990: Lutherans, 87·8; Greek Orthodox, 1·1; others, 0·9; not members of any religion, 10·2.

Education (1989–90). *Primary and Secondary Education:*

	Number of institutions	Teachers	Students
First-level Education (Lower sections of the comprehensive schools, grades I–VI)			391,599 [2]
Second-level Education General education (Upper sections of the comprehensive schools, grades VII–IX, and senior secondary schools)	5,333 [2]	48,343 [1]	305,730 [2]
Vocational education	546 [2]	18,082 [1]	113,650 [2]

[1] 1989   [2] 1990

Higher Education. Education at the third level (including universities and third level education at vocational and profession education institutions) was provided for 165,714 students. Education at universities was provided at 20 institutions with 7,788 teachers and 112,921 students.

University Education. Universities and university-type institutions with the number
of teachers and students in 1990:

	Founded	Teachers	Students Total	Women
Universities				
Helsinki	1640	1,760	30,740	18,377
Turku (Swedish)	1919	332	5,056	2,945
Turku (Finnish)	1922	807	11,437	7,020
Jyväskylä	1958	552	8,333	5,358
Oulu	1958	843	9,844	4,726
Tampere	1966	605	11,740	7,294
Joensuu	1969	348	5,348	3,376
Kuopio	1972	299	3,409	2,220
Lapland	1979	109	1,805	1,030
Vaasa	1968	126	2,256	1,223
Universities of Technology				
Lappeenranta	1969	176	2,360	405
Helsinki	1849	610	11,236	2,100
Tampere	1972	296	5,145	809
College of Veterinary Medicine, Helsinki	1946	50	373	287
Schools of Economics and Business Administration				
Helsinki (Finnish)	1911	158	4,120	2,014
Helsinki (Swedish)	1927	105	1,889	815
Turku (Finnish)	1950	86	1,823	933
Universities of Art				
Sibelius Academy	1939	289	1,452	848
University of Industrial Arts	1949	176	1,192	753
Theatre Academy	1979	61	270	136

General adult education (at civic institutes, folk high schools and study centres)
had 844,000 students in 1987–88.

Health. In 1989 there were 9,919 physicians, 3,794 dentists and (1988) 66,606 hospital beds.

Social Security. The Social Insurance Institution administers general systems of old
age pensions (to all persons over 65 years of age and disabled younger persons) and
of health insurance. An additional system of compulsory old age pensions paid for
by the employers is in force and works through the Central Pension Security Institute. Systems for child welfare, care of vagrants, alcoholics and drug addicts and
other public aid are administered by the communes and supervised by the National
Social Board and the Ministry of Social Affairs and Health.

The total cost of social security amounted to 127,091m. marks in 1989. Out of
this 36,279m. (28·5%) was spent for health, 2,323m. (1·8%) for industrial
accidents, 6,480m. (5·1%) for unemployment, 49,173m. (38·7%) old age and
disability, 21,991m. (17·3%) for family allowances and child welfare, 1,479m.
(1·2%) for general welfare purposes, 2,871m. (2·3%) for war-disabled, etc.,
2,320m. (1·8%) as tax reductions for children. Out of the total expenditure 27% was
financed by the State, 17% by local authorities, 45% by employers, 8% by the
beneficiaries and 4% by users.

DIPLOMATIC REPRESENTATIVES

Of Finland in Great Britain (38 Chesham Pl., London, SW1X 8HW)
Ambassador: Leif Blomquist.

Of Great Britain in Finland (16–20 Uudenmaankatu, Helsinki 00120)
Ambassador: G. Neil Smith, CMG.

Of Finland in the USA (3216 New Mexico Ave., NW, Washington, D.C., 20016)
Ambassador: Jukka Valtasaari.

Of the USA in Finland (Itäinen Puistotie 14A, Helsinki 00140)
Ambassador: John Giffen Weinmann.

Of Finland to the United Nations
Ambassador: Wilhelm Breitenstein.

Further Reading

Statistical Information: The Central Statistical Office (Tilastokeskus, Swedish: Statistikcentralen; address: PO Box 504, SF-00101 Helsinki 10) was founded in 1865 to replace earlier official statistical services dating from 1749 (in united Sweden–Finland). Statistics on foreign trade, agriculture, forestry, navigation, health and social welfare are produced by other state authorities. Its publications include: *Statistical Yearbook of Finland* (from 1879) and *Bulletin of Statistics* (monthly, from 1924). A bibliography of all official statistics of Finland was published in Finnish, Swedish and English in *Statistical publications 1856–1979.* Helsinki, 1980.

Constitution Act and Parliament Act of Finland. Helsinki, 1984
Suomen valtiokalenteri–Finlands statskalender (State Calendar of Finland). Helsinki. Annual
Facts About Finland. Helsinki. Annual (Union Bank of Finland)
Facts about Finland. Helsinki, 1988
Finland in Figures. Helsinki, Annual
Finland in Maps. Helsinki, 1979
Finnish Press Laws. Helsinki, 1984
Making and Applying Law in Finland. Ministry of Justice, 1983
Statistical Yearbook of Finland. Helsinki, Annual
Yearbook of Finnish Foreign Policy. Helsinki, Annual
The Finnish Banking System. Helsinki, 1987
Finnish Industry. Helsinki, 1988
Finnish Local Government. Helsinki, 1983
Health Care in Finland. Helsinki, 1987
Arter, D., *Politics and Policy-Making in Finland.* Brighton, 1987
Hurme-Malin-Syväoja, *Finnish-English General Dictionary.* Helsinki, 1984
Hurme-Pesonen, *English–Finnish General Dictionary.* Helsinki, 1982
Jakobson, M. *Myth and Reality.* Helsinki, 1987
Jutikkala, E. and Pirinen, K., *A History of Finland.* 3rd ed. New York, 1979
Kekkonen, U., *President's View.* London, 1982
Kirby, D. G., *Finland in the Twentieth Century.* 2nd ed. London, 1984
Klinge, M., *A Brief History of Finland.* Helsinki, 1987
Paasivirta, J., *Finland and Europe. The Period of Autonomy and the International Crises 1808–1914.* London, 1981
Polvinen, T., *Between East and West – Finland in International Politics 1944–1947.* Minnesota Univ. Press, 1986
Puntila, L. A., *The Political History of Finland, 1809–1966.* Helsinki, 1974
Screen, J. E. O., *Finland.* [Bibliography] Oxford and Santa Barbara, 1981
Singleton, F., *The Economy of Finland in the Twentieth Century.* Univ. of Bradford Press, 1987
University of Turku, *Political Parties in Finland.* Turku, 1987

FRANCE

République Française

Capital: Paris
Population: 56·61m. (1990)
GNP per capita: US$17,830 (1990)

HISTORY. The republic proclaimed on the fall of the Bourbon monarchy in 1792 lasted until the First Empire, under Napoleon I, was established in 1804. The Bourbon monarchy was restored in 1814 and (with an interval during 1815) lasted until the abdication of Louis Philippe in 1848. The Second Republic was established on 12 March 1848, the Second Empire (under Louis Napoleon) on 2 Dec. 1852. The Third Republic was established on 4 Sept. 1870 following the capture and imprisonment of Louis Napoleon in the Franco-Prussian war, and lasted until the German occupation of 1940. Power during the occupation was nominally exercised by the Vichy regime of Marshal Pétain. Following the liberation of 1944, the Fourth Republic was established on 24 Dec. 1946 but was dogged throughout by weak governments with unstable parliamentary support. It collapsed on 4 Oct. 1958 under the impetus of military revolt in Algeria, following which General de Gaulle assumed power. He subsequently inspired the constitution of the Fifth Republic, now in force.

AREA AND POPULATION. France is bounded in the north by the English Channel *(La Manche)*, north-east by Belgium and Luxembourg, east by Germany, Switzerland and Italy, south by the Mediterranean (with Monaco as a coastal enclave), south-west by Spain and Andorra, and west by the Atlantic Ocean The total area is 543,965 sq. km (210,033 sq. miles).

The population (present in actual boundaries) at successive censuses has been:

1801	27,349,003	1891	38,342,948	May 1954	42,777,174
1821	30,461,875	1901	38,961,945	Mar. 1962	46,519,997
1841	34,230,178	1911	39,604,992	Mar. 1968	49,778,540
1861	37,386,313	1921	39,209,518	Feb. 1975	52,655,802
1866	38,067,064	1931	41,834,923	Mar. 1982	54,334,871
1872	36,102,921	Mar. 1946	40,506,639	1990 [1]	56,614,500
1881	37,672,048				

[1] Provisional.

Controls on illegal immigration were tightened as from July 1991.
Vital statistics for calendar years:

	Marriages	Live births	Deaths
1985	269,300	768,431	552,500
1986	265,340	778,940	546,880
1987	265,177	767,828	527,466
1988	271,124	770,690	524,600

Live birth rate in 1989 was 13·6 per 1,000 inhabitants; death rate, 9·4; marriage rate, 5; divorce rate (1986), 2; infant mortality, 7·4 per 1,000 live births.

Abortions were legalized in 1975; there were 162,620 in 1990. Life expectation at birth (1989); men, 72·5; women, 80·7. Population growth rate (1989), 4·2 per 1,000. Average density (1990) 104 persons per sq. km.

The areas, populations and chief towns of the 22 Metropolitan regions were as follows:

Regions	Area (sq. km)	Census March 1982	Census 1990 [1]	Chief town
Alsace	8,280	1,566,048	1,624,400	Strasbourg
Aquitaine	41,308	2,656,544	2,795,800	Bordeaux
Auvergne	26,013	1,332,678	1,321,200	Clermont-Ferrand
Basse-Normandie	17,589	1,350,979	1,391,300	Caen
Bourgogne (Burgundy)	31,582	1,596,054	1,609,700	Dijon
Bretagne (Brittany)	27,208	2,707,886	2,795,600	Rennes
Centre	39,151	2,264,164	2,371,000	Orléans

Regions	Area (sq. km)	Census March 1982	Census 1990 [1]	Chief town
Champagne-Ardenne	25,606	1,345,935	1,347,800	Reims
Corse (Corsica)	8,680	240,178	249,700	Ajaccio
Franche-Comté	16,202	1,084,049	1,097,300	Besançon
Haute-Normandie	12,317	1,655,362	1,737,200	Rouen
Ile-de-France	12,012	10,073,059	10,660,600	Paris
Languedoc-Roussillon	27,376	1,926,514	2,115,000	Montpellier
Limousin	16,942	737,153	722,900	Limoges
Lorraine	23,547	2,319,905	2,305,700	Nancy
Midi-Pyrénées	45,348	2,325,319	2,430,700	Toulouse
Nord-Pas-de-Calais	12,414	3,932,939	3,965,100	Lille
Pays de la Loire	32,082	2,930,398	3,059,100	Nantes
Picardie	19,399	1,740,321	1,810,700	Amiens
Poitou-Charentes	25,810	1,568,230	1,595,100	Poitiers
Provence-Alpes-Côte d'Azur	31,400	3,965,209	4,257,900	Marseille
Rhône-Alpes	43,698	5,015,947	5,350,700	Lyon

[1] Provisional.

Populations of the principal conurbations and towns at Census 1990 (provisional):

	Conurbation	Town		Conurbation	Town
Paris	9,063,384 [1]	2,175,110	Avignon	181,136	89,440
Lyon	1,262,167 [2]	422,444	Limoges	170,165	136,407
Marseille	1,087,276	807,726	Amiens	155,580	136,358
Lille	950,265 [3]	178,301	Perpignan	138,735	108,049
Bordeaux	685,456	213,274	Nîmes	138,527	133,607
Toulouse	608,427	365,933	Bayonne	136,334	42,970[4]
Nantes	491,421	251,133	Pau	134,625	83,928
Nice	475,459	345,625	Thionville	132,386	41,448[4]
Toulon	437,553	170,167	Saint-Nazaire	131,565	66,087
Grenoble	400,141	153,973	Aix-en-Provence	130,888	126,854
Strasbourg	388,483	255,937	Troyes	122,763	60,755
Rouen	380,161	105,470	Besançon	122,623	119,194
Valenciennes	336,481	40,881[4]	Annecy	122,622	51,143
Cannes	335,647	69,363	Montbéliard	117,510	33,362[4]
Lens	323,174	38,307[4]	Hagondange-Briey	112,061	9,091[4]
Saint-Étienne	313,453	201,695	Valence	107,965	65,026
Nancy	310,718	102,410	Lorient	107,088	61,630
Tours	271,927	133,403	Poitiers	105,271	82,507
Béthune	259,679	26,105[4]	Maubeuge	102,772	36,156[4]
Clermont-Ferrand	254,416	140,167	Chambéry	102,548	55,603
Le Havre	253,627	197,219	Calais	101,768	75,836
Rennes	245,065	203,533	Angoulême	101,108	50,151
Orléans	243,153	107,965	La Rochelle	100,264	73,744
Montpellier	236,788	210,866	Forbach	97,847	27,231[4]
Dijon	226,025	151,636	Boulogne-sur-Mer	95,930	48,349[4]
Mulhouse	223,856	109,905	Bourges	92,720	78,773
Reims	206,362	185,164	Melun	92,425	36,218[4]
Angers	206,276	146,163	Cherbourg	92,045	30,112[4]
Brest	201,480	153,099	Creil	83,942	36,128[4]
Douai	199,562	44,515[4]	Saint-Brieuc	83,861	51,399[4]
Metz	193,117	123,920	Colmar	83,816	64,889
Dunkerque	192,852	71,071	Saint-Chamond	81,581	40,571[4]
Le Mans	189,107	148,465	Arras	79,607	45,364[4]
Mantes-la-Jolie	189,103	43,585[4]	Roanne	77,160	49,638[4]
Caen	188,799	115,624	Béziers	76,304	72,362

[1] Including towns of Boulogne-Billancourt (101,971), Montreuil (95,038), Argenteuil (94,162), Versailles (91,029), Saint-Denis (90,806), Nanterre (86,627) and Vitry-sur-Seine (82,820).
[2] Including towns of Villeurbanne (119,848) and Vénissieux (60,744).
[3] Including towns of Roubaix (98,179) and Tourcoing (94,425).
[4] Census 1982.

The official language is French. Regional languages are also spoken. In 1990 the Conseil Supérieur de la Langue Française (established 1989) recommended minor orthographic changes, to be introduced in schools in 1991.

CLIMATE. The north-west has a moderate maritime climate, with small temperature range and abundant rainfall, but inland, rainfall becomes more seasonal, with a summer maximum, and the annual range of temperature increases. Southern France has a Mediterranean climate, with mild moist winters and hot dry summers. Eastern France has a continental climate and a rainfall maximum in summer, with thunderstorms prevalent.

Paris. Jan. 37°F (3°C), July 64°F (18°C). Annual rainfall 22·9" (573 mm). Bordeaux. Jan. 41°F (5°C), July 68°F (20°C). Annual rainfall 31·4" (786 mm). Lyon. Jan. 37°F (3°C), July 68°F (20°C). Annual rainfall 31·8" (794 mm).

CONSTITUTION AND GOVERNMENT. The Constitution of the Fifth Republic, superseding that of 1946, came into force on 4 Oct. 1958. It consists of a preamble, dealing with the Rights of Man, and 92 articles.

France is a Republic, indivisible, secular, democratic and social; all citizens are equal before the law (Art. 2). National sovereignty resides with the people, who exercise it through their representatives and by referenda (Art. 3). Political parties carry out their activities freely, but must respect the principles of national sovereignty and democracy (Art. 4).

The *President* of the Republic sees that the Constitution is respected; he ensures the regular functioning of the public authorities, as well as the continuity of the state. He is the protector of national independence and territorial integrity (Art. 5). He is elected for 7 years by direct universal suffrage (Art. 6). He appoints a Prime Minister and, on the latter's advice, appoints and dismisses the other members of the Government (Art. 8). He presides over the Council of Ministers (Art. 9). He can dissolve the National Assembly, after consultation with the Prime Minister and the Presidents of the two Houses (Art. 12). He appoints to the civil and military offices of the state (Art. 13). In times of crisis, he may take such emergency powers as the circumstances demand; the National Assembly cannot be dissolved during such a period (Art. 16). The President's salary is 35,663 francs a month.

Previous Presidents of the Fifth Republic:

General Charles André Joseph de Gaulle, 8 Jan. 1959–28 April 1969 (resigned); Alain Poher (interim), 28 April 1969–20 June 1969; Georges Jean Raymond Pompidou, 20 June 1969–2 April 1974 (died); Alain Poher (interim), 2 April 1974–27 May 1974; Valéry Giscard d'Estaing, 27 May 1974–21 May 1981.

President of the Republic: François Mitterrand (elected 10 May 1981; took office 21 May 1981; re-elected 8 May 1988).

The government determines and conducts the policy of the nation (Art. 20). The Prime Minister directs the operation of the Government, is responsible for national defence and ensures the execution of laws (Art. 21). Members of the Government must not be members of Parliament (Art. 23).

Following a poor showing by the Socialist Party (PS) in local elections, Edith Cresson resigned as Prime Minister and a new government was formed in April 1992:

Prime Minister: Pierre Bérégovoy (PS).
Ministers of State:
National Education and Culture: Jack Lang (PS).
Foreign Affairs: Roland Dumas (PS).
Civil Service and Administrative Reform: Michel Delebarre (PS).

Ministers:
Justice, Keeper of the Seals: Michel Vauzelle (PS).
Interior and Public Security: Paul Quilès (PS).
Defence: Pierre Joxe (PS).
Economy and Finance: Michel Sapin.
Budget: Michel Charasse (PS).
Environment: Ségolène Royal.
Equipment, Transport and Housing: Jean-Louis Bianco (ind).

Industry and Foreign Trade: Dominique Strauss-Kahn (PS).
Labour, Employment and Vocational Training: Martine Aubry (UDF-PR).
Agriculture and Forestry: Louis Mermaz (PS).
Social Affairs and Integration: René Teulade (PS).
Health and Humanitarian Activities: Bernard Kouchner (ind).
Urban Affairs: Bernard Tapie (ind).
Overseas Departments and Territories: Louis Le Pensec (PS).
Research and Space: Hubert Curien (PS).
Post and Telecommunications: Emile Zuccarelli (MRG).
Youth and Sport: Frédérique Bredin (PS).

Ministers-Delegate:
Elisabeth Guigou (PS) *(European Affairs).*
Georges Kiejman (ind) *(Foreign Affairs).*
Marcel Debarge (PS) *(Foreign Co-operation and Development).*
Jean-Marie Rausch (France Unie) *(Trade and the Artisan Industry).*
Marie-Noëlle Lienemann (PS) *(Equipment, Housing and the Environment).*
Jean-Michel Baylet (MRG) *(Foreign Trade and Tourism).*

Parliament consists of the *National Assembly* and the *Senate*; the National Assembly is elected by direct suffrage by the second ballot system (by which, if no candidate obtains an absolute majority, there is a second round of voting between the 2 highest-placed candidates) and the Senate by indirect suffrage (Art. 24). It convenes as of right in two ordinary sessions per year, the first on 2 Oct. for 80 days and the second on 2 April for not more than 90 days (Art. 28).

The National Assembly comprises 577 Deputies, elected for a 5-year term from single-member constituencies – 555 in Metropolitan France and 22 in the various overseas departments and dependencies. The General Election, held in June 1988, resulted in a composition (by group, including 'affiliates') of 275 Socialist Party (PS) (including 9 Leftwing Radicals Movement (MRG) and 6 other 'affiliates'), 40 Centre Union (Social Democrats Centre), 132 *Rassemblement Pour la République* (RPR; Gaullists), 90 Union of French Democracy (UDF) (of which 58 Republican Party), 25 Communist Party (PCF) and 15 others. The composition in May 1991 was: PS, 264; RPR, 127; UDF, 90; UDC, 39; PC, 26; ind, 15. The *Speaker* is Henri Emmanuelli.

National Assembly elections are scheduled for March 1993.

The Senate comprises 321 Senators elected for 9-year terms (one-third every 3 years) by an electoral college in each Department or overseas dependency, made up of all members of the Departmental Council or its equivalent in overseas dependencies, together with all members of Municipal Councils within that area; there are 296 Senators for Metropolitan France, 13 for the Overseas Departments and dependencies, and 12 for French citizens residing outside France and its dependencies. Following the partial election held on 24 Sept. 1989, the Senate was composed of (by group, including 'affiliates') 91 RPR, 68 Centrist Union, 66 Socialist Group, 52 Republican and Independent Union, 23 Democratic and European Rally and 16 Communist Group. In Oct. 1989 Alain Poher was elected President of the Senate for an 8th 3-year term.

The *Constitutional Council* is composed of 9 members whose term of office is 9 years (non-renewable), one-third every 3 years; 3 are appointed by the President of the Republic, 3 by the President of the National Assembly, and 3 by the President of the Senate; in addition, former Presidents of the Republic are, by right, life members of the Constitutional Council (Art. 56). It oversees the fairness of the elections of the President (Art. 58) and Parliament (Art. 59) and of referenda (Art. 60), and acts as a guardian of the Constitution (Art. 61). Its President is Robert Badinter (appointed 1986).

The *Economic and Social Council* advises on Government and Private Members' Bills (Art. 69). It comprises representatives of employers', workers' and farmers' organizations in each Department and Overseas Territory.

National flag: The Tricolour of three vertical stripes of blue, white, red.

National anthem: La Marseillaise (words and music by C. Rouget de Lisle, 1792).

Local and Regional Government: France is divided into 22 regions for national development, planning and budgetary policy. Many of these regions are broadly comparable with the provinces of pre-revolutionary France, and give a measure of recognition to the distinctive personalities of peripheral areas such as Alsace and Brittany. In March 1982 state-appointed Regional Prefects were abolished and their executive powers transferred to the Presidents of the Regional Councils, which are directly elected. By a law of 13 May 1991 **Corsica** became a territorial collectivity. After the regional elections of March 1992 it had an assembly which elects an executive council.

There are 96 *départements* within the 22 regions each governed by a directly-elected *Conseil Général*. From 1982 their Presidents' powers were extended to take over local administration and expenditure from the former Departmental prefects, now called 'Commissioners of the Republic' with responsibility for public order. The *arrondissement* (325 in 1982) and the *canton* (3,714 in 1982), have little administrative significance.

The unit of local government is the *commune*, the size and population of which vary very much. There were, in 1990, in the 96 metropolitan departments, 36,551 communes. Most of them (30,790) had fewer than 1,500 inhabitants, and 15,623 had fewer than 300, while 235 communes had more than 30,000 inhabitants. The local affairs of the commune are under a Municipal Council, composed of from 9 to 36 members, elected by universal suffrage for 6 years by French citizens of 21 years or over after 6 months' residence. Each Municipal Council elects a mayor, who is both the representative of the commune and the agent of the central government.

At the local elections of March 1992 turn-out was 68·7%. The RPR-UDF coalition gained 33% of votes cast, the PS, 18·3% and the National Front, 13·9%.

Under a local taxation reform of 1990, some 11,000m. francs out of a total revenue of 42,000m. francs were based on income rather than rental values.

In Paris the *Conseil de Paris* is composed of 109 members elected from the 20 *arrondissements*. It combines the functions of departmental *Conseil Général* and Municipal Council.

DEFENCE. The President of the Republic exercises command over the Armed Forces. He is assisted by the High Council of Defence *(Conseil Supérieur de Défense)*, which studies defence problems, and by two Committees *(Comité de Défense* and *Comité de Défense restreint)* which formulate directives. The Prime Minister is responsible for national defence; he exercises his military responsibilities and co-ordinates inter-ministry defence activities through the General Secretariat of National Defence (SGDN). Under the Prime Minister's authority, the Minister of Defence is responsible for the execution of military policy, in particular the organization and administration of the Armed Forces.

On 5 July 1969 the Ministry of Defence assumed responsibility from the former individual service Ministries for the Army, Air Force and Navy. The Ministry prepares general directives for negotiations relating to defence. The preparation and control of the Armed Forces is exercised by the Chief of Staff of the Armed Forces, the Chiefs of Staff of the 3 services—Army, Navy and Air—and the head of the *Gendarmerie*.

French forces are not formally under the NATO command structure, although France signed the NATO strategic document on Eastern Europe in Nov. 1991. About 48,000 French service personnel are stationed in the Federal Republic of Germany, with a further 15,000 stationed in other overseas locations.

The General Directorate for Armament (DGA) is responsible for all aspects of the procurement of defence equipment. It employs about 73,000 personnel, and co-ordinates another 217,000 others employed in the defence industry.

Conscription was reduced from 12 to 10 months on 1 Jan. 1992.

Army. The Army consisted in 1992 of 280,300 personnel, of whom 6,000 were women and 173,500 are conscripts. Conscripts may not serve abroad unless war is declared.

The Territorial Defence Forces consist of 7 zone brigades, 23 joint-services divisional regiments (RIAD), an infantry division and a Rhine division. They provide the main operational defence of French territory.

The peace-time tactical units comprise the Mechanized Armoured Corps (CBM) and the Rapid Intervention Force (FAR). The CBM forms the 1st Army of 170,000 men, with headquarters in Strasbourg, and is organized, equipped and trained for action in the Central Europe theatre; it consists of 6 armoured divisions, 2 light armoured divisions and 2 motorized rifle divisions, plus artillery, engineering, signals, parachute, transport, supply and naval infantry and artillery units. It also includes 5 nuclear artillery regiments equipped with 30 launchers for 'Pluton' missiles.

The headquarters of the FAR are at Maisons-Laffite. It comprises 47,000 men organized, equipped and trained for rapid engagement either in Europe or over large distances elsewhere; it includes a parachute division, an air-portable marine division, a light armoured division, an alpine division and an air-mobile division, together with various specialized units.

Equipment includes 1,349 AMX-30 main battle tanks, 143 AMX-13 light tanks, 313 AMX-10RC armoured vehicles, 823 other armoured vehicles, 1,403 pieces of artillery, 181 *Roland* anti-aircraft missile systems and 1,440 *Milan* anti-tank weapons.

The *Aviation Légère de l'Armée de Terre* (ALAT) with about 7,000 personnel is an integral part of the Army, equipped with 700 helicopters of various types for observation, reconnaissance, combat area transport, liaison and supply duties.

The *Foreign Legion* was formed in 1831 for duty in North Africa. It is officered by French nationals and based at Aubagne, near Marseilles. About half the other ranks are French. It numbered 8,500 in 1991.

Gendarmerie. The para-military police force exists to ensure public security and maintain law and order, as well as participate in the operational defence of French territory as part of the armed forces. It consists of (1992) 89,300 personnel including 10,600 conscripts, 1,400 women and 967 civilians. It comprises a mobile force of 17,300 personnel and 120 departmental forces with 53,900 personnel, together with specialised units. It is equipped with 28 VBC-90 armoured gun-carriers, 121 light armoured cars, 155 armoured vehicles and 33 troop transport vehicles, as well as 44 helicopters and 6 light aircraft.

Navy. The missions of the French Navy are to provide the prime element of the French independent nuclear deterrent through its force of strategic submarines, to assure the security of the French offshore zones so as to contribute to NATO's logistic transatlantic re-supply, and to provide on-station and deployment forces overseas in support of French territories and interests.

French territorial seas and economic zones are organized into 3 maritime regions, each under the authority of a Maritime Prefect (with headquarters in Cherbourg, Brest and Toulon). Offshore, the seas and oceans are divided into 5 zones: Atlantic, Mediterranean, Indian Ocean, Pacific and Antilles-Guyana. Home-based forces are commanded by Commanders-in-Chief based in Brest and Toulon, those in the Indian Ocean and Pacific by Flag Officers based afloat in the Indian Ocean, and at Nouméa (in New Caledonia). Naval forces in the Caribbean come under a joint force commander based at Cayenne.

The following is a summary of the strength of the fleet at the end of the years shown:

	1986	1987	1988	1989	1990	1991
Aircraft carriers	2	2	2	2	2	2
Strategic-missile submarines	6	6	6	6	6	5
Other submarines	17	18	16	14	13	13
Cruisers	2	2	2	2	2	1
Destroyers	4	4	4	4	5	4
Frigates	38	38	36	36	35	34

The Navy operates 5 nuclear-powered strategic-missile submarines. The first 5 were of the Le Redoutable class, (*Redoutable, Terrible, Foudroyant, Indomptable* and *Tonnant*), 9,100 tonnes, completed between 1971 and 1980, and deploying 16 M-20 ballistic missiles. 3 have been, and a further 1 is being converted to carry 16 M-4 missiles. These missiles are also fitted in an intermediate ship, *L'Inflexible*, 9,100 tonnes, completed in 1985, while the first, *Le Redoutable*, has been decomissioned. A new, much larger class, (14,200 tonnes) is being built, of which the first, *Le Triomphant*, was laid down in 1988 for completion in 1995, and will deploy 16 M-4/5 missiles.

There are also 5 small (2,700 tonne) nuclear-powered submarines (1 new Amethyste and 4 Rubis class) and 8 operational diesel submarines.

The principal surface ships are the aircraft carriers *Clemenceau* and *Foch* of 33,300 tonnes each, completed in 1961 and 1963, and 1 cruiser. The 2 carriers embark an air group typically comprising 16 Super-Etendard strike aircraft, 7 F-8E Crusader, 6 Alize anti-submarine and warning and a flight of 4 utility helicopters. They are due to be withdrawn from service in 1998 and 2002, when nuclear-powered replacements are planned, although the second nuclear-powered ship may not now be built. The first, *Charles de Gaulle*, was laid down at Brest in 1988. The guided-missile cruiser *Colbert*, completed in 1959, was withdrawn from service in 1991. The helicopter cruiser *Jeanne d'Arc*, of 12,600 tonnes completed in 1963 is used in peacetime as a training vessel, but could perform amphibious or anti-submarine tasks in war. In these roles she could accommodate up to 8 Lynx helicopters, and 700 men. Her armament comprises 6 Exocet and 4 100mm guns.

Other surface combatants include 4 destroyers and 34 frigates. A modern mine countermeasure force consists of 10 tripartite coastal minehunters and 5 others, 3 old coastal minesweepers and 4 diver support vessels. The amphibious force includes 4 dock landing ships of which one is assigned to the Pacific nuclear test centre, 5 medium landing ships, and some 32 craft. Patrol forces include 1 ship (usually deployed in the South Indian Ocean), 21 coastal and 2 inshore patrol vessels. The Navy deploys a substantial support force which includes 7 large and 2 small tankers, 15 other maintenance and logistic ships, 5 weapon system trials ships and 6 survey and research ships. There are several hundred minor auxiliaries.

All warships, and a proportion of naval weapons, are produced by the government armaments service, of which the naval element, *Direction des Constructions Navales*, operates the shipbuilding yards as well as dockyards. Building takes place at Cherbourg, Brest and Lorient. In addition to units already mentioned, 2 more nuclear-powered fleet submarines and 6 patrol frigates are being built.

The naval air arm, known as *Aeronavale*, numbers some 10,000. Operational aircraft include 60 Super-Etendard nuclear-capable strike aircraft, 12 Etendard reconnaissance aircraft, 20 US-built Crusader F-8E all-weather fighters, 28 Alize turboprop anti-submarine aircraft, 35 Atlantique and 5 Gardian maritime reconnaissance aircraft. The Crusaders' fatigue safe life is being extended to keep about 15 operational until 1998, when the Rafale combat aircraft will enter service. Rotary wing strength includes 16 commando Super Frelon, and 36 anti-submarine and search-and-rescue Lynx helicopters. Numerous training, utility and transport aircraft bring the total strength to about 300 comprising 200 fixed-wing aircraft and 100 helicopters.

A small Marine force of 2,600 'Fusiliers Marins' provides 4 assault groups, an attack swimmer section as well as numerous naval base protection units.

Personnel in 1991 numbered 65,300 including 19,000 conscripts and a growing number of women, currently 1,800.

Air Force. Formed as the *Service Aéronautique* in April 1910, the *Armeé de l'Air* was reorganized in Sept. 1991. The *Commandement des Forces Aériennes Stratégiques* (CFAS) commands the airborne nuclear deterrent force and a group of land-based ballistic missiles. The *Commandement de la Force Aérienne Tactique* (FATAC) directs the tactical and air defence air forces. Under FATAC the 1st *Commandement Aérien Tactique* (1° CATAC) controls air units based in eastern France; the 2nd *Commandement Aérien Tactique* (2° CATAC) controls the reserve forces and the air component of the *Force d'Intervention*. The *Commandement du Transport Aérien Militaire* (COTAM) is responsible for air transport operations and participates also in the training and transport of airborne forces. The *Commandement de la*

Défense Aérienne (DA) controls French airspace, but has handed over all its figher aircraft to FATAC. The *Commandement des Écoles de l'Armée de l'Air* (CEAA) is responsible for training the personnel for all branches of the Air Force. The *Commandement des Transmissions* has responsibility for communications and electronic warfare. Finally, the *Commandement du Génie de l'Air*, made up mainly of Army personnel, undertakes airbase construction and maintenance under Air Force control.

The home-based French Air Force is divided territorially among 3 metropolitan air regions (Villacoublay, Bordeaux, Aix-en-Provence); overseas, small air units are integrated into the local joint-service commands. There are about 40 combat squadrons plus about 30 transport, helicopter and support squadrons, and the Air Force uses a total of 60 bases.

The strategic, tactical and air defence forces are equipped entirely with jet aircraft. The CFAS has 20 Mirage IV supersonic nuclear bombers, deployed in 2 squadrons, 45 Mirage 2000N fighter-bombers in 3 squadrons supported by 11 C-135F in-flight refuelling tanker transports. The FATAC deploys 9 wings (29 squadrons), with about 90 Mirage III-E and 5F ground-attack fighters, 120 Jaguar strike aircraft, 3 reconnaissance squadrons with Mirage F1-CRs, 8 squadrons with 120 Mirage F1-C and 4 squadrons with 60 Mirage 2000C interceptors. The COTAM is organized into 3 wings, equipped with 70 Transall C.160 turboprop transports, 5 DC-8s, 12 C-130s and 105 helicopters. Training aircraft include CAP-10/20/230 piston-engined primary trainers, Epsilon piston-engined and Fouga-Magister jet basic trainers, Alpha Jet advanced trainers, Mirage F1Bs, Mirage III-Bs, Mirage 2000Bs and two-seat Jaguars in wings for operational transformation; 25 Embraer 121-Xingus bought from Brazil are dual-purpose training/liaison aircraft. Total officers and other ranks (1991) 93,100 (5,600 women; 35,650 conscripts); 450 combat aircraft.

INTERNATIONAL RELATIONS

Membership. France is a member of the UN, the Council of Europe, NATO, WEU and the EC.

The Schengen Accord of June 1990 abolished border controls between France, Belgium, Germany, Luxembourg, Italy, Spain, Portugal and the Netherlands.

France is the focus of the *French Community* which formally links France with many of its former colonies in Africa. A wide range of agreements both with formal members of the Community and with other French-speaking countries extend to economic and technical matters and in particular to the disbursement of overseas aid.

ECONOMY

Policy. For the history of planning in France from 1947 to 1980, *see* THE STATESMAN'S YEAR-BOOK, 1982–83, p. 474. The Eighth Plan, covering the 1981–85 period, was set aside after the change of government in May 1981 and replaced by an interim plan for 1982–83, followed by a new Ninth Plan for 1984–88.

Private investors may acquire minority stakes in state-owned companies on condition that the government retains full control.

Budget. Receipts and expenditure in 1,000m. francs:

Receipts	1991	1992 [1]
Income tax	301	318
Corporation tax	162	163
Other direct taxes	110	110
Stamp duty	80	83
Excise	129	133
VAT	528	564
Other indirect taxes	39	43
EEC levies and local government subsidies	−216	−229
Fiscal reimbursements	−215	−225
Total gross budget receipts	1,191	1,241

Expenditure	1991	1992 [1]
Public debt	153	165
Administration and subsidies	796	820
Civil investment	93	92
Defence	238	240
Total expenditure	1,280	1,318

[1] Estimates.

The accounts of revenue and expenditure are examined by a special administrative tribunal (*Cour des Comptes*), instituted in 1807.

Currency. The unit of currency is the *franc* (FRF) of 100 *centimes*. Coins are issued for 5, 10, 20 and 50 centimes, 1, 2, 5 and 10 francs; and bank-notes for 10, 20, 50, 100, 200 and 500 francs. Annualized rate of inflation was 3·4% in 1990 and (provisionally) 3·1% in 1991. In March 1992, £1 sterling = 9·79 *francs*; US$1 = 5·58 *francs*.

14 former colonies are members of a *Franc Zone*: Benin, Burkina Faso, Cameroon, Central African Republic, Chad, Comoros, Congo, Côte d'Ivoire, Equatorial Guinea, Gabon, Mali, Niger, Senegal and Togo.

Banking and Finance. The Banque de France, founded in 1800, and nationalized on 2 Dec. 1945, has the monopoly (since 1848) of issuing bank-notes throughout France. Note circulation at 31 Dec. 1981 was 151,900m. francs. As a central bank, it puts monetary policy into effect and supervises its application. Its governor is appointed for 5 years (*Governor*, Jacques de Larosière).

The National Credit Council, formed in 1945 to regulate banking activity and consulted in all political decisions on monetary policy, comprises 45 members nominated by the Government; its president is the Minister for the Economy, its vice-president is the Governor of the Banque de France. Four principal deposit banks were nationalized in 1945 and the remainder in 1982 but the latter were privatized in 1987. The 10 chief banks in 1991 in order of their capital assets were: Crédit Agricole; Paribas (investment); Banque Nationale de Paris (state-owned); Crédit Lyonnais (state-owned); Société Générale; Caisses d'Epargne Ecureuil; Banques Populaires; CIC; Indosuez (investment); Crédit Commercial de France.

The state savings organization Caisse Nationale d'Epargne is administered by the post office on a giro system. On 31 Dec. 1981 the private savings banks (*Caisses d'epargne et de prévoyance*), numbering about 500 had 434,000m. francs in deposits; the state savings banks had 206,300m. francs in deposits. Deposited funds are centralized by a non-banking body, the *Caisse de Dépôts et Consignations*, which finances a large number of local authorities and state aided housing projects, and carries an important portfolio of transferable securities.

There is a stock exchange (Bourse) in Paris.

Weights and Measures. The metric system is in general use.

ENERGY AND NATURAL RESOURCES

Electricity. The state-owned monopoly Electricité de France is reponsible for power generation and supply under the Ministry of Industry. France is not rich in natural energy resources. In 1991 there were 57 nuclear reactors in operation, and some 80% of the electricity output was nuclear-produced, providing 33% of total energy consumption; a further 30% came from oil, 12% from gas and 8% from hydro-electric sources. Production (in 1m. kwh.): 1988, 373,318, of which 77,846 was hydroelectric and 295,472 nuclear. Supply 127 and 220 volts; 50 Hz.

Oil and Gas. In 1991 2·9m. tonnes of crude oil were produced. The greater part came from the Parentis oilfield in the Landes. Reserves (1985) total 221m. bbls. There is an important oil-refining industry, chiefly utilizing imported crude oil. In 1989, 76·37m. tonnes of petroleum products were refined. There are 7,802 km of pipelines.

The importation and distribution of natural gas is the responsibility of the government monopoly Gaz de France. Production of natural gas was 33,690m. cu. metres in 1989; reserves (1985) 41,000m. cu. metres.

Minerals. Principal minerals and metals produced in 1989, in 1,000 tonnes: Coal, 13,665; crude steel, 19,335; iron ore, 9,389; pig iron, 15,070; bauxite (1983), 1,660; potash salts (1983), 1,651.

Agriculture. Of the total area of France (54·9m. ha), the utilized agricultural area comprised 31·4m. ha in 1987, 18m. ha (57·1%) were arable, 11·9m. ha (37·9%) were pasture, and 1·3m. ha (4·2%) were under permanent crops including vines (0·98m. ha). In 1986 there were 1,484,900 tractors in use. In 1987 there were 981,722 holdings and in 1988 1·48m. persons (6·8% of the employed civilian workforce) were employed in agriculture, hunting, fishing and forestry.

The following table shows the area under the leading crops and the production for 3 years:

	Area (1,000 ha)			Produce (1,000 tonnes)		
	1986	1987	1988	1986	1987	1988
Wheat	4,859	4,932	4,825	26,475	27,415	29,677
Rye	81	82	79	229	299	276
Barley	2,090	1,992	1,916	10,063	10,489	10,086
Oats	312	281	273	1,066	1,122	1,074
Potatoes	201	197	183	6,267	6,720	6,344
Sugar-beet	448	446	432	25,830	26,471	28,606
Maize	1,884	1,743	1,936	11,641	12,470	13,996

Production (1988, in 1,000 tonnes): Centrifugal raw sugar, 4,424; beef and veal, 1,832; pork, 1,740; lamb and mutton, 152; poultry, 1,429; milk, 29,012; eggs, 0·94m.; wine, 69·34m. hectolitres.

The production of fruits (other than for cider making) for 3 years was (in 1,000 tonnes) as follows:

	1986	1987	1988		1986	1987	1988
Apples	2,739	2,424	2,357	Melons	274	286	275
Pears	370	439	355	Nuts	50	50	51
Plums	209	203	222	Grapes	9,340	9,164	7,419
Peaches	473	488	472	Strawberries	92	99	95
Apricots	121	98	97	Oranges	3	3	3

Livestock (in 1,000) in 1988 (and 1989): Horses, 292; cattle, 21,052 (20,122); sheep, 10,221; goats, 1,003; pigs, 11,915 (11,706); poultry, 220,000.

Forestry. In 1990 forest (36% coniferous, 31% oak) covered some 13·9m. ha, about 27% of the land area. 1·7m. ha are state property. Timber sold (1988), 32·9m. cu. metres valued at 10,500m. francs. 0·55m. persons were employed in forestry in 1990.

Fisheries. (1987). There were 23,426 fishermen, and 9,620 sailing-boats, steamers and motor-boats. Catch (in tonnes): Fish, total, 513,367; crustaceans, 24,111; shell fish, 226,890.

INDUSTRY. Industrial production (in 1,000 tonnes) for 3 years was as follows:

	1987	1988	1989
Sulphuric acid	3,960	4,081	4,187
Caustic acid	1,430	1,494	1,537
Sulphur	1,092	1,022	907
Polystyrene	527	536	542
Polyvinyl	933	1,017	1,103
Polyethylene	1,156	1,135	1,159
Wool	43	43	40
Cotton	189	136	185
Linen	1·2	1	...
Silk	67	73	...
Jute	4·9	4·6	4·7
Cheese	1,321	...	...
Chocolate	373	...	...
Biscuits	416	...	...

	1987	1988	1989
Sugar	3,655	...	...
Fish preparations	104	...	...
Jams and jellies	151	...	...
Cement and lime	23,557	25,273	25,884

Engineering production (in 1,000 units) for 3 years:

	1987	1988
Motor vehicles	3,493	3,666
Television sets	2,015	2,081
Radio sets	2,132	1,983
Tyres	56,450	60,366

Labour (1989). Out of an economically active population of 24,313,600 persons, 1,363,200 were engaged in agriculture, forestry and fishing, 1,576,500 in building, 1,183,100 in manufacturing industries, 931,700 in transport, 603,900 in banking and insurance, 4,259,000 in services, 2,662,700 in commerce. At 31 Dec. 1989, there were 21,809,900 employed.

On 1 July 1991 the minimum wage (SMIC) was raised to 32.66 francs an hour or 5,519.54 francs a months. SMIC affects about 1·6m. wage-earners.

Trade Unions. The main confederations recognized as nationally representative are: the CGT (Confédération Générale du Travail), founded in 1895; the CGT-FO (Confédération Générale du Travail–Force Ouvrière) which broke away from the CGT in 1948 as a protest against Communist influence therein; the CFTC (Confédération Française des Travailleurs Chrétiens), which was founded in 1919 and divided in 1964, with a breakaway group retaining the old name and the main body continuing under the new name of CFDT (Confédération Française Démocratique du Travail); and the CGC (Confédération Générale des Cadres) formed in 1944 which only represents managerial and supervisory staff.

Membership is estimated because unions are not required to publish figures; but at elections held on 8 Dec. 1982 for labour tribunals, the CGT was supported by 2·8m. members, the CGT–FO by 1·4m., the CFDT by 1·8m., the CFTC by 650,000 and the CGC by 740,000. Except for the CGC unions operate within the framework of industries and not of trades.

FOREIGN ECONOMIC RELATIONS

Commerce. Imports (c.i.f.) and exports (f.o.b.) in 1m. francs for 5 calendar years were (including gold):

	1985	1986	1987	1988	1989
Imports	962,747	887,502	944,999	1,053,799	1,216,663
Exports	870,811	825,417	857,936	963,748	1,102,411

The chief imports for home use and exports of home goods are to and from the following countries, in 1m. francs (including gold):

	Imports (c.i.f)		Exports (f.o.b.)	
Countries	1988	1989	1988	1989
Belgium-Luxembourg	96,313	111,767	86,273	97,736
Germany, Fed. Rep. of	208,012	235,169	157,741	176,527
Italy	122,779	140,340	117,706	133,410
Netherlands	55,836	62,969	54,007	62,371
Japan	44,388	54,245	51,774	63,017
Switzerland	26,496	29,949	40,066	46,289
UK	76,899	86,874	94,291	105,302

Foreign trade by sector, 1987, in 1m. francs:

	Imports (c.i.f)	Exports (f.o.b.)
Agriculture and agri-food industry	119,036	148,570
Energy	100,274	18,540
Raw materials and semi-products	246,431	230,023
Capital goods	229,838	212,039
Surface transport equipment	92,852	115,769
Consumer goods	153,325	127,306

Total trade between France and UK (British Department of Trade returns, in £1,000 sterling):

	1987	1988	1989	1990	1991
Imports to UK	8,381,984	9,390,207	10,785,429	11,758,481	11,066,081
Exports and re-exports from UK	7,781,546	8,270,408	9,461,648	10,885,803	11,591,139

Tourism. In 1987 there were 31·9m. tourists.

COMMUNICATIONS

Roads. In 1986 there were 345,000 km of departmental road network and, in 1989, 34,872 km of national road network of which 6,680 km were motorway. In 1987 there were 5,364,251 registered vehicles, including 4,373,675 private and commercial vehicles, 6,988 coaches and buses, 600,000 lorries and vans and 231,035 motorcycles.

Railways. As from 1 Jan. 1938 all the independent railway companies were merged with the existing state railway system in a Société Nationale des Chemins de Fer Français (SNCF), which became a public industrial and commercial establishment in 1983.

In 1990, SNCF totalled 34,322 km (12,430 km electrified) and carried 142m. tonnes of freight and 840m. passengers. A new railway for high-speed trains (TGV) was completed in 1983 between Paris and Lyon. 2 further routes opened in 1989 to Le Mans to serve Britanny and in 1990 to Tours to serve the south-west.

The Paris transport network consisted in 1990 of 302 km of underground railway (métro) and regional express railways. In 1990 it carried 1,547m. passengers. There are also métros in Lille (25 km), Lyon (28 km) and Marseille (18 km), and tram/light railway networks in Grenoble (13 km), Lille (23 km), Marseille (3 km), Nantes (12·5 km), Paris and St Étienne (7 km).

Boring of the Channel tunnel began in March 1988. A network (TGV Nord) is under construction linking Paris to the tunnel as well as to Lille, and this network will also connect Paris and the tunnel to Brussels and be extended to the Netherlands and Germany.

Civil Aviation. Air France, UTA and Air Inter, the national airlines, merged in 1990 to control 97% of French air traffic. In 1990 they operated some 200 aircraft, servicing Europe, North America, Central and South America, West and East Africa, Madagascar, the Near, Middle and Far East. 9 European routes were closed down in 1990. There are local networks in the West Indies and Central America. In 1988 Air France, UTA and Air Inter flew 3,693m. tonne-km (excluding mail) and 447,389m. passenger-km. There were (1984) 60 airports with scheduled services.

Shipping. Merchant ships, in 1990, numbered 223 vessels of 3,870,000 GRT (241 in 1989). During 1987, 186·87m. tonnes of cargo were unloaded, of which 92·2m. tonnes were crude and refined petroleum products, and 61·93m. tonnes were loaded; total passenger traffic, 21·5m.

Canals are administered by the public authority France Navigable Waterways (FVN). In 1989 there were 8,500 km of navigable rivers, waterways and canals (of which 1,647 km accessible to vessels over 3,000 tons), with a total traffic in 1989 of 63·9m. tonnes.

Telecommunications. In 1989 the telephone system (government-owned) had 25,609,000 subscribers, and there were 16,999 post offices. In Jan. 1991 France Télécom was removed from the control of the Ministry of Posts and Telecommunications and is now run as a public enterprise under autonomous management. La Poste is a similar body responsible for mail delivery and financial services.

Some 5·6m. Minitel videotext terminals have been distributed free to the public.

Radio and television broadcasting was reorganized under the Act of 7 Aug. 1974 which replaced the Office de Radiodiffusion Télévision Française with 4 broadcasting companies, a production company and an audio-visual institute. The broadcasting authority is the *Conseil Supérieur de l'Audiovisuel.* Radio programmes are broadcast from 874 VHF transmitters of which 418 belong to 4 stations: *France Info, France Inter, France Musique* and *France Culture.* There are 2 state-owned TV channels, Autenne-2 and FR3, which are partly financed by advertising, and 5 commercial channels (colour by SECAM). TV broadcasts must contain at least 60% EC-generated programmes and 50% of these must be French. There were about 49m. radio and 28·6m. TV sets in use in 1991.

Cinemas (1987). There were 5,063 cinemas; attendances totalled 132·5m.

Newspapers (1987). There were 72 daily papers published in the provinces with a circulation of 6·7m. copies, and 14 published in Paris with a national circulation of 2·5m. Among Paris dailies *France-Soir* sells 539,000; *Le Monde* 445,000; *Le Parisien Libéré* 421,000 and *Le Figaro* 465,000. Among provincial dailies *Ouest-France* (Rennes) sells 783,000; *Le Progrés* (Lyon) 447,000; *La Voix du Nord* (Lille) 372,000; *Sud-Ouest* (Bordeaux) 430,000; *La Dauphine Libérée* (Grenoble) 401,000 and *Le Provençal* (Marseilles) 345,000.

JUSTICE, RELIGION, EDUCATION AND WELFARE

Justice. The system of justice is divided into 2 jurisdictions: the judicial, and the administrative.

Within the judicial jurisdiction are common law courts including 473 lower courts (*tribunaux d'instance*, including 11 in overseas departments), 186 higher courts (*tribunaux de grande instance*, including 5 *tribunaux de première instance* in the overseas territories), and 454 police courts (*tribunaux de police*, including 11 in overseas departments).

The *tribunaux d'instance* are presided over by a single judge. The *tribunaux de grande instance* usually have a collegiate composition, although may be presided over by a single judge in some civil cases. The police courts, presided over by a judge on duty in the *tribunal d'instance*, deal with petty offences (*contraventions*); correctional chambers (*chambres correctionelles*, of which there is at least one in each *tribunal de grande instance*) deal with graver offences (*délits*), including cases involving imprisonment up to 5 years. Correctional chambers consist of 3 judges of a *tribunal de grande instance* (a single judge in some cases). Sometimes in cases of *délit*, and in all cases of more serious *crimes*, a preliminary inquiry is made in secrecy by one of 570 examining magistrates (*juges d'instruction*), who either dismisses the case or sends it for trial before a public prosecutor.

Still within the judicial jurisdiction are various specialised courts, including 229 commercial courts (*tribunaux de commerce*), composed of tradesmen and manufacturers elected for 2 years initially and then for 4 years; 282 conciliation boards (*conseils de prud'hommes*), composed of an equal number of employers and employees elected for 5 years to deal with labour disputes; 437 courts for settling rural landholding disputes (*tribunaux paritaires des baux ruraux*, including 11 in overseas departments); and 110 social security courts (*tribunaux des affaires de sécurité sociale*).

When the decisions of any of these courts are susceptible of appeal, the case goes to one of the 35 courts of appeal (*cours d'appel*) composed each of a president and a variable number of members. There are 102 courts of assize (*cours d'assises*), each composed of a president who is a member of the court of appeal, and 2 other magistrates, and assisted by a lay jury of 9 members. These try crimes involving imprisonment of over 5 years. The decisions of the courts of appeal and the courts of assize are final, However, the Court of Cassation (*Cour de cassation*) has discretion to verify if the law has been correctly interpreted and if the rules of procedure have been followed exactly. The Court of Cassation may annul any judgment, following which the cases must be retried by a court of appeal or a court of assizes.

The administrative jurisdiction exists to resolve conflicts arising between citizens and central and local government authorities. It consists of 33 administrative courts (*tribunaux administratifs*, including 7 in overseas departments and territories) and 5 administrative courts of appeal (*cours administratives d'appel*). The Council of State is the final court of appeal in administrative cases, though it may also act as a court of first instance.

Cases of doubt as to whether the judicial or administrative jurisdiction is competent in any case are resolved by a *Tribunal de conflits* composed in equal measure of members of the Court of Cassation and the Council of State.

Capital punishment was abolished in Aug. 1981.

On 24 Jan. 1973 the first Ombudsman (*médiateur*) was appointed for a 6-year period.

Penal institutions consist of: (1) *maisons d'arrêt*, where persons awaiting trial as well as those condemned to short periods of imprisonment are kept; (2) punishmnt institutions – (a) central prisons (*maisons centrales*) for those sentenced to long imprisonment, and (b) detention centres for offenders showing promise of rehabilitation; (3) hospitals for the sick. Special attention is being paid to classified treatment and the rehabilitation and vocational re-education of prisoners including work in open-air and semi-free establishments. There are 3 penal institutions for women.

Juvenile delinquents go before special judges in 135 (10 in overseas departments) juvenile courts (*tribunaux pour enfants*); they are sent to public or private institutions of supervision and re-education.

The population at 1 Oct. 1991 of all penal establishments was 47,308 men and 2,145 women.

Religion. No religion is officially recognized by the State. Under the law promulgated on 9 Dec. 1905, which separated Church and State, the adherents of all creeds are authorized to form associations for public worship (*associations culturelles*). The law of 2 Jan. 1907 provided that, failing *associations culturelles*, the buildings for public worship, together with their furniture, would continue at the disposition of the ministers of religion and the worshippers for the exercise of their religion; but in each case there was required an administrative act drawn up by the *préfet* as regards buildings belonging to the State or the departments and by the *maire* as regards buildings belonging to the communes.

There were (1985) 125 archbishops and bishops of the Roman Catholic Church, with (1974) 43,557 clergy of various grades and (1986) 42·35m. members. The Protestants of the Augsburg confession are, in their religious affairs, governed by a General Consistory, while the Reformed Church is under a Council of Administration, the seat of which is in Paris. In 1988 there were about 800,000 Protestants and 1·9m. Moslems.

The Chief Rabbi is Joseph Sitruk.

Education. The primary, secondary and higher state schools constitute the 'Université de France'. The Supreme Council of 84 members has deliberative, administrative and judiciary functions, and as a consultative committee advises respecting the working of the school system, the inspectors-general are in direct communication with the Minister. For local education administration France is divided into 25 academic areas, each of which has an Academic Council whose members include a certain number elected by the professors or teachers. The Academic Council deals with all grades of education. Each is under a Rector, and each is provided with academy inspectors, 1 for each department.

Compulsory education is now provided for children of 6–16. The educational stages are as follows:

1. Non-compulsory pre-school instruction for children aged 2–5, to be given in infant schools or infant classes attached to primary schools.

2. Compulsory elementary instruction for children aged 6–11, to be given in primary schools and certain classes of the *lycées*. It consists of 3 courses: Preparatory (1 year), elementary (2 years), intermediary (2 years). Physically or mentally handicapped children are cared for in special institutions or special classes of primary schools.

3. Lower secondary education (*Enseignement du premier cycle du Second Degré*) for pupils aged 11–15, consists of 4 years of study in the *lycées* (grammar schools), *Collèges d'Enseignement Technique* or *Collèges d'Enseignement Général*.

4. Upper secondary education (*Enseignement du second cycle du Second Degré*) for pupils aged 15–18:

　　　　Long, *général* or *professionel* provided by the *lycées* and leading to the *baccalauréat* or to the *baccalauréat de technicien* after 3 years.

Court, professional courses of 3, 2 and 1 year are taught in the *lycées d'enseignement professionel*, or the specialized sections of the *lycées*, CES or CEG.

The following table shows the number of schools in 1987–88 and the numbers of pupils in full-time education:

	State		Private	
	Schools	Pupils	Schools	Pupils
Nursery	17,900 ⎫		385 ⎫	
Primary	40,235 ⎬	5,732,931	6,038 ⎬	930,853
Secondary	7,342 ⎭	4,481,797	3,905 ⎭	1,192,813

Higher Instruction is supplied by the State in the universities and in special schools, and by private individuals in the free faculties and schools. The law of 12 July 1875 provided for higher education free of charge. This law was modified by that of 18 March 1880, which granted the state faculties the exclusive right to confer degrees. A decree of 28 Dec. 1885 created a general council of the faculties, and the creation of universities, each consisting of several faculties, was accomplished in 1897, in virtue of the law of 10 July 1896.

The law of 12 Nov. 1968 laying down future guidelines for higher education redefined the activities and working of universities. Bringing several disciplines together, 780 units for teaching and research (UER–Unités d'Enseignement et de Recherche) were formed which decided their own teaching activities, research programmes and procedures for checking the level of knowledge gained. They and the other parts of each university must respect the rules designed to maintain the national standard of qualifications.

The UERs form the basic units of 69 Universities and 3 National Polytechnic Institutes (with university status), grouped into 25 *académies* with 980,404 students in 1987.

There are also Catholic university facilities in Paris, Angers, Lille, Lyon and Toulouse with (1981–82) 34,118 students and private universities with (1984–85) 17,646 students.

Outside the university system, higher education (academic, professional and technical) is provided by over 400 schools and institutes, including the 177 Grandes Écoles, highly-selective public or private institutions offering mainly technological or commercial curricula, with an annual output of about 17,000 graduates. In 1984–85 there were 139,827 students in state establishments and 61,996 in private establishments. In 1986–87 there were also 48,811 students in preparatory classes leading to the Grandes Écoles, 129,942 in the Sections de Techniciens Supérieurs and 47,300 in the Écoles d'ingénieurs; there were also (1984-85) 18,951 students in Écoles normales d'instituteurs (teacher-training).

Health. On 1 Jan. 1988 there were 138,825 doctors, (1987) 49,610 chemists, (1986) 34,946 dentists, (1986) 294,260 nurses and (1986) 9,725 midwives. On 1 Jan. 1987 there were 3,730 hospitals with 574,000 beds.

Social Welfare. An order of 4 Oct. 1945 laid down the framework of a comprehensive plan of Social Security and created a single organization which superseded the various laws relating to social insurance, workmen's compensation, health insurance, family allowances, etc. All previous matters relating to Social Security are dealt with in the Social Security Code, 1956; this has been revised several times.

Contributions. All wage-earning workers or those of equivalent status are insured regardless of the amount or the nature of the salary or earnings. The funds for the general scheme are raised mainly from professional contributions, these being fixed within the limits of a ceiling and calculated as a percentage of the salaries. The calculation of contributions payable for family allowances, old age and industrial injuries relates only to this amount; on the other hand, the amount payable for sickness, maternity expenses, disability and death is calculated partly within the limit of the 'ceiling' and partly on the whole salary. These contributions are the responsibility of both employer and employee, except in the case of family allowances or industrial injuries, where they are the sole responsibility of the employer.

Self-employed Workers. From 17 Jan. 1948 allowances and old-age pensions were paid to self-employed workers by independent insurance funds set up within their own profession, trade or business. Schemes of compulsory insurance for sickness were instituted in 1961 for farmers and in 1966, with modifications in 1970, for other non-wage-earning workers.

Social Insurance. The orders laid down in Aug. 1967 ensure that the whole population can benefit from the Social Security Scheme; at present all elderly persons who have been engaged in the professions, as well as the surviving spouse, are entitled to claim an old-age benefit.

Sickness Insurance refunds the costs of treatment required by the insured and the needs of dependants.

Maternity Insurance covers the costs of medical treatment relating to the pregnancy, confinement and lying-in period; the beneficiaries being the insured person or the spouse.

Insurance for Invalids is divided into 3 categories: (1) those who are capable of working; (2) those who cannot work; (3) those who, in addition, are in need of the help of another person. According to the category, the pension rate varies from 30 to 50% of the average salary for the last 10 years, with additional allowance for home help for the third category.

Old-age Pensions for workers were introduced in 1910 and are now fixed by the Social Security Code of 28 Jan. 1972. Since 1983 people who have paid insurance for at least 37½ years (150 quarters) receive at 60 a pension equal to 60% of basic salary. People who have paid insurance for less than 37½ years but no less than 15 years can expect a pension equal to as many 1/150ths of the full pension as their quarterly payments justify. In the event of death of the insured person, the husband or wife of the deceased person receives half the pension received by the latter. Compulsory supplementary schemes ensure benefits equal to 70% of previous earnings.

Family Allowances. The system comprises: (*a*) Family allowances proper, equivalent to 25·5% of the basic monthly salary (1,246 francs) for 2 dependent children, 46% for the third child, 41% for the fourth child, and 39% for the fifth and each subsequent child; a supplement equivalent to 9% of the basic monthly salary for the second and each subsequent dependent child more than 10 years old and 16% for each dependent child over 15 years. (*b*) Family supplement (519 francs) for persons with at least 3 children or one child aged less than 3 years. (*c*) Antenatal grants. (*d*) Maternity grant equal to 260% of basic salary; increase for multiple births or adoptions, 198%; increase for birth or adoption of third or subsequent child, 457%. (*e*) Allowance for specialized education of handicapped children. (*f*) Allowance for orphans. (*g*) Single parent allowance. (*h*) Allowance for opening of school term. (*i*) Allowance for accommodation, under certain circumstances. (*j*) Minimum family income for those with at least 3 children. Allowances (*b*), (*g*), (*h*) and (*j*) only apply to those whose annual income falls below a specified level.

Workmen's Compensation. The law passed by the National Assembly on 30 Oct. 1946 forms part of the Social Security Code and is administered by the Social Security Organization. Employers are invited to take preventive measures. The application of these measures is supervised by consulting engineers (assessors) of the local funds dealing with sickness insurance, who may compel employers who do not respect these measures to make additional contributions; they may, in like manner, grant rebates to employers who have in operation suitable preventive measures. The injured person receives free treatment, the insurance fund reimburses the practitioners, hospitals and suppliers chosen freely by the injured. In cases of temporary disablement the daily payments are equal to half the total daily wage received by the injured. In case of permanent disablement the injured person receives a pension, the amount of which varies according to the degree of disablement and the salary received during the past 12 months.

Unemployment Benefits vary according to circumstances (full or partial unemployment) which are means-tested. Since 1926 unemployment benefits have been paid from public funds.

DIPLOMATIC REPRESENTATIVES

Of France in Great Britain (58 Knightsbridge, London, SW1X 7JT)
Ambassador: Bernard Dorin.

Of Great Britain in France (35 rue du Faubourg St Honoré, 75383 Paris Cedex 08)
Ambassador: Sir Ewen Fergusson, KCMG.

Of France in the USA (4101 Reservoir Rd., NW, Washington, D.C., 20007)
Ambassador: Jacques Andreani.

Of the USA in France (2 Ave. Gabriel, Paris)
Ambassador: Alan P. Larson.

Of France to the United Nations
Ambassador: Jean-Bernard Mérimée.

Further Reading

Statistical Information: The Institut National de la Statistique et des Études économiques (18, Boulevard Adolphe Pinard, 75014 Paris) is the central office of statistics. It was established by a law of 27 April 1946, which amalgamated the Service National des Statistiques (created in 1941 by merging the Direction de la Statistique générale de la France and the Service de la Démographie) with the Institut de Conjoncture (set up in 1938) and some statistical services of the Ministry of National Economy.

The main publications of the Institut include:

Annuaire statistique de la France (from 1878)
Annuaire statistique des Territoires d'Outre-Mer (from 1959)
Bulletin mensuel de statistique (monthly)
Documentation économique (bi-monthly)
Données statistiques africaines et Malgaches (quarterly)
Economie et Statistique (monthly)
Tableaux de l'Economie Française (biennially, from 1956)
Tendances de la Conjoncture (monthly)

Ambler, J. S. (ed.) *The French Welfare State: Surviving Social and Ideological Change.* New York Univ. Press, 1992
Braudel, F., *The Identity of France.* 2 vols. London, 1988–90
Caron, F., *An Economic History of Modern France.* London, 1979
Chambers, F. J., *France.* [Bibliography] Oxford and Santa Barbara, (rev. ed.) 1990
Hollifield, J. F. and Ross, G., *Searching for the New France.* London, 1991
McMillan, J. F., *Twentieth-Century France: Politics and Society in France, 1898–1991.* 2nd ed. [of *Dreyfus to De Gaulle*]. London, 1992
Mendras, H. and Cole, A., *Social Change in Modern France: towards a Cultural Anthopology of the Fifth Republic.* CUP, 1991
Monnier, A., *La Population de la France.* Paris, 1990
Peyrefitte, A., *The Trouble with France.* New York, 1981
Pinchemel, P., *France: A Geographical, Social and Economic Survey.* CUP, 1987
Schmidt, V. A., *Democratizing France: the Political and Administrative History of Decentralization.* CUP, 1991
Todd, E., *The Making of Modern France: Politics, Ideology and Culture.* Oxford, 1991
Verdié, M. (ed.) *L'Etat de la France et de ses habitants.* Paris, 1992
Weston, M., *English Reader's Guide to the French Legal System.* Oxford, 1991
Who's Who in France [in French]. Paris, annual

OVERSEAS DEPARTMENTS

On 19 March 1946 the French colonies of Guadeloupe, French Guiana, Martinique and Réunion each became an Overseas Department of France, with the same status as the departments comprising Metropolitan France. The former territory of Saint Pierre and Miquelon held a similar status from July 1976 until June 1985, when it became a *collectivité territorial.*

GUADELOUPE

HISTORY. Discovered by Columbus in Nov. 1493, the two main islands were then known as *Karukera* (Isle of Beautiful Waters) to the Carib inhabitants, who resisted Spanish attempts to colonize. A French colony was established on 28 June 1635, and apart from short periods of occupancy by British forces, Guadeloupe has since remained a French possession. On 19 March 1946 Guadeloupe became an Overseas Department; in 1974 it additionally became an administrative region.

AREA AND POPULATION. Guadeloupe consists of a group of islands in the Lesser Antilles. The two main islands, Basse-Terre to the west and Grande-Terre to the east, are separated by a narrow channel, called Rivière Salée. Adjacent to these are the islands of Marie Galante to the south-east, La Désirade to the east, and the Iles des Saintes to the south. The islands of St Martin and St Barthélemy lie 250 km to the north-west.

	Area in sq. km	Census 1982	Census 1990 [3]	Chief town
St Martin [1]	54 [2]	8,072	28,518	Marigot
St Barthélemy	21	3,059	5,038	Gustavia
Basse-Terre	848	135,341	149,943	Basse-Terre
Grande-Terre	590	163,668	177,570	Pointe-à-Pitre
Iles des Saintes	13	2,901	2,036	Terre-de-Bas
La Désirade	20	1,602	1,610	Grande Anse
Marie-Galante	158	13,757	13,463	Grand-Bourg
	1,705	328,400	378,178	

[1] Northern part only; the southern third is Dutch.   [2] Includes uninhabited Tintamarre.
[3] Preliminary results

Provision population figures at the census of March 1990, 378,178; 1991 estimate, 387,200. 77% are mulatto, 10% black and 10% mestizo, but the populations of St Barthélemy and Les Saintes are still mainly descended from 17th-century Breton and Norman settlers. French is the official language, but a Creole dialect is spoken by the vast majority except on St Martin.

The seat of government is Basse-Terre (13,796 inhabitants in 1988) at the south-west end of that island but the largest towns are Pointe-à-Pitre (25,312 inhabitants), the economic centre and main port, and its suburb, Les Abymes (56,237 inhabitants).

Vital statistics (1987): Live births, 6,855; deaths, 2,244; marriages, 1,880.

CLIMATE. Warm and humid. Pointe-à-Pitre. Jan. 74°F (23·4°C), July 80°F (26·7°C). Annual rainfall 71" (1,814 mm).

CONSTITUTION AND GOVERNMENT. Guadeloupe is administered by a *Conseil Général* of 42 members (assisted by an Economic and Social Committee of 40 members) and a Regional Council of 39 members, both directly elected for terms of 6 years. It is represented in the National Assembly by 4 deputies, in the Senate by 2 senators and on the Economic and Social Council by 2 councillors. There are 3 *arrondissements,* sub-divided into 34 communes, each administered by an elected municipal council. The French government is represented by an appointed Commissioner.

Commissioner: Yves Bonnet.
President of the Conseil Général: Dominique Larifla.
President of the Regional Council: Félix Proto.

ECONOMY

Budget. The budget for 1983 balanced at 1,633m. francs.

Banking. The main commercial banks are the Banque des Antilles Françaises (with 6 branches), the Banque Populaire de la Guadeloupe (with 6 branches), the Banque Nationale de Paris (14 branches), the Crédit Agricole (26), the Banque Française Commerciale (8), the Société Generale de Banque aux Antilles (5) and the Chase

Manhattan Bank (1). The Caisse Centrale de Coopération économique is the official bank of the department and issues its bank-notes.

ENERGY AND NATURAL RESOURCES

Electricity. Production in 1986 totalled 315m. kwh.

Agriculture. Chief products (1988) are bananas (120,000 tonnes), sugar-cane (891,000 tonnes), rum (64,883 hectolitres of pure alcohol in 1984). Other fruits and vegetables are grown for domestic consumption. 11·8m. flowers were grown in 1984.

Livestock (1988): Cattle, 74,000; goats, 33,000; sheep, 4,000; pigs, 43,000.

Forestry. In 1985, there were 395 sq. km of forests. In 1984, 51,848 cu. metres of wood were produced.

Fisheries. The catch in 1984 was 8,500 tonnes; crustacea (120 tonnes), shell fish (300 tonnes).

INDUSTRY. The major industry is food processing carried out by small and medium-sized businesses.

Labour. Economically active population in 1989 was 121,826. 31,077 persons (25·5% of the workforce) were registered unemployed in 1989. Of the estimated 17,600 jobs in the industrial sector, 9,152 persons were employed in the food processing business. About 69,000 persons (31,200 men, 38,700 women) were employed in the commercial sector. There were 16,761 persons in trade, 4,006 in transport and communications and 31,324 in services. The minimum wage (SMIC) was raised to 1,083.53 francs a week on 1 July 1991.

COMMERCE. Trade for 1985 (in 1m. francs) was imports 5,745 and exports 669, 60% of imports were from France, while 63% of exports went to France and 18% to Martinique. In 1985 bananas formed 43% of the exports, sugar 10% and rum 7%. St Martin and St Barthélemy are free ports.

Total trade between Guadeloupe and UK (British Department of Trade returns, £1,000 sterling):

	1989	1990	1991
Imports to UK	119	53	513
Exports and re-exports from UK	4,381	5,084	7,305

Tourism. Tourism is the chief economic activity, producing some 2,000m. francs in 1989. 320,000 tourists visited in 1989, of which 70% were French, 15% North American and 10% German.

COMMUNICATIONS

Roads. In 1984 there were 3,500 km of roads.

Aviation. Air France and 5 other airlines call at Guadeloupe. In 1984 there were 31,451 arrivals and departures of aircraft and 1,325,500 passengers at Raizet (Pointe-à-Pitre) airport and, 6,682 aircraft movements and 116,000 passengers at Marie-Galante airport. There are also airports at La Désirade and Saint-Barthélemy.

Shipping. Guadeloupe is in direct communication with France by means of 12 steam navigation companies. In 1983, 1,239 vessels arrived to disembark 74,921 passengers and 1,035,800 tonnes of freight and to embark 74,999 passengers and 470,600 tonnes of freight.

Telecommunications. In 1984 there were 47 post offices and 64,916 telephones. RFO broadcasts for 17 hours a day in French and television (2 channels: 1 regional and 1 by satellite) broadcasts for 6 hours a day. There were (1983) 25,000 radio and (1981) 32,886 TV receivers.

Newspapers. There was (1984) 1 daily newspaper *(France-Antilles)* with a circulation of 25,000.

JUSTICE, RELIGION, EDUCATION AND WELFARE

Justice. There are 4 *tribunaux d'instance* and 2 *tribunaux de grande instance* at Basse-Terre and Pointe-à-Pitre; there is also a court of appeal and a court of assizes at Basse-Terre.

Religion. The majority of the population are Roman Catholic.

Education. In 1988 there were 52,835 pupils at 304 primary schools and 46,414 at secondary schools. The University Antilles-Guyane had 4,817 students in 1988, of which Guadeloupe itself had 2,217.

Health. The medical services in 1989 included 17 public hospitals and 13 private clinics.

Further Reading

Information: Office du Tourisme du départemente, Point-à-Pitre. *Director:* Eric W. Rotin.
Lasserre, G., *La Guadeloupe, étude géographique.* 2 vols. Bordeaux, 1961

GUIANA

Guyane Française

HISTORY. A French settlement on the island of Cayenne was established in 1604 and the territory between the Maroni and Oyapock rivers finally became a French possession in 1817. Convicts settlements were established from 1852, that on off-shore Devil's Island being most notorious; all were closed by 1945. On 19 March 1946 the status of Guiana was changed to that of an Overseas Department and in 1974 also became an administrative region.

AREA AND POPULATION. French Guiana is situated on the north-east coast of Latin America, and has an area of about 83,533 sq. km (32,252 sq. miles). Population figure at the 1990 census: 114,808 (including 34,087 of foreign origin). The chief towns (1990 populations) are Cayenne, the capital (41,600), Kourou (11,208) and Saint-Laurent-du-Maroni (13,900).

In 1989, 66% of the inhabitants were of Creole origin.

Vital statistics (1988): Live births, 2,700; deaths, 562; marriages (1987), 365.

CONSTITUTION AND GOVERNMENT. French Guiana is administered by a General Council of 19 members and a Regional Council of 31 members, both directly elected for terms of 6 years. It is represented in the National Assembly by 2 deputies and in the Senate by 1 senator. The French government is represented by a Prefect. There are 2 *arrondissements* (Cayenne and Saint Laurent-du-Maroni) sub-divided into 21 communes.

Prefect: Jean-Pierre Lacroix.
President of the General Council: Elie Castor.
President of the Regional Council: Georges Othily.

ECONOMY

Budget. The budget for 1987 balanced at 847m. francs, excluding duplicated items and national expenditure.

Banking. The Banque de la Guyane has a capital of 10m. francs and reserve fund of 2·39m. francs. Loans totalled 2,762m. francs in 1987. Other banks include Banque National de Paris-Guyane, Crédit Populaire Guyanais and Banque Française Commerciale.

ENERGY AND NATURAL RESOURCES

Electricity. Production in 1988 totalled 243m. kwh. Supply 220 volts; 50 Hz.

Minerals. In 1988 530 kg of gold were produced.

Agriculture. Only 12,581 hectares are under cultivation. The crops (1988, in tonnes) consist of rice (1989, 14,310), manioc (6,263) and sugar-cane (1,740).
Livestock (1989): 16,500 cattle, 9,500 swine and (1987) 117,000 poultry.

Forestry. The country has immense forests (about 66,700 sq. km in 1988) rich in many kinds of timber. Roundwood production (1988) 101,273 cu. metres.

Fisheries. The fishing fleet for shrimps comprises 31 US and 41 French boats. The catch in 1988 totalled 4,256 tonnes of shrimps and 1,024 tonnes of fish. Production of *Macrobrachium Rosenbergii* (an edible river shrimp) totalled 62·8 tonnes.

INDUSTRY. A food processing industry has been created.

Labour. Economically active population in 1989 was 31,183. 3,827 persons (12·27% of the population) were registered unemployed in 1989. On 1 July 1991 the minimum wage (SMIC) was raised to 1,083.53 francs a week.

COMMERCE. Trade in 1m. francs:

	1985	1986	1987	1988
Imports	2,287	2,065	2,371	2,742
Exports	300	255	323	325

In 1986, 8% of imports came from Trinidad and Tobago, 65% from France and 11% from the EEC, while 36% of exports went to the USA, 16% to Japan, 22% to the French West Indies and 23% to France. In 1985, shrimps formed 53% of exports and timber, 9%.

Total trade between Guiana and UK (British Department of Trade returns, in £1,000 sterling):

	1987	1988	1989	1990	1991
Imports to UK	380	1,148	9,009	4,048	2,367
Exports and re-exports from UK	1,134	4,232	4,559	11,939	6,032

TOURISM. There were 14,500 tourists in 1987.

COMMUNICATIONS

Roads. Three chief and some secondary roads connect the capital with most of the coastal area by motor-car services. There are (1986) 372 km of national and 341 km of departmental roads. In 1989 there were 23,520 passenger cars, 1,568 trucks and 121 buses. Connexions with the interior are made by waterways which, despite rapids, are navigable by local craft.

Civil Aviation. In 1988, 123,792 passengers and 3,632 tonnes of freight arrived and 121,575 passengers and 1,572 tonnes of freight departed by air at Rochambeau International Airport (Cayenne). There are regular internal flights to 7 other airports.

The base of the European Space Agency (ESA) is located near Kourou and has been operational since 1979.

Shipping. The chief ports are: Cayenne, St-Laurent-du-Maroni and Kourou. Dégrad des Cannes (the port of Cayenne) is visited regularly by ships of the Compagnie Général Maritime, the Compagnie Maritime des Chargeurs Réunis and Marseille Fret. In 1988, 706 vessels arrived and departed. 189,000 tonnes of petroleum products arrived and 333,000 tonnes of other freight arrived and departed.

Telecommunications. Number of telephones (1989), 26,146. There are wireless stations at Cayenne, Oyapoc, Régina, St-Laurent-du-Maroni and numerous other locations.

RFO-Guyane (Guiana Radio) broadcasts for 133 hours each week on medium- and short-waves and FM in French. Television is broadcast for 135 hours each week on 2 channels. In 1986 there were 44,000 radio and 6,500 TV receivers.

Newspapers. There was (1988) 1 daily newspaper *(Presse de la Guyane)* with a circulation of 1,000 and a paper published 4 times a week *(France-Guyane)* with a circulation of 5,500.

JUSTICE, RELIGION, EDUCATION AND WELFARE

Justice. At Cayenne there is a *tribunal d'instance* and a *tribunal de grande instance*, from which appeal is to the regional *cour d'appel* in Martinique.

Religion. In 1984, 77·6% of the population was Roman Catholic and 4% Protestant.

Education. Primary education has been free since 1889 in lay schools for the two sexes in the communes and many villages. In 1988 public primary schools had 18,024 pupils and (1986) 890 teachers, 10,897 pupils and (1986) 793, the *lycées* and *collèges d'enseignement secondaire*, 793 teachers and 9,085 pupils. Private schools had 152 teachers and 2,224 pupils. The *Institut Henri Visioz* forms part of the *Université des Antilles-Guyane* (4,817 students in 1988) with 253 students.

Health. There were (1986) 160 physicians, 44 dentists, 33 pharmacists, 29 midwives and 496 nursing personnel. In 1989 there were 4 hospitals and 2 private clinics.

MARTINIQUE

HISTORY. Discovered by Columbus in 1493, the island was known to its inhabitants as *Madinina*, from which its present name was corrupted. A French colony was established in 1635 and, apart from brief periods of British occupation the island has since remained under French control. On 19 March 1946 its status was altered to that of an Overseas Department, and in 1974 it also became an administrative region.

AREA AND POPULATION. The island, situated in the Lesser Antilles between Dominica and St Lucia, occupies an area of 1,079 sq. km (417 sq. miles). Population at the 1990 Census: 359,572. Fort-de-France (1990 population, 101,540) is the capital and port. Other towns are Rivière-Pilote (11,261) and La Trinité (10,330).

French is the official language, but the majority of the population speak Creole.

Vital statistics (1988): Live births 6,397; deaths 2,099; marriages 1,537.

CLIMATE. Fort-de-France. Jan. 74°F (23·5°C), July 78°F (25·6°C). Annual rainfall 72" (1,840 mm).

CONSTITUTION AND GOVERNMENT. The island is administered by a General Council of 45 members and a Regional Council of 41 members, both directly elected for terms of 6 years. The French government is represented by an appointed Commissioner. There are 3 *arrondissements*, sub-divided into 34 communes, each administered by an elected municipal council. Martinique is represented in the National Assembly by 4 deputies, in the Senate by 2 senators and on the Economic and Social Council by 2 councillors.

At the Regional Council elections of Oct. 1990, the electorate was 223,658. 91,433 votes were cast. The Progressive Martinique Party (PPM) won 14 seats with 29,961 votes; the UDF-RPR 9, with 20,364 votes; the Martinique Independence Movement (MIM) 7, with 15,090 votes. 5 seats went to a left-wing, and 4 to a right-wing, coalition, and 2 to independents.

Commissioner: Michel Morin.
President of the General Council: Émile Maurice.
President of the Regional Council: Camille Darsieres.

ECONOMY

Budget. The budget, 1988, balanced at 2,451m. francs.

Banking. The Institut d'Émission des Départements d'Outre-Mer is the official bank of the department. The Caisse Centrale de Coopération Économique is used by the Government in assisting the economic development of the department.

The Banque des Antilles Françaises (with a capital of 32·5m. francs), the Crédit Martiniquais (30·4m. francs), the Société Générale de Banque aux Antilles (15m. francs), the Banque Française Commerciale (49m. francs), the Banque Nationale de Paris and the Crédit Agricole are operating in Fort-de-France.

ENERGY AND NATURAL RESOURCES

Electricity. Production in 1987 totalled 513m. kwh.

Agriculture. Bananas, sugar and rum are the chief products, followed by pineapples, food and vegetables. In 1988 there were 3,458 hectares under sugar-cane, 8,290 hectares under bananas and 400 hectares under pineapples. Production (1988): Sugar, 7,500 tonnes; rum, 85,987 hectolitres; cane for sugar, 93,535 tonnes; cane for rum, 121,835 tonnes; bananas 200,000 tonnes; pineapples, 24,000 tonnes.

Livestock (1988): 43,000 cattle, 90,000 sheep, 48,000 pigs, 46,000 goats and 2,000 horses.

Forestry. Production (1985) 11,000 cu. metres. Forests comprise 26% of the land area.

Fisheries. The catch in 1988 was 3,068 tonnes.

INDUSTRY. Some food processing and chemical engineering is carried out by small and medium-size businesses. There is an oil refinery with a treatment capacity of 550,000 tonnes annually.

Labour. Economically active population in 1989 was 128,072 (75% in trade and commerce and 10% in agriculture). 29,705 persons were registered unemployed in 1989. On 1 July 1991 the minimum wage (SMIC) was raised to 1,083.53 francs a week.

COMMERCE. Trade in 1m. francs:

	1985	1986	1987	1988
Imports	6,050	6,065	6,708	7,722
Exports	1,300	1,496	1,163	1,172

In 1987 the main items of import were crude petroleum and foodstuffs; main items of export were petroleum products (14%), bananas (46%) and rum (13%); 65% of imports came from France and 64% of exports went to France and 24% to Guadeloupe.

Total trade between Martinique and UK (British Department of Trade returns, in £1,000 sterling):

	1987	1988	1989	1990	1991
Imports to UK	712	83	158	1,071	752
Exports and re-exports from UK	10,705	3,886	8,815	26,315	6,127

Tourism. In 1988 there were 712,000 tourists, including 482,500 cruise visitors.

COMMUNICATIONS

Roads. In 1989 there were 7 km of motorway, 260 km of national roads, 620 km of district roads and 803 km of local roads. In 1987 there were 10,065 passenger cars and 2,361 commercial vehicles registered.

Aviation. In 1988, 1,273,376 passengers arrived and departed by Air France, Minerve, Aéromaritime, Air Martinique, Air Guadeloupe and Corso Air International at Fort-de-France–Lamentin international airport.

Shipping. The island is visited regularly by French, American and other lines. In 1987, 1,330 commercial vessels called at Martinique and discharged 8,970 passengers and (1988) 1,573,400 tonnes of freight and embarked 7,744 passengers and (1988) 711,000 tonnes of freight, excluding about 150,000 passengers calling in transit.

Telecommunications. There were, in 1985, 46 post offices and, 81,985 telephones. Radio-telephone service to Europe is available. R.F.O. broadcasts on FM wave, and operates 2 channels (1 satellite). In 1984 there were 46,000 radio and 42,500 TV receivers.

Newspapers. In 1989 there was 1 daily newspaper with a circulation of 19,000.

JUSTICE, RELIGION, EDUCATION AND WELFARE

Justice. Justice is administered by 2 lower courts (*tribunaux d'instance*), a higher court (*tribunal de grande instance*), a regional court of appeal, a commercial court, a court of assizes and an administrative court. For definitions *see* pp.494-95.

Religion. In 1982, 94% of the population was Roman Catholic.

Education. Education is compulsory between the ages of 6 and 16 years. In 1989, there were 49,920 pupils in primary schools, and 43,287 pupils in 46 secondary schools. There were 29 institutes of higher education. The *Université des Antilles-Guyane* had (1988) 4,817 students of which Martinique had about 2,600 students.

Health. In 1989 there were 17 hospitals, including 1 central, 10 general, 5 maternity, 1 psychiatric and 1 sanatorium. There were (1986) 3,427 hospital beds, 519 doctors, 160 pharmacists, 110 dentists and 134 midwives.

Further Reading

Annuaire statistique I.N.S.E.E. 1977–80. Martinique, 1982
La Martinique en quelques chiffres. Martinique, 1982
Guide Economique des D.O.M.-T.O.M., Paris, 1982

RÉUNION

HISTORY. Réunion (formerly Île Bourbon) became a French possession in 1638 and remained so until 19 March 1946, when its status was altered to that of an Overseas Department; in 1974 it also became an administrative region.

AREA AND POPULATION. The island of Réunion lies in the Indian Ocean, about 880 km east of Madagascar and 210 km south west of Mauritius. It has an area of 2,512 sq. km (968·5 sq. miles). Provisional population figures at the 1990 census: 596,693. The capital is Saint-Denis (population, 1990: 121,671); other towns are Saint-Paul (72,000) and Saint-Pierre (50,082). The official language is French. There is a creole vernacular.

Vital statistics (1989): Live births, 10,574; deaths, 3,306; marriages, (1988) 3,354.

The islands of Juan de Nova, Europa, Bassas da India, Îles Glorieuses and Tromelin, with a combined area of 32 sq. km, are uninhabited and lie at various points in the Indian Ocean adjacent to Madagascar. They remained French after Madagascar's independence in 1960, and are now administered by Réunion. Both Mauritius and the Seychelles claim Tromelin (transferred by the UK from the Seychelles to France in 1954), and Madagascar claims all 5 islands.

CLIMATE. A sub-tropical maritime climate, free from extremes of weather, though the island lies in the cyclone belt of the Indian Ocean. Conditions are generally humid and there is no well-defined dry season. Saint-Denis. Jan. 80°F (26·7°C), July 70°F (21·1°C). Annual rainfall 56" (1,400 mm).

CONSTITUTION AND GOVERNMENT. Réunion is administered by a General Council (*Conseil Général*) of 44 members and a Regional Council of 45 members, both directly elected for terms of 6 years. Réunion is represented in the National Assembly in Paris by 5 deputies, in the Senate by 3 senators, and in the

Economic and Social Council by 1 councillor. There are 4 *arrondissements*, subdivided into 24 communes each administered by an elected municipal council. The French government is represented by an appointed Commissioner.

Commissioner: Jacques Dewatre.
President of the General Council: Eric Boyer.
President of the Regional Council: Pierre Lagourgue.

ECONOMY

Production. GDP was estimated at 22·7m francs in 1988.

Budget. The budget for 1987 balanced at 2,938m. French francs.

Banking. The Institut d'émission des Départements d'Outre-mer has the right to issue bank-notes. Banks operating in Réunion are the Banque de la Réunion (Crédit Lyonnais), the Banque Nationale de Paris Internationale, the Caisse Régionale de Crédit Agricole Mutuel de la Réunion, the Banque Française Commerciale (BFC) CCP, Trésorerie Générale, and the Banque de la Réunion pour l'Economie et la Développement (BRED).

ENERGY AND NATURAL RESOURCES

Electricity. Production (1990) 905·4m. kwh.

Agriculture Production in tonnes: Sugar, 1990: 192,503; molasses, (1988): 79,500, bananas, 1988: 4,520; rum, 1990: 58,726 hectolitres; maize, 1988: 13,019; potatoes, 1989: 10,182; onions, 1989: 3,315; pineapples, 1989: 4,770; tomatoes, 1988: 3,155; vanilla, 1990: 9·6; tobacco, 1990: 99; geranium oil, 1990: 23·3.

Livestock (1988): 20,000 cattle, 75,000 pigs, 3,000 sheep, 44,000 goats and 4m. poultry. Meat production (in tonnes): Cattle (1990, 1,242), pigs (1989, 7,599), goats (1989, 13) and poultry (1990, 11,420). Milk production (1988), 200,743 hectolitres.

Forestry. There were (1989) 100,392 ha. of forest. Roundwood production (1985) 75,000 cu. metres.

Fisheries. In 1990 the catch was 1,698 tonnes.

INDUSTRY. The major industries are electricity and sugar. Food processing, chemical engineering, printing and the production of textiles, tobacco, wood and construction materials are carried out by small and medium-sized businesses.

Labour. The workforce was 220,000 in 1989. 60,034 persons were registered unemployed. The sugar industry employed 3,844. On 1 July 1991 the minimum wage (SMIC) was raised to 1,055.59 francs a week.

COMMERCE. Trade in 1m. French francs:

	1985	1986	1987	1988	1990
Imports	7,457	7,861	8,751	9,839	11,322
Exports	802	930	887	1,058	999

The chief export is sugar, forming (1989) 94% by value. In 1989 (by value) 25·5% of imports were from, and 80% of exports to, France.

Total trade between Réunion and UK (British Department of Trade returns, in £1,000 sterling):

	1988	1989	1990	1991
Imports to UK	1,372	4,389	1,204	1,668
Exports and re-exports from UK	8,536	7,529	11,732	11,878

Tourism. There were 200,300 visitors in 1990, including 143,300 from France and 163,800 tourists.

COMMUNICATIONS

Roads. There were, in 1989, 2,719 km of roads. There were some 126,000 registered vehicles in 1989.

Aviation. Réunion is served by Air France (from 9 to 12 flights a week) and 7 other airlines: South African Airways, Air Mauritius, Air Madagascar, Minerve, Air Liberté, Air Outre Mer, and Corse Air. In 1989, 368,170 passengers and 13,181 tonnes of freight arrived at, and 370,215 passengers and 3,429 tonnes of freight departed from Saint-Denis-Gillot airport.

Shipping. 6 shipping lines serve the island. In 1989, 455 vessels visited the island, unloading 1,712,653 tonnes of freight and loading 368,355 tonnes at Pointe-des-Galets.

Telecommunications. There are telephone and telegraph connexions with Mauritius, Madagascar and metropolitan France. There are 641 post offices and a central telephone office; number of telephones (1990), 170,000.

RFO broadcasts in French on medium- and short-waves for more than 18 hours a day. There are 3 television channels broadcasting for 70 hours a week and one independent channel.

Cinemas. In 1990 there were 17 cinemas.

Newspapers. There were (1990) 3 daily newspapers, 3 weeklies and 3 monthlies.

JUSTICE, RELIGION, EDUCATION AND WELFARE

Justice. There are 3 lower courts (*tribunaux d'instance*), 2 higher courts (*tribunaux de grande instance*), 1 appeal, 1 administrative court and 1 conciliation board. For definitions *see* pp.494-95.

Religion. In 1990, 95% of the population was Roman Catholic.

Education. In 1989-90 there were 107,537 pupils in primary, and 75,827 pupils in secondary, education. Secondary education was provided in (1989–90) 7 *lycées*, 56 *collèges*, and 12 technical *lycées*. There were 18 primary and secondary private schools, with 13,264 pupils. The *Université Française de l'Océan Indien* (founded 1971) had 5,000 students in 1989–90.

Health. In 1989 there were 19 hospitals with 3,270 beds, 928 physicians, 250 dentists, 185 pharmacists, 140 midwives and 2,070 nursing personnel.

Further Reading

Institut National de la Statistique et des Etudes Economiques. *Tableau Economique de la Réunion.* Paris, 1989
Bulletin de la Chambre de Commerce et de l'Industrie de la Réunion
Bertile, W., *Atlas Thématique et Régional.* Réunion, 1990

TERRITORIAL COLLECTIVITIES

MAYOTTE

HISTORY. Mayotte was a French colony from 1843 until 1914, when it was attached, with the other Comoro islands, to the government-general of Madagascar. The Comoro group was granted administrative autonomy within the French Republic and became an Overseas Territory.

When the other 3 islands voted to become independent (as the Comoro state) in 1974, Mayotte voted against this and remained a French dependency. In Dec. 1976, it became (following a further referendum) a Territorial Collectivity.

AREA AND POPULATION. Mayotte, east of the Comoro Islands, consists of a main island (362 sq. km) with 67,167 inhabitants at the 1985 Census (estimate mid-1991 85,000) containing the chief town, Mamoundzou (12,119); and the smaller island of Pamanzi (11 sq. km) lying 2 km to the east, with 9,775 inhabitants in 1985, containing the old capital of Dzaoudzi (5,675). The whole territory covers 373 sq. km (144 sq. miles). The spoken language is Mahorian (akin to Comoran, an Arabized dialect of Swahili), but French remains the official and commercial language.

CONSTITUTION AND GOVERNMENT. The island is administered by a *Conseil Général* of 17 members, directly elected for a 6-year term. The French government is represented by an appointed Commissioner. Mayotte is represented by 1 deputy in the National Assembly and by 1 member in the Senate. There are 17 communes, including 2 on Pamanzi.

Commissioner: Akli Khider.
President of the Conseil Général: Younoussa Bamana.

ECONOMY

Budget. In 1984, revenue was 137·1m. francs (44% being subsidies from France) and expenditure 148·4m. francs. The 1985 Budget balanced at 313m. francs.

Currency. Since Feb. 1976 the currency has been the (metropolitan) *French franc*.

Banking. The *Institut d'Emission d'Outre-mer* and the *Banque Française Commerciale* both have branches in Dzaoudzi.

ENERGY AND NATURAL RESOURCES

Electricity. Production (1982) 5m. kwh.

Agriculture. The area under cultivation in 1986 was some 8,000 ha. The main food crops (1985 production in tonnes) were mangoes (1,500), bananas (1,300), breadfruit (700), cassava (500) and pineapples (200). The chief cash crops (1986 output in tonnes) were: Essence of ylang-ylang (21), vanilla (35), coffee (9·2, 1985), copra, cinnamon and cloves.

Livestock (1986): Cattle, 3,000; goats, 15,000; pigs, 2,000. (1982): poultry, about 13,000.

Fisheries. A lobster and shrimp industry has recently been created. Annual catch is about 2,000 tonnes.

COMMERCE. In 1986 exports totalled 4·7m. francs (95% to France and 5% to Réunion) and imports 200m. francs, from France, South Africa, Bahrain, Thailand and Réunion.

Total trade between Mayotte and UK (British Department of Trade returns, in £1,000 sterling):

	1988	1989	1990	1991
Imports to UK	654	117	103	138
Exports and re-exports from UK	3,123	5,059	2,474	3,255

Tourism. In 1986 there were 1,200 visitors. There were about 100 tourist beds.

COMMUNICATIONS

Roads. In 1984 there were 93 km of main roads and 137 km of local roads, with 1,528 motor vehicles.

Aviation. Air France, and 2 other local air lines call at the airport on the island Pamandzi. In 1985, 17,426 passengers and 172 tonnes of freight arrived and departed by air.

Telecommunications. Since 1977 RFO broadcasts and in 1986, television was installed.

Post and Broadcasting. In 1984 there were 6,000 radio receivers. Telephones (1981) 400.

Newspapers. There is 1 daily newspaper, *le Journal de Mayotte*.

JUSTICE, RELIGION, EDUCATION AND WELFARE

Justice. There is a *tribunal de première instance* and a *tribunal supérieur d'appel*.

Religion. The population is 97% Sunni Moslem, with a small Christian (mainly Roman Catholic) minority.

Education. In 1987 there were 15,632 pupils and 366 teachers in 28 primary schools; 1,392 pupils in 1 secondary school; and 475 students in 2 technical and teacher-training establishments.

Health. In 1985 there were 9 doctors, 1 dentist, 1 pharmacist, 2 midwives and 51 nursing personnel. There were 2 hospitals with 77 beds.

ST PIERRE AND MIQUELON

Îles Saint-Pierre et Miquelon

HISTORY. The only remaining fragment of the once-extensive French possessions in North America, the archipelago was settled from France in the 17th century. It was a French territory from 1816 until 1976, an overseas department until 1985, and is now a territorial collectivity.

AREA AND POPULATION. The archipelago consists of 8 small islands off the south coast of Newfoundland, with a total area of 242 sq. km, comprising the Saint-Pierre group (26 sq. km) and the Miquelon-Langlade group (216 sq. km). The population (census, 1990) was 6,392 of whom 5,683 were on Saint-Pierre and 709 on Miquelon. The chief town is St Pierre.

Vital statistics (1990): Births, 75; marriages, 31; deaths, 33.

CONSTITUTION AND GOVERNMENT. The dependency is administered by a General Council of 19 members, directly elected for a 6-year term. It is represented in the National Assembly in Paris by 1 deputy, in the Senate by 1 senator and in the Economic and Social Council by 1 councillor. The French government is represented by an appointed Commissioner.

Prefect: Karnel Khrissate.
President of the General Council: Marc Plantegenest.

ECONOMY

Budget. The ordinary budget for 1990 balanced at 104·6m. francs.

Currency. The French franc is in use.

Banking. Banks include the Banque des Îles Saint-Pierre et Miquelon and the Crédit Saint-Pierrais.

ENERGY AND NATURAL RESOURCES

Electricity. Production (1990) 45·9m. kwh.

Agriculture. The islands, being mostly barren rock, are unsuited for agriculture, but some vegetables are grown and livestock kept for local consumption.

Fisheries. The catch amounted in 1990 to 12,149 tonnes, chiefly cod.

INDUSTRY. The island's main industry, from fishing is frozen fish production.

Labour. Economically active population in 1989 was 2,729 (41% in fish industry, electricity production and in services).

COMMERCE. Trade in 1m. francs:

	1987	1988	1989	1990
Imports	343·5	366·7	533·1	471·0
Exports	186·7	143·5	200·8	226·6

In 1990, 54% of imports came from Canada, while 63% of exports were to France, 18% to EEC and 19% to Canada.

The main exports are fish (74%), shellfish (18%) and fishmeal (8%).

Total trade between St Pierre and Miquelon and UK (British Department of Trade returns in £1,000 sterling):

	1987	1988	1989	1990	1991
Imports to UK	77	159	164	719	444
Exports and re-exports from UK	604	470	533	450	966

Tourism. There were (1990) 14,900 visitors.

COMMUNICATIONS

Roads. In 1988 there were 120 km of roads, of which 50 km were paved. In 1990 there were 1,866 passenger cars and 754 commercial vehicles.

Civil Aviation. Air Saint-Pierre connects St Pierre with Montreal, with Halifax and Sydney (Nova Scotia), and there are occasional flights to and from St John's (Newfoundland).

Shipping. St Pierre has regular services to Fortune and Halifax in Canada. In 1990, 118,253 tonnes of freight were unloaded and 66,794 tonnes loaded, while 1,272 ships (of 1·85m. gross tonnage) entered the harbour.

Telecommunications. There were 3,200 telephones in 1990. RFO broadcasts in French on medium-waves and on 2 television channels (1 satellite). St Pierre is connected by radio-telecommunication with most countries of the world.

JUSTICE, RELIGION, EDUCATION AND WELFARE

Justice. There is a court of first instance and a higher court of appeal at St Pierre. For definitions see pp.000-00.

Religion. The population is chiefly Roman Catholic.

Education. Primary instruction is free. There were, in 1990, 5 nursery and 5 primary schools with 875 pupils and 4 secondary schools (including 2 technical schools) with 702 pupils.

Health. There was (1990) 1 hospital on St Pierre with 100 beds; 12 doctors and 4 dentists.

Further Reading

De Curton, E., Saint-Pierre et Miquelon. Paris, 1944
De La Rüe, E. A., Saint-Pierre et Miquelon. Paris, 1963
Ribault, J. Y., Histoire de Saint-Pierre et Miquelon: Des Origines à 1814. St Pierre, 1962

OVERSEAS TERRITORIES

Among the 7 French Overseas Territories remaining since Algerian independence in 1962, the Comoro Islands declared their independence on 6 July 1975 (recognized by France on 31 Dec.), but the island of Mayotte remained French and in Dec. 1976 was classed as a 'territorial collectivity'. The territory of Saint Pierre and Miquelon became a fifth Overseas Department in July 1976, but in June 1985 it acquired the same status as Mayotte. The former French Somaliland (subsequently Territory of the Afars and Issas) became independent on 27 June 1977 as the Republic of Djibouti. The remaining French Overseas Territories are New Caledonia (with its dependencies), French Polynesia, Wallis and Futuna, and the French Southern and Antarctic Territories.

SOUTHERN AND ANTARCTIC TERRITORIES

Terres Australes et Antarctiques Françaises (TAAF)

The Territory of the TAAF was created on 6 Aug. 1955. It comprises the Kerguelen and Crozet archipelagoes, the islands of Saint Paul and Amsterdam (formerly Nouvelle Amsterdam), all in the southern Indian ocean, and Terre Adélie.

The Administrator is assisted by a 7-member consultative council which meets twice yearly in Paris; its members are nominated by the Government for 5 years. The 12 members of the Scientific Council are appointed by the Senior Administrator after approval by the Minister in charge of scientific research. A 15-member Consultative Committee on the Environment, created in Nov. 1982, meets at least once a year to discuss all problems relating to the preservation of the environment. The administration has its seat in Paris.

Administrateur supérieur: Bernard de Gouttes.

The staff of the permanent scientific stations of the TAAF (193 in 1991–92) is renewed annually and forms the only population.

Kerguelen islands, situated 48–50° S. lat., 68–70° E. long., consists of 1 large and 85 smaller islands and over 200 islets and rocks with a total area of 7,215 sq. km (2,786 sq. miles), of which Grande Terre occupies 6,675 sq. km (2,577 sq. miles). It was discovered in 1772 by Yves de Kerguelen, but was effectively occupied by France only in 1949. Port-aux-Français has several scientific research stations (85 members). Reindeer, trout and sheep have been acclimatized.

Crozet islands, situated 46° S. lat., 50–52° E. long., consists of 5 larger and 15 tiny islands, with a total area of 505 sq. km (195 sq. miles); the western group includes Apostles, Pigs and Penguins islands; the eastern group, Possession and Eastern islands. The archipelago was discovered in 1772 by Marion Dufresne, whose mate, Crozet, annexed it for Louis XV. A meteorological and scientific station (37 members) at Base Alfred-Faure on Possession Island was built in 1964.

Amsterdam Island and **Saint-Paul Island,** situated 38–39° S. lat., 77° E. long. Amsterdam, with an area of 54 sq. km (21 sq. miles) was discovered in 1522 by Magellan's companions; Saint-Paul, lying about 100 km to the south, with an area of 7 sq. km (2·7 sq. miles), was probably discovered in 1559 by Portuguese sailors. Both were first visited in 1633 by the Dutch explorer, Van Diemen, and were annexed by France in 1843. They are both extinct volcanoes. The only inhabitants are at Base Martin de Vivies, established in 1949 on Amsterdam Island, with several scientific research stations, hospital, communication and other facilities (37 members). Crayfish are caught commercially on Amsterdam.

Terre Adélie comprises that section of the Antarctic continent between 136° and 142° E. long., south of 60° S. lat. The ice-covered plateau has an area of about 432,000 sq. km (166,800 sq. miles), and was discovered in 1840 by Dumont d'Urville. A research station (34 members) is situated at Base Dumont d'Urville, which is maintained by the French Polar Expeditions.

NEW CALEDONIA

Nouvelle Calédonie et Dépendances

HISTORY. New Caledonia was annexed by France in 1853 and, together with most of its former dependencies, became an overseas territory in 1958.

AREA AND POPULATION. The territory comprises the island of New Caledonia and various outlying islands, all situated in the south-west Pacific with a total land area of 18,576 sq. km (7,172 sq. miles). In 1989 the population (census) was 164,173, including 55,085 Europeans (majority French), 73,598 Melanesians (Kanaks), 7,652 Vietnamese and Indonesians, 4,750 Polynesians, 14,186 Wallisians, 8,902 others. The capital, Nouméa had (1989) 65,110 inhabitants. Vital statistics (1990): Live births, 4,354; deaths, 895.

The main islands are:

1. The island of New Caledonia with an area of 16,372 sq. km, has a total length of about 400 km, and an average breadth of 50 km, and a population (census, 1989) of 144,051. The east coast is predominantly Melanesian, the Nouméa region predominantly European, and the rest of the west coast of mixed population.

2. The Loyalty Islands, 100 km (60 miles) east of New Caledonia, consisting of 3 large islands, Maré, Lifou and Uvéa, and many small islands with a total area of 1,981 sq. km and a population (census, 1989) of 17,912, nearly all Melanesians except on Uvéa, which is partly Polynesian. The chief culture in the islands is that of coconuts and the chief export, copra.

3. The Isle of Pines, 50 km (30 miles) to the south-east of Nouméa, with an area of 152 sq. km and a population of 1,465 (census 1989), is a tourist and fishing centre.

4. The Bélep Archipelago, about 50 km north-west of New Caledonia, with an area of 70 sq. km and a population of 745 (census 1989).

The remaining islands are all very small and none have permanent inhabitants. The largest are the Chesterfield Islands, a group of 11 well-wooded coral islets with a combined area of 10 sq. km, about 550 km west of the Bélep Archipelago. The Huon Islands, a group of 4 barren coral islets with a combined area of just 65 ha, are 225 km north of the Bélep Archipelago. Walpole, a limestone coral island of 1 sq. km, lies 150 km east of the Isle of Pines; Matthew Island (20 ha.) and Hunter Island (2 sq. km), respectively 250 km and 330 km east of Walpole, are spasmodically active volcanic islands also claimed by Vanuatu.

CLIMATE. Nouméa. Jan. 78°F (25·6°C), July 67°F (19·4°C). Annual rainfall 43" (1,083 mm).

CONSTITUTION AND GOVERNMENT. Following constitutional changes introduced by the French government in 1985 and 1988, the Territory is administered by a High Commissioner assisted by a 4-member Consultative Committee, consisting of the President of the Territorial Congress (as President) and the Presidents of the 3 Provincial Assemblies. The French government is represented by the appointed High Commissioner. In Sept. 1987 the electorate voted in favour of remaining a French possession.

There is a 54-member Territorial Congress consisting of the complete membership of the 3 Provincial Assemblies.

New Caledonia is represented in the National Assembly by 2 deputies, in the Senate by 1 senator and in the Economic and Social Council by 1 councillor.

The Territory is divided into 3 provinces, Nord, Sud and Iles Loyauté, each under a directly-elected Regional Council. They are sub-divided into 32 communes administered by locally-elected councils and mayors.

Agreement was reached in June 1988 between the French government and representatives of both the European and Melanesian communities on New Caledonia, and confirmed in Nov. 1988 by plebiscites in both France and New Caledonia, under which the territory has been divided into 3 autonomous provinces, and a further referendum on full independence will be held in 1998.

High Commissioner: Alain Christnacht.

ECONOMY

Budget. The budget for 1989 balanced at 51,786m. francs CFP.

Currency. The unit of currency is the *CFP franc* (XPF), with a parity of 18·18 to the French franc.

Banking. There are branches of the Westpac Banking Corporation, the Banque Nationale de Paris, the Banque de Paris et des Pays-Bas, the Société Générale, and the Banque de la Nouvelle-Calédonie (Crédit Lyonnais).

ENERGY AND NATURAL RESOURCES

Electricity. In 1990, production totalled 1,147m. kwh.

Minerals. The mineral resources are very great; nickel, chrome and iron abound; silver, gold, cobalt, lead, manganese, iron and copper have been mined at different times. The nickel deposits are of special value, being without arsenic. Production of nickel ore in 1990, 4·4m. tonnes and chrome ore 111,031 tonnes. In 1990 the furnaces produced 9,683 tonnes of matte nickel and 32,278 tonnes of ferro-nickel.

Agriculture. In 1989 7,646 persons worked in agriculture. In 1990 274,000 ha were pasture land; about 19,000 ha were commercially cultivated. The chief products are beef, pork, poultry, coffee, copra, maize, fruit and vegetables.

Livestock (1989): Cattle, 121,000; pigs, 35,000; goats, 18,000.

Forestry. There are about 0·4m. ha of forest. Roundwood production (1989) 6,675 cu. metres.

Fisheries. The catch in 1990 totalled 6,278 tonnes.

INDUSTRY. Local industries include chlorine and oxygen plants, cement, soft drinks, barbed wire, nails, pleasure and fishing boats, clothing, pasta, household cleaners and confectionery.

Labour. The working population (1989 census) was 54,230.

COMMERCE. Imports and exports in 1m. CFP francs:

	1986	1987	1988	1989	1990
Imports	62,939	63,349	65,386	88,608	86,929
Exports	26,249	20,653	50,805	77,900	43,931

In 1990, 47·5% of the imports came from France and 8·5% from Australia, while 33·1% of the exports went to France. Refined minerals (mainly ferro-nickel and nickel) formed 75% of exports by value, nickel ore 14·5% and chrome ore 0·04%. Imports to the UK (British Department of Trade returns, £1,000 sterling, 1991) 45; exports from the UK, 5,045.

Tourism. Tourists, 1989, 75,621 (14·7% French, 35·2% Japanese).

COMMUNICATIONS

Roads. There were, in 1987, 6,340 km of roads, of which 1,823·5 km were paved. There were (1989) 62,000 vehicles.

Civil Aviation. New Caledonia is connected by air routes with France and Tahiti (by UTA), Australia (UTA and Qantas), New Zealand (UTA and Air New Zealand), Fiji and Wallis and Futuna (by Air Cal International), Vanuatu (by UTA), and Nauru (by Air Nauru). In 1990, 132,218 passengers arrived and 131,819 departed via La Tontouta airport, near Nouméa. Internal services connect Nouméa with 21 domestic air fields.

Shipping. In 1990, 536 vessels entered Nouméa unloading 903,000 tonnes of goods and loading 2·26m. tonnes of which 1m. tonnes comprised mineral exports.

Telecommunications. There were (1989) 46 post offices and telex, telephone, radio and television services. There were (1990) 26,643 telephones. Radiodiffusion Française d'Outre-Mer broadcasts in French on medium- and short-wave radio (there are also 9 private stations) and on 2 television channels (colour by SECAM). There were about 90,000 radios in 1991 and 35,000 TV sets.

Cinemas. In 1991 there were 11 cinemas.

Newspapers. In 1992 there was 1 daily newspaper with a circulation of 20,000.

JUSTICE, RELIGION, EDUCATION AND WELFARE

Justice. There is a *Tribunal de Première Instance* and a *Cour d'Appel* in Nouméa.

Religion. In 1980 over 72% of the population was Roman Catholic, 16% Protestant and 4% Moslem.

Education. In 1990, there were 34,242 pupils and 1,696 teachers in 279 primary schools, 14,237 pupils in 43 secondary schools, 6,765 students in 31 technical and vocational schools, and 1,207 students and 72 teaching staff in 6 higher education establishments. The University of the Pacific had 603 students and 27 academic staff in 1991.

Health. In 1990 there were 216 physicians, 64 dentists, 46 pharmacists, 38 midwives and 1,038 paramedical personnel; 6 hospitals, 21 medical centres, 3 infirmaries and 19 dispensaries had a total of 1,118 beds.

Further Reading

Journal Officiel de la Nouvelle Calédonie
Tableaux de l'Economie Caledonienne, 1991
Information statistiques rapides. (monthly)

FRENCH POLYNESIA

Territoire de la Polynésie Française

HISTORY. French protectorates since 1843, these islands were annexed to France 1880–82 to form 'French Settlements in Oceania', which opted in Nov. 1958 for the status of an overseas territory within the French Community.

AREA AND POPULATION. The total land area of these 5 archipelagoes, scattered over a wide area in the Eastern Pacific is 3,265 sq. km (1,260 sq. miles). The population, Census, 1983, was 166,753; census (1988) 188,814.

The official languages are French and Tahitian.

Vital statistics (1987): Births, 5,384; marriages, 1,251; deaths, 980.

The islands are administratively divided into 5 *circonscriptions:*

1. The **Windward Islands** (Îles du Vent) (140,341 inhabitants in 1988) comprise Tahiti with an area of 1,042 sq. km and 115,820 inhabitants; Moorea with an area of 132 sq. km and 7,059 inhabitants; Maio (Tubuai Manu) with an area of 9 sq. km and 190 inhabitants, and the smaller Mehetia and Tetiaroa. The capital is Papeete (78,814 inhabitants including suburbs).

2. The **Leeward Islands** (Îles sous le Vent), comprise the volcanic islands of Raiatéa, Tahaa, Huahine, Bora-Bora and Maupiti, together with 4 small atolls, the group having a total land area of 404 sq. km and 22,232 inhabitants in 1988. The chief town is Uturoa on Raiatéa.

The Windward and Leeward Islands together are called the Society Archipelago (Archipel de la Société). Tahitian, a Polynesian language, is spoken throughout the archipelago and used as a *lingua franca* in the rest of the territory.

3. The **Tuamotu Archipelago**, consisting of two parallel ranges of 78 atolls lying north and east of the Society Archipelago, have a total area of 690 sq. km; the most populous atolls are Rangiroa, Hao and Turéia. Mururoa and Fangataufa atolls in the south-east of the group have been used by France for nuclear tests since 1966, having been ceded to France in 1964 by the Territorial Assembly.

The *circonscription* (12,374 inhabitants in 1988) also includes the **Gambier Islands** further east (of which Mangareva is the principal), with an area of 36 sq. km and a population of 582; the chief centre is Rikitea on Mangareva.

4. The **Austral or Tubuai Islands**, lying south of the Society Archipelago, comprise a 1,300 km chain of volcanic islands and reefs. They include Rimatara, Rurutu, Tubuai, Raivaevae and, 500 km to the south, Rapa-Iti, with a combined area of 148 sq. km and 6,509 (1988) inhabitants; the chief centre is Mataura on Tubuai.

5. The **Marquesas Islands**, lying north of the Tuamotu Archipelago, with a total area of 1,049 sq. km and 7,538 (1988) inhabitants, comprise Nukuhiva, Uapu, Uahuka, Hivaoa, Tahuata, Fatuhiva and 4 smaller (uninhabited) islands; the chief centre is Taiohae on Nukuhiva.

CLIMATE. Papeete. Jan. 81°F (27·1°C), July 75°F (24°C). Annual rainfall 83" (2,106 mm).

CONSTITUTION AND GOVERNMENT. Under the 1984 Constitution, the Territory is administered by a Council of Ministers, whose President is elected by the Territorial Assembly from among its own members; he appoints a Vice-President and 9 other ministers. There is an advisory Economic and Social Committee. French Polynesia is represented in the French Assembly by 2 deputies, in the Senate by 1 senator, and in the Economic and Social Council by 1 councillor. The French government is represented by a High Commissioner. The *Territorial Assembly* comprises 41 members elected every 5 years by universal suffrage using the same proportional representation system as in metropolitan French regional elections. To be elected a party must gain at least 5% of votes cast. The Assembly elects a head of local government.

Elections were held in March 1991. The electorate was 109,462; turn-out was 84,798 (78·35%).

Rassemblement pour le Peuple (RPP; affiliated to the French Rassemblement pour la République) won 18 seats with 31·41% of votes cast; Polynesian Union 14 with 23·27%; New Fatherland (NF) 5 with 12·28%; Independent Liberation Front of Polynesia 4 with 11·43%. An RPR-NF coalition was formed under Gaston Flosse (RPR).

High Commissioner: Jean Montpezat.
President of the Council of Ministers: Alexandre Leontieff.

Flag: Three horizontal stripes of red, white, red, with the white of double width containing the emblem of French Polynesia in yellow.

ECONOMY

Budget. The ordinary budget for 1987 balanced at 52,135m. francs CFP.

Currency. The unit of currency is the *franc CFP* (XPF), with a parity of *CFP francs* 18·18 to the French *franc*.

Banking. There are 5 commercial banks, the Bank Indosuez, the Bank of Tahiti, the Banque de Polynésie, Paribas Pacifique and Société de Crédit et de Développement de l'Océanie.

ENERGY AND NATURAL RESOURCES

Electricity. Production in 1987 amounted to 265m. kwh (18% hydro-electric).

Agriculture. An important product is copra (coconut trees covering the coastal plains of the mountainous islands and the greater part of the low-lying islands), production (1988) 15,000 tonnes. Tropical fruits, such as bananas, pineapples, oranges, etc., are grown only for local consumption.

Livestock (1988): Cattle, 10,000; horses, 2,000; pigs, 54,000; sheep, 2,000; goats, 3,000; poultry, 1m.

Fisheries. The catch in 1986 amounted to 1,703 tonnes of fish.

COMMERCE. Trade in 1m. francs CFP:

	1983	1984	1985	1986	1987
Imports	74,241	85,622	88,864	92,666	90,544
Exports	4,823	5,084	6,564	5,106	8,986

Total trade between French Polynesia and UK (British Department of Trade returns, in £1,000 sterling):

	1987	1988	1989	1990	1991
Imports to UK	18	56	416	16	58
Exports and re-exports from UK	5,275	3,421	3,996	4,763	4,362

Chief exports are coconut oil and cultured pearls. In 1987, France provided 52% of imports and USA 13%, while (1985) 44% of exports went to France and 21% to USA.

Tourism. Tourism is very important, earning almost half as much as the visible exports. There were 143,000 tourists in 1987.

COMMUNICATIONS

Roads. In 1985 there were 797 km of roads and 44,000 vehicles.

Aviation. Seven international airlines connect Tahiti with Paris, Los Angeles and many Pacific locations. There is also a regular air service between Faaa airport (on Tahiti), Moorea and the Leeward Isles with occasional connexions to the other groups. In 1987, 194,218 international passengers arrived and 197,301 departed *via* the airports at Faaa and on Mooréa and Bora-Bora. Thirty other airfields have regular domestic services.

Shipping. Several shipping companies connect France, San Francisco, New Zealand, Japan, Australia, South East Asia and most Pacific locations with Papeete.

Telecommunications. Number of telephones (1985), 28,192. *Radio Tele Tahiti* belongs to *Société de Radiodiffusion et de Télévision pour l'Outre-mer* (RFO) and broadcasts in French, Tahitian and English on medium- and short-waves and also broadcasts 1 television programme *via* 5 transmitters. There are also 9 private radio stations. Number of receivers (1986): Radio, 84,000; TV, 26,400.

Cinemas. In 1986 there were 8 cinemas in Papeete.

Newspapers. In 1988 there were 2 daily newspapers.

JUSTICE, RELIGION, EDUCATION AND WELFARE

Justice. There is a *tribunal de première instance* and a *cour d'appel* at Papeete.

Religion. In 1980 it was estimated that 46·5% of the inhabitants were Protestants, 39·4% Roman Catholic and 5·1% Mormon.

Education. There were, in 1987-88, 42,735 pupils in 264 primary schools, 15,002 pupils in 41 secondary schools, and 4,156 pupils in technical schools and teacher-training colleges.

Health. There were (1987) 273 physicians, 88 dentists, 35 pharmacists, 24 midwives and 464 nursing personnel. There was (1987) a main hospital at Mamao (on Tahiti), 7 secondary hospitals, 2 private clinics, 9 medical centres and 18 infirmaries, with together 1,048 beds.

DEPENDENCY. The uninhabited Clipperton Island, 1,000 km off the west coast of Mexico, is administered by the High Commissioner for French Polynesia but does not form part of the Territory; it is an atoll with an area of 5 sq. km.

Further Reading

Journal Officiel des Etablissements Françaises de l'Océanie, and *Supplement Containing Statistics of Commerce and Navigation*. Papeete
Andrews, E., *Comparative Dictionary of the Tahitian Language*. Chicago, 1944
Bounds, J. H., *Tahiti*. Bend, Oregon, 1978
Luke, Sir Harry, *The Islands of the South Pacific*. London, 1961
O'Reilly, P. and Reitman, E., *Bibliographie de Tahiti et de la Polynésie française*. Paris, 1967
O'Reilly, P. and Teissier, R., *Tahitiens. Répertoire bio-bibliographique de la Polynésie française*. Paris, 1963

WALLIS AND FUTUNA

HISTORY. French dependencies since 1842, the inhabitants of these islands voted on 22 Dec. 1959 by 4,307 votes out of 4,576 in favour of exchanging their status to that of an overseas territory, which took effect from 29 July 1961.

AREA AND POPULATION. The territory comprises two groups of islands (total area 274 sq. km) in the central Pacific, The Iles de Hoorn lie 240 km north-east of Fiji and consist of 2 main islands–Futuna (64 sq. km) and uninhabited Alofi (51 sq. km). The Wallis Archipelago lies another 160 km further north-east, and comprises one main island – Uvea (159 sq. km), with a surrounding coral reef. The capital is Mata-Utu (815 inhabitants, 1983) on Uvea.

The resident population, census March 1985, was 12,408 (Uvea, 8,084; Futuna, 4,324) (estimate, 1988, 15,400), comprising 7,843 on Uvea and 4,100 on Futuna. In 1990 11,943 Wallisians lived in New Caledonia. Wallisian and Futunian are distinct Polynesian languages.

CONSTITUTION AND GOVERNMENT. The Senior Administrator represents the French government and carries out the duties of head of the territory, assisted by a 20-member Territorial Assembly, directly elected for a 5-year term, and a 6-member Territorial Council, comprising the 3 traditional chiefs and 3 nominees of the Senior Administrator agreed by the Territorial Assembly. The territory is represented in Paris by 1 deputy in the National Assembly, by 1 senator in the Senate, and by 1 member on the Economic and Social Council. There are 3 districts: Singave and Alo (both on Futuna) and Wallis. In each tribal kings exercise customary powers assisted by ministers and district and village chiefs.

Senior Administrator: Jacques Le Ilénaff.
President of the Territorial Assembly: Falakiko Gata.

ECONOMY

Policy. A development plan was adopted in 1986.

Budget. The 1982 budget provided for expenditure of 303·8m. francs CFP.

Currency. The unit of currency is the *CFP franc* (XPF), with a parity of 18·18 to the French franc.

Banking. There is a branch of Indosuez at Mata-Utu.

ENERGY AND NATURAL RESOURCES

Electricity. There is a thermal power station at Mata-Utu. Supply is 220 volts; 50 Hz.

Agriculture. The chief products are copra, cassava, yams, taro roots and bananas.
Livestock: Pigs, 30,000 (1988); goats, 8,000 (1988).

COMMERCE. Imports (1984) amounted to 1,302m. CFP francs. There are few exports.

COMMUNICATIONS

Roads. In 1977 there were 100 km of roads on Uvea.

Civil Aviation. There is an airport on Wallis, at Hihifo, and another near Alo on Futuna. 3 flights a week link Wallis and Futuna. Air Calédonie International operates 2 flights a week to Nouméa.

Shipping. A regular cargo service links Mata-Utu (Wallis) and Singave (Futuna) with Nouméa (New Caledonia).

Telecommunications. In 1986 there were 2 radio stations and 6 post offices. In 1985 there were 340 telephones.

JUSTICE, RELIGION, EDUCATION AND WELFARE

Justice. There is a court of first instance, from which appeals can be made to the court of appeal in New Caledonia. For definitions *see* pp.494-95.

Religion. The majority of the population is Roman Catholic.

Education. In 1989, there were 4,080 pupils in primary classes and 542 in (some 90% of school-age children) lower secondary classes. Further education is available in New Caledonia.

Health. In 1990 there was 1 hospital with 45 beds and 4 dispensaries.

GABON

Capital: Libreville
Population: 1·22m. (1988)
GNP per capita: US$3,300 (1990)

République Gabonaise

HISTORY. First colonized by France in the mid-19th century, Gabon was annexed to French Congo in 1888 and became a separate colony in 1910 as one of the 4 territories of French Equatorial Africa. It became an autonomous republic within the French Community on 28 Nov. 1958 and achieved independence on 17 Aug. 1960.

AREA AND POPULATION. Gabon is bounded west by the Atlantic ocean, north by Equatorial Guinea and Cameroon and east and south by Congo. The area covers 267,667 sq. km; its population at the 1970 census was 950,007; estimate (1988) is 1,226,000. The capital is Libreville (350,000 inhabitants, 1983), other large towns being Port-Gentil (123,300), Masuku (formerly Franceville, 38,030), Lambaréné (26,257 in 1978) and Mouanda (22,909 in 1978).

Vital statistics (1975): Birth rate, 3·22%; death rate, 2·22%.

Provincial areas, populations (estimate 1978, in 1,000) and capitals are as follows:

Province	Sq. km	1978	Capital	Province	Sq. km	1978	Capital
Estuaire	20,740	359	Libreville	Nyanga	21,285	98	Tchibanga
Woleu-Ntem	38,465	166	Oyem	Ngounié	37,750	118	Mouila
Ogooué-Ivindo	46,075	53	Makokou	Ogooué-Lolo	25,380	49	Koulamoutou
Moyen-Ogooué	18,535	49	Lambaréné	Haut-Ogooué	36,547	213	Masuku
Ogooué-Maritime	22,890	194	Port-Gentil				

The largest ethnic groups are the Fang (30%) in the north, Eshira (25%) in the south-west, and the Adouma (17%) in the south-east. French is the official language.

CLIMATE. The climate is equatorial, with high temperatures and considerable rainfall. Mid-May to mid-Sept. is the long dry season, followed by a short rainy season, then a dry season again from mid-Dec. to mid-Feb., and finally a long rainy season once more. Libreville. Jan. 80°F (26·7°C), July 75°F (23·9°C). Annual rainfall 99" (2,510 mm).

CONSTITUTION AND GOVERNMENT. The 1967 Constitution (as subsequently revised) provides for an Executive President directly elected for a 7-year term, who appoints a Council of Ministers to assist him. The unicameral National Assembly consists of 120 members, directly elected for a 5-year term. Opposition parties were legalized in May 1990. Elections were held in Sept. 1990, but because of irregularities the results were partially anulled and a second round of voting took-place in Oct. In the final result the Gabonese Democratic Party (the former sole party permitted) won 63 seats. There are 7 opposition parties, including Morena-Bûcheron, with 20 seats, and the Gabonese Progress party, with 18.

Former President: Leon M'ba (17 Aug. 1960–died 30 Nov. 1967).

President: Omar Bongo (succeeded 2 Dec. 1967, re-elected in 1973, 1979 and 1986).

The Council of Ministers in Dec. 1990 consisted of 26 ministers and 10 secretaries of state.

Prime Minister: Vacant.

National flag: Three horizontal stripes of green, yellow, blue.
National anthem: Uni dans la concorde ('United in concord; words and tune by G. Damas).

Local government: The 9 provinces, each administered by a governor appointed by the President, are divided into 37 *départements*, each under a prefect.

DEFENCE

Army. The Army consists of 1 all-arms Presidential Guard battalion group with support units, totalling (1991), 3,250 men. There is also a paramilitary force of 2,000 personnel. France maintains an 800-strong marine infantry battalion.

Navy. The small naval flotilla in 1991 consisted of 1 French-built fast missile craft, 2 coastal and 4 inshore patrol craft. The flagship is a French-built medium landing ship, and there are about 3 minor service tenders. A separate Coast Guard operates some 10 small launches. Personnel in 1991 totalled 500. There is a coast guard of 2,800.

Air Force. The Air Force has 6 single-seat, 3 two-seat Mirage 5 and 3 Magister ground-attack aircraft, and 1 EMB-111 maritime patrol aircraft. Transport duties are performed primarily by 3 Hercules and 1 EMB-110 Bandeirante turboprop aircraft, 3 Nord 262s and 1 CN-235. Single Falcon 900, Gulfstream III, F.28 and DC-8 aircraft are used for VIP duties. Three T-34C-1 armed turboprop aircraft, an ATR.42 and an EMB-110 Bandeirante are operated for *La Garde Présidentiale.* Also in service are 2 Puma, 4 Gazelle, 1 Bell 212, 1 Bell 412 and 2 Alouette III helicopters. Personnel (1991) 1,000.

INTERNATIONAL RELATIONS

Membership. Gabon is a member of the UN, OAU and OPEC and is an ACP state of the EEC.

ECONOMY

Planning. The Fifth 5-year Plan (1984–88, later extended to 1990) envisaged public expenditure of 1,228,478m. francs CFA, of which 595,662m. were to develop the infrastructure.

Budget. The 1989 budget provided for expenditure of 358,000m. francs CFA and revenue of 260,000m.

Currency. The unit of currency is the franc CFA, with a parity value of 50 francs CFA to 1 French franc. There are coins of 1, 2, 5, 10, 25, 50, 100 and 500 *francs* CFA, and banknotes of 100, 500, 1,000, 5,000 and 10,000 *francs* CFA. In March 1992 £1 = 489·62 *francs* CFA; US$1 = 278·91 *francs* CFA.

Banking and Finance. The *Banque des États de l'Afrique Centrale* is the bank of issue. There are 9 commercial banks situated in Gabon. The *Banque Gabonaise de Développement* and the *Union Gabonaise de Banque* are Gabonese controlled.

ENERGY AND NATURAL RESOURCES

Electricity. The semi-public *Société d'energie et d'eau du Gabon* produced 886m. kwh. in 1986, mainly from thermal plants but increasingly from hydro-electric schemes at Kinguélé (near Libreville), Tchimbélé and Poubara (near Masuku). Supply 220 volts; 50 Hz.

Oil. Extraction from offshore fields totalled 14·9m. tonnes in 1991. Gabon operates 2 refineries, at Port-Gentil and at nearby Pointe Clairette. Proven reserves (1984) 490m. bbls.

Gas. Natural gas production (1985) was 201m. cu. metres.

Minerals. Production (1988) of manganese ore (from deposits around Moanda in the south-east) amounted to 2·25m. tonnes. Uranium is mined nearby at Mounana (850 tonnes in 1988). An estimated 850m. tonnes of iron ore deposits, discovered 1971 at Mékambo (near Bélinga in the north-east) await completion of the branch railway line to be exploited. Gold (18 kg in 1982), zinc and phosphates also occur.

Agriculture. The major crops (production, 1990, in 1,000 tonnes) are: Sugar-cane, 210; cassava, 220; plantains, 235; maize, 20; groundnuts, 15; bananas, 9; palm oil, 4·5; cocoa, 2; coffee, 2 and rice, 1.

Livestock (1988): 9,000 cattle, 84,000 sheep, 63,000 goats, 154,000 pigs.

Forestry. Equatorial forests cover 85% of the land area. Softwood production was 1·38m. cu. metres in 1985. Hardwoods (mahogany, ebony and walnut) are also produced.

Fisheries. The total catch (1986) amounted to 20,400 tonnes.

INDUSTRY. A sugar refinery at Masuku produced (1984) 15,000 tonnes raw sugar. Most manufacturing is based on the processing of food, timber and mineral resources.

Labour. The workforce in 1986 numbered 522,000 of whom 71% were agricultural.

FOREIGN ECONOMIC RELATIONS. Foreign debt was US$2,500m. in 1990.

Commerce. In 1985 imports totalled 384,000m. francs CFA and exports 876,000m. francs CFA. France and USA are Gabon's principal trading partners. In 1983 petroleum made up 83·5% of exports; metals, 7·5% and timber, 7%.

Total trade between Gabon and the UK (British Department of Trade returns, in £1,000 sterling):

	1987	1988	1989	1990	1991
Imports to UK	5,357	5,091	2,389	1,809	3,221
Exports and re-exports from UK	11,962	18,808	14,945	17,563	30,597

COMMUNICATIONS

Roads. There were (1987) 6,898 km of roads and in 1985 there were 16,093 passenger cars and 10,506 commercial vehicles.

Railways. A 1,435-mm gauge (Transgabonais) railway runs from Owendo via N'Djole to Booué and Lastourville, Mouanda and Masuku, opened throughout in 1986. Total 649 km of 1,437 mm gauge. In 1989, 54·4m. passenger-km and 189m. tonne-km were transported.

Civil Aviation. There are 3 international airports at Port-Gentil, Masuku, and Libreville; internal services link these to 65 domestic airfields.

Shipping. Owendo (near Libreville), Mayumba and Port-Gentil are the main ports. In 1987 there were 23 merchant vessels of 97,967 GNT. In 1986, 5·9m. tonnes were loaded and 968,000 tonnes unloaded at the ports.

Telecommunications. In 1985 there were 11,700 telephones. Broadcasting is the responsibility of the state-controlled Radiodiffusion Télévision Gabonaise. There are 2 radio programmes and provincial services. In 1991 there were 0·25m. radio and 40,000 TV sets (colour by SECAM).

Newspapers. There were (1984) 2 newspapers published in Libreville; *Gabon-Matin* (daily) has a circulation of 18,000 and *L'Union* (weekly) 15,000.

JUSTICE, RELIGION, EDUCATION AND WELFARE

Justice. There are *tribunaux de grande instance* at Libreville, Port-Gentil, Lambaréné, Mouila, Oyem, Masuku and Koulamoutou, from which cases move progressively to a central Criminal Court, Court of Appeal and Supreme Court, all 3 located in Libreville. Civil police number about 900.

Religion. In 1989 there were 0·81m. Roman Catholics, the majority of the balance following animist beliefs. There are about 10,000 Moslems.

Education. Education is compulsory between 6–16 years. In 1984–85 there were 178,111 pupils with 3,837 teachers in 940 primary schools; 25,815 pupils with

1,894 teachers in 51 secondary schools; 13,529 students with 720 teachers in 29 technical and teacher-training establishments.

The Université Omar Bongo, founded in 1970 in Libreville, had (1983–84) 3,228 students and 616 teaching staff.

Health. In 1985 there were 565 doctors, and in 1977, 20 dentists, 28 pharmacists, 99 midwives and 823 nursing personnel. In 1981 there were 16 hospitals and 87 medical centres, with a total of 4,815 beds, as well as 258 local dispensaries.

DIPLOMATIC REPRESENTATIVES

Of Gabon in Great Britain (27 Elvaston Place, London, SW7 5NL)
Ambassador: Vincent Boulé.

Of Great Britain in Gabon (resides at Kinshasa)
Ambassador: P. J. Priestley.

Of Gabon in the USA (2034 20th St., NW, Washington, D.C., 20009)
Ambassador: Alexandre Sambat.

Of the USA in Gabon (Blvd de la Mer, Libreville)
Ambassador: Keith L. Wauchope.

Of Gabon to the United Nations
Ambassador: Denis Dangue Rewaka.

Further Reading

Bory, P., *The New Gabon*. Monaco, 1978
Remy, M., *Gabon Today*. Paris, 1977
Saint Paul, M. A., *Gabon: The Development of a Nation*. London, 1989

THE GAMBIA

Capital: Banjul
Population: 875,000 (1990)
GNP per capita: US$290 (1989)

Republic of The Gambia

HISTORY. The Gambia was discovered by the early Portuguese navigators, but they made no settlement. During the 17th century various companies of merchants obtained trading charters and established a settlement on the river, which, from 1807, was controlled from Sierra Leone; in 1843 it was made an independent Crown Colony; in 1866 it formed part of the West African Settlements, but in Dec. 1888 it again became a separate Crown Colony. The boundaries were delimited only after 1890. The Gambia achieved full internal self-government on 4 Oct. 1963 and became an independent member of the Commonwealth on 18 Feb. 1965. The Gambia became a republic within the Commonwealth on 24 April 1970. The Gambia with Senegal formed the Confederation of Senegambia on 1 Feb. 1982; this was officially dissolved on 21 Sept. 1989.

AREA AND POPULATION. The Gambia takes its name from the River Gambia, and consists of a strip of territory never wider than 10 km on both banks. It is bounded in the west by the Atlantic Ocean and on all other sides by Senegal. Area of Banjul (formerly Bathurst) and environs, 87·8 sq. km. In the provinces (area, 10,601·5 sq. km) the settled population (1971) was 275,469, not including temporary immigrants. Total population (census, April 1983), 687,817; (estimate, 1990) 875,000. The largest tribe is the Mandingo (251,997), followed by the Fulas (117,092), Woloffs (91,004), Jolas (64,494) and Sarahulis (51,137). The country is administratively divided into the capital, Banjul, 1983 census (44,188), and the surrounding urban area, Kombo St Mary (101,504), and 5 divisions (with chief town): Lower River (Mansa Konko); MacCarthy Island (Georgetown); North Bank (Kerewan); Upper River (Basse Santa Su); Western (Brikama; population, 19,584 in 1983). Other principal towns are Serekunda (68,433), Bakau (19,309), Sukuta (7,227), Gunjur (7,115) and Farafenni (10,168).

Birth rate (1983) 49 per 1,000; death rate, 21.

CLIMATE. The climate is characterized by two very different seasons. The dry season lasts from Nov. to May, when precipitation is very light and humidity moderate. Days are warm but nights quite cool. The SW monsoon is likely to set in with spectacular storms and produces considerable rainfall from July to Oct., with increased humidity. Banjul. Jan. 73°F (22·8°C), July 80°F (26·7°C). Annual rainfall 52" (1,295 mm).

CONSTITUTION AND GOVERNMENT. Parliament consists of the House of Representatives which consists of a Speaker, Deputy Speaker and 36 elected members; in addition, 5 Chiefs are elected by the Chiefs in Assembly; 7 nominated members are without votes and the Attorney-General is appointed and has no vote.

A general election was held March 1987. State of parties (Jan. 1988): The People's Progressive Party 31 and the National Convention Party 5.

The Government was in Feb. 1992 composed as follows:

President and Minister of Defence: Sir Dawda Kairaba Jawara.
Vice-President, Education, Youth, Sports and Culture: Bakary B. Darbo. *External Affairs:* Alhaji Omar Sey. *Finance and Economic Affairs:* Saikou Sabally. *Agriculture:* Omar A. Jallow. *Health and Social Welfare:* Louise Njie. *Works and Communications:* Matthew Yaya Baldeh. *Trade, Industry and Employment:* Mbemba Jatta. *Justice and Attorney-General:* Hassan Jallow. *Natural Resources and the Environment:* Sarjo Touray. *Information and Tourism:* Alkali James Gaye. *Interior:* Alhaji Lamin Kiti Jabang. *Local Government and Lands:* Landing Jallow Sonko.

National flag: Three wide horizontal stripes of red, blue, green, with narrower stripes of white between them.

National anthem: For The Gambia, our homeland (words by V. J. Howe, tune traditional).

Local Administration. The Gambia is divided into 35 districts, each traditionally under a Chief, assisted by Village Heads and advisers. These districts are grouped into 6 Area Councils containing a majority of elected members, with the Chiefs of the district as *ex-officio* members. The city of Banjul is administered by a City Council.

DEFENCE. The Gambia National Army, 900 strong, has four infantry companies and an engineer squadron.

The marine unit of the Army consisted in 1991 of 100 personnel operating 2 ex-Chinese and 1 British-built inshore patrol craft and some boats based at Banjul.

There is also a paramilitary force of about 750.

INTERNATIONAL RELATIONS

Membership. The Gambia is a member of UN, OAU, the Commonwealth, ECOWAS, the Non-Aligned Conference and is an ACP state of EEC.

ECONOMY

Budget. Revenue and expenditure for years ending 30 June are (in dalasi):

	1983–84	1984–85	1985–86	1986–87
Revenue	150,500,000	172,300,050	218,080,000	266,730,000
Expenditure	164,908,621	189,279,550	207,524,639	262,531,520

Currency. The currency is the *dalasi* (GMD) and is divided into 100 *butut*. 15·59 *dalasi* = £1 sterling; 8·88 *dalasi* = US$1 (March 1992).

Banking. There are 4 banks: the Standard Chartered Bank of Gambia Ltd, Central Bank of The Gambia, Commercial and Development Bank and La Banque Internationale pour le Commerce et l'Industrie (BICI). On 30 Nov. 1978 the government savings bank had about 36,000 depositors holding approximately 992,496 dalasi.

ENERGY AND NATURAL RESOURCES

Electricity. Production (1986) 63m. kwh. Supply 230 volts; 50 Hz.

Minerals. Heavy minerals, including ilmenite, zircon and rutile, have been discovered (1m. tons up to 31 Dec. 1980) in Sanyang, Batokunku and Kartong areas.

Agriculture. Almost all commercial activity centres upon the marketing of groundnuts, which is the only export crop of financial significance; in 1990, 75,000 tonnes were produced. Cotton is also exported on a limited scale. Rice is of increasing importance for local consumption; production (1990) 20,000 tonnes.

Livestock (1990, in 1,000): 400 cattle, 200 goats, 170 sheep, 11 pigs and 100 poultry.

Forestry. Forests cover 200,000 ha, 17% of the land area.

Fisheries. Total catch (1986) 10,700 tonnes, of which 2,700 tonnes were from inland waters.

FOREIGN ECONOMIC RELATIONS

Commerce. Chief items of imports are textiles and clothing, vehicles and machinery, metal goods and petroleum products.

Imports and exports, in 1,000 dalasi:

	1984–85	1985–86	1986–87	1987–88 [1]
Imports	358,569	567,631	797,568	844,973
Exports	163,890	204,195	221,319	245,621

[1] Provisional.

Chief items of export (1985–86, in 1,000 dalasi): Groundnuts shelled, 33,570;

groundnut oil, 15,132; groundnut cake, 4,142; cotton lint, 3,862; fish and fish preparations, 2,507; hides and skins, 1,652. Main imports: Food and live animals, 175,280; basic manufactured goods, 113,916; machinery and transport equipment, 97,850; mineral fuels and lubricants, 56,630.

Total trade between the Gambia and UK (British Department of Trade returns, in £1,000 sterling):

	1987	1988	1989	1990	1991
Imports to UK	3,038	2,927	2,340	3,158	2,865
Exports and re-exports from UK	19,765	19,236	16,583	17,815	19,141

TOURISM. In 1988–89, 120,000 tourists visited The Gambia.

COMMUNICATIONS

Roads. There are 2,990 km of motorable roads, of which 1,718 km rank as all-weather roads including 306 km of bituminous surface and 531 km of laterite gravel. Number of licensed motor vehicles (1985): 5,200 private cars, 700 buses, lorries and coaches, 2,000 motorcycles, scooters and mopeds.

Civil Aviation. The Gambia is served by Minerve, Ghana Airways and Nigeria Airways. The national carrier is Gambia Airways. The number of aircraft landing at Yundum Airport in 1984–85 was 1,576.

Shipping. The chief port is Banjul. In 1985–86, 125,959 tonnes of goods were loaded and 300,212 tonnes unloaded. Internal communication is maintained by steamers and launches. The Gambia River Development Organization was founded in 1978 as a joint project with Senegal to develop the river and its basin. Guinea and Guinea-Bissau were also members in 1984.

Telecommunications. There are several post offices and agencies; postal facilities are also afforded to all river towns. Telephones numbered about 11,000 in 1991.

Radio Gambia, a government station, broadcasts for about 15 hours a day. There are 2 commercial stations. Number of radio receivers (1991, estimate), 135,000.

Cinemas. In 1984 there were 14 cinemas.

Newspapers. There is an official newspaper and several news-sheets.

JUSTICE, RELIGION, EDUCATION AND WELFARE

Justice. Justice is administered by a Supreme Court consisting of a chief justice and puisne judges. It has unlimited jurisdiction but there is a Court of Appeal. Two magistrates' courts and divisional courts are supplemented by a system of resident divisional magistrates. There are also Moslem courts, group tribunals dealing with cases concerned with customs and traditions, and one juvenile court.

Religion. About 90% of the population is Moslem. Banjul is the seat of an Anglican and a Roman Catholic bishop. There are some Methodist missions. A few sections of the population retain their original animist beliefs.

Education (1984–85). There were 189 primary schools (2,640 teachers, 66,257 pupils), 16 secondary technical schools (502 teachers, 10,102 pupils), 8 secondary high schools (235 teachers, 4,348 pupils). In 1982–83 there were 8 post-secondary schools (179 teachers, 1,489 pupils). Gambia College, which replaced Yundum College as a teacher-training and vocational centre, opened for agricultural and health students in 1979.

Health. In 1980 there were 43 government doctors, 23 private doctors and about 635 hospital beds.

DIPLOMATIC REPRESENTATIVES

Of The Gambia in Great Britain (57 Kensington Ct., London, W8 5DG)
High Commissioner: (Vacant).

Of Great Britain in The Gambia (48 Atlantic Rd., Fajara, Banjul)
High Commissioner: A. J. Pover, CMG.

Of The Gambia in USA (1030, 15th St, NW, Washington, D.C. 2005)
Ambassador: Ousman Ahmadou Sallah, also *Ambassador* to the United Nations.

Of the USA in The Gambia (Fajara (East), Kairaba Ave., Banjul)
Ambassador: Arlene Render.

Further Reading

The Gambia since Independence 1965–1980. Banjul, 1980
Gamble, D. P., *The Gambia*. [Bibliography] Oxford and Santa Barbara, 1988

GERMANY

Bundesrepublik Deutschland

(Federal Republic of Germany)

Capital: Berlin
Seat of Government: Bonn/Berlin
Population: 79·11m. (1990)
GNP per capita: US$20,750 (1989)

For the former **GERMAN DEMOCRATIC REPUBLIC (GDR)** as an independent state see THE STATESMAN'S YEAR-BOOK, 1990–91, pp. 526–32.

HISTORY. Following the unconditional surrender of the German armed forces on 8 May 1945 there was no central authority whose writ ran in the whole of Germany, and consequently no peace treaty was signed. France, the USSR, the UK and the USA assumed supreme authority over Germany by the Berlin Declaration of 5 June 1945. Each of the 4 signatories was allotted an occupation zone, in which the supreme power was to be exercised by the commander-in-chief in that zone (see map in THE STATESMAN'S YEAR-BOOK, 1947). Jointly these 4 commanders-in-chief constituted the Allied Control Council in Berlin, which was to be competent in all 'matters affecting Germany as a whole'. The territory of Greater Berlin, divided into 4 sectors, was to be governed as an entity by the 4 occupying powers.

At the Potsdam Conference (July–Aug. 1945) the northern part of the province of East Prussia, including its capital Königsberg (renamed Kaliningrad), was transferred to the USSR, and it was agreed that Poland should administer those parts of Germany east of a line running from the Baltic Sea west of Swinemünde along the river Oder to its confluence with the Western Neisse and thence along the Western Neisse to the Czechoslovak frontier (the 'Oder-Neisse line').

In June 1948 USA, UK and France agreed on a central government for the 3 western zones. An Occupation Statute, which came into force on 30 Sept. 1949, reduced the responsibilities of the occupation authorities. Formally, the Federal Republic of Germany came into existence on 21 Sept. 1949. The Petersberg Agreement of 22 Nov. 1949 freed the Federal Republic of numerous restrictions of the Occupation Statute. In 1951 the USA, the UK and France as well as other states terminated the state of war with Germany; the USSR followed on 25 Jan. 1955. On 5 May 1955 the High Commissioners of the USA, the UK and France signed a proclamation revoking the Occupation Statute. On the same day, the Paris and London treaties, signed in Oct. 1954, came into force and the Federal Republic of Germany became a sovereign independent country.

The eastern zone was administered by the USSR through a military government. A 'People's Chamber' (Volkskammer) was set up which promulgated a Soviet-type constitution in Oct. 1949 and proclaimed the German Democratic Republic. The GDR attained sovereignty in 1954 and obtained de facto diplomatic recognition from most countries. In 1961 the GDR built the mined and guarded 'Berlin Wall' to separate East from West Berlin. A treaty of 21 Dec. 1972 between the GDR and the Federal Republic agreed the basis of relations between the two countries.

Following public demonstrations in the GDR in favour of the democratization of political life in the autumn of 1989, and a mounting exodus of refugees to Federal Germany, Erich Honecker was replaced as Communist Party leader on 18 Oct. by Egon Krenz.

Exit restrictions were progressively eased until the border with Federal Germany, including the Berlin Wall, was opened on 9 Nov. On 13 Nov. the Volkskammer elected Hans Modrow as Prime Minister in place of Willi Stoph, and other Communist leaders were replaced. On 30 Nov. Egon Krenz and the entire Communist Party leadership resigned, amidst revelations of corruption under the former régime. Gregor Gysi was elected Party leader on 11 Dec.

On 1 Feb. 1990 Hans Modrow said 'Germany should again become the unified fatherland of all citizens of the German nation'.

Following the reforms in the GDR in Nov. 1989 the Federal Chancellor Helmut Kohl issued a 10-point plan for German confederation. The ambassadors of the 4 war-time allies met in Berlin in Dec. After talks with Chancellor Kohl on 11 Feb. 1990, President Gorbachev said the USSR had no objection to German re-unification in principle. On 13 Feb. 1990 Federal Germany, the GDR and the war-time allies agreed a formula ('two-plus-four') for re-unification talks to begin after the GDR elections on 18 March. 'Two-plus-four' talks began on 5 May 1990. On 18 May Federal Germany and the GDR signed a treaty transferring Federal Germany's currency, and its economic, monetary and social legislation, to the GDR as of 1 July. On 23 Aug. the Volkskammer by 294 votes to 62 'declared its accession to the jurisdiction of the Federal Republic as from 3 Oct. according to article 23 of the Basic Law', which provided for the Länder of pre-war Germany to accede to the Federal Republic.

On 12 Sept. the Treaty on the Final Settlement with Respect to Germany was signed by Federal Germany, the GDR and the 4 war-time allies: France, the USSR, the UK and the USA. This was ratified by the Volkskammer (by 200 votes to 80), the Bundestag (442 to 47) and the Bundesrat (unanimously). The treaty states *inter alia* 'that the unification of Germany as a state with definitive borders is a significant contribution to peace and stability in Europe' and that 'with the unification of Germany as a democratic and peaceful state, the rights and responsibilities of the Four Powers relating to Berlin and to Germany as a whole lose their function (Preamble); that the 'united Germany shall comprise the territory of the Federal Republic, the GDR and the whole of Berlin. Its external borders shall be the borders of the Federal Republic and the GDR' (Article 1.1); that 'the united Germany and Poland shall confirm the existing border between them in a treaty that is binding under international law' (Article 1.2); that 'the united Germany has no territorial claims whatsoever against other states and shall not assert any in the future' (Article 1.3); that the Federal Republic and the GDR declare 'that only peace will emanate from German soil' and 'acts to disturb peaceful relations between nations are unconstitutional and a punishable offence' (Article 2); that France, the USSR, the UK and the USA 'terminate their rights and responsibilities relating to Berlin and to Germany as a whole. As a result, the corresponding related quadripartite agreements, decisions and practices are dissolved' (Article 7.1); and that 'the united Germany shall have accordingly full sovereignty over its internal and external affairs' (Article 7.2).

AREA AND POPULATION. Germany is bounded in the north by Denmark and the North and Baltic Seas, east by Poland, east and south-east by Czechoslovakia, south-east and south by Austria, south by Switzerland and west by France, Luxembourg, Belgium and the Netherlands. Area: 356,958 sq. km. Population estimate, 1990: 79,112,800; density, 222 per sq. km. *In West Germany* there were 27·79m. households in 1989; 9·81m. were single-person, and 8·42m. had a female principal breadwinner. There were 842,000 unmarried couple households. 11·79m. persons were over 65 in 1987. There were some 110,000 Sorbs, a Slav minority, in 1985.

On 14 Nov. 1990 Germany and Poland signed a treaty confirming Poland's existing western frontier and renouncing German claims to territory lost as a result of the Second World War.

The capital is Berlin; after re-unification government offices began to move in phases to Berlin.

The Federation comprises 16 Länder (states). Area and population:

Länder	Area in sq. km	Population (in 1,000's) 1987 census	Population (in 1,000's) 1990 estimate	Per sq. km
Baden-Württemberg (BW)	35,751	9,286	9,619	269
Bavaria (BY)	70,554	10,903	11,221	159
Berlin (BE) [1]	883	...	3,410	3,862
Brandenburg (BB) [2]	29,059	...	2,641	91
Bremen (HB)	404	660	674	1,668
Hamburg (HH)	755	1,593	1,626	2,154

[1] 1987 census population of West Berlin: 2,013,000   [2] Reconstituted in 1990 in the GDR

Länder	Area in sq. km	Population (in 1,000's) 1987 census	1990 estimate	Per sq. km
Hessen (HE)	21,114	5,508	5,661	268
Lower Saxony (NI)	47,344	7,162	7,238	153
Mecklenburg-West Pomerania (MV) [2]	23,838	...	1,964	82
North Rhine-Westphalia (NW)	34,070	16,712	17,104	502
Rhineland-Palatinate (RP)	19,849	3,631	3,702	186
Saarland (SL)	2,570	1,056	1,065	414
Saxony (SN) [2]	18,337	...	4,901	267
Saxony-Anhalt (ST) [2]	20,445	...	2,965	145
Schleswig-Holstein (SH)	15,729	2,554	2,595	165
Thuringia (TH) [2]	16,251	...	2,684	165

[1] 1987 census population of West Berlin: 2,013,000   [2]Reconstituted in 1990 in the GDR

Birth rate in 1989, 11 per 1,000; death rate, 11·2.

Vital statistics:

	Marriages	Live births	Of these to single parents	Deaths	Divorces
1987	523,847	867,969	...	901,291	179,508
1988	534,903	892,993	...	900,627	178,277
1989	529,597	880,459	136,582	903,441	176,857

Rates per 1,000, 1989: Birth, 11·5; marriage, 7·2; divorce, 2·5; death, 11·6; infant mortality: 4 stillborn, 7·6 under 1 year. Expectation of life *in West Germany*, 1988: Men, 72·2; women, 78·7; *in the GDR*, 1987: Men, 69·8; women, 75·9.

On 31 Dec. 1989 there were 5,037,072 resident foreigners. 68,526 persons were naturalized *in West Germany* in 1989.

In West Germany in 1989 there were 545,000 emigrants and 1,522,200 immigrants. 842,227 refugees entered in 1989 (345,581 in 1988). These comprised 720,909 ethnic Germans (including 343,854 from GDR, 250,340 from Poland, 98,134 from USSR and 23,387 from Romania) and 121,318 non-Germans (mainly from Poland, Turkey, Yugoslavia, Sri Lanka, Lebanon and Iran). In 1990 ethnic German emigrants from East Europe numbered some 397,000, including 148,000 from the USSR, 113,000 from Poland and 107,000 from Romania.

Populations of towns of over 100,000 inhabitants in 1989 (in 1,000):

Town (and Land)	Population (in 1,000)	Ranking by population	Town (and Land)	Population (in 1,000)	Ranking by population
Aachen (NW)	234·1	34	Gelsenkirchen (NW)	288·0	22
Augsburg (BY)	248·3	30	Gera (TH)	134·5	54
Bergisch Gladbach (NW)	102·4	80	Göttingen (NI)	119·1	65
			Hagen (NW)	210·7	38
Berlin (BE)	3,376·8	1	Halle (ST)	234·8	33
Bielefeld (NW)	313·4	18	Hamburg (HH)	1,606·6	2
Bochum (NW)	390·1	16	Hamm (NW)	174·7	45
Bonn (NW)	283·7	23	Hanover (NI)	502·4	14
Bottrop (NW)	116·8	66	Heidelberg (BW)	132·4	55
Braunschweig (NI)	254·1	27	Heilbronn (BW)	112·8	69
Bremen (HB)	537·6	11	Herne (NW)	175·1	44
Bremerhaven (HB)	127·6	58	Hildesheim (NI)	103·4	77
Chemnitz (SN)	309·6	19	Ingolstadt (BY)	100·1	83
Cologne (NW)	940·2	4	Jena (TH)	107·5	72
Cottbus (BB)	129·1	57	Karlsruhe (BW)	267·2	24
Darmstadt (HE)	136·3	53	Kassel (HE)	189·5	39
Dessau (ST)	103·2	78	Kiel (SH)	241·2	31
Dortmund (ST)	589·2	7	Koblenz (RP)	107·3	74
Dresden (SN)	515·9	13	Krefeld (NW)	236·9	32
Duisburg (NW)	529·2	12	Leipzig (SN)	538·9	10
Düsseldorf (NW)	570·2	8	Leverkusen (NW)	158·2	48
Erfurt (TH)	220·0	36	Lübeck (SH)	211·0	37
Erlangen (BY)	100·8	82	Ludwigshafen am Rhein (RP)	158·9	47
Essen (NW)	620·9	6			
Frankfurt am Main (HE)	628·8	5	Magdeburg (ST)	290·4	21
Freiburg im Breisgau (BW)	185·3	41	Mainz (RP)	175·4	43
			Mannheim (BW)	302·7	20

Town (and Land)	Popula-tion (in 1,000)	Ranking by popu-lation	Town (and Land)	Popula-tion (in 1,000)	Ranking by popu-lation
Moers (NW)	102·4	79	Remscheid (NW)	121·1	63
Mönchengladbach (NW)	253·8	28	Reutlingen (BW)	101·2	81
Mülheim (NW)	176·0	42	Rostock (MV)	254·8	25
Munich (BY)	1,218·3	3	Saarbrücken (SL)	188·6	40
Münster (NW)	249·9	29	Salzgitter (NI)	111·8	70
Neuss (NW)	144·3	50	Schwerin (MV)	130·7	56
Nuremberg (BY)	481·9	15	Siegen (NW)	106·2	75
Oberhausen (NW)	221·4	35	Solingen (NW)	161·5	46
Offenbach am Main (HE)	113·0	68	Stuttgart (BW)	565·7	9
Oldenburg (NI)	141·0	52	Ulm (BW)	107·5	73
Osnabrück (NI)	156·9	49	Wiesbaden (HE)	254·6	26
Paderborn (NW)	115·3	67	Witten (NW)	103·9	76
Pforzheim (BW)	109·6	71	Wolfsburg (NI)	126·2	59
Potsdam (BB)	143·0	51	Wuppertal (NW)	372·4	17
Recklingshausen (NW)	122·1	61	Würzburg (BY)	125·6	60
Regensburg (BY)	119·2	64	Zwickau (SN)	121·2	62

CLIMATE. Oceanic influences are only found in the north-west where winters are quite mild but stormy. Elsewhere a continental climate is general. To the east and south, winter temperatures are lower, with bright frosty weather and considerable snowfall. Summer temperatures are fairly uniform throughout. Berlin. Jan. 31°F (–0·5°C), July 66°F (19°C). Annual rainfall 22·5" (563 mm). Dresden. Jan. 30°F (–0·1°C), July 65°F (18·5°C). Annual rainfall 27·2" (680 mm). Frankfurt. Jan. 33°F (0·6°C), July 66°F (18·9°C). Annual rainfall 24" (601 mm). Hamburg. Jan. 31°F (–0·6°C), July 63°F (17·2°C). Annual rainfall 29" (726 mm). Hanover. Jan. 33°F (0·6°C), July 64°F (17·8°C). Annual rainfall 24" (604 mm). Köln. Jan. 36°F (2·2°C), July 66°F (18·9°C). Annual rainfall 27" (676 mm). Munich. Jan. 28°F (–2·2°C), July 63°F (17·2°C). Annual rainfall 34" (855 mm). Stuttgart. Jan. 33°F (0·6°C), July 66°F (18·9°C). Annual rainfall 27" (677 mm).

CONSTITUTION. The Constituent Assembly (known as the 'Parliamentary Council') met in Bonn on 1 Sept. 1948, and worked out a Basic Law (*Grundgesetz*) which was approved by a two-thirds majority of the parliaments of the participating Länder and came into force on 23 May 1949. It is to remain in force until 'a constitution adopted by a free decision of the German people comes into being'.

The Basic Law consists of a preamble and 146 articles. There have been 35 amendments. The first section deals with the basic rights which are legally binding for legislation, administration and jurisdiction.

The Federal Republic is a democratic and social constitutional state on a parliamentary basis. The federation is constituted by the 16 Länder (states) (*see* p. 527). The Basic Law decrees that the general rules of international law form part of the federal law. The constitutions of the Länder must conform to the principles of a republican, democratic and social state based on the rule of law. Executive power is vested in the Länder, unless the Basic Law prescribes or permits otherwise. Federal law takes precedence over state law.

Legislative power is vested in the *Bundestag* (Federal Assembly) and the *Bundesrat* (Federal Council).

The Bundestag is composed of 662 members and is elected in universal, free, equal and secret elections for a term of 4 years. A party must gain 5% of total votes cast in order to gain representation in the Bundestag. The electoral system combines relative-majority and proportional voting; each voter has 2 votes, the first for the direct constituency representative, the second for the competing party lists in the Länder. This second proportional vote determines each party's share of the Bundestag seats.

The Bundesrat consists of 79 members appointed by the governments of the Länder in proportions determined by the number of inhabitants. Each Land has at least 3 votes.

The Head of State is the Federal President *(Bundespräsident)* who is elected for a 5-year term by a Federal Convention specially convened for this purpose. This Convention consists of all the members of the Bundestag and an equal number of members elected by the Länder parliaments in accordance with party strengths, but who need not themselves be members of the parliaments. No president may serve more than two terms. Presidents since 1949: Theodor Heuss (1949-59); Heinrich Lübke (1959-69); Gustav Heinemann (1969-74); Walter Scheel (1974-1979); Karl Castens (1979–84).

Executive power is vested in the Federal Government, which consists of the Federal Chancellor, elected by the Bundestag on the proposal of the Federal President, and the Federal Ministers, who are appointed and dismissed by the Federal President upon the proposal of the Federal Chancellor.

The Federal Republic has exclusive legislation on: (1) foreign affairs (2) federal citizenship; (3) freedom of movement, passports, immigration and emigration, and extradition; (4) currency, money and coinage, weights and measures, and regulation of time and calendar; (5) customs, commercial and navigation agreements, traffic in goods and payments with foreign countries, including customs and frontier protection; (6) federal railways and air traffic; (7) post and telecommunications; (8) the legal status of persons in the employment of the Federation and of public law corporations under direct supervision of the Federal Government; (9) trade marks, copyright and publishing rights; (10) co-operation of the Federal Republic and the Länder in the criminal police and in matters concerning the protection of the constitution, the establishment of a Federal Office of Criminal Police, as well as the combating of international crime; (11) federal statistics.

For concurrent legislation in which the Länder have legislative rights if and as far as the Federal Republic does not exercise its legislative powers, *see* THE STATESMAN'S YEAR-BOOK, 1956, p. 1038.

Federal laws are passed by the Bundestag and after their adoption submitted to the Bundesrat, which has a limited veto. The Basic Law may be amended only upon the approval of two-thirds of the members of the Bundestag and two-thirds of the votes of the Bundesrat.

The foreign service, federal finance, railways, postal services, waterways and shipping are under direct federal administration.

In the field of finance the Federal Republic has exclusive legislation on customs and financial monopolies and concurrent legislation on: (1) excise taxes and taxes on transactions, in particular, taxes on real-estate acquisition, incremented value and on fire protection; (2) taxes on income, property, inheritance and donations; (3) real estate, industrial and trade taxes, with the exception of the determining of the tax rates.

The Federal Republic can, by federal law, claim part of the income and corporation taxes to cover its expenditures not covered by other revenues. Financial jurisdiction is uniformly regulated by federal legislation.

National flag: Three horizontal stripes of black, red, gold.

National anthem: Einigkeit und Recht und Freiheit ('Unity and right and freedom' words by H. Hoffmann, 1841; tune by J. Haydn, 1797).

Local Government. Below *Land* level local government is carried on by elected councils to 426 counties *(Landkreise)* and 117 county boroughs *(Kreisfreie Städte)*, which form the electoral districts for the *Land* governments, and are subdivided into 16,127 communities *(Gemeinden)*.

GOVERNMENT. The 12th Bundestag was elected on 2 Dec. 1990. A special 5% threshold was applied to constituencies in the former GDR. Electoral turnout was 78·5%. The government is formed by a coalition of the Christian Democrat/Christian Socialist (CDU/CSU) alliance with the Free Democrats (FDP). (The CSU is a Bavarian party where the CDU does not stand). Percentage votes, and seats gained (1987 electoral results in brackets): CDU/CSU 43·8%, 319 (44·3%, 223); Social Democratic Party (SPD), 33·5%, 239 (37%, 186); FDP, 11%, 79 (9·1%, 46); Democratic Socialists (former Communists), 2·4%, 17; Alliance '90/Greens, 1·2%, 8.

After the elections of April 1991 in the *Land* of Rhineland-Palatinate the SPD gained a majority in the Bundesrat.

Federal President: Dr Richard von Weizsäcker (sworn in 1 July 1984); elected for a second term 23 May 1989).

Speaker of the Bundestag: Rita Süssmuth (elected Nov. 1988).

The Cabinet in March 1992 comprised:

Chancellor: Dr Helmut Kohl (CDU).
Deputy Chancellor, Minister of Foreign Affairs: Hans-Dietrich Genscher (FDP).
Interior: Rudolf Seiters (CDU).
Justice: Klaus Kinkel (ind).
Finance: Theo Waigel (CSU).
Economy: Jürgen Mölleman (FDP).
Defence: Dr Gerhard Stoltenberg (CDU).
Transport: Günther Krause (CDU).
Family and Elderly: Hannelore Rönsch (CDU).
Minister at the Chancellery: Friedrich Bohl (CDU).
Women and Youth: Angela Merkel (CDU).
Food, Agriculture and Forestry: Ignaz Kiechle (CSU).
Labour and Social Affairs: Dr Norbert Blüm (CDU).
Health: Gerda Hasselfeldt (CDU).
Environment, Nature Conservation and Reactor Safety: Klaus Töpfer (CDU).
Posts and Telecommunications: Dr Christian Schwarz-Schilling (CDU).
Construction: Irmgard Adam-Schwätzer (FDP).
Research and Technology: Dr Heinz Riesenhuber (CDU).
Education and Science: Rainer Ortleb (FDP).
Economic Co-operation: Carl-Dieter Spranger (CSU).

At the ultimate elections to the *GDR* Volkskammer in March 1990 turn-out was 93%. Percentage votes, and seats gained: Alliance for Germany (CDU, German Social Union and Democratic Awakening), 48·1%, 193; SPD, 21·8%, 87; Party of Democratic Socialism (former Communists), 16%, 65; Alliance of Free Democrats (German Forum Party, Liberal Democratic Party and Free Democratic Party), 5·3%, 21; Alliance '90, 2·9%, 12; Democratic Farmers, 2·2%, 9; Greens, 2%, 8; National Democrats, 0·4%, 2. 3 other parties won 1 seat each.

Lothar de Maizière (CDU) formed a government.

At the *GDR local elections* in May 1990 turn-out was 80%. The CDU gained 34·3% of the vote, the SPD 21·2%, the Party of Democratic Socialism, 14·5%, the Liberal Democratic Party, 6·6%, and the German Social Union, 3·4%.

DEFENCE. The Paris Treaties, which entered into force in May 1955, stipulated a contribution of the Federal Republic to western defence within the framework of NATO and the Western European Union. On 30 Oct. 1990 the Bundestag ratified 2 treaties providing for the withdrawal of all Soviet forces from the territory of the former GDR by 1994. The German government is defraying part of the expenses of this operation. There were some 380,000 Soviet troops in the GDR.

The Federal Armed Forces *(Bundeswehr)* had a total strength (1991) of 476,300 all ranks (203,000 conscripts) and a further 1,009,400 reserves. Conscription was reduced from 15 to 12 months in Oct. 1990.

On re-unification the GDR's forces (see THE STATESMAN'S YEAR-BOOK, 1990–91, p. 528) were reduced from 170,000 to 50,000, and these latter were integrated into the Federal forces.

Army. The Army is divided into the Field Army, 219,000 strong, containing the units assigned to NATO in event of war, the Territorial Army, 64,600 strong, and the Eastern Command, 51,400 strong. The Field Army is organized in 3 corps, comprising 6 armoured, 4 armoured infantry, 1 mountain and 1 airborne divisions. Equipment includes 648 M-48, 2,054 Leopard I and 2,024 Leopard II tanks. An air component operates 205 BO 105P anti-armour helicopters, 107 CH-53G and 187 UH-1D Iroquois transport helicopters, plus 100 Alouette II and 95 BO 105M liaison/observation helicopters. Most of the helicopters inherited from the GDR are being retired, although some 40 Mi-8s will be kept in service until at least the end of 1992. The Territorial Army is organized into 5 Military Districts, under 3 Territorial Commands. Its main task is to defend rear areas and remains under national control even in wartime. Total strength was (1991) 335,000 (conscripts 163,300).

Navy. The Federal Navy is tasked to maritime operations in support of the central European theatre in the Baltic and North Sea environments. The emphasis is thus on coastal and shallow-seas warfare. The Fleet Commander operates from a modern Maritime Headquarters at Glücksburg, close to the Danish border.

The fleet includes 24 diesel coastal submarines, 3 US-built guided-missile and 3 other destroyers, 8 frigates, 5 anti-submarine corvettes and 40 fast missile craft. There is a large mine-warfare force of 54 vessels, comprising 2 minelayer/transports, 32 coastal minesweepers and hunters of which 10 are new combined minelayer/hunters and 6 control ships for TROIKA minesweeping drones, 18 inshore minesweepers and 2 diver support ships. Major auxiliaries include 4 tankers, 2 repair ships, 5 oilers, 6 minesweeper/patrol craft support and HQ ships, 8 logistic transports, 8 large tugs, 3 intelligence collectors, 2 trial ships and a sail training vessel. There are several dozen minor auxiliaries and service craft, as well as, the units inherited from the GDR's navy.

The main naval bases are at Wilhemshaven, Bremerhaven, Kiel, Olpenitz, and Rostock; there are several lesser bases.

The Naval Air Arm, 6,700 strong, is organized into 4 wings and comprises 104 missile-armed Tornado strike aircraft. 19 Atlantic long range, plus 19 Dornier-28 coastal patrol aircraft, 22 shore-based Sea King helicopters, 19 Lynx (12 frigate-based) and 1 DO228 anti-pollution patrol aircraft are also in use. Of the ex-GDR aircraft, only the Mi-8 helicopters will be retained after 1992.

Procurement of 4 new frigates and 16 further replacement mine warfare craft is in hand. Modernization of the existing force proceeds. Personnel in 1991 numbered 38,000 including the Naval Air Arm.

The 15,000 strength of the GDR navy in 1989 has reduced to some 5,200 long service officers and men eligible for incorporation into the Federal Navy. This is likely to prove difficult given the total naval ceiling strength of the reformed *Bundeswehr* reducing to under 35,000. The Federal Navy has no operational requirement for the ships of the former GDR navy, and 2 frigates and two dozen patrol and mine warfare are to be sold or scrapped.

Air Force. Since 1970, the *Luftwaffe* has comprised the following commands: German Air Force Tactical Command, German Air Force Support Command (including two German Air Force Regional Support Commands—North and South) and General Air Force Office. Only aboaut 100 of the 400 or so aircraft acquired through the merger of the former GDR airforce are being retained. Its strength in 1991 was approximately 110,000 officers and other ranks and over 550 first-line combat aircraft. Combat units, including 12 heavy fighter-bomber squadrons, 6 light ground attack/reconnaissance squadrons, 4 reconnaissance squadrons, 8 surface-to-surface missile squadrons, and an air defence force of 4 interceptor squadrons, 24 batteries of *Nike-Hercules* and 36 batteries of *Improved Hawk* surface-to-air missiles, are assigned to NATO. There are 4 F-4F Phantom and 2 MiG-29 interceptor squadrons, 8 Tornado attack squadrons, 4 attack squadrons of F-4Fs, 4 RF-4E Phantom reconnaissance squadrons, and 6 light attack/reconnaissance squadrons of Alpha Jets, although these will be retired in 1992. Four transport squadrons (each 15 aircraft) with turboprop Transall C-160 aircraft and 1 wing of 5 helicopter squadrons with UH-1D Iroquois add to the air mobility of the *Bundeswehr*. There are also VIP, support and light transport aircraft. About 90 An-26, L-410, Il-62, Tu-134 and Tu-154 fixed-wing transports and Mi-2 and Mi-8 helicopters from the GDR air force are still in use, but will be withdrawn in the next few years. Guided weapons in service include 8 squadrons of *Pershing* surface-to-surface missiles and 6 battalions of *Nike-Hercules* and 9 battalions of *Improved Hawk* surface-to-air missiles.

INTERNATIONAL RELATIONS. A treaty of friendship with Poland signed on 17 June 1991 recognized the Oder-Neisse border and guaranteed minorities' rights in both countries.

Membership. Germany is a member of the UN, OECD, EC, WEU, NATO and the Council of Europe. The Schengen Accord of June 1990 abolished border controls between Germany, Belgium, France, Italy, Luxembourg, the Netherlands, Portugal and Spain.

ECONOMY

Budget. Since 1 Jan. 1979 tax revenues have been distributed as follows: Federal Government. Income tax, 42·5%; capital yield and corporation tax, 50%; turnover tax, 67·5%; trade tax, 15%; capital gains, insurance and accounts taxes, 100%; excise duties (other than on beer), 100%. Länder. Income tax, 42·5%; capital yield and corporation tax, 50%; turnover tax, 32·5%; trade tax, 15%; other taxes, 100%. Local authorities. Income tax, 15%; trade tax, 70%; local taxes, 100%. Income tax was reduced in 1990.

Budgets for 1990 and 1991 (in DM1m.):

Revenue	All public authorities		Federal portion	
	1990	1991	1990	1991
		Current		
Taxes	931,142	597,142	261,839	315,080
Economic activities	39,414	40,544	13,999	16,896
Interest	10,421	3,741	1,585	1,483
Current allocations and subsidies	202,311	138,018	1,532	2,310
Other receipts	73,210	40,690	4,776	5,839
minus equalising payments	189,745	125,839	...	...
	1,066,753	694,296	283,730	341.588
		Capital		
Sale of assets	7,437	6,920	311	950
Allocations for investment	32,326	28,869	7	5
Repayment of loans	9,090	8,686	3,127	3,671
Public sector borrowing	2,769	1,778	...	...
minus equalising payments	31,548	27,019	...	...
	20,084	19,244	3,445	...
Totals	1,086,837	713,540	287,175	4,626
Expenditure		Current		
Staff	245,864	223,404	43,021	50,574
Materials	254,767	111,026	42,445	46,048
Interest	65,586	78,629	34,235	42,515
Allocations and subsidies	641,195	416,721	150,800	210,738
minus equalising payments	189,745	125,839	...	...
	1,017,667	703,941	270,681	349,681
		Capital		
Construction	49,781	49,000	6,574	8,759
Acquisition of property	17,659	14,113	1,963	2,786
Allocations and subsidies	56,524	79,922	20,966	43,506
Loans	29,464	25,184	9,591	9,334
Acquisition of shares	3,460	3,970	1,291	1,703
Repayments in the public sector	1,669	1,473	...	...
minus equalising payments	31,548	27,019	...	...
Totals	127,008	146,643	40,385	66,088

Supplementary budgets were drawn up in 1990 to cover the costs of re-unification, and a further tax rise, including 7·5% on income tax, was imposed in July 1991 for 1 year.

Federal spending was expected to be DM 422,500m. in 1992, including: the former GDR, DM 109,000m. (DM 93,000m. in 1991; social affairs, DM 92,800m.; debt servicing, DM 55,400m.; defence, DM 52,500m.).

Currency. The unit of currency is the *deutsche Mark* (DEM) of 100 *pfennig* (pf.). There are 1, 2, 5, 10, 50 pf., 1, 2, 5 and 10 DM coins and 5, 10, 20, 50, 100, 200, 500 and 1,000 DM notes. Money in circulation in 1989, DM 154,538m. The deutsche Mark became the sole German currency on 2 July 1990, replacing the GDR's Mark at parity. In March 1992, £1 = 2·88 DM; US$1 = 1·64.

Banking and Finance. In 1948 the Bank deutscher Länder was established in Frankfurt as the central bank. This and the Berlin central bank were merged on 1 Aug. 1957 to form the Deutsche Bundesbank (German Federal Bank). The central bank's duty is to protect the stability of the currency. It is independent of the government but obliged to support the government's general policy. Its Governor is appointed by the government for 8 years. The *Governor* is Helmut Schlesinger (b.1924). Its assets were DM 349,598m. in 1990. The largest private banks are the Deutsche Bank, Dresdner Bank and Commerzbank. The public sector banks consist of 771 retail savings banks and the Länder banks which represent them in the wholesale markets. The former GDR central bank Staatsbank has become a public commercial bank. Its former credit arm Deutsche Kreditbank has been taken over by Deutsche Bank and Dresdner Bank.

Savings deposits were DM 765,374m. in 1990.

There are stock exchanges in Berlin, Bremen, Düsseldorf, Frankfurt and 4 other regional centres. Plans are under discussion to create a unified market.

Weights and Measures. The metric system is in force.

ENERGY AND NATURAL RESOURCES

Electricity. In 1990 some 50% of electricity was produced from coal in *West Germany*, and 34% from nuclear power. There is a moratorium on further nuclear plant construction. In 1989, 440,893m. kwh. were produced. In *the GDR* in 1989 sources of energy included 73% lignite (85% in 1988) and 9·9% nuclear power from a single plant which was closed in 1990. Production, 1988: 118,328 kwh. Supply 220 volts; 50 Hz.

Oil and Gas. The chief oilfields are in Emsland (Lower Saxony). In 1990, 3·61m. tonnes of crude, 7·53m. tonnes of petroleum, and 12·69m. tonnes of diesel oil were produced. Gas production was 14,783m. cu metres.

Minerals. The main production areas are: North Rhine-Westphalia (for coal, iron and metal smelting-works), Central Germany (for brown coal), and Lower Saxony (Salzgitter for iron ore; the Harz for metal ore).

Production (in 1,000 tonnes):

Minerals	1985	1986	1987	1988	1989	1990
Coal	82,398	80,801	76,300	73,304	71,428	70,159
Lignite	120,667	114,310	108,799	108,563	110,081	107,525
Potash	29,248	24,775	25,795	27,030	26,002	26,105

Production of iron and steel (in 1,000 tonnes):

	1985	1986	1987	1988	1989	1990
Pig-iron	31,919	29,443	28,918	33,016	32,777	30,097
Steel	40,497	37,134	36,248	41,023	41,073	38,434
Rolled products finished	28,919	27,409	27,437	30,385	31,702	29,729

The former *GDR* was a major producer of lignite (production in 1989: 311m. tonnes).

Agriculture. Area cultivated in, 1990: 11·97m. ha (arable, 6·95m.; pasture, 5·62m.). In 1990 the number of agricultural holdings classified by area farmed was:

	Total	1–5 ha	5–20 ha	20–100 ha	Over 100 ha
Schleswig-Holstein	27,875	6,236	4,958	15,068	1,613
Hamburg	1,173	700	263	198	12
Lower Saxony	96,779	24,470	25,234	44,368	2,707
Bremen	384	116	93	167	8
North Rhine-Westphalia	81,032	24,721	26,467	29,143	701
Hessen	47,442	16,703	17,692	12,665	382
Rhineland-Palatinate	46,539	18,841	15,986	11,366	346
Baden-Württemberg	106,273	41,422	40,479	23,890	482

	Total	1–5 ha	5–20 ha	20–100 ha	Over 100 ha
Bavaria	218,970	55,614	103,710	58,884	762
Saarland	3,164	1,196	914	967	87
Berlin (West)	109	60	29	20	...
West Germany	629,740	190,079	235,825	196,736	7,100

Area (in 1,000 ha) and yield (in 1,000 tonnes) of the main crops:

	Area			Yield		
	1988	1989	1990	1988	1989	1990
Wheat	2,509	2,554	2,430	15,620	14,511	15,242
Rye	985	1,006	1,055	3,364	3,900	3,988
Barley	2,710	2,640	2,612	13,386	14,399	13,992
Oats	622	562	472	2,545	2,010	2,105
Potatoes	642	632	548	18,980	16,617	14,039
Sugar-beet	597	601	608	23,215	26,987	30,600

8·28m. tonnes of fertilizers were used in Oct. 1988-Sept. 1989; 7·43m. tonnes in 1989/90 in West Germany.

Wine production (in 1,000 hectolitres): 15,094 in 1989; 19,078 in 1990.

Livestock (in 1,000s), 1990: Cattle, 20,048 (including 6,598 milch cows); sheep, 4,170; pigs, 32,346; horses 491; poultry 106,054. Milk production was 4·02m. tonnes in 1990 *in West Germany*.

In 1990 there were 1·17m. tractors *in West Germany*.

In *the GDR* in 1989 the agricultural area was 6·2m. ha including 4·7m. ha arable and 1·26m. ha grassland. There were 3,855 collective farms with 5·3m. ha of arable land, and 465 state farms with 448,895 ha of land in 1988. In 1987 private plots accounted for 9% of production. In 1988 there were 167,529 tractors and 18,404 combine harvesters.

In 1989 6·52m. tonnes of meat, 32·44m. tonnes of milk and 17,794m. eggs were produced.

Forestry. Forestry is of great importance, conducted under the guidance of the State on scientific lines. In recent years enormous depredation has occurred through pollution with acid rain. Forest area in *West Germany* in 1990 was 5·36m. ha, of which 2·26m. were owned by the State. In 1989 42·99m. cu. metres of timber were cut. In *the GDR* in 1988 there were 2,981,303 ha of forest. Timber production was 10·9m. cu. metres.

Fisheries. In *West Germany* in 1990 the yield of sea fishing was 154,146 tonnes live weight. The fishing fleet consisted of 15 trawlers (26,625 GRT) and 557 cutters. In *the GDR* in 1988 the sea catch was 244,900 tonnes; inland, 26,524 tonnes.

INDUSTRY. Public limited companies are managed on the 'co-determination' principle, and have 3 statutory bodies: a board of directors, a works council elected by employees, and a supervisory council which includes employee representatives but has an in-built management majority.

In *West Germany* in 1989 there were 53,654 firms (with 20 and more employees) employing 8·43m. persons, made up of 282,000 in energy and water services, 188,000 in mining, 1·37m. in raw materials processing, 3·9m. in the manufacture of producers' goods, 1·3m. in the manufacture of consumer goods, 472,000 in food and tobacco and 920,000 in building.

Production of major industrial products:

Products (1,000 tonnes)	1986	1987	1988	1989	1990
Aluminium	765	793	753	734	715
Artificial fertilizers	1,425	1,449	1,274	1,179	1,202
Sulphuric acid, SO_3	3,351	3,323	3,308	3,288	3,221
Soda, Na_2CO_3	1,442	1,448	1,404	1,443	1,436
Cement	26,580	25,268	26,215	28,499	30,456
Plastics	7,941	8,546	9,218	9,176	7,637
Cotton yarn	128	142	126	124	122
Woollen yarn	41	40	38	36	32
Passenger cars (1,000)	3,952	4,008	3,980	4,106	4,179
TV sets (1,000)	3,895	3,537	3,737	3,236	3,595

In *the GDR* industry produced about 70% of the national income in 1989. The major industries were energy, chemicals, metallurgy, mechanical and electrical engineering, electronics and instruments.

1988 production (in 1,000 tonnes): Rolled steel, 9,472; sulphuric acid, 799; chemical fertilizers, 5,192; petrol, 4,765; diesel fuel, 6,301; caustic soda, 627; plastics and synthetic resins, 1,149; cement, 12,510; antibiotics, 84·9 tonnes; passenger cars (no.), 218,045; television receivers (no.), 774,100; shoes, 91m. pairs.

Labour. In *West Germany* In 1990 the workforce was 30·34m., of whom 1·88m. were unemployed and 28·45m. working, including 2·97m. self-employed, 2·47m. officials and 23·1m. employees. 1·78m. foreign workers and 9·17m. women were employed. Major categories: Manufacturing industries, 11·31m.; services, 10·82m.; commerce and transport, 5·31m.; agriculture, forestry and fishing, 0·96m. In 1990 there were 319,531 unfilled vacancies and 55,808 part-time workers.

In *the GDR* in 1988 the workforce was 8·59m. (4·2m. females), of whom 7·59m. were employees, 629,100 worked on collective farms, 164,000 in co-operative workshops and 181,700 were self-employed. Workforce distribution by activity, 1988: Industry, 37·4%; services, 21·4%; agriculture, 10·8%; commerce, 10·3%; building, 6·6%; transport, 5·9%; handicrafts, 3·1%; posts and telecommunications, 1·5%; other products, 3%. *In the former GDR area* in March 1991 there were 756,480 unemployed, including 414,856 females.

Trade Unions. The majority of trade unions belong to the *Deutscher Gewerk-schaftsbund* (DGB, German Trade Union Federation), which had (women in brackets) 7·94m. (1·94m.) members in 1990, including 5·29m. (922,523) manual workers, 1·85m. (844,400) white-collar workers and 797,947 (172,677) civil servants. DGB unions are organized in industrial branches such that only one union operates within each enterprise. Outside the DGB lie several smaller unions: The *Deutscher Beamtenbund* (DBB) or civil servants union with 799,003 (221,701) members, the *Deutsche Angestellten-Gewerkschaft* (DAG) or union of salaried staff with 573,000 (281,094 members and the *Christlicher Gewerkschaftsbund Deutschlands* (CGD, Christian Trade Union Federation of Germany) with 309,364 (77,945) members.

Strikes are not legal unless called by a union with the backing of 75% of members. Certain public service employees are contractually not permitted to strike. 100,409 working days were lost through strikes in 1989, 363,547 in 1990.

The official GDR trade union organization (FDGB) was dissolved in Sept. 1990 and the 21 branch unions were merged in the Deutscher Gewerkschaftsbund.

FOREIGN ECONOMIC RELATIONS

Commerce. *West German* imports and exports in DM 1m.:

Imports				Exports			
1987	1988	1989	1990	1987	1988	1989	1990
409,641	439,609	506,645	550,628	527,377	567,654	641,041	642,785

Distribution of imports and exports by categories of countries in 1990 (in DM 1m.): EEC, 286,608, 350,442; developing countries, 66,193, 65,040; Communist countries, 29,602, 27,475. Most important trading partners in 1990 (trade figures in DM 1m.) Imports: France, 65,111; Netherlands, 55,965; Italy, 51,820; USA, 36,994; Belgium with Luxembourg, 39,749; UK, 37,042; Japan, 32,871; Switzerland, 23,304; Austria, 23,941. Exports: France, 83,835; Italy, 59,980; UK, 54,794; Netherlands, 54,314; USA, 46,870; Belgium with Luxembourg, 47,756; Switzerland, 38,443; Austria, 36,841.

Distribution by commodities in 1990 (in DM 1m.) Imports and exports: Live animals, 648 and 953; foodstuffs, 50,886 and 25,371; drinks and tobacco 7,721 and 4,819; raw materials, 33,544 and 7,204; semi-finished goods, 62,107 and 33,834; manufacturers, 388,014 and 568,424.

Trade with the former German Democratic Republic was not categorized as 'foreign'.

Total trade between the Federal Republic of Germany and UK (British Department of Trade returns, in £1,000 sterling):

	1987	1988	1989	1990	1991
Imports to UK	15,783,904	17,667,097	20,005,276	19,907,062	17,741,093
Exports and re-exports					
from UK	9,404,257	9,521,851	11,110,623	13,169,405	14,653,972

Total trade between the former *GDR* and UK (British Department of Trade returns, in £1,000 sterling):

	1986	1987	1988	1989	1990
Imports to UK	195,513	180,299	152,977	168,742	128,498
Exports and re-exports from UK	81,276	81,489	113,239	106,445	57,013

Tourism. In 1990 there were 47,859 places of accommodation with 1·8m. beds (including 10,164 hotels with 575,274 beds). In the summer of 1989 220·9m. overnight stays by Germans and 34·84m. by foreigners were registered.

COMMUNICATIONS

Roads. In 1989 the total length of classified roads was 220,853 km, including 10,571 km of motorway *(Autobahn)*. *In West Germany* in 1989 there were 35,732 km of federal highways, 63,229 km first-class and 70,677 km second-class country roads. In 1990 there were 35,501,800 passenger cars, 2,724,700 motorcycles, 1,652,900 lorries and 142,700 buses. In 1989 *in West Germany* 414m. tonnes of freight (113·4m. tonne-kilometres) and 5,294m. passengers were transported by long-distance road traffic.

Road casualties in 1989 totalled 448,158 injured and 7,906 killed *in West Germany*.

In *the GDR* there were, in 1988, 47,203 km of classified roads including 1,855 km of motorways. 3,531m. passengers and 143m. tonnes of goods were carried by public road transport. There were 3,743,554 cars, 228,872 lorries, 1,318,571 motorcycles and 60,744 buses. There were 46,804 road accidents in 1988, with 1,441 fatalities.

Railways. Length of railway in 1990 was 44,330 km (1,435 mm gauge) of which 15,737 km was electrified. West German railways in 1990 carried 1,020m. passengers and 282m. tonnes of freight. There were also 2,795 km of privately-owned and other minor railways.

In the *GDR* in 1990 469m. passengers and 234m. tonnes of freight were carried.

There are metros in Berlin (136 km), Hamburg (95 km), Frankfurt am Main (51 km), Munich (63 km) and Nuremberg (23 km), and tram/light rail networks in 55 cities.

Civil Aviation. Lufthansa was set up in 1953 with a capital of DM 900m. In 1990 51% was state-owned.

Lufthansa flies to 181 destinations in 86 countries, including 8 in Germany, London, Moscow and 11 other European cities, Tokyo and New York.

In *West Germany* in 1990 civil aviation had 306 aircraft over 20 tonnes. In 1990 there were 40·54. passenger arrivals and 40·77m. departures. 56m. passengers were carried (16,638 person-kilometres), including 21·60m. to destinations abroad. Major international airports include Frankfurt am Main, Düsseldorf, Munich, Hamburg and 2 at Berlin (Tegel and Schönefeld).

In the *GDR* in 1988 1·58m. passengers and 31,300 tonnes of freight were carried. The GDR carrier, Interflug, had 32 aircraft.

Shipping. In 1989 the West German mercantile marine comprised 1,812 ocean-going vessels of 5,822,000 GRT.

Navigable inland waterways *in West Germany* have a total length of 4,447 km. The inland-waterways fleet on 31 Dec. 1989 included 1,995 motor freight vessels totalling 1·92m. tonnes and 444 tankers of 598,149 tonnes.

Sea-going ships in 1989 carried 155·7m. tonnes of cargo. Inland waterways carried 255·3m. tonnes in 1988.

Telecommunications. Telecommunications were deregulated in 1989.

In *West Germany* in 1990 there were 17,379 post offices, 43·1m. telephones and 682,168 fax transmitters.

The post office savings banks had, in 1990, 23,269,000 depositors with DM 42,818m. to their credit.

In 1989 postal revenues amounted to DM 59,848m. and expenditure to DM 56,672m.

There were 9 regional broadcasting stations. The *Arbeitsgemeinschaft der öffentlich-rechtlichen Rundfunkanstalten der Bundesrepublik Deutschland* (ARD) organizes co-operation between them and also broadcasts a federal-wide TV programme of its own. Number of wireless licences, (1989) 27·43m.; of television licences, 24·14m.

In the *GDR* in 1988 there were 11,971 post offices, 3,976,844 telephones and 17,363 telex subscribers. There were 6·78m. radio and 6·2m. TV licences.

Cinemas and Theatres. In 1989 there were 4,021 cinemas and 522 theatres with seating capacities of 841,133 and 208,806 respectively. 68 feature films were made in 1989 in *West Germany.*

Newspapers and Books. In *West Germany* in 1989, 323 newspapers and 7,069 periodicals were published with respective circulations of 25·09m. and 309·04m. 65,980 book titles were published. In 1989 there were 1,018 learned libraries, and 10,925 public libraries, the latter with 6·57m. users.

In the *GDR* there were 543 newspapers and periodicals in 1989. 6,073 book titles were published in 136·87m. copies.

JUSTICE, RELIGION, EDUCATION AND WELFARE

Justice. Justice is administered by the federal courts and by the courts of the Länder. In criminal procedures, civil cases and procedures of non-contentious jurisdiction the courts on the Land level are the local courts *(Amtsgerichte),* the regional courts *(Landgerichte)* and the courts of appeal *(Oberlandesgerichte).* Constitutional federal disputes are dealt with by the Federal Constitutional Court *(Bundesverfassungsgericht)* elected by the Bundestag and Bundesrat. The Länder also have constitutional courts. In labour law disputes the courts of the first and second instance are the labour courts and the Land labour courts and in the third instance, the Federal Labour Court *(Bundesarbeitsgericht).* Disputes about public law in matters of social security, unemployment insurance, maintenance of war victims and similar cases are dealt with in the first and second instances by the social courts and the Land social courts and in the third instance by the Federal Social Court *(Bundessozialgericht).* In most tax matters the finance courts of the Länder are competent and in the second instance, the Federal Finance Court *(Bundesfinanzhof).* Other controversies of public law in non-constitutional matters are decided in the first and second instance by the administrative and the higher administrative courts *(Observerwaltungsgerichte)* of the Länder, and in the third instance by the Federal Administrative Court *(Bundesverwaltungsgericht).*

For the inquiry into maritime accidents the admiralty courts *(Seeämter)* are competent on the Land level and in the second instance the Federal Admiralty Court *(Bundesoberseeamt)* in Hamburg.

The death sentence has been abolished.

Religion. In *West Germany* at the 1987 census there were 26,232,000 (13,822,000 female) Roman Catholics, 25,412,600 Protestants (13,784,000 female) and 1,651,000 Moslems (722,700 females).

The Evangelical (Protestant) Church (EKD) consists of 24 member-churches including 7 Lutheran Churches, 8 United-Lutheran-Reformed, 2 Reformed Churches and 1 Confederation of United member Churches: 'Church of the Union'. Its organs are the Synod, the Church Conference and the Council under the chairmanship of Bishop Dr Eduard Lohse (Hanover). There are also some 12 Evangelical Free Churches. In 1988 there were 10,729 parishes, 18,729 priests and 25·2m. members in *West Germany.*

In *West Germany* in 1988 there were 26·48m. Catholics. There are 5 Catholic archbishoprics (Bamberg, Cologne, Freiburg, Munich and Freising, Paderborn) and 17 bishoprics. Chairman of the German Bishops' Conference is Cardinal Joseph

Höffner, Archbishop of Cologne. A concordat between Germany and the Holy See dates from 10 Sept. 1933.

There were 27,711 Jews in 1989 with 53 synagogues and 13 rabbis.

In the *GDR* according to the census of 1950, 80·5% of the population were Protestants and 11% were Roman Catholics. The Synod of Lutheran Churches was founded in 1969 and embraces 8 regional churches. There were some 1·5m. Lutherans in 1989 in 7,200 parishes with 4,300 priests. The Catholic Church is organized in 2 dioceses, 3 episcopal districts and one apostolic administration. In 1989 there were 1·05m. Catholics in 916 parishes with 1,155 priests. There were 300 monasteries. There were also 40 Free and other churches, including Methodists, Quakers and Seventh-Day Adventists. In 1989 there were 8 synagogues.

Education. Education is compulsory for children aged 6 to 15. After the first 4 (or 6) years at primary school *(Grundschulen)* children attend post-primary *(Hauptschulen)*, secondary modern *(Realschulen)*, grammar *(Gymnasien)*, or comprehensive schools *(Integrierte Gesamtschulen)*. Secondary modern school comprises 6, grammar school 9, years. Entry to higher education is by the final Grammar School Certificate (Abitur-Higher School Certificate). There are special schools *(Sonderschulen)* for handicapped or maladjusted children.

In *West Germany* in 1989–90 there were 3,249 kindergartens with 67,512 pupils and 4,555 teachers, 13,585 primary schools with 2,449,711 pupils and 7,013 post-primary schools with 1,254,061 pupils. There were 229,826 teachers at primary and post-primary schools. There were also 2,762 special schools with 246,278 pupils and 42,128 teachers, 2,573 secondary modern schools with 857,218 pupils and 57,632 teachers; 2,462 grammar schools with 1,545,577 pupils and 121,854 teachers; 422 comprehensive schools with 273,001 pupils and 31,132 teachers.

Vocational education is provided in part-time, full-time and advanced vocational schools *(Berufs-, Berufsaufbau-, Berufsfach-* and *Fachschulen,* including *Fachschulen für Technik* and *Schulen des Gesundheitswesens)*. Occupation-related, part-time vocational training of 6 to 12 hours per week is compulsory for all (including unemployed) up to the age of 18 years or until the completion of the practical vocational training. Full-time vocational schools comprise courses of at least one year. They prepare for commercial and domestic occupations as well as specialized occupations in the field of handicrafts. Advanced full-time vocational schools are attended by pupils over 18. Courses vary from 6 months to 3 or more years.

In 1989–90 there were 7,592 full- and part-time vocational schools with 2,256,951 pupils (1,014,807 female) and 90,461 teachers.

Higher Education. In *West Germany* in 1989–90 there were 62 institutes of university status: Universities proper at Augsburg, Bamberg, Bayreuth, Berlin (West), Bielefeld, Bochum, Bonn, Bremen, Cologne, Dortmund, Düsseldorf, Erlangen-Nuremberg, Frankfurt am Main, Freiburg im Breisgau, Giessen, Göttingen, Hamburg, Hanover, Heidelberg, Hohenheim, Kaiserslautern, Karlsruhe, Kiel, Konstanz, Mainz, Mannheim, Marburg, Munich, Münster, Oldenburg, Osnabrück, Passau, Regensburg, Saarbrücken, Stuttgart, Trier, Tübingen, Ulm and Würzburg; technical universities at Berlin (West), Braunschweig, Clausthal, Hamburg-Harburg and Munich; military universities at Hamburg and Munich; a medical university at Lübeck; a Catholic university at Eichstatt; a private Nordic university at Flensburg; and advanced schools *(Hochschulen)* at Aachen, Cologne (sport), Darmstadt (technical), Hamburg (economics and politics), Hanover (medical, veterinary), Hildesheim, Koblenz (private business), Lüneberg, Rhineland-Palatinate (education), Speyer (administration) and Witten-Herdecke (private). There were 182 other institutes of higher education.

Academic staff in 1988–89: Universities including teacher training and theological colleges, 113,235; other institutes, 37,744.

Students in 1990–91: Universities, 1,166,693; other institutes, 552,076. Female students totalled 668,050.

In the *GDR* 10-year comprehensive schooling had been compulsory and free. In 1988 764,423 children were in 13,402 pre-school educational institutions. General education schools numbered 5,907 with 167,207 teachers and 2,054,817 pupils. Of these schools 5,207 with 1,953,012 pupils offered 10 years schooling and the remainder 12.

In addition there were 955 vocational schools *(Berufsschulen)* with 16,256 teachers and 359,308 trainees, and 237 technical schools with 157,513 students. There were also 9 universities and 44 other higher education institutes with 132,423 full-time students, including 65,152 women.

Health. In 1990 there were 229,065 doctors (including 91,895 in *West German* hospitals) and 53,793 dentists. There were 3,585 hospitals (including 981 private) with 833,055 beds.

Social Welfare (figures are for *West Germany*). *Social Health Insurance* (introduced in 1883). Wage-earners and apprentices, salaried employees with an income below a certain limit and socialinsurance pensioners are compulsorily insured. Voluntary insurance is also possible.

Benefits: Medical treatment, medicines, hospital and nursing care, maternity benefits, death benefits for the insured and their families, sickness payments and out-patients' allowances.

37·23m. persons were insured in 1989 (21·88m. compulsorily) and 10·9m. persons (including 6·8m. women) were drawing pensions. Number of cases of incapacity for work totalled 28·18m., and the number of working days lost were 259·33 (men) and 167,143 (women). Total disbursements DM 129,927m.

Accident Insurance (introduced in 1884). Those insured are all persons in employment or service, apprentices and the majority of the self-employed and the unpaid family workers.

Benefits in the case of industrial injuries and occupational diseases: Medical treatment and nursing care, sickness payments, pensions and other payments in cash and in kind, surviving dependants' pensions.

Number of insured in 1989, 40·30m.; number of current pensions, 930,143; total disbursements, DM 14,546m.

Workers' and Employees' Old-Age Insurance Scheme (introduced in 1889). All wage-earners and salaried employees, the members of certain liberal professions and—subject to certain conditions—self-employed craftsmen are compulsorily insured. The insured may voluntarily continue to insure when no longer liable to do so or increase the insurance.

Benefits: Measures designed to maintain, improve and restore the earning capacity; pensions paid to persons incapable of work, old age and surviving dependants' pensions.

Number of insured in 1989, 32·73m. (15·79m. women); number of current pensions, 1988: 14·12m.; pensions to widows and widowers, 3·98m. (1990). Total disbursements in 1990, DM 217,419m.

There are also special retirement and unemployment pension schemes for miners and farmers, assistance for war victims and compensation payments to members of German minorities in East European countries expelled after the Second World War and persons who suffered damage because of the war or in connexion with the currency reform. Special benefits for refugees from the GDR were abolished in July 1990.

Family Allowances. The monthly allowance for the first child is DM 600, payable for 2 years. DM 10,203m. were dispersed to 6·21m. recipients in 1990. Paid child care leave is available for 3 years to mothers or fathers.

Unemployment Allowances. In 1990 799,000 persons (407,000 women) were receiving unemployment benefit and 386,000 (114,000 women) earnings-related benefit. Total expenditure on these and similar benefits (e.g. short-working supplement, job creation schemes) was DM 41,423m. in 1990.

Accommodation Allowances averaging DM 150 a month were paid in 1989 to 1·72m. persons.

Public Welfare (introduced in 1962). In 1989 DM 28·76m. were distributed to 3·62m. recipients (1·94m. women).

Public Youth Welfare. For supervision of foster children, official guardianship, assistance with adoptions and affiliations, social assistance in juvenile courts, educational assistance and correctional education under a court order. Total expenditure in 1989, DM 9,860m.

DIPLOMATIC REPRESENTATIVES

Of Germany in Great Britain (23 Belgrave Sq., London, SW1X 8PZ)
Ambassador: Baron Hermann von Richthofen.

Of Great Britain in Germany (Friedrich-Ebert-Allee 77, 5300 Bonn 1)
Ambassador: Sir Christopher Mallaby, KCMG.

Of Germany in the USA (4645 Reservoir Rd, NW, Washington, D.C., 20007)
Ambassador: Juergen Ruhfus.

Of the USA in Germany (Deichmanns Ave., 5300, Bonn)
Ambassador: Robert M. Kimmit.

Of Germany to the United Nations
Ambassador: Detlev Graf zu Rantzau.

Further Reading

Statistical Information: The central statistical agency is the Statistisches Bundesamt, 62 Wiesbaden 1, Gustav Stresemann Ring 11. *President:* Egon Hölder. Its publications include:

Statistisches Jahrbuch für die Bundesrepublik Deutschland; Wirtschaft und Statistik (monthly, from 1949); *Das Arbeitsgebiet der Bundesstatistik* (latest issue 1988; Abridged English version: *Survey of German Federal Statistics*).

Ardagh, J., *Germany and the Germans.* 2nd ed. London, 1991
Bark, D. L. and Gress, D. R., *A History of West Germany, 1945-1988.* 2 vols. Oxford, 1989
Berghahn, V. R., *Modern Germany: Society, Economy and Politics in the Twentieth Century.* CUP, 1982
Betz, H. G., *Postmodern Politics in Germany.* London, 1991
Die Bundesrepublik Deutschland: Staatshandbuch. Cologne, annual
Burdick, C., *et al.* (eds.) *Contemporary Germany: Politics and Culture*, Boulder, 1984
Carr, W., *A History of Germany, 1815-1990.* 4th ed. London, 1991
Childs, D., *Germany in the 20th Century.* London, 1991
Conradt, D. P., *The German Polity.* 2nd ed. New York, 1982
Craig, G. A., *Germany, 1866-1945.* Oxford Univ. Press, 1981—*The Germans.* Harmondsworth, 1984
Dennis, M., *German Democratic Republic.* London, 1987
Detwiler, D. S. and Detwiler, I. E., *West Germany.* [Bibliography] Oxford and Santa Barbara, 1988
Dittmers, M., *The Green Party in West Germany.* 2nd ed. Buckingham, 1988
Edinger, L. J., *West German Politics.* New York, 1986
Eley, G., *From Unification to Nazism: Reinterpreting the German Past.* London, 1986
Friese, F-J., *Investment and Business Establishments in the Federal Republic of Germany: A Guide for the Foreign Investor.* Frankfurt-am-Main, 1988
Fulbrook, M., *A Concise History of Germany.* CUP, 1991
Hardach, K., *The Political Economy of Germany in the Twentieth Century.* California Univ. Press, 1980
Hucko, E. M. (ed.) *The Democratic Tradition* [Texts of German Constitutions]. Leamington Spa, 1987
James, H. A., *A German Identity.* rev. ed. London, 1990
Johnson, N., *State and Government in the Federal Republic of Germany: the Executive at Work.* 2nd ed. Oxford, 1983
Jonas, M., *The United States and Germany: A Diplomatic History.* Cornell Univ. Press, 1984
Koch, H. W., *A Constitutional History of Germany in the Nineteenth and Twentieth Centuries.* London, 1984
König, K., *et al.* (eds.) *Public Administration in the Federal Republic of Germany.* Boston, 1983
Leaman, J., *The Political Economy of West Germany, 1945-1985.* Basingstoke, 1987
Marsh, D., *The New Germany: at the Crossroads.* London, 1990
Marshall, B., *The Origins of Post-War German Politics.* London, 1988
Pasley, M. (ed.) *Germany: a Companion to German Studies.* 2nd ed. London, 1982

Schweitzer, D.-C., (ed.) *Politics and Government in the Federal Republic of Germany: Basic Documents.* Leamington Spa, 1984
Smith, G., *Democracy in Western Germany.* 3rd ed. Aldershot, 1986
Smyser, W. R., *The Economy of United Germany.* New York, 1992
Thomaneck, J. and Mellis, J., (eds.) *Politics, Society and Government in the German Democratic Republic: Basic Documents.* Oxford, 1989
Wallace, I., *East Germany: the German Democratic Republic.* [Bibliography]. Oxford and Santa Barbara, 1987
Watson, A., *The Germans: Who Are They Now?* London, 1992
Weizsäcker, R. von, *A Voice from Germany: Speeches.* London, 1986

National Libraries: Deutsche Bibliothek, Zeppelinallee 4–8; Frankfurt-am-Main. *Director:* K.-D. Lehmann; (Berliner) Staatsbibliothek Preussischer Kulturbesitz, Potsdamer Str., Postfach 1407 D-1000 Berlin 30. *Director:* Dr. Richard Landwehrmeyer.

THE LÄNDER

BADEN–WÜRTTEMBERG

AREA AND POPULATION. Baden-Württemberg comprises 35,751 sq. km, with a population (at 30 Sept. 1990) of 9,787,383 (4,765,042 males, 5,022,341 females).

The Land is administratively divided into 4 areas, 9 urban and 35 rural districts, and numbers 1,111 communes. The capital is Stuttgart.

Vital statistics for calendar years:

	Live births	Marriages	Divorces	Deaths
1988	110,627	58,939	17,204	92,418
1989	111,600	58,835	16,953	94,262
1990	118,579	61,448	16,688	97,570

CONSTITUTION. The Land Baden-Württemberg is a merger of the 3 Länder, Baden, Württemberg-Baden and Württemberg-Hohenzollern, which were formed in 1945. The merger was approved by a plebiscite held on 9 Dec. 1951, when 70% of the population voted in its favour. It has 7 seats in the Bundesrat.

At the elections to the Diet of Jan. 1991, turn-out was 71%. The Social Democrats won 40·8% of the vote; the Christian Democrats, 40·2%; the Greens, 8·8% and the Free Democrats, 7·4%. Elections were scheduled for April 1992.

Erwin Teufel (CDU) is *Prime Minister*.

AGRICULTURE. Area and yield of the most important crops:

	Area (in 1,000 ha)			Yield (in 1,000 tonnes)		
	1988	1989	1990	1988	1989	1990
Rye	16·3	16·1	17·0	73·9	73·8	82·0
Wheat	214·0	216·9	210·2	1,326·8	1,315·3	1,279·6
Barley	202·7	201·6	200·4	1,025·4	1,022·1	1,100·9
Oats	77·6	72·0	63·8	406·5	325·8	304·4
Potatoes	12·4	10·8	10·6	399·6	338·9	308·6
Sugar-beet	22·6	22·1	23·5	1,215·1	1,192·9	1,221·3

Livestock (3 Dec. 1990): Cattle, 1,583,962 (including 573,744 milch cows); horses, 58,651; pigs, 2,224,062; sheep, 279,727; poultry, 5,511,676.

INDUSTRY. In 1990 9,854 establishments (with 20 and more employees) employed 1,521,022 persons; of these, 289,338 were employed in machine construction (excluding office machines, data processing equipment and facilities); 62,933 in textile industry; 262,910 in electrical engineering; 235,137 in car building.

LABOUR. The economically active persons totalled 4,447,000 at the 1%-EC-sample survey of April 1989. Of the total 486,900 were self-employed (including family workers), 3,960,100 employees; 142,500 were engaged in agriculture and forestry; 2,099,700 in power supply, mining, manufacturing and building, 664,700 in commerce and transport, 1,540,100 in other industries and services.

ROADS. On 1 Jan. 1991 there were 28.007 km of 'classified' roads, including 998 km of autobahn, 5,041 km of federal roads, 10,048 km of first-class and 11,920 km of second-class highways. Motor vehicles, at 1 Jan. 1991, numbered 5,763,124, including, 4,916,140 passenger cars, 9,359 buses, 212,616 lorries, 319,476 tractors and 232,484 motor cycles.

JUSTICE. There are a constitutional court *(Staatsgerichtshof)*, 2 courts of appeal, 17 regional courts, 108 local courts, a Land labour court, 9 labour courts, a Land social court, 8 social courts, a finance court, a higher administrative court *(Verwaltungsgerichtshof)*, 4 administrative courts.

RELIGION. On 1 Jan. 1990, 40·7% of the population were Protestants and 45·1% were Roman Catholics.

EDUCATION. In 1990–91 there were 2,615 primary schools *(Grund* and *Hauptschule)* with 32,117 teachers and 585,841 pupils; 539 special schools with 8,342 teachers and 43,978 pupils; 445 intermediate schools with 11,047 teachers and 172,920 pupils; 413 high schools with 18,515 teachers and 230,916 pupils; 33 *Freie Waldorf* schools with 1,234 teachers and 16,178 pupils. Other schools together had 709 teachers and 9,890 pupils; there were also 40 *Fachhochschulen* (colleges of engineering and others) with 50,583 students.

In the winter term 1990–91 there were 9 universities (Freiburg, 22,732 students; Heidelberg, 27,065; Konstanz, 8,977; Tübingen, 24,667; Karlsruhe, 20,638; Stuttgart, 20,402; Hohenheim, 5,730; Mannheim, 12,652; Ulm, 5,841); 6 teacher-training colleges with 11,851 students; 5 colleges of music with 2,963 students and 2 colleges of fine arts with 1,065 students.

Statistical Information: Statistisches Landesamt Baden-Württemberg (P.O.B. 10 60 33, D7000 Stuttgart 10) *(President:* Prof. Dr. Max Wingen), publishes: *'Baden-Württemberg in Wort und Zahl'* (monthly); *Jahrbücher für Statistik und Landeskunde von Baden-Württemberg; Statistik von Baden-Württemberg* (series); *Statistisch-prognostischer Bericht* (latest issue 1988–89); *Statistisches Taschenbuch* (latest issue 1988–89).

State Library: Württembergische Landesbibliothek, Konrad-Adenauer-Str. 8, 7000 Stuttgart 1. *Director:* Dr Hans-Peter Geh. Badische Landesbibliothek Karlsruhe, Lamm-Str. 16, 7500 Karlsruhe 1. *Director:* Dr Römer.

BAVARIA

Bayern

AREA AND POPULATION. Bavaria has an area of 70,554 sq. km. The capital is Munich. There are 7 areas, 96 urban and rural districts and 2,051 communes. The population (30 Sept. 1990) numbered 11,412,982 (5,535,524 males, 5,877,458 females).

Vital statistics for calendar years:

	Live births	Marriages	Divorces	Deaths
1988	126,409	71,742	19,496	118,450
1989	127,029	72,077	19,521	121,343
1990	136,122	74,387	19,168	123,726

CONSTITUTION. The Constituent Assembly, elected on 30 June 1946, passed a constitution on the lines of the democratic constitution of 1919, but with greater emphasis on state rights; this was agreed upon by the Christian Social Union (CSU) and the Social Democrats (SPD). Bavaria has 6 seats in the Bundesrat. The CSU replaces the Christian Democratic Party in Bavaria.

At the Diet elections of Oct. 1990 the CSU won 127 seats with 54·9% of the vote, the SPD, 58 with 26%, the Greens, 12 with 6·4% and the Free Democrats 7 with 5·2%. The *Prime Minister* is Max Streibl.

AGRICULTURE. Area and yield of the most important products:

	Area (in 1,000 ha)			Yield (in 1,000 tonnes)		
	1988	1989	1990	1988	1989	1990
Wheat	511·6	501·8	482·2	3,865·0	3,301·3	3,193·3
Rye	51·5	58·3	62·6	225·4	269·6	312·0
Barley	516·9	511·5	495·6	2,707·9	2,906·1	2,721·3
Oats	114·0	105·7	93·1	505·4	440·9	492·3
Potatoes	65·2	61·8	63·1	2,587·3	2,253·8	1,953·4
Sugar-beet	77·6	79·0	81·1	4,256·6	4,574·9	4,814·3

Livestock (2 Dec. 1988): 4,939,800 cattle (including 1,890,200 milch cows); 64,900 horses; 340,800 sheep; 3,781,900 pigs; 12,089,600 poultry.

INDUSTRY. In 1990, 9,892 establishments (with 20 or more employees) employed 1,443,385 persons; of these, 269,414 were employed in electrical engineering; 205,084 in mechanical engineering; 108,921 in clothing and textile industries.

LABOUR. The economically active persons totalled 5,731,400 at the 1% sample survey of the microcensus of April 1990. Of the total, 569,400 were self-employed, 234,400 unpaid family workers, 4,927,400 employees; 2,412,000 in power supply, mining, manufacturing and building; 936,400 in commerce and transport; 2,020,200 in other industries and services.

ROADS. There were, on 1 Jan. 1990, 41,258 km of 'classified' roads, including 2,037 km of autobahn, 7,127 km of federal roads, 13,801 km of first-class and 18,293 km of second-class highways. Number of motor vehicles, at 1 July 1990, was 6,927,999, including 5,666,577 passenger cars, 255,082 lorries, 13,846 buses, 589,358 tractors, 319,152 motor cycles.

JUSTICE. There are a constitutional court *(Verfassungsgerichtshof)*, a supreme Land court *(Oberstes Landesgericht)*, 3 courts of appeal, 22 regional courts, 72 local courts, 2 Land labour courts, 11 labour courts, a Land social court, 7 social courts, 2 finance courts, a higher administrative court *(Verwaltungsgerichtshof)*, 6 administrative courts.

RELIGION. At the census of 25 May 1987 there were 67·2% Roman Catholics and 23·9% Protestants.

EDUCATION. In 1990–91 there were 2,813 primary schools with 44,902 teachers and 750,320 pupils; 378 special schools with 6,507 teachers and 42,361 pupils; 333 intermediate schools with 8,900 teachers and 121,531 pupils; 395 high schools with 20,573 teachers and 272,240 pupils; 258 part-time vocational schools with 8,003 teachers and 292,853 pupils, including 52 special part-time vocational schools with 628 teachers and 7,942 pupils; 566 full-time vocational schools with 3,878 teachers and 46,519 pupils including 245 schools for public health occupations with 1,132 teachers and 15,445 pupils; 322 advanced full-time vocational schools with 2,446 teachers and 27,248 pupils; 84 vocational high schools *(Berufsoberschulen, Fachoberschulen)* with 2,021 teachers and 26,812 pupils.

In the winter term 1989–90 there were 11 universities with 179,031 students (Augsburg, 11,097; Bamberg, 6,238; Bayreuth, 7,215; Eichstätt, 2,451; Erlangen–Nürnberg, 27,176; München, 61,839; Passau, 6,902; Regensburg, 13,417; Würzburg, 18,432; the Technical University of München, 23,024; München University of the Federal Armed Forces (Universität der Bundeswehr), 2,291); the college of philosophy, München, 339 and 2 philosophical-theological colleges with together 438 students (Benediktbeuern, 120; Neuendettelsau, 318). There were also 2 colleges of music, 2 colleges of fine arts and 1 college of television and film, with together 2,375 students; 13 vocational colleges *(Fachhochschulen)* with 59,643 students including one for the civil service *(Bayerische Beamtenfachhochschule)* with 5,681 students.

Statistical Information: Bayerisches Landesamt für Statistik und Datenverarbeitung, 51 Neuhauser Str. 8000 Munich, was founded in 1833. *President:* Rudolf Giehl. It publishes: *Statistisches Jahrbuch für Bayern.* 1894 ff.—*Bayern in Zahlen.* Monthly (from Jan. 1947).—*Zeitschrift des Bayerischen Statistischen Landesamts.* July 1869–1943; 1948 ff.—*Beiträge zur Statistik Bayerns.* 1850 ff.—*Statistische Berichte.* 1951 ff.— *Schaubilderhefte.* 1951 ff.—*Kreisdaten.* 1972 ff.—*Gemeindedaten.* 1973 ff.

Nawiasky, H. and Luesser, C., *Die Verfassung des Freistaates Bayern vom 2. Dez. 1946.* Munich, 1948; supplement, by H. Nawiasky and H. Lechner, Munich, 1953

State Library: Bayerische Staatsbibliothek, Munich 22. *Director:* Dr Franz G. Kaltwasser.

BERLIN

Except for the population total, figures refer only to the former West Berlin.

HISTORY. Greater Berlin was under 4-power (France, USSR, UK and USA) Allied government (the *Kommandatura*) from 5 June 1945 until 1 July 1948, when the Soviet element withdrew. On 30 Nov. 1948 a separate municipal government was set up in the Soviet sector. The French, UK and US sectors coalesced to form the administrative unit of 'West Berlin', covering 480 sq. km. With the establishment of the German Democratic Republic, the Soviet sector ('East Berlin', 403 sq. km) was designated its capital.

East and West Berlin were amalgamated on the re-unification of Germany in Oct. 1990.

AREA AND POPULATION. The area is 883 sq. km. Population, 1990, 3·41m.

Vital statistics for calendar years:

	Live births	Marriages	Divorces	Deaths
1987	19,554	11,961	6,230	30,719
1988	20,980	12,385	5,995	30,021
1989	21,159	12,743	6,157	30,045

CONSTITUTION AND GOVERNMENT. According to the constitution of 1 Sept. 1950, Berlin is simultaneously a Land of the Federal Republic and a city. It is governed by a House of Representatives (of at least 200 members); executive power is vested in a Senate, consisting of the Governing Mayor, the Mayor and not more than 16 senators.

Berlin has 5 seats in the Bundesrat.

At the elections of Dec. 1990 the Christian Democrats won 100 seats in the House of Representatives with 40·3% of the vote; the Social Democrats, 76, with 30·5%; the Party of Democratic Socialism (former Communists), 23, with 9·2%; the Free Democrats, 18, with 7·1%; the Greens, 12, with 5%; Alliance '90/Greens, 11, with 4·4%.

In the Senate, the Christian Democrats gained 8 seats and the Social Democrats, 7. A coalition government was formed.

Governing Mayor: Eberhard Diepgen (Christian Democrat).

ECONOMY

Banking. On 20 March 1949 when the DM (West) became the only legal tender of the Western Sectors, the Zentralbank of Berlin was established. Its functions were similar to those of the Zentralbanks of the Länder of the Federal Republic. The Berlin Central Bank was merged with the Bank deutscher Länder as from 1 Aug. 1957, when the latter became the Deutsche Bundesbank.

AGRICULTURE. Agricultural area (April 1989), 1,245 ha, including 930 ha of arable land and 84 ha of gardens, orchards and nurseries.
Livestock (Dec. 1988): Cattle, 657; pigs, 3,027; horses, 3,461; sheep, 1,241.

INDUSTRY. In 1989 (monthly averages), 1,125 establishments (with 20 or more employees) employed 165,960 persons; of these, 55,603 were employed in electrical engineering, 4,413 in steel construction, 3,776 in textiles. In 1988, 15,312 persons were employed in machine construction and 12,849, in the manufacture of chemicals.

LABOUR. The economically active persons totalled 994,800 at the 1%-sample survey of the microcensus of April 1989. Of the total, 89,300 were self-employed including unpaid family workers, 905,500 employees; 7,500 were engaged in agriculture and forestry; 300,900 in power supply, manufacturing and building; 189,800 in commerce and transport; 496,600 in other industries and services.

ROADS. There were, on 1 Jan. 1990, 146·96 km of 'classified' roads, including 46·9 km of autobahn and 100·5 km of federal roads. On 1 July 1989, 820,323 motor vehicles were registered, including 646,399 passenger cars, 45,747 lorries, 37,712 motor cycles, and 2,138 buses (1988).

JUSTICE. There are a court of appeal *(Kammergericht)*, a regional court, 7 local courts, a Land Labour court, a labour court, a Land social court, a social court, a higher administrative court, an administrative court and a finance court.

EDUCATION. In 1989–90 (preliminary figures) there were 453 schools providing general education (excluding special schools) with 186,381 pupils; 55 special schools with 6,264 pupils. There were a further 179 vocational schools with 55,496 pupils.
In the winter term 1989–90 there was 1 university (58,181 students); 1 technical university (34,540); 1 theological (evangelical) college (508); 1 college of fine arts with 4,649 students; 1 vocational college (for economics) (1,695); 2 colleges for social work (1,406); 1 technical college (6,605), 1 college of the Federal postal administration (535) and 2 colleges for public administration (2,739).

Statistical Information: The Statistisches Landesamt Berlin was founded in 1862 (Fehrbelliner Platz 1, 1000 Berlin 31). *Director:* Prof. Günther Appel. It publishes: *Statistisches Jahrbuch* (from 1867): *Berliner Statistik* (monthly, from 1947).—*100 Jahre Berliner Statistik* (1962).

State Library: Amerika-Gedenkbibliothek-Berliner Zentralbibliothek-, Blücherplatz 1, D1000 Berlin 61. *Director:* Dr Klaus Bock.

BRANDENBURG

AREA AND POPULATION. The area is 29,056 sq. km. Population on 31 Dec. 1990 was 2,578,312 (1,331,852 females). The capital is Potsdam.

Vital statistics for calendar years:

	Live births	Marriages	Divorces	Deaths
1988	35,872	22,720	8,449	32,684
1989	32,997	21,151	8,401	31,535
1990	29,339	16,815	5,828	32,167

CONSTITUTION AND GOVERNMENT. The Land was reconstituted on former GDR territory on 14 Oct. 1990. Brandenburg has 4 seats in the Bundesrat.
At the Diet elections of Oct. 1990 the Social Democrats won 36 seats with 38·3% of the vote; the Christian Democrats, 27, with 29·4%; the Party of Democratic Socialism (former Communists), 13, with 13·4%; the Free Democrats, 6, with 6·4%; Alliance '90/Greens, 6 with 6%.
The *Prime Minister* is Dr Manfred Stolpe (Social Democrat).
There are 6 urban districts, 38 rural districts and 1,787 communes.

AGRICULTURE. Livestock in 1991: Cattle, 888,262 (including 286,684 milch cows); horses, 7,317; pigs, 1,314,514; sheep, 181,948; poultry 4,422,702.
Area and yield of the most important crops:

	Area (in 1,000 ha)			Yield (in 1,000 tonnes)		
	1988	1989	1990	1988	1989	1990
Rye	272·3	289·5	298·2	709·7	904·0	886·9
Wheat	94·4	96·6	94·9	344·4	368·8	469·4
Barley	149·3	153·3	157·2	499·7	647·4	673·6
Oats	31·7	32·4	28·7	88·2	83·5	107·7
Potatoes	127·0	124·1	100·9	3,210·8	2,242·9	1,828·2
Sugar-beet	19·9	21·9	21·6	539·2	660·0	790·1

INDUSTRY. In 1991, 1,167 establishments (20 and more employees) employed 272,389 persons; of these, 71,016 were employed in electrical engineering; 48,420 in mining; 29,951 in machine construction; 15,059 in chemical industries.

LABOUR. In Nov. 1990 1,190,461 persons were economically active, including 36,304 self-employed and family assistants, and 628,701 manual and 525,456 white-collar workers.

ROADS. In 1990 there were 830,939 passenger cars, 48,600 lorries, 13,765 buses, 56,880 tractors and 213,039 motorcycles.

EDUCATION. In 1991/92 there were 1,165 schools with 358,892 pupils, including 553 primary schools (with 183,247 pupils), 122 primary and comprehensive (53,589), 182 comprehensive (51,001), 157 secondary (52,213) and 135 special needs (15,312).
There were 2 universities and 1 college with 8,002 students and 4 technical institutes with 691.

BREMEN
Freie Hansestadt Bremen

AREA AND POPULATION. The area of the Land, consisting of the towns and ports of Bremen and Bremerhaven, is 404 sq. km. Population, 31 Dec. 1990, 681,665 (326,224 males, 355,441 females).
Vital statistics for calendar years:

	Live births	Marriages	Divorces	Deaths
1988	6,420	4,230	2,037	8,712
1989	6,513	4,156	1,919	8,463
1990	6,895	4,338	1,701	8,371

CONSTITUTION. Political power is vested in the 100-member House of Burgesses *(Bürgerschaft)* which appoints the executive, called the Senate. Bremen has 3 seats in the Bundesrat.
At the elections of 29 Sept. 1991 the Social Democratic Party won 41 seats with 38% of votes cast (54 with 50·5% in 1987); the Christian Democrats, 32 with 30·7% (25 with 23·4%); the Greens, 11 with 11·4% (10 with 10·2%); the Free Democrats, 10 with 9·5% (10 with 10%); and the Deutsche Volksunion 6 with 6·2% (1 with 3·4%). The Senate president is Klaus Wedemeier (Social Democrat).

AGRICULTURE. Agricultural area comprised (1990), 10,017 ha: yield of grain crops (1987), 6,059 tonnes; potatoes, 155 tonnes.
Livestock (2 Dec. 1990): 14,997 cattle (including 4,209 milch cows); 3,477 pigs; 483 sheep; 1,121 horses; 19,874 poultry.

INDUSTRY. In 1990, 334 establishments (20 and more employees) employed 79,476 persons; of these, 6,854 were employed in shipbuilding (except naval engineering); 6,735 in machine construction; 10,498 in electrical engineering; 2,265 in coffee and tea processing.

LABOUR. The economically active persons totalled 286,300 at the microcensus of April 1990. Of the total, 21,300 were self-employed, 265,000 employees; 71,400 in commerce and transport, 120,700 in other industries and services; 91,700 in power supply, mining, manufacturing and building, and 2,000 in agriculture and fishing.

ROADS. On 1 Jan. 1988 there were 108 km of 'classified' roads, including 46 km of autobahn, 62 km of federal roads. Registered motor vehicles on 1 July 1990 numbered 311,038, including 280,183 passenger cars, 13,973 trucks, 2,547 tractors, 620 buses and 9,412 motor cycles.

SHIPPING. Vessels entered in 1990, 9,453 of 41,987,000 net tons; cleared, 9,365 of 42,014,000 net tons. Sea traffic, 1990, incoming 18,847,000 tonnes; outgoing, 11,358,000 tonnes.

JUSTICE. There are a constitutional court *(Staatsgerichtshof)*, a court of appeal, a regional court, 3 local courts, a Land labour court, 2 labour courts, a Land social court, a social court, a finance court, a higher administrative court, an administrative court.

RELIGION. On 25 May 1987 (census) there were 61% Protestants and 10% Roman Catholics.

EDUCATION. In 1990 there were 306 new system schools with 5,297 teachers and 64,262 pupils; 32 special schools with 583 teachers and 2,754 pupils; 25 part-time vocational schools with 22,397 pupils; 31 full-time vocational schools with 4,619 pupils; 10 advanced vocational schools (including institutions for the training of technicians) with 721 pupils; 10 schools for public health occupations with 897 pupils.

In the winter term 1990–91 13,900 students were enrolled at the university. In addition to the university there were 4 other colleges in 1990–91 with 7,914 students.

Statistical Information: Statistisches Landesamt Bremen (An der Weide 14–16 (P.B. 101309), D2800 Bremen 1), founded in 1850. *Director:* Ltd Reg. Dir. Volker Hannemann. Its current publications include: *Statistische Mitteilungen Freie Hansestadt Bremen* (from 1948).—*Monatliche Zwischenberichte* (1949–53); *Statistische Monatsberichte* (from 1954).—*Statistische Berichte* (from 1956).—*Statistisches Handbuch für das Land Freie Hansestadt Bremen (1950–60,* 1961; *1960–64,* 1967; *1965–69,* 1971; *1970–74,* 1975; *1975–80,* 1982; *1981–85,* 1987).—*Bremen im statistischen Zeitvergleich 1950–1976.* 1977.—*Bremen in Zahlen.* 1991.

State and University Library: Bibliotheks Str., D2800 Bremen 33. *Director:* Prof. Dr Hans-Albrecht Koch.

HAMBURG
Freie und Hansestadt Hamburg

AREA AND POPULATION. In 1938 the territory of the town was re-organized by the amalgamation of the city and its 18 rural districts with 3 urban and 27 rural districts ceded by Prussia. Total area, 755·3 sq. km (1990), including the islands Neuwerk and Scharhörn (7·6 sq. km). Population (31 Dec. 1990), 1,652,400 (779,500 males, 872,900 females).

Vital statistics for calendar years:

	Live births	Marriages	Divorces	Deaths
1988	15,359	9,787	4,549	21,186
1989	15,335	9,484	4,245	21,241
1990	16,693	9,938	4,202	21,199

CONSTITUTION. The constitution of 6 June 1952 vests the supreme power in the House of Burgesses *(Bürgerschaft)* of 121 members. The executive is in the hands of the Senate, whose members are elected by the Bürgerschaft. Hamburg has 3 seats in the Bundesrat.

The elections of 2 June 1991 had the following results: Social Democrats, 61 seats with 48% of votes cast; Christian Democrats, 44 with 35·1%; Green Alternatives 9, with 7·2%; Free Democrats, 7 with 5·4%. The First Burgomaster is Dr Henning Voscherau (Social Democrat).

The territory has been divided into 7 administrative districts.

AGRICULTURE. The agricultural area comprised 14,986 ha in 1989. Yield, 1990, in tonnes, of cereals, 22,790; potatoes, 853.

Livestock (3 Dec. 1990): Cattle, 11,212 (including 2,527 milch cows); pigs, 5,249; horses, 2,588; sheep, 3,586; poultry, 19,333.

FISHERIES. In 1990 the yield of sea and coastal fishing was 108 tonnes valued at DM 0·3m.

INDUSTRY. In June 1990, 774 establishments (with 20 and more employees) employed 134,123 persons; of these, 20,930 were employed in electrical engineering; 17,392 in machine construction; 7,014 in shipbuilding (except naval engineering); 13,625 in chemical industry.

LABOUR. The economically active persons totalled 753,900 at the 1%-sample survey of the microcensus of April 1990. Of the total, 70,300 were self-employed or 683,700 unpaid family workers, 7,000 employees were engaged in agriculture and forestry, 187,500 in power supply, mining, manufacturing and building, 211,600 in commerce and transport, 347,800 in other industries and services.

ROADS. On 31 Dec. 1990 there were 3,893 km of roads, including 81 km of autobahn, 151 km of federal roads. Number of motor vehicles (1 July 1991), 764,103, including 686,706 passenger cars, 38,145 lorries, 1,479 buses, 5,383 tractors, 20,992 motor cycles and 11,398 other motor vehicles.

SHIPPING. Hamburg is the largest sea port in the Federal Republic.

Vessels		1987	1988	1989
Entered:	Number	14,154	13,374	12,710
	Tonnage	55,192,622	55,249,906	55,063,073
Cleared:	Number	14,099	13,406	12,736
	Tonnage	54,975,740	55,138,397	54,371,078

JUSTICE. There is a constitutional court *(Verfassungsgericht)*, a court of appeal *(Oberlandesgericht)*, a regional court *(Landgericht)*, 6 local courts *(Amtsgerichte)*, a Land labour court, a labour court, a Land social court, a social court, a finance court, a higher administrative court, an administrative court.

RELIGION. On 25 May 1987 (census) Evangelical Church and Free Churches 50·2%, Roman Catholic Church 8·6%.

EDUCATION. In 1989 there were about 360 schools of general education (not including *Internationale Schule*) with nearly 12,161 teachers and 160,133 pupils; 59 special schools with 1,080 teachers and 6,594 pupils; 47 part-time vocational schools with 43,192 pupils; 15 schools with 1,251 pupils in their vocational preparatory year; 25 schools with 2,273 pupils in manual instruction classes; 56 full-time vocational schools with 8,530 pupils; 10 economic secondary schools with 2,409 pupils; 2 technical *Gymnasien* with 455 pupils; 26 advanced vocational schools with 3,278 pupils; 36 schools for public health occupations with 2,699 pupils; 8 vocational introducing schools with 192 pupils and 20 technical superior schools with 2,699 pupils; all these vocational and technical schools have a total number of 3,477 teachers.

In the summer term 1991 there was 1 university with 42,330 students; 1 technical university with 1,565 students; 1 college of music and 1 college of fine arts with together 1,740 students; 1 university of the *Bundeswehr* with 1,950 students; 1 high school for economics and politics with 2,200 students; 3 private professional high schools with a total 15,665 students.

Statistical Information: The Statistisches Landesamt der Freien und Hansestadt Hamburg (Steckelhörn 12, D2000 Hamburg 11) publishes: *Hamburg in Zahlen, Statistische Berichte, Statistisches Taschenbuch, Statistik des Hamburgischen Staates.*

Klessmann, E., *Geschichte der Stadt Hamburg.* Hamburg, 1981
Meyer-Marwitz, B., *Das Hamburg Buch.* Hamburg, 1981
Möller, I., *Hamburg-Länderprofile.* Hamburg, 1985
Plagemann, V., *Industriekultur in Hamburg.* Hamburg, 1984
Studt, B. and Olsen, H., *Hamburg—eine kurzgefaßte Geschichte der Stadt.* Hamburg, 1964

State Library: Staats- und Universitätsbibliothek, Carl von Ossietzky, Von-Melle-Park 3, D2000 Hamburg 13. *Director:* Prof. Dr Horst Gronemeyer.

HESSEN

AREA AND POPULATION. The state of Hessen comprehends the areas of the former Prussian provinces Kurhessen and Nassau (excluding the exclaves belonging to Hessen and the rural counties of Westerwaldkreis and Rhine-Lahn) and of the former Volksstaat Hessen, the provinces Starkenburg (including the parts of Rheinhessen east of the river Rhine) and Oberhessen. Hessen has an area of 21,114 sq. km. Its capital is Wiesbaden. Since 1 Jan. 1981 there have been 3 areas with 5 urban and 21 rural districts and 421 communes. Population, 31 Dec 1990, was 5,763,178 (2,803,620 males, 2,959,558 females).

Vital statistics for calendar years:

	Live births	Marriages	Divorces	Deaths
1988	57,643	35,280	12,035	62,128
1989	58,803	35,124	12,089	62,873
1990	62,026	36,543	11,612	64,590

CONSTITUTION. The constitution was put into force by popular referendum on 1 Dec. 1946. Hessen has 6 seats in the Bundesrat. The Diet, elected in Jan. 1991, consists of 46 Christian Democrats, 46 Social Democrats, 10 Greens and 8 Free Democrats.

The Social Democrat/Green cabinet is headed by *Prime Minister* Hans Eichel (SPD).

AGRICULTURE. Area and yield of the most important crops:

	Area (in 1,000 ha)			Yield (in 1,000 tonnes)		
	1988	1989	1990	1988	1989	1990
Wheat	148·0	149·7	141·8	932·7	885·1	924·0
Rye	26·2	26·7	29·8	118·8	131·6	142·1
Barley	139·6	128·2	123·7	748·5	764·9	719·2
Oats	46·4	41·0	34·3	178·7	145·3	144·8
Potatoes	7·3	6·8	6·7	245·6	206·0	217·3
Sugar-beet	20·9	21·6	22·2	1,023·3	1,090·9	1,153·4
Rape	40·1	46·3	59·4	124·7	145·7	183·1

Livestock, Dec. 1990: Cattle, 713,546 (including 231,185 milch cows); pigs 1·03m.; sheep, 171,236; horses, 35,208; poultry, 2·76m.

INDUSTRY. In June 1991, 3,880 establishments (with 20 and more employees) employed 660,523 persons; of these, 100,998 were employed in chemical industry; 92,048 in electrical engineering; 95,660 in car building; 82,008 in machine construction; 36,230 in food industry.

LABOUR. The economically active persons totalled 2·71m. at the 1% sample survey of the microcensus of April 1990. Of the total, 235,300 were self-employed, 50,000 unpaid family workers, 2,422,700 employees; 75,300 were engaged in agriculture and forestry, 1,040,500 in power supply, mining, manufacturing and building, 518,200 in commerce and transport, 1,074,000 in other services.

ROADS. On 1 Jan. 1991 there were 16,654 km of 'classified' roads, including 930 km of autobahn, 3,493 km of federal highways, 7,192 km of first-class highways and 5,038 km of second-class highways. Motor vehicles licensed on 1 July 1991 totalled 3,456,441, including 3,019,580 passenger cars, 6,105 buses, 128,253 trucks, 141,103 tractors and 121,340 motor cycles.

JUSTICE. There are a constitutional court *(Staatsgerichtshof)*, a court of appeal, 9 regional courts, 58 local courts, a Land labour court, 12 labour courts, a Land social court, 7 social courts, a finance court, a higher administrative court *(Verwaltungsgerichtshof)*, 5 administrative courts.

RELIGION. In 1987 (census) there were 52·7% Protestants and 30·4% Roman Catholics.

EDUCATION. In 1990 there were 1,248 primary schools with 15,021 teachers and 267,154 pupils (including *Förderstufen*); 231 special schools with 2,677 teachers and 17,196 pupils; 162 intermediate schools with 2,395 teachers and 42,917 pupils; 158 high schools with 8,854 teachers and 121,454 pupils; 193 *Gesamtschulen* (comprehensive schools) with 10,291 teachers and 148,054 pupils; 120 part-time vocational schools with 4,581 teachers and 139,961 pupils; 253 full-time vocational schools with 2,353 teachers and 31,522 pupils; 107 advanced vocational schools with 655 teachers and 11,253 pupils; in 1988 there were 168 schools for public health occupations with 9,295 pupils.

In the winter term 1990–91 there were 3 universities (Frankfurt/Main, 34,832 students; Giessen, 19,292; Marburg–Lahn, 16,494); 1 technical university in Darmstadt (17,100); 1 private *Wissenschaftliche Hochschule, 722;* 1 *Gesamthochschule* (14,528); 14 *Fachhochschulen* (45,400); 2 Roman Catholic theological colleges and 1 Protestant theological college with together 410 students; 1 college of music and 2 colleges of fine arts with together 1,357 students.

Statistical Information: The Hessisches Statistisches Landesamt (Rheinstr. 35–37, D6200 Wiesbaden). *President:* Götz Steppuhn. Main publications: *Statistisches Taschenbuch für das Land Hessen* (zweijährlich; 1980–81 ff.).—*Staat und Wirtschaft in Hessen* (monthly).—*Beiträge zur Statistik Hessens.—Statistische Berichte.—Hessische Gemeindestatistik* (annual, 1980 ff.).

State Library: Hessische Landesbibliothek, Rheinstr. 55–57, D6200 Wiesbaden.

LOWER SAXONY

Niedersachsen

AREA AND POPULATION. Lower Saxony (excluding the town of Bremerhaven, and the districts on the right bank of the Elbe in the Soviet Zone) comprises 47,439 sq. km, and is divided into 4 administrative districts, 38 rural districts, 9 towns and 1,019 communes; capital, Hanover.

Estimated population, on 31 Dec. 1989, was 7,283,795 (3,526,598 males, 3,757,197 females).

Vital statistics for calendar years:

	Live births	Marriages	Divorces	Deaths
1988	76,036	46,500	13,500	82,920
1989	76,696	47,021	13,172	83,945
1990	82,452	49,330	12,876	86,356

GOVERNMENT. The Land Niedersachsen was formed on 1 Nov. 1946 by merging the former Prussian province of Hanover and the *Länder* Brunswick,

Oldenburg and Schaumburg-Lippe. Lower Saxony has 7 seats in the Bundesrat. The Diet, elected on 13 May 1990, consists of 67 Christian Democrats, 77 Social Democrats; Free Democrats, 9 and Greens, 8.

The cabinet of the Social Democratic Party is headed by *Prime Minister* Gerhard Schröder (SPD).

AGRICULTURE. Area and yield of the most important crops:

	Area (in 1,000 ha)			*Yield (in 1,000 tonnes)*		
	1988	*1989*	*1990*	*1988*	*1989*	*1990*
Wheat	347	352	311	2,293	1,892	2,187
Rye	155	158	175	587	726	791
Barley	411	380	361	1,983	1,945	1,098
Oats	99	83	60	379	255	247
Potatoes	83	89	97	3,019	3,506	3,539
Sugar-beet	140	143	157	5,929	6,728	8,205

Livestock, 1 Dec. 1990: Cattle, 3,277,237 (including 949,545 milch cows); pigs, 7,127,068; sheep, 257,866; horses, 80,574; poultry, 41,428,275.

FISHERIES. In 1989 the yield of sea and coastal fishing was 75,896 tonnes valued at DM 127m.

INDUSTRY. In Sept. 1990, 4,267 establishments (with 20 and more employees) employed 686,630 persons; of these 66,588 were employed in machine construction; 72,487 in electrical engineering.

LABOUR. The economically active persons totalled 3,250,600 in 1990. Of the total 281,600 were self-employed, 69,200 unpaid family workers, 2,899,800 employees; 159,600 were engaged in agriculture and forestry, 1,218,200 in power supply, mining, manufacturing and building, 591,800 in commerce and transport, 1,281,000 in other industries and services.

ROADS. At 1 Jan. 1990 there were 28,025 km of 'classified' roads, including 1,194 km of autobahn, 4,836 km of federal roads, 8,614 km of first-class and 13,381 km of second-class highways.

Number of motor vehicles, 1 Jan. 1991, was 4,177,689 including 3,570,395 passenger cars, 159,345 lorries, 8,657 buses, 246,812 tractors, 142,840 motor cycles.

JUSTICE. There are a constitutional court *(Staatsgerichtshof)*, 3 courts of appeal, 11 regional courts, 79 local courts, a Land labour court, 15 labour courts, a Land social court, 8 social courts, a finance court, a higher administrative court and 4 administrative courts.

RELIGION. On 25 May 1987 (census) there were 66·12% Protestants and 19·6% Roman Catholics.

EDUCATION. In 1990 there were 1,847 primary schools with 17,154 teachers and 295,368 pupils; 286 special schools with 4,638 teachers and 26,629 pupils; 317 stages of orientation with 9,075 teachers and 125,154 pupils; 398 intermediate schools with 6,737 teachers and 76,136 pupils; 393 secondary schools with 7,032 teachers and 94,584 pupils; 237 grammar schools with 12,644 teachers and 139,171 pupils; 5 evening high schools with 103 teachers and 935 pupils; 14 integrated comprehensive schools with 1,662 teachers and 15,594 pupils; 17 co-operative comprehensive schools with 1,583 teachers and 18,443 pupils. In 1989 there were 11,552 vocational training institutes (full and part-time) with 285,711 pupils.

In the winter term 1990–91 there were 6 universities (Göttingen, 30,133 students; Hanover, 29,352; Oldenburg, 10,732; Osnabrück, 11,332; Hildesheim, 2,971; Lüneburg, 4,767); 2 technical universities (Braunschweig, 16,798; Clausthal, 4,051); the medical college of Hanover (3,560), the veterinary college in Hanover (1,885).

Statistical Information: The Niedersächsisches Landesant für—Statistik' Postfach 4460, D3000 Hanover. *Head of Division:* President Dr Günter Koop. Main publications are: *Statistisches*

Jahrbuch Niedersachsen (from 1950).—*Statistische Monatshefte Niedersachsen* (from 1947).—*Statistik Niedersachsen.*—*Statistiches Taschenbuck Niedersachsen 1990 (biennial).*

State Library: Niedersächsische Staats- und Universitätsbibliothek, Prinzenstr. 1, 3400, Göttingen. *Director:* Helmut Vogt; Niedersächsische Landesbibliothek, Waterloostr. 8, D3000 Hannover 1. *Director:* Dr W. Dittrich.

MECKLENBURG-WEST POMERANIA
Mecklenburg-Vorpommern

AREA AND POPULATION. The area is 23,834 sq. km. It is divided into 6 urban districts, 31 rural districts and 1,124 communes. Population on 31 Dec. 1991 was 1,923,959 (989,038 females). The capital is Schwerin.

Vital statistics for calendar years:

	Live births	Marriages	Divorces	Deaths
1987	30,608	18,373	5,771	21,600
1988	28,495	17,726	5,889	21,506
1989	26,403	16,732	6,185	21,231

CONSTITUTION AND GOVERNMENT. The Land was reconstituted on former GDR territory in 1990. It has 4 seats in the Bundesrat.

At the Diet elections of Oct. 1990, the Christian Democrats won 29 seats with 38·3% of the vote; the Social Democrats, 21, with 27%; the Party of Democratic Socialism (former Communists), 12, with 15·7%; and the Free Democrats, 4, with 5·5%. The *Prime Minister* is Berndt Seite (Christian Democrats).

AGRICULTURE. Area and yield of the most important crops:

	Area (in 1,000 ha)			Yield (in 1,000 tonnes)		
	1985	1989	1990	1985	1989	1990
Wheat	137·2	158·6	160·3	652·1	802·9	921·6
Rye	202·2	178·0	179·4	750·9	690·8	623·3
Barley	187·7	204·8	211·9	848·4	1,083·8	1,052·0
Oats	78·0	64·7	62·5	313·8	234·4	267·8
Potatoes	112·5	100·6	72·8	2,925·1	2,291·2	1,572·8
Sugar-beet	52·3	49·8	48·0	1,527·8	1,584·2	1,847·2

Livestock in 1990: Cattle, 1,105,472 (including 345,426 milch cows); pigs, 1,970,469; sheep, 195,364; horses, 18,095; poultry, 5,950,754.

FISHERIES. Sea catch, 1990: 116,729 tonnes. Freshwater: 2,850 tonnes (mainly carp, trout and eels).

INDUSTRY. At the end of 1990 there were 484 enterprises (with 10 or more employees) employing 151,000 persons.

LABOUR. 940,086 persons were employed as at 30 Nov. 1990 (437,572 females), including 23,618 self-employed and family assistants, 490,031 manual and 426,437 white-collar workers. Employment by sector: Manufacturing, 191,910; agriculture, forestry and fisheries, 140,916; trade, 98,639; transport and communications, 86,679; construction, 75,631; energy, water resources and mining, 18,325.

ROADS. In 1990 there were 832,230 registered motor vehicles, including 560,403 passenger cars, 31,857 lorries, 8,812 buses and 155,820 motorcycles.

SHIPPING. There is a lake district of some 660 lakes. Before re-unification the ports of Rostock, Stralsund and Wismar were important for ship-building and fishing. In 1990 the cargo fleet consisted of 139 vesels (including 3 tankers) of 1,510,511 DWT. 12·83m. tonnes of cargo were carried.

JUSTICE. There are 3 circuit and 31 district courts.

RELIGION. In 1990 the Evangelical Lutheran Church of Mecklenburg had 405,700 adherents, 322 pastors and 387 parishes. Roman Catholics numbered 61,200, with 61 priests and 52 parishes. In 1988 the Pomeranian Evangelical Church had about 200 pastors in 356 parishes.

EDUCATION. In 1991-92 there were 313 primary schools, 18 comprehensives, 540 secondary schools and 100 special needs schools. There are universities at Rostock and Greifswald with (in 1991-92) 9,528 students and 2,226 academic staff, and 4 institutions of equivalent status with 3,632 students and 926 academic staff.

Statistical Office: Statistisches Landesamt Mecklenburg—Vorpommern, Lübecker Strasse 287, 0-2762 Schwerin. It publishes: *Statistische Monatshefte* (since 1991). —*Statistische Berichte* (since 1991). —*Statistisches Jahrbuch Mecklenburg-Vorpommern* (since 1992).

NORTH RHINE-WESTPHALIA

Nordrhein-Westfalen

AREA AND POPULATION. The Land comprises 34,070 sq. km. It is divided into 5 areas, 23 urban and 31 rural districts. Capital Düsseldorf. Population, 30 Nov. 1990, 17,341,903 (8,363,290 males, 8,978,613 females).

Vital statistics for calendar years:

	Live births	Marriages	Divorces	Deaths
1988	185,877	109,236	37,919	186,987
1989	186,714	110,420	37,116	190,078
1990	199,294	114,422	36,083	193,117

GOVERNMENT. Since Oct. 1990 the North Rhine-Westphalia has had 6 seats in the Bundesrat. It is governed by Social Democrats; *Prime Minister*, Johannes Rau (SPD). The Diet, elected on 13 May 1990, consists of 122 Social Democrats (50% of votes cast), 89 Christian Democrats (36·7%), 14 Free Democrats (5·8%) and 12 Greens (5%).

AGRICULTURE. Area and yield of the most important crops:

	Area (in 1,000 ha)			Yield (in 1,000 tonnes)		
	1988	1989	1990	1988	1989	1990
Wheat	257·8	268·6	256·8	1,772·7	1,673·8	1,603·4
Rye	53·0	51·7	52·4	224·6	244·9	245·8
Barley	305·1	281·2	274·7	1,694·9	1,723·9	1,415·8
Oats	66·0	56·6	40·7	263·5	164·3	157·0
Potatoes	16·5	17·1	18·4	702·0	720·7	724·5
Sugar-beet	78·7	79·4	79·7	4,195·8	4,262·1	4,500·6

Livestock, 3 Dec. 1990: Cattle, 1,990,166 (including 526,669 milch cows); pigs, 5,937,549; sheep, 257,766; horses, 87,003; poultry, 11,620,814.

INDUSTRY. In Sept. 1990, 11,720 establishments (with 20 and more employees) employed 2,045,724 persons; of these, 131,462 were employed in mining; 299,309 in machine construction; 128,112 in iron and steel production; 196,792 in chemical industry; 196,725 in electrical engineering; 58,346 in textile industry.

Output and/or production in 1,000 tonnes, 1990: Hard coal, 60,043; lignite, 102,181; pig-iron, 18,899; raw steel ingots, 22,143; rolled steel, 15,811; castings (iron and steel castings), 1,277; cement, 11,545; fireproof products, 849; sulphuric acid (including production of cokeries), 1,632; staple fibres and rayon, 352; metal-working machines, 122; equipment for smelting works and rolling mills, 121; machines for mining industry, 161; cranes and hoisting machinery, 74; installation implements, 1,860,866,472 (pieces); cables and electric lines, 308; springs of all kinds, 221; chains of all kinds, 69; locks and fittings, 461; spun yarns, 197; electric power, 168,170m. kwh. Of the total population, 11·7% were engaged in industry.

LABOUR. The economically active persons totalled 7,439,600 at the 1%-sample survey of the microcensus of April 1990. Of the total, 591,600 were self-employed, 79,600 unpaid family workers, 6·77m. employees; 162,000 were engaged in agriculture and forestry, 3,165,200 in power supply, mining, manufacturing and building, 1,336,500 in commerce and transport, 2,775,900 in other industries and services.

ROADS. There were (1 Jan. 1991) 29,860 km of 'classified' roads, including 2,090 km of autobahn, 5,347 km of federal roads, 12,449 km of first-class and 9,974 km of second-class highways. Number of motor vehicles, 1 July 1991, 9,275,448, including 7,295,421 passenger cars, 958,249 lorries, 358,722 motor lorries/trucks, 17,298 buses, 212,788 tractors and 313,528 motor cycles.

JUSTICE. There are a constitutional court *(Verfassungsgerichtshof)*, 3 courts of appeal, 19 regional courts, 130 local courts, 3 Land labour courts, 30 labour courts, a Land social court, 8 social courts, 3 finance courts, a higher administrative court, 7 administrative courts.

RELIGION. On 25 May 1987 (census) there were 35·2% Protestants and 49·4% Roman Catholics.

EDUCATION. In 1990 there were 4,365 primary schools with 60,467 teachers and 1,002,839 pupils; 715 special schools with 12,461 teachers and 78,275 pupils; 527 intermediate schools with 14,649 teachers and 239,598 pupils; 191 *Gesamtschulen* (comprehensive schools) with 10,903 teachers and 125,486 pupils; 624 high schools with 35,932 teachers and 471,796 pupils; in 1990 there were 280 part-time vocational schools with 392,276 pupils; vocational preparatory year 189 schools with 8,582 pupils; 286 full-time vocational schools with 68,110 pupils; 2 schools offering upgrading courses to raise the general level of education and quality for vocational colleges with 19 pupils; 209 full-time vocational schools leading up to vocational colleges with 19,381 pupils; 184 advanced full-time vocational schools with 27,599 pupils; 591 schools for public health occupations with 12,264 teachers and 32,695 pupils; 29 schools within the scope of a pilot system of courses with 63,299 pupils and 2,658 teachers.

In the winter term 1990–91 there were 8 universities (Bielefeld, 14,776 students; Bochum, 34,943; Bonn, 36,237; Dortmund, 21,289; Düsseldorf, 16,669; Cologne, 49,993; Münster, 43,528; Witten, 453); the Technical University of Aachen (36,547); 4 Roman Catholic and 2 Protestant theological colleges with together 1,050 students. There were also 4 colleges of music, 3 colleges of fine arts and the college for physical education in Cologne with together 10,868 students; 20 *Fachhochschulen* (vocational colleges) with 106,382 students, and 6 *Universitäten-Gesamthochschulen* with together 105,662 students.

Statistical Information: The Landesamt für Datenverarbeitung und Statistik Nordrhein-Westfalen (Mauerstr. 51, D4000 Düsseldorf 30) was founded in 1946, by amalgamating the provincial statistical offices of Rhineland and Westphalia. *President:* A. Benker. The Landesamt publishes: *Statistisches Jahrbuch Nordrhein-Westfalen.* From 1949. More than 550 other publications yearly.

Först, W., *Kleine Geschichte Nordrhein-Westfalens.* Münster, 1986.

Land Library: Universitätsbibliothek, Universitätsstr. 1, D4000 Düsseldorf. *Director:* Dr G. Gattermann.

RHINELAND-PALATINATE

Rheinland-Pfalz

AREA AND POPULATION. Rhineland-Pfalz comprises 19,849 sq. km. Capital, Mainz. Population (at 30 Sept. 1990), 3,753,829 (1,820,169 males, 1,933,660 females).

Vital statistics for calendar years:

	Live births	Marriages	Divorces	Deaths
1988	39,850	24,899	7,463	41,882
1989	39,650	24,261	7,467	42,536
1990	42,732	25,164	7,329	43,811

CONSTITUTION. The constitution of the Land Rheinland-Pfalz was approved by the Consultative Assembly on 25 April 1947 and by referendum on 18 May 1947, when 579,002 voted for and 514,338 against its acceptance. It has 4 seats in the Bundesrat.

At the elections of 21 April 1991 the Social Democratic Party won 47 seats of the 101 in the state parliament with 44·8% of votes cast; the Christian Democrats 40 with 38·7%; the Free Democrats 7 with 6·9%; and the Greens, 7 with 6·5%.

The coalition cabinet is headed by Rudolf Scharping (Social Democrat).

AGRICULTURE. Area and yield of the most important products:

	Area (1,000 ha)			Yield (1,000 tonnes)		
	1988	1989	1990	1988	1989	1990
Wheat	100·3	102·0	96·3	601·8	583·9	532·2
Rye	25·0	23·5	24·8	109·7	111·0	114·7
Barley	141·0	136·2	136·5	657·1	592·1	677·1
Oats	36·1	32·7	27·7	142·6	96·2	100·3
Potatoes	10·9	10·3	10·7	334·2	331·5	338·8
Sugar-beet	22·0	22·2	22·6	1,177·2	1,200·7	1,175·5
Wine (1,000						
hectolitres)	61·0	61·1	61·2	6,090·9	8,664·6	5,765·7

Livestock (3 Dec. 1990): Cattle, 542,300 (including 180,400 milch cows); horses, 21,300; sheep, 144,200; pigs, 509,600; poultry, 2,898,500.

INDUSTRY. In Sept. 1990, 2,622 establishments (with 20 and more employees) employed 390,680 persons; of these 81,501 were employed in chemical industry; electrical equipment, 21,654; 12,805 in production of leather goods and footwear; 53,872 in machine construction; 12,750 in processing stones and earthenware.

LABOUR. The economically active persons totalled 1,701,800 in 1990. Of the total, 153,400 were self-employed, 37,800 unpaid family workers, 1,510,600 employees; 70,400 were engaged in agriculture and forestry, 691,800 in power supply, mining, manufacturing and building, 288,800 in commerce and transport, 650,700 in other industries and services.

ROADS. There were (1 Jan. 1991) 18,375 km of 'classified' roads, including 801 km of autobahn, 3,117 km of federal roads, 7,110 km of first-class and 7,348 km of second-class highways. Number of motor vehicles, 1 July 1991, was 2,289,883, including 1,937,147 passenger cars, 84,637 lorries, 5,368 buses, 139,607 tractors and 94,093 motor cycles.

JUSTICE. There are a constitutional court *(Verfassungsgerichtshof)*, 2 courts of appeal, 8 regional courts, 47 local courts, a Land labour court, 5 labour courts, a Land social court, 4 social courts, a finance court, a higher administrative court, 4 administrative courts.

RELIGION. On 25 May 1987 (census) there were 37·7% Protestants and 54·5% Roman Catholics.

EDUCATION. In 1990 there were 1,179 primary schools with 14,507 teachers and 234,807 pupils; 151 special schools with 1,795 teachers and 12,112 pupils; 108 intermediate schools with 3,137 teachers and 47,686 pupils; 135 high schools with 7,147 teachers and 94,552 pupils; 84 vocational schools with 89,845 pupils; 163 advanced vocational schools and institutions for the training of technicians (full- and part-time) with 8,381 pupils; 102 schools for public health occupations with 348 teachers and 5,696 pupils.

In the winter term 1990–91 there were the University of Mainz (26,366 students), the University of Kaiserslautern (9,239 students), the University of Trier (9,461 students), the University of Koblenz-Landau (4,427 students), the *Hochschule für Verwaltungswissenschaften* in Speyer (492 students), the Koblenz School of Corporate Management *(Wissenschaftliche Hochschule für Unternahmensführung Koblenz in Vallendar)* with 211 students, the Roman Catholic Theological College in Trier (201 students) and the Roman Catholic College in Vallendar (72 students). There were also the *Fachhochschule des Landes Rheinland-Pfalz* with 18,455 students and 4 *Verwaltungsfachhochschulen* with 2,749 students; also 2 private colleges for social-pedagogy (872 students).

Statistical Information: The Statistisches Landesamt Rheinland-Pfalz (Mainzer Str., 14–16, D5427 Bad Ems) was established in 1948. *President:* Dr Weis. Its publications include: *Statistisches Jahrbuch für Rheinland-Pfalz* (from 1948); *Statistische Monatshefte Rheinland-Pfalz* (from 1958); *Statistik von Rheinland-Pfalz* (from 1949) 325 vols. to date; *Rheinland-Pfalz im Spiegel der Statistik* (from 1968); *Die kreisfreien Städte und Landkreise in Rheinland-Pfalz* (from 1977); *Rheinland-Pfalz heute* (from 1973); *Benutzerhandbuch des Landesinformationssystems* (1990); *Rheinland-Pfalz heute und morgen* (Mainz, 1985); *Raumordnungsbericht 1985 der Landesregierung Rheinland-Pfalz* (Mainz, 1985). *Landesentwicklungsprogramm 1980* (Mainz, 1980).

Klöpper, R. and Korber, J., *Rheinland-Pfalz in seiner Gliederung nach zentralörtlichen Bereichen.* Remagen, 1957

SAARLAND

HISTORY. In 1919 the Saar territory was placed under the control of the League of Nations. Following a plebiscite, the territory reverted to Germany in 1935. In 1945 the territory became part of the French Zone of occupation, and was in 1947 accorded an international status inside an economic union with France. In pursuance of the German–French agreement signed in Luxembourg on 27 Oct. 1956 the territory returned to Germany on 1 Jan. 1957. Its re-integration with Germany was completed by 5 July 1959.

AREA AND POPULATION. Saarland has an area of 2,570 sq. km. Population, 31 Dec. 1989, 1,064,906 (512,889 males, 552,017 females). The capital is Saarbrücken.

Vital statistics for calendar years:

	Live births	Marriages	Divorces	Deaths
1987	10,517	7,021	2,481	12,318
1988	10,748	7,446	2,781	12,388
1989	10,661	7,249	2,585	12,398

CONSTITUTION. Saarland has 3 seats in the Bundesrat.

The Saar Diet, elected on 28 Jan. 1990, is composed as follows: 30 Social Democrats, 18 Christian Democrats, 3 Free Democrats.

Saarland is governed by Social Democrats in Parliament. *Prime Minister:* Oskar Lafontaine (Social Democrat).

AGRICULTURE AND FORESTRY. The cultivated area (1989) occupied 118,793 ha or 46·2% of the total area; the forest area comprises nearly 33·1% of the total (256,991 ha).

Area and yield of the most important crops:

	Area (in 1,000 ha)			Yield (in 1,000 tonnes)		
	1988	1989	1990	1988	1989	1990
Wheat	7·1	7·0	6·8	36·0	36·8	37·3
Rye	5·7	5·6	6·2	23·4	25·5	27·5
Barley	9·9	9·9	9·8	44·2	42·7	45·7
Oats	5·6	5·3	5·6	22·7	19·2	19·9
Potatoes	0·4	0·4	0·3	13·0	13·0	10·9

Livestock, Dec. 1990: Cattle, 67,281 (including 20,731 milch cows); pigs, 35,710; sheep, 21,245; horses, 4,484; poultry, 257,633.

INDUSTRY. In June 1991, 627 establishments (with 20 and more employees) employed 138,080 persons; of these 19,313 were engaged in coalmining, 21,216 in manufacturing motor vehicles, parts, accessories, 16,300 in iron and steel production, 15,294 in machine construction, 9,103 in electrical engineering, 7,197 in steel construction. In 1990 the coalmines produced 9·7m. tonnes of coal. 5 blast furnaces and 9 steel furnaces produced 3·8m. tonnes of pig-iron and 4·4m. tonnes of crude steel.

LABOUR. The economically active persons totalled 437,000 at the 1%-sample survey of the microcensus of April 1990. Of the total, 33,700 were self-employed, 398,900 employees; 6,000 were engaged in agriculture and forestry, 183,000 in power supply, mining, manufacturing and building, 81,700 in commerce and transport, 166,400 in other industries and services.

ROADS. At 1 Jan. 1991 there were 2,199 km of 'classified' roads, including 226 km of autobahn, 354 km of federal roads, 831 km of first-class and 788 km of second-class highways. Number of motor vehicles, 31 Dec. 1990, 609,330, including 541,123 passenger cars, 23,091 lorries, 1,544 buses, 13,525 tractors and 24,203 motor cycles.

JUSTICE. There are a constitutional court *(Verfassungsgerichtshof)*, a court of appeal, a regional court, 11 local courts, a Land labour court, 3 labour courts, a Land social court, a social court, a finance court, a higher administrative court, an administrative court.

RELIGION. On 25 May 1987 (census) 72·7% of the population were Roman Catholics and 21·9% were Protestants.

EDUCATION. In 1990–91 there were 321 primary schools with 3,445 teachers and 56,682 pupils; 46 special schools with 436 teachers and 2,619 pupils; 33 intermediate schools with 996 teachers and 13,766 pupils; 37 high schools with 1,848 teachers and 24,561 pupils; 11 comprehensive high schools with 547 teachers and 6,252 pupils; 2 *Freie Waldorfschulen* with 71 teachers and 806 pupils; 4 evening intermediate schools with 230 pupils; 2 evening high schools and 1 Saarland College with 370 pupils; 42 part-time vocational schools with 23,887 pupils; year of commercial basic training: 62 institutions with 1,859 pupils; 21 advanced full-time vocational schools and schools for technicians with 3,272 pupils; 48 full-time vocational schools with 4,025 pupils; 9 *Berufsaufbauschulen* (vocational extension schools) with 411 pupils; 28 *Fachoberschulen* (full-time vocational schools leading up to vocational colleges) with 2,746 pupils; 42 schools for public health occupations with 1,935 pupils. The number of pupils visiting the vocational schools amounts to 38,540. They are instructed by 2,990 teachers.

In the winter term 1990–91 there was the University of the Saarland with 19,801 students; 1 academy of fine art with 193 students; 1 academy of music with 305 students; 1 vocational college (economics and engineering) with 3,217 students; 1 vocational college for social affairs with 201 students; 1 vocational college for public administration with 142 students; and 1 private vocational college for mining with 163 students.

Statistical Information: The Statistisches Landesamt Saarland (Hardenbergstrasse 3, D–6600 Saarbrücken 1) was established on 1 April 1938. As from 1 June 1935, it was an independent agency; its predecessor, 1920–35, was the Statistical Office of the Government Commission of the Saar. *Chief:* Direktor Josef Mailänder. The most important publications are: *Statistisches Handbuch für das Saarland,* from 1950.—*Statistisches Taschenbuch für das Saarland,* from 1959.—*Saarland in Zahlen* (special issues).—*Einzelschriften zur Statistik des Saarlandes,* from 1950—*Statistische Nachrichten,* from 1981.

Fischer, P., *Die Saar zwischen Deutschland und Frankreich.* Frankfurt, 1959

Osang, R.M., *Saarland ABC*. Saarbrücken, 1975
Schmidt, R. H., *Saarpolitik 1945–57*. 3 vols. Berlin, 1959–62

SAXONY
Sachsen

AREA AND POPULATION. The area is 18,337 sq. km. Population in 1990 was 4·9m. The capital is Dresden.

CONSTITUTION AND GOVERNMENT. The Land was reconstituted as the Free State of Saxony on former GDR territory in 1990. It has 5 seats in the Bundesrat.

At the Diet elections of Oct. 1990 the Christian Democrats won 92 seats, with 53·8% of the vote; the Social Democrats, 32, with 19·1%; the Party of Democratic Socialism (former Communists), 17, with 10·2%; New Forum/Alliance '90/Greens, 10, with 8%; and the Free Democrats, 9, with 5·3%.

The *Prime Minister* is Kurt Biedenkopf (b. 1930; Christian Democrat).

SAXONY-ANHALT
Sachsen-Anhalt

AREA AND POPULATION. The area is 20,444 sq. km. It is divided into 3 urban districts, 37 rural districts and 1,367 communes. Population in 1990 was 2,890,474 (1,511,749 females). The capital is Magdeburg.

Vital statistics for calendar years:

	Live births	Marriages	Divorces	Deaths
1988	38,462	24,887	9,097	40,009
1989	35,128	23,276	8,729	38,127
1990	31,292	18,397	6,056	37,395

CONSTITUTION AND GOVERNMENT. The Land was reconstituted on former GDR territory in 1990. It has 4 seats in the Bundesrat.

At the Diet elections of Oct. 1990 the Christian Democrats won 48 seats, with 39% of the vote; the Social Democrats, 27, with 26%; the Free Democrats, 14, with 13·5%; the Party of Democratic Socialism (former Communists), 12 with 12%; Alliance '90/Greens, 5, with 5·5%.

The *Prime Minister* is Dr Werner Münch (CDU).

AGRICULTURE. Area and yield of the most important crops:

	Area (in 1,000 ha)			Yield (in 1,000 tonnes)		
	1988	1989	1990	1988	1989	1990
Cereals	534·0	540·5	559·3	44·1	42·7	47·2
Potatoes	91·1	88·4	72·3	261·4	193·6	200·3
Sugar-beet	75·6	85·2	80·9	185·7	241·3	340·9
Legumes	7·2	7·3	7·5	26·8	26·6	24·5
Fodder	122·2	118·0	108·5	298·5	323·4	377·3
Maize	105·8	96·1	113·9	355·1	316·0	311·4

Livestock in 1990 (in 1,000): Cattle, 888·5 (including milch cows, 290·9); pigs, 1,955·9; sheep, 372·8; horses, 19·9; poultry, 4,125·8.

INDUSTRY. In 1990 there were 910 enterprises. Major sectors are machine and transport equipment, construction, chemicals and energy and fuel. On 30 Nov. 1990 there were 1,375,982 economically active persons, including 46,499 self-employed and family assistants, 751,305 manual and 578,178 white-collar workers. Of these, 479,938 worked in manufacturing, 279,267 in local authorities and social security,

124,581 in agriculture, forestry and fisheries, 123,941 in trade, 105,345 in mining and 103,483 in transport and communications.

ROADS. In 1990 there were 228 km of motorways, 2,324 km of main and 7,244 km of local roads. There were 1,557,862 registered motor vehicles, including: 822,459 passenger cars, 45,873 lorries, 10,141 buses and 246,747 motorcycles.

RELIGION. There are Saxon and Anhalt branches of the Evangelical Church. There were some 0·2m. Roman Catholics in 1990.

EDUCATION. In 1990–91 there were 1,123 schools with 354,658 pupils, including 88 special-needs schools with 12,053 pupils and 8 specialized schools with 3,363 pupils. There were 2 universities (Martin Luther at Halle, and Merseburg Technical University) with 12,463 students and 7 other institutes of equivalent status with 8,131 students.

Statistical office: Statistisches Landesamt Sachsen-Anhalt, Postfach 262, 0-4090 Halle. It publishes *Statistisches Jahrbuch des Landes Sachsen-Anhalt* (since 1991).

SCHLESWIG-HOLSTEIN

AREA AND POPULATION. The area of Schleswig-Holstein is 15,730 sq. km; it is divided into 4 urban and 11 rural districts and 1,131 communes. The capital is Kiel. The population (estimate, 31 Dec. 1989) numbered 2,594,606 (1,255,014 males, 1,339,592 females).

Vital statistics for calendar years:

	Live births	Marriages	Divorces	Deaths
1988	27,310	17,273	5,495	30,424
1989	27,377	17,238	5,428	30,546
1990	29,046	18,530	5,357	31,461

GOVERNMENT. The Land has 4 seats in the Bundesrat. The elections of 8 May 1988 gave the Christian Democrats 27, the Social Democratic Party 46 and the South Schleswig Association 1 seat. Elections were scheduled for April 1992.

Prime Minister: Björn Engholm.

AGRICULTURE. Area and yield of the most important crops:

	Area (in 1,000 ha)			Yield (in 1,000 tonnes)		
	1988	1989	1990	1988	1989	1990
Wheat	176·6	176·6	164·3	1,394·6	1,332·7	1,282·9
Rye	44·5	41·3	43·8	210·7	210·4	224·3
Barley	113·0	34·9	89·0	740·5	709·6	606·8
Oats	29·3	22·1	13·3	137·8	85·1	67·8
Potatoes	3·6	4·4	4·3	113·3	141·4	139·3
Sugar-beet	16·7	15·9	19·5	756·5	752·9	972·3

Livestock, 3 Dec. 1990: 1,525,411 cattle (including 471,584 milch cows), 1,444,950 pigs, 259,141 sheep; 37,096 horses, 3,578,764 poultry.

FISHERIES. In 1990 the yield of small-scale deep-sea and inshore fisheries was 38,644 tonnes valued at DM83·6m.

INDUSTRY. In 1990 (average), 1,614 establishments (with 20 and more employees) employed 177,163 persons; of these, 8,791 were employed in shipbuilding (except naval engineering); 34,480 in machine construction; 23,974 in food and kindred industry; 18,826 in electrical engineering.

LABOUR. The economically active persons totalled 1,234,100 in 1990. Of the total, 113,400 were self-employed, 19,000 unpaid family workers, 1,101,700 employees; 62,100 were engaged in agriculture and forestry, 351,500 in power supply, mining, manufacturing and building, 265,200 in commerce and transport and 555,400 in other industries and services.

ROADS. There were (1 Jan. 1991) 9,871·2 km of 'classified' roads, including 445 km of autobahn, 1,934·3 km of federal roads, 3,492·5 km of first-class and 3,999·4 km of second-class highways. Number of motor vehicles, 1 Jan. 1991, was 1,467,130, including 1,261,289 passenger cars, 58,234 lorries, 2,969 buses, 73,432 tractors, 50,729 motor cycles.

SHIPPING. The Kiel Canal, 98·7 km (51 miles) long, is on Schleswig-Holstein territory. In 1938, 53,530 vessels of 22·6m. net tons passed through it; in 1981, 52,641 vessels of 53·3m. net tons; in 1990, 47,810 vessels of 43·5m. net tons.

JUSTICE. There are a court of appeal, 4 regional courts, 30 local courts, a Land labour court, 6 labour courts, a Land social court, 4 social courts, a finance court, an upper administrative court and an administrative court.

RELIGION. On 25 May 1987 (census) there were 73·3% Protestants and 6·2% Roman Catholics.

EDUCATION. In 1990–91 there were 685 primary schools with 4,614 teachers and 138,456 pupils; 161 special schools with 1,177 teachers and 12,115 pupils; 172 intermediate schools with 2,272 teachers and 48,943 pupils; 99 high schools with 3,453 teachers and 63,065 pupils; 16 integrated comprehensive schools with 367 teachers and 6,593 pupils; 42 part-time vocational schools with 1,630 teachers and 70,942 pupils; 141 full-time vocational schools with 436 teachers and 9,697 pupils; 60 advanced vocational schools for foreigners with 302 teachers and 5,966 pupils; 65 schools for public health occupations with 4,160 pupils; 64 vocational grammar schools with 445 teachers and 7,395 pupils; 6 vocational colleges with 16,943 pupils in the summer term of 1991.

In the summer term of 1991 the University of Kiel had 18,218 students, 2 teacher-training colleges had 2,725 students; 1 music college had 378 students, 1 Medical University in Lübeck had 1,279 students.

Statistical Information: Statistisches Landesamt Schleswig-Holstein (Fröbel Str. 15–17, D2300 Kiel 1). *Director:* Dr Mohr. Publications: *Statistisches Taschenbuch Schleswig-Holstein,* since 1954.—*Statistisches Jahrbuch Schleswig-Holstein,* since 1951.—*Statistische Monatshefte Schleswig-Holstein,* since 1949.—*Statistische Berichte,* since 1947.—*Beitrage zur historischen Statistik Schleswig-Holstein,* from 1967.—*Lange Reihen,* from 1977.

Baxter, R. R., *The Law of International Waterways.* Harvard Univ. Press, 1964
Brandt, O., *Grundriss der Geschichte Schleswig-Holsteins.* 5th ed. Kiel, 1957
Handbuch für Schleswig-Holstein. 24th ed. Kiel, 1988

State Library: Schleswig-Holsteinische Landesbibliothek, Kiel, Schloss. *Director:* Prof. Dr Dieter Lohmeier.

THURINGIA

Thüringen

AREA AND POPULATION. The area is 16,251 sq. km. Population in 1990 was 2,637,261. The capital is Erfurt.

CONSTITUTION AND GOVERNMENT. The Land was reconstituted on former GDR territory in 1990. It has 4 seats in the Bundesrat.

At the Diet elections of Oct. 1990 the Christian Democrats won 44 seats, with 45·4% of the vote; the SPD, 21 with 22·8%; the Party of Democratic Socialism, 9, with 9·7%; the Free Democrats, 9, with 9·3%; New Forum/Greens/Democracy Now, 6 with 7·2%.

The *Prime Minister* is Bernhard Vogel (CDU).

GHANA

Capital: Accra
Population: 14·9m. (1990)
GNP per capita: US$380 (1989)

Republic of Ghana

HISTORY. The State of Ghana came into existence on 6 March 1957 when the former Colony of the Gold Coast and the Trusteeship Territory of Togoland attained Dominion status. The name of the country recalls a powerful monarchy which from the 4th to the 13th century A.D. ruled the region of the middle Niger.

The Ghana Independence Act received the royal assent on 7 Feb. 1957. The General Assembly of the United Nations in Dec. 1956 approved the termination of British administration in Togoland and the union of Togoland with the Gold Coast on the latter's attainment of independence.

The country was declared a Republic within the Commonwealth on 1 July 1960 with Dr Kwame Nkrumah as the first President. On 24 Feb. 1966 the Nkrumah regime was overthrown in a military *coup* and ruled by the National Liberation Council until 1 Oct. 1969 when the military regime handed over power to a civilian regime under a new constitution. Dr K. A. Busia was the Prime Minister of the Second Republic. On 13 Jan. 1972 the armed forces and police took over power again from the civilian regime in a *coup*.

In Oct. 1975 the National Redemption Council was subordinated to a Supreme Military Council (SMC). In 1979 the SMC was toppled in a *coup* led by Flight-Lieut. J. J. Rawlings. The new government permitted elections already scheduled and these resulted in a victory for Dr Hilla Limann and his People's National Party. However on 31 Dec. 1981 another *coup* led by Flight-Lieut. Rawlings dismissed the government and Parliament, suspended the Constitution and established a Provisional National Defence Council to exercise all government powers.

AREA AND POPULATION. Ghana is bounded west by the Côte d'Ivoire, north by Burkina Faso, east by Togo and south by the Gulf of Guinea. The area of Ghana is 92,456 sq. miles (239,460 sq. km); census population 1984, 12,296,081. Estimate (1990) 14,925,000.

Ghana is divided into 10 regions:

Regions	Area (sq. km)	Population census 1984	Capital	Population census 1984
Eastern	19,977	1,680,890	Koforidua	58,731
Western	23,921	1,157,807	Sekondi-Takoradi	93,400
Central	9,826	1,142,335	Cape Coast	57,224
Ashanti	24,390	2,090,100	Kumasi	376,246
Brong-Ahafo	39,557	1,206,608	Sunyani	38,834
Northern	70,383	1,164,583	Tamale	135,952
Volta	20,572	1,211,907	Ho	37,777
Upper East	8,842	772,744	Bolgatanga	32,495
Upper West	18,477	438,008	Wa	...
Greater Accra	2,593	1,431,099	Accra	867,459

The capital is Accra, other chief towns (population, census, 1970); Asamankese, 101,144; Tema, 99,608 (1984); Nsawam, 57,350; Tarkwa, 50,570; Oda, 40,740; Obuasi, 40,001; Winneba, 36,104; Keta, 27,461; Agona Swedru, 23,843.

Vital statistics (1985): Birth rate, 47 per 1,000; death rate 15 per 1,000.

In the south and centre of Ghana, the people are of the Kwa ethno-linguistic group, mainly Akan (Ashanti, Fante, etc.), Ewe (in the Volta region) and Ga, while the 20% living in the north belong to Gur peoples (Dagbane, Gurma and Grusi).

CLIMATE. The climate ranges from the equatorial type on the coast to savannah in the north and is typified by the existence of well-marked dry and wet seasons. Temperatures are relatively high throughout the year. The amount, duration and seasonal distribution of rain is very marked, from the south, with over 80" (2,000

634

mm) to the north, with under 50" (1,250 mm). In the extreme north, the wet season is from March to Aug., but further south it lasts until Oct. Near Kumasi, two wet seasons occur, in May and June and again in Oct. and this is repeated, with greater amounts, along the coast of Ghana. Accra. Jan. 80°F (26·7°C), July 77°F (25°C). Annual rainfall 29" (724 mm). Kumasi. Jan. 77°F (25°C), July 76°F (24·4°C). Annual rainfall 58" (1,402 mm). Sekondi-Takoradi. Jan. 79°F (25°C), July 76°F (24·4°C). Annual rainfall 47" (1,181 mm). Tamale. Jan. 82°F (27·8°C), July 78°F (25·6°C). Annual rainfall 41" (1,026 mm).

CONSTITUTION AND GOVERNMENT. Since the coup of 31 Dec. 1981, supreme power is vested in the Provisional National Defence Council (PNDC), which in Sept. 1991 consisted of: *Chairman:* Flight-Lieut. Jerry John Rawlings. *Vice Chairman:* Justice Daniel Annan. Mary Grant. Ebo Tawiah. Mahama Iddrisu. P. V. Obeng. Capt. Kojo Tsikata. Lieut.-Gen. Arnold Quainoo. Maj.-Gen. W. M. Mensa-Wood.

In Feb. 1992 PNDC Secretaries (Ministers) included: *Foreign Affairs:* Obed Y. Asamoah. *Internal Affairs:* Nii Okaija Adamafio. *Finance and Economic Planning:* Dr Kwesi Botchwey. *Justice and Attorney-General:* E. G. Tanoh. *Defence:* Mahama Iddrisu. *Trade and Tourism:* Huudu Yahaya. *Cocoa:* Adjei Marfo. *Information:* Kofi Totobi Quakyi.

National flag: Red, gold, green (horizontal); a black star in the centre.
National anthem: Hail the name of Ghana.

Local government: The 10 Regions, each under a Regional Secretary appointed by the PNDC, are divided into 110 districts.

DEFENCE.

Army. The Ghana Army consists of 7 infantry battalions, 1 reconnaissance battalion, 1 field engineer battalion, 1 parachute battalion, 1 mortar battalion, with armoured cars and ancillary units. Total strength, (1991) 10,000.

Navy. The Ghana Navy, based at Sekondi and Tema comprises 2 German-built coastal patrol, 2 inshore patrol craft and 2 small service craft. Naval strength in 1991 numbered 1,100 including support personnel.

Air Force. The Ghana Air Force was formed in 1959, when an Air Force Training School was established at Accra. Its first combat unit has 4 Italian-built Aermacchi M.B.326K light ground attack jets ordered in 1976. It has, for training, transport, search and rescue, and air survey operations, 4 Fokker Friendship twin-turboprop transports, a C-212 Aviocar and a twin-turbofan Fokker Fellowship for Presidential use, 8 Islander piston-engined light transports, 4 Shorts Skyvan twin-turboprop STOL transports, and 10 Bulldog primary trainers; 2 Bell 212 helicopters; 4 Alouette III helicopters, and 5 Aermacchi M.B.326F and 2 M.B.339 jet trainers. There are air bases at Takoradi and Tamale. Personnel strength (1991) about 800.

INTERNATIONAL RELATIONS

Membership. Ghana is a member of the UN, the Commonwealth, OAU, ECOWAS and is an ACP state of EEC.

ECONOMY

Budget. In 1989 budget provided for revenue estimated at ₵ 204,617m. and expenditure estimated at ₵ 196,191m.

Currency. The monetary unit is the *cedi* (GHC) of 100 *pesewas* (P). Notes are issued of 1, 2, 5, 10, 50, 200 and 500 ₵; cupro-nickel coins of 2¹/₂, 5, 10 and 20 P and 1₵. In March 1992, £1 = ₵ 682·10; US$1 = ₵ 388·5.

Banking and Finance. The Bank of Ghana was established in Feb. 1957 as the central bank of the country. The Ghana Commercial Bank, also established in Feb. 1957, is a purely commercial institution with agricultural financing as one of its priorities. It had 150 full branches in Sept. 1987, 1 in London and 1 subsidiary in

Lomé (Togo). Barclays Bank of Ghana Ltd has 39 branches and agencies and the Standard Bank (Ghana) Ltd has 38 branches.

The National Investment Bank, established in 1963, is an autonomous joint state-private development finance institution. The former post office savings bank has been transformed into the National Savings and Credit Bank. The Bank for Housing and Construction opened in 1973; The Merchant Bank (Ghana) Ltd in 1972; The Ghana Co-operative Bank was established and re-organized in 1974; The Agricultural Development Bank in 1967; The Consolidated Discount House Ltd in Nov. 1987.

ENERGY AND NATURAL RESOURCES

Electricity. Production (1986) 4,372m. kwh, mainly from 2 hydro-electric stations operated by the Volta River Authority, Akosombo (6 units) and Kpong (4 units), with a total capacity of 1,072 mw. Supply 240 volts; 50 Hz.

Oil. The Government announced in Jan. 1978 that oil had been found in commercial quantities with known reserves (1980) 7m. bbls and in Oct. 1983 formed the Ghanaian National Petroleum Corporation with exploration rights in all areas not covered by existing agreements.

Minerals. In 1987 gold production was 323,496 fine oz.; diamonds, 396,720 carats; manganese, 235,123 tonnes; bauxite, 226,415 tonnes.

Agriculture. In southern and central Ghana main food crops are maize, rice, cassava, plantain, groundnuts, yam and cocoyam, and in northern Ghana groundnuts, rice, maize, sorghum, millet and yams.

Production of main food crops (1990 in 1,000 tonnes) was: Maize, 553; rice, 81; millet, 75; sorghum, 136; cassava, 3,600; cocoyam, 650 (1988); yam, 700; plantain, 900.

Cocoa is by far Ghana's main cash crop. Production (1988) 290,000 tonnes. Output has fallen considerably since the 1970s, and Ghana has lost its long-held position as the world's leading producer to the Côte d'Ivoire. While there is smuggling to that country, Ghana's low cocoa production was due to ageing trees and declining interest in cocoa growing because of poor prices. Since 1982 the PNDC has carried out a rehabilitation programme for cocoa as well as increased producer prices for farmers, which has halted the decline and raised production considerably.

Among other cash crops, tobacco and coffee are important, and improved types of palm oil and coconuts are being planted on an increased scale; progress has been made with clonal rubber in the south-west; pepper, ginger, pineapple, avocado, citrus and other crops are being grown for export, and efforts are being made to increase local supplies of cotton, kenaf, tobacco, palm oil, mango, pineapple and sugar-cane for local industries.

Livestock, 1990: Cattle, 1·25m.; sheep, 2·4m.; goats, 2·6m.; horses, 2,000; pigs, 614,000; poultry, 10m.

Forestry. In 1988 the closed forest zone covered 8,225,900 hectares (36% of the land area), of which 2,559,400 hectares were reserves and 46,600 hectares unreserved forest lands. In 1986, 221,000 cu. metres of logs and 104,000 cu. metres of sawn timber were exported. Production (1987) 493,543 cu. metres.

Fisheries. Catch (1987) 324,630 tonnes (54,630 from inland waters).

INDUSTRY. The aluminium smelter at Tema is the centre of industrial development, mainly concentrated on Accra/Tema, Kumasi and Takoradi/Sekondi. In 1984 the Volta Aluminium Company (VALCO), which operates the smelter, reached an agreement with the government on the use of Volta dam electricity. Production (1986) 120,000 tonnes.

FOREIGN ECONOMIC RELATIONS

Commerce. In 1989 exports were US$880m.; imports, US$1,200m. Exports went mainly to USA, UK, Japan and Federal Republic of Germany. Imports came from

Nigeria, UK, USA and Federal Republic of Germany. Principal exports: Cocoa, timber and gold; imports were raw materials, capital equipment, petroleum and food.

Total trade between Ghana and UK (British Department of Trade returns, in £1,000 sterling):

	1987	1988	1989	1990	1991
Imports to UK	113,859	106,314	92,208	105,118	77,345
Exports and re-exports from UK	138,081	126,148	121,076	162,057	169,296

Tourism. In 1987 there were 103,440 tourists.

COMMUNICATIONS

Roads. In 1988 agencies of the Ministry of Roads and Highways maintained about 14,514 km of trunk roads, 14,000 km of feeder and 10,000 km of other rural roads, and 1,700 km of city and municipal roads. The number of vehicles in use (1986) was 54,196, of which private cars, 26,590.

Railways. Total length of railways in 1989 was 947 km of 1,067 mm gauge. In 1989 railways carried 0·76m. tonnes of freight and 3·3m. passengers.

Aviation. There is an international airport at Accra, domestic airports at Takoradi, Kumasi, Tamale and Sunyani and airstrips at Wa, Navrongo and Ho. Services are operated by Ghana Airways, Nigeria Airways, Swissair, KLM, British Airways, Egypt Air, Air India, Air Afrique and Bulgarian Airlines. Total aircraft freight in 1986 was 8,661,971 tonnes.

Shipping. The chief ports are Takoradi and Tema. In 1983, 1,299,146 tonnes of cargo were imported and 1,682,519 tonnes were exported by 663 ships.

Telecommunications. There were 444 telephone exchanges and 666 call offices with (1987) 74,935 telephones in use. There are internal wireless stations at Accra, Kumasi, Bawku, Lawra, Kete-Krachi, Tamale, Yendi, Kpandu, Tumu and Sekondi-Takoradi. In 1991 there were over 3·1m. radio and 175,000 television receivers (colour by PAL).

Cinemas. In 1987 there were 83 cinemas with an average seating capacity of 1,200.

Newspapers. There were (1989) 3 daily newspapers (circulation 180,000).

JUSTICE, RELIGION, EDUCATION AND WELFARE

Justice. The Courts were constituted as follows:

Supreme Court. The Supreme Court consists of the Chief Justice who is also the President and not less than 4 other Justices of the Supreme Court. The Supreme Court is the final court of appeal in Ghana. The final interpretation of the provisions of the constitution has been entrusted to the Supreme Court.

Court of Appeal. The Court of Appeal consists of the Chief Justice together with not less than 5 other Justices of the Appeal court and such other Justices of Superior Courts as the Chief Justice may nominate. The Court of Appeal is duly constituted by 3 Justices. The Court of Appeal is bound by its own previous decisions and all courts inferior to the Court of Appeal are bound to follow the decisions of the Court of Appeal on questions of law. Divisions of the Appeal Court may be created, subject to the discretion of the Chief Justice.

High Court of Justice. The Court has jurisdiction in civil and criminal matters as well as those relating to industrial and labour disputes including administrative complaints. The High Court of Justice has supervisory jurisdiction over all inferior Courts and any adjudicating authority and in exercise of its supervisory jurisdiction has power to issue such directions, orders or writs including writs or orders in the nature of habeas corpus, certiorari, mandamus, prohibition and quo qarrantto. The High Court of Justice has no jurisdiction in cases of treason. The High Court consists of the Chief Justice and not less than 12 other judges and such other Justices of the Superior Court as the Chief Justice may appoint.

The PNDC has established Public Tribunals in addition to the traditional courts of justice.

There is a Public Tribunal Board consisting of not less than 5 members and not more than 15 members of the public appointed by the PNDC, at least one of whom shall be a lawyer of not less than 5 years' standing as a lawyer. The Board is responsible for the administration of all tribunals.

A tribunal consists of at least three persons and not more than five persons, selected by the Board from among persons appointed by the Council as members of public tribunals.

Religion. In 1989 9·12m Christians represented 62·6% of the population and 2·29m Moslems, 19·8%.

Education. In 1985–86 there were 2,399 kindergartens for the age-groups 4–6 years with 171,182 pupils. Primary schools are free and attendance is compulsory. In 1985–86 there were 9,004 primary schools with 1,491,162 pupils. In 1986 there were 5,310 middle schools with 617,613 pupils; 110 junior secondary schools with 18,372 pupils and 233 secondary schools with 133,435 students. In 1986 there were 45 training colleges with 15,210 students and 26 vocational-technical schools with 19,547 students at the beginning of the academic year. In 1987–88 there were 8,847 students at the 3 universities (University of Ghana, the University of Science and Technology at Kumasi, and the University of Cape Coast). University education is free.

Health. In 1988 medical facilities included 46 government hospitals, 252 health centres and posts, 3 university hospitals, 3 mental hospitals, 35 mission hospitals, 34 mission clinics and 40 private hospitals. In addition, there are 26 nurses and mid-wives training schools. There were 600 doctors, 5,190 nurses and 2,830 midwives in 1986.

DIPLOMATIC REPRESENTATIVES

Of Ghana in Great Britain (13 Belgrave Sq., London, SW1X 8PR)
High Commissioner: K. B. Asante.

Of Great Britain in Ghana (Osu Link, off Gamel Abdul Nasser Ave., Accra)
High Commissioner: Anthony M. Goodenough, CMG.

Of Ghana in the USA (3512 International Dr., NW, Washington, D.C., 20008)
Ambassador: Joseph Abbey.

Of the USA in Ghana (Ring Rd. East, Accra)
Ambassador: Raymond C. Ewing.

Of Ghana to the United Nations
Ambassador: Dr. Kofi Nyidevu Awoonor.

Further Reading

Digest of Statistics. Accra. Quarterly (from May 1953)
Ghana. Official Handbook. Annual
Davidson, B., *Black Star.* London, 1973
Jones, T., *Ghana's First Republic 1960–1966.* London, 1975
Killick, T., *Development Economics in Action: A Study of Economic Policies in Ghana.* London, 1978
Myers, R. A., *Ghana:* [Bibliography]. Oxford and Santa Barbara, 1991
Ray, D. I., *Ghana: Politics, Economics and Society.* London, 1986
Rothchild., D. (ed.): *Ghana: the Political Economy of Recovery.* Boulder, (Colo.), 1991

GIBRALTAR

Population: 30,861 (1990)
GNP per capita: US$4,370 (1985)

HISTORY. The Rock of Gibraltar was settled by Moors in 711; they named it after their chief Jebel Tariq, 'the Mountain of Tarik'. In 1462 it was taken by the Spaniards, from Granada. It was captured by Admiral Sir George Rooke on 24 July 1704, and ceded to Great Britain by the Treaty of Utrecht, 1713. The cession was confirmed by the treaties of Paris (1763) and Versailles (1783).

On 10 Sept. 1967, in pursuance of a United Nations resolution on the de-colonization of Gibraltar, a referendum was held in Gibraltar in order to ascertain whether the people of Gibraltar believed that their interests lay in retaining their link with Britain or in passing under Spanish sovereignty. Out of a total electorate of 12,762, 12,138 voted to retain the British connexion, while 44 voted for Spain.

On 15 Dec. 1982 the border between Gibraltar and Spain was re-opened for Spaniards and Gibraltarian pedestrians who are residents of Gibraltar. The border had been closed by Spain in June 1969. Following an agreement signed in Brussels in Nov. 1984 the border was fully opened on 5 Feb. 1985.

AREA AND POPULATION. Area, 2½ sq. miles (6·5 sq. km). Total popula-tion, including port and harbour (census, 1981), 28,719. Estimate (31 Dec. 1990) 30,861 (of which 20,531 were British Gibraltarian, 5,550 Other British and 4,780 Non-British). The population is mostly of Genoese, Portuguese and Maltese as well as Spanish descent.

Vital statistics (1990): Births, 531; marriages, 781; deaths, 279.

CLIMATE. The climate is warm temperate, with westerly winds in winter bring-ing rain. Summers are pleasantly warm and rainfall is low. Frost or snow is very rare. Jan. 57°F (13·7°C), July 75°F (23·9°C). Annual rainfall 23" (584 mm).

CONSTITUTION AND GOVERNMENT. Following a Constitutional Conference held in July 1968, a new Constitution was introduced in 1969. The Legislative and City Councils were merged to produce an enlarged legislature known as the Gibraltar House of Assembly. Executive authority is exercised by the Governor, who is also Commander-in-Chief. The Governor, while retaining certain reserved powers, is normally required to act in accordance with the advice of the Gibraltar Council, which consists of 4 *ex-officio* members (the Deputy Governor, the Deputy Fortress Commander, the Attorney-General and the Financial and Development Secretary) together with 5 elected members of the House of Assembly appointed by the Governor after consultation with the Chief Minister. Matters of primarily domestic concern are devolved to elected Ministers, with Britain responsible for other matters, including external affairs, defence and internal security. There is a Council of Ministers presided over by the Chief Minister.

The House of Assembly consists of a Speaker appointed by the Governor, 15 elected and 2 *ex-officio* members (the Attorney-General and the Financial and Development Secretary). No more than 8 of the elected seats may go to the winning party at elections.

A Mayor of Gibraltar is elected by the elected members of the Assembly.

At the elections of Jan. 1992 the electorate was 17,800; turn-out was 72%. The Gibraltar Socialist and Labour Party (GSLP) gained 8 seats with 73% of votes cast (58% in 1988). The Gibraltar Social Democratic Party gained 7 with 20%.

Governor and C.-in-C.: Adm. Sir Derek Reffell, KCB.

Chief Minister: Joseph John Bossano (b.1940; GSLP).

Flag: White with a red strip along the bottom, a red triple-towered castle with a gold key depending from the gateway.

DEFENCE. The British Army handed over responsibility for land defence to an enhanced Gibraltar Regiment in March 1991. The Gibraltar Regiment is a part-time unit consisting of 4 infantry companies, 1 battery of 105 mm light guns and an air defence troop equipped with blowpipe missiles with a small regular cadre. There are also in support and specialist roles Royal Engineers, Royal Military Police and Royal Signals personnel. There is an RAF Base and a Naval Base.

ECONOMY

Budget. Revenue and expenditure (in £ sterling):

	1987–88	1988–89	1989–90	1990–91
Revenue	78,343,477	82,124,000	87,421,000	85,597,000
Expenditure	82,063,600	81,904,000	91,388,000	90,246,000

Currency. The unit of currency is the Gibraltar pound (GIP). There are Gibraltar Government notes in denominations of Gib£50, £20, £10, £5 and £1 and Gibraltar Government coinage. The amount in notes in circulation at 31 March 1990 was £12·01m. In March 1992 £1 = Gib£1; US$ = Gib£0·57.

Banking. In April 1991 domestic and offshore banking services are provided by 30 banks with total assets of some £2,500m.

INDUSTRY. There are a number of small firms engaged in the bottling of beverages. A building components factory supplies the local construction industry.

Labour. The total insured labour force at 31 Dec. 1989, was 14,311. There were (1989) 8 registered trade unions and 9 employers associations. Approximately 45% of the local labour force is employed by the UK departments of the Gibraltar Government. In the private sector the main sources of employment are the construction industry, ship repairing, hotel and catering services, shipping services, trading agencies and retail distribution.

FOREIGN ECONOMIC RELATIONS. Gibraltar has a special status within the EC which exempts it from the latter's fiscal policy.

Commerce. Imports and exports (in £ sterling):

	1986	1987	1988	1989
Imports	111,700,000	140,962,000	144,787,000	200,493,000
Exports	44,300,000	51,731,000	46,093,000	76,138,000

Britain and the Commonwealth provide the bulk of imports, but fresh vegetables and fruit come mainly from Morocco and Spain. Foodstuffs accounted for 12% of total imports (about £24m.) in 1988. About 44% of non-fuel imports originate from the UK. Other sources include Japan, Spain and USA. Value of non-fuel imports, 1989, £165m. Exports are mainly re-exports of petroleum and petroleum products supplied to shipping. Gibraltar depends largely on tourism, offshore banking and other financial sector activity, the entrepôt trade and the provision of supplies to visiting ships. Exports of local produce are negligible.

Total trade between Gibraltar and UK (British Department of Trade returns, in £1,000 sterling):

	1988	1989	1990	1991
Imports to UK	4,537	4,560	5,048	4,289
Exports and re-exports from UK	67,944	69,350	69,073	80,105

Tourism. The number of tourists in 1990 was 4,373,258.

COMMUNICATIONS

Roads. There are 31 miles of roads including 4·25 miles of pedestrian way.

Civil Aviation. Scheduled flights are operated by GB Airways and Dan Air to London and by GB Airways to Manchester.

Shipping. There is a deep harbour of 440 acres. A total of 3,395 merchant ships of 58·1m. GRT entered the port during 1990, including 2,521 deep-sea ships of 57·6m.

GRT. In 1990, 4,955 calls were made by yachts of 158,356 GRT. 82 cruise liners called during 1990.

Telecommunications. The local Telephone Service is operated by Gibraltar Nynex Communications, a joint venture of the Government of Gibraltar and Nynex International. The number of telephones (1990) was 16,759. A new Digital System X Exchange became operational in April 1990 with capacity for 14,000 lines. International direct dialling is available to over 130 countries *via* the Gibraltar Telecommunications Ltd (Gibtel) Earth Station and other international circuits. A direct air-mail service between Gibraltar and Tangier is run by GB Airways Ltd. Radio Gibraltar broadcasts for 24 hours daily, in English and Spanish, and GBC Television operates for 17 hours on weekdays and 12 hours at weekends. Number of TV receivers in 1991, 7,340.

Newspapers. There were (1991) 1 daily and 4 weeklies.

JUSTICE, RELIGION, EDUCATION AND WELFARE

Justice. The judicial system is based on the English system. There is a Court of Appeal, a Supreme Court, presided over by the Chief Justice, a court of first instance and a magistrates' court.

Religion. Religion of civil population mostly Roman Catholic; 1 Anglican and 1 Roman Catholic cathedral and 2 Anglican and 6 Roman Catholic churches; 1 Presbyterian and 1 Methodist church and 4 synagogues; annual subsidy to each communion, £500.

Education. Free compulsory education is provided for children between ages 5 and 15 years. The medium of instruction is English. The comprehensive system was introduced in Sept. 1972. There were (1990) 12 primary and 2 comprehensive schools. Primary schools are mixed and divided into first schools for children aged 4-8 years and middle schools for children aged 8-12 years. The comprehensives are single-sex. In addition, there are 2 Services primary schools and 1 private primary school. A new purpose-built Special School for severely handicapped children aged 2-16 years was opened in 1977, and there are 3 Special Units for children with special educational needs (1 attached to a first school, 1 to a middle school and 1 at secondary level), 2 nurseries for children aged 3-4 years and an occupational therapy centre for handicapped adults. Technical education is available at the Gibraltar College of Further Education managed by the Gibraltar Government. In Sept. 1990, there were 1,340 pupils at government first schools, 1,369 at government middle schools, 232 at private and 561 at Services schools; 22 at the special school; 976 at the boys' comprehensive school and 906 at the girls' comprehensive. In addition there were 114 full-time and 550 part-time students in the Gibraltar College of Further Education. Scholarships are made available for universities, teacher-training and other higher education in Britain. In 1989–90, government expenditure on education was £7,620,143.

Health. In 1990 there were 2 hospitals with 252 beds and 29 doctors. Total expenditure on medical and health services during year ended 31 March 1990 was £12,102,072.

Further Reading

Gibraltar Year Book. Gibraltar, (Annual)
Ellicott, D., *Our Gibraltar.* Gibraltar, 1975
Green, M. M., *A Gibraltar Bibliography.* London, 1980.—*Supplement.* London, 1982
Hills, G., *Rock of Contention: A History of Gibraltar.* London, 1974
Jackson, W. G. F., *The Rock of the Gibraltarians.* Farleigh Dickinson Univ. Press, 1987
Magauran, H. C., *Rock Siege: The Difficulties with Spain 1964–85.* Gibraltar, 1986
Morris, D. S. and Haigh, R. H., *Britain, Spain and Gibraltar, 1945-90: the Eternal Triangle.* London, 1992
Shields, G. J., *Gibraltar.* [Bibliography] Oxford and Santa Barbara, 1988

GREECE

Capital: Athens
Population: 10·26m. (1991)
GNP per capita: US$5,758 (1990)

Elliniki Dimokratia

(Hellenic Republic)

HISTORY. Greece gained her independence from Turkey in 1821–29, and by the Protocol of London, of 3 Feb. 1830, was declared a kingdom, under the guarantee of Great Britain, France and Russia. For details of the subsequent history to 1947 *see* THE STATESMAN'S YEAR-BOOK, 1957, pp. 1069–70. A coup took place on 21 April 1967, and a military government was formed which suspended the 1952 constitution. King Constantine went abroad in 1967, and a republic was established after referenda in 1973 and 1974. (For details of the monarchy *see* THE STATESMAN'S YEAR-BOOK, 1973–74, p. 1000).

The military government collapsed on 23 July 1974 and a new constitution was introduced in June 1975.

AREA AND POPULATION. Greece is bounded in the north by Albania, Yugoslavia and Bulgaria, east by Turkey and the Aegean Sea, south by the Mediterranean and west by the Ionian Sea. The total area is 131,957 sq. km (50,949 sq. miles), of which the inhabited islands account for 25,042 sq. km (9,669 sq. miles).

The population was 10,264,156 according to preliminary data of the census of March 1991.

Athens is the capital; population of Greater Athens, in 1991, 3,096,775.

In 1987 the territory of Greece was administratively reorganized into 13 *regions* comprising in all 51 *departments* (for previous regions *see* THE STATESMAN'S YEAR-BOOK, 1991–92, pp 569–70). Areas and populations according to the preliminary results of the 1990 census:

Region/Department	Area in sq. km	Population	Chief town
Attica [1]	*3,808*	*3,522,769*	*Athens*
Aegean North	*3,836*	*198,241*	*Mytilene*
Chios	904	52,691	Chios
Lesbos	2,154	103,700	Mytilene
Samos	778	41,850	Samos
Aegean South	*5,286*	*257,522*	*Hermoupolis*
Cyclades	2,572	95,083	Hermoupolis
Dodecanese	2,714	162,439	Rhodes
Crete	*8,336*	*536,980*	*Heraklion*
Canea	2,376	133,060	Canea
Heraklion	2,641	263,868	Heraklion
Lassithi	1,823	70,762	Aghios Nikolaos
Rethymnon	1,496	69,290	Rethymnon
Epirus	*9,203*	*339,210*	*Ioannina*
Arta	1,662	78,884	Arta
Ioannina	4,990	157,214	Ioannina
Preveza	1,036	58,910	Preveza
Thesprotia	1,515	44,202	Hegoumenitsa
Greece Central [2]	*15,549*	*583,876*	*Lamia*
Boeotia	2,952	134,034	Levadeia
Euboea	4,167	209,132	Chalcis
Evrytania	1,869	23,535	Karpenissi
Phocis	2,120	48,884	Amphissa
Phthiotis	4,441	168,291	Lamia
Greece West	*11,350*	*702,027*	*Patras*
Achaia	3,271	297,318	Patras
Elia	2,618	174,021	Pyrgos
Aetolia and Acarnania	5,461	230,688	Missolonghi

[1] Attica is both region and department.   [2] Without Attica.

Region/Department	Area in sq. km	Population	Chief town
Ionian Islands	2,307	191,003	Corfu
Cephalonia	904	32,314	Argostoli
Corfu	641	105,043	Corfu
Leucas	356	20,900	Leucas
Zante	406	32,746	Zante
Macedonia Central	19,147	1,736,066	Thessaloniki
Chalcidice	2,918	91,654	Polygyros
Imathia	1,701	138,068	Veroia
Kilkis	2,519	81,845	Kilkis
Pella	2,506	138,261	Edessa
Pieria	1,516	116,820	Katerini
Serres	3,968	191,890	Serres
Thessaloniki	3,683	977,528	Thessaloniki
Macedonia East and Thrace	14,157	570,261	Comotini
Cavalla	2,111	135,747	Cavalla
Drama	3,468	96,978	Drama
Evros	4,242	143,791	Alexandroupolis
Rhodope	2,543	103,295	Comotini
Xanthi	1,793	90,450	Xanthi
Macedonia West	9,451	292,749	Kozani
Florina	1,924	52,852	Florina
Grevena	2,291	37,017	Grevena
Kastoria	1,720	52,721	Kastoria
Kozani	3,516	150,159	Kozani
Peloponnese	15,490	605,663	Tripolis
Arcadia	4,419	103,840	Tripolis
Argolis	2,154	97,250	Nauplion
Corinth	2,290	142,365	Corinth
Laconia	3,636	94,916	Sparta
Messenia	2,991	167,292	Calamata
Thessaly	14,037	731,230	Larissa
Karditsa	2,636	126,498	Karditsa
Larissa	5,381	269,300	Larissa
Magnesia	2,636	197,613	Volo
Trikala	3,384	137,819	Trikala

In 1981 cities (*i.e.*, communes of more than 10,000 inhabitants, including Greater Athens) had 5,475,997 inhabitants (56·2%), towns (*i.e.*, communes with between 2,000 and 9,999 inhabitants), 1,154,567 (11·9%), villages and rural communities (under 2,000 inhabitants), 3,109,853 (31·9%).

The *Monastic Republic of Mount Athos*, the easternmost of the three prongs of the peninsula of Chalcidice, is a self-governing community composed of 20 monasteries. (*See* THE STATESMAN'S YEAR-BOOK, 1945, p. 983.) For centuries the peninsula has been administered by a Council of 4 members and an Assembly of 20 members, 1 deputy from each monastery. The Greek Government on 10 Sept. 1926 recognized this autonomous form of government; Articles 109–112 of the Constitution of 1927 gave legal sanction to the Charter of Mount Athos, drawn up by representatives of the 20 monasteries on 20 May 1924. Article 103 of the 1952 Constitution and Article 105 of the 1975 Constitution confirmed the special status of Mount Athos.

Vital statistics (1989): 101,657 live births; 735 still births; 8,095 births to unmarried mothers; 61,884 marriages; 92,720 deaths.

The modern Greek language had 2 contesting literary standard forms, the archaizing *Katharevousa* ('purist'), and a version based on the spoken vernacular, 'Demotic'. In 1976 Standard Modern Greek was adopted as the official language, with Demotic as its core.

CLIMATE. Coastal regions and the islands have typical Mediterranean conditions, with mild, rainy winters and hot, dry, sunny summers. Rainfall comes almost entirely in the winter months, though amounts vary widely according to position and relief. Continental conditions affect the northern mountainous areas, with severe winters, deep snow cover and heavy precipitation, but summers are hot. Athens. Jan. 48°F (8·6°C), July 82·5°F (28·2°C). Annual rainfall 16·6" (414·3 mm).

CONSTITUTION AND GOVERNMENT. Voting took place on 29 July 1973 in the referendum to change Greece from a monarchy to a republic and to elect a president. 77·2% of the valid votes were cast for a republican régime.

On 25 Nov. 1973, in a bloodless coup, President Papadopoulos was overthrown and Lieut.-Gen. Phaedon Ghizikis was sworn in. The military dictatorship collapsed on 23 July 1974 and the 1952 Constitution was reintroduced in a modified form. A new Constitution was introduced in June 1975. Parliamentary elections took place on 12 Nov. 1974. A further referendum on the Monarchy took place on 8 Dec. 1974 and 69·2% of the valid votes were cast for an 'uncrowned democracy'.

President: Constantine Karamanlis (b. 1907), elected for 5 years in May 1990.

Parliamentary elections were held in April 1990; 6·45m. votes were cast. Seats gained (and % of vote): New Democracy, 150 (46·9); Pasok (i.e. Panhellenic Socialist Movement), 123 (38·6); Left Coalition, 19 (10·3); independents, 4 (1) and 4 others (2·2), with the support of one of whom New Democracy formed a government.

In March 1992 the Cabinet comprised:
Prime Minister, Constantine Mitsotakis.
Deputy Prime Minister, Tzannis Tzannetakis; *Minister to the Prime Minister,* Sotiris Kouvelas; *Foreign Affairs,* Antonis Samaras; *Defence,* Ioannis Varvitsiotis; *Finance,* Ioannis Palaiokrassas; *Economy,* Stefanos Manos; *Agriculture,* Mihalis Papakonstantinou; *Labour,* Aristides Kalatzakos; *Health, Welfare and Social Security,* Marietta Ioannakou; *Education and Religious Affairs,* George Souflias; *Public Order,* Ioannis Vassiliadis; *Industry, Energy, Technology and Commerce,* Andreas Andrianopoulos; *Commerce,* Athanassios Xarhas; *Transport and Communications,* Nikolaos Gelesthasis; *Merchant Marine,* Aristotle Pavlides; *Environment and Public Works,* Achileas Karamanlis; *Macedonia and Thrace,* Georgios Tzitzikostas; *Aegean,* Georgios Misailides; Mikis Theodorakis, without portfolio.

National flag: Nine horizontal stripes of blue and white, with a canton of blue with a white cross.
National anthem: Hymn to Freedom, Imnos eis tin Eleftherian (words by Dionysios Solomos, 1824; tune by N. Mantzaros, 1828).

Local government: There are 359 large towns and 5,600 wards with fewer than 10,000 inhabitants. Elections for mayors were held in Nov. 1990. New Democracy won an overall majority.

DEFENCE. In Aug. 1950 the Ministries of War, Marine and Military Aviation were fused into a single Ministry of National Defence. The General Staff of National Defence is directly responsible to the Minister on general defence questions, besides the special staffs for Army, Navy and Air Force. Military service in the Armed Forces is compulsory and universal. Liability begins in the 21st year and lasts up to the 50th. The normal terms of service are Army 21 months, Navy 25 months, Air Force 23 months, followed by 19 years in the First Reserve and 10 years in the Second Reserve.

Army. The Army is organized into 3 Military Regions, comprising 1 armoured, 1 mechanized, 1 para-commando, 6 parachute and 10 infantry divisions; 5 armoured brigades; 2 mechanized brigades, 18 field artillery, 10 anti-aircraft, 2 surface-to-air missile, and 3 army aviation battalions; and 1 independent aviation company. Equipment includes 390 M-47, 1,300 M-48, 149 AMX-30 and 106 Leopard 1A3 main battle tanks. Hellenic Army Aviation has over 150 helicopters, including 43 AB-205 and 64 UH-1H Iroquois, 10 Chinooks, 20 Nardi-Hughes 300s, and 15 Cessna U-17A observation aircraft, 2 Aero Commander and 1 Super King Air transports. Strength (1991) 117,000 (101,000 conscripts), with a further 350,000 reserves. There is also a paramiltary gendarmerie of 26,500 men.

Navy. The Hellenic Navy consists mostly of ex-US ships dating from the 1940s, but a modernization programme is under way. Current strength includes 10 diesel submarines, 11 destroyers, 7 frigates (2 built in the Netherlands) and 16 missile craft dating from the 1970s. Smaller units include 10 fast torpedo craft, 2 coastal and 8 inshore patrol craft, 2 minelayers and 14 mine countermeasure vessels. Substantial amphibious lift is provided by 1 dock landing ship, 7 tank landing ships and 5 medium landing ships as well as about 60 landing craft. Major auxiliaries include 2 small replenishment tankers, 1 ammunition transport, 5 survey ships, 1 water tanker and a training ship. There are about 40 minor auxiliaries and service craft. Main bases are at Salamis, Patras, and Soudha Bay (Crete).

The Air Force operates 8 HU-16 Albatross maritime patrol amphibians on naval tasks; and the Navy 12 AB-212 anti-submarine helicopters and 4 Alouettes for search-and-rescue operations and liaison.

Replacement equipment on order includes new frigates to the West German 'MEKO' design, new amphibious ships, and a modernization programme for the submarines. Personnel in 1991 totalled 19,500 of whom 11,500 were conscripts.

The Coastguard and Customs service, 4,000 strong, operate about 100 small patrol craft and 4 reconnaissance aircraft.

Air Force. The Hellenic Air Force had a strength (1991) of about 26,000 officers and men and 350 combat aircraft, consisting of 4 squadrons of F-4E Phantom and 2 squadrons of Mirage 2000 air-superiority fighters, 2 squadrons of F-104G Starfighters, 2 squadrons of F-16 fighter-bombers, 2 squadrons of Mirage F.1 fighters, 3 squadrons of A-7H Corsair II attack aircraft, 3 squadrons of F-5 fighters, 1 squadron of RF-4E reconnaissance fighters and 1 squadron of HU-16B Albatross ASW amphibians (under Navy control). There are also transport squadrons equipped with C-130H Hercules (11), Noratlas, NAMC YS-11, DO28 and C-47 aircraft, 12 Canadair CL-215 twin-engined amphibians, 36 T-2E Buckeye training/attack aircraft, other training and helicopter equipment, and anti-aircraft units equipped with Nike-Hercules and Hawk surface-to-air missiles.

The HAF is organized into Tactical, Training and Air Materiel Commands.

INTERNATIONAL RELATIONS

Membership. Greece is a member of the UN, EEC, the Council of Europe and the military and political wings of NATO.

ECONOMY

Policy. In 1990 the Government embarked on a large-scale privatization of state industries, but by 1992 sales had proved fewer than anticipated.

Budget. The 1990 budget was delivered after a 6-month delay in May 1990: Estimated revenue Dr 3,460,000m.; expenditure, Dr 5,530,000m.

Currency. On 11 Nov. 1944 the Greek currency was stabilized at 1 new *drachma* equalling 50,000m. old *drachmai*. Further readjustments took place in 1946, 1949 and 1953. A 'new issue' of notes and coins was put into circulation on 1 May 1954, 1 new drachma equalling 1,000 old drachmai (72 drachmai = £1; 30 drachmai = US$1). The 'new issue' comprises notes of 50, 100, 500 and 1,000 drachmai and metal coins of 1, 2, 5, 10 and 20 drachmai and 10, 20 and 50 *lepta*. Rate of exchange, March 1992; £1 = 331·33 drachmai; US$1 = 188·74.

Banking and Finance. The central bank and bank of issue is the Bank of Greece. Its *Governor* is Dimitris Halikias. The National Investment Bank for industrial development was set up in Dec. 1963; of its capital of 180m. drachmai, the National Bank provided 60%. Other important banks are the Ionian and Popular Bank of Greece, the Commercial Bank of Greece, the National Mortgage Bank, the Hellenic Industrial Development Bank, the Investment Bank, the Commercial Credit Bank, the Agricultural Bank, the Bank of Central Greece and the General Bank of Greece.

There is a stock exchange in Athens.

Weights and Measures. The metric system was made obligatory in 1959; the use of other systems is prohibited. The Gregorian calendar was adopted in Feb. 1923.

ENERGY AND NATURAL RESOURCES

Electricity. The state-owned Public Power Corporation is the sole producer and distributor. Total installed capacity was 8,361,246 kw. as at 31 Dec. 1987. 75% of power is supplied by lignite-fired power stations. A national grid supplies the mainland, and islands near its coast. Power is produced in remoter islands by local generators. Total net production in 1990 was 31,283m. kwh. Supply 220 volts; 50 Hz.

Minerals. Greece produces a variety of ores and minerals, including (with production, 1987, in tonnes) iron-pyrites (148,972), bauxite (2,466,480), nickel (1,082,278), magnesite (841,604), asbestos (3,384,570), chromite (211,599), barytes, marble (white and coloured) and various other earths, chiefly from the Laurium district, Thessaly, Euboea and the Aegean islands. There is little coal, and the lignite is of indifferent quality (44·65m. tonnes, 1987). Salt production (1988) 181,324 tonnes.

Agriculture. Of the total area (131,957 sq. km) 39,452 sq. km is arable and fallow. Another 52,550 sq. km is grazing land.
Production (1989, in 1,000 tonnes):

Wheat	2,592	Grapes	1,565 [1]
Tobacco	133	Wine must	462
Seed cotton	754	Citrus fruit	1,012 [1]
Sugar-beet	3,043	Other fruit	2,947 [1]
Raisins	138	Milk	1,788
Olive oil	290 [1]	Meat	456

[1] 1988.

Olive production in 1988 was about 1·5m. tonnes.
Rice is cultivated in Macedonia, the Peloponnese, Epirus and Central Greece. Successful experiments have been made in growing rice on alkaline land previously regarded as unfit for cultivation. The main kinds of cheese produced are white cheese in brine (commercially known as Fetta) and hard cheese, such as Kefalotyri.
Livestock (1988): 800,000 cattle, 1,000 buffaloes, 1,190,000 pigs, 10,816,000 sheep, 3,488,000 goats, 60,000 horses, 83,000 mules, 175,000 asses, 31m. poultry.

Forest. Forest covers 29,511 sq. km.

Fisheries. In 1989, 20,072 fishermen were active and landed 130,500 tonnes of fish. 17,000 kg of sponges were produced in 1989.

INDUSTRY. Manufacturing contributed 1,498,727m. drachmai to GDP in 1990. The main products are canned vegetables and fruit, fruit juice, beer, wine, alcoholic beverages, cigarettes, textiles, yarn, leather, shoes, synthetic timber, paper, plastics, rubber products, chemical acids, pigments, pharmaceutical products, cosmetics, soap, disinfectants, fertilizers, glassware, porcelain sanitary items, wire and power coils and household instruments.
Production, 1986 (1,000 tonnes): Textile yarns, 230; cement, 12,494; fertilizers, 1,448; ammonia, 294; iron (concrete-reinforcing bars), 857; alumina, 470; aluminium, 176; beer, 310; bottled wine, 112; chemical acids, 1,789; iron wire, 106; glass products, 141; packing materials, 200; cigarettes (1,000 pieces) 27,118; petroleum, 12,369; detergents, 127.

Labour. Of the economically active population in 1989, 932,858 were engaged in agriculture, 744,998 in manufacturing and 2,289,014 in other employment. Automatic index-linking of wages was abolished at the end of 1990. Wage increases of 8% were made in the public sector in 1991. In the private sector trade unions agreed to a 12% increase in 1991 and one of 9% in 1992. Since 1989 a statutory minimum of wage-bills must be spent on training.

Trade Unions. The status of trade unions in Greece is regulated by the Associations Act 1914. Trade-union liberties are guaranteed under the Constitution, and a law of June 1982 altered the unions' right to strike.
The national body of trade unions is the Greek General Confederation of Labour.

FOREIGN ECONOMIC RELATIONS

Commerce. In 1990 exports totalled (in 1m. drachmai) 1,267,507 including: Clothing, 264,731; textile yarn, 45,029; petroleum products, 81,724; tobacco, 49,319; prepared fruits, 41,483; olive oil, 45,349; cement, 28,048. Imports totalled 3,137,524 including: Crude oil, 158,542; meat, 42,466; agricultural tractors, 18,654; medicines, 19,240.

Exports in 1990 (in 1m. drachmai) were mainly to the Federal Republic of Germany (277,494), Italy (211,087), France (121,942), UK (92,661) and USA (71,268). Imports were mainly from the Federal Republic of Germany (645,502), Italy (483,049), France (253,805) and the Netherlands (211,168).

Total trade between Greece and UK (British Department of Trade returns, in £1,000 sterling):

	1987	1988	1989	1990	1991
Imports to UK	355,320	356,974	395,086	400,476	378,146
Exports and re-exports from UK	444,500	468,032	571,409	682,887	667,741

Tourism. Tourists visiting Greece in 1990 numbered 8,873,310. They spent the equivalent of US$2,587m. In 1991 there were 433,000 hotel beds.

COMMUNICATIONS

Roads. There were, in 1988, 38,485 km of roads, of which 9,293 were national and 29,192 provincial roads. Number of motor vehicles in 1990: 2,522,628, of which 1,729,683 were passenger cars, 772,416 goods vehicles and 20,529 buses.

Railways. In 1989 the State network, Hellenic Railways (OSE), totalled 2,479 km comprising 1,565 km of 1,435 mm gauge, 892 km of 1,000 mm gauge, and 22 km of 750 mm gauge. Railways carried 4m. tonnes of freight and 12·3m. passengers in 1989.

Civil Aviation. In 1991 the state-owned Olympic Airways had 38 aircraft, including 6 Boeing 737-400s and 3 Boeing 727s. 6·7m. passengers were carried in 1989. It operates routes from Athens to all important cities of the country, Europe, the Middle East and USA. 34 foreign companies fly to Athens.

Shipping. In 1990 the merchant navy comprised 2,031 vessels of 22,526,000 GRT. Greek-owned ships under foreign flags totalled 3,555,637 GRT in 1989.

There is a canal (opened 9 Nov. 1893) across the Isthmus of Corinth (about 4 miles).

Telecommunications. In 1990 there were 4,128 telephone exchanges and 4,697,770 telephones.

Elliniki Radiophonia Tileorasis (ERT), the Hellenic National Radio and Television Institute, is the government broadcasting station. ERT broadcasts 2 TV programmes (colour by SECAM). Number of receivers in 1991: Radio, 4,085,000; television, 2,281,263.

Cinemas (1981). There were 1,150 cinemas.

Newspapers (1988). There were 35 daily newspapers published in Athens, 6 in Piraeus and 76 elsewhere.

JUSTICE, RELIGION, EDUCATION AND WELFARE

Justice. Under the 1975 Constitution judges are appointed for life by the President of the Republic, after consultation with the judicial council. Judges enjoy personal and functional independence. There are three divisions of the courts: Administrative, civil and criminal and they must not give decisions which are contrary to the Constitution. Final jurisdiction lies with a Special Supreme Tribunal.

Some laws, passed before the 1975 Constitution came into force, and which are not contrary to it, remain in force.

Religion. The Christian Eastern Orthodox faith is the established religion to which 98% of the population belong.

The Greek Orthodox Church is under an archbishop and 67 metropolitans, 1 archbishop and 7 metropolitans in Crete, and 4 metropolitans in the Dodecanese. The Roman Catholics have 3 archbishops (in Naxos and Corfu and, not recognized by the State, in Athens) and 1 bishop (for Syra and Santorin). The Exarchs of the Greek Catholics and the Armenians are not recognized by the State.

Complete religious freedom is recognized by the Constitution of 1968, but proselytizing from, and interference with, the Greek Orthodox Church is forbidden.

Education. Public education is provided in nursery, primary and secondary schools, starting at 6 years of age and (since 1963) free at all levels.

In 1987–88 there were 5,389 nursery schools with 7,942 teachers and 155,246 pupils; 8,178 primary schools with 39,125 teachers and 868,335 pupils; 1,734 high schools with 26,544 teachers and 446,963 pupils; 1,078 lycea with 18,343 teachers and 261,586 pupils and 505 technical and vocational schools with 9,286 teachers and 129,802 pupils. There were also 7 teacher training schools with 65 teachers and 3,547 students; 12 technical education schools with 4,577 teachers and 64,990 students; 45 vocational and ecclesiastical schools with 683 teachers and 3,443 students and 16 higher education schools with 7,435 teachers and 117,193 students.

In 1982–83 there were 13 universities with 94,574 students and 7,638 lecturers.

Health (1988). There were 430 hospitals and sanatoria with a total of 51,587 beds. There were 32,145 doctors and 9,206 dentists.

DIPLOMATIC REPRESENTATIVES

Of Greece in Great Britain (1A Holland Park, London, W11 3TP)
Ambassador: George D. Papoulias.

Of Great Britain in Greece (1 Ploutarchou St., 106 75 Athens)
Ambassador: Sir David Miers, KBE, CMG.

Of Greece in the USA (2221 Massachusetts Ave., NW, Washington, D.C., 20008)
Ambassador: Christos Zacharakis.

Of the USA in Greece (91 Vasilissis Sophias Blvd., 10160 Athens)
Ambassador: Michael G. Sotirhos.

Of Greece to the United Nations
Ambassador: Antonios Exarchos.

Further Reading

Clogg, R., *Greece in the 1980s.* London, 1983
Clogg, M. J. and R., *Greece.* [Bibliography] Oxford and Santa Barbara, 1980
Freris, A. F., *The Greek Economy in the Twentieth Century.* London, 1986
Holden, D., *Greece Without Columns: The Making of the Modern Greeks.* London, 1972
Sarafis, M. and Eve, M. (eds.) *Background to Contemporary Greece.* London, 1990
Tsakalotos, E., *Alternative Economic Strategies: the Case of Greece.* Aldershot, 1991
Woodhouse, C. M., *Karamanlis: The Restorer of Greek Democracy.* OUP, 1982.—*Modern Greece: a Short History.* rev. ed. London, 1991

National statistical office: National Statistical Service; 14–16 Lycourgou St., Athens.

GRENADA

Capital: St George's
Population: 91,000 (1991)
GNP per capita: US$1,431 (1990)

HISTORY. Grenada became an independent nation within the Commonwealth on 7 Feb. 1974. Grenada was formerly an Associated State under the West Indies Act, 1967. The 1973 Constitution was suspended in 1979 following a revolution.

On 19 Oct. 1983 the army took control after a power struggle led to the killing of Maurice Bishop the Prime Minister. At the request of a group of Caribbean countries, Grenada was invaded by US-led forces on 24–28 Oct. On 1 Nov. a State of Emergency was imposed which ended on 15 Nov. when an interim government was installed. The 1973 Constitution was restored.

AREA AND POPULATION. Grenada is the most southerly island of the Windward Islands with an area of 133 sq. miles (344 sq. km); the state also includes the Southern Grenadine Islands to the north, chiefly Carriacou and Petit Martinique, with an area of 13 sq. miles (34 sq. km). The total population (Census, 1988) was 99,205. Estimate (1991), 91,000. The Borough of St. George's, the capital, had 35,742 inhabitants in 1989. In 1991, 82% of the people were Black of African descent, 13% of mixed origins and 1% White.

Vital statistics (1987): Births, 3,102; deaths, 781.

The official language is English. A French-African patois is also spoken.

CLIMATE. The tropical climate is very agreeable in the dry season, from Jan. to May, when days are warm and nights quite cool, but in the wet season there is very little difference between day and night temperatures. On the coast, annual rainfall is about 60" (1,500 mm) but it is as high as 150–200" (3,750–5,000 mm) in the mountains. Average temperature, 24°C.

CONSTITUTION AND GOVERNMENT. The British sovereign is represented by an appointed Governor-General. There is a bicameral legislature, consisting of a 13-member *Senate,* appointed by the Governor-General, and a 15-member *House of Representatives,* elected by universal suffrage. At the elections of March 1990 for the House of Representatives, the National Democratic Congress (NDC) won 7 seats, the Grenada United Labour Party (GULP) 4, the National Party (NP) 2 and the New National Party (NNP) 2. The state of the parties in Nov. 1991 was: NDP, 8 seats; GULP, 3; NP, 2; NNP, 2.

Governor-General: Sir Paul Scoon, GCMG, GCVO, OBE.

In Nov. 1991 the government comprised:

Prime Minister and Minister of External Affairs: Hon. Nicholas Alexander Brathwaite.

Agriculture, Forestry, Lands and Fisheries: Phinsley St Louis. *Education, Culture, Youth and Sports:* Carlyle Glean. *Finance, Trade and Industry:* George Brizan. *Health, Housing and the Environment:* Michael Andrew. *Labour, Social Security, Co-operative and Community Development:* Hon. Edzil Thomas. *Attorney-General, Local Affairs and Local Government:* Dr Hon. Francis Alexis. *Tourism, Civil Aviation and Women's Affairs:* Joan Purcell. *Works, Communications and Public Utilities:* Tillman Thomas.

National flag: Divided into 4 triangles of yellow, top and bottom, and green, hoist and fly; in the centre a red disc bearing a gold star; along the top and bottom edged red stripes each bearing 3 gold stars; on the green triangle near the hoist a pod of nutmeg.

Local government: There are 7 district councils (including 1 for Carriacou/Petite Martinique) and the Borough Council of St. George's. Local Government Bills had their first reading in Parliament on 24 Oct. 1986. The second reading and final stages of the Bills were postponed. The Department of Local Government has subsequently submitted new proposals for the re-establishment of elected local councils in Grenada, Carriacou and Petit Martinique.

DEFENCE

Royal Grenadian Police Force. Modelled on the British system, the 650-strong police force includes an 80-member paramilitary unit and a 30-member coastguard.

INTERNATIONAL RELATIONS

Membership. Grenada is a member of the UN, OAS, Caricom, the Commonwealth and is an ACP state of EEC.

ECONOMY

Budget. Current revenue in 1990 was US$57·2m.; expenditure, US$58·6m. Capital expenditure was US$18·4m. Value added tax has replaced income tax.

Currency. The unit of currency is the *Eastern Caribbean dollar* (XCD). In March 1992, £1 = EC$4·74; US$ = EC$2·70.

Banking and Finance. In 1991 there were 5 commercial banks: The National Commercial Bank, Barclays Bank International, Grenada Bank of Commerce, Bank of Nova Scotia and the Grenada Co-operative Bank. The Grenada Agricultural Bank was established in 1965 to encourage agricultural development; in 1975 it became the Grenada Agricultural and Industrial Development Corporation. In 1987, bank deposits were EC$269·2m.

ENERGY AND NATURAL RESOURCES

Electricity. Production (1984) 40·5m. kwh.

Agriculture. The principal crops (1990 production in 1,000 tonnes) are: Cocoa, 2, bananas, 2 and coconuts, 1; (1998 production in 1,000 lb.) was nutmegs, 5,510 and mace, 567. Corn and pigeon peas, citrus, sugar-cane, root-crops and vegetables are also grown, in addition to small scattered cultivations of cotton, cloves, cinnamon, pimento, coffee and fruit trees.

Livestock (1990): Cattle, 5,000; sheep, 15,000; goats, 11,000; pigs, 11,000.

Fisheries. The catch (1989) was 3,769 081 lbs.

FOREIGN ECONOMIC RELATIONS

Commerce. (1990). Total value of imports of goods and non-factor services, US$103·7m., primarily composed of foods, machinery and transport equipment, manufactured goods, and fuels. Imports were mainly from the USA, UK, Canada, Trinidad and Tobago, North Korea and the Netherlands. Exports of goods and nonfactor services (1990) totalled US$47·8m., primarily composed of nutmeg, cocoa, bananas, mace and textiles. Exports were mainly to the UK, Trinidad and Tobago, the Netherlands and Germany.

Total trade between Grenada and UK (British Department of Trade returns, in £1,000 sterling):

	1987	1988	1989	1990	1991
Imports to UK	6,302	6,115	5,924	4,778	4,236
Exports and re-exports to UK	8,772	7,162	9,058	7,822	7,730

Tourism. In 1990, there were 307,422 visitors, including 198,320 cruise ship passengers.

COMMUNICATIONS

Roads. In 1991 there were 1,127 km of roads, of which 580 km were hard-surfaced. Vehicles registered (1988) 12,198.

Civil Aviation. Point Salines international airport has daily connexions to London, New York, Miami and South America via nearby islands. Lauriston Airport is on Carriacou.

Shipping. The main port is at St George's; there are 8 minor ports. Total shipping for 1987 was 1,004 motor and steamships and 140 sailing and auxiliary vessels, with a total net tonnage of 869,235 and 7,253 respectively.

Telecommunications. At 31 Oct. 1990 there were 11,632 telephone lines and 10,930 telephone stations. The government-owned Radio Grenada broadcasts from 2 radio stations and the commercial Grenada Television Service from 1 TV station. In 1991 there were 40,000 radio and 30,000 TV sets. Colour is by NTSC.

Newspapers. In 1991 there were 4 weekly (total circulation, 12,000), 1 monthly and 2 bi-monthly newspapers.

JUSTICE, RELIGION, EDUCATION AND WELFARE

Justice. The Grenada Supreme Court, situated in St George's, comprises a High Court of Justice, a Court of Magisterial Appeal (which hears appeals from the lower Magistrates' Courts exercising summary jurisdiction) and an Itinerant Court of Appeal (to hear appeals from the High Court). For police *see* Defence.

Religion. The majority of the population are Roman Catholic; the Anglican and Methodist churches are also well represented.

Education. In 1989 there were 71 pre-primary schools with 3,660 pupils, 58 primary schools with 19,963 pupils, 18 secondary schools with 6,437 pupils, 2 schools for special education and 5 day care centres. The Grenada National College, established in July 1988, incorporates the Institute for Further Education, the Grenada Teachers' College, the Grenada Technical and Vocational Institute, the School of Nursing, the Mirabeau Farm Institute, the Science and Technological Council, the Continuing Education Programme, the Public Service Training Division and the School of Pharmacy. There is also a branch of the University of the West Indies. Adult literacy was 90% in 1991.

Health. In 1990 there was 1 main hospital with 2 subsidiaries. In 1990 there were 36 clinics, 52 doctors, 7 dentists, 28 pharmacists, 36 midwives, 296 nursing personnel and 28 medical technologists (laboratory, radiography and biomedical).

DIPLOMATIC REPRESENTATIVES

Of Grenada in Great Britain (1 Collingham Gdns., London, SW5)
High Commissioner: L. C. Noel.

Of Great Britain in Grenada
High Commissioner: E. T. Davies, CMG (resides in Bridgetown).

Of Grenada in the USA (1701 New Hampshire Ave., NW, Washington, D.C., 20009)
Ambassador: Denneth Modeste.

Of the USA in Grenada (P.O. Box 54, St George's)
Ambassador: (Vacant).

Of Grenada to the United Nations
Ambassador: Eugene M. Pursoo.

Further Reading

Davidson, J. S., *Grenada: A Study in Politics and the Limits of International Law.* London, 1987
Ferguson, J., *Grenada: Revolution in Reverse.* London, 1991
Gilmore, W. G., *The Grenada Intervention: Analysis and Documentation.* London, 1984
Heine, J. (ed) *A Revolution Aborted: the Lessons of Grenada.* Pittsburgh Univ. Press, 1990
O'Shaughnessy, H., *Grenada: Revolution, Invasion and Aftermath.* London, 1984

Page, A., Sutton, P. and Thorndike, T., *Grenada and Invasion*. London, 1984
Sandford, G. and Vigilante, R., *Grenada: The Untold Story*. London, 1988
Schoenhals, K., *Grenada*: [Bibliography]. Oxford and Santa Barbara, 1990
Searle, C., *Grenada: The Struggle against Destabilization*. London, 1983
Searle, C. and Rojas, D. (eds) *To Construct from Morning*. Grenada, 1982
Sinclair, N., *Grenada: Isle of Spice*. London, 1987
Thorndike, T., *Grenada: Politics, Economics and Society*. London, 1985

GUATEMALA

Capital: Guatemala City
Population: 9m. (1989)
GNP per capita: US$920 (1989)

República de Guatemala

HISTORY. From 1524 to 1821 Guatemala was a Spanish captaincy-general, comprising the whole of Central America. It became independent from Spain in 1821 and formed part of the Confederation of Central America from 1823 to 1839, when Rafael Carrera dissolved the Confederation and Guatemala became independent.

AREA AND POPULATION. Guatemala is bounded on the north and west by Mexico, south by the Pacific ocean and east by El Salvador, Honduras and Belize, and the area is 108,889 sq. km (42,042 sq. miles). In March 1936 Guatemala, El Salvador and Honduras agreed to accept the peak of Mount Montecristo as the common boundary point.

The census population was 6,054,227 in 1981. Estimate (1989) 9m. (41·6% urban). In 1983, 53% were Amerindian, of 21 different groups descended from the Maya; most of the remainder are mixed Amerindian and Spanish. 45% of the population in 1990 spoke Mayan languages. Density of population, 1989, 82 per sq. km.

Vital statistics, 1984: Births, 302,921; deaths, 75,462; marriages, 31,351.

Guatemala is administratively divided into 22 departments, each with a governor appointed by the President. Population, 1985:

Departments	Area (sq. km)	Population	Departments	Area (sq. km)	Population
Alta Verapaz	8,686	393,446	Petén	35,854	118,116
Baja Verapaz	3,124	160,567	Quezaltenango	1,951	478,030
Chimaltenango	1,979	283,887	Quiché	8,378	460,956
Chiquimula	2,376	220,067	Retalhuleu	1,858	228,563
El Progreso	1,922	106,115	Sacatepéquez	465	148,574
Escuintla	4,384	565,215	San Marcos	3,791	590,152
Guatemala	2,126	2,050,673	Santa Rosa	2,955	263,060
Huehuetenango	7,403	571,292	Sololá	1,061	181,816
Izabal	9,038	330,546	Suchitepéquez	2,510	327,763
Jalapa	2,063	171,542	Totonicapán	1,061	249,067
Jutiapa	3,219	348,032	Zacapa	2,690	155,496

The capital is Guatemala City with about 2m. inhabitants (1989). Other towns are Quezaltenango (246,000), Puerto Barrios (338,000), Mazatenango (38,319), Antigua (26,631), Zacapa (35,769) and Cobán (120,000).

CLIMATE. A tropical climate, with little variation in temperature and a well marked wet season from May to Oct. Guatemala City. Jan. 63°F (17·2°C), July 69°F (20·6°C). Annual rainfall 53" (1,316 mm).

CONSTITUTION AND GOVERNMENT. A new Constitution, drawn up by the Constituent Assembly elected on 1 July 1984, was promulgated in June 1985 and came into force on 14 Jan. 1986. The President and Vice-President are elected for a term of 5 years by direct election (with a second round of voting if no candidate secures 50% of the first-round votes). The unicameral Legislative Assembly comprises 100 members. At the first round of the presidential elections in Nov. 1990 4 candidates stood: Jorge Carpio (National Centre Union, UCN) gained 25·7% of the votes cast, Jorge Serrano (Movement of Solidarity Action, MAS), gained 24·2%. At the second round in Jan. 1991 some 50% of the 3·2m. electorate voted. Serrano gained the presidency with 68% of the votes.

At the general elections in Nov. 1990 the UCN won 41 of the 116 seats; the Christian Democrats, 29; and MAS, 19. Jorge Serrano formed a government of national unity in Jan. 1991.

President: Jorge Serrano (sworn in 15 Jan. 1991).
Labour: Mario Solorzano (Social Democrat). *Defence:* Gen. José Domingo García.

National flag: Three vertical strips of blue, white, blue, with the national arms in the centre.

National anthem: ¡Guatemala! Feliz ('Happy Guatemala' words by J. J. Palma; tune by R. Alvarez).

DEFENCE. There is selective conscription into the armed forces for 30 months.

Army. The Army numbered (1992) 37,000, organized in 39 infantry, 2 airborne, 6 strategic reserve and 1 engineer battalions. Equipment includes 10 light tanks and armoured cars. Reserves, 1992, 4,500. Territorial militia, 500,000.

Navy. A naval element of the combined armed forces operates 8 inshore patrol craft, as well as 20 river patrol boats. The force was (1991) 1,200 strong of whom 600 are marines for maintenance of riverine security. Main bases are Puerto Barrios (on the Atlantic Coast), Puerto Quetzal and Puerto San José (Pacific).

Air Force. There is a small Air Force with 10 A-37B and 2 T-33 light attack aircraft, 1DC-6, 10 C-47, 3 F.27 and 7 Israeli-built Arava transports, 10 Pilatus PC-7 turboprop trainers, and a number of Cessna light aircraft and Bell helicopters, including a few armed UH-1 Iroquois. Strength was (1991) about 1,400 personnel and 80 aircraft.

INTERNATIONAL RELATIONS

Membership. Guatemala is a member of the UN, OAS and CACM.

ECONOMY

Planning. The 1988 National Economic Development Plan, called 'Guatemala 2000', calls for sustained GDP growth of at least 6% per annum until 2000.

Budget. 1991 budget estimates balance at Q5,500m.

Currency. The unit of currency is the *quetzal* (CTQ) of 100 *centavos*, established 7 May 1925. There are coins of 25, 10, 5 and 1 *centavos* and notes of 100, 50, 20, 10, 5, 1 and ¹/₂ *quetzales* (50 *centavos*). In March 1992, £1 = Q.8·92; US$1 = Q.5·08.

Banking and Finance. On 4 Feb. 1946 the Central Bank of Guatemala (founded in 1926 as a mixed central and commercial bank) was superseded by a new institution, the Banco de Guatemala, to operate solely as a central bank. Savings and term deposits at commercial banks were Q.3,885·2m. at 31 July 1988. Total currency in circulation on 31 July 1989 was Q.1,785m.; total net international reserves amounted to Q.50m. on 31 July 1989.

There are 24 banks, including the Banco de Guatemala, Banco Nacional de Desarrollo, set up in 1971 to promote agricultural development, its counterpart for small industries (Banco de los Trabajadores) set up in Jan. 1966 with initial capital of US$1·3m. and a subsidiary of Lloyds Bank plc.

Weights and Measures. The metric system has been officially adopted, but is little used in local commerce.

Libra of 16 oz.	=1·014 lb.	*League*	=3 miles
Arroba of 25 libras	=25·35 lb.	*Vara*	=32 in.
Quintal of 4 arrobas	=101·40 lb.	*Manzana*	=100 varas sq.
Tonelada of 20 quintals	=20·28 cwt	*Caballeria* of 64 man-	
Fanega	=1¹/₂ Imp. bushels	zanas	=110 acres

ENERGY AND NATURAL RESOURCES

Electricity. 2,800m. kwh. of electricity were generated in 1989. A large hydro-electric plant was inaugurated in Dec. 1985. Supply 110 and 220 volts; 60 Hz.

Oil. Guatemala began exporting crude oil in 1980; exports, 1984, were valued at US$34m. Production is from wells in Alta Verapaz department from where the oil is piped to Santo Tomas de Castilla. Further exploration is proceeding in the Petén.

Minerals. Mineral production includes zinc and lead concentrates, some antimony and tungsten, a small amount of cadmium and silver; some copper is also being mined. Exports (1988) Q.2m.

Agriculture. The Cordilleras divide Guatemala into two unequal drainage areas, of which the Atlantic is much the greater. The Pacific slope, though comparatively narrow, is exceptionally well watered and fertile between the altitudes of 1,000 and 5,000 ft, and is the most densely settled part of the republic. The Atlantic slope is sparsely populated, and has little of commercial importance beyond the chicle and timber-cutting of the Petén, coffee cultivation of Cobán region and banana-raising of the Motagua Valley and Lake Izabal district. Soil erosion is serious and a single week of heavy rains suffices to cause flooding of fields and much crop destruction.

The principal crop is coffee; there are about 12,000 coffee plantations with 138m. coffee trees on about 338,000 acres, but 80% of the crop comes from 1,500 large coffee farms employing 426,000 workers. Production (1988) 156,000 tonnes. Estimated production, 1990–91: 204,000 tonnes. Banana production was 780,000 tonnes in 1989. Cotton lint production was 44,000 tonnes in 1988. Guatemala is a major producer of chicle gum (used for chewing-gum manufacture in USA). Rubber development schemes are under way, assisted by US funds. Guatemala is one of the largest sources of essential oils (citronella and lemon grass).

Livestock (1990): Cattle, 1·8m.; pigs, 800,000; sheep, 670,000; horses, 113,000; poultry, 10m.

Forestry. The forest area had (1989) an extent of 4m. ha, 37% of the land area. The department of Petén is rich in mahogany and other woods. Production (1980) 11·23m. cu. metres.

Fisheries. Exports were about Q.11·8m. in 1984.

INDUSTRY. The principal industries are food and beverages, tobacco, chemicals, hides and skins, textiles, garments and non-metallic minerals. New industries include electrical goods, plastic sheet and metal furniture.

Trade Unions. There are 3 federations for private sector workers.

FOREIGN ECONOMIC RELATIONS. External debt was US$2,500m. in 1989.

Commerce. Values in US$1,000 were:

	1986	1987	1988	1989
Imports (c.i.f.)	804	1,230	1,250	1,695
Exports (f.o.b.)	825	824	875	1,155

Coffee exports in 1987 were valued at US$400m. mainly to USA and Federal Republic of Germany.

Bananas are still an important export crop, but exports have at times been seriously reduced, partly by labour troubles and by hurricanes. Exports in 1987 were worth US$67m.

Cotton exports in 1984 were valued at US$70·4m. Other important exports (1984) were sugar, US$74·5m.; beef, US$11·6m.

Exports of essential oils were worth US$1·7m. in 1984. Cardamom exports (mainly to Arab countries) were worth US$40m. in 1987.

Total trade between Guatemala and UK (British Department of Trade returns, in £1,000 sterling):

	1987	1988	1989	1990	1991
Imports to UK	7,536	10,678	6,950	42,034	10,458
Exports and re-exports from UK	13,926	15,387	52,324	17,551	16,224

Tourism. There were 287,000 foreign visitors in 1986.

COMMUNICATIONS

Roads. In 1989 there were 18,000 km of roads, of which 2,850 are paved. There is a highway from coast to coast via Guatemala City. There are 2 highways from the Mexican to the Salvadorean frontier: the Pacific Highway serving the fertile coastal plain and the Pan-American Highway running through the highlands and Guatemala City. Motor vehicles numbered about 300,000 in 1989.

Railways. The railway system is the government-owned *Ferrocarriles de Guatemala*. All railways are of 914 mm gauge. Total length of all lines was (1989) 953 km. Passengers carried, 1989, numbered 293,000, and freight carried, 426,000 tonnes.

Civil Aviation. The part-government-owned airline, Aviateca, and 2 private airlines furnish both domestic and international services; 6 other airlines handle international traffic from La Aurora airport in Guatemala City.

Shipping. The chief ports on the Atlantic coast are Puerto Barrios and Santo Tomás de Castilla: on the Pacific coast, Puerto Quetzal and Champerico. Total tonnage handled was, 1987, 7m. tons.

Telecommunications. The Government own and operate the telegraph and telephone services; there were 180,000 telephones in Sept. 1988. There are some 70 broadcasting stations. Radio receiving sets in use, 1991, numbered about 0·4m. There are 4 commercial TV stations, 1 government station and about 475,000 TV receivers (colour by NTSC). There is also reception by US television satellite.

Cinemas (1989). Cinemas numbered approximately 100.

Newspapers (1989). There are 4 daily newspapers.

JUSTICE, RELIGION, EDUCATION AND WELFARE

Justice. Justice is administered in a Constitution Court, a Supreme Court, 6 appeal courts and 28 courts of first instance. Supreme Court and appeal court judges are elected by Congress. Judges of first instance are appointed by the Supreme Court.

All holders of public office have to show on entering office, and again on leaving, a full account of their private property and income.

Religion. Roman Catholicism is the prevailing faith and there is a Roman Catholic archbishopric. Membership of the approximately 100 evangelical Protestant churches was estimated at 30% of the population in 1991 (75% Pentecostalist), with about 14,000 places of worship.

Education. In 1988 there were 11,587 schools with 45,611 teachers and an attendance of 1,331,294 pupils; these figures include private schools. There are 1,237 secondary and other schools having 13,891 teachers and an attendance of 194,484 pupils; the state-supported but autonomous University of San Carlos de Borromeo, founded in 1678, was reopened in 1910 with 7 faculties and schools and there are 4 private universities. Students at the state university (1989) numbered approximately 65,000. All education is in theory free, but owing to a grave shortage of state schools private schools flourish. The 1988 census estimates that 63% of those 10 years of age and older were illiterate.

Social Welfare. A comprehensive system of social security was outlined in a law of 30 Oct. 1946. Medical personnel include about 1,250 doctors and 275 dentists for the whole republic. There are about 60 public hospitals and about 100 dispensaries.

DIPLOMATIC REPRESENTATIVES

Of Guatemala in Great Britain (13 Fawcett St., London, SW10 9HN)
Ambassador: (Vacant).

Of Great Britain in Guatemala (7a Avenida 5-10, Zona 4, Guatemala City)
Ambassador: Justin Nason, OBE.

Of Guatemala in the USA (2220 R. St., NW, Washington, D.C., 20008)
Chargé d'affaires: Norma J. Vasquez.

Of the USA in Guatemala (7–01 Avenida de la Reforma, Zone 10, Guatemala City)
Ambassador: Thomas Frank Stroock.

Of Guatemala to the United Nations
Ambassador: Francisco Villagrán De Leon.

Further Reading

The official gazette is called *Diario de Centro America.*

Banco de Guatemala, *Memoria annual, Estudio económico* and *Boletín Estadístico*
Bloomfield, L. M., *The British Honduras–Guatemala Dispute.* Toronto, 1953
Franklin, W. B., *Guatemala.* [Bibliography] Oxford and Santa Barbara, 1981
Glassman, P., *Guatemala Guide.* Dallas, 1977
Immerman, R. H., *The CIA in Guatemala: The Foreign Policy of Intervention.* Univ. of Texas Press, 1982
Mendoza, J. L., *Britain and Her Treaties on Belize.* Guatemala, 1946
Morton, F., *Xeláhuh.* London, 1959
Plant, R., *Guatemala: Unnatural Disaster.* London, 1978
Schlesinger, S. and Kinzer, S., *Bitter Front: The Untold Story of the American Coup in Guatemala.* London and New York, 1982

National Library: Biblioteca Nacional, 5a Avenida y 8a Calle, Zona 1, Guatemala City.

GUINEA

Capital: Conakry
Population: 6·71m. (1989)
GNP per capita: US$430 (1989)

République de Guinée

HISTORY. Guinea was proclaimed a French protectorate in 1888 and a colony in 1893. It became a constituent territory of French West Africa in 1904. The independent republic of Guinea was proclaimed on 2 Oct. 1958, after the territory of French Guinea had decided at the referendum of 28 Sept. to leave the French Community. Following the death of the first President, Ahmed Sekou Touré on 27 March 1984, the armed forces staged a coup and dissolved the National Assembly.

AREA AND POPULATION. Guinea, a coastal state of West Africa, is bounded north-west by Guinea-Bissau and Senegal, north-east by Mali, south-east by the Côte d'Ivoire, south by Liberia and Sierra Leone, and west by the Atlantic Ocean.

The area is 245,857 sq. km (94,926 sq. miles), and the population, census, 1983, was 5,781,014; estimate, 1989, 6,710,000. The capital is Conakry. In 1989, 22% were urban.

The areas, populations and chief towns of the major divisions are:

	Sq. km	Census 1983	Chief town	Census 1983
Conakry (city)	308	705,280	Conakry	705,280
Guinée-Maritime	43,980	1,147,301	Kindia	55,904
Moyenne-Guinée	51,710	1,595,007	Labé	65,439
Haute-Guinée	92,535	1,086,679	Kankan	88,760
Guinée-Forestière	57,324	1,246,747	Nzérékoré	23,000 [1]

[1] 1972.

The ethnic composition is Fulani (40·3%, predominant in Moyenne-Guinée), Malinké (or Mandingo, 25·8%, prominent in Haute-Guinée), Susu (11%, prominent in Guinée-Maritime), Kissi (6·5%) and Kpelle (4·8%) in Guinée-Forestière, and Dialonka, Loma and others (11·6%).

CLIMATE. A tropical climate, with high rainfall near the coast and constant heat, but conditions are a little cooler on the plateau. The wet season on the coast lasts from May to Nov., but only to Oct. inland. Conakry. Jan. 80°F (26·7°C), July 77°F (25°C). Annual rainfall 172" (4,293 mm).

CONSTITUTION AND GOVERNMENT. Following the coup of 3 April 1984, supreme power rests with a *Comité Militaire de Redressement National* (CMRN), ruling through a Council of Ministers appointed by the President which included in March 1992:

President and Head of CMRN: Brig.-Gen. Lansana Conté.

Ministers-Delegate to Presidency: Lieut.-Gen. Abdourahmane Diallo *(National Defence)*, Hervé Vincent Bangoura *(Information, Culture and Tourism)*, Major Henri Foula *(Economy and Finance)*, René Alseny Gómez *(Interior and Public Security)*.

Resident (Regional) Ministers: Major Abou Camara *(Guinée-Maritime)*, Lieut.-Col. Sory Doumbouya *(Moyenne-Guinée)*, Major Alpha Oumar Barou Diallo *(Haute-Guinée)*, Major Alhousseini Fofana *(Guinée-Forestière)*.

Local Government: The administrative division comprises the capital Conakry and 33 provinces divided into 175 districts, grouped into 4 regions which correspond to the 4 major geographical and ethnic areas: Guinée-Maritime; Moyenne-Guinée; Haute-Guinée and Guinée-Forestière.

National flag: Three vertical strips of red, gold, green.

National anthem: 'Liberté' (no words; tune by A. Yaya).

Besides French, there are 8 official languages taught in schools: Fulani, Malinké, Susu, Kissi, Kpelle, Loma, Basari and Koniagi.

DEFENCE

Army. The Army of 8,500 men (1991), comprises 1 armoured, 5 infantry, 1 commando and 1 engineer, 1 artillery, 1 air defence and 1 special force battalions. Equipment includes 30 T-34, 8 T-54 and 20 PT-76 tanks. There are also 3 paramilitary forces: People's Militia (7,000), Gendarmerie (1,000) and Republican Guard (1,600).

Navy. A small force of 400 (1991) operate 2 French-built and 7 Soviet-built inshore patrol craft, and a number of riverine boats from bases at Conakry and Kakanda.

Air Force. The Air Force, formed with Soviet assistance, is reported to be equipped with 6 MiG-17 jet-fighters and 2 MiG-15UTI trainers, 4 An-14 and 4 Il-14 piston-engined transports and a Yak-40 jet aircraft for VIP duties, all Russian built, plus a few French-supplied helicopters, piston-engined Yak-18 and L-29 jet trainers. Personnel (1991) 800.

INTERNATIONAL RELATIONS

Membership. Guinea is a member of the UN, OAU and is an ACP state of the EEC.

ECONOMY

Budget. The budget for 1987: balanced at 377,000m. *Guinea francs*.

Currency. The monetary unit is the *Guinea franc*. There are banknotes of 25, 50, 100, 500, 1,000 and 5,000 *Guinea francs*. In March 1992, £1 = 1,424·75 *francs*; US$1 = 811·59 *francs*.

Banking. In 1986 the Central Bank was restructured and commercial banking returned to the private sector.

ENERGY AND NATURAL RESOURCES

Electricity. Production of electrical energy was 236m. kwh. in 1986.

Minerals. Bauxite is mined at Fria, Boké and Kindia; output (1986) 14·7m. tonnes, alumina 580,000 tonnes. Production of iron ore from the Nimba and Simandou mountains commenced in 1981, following exhaustion of the Kaloum peninsula deposits. Diamond mining output (1985) 105,000 carats of gem diamonds and 7,000 carats of industrial diamonds.

Agriculture. The chief crops (production, 1990, in 1,000 tonnes) are: Cassava, 450; rice, 500; plantains, 400; sugar-cane, 225; bananas, 110; groundnuts, 52; sweet potatoes, 105; yams, 100; maize, 100; palm-oil, 50; palm kernels, 40; pineapples, 10; pulses, 60; coffee, 25; coconuts, 2.

Livestock (1990): Cattle, 1·8m.; sheep, 510,000; goats, 460,000; pigs, 33,000.

Forestry: In 1988, 41% of the country was forested (10m. ha). Round-wood production (1986) 4·4m. cu. metres.

Fisheries: Catch (1986) 30,000 tonnes.

FOREIGN ECONOMIC RELATIONS

Commerce. In 1984 imports totalled 7,542m. *Guinea francs* (32% from France) and exports 11,009m. *Guinea francs* (28% to the USA). Alumina forms about 30% and bauxite 58% of the exports.

Total trade between Guinea and the UK (British Department of Trade returns, in £1,000 sterling):

	1987	1988	1989	1990	1991
Imports to UK	19,538	7,582	10,657	11,508	5,854
Exports and re-exports from UK	10,675	10,106	13,937	11,368	7,800

COMMUNICATIONS

Roads. There are 29,000 km of roads and tracks, of which 520 km are bitumenized. In 1985 there were 106,000 cars and 113,000 commercial vehicles.

Railways. A railway connects Conakry with Kankan (662 km) and is to be extended to Bougouni in Mali. A line 134 km long linking bauxite deposits at Sangaredi with Port Kamsar was opened in 1973 (carried 2·3m. tonnes in 1990) and a third line links Conakry and Fria (144 km).

Civil Aviation. There are airports at Conakry and Kankan; in 1982, 131,000 passengers disembarked and embarked.

Shipping. There are ports at Conakry and for bauxite exports at Kamsar (opened 1973). There were (1983) 18 vessels of 6,944 GRT registered in Guinea.

Telecommunications. Telephones, 1981, numbered about 10,000. Broadcasting is the responsibility of the state-controlled Radiodiffusion Télévision Guinéenne. There were 200,000 radio and 65,000 television receivers in 1991 (colour by PAL).

Newspapers. In 1979 there was 1 daily newspaper (circulation 20,000).

JUSTICE, RELIGION, EDUCATION AND WELFARE

Justice. There are *tribunaux du premier degré* at Conakry and Kankan, and a *juge de paix* at Nzérékoré. The High Court, Court of Appeal and Superior Tribunal of Cassation are at Conakry.

Religion. In 1989 there were 5·7m Moslems.

Education. In 1987–88, 290,000 pupils and 7,239 teachers in primary schools, 76,000 pupils and 3,600 teachers in secondary schools, 4,700 students in technical schools and 1,200 in teacher-training colleges and 5,915 in higher education.

Health. In 1976 there were 314 hospitals and dispensaries with 7,650 beds; there were also 277 doctors, 21 dentists, 159 pharmacists, 394 midwives and 1,533 nursing personnel.

DIPLOMATIC REPRESENTATIVES

Of Guinea in Great Britain (resides in Paris)
Ambassador: (Vacant).

Of Great Britain in Guinea
Ambassador: R. C. Beetham, LVO (resides in Dakar).

Of Guinea in the USA (2112 Leroy Pl., NW, Washington, D.C., 20008)
Ambassador: (Vacant).

Of the USA in Guinea (2nd Blvd. and 9th Ave., Conakry)
Ambassador: Dane F. Smith.

Of Guinea to the United Nations
Ambassador: Zainoul Abidine Sanoussi.

Further Reading

Bulletin Statistique et Economique de la Guinée. Monthly. Conakry
Adamolekun, L., *Sékou Touré's Guinea*. London, 1976
Camara, S. S., *La Guinée sans la France*. Paris, 1976
Taylor, F. W., *A Fulani-English Dictionary*. Oxford, 1932

GUINEA-BISSAU

Capital: Bissau
Population: 966,000 (1990)
GNP per capita: US$180 (1989)

Republica da Guiné-Bissau

HISTORY. Guinea-Bissau, formerly Portuguese Guinea, on the coast of Guinea, was discovered in 1446 by Nuno Tristão. It became a separate colony in 1879. It is bounded by the limits fixed by the convention of 12 May 1886 with France. In 1951 Guinea-Bissau became an overseas province of Portugal. The struggle against colonial rule began in 1963. Independence was declared on 24 Sept. 1973. In 1974 Portugal formally recognized the independence of Guinea-Bissau.

AREA AND POPULATION. Guinea-Bissau is bounded by Senegal in the north, the Atlantic ocean in the west and by Guinea in the east and south. It includes the adjacent archipelago of Bijagós. Area, 36,125 sq. km (13,948 sq. miles); population (census, 1979), 767,739, of whom 125,000 (estimate, 1988) resided in the capital, Bissau; (estimate, 1990) 966,000. Density, 26·7 per sq. km; 30% urban. Annual growth rate (1985–90), 2·1%; infant mortality, 132 per 1,000 live births; expectation of life, 45 years.

The areas and populations (census 1979) of the regions were as follows:

Region	Sq. km	Census 1979	Region	Sq. km	Census 1979
Bissau City	78	109,214	Gabú	9,150	104,315
Bafatá	5,981	116,032	Oio	5,403	135,114
Biombo	838	56,463	Quinara	3,138	35,532
Bolama-Bijagós	2,624	25,473	Tombali	3,736	55,099
Cacheu	5,175	130,227			

The main ethnic groups were (1979) the Balante (27%), Fulani (23%), Malinké 12%), Mandjako (11%) and Pepel (10%). Portuguese remains the official language, but Crioulo is spoken throughout the country.

CLIMATE. The tropical climate has a wet season from June to Nov., when rains are abundant, but the hot, dry Harmattan wind blows from Dec. to May. Bissau. Jan. 76°F (24·4°C), July 80°F (26·7°C). Annual rainfall 78" (1,950 mm).

CONSTITUTION AND GOVERNMENT. A new Constitution was promulgated on 16 May 1984. The Revolutionary Council, established following the 1980 coup, was replaced by a 15-member Council of State, while in April 1984 a new National People's Assembly was elected comprising 150 Representatives elected by and from the directly-elected regional councils. The sole political movement was the *Partido Africano da Independencia da Guiné e Cabo Verde* (PAIGC), but in Dec. 1990 a policy of 'integral multi-partyism' was announced, and in May 1991 the National Assembly voted unanimously to abolish the law making the PAIGC the sole party. The President is Head of State and Government, leading a Council of Ministers which in Oct. 1991 was composed as follows:

President: Brig-Gen. João Bernardo Vieira.
Ministers of State: Col. Iafai Camara *(Armed Forces)*, Dr Vasco Cabral *(Justice)*, Carlos Correia *(Rural Development and Fisheries)*, Tiago Alelua Lopes *(Presidency)*.
Foreign Affairs: Júlio Semedo. *Education, Culture and Sports:* Dr Fidelis Cabral d'Almada. *Commerce and Tourism:* Maj. Manuel dos Santos. *Public Works:* Avito da Silva. *National Security and Public Order:* Maj. José Pereira. *Natural Resources and Industry:* Filinto de Barros. *Finance:* Dr Vítor Freire Monteiro. *Public Health:* Adelino Nunes Correia. *Planning:* (Vacant). *Civil Service and Labour:* Henriqueta Godinho Gomes. *Information and Telecommunications:* Mussa Djassi. *Minister-Governor of Central Bank:* Dr Pedro A. Godinho Gomes.
There are 11 Secretaries of State.

National flag: Horizontally yellow over green with red vertical strip in the hoist bearing a black star.

Local government: The administrative division is in 8 regions (each under an elected regional council), in turn subdivided into 37 sectors; and the city of Bissau, an autonomous sector treated as a separate region.

DEFENCE

Army. The Army consisted in 1991 of 1 artillery and 5 infantry battalions, 1 engineer unit and 1 tank squadron. Equipment includes 10 T-34 tanks. Personnel, 6,800.

Navy. The naval flotilla, based at Bissau, is equipped with 11 inshore patrol craft of diverse origins; Soviet, Chinese and European. Personnel in 1991 totalled 300 officers and men.

Air Force. Formation of a small Air Force began in 1978 with the delivery of a French-built Cessna FTB-337 twin-engined counter-insurgency and general-purpose light transport. It has been followed by 2 Alouette III helicopters and 2 Dornier Do 27 utility aircraft. Personnel (1991) 100.

INTERNATIONAL RELATIONS

Membership. Guinea-Bissau is a member of the UN, OAU and is an ACP state of the EEC.

ECONOMY

Policy. The Development Plan ending 1990 aimed at self-sufficiency in food.

Budget. The budget for 1985 balanced at 1,000m. pesos.

Currency. The monetary unit is the *peso* (GWP) of 100 *centavos*. There are coins of 50 *centavos* and 1, 2, 5 and 20 *pesos*, and banknotes of 50, 100, 500 and 1,000 *pesos*. In March 1992, £1 = 8,770·00 *pesos*; US$1 = 4,995·73 *pesos*.

Banking and Finance. The Banco Nacional da Guiné-Bissau, founded 1976, is the bank of issue and also the commercial bank. There are also state-owned savings institutions.

ENERGY AND NATURAL RESOURCES

Electricity. Production (1986) 28m. kwh.

Minerals. Mining is very little developed although bauxite (200m. tonnes) has been located in the Boé area.

Agriculture. Chief crops (production, 1990, in 1,000 tonnes) are: Groundnuts, 30; sugar-cane, 6; plantains, 25; coconuts, 25; rice, 160; palm kernels, 8; millet, 20; palm-oil, 4·5; sorghum, 40; maize, 24; cashew nuts, 10; timber, hides, seeds and wax.

Livestock (1990): Cattle, 340,000; sheep, 205,000; goats, 210,000; pigs, 290,000; poultry, 1m.

Forestry. Production (1985) 559,000 cu. metres. 33% of the country is forested.

Fisheries. Total catch (1986) 3,620 tonnes. Fishing is an important export industry.

FOREIGN ECONOMIC RELATIONS. Foreign debt totalled approximately US$423m. in 1989.

Commerce. Imports in 1983, 1,586m. pesos of which 33% from Portugal; exports, 358m. of which 66% went to Portugal, 11% to Senegal and 10% to Guinea. In 1980, fish formed 33% of exports, groundnuts, 24% and coconuts, 17%.

Total trade between Guinea-Bissau and UK (British Department of Trade returns, in £1,000 sterling):

	1987	1988	1989	1990	1991
Imports to UK	17	22	29	833	36
Exports and re-exports from UK	1,152	925	1,185	924	1,201

COMMUNICATIONS

Roads. There were (1982) 5,058 km of roads and 4,100 vehicles.

Aviation. There is an international airport serving Bissau at Bissalanca.

Shipping. The main port is Bissau; minor ports are Boloma, Cacheu and Catió. In 1985 vessels entering the ports unloaded 129,000 tonnes.

Telecommunications. In 1986 there were 3,000 telephones and 26,000 radio receivers.

Cinemas. There were 4 cinemas (1988) with a seating capacity of 950.

Newspapers (1984). There was one weekly newspaper, with a circulation of 3,000.

RELIGION, EDUCATION AND WELFARE

Religion. In 1985 about 30% of the population were Moslem and about 5% Christian (mainly Roman Catholic).

Education. There were, in 1984, 81,444 pupils in 658 primary schools with 3,153 teachers; 11,710 pupils in 12 secondary schools with 718 teachers and 1,027 students in 4 technical schools and teacher-training establishments with 107 teachers.

Health. In 1981 there were 17 hospitals and clinics with 1,570 beds and in 1980 there were 108 doctors, 2 dentists, 3 pharmacists, 2 midwives and 56 nursing personnel.

DIPLOMATIC REPRESENTATIVES

Of Guinea-Bissau in Great Britain (resides in Brussels)
Ambassador: (Vacant).

Of Great Britain in Guinea-Bissau
Ambassador: R. C. Beetham, LVO (resides in Dakar).

Of Guinea-Bissau in the USA
Ambassador: Alfredo Lopes Cabral.

Of the USA in Guinea-Bissau (Ave. Domingos Ramos, Bissau)
Ambassador: William L. Jacobsen, Jr.

Of Guinea-Bissau to the United Nations
Ambassador: Boubacar Toure.

Further Reading

Relatório e Mapas do Movimento Comercial e Maritimo da Guiné. Bolama, Annual
Cabral, A., *Revolution in Guinea.* London, 1969.—*Return to the Source.* New York, 1973
Davidson, B., *Growing from the Grass Roots.* London, 1974
Galli, R., *Guinea-Bissau:* [Bibliography]. Oxford and Santa Barbara, 1991
Gjerstad, O. and Sarrazin, C., *Sowing the First Harvest: National Reconstruction in Guinea-Bissau.* Oakland, 1978
Rudebeck, L., *Guinea-Bissau: A Study of Political Mobilization.* Uppsala, 1974

GUYANA

Capital: Georgetown
Population: 990,000 (1989)
GNP per capita: US$310 (1989)

Co-operative Republic of Guyana

HISTORY. The territory, including the counties of Demerara, Essequibo and Berbice, named from the 3 rivers, was first partially settled by the Dutch West Indian Company about 1620. The Dutch retained their hold until 1796, when it was captured by the English. It was finally ceded to Great Britain in 1814 and named British Guiana. On 26 May 1966 British Guiana became an independent member of the Commonwealth under the name of Guyana and the world's first Co-operative Republic on 23 Feb. 1970.

AREA AND POPULATION. Guyana is situated on the north-east coast of South America on the Atlantic ocean, with Suriname on the east, Venezuela on the west and Brazil on the south and west. Area, 83,000 sq. miles (214,969 sq. km). Estimated population (1989), 990,000. The official language is English, and in 1980 the population comprised 51% (East) Indians, 30% Africans, 10% mixed race, 5% Amerindian and 4% others. The capital is Georgetown, whose metropolitan area had 188,000 inhabitants in 1983; other towns are New Amsterdam, Linden, Rose Hall and Corriverton.

Vital statistics (1988): Birth rate 26·1%; death rate 8%.

Venezuela demanded the return of the Essequibo region in 1963. It was finally agreed in March 1983 that the UN Secretary-General should mediate. There was also an unresolved claim (1984) by Suriname for the return of an area between the New river and the Corentyne river.

CLIMATE. A tropical climate, with rainy seasons from April to July and Nov. to Jan. Humidity is high all the year but temperatures are moderated by sea-breezes. Rainfall increases from 90" (2,280 mm) on the coast to 140" (3,560 mm) in the forest zone. Georgetown. Jan. 79°F (26·1°C), July 81°F (27·2°C). Annual rainfall 87" (2,175 mm).

CONSTITUTION AND GOVERNMENT. A new Constitution was promulgated in Oct. 1980. The National Assembly consists of 65 elected members. Elections are held under the single-list system of proportional representation, with the whole of the country forming one electoral area and each voter casting his vote for a party list of candidates. The legislature is elected for 5 years unless earlier dissolved.

The elections held on 9 Dec. 1985 gave the People's National Congress 42 seats, the People's Progressive Party 8 seats, the United Force 2 seats and the Working People's Alliance 1 seat.

The Cabinet was in Nov. 1991 composed as follows:

President: H. Desmond Hoyte (b.1929).
First Vice-President and Prime Minister: Hamilton Green.
Vice-President, Deputy Prime Minister, Culture and Social Affairs: Viola Burnham. *Attorney-General:* Keith Massiah. *Deputy Prime Ministers:* Robert H. O. Corbin (*Public Utilities*); William H. Parris (*Planning and Development*). *Foreign Affairs:* Rashleigh Jackson. *Finance:* Carl Greenidge. *Travel and Tourism:* Winston Murray.

National flag: Green with a yellow triangle based on the hoist, edged in white, charged with a red triangle edged in black.

National anthem: Dear land of Guyana (words by A. L. Luker, tune by R. Potter).

Local government: There are 10 administrative regions: Barima/Waini, Pomeroon/Supernaam, Essequibo Islands/West Demerara, Demerara/Mahaica, Mahaica/Berbice, East Berbice/Corentyne, Cuyuni/Mazaruni, Potaro/Siparuni, Upper Takutu/Upper Essequibo, Upper Demerara/Berbice.

DEFENCE

Army. The Guyana Army had (1991) a strength of 5,100. It comprises 2 infantry, 1 guards, 1 special forces, 1 support weapons and 1 engineer battalions.

Navy. The Maritime Corps is an integral part of the Guyana Defence Force. In 1991 it had 100 personnel and comprised 1 fast inshore patrol craft, a number of armed boats and a utility landing craft.

Air Force. The Air Command has no combat aircraft. It is equipped with light aircraft and helicopters, including 1 Super King Air 200 twin-turboprop transport, 6 Islander twin-engined STOL transports, a Cessna U206F utility lightplane, and 4 Bell 206/212/412 and 2 Mi-8 helicopters. Personnel (1991) 300.

INTERNATIONAL RELATIONS

Membership. Guyana is a member of the UN, Commonwealth, CARICOM, the Non-Aligned Movement and is an ACP state of the EEC.

ECONOMY

Policy. State control is being reduced, and some 30 enterprises were scheduled for privatization in 1991.

Budget. Revenue and expenditure for calendar years (in G$1,000):

	1984	1985	1986	1987	1988	1989
Revenue	1,537,928	1,200,208	1,667,708	2,004,391	2,296,587	7,012,345
Expenditure	1,585,840	1,562,858	2,551,380	2,976,517	3,528,120	8,796,129

Currency. The unit of currency is the *Guyana dollar* (GYD) of 100 *cents.* There are notes of $1, 5, 10, 20 and 100 and coins of 1-, 5-, 10-, 25- and 50-cent pieces. In March 1992: £1 = 212·70 G$; US$1 = 121·16 G$.

Banking and Finance. The bank of issue is the Bank of Guyana. Of the 5 commercial banks operating in Guyana 2 are foreign-owned (Bank of Baroda and Bank of Nova Scotia) and 3 locally controlled (Guyana National Co-operative Bank, the National Bank of Industry and Commerce and the Republic Bank). The Guyana Agricultural and Industrial Development Bank (Gaibank) for farmers and agri-based industries and the Guyana Co-operative Mortgage Finance Bank for housing. Barclays Bank plc became Guyana Bank of Trade and Commerce in 1988.

ENERGY AND NATURAL RESOURCES

Electricity. Production (1986) 500m. kwh. Supply 110 volts; 60 Hz and 240 volts; 50 Hz.

Minerals. Placer gold mining commenced in 1884, and was followed by diamond mining in 1887. Output of gold was 18,803 oz. in 1988. Production of diamonds was 36,717 stones in 1988. Total production of the 4 grades of bauxite (calcined, chemical, metallurgical and abrasive) was 1·39m. tonnes in 1988. Full-scale production of manganese began in 1960 and other minerals include uranium, oil, copper and molybdenum.

Agriculture. Production, 1989: Sugar, 164,800 tonnes (154,000 tonnes in 1990); rice, 133,900 tonnes. Important products are coconuts, 30,800 tonnes, 1989 and citrus, 7·4m. tonnes. Other tropical fruits and vegetables are grown mostly in scattered plantings; they include mangoes, papaws, avocado pears, melons, bananas and gooseberries. Other important crops are tomatoes, cabbages, black-eye peas, peanuts, carrots, onions, turmeric, ginger, pineapples, red kidney beans, soybeans, eschallot and tobacco. Large areas of unimproved land in the coastal region, which vary in width up to about 30 miles from the sea, are still available for agricultural and cattle-grazing projects.

Livestock estimate (1990): Cattle, 210,000; pigs, 185,000; sheep, 120,000; goats, 77,000; poultry, 15m.

Forestry. In 1988, 16·4m. hectares of the land area (83%) was forested. Production (1986) 4·7m. cu. ft.

Fisheries. Production (1989) of fish, 40,300 tons and shrimp, 1,872 tons.

FOREIGN ECONOMIC RELATIONS

Commerce. In 1986 imports were worth G$1,618m. and exports G$1,092m. Exports were worth US$237m. in 1989.

Chief imports (1983): Fuel and lubricants, 19,367,367 kg, $272,513,835; milk, 1,386,887 kg, $8,674,714.

Chief domestic exports (1983): Sugar, 210,734 tonnes, $195,814,993; rice, 41,721 tonnes, $64,939,971; bauxite, dried, 779,768 tonnes, $66,629,072; bauxite, calcined, 340,709 tonnes, $136,201,592; alumina, 29,301 tonnes, $7,019,133; rum, 20,442,180 litres, $6,987,107; timber, 49,720 cu. metres, $10,837,689; molasses, 53,938,864 litres, $2,019,371; shrimps, 7,318,145 kg, $14,067,860.

Imports (exclusive of transhipments), 1981, from CARICOM Territories, 35%; from USA, 25%; from UK, 16%; from Canada, 4%; exports (exclusive of transhipments) to UK, 26%; to CARICOM Territories, 17%; to Canada, 5%.

Total trade between Guyana and UK (British Department of Trade returns, in £1,000 sterling):

	1987	1988	1989	1990	1991
Imports to UK	58,502	43,518	54,523	53,892	50,479
Exports and re-exports from UK	15,371	10,590	13,216	15,294	19,275

COMMUNICATIONS

Roads. Roads and vehicular trails in the national, provincial and urban systems amount to 8,870 km. Motor vehicles, as of 31 Dec. 1987, totalled 53,446, including 8,401 passenger cars, 3,682 lorries and vans, 8,958 tractors and trailers, and 15,893 motor cycles. The main road on the Atlantic Coast, some 290 km (180 miles) long extends from Charity on the Pomeroon River to Crabwood Creek on the Corentyne, there are two unbridged gaps made by the Berbice and Essequibo Rivers, and the banks of the Demerara River are linked by a 1,853 metre (6,074 ft) floating bridge.

Railways. There is a government-owned railway in the North West District, while the Guyana Mining Enterprise operates a standard gauge railway of 133 km from Linden on the Demerara River to Ituni and Coomacka.

Civil Aviation. Guyana Airways Corporation operates 11 flights weekly on its international service and 21 flights locally. In 1985 Guyana Airways Corporation carried 108,936 passengers on its international service and 59,113 passengers locally. Other services in operation: British Airways 4 times weekly to the Caribbean, Europe and North America: PANAM 3 times weekly to North, Central and South America: Air France, to and from Guadeloupe, Paramaribo and Cayenne 4 times a week; British West Indian Airways, Ltd, to and from Trinidad twice a week, providing direct connexion with New York and London; Cubana Airlines once a fortnight; Suriname Airways and Tropical Airways once weekly. The International Airport at Timehri serves Arrow Air Airlines, BWIA, Cubana Airways, and Suriname Airways.

Shipping. There are 217 nautical miles of river navigation. There are ferry services across the mouths of the Demerara, Berbice and Essequibo rivers, the last providing a link between the islands of Leguan and Wakenaam and the mainland at Adventure, and a number of coastal and river-boat services carrying both passengers and cargo. A number of launch services are operated in the more remote areas by private concerns.

Georgetown harbour, about ¹/₂ mile wide and 2¹/₂ miles long, has a minimum depth of 24 ft. New Amsterdam harbour is situated at the mouth of the Berbice River; there are wharves for coastal vessels only. Bauxite is loaded on ocean-going freighters at Mackenzie, 67 miles up the Demerara River, and at Everton on the Berbice River, about 10 miles from the mouth of the waterway. The Essequibo River has several timber-loading berths ranging from 20 to 40 ft. Springlands on the Corentyne River is the point of entry and departure of passengers travelling by launch services to and from Suriname. In 1984 the merchant marine comprised 84 vessels of 20,248 GRT.

Telecommunications. The inland public telegraph and radio communication services are operated and maintained by the Telecommunication Corporation. On 31 Aug. 1988 there were 57 post offices and 28 agencies.

The telephone exchanges had at 31 Aug. 1988 a total of 28,450 direct exchange lines with (1988), 20,000 telephone instruments. The number of route miles in the coastal and inland areas was 2,982 km. 39 land-line stations were maintained at post offices in the coastal area, and 8 telegraph stations in the interior provide communication with the coastal area through a central telegraph office in Georgetown.

The Guyana Broadcasting Corporation, which came into operation on 1 July 1980, has 2 channels. In 1991 there were 307,467 radio and about 40,000 TV receivers (colour by NTSC). Guyana Television is government-controlled and there are 2 private stations relaying US satelite services.

Cinemas (1989). There are 51 cinemas.

Newspapers (1989). There is 1 daily newspaper with a circulation of 60,000, 1 twice-weekly paper with an estimated circulation of 40,000 and 4 weekly papers with a combined circulation of 40,000.

JUSTICE, RELIGION, EDUCATION AND WELFARE

Justice. The law, both civil and criminal, is based on the common and statute law of England, save that the principles of the Roman–Dutch law have been retained in respect of the registration, conveyance and mortgaging of land.

The Supreme Court of Judicature consists of a Court of Appeal and a High Court.

Religion. In 1980, 34% of the population were Hindu, 34% Protestant, 18% Roman Catholic and 9% Moslem.

Education. In Sept. 1976 the Government assumed total responsibility for education from nursery school to university. Private education was abolished. In Sept. 1988, the total number of schools was 866: Nursery, 351; primary, 432; community high, 37; general secondary, 55.

There are now 3 technical and vocational schools and 2 schools for the teaching of home economics and domestic crafts. Training in co-operatives is provided by the Kuru-Kuru Co-operative College and agriculture by the Guyana School of Agriculture and there is one teacher training complex, the Cyril Potter College of Education. In 1986-87 there were 6,440 students at these post-secondary institutions. Higher education is also provided by the University of Guyana which was established in 1963 with faculties of medicine, natural science, social science, art, technology and education as well as first year students in law. There were 2,250 students in 1987–88. The total number of pupils in all schools was 211,315 in 1986-87.

Health. In 1989 there were 213 health facilities including hospitals. There were (1989) 111 doctors, 15 dentists, 29 pharmacists, 172 midwives and 854 nursing personnel.

DIPLOMATIC REPRESENTATIVES

Of Guyana in Great Britain (3 Palace Ct., London, W2 4LP)
High Commissioner: Cecil S. Pilgrim (accredited 5 Dec. 1986).

Of Great Britain in Guyana (44 Main St., Georgetown)
High Commissioner: R. D. Gordon.

Of Guyana in the USA (2490 Tracy Pl., NW, Washington, D.C., 20008)
Ambassador: Dr Cedric Hilburn Grant.

Of the USA in Guyana (31 Main St., Georgetown)
Ambassador: (Vacant).

Of Guyana to the United Nations
Ambassador: Samuel R. Insanally.

Further Reading

Baber, C. and Jeffrey, H. B., *Guyana: Politics, Economics and Society.* London, 1986
Braveboy-Wagner, J. A., *The Venezuela-Guyana Border Dispute: Britain's Colonial Legacy in Latin America.* London, 1984
Chambers, F., *Guyana.* [Bibliography] Oxford and Santa Barbara, 1989
Daly, P. H., *From Revolution to Republic.* Georgetown, 1970
Daly, V. T., *A Short History of the Guyanese People.* 3rd. ed. London, 1992
Hope, K. R., *Development Policy in Guyana: Planning, Finance and Administration.* London, 1979
Latin American Bureau, *Guyana: Fraudulent Revolution.* London, 1984
Sanders, A., *The Powerless People.* London, 1987
Spinner, T. J., *A Political and Social History of Guyana, 1945–83.* Epping, 1985
Williams, B. F., *Stains on My Name, War in My Veins: Guyana and the Politics of Cultural Struggle.* Duke Univ. Press, 1992

HAITI

Capital: Port-au-Prince
Population: 5·69m. (1990)
GNP per capita: US$400 (1989)

République d'Haïti

HISTORY. Haiti occupies the western third of the large island of Hispaniola which was discovered by Christopher Columbus in 1492. The Spanish colony was ceded to France in 1697 and became her most prosperous colony. After the extirpation of the Indians by the Spaniards (by 1533) large numbers of African slaves were imported whose descendants now populate the country. The slaves obtained their liberation following the French Revolution, but Napoleon restored French authority and imprisoned Toussaint Louverture, the leader of the slaves who had been appointed a French general and governor. Subsequently the French surrendered to a blockading British squadron.

The country declared its independence on 1 Jan. 1804, and its successful leader, Gen. Jean-Jacques Dessalines, proclaimed himself Emperor of the newly-named Haiti. After the assassination of Dessalines (1806) a separate régime was set up in the north under Henri Christophe, a Black general who in 1811 had himself proclaimed King Henry. In the south and west a republic was constituted, with Alexander Pétion as its first President. Pétion died in 1818 and was succeeded by Jean-Pierre Boyer, under whom the country became re-united after Henry had committed suicide in 1820. From 1822 to 1844 Haiti and the eastern part of the island (later the Dominican Republic) were united. After one more monarchical interlude, under the Emperor Faustin (1847–59), Haiti has been a republic. From 1915 to 1934 Haiti was under United States occupation.

Following a military coup in 1950, and subsequent uprisings, Dr François Duvalier was elected President on 22 Oct. 1957 and subsequently became president for life in 1964. He died on 21 April 1971 and was succeeded as president for life by his son, Jean-Claude Duvalier who fled the country on 7 Feb. 1986. Gen. Henry Namphy formed a Council of Government. In Jan. 1988 Leslie Manigat was elected president, but Namphy again seized power in June 1988. In Sept. 1988 he was deposed and replaced by the military government of Lieut.-Gen. Prosper Avril. In March 1990 Ertha Pascal-Trouillot became head of an interim government. Father Jean-Bertrand Aristide was elected president in Dec. 1990

On 1 Oct. 1991 President Aristide was deposed in a military coup and went into exile abroad. On 7 Oct. soldiers stormed the parliament building and forced the deputies to nominate Supreme Court Judge Joseph Nerette as interim president. Under the aegis of the OAS in Feb. 1992 President Aristide and representatives of the Senate and National Assembly reached agreement on the formation of a new government led by René Théodore and his own reinstatement.

AREA AND POPULATION. The area is 27,750 sq. km (10,700 sq. miles), of which about three-quarters is mountainous. The population at the census in 1982 was 5,053,792 of which 21% were urban and 48·5% male. Estimate (1990) 5,690,000, of which 28% were urban. Population density, 205 per sq. km. Infant mortality, 1990, 91·5 per 1,000 live births. Expectation of life, 55·7 years.

The areas and populations of the 9 departments:

Département	Sq. km	1988	Chief town	1988
Nord-Ouest	2,094	326,361	Port-de-Paix	135,374
Nord	2,175	610,282	Cap Haïtien	133,233
Nord-Est	1,698	199,336	Fort-Liberté	34,043
L'Artibonite	4,895	801,115	Gonaïves	144,081
Centre	3,597	406,608	Hinche	122,003
Ouest	4,595	1,869,805	Port-au-Prince	1,143,626
Sud-Est	2,077	393,554	Jacmel	216,600
Sud	2,602	531,255	Les Cayes	214,606
Grande Anse	3,100	519,808	Jérémie	152,081

The Île de la Gonâve, some 40 miles long, lies in the gulf of the same name. Among other islands is La Tortue, off the north peninsula. Most of the population is of African or mixed origin.

The official language is French, but 90% of the people speak Créole.

CLIMATE. A tropical climate, but the central mountains can cause semi-arid conditions in their lee. There are rainy seasons from April to June and Aug. to Nov. Hurricanes and severe thunderstorms can occur. The annual temperature range is small. Port-au-Prince. Jan. 77°F (25°C), July 84°F (28·9°C). Annual rainfall 53" (1,321 mm).

CONSTITUTION AND GOVERNMENT. The 1987 Constitution, ratified by a referendum, provides for a bicameral legislature (*Chamber of Deputies, Senate*), and an executive *President*.

At the presidential, parliamentary and local elections of Dec. 1990 the electorate was some 3m.; turn-out was estimated at 55% by international observers. Father Jean-Bertrand Aristide (b. 1957) was elected president by about 66% of votes cast. He was sworn in on 7 Feb. 1991.

Following the coup of 1 Oct. 1991 Joseph Nerette was sworn in as interim president on 8 Oct. He named Jean-Jacques Honorat (b. 1931) *Prime Minister*; the latter formed a government including himself as *Foreign and Defence Minister* and Col. Garcia Jean as *Interior Minister*.

National flag: Horizontally blue over red with the national arms on a white panel in the centre.

National anthem: 'La Dessalinienne': Pour le pays, pour les ancêtres ('For the country, for the ancestors'; words by J. Lhérisson; tune by N. Geffrard, 1903).

DEFENCE. The Haitian Defence Force (*Forces Armées d'Haiti*) totalling about 7,400 is divided into Army, Navy, and Air Force. The President is Commander-in-Chief and appoints the officers.

Army. Total strength, about 7,000 (1992), organized into 9 military departments. Three of the Departments are in Port-au-Prince and consist of the Presidential Guard, 1 infantry battalion, 1 airport security company, 2 artillery battalions and 6 artillery elements.

Navy. The Coast Guard of (1991) 250 personnel operates 1 offshore patrol craft and some boats; all are based at Port-au-Prince.

Air Force. Personnel strength was (1992) about 150. Aircraft include 7 Summit/ Cessna O2-337 Sentry twin piston-engined counter-insurgency aircraft, 1 DC-3, 6 light transports, 10 training and liaison aircraft, including 4 turboprop-powered SF.260 TPs.

INTERNATIONAL RELATIONS

Membership. Haiti is a member of the UN and OAS and is an ACP state of the EEC.

ECONOMY

Budget. The budget for the fiscal year ending 30 Sept. 1991 was 1,350m. gourdes.

Currency. The unit of currency is the *gourde* (HTG) of 100 *centimes*. Its value is fixed at 5 gourdes = US$1. There are copper–nickel coins for 50, 20, 10 and 5 centimes and copper–zinc–nickel coins of 10 and 5 centimes. Money in circulation in 1989, 1,459m. gourdes. In March 1992, £1 = 8·77 gourdes.

Banking and Finance. Banque Nationale de Credit, owned by the State, was established in 1982. US dollars may be included in the minimum required reserves. The Citibank, the Bank of Nova Scotia, the Bank of Boston, the Banque de l'Union Haïtienne (mainly local capital with participation from American, Canadian and Dominican Republic Banks), Banque Nationale de Paris and SOGEBANK (formerly the Royal Bank of Canada, now Haitian-owned) have branches. The Banque Nationale de la République d'Haïti is the central bank and bank of issue. Total bank deposits were 1,175m. gourdes in 1989.

Weights and Measures. The metric system and British imperial and US measures are in use.

ENERGY AND NATURAL RESOURCES

Electricity. Production (1988) 337m. kwh. Supply 110 and 220 volts; 60 Hz.

Minerals. Copper exists but is at present uneconomic to exploit. Haiti may possess undeveloped mineral resources of oil, gold, silver, antimony, sulphur, coal and lignite, nickel, gypsum and porphyry.

Agriculture. The agricultural area is 1·4m. ha, of which 0·91m. ha are cultivated and 0·49m. ha pasture. Some 90% of the population, mainly smallholders, make a living by agriculture carried on in 7 large plains, from 200,000 to 25,000 acres, and in 15 smaller plains down to 2,000 acres. Irrigation is used in some areas. Haiti's most important product is coffee of good quality, classified as 'mild'. Production in 1989 totalled about 38,400 tonnes. The second most important crop is sugar-cane, used to make sugar and spirits. Sisal is grown for export and for cordage. Cotton and rice are also grown. Essential oils from vetiver, neroli and amyris are an important product. Output in 1989 (in 1,000 tonnes): Plantains, 499; sorghum, 142; rice, 119; beans, 57; cocoa, 5; and in 1988: Sugar-cane, 3,000; mangoes, 355; maize, 145; bananas, 230; sisal, 5; cotton, 6; sweet potatoes, 300.

Livestock (1988); Cattle, 1,605,000; sheep, 96,000; goats, 1,274,000; horses, 435,000; pigs, 950,000; poultry, 15m.

Forestry. The forest area was 50,000 ha in 1990.

Fisheries. Production (1986) 8,000 tonnes.

INDUSTRY. Light manufacturing industries assembling or finishing goods (mainly clothing, leather goods and electrical/electronic components) for re-export constitute the fastest growing sector. Soap factories produce laundry soap, toilet soap and detergent. A cement factory located near the capital produced 265,000 tonnes in 1987. A steel plant making rods, beams and angles was opened in 1974. There are also a pharmaceutical plant, a tannery, a plastics plant, 2 paint works, 5 shoe factories, a large factory producing enamel cookingware, 2 pastamaking factories, a tomato cannery and a flour-mill, all located in or near Port-au-Prince.

FOREIGN ECONOMIC RELATIONS

Commerce. In 1989 exports were US$184m. and imports, US$314m. The leading imports are petroleum products, foodstuffs, textiles, machinery, animal and vegetable oils, chemicals, pharmaceuticals, raw materials for transformation industries and vehicles.

Total trade between Haiti and UK (British Department of Trade returns, in £1,000 sterling):

	1987	1988	1989	1990	1991
Imports to UK	621	844	803	1,271	1,253
Exports and re-exports from UK	5,327	6,760	6,566	6,807	7,280

Tourism. In 1989, 68,000 tourists visited Haiti.

COMMUNICATIONS

Roads. Total length of roads is some 4,000 km, little of which is practicable in ordinary motors in the rainy season. There were (1984) about 50,000 vehicles.

Railways. The only railway is owned by the Haitian American Sugar Company.

Civil Aviation. An airport capable of handling jets was opened at Port-au-Prince in 1965. US and French carriers provide daily direct services to New York, Miami, Jamaica, Puerto Rico and the French Antilles. There are also services to the Dominican Republic and the Netherlands Antilles. A Haitian company provides a cargo service to the US and Puerto Rico. Air services connecting Port-au-Prince with other Haitian towns are operated by Haiti Air Inter.

Shipping. US, French, German, Dutch, British, Canadian and Japanese lines connect Haiti with the USA, Latin America (except Cuba), Canada, Jamaica, Europe and the Far East.

Telecommunications. Most principal towns are connected by the government telegraph system, telephones and wireless. The telephone company, of which the Haitian Government is now the majority stockholder, is in process of being modernized. Telephone subscribers totalled 34,000 in 1984.

The government-controlled Conseil National des Télécommunications and Télévision Nationale d'Haiti broadcast radio and TV programmes (colour by NTSC). There were 135,000 radio and 25,000 TV sets in 1991.

Cinemas (1984). There were 10 cinemas in Port-au-Prince.

Newspapers (1989). There were 6 daily newspapers in Port-au-Prince, also a monthly in English and 1 weekly newspaper in Cap Haïtien.

JUSTICE, RELIGION, EDUCATION AND WELFARE

Justice. Judges, both of the lower courts and the court of appeal, are appointed by the President. The legal system is basically French. The divorce law has recently been amended to permit parties to obtain 'quick and painless' divorces at a moderate cost, in the hope of attracting the US trade, now that the Mexican 'divorce mills' have closed down. This has developed a useful flow of dollar revenue.

Police. The Police number about 1,200 in Port-au-Prince and are part of the armed forces.

Religion. Since the Concordat of 1860, the official religion is Roman Catholicism, under an archbishop with 5 suffragan bishops. There are still quite a number of foreigners, French and French Canadians mainly, among the clergy but the first Haitian archbishop took office in 1966. The Episcopal Church now has its first Haitian bishop who was consecrated in 1971. Other Christian churches number perhaps 10% of the population. The folk religion is Voodoo.

Education. Education is divided into primary (6 years, compulsory), secondary (7 years) and university/higher education. The school system is based on the French system and instruction is in French. In 1990 Educational Reform calling for basic schooling (9 years, compulsory) using Creole and French, with a 3-year secondary cycle, was being implemented.

In 1988 primary schools had 24,800 teachers and 983,000 pupils and 455 secondary schools had 8,400 teachers and 177,000 pupils.

Higher education is offered at the University of Haiti with 5,000 students in 1988.

Health. There were, in 1989, 944 doctors and 98 dentists in practice, and 87 hospitals and health centres with 4,566 beds.

DIPLOMATIC REPRESENTATIVES

Of Haiti in Great Britain. The Embassy closed on 30 March 1987.

Of Great Britain in Haiti
Ambassador: D. F. Milton, CMG (resides in Kingston).

Of Haiti in the USA (2311 Massachusetts Ave., NW, Washington, D.C., 20008)
Ambassador: Louis Harold Joseph.

Of the USA in Haiti (Harry Truman Blvd., Port-au-Prince)
Ambassador: Alvin P. Adams, Jr.

Of Haiti to the United Nations
Ambassador: Fritz Longchamp.

Further Reading

The official gazette is *Le Moniteur.*

Revue Agricole d' Haïti. From 1946. Quarterly
Bellegarde, D., *Histoire du Peuple Haïtien*. Port-au-Prince, 1953
Chambers, F. J., *Haiti*. [Bibliography] Oxford and Santa Barbara, 1983
Ferguson, J., *Papa Doc, Baby Doc: Haiti and the Duvaliers*. Oxford, 1987
Laguerre, M. S., *The Complete Haitiana*. [Bibliography] London and New York, 1982.—
  Voodoo and Politics in Haiti. London, 1989
Lawless, R., *Haiti: a Research Guide*. New York, 1990
Lundahl, M., *The Haitian Economy: Man, Land and Markets*. London, 1983
Nicholls, D., *From Dessalines to Duvalier: Race, Colour and National Independence in Haiti.*
  CUP, rev., 1992.—*Haiti in Caribbean Context: Ethnicity, Economy and Revolt*. London,
  1985
Thomson, I., *Bonjour Blanc: a Journey through Haiti*. London, 1992
Weinstein, B. and Segal, A., *Haiti: the Failure of Politics*. New York, 1992
Wilentz, A., *The Rainy Season: Haiti since Duvalier*. New York, 1989

National Library: Bibliothèque Nationale, Rue du Centre, Port-au-Prince.

HONDURAS

Capital: Tegucigalpa
Population: 4·44m. (1988)
GNP per capita: US$530 (1990)

República de Honduras

HISTORY. Honduras celebrates 15 Sept. as the anniversary of its national independence from Spain in 1821. On 5 Nov. 1838 Honduras declared itself an independent sovereign state, free from the Federation of Central America, of which it had formed a part.

AREA AND POPULATION. Honduras is bounded in the north by the Caribbean, east and south-east by Nicaragua, west by Guatemala, south-west by El Salvador and south by the Pacific ocean. The area is 112,088 sq. km (43,277 sq. miles). At the Census of 1988 the population was 4,443,721 (2,237,498 female). 1·68m. of the population was urban in 1988. Population density, 37·2 per sq. km. in 1988.

The chief cities (populations in 1,000, 1988) were Tegucigalpa, the capital (678·7), San Pedro Sula (460·6), El Progreso (64·7), Choluteca (68·5), Danlí (20·2) and the Atlantic coast ports of La Ceiba (68·2), Puerto Cortés (43·3) and Tela (28·4); other towns include Olanchito (14·1), Juticalpa (14·3), Comayagua (32·9), Siguatepeque (27·7) and Santa Rosa de Copán (21·2).

Areas and 1988 census populations of the 18 departments and the Central District (Tegucigalpa):

Department	Sq. km	1988	Department	Sq. km	1988
Atlántida	4,251	238,742	Islas de la Bahía	261	22,062
Choluteca	4,211	295,484	La Paz	2,331	105,927
Colón	8,875	149,677	Lempira	4,290	177,055
Comayagua	5,196	239,859	Ocotepeque	1,680	74,276
Copán	3,203	219,455	Olancho	24,350	283,852
Cortés	3,954	662,772	Santa Bárbara	5,115	278,868
El Paraíso	7,218	254,295	Valle	1,565	119,645
Francisco Morazán	6,298	828,274	Yoro	7,939	333,508
Gracias a Dios	16,630	34,970	Central District	1,648	576,661
Intibucá	3,072	124,681			

The official language is Spanish. The Spanish-speaking population is of mixed Spanish and Amerindian descent. There are some 35,000 aborigines, mainly Miskito, Paya and Xicaque Indians with some African admixture.

Over the period 1974-88, population growth has averaged 3%: Infant mortality rate in 1985 was 70 per 1,000 live births; life expectancy, 62.

CLIMATE. The climate is tropical, with a small annual range of temperature but with high rainfall. Upland areas have two wet seasons, from May to July and in Sept. and Oct. The Caribbean Coast has most rain in Dec. and Jan. and temperatures are generally higher than inland. Tegucigalpa. Jan. 66°F (19°C), July 74°F (23·3°C). Annual rainfall 64" (1,621 mm).

CONSTITUTION AND GOVERNMENT. The Executive, Legislature and Judiciary have formally separate powers but the system is strongly Presidential in character. The present Constitution came into force in 1982.

The President is elected for a 4-year term. Members of the National Congress and municipal councillors are elected on a proportional basis, according to votes cast for the Presidential candidate of their party.

The Nov. 1989 election was won by Rafael Leonardo Callejas (sworn in on 27 Jan. 1990) for the National Party. The National Party gained 71 seats in the National Congress, the Liberals 55 and PINU-SD 2.

National flag: Three horizontal stripes of blue, white, blue, with 5 blue stars in the centre.

National anthem: Tu bandera ('Thy Banner'; words by A. C. Coello; tune by C. Hartling).

Local government: Honduras comprises a Central District (containing the cities of Tegucigalpa and Comayaguela) and 18 departments *'departamentos'*; (each administered by an appointed Governor), sub-divided into 289 municipalities.

DEFENCE. Conscription is for 24 months.

Army. The Army consists of 4 infantry and 1 artillery brigade and 1 engineer, 1 special forces and 1 air defence battalion. Equipment includes 12 Scorpion light tanks. Strength (1991) 15,600 (11,500 conscripts). There is also a paramilitary Public Security Force of 5,000 men.

Navy. A small flotilla operates 5 US-built fast inshore patrol craft, some 6 other inshore craft, 4 landing craft and a number of boats. Personnel (1991), 1,000, of whom 700 are conscripts, and the total includes 500 marines. Bases are at Puerto Cortés and Amapala.

Air Force. Equipment includes 12 F-5E/F Tiger IIs and a few F-86 fighters, 12 A-37B jet light attack aircraft, 4 Spanish-built CASA C-101BB armed jet trainers, 5 four-engined Douglas and Lockheed transports, 6 C-47, 4 Israeli-built Arava and 2 Westwind transports, about 30 helicopters and Tucano and T-41D trainers. Total strength was (1991) about 2,100 personnel (800 conscripts), of whom many are civilian maintenance staff.

INTERNATIONAL RELATIONS

Membership. Honduras is a member of the UN and OAS.

ECONOMY

Budget. Expenditure approved for 1990 was 3,504m. lempiras.
Total external debt (31 Dec. 1989) was US$3,300m.

Currency. The unit of the monetary system is the *lempira* (HNL) also known as a *peso*, comprising 100 *centavos*. Notes are issued by the Banco Central de Honduras which has the sole right to issue, in denominations of 100, 50, 20, 10, 5, 2 and 1 *lempiras*. Coins in circulation are 50 and 20 *centavos* in silver, 10 and 5 *centavos* in cupro-nickel and 2 and 1 *centavos* in copper. There was a devaluation of 50% in 1990.
Rate of exchange, March 1992: £1 = 9·58 *lempiras;* US$1 = 5·46 *lempiras.*

Banking. The central bank of issue is the Banco Central de Honduras. Sixteen other banks belong to the central clearing system. Banco Atlántida is the largest. Banco de Londres y Montreal has branches in Tegucigalpa, San Pedro Sula, Comayaguela and La Ceiba. Banco de Honduras is controlled by Citibank. The Central American Bank for Economic Integration (BCIE) has its head office in Tegucigalpa.

Weights and Measures. The metric system has been legal since 1 April 1897, although there are still some minor traces of the Imperial and old Spanish systems.

ENERGY AND NATURAL RESOURCES

Electricity. Production (1989) 1,886m. kwh. Supply 110 volts; 60 Hz. The El Cajón hydro-electric station at Rio Lindo serves the central and north coast areas. Capacity: 290 mw.

Minerals. Lead, zinc and silver are the main minerals exported.

Agriculture. Honduras is primarily an agricultural country, but only a quarter of the total land area is cultivated and by far the larger portion of this is on the Caribbean and Pacific coastal plains. The main agricultural crops are grains, bananas, coffee and sugar. Coffee production was 108,000 tonnes in 1989–90.
Livestock (1990): Cattle, 3,514,000; sheep, 8,000; pigs, 734,000; goats, 27,000; horses, 170,000; poultry, 8m.

Forestry. Forests in 1988 covered 31% of the total land area, but are not effectively exploited and deforestation is becoming a severe problem. Large stands of mahogany and other hard-woods—granadino, guayacán, walnut and rosewood—grow in the north-eastern part of the country, in the interior valleys, and near the southern coast. Stands of pine occur almost everywhere in the interior, but are severely damaged by bark beetle and fires.

Fisheries. Commercial fishing in territorial waters is restricted to Honduran nationals and Honduran-controlled companies. Shrimps and lobsters are important catches.

INDUSTRY. Small-scale local industries include beer and mineral waters, cement, flour, vegetable lard, coconut oil, sweets, cigarettes, cigars, textiles and clothing, panama hats, plastics, nails, matches, plywood, furniture, paper bags, soap, candles, fruit juices and household chemicals.

Labour. The workforce was (in 1,000) 1,218·2 in 1988, of whom 640·5 worked in agriculture, hunting and fishery; 160·6 in manufacturing; 117·5 in trade; 54·8 in building; 48·1 in transport and communications and 14·1 in finance. A 'Charter of Labour' was granted in Feb. 1955 and an advanced Labour Code and Social Security Bill passed into law in May 1959.

Trade Unions. The organization of trade unions was begun in 1954 with the assistance of ORIT (Inter-American Regional Organization) sponsored by the US trade unions. In 1988 there were 236 active trade unions with about 160,000 members.

FOREIGN ECONOMIC RELATIONS.

Commerce. Imports in 1986 were valued at 1,940m. lempiras and exports at 1,800m. lempiras.

Imports (1985) in 1m. lempiras: Fuel and lubricants, (1986) 565; consumer goods, 426; raw materials, 576; capital goods, 432.

Exports (1986) in 1m. lempiras: Bananas, 530; coffee, 612; timber, 74; refrigerated meats, 40; shrimp and lobster, 88.

Trade with main countries in 1m. lempiras (1986) was: USA, 1,518·8; Japan, 302·2; Federal Republic of Germany, 297·2; Italy, 157·1; Netherlands, 89; Belgium, 85·6; Spain, 55·2; UK, 49.

Total trade between Honduras and UK (British Department of Trade returns, in £1,000 sterling):

	1987	1988	1989	1990	1991
Imports to UK	4,703	8,295	12,121	11,661	9,065
Exports and re-exports from UK	10,449	7,891	5,518	7,345	6,784

Tourism. There were 218,253 foreign visitors in 1988; 154,880 Hondurans went abroad.

COMMUNICATIONS

Roads. Honduras is connected with Guatemala, El Salvador and Nicaragua by the Pan-American Highway. Out of a total of 18,494 km of road (1988), 2,262 were asphalted and 9,099 were unpaved but of all-weather construction. There are asphalted highways between Puerto Cortés in the north and Choluteca in the south passing through San Pedro Sula and Tegucigalpa with branches to Guatemala and El Salvador. In 1988 there were 129,115 motor vehicles.

Railways. The small railway system was built to serve the banana industry and is confined to the northern coastal region. it is run by a government agency. The total railways operating in 1986 were 955 km of 1,067 mm and 914 mm gauge, which carried 1m. passengers and 1·2m. tonnes of freight.

Civil Aviation. There are international airports at Tegucigalpa and San Pedro Sula and a domestic one at La Ceiba, with over 30 smaller airstrips in various parts of the country.

Shipping. Sailings to the Atlantic coast port of Puerto Cortés from Europe are frequent, mainly operated by the Harrison Line, Cia Generale Transatlantique, the Royal Netherlands Steamships Co., Hapag Lloyd and vessels owned or chartered by the Tela Railroad Co., a subsidiary of Chiquita International, and the Standard Fruit Co.

Telecommunications. Hondutel, a govenrment agency, had exchanges with a capacity of 121,000 lines in 1988. Some 66,000 telephones were in operation. The telegraph remains important and there were 364 offices in the country in 1988.

In 1988, there were 9 TV channels and 287 radio stations (mostly local) operating.

Cinemas (1982). Cinemas numbered about 60 with seating capacity of some 60,000.

Newspapers (1990). The 4 national daily papers are *El Heraldo* and *La Tribuna* in Tegucigalpa, *La Prensa* and *El Tiempo* in San Pedro Sula. Several local papers exist but their circulation is low and their influence is very limited.

JUSTICE, RELIGION, EDUCATION AND WELFARE

Justice. Judicial power is vested in the Supreme Court, with 9 judges elected by the National Congress for 4 years; it appoints the judges of the courts of appeal, and justices of the peace.

Religion. Roman Catholicism is the prevailing religion, but the constitution guarantees freedom to all creeds, and the State does not contribute to the support of any. Evangelical movements from North America are spreading their influence.

Education. Instruction is free, formally compulsory (from 7 to 13 years of age) and secular. There is a high drop out rate after the first years in Primary education. In 1986 the 6,710 primary schools had 805,504 children (20,732 teachers); the 354 secondary, normal and technical schools had 130,247 pupils (6,945 teachers); the teachers' training college had 3,389 students in 1986. In 1986, the three universities had a total of 31,455 students.

The illiteracy rate was 40% of those 10 years of age and older in 1983.

Health. In 1990 there were about 2,900 doctors. In 1988 there were 21 public hospitals and 25 private, with 5,601 beds, and 617 health centres.

DIPLOMATIC REPRESENTATIVES

Of Honduras in Great Britain (115 Gloucester Pl., London, W1H 3PJ)
Ambassador: Carlos M. Zerón.

Of Great Britain in Honduras (Edificio Palmira, 3er Piso, Colonia Palmira, Tegucigalpa)
Ambassador: Peter John Streams, CMG (accredited 22 Aug. 1989).

Of Honduras in the USA (3007 Tilden St., NW, Washington, D.C., 20008)
Ambassador: Dr Jorge Ramón Hernandez-Alcerro.

Of the USA in Honduras (Av. La Paz, Tegucigalpa)
Ambassador: Cresencio S. Arcos.

Of Honduras to the United Nations
Ambassador: Roberto Flores Bermudez.

Further Reading

The *Anuario Estadístico* (latest issue, *Comercio Exterior de Honduras*, 1983) is published by the Dirección de Estadísticas y Censos, Tegucigalpa. *Director:* Elizabeth Zavala de Turcios.

Monthly Bulletin.—Honduras en Cifras. Banco Central de Honduras, 1986-88
Anderson, T. P., *Politics in Central America.* Boston, Mass., 1988
Howard-Reguindin, P., *Honduras [bibliography].* Oxford and Santa Barbara, 1991
Morris, J. A., *Honduras: Caudillo Politics and Military Rulers.* Boulder, 1984
Sheehan, E. R. F., *Agony in the garden. A Stranger in Central America.* New York, 1989

HONG KONG

Population: 5·95m. (1991)
GNP per capita: US$13,400 (1991)

HISTORY. Hong Kong Island and the southern tip of the Kowloon peninsula were ceded by China to Britain after the first and second Anglo-Chinese Wars by the Treaty of Nanking 1842 and the Convention of Peking 1860. Northern Kowloon was leased to Britain for 99 years by China in 1898. Since then, Hong Kong has been under British administration, except from Dec. 1941 to Aug. 1945 during the Japanese occupation. Talks began in Sept. 1982 between Britain and China over the future of Hong Kong after the lease expiry in 1997. On 19 Dec. 1984, the two countries signed a joint declaration whereby China would recover sovereignty over Hong Kong (comprising Hong Kong Island, Kowloon and the New Territories) from 1 July 1997 and establish it as a Special Administrative Region where the existing social and economic systems, and the present life-style, would remain unchanged for another 50 years. This 'one country, two systems' principle was embodied in the Basic Law of 1990, and allows Hong Kong after 1997 to keep control of its external economic relations, to remain a separate customs area and retain the status of an international financial centre, with foreign exchange markets and a convertible currency. Hong Kong will also retain a legislature and judiciary.

AREA AND POPULATION. Hong Kong island is 32 km east of the mouth of the Pearl River and 130 km south-east of Guangzhou. The area of the island is 79·45 sq. km. It is separated from the mainland by a fine natural harbour. On the opposite side is the peninsula of Kowloon (11·44 sq. km), which was added to the Territory by the Convention of Peking, 1860. By a further convention, signed at Peking on 9 June 1898, about 979·23 sq. km, consisting of all the immediately adjacent mainland and numerous islands in the vicinity, were leased to Great Britain by China for 99 years. This area is known as the New Territories. Total area of the Territory is 1,071 sq. km (including recent reclamations), a large part of it being steep and unproductive hillside. Some 40% of the Territory is conserved as country parks. Shortage of land suitable for development for housing and industry is a serious problem. Since 1945, the Government has reclaimed about 2,396·8 hectares from the sea, principally from the seafronts of Hong Kong and Kowloon, facing the harbour. In the New Territories, the new town of Tsuen Wan, incorporating Tsuen Wan, Kwai Chung and Tsing Yi, already houses 690,000 of its planned ultimate population of 860,000. The construction of 7 further new towns at Sha Tin, Tuen Mun, Tai Po, Fanling, Yuen Long, Tseung Kwan O and Tin Shui Wai is now well underway, with planned ultimate population of about 750,000, 562,000, 306,000, 280,000, 190,000, 440,000 and 140,000 respectively.

The population was 5,613,000 at 1987 census. Estimate (30 June 1990) 5,800,600. Average annual growth rate, 1976–89 1·9%. Vital statistics, 1990: Known births, 67,911; known deaths, 28,688. Rates (per 1,000): Birth,11·8; death, 5; infant mortalith, 5·9. Life expectancy, 1990: Males, 74·6 years; females, 80·3. some 62,000 persons emigrated in 1990, mainly to Canada, Australia and the USA. About 59% of the population was born in Hong Kong. There were some 64,000 Vietnamese refugees 'boat people' in 1991 (*see also* p. 1593).

The official languages are Chinese and English

CLIMATE. The climate is warm sub-tropical being much affected by monsoons, the winter being cool and dry and the summer hot and humid, May to Sept. being the wettest months. Jan. 60°F (15·6°C), July 83°F (28·6°C). Annual rainfall 85" (2,224·7 mm).

CONSTITUTION AND GOVERNMENT. The administration is in the hands of a Governor, aided by an Executive Council, composed of the Chief Secretary, the Commander British Forces, the Financial Secretary, the Attorney General (who are members *ex officio*) and such other members as may be appointed by the Queen upon the Governor's nomination. In Nov. 1991 there were, in addition to the

4 *ex-officio* members, 1 nominated official and 9 appointed members. There is also a Legislative Council, presided over by the Governor. It has 60 seats, 21 appointed by the Governor (17 councillors and 4 officials), 21 representing 'functional' constituencies of interest groups elected by 49,000 specialists voters and 18 directly-elected on a first-past-the-post basis by an electorate of 1·8m. in 9 constituencies. At the elections of Sept. 1991 9 of the functional seats were contested; turn-out was 47%. Turn-out for the 18 directly-elected seats was 39·15%. 12 were gained by the United Democratic Party and 4 by its Pro-Democracy electoral allies. Two municipal councils with elected members are responsible on a regional basis for environmental hygiene, public health, recreational and cultural matters. Consultative district boards with 274 elected members were set up in 1982 in the 19 administrative districts. At the March 1991 elections turn-out to these was 32·5%. Pro-democracy candidates won 80 seats. At local council elections of May 1991 the United Democrats of Hong Kong won 11 out of 27 seats, independents 11, the Liberal Democratic Federation 3 and Communists 2. A first political party, the United Democratic Party, led by Martin Lee, was formed in April 1990. In June 1991 the Legislative Council approved a Bill of Rights. China (People's Republic) objected to it.

Governor and C.-in-C.: Chris Patten.
Commander British Forces: Maj.-Gen. Peter Royson Duffell, CBE, MC.
Chief Secretary: Sir David Ford, KBE, LVO, JP.
Financial Secretary: Hamish Macleod.
Flag: British Blue Ensign with the arms of the Territory on a white disc in the fly.

DEFENCE. The Hong Kong garrison, under the Commander British Forces, comprises units of all three services. Its principal rôle is to assist the Hong Kong Government in maintaining security and stability.

Army. The Army constitutes the bulk of the garrison. It comprises a UK battalion, based at Stanley Fort, and 3 Gurkha infantry battalions, all based in the New Territories; supporting units include the Queen's Gurkha Engineers, the Queen's Gurkha Signals, the Gurkha Transport Regiment, and 660 Squadron Army Air Corps.

Navy. The Royal Naval Hong Kong Squadron, partly funded by the Hong Kong government, comprises 3 Peacock class patrol craft and is based at HMS *Tamar* at Victoria. The Royal Hong Kong Police force also operates some 35 lightly-armed inshore patrol craft.

Air Force. The Royal Air Force is based at Shek Kong. No. 28 (Army Cooperation) Squadron operates Wessex helicopters. In addition to its operational rôle in support of the army and navy, the RAF carries out search and rescue and medical evacuation tasks. It is also responsible for air traffic control services at Shek Kong, and provides a territory-wide air traffic advisory service.

Auxiliary Forces. The local auxiliary defence units, consisting of the Royal Hong Kong Regiment and the Royal Hong Kong Auxiliary Air Force, are administered by the Hong Kong Government, but, if called out, would come under the command of the Commander British Forces. The Royal Hong Kong Regiment (The Volunteers) has a strength of about 950. It is fully mobile and its rôle is to operate in support of regular army battalions stationed in Hong Kong. The Royal Hong Kong Auxiliary Air Force is intended mainly for internal security and air-sea rescue duties. It has a strength of about 171, operating a fleet of 14 aircraft – 2 twin-engined Beech King Air 200s, 4 Slingsby T-67 trainers, and 8 Sikorsky S-76 helicopters.

ECONOMY

Budget. The public revenue and expenditure for financial years ending 31 March were as follows (in HK$1m.):

	1987–88	1988–89	1989–90	1990–91 [1]
Revenue	55,641	72,658	82,429	91,700
Expenditure	44,022	56,591	71,366	90,980

[1] Estimate.

Estimated operating revenue (in HK$1m.) for 1990–91, 83,670; capital revenue, 8,030. Estimated operating expenditure, 63,940; capital expenditure, 27,040.

Currency. The unit of currency is the *Hong Kong dollar* (HKD) of 100 *cents*. Banknotes (of denominations of $10 upwards) are issued by the Hongkong and Shanghai Banking Corporation, and the Standard Chartered Bank. Their combined note issue was, at 31 Dec. 1990, HK$40,866m. Subsidiary currency consisting of HK$5, HK$2, HK$1, 50-cent, 20-cent, 10-cent, 5-cent alloy coins and 1-cent notes is issued by the Hong Kong Government and at 31 Dec. 1988 totalled HK$1,889m.

The Hong Kong Government has issued a set of 14 Hong Kong commemorative HK$1,000 gold coins over the years. The set comprises 2 coins commemorating the Queen's visit to Hong Kong in 1975 and in 1986 and 12 coins depicting the animals of the Chinese lunar calendar. The last coin in the lunar series was issued in 1987 to commemorate the Year of the Rabbit.

Since Oct. 1983 the HK$ has been linked to the US$1 at a fixed exchange rate of US$1 = HK$7·78. In March 1992, £1 = HK$13·64.

Banking. In 1991: There were 168 banks licensed under the Banking Ordinance, 44 restricted licence banks and 152 representative offices of foreign banks. Licensed banks by country of ownership: Japan, 31; USA, 20; Hong Kong, 15; China, 15; Germany, 9; France, 8; UK, 7; Italy, 7; others, 56. Bank assets were HK$4,858,210m. and loans and advances HK$1,679,576. There were 190 deposit-taking companies registered under the Banking Ordinance with total assets of HK$190,500m.

Weights and Measures. Metric, British Imperial, Chinese and US units are all in current use in Hong Kong. However Government departments have now effectively adopted metric units; all new legislation uses metric terminology and existing legislation is being progressively metricated. Metrication is also proceeding in the private sector.

The statutory equivalent for the *chek* is 14 5/8 inches. The variation of the size of the *chek* with usage still persists in Hong Kong but the *chek* and derived units are now used much less than in the past.

ENERGY AND NATURAL RESOURCES

Electricity. Production (1988) 23,956m. kwh. Supply 220 volts; 50 Hz.

Water. The provision of sufficient reservoir capacity to store the summer rainfall in order to meet supply requirements has always been a serious problem. There are 17 impounding reservoirs with a total capacity of 586m. cu. metres.

There are no sites remaining suitable for development as storage reservoirs. The purchase of water from China has been of increasing importance and the future needs of Hong Kong will be met to a large extent from this source. In 1988-89 water purchased from China was in the order of 644m. cu. metres. The agreement with China allows for annual increases up to a total figure of 660m. cu. metres per annum by 1994–95 which will represent 60% of Hong Kong's demand. As a reserve resource a desalination plant can supply 181,000 cu. metres of fresh water a day.

Agriculture. Agriculture supplies about a third of domestic demand. Only 9% of the total land area is suitable for crop farming and most produce derives from intensive market gardening. In 1990, 112,000 tonnes of vegetables and 4,310 tonnes of fruit and nuts were produced. Poultry production was 27,200 tonnes, milk, 1,800 tonnes, eggs, 111,900. There were 0·41m. pigs in 1990.

Fisheries. The fishing fleet of 4,900 vessels supplies 75% of fresh marine fish consumed locally. In 1990 the marine fish catch was 169,070 tonnes. Inland freshwater farming and coastal marine farming provided 6,130 tonnes of freshwater fish.

INDUSTRY. An economic policy based on free enterprise and free trade; an industrious work force; an efficient and aggressive commercial infrastructure; modern and efficient sea-port (including container shipping terminals) and airport facilities; its geographical position relative to markets in North America and its traditional trading links with Britain have all contributed to Hong Kong's success as a modern industrial territory.

In Sept. 1990, there were 49,087 factories employing 730,217 persons. Factories by product type (and persons employed) in Sept. 1990: Textiles and clothing, 13,352 (320,384); plastics, 5,263 (53,137); electronics, 1,837 (85,468); watches and clocks, 1,690 (27,154); electrical appliances, 672 (19,153); ship-building and repair, 73 (5,087).

Labour. In 1989 the labour force totalled 2·78m. (1·01m. female), including 1·09m. manual labourers, 0·52m. clerical workers, 0·47m. in services, 0·33m. salespersons and 0·21m. professional workers. 0·46m. worked in manufacturing, 3·5m. in textiles, 0·69m. in trade and catering, and 0·5m. in services. Unemployment was 1·8% in 1991.

FOREIGN ECONOMIC RELATIONS

Commerce. Industry is mainly export-oriented. The total value of domestic exports in 1990 was HK$225,875m.; re-exports, HK$413,999m. The major markets were USA (29·4%), People's Republic of China (21%), Federal Republic of Germany (including the German Democratic Republic, Jan.–Oct. 1990) (8%), UK (6·5%), and Japan (5·8%). The total value of imports in 1990 was HK$642,530m., mainly from the People's Republic of China (36·8%), Japan (16·6%), Taiwan (9·2%), USA (8·2%), South Korea (4·5%) and Singapore (4%).

In 1990 73% of domestic exports were made up by (in HK$1): Textiles and clothing, 89,071; electronic products, 58,467; clocks and watches, 19,133; plastic products, 8,189; electrical appliances, 3,374. The chief import items were manufactured goods (330,669), machinery and transport equipment (179,383), chemicals (47,802) and foodstuffs (39,769).

Visible trade normally carries an adverse balance which is offset by a favourable balance of invisible trade, in particular transactions in connexion with air transportation, shipping, tourism and banking services.

Duties are levied only on tobacco, hydrocarbon oils, methyl alcohol, alcoholic liquors, non-alcoholic beverages and cosmetics, whether imported into or manufactured in Hong Kong for local consumption. All imports (apart from foodstuffs, which are subject to a flat declaration charge irrespective of the value of the consignment) and exports are subject to an *ad valorem* declaration charge at the rate of HK50 cents for every $1,000 value (or part thereof) of the goods shipped.

Hong Kong has a free exchange market. Foreign merchants may remit profits or repatriate capital. Import and export controls are kept to the minimum, consistent with strategic requirements.

Total trade between Hong Kong and UK (British Department of Trade returns, in £1,000 sterling) is given as follows:

	1987	1988	1989	1990	1991
Imports to UK	1,531,681	1,788,631	2,036,976	1,972,154	2,147,611
Exports and re-exports from UK	1,013,038	1,030,725	1,111,517	1,238,023	1,385,892

Tourism. 5·36m. tourists (1·13m. from Taiwan) spent HK$36,900m. in Hong Kong during 1989.

COMMUNICATIONS

Roads. In 1991 there were 1,484 km of roads, distributed as follows: Hong Kong Island, 403; Kowloon, 379, and New Territories, 702. There are 9 road tunnels, including 2 under Victoria Harbour. In 1990 there were 363,520 registered motor vehicles, including 130,045 goods vehicles. There were 15,471 road accidents in 1990, 311 fatal.

Railways. There is an electric tramway with a total track length of 30·4 km, and a cable tramway connecting the Peak district with the lower levels in Victoria. The electrified Kowloon-Canton Railway runs for 34 km from the terminus at Hung

Hom in Kowloon to the border point at Lo Wu. It carried 179m. passengers and 4·4m. tonnes of freight in 1990. A light rail system (23 km) is operated by the Kowloon-Canton Railway in the Tuen Mun area; it carried 86m. passengers in 1990.

An underground Mass Transit Railway system, comprising 43·2 km with 38 stations, is now in operation. The system consists of 4 lines, one linking the Central District of Hong Kong Island with Tsuen Wan in the west of Kowloon, the second linking Quarry Bay on Hong Kong Island with Kwun Tong in East Kowloon with Yau Ma Tei in Nathan Road, the third linking Sheung Wan and Chai Wan on Hong Kong Island. It carried 719m. passengers in 1990.

Civil Aviation. Hong Kong International Airport (Kai Tak) is situated on the north shore of Kowloon Bay. It is regularly used by some 40 airlines and many charter airlines which provide frequent services throughout the Far East to Europe, North America, Africa, the Middle East, Australia and New Zealand. British Airways operates 17 flights per week via India or the Gulf to the UK. Cathay Pacific Airways, one of the two Hong Kong-based airlines, operates more than 400 passenger and cargo services weekly to Europe (including 14 passenger and 5 cargo services per week to the UK), the Far and Middle East, Australia and North America. Hong Kong Dragon Airlines Ltd operates B-737 scheduled and non-scheduled services to a number of cities in Asia, the People's Republic of China and Micronesia. Air Hong Kong, an all-cargo operator, provides a scheduled twice-weekly service to Manchester, UK, and operates non-scheduled services around the region. About 1,000 scheduled flights are operated weekly to and from Hong Kong by various airlines. In 1990, 105,800 aircraft arrived and departed carrying 18·7m. passengers and 0·8m. tonnes of freight.

Shipping. The port of Hong Kong, which ranks among the top three container ports in the world, handled 5·04m. 20-ft equivalent units in 1990. The Kwai Chung Container Port has 8 berths with more than 3,000 metres of quay backed by about 120 hectares of cargo handling area. In 1989 17,763 ocean-going vessels called at Hong Kong and loaded and discharged 64·65m. tonnes of cargo.

Telecommunications. There were 106 post offices in 1988. In 1990 there were 3·3m. telephones and 107,000 fax transmitters. Telephone service is provided by the Hong Kong Telephone Co. Ltd. It provides local, and in association with Cable and Wireless (HK) Ltd., international voice, data and facsimile transmission services for Hong Kong. Cable and Wireless (HK) Ltd. provides the international telecommunication services as well as local telegram and telex services. These include public telegram, telex, telephone, television programmes transmission and reception, leased circuits, facsimile, switched data, ship-shore and air-ground communications. International facilities are provided through submarine cables, microwave and satellite radio systems. Hong Kong Telephone Co. Ltd. and Cable and Wireless (HK) Ltd. are wholly-owned subsidiaries of Hong Kong Telecommunications Ltd. which is jointly owned by the Cable and Wireless World Wide Communications Group, Hong Kong Government and public shareholders.

Broadcasting is regulated by the Broadcasting Authority. There is a government broadcasting station, Radio Television Hong Kong, which broadcasts on 7 channels (3 Chinese, 1 English and 2 bi-lingual services and 1 dedicated to BBC world service), 4 of which provide 24-hour service. A commercial station, the Commercial Broadcasting Co. Ltd, transmits daily in English and Cantonese. It operates 3 channels which provide 24-hour service.

Television Broadcasts Ltd and Asia Television Ltd transmit commercial television in English and Chinese on 4 channels, in colour.

Cinemas. In 1990 there were 161 cinemas; attendance was 50m. (59m. in 1989). 241 films were made in 1990.

Newspapers. In 1991 there were 69 daily or weekly newspapers,including 39 dailies in Chinese and 2 in English, and 610 periodicals. A number of news agency bulletins are registered as newspapers.

JUSTICE, EDUCATION AND WELFARE

Justice. There is a Supreme Court which comprises the Court of Appeal and the High Court. While the Court of Appeal hears appeals on all matters, civil and criminal from the lower courts, the High Court has unlimited jurisdiction in both civil and criminal matters including bankruptcy, company winding-up, adoptions, probate and lunacy matters. The District Court has civil jurisdiction to hear monetary claims up to HK$120,000 or, where the claims are for recovery of land, the annual rent or rateable value does not exceed HK$100,000. In its criminal jurisdiction, it may try more serious offences except murder, manslaughter and rape; the maximum term of imprisonment it can impose is seven years. The Magistrates' Court exercises criminal jurisdiction over a wide range of indictable and summary offences. Its powers of punishment are generally restricted to a maximum of two years' imprisonment, or a fine of HK$10,000, though cumulative sentences of imprisonment up to three years may be imposed. The Coroner's Court inquires into the identity of a deceased person and the cause of death. The Juvenile Court has jurisdiction to hear charges against young people aged under 16 for any offence other than homicide. Children under the age of seven are not deemed to have reached the age of criminal responsibility. The Lands Tribunal determines on statutory claims for compensation over land and certain landlord and tenant matters. The Labour Tribunal provides inexpensive and speedy settlements to individual monetary claims arising from disputes between employers and employees. The Small Claims Tribunal deals with monetary claims involving amounts not exceeding HK$15,000. The Obscene Articles Tribunal, established in 1987, has two judicial functions. It has exclusive jurisdiction to determine whether an article referred to it by a court or a magistrate is an obscene or indecent article and where the matter publicly displayed is indecent and it also has power to classify an article as Class I (neither obscene nor indecent), Class II (an indecent article) or Class III (an obscene article).

After being in abeyance for 25 years, the death penalty was abolished in 1992.

88,300 crimes were reported in 1990.

Police. At the end of 1990, the establishment of the Royal Hong Kong Police Force was 27,578. Detection rate, 1990, was 45·2%.

The Marine Police Region is responsible for patrolling some 1,850 sq. km of territorial waters and involved in the control of some 33,000 local craft with a maritime population of about 100,000. At the end of 1989, it consisted of a disciplined staff of more than 3,200 and a fleet of over 150 vessels.

Education. The majority of schools have to be registered with the Education Department under the Education Ordinance. They are required to comply with regulations as to staff, building, fire and health requirements. From Sept. 1971, free and compulsory primary education was introduced in government and the majority of government-aided schools. Free junior secondary education of 3 years' duration was introduced in 1978 and it was made compulsory in Sept. 1979.

In 1990–91 there were 196,466 pupils in kindergartens (all private), 526,720 in primary schools (including 51,666 in private schools) and 455,250 in secondary schools (92,021).

There are 8 technical institutes and 16 training centres with a total enrolment of 80,000, 1 technical teachers' college and 3 colleges of education with a total enrolment of 4,979.

The University of Hong Kong had 8,654 students in 1988-89 and the Chinese University of Hong Kong (founded 1963), 7,900. The Hong Kong University of Science and Technology admitted its first intakes in 1991-92 with 700 students. The Hong Kong Polytechnic, 1988-89, had about 26,000 students. In Oct. 1984, the City Polytechnic of Hong Kong was opened and had a total of 6,900 students in 1988-89. The Hong Kong Baptist College had 2,700 full-time students in 1988-89.

Health. In 1990 there were 6,260 doctors, 1,532 dentists and 25,286 hospital beds.

Social Security. The Government co-ordinates and implements expanding programmes in social welfare, which include social security, family services, child care, services for the elderly, youth and community work, probation and corrections and rehabilitation. 159 voluntary welfare agencies are subsidized by public funds.

The Government gives non-contributory cash assistance to needy families, unemployed able-bodied adults, the severely disabled and the elderly. Caseload in 1990 totalled 444,400. Victims of natural disasters, crimes of violence and traffic accidents are financially assisted.

Further Reading

Statistical Information: The Census and Statistics Department is responsible for the preparation and collation of Government statistics. These statistics are published mainly in the *Hong Kong Monthly Digest of Statistics* which is also available in a collected annual edition. The Department also publishes monthly trade statistics, economic indicators, annual review of overseas trade, etc. Statistical information is also published in the annual reports of Government departments. *Hong Kong 1991*, and other government publications, are available from the Hong Kong Government Publications Centre, GPO Building, Connaught Place, Hong Kong, and the Hong Kong Government Office in London, 6 Grafton Street, London, W1X 3LB.

The Hong Kong Trade Development Council, Convention Plaza, Tower Rd, Wan Chai, Hong Kong, issues a monthly *Hong Kong Enterprise* and other publications.

Hong Kong 1991. Hong Kong Government Press, 1991
Benton, G., *The Hong Kong Crisis.* London, 1983
Bonavia, D., *Hong Kong 1997.* London, 1984
Cameron, N., *An Illustrated History of Hong Kong.* OUP, 1991
Cheng, J. Y. S. (ed.) *Hong Kong: In Search of a Future.* OUP, 1984
Chill, H., *et al* (eds.) *The Future of Hong Kong: Toward 1997 and Beyond.* Westport, 1987
Endacott, G. B., *A History of Hong Kong.* 2nd ed. OUP, 1973.–*Government and People in Hong Kong, 1841–1962. A Constitutional History.* OUP, 1965
Morris, J., *Hong Kong: Xianggang.* London, 1988
Patrikeeff, F., *Mouldering Pearl: Hong Kong at the Crossroads.* London, 1989
Scott, I., *Hong Kong:* [Bibliography]. Oxford and Santa Barbara, 1990
Tregear, E. R., *Land Use in Hong Kong.* Hong Kong Univ. Press, 1958.—*Hong Kong Gazetteer.* Hong Kong Univ. Press, 1958.—*The Development of Hong Kong as Told in Maps.* Hong Kong Univ. Press, 1959
Wacks, R., *Civil Liberties in Hong Kong.* OUP, 1988
Wilson, D., *Hong Kong, Hong Kong.* London, 1991

HUNGARY

Magyar Köztársaság
(Hungarian Republic)

Capital: Budapest
Population: 10·45m. (1990)
GNP per capita: US$2,560 (1989)

HISTORY. Hungary first became an independent kingdom in 1001. On 1 Feb. 1946 the National Assembly proclaimed a republic. The Communist People's Republic was established in Aug. 1949 (for details *see* THE STATESMAN'S YEAR-BOOK, 1989–90, p. 615).

On 23 Oct. 1956 an anti-Stalinist revolution broke out, and the newly-formed coalition government of Imre Nagy on 1 Nov. withdrew from the Warsaw Pact and asked the UN for protection. János Kádár, formed a counter-government on 3 Nov. and asked the USSR for support. Soviet troops suppressed the revolution and abducted Nagy and his ministers; Nagy was secretly executed in 1958.

A gathering reformist tendency within the Hungarian Socialist Workers' (i.e. Communist) Party led by Imre Pozsgay culminated in its self-dissolution in Oct. 1989 and reconstitution as the Hungarian Socialist Party. The People's Republic was abolished on 23 Oct. 1989.

Nagy had been reburied with state honours on 16 Aug. 1989.

AREA AND POPULATION. Hungary is bounded north by Czechoslovakia, north-east by the USSR, east by Romania, south by Yugoslavia and west by Austria. The peace treaty of 10 Feb. 1947 restored the frontiers as of 1 Jan. 1938. The area of Hungary is 93,032 sq. km (35,911 sq. miles).

The official language is Hungarian (Magyar).

According to preliminary data of the census of 1 Jan. 1990 the population was 10,450,000 (5,427,000 females). Ethnic minorities, 1984: Germans, 1·6%; Slovaks, 1·1%; Romanians, 0·2%; others, 0·5%. There were about 0·7m. Gypsies in 1991 with a Gypsy Council.

68% of the population is urban (19·1% in Budapest). Population density, 112·4 per sq. km. Rates (per 1,000), 1989; Birth, 11·4; death, 13·3; marriage, 6·2; divorce, 2·3; infant mortality, 15·8. Since 1981 the population has been decreasing, by 1·9 per 1,000 in 1989; expectation of life (1988): males, 66; females, 74. There is a world-wide Hungarian diaspora, of 1·5m. in 1988 (730,000 in US; 220,000 in Israel; 140,000 in Canada), and Hungarian minorities (3·5m. in 1988) in Romania, Yugoslavia and Czechoslovakia.

Vital statistics, 1989: Births, 120,566; marriages, 65,712 (some 20,000 remarriages); divorces, 24,000 (estimate); deaths, 140,857; abortions, 90,000 (approx.). There were 4,494 suicides in 1988.

Hungary is divided into 19 counties (*megyék*) and the capital, Budapest, which has county status.

Area (in sq. km) and population (in 1,000) of counties and county towns (preliminary census data, 1 Jan. 1990, for counties; 1989 estimate for towns):

Counties (1990)	Area	Population	Chief town (1989)	Population
Baranya	4,487	430	Pécs	183
Bács-Kiskun	8,362	545	Kecskemét	106
Békés	5,632	410	Békéscsaba	71
Borsod-Abaúj-Zemplén	7,247	770	Miskolc	208
Csongrád	4,263	450	Szeged	189
Fejér	4,373	425	Székesfehérvár	114
Győr-Sopron	4,012	430	Győr	132
Hajdú-Bihar	6,211	550	Debrecen	220
Heves	3,637	335	Eger	67
Jász-Nagykún-Szolnok	5,607	430	Szolnok	82
Komárom-Esztergom	2,251	320	Tatabánya	77
Nógrád	2,544	230	Salgótarján	49
Pest	6,394	970	Budapest	2,115
Somogy	6,036	350	Kaposvár	74

Counties (1990)	Area	Population	Chief town (1989)	Population
Szabolcs-Szatmár-Bereg	5,938	570	Nyíregyháza	119
Tolna	3,704	260	Szekszárd	39
Vas	3,337	280	Szombathely	88
Veszprém	4,689	385	Veszprém	66
Zala	3,784	310	Zalaegerszeg	64
Budapest	525	2,000	(has county status)	

CLIMATE. A humid continental climate, with warm summers and cold winters. Precipitation is generally greater in summer, with thunderstorms. Dry, clear weather is likely in autumn, but spring is damp and both seasons are of short duration. Budapest. Jan. 32°F (0°C), July 71°F (21·5°C). Annual rainfall 25" (625 mm). Pécs. Jan. 30°F (–0·7°C), July 71°F (21·5°C). Annual rainfall 26·4" (661 mm).

CONSTITUTION AND GOVERNMENT. On 18 Oct. 1989 the National Assembly approved by an 88% majority a constitution which abolished the People's Republic. The preamble states 'The Hungarian Republic is an independent, democratic, law-based state in which the values of bourgeois democracy and democratic socialism hold good in equal measure. All power belongs to the people, which they exercise directly and through the elected representatives of popular sovereignty...No party may direct any organs of state'.

Ethnic minorities have equal rights and education in their own tongue.

The single-chamber National Assembly has 386 members, made up of 176 individual constituency winners, 120 allotted by proportional representation and 90 from a national list. It is elected for 4-year terms. A Constitutional Court was established in Jan. 1990 to review laws under consideration.

Elections were held in two rounds in March and April 1990. The Hungarian Democratic Forum (MDF) won 165 seats; the Alliance of Free Democrats, 92; the Independent Smallholders (ISP), 43; the Hungarian Socialist Party (former Communists), 33; the Federation of Young Democrats, 21; the Christian Democratic People's Party (KDNP), 21; others, 5; independents, 6.

An MDF-ISP-KDNP coalition government was formed, which in Jan. 1992 consisted of:

Prime Minister: József Antall (MDF).

Minister of Agriculture: Elemér Gergátz (ISP). *Culture and Education:* Bertalan Andrásfalvy (MDF). *Defence:* Lajos Für (MDF). *Environment:* Sándor Keresztes (MDF). *Finance:* Mihály Kupa (ind). *Foreign Affairs:* Géza Jeszenszky (MDF). *Industry and Commerce:* (Vacant). *Interior:* Péter Boross (ind). *International Economic Relations:* Béla Kádár (ind). *Justice:* István Balsai (MDF). *Labour:* Gyula Kiss (ISP). *Public Welfare:* László Surján (KDNP). *Transport and Communications:* Csaba Siklós (MDF). *Without portfolio:* Katalin Botos (MDF); András Gálszécsy (ind); Balázs Horváth (MDF); Ferenc Mádl (ind); Ferenc Nagy (ISP); Ernö Pungor (ind). *Government Spokesman:* László Balász (MDF).

The *Speaker* is György Szabad.

The head of state is the *President* of the Republic. Referenda of Nov. 1989 and July 1990 established that the president is elected for a 4-year term by the National Assembly.

On 3 Aug. 1990 Árpád Göncz (b. 1922; Alliance of Free Democrats) was elected President by 295 votes to 13 with no opponent.

National flag: Three horizontal stripes of red, white, green.

National anthem: Isten áldd meg a magyart–God bless the Hungarians (words by Ferenc Kölcsey, tune by Ferenc Erkel).

Local Government. Elections were held in Sept. 1990 to replace the former Soviet-style councils with multi-party self-governing bodies. Turn-out at 36% failed to reach a mandatory 40%, entailing a second round at which turn-out was 28%. The Alliance of Free Democrats gained 20·2% of the vote, the MDF, 18·3% and the Federation of Young Democrats, 15·2%.

DEFENCE. The President of the Republic is Commander-in-Chief of the armed forces.

Men between the ages of 18 and 23 are liable for 12 months' conscription. Compulsory military service age-limits are 18 to 55 (18 to 45 women).

All Soviet forces had withdrawn by 1991.

Army. Hungary is divided into 4 army districts: Budapest, Debrecen, Kiskunféle-gyháza, Pécs. The strength of the Army was (1992) 66,400 (including 36,400 conscripts). It is organized in 3 tank, 9 motor rifle, 4 artillery and 4 anti-tank brigades; 4 surface-to-air missile, 1 multiple rocket launcher and 1 air defence artillery regiments; and 1 airborne battalion. Equipment includes 1,139 T-55, 143 T-54, 138 T-72 and 62 T-34 main battle tanks.

There are also 18,000 border guards (13,500 conscripts).

Navy. The Danube Flotilla, the maritime wing of the Army, in 1992 consisted of some 400 personnel operating 6 river minesweepers and numerous boats and special-purpose vessels.

Air Force. The Air Force is an integral part of the Army, with a strength (1992) of 20,100 (9,500 conscripts) and 200 combat aircraft. The combat aircraft strength comprises 1 regiment of MiG-23 fighters, 1 of MiG-21 interceptors, 1 of Su-22 fighter-bombers, 1 of Su-25 ground attack aircraft, and a regiment of Mi-8 and Mi-24 armed helicopters. Transport units are equipped with An-2, An-24 and An-26 aircraft. Other types in service include Mi-2 and Mi-8 helicopters and L-29 Delfin trainers. In addition, 'Guideline' and 'Goa' surface-to-air missiles are operational.

INTERNATIONAL RELATIONS

Membership. Hungary is a member of the UN, Council of Europe, IMF, IBRD and is an associate of the EC and NATO's North Atlantic Council. With Austria, Czechoslovakia, Italy and Yugoslavia, Hungary was an inaugural member of the 'Pentagonale' meeting on economic and political co-operation in July 1990, enlarged in 1991 to include Poland and renamed 'Hexagonal'.

ECONOMY

Policy. For planning under the Communist government *see* THE STATESMAN'S YEAR-BOOK, 1989-90, p. 616-17. An emergency budget in Dec. 1989 opened the economy to market mechanisms, and called for drastic cuts in Government spending, the abolition of price subsidies and the closure of loss-making state industries. It is envisaged that one-third of industry will be privatized by 1992. Enterprise councils, which were established in 1984, are being transformed into limited companies; the State retains 20% of shares while the rest are for sale. Income tax and VAT were introduced in Jan. 1988. A State Property Agency is overseeing privatization. Legislation of June 1991 provides for compensating of former owners or their descendants for property nationalized after May 1939. Land is being restored whether or not it is intended to cultivate it, or bonds are issued for buying into privatization. Some 1·5m. families are expected to benefit.

Budget. The budget for calendar years was as follows (in 1,000 forints):

	1982	1983	1984	1985	1986	1987	1988
Revenue	485,792	543,735	572,920	632,800	682,000	760,600	898,200
Expenditure	498,007	549,822	576,580	646,600	727,300	795,000	908,400

1988 revenue included (1,000m. forints): Payments by enterprises, 423·6; consumer taxes, 210·5; personal taxes, 154·7. Expenditure included: Support of enterprises, 143·8; social security, 216·6; consumer price subsidies, 44·5; capital expenditure, 108; education and culture, 93; defence, 59. Budget estimate for 1991, 931m.

Currency. A decree of 26 July 1946 instituted a new monetary unit, the *forint* (HUF) of 100 *fillér*. There are coins of 10, 20 and 50 fillér and 1, 2, 5, 10, 20 forints, and notes of 10, 20, 50, 100, 500, 1,000 and 5,000 forints. The forint was made fully convertible in Jan. 1991. It was devalued by 15%, and again by 5·8% in

Nov. 1991. Inflation was 30% at the end of 1990. The rate of exchange (March 1992) 137·15 forints to the £1 sterling, 78·13 forints = US$1.

Banking and Finance. In 1987 a two-tier system was established. The National Bank (*Director*, Péter Akos Bod) remained the central state financial institution, responsible for the circulation of money and foreign currency exchange, but also became a central clearing bank, with general (but not operational) control over commercial banks and development banks. There were 32 commercial banks in 1991. A law of June 1991 sets capital and reserve requirements, and provides for foreign investment in Hungarian banks. Permission is needed for investments of more than 10%. A stock exchange was opened in Jan. 1989.

The Hungarian International Trade Bank opened in London in 1973. In 1980 the Central European International Bank was set up in Budapest with 7 Western banks holding 66% of the shares. The National Savings Bank handles local government as well as personal accounts. Total savings deposits in 1989: 286,624m. forints.

Weights and Measures. The metric system is in use.

ENERGY AND NATURAL RESOURCES

Electricity. Supply 220 volts; 50 Hz. Sources of energy in 1989: Oil, 30·4%, gas, 28·7%; coal and lignite, 22·2%; others, 18·7%. Imported, 51·4%. Capacity of power stations was 7,266 mw. There is an 880-mw nuclear power station at Paks. A 750-kv power line links up with the Soviet grid. 29,587m. kwh were produced in 1989 (13,891 kwh by nuclear power), and 12,959m. kwh imported. In May 1989 Hungary withdrew from the Czech-Austrian-Hungarian hydroelectric project on the Danube at Nagymáros.

Oil. Oil and natural gas are found in the Szeged basin and Zala county. Production in 1989: Oil, 1·97m. tonnes; gas, 6,175m. cu. metres.

Minerals. Production in 1989 (in 1,000 tonnes): Coal, 2,172; lignite, 5,883; brown coal, 12,020; bauxite, 2,664.

Agriculture. Agricultural land was collectivized in 1950. It was announced in 1990 that land would be restored to its pre-collectivization owners if they wished to cultivate it.

In 1989 the agricultural area was (in 1,000 ha) 6,483, of which 4,713 were arable, 1,197 meadows and pastures, 339 market gardens, and 235 orchards and vineyards.

In 1989 there were 136 state farms (self-governing under the Ministry of Agriculture) with 886,400 ha of land and 117,500 employees, 1,246 collective farms with 5m. ha of land and 470,900 members and 1,435 small-scale producers with 978,900 ha. Structure of production, 1987: Co-operative, 48·4%; private, 36·4%; state, 15·2%. The irrigated area was 177,000 ha in 1989; 52,000 tractors were in use.

Sown area, 1989: 4·62m. ha (cereals, 2·8m.; industrial crops, 0·66m.; pulses, 195,000; potatoes, 44,000)

Crop production (in 1,000 tonnes) in 1989: Wheat, 6,509; rye, 261; barley, 1,323; oats, 145; maize, 6,747; sugar-beet, 5,277; sunflower seed, 700; potatoes, 816.

Livestock in 1989 (in 1,000 head): Cattle, 1,598; pigs, 7,660; poultry (1988), 35,607; sheep, 2,069.

Livestock products (1989): Eggs, 4,450m.; milk, 2,840m. litres; wool, 9,800 tonnes; meat, 1·36m. tonnes.

The north shore of Lake Balaton and the Tokaj area are important wine-producing districts. Wine production in 1989 was 345m. litres.

Forestry. The forest area was 1,688,200 ha in 1989. 32,000 ha were afforested and 8·33m. cu. metres of timber were cut.

Fisheries. There are fisheries in the rivers Danube and Tisza and Lake Balaton. In 1988 there were 26,500 ha of commercial fishponds. Fish production was 27,000 tonnes in 1989.

INDUSTRY. In 1990 there were 1,168 co-operatives, 1,485 incorporated economic companies, 1,295 limited liability companies, 1.037 enterprises and 125 corporations. 1,067 firms employed less than 20 persons and 913 more than 300.

Production (in 1,000 tonnes) in 1989: Pig iron, 1,954; crude steel, 3,317; rolled steel, 2,534; alumina, 882; aluminium, 75; aluminium semi-finished products, 183; cement, 3,857; sulphuric acid, 482; petrol, 2,809; plastics, 638; chemical fertilizers, 903; synthetic fibres, 36; antibiotics (tonnes), 638; buses (units), 11,974; lorries, 174; TV receivers, 495,000; refrigerators, 415,000.

Labour. In 1989 there were 4,822,700 wage-earners (2,215,300 female) in the following categories: Working-class, 59·4%; white-collar, 26·9%; co-operative peasantry, 7·2%; self-employed tradesmen, 6·5%. Percentage distributions of the workforce: Industry, 30·4; agriculture, 18·4; social and cultural services, 12·9; trade, 10·8; transport and communications, 8·3; building, 7. A 40-hour 5-day week was introduced in 1984. Average monthly wages in 1989: 10,172 forints. Minimum subsistence level, 1989, was 3,940 forints per month. There were 351,000 unemployed in Nov. 1991. Unemployment benefit for one year became payable from Jan. 1989. Retirement age: Men, 60; women, 55. Leave entitlement, 15-24 days in 1985.

Trade Unions. The former official communist organization (National Council of Trade Unions), renamed the Confederation of Hungarian Trade Unions, groups 70 organizations and claimed 1·8m. members in 1992. A law of July 1991 distributed its assets among the other trade unions and abolished its obligatory levy on pay packets. 16 other unions form the Democratic League for Independent Trade Unions, which claimed 0·2m., mainly white-collar, members in 1991. Other unions operate outside these federations.

FOREIGN ECONOMIC RELATIONS. Foreign debt was US$21,000m. in 1990. An EEC loan of £700m. was granted in Oct. 1989. In 1991 there were some 7,300 joint ventures (mainly from Germany, Austria and the USA) with a capital worth of US$1,200m.

Commerce. The economy is heavily dependent on foreign trade. Trade for calendar years (in 1m. forints):

	1983	1984	1985	1986	1987	1988	1989
Imports	365,000	390,500	410,100	439,700	463,100	472,500	523,500
Exports	374,100	414,000	424,600	420,300	450,100	504,100	571,300

In 1989 Hungary's trade with communist countries (in 1,000m. forints): Imports, 200·8; exports, 355·4. In 1988 USSR was Hungary's major trading partner (22·1% of imports, 25·1% of exports), ahead of the Federal Republic of Germany (16%, 11·9%) and Austria (8·6%, 6·5%).

Commodity structure of foreign trade (%), 1988:

	Imports		Exports	
	Communist countries	Other countries	Communist countries	Other countries
Fuels and electricity	27·5	0·7	0·4	3·4
Raw materials	13·3	11·1	2·5	12·3
Semi-finished products	14·1	32·7	9·5	28·3
Spare parts	7·9	16·3	11·3	3·9
Machinery and capital goods	19·4	17·3	46·3	10·4
Industrial consumer goods	15·4	11·8	16·9	14·9
Agricultural produce	0·4	3·0	4·1	9·5
Food industry products	2·0	7·1	9·0	17·4

In 1989 the US granted Hungary most-favoured-nation status. In 1988 a trade agreement was signed with the EEC which will lower quotas by 1995.

Total trade between Hungary and UK (British Department of Trade returns, in £1,000 sterling):

	1987	1988	1989	1990	1991
Imports to UK	83,267	96,288	105,221	102,741	103,869
Exports and re-exports from UK	101,300	131,212	117,947	121,837	132,448

Tourism. In 1989, 24·92m. foreigners visited Hungary (12·17m. from the West), of whom 10·24m. were tourists (5·18m. from the West); and 14·48m. Hungarians travelled abroad. There were some 38m. visitors in 1990 (including 9m. Romanian,

8m. Yugoslav and 5m. Austrian). Revenue from foreign tourists in 1989 was 49,433m. forints.

COMMUNICATIONS

Roads. In 1989 there were 29,715 km of roads, including motorways, 218 km; highways, 93 km and other first class main roads, 1,893 km. Passenger cars numbered 1,848,200 (1,808,100 private), lorries 181,062 and buses 26,169. 184m. tonnes of freight and 609m. passengers were transported by road (excluding intra-urban passengers). In 1989 there were 24,367 road accidents with 2,162 fatalities.

Railways. Route length of public lines in 1990, 7,765 km, of which 2,162 km were electrified. 87·4m. tonnes of freight and 208m. passengers were carried. There is a metro in Budapest (26·5 km), and tram/light rail networks in Budapest (159 km), Debrecen, Miskolc and Szeged.

Civil Aviation. Budapest airport (Ferihegy) handled 2·42m. passengers in 1989. In 1989 Hungarian Air Lines (Malév) flew 40 routes to Europe, the Middle East and North America. 1·47m. passengers were carried. Malév had 12 TU154s, 6 TU134s and leased 6 Boeing 737s in 1991. British Airways, PANAM, Air France, SABENA, Swissair, OS, Lufthansa and KLM as well as Aeroflot and East European lines have services to Budapest. TNT operates an express freight service.

Shipping. Navigable waterways have a length of 1,688 km. In 1989 3·71m. tonnes of cargo and 3·57m. passengers were carried. The Hungarian Shipping Company (MAHART) has agencies at Amsterdam, Alexandria, Algiers, Beirut, Rijeka and Trieste. It has 11 sea-going ships.

Pipeline. Length of network, 1989: Oil, 1,204 km; gas, 4,379. Quantity transported, 20·61m. tonnes.

Telecommunications. In 1989 there were 3,191 post offices, 915,900 telephones, (639,600 private), and 13,480 telex subscribers. There were 6m. radios and 4,214,949 TV sets in use in 1991. The government network *Magyar Rádió* broadcasts 4 programmes on medium-waves and FM and also regional programmes, including transmissions in German, Romanian and Serbo-Croat. There are 2 other networks, one of them commercial. *Magyar Televizsió* operates 2 TV channels. Colour transmissions use the SECAM system.

Cinemas and Theatres (1989). There were 2,414 cinemas; attendance 46m. 47 full-length feature films were made. There were 41 theatres; attendance 5·2m.

Newspapers and Books. In 1988 there were 29 dailies, circulating in 952m. copies and 1,692 other periodicals. 7,599 book titles were published in 1989 in 108·4m. copies. There were 4,410 public libraries and 4,321 trade union libraries.

JUSTICE, RELIGION, EDUCATION AND WELFARE

Justice. The administration of justice is the responsibility of the Procurator-General, elected by Parliament for 6 years. There are 109 regional courts and courts of labour, 20 county courts, 5 district courts and a Supreme Court. Criminal proceedings are dealt with by the regional courts through 3-member councils and by the county courts and the Supreme Court in 5-member councils. A new Civil Code was adopted in 1978 and a new Criminal Code in 1979.

Regional courts act as courts of first instance; county courts as either courts of first instance or of appeal. The Supreme Court acts normally as an appeal court, but may act as a court of first instance in cases submitted to it by the Public Prosecutor. All courts, when acting as courts of first instance, consist of 1 professional judge and 2 lay assessors, and, as courts of appeal, of 3 professional judges. Local government Executive Committees may try petty offences.

Regional and county judges and assessors are elected by the appropriate local councils; members of the Supreme Court by Parliament.

There are also military courts of the first instance. Military cases of the second instance go before the Supreme Court.

The death penalty was abolished in Oct. 1990.

62,834 sentences were imposed on adults in 1989, including 21,744 of imprisonment. There were 9,661 juvenile offenders. 15,928 persons were in prison in 1989.

Religion. Church-state affairs are regulated by a law of Feb. 1990 which guarantees freedom of conscience and religion and separates church and state by prohibiting state interference in church affairs. Religious matters are the concern of the Department for Church Relations, under the auspices of the Prime Minister's Office. State aid to all churches was 308m. forints in 1990 and 1,100m. forints in 1991. 8·5m. of the population professed a religious faith in 1976; the number of active church members was put between 1m. and 1·5m.

In 1976 there were 5·25m. Roman Catholics with 4,400 churches, and 500,000 Uniates. In 1979 there were 3 seminaries and 1 Uniate seminary, a theological academy, and 8 secondary schools. There were 2,400 Roman Catholic priests in 1986. There are also lay co-operators of both sexes who perform some priestly duties. The Primate of Hungary is Archbishop László Pacskai, appointed Aug. 1986. There are 11 dioceses, all with bishops or archbishops. There is one Uniate bishopric.

In 1976 there were 2m. Calvinists with 4 dioceses, 1,300 ministers and 1,567 churches. There were 2 theological colleges (20% of students female) with 16 teachers, and 1 secondary school. There were 500,000 Lutherans with 16 dioceses, 374 ministers and 673 churches. There is a theological college with 6 teachers. The 10 denominations in the Association of Free Churches had 37,000 members, 230 ministers and 675 churches. There are 4 Orthodox denominations with 40,000 members in 1979. The Unitarian Church has 10,000 members, 11 ministers and 6 churches. In 1991 there were 100,000 Jews (825,000 in 1939) with 136 synagogues, 26 rabbis and a rabbinical college which enrols 10 students a year.

Education. Education is free and compulsory from 6 to 14. Primary schooling ends at 14; thereafter education may be continued at secondary, secondary technical or secondary vocational schools, which offer diplomas entitling students to apply for higher education, or at vocational training schools which offer tradesmen's diplomas. Students at the latter may also take the secondary school diploma examinations after 2 years of evening or correspondence study. Optional religious education was introduced in schools in 1990.

In 1989–90 there were 4,748 kindergartens with 33,835 teachers and 392,273 pupils; 3,527 primary schools with 90,602 teachers and 1,183,600 pupils; 675 secondary schools with 21,452 teachers and 273,500 pupils; and 299 vocational training schools with 12,044 teachers and 201,700 trainees. There are 4 universities proper (Budapest, Pécs, Szeged, Debrecen), and 14 specialized universities (6 technical, 4 medical, 3 arts, 1 economics). At these and at 40 other institutions of higher education there were 16,319 teachers and 72,400 full-time students (10% of the 18-22 year-old population). Corvin University, a private institution, was preparing to open in Budapest in 1990.

Health. In 1989 there were 36,800 doctors and dentists and 104,540 hospital beds.

Social Security. Medical treatment is free. Patients bear 15% of the cost of medicines. Sickness benefit is 75% of wages, old age pensions (at 60 for men, 55 for women) 60–70%. In 1989, 156,500m. forints were paid out in pensions to 2·48m. pensioners (including old age, 1·37m.; disabled, 0·5m.; widows, 0·3m.) In 1989 52·8 forints in family allowances were paid out. Monthly allowances (in forints) are: One child, 1,770; two, 4,140; three, 5,700; four, 7,600 (more for single parents).

DIPLOMATIC REPRESENTATIVES

Of Hungary in Great Britain (35 Eaton Pl., London, SW1X 8BY)
Ambassador: Tibor Antalpéter.

Of Great Britain in Hungary (Harmincad Utca 6, Budapest V)
Ambassador: J. A. Birch, CMG.

Of Hungary in the USA (3910 Shoemaker St., NW, Washington, D.C., 20008)
Ambassador: Pál Tár.

Of the USA in Hungary (Szabadság Tér 12, Budapest V)
Ambassador: Charles Thomas.

Of Hungary to the United Nations
Ambassador: Endre Erdös.

Further Reading

Statisztikai Évkönyv. Budapest, annual; since 1871, abridged English version, *Statistical Year-Book*
Statistical Pocket Book of Hungary (in English). Budapest, annual from 1959
State Budget. Budapest, annual from 1983
The Hungarian Economy: a Quarterly Economic and Business Review. Budapest, since 1972
Hungary 66 (67 etc.). Budapest, annual from 1966
Managers in Hungary: A Biographical Directory. Budapest, 1986
Marketing in Hungary. Budapest, quarterly
Quarterly Review of the National Bank of Hungary. From 1983
Information Hungary. Budapest, 1980

Bako, E., *Guide to Hungarian Studies.* 2 vols. Stanford Univ. Press, 1973
Batt, J., *Economic Reform and Political Change in Eastern Europe: A Comparison of the Czechoslovak and Hungarian Experiences.* Basingstoke, 1988
Berend, I. T. and Ranki, G., *Hungary: A Century of Economic Development.* New York and Newton Abbot, 1974.—*Underdevelopment and Economic Growth: Studies in Hungarian Social and Economic History.* Budapest, 1979.—*The Hungarian Economy in the Twentieth Century.* London, 1985
Bernat, T., (ed.) *An Economic Geography of Hungary.* Budapest, 1985
Bölöny, J., *Magyarország Kormányai, 1848–1975.* Budapest, 1978. [Lists governments and politicians]
Brown, D. M., *Towards a Radical Democracy: The Political Economy of the Budapest School.* Cambridge, 1988
Burawoy, M. and Lukács, J., *The Radiant Past: Ideology and Reality in Hungary's Road to Capitalism.* Chicago Univ. Press, 1992
Fekete, J., *Back to the Realities: Reflections of a Hungarian Banker.* Budapest, 1982
Hann, C. M. (ed.), *Market Economy and Civil Society in Hungary.* London, 1990
Hegedüs, A., *The Structure of Socialist Society.* London, 1977
Heinrich, H.-G., *Hungary: Politics, Economics and Society.* London, 1986
Kabdebó, T., *Hungary.* [Bibliography] Oxford and Santa Barbara, 1980
Kornai, J., *The Road to a Free Economy: Shifting from a Socialist System—the Example of Hungary.* New York and London, 1990
Lendvai, P., *Hungary: The Art of Survival.* London, 1989
Macartney, C. A., *Hungary: A Short History.* London, 1962
Pamlényi, E. (ed.) *A History of Hungary.* Budapest, 1975
Pécsi, M. and Sárfalvi, B., *Physical and Economic Geography of Hungary.* 2nd ed. Budapest, 1979
Sugar, P. F. (ed.) *A History of Hungary.* London, 1991
Vasary, I., *Beyond the Plan: Social Change in a Hungarian Village.* Boulder, 1987

The Szechényi Library is the national library.

ICELAND

Capital: Reykjavík
Population: 255,708 (1990)
GNP per capita: US$21,962 (1990)

Lýðveldið Ísland

(Republic of Iceland)

HISTORY. The first settlers came to Iceland in 874. Between 930 and 1264 Iceland was an independent republic, but by the 'Old Treaty' of 1263 the country recognized the rule of the King of Norway. In 1381 Iceland, together with Norway, came under the rule of the Danish kings, but when Norway was separated from Denmark in 1814, Iceland remained under the rule of Denmark. Since 1 Dec. 1918 it has been acknowledged as a sovereign state. It was united with Denmark only through the common sovereign until it was proclaimed an independent republic on 17 June 1944.

AREA AND POPULATION. Iceland is a large island in the North Atlantic, close to the Arctic Circle, and comprises an area of about 103,000 sq. km (39,758 sq. miles), with its extreme northern point (the Rifstangi) lying in 66° 32' N. lat., and its most southerly point (Kötlutangi) in 63° 23' N. lat., not including the islands north and south of the land; if these are included, the country extends from 67° 10' N. (the Kolbeinsey) to 63° 17' N. (Surtsey, one of the Westman Islands). It stretches from 13° 30' (the Gerpir) to 24° 32' W. long. (Látrabjarg). The skerry *Hvalbakur* (The Whaleback) lies 13° 16' W. long.

There are 8 regions:

Region	Inhabited land (sq. km)	Mountain pasture (sq. km)	Waste-land (sq. km)	Total area (sq. km)	Popula-tion (1 Dec. 1990)
Capital area	1,266	716	—	1,982	145,980
Southwest Peninsula					15,202
West	5,011	3,415	275	8,711	14,537
Western Peninsula	4,130	3,698	1,652	9,470	9,798
Northland West	4,867	5,278	2,948	13,093	10,446
Northland East	9,890	6,727	5,751	22,368	26,127
East	16,921	17,929	12,555	21,991	13,216
South				25,214	20,402
Iceland	42,085	37,553	23,181	102,819	255,708

The census population (1980) was 229,187. In 1990, 23,654 were domiciled in rural districts and 232,054 in towns and villages (of over 200 inhabitants). The population is almost entirely Icelandic.

In 1990 foreigners numbered 4,812; of these 1,030 were Danish, 717 US, 454 British, 319 Norwegian and 310 German nationals.

The capital, Reykjavík, had on 1 Dec. 1990, a population of 97,569; other towns were Akranes, 5,230; Akureyri, 14,174; Bolungarvík, 1,187; Dalvík, 1,481; Eskif-jörður, 1,056; Garðabær, 6,954; Grindavík, 2,172; Hafnarfjörður, 15,151; Húsavík, 2,503; Ísafjörður, 3,498; Keflavík, 7,525; Kópavogur, 16,186; Neskaupstaður, 1,738; Njarðvík, 2,405; Ólafsfjörður, 1,171; Sauðárkrókur, 2,534; Selfoss, 3,915; Seltjarnarnes, 4,143; Seyðisfjörður, 981; Siglufjörður, 1,815; Vestmannaeyjar, 4,926.

Vital statistics for calendar years:

	Living births	Still-born	Marriages	Divorces	Deaths	Infant deaths
1988	4,673	18	1,294	459	1,818	29
1989	4,560	6	1,176	520	1,715	24
1990	4,768	13	1,154	479	1,704	28

The official language is Icelandic *(íslenska).*

CLIMATE. The climate is cool temperate oceanic and rather changeable, but mild for its latitude because of the Gulf Stream and prevailing S.W. winds. Precipitation is high in upland areas, mainly in the form of snow. Reykjavik. Jan. 34°F (1°C), July 52°F (11°C). Annual rainfall 34" (860 mm).

CONSTITUTION AND GOVERNMENT. On 24 May 1944 the people of Iceland decided in a referendum to sever all ties with the Danish Crown. The voters were asked whether they were in favour of the abrogation of the Union Act, and whether they approved of the bill for a republican constitution: 70,725 voters were for severance of all political ties with Denmark and only 370 against it; 69,048 were in favour of the republican constitution, 1,042 against it and 2,505 votes were invalid. On 17 June 1944 the republic was formally proclaimed, and as the republic's first president the Alþingi elected Sveinn Björnsson for a 1-year term (re-elected 1945 and 1949; died 25 Jan. 1952). The President is now elected by direct, popular vote for a period of 4 years.

President of the Republic of Iceland: Vigdís Finnbogadóttir (elected 29 June 1980, with 43,611 out of 129,049 valid votes, inaugurated 1 Aug. 1980); re-elected unopposed in 1984; re-elected in 1988 with 94% of the valid votes.

National flag: Blue with a red white-bordered Scandinavian cross.

National anthem: Ó Guð vors lands (words by M. Jochumsson, 1874; tune by S. Sveinbjörnsson).

The *Alþingi* (Parliament) is divided into two Houses, the Upper House and the Lower House. The former is composed of one-third of the members elected by the whole Alþingi in common sitting. The remaining two-thirds of the members form the Lower House. The members of the Alþingi receive payment for their services.

The budget bills must be laid before the two Houses in joint session, but all other bills can be introduced in either of the Houses. If the Houses do not agree, they assemble in a common sitting and the final decision is given by a majority of two-thirds of the voters, with the exception of budget bills, where a simple majority is sufficient. The ministers have free access to both Houses, but can vote only in the House of which they are members.

The electoral law enacted in 1984 provides for an Alþingi of 63 members. Of these, 54 seats are distributed among the 8 constituencies as follows: 14 seats are allotted to Reykjavík, 8 to Reykjanes (i.e. the South-west excluding Reykjavík) and 5 or 6 to each of the remaining 6. From the 9 seats then left, 8 are divided beforehand among the constituencies according to the number of registered voters in the preceding elections. Finally, one seat is given to a constituency after the elections, to compensate the party with the fewest seats as compared to its number of votes.

Elections were held in April 1991. The electorate was 182,768. Turn-out was 157,769. 1,029 candidates stood. The Independence Party (IP) gained 26 seats with 38·6% of votes cast (18 with 27·2% in 1987); the Progressive Party gained 13 with 18·9% (13 with 18·9%); the Social Democratic Party gained 10 with 15·5% (10 with 15·2%); the People's Alliance gained 9 with 14·4% (8 with 13·3%); the Women's Alliance gained 5 with 8·3% (6 with 10·1%).

The executive power is exercised under the President by the Cabinet. The IP-SDP coalition Cabinet, as constituted in April 1991, was as follows:

Prime Minister: Davíð Oddsson (Ind.).
Foreign Affairs: Jón Baldvin Hannibalsson (Soc. Dem.). *Finance:* Friðrik Sophusson (Ind.). *Social Affairs:* Jóhanna Sigurðardóttir (Soc. Dem.). *Fisheries, Justice and Church:* Þorsteinn Pálsson (Ind.). *Agriculture and Communications:* Halldór Blöndal (Ind.). *Health and Social Security:* Sighvatur Björgvinsson (Soc. Dem.). *Commerce, Energy and Industry:* Jón Sigurðsson (Soc. Dem.). *Education:* Ólafur G. Einarsson (Ind.). *Environment:* Eiður Guðnason (Soc. Dem.).

Local Administration. Iceland was on 1 Dec. 1991 divided into 201 communes, of which 31 had the status of a town. The commune councils are elected by universal suffrage (men and women 18 years of age and over), in towns and other urban communes by proportional representation, in rural communes by simple majority. For general co-operation the communes are free to form district councils. All the communes except 10 towns are members in 20 district councils. The communes appoint one or more representatives to the district councils according to their population size. The commune councils are supervised by the Ministry of Social Affairs. For national government there are 27 divisions (*lögsagnarumdæmi*), consisting of towns and counties, single or combined, with the exception of Keflavík Airport (also a NATO base), which is a separate national government division consisting of parts of 5 communes. In the capital the different branches of national government are independent (jurisdictional power and executive power, i.e. courts, police, customs etc.), while in other national government divisions they are the charge of the sheriffs, also residing as the local magistrates.

DEFENCE. Iceland possesses neither an army nor a navy. Under the North Atlantic Treaty, US forces are stationed in Iceland as the Iceland Defence Force. 3 armed offshore patrol craft for fishery protection vessels are maintained by the Icelandic National Coastguard, with 1 patrol aircraft and 1 helicopter. Coastguard Service personnel in 1991 totalled 130.

INTERNATIONAL RELATIONS

Membership. Iceland is a member of the UN, EFTA, OECD, the Council of Europe, NATO and the Nordic Council.

ECONOMY

Budget. Total revenue and expenditure for calendar years (in 1m. kr.):

	1984	1985	1986	1987	1988	1989
Revenue	22,088	28,746	40,176	52,324	71,287	83,057
Expenditure	20,474	30,617	46,374	53,582	73,415	100,403

Main items of the Treasury accounts for 1989 (in 1m. kr.):

Revenue		Expenditure	
Direct taxes	12,588	Administration, justice and police	7,484
Indirect taxes	62,481	Foreign service	707
Other	7,988	Education, culture and	
		State Church	15,827
		Health and social security	36,008
		Subsidies	4,509
		Agriculture	4,820
		Fisheries	2,534
		Manufacturing and energy	4,921
		Communications	7,178
		Other	16,415

Central government debt was on 31 Dec. 1990, 110,020m. kr, of which the foreign debt amounted to 61,250m. kr.

Currency. The unit of currency is the *Icelandic króna* (ISK) of 100 *aurar*, (singular: *eyrir*). Foreign exchange markets were deregulated on 1 Jan. 1992. In March 1992, US$1 = kr. 52·75; £1 = kr. 108·53. Note and coin circulation, 31 Dec. 1990, was 3,083m. kr.

Banking and Finance. The *Seðlabanki Íslands* (The Central Bank of Iceland; *Governor:* Johannes Nordal), established in 1961, is responsible for note issue and carries out the central banking functions which before 1961 were carried out by the *Landsbanki Íslands* (The National Bank of Iceland, owned entirely by the State), currently (1991) the largest commercial bank. There are 2 other commercial banks: *Íslandsbanki* (The Iceland Bank Ltd), created in Jan. 1990 by a merger of 4 banks, and *Búnaðarbanki Íslands* (The Agricultural Bank of Iceland), a state-owned bank founded in 1930. Banking is being deregulated in stages to come into line with the EEC's internal market in Jan. 1993.

On 31 Dec. 1990 the accounts of the Central Bank balanced at 41,304m. kr.; commercial bank deposits were 103,399m. kr.; deposits in the 32 savings banks, 21,246m. kr.

There is a stock exchange.

Weights and Measures. The metric system of weights and measures is obligatory.

ENERGY AND NATURAL RESOURCES

Electricity. The installed capacity of public electrical power plants at the end of 1990 totalled 912,793 kw., of which 751,874 kw. comprised hydro-electric plants. Total electricity production in public-owned plants in 1990 amounted to 4,447m. kwh.; in privately-owned plants, 5m. kwh. Supply 220 volts; 50 Hz.

Agriculture. Of the total area of Iceland, about six-sevenths is unproductive, but only about 1·3% is under cultivation, which is largely confined to hay, potatoes and turnips. In 1990 the total hay crop was 3,256,405 cu. metres; the crop of potatoes, 14,893 tonnes, and of turnips, 808 tonnes. At the end of 1990 the livestock was as follows: Horses, 71,693; cattle, 74,889 (including 32,246 milch cows); sheep, 548,508; pigs, 3,116; poultry, 214,936.

Fisheries. Fishing vessels at the end of 1990 numbered 1,005 with a gross tonnage of 129,858. Total catch in 1989, 1,506,000 tonnes; 1990, 1,502,000 tonnes.

The Icelandic Government announced that the fishery limits off Iceland were extended from 12 to 50 nautical miles from Sept. 1972. An interim agreement for 2 years signed by the UK and Iceland in Nov. 1973 expired in Nov. 1975.

On 15 July 1975 the Icelandic Government issued a decree that from 15 Oct. 1975 the fishery limits of Iceland were extended from 50 to 200 nautical miles. The Icelandic Government maintain that this extension is necessary to protect the fish stocks in Icelandic waters because the fishing industry is of vital importance to the national economy.

INDUSTRY. Production, 1990, in 1,000 tonnes: Aluminium, 86·7; diatomite, 24·9; fertilizer, 48·3; ferro-silicon, 62·8. Sales of cement, 1990, 99·9 tonnes.

Labour. In Nov. 1991, 1·5% of the total labour force was registered as unemployed.

Trade Unions. In 1989 trade union membership was 76% of the workforce. Only union members receive unemployment benefit.

FOREIGN ECONOMIC RELATIONS. The economy is heavily trade-dependent.

Commerce. Total value of imports (c.i.f.) and exports (f.o.b.) in 1,000 kr.:

	1986	1987	1988	1989	1990
Imports	45,905,230	61,231,629	68,723,300	80,249,900	96,620,900
Exports	44,967,770	53,053,078	61,666,700	80,071,700	92,625,100

Leading exports (in 1,000 kg and 1,000 kr.):

	1989		1990	
	Quantity	Value	Quantity	Value
Marine products	637,971	56,811,800	607,227	69,897,400
Aluminium	89,657	10,289,600	86,392	9,587,100
Ferro-silicon	64,192	3,026,800	671,450	2,430,500

Leading imports (in 1,000 tonnes and 1,000 kr.):

	1989		1990	
	Quantity	Value	Quantity	Value
Ships (number)	18	2,770,400	12	1,261,400
Fuel oil	96,074	546,500	105,958	788,900
Gas oils	301,113	2,681,900	335,776	4,340,600
Jet fuel	109,143	1,151,400	78,664	1,123,900
Cereals	9,694	225,300	7,108	222,600
Animal feed	57,947	869,500	58,518	896,000
Gasoline	110,284	1,257,800	127,324	1,869,300
Motor vehicles (number)	7,430	3,485,100	9,148	5,374,500
Fishing nets and other gear	632	365,200	618	326,900

Value of trade with principal countries for 3 years (in 1,000 kr.):

	1988 Imports (c.i.f.)	Exports (f.o.b.)	1989 Imports (c.i.f.)	Exports (f.o.b.)	1990 Imports (c.i.f.)	Exports (f.o.b.)
Austria	474,100	63,500	633,000	77,200	706,500	176,700
Belgium	1,326,900	480,100	1,509,800	630,200	1,746,200	976,400
Brazil	250,500	70,900	256,800	262,600	256,300	189,400
Canada	290,900	174,000	429,600	429,600	510,200	286,700
Czechoslovakia	268,300	85,700	306,000	206,700	340,400	61,400
Denmark	6,357,700	2,032,600	7,262,800	2,927,400	8,324,800	4,676,500
Faroe Islands	9,500	544,500	19,600	1,042,500	47,100	1,438,500
Finland	1,693,300	763,700	1,617,800	1,200,200	1,602,500	897,600
France	2,150,100	2,978,700	2,496,300	4,594,900	2,942,700	8,311,400
German Dem. Rep.	117,500	81,200	164,200	8,900	145,700	25,000
Germany, Fed. Rep. of	9,783,700	6,367,000	10,497,700	9,506,300	12,011,700	11,752,200
Greece	58,500	483,800	74,800	819,900	83,900	860,400
Hungary	23,100	118,100	37,800	57,700	52,500	97,700
India	56,900	—	53,900	300	81,600	300
Ireland	233,300	29,100	307,300	6,900	391,000	75,800
Israel	31,900	1,200	142,500	66,500	50,500	74,500
Italy	3,010,200	1,560,300	2,486,600	2,552,500	2,993,200	2,690,600
Japan	4,756,500	4,706,500	3,916,900	5,674,800	5,419,300	5,545,600
Netherlands	5,607,300	704,300	8,358,300	1,373,300	10,022,400	1,955,900
Nigeria	400	241,800	—	347,900	100	588,700
Norway	6,166,200	1,489,400	5,295,800	1,742,400	4,869,600	1,348,800
Poland	979,900	851,700	1,313,900	1,192,500	1,098,300	184,900
Portugal	611,200	5,240,100	658,400	3,447,000	854,500	3,316,600
Spain	651,100	2,113,000	798,600	2,698,100	877,500	4,645,400
Sweden	6,025,000	1,094,200	6,592,400	1,384,600	7,388,700	1,695,400
Switzerland	785,900	2,783,600	1,155,300	4,409,700	1,174,900	3,871,600
USSR	2,396,400	2,194,100	3,382,600	2,489,700	4,786,500	2,347,100
UK	5,608,000	14,340,900	6,508,800	16,630,800	7,782,000	23,446,200
USA	5,185,800	8,372,600	8,823,300	11,435,500	13,949,500	9,176,900

Total trade between Iceland and UK (British Department of Trade returns, in £1,000 sterling):

	1987	1988	1989	1990	1991
Imports to UK	178,314	198,365	196,678	259,438	238,428
Exports and re-exports from UK	84,866	87,100	69,497	88,537	95,615

Tourism. There were 143,458 visitors to Iceland in 1991.

COMMUNICATIONS

Roads. On 31 Dec. 1990 the length of the public roads (including roads in towns) was 12,537 km. Of these 8,254 km were national main roads and 3,173 km were provincial roads. Total length of surfaced roads was 2,426 km. A ring road of 1,400 km runs just inland from much of the coast; about 60% of it is smooth-surfaced. Motor vehicles registered at the end of 1990 numbered 134,181, of which 121,059 were passenger cars and 13,122 trucks; there were also 1,113 motor cycles. There were 24 fatal road accidents in 1990.

Civil Aviation. Icelandair maintains regular domestic services from Reykjavík. (Icelandair 1990: 257,148 passengers). Icelandair is the only international carrier. It serves 14 destinations in west Europe and 3 in the USA. In 1991 it had 4 Boeing 737-400s, 3 757-200s and 3 757-400s. In 1990 Icelandair carried in scheduled foreign flights 476,835 passengers. There are international airports at Reykjavík and Keflavík (Leifsstöd).

Shipping. Total registered vessels, 1,155 (184,000 GRT) on 31 Dec. 1990, of these 1,005 were sea-going fishing vessels.

Telecommunications. At the end of 1990 the number of post offices was 123 and telephone and telegraph offices 82; number of telephone subscribers, 130,000. The State Broadcasting Service, *Ríkisútvarpid*, broadcasts 2 radio channels and 1 TV channel. On 1 Jan. 1986 the state monopoly on broadcasting was abolished by law and the field opened to others, if they fulfilled certain conditions. Besides *Rikisút-varpid* 8 privately owned radio stations and 1 TV station were in operation in 1991. Number of licensed receivers (1990): Radio, about 86,000; television, about 82,000.

Cinemas (1990). In the capital area there were 6 cinemas (22 cinema halls) with a seating capacity of about 5,472.

Newspapers (1991). There are 5 daily newspapers, 4 in Reykjavík and one in Akureyri, with a combined circulation of about 100,000.

JUSTICE, RELIGION, EDUCATION AND WELFARE

Justice. There were 22 judges in 1992. The lower courts of justice are those of the provincial magistrates (*sýslumenn*) and town judges (*bæjarfógetar*). From these there is an appeal to the Supreme Court (*hæstiréttur*) in Reykjavík, which has 8 judges. In July 1992 the judicial system was scheduled for reforms separating the judiciary from the prosecution.

Religion. The national church, and the only one endowed by the State, is Evangelical Lutheran. But there is complete religious liberty, and no civil disabilities are attached to those not of the national religion. The affairs of the national church are under the superintendence of a bishop. In 1990 92·6% of the population were members of it (93·2% in 1980). 7,311 persons (2·5%) were Dissenters and 3,373 persons (1·3%) did not belong to any religious community.

Education. Compulsory education for children began in 1907, and a university was founded in Reykjavík in 1911. There is in Reykjavík a teachers' training college and a technical high school; various specialized institutions of learning and a number of second-level schools are scattered throughout the country. There are many part-time schools of cultural activities, including music.

Compulsory education comprises 9 classes, 7-15 years of age. After completion of a facultative 9th class, attended by 93%-95% of the relevant age group, there is access to further schooling free of charge. Some 53%-74% of the age groups 16-19 years old attend schools. Around 15%-20% of each age group go into handicraft apprenticeship. About 30% pass matriculation examination, generally at the age of 20. Approximately one third-level student out of every four goes abroad for studies, two-thirds of them to Scandinavia, the rest mainly to English- and German-speaking countries.

Immatriculation in Iceland in autumn 1989: Preceding the first level, 4,400. First-level (1st-6th class) 25,500. Second-level first stage (7th-9th class) 12,400. Second-level second stage (4-year courses) 16,700. Third-level studies, 5,400.

Social Welfare. The main body of the Icelandic social welfare legislation is consolidated in six main acts:

(i) *The social security legislation* (a) health insurance, including sickness benefits; (b) social security pensions, mainly consisting of old age pension, disablement pension and widows' pension, and also children's pension; (c) employment injuries insurance.

(ii) *The unemployment insurance legislation,* where daily allowances are paid to those who have met certain conditions.

(iii) *The subsistence legislation.* This is controlled by municipal government, and social assistance is granted under special circumstances, when payments from other sources are not sufficient.

(iv) *The tax legislation.* Prior to 1988 children's support was included in the tax legislation, according to which a certain amount for each child in a family was subtracted from income taxes or paid out to the family. Since 1988 family allowances are paid directly to all children age 0-15 years. The amount is increased with the second child in the family, and children under the age of 7 get additional benefits. Single parents receive additional allowances.

(v) *The rehabilitation legislation.*

(vi) *Child and juvenile guidance.*

Health insurance covers the entire population. Citizenship is not demanded and there is no waiting period. Most hospitals are both municipally and state run, a few solely state run and all offer free medical help. Medical treatment out of hospitals is partly paid by the patient, the same applies to medicines, except medicines of life-long necessary use, which are paid in full by the health insurance. Dental care is free for the age groups 6-15, but is paid 75% for those five years or younger and the age group 16 but 50% for old age and disabled pensioners. Sickness benefits are paid to those who lose income because of periodical illness. The daily amount is fixed and paid from the 11th day of illness.

The pension system is composed of the public social security system and some 90 private pension funds. The social security system pays basic old age and disablement pensions of a fixed amount regardless of past or present income, as well as supplementary pensions to individuals with low present income. The pensions are index-linked, i.e. are changed in line with changes in wage and salary rates in the labour market. The private pension funds pay pensions that depend on past payments of premiums that are a fixed proportion of earnings. The payment of pension fund premiums is compulsory for all wage and salary earners. The pensions paid by the funds differ considerably between the individual funds, but are generally index-linked. In the public social security system, entitlement to old age and disablement pensions at the full rates is subject to the condition that the beneficiary has been resident in Iceland for 40 years at the age period of 16-67. For shorter period of residence, the benefits are reduced proportionally. Entitled to old age pension are all those who are 67 years old, and have been residents in Iceland for 3 years of the age period of 16-67. Entitled to disablement pension are those who have lost 75% of their working capacity and have been residents in Iceland for 3 years before application or have had full working capacity at the time when they became residents. Old age and disablement pension are of equally high amount, in the year 1990 the total sum was 133,500 kr. for an individual. Married pensioners are paid 90% of two individuals' pensions. In addition to the basic amount, supplementary allowances are paid according to social circumstances and income possibilities. Widows' pensions are the same amount as old age and disablement pension, provided the applicant is over 60 when she becomes widowed. Women at the age 50-60 get reduced pension. Women under 50 are not entitled to widows' pensions.

The employment injuries insurance covers medical care, daily allowances, disablement pension and survivors' pension and is applicable to practically all employees.

Social assistance is primarily municipal and granted in cases outside the social security legislation. Domestic assistance to old people and disabled is granted within this legislation, besides other services.

Child and juvenile guidance is performed by chosen committees according to special laws, such as home guidance and family assistance. In cases of parents' disablement the committees take over the guidance of the children involved.

DIPLOMATIC REPRESENTATIVES

Of Iceland in Great Britain (1 Eaton Terrace, London, SW1W 8EY)
Ambassador: Helgi Ágústsson (accredited 13 Dec. 1989).

Of Great Britain in Iceland (Laufásvegur 49, 101 Reykjavík)
Ambassador and Consul-General: Patrick Wogan, CMG.

Of Iceland in the USA (2022 Connecticut Ave., NW, Washington, D.C., 20008)
Ambassador: Tómas A. Tómasson.

Of the USA in Iceland (Laufásvegur 21, 101 Reykjavík)
Ambassador: Charles E. Cobb Jr.

Of Iceland to the United Nations
Ambassador: Helgi Gíslason.

Further Reading

Statistical Information: The Statistical Bureau of Iceland, Hagstofa Íslands (Reykjavík) was founded in 1914. *Director:* Hallgrímur Snorrason. Its main publications are:

Landshagir 1991. Statistical Abstract of Iceland
Hagskýrslur Íslands. Statistics of Iceland (from 1912)
Hagtíðindi (Monthly Statistics) (from 1916)
Hagtölur mánaðarins. Monthly Bulletin (from 1973). Central Bank of Iceland
Economic Statistics Quarterly. Central Bank of Iceland (quarterly from 1980)
Heilbrigðisskýrslur. Public Health in Iceland (latest issue for 1986-87; published 1991)
Yearbook of Nordic Statistics. Nordic Council of Ministers and the Nordic Statistical Secretariat, Copenhagen.

Foss, H. (ed.) *Directory of Iceland.* Annual. Reykjavík, 1907–40, 1948 ff.
Hermannsson, Halldór, *Islandica.* An annual relating to Iceland and the Fiske Icelandic Collection in Cornell University Library. Ithaca (from 1908)
Horton, J. J., *Iceland.* [Bibliography] Oxford and Santa Barbara, 1983
Magnússon, S. A., *Northern Sphinx: Iceland and the Icelanders from the Settlement to the Present.* London, 1977
Nordal, J. and Kristinsson, V. (eds) *Iceland 1986.* Central Bank of Iceland, Reykjavík, 1987
Þórðarson, Matthias, *The Althing, Iceland's Thousand-Year-Old Parliament, 930–1930.* Reykjavík, 1930

National Library: Landsbókasafnið, Reykjavík, *Librarian:* Dr Finnbogi Guðmundsson.

INDIA

Bharat

(Republic of India)

Capital: New Delhi
Population: 844·32m. (1991)
GNP per capita: US$350 (1989)

HISTORY. The Indus civilization was fully developed by *c.* 2500 B.C., and collapsed *c.* 1750 B.C. An Aryan civilization spread from the west as far as the Ganges valley by 500 B.C.; separate kingdoms were established and many of these were united under the Mauryan dynasty established by Chandragupta in *c.* 320 B.C. The Mauryan Empire was succeeded by numerous small kingdoms. The Gupta dynasty (A.D. 320–600) was followed by the first Arabic invasions of the north-west. Moslem, Hindu and Buddhist states developed together with frequent conflict until the establishment of the Mogul dynasty in 1526. The first settlements by the East India Company were made after 1600 and the Company established a formal system of government for Bengal in 1700. During the decline of the Moguls frequent wars between the Company, the French and the native princes led to the Company's being brought under British Government control in 1784; the first Governor-General of India was appointed in 1786. The powers of the Company were abolished by the India Act, 1858, and its functions and forces transferred to the British Crown. Representative government was introduced in 1909, and the first parliament in 1919. The separate dominions of India and Pakistan became independent within the Commonwealth in 1947 and India became a republic in 1950.

The leader of the Congress (I) Party, Rajiv Gandhi, was assassinated on 21 May 1991 at the beginning of national and state elections. The elections were suspended until June, and were ultimately won by Congress (I).

AREA AND POPULATION. India is bounded north-west by Pakistan, north by China, Tibet, Nepal and Bhutan, east by Burma, south-east, south and south west by the Indian ocean. The far eastern states and territories are almost separated from the rest by Bangladesh as it extends northwards from the Bay of Bengal. The area of the Indian Union (excluding the Pakistan and China-occupied parts of Jammu and Kashmir) is 3,165,596 sq. km. Its population (excluding occupied Jammu and Kashmir) according to the 1991 census was 844,324,222 (406,332,932 females). Population at the 1981 census was 683,329,097. Sex ratio was 929 females per 1,000 males (933 in 1981); density of population, 267 per sq. km. About 23·3% of the population was urban in 1981 (in Maharashtra, 35%; in Himachal Pradesh, 7·6%).

Many births and deaths go unregistered. Data from the office of the Registrar General of India suggest that the birth rate for 1988-89 was about 31·3 per 1,000 population, the death rate 10.9 per 1,000. In 1981 (census) the age-group 0–14 years represented 39·5% of the population and only 6·5% were over 60. In 1981 expectation of life was 54·4 years.

Marriages and divorces are not registered. The minimum age for a civil marriage is 18 for women and 21 for men; for a sacramental marriage, 14 for girls and 18 for youths.

The main details of the census of 1 March 1981 and of 1 March 1991 are:

Name of State	Area in sq. km	Population 1981	1991
States			
Andhra Pradesh	275,068	53,549,673	66,354,559
Arunachal Pradesh	83,743	...	858,392
Assam	78,438	19,896,843	22,294,562
Bihar	173,877	69,914,734	86,338,853
Goa	3,702	...	1,168,622
Gujarat	196,024	34,085,799	41,174,343

[1] Excludes the area occupied by Pakistan and China. [2] Projection.

701

	Area	Population	
Name of State	in sq. km	1981	1991
Haryana	44,212	12,922,618	16,317,715
Himachal Pradesh	55,673	4,280,818	5,111,079
Jammu and Kashmir[1]	100,569	5,987,389	7,718,700 [2]
Karnataka	191,791	37,135,714	44,806,468
Kerala	38,863	25,453,680	29,032,828
Madhya Pradesh	443,446	52,178,844	66,135,862
Maharashtra	307,690	62,684,171	78,748,215
Manipur	22,327	1,420,953	1,826,714
Meghalaya	22,429	1,325,819	1,760,626
Mizoram	21,081	...	686,217
Nagaland	16,579	774,930	1,215,573
Orissa	155,707	26,370,271	31,512,070
Punjab	50,362	16,788,915	20,190,795
Rajasthan	342,239	34,261,862	43,880,640
Sikkim	7,096	316,385	405,505
Tamil Nadu	130,058	48,408,077	55,638,318
Tripura	10,486	2,053,058	2,744,827
Uttar Pradesh	294,411	110,862,013	139,031,130
West Bengal	87,752	54,580,647	67,982,732
Union Territories			
Andaman and Nicobar Islands	8,249	188,741	279,111
Chandigarh	114	450,610	640,725
Dadra and Nagar Haveli	491	103,676	138,401
Daman and Diu	112	78,981	101,439
Delhi	1,483	6,220,406	9,370,475
Lakshadweep	32	40,249	51,681
Pondicherry	492	604,471	807,045
Grand total	3,165,596	685,184,692	844,324,222

Greatest density occurs in Delhi (6,319 per sq. km), Chandigarh (5,620), Lakshadweep (1,615) and Pondicherry (1,605). The lowest occurs in Arunachal Pradesh (10).

In 1991, 627m. were rural (74·28%) and 217m. were urban.

Cities and Urban Agglomerations (with states in brackets) having more than 250,000 population at the 1991 census were (1,000):

Agra (U.P.)	899	Delhi	7,175	Kanpur (U.P.)	1,958
Ahmedabad (Guj.)	2,873	Dhanbad (Bih.) [2]	818	Kochi (Ker.)	564
Ajmer (Raj.)	402	Dhule (Mah.)	277	Kolhapur (Mah.)	405
Akola (Mah.)	328	Durgapur (W.B.)	266	Kota (Raj.)	536
Aligarh (U.P.)	480	Faridabad Complex		Kozhikode (Ker.)	420
Allahabad (U.P.)	806	(Har.)	614	Lucknow (U.P.)	1,592
Amravati (Mah.)	434	Gaya (Bih.)	291	Ludhiana (Pun.)	1,012
Amritsar (Pun.)	709	Ghaziabad (U.P.)	461	Madras (T.N.)	3,795
Asansol (W.B.)	262	Gorakhpur (U.P.)	490	Madurai (T.N.)	952
Bangalore (Kar.)	2,651	Gulbarga (Kar.)	303	Malegaon (Mah.)	342
Bareilly (U.P.)	583	Guntur (A.P.)	471	Mangalore (Kar.)	273
Belgaum (Mah.)	326	Guwahati (Ass.)	578	Meerut (U.P.)	752
Bhagalpur (Bih.)	255	Gwalior (M.P.)	693	Moradabad (U.P.)	417
Bhatpara (W.B.)	304	Haora (W.B.)	947	Mysore (Kar.)	480
Bhavnagar (Guj.)	401	Hubli-Dharwad (Kar.)	648	Nagpur (Mah.)	1,622
Bhilainagar (M.P.)	390	Hyderabad (A.P.)	3,005	Nanded (Mah.)	275
Bhiwandi (Mah.)	379	Indore (M.P.)	1,087	Nashik (Mah.)	647
Bhopal (W.B.)	1,604	Jabalpur (M.P.)	740	Nellore (A.P.)	316
Bhubaneswar (Ori.)	412	Jaipur (Raj.)	1,455	New Bombay (Mah.)	307
Bikaner (Raj.)	415	Jalandhar (Pun.)	520	New Delhi (Del.)	294
Bombay (Mah.) [1]	9,990	Jamnagar (Guj.)	325	Panihati (W.B.)	275
Calcutta (W.B.) [2]	10,916	Jamshedpur (Bih.)	461	Patiala (Pun.)	253
Chandigarh (Ch.)	503	Jhansi (U.P.)	301	Patna (Bih.)	917
Coimbatore (T.N.)	853	Jodhpur (Raj.)	649	Pimpri-Chinchwad	
Cuttack (Ori.)	402	Kakinada (A.P.)	280	(Mah.)	516
Davangere (Kar.)	266	Kalyan (Mah.)	1,014	Pune (Mah.)	1,560
Dehra Dun (U.P.)	270	Kamarhati (W.B.)	266	Raipur (M.P.)	438

[1] Greater Bombay.   [2] Urban agglomeration.

Rajamundry (A.P.)	268	Surat (Guj.)	1,497	Ulhasnagar (Mah.)	369
Rajkot (Raj.)	556	Thane (Mah.)	797	Vadodara (Guj.)	1,021
Ranchi (Bih)	598	Thiruvananthapuram		Varanasi (U.P.)	926
Saharanpur (U.P.)	374	(Ker.)	524	Vijayawada (A.P.)	701
Salem (T.N.)	364	Tiruchirapalli (T.N.)	387	Visakhapatnam (A.P.)	750
Sholapur (Mah.)	604	Udaipur (Raj.)	308	Warangal (A.P.)	447
Srinagar (J. & K.)	595	Ujjain (M.P.)	367		

CLIMATE. India has a variety of climatic sub-divisions. In general, there are four seasons. The cool one lasts from Dec. to March, the hot season is in April and May, the rainy season is June to Sept., followed by a further dry season till Nov. Rainfall, however, varies considerably, from 4" (100 mm) in the N.W. desert to over 400" (10,000 mm) in parts of Assam.

Range of temperature and rainfall: New Delhi. Jan. 57°F (13·9°C), July 88°F (31·1°C). Annual rainfall 26" (640 mm). Bombay. Jan. 75°F (23·9°C), July 81°F (27·2°C). Annual rainfall 72" (1,809 mm). Calcutta. Jan. 67°F (19·4°C), July 84°F (28·9°C). Annual rainfall 64" (1,600 mm). Cherrapunji. Jan. 53°F (11·7°C), July 68°F (20°C). Annual rainfall 432" (10,798 mm). Darjeeling. Jan. 41°F (5°C), July 62°F (16·7°C). Annual rainfall 121" (3,035 mm). Hyderabad. Jan. 72°F (22·2°C), July 80°F (26·7°C). Annual rainfall 30" (752 mm). Kochi. Jan. 80°F (26·7°C), July 79°F (26·1°C). Annual rainfall 117" (2,929 mm). Madras. Jan. 76°F (24·4°C), July 87°F (30·6°C). Annual rainfall 51" (1,270 mm). Patna. Jan. 63°F (17·2°C), July 90°F (32·2°C). Annual rainfall 46" (1,150 mm).

CONSTITUTION AND GOVERNMENT. On 26 Jan. 1950 India became a sovereign democratic republic. India's relations with the British Commonwealth of Nations were defined at the London conference of Prime Ministers on 27 April 1949.

Unanimous agreement was reached to the effect that the Republic of India remains a full member of the Commonwealth and accepts the Queen as 'the symbol of the free association of its independent member nations and, as such, the head of the Commonwealth'. This agreement was ratified by the Constituent Assembly of India on 17 May 1949.

The constitution was passed by the Constituent Assembly on 26 Nov. 1949 and came into force on 26 Jan. 1950. It has since been amended 67 times.

India is a Union of States and comprises 25 States and 7 Union territories. Each State is administered by a Governor appointed by the President for a term of 5 years while each Union territory is administered by the President through a Lieut.-Governor or an administrator appointed by him.

The capital is New Delhi.

Presidency. The head of the Union is the President in whom all executive power is vested, to be exercised on the advice of ministers responsible to Parliament. He is elected by an electoral college consisting of all the elected members of Parliament and of the various state legislative assemblies. He holds office for 5 years and is eligible for re-election. He must be an Indian citizen at least 35 years old and eligible for election to the Lower House. He can be removed from office by impeachment for violation of the constitution.

There is also a Vice-President who is *ex-officio* chairman of the Upper House of Parliament.

Central Legislature. The Parliament for the Union consists of the President, the Council of States *(Rajya Sabha)* and the House of the People *(Lok Sabha)*. The Council of States, or the Upper House, consists of not more than 250 members; in Nov. 1991 there were 233 elected members and 12 members nominated by the President. The election to this house is indirect; the representatives of each State are elected by the elected members of the Legislative Assembly of that State. The Council of States is a permanent body not liable to dissolution, but one-third of the members retire every second year. The House of the People, or the Lower House, consists of 545 members, 543 directly elected on the basis of adult suffrage from territorial constituencies in the States, and the Union territories; in Nov. 1991 there were 520 elected members, 2 members nominated by the President and 23 vacancies. The House of the People unless sooner dissolved continues for a period of 5 years from the date appointed for its first meeting; in emergency, Parliament can extend the term by 1 year.

State Legislatures. For every State there is a legislature which consists of the Governor, and *(a)* 2 Houses, a Legislative Assembly and a Legislative Council, in the States of Bihar, Jammu and Kashmir, Karnataka, Madhya Pradesh (where it is provided for but not in operation), Maharashtra and Uttar Pradesh, and *(b)* 1 House, a Legislative Assembly, in the other States. Every Legislative Assembly, unless sooner dissolved, continues for 5 years from the date appointed for its first meeting. In emergency the term can be extended by 1 year. Every State Legislative Council is a permanent body and is not subject to dissolution, but one-third of the members retire every second year. Parliament can, however, abolish an existing Legislative Council or create a new one, if the proposal is supported by a resolution of the Legislative Assembly concerned.

Legislation. The various subjects of legislation are enumerated in three lists in the seventh schedule to the constitution. List I, the Union List, consists of 97 subjects (including defence, foreign affairs, communications, currency and coinage, banking and customs) with respect to which the Union Parliament has exclusive power to make laws. The State legislature has exclusive power to make laws with respect to the 66 subjects in list II, the State List; these include police and public order, agriculture and irrigation, education, public health and local government. The powers to make laws with respect to the 47 subjects (including economic and social planning, legal questions and labour and price control) in list III, the Concurrent List, are held by both Union and State governments, though the former prevails. But Parliament may legislate with respect to any subject in the State List in circumstances when the subject assumes national importance or during emergencies.

Other provisions deal with the administrative relations between the Union and the States, interstate trade and commerce, distribution of revenues between the States and the Union, official language, etc.

Fundamental Rights. Two chapters of the constitution deal with fundamental rights and 'Directive Principles of State Policy'. 'Untouchability' is abolished, and its practice in any form is punishable. The fundamental rights can be enforced through the ordinary courts of law and through the Supreme Court of the Union. The directive principles cannot be enforced through the courts of law; they are nevertheless fundamental in the governance of the country.

Citizenship. Under the Constitution, every person who was on the 26 Jan. 1950, domiciled in India and *(a)* was born in India or *(b)* either of whose parents was born in India or *(c)* who has been ordinarily resident in the territory of India for not less than 5 years immediately preceding that date became a citizen of India. Special provision is made for migrants from Pakistan and for Indians resident abroad. Under the Citizenship Act, 1955, which supplemented the provisions of the Constitution, Indian citizenship is acquired by birth, by descent, by registration and by naturalization. The Act also provides for loss of citizenship by renunciation, termination and deprivation. The right to vote is granted to every person who is a citizen of India and who is not less than 18 years of age on a fixed date and is not otherwise disqualified.

Parliament. Parliament and the state legislatures are organized according to the following schedule (figures show distribution of seats in Nov. 1991):

	Parliament		State Legislatures	
	House of the People (Lok Sabha)	Council of States (Rajya Sabha)	Legislative Assemblies (Vidhan Sabhas)	Legislative Councils (Vidhan Parishads)
States:				
Andhra Pradesh	42	18	294	–
Arunachal Pradesh	2	1	60	–
Assam	14	7	126	–
Bihar	54	22	324	96

| | Parliament | | State Legislatures | |
	House of the People (Lok Sabha)	Council of States (Rajya Sabha)	Legislative Assemblies (Vidhan Sabhas)	Legislative Councils (Vidhan Parishads)
States (continued):				
Goa	2	–	40	–
Gujarat	26	11	182	–
Haryana	10	5	90	–
Himachal Pradesh	4	3	68	–
Jammu and Kashmir	6	4	76[2]	36[4]
Karnataka	28	12	224	75
Kerala	20	9	140	–
Madhya Pradesh	40	16	320	–
Maharashtra	48	19	288	63
Manipur	2	1	60	–
Meghalaya	2	1	60	–
Mizoram	1	1	40	–
Nagaland	1	1	60	–
Orissa	21	10	147	–
Punjab	13	7	117	–
Rajasthan	25	10	200	–
Sikkim	1	1	32	–
Tamil Nadu	39	18	234	–
Tripura	2	1	60	–
Uttar Pradesh	85	34	425	108
West Bengal	42	16	294	–
Union Territories:				
Andaman and Nicobar Islands	1	–	–	–
Chandigarh	1	–	–	–
Dadra and Nagar Haveli	1	–	–	–
Delhi	7	3	56	–
Daman and Diu	1	–	–	–
Lakshadweep	1	–	–	–
Pondicherry	1	1	30	–
Nominated by the President under Article 80 (1) (a) of the Constitution	–	12	–	–
Total	545 [1]	244	4,047	378

[1] Includes 2 nominated members to represent Anglo-Indians.
[2] Excludes 24 seats for Pakistan-occupied areas of the State which are in abeyance.
[3] Nominated by the President.   [4] Excludes seats for the Pakistan-occupied areas.

The number of seats allotted to scheduled castes and scheduled tribes in the House of the People is 79 and 41 respectively. Out of the 4,047 seats allotted to the Legislative Assemblies, 557 are reserved for scheduled castes and 527 for scheduled tribes.

Composition of the House of the People after the election held in 1991: Congress (I) 232; Janata Dal, 59; Bharatiya Janata Party, 119; CPI (Marxist, 35; CPI, 14; AIADMK (All India Anna Dravida Munnetra Kazagam), 11; Shiv Sena, 4; Samajvadi Janata Party, 5; Revolutionary Socialist Party, 4; Bahujan Samaj Party, 2; Forward Bloc, 3; Jharkhand Mukti Morcha, 6; Muslim League, 2; Telugu Desam, 13; Independent and others, 11; nominated, 2; vacant, 23.

Composition of the Council of States in Feb. 1991: Congress (I) 108; Communist Party of India (Marxist), 17; All-India Anna DMK, 4; Janata Dal, 23; Bharatiya Janata, 17; Janata, 1; Telugu Desam, 10; Dravida Munnetra Kazagam, 10; Asom Gana Parishad, 5; Revolutionary Socialist Party, 2; J. & K. National Conference, 2; Communist Party, 3; Ind, 12; Janata Dal (S), 15, nominated, 5; vacant, 2.

National flag: Three horizontal stripes of saffron (orange), white and green, with the wheel of Asoka in the centre in blue.

National anthem: Jana-gana-mana ('Thou art the ruler of the minds of all people'; words by Rabindranath Tagore).

Language. The Constitution provides that the official language of the Union shall be Hindi in the Devanagari script. It was originally provided that English should continue to be used for all official purposes until 1965. But the Official Languages Act 1963 provides that, after the expiry of this period of 15 years from the coming into force of the Constitution, English might continue to be used, in addition to Hindi, for all official purposes of the Union for which it was being used immediately before that day, and for the transaction of business in Parliament. According to the Official Languages (Use for official purposes of the Union) Rules 1976, an employee may record in Hindi or in English without being required to furnish a translation thereof in the other language and no employee possessing a working knowledge of Hindi may ask for an English translation of any document in Hindi except in the case of legal or technical documents.

The 58th amendment to the Constitution (26 Nov. 1987) authorised the preparation of a Constitution text in Hindi.

The following 15 languages are included in the Eighth Schedule to the Constitution: Assamese, Bengali, Gujarati, Hindi, Kannada, Kashmiri, Malayalam, Marathi, Oriya, Punjabi, Sanskrit, Sindhi, Tamil, Telugu, Urdu.

There are numerous mother tongues grouped under each language. Hindi, Bengali, Telugu, Tamil and Marathi languages (including mother tongues grouped under each) are spoken by 264·2m., 51·5m., 54·2m., 44·7m. and 49·6m. of the population respectively.

Government. *President of the Republic:* R. Venkataraman (sworn in 25 July 1987). *Vice-President:* Shankar Dayal Sharma (elected 21 Aug. 1987).

There is a *Council of Ministers* to aid and advise the President of the Republic in the exercise of his functions; this comprises Ministers who are members of the Cabinet and Ministers of State who are not. A Minister who for any period of 6 consecutive months is not a member of either House of Parliament ceases to be a Minister at the expiration of that period. The Prime Minister is appointed by the President; other Ministers are appointed by the President on the Prime Minister's advice.

The salary of each Minister is Rs 27,000 per annum, and that of each Deputy Minister is Rs 21,000 per annum. Each Minister is entitled to the free use of a furnished residence and a chauffeur-driven car throughout his term of office. A Cabinet Minister has a sumptuary allowance of Rs 1,000 per month, Ministers of State, Rs 500 and Deputy Ministers, Rs 300. At the administrative head of each Ministry is a Secretary of the Government.

Following the resignation of Chandra Shekhar and his government in March 1991, elections were held in May-June 1991. No party got an absolute majority in the House of the People. As the leader of the largest party, P. V. Narasimha Rao formed a Congress (I) Government at the Centre.

The Cabinet was composed as follows in Feb. 1992:

Prime Minister: P. V. Narasimha Rao (b. 1921).

Portfolios held by the Prime Minister assisted by Ministers of State: *Personnel and Public Grievances, Science and Technology, Space, Ocean Development, Electronics, Atomic Energy, Chemicals and Fertilizers, Rural Development, Civil Supplies and Public Distribution System, and Industry.*

Defence: Sharad Pawar. *Human Resource Development:* Arjun Singh. *Agriculture:* Balram Jakhar. *Home Affairs:* S. B. Chavan. *Health and Family Welfare:* M. L. Fotedar. *Parliamentary Affairs:* Ghulam Nabi Azad. *Railways:* C. K. Jaffer Sharief. *Urban Development:* Sheila Kaul. *Welfare:* Sitaram Kesri. *Law, Justice and Company Affairs:* K. Vijaya Bhaskara Reddy. *Civil Aviation and Tourism:* Madhavrao Scindia. *Petroleum and Natural Gas:* B. Shankaranand. *Water Resources:* V. C. Shukla. *Finance:* Dr Manmohan Singh. *External Affairs:* Madhavsinh Solanki.

There were also 13 Ministers of State with independent responsibilities and 21 Ministers of State.

Local Government. There were in 1989-90, 72 municipal corporations, 1,770 municipal committees/boards/councils, 663 town area committees and 337 notified area committees. The municipal bodies have the care of the roads, water supply, drainage, sanitation, medical relief, vaccination, education, street lighting, etc. Their main sources of revenue are taxes on the annual rental value of land and buildings, octroi and terminal, vehicle and other taxes. The municipal councils enact their own bye-laws and frame their budgets, which in the case of municipal bodies other than corporations generally require the sanction of the State government. All municipal councils are elected on the principle of adult franchise.

For rural areas there is a 3-tier system of *panchayati raj* at village, block and district level, although the 3-tier structure may undergo some changes in State legislation to suit local conditions. All *panchayati raj* bodies are organically linked, and representation is given to special interests. Elected directly by and from among villagers, the *panchayats* are responsible for agricultural production, rural industries, medical relief, maternity and child welfare, common grazing grounds, village roads, tanks and wells, and maintenance of sanitation. In some places they also look after primary education, maintenance of village records and collection of land revenue. They have their own powers of taxation. There are some judicial *panchayats* or village courts.

Panchayati raj now cover almost all the States and Union Territories with variations in structural pattern. *Panchayati raj* involvels a 3-tier arrangement: Village level, block level and district level. Tenure of *Panchayati raj* institutions range from 3–5 years.

The powers and responsibilities of *Panchayati raj* institutions are derived from State Legislatures, and from the executive orders of State governments.

DEFENCE. The Supreme Command of the Armed Forces vests in the President of the Indian Republic. Policy is decided at different levels by a number of committees, including the Political Affairs Committee presided over by the Prime Minister and the Defence Minister's Committee. Administrative and operational control rests in the respective Service Headquarters, under the control of the Ministry of Defence.

The Ministry of Defence is the central agency for formulating defence policy and for co-ordinating the work of the three services. Among the organizations directly administered by the Ministry are the Research and Development Organization, the Production Organization, the National Defence College, the National Cadet Corps and the Directorate-General of Armed Forces Medical Services.

The Research and Development Organization (headed by the Scientific Adviser to the Minister) has under it about 30 research establishments. The Production Organization controls 8 public-sector undertakings and 39 ordnance factories.

The National Defence College, New Delhi, was established in 1960 on the pattern of the Imperial Defence College (UK): the 1-year course is for officers of the rank of brigadier or equivalent and for senior civil servants. The Defence Services Staff College, Wellington, trains officers of the three Services for higher command for staff appointments. There is an Armed Forces Medical College at Pune.

The National Defence Academy, Khadakvasla, gives a 3-year basic training course to officer cadets of the three Services prior to advanced training at the respective Service establishments.

Army. The Army Headquarters functioning directly under the Chief of the Army Staff is divided into the following main branches: General Staff Branch; Adjutant General's Branch; Quartermaster-General's Branch; Master-General of Ordnance Branch; Engineer-in-Chief's Branch; Military Secretary's Branch.

The Army is organized into 5 commands each divided into areas, which in turn are subdivided into sub-areas. Recruitment of permanent commissioned officers is through the Indian Military Academy, Dehra Dun. It conducts courses for ex-National Defence Academy, National Cadet Corps and direct-entry cadets, and for serving personnel and technical graduates.

The Territorial Army came into being in Sept. 1949, its role being to: (1) relieve the regular Army of static duties and, if required, support civil power; (2) provide anti-aircraft units, and (3) if and when called upon, provide units for the regular Army. The Territorial Army is composed of practically all arms of the Services.

The authorized strength of the Army was (1992) 1·1m., that of the Territorial Army, 160,000. There are 2 armoured, 1 mechanized, 21 infantry and 11 mountain divisions, 5 independent armoured brigades, 7 independent infantry, 3 independent artillery brigades, 1 parachute brigade, 1 mountain brigade, 6 air defence brigades and 4 engineer brigades. An Aviation Corps was formed in 1986 and operates locally-built Alouette and Lama helicopters.

Equipment includes some 500 T-55, 900 T-72/-M1 and 1,700 Vijayanta main battle tanks and 100 PT-76 light tanks.

Navy. The Navy has 3 commands; Eastern, Western and Southern, the latter a training and support command. The fleet is divided into two elements, Eastern and Western; and well-trained, all volunteer personnel operate a mix of Soviet and Western vessels. The continued build-up of the past 5 years may now have been halted due to budgetary difficulties.

The principal ships of the Indian Navy are the 2 light aircraft carriers, *Viraat* and *Vikrant*. The *Viraat*, formerly HMS *Hermes*, is of 29,000 tonnes and was completed in 1959. Having earlier been converted to vertical/short take-off and landing aircraft operations, she was transferred to the Indian Navy in 1987. *Vikrant*, 19,880 tonnes, (the former HMS *Hercules*), was transferred to India in 1961, and completed conversion to the vertical/short take-off and landing role in 1990. Both embark an air group of 8 Sea Harrier fighters and 8 Sea King anti-submarine helicopters.

The leased Soviet nuclear-powered missile submarine, *Chakra*, was returned to the USSR in 1991. The fleet now includes 8 'Kilo' and 7 'Foxtrot' Soviet-built diesel submarines and 3 smaller German-built. 5 new Soviet-built missile armed destroyers, 3 heavily modified and 6 rather less modified 'Leander' class frigates, all built in India, and 13 other frigates form the main surface force. Coastal forces include 9 Soviet-designed missile and 4 anti-submarine corvettes, 9 fast missile craft and 14 inshore patrol craft. There are 12 Soviet-built offshore minesweepers, and 8 much smaller inshore vessels. Amphibious lift for the 1,000 strong marine force is provided by 1 tank landing ship and 8 medium landing ships, as well as about 10 craft. Support forces include 3 tankers, 1 submarine depot ship, 1 transport, 8 survey and research, 2 tugs and 1 training ship.

The Naval Air force, 5,000 strong, operates 18 Sea Harriers, 5 Il-38 'May', 8 Tu-142M 'Bear-F' and 9 Britten-Norman Islander maritime patrol aircraft. Armed helicopters include 26 Chetak, 7 Ka-25, 12 Ka-27 and 38 Sea King, and the inventory is completed with some 22 training and communications aircraft.

Main bases are at Bombay (HQ Western Fleet, and main dockyard), Goa, Vishakhapatnam (HQ Eastern Fleet) and Calcutta on the sub-continent, and Port Blair in the Andaman Islands. HQ Southern Command is at Cochin.

Naval personnel in 1991 numbered 55,000 including 5,000 Naval Air Arm and 1,000 marines.

The Coast Guard is an independent para-military service 2,800 strong in 1991, which functions under Defence Ministry control, but is funded by the Revenue Department. The force comprises 8 offshore patrol vessels and 32 inshore patrol craft. Its 20 aircraft are of Dornier-228, Fokker F-27 and Britten-Norman Islander types and Chetak helicopters.

Air Force. The Indian Air Force Act was passed in 1932, and the first flight was formed in 1933.

The Air Headquarters, under the Chief of Air Staff, consists of 4 main branches, viz., Air Staff, Administration, Policy and Plans, and Maintenance. Units of the IAF are organized into 5 operational commands–Western at Delhi, Central at Allahabad, Eastern at Shillong, Southern at Thiruvananthapuram and South-Western at Jodhpur. Training Command HQ is at Bangalore, Maintenance Command at Nagpur. Nominal strength in 1992 was 110,000 personnel and 735 aircraft of all types, in over 50 squadrons of aircraft and helicopters and about 30 squadrons of 'Guideline' and 'Goa' surface-to-air missiles, and close-range missiles such as 'Gainful' and Tigercat.

Air defence units include 2 squadrons of MiG-23 variable-geometry interceptors, 2 squadrons of MiG-29s, 18 squadrons of MiG-21s and 3 of Mirage 2000s. Other combat units include 8 squadrons of MiG-27s, 2 of Canberras, 4 of Jaguars, 4 of MiG-23 supersonic fighter-bombers and one of MiG-25 reconnaissance aircraft plus a MiG-25U two seat trainer. Currently the main re-equipment programmes involve the licence-production of MiG-27 and Jaguar strike aircraft.

The large transport force includes An-12s, An-32s, Il-76s, Do 228s, HS 748s, 2 Boeing 737s, and smaller aircraft and helicopters for VIP and other duties. Helicopter units have Mi-8s and Mi-17s (10 squadrons), Mi-26s, and Mi-25 gunships, but the bulk of the Air Force's Chetaks (Alouette IIIs) and Cheetahs (Lamas) have been transferred to Army control, main training types are the Hindustan HPT-32 and Kiran, Polish-built TS-11 Iskra, Hunter T.66, MiG-21UT1 and MiG-23U.

Primary flying training is provided at the Elementary Flying School, Bidar, and advanced flying training at the Air Force Academy, Dundigal, Hyderabad. There is a Navigation and Signals School at Begumpet. The IAF Technical College, Jalahalli, imparts technical training, while the IAF Administrative College, Coimbatore, trains officers of the ground duty branch. There are also land-air warfare, flying instructors' and medical schools.

INTERNATIONAL RELATIONS

Membership. India is a member of the UN, the Commonwealth and the Colombo Plan.

Treaties. India pursues a general policy of non-alignment; the exception is a Treaty of Peace, Friendship and Cooperation with the USSR, 1971; the parties agreed to mutual support short of force in the event of either being attacked by a third party.

ECONOMY

Policy. The highest economic decision-making body is the *National Development Council*, of which all state chief ministers are members. There is also a *Planning Commission*.

The eighth 5-year plan (1992–97) emphasizes job creation and increases rural investment, and aims at an annual growth of 5·6% of GDP, 3% in employment and a domestic savings rate of 21·6% of GDP. Indicative planning, however, is tending to take the place of centralized planning.

As a first step towards partial privatization of the 248 state-owned corporations, selected public sector enterprises are being allowed to raise funds through equity issues.

Requirements for government approval of investment decisions were reduced in 1990. The eighth plan (1992–97) envisages an outlay of Rs 7,920,000m., with public sector investment of Rs 3,420,000m. Central plan outlay (1991–92), Rs 421,480m.

Budget. Revenue and expenditure (on revenue account) of the central government for years ending 31 March, in Rs 1m.:

	1989–90	1990–91 [1]	1991–92 [2]
Revenue	522,960	573,810	675,290
Expenditure	642,080	749,660	813,830

[1] Revised. [2] Budget estimates.

Important items of revenue and expenditure on the revenue account of the central government for 1991–92 (estimates), in Rs 1m.:

Revenue		Expenditure	
Net tax revenue	443,180	General Services	469,803
Non-tax revenue	130,630	Defence	115,954
		Major subsidies	78,240

Total capital account receipts (1991–92 budget), Rs 385,640m.; capital account disbursements, Rs 320,390m. Total (revenue and capital) receipts, Rs 1,057,030m.; disbursements, Rs 1,134,222m.

Under the Constitution (Part XII and 7th Schedule), the power to raise funds has been divided between the central government and the states. Generally, the sources of revenue are mutually exclusive. Certain taxes are levied by the Union for the sake of uniformity and distributed to the states. The Finance Commission (Art. 280 of the Constitution) advises the President on the distribution of the taxes which are distributable between the centre and the states, and on the principles on which grants should be made out of Union revenues to the states. The main sources of central revenue are: customs duties; those excise duties levied by the central government; corporation, income and wealth taxes; estate and succession duties on non-agricultural assets and property, and revenues from the railways and posts and telegraphs. The main heads of revenue in the states are: taxes and duties levied by the state governments (including land revenues and agricultural income tax); civil administration and civil works; state undertakings; taxes shared with the centre; and grants received from the centre.

Currency. A decimal system of coinage was introduced in 1957. The Indian *rupee* (INR) is divided into 100 *paise*. There are coins of 1, 2, 3, 5, 10, 20, 25 and 50 *paise*. The paper currency consists of: (1) Reserve Bank notes in denominations of Rs 2, 5, 10, 20, 50, 100 and 500; and (2) Government of India currency notes of denominations of Re 1 deemed to be included in the expression 'rupee coin' for the purposes of the Reserve Bank of India Act, 1934.

According to the Reserve Bank of India, the total money supply with the public on the last Friday of March 1991 was Rs 935,570m. crores. Foreign exchange reserves, Oct. 1991, Rs 59,600m.

The rupee is valued in relation to a package of main currencies. It was devalued by 18·74% against the dollar in July 1991. The £ is the currency of intervention. In March 1992 Rs 45.95 = £1; Rs 26.17 = US$1.

Banking and Finance. The Reserve Bank, the central bank for India, was established in 1934 and started functioning on 1 April 1935 as a shareholder's bank; it became a nationalized institution on 1 Jan. 1949. It has the sole right of issuing currency notes. Its *Governor* is S. Venkitaramanan. The Bank acts as adviser to the Government on financial problems and is the banker for central and state governments, commercial banks and some other financial institutions. The Bank manages the rupee public debt of central and state governments. It is the custodian of the country's exchange reserve and supervises repatriation of export proceeds and payments for imports. The Bank gives short-term loans to state governments and scheduled banks and short and medium-term loans to state co-operative banks and industrial finance institutions. The Bank has extensive powers of regulation of the banking system, directly under the Banking Regulation Act, 1949, and indirectly by the use of variations in Bank rate, variation in reserve ratios, selective credit controls and open market operations. Bank rate was raised to 10% in July 1981.

Except refinance for food credit and export credit, the Reserve Bank's refinance facility to commercial banks has been placed on a discretionary basis. The net profit of the Reserve Bank of India for the year ended June 1986, after making the usual or necessary provisions, amounted to Rs 2,100m.

The commercial banking system consisted of 274 scheduled banks (*i.e.*, banks which are included in the 2nd schedule to the Reserve Bank Act) and 4 non-scheduled banks on 30 June 1988; scheduled banks included 196 Regional Rural Banks. Total deposits in commercial banks, March 1991, stood at Rs 1,849,610m. The business of non-scheduled banks forms less than 0·1% of commercial bank business. Of the 274 scheduled banks, 22 are foreign banks which specialize in financing foreign trade but also compete for domestic business. The largest scheduled bank is the State Bank of India, constituted by nationalizing the Imperial Bank of India in 1955. The State Bank acts as the agent of the Reserve Bank and the subsidiaries of the State Bank act as the agents of the State Bank for transacting government business as well as undertaking commercial functions. Fourteen banks with aggregate deposits of not less than Rs 500m. were nationalized on 19 July 1969. Six banks were nationalized in April 1980. The 28 public sector banks (which comprise the State Bank of India and its seven associate banks and 20 nationalised banks) account for about 90% of deposits and bank credit of all scheduled commercial banks.

There are stock exchanges in Ahmedabad, Bombay, Calcutta, Delhi, Madras and 15 other centres.

Weights and Measures. Uniform standards of weights and measures, based on the metric system, were established for the first time by the Standards of Weights and Measures Act, 1956, which provided for a transition period of 10 years. So far the system has been fully adopted in trade transactions but there are a few fields such as engineering, survey and land records and the building and construction industry where it has not; efforts are being made to complete the change as early as possible.

In order to align this legislation with the latest international trends an expert committee (Weights and Measures (Law Revision) Committee) was set up by the central government to suggest a revised Bill which was passed by Parliament in April 1976. The new Standards of Weights and Measures Act, 1976, has recognized the International System of Units and other units recommended by the General Conference on Weights and Measures and is in line with the recommendations of the International Organisation of Legal Metrology (OIML). The new Act also covers the system of numeration, the approval of models of weights and measures, regulation and control of inter-state trade in relation to weights and measures. The Act also protects consumers through proper indication of weight, quantity, identity, source, date and price on packaged goods. A draft Standards of Weights and Measures (Enforcement) Bill has also been prepared by the committee for adoption either by Parliament or State legislatures, as enforcement is now in the 'concurrent' list of legislation.

The provisions of the 1976 Act came into force in Sept. 1977, as did the accompanying Standards of Weights and Measures (Packaged Commodities) Rules, 1977.

While the Standards of Weights and Measures are laid down in the Central Act, enforcement of weights and measures laws is entrusted to the state governments; the central Directorate of Weights and Measures is responsible for co-ordinating activities so as to ensure national uniformity.

An Indian Institute of Legal Metrology trains officials of the Weights and Measures departments of India and different developing countries. The Institute is being modernized with technical assistance from the Federal Republic of Germany.

There are 2 Regional Reference Standards laboratories at Ahmedabad and Bhubaneswar which (besides calibrating secondary standards of physical measurements) also provide testing facilities in metrological and industrial measurements. These laboratories are equipped with Standards next in line to the National Standards of physical measurements which are maintained at the National Physical Laboratory in New Delhi.

For weights previously in legal use under the Standards of Weight Act, 1956, *see* THE STATESMAN'S YEAR-BOOK, 1961, p. 171.

Calendar. The dates of the Saka era (named after the north Indian dynasty of the first century A.D.) are being used alongside Gregorian dates in issues of the *Gazette of India*, news broadcasts by All-India Radio and government-issued calendars, from 22 March 1957, a date which corresponds with the first day of the year 1879 in the Saka era.

ENERGY AND NATURAL RESOURCES

Electricity. In Dec. 1990 473,366 villages out of 579,132 had electricity. Production of electricity in 1989–90 was 245,400m. kwh., of which 183,330m. kwh. came from thermal and nuclear stations and 62,100m. kwh from hydro-electric stations. Supply 230 and 250 volts; 50 Hz.

Oil and Gas. The Oil and Natural Gas Commission and Oil India Ltd are the only producers of crude oil. Production 1990-91, 33·02m. tonnes, about 60% of consumption. The main fields are in Assam and Gujarat and offshore in the Gulf of Cambay (the Bombay High field). Natural gas production, 1990–91, 14,082m. cu. metres.

Water. The net area of 63·3m. ha (1987-88) under irrigation exceeds that of any other country except China, and equals about 38% of the total area under cultivation. Irrigation projects have formed an important part of all three Five-Year Plans. The possibilities of diverting rivers into canals being nearly exhausted, the emphasis is now on damming the monsoon surplus flow and diverting that. Ultimate potential of irrigation is assessed at 107m. ha, total cultivated land being 142m. ha. In 1985 India and Bangladesh reached an agreement to monitor the water of the Ganges at the Farakka barrage.

1987 was a year of severe drought, affecting both agriculture and water-supplies to cities.

Minerals. Bihar, West Bengal and Madhya Pradesh produce 42%, 25% and 19% of all coal, respectively. The coal industry was nationalized in 1973. Production, 1990, 216m. tonnes; reserves (including lignite) are estimated at 176,330m. tonnes. Production of other minerals, 1990 (in 1,000 tonnes): Iron ore, 53,697; bauxite, 5,277; chromite 1,084; copper ore, 5,212; manganese ore, 1,414; gold, 1,856 kg. Other important minerals are lead, zinc, limestone, apatite and phosphorite, dolomite, magnesite and silver. Value of mineral production, 1990, Rs 178,370m. of which mineral fuels produced Rs 153,620m., metallic minerals Rs 10,870m. and non-metallic Rs 13,880m.

Agriculture. The chief industry of India has always been agriculture. About 70% of the people are dependent on the land for their living. In 1988-89 it provided about 35% of net national product.

In 1989–90 agricultural commodities accounted for about 9·5% by value of Indian exports. In 1984–85 agricultural commodities, machinery and fertilizers accounted for about 20% of imports.

An increase in food production of at least 2% per annum is necessary to keep pace with the rising population. Foodgrain production, 1989-90 (estimate) 171m. tonnes.

The Indian Council of Agricultural Research works through 46 institutes, 20 national research centres, 9 project directorates, and 75 national research projects. There are 4 national research bureaux and 23 agricultural universities.

The farming year runs from July to June through three crop seasons: Kharif (monsoon); rabi (winter) and summer.

Agricultural production, 1989-90 (in 1,000 tonnes): Rice, 74,053; wheat, 49,652; total foodgrains, 170,626·5; maize, 9,410; pulses, 12,615; sugar-cane 222,628; oil-seeds, 18,033; cotton, 11·4m. bales (of 180 kg); jute is grown in West Bengal (70% of total yield), Bihar and Assam, total yield, 7·1m. bales (of 180 kg). The coffee industry is growing: The main cash varieties are Arabica and Robusta (main growing areas Karnataka, Kerala and Tamil Nadu).

The tea industry is important, with production concentrated in Assam, West Bengal, Tamil Nadu and Kerala. Total crop in 1989–90, 702,810 tonnes from 414,232 ha; exports in 1990–91 values at Rs 10,750m.

Livestock (1988): Cattle, 193m.; sheep, 51,684,000; pigs, 10·3m.; horses, 953,000; asses, 1,328,000m.; goats, 105m.; buffaloes, 72m.

Fertilizer consumption in 1990–91 was 12·7m. tonnes.

Land Tenure. There are three main traditional systems of land tenure: *Ryotwari* tenure, where the individual holders, usually peasant proprietors, are responsible for the payment of land revenues; *zamindari* tenure, where one or more persons own large estates and are responsible for payment (in this system there may be a number of intermediary holders); and *mahalwari* tenure, where village communities jointly hold an estate and are jointly and severally responsible for payment.

Agrarian reform, initiated in the first Five-Year Plan, being undertaken by the state governments includes: (1) The abolition of intermediaries under *zamindari* tenure. (2) Tenancy legislation designed to scale down rents to $^1/4$-$^1/5$ of the value of the produce, to give permanent rights to tenants (subject to the landlord's right to resume a minimum holding for his personal cultivation), and to enable tenants to acquire ownership of their holdings (subject to the landlord's right of resumption for personal cultivation) on payment of compensation over a number of years. (3) Fixing of ceilings on existing holdings and on future acquisition; the holding of a family is between 4·05 and 7·28 ha if it has assured irrigation to produce two crops a year; 10·93 ha for land with irrigation facilities for only one crop a year; and 21·85 ha for all other categories of land. Tea, coffee, cocoa and cardamom plantations have been exempted. (4) The consolidation of holdings in community project areas and the prevention of fragmentation of holdings by reform of inheritance laws. (5) Promotion of farming by co-operative village management (*see* p. 644).

The average size of holding for the whole of India is 2·63 ha. Andhra Pradesh, 2·87; Assam, 1·46; Bihar, 1·53; Gujarat, 4·49; Jammu and Kashmir, 1·43; Karnataka, 4·11; Kerala, 0·75; Madhya Pradesh, 3·99; Maharashtra, 4·65; Orissa, 1·98; Punjab, 3·85; Rajasthan, 5·5; Tamil Nadu, 1·49; Uttar Pradesh, 1·78; West Bengal, 1·56.

Of the total 71m. rural households possessing operational holdings, 34% hold on the average less than 0·20 ha of land each.

Opium. By international agreement the poppy is cultivated under licence, and all raw opium is sold to the central government. Opium, other than for wholly medical use, is available only to registered addicts.

Fisheries. Total catch (1990–91) was 3·8m. tons, of which Kerala, Tamil Nadu, and Maharashtra produced about half. Of the total catch, 2·3m. tonnes were marine fish. There were 225 deep-sea (20 metres and above) fishing boats in Oct. 1989. There were 23,500 mechanised boats (1987–88). There were 8,530 fishermen's co-operatives with 912,000 members in 1987–88; total sales, Rs 743m.

Forestry. The lands under the control of the state forest departments are classified as 'reserved forests' (forests intended to be permanently maintained for the supply of timber, etc., or for the protection of water supply, etc.), 'protected forests' and 'unclassed' forest land.

In 1988 the total forest area was 67·1m. ha. Main types are teak and sal. About 16% of the area is inaccessible, of which about 45% is potentially productive. In 1985–86 3m. saplings were planted. Some states have encouraged planting small areas around villages.

INDUSTRY. Railways, air transport, armaments and atomic energy are government monopolies. In a number of industries (including the manufacture of iron and steel and mineral oils, shipbuilding and the mining of coal, iron and manganese ores, gypsum, gold and diamonds) new units are set up only by the state. In a further group of industries (road transport, manufacture of chemicals such as drugs, dyestuffs, plastics and fertilizers) the state established new undertakings, but private enterprise may develop either on its own or with state backing, which may take the form of loans or purchase of equity capital. Nationalized industries employed 4m. in 1981. Under the Industries (Development and Regulation) Act, 1951, as amended, industrial undertakings are required to be licensed; 162 industries are within the scope of the Act. The Government are authorized to examine the working of any undertaking, to issue directions to it and to take over its control if this be deemed necessary. A Central Advisory Council has been set up consisting of representatives of industry, labour, consumers and primary producers. There are Development Councils for individual industries and (1981) 4 national development banks.

Oil refinery installed capacity, April 1990, was 51·85m. tonnes; production of petroleum refinery products (1989–90), 51·95m. tonnes. The Indian Oil Corporation was established in 1964 and had (1990) most of the market.

Industry, particularly steel, has suffered from a shortage of power and coal. There is expansion in petrochemicals, based on the oil and associated gas of the Bombay High field, and gas from Krishna-Godavari Basin, Rajasthan, Tripura, Assam and Bassein field. Small industries numbering 1·83m., (initial outlay on capital equipment of less than Rs 6m.) are important; they employ about 11·97m. and produced (1989–90) goods worth Rs 1,323,200m.

Industrial production, 1990-91 (in 1,000 tonnes): Pig-iron and ferro-alloys, 12,253; steel ingots, 14,194; finished steel, 11,118; aluminium, 443; 1,865,434 motor cycles, mopeds and scooters; 145,747 commercial vehicles; petroleum products, 48,567; cement, 46,609; board and paper, 2,062; nitrogen fertilizer, 7,068; phosphate fertilizer, 2,085; jute goods, 1,388; man-made fibre and yarn, 261; diesel engines, 158,270 engines; electric motors, 5·85m. h.p.; 220,768 passenger cars and jeeps; 24,111 railway wagons.

Labour. At the 1981 census there were 222·5m. workers, of whom 92·5m. were cultivators, 55·5m. agricultural labourers; in 1987-88 there were 6·3m. in manufacturing, 10·03m. in social, community and personal services, 1·3m. in construction and 3·07m. in transport, communications and storage. The bond labour system was abolished in 1975. Man-days lost by industrial disputes, 1989, 15·18m., of which 2·94m. were in the public sector. An ordnance of July 1981 gave the government power to ban strikes in essential services; the ordnance was to remain in force for six months and would then be renewable.

Companies. The total number of companies limited by shares at work in India, 31 Dec. 1990, was 214,429; aggregate paid-up capital was Rs 616,370m. There were 21,913 public limited companies with an aggregate paid-up capital of Rs 262,460m., and 192,516 private limited companies (Rs 353,900m.). There were also 307 companies with unlimited liability and 2,093 companies limited by guarantee and association not for profit.

During 1989–90, 21,597 new limited companies were registered in the Indian Union under the Companies Act 1956 with a total authorized capital of Rs 79,740m.; 20 were government companies (Rs 51,350m.) and 21,577 were non-government companies (Rs 28,390m.). There were 5 private companies with unlimited liability and 90 companies with liability limited by guarantee and association not for profit also registered in 1989–90. During 1989–90, 307 non-government companies with an aggregate paid-up capital of Rs 338·8m. went into liquidation or were struck off the register.

On 31 March 1990 there were 1,173 government companies at work with a total paid-up capital of Rs 459,240m.; 545 were public limited companies and 628 were private limited companies.

On 31 March 1990, 469 companies incorporated elsewhere were reported to have a place of business in India; 130 were of UK and 101 of US origin.

Department of Company Affairs, Govt. of India. *Annual Report.* New Delhi, 1990–91

Co-operative Movement. On 30 June 1989 there were about 350,000 co-operative societies with a total membership of 150m. These included Primary Cooperative Marketing Societies, State Co-operative Marketing Federations and the National Agricultural Co-operative Marketing Federation of India. There were also State Co-operative Commodity Marketing Federations, and 29 general purpose and 16 Special Commodites Marketing Federations.

There were, in 1986-87, 29 State Co-operative Banks, 353 Central Co-operative Banks, 115,781 Primary Agricultural Credit Societies, 19 State Land Development Banks, and 899 primary Land Development Banks/branches which provide long-term investment credit.

Total agricultural credit disbursed by Co-operatives in 1988–89 was Rs 54,420m. including Rs 38,330m. in short-term credit, Rs 3,810m. in medium-term credit and Rs 7,310m. in long-term credit.

Value of agricultural produce marketed by Co-operatives in 1988–89 was about Rs 54,160m.

In 1988–89 there were 2,422 agro-processing units; 214 sugar factories produced 5·07m. tons; 108 spinning mills (capacity 2·86m. spindles) produced 179m. kg. of yarn; there were 112 oilseed processing units; total storage capacity was 10·94m. tons.

In 1988–89 there were 67,000 retail depots distributing 3·5m. tons of fertilizers.

Co-operative Movement in India, Statistical Statements Relating to. Annual. Reserve Bank of India, Bombay

FOREIGN ECONOMIC RELATIONS. Foreign investment is encouraged by a tax holiday on income up to 6% of capital employed for 5 years. There are special depreciation allowances, and customs and excise concessions, for export industries. Proposals for investment ventures involving up to 51% foreign equity require only the Reserve Bank's approval under new liberalized policy. In Feb. 1991 India resumed trans-frontier trade with China, which had ceased in 1962.

Foreign debt was estimated at Rs 994,580m. in March 1991.

Commerce. The external trade of India (excluding land-borne trade with Tibet and Bhutan) was as follows (in Rs 100,000):

	Imports	Exports and Re-exports
1988-89	2,819,365	2,029,515
1989–90 [1]	3,541,188	2,768,147
1990–91 [1]	4,317,082	3,252,728

[1]Provisional.

The distribution of commerce by countries and areas was as follows in the year ended 31 March 1991 (in Rs 100,000):

Countries	Exports to	Imports from	Countries	Exports to	Imports from
Afghanistan	9,148	2,373	Malaysia	26,775	99,892
Argentina	853	11,897	Mexico	3,823	20,322
Australia	32,100	146,729	Morocco	1,968	27,151
Austria	12,488	14,780	Nepal	8,411	7,925
Bahrain	6,453	45,954	Netherlands	65,016	79,549
Bangladesh	54,738	3,143	New Zealand	4,008	11,919
Belgium	125,443	271,756	Nigeria	11,409	4,892
Brazil	2,632	43,722	Norway	5,672	6,299
Bulgaria	554	5,559	Pakistan	7,334	8,423
Burma	335	15,346	Poland	17,165	14,546
Canada	28,087	55,923	Qatar	3,082	36,303
Czechoslovakia	14,495	26,762	Romania	9,548	4,964
Denmark	15,208	13,409	Saudi Arabia	41,842	289,773
Egypt	17,732	7,986	Singapore	67,907	143,046
Finland	14,451	14,177	Spain	28,130	19,222
France	76,544	130,502	Sri Lanka	23,479	3,698
Germany	253,459	347,742	Sudan	3,852	285
Ghana	1,564	802	Sweden	15,892	35,039
Hong Kong	107,397	29,776	Switzerland	40,080	48,188
Hungary	8,339	14,340	Tanzania	5,310	6,110
Indonesia	19,544	14,488	Thailand	44,276	11,572
Iran	14,081	101,784	Turkey	9,492	17,732
Iraq	4,345	49,561	United Arab		
Italy	100,193	109,440	Emirates	78,045	189,950
Japan	302,525	324,553	USSR	526,629	255,173
Jordan	5,724	34,429	UK	212,280	291,985
Kenya	6,478	3,807	USA	479,552	523,698
Korea,			Yugoslavia	6,946	16,615
Republic of	32,742	64,871	Zaïre	500	10,728
Kuwait	7,370	36,303	Zambia	4,002	15,427

The value (in 100,000 rupees) of the leading articles of merchandise was as follows in the year ended 31 March 1991 (provisional):

Exports	Value
Meat and meat preparations	14,093
Marine products	95,968
Processed foods (miscellaneous)	21,293
Rice	43,995
Vegetables and fruits	66,409
Coffee and coffee substitutes	25,332
Tea and mate	107,482
Spices	23,321
Oilcake	62,490
Tobacco unmanufactured and tobacco refuse	19,266
Raw cotton	85,472
Iron ore	104,986
Ores and minerals (excluding iron, mica and coal)	60,108
Cotton yarn, fabrics and madeup articles	206,521
Ready-made garments	404,236
Jute manufactures including twist and yarn	29,991
Leather and leather manufactures	255,385
Natural silk textiles	21,915
Man-made textiles	40,567
Carpets, mill made	13,643
Plastic and manufactures thereof	19,819

Exports	*Value*
Sports goods	9,209
Gems and jewellery	521,004
Works of art	42,912
Handmade carpets	60,830
Engineering goods	390,158
Petroleum products	93,780
Chemicals and allied products	233,042

Imports	*Value*
Wheat	2,419
Rice	3,919
Raw wool	17,985
Pulp and waste paper	45,433
Crude rubber including synthetic and reclaimed	22,593
Synthetic and regenerated fibre	5,886
Fertilizers, crude	33,876
Sulphur and unroasted iron pyrites	26,721
Metalliferous ores and metal scrap	120,930
Petroleum, petroleum products and related materials	1,081,965
Edible oil	32,222
Organic chemicals	160,007
Inorganic chemicals	87,180
Medical and pharmaceutical products	32,502
Fertilizers, manufactured	109,081
Artificial resins, plastic materials etc	109,611
Chemical materials and products	27,919
Paper, paper board and manufactures thereof	46,242
Textile yarn, fabrics and madeup articles	44,884
Pearls, precious and semi-precious stones	373,229
Non-metallic mineral manufactures exclg. pearls	21,104
Iron and steel	220,958
Non-ferrous metal	110,867
Manufactures of metal	37,108
Machinery other than electric	666,550
Electrical machinery	174,075
Transport equipment	163,833
Professional, scientific, controlling instruments, photographic, optical goods, watches and clocks	108,210

Total trade between India and UK (British Department of Trade returns, in £1,000 sterling):

	1987	*1988*	*1989*	*1990*	*1991*
Imports to UK	536,704	559,684	701,985	799,438	776,976
Exports and re-exports from UK	1,090,146	1,111,740	1,382,436	1,264,189	1,017,398

Tourism. There were 1·33m. visitors (excluding nationals of Pakistan and Bangladesh) in 1990 bringing about Rs 24,440m. in foreign exchange; 230,893 from UK, 122,518 from USA, 68,238 from Sri Lanka.

COMMUNICATIONS

Roads. In 1989–90 there were 1·97m. km of roads, of which 0·96m. km were surfaced. Roads are divided into 5 main administrative classes, namely, national highways, state highways, major district roads, other district roads and village roads. The national highways (33,689 km in 1990) connect capitals of states, major ports and foreign highways. The national highway system is linked with the ESCAP (Economic and Social Commission for Asia and the Pacific) international highway system. The state highways are the main trunk roads of the states, while the major district roads connect subsidiary areas of production and markets with distribution centres, and form the main link between headquarters and neighbouring districts.

There were (31 March 1990) 16,605,000 motor vehicles in India, comprising 2,391,000 private cars, taxis and jeeps, 10·8m. motor cycles and scooters, 289,000 buses, 1,107,000 goods vehicles and 1,995,000 others.

Railways. The Indian railway system is government-owned and (under the control of the Railway Board) is divided into 9 zones; route-km at 31 March 1990:

Zone	Headquarters	Route-km
Central	Bombay	6,891 km (1,863 km elec.)
Eastern	Calcutta	4,270 km (1,231 km)
Northern	Delhi	10,975 km (884 km)
North Eastern	Gorakhpur	5,193 km
North East Frontier	Maligaon (Guwahati)	3,841 km (81 km)
Southern	Madras	6,756 km (598 km)
South Central	Secunderabad	7,204 km (514 km)
South Eastern	Calcutta	7,115 km (2,866 km)
Western	Bombay	9,899 km (939 km)

Principal gauges are 1,676 mm. and metre, with networks also of 762 and 610 mm. gauge.
Passengers carried in 1989–90 were 3,653m.; revenue earning freight, 310m. tonnes.
Revenue (1989–90) from passengers, Rs 26,690m.; from goods, Rs 74,610m.
Indian Railways pay to the central government a fixed dividend of 4·5% on capital-at-charge.
Railway finance in Rs 1m.:

Financial years	Gross traffic receipts	Working expenses	Net revenues (traffic and miscellaneous)	Net surplus or deficit (after dividend)
1988–89	92,593	86,330	7,373	+217
1989–90	107,394	98,877	9,821	+1,733
1990–91	120,965	111,539	11,138	+1,876

There is a metro (10 km) and tramway network (71 km) in Calcutta.

Civil Aviation. Air transport was nationalized in 1953 with the formation of 2 Air Corporations: Air India for long-distance international air services, and Indian Airlines for air services within India and to adjacent countries. A third airline, Vayudoot, was formed in 1981 as an internal feeder. There are 92 airports.

Air India runs Boeing 747s and 747 Combis, Airbus A-300 and A-310s; it operates from Bombay, Delhi, Madras, Trivandrum, Hyderabad, Goa and Calcutta to Africa (Nairobi, Lagos, Seychelles, Mauritius, Dar es Salaam, Lusaka and Harare); to Europe (London, Paris, Frankfurt, Geneva, Moscow and Rome); to western Asia (Doha, Abu Dhabi, Dharan, Dubai, Bahrain, Kuwait, Muscat, Jeddah, Ras al Khaymah, Sharjah, Tashkent, Tehran, Riyadh and Baghdad); to east Asia (Bangkok, Hong Kong, Tokyo, Osaka, Kuala Lumpur and Singapore); to North America (New York). In addition, freight services are operated to Zurich and Luxembourg. Air India carried 2·25m. passengers in 1989-90 and made a profit of Rs 433·1m.

Indian Airlines has a fleet of 56 aircraft consisting of Airbus A-300, Airbus-320, Boeing 737, F-27, and HS-748. During 1988–89 the airline carried 10·11m. passengers; net profit Rs 106·8m. Flights cover over 85,000 unduplicated route km. 9·85m passengers were carried in 1989-90.

Vayudoot serves remote areas of India; it has a network of 46 stations.

The National Airports Authority maintains and operates 88 civil aerodromes and 28 civil enclaves. The management of the 5 international airports at Bombay, Calcutta, Delhi, Madras and Thiruvananthapuram is vested in the International Airports Authority of India.

Shipping. In Dec. 1990, 416 ships totalling 6·03m. GRT were on the Indian Register; of these, 160 ships of 0·52m. GRT were engaged in coastal trade, and 256 ships of 5·51m. GRT in overseas trade. Traffic of major ports, 1989–90, was as follows:

Port	Ships cleared	Imports (1m. tonnes)	Exports (1m. tonnes)
Kandla	976	10·52	1·90
Bombay	2,035	11·19	6·92
Mormugao	387	0·92	12·54
New Mangalore	398	0·83	6·37
Cochin	676	2·49	0·56
Tuticorin	514	1·50	0·42
Madras	1,471	7·76	8·05
Vizag	781	7·82	7·81
Paradip	244	2·46	2·41
Haldia	583	6·25	0·38
Calcutta	750	2·78	0·75
Jawaharlal Nehru	99	0·52	0·18

The Hindustan shipyard at Vishakhapatnam is capable of building vessels of a maximum of 42,750 DWT. Present capacity is about 118,250 DWT per year. The Mazagon dock in Bombay and Goa shipyard build vessels primarily for defence purposes. The Cochin Shipyard can build ships of 85,000 DWT each and repair ships up to 100,000 DWT. The installed capacity of the shipyard is 84,000 DWT new construction and 1m. GRT ship repair, per annum. Garden Reach Shipbuilders and Engineers are building bulk carriers of 26,000 DWT, ferry ships (6,000 DWT), hydrographic research ships, tugs and fast patrol craft.

There are about 5,200 km of major rivers navigable by motorized craft, of which 1,700 km are used. Canals, 4,300 km, of which 485 km are navigable by motorized craft (335 km are used).

Telecommunications. On 31 March 1990 there were 147,236 post offices and 39,906 telegraph offices.

The telephone system is in the hands of the Telecommunications Department, except in Delhi, served by public corporation. In April 1990 the Department had 4·59m. telephones, 331 telex exchanges and 49,844 subscribers.

There were 104 radio stations in March 1991, and programmes were sent out from 190 transmitters. In March 1991 television reached some 75% of the population, through a network of 525 transmitters (colour by PAL). In 1991 there were estimated to be 55m. radio and 20m. TV sets.

Cinemas. In 1988-89 there were 13,355 cinemas and 948 feature films were produced in 1990–91.

Newspapers. There were 30,153 newspapers in 1989. In 1988 the total number of newspapers and periodicals was 25,536; about 30% were published in Delhi, Bombay, Calcutta and Madras. There were 2,281 daily and 7,813 weekly papers. Circulation of newspapers and periodicals (1988), 54·87m. Hindi papers have the highest number and circulation, followed by English, then Bengali, Urdu and Marathi.

Annual Report of the Register of Newspapers for India. New Delhi

JUSTICE, RELIGION, EDUCATION AND WELFARE

Justice. All courts form a single hierarchy, with the Supreme Court at the head, which constitutes the highest court of appeal. Immediately below it are the High Courts and subordinate courts in each state. Every court in this chain, subject to the usual pecuniary and local limits, administers the whole law of the country, whether made by Parliament or by the state legislatures.

The states of Andhra Pradesh, Assam (in common with Nagaland, Meghalaya, Manipur, Mizoram, Tripura and Arunachal Pradesh), Bihar, Gujarat, Himachal Pradesh, Jammu and Kashmir, Karnataka, Kerala, Madhya Pradesh, Maharashtra (in common with Goa and the Union Territories of Daman and Diu and Dadra and Nagar Haveli), Orissa, Punjab (in common with the state of Haryana and the Union Territory of Chandigarh), Rajasthan, Tamil Nadu, Uttar Pradesh, West Bengal and Sikkim have each a High Court. There is a separate High Court for Delhi. For the Andaman and Nicobar Islands the Calcutta High Court, for Pondicherry the High Court of Madras and for Lakshadweep the High Court of Kerala are the highest judicial authorities. The Allahabad High Court has a Bench at Lucknow, the Bombay High Court has Benches at Nagpur, Aurangabad and Panaji, the Gauhati High Court has Benches at Kohima and Aizwal, the Madhya Pradesh High Court has Benches at Gwalior and Indore, the Patna High Court has a Bench at Ranchi and the Rajasthan High Court has a Bench at Jaipur. Judges and Division Courts of the Gauhati High Court also sit in Meghalaya, Manipur and Tripura. Similarly, judges and Division Courts of the Calcutta High Court also sit in the Andaman and Nicobar Islands. Below the High Court each state is divided into a number of districts under the jurisdiction of district judges who preside over civil courts and courts of sessions. There are a number of judicial authorities subordinate to the district civil courts. On the criminal side magistrates of various classes act under the overall supervision of the High Court.

The Code of Criminal Procedure came into force with effect from 1 April 1974. It provides for complete separation of the Judiciary from the Executive throughout India.

In Oct. 1991 the Supreme Court upheld capital punishment by hanging.

Police. The states control their own police force through the state Home Ministers. The Home Minister of the central government co-ordinates the work of the states and controls the Central Detective Training School, the Central Forensic Laboratory, the Central Fingerprint Laboratory as well as the National Police Academy at Mount Abu (Rajasthan) where the Indian Police Service is trained. This service is recruited by competitive examination of university graduates and provides all senior officers for the state police forces. The Central Bureau of Investigation functions under the control of the Cabinet Secretariat.

The cities of Pune, Ahmedabad, Nagpur, Bangalore, Calcutta, Madras, Bombay, Delhi and Hyderabad have separate police commissionerates.

Religion. The principal religions in 1981 (census) were: Hindus, 549·7m. (82·63%); Moslems, 75·6m. (11·36%); Christians, 16·2m. (2·43%); Sikhs, 13·1m. (1·96%); Buddhists, 4·7m. (0·7%); Jains, 3·2m. (0·48%).

Education. Literacy. According to the 1991 census the literacy percentage in the country (excluding age-group, 0-6) was 52·11 (43·56 in 1981): 63·86% among males, 39·42% among females. Of the states and territories, Kerala and Chandigarh have the highest rates.

Educational Organization. Education is the concurrent responsibility of state and Union governments. In the union territories it is the responsibility of the central government. The Union Government is also directly responsible for the central universities and all institutions declared by parliament to be of national importance; the promotion of Hindi as the federal language; coordinating and maintaining standards in higher education, research, science and technology. Professional education rests with the Ministry or Department concerned, e.g., medical education, the Ministry or Department of Health. The Department of Education is a part of the Union Ministry of Human Resource Development, headed by a cabinet minister. There are several autonomous organizations attached to the Department of Education. These include the University Grants Commission, the National Institute of Educational Planning and Administration and the National Council of Educational Research and Training. There is a Central Advisory Board of Education to advise the Union and the State Governments on any educational question which may be referred to it.

School Education. The school system in India can be divided into four stages: Primary, middle, secondary and senior secondary.

Primary education is imparted either at independent primary (or junior basic) schools or primary classes attached to middle or secondary schools. The period of instruction in this stage varies from 4 to 5 years and the medium of instruction is in most cases the mother tongue of the child or the regional language. Free primary education is available for all children. Legislation for compulsory education has been passed by some state governments and Union Territories but it is not practicable to enforce compulsion when the reasons for non-attendance are socioeconomic. Residential schools are planned for country children.

The period for the middle stage varies from 2 to 3 years.

Higher Education. Higher education is given in arts, science or professional colleges, universities and all-India educational or research institutions. In 1988–89 there were 144 universities, 10 institutions of national importance and 25 institutions deemed as universities. Of the universities, 9 are central: Aligarh Muslim University; Banaras Hindu University; University of Delhi; University of Hyderabad; Jawaharlal Nehru University; North Eastern Hill University; Visva Bharati; Pondicherry; Indira Gandhi National Open. The rest are state universities. Total enrolment at universities, 1988–89, 3,947,922, of which 3,474,171 were undergraduates. Women students, 1,251,491.

Grants are paid through the University Grants Commission to the central universities and institutions deemed to be universities for their maintenance and development and to state universities for their development projects only; their maintenance is the concern of state governments. During 1988–89 the University Grants Commission sanctioned grants of Rs 1,943·3m.

Technical Education. The number of institutions awarding degrees in engineering and technology in 1988-89 was 267 (in 1947: 38), and those awarding diplomas in engineering and technology numbered 818 (in 1947: 53); the former admitted 205,282, the latter 286,397 students. Girls' Polytechnics had 32,137 students. For training high-level engineers and technologists 5 Institutes of Technology and the Indian Institute of Science, Bangalore. There are (1986) 4 national Management Institutions and 42 other management units, admitting about 3,000 annually.

Adult Education. In spite of the improvement in the literacy rate, the number of adult illiterates over 14 was over 424·26m. in 1981. Adult education is, therefore, being accorded a high priority; it formed part of the Minimum Needs Programme under the seventh Five-Year Plan (1985–90). The National Literacy Mission aims to cover all illiterate persons in the age-group 15–35 by 1990. The Directorate of Adult Education, established in 1971, is the national resource centre; with state resource centres it is responsible for producing teaching/learning materials, training and orientation, monitoring and evaluating the programme.

Educational statistics for the year 1988–89:

Type of recognized institution	No. of institutions	No. of students on rolls	No. of teachers
Primary/junior basic schools	548,059	95,739,976	1,603,058
Middle/senior basic schools	144,145	30,940,062	1,032,534
High/higher secondary schools [1]	68,665	16,229,942	1,235,530
Training schools and colleges	1,477	191,562 [2]	–
Arts, Science and Commerce colleges	4,670	3,474,171 [3]	194,095

[1] Including Junior Colleges.
[2] Enrolment by stages of teachers' training courses at school and college level.
[3] Enrolment by stages of all post-graduate and graduate courses.

Expenditure. Total public expenditure on education 1988–89 is estimated at Rs 98,890m. Total public expenditure on education, sport, arts and youth welfare during the Seventh Plan, Rs 63,826·5m.; Seventh Plan spending on adult education, Rs 1,300m. in the central and Rs 2,300m. in the state sectors.

Health. Health programmes are primarily the responsibility of the state governments. The Union Government has sponsored and supported major schemes for disease prevention and control which are implemented nationally. These include the prevention and control of malaria, filaria, tuberculosis, leprosy, venereal diseases, smallpox, trachoma and cancer. There are also Union Government schemes in connexion with water supply and sanitation, and with nutrition. The Nutrition Advisory Committee of the Indian Council of Medical Research sponsors schemes for research and advises the Government. The National Nutrition Advisory Committee is to formulate a national nutrition policy and recommend measures for improving national standards.

Medical relief and service is primarily the responsibility of the states. Medical education is also a state responsibility, but there is a co-ordinating Central Health Educational Bureau. Family planning is centrally sponsored and locally implemented. The goal is to reduce the birth-rate by means of education in family planning methods.

Total expenditure on health and family welfare in 1988-89 was Rs 50,480m.

DIPLOMATIC REPRESENTATIVES

Of India in Great Britain (India House, Aldwych, London, WC2B 4NA)
High Commissioner: Dr L. M. Singhvi.

Of Great Britain in India (Chanakyapuri, New Delhi 110021)
High Commissioner: Sir Nicholas Fenn, KCMG.

Of India in the USA (2107 Massachusetts Ave., NW, Washington, D.C., 20008)
Ambassador: Abid Hussain.

Of the USA in India (Shanti Path, Chanakyapuri, New Delhi 110021)
Ambassador: William Clark, Jr.

Of India to the United Nations
Ambassador: Chinmaya Rajaninath Gharekhan.

Further Reading

Special works relating to States are shown under their separate headings.

India: A Reference Annual. Delhi Govt. Printer. Annual
New Cambridge History of India. 4 vols. CUP, 1988–90
The Times of India Directory and Yearbook. Bombay and London. Annual
Akbar, M. J., *India: The Siege Within.* Harmondsworth, 1985
Balasubramanyam, V. N., *The Economy of India.* London, 1985
Bardham, P., *The Political Economy of Development in India.* Oxford, 1984
Bhambhri, C. P., *The Political Process in India, 1947–91.* Delhi, 1991
Brown, J., *Modern India: The Origins of an Asian Democracy.* OUP, 1985
Fishlock, T., *India File: Inside the Subcontinent.* London, 1983
Fürer-Haimendorf, C. von, *Tribes of India: the Struggle for Survival.* Univ. of California Press, 1983
Gupta, B. K. and Kharbas, D. S., *India.* [Bibliography] Oxford and Santa Barbara, 1984
Hall, A., *The Emergence of Modern India.* Columbia Univ. Press, 1981
Hart, D., *Nuclear Power in India: a Comparative Analysis.* London, 1983
Jalan, B., *India's Economic Crisis: the Way Ahead.* OUP, 1991
Kulke, H. and Rothermund, D., *A History of India.* rev. ed. London, 1990
Majumdar, R. C., Raychandhuri, H. C. and Datta, K., *An Advanced History of India.* 2nd ed. London, 1950
Mehra, P., *A Dictionary of Modern Indian History, 1707–1947.* Delhi, 1987
Mitra, H. N., *The Indian Annual Register.* Calcutta, from 1953
Moon, P., *The British Conquest and Dominion of India.* London and Indiana Univ. Press, 1989
Moore, R. J., *Making the New Commonwealth.* Oxford, 1987
Nanda, B. R. (ed.) *Socialism in India.* Delhi, Bombay, Bangalore, Kanpur, London, 1972
Pachauri, R. K., *Energy and Economic Development in India.* New York, 1977
Philips, C. H. (ed.) *The Evolution of India and Pakistan: Select Documents.* OUP, 1962 ff.—
    Politics and Society in India. London, 1963
Poplai, S. L. (ed.) *India, 1947–50* (select documents). 2 vols. Bombay and London, 1959
Ray, R. K., *Industrialisation of India.* OUP, 1983
Roach, J. R., (ed.) *India 2000: The Next Fifteen Years.* Riverdale, My, 1986
Smith, V. E., *Oxford History of India.* 3rd ed. OUP, 1958
Spear, P., *India: A Modern History.* 2nd ed. Univ. of Michigan Press, 1972
Thomas, R., *India's Emergence as an Industrial Power.* Royal Institute of International Affairs, London, 1982

STATES AND TERRITORIES

The Republic of India is composed of the following 25 States and 7 centrally administered Union Territories:

States	Capital	States	Capital
Andhra Pradesh	Hyderabad	Manipur	Imphal
Arunachal Pradesh	Itanagar	Meghalaya	Shillong
Assam	Dispur	Mizoram	Aizawl
Bihar	Patna	Nagaland	Kohima
Goa	Panaji	Orissa	Bhubaneswar
Gujarat	Gandhinagar	Punjab	Chandigarh
Haryana	Chandigarh	Rajasthan	Jaipur
Himachal Pradesh	Shimla	Sikkim	Gangtok
Jammu and Kashmir	Srinagar	Tamil Nadu	Madras
Karnataka	Bangalore	Tripura	Agartala
Kerala	Thiruvananthapuram	Uttar Pradesh	Lucknow
Madhya Pradesh	Bhopal	West Bengal	Calcutta
Maharashtra	Bombay		

Union Territories

Andaman and Nicobar Islands; Chandigarh; Dadra and Nagar Haveli; Daman and Diu; Delhi; Lakshadweep; Pondicherry.

States Reorganization. The Constitution, which came into force on 26 Jan. 1950, provided for 9 Part A States (Assam, Bihar, Bombay, Madhya Pradesh, Madras, Orissa, Punjab, Uttar Pradesh and West Bengal) which corresponded to the previous governors' provinces; 8 Part B States (Hyderabad, Jammu and Kashmir, Madhya Bharat, Mysore, Patiala-East Punjab (PEPSU), Rajasthan, Saurashtra and Travancore-Cochin) which corresponded to Indian states or unions of states; 10 Part C States (Ajmer, Bhopal, Bilaspur, Coorg, Delhi, Himachal Pradesh, Kutch, Manipur, Tripura and Vindhya Pradesh) which corresponded to the chief commissioners' provinces; and Part D Territories and other areas (*e.g.*, Andaman and Nicobar Islands). Part A States (under governors) and Part B States (under rajpramukhs) had provincial autonomy with a ministry and elected assembly. Part C States (under chief commissioners) were the direct responsibility of the Union Government, although Kutch, Manipur and Tripura had legislatures with limited powers. Andhra was formed as a Part A State on its separation from Madras in 1953. Bilaspur was merged with Himachal Pradesh in 1954.

The States Reorganization Act, 1956, abolished the distinction between Parts A, B and C States and established two categories for the units of the Indian Union to be called States and Territories. The following were the main territorial changes: the Telugu districts of Hyderabad were merged with Andhra; Mysore absorbed the whole Kannada-speaking area (including Coorg, the greater part of 4 districts of Bombay, 3 districts of Hyderabad and 1 district of Madras); Bhopal, Vindhya Pradesh and Madhya Bharat were merged with Madhya Pradesh, which ceded 8 Marathi-speaking districts to Bombay; the new state of Kerala, comprising the majority of Malayalam-speaking peoples, was formed from Travancore-Cochin with a small area from Madras; Patiala-East Punjab was included in Punjab; Kutch and Saurashtra in Bombay; and Ajmer in Rajasthan; Hyderabad ceased to exist.

On 1 May 1960 Bombay State was divided into two parts: 17 districts (including Saurashtra and Kutch) in the north and west became the new state of Gujarat; the remainder was renamed the state of Maharashtra.

In Aug. 1961 the former Portuguese territories of Dadra and Nagar Haveli became a Union territory. The Portuguese territory of Goa and the smaller territories of Daman and Diu, occupied by India in Dec. 1961, were constituted a Union territory in March 1962. In Aug. 1962 the former French territories of Pondicherry, Karikal, Mahé and Yanaon were formally transferred to India and became a Union territory. In Sept. 1962 the Naga Hills Tuensang Area was constituted a separate state under the name of Nagaland. On 1 Nov. 1966, under the Punjab Reorganization Act 1966, a new state of Haryana and a new Union Territory of Chandigarh were created from parts of Punjab (India); for details, *see* pp. 662 and 695. On 26 Jan. 1971 Himachal Pradesh became a state. In 1972 the North East Frontier Agency and Mizo hill district were made Union territories (as Arunachal Pradesh and Mizoram) and Manipur, Meghalaya and Tripura full states. Sikkim became a state in 1975. Statehood for Mizoram was passed by parliament in July 1986; for Arunachal Pradesh in Dec. 1986; for Goa in May 1987.

Report of the States Reorganization Commission. Government of India. Delhi, 1956

ANDHRA PRADESH

HISTORY. Andhra was constituted a separate state on 1 Oct. 1953, on its partition from Madras, and consisted of the undisputed Telugu-speaking area of that state. To this region was added, on 1 Nov. 1956, the Telangana area of the former Hyderabad State, comprising the districts of Hyderabad, Medak, Nizamabad, Karimnaga, Warangal, Khammam, Nalgonda and Mahbubnaga, parts of the Adilabad district and some taluks of the Raichur, Gulbarga and Bidar districts, and some revenue circles of the Nanded district. On 1 April 1960, 221·4 sq. miles in the Chingleput and Salem districts of Madras were transferred to Andhra Pradesh in exchange for 410 sq. miles from Chittoor district. The district of Prakasam was formed on 2 Feb. 1970. Hyderabad was split into 2 districts on 15 Aug. 1978, (Ranga Reddy and Hyderabad). A new district, Vizianagaram, was formed in 1979.

AREA AND POPULATION. Andhra Pradesh is in south India and is bounded south by Tamil Nadu, west by Karnataka, north and northwest by Maharashtra, northeast by Madhya Pradesh and Orissa, east by the Bay of Bengal. The state has an area of 275,068 sq. km and a population (1991 census) of 66·4m. Density, 241 per sq. km. Growth rate 1981–91, 23·82%. The principal language is Telugu. Cities with over 250,000 population (1991 census), see p. 629. Other large cities (1991): Nizamabad (240,924); Kurnool (240,924); Eluru (212,918); Anantapur (174,792); Tirupati (174,393); Vizianagaram (159,461); Machilipatnam (159,007); Karimnagar (148,349); Tenali (143,836); Adoni (135,718); Proddatur (133,860); Chittoor (133,233); Khammam (127,812); Bheemavaram (125,495); Cuddapah (121,422).

CONSTITUTION AND GOVERNMENT. Andhra Pradesh has a unicameral legislature; the Legislative Council was abolished in June 1985. There are 295 seats in the Legislative Assembly. At the election of Nov. 1989, the Congress I party took office.

For administrative purposes there are 23 districts in the state. The capital is Hyderabad.

Governor: Krishna Kant.
Chief Minister: N. Janardhan Reddy.

BUDGET. Budget estimate, 1990–91: receipts on revenue account, Rs 49,153m.; expenditure, Rs 52,393m. Annual plan, 1991-92: Rs 14,100m.

ENERGY AND NATURAL RESOURCES

Electricity. There are 6 hydro-electric plants including Machkund, Upper Sileru and Nizam Sagar, 5 thermal stations including Nellore and Kothagudam, and 2 gas-based units. Several new thermal and gas-based power plants will be set up during the eighth 5-year plan period (1992–97). Installed capacity, 1989–90, 4,542 mw., power generated 15,031m. kwh. In 1989–90 there were 27,379 electrified villages and 1·1m. electric pump sets.

Oil and Gas. Oil/gas structures have been discovered at Lingala in the Krishna–Godavari basin. Three gas-powered generating stations are proposed.

Water. In 1989–90, 15 large and 36 medium irrigation projects were in hand. The Telugu Ganga joint project with Tamil Nadu, now in execution, will irrigate about 233,000 hectares, besides supplying drinking water to Madras city (Tamil Nadu).

Minerals The state is an important producer of asbestos and barytes. Other important minerals are copper ore, coal, iron and limestone, steatite, mica and manganese.

Agriculture. There were (1987–88) about 12·1m. ha of cropped land, of which 7·57m. ha were under food-grains. Production in 1989–90 (in tonnes): Foodgrains, 12·63m. (rice, 10·1m., wheat, 9,100); pulses, 0·7m.; sugar-cane, 11·6m.; oil seeds, 2·25m.

Livestock (1983 provisional): Cattle, 13·12m.; buffaloes, 8·7m.; goats, 5·5m.; sheep, 7·5m.

Forests. In 1989 it was estimated that forests occupy 23·2% of the total area of the state or 63,771 sq. km; main forest products are teak, eucalyuptus, cashew, casuarina, softwoods and bamboo.

Fisheries. Production 1989–90, 111,000 tonnes of marine fish and 134,000 tonnes of inland water fish. The state has a coastline of 974 km.

INDUSTRY. The main industries are textile manufacture, sugar-milling machine tools, pharmaceuticals, cement, chemicals, glass, fertilizers, electronic equipment, heavy electrical machinery, aircraft parts and paper-making. There is an oil refinery at Vishakhapatnam, where India's major shipbuilding yards are situated. In 1990 a steel plant was inaugurated at Vishakhapatnam and a railway repair shop at Tirupathi is functioning.

In 1991 there were 828 large and medium industries employing 0·5m. persons, and 91,000 small businesses employing 0·8m.

Cottage industry includes the manufacture of carpets, wooden and lacquer toys, brocades, bidriware, filigree and lace-work. The wooden toys of Nirmal and Kondapalli are particularly well known. Sericulture is developing rapidly. District Industries Centres have been set up to promote small-scale industry.

Tourism is growing; the main centres are Hyderabad, Nagarjunasagar, Warangal, Araku Valley, Horsley Hills and Tirupathi.

COMMUNICATIONS

Roads. In 1989–90 there were 2,587 km of national highways, 8,985 km of state highways and 25,267 km of major district roads. Number of vehicles during 1988–89 were 1,089,286 out of which were 849,332 motor cycles and scooters, 79,479 cars and jeeps, 59,504 goods vehicles and 14,587 buses.

Railways. In 1988–89 there were 5,021 route-km of railway, of which 3,032 km were broad gauge.

Aviation. There are airports at Hyderabad, Tirupathi, Vijayawada and Vishaka-patnam, with regular scheduled services to Bombay, Delhi, Calcutta, Bangalore and Madras. A feeder airline serves Rajahmundry and Cuddapah.

Shipping. The chief port is Vishakhapatnam. There are minor ports at Kakinada, Machilipatnam, Bheemunipatnam, Narsapur, Krishnapatnam, Vadarevu and Kalingapatnam.

JUSTICE, RELIGION, EDUCATION AND WELFARE

Justice. The high court of Judicature at Hyderabad has a Chief Justice and 25 puisne judges.

Religion. At the 1981 census Hindus numbered 47,525,681; Moslems, 4,533,700; Christians, 1,433,327; Jains 18,642; Sikhs, 16,222; Buddhists, 12,930.

Education. In 1991, 45·11% of the population were literate (56·24% of men and 33·71% of women). There were, in 1988–89 46,891 primary schools (5,684,237 students); 5,878 upper primary (1,879,838); 5,329 high schools (2,347,522). Education is free for children up to 14.

In 1988–89 there were 931 junior colleges (221,400 students); 368 degree colleges (303,000 students); 54 oriental colleges (6,021 students) and 13 universities: Osmania University, Hyderabad; Andhra University, Waltair; Sri Venkateswara University, Tirupathi; Kakatiya University, Warangal; Nagarjuna University, Guntur; Sri Jawaharlal Nehru Technological University, Hyderabad; Central Institute of English and Foreign Languages, Hyderabad; A.P. Agricultural University, Hyderabad; Sri Krishnadevaraya University, Anantapur; Smt. Padmarathi Mahila Vishwavidyalayam (University for Women), Tirupathi; A. P. Open University, Hyderabad; Telugu University, Hyderabad and A. P. Medical University, Vijayawada.

Health. There were (1989-90) 1,486 allopathic hospitals and dispensaries, 348 Ayurvedic hospitals and dispensaries, 196 Unani and 284 homeopathy dispensaries. There were also 181 nature cure hospitals (1988), and 1,243 primary health centres. Number of beds in hospitals was 29,263 (1988).

ARUNACHAL PRADESH

HISTORY. In Jan. 1972 the former North East Frontier Agency of Assam was created a Union Territory. In Dec. 1986, by the Constitution (55th Amendment) and State of Arunachal Pradesh Acts, the Territory became the 24th state of India.

AREA AND POPULATION. The state is in north-east India and is bounded by Assam, Bhutan, China and Burma; it has 11 districts and comprises the former frontier divisions of Kameng, Tirap, Subansiri, Siang and Lohit; it has an area of 83,743 sq. km and a population (1991 census) of 858,392; growth, 1981–91, 35·86%; density, 10 per sq. km.

The state is mainly tribal; there are over 80 tribes using about 50 tribal dialects.

CONSTITUTION AND GOVERNMENT. There is a Legislative Assembly of 60 members. The capital is Itanagar.

Governor: Surendranath Dwivedi.
Chief Minister: Gegong Apang.

BUDGET. Estimates for 1991–92, Rs 4,800m. Plan outlay, 1990–91, Rs 1,830m.

ENERGY AND NATURAL RESOURCES

Electricity. Power generated (1988): 42·01m. units. 1,374 out of 3,257 villages have electricity.

Oil, Gas and Coal. Production, 1988–89, 35,000 tonnes of crude oil and 18m. cu. metres of gas. Crude oil reserves are estimated at 1·5m. tonnes and coal 850,000 tonnes.

Agriculture. Production of foodgrains, 1989–90, 207,600 tonnes.

Forestry. Area under forest, 51,540 sq. km; revenue from forestry (1988) Rs 141m.

Industries. The state has a light roofing-sheet factory, a fruit processing plant and a cement plant. There are 15 medium and 1,887 small industries. Most of the medium industries are forest-based.

Roads. Total length of roads in the state, 12,778 km of which 2,050 km are surfaced. There were 502 vehicles in 1986–87. The state has 330 km of national highway.

EDUCATION AND WELFARE

Education. In 1991, 41·22% of the population were literate (51·1% of men and 29·37% of women). There were (1988–89) 1,079 primary schools with 103,313 students, 228 middle schools with 22,522 students, 99 high and higher secondary schools with 12,319 students and 4 colleges. Arunachal University was established in 1985.

Health. There are (1990) 13 hospials, 5 community health centres, 20 primary health centres and 125 sub-centres. There are also 2 TB hospitals and 4 leprosy hospitals. Total number of beds, 2,158.

ASSAM

HISTORY. Assam first became a British Protectorate at the close of the first Burmese War in 1826. In 1832 Cachar was annexed; in 1835 the Jaintia Hills were included in the East India Company's dominions, and in 1839 Assam was annexed to Bengal. In 1874 Assam was detached from Bengal and made a separate chief commissionership. On the partition of Bengal in 1905, it was united to the Eastern Districts of Bengal under a Lieut.-Governor. From 1912 the chief commissionership of Assam was revived, and in 1921 a governorship was created. On the partition of India almost the whole of the predominantly Moslem district of Sylhet was merged with East Bengal (Pakistan). Dewangiri in North Kamrup was ceded to Bhutan in 1951. The Naga Hill district, administered by the Union Government since 1957, became part of Nagaland in 1962. The autonomous state of Meghalaya within Assam, comprising the districts of Garo Hills and Khasi and Jaintia Hills, came into existence on 2 April 1970, and achieved full independent statehood in Jan. 1972, when it was also decided to form a Union Territory, Mizoram (now a state), from the Mizo Hills district.

AREA AND POPULATION. Assam is in eastern India, almost separated from central India by Bangladesh. It is bounded west by West Bengal, north by Bhutan and Arunachal Pradesh, east by Nagaland, Manipur and Burma, south by Meghalaya, Bangladesh, Mizoram and Tripura. The area of the state is now 78,438 sq. km. Population (census 1991) 22·3m. Density, 284 per sq. km. Growth rate 1981–91, 23·58%. Principal towns with population (1991) are; Guwahati, 577,591; Dibrugarh, 118,374; Silchar, 115,045; Nagaon, 93,324; Tinsukia, 73,760; Dhubri, 65,861; Tezpur, 54,999. The principal language is Assamese.

The central government is surveying the line of a proposed boundary fence to prevent illegal entry from Bangladesh.

CONSTITUTION AND GOVERNMENT. Assam has a unicameral legislature of 126 members. In the 1991 elections a Congress (I) government was returned. The temporary capital is Dispur. The state has 23 districts.

Governor: Lok Nath Mishra.
Chief Minister: Hiteswar Saikia.

BUDGET. The budget estimates for 1991–92 showed receipts of Rs 48,445·6m. and expenditure of Rs 50,860m. Plan allocation, 1991-92, Rs 22,510m.

ENERGY AND NATURAL RESOURCES

Electricity. In 1988–89 there was an installed capacity of 514·4 mw. In Dec. 1990, 21,010 villages (out of 21,995) had electricity. New power stations are under construction at Lakwa, and Karbi-Langpi hydro-electricity project.

Oil and Gas. Assam contains important oilfields and produces about 15% of India's crude oil. Production (1990-91): Crude oil, 5·08m. tonnes; gas, 2·01m. tonnes.

Water. In 1989–90, 232,744 ha were irrigated; 2 major and 11 medium projects were in hand.

Minerals. Coal production (1988), 1,017,103 tonnes. The state also has limestone, refractory clay, dolomite, and corundum.

Agriculture. There are 845 tea plantations, and growing tea is the principal industry. Production in 1988-89, 371m. kg, over 50% of Indian tea. Over 72% of the cultivated area is under food crops, of which the most important is rice. Total foodgrains, 1989–90, 2·95m. tonnes. Main cash crops: Jute, tea, cotton, oilseeds, sugarcane, fruit and potatoes. Wheat production 87,500 tonnes in 1989–90; rice, 2·79m. tonnes; pulses, 51,000 tonnes. Cattle are important.

Forestry. There are 17,423·4 sq. km of reserved forests under the administration of the Forest Department and 9,187·24 sq. km of unclassed forests, altogether about 30% of the total area of the state. Revenue from forests, 1988–89, Rs 148,800,000.

INDUSTRY. Sericulture and hand-loom weaving, both silk and cotton, are important home industries together with the manufacture of brass, cane and bamboo articles. Hand-loom weaving of silk is stimulated by state and central development schemes. There are two silk-spinning mills and 26 cotton-mills. The main heavy industry is petro-chemicals; there are 3 oil refineries with 1 under construction in 1991. Other industries include manufacturing paper, nylon, fertilizers, sugar, jute and plywood products, rice and oil milling.

There were 15,392 small businesses in 1990. The state in 1991 ran 480,622 enterprises employing 1·3m. persons.

COMMUNICATIONS

Roads. In 1987–88 there were 28,930 km of road maintained by the Public Works Department. There were 2,026 km of national highway in 1990. There were 216,475 motor vehicles in the state in 1988.

Railways. The route km of railways in 1989–90 was 2,451 km, of which 262·09 km are broad gauge.

Aviation. Daily scheduled flights connect the principal towns with the rest of India. There are airports at Guwahati, Tezpur, Jorhat, North Lakhimpur, Silchar and Dibrugarh.

Shipping. Water transport is important in Lower Assam; the main waterway is the Brahmaputra River. Cargo carried in 1988–89 was 109,051 tonnes.

JUSTICE, RELIGION, EDUCATION AND WELFARE

Justice. The seat of the High Court is Guwahati. It has a Chief Justice and 6 puisne judges.

Religion. At the 1971 census Hindus numbered 10,604,618; Moslems, 3,592,124; Christians, 381,010; Buddhists, 22,565; Jains, 12,914; Sikhs, 11,920.

Education. In 1991, 53·42% of the population were literate (62·34% of men and 43·7% of women). In 1988–89 there were 28,807 primary/junior basic schools with 3,433,077 students; 5,635 middle/senior basic schools with 1,231,297 students; 3,110 high/higher secondary schools with 601,523 students. There were 175 colleges for general education, 3 medical colleges, 3 engineering and 1 agricultural, 9 teacher-training colleges and 3 universities. The universities are Assam Agricultural University, Jorhat, Dibrugarh University, Dibrugarh and Gauhati University, Gauhati. There is a fisheries college at Raha. Two central universities will be established at Silchar and Tezpur during 1992–97.

Health. In 1989–90 there were 118 hospitals (11,768 beds) and 444 primary health centres and 4,989 sub-centres.

BIHAR

The state contains the ethnic areas of North Bihar, Santhalpargana and Chota Nagpur. In 1956 certain areas of Purnea and Manbhum districts were transferred to West Bengal.

AREA AND POPULATION. Bihar is in north India and is bounded north by Nepal, east by West Bengal, south by Orissa, south-west by Madhya Pradesh and west by Uttar Pradesh. The area of Bihar is 173,877 sq. km and its population (1991 census), 86,338,853, a density of 497 per sq. km. Growth rate since 1981, 23·49%. Population of principal towns, see p. 629. Other large towns (1991): Muzaffarpur, 240,450; Darbhanga, 218,274; Biharsharif, 200,976; Arrah, 156,871; Dhanbad, 151,334; Munger, 150,042; Chapra, 136,824; Katihar, 135,348; Purnea, 114,189.

The official language is Hindi (55·8m. speakers at the 1981 census), the second, Urdu (6·9m.), the third, Bengali (2m.).

CONSTITUTION AND GOVERNMENT. Bihar has a bicameral legislature. The Legislative Assembly consists of 324 elected members and the Council, 96. After the elections in Feb. 1990 a Janata Dal government, supported by Bharatiya Janata Party, Communist Party of India, Jharkhand Mukti Morcha and Communist-Marxist, came to power. Total seats, 324: Janata Dal, 122; Congress-I, 71; Bharatiya Janata Party, 37; Communist Party of India, 23; Jharkhand Mukti Morcha, 19; Communist-Marxist, 6; Indian People's Front, 7; Independent and others, 36; vacant, 3. For the purposes of administration the state is divided into 10 divisions covering 42 districts. The capital is Patna.

Governor: Mohammed Shafi Qureshi.
Chief Minister: Laloo Prasad Yadav.

BUDGET. The budget estimates for 1990–91 show total receipts of Rs 56,256·9m and expenditure of Rs 59,875·9m. Plan allocation, 1991–92, Rs 22,510m.

ENERGY AND NATURAL RESOURCES

Electricity. Installed capacity (1988–89) 1,530 mw. Power generated (1989–90), 3,924m. kw.; there were (1990) 46,270 villages with electricity. Hydro-electric projects in hand will add about 149·2mw. capacity.

Minerals. Bihar is very rich in minerals, with about 40% of national production. There are huge deposits of copper, capatite and kyanite and sizeable deposits of coal, mica and china clay. Bihar is a principal producer of iron ore. Other important minerals: Manganese, limestone, graphite, chromite, asbestos, barytes, dolomite, feldspar, columbite, pyrites, saltpetre, glass sands, slate, lead, silver, building stones and radio-active minerals. Value of production (1988) Rs 17,330m.

Agriculture. The irrigated area was 4·05m. ha in 1991. Cultivable land, 11·6m. ha, of a total area of 17·4m. ha. Total cropped area, 1989–90, 10·3m. ha. Production (1989–90): Rice, 6·4m. tonnes; wheat, 3·2m.; total foodgrains, 11·8m. Other food crops are maize, rabi and pulses. Main cash crops are jute, sugar-cane, oilseeds, to-bacco and potato.

Forests in 1990 covered 2·9m. ha. There are 12 protected forests.

INDUSTRY. Main plants are the Tata Iron and Steel Co., the Tata Engineering and Locomotive Co., the steel plant at Bokaro, oil refinery at Barauni, Heavy Engineering Corporation and Foundry Forge project at Ranchi, and aluminium plant at Muri. Other important industries are machine tools, fertilizers, electrical engineering, sugar-milling, paper-milling, silk-spinning, manufacturing explosives and cement. There is a copper smelter at Ghatsila and a zinc plant at Tundo. There were 75,149 small industries in 1988.

TOURISM. The main tourist centres are Bodh Gaya, Patna, Nalanda, Jamshedpur, Sasaram, Betla, Hazaribagh and Vaishali.

COMMUNICATIONS

Roads. In March 1989 the state had 35,411 km of metalled roads, including 2,118 km of national highway, and 50,259 km of unmetalled roads. Passenger transport has been nationalized in 7 districts. There were 452,537 motor vehicles in March 1991.

Railways. The North Eastern, South Eastern and Eastern railways traverse the state; route-km, 1989–90, 5,326.

Civil Aviation. There are airports at Patna and Ranchi with regular scheduled services to Calcutta and Delhi.

Shipping. The length of waterways open for navigation is 900 miles.

JUSTICE, RELIGION, EDUCATION AND WELFARE

Justice. There is a High Court (constituted in 1916) at Patna, and a bench at Ranchi, with a Chief Justice, 32 puisne judges and 4 additional judges.

Police. The police force is under a Director General of Police; in 1986 there were 1,036 police stations.

Religion. At the 1981 census Hindus numbered 58,011,070; Moslems, 9,874,993; Christians, 740,186; Sikhs, 77,704; Jains, 27,613; Buddhists, 3,003.

Education. At the census of 1991 the number of literates was 26·85m. (38·54%: males 52·63%; females, 23·1%). There were, 1988–89, 3,875 high and higher secondary schools with 820,687m. pupils, 12,530 middle schools with 1·94m. pupils, 52,181 primary schools with 8,301,386 pupils. Education is free for children aged 6-11.

There were 10 universities in 1990: Patna University (founded 1917) with 18,895 students (1984–85); Bihar University, Muzaffarpur (1952) with 60 constituent colleges, 7 affiliated colleges and 75,370 students (1984–85); Bhagalpur University (1960) with 50,473 students (1985–86); Ranchi University (1960) with 88,771 students (1985–86); Kameswar Singh Darbhanga Sanskrit University (1961); Magadha University, Gaya (1962) and Lalit Narayan Mithila University (1972), Darbhanga, Bisra Agricultural University, Ranchi (1980), Rajendra Agricultural University, Samastipur (1970), Nalanda Open University, Nalanda.

Health. In 1985 there were 1,289 hospitals and dispensaries.

Das, A. N., *Agrarian Movements in India: Studies in 20th Century Bihar*. London, 1982

GOA

HISTORY. The coastal area was captured by the Portuguese in 1510 and the inland area was added in the 18th century. In Dec. 1961 Portuguese rule was ended and Goa incorporated into the Indian Union as a Territory together with Daman and Diu. Goa was granted statehood as a separate unit on 30 May 1987. Daman and Diu remained Union Territories.

AREA AND POPULATION. Goa, bounded on the north by Maharashtra and on the east and south by Karnataka, has a coastline of 105 km. The area is 3,702 sq. km. Population, 1991 census, 1,168,622. Density, 316 per sq. km. Mormugao is the largest town; population (urban agglomeration, 1991) 91,285. The languages spoken are Konkani (official language), Marathi, Hindi, English.

GOVERNMENT. The Indian Parliament passed legislation in March 1962 by which Goa became a Union Territory with retrospective effect from 20 Dec. 1961. On 30 May 1987 Goa attained statehood. It is represented by 2 elected and 2 nominated representatives in Parliament. There is a Legislative Assembly of 40 members. The capital is Panaji; population (urban agglomeration 1991) 85,199. The state has 2 districts. There are 183 village Panchayats.

Governor: Bhanu Prakash Singh.
Chief Minister: Ravi Naik.

BUDGET. The total budget for 1990–91 was Rs 4,888·7m. Annual plan 1991–92, Rs 1,725m.

ENERGY AND NATURAL RESOURCES

Electricity. Fifteen towns and 377 villages were supplied with electric power by March 1990. Goa receives its power supply from the states of Maharashtra, Karnataka and Madhya Pradesh.

Minerals. Resources include manganese ore and iron ore, both of which are exported. Iron ore production (1989-90) 9,873,333 tonnes. There are also reserves of ferro-manganese, bauxite, lime stone and clay.

Agriculture. Agriculture is the main occupation, important crops are rice, pulses, ragi, mango, cashew and coconuts. Area under high yielding variety paddy (1989–90) 43,825 ha; production, 207,069 tonnes. Area under pulses 10,705 ha, sugar-cane 1,700 ha, groundnut 997 ha. Total production of foodgrains, 1989–90, 0·16m. tonnes.

Government poultry and dairy farming schemes produced 92m. eggs and 27,000m. litres of milk in 1989–90.

Fisheries. Fish is the state's staple food. In 1989–90 the catch of seafish was 54,550 tonnes (value Rs 201,981,000). There is a coastline of about 104 km and about 4,442 active fishing vessels.

INDUSTRY. In 1989–90 there were 42 large and medium industrial projects and 4,552 small units registered. Production included: Nylon fishing nets, ready made clothing, electronic goods, pesticides, pharmaceuticals, tyres and footwear.

In 1989-90 4552 small-scale industry units employed 28,822 persons.

ROADS. In 1989-90 there were 4,163 km of motorable roads (National Highway, 224 km).

RAILWAYS. In 1990 there were 79 km. of route.

JUSTICE, EDUCATION AND WELFARE

Justice. There is a bench of the Bombay High Court at Panaji.

Education. In 1991, 76·96% of the population were literate (85·48% of men and 68·2% of women). In 1989-90 there were 1,250 primary schools (144,227 students in 1988–89), 436 middle schools (81,493 students in 1988–89) and 368 high and higher secondary schools (53,595 students in 1988–89). There were also 2 engineering colleges, 1 medical college, 1 teacher-training college and 22 other colleges. Goa University, Bambolin (1985) has 28 colleges affiliated to it.

Health. There were (1989-90) 119 hospitals (3,834 beds), 251 rural medical dispensaries, health and sub-health centres and 261 family planning units.

Hutt, A., *Goa: A Traveller's Historical and Architectural Guide*. Buckhurst Hill, 1988

GUJARAT

HISTORY. On 1 May 1960, as a result of the Bombay Reorganization Act, 1960, the state of Gujarat was formed from the north and west (predominantly Gujarati-speaking) portion of Bombay State, the remainder being renamed the state of Maharashtra. Gujarat consists of the following districts of the former state of Bombay: Banas Kantha, Mehsana, Sabar Kantha, Ahmedabad, Kaira, Panch Mahals, Vadodara, Bharuch, Surat, Dangs, Amreli, Surendranagar, Rajkot, Jamnagar, Junagadh, Bhavnagar, Kutch, Gandhinagar and Bulsar.

AREA AND POPULATION. Gujarat is in western India and is bounded north by Pakistan and Rajasthan, east by Madhya Pradesh, south-east by Maharashtra, south and west by the Indian ocean and Arabian sea. The area of the state is 196,024 sq. km and the population at the 1991 census was 41,174,343; a density of 210 per sq. km. Growth rate 1981–91, 20·8%. The chief cities, *see* p. 629. Other important towns (1991) are: Nadiad (166,852), Bharuch (132,312), Junagadh (130,132), Navsari (125,980), Gandhinagar (121,746), Porbandar (116,546), Anand (110,144). Gujarati and Hindi in the Devanagari script are the official languages.

CONSTITUTION AND GOVERNMENT. Gujarat has a unicameral legislature, the Legislative Assembly, which has 182 elected members. After the elections in Feb. 1990 a coalition government of Janata Dal and Bharatiya Janata Party came to power. Total seats, 182: Janata Dal, 4; Janata Dal (Gujarat), 66; Bharatiya Janata Party, 67; Congress (I), 33; Independents, 12.

The capital is Gandhinagar. There are 19 districts.

Governor: Dr Swarup Singh.
Chief Minister: Chimanbhai Patel.

BUDGET. The budget estimates for 1990–91 showed revenue receipts of Rs 37,840·3m. and revenue expenditure of Rs 37,921·5m. Plan outlay for 1990–91, Rs 14,510m.

ENERGY AND NATURAL RESOURCES

Electricity. In 1989-90 the total generating capacity was 5,025 mw of electricity. In Dec. 1990, 17,892 villages out of 18,114 were electrified.

Water. The Karjan Dam, under construction, will provide a reservoir of 630m. cu. metres capacity; it is designed to irrigate 56,000 hectares through 2 main canals.

Oil and Gas. There are large crude oil and gas reserves. Production, 1990–91: Crude oil, 6·4m. tonnes; gas, 1,696,000 tonnes.

Minerals. Chief minerals produced in 1989-90 (in tonnes) included lime stone (7·19m.), agate stone (856), calcite (756), quartz and silica (178,000), bauxite (527,400), crude china clay (20,699), refined china clays (6,708), dolomite (473,900), crude fluorite (150,914), calcareous and sea sand (112,000) and lignite (1·62m.). Value of production (1989-90) Rs 15,082m. Enormous reserves of coal were found under the Kalol and Mehsana oil and gas fields in May 1980. The deposit, mixed with crude petroleum, is estimated at 100,000m. tonnes, extending over 500 km.

Agriculture. Cropped area, 1989–90, was 19·6m. ha. 24% of the cropped area is irrigated. Production of principal crops, 1989–90: Rice, 817,300 tonnes from 601,000 ha; foodgrains, 4·8m. tonnes (wheat, 1,101,700 tonnes); pulses, 567,400 tonnes; cotton, 1·76m. bales of 170 kg.

Livestock (1982): Buffaloes, 4·43m.; other cattle, 6·93m.; sheep, 2·33m.; goats, 3·26m.; horses and ponies, 24,000.

Fisheries. There were (1987) 80,204 people engaged in fisheries. There were 13,811 fishing vessels (5,313 motor vessels). The catch for 1988–89 was 381,000 tonnes.

INDUSTRY. Gujarat is one of the 4 most industrialized states. In 1989 there were 105,685 small-scale units and 13,000 factories including 1,757 textile factories, 1,585 chemical and chemical products factories, 1,381 non-metallic mineral products factories and 1,324 machinery, machine tools and parts factories. There were 167 industrial estates. Principal industries are textiles, general and electrical engineering, petrochemicals, machine tools, heavy chemicals, pharmaceuticals, dyes, sugar, soda ash, cement, man-made fibres, salt, sulphuric acid, paper and paperboard. Large fertilizer plants have been set up and there is an oil refinery at Koyali near Vadodara, with a developing petro-chemical complex at Gandhar.

State production of soda-ash is 90·4% of national output, and of salt, about 60%. Salt production (1986) 6·6m. tonnes; cement production, 2·4m. tonnes.

COMMUNICATIONS

Roads. In 1989-90 there were 65,565 km of roads. Gujarat State Transport Corporation operated 16,257 routes. Number of vehicles, 1,522,169.

Railways. In 1989-90 the state had 5,287 route km of railway line.

Aviation. Ahmedabad is the main airport. There are regular services between Ahmedabad and Bombay, Jaipur and Delhi. There are 8 other airports: Baroda, Bhavnagar, Bhuj, Jamnagar, Kandla, Keshod, Porbandar and Rajkot.

Shipping. The largest port is Kandla. There are 39 other ports, 11 intermediate, 28 minor.

Post. There were (1989–90) 8,690 post offices, 1,813 telegraph offices. There were 415,008 telephone connexions in the state.

JUSTICE, RELIGION, EDUCATION AND WELFARE

Justice. The High Court of Judicature at Ahmedabad has a Chief Justice and 18 puisne judges.

Religion. At the 1981 census Hindus numbered 30,518,500; Moslems, 2,907,744; Jains, 467,768; Christians, 132,703; Sikhs, 22,438; Buddhists, 7,550.

Education. In 1991 the number of literates was 21·27m. (60·91%; male, 72·45%, female 48·5%). Primary and secondary education up to Standard XI are free. Education above Standard XII is free for girls. In 1989–90 there were 29,937 primary schools with 6,663,000 students and 5,427 secondary schools with 1,852,000 students including 419 higher secondary schools.

There are 9 universities in the state. Gujarat University, Ahmedabad, founded in 1949, is teaching and affiliating; it has 147 affiliated colleges. The Maharaja Sayajirao University of Vadodara (1949) is residential and teaching. The Sardar

Patel University, Vallabh-Vidyanagar, (1955) has 16 constituent and affiliated colleges, Saurashtra University at Rajkot with 64 affiliated colleges, and South Gujarat at Surat with 39. Bhavnagar University (1978) is residential and teaching with 8 affiliated colleges. North Gujarat University was established at Patan in 1986. Gujarat Vidyapith at Ahmedabad is deemed a university under the University Grants Commission Act. There are also Gujarat Agricultural University, Banaskantha and Gujarat Ayurved University, Jamnagar.

There are 11 engineering colleges, 24 polytechnics, 6 medical colleges, 6 agricultural, 3 pharmaceutical and 2 veterinary. There are also 223 arts, science and commerce colleges and 40 teacher-training colleges.

Health. In 1987 there were 1,854 hospitals (22,595 beds), 457 primary health centres and 5,551 sub-centres.

Rushbrook Williams, L. F., *The Black Hills: Kutch in History and Legend*. London, 1958
Desai, I. F., *Untouchability in Rural Gujarat*. Bombay, 1977

HARYANA

HISTORY. The state of Haryana, created on 1 Nov. 1966 under the Punjab Reorganization Act, 1966, was formed from the Hindi-speaking parts of the state of Punjab (India). It comprises the districts of Hissar, Mahendragarh, Gurgaon, Rohtak, Yamunanagar, Rewari, Kaithal, Karnal; Bhiwani, Faridabad, Jind, Kurukshetra, Sirsa, Sonipat, Ambala.

AREA AND POPULATION. Haryana is in north India and is bounded north by Himachal Pradesh, east by Uttar Pradesh, south and west by Rajasthan and north-west by Punjab. Delhi forms an enclave on its eastern boundary. The state has an area of 44,212 sq. km and a population (1991) of 16,317,715; density, 369 per sq. km. Growth rate, 1981–91, 26·28%. Principal cities, *see* p.629. Other large towns (1991) are: Rohtak (215,844), Panipat (191,010), Karnal (173,742), Hisar (172,873), Yamunanagar (144,250), Sonipat (142,992), Bhiwani (121,449), Gurgaon (120,790), Ambala (119,735), Sirsa (112,542). The principal language is Hindi.

CONSTITUTION AND GOVERNMENT. The state has a unicameral legislature with 90 members. In Nov. 1991 Congress (I) held 51 seats; Janata Dal (S), 16; Haryana Vikas Party, 12; Janata Dal, 3; Bharatiya Janata, 2; others, 6. The state shares with Punjab (India) a High Court, a university and certain public services. The capital (shared with Punjab) is Chandigarh (*see* p. 693). Its transfer to Punjab, intended for 1986, has been postponed. There are 15 districts.

Governor: Dhanik Lal Mandal.
Chief Minister: Bhajan Lal.

BUDGET. Budget estimates for 1991–92 show income of Rs 22,570m. and expenditure of Rs 23,050m. Annual plan 1990–91, Rs 7,000m.

ENERGY AND NATURAL RESOURCES

Electricity. Approximately 1,000 mw are supplied to Haryana, mainly from the Bhakra Nangar system. In 1990–91 installed capacity was 2,234 mw and all the villages had electric power.

Minerals. Minerals include placer gold, barytes and rare earths. Value of production, 1987–88, Rs 40m.

Agriculture. Haryana has sandy soil and erratic rainfall, but the state shares the benefit of the Sutlej-Beas scheme. Agriculture employs over 82% of the working population; in 1981 there were about 900,000 holdings (average 3·7 ha), and the gross irrigated area was 2·04m. ha. Area under foodgrains, 1989–90, 3·9m. ha; foodgrain production was 8·65m. tonnes (rice 1·7m. tonnes, wheat 5·9m. tonnes);

pulses, 428,600 tonnes; cotton, 1·18m. bales of 170 kg; sugar (gur) and oilseeds are important.

Forests cover 3·3% of the state.

INDUSTRY. Haryana has a large market for consumer goods in neighbouring Delhi. In 1990–91 there were 461 large and medium scale industries employing 120,000 and producing goods worth over Rs 10,000m. There were 106,421 small units. The main industries are cotton textiles, agricultural machinery, woollen textiles, scientific instruments, glass, cement, paper and sugar milling, cars, tyres and tubes, motor cycles, bicycles, steel tubes, engineering goods, electrical and electronic goods. An oil refinery is being set up at Karnal, capital outlay, Rs 18,000.

COMMUNICATIONS

Roads. There were (1988–89) 21,250 km of metalled roads, linking all villages. Road transport is nationalized. There were 282,294 motor vehicles in 1986–87. In 1990-91 road transport caried 1·64m. passengers.

Railways. The state is crossed by lines from Delhi to Agra, Ajmer, Ferozepur and Chandigarh. Route km, 1989–90, 1,500. The main stations are at Ambala and Kurukshetra.

Aviation. There is no airport within the state but Delhi is on its eastern boundary.

JUSTICE, EDUCATION AND WELFARE

Justice. Haryana shares the High Court of Punjab and Haryana at Chandigarh.

Education. In 1991 the number of literates was 7·43m. (55·33%); 67·85% of men and 40·94% of women. In 1988-89 there were 5,032 primary schools with 1,628,716 students, 2,118 high and higher secondary schools with 366,741 students, 1,232 middle schools with 686,718 students and 114 colleges of arts, science and commerce, 3 engineering colleges and 2 medical colleges. There are 3 universities. The universities are Haryana Agricultural University, Hisar, Kurukshetra University, Kurukshetra and Maharshi Dayanand University, Rohtak.

Health. There were (1990-91) 79 hospitals (10,621 beds), 166 community health centres and dispensaries, 394 primary health centres and 2,293 sub-centres.

HIMACHAL PRADESH

HISTORY. The territory came into being on 15 April 1948 and comprised 30 former Hill States. The state of Bilaspur was merged with Himachal Pradesh in 1954. The 6 districts were: Mahasu, Sirmur, Mandi, Chamba, Bilaspur and Kinnuar. On 1 Nov. 1966, under the Punjab Reorganization Act, 1966, certain parts of the State of Punjab (India) were transferred to Himachal Pradesh. These comprise the districts of Shimla, Kullu, Kangra, and Lahaul and Spiti; and parts of Hoshiarpur, Ambala and Gurdaspur districts.

AREA AND POPULATION. Himachal Pradesh is in north India and is bounded north by Kashmir, east by Tibet, south-east by Uttar Pradesh, south by Haryana, south-west and west by Punjab. The area of the state is 55,673 sq. km and it had a population at the 1991 census of 5,111,079. Density, 92 per sq. km. Growth rate, 1981–91, 19·39%. Principal languages are Hindi and Pahari.

CONSTITUTION AND GOVERNMENT. Full statehood was attained, as the 18th state of the Union, on 25 Jan. 1971.

On 1 Sept. 1972 districts were reorganized and 2 new districts created, Hamirpur and Una, making a total of 12. The capital is Shimla; 1991 census population (urban agglomeration) 109,860.

There is a unicameral legislature. After the elections in Feb. 1990 a Bharatiya

Janata Party government came to power. Total seats, 68: Bharatiya Janata Party, 44; Janata Dal, 11; Congress (I), 10; Independents and others, 3.

Governor: Virendra Verma.
Chief Minister: Shanta Kumar.

BUDGET. Budget estimates for 1991–92 showed revenue receipts of Rs 9,364m. and expenditure on revenue account of Rs 10,090m. Annual plan, 1991–92, Rs 4,100m.

ENERGY AND NATURAL RESOURCES

Electricity. In 1990, all the 16,807 villages had electricity. Electricity generated (1989-90), 935·5m. kwh.

Water. An artificial confluence of the Sutlej and Beas rivers has been made, directing their united flow into Govind Sagar Lake. Other major rivers are Ravi, Chenab and Yamuna.

Minerals. The state has rock salt, slate, gypsum, limestone, barytes, dolomite and pyrites.

Agriculture. Farming employs 71% of the people. Irrigated area is 17% of the area sown. Main crops are seed potatoes, wheat, maize, rice and fruits such as apples, peaches, apricots, nuts, pomegranates; 0·46m. tonnes of fruits were produced in 1989-90.

Production (1989-90): Rice, 945,000 tonnes, wheat, 600,400 tonnes; pulses, 10,600 tonnes.

Livestock (1982 census): Buffaloes, 617,000; other cattle, 2,174,000; goats and sheep, 2·15m.

Forestry. (1991) Himachal Pradesh forests cover 67·5% of the state and supply the largest quantities of coniferous timber in northern India. The forests also ensure the safety of the catchment areas of the Yamuna, Sutlej, Beas, Ravi and Chenab rivers. Commercial felling of green trees has been totally halted and forest working nationalized. Area under forests in 1988-89, 37,591 sq. km, of which 1,896 sq. km are reserved and 33,350 sq. km are protected.

INDUSTRY. The main sources of employment are the forests and their related industries; there are factories making turpentine and rosin. The state also makes fertilizers, cement, electronic items and TV sets. There is a foundry and a brewery. Other industries include salt production and handicrafts, including weaving. The state has 130 large and medium units, 20,173 small scale units and 5 industrial estates.

COMMUNICATIONS

Roads. The national highway from Chandigarh runs through Shimla; other main highways from Shimla serve Kullu, Manali, Kangra, Chemba and Pathankot. The rest are minor roads. Pathankot is also on national highways from Punjab to Kashmir. Length of roads (1990), 29,958 km; number of vehicles (1986–87), 45,175.

Railways. There is a line from Chandigarh to Shimla, and the Jammu-Delhi line runs through Pathankot. A Nangal-Talwara rail link has been approved by the central government and was in an advanced stage of completion in 1989. Route-km in 1989-90, 256 km.

Aviation. The state has airports at Bhuntar near Kullu and at Jubbarharthi near Shimla. Another airport, at Gaggal in Kangra district, was nearing completion in 1989.

JUSTICE, EDUCATION AND WELFARE

Justice. The state has its own High Court at Shimla.

Education. In 1991, 63·54% of the population were literate (74·57% of men and

52·46% of women). There were (1988-89) 7,182 primary schools with 663,000 students, 1,066 middle schools with 337,200 students, 941 high and higher secondary schools with 153,300 students, 39 arts, science and commerce colleges, 1 engineering college, 1 medical college, 2 teacher training colleges and 3 universities. The universities are Himachal Pradesh University, Shimla (1970) with 27 affiliated colleges, Himachal Pradesh Agricultural University, Palanpur (1978) and Dr Y. S. Parmar University of Horticulture and Forestry, Solan (1985). In 1981, 42·48% of the population was literate.

Health. There were (1990) 69 hospitals (7,424 beds), 225 primary health centres and 735 allopathic and Ayurvedic dispensaries.

JAMMU AND KASHMIR

HISTORY. The state of Jammu and Kashmir, which had earlier been under Hindu rulers and Moslem sultans, became part of the Mogul Empire under Akbar from 1586. After a period of Afghan rule from 1756, it was annexed to the Sikh kingdom of the Punjab in 1819. In 1820 Ranjit Singh made over the territory of Jammu to Gulab Singh. After the decisive battle of Sobraon in 1846 Kashmir also was made over to Gulab Singh under the Treaty of Amritsar. British supremacy was recognized until the Indian Independence Act, 1947, when all states decided on accession to India or Pakistan. Kashmir asked for standstill agreements with both. Pakistan agreed, but India desired further discussion with the Government of Jammu and Kashmir State. In the meantime the state became subject to armed attack from the territory of Pakistan and the Maharajah acceded to India on 26 Oct. 1947, by signing the Instrument of Accession. India approached the UN in Jan. 1948; India-Pakistan conflict ended by ceasefire in Jan. 1949. Further conflict in 1965 was followed by the Tashkent Declaration of Jan. 1966. Following further hostilities between India and Pakistan a ceasefire came into effect on 17 Dec. 1971, followed by the Simla Agreement in July 1972, whereby a new line of control was delineated bilaterally through negotiations between India and Pakistan and came into force on 17 Dec. 1972.

AREA AND POPULATION. The state is in the extreme north and is bounded north by China, east by Tibet, south by Himachal Pradesh and Punjab and west by Pakistan. The area is 222,236 sq. km, of which about 78,932 sq. km is occupied by Pakistan and 42,735 sq. km by China; the population of the territory on the Indian side of the line, 1991 projection, was 7,718,700. Growth rate, 1981–89, 28·92%. The official language is Urdu; other commonly spoken languages are Kashmiri (3·1m. speakers at 1981 census), Hindi (1m.), Dogri, Balti, Ladakhi and Punjabi.

CONSTITUTION AND GOVERNMENT. The Maharajah's son, Yuvraj Karan Singh, took over as Regent in 1950 and, on the ending of hereditary rule (17 Oct. 1952), was sworn in as Sadar-i-Riyasat. On his father's death (26 April 1961) Yuvraj Karan Singh was recognized as Maharajah by the Indian Government; he decided not to use the title while he was elected head of state.

The permanent Constitution of the state came into force in part on 17 Nov. 1956 and fully on 26 Jan. 1957. There is a bicameral legislature; the Legislative Council has 36 members and the Legislative Assembly has 76. Since the 1967 elections the 6 representatives of Jammu and Kashmir in the central House of the People are directly elected; there are 4 representatives in the Council of States. After a period of President's rule, a National Conference–Indira Congress coalition government was formed in March 1987. The government was dismissed and the state was brought under President's rule on 18 July 1990.

Kashmir Province has 8 districts and Jammu Province has 6 districts. Srinagar (population, 1981, 586,038) is the summer and Jammu (206,135) the winter capital.

Governor: Girish Saksena.
Chief Minister: (Vacant).

BUDGET. Total expenditure (1991-92) Rs 20,026·8m.; total revenue, Rs 18,250·9m.

ENERGY AND NATURAL RESOURCES

Electricity. Installed capacity (1987–88) 212 mw.; 6,119 villages had electricity in 1990.

Minerals. Minerals include coal, bauxite and gypsum.

Agriculture. About 80% of the population are supported by agriculture. Rice, wheat and maize are the major cereals. The total area under foodgrains (1989-90) was estimated at 878,400 ha. Total foodgrains produced, 1989–90, 1·3m. tonnes (rice, 579,600 tonnes; wheat, 245,600 tonnes); pulses, 24,800 tonnes. Fruit is important: Production, 1989–90, 800,000 tonnes; exports, Rs 3,000m.

The Agrarian Reforms Act came into force in July 1978; the Debtors Relief Act and the Restriction of Mortgage Properties Act also alleviate rural distress. The redistribution of land to cultivators is continuing.

Livestock (1982): Cattle, 2,325,200; buffaloes, 5,631,000; goats, 1,003,900; sheep, 1,908,700; horses, 973,000, and poultry, 2,406,760.

Forestry. Forests cover about 20,891·89 sq. km., forming an important source of revenue, besides providing employment to a large section of the population. About 20,174 sq. km of forests yield valuable timber; state income in 1985–86 was Rs 477m.

INDUSTRY. There are 2 central public sector industries and 30 medium-scale (latter employing 6,468 in 1984). The largest industrial complex is the Bari Brahmara estate in Jammu which covers 320 acres and accommodates diverse manufacturing, as does the Khanmuh estate. The Sopore industrial area in Kashmir Division is intended for industries based on horticulture. There are 26,332 small units (1988–89) employing 115,243. The main traditional handicraft industries are silk spinning, wood-carving, papier-maché and carpet-weaving.

COMMUNICATIONS

Roads. Kashmir is linked with the rest of India by the motorable Jammu-Pathankot road. The Jawahar Tunnel, through the Banihal mountain, connects Srinagar and Jammu, and maintains road communication with the Kashmir Valley during the winter months. In 1988-89 there were 10,260 km of roads.

There were 104,864 motor vehicles in 1989.

Railways. Kashmir is linked with the Indian railway system by the line between Jammu and Pathankot; route km of railways in the state, 1989–90, 77 km.

Aviation. Major airports, with daily service from Delhi, are at Srinagar and Jammu. There is a third airport at Leh. Srinagar airport is being developed as an international airport.

Post. There were 1,457 post offices in 1985, 82 telephone exchanges and approximately 18,000 private telephones.

JUSTICE, RELIGION, EDUCATION AND WELFARE

Justice. The High Court, at Srinagar and Jammu, has a Chief Justice and 4 puisne judges.

Religion. The majority of the population, except in Jammu, are Moslems. At the 1981 census Moslems numbered 3,843,451; Hindus, 1,930,448; Sikhs, 133,675; Buddhists, 69,706; Christians, 8,481; Jains, 1,576.

Education. The proportion of literates was 32·68% in 1991 (44·18% of men and 19·55% of women). Education is free. There were (1988–89) 1,097 secondary schools with 181,313 students, 2,320 middle schools with 291,738 students and 8,712 primary schools with 738,760 students. Jammu University (1969) has 3 constituent and 11 affiliated colleges, with 8,903 students (1985–86); Kashmir University (1948) has 6 constituent, 15 affiliated and 6 oriental institutions (11,900 students); the third university is Sher-E-Kashmir University of Agricultural Sciences and Technology. There are 2 medical colleges, 4 engineering and technology colleges, 2 polytechnics, 8 oriental colleges and an Ayurvedic college, and 3 teacher training colleges.

Health. In 1984–85 there were 50 hospitals, 93 primary health centres and 425 units, 679 clinics and dispensaries, and 483 other units. There were (1986) 3,442 doctors. There is a National Institute of Medical Sciences.

Bamzai, P. N. K., *A History of Kashmir*. Delhi, 1962
Gupta, S., *Kashmir: A Study in India-Pakistan Relations*. London, 1967
Lamb, A., *Kashmir: a Disputed Legacy, 1846–1990*. Hertingfordbury, 1991

KARNATAKA

HISTORY. The state of Karnataka, constituted as Mysore under the States Reorganization Act, 1956, brought together the Kannada-speaking people distributed in 5 states, and consisted of the territories of the old states of Mysore and Coorg, the Bijapur, Kanara and Dharwar districts and the Belgaum district (except one taluk) in former Bombay, the major portions of the Gulbarga, Raichur and Bidar districts in former Hyderabad, and South Kanara district (apart from the Kasaragod taluk) and the Kollegal taluk of the Coimbatore district in Madras. The state was renamed Karnataka in 1973.

AREA AND POPULATION. The state is in south India and is bounded north by Maharashtra, east by Andhra Pradesh, south by Tamil Nadu and Kerala, west by the Indian ocean and north-east by Goa. The area of the state is 191,791 sq. km, and its population (1991 census), 44,806,468, an increase of 20·69% since 1981. Density, 234 per sq. km. Kannada is the language of administration and is spoken by about 66% of the people. Other languages include Telugu (8·17%), Urdu (9%), Marathi (4·5%), Tamil (3·6%), Tulu and Konkani. Principal cities, *see* p. 629. Other large towns (1991) are: Bellary (245,758), Bijapur (186,846), Shimoga (178,882), Raichur (157,477), Tumkur (138,598), Gadag-Batigeri (133,918), Bidar (107,542).

CONSTITUTION AND GOVERNMENT. Karnataka has a bicameral legislature. The Legislative Council has 75 members. The Legislative Assembly consists of 224 elected members. After elections in Nov. 1989 the Congress-I party formed a government.

The state has 20 districts (of which Bangalore Rural is one) in 4 divisions: Bangalore, Mysore, Belgaum and Gulbarga. The capital is Bangalore.

Governor: Khurshid Alam Khan.
Chief Minister: S. Bangarappa.

BUDGET. Budget estimates, 1991–92: Revenue receipts, Rs 48,179·1m.; revenue expenditure, Rs 48,154·6m. Plan allocation 1991-92, Rs 15,100m.

ENERGY AND NATURAL RESOURCES

Electricity. In 1990-91 the state's installed capacity was 2,760 mw. Electricity generated, 1987–88, 7,434m. kwh. 26,483 villages out of 27,028 had electricity in Dec. 1990.

Water. About 2·09m. ha were irrigated in 1988-89.

Minerals. Karnataka is an important source of gold and silver. The estimated reserves of high grade iron ore are 5,000m. tonnes. These reserves are found mainly in the Chitradurga belt. The National Mineral Development Corporation of India has indicated total reserves of nearly 1,000m. tonnes of magnesite and iron ore (with an iron content ranging from 25 to 40) which have been found in Kudremukh

Ganga-Mula region in Chickmagalur District. Value of production (1988-89) Rs 2,590m. The estimated reserves of manganese are over 275m. tonnes.

Limestone is found in many regions; deposits (1986) are about 4,248m. tonnes.

Karnataka is the largest producer of chromite. It is one of the only two states of India producing magnesite. The other minerals of industrial importance are corundum and garnet.

Agriculture. Agriculture forms the main occupation of more than three-quarters of the population. Physically, Karnataka divides into 4 regions–the coastal region, the southern and northern plains, comprising roughly the districts of Bangalore, Tumkur, Chitaldrug, Kolar, Bellary, Mandya and Mysore, and the hill country, comprising the districts of Chickmagalur, Hassan and Shimoga. Rainfall is heavy in the hill country, and there is dense forest. The greater part of the plains are cultivated. Coorg district is essentially agricultural.

The main food crops are rice and jowar, and ragi which is also about 30% of the national crop. Total foodgrains production (1989–90), 7·13m. tonnes (rice 2·38m. tonnes, wheat 126,500 tonnes); pulses 536,300 tonnes. Sugar, groundnut, castorseed, safflower, mulberry silk and cotton are important cash crops. The state grows about 70% of the national coffee crop.

Production, 1989–90 (1,000 tonnes): Sugar-cane, 17,648; cotton, 887 bales (170 kg).

Livestock (1986): Buffaloes, 3,647,967; other cattle, 11,300,223; sheep, 4,791,650; goats, 4,546,928.

Forestry. Total forest in the state (1988–89) is 3,071,000 ha, producing sandal wood, bamboo and other timbers, and ivory.

Fisheries. Production, 1988–89, 242,000 tonnes.

INDUSTRY. There were 12,746 factories employing 816,900 in March 1989. The Vishweswaraya Iron and Steel Works is situated at Bhadravati, while at Bangalore are national undertakings for the manufacture of aircraft, machine tools, light engineering and electronics goods. Other industries include textiles, vehicle manufacture, cement, chemicals, sugar, paper, porcelain and soap. In addition, much of the world's sandalwood is processed, the oil being one of the most valuable productions of the state. Sericulture is a more important cottage industry giving employment, directly or indirectly, to about 2·7m. persons; production of raw silk, 1986–87, 4,671 tonnes, over two-thirds of national production.

COMMUNICATIONS

Roads. In 1988–89 the state had 110,947 km of roads, including 1,968 km of national highway. There were (31 March 1989) 1,299,905 motor vehicles.

Railways. In 1989-90 there were 3,065 km of railway (including 154 km of narrow gauge) in the state.

Aviation. There are airports at Bangalore, Mangalore, Bellary and Belgaum, with regular scheduled services to Bombay, Calcutta, Delhi and Madras.

Shipping. Mangalore is a deep-water port for the export of mineral ores. Karwar is being developed as an intermediate port.

JUSTICE, RELIGION, EDUCATION AND WELFARE

Justice. The seat of the High Court is at Bangalore. It has a Chief Justice and 24 puisne judges.

Religion. At the 1981 census there were 31,906,793 Hindus; 4,104,616 Moslems; 764,449 Christians; 297,974 Jains; 42,147 Buddhists; 6,401 Sikhs.

Education. The number of literates, according to the 1991 census, was 21·07m. (55·98%; 67·25% of men and 44·34% of women). In 1988–89 the state had 23,337 primary schools with 5,428,714 students, 15,725 middle schools with 1,687,515 students, 4,799 high and higher secondary schools with 829,205 students, 173 polytechnic and 18 medical colleges, 50 engineering and technology colleges, 403 arts, science and commerce colleges and 9 universities. Education is free up to pre-university level.

Universities: Mysore (1916); Karnatak (1950) at Dharwar; University of Agricultural Sciences (1964) at Hebbal, Bangalore; Gulbarga, and Mangalore; University of Agricultural Sciences, Dharwad; Kuvempu University, Shimoga. Mysore has 6 university and 117 affiliated colleges (1983–84); Karnatak, 5 and 115; Bangalore, 126 affiliated; Hebbal, 8 constituent colleges.

The Indian Institute of Science, Bangalore, has the status of a university.

Health. There were in 1988-89, 288 hospitals, 208 dispensaries, 1,142 primary health centres and 467 family welfare centres. Total number of beds, 41,607.

KERALA

HISTORY. The state of Kerala, created under the States Reorganization Act, 1956, consists of the previous state of Travancore-Cochin, except for 4 taluks of the Thiruvananthapuram (Trivandrum) district and a part of the Shencottah taluk of Kollam (Quilon) district. It took over the Malabar district (apart from the Laccadive and Minicoy Islands) and the Kasaragod taluk of South Kanara (apart from the Amindivi Islands) from Madras State.

AREA AND POPULATION. Kerala is in south India and is bounded north by Karnataka, east and south-east by Tamil Nadu, south-west and west by the Indian ocean. The state has an area of 38,863 sq. km. The 1991 census showed a population of 29,032,828; density of population was 747 per sq. km. Growth rate, 1981–91, 13·98%. Other principal towns (1991): Alappuzha (174,606), Kollam (139,717), Palakkad (122,964), Thalassery (103,577).

Languages spoken in the state are Malayalam, Tamil and Kannada.

The physical features of the land fall into three well-marked divisions: (1) the hilly tracts undulating from the Western Ghats in the east and marked by long spurs, extensive ravines and dense forests; (2) the cultivated plains intersected by numerous rivers and streams; and (3) the coastal belt with dense coconut plantations and rice fields.

CONSTITUTION AND GOVERNMENT. The state has a unicameral legislature of 140 elected (and one nominated) members including the Speaker. After the elections of June 1991 the Indian National (I) Congress Party and allies held 90 seats, the Left Front (CPI, CPI (M) and allies), 50.

The state has 14 districts. The capital is Thiruvananthapuram.

Governor: B. Rachiah.
Chief Minister: K. Karunakaran.

BUDGET. Budget estimates for 1991–92 showed total receipts of Rs 26,900m. expenditure Rs 30,895m. Annual Plan expenditure, 1991–92, Rs 8,070m.

ENERGY AND NATURAL RESOURCES

Electricity. Installed capacity (March 1988), 1,476·5 mw.; energy generated in 1987–88 was 4,094m. kw. The Idukki hydro-electric plant produced 2,314·4m. kwh, the Sabarigiri scheme 962·99m. kwh. All villages are electrified.

Minerals. The beach sands of Kerala contain monazite, ilmenite, rutile, zircon, sillimanite, etc. There are extensive whiteclay deposits; other minerals of commercial importance include mica, graphite, limestone, quartz sand and lignite. Iron ore has been found at Kozhikode (Calicut).

Agriculture. Area under irrigation in 1988-89 was 536,000 ha; 19 irrigation projects were under execution in 1987-88. The chief agricultural products are rice, tapioca, coconut, arecanut, cashewnut, oilseeds, pepper, sugar-cane, rubber, tea, coffee and cardamom. About 98% of Indian black pepper and about 95% of Indian rubber is produced in Kerala. Production of principal crops, 1989–90: Total foodgrains, 1·1m. tonnes (of which rice 1,048,000 tonnes from 572,000 ha); pulses, 18,900 tonnes; sugar-cane, 535,700 tonnes.

Livestock (1982); Buffaloes, 408,584; other cattle, 3·1m.; goats, 2m. In 1985–86 milk production was 1·34m. tonnes; egg production, 1,397m.

Forestry. Forest occupied 1,123,000 ha in 1989–90. About 24% of the area is comprised of forests, including teak, sandal wood, ebony and blackwood and varieties of softwood. Net forest revenue, 1986–87, Rs 481·8m., from timber, bamboos, reeds and ivory.

Fisheries. Fishing is a flourishing industry; the catch in 1988-89 was about 365,400 tonnes. Fish exports, Rs 1,839·4m. in 1987-88.

INDUSTRIES. Most of the major industrial concerns are either owned or sponsored by the Government. Among the privately owned factories are the numerous cashew and coir factories. Other important factory industries are rubber, tea, tiles, electronics, oil, textiles, ceramics, fertilizers and chemicals, zinc-smelting, sugar, cement, rayon, glass, matches, pencils, monazite, ilmenite, titanium oxide, rare earths, aluminium, electrical goods, paper, shark-liver oil, etc. The state has a refinery and a shipyard at Kochi (Cochin).

The number of factories registered under the Factories Act 1948 on 1 July 1990 was 12,557, with daily average employment of 292,000.

Among the cottage industries, coir-spinning and handloom-weaving are the most important, forming the means of livelihood of a large section of the people. Other industries are the village oil industry, ivory carving, furniture-making, bell metal, brass and copper ware, leather goods, screw-pines, mat-making, rattan work, beekeeping, pottery, etc. These have been organized on a co-operative basis.

COMMUNICATIONS

Roads. In 1989–90 there were 125,633 km of roads in the state; national highways, 839 km. There were 581,054 motor vehicles at 31 March 1990.

Railways. There is a coastal line from Mangalore in Karnataka which serves Kannur (Cannanore), Mahé, Kozhikode (Calicut), Ernakulam (for Kochi (Cochin)), Aleppuzha (Aleppy), Kollam (Quilon) and Thiruvananthapurum (Trivandrum), and connects them with main towns in Tamil Nadu. In 1989–90 there were 984 route-km of track.

Civil Aviation. There are airports at Kozhikode, Kochi and Thiruvananthapuram with regular scheduled services to Delhi, Bombay and Madras; international flights leave from Thiruvananthapuram.

Shipping. Port Kochi, administered by the central government, is one of India's major ports; in 1983 it became the out-port for the Inland Container Depot at Coimbatore in Tamil Nadu. There are 13 other ports and harbours.

JUSTICE, RELIGION, EDUCATION AND WELFARE

Justice. The High Court at Ernakulam has a Chief Justice and 14 puisne judges and 3 additional judges.

Religion. At the 1981 census there were 14,801,347 Hindus; 5,409,687 Moslems; 5,233,865 Christians; 3,605 Jains; 1,295 Sikhs.

Education. Kerala is the most literate Indian State with 22·66m. literates at the 1991 census (90·59%); 94·45% of men and 86·93% of women). Education is free up to the age of 14.

In 1988–89 there were 6,817 primary schools with 3.22m. students, 2,885 middle schools with 1.76m students and 2,456 high schools with 0.89m students.

Kerala University (established 1937) at Trivandrum, is affiliating and teaching; in 1986–87 it had 43 affiliated arts and science colleges. The University of Cochin is federal, and for post-graduate studies only. The University of Calicut (established

1968) is teaching and affiliating and has 92 affiliated colleges. Kerala Agricultural University (established 1971) has 8 constituent colleges. Mahatma Gandhi University at Kottayam was established in 1983 and has 56 affiliated colleges.

Health. There were 140 allopathic, 101 Ayurvedic and 279 homeo hospitals, and 881 health centres in 1990.

Further Reading

Jeffrey, R., *Politics, Women and Well-being: How Kerala became a Model.* London, 1992

MADHYA PRADESH

HISTORY. Under the provisions of the States Reorganization Act, 1956, the State of Madhya Pradesh was formed on 1 Nov. 1956. It consists of the 17 Hindi districts of the former state of Madhya Pradesh, the former state of Madhya Bharat (except the Sunel enclave of Mandsaur district), the former states of Bhopal and Vindhya Pradesh and the Sironj subdivision of Kotah district, which was an enclave of Rajasthan in Madhya Pradesh.

For information on the former states, *see* THE STATESMAN'S YEAR-BOOK , 1958, pp. 180–84.

AREA AND POPULATION. The state is in central India and is bounded north by Rajasthan and Uttar Pradesh, east by Bihar and Orissa, south by Andhra Pradesh and Maharashtra, west by Gujarat. Madhya Pradesh is the largest Indian state in size, with an area of 443,446 sq. km. In respect of population it ranks sixth. Population (1991 census), 66,135,862, an increase of 26·75% since 1981. Density, 149 per sq. km.

Cities with over 250,000 population, *see* p. 629. Other large cities (1991): Sagar, 195,106; Bilaspur, 190,911; Ratlam, 183,370; Burhanpur, 172,809; Dewas, 163,699; Murwara, 163,390; Satna, 156,321; Durg, 150,513; Morena, 147,095; Khandwa, 145,111; Rewa, 128,918; Rajnandgaon, 125,394; Korba, 124,365; Bhind, 109,731; Shivpuri, 108,271.

The number of persons speaking each of the more prevalent languages (1981 census) were: Hindi, 43,870,242; Urdu, 1,131,288; Marathi, 1,184,128; Gujarati, 581,084. In April 1990 Hindi became the sole official language.

CONSTITUTION AND GOVERNMENT. Madhya Pradesh is one of the 9 states for which the Constitution provides a bicameral legislature, but the Vidhan Parishad or Upper House (to consist of 90 members) has yet to be formed. The Vidhan Sabha or Lower House has 320 elected members. Following the election of Feb. 1990, a Bharatiya Janata Party government was returned, with 220 out of 320 seats. State of the parties following the Nov. 1991 by-elections: Bharatiya Janata Party, 220; Congress (I), 54; Janata Dal, 17; (Samajvadi) Janata Dal, 5; independents and others, 17; vacant, 7.

For administrative purposes the state has been split into 12 divisions with a Commissioner at the head of each; the headquarters of these are located at Bhopal, Bilaspur, Gwalior, Hoshangabad, Indore, Jabalpur, Jagdalpur, Morena, Raipur, Rewa, Sagar and Ujjain. There are 45 districts.

The seat of government is at Bhopal.

Governor: Kunwar Mehmood Ali Khan.
Chief Minister: Sundarlal Patwa.

BUDGET. Budget estimates for 1991–92 showed revenue receipts of Rs 55,360·1m. and expenditure of Rs 54,226·8m. Annual plan, 1991–92, Rs 24,260m.

ENERGY AND NATURAL RESOURCES

Electricity. Madhya Pradesh is rich in low-grade coal suitable for power generation, and also has immense potential hydro-electric energy. Total installed capacity,

1990: 3,158·7 mw. Power generated, 29,470m. kwh. in 1990–91. The thermal power stations are at Korba in Bilaspur district, Amarkantak in Shahdol district and Satpura in Betul district; new stations are being built. The only hydro-electric power station is at Gandhi Sagar lake in Mandsaur district; this, with a maximum water surface of 165 sq. miles, is the biggest man-made lake in Asia. 63,007 out of 71,352 villages were electrified in 1991.

Water. Major irrigation projects include the Chambal Valley scheme (started in 1952 with Rajasthan), the Tawa project in Hoshangabad district, the Barna and Hasdeo schemes, the Mahanadi canal system and schemes in the Narmada valley at Bargi and Narmadasagar.

Minerals. The state has extensive mineral deposits. Nearly 0·4m. sq. km have been surveyed and known deposits include 800·1m. tonnes of limestone, 126·8m. tonnes of bauxite, 26,852m. tonnes of coal and 2,186·2m. tonnes of iron ore. Other deposits include manganese, ochre, sillimanite, dolomite, rock phosphate, copper, lead, tin, fluorite, barytes, china clay and fireclay, corundum, gold, diamonds, pyrophyllite and diaspore, lepidolite, asbestos, vermiculite, mica, glass sand, quartz, felspars, bentonite and building stone. New and very large reserves of copper were found in the Malanjkhand area in 1986.

In 1987 the output of major minerals was (in tonnes): Limestone, 11·2m.; diamonds, 15,000 carats; iron ore, 7·7m.; manganese ore, 200,000. Value of production, 1987, Rs 11,120m. Coal output was 67·52m. tonnes in 1990.

Agriculture. Agriculture is the mainstay of the state's economy and 80% of the people are rural. 43·7% of the land area is cultivable, of which 16·6% is irrigated. The Malwa region abounds in rich black cotton soil, the low-lying areas of Gwalior, Bundelkhand and Baghelkhand and the Chhatisgarh plains have a lighter sandy soil, while the Narmada valley is formed of deep rich alluvial deposits. Production of principal crops, 1990–91 (in tonnes): Foodgrains, 17·8m. (rice, 6m., wheat 5.5m.); pulses 2.9m.; cotton (1989–90), 0·4m. bales of 170 kg.

Livestock (1989–90): Buffaloes, 7,262,022; other cattle, 27,612,636; sheep, 912,147; goats, 7,398,406; horses and ponies, 96,556.

Forestry. In 1991, 155,411 sq. km, or about 35% of the state's area was covered by forests. The forests are chiefly of sal, saja and teak species. They are the chief source in India of best-quality teak; they also provide firewood for about 60% of domestic fuel needs, and form valuable watershed protection. Forest revenue, 1988–89, Rs 3,390m.

INDUSTRY. The major industries are the steel plant at Bhilai, Bharat Heavy Electricals at Bhopal, the aluminium plant at Korba, the security paper mills at Hoshangabad, the Bank Note Press at Dewas, the newsprint mill at Nepanagar and alkaloid factory at Neemuch, cement factories, vehicle factory, ordnance factory, and gun carriage factory. There are also 23 textile mills, 7 of them nationalized.

The Bhilai steel plant near Durg is one of the 6 major steel mills. A power station at Korba (Bilaspur) with a capacity of 420 mw serves Bhilai, the aluminium plant and the Korba coalfield.

The heavy electrical factory was set up by the Government of India at Bhopal during the second-plan period. This is India's first heavy electrical equipment factory.

Other industries include cement, sugar, fertilizers, straw board, paper, vegetable oil, refractories, potteries, textile machinery, steel casting and rerolling, industrial gases, synthetic fibres, drugs, biscuit manufacturing, engineering, electronics, optical fibres, plastics, tools, rayon and art silk. The number of heavy and medium industries in the state is 518, with 181 ancillary industries; the number of small-scale establishments in production is 275,000. 39 out of 45 districts in the state are categorized as industrially backward.

There are 22 'growth centres' in operation, and 5 under development.

The main industrial development agencies are Madhya Pradesh Financial Corporation, Madhya Pradesh Audyogik Vikas Nigam Ltd, Madhya Pradesh State Industries Corporation, Madhya Pradesh Laghu Udyog Nigam, Madhya Pradesh State

Textile Corporation, Madhya Pradesh Handicrafts Board, Khadi and Village Industries Board and Madhya Pradesh State Mining Corporation.

The state is known for its traditional village and home crafts such as handloom weaving, best developed at Chanderi and Maheshwar, toys, pottery, lacework, woodwork, zari work, leather work and metal utensils. The ancillary industries of dyeing, calico printing and bleaching are centred in areas of textile production.

COMMUNICATIONS

Roads. Total length of roads in 1990–91 was 902,580 km, of which 70,849 km were surfaced. In 1989–90 there were 1,251,411 motor vehicles.

Railways. Bhopal, Bilaspur, Katni, Khandwar and Ratlam are junctions for the central, south, eastern and western networks. Route km of railways (1989–90), 5,838 km.

Aviation. There are airports at Bhopal, Gwalior, Indore, Khajuraho and Raipur with regular scheduled services to Bombay and Delhi, Varanasi and Nagpur.

JUSTICE, RELIGION AND EDUCATION

Justice. The High Court of Judicature at Jabalpur has a Chief Justice and 24 puisne judges. Its benches are located at Gwalior and Indore.

Religion. At the 1981 census Hindus numbered 48,504,575; Moslems, 2,501,919; Christians, 351,972; Buddhists, 75,312; Sikhs, 143,020, Jains, 444,960.

Education. The 1991 census showed 23·49m. people to be literate (43·45%; 57·43% of men; 28·39% of women). Education is free for children aged up to 14.

In 1990–91 there were 66,849 primary schools with 7,994,000 students, 13,977 middle schools with 2,653,000 students, 1,695 high schools with 710,000 students and 2,278 secondary schools with 294,000 students.

There are 14 universities in Madhya Pradesh: Dr. Hari Singh Gour University (established 1946), at Sagar, had 92 affiliated colleges and 30,487 students in 1990–91; Rani Durgavati University at Jabalpur (1957) had 36 affiliated colleges and 20,101 students; Vikram University (1957), at Ujjain, had 80 affiliated colleges and 24,226 students; Indira Kala Sangeet Vishwavidyalaya (1956), at Khairagarh, had 33 affiliated colleges and 6,720 students on roll (this university teaches music and fine arts); Devi Ahilya University at Indore (1964) had 26 affiliated colleges and 20,332 students; Jiwaji University (1963), at Gwalior, had 58 affiliated colleges and 25,766 students; Jawaharlal Nehru Krishi University (1964), at Jabalpur, had 10 constituent colleges and 2,994 students in 1985–86; Ravishankar University (1964), at Raipur, had 84 affiliated colleges; Indira Gandhi Krishi Vishwavidyalaya, Raipur; A. P. Singh University, Rewa; Barkatullah Vishwavidyalaya, Bhopal; Guru Ghasidas University, Bilaspur; Makhanlal Chaturvedi Rashtriya Patrakarita Vishwavidhyalaya Bhopal; Chitrakoot Gramodoya Vishwavidhayalaya Chitrakoot. In 1990-91 there were 554 colleges of arts, science and commerce, 19 teacher-training colleges, and 13 engineering and technology colleges, 6 medical colleges, 32 polytechnics and 63 technical-industrial arts and craft schools.

Health. In 1988–89 there were 717 hospitals with 27,800 beds, and 1,436 primary health centres.

MAHARASHTRA

HISTORY. Under the States Reorganization Act, 1956, Bombay State was formed by merging the states of Kutch and Saurashtra and the Marathi-speaking areas of Hyderabad (commonly known as Marathwada) and Madhya Pradesh (also called Vidarbha) in the old state of Bombay, after the transfer from that state of the Kannada-speaking areas of the Belgaum, Bijapur, Kanara and Dharwar districts which were added to the state of Mysore, and the Abu Road taluka of Banaskantha district, which went to the state of Rajasthan.

By the Bombay Reorganization Act, 1960, which came into force 1 May 1960, 17 districts (predominantly Gujarati-speaking) in the north and west of Bombay State became the new state of Gujarat, and the remainder was renamed Maharashtra.

The state of Maharashtra consists of the following districts of the former Bombay State: Ahmednagar, Akola, Amravati, Aurangabad, Bhandara, Bhir, Buldana, Chanda, Dhulia (West Khandesh), Greater Bombay, Jalgaon (East Khandesh), Kolaba, Kolhapur, Nagpur, Nanded, Nasik, Osmanabad, Parbhani, Pune, Ratnagiri, Sangli, Satara, Sholapur, Thana, Wardha, Yeotmal; certain portions of Thana and Dhulia districts have become part of Gujarat.

AREA AND POPULATION. Maharashtra is in central India and is bounded north and east by Madhya Pradesh, south by Andhra Pradesh, Karnataka and Goa, west by the Indian ocean and north-west by Daman and Gujarat. The state has an area of 307,690 sq. km. The population at the 1991 census was 78,748,215 (an increase of 25·36% since 1981), of whom about 30m. were Marathi-speaking. Density, 256 per sq. km. The area of Greater Bombay was 603 sq. km. and its population 9·99m. For other principal cities, *see under* India: Area and Population. Other large towns (1991): Jalgaon (241,603), Chandrapur (225,841), Ichalkaranji (214,835), Latur (197,164), Sangli (193,181), Parbhan (190,235), Ahmadnagar (181,015), Jalna (174,958), Bhusawal (144,804), Miraj (121,564), Bid (112,351), Gondiya (109,271), Yavatmul (108,591), Wardha (102,974).

CONSTITUTION AND GOVERNMENT. Maharashtra has a bicameral legislature. The Legislative Council has 78 members. The Legislative Assembly has 288 elected members and 1 member nominated by the Governor to represent the Anglo-Indian community. Following the election of Feb. 1990 Congress (I) retained power with the support of some independent members. Total seats, 288: Congress (I), 141; Shiv Shena, 52; Bharatiya Janata Party, 42; Janata Dal, 24; People's and Workers' Party, 8; Independents and others, 21.

The Council of Ministers consists of the Chief Minister, 16 other Ministers, and 19 Ministers of State.

The capital is Bombay. The state has 30 districts.

Governor: C. Subramaniam
Chief Minister: Sudhakarrao Naik.

BUDGET. Budget estimates, 1991–92: receipts, Rs 125,685m.; expenditure; Rs 127,150·7m. Plan outlay, 1991-92, Rs 30,000m.

ENERGY AND NATURAL RESOURCES

Electricity. Installed capacity, 1988-89, 7,658 mw. (5,634 mw. thermal, 1,436 mw. hydro-electricity and 160 mw. nuclear). 39,106 villages out of 39,354 were electrified in 1990. Electricity generated, 1989-90, 35,260m. kwh.

Oil and Gas. Bombay High (offshore) produced 21·1m. tonnes of crude oil and 9·7m. cu. metres of natural gas in 1988–89.

Minerals. The state has coal, silica, sand, dolomite, kyanite, sillimanite, limestone, iron ore, manganese, bauxite. Value of mineral production, 1989, Rs 4,860m.

Agriculture. About 12·1% of the cropped area is irrigated. In normal seasons the main food crops are rice, wheat, jowar, bajri and pulses. Main cash crops: Cotton, sugar-cane, groundnuts. Production, 1989-90 (in tonnes): Foodgrains, 13·2m. (rice, 2·32m., wheat, 0·91m.); pulses, 1·73m.; cotton, 2·21m. bales of 170 kg.

Livestock (1982 census): Buffaloes, 3,972,000; other cattle, 16,162,000; sheep, 2,671,000; goats, 7,705,000; horses and ponies, 49,000; poultry, 19,844,000.

Forestry. Forests occupy 63,812 sq. km.

Fisheries. In 1989-90 the marine fish catch was estimated at 403,000 tonnes and the inland fish catch at 50,000 tonnes; 15,442 boats, including 6,953 mechanized, were used for marine fishing.

INDUSTRY. Industry is concentrated mainly in Bombay, Pune and Thane. The main groups are chemicals and products, textiles, electrical and non-electrical machinery, petroleum and products, aircraft, rubber and plastic products, transport equipment and food products. The state industrial development corporation had invested Rs 56,000m. in 8,800 industrial units by 1989. In 1989-90 there were 23,058 working factories employing 1·16m. people.

COMMUNICATIONS

Roads. On 31 March 1990 there were 208,077 km of roads, of which 142,635 km were surfaced. There were 2,641,000 motor vehicles on 1 Jan. 1991, of which 25% were in Greater Bombay. Passenger and freight transport has been nationalized.

Railways. The total length of railway on 31 March 1990 was 5,434 km; 61% was broad gauge, 18% metre gauge and 20% narrow gauge. The main junctions and termini are Bombay, Manmad, Akola, Nagpur, Pune and Sholapur.

Aviation. The main airport is Bombay, which has national and international flights. Nagpur airport is on the route from Bombay to Calcutta and there are also airports at Pune and Aurangabad.

Shipping. Maharashtra has a coastline of 720 km. Bombay is the major port, and there are 48 minor ports.

JUSTICE, RELIGION, EDUCATION AND WELFARE

Justice. The High Court has a Chief Justice and 45 judges. The seat of the High Court is Bombay, but it has benches at Nagpur, Aurangabad and Panaji (Goa).

Religion. At the 1981 census Hindus numbered 51,109,457; Moslems, 5,805,785; Buddhists, 3,946,149; Christians, 795,464; Jains, 939,392; Sikhs, 107,255. Other religions, 155,692; religion not stated, 1,394.

Education. The number of literates, according to the 1991 census, was 42.8m. (63·05%; men 74·84%, women 50·51%). In 1990–91, there were 9,830 high and higher secondary schools with 5,865,000 pupils and 57,444 primary schools, with 10,292,000 pupils. There are 75 engineering and technology colleges, 16 medical colleges, 88 teacher training colleges, 140 polytechnics and 540 arts, science and commerce colleges.

Bombay University, founded in 1857, is mainly an affiliating university. It has 159 colleges with a total (1988–89) of 162,000 students. Colleges in Goa can affiliate to Bombay University. Nagpur University (1923) is both teaching and affiliating. It has 117 colleges with 55,000 students. Pune University, founded in 1948, is teaching and affiliating; it has 191 colleges and 97,000 students. The SNDT Women's University had 25 colleges with a total of 26,000 students. Marathwada University, Aurangabad, was founded in 1958 as a teaching and affiliating body to control colleges in the Marathwada or Marathi-speaking area, previously under Osmania University; it has 133 colleges and 55,000 students. Shiwaji University, Kolhapur, was established in 1963 to control affiliated colleges previously under Pune University. It has 138 colleges and 56,000 students. Amravati University has 88 colleges and 35,000 students.Other universities are: Marathwada Krishi Vidyapeeth, Parbhani; Y. Chavan Maharashtra Open University, Nashik; North Maharashtra University, Jalgaon; Tilak Vidyapeeth, Pune.

Health. In 1989-90 there were 768 hospitals (108,469 beds), 1,896 dispensaries and 1,539 primary health centres.

Statistical Information: The Director of Publicity, Sachivalaya, Bombay.
Tindall, G., *City of Gold*, London, 1982

MANIPUR

HISTORY. Formerly a state under the political control of the Government of India, Manipur, on 15 Aug. 1947, entered into interim arrangements with the Indian

Union and the political agency was abolished. The administration was taken over by the Government of India on 15 Oct. 1949 under a merger agreement, and it is centrally administered by the Government of India through a Chief Commissioner. In 1950–51 an Advisory form of Government was introduced. In 1957 this was replaced by a Territorial Council of 30 elected and 2 nominated members. Later in 1963 a Legislative Assembly of 30 elected and 3 nominated members was established under the Government of Union Territories Act 1963. Because of the unstable party position in the Assembly, it had to be dissolved on 16 Oct. 1969 and President's Rule introduced. The status of the administrator was raised from Chief Commissioner to Lieut.-Governor with effect from 19 Dec. 1969. On the 21 Jan. 1972 Manipur became a state and the status of the administrator was changed from Lieut.-Governor to Governor.

AREA AND POPULATION. The state is in north-east India and is bounded north by Nagaland, east by Burma, south by Burma and Mizoram, and west by Assam. Manipur has an area of 22,327 sq. km and a population (1991) of 1,826,714. Density, 82 per sq. km. Growth rate, 1981–91, 28·56%. The valley, which is about 1,813 sq. km, is 2,600 ft above sea-level. The hills rise in places to nearly 10,000 ft, but are mostly about 5,000–6,000 ft. The average annual rainfall is 65 in. The hill areas are inhabited by various hill tribes who constitute about one-third of the total population of the state. There are about 40 tribes and sub-tribes falling into two main groups of Nagas and Kukis. Manipuri and English are the official languages. A large number of dialects are spoken, while Hindi is gradually becoming prevalent.

CONSTITUTION AND GOVERNMENT. With the attainment of statehood, Manipur has a Legislative Assembly of 60 members, of which 19 are from reserved tribal constituencies. There are 8 districts. Capital, Imphal (population, 1991, 196,268). Presidential rule was imposed in Feb. 1981. Following the election in Feb. 1990, a United Legislature Front government led by Manipur People's Party came to power. Total seats, 60: Congress (I), 28; Manipur People's Party, 10; Janata Dal, 10; Congress (S), 6; Independents and others, 6.

Governor: Chintamani Panigrahi.
Chief Minister: R. K. Ranvir Singh.

BUDGET. Budget estimates for 1988–89 show revenue of Rs 3,540m. and expenditure of Rs 3,460m. Plan allocation 1991–92, Rs 1,950m.

ENERGY AND NATURAL RESOURCES

Electricity. Installed capacity (1988-89) is 10,715 Kw. from diesel and hydro-electric generators. This has been augmented since 1981 by the North Eastern Regional Grid. In 1989-90 there were 1,292 villages with electricity.

Water. The main power, irrigation and flood-control schemes are the Loktak Lift Irrigation scheme (irrigation potential, 40,000 ha; the Singda scheme (potential 4,000 ha, and improved water supply for Imphal); the Thoubal scheme (potential 34,000 ha, 7·5 mw. of electricity and 10 MGD of water supply), and four other large projects. By 1986–87 more than 43,500 ha had been irrigated.

Agriculture. Rice is the principal crop; with wheat, maize and pulses. Total foodgrains, 1989–90, 0·26m. tonnes (rice, 245,100 tonnes).
Agricultural work force, about 348,000. Only 210,000 ha are cultivable, of which 186,000 are under paddy. Fruit and vegetables are important in the valley, including pineapple, oranges, bananas, mangoes, pears, peaches and plums. Soil erosion, produced by shifting cultivation, is being halted by terracing.

Forests. Forests occupy about 15,154 sq km. The main products are teak, jurjan, pine; there are also large areas of bamboo and cane, especially in the Jiri and Barak river drainage areas, yielding about 300,000 tonnes annually. Total revenue from forests, 1987–88, Rs 17·1m.

Fisheries. Landings in 1981–82, 3,450 tonnes.

INDUSTRY. Handloom weaving is a cottage industry. Larger-scale industries include the manufacture of bicycles and TV sets, sugar, cement, starch, vegetable oil and glucose. Sericulture produces about 45 tonnes of raw silk annually. Estimated non-agricultural work force, 240,000.

COMMUNICATIONS. A national highway from Kaziranga (Assam) runs through Imphal to the Burmese frontier. A railway link was opened in 1990. There is an airport at Imphal with regular scheduled services to Delhi and Calcutta. Length of road (1987) 3,971 km; number of vehicles (1988) 29,760.

EDUCATION AND HEALTH

Education. The 1991 census gave the number of literates as 895,223 (60·96%; men 72·98%, women 48·64%). In 1988–89 there were 2,771 primary schools with 268,800 students, 443 middle schools with 73,000 students, 388 high and higher secondary schools and 33 colleges with 50,400 students, 1 medical college, 3 teacher training colleges, 1 polytechnic as well as Manipur University.

Health. In 1987–88 there were 11 hospitals, 52 dispensaries, 8 community health centres, 49 primary health centres and 389 sub-centres.

MEGHALAYA

HISTORY. The state was created under the Assam Reorganization (Meghalaya) Act 1969 and inaugurated on 2 April 1970. Its status was that of a state within the State of Assam until 21 Jan. 1972 when it became a fully-fledged state of the Union. It consists of the former Garo Hills district and United Khasi and Jaintia Hills district of Assam.

AREA AND POPULATION. Meghalaya is bounded north and east by Assam, south and west by Bangladesh. In 1991 (census figure) the area was 22,429 sq. km and the population 1,760,626. Density 78 per sq. km. Growth rate, 1981–91, 31·8%. The people are mainly of the Khasi, Jaintia and Garo tribes.

CONSTITUTION AND GOVERNMENT. Meghalaya has a unicameral legislature. The Legislative Assembly has 60 seats. Party position in Nov. 1990: Meghalaya United Parliamentary Party, 30; United Meghalaya Parliamentary Forum, 26. President's rule was imposed on 11 Oct. 1991.

There are 5 districts. The capital is Shillong (population, 1991, 130,691).

Governor: Madhukar Dighe.
Chief Minister: (Vacant).

BUDGET. Budget estimates for 1986–87 showed revenue receipts of Rs 2,177m. and expenditure of Rs 1,639m. Annual Plan expenditure, 1991–92, Rs 2,100m.

ENERGY AND NATURAL RESOURCES

Electricity. Total installed capacity (1988–89) was 128.72 mw. 2,206 villages out of 4,902 had electricity in Dec. 1990.

Minerals. The East and West Khasi and Jaintia Hills districts produce coal, sillimanite (95% of India's total output), limestone, fire clay, dolomite, felspar, quartz and glass sand. The state also has deposits of coal (estimated reserves 500m. tonnes), limestone (4,000m.), fire clay (100,000) and sandstone which are virtually untapped because of transport difficulties.

Agriculture. About 80% of the people depend on agriculture. Principal crops are rice, maize, potatoes, cotton, oranges, ginger, tezpata, areca nuts, jute, mesta, bananas and pineapples. Production 1989–90 (in tonnes) of principal crops: Rice, 108,500; potatoes, 115,800; maize, 20,100; jute, 6,600; wheat, 6,700; cotton, 867; rape and mustard, 3,400; pulses, 2,300.

Forest products are the state's chief resources.

INDUSTRY. Apart from agriculture the main source of employment is the extraction and processing of minerals; there are also important timber processing mills. The state has a plywood factory, a cement factory (production capacity, 930 tonnes per day), a beverage plant and watch and match splint factories. Meghalaya Industrial Development Corporation has set up industrial units. There is a new industrial area in Byrnihat, and two industrial estates in Shillong and Mendipathar. Tantalum capacitors are manufactured in the Khwan Industrial Area near Shillong. In 1988–89 there were 58 registered factories and 1,231 small-scale industries.

COMMUNICATIONS. Three national highways run through the state. The state has no railways. Umroi airport (20 km from Shillong) connects the state with main air services. In 1989 there were 461 km of national highway and (1988-89) 5,399 km of surfaced and unsurfaced roads. Total number of motor vehicles, 1986–87, 14,202.

JUSTICE, EDUCATION AND WELFARE

Justice. The Guwahati High Court is common to Assam, Meghalaya, Nagaland, Manipur, Mizoram, Tripura and Arunachal Pradesh. There is a bench of the Guwahati High Court at Shillong.

Education. In 1991, 48·26% of the population were literate (51·57% of men and 44·78% of women). In 1988–89 the state had 4,175 primary schools with 239,291 students, 749 middle schools with 68,370 students, 342 high schools with 42,260 students, 1 teacher training college, 1 polytechnic and 23 colleges. The North-eastern Hill University started functioning at Shillong in 1973.

Health. In 1989–90 there were 8 government hospitals, 56 primary health centres, 24 government dispensaries and 247 sub-centres. Total beds (hospitals and health centres), 1,714.

MIZORAM

HISTORY. On 21 Jan. 1972 the former Mizo Hills District of Assam was created a Union Territory. A long dispute between the Mizo National Front (originally Seperatist) and the central government was resolved in 1985. Mizoram became a state by the Constitution (53rd Amendment) and the State of Mizoram Acts, July 1986.

AREA AND POPULATION. Mizoram is one of the eastern-most Indian states, lying between Bangladesh and Burma, and having on its northern boundaries Tripura, Assam and Manipur. The area is 21,081 sq. km and the population (1991 census) 686,217. Density, 33 per sq. km; growth rate 1981–91, 38·98%.

CONSTITUTION AND GOVERNMENT. Mizoram has a unicameral Legislative Assembly with 40 seats: Congress I, 22; Mizo National Front, 14; others, 4. The capital is Aizawl (population, 1991, 154,343).

Governor: Swaraj Kaushal.
Chief Minister: Lalthnahawla.

BUDGET. Budget estimates for 1991-92 show revenue receipts of Rs 3,496·1m. and revenue expenditure of Rs 2,692·2m. Annual plan outlay (1991-92) Rs 1,500m.

ELECTRICITY. Installed capacity (1986–87), 16,109 kw. 407 out of 721 villages had electricity in 1990.

AGRICULTURE. About 90% of the people are engaged in agriculture, either on terraced holdings or in shifting cultivation. Area under rice, 1989–90, 60,100 ha; production, 69,000 tonnes.
    Total forest area, 15,935 sq. km.

INDUSTRY. Hand loom weaving and other cottage industries are important.

COMMUNICATIONS. Aizawl is connected by road and air with Silchar in Assam. Total length of roads, 31 March 1984, 2,665 km. There were 5,467 motor vehicles in 1986–87.

RELIGION. The mainly tribal population is 83·81% Christian.

EDUCATION. The number of literates in 1991 was 462,246 (81·23%; 84·06% of men and 78·09% of women). In 1988–89 there were 1,053 primary schools with 106,176 students, 498 middle schools with 33,750 students and 185 high schools with 12,436 students; there were 13 colleges and one university.

HEALTH. In 1986–87 there were 9 hospitals, 22 primary and 25 subsidiary health centres. Total beds, 893.

NAGALAND

HISTORY. The territory was constituted by the Union Government in Sept. 1962. It comprises the former Naga Hills district of Assam and the former Tuensang Frontier division of the North-East Frontier Agency; these had been made a Centrally Administered Area in 1957, administered by the President through the Governor of Assam. In Jan. 1961 the area was renamed and given the status of a state of the Indian Union, which was officially inaugurated on 1 Dec. 1963.

For some years a section of the Naga leaders sought independence. Military operations from 1960 and the prospect of self-government within the Indian Union led to a general reconciliation, but rebel activity continued. A 2-month amnesty in mid 1963 had little effect. A 'ceasefire' in Sept. 1964 was followed by talks between a Government of India delegation and rebel leaders. The peace period was extended and the 'Revolutionary Government of Nagaland' (a breakaway group from the Naga Federal Government) was dissolved in 1973. Further talks with the Naga underground movement resulted in the Shillong Peace Agreement of Nov. 1975.

AREA AND POPULATION. The state is in the extreme north-east and is bounded west and north by Assam, east by Burma and south by Manipur. Nagaland has an area of 16,579 sq. km and a population (1991 census) of 1,215,573. Density, 73 per sq. km. Growth rate, 1981–91, 56·86%. The major towns are the capital, Kohima (1991 population, 53,122) and Dimapur (56,918). Other towns include Mokokchung and Tuensang. The chief tribes in numerical order are: Angami, Ao, Sema, Konyak, Chakhesang, Lotha, Phom, Khiamngan, Chang, Yimchunger, Zeliang-Kuki, Rengma and Sangtam.

CONSTITUTION AND GOVERNMENT. An Interim Body (Legislative Assembly) of 42 members elected by the Naga people and an Executive Council (Council of Ministers) of 5 members were formed in 1961, and continued until the State Assembly was elected in Jan. 1964. The Assembly has 60 members, and includes: Congress I, 24; Nagaland People's Council, 17. The Governor has extraordinary powers, which include special responsibility for law and order.

The state has 7 districts (Kohima, Mon, Zunheboto, Wokha, Phek, Mokokchung and Tuensang). The capital is Kohima.

Governor: M. M. Thomas.
Chief Minister: S. Vamuzo.

BUDGET. Total budget for 1990–91 was Rs 4,692·8m. Annual Plan, 1991–92, Rs 1,700m.

ENERGY AND NATURAL RESOURCES

Electricity. Installed capacity (1984) 5·12 mw; all towns and villages are electrified.

Agriculture. 90% of the people derive their livelihood from agriculture. The Angamis, in Kohima district, practise a fixed agriculture in the shape of terraced slopes, and wet paddy cultivation in the lowlands. In the other two districts a traditional form of shifting cultivation (*jhumming*) still predominates, but some farmers have begun tea and coffee plantations and horticulture. About 27,133 ha were under terrace cultivation and 76,512 ha under *jhumming* in 1988–89. Production of rice (1989–90) was 0·15m. tonnes, total foodgrains 175,900 tonnes, pulses 5,900 tonnes. Forests covered 2,875 sq. km in 1988.

INDUSTRY. There is a forest products factory at Tijit; a paper-mill (100 tonnes daily capacity) at Tuli, a distillery unit and a sugar-mill (1,000 tonnes daily capacity) at Dimapur. Bricks and TV sets are also made, and there are over 1,000 small units. Oil has been located in 3 districts. Other minerals include: Coal, limestone, clay, glass sand and slate.

COMMUNICATIONS. There is a national highway from Kaziranga (Assam) to Kohima and on to Manipur. There are state highways connecting Kohima with the district headquarters. Total length of roads in 1989, 9,345 km.; 1,538 km were surfaced in 1988. Dimapur has a rail-head and a daily air service to Calcutta. Railway route-km in 1989-90, 9km. There were 8,101 motor vehicles in 1986–87.

RELIGION, EDUCATION AND WELFARE

Religion. At the 1981 census there were 621,590 Christians; 111,266 Hindus; 11,806 Moslems; 1,153 Jains; 743 Sikhs.

Education. The 1991 census records 621,048 literates, or 61·3%: 66·09% of men and 55·72% of women. In 1988-89 there were 1,286 primary schools with 153,800 students, 343 middle schools with 48,000 students, 120 high schools with 17,500 students, 20 colleges, 1 teacher training college and 1 polytechnic. The North Eastern Hill University opened at Kohima in 1978.

Health. In 1988 there were 33 hospitals (1,409 beds), 23 primary and 3 community health centres, 73 dispensaries, 218 sub-centres.

Aram, M., *Peace in Nagaland,* New Delhi, 1974

ORISSA

HISTORY. Orissa, ceded to the Mahrattas by Alivardi Khan in 1751, was conquered by the British in 1803. In 1803 a board of 2 commissioners was appointed to administer the province, but in 1805 it was designated the district of Cuttack and was placed in charge of a collector, judge and magistrate. In 1829 it was split up into 3 regulation districts of Cuttack, Balasore and Puri, and the non-regulation tributary states which were administered by their own chiefs under the aegis of the British Government. Angul, one of these tributary states, was annexed in 1847, and with the Khondmals, ceded in 1835 by the tributary chief of the Boudh state, constituted a separate non-regulation district. Sambalpur was transferred from the Central Provinces to Orissa in 1905. These districts formed an outlying tract of the Bengal Presidency till 1912, when they were transferred to Bihar, constituting one of its divisions under a commissioner. Orissa was constituted a separate province on 1 April 1936, some portions of the Central Provinces and Madras being transferred to the old Orissa division.

The rulers of 25 Orissa states surrendered all jurisdiction and authority to the Government of India on 1 Jan. 1948, on which date the Provincial Government took over the administration. The administration of 2 states, viz., Seraikella and Kharswan, was transferred to the Government of Bihar in May 1948. By an agreement with the Dominion Government, Mayurbhanj State was finally merged with the province on 1 Jan. 1949. By the States Merger (Governors' Provinces) Order, 1949, the states were completely merged with the state of Orissa on 19 Aug. 1949.

AREA AND POPULATION. Orissa is in eastern India and is bounded north by Bihar, north-east by West Bengal, east by the Bay of Bengal, south by Andhra Pradesh and west by Madhya Pradesh. The area of the state is 155,707 sq. km, and its population (1991 census), 31,512,070, density 202 per sq. km. Growth rate, 1981–91, 19·5%. Cities with over 250,000 population at 1991 census, *see* p.629. Other large cities (1991): Rourkela (urban agglomeration), 398,692; Brahmapur, 210,585; Sambalpur, 130,766; Puri, 124,835. The principal and official language is Oriya.

CONSTITUTION AND GOVERNMENT. The Legislative Assembly has 147 members. After the election in Feb 1990 a Janata Dal government came to power. Total seats, 147: Janata Dal, 123; Congress (I), 10; Communist Party of India, 5; Independents and others, 9.

The state consists of 16 districts.

The capital is Bhubaneswar (18 miles south of Cuttack).

Governor: Yagya Dutt Sharma.

Chief Minister: Biju Patnaik.

BUDGET. Budget estimates, 1991–92, showed total revenue of Rs 67,223·4m. and expenditure of Rs 67,639·6m. Annual plan outlay, 1991-92, Rs 14,000m.

ENERGY AND NATURAL RESOURCES

Electricity. The Hirakud Dam Project on the river Mahanadi irrigates 628,000 acres and has an installed capacity of 1,394 mw. There are other projects under construction: The upper Kolab; Indrabati; Rengali Dam; hydro-electric power is now serving a large part of the state. There were 30,299 electrified villages in Dec. 1990.

Minerals. Orissa is India's leading producer of chromite (95% of national output), dolomite (50%), manganese ore (25%), graphite (80%), iron ore (16%), fire-clay (34%), limestone (20%), and quartz-quartzite (18%). Production in 1986 (1,000 tonnes): Iron ore, 8,030; manganese ore, 464; chromite, 561; coal, 6,844; limestone, 2,954; dolomite, 980; bauxite, 239. Value of production in 1987 was Rs 3,290m.

Agriculture. The cultivation of rice is the principal occupation of nearly 75% of the population, and only a very small amount of other cereals is grown. Production of foodgrains (1989–90) totalled 7·87m. tonnes from 7m. ha (rice 6·3m. tonnes, wheat 65,100 tonnes); pulses 1·01m. tonnes; oilseeds, 830,100 tonnes; sugar-cane 3·33m. tonnes. Turmeric is cultivated in the uplands of the districts of Ganjam, Phulbani and Koraput, and is exported.

Livestock (1988): Buffaloes, 1·33m.; other cattle, 12·92m.; sheep, 1·98m.; goats, 4·93m.; 10·55m. poultry including ducks.

Forests. Forests occupy about 35·8% of the area of the state, the most important species being sal, teak, kendu, sandal, sisu, bija, kusum, kongada and bamboo.

Fisheries. There were, in 1985, 574 fishery co-operative societies. Fish production in 1988-89 was 129,865 tonnes. A fishing harbour has been developed at Dhamara.

INDUSTRY. 184 large and medium industries have been established (1988-89), mostly based on minerals, including the steel plant of Steel Authority of India Ltd at Rourkela, a pig-iron plant near Barbil, 3 ferrochrome plants, 2 ferromanganese plants at Joda and Rayagada, 1 ferrosilicon plant at Theruvelli and an aluminium smelter plant at Hirakud, 4 refractory plants and 2 cement plants. There are 3 large paper mills at Rayagada, Chowdwar and Brajrajnagar, three fertilizer plants, a caustic soda plant, a salt manufacturing unit and an industrial explosives plant. There are aluminium-alumina plants at Damanjodi and Angul.

Other industries of importance are sugar, glass, aluminium, heavy machine tools, a coach-repair factory, a re-rolling mill, textile mills and electronics. Also, there were 31,922 small-scale industries employing 245,000 persons. There were 771,686 cottage industries providing employment to 1·26m. persons; handloom weaving and the manufacture of baskets, wooden articles, hats and nets; silver filigree work and hand-woven fabrics are specially well known.

TOURISM. Tourist traffic is concentrated mainly on the 'Golden Triangle', Konark, Puri and Bhubaneswar, and its temples. Tourists also visit Gopalpur, the Similipal National Park, Nandankanan and Chilka Lake.

COMMUNICATIONS

Roads. On 31 March 1984–85 length of roads was: State highway, 2,846 km; national highway, 1,625 km; other Public Works Department roads, 61,330 km; council roads, 5,048 km. There were 164,726 motor vehicles in 1987. A 144-km expressway, part national highway, connects the Daitari mining area with Paradip Port.

Railways. The route-km of railway in 1989–90 was 2,002 km, of which 1,310 km was single line.

Civil Aviation. There is an airport at Bhubaneswar with regular scheduled services to New Delhi, Calcutta, Visakhapatnam and Hyderabad.

Shipping. Paradip was declared a 'major' port in 1966 and has been developed to handle 4m. tons of traffic. Other minor ports at Chandbali and Gopalpur.

JUSTICE, RELIGION, EDUCATION AND WELFARE

Justice. The High Court of Judicature at Cuttack has a Chief Justice and 10 puisne judges.

Religion. There were in 1981: Hindus (including scheduled castes and scheduled tribes), 25,161,725; Christians, 480,426; Moslems, 422,266; Sikhs, 14,270; Buddhists, 8,028; Jains, 6,642.

Education. The percentage of literates in the population in 1991 was 48·55% (males, 62·37%, females, 34·4%).

In 1988–89 there were 39,293 primary schools with 3,505,000 students, 9,396 middle schools with 870,000 students and 4,468 high and higher secondary schools with 501,083 students. There are 6 engineering and technology colleges, 3 medical colleges, 21 teacher training colleges, 4 polytechnics and 431 colleges.

Utkal University was established in 1943 at Cuttack and moved to Bhubaneswar in 1962; it is both teaching and affiliating. It has 2 university colleges (law) and 150 affiliated colleges. Berhampur University has 31 affiliated colleges and Orissa University of Agriculture and Technology 8 constituent colleges. Sambalpur University has 84 affiliated colleges. Sri Jagannath Sanskrit Viswavidyalaya at Puri was established in 1981 for oriental studies.

Health. There were (1988) 13 district hospitals and 7,479 institutions for health care.

PUNJAB (INDIA)

HISTORY. The Punjab was constituted an autonomous province of India in 1937. In 1947, the province was partitioned between India and Pakistan into East and West Punjab respectively, under the Indian Independence Act, 1947, the boundaries being determined under the Radcliffe Award. The name of East Punjab was changed to Punjab (India) under the Constitution of India. On 1 Nov. 1956 the erstwhile states of Punjab and Patiala and East Punjab States Union (PEPSU) were integrated to form the state of Punjab. On 1 Nov. 1966, under the Punjab Reorganization Act, 1966, the state was reconstituted as a Punjabi-speaking state comprising the districts of Gurdaspur (excluding Dalhousie), Amritsar, Kapurthala, Jullundur, Ferozepore, Bhatinda, Patiala and Ludhiana; parts of Sangrur, Hoshiarpur and Ambala districts; and part of Kharar tehsil. The remaining area comprising an area of 18,000 sq. miles and an estimated (1967) population of 8·5m. was shared between the new state of Haryana and the Union Territory of Himachal Pradesh. The existing capital of Chandigarh was made joint capital of Punjab and Haryana;

its transfer to Punjab alone (due in 1986) has been delayed while the two states seek agreement as to which Hindi-speaking districts shall be transfered to Haryana in exchange.

AREA AND POPULATION. The Punjab is in north India and is bounded at its northernmost point by Kashmir, north-east by Himachal Pradesh, south-east by Haryana, south by Rajasthan, west and north-west by Pakistan. The area of the state is 50,362 sq. km, with census (1991) population of 20,190,795. Density, 401 per sq. km. Growth rate, 1981-91, 20·26%. Cities with over 250,000 population at 1991 census, *see* p. 629. Other principal towns (1991): Bathinda (159,114), Pathankot (142,862), Moga (108,213), Abohar (107,016). The official language is Punjabi.

CONSTITUTION AND GOVERNMENT. Punjab (India) has a unicameral legislature, the Legislative Assembly, of 117 members. Presidential rule was imposed in May 1987 after outbreaks of communal violence. In March 1988 the Assembly was officially dissolved. Elections were held in Feb. 1992. Turn-out was 28%. Congress (I) gained 87 seats in the Legislative Assembly, and 11 of Punjab's 13 seats in the Indian federal parliament.

There are 12 districts. The capital is Chandigarh. There are 106 municipalities, 118 community development blocks and 9,331 elected village *panchayats*.

Governor: Gen. O. P. Malhotra.
Chief Minister: Beant Singh.

BUDGET. Budget estimates, 1991–92, showed revenue receipts of Rs 37,790·3m. and revenue expenditure of Rs 43,557·4m. Plan outlay, 1991-92, Rs 10,000m. Per capita income was Rs 7,081 in 1991.

ENERGY AND NATURAL RESOURCES

Electricity. Installed capacity, 1990–91, was 3,050 mw; all villages had electricity.

Agriculture. About 75% of the population depends on agriculture which is technically advanced. The irrigated area rose from 2·21m. ha in 1950–51 to 3·8m. ha in 1990–91. In 1989–90, wheat production was 11·7m. tonnes; rice, 6·7m.; maize, 399,000; oilseeds, 107,600; cotton, 2·45m. bales of 170 kg.

Livestock (1977 census): Buffaloes, 4,110,000; other cattle, 3·31m.; sheep and goats, 1,219,600; horses and ponies, 75,900; poultry, 5·5m.

Forestry. In 1988–89 there were 284,237 ha of forest land, of which 134,804 ha belonged to the Forest Department.

INDUSTRY. In March 1991 the number of registered industrial units in the Punjab (India) was 160,724, employing about 0·85m. people. On 31 March 1991 there were (provisional) 160,352 small industrial units, investment Rs 13,460m. The chief manufactures are textiles (especially hosiery), sewing machines, sports goods, sugar, bicycles, electronic goods, machine tools, hand tools, vehicle parts, surgical goods, vegetable oils, tractors, chemicals and pharmaceuticals. Recent (1989) large projects include food processing, electronics, railway coaches, paper and newsprint.

COMMUNICATIONS

Roads. The total length of metalled roads on 31 March 1991 was 38,307 km. State transport services cover 1·9m. effective km daily with a fleet of 2,326 buses carrying a daily average of over 1m. passengers. Coverage by private operators is estimated as 40%.

Railways. The Punjab possesses an extensive system of railway communications, served by the Northern Railway. Route-km (1989-90) 2,151 km.

Civil Aviation. There is an airport at Amritsar, and Chandigarh airport is on the north-eastern boundary; both have regular scheduled services to Delhi, Jammu, Srinagar and Leh. There are also Vayudoot services to Ludhiana.

JUSTICE, RELIGION, EDUCATION AND WELFARE

Justice. The Punjab and Haryana High Court exercises jurisdiction over the states of Punjab and Haryana and the territory of Chandigarh. It is located in Chandigarh. It consists (1988) of a Chief Justice and 21 puisne judges.

Religion. At the 1981 census Hindus numbered 6,200,195; Sikhs, 10,199,141; Moslems, 168,094; Christians, 184,934; Jains, 27,049.

Education. Compulsory education was introduced in April 1961; at the same time free education was introduced up to 8th class for boys and 9th class for girls as well as fee concessions. The aim is education for all children of 6-11. In 1991, 57·14% of the population were literate (63·68% of men and 49·72% of women).

In 1988-89 there were 12,357 primary schools with 2,092,295 students, 1,413 middle schools with 809,795 students, 2,353 high schools with 373,124 students and 387 senior secondary schools with 165,112 students.

Punjab University was established in 1947 at Chandigarh as an examining, teaching and affiliating body. In 1962 Punjabi University was established at Patiala and Punjab Agricultural University at Ludhiana. Guru Nanak Dev University has been established at Amritsar to mark the 500th anniversary celebrations for Guru Nanak Dev, first Guru of the Sikhs. Altogether there are 197 affiliated colleges, 171 for arts and science, 18 for teacher training, 5 medical, 4 engineering and 11 for other studies.

Health. Punjab claims the longest life expectancy (60·6 years for women, 60·7 for men) and lowest death rate (9 per 1,000). There were (1990-91) 278 hospitals, 2,170 allopathic, homeopathic, Ayurvedic and Unani hospitals and dispensaries, and 460 primary health centres. Total number of beds, 24,179.

Singh, Khushwant, *A History of the Sikhs*. 2 vols. Princeton and OUP, 1964–67

RAJASTHAN

HISTORY. As a result of the implementation of the States Reorganization Act, 1956, the erstwhile state of Ajmer, Abu Taluka of Bombay State and the Sunel Tappa enclave of the former state of Madhya Bharat were transferred to the state of Rajasthan on 1 Nov. 1956, whereas the Sironj subdivision of Rajasthan was transferred to the state of Madhya Pradesh.

EVENTS. An instance of *suttee* on 4 Sept. 1987 brought about state legislation (Rajasthan Sati (Prevention) Ordinance) promulgated on 1 Oct., and the central government's Sati Prevention Act (strengthening existing penalties) in Dec. 1987.

AREA AND POPULATION. Rajasthan is in north-west India and is bounded north by Punjab, north-east by Haryana and Uttar Pradesh, east by Madhya Pradesh, south by Gujarat and west by Pakistan. The area of the state is 342,239 sq. km and its population (census 1991), 43,880,640, density 128 per sq. km. Growth rate, 1981–91, 28·07%. The chief cities, *see* p. 629. Other major towns (1991); Bhilwara (183,791), Ganganagar (161,377), Bharatpur (148,506), Sikar (148,235), Pali (136,797), Beawar (105,357), Tonk (100,020).

CONSTITUTION AND GOVERNMENT. There is a unicameral legislature, the Legislative Assembly, having 200 members. After the election in Feb 1990 a coalition government of Bharatiya Janata Party and Janata Dal come to power. Bharatiya Janata party, 85; Janata Dal, 54; Congress (I), 50; Independents and others, 10; vacant, 1..

The capital is Jaipur. There are 27 districts.

Governor: Dr Swarup Singh.
Chief Minister: Bhairon Singh Shekhawat.

BUDGET. Estimates for 1991–92 show total revenue receipts of Rs 38,254.4m., and expenditure of Rs 40,200.4m. Annual plan 1991–92, Rs 11,660m.

ENERGY AND NATURAL RESOURCES

Electricity. Installed capacity in Feb. 1988, 1,978 mw.; 26,320 villages (1990) and 318,000 wells had electric power.

Water. In 1984 the Bhakra Canal irrigated 300,000 ha, the Chambal Canal, 200,000 and the Rajasthan Canal, 450,000. The Rajasthan (now the Indira Gandhi canal) is the main canal system, of which (1984) 189 km. of main canal and 2,950 km of distributors had been built. Cost, at 1 March 1984, Rs 4,190m. There were 28,739 villages with drinking water in March 1987, out of 34,968.

Minerals. The state is rich in minerals. In 1987, 1·7m. tonnes of gypsum and 300,000 tonnes of rock phosphate were produced. Other minerals include silver (21,550 kg., 1987 estimate), asbestos, felspar, copper, limestone and salt. Total sale value of mineral production in 1987 (estimate) was about Rs 3,500m. Lead-zinc reserves have been found near Rampura-Agucha, estimated at 61m. tonnes.

Agriculture. The state has suffered drought and encroaching desert for several years. The cultivable area is (1988–89) about 26·6m. ha, of which 4.3m. is irrigated. Production of principal crops (in tonnes), 1989–90: Pulses, 1·16m.; total foodgrains, 8·53m. (rice, 151,100; wheat, 3·4m.); cotton, 1m. bales of 170 kg.

Livestock (1983): Buffaloes, 6,034,743; other cattle, 13,466,474; sheep, 15,389,100; goats, 15,397,993; horses and ponies, 45,381; camels, 7,528,287.

INDUSTRY. In Dec. 1987 there were 9,665 registered factories and 122,304 small industrial units. There were 171 industrial estates. Total capital investment Rs 4,750·7m. Chief manufactures are textiles, cement, glass, sugar, sodium, oxygen and acetylene units, pesticides, insecticides, dyes, caustic soda, calcium, carbide, nylon tyre cords and refined copper.

COMMUNICATIONS

Roads. In 1988-89 there were 55,123 km of roads including 42,478 km of good and surfaced roads in Rajasthan; there were 2,521 km of national highway. Motor vehicles numbered 719,364 in Dec. 1987.

Railways. Jodhpur, Marwar, Udaipur, Ajmer, Jaipur, Kota, Bikaner and Sawai Madhopur are important junctions of the north-western network. Route km (1989-90) 5,769.

Aviation. There are airports at Jaipur, Jodhpur, Kota and Udaipur with regular scheduled services by Indian Airlines.

JUSTICE, RELIGION, EDUCATION AND WELFARE

Justice. The seat of the High Court is at Jodhpur. There is a Chief Justice and 11 puisne judges. There is also a bench of High Court judges at Jaipur.

Religion. At the 1981 census Hindus numbered 30,603,970; Moslems, 2,492,145; Jains, 624,317; Sikhs, 492,818; Christians, 39,568; Buddhists, 4,427.

Education. The proportion of literates to the total population was 38·81% at the 1991 census; men 55·07% and women 20·84%.

In 1988–89 there were 28,507 primary schools with 4,399,839 students, 8,355 middle schools with 1,252,350 students, 2,171 high schools with 492,653 students and 897 higher secondary schools with 133,143 students. Elementary education is free but not compulsory.

In 1988–89 there were 179 colleges. Rajasthan University, established at Jaipur in 1947, is teaching and affiliating (6 affiliated colleges); Jodhpur University and Udaipur University were founded in 1962. There are 6 other universities: Rajasthan Vidyapeeth, Udaipur; Rajasthan Agricultural University, Bikaner; Mohanlal Sukhadia University, Udaipur; Ajmer University, Ajmer; Banasthali Vidyapith, Banasthali; Kota Open University, Kota. There are also 5 medical and nursing colleges, 3 engineering colleges, 21,436 adult and other education centres, 32 sanskrit institutions, 33 teacher-training colleges and 14 polytechnics.

Health. In 1987 there were 899 hospitals and dispensaries, 498 primary health centres. In addition there were 3,228 Ayurvedic, Unani, homoepathic and naturopathy hospitals. There were 116 maternity centres.

SIKKIM

HISTORY. Sikkim became the twenty-second state of the Indian Union in May 1975. It is inhabited chiefly by the Lepchas, who are a tribe indigenous to Sikkim with their own dress and language, the Bhutias, who originally came from Tibet, and the Nepalis, who entered from Nepal in large numbers in the late 19th and early 20th century. The main languages spoken are Bhutia, Lepcha and Nepali. Being a small country Sikkim had frequently been involved in struggles over her territory, and as a result her boundaries have been very much reduced over the centuries. In particular the Darjeeling district was acquired from Sikkim by the British East India Company in 1839. The Namgyal dynasty had been ruling Sikkim since the 14th century; the first consecrated ruler was Phuntsog Namgya I who was consecrated in 1642 and given the title of 'Chogyal', meaning 'King ruling in accordance with religious laws', derived from Cho–religion and Gyalpo–king. The last Chogyal was deposed in 1975 and died in America in 1982.

Sikkim is a land of wide variation in altitude, climate and vegetation, and is known for the great number and variety of birds, butterflies, wild flowers and orchids to be found in the different regions. It is a fertile land and to the Sikkimese is known as Denjong, The Valley of Rice.

AREA AND POPULATION. Sikkim is in the Eastern Himalayas and is bounded north by Tibet, east by Tibet and Bhutan, south by West Bengal and west Nepal. Area, 7,096 sq. km. Census population (1991), 405,505, of whom 24,971 lived in the capital, Gangtok. Density, 57 per sq km. Growth rate, 1981–91, 27·57%.

CONSTITUTION AND GOVERNMENT. Sikkim was joined to the British Empire by a treaty in 1886 until 1947, but that relationship ceased when Britain withdrew from India in 1947. Thereafter there was a standstill agreement between India and Sikkim until a treaty was signed on 5 Dec. 1950 between India and Sikkim by which Sikkim became a protectorate of India and India undertook to be responsible for Sikkim's defence, external relations and strategic communications. The Chogyal had governed Sikkim with the help of the Sikkim Council, consisting of 18 elected members and 6 members nominated by the Chogyal. Sikkim parties represented were: National Party, Sikkim National Congress and, later, Sikkim Janta Congress.

Political reforms were demanded by the National Congress and the Janta Congress in March-April 1973 and Indian police took over control of law and order at the request of the Chogyal. On 13 April it was announced that the Chogyal had agreed to meet most of the political demands. Elections were held in April 1974 to a popularly-elected assembly. By the Government of Sikkim Act, June 1974, the Chogyal became a constitutional monarch with power of assent to the Assembly's legislation. By the Constitution (Thirty-Sixth Amendment) Act 1974 Sikkim became a state associated with the Indian Union. The office of Chogyal was abolished in April 1975. By the Constitution (Thirty-Eighth Amendment) Act 1975 Sikkim became the twenty-second state of the Indian Union. The Assembly has 32 members. After the election of Nov. 1989 the Sangram Parishad government continued in power.

Governor: Adm. R. H. Tahiliani.
Chief Minister: Nar Bahadur Bhandari.

The official language of the Government is English. Lepcha, Bhutia, Nepali and Limboo have also been declared official languages.

Sikkim is divided into 4 districts for administration purposes, Gangtok, Mangan, Namchi and Gyalshing being the headquarters for the Eastern, Northern, Southern and Western districts respectively. Each district is administered by a District Collector. Within this framework are the Panchayats or Village Councils.

ECONOMY

Budget. Budget estimates for 1991-92 show revenue receipt of Rs 2,168·5m. and total disbursements of Rs 2,299·3m. Annual plan outlay for 1991-92 is Rs 950m.

ENERGY AND NATURAL RESOURCES

Electricity. There are 4 hydro-electric power stations. All villages had electricity in 1991.

Agriculture. The economy is mainly agricultural; main food crops are rice, maize, millet, wheat and barley; cash crops are cardamom (a spice), mandarin oranges, apples, potatoes, and buckwheat. Foodgrain production, 1989-90, 116,300 tonnes (rice 20,400 tonnes, wheat 20,300 tonnes); pulses, 6,500 tonnes. Tea is grown. Forests occupy about 1,000 sq. km. and the potential for a timber and wood-pulp industry is being explored. Medicinal herbs are exported.

INDUSTRY AND TRADE

Industry. There is a state Industrial Development Investment Corporation and an Industrial Training Institute offering 7 trades. There are two cigarette factories (at Gangtok and Rangpo), two distilleries and a tannery at Rangpo and a fruit preserving factory at Singtam. Copper, zinc and lead are mined by the Sikkim Mining Corporation. A recent survey by the Geological Survey of India and the Indian Bureau of Mines has confirmed further deposits of copper, zinc, silver and gold in Dikchu, North Sikkim. There is a jewel-bearing factory for the production of industrial jewels. A watch factory has been set up in collaboration with Hindustan Machine Tools (India). A number of small manufacturing units for leather, wire nails, storage cells batteries, candles, safety matches and carpets, are already producing in the private sector. Local crafts include carpet weaving, making handmade paper, wood carving and silverwork. To encourage trading in indigenous products, particularly agricultural produce, the State Trading Corporation of Sikkim has been established.

Tourism. There is great potential for the tourist industry; a 78-bed lodge at Gangtok and a 50-bed tourist lodge in West Sikkim have been opened. Tourism has been stimulated by the opening of new roads from Pemayangtse to Yuksam in West Sikkim and from Yuksam to the Dzongri Glacier.

COMMUNICATIONS

Roads. There are 1,456 km. of roads, all on mountainous terrain, and 18 major bridges under the Public Works Department. Public transport and road haulage is nationalized. There were 2,174 motor vehicles in 1986–87.

Railways. The nearest railhead is at Siliguri (115 km from Gangtok).

Aviation. The nearest airport is at Bagdogra (128 km from Gangtok), linked to Gangtok by helicopter service.

Post and Broadcasting. There are 1,445 telephones (1987) and 37 wireless stations. A radio broadcasting station, Akashvani Gangtok, was built in 1982, and a permanent station in 1983. Gangtok also has a low-power TV transmitter.

RELIGION, EDUCATION AND WELFARE

Religion. At the 1981 census there were 212,780 Hindus; 3,241 Moslems; 7,015 Christians; 90,848 Buddhists; 322 Sikhs; 108 Jains.

Education. At the 1991 census there were 186,789 literates (56·53%; men 64·34% and women 47·23%). Sikkim had (1988-89) 528 pre-primary schools with 17,981 students, 489 primary schools with 62,917 students, 123 middle schools with 15,226 students, 54 high schools with 5,139 students and 14 higher secondary schools with 1,490 students. Education is free up to class XII; text books are free up to class V. There are 500 adult education centres. There is also a training institute for primary teachers and a degree college.

Health. There are (1983) 4 district hospitals at Singtam, Gyalshing, Namchi and Mangan, and one central referral hospital at Gangtok, besides 20 primary health centres, 109 sub-centres and 8 dispensaries, a maternity ward, chest clinic and 2 blocks for tuberculosis patients. There is a blood bank at Gangtok. There are 110 doctors. Medical and hospital treatment is free; there is a health centre for every 20,000 of the population. Small-pox and Kala-azar have been completely eliminated and many schemes for the provision of safe drinking water to villages and bazaars have been implemented. A leprosy hospital (20 beds) has been built near Gangtok.

TAMIL NADU

HISTORY. The first trading establishment made by the British in the Madras State was at Peddapali (now Nizampatnam) in 1611 and then at Masulipatnam. In 1639 the English were permitted to make a settlement at the place which is now Madras, and Fort St George was founded. By 1801 the whole of the country from the Northern Circars to Cape Comorin (with the exception of certain French and Danish settlements) had been brought under British rule.

Under the provisions of the States Reorganization Act, 1956, the Malabar district (excluding the islands of Laccadive and Minicoy) and the Kasaragod district taluk of South Kanara were transferred to the new state of Kerala; the South Kanara district (excluding Kasaragod taluk and the Amindivi Islands) and the Kollegal taluk of the Coimbatore district were transferred to the new state of Mysore; and the Laccadive, Amindivi and Minicoy Islands were constituted a separate Territory. Four taluks of the Trivandrum district and the Shencottah taluk of Quilon district were transferred from Travancore-Cochin to the new Madras State. On 1 April 1960, 405 sq. miles from the Chittoor district of Andhra Pradesh were transferred to Madras in exchange for 326 sq. miles from the Chingleput and Salem districts. In Aug. 1968 the state was renamed Tamil Nadu.

AREA AND POPULATION. Tamil Nadu is in south India and is bounded north by Karnataka and Andhra Pradesh, east and south by the Indian ocean and west by Kerala. Area, 130,058 sq. km. Population (1991 census), 55,638,318, density of 428 per sq. km. Growth rate, 1981–91, 14·94%. Tamil is the principal language and has been adopted as the state language with effect from 14 Jan. 1958. For the principal towns, *see* India: Area and Population. Other large towns (1991): Tuticorin (205,105), Thanjavur City (200,216), Nagercoil City (189,482), Dindigul City (182,293), Vellore (172,467), Cuddalore City (143,774), Kanchipuram (139,449), Neyveli (117,471), Rajapalaiyam City (114,142). There are 21 districts. The capital is Madras.

CONSTITUTION AND GOVERNMENT. The Governor is aided by a Council of 16 ministers. There is a unicameral legislature; the Legislative Assembly has 235 members: DMK, 144; AIADMK, 29; Congress I, 26; others, 36.

Presidential rule was imposed in Jan. 1991 and the Assembly was dissolved.

Governor: Bishma Narain Singh.
Chief Minister: J. Jayalalitha.

BUDGET. Budget estimates for 1991-92, revenue receipts, Rs 53,473·4m., revenue expenditure, Rs 62,498·3m. Annual plan 1991–92, Rs 16,000m.

ENERGY AND NATURAL RESOURCES

Electricity. Installed capacity 1987–88 amounted to 4,558 mw of which 1,799 mw was hydro-electricity and 2,408 mw thermal. 99·9% of villages were supplied with electricity. The Kalpakkam nuclear power plant became operational in 1983; capacity, 350 mw.

Water. A joint project with Andhra Pradesh was agreed in 1983, to supply Madras with water from the Krishna river, also providing irrigation, *en route,* for Andhra Pradesh. In 1986–87 2·84m. ha were irrigated.

Minerals. Value of mineral production, 1987, Rs 1,760m. The state has magnesite, salt, coal, chromite, bauxite, limestone, manganese, mica, quartz, gypsum and feldspar.

Agriculture. In 1981 there were 5·5m. cultivators and 5·9m. agricultural labourers. The land is a fertile plain watered by rivers flowing east from the Western Ghats, particularly the Cauvery and the Tambaraparani. Temperature ranges between 6°C. and 39°C., rainfall between 442 mm. and 1,307 mm. Of the total land area (13m. ha), 6,508,349 ha were cropped and 298,659 ha of waste were cultivable. The staple food crops grown are paddy, maize, jawar, bajra, pulses and millets. Important commercial crops are sugar-cane, oilseeds, cashew-nuts, cotton, tobacco, coffee, tea, rubber and pepper. Production, 1989–90, in 1,000 tonnes, (and area, 1,000 ha): Rice 6,232 (2,015); small millet 113 (210); sugar-cane 23,444 (232); pulses 388 (974); cotton 0·5m. bales of 170 kg (268); groundnuts, 1,246 (1,081).

Livestock (1982 census): Buffaloes, 3,212,242; other cattle, 10,365,500; sheep, 5,536,514; goats, 5,246,192; swine, 693,735; horses, ponies, mules, camels and donkeys, 90,632; poultry, 18,283,720.

Forestry. Forest area, 1986–87, 2,250,670 ha, of which 1,854,944 ha were reserved forest. Forests cover about 27% of land area. Main products are teak, soft wood, wattle, sandalwood, pulp wood, cashew and cinchona bark.

Fisheries. There were 105,466 active marine fishermen working the 1,000 km coastline in 1987–88.

INDUSTRY AND TRADE

Industry. The number of working factories was 12,599 in 1989, employing 813,290 workers. The consumption of power in the industrial sector was 43% of total state consumption in 1982–83. The biggest central sector project is Salem steel plant.

Cotton textiles is one of the major industries. There are nearly 180 cotton textile mills and many spinning mills supplying yarn to the decentralized handloom industry. Other important industries are cement, sugar, manufacture of textile machinery, power-driven pumps, bicycles, electrical machinery, tractors, motor-cars, rubber tyres and tubes, bricks and tiles and silk.

Public sector undertakings include the Neyveli lignite complex, petrochemicals, integral coach factory, high-pressure boiler plant, photographic film factory, surgical instruments factory, teleprinter factory, oil refinery, continuous casting plant and defence vehicles manufacture. Main exports: Cotton goods, tea, coffee, spices, engineering goods, motor-car ancillaries, leather and granite.

In 1988 there were 4,468 registered trade unions. Man-days lost by strikes, 2,618,993; by lockouts, 631,230.

Tourism. In 1989, 369,883 foreign tourists visited the state.

COMMUNICATIONS

Roads. On 31 March 1987 the state had approximately 170,652 km of national and state highways, major and other district roads. In 1988 there were 1,005,240 registered motor vehicles.

Railways. On 31 March 1990 there were 6,555·45 km of railway track (4,012 route km). Madras and Madurai are the main centres.

Aviation. There are airports at Madras, Tiruchirapalli and Madurai, with regular scheduled services to Bombay, Calcutta and Delhi. Madras is the main centre of airline routes in South India.

Shipping. Madras and Tuticorin are the chief ports. Important minor ports are Cuddalore and Nagapattinam. Madras handled 23·9m. tonnes of cargo in 1988-89, Tuticorin, 5·2m. The Inland Container Depot at Coimbatore has a capacity of 50,000 tonnes of export traffic; it is linked to Cochin (Kerala).

JUSTICE, RELIGION, EDUCATION AND WELFARE

Justice. There is a High Court at Madras with a Chief Justice and 16 judges. *Police:* Strength of police force, 1 Jan. 1990, 67,094.

Religion. At the 1981 census Hindus numbered 43,016,546 (88·86%), Christians, 2,798,048 (5·78%); Moslems, 2,519,947 (5·21%).

Education. At the 1991 census 30·38m. people were literate (63·72%; men 74·88% and women 52·29%).

Education is free up to pre-university level. In 1989-90 there were 40,091 schools for general education, 12·3m. students and 297,918 teachers. There were 212 general colleges (203,215 students and (1986–87) 15,155 teachers); 119 professional colleges (62,498 and 14,759); (1986–87) 19 special education colleges (2,366 and 316).

There are 14 universities. Madras University (founded in 1857) is affiliating and teaching. Annamalai University, Annamalainagar (founded 1928) is residential; Madurai Kamaraj University (founded 1966) is an affiliating and teaching university; 11 others include one agricultural and one rural university, Mother Theresa Women's University, and Tamil University, Tanjavur.

Health. There were (1988-89) 410 hospitals, 1,160 dispensaries, 1,094 primary health centres and 8,243 health sub-centres.

Statistical Information: The Department of Statistics (Fort St George, Madras) was established in 1948 and reorganized in 1953. *Director:* C. Sethu. Main publications:
Annual Statistical Abstract; Decennial Statistical Atlas; Season and Crop Report; Quinquennial Wages Census; Quarterly Abstract of Statistics.

TRIPURA

HISTORY. A Hindu state of great antiquity having been ruled by the Maharajahs for 1,300 years before its accession to the Indian Union on 15 Oct. 1949. With the reorganization of states on 1 Sept. 1956 Tripura became a Union Territory, and was so declared on 1 Nov. 1957. The Territory was made a State on 21 Jan. 1972.

EVENTS. Tripura National Volunteers (tribal guerillas) signed an agreement with Union and State governments in Aug. 1988, to end an 8-month campaign of insurgency.

AREA AND POPULATION. Tripura is bounded by Bangladesh, except in the north-east where it joins Assam and Mizoram. The major portion of the state is hilly and mainly jungle. It has an area of 10,486 sq. km and a population of 2,744,827 (1991 census); Density, 262 per sq. km. Growth rate, 1981-91, 33·69%.

The official languages are Bengali and Kokbarak. Manipuri is also spoken.

CONSTITUTION AND GOVERNMENT. There is a Legislative Assembly of 60 members. The territory has 3 districts, divided into 10 administrative subdivisions, namely, Sadar, Khowai, Kailasahar, Dharmanagar, Sonamura, Udaipur, Belonia, Kamalpur, Sabroom and Amarpur.

The capital is Agartala (population, 1991, 157,636).

Governor: Raghunath Reddy.
Chief Minister: Sudhir Ranjan Majumdar.

BUDGET. Budget estimates, 1991-92, show an expenditure of Rs 6,840m. Annual plan outlay for 1991-92 is Rs 2,250m.

ENERGY AND NATURAL RESOURCES

Electricity. Installed capacity (1988), 25 mw; there were (Dec. 1990) 2,734 electrified villages out of a total of 4,727.

Agriculture. About 24% of the land area is cultivable. The tribes practise shifting cultivation, but this is being replaced by modern methods. The main crops are rice, wheat, jute, mesta, potatoes, oilseeds and sugar-cane. Foodgrain production (1989-90), 471,800 tonnes. There are 54 registered tea gardens producing 3,339,000 kg per year, and employing 8,945.

Forestry. Forests cover about 55% of the land area. They have been much depleted by clearance for shifting cultivation and, recently, for refugee settlements of Bangladeshis. About 8% of the forest area still consists of dense natural forest; losses elsewhere are being replaced by plantation. Commercial rubber plantation has also been encouraged. In 1988, 7,597 ha were under new rubber plantations.

INDUSTRY. Tea is the main industry. There is also a jute mill producing about 15 tonnes per day and employing about 2,000. The main small industries: Aluminium utensils, rubber, saw-milling, soap, piping, fruit canning, handloom weaving and sericulture. Handloom weaving products (1983–84) were valued at Rs 9·75 crores.

COMMUNICATIONS

Roads. Total length of motorable roads (1989) 6,348 km, of which 2,731 km were surfaced. Vehicles registered, 31 March 1988, 13,963, of which 3,542 were lorries.

Railways. There is a railway between Dharmanagar and Kalkalighat (Assam). Route-km in 1989-90, 45 km.

Civil Aviation. There is 1 airport and 2 airstrips. The airport (Agartala) has regular scheduled services to Calcutta.

EDUCATION AND WELFARE

Education. In 1991, 60·39% of the population were literate (70·08% of men and 50·01% of women). In 1988-89 there were 1,989 primary schools (371,372 pupils); 419 middle schools (116,998); 381 high and higher secondary schools (66,142). There were 13 colleges of general education, 1 engineering college, 1 teacher training college and 1 polytechnic.

Health. There were (1988) 21 hospitals, with 1,810 beds, 317 dispensaries, 539 doctors and 618 nurses. There were 47 primary health centres and 66 family planning centres.

UTTAR PRADESH

HISTORY. In 1833 the then Bengal Presidency was divided into two parts, one of which became the Presidency of Agra. In 1836 the Agra area was styled the North-West Province and placed under a Lieut.-Governor. The two provinces of Agra and Oudh were placed, in 1877, under one administrator, styled Lieut.-Governor of the North-West Province and Chief Commissioner of Oudh. In 1902 the name was changed to 'United Provinces of Agra and Oudh', under a Lieut.-Governor, and the Lieut.-Governorship was altered to a Governorship in 1921. In 1935 the name was shortened to 'United Provinces'. On Independence, the states of Rampur, Banaras and Tehri-Garwhal were merged with United Provinces. In 1950 the name of the United Provinces was changed to Uttar Pradesh.

AREA AND POPULATION. Uttar Pradesh is in north India and is bounded north by Himachal Pradesh, Tibet and Nepal, east by Bihar, south by Madhya Pradesh and west by Rajasthan, Haryana and Delhi. The area of the state is 294,411 sq. km. Population (1991 census), 139,031,130, a density of 471 per sq. km. Growth rate, 1981–91, 25·16%. Cities with more than 250,000 population, *see* India: Area and Population. Other important towns (1991): Rampur (242,752), Muzaffarnagar (240,057), Shahjahanpur (237,663), Mathura (226,850), Firozabad (215,089), Farrukhabad-Cum-Fatehgarh (193,624), Mirzapur-Cum-Vindhyachal (169,368), Noida (167,440), Sambhal (150,012), Hardwar (148,882), Hapur (146,591), Amroha (136,893), Maunath Bhanjan (136,447), Jaunpur (136,287), Bahraich (135,352), Rae Bareli (130,101), Bulandshahr (126,737), Faizabad (125,012), Etawah (124,032), Sitapur (120,595), Fatehpur (117,203), Budaun (116,706), Hathras (113,653), Unnao (107,246), Pilibhit (106,329), Gonda (106,078), Haldwani-Cum-Kathgodam (102,744), Modinagar (102,307). The sole official language has been Hindi since April 1990.

CONSTITUTION AND GOVERNMENT. Uttar Pradesh has had an autonomous system of government since 1937. There is a bicameral legislature. The Legislative Council has 108 members; the Legislative Assembly has 426, of which 425 are elected. After the elections in 1991 a Bharatiya Janata Party government was returned.

There are 13 administrative divisions, each under a Commissioner, and 63 districts.

The capital is Lucknow.

Governor: B. Satya Narain Reddy.
Chief Minister: Kalyan Singh.

BUDGET. Budget estimates 1991–92 show revenue and capital receipts of Rs 131,876m.; revenue and capital account expenditure, Rs 143,845m. Annual plan outlay (1991-92) Rs 37,100m.

ENERGY AND NATURAL RESOURCES

Electricity. The State Electricity Board had, 1988–89, an installed capacity of 5,376·35 mw. There were 80,617 villages with electricity in Dec. 1990, out of a total 112,566.

Minerals. The state has magnesite, fire-clay, coal, copper, dolomite, limestone, soapstone, gypsum, bauxite, diaspore, ochre, phosphorite, pyrophyllite, silica sand and steatite among others.

Agriculture. Agriculture occupies 78% of the work force. 10·13m. ha are irrigated. The state is India's largest producer of foodgrains; production (1989–90), 33·7m. tonnes (rice 9·4m. tonnes, wheat 17·8m. tonnes); pulses, 2·42m. tonnes. The state is one of India's main producers of sugar; production of sugar-cane (1989-90), 97·1m. tonnes. There were (1987-88) 1,605 veterinary centres for cattle.

Forests cover (1987) about 5·13m. sq. km.

The state government in 1985 began a management programme for the ravines of the Chambal river catchment area. The programme includes stabilizing ravines, soil conservation, afforestation, pasture development and ravine reclamation. Estimated cost of a six-year programme, Rs 453·96m.

INDUSTRY. Sugar production is important; other industries include edible oils, textiles, distilleries, brewing, leather working, agricultural engineering, paper and chemicals. There is an aluminium smelter at Renukoot. An oil refinery at Mathura has capacity of 6m. tonnes per annum. Large public-sector enterprises have been set up in electrical engineering, pharmaceuticals, locomotive building, general engineering, electronics and aeronautics. Village and small-scale industries are important; there were 130,061 small units in 1987-88. A petrochemical complex and a fertilizer complex are being implemented at Auriya and Shahjahanpur respectively. About one-third of cloth output is from hand-looms. Total working population (1981) 30·8m., of whom 6·8m. were non-agricultural.

COMMUNICATIONS

Roads. There were, 31 March 1989, 97,559 km of motorable roads. In 1987–88 there were 1,240,939 motor vehicles of which 829,230 were motorcycles.

Railways. Lucknow is the main junction of the northern network; other important junctions are Agra, Kanpur, Allahabad, Mughal Sarai, Dehra Dun and Varanasi. Route-km in 1989-90, 8,888 km.

Civil Aviation. There are airports at Lucknow, Kanpur, Varanasi, Allahabad, Agra and Gorakhpur.

JUSTICE, RELIGION, EDUCATION AND WELFARE

Justice. The High Court of Judicature at Allahabad (with a bench at Lucknow) has a Chief Justice and 49 puisne judges including additional judges. There are 56 sessions divisions in the state.

Religion. At the 1981 census Hindus numbered 92,365,968; Moslems, 17,657,735; Sikhs, 458,647; Christians, 162,199; Jains, 141,549; Buddhists, 54,542.

Education. At the 1991 census 46·87m. people were literate (41·71%; 55·35% of men and 26·02% of women). In 1988–89 there were 74,705 primary schools with 12,618,000 students, 16,652 middle schools with 3,931,000 students, 2,366 high schools with 1,935,514 students and 3,380 intermediate/junior colleges with 2,436,531 students.

Uttar Pradesh has 19 universities: Allahabad University (founded 1887); Agra University (1927); the Banaras Hindu University, Varanasi (1916); Lucknow University (1921); Aligarh Muslim University (1920); Roorkee University (1948), formerly Thomason College of Civil Engineering (established in 1847); Gorakhpur University (1957); Sampurnanand Sanskrit Vishwavidyalaya, Varanasi (1958). Kanpur University and Meerut University were founded in 1966. Govind Ballabh Pant University of Agriculture and Technology, Pantnagar (1960); H. N. Bahuguna Garhwal University, Srinagar, (1973). C. S. Azad University of Agriculture and Technology, Kaupur, and Narendra Deva University of Agriculture and Technology, Faizabad, were founded in 1974–75 and Avadh, Kumaon, Rohilkhand and Bundelkhand Universities in 1975. Jaunpur University (Purvanchal Vishwavidyalaya) was founded in 1987.

There are also 3 institutions with university status: Gurukul Kangri Vishwavidyalaya, Hardwar, Kashi Vidyapith, Varanasi and Dayal Bagh Educational Institute. There are 8 medical colleges, 3 engineering colleges, 13 teacher-training colleges and 407 arts, science and commerce colleges.

Health. In 1987–88 there were 4,034 allopathic, 2,448 ayurvedic and unani and 980 homoepathic hospitals. There were also TB hospitals and clinics.

WEST BENGAL

HISTORY. For the history of Bengal under British rule, from 1633 to 1947, *see* THE STATESMAN'S YEAR-BOOK , 1952, p. 183.

Under the terms of the Indian Independence Act, 1947, the Province of Bengal ceased to exist. The Moslem majority districts of East Bengal, consisting of the Chittagong and Dacca Divisions and portions of the Presidency and Rajshahi Divisions, became what was then East Pakistan (now Bangladesh).

EVENTS. Gorkha seperatists have campaigned for a Gorkha state in the hill areas; there has been strike and terrorist action. In Aug. 1988 an agreement was signed establishing a Darjeeling Gorkha Hill Council with limited autonomy.

AREA AND POPULATION. West Bengal is in north-east India and is bounded north by Sikkim and Bhutan, east by Assam and Bangladesh, south by the Bay of Bengal and Orissa, west by Bihar and north-west by Nepal. The total area of West Bengal is 88,752 sq. km. At the 1991 census its population was 67,982,732, an increase of 24·55% since 1981, the density of population 766 per sq. km. Population of chief cities, *see* India: Area and Population. Other major towns (1991): Barddhaman (244,789), South Dum Dum (230,507), Siliguri (226,677), Baranagar

(223,770), Kharagpur (189,010), Bally (181,978), Burnpur (174,704), Uluberia (155,188), Raiganj (151,454), North Dum Dum (151,298), Dabgram (146,917), Hugli-Chinsura (142,388), English Bazar (139,018), Serampur (137,087), Barrack-pur (133,429), Naihati (132,032), Nabhdwip (125,247), Medinipur (125,098), Chandannagar (122,351), Krishnanagar (120,918), Balurghat (119,829), Baha-rampur (115,036), Bankura (114,927), Titagarh (113,831), Halisahar (113,670), Santipur (109,911), Kulti-Barakar (108,930), Basirhat (101,652), Habra (100,142), Haldia (100,109), Kanchrapara (100,059). The principal language is Bengali.

CONSTITUTION AND GOVERNMENT. The state of West Bengal came into existence as a result of the Indian Independence Act, 1947. The territory of Cooch-Behar State was merged with West Bengal on 1 Jan. 1950, and the former French possession of Chandernagore became part of the state on 2 Oct. 1954. Under the States Reorganization Act, 1956, certain portions of Bihar State (an area of 3,157 sq. miles with a population of 1,446,385) were transferred to West Bengal.

The Legislative Assembly has 295 seats. Distribution, Nov. 1991: Communist Party of India (Marxist), 188; Forward Bloc, 29; Revolutionary Socialist Party, 18; Communist Party of India, 6; Indian National Congress, 43; Independents and others, 10.

The capital is Calcutta.

For administrative purposes there are 3 divisions (Jalpaiguri, Burdwan and Presidency), under which there are 17 districts, including Calcutta. The Calcutta Metropolitan Development Authority has been set up to co-ordinate development in the metropolitan area (1,350 sq. km). For the purposes of local self-government there are 16 *zila parishads* (district boards) excluding Darjeeling, 331 *panchayat samities* (regional boards), and 3,246 *gram* (village) *panchayats*. There are 111 municipalities, 3 Corporations and 9 Notified Areas. The Calcutta Corporation has a mayor and deputy mayor, a commissioner, aldermen and standing committees.

Governor: Nurul Hasan.
Chief Minister: Jyoti Basu.

BUDGET. Budget estimates for 1991–92, revenue receipts Rs 49,328,594 and expenditure Rs 60,959,384m. Plan outlay for 1990-91 was Rs 14,860m.

ENERGY AND NATURAL RESOURCES

Electricity. Installed capacity, 1990–91, 3,045 mw; 27,584 villages had electricity at 31 March 1991.

Water. The largest irrigation and power scheme under construction is the Teesta Barrage (9,000 ha). Other major irrigation schemes are the Mayurakshi Reservoir, Kanshabati Reservoir, Mahananda Barrage and Aqueduct and Damodar Valley. At March 1988 there were 10,896 tubewells and 3,198 riverlift irrigation schemes.

Minerals. Value of production, 1988, Rs 6,278m. The state has coal (the Ranijunj field is one of the 3 biggest in India) including coking coal. Coal production (1989, provisional) 21m. tonnes.

Agriculture. About 11m. ha were under rice-paddy in 1989-90. Total foodgrain production, 1989–90, 11·86m. tonnes (rice 10·9m. tonnes, wheat 569,000 tonnes); pulses 181,000 tonnes; oilseeds, 418,300 tonnes; jute, 5m. bales of 180 kg; tea (1989 estimate), 146,943,000m. kg. The state produces 60·4% of the national output of jute and *mesta* (1989-90).

Livestock (1976 census): 11,968,000 cattle, 758,000 buffaloes; 1981 census, 758,000 sheep and goats, and 15,052,000 poultry.

Forests cover 13·49% of the state.

Fisheries. Landings, 1989–90, 601,000 tonnes, of which inland 523,000 tonnes. During 1986–87 Rs 78m. was invested in fishery schemes. The state is the largest inland fish producer in the country.

INDUSTRY. The total number of registered factories, 1989, was 8,746 (excluding defence factories); average daily employment in public sector industries, 1988, 2·1m. The coalmining industry, 1988, had 114 units with average daily employment of 98,000.

There is a large automobile factory at Uttarpara, and there are aluminium rolling-mills at Belur and Asansol. Durgapur has a large steel plant and other industries under the state sector—a thermal power plant, coke oven plant, fertilizer factory, alloy steel plant and ophthalmic glass plant. There are a locomotive factory and cable factory at Chittaranjan and Rupnarayanpur. A refinery and fertilizer factory are operating at Haldia. Other industries include chemicals, engineering goods, electronics, textiles, automobile tyres, paper, cigarettes, distillery, aluminium foil, tea, pharmaceuticals, carbon black, graphite, iron foundry, silk and explosives.

Small industries, including the silk industry, are important; 337,941 units were registered at 31 March 1990, (estimated employment, 2,280,857).

COMMUNICATIONS

Roads. In 1988 the length of national highway was 1,631 km. On 31 March 1989 the state had 776,301 motor vehicles.

Railways. The route-km of railways within the state (1989–90) is 3,809 km. The main centres are Howrah, Sealdah, Asansol and New Jalpaiguri. The Calcutta Metro is under construction.

Aviation. The main airport is Calcutta which has national and international flights. The second airport is at Bagdogra in the extreme north, which has regular scheduled services to Calcutta. Vayudoot domestic airline also operates in the state.

Shipping. Calcutta is the chief port: A barrage has been built at Farakka to control the flow of the Ganges and to provide a rail and road link between North and South Bengal. A second port is being developed at Haldia, between the present port and the sea, which is intended mainly for bulk cargoes. West Bengal possesses 779 km of navigable canals.

JUSTICE, RELIGION, EDUCATION AND WELFARE

Justice. The High Court of Judicature at Calcutta has a Chief Justice and 44 puisne judges. The Andaman and Nicobar Islands *(see below)* come under its jurisdiction.

Police. In 1989 the police force numbered 57,599, under a director-general and an inspector-general. Calcutta has a separate force under a commissioner directly responsible to the Government; its strength was 21,535 at 1 Oct. 1989.

Religion. At the 1981 census Hindus numbered 42,007,159; Moslems, 11,743,259; Christians, 319,670; Buddhists, 156,296; Sikhs, 49,054; Jains, 38,663.

Education. At the 1991 census 32·72m. people were literate (57·72%; 67·24% of men and 47·15% of women). In 1988–89 there were 50,827 primary schools with 9,274,121 students, 4,179 junior high schools with 2,742,767 students and 6,804 high and higher secondary schools with 1,598,616 students. Education is free up to higher secondary stage. There are 8 universities.

The University of Calcutta (founded 1857) is affiliating and teaching; in 1983–84 it had 150,000 students. Visva Bharati, Santiniketan, was established in 1951 and is residential and teaching; it had 3,943 students in 1985–86. The University of Jadavpur, Calcutta (1955), had 6,000 students in 1990–91. Burdwan University was established in 1960; in 1985–86 there were 84,095 students. Kalyani University was established in 1960 (2,306 students in 1985–86). The University of North Bengal (1962) had 22,504 students in 1984–85. Rabindra Bharati University had 4,273 students in 1985–86. Bidhan Chandra Krishi Viswavidyalaya (1974) had 540 students in 1985–86. There is also Vidyasagar University, Medinipur. There are 9 engineering and technology colleges, 10 medical colleges, 43 teacher training colleges, 46 polytechnics and 302 arts, science and commerce colleges.

Health. There were (1989) 410 hospitals, 1,177 clinics, 1,194 health centres and 551 dispensaries.

UNION TERRITORIES

ANDAMAN AND NICOBAR ISLANDS. The Andaman and Nicobar Islands are administered by the President of the Republic of India acting through a Lieut.-Governor. There is a 30-member Pradesh Council, 5 members of which are selected by the Administrator as advisory counsellors. The seat of administration is at Port Blair, which is connected with Calcutta (1,255 km away) and Madras (1,190 km) by steamer service which calls about every 10 days; there are air services from Calcutta and Madras. Roads in the islands, 733 km black-topped and 48 km others. There are 2 districts.

The population (1991 census) was 279,111; Area, 8,249 sq. km; density 34 per sq. km. Growth rate 1981-91, 47·29%. Port Blair (1991), 74,810.

The climate is tropical, with little variation in temperature. Heavy rain (125" annually) is mainly brought by the south-west monsoon. Humidity is high.

Budget figures for 1989–90 show total revenue receipts of Rs 2,367,000, and total expenditure on revenue account of Rs 14,233,000. Plan outlay, 1990-91, Rs 970m.

In 1988-89 there were 185 primary schools with 37,176 students, 42 middle schools with 17,451 students, 29 high schools with 7,877 students and 31 higher secondary schools with 3,450 students. There is a teachers' training college, a polytechnic and a college. Literacy (1991 census), 73·74% (79·68% of men and 66·22% of women).

Lieut.-Governor: Lieut.-Gen. R. S. Dayal.

The **Andaman Islands** lie in the Bay of Bengal, 193 km from Cape Negrais in Burma, 1,255 from Calcutta and 1,190 from Madras. Five large islands grouped together are called the Great Andamans, and to the south is the island of Little Andaman. There are some 204 islets, the two principal groups being the Ritchie Archipelago and the Labyrinth Islands. The Great Andaman group is about 467 km long and, at the widest, 51 km broad.

The original inhabitants live in the forests by hunting and fishing; they are of a small Negrito type and their civilization is about that of the Stone Age. Their exact numbers are not known, as they avoid all contact with civilization. The total population of the Andaman Islands (including about 430 aboriginals) was 158,287 in 1981. Main aboriginal tribes, Andamanese, Onges, Jarawas and Sentinelese. Under a central government scheme started in 1953, some 4,000 displaced families, mostly from East Pakistan, had been settled in the islands by May 1967.

Japanese forces occupied the Andaman Islands on 23 March 1942. Civil administration of the islands was resumed on 8 Oct. 1945.

From 1857 to March 1942 the islands were used by the Government of India as a penal settlement for life and long-term convicts, but the penal settlement was abolished on re-occupation in Oct. 1945.

The Great Andaman group, densely wooded, contains many valuable trees, both hardwood and softwood. The best known of the hardwoods is the *padauk* or Andaman redwood; *gurjan* is in great demand for the manufacture of plywood. Large quantities of softwood are supplied to match factories. Annually the Forest Department export about 25,000 tons of timber to the mainland. Coconut, coffee and rubber are cultivated. The islands are slowly being made self-sufficient in paddy and rice, and now grow approximately half their annual requirements. Livestock (1982): 27,400 cattle, 9,720 buffaloes, 17,600 goats and 21,220 pigs. Fishing is important. There is a sawmill at Port Blair and a coconut-oil mill. Little Andaman has a palm-oil mill.

The islands possess a number of harbours and safe anchorages, notably Port Blair in the south, Port Cornwallis in the north and Elphinstone and Mayabandar in the middle.

The **Nicobar Islands** are situated to the south of the Andamans, 121 km from Little Andaman. The British were in possession 1869–1947. There are 19 islands, 7 uninhabited; total area, 1,841 sq. km. The islands are usually divided into 3 sub-groups (southern, central and northern), the chief islands in each being respectively, Great Nicobar, Camotra with Nancowrie and Car Nicobar. There is a fine land-locked harbour between the islands of Camotra and Nancowrie, known as Nancowrie Harbour.

The population numbered, in 1981, 30,454, including about 22,200 of Nicobarese and Shompen tribes. The coconut and arecanut are the main items of trade, and coconuts are a major item in the people's diet.

The Nicobar Islands were occupied by the Japanese in July 1942; and Car Nicobar was developed as a big supply base. The Allies reoccupied the islands on 8 Oct. 1945.

CHANDIGARH. On 1 Nov. 1966 the city of Chandigarh and the area surrounding it was constituted a Union Territory. Population (1991), 640,725; density, 5,620 per sq. km.; growth rate, 1981–91, 41·88%. Area, 114 sq. km. It serves as the joint capital of both Punjab (India) and the state of Haryana, and is the seat of a High Court and of a university serving both states. The city will ultimately be the capital of just the Punjab; joint status is to last while a new capital is built for Haryana.

There is some cultivated land and some forest (27·5% of the territory).

In 1991, 78·73% of the population were literate (82·67% of men and 73·61% of women).

Administrator: Surendra Nath.

DADRA AND NAGAR HAVELI. Formerly Portuguese, the territories of Dadra and Nagar Haveli were occupied in July 1954 by nationalists, and a pro-India administration was formed; this body made a request for incorporation into the Union, 1 June 1961. By the 10th amendment to the constitution the territories became a centrally administered Union Territory with effect from 11 Aug. 1961, forming an enclave at the southernmost point of the border between Gujarat and Maharashtra. Area 491 sq. km.; population (1991), 138,542 (males 70,927, females 67,615); density 288 per sq. km; growth rate, 1981–91, 33·63%. There is an Administrator appointed by the Government of India. The day-to-day business is done by various departments, co-ordinated by the Administrator's secretary and headed by a Collector. Headquarters are at Silvassa. The territory and 78·82% of the population is tribal and organized in 72 villages. Languages used are Bhilli, Gujarati, Bhilodi (91·1%), Marathi and Hindi.

Administrator: Bhanu Prakash Singh.
Chief Secretary: R. P. Rai.

Electricity. Electricity is supplied by Gujarat, and all villages have been electrified.

Water. As the result of a joint project with the governments of Gujarat, Goa, Daman and Diu there is a reservoir at Damanganga with irrigation potential of 8,280 ha.

Agriculture. Farming is the chief occupation, and about 25,000 hectares were under crops in 1988–89. Much of the land is terraced and there is a 100% subsidy for soil conservation. The major food crops are rice and ragi; wheat, small millets and pulses are also grown. There is little irrigation (1,280 hectares). There are 9 veterinary centres, a veterinary hospital, an agricultural research centre and breeding centres to improve strains of cattle and poultry. During 1988–89 the Administration distributed 250 tonnes of high yielding paddy seed, and high yielding wheat seed, and 611 tonnes of fertilizer.

Forests. About 20,311 hectares or 41·2% of the total area is forest, mainly of teak, sadad and khair. Timber production provides the largest simple contribution to the territory's revenue. There was (1985) a moratorium on commercial felling, to preserve the environmental function of the forests and ensure local supplies of firewood, timber and fodder.

Industry. There is no heavy industry, and the Territory is a "No Industry District". Industrial estates for small and medium units have been set up at Piparia, Masat and Khadoli. There were (1989) 322 small units, and 89 medium scale, employing about 7,000. Concessions (25% subsidy, 15 years' sales tax holiday) are available for small industries.

Communications. There are (1989) 326 km of motorable road. The railway line from Bombay to Ahmedabad runs through Vapi near Silvassa. The nearest airport is Bombay. There were 424 motor vehicles in 1986–87.

Tourism. The territory is a rural area between the industrial centres of Bombay and Surat-.Vapi. The Tourism Department is developing areas of natural beauty to promote acceptable tourism.

Justice. The territory is under the jurisdiction of the Bombay (Maharashtra) High Court. There is a District and Sessions Court and one Junior Division Civil Court at Silvassa.

Education. Literacy was 39·45% of the population at the 1991 census (52·07% of men and 26·1% of women). In 1988–89 there were 150 adult education centres (4,500 students); there were 122 primary schools, 39 middle schools (4,058 students); 3 higher secondary schools and 5 high schools. Total primary enrolment was 15,002; high-school and higher secondary, 1,905.

Health. The territory had (1989) 1 cottage hospital, 5 primary health centres and 4 dispensaries; there is also a mobile dispensary.

DAMAN AND DIU. Daman (Damão) on the Gujarat coast, 100 miles (160 km) north of Bombay, was seized by the Portuguese in 1531 and ceded to them (1539) by the Shar of Gujarat. The island of Diu, captured in 1534, lies off the south-east coast of Kathiawar (Gujarat); there is a small coastal area. Former Portuguese forts on either side of the entrance to the Gulf of Cambay, in Dec. 1961 the territories were occupied by India and incorporated into the Indian Union; they were administered as one unit together with Goa, to which they were attached until 30 May 1987, when Goa was seperated from them and became a state.

Area and Population. Daman, 72 sq. km, population (1991) 61,951; Diu, 40 sq. km, population 39,488. Density, 906 per sq. km. Growth rate 1981-91, 28·43%. The main language spoken is Gujarati.

The chief towns are Daman (population, 1991, 26,895) and Diu (20,643).

Daman and Diu have been governed as parts of a Union Territory since Dec. 1961, becoming the whole of that Territory on 30 May 1987.

The main activities are tourism, fishing and tapping the toddy palm. In Daman there is rice-growing, some wheat and dairying. Diu has fine tourist beaches, grows coconuts and pearl millet, and processes salt.

Administrator: Bhanu Prakash Singh.

Education. In 1991, 73·58% of the population were literate (85·67% of men and 61·38% of women). In 1988-89 there were 39 primary schools with 10,345 students, 39 middle schools with 7,695 students, 17 high schools with 4,650 students and 2 higher secondary schools with 819 students. There is a degree college.

DELHI. Delhi became a Union Territory on 1 Nov. 1956.

Area and Population. The territory forms an enclave inside the eastern frontier of Haryana in north India. Delhi has an area of 1,483 sq. km. At the 1991 census its population was 9,370,475 (density per sq. km, 6,319). Growth rate, 1981–91, 50·64%. In the rural area of Delhi there are 214 inhabited and 17 deserted villages and 27 census towns. They are distributed in 5 community development blocks.

Government. The Lieut-Governor is the Administrator. Delhi Metropolitan Council stands dissolved with effect from 13 Jan. 1990 and the Chief Executive Councillor and other Executive Councillors ceased to hold their offices. The Territory is covered by 3 local bodies: Delhi Municipal Corporation, New Delhi Municipal Committee and Delhi Cantonment Board.

Lieut.-Governor: Markandey Singh.

Budget. Revised estimates 1989–90 show total revenue of Rs 11,729m. and expenditure including plan expenditure: Rs 15,123m. of which plan, Rs 6,373m.;

power, Rs 1,676m.; transport, Rs 852m.; water and sewerage, Rs 930m.; urban development, Rs 814m.; medical services and public health, Rs 584m. Plan outlay (1991-92) Rs 13,509m.

Agriculture. The contribution to the economy is not significant. In 1988-89 about 77,087 ha were cropped (of which 57,509 are irrigated). Animal husbandry is increasing and mixed farms are common. Chief crops are wheat, jowar, bajra, grain, sugar-cane and vegetables.

Industry. The modern city is the largest commercial centre in northern India and an important industrial centre. Since 1947 a large number of industrial concerns have been established; these include factories for the manufacture of razor blades, sports goods, radios and television and parts, bicycles and parts, plastic and PVC goods including footwear, textiles, chemicals, fertilizers, medicines, hosiery, leather goods, soft drinks, hand tools. There are also metal forging, casting, galvanising, electroplating and printing enterprises. The number of industrial units functioning was about 85,000 in 1990–91; average number of workers employed was 0·75m. Production was worth Rs 50,000m. and investment was about Rs 15,000m.

Some traditional handicrafts, for which Delhi was formerly famous, still flourish; among them are ivory carving, miniature painting, gold and silver jewellery and papier mâché work. The handwoven textiles of Delhi are particularly fine; this craft is being successfully revived.

Delhi publishes major daily newspapers, including the *Times of India, Hindustan Times, The Hindu, Indian Express, National Herald, Patriot, Economic Times, Business & Political Observer, Financial Express* and *Statesman* (all in English); *Nav Bharat Times, Jansatta* and *Hindustan* (in Hindi), and 3 Urdu dailies.

Roads. Five national highways pass through the city. There were (1989) 1,589,795 registered motor vehicles in Delhi. The Transport Corporation had 4,399 buses in daily service in 1989-90.

Railways. Delhi is an important rail junction with three main stations: Delhi, New Delhi, Hazarat Nizamuddin. There is an electric ring railway for commuters.

Aviation. Indira Gandhi International Airport operates international flights; Palam airport operates internal flights.

Religion. At the 1981 census Hindus numbered 5,200,432; Sikhs, 393,921; Moslems, 481,802; Jains, 73,917; Christians, 61,609; Buddhists, 7,117; others, 1,608.

Education. The proportion of literates to the total population was 76·09% at the 1991 census (82·63% of males and 68·01% of females). In 1988-89 there were 1,849 primary schools with 888,417 students, 384 middle schools with 479,095 students, 282 high schools with 226,394 students and 735 higher secondary schools with 129,786 students. There are 2 engineering and technology colleges, 4 medical colleges and 5 polytechnics.

The University of Delhi was founded in 1922; it had 69 constituent colleges and institutions in 1988–89, and a total of 121,445 students in 1987-88. There are also Jawaharlal Nehru University, Indira Gandhi National Open University and the Jamia Millia Islamia University; the Indian Institute of Technology at Haus Khas; the Indian Agricultural Research Institute at Pusa; the All India Institute of Medical Science at Ansari Nagar and the Indian Institute of Public Administration are the other important institutions.

Health. In 1989 there were 79 hospitals including 43 general, 27 special, 5 Ayurvedic, 2 Unani, 2 Homeopathic. There were 609 dispensaries.

LAKSHADWEEP. The territory consists of an archipelago of 36 islands (10 inhabited), about 300 km off the west coast of Kerala. It was constituted a Union Territory in 1956 as the Laccadive, Minicoy and Amindivi Islands, and renamed in Nov. 1973. The total area of the islands is 32 sq. km. The northern portion is called the Amindivis. The remaining islands are called the Laccadives (except Minicoy Island). The inhabited islands are: Androth (the largest), Amini, Agatti, Bitra, Chetlat, Kadmat, Kalpeni, Kavaratti, Kiltan and Minicoy. Androth is 4·8 sq. km, and is nearest to Kerala. An Advisory Committee associated with the Union Home Minister and an Advisory Council to the Administrator assist in the administration of the islands; these are constituted annually. Population (1991 census), 51,681, nearly all Moslems. Density, 1,615 per sq. km.; growth rate, 1981–91, 28·4%. The language is Malayalam, but the language in Minicoy is Mahl. Plan outlay, 1990-91, Rs 211·3m. In 1991, 79·23% of the population were literate (87·06% of men and 70·88% of women). There were, in 1988-89, 9 high schools (1,181 students) and 9 nursery schools (932 students), 19 junior basic schools (8,418 students), 4 senior basic schools (3,087 students) and 2 junior colleges. There are 2 hospitals and 7 primary health centres. The staple products are copra and fish. There is a tourist resort at Bangarem, an uninhabited island with an extensive lagoon. Headquarters of administration, Kavaratti Island. An airport, with Vayudoot services, opened on Agatti island in April 1988. The islands are also served by ship from the mainland and have helicopter inter-island services.

Administrator: Pradeep Singh.

PONDICHERRY. Formerly the chief French settlement in India, Pondicherry was founded by the French in 1674, taken by the Dutch in 1693 and restored to the French in 1699. The English took it in 1761, restored it in 1765, re-took it in 1778, restored it a second time in 1785, retook it a third time in 1793 and finally restored it to the French in 1814. Administration was transferred to India on 1 Nov. 1954. A Treaty of Cession (together with Karaikal, Mahé and Yanam) was signed on 28 May 1956; instruments of ratification were signed on 16 Aug. 1962 from which date (by the 14th amendment to the Indian Constitution) Pondicherry, comprising the 4 territories, became a Union Territory.

Area and Population. The territory is composed of enclaves on the Coromandel Coast of Tamil Nadu and Andhra Pradesh, with Mahé forming an enclave on the coast of Kerala. The total area of Pondicherry is 492 sq. km, divided into 4 Districts. On Tamil Nadu coast: Pondicherry (293 sq. km; population, 1991 census, 607,600), Karaikal (160; 145,723). On Kerala coast: Mahé (9; 33,425). On Andhra Pradesh coast: Yanam (30; 20,297). Total population (1991 census), 807,045; density, 1,605 per sq. km.; growth rate, 1981–91, 28·15%. Pondicherry Municipality had (1991) 202,648 inhabitants. The principal languages spoken are Tamil, Telugu, Malayalam, French and English.

Government. By the Government of Union Territories Act 1963 Pondicherry is governed by a Lieut.-Governor, appointed by the President, and a Council of Ministers responsible to a Legislative Assembly. A Congress (I) government was formed after the election in June 1991. Total seats, 30: Congress (I), 15; DMK, 4; Janata Dal, 1; All India Anna DMK, 6; CPI, 1; Independents, 3.

Lieut.-Governor: Dr Har Swarup Singh.

Planning. Approved outlay for 1990–91 was Rs 700m. Of this, Rs 27·2m. was for agriculture, Rs 17m. for rural development, Rs 10·5m. for co-operatives, Rs 145m. for education, Rs 11·8m. for public works, Rs 115m. for power, Rs 13·4m. for fisheries.

Budget. Budget estimates for 1991–92 show revenue receipts of Rs 2,272.2m. and expenditure of Rs 2,272·2m. Plan outlay, 1991-92, Rs 850m.

Electricity. Power is bought from neighbouring states. All 292 villages have electricity. Consumption, 1989–90, 585 units per head. Peak demand, 91 mw.; total consumption, 443m. units.

Agriculture. Over 65% of the population is engaged in agriculture and allied pursuits; 90% of the cultivated area is irrigated. The main food crop is rice. Foodgrain production, 103,000 tonnes from 33,293 ha in 1990–91, of which 93,295 tonnes was rice; cash crops include oilseeds (12,895 tonnes), cotton (8,367 bales of 180 kg) and sugar-cane (247,548 tonnes).

Industry. There are (Aug. 1991) 18 large and 53 medium-scale industries manufacturing items such as textiles, sugar, cotton yarn, spirits and beer, potassium chlorate, rice bran oil, vehicle parts, soap, amino acids, disposable syringes, red mud sheets, nylon mono filaments, hard gelatine capsules, washing machines, glass and tin containers and bio polymers. There were also 3,903 small industrial units engaged in varied manufacturing.

Roads. There were (1990, provisional) 2,328 km of roads of which 1,398 km were surfaced. Motor vehicles (1990, provisional) 68,700.

Railways. Pondicherry is connected to Villupuram Junction.

Aviation. The nearest main airport is Madras. Vayudoot domestic airline connects Pondicherry with Madras.

Education. In 1991, 74·91% of the population were literate (83·91% of men and 65·79% of women). There were, in Sept. 1990, 111 pre-primary schools (10,453 pupils), 341 primary schools (50,930), 107 middle schools (50,235), 77 high schools (53,358) and 28 higher secondary schools (33,343). There were (1991) 19 general education colleges, including a medical college, a law college, an engineering college, an agricultural college and a dental college, 3 polytechnics and a university.

Health. In 1991 there were 8 hospitals, 51 health centres and dispensaries and 73 sub-centres. In 1989 family schemes had reduced the birth rate to 21 per 1,000 and the infant mortality rate to 34·5 per 1,000 live births.

INDONESIA

Capital: Jakarta
Population: 179·1m. (1989)
GNP per capita: US$490 (1989)

Republik Indonesia

HISTORY. In the 16th century Portuguese traders in quest of spices settled in some of the islands, but were ejected by the British, who in turn were ousted by the Dutch (1595). From 1602 the Netherlands East India Company conquered the Netherlands East Indies, and ruled them until the dissolution of the company in 1798. Thereafter the Netherlands Government ruled the colony from 1816 to 1941, when it was occupied by the Japanese until 1945. An independent republic was proclaimed by Dr Sukarno and Dr Hatta on 17 Aug. 1945.

Complete and unconditional sovereignty was transferred to the Republic of the United States of Indonesia on 27 Dec. 1949, except for the western part of New Guinea, the status of which was to be determined through negotiations between Indonesia and the Netherlands within one year after the transfer of sovereignty. A union was created to regulate the relationship between the two countries. A settlement of the New Guinea (Irian Jaya) question was, however, delayed until 15 Aug. 1962, when, through the good offices of the United Nations, an agreement was concluded for the transfer of the territory to Indonesia on 1 May 1963. In Feb. 1956 Indonesia abrogated the union and in Aug. 1956 repudiated Indonesia's debt to the Netherlands.

During 1950 the federal system which had sprung up in 1946–48 (*see* THE STATESMAN'S YEAR-BOOK, 1950, p. 1233) was abolished, and Indonesia was again made a unitary state. The provisional constitution was passed by the Provisional House of Representatives on 14 and came into force on 17 Aug. 1950. On 5 July 1959 by Presidential decree, the Constitution of 1945 was reinstated and the Constituent Assembly dissolved. For history 1960–66 *see* THE STATESMAN'S YEAR-BOOK, 1982–83, p. 678.

On 11–12 March 1966 the military commanders under the leadership of Lieut.-Gen. Suharto took over the executive power while leaving President Sukarno as the head of State. The Communist Party was at once outlawed and the National Front was dissolved in Oct. 1966. On 22 Feb. 1967 Sukarno handed over all his powers to Gen. Suharto.

AREA AND POPULATION. Indonesia, covering a total land area of 741,098 sq. miles (1,919,443 sq. km), consists of 13,677 islands (6,000 of which are inhabited) extending about 3,200 miles east to west through three time-zones (East, Central and West Indonesian Standard time) and 1,250 miles north to south. The largest islands are Sumatra, Java, Kalimantan (Indonesian Borneo), Sulawesi (Celebes) and Irian Jaya (the western part of New Guinea). Most of the smaller islands except Madura and Bali are grouped together. The two largest groups of islands are Maluku (the Moluccas) and Nusa Tenggara (the Lesser Sundas).

Population at the 1980 census was 147,490,298. For breakdown by province, *see* THE STATESMAN'S YEAR-BOOK, 1990-91, p. 700.

The estimated population in 1989 was 179,136,110, distributed as follows:

Province	Sq. km	Estimate 1989	Chief town	Census 1980
Aceh (D.I.)	55,392	3,323,664	Banda Aceh	72,090
Sumatera Utara	70,787	10,330,091	Medan	1,378,955
Sumatera Barat	49,778	3,904,725	Padang	480,922
Riau	94,562	2,882,826	Pakanbaru	186,262
Jambi	44,924	2,022,560	Telanaipura	230,373
Sumatera Selatan	103,688	6,072,526	Palembang	787,187
Bengkulu	21,168	1,114,219	Bengkulu	64,783
Lampung	33,307	7,231,379	Tanjungkarang	284,275
Sumatera	473,606	36,881,990		

Province	Sq. km	Estimate 1989	Chief town	Census 1980
Jakarta Raya (D.C.I.)	590	9,104,786	Jakarta	6,503,449
Jawa Barat	46,300	33,769,422	Bandung	1,462,637
Jawa Tengah	34,206	28,644,330	Semarang	1,026,671
Yogyakarta (D.I.)	3,169	3,126,969	Yogyakarta	398,727
Jawa Timur	47,922	32,868,291	Surabaya	2,027,913
Jawa and Madura	132,187	107,513,798		
Kalimantan Barat	146,760	3,148,169	Pontianak	304,778
Kalimantan Tengah	152,600	1,273,948	Palangkaraya	60,447
Kalimantan Selatan	37,660	2,463,782	Banjarmasin	381,286
Kalimantan Timur	202,440	1,791,560	Samarinda	264,718
Kalimantan	539,460	8,677,459		
Sulawesi Utara	19,023	2,472,942	Menado	217,159
Sulawesi Tengah	69,726	1,734,229	Palu	298,584
Sulawesi Selatan	72,781	7,001,751	Ujung Padang	709,038
Sulawesi Tenggara	27,686	1,298,728	Kendari	41,021
Sulawesi	189,216	12,507,650		
Bali	5,561	2,782,038	Denpasar	261,263
Nusa Tenggara Barat	20,177	3,305,006	Mataram	68,964
Nusa Tenggara Timur	47,876	3,383,490	Kupang	403,110
Timor Timur [1]	14,874	714,847	Dili	60,150
Maluku	74,505	1,814,150	Amboina	208,898
Irian Jaya	421,981	1,555,682	Jayapura	149,618
Pulau–Pulau Lain	584,974	13,555,213		

[1] Formerly Portuguese East Timor.

Other major cities (census 1980): Malang, 511,780; Surakarta, 469,888; Bogor, 247,409; Cirebon, 223,776; Kediri, 221,830; Madiun, 150,562; Pematangsiantar, 150,376; Pekalongan, 132,558; Tegal, 131,728; Magelang, 123,484; Jember, 122,712; Sukabumi, 109,994 and Probolinggo, 100,296 (all on Java); Balikpapan (on Kalimantan), 280,875.

Vital statistics, 1988: Birth rate, 28·7 per 1,000; death rate, 7·9.

The principal ethnic groups are the Acehnese, Bataks and Minangkabaus in Sumatra, the Javanese and Sundanese in Java, the Madurese in Madura, the Balinese in Bali, the Sasaks in Lombok, the Menadonese, Minahasans, Torajas and Buginese in Sulawesi, the Dayaks in Kalimantan, Irianese in Irian Jaya, the Ambonese in the Moluccas and Timorese in Timor Timur. There were some 6m. Chinese resident in 1991.

Bahasa Indonesia, a Malay dialect, is the official language of the Republic although Dutch is spoken as an unofficial language.

CLIMATE. Conditions vary greatly over this spread of islands, but generally the climate is tropical monsoon, with a dry season from June to Sept. and a wet one from Oct. to April. Temperatures are high all the year and rainfall varies according to situation on lee or windward shores. Jakarta. Jan. 78°F (25·6°C), July 78°F (25·6°C). Annual rainfall 71" (1,775 mm). Padang. Jan. 79°F (26·7°C), July 79°F (26·7°C). Annual rainfall 177" (4,427 mm). Surabaya. Jan. 79°F (27·2°C), July 78°F (25·6°C). Annual rainfall 51" (1,285 mm).

CONSTITUTION AND GOVERNMENT. The political system is based on *pancasila*, in which deliberations lead to a consensus. 400 members of the *House of People's Representatives* are elected every 5 years, and the remaining 100 are appointed from the armed forces. Together with 500 government appointees they make up the *People's Consultative Assembly* which meets every 5 years to choose a president. The military perform a dual function enshrined in law, combining conventional defence duties with participation in all areas of political and social life. Golkar is a 'functional group'. There are 2 officially-sanctioned parties also in the House of People's Representatives: the United Development Party (largely Moslem), and the Indonesian Democratic Party (nationalist Christian).

General elections to the 400 elected seats in the House of Representatives were held on 23 April 1987 and 299 seats were won by the Golkar Party.

The Cabinet was as follows in Nov. 1991:

President, Prime Minister and Minister of Defence: Gen. Suharto (b. 1920), elected by the People's Consultative Assembly in 1968 and re-elected in 1973, 1978, 1983 and 1988.

Vice-President: Sudharmono. *Internal Affairs:* Rudini. *Foreign Affairs:* Ali Alatas. *Defence and Security:* L. B. Murdani. *Justice:* Ismail Saleh. *Information:* Harmoko. *Finance:* Dr J. B. Sumarlin. *Trade:* Dr Arifin Siregar. *Industry:* Hartarto. *Agriculture:* Wardoyo. *Mines and Energy:* Dr Ginandjar Kartasasmita. *Public Works:* Radinal Mochtar. *Communications:* Azwar Anas. *Co-operatives:* Bustanil Arifin. *Manpower:* Cosmas Batubara. *Transmigration:* Sugiarto. *Tourism, Post and Telecommunications:* Susilo Sudarman. *Education and Culture:* Dr Fuad Hassan. *Health:* Dr Adhyatma. *Religious Affairs:* H. Munawir Sjadzali. *Social Affairs:* Dr Haryati Soebadio. *Forestry:* Hasrul Harahap. *Co-ordinator Minister of Political and Security Affairs:* Sudomo. *Co-ordinator Minister of Economic, Financial and Industrial Affairs and Development Supervision:* Radius Prawiro. *Co-ordinator Minister of People's Welfare:* Supardjo Rustam. *State Minister and Secretary of State:* Moerdiono. *State Minister of National Development Planning and Chairman of the National Development Planning Board:* Dr Saleh Afiff. *State Minister of Population Affairs and Environment:* Dr Emil Salim. *State Minister of Housing Affairs:* Siswono Yudohusodo. *State Minister of Youth Affairs and Sports:* Akbar Tandjung. *State Minister of Research and Technology and Chairman of the Agency for the Assessment and Application of Technology:* Dr B. J. Habibe. *State Minister of Administrative Reform:* Sarwono Kusumaatmadja. *State Minister of Women's Affairs:* Sulasikin Murpratomo. *Commander-in-Chief of the Armed Forces:* Gen. Try Sutrisno. *Attorney-General:* Sukarton Marmosudjono. *Governor of Central Bank:* Dr Adrianus Moy.

There are 6 junior ministers.

National flag: Horizontally red over white.

National anthem: Indonesia Raya ('Indonesia the Great'; tune by Wage Rudolf Supratman, 1928).

Local government: There are 27 provinces, 3 of which are special territories (the capital city of Jakarta, Yogyakarta and Aceh), each administered by a Governor appointed by the President; they are divided into 246 districts (*kabupatens*), each under a district head (*bupati*), and 55 municipalities (*kotamadya*), each under a mayor (*wali kota*). The districts are divided into 3,592 sub-districts (*kecamtans*), each headed by a *camat*. There are 66,594 villages (1988).

DEFENCE. The Indonesian Armed Forces were formally set up on 5 Oct. 1945. On 11 Oct. 1967 the Army, Navy, Air Force and Police were integrated under the Department of Defence and Security. Their commanders no longer hold cabinet rank. There is selective conscription for 2 years.

Army. There are 3 infantry divisions, 1 armoured cavalry brigade, 3 infantry brigades, 3 airborne infantry brigades, 3 artillery regiments, 1 air defence regiment, 10 engineer battalions and 4 special warfare groups. There are 65 independent infantry battalions, 17 independent artillery battalions and 8 independent cavalry battalions. Equipment includes 125 AMX-13 and 41 PT-76 light tanks. The Army has over 80 aircraft, including 1 Islander, 2 C-47s and 25 other fixed-wing types, 16 Bell 205, 18 BO 105, 10 Hughes 300, 28 locally-built Bell 412 helicopters. Total strength in 1992 was 212,000.

Navy. The Indonesian navy in 1991 numbered 42,000, including 12,000 in the Commando Corps, and 1,000 in the Naval Air Arm. Combatant strength includes 2

German-built diesel submarines and 14 frigates of which 6 are former Dutch Van Speijk class, and 3 former British Ashanti class. There are also 4 fast missile craft, 2 torpedo-armed craft and 37 miscellaneous patrol craft as well as 2 Dutch-built tripartite coastal minehunters. Amphibious lift is provided by 14 tank landing ships (4 with helicopter facilities) and 50 craft. The auxiliary force includes 1 tanker, 6 surveying vessels, 1 command and submarine support ship, 1 repair ship, 3 training ships and some dozens of minor auxiliaries and service craft.

The Naval Air Arm operates 70 aircraft, including 18 Searchmaster maritime reconnaissance and BNC-212 Aviocar transport aircraft, and 15 anti-submarine helicopters as well as miscellaneous communications and utility aircraft.

A separate Military Sealift Command operates about 25 inter-island transport ships (which number includes 3 of the tank landing ships in the navy listing) totalling approximately 30,000 tonnes. The Maritime Security Agency operates 10 cutters, the Customs about 70 and the armed Marine Police 60 craft.

Air Force. Operational combat units comprise two squadrons of A-4E Skyhawk attack aircraft, and single squadrons of F-5E Tiger II and of F-16 fighters and OV-10F Bronco twin-turboprop counter-insurgency aircraft. There are 3 transport squadrons, equipped with turboprop C-130 Hercules, Nurtanio/CASA NC-212 Aviocar and F27 Friendship aircraft, and piston-engined C-47s, plus 3 specially-equipped Boeing 737 dual-purpose maritime surveillance/transports; and an assortment of other aircraft in transport, helicopter and training units including 16 Hawk attack/trainers, 23 T-34C-1 armed turboprop trainers, and 40 Swiss-built AS 202 Bravo piston-engined primary trainers. On order are 32 CN-235 twin-turboprop transports from IPTN of Indonesia. Personnel (1991) approximately 25,000.

INTERNATIONAL RELATIONS

Membership. Indonesia is a member of the UN, OPEC and ASEAN.

ECONOMY

Policy. The fifth Five-Year Development Plan (1990-94) constitutes the final 5 years of the Government's first 25-Year Long Term Development Plan. It places emphasis on the structural diversification of the economy to reduce dependence on crude oil and, in particular, it places importance on the development of export-oriented and labour-intensive industries in the agricultural and manufacturing sectors.

Budget. By law the budget must balance. The fiscal year starts 1 April. Revenue and expenditure for 1992–93 were estimated at US$28,000m.

Currency. The monetary unit is the *rupiah* (IDR) of 100 *sen*. There are banknotes of 1, 2·5, 5, 10, 25, 50, 100, 500, 1,000, 5,000 and 10,000 rupiahs and aluminium coins of 1, 5, 10, 25 and cupro-nickel coins of 50 sen.

In March 1992 3,529·70 rupiahs = £1 sterling; 2,010·65 rupiahs = US$1.

Banking and Finance. The Bank Indonesia, successor to De Javasche Bank established by the Dutch in 1828, was made the central bank of Indonesia on 1 July 1953. Its *Governor* is Dr Adrianus Moy. It had an original capital of Rp. 25m.; a reserve fund of Rp. 18m. and a special reserve of Rp. 84m. Total assets and liabilities at 31 March 1988, Rp. 36,252,000m.

There are 117 commercial banks, 28 development banks and other financial institutions, 8 development finance companies and 9 joint venture merchant banks. Commercial banking is dominated by 5 state-owned banks: Bank Rakyat Indonesia provides services to smallholder agriculture and rural development; Bank Bumi Daya, estate agriculture and forestry; Bank Negara Indonesia 1946, industry; Bank Dagang Negara, mining; and Bank Expor-Impor Indonesia, export commodity sector. All state banks are authorized to deal in foreign exchange.

There are 70 private commercial banks owned and operated by Indonesians. The 11 foreign banks, which specialize in foreign exchange transactions and direct lending operations to foreign joint ventures, include the Chartered Bank, the Hongkong and Shanghai Banking Corporation, the Bank of America, the City Bank, the Bank of Tokyo, Chase Manhattan and the American Express International Banking Corporation. The government owns one Savings Bank, Bank Tabungan Negara, and 1,000 Post Office Savings Banks. There are also over 3,500 rural and village savings bank and credit co-operatives.

The state-run stock exchange in Jakarta was scheduled for privatization in 1991.

Weights and Measures. The metric system is is use.

The following are the old weights and measures: *Pikol* = 136·16 lb. avoirdupois; *Katti* = 1·36 lb. avoirdupois; *Bau* = 1·7536 acres; *Square Pal* = 227 hectares = 561·16 acres; *Jengkal* = 4 yd; *Pal* (Java) = 1,506 metres; *Pal* (Sumatra) = 1,852 metres.

ENERGY AND NATURAL RESOURCES

Electricity. There were 7 hydro-electric plants in 1989; 19,044 out of 66,594 villages are supplied with electricity in Java and Sumatra. Electricity produced (1986) 30,000m. kwh. Supply 127 and 220 volts; 50 Hz.

Oil. Indonesia is the principal producer of petroleum in the Far East, production coming from Sumatra, Kalimantan (Indonesian Borneo) and Java. Proven reserves (1986) 8,500m. bbls. The 1989 output of crude oil was 66m. tonnes.

Gas. Pertamina, the state oil company, started to pump natural gas to Jakarta in 1979. Production (1988–89) 1,787,000m. cu. ft.

Water. In 1988–89, 23,677 ha of new irrigation networks were constructed and 377,461 ha rehabilitated and maintained.

Minerals. The high cost of extraction means that little of the large mineral resources outside Java is exploited; however, there is copper mining in Irian Jaya, nickel mining and processing on Sulawesi, aluminium smelting in northern Sumatra. Open-cast coal mining has been conducted since the 1890s, but since the 1970s coal production has been developed as an alternative to oil. Reserves are estimated at 28,000m. tonnes. Coal production (1990–91) 13·5m. tonnes; bauxite (1988–89), 514,100 tonnes. Output (in 1,000 tonnes, 1988–89) of iron ore was 210·5; copper, 302·7; silver (1987–88), 5,178·6 kg; gold, 5,050 kg; nickel ore, 1,881·6. In 1988–89 tin production was 28,900 tonnes.

Agriculture. Production (1988, in 1,000 tonnes): Rice, 41,769; cassava, 15,166; maize, 6,229; sweet potatoes, 2,166; sugar-cane, 20,800; coconuts and copra, 12,750; palm oil, 1,370; soybeans, 1,260; rubber, 1,094; coffee, 358; groundnuts, 585; vegetables, 3,180; fruits, 5,598; tea, 144; tobacco, 147. In 1991 6,750 tonnes of nutmeg were produced, about 75% of world production.

Livestock (1988): Cattle, 6·5m.; buffaloes, 3m.; horses, 722,000; sheep, 5·4m.; goats, 12·7m.; pigs, 6·5m.; poultry, 439m.

Forestry. The forest area was (1988) 122m. ha, 67% of the land area. Production (1988–89), provisional: Sawn timber, 4·3m. cu. metres; plywood, 7·5m. cu. metres. Exports (1988–89, provisional) of sawn timber, 2,874,000 cu. metres; plywood, 6·86m. cu. metres.

Fisheries. In 1988 the catch of sea fish was 2,166,000 tonnes; inland fish was 715,000 tonnes. In 1988 there were 117,526 motorized and 222,233 other fishing vessels. Exports (1988, provisional) included 56,552 tonnes of shrimps, 59,049 tonnes of fresh fish and 955 tonnes of ornamental fish.

INDUSTRY. There are shipyards at Jakarta Raya, Surabaya, Semarang and Amboina. There were (1985) more than 2,000 textile factories (total production in 1987–88, 2,925·6m. metres), large paper factories (817,200 tonnes, 1986–87), match factories, automobile and bicycle assembly works, large construction works, tyre factories, glass factories, a caustic soda and other chemical factories. Production (1987–88): Cement, 22,419,000 tonnes; fertilizers, 5,811,000 tonnes; 160,372 motor vehicles and 249,573 motorcycles; 2·36m. boxes of matches; glasses and bottles, 126,060 tonnes; steel ingots, 1,337,000 tonnes; 640 TV sets and 159,020 refrigerators.

Labour. In 1985 there were 62,457,138 people employed: 34,141,809 in agriculture; 9,345,210 in commerce; 8,317,285 in public services; 5,795,919 in industry; 2,095,577 in construction; 1,958,333 in transport and communications; 415,512 in mining and quarrying; 250,481 in finance and insurance; 69,715 in electricity, gas and water.

Trade Unions. Workers have a constitutional right to organize. Unions are expected to affiliate to the All Indonesia Labour Federation (FBSI) which enjoys government approval, but in Nov. 1990 an independent union, Setia Kawan (Solidarity) was set up. About 40% of the labour force belong to unions. Strikes are forbidden by law.

FOREIGN ECONOMIC RELATIONS

Commerce. Imports and exports (including oil and gas) in US$1m. for year ending March:

	1985–86	1986–87	1987–88	1988–89
Imports f.o.b.	12,522	11,451	12,952	14,311
Exports f.o.b.	18,612	13,697	18,343	19,824

The main export items (in US$1m.) in 1987 were: Gas and oil, 8,556; forestry products, 2,504; manufactured goods, 1,262; rubber, 961; coffee, 535; fishery products, 430; copper, 159; tin, 155; pepper, 148; palm products, 144; tea, 119. Exports went mainly to Japan (43·1%), USA (19·5%), Singapore (8·4%), Netherlands (2·9%), Federal Republic of Germany (2·1%) and Australia (2·1%).

The main import items are non-crude oil, rice, consumer goods, fertilizer, chemicals, weaving yarn, iron and steel, industrial and business machinery. In 1987 imports came mainly from Japan (28·7%), USA (11·3%), Singapore (8·7%), Federal Republic of Germany (6·7%), Australia (4·4%), Taiwan (3·7%), China (3·3%) and France (3·1%).

Coal exports were 5·3m. tonnes in 1990.

Total trade between Indonesia and UK (British Department of Trade returns, in £1,000 sterling):

	1987	1988	1989	1990	1991
Imports to UK	144,819	233,807	273,102	327,877	415,340
Exports and re-exports from UK	236,027	203,275	184,032	194,274	197,991

Tourism. In 1988 1,301,249 tourists visited Indonesia.

COMMUNICATIONS

Roads. The total length of the artery and connecting road network in 1988-89 was 44,552 km, of which 27,480 km were in good condition. Motor vehicles, at 31 Dec. 1989, totalled 9,674,246.

Railways. In 1987 the State Railways totalled 6,458 km of 1,067 mm gauge, comprising 4,967 km on Java (of which 125 km electrified) and 1,491 km on Sumatra. In 1989–90 they carried 55·3m. passengers and 12·2m. tonnes of freight. In addition some narrow gauge lines are still operated.

Civil Aviation. Garuda Indonesia is the national flag carrier. Merpati Nusantara Airways is their domestic subsidiary. There are international airports at Jakarta (Sukarno-Hatta), Denpasar (on Bali), Medan (Sumatra), Pekanbaru (Sumatra), Ambon (Maluku), Biak (Irian Jaya) and Batu Ampar (Batam). In 1988-89 there were 797 aircraft in operation with 175 scheduled and 622 non-scheduled flights. The total number of passengers carried was 6,679,438, total freight 76,486 tonnes.

Shipping. There are 16 ports for oceangoing ships, the largest of which is Tanjung Priok, which serves the Jakarta area and has a container terminal. The national shipping company Pelajaran Nasional Indonesia (PELNI) maintains interinsular communications. The Jakarta Lloyd maintains regular services between Jakarta, Amsterdam, Hamburg and London. In 1988–89, 35 ocean-going ships with a capacity of 446,980 DWT carried 17,887,500 tonnes of freight.

Telecommunications. In 1979 the postal and telegraph services of Indonesia included 2,796 post offices. There were 660 telegraph offices which handled 3·9m. domestic and 488,000 international cables. Post offices handled 396·63m. letters, Rp. 388,700m. in money orders and 4,550,000m. in postal cheques in 1987–88. Deposits with post office savings accounts, Rp. 31,210m. Number of telephones (1988), 999,321.

Radio Republik Indonesia, under the Department of Information, operates 49 stations. In 1988–89 there were 8,948,195 TV receivers, and 54,318 public TV sets had been placed in villages within reach of the state-owned Televisi Republik Indonesia telecast.

Newspapers (1986–87). There were about 252 newspaper publishers with estimated circulation (1988-89) of 10,783,009, of which 3,716,056 daily newspapers. There were 270 publishers of weekly papers and magazines with a circulation (1988–89) of 3,444,802 and 1,721,130 respectively.

JUSTICE, RELIGION, EDUCATION AND WELFARE

Justice. There are courts of first instance, high courts of appeal in every provincial capital and a Supreme Court of Justice for the whole of Indonesia in Jakarta. Administrative matters on judicial organization are under the direction of the Department of Justice.

In civil law the population is divided into three main groups: Indonesians, Europeans and foreign Orientals, to whom different law systems are applicable. When, however, people from different groups are involved, a system of so-called 'intergentile' law is applied.

The present criminal law, which has been in force since 1918, is codified and is based on European penal law. This law is equally applicable to all groups of the population. For private and commercial law, however, there are various systems applicable for the various groups of the population. For the Indonesians, a system of private and agrarian law is applicable; this is called Adat Law, and is mainly uncodified. For the other groups the prevailing private and commercial law system is codified in the Private Law Act (1847) and the Commercial Law Act (1847). These Acts have their origins in the French *Code Civile* and *Code du Commerce* through the similar Dutch codifications. These Acts are entirely applicable to Indonesian citizens and to Europeans, whereas to foreign Orientals they are applicable with some exceptions, mainly in the fields of family law and inheritance. Penal law was in the process of being codified in 1981.

Religion. Religious liberty is granted to all denominations. About 87% of the Indonesians were Moslems in 1988 and 9% Christians. There are also about 1·6m. Buddhists, probably for the greater part Chinese. Hinduism has 3·5m. members, of whom 2·5m. are on Bali.

Education. In 1987–88 there were 30,960,000 pupils in primary schools and, in 1988–89, 6,679,700 students in junior high schools and 4,146,900 students in senior high schools, vocational schools, higher training and sports teachers' training colleges.

English is the first foreign language taught in schools. Literacy rate was 72% in 1984.

Total number of students in higher education (1988–89) 1,663,900. In 1987–88 there were 49 state and 637 private universities and technical institutes.

Health. In 1988 there were 23,084 doctors, 64,087 nurses, 5,472 public health centres, 12,562 sub-public health centres and 3,521 mobile units.

DIPLOMATIC REPRESENTATIVES

Of Indonesia in Great Britain (38 Grosvenor Sq., London W1X 9AD)
Ambassador: T.M Hadi Thayeb.

Of Great Britain in Indonesia (Jalan M.H. Thamrin 75, Jakarta 10310)
Ambassador: R. J. Carrick, CMG, LVO.

Of Indonesia in the USA (2020 Massachusetts Ave., NW, Washington, D.C., 20036)
Ambassador: A. R. Ramly.

Of the USA in Indonesia (Medan Merdeka Selatan 5, Jakarta)
Ambassador: John C. Monjo.

Of Indonesia to the United Nations
Ambassador: Nana Sutresna.

Further Reading

Indonesia 1989. Department of Information, Jakarta, 1989

Bee, O. J., *The Petroleum Resources of Indonesia.* OUP, 1982

Bemmelen, R. W. van, *Geology of Indonesia.* 2 vols. The Hague, 1949

Echols, J. M. and Shadily, H., *An Indonesian–English Dictionary.* 3rd ed. Cornell Univ. Press, 1989

International Commission of Jurists, *Indonesia and the Rule of Law.* London, 1987

Leifer, M., *Indonesia's Foreign Policy.* London, 1983

McDonald, H., *Suharto's Indonesia.* Univ. Press of Hawaii, 1981

Palmier, L., *Understanding Indonesia.* London, 1986

Papenek, G., *The Indonesian Economy.* Eastbourne, 1980

Polomka, P., *Indonesia Since Sukarno.* London, 1971

Robison, R., *Indonesia: The Rise of Capital.* Sydney, 1986

Thoolen, H., *Indonesia and the Rule of Law.* London, 1987

IRAN

Capital: Tehran
Population: 53·92m. (1988)
GNP per capita: US$1,690 (1986)

Jomhori-e-Islami-e-Iran

(Islamic Republic of Iran)

HISTORY. Persia was ruled by the Shahs as an absolute monarchy until 30 Dec. 1906 when the first Constitution was granted. Reza Khan took control after a coup on 31 Oct. 1925 deposed the last Shah of the Qajar Dynasty, and became Reza Shah Pahlavi on 12 Dec. 1925. The country's name was changed to Iran on 21 March 1935. Reza Shah abdicated on 16 Sept. 1941 in favour of his son, Mohammad Reza Pahlavi.

Following widespread civil unrest, the Shah left Iran on 17 Jan. 1979. The Ayatollah Ruhollah Khomeini, spiritual leader of the Shi'a Moslem community, returned from 15 years' exile on 1 Feb. 1979 and appointed a provisional government on 5 Feb. An Islamic Republic was proclaimed on 1 Apr. 1979.

In Sept. 1980 war began with Iraq with destruction of some Iranian towns and damage to the oil installations at Abadan. A UN-arranged ceasefire took place on 20 Aug. 1988 and UN-sponsored peace talks continued in 1989. On 15 Aug. 1990 the Iraqi President Saddam Hussein offered peace terms and began the withdrawal of Iraqi forces. Iran and Iraq exchanged prisoners of war in the last quarter of 1990.

AREA AND POPULATION. Iran is bounded north by the USSR and the Caspian Sea, east by Afghanistan and Pakistan, south by the Gulf of Oman and the Persian Gulf, and west by Iraq and Turkey. It has an area of 1,648,000 sq. km (634,724 sq. miles), but a vast portion is desert, and the average density is only (1987) 31 inhabitants to the sq. km. Refugees in Iran (Jan. 1988) 2·6m. (of which 2·2m. Afghans).

The population at recent censuses was as follows: (1956) 18,944,821; (1966) 25,781,090; (1976) 33,708,744; (1986) 49,445,010. Population estimate in 1988 (tentative because of unquantified losses in the war with Iraq): 53·92m.

The areas, populations and capitals of the 24 provinces *(ostan)* were:

Province	Area (sq. km)	Census 1976	Census 1986	Capital
Azarbaijan, East	67,102	3,197,685	4,114,084	Tabriz
Azarbaijan, West	38,850	1,407,604	1,971,677	Orumiyeh [2]
Bakhtaran [1]	23,667	1,030,714	1,462,965	Bakhtaran [3]
Boyer ahmadi and Kohkiluyeh	14,261	244,370	411,828	Yasuj
Bushehr	27,653	347,863	612,183	Bushehr
Chahar Mahal and Bakhtiari	14,870	394,357	631,179	Shahr-e-Kord
Esfahan	104,650	2,176,694	3,294,916	Esfahan
Fars	133,298	2,035,582	3,193,769	Shiraz
Gilan	14,709	1,581,872	2,081,037	Rasht
Hamadan	19,784	1,088,024	1,505,826	Hamadan
Hormozgan	66,870	462,440	762,206	Bandar-e-Abbas
Ilam	19,044	246,024	382,091	Ilam
Kerman	179,916	1,091,148	1,622,958	Kerman
Khorasan	313,337	3,264,398	5,280,605	Mashhad
Khuzestan	67,282	2,187,118	2,681,978	Ahvaz
Kordestan	24,998	782,440	1,078,415	Sanandaj
Lorestan	28,803	933,939	1,367,029	Khorramabad
Markazi	29,080	796,754	1,082,109	Arak
Mazandaran	46,456	2,387,171	3,419,346	Sari
Semnan	90,905	289,463	417,035	Semnan
Sistan and Baluchestan	181,578	664,292	1,197,059	Zahedan
Tehran (formed from Markazi)	29,993	5,624,784	8,712,087	Tehran
Yazd	70,011	356,849	574,028	Yazd
Zanjan	36,398	1,117,157	1,588,600	Zanjan

[1] Formerly Kermanshahan.　　[2] Formerly Rezayeh.　　[3] Formerly Kermanshah.

The principal cities were:

	Census 1976	Census 1986		Census 1976	Census 1986
Tehran	4,530,223	6,042,584	Ardabil	147,865	281,973
Esfahan	661,510	986,753	Khorramshahr	140,490	...
Mashhad	667,770	1,463,508	Kerman	140,761	257,284
Tabriz	597,976	971,482	Karaj	137,926	275,100
Shiraz	425,813	848,289	Qazvin	139,258	248,591
Ahvaz	334,399	579,826	Yazd	135,925	230,483
Abadan	294,068	...	Arak	116,832	265,349
Bakhtaran	290,600	560,514	Desful	121,251	151,420
Qom	247,219	543,139	Khorramabad	104,912	208,592
Rasht	188,957	290,897	Borujerd	101,345	183,879
Orumiyeh	164,419	300,746	Zanjan	100,351	215,261
Hamadan	165,785	272,499			

The national language is Farsi or Persian, spoken by 45% of the population. 23% spoke related languages, including Kurdish and Luri in the west and Baluchi in the south-east, while 26% spoke Turkic languages, primarily the Azerbaijani-speaking peoples of the north-west and the Turkomen of Khorasan in the north-east.

CLIMATE. Mainly a desert climate, but with more temperate conditions on the shores of the Caspian Sea. Seasonal range of temperature is considerable. Abadan. Jan. 54°F (12·2°C), July 97°F (36·1°C). Annual rainfall 8" (204 mm). Tehran. Jan. 36°F (2·2°C), July 85°F (29·4°C). Annual rainfall 10" (246 mm).

CONSTITUTION AND GOVERNMENT. The Constitution of the Islamic Republic was approved by a national referendum in Dec. 1979. It gives supreme authority to the *Spiritual Leader* (*wali faqih*), which position was held by Ayatollah Khomeini until his death on 3 June 1989. Seyed Ali Khamenei was elected to succeed him on 4 June 1989.

The 83-member *Assembly of Experts* was established in 1982. it is popularly elected every 8 years. Its mandate is to interpret the constitution and select the Spiritual Leader. Candidates for election are examined by the Council of Guardians. At the elections of Oct. 1990 turn-out was 46%.

The *President* of the Republic is popularly-elected for a 4-year term and is head of the executive; he appoints Ministers, subject to approval by the *Majlis*.

Presidents since the establishment of the Islamic Republic:

Abolhassan Bani-Sadr. 4 Feb. 1980–22 June 1981 (deposed).
Mohammad Ali Raja'i, 24 July 1981–30 Aug. 1981 (assassinated).

Sayed Ali Khamenei, 12 Oct. 1981-4 June 1989.

The Cabinet was composed as follows in 1991:

President: Hojatolislam Ali Akbar Hashemi Rafsanjani (sworn in on 3 Aug. 1989).

Vice President: Hassan Habibi.

Foreign Affairs: Ali Akbar Vellayati. *Oil:* Gholamreza Aghazadeh. *Interior:* Abdollah Nouri. *Economic Affairs and Finance:* Mohsen Nourbakhsh. *Agriculture and Rural Affairs:* Isa Kalantari. *Commerce:* Abdol-Hossein Vahaji. *Energy:* Namdar Zanganeh. *Roads and Transport:* Mohammed Saeedi Kya. *Construction Jihad:* Gholamreza Foruzesh. *Heavy Industries:* Mohammad Hadi Nezhad-Hosseinian. *Industry:* Mohammad Reza Nematzadeh. *Housing and Urban Development:* Sarajuddin Kazeruni. *Labour and Social Affairs:* Hossein Kamali. *Posts, Telephones and Telegraphs:* Mohammed Gharazi. *Health, Treatment and Medical Education:* Iraj Fazel. *Education and Training:* Mohammad Ali Najafi. *Higher Education and Culture:* Mostafa Moin. *Justice:* Hojatolislam Ismail Shostari. *Defence and Armed Forces Logistics:* Akbar Torkan. *Intelligence and Security:* Hojatolislam Ali Fallahiyan. *Culture and Islamic Guidance:* Seyyed Mohammad Khatami. *Mines and Metals:* Mohammad Hossein Mahloji.

Legislative power is held by the 270-member *(Majlis)* Islamic Consultative

Assembly, directly elected on a non-party basis for a 4-year term in May-April 1988. The *Speaker* is Hojatoleslam Karrubi. All legislation is subject to approval by a 12-member *Council of Guardians* who ensure it is in accordance with the Islamic code and with the Constitution. Six members are appointed by the *Spiritual Leader* and six by the judiciary.

National flag: Three horizontal stripes of green, white and red; on the borders of the green and red stripes the legend *Allah Akbar* in white Kufi script repeated 22 times in all; in the centre of the white stripe the national emblem in red.

Local Government. The country is divided into 24 provinces *(ostan)*, these are sub-divided into 195 *shahrestan* (counties), each under a *farmandar* (governor) and thence into 500 *bakhsh* (districts), each under a *bakhshdar*. The districts are sub-divided into *dehistan* (groups of villages) each under a *dehdar*, each village having its elected *kadkhoda* (headman).

DEFENCE. Two years' military service is compulsory.

Army. The Army consisted (1991) of 305,000 men (about 250,000 conscripts). It is organized in 4 mechanized, 1 special force, 7 infantry and 1 airborne divisions, and auxiliary units. Equipment includes some 700 T-54/-55/-62, T-72, Chieftain, M-47/-48 and M-60A1 main battle tanks. There is also a 300,000-strong Revolutionary Guard Corps. The Army is estimated to have an inventory of 50 fixed-wing aircraft and over 400 helicopters but the effective strength is not known.

Revolutionary Guard. This in 1991 numbered some 150,000 ground forces and 20,000 naval. The ground forces are divided into 11 regional commands loosely organized in battalions of no fixed size and grouped into 24 infantry and 4 armoured divisions and other units. It controls the Basij, a volunteer 'popular mobilization army', which may reach 1m. strong in war-time.

Navy. The Navy continues to recover from the effects of the war with Iraq, but remains weaker than before the war. The combatant fleet is currently believed to comprise 1 ex-British 'Battle' class and 2 ex-US Sumner class destroyers, 3 UK-built frigates, 2 old ex-US patrol frigates and about 10 missile craft (for which there may be no missiles). Other units include 19 inshore patrol craft (some of them hovercraft), 3 small minesweepers and a substantial amphibious force of 7 tank landing ships and 4 tank landing craft. Auxiliaries include 3 tankers, 1 repair ship, 2 water tankers and 2 accommodation ships.

Naval Aviation comprises 1 anti-submarine helicopter squadron with perhaps 15 Sea King and AB-212 helicopters, a mine counter-measures squadron with 2 RH-53D helicopters and a transport squadron with about a dozen various aircraft. Main naval bases are at Bandar-e-Abbas, Bushehr and Chah Bahar.

The naval forces of the Revolutionary Guard were until 1989 organizationally separate, but now fall under Naval Operational command, and integrated operations are regularly exercised. The naval elements of the Revolutionary Guard number about 20,000 and operate some 40-60 fast boats armed with portable weapons. They control the offshore oil rigs used as bases, and coastal artillery and missile batteries.

Air Force. In Aug. 1955 the Air Force became a separate and independent arm, and had a strength of about 23 first-line squadrons (each 15 aircraft, plus reserves), with 100,000 personnel before the 1979 revolution. Strength (1991) was estimated at 35,000 personnel and 200 serviceable combat aircraft. The latter include some MiG-19/Chinese-built F-6 fighter-bombers, supplied via North Korea, and surviving US fighters that include F-14 Tomcat, F-5E Tiger II and F-4D/E Phantom II fighter-bombers, plus a few RF-4E reconnaissance-fighters. Transport aircraft include F27s, C-130 Hercules, PC-6 Turbo-Porters, Boeing 707s and 747s, some equipped as flight refuelling tankers. The status of the large fleet of CH-47C Chinook, Bell Model 214 and other helicopters is not known; but two P-3F Orion maritime patrol aircraft remain operational. Training aircraft include Bonanza basic trainers, 35 PC-7 Turbo-Trainers and 15 Tucanos for advanced training.

INTERNATIONAL RELATIONS

Membership. Iran is a member of the UN, OPEC and the Colombo Plan.

ECONOMY

Policy. A development plan is running 1989–93. At the beginning of 1991 about 70% of industry was state-owned, much of it nationalized after the 1979 revolution, but the government is now committed to partial privatization. Strategic heavy industry will remain in the public sector.

Budget. The budget for 1989 (public funds) balanced at 4,766,000m. *rials*.

Currency. The unit of currency is the *rial* (IRR) of which 10 = 1 *toman*.

Notes in circulation are of denominations of 100, 200, 500, 1,000, 2,000, 5,000 and 10,000 *rials*. Coins in circulation are silver alloy, 1, 2, 5, 10, 20 and 50 *rials*. There is a 2-tier exchange rate: an official rate, and a market rate offered to tourists and the private sector. The official rate in March 1992, US$1 = 66·22 *rials*; £1 = 116·25 *rials*.

Banking and Finance. The *Bank Markazi Iran* was established in 1960 as the note-issuing authority and government bank. Its *Governor* is Mohammad Adeli. All other banks and insurance companies were nationalized in June 1979, and re-organized into 8 new state banking corporations. The 'Law for Usury-Free Banking' was given final approval in Aug.-Sept. 1983. From 21 March 1985 interest on accounts was abolished.

Weights and Measures. The metric system is in force.

The Iranian year is a solar year running from 21 March to 20 March; the Hejira year 1362 corresponds to the Christian year 21 March 1984–20 March 1985.

ENERGY AND NATURAL RESOURCES

Electricity. Total installed capacity, 1989, was 16,619,000 kw., and 52,712m. kwh. were generated. Supply 220 volts; 50 Hz.

Oil. For a history of Iran's oil industry 1951–79, *see* THE STATESMAN'S YEAR-BOOK, 1982–83.

The petroleum industry was seriously disrupted by the 1979 revolution, and many facilities, including the vast refinery at Abadan, the new refinery at Bandar Khomeini and the tanker terminal at Kharg Island, have been destroyed or put out of action during the Gulf war with Iraq. All operating companies were nationalized in 1979 and operations are now run by the National Petrochemical Company.

Crude oil production, 166m. tonnes, 1991.

Gas. Natural gas production (1986) was 25,311m. cu. metres.

Minerals. Iran has substantial mineral deposits relatively underdeveloped. Production figures for 1988 (in 1,000 tonnes): Iron ore, 1,867; coal, 885; zinc concentrate, 17; lead concentrate, 26; copper concentrate, 170; manganese, 31; chromite, 70; salt, 1,236. There is also bauxite, copper and decorative stone.

Agriculture. In 1991, cultivatable land totalled 17,150,140 ha: 10,706,380 ha were under annual crops (of which 4,878,220 ha were irrigated), 1,095,700 ha orchards and nurseries (965,040 ha irrigated) and 5,348,150 ha fallow land (1,782,540 ha irrigated).

Crop production for 1991 (in tonnes): Wheat, 5,876,960; barley, 2,636,470; rice, 1,222,370; sugar-beet, 3,649,330; tobacco, 21,220.

Wool comes principally from Khorasan, Bakhtaran, Mazandaran and Azarbaijan. Production, 1988, 16,000 tonnes greasy, 8,800 tonnes scoured.

Rice is grown largely on the Caspian shores.

Cigarette tobacco is grown mainly in Gilan, Mazandaran and West Azarbaijan *ostans*. It is purchased by the Tobacco Monopoly and manufactured in the government factory at Tehran.

Opium, until 1955, was an important export commodity in Iran. On 7 Oct. 1955 an Act was approved by Parliament to prohibit the cultivation and usage of opium.

Livestock (1991): 40,707,000 sheep, 22,244,000 goats, 6,126,000 cattle, 155,172 horses, 86,000 camels, 289,000 buffaloes, and 1,422,672 donkeys.

Fisheries. The North Fisheries Co. (Shilat) is a government monopoly. Total catch (1986) 152,000 tonnes.

INDUSTRY. Production of selected commodites in manufacturing establishments with 50 workers and more, 1989: Vegetable shortening, 479,000 tonnes; sugar, 535,000 tonnes; stockings, 55,188,000 pairs; machine-made bricks, 2,469m.; cement, 12,587,000 tonnes; gas ranges and rings, 81; sedans, 6,829; small vans, 5,291; lorries and trucks, 2,795; buses, 691; mini-buses, 2,176; jeeps, station wagons and ambulances, 6,396; motor cycles, 23,469. In 1989 there were 1,271 large-scale manufacturing establishments and the number of employees was 447,884.

FOREIGN ECONOMIC RELATIONS. In May 1990 Iran and the USA signed a US$50m. agreement to settle 2,750 US small claims arising from the Iranian revolution in 1979.

EEC sanctions were lifted in Oct. 1990.

The 1989–93 development plan calls for US$17,700m. direct foreign financing and US$10,000 foreign investment. Foreign investors may own only up to 49% of Iranian companies.

Commerce. Imports totalled 927,257m. rials in 1989. Exports totalled 74,736m. rials in 1989, excluding oil and hydrocarbon solvents obtained from oil.

Total trade between Iran and UK (British Department of Trade returns, in £1,000 sterling):

	1987	1988	1989	1990	1991
Imports to UK	187,572	140,207	250,548	279,135	158,354
Exports and re-exports from UK	307,853	247,768	257,149	384,713	511,532

US imports were worth US$166m. in 1990. Germany is Iran's main trading partner: imports were worth US$2,500m. in 1990.

Tourism. Total number of visitors (1989) 153,783.

COMMUNICATIONS

Roads. In 1986 the total length of roads was 151,485 km, of which 459 km were freeways, 21,577 km main roads, 36,343 km by-roads, 37,793 km rural roads and 55,316 km other roads.

In 1989 vehicles numbered 2,870,428, including 1,957,978 sedans, 42,722 taxis, 263,781 trucks, 105,528 buses and minibuses, 500,409 vans and 993,242 motorcycles.

Railways. The State Railways totalled 4,569 km of main lines in 1989, of which 146 km were electrified. In 1989 the railways carried 6,672,000 passengers and 12,834,000 tonnes of freight. An isolated 1,676 mm gauge line in the south-east links with Pakistan Railways.

Aviation. In 1989, 2,518,000 passengers arrived at Mehrabad Airport (2,074,000 on domestic flights and 444,000 on international flights) and 2,441,000 passengers departed (2,016,000 domestic and 425,000 international). The state airline carried 4,594,000 passengers and 52,715 tons of cargo and mail in 1989.

Shipping. In 1989, 1,314 ships, capacity 8,508,000 tonnes, entered commercial ports, unloading 16,277,000 tonnes and loading 1,214,000 tonnes of goods (excluding oil products).

Telecommunications. Postal, telegraph and telephone services are administered by the Ministry of Posts, Telegraphs and Telephones.

In 1989 the number of telephones was 2,026,106; in 1985 some 488,516 were in Tehran province. Radio stations numbered 69 in 1989, and television stations, 671.

Cinemas (1988). There were 260 cinemas with 162,051 seats.

Newspapers. There were in 1989, 17 newspapers issued nationwide. Their circulation is relatively small.

JUSTICE, RELIGION, EDUCATION AND WELFARE

Justice. A new legal system based on Islamic law was introduced by the new constitution in 1979. The President of the Supreme Court and the public Prosecutor-General are appointed by the Spiritual Leader. The Supreme Court has 16 branches and 109 offences carry the death penalty. To these were added economic crimes in July 1990.

Religion. The official religion is the Shi'a branch of Islam, known as the *Ithna-Ashariyya,* which recognizes 12 Imams or spiritual successors of the Prophet Mohammad. Of the total population in 1986, 98·38% were Moslem.

Education. The great majority of primary and secondary schools are state schools. Elementary education in state schools and university education is free; small fees are charged for state-run secondary schools. Text-books are issued free of charge to pupils in the first 4 grades of elementary schools.

In 1988–89 there were 8,262,441 pupils in primary schools, 2,724,606 in orientation schools and 1,363,130 in high schools; there were 209,887 students in technical and vocational schools, 41,884 in teacher-training schools, 29,127 gifted children, and 921,152 in adult education courses. Universities and other institutes of higher education had 250,709 students in 1988–89. The Free Islamic University was established after the revolution and in 1983 the International University of Islamic Studies was being organized.

A literacy movement was established in 1981 and by 1985, 3m. citizens had participated.

Health. In 1988, 77,804 hospital beds were available in 609 hospitals. Medical personnel included 13,898 physicians and 954 dentists in 1988.

DIPLOMATIC REPRESENTATIVES

Of Iran in Great Britain (27 Prince's Gate, London, SW7 1PX)
Chargé d' Affaires: Seyed Shamseddin Khareghani.

Of Great Britain in Iran (Ave. Ferdowski Tehran)
Chargé d' Affaires: David Reddaway, MBE.

Of Iran in the USA (3005 Massachusetts Ave., NW, Washington, D.C., 20008)
Ambassador: (Vacant).

Of the USA in Iran (260 Takhte Jamshid Ave., Tehran)
Ambassador: (Vacant).

Of Iran to the United Nations
Ambassador: Dr Kamal Kharrazi.

Further Reading

Statistical Information. Statistical Centre of Iran, Dr Fakemi Avenue, Tehran, Iran, 14144.

Afshar, H., *Iran: A Revolution in Turmoil.* London, 1985
Bakhash, S., *The Reign of the Ayatollahs.* London, 1984
Benard, C. and Zalmay, K., *'The Government of God': Iran's Islamic Republic.* Columbia Univ. Press, 1984
Bina, C. and Zanganeh, H. (eds.), *Modern Capitalism and Islamic Ideology in Iran.* London, 1991
The Cambridge History of Iran. 7 vols. CUP, 1968–91
Fuller, G. E., *Centre of the Universe: Geopolitics of Iran.* Boulder (Colo.), 1992
Heikal, M., *Iran: The Untold Story.* New York, 1982
Hiro, D., *Iran under the Ayatollahs.* London, 1985
Hussain, A., *Islamic Iran: Revolution and Counter-Revolution.* London, 1985
Karshenas, M., *Oil, State and Industry in Iran.* CUP, 1990
Katouzian, H., *The Political Economy of Iran.* London, 1981
Keddie, N., *Roots of Revolution.* Yale Univ. Press, 1981

Navabpour, A. R., *Iran*. [Bibliography] Oxford and Santa Barbara, 1988

Rahnema, A. and Nomani, F., *The Secular Miracle: Religion, Politics and Economic Activity*. London, 1990

Sick, G., *All Fall Down*. London, 1985

Stempel, J. D., *Inside the Iranian Revolution*. Indiana Univ. Press, 1981

Zabih, S., *Iran's Revolutionary Upheaval: An Interpretive Essay*. San Francisco, 1979.—*The Mosadegh Era: Roots of the Iranian Revolution*. Chicago, 1982.—*Iran since the Revolution*. London, 1982.—*The Left in Contemporary Iran*. London and Stamford, 1986

IRAQ

Capital: Baghdad
Population: 17·86m. (1990)
GNP per capita: US$2,140 (1986)

Jumhouriya al 'Iraqia

(Republic of Iraq)

HISTORY. Part of the Ottoman Empire from the 16th century, Iraq was captured by British forces in 1916 and became in 1921 a Kingdom under a League of Nations mandate, administered by Britain. It became independent on 3 Oct. 1932 under the Hashemite Dynasty, which was overthrown on 14 July 1958 by a military coup which established a Republic. In 1968 the Ba'ath Party seized power and established the Revolutionary Command Council as government.

Fighting between government forces and secessionist Kurds in the north-east has continued despite settlements announced in 1970 and subsequently.

In Sept. 1980 Iraq invaded Iran in a dispute over territorial rights in the Shatt-al-Arab waterway which developed into a full-scale war. A UN-arranged ceasefire took place on 20 Aug. 1988 and UN-sponsored peace talks continued in 1989. On 15 Aug. 1990 Iraq offered peace terms and began the withdrawal of troops from Iranian soil.

Early on 2 Aug. 1990 Iraqi forces without warning invaded and rapidly overran Kuwait, meeting little resistance. The Amir escaped to Saudi Arabia. President Saddam of Iraq declared the annexation of Kuwait on 8 Aug.

On 6 Aug. the UN Security Council voted by 13 to nil with 2 abstentions (Cuba and Yemen) to impose total economic sanctions on Iraq until it withdrew from Kuwait. On 7 Aug. the USA announced it was sending a large military force to Saudi Arabia at the latter's request to prevent a further Iraqi invasion of the area, and the UK made a similar commitment the following day. Various other countries announced the despatch of forces and equipment to this coalition force, including 12 Arab League countries on 10 Aug.

Measures to secure Iraq's withdrawal from Kuwait were given international legal sanction by a UN Security Council resolution of 25 Aug. (by 13 votes to nil), authorizing a naval blockade of Iraq under UN auspices. Further Security Council resolutions included (25 Sept., by 14 votes to 1) an air embargo of Iraq and (29 Oct., 13-nil) a call for compensation to be paid by Iraq to states for losses resulting from the invasion of Kuwait. A 12th resolution of 29 Nov. (12 in favour, Cuba and Yemen against, China abstaining) authorized the use of military force if Iraq did not withdraw by 15 Jan. 1991.

Iraq accepted an offer of talks between its Foreign Minister and the US Secretary of State at Geneva on 9 Jan. 1991. Following the failure of these talks to secure Iraq's withdrawal from Kuwait, the UN Secretary-General went to Baghdad, but was unable to secure a peaceful solution.

On the night of 16-17 Jan. coalition forces began an air attack on strategic targets in Iraq. Iraqi counter-attacks included missile strikes against Israel, which caused fatal casualties.

After a last-minute Soviet peace initiative had failed to secure an unconditional Iraqi withdrawal from Kuwait, coalition forces launched a land offensive on 24 Feb. The Iraqi army was routed and sustained massive destruction. Kuwait City was liberated on 27 Feb. and on 28 Feb. Iraq agreed to the conditions of a provisional ceasefire, including withdrawal from Kuwait. Coalition forces advanced into Iraq and held positions up to the lower River Euphrates.

A UN resolution of 2 March setting out the conditions of a permanent ceasefire was carried by 11 votes to 1 (Cuba) with 3 abstentions (China, India, Yemen). Iraq accepted it.

On 3 April 1991 the UN Security Council adopted a permanant ceasefire resolution by 12 votes to 1 (Cuba) with 2 abstentions (Ecuador, Yemen). This provided for Iraq and Kuwait to respect the disputed border, the UN to demarcate it, and the Security Council to guarantee it. A UN observer force is to monitor a demilitarized zone extending 10 km into Iraq and 5 km into Kuwait, the deployment of this force allowing the withdrawal of the coalition forces. Iraq is to accept the destruction of all chemical and biological weapons and nuclear weapons-usable material, under international supervision, and is liable for damages arising from its invasion of Kuwait. Sanctions on Iraqi exports are to be lifted. This resolution was accepted by Iraq on 11 April. The UN observer force arrived in South Iraq in May, and coalition forces completed their withdrawal

Insurrections which began in March amongst Shi'ites in the south and Kurds in the north were put down by govenrment forces. A massive exodus of Kurdish refugees to the borders of Iran and Turkey followed. International relief operations were succeeded in April by the establishment of 'safe havens' for refugees within Iraqi borders policed by US and other coalition troops. Kurdish opposition leaders began talks with the Iraqi government at the end of April, and refugees began to move from the border areas into camps in north Iraq under the supervision of US, UK and other coalition forces. In May 1991 a UN Security Council resolution adopted by 14 votes to 1 (Cuba) provided for a fund to compensate victims for damage caused during the Iraqi invasion of Kuwait. The fund is based at Geneva, administered by a council of representatives of all the Security Council members, and supplied from not more than 30% of Iraqi oil-export earnings. Iraq denounced the resolution as illegal, but said it would comply with it as it had no choice. Following a UN-Iraqi agreement, about 500 UN security guards were brought in in June 1991 to protect Kurds in the north. Coalition forces in Iraq had withdrawn by 15 July, but a Coalition 'rapid reaction force' of some 3,000 troops remained in Turkey to continue protecting the Kurds in Iraq till Oct., when ground troops were withdrawn, leaving only air forces, which Turkey permitted to remain until June 1992.

In Sept. a UN Security Council resolution adopted by 13 votes to 1 (Cuba) with 1 abstention (Yemen) permitted Iraq to sell oil worth US1,600m. to pay for food and medical supplies and start a reparations fund. In Oct. the Security Council voted unanimously to prohibit Iraq from all nuclear activities except medical. Imports of materials used in the manufacture of nuclear, biological or chemical weapons are banned, and UN inspectors have received wide powers to examine and retain data throughout Iraq.

AREA AND POPULATION. Iraq is bounded north by Turkey, east by Iran, south-east by the Gulf, south by Kuwait and Saudi Arabia, and west by Jordan and Syria. The country has an area of 438,317 sq. km. Population, 1987 census, 16,335,198; 1990 estimate, 17,856,000. Density, 42 per sq. km.

The areas, populations and capitals of the governorates:

Governorate	sq. km	Population (1987 census)	Capital	Population (1985 estimate)
Al-Anbar	138,501	820,690	Ar-Ramadi	137,388
Babil (Babylon)	6,468	1,109,574	Al-Hillah	215,249
Baghdad	734	3,841,268	Baghdad	4,648,609
Al-Basrah	19,070	872,176	Al-Basrah	616,700
Dahuk	6,553	293,304	Dahuk	19,736 [2]
Dhi Qar	12,900	921,066	An-Nasiriyah	138,842
Diyala	19,076	961,073	Ba'qubah	114,516
Irbil	14,471	770,439	Irbil	333,903
Karbala	5,034	469,282	Karbala	184,574
Maysan	16,072	487,448	Al-Amarah	131,758
Al-Muthanna	51,740	315,815	As-Samawah	33,473 [1]
An-Najaf	28,824	590,078	An-Najaf	242,603
Ninawa (Nineveh)	37,323	1,479,430	Mosul	570,926
Al-Qadisiyah	8,153	559,805	Ad-Diwaniyah	60,553 [1]
Salah ad-Din	24,751	726,138	Samarra	62,008 [2]
As-Sulaymaniyah	17,023	951,723	As-Sulaymaniyah	279,424
Ta'mim	10,282	601,219	Kirkuk	207,852 [2]
Wasit	17,153	564,670	Al-Kut	58,647 [2]

[1] Census 1965.   [2] Estimate 1970.

The Bagdad conurbation had 3·85m. inhabitants in 1987.
There were in 1991 some 3·5m. Kurds. The national language is Arabic.

CLIMATE. The climate is mainly arid, with small and unreliable rainfall and a large annual range of temperature. Summers are very hot and winters cold. al-Basrah. Jan. 55°F (12·8°C), July 92°F (33·3°C). Annual rainfall 7" (175 mm). Baghdad. Jan. 50°F (10°C), July 95°F (35°C). Annual rainfall 6" (140 mm). Mosul. Jan. 44°F (6·7°C), July 90°F (32·2°C). Annual rainfall 15" (384 mm).

CONSTITUTION AND GOVERNMENT. The Provisional Constitution was promulgated on 16 July 1970. The highest state authority is the 8-member Revolutionary Command Council (RCC) but some legislative power has now been given to the 250-member National Assembly, elected in April 1989 for a 4-year term.

The only legal political grouping was the National Progressive Front (founded 1973) comprising the Arab Socialist Renaissance (Ba'ath) Party and various Kurdish groups, but a law of Aug. 1991 legalized political parties provided they are not based on religion, racism or ethnicity.

The President and Vice-President are elected by the RCC; the President appoints and leads a Council of Ministers responsible for administration.

President: Saddam Hussein at-Takriti (assumed office 17 July 1979).

In Nov. 1991 the RCC comprised: President Saddam; Mohamed Hamza El Zoubaidi (*Prime Minister*); Watban Ibrahim Al Hassan (*Interior*); Mazbane Khedr Hadi; Ezzat Ibrahim; Taha Yassin Ramadan; Mohieddin Masarouf; Tarek Aziz (*Deputy Prime Minister*).

Ministers not in the RCC include: *Foreign Affairs*, Ahmed Hussein. *Trade*, Mohamed Mehdi Saleh. *Oil*, Osama Abdul-Razzak Al Hiti. *Information*, Hamad Youssef Hammadi. *Defence*, Gen. Ali Hassan El Majid.

National flag: Three horizontal stripes of red, white, black, with 3 green stars on the white stripe.

Local Government. Iraq is divided into 18 governorates *(liwa),* each administered by an appointed Governor; three of the governorates form a (Kurdish) Autonomous Region, with an elected 57-member Kurdish Legislative Council. Each governorate is divided into *qadhas* (under Qaimaqams) and *nahiyahs* (under Mudirs).

DEFENCE. Reliable data was not available after the losses sustained by the Iraqi forces during their expulsion from Kuwait in Feb. 1991. The figures below reflect strengths at the end of 1990. Peace-time conscription is 21-24 months at age 18.

Army. The Army is organized into 7 armoured/mechanized and 40 infantry divisions including People's Army and Reserve brigades; 6 Republican Guard divisions, 20 special forces and 2 missile brigades. Equipment includes 1,500 T-54/-55/-77, 1,500 Chinese T-59/-69, 1,500 T-62, 1,000 T-72 and 30 Chieftian main battle tanks, and 100 PT-76 light tanks. Strength (1990 estimate) 955,000, including 480,000 active reserves.

Navy. The navy, which played little part in the war with Iran sought unsuccessfully to intervene in the operations to retain Kuwait in 1991. The 11 ships ordered from Italy in 1981, although completed, remain undelivered, and their future is in doubt. The forces in the country at the time of the invasion of Kuwait (1 frigate, 8 missile craft, 6 torpedo boats and numerous inshore craft) amounting to some 90 units, together with the majority of the Kuwait flotilla captured in Aug. 1990, were destroyed in early 1991 during Operation Desert Storm. The sole successes of the Iraqi navy were achieved through a relatively sophisticated mining campaign in the Kuwait approaches.

In 1990 naval personnel totalled 5,000 officers and ratings, but current strength cannot be estimated. The main base at Basra remains unusable, due to mines and obstructions in the Shatt al 'Arab, but that at Umm Qasr could be used by any newly-acquired naval units.

Air Force. The Iraqi Air Force suffered heavy losses during the Gulf War; over 60 aircraft were destroyed by the opposing Allied forces, many more were damaged beyond repair on the ground in Iraq and at least 100 aircraft are impounded in Iran. Reliable data on the status of the service are not available and the following are estimates. The combact aircraft are mostly of Soviet manufacture, although there are French-supplied Mirage F1-E/B fighters, Alouette, Super Frelon and Super Puma helicopters, F-6 and F-7 fighters from China, Bell 214ST helicopters from the USA, Czech-built L-39 light attack/trainer aircraft, and BO 105 and BK-117 helicopters from Germany.

There are about a dozen Tu-16 and Tu-22 bombers, over 150 MiG-21, MiG-23, MiG-25, MiG-29 and F-7 interceptors, at least 150 Mirage F1-EQ, L-39 Albatros, Su-7, Su-22, Su-25 and F-6 fighter-bomber and strike aircraft, and a few MiG-21 and MiG-25 reconnaissance aircraft. The combat helicopter inventory comprises anti-armour Gazelles, Mi-24s and BO 105s, and Super Pumas equipped for anti-shipping duties. Transports include fixed-wing An-12s, An-26s and Il-76s, and Puma, Bell 214ST, BO 105, BK-117, MiL Mi-4, Mi-6, Mi-8/17, AB.212 and AS-61 transport and liaison helicopters. Training aircraft comprise AS.202 Bravo primary trainers, Tucano, PC-7 and PC-9 basic trainers and two-seat models of most combat types.

INTERNATIONAL RELATIONS

Membership. Iraq is a member of the UN, Arab League and the Non-Aligned Movement.

ECONOMY

Budget. Revenue and expenditure for 1989 balanced at I.D. 19,434m.

Oil revenues account for nearly 50%, customs and excise for about 26% of the total revenue.

Currency. The monetary unit is the *Iraqi dinar* (IQD) of 1,000 *fils*. Silver alloy coins for 100 and 50 fils (*dirham*) and 25 fils are in circulation, and other coins for 10, 5 and 1 fils. Notes are for $\frac{1}{4}$, $\frac{1}{2}$ and 1 dinar, and for 5 and 10 dinars. In March 1992, £1 = 0·59 *dinar*; US$1 = 0·34 *dinar*.

Banking. All banks were nationalized on 14 July 1964. The Central Bank of Iraq is the sole bank of issue. In 1941 the Rafidain Bank, financed by the Iraqi Government, was instituted to carry out normal banking transactions. Its head office is in Baghdad and it has 239 branches, 11 abroad, including London. Its assets were US$47,000m. in Sept. 1990. In addition, there are 4 government banks which are authorized to issue loans to companies and individuals: the Industrial Bank, the Agricultural Bank, the Estate Bank, and the Mortgage Bank.

Weights and Measures. The metric system is in general use.

ENERGY AND NATURAL RESOURCES

Electricity. Production in 1986 amounted to 22,560m. kwh. Supply 220 volts; 50 Hz.

Oil. The total crude petroleum production was (1991) 14·88m. tonnes.

Agriculture. In 1990 there were 5·45m. ha of arable land and 4m. ha of permanent cropland. The chief winter crops (1988) are wheat, 1·2m. tonnes and barley, 1·25m. tonnes. The chief summer crop is rice, 250,000 tonnes. The date crop is important (350,000 tonnes), the country furnishing about 80% of the world's trade in dates; the chief producing area is the totally irrigated riverain belt of the Shatt-el-Arab. Wool and cotton are also important exports.

Livestock (1988): Cattle, 1·6m.; buffaloes, 145,000; sheep, 9·2m.; goats, 1·55m.; horses, 55,000; camels, 55,000; chickens, 76m.

Fisheries. Catch (1986) 20,600 tonnes.

INDUSTRY. Iraq is still relatively under-developed industrially but work has begun on new industrial plants.

FOREIGN ECONOMIC RELATIONS

Commerce. Imports and exports for 4 calendar years were (in US$1m.):

	1983	1984	1986	1987
Imports	9,785	11,260	6,360	3,854
Exports	12,275	11,720	…	…

In 1983, crude oil formed 98·6% of all exports, of which 23% to Brazil and 12·5% to Italy. 13·8% of imports came from Federal Republic of Germany and 11% from Kuwait.

Total trade between Iraq and UK (British Department of Trade returns, in £1,000 sterling):

	1987	1988	1989	1990	1991
Imports to UK	33,871	43,406	55,175	101,557	2,548
Exports and re-exports from UK	271,655	412,091	450,495	293,393	4,399

Tourism. About 1,004,000 tourists visited Iraq in 1986.

COMMUNICATIONS

Roads. There were 25,500 km of main roads in 1985. Vehicles registered in 1986 totalled 492,000 passenger cars and 246,000 commercial vehicles.

Railways. Following closure of metre-gauge operations in 1988, Iraqi Republic Railways comprised in 1990 2,032 km of 1,435 mm gauge route. In 1989 it carried 4·3m. passengers and 7·4m. tonnes of freight.

Civil Aviation. Baghdad airport is served by British Airways, Lufthansa, Alitalia, SAS, Swissair, KLM, Middle East Air Lines, PIA, Iraqi Airways, Air Liban, United Arab Airlines and Aeroflot. In 1982 passenger-km were 1,476m. and cargo, 37·5m. tonne-km.

Shipping. The merchant fleet in 1980 comprised 142 vessels (over 100 gross tons) with a total tonnage of 1,465,949. The ports of Basra and Um Qasr have been closed since Sept. 1980.

Telecommunications. Wireless telegraph services exist with UK, USA, UAR, Lebanon and Saudi Arabia, and wireless telephone services with UK, USA, Italy, UAR and USSR. Telephones, 1983, 624,685 (Baghdad, 302,219). In 1986 there were 2·5m. radio and 750,000 television receivers.

Newspapers (1989). In Baghdad there are 4 main daily newspapers (one of which is in English with a circulation of 550,000).

JUSTICE, RELIGION, EDUCATION AND WELFARE

Justice. The courts are established throughout the country as follows: For civil matters: The court of cassation in Baghdad; 6 courts of appeal at Baghdad (2), Basra, Babylon, Mosul and Kirkuk; 18 courts of first instance with unlimited powers and 150 courts of first instance with limited powers, all being courts of single judges. In addition, 6 peace courts have peace court jurisdiction only. 'Revolutionary courts' deal with cases affecting state security.

For *Shara'* (religious) matters: The Shara' courts at all places where there are civil courts, constituted in some places of specially appointed Qadhis (religious judges) and in other places of the judges of the civil courts. For criminal matters: The court of cassation; 6 sessions courts (2 being presided over by the judge of the local court of first instance and 4 being identical with the courts of appeal). Magistrates' courts at all places where there are civil courts, constituted of civil judges exercising magisterial powers of the first and second class. There are also a number of third-class magistrates' courts, powers for this purpose being granted to municipal councils and a number of administrative officials. Some administrative officials are granted the powers of a peace judge to deal with cases of debts due from cultivators.

The death penalty was introduced for serious theft in Jan. 1992.

Religion. The constitution proclaims Islam the state religion, but also stipulates freedom of religious belief and expression. In 1989 there were 10·76m. Shi'ite Moslems and 5·94m. Sunni Moslems. In 1991 there were some 1m. Christians in 14 sects, including: 0·8m. Chaldean Church, with some 100 priests in 9 dioceses; 0·25m. Apostolic Assyrian (Nestorian) Church, with 29 priests in 3 dioceses and 70,000 Syriac Orthodox in 2 dioceses. There were some 10,000 in various Protestant sects.

Education. Primary and secondary education is free and primary education became compulsory in Sept. 1976. Primary school age is 6–12. Secondary education is for 6 years, of which the first 3 are termed intermediate. The medium of instruction is Arabic; Kurdish is used in primary schools in northern districts.

There were, in 1987, 8,210 primary schools with 2,917,474 pupils, and 2,315 secondary schools with 1,012,426 pupils. 245 vocational schools had 133,568 students and 43 teacher-training colleges had 28,164 students.

There were (1987) 6 universities with 110,173 students and 19 other higher educational establishments with 32,322 students.

Health. In 1981 there were 7,634 doctors, and 25,443 hospital beds.

DIPLOMATIC REPRESENTATIVES

On 6 Feb. 1991 Iraq broke off diplomatic relations with Great Britain and the USA.

Of Iraq to the United Nations
Ambassador: Dr Abdul Amir A. Al-Anbari.

Further Reading

Abdulrahman, A. J., *Iraq* [Bibliography]. Oxford and Santa Barbara, 1984
Al-Khalil, S., *Republic of Fear: the Politics of Modern Iraq.* Univ. of California Press, 1989
Axelgrad, F. W., *Iraq in Transition: A Political, Economic and Strategic Perspective.* London, 1986
Baram, A., *Cultural History and Ideology in the Formation of Ba'athist Iraq, 1968–89.* London, 1991
Bulloch, J. and Morris, H., *Saddam's War: the Origins of the Kuwait Conflict and the International Response.* London, 1991
Chubin, S. and Tripp, C., *Iran and Iraq at War.* London, 1988
Farouk-Sluglett, M., and Sluglett, P., *Iraq since 1958: from Revolution to Dictatorship.* London, 1991
Ghareeb, E., *The Kurdish Question in Iraq.* Syracuse Univ. Press, 1981
Postgate, E., *Iraq: International Relations and National Development.* London, 1983

National statistical office: Central Statistical Organization, Ministry of Planning, Baghdad.

IRELAND

Capital: Dublin
Population: 3·52m. (1991)
GNP per capita: US$8,500 (1990)

Éire

HISTORY. In April 1916 an insurrection against British rule took place and a republic was proclaimed. The armed struggle was renewed in 1919 and continued until 1921. The independence of Ireland was reaffirmed in Jan. 1919 by the National Parliament (*Dáil Éireann*), elected in Dec. 1918.

In 1920 an Act was passed by the British Parliament, under which separate Parliaments were set up for 'Southern Ireland' (26 counties) and 'Northern Ireland' (6 counties). The Unionists of the 6 counties accepted this scheme, and a Northern Parliament was duly elected on 24 May 1921. The rest of Ireland, however, ignored the Act.

On 6 Dec. 1921 a treaty was signed between Great Britain and Ireland by which Ireland accepted dominion status subject to the right of Northern Ireland to opt out. This right was exercised, and the border between *Saorstát Éireann* (26 counties) and Northern Ireland (6 counties) was fixed in Dec. 1925 as the outcome of an agreement between Great Britain, the Irish Free State and Northern Ireland. The agreement was ratified by the three parliaments.

Subsequently the constitutional links between *Saorstát Éireann* and the UK were gradually removed by the *Dáil*. The remaining formal association with the British Commonwealth by virtue of the External Relations Act, 1936, was severed when the Republic of Ireland Act, 1948, came into operation on 18 April 1949.

AREA AND POPULATION. The Republic of Ireland lies in the Atlantic ocean, separated from Great Britain by the Irish Sea to the east, and bounded northeast by Northern Ireland.

Counties and county boroughs	Area in ha [1]	Population, 1991 [2] Males	Females	Total
Province of Leinster				
Carlow	89,635	20,786	20,160	40,946
Dublin County Borough	11,499	225,532	252,143	477,675
Dublin-Belgard		102,769	105,897	208,666
Dublin-Fingal	80,657	75,325	77,401	152,726
Dun Laoghaire-Rathdown		88,468	96,894	185,362
Kildare	169,425	62,160	60,356	122,516
Kilkenny	206,167	37,449	36,164	73,613
Laois	171,954	26,910	25,415	52,325
Longford	104,387	15,523	14,770	30,293
Louth	82,334	44,792	45,915	90,707
Meath	233,587	53,510	52,030	105,540
Offaly	199,774	29,876	28,572	58,448
Westmeath	176,290	31,018	30,864	61,882
Wexford	235,143	51,425	50,620	102,045
Wicklow	202,483	48,074	49,219	97,293
Total of Leinster	1,963,335	913,617	946,420	1,860,037
Province of Munster				
Clare	318,784	46,322	44,504	90,826
Cork County Borough	3,731	61,260	65,764	127,024
Cork	742,257	143,080	139,710	282,790
Kerry	470,142	61,792	59,927	121,719
Limerick County Borough	1,904	25,309	26,731	52,040
Limerick	266,676	55,768	54,048	109,816
Tipperary, N. R.	199,622	29,352	28,477	57,829
Tipperary, S. R.	225,836	37,970	36,821	74,791

[1] Exclusive of certain rivers, lakes and tideways.   [2] Preliminary.

Counties and county boroughs	Area in ha [1]	Population, 1991 [1]		Total
		Males	Females	
Province of Munster—contd.				
Waterford County Borough	3,809	19,721	20,624	40,345
Waterford	179,977	25,996	25,267	51,263
Total of Munster	2,412,738	506,570	501,873	1,008,443
Province of Connacht				
Galway County Borough	...	24,282	26,560	50,842
Galway	593,966	66,637	62,825	129,462
Leitrim	152,476	13,190	12,107	25,297
Mayo	539,846	55,963	54,733	110,696
Roscommon	246,276	26,687	25,189	51,876
Sligo	179,608	27,230	27,506	54,736
Total of Connacht	1,712,172	213,989	208,920	422,909
Province of Ulster (part of)				
Cavan	189,060	27,307	25,449	52,756
Donegal	483,058	64,734	63,260	127,994
Monaghan	129,093	26,172	25,090	51,262
Total of Ulster (part of)	801,211	118,213	113,798	232,011
Total	6,889,456	1,752,389	1,771,011	3,523,400

[1] Exclusive of certain rivers, lakes and tideways. [2] Preliminary.

The capital is Dublin (Baile Átha Cliath). Town populations, 1986: Greater Dublin including Dún Laoghaire, 920,956; Cork, 173,694; Limerick, 76,557; Galway, 47,104; Waterford, 41,054.

Vital statistics for 6 calendar years:

	Births	Marriages	Deaths		Births	Marriages	Deaths
1985	62,388	18,791	33,213	1988	54,606	18,382	31,580
1986	61,620	18,573	33,630	1989	51,659	18,174	32,111
1987	58,433	18,309	31,413	1990 [1]	52,952	17,490	31,903

[1] Provisional

In 1989-90, 31,000 people emigrated. Total 1982-90 (estimate) 210,000.

CLIMATE. Influenced by the Gulf Stream, there is an equable climate with mild south-west winds, making temperatures almost uniform over the whole country. The coldest months are Jan. and Feb. (39–45°F, 4–7°C) and the warmest July and Aug. (57–61°F, 14–16°C). May and June are the sunniest months, averaging 5·5 to 6·5 hours each day, but over 7 hours in the extreme S.E. Rainfall is lowest along the eastern coastal strip. The central parts vary between 30–44" (750–1,125 mm), and up to 60" (1,500 mm) may be experienced in low-lying areas in the west. Dublin. Jan. 40°F (4·7°C), July 59°F (15°C). Annual rainfall 30" (750 mm). Cork. Jan. 42°F (5·6°C), July 61°F (16°C). Annual rainfall 41" (1,025 mm).

CONSTITUTION AND GOVERNMENT. Ireland is a sovereign independent, democratic republic. Its parliament exercises jurisdiction in 26 of the 32 counties of Ireland.

The first Constitution of the Irish Free State came into operation on 6 Dec. 1922. Certain provisions which were regarded as contrary to the national sentiments were gradually removed by successive amendments, with the result that at the end of 1936 the text differed considerably from the original document. On 14 June 1937 a new Constitution was approved by Parliament (*Dáil Éireann*) and enacted by a plebiscite on 1 July 1937. This Constitution came into operation on 29 Dec. 1937. Under it the name Ireland (Éire) was restored.

The Constitution provides that, pending the reintegration of the national territory, the laws enacted by the Parliament established by the Constitution shall have the same area and extent of application as those of the Irish Free State.

The head of state is the *President*, whose role is largely ceremonial, but who has the power to refer proposed legislation which might infringe the constitution to the Supreme Court.

The *Oireachtas* or National Parliament consists of a House of Representatives, (*Dáil Éireann*) and a Senate (*Seanad Éireann*). The *Dáil*, consisting of 166 members, is elected by adult suffrage on the Single Transferable Vote system, which involves constituencies of 4 or 5 members. Each elector has the same number of votes as there are seats, and numbers preferences in order. A quota is calculated from the minimum number of votes required to win. When a candidate obtains this quota, further votes are transferred to other candidates according to second and further preferences. Candidates with the least votes are eliminated and their votes redistributed. Of the 60 members of the Senate, 11 are nominated by the *Taoiseach* (Prime Minister), 6 are elected by the universities and the remaining 43 are elected from 5 panels of candidates established on a vocational basis, representing the following public services and interests: (1) national language and culture, literature, art, education and such professional interests as may be defined by law for the purpose of this panel; (2) agricultural and allied interests, and fisheries; (3) labour, whether organized or unorganized; (4) industry and commerce, including banking, finance, accountancy, engineering and architecture; (5) public administration and social services, including voluntary social activities. The electing body is a college of 1,109 members, comprising members of the *Dáil*, Senate, county boroughs and county councils. There are no formal party divisions in the Senate.

A maximum period of 90 days is afforded to the Senate for the consideration or amendment of Bills sent to that House by the *Dáil*, but the Senate has no power to veto legislative proposals.

No amendment of the Constitution can be effected except with the approval of the people given at a referendum.

Irish is the first official language; English is recognized as a second official language. For further details of the Constitution *see* THE STATESMAN'S YEAR-BOOK , 1952, pp. 1123–34.

President: Mary Robinson (b. 1944), elected out of 3 candidates by 817,000 votes to 731,000 on 7 Nov. 1990, inaugurated 3 Dec. 1990.

Former Presidents: Dr Douglas Hyde (1938–45); Seán T. O. Ceallaigh (1945–59; 2 terms); Éamon de Valéra (1959–73; 2 terms); Erskine Childers (1973–74; died in office); Cearbhall Ó Dálaigh (1974–76; resigned). Pádraig Ó hIrighile (Patrick Hillery) (1976–90; 2 terms).

A general election was held in June 1989: Fianna Fáil, 77 (Feb. 1987 election, 81); Fine Gael, 55 (51); Labour Party, 15 (12); Progressive Democrats, 6 (14); Workers' Party, 7 (4); Others 6 (4).

The Government consisted of the following members in March 1992:

Taoiseach (Prime Minister): Albert Reynolds.

Tánaiste (Deputy Prime Minister), Minister for Defence and for the Gaeltacht: John P. Wilson. *Foreign Affairs:* David Andrews. *Finance:* Bertie Ahern. *Agriculture and Food:* Joe Walsh. *Industry and Commerce:* Desmond J. O'Malley. *Labour:* Brian Cowen. *Energy:* Bobby Molloy. *Social Welfare:* Charlie McCreevy. *Justice:* Pádraig Flynn. *Environment:* Michael Smith. *Health:* John O'Connell. *Education:* Séamus Brennan. *Marine:* Michael J. Woods. *Tourism, Transport and Communications:* Máire Geoghegan-Quinn.

There were 15 Ministers of State.
Attorney-General: Harold A. Whelehan.

National flag: Three vertical strips of green, white, orange.
National anthem: The Soldier's Song (words by P. Kearney; music by P. Heaney).

Local Government. The elected local authorities comprise 27 county councils, 5 county borough corporations, 6 borough corporations, 49 urban district councils and 26 Boards of Town Commissioners. All the members of these authorities are elected under a system of proportional representation, normally every 5 years. All residents of an area who have reached the age of 18 are entitled to vote in the local election for their area. Elected members are not paid, but provision is made for the payment of travelling expenses and subsistence allowances.

The range of services for which local authorities are responsible is broken down into 4 main programme groups as follows: Housing, Roads, Environment and General Local Services, and Sanitary Services. Because of the small size of their administrative areas the functions carried out by town commissioners and some of the smaller urban district councils have tended to become increasingly limited, and the more important tasks of local government have tended to become the responsibility of the county councils.

The local authorities have a system of government which combines an elected council and a whole-time manager. The elected members have specific functions reserved to them which include the striking of rates (local tax), the borrowing of money, the adoption of development plans, the making, amending or revoking of bye-laws and the nomination of persons to other bodies. The managers, who are paid officers of their authorities, are responsible for the performance of all functions which are not reserved to the elected members, including the employment of staff, making of contracts, management of local authority property, collection of rates and rents and the day-to-day administration of local authority affairs. The manager for a county council is manager also for every borough corporation, urban district council and board of town commissioners whose functional area is wholly within the county.

At the elections of June 1991, 883 seats were contested. Fianna Fáil won 358 seats with 38% of votes cast. Fine Gael 270 with 26%. Labour 90 with 12%, the Progressive Democrats 37 with 5%, the Workers' Party 24 with 4%, the Greens 14 with 2%, and Sinn Fein 7 with 2%. Independents gained 83 seats.

DEFENCE. Under the direction of the President, and subject to the provisions of the Defence Act, 1954, the military command of the Defence Forces is exercisable by the Government through the Minister for Defence. To aid and counsel the Minister for Defence on all matters in relation to the business of the Department of Defence on which he may consult it, there is a Council of Defence consisting of the Minister of State at the Department of Defence, the Secretary of the Department of Defence, the Chief of Staff, the Adjutant-General and the Quartermaster-General. At present the Permanent Defence Force strength is approximately 13,000 all ranks including the Air Corps and the Naval Service. The Reserve Defence Force strength is approximately 16,400 all ranks. Recruitment is on a voluntary basis. The minimum terms of enlistment are 3 years in the Permanent Defence Force and 6 years in the Reserve. There is no conscription.

United Nations Contingent. Defence Forces personnel are currently (1992) serving in other overseas missions as follows: Middle East (UNTSO), 20 of whom 3 are currently detached for duty in Yugoslavia; El Salvador (ONUSAL), 3; Cyprus (UNFICYP), 8; Kuwait (UNIKOM), 8; Angola (UNAVEM), 15; Cambodia (UNAMIC), 2; Western Sahara (MINURSO), 6; Afghanistan/Pakistan (OSGAP), 1; CSCE Vienna, 1; Yugoslavia, 2 + 3 ex UNTSO.

Army. The Army has 4 infantry brigades and an infantry force of 2 battalions. 3 of the brigades have 2 infantry battalions and 1 brigade has 3 infantry battalions. Each brigade has a field artillery regiment and a squadron/company size unit for each of the support corps. Equipment includes 14 Scorpion light tanks. The current (1991) strength of the Army is 11,200 all ranks.

Navy. The Naval Service comprises 6 offshore patrol vessels and 1 helicopter patrol vessel. The Air Corps operates 2 Dauphin helicopters for use from the helicopter patrol vessel and 3 maritime reconnaissance aircraft. The Naval Base is at Haulbowline Island, in Cork. The 1991 strength of the Naval Service was 1,000.

Air Corps. The Air Corps has a current (end 1991) strength of 900 all ranks. It has a total of 41 aircraft, comprised of 6 Fouga Magister armed jet trainers, 8 SF 260W armed piston-engined trainers, 8 Rheims-Cessna Rockets, 8 Alouette III, 5 Dauphin and 2 Gazelle helicopters, 1 Casa CN-235 for sea fisheries patrol, 1 British Aerospace HS-125/700, 1 Beech Super Kingair and 1 Gulfstream IV transports.

INTERNATIONAL RELATIONS

Membership. Ireland is a member of the UN, OECD, the Council of Europe and the EC.

ECONOMY

Budget. Current revenue and expenditure (in IR£1m.):

Current revenue	1990	1991
Customs duties	147	120
Excise duties	1,684	1,722
Capital taxes	64	103
Stamp duties	286	250
Income tax	2,920	3,231
Income levy	–	–
Corporation tax	338	593
Value-added tax	2,015	2,010
Agricultural levies (EC)	13	10
Motor vehicle duties	149	184
Employment and training levy	124	134
Non-Tax Revenue	390	419
Total	8,130	8,776

Current expenditure		
Debt service	2,310	2,353
Industry and Labour	224	248
Agriculture	356	490
Fisheries, Forestry, Tourism	54	57
Health	1,312	1,530
Education	1,303	1,419
Social Welfare	2,793	3,192
Less: Receipts, e.g. social security	(–)1,837	(–)2,233
Total (including other items)	6,479	7,056

Capital expenditure amounted to IR£684m. in 1990, and IR£1,750m. in 1991.

On 31 Dec. 1990 the National Debt amounted to IR£25,116·6m. of which IR£16,255m. was denominated in Irish pounds and IR£8,862m. in foreign currencies and the official external reserves of the Central Bank of Ireland amounted to IR£2,892m.

Currency. The unit of currency is the *Irish pound* (IEP) or *punt Éireannach* of 100 *pence*. From 10 Sept. 1928 when the first Irish legal-tender notes were issued, the Irish currency was linked to Sterling on a one-for-one basis. This relationship was discontinued on 30 March 1979 when, following Ireland's adherence to the European Monetary System, it became inconsistent with Ireland's obligations under that system.

The Central Bank has the sole right of issuing legal tender notes; token coinage is issued by the Minister for Finance through the Bank. In March 1992, £1 = IR£1·08; US$1 = IR£0·61.

The volume of legal-tender notes outstanding in Sept. 1991 was IR£1,282m.

Banking and Finance. The Central Bank, which was established as from 1 Feb. 1943, in accordance with the Central Bank Act, 1942, replaced the Currency Commission, which was set up under the Currency Act, 1927, and had been responsible *inter alia* for the regulation of the note issue. In addition to the powers and functions of the Currency Commission the Central Bank has the power of receiving deposits from banks and public authorities, of rediscounting Exchequer bills and bills of exchange, of making advances to banks against such bills or against Government securities, of fixing and publishing rates of interest for rediscounting bills, or buying and selling certain Government securities and securities of any international bank or financial institution formed wholly or mainly by governments. The Bank also collects and publishes information relating to monetary and credit matters. The Central Bank Acts, 1971 and 1989, give further powers to the Central Bank in the regulation of banking including licensing of banks, the supervision of their operations and control of liquidity and reserve ratios. The capital of the Bank is IR£40,000, of which IR£24,000 has been paid up and is held by the Minister for Finance.

The Board of Directors of the Central Bank consists of a Governor, appointed by the President on the advice of the Government, and 9 directors, all appointed by the Minister for Finance.

The principal independent commercial banks are Allied Irish Banks PLC., Bank of Ireland and two smaller banks, Ulster Bank and National Irish Bank. They operate the branch banking system; on 30 Sept. 1991 their total deposit and current accounts within Ireland amounted to IR£9,069·9m. and their total gross assets in Ireland, IR£18,635·4m.

There are also 32 Non-Associated Banks of which 24 are merchant and commercial banks and 8 are industrial banks whose main activity is instalment credit. Four of the merchant or commercial banks are subsidiaries of the Associated Banks; 11 are from other EC countries and 7 from outside the EC (mainly US) and the remainder are Irish. On 30 Sept. 1991 their current and deposit accounts and interbank borrowings amounted to IR£14,986·2m. (42% of total bank resources) and their lending to IR£16,037m. (68% of lending to residents); total gross assets in Ireland, IR£16,259·5m.

There are two state-owned credit corporations, one industrial and one agricultural, and 8 building societies. There are 2 Trustee Savings Banks and the Post Office Savings Bank which together had deposits of IR£1,301m. on 31 Dec. 1990.

The Dublin stock exchange, affiliated to the London exchange since 1973, came under the regulation of the Bank of Ireland in 1991. Operational links were unchanged.

Weights and Measures. Conversion to the metric system is in progress; with some exceptions which are confined to the domestic market, all imperial units of measurement will cease to be legal, for general use, after 31 Dec. 1994.

ENERGY AND NATURAL RESOURCES

Electricity. The total generating capacity was (1990) 3,932 mw. In 1990 the total sales of electricity amounted to 11,678m. units supplied to 1,278,870 customers. Electricity generated by fuel source 1990: Coal, 42%; oil, 10%; gas, 27%; peat, 16%; hydro, 5%. Supply 220 volts; 50 Hz.

Oil. About 618,000 sq. km of the Irish continental shelf has been designated an exploration area for oil and gas; at the furthest point the limit of jurisdiction is 520 nautical miles from the coast. Since 1970, 111 exploratory offshore wells have been drilled. A number of encouraging oil and gas flows have been recorded. In 1991, 51 blocks were held under exclusive offshore exploration licences and offshore petroleum leases.

Gas. (1991) All of Ireland's natural gas requirements are met by the Kinsale Head gas field 50 km off the south coast. In March 1989 additional natural gas was discovered about 10 miles north-west of this field at Ballycotton, a field of modest proportions which went into production in July 1991. Existing gas reserves should be depleted in approximately 15 years. Gas Transmission is controlled by the Irish Gas Board (BGE), which sells the gas into electricity generation, fertilizer production, and distribution systems for domestic, commercial and industrial use.

Peat. The country has very little indigenous coal, but possesses large reserves of peat, the development of which is handled largely by Bord na Mona (Peat Board). To date, the Board has acquired over 200,000 acres of bog and has 15 locations around the country. In the year ending 31 March, 1990, the Board sold 148,000 tonnes of sod peat to the domestic market and 63,000 tonnes for use in 7 sod peat electricity generating stations. The Board also sold 3,182,403 tonnes of milled peat for use in 7 milled peat generating stations. A further 946,000 tonnes was used by the Board in its factories to produce 355,000 tonnes of briquettes for sale to the domestic heating market. The Board also sold 1·2m. cu. metres of horticultural peat.

Minerals. Lead and zinc concentrates are important. In 1991, 2 discoveries increased reserves by 2·5m. tonnes of zinc and 0·3m. tonnes of lead. Metal content of production, 1991: Zinc, 187,500 tonnes; lead, 39,900 tonnes. Barytes, gypsum, limestone and aggregates are also important, and there is some slate coal, silver, dolomite and silica sand. Exploration activity is centred on base metals, precious metals, industrial minerals and coal and about 50 companies are prospecting.

Agriculture. Although in 1991 13·8% of the employed workforce made a living from agriculture, population is tending to migrate from rural areas, and in 1990 50% of farmers were over 50 years old. General distribution of surface (in ha) in 1990: Crops and pasture, 4,682,500; other land, including grazed mountain, 2,206,700; total, 6,889,200.

Estimated area (ha) under certain crops calculated from sample returns:

			Area		
Crops	*1986*	*1987*	*1988*	*1989*	*1990*
Wheat	76,100	56,900	60,400	62,300	72,100
Oats	20,900	20,400	19,600	19,100	18,300
Barley	282,800	276,000	266,100	263,400	236,900
Potatoes	30,500	30,300	28,100	25,900	25,400
Sugar-beet	37,000	37,100	33,300	32,100	32,300

Gross agricultural output (including value of changes in stocks) for the year 1990 was valued at £3,215·9m.

Livestock (1990): Cattle, 6,996,600; sheep, 8·69m.; pigs, 1,047,200; horses and ponies, 53,500; poultry, 8,933,400.

Forestry. The total area under forest at 31 Dec. 1989 was some 0·42m. ha, of which 83% was owned by the Coillte Teoranta (state forestry company) and 17% privately-owned. Timber production, 1990, 1·6m. cu. metres.

Fisheries. In 1989 approximately 13,500 people were engaged full- or part-time in the sea fishing industry; 5,850 full-time and 6,250 part-time in the fish catching, farming and processing industries. The number of vessels engaged in fishing in 1990 was 3,900, of which 1,100 accounted for the greater part of the fishing effort. The quantities and values of fish landed during 1988 were: Demersal fish, 44,450 tonnes, value IR£44,445,000; pelagic fish, 159,023 tonnes; shellfish, 22,783 tonnes. Total quantity: 226,256 tonnes; total value, IR£83,932,000.

INDUSTRY. The census of industrial production for 1987 gives the following details of the values (in IR£1m.) of gross and net output for the principal manufacturing industries. The figures for net output are those of gross output minus cost of materials, including fuel, light and power, repairs to plant and machinery and amounts paid to others in connexion with products made.

	Gross output	*Net output*
Slaughtering, preparing and preserving meat	1,658·9	231·7
Manufacture of dairy products	1,677·6	292·7
Bread, biscuit and flour confectionery	214·8	100·4
Cocoa, chocolate and sugar confectionery	240·4	72·9
Animal and poultry foods	410·7	76·7
Brewing and malting	277·4	187·0
Spirit distilling and compounding	147·3	77·4
Paper and paper products	213·9	82·7
Printing and publishing	387·2	246·9
Manufacture of metal articles	482·4	214·0
Manufacture of non-metallic mineral products	487·4	207·3
Chemicals, including manmade fibres	1,647·9	902·0
Mechanical engineering	403·9	198·7

	Gross output	Net output
Office machinery and data-processing machinery	1,772·6	826·3
Electrical engineering	1,206·1	666·1
Manufacture and assembly of motor vehicles, parts and accessories	102·6	47·6
Manufacture of other means of transport	159·5	80·8
Instrument engineering	423·2	251·7
Textiles	443·1	180·7
Manufacture of footwear and clothing	302·9	141·7
Timber and wooden furniture	278·2	116·2
Processing rubber and plastics	417·7	195·7
Mineral oil refining	193·1	28·1
Gas, water and electricity	949·5	639·2
All other industries	2,130·3	1,285·7
Total (all industries)	16,628·6	7,350·2

Labour. The total labour force at mid-April 1990 was about 1,305,000, of which about 179,000 persons were out of work. Of the estimated 1·13m. persons at work, 167,000 were in the agricultural sector, 320,000 in industry and 639,000 in services.

Trade Unions. The number of trade unions in Dec. 1989 was 69; total membership, 487,000. About 229,000 were organized in 3 general unions catering both for white collar and manual workers. There were 16 employers' associations holding negotiation licences, with membership of 11,200.

FOREIGN ECONOMIC RELATIONS

Commerce. Value of imports and exports of merchandise for calendar years (in IR£1,000):

	1987	1988	1989	1990
Imports	9,155,207	10,214,758	12,284,266	12,479,471
Exports	10,723,498	12,304,848	14,597,041	14,342,997

The values of the chief imports and total exports are shown in the following table (in IR£1,000):

	Imports		Exports	
	1989	1990	1989	1990
Live animals and food	1,153,753	1,121,191	3,208,932	2,859,705
Raw materials	392,392	379,121	642,155	528,066
Mineral fuels and lubricants	674,307	802,279	68,656	90,635
Chemicals	1,524,711	1,554,140	2,084,873	2,274,398
Manufactured goods	1,847,176	1,925,738	1,148,755	1,152,172
Machinery and transport				
equipment	4,646,668	4,482,008	4,652,454	4,488,051
Manufactured articles	1,552,767	1,703,360	1,965,691	2,039,593

Exports, in IR£1m., for 1990 (and 1989): UK, 4,834 (4,896); Federal Republic of Germany, 1,679 (1,610); France, 1,510 (1,455); USA, 1,175 (1,153); Netherlands, 831 (1,031); Belgium and Luxembourg, 631 (661); Italy, 634 (647); Japan, 264 (317); Spain, 308 (287); Sweden, 276 (269); Switzerland, 243 (218); Norway, 116 (163); Denmark, 149 (132). Imports: UK, 5,266 (5,028); USA, 1,815 (1,973); Federal Republic of Germany, 1,041 (1,075); Japan, 700 (719); Netherlands, 515 (509); France, 570 (503); Italy, 319 (324); Belgium and Luxembourg, 269 (267); Sweden, 190 (199); Spain, 143 (151); Denmark, 113 (114); Norway, 103 (47).

Total trade between Ireland and UK (British Department of Trade returns, in £1,000 sterling):

	1987	1988	1989	1990	1991
Imports to UK	3,488,406	3,876,630	4,279,202	4,498,571	4,416,151
Exports and re-exports from UK	3,831,737	4,057,046	4,714,780	5,311,539	5,295,949

Tourism. Total number of overseas tourists in 1990 was 3,069,000. These, together with cross-border visitors, spent IR£1,139m.

COMMUNICATIONS

Roads. At 31 Dec. 1991 there were 92,303 km of public roads, consisting of 32 km of motorway, 2,630 km of national primary roads, 2,625 km of national secondary roads, 10,566 km of regional roads, 73,975 km of county roads and 2,499 km of urban roads.

Number of licensed motor vehicles at 30 Sept. 1990: Private cars, 796,408; public-service vehicles, 9,024; goods vehicles, 143,166; agricultural vehicles, 70,011; motor cycles, 22,744; other vehicles, 12,906.

The total number of km run by road motor passenger vehicles of the omnibus type during 1989 was 94·85m. Passengers carried numbered 220,609,000 and the gross receipts from passengers were IR£125,827,000.

Railways. The total length of railway open for traffic at 31 Dec. 1989 was 1,944 km (38 km electrified), all 1,600 mm gauge.

Railway statistics for years ending 31 Dec.	1989	1990
Passengers (journeys)	24,595,000	25,010,000
Km run by coaching trains	9,534,000	9,869,000
Freight (tonne-km)	555,940,000	588,550,000
Km run by freight trains	4,136,000	4,369,000
Receipts (IR£)	133,464,000	133,255,000
Expenditure (IR£)	124,888,000	130,174,000

Civil Aviation. The state-owned Aer Lingus Group comprises Aer Lingus plc, incorporated in 1936, which operates services within Ireland and between Ireland and Britain and Europe, and Aerlinte Eireann plc, incorporated in 1947, which operates services to the USA. Although separate legal entities, the two companies share a common management and board of directors and their services are integrated under the marketing name of Aer Lingus as the national airline. During the year ended 31 March 1991 Aer Lingus carried 3,775,096 passengers and 29,567 tonnes of cargo/mail on its European services and 472,817 passengers and 21,226 tonnes of cargo/mail on its trans-Atlantic services.

In addition to Aer Lingus, there were in 1991 10 independent air transport operators, the largest of which, Ryanair, operated air services on a number of international routes (Ireland/UK, Ireland/Germany).

The principal airports are at Dublin, Shannon and Cork.

Shipping. The Irish merchant fleet, of vessels of 100 gross tonnes or over, consisted of 67 vessels totalling 125,359 GRT at 30 June 1990. Total cargo traffic passing through the country's ports amounted to 24·9m. tonnes in 1990.

Inland Waterways. The principal inland waterways open to navigation are the Shannon Navigation (208 km) and the Grand Canal and Barrow Navigation (249 km). The Office of Public Works is responsible for the waterways system as a public amenity. Merchandise traffic has now ceased and navigation is confined to pleasure craft operated either privately or commercially.

Telecommunications. Telecommunication services are provided by Telecom Eireann, a statutory body set up under the Postal and Telecommunications Services Act, 1983. Number of working lines (March 1991), 983,000; telex lines, 3,735; data lines, over 10,660; Eirpac (public packet-switched network), 2,463 customers; Eircell (mobile telephone network), 25,000 customers; Eirpage (radio paging network), 6,814 customers.

Postal services are provided by An Post, a statutory body established under the Postal and Telecommunications Services Act, 1983. Number of Post Offices as of Dec. 1990, 2,075. Delivery points, 1·17m. Number of items delivered during year ended 31 Dec. 1990, 482m. An Post also offers a range of services throughout its Post Office network including National Savings Services and payment of Social Welfare Benefits/Pensions on an agency basis for the State.

Public service broadcasting is provided by Radio Telefis Eireann, a statutory body established under the Broadcasting Authority Acts 1960–79 to provide the national TV and radio services. RTE is financed by advertising and by TV licences. On 31 Dec. 1991 there were 829,244 current TV licences. Legislation enacted in 1988 provided for the establishment of the Independent Radio and Television Commission to arrange provision of independent commercial radio services and an independent TV service. There are (1992) 22 radio stations in operation. The awarding of the contract for the TV service is under consideration by the Commission.

Cinemas. There were (1986) 124 cinemas and 169 (estimate) screens.

Newspapers (1986). There are 7 daily newspapers (all in English) with a combined circulation of 647,912; 5 of them are published in Dublin (circulation, 555,282).

JUSTICE, RELIGION, EDUCATION AND WELFARE

Justice. The Constitution provides that justice shall be administered in public in Courts established by law by Judges appointed by the President on the advice of the Government. The jurisdiction and organization of the Courts are dealt with in the Courts (Establishment and Constitution) Act, 1961 and the Courts (Supplemental Provisions) Acts, 1961–88. These Courts consist of Courts of First Instance and a Court of Final Appeal, called the Supreme Court. The Courts of First Instance are the High Court with full original jurisdiction and the Circuit and the District Courts with local and limited jurisdiction. A judge may not be removed from office except for stated misbehaviour or incapacity and then only on resolutions passed by both Houses of the *Oireachtas*. Judges of the Supreme, High and Circuit Courts are appointed from among practising barristers. Judges of the District Court may be appointed from among practising barristers or practising solicitors.

The Supreme Court, which consists of the Chief Justice (who is *ex officio* an additional judge of the High Court) and 4 ordinary judges, has appellate jurisdiction from all decisions of the High Court. The President may, after consultation with the Council of State, refer a Bill, which has been passed by both Houses of the *Oireachtas* (other than a money bill and certain other bills), to the Supreme Court for a decision on the question as to whether such Bill or any provision thereof is repugnant to the Constitution.

The High Court, which consists of a President (who is *ex officio* an additional Judge of the Supreme Court) and 17 ordinary judges, has full original jurisdiction in and power to determine all matters and questions, whether of law or fact, civil or criminal. In all cases in which questions arise concerning the validity of any law having regard to the provisions of the Constitution, the High Court alone exercises original jurisdiction. The High Court on Circuit acts as an appeal court from the Circuit Court.

The Court of Criminal Appeal consists of the Chief Justice or an ordinary Judge of the Supreme Court, together with either 2 ordinary judges of the High Court or the President and one ordinary judge of the High Court. It deals with appeals by persons convicted on indictment where the appellant obtains a certificate from the trial judge that the case is a fit one for appeal, or, in case such certificate is refused, where the court itself, on appeal from such refusal, grants leave to appeal. The decision of the Court of Criminal Appeal is final, unless that court, the Attorney-General or the Director of Public Prosecutions certifies that the decision involves a point of law of exceptional public importance, in which case an appeal is taken to the Supreme Court.

The Offences against the State Act, 1939 provides in Part V for the establishment of Special Criminal Courts. A Special Criminal Court sits without a jury. The rules of evidence that apply in proceedings before a Special Criminal Court are the same as those applicable in trials in the Central Criminal Court. A Special Criminal Court is authorised by the 1939 Act to make rules governing its own practice and procedure. An appeal against conviction or sentence by a Special Criminal Court may be taken to the Court of Criminal Appeal. On 30 May 1972 Orders were made establishing a Special Criminal Court and declaring that offences of a particular class or kind (as set out) were to be scheduled offences for the purposes of Part V of the Act, the effect of which was to give the Special Criminal Court jurisdiction to try persons charged with those offences.

The High Court exercising criminal jurisdiction is known as the Central Criminal Court. It consists of a judge or judges of the High Court, nominated by the President of the High Court. The Court sits in Dublin and tries criminal cases which are outside the jurisdiction of the Circuit Court.

The country is divided into a number of circuits for the purposes of the Circuit Court. The President of the Circuit Court is *ex officio* an additional judge of the

High Court. The jurisdiction of the court in civil proceedings is limited to IR£30,000 in contract and tort, IR£30,000 in actions founded on hire-purchase and credit-sale agreements, IR£15,000 in equity and IR£15,000 in probate and administration, save by consent of the parties, in which event the jurisdiction is unlimited. In criminal matters it has jurisdiction in all cases except murder, treason, piracy and allied offences. The Circuit Court acts as an appeal court from the District Court.

The District Court has summary jurisdiction in a large number of criminal cases where the offence is not of a serious nature. In civil matters the Court has jurisdiction in contract and tort (except slander, libel, seduction, slander of title and false imprisonment) where the claim does not exceed IR£5,000; in proceedings founded on hire-purchase and credit-sale agreements, the jurisdiction is IR£5,000.

All criminal cases, except those of a minor nature, and those tried in the Special Criminal Court, are tried by a judge and a jury of 12. A majority vote of the jury (10 must agree) is necessary to determine a verdict.

Religion. According to the census of population taken in 1981 the principal religious professions were as follows:

	Leinster	Munster	Connacht	Ulster (part of)	Total
Roman Catholics	1,645,489	949,938	406,811	202,238	3,204,476
Church of Ireland (Anglican)	58,356	18,076	5,973	12,961	95,366
Presbyterians	4,337	542	345	9,031	14,255
Methodists	3,339	1,285	324	842	5,790
Other religious denominations	9,148	2,586	753	483	12,970
Not stated or no religion	69,852	25,888	10,204	4,604	110,548

Cahal Daly (b. 1917) is the Roman Catholic Cardinal of Armagh and Primate of All Ireland.

In May 1990 the General Synod of the Church of Ireland voted to ordain women.

Education. *Elementary.* Elementary education is free and was given in about 3,352 national schools (including 117 special schools) in 1990–91. The total number of pupils on rolls in 1990–91 was 543,724, including pupils in special schools and classes; the number of teachers of all classes was about 20,430 in 1990–91, including remedial teachers and teachers of special classes. The net state expenditure on elementary education for 1991 was IR£500,046,000, excluding the cost of administration.

Special. Special provision is made for handicapped and deprived children in special schools which are recognized on the same basis as primary schools, in special classes attached to ordinary schools and in certain voluntary centres where educational services appropriate to the needs of the children are provided. Categories of children include visually handicapped, hearing impaired, physically handicapped, mentally handicapped, emotionally disturbed, travelling children and other socially disadvantaged children. Provision is also made, on an increasing scale, for children with dual or multiple handicaps. In each case a programme suited to the needs of a particular handicap is provided. Each class is very much smaller than ordinary classes in a primary school and, because of the size of the catchment areas involved, an extensive system of school transport has been developed. Many handicapped children who have spent some years in a special school or class are integrated into normal schools for part of their school career, if necessary with special additional facilities such as nursing services, special equipment, etc. For others who cannot progress within the ordinary school system the special schools or classes provide both the primary and post-primary level of education. There are also part-time teaching facilities in hospitals, child guidance clinics, rehabilitation workshops, special 'Saturday-morning' centres and home teaching schemes.

Special schools (1990–91) numbered 117 with approximately 8,269 pupils. There were also some 3,235 pupils enrolled in about 291 special classes, and 797 remedial teachers were employed for backward pupils in ordinary national schools. 30 peripatetic teachers were employed for children with hearing or visual impairments, and for travelling children.

Secondary. Voluntary secondary schools are under private control and are conducted in most cases by religious orders. These schools receive grants from the State and are open to inspection by the Department of Education. The number of recognized secondary schools during the school year 1990–91 was 476, and the number of pupils in attendance was 212,903.

Vocational Education Committee schools provide courses of general and technical education. The number of vocational schools during the school year 1990–91 was 248, and the number of full-time students in attendance was 86,495. These schools are controlled by the local Vocational Education Committees; they are financed mainly by state grants and also by contributions from local rating authorities and VEC receipts.

Comprehensive. Comprehensive schools which are financed by the State combine academic and technical subjects in one broad curriculum so that each pupil may be offered educational options suited to his needs, abilities and interests available to him. Pupils are prepared for State examinations and for entrance to universities and institutes of further education. The number of comprehensive schools during the school year 1990–91 was 16 and the number of students in attendance was 8,861.

Community. Community schools continue to be established through the amalgamation of existing voluntary secondary and Vocational Education Committee schools, where this is found feasible and desirable, and in new areas where a single larger school is considered preferable to 2 smaller schools under separate managements. These schools provide second-level education and also provide adult education facilities for their own areas. They also make facilities available to voluntary organizations and to the adult community generally. The number of community schools during the school year 1990–91 was 52 and the number of students in attendance was 34,080.

The net State expenditure for post-primary education for 1991 was IR£482,361,000.

Education Third-Level. University education is provided by the National University of Ireland, founded in Dublin in 1908, by the University of Dublin (Trinity College), founded in 1592, and by the Dublin City University and the University of Limerick established in 1989. The National University comprises 3 constituent colleges–University College, Dublin, University College, Cork, and University College, Galway.

St Patrick's College, Maynooth, Co. Kildare, is a national seminary for Catholic priests and a pontifical university with the power to confer degrees up to doctoral level in philosophy, theology and canon law. It also admits lay students (men and women) to the courses in arts, science and education which it provides as a recognized college of the National University.

Besides the University medical schools, the Royal College of Surgeons in Ireland (a long-established independent medical school) provides medical qualifications which are internationally recognized. Courses to degree level are available at the National College of Art and Design, Dublin.

Regional Technical Colleges in 9 centres (Athlone, Carlow, Cork, Dundalk, Galway, Letterkenny, Sligo, Tralee and Waterford) provide vocational education and training for trade and industry from craft to professional level, operating under the aegis of the Vocational Education Committees (VECs) for their areas. Six colleges in Dublin provide degree and diploma level courses in engineering, architecture, business studies, catering, music, etc., operating under the aegis of the City of Dublin VEC. A College of Art, Commerce and Technology in Limerick and a School of Art and a School of Music in Cork operate under the aegis respectively of the cities of Limerick and Cork VECs. Total full-time enrolments in 1990–91 were approximately 27,300.

There are 5 Colleges of Education for training primary school teachers. For degree awarding purposes, 3 of these colleges are associated with Trinity College and 2 with The National University of Ireland. Thomond College of Education, Limerick, trains post-primary teachers in the areas of physical education, metalwork and engineering technology, wood building and technology and commercial and secretarial subjects. There are also 2 Home Economics Colleges for teacher training, one associated with Trinity College and the other with University College, Galway.

The total full-time enrolment at third-level for 1990–91 was approximately 70,100 and net State expenditure on third-level education for 1991 was IR£205,874,000. The National Council for Educational Awards, established on a statutory basis in 1979, is the validating and awarding authority for courses in the third-level sector outside the universities.

Agricultural. Teagasc – the Agriculture and Food Development Authority is the agency responsible for providing agricultural advisory, training, research and development services. Full-time instruction in agriculture is provided for all sections of the farming community. There are 4 agricultural colleges for young people, administered by Teagasc, and 7 private Teagasc-aided agricultural colleges, at each of which a 1-year course in agriculture is given. A second-year course in farm machinery is provided at one college. Scholarships tenable at these colleges, all of which are residential, are awarded by Teagasc which also provides a comprehensive agricultural advisory service and operates an intensive programme of short courses for adult farmers in agriculture and horticulture at local centres.

Horticultural. Two of the agricultural colleges mentioned above also provide a commercial horticultural course. A third college aided by Teagasc also provides this course. A 3-year course in amenity horticulture is provided at the National Botanic Gardens in Dublin.

A comprehensive 3-year training programme for young entrants to farming leading to a 'Certificate in Farming', the main training programme for young people entering farming, involving both formal instruction and a period of supervised on-farm work experience, was introduced by ACOT in 1982. Students taking the Certificate in Farming can follow a course in general agriculture, pigs, poultry or horticulture. In the case of horticulture, the major part of this course is taken at one of the three horticultural colleges.

Health Services. There are 3 categories of entitlement, based on a person's income:
(i) Persons on a low income and their dependants, who qualify for the full range of health services, free of charge, i.e. family doctor, drugs and medicines, hospital and specialist services as well as dental, aural and optical services. Maternity care and infant welfare services are also provided. There is no fixed limit, but guidelines laid down by health boards, determine eligibility – each application is considered on its merit. There is provision for hardship cases.
(ii) Persons whose income for the year ended 5 April 1990 was under IR£16,700. They and their dependants are entitled to hospital services, subject to certain charges, both as an in-patient and an out-patient, a full maternity and infant welfare service and assistance towards the cost of prescriptions. The latter limits the nett outlay on medicines used in a calendar month to IR£28.
(iii) Persons whose income for the year ended 5 April 1990 was IR£16,700 or more. They are entitled to in-patient and out-patient hospital services, subject to certain charges, but they are liable for the fees of consultants. They are also entitled to assistance towards the cost of prescriptions. Drugs and medicines are made available free of charge to all persons suffering from specified long-term ailments such as diabetes, multiple sclerosis, epilepsy, etc. Hospital in-patient and out-patient services are free of charge to all children under 16 years of age, suffering from specified long-term conditions such as cystic fibrosis, spina bifida, cerebral palsy, etc. Immunization and diagnostic services as well as hospital services are free of charge to everyone suffering from an infectious disease. A maintenance allowance is also payable in necessitous cases.

From 18 May 1987 persons in categories *(ii)* and *(iii)* are liable for in-patient and out-patient charge. A charge of IR£10 is made for each day or part of a day during which in-patient services are availed of subject to a maximum payment of IR£100 in any period of 12 consecutive months. A charge of IR£10 for out-patient services is made for the first and subsequent instances relating to the same matter. Persons in category *(i)*, women receiving service in respect of motherhood, children suffering from certain diseases etc. are not liable for these charges.

Services for Children: Health Boards are involved, with the co-operation of a wide network of voluntary organizations, in the provision of a range of child care services including adoption, fostering, residential care, day care and social work services for families in need of support.

Welfare Services: There are various services provided for the elderly, the chronic sick, the disabled and families in stress, such as social support service, day care services for children, home helps, home nursing, meals-on-wheels, day centres, cheap fuel, etc. Health Boards also provide disabled persons, without charge, with training for employment and place them in jobs.

Grants and Allowances: Disabled Persons' Maintenance Allowance is payable to the chronically disabled over the age of 16 who are not in long term care. Recipients are entitled to free travel and subject to certain conditions to electricity allowance, free TV licence, telephone rental and fuel vouchers. Mobility allowance is payable to severely disabled persons between 16 and 66 years who are unable to walk. Allowance for the Domiciliary Care of Severely Handicapped Children is payable to the mother of a severely handicapped child, maintained at home, but needing constant care and supervision. Blind welfare allowance: This allowance is in addition to the benefits for the blind operated by the Department of Social Welfare. Grants up to IR£1,500 are paid, subject to a means test, to disabled persons towards the purchase of a car, in order that they might obtain or retain employment.

Health contributions: A health contribution of 1·25% of income up to a ceiling of IR£16,700 is payable by all.

Social Welfare Services. The Department of Social Welfare provides a range of payments and benefits in kind. The payments can be divided into two categories, social insurance and social assistance. The Department also administers a scheme of grants for voluntary organizations working in the social services area.

Social Insurance Payments. Payments under social insurance are funded by employers, their employees and the self-employed. Any deficit in the fund is met by Exchequer subvention. Employees and self-employed people between the ages of 16 and 66 are liable for pay-related social insurance contributions. The majority of employees must pay a contribution which gives cover for the full range of social insurance benefits while self-employed people must pay a contribution which gives cover for widows and orphans pensions and old age contributory pension. Entitlement to social insurance benefits depends on the claimant having a number of contributions paid or credited in a specific time period. The contribution conditions vary according to the different schemes. The social insurance schemes are: Old Age Contributory Pension; Widow's Contributory Pension; Orphan's Contributory Allowance; Disability Benefit; Pay-related Benefit, Dental and Optical Benefit; Retirement Pension; Deserted Wife's Benefit; Invalidity Pension, Unemployment Benefit; Maternity Benefits; Death Grant. There is also a scheme of occupational injuries benefits which is not strictly a social insurance scheme as there are no contribution conditions for entitlement. Expenditure on this scheme is paid from a fund which is financed by employers' contributions and income from investments.

Social Assistance Payments. Social assistance schemes are financed entirely by the Exchequer. One of the basic qualifying conditions for payment is that the applicant satisfies a means test. The social assistance payments are: Old Age Non-Contributory Pension; Blind Person's Pension; Lone Parent's Allowance; Widow's Non-Contributory Pension [1]; Deserted Wife's Allowance [1]; Prisoner's Wife's Allowance [1]; Unemployment Assistance; Supplementary Welfare Allowance; Orphan's Non-Contributory Pension; Single Woman's Allowance [2]; Rent Allowance; Family Income Supplement; Carer's Allowance. Child benefit is payable without a means test in respect of each child under age 16 and children between 16 and 18 who are at school or incapacitated for a prolonged period. it is funded from the Exchequer.

Other Schemes. The Department also provides a range of benefits in kind, princi-

[1] For certain women who do not qualify for the lone parent's allowance.
[2] For women between ages 58 and 66.

pally for the elderly and disabled. These are: Free travel; free electricity allowance; free gas allowance; free telephone rental; free TV licence; fuel allowance.

DIPLOMATIC REPRESENTATIVES

Of Ireland in Great Britain (17 Grosvenor Pl., London, SW1X 7HR)
Ambassador: Joseph Small.

Of Great Britain in Ireland (33 Merrion Rd., Dublin, 4)
Ambassador: David Blatherwick, CMG, OBE.

Of Ireland in the USA (2234 Massachusetts Ave., NW, Washington, D.C., 20008)
Ambassador: Dermot Gallagher.

Of the USA in Ireland (42 Elgin Rd., Ballsbridge, Dublin)
Ambassador: Richard A. Moore.

Of Ireland to the United Nations
Ambassador: Francis Mahon Hayes.

Further Reading

Statistical Information: The Central Statistics Office (Earlsfort Terrace, Dublin, 2) was established in June 1949, and is attached to the Department of the Taoiseach. *Director:* Donal Murphy, M.Sc., M.Econ.Sc., M.Sc. (Mgt.).

Principal publications of the Central Statistics Office are *National Income and Expenditure* (annually), *Statistical Abstract* (annually), *Census of Population Reports, Census of Industrial Production Reports, Trade and Shipping Statistics* (annually and monthly), *Trend of Employment and Unemployment* (annually), *Reports on Vital Statistics* (annually and quarterly), *Irish Statistical Bulletin* (quarterly), *Labour Force Surveys* (annually), *Trade Statistics* (monthly), *Economic Series* (monthly).

Aspects of Ireland. (Series). Dublin Department of Foreign Affairs.
Atlas of Ireland. Royal Irish Academy, Dublin, 1979
Facts About Ireland. Dublin Department of Foreign Affairs, 6th ed. 1985
The Gill History of Ireland. 11 vols. Dublin
Bartholomew, P. C., *The Irish Judiciary.* Dublin, Institute of Public Administration, 1974
Chubb, B., *The Constitution and Constitutional Change in Ireland.* Dublin, reprinted 1988
Coolahan, J., *Irish Education: Its History and Structure.* Dublin, 1981
Eager, A. R., *A Guide to Irish Bibliographical Material.* 2nd ed. London, 1980
Encyclopaedia of Ireland. Dublin, 1968
Fitzgerald, G., *All in a Life: an Autobiography.* London, 1991
Foster, R. F., *Modern Ireland 1600–1972.* London, 1988.—(ed.) *The Oxford Illustrated History of Ireland.* OUP, 1991
Hensey, B., *The Health Services of Ireland.* 4th ed. Dublin, 1988
Hickey, D. J. and Doherty, J. E., *A Dictionary of Irish History since 1800.* Dublin, 1980
Johnston, T. J. and others, *A History of the Church of Ireland.* Dublin, 1953
Lee, J. J., *Ireland 1912-1985: Politics and Society.* CUP, 1989
McDunphy, Michael, *The President of Ireland: His Powers, Functions and Duties.* Dublin, 1945
Miller, K. A., *Emigrants and Exiles: Ireland and the Irish Exodus to North America.* OUP, 1988
Page, R., *Sources of Economic Information: Ireland.* Dublin, 1985
Shannon, M. O., *Irish Republic.* [Bibliography] Oxford and Santa Barbara, 1986

ISRAEL

Capital: Jerusalem
Population: 4·98m. (1991)
GNP per capita: US$8,650 (1988)

Medinat Israel

(State of Israel)

HISTORY. During the First World War the then Turkish province of Palestine, populated mainly by Arabs, was occupied by the British, who in 1917 issued the Balfour Declaration, viewing 'with favour the establishment in Palestine of a national home for the Jewish people'. This position was endorsed by the League of Nations. In Nov. 1947 the UN called for the establishment of both a Jewish and an Arab state. Jewish settlement had been taking place throughout the British mandate.

The State of Israel was proclaimed on 14 May 1948. No Arab state was established. Neighbouring Arab states invaded Israel on 15 May without success. At the ceasefire in Jan. 1949 Israel had increased its territory by one-third.

There have been conflicts with Egypt (sometimes with the involvement of other Arab states) in the 1956 Suez crisis; the 1967 'Six-Day War', which left Israel in possession of the Gaza Strip, the West Bank (of the River Jordan) and the Sinai Peninsula; and in 1973. (For details *see* THE STATESMAN'S YEAR-BOOK, 1990–91, p. 734).

Negotiations began between Israel and Egypt at Camp David in the USA in Oct. 1978 and a peace treaty was signed on 26 March 1979. Israel had withdrawn from Sinai by April 1982.

Early in 1991, in the course of the air attack on Iraq by the UN-supported coalition enforcing Iraq's withdrawal from Kuwait, Iraq made a series of missile attacks on Israel, causing fatal casualties among the civilian population.

AREA AND POPULATION. The area of Israel, within the boundaries defined by the 1949 armistice agreements with Egypt, Jordan, the Lebanon and Syria, is 20,770 sq. km (8,017 sq. miles), with a population (June 1983 census) of 4,037,600 (estimated, 1991, 4,977,200). Population of areas under Israeli administration as a result of the Six-Day War was, in 1989: Judaea and Samaria (West Bank), 915,000, Gaza Strip, 612,000.

Crude birth rate per 1,000 population of Jewish population (1989), 19·7; non-Jewish: Moslems, 36·2; Christians, 22·8; Druzes and others, 30·8. Crude death rate, Jewish, 7; non-Jewish: Moslems, 3·3; Christians, 5·4; Druzes and others, 3·6. Infant mortality rate per 1,000 live births, Jewish, 8·3; non-Jewish: Moslems, 15; Christians, 12·4; Druzes and others, 13·1. Life expectancy (1987): Males, 73·6 years; females, 77. Average population growth rate, 1980–89, 1·8%. Growth rate in 1990 was 5·8%, largely due to increased immigration from the USSR.

Israel is administratively divided into 6 districts:

District	Area (sq. km)	Population [1]	Chief town
Northern	4,501	739,500	Nazareth
Haifa	854	602,800	Haifa
Central	1,242	938,600	Ramla
Tel Aviv	170	1,029,700	Tel Aviv
Jerusalem [2]	627	538,300	Jerusalem
Southern	14,107	529,300	Beersheba

[1] 1988.   [2] Includes East Jerusalem.

On 23 Jan. 1950 the Knesset proclaimed Jerusalem the capital of the State and on 14 Dec. 1981 extended Israeli law into the Golan Heights. Population of the main towns (1988): Tel-Aviv/Jaffa, 317,800; Jerusalem, 493,500; Haifa, 222,600; Ramat Gan, 115,700; Bat-Yam, 133,100; Holon, 146,100; Petach-Tikva, 133,600; Beersheba, 113,200.

The official languages are Hebrew and Arabic.

Areas under Israeli occupation as a result of the 6-day war:

The **West Bank** has an area of 5,879 sq. km (2,270 sq. miles) and a population (1989) of 915,000 97% of the population in 1988 were Palestinian Arabs of whom some 85% were Muslims, 7·4% Jewish and 8% Christian. In 1984, the birth rate was 3·9% and the death rate 8%. In 1987, there were 39,091 private cars and 13,710 commercial vehicles registered. There were (1988) 183,041 pupils in primary schools and 105,007 in secondary schools, while (1983) there were 7,066 students in higher education. In 1988 there were 16 hospitals and clinics with 1,336 beds.

The **Gaza Strip** has an area of 363 sq. km (140 sq. miles) and a population (1989) of 612,000. The chief town is Gaza itself, with (1979) 120,000 inhabitants. In 1984, over 98% of the population were Arabic-speaking Muslims; the birth rate was 4·8% and the death rate 0·8%. Citrus fruits, wheat and olives are grown, with farm land covering 193 sq. km (1980) and occupying most of the active workforce. Some 1,600 tonnes of fish (1984) was also caught. In 1987 there were 18,761 private cars and 4,374 commercial vehicles registered. There were (1988) 112,959 pupils in primary schools and 64,699 in secondary schools, with (1983) 2,387 students in higher education. In 1988 there were 7 hospitals and clinics with 895 beds.

Immigration. The following table shows the numbers of Jewish immigrants entering Palestine (Israel), including persons entering as travellers who subsequently registered as immigrants. For a year-by-year breakdown, *see* THE STATESMAN'S YEAR-BOOK, 1951, p. 1167.

1919–48	482,857	1958–68	384,870	1980–88	129,789
1948–57	905,740	1969–79	384,066	1989–90	223,566

During 1948–68, 45·5% of the immigrants came from Europe and America and 54·5% from Asia and Africa; in 1988, 74% came from Europe and America and 25·7% from Asia and Africa. With the liberalization of Soviet emigration policy, there was a marked increase in immigrants from the USSR (185,000 in 1990). In all some 360,000 immigrants were expected in 1990–91.

The Jewish Agency, which, in accordance with Article IV of the Palestine Mandate, played a leading role in establishing the State of Israel continues to organize immigration.

CLIMATE. From April to Oct., the summers are long and hot, and almost rainless. From Nov. to March, the weather is generally mild, though colder in hilly areas, and this is the wet season. Jerusalem. Jan. 48°F (9°C), July 73°F (23°C). Annual rainfall, 563 mm. Tel Aviv. Jan. 57°F (14°C), July 81°F (27°C). Annual rainfall, 541 mm.

CONSTITUTION AND GOVERNMENT. Israel is an independent sovereign republic, established by proclamation on 14 May 1948.

In 1950 the Knesset (*Parliament*), which in 1949 had passed the Transition Law dealing in general terms with the powers of the Knesset, President and Cabinet, resolved to enact from time to time fundamental laws, which eventually, taken together, would form the Constitution. Fundamental laws that have been passed are: The Knesset (1958), Israel Lands (1960), the President (1964), the Government (1968), the State Economy (1975), the Army (1976), Jerusalem, capital of Israel (1980), and the Judicature (1984).

National flag: White with 2 horizontal blue stripes, the blue Shield of David in the centre.

National anthem: Hatikvah (The Hope). Words by N. N. Imber (1878); adopted as the Jewish National Anthem by the first Zionist Congress (1897).

The Knesset, a one-chamber Parliament, consists of 120 members. It is elected for a 4-year term by secret ballot and universal direct suffrage. The system of election is by proportional representation. Voters choose between party lists of candidates in multi-member constituencies. After the Nov. 1988 elections the Knesset was composed as follows: Likud (Lik), 40; Labour Alignment (Lab), 39; Shas (Oriental

Religious Jews), 6; National Religious Party, 5; Agudat Yisrael, 5; Citizens Rights Movement, 5; Communists, 4; Mapam, 3; Tehiya, 3; Shinui, 2; Moledet, 2; Degel Hatora, 2; Tsomet, 2; Arab Democratic List, 1; Progressive List for Peace, 1. The *President* (head of state) is elected by the Knesset by secret ballot by a simple majority; his term of office is 5 years. He may be re-elected once.

Former Presidents of the State: Chaim Weizmann (1949–52); Izhak Ben-Zvi (1952–63); Zalman Shazar (1963–68); Ephraim Katzir (1968–78); Yitzhak Navon (1978–83).

President: Chaim Herzog, elected 1983; re-elected 1988.

In June 1990 Yitzhak Shamir formed a new Likud government. In Nov. 1990 the government entered into a coalition with Agudat Israel, an orthodox religious party. In Feb. 1992 the Cabinet consisted of:

Prime Minister: Yitzhak Shamir (b. 1916, Lik).

Deputy Prime Minister and Foreign Minister: David Levy (Lik). *Deputy Prime Minister and Minister of Industry and Commerce:* Moshe Nissim (Lik). *Defence:* Moshe Arens (Lik). *Finance:* Yitzhak Moda'i (Zionist Renewal). *Environment:* Ariel Sharon (Lik). *Justice:* Dan Meridor (Lik). *Transport:* Moshe Katzav (Lik). *Economy:* David Magen (Lik). *Police:* Ronni Milo (Lik). *Tourism:* Gideon Patt (Lik). *Health:* Ehud Olmert (Lik). *Education:* Zevulun Hammer (National Religious Party). *Religious Affairs:* Avner Shaki (National Religious Party). *Science and Energy:* (vacant). *Agriculture:* (vacant). *Interior:* Arie Der'i (Shas). *Communications:* Raphael Pinhasi (Shas). *Immigration:* Yitzhak Peretz (Shas).

Ministerial resignations in Jan. 1992 put this government in a minority, and elections were scheduled for 23 June 1992.

Local Government. Local authorities are of three kinds, namely, municipal corporations, local councils and regional councils. Their status, powers and duties are prescribed by statute. Regional councils are local authorities set up in agricultural areas and include all the agricultural settlements in the area under their jurisdiction. All local authorities exercise their authority mainly by means of bye-laws approved by the Minister of the Interior. Their revenue is derived from rates and a surcharge on income tax. Local authorities are elected for a 4-year term of office concurrently with general elections.

There were (1989) 42 municipalities (3 Arab), 136 local councils (63 Arab and Druze) and 54 regional councils.

DEFENCE. The Defence Service Law, provides a compulsory 36-month conscription for men (Jews and Druze only). Unmarried women (Jews only) serve 30 months.

The Israel Defence Force is a unified force, in which army, navy and air force are subordinate to a single chief-of-staff. The Minister of Defence is *de facto* commander-in-chief but from Oct. 1973 the cabinet formed a defence committee with authority to make decisions on military operations.

Army. The Army is organized in 3 armoured divisions, 3 infantry divisions, 5 mechanized infantry brigades, 3 artillery battalions and 1 surface-to-surface missile battalion. The Reserves are organized in 9 armoured divisions, 1 mechanized (air mobile) division, 10 infantry and 4 artillery brigades. Equipment includes 1,080 Centurion, 550 M-48A5, 1,400 M-60/A1/A3, 488 T-54/-55, 110 T-62 and 660 Merkava main battle tanks and 6,000 other armoured fighting vehicles. Strength (1991) 104,000 (conscripts 88,000), rising to 598,000 on mobilization.

Navy. The Navy, tasked primarily for coastal protection and based at Haifa, Ashdod and Eilat, includes 3 small diesel submarines, 20 missile craft, 19 of which are of the evolving SA'AR types, from 250 to 500 tonnes, and 3 missile-armed hydrofoils. There are an additional 40 fast inshore patrol craft, 7 amphibious craft and a few minor auxiliaries.

Planned construction includes 2 corvettes and 2 submarines, to be built through the US foreign military sales programme.

Naval personnel in 1991 totalled 9,000 officers and men, of whom 3,000 are conscripts, including a Naval Cammando of 300. There are also 1,000 naval reservists available on mobilization.

Air Force. The Air Force has a personnel strength (1991) of 28,000 (19,000 conscripts), rising to 37,000 on mobilization, with about 629 first-line aircraft, all jets, of Israeli and US manufacture. There are 4 squadrons with about 70 F-15s, and 6 squadrons with the first 150 of a planned 250 F-16s in an interceptor role; 4 squadrons with 110 F-4E Phantoms, 4 squadrons with about 120 Kfirs, and 3 squadrons with A-4E/H/N Skyhawks in the fighter-bomber/attack role; and 15 RF-4E reconnaissance fighters; supported by 4 E-2C Hawkeye airborne early warning and control aircraft, RC-12 and RU-21 Elint aircraft. There are transport squadrons of turboprop C-130/KC-130 Hercules, C-47, Arava, Islander, and Boeing 707 (some equipped for tanker or ECM duties) aircraft, helicopter squadrons of CH-53, AH-64A Apache, AH-1 Huey-Cobra, Hughes 500MD/TOW Defender, JetRanger, Dauphin, Agusta-Bell 205, 206 and 212 aircraft, and training units with locally-built Magister jet trainers, which can be used also in a light ground attack role. Missiles in service include surface-to-air Hawks and surface-to-surface Lances.

INTERNATIONAL RELATIONS
Membership. Israel is a member of UN.

ECONOMY
Policy. 30 to 40 of some 150 state-owned companies are scheduled for privatization under a scaled-down programme of 1991. Efforts to generate some 0·5m. jobs are being made to cope with the influx of Soviet immigrants.

Budget. The budget year runs from 1 Jan to 31 Dec. beginning with 1992. Previously it ran from 1 April to 31 March. Government revenue in 1987-88 amounted to 44,539m. new shekels; expenditure, 44,021m. new shekels.

Currency. The unit of currency is the *shekel* (ILS) of 100 *agorot*. Currency in circulation on 31 Dec. 1984 was I£161,651m. (bank-notes and coins). In March 1992, £1 = 4·13 *shekel*; US$ = 2·35 *shekel*.

Banking and Finance. The Bank of Israel was established by law in 1954 as Israel's central bank. Its *Governor* is appointed by the President on the recommendation of the Cabinet for a 5-year term. He acts as economic adviser to the Government and has ministerial status. The *Governor* is Jacob Frenkel, appointed till 1996. There are 26 commercial banks headed by Bank Leumi Le Israel, Bank Hapoalim and Israel Discount Bank, 2 merchant banks, 1 foreign bank, 15 mortgage banks and 9 lending institutions specifically set up to aid industry and agriculture. The government holds a majority stake in the 4 largest banks, but there are plans to privatize them by 1992.

There is a stock exchange in Tel Aviv.

Weights and Measures. The metric system is in general use. The (metrical) *dunam* = 1,000 sq. metres (about 0·25 acre).

Jewish Year. The Jewish year 5750 corresponds to 30 Sept. 1989–19 Sept. 1990; 5751 20 Sept. 1990–8 Sept. 1991; 5752 9 Sept. 1991–27 Sept. 1992.

ENERGY AND NATURAL RESOURCES
Electricity. Electric-power production amounted during 1988 to 18,761m. kwh. Supply 230 volts; 50 Hz.

Oil and Gas. The only significant indigenous hydrocarbon known to be found is oil shale. In 1988 recoverable potential was estimated to be 250m. tons of oil.

Minerals. The most valuable natural resources of the country are the potash, bromine and other salt deposits of the Dead Sea, which are exploited by the Dead Sea Works, Ltd. Geological research and exploration of the natural resources in the Negev are undertaken by the Israel Mining Corporation. Potash production in 1986 was 2,035,000 tons.

Agriculture. In the coastal plain (Sharon, Emek Hefer and the Shephelah) mixed farming, poultry raising, citriculture and vineyards are the main agricultural activities. The Emek (the Valley of Jezreel) is the main agricultural centre of Israel. Mixed farming is to be found throughout the valleys; the sub-tropical Beisan and Jordan plainlands are also centres of banana plantations and fish breeding. In Galilee mixed farming, olive and tobacco plantations prevail. The Hills of Ephraim are a vineyard centre; many parts of the hill country are under afforestation. In the northern Negev farming has been aided by the Yarkon–Negev water pipeline. This has become part of the overall project of the 'National Water Carrier', which is to take water from the Sea of Galilee (Lake Kinnereth) to the south. The plan includes a number of regional projects such as the Lake Kinnereth–Negev pipeline which came into operation in 1964; it has an annual capacity of 320m. cu. metres.

The area under cultivation (in 1,000 dunams) in 1990 was 4,371, of which 2,057 were under irrigation. Of the total cultivated area 2,221 dunams were under field crops, 449 under vegetables, potatoes, pumpkins and melons, 344 under citrus and plantations, 29 under fish ponds and the rest under miscellaneous crops, including auxiliary farms, nurseries, flowers, etc.

Industrial crops, such as cotton, have successfully been introduced. In 1990 the area under cotton totalled 319,800 dunams.

Production, 1990 (in 1,000 tonnes): Wheat, 291; barley, 8; maize, 119; potatoes, 214; melons, 67; tomatoes, 524; citrus fruit, 1,506; cotton, 134.

Livestock (1990) included 331,000 cattle, 375,000 sheep, 110,000 goats, 27·1m. poultry.

Characteristic types of rural settlement are, among others, the following: (1) The *Kibbutz* and *Kvutza* (communal collective settlement), where all property and earnings are collectively owned and work is collectively organized. (125,100 people lived in 270 *Kibbutzim* in 1990). (2) The *Moshav* (workers' co-operative smallholders' settlement) which is founded on the principles of mutual aid and equality of opportunity between the members, all farms being equal in size. (149,100 in 409). (3) The *Moshav Shitufi* (co-operative settlement), which is based on collective ownership and economy as in the *Kibbutz*, but with each family having its own house and being responsible for its own domestic services. (11,300 in 45). (4) Other rural settlements in which land and property are privately owned and every resident is responsible for his own well-being. In 1990 there were 232 villages with a population of 114,000.

INDUSTRY. A wide range of products is manufactured, processed or finished in the country, including chemicals, metal products, textiles, tyres, diamonds, paper, plastics, leather goods, glass and ceramics, building materials, precision instruments, tobacco, foodstuffs, electrical and electronic equipment.

Labour. The workforce was 1·65m. in 1990. A 'social-economic pact' between government, employers and trade unions in May 1991 aimed to create some 32,000 new jobs to lessen the impact of increased immigration.

Trade Unions. The General Federation of Labour (Histadrut) founded in 1920, had, in 1987, 1·6m. members (including 170,000 Arab and Druze members); including workers' families, this membership represents 71·5% of the population covering 87% of all wage-earners. Several trades unions also exist representing other political and religious groups.

FOREIGN ECONOMIC RELATIONS

Commerce. External trade, in US$1m., for calendar years:

	1986	1987	1988	1989	1990
Imports	9,550	11,916	12,960	13,027	15,104
Exports	7,712	8,475	9,739	10,669	11,576

The main exportable commodities are citrus fruit and by-products, fruit-juices, flowers, wines and liquor, sweets, polished diamonds, chemicals, tyres, textiles, metal products, machinery, electronic and transportation equipment. The main exports were, in 1988 (US$1m.): Diamonds, 2,837; chemical and oil products, 1,122·6; agricultural products including citrus fruit, 573; manufactured goods, machinery and transport equipment, 4,328. In 1987 64·1% of imports came from Europe, 17·2% from Canada and USA, 8·3% from Africa and Asia. Of exports, 36·4% went to Europe, 33·5% to Canada and USA, 14·2% to Africa and Asia.

Total trade between Israel and UK (British Department of Trade returns, in £1,000 sterling):

	1987	1988	1989	1990	1991
Imports to UK	437,014	460,289	479,840	506,106	455,765
Exports and re-exports from UK	523,591	487,255	502,411	567,712	529,484

Tourism. In 1990 there were about 1,131,700 tourists.

COMMUNICATIONS

Roads. There were 13,181 km of paved roads in 1990. Registered motor vehicles in 1990 totalled 1,015,404, including 8,886 buses, 153,058 trucks and 803,021 private cars.

Railways. Internal communications (1990) are provided by 574 km of standard gauge line. In 1990, 2·5m. passengers and 7·2m. tonnes of freight were carried.

Civil Aviation. Air communications are centred in the airport of Ben Gurion, near Tel Aviv. In 1990, 13,401 planes landed at Israeli airports on international flights; 1,923,000 passengers arrived, 1,797,000 departed. In 1990, 106,466 tons of freight were loaded and 87,697 tons unloaded. The Israeli airline El Al maintains regular flights to London, Manchester, Paris, Rome, Berlin, Frankfurt, Munich, Amsterdam, Brussels, Cairo, Madrid, Lisbon, Bucharest, Athens, Vienna, New York, Boston, Chicago, Los Angeles, Montreal, Zurich, Munich, Istanbul, Johannesburg, Nairobi, Budapest, Prague, Moscow, Warsaw and Copenhagen. In 1986–87 El Al carried 1·5m. passengers.

Shipping. Israel has 3 commercial ports, Haifa, Ashdod and Eilat. In 1990, 3,629 ships departed from Israeli ports; 21·7m. tons. of freight were handled. The merchant fleet consisted in 1988 of 72 vessels, totalling 1,573,000 GRT.

Telecommunications. The Ministry of Communications controls the postal service, and a public company responsible to the Ministry administers the telecommunications service. In 1986 there were 594 post offices and postal agencies, 50 mobile post offices and (1988) 1·94m. telephones.

Israeli television and the state radio station, *Kol Israel* are controlled by the Israel Broadcasting Authority, established in 1965. Radio licences in 1985 numbered approximately 1·12m. and television licences (1986) 936,000.

Cinemas. In 1987 there were 162 cinemas.

Newspapers (1987). There were 23 daily newspapers.

JUSTICE, RELIGION, EDUCATION AND WELFARE

Justice. *Law.* Under the Law and Administration Ordinance, 5708/1948, the first law passed by the Provisional Council of State, the law of Israel is the law which was obtaining in Palestine on 14 May 1948 in so far as it is not in conflict with that Ordinance or any other law passed by the Israel legislature and with such modifications as result from the establishment of the State and its authorities.

Capital punishment was abolished in 1954, except for support given to the Nazis and for high treason.

The law of Palestine was derived from three main sources, namely, Ottoman law, English law (Common Law and Equity) and the law enacted by the Palestine legislature, which to a great extent was modelled on English law. The Ottoman law in its turn was derived from three main sources, namely, Moslem law which had survived in the Ottoman Empire, French law adapted by the Ottomans and the personal law of the non-Moslem communities.

Civil Courts. Municipal courts, established in certain municipal areas, have criminal jurisdiction over offences against municipal regulations and bye-laws and certain specified offences committed within a municipal area.

Magistrates courts, established in each district and sub-district, have limited jurisdiction in both civil and criminal matters.

District courts, sitting at Jerusalem, Tel-Aviv and Haifa, have jurisdiction, as courts of first instance, in all civil matters not within the jurisdiction of magistrates courts, and in all criminal matters, and as appellate courts from magistrates courts and municipal courts.

The Supreme Court has jurisdiction as a court of first instance (sitting as a High Court of Justice dealing mainly with administrative matters) and as an appellate court from the district courts (sitting as a Court of Civil or of Criminal Appeal).

In addition, there are various tribunals for special classes of cases, such as the Rents Tribunals and the Tribunals for the Prevention of Profiteering and Speculation. Settlement Officers deal with disputes with regard to the ownership or possession of land in settlement areas constituted under the Land (Settlement of Title) Ordinance.

Religious Courts. The rabbinical courts of the Jewish community have exclusive jurisdiction in matters of marriage and divorce, alimony and confirmation of wills of members of their community other than foreigners, concurrent jurisdiction with the civil courts in such matters of members of their community who are foreigners if they consent to the jurisdiction, and concurrent jurisdiction with the civil courts in all other matters of personal status of all members of their community, whether foreigners or not, with the consent of all parties to the action, save that such courts may not grant a decree of dissolution of marriage to a foreign subject.

The courts of the several recognized Christian communities have a similar jurisdiction over members of their respective communities.

The Moslem religious courts have exclusive jurisdiction in all matters of personal status over Moslems who are not foreigners, and over Moslems who are foreigners, if under the law of their nationality they are subject in such matters to the jurisdiction of Moslem religious courts.

Where any action of personal status involves persons of different religious communities, the President of the Supreme Court will decide which court shall have jurisdiction, and whenever a question arises as to whether or not a case is one of personal status within the exclusive jurisdiction of a religious court, the matter must be referred to a special tribunal composed of 2 judges of the Supreme Court and the president of the highest court of the religious community concerned in Israel.

Religion. Religious affairs are under the supervision of a special Ministry, with departments for the Christian and Moslem communities. The religious affairs of each community remain under the full control of the ecclesiastical authorities concerned: in the case of the Jews, the Sephardi and Ashkenazi Chief Rabbis, in the case of the Christians, the heads of the various communities, and in the case of the Moslems, the Qadis. The Druze were officially recognized in 1957 as an autonomous religious community.

In 1990 there were: Jews, 3,946,700; Moslems, 677,700; Christians, 114,700; Druze and others, 82,600.

The Jewish Sabbath and Holy Days are observed as days of rest in the public services. Full provision is, however, made for the free exercise of other faiths, and for the observance by their adherents of their respective days of rest and Holy Days.

Education. Laws passed by the Knesset in 1949 and 1978 provide for free and compulsory education from 5 to 16 years of age. There is free education until 18 years of age.

The State Education Law of 12 Aug. 1953 established a unified state-controlled elementary school system with a provision for special religious schools. The standard curriculum for all elementary schools is issued by the Ministry with a possibility of adding supplementary subjects comprising not more than 25% of the total syllabus. Most schools in towns are maintained by municipalities, a number are private and some are administered by teachers' co-operatives or trustees.

Statistics relating to schools under government supervision, 1990–91:

Type of School [1]	Schools	Teachers	Pupils
Hebrew Education			
Primary schools	1,379	33,656	476,055
Schools for handicapped children	187	3,394	11,024
Schools of intermediate division	323	14,994	129,591
Secondary schools	546		215,720
Vocational schools	302	26,333	99,173
Agricultural schools	23		5,091
Arab Education			
Primary schools	313	6,620	139,409
Schools for handicapped children	25	318	1,367
Schools of intermediate division	74	2,332	31,293
Secondary schools	90		40,271
Vocational schools	49	3,071	8,574
Agricultural schools	2		600

[1] Schools providing more than one type of education are included more than once.

There are also a number of private schools maintained by religious foundations—Jewish, Christian and Moslem—and also by private societies.

The Hebrew University of Jerusalem, founded in 1925, comprises faculties of the humanities, social sciences, law, science, medicine and agriculture. In 1989–90 it had 17,700 students. The Technion in Haifa had 9,770 students. The Weizmann Institute of Science in Rehovoth, founded in 1949, had 640 students.

Tel Aviv University had 19,440 students. The religious Bar-Ilan University at Ramat Gan, opened in 1965 had 10,200 students. The Haifa University had 7,030 students. The Ben Gurion University had 6,410 students.

Health. In 1990 Israel had 187 hospitals with 29,094 beds and 9,500 doctors.

The National Insurance Law, which took effect in April 1954, provides for old-age pensions, survivors' insurance, work-injury insurance, maternity insurance, family allowances and unemployment benefits.

DIPLOMATIC REPRESENTATIVES

Of Israel in Great Britain (2 Palace Green, London, W8 4QB)
Ambassador: Yoav Biran (accredited 24 Nov. 1988).

Of Great Britain in Israel (192 Hayarkon St., Tel Aviv 63405)
Ambassador: Mark Elliott, CMG.

Of Israel in the USA (3514 International Dr., NW, Washington, D.C., 20008)
Ambassador: Zalman Shoval.

Of the USA in Israel (71 Hayarkon St., Tel Aviv)
Ambassador: William A. Brown.

Of Israel to the United Nations
Ambassador: Yoram Aridor.

Further Reading

Statistical Information: There is a Central Bureau of Statistics at the Prime Minister's Office, Jerusalem. It publishes monthly and annual publications of statistics (economic and social), foreign trade statistics and price statistics.
Atlas of Israel. 3rd ed. 1985
Government Yearbook. Government Printer, Jerusalem. 1951 ff. (latest issue, 1971/72)
Facts about Israel. Ministry of Foreign Affairs, Jerusalem, 1985
Statistical Abstract of Israel. Government Printer, Jerusalem (from 1949/50)
Israel Yearbook. Tel-Aviv, 1948–49 ff.
Statistical Bulletin of Israel. 1949 ff.
Reshumoth (Official Gazette)
Middle East Record. London, 1960 ff.
Laws of the State of Israel. Authorized translation. Government Printer, Jerusalem, 1958 ff.
Aharoni, Y., *The Israeli Economy: the Dreams and Realities.* London, 1991
Ben-Gurion, D., *Ben-Gurion Looks Back.* London, 1965.—*The Jews in Their Land.* London, 1966.—*Israel: A Personal History.* New York, 1971
Harkabi, Y., *Israel's Fateful Decisions.* London, 1989

Harris, W., *Taking Root: Israeli Settlement in the West Bank, The Golan and Gaza Sinai 1967–1980*. Chichester, 1981

Kieval, G. R., *Party Politics in Israel and the Occupied Territories*. Westport, 1983

Louis, W. R. and Stookey, R. W., *The End of the Palestine Mandate*. London, 1986

O'Brien, C. C., *The Siege*. London, 1986

Peri, Y., *Between Battles and Ballots: Israeli Military in Politics*. CUP, 1983

Reich, B., *Israel: Land of Tradition and Conflict*. London, 1986.— and Kieval (eds.) *Israeli Politics in the 1990s: Key Domestic and Foreign Policy Factors*. London, 1991

Sachar, H. M., *A History of Israel*. 2 vols. OUP, 1976–87

Sager, S., *The Parliamentary System of Israel*. Syracuse Univ. Press, 1986

Segev, T., *1949: The First Israelis*. New York, 1986

Sharkansky, I., *The Political Economy of Israel*. Oxford and Santa Barbara, 1986

Shimshoni, D., *Israeli Democracy: The Middle of the Journey*. New York, 1982

Snyder, E. M. and Kreiner, E., *Israel*. [Bibliography] Oxford and Santa Barbara, 1985

Wolffsohn, M., *Politik in Israel*. Opladen, 1983

National Library: The Jewish National and University Library, Jerusalem.

ITALY

Repubblica Italiana

Capital: Rome
Population: 57·7m. (1990)
GNP per capita: US$15,150 (1989)

HISTORY. On 10 June 1946 Italy became a republic on the announcement by the Court of Cassation that a majority of the voters at the referendum held on 2 June had voted for a republic. The final figures, announced on 18 June, showed: For a republic, 12,718,641 (54·3% of the valid votes cast, which numbered 23,437,143); for the retention of the monarchy, 10,718,502 (45·7%); invalid and contested, 1,509,735. Total 24,946,878, or 89·1% of the registered electors, who numbered 28,005,449. For the results of the polling in the 13 leading cities, *see* THE STATESMAN'S YEAR-BOOK , 1951, p. 1175. Voting was compulsory, open to both men and women 21 years of age or older, including members of the Civil Service and the Armed Forces; former active Fascists and a few other categories were excluded.

On 18 June the then Provisional Government without specifically proclaiming the republic, issued an 'Order of the Day' decreeing that all court verdicts should in future be handed down 'in the name of the Italian people', that the *Gazzetta Ufficiale del Regno d'Italia* should be re-named *Gazzetta Ufficiale della Repubblica Italiana,* that all references to the monarchy should be deleted from legal and government statements and that the shield of the House of Savoy should be removed from the Italian flag.

Thus ended the reign of the House of Savoy, whose kings had ruled over Piedmont for 9 centuries and as Kings of Italy since 18 Feb. 1861. (For fuller account of the House of Savoy, *see* THE STATESMAN'S YEAR-BOOK, 1946, p. 1021.) The Crown Prince Umberto, son of King Victor Emmanuel III, became Lieut.-Gen. (*i.e.,* Regent) of the kingdom on 5 June 1944. Following the abdication and retirement to Egypt of his father on 9 May 1946, Umberto was declared King Umberto II; his reign lasted to 13 June, when he left the country. King Victor Emmanuel III died in Alexandria on 28 Dec. 1947.

AREA AND POPULATION. Italy is bounded north by Switzerland and Austria, east by Yugoslavia and the Adriatic Sea, south-east by the Ionian Sea, south by the Mediterranean Sea, south-west by the Tyrrhenian Sea and Ligurian Sea and west by France. The population (present in actual boundaries) at successive censuses were as follows:

31 Dec. 1881	29,277,927	21 April 1936	42,302,680
10 Feb. 1901	33,370,138	4 Nov. 1951	47,158,738
10 June 1911	35,694,582	15 Oct. 1961	49,903,878
1 Dec. 1921	37,403,956	24 Oct. 1971	53,744,737
21 April 1931	40,582,043	25 Oct. 1981	56,243,935

The following table gives area and population of the Regions (census 1981 and estimate, 1990):

Regions	Area in sq. km (1981)	Resident pop. census, 1981	Resident pop. estimate, 1990	Density per sq. km (1981)
Piemonte	25,399	4,479,031	4,356,227	175
Valle d'Aosta	3,262	112,353	115,996	35
Lombardia	23,856	8,891,652	8,939,429	373
Trentino-Alto Adige	13,613	873,413	891,421	64
Bolzano-Bozen	7,400	430,568	441,671	58
Trento	6,213	442,845	449,750	71
Veneto	18,364	4,345,047	4,398,114	235
Friuli-Venezia Giulia	7,846	1,233,984	1,201,027	157
Liguria	5,416	1,807,893	1,719,202	332
Emilia Romagna	22,123	3,957,513	3,928,744	178
Toscana	22,992	3,581,051	3,562,525	155
Umbria	8,456	807,552	822,765	95
Marche	9,694	1,412,404	1,435,574	145
Lazio	17,203	5,001,684	5,191,482	289
Abruzzi	10,794	1,217,791	1,272,387	113
Molise	4,438	328,371	336,456	73

Regions	Area in sq. km (1981)	Resident pop. census, 1981	Resident pop. estimate, 1990	Density per sq. km (1981)
Campania	13,595	5,463,134	5,853,902	398
Puglia	19,347	3,871,617	4,081,542	199
Basilicata	9,992	610,186	624,519	60
Calabria	15,080	2,061,182	2,153,656	135
Sicilia	25,708	4,906,878	5,196,822	189
Sardegna	24,090	1,594,175	1,664,373	66
Total	301,268	56,556,911	57,746,163	187

Vital statistics for calendar years:

| | | Living births | | | | Deaths |
| | | Married | Single | | | excl. of |
	Marriages	parent	parent	Total	Still-born	still-born
1983	303,663	572,641	29,287	601,928	4,396	564,330
1984	300,889	557,773	30,098	587,871	4,175	534,676
1985	298,523	546,224	31,121	577,345	3,871	547,436
1986	297,540	523,876	31,569	555,445	3,584	544,489
1987	306,264	519,406	32,133	551,539	3,483	532,771
1988	318,296	536,472	33,226	569,698	3,453	539,426
1989	311,613 [1]	521,886 [1]	33,800 [1]	555,686 [1]	3,306 [1]	523,888
1990 [1]	314,585	527,773	35,246	563,019	3,157	536,717

[1] Provisional.

Emigrants to non-European countries, by sea and air: 1978, 23,589; 1979, 21,302; 1980, 20,360; 1981, 20,628; 1982, 22,324; 1983, 20,443; 1984, 16,776; 1985, 16,151; 1986, 13,215; 1987, 12,796; 1988, 11,457; 1989, 8,820. Since 1960 nearly nine-tenths of these emigrants have gone to Canada, USA and Australia.

Communes of more than 100,000 inhabitants, with population resident at the census of 25 Oct. 1981 and on 31 Dec. 1990:

	1981	1990		1981	1990
Roma (Rome)	2,840,259	2,791,354	Perugia	142,348	150,576
Milano (Milan)	1,604,773	1,432,184	Ravenna	138,034	136,724
Napoli (Naples)	1,212,387	1,206,013	Pescara	131,330	128,553
Torino (Turin)	1,117,154	991,870	Reggio nell'E.	130,376	131,880
Genova (Genoa)	762,895	701,032	Rimini	127,813	130,896
Palermo	701,782	734,238	Monza	123,145	123,188
Bologna	459,080	411,803	Bergamo	122,142	117,886
Firenze (Florence)	448,331	408,403	Sassari	119,596	120,011
Catania	380,328	364,176	Siracusa (Syracuse)	117,615	125,444
Bari	371,022	353,032	La Spezia	115,392	103,008
Venezia (Venice)	346,146	317,837	Vicenza	114,598	109,333
Verona	265,932	258,946	Terni	111,564	109,809
Messina	260,233	274,846	Forli	110,806	109,755
Trieste	252,369	231,047	Piacenza	109,039	103,536
Taranto	244,101	244,033	Cosenza	106,801	104,483
Padova (Padua)	234,678	218,186	Ancona	106,498	103,268
Cagliari	233,848	211,719	Bolzano	105,180	100,380
Brescia	206,661	196,766	Pisa	104,509	101,500
Modena	180,312	177,501	Torre del Greco	103,605	102,647
Parma	179,019	193,991	Novara	102,086	103,349
Livorno (Leghorn)	175,741	171,265	Udine	102,021	98,322
Reggio di C.	173,486	178,496	Catanzaro	100,832	103,802
Prato	160,220	166,688	Alessandria	100,523	93,351
Salerno	157,385	151,374	Trento	99,179	102,124
Foggia	156,467	159,541	Lecce	91,289	102,344
Ferrara	149,453	140,600			

CLIMATE. The climate varies considerably with latitude. In the south, it is warm temperate, with little rain in the summer months, but the north is cool temperate with rainfall more evenly distributed over the year.

Florence, Jan. 42°F (5·6°C), July 76°F (25°C). Annual rainfall 36" (901 mm). Milan, Jan. 35°F (2°C), July 75°F (24°C). Annual rainfall 32" (802 mm). Naples, Jan. 48°F (8·9°C), July 77°F (25·6°C). Annual rainfall 34" (850 mm). Palermo, Jan. 52°F (11·1°C), July 79°F (26·1°C). Annual rainfall 28" (702 mm). Rome, Jan. 44·5°F (7°C), July 77°F (25°C). Annual rainfall 26" (657 mm). Venice, Jan. 38°F (3·3°C), July 75°F (23·9°C). Annual rainfall 29" (725 mm).

CONSTITUTION AND GOVERNMENT. The new Constitution was passed by the constituent assembly by 453 votes to 62 on 22 Dec. 1947; it came into force on 1 Jan. 1948. The Constitution consists of 139 articles and 18 transitional clauses. Its main dispositions are as follows:

Italy is described as 'a democratic republic founded on work'. Parliament consists of the *Chamber of Deputies* and the *Senate*. The Chamber is elected for 5 years by universal and direct suffrage and it consists of 630 deputies. The Senate is elected for 5 years on a regional basis; each Region having at least 7 senators, consisting of 315 elected senators; the Valle d'Aosta is represented by 1 senator only, the Molise by 2. The President of the Republic can nominate 5 senators for life from eminent men in the social, scientific, artistic and literary spheres. On the expiry of his term of office, the President of the Republic becomes a senator by right and for life, unless he declines. The *President* of the Republic is elected in a joint session of Chamber and Senate, to which are added 3 delegates from each Regional Council (1 from the Valle d'Aosta). A two-thirds majority is required for the election, but after a third indecisive scrutiny the absolute majority of votes is sufficient. The President must be 50 years or over; his term lasts for 7 years. The President of the Senate acts as his deputy. The President can dissolve the chambers of parliament, except during the last 6 months of his term of office.

The Cabinet can be forced to resign only on a motivated motion of censure; the defeat of a government bill does not involve the resignation of the Government.

The salary of the President in 1990 was 248·41m. lira a year; of the Prime Minister, 240m. lira; and of members of the Chamber of Deputies, 180m. lira.

A *Constitutional Court*, consisting of 15 judges who are appointed, 5 each, by the President of the Republic, Parliament (in joint session) and the highest law and administrative courts, can decide on the constitutionality of laws and decrees, define the powers of the State and Regions, judge conflicts between the State and Regions and between the Regions, and try the President of the Republic and the Ministers. The court was set up in Dec. 1955.

The reorganization of the Fascist Party is forbidden. Direct male descendants of King Victor Emmanuel are excluded from all public offices, have no right to vote or to be elected, and are banned from Italian territory; their estates are forfeit to the State. Titles of nobility are no longer recognized, but those existing before 28 Oct. 1922 are retained as part of the name.

A referendum was held in June 1991 to decide whether the system of preferential voting by indicating 4 candidates by their listed number should be changed to a simpler system, less open to abuse, of indicating a single candidate by name. The electorate was 46m. Turn-out was 62·5% (there was a 50% quorum). 95·6% of votes cast were in favour of the change.

National flag: Three vertical strips of green, white, red.

National anthem: Fratelli d'Italia ('Brothers of Italy'; words by G. Mameli; tune by M. Novaro, 1847).

Head of State: On 3 July 1985 Chamber and Senate in joint session elected by an absolute majority (752 votes out of 977 votes cast) Francesco Cossiga (Christian Democrat; b. 1928), President of the Republic.

Former Presidents of the Republic: Luigi Einaudi (1948–55); Giovanni Gronchi (1955–62); Antonio Segni (1962–64); Giuseppe Saragat (1964–71); Giovanni Leone (1971–78); Alessandro Pertini (1978–85).

General elections for the Senate and Chamber of Deputies took place on 14 June 1987.

Senate. Christian Democrats, 125; Communists, 101; Socialists, 36; Italian Social Movement, 16; Social Democrats, 5; Republicans, 8; Liberals, 3; other groups, 21. Total: 315.

Chamber. Christian Democrats, 234; Communists, 177; Socialists, 94; Italian Social Movement, 35; Republicans, 21; Social Democrats, 17; Liberals, 11; Radical Party, 13; Green Party, 13; other groups, 15. Total: 630.

The coalition government was composed as follows in Feb. 1992.

Prime Minister: Giulio Andreotti (DC).

Vice Prime Minister: Claudio Martelli (PSI).
Foreign Affairs: Gianni De Michelis (PSI).
Interior: Vincenzo Scotti (DC).
Justice: (Vacant).
Southern Affairs: Giovanni Maroggio (DC).
Treasury: Guido Carli (DC).
Budget: Paolo Cirino Pomicino (DC).
Finance: Rino Formica (PSI).
Defence: Virginio Rognoni (DC).
Education: Gerardo Bianco (DC).
Public Works: Giovanni Prandini (DC).
Agriculture: Vito Saccamandi (DC).
Transport: Carlo Bernini (DC).
Post: Oscar Mammi (PRI).
Industry: Adolfo Battaglia (PRI).
Labour: Carlo Donat Cattin (DC).
Foreign Trade: Renato Ruggiero (PSI).
Merchant Navy: Carlo Vizzini (PSDI).
State Shareholdings: vacant.
Health: Francesco De Lorenzo (PLI).
Tourism: Carlo Tognoli (PSI).
Culture: Ferdinando Facchiano (PSDI)
EEC Affairs: Pierluigi Romita (PSI).
Public Administration: Remo Gaspari (DC).
Scientific Research and Universities: Antonio Ruberti (PSI).
Regional and Institutional Affairs: Antonio Maccanico (PRI).
Relations with Parliament: Egidio Sterpa (PLI).
Civil Protection: Vito Lattanzio (DC).
Ecology: Giorgio Ruffolo (PSI).
Urban Problems: Carmelo Conte (PSI).
Special Affairs: Rosa Russo Jervolino (DC).

General elections were scheduled for 5 and 6 April 1992.

Regional Administration. Italy is administratively divided into 15 autonomous regions, 5 autonomous regions with special statute, regions, provinces and municipalities. The regions have their own parliaments (*consiglio regionale*) and governments (*giunta regionale e presidente*) with certain legislative and administrative functions adapted to the circumstances of each region. A government commissioner co-ordinates regional and national activities.

Measures for the autonomy of the largely German-speaking Alto Adige (South Tyrol) were granted in Jan. 1992.

Regional elections were held in May 1990. Turn-out was 87·1%. Share of votes cast: Christian Democrats, 33·4%; Communists, 24%; Socialists, 15·3%; various regional autonomy movements, 7%; Greens, 5%; Italian Social Movement (MSI), 4%. These and other results by region:

Regions	Election date	Christ-ian Demo-crats	Com-mun-ists	Social-ists	Social Move-ment	Social Demo-crats	Repub-licans	Lib-erals	Others	Total
Piemonte	6 May 1990	18	14	9	2	2	2	2	11	60
Valle d'Aosta [1]	26 June 1988	7	5	3	1	–	1	–	18	35
Lombardia	6 May 1990	25	15	12	2	1	2	1	22	80
Trentino-Alto Adige [1]	20 Nov. 1988	20	4	5	5	1	1	1	33	70
Veneto	6 May 1990	27	10	8	1	1	1	1	11	60
Friuli-Venezia Giulia [1]	26 June 1988	24	11	12	3	2	1	1	8	62
Liguria	6 May 1990	12	12	6	1	1	1	1	6	40
Emilia-Romagna	6 May 1990	13	23	6	1	1	2	1	3	50
Toscana	6 May 1990	14	22	6	1	1	1	1	4	50
Umbria	6 May 1990	9	12	5	1	–	1	–	2	30
Marche	6 May 1990	15	13	5	1	1	1	1	3	40
Lazio	6 May 1990	22	15	9	4	2	3	1	4	60

Regions	Election date	Christ-ian Demo-crats	Com-mun-ists	Social-ists	Social Move-ment	Social Demo-crats	Repub-licans	Lib-erals	Others	Total
Abruzzi	6 May 1990	20	8	6	1	1	1	1	2	40
Molise	6 May 1990	19	4	4	1	1	1	–	–	30
Campania	6 May 1990	25	10	12	3	3	3	1	3	60
Puglia	6 May 1990	22	10	10	3	2	1	1	1	50
Basilicata	6 May 1990	15	6	6	1	2	–	–	–	30
Calabria	6 May 1990	16	8	9	2	2	1	1	1	40
Sicilia [1]	16 June 1991	39	13	13	5	6	3	2	9	90
Sardegna [1]	11 June 1989	29	19	12	3	4	3	–	10	80

[1] Autonomous regions with special statute.

DEFENCE. Head of the armed forces is the Defence Chief of Staff. There is conscription for 12 months.

Army. The Army consists of 3 corps, one of which is mountain, consisting of 8 mechanized, 4 armoured, 5 mountain and 1 motorized brigades. In addition there is a rapid intervention force, 2 amphibious battalions and a support brigade with missiles. Equipment includes 300 M-60A1 and 920 Leopard main battle tanks. The Army air corps operates 8 DO228 transports, over 60 light aircraft and 380 helicopters. Strength (1992) 234,200 (170,000 conscripts), with 520,000 reserves. The paramilitary Carabinieri number 111,400.

Navy. The principal ships of the Navy are the light aircraft carrier *Giuseppe Garibaldi*, the helicopter-carrying cruiser *Vittorio Veneto*, and the guided missile cruiser *Andrea Doria*. The *Giuseppe Garibaldi*, 13,450 tonnes, was completed in 1985 and currently operates an air group of 16 SH-3D Sea King anti-submarine helicopters. She is also armed with 4 Teseo anti-ship missiles. The *Vittorio Veneto*, completed in 1969, is of 9,650 tonnes, and operates a squadron of 6 AB-212 anti-submarine helicopters as well as a twin launcher for ASROC and US Standard SM-1 surface-to-air missiles, and 4 Teseo. The *Andrea Doria* displaces 7,400 tonnes, was completed in 1964, is armed with Standard SM-1 missiles, and operates 3 AB-212 anti-submarine helicopters.

The combatant forces also include 9 diesel submarines, 3 guided-missile destroyers armed with Standard SM-I, 26 frigates, of which 14 carry one or more AB-212 helicopters, 3 corvettes and 7 missile-armed patrol hydrofoils. Mine countermeasure forces comprise 2 ocean minesweepers, 11 coastal minehunters and 2 coastal sweepers. There are 4 new offshore patrol vessels for the protection of economic resources. Amphibious lift for the San Marco commando group (800 men) is provided by 2 dock landing ships and 40 craft. Auxiliaries include 2 replenishment oilers, 4 water carriers, 3 survey ships, 3 trial vessels, 2 training ships and 9 large tugs.

The Naval Air Arm, 1,500 strong, operates 98 anti-submarine and training helicopters and has acquired the first 2 training Harrier-type TAV-8B short take off/ vertical landing aircraft for the carrier squadron now on order. There is a Special Forces commando of some 600 assault swimmers.

Main naval bases are at Spezia, Naples, Taranto and Ancona, with minor bases at Brindisi and Venice. The personnel of the Navy in 1991 numbered 49,000, including the naval air arm and the marine battalion.

Paramilitary maritime tasks are carried out by the Financial Guards fleet of some 70 patrol craft and a harbour control force with 25 inshore patrol craft and numerous boats.

Air Force. Control is exercised through 2 regional HQ near Taranto and Milan. Units assigned to NATO comprise the 1st air brigade of Nike-Hercules surface-to-air missiles, 5 fighter-bomber, 2 light attack, 8 interceptor and 2 tactical reconnaissance squadrons, with supporting transport, search and rescue, and training units. Two of the fighter-bomber squadrons have Tornados, others have Aeritalia G91Ys. The light attack squadrons operate AM-X Centauros, of which 187 are being delivered to repalce G91R, G91Y and F-104G aircraft. F-104S Starfighters have been standardized throughout the interceptor squadrons. The reconnaissance force operates RF-104G Starfighters.

One transport squadron has turboprop C-130H Hercules aircraft; 2 others have turboprop Aeritalia G222s. There is a VIP and personnel transport squadron, equipped with AS-61, DC-9, Gulfstream III and Falcon 50 aircraft. Electronic warfare duties are performed by specially equipped G222s, PD-808s and MB 339s. Two land-based anti-submarine squadrons operate Breguet Atlantics. Search and rescue are performed by 30 Agusta-Sikorsky HH-3F helicopters and smaller types. There are also strong support and training elements; some MB 339 jet trainers have armament provisions for secondary close air support and anti-helicopter roles.

Air Force strength in 1992 was about 78,200 (26,000 conscripts) with 449 combat aircraft.

INTERNATIONAL RELATIONS

Membership. Italy is a member of the UN, NATO, EC and WEU. With Austria, Czechoslovakia, Hungary and Yugoslavia, Italy was an inaugural member of the 'Pentagonal' meeting on economic and political co-operation in July 1990. On Poland's accession in May 1991, it was renamed 'Hexagonal'. In Nov. 1990 Italy acceded to the Schengen Accord of June 1990 which abolishes border controls between Belgium, France, Germany, Luxembourg, the Netherlands, Portugal and Spain.

ECONOMY

Budget. Total revenue and expenditure for fiscal years, in 1m. lire:

	Revenue	Expenditure		Revenue	Expenditure
1984	199,986,000	292,348,000	1987	283,875,850	442,965,463
1985	218,973,000	319,099,000	1988	312,790,760	474,587,541
1986	266,301,009	384,344,429	1989	346,428,493	464,650,218

In the revenue for 1989 turnover and other business taxes accounted for 81,140,380m. lire, customs duties and indirect taxes for 30,111,544m. lire.

The public debt at 31 Dec. 1989 totalled 1,047,952,764m. lire, including consolidated debt of 40,436m. lire and the floating debt 429,799,875m. lire.

Currency. The unit of currency is the *lira* (ITL). From 30 March 1960 the gold standard was formally established as equal to 0·00142187 gramme of gold per lira.

State metal coins are of 5, 10, 20, 50, 100, 200, and 500 lire. There are in circulation bank-notes of 1,000, 2,000, 5,000, 10,000, 20,000, 50,000 and 100,000 lire; they are neither convertible into gold as foreign moneys nor exportable abroad, nor importable from abroad into Italy (except for certain specified small amounts).

Circulation of money at 31 Dec. 1989: State coins and notes, 1,436,796m. lire; bank-notes, 73,376,000m. lire.

Foreign reserves (excluding gold) totalled US$46,700m. in 1989.

In March 1992 the rate of exchange was 1,230·99 lire = US$1 and 2,161 lire = £1 sterling.

Banking and Finance. The Bank of Italy was founded in 1893 and became the sole bank of issue in 1926. It is owned by public-sector banks. Its *governor* (Carlo Ciampi) is selected without fixed term by the 13 directors of the Bank's non-executive board. In 1991 it received increased responsibility for the supervision of banking and stock exchange affairs. Its gold reserve amounted to 30,580,000m. lire in Dec. 1990; the foreign credit reserves of the Exchange Bureau (*Ufficio Italiano Cambi*) amounted to 63,810,000m. lire at the same date.

Since 1936, all credit institutions have been under the control of a State organ, named 'Inspectorate of Credit'; the Bank of Italy has been converted into a 'public institution', whose capital is held exclusively by corporate bodies of a public nature. Other credit institutions, totalling 1,064, are classified as: (1) 6 chartered banks (Banco di Napoli, Banco di Sicilia, Banca Nazionale del Lavoro, Monte dei Paschi di Siena, Istituto di S. Paolo di Torino, Banca di Sardegna); (2) 3 banks of national interest (Banca Commerciale Italiana in Milan, Credito Italiano in Genoa and Banco di Roma); (3) banks and credit concerns in general, including 143 joint-stock banks and 108 co-operative banks; (4) 82 savings banks and Monti di pegno (institutions granting loans against personal chattels as security); (5) 717 *Casse rurali e agrarie* (agricultural banks, established as co-operative institutions with unlimited liability of associates); (6) 5 Istituti di Categoria.

The 'Amato' law of July 1990 gave public sector banks the right to become joint stock companies and permitted the placing of up to 49% of their equity with private shareholders.

At 31 Dec. 1990 there were 292 credit institutes handling 94% of all deposits and current accounts, with capital and reserves of 95,594,000m. lire.

On 31 Dec. 1990 the post office savings banks had deposits and current accounts of 143,977,000m. lire; credit institutions, 692,185,000m. lire.

Legislation reforming stock markets came into effect in Dec. 1990. There are stock exchanges in Milan, Rome, Turin and Genoa.

By a decree of 29 April 1923 life-assurance business is carried on only by the National Insurance Institute and by other institutions, national and foreign, authorized by the Government. At 31 Dec. 1989 the insurances vested in the *Istituto Nazionale delle Assicurazioni* amounted to 28,990,671m. lire, including the decuple of life annuities.

Weights and Measures. The metric system is in general use.

ENERGY AND NATURAL RESOURCES

Electricity. Italy has greatly developed its hydro-electric resources. In 1990 the total power generated was 216,891m. kwh., of which 35,079m. kwh. were generated by hydro-electric plants. Supply 220 volts; 50 Hz and 120, 125, 160 and 260 volts; 60 Hz.

Oil. Production in 1990 amounted to 4,623,694 tonnes, of which 806,733 came from Sicily. Natural gas production (1990) 597,326m. cu. ft.

Minerals. Mining is most developed in Sicily (Caltanissetta), Tuscany (Arezzo, Florence and Grosseto), Sardinia (Cagliari, Sassari and Iglesias), Lombardy (particularly near Bergamo and Brescia) and Piedmont.

Italy's fuel and mineral resources are wholly inadequate. Only sulphur and mercury outputs yield a substantial surplus for exports. In 1989 outputs, in tonnes, of raw steel were 25,180,676; rolled iron, 22,772,238; cast-iron ingots, 11,761,000.

Production of metals and minerals (in tonnes) was as follows:

	1985	1986	1987	1988	1989	1990
Iron pyrites	690,395	760,860	784,924	720,132	835,713	805,825
Manganese	8,621	6,396	3,802	9,701	5,899	6,654
Zinc	87,380	50,515	67,798	71,979	80,960	83,077
Crude sulphur	4,911	–	–	–	–	–
Bauxite	–	2,250	15,057	17,864	14,864	–
Lead	37,051	27,219	58,515	68,946	71,240	64,591
Aluminium	226,300	262,562	258,051	257,995	233,046	246,346

Agriculture. The area of Italy in 1988 comprised 301,278 sq. km, of which 262,780 sq. km was agricultural and forest land and 38,498 sq. km was unproductive; the former was mainly distributed as follows (in 1,000 ha): Forage and pasture, 7,881; woods, 6,756; cereals, 4,590; vines, 1,165; olive trees, 994; garden produce, 680; leguminous plants, 289.

At the third general census of agriculture (24 Oct. 1982) agricultural holdings numbered 3,270,560 and covered 23,559,924 ha. 3,063,010 owners (93·6%) farmed directly 16,597,798 ha (70·4%); 152,250 owners (4·7%) worked with hired labour on 6,209,702 ha (26·4%); 130,648 share-croppers (3·6%) tilled 1,271,485 ha (5·1%); the remaining 55,300 holdings (1·7%) of 752,424 ha (3·2%) were operated in other ways.

According to the labour force survey in July 1990 persons engaged in agriculture numbered 1·9m. (1·22m. males and 0·68m. females).

In 1989, 1,399,375 farm tractors were being used.

The production of the principal crops (in 1,000 metric quintals) in 1990: Sugar beet, 117,684; wheat, 80,478; maize, 58,639; tomatoes, 54,691; potatoes, 23,172;

oranges, 17,607; rice, 12,907; barley, 17,034; lemons, 6,374; oats, 2,984; olive oil, 9,125; tangerines, mandarines and clementines, 3,864; other citrus fruit, 329; rye, 208.

Production of wine, 1990, 54,866,100 hectolitres; of tobacco (1989), 188,000 tonnes.

In 1989 consumption of chemical fertilizers in Italy was as follows (in 1,000 tons): Perphosphate, 574·3; nitrate of ammonia, 713·3; sulphate of ammonium, 308·3; potash salts, 311; nitrate of calcium$^{15/16}$, 62·5; deposed slags, 28·6.

Livestock estimated in 1990: Cattle, 8,234,500; pigs, 8,837,000; sheep, 10,847,600; goats, 1,297,500; horses, 288,000; donkeys, 51,000; mules, 33,000.

Fisheries. The Italian fishing fleet comprised, in 1989, 18,433 motor boats of 263,164 gross tonnes and 5,629 sailing vessels of 7,008 gross tonnes. The catch in 1989 was 3,609,629 metric quintals.

INDUSTRY. The main branches of industry are: (% of industrial value added at factor cost in 1990) Textiles, clothing, leather and footwear (14·2%), food, beverages and tobacco (8%), energy products (9·1%), agricultural and industrial machines (8·9%), metal products except machines and means of transport (9%), mineral and non-metallic mineral products (7·1%), timber and wooden furniture (4·8%), electric plants and equipment (6·6%), chemicals and pharmaceuticals (8·5%), means of transport (7·3%).

Production, 1990: Steel, 25,466,928 tonnes; motor vehicles, 2,133,879; cement, 40,544,149 tonnes; artificial and synthetic fibres (including staple fibre and waste), 727,122 tonnes; polyethylene resins, 931,143 tonnes.

Labour. In 1988, 20·8m. persons were employed and 2m. unemployed. Unemployment was 12% in 1990. Pensionable retirement age was 60 for men and 55 for women in 1991, but this is being progressively raised to 65 for both sexes.

Trade Unions. There are 4 main groups: Confederazione Generale Italiana del Lavoro (Communist-dominated); Confederazione Italiana Sindacati Lavoratori (Catholic); Unione Italiana del Lavoro and Confederazione Italiana Sindacati Nazionali Lavoratori.

FOREIGN ECONOMIC RELATIONS. Foreign debt was US$74,000m. in Nov. 1990.

Commerce. The territory covered by foreign trade statistics includes Italy and San Marino, but excludes the municipalities of Livigno and Campione.

The following table shows the value of Italy's foreign trade (in 1m. lire):

	1985	1986	1987	1988	1989	1990
Imports	172,809,202	148,993,862	161,596,640	180,064,049	209,910,059	217,724,798
Exports	149,723,608	145,331,231	150,454,324	167,189,222	192,797,156	203,586,272

The following table shows trade by countries in 1m. lire:

	Imports into Italy from			Exports from Italy to		
Countries	1988	1989	1990	1988	1989	1990
Argentina	591,995	612,593	770,399	453,033	398,195	400,655
Australia	1,272,254	1,372,744	1,172,911	1,298,182	1,636,012	1,279,068
Austria	4,320,180	4,846,701	4,967,965	4,129,405	4,637,114	4,966,958
Belgium-Luxembourg	8,801,012	10,391,355	11,084,491	5,712,674	6,306,245	6,937,121
France	26,733,833	30,841,861	30,981,175	27,677,255	31,412,527	33,340,992
Germany, Fed. Rep. of	39,217,256	44,496,397	46,192,114	30,211,166	32,717,634	38,699,047
Japan	4,549,940	4,840,880	5,069,383	3,165,492	4,404,147	4,772,388
Netherlands	10,299,944	11,532,003	12,483,940	5,136,207	5,972,640	6,351,270
Switzerland	8,062,673	9,089,017	9,934,733	7,868,418	8,617,249	9,219,850
USSR	4,091,736	4,940,999	4,938,393	2,733,745	3,529,233	3,184,899
UK	9,168,468	10,172,712	11,381,274	13,416,658	15,204,471	14,408,076
USA	10,053,542	11,443,604	11,102,585	14,834,391	16,614,970	15,526,269
Yugoslavia	2,959,017	3,497,279	3,595,171	2,041,451	2,604,925	3,565,909

In 1988 the main imports were maize, wood, greasy wool, metal scrap, pit-coal, petroleum, raw oils, meat, paper, rolled iron and steel, copper and alloys, mechanical and electric equipment, motor vehicles. The main exports were fruit and vegetables, fabrics, footwear and other clothing articles, rolled iron and steel, machinery, motor vehicles, plastic materials and petroleum by-products.

Italy's balance of trade (in 1,000m. lire) has been estimated as follows:

		Goods and services		Income from investments and	Net
	Export	Import	Balance	work, balance	balance
1980	83,705	94,276	−10,571	790	−9,781
1988	208,816	206,734	+1,482	−7,888	−5,806
1989	241,898	243,664	−1,766	−10,323	−12,089

Remittances from Italians abroad (in US$1m. until 1969 and then 1,000m. lire): 1950, 72; 1960, 214; 1970, 289; 1980, 1,059; 1989, 1,858.

Total trade between Italy and UK (British Department of Trade returns, in £1,000 sterling):

	1987	1988	1989	1990	1991
Imports to UK	5,216,751	5,817,445	6,701,683	6,735,496	6,378,908
Exports and re-exports from UK	4,145,659	4,106,417	4,630,896	5,612,751	6,145,014

Tourism. In 1989, 55·1m. foreigners visited Italy; they included 10·1m. German, 10·2m. Swiss, 9·4m. French, 6·1m. Austrian, 5·9m. Yugoslav, 1·9m. British, 1·8m. Dutch and 1·4m. US citizens. They spent about 16,443,000m. lire.

COMMUNICATIONS

Roads. Italy's roads totalled (31 Dec. 1988) 302,403 km, of which 50,843 km were state roads and highways, 109,894 km provincial roads, 141,666 km communal roads. Motor vehicles, Dec. 1987: Cars, 24,320,167m.; buses, 74,114; lorries, 1,994,661; motor cycles, light vans, etc., 6,890,339.

Railways. Railway history in Italy begins in 1839, with a line between Naples and Portici (8 km). Length of railways (31 Dec. 1990), 19,595 km, including 16,066 km of state railways (9,799 km electrified). In 1990 the state railways carried 429m. passengers and 65m. tonnes of goods. There are metros in Milan (68 km) and Rome (33·5 km), and tram/light rail networks in Genoa (2·3 km), Milan (240 km), Naples (23 km) and Turin (119 km).

Civil Aviation. The Italian airline Alitalia (with a capital of 585,000m. lire, of which 99·1% is owned by the State) operates flights to every part of the world. Airports include 25 international, 36 national and 75 club airports. Domestic and international traffic in 1989 registered 20,784,413 passengers arrived and 20,846,342 departed, while freight and mail (excluding luggage) amounted to 205,842 tonnes unloaded and 229,787 tonnes loaded.

Shipping. The mercantile marine at 31 Dec. 1986 consisted of 2,031 vessels of 8,060,067 gross tons, not including pleasure boats (yachts, etc.), sailing and motor vessels. There were 1,371 motor vessels of 100 gross tons and over.

In 1988, 271,266,000 tonnes of cargo were unloaded, and 104,211,000 tonnes of cargo were loaded in Italian ports.

Telecommunications. On 31 Dec. 1985 there were 14,276 post offices and 13,759 telegraph offices. The maritime radio-telegraph service had 20 coast stations. On 1 Jan. 1987 the telephone service had 26,873,730 apparatus. *Radiotelevisione Italiana* broadcasts 3 programmes and additional regional programmes, including transmissions in English, French, German and Slovenian on medium- and short-waves and on FM. It also broadcasts 2 TV programmes. In 1991 there were 14,817,197 radio and 15,089,500 TV sets (colour by PAL).

Cinemas. There were 3,587 cinemas in 1989.

Newspapers. There were (1988) 73 daily newspapers with a combined circulation of 6,005,000 copies; of the papers 12 are published in Rome and 7 in Milan. One daily each is published in German and Slovene.

JUSTICE, RELIGION, EDUCATION AND WELFARE

Justice. Italy has 1 court of cassation, in Rome, and is divided for the administration of justice into 26 appeal court districts, subdivided into 160 tribunal *circondari* (districts), and these again into *mandamenti* each with its own magistracy (*Pretura*), 628 in all. There are also 90 first degree assize courts and 26 assize courts of appeal. For civil business, besides the magistracy above mentioned, *Conciliatori* have jurisdiction in petty plaints (those to a maximum amount of 1m. lire).

On 31 Dec. 1990 there were 18,137 male and 1,278 female prisoners in establishments for preventive custody, 5,390 males and 39 females in penal establishments and 1,250 males and 56 females in establishments for the execution of safety measures.

Religion. The treaty between the Holy See and Italy, of 11 Feb. 1929, confirmed by article 7 of the Constitution of the republic, lays down that the Catholic Apostolic Roman Religion is the only religion of the State. Other creeds are permitted, provided they do not profess principles, or follow rites, contrary to public order or moral behaviour.

The appointment of archbishops and of bishops is made by the Holy See; but the Holy See submits to the Italian Government the name of the person to be appointed in order to obtain an assurance that the latter will not raise objections of a political nature.

Catholic religious teaching is given in elementary and intermediate schools. Marriages celebrated before a Catholic priest are automatically transferred to the civil register. Marriages celebrated by clergy of other denominations must be made valid before a registrar. In 1972 there were 279 dioceses with 28,154 parishes and 43,714 priests. There were 187,153 members (154,796 women) of about 20,000 religious houses.

In 1962 there were about 100,000 Protestants and about 50,000 Jews.

Education. Education is compulsory from 6 to 14 years of age. An optional pre-school education is given to the children between 3 and 5 years in the preparatory schools (kindergarten schools). Illiteracy of males over 6 years was 2·2% in 1981, of females 3·9%.

Compulsory education can be classified as primary education (5-year course) and junior secondary education (3-year course).

Senior secondary education is subdivided in classical (*ginnasio* and classical *liceo*), scientific (scientific *liceo*), language lyceum, professional institutes and technical education: agricultural, industrial, commercial, technical, nautical institutes, institutes for surveyors, institutes for girls (5-year course) and teacher-training institutes (4-year course).

University education is given in Universities and in University Higher Institutes (4, 5, 6 years, according to degree course).

Statistics for the academic year 1990–91:

Elementary schools	No.	Pupils
Kindergarten	27,716	1,552,694
Public elementary schools	22,015	2,809,412
Private elementary schools	2,253	246,471
Private elementary recognized schools (*parificate*)		

Government secondary schools		Total students
Junior secondary schools	9,986	2,265,947
Classical lyceum	745	229,548
Lyceum for science	1,031	460,297
Language lyceum	375	45,657
Teachers' schools	175	23,340
Teachers' institutes	652	162,464
Professional institutes	1,706	541,576
Technical institutes, of which:		
Industrial institutes	626	329,657
Commercial institutes	1,339	667,743
Surveyors' institutes	542	168,710
Agricultural institutes	94	28,717

Government secondary schools	Total students
Technical institutes (continued):	

Government secondary schools	Total students	
Technical institutes (continued):		
Nautical institutes	50	12,706
Technical institutes for tourism	48	18,855
Managerial institutes	161	49,281
Girls technical schools	72	24,859
Artistic studies	294	97,573

Universities and higher institutes	Date of foundation	Students 1989–90	Teachers 1989–90	Universities and higher institutes	Date of foundation	Students 1989–90	Teachers 1989–90
Ancona	1965	7,812	380	Modena	1678	8,758	622
Arezzo	1971	1,065	84	Napoli	1224	116,871	4,553
Bari	1924	68,351	1,866	Padova	1222	50,364	2,398
Bergamo	1970	4,612	125	Palermo	1805	42,938	2,246
Bologna	1200	73,982	2,827	Parma	1502	17,593	1,009
Brescia	1970	8,596	372	Pavia	1390	22,685	1,240
Cagliari	1626	26,733	1,229	Perugia	1276	20,411	1,227
Camerino				Pescara	1965	12,533	330
(Macerata)	1727	4,547	232	Piacenza	1924	612	100
Campobasso	1986	1,768	196	Pisa	1338	30,373	2,077
Cassino				Potenza	1983	2,427	293
(Frosinone)	1968	6,555	168	Reggio di C.	1968	4,396	189
Catania	1434	35,048	1,650	Roma	1303	186,077	7,067
Catanzaro	1983	4,568	213	Salerno	1944	26,362	609
Chieti	1965	4,210	232	Sassari	1677	9,156	517
Cosenza	1972	7,213	505	Siena	1300	12,659	754
Feltre (Belluno)	1969	579	36	Teramo	1965	6,629	141
Ferrara	1391	5,270	495	Torino	1404	73,304	2,709
Firenze	1924	50,664	2,254	Trento	1965	7,594	412
Foggia	1986	564	122	Trieste	1924	16,030	946
Genova	1243	35,696	1,893	Udine	1969	6,763	475
L'Aquila	1956	6,614	643	Urbino	1564	16,309	578
Lecce	1959	11,851	375	Venezia	1868	27,458	691
Macerata	1290	6,241	164	Verona	1969	10,569	626
Messina	1549	31,289	1,546	Viterbo	1980	2,139	233
Milano	1924	157,153	4,111				

Health. The provision of health services is a regional responsibility, but they are funded by central government. Medical consultations are free, but a portion of prescription costs have been payable since April 1989. In 1986 there were 245,116 doctors and (1988) 424,417 hospital beds.

Social Security. Social expenditure is made up of transfers which the central public departments, local departments and social security departments, make to families. Payment is principally for pensions, family allowances and health services. Expenditure on subsidies, public assistance to various classes of people and people injured by political events or national disasters are also included.

State pensions are indexed to prices, 19m. pensions were paid in 1990.

DIPLOMATIC REPRESENTATIVES

Of Italy in Great Britain (14 Three Kings Yard, London, W1Y 2EH)
Ambassador: Count Giacomo Attolico.

Of Great Britain in Italy (Via XX Settembre 80A, 00187, Rome)
Ambassador: Sir Stephen Egerton, KCMG.

Of Italy in the USA (1601 Fuller St., NW, Washington, D.C., 20009)
Ambassador: Rinaldo Petrignani.

Of the USA in Italy (Via Veneto 119/A, Rome)
Ambassador: Peter Secchia.

Of Italy to the United Nations
Ambassador: Vieri Traxler.

Further Reading

Statistical Information: The Istituto Nazionale di Statistica (16 Via Cesare Balbo 00100 Rome) was set up by law of 9 July 1926 as the national institute in charge of census and all statistical information. *President:* Prof. Guido Mario Rey. *Director-General:* Vincenzo Siesto. Its publications include:

Annuario statistico italiano. 1989, *Compendio statistico italiano.* 1990, *Bollettino mensile di statistica.* Monthly, from 1950, *Statistiche industriali.* 1987, *Statistiche demografiche.* 1988, *Statistiche agrarie.* 1988, *Statistiche della navigazione marittima.* 1990, *Statistiche del commercio interno.* 1990, *Statistiche annuale del commercio con l'estero.* 1988, *Statistiche del commercio con l'estero.* Quarterly, *Statistiche del lavoro.* 1986, *Censimento generale dell'agricoltura.* 1982, *Censimento generale della popolazione, 1981.* Vol. I, II and III, *Censimento generale dell'industria e del commercio.* 1981 *Sommario di statistiche storiche, 1926–1988.*

Italy. Documents and Notes. Servizi delle Informazioni, Rome. 1952 ff.
Italian Books and Periodicals. Bimonthly from 1958
Banco di Roma, *Review of the Economic Condition in Italy* (in English). Bimonthly, 1947 ff.
Credito Italiano, *The Italian Economic Situation.* Bimonthly. Milan, from June 1961 (in Italian), from June 1962 (in English)
Compendio Economico Italiano. Rome, Unione Italiana delle Camere di Commercio. Annually from 1954
Clark, M., *Modern Italy 1871–1982.* London, 1984
Finer, S. E. and Mastropaolo, A. (eds.), *The Italian Party System, 1945–80.* London, 1985
Ginsborg, P., *A History of Contemporary Italy: Society and Politics, 1943–1988.* London, 1990
Hearder, H., *Italy: a Short History.* CUP, 1991
Smith, D. M., *The Making of Italy 1796–1866.* London, 1988
Spotts, F. and Wieser, T., *Italy: A Difficult Democracy.* CUP, 1986

National Library: Biblioteca Nazionale Centrale Vittorio Emanuele II Viale Castro Pretorio, Rome. *Director:* Dr L. M. Crisari.

JAMAICA

Capital: Kingston
Population: 2·4m. (1989)
GNP per capita: US$1,260 (1989)

HISTORY. Jamaica was discovered by Columbus in 1494, and was occupied by the Spaniards between 1509 and 1655, when the island was captured by the English; their possession was confirmed by the Treaty of Madrid, 1670. Self-government was introduced in 1944 and gradually extended until Jamaica achieved complete independence within the Commonwealth on 6 Aug. 1962.

AREA AND POPULATION. The island of Jamaica lies in the Caribbean Sea about 150 km south of Cuba. The area is 4,411 sq. miles (11,425 sq. km). The population at the census of 8 June 1982 was 2,095,878, distributed on the basis of the 14 parishes of the island as follows: Kingston and St Andrew, 565,487; St Thomas, 76,347; Portland, 70,787; St Mary, 101,442; St Ann, 132,475; Trelawny, 65,038; St James, 127,994; Hanover, 60,420; Westmoreland, 116,163; St Elizabeth, 132,353; Manchester, 136,517; St Catherine, 315,970; Clarendon, 194,885.

Chief towns (census, 1982): Kingston and St Andrew, 524,638, metropolitan area; Spanish Town, 89,097; Montego Bay, 70,265; May Pen, 40,962; Mandeville, 34,502.

Estimated population, in 1989, was 2·4m. The population is 76% of African ethnic origin, 3% European and 21% mixed and other groups.

Vital statistics (1989): Births, 59,100 (24·9 per 1,000 population); deaths, 14,300 (6·0); migration loss, 23,305.

CLIMATE. A tropical climate but with considerable variation. High temperatures on the coast are usually mitigated by sea breezes, while upland areas enjoy cooler and less humid conditions. Rainfall is plentiful over most of Jamaica, being heaviest in May and from Aug. to Nov. The island lies in the hurricane zone. Kingston. Jan. 76°F (24·4°C), July 81°F (27·2°C). Annual rainfall 32" (800 mm).

CONSTITUTION AND GOVERNMENT. Under the Constitution of Aug. 1962 the Crown is represented by a Governor-General appointed by the Crown on the advice of the Prime Minister. The Governor-General is assisted by a Privy Council. The Legislature comprises two chambers, an elected House and a nominated Senate. The executive is chosen from both chambers.

The Executive comprises the Prime Minister, who is the leader of the majority party, and Ministers appointed by the Prime Minister. Together they form the Cabinet, which is the highest executive power. An Attorney-General is a member of the House and is legal adviser to the Cabinet.

The Senate consists of 21 senators appointed by the Governor-General, 13 on the advice of the Prime Minister, 8 on the advice of the Leader of the Opposition. The House of Representatives (60 members, Feb. 1991) is elected by universal adult suffrage for a period not exceeding 5 years. Electors and elected must be Jamaican or Commonwealth citizens resident in Jamaica for at least 12 months before registration. The powers and procedure of Parliament correspond to those of the British Parliament.

The Privy Council consists of 6 members appointed by the Governor-General in consultation with the Prime Minister.

Governor-General: Sir Florizel Glasspole, GCMG, GCVO.
National flag: A yellow diagonal cross dividing triangles of green, top and bottom, and black, hoist and fly.
National anthem: Eternal Father, bless our land (words by H. Sherlock, tune by R. Lightbourne).

The elections to the House of Representatives, held on 9 Feb. 1989, returned 45 members of the People's National Party and the Jamaica Labour Party, 15 seats.

The Cabinet in March 1992 was comprised as follows:

Prime Minister: Percival Patterson (b. 1935).

Deputy Prime Minister and Minister of Finance, Development and Planning: Hugh Small, QC. *Foreign Affairs and Foreign Trade:* David Coore, QC. *National Security:* K. D. Knight. *Justice and Attorney-General:* Carl Rattray, QC. *Education:* Carlyle Dunkley. *Health:* Easton Douglas. *Labour, Welfare and Sports:* Portia Simpson. *Construction:* O. D. Ramtallie. *Public Utilities and Transport:* Robert Pickersgill. *Agriculture:* Seymour Mullings. *Local Government:* Ralph Brown. *Tourism:* Frank Pringle. *Mining and Energy:* Vacant. *Youth, Culture and Community Development:* Dr Douglas Manley. *Public Service and Leader of the House (with special responsibility for Parliamentary Affairs):* Dr Kenneth McNeil. *Information and Culture:* Dr Paul Robertson.

There are 12 Ministers of State.

DEFENCE

Army. The Jamaica Defence Force consists of a Regular and a Reserve Force. The Regular Force is comprised of the 1st battalion, Jamaica Regiment and Support Services which include the Air Wing and Coast Guard. The Coast Guard, numbering 180 in 1991, operates 5 inshore patrol craft based at Port Royal. The Reserve Force consists of the 3rd battalion, Jamaica Regiment. Total strength (army, 1991), 3,000. Reserves, 800.

Air Force. The Air Wing of the Jamaica Defence Force was formed in July 1963 and has since been expanded and trained successively by the British Army Air Corps and Canadian air force personnel. Equipment for army liaison, search and rescue, police co-operation, survey and transport duties includes 2 Defender armed STOL transports; 1 Beech King Air and 1 Cessna 337 light transports; 4 JetRanger and 2 Bell 212 helicopters. Personnel (1990) 150.

INTERNATIONAL RELATIONS

Membership. Jamaica is a member of UN, the Commonwealth, OAS, CARICOM and is an ACP state of EEC.

ECONOMY

Budget. Revenue and expenditure for fiscal years ending 31 March (in J$1m.):

	1986–87	1987–88	1988–89	1989–90
Revenue	4,467	5,429	6,020	7,895
Expenditure	5,631	6,509	8,199	7,738

The chief heads of recurrent revenue are income tax; consumption, customs and stamp duties. The other major share of current resources is generated by the Bauxite levy. The chief items of recurrent expenditure are public debt, education and health.

Currency. The unit of currency is the *Jamaican dollar* (JMD), divided into 100 *cents.* The Jamaican dollar was floated in Sept. 1990. Currency circulation at 30 June 1989 was J$1,129·8m. Inflation was 57% in 1991. In March 1992, £1 = J$36·10; US$1 = J$20·56.

Banking and Finance. The central bank is the Bank of Jamaica. It has the sole right to issue notes and coins, acts as Banker to the Government and to the commercial banks, and administers the island's external reserves and exchange control.

There are 10 commercial banks with about 171 branches and agencies in operation. 6 of these banks are subsidiaries of major British and North American banks, of which 4 are incorporated locally. The Workers' Savings and Loan Bank is owned by the Government, Trade Unions and the private sector. The National Commercial Bank (Jamaica) Ltd, is 49% government-owned. The other 8 banks which operate are: The Bank of Nova Scotia (Jamaica) Ltd, City Bank of North America, Mutual Security Bank, Canadian Imperial Bank of Commerce, Jamaica Citizens Bank Ltd, Eagle Commercial Bank, Bank of Credit and Commerce International and Century National Bank.

There is a stock exchange in Kingston, which participates in the regional Caribbean exchange.

Total deposits in commercial banks, 30 June 1990, J$11,083·2m., of which J$3,202·1m. were time deposits and J$5,695·8m. (51·4%) were savings.

ENERGY AND NATURAL RESOURCES

Electricity. The Jamaica Public Service Co. is the public supplier of electricity. The bauxite companies, sugar estates and the Caribbean Cement Co. and Goodyear generate their own electricity. Total installed capacity, 1989, 485·7 mw. Production (1989) 1,878m. kwh. Supply 110 and 220 volts; 50 Hz.

Minerals. Bauxite, ceramic clays, marble, silica sand and gypsum are commercially viable. Jamaica has become the world's third largest producer of bauxite and alumina. The bauxite deposits are worked by a Canadian, an American and a Jamaican company. In 1989, 9·6m. tonnes of bauxite ore was mined; gypsum, 178,000 tonnes; marble, 5,000 tonnes; sand and gravel, 900,000 cu. metres; industrial lime, 2·5m. cu. metres.

Agriculture (1989). Production: Sugar-cane, 2,257,000 tons; sugar, 197,000 tons; rum, 5,556,000 proof gallons; molasses, 85,000 tons; bananas, 43,000 tons; citrus fruit, 591,000 boxes; cocoa, 1,442 tons; spices, 1,932 tons; copra, 256 short tons; domestic food crops, 387,652 short tons.

Livestock (1988): Cattle, 290,000; goats, 440,000; pigs, 250,000; poultry, 6m. Slaughtered livestock (1989): Cattle, 62,090 heads: goats, 44,083 heads: pigs, 125,601; poultry, 86,000 lbs.

INDUSTRY. Three bauxite-mining companies also process bauxite into alumina; production, 1989, 2·2m. tonnes. From processing only a few agricultural products—sugar, rum, condensed milk, oils and fats, cigars and cigarettes—the island is now producing clothing, footwear, textiles, paints, building materials (including cement), agricultural machinery and toilet articles. There is an oil refinery in Kingston. In 1989 manufacturing contributed J$4,497·5m. to the total GDP at current prices.

Labour. Average total labour force (1989), 1,062,900, of whom 871,800 were employed. Government and other services employed 247,000; agriculture, forestry and fishing, 247,700; manufacturing, 133,800; construction and installation, 54,900.

FOREIGN ECONOMIC RELATIONS

Commerce. Value of imports and domestic exports for calendar years (in US$1m.):

	1986	1987	1988	1989	1990
Imports	969	1,234	1,435	1,826	1,782
Domestic exports	567	692	812	970	1,112

Principal imports in 1990 (in US$1m.): Manufactured goods classified by materials, 289·9 (16·3%); machinery and transport equipment, 469·5 (26·3%); food, 206·7 (11·8%); minerals, fuels, lubricants and related materials, 342·0 (19·2%); chemicals, 206·8 (11·6%).

Principal domestic exports in 1990 (in US$1m.): Crude materials, inedible oils except fuels, 718·5 (64·6%), of which alumina, 632·6 (56·9%) and bauxite, 103·1 (9·3%); food, 174·2 (15·6%), of which sugar, 73·0 (6·5%); miscellaneous materials, 98·7 (8·9%).

Total trade between Jamaica and UK (British Department of Trade returns, in £1,000 sterling):

	1987	1988	1989	1990	1991
Imports to UK	85,655	89,693	95,516	136,535	123,773
Exports and re-exports from UK	54,644	48,855	61,355	58,702	54,669

Tourism. In 1990, 1,236,089 tourists arrived in Jamaica, spending about US$700m.

COMMUNICATIONS

Roads (1989). The island has 3,000 miles of main roads, and over 7,000 miles of secondary and tertiary roads. Main roads are constructed and maintained by the

Ministry of Construction (Works), while other roads are constructed and maintained by parish councils. In 1989 there were 98,857 licensed vehicles.

Railways. There are 294 km of railway open of 1,435 mm gauge, operated by the Jamaica Railway Corporation. In 1988 the railway carried 38,540 tonnes and in 1989, carried 1·08m. passengers.

Civil Aviation. Scheduled commercial international airlines operate through the Norman Manley and Sangster international airports at Palisadoes and Montego Bay. In 1989 Norman Manley airport had 25,258 aircraft movements, handled 1·18m. passengers and 25,443 tonnes of freight. Sangster had 20,404 movements, with 1·7m. passengers and 4,164 tonnes of freight. Trans-Jamaica Airlines Ltd operates internal flights; in 1987 it carried 37,600 passengers. Air Jamaica, originally set up in conjunction with BOAC and BWIA in 1966, became a new company, Air Jamaica (1968) Ltd, and is affiliated to Air Canada. In 1969 it began operations as Jamaica's national airline. In 1989 Air Jamaica carried 1·13m. passengers.

Shipping. In 1989 there were 2,456 visits to all ports; 11·6m. tons of cargo were handled. Kingston had 1,411 visits and handled 1·9m. tons. The outports had 1,045 visits and handled 9·6m. tons, of which 7·3m. was loaded and 2·3m. landed.

Telecommunications. In 1989 there were 824 postal points. In Dec. 1989 there were 177,808 telephones.

There were (1989) 2 commercial and 1 publicly owned broadcasting stations; the latter also operates a television service (colour by NTSC). In 1991 there were 1,481,000 radio and 484,000 TV sets.

Cinemas. In 1989 there were 35 cinemas and 2 drive-in cinemas.

JUSTICE, RELIGION, EDUCATION AND WELFARE

Justice. The Judicature comprises a Supreme Court, a court of appeal, resident magistrates' courts, petty sessional courts, coroners' courts, a traffic court and a family court which was instituted in 1975. The Chief Justice is head of the judiciary. All prosecutions are initiated by the Director of Public Prosecutions.

Police. The Constabulary Force in 1989 stood at approximately 5,460 officers, sub-officers and constables (men and women).

Religion. Freedom of worship is guaranteed under the Constitution. The main Christian denominations are Anglican, Baptist, Roman Catholic, Methodist, Church of God, United Church of Jamaica, and Grand Cayman (Presbyterian–Congregational) Moravian, Seventh-Day Adventists, Pentecostal, Salvation Army, Quaker, and Disciples of Christ. Pocomania is a mixture of Christianity and African survivals. Non-Christians include Hindus, Jews, Moslems, Bahai followers and Rastafarians.

Education. In Sept. 1973 education became free for all government grant-aided schools (the majority of all schools) and for all Jamaicans entering the University of the West Indies, the College of Arts, Science and Technology and the Jamaica School of Agriculture. In 1988–89 there were 1,307 pre-primary schools and departments (130,355 pupils); 298 primary schools (172,416 pupils); 493 all-age schools (154,908 pupils).

There were 141 secondary and vocational schools (104,774 students). Teacher-training colleges had 3,190 students; community colleges had 5,508; the College of Arts, Science and Technology had 4,964; the College of Agriculture, 236 and the University of the West Indies, 4,512.

Health. In 1989 the public health service had 3,742 staff in medicine, nursing and pharmacology; 305 in dentistry; 262 public health inspectors; 61 in nutrition. In 1989 there were 359 primary health centres, 5,021 public hospital beds and 282 private beds.

DIPLOMATIC REPRESENTATIVES

Of Jamaica in Great Britain (1-2 Prince Consort Rd., London, SW7 2BZ)
High Commissioner: Ellen Bogle, CD (accredited 27 Oct. 1989).

Of Great Britain in Jamaica (Trafalgar Rd., Kingston 10)
High Commissioner: Derek Milton, CMG.

Of Jamaica in the USA (1850 K. St., NW, Washington, D.C., 20006)
Ambassador: Richard L. Bernal.

Of the USA in Jamaica (2 Oxford Rd., Kingston 5)
Ambassador: Glen A. Holden.

Of Jamaica to the United Nations
Ambassador: Herbert S. Walker.

Further Reading

Statistical Information: The Department of Statistics, now Statistical Institute of Jamaica (25 Dominica Dr., Kingston), was set up in 1945—the nucleus being the Census Office, which undertook the operations of the 1943 Census of Jamaica and its Dependencies. *Director:* Vernon James. Publications of the Institute include the *Bulletin of Statistics on External Trade* and the *Annual Abstract of Statistics.*

Economic and Social Survey, Jamaica. Planning Institute of Jamaica, Kingston (Annual)
Social and Economic Studies. Institute of Social and Economic Research, Univ. of the West Indies. Quarterly
A Review of the Performance of the Jamaican Economy 1981–1983. Jamaica Information Service, 1985
Quarterly Economic Report. Planning Institute of Jamaica, Kingston
Bakan, A. B. *Ideology and Class Conflict in Jamaica: the Politics of Rebellion.* Montreal, 1990
Beckford, G. and Witter, M., *Small Garden... Bitter Weed. The Political Struggle and Change in Jamaica.* 2nd ed. London, 1982
Cassidy, F. G. and Le Page, R. B., *Dictionary of Jamaican English.* CUP, 1966
Floyd, B., *Jamaica: An Island Microcosm.* London, 1979
Goulbourne, H., *Teachers, Education and Politics in Jamaica, 1892–1972.* London, 1988
Ingram, K. E., *Jamaica.* [Bibliography] Oxford and Santa Barbara, 1984
Manley, M., *A Voice at the Work Place.* London, 1975.—*Jamaica: Struggle in the Periphery.* London, 1983
Payne, A. J., *Politics in Jamaica.* London and New York, 1988
Post, K., *Strike the Iron, A Colony at War: Jamaica 1939–1945.* 2 vols. Atlantic Highlands, N.J., 1981
Sherlock, P., *Keeping Company with Jamaica.* London, 1984
Stephens, E. H. and Stephens, J. D., *Democratic Socialism in Jamaica.* London, 1986
Stone, C., *Class, Race and Political Behaviour in Urban Jamaica.* Kingston, 1973—*Democracy and Clientelism in Jamaica.* London and New Brunswick, N.J., 1981
Bibliography of Jamaica, 1900–1963. Jamaica Library Service, 1963

Libraries: National Library of Jamaica, Kingston. Jamaica Library Service, Kingston.

JAPAN

Nippon (*or* Nihon)

Capital: Tokyo
Population: 123·61m. (1990)
GNP per capita: US$23,472 (1989)

HISTORY. The house of Yamato, from about 500 B.C. the rulers of one of several kingdoms, in about A.D. 200 united the nation; the present imperial family are their direct descendants. From 1186 until 1867 successive families of Shoguns exercised the temporal power. In 1867 the Emperor Meiji recovered the imperial power after the abdication on 14 Oct. 1867 of the fifteenth and last Tokugawa Shogun Keiki (in different pronunciation: Yoshinobu). In 1871 the feudal system (Hoken Seido) was abolished; this was the beginning of the rapid westernization.

At San Francisco on 8 Sept. 1951 a Treaty of Peace was signed by Japan and representatives of 48 countries. For details *see* THE STATESMAN'S YEAR-BOOK, 1953, p. 1169. On 26 Oct. 1951 the Japanese Diet ratified the Treaty by 307 votes to 47 votes with 112 abstentions. On the same day the Diet ratified a Security Treaty with the US by 289 votes to 71 votes with 106 abstentions. The treaty provided for the stationing of American troops in Japan until she was able to undertake her own defence. The peace treaty came into force on 28 April 1952, when Japan regained her sovereignty. In 1960 Japan signed the Japan–US Mutual Security Treaty, valid for 10 years, which was renewed in 1970. Of the islands under US administration since 1945, the Bonin (Ogasawara), Volcano, and Daito groups and Marcus Island were returned to Japan in 1968, and the southern Ryukyu Islands (Okinawa) in 1972.

AREA AND POPULATION. Japan consists of 4 major islands, Honshu, Hokkaido, Kyushu and Shikoku, and many small islands, with an area of 377,727 sq. km. Census population (1 Oct. 1990) 123,611,541 (males 60,691,561, females 62,919,980). Population density, 372·2 per sq. km. Foreigners registered 31 Dec. 1990 were 1,075,317, of whom 689,940 were Koreans, 150,339 Chinese, 56,429 Brazilians, 49,092 Filipinos, 38,364 Americans, 10,279 Peruvians, 10,206 British, 6,724 Thais, 6,233 Vietnamese, 1,476 stateless persons. In 1988 there were 3,542 Malaysians and 3,222 West Germans; in 1989 there were 4,172 Canadians.

Japanese overseas, Oct. 1989, 586,972; of these 213,100 lived in USA, 109,311 in Brazil, 37,335 in the UK, 21,361 in the Federal Republic of Germany, 20,565 in Canada, 16,702 in France, 15,118 in Argentina, 13,113 in Thailand, 12,307 in Australia, 11,696 in Hong Kong.

The areas, populations and chief cities of the principal islands (and regions) are:

Island/Region	Sq. km	Census 1990	Chief cities
Hokkaido	83,408	5,644,000	Sapporo
Honshu/Tohoku	66,942	9,738,000	Sendai
/Kanto	32,413	38,543,000	Tokyo
/Chubu	65,770	21,021,000	Nagoya
/Kinki	33,080	22,207,000	Osaka
/Chugoku	31,905	7,745,000	Hiroshima
Shikoku	18,795	4,195,000	Matsuyama
Kyushu	42,144	13,296,000	Fukuoka
Okinawa	2,264	1,222,000	Naha

The leading cities, with population, 1 Oct. 1990 (in 1,000), are:

Akashi	271	Fukuyama	366	Ibaraki	254
Akita	302	Funabashi	533	Ichihara	258
Amagasaki	499	Gifu	410	Ichinomiya	262
Aomori	288	Hachioji	466	Ichikawa	437
Asahikawa	359	Hakodate	307	Iwaki	356
Chiba	829	Hamamatsu	535	Kagoshima	537
Fujisawa	350	Higashiosaka	518	Kanazawa	443
Fukui	253	Himeji	454	Kashiwa	305
Fukuoka	1,237	Hirakata	391	Kasugai	267
Fukushima	278	Hiroshima	1,086	Kawagoe	305

Kawaguchi	439	Naha	305	Suita	345
Kawasaki	1,174	Nara	349	Takamatsu	330
Kitakyushu	1,026	Neyagawa	257	Takatsuki	360
Kobe	1,477	Niigata	486	Tokorozawa	303
Kochi	317	Nishinomiya	427	Tokushima	263
Koriyama	315	Oita	409	Tokyo	8,163
Koshigaya	285	Okayama	594	Toyama	321
Kumamoto	579	Okazaki	307	Toyohashi	338
Kurashiki	415	Omiya	404	Toyonaka	410
Kyoto	1,416	Osaka	2,642	Toyota	332
Machida	349	Sagamihara	532	Urawa	418
Maebashi	286	Sakai	808	Utsunomiya	427
Matsudo	456	Sapporo	1,672	Wakayama	397
Matsuyama	443	Sasebo	245	Yao	278
Miyazaki	287	Sendai	918	Yokkaichi	274
Nagano	347	Shimonoseki	263	Yokohama	3,220
Nagasaki	445	Shizuoka	472	Yokosuka	433
Nagoya	2,155				

Vital statistics (in 1,000) for calendar years:

	1983	1984	1985	1986	1987	1988	1989
Births	1,509	1,490	1,432	1,383	1,347	1,314	1,247
Deaths	740	740	752	751	751	793	789

Crude birth rate of Japanese nationals in present area, 1989, was 10·2 per 1,000 population (1947: 34·3); crude death rate, 6·4; crude marriage rate, 5·8; infant mortality rate per 1,000 live births, 4·6. Population growth rate was 3·7 per 1,000 in 1989. Expectation of life was 75·91 years for men, 81·77 years for women.

CLIMATE. The islands of Japan lie in the temperate zone, north-east of the main monsoon region of S.E. Asia. The climate is temperate with warm, humid summers and relatively mild winters except in the island of Hokkaido and northern parts of Honshu facing the Japan Sea. There is a month's rainy season in June-July, but the best seasons are spring and autumn, though Sept. may bring typhoons. There is a summer rainfall maximum. Tokyo. Jan. 40·5°F (4·7°C), July 77·4°F (25·2°C). Annual rainfall 63" (1,460 mm). Hiroshima. Jan. 39·7°F (4·3°C), July 78°F (25·6°C). Annual rainfall 61" (1,603 mm). Nagasaki. Jan. 43·5°F (6·4°C), July 79·7°F (26·5°C). Annual rainfall 77" (2,002 mm). Osaka. Jan. 42·1°F (5·6°C), July 80·6°F (27°C). Annual rainfall 53" (1,400 mm). Sapporo. Jan. 23·2°F (−4·9°C), July 68·4°F (20·2°C). Annual rainfall 47" (1,158 mm).

EMPEROR. The Emperor bears the title of Nihon-koku Tenno ('Emperor of Japan'). **Akihito**, born in Tokyo, 23 Dec. 1933; succeeded his father, Hirohito, 7 Jan. 1989 (enthroned, 12 Nov. 1990); married 10 April 1959, to Michiko Shoda, born 20 Oct. 1934. *Offspring:* Crown Prince Naruhito (Hironomiya), born 23 Feb. 1960; Prince Fumihito (Akishinomiya), born 30 Nov. 1965; Princess Sayako (Norinomiya), born 18 April 1969.

By the Imperial House Law of 11 Feb. 1889, revised on 16 Jan. 1947, the succession to the throne was fixed upon the male descendants.

CONSTITUTION AND GOVERNMENT. Japan's Government is based upon the Constitution of 1947 which superseded the Meiji Constitution of 1889. In it the Japanese people pledge themselves to uphold the ideas of democracy and peace. The Emperor is the symbol of the States and of the unity of the people. Sovereign power rests with the people. The Emperor has no powers related to government. Fundamental human rights are guaranteed.

National flag: White, with a red disc.

National anthem: Kimi ga yo wa ('May your peaceful reign long last'; words 9th century, tune by Hiromori Hayashi, 1881).

Legislative power rests with the *Diet*, which consists of the *House of Representatives* (of 512 members), elected by men and women over 20 years of age for a 4-year term, and the *House of Councillors* of 252 members (100 elected by party list system with proportional representation according to the d'Hondt method and 152 from prefectural districts), one-half of its members being elected every 3 years. The House of Representatives controls the budget and approves treaties with foreign powers.

The former House of Peers is replaced by the House of Councillors, whose members, like those of the House of Representatives, are elected as representatives of all the people. The House of Representatives has pre-eminence over the House of Councillors.

In 1990 the Prime Minister's salary was 2,062,280 yen per month.

On 8 Jan. 1992 the House of Representatives consisted of 279 Liberal Democrats (LDP), 138 Socialists, 46 Komeito (Buddhist), 16 Communists, 14 Democratic Socialists, 9 others.

The Cabinet, as constituted in Feb. 1992, was as follows:

Prime Minister: Kiichi Miyazawa (b. 1919; LDP).
Justice: Takashi Tawara.
Foreign Affairs: Michio Watanabe (b. 1923).
Finance: Tsutomu Hata.
Education: Kunio Hatoyama.
Health and Welfare: Tokuo Yamashita.
Agriculture, Forestry and Fishery: Masami Tanabu.
Internal Trade and Industry (MITI): Kozo Watanabe.
Transport: Keiwa Okuda.
Postal Service: Hideo Watanabe.
Labour: Tetsuo Kondo.
Construction: Taku Yamasaki.
Home Affairs: Masajuro Shiokawa.
Science and Technology: Kanzo Tanigawa.
Chief Cabinet Secretary: Koichi Kato.

Local Government. The country is divided into 47 prefectures (*Todofuken*), including Tokyo-to (the capital), Osaka-fu and Kyoto-fu, Hokkai-do, and 43 *Ken*. Each *Todofuken* has its governor (*Chiji*) elected by the voters in the area. The prefectural government of Tokyo-to is also responsible for the urban part (formerly Tokyo-shi) of the prefecture. Each prefecture, city, town and village has a representative assembly elected by the same franchise as in parliamentary elections. There were 3,268 local authorities in 1990.

Elections were held in April 1991 for 2,693 seats in 44 prefectures. The LDP gained 1,543 seats (1,382 in 1987), the Socialists 345 (443), Komeito 159 (186), the Communists 98 (118) and the Democratic Socialists 82 (104).

DEFENCE. Japan has renounced war as a sovereign right and the threat or the use of force as a means of settling disputes with other nations. Its troops may not serve abroad, a stipulation upheld by the Diet in 1990.

In Jan. 1991 Japan and the USA signed a renewal agreement under which Japan pays 40% of the costs of stationing US forces and 100% of the associated labour costs.

Army. The 'Ground Self-Defence Force' had in 1991 an authorized strength of 156,200 uniformed personnel, plus a reserve of 46,000 men. The Army is organized in 12 infantry divisions, 1 armoured division, 1 airborne brigade, 2 air defence brigades, 1 artillery, 2 combined and 1 helicopter brigades in addition to 4 anti-aircraft artillery groups. Equipment includes 1,200 main battle tanks, approximately 450 anti-armour, observation and training helicopters, as well as 19 fixed-wing aircraft.

The Northern Army, stationed in Hokkaido, consists of 4 divisions (1 of which is armoured), an artillery brigade, an anti-aircraft artillery brigade, a tank group and an engineering brigade. The Western Army, stationed in Kyushu, consists of 2 divisions and 1 combined brigade. The North-Eastern Army (2 divisions), the Eastern Army (2 divisions and 1 airborne brigade), the Middle Army (3 divisions and 1 combined brigade). The infantry division establishment is approximately 9,000 with

4 infantry regiments or 7,000 (lower establishment) with 3 infantry regiments. Each infantry division has an artillery regiment, an anti-tank unit, a tank battalion and an engineering battalion in addition to administrative units.

Navy. The 'Maritime Self-Defence Force' is tasked with coastal protection and defence of the sea lanes to 1,000 nautical miles range from Japan. The modern and well-equipped combatant forces are mainly equipped with American weapon systems, which in many cases have been re-engineered and improved in Japan.

The combatant fleet, all home-built, comprises 15 diesel submarines and 2 trials and training boats, 6 guided-missile destroyers armed with US Standard SM1 surface to air missiles, 24 helicopter-carrying frigates, with one or more Sea King anti-submarine helicopters, and 36 other frigates of which 5 are employed on non-military tasks. Light forces comprise 2 torpedo craft and 9 small inshore patrol craft. There are 47 mine warfare vessels, 1 minelayer, 1 layer/command ship, 32 coastal minesweepers and 12 smaller vessels. A substantial amphibious capability is provided by 6 tank landing ships supported by some 40 smaller craft. 12 major auxiliaries include 4 combined oiler/ammunition ships, 5 survey vessels and 3 training support vessels, and there are several hundred minor auxiliaries and service craft.

The Air Arm, organized into 7 operational Air Groups, includes 95 Orion and Neptune anti-submarine patrol aircraft, 7 US-1 rescue flying boats, 72 Sea King anti-submarine helicopters, 17 mine countermeasures helicopters as well as numerous transport, training and utility aircraft.

The main elements of the fleet are organized into 4 escort flotillas based at Yokosuka (2), Sasebo and Maizuru. The submarines are based at Sasebo and Kure.

Personnel in 1991 numbered 44,000 including about 12,000 in the Naval Air Arm.

The Maritime Safety Agency (coastguard) regulates and safeguards all coastal navigation, providing a comprehensive search-and-rescue and navigation service. It operates 81 offshore patrol vessels, 11 coastal patrol vessels, and some 240 inshore patrol craft, as well as numerous boats and service vessels. There are numerous shore command and support facilities, and 24 fixed-wing aircraft and 38 helicopers complete the equipment inventory. Personnel in 1991 numbered 12,000.

Air Force. An 'Air Self-Defence Force' was inaugurated on 1 July 1954. In 1991 its equipment included 7 interceptor squadrons of F-15J/DJ Eagles (total of 168 aircraft to be acquired by 1992) and 4 of F-4EJ Phantoms; 3 squadrons of Mitsubishi F-1 close-support fighters; 1 squadron of RF-4E reconnaissance fighters; 8 E-2C Hawkeye AWACS aircraft; ECM flight with 2 YS-11Es; 3 squadrons of turbofan Kawasaki C-1 and turboprop C-130H Hercules and NAMC YS-11 transports. About 55 helicopters, mostly KV-107s (now being replaced with CH-47 Chinooks), and MU-2 twin-turboprop aircraft perform search, rescue and general duties. Training units use piston-engined Fuji T-3 basic trainers, Fuji T-1 jet intermediate trainers, Kawasaki T-4 jet trainers and supersonic Mitsubishi T-2 jet advanced trainers. Six surface-to-air missile groups (19 squadrons) are in service. Total strength (1991) 390 combat aircraft and 46,400 officers and men.

INTERNATIONAL RELATIONS

Membership. Japan is a member of the UN, Colombo Plan and OECD.

ECONOMY

Policy. The 1988–92 Plan envisages an onward real growth rate of 3·75% and a nominal 4·75%. The real growth rate for 1992 was envisaged at 3·5% and the nominal 5%.

Budget. Ordinary revenue and expenditure for fiscal year ending 31 March 1992 balanced at 70,347,400m. yen.

Of the proposed revenue in 1991, 61,772,000m. was to come from taxes and stamps, 5,343,000m. from public bonds. Main items of expenditure: Social security, 12,212,200m.; public works, 6,589,700m.; local government, 15,974,900m.; education, 5,394,400m.; defence, 4,387,000m.

The outstanding national debt incurred by public bonds was estimated in March 1990 to be 163,098,000m. yen.

The estimated 1991 budgets of the prefectures and other local authorities forecast a total revenue of 70,885,000m. yen, to be made up partly by local taxes and partly by government grants and local loans.

Currency. The unit of currency is the *yen* (JPY). Coins of 1, 5, 10, 50, 100 and 500 *yen* are in circulation as well as notes of the Bank of Japan, of 1,000, 5,000 and 10,000 *yen*. Bank-notes for 500 *yen* are still in circulation but are gradually being replaced by coins. In March 1992, £1 = 227·50 *yen*; US$1 = 129·59 *yen*.

In Dec. 1990 the currency in circulation consisted of 39,797,800m. yen Bank of Japan notes and 3,219,300m. yen subsidiary coins.

Banking and Finance. The modern banking system dates from 1872. The Nippon Ginko (Bank of Japan) was founded in 1882. The Bank of Japan has undertaken to finance the Government and the banks; its function is similar to that of a Central Bank in other countries. The Bank undertakes the actual management of Treasury funds and foreign exchange control. Its *Governor* is Yasushi Mieno.

Gold bullion and cash holdings of the Bank of Japan at 31 Dec. 1990 stood at 571,000m. yen.

There were on 31 Dec. 1990, 12 city banks, 64 regional banks, 7 trust banks, 3 long-term credit banks, 68 member banks of the second association of regional banks, 451 Shinkin banks (credit associations), 407 credit co-operatives, and 85 foreign banks. There are also various governmental financial institutions, including postal savings which amounted to 145,311,800m. yen in Sept. 1991. Total savings by individuals, including insurance and securities, stood at 776,848,300m. yen on 30 Sept. 1991, and about 62% of these savings were deposited in banks and the post-office.

Many foreign banks operate branches in Japan including: Bank of Indo-China, Hongkong & Shanghai Banking Corporation, Chartered Bank of India, Australia and China, Bank of India, Mercantile Bank of India, Bank of Korea, Bank of China, Algemene Bank Nederland NV, National Handelsbank NV, Bank of America, National City Bank of New York, Chase Manhattan Bank, Bangkok Bank and American Express Co.

There are 8 stock exchanges, the largest being in Tokyo, Osaka and Nagoya.

Weights and Measures. The metric system was made obligatory by a law passed in March 1921, and the period of grace for its compulsory use ended on 1 April 1966.

ENERGY AND NATURAL RESOURCES

Electricity. Japan is poor in energy resources, and nuclear power generation is important in reducing dependence on foreign supplies. In 1989 generating facilities were capable of an output of 186,231,000 kw.; electricity produced was 798,756m. kwh. There were 38 nuclear reactors in 17 power plants in 1990, producing about 30% of electricity, and 13 more were under construction in 1991. 9 regional publicly-held supply companies produce about 75% of output. Supply 100 and 200 volts; 50 or 60 Hz.

Oil and Gas. Output of crude petroleum, 1989, was 641,000 kl, almost entirely from oilfields on the island of Honshu, but 209,692,000 kl crude oil had to be imported. Output of natural gas, 1989, 2,009m. cu. metres.

Minerals. Ore production in tonnes, 1989, of chromite, 11,674; coal, 10,187,000; iron, 41,425; zinc, 131,794; copper, 16,650; lead, 18,595; tungsten, 488; silver, 155,792 kg.; gold, 6,097 kg.

Agriculture. Agricultural workers in 1990 were 5,653,000, including 503,000 subsidiary and seasonal workers; 8·4% (1985) of the labour force as opposed to 24·7% in 1962. The arable land area in 1990 was 5,243,000 ha. Rice is the staple food, but its consumption is declining. Rice cultivation accounted for 2,055,000 ha in 1990. The area planted with industrial crops such as rapeseed, tobacco, tea, rush, etc., was 235,000 ha in 1989.

Average farm size was just over 1 ha in 1990. Farmers are represented by the co-operative organization in Nokyo.

In 1990 there were 4,327,000 power cultivators and tractors and 1,983,000 rice power planters. (1988): 1,408,000 power sprayers and 1,674,000 power dusters.

Output of rice was 11,878,000 in 1984, 11,662,000 in 1985, 11,647,000 in 1986, 10,627,000 in 1987, 9,935,000 in 1988 and 10,347,000 in 1989.

Production in 1990 (in 1,000 tonnes) of barley was 346; wheat, 952; soybeans, 220. Sweet potatoes, which in the past mitigated the effects of rice famines, have, in view of rice over-production, decreased from 4,955,000 tonnes in 1965 to 1,402,000 tons in 1990. Domestic sugar-beet and sugar-cane production accounted for only 34·6% of requirement in 1989. In 1989, 1,791,000 tonnes were imported, 37·6% of this being imported from Australia, 18·4% from South Africa, 28·3% from Thailand, 12·7% from Cuba.

Fruit production, 1989 (in 1,000 tonnes): Mandarins, 2,015; apples, 1,405; pears, 449; grapes, 296; peaches, 203; and persimmons, 288.

Livestock (1990): 4·76m. cattle (including about 2m. milch cows), 23,000 horses, 11,817,000 pigs, 31,000 sheep, 35,000 goats, 338m. chickens. Milk (1989), 8·06m. tonnes.

Forestry. Forests and grasslands cover about 25m. ha (nearly 70% of the whole land area), with an estimated timber stand of 2,862m. cu. metres in 1986. In 1988, 38,554,000 cu. metres were felled.

Fisheries. Before the War, Japanese catch represented one-half to two-thirds of the world's total fishing, in 1988 it was 12·1%. The catch in 1989 was 11·91m. tonnes, excluding whaling.

INDUSTRY. The industrial structure is dominated by corporate groups (*keiretsu*) either linking companies in different branches or linking individual companies with their suppliers and distributors.

Japan's industrial equipment, 1988, numbered 745,108 plants of all sizes, employing 11,554,000 production workers.

Since 1920 there has been a shift from light to heavy industries. The production of electrical appliances and electronic machinery has made great strides: Television sets (1990: 15,132,000), radio sets (1989: 10·69m.), cameras (1989: 16,961,000), computing machines and automation equipment are produced in increasing quantities. The chemical industry ranks third in production value after machinery and metals (1988). Production, 1989, included (in tonnes): Sulphuric acid, 6,885,000; caustic soda, 3,564,000; ammonium sulphate, 1,718,000; calcium superphosphate, 454,000.

Output (1989), in 1,000 tonnes, of pig iron was 80,197; crude steel, 107,908; ordinary rolled steel, 86,687.

In 1989 paper production was 15,726,000 tonnes; paperboard, 11,083,000 tonnes.

Japan's textile industry before the War had 13m. cotton-yarn spindles. After the War she resumed with 2·78m. spindles; in 1964, 8·42m. spindles were operating. Output of cotton yarn, 1989, 459,000 tonnes, and of cotton cloth, 1,915m. sq. metres.

In wool, Japan aims at wool exports sufficient to pay for the imports of raw wool. Output, 1989, 118,000 tonnes of woollen yarns and 351m. sq. metres of woollen fabrics.

Output, 1989, of rayon woven fabrics, 629m. sq. metres; synthetic woven fabrics, 2,670m. sq. metres; silk fabrics, 97m. sq. metres.

Shipbuilding has been decreasing and in 1989, 5,253,000 gross tons were launched, of which 2,206,000 GRT were tankers.

Labour. Total labour force, 1990, was 62·49m., of which 4·1m. were in agriculture and forestry, 400,000 in fishing, 60,000 in mining, 5·9m. in construction, 15·05m. in manufacturing, 17m. in commerce and finance, 3·75m. in transport and other public utilities, 13·94m. in services (including the professions) and 1·95m. in government work. Normal retirement age is 60, but some 40% of the workforce retire earlier.

Trade Unions. In 1990 there were 12,265,000 workers organized in 72,202 unions.

The largest federation is the 'Japanese Private Sector Trade Union Confederation' (Rengo) with 7·58m. members. Rengo was organized in Nov. 1987 by dissolving the 'Japanese Confederation of Labour' (Domei Kaigi) and the 'Federation of Independent Unions' (Churitsu Roren). The 'National Confederation of Trade Unions' (Zenroren) with 833,000 members and the 'National Trade Union Council' (Zenrokyo) with 303,000 members were both organized in 1989. The 'General Council of Japanese Trade Unions' (Sohyo) with 3,907,000 members in 1989 was dissolved in 1990.

In 1990, 1·34m. (2·1%) were unemployed. In 1990, 145,000 working days were lost in industrial stoppages.

FOREIGN ECONOMIC RELATIONS

Commerce. Trade (in US$1m.):

	1984	1985	1986	1987	1988	1989	1990
Imports	136,503	129,539	126,408	149,515	187,354	210,847	234,799
Exports	170,114	175,638	209,151	229,221	264,917	275,175	286,948

Distribution of trade by countries (customs clearance basis) (US$1m.):

	Exports		Imports	
	1989	1990	1989	1990
Africa	4,609	4,886	4,078	3,720
Australia	7,805	6,900	11,605	12,369
Canada	6,807	6,726	8,645	8,392
China	8,516	6,130	11,146	12,054
Fed. Rep. of Germany	15,920	17,782	8,995	11,487
Hong Kong	11,526	13,072	2,219	2,173
Latin America	9,381	10,280	8,871	9,851
South-east Asia	73,516	82,721	52,906	54,601
Korea, Republic of	16,561	17,457	12,994	11,707
Taiwan	15,421	15,430	8,979	8,496
USSR	3,082	2,563	3,005	3,351
UK	10,741	10,786	4,466	5,239
USA	93,188	90,322	48,246	52,369

Principal items in 1990, with value in 1m. yen were:

Imports, c.i.f.		Exports, f.o.b.	
Mineral fuels	8,083,000	Machinery and transport equipment	31,071,000
Foodstuffs	4,572,000		
Metal ores and scrap	1,321,000	Metals and metal products	2,825,000
Machinery and transport equipment	5,903,000	Textile products	1,042,000
		Chemicals	2,295,000

Total trade between Japan and UK (British Department of Trade returns, in £1,000 sterling):

	1987	1988	1989	1990	1991
Imports to UK	5,463,116	6,509,137	7,108,441	6,761,592	6,753,642
Exports and re-exports from UK	1,495,111	1,742,747	2,259,823	2,631,326	2,257,552

Tourism. In 1990, 3,504,470 foreigners visited Japan, 564,958 of whom came from USA, 212,043 from UK. Japanese travelling abroad totalled 10,997,431 in 1990.

COMMUNICATIONS

Roads. The total length of roads (including urban and other local roads) was 1,109,981 km at 1 April 1989. There were 46,805 km of national roads, of which 45,847 km were paved. Motor vehicles, at 31 Dec. 1990, numbered 56,491,000, including 34,924,000 passenger cars and 21,321,000 commercial vehicles.

Railways. The first railway was completed in 1872, between Tokyo and Yokohama (29 km). Railway gauge was originally narrow (1,069 mm.), but the high-speed 'Shinkansen' lines are standard 1,435 mm gauge. In April 1987 the Japanese National Railways was reorganized into 7 private companies, the Japanese Railways (JR) Group – 6 passenger companies and 1 freight company. Total length of railways, in March 1989, was 25,346 km, of which the JR had 18,307 km and other private railways, 7,039 km. In 1989 the JR carried 7,979m. passengers (other private, 13,230m.) and 56m. tons of freight (other private, 27m.). An undersea tunnel linking Honshu with Hokkaido was opened to rail services in 1988.

There are metros in Tokyo (2 systems total 218 km), Fukuoka (15 km), Kobe (23 km), Kyoto (11 km), Nagoya (67 km), Osaka (104 km), Sapporo (40 km), Sendai (14 km) and Yokohama (22 km), and tram/light rail networks in 19 cities.

Civil Aviation. The principal airlines are Japan Airlines (JAL) and All Nippon Airways. Japan Airlines, founded in 1953 and privatized in 1987, had 63 Boeing-747s in 1990. It operates international services from Tokyo to the USA, Europe, the Middle East and Southeast Asia, including flights to London over the North Pole and to Moscow by way of Siberia. In 1989 Japanese companies carried 60m. passengers in domestic services and 10,616,000 passengers in international services.

Shipping. On 1 July 1990 the merchant fleet consisted of 7,668 vessels of 100 gross tons and over; total tonnage 25m. gross tons; there were 714 ships for passenger transport (1·36m. gross tons), 2,408 cargo ships (1,228,000 gross tons) and 1,209 oil tankers (7,586,000 gross tons).

Coastguard. The 'Maritime Safety Agency' (Coastguard) consists of 11 regional MS headquarters, 66 MS offices, 51 MS stations, 14 air stations, 1 special rescue station, 9 district communications centres, 3 traffic advisory service centres, 4 hydrographic observatories and 116 navigation aids offices (with 5,299 navigation aids facilities) and controls 47 large patrol vessels, 47 medium patrol vessels, 19 small patrol vessels, 225 patrol craft, 21 hydrographic service vessels, 5 firefighting vessels, 10 firefighting boats, 69 guard and rescue boats and 78 navigation aids service supply vessels. Personnel in 1991 numbered 12,134 officers and men.

The Coastguard aviation service includes 21 fixed-wing aircraft and 41 helicopters.

Telecommunications. Telephone services have been operated by a private company (NTT) since 1985. In 1989 there were 52m. instruments.

In 1991 there were 97m. radio and 68·6m. TV sets (colour by NTSC).

Cinemas (1990). Cinemas numbered 1,836 with an annual attendance of 146m. (1960: 1,014m.).

Newspapers (1989). Daily newspapers numbered 124 with aggregate circulation of 71,457,000, including 4 major English-language newspapers.

JUSTICE, RELIGION, EDUCATION AND WELFARE

Justice. The Supreme Court is composed of the Chief Justice and 14 other judges. The Chief Justice is appointed by the Emperor, the other judges by the Cabinet. Every 10 years a justice must submit himself to the electorate. All justices and judges of the lower courts serve until they are 70 years of age.

Below the Supreme Court are 8 regional higher courts, district courts (*Chihosaibansho*) in each prefecture (4 in Hokkaido) and the local courts.

The Supreme Court is authorized to declare unconstitutional any act of the Legislature or the Executive which violates the Constitution.

The police are under central government control.

Religion. There has normally been religious freedom, but Shinto (literally, The Way of the Gods) was given the status of quasi-state-religion in the 1930s; in 1945 the Allied Supreme Command ordered the Government to discontinue state support of Shinto. State subsidies have ceased for all religions, and all religious teachings are forbidden in public schools.

In Dec. 1989 Shintoism claimed 107,068,000 adherents, Buddhism 91,048,000; these figures obviously overlap. Christians numbered 1,467,000.

Education. Education is compulsory and free between the ages of 6 and 15. Almost all national and municipal institutions are co-educational. On 1 May 1990 there were 14,988 kindergartens with 100,937 teachers and 2,007,964 pupils; 24,021 elementary schools with 444,218 teachers and 9,373,295 pupils; 11,182 junior high schools with 286,065 teachers and 5,369,162 pupils; 5,342 senior high schools with

286,006 teachers and 5,623,336 pupils; 593 junior colleges with 20,489 teachers and 479,389 pupils.

There were also 852 special schools for handicapped children (44,798 teachers, 93,497 pupils).

Japan has 7 main state universities, formerly known as the Imperial Universities: Tokyo University (1877); Kyoto University (1897); Tohoku University, Sendai (1907); Kyushu University, Fukuoka (1910); Hokkaido University, Sapporo (1918); Osaka University (1931), and Nagoya University (1939). In addition, there are various other state and municipal as well as private universities of high standing, such as Keio (founded in 1859), Waseda, Rikkyo, Meiji universities, and several women's universities, among which Tokyo and Ochanomizu are most notable. There are 507 colleges and universities with (1 May 1990) 2,133,362 students and 123,838 teachers.

Social Welfare. Hospitals on 1 Oct. 1989 numbered 10,081 with 1,661,952 beds. Physicians at the end of 1988 numbered 201,658; dentists, 70,572.

There are in force various types of social security schemes, such as health insurance, unemployment insurance and old-age pensions. The total population come under one or more of these schemes.

In 1989, 13,194,245 persons and 7,858,977 households received some form of regular public assistance, the total of which came to 1,395,873m. yen.

14 weeks maternity leave is statutory.

DIPLOMATIC REPRESENTATIVES

Of Japan in Great Britain (101 Piccadilly, London, W1V 9FN)
Ambassador: Hiroshi Kitamura.

Of Great Britain in Japan (1 Ichiban-cho, Chiyoda-ku, Tokyo 102)
Ambassador: Sir John Whitehead, GCMG, CVO.

Of Japan in the USA (2520 Massachusetts Ave., NW, Washington, D.C., 20008)
Ambassador: Ryohei Murata.

Of the USA in Japan (10–1, Akasaka 1-chome, Minato-Ku, Tokyo)
Ambassador: Michael Armacost.

Of Japan to the United Nations
Ambassadors: Yoshio Hatano and Katsumi Sezaki.

Further Reading

Statistics Bureau of the Prime Minister's Office: *Statistical Year-Book* (from 1949).—*Statistical Abstract* (from 1950).—*Statistical Handbook of Japan 1977.—Monthly Bulletin* (from April 1950)

Economic Planning Agency: *Economic Survey* (annual), *Economic Statistics* (monthly), *Economic Indicators* (monthly)

Ministry of International Trade: *Foreign Trade of Japan* (annual)

Kodansha Encyclopedia of Japan. 9 vols. Tokyo, 1983

Japan Times Year Book. (I. Year Book of Japan. II. Who's Who in Japan. III. Business Directory of Japan.) Tokyo, first issue 1933

Labor in Tokyo. Tokyo Metropolitan Government, 1986

Allen, G. C., *The Japanese Economy.* London, 1981

Baerwald, H. H., *Japan's Parliament.* CUP, 1974.—*Party Politics in Japan.* Boston, 1986

Beasley, W. T., *The Rise of Modern Japan.* London, 1990

Cambridge History of Japan. vols. 3-5. CUP, 1990

Cortazzi, H., *The Japanese Achievement.* London, 1990

Francks, P., *Japanese Economic Development: Theory and Practice.* London, 1991

Goodhart, C. A. E. and Sutija, G. (eds.) *Japanese Financial Growth.* London, 1990

Horsley, W. and Buckky, R., *Nippon, New Superpower: Japan since 1945.* London, 1990

Ito, T., *The Japanese Economy.* Boston (Mass.), 1992

Morishima, U. *Why has Japan 'Succeeded'?* CUP, 1984

Murata, K., *An Industrial Geography of Japan.* London, 1980

Nester, W. R., *The Foundation of Japanese Power: Continuities, Changes, Challenges.* London, 1990

Newland, K., (ed.) *The International Relations of Japan.* London, 1990

Nippon: A Chartered Survey of Japan. Tsuneta Yano Memorial Society. Tokyo, annual
Okita, S., *The Developing Economics of Japan: Lessons in Growth.* Univ. of Tokyo Press, 1983
Perren, R., *Japanese Studies From Pre-history to 1990.* Manchester Univ. Press, 1992
Prindl, A., *Japanese Finance: Guide to Banking in Japan.* Chichester, 1981
Reischauer, E. O., *The Japanese Today: Change and Continuity.* Harvard Univ. Press, 1991
Sansom, G. B., *A History of Japan.* 3 vols. London, 1958–64
Shulman, F. J., *Japan.* [Bibliography] Oxford and Santa Barbara, 1990
Steven, R., *Japan's New Imperialism.* London, 1990
Tsoukalis, L., (ed.) *Japan and Western Europe.* London, 1982
Ward, P., *Japanese Capitals.* Cambridge, 1985

JORDAN

Capital: Amman
Population: 3·17m. (1990)
GNP per capita: US$1,500 (1988)

Mamlaka al Urduniya al Hashemiyah

(Hashemite Kingdom of Jordan)

HISTORY. By a Treaty, signed in London on 22 March 1946, Britain recognized Transjordan as a sovereign independent state. On 25 May 1946 the Amir Abdullah assumed the title of King, and when the treaty was ratified on 17 June 1946 the name of the territory was changed to that of 'The Hashemite Kingdom of Jordan' in 1949. A new Anglo-Transjordan treaty was signed in Amman on 15 March 1948. The treaty was to remain in force for 20 years, but by mutual consent was terminated on 13 March 1957.

The Arab Federation between the Kingdoms of Iraq and Jordan, which was concluded on 14 Feb. 1958, lapsed after the revolution in Iraq of 14 July 1958, and was officially terminated by royal decree on 1 Aug. 1958.

Since the occupation of the West Bank in June 1967 by Israeli forces, that part of Palestine has not been administratively controlled by the Jordanian government.

On 31 July 1988, King Hussein announced that Jordan was to abandon its efforts to administer the Israeli-occupied West Bank and surrendered its claims to the territory to the Palestine Liberation Organization.

AREA AND POPULATION. The part of Palestine remaining to the Arabs under the armistice with Israel on 3 April 1949, with the exception of the Gaza strip, was in Dec. 1949 placed under Jordanian rule and formally incorporated in Jordan on 24 April 1950. For the frontier lines *see* map in THE STATESMAN'S YEAR-BOOK, 1951. In June 1967 this territory, known as the West Bank, was occupied by Israeli forces. For details *see* p. 734.

The area formerly administered by the Jordanian government, known as the East Bank, comprised 89,206 sq. km (34,443 sq. miles) following an exchange of territory with Saudi Arabia on 10 Aug. 1965. Its population at the 1979 Census was 2,132,997; latest estimate (1990) 3,165,000. In 1989 2·18m. of the 3·11m. population were urban and 1·48m. female. Population of the 8 governorates:

Governorate	1989	Governorate	1989
Amman	1,297,100	Ma'an	108,300
Balqa	214,700	Mafraq	109,000
Irbid	753,400	Tafilah	45,800
Karak	132,800	Zarqa	449,900

The largest towns with suburbs, with estimated population, 1986: Amman, the capital, 1,160,000; Irbid, 680,200; Zarqa, 404,500;.

Vital statistics, 1989: Births, 115,742; deaths, 9,695; marriages, 31,508; divorces, 4,694.

CLIMATE. Predominantly a Mediterranean climate, with hot dry summers and cool wet winters, but in hilly parts summers are cooler and winters colder. Those areas below sea-level are very hot in summer and warm in winter. Eastern parts have a desert climate. Amman. Jan. 46°F (7·5°C), July 77°F (24·9°C). Annual rainfall 12" (290 mm). Aqaba. Jan. 61°F (16°C), July 89°F (31·5°C). Annual rainfall 1·5" (35 mm).

KING. The Kingdom is a constitutional monarchy headed by HM King **Hussein**, GCVO, eldest son of King Talal, who, being incapacitated by mental illness, was deposed by Parliament on 11 Aug. 1952 and died 8 July 1972. The King was born 14 Nov. 1935, and married Princess Dina Abdul Hamid on 19 April 1955 (divorced 1957), Toni Avril Gardiner (Muna al Hussein) on 25 May 1961 (divorced 1972), Alia Toukan on 26 Dec. 1972 (died in air crash 1977) and Elizabeth Halaby on 15 June 1978. *Offspring:* Princess Alia, born 13 Feb. 1956; Prince Abdulla, born 30 Jan. 1962; Prince Faisal, born 11 Oct. 1963; Princesses Zein and Aisha, born 23 April 1968; Princess Haya, born 3 May 1974; Prince Ali, born 23 Dec. 1975; Prince Hamzah, born 1 April 1980; Prince Hashem, born 10 June 1981; Princess Iman, born 4 April 1983; Princess Raya, born 9 Feb. 1986. *Crown Prince* (appointed 1 April 1965): Prince Hassan, younger brother of the King.

CONSTITUTION AND GOVERNMENT. The Constitution passed on 7 Nov. 1951 provides that the Cabinet is responsible to Parliament.

The legislature consists of a lower house of 80 members elected by universal suffrage and a senate of 30 members nominated by the King.

On 5 Feb. 1976 both Houses of Parliament approved amendments to the Constitution by which the King was empowered to postpone calling elections until further notice. The lower house was dissolved. This step was taken because no elections could be held in the West Bank which has been under Israeli occupation since June 1967.

Parliament was reconvened on 9 Jan. 1984. By-elections were held in March 1984 and 6 members were nominated for the West Bank bringing Parliament to 60 members. Women voted for the first time in 1984. Elections were held on 8 Nov. 1989; the Moslem Brotherhood won 22 of the 80 seats.

On 9 June 1991 the king and the main political movements signed a national charter which legalized political parties in return for the acceptance of the constitution and monarchy. Movements linked to, or financed by, other Arab governments are banned. Martial law, imposed in 1967, was lifted in July 1991.

A coalition government of 29 ministers and excluding the Moslem Brotherhood was formed in Nov. 1991, including:

Prime Minister: Sharif Zeid bin Shaker.

Deputy Prime Ministers: Ali Suheimat, Dhukan Hindawi. *Foreign Affairs:* Kamel Abu Jaber. *Interior:* Jawdat al Sbould. *Finance:* Basil Jardaneh. *Parliamentary Affairs:* Atef Btush.

National flag: Three horizontal stripes of black, white, green, with a red triangle based on the hoist, bearing a white 7-pointed star.

Local government. The 8 governorates are divided into cities, towns, districts and sub-districts.

The official language is Arabic.

DEFENCE

Army. The Army is organized in 2 armoured and 2 mechanized infantry divisions, 1 Royal Guard and 1 special forces brigade, and 1 field artillery brigade. Equipment includes 1,131 main battle tanks. Total strength (1991) 74,000 men.

Navy. The Jordan Coastal Guard numbered 300 in 1991 and operates 3 small patrol boats.

Air Force. The Air Force has 2 interceptor and 3 ground attack squadrons equipped respectively with Mirage F1 and F-5E Tiger II fighters, and 2-seat F-5Fs, plus an OCU equipped with F-5A fighters and 2-seat F-5Bs. Two anti-armour squadrons have Bell AH-1S Huey Cobra helicopters. There are 6 C-130B/H Hercules and 2 CASA Aviocar turboprop transports, S-70 Blackhawk, S-76, Gazelle, Alouette III and Hughes 500D helicopters, piston-engined Bulldog basic trainers and CASA Aviojet jet trainers. Hawk surface-to-air missiles equip 14 batteries. Strength (1990) about 10,000 officers and men and 94 combat aircraft and 24 armed helicopters.

INTERNATIONAL RELATIONS

Membership. Jordan is a member of the UN and the Arab League.

ECONOMY

Policy. An economic readjustment programme was instituted in 1988.

Budget. Revenue, 1989, JD.883,210; expenditure, JD.1,002,345, Defence expenditure, JD.168,000; social services and culture, JD.96,435.

Currency. The unit of currency is the *Jordan dinar,* (JOD) of 1,000 *fils.* The following bank-notes and coins are in circulation: 10, 5 dinars, 1 dinar, 500 fils (notes), 250, 100, 50, 25, 20 fils (cupronickel), 10, 5, 1 fils (bronze). In March 1992, £1 = JD.1·18; US$ = JD.0·67.

Banking and Finance. The Central Bank of Jordan was established in 1964. In 1989 there were 33 banks. Assets and liabilities of the banking system (including the Central Bank, commercial banks and the Housing Bank) totalled JD.4,091·4m.

Weights and Measures. The metric system is in force. Land area is measured in *dunums* (1 dunum = approx. 10 ha).

ENERGY AND NATURAL RESOURCES

Electricity. Production (1989) 3,433m. kwh. Supply 220 volts; 50 Hz.

Minerals. Phosphates production in 1989 was 6·64m. tonnes; potash, 1·32m tonnes.

Agriculture. The country east of the Hejaz Railway line is largely desert; north-western Jordan is potentially of agricultural value and an integrated Jordan Valley project began in 1973. Arable land was 308,000 ha. in 1989; permanent crops, 66,000 ha.; permanent pasture, 791,000 ha. The agricultural cropping pattern for irrigated vegetable cultivation was introduced in 1984 to regulate production and diversify the crops being cultivated. In 1986 the government began to lease state-owned land in the semi-arid southern regions for agricultural development by private investors, mostly for wheat and barley.

Production in 1989 (in tonnes): Wheat, 54,520; barley, 20,571; maize, 5,584; clover trifoil, 14,037; tobacco, 2,827; tomatoes, 524,200; potatoes, 692,200; olives, 25,683; citrus fruits, 166,670; grapes, 21,840.

Livestock (1989): 1·52m. sheep; 0·47m. goats; 28,953 cattle; 18,254 camels. Red meat production was 9,372 tonnes in 1989; milk, 69,426 tonnes.

There were 5,673 tractors in 1989.

Forestry. There were 71,000 ha. of forest and woodland in 1989.

INDUSTRY. There were 2,922 firms in 1988, 1,502 of which employed fewer than 10 persons and 269 were state-owned. 1,247 firms were engaged in manufacturing, 790 in services and administration and 500 in commerce. Production (1989, in 1,000 tonnes): Fertilizers, 2,498; cement, 1,930; petroleum products, 2,103; salt, 57.

Labour. The workforce in 1989 was 523,505, of whom 257,564 worked in social and public administration, 54,445 in mining and manufacturing, 53,398 in commerce, 46,068 in transport and communications and 37,692 in agriculture. In 1987 277,200 Jordanians worked abroad.

FOREIGN ECONOMIC RELATIONS

Commerce. Imports in 1989 were valued at JD.1,230·14m. and exports and re-exports at JD.632·99m.

Major exports in 1989 (in JD.1m.) included phosphates, 146; chemicals, 156; food and live animals, 48·6; manufactured goods, 63·65.

Exports in 1989 (in JD.1m.) were mainly to Iraq, 122·37; Saudi Arabia, 49 and India, 95. Imports were mainly from Federal Germany, 77·36 and the USA, 170.

Total trade between Jordan and UK (British Department of Trade returns, in £1,000 sterling):

	1987	1988	1989	1990	1991
Imports to UK	29,285	21,310	16,462	14,788	10,984
Exports and re-exports from UK	188,998	183,555	110,684	109,483	89,411

Tourism. In 1989 there were 2·28m. foreign visitors.

COMMUNICATIONS

Roads. Total length of roads, 1989, 5,865 km, of which 2,548 km were main roads. Motor vehicles in 1989 included 148,380 motor cars (133,273 private), 6,520 motorcycles, 1,510 buses, 11,230 lorries and 43,206 vans. There were 18,336 road accidents in 1989 (355 fatalities).

Railways. The 1,050 mm gauge Hejaz Jordan and Aqaba Railway runs from the Syrian border at Nassib to Ma'an and Naqb Ishtar and Aqaba Port (total, 618 km). In 1988 the railways carried some 20,000 passengers and 614m. tonne-km of freight.

Civil Aviation. The Queen Alia International airport is at Zizya, 30 km south of Amman. There are also international airports at Amman and Aqaba. Jordan is served by over 20 international airlines. The national carrier is Royal Jordanian Airlines, which carried 1·2m. passengers and 49,717 tonnes of freight in 1989.

Shipping 18·68m. tonnes of cargo were handled by the port of Aqaba in 1989; 2,446 ships put in.

Telecommunications. In 1989 there were 769 post offices and agencies, 236,673 telephones and 2,191 telexes. There were 250,000 TV receivers and 1·1m. radios in 1988.

Newspapers (1989). There were 4 daily (including 1 in English) and 4 weekly papers, with a total circulation (1987) of 188,000. Newspapers were denationalized in 1990, though government institutions still hold majority ownership.

RELIGION, EDUCATION AND WELFARE

Religion. About 80% of the population are Sunni Moslems.

Education. In 1988–89 there were 515 kindergartens (513 private) with 1,833 teachers and 36,776 pupils; 1,435 elementary schools (234 private) with 20,265 teachers and 581,412 pupils; 1,033 preparatory schools (35 private) with 12,735 teachers and 225,379 pupils; 622 secondary schools (60 private) with 10,264 teachers and 118,462 pupils and 30 vocational schools with 2,288 teachers and 24,859 pupils. In 1988–89 there were 4 universities with 27,885 students (12,324 women) and 1,588 academic staff (198 women). The University of Jordan, (founded in 1962) had 12,994 students, Yarmouk University (1976), 9,630; Mu'tah University (1981), 2,545 and Jordan University of Science and Technology (1987), 2,716. 33,566 Jordanians were studying abroad.

Health In 1989 there were 2,280 doctors, 206 dentists and 4,080 hospital beds.

DIPLOMATIC REPRESENTATIVES

Of Jordan in Great Britain (6 Upper Phillimore Gdns., London, W8 7HB)
Ambassador: Fouad Ayoub.

Of Great Britain in Jordan (Abdoun, Amman)
Ambassador: Patrick Eyers, CMG, LVO.

Of Jordan in the USA (3504 International Dr., NW, Washington, D.C., 20008)
Ambassador: Hussein Hamami.

Of the USA in Jordan (Jebel Amman, Amman)
Ambassador: Roger G. Harrison.

Of Jordan to the United Nations
Ambassador: Abdullah Salah.

Further Reading

Central Bank of Jordan. *Monthly Statistical Bulletin*
Department of Statistics. *Statistical Yearbook*

The Constitution of the Hashemite Kingdom of Jordan. Amman, 1952
Gubser, P., *Jordan.* Boulder, Colo., 1982
Seccombe, I., *Jordan.* [Bibliography] Oxford and Santa Barbara, 1984
Toni, Y. T. and Mousa, S., *Jordan: Land and People.* Amman, 1973
Wilson, M. C., *King Abdullah, Britain and the making of Jordan.* CUP, 1987

National statistical office: Department of Statistics, Amman

KENYA

Capital: Nairobi
Population: 24·03m. (1990)
GNP per capita: US$380 (1989)

Jamhuri ya Kenya

(Republic of Kenya)

HISTORY. Until Kenya became independent it consisted of a colony and a protectorate. The protectorate comprised the mainland dominions of the Sultan of Zanzibar, a coastal strip of territory 10 miles wide to the northern branch of the Tana River, Mau, Kipini and the Island of Lamu, and all adjacent islands between the rivers Umba and Tana. The Sultan on 8 Oct. 1963 ceded the coastal strip to Kenya with effect from 12 Dec. 1963. The colony and protectorate, formerly known as the East African Protectorate were in 1905, transferred from the Foreign Office to the Colonial Office and in 1906 the protectorate was placed under the control of a governor and C.-in-C. and (except the Sultan of Zanzibar's dominions) became a Crown Colony in 1920 under the name of the Colony of Kenya. The territories on the coast became the Kenya Protectorate. In 1925 the UK ceded the Juba River and a strip from 50 to 100 miles wide on its west bank to Italian Somaliland (now Somalia). The northern boundary is defined by an agreement with Ethiopia in 1947.

A Constitution conferring internal self-government was brought into force on 1 June 1963, and full independence was achieved on 12 Dec. 1963. On 12 Dec. 1964 Kenya became a republic.

AREA AND POPULATION. Kenya is bounded by Sudan and Ethiopia in the north, Uganda in the west, Tanzania in the south and Somalia and the Indian ocean in the east. The total area is 582,646 sq. km, of which 571,416 sq. km is land area. In the 1979 census, the population was 15,327,061, of which 15,101,540 were Africans, 78,600 Asians, 39,900 Europeans, 39,140 Arabs. Estimate (1990), 24·03m. (22·8% urban). Expectation of life, 1989, 59 years.

The land areas, populations and capitals of the provinces are:

Province	Sq. km	Census 1979	Estimate 1987	Capital	Census 1979
Rift Valley	171,108	3,240,402	4,702,400	Nakuru	92,851
Eastern	155,760	2,719,851	3,864,700	Embu	15,986
Nyanza	12,526	2,643,956	3,892,600	Kisumu	152,643
Central	13,173	2,345,833	3,284,800	Nyeri	35,753
Coast	83,040	1,342,794	1,904,100	Mombasa	425,634 [1]
Western	8,223	1,832,663	2,535,900	Kakamega	32,025
Nairobi Municipality	684	827,775	1,288,700	Nairobi	1,103,554 [1]
North-Eastern	126,902	373,787	554,000	Garissa	14,076

[1] Estimate, 1984.

Other towns (1979): Machakos (84,320), Meru (70,439), Eldoret (59,503), Thika (41,324).

Kiswahili is the official language, but 21% speak Kikuyu as their mother tongue, 14% Luhya, 13% Luo, 11% Kamba, 11% Kalenjin, 6% Gusii, 5% Meru and 5% Mijikenda. English is spoken in commercial centres.

CLIMATE. The climate is tropical, with wet and dry seasons, but considerable differences in altitude make for varied conditions between the hot, coastal lowlands and the plateau, where temperatures are very much cooler. Heaviest rains occur in April and May, but in some parts there is a second wet season in Nov. and Dec. Nairobi. Jan. 65°F (18·3°C), July 60°F (15·6°C). Annual rainfall 39" (958 mm). Mombasa. Jan. 81°F (27·2°C), July 76°F (24·4°C). Annual rainfall 47" (1,201 mm).

CONSTITUTION AND GOVERNMENT. There is a unicameral National Assembly of 200 members, comprising 188 elected by universal suffrage for a 5-

year term, 10 members appointed by the President, and the Speaker and Attorney-General ex-officio. The President is also directly elected for 5 years; he appoints a Vice-President and other Ministers to a Cabinet over which he presides. The sole legal political party is the Kenya African National Union (KANU). In Dec. 1990 KANU restored the secret ballot and security of tenure for judges, but remained committed to the principle of 'democracy with a sole party'. However, in Dec. 1991 KANU agreed to legalize opposition parties.

Elections to the National Assembly took place by secret ballot on 21 March 1988. Only 123 seats were contested, the rest were unopposed.

President: Daniel T. arap Moi (b. 1924, elected 1978, re-elected 1983 and 1988). Ministers proclaimed him president for life at a rally in Sept. 1991.

In Feb. 1992 the government comprised:

Vice-President and Minister of Finance: George Saitoti. *Environment and Natural Resources:* Nioroge Mungai. *Lands and Housing:* Darius Mbela. *Water Development:* John Okwanyo. *Home Affairs and National Heritage:* Davidson Kuguru. *Planning and National Development:* Zachary Onyonka. *Transport and Communications:* Joseph Kamotho. *Local Government and Physical Planning:* William Ntimama. *Foreign Affairs and International Co-operation:* Wilson Ayah. *Commerce:* Arthur Magugu. *Tourism and Wildlife:* Katana Ngala. *Culture and Social Services:* James Niiru. *Agriculture:* Elijah Mwangale. *Health:* vacant. *Public Works:* Timothy Mibei. *Co-operative Development:* John Cheruiyot. *Labour:* Philip Masinde. *Education:* vacant. *Information and Broadcasting:* Nahashon Kanyi. *Livestock Development:* Jeremiah Nvagah. *Industry:* John Kyalo. *Supplies and Marketing:* Wycliffe Mudavadi. *Technical Training and Applied Technology:* S. K. Ongeri. *Manpower Development and Employment:* Dalmas Otieno. *Reclamation and Development of Arid, Semi-Arid and Wasteland:* George Ndoto. *Regional Development:* Onyango Midika. *Attorney-General:* Amos Wako.

National flag: Three horizontal stripes of black, red, green, with the red edged in white; bearing in the centre an African shield in black and white with 2 crossed spears behind.

National anthem: Ee Mungu nguvu yetu (Oh God of all creation; tune traditional).

Local government. The country is divided into the Nairobi Municipality and 7 provinces and there are 40 districts.

DEFENCE

Army. The Army consists of 1 armoured, 1 engineer and 2 infantry brigades; 2 engineer, 1 air cavalry, 1 airborne, 1 anti-aircraft, 2 artillery and 5 infantry battalions. Equipment includes 76 Vickers Mk3 main battle tanks. Total strength (1992) 19,000.

Navy. The Navy, based in Mombasa, in 1991 consisted of 2 56-metre fast missile craft, 4 smaller missile craft, and 1 inshore patrol craft, all built in Britain, and 1 tug. Personnel in 1991 totalled 1,100.

The Marine police and Customs operate an additional 15 patrol boats.

Air Force. An air force, formed 1 June 1964, was built up with RAF assistance and is under Army command. Equipment includes 11 F-5E/F-5F supersonic combat aircraft/trainers, 12 Hawk and 5 BAC 167 Strikemaster light jet attack/trainers, 7 twin-turboprop Buffaloes and Dash-8s for transport, air ambulance, anti-locust spraying and security duties, 7 Skyservant light twins, 12 Bulldog piston-engined primary trainers and Puma, Gazelle and Hughes 500 helicopters. Personnel (1992) 3,500, with 28 combat aircraft and 38 armed helicopters.

INTERNATIONAL RELATIONS

Membership. Kenya is a member of the UN, Commonwealth, OAU and is an ACP state of EEC.

ECONOMY

Planning. The sixth national development plan (1989-93) aims to expand the economy and create 2m. jobs.

Budget. The fiscal year ends on 30 June. Current revenue (in K£1m.), 1989–90, 2,174; capital revenue, 756; current expenditure, 2,339; capital expenditure, 1,167.

Currency. The monetary unit is the *Kenya shilling* (KES) of 100 *cents*; 20 shillings = K£1. There are notes of KSh.5, 10, 20, 50, 100, 200 and 500 and coins of 5, 10 and 50 cents and KSh.1 and 5. Currency in circulation, 1990: Notes, K£525·77m.; coins, K£16m. Inflation was 20% in 1991. Foreign exchange reserves were K£242m. in March 1990. In March 1992, £1 = 51·58 *shilling*; US$1 = 29·37 *shilling*.

Banking and Finance. The central bank and bank of issue is the Central Bank of Kenya. There were 28 banks and 50 other financial institutions operating in 1991. In March 1990 their combined assets totalled K£3,545m. The Kenya Commercial Bank is 70% state-owned.

Savings deposits totalled K£724m. in March 1990.

There is a stock exchange in Nairobi.

ENERGY AND NATURAL RESOURCES

Electricity. Installed generating capacity was 706 mw in 1989; two-thirds was provided by hydropower from power stations on the Tana river, 30% by oil-fired power stations and the rest by geothermal power. Production (1989) 2,840m. kwh. Supply 220 volts; 50 Hz.

Minerals. In 1989 there were 49 mines and quarries. Production, 1989 (in 1,000 tonnes): Soda ash, 241; fluorspar, 94·7; salt, 41. Other minerals included gold, raw soda, lime and limestone, diatomite, garnets and vermiculite.

Agriculture. As agriculture is possible from sea-level to altitudes of over 9,000 ft, tropical, sub-tropical and temperate crops can be grown and mixed farming is pursued. Agriculture produces 30% of GDP. There were 52·05m. ha of agricultural land in 1989. Four-fifths of the country is range-land which produces mainly livestock products and the wild game which constitutes a major attraction of the tourist industry.

In 1989 there were 2,572 enterprises engaged in agriculture and forestry, including 772 mixed farms, 448 ranches, 400 coffee plantations and 105 tea plantations. 619 enterprises employed more than 50 persons. The main areas of crop production are the Central, Rift Valley, Western and Nyanza Provinces and parts of Eastern and Coast Provinces. Coffee, tea, sisal, pyrethrum, maize and wheat are crops of major importance in the Highlands, while coconuts, cashew nuts, cotton, sugar, sisal and maize are the principal crops grown at the lower altitudes. Production, 1989 (in 1,000 tonnes): Maize, 625·9; wheat, 233·2; rice, 31·5; barley, 20; millet, 60; sorghum, 143; potatoes, 300; sweet potatoes, 550; cassava, 620; sugar-cane, 4,261; tobacco, 9; coffee, 113·1; tea, 180·6; vegetables, 491; fruit, 764; seed cotton, 13·8; sisal, 37·4.

Livestock (1989): Cattle, 13·46m.; sheep, 6·33m.; goats, 7·5m.; pigs, 100,000; poultry, 24m.

10,787 ha were irrigated in 1988–89.

Forestry. The total area of gazetted forest reserves amounts to 16,800 sq. km, mainly between 6,000 and 11,000 ft above sea-level. There are coniferous, broadleaved, hardwood and bamboo forests. The forest area in 1989 was (in 1,000 ha) 1,750, of which 1,691 were gazetted, 1,338 in state ownership, 412 in local authority ownership and 124 in private ownership. 493,000 cu. metres of timber were cut in 1989.

Fisheries. Landings in 1989 were 138,791 tonnes of fresh water fish, 6,708 tonnes of marine fish, 715 tonnes of crustaceans and 187 tonnes of other marine products; total value K£40,957,600.

INDUSTRY. In 1989 there were 1,971 manufacturing firms, 586 of which employed more than 50 persons. In 1986 industry accounted for some 13% of GDP and employed about one-fifth of the wage-earning labour force. The main activities were textiles, chemicals, vehicle assembly and transport equipment, leather and footwear, printing and publishing, food and tobacco processing. An important sub-sector was the refining of crude petroleum at Mombasa. Production in 1988 included (in tonnes): Sugar, 407,371; maize meal, 261,181; wheat flour, 266,625; animal feed, 184,266; cotton yarn, 4,767; cotton fabrics, 45·69m. sq. metres.

FOREIGN ECONOMIC RELATIONS

Commerce. Exports were valued at K£999·84m. in 1989; imports, K£2,238·63m.

Principal exports (% of value) 1989: Tea, 27·2; coffee, 20·4; horticultural produce, 11·2; petroleum products, 10·2; hides and furs, 3·3. Coffee exports were worth US$191m., tea US$273m. and manufactures US$94m. in 1990. Imports: Machinery and transport equipment, 39·3; mineral fuels, 15·9; chemicals, 15·8; manufactures, 15·7.

Main export markets in 1989 (in K£1m.): UK, 198·7; Federal Republic of Germany, 88·8; Pakistan, 72; Uganda, 65·9. Main import suppliers: UK, 351; United Arab Emirates, 253·3; Japan, 245·6; Federal Republic of Germany, 198·8; France, 196·7.

Total trade between Kenya and UK (British Department of Trade returns, in £1,000 sterling):

	1987	1988	1989	1990	1991
Imports to UK	129,236	142,455	154,313	149,474	141,996
Exports and re-exports from UK	199,059	202,094	208,464	223,080	206,927

Tourism. In 1990 there were 889,000 business and holiday visitors. Tourist earnings totalled US$467m.

COMMUNICATIONS

Roads. In 1989 there were 7,687 km of bitumen-surfaced roads and 54,000 km of gravel-surfaced roads. There were, in 1989, 150,681 motor cars, 22,368 motor cycles, 83,348 vans, 31,528 lorries and 12,340 buses. There were 10,106 road accidents in 1989 (2,014 fatal).

Railways. in 1989 route length was 1,919 km of metre-gauge. 3·96m. passengers and 3·31m. tonnes of freight were carried.

Civil Aviation. The national carrier is Kenya Airways, which carried 812,200 passengers and 16,229 tonnes of freight in 1989. Jomo Kenyatta Airport at Nairobi is the main international airport. South African Airways began a weekly flight from Johannesburg to Nairobi in Dec. 1990.

Shipping. The main port is Mombasa, which handled 7·24m. tonnes of cargo in 1989.

Telecommunications. The Voice of Kenya operates 2 national services (Swahili–English) from Nairobi and regional services in Kisumu, Nairobi and Mombasa. The television service provides programmes mainly in English and Swahili. Colour by PAL. Telephones (1989) 357,251; television sets (1990) 0·26m.; radios (1990) 4m.

Newspapers. In 1989 English-language dailies had an average circulation of 271,100, and Swahili, 54,200.

JUSTICE, RELIGION, EDUCATION AND WELFARE

Justice. The courts of Justice comprises the court of Appeal, the High Court and a large number of subsidiary courts. The court of Appeal is the final Apellant court in the country and is based in Nairobi. It comprises of 7 Judges of Appeal. In the course of its Appellate duties the court of Appeal visits Mombasa, Kisumu, Nakuru and Nyeri. The High court with full jurisdiction in both civil and criminal matters comprises of a total of 28 puisne Judges. Puisne Judges sit in Nairobi (16), Mombasa (2), Nakuru, Kisumu, Nyeri, Eldoret Meru and Kisii (1 each).

The Magistracy consists of approximately 300 magistrates of various cadres based in all provincial, district and some divisional centres. In addition to the above there are the Kadhi courts established in areas of concentrated Muslim populations: Mombasa, Nairobi, Malindi, Lamu, Garissa, Kisumu and Marsabit. They exercise limited jurisdiction in matters governed by Islamic Law.

There were 20,961 criminal convictions in 1989; the prison population was 106,107.

Religion. In 1987, the Roman Catholic Church had nearly 6m. adherents (27% of the population), Protestants 4m. (19%) and other Christian churches over 6m. (27%), while Islam had 1·3m. (6%), traditional tribal religions 4m. (19%) and others 400,000 (2%).

Education. In 1989-90 there were 14,691 primary schools with 5,389,148 pupils and 163,609 teachers; 2,654 secondary schools with 640,735 pupils and 18,236 teachers; 24 teacher training schools with 20,105 students and 1,541 teachers; 19 technical training institutes with 4,100 students and 477 teachers. There were 2 polytechnics with 5,374 students, and 5 universities (Nairobi, Moi, Kenyatta, Egerton and Jomo Kenyatta University College of Agriculture and Technology) with 27,294 students.

Health. In 1989 there were 3,266 doctors and 561 dentists. There were 264 hospitals (with 32,534 beds), 294 health centres and 1,555 sub-centres and dispensaries. Free medical service for all children and adult out-patients was launched in 1965.

DIPLOMATIC REPRESENTATIVES

Of Kenya in Great Britain (45 Portland Pl., London, W1)
High Commissioner: Simon B. Arap Bullut.

Of Great Britain in Kenya (Bruce Hse., Standard St., Nairobi)
High Commissioner: Sir Roger Tomkys, KCMG.

Of Kenya in the USA (2249 R. St., NW, Washington, D.C., 20008)
Ambassador: Denis D. Afande.

Of the USA in Kenya (Moi/Haile Selassie Ave., Nairobi)
Ambassador: Smith Hempstone, Jr.

Of Kenya to the United Nations
Ambassador: Michael George Okeyo.

Further Reading

Central Bureau of Statistics. *Statistical Abstract*. (Annual)
Kenya Economic Survey, 1988. Nairobi, 1988
Arnold, G., *Modern Kenya*. London, 1982
Bigsten, A., *Education and Income Distribution in Kenya*. Brookfield, Vermont, 1984
Collison, R. L., *Kenya*. [Bibliography] London and Santa Barbara, 1982
Ochieng, W. R., (ed.) *Themes in Kenyan History*. Nairobi and Ohio Univ. Press, 1990
Who's Who in Kenya 1982–1983. London, 1983

National statistical office: Central Bureau of Statistics, Ministry of Planning and National Development, POB 30266, Nairobi

KIRIBATI

Capital: Tarawa
Population: 72,298 (1990)
GNP per capita: US$600 (1990)

Republic of Kiribati

HISTORY. The Gilbert and Ellice Islands were proclaimed a protectorate in 1892 and annexed (at the request of the native governments) as the Gilbert and Ellice Islands Colony on 10 Nov. 1915 (effective on 12 Jan. 1916). On 1 Oct. 1975 the former Ellice Islands severed its constitutional links with the Gilbert Islands and took a new name Tuvalu.

Internal self-government was obtained on 1 Nov. 1976 and independence achieved on 12 July 1979 as the Republic of Kiribati.

AREA AND POPULATION. Kiribati (pronounced Kiribass) consists of 3 groups of coral atolls and one isolated volcanic island, spread over a large expanse of the Central Pacific with a total land area of 717·1 sq. km (276·9 sq. miles). It comprises Banaba or Ocean Island (5 sq. km), the 16 Gilbert Islands (295 sq. km), the 8 Phœnix Islands (55 sq. km), and 8 of the 11 Line Islands (329 sq. km), the other 3 Line Islands (Jarvis, Palmyra and Kingman Reef) being uninhabited dependencies of the US. Population, 1990 census, 72,298. It was announced in 1988 that 4,700 people were to be resettled on Teraina and Tabuaeran atolls because the main island group was overcrowded. In 1989, the second phase was completed, with 1,500 people settled on Teraina and Tabuaeran, and the resettlement scheme will be completed in 1993. Banaba, all 16 Gilbert Islands, and 3 atolls in the Line Islands (Teraina, Tabuaeran and Kiritimati—formerly Washington, Fanning and Christmas Islands respectively) are inhabited; their populations in 1990 (census) were as follows:

Banaba (Ocean Is.)	284	Abemama	3,218	Onotoa	2,112
Makin	1,762	Kuria	985	Tamana	1,396
Butaritari	3,786	Aranuka	1,002	Arorae	1,440
Marakei	2,863	Nonouti	2,766	Kanton	45
Abaiang	5,314	North Tabiteuea	3,275	Teraina	936
North Tarawa	3,648	South Tabiteuea	1,325	Tabuaeran	1,309
South Tarawa	25,154	Beru	2,909	Kiritimati	2,537
Maiana	2,184	Nikunau	2,048		

The remaining 12 atolls have no permanent population; the 8 Phoenix Islands comprise Birnie, Rawaki (formerly Phoenix), Enderbury, Kanton (or Abariringa), Manra (formerly Sydney), Orona (formerly Hull), McKean and Nikumaroro (formerly Gardner), while the others are Malden and Starbuck in the Central Line Islands and Caroline, Flint and Vostok in the Southern Line Islands. The population is almost entirely Micronesian.

CLIMATE. The Line Islands, Phoenix Islands and Banaba have a maritime equatorial climate, but the islands further north and south are tropical. Annual and daily ranges of temperature are small and mean annual rainfall ranges from 50" (1,250 mm) near the equator to 120" (3,000 mm) in the north. Tarawa. Jan. 83°F (28·3°C), July 82°F (27·8°C). Annual rainfall 79" (1,977 mm).

CONSTITUTION AND GOVERNMENT. Under the independence Constitution the republic has a unicameral legislature, comprising 36 members elected from 20 constituencies for a 4-year term. The *President* is both Head of State and of Government.

In Oct. 1991 the government was composed as follows:

President, Foreign Affairs and International Trade: Teatao Teannaki.
Vice-President, Finance and Economic Planning: Taomati T. Iuta. *Environment and Natural Resource Development:* Ieremia T. Tabai, GCMG. *Health, Family Planning and Social Welfare:* Baitika Toum. *Line and Phoenix Islands Development:* Boanareke Boanareke. *Home Affairs and Rural Development:* Binata Tetaeka.

Transport, Communications and Tourism: Inatoa Tebania. *Education, Science and Technology:* Anterea Kaitaake. *Commerce, Industry and Employment:* Remuera Tateraka. *Works and Energy:* Teaiwa Tenieu. *Attorney-General:* Michael Takabwebwe.

National flag: Red, with blue and white wavy lines in base, and in the centre a gold rising sun and a flying frigate bird.

National anthem: Teirake Kain Kiribati.

INTERNATIONAL RELATIONS

Membership. Kiribati is a member of the UN, Commonwealth, South Pacific Forum and is an ACP state of the EEC.

ECONOMY

Budget. Budget estimates for 1991 show revenue, $A22·8m.; principal items: Fishing licences, $A2·9m.; customs duties, $A6·3m.; direct taxation, $A3·5m. Expenditure amounted to $A22·8m.

Currency. The currency in use is the Australian *dollar*.

ENERGY AND NATURAL RESOURCES

Electricity. Electric power production (1990) was 7,872,000 kwh.

Agriculture. The land is basically coral reefs upon which coral sand has built up, and then been enriched by humus from rotting vegetation and flotsam which has drifted ashore. About half the total land area is cultivated. The principal tree is the coconut, which grows on most of the islands. Other food-bearing trees are the pandanus palm and the breadfruit. The only vegetable which grows in any quantity is a coarse calladium (alocasia) with the local name 'bwabwai', which is cultivated in pits. Pigs and fowls are kept. Copra production (1988), 12,000 tonnes; coconuts, 90,000 tonnes.

Livestock (1988): Pigs, 10,000; poultry (1982), 163,000.

Fisheries. Tuna fishing is an important industry and licenses have been granted to the USA, Japan and South Korea.

FOREIGN ECONOMIC RELATIONS

Commerce. The principal imports (1990, in A$1m.) are: Food, 9·1; machinery and transport equipment, 6·6; manufactured goods, 4·1; fuels, 3·7. The value of exports for 1990 amounted to $A3·7m. Exports are almost exclusively copra.

Total trade between Kiribati and UK (British Department of Trade returns, in £1,000 sterling):

	1988	1989	1990	1991
Imports to UK	128	26	21	9
Exports and re-exports from UK	522	378	604	253

Tourism. Tourism is in the early stages of development.

COMMUNICATIONS

Roads. There were (1988) 640 km of roads, of which 483 km suitable for vehicles.

Civil Aviation. Air Tungaru is the national carrier. It operates services from Tarawa to the other 15 outer Islands in the Gilbertese Group, services varying between one and four flights each week. A fortnightly service operates to Funafuti and weekly to Majuro and Nandi. Air Nauru has a weekly flight between Nauru and Tarawa.

Shipping. The main port is at Betio (Tarawa). Other ports of entry are Christmas Island and Banaba. In 1989, 58 vessels were handled at Betio.

Telecommunications. In 1991 there were 12,000 telephones on South Tarawa and Betio, and a direct link service for 7 other islands. Radio Kiribati, a division of the Broadcasting and Publications Authority, transmits daily in English and I-Kiribati from Tarawa. A satellite link to Australia was established in 1985. There were (1990 estimate) 30,000 radio receivers.

Cinemas. In 1990 there were 4 cinemas.

Newspapers. There was (1991) 1 bi-lingual fortnightly newspaper.

JUSTICE, RELIGION, EDUCATION AND WELFARE

Justice. In 1989 Kiribati had a police force of 232 under the command of a Commissioner of Police. The Commissioner of Police is also responsible for prisons, immigration, fire service (both domestic and airport) and firearms licensing.

Religion. The majority of the population belong to the Roman Catholic or Protestant (Congregational) church; there are small numbers of Seventh-day Adventist, Mormons, Baha'i and Church of God.

Education. In 1990 the government maintained boarding school had an enrolment of 593 pupils and there were 104 primary schools, with a total of 14,709 pupils, 8 secondary schools with 2,713 pupils, and 1 community high school with 117 pupils. The Government also maintains a teachers' training college with 39 students in 1990 and a marine training centre which offers training for about 100 merchant seamen each year. The Tarawa Technical Institute at Betio offers a variety of part-time and evening technical and commercial courses and had 389 students in 1986.

In 1990, 54 islanders were in overseas countries for secondary and further education or training.

Welfare. Government maintains free medical and other services. There were 16 doctors in 1990. There is a general hospital on Tarawa and dispensaries on other islands, with 283 beds.

DIPLOMATIC REPRESENTATIVES

Of Kiribati in Great Britain
High Commissioner: Margaret Baaro (resides in Tarawa).

Of Great Britain in Kiribati (Tarawa)
High Commissioner: Derek White.

Of Kiribati in the USA
Ambassador: Margaret Baaro (resides in Tarawa).

Of USA in Kiribati
Ambassador: Evelyn I. Teegen.

Further Reading

Kiribati: Aspects of History. Univ. of South Pacific, 1979
Bailey, E., *The Christmas Island Story.* London, 1977
Grimble, A., *A Pattern of Islands.* London, 1953.—*Return to the Islands.* London, 1957
Sabatier, E., *Astride the Equator.* Melbourne, 1978
Tearo, T., *Coming of Age.* Tarawa, 1989
Whincup, T., *Nareau's Nation.* London, 1979

KOREA

Daehan Min-kuk

(Republic of Korea)

Capital: Seoul
Population: 42·79m. (1990)
GNP per capita: US$3,336 (1989)

HISTORY. Korea was united in a single kingdom under the Silla dynasty from 668. China, which claimed a vague suzerainty over Korea, recognized Korea's independence in 1895. Korea concluded trade agreements with the USA (1882), Great Britain, Germany (1883). After the Russo-Japanese war of 1904–5 Korea was virtually a Japanese protectorate until it was formally annexed by Japan on 29 Aug. 1910 thus ending the rule of the Choson kingdom, which had begun in 1392.

For the partition of Korea after the Second World War and the Korean War of 1950–53, *see* THE STATESMAN'S YEAR-BOOK, 1991–92, p. 781.

A North Korean–UN agreement of 6 Sept. 1976 established a joint security area 850 metres in diameter, divided into 2 equal parts to ensure the separation of the two sides.

On 13 Dec. 1991 the prime ministers of North and South Korea signed a declaration of non-aggression and reconciliation, agreeing to respect each other's political systems, not to interfere in each other's internal affairs or slander each other.

AREA AND POPULATION. South Korea is bounded north by the demilitarized zone (separating it from North Korea), east by the Sea of Japan (East Sea), south by the Korea Strait (separating it from Japan) and west by the Yellow Sea. The area is 99,263 sq. km. The population (census, 1 Nov. 1985) was 40,466,577 (male, 20,280,857). Estimate (1990) 42,793,000 (male, 21,564,000; 74% urban). Density, 431 per sq. km. Vital statistics rates per 1,000 in 1990: Birth, 16·29; death, 5·8; infant mortality, 12·82; growth, 9·7%. Expectation of life, 1990: Males, 66·9; females, 74·9.

There are 9 provinces (*do*) and 6 cities with provincial status. Area in 1989 and 1985 census population:

Province	Area (in sq. km)	Population (in 1,000)	Province	Area (in sq. km)	Population (in 1,000)
Seoul (city)	605	9,645,824	North Chungchong	7,437	1,391,084
Pusan (city)	526	3,516,768	South Chungchong	8,317	3,001,538
Taegu (city)	456	2,030,649	North Cholla	8,052	2,202,218
Inchon (city)	313	1,387,475	South Cholla	11,812	3,748,442
Kwangju (city)	501	–	North Kyongsang	19,443	3,013,276
Taejon (city)	537	–	South Kyongsang	11,771	3,519,121
Kyonggi	10,769	4,794,240	Cheju	1,825	489,458
Kangwon	16,898	1,726,029			

The chief cities (populations, census 1985) are:

Seoul	9,645,824	Kwangchu	905,896	Masan	449,236
Pusan	3,516,768	Taejon	866,303	Seongnam	447,832
Taegu	2,030,649	Ulsan	551,219	Suweon	430,827
Inchon	1,387,475	Puch'on	456,311	Chonchu	426,490

CLIMATE. The extreme south has a humid warm temperate climate while the rest of the country experiences continental temperate conditions. Rainfall is concentrated in the period April to Sept. and ranges from 40" (1,020 mm) to 60" (1,520 mm). Pusan. Jan. 36°F (2·2°C), July 76°F (24·4°C). Annual rainfall 56" (1,407 mm). Seoul. Jan. 23°F (–5°C), July 77°F (25°C). Annual rainfall 50" (1,250 mm).

CONSTITUTION AND GOVERNMENT. A new constitution was approved by national referendum in Oct. 1987 and came into force on 25 Feb. 1988. It provides for a President, to be directly elected for a single 5-year term, a State

Council of ministers whom he appoints and leads, and a National Assembly (299 members) directly elected for 4 years (237 from constituencies and 62 from party lists in proportion to the overall vote).

Elections to the National Assembly were held in March 1992. The Democratic Liberal Party gained 149 seats, the Democratic Party 97, the Party for National Unification 32 and independents 22.

President of the Republic: Roh Tae-woo (took office 25 Feb. 1988).
The Cabinet in Feb. 1992 was composed as follows:
Prime Minister: Chung Won Shik (b.1928).
Deputy Prime Minister and Minister of National Unification: Choi Ho-Joong. *Deputy Prime Minister and Minister of Economic Planning:* Choi Kak Kyu. *Foreign Affairs:* Lee Sang Ok. *Home Affairs:* Lee Sang Yeon. *Finance:* Rhee Yong Man. *Justice:* Kim Ki Choon. *Defence:* Gen. Choi Sae Chang. *Youth and Sport:* Lee Jin Sam. *Agriculture, Forestry and Fisheries:* Cho Kyun Shik. *Commerce and Industry:* Hahn Bong Suh. *Construction:* Seo Yeong Taek. *Health and Social Affairs:* Ahn Pil Joon. *Labour Affairs:* Choe Byung Yul. *Transport:* Kim Chang Keun. *Communications:* Lee Woo Jae. *Culture and Information:* Lee Soo Jung. *Government Administration:* Lee Sang Bae. *Science and Technology:* Rhee Sang Hi. *Minister for State Affairs:* Kim Yung Chung. *Office of Legislation:* Hyun Hong Joo. *Patriots and Veterans Affairs Agency:* Lee Sahng Yeon. *Environment:* Kwon Hwi Hyuk. *Energy and Natural Resources:* Jim Nyum.

National flag: White charged in the centre with the *yang-um* in red and blue and with 4 black *p'algwae* trigrams.

Local government: The 15 provinces are divided into 137 districts *(Gun)* and 67 cities *(Shi)*.

A first round of elections was held in March 1991 in 3,562 electoral districts for 4,304 seats to form legislative councils in districts, towns and municipal wards. 10,119 candidates stood. Turn-out was 55%. A second round was held in June for 866 seats on the provincial and city councils. The DLP won 564 seats and gained control of 11 councils; the NDP won 165 seats and 3 councils.

DEFENCE. Military service is compulsory for 18 months. Conscripts may exchange military service for a 5-year period in civilian industry.

Army. The Army is organized in 19 infantry divisions, 2 mechanized infantry divisions, 2 independent infantry brigades, 7 special forces brigades, 2 anti-aircraft artillery brigades, 2 surface-to-air missile brigades, 1 army aviation brigade and 2 surface-to-surface missile battalions. Equipment includes 250 Type 88, 350 M-47 and 950 M-48A5 main battle tanks. Army aviation equipment includes 50 Hughes 500 and 48 AH-1F/J/S helicopters for anti-armour operations, observation and liaison, and 18 CH-47D transport helicopters and 270 utility helicopters. Delivery of 81 UN-60 Black Hawk transport helicopters began in 1991 and is scheduled to continue until 1995. Strength (1992) 650,000, with a Regular Army Reserve of 1·5m. and a Homeland Reserve Defence Force of 3·3m. Para-military Civilian Defence Corps, 3·5m.

Navy. A substantial force of 60,000 (19,000 conscripts), including 25,000 marines (1991), continues its rapid modernization programme. Current strength includes the first of a class of German-designed ocean-going diesel submarine, 3 midget submarines (175 tonnes), 8 aged (1943–46) ex-US destroyers, and 26 locally-built frigates with new US and European weapons, 4 corvettes, 11 fast missile craft, together with a patrol force of 68 inshore craft. There are 9 coastal minesweepers and an amphibious force of 7 tank landing ships, 7 medium landing ships, together with 35 amphibious craft. Major auxiliaries include 3 tankers, 2 large tugs, 4 survey vessels and 35 service craft. The Navy has a small aviation element with 24 shore-based S-2F Tracker anti-submarine aircraft and 25 Hughes 500MD, 12 Lynx and 10 Alouette helicopters, some of which embark in frigates and destroyers.

A further 2 German-designed diesel submarines are under construction; and the squadron may in due course reach a total of 6.

Construction of the first indigenous guided-missile destroyer started in mid-1991. Main bases are at Chinhae, Inchon and Pusan.

The Coastguard numbering some 12,000 (mostly shore-based) operates 14 off-shore, 24 coastal and 40 inshore patrol craft as well as 9 light helicopters.

Air Force. With a 1992 strength of about 40,000 men and 450 combat aircraft, the Air Force is undergoing rapid expansion with US assistance. Its combat aircraft include 36 F-16C/D Fighting Falcons, about 120 F-4D/E Phantoms, 50 F-5A/B tactical fighters, 200 F-5E/F tactical fighters, 6 RF-5A reconnaissance fighters, 10 O-2A forward air control aircraft and 10 Hughes 500-D Defender helicopters. There are also 10 C-54 and 10 C-123 piston-engined transports, 10 C-130 Hercules turboprop-engined transports, 2 HS.748s, 1 Boeing 737 and 1 DC-6 for VIP transport; UH-1, Bell 212 and Bell 412 transport helicopters, and T-41, T-28, T-33 and T-37C trainers.

INTERNATIONAL RELATIONS

Membership. The Republic of Korea is a member of the UN.

ECONOMY

Policy. Under the sixth 5-year social and economic plan (1987–91) the 1988 growth rate was 12·2% and the forecast annual rate for 1989–91 was 7·3%. A task force responsible to the president is co-ordinating a large-scale long-term programme of infrastructural development. The seventh 5-year social and economic plan is scheduled to start in 1992.

Budget. Revenue and expenditure (in 1,000m. won) at the 1991 budget (and estimates for 1992): 31,382 (33,505). Sources of revenue: National tax, 27,720 (32,462); non-tax, 848 (1,042); carry-over, 2,814. Expenditure: Administration, 1,390·2 (1,462·8); legislation and elections, 130·7 (146·1); judiciary and police, 2,079·5 (2,457·2); economic development, 5,081·5 (6,189); social development, 3,204·3 (3,229·8); education, 5,559·5 (6,433); defence, 7,767 (8,753); local authority grants, 3,358·7 (3,830·1); loan payments, 563·2 (640·7); investments, 2,247·7 (8,350·1).

Currency. The unit of currency is the *won* (KRW) of 100 *chon*. Notes are in denominations of 10,000, 5,000, 1,000 and 500 *won* and coins in denominations of 500, 100, 50, 10, 5 and 1 *won*. 1,006,200m. *won* were in circulation in 1989. Inflation was 10% in 1991. In March 1992, 766·11 *won* = US$1; 1,344·90 *won* = £1 sterling.

Banking and Finance. The central bank and bank of issue is the Bank of Korea (*Governor*, Kim Kun). State-run banks include the Korean Development Bank, the Medium & Small Industry Bank, the Citizen's National Bank, the Korea Exchange Bank, the National Livestock Co-operatives Federation and the Federation of Fisheries Co-operatives serving as banking and credit institutions for farmers and fishermen, the Korea Housing Bank, the Export and Import Bank of Korea.

There are 8 commercial banks: The Bank of Seoul & Trust Co. Ltd, the Cho Heung Bank Ltd, the Commercial Bank of Korea, the Korea First Bank, the Hanil Bank, the Shinhan Bank, the Koram Bank, the Donghwa Bank; and 10 local banks. Foreign banks were granted parity of treatment with domestic banks in July 1991, and the ceiling on their funds was lifted.

In addition, there are non-bank financial institutions consisting of 20 insurance companies, the Land Bank of Korea, the Credit Guarantee Fund, 32 short-term financial companies, 237 mutual credit companies, and the Merchant Banking Corporation.

There is a stock exchange in Seoul.

Weights and Measures. The metric system is in use alongside traditional measures. 1 *sok* = 144 kg.

ENERGY AND NATURAL RESOURCES

Electricity. Electricity generated (1989) was 94,471m. kwh. Supply 100 and 220 volts; 60 Hz.

Minerals. In 1988, 1,795 mining companies employed 87,614 people. Mineral deposits are small except tungsten. Output, 1989, included (in tonnes): Anthracite coal, 19m.; iron ore, 0·68m.; tungsten ore, 3,265; limestone, 46·9m.; graphite, 97,882; lead ore, 25,868; zinc ore, 45,123.

Agriculture. Arable land was 12·13m. ha in 1989, of which 1·35m. ha were rice paddies. The farming population was 6·79m. in 1989; there were 1·77m. farms. The agricultural workforce was 3·03m.

Production (1989, in 1,000 tonnes): Rice, 7,174; barley, 738; wheat, 20,579 sok; potatoes, 302; maize, 6,555. There were 31,328 tractors in 1989.

Livestock in 1989 (in 1,000): Draught cattle, 1,536; milch cows, 515; pigs, 4,801; sheep, 3,410; chickens, 61,689; ducks, 596.

Forestry. Forest area was 6·49m. ha in 1989. 1m. cu. metres of timber were cut.

Fisheries. In 1989, there was a total of 98,455 boats (963,231 gross tons). 799 deep-sea fishing vessels were operating overseas. The fish catch (inland and marine) was 3,319,395 tonnes.

INDUSTRY. Manufacturing industry is concentrated primarily on oil, petrochemicals, chemical fibres, construction, iron and steel, cement, machinery, shipbuilding, automobiles and electronics. Tobacco manufacture is a government monopoly. Industry is dominated by giant conglomerates (*chaebol*).

Production in 1989 (in 1,000 tonnes): Paper and products, 1,862; artificial fertilizers, 2,872; plastic products, 628; pig-iron, 14,949; steel bars, 809; steel angles, 1,655; (in 1,000 sq. metres): Cotton fabrics, 646; silk fabrics, 20; synthetic fabrics, 2,908; petrol, 2,910,952 kilolitres; shoes, 11·49m. pairs; 64,578 cars; 16,056 lorries; 9·33m. microwave ovens; 2·18m. electronic calculators.

Labour. In 1989 the population of working age (15 years and over) was 30·22m. (15·6m. females), of whom 17·97m. (7·25m. female) were economically active and 0·46m. (0·13m. females) unemployed.

In 1989 4·73m. persons were employed in manufacturing, 1·25m. in building, 1·49m. in the professions and 8·32m. in services. There were 1,322 strikes in 1990 (1,616 in 1989). Unemployment was 2·9% in May 1991.

FOREIGN ECONOMIC RELATIONS. Since March 1991 foreign partners in joint ventures holding less than 50% of the capital have needed only to report, instead of seek approval for, their projects. Tax concessions for foreign investments have been reduced. Since 1992 foreign investors have been able to buy 10% of the equity of most Korean companies.

Commerce. In 1989 exports were US$62,377m., imports US$61,465m. Trade in 1989 with major partners (in US$1m.): Imports: Japan, 17,449; USA, 15,911; EC, 6,472. Exports: USA, 20,639; Japan, 13,457; EC, 7,394. Rice may not be imported.

Major exports are textiles, electronics, iron and steel and machinery, and in 1988 included (in US$1m.): Heavy chemical products, 33,462; light industrial products, 24,782. Major imports included: Crude oil, 15,088; raw materials, 18,786; capital goods, 15,436; consumer goods, 4,860.

Total trade between Korea and UK (British Department of Trade returns, in £1,000 sterling):

	1987	1988	1989	1990	1991
Imports to UK	936,038	1,135,107	1,164,723	963,829	924,615
Exports and re-exports from UK	427,229	1,742,747	493,945	620,690	786,162

Tourism. In 1989 there were 2,728,100 foreign tourists. Age limits for foreign travel were lifted in Jan. 1989, and in 1989 1·2m. Koreans travelled abroad.

COMMUNICATIONS

Roads. In 1989 there were 56,481 km of roads, including 1,552 km of expressway. 11·95m. passengers and 200m. tonnes of freight were carried in 1989. In 1989 motor vehicles totalled 2,660,212 (2,337,380 private) including 768,943 trucks, 323,402 buses, and 1,558,650 passenger cars (1,405,314 private).

Railways. In 1989 the National Railroad totalled 3,120 km of 1,435 mm gauge (525 km electrified) and 46 km of 762 mm gauge. In 1989 railways carried 585m. passengers and 58·7m. tonnes of freight.

Civil Aviation. In 1989, 40 countries maintained aviation agreements with Korea and had 47 air routes with 28 cities in 18 countries. The Ministry of Transportation opened the Seoul-Singapore-Jakarta passenger route in 1989.

In Sept. 1989 Korea had 159 commercial aircraft (62 Korean Air passenger-cargo planes, 9 Asiana Airlines passenger-cargo planes, 38 light planes and 43 helicopters). In 1989, 8·73m. passengers and 150,381 tons of cargo were carried on domestic routes and 4,033,300 passengers and 319,053 tonnes of cargo on international routes.

Shipping. There are 25 first-grade ports and 22 second-grade ports. There were 4,610 vessels registered in 1989, including 151 passenger ships, 1,049 cargo ships and 529 oil tankers. Total tonnage, 7,305,956. 8·85m. passengers and 54·87m. tonnes of freight were carried in 1989.

Telecommunications. Post offices totalled 3,216 in 1989; telephones, 4,194,900. The fifth satellite earth station was opened in June 1988, bringing the number of communications circuits via satellite to 2,866. There were 41,958,516 radio and 8·7m. television receivers in 1990 (colour by NTSC).

Cinemas. In 1988 there were 696 with a seating capacity of 240,000.

Newspapers (1989). There were 68 daily papers, including 2 in English appearing in Seoul and 2 news agencies.

RELIGION, EDUCATION AND WELFARE

Justice. Judicial power is vested in the Supreme Court, High Courts, District Courts and Family Court. The Justices of the Supreme Court are appointed by the President of the Republic; the Chief Justice appoints other judges. The President appoints the Prosecutor-General.

Religion. Basically the religions of Korea have been Shamanism, Buddhism (introduced A.D. 372) and Confucianism, which was the official faith from 1392 to 1910. Catholic converts from China introduced Christianity in the 18th century, but the ban on Roman Catholicism was not lifted until 1882. Protestantism was introduced in the late 19th century. Religious affiliations of the population in 1991 (and 1985): Buddhism, 23·7% (27·7%); Protestantism, 16·3% (18·6%); Roman Catholicism, 4·8% (5·7%); Confucianism, 1·5% (1%); others, 0·9% (1%); no religion, 52·9% (46%).

Education. After 1 or 2 years of kindergarten, education is compulsory from 6 to 12, followed by the options of middle school till 15 and general or vocational high school to 18.

In 1989–90 there were 8,246 kindergartens with 410,824 pupils and 14,886 teachers; 6,396 elementary schools with 4,894,261 pupils and 134,898 teachers; 2,450 middle schools with 2,371,215 pupils and 81,699 teachers; 1,084 high schools with 1,490,846 pupils and 54,333 teachers; 588 vocational high schools with 835,216 students and 32,944 teachers; 117 junior colleges with 291,041 students and 6,999 teachers; 11 teacher training colleges with 17,182 students and 679 teachers; and 104 colleges and universities with 1,020,771 students and 31,675 teachers.

Health. In 1989 there were 213 general hospitals (with 62,832 beds), 323 other hospitals (29,760), 3,609 oriental medical hospitals and clinics (1,151) and 4,004 dental hospitals and clinics. There were 39,769 physicians, 5,435 oriental medical doctors, 8,630 dentists, 7,397 midwives, 82,657 nurses, and 35,756 pharmacists.

DIPLOMATIC REPRESENTATIVES

Of Korea in Great Britain (4 Palace Gate, London, W8 5NF)
Ambassador: Dr Lee Hong Koo.

Of Great Britain in Korea (4 Chung-Dong, Chung-Ku, Seoul)
Ambassador: David J. Wright, CMG, LVO.

Of Korea in the USA (2370 Massachusetts Ave., NW, Washington, D.C., 20008)
Ambassador: Hyun Hong Choo.

Of the USA in Korea (Sejong-Ro, Seoul)
Ambassador: Donald Gregg.

Of Korea at the United Nations:
Ambassador: Yoo Chong Ha.

Further Reading

Korean Overseas Information Office. *A Handbook of Korea*. 8th ed. Seoul, 1990
National Bureau of Statistics. *Korea Statistical Yearbook*
Das, D. K., *Korean Economic Dynamism*. London, 1991
Eckert, C. J. *et al.*, *Korea Old and New: a History*. Harvard Univ. Press, 1991
Hastings, M., *The Korean War*. London, 1987
Korea Annual. Seoul

National statistical office: National Bureau of Statistics, Economic Planning Board, Seoul

NORTH KOREA

Capital: Pyongyang
Population: 22·42m. (1989)
GNP per capita: US$2,460 (1991)

Chosun Minchu-chui
Inmin Konghwa-guk

(People's Democratic Republic
of Korea)

HISTORY. In northern Korea the Russians, arriving on 8 Aug. 1945, one month ahead of the Americans, established a Communist-led 'Provisional Government'. The newly created Korean Communist Party merged in 1946 with the New National Party into the Korean Workers' Party. In July 1946 the KWP, with the remaining pro-Communist groups and non-party people, formed the United Democratic Patriotic Front. On 25 Aug. 1948 the Communists organized elections for a Supreme People's Assembly, both in Soviet-occupied North Korea (212 deputies) and in US-occupied South Korea (360 deputies, of whom a certain number went to the North and took their seats). A People's Democratic Republic was proclaimed on 9 Sept. 1948. On 13 Dec. 1991 the prime ministers of North and South Korea signed a declaration of non-aggression, agreeing to respect each other's political systems, not to interfere in each other's internal affairs or slander each other.

AREA AND POPULATION. North Korea is bounded north by China, east by the sea of Japan, west by the Yellow Sea and south by South Korea, from which it is separated by a demilitarized zone of 1,262 sq. km. Its area is 120,538 sq. km. Population estimate in 1989, 22·42m. (64% urban). Population density, 186 per sq. km. Rate of population increase, 1989, 1·64%; birth rate, 1985, 3%; death rate, 0·6%. Marriage is discouraged before the age of 32 for men and 29 for women. Expectation of life in 1990 was: Males, 69; females, 75 years. Large towns (estimate, 1984): Pyongyang, the capital (2,639,448); Chongjin (754,128); Nampo (691,284); Sinuiju (500,000); Wonsan (350,000); Kaesong (345,642); Kimchaek (281,000); Haeju (131,000); Sariwon (130,000); Hamhung (775,000 in 1981).

CLIMATE. There is a warm temperate climate, though winters can be very cold in the north. Rainfall is concentrated in the summer months. Pyongyang. Jan. 18°F (−7·8°C), July 75°F (23·9°C). Annual rainfall 37" (916 mm).

CONSTITUTION AND GOVERNMENT. The political structure is based upon the Constitution of 27 Dec. 1972. The Constitution provides for a *Supreme People's Assembly* elected every 4 years by universal suffrage. Citizens of 17 years and over can vote and be elected. Elections were held in April 1990. It was claimed that 99·78% of the electorate voted for the list of single candidates presented. There are 687 deputies. The government consists of the *Administration Council* directed by the Central People's Committee (*Secretary,* Chi Chang Ik).

The head of state is the *President,* elected for 4-year terms. On 24 May 1990 the National Assembly unanimously elected Kim Il Sung (b. 1912) for a fifth term.

In practice the country is ruled by the Korean Workers' (*i.e.*, Communist) Party which elects a Central Committee which in turn appoints a Politburo. In Nov. 1991 this was composed of: Marshal Kim Il Sung, (*General Secretary of the Party, President of the Republic, Chairman of the Central People's Committee, Supreme Commander of the Armed Forces*); Kim Jong Il (b. 1943; Kim Il Sung's son and designated successor) (*Vice-President of the Republic*); O Jin U (*Armed Forces' Minister*) (The latter 3 constituting the Politburo's Presidium); Kang Song San; Li Jong Ok (*Vice-President of the Republic*); Pak Sung Chul (*Vice-President of the*

863

Republic); So Chol; Kim Yong Nam *(Deputy Prime Minister and Foreign Minister)*; Kim Hwan *(Deputy Prime Minister, Minister of the Chemical Industry)*; Yon Hyong Muk *(Prime Minister)*; O Guk Ryol; So Yun Sok; Yun Ki Bok *(Deputy Prime Minister with responsibility for Re-unification)*; Hong Song Nam *(First Deputy Prime Minister, Chairman, State Planning Commission)*; Kye Ung Tae; Hwang Chang Yop. There were also 9 candidate members.

Ministers not full members of the Politburo include Kim Yun Hyok *(Deputy Prime Minister)*; Cho Se Ung *(Deputy Prime Minister)*; Yun Gi Jong *(Finance)*; Chong Song Nam *(Foreign Economic Affairs)*; Kim Bok Sin; Chong Jun Gi, Kim Yun Hyok, Kim Chang Ju *(Deputy Prime Ministers)*; Choe Jong Gun *(Foreign Trade)*; Paek Hak Rim *(Public Security)*.

In 1981 the Party had some 2m. members.

There are also the puppet religious Chongu and Korean Social Democratic Parties and various organizations combined in a Fatherland Front.

National flag: Blue, red and blue horizontal stripes separated by narrow white bands. The red stripe bears a white circle within which is a red 5-pointed star.

National anthem: 'A chi mun bin na ra i gang san' ('Shine bright, o dawn, on this land so fair'). Words by Pak Se Yong; music by Kim Won Gyun.

Local government: The country is divided into 13 administrative units: 4 cities (Pyongyang, Chongjin, Hamhung and Kaesong) and 9 provinces (capitals in brackets): South Pyongan (Nampo), North Pyongan (Sinuiju), Jagang (Kanggye), South Hwanghai (Haeju), North Hwanghai (Sariwon), Kangwon (Wonsan), South Hamgyong (Hamheung), North Hamgyong (Chongjin), Yanggang (Hyesan). These are sub-divided into 152 counties. There are 26,539 deputies in People's Assemblies at city/province, county and commune level. Elections were held in Nov. 1991. Turn-out was said to be 99·5%.

DEFENCE. There is a *National Defence Commission* headed by Kim Il Sung. Chief of the General Staff is Choe Gwang (appointed 1988). Military service is compulsory at the age of 16 for periods of 5-8 years in the Army, 5-10 years in the Navy and 3–4 years in the Air Force. In 1990 defence spending was 21% of GNP. North Korea adhered to the 1968 Non-Proliferation Treaty on nuclear weapons in 1985, but was unwilling to permit international inspection of its nuclear plants in 1991.

Army. The Army is organized in 25 infantry divisions (some motorized); 15 armoured, 30 motorized infantry and 3 independent infantry brigades; 1 special purpose corps numbering 60,000; and an artillery corps with multiple rocket launchers and 6 surface-to-surface missile battalions. Equipment includes 200 T-34, 1,600 T-54/55, 1,500 T-62 and 175 Type-59 main battle tanks. Strength (1992) 868,000, with 0·5m. reserves. There is also a paramilitary militia of some 4m. men and a Ministry of Public Security force of 200,000 including border guards.

Navy. The Navy, principally tasked to coastal patrol and defence, comprises 24 diesel submarines (20 of Chinese design and 4 ex-Soviet). Surface forces include 3 small frigates, (1 missile-armed), 3 corvettes, 36 missile craft, 170 fast torpedo craft, 6 anti-submarine patrol craft and some 150 inshore patrol craft. Amphibious forces consist of some 130 small craft. Support is provided by 2 ex-Soviet ocean tugs and 100 service craft. There is a coastal defence element equipped with some 6 missile batteries and old 122 mm, 130 mm and 152 mm guns. Personnel in 1991 totalled 41,000 officers and men with 40,000 reserves.

Air Force. The Air Force had a total of about 690 combat aircraft and 60 armed helicopters and 82,000 personnel in 1992. Since 1985 the USSR has supplied 50 MiG-23 supersonic and 30 MiG-29 interceptors, 40 Su-25 fighter-bombers and 30 SA3 surface-to-air missiles. Other equipment is believed to include about 160 supersonic MiG-21 interceptors, more than 100 F-6s (Chinese-built MiG-19s), 150 MiG-17s for ground attack and reconnaissance, 30 Su-7 fighter-bombers, 40 Chinese-built A5 fighter-bombers, 50 Il-28 twin-jet light bombers, 200 An-2 light transport aircraft, 40 Mi-4 and Mi-8 transport helicopters and 80 US Hughes 300 and 500 helicopters.

INTERNATIONAL RELATIONS

Membership. North Korea is a member of the UN and WHO.

ECONOMY

Policy. For previous plans *see* THE STATESMAN'S YEAR-BOOK, 1987–88. After a hiatus it was announced in Oct. 1986 that a third 7-year plan would run from 1987 to 1993. Steel production targets have been reduced (to 10m. tonnes) and more emphasis placed on export items, non-ferrous metals and fishery products.

Budget (in 1m. won) for calendar years:

	1984	1985	1986	1987	1988
Revenue	26,305	27,439	28,539	30,337	31,852
Expenditure	26,158	27,329	28,396	30,085	31,852

Defence spending was 13·8% of the budget in 1987 (14% in 1986). Local government revenue in 1987: 4,185m. *won*; expenditure, 3,427m. *won*.

Currency. The monetary unit is the *won* (KPW) of 100 *jun*. There are coins of 1, 5, 10 and 50 *jun* and 1, 5, 10, 50 and 100 *won*. In March 1992, US$1 = 0·97 *won*; £1 = 1·70 *won*.

Weights and Measures. While the metric system is in force traditional measures are in frequent use. The *jungbo* = 1 ha; the *ri* = 3,927 metres.

ENERGY AND NATURAL RESOURCES

Electricity. There are 3 thermal power stations and 4 hydro-electric plants. A nuclear power plant is being built. Output in 1990, was 27,890m. kwh. Installed capacity was 6·9m. kw in 1990. Hydro-electric potential exceeds 8m. kw. A hydro-electric plant and dam under construction on the Pukhan near Mount Kumgang has been denounced as a flood threat by the South Koreans, who constructed a defensive 'Peace Dam' in retaliation.

Oil. Oilwells went into production in 1957. An oil pipeline from China came on stream in 1976. Crude oil refining capacity was 70,000 bbls. a day in 1990.

Minerals. North Korea is rich in minerals. Estimated reserves in tonnes: Iron ore, 3,300m.; copper, 2·15m.; lead, 6m.; zinc, 12m.; coal, 11,990m.; uranium, 26m.; manganese, 6,500m. 40·7m. tonnes of coal were mined in 1990, 8m. tonnes of iron ore and 15,000 tonnes of copper ore in 1986. 1986 production of gold was 160,000 fine troy oz; silver, 1·6m. fine troy oz; salt, 570,000 tonnes.

Agriculture. In 1990 there were 2·14m. ha. of cultivated land, including 0.6m. ha of paddy fields. In 1990, 7·99m. persons made a living from agriculture.

Collectivization took place between 1954 and 1958. 90% of the cultivated land is farmed by co-operatives. Land belongs either to the State or to co-operatives, and it is intended gradually to transform the latter into the former, but small individually-tended plots producing for 'farmers' markets' are tolerated as a 'transition measure'. Livestock farming is mainly carried on by large state farms.

There is a large-scale tideland reclamation project. There were 37,600 km of irrigation canals in 1976, making possible 2 rice harvests a year. In 1988 there were 77,000 tractors. The technical revolution in agriculture (nearly 95% of ploughing, etc., is mechanized) has considerably increased the yield of grain (sown on 2·3m. *jungbo* of land); rice production, 1990, was 5·5m. tonnes, maize, 4·4m. tonnes; potatoes, 2·1m. tonnes; soya beans, 0·46m. tonnes.

Livestock, 1990: 1·3m. cattle, 3·2m. pigs, 0·39m. sheep, 0·29m. goats and 21m. poultry.

Forestry. Forest area in 1988 was 8·97m. ha. 4·6m. cu metres of timber were cut in 1986.

Fisheries. Catch in 1990: 2·15m. tonnes. There is a fishing fleet of 30,600 vessels including 20,000 motor vessels.

INDUSTRY. Industries were intensively developed by the Japanese, notably cotton spinning, hydro-electric power, cotton, silk and rayon weaving, and chemical fertilizers. Production (in tonnes) in 1982: Pig-iron, 4m.; crude steel, 4m.; rolled steel, 3·2m.; lead, 30,000; zinc, 140,000; copper, 48,000; ship-building, 400,000; chemical fertilizers, 620,000; chemicals, 20,000; synthetic resins, 90,000; cement (1986), 9,040; textiles (1986), 600m. metres; woven goods, 600m. metres; shoes, 40m. pairs; motor-cars (1986), 20,000; TV sets (1986), 240,000; refrigerators, 10,000. Annual steel production capacity was 4·3m. tonnes in 1987.

Labour. The economically-active population was 9·27m. in 1989. Industrial workers make up some 60% of the work force. Average monthly wage, 1984: 90 won.

FOREIGN ECONOMIC RELATIONS. Joint ventures with foreign firms have been permitted since 1984. In 1990 foreign debt was estimated at US$4,500m. (of which US$3,800m. were to the USSR). The USA imposed sanctions in Jan. 1988 for alleged terrorist activities.

Commerce. Exports in 1990 were US1,990m.; imports, US$3,160m. 58% of trade was with the USSR in 1989, 13% with China, 10% with Japan. The chief exports are metal ores and products, the chief imports machinery and petroleum products.

An agreement with the USSR of Nov. 1990 provided for trade to be conducted in hard currency from 1991.

Total trade between North Korea and UK (British Department of Trade returns, in £1,000 sterling):

	1987	1988	1989	1990	1991
Imports to UK	641	824	1,095	373	349
Exports and re-exports from UK	2,198	3,125	3,087	4,774	5,503

Tourism. A 40-year ban on non-Communist tourists was lifted in 1986.

COMMUNICATIONS

Roads. There were 23,000 km of road in 1990, including 240 km of motorways. There were 248,000 motor cars in 1990.

Railways. In 1990 there were 4,927 km of track, (2,706 km were electrified in 1984). In 1986, 89% of trains were hauled by electricity. In 1987 86% of all freight was transported by rail. In 1990 there were 30·5 km of urban local transit systems.

Civil Aviation. There are services to Moscow, Khabarovsk, Beijing and Hong Kong. An agreement envisaging a service from Pyongyang to Tokyo was signed in 1990. There are domestic flights from Pyongyang to Hamhung and Chongjin.

Shipping. The leading ports are Chongjin, Wonsan and Hungnam. Nampo, the port of Pyongyang, has been dredged and expanded. Pyongyang is connected to Nampo by railway and river. In 1987 the ocean-going merchant fleet numbered 71 vessels totalling 407,253 GRT.

The biggest navigable river is the Yalu, 698 km up to the Hyesan district.

Telecommunications. There were some 30,000 telephones in 1990. An agreement to share in Japan's telecommunications satellites was reached in Sept. 1990. The government-controlled Korean Central Broadcasting Station and Korean Central Television Station are responsible for radio and TV broadcasting. In 1991 there were 34 radio and 11 TV stations (colour by PAL). There were 3·75m. radio and 0·25m. TV sets in 1991.

Cinemas. There were 1,778 cinemas in 1985 and 3,515 mobile cinemas.

Newspapers. There were 11 newspapers in 1984. The party newspaper is *Nodong* (or *Rodong*) *Sinmun* (Workers' Daily News). Circulation about 600,000.

JUSTICE, RELIGION, EDUCATION AND WELFARE

Justice. The judiciary consists of the Supreme Court, whose judges are elected by the Assembly for 3 years; provincial courts; and city or county people's courts. The procurator-general, appointed by the Assembly, has supervisory powers over the judiciary and the administration; the Supreme Court controls the judicial administration.

Religion. The Constitution provides for 'freedom of religion as well as the freedom of anti-religious propaganda'. In 1986 there were 3m. Chondoists, 400,000 Buddhists and 200,000 Christians. Another 3m. followed traditional beliefs.

Education. Free compulsory universal technical education lasts 11 years: 1 pre-school year, 4 years primary education starting at the age of 6, followed by 6 years secondary.

In 1988 there were 47,600 kindergartens. In 1980 there were some 10,000 11-year schools. In 1982–83 there were 5·2m. pupils and 110,000 teachers, and nearly 1m. students in higher education. In 1985 there were 216 institutes of higher education, including 3 universities—Kim Il Sung University (founded 1946), Kim Chaek Technical University, Pyongyang Medical School—and an Academy of Sciences (founded 1952).

In 1977–78 Kim Il Sung University had some 17,000 students.

Health. Medical treatment is free. In 1982 there were 1,531 general hospitals, 979 specialized hospitals and 5,414 clinics. There were 24 doctors and 130 hospital beds per 10,000 population in 1983.

DIPLOMATIC REPRESENTATIVE

Of North Korea to the United Nations
Ambassador: Pak Gil Yon.

Further Reading

North Korea Directory. Tokyo, annual since 1988
An, T. S., *North Korea in Transition*. Westport, 1983;–*North Korea: a Political Handbook*. Washington, 1983
Baik Bong, *Kim Il Sung: Biography*. 3 vols. New York, 1969–70
Chung, C.-S., (ed.) *North Korean Communism: A Comparative Analysis*. Seoul, 1980
Kihl, Y. W., *Politics and Policies in Divided Korea*. Boulder, 1984
Kim Han Gil, *Modern History of Korea*. Pyongyang, 1979
Kim Il Sung, *Works*. Pyongyang, 1980–83
Kim, Y. S., (ed.) *The Economy of the Korean Democratic People's Republic, 1945–1977*. Kiel, 1979
Koh, B. C., *The Foreign Policy Systems of North and South Korea*. Berkeley, 1984
Park, J. K. and Kim, J.-G., *The Politics of North Korea*. Boulder, 1979
Scalapino, R. A. and Lee, C.-S., *Communism in Korea. Part I: The Movement. Part II: The Society*. Univ. of Calif. Press, 1972—and Kim, J-Y. (eds.), *North Korea Today: Strategic and Domestic Issues*. Univ. of California Press, 1983
Suh, D.-S., *Korean Communism, 1945–1980: A Reference Guide to the Political System*. Honolulu, 1981

KUWAIT

Capital: Kuwait
Population: 2·04m. (1990)
GNP per capita: US$16,380 (1989)

Dowlat al Kuwait

(State of Kuwait)

HISTORY. The ruling dynasty was founded by Shaikh Sabah al-Owel (ruled 1756-72). In 1899 Shaikh Mubarak concluded a treaty with the UK: in return for British protection, he undertook not to alienate any of his territory without British agreement. In 1914 the UK recognized Kuwait as an independent government under British protection. On 19 June 1961 an agreement reaffirmed the independence and sovereignty of Kuwait and recognized the Government of Kuwait's responsibility for the conduct of internal and external affairs; the agreement of 1899 was terminated and the UK agreed to assist Kuwait should it request it.

Early on 2 Aug. 1990 Iraqi forces without warning invaded and rapidly overran the country, meeting little resistance. The Amir escaped to Saudi Arabia, but his brother Sheikh Fahd, was killed. President Saddam of Iraq declared the annexation of Kuwait on 8 Aug. The Kuwaiti government established itself in exile at Taif (Saudi Arabia) during the Iraqi occupation.

Following the expiry of the date required by the UN for the withdrawal of Iraqi forces on 15 Jan. 1991, an air offensive was launched by coalition forces against targets in Kuwait, followed by a land attack on 24 Feb. Iraqi forces were routed, and Kuwait City was liberated on 27 Feb. In compliance with the provisional ceasefire of 28 Feb., Iraq withdrew all its forces from Kuwait.

AREA AND POPULATION. Kuwait is bounded in the east by the Persian Gulf, north and west by Iraq and south and south-west by Saudi Arabia, with an area of about 6,880 sq. miles (17,819 sq. km); the total population at the census of 1985 was 1,697,301, of which about 60% were non-Kuwaitis. Estimate (1990) 2·04m., including 1·1m. non-Kuwaitis. Population density, 110 per sq. km.

Following the Iraqi occupation of 1990-91, the government announced plans to reduce its population to about 1m. to ensure that Kuwaitis formed a majority at about 0·55m. Many foreign workers who fled during the occupation would not be permitted to return. A Palestinian community of 0·2m. was envisaged as the second-largest group. Life expectancy was 74 years in 1989.

Over 78% speak Arabic, the official language, 10% speak Kurdish and 4% Iranian (Farsi). English is also used as a second language.

The country is divided into 4 governorates: The capital (comprising Kuwait City, Kuwait's 9 islands and territorial and shared territorial waters), with an area of 983 sq. km (population 167,750 at 1985 census); Hawalli, 620 sq. km (943,250); Ahmadi, 4,665 sq. km (304,662) and Jahra, 11,550 sq. km (279,466).

The chief cities were (census, 1985) Kuwait, the capital (44,335), and its suburbs Hawalli (145,126), as-Salimiya (153,369) and Jahra (111,222).

The Neutral Zone (3,560 sq. miles, 5,700 sq. km), jointly owned and administered by Kuwait and Saudi Arabia from 1922 to 1966, was partitioned between the two countries in May 1966, but the exploitation of the oil and other natural resources continues to be shared.

CLIMATE. Kuwait has a dry, desert climate which is cool in winter but very hot and humid in summer. Rainfall is extremely light. Kuwait. Jan. 56°F (13·5°C), July 99°F (36·6°C). Annual rainfall 5" (125 mm).

RULER. HH Shaikh Jabir al-Ahmad al-Jabir al-Sabah the 13th Amir of Kuwait, succeeded on 31 Dec. 1977.

CONSTITUTION AND GOVERNMENT. In 1976 the Amir dissolved the Assembly and at the same time parts of the Constitution were suspended. In April 1990 the National Assembly was re-established, consisting of 50 elected members and 25 appointed by the Amir. The franchise, limited to men over 21 whose families have been of Kuwaiti nationality for at least one generation, produced an electorate of 62,000. Elections were held in June 1990 and further elections are scheduled for Oct. 1992. Executive authority is vested in the Council of Ministers. A new 20-member Cabinet was formed in April 1991 including:

Prime Minister: HRH Crown Prince Shaikh Saad al-Abdullah as Salim as Sabah.

Deputy Prime Minister, Foreign Affairs: Shaikh Sabah al Ahmad al Jabir as Sabah. *Defence:* Shaikh Ali as Salim as Sabah. *Justice:* Ghazi Obeid as Sammar. *Finance:* Nasser al Rowdhan. *Oil:* Hamoud Abdulla al Raqba. *Electricity and Water:* Ahmed al Adsany.

Elections were scheduled for Oct. 1992.

National flag: Three horizontal stripes of green, white, red, with a black trapezium based on the hoist.

DEFENCE. In Sept. 1991 the USA signed a 10-year agreement with Kuwait to store equipment, use ports and carry out joint training exercises. In Feb. 1992 the UK signed an agreement with Kuwait to provide advisers and equipment. Military service is compulsory for 24 months (university students, 12 months).

Army. The army consists of 2 mechanized infantry brigades. Equipment includes 15 Chieftain and 21 M-84 main battle tanks. Strength (1992) about 7,000.

Navy. Only 2 units of the combatant flotilla, both German-built fast missile craft, survived the 1991 war. The remainder fell into Iraqi hands and were destroyed in action. Personnel probably number about 500.

Air Force. From a small initial combat force the Air Force has grown rapidly, although it suffered heavy losses after the Iraqi invasion of 1990–91. It has 1 squadron with 15 Mirage F1-C fighters and 1 Mirage F1-B 2-seat trainer; and 1 squadron with 15 A-4KU/TA-4KU Skyhawk attack aircraft. Other equipment includes 1 DC-9 jet transport, 2 L-100-30 Hercules turboprop transports and 6 Hawk jet trainers, 6 Puma, 4 Exocet missile-armed Super Puma and 20 missile-armed Gazelle helicopters. The Air Force is taking delivery of 40 F-18 Hornet combat aircraft and 16 Tucano basic trainers. Hawk surface-to-air missiles are in service. Personnel strength (1992) about 1,000, with 30 combat aircraft and 20 armed helicopters.

INTERNATIONAL RELATIONS

Membership. Kuwait is a member of the UN, Arab League, Gulf Co-operation Council, OPEC and OAPEC.

ECONOMY

Policy. The 5-year development plan ran from 1986–90.

Budget. In 1985–86 revenue, KD1,979m.; expenditure, KD3,158m.

Currency. The unit of currency is the *Kuwaiti dinar* (KWD) of 1,000 *fils*, which replaced the Indian external rupee on 1 April 1961. Coins in circulation are, 1, 5, 10, 20, 50 and 100 fils and notes of KD, 20, 10, 5, 1, $^1\!/_2$ and $^1\!/_4$. Official reserves were some US$80,000m. in 1990. In March 1992, £1 sterling = KD 0·518; US$1 = KD 0·295.

Banking and Finance. The *Governor* of the Central Bank is Shaikh Salem Abdul-Aziz al Sabah. There is also the Kuwait Finance House, which is not subject to the control of the Central Bank. Before the Iraqi invasion in Aug. 1990 there were 12 banks with 181 branches. By July 1991 only 76 had resumed operations and the Central Bank announced a series of mergers would take place.

Weights and Measures. The metric system is in force.

ENERGY AND NATURAL RESOURCES

Electricity. There are 2 2,400mw power stations. 16,360m. kwh. were produced in 1986. Supply 240 volts; 50 Hz.

Oil. The Kuwait Petroleum Corporation (KPC) was set up in 1980 to reorganize, integrate and develop the oil sector. The functions of the operating oil companies have been reallocated: Kuwait Oil Company (KOC) specializes in exploration, drilling and production in all areas; Kuwait National Petroleum Company (KNPC) is responsible for refining, local marketing and gas liquefaction operations; Kuwait Oil Tankers Company (KOTC) is in charge of transporting crude oil, liquefied gas and oil products to various world markets; Petrochemical Industries Company is in charge of use of hydrocarbon resources to set up diverse petrochemical industries, and the International Marketing Department of KPC markets and sells oil and gas worldwide.

Oil revenues in 1983–84 were KD2,787·6m. Crude oil production in 1991, 9·57m. tonnes (58·72m. in 1990; 91·89m. in 1989). Kuwait is also refining, marketing refined products, and producing abroad. 732 of the approximately 950 oil wells were fired by the Iraqi occupation forces in 1990-91. All were extinguished by Nov. 1991. By the end of 1991 production of crude oil had recovered to 0·5m. bbls a day (refined, 0·38m. bbls a day). Pre-invasion output of crude was 2·3m. bbls a day.

Gas. Production (1983) 170,200m. cu. ft.

Water. The country depends upon desalination plants. In 1986 there were 5 plants with a daily total capacity of 215m. gallons. Fresh mineral water is pumped and bottled at Rawdhatain. Underground brackish water is used for irrigation, street cleaning and livestock; production, 1985, 18,000m. gallons.

Agriculture. In 1985 the area of cultivated land was 20m. sq. metres and there were 27 dairy farms with a total production capacity of about 30,000 tonnes of fresh milk. Major crops (production, 1988, in tonnes) were melons (6,000), tomatoes (39,000), onions (25,000), dates (1,000), radishes, clover.

Livestock (1988): Cattle, 26,000; sheep, 300,000; goats, 20,000; poultry, 28m.

Fisheries. Shrimp fishing is becoming one of the important non-oil industries.

INDUSTRY. In 1985 there were 600 industrial establishments and 50,000 workers in the industrial sector. Industries, apart from oil, include boat building, fishing, food production, petrochemicals, gases and construction. The manufacture or import of alcoholic drinks is prohibited.

Labour. In 1985 the labour force totalled 670,385, with 530,996 employed.

Trade Unions. In 1986 there were 16 trade unions and 17 labour federations.

FOREIGN ECONOMIC RELATIONS

Commerce. The port of Kuwait formerly served mainly as an entrepôt for goods for the interior, for the export of skins and wool, and for pearl fishing. Entrepôt trade continues but, with the development of the oil industry, is declining in importance. Pearl fishing is now on a small scale.

Imports were valued at US$6,303m. in 1989 and exports at US$11,476m. Oil accounted for some 85% of exports.

Major domestic exports include chemical fertilizers and other chemicals, shrimps, metal pipes and building materials, which represent about 33% of total non-oil products. The other 66% come from re-exports, particularly of machinery, transport equipment, foodstuffs and some industrial goods, which go mainly to neighbouring Arab countries.

Main imports include machinery, electrical generators, appliances, cars and medicines.

Total trade between Kuwait and UK (British Department of Trade returns, in £1,000 sterling):

	1987	1988	1989	1990	1991
Imports to UK	81,530	72,318	150,354	109,970	29,386
Exports and re-exports from UK	225,168	237,515	228,711	181,480	178,248

Tourism. There were 116,000 visitors in 1985.

COMMUNICATIONS

Roads. In 1986 there were 3,800 km of roads. Number of vehicles (1989) was 615,000 (private cars 499,000; buses, 11,000; lorries, 100,000; motorcycles, 5,000).

Civil Aviation. There were 29,000 scheduled and unscheduled flights to and from Kuwait International Airport in 1985, carrying 2,257,000 passengers and 74,000 tonnes of freight. The 23 Kuwait Airways aircraft destroyed or stolen during the Iraqi invasion are being replaced with new purchases including 15 Airbuses. Iran Air resumed 4 weekly flights in Sept. 1991.

Shipping. The largest oil terminal is at Mina Ahmade, which received 348 oil tankers in 1984. Three small oil ports lie to the south of Mina Ahmade: Mina Shuaiba (250 oil tankers in 1984); Mina Abdullah (25) and Mina Al-Zor (40). The main ports for other traffic are at Shuwaikh, where 1,585 ships docked in 1985, discharging 5m. tonnes of goods; Shuiaba, about 3·75m. tonnes were handled in 1985 (3·1m. imported, 650,000 exported), and Doha. The merchant fleet totalled 7,783,000 GRT in 1990, of which 593,000 GRT were tankers.

Telecommunications. There were (1984), 419,200 telephones. Radio Kuwait and Kuwait Television broadcast from 3 stations each (colour by PAL).In 1986 there were 0·8m. TV receivers and 0·75m. radios.

Cinemas. In 1984 there were 14 cinemas, including 2 drive-ins.

Newspapers. In 1987 there were 5 daily newspapers in Arabic and 2 in English, with a combined circulation of about 418,000. Formal press censorship was lifted in Jan. 1992.

JUSTICE, RELIGION, EDUCATION AND WELFARE

Justice. In 1960 Kuwait adopted a unified judicial system covering all levels of courts. These are: Courts of Summary Justice, Courts of the First Instance, Supreme Court of Appeal, Court of Cassation, Constitutional Court and State Security Court. Islamic Sharia is a major source of legislation.

Religion. In 1980 about 78% of the population were Sunni Moslems, 14% Shia Moslems, 6% Christians and 2% others. In 1988 there were 1·43m. Moslems in all.

Education. In 1987–88 there were 33,375 pupils in kindergartens, 119,932 in primary schools, 120,961 in intermediate schools and 93,317 in secondary schools. In 1988 there were 836 students in the Religious Institute and 1,898 in special training institutes. The University of Kuwait had 15,990 students and 877 teachers in 1985–86.

Health. Medical services are free to all residents. There were (1985) 25 hospitals and sanatoria with 5,886 beds, 64 clinics and 25 health centres. In 1985 there were 2,692 doctors, 291 dentists and 8,557 nursing staff.

DIPLOMATIC REPRESENTATIVES

Of Kuwait in Great Britain (45 Queen's Gate, London, SW7)
Ambassador: Ghazi Mohammed Amin Al-Rayes (accredited 12 Feb. 1981).

Of Great Britain in Kuwait (Arabian Gulf St., Kuwait)
Ambassador: Sir Michael Weston, KCMG, CVO.

Of Kuwait in the USA (2940 Tilden St., NW, Washington, D.C., 20008)
Ambassador: Shaikh Saud Nasir Al-Sabah.

Of the USA in Kuwait (PO Box 77, Safat, Kuwait)
Ambassador: Edward Gneim.

Of Kuwait to the United Nations
Ambassador: Mohammad A. Abulhasan.

Further Reading

Annual Statistical Abstract of Kuwait. Kuwait
Kuwait Facts and Figures. Ministry of Information
Clements, F. A., *Kuwait*. [Bibliography] Oxford and Santa Barbara, 1985
Girgis, M., (ed.) *Industrial Progress in Small Oil-Exporting Countries: The Prospect for Kuwait*. Harlow, 1984
Mansfield, P., *Kuwait: Vanguard of the Gulf*. London, 1991
Sabah, Y. S. F., *The Oil Economy of Kuwait*. London, 1980

LAOS

Capital: Vientiane
Population: 4·05m. (1989)
GNP per capita: US$180 (1990)

Saathiaranarath Prachhathipatay
Prachhachhon Lao

(Lao People's Democratic Republic)

HISTORY. The Lao People's Democratic Republic was founded on 2 Dec. 1975. Until that date Laos was a Kingdom, once called Lanxang (the land of a million elephants).

In 1893 Laos became a French protectorate and in 1907 acquired its present frontiers. In 1941 French authority was suppressed by the Japanese. When the Japanese withdrew in 1945 an independence movement known as Lao Issara (Free Laos) set up a government under Prince Phetsarath, the Viceroy of Luang Prabang. This government collapsed with the return of the French in 1946 and the leaders of the movement fled to Thailand.

Under a new Constitution of 1947 Laos became a constitutional monarchy under the Luang Prabang dynasty, and in 1949 became an independent sovereign state within the French Union. Most of the Lao Issara leaders returned to Laos but a few remained in dissidence under Prince Souphanouvong, who allied himself with the Vietminh and subsequently formed the 'Pathet Lao' (Lao State) rebel movement.

The war in Laos from 1953 to 1973 between the Royal Lao Government (supported by American bombing and Thai mercenaries) and the Patriotic Front *Pathet Lao* (supported by large numbers of North Vietnamese troops) ended in 1973 when an agreement and a protocol were signed. A provisional coalition government was formed by the two sides in 1974. However, after the communist victories in neighbouring Vietnam and Cambodia in April 1975, the *Pathet Lao* took over the running of the whole country, although maintaining the façade of a coalition. On 29 Nov. 1975 HM King Savang Vatthana abdicated and a 264-member People's Congress proclaimed a People's Democratic Republic of Laos on 2 Dec. For the history of *Pathet Lao* and the military intervention of the Vietminh, *see* THE STATESMAN'S YEAR-BOOK, 1971–72, pp. 1126–28 and 1975–76, pp. 1115–16.

AREA AND POPULATION. Laos is a landlocked country of about 91,400 sq. miles (236,800 sq. km) bordered on the north by China, the east by Vietnam, the south by Cambodia and the west by Thailand and Burma. Apart from the Mekong River plains along the border of Thailand, the country is mountainous, particularly in the north, and in places densely forested.

The population (census, 1986) was 3,722,000 (1,824,000 male); estimate (1990) 4·14m (18·6% urban). Growth rate (1989), 2·9%. Population density, 17·5 per sq. km. Infant mortality was 103·5 per 1,000 live births in 1990. Expectation of life was 49·7 years. The most heavily populated areas are the Mekong River plains by the Thailand border. The majority of the population is officially divided into 3 groups: about 56% Lao-Lum (Valley-Lao), 34% Lao-Theung (Lao of the mountain sides); and 9% Lao-Soung (Lao of the mountain tops), who comprise the Meo and Yaoe. Other minorities include Vietnamese, Chinese, Europeans, Indians and Pakistanis.

There are 17 provinces. There are few towns. The capital and largest town is Vientiane, with a population of (census 1985) 377,409. Other important towns (1973) are Luang Prabang, 44,244; Pakse, 44,860, in the extreme south, and Savannakhet, 50,690.

Lao is the official language. French and English are spoken.

873

CLIMATE. A tropical monsoon climate, with high temperatures throughout the year and very heavy rains from May to Oct. Vientiane. Jan. 70°F (21·1°C), July 81°F (27·2°C). Annual rainfall 69" (1,715 mm).

CONSTITUTION AND GOVERNMENT. On 14 Aug. 1991 the National Assembly adopted a new constitution, and elected Kaysone Phomvihane (b.1920) *President* with enhanced powers.

Under the constitution the Lao People's Revolutionary Party (LPRP) remains the 'central nucleus ' of the 'people's democracy'; other parties are not permitted. The LPRP's Politburo was reconstituted in March 1991 to comprise 11 members, including Kaysone Phomvihane (*LPRP President*), Kamphoui Keobouaplapha, Thongsing Thamavong.

In Nov. 1991 the *Prime Minister* was Gen. Khamtay Siphandon.

National flag: Three horizontal stripes of red, blue, red, with blue of double width with in the centre a large white disc bearing a Buddhist shrine (stupa).
National anthem: Peng Sat Lao (Hymn of the Lao People).

Provincial Administration: All provincial administration is in the hands of the Lao People's Revolutionary Party. Orders come from the Central Committee through a series of 'People's Revolutionary Committees' at the province, town and village level.

DEFENCE. Military service is compulsory for a minimum of 18 months.

Army. The Army is organized in 5 infantry divisions; 3 engineering regiments, 7 independent infantry regiments and 65 independent infantry companies; and 5 artillery and 9 anti-aircraft battalions. Equipment includes 30 T-54/-55 main battle tanks. Strength (1992) about 50,500.

Navy. There is believed to be a riverine force of about 600 personnel organized into 4 squadrons running some 40 river patrol craft for operations on the Mekong.

Air Force. Since 1975, the Air Force has received aircraft from the USSR, including 40 MiG-21 fighters, 6 An-24 and 3 An-26 turboprop transports and 10 Mi-8 helicopters. They may be supplemented by a few of the C-47 and C-123 transports, and UH-1 Iroquois, supplied by the USA to the former régime. Personnel strength, about 2,000 in 1992, with 34 combat aircraft.

INTERNATIONAL RELATIONS
Membership. Laos is a member of the UN.

ECONOMY
Policy. The priorities of the second Five Year Plan, 1986–90, continued to be infrastructure projects (telecommunications and transport), agriculture (crop diversification and improving paddy production), and agro-industrial processing. In 1989, in an attempt to stimulate the economy, the Government introduced a 'New Economic Management Mechanism' introducing managerial autonomy into state enterprises and a limited increase of private sector activities. Further moves towards a free market were announced in Dec. 1990.

The third Five Year Plan is running from 1991 to 1995. The state is playing a smaller role, though retaining control of water supplies, energy and communications. The constitution of Aug. 1991 affirms the right to a market economy, private property and private investment, including foreign.

Budget. Total revenue 1986, K.14,127m.; total expenditure, K.24,900m. including capital expenditure of K.12,800m.

Currency. The unit of currency is the *kip* (LAK) of 100 *att*. Coinage, 1, 2 and 5 *att*; banknotes, 1, 5, 10, 20, 50, 100 and 500 *kip*. The official rate of exchange was (March 1992) K.704·39 = US$1; £1 = K1,236·55.

Banking and Finance. The head of the State Bank is Pani Vangkhamatou.

ENERGY AND NATURAL RESOURCES

Electricity. Hydro-electric resources are important. Total installed capacity (1985) was 168,000 kw. Transmission lines to Vientiane and to Thailand have been constructed, but few towns have electricity. Production (1986) 900m. kwh. Supply 127 and 220 volts; 50 Hz.

Minerals. Various minerals are found, but only tin is mined to any significant extent at present, and only at 2 mines. Production of tin concentrates (1986) 559 tonnes. There are deposits of high-quality iron in Xieng Khouang province, potash near Vientiane, gypsum and coal.

Agriculture. About 80% of the population make a living from agriculture, which accounts for 60% of GDP. In 1988 the agricultural area was 1·7m, ha, of which 0·9m. ha were arable and 0·8m. pasture. The chief products (1990 output in 1,000 tonnes) are rice (1,491), maize (67), tobacco (5), seed-cotton (15), coffee (5) and sugar-cane (96). Opium is produced but its manufacture is controlled by the state.

Livestock (1990): Cattle, 842,000; buffaloes, 1,072,000; horses, 44,000; pigs, 1,372,000; goats, 139,000; poultry, 8m.

Forestry. The forests, which cover 12·9m. ha, produce valuable woods such as teak. Logging was suspended in Sept. 1991 to conserve the forest area.

INDUSTRY. Industry accounts for 14% of GDP. Industry is limited to wood-processing, textiles and light industry. Most factories have been working at limited capacity in recent years.

Labour. The workforce was 1·95m. in 1990. Unemployment was 21%.

FOREIGN ECONOMIC RELATIONS. Since 1988 foreign companies have been permitted to participate in Lao enterprises. In 1990 foreign investments amounted to US$189m., mainly in hotels and textiles.

Commerce. In 1989 (and 1988) imports amounted to US$162 (125)m. and exports to US$54 (49)m. The main imports in 1988 (in US$1m.) were: Machinery and raw materials, 8·8; rice and other food, 5·7; petroleum products, 5·3. The chief trading partners were the USSR, Thailand and Japan. The main exports in 1988 (in US$1m.) were: Timber, 350; electricity, 11·1; gypsum, 1; tin, 0·9.

Total trade between Laos and UK (British Department of Trade returns, in £1,000 sterling):

	1987	1988	1989	1990	1991
Imports to UK	621	2	1,369	54	39
Exports and re-exports from UK	1,742	1,332	908	1,261	1,173

COMMUNICATIONS

Roads. In 1986 the national road network, consisted of 2,350 km paved, 3,250 km gravel and 6,780 km earth roads.

Railways. There is no railway in Laos, but the Thai railway system extends to Nongkhai, on the Thai bank of the Mekong, which is connected by ferry with Thadeua about 12 miles east of Vientiane.

Civil Aviation. Lao Aviation provides scheduled domestic air services linking major towns in Laos and international services to Bangkok, Phnom Penh and Hanoi. Thai International, Aeroflot and Air Vietnam provide flights from Bangkok, Hanoi, Rangoon, Ho Chi Min City and Moscow.

Shipping. The river Mekong and its tributaries are an important means of transport, but rapids, waterfalls and narrow channels often impede navigation and make trans-shipments necessary.

Telecommunications. The government-controlled National Radio of Laos broadcasts from 19 radio transmitters and Lao National TV from 2 transmitters (colour by PAL). There are regional radio services, an external service and a European service (in French). There were (1991) about 425,000 radio and 32,000 television receivers.

In 1985 there were 8,136 telephones.

RELIGION, EDUCATION AND WELFARE

Justice. Criminal legislation of 1990 established a system of courts and a prosecutor's office. Polygamy became an offence.

Religion. In 1989 some 2·28m. were Buddhists (Hinayana), but about a third of the population follow tribal religions.

Education. In 1985–86 school year there were 8,000 elementary schools (523,000 pupils); 420 secondary schools (97,000 pupils); 60 senior high schools (4,900 pupils); and 55 vocational schools (6,800 students). There is 1 teachers' training college, 1 college of education, 1 school of medicine, 1 agricultural college and an advanced school of Pali.

Sisavangvong University in Vientiane (founded 1958) had 1,600 students in 1984, and there are regional technical colleges in Luang Prabang, Savannakhét and Champasak.

65% literacy was claimed in 1990.

Health. In 1985 there were 430 doctors and 11,650 hospital beds.

DIPLOMATIC REPRESENTATIVES

Of Laos in Great Britain (resides in Paris)
Ambassador: vacant.

Of Great Britain in Laos
Ambassador: Ramsay Melhuish, CMG (resides in Bangkok).

Of Laos in USA (2222 S. St., NW, Washington, D.C., 20008)
Chargé d'Affaires: Linthong Phetsavan.

Of USA in Laos (Rue Bartholonie, Vientiane)
Chargé d'Affaires: Charles B. Salmon, Jr.

Of Laos to the United Nations
Ambassador: Saly Khamsy.

Further Reading

Cordell, H., *Laos.* [Bibliography] Oxford and Santa Barbara, 1990
Stuart-Cox, M., *Laos: Politics, Economics and Society.* London, 1986
Zasloff, J. J., and Unger, L. (eds.) *Laos: Beyond the Revolution.* London, 1991

LATVIA

Capital: Riga
Population: 2·69m. (1990)

Latvijas Republika

HISTORY. Latvian tribes were under the hegemony of the German Order of Livonian Knights until 1561, when Latvia fell into Polish and Swedish hands. Between 1721 and 1795 Latvia was absorbed into the Russian empire. In the part of Latvia unoccupied by the Germans during the first World War, the Bolsheviks won 72% of the votes in the Constituent Assembly elections (Nov. 1917). Soviet power was proclaimed in Dec. 1917, but was overthrown when the Germans occupied all Latvia (Feb. 1918). Restored when they withdrew (Dec. 1918), it was overthrown once more by combined British naval and German military forces (May–Dec. 1919), and a democratic government set up. This régime was in turn replaced when a coup took place in May 1934.

The secret protocol of the Soviet–German agreement of 23 Aug. 1939 assigned Latvia to the Soviet sphere of interest. An ultimatum (16 June 1940) led to the formation of a government acceptable to the USSR. On 21 July a People's Diet proclaimed the establishment of the Latvian Soviet Socialist Republic and applied to join the USSR, whose Supreme Soviet accepted the application on 5 Aug. The incorporation was accorded *de facto* recognition by the UK, but not by the USA, which continued to recognize the Chargé d'Affaires in Washington, D.C.

On 4 May 1990 the Latvian Supreme Soviet declared, by 138 votes to nil with 58 abstentions, that the Soviet occupation of Latvia on 17 June 1940 was illegal, and resolved to re-establish the authority of the Constitution of 1922. A transition period was set for the restoration of independence. In a referendum in March 1991 the principle of independence was supported by 73·6% of votes cast. A fully independent status was conceded by the USSR State Council in Sept. 1991 and Latvia was subsequently admitted into the UN and other international bodies.

AREA AND POPULATION. Latvia is bounded in the north by Estonia and the Baltic Sea, west by the Baltic, south by Lithuania and Belorussia and east by Russia. Latvia has a total area of 63,700 sq. km (24,595 sq. miles). Population, Jan. 1990, 2,687,000. The 1989 census population was 2,666,567, of whom Latvians accounted for 52%, Russians 34%, Belorussians, 4·5%, Ukrainians 3·5%, Poles 2·3%, Lithuanians 1·3% and Jews 0·9%. There are 26 districts, 56 towns and 37 urban settlements.

The capital is Riga (915,000 in 1990); other principal towns are Daugavpils (Dvinsk), Liepāja, Jurmala, Jelgava (Mitau) and Ventspils (Windau).

CONSTITUTION AND GOVERNMENT. On 18 March 1990 elections were held to the 201-member Supreme Soviet. The Popular Front won a majority. A Congress of Latvia, elected by ethnic Latvians, has been set up alongside the Supreme Soviet. The declaration of independence of 21 Aug. 1991 states that Latvia is an independent democratic republic whose status is defined by the constitution of 1922.

Chairman, Presidium of the Supreme Soviet (i.e. President of the Republic): A. V. Gorbunovs (b. 1942); *Vice-President:* Dainis Ivans (b. 1955).

Prime Minister: Ivars Godmanis (b. 1951). *Foreign Minister:* Janis Jurkans.

National flag: Dark red, with a narrow horizontal white stripe across the centre.

Local government. In Dec. 1989 elections were held to district, urban and rural Soviets.

DEFENCE. Russian (ex-Soviet) troops began withdrawing in March 1992.

INTERNATIONAL RELATIONS

Membership. Latvia is a member of the UN.

ECONOMY

Finance. Budget estimates (in 1m. rubles), 1988, 2,733; 1989 (plan), 3,133.

Banking and Finance. There is a stock exchange in Riga.

ENERGY AND NATURAL RESOURCES

Electricity. Output in 1989 was 5,800m. kwh.

Minerals. Peat deposits extend over 645,000 ha or about 10% of the total area, and it is estimated that total deposits are 3,000–4,000m. tons; output of briquettes in 1988, 55,200 tonnes. There are also gypsum deposits; amber is frequently found in the coastal districts.

Agriculture. Latvia is now no longer mainly an agricultural country. The urban population, 35% of the total in 1939, was 71% in Jan. 1990.

Area under cultivation was 3·9m. ha in 1990. 1·8m. ha of marsh land had been drained (1983). Cattle and dairy farming are the chief agricultural occupations. Oats, barley, rye, potatoes and flax are the main crops.

On 1 Jan. 1989 there were 248 state farms and 331 (including 11 fishery) collective farms. There were 38,100 tractors and 7,400 grain combine harvesters. Large state and collective farms are being converted into shareholding enterprises; the remainder are being divided into small private holdings for collective farm workers or former owners. There were 12,500 such farms in 1991.

Livestock (Jan. 1990): Cattle, 1·5m; sheep and goats, 167,000; pigs, 1·6m.

Output of main agricultural products (in 1,000 tonnes) in 1989: Grain, 1,600; sugar-beet, 395; potatoes, 1,316; vegetables, 219; meat, 331; milk, 1,977; eggs, 890m.

Forestry. In 1983 forest covered 3·9m. ha. Timber output was 4·2m. cu. metres.

INDUSTRY. Latvia is a major producer of electric railway passenger cars and long-distance telephone exchanges, paper and woollen goods, sawn timber, and mineral fertilizers.

Industrial output in 1989 (in 1,000 tonnes) included: Steel, 555; rolled ferrous metals, 800; timber, 2·4m. cu. metres; paper, 138; cement, 776; fabrics, 125m. sq. metres; hosiery, 78·8m. pairs; knitwear, 43m. items; footwear, 10·2m. pairs; butter, 47; granulated sugar, 248; preserves, 504m. standard jars.

Labour. In 1989 employees in the state sector numbered 1,171,000.

Trade Unions. The Latvian Free Trade Union has Andris Siliņš as chairman.

FOREIGN ECONOMIC RELATIONS. On 20 April 1990 Latvia, Estonia and Lithuania concluded a Baltic Economic Co-operation Agreement.

COMMUNICATIONS

Roads. In 1990 there were 58,600 km of roads (32,500 km hard-surfaced).

Railways. In 1990 the length of railways was 2,400 km.

Shipping. Riga is the second-largest port on the Baltic. In 1989, 302m. tonne-km of freight were carried on inland waterways.

Newspapers (1989). There were 129 newspapers (78 in Latvian). Daily circulation of Latvian-language newspapers, 2m., other languages 764,000.

JUSTICE, RELIGION, EDUCATION AND WELFARE

Religion. Church-state affairs are the concern of the Department of Religious Affairs attached to the Council of Ministers. Traditionally, Lutherans constituted the largest church, but their numbers have declined from some 0·6m. in 1956 to 0·1m. in 1991. Estimates of Roman Catholics in 1991 varied from 0·3m. to 0·5m. Congregations in March 1991: Lutherans, 256; Roman Catholics, 186; Russian Orthodox, 90; Old Believers, 65; Baptists, 61; and in Oct. 1990: Adventists, 28; Pentecostalists, 6; Jews, 4.

Education. In 1989–90 there were 900 primary and secondary schools, with a total of 400,000 pupils: 59% of eligible children attended pre-school institutions. 10 places of higher education had 45,600 students, 57 technical colleges had 38,100 students; there were also 21 music and art schools, 3 teachers' training colleges and an agricultural academy. In 1946 an Academy of Sciences was opened which in Jan. 1989 had 15 research institutes with a staff of 1,812 scientific workers; there were over 14,000 scientific workers in 101 research institutions.

Health. There were 13,400 doctors and 39,300 hospital beds in 1989.

DIPLOMATIC REPRESENTATIVES
Diplomatic relations between Latvia and Great Britain were restored on 8 Oct. 1991.

Of Great Britain in Latvia
Ambassador: Richard Samuel, CMG, CVO.

Of Latvia in Great Britain (72 Queensborough Terrace, London, W2 3SP)
Chargée d'affaires: Marie-Anne Zarine.

Of Latvia in the USA and to the United Nations (115 West 183rd St., NY 10453)
Ambassador: Dr Anatol Dinbergs.

Further Reading
Latvian Academy of Sciences, *Istoriya Latviiskoi SSR*. Riga. 3 vols. 1952–58
Bilmanis, A., *A History of Latvia*. Princeton Univ. Press, 1951
Spekke, A., *History of Latvia*. Stockholm, 1951

LEBANON

Capital: Beirut
Population: 3m. (1989)

Jumhouriya
al-Lubnaniya

(Republic of Lebanon)

HISTORY. After 20 years as a mandate of France, Lebanon was proclaimed independent on 26 Nov. 1941. The evacuation of foreign troops was completed in Dec. 1946.

For events between the insurrection of 1958 and the intervention of the Arab Deterrent Force *see* THE STATESMAN'S YEAR-BOOK, 1990-91, p.799.

By Nov. 1976 the Syrian-dominated Arab Deterrent Force had ensured sufficient security to permit Lebanon to establish quasi-normal conditions under President Sarkis. Large areas of the country, however, remained outside government control, including West Beirut which was the scene of frequent conflict between opposing militia groups. The South, where the Arab Deterrent Force could not deploy, remained unsettled and subject to frequent Israeli attacks. In March 1978 there was an Israeli invasion following a Palestinian attack inside Israel. Israeli troops eventually withdrew in June, but instead of handing over all their positions to UN Peacekeeping Forces they installed Israeli-controlled Lebanese militia forces in border areas. Severe disruption continued in the South. In June 1982, following on the attempted assassination of the Israeli ambassador in London, Israeli forces once again swept through the country, eventually laying siege to and bombing Beirut. In Sept. Palestinian forces evacuated Beirut.

On 23 Aug. 1982 Bachir Gemayel was elected President of Lebanon. On 14 Sept. he was assassinated. His brother, Amin Gemayel, was elected in his place on 21 Sept. There followed a state of 'no peace, no war' with intermittent clashes between the various forces. Israeli forces began a phased withdrawal in 1985 and have now relinquished control of all but their so-called security zone in the South of the country. The heads of the 3 leading militia forces signed an agreement on political reform and relations with Syria in 1985 but this was never implemented; Syrian forces remain deployed in most areas of Lebanon.

The term of office of President Amin Gemayel expired in September 1988 and efforts to elect a successor failed. Gemayel appointed the Commander of the Army, Gen. Michel Aoun, Prime Minister until such time as a President could be elected. His appointment was disputed by the Moslems and the Syrians, and the existing Prime Minister, Selim Hoss, remained in office heading a rival administration in West Beirut. In 1989 Gen. Aoun launched his 'war of liberation' against the Syrians. The resulting damage and death toll prompted the Arab League to take action and in Oct. 1989 Lebanese parliamentarians gathered in Taif in Saudi Arabia to sign an agreement on political reform and relations with Syria formulated by a tripartite committee of the Arab League. In Nov. 1989 Rene Moawwad was elected President, but he was assassinated later that month and Elias Hrawi elected in his place. Gen. Aoun refused to accept the Taif accords or recognise the legitimacy of the Hrawi presidency. Aoun was dismissed as head of the Lebanese Armed Forces and replaced by Gen. Emile Lahoud. In Feb. 1990 full-scale hostilities broke out between elements of the Lebanese army loyal to Aoun and the principal Christian militia, the Lebanese Forces. As a result Lebanon's remaining commercial and industrial infrastructure was severely damaged. In Sept. 1990 constitutional changes establishing the Second Republic were made, enabling the implementation of the political reform provisions of the Taif accords. In Oct. 1990 Syrian forces in support of the Lebanese government ousted Gen. Aoun, who took refuge first in the French embassy and eventually in exile in France. In Nov. and Dec. the various militias which had held sway in Beirut withdrew. A new Government of National Reconciliation was announced on 24 Dec. 1990. In Feb. 1991 the army began to move south. The dissolution of all militias was decreed by the National Assembly in April 1991. In July the army defeated the Palestine Liberation Organization at Sidon, depriving the latter of their territorial base in South Lebanon, and bringing the army up to the Israeli occupied southern strip.

AREA AND POPULATION. Lebanon is a mountainous country about 135 miles long and varying between 20 and 35 miles wide, bounded on the north and east by Syria, on the west by the Mediterranean and on the south by Israel. Between the two parallel mountain ranges of Lebanon and Anti-Lebanon lies the fertile Bekaa Valley. About one-half of the country lies at an altitude of over 3,000 ft.

The area of Lebanon is estimated at 10,452 sq. km (4,036 sq. miles) and the population at 2,897,000. (1989) 83·7% was urban. The principal towns, with estimated population (1988), are: Beirut (the capital), 1·5m.; Tripoli, 160,000; Zahlé, 45,000; Saida (Sidon), 38,000; Tyre, 14,000. Population density, 279 per sq. km. Infant mortality was 44 per 1,000 live births in 1990; expectation of life, 66·1 years.

The official language is Arabic. French and, increasingly, English are widely spoken in official and commercial circles.

CLIMATE. A Mediterranean climate with short, warm winters and long, hot and rainless summers, with high humidity in coastal areas. Rainfall is largely confined to the winter months and can be torrential, with snow on high ground. Beirut. Jan. 55°F (13°C), July 81°F (27°C). Annual rainfall 35·7" (893 mm).

CONSTITUTION AND GOVERNMENT. Lebanon is an independent republic. The first Constitution was established under the French Mandate on 23 May 1926. It has since been amended in 1927, 1929, 1943 (twice), 1947 and 1990. It is a written constitution based on the classical separation of powers, with a President, a single-chamber *National Assembly* elected by universal adult suffrage, and an independent judiciary. The executive consists of the President and a Prime Minister and Cabinet appointed after consulation between the President and the Chamber of Deputies. The system is, however, adapted to the peculiar communal balance on which Lebanese political life depends. This is done by the electoral law which allocates deputies according to the confessional distribution of the population, and by a series of constitutional conventions whereby, *e.g.*, the President is always a Maronite Christian, the Prime Minister a Sunni Moslem and the Speaker of the Assembly a Shia Moslem. There is no highly developed party system other than on religious confessional lines. In Aug. 1990 the National Assembly voted to enlarge itself from 99 to 108 members with equal numbers of Christians and Moslems.

On 21 Sept. President Hrawi formally established the Second Republic by signing constitutional amendments which had been negotiated at Taif (Saudi Arabia) in Oct. 1989. These institute an executive collegium between the President, Prime Minister and Speaker, and remove from the President the right to recall the Prime Minister, dissolve the Assembly and vote in the Council of Ministers.

President: Elias Hrawi (Maronite; elected 24 Nov. 1989).

In Nov. 1991 the cabinet consisted of: *Prime Minister,* Omar Karame. *Foreign Affairs,* Farez Bouez. *Defence,* Michel Al Murr. *Interior,* Brig. Sami Al Khatib. *Other ministers:* Walid Joumblatt, Soleiman Frangie, Elie Hobeika, Marwan Hamadi, Mohamed Jaroudi, Talal Arslan, Abdalla Amin, Mohsen Dalloul.

National flag: Three horizontal stripes of red, white, red, with the white of double width and bearing in the centre a green cedar of Lebanon.

National anthem: Kulluna lil watan lil 'ula lil 'alam ('All of us for our country, flag and glory'; words by Rashid Nachleh, tune by Flaïfel brothers).

Local government: The 6 governorates (including the city of Beirut) are subdivided into 26 districts.

DEFENCE

Army. The strength of the Army was about 17,500 in 1992 but it is in a state of flux and most of its units are well below strength. Its equipment includes 175 M-48A and 70 T-54 tanks T-55 main battle. An internal security force, run by the Ministry of the Interior, some 9,000 strong is being reorganized.

Navy. Following the partial normalization of the Lebanese situation, the flotilla is believed to consist of 1 inshore patrol craft, 2 tank landing craft and some boats, manned and supported by some 500 personnel.

Air Force. The Air Force had (1992) about 800 men and 50 aircraft. In addition to 5 Hunter jet fighter-bombers, it has (in storage) 9 Mirage III supersonic fighters and 1 Mirage 2-seat trainer. Other aircraft include 12 Alouette II and III, 4 Gazelle, 9 Puma and 8 Agusta-Bell 212 helicopters, and 5 Fouga Magister jet and 5 piston-engined Bulldog trainers. Serviceability of most aircraft is low following the years of civil war.

INTERNATIONAL RELATIONS. A Treaty of Brotherhood, Co-operation and Co-ordination with Syria of May 1991 provides for close relations in the fields of foreign policy, the economy, military affairs and security. The treaty stipulates that Lebanese government decisions are subject to review by 6 joint Syrian-Lebanese bodies.

Membership. Lebanon is a member of the UN and Arab League.

ECONOMY

Budget. The budget for 1986 provided for a total expenditure of £Leb.17,937m.

Currency. The unit of currency is the *Lebanese pound* (LBP) of 100 *piastres*. There is a fluctuating official rate of exchange, fixed monthly (March 1992: £Leb.1,930·20 = £1 sterling; £Leb.1,099·52 = US$1); it in practice is used only for the calculation of *ad-valorem* customs duties on Lebanese imports and for import statistics. For other purposes the free market is used.

Banking and Finance. The Bank of Lebanon (*Governor*, Edmond Naim) is the bank of issue. It commenced operating in 1964. As a result of the civil war, Beirut has lost much of its former status as an international and regional banking centre; in general only local offices for banks remain.

Weights and Measures. The use of the metric system is legal. In outlying districts the former weights and measures may still be in use. They are: 1 *okiya* = 0·47 lb.; 6 *okiyas* = 1 *oke* = 2·82 lb.; 2 *okes* = 1 *rottol* = 5·64 lb.; 200 *okes* = 1 *kantar*.

ENERGY AND NATURAL RESOURCES

Electricity. Electric power production (1986) was 2,270m. kwh. Supply 110 and 120 volts; 50 Hz.

Oil. There are 2 oil refineries: at Tripoli, which refines oil brought by ship from Iraq, and at Sidon, which refines oil brought from Saudi Arabia by a pipeline owned by the Trans-Arabian Pipeline Co. These refineries have not been fully active since the late 1970s, and the country depends on imports.

Minerals. Iron ore exists but is difficult to work. Other minerals known to exist are iron pyrites, copper, bituminous shales, asphalt, phosphates, ceramic clays and glass sand; but the available information is of doubtful value.

Agriculture. Lebanon is essentially an agricultural country, although owing to its physical character only about 38% of the total area of the country is at present cultivated.

The estimated production (in 1,000 tonnes) of the main crops in 1990 was as follows: Citrus fruits, 451; apples, 199; grapes, 218; potatoes, 237; sugar-beet, 3·8; wheat, 52; bananas, 37; olives, 62.

Livestock (estimated, 1990): Goats, 410,000; sheep, 210,000; cattle, 60,000; pigs, 49,000; donkeys, 12,000; mules, 5,000.

Forestry. The forests of the past have been denuded by exploitation and in 1988 covered 100,000 ha.

Fisheries. Total catch (1986) 1,600 tonnes.

INDUSTRY. Industry has suffered badly during the civil war. The manufacturing industry was small but had doubled in size in the 10 years before the war. Some concerns have closed, others are working at reduced capacity.

Labour. The workforce was some 823,000 in 1990, of whom 72,000 worked in agriculture.

FOREIGN ECONOMIC RELATIONS. Foreign and domestic trade is the principal source of income. In 1990 imports were valued at US$2,390m.; exports, US$492m.

Commerce. Total trade between Lebanon and UK (British Department of Trade returns, in £1,000 sterling):

	1987	1988	1989	1990	1991
Imports to UK	9,528	14,172	11,054	6,249	8,465
Exports and re-exports from UK	40,707	55,575	48,474	53,266	87,760

COMMUNICATIONS

Roads. There were (1987) 7,000 km of roads of which main roads (2,000 km) are not good by international standards. The surface is normally of asphalt and they are well maintained in normal times.

In 1985 there were about 300,000 cars and taxis.

Railways. There are 3 railway lines, all operated by the *Office des Chemins de Fer de l'Etat Libanais* (CFL): (1) Nakoura–Beirut–Tripoli (standard gauge); (2) a narrow-gauge line running from Beirut to Riyak in the Bekaa Valley and thence to Damascus, Syria; (3) a standard-gauge line from Tripoli to Homs and Aleppo in Syria, providing access to Ankara and Istanbul. From Homs a branch of the CFL line extends south and re-enters Lebanon, terminating at Riyak. The total length is 417 km. Apart from a short section near Beirut these lines have been closed since the civil war began.

Civil Aviation. Beirut International Airport is used by a few international airlines. There are 2 national airlines, Middle East Airlines and Trans-Mediterranean Airways.

Shipping. Beirut is the largest port, followed by Tripoli, Jounieh and Sidon.

Telecommunications. There is an automatic telephone system in Beirut which is being extended to other parts of the country. There are no communications with Israel. Number of telephones (1986), 150,000.

The government-controlled Radio Lebanon transmits in Arabic, French, English and Armenian. Tele-Liban, which is government-owned, transmits 3 programmes from 6 stations. Colour is by SECAM. There were 838,037 TV sets in 1990 and 2·15m. radios.

Newspapers (1989). There were about 30 daily newspapers in Arabic, 2 in French, 1 in English and 4 in Armenian, and 30 weekly periodicals.

RELIGION, EDUCATION AND WELFARE

Religion. The Christian faith has been indigenous since the earliest times. The Christians include the Maronites, Greek Orthodox, Armenians, Greek and Roman Catholics, Armenian Catholics and the Protestants. Moslems include the Sunnis, the Shi'ites and the Druzes. In 1990 it was estimated that the population was 62% Moslem (including 31% Shi'ite and 27% Sunni) and 38% Christian (including 22% Maronite).

Education. Government schools comprise primary and secondary schools. There were also private primary and secondary schools. There are also 5 universities, namely the Lebanese (State) University, the American University of Beirut, the French University of St Joseph (founded in 1875), the Arab University, a branch of Alexandria University and Beirut University College. The French Government runs the École Supérieure de Lettres and the Centre d'Études Mathématiques. The Maronite monks run the University of the Holy Spirit at Kaslik.

The Lebanese Academy of Fine Arts includes schools of architecture, art, music, political and social science.

Health. There are several government-run hospitals, and many private ones.

DIPLOMATIC REPRESENTATIVES

Of Lebanon in Great Britain (21 Kensington Palace Gdns., London, W8 4QM)
Ambassador: Mahmoud Hammoud.

Of Great Britain in Lebanon (Shamma Bldg., Raouché, Ras Beirut)
Ambassador: D. E. Tatham, CMG.

Of Lebanon in the USA (2560 28th St., NW, Washington, D.C., 20008)
Ambassador: Nassib Lahoud.

Of the USA in Lebanon
Ambassador: Ryan Crocker.

Of Lebanon to the United Nations
Acting Ambassador: Khalil Makkawi.

Further Reading

Bleaney, C. H., *Lebanon.* [Bibliography]. 2nd ed. Oxford and Santa Barbara, 1991
Cobban, H., *The Making of Modern Lebanon.* London, 1985
Fisk, R., *Pity the Nation: Lebanon at War.* London, 1990
Gilmour, D., *Lebanon: The Fractured Country.* Oxford and New York, 1983
Gordon, D. C., *The Republic of Lebanon: Nation in Jeopardy.* London, 1983
Norton, A. R., *Amal and the Shi'a: Struggle for the Soul of Lebanon.* Univ. of Texas Press, 1987
Rabanovich, I., *The War for Lebanon, 1970–1983.* Cornell Univ. Press, 1984
Shehadi, N. and Mills, D.H., *Lebanon: A History of Conflict and Consensus.* London, 1988
Weinberger, N. J., *Syrian Intervention in Lebanon.* New York, 1986

National library: Dar el Kutub, Parliament Sq., Beirut.
National statistical office: Service de Statistique Générale, Beirut.

LESOTHO

Kingdom of Lesotho

Capital: Maseru
Population: 1·72m. (1989)
GNP per capita: US$470 (1989)

HISTORY. Basutoland first received the protection of Britain in 1868 at the request of Moshoeshoe I, the first paramount chief. In 1871 the territory was annexed to the Cape Colony, but in 1884 it was restored to the direct control of the British Government through the High Commissioner for South Africa.

On 4 Oct. 1966 Basutoland became an independent and sovereign member of the Commonwealth under the name of the Kingdom of Lesotho.

King Moeshoeshoe II was deposed by the Military Council in Nov. 1990 and replaced by King Letsie III. Maj.-Gen. Lekhanya was deposed from the chairmanship of the Military Council in a bloodless coup on 30 April 1991.

AREA AND POPULATION. Lesotho, an enclave within the Republic of South Africa is bounded on the west by the Orange Free State, on the north by the Orange Free State and Natal, on the east by Natal, and on the south by Transkei. The altitude varies from 1,500 to 3,482 metres. The area is 11,720 sq. miles (30,355 sq. km). Lesotho is a purely African territory, and the few European residents are government officials, traders, missionaries and artisans.

The census in 1986 showed a total population of 1,577,536 persons. Estimate (1989) 1,724,000. The capital is Maseru (population, 1986, 109,382).

The official languages are Sesotho and English.

CLIMATE. A healthy and pleasant climate, with variable rainfall, but averaging 29" (725 mm) a year over most of the country. The rain falls mainly in the summer months of Oct. to April, while the winters are dry and may produce heavy frosts in lowland areas and frequent snow in the highlands. Temperatures in the lowlands range from a maximum of 90°F (32·2°C) in summer to a minimum of 20°F (–6·7°C) in winter.

CONSTITUTION AND GOVERNMENT. Lesotho is a constitutional monarchy with HM the King as Head of State, but the constitution adopted at independence was suspended and the elections of 27 Jan. 1970 were declared invalid on 31 Jan. 1970. Parliamentary rule, with a National Assembly of nominated members, was reintroduced in April 1973, but the National Assembly was dissolved on 1 Jan. 1985 by the first Prime Minister, Chief Joseph Leabua Jonathan.

Chief Jonathan was deposed in a bloodless military coup on 20 Jan. 1986. HM the King, acts through a *Council of Ministers* on the advice of a *Military Council.*

Ruler: Mohato Seeisa, King Letsie III, (b.1963), eldest son of Moeshoeshoe II, was proclaimed King by an assembly of traditional chiefs on 9 Nov. 1990.

Chairman of the Military Council and Council of Ministers: Col. Elias Pishona Ramaema. *Members:* Brig. Benedict Lerotholi; Col. Jacob Jane; Lieut.-Col. Ernest Mokete; Lieut.-Col. Tseliso Lehohla; Lieut.-Col. Maobi Mothibeli.

In Dec. 1991 the Council of Ministers comprised: *Minister of Finance, Planning and Economic Development:* Abel Thoahlane. *Foreign Affairs, Information and Broadcasting:* Pius Malapo. *Justice, Prisons, Law and Constitutional Affairs:* A. K. Maope. *Water, Energy and Mining:* Col. A. I. Jane. *Employment, Social Security and Pensions:* Col. Leonard Mothakathi. *Highlands Water and Energy:* Maj. R. Habi. *Works, Transport and Telecommunications:* Col. V. M. Mokone. *Interior, Chieftainship Affairs and Rural Development:* Chief Mphosi Matete. *Health:* William Khuele. *Tourism, Sports and Culture:* Chief Lechesa Mathealira. *Trade and Industry:* Chief Moletsane Mokroane. *Minister in the Office of the Military Council:* Patrick Molapo.

The *College of Chiefs* settles the recognition and succession of Chiefs and adjudicates cases of inefficiency, criminality and absenteeism among them.

National flag: Diagonally white over blue over green with the white of double width charged with a brown Basotho shield in the upper hoist.

National anthem: 'Lesotho fatsela bontat'a rona' ('Lesotho, land of our fathers'; words by F. Coillard, tune by L. Laur).

Local Government. The country is divided into 10 districts, subdivided into 22 wards, as follows: Maseru, Qacha's Nek, Mokhotlong, Leribe, Butha–Buthe, Teyateyaneng, Mafeteng, Mohale's Hoek, Quthing, Thaba–Tseka. Most of the wards are presided over by hereditary chiefs allied to the Moshoeshoe family.

DEFENCE

The Royal Lesotho Defence Force has 2,000 personnel. Formed in 1978, to facilitate deployment of men and equipment to less accessible regions, the service has 2 Aviocar transports, and 3 Bell 412 and 2 BO-105 helicopters.

INTERNATIONAL RELATIONS

Membership. Lesotho is a member of the UN, OAU, the Commonwealth and is an ACP state of the EEC.

ECONOMY

Budget. Expenditure (1986–87) M463m.; revenue, M385m.

Currency. The unit of currency is the *loti* (plural *maloti*) (LSM) of 100 *lisente* which is at par with the South African *rand*. In March 1992, £1 = 5 *maloti*; US$1 = 2·85 *maloti*.

Banking and Finance. The Standard Bank of South Africa and Barclays Bank International have branches at Maseru, Mohale's Hoek and Leribe. The Lesotho Bank has branches throughout the country.

ENERGY AND NATURAL RESOURCES

Electricity. Production (1985) 1m. kwh. Supply 230 volts; 50 Hz.

Agriculture. The chief crops were (1990 production in 1,000 tonnes): Wheat, 20; maize, 111; sorghum, 28; barley, oats, beans, peas and other vegetables are also grown. Soil conservation and the improvement of crops and pasture are matters of vital importance.

Livestock (1990): Cattle, 530,000; horses, 122,000; donkeys, 130,000; pigs, 74,000; sheep, 1·48m.; goats, 1·07m.; poultry, 1m.

INDUSTRY. Industrial development is progressing under the National Development Corporation.

FOREIGN ECONOMIC RELATIONS. Lesotho, Botswana and Swaziland are members of the South African customs union, by agreement dated 29 June 1910.

Commerce. Total values of imports and exports into and from Lesotho (in Mm.):

	1983	1984	1985	1986
Imports	627	725	797	893
Exports	35	42	50	58

Principal imports are food, livestock, drink and tobacco, machinery and transport equipment, mineral fuels and lubricants; principal exports were wool and mohair and diamonds.

The majority of international trade is with South Africa.

Total trade between Lesotho and UK (British Department of Trade returns, in £1,000 sterling):

	1987	1988	1989	1990	1991
Imports to UK	486	977	734	1,288	2,799
Exports and re-exports from UK	1,112	1,260	795	642	3,258

Tourism. In 1986 there were 213,000 visitors.

COMMUNICATIONS

Roads. There were (1988) 572 km of tarred roads and 2,300 km of gravel-surfaced roads. In addition to the main roads there were (1983) 931 km of food aid tracks leading to trading stations and missions. Communications into the mountainous interior are by means of bridlepaths suitable only for riding and pack animals, but a mountain road of 80 miles has been constructed, and some parts are accessible by air transport, which is being used increasingly. In 1983 there were 10,200 commercial vehicles and 4,359 passenger cars.

Railways. A railway built by the South African Railways, 1 mile long, connects Maseru with the Bloemfontein–Natal line at Marseilles.

Civil Aviation. There is a scheduled passenger service between Maseru and Jan Smuts Airport, Johannesburg, operated jointly by Lesotho National Airways and South African Airways. There are also 30 airstrips for light aircraft.

Telecommunications. There were 5,409 telephones in 1983. Radio Lesotho transmits daily in English and Sesotho. Radio receivers (1987), 400,000.

Newspapers. In 1985, 3 daily newspapers had a combined circulation of 44,000.

JUSTICE, RELIGION, EDUCATION AND WELFARE

Justice. The Lesotho High Court and the Court of Appeal are situated in Maseru, and there are Magistrates' Courts in the districts.

Religion. About 93% of the population are Christians, 44% being Roman Catholics.

Education. Education is largely in the hands of the 3 main missions (Paris Evangelical, Roman Catholic and English Church), under the direction of the Ministry of Education. In 1984–85 the total enrolment in 1,141 primary schools was 314,003; in 143 secondary schools, 35,423; in the National Teacher-Training College and 8 technical schools enrolment 2,221. University education is provided at the National University of Lesotho established in 1975 at Roma; enrolment in 1985, 1,119 and 146 teaching staff.

Health. The government medical staff of the territory consists of 1 Permanent Secretary for Health, 1 Director of Health Services, 1 medical superintendent, 8 district medical officers and a total of 102 doctors including 20 specialists.

There are 11 government hospitals staffed by 308 matrons, sisters and nurses. There is accommodation for 2,175 patients in government hospitals.

DIPLOMATIC REPRESENTATIVES

Of Lesotho in Great Britain (10 Collingham Rd., London, SW5 0NR)
High Commissioner: M. K. Tsekoa (accredited 15 Nov. 1989).

Of Great Britain in Lesotho (PO Box MS 521, Maseru 100)
High Commissioner: J. C. Edwards, CMG.

Of Lesotho in the USA (2511 Massachusetts Ave., NW, Washington, D.C., 20008)
Ambassador: W. T. Van Tonder.

Of the USA in Lesotho (PO Box 333, Maseru, 100)
Ambassador: Leonard H. Spearman.

Of Lesotho to the United Nations
Ambassador: Monyane P. Phoofolo.

Further Reading

Statistical Information: Bureau of Statistics, PO Box 455, Maseru, Lesotho.
Ashton, H., *The Basuto.* 2nd ed. OUP, 1967
Bardill, J. E. and Cobbe, J. H., *Lesotho: Dilemmas of Dependence in South Africa.* London, 1986
Murray, C., *Families Divided: The Impact of Migrant Labour in Lesotho.* OUP, 1981
Willet, S. M. and Ambrose, D. P., *Lesotho.* [Bibliography] Oxford and Santa Barbara, 1981

LIBERIA

Republic of Liberia

Capital: Monrovia
Population: 2·44m. (1988)
GNP per capita: US$440 (1987)

HISTORY. The Republic of Liberia had its origin in the efforts of several American philanthropic societies to establish freed American slaves in a colony on the West African coast. In 1822 a settlement was formed near the spot where Monrovia now stands. On 26 July 1847 the State was constituted as the Free and Independent Republic of Liberia.

On 12 April 1980, President Tolbert was assassinated and his government overthrown in a coup led by Master-Sergeant Samuel Doe, who was later installed as Head of State and Commander-in-Chief of the army.

At the beginning of 1990 rebel forces entered Liberia from the north and fought their way successfully southwards to confront President Doe's forces in Monrovia. The rebels comprised the National Patriotic Front of Liberia led by Charles Taylor, and the hostile breakaway Independent National Patriotic Front led by Prince Johnson. A peacekeeping force dispatched by the Economic Community of West African States (ECOWAS) disembarked at Monrovia on 25 Aug. 1990, and attempts to form a new provisional government were made.

On 9 Sept. President Doe was assassinated by Prince Johnson's rebels. At an ECOWAS summit at Bamako (Mali) on 28 Nov. government forces and the two rebel factions signed a ceasefire. ECOWAS installed a provisional government led by Amos Sawyer. Charles Taylor also declared himself president, as did the former vice-president, Harry Moniba.

On 13 Feb. 1991 Taylor, Johnson and the commander of the Liberian armed forces signed a second ceasefire. After a West African 12-nation summit meeting from July to Oct. 1991 Taylor signed an agreement to allow ECOWAS to disarm his troops and organize elections.

AREA AND POPULATION. Liberia has about 350 miles of coastline, extending from Sierra Leone, on the west, to the Côte d'Ivoire, on the east. It stretches inland to a distance, in some places, of about 250 miles and is bounded in the north by Guinea.

The total area is about 42,989 sq. miles (111,370 sq. km). At the census (1984) population 2,101,628. Estimate (1988) 2,436,000. English is the official language spoken by 15% of the population. The rest belong in the main to 3 linguistic groups: Mande, West Atlantic, and the Kwa. These are in turn subdivided into 16 ethnic groups: Bassa, Bella, Gbandi, Mende, Gio, Dey, Mano, Gola, Kpelle, Kissi, Krahn, Kru, Lorma, Mandingo, Vai and Grebo.

Monrovia, the capital, had (1984) a population of 425,000; other towns include Buchanan (24,000).

There are 13 counties, whose areas, populations (1984 census) and capitals are as follows:

County	Sq. km	1984	Chief town
Bomi	1,955	66,420	Tubmanburg
Bong	8,099	255,813	Gbarnga
Grand Bassa	8,759	159,648	Buchanan
Grand Cape Mount	5,827	79,322	Robertsport
Grand Gedeh	17,029	102,810	Zwedru
Lofa	19,360	247,641	Voinjama
Margibi	3,263	97,992	Kakata
Maryland	5,351	132,058	Harper
Montserrado	2,740	544,878	Bensonville
Nimba	12,043	313,050	Saniquillie
Rivercess	4,385	37,849	Rivercess
Sinoe	10,254	64,147	Greenville

The county of Grand Kru (chief town, Barclayville) was created in 1985 from the former territories of Kru Coast and Sasstown.

CLIMATE. An equatorial climate, with constant high temperatures and plentiful rainfall, though Jan. to May is drier than the rest of the year. Monrovia. Jan. 79°F (26·1°C), July 76°F (24·4°C). Annual rainfall 206" (5,138 mm).

CONSTITUTION AND GOVERNMENT. A new Constitution was approved by referendum in July 1984 and came into force on 6 Jan. 1986. The National Assembly consists of a 26-member Senate and a 64-member House of Representatives. General elections were held on 15 Oct. 1985. The National Democratic Party of Liberia gained 21 seats in the Senate; the Liberal Action Party, 3 seats and the Liberian Unification Party and the Unity Party one each. In the House of Representatives, the NDPL won 45 seats and others 19 seats.

A National Conference re-elected Amos Sawyer interim president in April 1991.

National flag: Six red and 5 white horizontal stripes alternating. In the upper corner, nearest the staff, is a square of blue covering a depth of 5 stripes. In the centre of this blue field is a 5-pointed white star.

National anthem: All hail, Liberia, hail! (words by President Warner; tune by O. Lucas, 1860).

DEFENCE. Since the assassination of President Doe, Liberian armed forces have effectively ceased to exist. Their previous status was:

Army. The establishment was organized on a militia basis numbering 7,300 (1990), divided into 6 infantry battalions with support units.

Navy. A coast-guard force of (1990) about 500 operated 5 inshore patrol craft, none exceeding 50 tonnes.

Air Force. The Air Reconnaissance Unit supported the Liberian Army. Equipment included 2 C-47 transports, 4 Israeli-built Arava twin-turboprop light transports, 1 Cessna 208 Caravan transport and a small number of Cessna 172, 185 and 337G light aircraft. Personnel (1990) about 250.

INTERNATIONAL RELATIONS

Membership. Liberia is a member of the UN, OAU, ECOWAS and is an ACP state of the EEC.

ECONOMY

Budget. Revenue and expenditure was as follows (in US$1,000):

	1984–85	1985–86	1986–87
Revenue	315,000	237,600	366,400
Expenditure	371,000	366,700	366,400

Currency. The legal currency is the *Liberian dollar* (LRD) which is equivalent to US$1 which itself has been in circulation since 3 Nov. 1942, but there is a Liberian coinage in silver and copper. Official accounts are kept in dollars and cents. The Liberian coins are as follows: Silver, $5, $1, 50-, 25-, 10- and 5-cent pieces; alloy, 2-cent and copper 1-cent pieces. The Government has not yet issued paper money. In March 1992, £1 = 1·76 Liberian $; US$1 = 1 Liberian $.

Banking and Finance. The First National City Bank (Liberia) was founded in 1935. An Italian bank, Tradevco, started business in 1955. The International Trust Co. of Liberia opened a commercial banking department at the end of 1960. The Liberian Bank of Development and Investment (LBDI) was founded in 1964 and began operations in 1965. The National Bank of Liberia opened on 22 July 1974, to act as a central bank. The National Housing and Savings Bank opened on 20 Jan. 1972. The Liberian Finance & Trust Corporation was incorporated Oct. 1976 and began operations in May 1977. The Liberian Agricultural and Co-operative Development Bank started operations in 1978. The Bank of Credit & Commerce International opened in Sept. 1978 and Meridien Bank of Liberia in July 1985.

Weights and Measures. Weights and measures are the same as in UK and USA.

ENERGY AND NATURAL RESOURCES

Electricity. Production (1986) was 655m. kwh. Supply 120 volts; 60 Hz.

Minerals. Iron ore production was 8·9m. tonnes in 1985. Gold production (1986) 21,125 oz valued at US$7·3m. and diamond production (1985) 66,000 carats.

Agriculture. Over 65% of the labour force is engaged in agriculture. The soil is productive, but due to excessive rainfall (from 160 to 180 in. per year), there are large swamp areas. Rice, cassava, coffee, citrus and sugar-cane are cultivated. The Government is negotiating the financing of large-scale investment in rice production aimed at making the country self-sufficient in rice production. Coffee, cocoa and palm-kernels are produced mainly by the traditional agricultural sector.

The Liberia Produce Marketing Corporation (LPMC) operates an oil-mill in Monrovia, processing most of the palm-kernels. There were 2 large commercial oil-palm plantations in the country. The Liberia Industrial Co-operative (LBINC) has 6,000 acres of oil-palm (of which 5,000 acres are in production) in Grand Bassa County, and West Africa Agricultural Co. (WAAC) has 4,020 acres in production in Grand Cape Mount County.

Production (1988, in 1,000 tonnes): Rice, 279; cassava, 310; coffee, 5; oranges, 7; sugar-cane, 225; cocoa, 5; palm-kernels, 8.

Livestock (1988): Cattle, 42,000; pigs, 140,000; sheep, 240,000; poultry, 4m.

Forestry. The Firestone Plantation Co. have large rubber plantations, employing over 40,000 men. Their concession comprises about 1m. acres and expires in the year 2025. About 100,000 acres have been planted. Independent producers have a further 65,000 acres planted.

Production in 1986 was 4·75m. cu. metres.

Fisheries. Catch (1986) 16,100 tonnes.

INDUSTRY. There are a number of small factories (brick and tile, soap, nails, mattresses, shoes, plastics, paint, oxygen, acetylene, tyre retreading, a brewery, soft drinks, cement, matches, candy and biscuits).

FOREIGN ECONOMIC RELATIONS

Commerce. Imports in 1986 totalled US$259,037,900 (1985, US$284,377,000) and exports US$408,374,099 (1985, US$435,570,000). Liberia's main trading partners are the USA and the Federal Republic of Germany.

In 1987, iron ore accounted for about 70% of total export earnings, rubber 15% and sawn timber over 5%. Other exports were coffee, cocoa, palm-kernel oil, diamonds and gold.

Total trade between Liberia and UK (British Department of Trade returns, in £1,000 sterling):

	1987	1988	1989	1990	1991
Imports to UK	7,284	9,574	12,776	13,240	972
Exports and re-exports from UK	13,538	11,684	15,148	8,639	8,865

The figures for exports from the UK include the value of shipping transferred to the Liberian flag; the genuine exports are considerably lower.

COMMUNICATIONS

Roads. In 1981, there were 4,794 miles of public roads (1,165 primary, 366 paved, 799 all-weather, 3,629 secondary and feeder) and 1,474 miles of private roads (93 paved, 1,381 laterite and earth). The principal highway connects Monrovia with the road system of Guinea, with branches leading into the Eastern and Western areas of Liberia. The latter branch reaches the Sierra Leone border and joins the Sierra Leone road system. A bridge over the St Paul River carries road traffic to the iron-ore mines at Bomi Hills.

Railway. A railway (for freight only) was built in 1951, connecting Monrovia with the Bomi Hills iron-ore mines about 69 km distant; this has been extended to the

National Iron Ore Co. area by 79 km. There is a line from Bong to Monrovia (78 km).

Civil Aviation. The airport for Liberia is Roberts International Airport (30 miles from Monrovia). The James Spriggs Payne Airfield, 5 miles from Monrovia, can be used by light aircraft and mini jumbo jets. Air services are maintained by Ghana Airways, Swissair, British Caledonian, Air Guinea, SABENA, Iberia Airlines, Romanian Airlines and Air Liberia.

Shipping. Over 2,000 vessels enter Monrovia each year. The Liberian Government requires only a modest registration fee and an almost nominal annual charge and maintains no control over the operation of ships flying the Liberian flag. In 1990, 1,370 ships were registered totalling 88·3m. DWT, of which some 56m. DWT represented oil tankers.

Telecommunications. There is cable communication with Europe and America via Dakar, and a wireless station is maintained by the Government at Monrovia. There is a telephone service (8,510 telephones, 1983), in Monrovia, which is gradually being extended over the whole country. There were (1988) 570,000 radio and 43,000 television receivers.

JUSTICE, RELIGION, EDUCATION AND WELFARE

Justice. Justice is administered by a Supreme Court of 5 judges, 14 circuit courts and lower courts.

Religion. The main denominations represented in Liberia are Methodist, Baptist, Episcopalian, African Methodist, Pentecostal, Seventh-day Adventist, Lutheran and Roman Catholic, working through missionaries and mission schools. There were (1985) about 670,000 Moslems.

Education. Schools are classified as: (1) Public schools, maintained and run by the Government; (2) Mission schools, supported by foreign Missions and subsidized by the Government, and operated by qualified Missionaries and Liberian teachers; (3) Private schools, maintained by endowments and sometimes subsidized by the Government.

In 1986 there were estimated to be 1,830 schools with 8,744 teachers and 443,786 pupils.

Health. There were 236 doctors in 1981 and about 3,000 hospital beds.

DIPLOMATIC REPRESENTATIVES

Of Liberia in Great Britain (2 Pembridge Pl., London, W2 4XB)
Ambassador: (Vacant).

Of Great Britain in Liberia (PO Box 10-0120, 1000, Monrovia)
The embassy closed on 8 March 1991.

Of Liberia in the USA (5201 16th St., NW, Washington, D.C., 20011)
Ambassador: Eugenia Wordsworth-Stevenson.

Of the USA in Liberia (United Nations Drive, Monrovia)
Ambassador: Peter J. de Vos.

Of Liberia to the United Nations
Ambassador: William Bull.

Further Reading

Economic Survey of Liberia, 1981. Ministry of Planning and Economic Affairs
Dunn, D. E., *The Foreign Policy of Liberia during the Tubman Era, 1944–71.* London, 1979
Fraenkel, M., *Tribe and Class in Monrovia.* OUP, 1964
Wilson, C. M., *Liberia: Black Africa in Microcosm.* New York, 1971

LIBYA

Capital: Tripoli
Population: 4m. (1990)
GNP per capita: US$5,410 (1988)

Jamahiriya Al-Arabiya
Al-Libiya Al-Shabiya
Al-Ishtirakiya Al-Uzma

(Great Socialist People's
Libyan Arab Republic)

HISTORY. Tripoli fell under Turkish domination in the 16th century, and though in 1711 the Arab population secured some measure of independence, the country was in 1835 proclaimed a Turkish vilayet. In Sept. 1911 Italy occupied Tripoli and on 17 Oct. 1912, by the Treaty of Ouchy, Turkey recognized the sovereignty of Italy in Tripoli.

After the expulsion of the Germans and Italians in 1942 and 1943, Tripolitania and Cyrenaica were placed under British, and the Fezzan under French, military administration. Britain recognized the Amir Mohammed Idris Al-Senussi as Amir of Cyrenaica in June 1949.

Libya became an independent, sovereign, federal kingdom under the Amir of Cyrenaica, Mohammed Idris Al-Senussi, as King of the United Kingdom of Libya, on 24 Dec. 1951, when the British Residents in Tripolitania and Cyrenaica and the French Resident in the Fezzan transferred their remaining powers to the federal government of Libya, in pursuance of decisions passed by the United Nations in 1949 and 1950.

On 1 Sept. 1969 King Idris was deposed by a group of army officers. Twelve of the group of officers formed the Revolutionary Command Council chaired by Col. Muammar Qadhafi and proclaimed a republic.

AREA AND POPULATION. Libya is bounded north by the Mediterranean Sea, east by Egypt and Sudan, south by Chad and Niger and west by Algeria and Tunisia. The area is estimated at 1,759,540 sq. km (679,358 sq. miles). The population, at the census on 31 July 1984, was 3,637,488; estimate (1990), 4m.

In 1985, 65% of the population was urban. The chief cities (1981) were: Tripoli, the capital (858,000), Benghazi (368,000) and Misurata (117,000).

The populations (1984) of the municipalities were as follows:

Ajdabiya	100,547	Jabal al-Akhdar	120,662	Shati	46,749
Awbari	48,701	Khums	149,642	Surt	110,996
Aziziyah	85,068	Kufrah	25,139	Tarhunah	84,640
Benghazi	485,386	Marzuq	42,294	Tobruk	94,006
Derna	105,031	Misurata	178,295	Tripoli	990,697
Fatah	102,763	Niqat al-Khums	181,584	Yafran	73,420
Ghadames	52,247	Sabha	76,171	Zawia	220,075
Gharyan	117,073	Sawfajjin	45,195	Zlitan	101,107

CLIMATE. The coastal region has a warm temperate climate, with mild wet winters and hot dry summers, though most of the country suffers from aridity. Tripoli. Jan. 52°F (11·1°C), July 81°F (27·2°C). Annual rainfall 16" (400 mm). Benghazi. Jan. 56°F (13·3°C), July 77°F (25°C). Annual rainfall 11" (267 mm).

CONSTITUTION AND GOVERNMENT. In March 1977 a new form of direct democracy, the 'Jamahiriya' (state of the masses) was promulgated and the official name of the country was changed to Socialist Peoples Libyan Arab Jamahiriya. Under this system, every adult is supposed to be able to share in policy making through the Basic People's Congresses of which there are some 2,000 throughout Libya. These Congresses appoint Popular Committees to execute policy. Provincial and urban affairs are handled by Popular Committees responsible to Municipality People's Congresses, of which there are 13. Officials of these Congresses and Committees form at national level the General People's Congress which now normally meets for about a week early each year (usually in March). This is the highest policy-making body in the country. The General People's Congress appoints its own General Secretariat and the General People's Committee, whose members (the equivalents of ministers under other forms of government) head the 10 government departments which execute policy at national level.

Until 1977 Libya was ruled by a Revolutionary Command Council headed by Col. Muammar Qadhafi. Upon its abolition in that year the 5 surviving members of the RCC became the General Secretariat of the General People's Congress, still under Qadhafi's direction. In 1979 they stood down to be replaced by elected officials. Since then, Col. Qadhafi has retained his position as Leader of the Revolution. But neither he nor his former RCC colleagues have any formal posts in the present administration, although they continue to wield considerable authority.

The government of 12 members appointed in Oct. 1990 included:

Secretary of the General People's Congress (Prime Minister): Abu Zaid Omar Burda.

Foreign Affairs: Ibrahim Mohammed Bishari. *Planning and Economy:* Omar Mustapha Al-Muntasir. *Vocational Training:* Maatooq Mohammed. *Information and Culture:* Ali Milad Abu Jaziyah.

The *Speaker* of the Congress is Abd Al-Raziq Sawsa.

National flag: Plain green.
Arabic is the official language

DEFENCE. There is selective conscription for 2-4 years. Enrolment in the reserves, numbering about 40,000, continues until age 49. On 31 Aug. 1989 it was announced that the traditional armed forces were abolished and in future would be known as the 'Armed People'.

Army. The Army is organized into 1 tank and 2 mechanized infantry divisions in addition to 42 tank battalions, 48 mechanized infantry, 1 National Guard, 41 artillery, 2 anti-aircraft and 10 parachute commando battalions, 7 surface-to-surface and 3 surface-to-air brigades. Equipment includes 1,500 T-54/-55, 350 T-62 and 300 T-72 main battle tanks. The Army has an aviation component with 13 transport and 60 anti-armour liaison helicopters, as well as 10 Cessna D-1 fixed-wing aircraft. Strength (1991) 55,000. The paramilitary Pan-African Islamic Legion numbers approximately 2,500, the Revolutionary Guard, 3,000.

Navy. The fleet, a mixture of Soviet and West European-built ships, comprises 6 Soviet-built diesel submarines, 3 missile-armed frigates, 7 missile-armed corvettes, 24 fast missile craft and 14 inshore patrol craft. There are 2 tank landing ships and 3 medium landing ships as well as 2 landing craft. Auxiliaries include 1 logistic support ship, 1 salvage ship, 1 transport and a diving support ship.

There is a small Naval Aviation wing operating 12 Mi-14 Haze and 12 Super-Frelon helicopters from shore bases.

Personnel in 1991 totalled 8,000, including coastguard. The forces are based at Tripoli, Benghazi, Darnah, Tobruk, Sidi Bilal and Al Khums.

Air Force. The creation of an Air Force began in 1959. In 1974, delivery was completed of a total of 110 Mirage 5 combat aircraft and trainers, of which about 60 remain. They have been followed by 10 Tu-22 supersonic reconnaissance bombers, 70 MiG-25 interceptors and reconnaissance aircraft, 100 Su-22 ground attack fighters, 94 MiG-21s, and about 140 MiG-23 variable-geometry fighters and fighter-bombers from the USSR. In 1989 the first of 15 Su-24D supersonic bombers were delivered. Other equipment includes 50 Mirage F1 fighters from France, 6 Mirage F1-B two-seat trainers, 20 Mi-24 gunship helicopters, Mi-14 anti-submarine helicopters, 10 C-130/L-100 Hercules and 20 Aeritalia G222T transports, 8 Super Frelon and 6 Agusta-built CH-47C Chinook heavy-lift helicopters, and a total of 16 Bell 212, Bell 47, Alouette III and Mi-8 helicopters. Training is performed on piston-engined SF.260Ms (some of which are armed for light attack duties) from Italy; L-39 Albatros, Galeb and Magister jet aircraft; and twin-engined L-410s built in Czechoslovakia. Personnel total (1991) about 22,000, with many of the combat aircraft operated by foreign aircrew, with 513 combat aircraft and 35 armed helicopters.

INTERNATIONAL RELATIONS

Membership. Libya is a member of the UN, OAU, OPEC, Arab Maghreb Union and the Arab League.

ECONOMY

Policy. Declining oil revenues (60% down on 1980 levels) has meant postponing most projects envisaged in the 5-year development plan (1981–85) though the Great-Man-Made River Project has not been affected.

Budget. A budget of LD3,240m. was announced for 1991.

Currency. The unit of currency is the *Libyan dinar* (LYD) of 1,000 *millemes*. Rate of exchange, March 1992: LD 0·491 = £1; LD 0·280 = US$1.

Banking and Finance. A National Bank of Libya was established in 1955; it was renamed the Central Bank of Libya in 1972. The *Governor* is Said Al-Zilitny. All foreign banks were nationalized by Dec. 1970. In 1972 the government set up the Libyan Arab Foreign Bank whose function is overseas investment and to participate in multinational banking corporations. The National Agricultural Bank, which has been set up to give loans and subsidies to farmers to develop their land and to assist them in marketing their crops, has offices in Tripoli, Benghazi, Sebha and other agricultural centres.

Weights and Measures. Although the metric system has been officially adopted and is obligatory for all contracts, the following weights and measures are still used: *oke* = 1·282 kg; *kantar* = 51·28 kg; *draa* = 46 cm; *handaza* = 68 cm.

ENERGY AND NATURAL RESOURCES

Electricity. Electricity capacity (1985) 5,615 mw. Production (1986) 2,126m. kwh. Supply 110, 115 and 220 volts; 50 Hz.

Oil. Oil revenues provided 28·2% of GDP in 1990. Production (1991) 74m. tonnes. Reserves (1988) 23,000m. bbls. The Libyan National Oil Corporation (NOC) was established in March 1970 to be the state's organization for the exploitation of Libya's oil resources. NOC does not participate in the production of oil but has a majority share in all the operating companies with the exception of two small producers Aquitaine-Libya and Wintershall Libya.

The largest producers are Waha (formerly Oasis, until the withdrawal of US oil companies at the end of June 1986) and AGECO who together produce more than 50% of total production. The other significant producers are Zuweitina (formerly Occidental Libya), AGIP, Sirte Oil Company, and Veba.

Gas. Reserves (1988) 620,000m. cu. metres. Production (1982) 29,000m. cu. metres. In 1983 a gas pipeline was under construction which will take gas from Brega, along the coast to Misurata. In 1987 agreement was reached with Algeria and Tunisia to construct a gas pipeline to supply western Libya with Algerian gas.

Water. Since 1984 a major project has been under way to bring water from wells in southern Libya to the coast. This scheme, called the 'Great Man-made River', is planned, on completion, to irrigate some 185,000 acres of land with water brought along some 4,000 km of pipes. Phase I was completed in Aug. 1991 at a cost of US$3,300m; Phase II of the project (covering the west of Libya) was announced in Sept. 1989. This contract is valued at US$5,300m. and is expected to last 74 months.

Minerals. Cement production (1987) 2·7m. tonnes. Gypsum output (1982) 172,400 tonnes. Iron ore deposits have been found in the south and uranium has reportedly been found in the region of Ghat in the south-west.

Agriculture. Tripolitania has 3 zones from the coast inland—the Mediterranean, the sub-desert and the desert. The first, which covers an area of about 17,231 sq. miles, is the only one properly suited for agriculture, and may be further subdivided into: (1) the oases along the coast, the richest in North Africa, in which thrive the date palm, the olive, the orange, the peanut and the potato; (2) the steppe district, suitable for cereals (barley and wheat) and pasture; it has olive, almond, vine, orange and mulberry trees and ricinus plants; (3) the dunes, which are being gradually afforested with acacia, robinia, poplar and pine; (4) the Jebel (the mountain district, Tarhuna, Garian, Nalut-Yefren), in which thrive the olive, the fig, the vine and other fruit trees, and which on the east slopes down to the sea with the fertile hills of Msellata. Of some 25m. acres of productive land in Tripolitania, nearly 20m. are used for grazing and about 1m. for static farming. The sub-desert zone produces the alfa plant. The desert zone and the Fezzan contain some fertile oases, such as those of Ghadames, Ghat, Socna, Sebha, Brak.

Cyrenaica has about 10m. acres of potentially productive land, most of which, however, is suitable only for grazing. Certain areas, chief of which is the plateau known as the Barce Plain (about 1,000 ft above sea-level), are suitable for dry farming; in addition, grapes, olives and dates are grown. With improved irrigation, production, particularly of vegetables, could be increased, but stock raising and dry farming will remain of primary importance. About 143,000 acres are used for settled farming; about 272,000 acres are covered by natural forests. The Agricultural Development Authority plans to reclaim 6,000 ha each year for agriculture. In the Fezzan there are about 6,700 acres of irrigated gardens and about 297,000 acres are planted with date palms.

Production (1988, in tonnes): Wheat, 193,000; barley, 99,000; milk, 143,000; meat, 154,000. Olive trees number about 3·4m. and productive date-palm trees about 3m.

Livestock (1988): 5·7m. sheep, 965,000 goats, 215,000 cattle, 37m. poultry.

Fisheries. The catch in 1986 was 7,800 tonnes.

INDUSTRY. Since the revolution there has been an ambitious programme of industrial development aimed at the local manufacture of building materials (steel and aluminium pipes and fittings, electric cables, cement, bricks, glass, etc.), foodstuffs (dairy products, flour, tinned fruits and vegetables, dates, fish processing and canning, etc.), textiles and footwear (ready-made clothing, woollen and cotton cloth, blankets, leather footwear, etc.) and development of mineral deposits (iron ore, phosphates, mineral salts). Many projects have been delayed or reduced in recent years, owing to fall in oil revenues since 1980. Small scale private sector industrialization in the form of partnerships is permitted. From 21 Sept. 1969 all businesses, except oil and banks, were Libyan-owned; subsequently all banks and most oil companies were nationalized.

FOREIGN ECONOMIC RELATIONS. In Feb. 1989 Libya signed a treaty of economic co-operation with the 4 other Maghreb countries, Algeria, Mauritania, Morocco and Tunisia.

Commerce. Total imports in 1987 were valued at US$4,969 (f.o.b.) and exports at US$6,612 (f.o.b.), virtually all crude oil. In 1987, 25% of imports came from Italy, while 33% of exports were to Italy, 16% to the Federal Republic of Germany and 11% to Spain.

Total trade between Libya and UK (British Department of Trade returns, in £1,000 sterling):

	1987	1988	1989	1990	1991
Imports to UK	133,649	111,812	104,546	151,605	121,220
Exports and re-exports from UK	220,626	235,957	239,191	244,850	255,719

COMMUNICATIONS

Roads. In 1986 there were 25,675 km of roads. In 1982 there were 415,509 passenger cars and 334,405 commercial vehicles.

Railways. In 1990 there were no operating railways.

Civil Aviation. A national airline, the Libyan Arab Airlines (LAA), was inaugurated on 30 Sept. 1965. Benghazi and Tripoli are linked by LAA and other international airlines to Athens, Rome, Madrid, Malta, Moscow, Frankfurt, Paris, Amsterdam, Vienna and Zurich. In 1990 the 5 Maghreb countries announced they would merge their airlines in an Air Maghreb.

Telecommunications. Radio-telephone services connect Libya with most countries of western Europe. In 1982 some 102,000 telephones were in use. Broadcasting is controlled by the government Libyan Jamihiriya Broadcasting and People's Revolution Broadcasting-Television. Radio has a home service, external services in English, French and Arabic and a Holy Koran programme. In 1991 there were estimated to be 1m. radio and 0·5m. TV receivers (colour by PAL).

Newspapers. There was (1990) 1 daily in Tripoli with a circulation of about 40,000 and a number of weeklies.

JUSTICE, RELIGION, EDUCATION AND WELFARE

Justice. The Civil, Commercial and Criminal codes are based mainly on the Egyptian model. Matters of personal status of family or succession matters affecting Moslems are dealt with in special courts according to the Moslem law. All other matters, civil, commercial and criminal, are tried in the ordinary courts, which have jurisdiction over everyone.

There are civil and penal courts in Tripoli and Benghazi, with subsidiary courts at Misurata and Derna; courts of assize in Tripoli and Benghazi, and courts of appeal in Tripoli and Benghazi.

Religion. Islam is declared the State religion, but the right of others to practise their religions is provided for. In 1990, 97% were Sunni Moslems.

Education. There were (1981–82) 718,124 pupils in primary schools, 286,414 in preparatory and secondary schools, 44,789 pupils in technical schools and 25,700 students in higher education. There are 3 universities of Al Fatah (in Tripoli), Garyounes (in Benghazi) and Sabha.

Health. In 1981 there were 74 hospitals with 15,375 beds, 4,690 physicians, 314 dentists, 420 pharmacists, 1,080 midwives and 5,346 nursing personnel.

DIPLOMATIC REPRESENTATIVES

UK broke off diplomatic relations with Libya on 22 April 1984. Saudi Arabia looks after Libyan interests in UK and Italy looks after UK's interests in Libya.

USA suspended all embassy activities in Tripoli on 2 May 1980.

Of Libya to the United Nations
Ambassador: Dr Ali Treiki.

Further Reading

Allen, J. A., *Libya: The Experience of Oil*. London and Boulder, 1981.—*Libya since Independence*. London, 1982
Bearman, J., *Qadhafi's Libya*. London, 1986
Blundy, D. and Lycett, A., *Qadhafi and the Libyan Revolution*. London, 1987
Cooley, J. K., *Libyan Sandstorm: The Complete Account of Qaddafi's Revolution*. London and New York, 1983
Davis, J., *Libyan Politics: Tribe and Revolution*. London, 1988
Fergiani, M. B., *The Libyan Jamahiriya*. London, 1984
Hahn, L., *Historical Dictionary of Libya*. London, 1961
Harris, L. C., *Libya: Qadhafi's Revolution and the Modern State*. Boulder and London, 1986
Lawless, R. I., *Libya*. [Bibliography] Oxford and Santa Barbara, 1987
St John, R. B., *Qaddafi's World Design: Libyan Foreign Policy, 1969-1987*. London, 1987
Waddhams, F. C., *The Libyan Oil Industry*. London, 1980
Wright, J., *Libya: A Modern History*. London, 1982

LIECHTENSTEIN

Capital: Vaduz
Population: 28,877 (1990)

Fürstentum Liechtenstein

(Principality of Liechtenstein)

HISTORY. Liechtenstein is a sovereign state whose history dates back to 3 May 1342, when Count Hartmann III became ruler of the county of Vaduz. Additions were later made to the count's domains, and by 1434 the territory reached its present boundaries. It consists of the two former counties of Schellenberg and Vaduz (until 1806 immediate fiefs of the Holy Roman Empire). The former in 1699 and the latter in 1712 came into the possession of the house of Liechtenstein. On 23 Jan. 1791 the Emperor Charles VI constituted the two counties as the Principality of Liechtenstein.

AREA AND POPULATION. Liechtenstein is bounded on the east by Austria and the west by Switzerland. Area, 160 sq. km (61·8 sq. miles); population (census 1980), 25,215; estimate, 1989, 28,452 (14,533 females), including 10,354 resident foreigners. Estimate, 1990, 28,777. In 1990 there were 379 births and 195 deaths. Population of Vaduz (census 1980), 4,606; estimate, 1990, 4,870. The language is German.

REIGNING PRINCE. Hans-Adam II, born 14 Feb. 1945; succeeded his father Prince Francis-Joseph, 13 Nov. 1989 (he exercised the prerogatives to which the Sovereign is entitled from 26 Aug. 1984); married on 30 July 1967 to Countess Marie Kinsky; there are 3 sons, Hereditary Prince Alois (born 11 June 1968), Prince Maximilian (born 16 May 1969) and Prince Constantin (born 15 March 1972), and one daughter, Princess Tatjana (born 10 April 1973). The monarchy is hereditary in the male line.

CONSTITUTION AND GOVERNMENT. Liechtenstein is a constitutional monarchy ruled by the princes of the House of Liechtenstein. The present constitution of 5 Oct. 1921 provided for a unicameral parliament (Diet) of 15 members elected for 4 years, but this was amended to 25 members in 1988. Election is on the basis of proportional representation. The prince can call and dismiss the parliament. On parliamentary recommendation, he appoints the prime minister and the 4 councillors for a 4-year term. Any group of 1,000 persons or any 3 communes may propose legislation (initiative). Bills passed by the parliament may be submitted to popular referendum. A law is valid when it receives a majority approval by the parliament and the prince's signed concurrence. The capital is Vaduz.

At the elections for the Diet, on 5 March 1989, the Fatherland Union obtained 13 seats, the opposition Progressive Citizens' Party, 12 seats.

Head of Government and Foreign Minister: Hans Brunhart.

National flag: Horizontally blue over red, with a gold coronet in the first quarter.
National anthem: Oben am jungen Rhein (words by H. H. Jauch, 1850; tune, 'God save the Queen').

Local government. There are 11 communes, fully independent administrative bodies within the laws of the principality. They levy additional taxes to the state taxes.

INTERNATIONAL RELATIONS

Membership. Liechtenstein is a member of the UN, EFTA, the Council of Europe and the International Court of Justice.

ECONOMY

Budget. Budget (in Swiss francs), 1990: Revenue, 365,763,331; expenditure, 405,287,969. There is no public debt.

Currency. Swiss currency has been in use since 1921.

Banking and Finance. There were (1992) 5 banks. There were 1,395m. Swiss francs in 81,104 savings accounts in 1989.

Weights and Measures. The metric system is in force.

ENERGY AND NATURAL RESOURCES

Electricity. Electricity produced in 1989 was 63,992,000 kwh.

Agriculture. In 1990 there were 3,890 ha of cultivated land, 2,510 ha of Alpine pasture and 5,560 ha of forest. 13,479 cu. metres of timber were cut in 1989. The rearing of cattle, for which the fine alpine pastures are well suited, is highly developed. In 1990 there were 6,328 cattle (including 2,850 milk cows), 239 horses, 2,781 sheep, 171 goats, 3,251 pigs. Total production of dairy produce, 1989, 13,367,031 kg.

INDUSTRY. The country has a great variety of light industries (textiles, ceramics, steel screws, precision instruments, canned food, pharmaceutical products, heating appliances, etc.).

Since 1945 Liechtenstein has changed from a predominantly agricultural country to a highly industrialized country.

Labour. The farming population has gone down from 70% in 1930 to 1·8% in 1990. The rapid change-over has led to the immigration of foreign workers (Austrians, Germans, Italians, Spaniards). The workforce was 13,764 in 1989, and a further 6,482 employees commuted from abroad. Industrial undertakings affiliated to the Liechtenstein Chamber of Commerce in 1990 employed 7,166 workers earning 416m. Swiss francs.

FOREIGN ECONOMIC RELATIONS. Liechtenstein has been in a customs union with Switzerland since 1923.

Commerce. Exports of home produce in 1990 (in Swiss francs), for member companies affiliated to the Chamber of Industry and Commerce, amounted to 2,213·1m.: 463·3m. (20·9%) went to EFTA countries, of which Switzerland took 341·5m. (15·4%), and 944·5m. (42·7%) went to EEC countries. Imports in 1989 amounted to 876m. Swiss francs.

Total trade with UK is included with Switzerland from 1968.

Tourism. In 1990, 77,735 overnight visitors arrived in Liechtenstein.

COMMUNICATIONS

Roads. There are 250 km of roads. Postal buses are the chief means of public transportation within the country and to Austria and Switzerland. There were 16,891 cars in 1990. There were 363 road accidents in 1989 (2 fatal).

Railways. The 18·5 km of main railway passing through the country is operated by Austrian Federal Railways.

Telecommunications. In 1990 there were 16,538 telephones, 276 telex, 10,279 radios and 9,787 TV sets. Post and telegraphs are administered by Switzerland.

Cinemas. There were 2 cinemas in 1988.

Newspapers. In 1990 there were 2 daily newspapers with a total circulation of 17,195.

JUSTICE, RELIGION, EDUCATION AND WELFARE

Justice. The principality has its own civil and penal codes. The lowest court is the county court, *Landgericht*, presided over by one judge, which decides minor civil cases and summary criminal offences. The criminal court, *Kriminalgericht*, with a bench of 5 judges is for major crimes. Another court of mixed jurisdiction is the court of assizes (with 3 judges) for misdemeanours. Juvenile cases are treated in the Juvenile Court (with a bench of 3 judges). The superior court, *Obergericht*, and Supreme Court, *Oberster Gerichtshof*, are courts of appeal for civil and criminal cases (both with benches of 5 judges). An administrative court of appeal from government actions and the State Court determines the constitutionality of laws.

The death penalty was abolished in 1989.

Police. The principality has no army. Police force, 45; auxiliary police, 23 (1989).

Religion. In 1990 there were 24,756 Roman Catholics and 2,256 Protestants.

Education (1990–91). In 14 primary, 3 upper, 5 secondary, 1 grammar and 2 (for backward children) schools there were 3,569 pupils and 387 teachers. There is also an evening technical school, a music school and a children's pedagogic-welfare day school.

Health. There is an obligatory sickness insurance scheme. In 1989 there was 1 hospital, but Liechtenstein has an agreement with the Swiss cantons of St Gallen and Graubünden and the Austrian Federal State of Vorarlberg that her citizens may use certain hospitals.

DIPLOMATIC REPRESENTATIVES

In 1919, Switzerland agreed to represent the interests of Liechtenstein in countries where it has diplomatic missions and where Liechtenstein is not represented in its own right. In so doing Switzerland always acts only on the basis of mandates of a general or specific nature, which it may either accept or refuse, while Liechtenstein is free to enter into direct relations with foreign states or to set up its own additional diplomatic missions.

British Consul-General: T. Bryant, CMG. (resident in Zürich).
USA Consul-General: Ruth N. van Heuven (resident in Zürich).

Of Liechtenstein to the United Nations
Ambassador: Claudia Fritsche

Further Reading

Amt für Volskwirtschaft Information. *Statistiches Jahrbuch.* Vaduz

Rechenschaftsbericht der Fürstlichen Regierung. Vaduz. Annual, from 1922
Jahrbuch des Historischen Vereins. Vaduz. Annual since 1901
Green, B., *Valley of Peace.* Vaduz, 1967
Larke, T. A. T., *Index and Thesaurus of Liechtenstein.* 2nd ed. Berkeley, 1984
Raton, P., *Liechtenstein: History and Institutions of the Principality.* Vaduz, 1970
Seger, O., *A Survey of Liechtenstein History.* 4th English ed. Vaduz, 1984

National statistical office: Amt für Volkwirtschaft, Vaduz
National Library: Landesbibliothek, Vaduz

LITHUANIA

Capital: Vilnius
Population: 3·72m. (1990)

Lietuvos Respublika

HISTORY. Lithuanian tribes, organized into state units in the 9th century, unified in the face of encroachment by the German order of Teutonic Knights. At the time of Tatar-Mongol domination of Russia, Lithuania annexed Russian lands until by the middle of the 15th century Belorussia, parts of Russia and the Ukraine as far as the Black Sea were under its rule. Lithuania united with Poland dynastically in 1385 and politically in 1569. During the Russian partitions of Poland in the 18th century Lithuania yielded its Russian territories and was itself absorbed into the Russian empire in 1795.

Germany occupied Lithuania during the First World War. Following the Russian revolution a Lithuanian government was formed on 7 Feb. 1918, but Soviet troops reoccupied Lithuania in Jan. 1919. These were expelled (having ceded Vilnius to Lithuania) by Polish forces in April 1919; the Lithuanian government re-formed and a democratic republic was established. In Oct. 1919 Poland occupied Vilnius and incorporated it into Poland in 1923. (This was acknowledged by Lithuania only in 1938). In Dec. 1926 the democratic regime was overthrown by a coup.

The secret protocol of the Soviet–German frontier treaty of 28 Sept. 1939 assigned the greater part of Lithuania to the Soviet sphere of influence. In Oct. 1939 the province and city of Vilnius (in Polish occupation 1920–39) were ceded by the USSR. An ultimatum (16 June 1940) led to the formation of a government acceptable to the USSR. A people's Diet, elected on 14–15 July, proclaimed the establishment of the Lithuanian Soviet Socialist Republic on 21 July and applied for admission to the USSR, which was effected by decree of the USSR Supreme Soviet on 3 Aug. and included also those parts of Lithuania which had been reserved for inclusion in Germany. This incorporation has been accorded *de facto* recognition by the UK, but not by the USA, which continues to recognize a Lithuanian Chargé d'Affaires in Washington, D.C. On 11 March 1990 the newly-elected Lithuanian Supreme Soviet, by 120 votes to nil, proclaimed independence based on the continuing validity of the act of independence of 16 Feb. 1918. This decision was not accepted by the USSR government.

Massive price rises in Jan. 1991 triggered demonstrations from ethnic Russians and led the Prime Minister, Kazimiera Prunskiene, to resign, a decision approved by parliament by 72 votes to 8 with 22 abstentions. Initially dispatched to Vilnius to enforce conscription, Soviet army units occupied key buildings in the face of mounting popular unrest. On 13 Jan. the army fired on demonstrators and there were fatal casualties. A referendum on independence was held in Feb. 1991 at which 90·5% voted in favour.

A fully independent status was conceded by the USSR State Council on 6 Sept. 1991 and Lithuania was subsequently admitted into the UN and other international bodies.

AREA AND POPULATION. Lithuania is bounded in the north by Latvia, east and south by Belorussia, and west by Poland, the Kaliningrad area of Russia and the Baltic Sea. The total area is 65,200 sq. km (25,170 sq. miles) and the population (Jan. 1990) 3,723,000. The 1989 census population was 3,674,802, of whom Lithuanians accounted for 79·6%, Russians 9·4%, Poles 7%, Belorussians 1·7% and Ukrainians 1·2%.

The capital is Vilnius (593,000). Other large towns are Kaunas (Kovno), Klaipeda (Memel), Siauliai (145,000) and Panevežys (126,000). The official language is Lithuanian, but ethnic minorities have the right to official use of their language where they form a substantial part of the population.

Residents who applied by 3 Nov. 1991 received Lithuanian citizenship.

CONSTITUTION AND GOVERNMENT. At the elections to the 141-member Supreme Soviet of 24 Feb. 1990, the nationalist movement Sajudis won a large majority.

Chairman, Presidium of the Supreme Soviet (i.e. President of the Republic): Vytautas Landsbergis (b. 1932).
Prime Minister: Gediminas Vagnorius (b. 1957).
First Deputy Prime Minister: Zigmas Vaišvila. *Second Deputy Prime Minister and Minister of Justice:* Vytautas Pakalniskis. *Third Deputy Prime Minister and Minister of Social Security:* Algis Dobravolskas.

National flag: 3 horizontal strips of yellow, green and red.
National anthem: Lietuva tėvynė mū sų (words and tune by V. Kurdirka).

Local Government: There are 22 urban and 44 rural districts and 92 towns.

DEFENCE. Russian (ex-Soviet) troops began to withdraw in Feb. 1992.

INTERNATIONAL RELATIONS

Membership. Lithuania is a member of the UN.

ECONOMY

Policy. Prices on most consumer goods were raised 25%–100% in Nov. 1991; pensions and low wages were raised as a compensatory measure. There is a privatization programme: 114 enterprises were offered for hard-currency sale at the beginning of 1992. Each citizen was given a 10,000-ruble voucher for house or equity purchase.

Budget. Budget estimates (in 1m. rubles), 1988, 3,962; 1989 (plan), 4,581.

Currency. It is planned to replace the ruble with the *litas* as the unit of currency eventually.

ENERGY AND NATURAL RESOURCES

Electricity. Output was 29,200m. kwh in 1989. There is a nuclear power station responsible for about 25% of total output in 1991.

Oil. Production started from a small field at Kretinga in 1990. Tenders have been invited to explore the Genciai field.

Agriculture. Lithuania before 1940 was a mainly agricultural country, but has since been considerably industrialized. The population was 69% urban in Jan. 1990. Resources consist of timber and agricultural produce. Farming is focussed on milk and meat production. Of the total area, 49·1% is arable, 22·2% meadow and pasture, 16·3% forests and 12·4% unproductive.

Area under cultivation in Nov. 1990, 4·6m. ha. By 1981 over 2·7m. ha of swamps had been drained. Output of main agricultural products (in 1,000 tonnes) in 1989: Grain, 3,300; potatoes, 1,927; sugar-beet, 1,075; vegetables, 326; meat, 534; milk, 3,235; eggs, 1,331m. On 1 Jan. 1990 there were 2·4m. cattle, 2·7m. pigs and 78,000 sheep and goats.

There were 311 state and 737 collective farms in the last year of the Communist regime. These are being converted into shareholding businesses. The remainder are being divided into smallholdings for collective farm workers or former owners. There were 3,000 such farms in 1991.

Forestry. Forests cover 1·55m. ha; 70% of the forests consist of conifers, mostly pines. Peat reserves total 4,000m. cubic metres.

INDUSTRY. There are heavy engineering, shipbuilding and building material industries. Industrial output included, in 1989, steel, 7,400 tonnes; timber, 2m. cu. metres; cement, 3·4m. tonnes; paper, 117,000 tonnes; fabrics, 218m. sq. metres; knitwear, 62·3m. items; hosiery, 105m. pairs; footwear, 11·9m. pairs; granulated sugar, 239,000 tonnes; butter, 78,000 tonnes; preserves, 423m. standard jars.

Labour. In 1989 there were 1,553,000 employees in the state sector.

FOREIGN ECONOMIC RELATIONS. On 20 April 1990 Lithuania, Estonia and Latvia concluded a Baltic Economic Co-operation Agreement. A 10-year treaty signed with Russia in July 1991 guarantees the future of the Russian enclave of Kaliningrad. Lithuania has undertaken to supply Kaliningrad with gas and electricity with the help of Russian energy imports, and promised a free flow of goods through its territory.

COMMUNICATIONS

Roads. In 1990 there were 43,100 km of motor roads (34,100 km hard surfaced).

Railways. Length of railways in 1990 was 2,010 km.

Civil Aviation. The national carrier is Lithuanian Airlines. There is an international airport at Vilnius, with flights to Copenhagen, Berlin and Frankfurt and 43 cities in the CIS. It has 21 aircraft. SAS operates a flight to Copenhagen.

Newspapers (1989). Of 240 newspapers, 192 were in Lithuanian. Daily circulation of Lithuanian-language newspapers, 4m.; other languages, 488,000.

JUSTICE, RELIGION, EDUCATION AND WELFARE

Justice. Trial by jury has been introduced for capital offences.

Religion. 80% of the population are Roman Catholic. There is an archbishopric of Vilnius and 10 bishops. In 1956, the Lithuanian Lutheran Church had 215,000 members.

Education. In 1989–90 there were 500,000 pupils in 2,200 primary and secondary schools. The University of Vytautas the Great, at Kaunas, was opened on 16 Feb. 1922. On 15 Jan. 1940 certain faculties were transferred to Vilnius to join the ancient University of Vilnius (founded 1570). In 1989–90 there were 12 higher educational institutions with 69,400 students: in 66 technical colleges of all kinds there were 51,700 students. The Lithuanian Academy of Sciences, founded in 1941, had 12 institutions with a total scientific staff of 1,966 in Jan. 1989; there were 88 scientific institutions with 15,400 research personnel. 54% of eligible children in Jan. 1990 were attending pre-school institutions.

Optional religious instruction was introduced in schools in 1991.

Health. In 1989 there were 16,900 doctors and 46,700 hospital beds.

DIPLOMATIC REPRESENTATIVES

Diplomatic relations with Great Britain were restored on 8 Oct. 1991.

Of Lithuania in Great Britain (17 Essex Villas, London, W8 7BP)
Ambassador: Vinčas Baličkas.

Of Great Britain in Lithuania
Ambassador: Michael Peart, LVO.

Of Lithuania in the USA
Ambassador: Stasys Lozoraitis.

Of Lithuania to the United Nations
Ambassador: Anicetas Simutis.

Further Reading

Jurgela, C. R., *History of the Lithuanian Nation.* New York, 1948
Kantantas, A. and F., *A Lithuanian Bibliography.* Univ. of Alberta Press, 1975
Suziedlis, S., (ed.) *Encyclopedia Lituanica.* 6 vols. Boston, 1970–78
Vardys, S., (ed.) *Lithuania under the Soviets: Portrait of a Nation, 1940–45.* New York, 1965

LUXEMBOURG

Capital: Luxembourg
Population: 378,400 (1990)
GNP per capita: US$22,856 (1989)

Grand-Duché de Luxembourg

HISTORY. The country formed part of the Holy Roman Empire until it was conquered by the French in 1795. In 1815 the Grand Duchy of Luxembourg was formed under the house of Orange-Nassau, also sovereigns of the Netherlands. In 1839 the Walloon-speaking area was joined to Belgium. In 1890 the personal union with the Netherlands ended with the accession of a member of another branch of the house of Nassau, Grand Duke Adolphe of Nassau-Weilburg.

AREA AND POPULATION. Luxembourg has an area of 2,586 sq. km (999 sq. miles) and is bounded on the west by Belgium, south by France, east by the Federal Republic of Germany. The population (1990) was 378,400. The capital, Luxembourg, had (1990) 74,400 inhabitants; Esch-Alzette, the centre of the mining district, 23,890; Differdange, 16,050; Dudelange, 14,230, and Petange, 11,900. In 1990 the foreign population was about 104,000.

Vital statistics (1989): 4,665 births, 3,984 deaths, 2,184 marriages.

Luxembourgish is spoken by most of the population, and since 1985 has been an official language with French and German.

CLIMATE. Cold, raw winters with snow covering the ground for up to a month are features of the upland areas. The remainder resembles Belgium in its climate, with rain evenly distributed throughout the year. Jan. 33·3°F (0·7°C), July 63·5°F (17·5°C). Annual rainfall 30·1" (764 mm).

REIGNING GRAND DUKE. Jean, born 5 Jan. 1921, son of the late Grand Duchess Charlotte and the late Prince Felix of Bourbon-Parma; succeeded 12 Nov. 1964 on the abdication of his mother; married to Princess Joséphine-Charlotte of Belgium, 9 April 1953. *Offspring:* Princess Marie-Astrid, born 17 Feb. 1954, married Christian of Habsbourg-Lorraine 6 Feb. 1982 (*Offspring:* Marie Christine, born 31 July 1983; Imre, born 8 Dec. 1985); Prince Henri, *heir apparent,* born 16 April 1955, married Maria Teresa Mestre 14 Feb. 1981; (*Offspring:* Prince Guillaume, born 11 Nov. 1981, Prince Felix, born 3 June 1984, Prince Louis, born 3 Aug. 1986, Princess Alexandra, born 16 Feb. 1991). Prince Jean, born 15 May 1957, married Hélène Vestur; Princess Margaretha, born 15 May 1957, married Prince Nikolaus of Liechtenstein 20 March 1982; Prince Guillaume, born 1 May 1963.

The civil list is fixed at 300,000 gold francs per annum, to be reconsidered at the beginning of each reign.

On 28 Sept. 1919 a referendum was taken in Luxembourg to decide on the political and economic future of the country. The voting resulted as follows: For the reigning Grand Duchess, 66,811; for the continuance of the Nassau-Braganza dynasty under another Grand Duchess, 1,286; for another dynasty, 889; for a republic, 16,885; for an economic union with France, 60,133; for an economic union with Belgium, 22,242. But France refused in favour of Belgium, and on 22 Dec. 1921 the Chamber of the Grand Duchy passed a Bill for the economic union between Belgium and Luxembourg. The agreement, which is for 60 years, provides for the disappearance of the customs barrier between the two countries and the use of Belgian, in addition to Luxembourg, currency as legal tender in the Grand Duchy. It came into force on 1 May 1922.

The Grand Duchy was under German occupation from 10 May 1940 to 10 Sept. 1944. The Grand Duchess Charlotte and the Government carried on an independent administration in London. Civil government was restored in Oct. 1944.

National flag: Three horizontal stripes of red, white and light blue.

National anthem: Ons Hemecht ('Our Homeland'; words by M. Lentz, 1859; tune by J. A. Zinnen).

CONSTITUTION AND GOVERNMENT. The Grand Duchy of Luxembourg is a constitutional monarchy, the hereditary sovereignty being in the Nassau family. The constitution of 17 Oct. 1868 was revised in 1919, 1948, 1956, 1972, 1979, 1983, 1988 and 1989. The revision of 1948 has abolished the 'perpetually neutral' status of the country and introduced the concepts of right to work, social security, health services, freedom of trade and industry, and recognition of trade unions. The revision of 1956 provides for the devolution of executive, legislative and judicial powers to international institutions.

The country forms 4 electoral districts. An elector must be a citizen (male or female) of Luxembourg and have completed 18 years of age; to be eligible for election the citizen must have completed 21 years of age. Voters choose between party lists of candidates in multi-member constituencies.

The Chamber of Deputies consists of 22 Christian Social, 18 Socialists, 12 Democrats, 1 Communist, 2 Green Alternatives, 2 Green Ecologists and 3 5/6 Action Committee (elections of 18 June 1989). A maximum of 60 members are elected for 5 years; they receive a salary and a travelling allowance.

The head of the state takes part in the legislative power, exercises the executive power and has a certain part in the judicial power. The constitution leaves to the sovereign the right to organize the Government, which consists of a Minister of State, who is President of the Government, and of at least 3 Ministers.

The Cabinet was, in Dec. 1991, composed as follows:

Prime Minister, Minister of State, Minister for Exchequer, Cultural Affairs: Jacques Santer.

Vice-Prime Minister, Foreign Affairs, Foreign Trade and Cooperation, Armed Forces: Jacques F. Poos. *Family Affairs and Social Solidarity, Middle Classes and Tourism:* Fernand Boden. *Interior, Housing and Town Planning:* Jean Spautz. *Finance, Labour:* Jean-Claude Juncker. *National Education, Justice, Civil Service:* Marc Fischbach. *Health, Social Security, Physical Education and Sports, Youth:* Johny Lahure. *Agriculture, Viticulture and Country Planning:* René Steichen. *Economy, Public Works, Transport:* Robert Goebbels. *Land Planning and Environment, Energy, Communications:* Alex Bodry. *Secretary of State for Foreign Affairs, Foreign Trade and Co-operation, Armed Forces:* Georges Wohlfart. *Secretary of State for Health, Social Security, Physical Education and Sports, Youth:* Mady Delvaux-Stehres.

Besides the Cabinet there is a Council of State. It deliberates on proposed laws and Bills, and on amendments; it also gives administrative decisions and expresses its opinion regarding any other question referred to it by the Grand Duke or the Government. The Council of State is composed of 21 members chosen for life by the sovereign, who also chooses a president from among them each year.

DEFENCE. A law passed by Parliament on 29 June 1967 abolished compulsory service and instituted a battalion-size army of volunteers enlisted for 3 years. Strength (1991) 800. The defence estimates for 1989 amounted to 2,346m. francs. Luxembourg is an original member of NATO and the battalion is committed to NATO ACE mobile force.

INTERNATIONAL RELATIONS

Membership. Luxembourg is a member of the UN, Benelux, the European Communities, OECD, the Council of Europe, NATO and WEU.

The Schengen Accord of June 1990 abolishes border controls between Luxembourg, Belgium, France, Germany, Italy, the Netherlands, Portugal and Spain.

ECONOMY

Budget. Revenue and expenditure (including extraordinary) for years ending 30 April (in 1m. francs):

	1985	1986	1987	1988	1989	1990
Revenue	81,363·8	82,385·3	86,313·0	85,047·5	89,593·5	97,162·7
Expenditure	79,536·8	81,863·3	86,239·7	88,913·8	88,922·3	94,414·5

Consolidated debt at 31 Dec. 1989 amounted to 11,088m. francs (long-term) and 3,437m. francs (short-term).

Currency. The unit of currency is the *Luxembourg franc* (LUF), fixed at par value with the Belgian franc on 14 Oct. 1944. Notes of the Belgian National Bank are legal tender in Luxembourg.

Banking and Finance. Luxembourg's equivalent of a central bank is its Monetary Institute (*Director-General*, Pierre Jaans). On 31 Dec. 1989 depositors in the State Savings Bank had a total of 54,949m. francs to their credit. In 1991 there were 185 banks and 24 non-bank credit institutions established in Luxembourg, which has become an international financial centre. There is a stock exchange. The financial sector accounted for 15% of GDP in 1991.

Weights and Measures. The metric system is in force.

ENERGY AND NATURAL RESOURCES

Electricity. Power production was 1,380m. kwh. in 1989.

Minerals. In 1989 production (in tonnes) of pig-iron, 2,683,800; of steel, 3,720,920.

Agriculture. Agriculture is carried on by about 6,200 of the population on (1989) 3,945 farms with an average area of 37·18 ha; 126,514 ha were under cultivation in 1989. Production, 1989 (in tonnes) of main crops: Maize, 385,830; roots and tubers, 36,150; bread crops, 34,900; other crops, 87,340; forage crops, 69,350; pulses, 1,400; grassland, 137,630. Production, 1989 (in 1,000 tonnes) of meat, 21·9; milk, 279·8; butter, 5·9; cheese, 4·1. In 1989, 232,100 hectolitres of wine were produced from 1,288 ha. In 1989 there were 9,781 tractors, 1,428 harvester-threshers, 2,559 manure spreaders and 2,685 gatherer-presses.

Livestock (1989): 1,669 horses, 214,987 cattle, 76,553 pigs, 7,511 sheep.

Forestry. In 1987 there were 88,600 ha of forests, which produced 154,000 cu. metres of broadleaved and 159,050 cu. metres of coniferous wood.

INDUSTRY. Production, 1989 (in 1,000 tonnes); Steel, 3,721; rolled steel products, 4,113. At 1 Nov. 1989 there were 2,074 industrial enterprises.

Labour. The government fixes a legal minimum wage.

FOREIGN ECONOMIC RELATIONS. By treaties of 5 Sept. 1944 and 14 March 1947 Luxembourg with Belgium and the Netherlands, became a party to the Benelux Customs Union, which came into force on 1 Jan. 1948. For further particulars *see* Belgium: Foreign Economic Relations.

Commerce. Trade between Luxembourg and the UK has been included with Belgium since 1974.

Tourism. In 1989 there were 792,322 tourists.

COMMUNICATIONS

Roads. In 1989 there were 5,091 km of roads of which 78 km were motorways. Motor vehicles registered on 1 Jan. 1990 included 183,404 passenger cars, 11,275 trucks, 734 buses, 3,334 motorcycles, 20,546 tractors and special vehicles.

Railways. In 1990 there were 270 km of railway (standard gauge) of which 162 km were electrified. It carried 12·7m. passengers and 17·6m. tonnes of freight.

Civil Aviation. Findel is the airport for Luxembourg. 945,454 passengers and 126,933 tonnes of freight were handled in 1989.

Shipping. A shipping register was set up in 1990. 54 vessels were registered at the end of 1991.

Telecommunications. In 1989 there were 167,363 telephones and 107 post and telegraph offices. *Compagnie Luxembourgeoise de Télédiffusion* broadcasts 1 programme in Letzebuergesch on FM. Powerful transmitters on long-, medium- and short-waves are used for commercial and religious programmes in French, Dutch, German, English and Italian. Ten TV programmes are broadcast. Colour transmission is by the SECAM system. 2 Astra satellites are based on Luxembourg City.

Cinemas (1990). There were 17 cinemas.

Newspapers (1990). There were 5 daily newspapers with a circulation of 130,000.

RELIGION, EDUCATION AND WELFARE

Religion. The population is 95% Roman Catholic. The remaining 5% is mainly Protestant or Jewish, or does not belong to any religion. The Protestant Church is organized on an interdenominational basis.

Education. Education is compulsory for all children between the ages of 6 and 15. In 1988-89 nursery schools had 7,867 pupils; primary schools, 25,725 pupils. In 1988-89 technical secondary schools had 14,367 pupils; secondary schools, 7,885 pupils. In higher eduction the Higher Institute of Technology, 251 students. 174 students were in teacher training, and 572 pursued university studies.

Health. In 1987 there were 666 doctors and 4,661 hospital beds.

DIPLOMATIC REPRESENTATIVES

Of Luxembourg in Great Britain (27 Wilton Crescent, London, SWIX 8SD)
Ambassador: Edouard Molitor, KCMG (accredited 13 June 1989).

Of Great Britain in Luxembourg (14 Blvd Roosevelt, Luxembourg)
Ambassador and Consul-General: The Hon. Michael Pakenham.

Of Luxembourg in the USA (2200 Massachusetts Ave., NW, Washington, D.C., 20008)
Ambassador: Alphonse Burns.

Of the USA in Luxembourg (22 Blvd. Emmanuel Servais, Luxembourg)
Ambassador: Edward Morgan Rowell.

Of Luxembourg to the United Nations
Ambassador: Jean Feyder.

Further Reading

Statistical Information: The Service Central de la Statistique et des Études Économiques (STATEC) was founded in 1900 and reorganized in 1962 (19–21 boulevard Royal, C.P. 304 Luxembourg-City). *Director:* Robert Weides. Main publications: *Bulletin du STATEC.— Annuaire statistique.—Cahiers économiques.*

Bulletin de Documentation. Government Information Service. From 1945 (monthly)
The Institutions of the Grand Duchy of Luxembourg. Information and Press Service, Luxembourg, 1989
La Vie Politique au Grand-Duché de Luxembourg. Information and Press Service, Luxembourg, 1990
Als, G., *Le Luxembourg: Statistiques Historiques 1839-1989.* Luxembourg, 1989
Calmes, C., *The Making of a Nation from 1815 up to our Days.* Luxembourg, 1989
Hury, C. and Christophory, J., *Luxembourg.* [Bibliography] Oxford and Santa Barbara, 1981
Newcomer, J., *The Grand Duchy of Luxembourg: The Evolution of Nationhood, 963 A.D. to 1983.* Washington, 1983
Trausch, G., *The Significance of the Historical Date of 1839.* Luxembourg, 1989

Archives of the State: Luxembourg-City. *Director:* Cornel Meder.
National Library: Luxembourg-City, 37 Boulevard Roosevelt. *Director:* Jules Christophory.

MADAGASCAR

Capital: Antananarivo
Population: 11·44m. (1990)
GNP per capita: US$230 (1989)

Repoblika Demokratika Malagasy

HISTORY. Madagascar was discovered by the Portuguese, Diego Diaz, in 1500. The island was unified under the Imérina monarchy between 1797 and 1861, but French claims to a protectorate led to hostilities culminating in the establishment of a protectorate on 30 Sept. 1895. Madagascar became a French Colony on 6 Aug. 1896 and the monachy was abolished on 26 Feb. 1897.

Madagascar became an Overseas Territory in 1946, and on 14 Oct. 1958, following a referendum, was proclaimed the autonomous Malagasy Republic within the French Community, achieving full independence on 26 June 1960.

The government of Philibert Tsiranana, President from independence, resigned on 18 May 1972 and executive powers were given to Maj.-Gen. Gabriel Ramanantsoa, who replaced Tsiranana as President on 11 Oct. 1972. On 5 Feb. 1975, Col. Richard Ratsimandrava became Head of State, but was assassinated 6 days later. A National Military Directorate under Brig.-Gen. Gilles Andriamahazo was established on 12 Feb. On 15 June it handed over power to a Supreme Revolutionary Council (SRC) under Didier Ratsiraka.

After 6 months of anti-government unrest, during which the opposition formed an alternative 'government', in Oct. 1991 the government and the Committee of Living Forces, a coalition of 16 opposition parties led by Albert Zafy, agreed to form an 18-month transitional administration. However, Zafy refused to join a government formed on 13 Nov., and was instead appointed chairman of the High State Authority for a Provisional Government formed on 23 Nov.

AREA AND POPULATION. Madagascar is situated off the south-east coast of Africa, from which it is separated by the Mozambique channel, the least distance between island and continent being 250 miles (400 km); its length is 980 miles (1,600 km); greatest breadth, 360 miles (570 km).

The area is 587,041 sq. km (226,658 sq. miles). In 1975 (census) the population was 7,603,790. Estimate (1990) 11,443,000.

Province	Area in Sq. km	Population 1990	Chief town	Population 1990
Antsiranana	43,046	715,000	Antsiranana	54,418
Mahajanga	150,023	1,253,000	Mahajanga	121,967
Toamasina	71,911	1,585,000	Toamasina	145,431
Antananarivo	58,283	3,811,000	Antananarivo	802,390
Fianarantsoa	102,373	2,420,000	Fianarantsoa	124,489
Toliary	161,405	1,659,000	Toliary	61,460

Vital statistics, 1984: Births, 456,000; deaths, 146,000. Growth rate, 1989: 3 per 1,000.

The indigenous population are of Malayo-Polynesian stock, divided into 18 ethnic groups of which the principal are Merina (26%) of the central plateau, the Betsimisaraka (15%) of the east coast, and the Betsileo (12%) of the southern plateau. Foreign communities include Europeans, mainly French (30,000), Indians (15,000), Chinese (9,000), Comorians and Arabs.

CLIMATE. A tropical climate, but the mountains cause big variations in rainfall, which is very heavy in the east and very light in the west. Antananarivo. Jan. 70°F (21·1°C), July 59°F (15°C). Annual rainfall 54" (1,350 mm). Toamasina. Jan. 80°F (26·7°C), July 70°F (21·1°C). Annual rainfall 128" (3,256 mm).

CONSTITUTION AND GOVERNMENT. The new Constitution of the

Democratic Republic of Madagascar was approved by referendum on 21 Dec. 1975 and came into force on 30 Dec. It provides for a National People's Assembly of 137 members elected by universal suffrage for a 5-year term from the single list of the *Front National pour la Défense de la Révolution Socialiste Malgache*. Executive power is vested in the President, directly elected for 7 years, who appoints a Council of Ministers to assist him, with the guidance of the 27-member Supreme Revolutionary Council.

Under a convention of 31 Oct. 1991 the powers of the National People's Assembly and the Supreme Revolutionary Council were delegated to a High State Authority for a Provisional Government.

President: Adm. Didier Ratsiraka (re-elected 12 March 1989).

A government of 24 ministers was formed on 13 Nov. 1991 which included:

Prime Minister: Guy Willy Razanamasy.

Interior: Col. Charles Sylvain Rabotoarison. *Defence:* Gen. Gerard Raveomtsanga. *Industry and Mines:* Jean-Jacques Rakotoniaina (Democratic Christian Movement). *Finance:* Gerard Rabevohitra (Movement for Proletarian Power, MFM). *Decentralization:* Francisque Ravony (MFM). *Education:* Jacques Vestalys (MFM).

National flag: Horizontally red over green, in the hoist a vertical white strip.

National anthem: Ry tanindrazanay malala ô!

Malagasy, which is a language of Malayo-Polynesian origin, is the official language. French and English are understood and taught in Malagasy schools.

Local Government: The six provinces (*faritany*) are sub-divided into 111 *fivondronana*, which in turn are divided into 13,476 *fokontany* (the traditional communal divisions). Each level is governed by an elected council.

DEFENCE

Army. The Army is organized in 2 battalion groups, and 1 engineer, 1 signals, 1 service and 7 construction regiments. Equipment includes PT-76 light tanks and M-8 armoured cars. Strength (1991) 20,000 and gendarmerie 7,500.

Navy. In 1991 the small maritime force had a strength of 500 (including 100 marines), and was equipped with 1,250-tonne patrol craft, 1 medium landing ship, a few small landing craft, together with a 600-tonne former trawler used for transport and training.

Air Force. Created in 1961, the Malagasy Air Force received its first combat equipment in 1978, with the arrival of 8 MiG-21 and 4 MiG-17 fighters, plus flying and ground staff instructors, from North Korea. Other equipment includes 5 An-26 turboprop transports, 1 Britten-Norman Defender armed transport, 2 C-47s, 1 HS.748 and 1 Yak-40 for VIP use, 1 Aztec, 2 Cessna Skymasters, 4 Cessna 172Ms and 6 Mi-8 helicopters. Personnel (1991), 500, with 12 combat aircraft.

INTERNATIONAL RELATIONS

Membership. Madagascar is a member of the UN, OAU and is an ACP state of the EEC.

ECONOMY

Policy. A programme of privatization was launched in 1989.

Budget. The 1990 budget envisaged expenditure of MGFr1,124,400m.

Currency. The unit of currency is the *Malagasy franc* (MGF). There are coins of MGFr1, 2, 5, 10, 50 and 100 and banknotes of MGFr50, 100, 500, 1,000, 5,000 and 10,000. In March 1992, £1 = MGFr3,134; US$1 = MGFr1,785.

Banking and Finance. A Central Bank was formed in 1973, replacing the former *Institut d'Emission Malgache* as the central bank of issue. All commercial banking and insurance was nationalized in 1975 and privatized in 1988. Industrial development is financed through the *Bankin'ny Indostria*. Other commercial banking is undertaken by the *Bankin'ny Tantsaha Mpamokatra*, the *Banky Fampandrosoana ny Varotra*. The Malagasy Bank of the Indian Ocean was set up in Sept. 1990 as part of a bank privatization programme.

Weights and Measures. The metric system is in use.

ENERGY AND NATURAL RESOURCES

Electricity. Production (1986) 479m. kwh. Supply 127 and 220 volts; 50 Hz.

Oil. The oil refinery at Toamasina has a capacity of 12,000 bbls a day.

Minerals. Mining production in 1989 included: Graphite, 15,865 tonnes; chromite, 165,397 tonnes; zircon, 220 kg; beryl (industrial), 30,434 kg; mica, 1,182 kg; gold, 61 grammes; industrial garnet, 407 kg.

Agriculture. 80–85% of the workforce is employed in agriculture. The principal agricultural products in 1988 were (in 1,000 tonnes): Rice, 2,380; cassava, 2,277; mangoes, 180; bananas, 217; potatoes, 271; sugar-cane, 1,990; maize, 160; sweet potatoes, 483; coffee, 85; citrus fruits, 81; pineapples, 50; seed cotton, 42; ground-nuts, 30; sisal, 20; tobacco, 9.

Cattle breeding and agriculture are the chief occupations. There were, in 1989, 10,243,000 cattle, 1·4m. pigs, 1,950,000 sheep and goats and 30m. poultry.

Forestry. The forests covered (1989) 14·7m. hectares (about 25% of the land surface) and contain many valuable woods, while gum, resins and plants for tanning, dyeing and medicinal purposes abound. Production (1984) 6·26m. cu. metres.

Fisheries. The fish catch in 1984 was 56,000 tonnes.

INDUSTRY. Industry, hitherto confined mainly to the processing of agricultural products, is now extending to cover other fields.

FOREIGN ECONOMIC RELATIONS

Commerce. Trade in MGFr1m.:

	1984	1985	1986	1987	1988	1989
Imports (c.i.f)	213,531	265,916	238,458	376,792	512,063	545,399
Exports (f.o.b)	192,267	181,630	205,875	348,025	385,080	506,193

Chief exports, in tonnes (and value): Coffee, 1989, 43,105 (MGFr104,080m.); cloves, 1989, 16,449 (MGFr51,408m.); vanilla, 1988, 625 (MGFr58,531m.). In 1985 France took 37% of exports, the USA, 14% and Japan, 11%, while France supplied 33% of imports, the USSR, 9%, Federal Republic of Germany, 6%, Qatar, 6% and the USA, 6%.

Total trade between Madagascar and UK (British Department of Trade returns, in £1,000 sterling):

	1988	1989	1990	1991
Imports to UK	7,154	5,865	5,952	7,707
Exports and re-exports from UK	4,747	3,352	16,093	6,945

Tourism. There were 38,954 tourists in 1989.

COMMUNICATIONS

Roads. In 1986 there were about 50,000 km of roads (10% bitumenized). In 1986 there 42,131 motor vehicles.

Railways. In 1989 there were 883 km of railways, all metre gauge. In 1989, 2·4m. passengers and 528,000m. tonnes of cargo were transported.

Civil Aviation. Air France and Air Madagascar connect Antananarivo (International airport, Ivato) with Paris, Alitalia connects with Rome. Several weekly services operated by Air Madagascar connect the capital with the ports and the chief inland towns. In 1987, 129,736 passengers and 4,734 tonnes of cargo arrived and departed.

Shipping. In 1987, 692,270 tonnes were loaded and 1,261,205 tonnes unloaded at Toamasina, Mahajanga and other ports. In 1980, registered merchant marine was 56 vessels (of more than 100 GRT) with a total of 91,211 GRT.

Telecommunications. There were in 1986, 724 post offices and agencies. There were (1983) 37,100 telephone subscribers, and (1989) 0·8m. radio receivers and 0·15m. television receivers.

Newspapers. In 1985 there were 7 daily newspapers with a total circulation of 68,000.

Cinemas. There were, in 1974, 31 cinemas with a seating capacity of 12,500.

JUSTICE, RELIGION, EDUCATION AND WELFARE

Justice. The Supreme Court and the Court of Appeal are in Antananarivo. In most towns there are Courts of First Instance for civil and commercial cases. For criminal cases there are ordinary criminal courts in most towns.

Religion. In 1989 47% of the population practised the traditional religion; 26% were Roman Catholic, 22% Protestant (mainly belonging to the Fiangonan'i Jesosy Kristy eto Madagaskar) and 1·7% Moslem.

Education. Education is compulsory from 6 to 14 years of age in the primary schools. In 1988-89 there were 1,534,142 pupils and 37,894 teachers in 13,672 primary schools, 257,377 pupils and 11,200 teachers in 1,142 secondary schools and 87,925 students and 4,976 teachers in 366 *lycées*. The University of Madagascar has a main campus at Antananarivo and 5 university centres in the other provincial capitals, with 35,106 students and 884 academic staff in 1987. There are also 4 agricultural schools at Nanisana, Ambatondrazaka, Marovoay and Ivoloina.

Health. In 1980 there were 749 hospitals and dispensaries with 18,485 beds; there were (1985) 1,189 doctors, 100 dentists, 37 pharmacists, 1,638 midwives and 3,323 nursing personnel.

DIPLOMATIC REPRESENTATIVES

Of Madagascar in Great Britain
Ambassador: François de Paul Rabotoson (resides in Paris)

Of Great Britain in Madagascar (Immeuble Ny Havana, Cite de 67 Ha, Antananarivo)
Ambassador: D. O. Amy, OBE.

Of Madagascar in the USA (2374 Massachusetts Ave., NW, Washington, D.C., 20008)
Ambassador: Pierrot J. Rajaonarivelo.

Of the USA in Madagascar (14 rue Rainitovo, Antsahavola, Antananarivo)
Ambassador: Howard K. Walker.

Of Madagascar to the United Nations
Ambassador: Blaise Rabetafika.

Further Reading

Official sources: Publications of the Banque des Donnés de l'Etat include the *Bulletin mensuel de Madagascar* (from 1971); *Situation Économique de Madagascar au 1 Janvier 1988*; *Inventaire Socio-Economique 1976–86* 2 vols; *Recensement Industriel Annuel* (latest 1986). The Government has published an *Annuaire Officiel, 1987–88*.
Brandt, H., *Guide to Madagascar*. Chalfont St Peter, 1988
Brown, M., *Madagascar Rediscovered*. London, 1978
Deschamps, H., *Histoire de Madagascar*. Paris, 4th ed. 1972
Rabetafika, R., *Réforme Fiscal et Révolution Socialiste à Madagascar*. Paris, 1990
Rajoelina, P. and Ramelet, A., *Madagascar, la Grande Ile*. Paris, 1989
Ramahatra, O., *Madagascar: une Economie en Phase d'Ajustement*. Paris, 1989

MALAŴI

Republic of Malaŵi

Capital: Lilongwe
Population: 7·98m. (1987)
GNP per capita: US$180 (1989)

HISTORY. Malaŵi was formerly the Nyasaland (until 1907 British Central Africa) Protectorate, constituted on 15 May 1891.

Nyasaland became a self-governing country on 1 Feb. 1963, and on 6 July 1964 an independent member of the Commonwealth under the name of Malaŵi. It became a republic on 6 July 1966.

AREA AND POPULATION. Malaŵi lies along the southern and western shores of Lake Malaŵi (the third largest lake in Africa), and is otherwise bounded north by Tanzania, south by Mozambique and west by Zambia. Land area (excluding inland water of Lakes Malombe, Chilwa and Chiuta) 36,325 sq. miles, divided into 3 regions and 24 districts, each administered by a District Commissioner.

Lake Malaŵi waters belonging to Malaŵi are 9,250 sq. miles and the whole Lake Malaŵi (including the waters under Mozambique by an agreement made between the two countries in 1950) is 11,650 sq. miles.

Population at census 1987, 7,982,607. Over 90% of the population live in rural areas.

Population of main towns (census 1987) was as follows: Blantyre, 331,588; Lilongwe, 233,973; Mzuzu, 44,238; Zomba, 42,878.

Population of the regions, census 1987 (and census 1977): Northern, 907,121 (648,853); Central, 3,116,038 (2,143,716); Southern, 3,959,448 (2,754,891).

The official languages are Chichewa, spoken by over 50% of the population, and English.

CLIMATE. The tropical climate is marked by a dry season from May to Oct. and a wet season for the remaining months. Rainfall amounts are variable, within the range of 29–100" (725–2,500 mm), and maximum temperatures average 75–89°F (24–32°C), and minimum temperatures 58–67°F (14·4–19·4°C). Lilongwe. Jan. 73°F (22·8°C), July 60°F (15·6°C). Annual rainfall 36" (900 mm). Blantyre. Jan. 75°F (23·9°C), July 63°F (17·2°C). Annual rainfall 45" (1,125 mm). Zomba. Jan. 73°F (22·8°C), July 63°F (17·2°C). Annual rainfall 54" (1,344 mm).

CONSTITUTION AND GOVERNMENT. The President of the republic is also head of Government and of the Malaŵi Congress Party. Malaŵi is a one-party state. Parliament is composed of 120 members: 104 elected for up to 5 years, and 16 nominated by the President.

Life President, External Affairs, Agriculture, Justice, Works: Ngwazi Dr Hastings Kamuzu Banda. (Took office 6 July 1966 and became Life President on 6 July 1971).

The Cabinet in Nov. 1991 was composed as follows:

Without Portfolio, Administrative Secretary of Malaŵi Congress Party: Maxwell Pashane. *Labour:* Wadson B. Deleza. *Health:* Dr H. M. Niaba. *Trade, Industry and Tourism:* Robson W. Chirwa. *Finance:* Louis J. Chimango. *Forestry and Natural Resources:* Stanford Demba. *Transport and Communications:* Dalton S. Katopola. *Education and Culture:* Michael Mlambala. *Local Government:* E. C. Katola Phiri. *Community Services:* Mfunjo Mwanjasi Mwakikunga.

National flag: Three equal horizontal stripes of black, red, green, with a red rising sun on the centre of the black stripe.

DEFENCE. All services form part of the Army and have a strength (1991) 7,250.

Army. The army is organized into 3 infantry battalions and 1 support battalion. Equipment includes scout cars.

Navy. A single patrol craft and some 3 boats operated by about (1991) 100 personnel based at Chilumba on Lake Nyasa.

Air Wing. To support the infantry battalion, the Air Wing has 2 C-47 transports, 1 Do 28D Skyservant and 4 Do 228 light transports, and 2 Puma, 1 Ecureuil, 1 Dauphin, and 1 Alouette III helicopters. An HS 125 jet is used for VIP transport. Personnel (1991), 150.

INTERNATIONAL RELATIONS

Membership. Malawi is a member of the UN, the Commonwealth, the Non-Aligned States, OAU, SADCC and is an ACP state of the EEC.

ECONOMY

Policy. The government operates a 3-year 'rolling' public-sector investment programme, revised annually to take into account changing needs and the expected level of resources available. The greatest part of the development programme is annually financed from external aid, and priority in the use of resources has always been given to providing the counterpart contributions to funds received from external sources. The balance of these local resources is used for financing projects commanding high national priority for which no external funds can be secured.

Budget. Revenue Account receipts and expenditure (in K.1,000) for years ending 31 March:

	1987–88	1988–89	1989–90	1990–91
Revenue	583,382	681,800	941,733	1,066,360
Expenditure	728,834	784,300	1,056,606	1,168,738

Currency. The unit of currency is the *kwacha* (MWK) of 100 *tambala*. From 9 June 1975 the kwacha has been pegged to Special Drawing Rights. In March 1992: £1 sterling = K.4·82, US$1 = K.2·75.

Banking and Finance. In July 1964 the Reserve Bank of Malawi was set up with a capital of K.1m. to be responsible for the issue of currency and the holding of external reserves and to issue treasury bills and local registered stock on behalf of the Government. Since then, the Reserve Bank has fully assumed the responsibilities of a Central Bank.

The National Bank of Malawi has a total of 14 branches in major urban areas and 25 static and 41 mobile agencies in rural areas. The Commercial Bank of Malawi Ltd opened in 1970 and has branches at Limbe, Lilongwe, Mzuzu and Zomba and an agency in Dedza and headquarters at Blantyre. It has 4 permanent and 65 mobile agencies.

In 1972 The Investment Development Bank of Malawi was established in Blantyre. Its resources are derived from domestic and foreign official sources and its objective is to provide medium and long-term credits to private entities considered of importance to the economy.

The Post Office Savings Bank had (1985) 257 offices conducting savings business throughout the country, and the New Building Society has agencies in Limbe, Mzuzu, Zomba, Muloza and Blantyre with its head office in Lilongwe.

Weights and Measures. The metric system became fully operational in 1982.

ENERGY AND NATURAL RESOURCES

Electricity. The Electricity Supply Commission of Malawi is the sole supplier of electrical power and energy and the demand and supply of electricity and power on the inter-connected system was met from the hydro-electric generator sets installed at Tedzani Falls and Nkula Falls stations which together have a total capacity of 124 mw as at 1984. The inter-connected system extends from the Shire River hydro stations and covers most areas of the Southern and Central Regions, and part of the Northern Region. Production (1986) 466m. kwh. Supply 230 volts; 50 Hz.

Thermal plant of 23·8 mw capacity is available on the inter-connected system and there are stations at Blantyre, Lilongwe, Mtunthama, Kasungu, and Mzuzu. The capacity of the isolated station at Karonga was increased to 480 kw with the installation of 120 kw diesel generator set.

Minerals. The main product in 1976 was marble (149,254 tonnes) for the manufacture of cement. Coal mining began in 1985.

Agriculture. Malaŵi is predominantly an agricultural country. In 1983 agriculture contributed about 43% to the GDP, and agricultural produce accounted for 90% of total exports. Maize is the main subsistence crop and is grown by over 95% of all smallholders; production (1990) 1,343,000 tonnes. Tea cultivation is of growing importance; in 1990, 20,000 tonnes were produced. Almost all the surplus crops produced by smallholders are sold to the Agricultural Development and Marketing Corporation. Production (1990): Tobacco, 91,000 tonnes; sugar-cane, 1·8m. tonnes.

Livestock in 1990: Cattle, 1·1m.; sheep, 0·22m.; goats, 1m.; pigs, 0·27m.

Forestry. There were (1989) 4·3m. ha of forests; 46% of the land area. In 1983–84, 11,108 cu. metres of sawn timber were removed.

Fisheries. Landings in 1987 were 88,400 tonnes.

INDUSTRY. Index of manufacturing output in 1987 (1984 = 100): manufacturing for domestic consumption, excluding mining and quarrying, 290·8; of this consumer goods were at 109 and intermediate goods for building and construction were at 99·9. Manufacturing for export, 97·4.

FOREIGN ECONOMIC RELATIONS

Commerce. Exports 1987 (in K.1m.): Tobacco, 373·7; tea, 61; sugar, 63·5; pulses, 25·6; groundnuts, 13·2; rice (1985), 3; other crops including manufactures, 41·5.

Trade statistics for calendar years are (in K.1m.):

	1984	1985	1986	1987
Imports	381·5	492·5	480·0	653·9
Exports	446·2	419·6	445·9	602·5

Total trade between Malaŵi and UK (British Department of Trade returns, in £1,000 sterling):

	1988	1989	1990	1991
Imports to UK	30,183	27,890	24,666	25,381
Exports and re-exports from UK	27,618	30,604	33,575	31,462

Tourism. There were 76,134 visitors to Malaŵi in 1987.

COMMUNICATIONS

Roads. In 1988 there were 2,701 km of main road, of which 1,857 km were bitumen surfaced and 410 km gravel; 2,782 km of secondary roads, of which 285 km were surfaced and 239 km gravel; 5,354 km of district roads, of which 24 km were surfaced and 16 km gravel, and 8,008 km of earth roads. In 1987 there were 14,911 cars and 15,643 commercial vehicles.

Railways. Malaŵi Railways (789 km–1,067 mm gauge) operates a main line from Salima to the Mozambique border near Nsanje, from which running powers over the Trans-Zambezia Railway allow access to the port of Beira; a branch opened in 1970 runs eastwards from a point 16 km south of Balaka to the Mozambique border to give a direct route to the deep-water port of Nacala. The 26-km section from Nsanje to the border is operated by the Central Africa Railway Co. Ltd. An extension of 111 km from Salima to the new state capital of Lilongwe was opened in Feb. 1979, and a further extension to Mchinji on the Zambian border (120 km) was completed in 1981. In 1989–90, 70 tonne-km of freight and 115m. passenger-km were carried.

Civil Aviation. In 1983 the Kamuzu International Airport at Lilongwe was inaugurated. It handled (1989-90) 320,505 passengers and 5,646·6 tonnes. In 1989-90 Chileka Airport handled 80,116 passengers and 1,228 tonnes of freight.

Shipping. In 1987–88 lake ships carried 210,103 passengers and 28,983 tonnes of freight.

Telecommunications. Number of telephones (1987) 25,000. The Malaŵi Broadcasting Corporation broadcasts in English and Chichewa. There were 1m. radio sets in 1983.

Newspapers (1989). *The Daily Times* (English, Monday to Friday); 17,000 copies daily. *Malaŵi News* (English and Chichewa, Saturdays); 23,000 copies weekly. *Odini* (English and Chichewa); 8,500 copies fortnightly. *Boma Lathu* (Chichewa); 80,000 copies monthly. *Za Alimi* (English and Chichewa); 10,000 copies monthly.

JUSTICE, RELIGION, EDUCATION AND WELFARE

Justice. Justice is administered in the High Court, the magistrates' courts and traditional courts. There are 23 magistrates' courts, 176 traditional courts and 23 local appeal courts.

Appeals from traditional courts are dealt with in the traditional appeal courts and in the national traditional appeal court. Appeals from magistrates' courts lie to the High Court, and appeals from the High Court to Malaŵi's Supreme Court of Appeal.

Religion. In 1988 the Roman Catholic Church claimed 1·5m. members; Church of Central Africa Presbyterian, 500,000; Diocese of Southern Malaŵi and Lake Malaŵi (part of the Province of Central Africa (the Anglican Communion) (1983), 70,606; Seventh Day Adventist Church (1984), 59,319. Zambezi Evangelical Church (formerly Zambezi Industrial Mission) (1987), 30,000; Assembly of God, 13,740; Seventh Day Baptist (Central Africa Conference) (1987), 4,861; Church of Christ, 60,000; African Evangelical Church (1983), 6,000. Moslems were estimated to number about 500,000 in 1983.

Education In 1986–87 the number of pupils in primary schools was 1,022,765; in secondary schools, 25,681. There were 25,013 teachers in primary schools and 1,229 in secondary schools. The primary school course is of 8 years' duration, followed by a 4-year secondary course. English is taught from the 1st year and becomes the general medium of instruction from the 4th year. There were 1,802 students in teacher training schools and 777 in government technical schools.

The University of Malaŵi was inaugurated in 1965. In 1988–89 there were 2,323 students taking degree and diploma courses.

Health. In 1989 there were two central hospitals, one general hospital, one mental hospital, two leprosaria and 45 hospitals of which 21 were government district hospitals. In 1986 there were 7,081 hospital beds of which 1,612 were for maternity.

DIPLOMATIC REPRESENTATIVES

Of Malaŵi in Great Britain (33 Grosvenor St., London, W1X 0DE)
High Commissioner: Tony Kandiero.

Of Great Britain in Malaŵi (Lingadzi Hse., Lilongwe, 3)
High Commissioner: W. N. Wenban-Smith, CMG.

Of Malaŵi in the USA (2408 Massachusetts Ave., NW, Washington, D.C., 20008)
Ambassador: Robert Mbaya.

Of the USA in Malaŵi (PO Box 30016, Lilongwe, 3)
Ambassador: George A. Trail III.

Of Malaŵi to the United Nations
Ambassador: Robert Mbaya.

Further Reading

General Information: The Chief Information Officer, PO Box 494, Blantyre.
Boeder, R. B., *Malaŵi.* [Bibliography] Oxford and Santa Barbara, 1980

MALAYSIA

Federation of Malaysia

Capital: Kuala Lumpur
Population: 17·81m. (1990)
GNP per capita: US$2,130 (1989)

HISTORY. On 16 Sept. 1963 Malaysia came into being, consisting of the Federation of Malaya, the State of Singapore and the colonies of North Borneo (renamed Sabah) and Sarawak. The agreement between the UK and the 4 territories was signed on 9 July (Cmnd. 2094); by it, the UK relinquished sovereignty over Singapore, North Borneo and Sarawak from independence day and extended the 1957 defence agreement with Malaya to apply to Malaysia. Malaysia became automatically a member of the Commonwealth of Nations. *See* map in THE STATESMAN'S YEAR-BOOK, 1964–65.

On 9 Aug. 1965, by a mutual agreement dated 7 Aug. 1965 between Malaysia and Singapore, Singapore seceded from Malaysia to become an independent Sovereign nation.

AREA AND POPULATION. The federal state of Malaysia comprises the 11 states and 1 federal territory of Peninsular Malaysia on the Malay Peninsula, bounded in the north by Thailand, and with the island of Singapore as an enclave on its southern tip; and, on the island of Borneo to the east, the state of Sabah (which includes the federal territory of the island of Labuan), and the state of Sarawak, with Brunei as an enclave, both bounded in the south by Indonesia and in the north-west and north-east by the South China and Sulu Seas.

The area of Malaysia is 329,758 sq. km (127,317 sq. miles) and the population (1990 estimate) is 17,812,000. The growth of Census population has been:

Year	Peninsular Malaysia	Sarawak	Sabah/Labuan	Total Malaysia
1970	8,809,557	975,918	655,295	10,440,770
1980	11,426,613	1,307,582	1,011,046	13,745,241

The areas, populations and chief towns of the states and federal territories are:

State	Sq. km	Census 1980 [1]	Capital	Census 1980
Johor	18,985	1,638,229	Johor Baharu	249,880
Kedah	9,425	1,116,140	Alor Setar	71,682
Kelantan	14,931	893,753	Kota Baharu	170,559
Kuala Lumpur [2]	243	977,102	Kuala Lumpur	937,875
Melaka	1,658	464,754	Melaka	88,073
Negeri Sembilan	6,646	573,578	Seremban	136,252
Pahang	35,960	798,782	Kuantan	136,625
Perak	21,005	1,805,198	Ipoh	300,727
Perlis	795	148,276	Kangar	12,956
Pinang	1,033	954,638	Pinang (Georgetown)	250,578
Selangor	7,956	1,515,536	Shah Alam	24,138
Terengganu	12,955	540,627	Kuala Terengganu	186,608
Peninsular Malaysia	131,592	11,426,613		
Labuan [2]	98	26,413	Victoria	...
Sabah	73,613	984,633	Kota Kinabalu	55,997
Sarawak	124,449	1,307,582	Kuching	74,229
East Malaysia	198,160	2,318,628		

[1] Revised figures   [2] Federal Territories.

Other large cities (1980 Census): Petaling Jaya (207,805), Kelang (192,080), Taiping (146,002), Sibu (85,231), Sandakan (70,420) and Miri (52,125).

Vital statistics (1989): Crude birth rate, 29·8 per 1,000 population; crude death rate 4; infant mortality rate 13·87 per 1,000 live births; natural increase, 24·7 per 1,000. Life expectancy in 1989: Males, 68·8 years; females, 73·3.

Of the total population in 1980, 47% were Malay, 32% Chinese, 8% Indian and 13% others.

Over 58% speak Bahasa Malaysia, the official language, 9% Chinese, 4% Tamil and 3% Iban.

CLIMATE. Malaysia is affected by the monsoon climate. The N.E. monsoon prevails from Oct. to Feb., bringing rain to the east coast of the peninsula. The S.W. monsoon lasts from mid-May to Sept. and affects the opposite coastline the most. Temperatures are uniform throughout the year. Kuala Lumpur. Jan. 81°F (27·2°C), July 81°F (27·2°C). Annual rainfall 97·6" (2,441 mm). Penang. Jan. 82°F (27·8°C), July 82°F (27·8°C). Annual rainfall 109·4" (2,736 mm).

CONSTITUTION AND GOVERNMENT. The Constitution of Malaysia is based on the Constitution of the former Federation of Malaya, but includes safeguards for the special interests of Sabah and Sarawak. It was amended in 1983.

The federal capital is Kuala Lumpur, established on 1 Feb. 1974 with an area of approximately 94 sq. miles. The official language is Bahasa Malaysia.

The Constitution provides for one of the 9 Rulers of the Malay States to be elected from among themselves to be the *Yang di-Pertuan Agong* (Supreme Head of the Federation). He holds office for a period of 5 years. The Rulers also elect from among themselves a Deputy Supreme Head of State, also for a period of 5 years.

Supreme Head of State (Yang di-Pertuan Agong): HM Sultan Azlan Shah Muhibbuddin Shah ibni Almarhum Sultan Yussuf Izzuddin Ghafarullahu-lahu Shah, DK, DMN, PMN, SPCM, SPMP, elected as 9th *Yang di-Pertuan Agong* from 2 March 1989, succeeded 26 April 1989 and installed 18 Sept. 1989.

Raja of Perlis: HRH Tuanku Syed Putra ibni Al-Marhum Syed Hassan Jamalullail, DK, DKM, DMN, SMN, SPMP, SPDK, acceded 12 March 1949.

Sultan of Kedah: HRH Tuanku Haji Abdul Halim Mu'adzam Shah ibni Al-Marhum Sultan Badlishah, DK, DKH, DKM, DMN, DUK, SPMK, SSDK, acceded 20 Feb. 1959.

Sultan of Johor: HRH Sultan Mahmood Iskandar ibni Al-Marhum Sultan Ismail, DK, SPMJ, SPDK, DK (Brunei), SSIJ, PIS, BSI, acceded 11 May 1981 (Supreme Head of State from 26 April 1984 to 25 April 1989), returned as Sultan of Johor 26 April 1989.

Sultan of Selangor: HRH Sultan Salahuddin Abdul Aziz Shah ibni Al-Marhum Sultan Hisamuddin 'Alam Shah Al-Haj, DK, DMN, SPMS, SPDK, acceded 3 Sept. 1960.

Regent of Perak: HRH Raja Nazrin, appointed April 1989.

Yang di-Pertuan Besar of Negeri Sembilan: HRH Tuanku Ja'afar ibni Al-Marhum Tuanku Abdul Rahman, DMN, DK, acceded 8 April 1968.

Sultan of Kelantan: HRH Sultan Ismail Petra ibni Al-Marhum Sultan Yahya Petra, DK, SPMK, SJMK, SPSM, appointed 29 March 1979.

Sultan of Trengganu: HRH Sultan Mahmud Al-Marhum ibni Al-Marhum Tuanku Al-Sultan Ismail Nasiruddin Shah, DK, SPMT, SPCM, appointed 2 Sept. 1979.

Sultan of Pahang: Sultan Haji Ahmad Shah Al-Musta'in Billah ibni Al-Marhum Sultan Abu Bakar Ri'Ayatuddin Al-Mu'Adzam Shah, DKM, DKP, DK, SSAP, SPCM, SPMJ.

Yang di-Pertua Negeri Paau Pinang: HE Tun Haji Hamdan Sheikh Tahir, appointed 2 May 1989.

Yang di Pertua Negeri Melaka: HE Tun Datuk Seri Utama Syed Ahmad Al-Haj bin Syed Mahmud Shahabudin, SSM, PSM, DUNM, SPMK, SSDK, PGDK, PNBS, JMN, JP, appointed 4 Dec. 1984.

Yang di-Pertua Negeri Sarawak: HE Datuk Patinggi Haji Ahmad Zaidi Adruce bin Muhammed Noor, SSM, DP, DUNM, PNBS, BM Adipradana (Indonesia) appointed 2 April 1985.

Yang di-Pertua Negeri Sabah: HE Tan Sri Datuk Haji Mohd Said bin Keruak, PMN, SPDK, appointed 31 Dec. 1986.

Parliament consists of the *Yang di-Pertuan Agong* and two *Majlis* (Houses of Parliament) known as the *Dewan Negara* (Senate) of 69 members and *Dewan Rakyat* (House of Representatives) of 180 members, allocated by state as follows: Perlis, 2; Kedah, 14; Kalantan, 13; Terengganu, 9; Penang, 11; Perak, 23; Pahang, 10; Selangor, 14; Kuala Lumpur Federal Territory, 7; Negri Sembilan, 7; Melaka, 5; Johor, 18; Labuan Federal Territory, 1; Sabah, 20; Sarawak, 27. Appointment to the Senate is for 3 years. The maximum life of the House of Representatives is 5 years, subject to its dissolution at any time by the *Yang di-Pertuan Agong* on the advice of his Ministers.

National flag: Fourteen horizontal stripes of red and white, with a blue quarter bearing a crescent and a star of 14 points, all in gold.

National Anthem: Negara-Ku ('My Country').

Elections to the House of Representatives were held on 21 Oct. 1990. In Sept. 1991 the allocation of seats by party was: National Front coalition, 132 (consisting of United Malays National Organization, 73; the Sarawak parties, 25; Malaysian Chinese Association, 18; Malaysian Indian Congress, 6; Sabah parties, 6; Gerakan, 4); opposition, 48 (consisting of Democratic Action Party, 20; Parti Bersatu Sabah, 14; Islam Party, 7; Spirit of 1946 Party, 7).

The Cabinet formed on 15 March 1991 consisted of:

Prime Minister and Minister for Home Affairs: Dato Seri Dr Mahathir Mohamad.

Deputy Prime Minister and Minister for Rural Development: Abdul Ghafar Baba. *Transport:* Dato Seri Dr Ling Liong Sik. *Energy, Telecommunications and Posts:* Dato Seri S. Samy Vellu. *Primary Industries:* Dato Seri Dr Lim Keng Yaik. *Works:* Dato Leo Moggie Anak Irok. *International Trade and Industry:* Dato Seri Rafidah Aziz. *Domestic Trade and Consumer Affairs:* Dato Haji Abu Hassan bin Haji Omar. *Agriculture:* Datuk Seri Sanusi bin Haji Junid. *Education:* Dato Dr Haji Sulaiman bin Haji Daud. *Foreign Affairs:* Dato Abdullah bin Haji Ahmad Badawi. *Finance:* Dato Seri Anwar bin Ibrahim. *Health:* Dato Lee Kim Sai. *Defence:* Dato Seri Haji Mohd Najib bin Tun Haji Abdul Razak. *Information:* Dato Mohamed bin Rahmat. *Culture, Arts and Tourism:* Dato Sabbaruddin bin Chik. *National Unity and Community Development:* Dato Napsiah binti Omar. *Public Enterprises:* Dato Dr Mohamad Yusof bin Haji Mohamad Nor. *Human Resources:* Dato Lim Ah Lek. *Science, Technology and Environment:* Law Hieng Ding. *Housing and Local Government:* Dr Ting Chew Peh. *Land and Co-operative Development:* Tan Sri Datuk Haji Sakaran bin Dandai. *Justice:* Syed Hamid bin Syed Jaafar Albar. *Minister in the Prime Minister's Department, Youth and Sports:* Haji Annuar bin Musa. *Minister in the Prime Minister's Department:* Datuk Abang Abu Bakar bin Datu Bandar Abang Haji Mustapha.

DEFENCE. The Malaysian Constitution provides for the *Yang di-Pertuan Agong* (Supreme Head of State) to be the Supreme Commander of the Armed Forces who exercises his powers and authority in accordance with the advice of the Cabinet. Under the general authority of the Yang di-Pertuan Agong and the Cabinet, there is the Armed Forces Council which is responsible for the command, discipline and administration of all other matters relating to the Armed Forces, other than those relating to their operational use.

The Armed Forces Council is chaired by the Minister of Defence and its membership consists of the chief of the Defence Forces, the 3 Service Chiefs and 2 other senior military officers, the Secretary-General of the Ministry of Defence, a representative of State Rulers and an appointed member.

The chief of the Armed Forces Staff is the professional head of the Armed Forces and the senior military member in the Armed Forces Council. He is the principal adviser to the Minister of Defence on the military aspects of all defence matters. The chief of the Armed Forces Staff's committee, established under the authority of the Armed Forces Council, is the highest level at which joint planning and coordination with the Armed Forces are carried out. The Committee is chaired by the chief of the Armed Forces Staff and its membership consists of the chief of the Army, Navy and Air Force, the chief of Personnel Staff, the chief of logistic Staff and the chief of Staff of the Ministry of Defence.

Malaysia is a member of the Five Powers Defence Arrangement with Australia, New Zealand, Singapore and the UK.

Army. The Army is organized into 4 divisions, comprising 9 infantry brigades made up of 36 infantry battalions; 4 armoured, 5 field artillery, 5 engineer and 5 signals regiments and 2 anti-aircraft battalions. There is also a special service regiment. Equipment includes 26 Scorpion light tanks. Strength (1992) about 97,000, with as reserves the Malaysian Territorial Army and the regular reservists who have completed their full-time service (38,000).

Navy. The Royal Malaysian Navy is commanded by the Chief of the Navy from the integrated Ministry of Defence in Kuala Lumpur. Main bases are at Lumut, and on Labuan Island which are also the headquarters for the Malay Peninsula and Borneo operational areas respectively. The peace-time tasks include fishery protection and anti-piracy patrols.

The combatants include 2 German-built and 2 British-built frigates all with helicopter platforms, 8 fast missile craft, 2 offshore and 27 inshore patrol craft. There are also 4 Italian-type offshore mine countermeasure vessels and 2 tank landing ships normally employed in support of patrol and missile craft. Auxiliaries include 2 multi-purpose support ships, 1 survey ship, 1 diving support ship and 33 amphibious craft.

A Naval aviation squadron was formed in 1988 and operates 6 ex-British Wasp helicopters. Navy personnel in 1991 totalled 10,500 and 2,000 reserves.

Paramilitary maritime forces include 50 armed patrol launches, 48 operated by the Royal Malaysian Police and 2 by the Government of Sabah which also operates 4 other patrol boats, 1 landing craft and a yacht.

Air Force. Formed on 1 June 1958, the Royal Malaysian Air Force is equipped primarily to provide air defence and air support for the Army, Navy and Police. Its secondary rôle is to render assistance to Government departments and civilian organizations. There are 13 squadrons, of which 9 operate transport aircraft and helicopters. Some 35 A-4 Skyhawks equip 2 squadrons. Other equipment includes 14 F-5E Tiger II jet fighterbombers, 2 RF-5E reconnaissance-fighters, and 3 F-5F trainers, 1 F.28 Fellowship and 1 Falcon 900 VIP transports, 8 C-130 Hercules four-engined transport and patrol aircraft, 12 Caribou twin-engined STOL transports, 2 HU-16 amphibians, 33 Sikorsky S-61A-4 Nuri heavy troop and cargo transport helicopters, 20 Alouette III, and 6 Bell 47 helicopters, 10 Cessna 402Bs for twin-engine training and liaison, 42 PC-7 Turbo-Trainers, 11 MB.339 jet trainers, 2 H.S. 125 Merpati twin-jet executive transports and 1 Super Puma VIP transport helicopter. Personnel (1992) totalled about 12,400, with 67 combat aircraft.

Volunteer Forces. The Army Volunteer Force (Territorial Army) consists of first-line infantry, signals, engineer and logistics units able to take the field with the active army, and a second-line organization to provide local defence. There is also a small Naval Volunteer Reserve with Headquarters in Penang and Kuala Lumpur. The Royal Malaysian Air Force Volunteer Reserve has both air and ground elements.

INTERNATIONAL RELATIONS

Membership. Malaysia is a member of the UN, the Commonwealth, Non-Aligned movement, the Colombo Plan, Organization of Islamic Conference and ASEAN.

ECONOMY

Policy. The fifth 5-year Malaysia Plan, 1986–90, envisaged an expenditure of M$74,000m. and aimed the development of manufacturing industries, revitalization of agriculture and improvement of productivity. The Second Outline Perspective Plan of 1991 set targets for the coming decade to be implemented by the New

Development Policy. The sixth Malaysia Plan is the first of 2 5-year programmes under the Policy. It envisages public spending of M$104,000m.: M$55,000m. on federal improvements to communications, education, health and defence, and M$49,000m. by state and local authorities. There are privatization programmes involving telecommunications, railways, airports, electricity and shipping.

Budget. Revenue and expenditure for calendar years, in M$1m.:

	1987	1988	1989	1990	1991 [1]
Revenue	24,366	28,730	31,966	34,061	37,064
Operating expenditure	23,187	25,116	26,989	29,017	32,097

[1] Estimate

Sources of revenue in 1991: Income taxes, 28%; non-tax revenue and other taxes, 23·8%; borrowing and use of government assets, 21·3%; other indirect taxes, 13·4%; import duties, 8·3%; export duties, 5·2%. Expenditure: Emoluments, 25·6%; debt service charges, 19%; economic services, 11·8%; supply and services, 9%; social services, 5·4%; defence, 4·5%; pensions, 4·4%; grants to state governments, 3·4%; other, 17%.

The 1991 budget abolished export and import taxes on rubber, tin and pepper, reduced corporate taxes from 40% to 35%, and reduced income tax by 1–5%.

Currency. Bank Negara Malaysia (Central Bank of Malaysia) assumed sole currency issuing authority in Malaysia on 12 June 1967. The unit of currency is the Malaysian *ringgit* (MYR) of 100 *sen*. Currency notes are of denominations of M$1, 5, 10, 20, 50, 100, 500 and 1,000. Coins are of denominations of 1 *sen*, 5, 10, 20, 50 *sen* and M$1, 5 and 100. Total amount of currency in circulation at 30 June 1988, M$7,497m. Inflation was 6·7% in 1990 (5·5% in 1989). In March 1992 £1 = M$4·53; US$1 = M$2·58.

Banking and Finance. 38 commercial banks were operating at 31 Dec. 1988; of these 22 were incorporated locally, with 911 banking offices. Total deposits with commercial banks at 30 Aug. 1990 were M$79,373m. There were 12 merchant banks at 31 Dec. 1988. Their total income was M$157m. in 1988. The Islamic Bank of Malaysia began operations in July 1983. The National Savings Bank (formerly known as the post office savings bank) held M$973·8m. due to 3,600,948 depositors at 31 Dec. 1978.

There were 47 finance companies with 486 offices in 1988.

There is a stock exchange at Kuala Lumpur.

Weights and Measures. The metric system is standard, but British imperial units are still in residual use.

ENERGY AND NATURAL RESOURCES

Oil. Production (1991) 30·91m. tonnes.

Gas. Natural gas reserves, 1987, 1,400,000m. cu. metres. Production of liquefied natural gas in 1990 was 6·61m. tonnes.

Minerals. In 1990 mining contributed 9·8% of GDP. Production (1986, in 1,000 tonnes): Bauxite, 566; iron ore, 208; copper, 115; tin, 29. Tin production was at 29,000 tonnes in 1990.

Agriculture. In 1990 agriculture contributed 19·4% of GDP. Production (1990): Fruit, 722,485 tonnes (of which pineapples, 167,900 tonnes); tobacco, 97,900 cocoa, 270,000 tonnes; rubber, 1,350,000 tonnes from 1,819,300 ha.; palm oil, 6,550,000 tonnes from 2,011,000 ha.

Livestock (1988): Cattle, 625,000, buffaloes, 220,000; sheep, 99,000; pigs, 2,258,000; goats, 347,000.

Forestry. In 1990 there were 19·6m. ha of forests. The total output of saw logs was 40m. cu. metres; sawn timber (1988), 6·6m. cu. metres.

Fisheries. Total landings of marine fish, 1990, 907,300 tonnes.

INDUSTRY. In 1990 manufacturing contributed 26·6% of GDP.

Labour. 1990: 6,603,400 were employed: 1,995,700 in agriculture, forestry and fishing; 1,159,300 in manufacturing; 850,200 in government services; 1,646,100 in other services; 39,100 in mining and quarrying; 424,200 in construction; 231,300 in finance, insurance, business services and real estate; 278,100 in transport, storage and communication. Unemployment was 7·1%.

Trade Unions. Membership was 617,000 in 1988, of which the Malaysian Trades Union Congress, an umbrella organization of 138 unions, accounted for 0·5m.

FOREIGN ECONOMIC RELATIONS. Privatization policy permits foreign investment of 25–30% generally; total foreign ownership is permitted of export-oriented projects.

Commerce. In 1990 exports totalled M$79,548m. and imports M$79,122m.

Chief imports: Machinery and transport equipment, M$26,352m.; manufactured goods, M$9,278m.; food, beverages and tobacco M$4,763m.; crude petroleum and related products, M$2,405m.

Chief exports (1990): Manufactured goods (M$36,592m.); crude petroleum (M$10,190m.); palm oil (M$4,312m.); rubber (M$3,128m.); saw logs (M$4,200m.); tin, M$800; liquefied natural gas, M$2,427; cocoa, M$451m.

In 1988 imports (in M$1m.) came chiefly from Japan (10,170); USA (7,669) and Singapore (5,730). Exports went chiefly to Singapore (10,697), USA (9,611) and Japan (9,395).

Total trade of Malaysia with UK (British Department of Trade returns, in £1,000 sterling):

	1988	1989	1990	1991
Imports to UK	525,017	676,258	775,667	930,036
Exports and re-exports from UK	310,462	441,762	601,909	582,239

Tourism. 7·4m. tourists visited Malaysia in 1990.

COMMUNICATIONS

Civil Aviation. In 1990 there were 4 international airports and 15 other aerodromes at which regular public air transport was operated. About 20 international airlines operate through Kuala Lumpur. Malaysia Airlines, the national airline, operates domestic flights within Peninsular Malaysia as well as between Kuala Lumpur and Sabah and Sarawak, and flies to international destinations in Asia, Australia, Europe and the USA. In 1987 there were 204,155 landings and take-offs, carrying 5,445,610 passengers.

Shipping. The major ports are Port Kelang, Labuan, Pulau Pinang, Pasir Gudang, Kuantan, Kota Kinabalu, Sandakan, Kuching, Sibu and Bintulu. The Malaysian International Shipping Corporation operates a fleet of vessels.

Telecommunications. Postal services are under the Ministry of Energy, Telecommunications and Post and are headed by a Director-General. There were 1,579,634 telephone and 8,115 telex subscribers in 1990. As at 31 Dec. 1986, 525 post offices, 1,586 postal agencies, 236 mobile post offices and 1 riverine postal office were operating.

In 1987, 378,314 radio licences and 1,658,566 television licences were issued. The government-controlled Radio Television Malaysia broadcasts radio and TV programmes in Peninsular Malaysia, Sabah and Sarawak. System TV Malaysia Berhad transmits from Kuala Lumpur, TV Malaysia Sabah and Sarawak to east Malaysia. (Colour by PAL). In 1990 there were 7·1m. radio and 2m. TV sets.

Newspapers. Papers are published in Malay, English, Chinese and Tamil The national news agency Bernama has the sole right to receive and distribute news.

JUSTICE, RELIGION, EDUCATION AND WELFARE

Justice. By virtue of Art. 121(1) of the Federal Constitution judicial power in the Federation is vested on 2 High Courts of co-ordinate jurisdiction and status namely the High Court of Malaya and the High Court of Borneo, and the inferior courts. The Federal Court with its principal registry in Kuala Lumpur is the Supreme Court in the country.

The Lord President as the supreme head of the Judiciary, the 2 Chief Justices of the High Courts and 6 other Judges form the constitution of the Federal Court. Apart from having exclusive jurisdiction to determine appeals from the High Court the Federal Court is also conferred with such original and consultative jurisdiction as is laid out in Articles 128 and 130 of the Constitution.

A panel of 3 Judges or such greater uneven number as may be determined by the Lord President preside in every proceeding in the Federal Court.

The right of appeal to the Yang di-Pertuan Agong (who in turn refers the appeal to the Judicial Committee of the British Privy Council) from a decision of the Federal Court in respect of criminal and constitutional matters was abolished on 1 July 1978.

Religion. Islam is the official religion but there is freedom of worship.

Education. In 1989 there were 2,390,000 pupils enrolled in primary schools with 111,729 teachers and 1,353,000 in lower and 53,476 in upper secondary schools with 66,937 teachers. There were 53,476 university students.

Health. In 1990 there were 6,577 private and government doctors, (1986) 1,130 dentists, 12,721 government nurses, 102 hospitals and 2,681 government clinics.

Social Security. The Employment Injury Insurance Scheme provides medical and cash benefits and the Invalidity Pension Scheme provides protection to employees against invalidity due to disease or injury from any cause. Other supplementary measures are the Employees' Provident Fund, the pension scheme for government employees, free medical benefits for all who are unable to pay and the provision of medical benefits particularly for workers under the Labour Code.

DIPLOMATIC REPRESENTATIVES

Of Malaysia in Great Britain (45 Belgrave Sq., London, SW1X 8QT)
High Commissioner: Tan Sri Dato Wan Sidek bin Haji Abdul Rahman.

Of Great Britain in Malaysia (185, Jalan Semantan, Ampang, Kuala Lumpur)
High Commissioner: Duncan Slater, CMG.

Of Malaysia in the USA (2401 Massachusetts Ave., NW, Washington, D.C., 20008)
Ambassador: A. R. Ahmad Fuzi.

Of the USA in Malaysia (376 Jalan Tun Razak, Kuala Lumpur)
Ambassador: Paul M. Cleveland.

Of Malaysia to the United Nations
Ambassador: Razali Ismail.

Further Reading

Statistical Information: The Department of Statistics, Malaysia, Kuala Lumpur, was set up in 1963, taking over from the Department of Statistics, States of Malaya. *Chief Statistician:* Khoo Teik Huat. Main publications: *Peninsular Malaysia Monthly* and *Annual Statistics of External Trade; Malaysia External Trade* (quarterly); *Peninsular Malaysia Statistical Bulletin* (monthly); *Rubber Statistics* (monthly); *Rubber Statistics Handbook* (annual); *Oil Palm Statistics* (monthly); *Oil Palm, Coconut and Tea Statistics* (annual). *Malaysia 1985,* The Department of Information, Kuala Lumpur, 1986

Anand, S., *Inequality and Poverty in Malaysia.* OUP, 1983
Brown, I. and Ampalavanar, R., *Malaysia.* [Bibliography] Oxford and Santa Barbara, 1986
Gullick, J., *Malaysia: Economic Expansion and National Unity.* Boulder and London, 1982
Jomo, K. S., *Growth and Structural Change in the Malaysian Economy.* London, 1990
King, V. T. and Parnwell, M. J. (eds), *Margins and Minorities: the Peripheral Areas and People of Malysia.* Hull Univ. Press, 1990
Means, G. P., *Malaysian Politics: the Second Generation.* OUP, 1991
Snodgrass, D. R., *Inequality and Economic Development in Malaysia.* OUP, 1982
Zakaria, A., *Government and Politics in Malaysia.* OUP, 1987

PENINSULAR MALAYSIA

AREA AND POPULATION. The total area of Peninsular Malaysia is about 50,810 sq. miles (131,598 sq. km). Population (1990 estimate) 14,667,000. The federal capital is Kuala Lumpur (244 sq. km).

CONSTITUTION AND GOVERNMENT. The States of the Federation of Malaya, now known as Peninsular Malaysia, comprises the 11 States of Johor, Pahang, Negeri Sembilan, Selangor, Perak, Kedah, Perlis, Kelantan, Trengganu, Penang and Melaka.

For earlier history of the States and Settlements *see* THE STATESMAN'S YEAR-BOOK, 1957, p. 241.

The Constitution is based on the agreements reached at the London conference of Jan.-Feb. 1956, between HM Government in the UK, the Rulers of the Malay states and the Alliance Party (which at the first federal elections on 27 July 1955 obtained 51 of the 52 elected members), and subsequently worked out by the Constitutional Commission appointed after that conference.

ECONOMY

Budget. *See* p. 919.

ENERGY AND NATURAL RESOURCES

Electricity. In 1987, 16,287m. kwh. were generated. Supply 240 volts; 50 Hz.

Oil. Production (1987) 23·6m. tonnes of crude oil.

Minerals. Production (in tonnes): Tin-in-concentrates: 1986, 29,134; 1987, 30,388. Iron ore: 1986, 207,963; 1987, 161,287. Bauxite: 1986, 566,170; 1987, 482,125. Copper: 1986, 115,304; 1987, 122,206. Gold: 1986, 2,221 troy oz.; 1987, 2,716.

Agriculture. Production in 1986 (in tonnes): Rice (1985), 1,122,400 from (1986) 627,000 ha; rubber, 1·54m.; palm oil, 4·54m.; palm kernels, 1·34m.; cocoa, 102,000; coconuts, 33,900; (the following all 1985) copra, 216,000; vegetables, 481,000; fruit, 898,000; sugar-cane, 1·2m.; tea, 4,000; cassava, 370,000; sweet potatoes, 50,000; roots and tubers, 505,000; maize, 24,000.

Forestry (1984). Reserved forests, 4·7m. ha. Production of logs (1986), 30m. cu. metres; sawn timber, 5·15m. cu. metres; plywood (1984), 630,000 cu. metres.

Fisheries. Landings in 1983 493,117 tonnes. Fishermen (1985) 87,000; 70% off-shore.

INDUSTRY AND TRADE

Trade Unions. There were, in 1987, 311 trade unions with 560,800 members in Peninsular Malaysia.

Tourism. In 1987 there were 3,285,166 tourists.

COMMUNICATIONS

Roads. In 1986 the Public Works Department maintained 39,915 km of roads. In 1985 the 8-mile road bridge between the mainland and Penang island opened.

In 1987, 4,591,472 motor vehicles were registered, including 1,475,760 private cars, 22,134 buses, 316,846 lorries and vans, 2,611,584 motor cycles.

Railways. The Malayan Railway main line runs from Singapore to Butterworth opposite Penang Island. From Bukit Mertajam 8 miles south of Butterworth a branch line connects Peninsular Malaysia with the State Railways of Thailand at the frontier station of Padang Besar. Other branch lines connect the main line with Port of Klang, Teluk Anson, Port Dickson and Ampang. The east-coast line, branching off the main line at Gemas, runs for over 300 miles to Tumpat, Kelantan's northern-most coastal town; a 13-mile branch line linking Pasir Mas with Sungei Golok makes a second connexion with Thailand.

In 1990 there were 1,672 km (metre gauge) which carried 8,019m. passenger-km and 4m. tonnes of freight.

Civil Aviation (1985). International air services are operated into Kuala Lumpur, Johor and Penang airports. The national carrier, Malaysian Airlines System (MAS), began operation on 1 Oct. 1972 to provide both domestic and international services.

Civil aviation statistics for airports in Peninsular Malaysia (1984): Aircraft movements, 97,890; terminal passengers, 6,078,273; freight, 80,232 tonnes; mail, 7,163 tonnes.

Shipping. The major ports of Peninsular Malaysia are Port Kelang, Penang, Johor and Kuantan. In 1984 Port Kelang handled 12,357,262 tonnes of cargo valued at M$16,318·4m., of which imports totalled 7,744,789 tonnes (M$9,532·9m.) and exports 4,612,473 tonnes (M$6,785·5m.). A total of 4,630 ships, GRT 35m. tonnes, called in 1984. In 1984 the Port of Penang handled 7,960,506 tonnes of cargo, of which 5,220,550 tonnes were imports and 2,739,956 tonnes exports. The total cargo handled in all ports during 1984 was 31,986,000 tonnes.

JUSTICE, RELIGION, EDUCATION AND WELFARE

Justice. Unlike the Federal Court and the High Court which were established under the Constitution, the subordinate courts in Peninsular Malaysia comprising the sessions court, the Magistrates' court and the Penghulu's court were established under a Federal Law (the subordinate Courts Act, 1948 (Revised 1972)).

All offences other than those punishable with death are tried before a Sessions Court President who is empowered to pass any sentence allowed by law other than the sentence of death. In civil matters, the sessions court has jurisdiction to hear all actions and suits where the amount in dispute does not exceed M$25,000.

A First Class Magistrate's criminal jurisdiction is limited to offences for which the maximum term provided by law does not exceed 10 years' imprisonment and to certain specified offences where the term of imprisonment provided for may be extended to 14 years' imprisonment or which are punishable with fine only.

Juvenile courts established under the Juvenile Courts Act, 1947 for juvenile offenders below the age of 18 are presided over by a First Class Magistrate assisted by 2 advisers. There are 30 penal institutions, including Borstal establishments and an open prison camp.

Religion. More than half the population are Moslems, and Islam is the official religion. In 1970 there were 4,673,670 Moslems, 765,250 Hindus, 220,897 Christians and 2,495,739 Buddhists.

Education. In 1987 there were 6,703 state assisted primary schools with 2,325,462 pupils and 103,983 teachers and in 1980, 208 private primary schools with 5,130 pupils and 224 teachers.

In 1986 there were 1,226 secondary schools with 1,329,399 pupils and 60,863 teachers.

There were (1980): 10 special schools with 1,312 pupils and 104 teachers; 401 classes for further education with 10,281 students and 997 teachers; 25 teacher training colleges with over 12,000 students.

In 1989–90 there were 11 institutions of higher education: Utara Malaysia University; University of Malaya, Kuala Lumpur; University of Kebangsaan, Bangi; International Islamic University; University of Science, Penang; University of Agriculture, Serdang; University of Technology, Kuala Lumpur; Ungku Omar Polytechnic, Ipoh; Kuantan Polytechnic; MARA Institute of Technology, Shah Alam; Tunku Ab. Rahman College, Kuala Lumpur.

Health. In 1989 there were 69 hospitals and 2,180 clinics. In 1983 there were 4,082 doctors, 774 dentists, 13,874 midwives and 17,916 nurses.

Further Reading

Morris, M. W., *Local Government in Peninsular Malaysia*. London, 1980
Winstedt, Sir R., *Malaya and Its History*. 3rd ed. London, 1953.—*The Malays: A Cultural History*. London, 1959

SABAH

HISTORY. The territory now named Sabah, but until Sept. 1963 known as North Borneo, was in 1877-78 ceded by the Sultans of Brunei and Sulu and various other rulers to a British syndicate, which in 1881 was chartered as the British North Borneo (Chartered) Company. The Company's sovereign rights and assets were transferred to the Crown with effect from 15 July 1946. On that date, the island of Labuan (ceded to Britain in 1846 by the Sultan of Brunei) became part of the new Colony of North Borneo. On 16 Sept. 1963 North Borneo joined the new Federation of Malaysia and became the State of Sabah.

AREA AND POPULATION. Area, about 28,460 sq. miles (73,711 sq. km), with a coastline of 973 miles (1,577 km). The interior is mountainous, Mount Kinabalu being 13,455 ft (4,175 metres) high. Population, 1980 census 1,011,046, of whom 838,141 were Pribumis, 163,996 Chinese, 5,613 Indians, 3,296 others. The native population comprises Kadazans (largest and mainly agricultural, Christians since the 16th century), Bajaus and Bruneis (agriculture and fishing), Muruts (hill tribes), Suluks (mainly seafaring) and several smaller tribes (1990 estimate, 1,498,698).

The island of Labuan became Federal territory on 16 April 1984, 35 sq. miles (75 sq. km) in area, lying 6 miles (9·66 km) off the north-west coast of Borneo is a free port.

The principal towns are situated on or near the coast. They include Kota Kinabalu, the capital (formerly Jesselton), 1980 census population, 108,725, Tawau (113,708), Sandakan (113,496), Keningau in the hinterland (41,204), and Kudat (38,397).

CLIMATE. The climate is tropical monsoon, but on the whole is equable, with temperatures around 80°F (26·5°C) throughout the year. Annual rainfall varies, according to locality, from 10" (250 mm) to 148" (3,700 mm). The north-east monsoon lasts from Dec. to April and chiefly affects the east coast, while the south-west monsoon from May to Aug. gives the west coast its wet season.

CONSTITUTION AND GOVERNMENT. The Constitution of the State of Sabah provides for a Head of State, called the *Yang Dipertua Negeri Sabah*. Executive authority is vested in the State Cabinet headed by the Chief Minister.

At the elections of July 1990 the electorate was 0·49m. 253 candidates from 9 parties stood. The Bersatu Sabah Party (Christian) won 36 of the 48 electable seats; the United Sabah National Organization (mainly Moslem) won 12.

Head of State: Tan Seri Mohamad Said Keruak.
Chief Minister: Datuk Joseph Pairin Kitingan.
Deputy Chief Minister: Bernard Dompok.

Flag: Three horizontal stripes of blue, white and red with a large light blue canton bearing an outline of Mount Kinabalu in dark blue.

The Legislative Assembly consists of the Speaker, 48 elected members and not more than 6 nominated members.

The official language is Bahasa Malaysia. English is widely used especially for business.

ECONOMY

Budget. Budgets (not including the Federal Territory of Labuan) for calendar years, in M$1,000:

Ordinary Budget	1986	1987	1988	1989	1990
Revenue	1,099,475	1,411,509	2,037,913	1,743,998	1,691,924
Expenditure	1,017,981	1,061,724	1,715,387	1,740,731	1,996,174
Development Budget					
Revenue	219,067	183,680	333,574	426,665	672,445
Expenditure	206,510	212,710	306,325	409,202	793,318

Banking and Finance. 12 banks were operating in 1990.

The National Savings Bank had (1989) M$45·7m. due to depositors. It also provides additional services to depositors including the granting of loans for housing.

COMMERCE. The main imports are machinery and transport equipment, manufactured goods and food. The main exports are crude oil, saw logs and sawn timber. Statistics for calendar years, in M$1,000:

	1986	1987	1988	1989	1990
Imports	3,432,768	3,604,801	4,127,769	5,344,688	6,614,232
Exports	4,967,423	6,477,242	6,809,728	7,640,191	8,822,601

Tourism. In 1990 68,671 tourists visited Sabah, excluding foreign visitors arriving via Peninsular Malaysia, Sarawak and Labuan.

COMMUNICATIONS

Roads (1990). There were 9,116 km of roads, of which 2,600 km were bitumen surfaced, 5,709 km gravel surfaced and 807 km of earth.

Railways. A metre-gauge railway, 134 km, runs from Kota Kinabalu to Tenom in the interior. It carried 451,200 passengers and 199,000 tonnes of freight in 1990.

Civil Aviation. External communications are provided from the international airport at Kota Kinabalu by Cathay Pacific Airways Ltd to Hong Kong; Malaysian Airways to Hong Kong, Manila, Brunei, Kuching, Singapore, Tokyo, Seoul and Kuala Lumpur; Brunei Airways to Brunei and Kuching and Philippine Airlines to Manila.

The total air traffic handled at Sabah airports during 1990 was 2,981,039 passengers, 26,137 tonnes of freight and 5,080 tonnes of mail.

Shipping (1990). Merchant shipping totalling 22,329,712 NRT used the ports, handling 22,193,831 tonnes of cargo.

Telecommunications. As at 31 Dec. 1990 there were 41 post offices. There were 117,622 telephones on 31 Dec. 1990, and 95,796 television licences were issued.

JUSTICE, EDUCATION AND WELFARE

Justice. Pursuant to the Subordinate Courts Ordinance (Cap. 20) (1951) Courts of a Magistrate of the First Class, Second Class and Third Class were established to adjudicate upon the administration of civil and criminal law. The civil jurisdiction of a First Class Magistrate is limited to cases where the amount in dispute does not exceed M$1,000. but provision is made for the Chief Justice to enlarge that jurisdiction to M$3,000. This has been established so as to confer this jurisdiction on all stipendiary magistrates. A Second Class Magistrate can only try suits where the amount involved does not exceed M$500 and a Third Class Magistrate where it does not exceed M$100.

The criminal jurisdiction of these Magistrates' Courts is limited to offences of a less serious nature although stipendiary magistrates have enhanced jurisdiction. There are no Juvenile Courts.

There are also Native Courts with jurisdiction to try cases arising from breach of native law and custom (including Moslem Law and custom) where all parties are natives or one of the party is a native (if the matter is a religious, matrimonial or sexual one). Appeals from Native Courts lie to a District Judge or a Native Court of Appeal presided over by a Judge.

In 1989, 3,144 convictions were obtained in 485 cases taken to court.

Education. In 1990, there were 237,664 primary and 111,661 secondary pupils. There were 977 primary schools (801 government, 161 grant-aided and 15 private), and 139 general secondary schools (89 government, 37 grant-aided and 13 private) the State. There were 4 teacher-training colleges, with (1990) 2,100 students.

The Government also runs 7 vocational schools and further education classes in most towns and districts. The main medium of instruction in primary schools is Bahasa Malaysia although there are some Chinese medium primary schools. Secondary education is principally in English but this is being replaced by Bahasa Malaysia.

Health. As at 31 Dec. 1990 there were 16 hospitals (2,803 beds) and 265 clinics. 65 fixed dispensaries in outlying districts providing in-patient and out-patient care are staffed by hospital assistants under the supervision of district medical officers. There is 1 mental hospital at Kota Kinabalu. There are 18 maternity and child health centres.

Further Reading

Statistical Information: Director, Federal Department of Information, Kota Kinabalu.

Tregonning, K. G., *North Borneo*. HMSO, 1960

SARAWAK

HISTORY. The Government of part of the present territory was obtained on 24 Sept. 1841 by Sir James Brooke from the Sultan of Brunei. Various accessions were made between 1861 and 1905. In 1888 Sarawak was placed under British protection. On 16 Dec. 1941 Sarawak was occupied by the Japanese. After the liberation the Rajah took over his administration from the British military authorities on 15 April 1946. The Council Negeri, on 17 May 1946, authorized the Act of Cession to the British Crown by 19 to 16 votes, and the Rajah ceded Sarawak to the British Crown on 1 July 1946.

On 16 Sept. 1963 Sarawak joined the Federation of Malaysia.

AREA AND POPULATION. The area is about 48,050 sq. miles (124,449 sq. km), with a coastline of 450 miles and many navigable rivers.

The population at 1980 census was 1,307,582 (1989 estimate, 1,633,069, including 481,960 Ibans; 474,176 Chinese; 339,368 Malays; 136,741 Bidayuhs; 93,946 Melanaus; 88,260 other indigenous; 18,618 others). 1990 estimate, 1·7m.

The capital, Kuching City, is about 34 km inland, on the Sarawak River (1989 population: 157,000). The other major towns (with 1989 population) are Sibu, 128 km up the Rejang River, which is navigable by large steamers (114,000) and Miri, the headquarters of the Sarawak Shell Ltd (91,000).

CONSTITUTION AND GOVERNMENT. On 24 Sept. 1941 the Rajah began to rule through a constitution. Since 1855 two bodies, known as Majlis Mesyuarat Kerajaan Negeri (Supreme Council) and the Dewan Undangan Negeri (State Legislature), had been in existence. By the constitution of 1941 they were given, by the Rajah, powers roughly corresponding to those of a colonial executive council and legislative council respectively. Sarawak has retained a considerable measure of local autonomy in state affairs. The State Legislature consists of 56 elected members and sits for 5 years unless sooner dissolved.

A ministerial system of government was introduced in 1963. The Chief Minister presides over the Supreme Council, which contains no more than 8 other members, all of whom are Ministers.

Elections to the State Legislature were held in Oct. 1991. The electorate was 0·7m. The National Front Coalition Three won 49 seats, the tribal nationalist Bangsa Dayak Sarawak Party, 7.

Sarawak has 27 seats in the Malaysia House of Representatives and 5 seats in the Senate.

Sarawak has 9 divisions each under a Resident.

Head of State: Tun Datuk Patinggi Haji Ahmad Zaidi Adruce bin Muhammed Noor, SMN, SSM, DP, PNBS, Bintang Mahaputera Adipradana (Indonesia), PSLJ (Brunei).

Chief Minister: Datuk Patinggi Tan Sri Haji Abdul Taib Mahmud, DP, PSM, SPMJ, DGSM, PGDK, Kt. WE (Thailand) KOU (Korea), KEPN (Indonesia).

Deputy Chief Ministers: Datuk Amar Tan Sri Sim Kheng Hong, DA, PSM, PGDK, JMN. Datuk Amar Alfred Jabu Anak Numpang, DA, PNBS, KMN. *Environment and Tourism:* Datuk Amar James Wong Kim Min, DA, PNBS. *Infrastructure Development:* Datuk Amar Dr Wong Soon Kai, DA, PNBS, PBS.

Housing: Datuk Celestine Ujang Anak Jilan, PNBS. *Industrial Development:* Abang Abdul Rahman Zohari bin Tun Datuk Abang Haji Openg, JBS. *Land Development:* Datuk Adenan bin Haji Satem, JBS. *Special Functions:* Datuk Dr George Chan Hong Nam, KMN, PBS. *State Secretary:* Tan Sri Datuk Amar Haji Bujang Mohd. Nor, DA, PNBS, JSM, AMN. *Acting State Attorney-General:* Encik Abdul Hamid Mohammed Yusof, PPB. *State Financial Secretary:* Datuk Liang Kim Bang, PNBS, JBS, PPC, KMN.

The official language is Bahasa Malaysia. The use of English as official language in Sarawak was abolished in 1985.

Flag: Yellow with a diagonal stripe divided black over red charged with a yellow star of nine points.

ECONOMY

Planning. The sixth Malaysia 5-year development plan (1991-95) provides for Sarawak an expenditure of M$8,100m.; of this amount, 78% is allocated to the economic sector (of which 53% to transport and communication and public utilities, 14% to the agricultural sector and 10% to commerce and industry), 15% to the social sector, 6% to administration and 1% to security and defence.

Budget. In 1992 State revenue was estimated at M$1,624·3m.; expenditure, M$1,399·1m. The revenue is mainly derived from royalties on oil, timber and gas.

Currency. The monetary unit is the Malaysian *ringgit*.

Banking. The National savings bank had 166,714 depositors in July 1988; the amount to their credit was M$75m. There are branches of Bank Negara Malaysia in Kuching, and branches of the Chartered Bank, the Hongkong & Shanghai Bank, Bank Bumiputera Malaysia, the Overseas Chinese Banking Corporation, the Malayan Bank.

Nine local banks have branches in major towns. Sibu is the centre for local commercial banking with Hock Hua Bank (established in 1951, 13 branches and assets of M$872·4m. in 1983) and Kwong Ming Bank (established in 1964, 8 branches and assets of M$170m. in 1983). Both are locally owned and have branches in Kuala Lumpur and other towns.

INDUSTRY AND TRADE

Industry. Industry includes petroleum and petroleum products, natural gas, timber and timber products and rubber. Emphasis is being given to the development of petro-chemical, timber-based and agro-based industries.

Commerce. Exports in 1990 totalled M$10,876·6m. The main exports in 1989 were: Saw logs, which accounted for 29·7% of the total, with 14,960,000 cu. metres, value M$2·67m.; liquefied natural gas, 22·9% of the total, with 6,629,000 cu. metres, value, M$2·1m.; crude petroleum, 22·5% of the total, with 5,792,000 tonnes, value M$2·03m.; petroleum products, 6·1% of the total, with 1,302,000 tonnes, value M$549,018; sawn timber, 2·2% of the total, with 27,900 cu. metres, value M$197,060. The major agricultural exports, which together accounted for M$355·9m. or 3·9% of the total in 1989, were pepper, cocoa beans, palm oil and rubber.

Total import value, 1990, M$6,479m.

Sarawak's major trading partners in 1989 were Japan (export, 45·5%; import, 15·7%), Peninsular Malaysia (export, 11·4%, import, 41·7%); Republic of Korea (export, 12·1%, import, 0·3%); Singapore (export, 10·9%, import, 0·6%); USA (export, 1·4%, import, 14·1%); Sabah (export, 5·8%, import, 1·2%).

Tourism. In 1990 there were 264,756 tourists.

COMMUNICATIONS

Roads. In 1988 there were 6,902 km of roads, consisting of 2,878 km of bitumen surfaced, 3,062 km of gravel or stone surfaced and 962 km of earth roads. There are no railways.

Civil Aviation. There are daily Malaysian Airline System (MAS) B737 and Airbus flights between Kuching and Kuala Lumpur via Singapore, and also scheduled flights between Pontianak, Kuching, Brunei, Hong Kong and Singapore. Major towns in Sarawak are linked up by internal air routes.

Shipping. In 1989 Sarawak ports handled a total of 27m. tonnes of cargo. Kuching Port, operational since 1974, can accommodate vessels up to 15,000 tonnes. The Bintulu Port, the largest in the State, handled more than 11m. tonnes in 1989.

Telecommunications. There are 55 post offices, 18 mobile offices, 7 mini post offices and 213 postal agencies. The Telecommunications department was privatized in 1986 and renamed Telekom Malaysia Berhad. A telephone system with 65 automatic exchanges (118,000 telephone lines) covers the country. There are International Subscribers Dialling (ISD) links with 75 countries and Atur system was introduced in 1985. The government radio and television service had, in 1989, 37,286 electric radio sets and, in 1990, 92,189 TV receivers registered.

Newspapers (1991). There are 2 Malay newspapers (1 weekly and 1 monthly), 3 English and 8 Chinese dailies. 1 Malay and 1 Iban monthly newspaper are published by the Government.

JUSTICE, RELIGION, EDUCATION AND WELFARE

Justice (1992). In Sarawak there are the High Court and the Subordinate Court. High Court cases go on appeal to the Supreme Court which sits in Sarawak and Sabah twice a year. The Subordinate Courts (Amendment) Act 1987 was extended to Sarawak on 2 Sept. 1987 in which the jurisdiction of the Sessions Court judges and magistrates of the First Class and Second Class was enhanced.

In 1986 a Syariah Court was established, and the Juvenile Court was extended to Sarawak.

Police. There is a Royal Malaysia Police, Sarawak Component, with a total establishment of about 9,000 regular officers and men.

Religion. There is a large Moslem population and many Buddhists. Islam is the national religion.

Education (1991). There were 1,264 government and government-aided primary schools with 230,843 pupils and 13,523 teachers, and 137 secondary schools with 131,143 pupils and 6,276 teachers. There were 3 teacher-training colleges with (1989) 2,945 students and an agricultural university campus conducting pre-university courses. The MARA Institute of Technology campus, established in 1973, had 960 students in 1987 and offers 3-year courses leading to diploma in accountancy, stenography and business studies and a 6-month pre-commerce course.

The Kuching Polytechnic campus, established in 1989, offers 2 and 3-year courses leading to a diploma in accountancy and certificates in book-keeping, general mechanical, civil works, electronic and computer engineering.

Health. In 1990 there were 17 government hospitals, 4 polyclinics, 12 health centres, 115 rural clinics, 3 dispensaries and 38 sub-dispensaries, 180 maternal and child clinics and 120 mobile clinics. There were 358 doctors and 51 dentists. There is a flying doctor service for the interior.

Further Reading

Population and Housing Census of Malaysia, 1980. Dept. of Statistics, Kuala Lumpur
Sarawak Annual of Statistics. Dept. of Statistics, Kuching
Sarawak Annual External Trade Statistics. Dept. of Statistics, Kuching
Runciman, S., *The White Rajahs.* CUP, 1960

National Library: The Sarawak Central Library, Kuching.

MALDIVES

Dhivehi Raajjeyge Jumhooriyyaa

(Republic of the Maldives)

Capital: Malé
Population: 213,215 (1990)
GNP per capita: US$420 (1989)

HISTORY. The islands were under British protection from 1887 until complete independence was achieved on 26 July 1965. The Maldives became a republic on 11 Nov. 1968.

AREA AND POPULATION. The Republic of the Maldives, some 400 miles to the south-west of Sri Lanka, consists of 1,200 low-lying (the highest point is 6 feet above sea-level) coral islands, grouped into 12 clearly defined clusters of atolls. 200 are inhabited. Area 115 sq. miles (298 sq. km). According to the 1990 census, the population was 213,215 (103,879 females). Expectation of life was 60 years in 1989. Capital, Malé (55,130).

CLIMATE. The islands are hot and humid, and affected by monsoons. Malé: Average temperature 81°F (27°C), annual rainfall 59" (1,500 mm).

CONSTITUTION AND GOVERNMENT. The President is elected every 5 years by universal adult suffrage. He is assisted by the Ministers' *Majlis*, a cabinet of ministers of his own choice whom he may dismiss at will. There is also a Citizens' *Majlis* (Parliament) which consists of 48 members, 8 of whom are nominated by the President and 40 directly elected (2 each from Malé and the 19 administrative districts) for a term of 5 years. There are no political parties.

President, Minister of Defence, National Security and Minister of Finance: Maumoon Abdul Gayoom (re-elected unopposed for a third term on 23 Sept. 1988).

In Sept. 1991, the Government consisted of: *Home Affairs and Sports:* Umar Zahir. *Education:* Abdulla Hameed. *Health and Welfare:* Abdul Sattar Moosa Didi. *Fisheries and Agriculture:* Abbas Ibrahim. *Tourism:* Abdullah Jameel. *Foreign Affairs:* Fathulla Jameel. *Atolls Administration:* Ilyas Ibrahim. *Trade and Industries:* Vacant. *Justice:* Mohamed Rasheed Ibrahim. *Public Works and Labour:* Abdulla Kamaludeen. *Transport and Shipping:* Ahmed Zahir. *Acting Attorney-General:* Mohamed Zahir Hussain. *Speaker of Citizens' Majlis:* Ahmed Zaki.

The official and spoken language is Dhivehi.

National flag: Red with a green panel bearing a white crescent.

Local government: The Maldives is divided into the capital and 19 other administrative districts, each under an appointed governor *(atholhu verin)* assisted by local chiefs *(katheebun)*, who are also appointed.

INTERNATIONAL RELATIONS

Membership. The Maldives is a member of the UN, the Commonwealth and the Colombo Plan.

ECONOMY

Budget. 1990 estimates: Revenue, 429·6m. rufiyaas; expenditure 598·4m. rufiyaas.

Currency. The unit of currency is the *rufiyaa* of 100 *laari.* There are notes of 2, 5, 10, 20, 50, 100, 500 *rufiyaa.* In March 1992, £1 = 18·57 *rufiyaa*; US$1 = 10·58 *rufiyaa.*

ENERGY AND NATURAL RESOURCES

Electricity. Production, 1990, 29·5m. kwh.

Minerals. Inshore coral mining has been banned as a measure against the encroachment of the sea.

Agriculture. The islands are covered with coconut palms and yield millet, cassava, yams, melons and other tropical fruit as well as coconut produce.

Principal crops in 1989 (in tonnes): Coconuts (number of nuts), 12,491,724; areca nuts, 109; maize, 3·4; cassava, 22; sweet potatoes, 30; onions, 8; chillies, 13.

Fisheries. Catch, 1990, 76,400 tonnes.

INDUSTRY. The main industries are fishing, tourism, shipping, lacquerwork and garment manufacturing.

FOREIGN ECONOMIC RELATIONS

Commerce. In 1990 imports amounted to 1,315,406,000 rufiyaas and exports to 502,716,895 rufiyaas. Bonito ('Maldive fish') is the main export commodity. It is exported principally to Thailand, Singapore, Sri Lanka, Japan, and some European markets.

Total trade between the Republic of the Maldives and UK (British Department of Trade returns, in £1,000 sterling):

	1987	1988	1989	1990	1991
Imports to UK	440	1,859	5,224	6,573	7,909
Exports and re-exports from UK	2,772	1,689	3,412	3,458	2,862

Tourism. Tourism is the major foreign currency earner. There were 195,156 visitors in 1990.

COMMUNICATIONS

Roads. In 1990 there were 623 cars, 2,943 motorbikes, 937 handcarts, 28,252 bicycles and 813 other vehicles.

Civil Aviation. There are direct flights from Colombo, Trivendrum, Dubai, Karachi, Singapore, Paris and Zurich. In 1990, 1,650 aircraft, 217,953 passengers and 7,041,586 kg of freight were handled at Malé International Airport. There are 4 domestic airports. Air Maldives operates domestic flights only.

Shipping. The Maldives Shipping Line operated (1984) 32 vessels.

Telecommunications. There were (1990) 6,241 telephones. There is one AM and one FM radio station broadcasting. There were (1990) 26,532 radio receivers and 6,126 television sets.

Newspapers. There were (1991) 2 daily newspapers, 2 weekly, 2 fortnightly and a number of monthly periodicals.

JUSTICE, RELIGION, EDUCATION AND WELFARE

Justice. Justice is based on the Islamic Shari'ah.

Religion. The State religion is Islam.

Education. Education is not compulsory. In 1987 there were 300 primary schools with 53,412 pupils and 1,134 teachers and 6 secondary schools with 1,313 students and 116 teachers. In 1990, there were 50 government schools (25,608 pupils) and 213 community and private schools (36,985 pupils).

Health. In 1990 there was a 95-bed hospital in Malé, 4 regional hospitals (72 beds) and 225 health centres. In 1990 there were 40 doctors, 1 dentist and 137 nurses.

DIPLOMATIC REPRESENTATIVES

Of Great Britain in the Republic of the Maldives
High Commissioner: Vacant.

Of the Republic of the Maldives to the United Nations
Ambassador: (Vacant).

Further Reading

Bell, H. C. P., *History, Archaeology and Epigraphy of the Maldive Islands.* Ceylon Govt. Press, Colombo, 1940
Bernini, F. and Corbin, G., *Maldives.* Turin, 1973
Forbes, A. D. W., *The Maldives.* [Bibliography] Oxford and Santa Barbara, 1989

MALI

Capital: Bamako
Population: 9·09m. (1989)
GNP per capita: US$230 (1988)

République du Mali

HISTORY. Annexed by France between 1881 and 1895, the region became the territory of French Sudan as a part of French West Africa. It became an autonomous state within the French Community on 24 Nov. 1958, and on 4 April 1959 joined with Senegal to form the Federation of Mali. The Federation achieved independence on 20 June 1960, but Senegal seceded on 22 Aug. and Mali proclaimed itself an independent republic on 22 Sept. The National Assembly was dissolved on 17 Jan. 1968 by President Modibo Keita, whose government was then overthrown by an Army coup on 19 Nov. 1968; power was assumed by a Military Committee for National Liberation led by Moussa Traoré, who became President on 19 Sept. 1969. He was deposed on 26 March 1991 in a military coup. Lieut.-Col. Amadou Touré was named head of a Transitional Committee of Public Safety.

In Jan. 1991 a ceasefire was signed with Tuareg insurgents in the north, but sporadic skirmishing continued. A further agreement was reached at a Special Conference on the North held in Dec. 1991.

AREA AND POPULATION. Mali is a landlocked state, consisting of the Middle and Upper Niger basin in the south, the Upper Senegal basin in the southwest, and the Sahara in the north. It is bounded west by Senegal, north-west by Mauritania, north-east by Algeria, east by Niger and south by Burkina Faso, Côte d'Ivoire and Guinea. The republic covers an area of 1,240,192 sq. km (478,841 sq. miles) and had a population of 7,620,225 at the 1987 Census; estimate (1989) 9,092,000. In 1985, 21% lived in urban areas.

The areas, populations and chief towns of the regions are:

Region	Sq. km	Census 1987	Chief town	Census 1976
Kayes	197,760	1,058,575	Kayes	44,736
Koulikoro	89,833	1,180,260	Koulikoro	16,876
Capital District	267	646,153	Bamako	404,022
Sikasso	76,480	1,308,828	Sikasso	47,030
Ségou	56,127	1,328,250	Ségou	64,890
Mopti	88,752	1,261,383	Mopti	53,885
Tombouctou	408,977	453,032	Tombouctou	20,483
Gao	321,996	383,734	Gao	30,714

An 8th region, Kidal, was instituted in the north in 1991.

The various indigenous languages belong chiefly to the Mande group; of these the principal are Bambara (spoken by 60% of the population), Soninké, Malinké and Dogon; non-Mande languages include Fulani, Songhai, Senufo and Tuareg. The official language is French.

CLIMATE. A tropical climate, with adequate rain in the south and west, but conditions become increasingly arid towards the north and east. Bamako. Jan. 76°F (24·4°C), July 80°F (26·7°C). Annual rainfall 45" (1,120 mm). Kayes. Jan. 76°F (24·4°C), July 93°F (33·9°C). Annual rainfall 29" (725 mm). Tombouctou. Jan. 71°F (21·7°C), July 90°F (32·2°C). Annual rainfall 9" (231 mm).

CONSTITUTION AND GOVERNMENT. A constitution was approved by a national referendum on 2 June; it was amended by the National Assembly on 2 Sept. 1981. The sole legal party was the *Union démocratique du peuple malien* (UDPM).

A national conference of 1,800 delegates agreed a draft constitution enshrining multi-party democracy in Aug. 1991, and this was approved by 99·76% of votes cast at a referendum in Jan. 1992. Turn-out was 43%.

Elections were held in Feb.–March 1992 for the 129-member National Assembly. The Alliance for Democracy in Mali won 76 seats. The electorate is 5m.

National flag: Three vertical stripes of green, yellow, red.

Local Government: Mali is divided into the Capital District of Bamako and 7 regions, sub-divided into 46 *cercles* and then into 279 *arrondissements*.

At the elections of Jan. 1992 turn-out was 35%. The Alliance for Democracy in Mali (ADEMA) gained 214 of the 751 seats contested, the Sudanese Union-RDA (US-RDA), 130, and the National Committee for Democratic Initiative (CNID), 96.

DEFENCE. There is a selective system of 2 years' military service.

Army. The Army consists of 4 infantry battalions, 2 tank, 1 engineer, 1 parachute, 1 special force, 2 artillery battalions and support units. Equipment includes 21 T-34 tanks. Strength (1991) 6,900. There are also paramilitary forces of 7,800 men.

Air Force. The Air Force has 10 MiG-21 and 3 MiG-17 jet fighters, 1 MiG-15UTI jet trainer, some Yak-18 piston-engined trainers, 2 An-24, 2 An-26 and 2 An-2 transports, and 3 Mi-8 and Mi-4 helicopters from USSR. A twin-turbofan Corvette is used for VIP transport. Personnel (1991) total about 400, with 13 combat aircraft.

INTERNATIONAL RELATIONS

Membership. Mali is a member of the UN, OAU and is an ACP state of the EEC.

ECONOMY

Budget. The budget for 1988 provided for revenue of 112,100m. francs CFA and expenditure of 146,500m. francs CFA.

Currency. Mali introduced its own currency, the *Mali franc,* in July 1962 but reverted to the *franc CFA* on 1 June 1984 at a rate of 2 *Mali francs* to 1 *franc CFA.* There are coins of 1, 2, 5, 10, 25, 50 and 100 *francs CFA,* and notes of 50, 100, 500, 1,000, 5,000 and 10,000 *francs CFA.*

Banking. The *Banque Centrale du Mali* (founded in 1968) is the bank of issue. There are 4 domestic and 2 French-owned banks.

ENERGY AND NATURAL RESOURCES

Electricity. Production (1986) totalled 161m. kwh. Supply 220 volts; 50 Hz.

Minerals. Mineral resources are limited, but marble (at Bafoulabé) and limestone (at Diamou) are being extracted in the Upper Senegal valley; iron ore deposits in this area await development. Salt is mined at Taoudenni in the far north (4,500 tonnes in 1986) and phosphates at Bouren (10,000 tonnes).

Agriculture. Production in 1990 included (in 1,000 tonnes): Millet, 695; sugarcane, 270; groundnuts, 160; rice, 376; maize, 214; seed cotton, 245; cotton lint, 97; cassava, 73; sweet potatoes, 56.

Livestock, 1990: Cattle, 5m.; horses, 62,000; asses, 550,000; sheep, 5,850,000; goats, 5,850,000; camels, 241,000; chickens, 22m.

Forestry. Production (1986) 5·05m. cu. metres. 7% of the land is forested.

Fisheries. In 1986 60,000 tonnes of fish were caught in the rivers.

FOREIGN ECONOMIC RELATIONS

Commerce. Exports in 1985 totalled 77,200m. francs CFA. Chief imports are foodstuffs, automobiles, petrol, building material, sugar, salt and beer. France and Côte d'Ivoire are the main sources of imports. Cotton formed 41% of exports and livestock in 1983; 25% went to Belgium and 16% to France.

Total trade between Mali and UK (British Department of Trade returns, in £1,000 sterling):

	1987	1988	1989	1990	1991
Imports to UK	6,937	2,240	2,305	1,835	1,631
Exports and re-exports from UK	5,573	12,732	7,102	8,819	9,589

Tourism. There were 54,000 foreign tourists in 1986.

COMMUNICATIONS

Roads. There were (1985) 15,700 km of roads, 23,209 passenger cars and 6,802 commercial vehicles.

Railways. Mali has a railway from Kayes to Koulikoro by way of Bamako, a continuation of the Dakar–Kayes line in Senegal. Total length 642 km (metre-gauge) and in 1987 carried 196m. passenger-km and 199m. tonne-km of freight.

Civil Aviation. Air services connect the republic with Paris, Dakar and Abidjan. There are international airports at Bamako and Mopti, and Air Mali operates domestic services to 10 other airports.

Shipping. For about 7 months in the year small steamboats perform the service from Koulikoro to Tombouctou and Gao, and from Bamako to Kouroussa.

Telecommunications. There were, in 1984, 9,537 telephones. Broadcasting is the responsibility of the government-controlled Radiodiffusion Télévision du Mali. In 1991 there were estimated to be 0·15m. radio and 10,000 TV sets (colour by SECAM).

JUSTICE, RELIGION, EDUCATION AND WELFARE

Justice. The Supreme Court was established at Bamako in 1969 with both judicial and administrative powers. The Court of Appeal is also at Bamako, at the apex of a system of regional tribunals and local *juges de paix*.

Religion. In 1983, 90% of the population were Sunni Moslems, 9% animists and 1% Christians.

Education. In 1982–83 there were 364,382 pupils and 10,912 teachers in 1,558 primary and intermediate schools, 13,227 pupils and 890 teachers in 20 senior schools, 12,612 students in 11 technical schools. There were 5,792 students and 491 teaching staff in 7 higher educational establishments in 1979.

Health. In 1980 there were 12 hospitals, 327 health centres and 445 dispensaries, with a total of 3,200 beds; there were 319 doctors, 18 surgeons, 14 dentists (1978), 24 pharmacists (1978), 250 midwives and 1,312 nursing personnel.

DIPLOMATIC REPRESENTATIVES

Of Mali in Great Britain (resides in Brussels)
Ambassador: Vacant.

Of Great Britain in Mali
Ambassador: R. C. Beetham, LVO (resides in Dakar).

Of Mali in the USA (2130 R. St., NW, Washington, D.C., 20008)
Ambassador: Mohamed Alhousseyni Toure.

Of the USA in Mali (Rue Testard and Rue Mohamed V, Bamako)
Ambassador: Herbert D. Gelber.

Of Mali to the United Nations
Ambassador: Noumou Diakite.

MALTA

Capital: Valletta
Population: 355,910 (1990)
GNP per capita: US$6,996 (1990)

Repubblika ta' Malta

HISTORY. Malta was held in turn by Phoenicians, Carthaginians and Romans, and was conquered by Arabs in 870. From 1090 it was subject to the same rulers as Sicily until 1530, when it was handed over to the Knights of St John, who ruled until dispersed by Napoleon in 1798. The Maltese rose in rebellion against the French and the island was subsequently blockaded by the British aided by the Maltese from 1798 to 1800. The Maltese people freely requested the protection of the British Crown in 1802 on condition that their rights and privileges be preserved. The islands were finally annexed to the British Crown by the Treaty of Paris in 1814.On 15 April 1942, in recognition of the steadfastness and fortitude of the people of Malta during the Second World War, King George VI awarded the George Cross to the island. Malta became independent on 21 Sept. 1964 and became a republic within the Commonwealth on 13 Dec. 1974. For earlier constitutional and government history *see* THE STATESMAN'S YEAR-BOOK, 1980–81, p. 837.

In 1971 Malta began to follow a policy of non-alignment and closed the NATO base. The British military base which was closed in 1979.

AREA AND POPULATION. The area of Malta is 246 sq. km (94·9 sq. miles); Gozo, 67 sq. km (25·9 sq. miles); Comino, 3 sq. km (1·1 sq. miles); total area, 316 sq. km (121·9 sq. miles). Population, census 16 Nov. 1985, 345,418; estimate (Dec. 1990) 355,910. Malta island (1990), 329,846; Gozo and Comino, 26,064. Chief town and port, Valletta, population 9,199 but the urban harbour area, 101,749.

Vital statistics, 1990, estimate: Births, 5,368; deaths, 2,745; marriages, 2,498; emigrants, 160; returned emigrants, 858.

CLIMATE. The climate is Mediterranean, with hot, dry and sunny conditions in summer and very little rain from May to Aug. Rainfall is not excessive and falls mainly between Oct. and March. Average daily sunshine in winter is 6 hours and in summer over 10 hours. Valletta. Jan. 55°F (12·8°C), July 78°F (25·6°C). Annual rainfall 23" (578 mm).

CONSTITUTION AND GOVERNMENT. Malta is a democracy. The Constitution provides for a *President* of the Republic, a *House of Representatives* of elected members and a Cabinet consisting of the Prime Minister and such number of Ministers as may be appointed. The Constitution, which is founded on work, makes provision for the protection of fundamental rights and freedom of the individual, and for freedom of conscience and religious worship. In Jan. 1987 the 2 political parties agreed to amend the Constitution to provide that any political party winning more than 50% of all valid votes (but less than 50% of elected members) shall have the number of its members increased in order to have a majority in the House of Representatives. In 1992 the House of Representatives had 65 seats. At the elections of 22 Feb. 1992 the electorate was 0·26m. Turn-out was 96·08%. The Nationalist Party (NP) gained 51·8% of votes cast, the Labour Party 46·5% and the Democratic Alternative lost its single seat with 1·7%. The NP had a 3-seat majority.

Maltese and English are the official languages.

President: Dr Censu Tabone (sworn in April 1989).

The Cabinet (Nationalist Party) was as at Nov. 1991:

Prime Minister: Dr Edward Fenech-Adami.
Deputy Prime Minister, Minister of Foreign Affairs and Justice: Dr Guido de

Marco. *Education and the Interior:* Dr Ugo Mifsud-Bonnici. *Social Policy:* Dr
Louis Galea. *Finance:* Dr George Bonello Du Puis. *Development of Infrastructure:*
Michael Falzon. *Agriculture and Fisheries:* Lawrence Gatt. *Development of Ter-
tiary Sector:* Dr Emmanuel Bonnici. *Gozo:* Anton Tabone. *Economic Affairs:* John
Dalli.

National flag: Vertically white and red, with a representation of the George Cross
medal in the canton.

DEFENCE. The Armed Forces of Malta in 1992 were made up of 1,700 all ranks
organized into a Depot and 2 regiments. The major sub-units are the Infantry Company, the Airport Security Company, the Air Defence Battery, the Maritime Squadron (5 inshore patrol craft and a number of boats in 1991), the Helicopter Flight (4
Bell 47G light helicopters and 1AB206A JetRanger), the Engineer Company, the
General Duties Company, the Ammunition and Explosives Company, the Air Traffic Control Corps and the Revenue Security Corps.

A reorganization is in progress whereby 1st Regiment will become an Infantry
Battalion, 2nd Regiment will be a Support Regiment comprising artillery, air and
maritime elements, while Depot will provide logistical support. Amongst other
equipment, 2nd Regiment will hold a number of patrol craft of varying sizes and
both helicopters and light fixed-wing aircraft.

INTERNATIONAL RELATIONS

Membership. Malta is a member of the UN, the Commonwealth, the Council of
Europe and the Non-Aligned Movement. An application to join the EC was made in
1991.

ECONOMY

Policy. After a lengthy commitment to state ownership, overall policy now is to dispose of government shareholdings in non-strategic sectors as rapidly as possible.
National economic strategy aims especially at the attraction of new investment and
the creation of new employment in the directly productive and market services
(tertiary) sectors as a means of stimulating export-oriented growth. The objective is
to promote the location in Malta of new manufacturing industry with higher skill
production, develop the island as an offshore financial centre, and enter the EC as a
full member under suitable conditions. With this in mind an industrial incentive
package has been announced, and a scheme introduced for the retraining of workers
for productive employment in the private sector. Besides manufacturing (food,
clothing, chemicals and electrical machinery parts), ship repair and shipbuilding
and tourism are the mainstays of the economy.

Budget. Revenue and expenditure (in Lm):

	1987	1988	1989	1990
Revenue	221,160,214	308,747,572	291,779,385	385,606,694
Expenditure	263,619,931	274,003,588	320,743,721	381,690,455

The most important sources of revenue are customs and excise duties, income tax,
social security and receipts from the Central Bank of Malta.

Currency. The unit of currency is the *Maltese pound* (MTP) of 100 *cents* of 10
mils. Central Bank of Malta notes of Lm2, Lm5, Lm10 and Lm20 denominations
are in circulation. Malta coins are issued in the following denominations: Lm1, 50,
25, 10, 5, 2 and 1 cents; 5, 3 and 2 *mils.* Total notes and coins in circulation on 30
Sept. 1991, Lm348m. In March 1992, £1 sterling = Lm 0·56; US$1 = Lm 0·32.

Banking and Finance. The Central Bank of Malta was founded in 1968. Commercial banking facilities are provided by Bank of Valletta Ltd, Lombard Bank (Malta)
Ltd, the Apostleship of Prayer Savings Bank Ltd, and Mid-Med Bank Ltd. The
other domestic banking institutions are the Investment Finance Bank and Valletta
Investment Bank (long-term industrial loans), Lohombus Corporation Ltd (house
mortgage) and Melita Bank International Ltd (offshore bank).

Malta is developing as a financial and offshore business centre. The Malta International Business Authority is responsible for the registration and supervision of offshore companies carrying on business in Malta. About 600 such companies have been registered since the offshore legislation came into force in July 1989.

ENERGY AND NATURAL RESOURCES

Electricity. Electricity is generated at 2 interconnected power stations located at Marsa, having a total generating capacity of 289 mw. The larger station with an installed capacity of 235 mw is also equipped to produce potable water as a co-generation process. A new power station, initially of 120 mw, was under construction in 1991. Supply 240 volts; 50 Hz.

The gross electricity generated in 1990–91 was 1,278m. kwh.

Oil. The government announced an offshore exploration campaign in March 1988 and a number of companies were awarded contracts in 1990. In April 1991 the government opened a new area for exploration to the south of Malta; a number of applications from major oil companies were received and new contracts were expected to be awarded in 1992.

Agriculture. Out of a total area of 316 sq. km, about 135 sq. km may be described as agricultural. According to the latest Census (for agricultural year 1985–86) there were 12,173 holdings, inclusive of full-time and part-time farmers, encompassing some 11,490 ha of intensively cultivated land. For various socio-economic reasons a faster process of land alienation takes place, but land reclamation through both the private and public initiative helps to recover some of the loss. The envisaged Structural Plan for the Maltese Islands will in future safeguard the national land resource suitable for agriculture.

In 1990, the total output of agriculture and fisheries rose to Lm22·6m., representing 3·4% in the GDP. Gross capital formation by this sector stood at 9·9% of the sectoral value added, while employment was 2·48% of the national labour force.

Free market characterizes the economic organization in both the agricultural and fisheries spheres. With trade liberalization as a major policy goal, the domestic price level of local agricultural produce and fish is expected gradually to approach international price levels enhancing the competitiveness and productivity of Malta's primary sector.

Livestock (1990): Cattle, 21,330; pigs, 61,970; sheep, 5,945; goats 5,094; poultry, 1,612,512.

Fisheries. In 1989 the fishing industry employed 1,164 power propelled and 42 other fishing boats, engaging 227 full-time and 1,021 part-time fishermen. The catch in 1989 was 819 tonnes valued at Lm853,799.

INDUSTRY. Over 500 state-aided manufacturing enterprises are in operation in various industrial sectors, of which the majority are foreign-owned or have foreign interests. The Malta Development Corporation is the Government agency responsible for promoting and implementing new industrial projects.

Labour. The total labour force in Sept. 1991 was 135,635 (females, 34,839), distributed as follows: Agriculture and fisheries, 3,292; manufacturing, 32,148; building, construction and quarrying, 6,916; services, 46,158; electricity, gas and drydocks, 5,769; government, 33,200; training scheme and auxiliary workers, 2,915. Unemployment was 5,237 in Sept. 1991.

Trade Unions. There were 30 trade unions registered as at 30 Oct. 1991, with a total membership of 70,463 and 21 employers' associations with a total membership of 5,558.

FOREIGN ECONOMIC RELATIONS. Imports are being gradually liberalized, and plans are under way to turn Marsaxlokk all weather port into a free port zone for transhipment activities.

Commerce. Imports and exports including bullion and specie (in Lm1,000):

	1985	1986	1987	1988	1989	1990
Imports	354,139	347,909	392,874	447,431	515,805	620,511
Exports	187,099	194,668	208,590	235,920	294,405	357,890

In 1990 the principal items of imports were: Semi-manufactures, Lm120·1m.; machinery and transport, Lm284·1m.; food, Lm53·9m.; fuels, Lm31·8m.; manufactures, Lm54·5m.; chemicals, Lm42·7m.; others, Lm33·4m. Of domestic exports: Manufactures, Lm111·7m.; machinery and transport, Lm174m.; semi-manufactures, Lm29·8m.; beverages and tobacco, Lm2·3m.; food, Lm4·7m.; chemicals, Lm3·9m.

In 1990, Lm202·4m. of the imports came from Italy, Lm92·2m. from UK, Lm72·8m. from Federal Republic of Germany, Lm22·4m. from USA, Lm56·2m. from Asia, Lm18·3m. from the EFTA, Lm22·5m. from Africa, Lm2·1m. from Australia/Oceania, Lm24·6m. from other European countries; of domestic exports, Lm122·5m. to Italy, Lm70·1m. to Federal Republic of Germany, Lm28·2m. to UK, Lm19m. to Africa, Lm17·1m. to Asia, Lm12·7m. to USA, Lm3·8m. to EFTA and Lm12·7m. to other European countries.

Total trade between Malta and UK (British Department of Trade returns, in £1,000 sterling):

	1987	1988	1989	1990	1991
Imports to UK	52,105	40,189	42,194	50,541	40,771
Exports and re-exports from UK	107,941	121,696	132,287	141,298	162,454

Tourism. Tourism is the major foreign currency earner. In 1990, 871,675 tourists (51·6% from the UK) produced earnings of Lm157m. Estimated number of tourists in 1991 was 880,000.

COMMUNICATIONS

Roads. Every town and village is served by motor omnibuses. There are ferry services running between Malta and Gozo; cars can be transported on the ferries. In 1990 there were 1,405 km of roads. Motor vehicles registered at 31 Oct. 1991 totalled 123,565, of which 93,749 were private cars, 3,860 hire cars, 18,097 commercial vehicles, 417 buses and minibuses and 7,442 motor cycles.

Civil Aviation. In 1991 the main scheduled airlines, Air Malta, Alitalia, Corse Air, JAT, UTA, Lufthansa, Libyan Arab Airlines, Balkan Bulgarian Airlines, Czechoslovakian Airlines, Austrian Airlines, Swissair, Aeroflot and Tunisavia, operated scheduled services between Malta and UK, Germany, France, Italy, Libya, Switzerland, Yugoslavia, Bulgaria, Czechoslovakia, Austria, USSR, Tunisia, Greece, Spain, Hungary, Sicily, Egypt and Belgium. In 1990 there were 18,805 civil aircraft movements at Luqa Airport (Valletta). A new terminal with a capacity for 2·5m. passengers was due to open in 1992. 1,751,897 passengers, 6,792 tonnes of freight and 604 tonnes of mail were handled.

Shipping. The number of yachts and ships registered in Malta on 31 Dec. 1990 was 1,167; 5,571,404 GRT. Ships entering harbour, excluding yachts and fishing vessels, during 1989, 2,469. In 1991 3m. tonnes of international shipping was registered in Malta.

Telecommunications. Telephone services are administered by Telemalta Corporation with exchanges at Malta and Gozo. Broadcasting was nationalized in 1975, but independent radio and TV were re-introduced in 1991. There are 10 radio stations as well as non-profit-making community stations, and a cable TV operation. On 30 Sept. 1991 there were 191,000 telephones, 146,107 television sets and (31 Dec. 1988) 27,226 radio sets.

Cinemas (1990). There were 10 cinemas with a seating capacity of 7,000.

Newspapers. There were (1991) 1 English, 2 Maltese daily newspapers and 6 weekly and 1 fortnightly papers.

JUSTICE, RELIGION, EDUCATION AND WELFARE

Justice. The number of persons convicted of crimes in 1989 was 1,086; those convicted for contraventions against various laws and regulations numbered 4,832. 95 were committed to prison and 5,825 were awarded fines.

Police. On 30 Oct. 1991 police numbered 95 officers (including 3 women) and 1,527 other ranks (including 146 women).

Religion. The majority of the population (98%) belong to the Roman Catholic Church, which is established by law as the religion of the country, though full liberty of conscience and freedom of worship are guaranteed.

Education. Education is compulsory between the ages of 5 and 16 and free in government schools. Kindergarten education is provided for 3- and 4-year old children. The primary level enrols children between 5 and 11 years in a 6-year course. In 1990, there were 24,924 children (12,964 boys and 11,960 girls) in 81 primary schools. At the end of the course students are transferred automatically to secondary school, some of which (Junior Lyceums) are selective. In 1990, 10 Junior Lyceums had a total of 16,741 students (7,136 boys, 9,605 girls). There were 28 other secondary schools with a total of 12,427 (6,717 boys, 5,710 girls) in 1989. Secondary schools run 5-year courses leading to GCE 'O' level. Two-year GCE 'A' level courses leading to university entrance, during which students are paid an allowance and expected to gain work experience, are offered by the New Lyceums, *i.e.* upper secondary schools (2 in Malta and 1 in Gozo, with a total of 1,831 students in 1989). A higher Secondary School catering for students at GCE 'O' and 'A' level enrolled 921 students in 1990. Enrolment in vocational and technician courses in 3 technical institutes and 5 specialized training centres was 900 in 1989. Trade schools provide a technical and vocational education at craft level and are open to students who finish their second year of secondary education. Extended skills training schemes are also available for trade school graduates. The number of students of all ages in special education was 444.

There were (1991) about 94 private schools with a population of 4,145 at the nursery level, 10,807 at the primary level and 7,604 at the secondary level.

About 550 students in 1990 attended evening courses in academic, commercial, technical and practical subjects established in various centres. Other schools run on a mainly part-time basis by the Education Department for adult students are the School of Art, the School of Music, the School of Art and Design and the School of Drama (in Gozo).

The University of Malta consists of 10 faculties: Law; Medicine and Surgery; Architecture and Civil Engineering; Dental Surgery; Education; Economics, Management and Accountancy; Mechanical and Electrical Engineering; Theology; Arts; Science. There were 3,150 full-time students in 1990–91.

Social Security. The Social Security Act, 1987, provides cash benefits for marriage, maternity, sickness, unemployment, widowhood, orphanhood, invalidity, old age, children's allowances and industrial injuries.

The total number of persons in receipt of benefits on 31 Dec. 1991 was 159,780, viz., 1,098 in receipt of sickness benefit, 324 unemployment benefit, 171 special unemployment benefit, 71 injury benefit, 337 disablement benefit, 92 death benefit, 24,615 retirement pensions, 10,216 widows' pensions, 6 widows' special allowance, 7 orphan's allowance, 4,461 invalidity pensions, 51,184 children's allowances and 586 maternity benefit, 630 handicapped child allowance, 14,123 parental allowance and 51,859 family bonus.

The Act further provides for the payment of social assistance, medical assistance and non-contributory pensions to persons over 60 years of age, to blind persons over the age of 14 years and to handicapped persons over the age of 16 years.

The number of households in receipt of social assistance and of medical assistance on 31 Dec. 1991 was 7,715 and 9,357 respectively, and the number of pensioners in receipt of a non-contributory pension was 6,490.

Health. In 1991 there were 805 doctors, 98 dentists, 440 pharmacists, 274 midwives, 3,905 nursing personnel and 6 hospitals with 3,326 beds.

DIPLOMATIC REPRESENTATIVES

Of Malta in Great Britain (16 Kensington Sq., London, W8 5HH)
High Commissioner: Salv Stellini.

Of Great Britain in Malta (7 St Anne St., Floriana)
High Commissioner: Peter Wallis, CMG.

Of Malta in the USA (2017 Connecticut Ave., NW, Washington, D.C., 20008)
Ambassador: Dr Albert Borg Olivier de Puget.

Of the USA in Malta (Development Hse., St Anne St., Floriana)
Ambassador: Sally J. Novetzke.

Of Malta to the United Nations
Ambassador: Victor Camilleri.

Further Reading

Statistical Information: The Central Office of Statistics (Auberge d'Italie, Valletta) was set up in 1947. It publishes *Statistical Abstracts of the Maltese Islands*, a quarterly digest of statistics, quarterly and annual trade returns, annual vital statistics and annual publications on shipping and aviation, education, agriculture, industry, National Accounts and Balance of Payments.

Government publications: Department of Information (Auberge de Castille, Malta), set up in 1955, publishes *The Malta Government Gazette, Malta Information, Economic Survey 1991, Reports on the Working of Government Departments for the year 1989, Malta: Weekly Review of the Press, Report on the Organisation of the Public Service, Acts of Parliament and Subsidiary Legislation for the year 1990, Laws of Malta.*

Annual Reports. Central Bank of Malta
Trade Directory. Chamber of Commerce (annual)
The Malta Year Book. Sliema (annual)
Malta Independence Constitution (Cmnd 2406). HMSO, 1964
Constitution of the Republic of Malta. Department of Information, 1975
Made in Malta. METCO, 1991
Blouet, B., *The Story of Malta.* London, Rev. ed. 1981
Cremona, J. J., *The Constitutional Developments of Malta under British Rule.* Malta Univ. Press, 1963.—*Human Rights Documentation in Malta.* Malta Univ. Press, 1966
Gerada, E. and Zuber, C., *Malta: An Island Republic.* Paris, 1979
Thackrah, J. R., *Malta.* [Bibliography] Oxford and Santa Barbara, 1985

MARSHALL ISLANDS

Capital: Majuro
Population: 45,563 (1990)

Republic of the Marshall Islands

HISTORY. A German protectorate was formed in 1886 which was occupied at the beginning of the First World War by Japan. Japan was awarded a mandate by the League of Nations in 1919. During the Second World War the Islands were occupied by Allied forces in 1944, and became part of the UN Trust Territory of the Pacific Islands created on 18 July 1947 and administered by the USA. On 21 Oct. 1986 a Compact of Free Association with the USA came into force. The UN recognized the termination of the US Trusteeship on 22 Dec. 1990, and the Islands became a full UN member state on 17 Sept. 1991.

AREA AND POPULATION. The Marshall Islands lie in the Pacific Ocean north of Kiribati and east of Micronesia, and consist of an archipelago of 31 coral atolls, 5 single islands and 1,152 islets strung out in 2 chains, eastern and western. The land area is 181 sq. km (70 sq. miles). The capital is Majuro in the eastern chain (population, 1990, 20,000). Principal atolls in the western chain include Jaluit, Kwajalein and Eniwetok.

At the census of 1980 the population was 30,873 (48% urban); 1990 estimate, 45,630. About 92% of the population are Marshallese, a Micronesian people. Marshallese and English are both official languages.

CLIMATE. Jaluit, Jan. 81°F (27·2°C), July 82°F (27·8°C). Annual rainfall 161" (4,034 mm).

CONSTITUTION AND GOVERNMENT. For the US Trusteeship arrangements *see* THE STATESMAN'S YEAR-BOOK, 1991–92, p. 1556. Under the constitution which came into force on 1 May 1979 the Marshall Islands form a republic with a bicameral legislature and a *President* as head of state and executive, all elected for 4-year terms. The *Senate* comprises 12 members and the *House of Assembly* 33.

President: Amata Kabua.

National flag: Blue with a diagonal strip divided orange over white, and a white sun of 25 rays in the canton.

DEFENCE. The compact of free association gave the USA responsibility for defence in return for US assistance.

INTERNATIONAL RELATIONS

Membership. The Marshall Islands is a member of the UN and the South Pacific Forum.

ENERGY AND NATURAL RESOURCES

Minerals. High-grade phosphate deposits are mined on Ailinglaplap Atoll.

Agriculture. Coconuts, tomatoes, melons and breadfruit are grown for export.

FOREIGN ECONOMIC RELATIONS

Commerce. A small amount of agricultural produce is exported. Imports (mainly oil) totalled US$33·5m. in 1987.

COMMUNICATIONS

Civil Aviation. Air Marshall Islands operates flights to Fiji, Kiribati, Micronesia and Tuvalu as well as domestic services.

Telecommunication. In 1988 there were 800 telephones on Majuro and Ebeye. There is a US communications satellite earth station on Kwajalein. There is a TV and 3 radio stations.

JUSTICE, RELIGION, EDUCATION AND WELFARE

Justice. The Supreme Court is situated on Majuro. There is a Traditional Rights Court for customary disputes.

Religion. The population is mainly Protestant, but there are Roman Catholic and Baha'i communties.

Education. In 1985 there were 9,777 pupils in 86 primary schools, and 1,727 pupils in 7 secondary schools.

Health. In 1985 there were 17 doctors, 2 dentists, 51 nurses and 2 hospitals with a total of 54 beds.

DIPLOMATIC REPRESENTATIVES

Great Britain recognized the Marshall Islands in Aug. 1991.

Of the Marshall Islands to the United Nations
Ambassador: Wilfred I. Kendall.

MAURITANIA

Capital: Nouakchott
Population: 1·97m. (1989)
GNP per capita: US$490 (1989)

République Islamique Arabe et Africaine de Mauritanie

HISTORY. Mauritania became a French protectorate in 1903 and a colony in 1920. It became an autonomous republic within the French Community on 28 Nov. 1958 and achieved full independence on 28 Nov. 1960. Under its first President, Moktar Ould Daddah, Mauritania became a one-party state in 1964, but following his deposition by a military coup on 10 July 1978, the ruling *Parti du peuple mauritanien* was dissolved.

Following the Spanish withdrawal from Western Sahara on 28 Feb. 1976, Mauritania occupied the southern part (88,667 sq. km) of this territory and incorporated it under the name of Tiris el Gharbia. In Aug. 1979 Mauritania renounced sovereignty and withdrew from Tiris el Gharbia.

Following the *coup* of 10 July 1978, power was placed in the hands of a Military Committee for National Recovery (CMRN); the constitution was suspended and the 70-member National Assembly dissolved. On 6 April 1979 the CMRN was renamed the Military Committee for National Salvation (CMSN).

AREA AND POPULATION. Mauritania is bounded west by the Atlantic ocean, north by Western Sahara, north-east by Algeria, east and south-east by Mali, and south by Senegal. The total area is 1,030,700 sq. km (398,000 sq. miles) of which 47% is desert, and the population at the Census of 1976 was 1,419,939 including 12,897 in Tiris el Gharbia; latest estimate (1989) 1,969,000. The capital Nouakchott had a population of over 500,000 in 1985; other towns (1976) were Nouâdhibou (21,961), Kaédi (20,848), Zouérate (17,474), Rosso (16,466) and Atâr (16,326).

The areas and populations of the Capital District and 12 Regions are:

Region	Sq. km	Estimate 1982	Region	Sq. km	Estimate 1982
Nouakchott District	120	150,000	Adrar	215,300	60,000
Hodh ech-Chargui	182,700	235,000	Dakhlet Nouâdhibou	22,300	30,000
Hodh el-Gharbi	53,400	154,000	Tagant	95,200	84,000
Açâba	36,600	152,000	Guidimaka	10,300	102,000
Gorgol	13,600	169,000	Tiris Zemmour	252,900	28,000
Brakna	33,000	171,000	Inchiri	46,800	23,000
Trarza	67,800	242,000			

In 1983, 34% of the population were urban and 25% were nomadic. In 1980 81% of the inhabitants were Moorish, speaking the Hassaniyah dialect of Arabic, while the other 19% consist of Negro peoples, mainly Fulfulde-speaking Tukulor (8%) and Fulani (5%) who together with the Soninike (Sarakole) and Wolof groups all inhabit the Senegal valley in the extreme south.

Arabic is the official language; Pulaar, Soninke and Wolof are national languages.

CLIMATE. A tropical climate, but conditions are generally arid, even near the coast, where the only appreciable rains come in July to Sept. Nouakchott. Jan. 71°F (21·7°C), July 82°F (27·8°C). Annual rainfall 6″ (158 mm).

CONSTITUTION AND GOVERNMENT. A referendum was held in July 1991 to approve a new constitution instituting multi-party politcs. Turn-out was 85·34%; 97·94% of votes cast were in favour.

The new constitution envisages that the president is elected by universal suffrage for renewable 6-year terms. The government is headed by a prime minister. There will be a Senate and a National Assembly. Parties specifically Islamic are not permitted.

Presidential elections were held 24 Jan. 1992. There were 4 candidates. Col. Maaouiya Ould Sidi Ahmed Taya was elected with 62·8% of votes cast.

President, Prime Minister, Minister of Defence and Chairman of CMSN: Col. Maaouiya Ould Sidi Ahmed Taya (assumed office 12 Dec. 1984; re-elected Jan. 1992).

Foreign Affairs: Ismael Ould Yahi. *Finance:* Mohamed Ould Nany.

National flag: Green, with a crescent beneath a star in yellow in the centre.

Local Government: Mauritania is divided into a capital district and 12 regions and sub-divided into 49 *départements*.

DEFENCE

Army. The Army consists of 7 motorized infantry, 1 parachute, 1 artillery, and 2 Camel Corp battalions, 1 armoured car squadron, 4 artillery batteries and an engineer company; total strength, 11,000 in 1992.

Navy. The Navy, some 500 strong in 1991, is based at Nouadhibou and consists of 4 fast patrol craft and a few boats.

Air Force. The Air Force has 5 Britten-Norman Defender armed light transports, 2 Maritime Surveillance Cheyennes for coastal patrol, 2 Buffalo and 1 Skyvan transports, 4 Reims-Cessna 337 Milirole twin-engined counter-insurgency, forward air control and training aircraft and 4 Hughes 500 helicopters for communications. Personnel (1992) 250.

INTERNATIONAL RELATIONS

Membership. Mauritania is a member of the UN, OAU, the Arab League and is an ACP state of the EEC.

ECONOMY

Budget. The ordinary budget for 1989 balanced at 22,000m. ouguiyas.

Currency. The monetary unit is the *ouguiya* (MRO) which is divided into 5 *khoums*. Banknotes of 1,000, 500, 200 and 100 *ouguiya* and coins of 20, 10, 5 and 1 *ouguiya* and 1 *khoum* are in circulation. In March 1992, £1 = 142·85 *ouguiya*; US$1 = 81·37 *ouguiya*.

Banking and Finance. *The Banque Centrale de Mauritanie* (created 1973) is the bank of issue, and there are 5 commercial banks situated in Nouakchott.

ENERGY AND NATURAL RESOURCES

Electricity. Production (1986) 74m. kwh.

Minerals. Iron ore production (1984) 9·5m. tonnes. Copper mining at Akjoujt (by the state-owned SOMIMA), suspended in 1978, resumed in 1983.

Agriculture. Agriculture is mainly confined to the south, in the Senegal river valley. Production in tonnes (1990) of millet, 3,000; dates, 13,000; potatoes, 1,000; maize, 3,000; sweet potatoes, 3,000; rice, 52,000; groundnuts, 2,000.

In 1990 there were 820,000 camels, 1,263,000 cattle, 151,000 asses, 18,000 horses, 4·2m. sheep, 3,320,000 goats.

Forestry. There were 15m. ha of forests, chiefly in the southern regions, where wild acacias yield the main product, gum arabic.

Fisheries. Total catch (1986) 104,100 tonnes.

FOREIGN ECONOMIC RELATIONS. In Feb. 1989 Mauritania signed a treaty of economic co-operation with the 4 other Maghreb countries, Algeria, Libya, Morocco and Tunisia.

Commerce. In 1986 imports totalled 17,392m. ouguiya, and exports, 25,950 ouguiya of which iron ore comprised 40% of exports and salted and dried fish 60%;

24% of all exports went to Italy, 22% to Japan, 18% to Belgium and 15% to France, while France provided 22% of imports and Spain 20%.

Total trade between Mauritania and UK (British Department of Trade returns, in £1,000 sterling):

	1987	1988	1989	1990	1991
Imports to UK	8,724	7,259	15,387	14,525	15,313
Exports and re-exports from UK	3,862	3,048	4,005	2,997	2,336

Tourism. In 1986 there were 13,000 tourists.

COMMUNICATIONS

Roads. There were 8,900 km of roads in 1983. In 1985 there were 15,017 passenger cars and 2,188 commercial vehicles.

Railways. A 652-km railway links Zoué rate with the port of Point-Central, 10 km south of Nouâdhibou, and is used primarily for iron ore exports. In 1989 it carried 12·1m. tonnes of freight and (in 1986) 19,353 passengers.

Aviation. There are international airports at Nouakchott, Nouâdhibou and Néma. In 1990 the 5 Maghreb countries agreed to merge their airlines into Air Maghreb.

Shipping. The major ports are at Point-Central (for mineral exports), Nouakchott and Nouâdhibou.

Telecommunications. There were, in 1985, 3,161 telephones. The government-controlled Office de Radiodiffusion-Télévision de Mauritaine is responsible for broadcasting. In 1991 there were estimated to be 0·25m. radio and 1,100 TV sets (colour by SECAM).

JUSTICE, RELIGION, EDUCATION AND WELFARE

Justice. There are *tribunaux de première instance* at Nouakchott, Atâr, Kaédi, Aïoun el Atrouss and Kiffa. The Appeal Court and Supreme Court are situated in Nouakchott. Islamic jurisprudence was adopted in Feb. 1980.

Religion. Over 99% of Mauritanians are Sunni Moslem, mainly of the Qadiriyah sect.

Education. In 1986 there were 150,605 pupils in primary schools, 35,129 in secondary schools, 2,808 in technical schools and teacher-training establishments and 4,830 students in higher education. The University of Nouakchott (founded 1983) had 974 students in 1984.

Health. In 1984 there were 13 hospitals and clinics with 1,325 beds. In 1984 there were 170 doctors, 8 dentists, 16 pharmacists, 129 midwives and 582 nursing personnel.

DIPLOMATIC REPRESENTATIVES

Of Mauritania in Great Britain
Ambassador: Mohamed El Hanchi Ould Mohamed Saleh (resides in Paris).

Of Great Britain in Mauritania
Ambassador: John Macrae, CMG (resides in Rabat).

Of Mauritania in the USA
Ambassador: Abdellah Ould Daddah.

Of the USA in Mauritania (PO Box 222, Nouakchott)
Ambassador: William H. Twaddell.

Of Mauritania to the United Nations
Ambassador: Mohamedou Ould Mohamed Mahmoud.

Further Reading

Stewart, C. C. and Stewart, E. K., *Islam and Social Order in Mauritania.* New York, 1970
Westebbe, R. M., *The Economy of Mauritania.* New York, 1971

MAURITIUS

Capital: Port Louis
Population: 1,091,682 (1990)
GNP per capita: US$2,600 (1990)

Republic of Mauritius

HISTORY. Mauritius was known to Arab navigators by the 10th century. It was rediscovered by the Portuguese between 1507 and 1512, but the Dutch were the first settlers (1598). In 1710 they abandoned the island, which was occupied by the French under the name of Ile de France (1715). The British occupied the island in 1810, and it was formally ceded to the UK in 1814. In 1965 the Chagos Archipelago was transferred to the British Indian Ocean Territory. Mauritius became an independent state and a monarchical member of the Commonwealth on 12 March 1968 after 7 months of internal self-government, and a republic on 12 March 1992.

AREA AND POPULATION. Mauritius, the main island, lies 500 miles (800 km) east of Madagascar. Rodrigues (formerly a dependency and now a part of Mauritius) is about 350 miles (560 km) east of Mauritius. The outer islands consist of Agalega and the St Brandon Group. Population estimate (1989) 1,081,669.

Island	Area in sq. km	Census 1983	Estimate 1990
Mauritius	1,865	966,863	1,053,400
Rodrigues	104	33,082	37,782
Dependencies			
Agalega	70	487	500
St Brandon	1	–	–
Total	2,040	1,000,432	1,091,682

Port Louis is the capital (141,870, 1989). Other towns, Beau Bassin-Rose Hill, 94,236; Curepipe, 66,704; Quatre Bornes, 67,759; Vacoas-Phoenix, 56,335.

Vital statistics, 1989: Births, 20,955 (20·4 per 1,000); marriages, 11,040; deaths, 6,946 (6·8 per 1,000).

The official language is English.

CLIMATE. The sub-tropical climate produces quite a difference between summer and winter, though conditions are generally humid. Most rain falls in the summer so that the pleasantest months are Sept. to Nov. Rainfall amounts vary between 40" (1,000 mm) on the coast to 200" (5,000 mm) on the central plateau, though the west coast only has 35" (875 mm). Mauritius lies in the cyclone belt, whose season runs from Nov. to April, but is seldom affected by intense storms. Port Louis. Jan. 73°F (22·8°C), July 81°F (27·2°C). Annual rainfall 40" (1,000 mm).

CONSTITUTION AND GOVERNMENT. The Governor-General was the representative of HM the Queen, the Head of the State. A law of Dec. 1991 provided for Mauritius to become a republic on 12 march 1992 and the Governor-General a *President*.

The *Cabinet* is presided over by the Prime Minister. Each of the other 24 members of the Cabinet is responsible for the administration of specified departments or subjects and is bound by the rule of collective responsibility. Parliamentary Secretaries may also be appointed by the Governor-General on the advice of the Prime Minister.

The *Legislative Assembly* consists of a Speaker, elected from its own members, and 62 elected members (3 each for the 20 constituencies of Mauritius and 2 for Rodrigues) and 8 additional seats in order to ensure a fair and adequate representation of each community within the Assembly. General Elections are held every 5 years on the basis of universal adult suffrage.

The Constitution also provides for the Public Service Commission and the Judicial and Legal Service Commission which have both assumed executive powers for appointments to the Public Service. An Ombudsman assumed office on 2 March 1970.

945

At the General Election held on 15 Sept. 1991, 57 of the 60 seats on mainland Mauritius were won by the ruling *Alliance* (Mouvement Socialiste Militant, 29; Mouvement Militant Mauricien, 26; Mouvement Travailliste Démocrate, 2) and 3 by the opposition Labour Party/Parti Mauricien Social Démocrate *Alliance*. The 2 seats for the island of Rodrigues were won by the Organisation du Peuple Rodriguais. The electorate was 628,000; turn-out was high. Of the 8 additional seats awarded to the highest losers in each community, only the first set of 4 were allocated, and these went to the opposition *Alliance*.

President: Sir Veerasamy Ringadoo, GCMG, QC.
The Cabinet was composed as follows in Oct. 1991:

Prime Minister, Defence and Internal Security, Information, Internal and External Communications and the Outer Islands: Rt. Hon. Sir Anerood Jugnauth, PC, KCMG, QC.
Deputy Prime Minister and Health: Dr Paramhamsa Nababsing. *Trade and Shipping:* Anil Kumar Bachoo. *Women's Rights, Child Development and Family Welfare:* Sheilabhai Bappoo. *External Affairs:* Paul Raymond Berenger. *Arts, Culture, Leisure and Reform Institutions:* Mookhesswur Choonee. *Rodrigues:* Louis Serge Clair. *Housing, Lands and Town and Country Planning:* Jaya Krishna Cuttaree. *Economic Planning and Development:* Jean Claude Gervais Raoul de L'Estrac. *Agriculture, Fisheries and Natural Resources:* Murlidas Dulloo. *Local Government:* Jean Regis Finette. *Labour and Industrial Relations:* Dharmanand Goopt Fokeer. *Attorney-General and Justice:* Alan Ganoo. *Youth and Sports:* Michael James Kevin Glover. *Co-operatives, Handicraft and Small Scale Industries:* Jagdishwar Goburdhun. *Works:* Dwarkanath Gungah. *Manpower Resources and Vocational and Technical Training:* Ramduthsing Jaddoo. *Environment and Quality of Life:* Dr Ahmud Swalay Kasenally. *Tourism:* Noe Ah-Qwet Lee Cheong Lem. *Social Security and National Solidarity:* Karl Auguste Offman. *Education and Science:* Armoogum Parsuraman. *Civil Service Affairs and Employment:* Keerteecoomar Ruhee. *Finance:* Ramakrishna Sithanen. *Energy, Water Resources and Postal Services:* Mahyendrah Utchanah. *Industry and Industrial Technology:* Cassam Uteem.

National flag: Horizontally 4 stripes of red, blue, yellow and green.

Local government: The Island of Mauritius (only) is divided into 9 administrative districts.

DEFENCE. The Mauritius Police, which is responsible for defence, is equipped with arms; its strength was (1990) 6,584 officers and men.

INTERNATIONAL RELATIONS

Membership. Mauritius is a member of the UN, Commonwealth, OAU, Non-Aligned Movement and is an ACP state of the EEC.

ECONOMY

Budget. Revenue and expenditure (in Rs1m.) for years ending 30 June:

	1988–89	1989–90	1990–91	1991–92
Revenue	7,193	8,367	9,899	10,981
Expenditure	7,655	8,199	9,230	10,070

Principal sources of revenue, 1991–92 (estimate): Direct taxes, Rs 2,306·4m.; indirect taxes, Rs 7,592·7m.; receipts from public utilities, Rs 201·6m.; receipts from public services Rs 261·5m.; interest and reimbursement, Rs 601·8m. Capital expenditure was Rs 3,360m. Capital revenue, Rs 2,261m. On 30 June 1990 the public debt of Mauritius was Rs 2,173m.

Currency. The unit of currency is the *Mauritius rupee* (MUR) of 100 *cents*.
The currency consists of: (i) Bank of Mauritius notes of Rs 1,000, 500, 200, 100, 50, 10 and 5; (ii) Cupro-nickel coins of 5 rupees and 1 rupee; (iii) nickel-plated steel coins of 50 cents, 25 cents, 20 cents and 10 cents; (iv) copper-plated steel coins of 5 cents and 1 cent. In March 1992, £1 = 27·69 *rupees*; US$1 = 15·77.

Banking and Finance. The Bank of Mauritius was established in 1966, with an authorized capital of Rs 10m., to exercise the function of a central bank. The *Governor* is Sir Indurduth Ramphul. There are 12 commercial banks, the Mauritius Commercial Bank Ltd (established 1838), Barclays Bank PLC, the Bank of Baroda Ltd, The HongKong and Shanghai Banking Corporation, the Mauritius Co-operative Central Bank Ltd, Banque Nationale de Paris (Intercontinentale), the Habib Bank Ltd, the State Commercial Bank Ltd, Indian Ocean International Bank Ltd, Union International Bank Ltd, South East Asia Bank and Delphis Bank. Other financial institutions include the Mauritius Housing Corporation Ltd, the Development Bank of Mauritius, the Post Office Savings Bank and the State Investment Corporation.

On 31 Dec. 1990 the Post Office Savings Bank held 213,400 deposits amounting to Rs 295·4m.

ENERGY AND NATURAL RESOURCES

Electricity. Electric power production (1990) was 667m. kwh. Supply 230 volts; 50 Hz.

Agriculture. In 1989, 77,000 ha were planted with sugar-cane. There were 19 factories and sugar production (1990 in tonnes) was 624,302, molasses, 179,000.

The main secondary crops in 1990 were tea (3,070 ha from which 5,500 tonnes were produced), tobacco (1,040 tonnes), potatoes (18,210 tonnes) and maize (5,751 tonnes).

In 1989 beef production totalled 784 tonnes, pork 595 tonnes and goat meat 131 tonnes.

Livestock (1989): Cattle, 10,836; goats, 15,892; poultry, 2m.

Forestry. The total forest area was estimated (1989) at 65,400 ha including some 6,775 ha of plantations. In 1988 production totalled 27,954 cu. metres of timber, poles and fuel wood.

Fisheries. Production (1989) 14,861 tonnes.

INDUSTRY. Manufactures include: Knitwear, clothing, footwear, diamond cutting, jewellery, furniture, watchstraps, sunglasses, plastic ware and chemical products.

Labour. In 1990 the labour force was 279,410, of whom 107,755 were employed in manufacturing.

Trade Unions. In 1989 there were 291 registered trade unions and 11 federations with a total membership of about 100,000.

FOREIGN ECONOMIC RELATIONS

Commerce. Total trade (in Rs1m.) for calendar years:

	1987	1988	1989	1990 [1]
Imports c.i.f.	13,042	17,247	20,217	24,019
Exports f.o.b.	11,497	13,454	15,049	17,569

[1] Provisional.

In 1990, Rs 3,525m. of the imports came from France, Rs 2,110m. from the Republic of South Africa, Rs 1,702m. from UK, Rs 581m. from Australia. In 1990 Rs 6,289m. of the exports went to UK, Rs 3,981m. to France, Rs 2,307m. to USA and Rs 1,528m. to the Federal Republic of Germany.

Sugar exports in 1990 were 578,000 tonnes, Rs 5,104m. Other major exports (1990) included clothing, Rs 9,096m.; tea, Rs 82m. and toys, games and sporting goods, Rs 124m. Major imports included (1990) textiles and fabrics, Rs 4,187m. and machinery and transport equipment, Rs 6,273m.

Total trade between Mauritius and UK (British Department of Trade returns, in £1,000 sterling):

	1987	1988	1989	1990	1991
Imports to UK	163,271	186,240	216,190	233,936	250,218
Exports and re-exports from UK	44,395	38,553	43,528	50,746	52,360

Tourism. In 1990, 291,550 tourists visited Mauritius.

COMMUNICATIONS

Roads. In 1989 there were 29 km of motorway, 856 km of main roads, 816 km of secondary and other roads. At 31 Dec. 1990 there were 29,401 cars, 1,929 buses, 11,650 motor cycles, 44,969 auto cycles and 12,076 lorries and vans.

Civil Aviation. Mauritius is linked by air with Europe, Africa, Asia and Australia by the following airlines: Air France, Air India, Air Madagascar, Air Mauritius, Air Zimbabwe, British Airways, Cathay Pacific Airways, Lufthansa, Malaysian Airline System, Singapore Airlines, South African Airways and Zambia Airways. In addition to passenger services a weekly cargo flight is operated by Air France to Paris. In 1990, 412,200 passengers arrived at Sir Seewoosagur Ramgoolam international airport and 12,316 tonnes of freight were unloaded. Air Mauritius operates a joint regional service with Air Madagascar on the Mauritius–Antananarivo–Moroni–Nairobi route, a twice weekly service jointly with Air India to Bombay, and a joint weekly service to Hong Kong with Cathay Pacific Airlines.

Shipping. A free port was established at Saint Louis in Sept. 1991. In 1990, 955 vessels entered Port Louis with a total gross tonnage of 4·2m. tonnes.

Telecommunications. In 1989 there were 33 telephone exchanges and 74,118 individual telephone installations in Mauritius and Rodrigues. Communication with other parts of the world is established *via* satellite.
At 31 Dec. 1990 there were 146,737 television sets.

Cinemas (1990). There were 16 cinemas, with a seating capacity of about 20,000.

Newspapers. There were (1990) 5 French daily papers (with occasional articles in English) and 2 Chinese daily papers with a combined circulation of about 80,000.

RELIGION, EDUCATION AND WELFARE

Religion. At the 1983 Census (excluding Rodrigues) there were 247,723 Roman Catholics, 6,049 Protestants (Church of England and Church of Scotland), 506,270 Hindus and 160,190 Moslems.

Education. Primary education is free and compulsory. About 96% of children aged 5 to 11 years attend schools. In 1990 there were 131,203 pupils at 277 primary schools and 76,440 pupils at 122 secondary schools. There were 8 special schools and 870 students in 3 technical institutions and 5 handicraft training centres and 501 teachers in training in 1989.
In 1989, 1,241 students were enrolled at the University of Mauritius.

Health. In 1990 there were 950 doctors, including 152 specialists, and 2,900 hospital beds.

DIPLOMATIC REPRESENTATIVES

Of Mauritius in Great Britain (32–33 Elvaston Pl., London, SW7)
High Commissioner: Babooram Mahadoo.

Of Great Britain in Mauritius (King George V Ave., Floreal, Port Louis)
High Commissioner: M. E. Howell, CMG, OBE.

Of Mauritius in the USA (4301 Connecticut Ave., NW, Washington, D.C., 20008)
Ambassador: Chitmansing Jesseramsing.

Of the USA in Mauritius (Rogers Bldg., John Kennedy St., Port Louis)
Ambassador: Penne Percy Korth.

Of Mauritius to the United Nations
Ambassador: Dr S. Peerthum.

Further Reading

Central Statistical Information Office, *Bi-annual Digest of Statistics.* Ministry of Information,—*The Mauritius Handbook 1989*
Bennett, P. R., *Mauritius.* [Bibliography] Oxford and Santa Barbara, 1992
Bowman, L. W., *Mauritius: Democracy and Development in the Indian Ocean.* Aldershot, 1991
Library: The Mauritius Institute Public Library, Port Louis.
National statistical office: Central Statistical Information Office, Rose Hill.

MEXICO

Capital: Mexico City
Population: 81·14m. (1990)
GNP per capita: US$1,990 (1989)

Estados Unidos Mexicanos

(United States of Mexico)

HISTORY. Mexico's history falls into four epochs: the era of the Indian empires (before 1521), the Spanish colonial phase (1521–1810), the period of national formation (1810–1910), which includes the war of independence (1810–21) and the long presidency of Porfirio Díaz (1876–80, 1884–1911), and the present period which began with the social revolution of 1910–21 and is regarded by Mexicans as the period of social and national consolidation.

AREA AND POPULATION. Mexico is bounded in the north by the USA, west and south by the Pacific Ocean, southeast by Guatemala, Belize and the Caribbean Sea, and north-east by the Gulf of Mexico. It comprises 1,958,201 sq. km (756,198 sq. miles), including uninhabited islands (5,073 sq. km) offshore. Population density, 41·25 per sq. km.

Population at recent censuses: 1900, 13,607,272; 1950, 25,791,017; 1960, 34,923,129; 1970, 48,225,288; 1980, 66,846,833; 1990, 81,140,922.

Area population and capitals of the Federal District and 31 states:

	Area (Sq. km)	Population (1990 census)	Capital
Federal District	1,479	8,236,960	Mexico City
Aguascalientes	5,471	719,650	Aguascalientes
Baja California	69,921	1,657,927	Mexicali
Baja California Sur	73,475	317,326	La Paz
Campeche	50,812	528,824	Campeche
Chiapas	74,211	3,203,915	Tuxtla Gutiérrez
Chihuahua	244,938	2,439,954	Chihuahua
Coahuila	149,982	1,971,344	Saltillo
Colima	5,191	424,656	Colima
Durango	123,181	1,352,156	Victoria de Durango
Guanajuato	30,491	3,980,204	Guanajuato
Guerrero	64,281	2,622,067	Chilpancingo
Hidalgo	20,813	1,880,636	Pachuca de Soto
Jalisco	80,836	5,278,987	Guadalajara
México	21,355	9,815,901	Toluca de Lerdo
Michoacán	59,928	3,534,042	Morelia
Morelos	4,950	1,195,381	Cuernavaca
Nayarit	26,979	816,112	Tepic
Nuevo Léon	64,924	3,086,466	Monterrey
Oaxaca	93,952	3,021,513	Oaxaca de Juárez
Puebla	33,902	4,118,059	Puebla de Zaragoza
Querétaro	11,449	1,044,227	Querétaro
Quintana Roo	50,212	493,605	Chetumal
San Luis Potosí	63,068	2,001,966	San Luis Potosí
Sinaloa	58,328	2,210,766	Culiacán Rosales
Sonora	182,052	1,822,247	Hermosillo
Tabasco	25,267	1,501,183	Villahermosa
Tamaulipas	79,384	2,244,208	Ciudad Victoria
Tlaxcala	4,016	763,683	Tlaxcala
Veracruz	71,699	6,215,142	Jalapa Enríquez
Yucatán	38,402	1,363,540	Mérida
Zacatecas	73,252	1,278,279	Zacatecas

At the 1980 census 33,039,307 were males, 33,807,526 females. Urban population was 66·3% in 1988. The official language is Spanish, the mother tongue of over 92% of the population, but there are 5 indigenous language groups (Náhuatl,Maya, Zapotec, Otomi and Mixtec) from which are derived a total of 59 dialects spoken by 5,181,038 inhabitants (1980 census). In 1980, about 16% of the population were of European ethnic origin, 55% mestizo and 29% Amerindian.

The populations (1990 Census) of the largest cities were:

México [1]	13,636,127	Hermosillo	449,472	Guasave	257,821
Guadalajara [1]	2,846,720	Saltillo	440,845	Tepic	238,101
Monterrey [1]	2,521,697	Victoria de Durango	414,015	Gómez Palacio	232,550
Puebla de Zaragoza	1,054,921	Villa Hermosa	390,161	Coatzacoalcos	232,314
Léon de los Aldama	872,453	Irapuato	362,471	Tapachula	222,282
Ciudad Juárez	797,679	Veracruz Llave	327,522	Nuevo Laredo	217,914
Tijuana	742,686	Celaya	315,577	Uruapán	217,142
Mexicali	602,391	Atizapán de Zaragoza	315,413	Oaxaca de Juárez	212,943
Culiacán Rosales	602,114	Mazatlán	314,249	Ciudad Victoria	207,830
Acapulco de Juárez	592,187	Ciudad Obregón	311,078	Salamanca	206,275
Mérida	557,340	Los Mochis	305,507	Minatitlán	199,840
Chihuahua	530,487	Matamoros	303,392	Pachuca de Soto	179,440
San Luis Potosí	525,819	Tuxtla Gutiérrez	295,615	Monclova	178,023
Aguascalientes	506,384	Jalapa Enríquez	288,331	Campeche	172,208
Morelia	489,758	Cuernavaca	281,752	Ciudad Madero	159,644
Toluca de Lerdo	487,630	Reynosa	281,392	Poza Rica de Hidalgo	151,201
Torreón	459,809	Tampico	271,636	Córdoba	150,428
Querétaro	454,049	Ensenada	260,905		

[1] Metropolitan Area.

Vital statistics for calendar years:

	Births	Deaths	Marriages	Divorces
1989	2,586,708	428,667	633,424	45,907
1990	2,262,863	434,069	637,460	44,160

CLIMATE. Latitude and relief produce a variety of climates. Arid and semi-arid conditions are found in the north, with extreme temperatures, whereas in the south there is a humid tropical climate, with temperatures varying with altitude. Conditions on the shores of the Gulf of Mexico are very warm and humid. In general, the rainy season lasts from May to Nov. Mexico City. Jan. 55°F (12·6°C), July 61°F (16·1°C). Annual rainfall 30" (747 mm). Guadalajara. Jan. 59°F (15·2°C), July 69°F (20·5°C). Annual rainfall 36" (902 mm). La Paz. Jan. 64°F (17·8°C), July 85°F (29·4°C). Annual rainfall 6" (145 mm). Mazatlan Jan. 66°F (18·9°C), July 82°F (27·8°C). Annual rainfall 33" (828 mm). Merida. Jan. 72°F (22·2°C), July 83°F (28·3°C). Annual rainfall 38" (957 mm). Monterrey. Jan. 58°F (14·4°C), July 81°F (27·2°C). Annual rainfall 23" (588 mm). Puebla de Zaragoza. Jan. 54°F (12·2°C), July 63°F (17·2°C). Annual rainfall 34" (850 mm).

CONSTITUTION AND GOVERNMENT. A new Constitution was promulgated on 5 Feb. 1917 and has been amended from time to time. Mexico is a representative, democratic and federal republic, comprising 31 states and a federal district, each state being free and sovereign in all internal affairs, but united in a federation established according to the principals of the Fundamental Law. Citizenship, including the right of suffrage, is vested in all nationals of 18 years of age and older who have 'an honourable means of livelihood'.

There is complete separation of legislative, executive and judicial powers (Art. 49). Legislative power is vested in a General Congress of 2 chambers, a Chamber of Deputies and a Senate (Art.50). The Chamber of Deputies consists of 500 members directly elected for 3 years, 300 of them from single-member constituencies and 200 chosen under a system of proportional representation (Arts.51–55). In July 1990 Congress voted a new Electoral Code by 369 votes to 65. This establishes a body to organize elections (IFE), an electoral court (TFE) to resolve disputes, new electoral rolls and introduces a voter's registration card. Priests were enfranchised in Nov. 1991.

At the general elections held on 7 July 1988, 234 of the single-member seats were won by the Institutional Revolutionary Party (PRI), 38 by the Party of National Action (PAN). At the mid-term elections of Aug. 1991 for 300 electoral districts, 32

Senate seats and 6 governorships, the PRI gained 61·4% of votes cast and won 290 Congress seats, 31 Senate seats and all 6 governorships. PAN gained 17·7% of votes cast, and the Party of Democratic Revolution, 8·3%.

The Senate comprises 64 members, 2 from each state and 2 from the federal district, directly elected for 6 years (Arts.56–58). At the elections of 7 July 1988, the PRI won 60 seats and the FDN 4 seats. Members of both chambers are not immediately re-eligible for election (Art.59). Congress sits from 1 Sept. to 31 Dec. each year; during the recess there is a permanent committee of 15 deputies and 14 senators appointed by the respective chambers.

The President is the supreme executive authority. He appoints the members of the Council of Ministers and the senior military and civilian officers of the state. He is directly elected for a single 6-year term.

The names of the presidents from 1958 are as follows:

Adolfo López Mateos, 1 Dec. 1958–30 Nov. 1964.

José López Portillo y Pacheco, 1 Dec. 1976–30 Nov. 1982.

Gustavo Díaz Ordaz, 1 Dec. 1964–30 Nov. 1970.

Miguel de la Madrid Hurtado, 1 Dec. 1982–30 Nov. 1988.

Luis Echeverría Alvarez, 1 Dec. 1970–30 Nov. 1976.

President: Carlos Salinas de Gortari (b. 1948; assumed office 1 Dec. 1988).

In Jan. 1992 the Council of Ministers was composed as follows: *Interior:* Fernando Gutiérrez Barrios. *Foreign Relations:* Fernando Solana Morales. *Defence:* Gen. Antonio Riviello Bazan. *Navy:* Adm. Luis Carlos Ruano Angulo. *Finance and Public Credit:* Dr Pedro Aspe Armella. *Comptroller-General:* María Elena Vásquez Nava. *Energy, Mines and Public Industries:* Fernando Hiriart Balderrama. *Commerce:* Dr Jaime Serra Puche. *Agriculture and Water Resources:* Carlos Hank González. *Communications and Transport:* Andres Caso Lombardo. *Urban Development and Ecology:* Patricio Chirinos. *Education:* Ernesto Zedillo Ponce de Léon. *Health:* Dr Jesús Kumate. *Labour and Social Welfare:* Arsenio Farell Cubillas. *Agrarian Reform:* Victor Cervera Pacheco. *Tourism:* Pedro Joaquín Coldwell. *Fisheries:* Maria de los Angeles Moreno Uruegas. *Governor of Federal District:* Manuel Camacho Solis. *Attorney-General:* Ignacio Morales Lechuga. *Attorney-General of the Federal District:* Miguel Montes Garcia. *Chief of the Presidential Staff:* Brig.-Gen. Arturo Cardona Marino. *Director-General of the Technical Cabinet Secretariat:* Dr José Córdoba Montoya. *Presidential Secretary:* Andrés Massieu Berlanga. *Director-General of Legal Affairs of the Presidency:* Ruben Valdéz Abascal. *Director-General of Presidential Public Relations:* Otto Granados Roldán.

National flag: Three vertical strips of green, white, red, with the national arms in the centre.

National anthem: Mexicanos, al grito de guerra ('Mexicans, at the war-cry'; words by F. González Bocanegra; tune by Jaime Nunó, 1854).

Local Government. Mexico is divided into 31 states and a Federal District. The latter is co-extensive with Mexico City and is administered by a Governor appointed by the President. Each state has its own constitution, with the right to legislate and to levy taxes (but not inter-state customs duties); its Governor is directly elected for 6 years and its unicameral legislature for 3 years; judicial officers are appointed by the state governments. Mexico City is sub-divided into 16 municipalities and the 31 states into 2,378 municipalities.

DEFENCE

Army. Enlistment into the regular army is voluntary, but there is also one year of conscription by lottery. The army consists of 3 infantry brigades (one of which is mechanized), 3 armoured regiments, a garrison for each of the country's 36 military zones (with motorized cavalry, artillery and infantry), and support units. Equipment includes 45 M-3/-8 tanks and some 140 armoured cars. Strength of the regular army (1991) 105,500; conscripts, 60,000.

Navy. The Navy is primarily equipped and organized for offshore and coastal patrol duties. It comprises 3 old ex-US destroyers, 8 modern offshore patrol vessels with small helicopter decks and hangars, and 35 older offshore ships, mostly ex-US. There are also 34 inshore patrol vessels and 20 riverine patrol craft. Auxiliaries include 3 survey ships, 1 repair ship, 2 training ships, 6 tugs and some 24 service craft.

The naval air force, 500 strong, operates 10 Aviocars for maritime patrol and rescue, 12 Bo-105 helicopters for service afloat, and some 40 fixed wing and 5 helicopters for transport, liaison and training duties.

Naval personnel in 1991 totalled 37,000, including the naval air force and 9,000 marines.

Air Force. The Air Force had (1991) a strength of about 8,000 with 113 combat aircraft and 23 armed helicopters, and has nine operational groups, each with one or two squadrons. No. 1 Group comprises No. 208 Squadron with 9 IAI Aravas for transport, search and rescue and counter-insurgency duties; and No. 209 Squadron with Bell 205A, 206B JetRanger, Alouette III and Puma helicopters. No. 2 Group has two Squadrons (Nos. 206 and 207) of Swiss-built Pilatus PC-7 Turbo-Trainers for light attack duty. No. 3 Group (203 and 204 Squadrons) also operates PC-7s; No. 4 Group (201 and 205 Squadrons) is equipped with PC-7s. No. 5 Group consists of No. 101 communications Squadron and a photo-reconnaissance unit, both equipped with Aero Commander 500S piston-engined light twins. Nos. 301 and 302 Squadrons, in No. 6 Group, operate a total of 8 turboprop-powered Lockheed C-130 Hercules and 5 C-54, 2 C-118A and 1 DC-7 piston-engined transports. The main combat Group, No. 7, comprises No. 401 Squadron with 11 F-5E Tiger II and F-5F 2-seat fighters; and No. 202 Squadron with AT-33A jet trainer/fighter-bombers. No. 8 Group has 7 C-47s in a VIP transport squadron. No. 9 Group operates the Air Force's remaining 12 or more C-47s in Nos. 311 and 312 transport Squadrons. There is a Presidential Squadron with 7 Boeing 727s, 1 757, 2 737s, 1 HS.125, 1 Electra, 1 JetStar, 1 Islander, 2 Super Pumas and 1 Bell 212. Other training aircraft include 20 Mudry CAP-10Bs, 20 Beech Musketeers, 40 Bonanzas and over 20 T-28 Trojans.

INTERNATIONAL RELATIONS

Membership. Mexico is a member of UN, OAS, SELA and LAIA.

ECONOMY

Policy. An economic development plan (1989-94) was announced in June 1989 aimed at restoring growth and improving living standards. A privatization programme includes banks, steel and telecommunications.

Budget. The 1988 budget provided for expenditure of 103,348,500m. pesos and revenue of 65,505,900m. pesos. Budget estimate for 1991: 234,000,000m. pesos.

Currency. The unit of currency is the *Mexican peso* (MXP). There are coins of 1, 5, 10, 20, 50, 100, 200, 500, 1,000 and 5,000 *pesos*; and banknotes of 1,000, 2,000, 5,000, 10,000, 20,000 and 50,000 *pesos*. In Oct. 1991 the annualized rate of inflation was 16%. Beginning in 1990 the peso was progressively devalued against the US dollar at an annual rate first of 10.5%, then of 5%. In Nov. 1991 this was halved to 20 centavos per day. International exchange reserves were US$16,270m. in Sept. 1991. Total currency in circulation (1988) was 13,164,400m. *pesos*. Rate of exchange (controlled rate), March 1992: 3,029 pesos = US$1; 5,318 pesos = £1. There is a higher rate, for 'essential imports'.

Banking and Finance. The Bank of Mexico, established 1 Sept. 1925, is the central bank of issue; it is modelled on the Federal Reserve system, with large powers to 'manage' the currency. Banks were nationalized in 1982, but in May 1990 the government approved their reprivatization. The state continues to have a majority holding in foreign trade and rural development banks. Foreign holdings are limited to 30%.

There is a stock exchange in Mexico City.

Weights and Measures. The metric system is legal.

ENERGY AND NATURAL RESOURCES

Electricity. Output in 1990 was 116,892 kwh, of which 23,757 kwh was hydro-electric. Supply 120 volts; 50 Hz and some 120 volts; 60 Hz.

Oil. Mexico has the largest oil deposits in Latin America. Crude petroleum output was 155·4m. tonnes in 1991.

Gas. Natural gas production 3,478m. cu. feet in 1988.

Minerals. Mexico is a leading producer of strontium and fluorite. Uranium reserves, 1982: 15,000 tonnes proven, 150,000 tonnes potential. Coal reserves, 5,448m. tonnes, including 1,675m. tonnes (65% cokeable) high-grade coking coal in Coahuila. Coal output in 1989 was 6,460m. tonnes.

A 1990–94 development plan for minerals envisages an expansion of foreign investment and a full inventorization of mineral reserves.

Output, (in 1,000 tonnes) 1989: Lead, 62·8; 1990: Copper, 29·1; zinc, 29·8; fluorite, 67·2; pig iron, 6,194·0; sulphur, 2,135·6; manganese, 136·7; barite, 310·6; graphite, 25·3; silver (tonnes), 2,324; gold, 8.

Agriculture. In 1981 Mexico had 21·9m. ha of arable land, 74·4m. ha of meadows and pastures, 48·1m. ha of forests, 1·6m. ha of permanent crops and 40·6m. ha of other land. Agriculture provided 8% of GDP in 1991. Some 60% of agricultural land belongs to about 28,000 *ejidos*, communal lands with each member farming his plot independently. *Ejidos* can be inherited but not sold or rented. Other private farmers may not own more than 100 ha of irrigated land or an equivalent in unirrigated land. There is a theoretical legal minimum of 10 ha for holdings, but some 60% of private farms were less than 5 ha in 1990. Laws abolishing the *ejido* system were passed in 1992. Grains occupy most of the cultivated land, with about 43% given to maize, 10% to sorghum and 5% to wheat. In 1982 there were 146,083 tractors.

Livestock (1990): Cattle, 32·0m.; sheep, 5·8m.; pigs, 15·2m.; goats, 10·4m.; (1988) horses, 6·16m.; mules, 3·13m.; donkeys, 3·18; (1988) poultry, 243m.

Production of crops in 1990 (in 1,000 tonnes): Wheat, 3,759; rice, 229; barley, 468; maize, 12,019; sorghum, 5,754; cotton-seed, 263; tomatoes, 1,746; grapes, 506; apples, 416; oranges, 708; lemons and limes, 612; mangoes, 816; pineapples, 337; bananas, 1,065; coffee, 413; (1989) sugar-cane, 25,112; (1988) potatoes, 960; cotton-yarn, 253.

Forestry. Forests extended over 44m. ha in 1984, representing 23% of the land area, containing pine, spruce, cedar, mahogany, logwood and rosewood. There are 14 forest reserves (nearly 0·8m. ha) and 47 national park forests of 0·75m. ha. In 1990 total roundwood production amounted to 8·12m. cu. metres.

Fisheries. Catch (1990, in 1,000 tonnes), 1,283·7, including: Sardines, 347·9; anchovies, 85·5 (1988 industrial consumption); shrimp, 44·8; oysters, 52·0; tuna, including crab, tunny and jurel, 138·6; dog-fish and shark, 34·4; sea perch (*mojarras*), 90·5; sea bass, 13·2; saw-fish, 15·4; carp, 26·1; freshwater fish, 11·9.

INDUSTRY. In 1989 manufacturing industry provided 22·8% of GDP.

Labour. In 1987 unemployment was estimated to be over 50%. The legal minimum wage was raised 12% in Nov. 1991.

Trade Unions. The Mexican Labour Congress (CTM), leader Fidel Velazquez (b. 1900), is incorporated into the Institutional Revolutionary Party, and is an umbrella organization numbering some 5m. In 1990 there were attempts to form independent unions. A 'Pact for Economic Stability and Growth' between government, business and labour restrained prices and wages in the private sector throughout 1991. In Nov. 1991 the Pact was extended to Jan. 1993.

FOREIGN ECONOMIC RELATIONS. In Sept. 1991 Mexico signed the free trade Treaty of Santiago with Chile, envisaging an annual 10% tariffs reduction from Jan. 1992. Nominal foreign debt was US$79,000m. in 1990.

Commerce. Trade for calendar years in US$1m.:

	1986	*1987*	*1988*	*1989*	*1990*
Imports	11,918	12,761	19,720	18,202	22,454
Exports	16,031	20,656	20,565	16,950	20,618

Of total imports in 1990, 69·1% came from USA, 6·0% from Federal Republic of Germany, 5·0% from Japan and 1·7% from UK.

Of total exports in 1990, 74·7% went to USA, 5·2% to Japan, 5·4% to Spain and 0·7% to UK.

The in-bond (*maquiladora*) assembly plants along the US border generate the largest flow of foreign exchange with oil (40% of exports in 1990) and tourism.

Total trade between Mexico and UK (British Department of Trade returns, in £1,000 sterling):

	1987	*1988*	*1989*	*1990*	*1991*
Imports to UK	244,719	144,947	165,295	172,144	147,214
Exports and re-exports from UK	198,992	190,011	205,130	262,952	276,557

Tourism. In 1990, there were 6·6m. tourists; gross revenue, including border visitors, amounted to US$3,000m.

COMMUNICATIONS

Roads. Total length, (1990) 239,235 km, of which 47,504 km were main roads, 61,108 km were secondary roads and 130,623 km by-roads. In 1990 6,754,096 motor vehicles (6,439,620 private), 4,892,848 lorries, 94,004 buses and 231,503 motorcycles were registered.

Railways. The sole common carrier is National Railways, *Ferrocarriles Nacionales de Mexico* (NdeM). It comprises 20,216 km of 1,435 mm gauge and 90 km of 914 mm gauge. In 1989 it carried 53.9m. tonnes of freight and in 1990, 17.1m. passengers. In Mexico City an urban railway system opened in 1969 had 141 km of route and 8 lines in 1989 and carried 1,543m. passengers. There are light rail lines in Guadalajara (15 km) and Monterrey (17·5 km).

Civil Aviation. There are 32 international and 41 national airports. Each of the larger states has a local airline which links them with main airports. Thirty-four companies maintained international services, of which *Aeromexíco* and *Mexicana de Aviacíon* are Mexican. In 1989 there were 17·78m. passengers on domestic flights and 8·67m. on international flights.

Shipping. Mexico has 49 ocean ports, of which, on the Gulf coast, the most important include Coatzacoalcos, Carmen (Campeche), Tampico, Veracruz and Tuxpan. On the Pacific Coast are Salina Cruz, Isla de Cedros, Guaymas, Santa Rosalia, Manzanillo, Lázaro Cárdenas and Mazatlán.

Merchant shipping loaded 122·73m. tonnes and unloaded 52·89m. tonnes of cargo in 1990. In 1982, the merchant marine comprised 545 vessels (of over 100 GRT) with a total tonnage of 1,251,630 GRT.

Telecommunications. In 1980 the telegraph and telephone system had 7,140 offices. Telmex, previously a state-controlled company, was privatized in 1991. It controls about 98% of all the telephone service. Telephones in use, Jan. 1985, 7,329,416.

In 1989 there were 1,524 radio stations while (1986) 21m. homes had receiving sets. In 1989 commercial television stations numbered 537; there were 9·5m. homes with receiving sets in 1988.

Cinemas (1987). Cinemas numbered 2,226.

Newspapers (1986). There were 308 dailies with a combined circulation of 10·36m., 25 newspapers of lesser frequency (0·72m.) and 98 journals (16·94m.).

JUSTICE, RELIGION, EDUCATION AND WELFARE

Justice. Magistrates of the Supreme Court are appointed for 6 years by the President and confirmed by the Senate; they can be removed only on impeachment. The courts include the Supreme Court with 21 magistrates, 12 collegiate circuit courts with 3 judges each and 9 unitary circuit courts with 1 judge each, and 68 district courts with 1 judge each.

The penal code of 1 Jan. 1930 abolished the death penalty, except for the armed forces.

Religion. The prevailing religion is the Roman Catholic (80% of the population in 1991); with (1983) 3 cardinals, 12 archbishops and 87 bishops, but by the constitution of 1857, the Church was separated from the State, and the constitution of 1917 provided strict regulation of this and all other religions. In Nov. 1991 Congress approved an amendment to the 1917 constitution permitting the recognition of churches by the state, the possession of property by churches and the enfranchisement of priests. State and church remain separated, and church buildings remain state property. At the 1980 census there were also 3·3% Protestants, and 4·1% members of other religions.

Education. Primary and secondary education is free and compulsory, and secular, although religious instruction is permitted in private schools.

In 1988–89 there were:

	Establishments	Teachers	Students
Nursery	43,339	98,521	2,662,588
Primary	80,636	466,532	14,493,763
Secondary	18,686	233,042	4,267,156
Vocational training	3,240	22,153	436,128
Professional	1,807	37,303	413,481
Other advanced	6,281	241,794	2,937,164

The most important university is the Universidad Nacional Autónoma de México (UNAM) in México City which, with its associated institutions, had, in 1982, 136,534 students (excluding post-graduates). UNAM was founded in 1551, re-organized in 1910, and granted full autonomy in 1920. Other universities of particular importance in México City are the Instituto Politécnico Nacional, specializing in technology and applied science, with 52,694 students, and the Universidad Autónoma Metropolitana with 27,452 students, opened in 1973.

Outside México City the principal universities are the Universidad de Guadalajara (in Guadalajara) with 65,799 students; the Universidad Veracruzana (in Jalapa) with 57,755 students; the Universidad Autónoma de Nueva León (in Monterrey) with 48,124 students; the Universidad Autónoma de Puebla (in Puebla) with 39,505 students; the Universidad Auto noma de Sinaloa (in Culiacán) with 33,366 students; and the Universidad Michoacana (in Morelia) with 23,935 students.

Health. In 1986 Mexico had 71,058 physicians; there were 11,072 state and private hospitals and clinics with 57,391 beds.

DIPLOMATIC REPRESENTATIVES

Of Mexico in Great Britain (8 Halkin St., London, SW1X 7DW)
Ambassador: Bernardo Sepúlveda, GCMG.

Of Great Britain in Mexico (Lerma 71, Col. Cuauhtémoc, México City 06500, D.F.)
Ambassador: Sir Roger Hervey, KCMG.

Of Mexico in the USA (2829 16th St., NW, Washington, D.C., 20009)
Ambassador: Gustavo Petricioli.

Of the USA in Mexico (Paseo de la Reforma 305, México City 5, D.F.)
Ambassador: John D. Negroponte.

Of Mexico to the United Nations
Ambassador: Dr Jorge Montaño

Further Reading

Anuario Estadístico de los Estados Unidos Mexicanos. Annual
Revista de Estadística (Monthly); *Revista de Economia* (Monthly)
Banco de México S.A., Annual report

Banco Nacional de Comercio Exterior. *Comercio Exterior,* monthly.—*Mexico.* Annual (in Spanish or English)

Bailey, J. J., *Governing Mexico: The Statecraft of Crisis Management.* London and New York, 1988

Bazant, J., *A Concise History of Mexico.* CUP, 1977

Bethell, L. (ed.) *Mexico since Independence.* CUP, 1992

Grayson, G. W., *Oil and Mexican Foreign Policy.* Univ. of Pittsburgh Press, 1988

Hamilton, N. and Harding, T. F., (eds.) *Mexico: State, Economy and Social Conflict.* London, 1986

Philip, G., (ed.) *Politics in Mexico.* London, 1985.—*The Presidency in Mexican Politics.* London, 1991

Riding, A., *Distant Neighbours.* London, 1985.—*Mexico: Inside the Volcano.* London, 1987

Robbins, N. C., *Mexico.* [Bibliography] Oxford and Santa Barbara, 1984

Ruíz, R. E. *Triumphs and Tragedy: a History of the Mexican People.* New York, 1992

MICRONESIA

Capital: Kolonia
Population: 107,900 (1990)
GNP per capita: US$1,500 (1989)

Federated States of Micronesia

HISTORY. Spain acquired sovereignty over the Caroline Islands in 1885–86, but sold the archipelago to Germany in 1899. Japan occupied the Islands at the beginning of the First World War, and in 1921 they were mandated to Japan by the League of Nations. Captured by Allied Forces in the Second World War in 1944, the Islands became part of the UN Trust Territory of the Pacific Islands created on 18 July 1947 and administered by the USA. The Federated States of Micronesia came into being on 10 May 1979 comprising all of the Caroline Islands except the Belau (Palau) group, and on 3 Nov. 1986 entered into a 15-year Compact of Free Association with the USA. The UN recognized the termination of the Trusteeship Agreement on 22 Dec. 1990, and Micronesia became a full UN member state on 17 Sept. 1991.

AREA AND POPULATION. The Federated States lie in the Western Pacific between 137° and 163° E, comprising 607 islands with a total land area of 701 sq. km (271 sq. miles). The population (Census 1980) was 73,160; estimate (1990) 107,900. There are 8 indigenous languages spoken in the archipelago; English is used in the schools and is the official language.

The areas and populations of the 4 states (east to west) are as follows:

State	Sq. km	1980 Census	1990 Estimate	Headquarters
Kosrae	109	5,491	7,200	Lelu
Pohnpei	344	22,081	33,100	Kolonia
Truk	127	37,488	53,700	Moen
Yap	119	8,100	13,900	Kolonia

Kosrae (formerly Kusaie) consists of a single volcanic island; its inhabitants are Kosraeans, with their own Micronesian language.

Pohnpei comprises a single volcanic island, Pohnpei (formerly Ponape, covering 334 sq. km with 30,000 inhabitants in 1990), and 8 scattered coral atolls; among the atolls, Mokil and Pingelap in the east have their own Micronesian language and Nukuoro and Kapingamarangi in the south speak a Polynesian language, while Pohnpeian is spoken throughout the rest of the state.

Truk consists of a group of 14 volcanic islands within a large reef-fringed lagoon, with 45,000 inhabitants in 1990; the state also included a dozen coral atolls, the most important being the Mortlock Islands; 83% of the state's population speak Trukese and 16% Mortlockese.

Yap also comprises a main group of 4 islands (covering 101 sq. km with 9,200 inhabitants in 1990),and 13 coral atolls, the main ones being Ulithi and Woleai; 50% of the state's inhabitants speak Yapese and 34% Ulithian (or Woleaian).

The chief towns (1980) are Moen (10,351) and Tol (6,705), both in the main Truk group, and the federal capital Kolonia (5,549) on Pohnpei.

CLIMATE. Kolonia, Pohnpei, Jan. 80°F (26·7°C), July 79°F (26·1°C). Annual rainfall 194" (4,859 mm).

CONSTITUTION AND GOVERNMENT. Under the Constitution adopted on 18 July 1978, there is a 14-member National Congress, comprising 10 members elected for 2-year terms from single-member constituencies of similar electorates, and 4 Senators elected one from each State for a 4-year term. The Federal President and Vice-President are directly elected for 4-year terms:

President: Bailey Olter (b. 1932)
Vice-President: Hiroshi Ismael.

957

Each State has a Governor and a unicameral State Legislature, all directly elected for terms of 4 years.

National flag: Blue, with a ring of 4 white stars in the centre.

INTERNATIONAL RELATIONS

Membership. Micronesia is a member of the UN.

ECONOMY

Budget. The budget for 1985 amounted to US$80,966,000.

ENERGY AND NATURAL RESOURCES

Fisheries. In 1988 the catch amounted to 3,600 tons.

FOREIGN ECONOMIC RELATIONS

Commerce. In 1986 imports totalled US$44·2m., and exports (mainly copra) US$2·3m. Major trading partners are the USA and Japan.

Tourism. In 1985 there were 11,805 visitors.

COMMUNICATIONS

Roads. In 1987 there were 226 km of roads (39 km paved).

Civil Aviation. There are international airports on Pohnpei, Truk (Moen), Yap and Kosrae.

Shipping. The main ports are at Kolonia, Truk and Okat.

Telecommunications. In 1986 there were 1,556 telephones. There are 6 radio and 6 TV stations, and in 1986 there were estimated to be 17,000 radio and 1,100 TV sets.

JUSTICE, RELIGION, EDUCATION AND WELFARE

Justice. There is a Supreme Court in Kolonia, and a State Court in each of the 4 states.

Religion. Yap is mainly Roman Catholic, while Protestantism is prevalent elsewhere.

Education. In 1983–84 there were 23,345 in 151 primary schools, 4,159 pupils in 14 high schools and 920 students in the 2-year College of Micronesia in Kolonia.

Health. In 1985 there were 36 doctors, 13 dentists, 7 pharmacists and 257 nurses. There were 4 hospitals with 325 beds.

DIPLOMATIC REPRESENTATIVES

Great Britain recognized Micronesia in Aug. 1991.

Of Micronesia in the USA and to the United Nations
Ambassador: Jesse B. Marehalau.

Further Reading

Kluge, P. F., *The Edge of Paradise: America in Micronesia.* New York, 1991

MONACO

Capital: Monaco
Population: 29,876 (1990)

Principauté de Monaco

HISTORY. Monaco is a small Principality on the Mediterranean, surrounded by the French Department of Alpes Maritimes except on the side towards the sea. From 1297 it belonged to the house of Grimaldi. In 1731 it passed into the female line, Louise Hippolyte, daughter of Antoine I, heiress of Monaco, marrying Jacques de Goyon Matignon, Count of Torigni, who took the name and arms of Grimaldi. The Principality was placed under the protection of the Kingdom of Sardinia by the Treaty of Vienna, 1815, and under that of France in 1861. Prince Albert I (reigned 1889–1922) acquired fame as an oceanographer; and his son Louis II (1922–49) was instrumental in establishing the International Hydrographic Bureau.

AREA AND POPULATION. The area is 195 ha (481 acres). The Principality is divided into 4 districts: Monaco-Ville, la Condamine, Monte-Carlo and Fontvieille. Population (1990), 29,876, of whom 6,200 were Monegasques. The official language is French.

CLIMATE. A Mediterranean climate, with mild moist winters and hot dry summers. Monaco. Jan. 50°F (10°C), July 74°F (23·3°C). Annual rainfall 30" (758 mm).

REIGNING PRINCE. Rainier III, born 31 May 1923, son of Princess Charlotte, Duchess of Valentinois, daughter of Prince Louis II, 1898–1977 (married 19 March 1920 to Prince Pierre, Comte de Polignac, who had taken the name Grimaldi, from whom she was divorced 18 Feb. 1933). Prince Rainier succeeded his grandfather Louis II, who died on 9 May 1949. He married on 19 April 1956 Miss Grace Kelly, a citizen of the USA (died 14 Sept. 1982). *Issue:* Princess Caroline Louise Marguerite, born 23 Jan. 1957; married Philippe Junot on 28 June 1978, divorced, 9 Oct. 1980, married Stefano Casiraghi on 29 Dec. 1983 (died, 3 Oct. 1990), offspring: Andrea, born 8 June 1984, Charlotte, born 3 Aug. 1986, Pierre, born 7 Sept. 1987. Prince Albert Alexandre Louis Pierre, born 14 March 1958 *(heir apparent)*. Princess Stephanie Marie Elisabeth, born 1 Feb. 1965.

CONSTITUTION AND GOVERNMENT. Prince Rainier III on 28 Jan. 1959 suspended the Constitution of 5 Jan. 1911, thereby dissolving the National Council and the Communal Council. On 28 March 1962 the National Council (18 members elected every 5 years, last elections 1988) and the Communal Council (15 members elected every 4 years, last elections 1987) were re-established as elected bodies. On 17 Dec. 1962 a new constitution was promulgated. It maintains the hereditary monarchy, though Prince Rainier renounces the principle of divine right. The supreme tribunal becomes the custodian of fundamental liberties, and guarantees are given for the right of association, trade union freedom and the right to strike. It provides for votes for women and the abolition of the death penalty.

The constitution can be modified only with the approval of the elected National Council. Women were given the vote in 1945.

Monegasque relations with France are based on conventions of 1963. French citizens are treated as if in France.

National flag: Horizontally red over white.

ECONOMY

Planning. A 22-ha site reclaimed from the sea at Fontvieille has been earmarked for office and residential development. The present industrial zone is to be reorganized and developed with a view to attracting new light industry.

Budget. The budget (in 1,000 francs) was as follows:

	1987	1988	1989	1990	1991
Revenue	2,232,032	2,542,175	2,436,246	2,666,568	2,844,940
Expenditure	2,229,806	2,494,307	2,427,436	2,657,565	2,840,040

Currency. Monaco is a member of the French Franc Zone.

Banking and Finance. There were 39 banks in 1991. Financial services represent about 35% of economic activity.

Weights and Measures. The metric system is in use.

INDUSTRY. Light industry makes up about 25% of economic activity. There are some 700 small businesses, including chemicals, plastics, electronics, engineering and paper.

Labour. There were 28,590 persons employed on 1 June 1991.

Trade Unions. Membership of trade unions was estimated at 2,000 out of a work force of 25,600 (1989).

EXTERNAL ECONOMIC RELATIONS

Commerce. There is a customs union with France, and international trade is included with France.

Tourism. Tourism is the main industry. There were 244,640 overnight tourists in 1990, who spent a total of 726,561 nights.

COMMUNICATIONS

Roads. There were 50 km of roads in 1991.

Railways. The 1·6 km of main line passing through the country is operated by the French National Railways (SNCF).

Civil Aviation. The nearest airport is at Nice, France. At the Heliport of Monaco (Fontvieille) there were 125,651 passengers in the year ending Sept. 1991 (98,550 in the year ending Sept. 1990).

Shipping. The harbour has an area of 15 ha; depth at the entrance is 26 metres, and alongside the quays, 7 metres. Length of the quays: 2,290 metres.

Telecommunications. Telephone subscribers numbered 26,240 in 1990 and telex subscribers, 676. Monaco issues its own postage stamps.

Radio Monte Carlo broadcasts FM commercial programmes in French (long- and medium-waves). Radio Monte Carlo owns 55% of Radio Monte Carlo Relay Station on Cyprus. The foreign service is dedicated exclusively to religious broadcasts and is maintained by voluntary contributions. It operates in 36 languages under the name 'Trans World Radio' and has relay facilities on Bonaire, West Indies, and is planning to build relay facilities in the southern parts of Africa. *Télé Monté-Carlo* broadcasts TV programmes in French, Italian and English. There is a 30-channel cable service.

Cinemas. In 1989 there were 4 cinemas (one open air) with seating capacity of 1,000.

JUSTICE, RELIGION, EDUCATION AND WELFARE

Justice. There are the following courts, *Juge de Paix*, Tribunal of the First Instance, a Court of Appeal, Criminal Tribunal, *Cour de Révision Judiciaire* and a Supreme Tribunal.

Police: There is an independent police force *(Sûreté Publique)* which comprised (1989) 236 policemen and inspectors.

Religion. There has been since 1887 a Roman Catholic bishop elevated since 1982 to an archbishop, directly dependent on the Holy See.

Education. In 1990 there were 5,523 pupils with over 735 teachers.

Health. In 1990 there were 537 hospital beds and 80 physicians.

DIPLOMATIC REPRESENTATIVES

British Consul-General (resident in Marseilles): John Illman.
British Honorary Consul (resident in Nice): Lieut.-Col. R. W. Challoner, OBE.
Consul-General for Monaco in London: I. S. Ivanovic.

Further Reading

Journal de Monaco. Bulletin Officiel. 1858 ff.
Handley-Taylor, G., *Bibliography of Monaco.* London, 1968
Hudson, G. L. *Monaco*: [Bibliography]. Oxford and Santa Barbara, 1990

MONGOLIA

Capital: Ulan Bator
Population: 2·15m. (1990)
GNP per capita: US$112 (1990)

(State of Mongolia)

HISTORY. Outer Mongolia was a Chinese province from 1691 to 1911, an auto-nomous state under Russian protection from 1912 to 1919 and again a Chinese pro-vince from 1919 to 1921. On 13 March 1921 a Provisional People's Government was established which declared the independence of Mongolia and on 5 Nov. 1921 signed a treaty with Soviet Russia annulling all previous unequal treaties and estab-lishing friendly relations. On 26 Nov. 1924 the Government proclaimed the country the Mongolian People's Republic.

On 5 Jan. 1946 China recognized the independence of Outer Mongolia after a plebiscite in Mongolia (20 Oct. 1945) had resulted in an overwhelming vote for in-dependence. A Sino-Soviet treaty of 14 Feb. 1950 guaranteed this independence. In Aug. 1986 a consular agreement, in June 1987 a boundary agreement, and in Nov. 1988 a border treaty, were signed with China.

Until 1990 sole power was in the hands of the Mongolian People's Revolutionary (*i.e.*, Communist) Party (MPRP), but an opposition Mongolian Democratic Party, founded in Dec. 1989, achieved tacit recognition and held its first congress in Feb. 1990. Following demonstrations and hunger-strikes, on 12 March the entire MPRP Politburo resigned and political opposition was legalized.

AREA AND POPULATION. Mongolia is bounded in the north by the Russian Federation, and in the east and south and west by China. Area, 1,566,500 sq. km (604,250 sq. miles). Population (1989 census), 2,095,600; 1990 estimate, 2,149,300 (57% urban; 49·9% male). Density, 1·35 per sq. km. Birth rate, 35·3 per 1,000; death rate, 8·5 per 1,000; marriage rate, 8·6 per 1,000; divorce rate, 0·5 per 1,000. Rate of increase, 26·8 per 1,000. The population is predominantly made up of Mongolian peoples (78·8% Halh). There is a Turkic Kazakh minority (5·9% of the population) and 20 Mongol minorities. The official language is Halh Mongol. Expectation of life in 1987 was 63 years. 43·6% of the population is under 16.

The republic is administratively divided into 3 cities: Ulan Bator, the capital, (1990 population, 575,000), Darhan, (88,600) and Erdenet (58,200), and 18 pro-vinces *(aimag)*. The provinces are sub-divided into 306 districts *(suums)*.

CLIMATE. A very extreme climate, with six months of mean temperatures below freezing, but much higher temperatures occur for a month or two in summer. Rain-fall is very low and limited to the months mid-May to mid-Sept. Ulan Bator. Jan. −14°F (−25·6°C), July 61°F (16·1°C). Annual rainfall 8" (208 mm).

CONSTITUTION AND GOVERNMENT. For the Communist régime be-fore 1990 *see* THE STATESMAN'S YEAR-BOOK 1990–91, p. 872. The Constitution of 13 Jan. 1992 abolished the 'People's Democracy', introduced democratic institu-tions and a market economy and guarantees freedom of speech.

Since May 1990, the legislature has consisted of the 430-member *Great People's Hural* elected from 306 rural constituencies *(suums)* and 10,000-strong urban con-stituencies; and the 50-member *Small State Hural*. Suffrage is universal at 18. The Great Hural meets 4 times in its 5-year term. The Small Hural meets twice a year for 75-day periods during its 5-year term; it is elected partly by the Great Hural and partly directly, and its Chairman is Vice-President of the Republic. The *President* of the Republic is elected by the Great Hural. Elections were scheduled for June 1992 for a new single-chamber 76-seat parliament.

At the election of July 1990 the electorate was 1m.; turn-out was 91·9%. The Mongolian People's Revolutionary Party (Communists) won 357 seats in the Great

Hural and 31 in the Small Hural. In the Great Hural the Democratic Party won 20 seats, the National Progress Party, 6, and the Social Democratic Party, 4.

In Sept. 1990 the Great Khural elected Punsalmaagiin Ochirbat (b. 1942) *President* of the Republic, Radnaasumberelin Gonchigdorj (b. 1954) *Vice-President*, and Dashiin Byambasuren (b. 1942) *Prime Minister*.

Other members of the government include:

First Deputy Prime Minister: Davaadorjiya Gambold. *Minister of National Development:* Jamiyangin Batsuri. *Foreign Minister:* Tserenpiliyn Gombosuren (b. 1943).

National flag: Red–sky-blue–red (vertical), with a golden 5-pointed star and under it the golden *soyombo* emblem on the red stripe nearest to the flagpole.

National anthem: Was being revised in 1991 to expunge references to the USSR.

Local government is carried out by 380 People's Deputies' Hurals. Some 13,000 deputies were elected in July 1990.

DEFENCE. Military service is 2 years.

Army. The Army comprises 4 motorized infantry divisions. Equipment includes 650 T-54/-55/-62 main battle tanks. Strength (1992) 14,000 (11,000 conscripts). There is a paramilitary Ministry of Public Security force of about 10,000 men.

Air Force. The Air Force has about 100 pilots and more than 70 aircraft, including 12 MiG-21 and 10 MiG-17 fighters; a total of about 30 An-2, An-24 and An-26 transports used mainly on civil air services; 3 Wilga utility aircraft; 6 Mi-4 and 10 Mi-8 helicopters; and 12 Yakovlev trainers. Personnel (1991), 500 with 22 combat aircraft.

INTERNATIONAL RELATIONS

Membership. Mongolia is a member of the UN and OIEC.

ECONOMY

Policy. Mongolia has had for centuries a traditional nomadic pastoral economy, which the Government aims to transform into a market economy. A law of May 1991 envisages privatization by the issue of vouchers to all citizens to acquire holdings in about 40% of state industrial property.

Budget (in 1m. tugriks):

	1982	1983	1985	1987	1989	1990
Revenue	4,830	5,156	5,741	6,442	6,902	6,494
Expenditure	3,131	5,126	5,701	6,409	7,062	6,812

Sources of revenue, 1990: Turnover tax, 54%; profits tax, 31%; social insurance, 3·7%. Expenditure: Economy, 46%; social and cultural, 45%.

Currency. The unit of currency is the *tugrik* (MNT) of 100 *möngö*. Notes are issued for 1, 2, 5, 10, 20, 50 and 100 *tugriks*; and coins for 1, 2, 5, 10, 15, 20, 50 *möngö* and 1 *tugrik*. The tugrik was devalued in June 1991 as a first step to convertibility. In March 1992, £1 = 73·67 *tugriks*; US$1 = 41·96 *tugriks*.

Banking and Finance. The Mongolian State Bank (established 1924) is the bank of issue, being also a commercial, savings and development bank. It has 21 main branches. There are also a Trade and Industry Bank, an Insurance Bank and a Co-operative Bank. A stock exchange opened in Ulan Bator in 1992.

Weights and Measures. The metric system is in use.

ENERGY AND NATURAL RESOURCES

Electricity. There are 6 thermal electric power stations. Production of electricity, 1990, 3,348m. kwh.

Minerals. There are large deposits of copper, nickel, zinc, molybdenum, phosphorites, tin, wolfram and fluorspar; production of the latter in 1990, 512,100 tonnes, entirely exported to the USSR. The copper/molybdenum ore-dressing plant at Erdenet was completed in 1981. There are major coalmines near Ulan Bator and Darhan. Coal (mainly lignite) production in 1990 was 7m. tonnes.

Agriculture. 73% of agricultural production derives from cattle-raising. In 1990 there were 2,262,000 horses, 2,848,700 cattle, 15,083,000 sheep, 537,500 camels and 5,125,700 goats.

Ownership of livestock (in 1m.) in 1990:

	Collective farms	State farms	Private
Cattle	1·09	0·30	1·46
Camels	0·44	0·01	0·09
Horses	1·00	0·15	1·11
Sheep	9·69	1·71	3·68
Goats	3·04	0·18	1·90

In 1990 there were 134,700 pigs and 326,200 poultry. 248,900 tonnes of meat and 25m. litres of fermented mare's milk. Milk production was 306m. litres. In 1990 there were 255 collective farms, 36 inter-farm associations, 20 fodder supply farms and 53 state farms.

All cultivated land belongs to collective or state farms. The total agricultural area in 1990 was 125·7m. ha, of which 1·4m. were arable (0·8m. sown) and 124·3m. meadows and pastures. 60·3% of the sown area belongs to state farms, 23% to collectives. In 1990, 83% was sown to cereals, 18% to fodder and 2% to vegetables. The 1990 crop was 596,200 tonnes of wheat; 2,300 tonnes of rye; 30,200 tonnes of oats; 88,900 tonnes of barley. In 1990, 131,100 tonnes of potatoes were harvested. In 1990 there were 7,500 tractors (15 h.p. units) and 2,300 combine harvesters.

Forestry. Forests, chiefly larch, cedar, fir and birch, occupy 15·1m. ha, 9·5% of the land area. Production, 1990: 471,600 cu. metres of sawn wood.

INDUSTRY. Industry though still small in scale and local in character, is being vigorously developed and now accounts for a greater share of GNP than agriculture. The food industry accounts for 25% of industrial production. The main industrial centre is Ulan Bator; others are at Erdenet and Baga-Nur, and a northern territorial industrial complex is being developed based on Darhan and Erdenet to produce copper and molybdenum concentrates, lime, cement, machinery and wood- and metal-worked products. Production figures (1990): Scoured wool, 9,700 tonnes; cement, 440,800 tonnes; leather footwear, 4·8m. pairs; meat, 59,000 tonnes; soap, 2,600 tonnes.

Labour. The labour force was 648,700 in 1990, including 123,400 in industry, 189,400 in agriculture, 44,600 in building, 48,000 in transport and communications and 49,200 in trade. In 1990, 49% of the labour force was female. Average wage was 557 tugriks per month in 1990.

Trade Unions. Membership was 0·53m. in 1988.

FOREIGN ECONOMIC RELATIONS. Relations with the USSR have been based on a 1985 treaty of economic co-operation.

Joint ventures with foreign firms are permitted. Foreign investors may acquire up to 49% of the equity in Mongolian companies.

Commerce. Since 1989 some enterprises have been able to trade directly abroad. Trade figures for 1990 (in 1m. tugriks): Exports, 1,967; imports, 2,751. Exports in 1990 included 48% minerals and fuels, 27% food and consumer goods and 15% non-food raw materials. 93% of foreign trade was with Communist countries. Main imports are machinery and fuel. Imports from the USSR totalled 480m. roubles in 1990, exports to the USSR, 347m. roubles. The main non-Communist trading partner was Japan.

Total trade between Mongolia and UK (British Department of Trade returns, in £1,000 sterling):

	1988	1989	1990	1991
Imports to UK	1,857	405	1,674	1,430
Exports and re-exports from UK	1,637	979	1,636	1,148

Tourism. 147,200 tourists visited Mongolia in 1990.

COMMUNICATIONS

Roads. There are 1,185 km of surfaced roads running around Ulan Bator, from Ulan Bator to Darhan, at points on the frontier with the Russian Federation and towards the south. Truck services run where there are no surfaced roads. 36·8m. tonnes of freight were carried in 1990, and 228·3m. passengers.

Railways. The Trans-Mongolian Railway (1,100 km in 1990) connects Ulan Bator with the Russian Federation and China. The Moscow–Ulan Bator–Beijing express runs each way once a week, and there are services to Irkutsk, Moscow and Beijing. There are spur lines to Erdenet and to the coalmines at Nalayh and Sharyn Gol. A separate line connects Choybalsan in the east with Borzaya on the Trans-Siberian Railway. 2·4m. passengers and 1·5m. tonnes of freight were carried in 1990.

Civil Aviation. Mongolian Airlines (MIAT) operates internal services, a flight to Irkutsk which links with a stopping service to Moscow, and a daily non-stop service to Moscow from Ulan Bator. There are weekly flights to Beijing. 10,000 tons of freight were carried in 1990 and 0·8m. passengers. Ulan Bator airport (Buyant Uhaa) was modernized and expanded in 1985.

Shipping. There is a steamer service on the Selenge River and a tug and barge service on Hövsgöl Lake. 70,000 tonnes of freight were carried in 1990.

Telecommunications. There were, in 1990, 428 post offices and 341 telephone exchanges. Number of telephones (1990), 66,400.

There are wireless stations at Ulan Bator, Gobi Altai and Olgii. In 1990 there were 205,600 radio and 137,400 television receivers. Television services began in 1967. A Mongolian television station opened in 1970. Mongolia is a member of the international TV organization Intervision.

Cinemas. In 1990 there were 30 cinemas, 522 mobile cinemas and 30 theatres.

Newspapers and books. In 1990, 56 newspapers and 45 journals were published. 717 book titles were published in 1990 in 6·4m. copies.

JUSTICE, RELIGION, EDUCATION AND WELFARE

Justice. The Procurator-General is appointed, and the Supreme Court elected, by the *Hural* for 5 years. There are also courts at province, town and district level. Lay assessors sit with professional judges.

Religion. Tibetan Buddhist Lamaism was the prevalent form of religion. It was suppressed in the 1930s, 40 monasteries with some 500 lamas (monks) function today.

Education. In 1990 there were 872 nurseries with 97,200 children. Schooling begins at the age of 7. In 1990 there were 634 general education schools with 440,900 pupils and 20,600 teachers, 31 specialized secondary schools with 18,500 students and 1,300 teachers and 44 vocational technical schools with 29,100 pupils. There is a state university (founded 1942) at Ulan Bator (4 professors, 271 lecturers and 1,900 students in 1990), and 7 other institutes of higher learning (teacher training, medicine, agriculture, economics, etc.) with 11,929 students in 1990 and 1,190 teachers. The Academy of Sciences (founded 1961) has 16 institutes and 715 research workers. In 1990, 3,513 students were sent to study abroad, principally in the USSR.

In 1946 the Mongolian alphabet was replaced by Cyrillic, but its teaching has now been resumed.

Health and Welfare. In 1990, 82·5m. tugriks were spent on maternity benefits.

Annual average per capita consumption (in kilogrammes) of foodstuffs in 1990:

Meat, 97; milk and products, 118; sugar, 23; flour, 97; potatoes, 23; fresh vegetables, 20. In 1990 there were 29 doctors and 126 hospital beds per 10,000 population.

DIPLOMATIC REPRESENTATIVES

Of Mongolia in Great Britain (7 Kensington Ct., London, W8 5DL)
Ambassador: Choisurengyn Baatar.

Of Great Britain in Mongolia (30 Enkh Taivny Gudamzh, Ulan Bator)
Ambassador: Anthony Morey.

Of Mongolia in the USA
Ambassador: Gendengiin Nyamdoo.

Of the USA in Mongolia
Ambassador: Joseph Edward Lake.

Of Mongolia to the United Nations
Ambassador: (Vacant).

Further Reading

The Central Statistical Office; *National Economy of the MPR, 1924–1984: Anniversary Statistical Collection.* Ulan Bator, 1984

Bawden, C. R., *The Modern History of Mongolia.* London, 1968
Butler, W. E., (ed.) *The Mongolian Legal System: Contemporary Legislation and Documentation.* The Hague, 1982
Jagchid, S. and Hyer, P., *Mongolia's Culture and Society.* Folkestone, 1979
Lattimore, O., *Nationalism and Revolution in Mongolia.* Leiden, 1955.—*Nomads and Commissars.* OUP, 1963
Lörinc, L., *Histoire de la Mongolie des Origines à nos Jours.* Budapest, 1984
News from Mongolia. Ulan Bator, fortnightly, Jan. 1980
Sanders, A. J. K., *The People's Republic of Mongolia: A General Reference Guide.* OUP, 1968.—*Mongolia: Politics, Economics and Society.* London, 1987
Shirendev, B. and Sanjdorj, M. (eds.) *History of the Mongolian People's Republic.* Vol. 3 (vols. 1 and 2 not translated). Harvard Univ. Press, 1976

MONTSERRAT

Capital: Plymouth
Population: 11,852 (1985)
GNP per capita: US$3,127 (1985)

HISTORY. Montserrat was discovered by Columbus in 1493 and colonized by Britain in 1632 who brought Irish settlers to the island. Montserrat formed part of the federal colony of the Leeward Islands from 1871 until 1956, when it became a separate colony following the dissolution of the Federation. The island's Constitution came into force in 1960 and the title Administrator was changed to that of Governor in 1971. On 17 Sept. 1989 hurricane 'Hugo' caused damage estimated at US$330m.

AREA AND POPULATION. Montserrat is situated in the Caribbean Sea 25 miles south-west of Antigua. The area is 39·5 sq. miles (106 sq. km). Population, 1985, 11,852. Chief town, Plymouth, 3,500 inhabitants.

CLIMATE. A tropical climate but with no well-defined rainy season, though July to Dec. shows slightly more rainfall, with the average for the year being about 60" (1,500 mm). Dec. to March is the cooler season while June to Nov. is the hotter season, when hurricanes may occur. Plymouth. Jan. 76°F (24·4°C), July 81°F (27·2°C). Annual rainfall 65" (1,628 mm).

CONSTITUTION AND GOVERNMENT. Montserrat is a crown colony. The Executive Council is composed of 4 elected Ministers (the Chief Minister and 3 other Ministers) and 2 civil service officials (Attorney-General and Financial Secretary). The Legislative Council consists of 7 elected and 2 civil service officials (the Attorney-General and Financial Secretary) and 2 nominated members. The Executive Council is presided over by the Governor and the Legislative Council by the Speaker.

In elections to the Legislative Council in 1990, 4 seats were won by the National Progressive Party, 1 by the National Development Party, 1 by the People's Liberation Movement and 1 by an independent.

Governor: David Taylor.
Chief Minister: Reuben Meade.
Flag: The British Blue Ensign with the shield of Montserrat in the fly.

ECONOMY

Budget. In 1990 budget expenditure was EC$38m. (EC$35m. in 1989).

Currency. 100 cents = 1 Eastern Caribbean dollar (XCD). Coins: 1, 2, 5, 25, 50 cents. Notes: 1, 5, 10, 20 and 100 dollars.

Banking and Finance. There is a Bank of Montserrat, a Government Savings Bank; Barclays Bank, the Guardian International Bank and the Royal Bank of Canada maintain branches and the Montserrat Building Society. Responsibility for overseeing offshore banking rests with the Governor.

ENERGY AND NATURAL RESOURCES

Electricity. Production (1987) 16·3m. kwh.

Agriculture. Self-sufficiency in fruit, ground provisions and vegetables though canned and preserved foodstuffs were imported was achieved in 1988. The processing and packaging of tropical fruits and herbal teas for export are being encouraged together with the growing of ornamental plants for export.

Livestock (1988); Cattle, 3,000; pigs, 1,000; sheep and goats, 11,005; poultry, 50,500.

Fisheries. Catch (1988) 100 tonnes.

INDUSTRY. Manufacturing contributes about 6% to GDP and accounts for 10%

967

of employment, but is responsible for up to 85% of exports. It is limited to small scale industries producing light consumer goods such as electronic components, plastic bags, leather goods and various items made from locally grown cotton.

FOREIGN ECONOMIC RELATIONS

Commerce. Imports in 1990 totalled EC$118·5m.; domestic exports, EC$4·3m. Chief imports were manufactured goods, food and beverages, machinery and transport equipment and fuel. Chief exports were cotton clothing, electronic parts and lighting fittings.

Total trade between Montserrat and UK (British Department of Trade returns, in £1,000 sterling):

	1987	1988	1989	1990	1991
Imports to UK	139	125	494	425	39
Exports and re-exports from UK	2,432	2,524	3,092	3,515	2,720

Tourism. In 1988, 29,736 tourists arrived in Montserrat.

COMMUNICATIONS

Roads. In 1987 there were 290 km of roads, 212 km paved, 1,368 passenger cars and 270 commercial vehicles.

Aviation. At Blackburne airport 4,447 aircraft landed in 1988, disembarking 30,272 passengers and 214 tonnes of cargo.

Shipping. In 1988, 270 cargo vessels arrived, landing 47,026 and loading (1987) 663 tonnes of cargo.

Post and Broadcasting. Number of telephones (1988), 3,938; telex, 46 and 44 facsimile subscribers. In 1984 there were 4,000 radio and 1,100 TV receivers.

JUSTICE, RELIGION, EDUCATION AND WELFARE

Justice. There are 2 magistrates' courts, at Plymouth and Cudjoe Head. Strength of the police force (1987), 2 gazetted officers, 3 inspectorate and 89 other ranks.

Religion. In 1980 (census) there were 1,368 Roman Catholics, 3,676 Anglicans, 2,742 Methodists, 1,041 Seventh Day Adventists, 1,503 Pentecostals and 285 members of the Church of God. There is also a Christian Council of Churches.

Education. There were (1989) 2 day-care centres, 12 nursery schools, 12 primary schools, a comprehensive secondary school with 3 campuses, and a technical training college. Schools are run by the Government, the churches and the private sector. In 1988 there were 460 pupils at nursery schools; 1,403 at primary school, 1,043 at secondary school and 72 at the technical training college. There is an Extra Mural Department of the University of the West Indies in Plymouth with about 200 students and 15 part-time and 1 full-time lecturers.

Health. In 1990 there were 8 doctors and 67 hospital beds.

Further Reading

Population Census 1980. Montserrat
Overseas Trade 1983. Montserrat Government
Vital Statistics Report. Montserrat Government, 1983
Statistical Digest 1984. Montserrat Government
Fergus, H.A., *Montserrat: Emerald Isle of the Caribbean.* London, 1983

Library: Public Library, Plymouth. *Librarian:* Miss Ruth Allen.

MOROCCO

Mamlaka al-Maghrebia
(Kingdom of Morocco)

Capital: Rabat
Population: 24.37m. (1989)
GNP per capita: US$900 (1989)

HISTORY. From 1912 to 1956 Morocco was divided into a French protectorate (established by the treaty of Fez concluded between France and the Sultan on 30 March 1912), a Spanish protectorate (established by the Franco-Spanish convention of 27 Nov. 1912) and the international zone of Tangier (set up by France, Spain and Great Britain on 18 Dec. 1923).

On 2 March 1956 France and the Sultan terminated the treaty of Fez; on 7 April 1956 Spain relinquished her protectorate, and on 29 Oct. 1956 France, Spain, Great Britain, Italy, USA, Belgium, the Netherlands, Sweden and Portugal abolished the international status of the Tangier Zone. The northern strip of Spanish Sahara was ceded by Spain on 10 April 1958, and on 30 June 1969 the former Spanish province of Ifni was returned to Morocco.

A tripartite agreement was announced on 14 Nov. 1975 providing for the transfer of power from Spanish Sahara (Western Sahara) to the Moroccan and Mauritanean governments on 28 Feb. 1976. Spanish troops left El-Aaiún on 20 Dec. 1975. On 14 April 1976 a Convention was signed by Mauritania and Morocco in which the 2 countries agreed to partition the former Spanish territory, but on 14 Aug. 1979 Mauritania renounced its claim to its share of the territory (Tiris El-Gharbiya) which was added by Morocco to its area. For Western Sahara *see* pp. 1220–21.

AREA AND POPULATION. Morocco is bounded by Algeria to the east and south-east, Western Sahara to the south-west, the Atlantic ocean to the north-west and the Mediterranean to the north. Excluding the Western Saharan territory claimed and occupied since 1976 by Morocco, the area is 458,730 sq. km and population at the 1982 census was 20,255,687. Western Sahara had an area of 252,120 sq. km and 163,868 population. Population in 1989: Morocco without Western Sahara, 24·37m. (11·2m. urban); Western Sahara, 194,000. Density, 34·6 per sq. km.

The 49 provinces and prefectures are grouped into 7 non-administrative regions. Area and population in 1989 (*italicized* provinces are in Western Sahara):

Province	Area in sq. km	Population in 1,000	Province	Area in sq. km	Population in 1,000
Agadir	5,910	751	Khouribga	4,250	526
Boujdour	100,120	10	Settat	9,750	781
Es-Semara	61,760	24	Kénitra	4,745	356
Guelmim	28,750	160	Chefchaouen	4,350	880
El-Aaiún	39,360	135	Khémisset	8,305	464
Ouarzazate	41,550	630	Rabat		642
Oued Eddahab	50,880	25	Salé	1,275	575
Tan-Tan	17,295	56	Skhirate-Témara		188
Taroudannt	16,460	645	Sidi Kacem	4,060	590
Tata	25,925	109	Tanger	1,195	539
Tiznit	6,960	370	Tétouan	0,000	000
El Kelâa Srahna	10,070	669	Larache	6,025	837
Essaouira	6,335	430	Al Hoceima	3,550	362
Marrakesh	14,775	1,485	Boulemane	14,395	151
Safi	7,285	827	Fes	5,400	985
Azilal	10,050	420	Taounate	5,585	597
Béni Mellal	7,075	873	Taza	15,020	704
Ben Slimane	2,760	199	Figuig	55,990	111
Aïn Chok-Hay Hassani		409	Nador	6,130	750
Aïn Sebaâ-Hay Mohammadi		547	Oujda	20,700	940
Ben Msik-Sidi Othmane	1,615	890	Errachidia	59,585	490
Casablanca-Anfa		1,054	Ifrane	3,310	115
Mohammadia-Znata		202	Khenifra	12,320	429
El Jadida	6,000	901	Meknes	3,995	734

969

The chief cities (with Census populations, 1982) are as follows:

Casablanca	2,139,204	Tangier	266,346	Agadir	110,479
Rabat	518,616	Oujda	260,082	Mohammedia	105,120
Fez	448,823	Tétouan	199,615	Beni Mellal	95,003
Marrakesh	439,728	Safi	197,616	Al Jadida	81,455
Meknès	319,783	Kénitra	188,194	Taza	77,216
Salé	289,391	Khouribga	127,181	Ksar al Kabir	73,541

The official language is Arabic, spoken by 75% of the population; the remainder speak Berber. French and Spanish are considered subsidiary languages.

CLIMATE. The climate ranges from semi-arid in the south to warm temperate Mediterranean conditions in the north, but cooler temperatures occur in the mountains. Rabat. Jan. 55°F (12·9°C), July 72°F (22·2°C). Annual rainfall 23" (564 mm). Agadir. Jan. 57°F (13·9°C), July 72°F (22·2°C). Annual rainfall 9" (224 mm). Casablanca. Jan. 54°F (12·2°C), July 72°F (22·2°C). Annual rainfall 16" (404 mm). Marrakesh. Jan. 52°F (11·1°C), July 84°F (28·9°C). Annual rainfall 10" (239 mm). Tangier. Jan. 53°F (11·7°C), July 72°F (22·2°C). Annual rainfall 36" (897 mm).

REIGNING KING. Hassan II, born on 9 July 1929, succeeded on 3 March 1961, on the death of his father Mohammed V, who reigned 1927–61. The royal style was changed from 'His Sherifian Majesty the Sultan' to 'His Majesty the King' on 18 Aug. 1957. *Heir apparent:* Crown Prince Sidi Mohammed, born 21 Aug. 1963.

The King holds supreme civil and religious authority; the latter in his capacity of Emir-el-Muminin or Commander of the Faithful. He resides usually at Rabat, but occasionally in one of the other traditional capitals, Fez (founded in 808), Marrakesh (founded in 1062), or at Skhirat.

CONSTITUTION AND GOVERNMENT. A new Constitution was approved by referendum in March 1972 and amendments were approved by referendum in May 1980. The Kingdom of Morocco is a constitutional monarchy with a legislature of a single chamber composed of 306 deputies. Deputies for 102 seats are elected by indirect vote through an electoral college representing the town councils, the regional assemblies, the chambers of commerce, industry and agriculture, and the trade unions. Deputies for the remaining 204 seats are by general election. The King, as sovereign head of State, appoints the Prime Minister and other Ministers, has the right to dissolve Parliament and approves legislation.

In the General Elections held on 14 Sept. 1984, the new *Union constitutionelle* (founded Jan. 1983) won 83 seats, the *Rassemblement nationale des indépendants* 61 seats, the *Union socialiste des forces populaires* 36 seats, the *Mouvement populaire* 47 seats, *Istiqlal* (Independence) 41 seats; others 38 seats.

Elections due in 1990 have been postponed to 1992.

National flag: Red, with a green pentacle star in the centre.

The cabinet in 1992 was composed as follows:

Prime Minister: N. Azzeddine Laraki.
Justice: Moulay Mustapha Belarbi Alaoui. *Interior and Information:* Driss Basri. *Foreign Affairs and Co-operation:* Abdellatif Filali. *Planning:* Rachid Ghazouani. *National Education:* Mohamed Hilali. *Economic Affairs:* Moulay Zine Zahidi. *Finance:* Abdellatif Jouahri. *Trade, Industry and Tourism:* Abdallah al-Azmani. *Handicrafts and Social Affairs:* Mohamed Labied. *Transport:* Mohamed Bouamoud. *Energy and Mining:* Mohamed Fettah. *Health:* Tayeb Bencheikh. *Maritime Fishing and Merchant Navy:* Bensalem Smili. *Secretary-General of the Government:* Abbas Kaissi. *Cultural Affairs:* Mohamed Benaissa. *Housing and Land Management:* Abderrahmane Boufettas. *Equipment, Executive and Professional Training:* Mohamed Kabbaj. *Posts and Telecommunications:* Mohand Laensar. *Agriculture and Land Reform:* Otman Demnati. *Relations with Parliament:* Tahar Afifi. *Youth and Sports:* Abdellatif Semlali. *Labour:* Hassan Abbadi. *Islamic Affairs:* Abdelkbar Alaoui Medaghri. *Administrative Affairs:* Abderrahim Ben

Abdeljalil. *Saharan Province:* Khali H. Ould Rachid. *Relations with the European Community:* Azzedine Guessous. There was 1 Minister of State.

Local Government: The country is administratively divided into 49 provinces and prefectures divided into 59 municipalities and 133 circles, which are subdivided into 760 rural communes and 40 autonomous centres.

DEFENCE. Military service is compulsory for 18 months.

Army. The Army is deployed in 3 commands: North-West Atlas, Border and South. It comprises 3 mechanized infantry and 2 parachute brigades; 11 mechanized infantry regiments; 10 artillery, 1 air defence and 9 armed squadron groups; and 37 infantry, 3 camel corps, 3 cavalry, 1 mountain and 4 engineer battalions. There is a Royal guard of 1,500. Equipment includes 224 M-48A5 and 60 M-60A1 main battle tanks and 58 AMX-13 light tanks. Strength (1992), 175,000. There are also 40,000 paramilitary troops.

Navy. The Navy includes 1 missile-armed Spanish-built frigate, 4 fast missile craft, 13 coastal patrol craft and 10 inshore patrol craft. There are additionally 3 medium landing ships of French origin, 2 transports and 1 Ro-Ro ferry in naval use. Personnel in 1991 numbered 7,000, including a 1,500 strong brigade of Naval Infantry. Bases are located at Casablanca, Agadir, Al-Hoceima and Dakhla.

The Coast Guard wing of the Royal Gendarmerie operates 18 patrol craft.

Air Force. The Air Force was formed in Nov. 1956. Equipment in current use is mainly of US and West European origin. It includes 40 Mirage F1s, a total of 35 F-5A/B/E/F fighter-bombers and RF-5A reconnaissance-fighters, 3 OV-10 Bronco counter-insurgency aircraft, 2 Falcon 20s for electronic warfare, and 24 Gazelle armed helicopters, 24 Alpha Jet advanced trainers, 22 Magister armed jet basic trainers, 12 T-34C-1 turboprop basic trainers, 10 Swiss-built Bravo primary trainers, 2 Mudry CAP 10B and 4 CAP 230 aerobatic trainers, 4 Broussard liaison aircraft, 90 Agusta-Bell 205 and 212, Puma and JetRanger helicopters, 2 Do 28D Skyservants for coastal patrol, 11 CH-47C heavy-lift helicopters, 18 C-130H turboprop transport aircraft, 2 KC-130H tanker/transports, a Falcon 50 and a Gulfstream II VIP transport, 2 Boeing 707s, 7 CN-235s and 8 turboprop King Air light transports. Personnel strength (1992) about 13,500, with 93 combat aircraft and 24 armed helicopters.

INTERNATIONAL RELATIONS

Membership. Morocco is a member of the UN, the Non-Aligned Movement, the Islamic Conference and the Arab League.

ECONOMY

Policy. An economic and social development plan ran from 1988 to 1992.

Budget. 1989 revenue was DH49,795m.; expenditure, DH54,145m.

Currency. The unit of currency is the *dirham* (MAD) of 100 *centimes*, introduced in 1959. Notes: 10, 50, 100 DH; coins: 0·10, 0·20, 0·50, 1 DH. The exchange rate in March 1992 was £1 sterling = 14·90 DH; US$1 = 8·49 DH.

Banking and Finance. The central bank is the Banque al Maghrib. Authorized banks are: La Banque Marocaine du Commerce Extérieur, La Banque Marocaine pour le Commerce et l'Industrie, La Banque Commerciale du Maroc, Compagnie Marocaine du Crédit et de Banque, Société Générale Marocaine de Banque, Crédit du Maroc, Union Marocaine de Banque, Société de dépôt et de crédits, Arab Bank Ltd, Bank of America, Banco Espagnol en Maruecos, Banque de Paris et des Pays-Bas, First National City Bank, Société Hollandaise de Banque et de Gestion, The British Bank of the Middle East, Société de Dépôt et de Crédits, Wafabank, Citibank, Algemene Bank Nederland and Banque Américano-Suisse pour le Maroc. The Banque Centrale Populaire and regional Banques populaires also provide banking services for small and medium businesses. There are 3 development banks:

Banque Nationale du Development Economique, whose major area of investment has been industry; Credit Industrial et Hotelier, which finances housing on easy terms; Caisse Nationale du Credit Agricole, which specializes in agriculture. La Banque National pour le Développement économique grants loans to the industrial sector. Le Crédit Immobilier et Hôtelier grants loans for construction. La Caisse de Dépôt et de Gestion is responsible for the centralization of savings and their management.

Weights and Measures. The metric system is legal.

ENERGY AND NATURAL RESOURCES

Electricity. Installed capacity was 2,199,400 kw. in 1989. Production was 8,507,300 kwh. (1,133,900 hydroelectric). Supply 110, 127 and 220 volts; 50 Hz.

Minerals. The principal mineral exploited is phosphate, the output of which was 18·7m. tonnes in 1989. Other minerals (in tonnes, 1989) are: Anthracite (504,300), iron ore (158,780), lead (95,513), copper (41,417), zinc (33,913), manganese (32,000), baryt (341,743), fluorine (105,000), salt (89,075), silver (317).

Agriculture. Land suitable for cultivation, 1989, 8·66m. ha, of which (in 1,000 ha): Cereals, 5,513; leguminous vegetables, 489; market gardening, 188; oil-producing, 136, industrial cultivation, 128; fodder, 145; dense fruit plantations, 612.

Production in 1989 (in 1,000 tonnes): Wheat, 3,927; barley, 2,999; maize, 403; fruit, 1,787 (of which citrus fruits, 1,275); pulses, 347; sunflower seeds, 96; ground-nuts, 23; sugar beets, 2,876; sugar-cane, 985; cotton, 29.

Dairy production in 1988 included: Milk, 923,000 tonnes; butter, 13,629 tonnes; cheese, 7,221 tonnes. Meat production (1989) 364,196 tonnes.

Livestock (in 1,000 head), 1989: Cattle, 3,400; sheep, 17,500; goats, 6,071.

Forestry. Natural forests covered (1989) 8·27m. ha, 526,262 ha were reafforested in 1988–89. They produce mainly firewood, building and industrial timber, some cork and charcoal.

Fisheries. The fishing fleet numbered 2,578 vessels in 1989 (of which 347 were deep-sea). The industry employed 83,000 workers in 1987. Total catch in 1989 was 517,714 tonnes, (deep-sea, 107,644 tonnes). Total catch value was DH2,891m.

INDUSTRY. In 1988 there were 4,874 industrial firms employing 355,104 persons. 1,601 of these employed fewer than 10 persons; 76, more than 500. Production, 1989 (in tonnes): Sugar, 470,347; olive oil, 30,000; cement, 4,605,000.

Labour. An increase of 15% in the minimum wage was decreed in 1991.

Trade Unions. In 1984 there were 8 trade unions.

FOREIGN ECONOMIC RELATIONS. In Feb. 1989 Morocco signed a treaty of economic co-operation with the 4 other Maghreb countries: Algeria, Libya, Mauritania and Tunisia.

Foreign debt was US$21,000m. in Sept. 1990.

Commerce. Imports and exports were (in DH1m.):

	1985	1986	1987	1988	1989
Imports	38,675	34,608	35,271	39,132	46,594
Exports	21,740	22,103	23,390	29,751	28,271

Exports (1989) of phosphates 12·4m. tonnes, value DH4,148m.

Exports in 1989 (in DH1m.) went mainly to France (8·3%), Spain (2·4%), and Italy (1·8%). Imports were mainly from France (11·4%), Spain (4·1%), and Iraq (3·3%).

Total trade between Morocco and UK (British Department of Trade returns, in £1,000 sterling):

	1987	1988	1989	1990	1991
Imports to UK	61,108	78,896	96,138	106,425	95,522
Exports and re-exports from UK	94,487	79,017	84,475	118,599	152,245

Tourism. In 1989, 3,468,456 visitors stayed 18·6m. nights, spending DH9,600m.

COMMUNICATIONS

Roads. In 1989 there were 59,452 km of classified roads, of which 29,141 km were surfaced and including 9,577 km of surfaced main roads. A motorway links Rabat to Casablanca. 2·83m. passengers and 15·23m. tonnes of freight were carried in 1989. In 1989 there were in use 272,393 commercial vehicles, 634,431 private cars and 19,286 motor cycles. There were 22,668 road accidents in 1989 (839 fatalities).

Railways. In 1989 there were 1,893 km of railways, of which 974 km were electrified. The principal standard-gauge lines are from Casablanca eastward to the Algerian border, forming part of the continuous rail line to Tunis; Casablanca to Marrakesh with 2 important branches, one eastward to Oued Zem tapping the Khouribga phosphate mines, the other westward to the port of Safi. Another branch serves the manganese mines at Bou Arfa. Two new double-track electrified lines are to serve a new deep-water port at Jorf Lasfar.

In 1989 the railways carried 11·78m. passengers and 24·21m. tonnes of freight.

Civil Aviation. The national carrier is Royal Air Maroc. The major international airport is Mohammed V at Casablanca; there are also airports at Agadir, Al Hoceima, Marrakesh, Oujda, Rabat-Salé, Tangiers, Tetouan, Fez-Sais, Ouarzazate and El-Aaiún. 4,256,375 passengers and 44,150 tonnes of freight were carried in 1989. In 1990 the 5 Maghreb countries agreed to merge their national airlines into Air Maghreb.

Shipping. There are 12 ports, the largest being Casablanca, Tangiers and Agadir. 596,730 passengers and 19·49m. tonnes of freight were carried in 1989.

Telecommunications. In 1984 there were 578 post offices. Telephone subscribers totalled 335,000 in 1989.

There are broadcasts in Arabic, Berber, French, Spanish and English from Rabat and Tangier; television in Arabic and French began in 1962. In 1988 there were 4·4m. radio receivers and 1·2m. television receivers.

Cinemas. There were 252 cinemas in 1989 and 30·23m. attendances.

Newspapers. In 1984 there were 12 daily newspapers (7 Arabic, 5 French) and 18 main weeklies and monthlies (10 Arabic, 8 French).

JUSTICE, RELIGION, EDUCATION AND WELFARE

Justice. The legal system is based on French and Islamic law codes.

Religion. Islam is the established state religion. 98% are Sunni Moslems of the Malekite school and 2% are Christians, mainly Roman Catholic. The judiciary consists of a Supreme Court, courts of appeal, regional tribunals and magistrates' courts.

Education. Education is compulsory from the age of 7 to 13. In 1989–90 there were 32,698 Koranic schools with 36,891 teachers and 755,438 pupils; 290 pre-primary schools with 1,430 teachers and 32,034 pupils; 3,558 primary schools with 83,497 teachers and 2,085,105 pupils; 1,068 secondary schools with 72,434 teachers and 1,387,216 pupils. There were 11 universities with 6,187 teachers and 198,054 students (73,089 women), 9,506 students (3,391 women) in teacher training and 8,431 students (2,025 women) in other higher education.

Health. In the public sector, 1990, 2,619 doctors, and 36 dentists. In the private sector there were 2,243 doctors, and 473 dentists. In 1989 there were 76 hospitals, 16 maternity hospitals, 377 health centres and 1,243 dispensaries. In the public sector there were 24,054 hospital beds.

DIPLOMATIC REPRESENTATIVES

Of Morocco in Great Britain (49 Queen's Gate Gdns., London, SW7 5NE)
Ambassador: Khalil Haddaoui.

Of Great Britain in Morocco (17 Blvd de la Tour Hassan, Rabat)
Ambassador: John Macrae, CMG.

Of Morocco in the USA (1601 21st St., NW, Washington, D.C., 20009)
Ambassador: Mohammod Belkhayat.

Of the USA in Morocco (2 Ave. de Marrakech, Rabat)
Ambassador: E. Michael Ussery.

Of Morocco to the United Nations
Ambassador: Ali Skalli.

Further Reading

Direction de la Planification. *Plan d'Orientation pour le Développement Économique et Sociale, 1988–1992.* 1987
Direction de la Statistique. *Annuaire Statistique du Maroc.—Conjoncture Économique.* Quarterly *Bulletin Official.* Rabat. Weekly
Findlay, A. M. and A. M. and Lawless, R. I., *Morocco.* [Bibliography] Oxford and Santa Barbara, 1984
Kinross, Lord and Hales-Gary, D., *Morocco.* London, 1971

National library: Bibliothèque Générale et Archives, Rabat.
National statistical office: Direction de la Statistique, BP178, Rabat.

MOZAMBIQUE

Capital: Maputo
Population: 16·11m. (1991)
GNP per capita: US$80 (1989)

República de Moçambique

HISTORY. Trading settlements were established by Arab merchants at Sofala (Beira), Quelimane, Angoche and Mozambique Island in the fifteenth century. Mozambique Island was visited by Vasco da Gamba's fleet on 2 March 1498, and Sofala was occupied by Portuguese in 1506. At first ruled as part of Portuguese India, a separate administration was created in 1752, and on 11 June 1951 Mozambique became an Overseas Province of Portugal. Following a decade of guerrilla activity, Portugal and the nationalists jointly established a transitional government on 20 Sept. 1974. Independence was achieved on 25 June 1975. In March 1984 the Republic of South Africa and Mozambique signed a non-agression pact.

Since July 1990 the government and the RENAMO rebel movement have signed 3 agreements setting out conditions to end guerrilla warfare and organize elections.

AREA AND POPULATION. Mozambique is bounded east by the Indian ocean, south by South Africa, south-west by Swaziland, west by South Africa and Zimbabwe and north by Zambia, Malawi and Tanzania. It has an area of 799,380 sq. km (308,642 sq. miles) and a population, according to the census of 1980, of 11,673,725. Estimate (1991) 16,110,000 of whom 1,098,000 lived in the capital, Maputo. Other chief cities are Beira (1990 population, 299,300), Nampula (202,600) and Nacala (104,300). The areas, populations and capitals of the provinces are:

Province	Sq. km	Census 1980	Estimate 1987	Capital
Cabo Delgado	82,625	940,000	1,109,921	Pemba
Niassa	129,056	514,100	607,670	Lichinga
Nampula	81,606	2,402,700	2,837,856	Nampula
Zambézia	105,008	2,500,200	2,952,251	Quelimane
Tete	100,724	831,000	981,319	Tete
Manica	61,661	641,200	756,886	Chimoio
Sofala	68,018	1,065,200	1,257,710	Beira
Inhambane	68,615	997,600	1,167,022	Inhambane
Gaza	75,709	990,900	1,138,724	Xaixai
Province of Maputo	25,756	491,800	544,692	Maputo
City of Maputo	602	755,300	1,006,765	

The main ethnolinguistic groups are the Makua/Lomwe (52% of the population), mainly in the 4 provinces in the north, the Malawi (12%), Shona (6%) and Yao (3%) in Tete, Manica and Sofala, and the Thonga (24%) in the 3 provinces in the south. Portuguese remains the official language, but vernaculars are widely spoken throughout the country.

CLIMATE. A humid tropical climate, with a dry season from June to Sept. In general, temperatures and rainfall decrease from north to south. Maputo. Jan. 78°F (25·6°C), July 65°F (18·3°C). Annual rainfall 30" (760 mm). Beira. Jan. 82°F (27·8°C), July 69°F (20·6°C). Annual rainfall 60" (1,522 mm).

CONSTITUTION AND GOVERNMENT. Under the Constitution adopted at independence on 25 June 1975, the directing power of the state was vested in the Mozambique Liberation Front (*Frente de Liberação de Moçambique*, FRELIMO), the liberation movement, which in Feb. 1977 was reconstituted as sole political Party.

On 2 Nov. 1990 the People's Assembly unanimously voted a new constitution, which came into force on 30 Nov. This changed the name of the state to 'Republic of Mozambique' and that of the parliament to 'Assembly of the Republic', legalized opposition parties, provided for universal secret elections and introduced a bill of rights including the right to strike, press freedoms and habeas corpus. The

250-member People's Assembly had been elected in Dec. 1986. The Speaker is Marcelino dos Santos.

The Council of Ministers in March 1992 consisted of:

President, and Commander-in-Chief of the Armed Forces: Joaquim Alberto Chissano.
Prime Minister: Mário da Graça Machungo.
Foreign Affairs: Pascoal Manuel Mocumbi. *Finance:* Abdul Magid Osman.
Defence: Gen. Alberto Chipande.

National flag: Horizontally green, black, yellow with the black fimbriated in white; a red triangle based on the hoist, charged with a yellow star surmounted by an open white book and a crossed rifle and hoe in black.

Local Government. The capital of Maputo and 10 provinces, each under a Governor who is automatically a member of the Council of Ministers, are sub-divided into 112 districts.

DEFENCE. Selective conscription for 2 years is in force.

Army. The Army consists of 1 tank brigade and 7 infantry brigades, 6 anti-aircraft artillery battalions and many support units. A light infantry brigade is forming. Equipment includes 80 T-54/-55 main battle tanks. Strength (1992) 45,000. There are also 5,000 Border Guards and provincial militias.

Navy. The small flotilla based principally at Maputo, with subsidiary bases at Beira, Nacala, Pemba and Inhambane comprises 12 inshore patrol craft of mixed origins, 2 ex-Soviet inshore minesweepers and 2 landing craft. 4 of the patrol craft are based at Metangula on Lake Nyasa. Naval personnel in 1991 were believed to total 1,000.

Air Force. The Air Force is reported to have about 20 MiG-17 and 20 MiG-21 fighters, An-26 turboprop transports, and a few C-47 piston-engined transports. About 6 Mi-24 armed helicopters and 10 Mi-8 transport helicopters, a small number of L-39 jet trainers, Zlin 326 primary trainers and a few ex-Portuguese Air Force Alouette liaison helicopters. Personnel (1991) 6,000, with 40 combat aircraft and 6 armed helicopters.

INTERNATIONAL RELATIONS

Membership. Mozambique is a member of UN, OAU, SADCC and is an ACP state of EEC.

ECONOMY

Policy. In 1990 the government abandoned economic planning in favour of a market economy.

Budget. In 1987 the revenue was US$277·87m.; expenditure, US$427·91m. Foreign debt (1986) US$3,200m.

Currency. The unit of currency is the *metical* (MZM) of 100 *centavos*. The *metical* was established at par with the former *escudo* in 1980. In March 1992, £1 = 3,395 *meticais*; US$1 = 1,933·90 *meticais*.

Banking. Most banks had been nationalized by 1979. The *Banco de Moçambique* (bank of issue) and the *Banco Popular de Desenvolvimento* (state investment bank) each have a capital of 1,000m. meticais.

Weights and Measures. The metric system is in force.

ENERGY AND NATURAL RESOURCES

Electricity. Production (1986) 1,640m. kwh. Capacity (1986) 2,225,000 kw. Supply 220 volts; 50 Hz. The hydro-electric dam at Cabora Bassa on the Zambezi is the largest producer in Africa.

Minerals. Coal is the main mineral being exploited. Output was 380,000 tonnes in

1983. Coal reserves (estimate) 400m. tonnes. Small quantities of bauxite, gold, titanium, fluorite and colombo-tantalite are produced. Iron ore deposits and natural gas are known to exist.

Agriculture. Production in tonnes (1990): Cereals, 734,000; maize, 453,000; bananas, 85,000; sisal, 1,000; rice, 96,000; groundnuts, 70,000; copra, 70,000; vegetables, 32,000; citrus, potatoes, 70,000; cashews, 49,000; sunflower seed, 20,000; cotton (lint), 28,000.

Livestock 1990: 1·37m. cattle, 385,000 goats, 122,000 sheep, 170,000 pigs, 20,000 asses.

Forestry. Forests covered (1988) 19% of land area. Production (1985) 35,000 cu. metres of cut timber.

Fisheries. In 1984 the prawn catch was 5,800 tonnes; other fish (1986) 31,900 tonnes.

INDUSTRY. Although the country is overwhelmingly rural, there is some substantial industry in and around Maputo (steel, engineering, textiles, processing, docks and railways).

FOREIGN ECONOMIC RELATIONS

Commerce. Imports in 1987 totalled US$645m. and exports US$96m. In 1986 12% of imports came from the USSR, 12% from the Republic of South Africa and 12% from the USA. 21% of exports were to Spain, 22% to the USA and 23% to Japan. Shrimps made up 48% of exports; cashews, 12%; sugar, 10%; copra, 3% and petroleum products, 5%.

Total trade between Mozambique and UK (British Department of Trade returns, in £1,000 sterling):

	1987	1988	1989	1990	1991
Imports to UK	6,580	5,574	14,582	10,709	2,393
Exports and re-exports from UK	21,168	24,218	20,268	28,992	18,351

COMMUNICATIONS

Roads. There were, in 1984, 20,000 km of roads, of which 5,000 km were tarred. Motor vehicles, in 1980, included 99,400 passenger cars and 24,700 lorries and buses. The Government is devoting effort to constructing a new North/South road link, and to improving provincial rural feeder road systems.

Railways. The Mozambique State Railways consist of 5 independent networks known as the Maputo, Mozambique, Sofala (Beira), Inhambane and Gaza, and Quelimane systems. The Maputo system has a link at Komatipoort with the Republic of South Africa, Swaziland and Zimbabwe railways; the Sofala system links with Zimbabwe at Machipanda (near Umtali); and the Mozambique system links with Malawi at Entre Lagos. Total route-km (1986), 2,988 km (1,067 mm gauge), and 143 km (762 mm gauge). In 1989, 6·8m. passengers and 400m. tonne-km of goods were carried.

Civil Aviation. There are international airports at Maputo, Beira and Nampula with regular services to European and Southern African destination by several foreign airlines and by *Linhas Aéreas de Moçambique*, who also serve 13 domestic airports.

Shipping. The total tonnage handled by Mozambique ports (1987) was 2·7m. The principal ports are Maputo, Beira, Nacala and Quelimane.

Telecommunications. Maputo is connected by telegraph with the Transvaal system. Quelimane has telegraphic communication with Chiromo. Number of telephones (1983), 59,000.

Radio Moçambique is part state-owned and part commercial. There are 3 national programmes in Tsonga and Portuguese and an external service in English. Television is at a trial stage (colour by PAL). In 1991 there were about 0·5m. radio and 35,000 TV receivers.

Cinemas. There were 60 in 1987.

Newspapers. There are 2 daily newspapers: *Noticias,* published in Maputo, and *Diario de Mozambique* in Beira.

JUSTICE, RELIGION, EDUCATION AND WELFARE

Justice. The 1990 constitution provides for an independent judiciary, habeas corpus, and an entitlement to legal advice on arrest. The death penalty was abolished in Nov. 1990.

Religion. About 60% of the population follow traditional animist religions, while some 18% are Christian (mainly Roman Catholic) and 16% Moslem.

Education. In 1987 there were 1,370,528 pupils in 4,105 primary schools and (1986) 144,015 in 171 secondary schools. Private schools were permitted to function in 1990. The *Universidade Eduardo Mondlane* had 2,500 students in 1985. Literacy rate (1986) 30%.

Health. There were (1987) 1,156 hospitals and medical centres with 11,671 beds; there were 327 doctors, 1,112 midwives and 2,871 nursing personnel. In 1987 there were 138 dentists and 301 pharmacists.

DIPLOMATIC REPRESENTATIVES

Of Mozambique in Great Britain (21 Fitzroy Sq., London W1P 5HJ)
Ambassador: Armando Alexandre Panguene.

Of Great Britain in Mozambique (Ave. Vladimir I. Lenine 310, Maputo)
Ambassador: Maeve G. Fort, CMG.

Of Mozambique in the USA (1990 M. St., NW, Washington, D.C., 20036)
Ambassador: Hipolito Patrício.

Of the USA in Mozambique (Ave Kaunda 193, Maputo)
Ambassador: Townsend B. Friedman.

Of Mozambique to the United Nations
Ambassador: Pedro Comissario Afonso.

Further Reading

Darch, C., *Mozambique.* [Bibliography] Oxford and Santa Barbara, 1987
Hanlon, J., *Mozambique: The Revolution under Fire.* London, 1984
Henriksen, T. H., *Mozambique: A History.* London and Cape Town, 1978
Houser, G. and Shore, H., *Mozambique: Dream the Size of Freedom.* New York, 1975
Mondlane, E., *The Struggle for Mozambique.* London, 1983
Munslow, B., *Mozambique: The Revolution and its Origins.* London and New York, 1983

NAMIBIA

Capital: Windhoek
Population: 1·29m. (1988)
GNP per capita: US$1,020 (1986)

Republic of Namibia

HISTORY. Britain annexed Walvis Bay in 1878, and incorporated it in the Cape of Good Hope in 1884. In 1884 South West Africa was declared a German protectorate. In 1915 the Union of South Africa occupied German South West Africa at the request of the Allied powers. On 17 Dec. 1920 the League of Nations entrusted South West Africa as a Mandate to the Union of South Africa, to be administered under the laws of the mandatory power. After World War II South Africa refused to place the territory under the UN Trusteeship system, and formally applied for its annexation to the Union. In Oct. 1966 the General Assembly of the UN terminated South Africa's mandate, and established a UN Council for South West Africa in May 1967. However, South Africa continued to administer the territory, in defiance of various UN resolutions. In June 1968 the UN changed the name of the territory to Namibia. In 1971 the International Court of Justice ruled in an advisory opinion that South Africa's presence in Namibia was illegal. In Dec. 1973 the UN appointed a UN Commissioner for Namibia.

After negotiations between South Africa and the UN, a multi-racial Advisory Council was appointed in 1973. Representatives of all the population groups assembled in Windhoek for the Constitutional Conference, which in Aug. 1976 resolved that a multi-racial interim government be formed by early 1977, and that the country should become independent by 31 Dec. 1978. This resolution was rejected by the UK, the USA, the Federal Republic of Germany, France and Canada, after which South Africa agreed to universal suffrage elections. An Administrator-General was appointed in Sept. 1977 to govern the territory until independence, and he moved to abolish all laws based on racial discrimination – a precondition for elections. In April 1978 South Africa accepted a plan for UN-supervised elections leading to independence, which was endorsed in UN Security Council Resolution 435 of 27 July 1978. After the final plans for the UN-supervised elections were published, South Africa announced on 20 Sept. 1978 that it was going ahead with internally sponsored elections for a Constituent Assembly. In the elections held on 4-8 Dec. 1978 the Democratic Turnhalle Alliance (DTA) gained 41 of the 50 seats in a percentage poll of 82%, in spite of the fact that the South West Africa People's Organisation (SWAPO) instructed its members not to take part in the elections.

A 12-member Ministers' Council was instituted, and in Sept. 1981 it was enlarged to 15 members and given executive authority on all matters except constitutional issues, security and foreign affairs. On 11-13 Nov. 1980 elections were held for the second-tier Representative Authorities, which each controlled certain administrative functions for a specific ethnic group, but no specific geographical area. In Jan. 1983 the Ministers' Council and the National Assembly were dissolved and executive and legislative powers reverted to the Administrator-General.

In Sept. 1983 the Multi-Party Conference (MPC) was formed. In May 1984 talks were held in Lusaka between the MPC and SWAPO, which were followed in July 1984 by talks between the Administrator-General and SWAPO. SWAPO refused to take part in further constitutional talks with the MPC. The MPC then petitioned South Africa for a form of self-government for Namibia, and on 17 June 1985 the Transitional Government of National Unity was installed. Negotiations began again in May and July 1988 between Angola, Cuba and South Africa. A peaceful settlement was agreed and the Geneva Protocol was signed on 5 Aug. 1988. In Dec. it was agreed that Cuban troops should withdraw from Angola and South African troops from Namibia by 1 April 1989. The Transitional Government of National Unity resigned on 28 Feb. 1988 to make provision for the implementation of UN Security Council Resolution 435. The UN Transition Assistance Group (UNTAG) supervised elections for the constituent assembly in Nov. 1989. Independence was achieved on 21 March 1990.

AREA AND POPULATION. The area, including the Caprivi-Strip, is 823,145 sq. km. Namibia lays claim to the enclave of Walvis Bay, administered by South Africa (1,124 sq. km.).

The country is bounded in the north by Angola and Zambia, west by the Atlantic ocean, south and south-east by South Africa and east by Botswana. The Caprivi Strip, about 300 km long, extends eastwards up to the Zambezi river, projecting into Zambia and Botswana and touching Zimbabwe. The rainfall increases steadily from less than 50 mm. in the west and south-west up to 600 mm. in the Caprivi Strip.

The population at the censuses in 1970 and 1981 and estimates 1988, were:

	1970	1981	1988
Ovambos	342,455	506,114	641,000
Whites	90,658	76,430	82,000
Damaras	64,973	76,179	97,000
Hereros	55,670	76,296	97,000
Namas	32,853	48,541	62,000
Kavangos	49,577	95,055	120,000
Caprivians	25,009	38,594	48,000
Coloureds	28,275	42,254	52,000
Basters	16,474	25,181	32,000
Bushmen	21,909	29,443	37,000
Tswanas	4,407	6,706	8,000
Other	...	12,403	12,000
	732,260	1,033,196	1,288,000

Namibia is divided into 26 districts of which one is the capital, Windhoek (population 114,500, estimate 1988). Towns with populations over 5,000: Swakopmund, 15,500; Rehoboth, 15,000; Rundu, 15,000; Keetmanshoop, 14,000; Tsumeb, 13,500; Otjiwarongo, 11,000; Grootfontein, 9,000; Okahandja, 8,000; Mariental, 6,500; Gobabis, 6,500; Khorixas, 6,500; Lüderitz, 6,000.

The other districts are (with chief town where name differs): Bethanian, Bushmanland (Tsumkwe), Caprivi East (Katima Mulilo), Damaraland (Khorixas), Gobabis, Grootfontein, Hereroland East (Otjinene), Hereroland West (Okakarara), Kaokoland (Opuwo), Karasburg, Karibib, Kavango (Rundu), Keetmanshoop, Lüderitz, Maltahöhe, Mariental, Namaland (Gibeon), Okahandja, Omaruru, Otjiwarongo, Outjo, Owambo (Ondangwa), Rehoboth, Swakopmund, Tsemeb.

English and Afrikaans are the official languages. German is also spoken.

CONSTITUTION AND GOVERNMENT. For history of the administration from 1949–1985 *see* THE STATESMAN'S YEAR-BOOK 1986–87 p. 1087.

At the elections 7–11 Nov. 1989 voting was for the 72 seats in the Constituent Assembly. South West Africa People's Organization (SWAPO) won 41 seats; Democratic Turnhalle Alliance (DTA) 21; United Democratic Front, 4; Action Christian Nation (ACN) 3; Namibia Patriotic Front (NPF) 1; Federal Convention of Namibia (FCN) 1; Namibia National Front (NNF) 1. Swapo-Democrats (SWAPO-D), Christian Democratic Action (CDA) and Namibia National Democratic Party (NNDP) won no seats.

On 9 Feb 1990 a unanimous vote the Constituent Assembly approved the Constitution which stipulated a multi-party republic, an independent judiciary and an executive *President* who may serve a maximum of two 5-year terms. The bicameral legislature consists of a 78-member *National Assembly*, elected for 5-year terms by proportional representation, and a *National Council* consisting of 2 members from each geographical region elected for 6-year terms from members of regional councils.

President: Sam Nujoma.

In Nov. 1991 the Government consisted of:

Prime Minister: Hage Geingob.

Minister of Home Affairs: Hifikepunye Pohamba. *Foreign Affairs:* Theo-Ben Gurirab. *Defence:* Peter Mueshihange. *Finance:* Otto Herrigel. *Education, Culture Youth and Sport:* Nahas Angula. *Information and Broadcasting:* Hidipo Hamutenya. *Health and Social Services:* Nicky Iyambo. *Labour, Public Service and Manpower*

Development: Hendrik Witbooi. *Mines and Energy*: Andimba Toivo ya Toivo. *Justice*: Ngarikutuke Tjiriange. *Local Government and Housing*: Libertine Amathila. *Wildlife, Conservation and Tourism:* Nico Bessinger. *Trade and Industry:* Ben Amathila. *Agriculture, Fisheries, Water and Rural Development*: Gerhard Hanekom. *Works, Transport and Communications*: Richard Kapelwa Kabajani. *Lands, Resettlement and Rehabilitation*: Marco Hausiku. *Attorney-General*: Hartmut Ruppel.

National Flag: Divided diagonally blue over green by a red white-edged stripe; in the canton a yellow sun of 12 rays.

Local government is carried out by elected regional and local authority councils. A *Council of Traditional Chiefs* advises the President on the utilization and control of communal land.

DEFENCE. The UK is training a National Defence Force, which is composed of former members of the South West African Territorial Force and the People's Liberation Army of Namibia. Initial strength was about 10,000.

INTERNATIONAL RELATIONS

Membership. Namibia is a member of the UN, Commonwealth, IMF, SADCC and OAU.

ECONOMY

Budget. In 1991-92 revenue was R2,394·1m. and expenditure, R2,819·3m. Tax revenue totalled R1,985·1m. and included taxes on income and profits, R536·4m.

Currency. The monetary unit is the South African *Rand*. There are plans to introduce a Namibian dollar in 1993.

Banking and Finance. The Bank of Namibia is the central bank. Its *Governor* is Dr Wouter Benard. Commercial banks include First National Bank of Namibia, Namibian Banking Corporation, Standard Bank Namibia, Commercial Bank of Namibia and Bank Windhoek (the only locally-owned bank). There is an Agricultural Bank in Windhoek. Total assets of commercial banks were R2,059·9m. at 31 Dec. 1990.

There are 2 building societies with total assets (31 March 1990) R424.9m. A Post Office Savings Bank was established in 1916. In March 1991 its total assets were R21·8m.

ENERGY AND NATURAL RESOURCES

Electricity. Production (1986) 692m. kwh.

Water. The 12 most important dams have a total capacity of 589·2m. cu. metres. Rainfall increases steadily from less than 50 mm. in the west and south-west up to 600 mm. in the Caprivi Strip.

The Kunene River and the Okavango, which form portions of the northern border of the country, the Zambezi, which forms the eastern boundary of the Caprivi-Strip, the Kwando or Mashi, which flows through the Caprivi-Strip from the north between the Okavango and the Zambezi, and the Orange River in the south, are the only permanently running streams. But there is a system of great, sandy, dry riverbeds throughout the country, in which water can generally be obtained by sinking shallow wells. In the Grootfontein area there are large supplies of underground water, but except for a few springs, mostly hot, there is no surface water in the country.

Minerals. Diamonds of 1,009,520 carats were recovered in 1986 from open cast mines north of the Orange river. A new open-cast diamond mining area will start production here in 1990, with another to be developed near Elizabeth Bay, south of Lüderitz. The largest open groove uranium mine in the world started operations near Swakopmund in 1976. The mine has a production capacity of 5,000 short tons of uranium oxide concentrate per year and an estimated average of 60m. tons of ore has been processed annually since 1979. Total value of mineral exports, 1988, R1,542·6m.; diamonds, R653·5m.

Agriculture. Namibia is essentially a stock-raising country, the scarcity of water and poor rainfall rendering crop-farming, except in the northern and north-eastern parts, almost impossible. Generally speaking, the southern half is suited for the raising of small stock, while the central and northern parts are more suited for cattle. In 1986 there were 314 registered hunting farms, 25 guest farms and 20 safari farms. Guano is harvested from the coast, converted into fertilizer in the Republic of South Africa and most of it exported to Europe. In 1986, 16% of the active labour force worked in the agricultural sector, while 70% of the population was directly or indirectly dependent on agriculture for their living.

Livestock (1990): 2·07m. cattle, 6·7m. sheep, 0·5m. goats.

In 1990, 70,000 tonnes of cows' milk and (in 1988) 70,000 tonnes of cheese were produced. Principal crops (1990 in tonnes): Wheat, 2,000; maize, 65,000; sunflower seed (1987), 525, sorghum; 8,000; vegetables, 32,000.

Forestry. Forests cover 18m. ha (22% of the land area).

Fisheries. Value of catches, 1988-89: Pelagic fish, R182·7m.; crayfish, R53,298,968. After independence a 200-mile exclusive economic zone was declared. The allowable hake catch for 1991 was set at 60,000 tonnes, 15% of this being open to foreign fleets.

INDUSTRY. Of the estimated total of 259 undertakings, the most important are meat processing, the supply of specialized equipment to the mining industry, the assembly of goods from predominantly imported materials and the manufacture of metal products and construction material. Small industries, including home industries, textile mills, leather and steel goods, have expanded. Products manufactured locally include chocolates, beer, leather shoes and delicatessen meats and game meat products.

Labour. In 1988 there were 184,983 economically active persons, 67·2% male. The estimated unemployment rate was 20%. The main employers were government services, agriculture and mining.

FOREIGN ECONOMIC RELATIONS

Commerce. Total imports (in R1,000), 1989, R2,339·6. Total exports, 1989: 2,671·6 including agricultural exports, 293·7; fish, 64·9; diamonds, 814; other minerals, 1212·8.

Total trade between Namibia and UK (British Department of Trade returns, in £1,000 sterling):

	1987	1988	1989	1990	1991
Imports to UK	7,681	10,729	4,568	349	19,606
Exports and re-exports from UK	3,909	3,259	4,264	4,246	3,981

COMMUNICATIONS

Roads. In 1991 the total national road network was 41,815 km, including 4,572 km of tarred roads. In 1991 there were 132,331 registered motor vehicles.

Railways. The Namibia system connects with the main system of the South African railways at Aramsvlei. The total length of the line inside Namibia was 2,382 km of 1,065 mm gauge in 1990/91. In 1990/91 railways carried 215,175 passengers and 16·78m. tonnes of freight.

Civil Aviation. In 1990-91 the 2 major airports handled about 215,175 passengers and 2·8m. kg of freight on international flights and 7,117 passengers and 211,218 kg of freight on internal flights.

Shipping. The bulk of the direct imports into the country is landed at Walvis Bay. There is a harbour at Inderitz which handles a small number of fishing vessels.

Telecommunications. In 1991 there were 72 post offices and 16 postal agencies which served 43,000 private box renters and 1,175 private bag services distributed by rail or road transport.

There were (1991) 85,036 telephones. There were 534 telex users.

In 1987, 57,683 radios and 28,500 TV licences were issued. TV colour is by PAL.

The Namibian Broadcasting Corporation operates a national radio service from 3 stations and vernacular services. It also operates 10 TV stations.

Newspapers (1989). There were 5 daily and 6 weekly newspapers.

JUSTICE, RELIGION, EDUCATION AND WELFARE

Justice. There is a Supreme Court, a High Court and a number of magistrates' and lower courts. An Ombudsman is appointed. Judges' are appointed by the president on the recommendation of the Judicial Service Commission.

Religion. About 90% of the population is Christian.

Education (1988). In 1989–90, R143·6m. was spent on education. There were 1,153 schools for all races, 374,269 pupils and 12,525 teachers. This included 1,118 primary and senior secondary schools, 3 centres for the handicapped, 1 technical school and 2 agricultural schools, 3 technical institutes and 3 agricultural colleges. There were 4 teachers' training colleges and an academy.

Health (1988). There were 68 hospitals and 171 clinics. The ratio of beds per population was 5·5 per 1,000. There were 270 general practitioners, 30 specialists and 40 dentists. Nursing staff numbered 4,350.

DIPLOMATIC REPRESENTATIVES

Of Namibia in Great Britain (34 South Molton St., London W1P 5HJ)
High Commissioner: Veiccoh K. Nghiwete.

Of Great Britain in Namibia (116A Leutwein St., Windhoek)
High Commissioner: Francis Richards.

Of Namibia in the USA
Ambassador: (Vacant).

Of the USA in Namibia (14 Lossen St., Windhoek)
Ambassador: Jenta H. Holmes.

Of Namibia to the United Nations
Ambassador: Dr Tunguru Huaraka.

Further Reading

Namibia Information Services, *Namibia: The Economy*. Windhoek, 1987
Gupta, V., *Independent Namibia: Problems and Prospects*. Delhi, 1990
Human Rights and Namibia. London, 1986
Herbstein, D. and Evenston, J., *The Devils are Among Us: The War for Namibia*. London, 1989
Katjavivi, P.H., *A History of Resistance in Namibia*. London, 1988
Rotberg, R. I., *Namibia: Political and Economic Prospects*. Lexington, 1983
Schoeman, E. R. and H. S., *Namibia*. [Bibliography] Oxford and Santa Barbara, 1984
Soggot, D., *Namibia: The Violent Heritage*. New York, 1986
van der Merwe, J. H., *National Atlas of South West Africa*. Windhoek, 1983

NAURU

Population: 8,100 (1990)
GNP per capita: US$9,091 (1985)

Republic of Nauru

HISTORY. The island was discovered by Capt. Fearn in 1798, annexed by Germany in Oct. 1888, and surrendered to Australian forces in 1914. It was administered under a mandate, effective from 17 Dec. 1920, conferred on the British Empire and approved by the League of Nations until 1 Nov. 1947, when the UN General Assembly approved a trusteeship agreement with the governments of Australia, New Zealand and the UK as joint administering authority. Independence was gained in 1968.

AREA AND POPULATION. The island is situated 0° 32' S. lat. and 166° 56' E. long. Area, 5,263 acres (2,130 hectares). It is an oval-shaped upheaval coral island of approximately 12 miles in circumference, surrounded by a reef which is exposed at low tide. There is no deep water harbour but offshore moorings, reputedly the deepest in the world, are capable of holding medium-sized vessels, including 30,000 tonne capacity bulk carriers. There is an extensive plateau bearing phosphate of a high grade, the mining rights of which were vested in the British Phosphate Commissioners until 1 July 1970, subject to the rights of the Nauruan landowners. In July 1970 the Nauru Phosphate Corporation assumed control and management of the enterprise. It is chiefly on the fertile section of land between the sandy beach and the plateau that the Nauruans have established themselves, as the plateau has been mined out, and the near absence of top soil prevents regeneration of fruit-bearing trees or crops.

At the census held on 13 May 1983 the population totalled 8,100, of whom 5,285 were Nauruans.

Vital statistics rates, 1989: Births, 21 (per 1,000 population); deaths, 5; infant mortality, 41 (per 1,000 live births).

CLIMATE. A tropical climate, tempered by sea breezes, but with a high and irregular rainfall, averaging 82" (2,060 mm). Jan. 81°F (27·2°C), July 82°F (27·8°C). Annual rainfall 75" (1,862 mm).

CONSTITUTION AND GOVERNMENT. A Legislative Council was established by the Nauru Act, passed by the Australian Parliament in Dec. 1965 and was inaugurated on 31 Jan. 1966. The trusteeship agreement terminated on 31 Jan. 1968, on which day Nauru became an independent republic but having special relationship with the Commonwealth. An 18-member Parliament is elected on a 3-yearly basis.

The government in Nov. 1991 comprised:

President and Minister for Island Development and Industry, Civil Aviation, Foreign Affairs, Internal Affairs and the Public Service: Bernard Dowiyogo.

Finance: Kinza Clodumar. *Works and Community Services:* Vinson Detenamo. *Justice:* Nimes Ekwona. *Health and Education:* Vinci Clodumar.

National flag: Blue with a narrow horizontal gold stripe across the centre, beneath this near the hoist a white star of 12 points.

INTERNATIONAL RELATIONS

Membership. Nauru is a member of the South Pacific Forum.

ECONOMY

Currency. The Australian dollar is in use.

Budget. For year ending 30 June 1989 (estimate): revenue, $A57·35m.; expenditure, $A59·23m., including on health, $A3·12m.; education, $A3·5m.

INDUSTRY. The interests in the phosphate deposits were purchased in 1919 from the Pacific Phosphate Company by the governments of the UK, Australia and

New Zealand at a cost of £3·5m., and a Board of Commissioners representing the three governments was appointed to manage and control the working of the deposits. In 1967 the British Phosphate Corporation agreed to hand over the phosphate industry to Nauru for approximately $A20m. over 3 years. Nauru took over the industry in July 1969. It is estimated that the deposits will be exhausted by 1995–97. Phosphate sales amounted to $A1·4m. in 1988-89. In May 1989 Nauru filed a claim against Australia for environmental damage caused by the mining.

FOREIGN ECONOMIC RELATIONS

Commerce. The export trade consists almost entirely of phosphate shipped to Australia, New Zealand, the Philippines and Japan. The imports: food, building construction materials, machinery for the phosphate industry and medical supplies.

Total trade between Nauru and UK (British Department of Trade returns, in £1,000 sterling):

	1987	1988	1989	1990	1991
Imports to UK	674	642	662	54	718
Exports from UK	394	759	549	1,145	1,189

COMMUNICATIONS

Civil Aviation. There is an airfield on the island capable of accepting medium size jet aircraft. Air Nauru, a wholly owned government subsidiary, operates services with Boeing 737 aircraft to Melbourne, Sydney, Honiara, Guam, Tarawa, Port Vila, Suva, Nadi, Manila, Truk, Palau and Auckland.

Shipping. The Nauru Local Government Council, through its agency the Nauru Pacific Shipping Line, owns 3 ships and 1 fishing boat. These ships ply between Australia, the Pacific Islands, the USA, New Zealand, Japan and Singapore. Other shipping coming to the island consists of vessels under charter to the phosphate industry.

Telecommunications. There were 2,000 telephones in 1989 and 5,500 radio receivers in 1984. International telephone, telex and fax communications are maintained by Intelsat satellite. a satellite earth station was commissioned in 1990.

Cinemas. In 1989 there were 3 cinemas with seating capacity of 500.

JUSTICE, RELIGION AND EDUCATION

Justice. The highest Court is the Supreme Court of Nauru. It is the Superior Court of record and has the jurisdiction to deal with constitutional matters in addition to its other jurisdiction. There is also a District Court which is presided over by the Resident Magistrate who is also the Chairman of the Family Court and the Registrar of Supreme Court. The laws applicable in Nauru are its own Acts of Parliament. A large number of British statutes and much common law has been adopted insofar as is compatible with Nauruan custom.

Religion. The population is mainly Roman Catholic or Protestant.

Education. Attendance at school is compulsory for all children between the ages of 6 and 17. In June 1989 there were 10 infant and primary schools and 2 secondary schools. There were 165 teachers and 2,707 pupils in infant, primary and secondary schools. In addition, there is a trade school with 4 instructors and an enrolment of 88 trainees. Scholarships are available for Nauruan children to receive secondary and higher education and vocational training in Australia and New Zealand. In 1989, 99 Nauruans were receiving secondary and tertiary education abroad.

DIPLOMATIC REPRESENTATIVES

Of Great Britain in Nauru
High Commissioner: A. B. P. Smart (resides in Suva).
Of Nauru in the USA
Ambassador: (Vacant; resides in Melbourne).

Further Reading

Macdonald, B., *Trusteeship and Independence in Nauru.* Wellington, 1988
Packett, C. N., *Guide to the Republic of Nauru.* Bradford, 1970
Viviani, N., *Phosphate and Political Progress.* Canberra, 1970
Williams, M. and Macdonald, B., *The Phosphateers.* Melbourne Univ. Press, 1985

NEPAL

Nepal Adhirajya

(Kingdom of Nepal)

Capital: Kathmandu
Population: 18·9m. (1990)
GNP per capita: US$170 (1989)

HISTORY. From 1846 to 1951 Nepal was virtually ruled by the Rana family, a member of which always held the office of prime minister, the succession being determined by special rules. The last Rana prime minister (and, until 18 Feb. 1951, Supreme C.-in-C.) was HH Maharaja Mohan Shumsher Jung Bahadur Rana, who resigned in Nov. 1951. The 15 feudal chieftanships were integrated into the kingdom on 10 April 1961.

Following two months of popular pro-democracy demonstrations, on 16 April 1990 King Birendra dismissed the government and proclaimed the abolition of the *panchayat* system of nominated councils. On 9 Nov. 1990 the King proclaimed a constitution which relinquished his absolute powers.

AREA AND POPULATION. Nepal, is bounded on the north by Tibet, on the east by Sikkim and West Bengal, on the south and west by Bihar and Uttar Pradesh. There are 3 geographical regions: The fertile Tarai plain in the south; a central belt containing the Mahabharat Lekh and Churia Hills and the basins of the Inner Tarai; and the Himalayas in the north. Area 140,797 sq. km; population (estimate, 1990), 18·9m.; (census, 1981) 15,022,839 of whom 52·4% were Nepali-speaking and 18·5% Bihari-speaking. Population density, 134 per sq. km. Expectation of life was 52 years in 1989.

Capital, Kathmandu, 75 miles from the Indian frontier; population (census 1981) 235,160. Other towns include Patan (also called Lalitpur), 79,875; Morang (Biratnagar), 93,544; Bhadgaon (Bhaktapur), 48,472.

The aboriginal stock is Tibetan with a considerable admixture of Hindu blood from India. They were originally divided into numerous hill clans and petty principalities, one of which, Gurkha, became predominant in 1559 and has since given its name to men from all parts of Nepal.

CLIMATE. The rainfall is high, with maximum amounts from May to Sept., but conditions are very dry from Nov. to Jan. The range of temperature is moderate. Káthmándu. Jan. 50°F (10°C), July 76°F (24·4°C). Annual rainfall 57" (1,428 mm).

RULING KING. The sovereign is HM Maharajadhiraja **Birendra Bir Bikram Shah Dev** (b. 1946), who succeeded his father Mahendra Bir Bikram Shah Dev on 31 Jan. 1972.

CONSTITUTION AND GOVERNMENT. On 18 Feb. 1951 the King proclaimed a constitutional monarchy, and on 16 Dec. 1962 a new Constitution which instituted the *panchayat* system of nominated national and local councils.

This was abolished in 1990 and a 30-year ban on opposition parties was lifted. Under the constitution of 9 Nov. 1990 Nepal became a constitutional monarchy based on multi-party democracy. *Parliament* has 2 chambers: a 205-member House of Representatives (*Pratinidhi Sabha*) elected for 5-year terms, and a 60-member House of Estates (*Rashtriya Sabha*), of which 10 members are nominated by the king. Voting age is 18.

Elections were held in May 1991. The electorate was 11m.; turn-out was about 60%. The Nepali Congres won 110 seats and the Communist Party-United Marxist-Leninist Party, 69. In Feb. 1992 the cabinet comprised:

Prime Minister, Minister of Finance, Foreign Affairs, Defence and Royal Palace Affairs: Girija Prasad Koirala (b.1925).

Interior: Sher Bahadur Deupa. *Agriculture:* Shailaja Acharya. *Housing and Physical Planning:* Bal Bahadur Rai. *Land Reforms and Management:* Jagannath Acharya. *Tourism:* Ram Hari Joshi. *Local Development:* Ramchandra Poudel. *General Administration, Law and Justice, and Parliamentary Affairs:* Maleshwor Prasad Singh. *Works and Transport:* Khum Bahadur Khadka. *Education, Culture and Social Welfare:* Govinda Raj Joshi.

National flag: Two triangular parts of red, with a blue border all round, bearing symbols of the moon and the sun in white.

National anthem: 'May glory crown our illustrious sovereign' (1952).

Local Government: The country is administratively divided into 14 zones (Bagmati, Bheri, Dhaulagiri, Gandaki, Janakpur, Karnali, Kosi, Lumbini, Mahakali, Mechi, Narayani, Rapti, Sagarmatha and Seti) and thence into 75 districts and over 3,500 villages.

DEFENCE. The King is commander-in-chief of the armed forces, but shares supreme military authority with the National Defence Council, of which the Prime Minister is chairman.

Army. The Army consists of 1 Royal Guard including 1 cavalry squadron and 1 garrison battalion, 5 infantry brigades, 1 support brigade, 1 artillery regiment and an engineer battalion. Strength (1992) 34,800, and there is also a 28,000-strong paramilitary police force.

Air Force. Independent of the army since 1979, the Air Force has 1 Twin Otter and 3 Skyvan transport aircraft, 1 Puma helicopter and 4 Chetak helicopters. An H.S. 748 turboprop transport and 1 Super Puma and 1 Puma helicopter are operated by the Royal Flight. There are no combatant aircraft. Personnel, 1992, 200.

INTERNATIONAL RELATIONS

Membership. Nepal is a member of the UN and the Colombo Plan.

ECONOMY

Budget. The general budget for the fiscal year 1987–88 envisaged current expenditure of NRs 4,307m. Domestic revenue were estimated at NRs 5,875m.

Currency. The unit of currency is the *Nepalese rupee* (NPR) of 100 *pais*. 50 *pais* = 1 *mohur*. The rupee is 171 grains in weight, as compared with the Indian rupee, which weighs 180 grains. Coins of all denominations are minted. The Rastra Bank also issues notes of 1, 5, 10, 100 and 1,000 rupees. In March 1992, US$1 = 42·66 *rupees*; £1 = 74·90 *rupees*.

ENERGY AND NATURAL RESOURCES

Electricity. Production (1986) 395m. kwh.

Agriculture. In the northern part of the country, on the slopes of the Himalayas, large quantities of medicinal herbs grow which find a world-wide market. 5·4m. acres is covered by perpetual snow; 9·6m. acres is under paddy, 2·9m. maize and millet, 800,000 wheat. Production (1990 in 1,000 tonnes): Rice, 3,300; maize, 950; wheat, 855; sugar-cane, 988; potatoes, 672; millet, 240.

Livestock (1990); Cattle, 6,281,000; 3,013,000 buffaloes; sheep, 892,000; goats, 5,324,000; pigs, 730,000; poultry, 7m.

Forestry. There are valuable forests in the southern part of the country. Forest area was 2·3m. ha. in 1988.

Fisheries. Catch (1986) 9,400 tonnes.

INDUSTRY. Industries, such as jute- and sugar-mills, match, leather, cigarette, and shoe factories, and chemical works have been established, including two industrial estates at Patan and Balaju. Production (1986 in 1,000 tonnes): Jute goods, 20·5; sugar, 18·5; cement, 10·4.

FOREIGN ECONOMIC RELATIONS

Commerce. The principal articles of export are food grains, jute, timber, oilseeds, ghee (clarified butter), potatoes, medicinal herbs, hides and skins, cattle. The chief imports are textiles, cigarettes, salt, petrol and kerosene, sugar, machinery, medicines, boots and shoes, paper, cement, iron and steel, tea.

Imports and exports in NRs 1,000:

	1985	1986	1987	1988
Imports	7,742,000	9,341,200	11,020,300	13,940,000
Exports	2,741,000	3,079,000	3,059,700	4,080,000

Total trade between Nepal and UK (British Department of Trade returns, in £1,000 sterling):

	1987	1988	1989	1990	1991
Imports to UK	8,331	9,384	8,306	7,039	4,531
Exports and re-exports from UK	8,707	4,968	7,802	4,099	4,938

Tourism. There were 248,000 tourists in 1987.

COMMUNICATIONS

Roads. With the co-operation of India and the USA 900 miles of motorable roads are being constructed, including the East-West Highway through southern Nepal. A road from the Tibetan border to Káthmándu was recently completed with Chinese aid. There are about 1,300 miles motorable roads. A ropeway for the carriage of goods covers the 14 miles from Dhursing above Bhimphedi into the Káthmándu valley. A road connects Káthmándu with Birgung.

Railways. Railways (762 mm gauge) connect Jayanagar on the North Eastern Indian Railway with Janakpur and thence with Bizalpura (54 km).

Civil Aviation. The Royal Nepal Airline Corporation has linked Kathmandu with 11 districts of Nepal and has services between Kathmandu and Calcutta, Patna, New Delhi, Bangkok, Rangoon and Dacca, employing Boeing 727 jet aircraft.

Telecommunications. Kathmandu is connected by telephone with Birganj and Raxaul (North Eastern Indian Railway) on the southern frontier with Bihar; and with the eastern part of the Terai foothills; an extension to the western districts is being completed. Number of telephones (1980) 11,800. Radio Nepal is part government-owned and part commercial. It broadcasts in Nepali and English from 3 stations. The government-owned Nepal Television Corporate transmits from 1 station (colour by PAL). In 1990 there were 0·6m. radio and 35,100 TV sets.

Newspapers. In 1987 there were 58 daily newspapers, including the official English-language *Rising Nepal*. Press censorship was relaxed in June 1991.

JUSTICE, RELIGION, EDUCATION AND WELFARE

Justice. The Supreme Court Act, established a uniform judicial system, culminating in a supreme court of a Chief Justice and no more than 6 judges. Special courts to deal with minor offences may be established at the discretion of the Government.

Religion. Hinduism is the religion of 90% of the people. Buddhists comprise 5% and Moslems 3%. Christian missions are permitted, but conversion is forbidden.

Education. In 1985 there were 1,818,668 primary school pupils, 501,063 secondary school pupils and in 1984, 55,555 students at the Tribhuvan University (founded 1960).

In 1981, 23% of the population were literate.

Health. There were about 420 doctors and 2,586 hospital beds in 1979.

DIPLOMATIC REPRESENTATIVES

Of Nepal in Great Britain (12a Kensington Palace Gdns., London, W8 4QU)
Ambassador: Maj.-Gen. Bharat Kesher Simha (accredited 14 July 1988).

Of Great Britain in Nepal (Lainchaur, Kathmandu)
Ambassador: T. J. B. George, CMG.

Of Nepal in the USA (2131 Leroy Pl., NW, Washington, D.C., 20008)
Ambassador: Mohan Man Sainju.

Of the USA in Nepal (Pani Pokhari, Kathmandu)
Ambassador: Julia Chang Bloch.

Of Nepal to the United Nations
Ambassador: Dr. Jayaraj Acharya.

Further Reading

Statistical Information: A Department of Statistics was set up in Kathmandu in 1950.

Baral, L. S., *Political Development in Nepal*. London, 1980
Pant, Y. P., *Trade and Co-operation in South Asia: a Nepalese Perspective*. Delhi, 1991
Whelpton, J., *Nepal*. [Bibliography] Oxford and Santa Barbara, 1990

THE NETHERLANDS

Capital: Amsterdam
Seat of Government: The Hague
Population: 15·01m. (1991)
GNP per capita: US$16,010 (1989)

Koninkrijk der Nederlanden

(Kingdom of the Netherlands)

HISTORY. William of Orange (1533–84), as the German count of Nassau, inherited vast possessions in the Netherlands and the Princedom of Orange in France. He was the initiator of the struggle for independence from Spain (1568–1648); in the Republic of the United Netherlands he and his successors became the 'first servants of the Republic' with the title of 'Stadhouder' (governor). In 1689 William III acceded to the throne of England, becoming joint sovereign with Mary II, his wife. William III died in 1702 without issue, and after a stadhouderless period a member of the Frisian branch of Orange–Nassau was nominated hereditary stadhouder in 1747; but his successor, Willem V, had to take refuge in England, in 1795, at the invasion of the French Army. In Nov. 1813 the United Provinces were freed from French domination.

The Congress of Vienna joined the Belgian provinces, the 'Austrian Netherlands' before the French Revolution, to the Northern Netherlands. The son of the former stadhouder Willem V was proclaimed King of the Netherlands at The Hague on 16 March 1815 as Willem I. The union was dissolved by the Belgian revolution of 1830, and the treaty of London, 19 April 1839, constituted Belgium an independent kingdom.

Netherlands Sovereigns

Willem I	1815–1840 (died 1843)	Wilhelmina	1890–1948 (died 1962)
Willem II	1840–1849	Juliana	1948–1980
Willem III	1849–1890	Beatrix	1980–

AREA AND POPULATION. The Netherlands is bounded in the north and west by the North Sea, south by Belgium and east by Germany.

The total area of the Netherlands is 41,547 sq. km, of which 33,936 sq. km is land area.

On 14 June 1918 a law was passed concerning the reclamation of the Zuiderzee. The work was begun in 1920; the following sections have been completed: 1. The Noordholland–Wieringen Barrage (2·5 km), 1924; 2. The Wieringermeer Polder (210 sq. km), 1930 (inundated by the Germans in 1945, but drained again in the same year); 3. The Wieringen–Friesland Barrage (30 km), 1932; 4. The Noordoost Polder (501 sq. km), 1942; 5. Oost Flevoland (604 sq. km), 1957; 6. Zuidelijk Flevoland (499 sq. km), 1967.

The reclamation of the Markerwaard is still a subject of political discussion. A portion of what used to be the Zuiderzee behind the barrage will remain a freshwater lake: Ijsselmeer (1,400 sq. km). The 'Delta-project', completed in 1986, comprises (semi) enclosure dams in the estuaries between the islands in the southwestern part of the country, excluding the sea-entrances to the ports of Rotterdam and Antwerp. *See* map in THE STATESMAN'S YEAR-BOOK, 1959.

Growth of census population:

1829	2,613,298	1909	5,858,175	1960	11,461,964
1849	3,056,879	1920	6,865,314	1971	13,060,115
1869	3,579,529	1930	7,935,565		
1889	4,511,415	1947	9,625,499		

Area, density and estimated population on 1 Jan. 1991:

Province	Land area (in sq. km) 1991	Population 1991	Density per sq. km 1991
Groningen	2,346·69	554,604	236
Friesland	3,356·58	600,013	179
Drenthe	2,655·31	443,510	167
Overijssel	3,339·68	1,026,325	307
Flevoland [1]	1,411·52	221,505	157
Gelderland	5,015·27	1,816,935	362
Utrecht	1,358·66	1,026,841	756
Noord-Holland	2,667·21	2,397,088	899
Zuid-Holland	2,871·47	3,245,447	1,130
Zeeland	1,796·19	357,454	199
Noord-Brabant	4,948·53	2,209,047	446
Limburg	2,168·61	1,109,841	512
Central Population Register [2]	—	1,835	—
Total	33,935·71	15,010,445 [3]	442

[1] The province of Flevoland, formerly Ijsselmeerpolders, was established on 1 Jan. 1986. The Noordoostpolder (drained in 1942) and the Zuidelijke Ijsselmeerpolders (drained in 1957) are parts of the former Zuiderzee, now called Ijsselmeer.
[2] The Central Population Register includes persons who have no fixed residence (e.g. resident in caravans or on inland vessels).
[3] 7,419,501 males; 7,590,944 females.

Vital statistics for calendar years:

	Live births						Net
	Total	Single parent	Still births	Marriages	Divorces	Deaths	migration
1985	178,136	14,766	1,054	82,747	34,044	122,704	+ 24,147
1986	184,513	16,220	1,060	87,337	29,836	125,307	+ 32,669
1987	186,667	17,385	1,036	87,400	27,788	122,199	+ 43,924
1988	186,647	18,951	1,038	87,843	27,870	124,163	+ 35,447
1989	188,979	20,177	1,100	90,248	28,250	128,905	+ 39,207
1990	197,965	22,525	1,139	95,649	28,419	128,824	+ 60,006

Population of municipalities with over 20,000 inhabitants on 1 Jan. 1991:

Aalsmeer	22,196	Culemborg	22,052	Haaksbergen	22,899
Achtkarspelen	27,632	Delft	89,365	Haarlem	149,474
Alkmaar	90,778	Delfzijl	31,655	Haarlemmermeer	98,073
Almelo	62,668	Deurne	29,681	The Hague	444,242
Almere	78,100	Deventer	67,471	Hardenberg	32,438
Alphen a/d Rijn	62,401	Doetinchem	42,060	Harderwijk	35,804
Amersfoort	101,974	Dongen	21,214	Heemskerk	33,739
Amstelveen	70,340	Dongeradeel	24,288	Heemstede	26,660
Amsterdam	702,444	Dordrecht	110,473	Heerenveen	38,270
Apeldoorn	148,204	Dronten	25,577	Heerhugowaard	35,822
Arnhem	131,703	Edam-Volendam	24,839	Heerlen	94,344
Assen	50,357	Ede	94,754	Heiloo	20,523
Baarn	24,847	Eindhoven	192,895	Den Helder	61,468
Barendrecht	20,202	Elburg	20,733	Hellendoorn	34,628
Barneveld	42,866	Emmen	92,895	Hellevoetsluis	35,388
Bergen op Zoom	46,900	Enschede	146,509	Helmond	69,967
Best	22,361	Epe	33,995	Hengelo	76,371
Beuningen	22,547	Ermelo	26,063	's-Hertogenbosch	92,057
Beverwijk	35,165	Etten-Leur	32,651	Hilversum	84,606
De Bilt	32,518	Franekeradeel	20,689	Hoogeveen	46,207
Borne	21,696	Geldermalsen	22,259	Hoogezand-	
Borsele	20,397	Geldrop	25,967	Sappemeer	34,311
Boxtel	25,385	Geleen	33,827	Hoorn	58,225
Breda	124,794	Gendringen	20,393	Houten	26,880
Brummen	20,766	Gilze en Rijen	22,937	Huizen	42,001
Brunssum	29,901	Goes	32,244	Ijsselstein	21,017
Bussum	31,572	Gorinchem	28,911	Kampen	32,679
Capelle a/d Ijssel	58,307	Gouda	65,926	Katwijk	40,096
Castricum	22,277	Groningen	168,702	Kerkrade	53,282

Krimpen a/d		Oud-Beijerland	20,681	Uithoorn	22,908
Ijssel	27,476	Papendrecht	27,677	Utrecht	231,231
Landgraaf	40,352	Purmerend	60,876	Valkenswaard	30,220
Langedijk	21,305	Putten	21,175	Veendam	28,292
Leeuwarden	85,693	Raalte	27,440	Veenendaal	49,687
Leiden	111,949	Renkum	33,315	Veghel	26,230
Leiderdorp	22,630	Rheden	45,562	Veldhoven	39,093
Leidschendam	33,192	Ridderkerk	45,989	Velsen	60,135
Lelystad	58,062	Rijssen	24,366	Venlo	64,392
Leusden	27,462	Rijswijk	47,705	Venray	34,414
Lisse	21,312	Roermond	42,556	Vlaardingen	73,719
Loon op Zand	22,139	De Ronde Venen	31,799	Vlissingen [1]	43,800
Losser	22,625	Roosendaal c.a.	60,725	Voorburg	39,813
Maarssen	39,423	Rosmalen	27,631	Voorschoten	22,207
Maassluis	33,272	Rotterdam	582,266	Voorst	23,731
Maastricht	117,417	Rucphen	21,505	Vught	24,141
Meerssen	20,556	Schiedam	70,207	Waalwijk	28,821
Meppel	23,993	Schijndel	21,585	Waddinxveen	25,172
Middelburg	39,617	Sittard	45,883	Wageningen	32,818
Naaldwijk	27,987	Skarsterlân	24,386	Wassenaar	26,218
Nieuwegein	58,916	Sliedrecht	23,213	Weert	40,560
Nijkerk	25,836	Smallingerland	50,072	Weststellingwerf	24,353
Nijmegen	145,782	Sneek	29,282	Wierden	22,411
Noordoostpolder	38,278	Soest	41,420	Wijchen	34,513
Noordwijk	25,256	Spijkenisse	69,104	Winterswijk	27,954
Nuenen c.a.	21,110	Stadskanaal	32,936	Woerden	35,003
Nunspeet	25,064	Steenwijk	20,960	Zaanstad	130,705
Oldebroek	21,562	Stein	26,687	Zeist	59,357
Oldenzaal	29,835	Terneuzen	35,065	Zevenaar	26,920
Oosterhout	48,673	Tiel	32,395	Zoetermeer	99,092
Ooststellingwerf	24,934	Tilburg	158,846	Zutphen	31,064
Opsterland	26,753	Tytsjerksteradiel	30,291	Zwijndrecht	42,046
Oss	51,685	Uden	36,013	Zwolle	95,572

[1] Also known as Flushing

Urban agglomerations as at 1 Jan. 1991: Amsterdam, 1,061,766; Rotterdam, 1,050,833; The Hague, 690,262; Utrecht, 534,967; Eindhoven, 386,232; Arnhem, 303,424; Heerlen-Kerkrade, 267,989; Enschede-Hengelo, 252,065; Nijmegen, 244,385; Tilburg, 231,620; Haarlem, 214,451; DordrechtZwijndrecht, 208,278; Groningen, 207,637; 's-Hertogenbosch, 198,206; Leiden, 189,075; Geleen-Sittard, 182,034; Maastricht, 162,822; Breda, 160,905; Zaanstreek, 144,575; Velsen-Beverwijk, 129,039; Hilversum, 102,232.

CLIMATE. A cool temperate maritime climate, marked by mild winters and cool summers, but with occasional continental influences. Coastal temperatures vary from 37°F (3°C) in winter to 61°F (16°C) in summer, but inland the winters are slightly colder and the summers slightly warmer. Rainfall is least in the months Feb. to May, but inland there is a well-defined summer maximum in July and Aug.

The Hague. Jan. 37°F (2·7°C), July 61°F (16·3°C). Annual rainfall 32·8" (820 mm). Amsterdam. Jan. 36°F (2·3°C), July 62°F (16·5°C). Annual rainfall 34" (850 mm). Rotterdam. Jan. 36·5°F (2·6°C), July 62°F (16·6°C). Annual rainfall 32" (800 mm).

REIGNING QUEEN. Beatrix Wilhelmina Armgard, born 31 Jan. 1938 daughter of Queen Juliana and Prince Bernhard; married to Claus von Amsberg on 10 March 1966; succeeded to the crown on 1 May 1980, on the abdication of her mother. *Offspring:* Prince Willem-Alexander, born 27 April 1967; Prince Johan Friso, born 25 Sept. 1968; Prince Constantijn, born 11 Oct. 1969.

The Queen receives an allowance from the civil list. This was 6·1m. guilders in 1991; that of Prince Claus was 1·2m. guilders and that of Crown Prince Willem Alexander, 1·4m. guilders.

Mother of the Queen: Queen Juliana Louise Emma Marie Wilhelmina, born 30 April 1909, daughter of Queen Wilhelmina (born 31 Aug. 1880, died 28 Nov. 1962) and Prince Henry of Mecklenburg-Schwerin (born 19 April 1876, died 3 July 1934); married to Prince Bernhard Leopold Frederick Everhard Julius Coert Karel

Godfried Pieter of Lippe-Biesterfeld (born 29 June 1911) on 7 Jan. 1937. Abdicated in favour of her daughter, the Reigning Queen, on 30 April 1980.

Sisters of the Queen: Princess Irene Emma Elisabeth, born 5 Aug. 1939, married to Prince Charles Hugues de Bourbon-Parma on 29 April 1964, divorced 1981 (*sons:* Prince Carlos Javier Bernardo, born 27 Jan. 1970; Prince Jaime Bernardo, born 13 Oct. 1972; *daughters:* Princess Margarita Maria Beatriz, born 13 Oct. 1972; Princess Maria Carolina Christina, born 23 June 1974); Princess Margriet Francisca, born in Ottawa, 19 Jan. 1943, married to Pieter van Vollenhoven on 10 Jan. 1967 (*sons:* Prince Maurits, born 17 April 1968; Prince Bernhard, born 25 Dec. 1969; Prince Pieter-Christiaan, born 22 March 1972; Prince Floris, born 10 April 1975); Princess Maria Christina, born 18 Feb. 1947, married to Jorge Guillermo on 28 June 1975 (*sons:* Bernardo, born 17 June 1977; Nicolas Daniel Mauricio, born 6 July 1979; *daughter:* Juliana, born 8 Oct. 1981).

CONSTITUTION AND GOVERNMENT. According to the Constitution of the Kingdom of the Netherlands, the Kingdom consists of the Netherlands, Aruba and the Netherlands Antilles. Their relations are regulated by the 'Statute' for the Kingdom, which came into force on 29 Dec. 1954. Each part enjoys full autonomy; they are united, on a footing of equality, for mutual assistance and the protection of their common interests.

The first Constitution of the Netherlands after its restoration as a Sovereign State was promulgated in 1814. It was revised in 1815 (after the addition of the Belgian provinces, and the assumption by the Sovereign of the title of King), 1840 (after the secession of the Belgian provinces), 1848, 1884, 1887, 1917, 1922, 1938, 1946, 1948, 1953, 1956, 1963, 1972 and 1983.

The Netherlands is a constitutional and hereditary monarchy. The royal succession is in the direct male or female line in the order of primogeniture. The Sovereign comes of age on reaching his/her 18th year. During his/her minority the royal power is vested in a Regent—designated by law—and in some cases in the Council of State.

The central executive power of the State rests with the Crown, while the central legislative power is vested in the Crown and Parliament (the *Staten-Generaal*), consisting of 2 Chambers. After the 1956 revision of the Constitution the Upper or First Chamber is composed of 75 members, elected by the members of the Provincial States, and the Second Chamber consists of 150 deputies, who are elected directly from all Netherlands nationals who are aged 18 or over on polling day. Members of the States-General must be Netherlanders or recognized as Netherlands subjects and 21 years of age or over; they may be men or women. They receive an allowance.

First Chamber (as constituted in 1987): Labour Party, 26; Christian Democratic Appeal, 26; People's Party for Freedom and Democracy, 12; Democrats '66, 5; Party of Political Radicals, 1; Communist Party, 1; Pacifist Socialist Party, 1; Calvinist Party, 1; Reformed Political Federation, 1; Calvinist Political Union, 1.

Second Chamber (elected on 6 Sept. 1989): Christian Democratic Appeal (CDA), 54; Labour Party (PVDA), 49; People's Party for Freedom and Democracy, 22; Democrats '66, 12; Green Left, 6; Calvinist Party, 3; Reformed Political Federation, 1; Calvinist Political Union, 2; Centre Democrats, 1.

The revised Constitution of 1917 has introduced an electoral system based on universal suffrage and proportional representation. Under its provisions, members of the Second Chamber are directly elected by citizens of both sexes who are Netherlands subjects not under 18 years (since 1972).

The members of the First Chamber and of the Second Chamber are elected for 4 years, and retire in a body. The Sovereign has the power to dissolve both Chambers of Parliament, or one of them, subject to the condition that new elections take place within 40 days, and the new House or Houses be convoked within 3 months.

Both the Government and the Second Chamber may propose Bills; the First Chamber can only approve or reject them without inserting amendments. The meetings of both Chambers are public, though each of them may by a majority vote decide on a secret session. It is a fixed custom, that Ministers and Secretaries of State, on their own initiative or upon invitation of the Parliament, attend the sessions to defend their policy, their budget, their proposals of Bills, etc., when these are in discussion. A Minister or Secretary of State, however, cannot be a member of Parliament at the same time.

The Constitution can be revised only by a Bill declaring that there is reason for introducing such revision and containing the proposed alterations. The passing of this Bill is followed by a dissolution of both Chambers and a second confirmation by the new States-General by two-thirds of the votes. Unless it is expressly stated, all laws concern only the realm in Europe, and not the oversea part of the kingdom, the Netherlands Antilles.

Every act of the Sovereign has to be covered by a responsible Minister.

The Ministry, a coalition of Christian Democrats and Social Democrats, was composed as follows in Dec. 1991:

Prime Minister: Ruud Lubbers (CDA).

Deputy Prime Minister and Finance: Wim Kok (PVDA). *Foreign Affairs:* Hans van den Broek (CDA). *Economic Affairs:* J. Andriessen (CDA). *Defence:* Relus ter Beek (PVDA). *Development Aid Co-operation:* Jan Pronk (PVDA). *Home Affairs:* Ien Dales (PVDA). *Justice:* E. Hirsch-Ballin (CDA). *Agriculture and Fisheries:* P. Bukman. *Welfare, Public Health and Culture:* Hedy d'Ancona (PVDA). *Education and Science:* Jo Ritzen (PVDA). *Transport and Public Works:* Hanja Maij-Weggen (CDA). *Housing, Physical Planning and Environment:* Hans Alders (PVDA). *Social Affairs and Employment:* Bert de Vries (CDA).

There are also 11 state secretaries.

The Council of State *(Raad van Staat)*, appointed by the Crown, is composed of a vice-president and not more than 28 members. The Queen is president, but the day-to-day running of the council is in the hands of the vice-president. The Council can be consulted on all legislative matters. Decisions of the Crown in administrative disputes are prepared by a special section of the Council.

The Hague is the seat of the Court, Government and Parliament; Amsterdam is the capital.

National flag: Three horizontal stripes of red, white, blue.

National anthem: Wilhelmus van Nassoue (words by Philip Marnix van St Aldegonde, *c.* 1570).

Local Government. The kingdom is divided into 12 provinces and 647 municipalities. Each province has its own representative body, the Provincial States. The members must be 21 years of age or over; they are directly elected for 4 years. The electoral register is the same as for the Second Chamber. The members retire in a body and are subject to re-election. The total number of members is 748; provincial membership varies according to the population of the province, from 83 for Zuid-Holland to 39 for Flevoland. The Provincial States are entitled to issue ordinances concerning the welfare of the province, and to raise taxes pursuant to legal provisions. The provincial budgets and the provincial ordinances and resolutions relating to provincial property, loans, taxes, etc., must be approved by the Crown. The members of the Provincial States elect the First Chamber of the States-General. They meet twice a year, as a rule in public. A permanent commission composed of 6 of their members, called the 'Deputy States', is charged with the executive power and, if required, with the enforcement of the law in the province. Deputy as well as Provincial States are presided over by a Commissioner of the Queen, appointed by the Crown, who in the former assembly has a deciding vote, but attends the latter in only a deliberative capacity. He is the chief magistrate in the province. The Commissioner and the members of the Deputy States receive an allowance.

Elections to the Provincial States were held in March 1991; turn-out was 58.1%.

Each municipality forms a Corporation with its own interests and rights, subject to the general law, and is governed by a Municipal Council, directly elected from the Netherlands inhabitants, and, under certain circumstances, non-Netherlands inhabitants of the municipality who are 18 years of age or over, for 4 years. All Netherlands inhabitants and non-Netherlands inhabitants who meet certain requirements aged 21 or over are eligible, the number of members varying from 7 to 45, according to the population. The Municipal Council has the right to issue bye-laws concerning the communal welfare. The Council may levy taxes pursuant to legal provisions; these ordinances must be approved by the Crown. All bye-laws may be vetoed by the Crown. The Municipal Budget and resolutions to alienate municipal property require the approbation of the Deputy States of the province. The Council meets in public as often as may be necessary, and is presided over by a Burgomaster, appointed by the Crown. The day-to-day administration is carried out by the Burgomaster and 2–7 Aldermen *(wethouders)*, elected by and from the Council; this body is also charged with the enforcement of the law. The Burgomaster may suspend the execution of a resolution of the council for 30 days, but is bound to notify the Deputy States of the province. In maintaining public order, the Burgomaster acts as the chief of police. The Burgomaster and Aldermen receive allowances.

DEFENCE. Conscription is legally 20-22 months but the period actually served is 14 months for reserve-officers and n.c.o.s (15 months in the Navy) and 12 months for other ranks. The balance is spent as 'short leave'. After their period of actual service or short leave, conscript personnel are granted long leave. However, they are liable to being called up for refresher training or in case of mobilization until they have reached the age of 35 (n.c.o.s 40, reserve officers 45).

Army. The 1st Netherlands Army Corps is assigned to NATO. It consists of 10 brigades and Corps troops. The active part of the Corps comprises 2 armoured brigades and 4 armoured infantry brigades, grouped in two divisions and 40% of the Corps troops. Part of this force is stationed in Germany. The peacetime strength of the active brigades is 80% of the war-authorized strength.

The mobilizable part of the Corps comprises 1 armoured brigade, 2 armoured infantry brigades, 1 infantry brigade and the remaining Corps troops.

The mechanized brigades comprise tank battalions (Leopard I improved and Leopard 2), armoured infantry battalions (YPR-765), medium artillery battalions (155 mm self-propelled), armoured engineer units and armoured anti armour units. The Corps troops comprise headquarters units, combat-support units, including Engineer and Corps artillery and service-support units. Helicopter squadrons are also available. Personnel in 1992 numbered 64,100 (45,500 conscripts).

The National Territorial Command forces consist of territorial brigades, security forces, some logistical units and staffs. The major part of these units is mobilizable. Some units in the Netherlands may be assigned to the UN as peace-keeping forces. The army is responsible for the training of these units. In time of war, the civil defence operations will be closely co-ordinated with the local civilian authorities.

Navy. The principal headquarters and main base of the Royal Netherlands Navy is at Den Helder, with minor bases at Vlissingen (Flushing), Curaçao (Netherlands Antilles) and Oranjestad (Aruba).

The modern and effective combatant fleet, all built in home shipyards, and largely equipped with indigenous sensors and imported weapons, comprises 5 diesel submarines including the first 2 of the new Zeeleeuw class, 4 guided-missile destroyers armed with US Standard SM1-MR surface-to-air missiles, 11 frigates each with 1 or 2 Lynx anti-submarine helicopters, 15 coastal minehunters and 11 coastal minesweepers. There are 2 multi-purpose support ships (each carrying up to 3 helicopters), 3 survey ships, 2 training ships and a torpedo tender, as well as numerous service vessels.

The Marine corps has 12 small amphibious craft, but is integrated operationally with the UK Marines for its NATO tasks.

The Naval Air Service operates 13 Orion P-3C, 2 F-27, 17 Westland Lynx SH-14B for embarked service and 5 Lynx UH-14A for search and rescue, utility and transport.

In 1991 personnel totalled 16,500 officers and other ranks, including 1,600 in the Naval Air Service, 560 women (who serve in all classes of ships except submarines) and 2,800 in the Royal Netherlands Marine Corps.

Air Force. The Royal Netherlands Air Force (RNLAF) was established 1 July 1913. Its strength (1992) was 16,000 personnel (3,500 conscripts) and it has a first-line combat force of 9 squadrons of aircraft and 2 groups of surface-to-air missiles in Germany. All squadrons are operated by Tactical Air Command. The only combat types are F-16A/B (8 squadrons for air defence and ground attack, 1 for tactical reconnaissance). Also under control of Tactical Air Command is 1 squadron of the USAF, flying F-15C/D Eagles in the air defence role. 3 squadrons of Alouette III and Bölkow Bö 105C helicopters are under control of the Royal Netherlands Army, but flown and maintained by the RNLAF for use in the communications and observation roles. Also operated is 1 squadron of F.27 Friendship/Troopship transport aircraft, and another (based in Curaçao) with F.27 maritime patrol aircraft.

Basic training is carried out on the PC-7 Turbo-Trainer; pilots then go to the USA for advanced training. The surface-to-air missile force consists of 4 squadrons of Patriot with 160 missiles and 11 squadrons with Hawks, of which 7 are for airfield defence.

INTERNATIONAL RELATIONS

Membership. The Netherlands is a member of the UN, EC, OECD, Council of Europe, WEU and NATO. The Schengen Accord of June 1990 abolished border controls between the Netherlands and Belgium, France, Germany and Luxembourg. Italy, Portugal and Spain acceded subsequently.

ECONOMY

Budget. The revenue and expenditure of the central government (ordinary and extraordinary) were, in 1m. guilders, for calendar years:

	1984	1985	1986	1987	1988	1989	1990
Revenue [1]	127,918	138,605	159,689	156,111	151,904	145,034	155,623
Expenditure [2]	157,709	162,085	167,321	170,275	173,097	168,806	178,515

[1] Without the revenue of loans.   [2] Without redemption of loans.

The revenue and expenditure of the Agriculture Equalization Fund, the Fund for Central Government roads, the Property Acquisition Fund and of the Investment Account Fund (established in 1978) have been incorporated in the general budget.

The national debt, in 1m. guilders, was on 31 Dec.:

	1986	1987	1988	1989	1990
Internal funded debt	219,466	234,474	263,949	287,155	312,110
„ floating „	19,969	16,683	10,524	6,544	5,558
Total	239,435	251,157	274,473	293,699	317,668

Currency. The monetary unit is the *gulden* (NLG; written as fl[orin]; in English, 'guilder') of 100 *cents*. It is tied to the German Deutschmark. In March 1992 the rate of exchange was US$1 = 1·85 guilders; £1 = 3·24 guilders.

Legal tender are bank-notes, silver 10-guilder pieces, 5-guilder pieces, nickel $2^1/_2$- and 1-guilder pieces, 25-cent, 10-cent pieces and bronze 5-cent pieces.

Banking and Finance. The central bank and bank of issue is the Netherlands Bank (*Governor* Willem Duisenberg), founded in 1814 and nationalized in 1948. Its Governor is appointed by the government for 7-year terms. The capital amounts to 75m. guilders.

There is a stock exchange in Amsterdam.

Weights and Measures. The metric system is in use.

ENERGY AND NATURAL RESOURCES

Electricity. Production of electrical energy in 1990, 71,852m. kwh. Some 3,000 windmills were installed in 1991 to produce 1,000 mw. Supply 220 volts; 50 Hz.

Gas. Production of natural gas in 1990, 72,238m. cu. metres.

Minerals. The production of crude petroleum (in 1,000 tonnes) amounted in 1943 (first year) to 0·2; 1953, 820; 1970, 1,919; 1978, 1,402; 1979, 1,316; 1980, 1,280; 1981, 1,348; 1982, 1,637; 1983, 2,589; 1984, 3,102; 1985, 3,729; 1986, 4,628; 1987, 4,291; 1988, 3,909; 1989, 3,391; 1990, 3,976; 1991; 3,772.

There are saltmines at Hengelo and Delfzijl; production (in 1,000 tonnes), 1950, 412·6; 1960, 1,096; 1970, 2,871; 1978, 2,939; 1979, 3,951; 1980, 3,464; 1981, 3,578; 1982, 3,191; 1983, 3,124; 1984, 3,674; 1985, 4,154; 1986, 3,763; 1987, 3,979; 1988, 3,693; 1989, 3,756; 1990, 3,653.

Agriculture. The net area of all holdings was divided as follows (in ha):

	1987	1988	1989	1990	1991 [1]
Field crops	787,078	789,798	795,822	799,436	797,187
Grass	1,124,472	1,114,009	1,098,823	1,096,496	...
Market gardening	66,971	70,415	71,281	71,291	75,494
Land for flower bulbs	16,432	16,420	16,698	16,318	16,411
Flower cultivation	6,377	6,623	7,054	7,243	7,364
Nurseries	7,523	7,911	8,478	8,886	9,061
Fallow land	5,410	6,493	5,722	5,934	...
Total	2,014,263	2,011,669	2,003,878	2,005,608	...

[1] Provisional figures.

The net areas under special crops were as follows (in ha):

Products	1990	1991 [1]	Products	1990	1991 [1]
Autumn wheat	135,104	115,196	Colza	8,415	7,073
Spring wheat	5,499	8,039	Flax	5,535	4,414
Rye	8,604	7,049	Agricultural seeds	26,314	27,980
Autumn barley	9,941	7,120	Potatoes, edible [2]	112,481	116,791
Spring barley	30,447	34,813	Potatoes, industrial [3]	62,838	63,142
Oats	3,401	3,335	Sugar-beet	124,995	123,361
Peas	11,703	7,536	Fodder-beet	3,023	2,842

[1] Provisional figures. [2] Including early and seed pototoes. [3] Including seed potatoes.

The yield of the more important products, in tonnes, was as follows:

Crop	Average 1970–79	Average 1980–89	1989	1990	1991 [1]
Wheat	701,934	933,966	1,046,770	1,075,853	911,000
Rye	103,442	26,916	33,424	36,219	37,500
Barley	327,345	239,683	250,712	218,834	226,900
Oats	144,855	70,036	32,055	16,104	16,800
Field beans	...	19,205	29,823	15,067	9,600
Peas	19,972	64,674	72,595	61,134	33,300
Colza	32,797	30,358	22,953	25,508	20,800
Flax, unrippled	43,620	28,860	31,341	39,598	35,500
Potatoes, edible	3,084,356	4,297,587	4,376,244	4,658,423	4,735,000
Potatoes, industrial	2,554,555	2,312,059	2,479,372	2,377,816	...
Sugar-beet	5,546,689	6,871,557	7,678,508	8,623,400	...
Fodder-beet	348,117	179,506	232,519	292,086	...

[1] Provisional figures.

Livestock, May 1991: 5,056,597 cattle, 13,196,000 pigs; 76,719 horses and ponies; 1,878,003 sheep, 96,548,700 poultry (provisional).

In 1990 the production of butter, under state control, declined to 178,015 tonnes; in 1990, that of cheese, under state control, increased to 616,160 tonnes. Export value (processed and unprocessed) of arable crops: 20,365m. guilders; animal produce, 20,248m. guilders and horticultural produce, 14,887m. guilders.

Fisheries. Catch in 1989: Marine, 416,260 tonnes; inland, 5,353 tonnes.

INDUSTRY. Numbers employed (in 1,000) and turnover (in 1,000m. guilders) in manufacturing enterprises with 10 employees and more, excluding building:

Class in industry	Numbers employed		Turnover	
	1989	1990	1989	1990
Mining and quarrying	8·8	8·7	15·3	17·1
Manufacturing industry	830·2	845·6	276·3	282·5
Foodstuffs and tobacco products	133·1	136·2	73·4	73·2
Textile industry	22·3	22·8	5·3	5·3
Clothing	9·9	9·2	1·2	1·2
Leather and footwear	5·4	5·1	0·9	1·0

Class in industry	Numbers employed		Turnover	
	1989	1990	1989	1990
Wood and furniture industry	27·9	28·7	4·9	5·2
Paper industry	25·1	25·3	8·5	9·0
Graphic industry, publishers	67·4	68·2	15·1	16·3
Petroleum industry	8·7	8·0	18·9	18·1
Chemical industry, artificial yarns and fibre industry	89·7	91·6	44·6	45·4
Rubber and synthetic materials processing industry	31·4	32·9	8·5	8·6
Building industry, earthenware and glass	31·0	31·7	7·7	8·1
Basic metal industry	29·2	28·8	10·8	9·4
Metal products (excl. machinery and means of transport)	78·2	81·1	15·6	17·3
Machinery	82·1	86·3	16·3	18·0
Electrical industry	115·7	114·5	26·3	26·8
Means of transport	58·5	61·3	16·0	17·4
Instrument making and optical industry	7·5	8·3	1·1	1·2
Other industries	5·0	5·6	0·8	0·9
Public utilities	...	...	17·4	19·5

Labour. In 1991 there was a legal minimum wage of 2,100 guilders a month. Retirement age is 65 years. In Jan. 1991 job exchanges were moved from government control to joint control by employers, trade unions and local authorities.

Unemployment was 343,000 at the end of 1990, with 98,000 job vacancies.

FOREIGN ECONOMIC RELATIONS. On 5 Sept. 1944 and 14 March 1947 the Netherlands signed agreements with Belgium and Luxembourg for the establishment of a customs union. On 1 Jan. 1948 this union came into force and the existing customs tariffs of the Belgium–Luxembourg Economic Union and of the Netherlands were superseded by the joint Benelux Customs Union Tariff. It applied to imports into the 3 countries from outside sources, and exempted from customs duties all imports into each of the 3 countries from the other two.

Commerce. Imports and exports for calendar years (in 1,000 guilders):

	Imports	Exports		Imports	Exports
1959	14,968,454	13,702,927	1987	184,843,632	188,017,411
1969	39,955,406	36,205,110	1988	195,801,221	203,777,722
1979	134,885,386	127,689,416	1989	221,352,737	229,409,169
1986	185,052,790	197,286,108	1990	229,207,832	239,282,481

Value of trade with major partners (in 1,000 guilders):

	Imports		Exports	
Country	1989	1990	1989	1990
Belgium–Luxembourg	31,265,225	31,958,679	33,552,870	35,097,568
France	16,815,468	17,692,771	24,981,593	26,716,272
Germany (Fed. Rep.)	56,902,792	58,806,683	59,175,607	66,140,547
Italy	8,057,345	8,585,719	15,146,711	15,856,286
Japan	6,675,939	7,309,991	2,245,592	2,038,810
Spain	2,790,174	3,337,379	5,330,057	5,913,285
Sweden	4,859,285	4,963,900	4,522,651	4,296,175
Switzerland	2,907,821	3,196,588	3,991,511	4,385,513
UK	17,438,673	18,761,355	25,412,917	24,335,615
USA	18,714,238	18,046,269	10,433,281	9,562,543

Total trade between the Netherlands and UK (British Department of Trade returns, in £1,000 sterling):

	1987	1988	1989	1990	1991
Imports to UK	7,148,036	8,279,747	9,585,699	10,483,576	9,969,981
Exports and re-exports from UK	5,856,164	5,583,280	6,515,325	7,516,576	8,258,475

Tourism. There were 3·9m. foreign visitors in 1990 to hotels: 0·73m. from the Federal Republic of Germany, 0·72m. from the UK and 0·45m. from the USA. Total income from tourism (1989) US$3,020m.

COMMUNICATIONS

Roads. In 1988 the length of the Netherlands network of surfaced inter-urban roads was 55,100 km, of which 2,060 km were motor highways. Number of private cars (1991), 5·6m.

Railways. All railways are run by the mixed company 'N.V. Nederlandse Spoorwegen'. Route length in 1990 was 2,798 km, of which 1,957 km were electrified. Passengers carried (1990), 256m.; goods transported, 18·4m. tonnes. There is a metro (18 km) and tram/light rail network (124 km) in Amsterdam and in Rotterdam (940 km and 94 km). Tram/light rail networks operate in The Hague (117 km) and Utrecht (21·5 km).

Civil Aviation. The Royal Dutch Airlines (KLM) was founded on 7 Oct. 1919. Revenue traffic, 1990–91: Passengers, 7·5m.; freight and mail, 371m. kg.

Sea-going Shipping. Survey of the Netherlands mercantile marine as at 1 Jan. (capacity in 1,000 GRT):

	1990		1991	
Ships under Netherlands flag	Number	Capacity	Number	Capacity
Passenger ships [1]	4	77	5	84
Freighters (100 GRT and over)	359	2,047	352	2,093
Tankers	55	646	55	667
	418	2,771	412	2,845

[1] With accommodation for 13 or more cabin passengers.

In 1990, 45,389 sea-going ships of 421m. gross tons entered Netherlands ports.

Total goods traffic by sea-going ships in 1990 (with 1989 figures in brackets), in 1m. tonnes, amounted to 281 (280) unloaded, of which 128 (128) tankshipping, and 92 (93) loaded, of which 32 (33) tankshipping. The total seaborne freight traffic at Rotterdam was 288m. (290m.) and at Amsterdam 31m. (29m.) tonnes.

The number of containers (including flats) at Rotterdam in 1990 (with 1989 figures in brackets) was: Unloaded from ships, 1,227,795 (1,183,961) and 1,226,086 (1,222,728) loaded into ships.

Inland Shipping. The total length of navigable rivers and canals is 5,052 km, of which 2,398 km is for ships with a capacity of 1,000 and more tonnes. On 1 Jan. 1991 the inland fleet used for transport (with carrying capacity in 1,000 tonnes) was composed as follows:

	Number	Capacity
Self-propelled barges	5,074	4,247
Dumb barges	262	257
Pushed barges	675	1,490
	6,011	5,994

In 1990, 286m. (1989: 293m.) tonnes of goods were transported on rivers and canals, of which 202m. (203m.) was international traffic. Goods transport on the Rhine across the Dutch–German frontier near Lobith amounted to 143m. (142m.) tonnes.

Telecommunications. On 1 Jan. 1991 there were 6·9m. telephone connexions (46 per 100 inhabitants). Number of telex lines, 22,000. *Nederlandse Omroepprogramma Stichting* (NOS) provides 5 programmes on medium-waves and FM in co-operation with broadcasting organizations. Regional programmes are also broadcast.

Advertisements are transmitted. NOS broadcasts 3 TV programmes (colour by PAL). Television sets (1 Jan. 1991) totalled 4·9m.; holders of television licences may, in addition, have radio sets. There were 12,146,299 radio sets in 1990.

Cinemas (1990). There were 443 cinemas with a seating capacity of 104,000.

Newspapers (1990). There were 75 daily newspapers with a total circulation of 4·7m.

JUSTICE, RELIGION, EDUCATION AND WELFARE

Justice. Justice is administered by the High Court of the Netherlands (Court of Cassation), by 5 courts of justice (Courts of Appeal), by 19 district courts and by 63 cantonal courts; trial by jury is unknown. The Cantonal Court, which deals with minor offences, is formed by a single judge; the more serious cases are tried by the district courts, formed as a rule by 3 judges (in some cases one judge is sufficient); the courts of appeal are constituted of 3 and the High Court of 5 judges. All judges are appointed for life by the Sovereign (the judges of the High Court from a list prepared by the Second Chamber of the States-General). They can be removed only by a decision of the High Court.

At the district court the juvenile judge is specially appointed to try children's civil cases and at the same time charged with administration of justice for criminal actions committed by young persons between 12 and 18 years old, unless imprisonment of more than 6 months ought to be inflicted; such cases are tried by 3 judges.

Number of sentences, and cases in which prosecution was evaded by paying a fine to the public prosecutor (excluding violation of economic and tax laws):

Major offences		Minor offences	
1987	97,361	1987	915,329
1988	102,348	1988	825,190
1989	107,059	1989[1]	751,401

In addition, prosecution was evaded by paying a fine to the police in about 1·95m. cases in 1988.

[1] Provisional.

Police. There are both State and Municipal Police. In 1989 the State Police, about 7,500 strong, served 554, and the Municipal Police, about 20,400 strong, served 148 municipalities. The State Police includes ordinary as well as water, mounted and motor police. The State Police Corps is under the jurisdiction of the Police Department of the Ministry of Justice, which also includes the Central Criminal Investigation Office, which deals with serious crimes throughout the country, and the International Criminal Investigation Office, which informs foreign countries of international crimes.

Religion. Entire liberty of conscience is granted to the members of all denominations. The royal family belong to the Dutch Reformed Church.

The number of adherents of the Churches according to survey estimates of 1990 was: Roman Catholics, 4,210,000; Dutch Reformed Church, 2,502,000; Reformed Churches, 1,236,000; other creeds, 715,000; no religion, 5,629,000.

The government of the Reformed Church is Presbyterian. On 1 July 1972 the Dutch Reformed Church had 1 synod, 11 provincial districts, 54 classes, 147 districts and 1,905 parishes.

Their clergy numbered 2,000. The Roman Catholic Church had, Jan. 1973, 1 archbishop (of Utrecht), 6 bishops and 1,815 parishes and rectorships. The Old Catholics had (1 July 1972) 1 archbishop (Utrecht), 2 bishops and 29 parishes. The Jews had, in 1970, 46 communities.

Education. Statistics for the scholastic year 1989–90:

	Full-time Pupils/Students			Part-time [1] Pupils/Students		
	Schools	Total	Female	Schools	Total	Female
Basic schools	8,442	1,432,777	709,061	—	—	—
Special schools	1,001	106,712	34,081	—	—	—
Secondary general schools	1,284	697,354	364,589	78	89,337	62,784
Secondary vocational schools:						
Junior—						
Technical, nautical	577	103,474	6,065	5	827	71
Agricultural	193	20,988	6,676	93	8,804	2,212
Domestic science	697	54,898	50,550	—	—	—
Other	248	72,858	36,113	—	—	—
Senior—						
Technical, nautical	129	83,693	9,971	21	5,350	344
Agricultural	66	17,531	3,686	41	7,363	1,576
Service trade and health care training	132	68,973	61,289	15	9,389	6,563
Other	212	124,235	59,604	462	190,407	65,997

[1] Including apprenticeship schemes, young workers' educational institutes.

		Full-time Pupils/Students			Part-time [1] Pupils/Students	
	Schools	Total	Female	Schools	Total	Female
Third level non-university training:						
Technical, nautical	55	44,945	5,724	15	4,843	522
Agricultural	13	8,620	2,136	1	173	26
Arts	46	16,913	9,518	33	4,827	2,474
Teachers' training	65	28,205	19,316	29	20,496	10,385
Other	144	81,536	46,996	75	24,806	12,834

[1] Including apprenticeship schemes, young workers' educational institutes.

Academic Year 1989–90

		Full-time Students		Part-time Students	
	Schools	Total	Female	Total	Female
University education:					
Arts and humanities		27,801	17,560	1,853	1,023
Social sciences		72,667	30,475	11,556	5,090
Mathematic and natural sciences	22	12,558	3,624	396	76
Engineering sciences		24,887	2,991	34	1
Medical sciences		16,233	8,694	368	231
Agricultural sciences		5,599	2,285	75	27

Health. On 1 Jan. 1991 there were 37,461 doctors and about 64,879 licensed hospital beds.

Social Security. Under the Incapable of Work scheme ('WAO') some 0·9m. persons received 24,000m. guilders in 1990, when benefits were paid up to 70% of former salary until the retirement age of 65. In 1991 the period of eligibility was capped according to the number of years beneficiaries had been in employment.

DIPLOMATIC REPRESENTATIVES

Of the Netherlands in Great Britain (38 Hyde Park Gate, London, SW7 5DP)
Ambassador: Joop Hoekman.

Of Great Britain in the Netherlands (Lange Voorhout, 10, The Hague)
Ambassador: Sir Michael Jenkins, KCMG.

Of the Netherlands in the USA (4200 Linnean Ave., NW, Washington, D.C., 20008)
Ambassador: Johan H. Meesman.

Of the USA in the Netherlands (Lange Voorhout, 102, The Hague)
Ambassador: C. Howard Wilkins Jr.

Of the Netherlands to the United Nations
Ambassador: Robert J. Van Schaik.

Further Reading

Centraal Bureau voor de Statistiek. *Statistical Yearbook of the Netherlands.* From 1923/24 (preceded by *Jaarcijfers voor het Koninkrijk der Nederlanden, 1898–1922).—Statistisch Jaarboek.* From 1899/1924.—*CBS Select (Statistical Essays).* From 1980.—*Statistisch Bulletin.* From 1945; weekly.—*Maandschrift.* From 1944; monthly bulletin.—*90 Jaren Statistiek in Tijdreeksen* (historical series of the Netherlands 1899–1989)
Nationale Rekeningen (National Accounts). From 1948–50.—*Statistisch Magazine.* From 1981.—*Statistische onderzoekingen.* From 1977.—*Regionaal Statistisch Zakboek* (Regional Pocket Yearbook). From 1972.—*Environmental Statistics of the Netherlands,* 1987
Staatsalmanak voor het Koninkrijk der Nederlanden. Annual. The Hague, from 1814
Staatsblad van het Koninkrijk der Nederlanden. The Hague, from 1814
Staatscourant (State Gazette). The Hague, from 1813
Atlas van Nederland. Government Printing Office, The Hague, 1970 and supplements up to and including 1973
Gladdish, K., *Governing from the Centre: Politics and Policy-Making in the Netherlands.* London, 1991

King, P. K. and Wintle, M., *The Netherlands*. [Bibliography] Oxford and Santa Barbara, 1988
Pyttersen's Nederlandse Almanak. Zaltbommel, annual, from 1899
A Compact Geography of the Netherlands. Utrecht, 1980

National library: De Koninklijke Bibliotheek, Prinz Willem Alexanderhof 5, The Hague.
  Director: Dr C. Reedijk.
National statistical office: Centraal Bureau voor de Statistiek, POB 959, 2270 AZ Voorburg.

ARUBA

HISTORY. Discovered by Alonzo de Ojeda in 1499, the island of Aruba was claimed for Spain but not settled. It was acquired by the Dutch in 1634, but apart from garrisons was left to the indigenous Caiquetios (Arawak) Indians until the 19th century. From 1828 it formed part of the Dutch West Indies and, from 1845, part of the Netherlands Antilles, with which on 29 Dec. 1954 it achieved internal self-government.

Following a referendum in March 1977, the Dutch government announced on 28 Oct. 1981 that Aruba would proceed to independence separately from the other islands. Aruba was constitutionally separated from the Netherlands Antilles from 1 Jan. 1986, and full independence has been promised by the Netherlands after a 10-year period.

AREA AND POPULATION. The island, which lies in the southern Caribbean 24 km north of the Venezuelan coast and 68 km west of Curaçao, has an area of 193 sq. km (75 sq. miles) and a population at the 1981 census of 60,312; estimate (1988) 62,500. The chief towns are Oranjestad, the capital (20,000) and Sint Nicolaas, site of the former oil refinery (17,000). Dutch is the official language, but the language usually spoken is Papiamento, a creole language. Unlike other Caribbean islands, over half the population is of Indian stock, with the balance chiefly of Dutch, Spanish and mestizo origin.

CLIMATE. Aruba has a tropical marine climate, with a brief rainy season from Oct. to Dec. Oranjestad. Jan. 79°F (26·0°C), July 84°F (29·0°C). Annual rainfall 17" (432 mm).

CONSTITUTION AND GOVERNMENT. Under the separate constitution inaugurated on 1 Jan. 1986, Aruba is an autonomous part of the Kingdom of the Netherlands with its own legislature, government, judiciary, civil service and police force. The Netherlands is represented by a Governor appointed by the monarch. The unicameral legislature *(Staten)* consists of 21 members; at the general elections held on 6 Jan. 1989, 10 seats were won by the *(Movimento Electoral di Pueblo)*, 8 by the *Arubaanse Volks Partij*, and 1 each by 3 smaller parties with whom the AVP formed a coalition government.

Governor: Felipe B. Tromp.
Prime Minister, Minister of General Affairs: Nelson O. Oduber.
Deputy Prime Minister, Public Works and Health: Pedro P. Kelly.
Economic Affairs and Tourism: Daniel I. Leo. *Justice:* Hendrik S. Croes. *Social Affairs and Education:* Fredis J. Refunjol. *Transport and Communications:* Euladio D. Nicolaas. *Finance:* Guillermo P. Trinidad.

Flag: Blue, with 2 narrow horizontal yellow stripes, and in the canton a red 4-pointed star fimbriated in white.

ECONOMY

Budget. The 1984 budget totalled 207m. guilders revenue and 278m. guilders expenditure.

Currency. From 1 Jan. 1986 the currency has been the Aruban florin, at par with the Netherlands Antilles guilder. In March 1992, £1 = 3·14 *Aruban florins*; US$1 = 1·79 *Aruban florins*.

Banking. As well as the Aruba Bank, there are local branches of the Algemene Bank Nederland, Barclays Bank International, Caribbean Mercantile Bank and Citibank.

ENERGY AND NATURAL RESOURCES

Electricity. Generating capacity totals 310,000 kw. Production (1986) 945m. kwh.

Oil. The Exxon refinery dominated the economy from 1929–85, when it was closed, resulting in unemployment reaching 40% by the end of 1985.

Minerals. Gold, first discovered in 1825, is still found but in uneconomic quantities.

EXTERNAL ECONOMIC RELATIONS

Commerce. Total trade between Aruba and UK (British Department of Trade returns, in £1,000 sterling):

	1989	1990	1991
Imports to UK	653	50	6,365
Exports and re-exports from UK	12,751	11,386	18,934

Tourism. Tourism is now the main economic sector. In 1986 there were 181,000 tourists.

COMMUNICATIONS

Roads. In 1984 there were 380 km of surfaced highways. In 1984 there were 23,409 passenger cars and 582 commercial vehicles.

Aviation. There is an international airport (Prinses Beatrix) served by numerous airlines.

Telecommunications. In 1983 there were 5 radio stations and 1 television station. In 1983 there were 17,000 telephones.

JUSTICE RELIGION, EDUCATION AND WELFARE

Justice. The Aruban judiciary is now separated from that of the Netherlands Antilles. There is a Court of First Instance and a Court of Appeal situated in Oranjestad.

Religion. In 1981, 89% of the population were Roman Catholic and 7% Protestant.

Education. In 1983 there were 33 elementary schools with 6,763 pupils, 10 junior high schools with 3,082 pupils and 4 senior schools and colleges with 881 students.

Health. In 1985 there were 59 doctors, 16 dentists, 9 pharmacists, 189 nursing personnel and one hospital with 279 beds.

THE NETHERLANDS ANTILLES

De Nederlandse Antillen

HISTORY. Bonaire and Curaçao islands, originally populated by Arowak Indians, were discovered in 1499 by Alonso de Ojeda, and claimed for Spain. They were settled in 1527, and the indigenous population exterminated and replaced by a slave-worked plantation economy. The 3 Windward Islands, inhabited by Caribs, were discovered by Columbus in 1493. They were taken by the Dutch in 1632 (Saba and Sint Eustatius), 1634 (Curaçao and Bonaire) and 1648 (the southern part of Sint Maarten, with France acquiring the northern part). With Aruba, the islands formed part of the Dutch West Indies from 1828, and the Netherlands Antilles from 1845, with internal self-government being granted on 29 Dec. 1954. Aruba was separated from 1 Jan. 1986.

AREA AND POPULATION. The Netherlands Antilles comprise two groups of islands, the Leeward group (Curaçao and Bonaire) being situated 100 km north of the Venezuelan coast and the Windward Islands situated 800 km away to the north-east, at the northern end of the Lesser Antilles. The total area is 800 sq. km (308 sq. miles) and the Census population in 1981 was 235,707. Estimate (1990) 190,577 (excluding Aruba). Willemstad is the capital.

The areas, populations and chief towns of the islands are:

Island	Sq. km	1990 Estimate	Chief town	1981 Census
Bonaire	288	11,058	Kralendijk	1,200
Curaçao	444	144,962	Willemstad	50,000
Saba	13	1,119	The Bottom	–
Sint Eustatius	21	1,716	Oranjestad	–
Sint Maarten [1]	34	31,722	Philipsburg	6,000

[1] The southern part belongs to the Netherlands Antilles, the northern to France.

Dutch is the official language, but the languages usually spoken are Papiamento (derived from Dutch, Spanish and Portuguese) on Curaçao and Bonaire, and English in the Windward Islands.

Vital statistics (1990), Live births, 3,602; marriages, 1,267; divorces, 409; deaths, 1,217.

CLIMATE. All the islands have a tropical marine climate, with very little difference in temperatures over the year. There is a short rainy season from Oct. to Jan. Willemstad. Jan. 79°F (26·1°C), July 82°F (27·8°C). Annual rainfall 23" (582 mm).

CONSTITUTION AND GOVERNMENT. On 29 Dec. 1954, the Netherlands Antilles became an integral part of the Kingdom of the Netherlands but are fully autonomous in internal affairs, and constitutionally equal with the Netherlands and Aruba. The Sovereign of the Kingdom of the Netherlands is Head of State and Government, and is represented by a Governor.

The executive power in internal affairs rests with the Governor and the Council of Ministers, who together form the Government. The Ministers are responsible to a unicameral legislature *(Staten)* consisting of 22 members (since 1986, 14 from Curaçao, 3 from Bonaire, 3 from Sint Maarten, and 1 each from Saba and Sint Eustatius) elected by universal suffrage. In general elections held for the *Staten* on 16 March 1990, 1 seat was won by the *Democratische Partij* (DP), 7 by the *Nationale Volks Partij* (NVP), 2 by the *Movimento Antias Nobo* (MAN), 3 by the combination *Sosial Independiente/Frente Obrero y Liberashon* (SI/FOL), 3 by the *Union Patriotico Bonairiano* (UPB), 2 by the *Democratic Party of St. Maarten Patriotic Alliance* (DP of St. Maarten), 1 for *Nos Patria*, 1 for *St. Maarten Patriotic Alliance* (SPA), 1 for the *Windward Island People's Movement* (WIPM), and 1 for the *Democratic Party of St. Eustatius* (DP of St. Eustatius).

The executive power in external affairs is vested in the Council of Ministers of the Kingdom, in which the Antilles is represented by a Minister Plenipotentiary with full voting powers. On each of the insular communities, local autonomous power is divided between an Island Council (elected by universal suffrage), the Executive Council and the Lieut.-Governor, responsible for law and order.

Governor: Dr Jaime M. Saleh.

The Cabinet in Sept. 1991 was composed as follows:
Prime Minister: Maria-Liberia Peters (NVP).

Deputy Prime Minister and Finance: Gilbert de Paula (NVP). *Justice:* Ivo Knoppel (NVP). *Economic Affairs and Education:* Cornelius Smits (NVP). *Social and Labour Affairs:* Eithel Pietersz (SI/FOL). *Developmental Affairs:* Rudy Ellis (UPB). *Public Health and Environmental Affairs:* Stanley Inderson (SI/FOL). *Transport and Communications:* Dester Nisbet (DP of St. Maarten).

Flag: White, with a red vertical strip crossed by a blue horizontal strip bearing 5 white stars.

ECONOMY

Budget. The central budget for 1990 envisaged 337·4m. NA guilders revenue and 356m. NA guilders expenditure.

Currency. The unit of currency is the *Netherlands Antilles guilder* (ANG) of 100 *cents*. There are notes of 500, 250, 100, 50, 25, 10 and 5 *guilder*, and coins of 2¹/₂ and 1 *guilder* and 50, 25, 10, 5, 2¹/₂ and 1 *cent*. The official rate of exchange was £1 = 3·14 *NA guilder* in March 1992. The *NA guilder* has been pegged to the US dollar at US$1 = 1·79 *NA guilder* since 12 Dec. 1971.

Banking. At 31 Dec. 1990 the Bank of the Netherlands Antilles had total assets and liabilities of 549·3m. NA guilders; commercial banks, 2,891·6m. NA guilders.
Post office savings banks had deposits of 11,730m. NA guilders in 1990.

ENERGY AND NATURAL RESOURCES

Electricity. Production (1990) totalled 785m. kwh.

Oil. The economy was formerly based largely on oil refining at the Shell refinery on Curaçao, but following an announcement by Shell that closure was imminent, this was sold to the Netherlands Antilles government in Sept. 1985, and leased to Petróleos de Venezuela to operate on a reduced scale.

Minerals. Calcium carbonate (limestone) has been mined since 1980; mining of calcium phosphate ceased in 1979. Production of limetone, 1990 (estimate), 0·36m. tons.

Agriculture. Livestock (1990 estimate): Cows, 425; goats, 58,000; pigs, 7,000. Figures exclude Aruba. (Curaçao, 1990 estimate: cows, 300; goats, 48,000; pigs, 6,300; sheep, 10,700).

Fisheries. Catch (1990 estimate) 8,500 tonnes.

INDUSTRY AND TRADE

Industry. Curaçao has an oil refinery and one of the largest ship-repair dry docks in the western hemisphere, which together form the main industrial activities. Curaçao also has a paint factory, a cigarette factory, a rice factory, a brewery and some smaller industries. Bonaire has a textile factory and a modern equipped salt plant. Sint Maarten's industrial activities are primarily based on a rum factory and a fishing factory. Saba has an oil terminal operating in its territorial waters.

Labour. In 1988 the economically active population numbered 73,101 (Curaçao, 1991: 57,310), the working population 58,165, (Curaçao, 1988: 43,770).

Commerce. There is a Free Zone on Curaçao, Total imports (1990) amounted to 3,162·1m. (crude and petroleum products, 329·1m.) NA guilders, total exports to 2,985·9m. (crude and petroleum products, 60·1m.) NA guilders.
Total trade between the Netherlands Antilles and UK (British Department of Trade returns, in £1,000 sterling):

	1987	1988	1989	1990	1991
Imports to UK	5,133	7,823	5,115	43,552	29,049
Exports and re-exports from UK	19,635	20,089	19,396	23,800	18,954

Tourism. In 1990, 795,833 tourists visited the islands (Sint Maarten, 546,842; Curaçao, 207,673; Bonaire, 41,318) excluding 678,006 cruise passengers (Curaçao, 158,552; Sint Maarten, 514,974; Bonaire, 4,480).

COMMUNICATIONS

Roads. In 1989, the Netherlands Antilles had 845 km of surfaced highway distributed as follows: Curaçao, 590; Bonaire, 226; Sint Maarten, 19. Number of motor vehicles (31 Dec. 1990): 56,589.

Aviation. There are international airports on Curaçao (Curaçao International Airport), Bonaire (Flamingo Airport) and Sint Maarten (Princess Juliana Airport). In 1990 Curaçao handled 916,000 passengers, Bonaire 219,000, Sint Maarten 1,015,000, Sint Eustatius 26,562 and Saba 18,298.

Shipping (1990). 5,032 ships (totalling 31,595,000 GRT) entered the port of Curaçao; 1,024 ships (4,048,000 GRT) entered the port of Bonaire: 2,162 ships (14,968,000 GRT) entered the port of St. Maarten. In 1990 Curaçao handled 177,185 passengers, Bonaire 4,877 and Sint Maarten 523,786.

Telecommunications. Number of telephones, 31 Dec. 1990, 54,150. At 31 Dec. 1990 there were 20 radio transmitters (6 on Bonaire, 9 on Curaçao, 2 each on Saba and Sint Maarten and 1 on Sint Eustatius) and each island had 1 cable television station. These stations broadcast in *Papiamento*, Dutch, English and Spanish and are mainly financed by income from advertisements. In addition, Radio Nederland and Trans World Radio have powerful relay stations operating on medium- and short-waves from Bonaire. In 1989, excluding Aruba, there were approximately 147,000 radio and 69,000 TV receivers.

Newspapers. In 1990 there were 10 daily newspapers. Total daily circulation 95,000 (1990).

JUSTICE, RELIGION, EDUCATION AND WELFARE

Justice. There is a Court of First Instance, which sits in each island, and a Court of Appeal in Willemstad.

Religion. In 1986, 84% of the population were Roman Catholics, 9·5% were Protestants (Sint Maarten and Sint Eustatius being primarily Protestant).

Education. In 1989 there were 21,778 pupils in primary schools, 8,698 pupils in general secondary schools, 6,526 pupils in junior and senior secondary vocational schools, and 578 students in vocational colleges and universities.

Health. In 1990 there were 278 doctors, 57 dentists, 1,494 hospital beds and an estimated 1,706 nursing personnel.

DIPLOMATIC REPRESENTATIVE

USA Consul-General: Sharon Wilkinson.

Further Reading

Central Bureau of Statistics. *Statistical Yearbook of the Netherlands Antilles*
Bank of the Netherlands Antilles. *Annual Report.*

NEW ZEALAND

Capital: Wellington
Population: 3·42m. (1991)
GNP per capita: US$11,800 (1989)

HISTORY. Polynesian Maoris immigrated from the eastern Pacific before and during the 14th century. The first European to discover New Zealand was Tasman in 1642. The coast was explored by Capt. Cook in 1769. From about 1800 onwards, New Zealand became a resort for whalers and traders, chiefly from Australia. By the Treaty of Waitangi in 1840 the Maori chiefs ceded sovereignty to the British Crown and the islands became a British colony. Then followed a steady stream of British settlers.

Between 1845 and 1848, and between 1860 and 1870, misunderstandings over land led to war, but peace was permanently established in 1871.

AREA AND POPULATION. New Zealand lies south-east of Australia in the south Pacific, Wellington being 1,983 km from Sydney by sea. There are two principal islands, the North and South Islands, besides Stewart Island, Chatham Islands and small outlying islands, as well as the territories overseas (see pp. 000–00).

New Zealand (i.e., North, South and Stewart Islands) extends over 1,750 km from north to south. Area, excluding territories overseas, 267,844 sq. km comprising North Island, 114,821 sq. km; South Island, 149,463 sq. km; Stewart Island, 1,746 sq. km; Chatham Islands, 963 sq. km; minor islands, 833 sq. km. Growth in census population, exclusive of territories overseas:

	Total population	Average annual increase %		Total population	Average annual increase %
1858	115,462	—	1926	1,408,139	2·06
1874	344,984	—	1936	1,573,810	1·13
1878	458,007	7·33	1945[1]	1,702,298	0·83
1881	534,030	5·10	1951[1]	1,939,472	2·37
1886	620,451	3·05	1956[1]	2,174,062	2·31
1891	668,632	1·50	1961[1]	2,414,984	2·12
1896	743,207	2·13	1966[1]	2,676,919	2·10
1901[1]	815,853	1·89	1971[1]	2,862,631	1·34
1906	936,304	2·75	1976[1]	3,129,383	1·71
1911	1,058,308	2·52	1981[1]	3,175,737	0·20
1916[1]	1,149,225	1·50	1986[1]	3,307,084	0·82
1921	1,271,644	2·27			

The census of New Zealand is quinquennial, but the census falling in 1931 was abandoned as an act of national economy, and owing to war conditions the census due in 1941 was not taken until 25 Sept. 1945. There was a census on 5 March 1991.

[1] Excluding members of the Armed Forces overseas.

The areas and populations of local government regions (with principal centres) at 4 March 1986 were as follows [1]:

Local Government Region (and principal centre)	Area[2] (sq. km)	Total Population 1981 census	1986 census	Intercensal change (%)
Northland (Whangarei)	12,604	113,994	126,999	11·4
Auckland (Auckland) [1]	5,201	827,408	887,448	7·3
Thames Valley (Thames–Coromandel)	4,666	54,343	58,665	8·0
Bay of Plenty (Tauranga)	9,126	172,480	187,462	8·7
Waikato (Hamilton)	13,241	221,850	228,303	2·9
Tongariro (Taupo)	12,085	40,089	40,793	1·8
East Cape (Gisborne)	11,461	53,295	53,968	1·3
Hawke's Bay (Napier, Hastings)	12,396	137,840	140,709	2·1
Taranaki (New Plymouth)	7,876	103,798	107,600	3·7
Wanganui (Wanganui)	9,171	68,702	69,439	1·1
Manawatu (Palmerston North)	6,669	113,238	115,500	2·0

Local Government Region (and principal centre)	Area [2] (sq. km)	Total Population 1981 census	1986 census	Intercensal change (%)
Horowhenua (Levin)	1,614	49,296	53,592	8·7
Wellington (Wellington)	1,379	323,162	328,163	1·5
Wairarapa (Masterton)	6,894	39,689	39,608	−0·2
Total, North Island [2]	114,383	2,319,184	2,438,249	5·1
Nelson Bays (Nelson)	10,197	65,934	69,648	5·6
Marlborough (Blenheim)	12,882	37,557	38,225	1·8
West Coast (Greymouth)	22,893	34,178	34,942	2·2
Canterbury (Christchurch)	17,465	336,846	348,712	3·5
Aorangi (Timaru)	19,910	84,772	81,294	−4·1
Clutha–Central Otago	28,982	45,402	48,771	7·4
Coastal–North Otago (Dunedin)	10,590	138,164	137,393	−0·6
Southland (Invercargill)	27,716	107,905	104,618	−3·0
Total, South Island [2]	150,635	850,758	863,603	1·3
Total, New Zealand [2]	265,018	3,169,942	3,301,852	4·2

[1] Excludes Great Barrier Island and Chatham Island Counties.
[2] Excludes Extra County Islands.

New Zealand-born residents made up 84·5% of the population at the 1986 census. Foreign-born (provisional): UK, 196,872; Australia, 46,839; Netherlands, 24,159; Samoa, 33,864; Cook Islands, 15,540; others (including USA and Ireland), 187,644.

Estimated population on 31 Dec. 1990, 3,429,100 (1,729,600 females).

Maori population: 1896, 42,113; 1936, 82,326; 1945, 98,744; 1951, 115,676; 1961, 171,553; 1971, 227,414; 1976, 270,035; 1981, 279,255; 1986, 294,201. Estimate, 1990: 309,000 (153,400 females). Population increase, 1990, 0·9%.

Populations of main urban areas as at 31 March 1990 were as follows:

Christchurch	303,400	Nelson	45,800
Dunedin	106,400	New Plymouth	48,300
Hamilton	105,000	Rotorua	54,200
Hastings	55,800	Tauranga	64,000
Napier	52,300	Timaru	28,200
Palmerston North	69,300	Wanganui	41,100
Gisborne	31,900	Whangarei	44,100
Invercargill	51,700		

In 1991, the population of Wellington (the capital) was 324,792 and of Auckland was 953,085. Vital statistics for calendar years:

	Total live births	Ex-nuptial births	Deaths	Marriages	Divorces (decrees absolute)
1988	57,546	17,623	27,408	23,485	8,674
1989	58,091	19,230	27,042	22,733	...
1990	60,153	20,479	26,531	...	9,036

Birth rate, 1990, 17·80 per 1,000; death rate, 7·85 per 1,000; marriage rate, 22·08 (1989) per 1,000; infant mortality, 8·31 per 1,000 live births. Population increase 1990, 1·3%. Expectation of life, 1990: Males 71 years; females, 77.

In 1991 there were 57,088 immigrants (52,001 in 1990) and 45,472 emigrants (56,019 in 1990).

CLIMATE. Lying in the cool temperate zone, New Zealand enjoys very mild winters for its latitude owing to its oceanic situation, and only the extreme south has cold winters. The situation of the mountain chain produces much sharper climatic contrasts between east and west than in a north-south direction. Observations for 1983: Auckland. Jan. 65·5°F (18·6°C), July 50°F (10·2°C). Annual rainfall 41·5" (1,053 mm). Christchurch. Jan. 61·3°F (16·3°C), July 42·4°F (5·8°C). Annual rainfall 29" (737 mm). Dunedin. Jan. 57·4°F (14·1°C), July 43·2°F (6·2°C). Annual rainfall 38·1" (968 mm). Hokitika. Jan. 56·1°F (13·4°C), July 43·5°F (6·4°C). Annual rainfall 132·2" (3,357 mm). Rotorua. Jan. 61·2°F (16·2°C), July 43·7°F (6·5°C). Annual rainfall 49·9" (1,268 mm). Wellington. Jan. 59·9°F (15·5°C), July 46·4°F (8·0°C). Annual rainfall 51·2" (1,300 mm).

CONSTITUTION AND GOVERNMENT. Definition was given to the status of New Zealand by the (Imperial) Statute of Westminster of Dec. 1931, which had received the antecedent approval of the New Zealand Parliament in July 1931. The Governor-General's assent was given to the Statute of Westminster Adoption Bill on 25 Nov. 1947.

The powers, duties and responsibilities of the Governor-General and the Executive Council under the present system of responsible government are set out in Royal Letters Patent and Instructions thereunder of 11 May 1917, published in the *New Zealand Gazette* of 24 April 1919. In the execution of the powers vested in him the Governor-General must be guided by the advice of the Executive Council.

The following is a list of Governors-General, the title prior to June 1917 being Governor:

Earl of Liverpool	1917–20	Viscount Cobham	1957–62
Viscount Jellicoe	1920–24	Sir Bernard Fergusson	1962–67
Sir Charles Fergusson, Bt	1924–30	Sir Arthur Porrit, Bt	1967–72
Lord Bledisloe	1930–35	Sir Denis Blundell	1972–77
Viscount Galway	1935–41	Sir Keith Holyoake	1977–80
Sir Cyril Newall	1941–46	Sir David Beattie	1980–85
Lord Freyberg, VC	1946–52	Sir Paul Reeves	1985–90
Lord Norrie	1952–57		

National flag: The British Blue Ensign with 4 stars of the Southern Cross in red, edged in white, in the fly.

National anthems: God Save the Queen; God Defend New Zealand (words by Thomas Bracken, music by John J. Woods).

Since Nov. 1977 both 'God Save the Queen' and 'God Defend New Zealand' have equal status as national anthems.

Parliament consists of the House of Representatives, the former Legislative Council having been abolished since 1 Jan. 1951.

The statute law on elections and the life of Parliament is contained in the Electoral Act, 1956. In 1974 the voting age was reduced from 20 to 18 years.

The House of Representatives from Aug. 1987 consists of 97 members, including 4 members representing Maori electorates, elected by universal adult suffrage for 3-year terms. (At a referendum of 27 Oct. 1990 continuation of the 3-year term was favoured by a large majority). The 4 Maori electoral districts cover the whole country and adult Maoris of half or more Maori descent are the electors. From 1976 a descendant of a Maori is entitled to register either for a general or a Maori electoral district.

At the elections of 27 Oct. 1990, 677 candidates stood. The National Party won 68 seats with 48·7% of the votes cast; the Labour Party, 28, with 34·5%; the New Labour Party, 1, with 5·2%.

Governor-General: Dame Catherine Tizard, GCMG, DBE.

The National Party government formed in Dec. 1990, in Oct. 1991 consisted of:

Prime Minister: Jim Bolger (b.1935).

Deputy Prime Minister, Minister for External Relations and Trade, Foreign Affairs: Don McKinnon. *Labour, Immigration, State Services, Pacific Island Affairs:* Bill Birch. *Finance:* Ruth Richardson. *Attorney-General, Leader of the House:* Paul East. *Agriculture, Forestry, Racing:* John Falloon. *State-owned Enterprises:* Doug Kidd. *Commerce and Industry:* Philip Burdon. *Health, Environment, Research, Science and Technology:* Simon Upton. *Police, Tourism, Recreation and Sport:* John Banks. *Social Welfare and Womens Affairs:* Jenny Shipley. *Defence, Local Government, Television and Radio:* Warren Cooper. *Justice, Disarmament and Arms Control, Arts and Culture:* Doug Graham. *Education:* Lockwood Smith. *Employment:* Maurice McTigue. *Transport, Environment and Lands:* Rob Storey. *Maori Development:* Doug Kidd. *Conservation and Science:* Denis Marshall. *Housing and Energy:* John Luxton. *Revenue, Customs and Government Superannuation Fund:* Wyatt Creech. *Communications, Broadcasting and Statistics:* Maurice Williamson.

There are also 5 Ministers outside the Cabinet.

The Prime Minister (provided with residence) had in 1989 a salary of NZ$147,000 plus a tax-free expense allowance of NZ$26,000 per annum; Ministers with portfolio, NZ$103,000 plus a tax-free expense allowance of NZ$10,750 per annum; Minister without portfolio, NZ$83,000 plus a tax-free expense allowance of NZ$8,500 per annum; Parliamentary Under-Secretaries, NZ$80,000 plus an expense allowance of NZ$8,500 per annum. In addition, Ministers and Parliamentary Under-Secretaries not provided with residence at the seat of Government receive NZ$2,000 per annum house allowance. An allowance of up to NZ$220 per day while travelling within New Zealand on public service is payable to Ministers.

The Speaker of the House of Representatives receives NZ$97,000 plus an expense allowance of NZ$14,250 per annum in addition to his electorate allowance, and residential quarters in Parliament House, and the Leader of the Opposition NZ$103,000 plus expense allowance of NZ$10,750 per annum, and allowances for travelling and housing.

Members were paid NZ$57,000 per annum, plus an expense allowance of NZ$5,500 plus an electoral allowance varying from NZ$7,600 to NZ$18,600 according to the area of electorate represented.

There is a compulsory contributory superannuation scheme for members; retiring allowances are payable to a member after 9 years' service and the attainment of 45 years of age.

Dollimore, H. N., *The Parliament of New Zealand and Parliament House*. 3rd ed. Wellington, 1973

Scott, K. J., *The New Zealand Constitution*. OUP, 1962

Local Government. Since the local government reform of Nov. 1989, territorial local authorities consist of 20 cities and 59 districts. There are also 14 regional authorities. Chatham Islands remains outside this system. Territorial and regional councils are directly elected. A city must have a minimum of 50,000 persons, be predominantly urban in character, be a distinct entity and a major centre of activity within the region. A district, on the other hand, serves a combination of rural and urban communities. There is no distinction in structural status or responsibility between a city council and a district council. There are a few other local authorities created for specific functions.

DEFENCE. The control and co-ordination of defence activities is obtained through the Ministry of Defence. This is a unitary department combining not only all joint-Service functions but also the former Departments of Army, Navy and Air.

Defence spending was reduced by 4% at the budget of July 1990, and by a further NZ$20m. in Dec. 1990.

Army. The Chief of the General Staff commands the Army, assisted by the General Staff and the staffs of Defence Headquarters. A regular force battalion is stationed in Singapore.

There are 2 infantry battalions, 1 artillery battery and 1 light armoured squadron. Equipment includes 26 Scorpion light tanks.

Regular personnel, in 1992, totalled 4,900; territorial personnel totalled 6,696.

Navy. The Royal New Zealand Navy was 2,500 strong (with 1,500 Reserve personnel) in 1991 and includes 4 frigates of British Leander type, 1 12,400-tonne fleet replenishment ship with helicopter facilities, 4 inshore patrol craft, 2 survey vessels, and 1 diver support ship. The 7 Wasp helicopters for embarked service are Air Force owned and operated. The main base and Fleet headquarters is at Auckland.

Air Force. The Chief of Air Staff and Air Officer Commanding commands the Royal New Zealand Air Force (RNZAF). Maritime (P-3B Orion), long and medium-range transport (Boeing 727, C-130H Hercules, Andover, F.27 Friendship) and helicopter (Iroquois, Wasp) squadrons are based at RNZAF Base Auckland, and Hobsonville; and offensive support (A-4 Skyhawk) at RNZAF Base Ohakea. Flying training units (Airtrainer, Strikemaster, MB 339, TA-4 Skyhawks, Sioux) are located at RNZAF Bases Wigram and Ohakea; ground training is carried out at RNZAF Bases Auckland, Woodbourne and Wigram.

The strength in 1992 was 3,900 regular personnel with 36 combat aircraft.

INTERNATIONAL RELATIONS

Membership. New Zealand is a member of the UN, the Commonwealth, OECD, South Pacific Forum and the Colombo Plan.

ECONOMY

Budget. The following tables of revenue and expenditure relate to the Consolidated Account, which covers the ordinary revenue and expenditure of the government—*i.e.*, apart from capital items, commercial and special undertakings, advances, etc. Total revenue and expenditure of the Consolidated Account, which covers ordinary revenue and expenditure of the New Zealand government (*i.e.* apart from capital items, commercial and special undertakings, advances, etc.), in NZ$1m., year ended 30 June:

	1989	1990	1991
Revenue	32,150·6	28,351·0	28,911·0
Expenditure	32,151·2	25,108·0	27,658·0

Taxation receipts in 1990–91 for all purposes amounted to NZ$25,675m., giving an average of NZ$7,780 per head of mean population. Included in the total taxation is NZ$733m. National Roads Fund taxation.

The gross public debt at 30 June 1991 was NZ$43,931m., of which NZ$23,440m. was held in New Zealand, NZ$5,017m. in Europe, NZ$12,292m. in USA, NZ$3,182m. in Japan and NZ$1m. in other sources. The gross annual interest charge on the public debt at 30 June 1990 was NZ$4,842m.

New Zealand System of National Accounts. This replaces the National Income and Expenditure Accounts which have been produced since 1948.

National Accounts aggregates for 4 years are given in the following table (in NZ$1m.):

Year ended 31 March	Gross domestic product	Gross national product	National income
1986	44,861	42,817	39,180
1987	53,079	50,865	46,768
1988	59,257	56,506	51,944
1989	63,805	61,075	55,960
1990	69,785	65,853	60,039

Currency. The monetary unit is *the New Zealand dollar* (NZD), of 100 *cents*. There are notes of NZ$5, 10, 20, 50 and 100; and coins of 5c, 10c, 20c, 50c, NZ$1 and NZ$2. Inflation was 1% at the end of 1991. In March 1992, £1 = 3·21NZ$; US$1 = 1·83NZ$.

Banking and Finance. The central bank and bank of issue is the Reserve Bank (*Governor*, Dr Don Brash).

The financial system comprises a central bank (the Reserve Bank of New Zealand), registered banks, and other financial institutions. Registered banks including banks from abroad, which have to satisfy capital adequacy and managerial quality requirements. Other financial institutions include the regional trustee banks, now grouped under Trust Bank, building societies, finance companies, merchant banks and stock and station agents. The number of registered banks (1990, 22) grows as other financial institutions apply for, and satisfy the requirements for registration as a bank.

The primary functions of the Reserve Bank are the formulation and implementation of monetary policy to achieve the economic objectives set by the Government, and the promotion of the efficiency and soundness of the financial system, through the registration of banks, and supervision of financial institutions. The state owns 52% of the Bank of New Zealand, whose assets were NZ$17,900m. in 1989-90; deposits amounted to NZ$16,210m.

On 30 June 1991 the funding (financial liabilities including deposits) and claims (financial assets including loans) for all registered banks and other financial institutions were: Funding, NZ$61,960m. (foreign currency, NZ$9,564); claims, NZ$63,329m. (foreign currency, NZ$2,942m.).

The stock exchange in Wellington conducts on-screen trading, unifying the 3 former trading floors in Auckland, Christchurch and Wellington.

Weights and Measures. The metric system of weights and measures operates.

ENERGY AND NATURAL RESOURCES

Electricity. On 1 April 1987 the former Electricity Division of the Ministry of Energy became a state-owned enterprise, the Electricity Corporation of N.Z. Ltd., which has 39 power stations (30 hydro-electric and 9 thermal, with a total nominal capacity of 7,247 mw) producing 96% of the country's electricity. The other 4% comes from supply authorities' own generation schemes. Supply 230 volts; 50 Hz.

Statistics for 4 years ended 31 March are:

	1986	1987	1988	1989
Total sales revenue ($1m.)	1,022	1,196	1,317	1,434
Total sales volume (gwh)	24,241	25,187	25,772	26,436
Generation (gwh) (nett)	25,957	26,948	27,498	28,189
Number of employees	5,107	5,079	4,403	4,106
Production/total staff employed (gwh/person)	5·15	5·30	5·80	6·63

In 1991, 29,556 gwh. were generated.

Natural Gas. In 1989 there were 4 gasfields in production: Kapuni (on stream 1970), Maui (1979), McKee (mainly crude oil) (1984), Kaimiro (1984).

Minerals. Production of minerals in 1990 (in tonnes) included 4·62 of gold, 1,393 of bentonite, 65,644 of clay for bricks, tiles, etc., 25,435 of potters' clays, 2,296,153 of iron sand concentrate, 1,048,829 of limestone for agriculture and 357,721 of limestone for industry, 1,360,401 of limestone, marl, etc., for cement, 2,521 of pumice, 20,157 of serpentine, 100,280 of silica sand and 2,581,783 of coal. Macraes hard rock gold mine started production in Nov. 1990. Deposits were some 1,235m. troy oz.; annual initial output 55,000 troy oz.

Agriculture. Two-thirds of the land area is suitable for agriculture and grazing. The total area under cultivation at 30 June 1989 was 17,653,291 ha. (including residential area and domestic orchards). There were 13,677,225 ha. of grassland, lucerne and tussock, 89,825 ha. of land for horticulture, 335,245 ha. of grain or fodder crops and 1,249,154 ha. of plantations.

The largest freehold estates are held in the South Island. The number of occupied holdings as at 30 June 1990, and their aggregate area in 1988 (exclusive of holdings within borough boundaries) were as follows:

Size of holdings (ha.)	Number of farms	Aggregate area (ha.)	Size of holdings (ha.)	Number of farms	Aggregate area (ha.)
Under 5	10,203	31,182	400–799	4,373	2,389,912
5–19	16,748	157,622	800–1,199	1,212	1,160,296
20–39	8,701	235,550	1,200–1,999	905	1,398,745
40–59	7,167	359,649	2,000–3,999	567	1,544,234
60–99	9,895	777,712	4,000 and over	481	5,415,761
100–199	11,317	1,639,339			
200–399	9,335	2,685,111	Total	80,904	17,795,113

The area and yield for each of the principal crops are given as follows (area and yield for threshing only, not including that grown for chaff, hay, silage, etc.):

Crop years	Wheat Area (1,000 ha.)	Yield (1,000 tonnes)	Maize Area (1,000 ha.)	Yield (1,000 tonnes)	Barley Area (1,000 ha.)	Yield (1,000 tonnes)
1987 [1]	83·0	336·8	19·0	176·1	102·5	400·6
1988 [1]	50·6	206·0	16·0	136·9	83·0	356·1
1989 [1]	37·8	135·0	14·9	138·7	86·5	326·8
1990	40·6	18·8	17·6	161·7	96·7	434·9

[1] Area sown.

In 1990, 1,927,804 tonnes of fertilizer was spread.

Livestock 1990 (in 1,000): Dairy cattle, 3,422; beef cattle, 4,651; sheep, 58,334;

deer, 951; goats, 1,108; pigs (1989), 411. Total meat produced in the year ended 30 Sept. 1989 was estimated at 1·22m. tonnes (including 542,200 tonnes of beef and 393,500 tonnes of lamb). Total liquid milk produced in the year ended 31 May 1989 was 6,545m. litres.

Production of wool for 1988–89, 283,457 tonnes.

Agricultural Statistics. Dept. of Statistics, Wellington. Annual.

Forestry. Of the 6·2m. ha of indigenous forest, most is protected in National Parks or State Forests. Declining quantities of indigenous timber are being produced from restricted areas of State Forest and from privately owned forest. There are just over 1m. ha of productive exotic forest, and this produces far more timber than the indigenous forests. Introduced pines form the bulk of the large exotic forest estate and among these radiata pine is the best multi-purpose tree, reaching log size in 25–30 years. Other species planted are Douglas fir and Eucalyptus species. The table below shows production of rough sawn timber in 1,000 cu. metres for years ending 31 March:

	Indigenous			Exotic			All Species
	Rimu and			Exotic	Douglas		
	Miro	Beech	Total	Pines	Fir	Total	Total
1986–87	85	8	112	1,764	174	1,966	2,079
1987–88	62	9	85	1,557	163	1,737	1,822
1988–89	58	10	75	1,585	191	1,802	2,119

Forest industries consist of 300 saw-mills, 6 plywood and veneer plants, 3 particle board mills, 8 pulp and paper mills and 4 fibreboard mills.

The basic products of the pulp and paper mills are mechanical and chemical pulp which are converted into newsprint, kraft and other papers, paperboard and fibreboard. Production of woodpulp, 31 March 1989, amounted to 1·26m. tonnes and of paper (including newsprint paper and paperboard) to 735,207 tonnes.

Fisheries. The total value of New Zealand Fisheries exports during the year ended 30 June 1991 was NZ$624·9m. Exports (1991): Fish, 160,902 tonnes, value NZ$537·5m.; crustaceans, 2,530 tonnes, value NZ$87·4m.

INDUSTRY. Statistics of manufacturing industries:

Production year	Persons engaged	Salaries and wages paid (NZ$1,000)	Cost of materials (NZ$1,000)	Sales and other income (NZ$1,000)	Value added (NZ$1,000)
1988–89	260,803	6,007,336	19,018,393	36,158,470	11,015,568

The following is a statement of the provisional value of the products (including repairs) of the principal industries for the year 1990–91 (in NZ$1,000):

Industry group	Purchases & operating expenses	Sales and other income (NZ$1,000)	Additions to fixed tangible assets
Primary and other food manufacturing	10,434,700	13,026,900	559,900
Textile, wearing apparel	1,922,500	2,703,100	35,400
Wood and wood products (including furniture)	1,582,100	2,220,900	125,000
Paper and paper products, printing and publishing	3,159,700	4,639,200	259,700
Chemicals and chemical, petroleum, coal, rubber and plastic products	3,199,200	4,335,500	165,900
Non-metallic mineral products	714,300	972,100	61,900
Basic metal industries	1,198,700	1,535,500	52,200
Fabricated metal products, machinery and equipment	4,989,800	6,914,700	243,000
Other manufacturing industries	255,200	358,900	9,000
Total	27,455,900	36,706,900	1,511,900

Labour. There were 961,700 full-time jobs in Nov. 1990. Unemployment was 9·6% of the workforce in Feb. 1991. The weekly average wage in Feb. 1991 was NZ$587·93 for men, NZ$458·70 for women.

Trade Unions. In March 1989 there were 168 industrial unions of workers with a total of 649,857 members. Compulsory trade union membership was made illegal in 1991, and the national wage award system was replaced by local wage agreements.

FOREIGN ECONOMIC RELATIONS. Foreign debt was NZ$47,600m. at the end of 1989. In 1990 New Zealand and Australia completed the Closer Economic Relations Agreement (initiated in 1983), which provides for mutual free trade in goods.

Commerce. Trade (excluding specie and bullion) in NZ$1m. for 12 months ended 30 June:

	Total merchandise imported (v.f.d.) [1]	Exports of domestic produce	Re-exports	Total merchandise exported (f.o.b.)
1986–87	10,803·4	11,723·9	383·3	12,107·2
1987–88	10,625·1	12,104·1	347·4	12,451·5
1988–89	11,402·4	14,484·7	422·5	14,907·2
1989–90	14,420·1	14,588·9	638·9	15,277·8

[1] Value for duty.

The principal imports for the 12 months ended 30 June 1990:

Commodity	Value (NZ$1m. v.f.d.)
Fruit	101·2
Sugar and sugar confectionery	118·5
Beer, wine and spirits	105·6
Crude petroleum oil	682·2
Inorganic chemicals (excluding aluminium oxide)	157·7
Aluminium oxide	203·8
Knitted or crocheted fabrics and articles	145·5
Glass and glassware	110·5
Iron and steel	311·8
Articles of iron and steel	203·7
Copper and articles of copper	96·4
Aluminium and articles of aluminium	158·7
Tools, implements and articles of base metals	162·3
Machinery and mechanical appliances	2,049·9
Organic chemicals	220·4
Pharmaceutical products	341·1
Plastics and articles of plastic	581·3
Rubber and articles of rubber	173·7
Paper, paperboard and articles thereof	316·5
Printed books, newspapers etc.	241·8
Cotton yarn and fabrics	109·3
Man-made filaments and fibres	224·1
Electrical machinery and equipment	1,464·5
Motor cars, station wagons, utilities	1,076·3
Trucks, buses and vans	246·2
Aircraft	882·7
Ships and boats	152·0
Optical, photographic, technical and surgical equipment	469·5

The principal exports of New Zealand produce for the 12 months ended 30 June 1990 were:

Commodity	Value (NZ$1m.f.o.b.)	Commodity	Value (NZ$1m.f.o.b.)
Live animals	193·7	Sausage casings	105·5
Meat, fresh, chilled or frozen		Fish, fresh, chilled	
Beef and veal	1,091·6	or frozen	503·7
Lamb and mutton	1,093·5	Vegetables	198·4
Dairy products		Fresh kiwifruit	539·1
Milk, cream and yoghurt	998·4	Fresh apples	212·6
Butter	710·5	Forest products	
Cheese	341·0	Sawn timber and logs	402·4
Raw hides, skins and leather	658·2	Paper and paper products	352·1
Wool	1,315·9	Wood pulp	387·2

Commodity	Value (NZ$1m.f.o.b.)	Commodity	Value (NZ$1m.f.o.b.)
Aluminium and articles thereof	439·1	Iron and steel and articles thereof	328·7
Casein and caseinates	742·0	Machinery and mechanical appliances	377·0
Plastic materials and articles thereof	126·3	Electrical machinery and equipment	227·2

The following table shows the trade with different countries for the year ended 30 June (in NZ$1m.):

Countries	Imports v.f.d. from 1989	1990	Exports and re-exports f.o.b. to 1989	1990
EC countries	25·2	29·3	43·8	47·1
Australia	2,459·9	2,990·0	2,609·6	2,985·2
Bahrain	3·3	0·1	–	–
Belgium	75·3	100·7	272·1	186·4
Canada	227·7	265·1	261·2	274·9
China	125·2	153·1	539·1	157·1
Fiji	–	–	141·6	249·1
France	165·8	236·3	204·8	176·9
Germany, Fed. Rep. of	497·0	634·1	307·6	353·2
Hong Kong	202·6	196·2	247·8	215·7
Iran	–	–	130·6	178·1
Italy	196·0	291·4	316·8	268·2
Japan	2,109·6	2,371·7	2,661·2	2,483·4
Korea, Republic of	280·0	267·8	468·8	502·0
Malaysia	72·2	43·5	247·5	246·3
Netherlands	124·7	159·1	171·1	160·1
Peru	–	–	22·9	50·0
Philippines	–	–	159·7	144·5
Saudi Arabia	343·9	440·8	–	–
Singapore	138·2	187·0	174·9	171·4
Sweden	169·7	159·6	–	–
Switzerland	106·5	153·7	–	–
Taiwan	372·8	400·9	281·4	248·8
UK	882·6	1,303·2	1,036·4	1,094·0
USSR	–	–	351·4	354·2
USA	1,906·0	2,615·4	2,008·2	2,029·7

Total trade between New Zealand and UK was as follows (British Department of Trade returns, in £1,000 sterling):

	1987	1988	1989	1990	1991
Imports to UK	487,332	443,081	436,772	438,615	391,643
Exports and re-exports from UK	378,368	300,016	399,295	439,608	260,052

Tourism. There were 1,772,524 tourists in the year to March 1991 (including 362,134 from Australia. 141,360 from the USA, 107,770 from Japan and 100,546 from the UK). Tourist earnings for the year ended 31 March 1990 were NZ$2,551m. (NZ$2,277m. in 1988-89).

COMMUNICATIONS

Roads. Total length of formed roads and streets at 31 March 1989 was 92,974 km. There were 14,057 bridges of over 3 metres in length with a total length of 314,000 metres. The network of state highways comprised 11,523 km, including the principal arterial traffic routes.

Total expenditure on roads, streets and bridges by the central government and local authorities combined for the financial year 1988–89 amounted to $849m.

At 31 March 1991 motor vehicles licensed numbered 2,348,410, of which 1,539,809 were cars and 10,756 omnibuses, public taxis and service vehicles. Included in the remaining numbers were 73,546 motor cycles, 1,207 power cycles, 298,801 trucks, 369,301 trailers and caravans and 8,630 farm tractors and other farm equipment.

In 1990 there were 11,977 traffic casualties, of which 761 were fatal.

Railways. In 1990 there were 4,029 km of 1,067 mm gauge railway open for traffic

(519 km electrified). In 1989–90, railways carried 8·3m. tonnes and 26·2m. passengers. Operating revenue during 1987–88, $646,821,000 and operating expenses $684,117,000. Three rail/road ferries maintain a regular service between the North and South Islands.

Civil Aviation. International services are operated to and from New Zealand by a previously state-owned company, Air New Zealand National, and by a number of overseas companies. There are various flights from Auckland to Los Angeles taking in Fiji, Hawaii, Rarotonga and Tahiti, and flights to Japan, Thailand and South Korea. In Nov. 1990 Air New Zealand's fleet included 8 Boeing 767s and 5 Boeing 747s. Air New Zealand Ltd, Mt Cook Airlines and Ansett are the major domestic carriers.

Domestic scheduled services during the 12 months ended Dec. 1988: Passengers carried, 4,125,000; freight, 39,300 tonnes. International services: Passengers carried, 3,279,000; freight, 130,295 tonnes.

Shipping. Container ships operate from all major ports, serving all the major trading areas.

Entrances and clearances of vessels from overseas:

	Entrances		Clearances	
	No.	Tons	No.	Tons
1986	2,519	13,388,000	2,527	13,365,000
1987	3,060	14,113,000	3,050	14,107,000
1988	3,298	27,844,000	3,334	27,247,000
1989	3,741	30,940,000	3,730	30,190,000

Telecommunications. The provision of postal and telecommunication services is the responsibility of two state-owned enterprises: New Zealand Post, which began operations on 1 April 1987; the Telecom Corporation of New Zealand, formed in 1987 was privatised in 1991. There were 58,000 cellular telephone users in 1991 (2,300 in 1988). New Zealand Post restarted a telegram service in 1990. There are also 2 independent telegraph companies. In 1989 there were 470 post offices, and 336 post shops with 8,700 staff.

The New Zealand Broadcasting Corporation has been superseded. Radio New Zealand operates sound services. Television New Zealand operates 2 channels. A third, TV3, is commercial. There are also regional TV networks. Radio New Zealand International broadcasts in 14 languages. There are (1990) 59 medium-wave broadcasting stations, 28 FM broadcasting transmitters and 1 100 kw short-wave transmitter. Some commercial material is broadcast by both sound and TV services. Number of TV receiving licences at 31 March 1988 was 949,810.

Cinemas. There were in 1987, 121 cinemas.

Newspapers. There were (1989), 32 daily newspapers (9 morning and 23 evening). The New Zealand Herald published in Auckland has the largest daily circulation of 250,118. Other dailies range from 3,000–100,000 copies.

JUSTICE, RELIGION, EDUCATION AND WELFARE

Justice. The judiciary consists of the Court of Appeal, the High Court and District Courts. All exercise both civil and criminal jurisdiction. Other special courts include the Maori Land Court, Family Courts and Children's and Young Persons' Courts. In Aug. 1990 prisons and corrective training institutions contained 4,062 prisoners. Some 0·49m. criminal offences, including 67 murders were reported in 1990. The death penalty for murder was replaced by life imprisonment in 1961.

The Criminal Injuries Compensation Act, 1963, which came into force on 1 Jan. 1964, provided for compensation of persons injured by certain criminal acts and the dependants of persons killed by such acts. However, this has now been phased out in favour of the Accident Compensation Act, 1972, except in the residual area of property damage caused by escapers. The Offenders Legal Aid Act 1954 provides that any person charged or convicted of any offence may apply for legal aid which may be granted depending on the person's means and the gravity of the offence etc.

Since 1970 legal aid in civil proceedings (except divorce) has been available for persons of small or moderate means.

Police. The police in New Zealand are a national body maintained wholly by the central government. The total authorized establishment at June 1991 was 4,991, the proportion of police to population being 1 to 675. The total cost of police services for the year 1990–91 was NZ$502·7m., equivalent to $149 per head of population. In 1991 1,100 traffic officers merged with the police, who previously did not control traffic.

Ombudsmen. The office of Ombudsman was created in 1962. From 1975 additional Ombudsmen have been authorized. There are currently two. Ombudsmen's functions are to investigate complaints under the Ombudsman Act, the Official Information Act and the Local Government Official Information and Meetings Act from members of the public relating to administrative decisions of central, regional and local government.

During the year ended 30 June 1990, a total of 3,009 complaints were received, 592 of which were sustained.

Religion. No direct state aid is given to any form of religion. For the Church of England the country is divided into 7 dioceses, with a separate bishopric (Aotearoa) for the Maoris. The Presbyterian Church is divided into 23 presbyteries and the Maori Synod. The Moderator is elected annually. The Methodist Church is divided into 10 districts; the President is elected annually. The Roman Catholic Church is divided into 4 dioceses, with the Archbishop of Wellington as Metropolitan Archbishop.

Religious denomination	Number of clergy (April 1977)	Number of adherents 1981 census	1986 census [1]
Church of England	780	814,740	784,059
Presbyterian	686	523,221	586,530
Roman Catholic (including 'Catholic' undefined)	931	456,858	495,300
Methodist	349	148,512	152,955
Baptist	254	50,043	67,716
Brethren	187	24,324	
Ratana	142	35,781	
Protestant (undefined)	—	16,986	
Salvation Army	241	20,490	
Latter-day Saints (Mormon)	162	37,686	
Congregationalist	10	3,825	
Seventh-day Adventist	55	11,523	
Ringatu	88	6,114	871,689
Christian (undefined)	—	101,901	
Jehovah's Witnesses	125	13,737	
Hebrew	7	3,360	
All other religious professions	—	279,768	
Agnostic	—	24,201	
Atheist	—	21,528	
Not specified	—	108,015	59,385
Object to state	—	473,115	244,152
Total	4,712	3,175,737	3,261,786

[1] Provisional.

Education. New Zealand has 7 universities, the University of Auckland, University of Waikato (at Hamilton), Victoria University of Wellington, Massey University (at Palmerston North), the University of Canterbury (at Christchurch), the University of Otago (at Dunedin) and Lincoln University (near Christchurch). The number of students in 1988 was 72,313. There were 6 teachers' training colleges with 4,502 students in 1988.

At 1 July 1988 there were 315 state secondary schools with 14,506 full-time teachers and 217,272 pupils. There were also 35 area high schools with 3,208 scholars in the secondary division. At 1 July 1988, 70,045 part-time pupils attended technical classes, and 33,601 received part-time instruction from the technical correspondence institute. At 1 July 1988, 1,171 pupils received tuition from the secondary department of the correspondence school. There were 18 registered private secondary schools with 451 teachers and 12,132 pupils.

At 1 July 1988, there were 2,316 state primary schools (including intermediate schools and departments), with 398,189 pupils; the number of teachers was 18,214. A correspondence school for children in remote areas and those otherwise unable to attend school had 1,683 primary pupils. There were 78 registered private primary schools with 356 teachers and 12,053 pupils.

Education is compulsory between the ages of 6 and 15. Children aged 3 and 4 years may enrol at the 568 free kindergartens maintained by Free Kindergarten Associations, which receive government assistance. There are also 644 play centres which also receive government subsidy. In July 1988 there were 42,537 and 14,628 children on the rolls respectively. There are also 618 childcare centres with 15,701 children, 534 *kohanga reo* (providing early childhood education in the Maori language) with 11,125 children, and a number of other smaller providers of early childhood care and education.

Total budgeted expenditure in 1989–90 on education was NZ$4,374m.

The universities are autonomous bodies. All state-funded primary and secondary schools are controlled by boards of trustees. Education in state schools is free for children under 19 years of age. All educational institutions are reviewed every 3 years by teams of educational reviewers.

A series of reforms is being implemented by the government following reports of 18 working groups on tertiary education. These include a new funding system, began in 1991 and based solely on student numbers.

Report of the Minister of Education ('E.1. Report'). Annually. Wellington, Government Printer

NZ Committee on Secondary Education. *Towards Partnership*. Dept. of Education, 1976

Health. At 30 June 1989 there were 9,453 doctors on the medical register. In 1991 there were 19,350 public hospital beds (1989: 1,277 maternity beds). The 14 area health boards have been replaced by 4 regional health authorities.

Social Welfare. New Zealand's record for progressive legislation reached back to 1898, when it was second to Denmark in introducing non-contributory old-age pensions. Large reductions in welfare expenditure were introduced by the government in Dec. 1990. (For previous provisions *see* THE STATESMAN'S YEAR-BOOK, 1990–91, pp. 928–30).

The July 1990 budget announced that in April 1991 a new Universal Benefit would replace the former Unemployment, Widows' and Domestic Purposes Benefits. A Family Benefit for families on the lowest incomes was to be NZ$49·36 for the first child and NZ$28·31 for subsequent children. Child allowance for single persons with one child was to be NZ$213·14 per week; with two or more children, NZ$228·87 per week.

Benefit reductions in Dec. 1990 included the abolition of the universal NZ$6 per week child allowance, and a cut in unemployment benefit for a single man from NZ$135 to NZ$108 per week (NZ$100 to persons under 25 years). Persons made redundant become eligible for benefit only after 26 weeks. In 1991 subsidised housing was replaced by cash subsidies.

In 1991 earners of NZ$17,280 a year and less receive subsidized health care; a lesser subsidy applies up to NZ$23,000; over that health care must be paid by patients.

Under the Guaranteed Retirement Income scheme (GRI) introduced in April 1990, a married couple received NZ$288·10 per week; a single person, NZ$172·86. Persons living alone received an additional NZ$14·40 per week from Oct. 1990. In 1991 there were some 0·53m. GRI recipients.

In the budget of July 1991 it was announced that current rates of GRI payment would be frozen until 1 April 1993, thereafter to be on the previous year's consumer price index. On 1 April 1992 GRI will be replaced by the National superannuation scheme which will be income tested. Eligibility will be gradually increased to 65 years by 2001. Universal eligibility is available at 70 years.

Social Welfare Benefits and War Pensions:

Benefits	Number in force at 31 March 1990	Total payments 1989–90 (NZ$1,000)
SOCIAL WELFARE:		
Monetary—		
Retirement pension	493,715	4,539,578
Widows	12,847	132,111
Invalids	27,550	287,762
Miners and orphans	5,189	21,652
Domestic purposes	94,381	1,326,604
Unemployment	134,328	1,411,390
Sickness	18,944	258,445
War pensions	25,412	111,927
Total	812,366	8,089,469

Family benefits in 1990: 440,168 were in force; expenditure was NZ$446,487,000.

Health benefits in 1990: Payments for private hospitals, NZ$55,023,000; health benefits, NZ$321,235,000; pharmaceutical, NZ$516,822.

Reciprocity with Other Countries. There are reciprocal arrangements between New Zealand and Australia in respect of age, invalids', widows', family, unemployment and sickness benefits, and between New Zealand and the UK in respect of family, age, superannuation, widows', orphans', invalids', sickness and unemployment benefits.

MINOR ISLANDS

The minor islands (total area, 320 sq. miles, 829 sq. km) included within the geographical boundaries of New Zealand (but not within any local government area) are the following: Kermadec Islands (34 sq. km), Three Kings Islands (8 sq. km), Auckland Islands (62 sq. km), Campbell Island (114 sq. km), Antipodes Islands (606 sq. km), Bounty Islands (1 sq. km), Snares Islands (3 sq. km), Solander Island (1 sq. km). With the exception of meteorological station staff on Raoul Island in the Kermadec Group (5 in 1986) and Campbell Island (10 in 1986) there are no inhabitants.

The **Kermadec Islands** were annexed to New Zealand in 1887, have no separate administration and all New Zealand laws apply to them. Situation, 29° 10' to 31° 30' S. lat., 177° 45' to 179° W. long., 1,000 miles NNE of New Zealand. The largest of the group is Raoul or Sunday Island, 29 sq. km, smaller islands being Macaulay and Curtis, while Macaulay Island is 3 miles in circuit.

TERRITORIES OVERSEAS

Territories Overseas coming within the jurisdiction of New Zealand consist of Tokelau and the Ross Dependency.

Tokelau. Situated some 480 km to the north of Western Samoa between 8° and 10° S. lat., and between 171° and 173° W. long., are the 3 atoll islands of Atafu, Nukunonu and Fakaofo of the Tokelau (Union) group. Formerly part of the Gilbert and Ellice Islands Colony, the group was transferred to the jurisdiction of New Zealand on 11 Feb. 1926. By legislation enacted in 1948, the Tokelau Islands were declared part of New Zealand as from 1 Jan. 1949. The area of the group is 1,011 ha; the population at 10 Oct. 1986 was 1,690.

By the Tokelau Islands Act 1948 the Tokelau Group was included within the territorial boundaries of New Zealand; legislative powers are now invested in the Governor-General in Council. The inhabitants are British subjects and New Zealand citizens. In Dec. 1976 the territory was officially renamed 'Tokelau', the name by which it has customarily been known to its inhabitants.

From 8 Nov. 1974 the office of Administrator was invested in the Secretary of Foreign Affairs. Certain powers are delegated to the district officer in Apia, Western Samoa.

Because of the very restricted economic and social future in the atolls, the islanders agreed to a proposal put to them by the Minister of Island Territories in 1965 that over a period of years most of the population be resettled in New Zealand. Up to March 1975, 528 migrants entered New Zealand as permanent residents under Government sponsorship. At the request of the people the scheme has now been suspended.

New Zealand Government aid to Tokelau totalled NZ$4·1m. for the year ended 31 March 1990. There was a cyclone grant of NZ$1·2m.

Ross Dependency. By Imperial Order in Council, dated 30 July 1923, the territories between 160° E. long. and 150° W. long. and south of 60° S. lat. were brought within the jurisdiction of the New Zealand Government. The region was named the Ross Dependency. From time to time laws for the Dependency have been made by regulations promulgated by the Governor-General of New Zealand.

The mainland area is estimated at 400,000–450,000 sq. km and is mostly ice-covered. In Jan. 1957 a New Zealand expedition under Sir Edmund Hillary established a base in the Dependency. In Jan. 1958 Sir Edmund Hillary and 4 other New Zealanders reached the South Pole.

The main base—Scott Base—at Pram Point, Ross Island—is manned throughout the year, about 12 people being present during winter. Vanda Station in the dry ice-free Wright Valley is manned every summer.

Quartermain, L. B., *New Zealand and the Antarctic*. Wellington, 1971

SELF-GOVERNING TERRITORIES OVERSEAS

THE COOK ISLANDS

HISTORY. The Cook Islands, which lie between 8° and 23° S. lat., and 156° and 167° W. long., were proclaimed a British protectorate in 1888, and on 11 June 1901 were annexed and proclaimed part of New Zealand. In 1965 the Cook Islands became a self-governing territory in 'free association' with New Zealand.

AREA AND POPULATION. The islands within the territory fall roughly into two groups—the scattered islands towards the north (Northern group) and the islands towards the south known as the Lower group. The names of the islands with their populations as at the census of 1986 were as follows:

Lower Group—	Area sq. km	Population	Northern Group—	Area sq. km	Population
Rarotonga	67·2	9,678	Nassau	1·2	118
Mangaia	51·8	1,235	Palmerston (Avarau)	2·0	66
Atiu	26·9	955	Penrhyn (Tongareva)	9·8	496
Aitutaki	18·0	2,391	Manihiki (Humphrey)	5·4	508
Mauke (Parry Is.)	18·4	637	Rakahanga (Reirson)	4·1	283
Mitiaro	22·3	272	Pukapuka (Danger)	5·1	760
Manuae and Te au-o-tu	6·2	–	Suwarrow (Anchorage)	0·4	6
Takutea	1·3	–			
			Total	293	17,463

The population in 1988 was 17,700. Birth rate (per 1,000), 24·3; death rate, 5·3.

CONSTITUTION AND GOVERNMENT. The Cook Islands Constitution Act 1964, which provides for the establishment of internal self-government in the Cook Islands, came into force on 4 Aug. 1965.

The Act establishes the Cook Islands as fully self-governing but linked to New

Zealand by a common Head of State, the Queen, and a common citizenship, that of New Zealand. It provides for a ministerial system of government with a Cabinet consisting of a Premier and 6 other Ministers. The New Zealand Government is represented by a New Zealand Representative and the position of a Queen's Representative has recently been created by changes in the Constitution. New Zealand continues to be responsible for the external affairs and defence of the Cook Islands, subject to consultation between the New Zealand Prime Minister and the Prime Minister. The changed status of the Islands does not affect the consideration of subsidies or the right of free entry into New Zealand for exports from the group. The capital is Rarotonga, which was devastated by a hurricane in Jan. 1987.

The unicameral Parliament comprises 24 members elected for a term of 5 years; at general elections held in Jan. 1989, the Cook Islands Party won 12 seats, the Democratic Coalition Party 10, and the Democratic Tumu Party, 2 seats. There is also an advisory council composed of hereditary chiefs, the 15-member House of Ariki, without legislative powers.

Prime Minister: Hon. Geoffrey A. Henry.

ECONOMY AND TRADE

Budget. Revenue, 1988–89, NZ$55·08m. (NZ$28·23m. from taxation); expenditure, NZ$55·83m. Revenue is derived chiefly from customs duties which follow the New Zealand customs tariff, income tax and stamp sales.

Grants from New Zealand, mainly for medical, educational and general administrative purposes totalled NZ$7m. in 1982–83.

Currency. The Cook Island *dollar* is at par with the New Zealand *dollar*.

Electricity. 14·31m. KWH were generated in 1988.

Agriculture. Livestock (1988): Pigs, 18,000; goats, 3,000.

Fisheries. Catch (1984) 800 tonnes.

Commerce. Exports, mainly to New Zealand, were valued at NZ$6·6m. in 1988. Main items exported were fresh fruit and vegetables, clothing and footwear. Imports totalled NZ$64·5m. in 1988. Main items imported were foodstuffs, manufactured goods (including transport equipment), petrol and petroleum products.

COMMUNICATIONS

Roads. In 1984 there were 280 km of roads and 1,417 vehicles.

Aviation. New Zealand has financed the construction of an international airport at Rarotonga which became operational for jet services in Sept. 1973.

Shipping. A fortnightly cargo shipping service is provided between New Zealand, Niue and Rarotonga.

Telecommunications. Wireless stations are maintained at all the permanently inhabited islands. In 1983 there were 2,052 telephones. There are 2 radio stations on Rarotonga with (1983) 10,000 receivers.

Newspapers. The *Cook Islands News* (circulation 2,000) is the sole daily newspaper.

JUSTICE, RELIGION, EDUCATION AND HEALTH

Justice. There is a High Court and a Court of Appeal, from which further appeal is to the Privy Council in the UK.

Religion. Some 69% of the population belong to the Cook Islands Christian Church, about 15% are Roman Catholics, and the rest chiefly Latter Day Saints and Seventh-Day Adventists.

Education. In 1986 there were 30 primary schools with 165 teachers and 3,183 pupils, and 8 secondary schools with 146 teachers and 2,156 pupils on Rarotonga, Aitutaki, Mangaia, Atiu, Mauke and Pukapuka.

Health. All Cook Islanders receive free medical and surgical treatment in their villages, the hospital and the tuberculosis sanatorium. Cook Islands Maori patients in the hospital and the sanatorium and all schoolchildren receive free dental treatment. In 1982 there were 18 doctors, 8 dentists and 65 nursing personnel. In 1981 there were 8 hospitals and clinics with 154 beds.

NIUE

History. Captain James Cook sighted Niue in 1774 all called it Savage Island. Christian missionaries arrived in 1846. Niue became a British Protectorate in 1900 and was annexed to New Zealand in 1901. Internal self-government was achieved in free association with New Zealand on 19 Oct. 1974, New Zealand taking responsibility for external affairs and defence. Niue is a member of the South Pacific Forum.

Area and Population. Niue is the largest uplifted coral island in the world. Distance from Auckland, New Zealand, 1,343 miles; from Rarotonga, 580 miles. Area, 258 sq. km; height above sea-level, 220 ft. Population (census, 1986) 2,531; estimate 31 Dec. 1988 was 2,190. During 1988 births registered numbered 55, deaths 14. Migration to New Zealand is the main factor in population change. The capital is Alofi (811 inhabitants in census, 1986).

Constitution and Government. There is a Legislative Assembly of 20 members, 14 elected from 14 constituencies and 6 elected by all constituencies.

Premier: Sir Robert R. Rex, CMG, OBE.

Budget. Financial aid from New Zealand, 1987–88, totalled $8,500,000.

Agriculture. The most important products of the island are coconuts, honey, limes and root crops.

Trade. Exports, 1985, $175,924 (main export, coconut cream); imports, $3,753,384.

Civil Aviation. A weekly commercial air service links Niue with New Zealand.

Telecommunications. There is a wireless station at Alofi, the port of the island. Cable television is available. A weekly newspaper is published in English and Niuean. Telephones (1986) 460.

Justice. There is a High Court under a Chief Justice, with a right of appeal to the New Zealand Supreme Court.

Religion. 75% of the population belong to the Congregational (Ekalesia Niue); 10% are Mormons and 5% Roman Catholics.

Education. There were 7 government schools with 702 pupils in 1987.

Health. In 1986 there were 3 doctors, 3 dentists, 7 midwives and 27 nursing personnel. There is a 30-bed hospital at Alofi.

DIPLOMATIC REPRESENTATIVES

Of New Zealand in Great Britain (New Zealand Hse, Haymarket, London, SW1Y 4TQ)
High Commissioner: George Gair, QSO.

Of Great Britain in New Zealand (Reserve Bank of New Zealand Bldg., 2 The Terrace, Wellington, 1)
High Commissioner: D. J. Moss, CMG.

Of New Zealand in the USA (37 Observatory Cir., NW, Washington, D.C., 20008)
Ambassador: Denis McLean.

Of the USA in New Zealand (29 Fitzherbert Terrace, Wellington)
Ambassador: Della M. Newman.

Of New Zealand to the United Nations
Ambassador: Terence O'Brien.

Further Reading

Department of Statistics. *New Zealand Official Yearbook.* (not published every year).—*Key Statistics: a monthly Abstract of Statistics.—Pocket Digest of Statistics.*
Dictionary of New Zealand Biography. vol 1 (to 1868). Wellington, 1990
Encyclopaedia of New Zealand. 3 vols. Wellington, 1966
Alley, R., *New Zealand and the Pacific.* Boulder, 1984
Bedggood, D., *Rich and Poor in New Zealand.* Sydney, 1980
Bush, G., *Local Government and Politics in New Zealand.* Sydney, 1980
Easton, B., *Social Policy and the Welfare State in New Zealand.* Auckland, 1980
Grover, R. R., *New Zealand.* [Bibliography] Oxford and Santa Barbara, 1981
Hawke, G. R., *The Making of New Zealand: An Economic History.* CUP, 1985
McLeay, E. (ed.) *The 1990 General Election: Perspective on Political Change in New Zealand.* Victoria Univ. Press, 1991
Morrell, W. P. and Hall, D. O. W., *A History of New Zealand Life.* Christchurch and London, 1957
Oliver, W. H. (ed.) *The Oxford History of New Zealand.* OUP, 1981
Robson, J. L. (ed.) *New Zealand: The Development of its Laws and Constitution.* 2nd ed. London, 1967
Sinclair, K., *A History of New Zealand.* Rev. ed. London, 1980 –. (ed.) *The Oxford Illustrated History of New Zealand.* OUP, 1990
Thakur, R., *In Defence of New Zealand.* Wellington, 1984
Wards, I., *A Descriptive Atlas of New Zealand.* Wellington, Government Printer, 1976

National statistical office: Department of Statistics, Wellington, 1.

NICARAGUA

Capital: Managua
Population: 3·87m. (1991)
GNP per capita: US$830 (1987)

República de Nicaragua

HISTORY. Active colonization of the Pacific coast was undertaken by Spaniards from Panama, beginning in 1523. After links with other Central American territories, and Mexico, Nicaragua became completely independent in 1838, but subject to a prolonged feud between the 'Liberals' of León and the 'Conservatives' of Granada. Mosquitia remained an autonomous kingdom on the Atlantic coast, under British protection until 1860.

On 5 Aug. 1914 the Bryan–Chamarro treaty between Nicaragua and the US was signed, under which the US in return for US$3m. acquired a permanent option for a canal route through Nicaragua and a 99-year option for a naval base in the Bay of Fonseca on the Pacific coast and Corn Islands on the Atlantic coast. It was ratified by Nicaragua on 7 April 1916 and by the US on 22 June 1916. US Marines finally left in 1933. The Bryan–Chamarro treaty was abrogated on 14 July 1970 and the Corn Islands handed back in 1971.

The 46-year political domination of Nicaragua by the Somoza family ended on 17 July 1979, after the 17 years long struggle by the Sandinista National Liberation Front flared into civil war. A Government Junta of National Reconstruction was established by the revolutionary government on 20 July 1979 and a 51-member Council of State later created; both were dissolved on 10 Jan. 1985 following new Presidential and legislative elections.

On 9 Jan. 1987 the President signed the new Constitution, but immediately reimposed a state of emergency, suspending many of the liberties granted under the Constitution.

In Nov. 1989, following infiltration into Nicaragua by some 2,000 Contras, the ceasefire was ended. On 7 Nov. 1989 the Security Council of the UN voted to establish a UN Observer Group in Central America.

AREA AND POPULATION. Nicaragua is bounded north by Honduras, east by the Caribbean, south by Costa Rica and west by the Pacific. Area, 130,682 sq. km (120,349 sq. km dry land). The coastline runs 540 km on the Atlantic and 350 km on the Pacific. Population at the census of April 1971 was 1,877,972. Estimate (1991) 3·87m. (1·93m. female; 2·31m. urban). Population density was 29·6 per sq. km in 1991.

Vital statistics rates (per 1,000), 1985–90: Birth, 41·8; death, 8; infant mortality (per 1,000 live births) 61·7. Expectation of life in 1988: Males, 62 years; females, 65.

The population is of Spanish and Amerindian origins with an admixture of Afro-Americans on the Caribbean coast. Ethnic groups in 1980: Mestizo, 69%; white, 14%; black, 13%; Amerindian, 4%. The official language is Spanish.

16 administrative departments are grouped in 3 zones. Areas (in sq. km.), populations (in 1,000) and chief towns in 1990:

	Area	Population	Chief town
Pacific Zone	18,369	2,394·3	
Chinandega	4,789	330·5	Chinandega
León	5,243	344·5	León
Managua	3,368	1,026·1	Managua
Masaya	690	230·8	Masaya
Granada	992	162·6	Granada
Carazo	1,097	150·0	Jinotepe
Rivas	2.190	149·8	Rivas
Central-North Zone	34,543	1,125·3	
Chontales	6,324	129·6	Juigalpa
Boaco	4,271	117·9	Boaco
Matagalpa	6,929	322·3	Matagalpa

	Area	Population	Chief town
Jinotega	9,640	175·6	Jinotega
Estelí	2,173	169·1	Estelí
Madriz	1,612	88·7	Somoto
Nueva Segovía	3,594	122·1	Ocotal
Atlantic Zone	67,437	351·1	
Rio San Juan	7,402	52·2	San Carlos
Zelaya	60,035	298·9	Bluefields

The capital is Managua with (1985) 682,111 inhabitants. Other cities: León, 100,982; Granada, 88,636; Masaya, 74,946; Chinandega, 67,792; Matagalpa, 36,983; Estelí, 30,635; Tipitapa, 30,078; Chichigalpa, 28,889; Juigalpa, 25,625; Corinto, 24,250; Jinotepe, 23,538.

CLIMATE. The climate is tropical, with a wet season from May to Jan. Temperatures vary with altitude. Managua. Jan. 79°F (26°C), July 86°F (30°C). Annual rainfall 45" (1,140 mm).

CONSTITUTION AND GOVERNMENT. The National Assembly drafted and approved on 19 Nov. 1986 the new Constitution which was promulgated on 9 Jan. 1987. It provided for a unicameral *National Assembly* comprising 92 members directly elected by proportional representation, together with unsuccessful presidential election candidates obtaining a minimum level of votes.

The *President* and Vice-President are directly elected for a 6-year term commencing on the 10 Jan. following their date of election.

Under Article 185 of the Constitution, the President is empowered to declare a state of emergency and suspend certain of the civil rights provisions enshrined therein; this was done by the President immediately upon the promulgation of the Constitution.

Elections were held on 25 Feb 1990. The National Opposition Union (UNO) gained 51 seats, the Sandinista National Liberation Front (FSLN) 39 and independents 2.

President and Minister of Defence: Violeta Barrios de Chamorro (UNO; elected 25 Feb. 1990, took office 25 April 1990).

Minister of the Interior: Carlos Hurtado Cabrera. *Foreign Affairs:* Ernesto Leal. *Finance:* Emilio Pereira Alegria. *Education:* Sofonias Cisneiros Leiva. *Agriculture:* Roberto Rondón Sacasa. *Economy and Development:* Julio Cardenas. *Construction and Transport:* Jaime Icabalceta Mayorga. *Health:* Ernesto Salmarón Bermudez. *Labour:* Francisco Rosales Arguello. *Presidency Minister:* Antonio Lacayo Oyanguren. *Agrarian Reform:* Boanerges Matus. *Director of the Nicaraguan Repatriation Institute:* Jaime Cuadra.

National flag: Three horizontal stripes of blue, white, blue, with the national arms in the centre.

National anthem: Salve a ti Nicaragua ('Hail to thee, Nicaragua'; words by S. Ibarra Mayorga, 1937).

Local government. There are 16 departments (chief town in brackets if name differs): Boaco; Carazo (Jinotepe); Chinandega; Chontales (Juigalpa); Esteli; Granada; Jinotega; León; Madriz (Samoto); Managua; Masaya; Matagalpa; Nueva Segovia (Ocotal); Río San Juan (San Carlos); Rivas; Zelaya (Bluefields) and 134 municipalities.

DEFENCE. Conscription was ended in 1990, and the armed forces cut from 70,000 to 28,000. The 1991 budget cut defence spending by 10%.

Army. The Army is being reorganized. There are 7 military regions, and in 1991 the Army comprised 2 armoured, 2 motorized infantry, 2 frontier and 1 artillery brigades, 20 infantry and 4 engineer battalions. Equipment included 130 T-54/-55 main battle tanks. Strength (1992) probably about 27,000.

Navy. The Nicaraguan Navy was in 1991 some 1,500 strong and operates 26 inshore patrol craft of mixed Soviet and North Korean origins, 8 small inshore mine-sweepers and 3 minor landing craft.

Air Force. Formed in June 1938 as the Nicaraguan Army Air Force, the Air Force has been semi-independent since 1947. Its combat units are reported to have 4 L-39 Albatros light jet attack/trainers and 4 T-33 armed jet trainers. Other equipment includes 2 C-47s, 2 Spanish-built Aviocar and 2 Soviet-supplied An-26 transports and smaller communications aircraft and helicopters, including 20 Mi-8/17s, 2 Mi-2s and 5 Mi-24 gunships and 6 SF.260s for counter-insurgency duties. Personnel (1992) 2,000, with 14 combat aircraft and 7 armed helicopters.

INTERNATIONAL RELATIONS

Membership. Nicaragua is a member of the UN, OAS, SELA and the Central American Common Market.

ECONOMY

Budget. Estimates for 1991: Revenue, US$349m.; expenditure, US$499m. US$91m. of the deficit was to be covered by foreign loans.

Currency. The monetary unit is the *córdoba* (NIC), of 100 *centavos*. There are notes in denominations from 1,000 córdobas to 1 córdoba. Coins are 5 and 1 *córdobas* and 50, 25, 10 and 5 *centavos*. A 'gold córdoba', with parity with the US dollar, was introduced in 1990, and devalued to 5 = US$1 in March 1991. In a series of devaluations in 1990 the value of the ordinary currency was reduced by 98·4%. In March 1992, US$1 = 4·99m. *córdobas*; £1 = 8·77m. new *córdobas*.

Banking and Finance. The Central Bank of Nicaragua came into operation on 1 Jan. 1961 as an autonomous bank of issue, absorbing the issue department of the National Bank. Its *Governor* is Silvio de Franco Montalván. In July 1979 private financial banking was nationalized and branches of foreign banks were prohibited from receiving deposits, but in 1991 private banking was again permitted.

Weights and Measures. The metric system is recommended. 1 manzana = 1·73 acres.

ENERGY AND NATURAL RESOURCES

Electricity. Installed capacity was 395,000 kw. in 1986 and 1,197 kwh. was produced. Supply 120 volts; 60 Hz.

Minerals. Production of gold in 1988 was 28,000 troy oz.; of silver, 16,000 troy oz.; of limestone, 3,800 tonnes.

Agriculture. Agriculture is the principal source of national wealth.

The agricultural area in 1987 was 6,518,000 ha, of which 1,095,000 ha were arable, 173,000 ha permanent cropland and 5,250,000 ha pasture. Production (in 1,000 tonnes) in 1988: Rice, 168; maize, 280; sorghum, 113; potatoes, 22; manioc, 66; beans, 50; soya beans, 17; sesame seed, 4; cotton seed, 76; coconuts, 3; cabbage, 11; tomatoes, 29; raw sugar, 1,932; oranges, 56; pineapples, 39; bananas, 229; green coffee, 43; green tobacco, 4; raw cotton, 42.

There were about 1·68m. head of cattle in 1990 and 690,000 pigs. Animal products (in 1,000 tonnes), 1988: Beef, 30; pork, 16; poultry, 12; milk, 100; eggs, 29·5.

Forestry. The forest area in 1987 was 3·71m. ha. The forests contain mahogany and cedar, three varieties of rosewoods, lignum vitae and dye-woods. Production of sawn wood in 1987, 3·77m. cu. metres (2·89m. cu. metres for fuel).

Fisheries. In 1988 the fishing fleet comprised 17 vessels of 1,917 GRT. The catch was 4,983 tonnes (170 tonnes freshwater).

INDUSTRY. Production in 1987: Sawn timber, 0·22m. cu. metres; plywood, 14,000 cu. metres; refined sugar, 198,000 tonnes; butter, 1,892 tonnes; cheese, 8,095 tonnes. In 1986 (in 1,000 tonnes): Cement, 285; plastics, 2·3; soap, 29·8; wheat flour, 43·6; leather shoes, 3·22m. pairs; cotton fabric, 14·76m. metres.

Labour. In 1990 the workforce was 1,204,000 (303,000 females, 52,000 between 10 and 15 years of age). 0·34m. worked in agriculture and forestry, 0·3m. in manufacturing, 0·18m. in services and 0·13m. in trade. There were 0·31m. unemployed in 1988.

FOREIGN ECONOMIC RELATIONS

Commerce. Foreign trade in US$1m. (1988): Exports, 236m. consisting of cotton, coffee, chemical products, meat, sugar; imports, 900m.

Total trade between Nicaragua and UK (British Department of Trade returns, in £1,000 sterling):

	1987	1988	1989	1990	1991
Imports to UK	717	725	918	1,899	492
Exports and re-exports from UK	7,883	6,856	6,985	6,515	8,029

Main import suppliers (in US$1m.) in 1988: USSR, 67·7; Cuba, 53·4; Netherlands, 35·5; Italy, 33·8; Spain, 32·1. Main export markets: Canada, 51·7; Federal Republic of Germany, 45; Japan, 39.

Tourism. In 1987 there were about 169,000 visitors.

COMMUNICATIONS

Roads. Road length in 1988was 14,997 km, of which 1,569 km were asphalted. In 1986 there were 46,200 motor cars, 4,700 buses, 25,800 lorries and 12,400 motor cycles.

Railways. The Pacific Railroad of Nicaragua, owned and operated by the Government, has a total length of 334 km, all single-track, and connects Corinto, Chinandega, León, Managua, Masaya and Granada. Passengers carried (1986) 3·5m. and 2·5m. tonnes of freight.

Civil Aviation. The national carrier is Aeronica. 87,000 passengers were carried in 1988. The Augusto Sandino international airport at Managua handled 265,800 passengers in 1985.

Shipping. The Pacific ports are Corinto (the largest), San Juan del Sur and Puerto Sandino through which pass most of the external trade. The chief eastern ports are El Bluff (for Bluefields) and Puerto Cabezas. The merchant marine in 1988 comprised 23 vessels totalling 13,700 GRT. 455 vessels put in in 1985; 0·31m. tonnes of cargo were loaded, 1·19m. tonnes discharged.

Telecommunications. In 1987 there were 46,300 telephones.

The Tropical Radio Telegraph Company maintains a powerful station at Managua, and branch stations at Bluefields and Puerto Cabezas. The Government operates the National Radio with 47 broadcasting stations: There are 31 commercial stations and some 70 others. Number of radio sets in 1987 was 830,000 and television sets 210,000. There are 2 television stations at Managua.

Newspapers. In 1984 there were 3 daily newspapers (2 in Managua and 1 in León), with a total circulation of about 105,000.

JUSTICE, RELIGION, EDUCATION AND WELFARE

Justice. The judicial power is vested in a Supreme Court of Justice at Managua, 5 chambers of second instance (León, Masaya, Granada, Matagalpa and Bluefields) and 153 judges of inferior tribunals.

Religion. The prevailing form of religion is Roman Catholic, but religious liberty is guaranteed by the Constitution. The republic constitutes 1 archbishopric (seat at Managua) and 7 bishoprics (León, Granada, Estelí, Matagalpa, Juigalpa, Masaya and Puerto Cabezas). Protestants, established principally on the Atlantic coast, numbered 54,100 in 1966.

Education. There were, in 1986, 4,526 primary schools, with a total of 556,684 pupils and 17,199 teachers; and 119,000 pupils in secondary schools. The illiteracy rate was 12% in 1983. In 1987 there were 26,878 students in higher education. Universities were restructured in 1990 to form 2 state universities and 2 religious universities (the Jesuit UCA and the Protestant UPOLI).

Health. In 1986 there were 2,026 doctors, and in 1984 222 dentists and 5,649 nursing personnel. In 1986 there were 30 hospitals with 4,925 beds, 107 health centres (20 with beds) and 431 medical posts.

DIPLOMATIC REPRESENTATIVES

Of Nicaragua in Great Britain (8 Gloucester Rd., London, SW7 4PP)
Ambassador: Roberto Parrales.

Of Great Britain in Nicaragua (Los Robles, Entrada Principal de la Carretera a
Masaya, Cuarta Casa a Mano Derecha, Managua)
Ambassador and Consul-General: Roger Brown.

Of Nicaragua in the USA (1627 New Hampshire Ave., NW, Washington, D.C.,
20009)
Ambassador: Ernesto Palizio.

Of the USA in Nicaragua (Km. 4¹/₂ Carretera Sur., Managua)
Ambassador: Harry W. Schlaudeman.

Of Nicaragua to the United Nations
Ambassador: Dr Roberto Mayorga-Cortes.

Further Reading

Booth, J. A., *The End of the Beginning: The Nicaraguan Revolution*. Boulder, 1982
Christian, S., *Nicaragua: Revolution in the Family*. New York, 1985
Dematteis, L. and Vail, C., *Nicaragua: a Decade of Revolution*, New York, 1991
Gilbert, D., *Sandinistas: The Party and the Revolution*. Oxford, 1988
Rosset, P. and Vandermeer, J., (eds.) *The Nicaragua Reader: Documents of a Revolution
   under Fire*. New York, 1984
Spalding, R. J., *The Political Economics of Revolutionary Nicaragua*. London, 1987
Walker, T. W., *Nicaragua: The Land of Sandino*. 2nd ed. Boulder (Colo.), 1991
Woodward, R. L., *Nicaragua*. [Bibliography] Oxford and Santa Barbara, 1983

National library: Biblioteca Nacional, Managua
National statistical office: Dirección General de Estadística y Censos, Managua

NIGER

République du Niger

Capital: Niamey
Population: 8·04m. (1991)
GNP per capita: US$290 (1989)

HISTORY. Niger was occupied by France between 1883 and 1899, and constituted a military territory in 1901, which became a part of French West Africa in 1904. It became an autonomous republic within the French Community on 18 Dec. 1958 and achieved full independence on 3 Aug. 1960.

On 15 April 1974 the first President, Hamani Diori, was overthrown in a military coup led by Lieut.-Col. Seyni Kountché, who suspended the constitution, dissolved the National Assembly and banned political groups.

AREA AND POPULATION. Niger is bounded north by Algeria and Libya, east by Chad, south by Nigeria, south-west by Benin and Burkina Faso, and west by Mali. Area, 1,267,000 sq. km, with a population at the 1988 census of 7,250,383. Estimate (1991) 8·04m., of which 21.1% live in urban areas. Population density 6.8 per sq. km. The major towns (populations, census, 1988) are: Niamey, the capital (398,265 inhabitants), Zinder (120,900), Maradi (113,000), Tahoua (51,600) and Agadez (50,200). The population is composed chiefly of Hausa (54%), Songhai and Djerma (23%), Fulani (10%), Beriberi-Manga (9%) and Tuareg (3%).

The country is divided into the capital, Niamey, an autonomous district, and 7 departments. Area, population and chief towns at the 1988 census:

Department	Sq. km	Population	Chief town	Population
Niamey	670	398,265	Niamey	398,265
Agadez	634,209	203,959	Agadez	50,200
Diffa	140,216	189,316	Diffa	–
Dosso	31,002	1,019,997	Dosso	–
Maradi	38,581	1,388,999	Maradi	113,000
Tahoua	106,677	1,306,652	Tahoua	51,600
Tillabéry	89,623	1,332,398	Tillabéry	–
Zinder	145,430	1,410,797	Zinder	120,900

The official language is French. Hausa is understood by 85% of the population. Growth rate, 1985-90, 3%; infant mortality, 135 per 1,000; expectation of life, 44.5 years.

Vital statistics (1985): Births, 330,000; deaths, 150,000.

CLIMATE. Precipitation determines the geographical division into a southern zone of agriculture, a central zone of pasturage and a desert-like northern zone. The country lacks water, with the exception of the south-western districts, which are watered by the Niger and its tributaries, and the southern zone, where there are a number of wells. Niamey, 95°F (35°C). Annual rainfall varies from 22" (560 mm) in the south to 7" (180 mm) in the Sahara zone.

CONSTITUTION AND GOVERNMENT. The country was administered by a Supreme Military Council of 12 officers led by the President, who appointed a Council of Ministers to assist him. A system of elected Development Councils at all levels was created, culminating in a 150-member National Development Council with limited legislative powers.

A national conference of 1,204 delegates sat from July to Nov. 1991. In Aug. it declared its sovereignty and suspended the constitution; on 10 Sept it dissolved the government; and in Oct. it elected Amadou Cheffou (b. 1942) against 15 opponents as prime minister of a transitional government until Jan. 1993. The president has been stripped of most of his executive powers, and a High Council of the Republic chaired by André Salifou has been established as a provisional legislative assembly.

President of the Republic: Col. Ali Seybou (took office 14 Nov. 1987).

A 13-member government was formed in Nov. 1991, including:

Minister of the Interior: Mohamed Moussa. *Foreign Affairs:* Hassane Hamidou. *Economy and Finance:* Laoual Chaffani.

National flag: Three horizontal strips of orange, white and green, with an orange disc in the middle of the white strip.

National anthem: 'La Nigérienne' (words by M. Thirlet, tune by R. Jacquet and N. Frionnet).

Local government: The 8 departments are each under a prefect, sub-divided into 32 *arrondissements*, each under a sub-prefect, and some 150 communes.

DEFENCE. Selective military service for 2 years operates.

Army. The Army consists of 2 armoured reconnaissance squadrons, 6 infantry, 1 engineer and 1 parachute company. Equipment includes 10 M-8, 18 AML-90 and 18 AML-60-7 armoured cars. Strength (1991) 3,200. There are additional paramilitary forces of some 4,500 men.

Air Force. The Air Force had (1991) over 100 officers and men, 2 C-130H and 3 Noratlas transports, 1 Boeing 737 VIP transport, 2 Cessna Skymasters and 3 Do 28D Skyservants and 1 Do 228 for communications duties. There are no combat aircraft.

INTERNATIONAL RELATIONS

Membership. Niger is a member of the UN, OAU and is an ACP state of the EEC.

ECONOMY

Policy. The 10-year plan (1981–90) provided for an investment of 520,000m. francs CFA in the first phase (1981–85) with a prime aim of obtaining selfsufficiency in food and developing the mining sector.

Budget. The 1988 budget balanced at 114,310 francs CFA.

Currency. The unit of currency is the *franc CFA* (XAF), with a parity rate of 50 francs CFA to 1 French franc.

Banking. The *Banque Centrale des États de l'Afrique de l'Ouest* is the bank of issue, and there are 9 commercial banks in Niamey.

ENERGY AND NATURAL RESOURCES

Electricity. Production (1986) amounted to 265m. kwh. Supply 220 volts; 50 Hz.

Minerals. Large uranium deposits are mined at Arlit and Akouta. Concentrate production (1986) 3,108 tonnes. Phosphates are mined in the Niger valley, and coal reserves are being exploited by open-cast mining (production, 1985, 61,000 tonnes). Salt and natron are produced at Manga and Agadez, tin ore in Aïr, iron ore at Say.

Agriculture. Production in 1991 (in 1,000 tonnes) were: Millet, 1,853; maize, 942; sorghum, 468; in 1990: Groundnuts, 27·4; in 1989: Cassava, 62·2; sugar-cane, 31·4; sweet potatoes, 33·2; cotton, 5·9; potatoes, 25·8.

Livestock (1990): Cattle, 3·6m.; horses, 302,000; asses, 512,000; sheep, 3·5m.; goats, 7·62m.; camels, 420,000; chickens, 18m.

Forestry. There were (1988) 2·5m. ha of forest. Production (1986) 4·01m. cu. metres.

Fisheries. Catch (1986) 2,400 tonnes.

INDUSTRY.
Some small manufacturing industries, mainly in Niamey, produce textiles, food products, furniture and chemicals.

Trade Unions. The sole national body is the *Union Nationale des Travailleurs du Niger*, which has 15,000 members in 31 unions.

FOREIGN ECONOMIC RELATIONS

Commerce. In 1986 imports were valued at US$316m. and exports at US$260m. Uranium is an important export. Major trading partners are France, Nigeria and Japan.

Total trade between Niger and UK (British Department of Trade returns, in £1,000 sterling):

	1987	1988	1989	1990	1991
Imports to UK	10,556	1,359	1,472	1,161	882
Exports and re-exports from UK	7,026	7,552	6,862	10,780	10,838

Tourism. There were 27,000 tourists in 1986.

COMMUNICATIONS

Roads. In 1987 there were 19,000 km of roads. Niamey and Zinder are the termini of two trans-Sahara motor routes; the Hoggar–Aïr–Zinder road extends to Kano and the Tanezrouft-Gao-Niamey road to Benin. A 648-km 'uranium road' runs from Arlit to Tahoua. There were (1987), 9,000 private cars and 21,000 goods vehicles and vans.

Civil Aviation. There are international airports at Niamey, Zinder and Maradi. Air Niger operates domestic services to over 20 other public airports.

Shipping. Sea-going vessels can reach Niamey (300 km. inside the country) between Sept. and March.

Telecommunications. There were (1983) 159 post offices and (1985) 11,824 telephones. La Voix du Sahel and Télé-Sahel under the government's Office de Radiodiffusion Télévision du Niger are responsible for radio and TV broadcasting (colour by SECAM). In 1991 there were estimated to be 0·4m. radio and 25,000 TV sets.

Newspapers. In 1986 there was 1 daily newspaper, *Le Sahel*, with a circulation of 3,000.

JUSTICE, RELIGION, EDUCATION AND WELFARE

Justice. There are Magistrates' and Assize Courts at Niamey, Zinder and Maradi, and justices of the peace in smaller centres. The Court of Appeal is at Niamey.

Religion. In 1989 there were 5·72m. Sunni Moslems. There are some Christians, and traditional animist beliefs survive.

Education. There were, in 1986, 294,000 pupils and 7,600 teachers in 2,000 primary schools, 51,000 and 1,900 teachers in secondary schools, and 2,400 students and 120 teachers in the technical and teacher-training colleges. In 1984 there were 2,863 students and 314 teaching staff at the University of Niamey.

Health. In 1982 there were 2 hospitals, 36 medical centres and 116 dispensaries. In 1980 there were 136 doctors, and (in 1978) 10 dentists, 12 pharmacists, 88 midwives and 1,080 nursing personnel.

DIPLOMATIC REPRESENTATIVES

Of Niger in Great Britain
Ambassador: Sandi Yacouba (resides in Paris).

Of Great Britain in Niger
Ambassador: Margaret Rothwell (resides in Abidjan).

Of Niger in the USA (2204 R. St., NW, Washington, D.C., 20008)
Ambassador: Col. Moumouni Adamou Djermakoye.

Of the USA in Niger (PO Box 11201, Niamey)
Ambassador: Carl C. Cundiff.

Of Niger to the United Nations
Ambassador: Col. Moumouni Adamo Djermakoye.

Further Reading
Bonardi, P., *La République du Niger*. Paris, 1960
Fugelstad, F., *A History of Niger, 1850–1960*. OUP, 1984
Séré de Rivières, E., *Histoire du Niger*. Paris, 1965

NIGERIA

Capital: Abuja
Population: 88·5m. (1991)
GNP per capita: US$250 (1989)

Federal Republic of Nigeria

HISTORY. The Federal Republic comprises a number of areas formerly under separate administrations. Lagos, ceded in Aug. 1861 by King Dosunmu, was placed under the Governor of Sierra Leone in 1866. In 1874 it was detached, together with Gold Coast Colony, and formed part of the latter until Jan. 1886, when a separate 'colony and protectorate of Lagos' was constituted. Meanwhile the United African Company had established British interests in the Niger valley, and in July 1886 the company obtained a charter under the name of the Royal Niger Company. This company surrendered its charter to the Crown on 31 Dec. 1899, and on 1 Jan. 1900 the greater part of its territories was formed into the protectorate of Northern Nigeria. Along the coast the Oil Rivers protectorate had been declared in June 1885. This was enlarged and renamed the Niger Coast protectorate in 1893; and on 1 Jan. 1900, on its absorbing the remainder of the territories of the Royal Niger Company, it became the protectorate of Southern Nigeria. In Feb. 1906 Lagos and Southern Nigeria were united into the 'colony and protectorate of Southern Nigeria', and on 1 Jan. 1914 the latter was amalgamated with the protectorate of Northern Nigeria to form the 'colony and protectorate of Nigeria', under a Governor. On 1 Oct. 1954 Nigeria became a federation under a Governor-General. In 1967, 12 states were created and in 1976 this was increased to 19 and to 21 in 1987. On 1 Oct. 1960 Nigeria became sovereign and independent and a member of the Commonwealth and on 1 Oct. 1963 Nigeria became a republic.

Military coups took place in Dec. 1983 and Aug. 1985.

AREA AND POPULATION. Nigeria is bounded north by Niger, east by Chad and Cameroon, south by the Gulf of Guinea and west by Benin. It has an area of 356,669 sq. miles (923,773 sq. km). Census population, Nov. 1991, 88,500,000. The results of the 1973 census were officially repudiated. There had been considerable uncertainty over the size of the population, and the 1991 census results show that previous estimates, such as that of 95m. based on electoral registration in 1978, were exaggerated.

There were (1992) 30 states and a Federal Capital Territory (Abuja). 9 states were created in 1991: Abia, Anambra, Delta, Jigawa, Kebbi, Keffie, Osun, Taraba and Yobe. States, area and population in 1988:

States	Area (in sq. km)	Population	States	Area (in sq. km)	Population
Akwa Ibom	7,081	5,077,540	Katsina	24,192	5,389,950
Anambra	17,675	7,879,900	Kwara	66,869	3,685,100
Bauchi	64,605	5,326,800	Lagos	3,345	4,569,400
Bendel	35,500	5,391,700	Niger	65,037	2,214,700
Benue	45,174	5,317,500	Ogun	16,762	3,397,900
Borno	116,400	6,567,200	Ondo	20,959	5,980,700
Cross River	20,156	2,505,766	Oyo	37,705	11,412,300
Gongola	91,390	5,708,200	Plateau	58,030	4,385,100
Imo	11,850	8,046,500	Rivers	21,850	3,768,100
Kaduna	46,053	3,689,850	Sokoto	102,535	9,944,100
Kano	43,285	12,351,100	Abuja (FCT)	7,315	379,000 [2]

The populations (1983) of the largest towns were as follows:

Lagos	1,097,000	Abeokuta	308,800	Kaduna	247,100
Ibadan	1,060,000	Port Harcourt	296,200	Mushin	240,700
Uyo	1,000,000 [1]	Zaria	274,000	Maiduguri	230,900
Ogbomosho	527,400	Ilesha	273,400	Enugu	228,400
Kano	487,100	Onitsha	268,700	Ede	221,900
Oshogbo	344,500	Ado-Ekiti	265,800	Aba	216,000
Ilorin	343,900	Iwo	261,600	Ife	214,500

[1] 1988.   [2] At the 1991 census.

Ila	189,700	Offa	142,300	Effon-Alaiye	110,600
Oyo	185,300	Owo	132,600	Kumo	107,000
Ikerre-Ekiti	176,800	Calabar	126,000	Shomolu	106,800
Benin City	165,900	Shaki	125,800	Oka-Akoko	103,500
Iseyin	157,000	Ondo	122,600	Ikare	101,700
Katsina	149,300	Akure	117,300	Sapele	100,600
Jos	149,000	Gusau	114,100	Minna	98,900
Sokoto	148,000	Ijebu-Ode	113,100	Warri	91,100
Ilobu	143,800				

Abuja replaced Lagos as the federal capital and seat of government in Dec. 1991.

CLIMATE. Lying wholly within the tropics, temperatures everywhere are high. Rainfall varies very much, but decreases from the coast to the interior. The main rains occur from April to Oct. Lagos. Jan. 81°F (27·2°C), July 78°F (25·6°C). Annual rainfall 72" (1,836 mm). Ibadan. Jan. 80°F (26·7°C), July 76°F (24·4°C). Annual rainfall 45" (1,120 mm). Kano. Jan. 70°F (21·1°C), July 79°F (26·1°C). Annual rainfall 35" (869 mm). Port Harcourt. Jan. 79°F (26·1°C), July 77°F (25°C). Annual rainfall 100" (2,497 mm).

CONSTITUTION AND GOVERNMENT. Under the Constitution drafted and ratified in 1977–78, Nigeria is a sovereign, federal republic comprising states and a federal capital district. Following the coup of Aug. 1985 a 29-member Armed Forces Ruling Council (AFRC) was sworn in on 30 Aug. 1985. As part of the process of demilitarization and democratization the government has created 2 parties, the Social Democratic Party (SDP) and the National Republican Convention (NRC). Voting has not been secret since March 1991; voters indicate a poster of the candidate of their choice.

At the legislative and gubernatorial elections of Dec. 1991 the NRC gained 16 state governorships and the SDP 14. Parliamentary elections have been announced for Nov. 1992; Presidential elections for Dec. 1992.

President, Chairman of AFRC and C.-in-C. of the Armed Forces: Gen. Ibrahim Badamisi Babangida; *Vice-President:* Vice-Adm. Augustus Aikhomu.

On 12 Sept. 1985 the AFRC appointed a National Council of Ministers comprising the following in Dec. 1991:

Agriculture and Natural Resources: Shettima Mastapha. *Aviation:* Tonye Graham-Douglas. *Budget and Planning:* Chu Okongwu. *Communications:* A. O. Ige. *Culture and Social Welfare:* Cdre. L. Gwom. *Defence:* Lieut.-Gen. Sani Abacha. *Education:* Babs Fafunwa. *Employment, Labour and Productivity:* Bunu Sherif Musa. *External Affairs:* Maj.-Gen. Ike Nwachukwu. *Federal Capital Territory:* Maj.-Gen. Gado Nasko. *Finance and Economic Development:* Alhaji Abubakar Alhaji. *Health:* Olikoye Ransome-Kuti. *Industries:* Air Vice-Marshal M. Yahaya. *Information:* Vacant. *Internal Affairs:* Maj.-Gen. A. B. Mamman. *Justice:* Prince Bola Ajibola. *Mines, Power and Steel:* Air Vice-Marshal Nura M. Imam. *Petroleum Resources:* Jubril Aminu. *Science and Technology:* Gordian Ezekwe. *Youth and Sports:* Maj.-Gen. Y. Y. Kure. *Water Resources:* Alhaji Abubakar Hashidu. *Trade and Tourism:* S. J. Ukpanah. *Transport:* Cmdre. L. Gworm. *Works and Housing:* Brig. Mamman Kontagora.

National flag: Three vertical strips of green, white, green.
National anthem: Arise, O compatriots, Nigeria's call obey (tune by B. Odiase).

Local Government: Each of the states is administered by a military governor, who appoints and presides over a State Executive Council. Local elections took place in Dec. 1990. Turn-out was 20%. The SDP won control of 232 authorities, the NRC of 206.

DEFENCE. Restructuring of the armed forces began in Sept. 1990 with the retirement of 22 senior officers. The total number of the armed forces is being reduced.

Army. The Army consists of 1 armoured division, 2 mechanized divisions, 1 air defence brigade and 1 airborne and amphibious forces division, each with supporting artillery and engineer and reconnaissance units. Equipment includes 60 T-55 and 97 Vickers Mk 3 main battle tanks. Strength (1991) 80,000.

Navy. The Nigerian Navy comprises 1 German-built MEKO-type frigate with a helicopter and 1 frigate-type training ship, 3 British-built corvettes, 6 fast missile craft, 2 minehunters, and some 45 inshore patrol craft. There are also 2 German-built tank landing ships, 1 survey ship and some 15 service craft. The Navy has a small aviation element equipped with 2 Lynx anti-submarine helicopters. Naval personnel in 1991 totalled 5,000.

The Nigerian Coast Guard also operate about 10 patrol craft launches, and the police numerous boats.

Air Force. The Nigerian Air Force was established in Jan. 1964. Pilots were trained initially in Canada, India and Ethiopia. The Air Force was built up subsequently with the aid of a Federal Republic of Germany mission; much first-line equipment has since been received from the Soviet Union.

It has 14 MiG-21 supersonic jetfighters, 15 Jaguar attack aircraft and MiG-21U fighter-trainers, and 22 Alpha Jet light attack/trainers. About 20 BO 105 twin-turbine helicopters have been acquired from the Federal Republic of Germany for search and rescue, while 2 F.27MPAs are used for maritime patrol. Transport units operate 9 C-130H-30 and C-130H Hercules 4-turboprop heavy transports, 5 twin-turboprop Aeritalia G222s, 2 Puma and 12 Super Puma helicopters, 3 DO 228s, a Boeing 727 and a Gulfstream II for VIP use, 18 Dornier 128-6 twin-turboprop and 18 DO 28D twin-piston utility aircraft, 2 Navajos and a Navajo Chieftain. Training types include 25 Bulldog primary trainers, 12 MB 339 jets for instrument training, and 22 L-39 Albatros advanced trainers. Personnel (1991) total about 9,500, with 50 combat aircraft.

INTERNATIONAL RELATIONS

Membership. Nigeria is a member of the UN, the Commonwealth, ECOWAS, OAU, OPEC and is an ACP state of the EEC.

ECONOMY

Budget. 1991 revenue, ₦35,100m.; expenditure, ₦68,000m. 1992 estimated revenue, ₦54,000m.; expenditure, ₦52,000m.

Currency. The unit of currency is the *naira* (NGN) of 100 *kobo*. Notes in circulation ₦20, ₦10, ₦5, ₦1, 50k. Coins, 25k, 10k, 5k, 1k, ½ k. In March 1992 the Central Bank ceased to fix the exchange rate and the naira was allowed to float. In March 1992, £1 = ₦18·42; US$1 = ₦10·49.

Banking and Finance. The Central Bank is the bank of issue. There were 120 banks in 1992 (81 in 1989), in 20 of which central or state governments held a controlling interest.

There is a stock exchange.

Weights and Measures. The metric system is in force.

ENERGY AND NATURAL RESOURCES

Electricity. The National Electric Power Authority generated 10,730m. kwh. in 1986. Supply 230 volts; 50 Hz.

Oil. There are refineries at Port Harcourt, Warri and at Kaduna. Oil represents 95% of exports. Production, 1991, 96·35m. tonnes.

Gas. Natural gas is being used at electric power stations at Afam, Ughelli and Utorogu. Reserves: 2,600,000m. cu. metres. Production, 1990, 27,593m. cu. metres.

Water. Eleven River Basin Development Authorities have been established for water resources development.

Minerals. Production: Tin, 1980, 2,527 tonnes; columbite, 1977 (the world's largest producer), 800 tonnes; coal (1981) 114,875 tonnes. There are large deposits of iron ore, coal (reserves estimate 245m. tonnes), lead and zinc. There are small quantities of gold and uranium.

Agriculture. Of the total land mass, 75% is suitable for agriculture, including arable farming, forestry, livestock husbandry and fisheries. Main food crops are millet and sorghum in the north, plantains and oil palms in the south, and maize, yams, cassava and rice in much of the country, the north being, however, the main food producing area. Production, 1990 (in 1,000 tonnes): Millet, 4,000; sorghum, 4,000; plantains, 1,257; maize, 1,832; yams, 22,000; cassava, 213,000; rice, 1,900; groundnuts, 1,166; cotton lint, 27; palm kernel, 330; palm oil, 900.

Cocoa production was an estimated 160,000 tonnes in 1990; cocoa processing capacity is 90,000 tonnes a year.

Livestock (1990). There were 12m. cattle, 9m. sheep, 22m. goats, 1·1m. pigs and 165m. poultry.

Forestry. In 1988 there were 14m. ha of woodland, 16% of the total land area. There are plywood factories at Epe, Sapele and Calabar, and numerous saw-mills. The most important timber species include mahogany, iroko, obeche, abwa, ebony and camwood.

Fisheries. The total catch (1984) was 373,800 tonnes.

INDUSTRY. Timber and hides and skins are major export commodities. Industrial products include soap, cigarettes, beer, margarine, groundnut oil, meat and cake, concentrated fruit juices, soft drinks, canned food, metal containers, plywood, textiles, ceramic products and cement (3m. tonnes, 1985). Of growing importance is the local assembly of motor vehicles, bicycles, radio equipment, electrical goods and sewing machines. In 1982, the Delta Steel Plant opened at Ovwian—Aladja.

Two petrochemical plants (one at Ekpan near Warri in Bendel State producing about 35,000 tonnes of polypropylene and 18,000 tonnes of carbon black annually, and one at Kaduna producing 30,000 tonnes of linear-alkyl benzene annually) were commissioned in 1988.

Labour. The government doubled the minimum wage to ₦230 per month in 1991.

Trade Unions. There is a central labour Trade Union, the Nigerian Labour Congress.

FOREIGN ECONOMIC RELATIONS. Foreign exchange reserves were US$3,000m. in 1990. Foreign debt was US$33,360m. in Nov. 1991.

Commerce. Exports in 1990 were valued at US$13,700m. (including oil, US$13,300m.). Estimates for 1991: US$10,600m. (including oil, US$10,200m.); 1992: US$9,500m. (including oil, US$9,000m.). Imports in 1990: US$4,900m. Estimates for 1991: US$5,100m.; 1992: US$5,400m.

Total trade between Nigeria and UK (according to British Department of Trade returns, in £1,000 sterling):

	1987	1988	1989	1990	1991
Imports to UK	159,386	128,123	129,406	297,436	249,254
Exports and re-exports from UK	481,568	330,476	388,777	499,838	544,553

Tourism. There were 340,000 foreign visitors in 1985.

COMMUNICATIONS

Roads (1980). There were 108,000 km of maintained roads and 633,268 vehicles were registered.

Railways. There are 3,505 route-km of line 1,067 mm gauge, which in 1990 carried 0.4m. tonnes of freight and 5·5m. passengers.

Civil Aviation. There is an extensive system of internal and international air routes, serving Europe, USA, Middle East and South and West Africa. Regular services are operated by Nigerian Airways (WAAC), British Caledonian, UTA, KLM, SABENA,

Swissair, PANAM and other lines. In 1981, 2·3m. passengers were carried on domestic and international routes.

Shipping. The principal ports are Lagos, Port Harcourt, Warri and Calabar. There is an extensive network of inland waterways.

Telecommunications. Postal facilities are provided at 1,667 offices and agencies; telegraph, money order and savings bank services are provided at 280 of these. Most internal letter mail is carried by air at normal postage rates. External telegraph services are owned and operated by Nigerian External Telecommunications (NITEL), at Lagos, from which telegraphic communication is maintained with all parts of the world. There were 708,390 telephones in use in 1982, of which 249,150 were in Lagos and 33,138 in Ibadan. There is also a telex service.

Federal and some state governments have established commercial corporations for sound and television broadcasting, which are widely used in schools. In 1991 there were an estimated 10m. radio and 10m. TV sets (colour by PAL) and 500,000 television receivers.

Cinemas (1974). There were 120 cinemas, with a seating capacity of 60,000. Mobile cinemas are used by the Federal and States Information Services.

Newspapers. In 1989 there were 18 daily and 30 weekly newspapers. The aggregate circulation is about 1m., of which the *Daily Times* (Lagos) has about 400,000. (Another 4 dailies were published in Lagos, 4 in Ikeja, 3 in Enugu, and 4 in Ibadan.)

JUSTICE, RELIGION, EDUCATION AND WELFARE

Justice. The highest court is the Federal Supreme Court, which consists of the Chief Justice of the Republic, and up to 15 Justices appointed by AFRC. It has original jurisdiction in any dispute between the Federal Republic and any State or between States; and to hear and determine appeals from the Federal Court of Appeal, which acts as an intermediate appellate Court to consider appeals from the High Court.

High Courts, presided over by a Chief Justice, are established in each state. All judges are appointed by the AFRC. Magistrates' courts are established throughout the Republic, and customary law courts in southern Nigeria. In each of the northern States of Nigeria there are the Sharia Court of Appeal and the Court of Resolution. Moslem Law has been codified in a Penal Code and is applied through Alkali courts.

Religion. Moslems, 48%; Christians, 34% (17% Protestants and 17% Roman Catholic); others, 18%. Northern Nigeria is mainly Moslem; Southern Nigeria is predominantly Christian and Western Nigeria is evenly divided between Christians, Moslems and animists.

Education. In 1982–83 there were 15,021,100 primary school pupils, and 2,421,625 secondary grammar/commercial school pupils.

In 1989 there were 9 teacher training colleges, 41 government 'Unity' colleges and 10 polytechnics.

In 1989 there were 16 federal and 8 state universities.

Health. Most tropical diseases are endemic to Nigeria. Blindness, yaws, leprosy, sleeping sickness, worm infections, malaria are major health problems which, however, are yielding to remedial and preventative measures. In co-operation with the World Health Organization river blindness and malaria are being tackled on a large scale, while annual campaigns are undertaken against the danger of smallpox epidemics. Dispensaries and travelling dispensaries are found in most parts of the country.

In 1980 there were 8,000 doctors and 75,000 hospital beds.

DIPLOMATIC REPRESENTATIVES

Of Nigeria in Great Britain (9 Northumberland Ave., London, WC2 5BX)
High Commissioner: Christopher MacRae, CMG.

Of Great Britain in Nigeria (11 Eleke Cres., Victoria Island, Lagos)
High Commissioner: George Dove-Edwin, GCVO.

Of Nigeria in the USA (2201 M. St., NW, Washington, D.C., 20037)
Ambassador: Kevin Efretei.

Of the USA in Nigeria (2 Eleke Cres., Lagos)
Ambassador: Lannon Walker.

Of Nigeria to the United Nations
Ambassador: Prof. Ibrahim A. Gambari.

Further Reading

Nigeria Digest of Statistics. Lagos, 1951 ff. (quarterly)
Annual Abstract of Statistics. Federal Office of Statistics. Lagos, 1960 ff.
Nigeria Trade Journal. Federal Ministry of Commerce and Industries (quarterly)
Achebe, C., *The Trouble with Nigeria.* London, 1984
Adamolekun, L., *Politics and Administration in Nigeria.* Ibadan, 1986
Barbour, K. M. (ed.) *Nigeria in Maps.* London, 1982
Burns, A., *History of Nigeria.* 8th ed. London, 1978
Crowder, M. and Abdullahi, G., *Nigeria, an Introduction to its History.* London, 1979
Kirk-Greene, A. and Rimmer, D., *Nigeria since 1970.* London, 1981
Myers, R. A., *Nigeria.* [Bibliography] Oxford and Santa Barbara, 1989
Nwabueze, B. O., *The Presidential Constitution of Nigeria.* Lagos and London, 1982
Oyediran, O., *Nigerian Government and Politics under Military Rule, 1966–1979.* New York, 1980
Oyovbaine, S.E., *Federalism in Nigeria: A Study in the Development of the Nigerian State.* London, 1985
Shaw, T. M. and Aluko, O., *Nigerian Foreign Policy: Alternative Perceptions and Projections.* London, 1984
Williams, D., *President and Power in Nigeria.* London, 1982
Zartman, I. W., *The Political Economy of Nigeria.* New York, 1983

NORWAY

Kongeriket Norge

(Kingdom of Norway)

Capital: Oslo
Population: 4·24m. (1990)
GNP per capita: US$21,850 (1989)

HISTORY. By the Treaty of 14 Jan. 1814 Norway was ceded to the King of Sweden by the King of Denmark, but the Norwegian people declared themselves independent and elected Prince Christian Frederik of Denmark as their king. The foreign Powers refused to recognize this election, and on 14 Aug. a convention proclaimed the independence of Norway in a personal union with Sweden. This was followed on 4 Nov. by the election of Karl XIII (II) as King of Norway. Norway declared this union dissolved, 7 June 1905, and Sweden agreed to the repeal of the union on 26 Oct. 1905. The throne was offered to a prince of the reigning house of Sweden, who declined. After a plebiscite, Prince Carl of Denmark was formally elected King on 18 Nov. 1905, and took the name of Haakon VII.

Norwegian Sovereigns

Inge Baardssøn	1204	Erik of Pomerania	1389
Haakon Haakonssøn	1217	Kristofer af Bavaria	1442
Magnus Lagabøter	1263	Karl Knutssøn	1449
Eirik Magnussøn	1280	Same Sovereigns as in Denmark	1450–1814
Haakon V Magnussøn	1299	Christian Frederik	1814
Magnus Erikssøn	1319	Same Sovereigns as in Sweden	1814–1905
Haakon VI Magnussøn	1343	Haakon VII	1905
Olav Haakonssøn	1381	Olav V	1957
Margrete	1388		

AREA AND POPULATION. Norway is bounded north by the Arctic ocean, east by the USSR, Finland and Sweden, south by the Skagerrak Straits and west by the North Sea.

Fylker (counties)	Area (sq. km)	Census population 1 Nov. 1980	Population 1 Jan. 1990	Pop. per sq. km (total area) 1990
Oslo (City)	454·0	452,023	458,364	1,009·6
Akershus	4,916·5	369,193	414,503	84·3
Østfold	4,183·4	233,301	237,981	56·9
Hedmark	27,388·4	187,223	186,884	6·8
Oppland	25,259·7	180,765	182,350	7·2
Buskerud	14,927·3	214,571	224,701	15·1
Vestfold	2,215·9	186,691	197,207	89·0
Telemark	15,315·1	162,050	162,981	10·6
Aust-Agder	9,211·7	90,629	96,880	10·5
Vest-Agder	7,280·3	136,718	144,026	19·8
Rogaland	9,140·7	305,490	335,753	36·7
Hordaland	15,633·8	391,463	409,124	26·2
Sogn og Fjordane	18,633·5	105,924	106,540	5·7
Møre og Romsdal	15,104·2	236,062	238,346	15·8
Sør-Trøndelag	18,831·4	244,760	250,344	13·3
Nord-Trøndelag	22,463·4	125,835	126,858	5·6
Nordland	38,327·1	244,493	239,532	6·2
Troms	25,953·8	146,818	146,594	5·6
Finnmark	48,637·3	78,331	74,148	1·5
Mainland total	323,877·5 [1]	4,092,340	4,233,116	13·1

Svalbard and Jan Mayen have an area of 63,080 sq. km. Persons staying on Svalbard and Jan Mayen are registered as residents of their home Norwegian municipality.

[1] 125,049 sq. miles.

On 1 Nov. 1980, 2,874,990 persons lived in densely populated areas and 1,197,939 in sparsely populated areas.

Population of the principal towns at 1 Jan. 1990:

Oslo	458,364	Sandnes	43,340	Gjøvik	27,275
Bergen	211,826	Sandefjord	38,019	Halden	26,527
Trondheim	137,346	Bodø	36,536	Moss	26,083
Stavanger	97,570	Ålesund	35,888	Lillehammer	25,816
Kristiansand	64,888	Porsgrunn	35,751	Harstad	24,657
Drammen	51,978	Haugesund	31,275	Molde	22,782
Tromsø	50,548	Ringerike	31,209	Kongsberg	22,507
Skien	47,679	Fredrikstad	27,600	Steinkjer	22,384

Vital statistics for calendar years:

	Marriages	Divorces	Births	Still-born	Outside marriage [1]	Deaths
1986	20,513	7,891	52,514	268	14,673	43,560
1987	21,081	8,417	54,027	237	16,705	44,959
1988	21,744	8,772	57,526	270	19,407	45,354
1990	...	9,238	59,303	292	21,588	45,173

[1] Excluding still-born.

Expectation of life, 1989: Males, 73·34 years; females, 79·85.

CLIMATE. There is considerable variation in the climate because of the extent of latitude, the topography and the varying effectiveness of prevailing westerly winds and the Gulf Stream. Winters along the whole west coast are exceptionally mild but precipitation is considerable. Oslo. Jan. 24°F (–4·7°C), July 63°F (17·3°C). Annual rainfall 29·1" (740 mm). Bergen. Jan. 35°F (1·4°C), July 60°F (15·3°C). Annual rainfall 83" (2,108 mm). Trondheim. Jan. 26°F (–3·5°C), July 57°F (14°C). Annual rainfall 32·1" (870 mm).

REIGNING KING. Harald V, born 21 Feb. 1937, married on 29 Aug. 1968 to Sonja Haraldsen. He succeeded on the death of his father, King Olav V, on 21 Jan. 1991. *Offspring:* Princess Märtha Louise, born 22 Sept. 1971; Crown Prince Haakon Magnus, born 20 July 1973.

The king receives a tax-free annual allowance of 19·8m. kroner from the civil list. Women have been eligible to succeed to the throne since 1990. There is no coronation ceremony.

CONSTITUTION AND GOVERNMENT. Norway is a constitutional and hereditary monarchy. The royal succession is in direct male line in the order of primogeniture. In default of male heirs the King may propose a successor to the Storting, but this assembly has the right to nominate another, if it does not agree with the proposal.

The Constitution, voted by the constituent assembly at Eidsvoll on 17 May 1814 and modified at various times, vests the legislative power of the realm in the *Storting* (Parliament). The royal veto may be exercised; but if the same Bill passes two Stortings formed by separate and subsequent elections it becomes the law of the land without the assent of the sovereign. The King has the command of the land, sea and air forces, and makes all appointments.

National flag: Red with a blue white-bordered Scandinavian cross.
National anthem: Ja, vi elsker dette landet (Yes, we love this land; words by B. Bjørnson, 1865; tune by R. Nordraak, 1865).

The 165-member Storting assembles every year. The meetings take place *suo jure*, and not by any writ from the King or the executive. They begin on the first weekday in Oct. each year, until June the following year. Every Norwegian subject of 18 years of age is entitled to vote, unless he is disqualified for a special cause. The mode of election is direct and the method of election is proportional. The country is divided into 19 districts, each electing from 4 to 15 representatives.

At the elections for the Storting held in 1989 the following parties were elected: Labour, 63; Conservative, 37; Centre Party, 11; Christian Democratic Party, 14; Socialist Left Party, 17; Party of Progress, 22; Future for Finmark, 1.

The Storting, when assembled, divides itself by election into the *Lagting* and the *Odelsting*. The former is composed of one-fourth of the members of the Storting, and the other of the remaining three-fourths. Each Ting (the Storting, the Odelsting and the Lagting) nominates its own president. Most questions are decided by the Storting, but questions relating to legislation must be considered and decided by the Odelsting and the Lagting separately. Only when the Odelsting and the Lagting disagree, the Bill has to be considered by the Storting in plenary sitting, and a new law can then only be decided by a majority of two-thirds of the voters. The same majority is required for alterations of the Constitution, which can only be decided by the Storting in plenary sitting. The Storting elects 5 delegates, whose duty it is to revise the public accounts. The Lagting and the ordinary members of the Supreme Court of Justice (the *Høyesterett*) form a High Court of the Realm (the *Riksrett*) for the trial of ministers, members of the *Høyesterett* and members of the Storting. The impeachment before the *Riksrett* can only be decided by the Odelsting.

The executive is represented by the King, who exercises his authority through the Cabinet or Council of State *(Statsråd)*, composed of a Prime Minister *(Statsminster)* and (at present) 17 ministers *(Statsråder)*. The ministers are entitled to be present in the Storting and to take part in the discussions, but without a vote.

A Coalition Government was formed and took office on 16 Oct. 1989. This government resigned on 29 Oct. 1990 over the question of joining the EEC, and Gro Harlem Brundtland (b. 1949) formed a minority Labour government, which consisted of the following ministers in Nov. 1991:

Prime Minister: Gro Harlem Brundtland.
Foreign Affairs: Thorvald Stoltenberg. *Education, Research and Church Affairs:* Gudmund Hernes. *Environment:* Torbjørn Berntsen. *Industry:* Ole Knapp. *Petroleum and Energy:* Finn Kristensen. *Local Government and Labour:* Kjell Borgen. *Development Cooperation:* Grete Faremo. *Trade and Shipping:* Eldrid Nordbøe. *Fisheries:* Oddrun Pettersen. *Defence:* Johan Jørgen Holst. *Transport and Communications:* Kjell Opseth. *Justice and the Police:* Kari Gjesteby. *Finance:* Sigbjørn Johnsen. *Child and Family Affairs:* Matz Sandmann. *Health and Social Affairs:* Tove Veierød. *Agriculture:* Gunhild Øyangen. *Cultural Affairs:* Åse Kleveland. *Government Administration:* Tove Strand Gerhardsen.

The official language is Norwegian, which has 2 versions: Bokmål (or Riksmål) and Nynorsk (or Landsmål).

Local Government. For the purposes of administration the country is divided into 19 counties *(fylker)*, in each of which the central government is represented by a county governor *(fylkesmannen)*. The counties are divided into 448 municipalities, each of which usually corresponds in size to a parish *(prestegjeld)*. The municipalities are administered by municipal councils *(kommunestyrer)*, whose membership may vary between 13 and 85 councillors, and by a committee *(formannskap)* which is elected by and from the members of the council. The council is four times the size of the committee. The council elects a chairman and a vice-chairman from among the committee members. Elections were held in Sept. 1991. The Labour Party gained 30·4% of all votes cast, the Centre Party, 12·1% and the Socialist Left Party, 12·1%.

18 of the counties form a county district *(fylkeskommune)* each, while the remaining one, Oslo, comprises an urban district. The supreme authority in a county district is the county council *(fylkesting)*. The members of the county council are elected directly by the electors of the county and the number of representatives varies between 25 and 85. In a county district the county committee *(fylkesutvalg)* occupies a position corresponding to that of the committee *(formannskap)* in the primary districts. The county committee is elected by and from among the members of the county council. The number of county committee members is one-fourth of the membership of the county council, but must be not more than 15. The county council elects from among the members of the county committee a county sheriff *(fylkesordfører)* and a deputy sheriff.

DEFENCE. Service is universal and compulsory, liability in peace-time commencing at the age of 19 and continuing till the age of 44. The service period in the Army, Coastal Artillery and the Air Force is 12 months, and periodic refresher training, in the Navy, 15 months and limited refresher training. The Norwegian Defence forces are organized into 2 integrated regional commands, Northern and Southern.

Army. Under the 2 principal subordinate commands (Commander Land Forces North Norway COMLANDNON, and Commander Allied Land Forces South Norway COMLANDSONOR), the Army is organized in 5 regional commands and 16 territorial commands.

In Defence Command North Norway the largest standing element is Brigade North. There are also 2 infantry battalions and 1 tank platoon, 1 self-propelled field artillery battery and 1 AD battery in the north. Defence Command South Norway comprises 1 infantry battalion, 1 tank company and 1 self-propelled field artillery battery. Equipment includes 78 Leopard I/A5 and 55 M-48A5 main battle tanks. Strength (1992) 15,900 (including 13,000 conscripts). The fast mobilization force numbers 165,000, organized under the 2 principal subordinate commands, (North and South Norway).

In the war time command structure there are 5 regional commands, 16 territorial commands, 13 brigades, 28 independent infantry battalions, 7 independent artillery battalions and 50–60 independent units as tank squadrons, infantry companies, engineer companies and signal units.

Navy. The Royal Norwegian Navy has 3 components: The Navy, Coast Guard and Coastal Artillery. Main Naval combatants include 12 coastal submarines (including the first 4, of a new German-built Ula class), 5 frigates, 35 missile torpedo-boats, 3 coastal minesweepers, 1 minehunter and 2 minelayers. Auxiliaries comprise 1 submarine/missile craft support ship, 1 Royal Yacht and some 10 small general-purpose tenders. The Coastal Artillery man 32 coastal batteries and other static defence systems.

The personnel of the navy totalled 7,300 in 1991, of whom 4,500 were conscripts, and 2,000 served in coast artillery. The main naval base is at Bergen (Håkonsvern), with subsidiary bases at Horten, Ramsund and Tromsø.

The naval elements of the Home Guard on mobilization can muster some 7,000 personnel, and man 2 tank landing craft and about 400 requisitioned fishing vessels.

The 13 Coast Guard offshore patrol vessels (of which 3 are armed, and of frigate capability) are Navy-subordinated, and assist other government agencies in rescue service, environmental patrols, surveillance and police duties. The coast guard numbered 675 in 1991.

Air Force. The Royal Norwegian Air Force comprises the Air Force and the Anti-air Artillery. The Air Force consists of 4 squadrons of F-16 Fighting Falcons, 1 squadron of F-5 fighter-bombers, 1 maritime patrol squadron of P-3N and P-3C Orions, 1 squadron of C-130 Hercules transports and Falcon 20s equipped for EW duties, 1 squadron with DHC-6 Twin Otter light transports and 2 squadrons of Bell 412SP helicopters. The Anti-air Artillery deploy 4 Nike surface-to-air missile batteries and several light anti-aircraft artillery units. 6 NOAH (Norwegian adapted Hawk missiles) batteries provide area and airfield defence co-ordinated with 10 SAM batteries with the mobile missile system RBS-70. Finally 27 batteries with 40 mm Bofors AA-guns and 12·7 mm machine guns. 9 Westland Sea King helicopters are used for search and rescue duties; 6 Lynx helicopters are operated for the Coast Guard; 17 Saab Safaris are used for primary training; pilots then go to the USA for advanced training. The O-1 Bird Dogs operated for the Army are being retired.

Total strength (1992) is about 9,500 personnel, including 5,300 conscripts.

Home Guard. The Home Guard is organized in small units equipped and trained for special tasks. Service after basic training is 1 week a year. The total strength is approximately 80,000.

The Home Guard consists of the Land Home Guard (LHG), Sea Home Guard (SHG) and Anti-Air Home Guard (AAHG) organized in 18 Home Guard Districts. The LHG is divided into 83 LHG sub-districts and 470 local units. The SHG is divided into 5 SHG sub-districts and 33 local units. The AAHG is divided into 2 AAHG sub-districts organized in 8 AAHG batteries and 1 reinforced battery.

In case of preparedness, mobilization or war, the Land HG is subordinate to The

Land Defence District or The Land Defence, Sea HG is subordinate to The Naval District and the Anti-Air HG is subordinate to the Air Station.

INTERNATIONAL RELATIONS

Membership. Norway is a member of UN, NATO, EFTA, OECD, the Council of Europe and the Nordic Council.

ECONOMY

Budget. Current central government revenue and expenditure for years ending 31 Dec. (in 1m. kroner):

	1988	1989	1990
Revenue	276,329	288,672	316,964
Expenditure	249,393	270,000	295,448

Currency. The unit of currency is the *Norwegian krone* (NOK) of 100 *øre*. National bank-notes of 50, 100, 500 and 1,000 *kroner* are legal means of payment. On 30 June 1990 the nominal value of the coin in circulation was 1,956m. kroner; notes in circulation, 27,690m. kroner.

Since Oct. 1990 the krone has been fixed to the ecu in the European Monetary System of the EEC in the narrow band of 2·25%. In March 1992, US$1 = 6·44 *kroner*; £1 = 11·31 *kroner*.

Banking and Finance. Norges Bank is the central bank and bank of issue. Supreme authority is vested in the Executive Board consisting of 7 members appointed by the King and the Supervisory Council consisting of 15 members elected by the Storting. The *Governor* is Hermod Skanland.

There are 3 major commercial banks: Den Norske Bank, Christiana and Fokus. Following the collapse of the Christiana Bank in Oct. 1991 the government introduced a rescue programme.

At the end of 1989 there were 28 private joint-stock banks. Their total amount of capital and funds was 14,923m. kroner (capital 9,230m., funds 5,693m.). Deposits amounted to 245,824m. kroner, of which 184,118m. kroner were on ordinary notice, and 161,706m. kroner on special terms.

The number of savings banks at the end of 1989 was 151. The total amount of capital and funds of the savings banks amounted to 10,840m. kroner, of which 638m. kroner were capital certificate funds. Total deposits amounted to 183,716m. kroner, of which 143,193m. kroner were on ordinary terms and 40,523m. kroner on special terms.

There is a stock exchange in Oslo.

Weights and Measures. The metric system is obligatory.

ENERGY AND NATURAL RESOURCES

Electricity. Norway is a large producer of hydro-electric energy. The potential total hydro-electric power at regulated mean water flow is estimated at 170,000m. kwh. annually.

By the end of 1988 the capacity of the installations for production of thermo-electric energy was 251 mw. and the capacity for production of hydro-electric energy was 25,841 mw. In 1990 the total production of electricity amounted to 121,601m. kwh. of which 99·6% was produced by hydro-electric plants.

Most of the electricity is used for industrial purposes, especially by the chemical and basic metal industries for production of nitrate of calcium and other nitrogen products, carbide, ferrosilicon and other ferro-alloys, aluminium and zinc. The paper and pulp industries are also big consumers of electricity. Supply 130, 150, 220 and 230 volts; 50 Hz.

Oil. In 1963 sovereignty was proclaimed over the Norwegian continental shelf and in 1966 the first exploration well was drilled. By 1989 production was almost 7 times the domestic consumption of petroleum and is valued at about 12% of the GNP. Production (1990) 81m. tonnes.

Gas. Production (1989) 1,128,330m. cu. ft.

Minerals. Production and value of the chief concentrates, metals and alloys were:

	1987		1988	
Concentrates and minerals	*Tonnes*	*1,000 kroner*	*Tonnes*	*1,000 kroner*
Copper concentrates	102,471	303,282	82,830	287,173
Pyrites	355,686	77,819	306,842	62,704
Titanium ore	852,323	...	898,035	...
Zinc and lead concentrates	47,471	69,369	38,195	84,465
Metals and alloys				
Copper	30,101	...	31,730	...
Nickel	44,564	...	52,545	...
Aluminium	853,213	8,880,670	838,224	11,331,473
Ferro-alloys	776,945	2,705,960	863,682	3,973,330
Pig-iron	377,671	...	390,751	...
Zinc	116,593	...	122,203	...
Lead and tin	17	...	9	...

Agriculture. Norway is a barren and mountainous country. The arable soil is found in comparatively narrow strips, gathered in deep and narrow valleys and around fiords and lakes.

In 1990 the agricultural area was 976,400 ha, of which 540,800 ha were meadow and pasture, 174,500 ha were sown to barley, 126,100 ha to oats, 47,300 ha to wheat and 18,600 ha to potatoes. Production (in 1,000 tonnes) in 1990: Barley, 731; oats, 570; wheat, 237; potatoes, 482; hay, 3,329; vegetables, 143; meat, 210.

Livestock, 1990 [1]: 953,100 cattle (333,500 milch cows), 896,400 sheep, 61,000 goats, 709,700 pigs, 3,763,400 hens.

Fur production in 1988–89 was as follows (1987–88 in brackets): Silver fox, 320,400 (223,300); silver-blue fox, 59,300 (170,300); blue fox, 359,200 (295,700); mink, 566,800 (509,000).

[1] Holdings with at least 5 decares agricultural area in use.

Forestry. Productive forest area, 1989, 63,528 sq. km. About 80% of the productive forest area consists of conifers and 20% of broadleaves. The annual increment (in 1989) was 15,538,000 cu. metres with bark. In 1988–89 10·66m. cu. metres of roundwood were cut (9·9m. cu. metres coniferous, 0·38m. cu. metres broadleaf). 4·28m. cu. metres went to sawmills and wood industries, 4·92m. cu. metres to pulp industries and 0·43m. cu. metres went for fuel.

Fisheries. The total number of registered fishermen in 1990 was 27,518, of whom 7,043 had another chief occupation. In 1990, the number of fishing vessels (all with motor) was 17,393, and of these 8,956 were open boats.

The value of sea fisheries in 1m. kroner in 1989 was: Cod, 1,264; capelin, 86; mackerel, 284; coal-fish (saithe), 430; deep-water prawn, 780; haddock, 212; herring, 388; dogfish, 22. The catch in 1990 totalled 1,568,371 tonnes. 15,232 seals were caught in 1990. Small-whale catching was prohibited in 1988.

Fish farming is a growth industry, exports (1989) 3,486m. kroner.

INDUSTRY. Industry is chiefly based on raw materials produced within the country (wood, fish, etc.) and on water power, of which the country possesses a large amount. Crude petroleum and natural gas production, the manufacture of paper and paper products, industrial chemicals and basic metals are the most important export manufactures. In the following table are given figures for industrial establishments in 1988, excluding one-man units. Electrical plants, construction and building industry are not included. The values are given in 1m. kroner.

Industries	*Establish-ments*	*Number of Employees*	*Gross value of produc-tion*	*Value added*
Coalmining	1	557	134·2	–8·4
Crude petroleum and natural gas	15	14,138	65,489·9	45,769·0
Metal-mining	9	2,278	1,309·0	397·4
Other-mining	449	3,256	2,629·5	1,140·0
Food manufacturing	2,159	48,758	59,971·3	7,992·3
Beverages	56	4,669	5,628·4	3,677·2

Industries	Establishments	Number of Employees	Gross value of production	Value added
Tobacco	3	936	3,197·3	2,635·7
Textiles	417	7,476	3,395·6	1,278·8
Clothing, etc.	258	3,191	1,185·4	502·9
Footwear	27	542	192·6	84·7
Leather	45	608	285·8	89·7
Wood	1,412	19,470	13,637·3	4,219·6
Furniture and fixtures	511	8,501	4,468·5	1,579·1
Pulp and paper	128	12,369	16,602·9	4,592·5
Printing and publishing	1,918	35,673	20,602·7	8,762·1
Chemical, industrial	56	8,040	14,216·1	4,906·0
Chemical, other	149	5,954	6,004·4	2,256·7
Petroleum, refined	3	1,189	8,022·0	819·6
Petroleum and coal	74	1,466	1,995·1	435·5
Rubber	73	1,582	981·7	398·0
Plastics	325	6,534	4,934·7	1,638·6
Ceramics	39	1,034	341·4	193·6
Glass	67	1,996	1,265·2	493·4
Other mineral products	501	8,083	7,442·3	2,643·0
Iron, steel and ferro-alloys	45	9,253	10,615·3	3,209·4
Non-ferrous metals	57	12,364	23,852·3	7,930·3
Metal products, except machinery	1,782	26,785	13,541·6	5,650·2
Machinery and equipment	1,245	37,725	42,656·5	10,126·1
Electrical apparatus and supplies	500	19,596	13,985·7	5,162·0
Transport equipment	861	23,810	16,755·2	5,302·5
Professional and scientific instruments, photographic and optical goods	75	1,720	1,170·9	490·3
Other manufacturing industries	294	2,883	1,241·0	545·3
Total (all included)	13,554	332,436	367,751·8	134,913·0

Income at factor cost (in 1m. kroner):

	1986	1987	1988
Net domestic product	441,157	480,497	501,942
Less Indirect taxes	99,922	107,059	107,042
Add Subsidies	29,569	31,515	33,638
	370,804	404,953	428,538
Industries			
Agriculture	10,198	11,684	11,175
Forestry	2,788	3,182	3,675
Fishing and fish breeding	3,519	3,187	3,707
Crude petroleum and natural gas production	27,066	24,755	15,529
Manufacturing, mining and quarrying	71,366	78,011	87,361
Electricity supply	11,429	12,385	14,659
Construction	25,374	32,534	33,593
Wholesale and retail trade	41,649	43,919	44,275
Hotels and restaurants	7,709	8,730	9,413
Financial services	24,287	29,691	29,875
Business services	22,292	25,008	27,450

Labour. The labour force (i.e. employed persons plus non-employed persons seeking work aged 16–74) averaged 2,030,000 (6%) persons in 1990 (915,000 females).

Distribution of employed persons by occupation in 1989 showed 459,000 (22%) in technical, physical science, humanistic and artistic work; 131,000 (6%) administrative executive work; 228,000 (11%) clerical; 215,000 (10%) sales; 131,000 (6%) agriculture, forestry, fishing etc.; 9,000 (0·4%) mining and quarrying; 134,000 (7%) transport and communication; 423,000 (21%) manufacturing; 273,000 (13%) service, and 46,000 (2%) military and occupation not specified.

There were 92,695 registered unemployed in 1990 (35,584 females).

There were 15 work stoppages in 1990; 139,047 working days were lost.

Trade Unions. There were 1,289,547 union members in 1990.

FOREIGN ECONOMIC RELATIONS

Commerce. Total imports and exports in calendar years (in 1,000 kroner):

	1986	1987	1988	1989	1990
Imports	150,052,325	152,041,081	151,100,812	163,380,270	169,998,400
Exports	133,847,404	144,543,413	146,165,546	187,146,395	211,579,400

Major import suppliers in 1990 (value in 1m. kroner): Sweden, 26,492·5; Federal Republic of Germany, 23,570·8; UK, 15,109·8; USA, 14,952·3; Denmark, 11,226; Japan, 7,328·1; Netherlands, 6,702·3; France, 6,327·4; Liberia, 5,712·7; Italy, 5,388·6; Finland, 5,263·8. Imports from economic areas: EC, 77,755·6; Nordic countries, 43,172·9; EFTA, 36,154·7.

Major export markets: UK, 55,369·4; Sweden, 24,572·2; Federal Republic of Germany, 23,447; Netherlands, 16,539·8; France, 16,315·3; USA, 13,374; Denmark, 10,246·9; Finland, 5,803·8; Italy, 5,533·9. Exports to economic areas: EC, 136,768·4; Nordic countries, 41,574·1; EFTA, 33,437·9.

Principal items of import in 1990 (in 1m. kroner): Machinery, 18,082·1; iron and steel, 6,757·7; non-ferrous metals, 2,716·5; office machines, 6,535·6; electrical-machinery, 8,131·2; motor vehicles, 9,571; aircraft, 4,312·5; chemicals, 3,073·6; medical products, 2,274·6; primary plastics, 1,952; non-primary plastics, 1,389; textiles, 3,460. Principal items of export in 1990 (in 1m. kroner): Fish, 12,597·7; wood, 1,365·7; pulp, 2,489·9; metal ores, 1,608·1; oil and products, 84,621; gas, 29,272·4; chemicals, 4,406; paper, 6,721·4; iron and steel, 6,161·1; non-ferrous metals, 18,449·1; ships over 100 tonnes, 10,092·6.

Total trade between Norway and UK (British Department of Trade returns, in £1,000 sterling):

	1987	1988	1989	1990	1991
Imports to UK	3,290,339	3,074,000	3,637,119	4,235,348	4,232,827
Exports and re-exports from UK	1,220,844	1,053,613	1,056,506	1,289,789	1,357,299

Tourism. In 1990 there were 1,135 hotels. There were 3·91m. foreign tourists staying 7·07m. nights.

COMMUNICATIONS

Roads. In 1991 the length of public roads (including roads in towns) totalled 88,800 km. Of these, 62,101 km were hard-surfaced. Total road length included: National roads, 26,221 km; provincial roads, 26,975 km; local roads, 35,605 km.

Number of registered motor vehicles, 1991: 1,612,674 passenger cars (including taxis), 21,222 buses, 164,738 vans, 68,910 combined vehicles, 74,651 lorries, 211,179 tractors, 35,551 snow scooters and 167,954 motor cycles and mopeds. The scheduled bus and lorry services in 1987 drove 4,199m. passenger-km. In 1989 there were 8,494 road accidents with 381 fatalities.

Railways. The length of state railways in 1991 was 4,044 km (2,426 km electrified); of private companies, 16 km (electrified). Total receipts of the state railways in 1990 were 4,342m. kroner; total expenses, 5,996m. kroner. The state railways carried 21·5m. tonnes of freight and 34·5m. passengers.

There is a metro (98 km) and tram/light rail line (54 km) in Oslo.

Civil Aviation. Denmark and Norway hold each two-sevenths and Sweden three-sevenths of the capital of SAS (Scandinavian Airlines System), but they have joint responsibility towards third parties.

In 1991 there were 840 registered aircraft.

Air transport on domestic routes:

	1,000 km flown	Passengers carried	1,000 passenger-km	Post, luggage, freight and passengers (1,000 ton-km)	
				Total	Of which post
1987	45,882	6,360,417	2,495	231,000	8,000
1988	47,436	6,421,708	2,553	239,000	8,000
1989	44,050	6,003,917	2,442	229,000	7,000
1990	48,917	6,616,154	2,666	249,000	7,000

Shipping. The Norwegian International Shipping Registry was set up in 1987. In 1991 870 ships were registered (737 Norwegian) totalling 22·11m. GRT. In 1991 there were also 1,016 ships totalling 1·5m. GRT on the Norwegian Ordinary Register. These figures do not include fishing boats, tugs, salvage vessels, icebreakers and similar special types of vessels.

Goods (in 1,000 tonnes) in 1989 discharged, 18,369; loaded, 82,886.

In 1989 53,449 passengers and 36,091 tonnes of cargo were carried by coastwise shipping.

Telecommunications. There were 2,536 post offices in 1990. Number of telephone connexions on 31 Dec. 1990 was 2,132,290. Receipts, 16,020m. kroner; expenses, 14,078m. kroner (interest on capital included) for State Telecommunications. The Norwegian Broadcasting Corporation is a non-commercial enterprise operated by an independent state organization and broadcasts 1 programme (P1) on long-, medium-, and short-waves and on FM and 1 programme (P2) on FM. Local programmes are also broadcast. It broadcasts 1 TV programme from 2,259 transmitters. Colour programmes are broadcast by PAL system. Number of television licences, 1991, 1,496,409.

Cinemas. There were 403 cinemas with a seating capacity of 103,283 in 1989, and 14 theatres and operas.

Newspapers. There were 61 daily newspapers with a combined circulation of 2·16m. in 1989, and 98 weeklies and semi-weeklies with 0·77m.

JUSTICE, RELIGION, EDUCATION AND WELFARE

Justice. The judicature is common to civil and criminal cases. The same professional judges, who are legally educated, preside over both kinds of cases. These judges are as such state officials. The participation of lay judges and jurors, both summoned for the individual case, varies according to the kind of court and kind of case.

The 96 city or district courts of first instance are in criminal cases composed of one professional judge and 2 lay judges, chosen by ballot from a panel elected by the local authority. In civil cases 2 lay judges may participate. These courts are competent in all cases except criminal cases where the maximum penalty exceeds 6 years imprisonment.

In every community there is a Conciliation Board *(Forliksråd)* composed of 3 lay persons elected by the district council. A civil lawsuit usually begins with mediation by the Board which can pronounce judgement in certain cases.

The 5 high courts, or courts of second instance are composed of 3 professional judges. Additionally, in civil cases 2 or 4 lay judges may be summoned. In serious criminal cases, which are brought before high courts in the first instance a jury of 10 lay persons is summoned to determine whether the defendant is guilty according to the charge. In less serious criminal cases the court is composed of 2 professional and 3 lay judges. In civil cases, the court of second instance is an ordinary court of appeal. In criminal cases in which the lower court does not have judicial authority, it is itself the court of first instance. In other criminal cases it is an appeal court as far as the appeal is based on an attack against the lower court's assessment of the facts when determining the guilt of the defendant. An appeal based on any other alleged mistakes is brought directly before the Supreme Court.

The Supreme Court *(Høyesterett)* is the court of last resort. There are 18 Supreme Court judges. Each individual case is heard by 5 judges. Some major cases are determined in plenary session. The Supreme Court may in general examine every aspect of the case and the handling of it by the lower courts. However, in criminal cases the Court may not overrule the lower court's assessment of the facts as far as the guilt of the defendant is concerned.

The Court of Impeachment *(Riksretten)* is composed of 5 judges of the Supreme Court and 10 members of Parliament.

All serious offences are prosecuted by the State. The Public Prosecution Authority *(Påtalemyndigheten)* consists of the Attorney General *(Riksadvokaten)*, 18 district attorneys *(statsadvokater)* and legally qualified officers of the ordinary police force. Counsel for the defence is in general provided for by the State.

Religion. There is freedom of religion, the Church of Norway (Evangelical Lutheran), however, being the national church, endowed by the State. Its clergy are nominated by the King. Ecclesiastically Norway is divided into 11 *Bispedømmer* (bishoprics), 96 *Prostier* (provostships or archdeaconries) and 624 *Prestegjeld* (clerical districts). There were 197,645 members of registered and unregistered religious communities outside the Evangelical Lutheran Church, subsidized by central government and local authorities in 1990. The Roman Catholics are under a Bishop at Oslo, a Vicar Apostolic at Trondheim and a Vicar Apostolic at Tromsø.

Education. There is free compulsory schooling in primary and lower secondary schools for 9 years starting at age 7. In 1989 there were 4,310 nursery schools for children under 7 with 128,237 children and 33,075 staff. In 1989–90 there were 3,442 primary and lower secondary schools with 482,961 pupils and 34,021 teachers; 84 schools for the disabled with 2,427 pupils and 1,049 teachers; 854 upper secondary schools with 223,989 pupils and 19,146 teachers; and 213 colleges, with 70,000 students and 3,187 teachers.

There are 4 universities (Bergen, founded 1948; Oslo, 1811; Tromsø, 1968; and Trondheim, 1910) and 10 specialized institutions of equivalent status. In 1989–90 these had 56,622 students and 4,024 academic staff.

Health. In 1990 there were 12,952 doctors, 4,949 dentists and 55,968 nurses.

Social Security. In 1989, about 120,800m. kroner were paid under different social insurance schemes, amounting to approximately 23% of the net national income.

The National Insurance Act of 17 June 1966, which came into force on 1 Jan. 1967, replaced the schemes relating to old age pensions, disability benefits, widows' and mothers' pensions, benefits to unmarried women, 'survivors' benefit for children and rehabilitation aid. Schemes relating to health insurance, unemployment insurance and occupational injury insurance were revised and incorporated in National Insurance Scheme on 1 Jan. 1971. As from 1 Jan. 1981, benefits to divorced and separated supporters also are covered by the National Insurance Scheme.

The following conspectus gives a survey of schemes established by law. Some municipalities grant additional benefits to old-age, disablement and survivor's pensions.

Type of scheme	Intro- duced [1]	Scope	Principal benefits as from 1 Oct. 1990
National insurance	1967 (1990)		
Medical care and sickness cash benefits [2]	1911	All residents	Medical benefits: all hospital expenses; cost share of expense of medical consultation, important medicines, travel expenses, etc. (such costs exceeding 880kr. a calendar year are paid in full by the National Insurance).
		Nearly all wage-earners	Daily sickness allowances: kr. 65 to 72·85 per day cash (5 days a week). The present sickness allowance scheme (established 1972) entitles employees to a daily allowance equal to 100% of their gross earned income (within certain limits) from and including the first day of absence; self-employed persons, ordinarily 65% of gross earned income as from the 15th day. Supplementary insurance available
		All female residents giving birth	Maternity allowances: same as sickness allowances for 140 days (or 80% of allowance for 172 days) (time sharing with the father is possible) or a lump sum of kr. 8,725 per child
Unemployment benefits [2]	1939	Nearly all wage-earners	Daily allowance during unemployment kr. 52 to 408 per day, excluding supplement for supported child(ren) (six days a week). Contributions to training and retraining, removal expenses, wage subsidies

For notes *see* p. 1048.

Type of scheme	Intro- duced [1]	Scope	Principal benefits as from 1 Oct. 1990
Rehabilitation bene- fits [3]	1961	Persons unfit for work because of disablement and persons who have a substantially limited general functional ca- pacity	Training; treatment; rehabilitation al- lowance grants and loans Full rehabilitation allowance equals old age pension (however, no special supplement is granted, see below.)
Disability benefits [3]	1961	All residents	*A basic grant* and *an assistance grant* to persons with special needs. Basic grant: kr. 4,800 to kr. 15,960 per annum. Assistance grant: kr. 7.2,980, may be increased for children below 18 years of age to a maximum of kr. 44,688 per annum
		All residents between 16 and 67 years of age	Disability pension to persons between 16 and 67 years of age, occu- pationally disabled by at least 50%, unfit for rehabilitation. Full disability pension equals old age pension
Occupational injury benefits [1] (industrial workers 1895; fishermen 1909; seamen 1913; military personnel 1953, combined in the act of occupational injury insurance 1960)	1895	All employed persons, drafted military per- sonnel, school children and students; self- employed on a volun- tary basis	The ordinary benefits of the National Insurance, alternative calculation of pensions etc. which in many cases are more favourable for the insured per- son—or his survivors than the or- dinary rules *An occupational injury compensation,* alone or in addition to a disability pension
Old age pensions [3]	1937	All persons above 67 years of age	Basic pensions: Single, kr. 34,000; couples, kr. 51,000 per annum; sup- plementary pensions based on pre- vious pensionable income; supple- ment for supported spouse kr. 17,000 per annum; supplement for supported child(ren) kr. 8,500 to kr. 4,250 per child per annum; *see below* under 'Special supplement' and 'Compensa- tion supplement'
Death grants	1967	All residents	A certain amount fixed by the Stort- ing, for the time being kr. 4,000
Survivors' benefits [3]	1965	All residents	Full pension = kr. 34,000 per annum + 55% of the supplementary pension due to the deceased, *transitional benefits,* child care allowance and ed- ucational allowances (*see below* under 'Special supplement' and 'Compensation supplement')
Children's pension [3]	1958	Under 18 (20) years of age, after loss of one or both parents	40% of basic amount (kr. 13,600) for first child, 25% (kr. 8,500) for each additional child. If both parents are dead, full survivors' pension for first, 40% of basic amount for second, 25% third, etc., child
Benefits to unmarried supporters [3]	1965	Unmarried mothers or fathers	An additional maternity benefit of kr. 9,680, transitional benefit, full amount kr. 34,000 per annum, child care allowance and educational al- lowances (*see below* under 'Special supplement' and 'Family allow- ances')
Benefits to divorced and separated supporters [4] For notes *see* p. 1048.	1972	Divorced and separat- ed supporters	Same kind of benefits as unmarried supporters above

Type of scheme	Intro- duced [1]	Scope	Principal benefits as from 1 Oct. 1990
Benefits to unmarried persons forced to live at home [3]	1965	Unmarried persons under 67 years of age having stayed at home for at least 5 years to give necessary care and attention to parents or other near relatives	Transitional benefit or a pension kr. 34,000 per annum, educational allowances (*see below* under 'Special supplement' and 'Compensation supplement')
Special supplement to National Insurance pensions or transitional benefits	1969 (1989)	Pensioners and persons with transitional allowance on basic rates	Full special supplement, 58% of basic amount, *i.e.* kr. 19,720. For a married pensioner the rate may be different. If the pensioner supports a spouse who is 60 years or older, the rate is 106·5%, *i.e.* kr. 36,210. If the spouse has a pension of his/her own, the rate is 53·25%, *i.e.* kr. 18,105
Compensation supplement to National Insurance pensions or transitional benefits	1970 (1989)	Pensioners, persons with transitional benefits (except unmarried, divorced and separated supporters) or rehabilitation allowances	Full compensation supplement kr. 500 for single persons and kr. 750 for married couples per annum
Family allowances	1946 (1989)	All families with children under 16 years of age	Kr. 8,748 per annum for the first child, kr. 9,240 for the second, kr. 10,656 for the third, kr. 11,280 for the fourth and kr. 11,664 for the fifth and each additional child. Single supporters receive benefits for one child more than the actual number. Families resident in certain districts north of the Arctic Circle receive an additional amount of kr. 3,600 per child
War pensions	1946 (1989)	War victims, 1939—45	Pensions up to kr. 150,720 per annum for single pensioners/couples (excluding supplement for supported child(ren); widows' and children's pensions)
Special pension schemes:		Persons with at least: [5]	Maximum old-age pension:
Forestry workers	1952 (1989)	750 premium weeks (1,500 ,, ,,)	Kr. 34,000 per annum (for supported spouse an additional 33^1/3%, 10% supplement per child, maximum 5 children)
Fishermen	1958 (1989)	750 premium weeks (1,500 ,, ,,)	Kr. 34,000 per annum (for supported spouse an additional 50%, 30% supplement per child)
Seamen	1948 (1989)	150 months service (360 ,, ,,)	Kr. 111,409 [6] per annum (officers) Kr. 79,578 [6] ,, ,, (others) (no spouse supplement, an additional 10% per child)

[1] Date of latest revision of law in brackets.
[2] Transferred to national insurance scheme and revised in 1971.
[3] Transferred to national insurance scheme and revised in 1967.
[4] Transferred to national insurance scheme and revised in 1981.
[5] Requirements for maximum pensions in brackets.
[6] Supplements for service during war not included.

Provisions have been laid down for the integration of more than one benefit, pension, etc., so as to limit the total amount.

As a main rule all running benefits are taxable, while lump sums are not taxed. Certain tax modifications apply to all pensioners and pensioners with no other income than minimum benefits are not charged for tax.

SVALBARD

An archipelago situated between 10° and 35° E. long. and between 74° and 81° N. lat. Total area, 62,000 sq. km (24,000 sq. miles).

The main islands of the archipelago are Spitsbergen (formerly called Vestspitsbergen), Nordaustlandet, Edgeøya, Barentsøya, Prins Karls Forland, Bjørnøya, Hopen, Kong Karls Land, Kvitøya, and many small islands. The arctic climate is tempered by mild winds from the Atlantic.

The archipelago was probably discovered by Norsemen in 1194 and rediscovered by the Dutch navigator Barents in 1596. In the 17th century the very lucrative whale-hunting caused rival Dutch, British and Danish–Norwegian claims to sovereignty and quarrels about the hunting-places. But when in the 18th century the whale-hunting ended, the question of the sovereignty of Svalbard lost its significance; it was again raised in the 20th century, owing to the discovery and exploitation of coalfields. By a treaty, signed on 9 Feb. 1920 in Paris, Norway's sovereignty over the archipelago was recognized. On 14 Aug. 1925 the archipelago was officially incorporated in Norway.

Total population on 31 Dec. 1989 was 3,544, of whom 1,125 were Norwegians, 2,407 Soviet citizens, and 12 Poles. Coal is the principal product. There are 2 Norwegian and 2 Soviet mining camps. 259,183 tonnes of coal were produced from Norwegian mines in 1989 values at 100·91m. kroner.

Norwegian and foreign companies have been prospecting for oil. So far 5 deep drillings have been made, but oil and gas finds have not been reported.

There are Norwegian meteorological and/or radio stations at the following places: Bjørnøya (since 1920), Hopen (1945), Isfjord Radio (1933), Longyearbyen (1930), Svalbard Lufthavn (1975) and Ny-Ålesund (1961). A research station, administered by Norsk Polarinstitutt, was erected at Ny-Ålesund in 1968 for various observations and investigations. An airport near Longyearbyen (Svalbard Lufthavn) opened in 1975.

Norsk Polarinstitutt, Skrifter, Oslo, from 1948 (under different titles from 1922)
Greve, T., *Svalbard: Norway in the Arctic.* Oslo, 1975
Hisdal, V., *Geography of Svalbard.* Norsk Polarinstitutt, Oslo, rev. ed., 1984
Orvin, A. K., 'Twenty-five Years of Norwegian Sovereignty in Svalbard 1925–1950' (in *The Polar Record,* 1951)

JAN MAYEN

This bleak, desolate and mountainous island of volcanic origin and partly covered by glaciers, is situated 71° N. lat. and 8° 30' W. long., 300 miles NNE of Iceland. The total area is 380 sq. km (147 sq. miles). Beerenberg, its highest peak, reaches a height of 2,277 metres. Volcanic activity, which had been dormant, was reactivated in Sept. 1970.

The island was possibly discovered by Henry Hudson in 1608, and it was first named Hudson's Tutches (Touches). It was again and again rediscovered and re-named. Its present name derives from the Dutch whaling captain Jan Jacobsz May, who indisputably discovered the island in 1614. It was uninhabited, but occasionally visited by seal hunters and trappers, until 1921 when Norway established a radio and meteorological station. On 8 May 1929 Jan Mayen was officially proclaimed as incorporated in the Kingdom of Norway. Its relation to Norway was finally settled by law of 27 Feb. 1930. A LORAN station (1959) and a CONSOL station (1968) have been established.

BOUVET ISLAND
Bouvetøya

This uninhabited volcanic island, mostly covered by glaciers and situated 54° 25' S. lat. and 3° 21' E. long., was discovered in 1739 by a French naval officer, Jean Baptiste Loziert Bouvet, but no flag was hoisted till, in 1825, Capt. Norris raised the

Union Jack. In 1928 Great Britain waived its claim to the island in favour of Norway, which in Dec. 1927 had occupied it. A law of 27 Feb. 1930 declared Bouvetøya a Norwegian dependency. The area is 50 sq. km (19 sq. miles). From 1977 Norway has had an automatic meteorological station on the island, and 5 men operated a meteorological station there during the 1978–79 season.

PETER I ISLAND
Peter I Øy

This uninhabited island, situated 68° 48' S. lat. and 90° 35' W. long., was sighted in 1821 by the Russian explorer, Admiral von Bellingshausen. The first landing was made in 1929 by a Norwegian expedition which hoisted the Norwegian flag. On 1 May 1931 Peter I Island was placed under Norwegian sovereignty, and on 24 March 1933 it was incorporated in Norway as a dependency. The area is 180 sq. km (69 sq. miles).

QUEEN MAUD LAND
Dronning Maud Land

On 14 Jan. 1939 the Norwegian Cabinet placed that part of the Antarctic Continent from the border of Falkland Islands dependencies in the west to the border of the Australian Antarctic Dependency in the east (between 20° W. and 45° E.) under Norwegian sovereignty. The territory had been explored only by Norwegians and hitherto been ownerless. Since 1949 expeditions from various countries have explored the area. In 1957 Dronning Maud Land was given the status of a Norwegian dependency.

DIPLOMATIC REPRESENTATIVES

Of Norway in Great Britain (25 Belgrave Sq., London, SW1X 8QD)
Ambassador: Kjell Eliassen, GCMG (accredited 15 Feb. 1989).

Of Great Britain in Norway (Thomas Heftyesgate 8, 0244 Oslo, 2)
Ambassador: David Ratford, CMG, CVO.

Of Norway in the USA (2720 34th St., NW, Washington, D.C., 20008)
Ambassador: Kjeld Vibe.

Of the USA in Norway (Drammensveien 18, 0244 Oslo, 2)
Ambassador: Loret Miller Ruppe.

Of Norway to the United Nations
Ambassador: Martin Huslid.

Further Reading

Central Bureau of Statistics. *Statistisk Årbok*; *Statistical Yearbook of Norway.—Economic survey* (annual, from 1935; with English summary from 1952, now published in *Økonomiske Analyser*, annual).—*Historisk Statistikk*; *Historical Statistics.—Statistisk Månedshefte* (with English index)
Norges Statskalender. From 1816; annual from 1877
Facts about Norway. Ed. by Aftenposten. 20th ed. Oslo, 1986–87
Arntzen, J. G. and Knudsen, B. B., *Political Life and Institutions in Norway.* Oslo, 1981
Derry, T. K., *A History of Modern Norway, 1814–1972.* OUP, 1973.—*A History of Scandinavia.* London, 1979
Greve, T., *Haakon VI of Norway, Founder of a New Monarchy.* London, 1983
Imber, W., *Norway.* Oslo, 1980
Larsen, K., *A History of Norway.* New York, 1948
Midgaard, J., *A Brief History of Norway.* Oslo, 1969

Orvik, N. (ed.) *Fears and Expectations: Norwegian Attitudes Toward European Integration*. Oslo, 1972
Popperwell, R. G., *Norway*. London, 1972
Sather, L. B., *Norway*. [Bibliography] Oxford and Santa Barbara, 1986
Selbyg, A., *Norway Today: An Introduction to Modern Norwegian Society*. Oslo, 1986

National library: The University Library, Drammensvein 42b, 0255 Oslo.
National statistical office: Central Bureau of Statistics, PB 8131 Dep., 0033 Oslo 1.

OMAN

Capital: Muscat
Population: 1·5m. (1991)
GNP per capita: US$4,770 (1990)

Saltanat 'Uman

(Sultanate of Oman)

HISTORY. Oman was dominated by Portugal from 1507–1649. The Al-Busaid family assumed power in 1744 and have ruled to the present day. The Sultanate of Oman was known as the Sultanate of Muscat and Oman until 1970.

AREA AND POPULATION. Oman is bounded in the north-east by the Gulf of Oman and south-east by the Arabian Sea (a coastline of some 1,700 km), south-west by Yemen and north-west by Saudi Arabia and the United Arab Emirates. There is an enclave at the northern tip of the Musandam Peninsula between the United Arab Emirates of Ras al-Khaimah in the west and Fujairah in the south-east.

The port of Gwadur and a small tract of country on the Baluchistan coast of the Gulf of Oman were handed over to Pakistan on 8 Sept. 1958.

The **Kuria Muria** islands were ceded to the UK in 1854 by the Sultan of Muscat and Oman. On 30 Nov. 1967 the islands were retroceded to the Sultan of Muscat and Oman, in accordance with the wishes of the population.

The Sultanate extends inland to the borders of the Rub' al Khali ('Empty Quarter') across three geographical divisions—a coastal plain, a range of hills and a plateau. The coastal plain varies in width from 10 miles near Suwaiq to practically nothing in the vicinity of Mutrah and Muscat, where the hills descend abruptly into the sea. These hills are for the most part barren. The plateau has an average height of 1,000 ft.

The area is 0·3m. sq. km. Estimated population (1991) 2,142,450, chiefly Arabs, and including 0·35m. foreign workers. The capital is Muscat. Estimated population of the Capital area (comprising Bausher, Al Hajar, Muscat, Mutrah, Quriyat, Ruwi and Seeb), 1990, 0·38m.

The country is divided into 7 planning regions:

Region	Population 1990	Regional centres	Population 1990
Muscat	444,472	Muscat	...
Southern (Janubiah)	216,546	Salalah	...
Interior (Dakhiliah)	253,684	Nizwa,	62,880
		Sumail	44,721
Sharqiyah	290,784	Ibra,	21,967
		Sur	59,963
Batinah	581,968	Sohar,	91,521
		Rustaq	66,205
Dhahirah	180,781	Al-Buraimi	40,160
Musandam	31,766	Khasab	19,702

CLIMATE. Oman has a desert climate, with exceptionally hot and humid months from April to Oct., when temperatures may reach 117°F (47°C). From Dec. to the end of March, the climate is more pleasant. Light monsoon rains fall in the south from June to Sept., with highest amounts in the western highland region. Muscat. Jan. 72°F (22·2°C), July 91°F (33·3°C). Annual rainfall 4·0" (99·1 mm). Salalah. Jan. 72°F (22·2°C), July 78°F (25·6°C). Annual rainfall 3·3" (81·3 mm).

RULER. The present Sultan is Qaboos bin Said (born Nov. 1940). He took over from his father Said bin Taimur, on 23 July 1970 in a Palace coup.

CONSTITUTION AND GOVERNMENT. Oman is an absolute monarchy and there is no formal constitution. The Sultan legislates by decree and appoints a Cabinet to assist him; and he is nominally Prime Minister and Minister of Foreign Affairs, Defence and Finance. The other Ministers were in Oct. 1991:

Deputy Prime Ministers: Sayyid Fahr bin Taimur bin Faisal Al Said (*Security and Defence*), Sayyid Fahd bin Mahmud bin Muhammad Al Said (*Legal Affairs*), Qais bin Abdul Mun'im al Zawawi (*Financial and Economic Affairs*). *Agriculture and Fisheries:* Muhammed bin Abdullah bin Zaher al Hinai. *Civil Service:* Ahmad bin Abdul Nabi Macki. *Commerce and Industry:* Salim bin Abdullah al Ghazali. *Communications:* Hamud bin Abdullah al Harthy. *Education and Youth:* Yahya bin Mahfudh al Manthari. *Electricity and Water:* Mohamed bin Ali al Qatabi. *Environment:* Sayyid Shabib bin Taimur Al Said. *Health:* Ali bin Muhammed bin Musa al Raisi. *Housing:* Malik bin Sulaiman al Ma'mari. *Information:* Abdul Aziz bin Muhammed al Rowas. *Interior:* Sayyid Badr bin Saud bin Harib Al Bu Saidi. *Justice, Awqaf and Islamic Affairs:* Sayyid Hilal bin Saud bin Harib Al Bu Saidi. *National Heritage and Culture:* Sayyid Faisal bin Ali Al Said. *Petroleum and Minerals:* Said bin Ahmad al Shanfari. *Posts, Telegraphs and Telephones:* Ahmad bin Suweidan al Baluchi. *Regional Municipalities:* Amour bin Shuwin al Hosni. *Social Affairs:* Mustahail bin Ahmed al Ma'ashani. *Labour and Vocational Training:* Sayid Mutasim bin Hamood al Busaidy. *President, Diwan of the Royal Court:* Sayyid Saif bin Hamad bin Saud. *President of the Palace Office:* Maj.-Gen. Ali bin Majid al Mamari.

In 1991 a new consultative assembly, the *Majlis al Shura*, replaced the former State Consultative Chamber. The Majlis consists of a president and 59 representatives who are nominated one from each governorate, and ultimately approved by the Sultan. It debates domestic issues, but has no legislative or veto powers.

National flag: Red, with a white panel in the upper fly and a green one in the lower fly, and in the canton the national emblem in white.

Local government: Oman is divided into 7 regions *(see above)* and sub-divided into 59 governorates *(wilayats)*, each under a governor.

DEFENCE

Army. The Army consists of 1 headquarter division and 2 headquarter brigades; 1 armoured, 1 reconnaissance, 2 artillery, 8 infantry, 1 infantry reconnaissance, 1 field engineer and 1 airborne regiment. Equipment includes 6 M-60A1 and 33 Chieftain main battle tanks. Strength (1992) about 20,000. (Regiments are of battalion size.)

Navy. The Navy, which is based principally at Seeb (HQ) and Wudam comprises 4 fast missile craft, 4 coastal and 4 inshore patrol craft. Auxiliaries include 1 training ship, 1 logistic support ship, 1 troop transport and 1 survey craft. There are also 2 specially adapted amphibious ships and 3 craft. Naval personnel in 1991 totalled 3,400.

The marine police coastguard, 400 strong in 1991, operate 8 coastal patrol craft and 2 logistics support craft.

The wholly separate Royal Yacht Squadron consists of a 3,800-tonne yacht and an 11,000-tonne support ship.

Air Force. The Air Force, formed in 1959, had in 1987 two strike/interceptor squadrons of Jaguars, a ground attack/interceptor squadron of Hunters, a squadron of Strikemaster light jet training/attack aircraft, 1 DC-8, 3 BAC One-Eleven and 2 Gulfstream VIP transports, 3 C-130H Hercules, 6 Defender and 15 Skyvan light transports, 35 Agusta-Bell 205, 212, 214B and JetRanger, and Bell 214 ST helicopters for security duties, 2 Super Puma VIP helicopters and 2 Bravo piston-engined trainers. Air defence force has batteries of Rapier low-level surface-to-air missiles. Personnel (1992) about 3,000, with 50 combat aircraft.

INTERNATIONAL RELATIONS

Membership. Oman is a member of the UN, the Arab League, the Islamic Conference Organisation and the Gulf Co-operation Council.

Treaties. The Treaty of Friendship, Commerce and Navigation between Britain and the Sultan signed on 20 Dec. 1951, reaffirmed the close ties which have existed between the British Government and the Sultanate of Oman for over a century and a half. A Memorandum of Understanding signed in June 1982 provided for regular consultations on international and bilateral issues.

ECONOMY

Policy. The fourth 5-year plan is running from 1991 to 1995.

Budget. Revenue (1990) OR 2,040m.; expenditure, OR 1,887m.

Currency. The unit of currency is the *Omani rial* (OMR), which replaced the *rial saidi* in 1972. It is divided into 1,000 *baiza*. There are notes of 100, 200 and 500 *baiza* and OR 1, 5, 10, 20 and 50 and coins of 5, 10, 25, 50, 100, 250 and 500 *baiza*. The rial is pegged to the US dollar. The exchange rate in March 1992 was £1 = 675 *baiza*; US$1 = 384 *baiza*.

Banking and Finance. In 1991 there were 25 commercial banks operating, of which 12 were foreign institutions. There are 3 specialized banks: The Oman Development Bank, the Oman Housing Bank and the Oman Bank for Agriculture and Fisheries. The Central Bank of Oman commenced operations in 1975.

Weights and Measures. The metric system is in operation. Transactions in the former measurements are now illegal.

ENERGY AND NATURAL RESOURCES

Electricity. Production (1990) 4,504m. kwh. Supply 240 volts; 50 Hz.

Oil. The economy is dominated by the oil industry, which provided 83% of Government revenue in 1990 and 49·2% of GDP. In 1937 Petroleum Concessions (Oman) Ltd, a subsidiary of the Iraq Petroleum Co. (IPC), was granted a 75-year oil concession over the whole of Oman, although it relinquished Dhofar in 1950. In 1951 the company's name was changed to Petroleum Development (Oman) Ltd (PDO). The company (PDO) regained the Dhofar concession area in 1969. When some of the IPC partners withdrew from Oman in 1960, Shell took over the management of PDO with an 85% interest (minority interests were held by Compagnie Française des Pétroles, 10% and Gulbenkian, 5%). At the beginning of 1974 the Oman Government bought a 25% share in PDO, increasing this retroactively to 60% in July. A Joint Management Committee was established. Other companies active in exploration activities in Oman, with mixed success, include Amoco, Elf-Acquitaine and a consortium of Deminex, Agip and Hispanoil with BP as operator.

Oil in commercial quantities was discovered in 1964 and production began in 1967. Production in 1991 was 34·9m. tonnes. Total proven reserves were estimated in 1991 to be 4,300m. bbls. Since the first oil refinery became operational in 1982, Oman has been self-sufficient in most oil-derived products.

Gas. Production (1990) 4·8m. cu. metres per day. In 1989 reserves were estimated at 283,000m. cu. metres.

Water Resources. Oman relies on a combination of aquifers and desalination plants for its water. Two desalination plants at Ghubriah, built in 1972 and 1982, provide most of the water needs of the capital area.

Minerals. Production of refined copper at the smelter at Sohar was 12,015 tonnes in 1990.

Agriculture. About 0·1m. ha are cultivable. The coastal plain (Batinah) north-west of Muscat is fertile, as are the Dhofar highlands in the south. In the valleys of the interior, as well as on the Batinah coastal plain, date cultivation has reached a high level, and there are possibilities of agricultural development subject to present water resources and soil surveys. The crop of dates was 121,000 tonnes in 1989. Vegetable and fruit production are also important, and livestock are raised in the south where there are monsoon rains. Camels (82,000 in 1988) are bred by the inland tribes.

Fisheries. Catch (1990) 118,640 tonnes. 15% of the catch is taken by industrial ships, the rest by some 85,000 self-employed fishermen.

INDUSTRY. In 1990 manufacturing accounted for only 3·7% of GDP. Apart from oil production, copper mining and smelting and cement production there are light industries, mainly food processing and chemical products. The government gives priority to import substitute industries.

FOREIGN ECONOMIC RELATIONS

Commerce. Main imports include machinery and transport equipment, manufactured goods, food and live animals, petroleum products and chemicals.

Total imports, 1989: OR 868m.; exports (1990), OR 1,481m. (of which oil: OR 1,313m.). The biggest non-oil export is fish, OR 17·8m. in 1990.

Total trade between Oman and UK (British Department of Trade returns, in £1,000 sterling):

	1987	1988	1989	1990	1991
Imports to UK	49,487	146,751	84,009	89,445	73,574
Exports and re-exports from UK	249,916	344,875	298,974	272,072	237,890

COMMUNICATIONS

Roads. A network of adequate graded roads links all the main sectors of population, and only a few mountain villages are not accessible by motor vehicles. In 1991 there were 4,995 km of asphalt roads and 22,443 km of graded roads. In 1990 there were 215,226 vehicles on the road.

Civil Aviation. Gulf Air run regional services in and out of Seeb international airport (20 miles from Muscat) to Bahrain, Doha, Abu Dhabi, Dubai, Karachi, Bombay and operate daily flights to and from London. Other airlines serving Muscat are British Airways, KLM, Thai International, British Caledonian, Air Tanzania, MEA, Kuwait Airlines, PIA, Air India, Iran Air, TMA (cargo) and Trade Winds (cargo). Domestic flights are provided by Oman Aviation Services.

Shipping. In Mutrah a deep-water port (named Mina Qaboos) was completed in 1974. It provides 12 berths, 9 of which are deep-water berths, warehousing facilities and a harbour for dhows and coastal vessels. The annual handling capacity has been raised to 1·5m. tons. Mina Raysut, the port of Salalah, has a capacity of 1m. tons per year.

Telecommunications. In 1989 there were 71 post offices and sub-post offices. The General Telecommunications Organization maintains a telegraph office at Muscat and an automatic telephone exchange (107,409 lines, 1990) which includes Mutrah, Bait-al-Falaj and Mina al-Fahal, the oil company terminal. A high-frequency radio link with Bahrain was opened in Aug. 1972 providing communications with other parts of the world. Internally, there are radio telephone, telex and telegraph services direct between Salalah and Muscat, and a VHF radio link between Seeb international airport and Muscat. The airport is also served by a SITA telex system.

The government-owned Radio Oman broadcasts daily for 19 hours in Arabic and 15 hours in English. A colour (PAL) television service, the government-owned Oman Television, covering Muscat and the surrounding area started transmission in 1974. A television service for Dhofar opened in 1975. In 1991 there were 7 television stations. Total number of televisions, 1,000,033 and radios, 0·9m. in 1991.

Newspapers. There were (1991) 2 Arabic-language and 2 English-language daily newspapers.

EDUCATION AND WELFARE

Education. In 1989–90, there were 741 schools with 323,468 pupils and 13,695 teachers. Plans have been implemented for the development of technical and agricultural training and craft training at intermediate and secondary level. Oman's first university, the Sultan Qaboos University, opened in 1986 and in 1990–91 there were 2,473 students and 337 teachers. There are programmes to combat adult illiteracy.

Health. In 1990 there were 52 hospitals with 3,952 beds, 99 health centres, 1,393 doctors, 97 dentists, 239 pharmacists and 3,944 nursing staff.

DIPLOMATIC REPRESENTATIVES

Of Oman in Great Britain (44A Montpelier Sq., London, SW7 1JJ)
Ambassador: Abdalla Bin Mohamed Al-Dhahab.

Of Great Britain in Oman (PO Box 300, Muscat)
Ambassador: Sir Terence Clark, KBE, CMG, CVO.

Of Oman in the USA (2342 Massachusetts Ave., NW, Washington, D.C., 20008)
Ambassador: Awadh Bader Al-Shanfari.

Of the USA in Oman (PO Box 50202 Madinat Qabos, Muscat)
Ambassador: Richard Boehm.

Of Oman to the United Nations
Ambassador: Salim Bin Mohammed Al-Khussaiby.

Further Reading

Carter, J. R. L., *Tribes of Oman.* London, 1981
Clements, F. A., *Oman: The Reborn Land.* London and New York, 1980.—*Oman.* [Bibliography] Oxford and Santa Barbara, 1981
Graz, L., *The Omani's: Sentinels of the Gulf.* London, 1982
Hawley, D., *Oman and its Rennaissance.* London, 1977
Peterson, J. E., *Oman in the Twentieth Century.* London and New York, 1978
Peyton, W. D., *Oman before 1970: The End of an Era.* London, 1985
Pridham, B. R., (ed.) *Oman: Economic, Social and Strategic Developments.* London, 1987
Shannon, M. O., *Oman and South-Eastern Arabia: A Bibliographic Survey.* Boston, 1978
Skeet, I., *Muscat and Oman: The End of an Era.* London, 1974
Thesiger, W., *Arabian Sands.* London, 1959
Townsend, J., *Oman.* London, 1977
Ward, P., *Travels in Oman.* Cambridge, 1987
Wikan, U., *Behind the Veil in Arabia: Women in Oman.* Johns Hopkins Univ. Press, 1982
Wilkinson, J. C., *The Imanate Tradition of Oman.* CUP, 1987

PAKISTAN

Capital: Islamabad
Population: 114m. (1991)
GNP per capita: US$370 (1989)

Islami Jamhuriya e Pakistan

(Islamic Republic of Pakistan) [1]

HISTORY. Pakistan was constituted as a Dominion on 14 Aug. 1947, under the provisions of the Indian Independence Act, 1947. The Dominion consisted of the following former territories of British India: Baluchistan, East Bengal (including almost the whole of Sylhet, a former district of Assam), North-West Frontier, West Punjab and Sind; and those States which had acceded to Pakistan.

On 23 March 1956 an Islamic republic was proclaimed after the Constituent Assembly had adopted the draft constitution on 29 Feb.

On 7 Oct. 1958 President Mirza declared martial law in Pakistan, dismissed the central and provincial Governments, abolished all political parties and abrogated the constitution of 23 March 1956. Field Marshal Mohammad Ayub Khan, the Army Commander-in-Chief, was appointed as chief martial law administrator and assumed office on 28 Oct. 1958, after Maj.-Gen. Iskander Mirza had handed all powers to him. His authority was confirmed by a ballot in Feb. 1960. He proclaimed a new constitution on 1 March 1962.

On 25 March 1969 President Ayub Khan resigned and handed over power to the army under the leadership of Maj.-Gen. Agha Muhammad Yahya Khan who immediately proclaimed martial law throughout the country, appointing himself chief martial law administrator on the same day. On 29 March 1970 the Legal Framework Order was published, defining a new constitution: Pakistan to be a federal republic with a Moslem Head of State; the National Assembly and Provincial Assemblies to be elected in free and periodical elections, the first of which was held on 7 Dec. 1970.

At the general election the Awami League based in East Pakistan and led by Sheikh Mujibur Rahman gained 167 seats and the Peoples' Party 90. Martial law continued pending the settlement of differences between East and West, which developed into civil war in March 1971. The war ended in Dec. 1971 and the Eastern province declared itself an independent state, Bangladesh. On 20 Dec. 1971 President Yahya Khan resigned and Z. A. Bhutto became President and chief martial law administrator. On 30 Jan. 1972, Pakistan withdrew from the Commonwealth, rejoining on 1 Oct. 1989.

A new Constitution was adopted by the National Assembly on 10 April 1973 and enforced on 14 Aug. 1973. It provided for a federal parliamentary system with the President as constitutional head and the Prime Minister as chief executive. President Bhutto stepped down to become Prime Minister and Fazal Elahi Chaudhry was elected President.

The Chief of the Army Staff, Gen. M. Zia-ul-Haq, proclaimed martial law on 5 July 1977 and the armed forces took control of the administration; scheduled elections were postponed. Mr Bhutto was hanged (for conspiracy to murder) on 4 April 1979. Gen. M. Zia-ul-Haq succeeded Fazal Elahi Chaudhry as President in Sept. 1978.

With the proclamation of martial law the Constitution was kept in abeyance, but not abrogated.

National elections were held in Feb. 1985 on the basis of the 1973 Constitution, amended to provide wider presidential powers. On 19 Dec. 1984 a referendum had been held to determine whether the President should continue in office for a 5-year term, following the elections; results were announced as 98% in favour.

[1] The name 'Pakistan' is a coinage representing 'Punjab, the Afghan border states, Kashmir, Sind and Baluchistan'.

The Pakistan People's Party won 47 seats in the new Assembly, the Muslim League 17 and the Jamaat Islami Party, 9. In March 1985 the President set up a new National Security Council, led by himself; he assumed power to appoint and dismiss ministers and retained the final decision on legislation.

In April 1985 the Council was replaced by a Federal Cabinet. On 30 Dec. 1985 martial law ended. On 6 Aug. 1990 the President, accusing the government of corruption and undermining the constitution, dismissed the Prime Minister, Benazir Bhutto, and all her cabinet, dissolved the National Assembly and declared a state of emergency. New governors were appointed for all four provinces. In Sept. Benazir Bhutto was brought to trial on charges of misconduct and abuse of power.

Governors-General of Pakistan: Quaid-I-Azam Mohammed Ali Jinnah (14 Aug. 1947–11 Sept. 1948); Khawaja Nazimuddin (14 Sept. 1948–18 Oct. 1951; took over the premiership after the assassination of Liaquat Ali Khan); Ghulam Mohammad (19 Oct. 1951–6 Aug. 1955); Maj.-Gen. Iskander Mirza (assumed office of President on 6 Oct. 1955, elected President on 5 March 1956).

Presidents of Pakistan: Maj.-Gen. Iskander Mirza (23 March 1956–28 Oct. 1958); Field Marshal Mohammad Ayub Khan (28 Oct. 1958–25 March 1969); Maj.-Gen. Agha Muhammad Yahya Khan (31 March 1969–20 Dec. 1971); Zulfiqar Ali Bhutto (20 Dec.1971–14 Aug. 1973); Fazal Elahi Chaudhry (14 Aug. 1973–16 Sept. 1978); Gen. Mohammad Zia ul-Haq (16 Sept. 1978–17 Aug. 1988); Ghulam Ishaq Khan (acting 17 Aug. 1988, confirmed 12 Dec. 1988).

AREA AND POPULATION. Pakistan is bounded in the north-west by Afghanistan, north by China, east by India and south by the Arabian Sea. The total area of Pakistan is 307,293 sq. miles (796,095 sq. km); population (1981 census), 84·25m.; males, 44,232,000; females, 40,021,000. Density, 105·8 per sq. km. Estimate (1991) 114m. Urban population (1987), 28·3%. Vital statistics, 1990 (rates per 1,000 population: Birth, 43·3; growth, 0·3. Population density, 1990, 138 per sq. km. Expectation of life was 55 years in 1989.

The population of the principal cities:

Census of 1981

Islamabad	201,000	Multan	730,000	Jhang	195,000
Karachi	5,103,000	Gujranwala	597,000	Sukkur	191,000
Lahore	2,922,000	Peshawar	555,000	Bahawalpur	178,000
Faisalabad	1,092,000	Sialkot	296,000	Kasur	155,000
Rawalpindi	928,000	Sargodha	294,000	Gujrat	154,000
Hyderabad	795,000	Quetta	285,000	Okara	154,000

Population of the provinces (census of 1981) was (1,000):

	Area (sq. km)	1981 census population Total	Male	Female	Urban	1981 density per sq. km (number)	Estimated total 1985
North-West Frontier Province	74,521	11,061	5,761	5,300	1,665	148	12,287
Federally admin. Tribal Areas	27,219	2,199	1,143	1,056	–	81	2,467
Fed. Cap. Territory Islamabad	907	340	185	155	204	376	379
Punjab	205,344	47,292	24,860	22,432	13,051	230	53,840
Sind	140,914	19,029	9,999	9,030	8,243	135	21,682
Baluchistan	347,190	4,332	2,284	2,048	677	12	4,908

There are some 3m. Afghan refugees mainly in the North-West Frontier Province.
Urdu is the national language; English is used in business, higher education and in central government.

CLIMATE. A weak form of tropical monsoon climate occurs over much of the country, with arid conditions in the north and west, where the wet season is only from Dec. to March. Elsewhere, rain comes mainly in the summer. Summer temperatures are high everywhere, but winters can be cold in the mountainous north. Islamabad. Jan. 50°F (10°C), July 90°F (32·2°C). Annual rainfall 36" (900 mm). Karachi. Jan. 61°F (16·1°C), July 86°F (30°C). Annual rainfall 8" (196 mm).

Lahore. Jan. 53°F (11·7°C), July 89°F (31·7°C). Annual rainfall 18" (452 mm).
Multan. Jan. 51°F (10·6°C), July 93°F (33·9°C). Annual rainfall 7" (170 mm).
Quetta. Jan. 38°F (3·3°C), July 80°F (26·7°C). Annual rainfall 10" (239 mm).

CONSTITUTION AND GOVERNMENT. Under the Constitution of 1973 Parliament is bi-cameral, comprising a Senate of 63 members (14 from each province elected by the members of the Provincial Assemblies 2 from the federal capital area elected by the National Assembly and 5 from tribal areas), and a National Assembly of 207 directly elected Moslem males, 20 women elected by the National Assembly and 10 religious minority representatives.

The Constitution obliges the Government to enable the people to order their lives in accordance with Islam. The Constitution (Ninth Amendment) Bill, 1986, consolidated Islam as the basis of law. An Ombudsman was appointed in Jan. 1983.

Following the President's dismissal of Benazir Bhutto's government in Aug. 1990, elections were held in Oct. 1990 for the 217 contestable seats in the National Assembly. The 8-party coalition of the Islamic Democratic Alliance (IDA) won 105 seats, and the Pakistan Democratic Alliance, headed by Benazir Bhutto's Pakistan People's Party (PPP), won 45. The electorate was 49m.; turn-out was low. There were 1,331 candidates.

Elections to 42 seats of the Senate were held in March 1991. The IDA won 30 seats, the PPP, 5.

President, Head of State: Ghulam Ishaq Khan.

On 6 Nov. 1990 Nawaz Sharif (b.1949) was elected *Prime Minister* by 153 votes to 39. In March 1992 his cabinet included:

Minister of Communications: Murtaza Khan Jatoi. *Railways:* Gulam Ahmed Bilour. *Production:* Islam Nabi. *Housing and Works:* Tariq Mahmood. *Narcotics Control:* Chandar Singh. *Finance:* Sartaj Aziz. *Environment and Urban Affairs:* Anwar Saifullah. *Defence:* Ghous Ali Shah. *Interior:* Shujat Hussain. *Education:* Syed Fakhar Imam. *Commerce:* Naeem Khan. *Petroleum and Natural Resources:* Nisar Ali Khan. *Planning and Development:* Hamid Nasir Chatta. *Health:* Nawaz Food, Agriculture and Co-operatives: Lieut.-Gen. Abdul Majid Malik. *Labour, Manpower and Overseas Pakistanis:* Muhammad Ijaz-ul-Haq. *Kashmir and Northern Affairs:* Mehtab Ahmed Khan. *States and Frontier Regions:* Yaqub Khan Nasser. *Religious Affairs:* Sattar Khan Niazi. *Industry:* Rashid Ahmed. *Law and Justice:* Abdul Ghafoor. *Local Government and Rural Development:* Ghulam Dastagir Khan. *Water and Power:* Mohammad Yousaf. *Inter-Provincial Co-ordination:* Aslam Khan Khattak. *Science and Technology:* Bukhash Soomro.

National flag: Green, charged at the centre, with a white crescent and white 5-pointed star, a white vertical stripe at the mast to one-quarter of the flag.

Provincial and local government. Pakistan comprises the Federal Capital Territory (Islamabad), the provinces of the Punjab, the North-West Frontier (NWFP), Sind and Baluchistan, and the tribal areas of the north-west. The provincial capitals are Peshawar (NWFP), Lahore (Punjab), Karachi (Sind) and Quetta (Baluchistan). Provincial governors are appointed by the President and are assisted by elected provincial assemblies. Elections for all 4 assemblies were held in Oct. 1990. Municipal elections were held in the Punjab in Dec. 1991.

Within the provinces there are divisions administered by Commissioners appointed by the President; the divisions are divided into districts and agencies administered by Deputy Commissioners or Political Agents who are responsible to the Provincial Governments.

The tribal areas (Khyber, Kurram, Malakand, Mohmand, North Waziristan, South Waziristan) are administered by political agents responsible to the federal government.

Kashmir. Pakistan controls the northern and western portions of Kashmir, an area of about 84,160 sq. km with a population of about 2·8m. in 1985. Under a United Nations resolution of 1949 its future was to be decided by plebiscite; it is still a disputed territory.

The people of Azad Kashmir (the west) have their own Assembly (48 members including 2 women), their own Council (of 14 members), High Court and Supreme Court. There is a Parliamentary form of Government with a Prime Minister as the executive head and the President as the Constitutional head. Elections to the Legislative's 40 general seats are to be held within 10 days of the general elections in Pakistan, according to a presidential proclamation of 8 Oct. 1977. The seat of government is Muzaffarabad. The elections held in June 1991 were declared invalid by the Prime Minister, Mumtaz Rathore (PPP). He was arrested in July and replaced by the President, Sardar Abdul Qayyum Khan (Islamic Conference).

The Pakistan Government is directly responsible for Gilgit, Diamir and Baltistan (the north).

Local government elections scheduled for Nov. 1991 were postponed to April 1992.

DEFENCE

Army. The Army consists of 2 armoured and 19 infantry divisions; 6 independent armoured, 6 independent infantry, 7 artillery, 5 engineer and 4 anti-aircraft brigades; 3 armoured reconnaissance regiments and 1 Special Services Group. Equipment includes 150 M-47, 50 T-54/-55, 280 M-48 and 1,500 Chinese Type-59 and -69 main battle tanks. The Army has an air component with about 150 fixed-wing aircraft for transport, reconnaissance and observation duties and 110 helicopters for anti-armour operations, transport, liaison and training. Strength (1992) 500,000, with a further 500,000 reservists. There are also 238,000 men in paramilitary units: National Guard, Frontier Corps, Pakistan Rangers, Coast Guard and Frontier Constabulary.

Navy. 8 ex-US frigates form the core of the surface fleet. The smaller craft are mostly of Chinese origin.

The combatant fleet comprises 6 French-built diesel submarines, about 6 midget submarines for swimmer delivery, 1 UK-built 'County' class destroyer, *Babur*, converted to carry up to to 4 Sea King anti-submarine helicopters, 2 ex-US Second World War vintage destroyers, 4 ex-US Brooke class guided missile frigates armed with Standard SM-1 surface-to-air missiles, 6 other frigates, 8 fast missile craft, 4 hydrofoil torpedo craft, 4 coastal and 9 inshore patrol craft, and 2 coastal minesweepers. Auxiliaries include 2 fleet replenishment tankers, 1 survey ship and 1 salvage tug, as well as a static ex-US repair ship. There are about a dozen minor auxiliaries.

The Air force operates 6 Atlantic aircraft under naval control for maritime patrol duties, whilst the Navy operates 2 F27 patrol aircraft, 6 Sea King helicopters and 4 Alouette III anti-submarine and liaison helicopters. All destroyers and frigates have helicopter decks capable of operating an Alouette.

The principal naval base and dockyard are at Karachi. Naval personnel in 1991 totalled 20,000.

A navy-subordinated Maritime Safety Agency 2,000 strong (1991) operates 1 ex-naval destroyer and 4 fast inshore patrol craft on economic exclusion zone protection duties.

Air Force. The Pakistan Air Force came into being on 14 Aug. 1947. It has its headquarters at Peshawar and is organized within 3 air defence sectors, in the northern, central and southern areas of the country. Air defence units include 2 squadrons of F-16 Fighting Falcons, 3 squadrons of F-7P Skybolts and 4 squadrons of Chinese-built F-6s (MiG-19). Tactical units include 3 squadrons of Mirage III-EP/5 supersonic fighters and 3 with A-5 fighter-bombers, 1 squadron equipped with Mirage III-RP reconnaissance aircraft, and 1 with C-130 Hercules turboprop transports. Flying training schools are equipped with Masshaq (Saab Supporter) armed piston-engined primary trainers, T-33 and T-37B/C jet trainers supplied by the USA, Mirage III-DPs and Chinese-built FT-5s (two-seat MiG-17s) and FT-6s (two-seat MiG-19s). A VIP transport squadron operates the Presidential F27 turboprop aircraft, 3 four-jet Boing 707s, 3 twin-jet Falcon 20s and a Puma helicopter. There is a flying college at Risalpur and an aeronautical engineering college at Korangi Creek. Total strength in 1992 was 470 combat aircraft and 45,000 personnel.

INTERNATIONAL RELATIONS

Membership. Pakistan is a member of the UN, the Commonwealth, the Colombo Plan, and Regional Co-operation for Development.

External Debt (30 June 1989), US$19,983·17m.

ECONOMY

Policy. The 7th Five-Year Plan is running from 1988 to 1993. It envisages a fixed investment of Rs 642,000m. Since 1991 investors have no longer been required to seek government permission to set up industrial units, except in arms and alcohol production.

Budget. Total outlay of the 1990–91 budget, Rs 230,185·4m. Revenue receipts, Rs 141,188·9m. (including Rs 115,477·6m. tax revenue); capital receipts, Rs 25,648·9m. Current expenditure, Rs 161,779·1m., including defence, Rs 63,173·1m., domestic debt servicing, Rs 39,822·3m., foreign debt servicing, Rs 13,544·5m., administration, Rs 7,016·8m., law and order, Rs 3,302·5m., community and social services, 7,344·5m.

The 1991-92 budget envisaged revenue of Rs 153,400m. and current expenditure of Rs 185,600m. Defence spending, Rs 71,000m.

Currency. The monetary unit is the *Pakistan rupee* (PKR) of 100 *paisas*. There are notes of R1, 5, 10, 50 and 100; and coins of 1, 5, 10, 25 and 50 paisas. Currency in circulation in March 1992, Rs 116,856m. In March 1991 Rs 43·20 = £1; Rs 24·60 = US$1.

Banking and Finance. As from 1 Jan. 1985, banks and other financial institutions abandoned, in conformity with Islamic doctrine, the payment of interest on new transactions. This does not apply to international business, but does apply to the domestic business of foreign banks operating in Pakistan. Investment partnerships, between bank and customer, replaced straight loans at interest. In Dec. 1991 the Federal Shariat Court pronounced that interest or usury (*riba*) is un-Islamic and therefore illegal.

The State Bank of Pakistan is the central bank; it came into operation as the Central Bank on 1 July 1948 with an authorized capital of Rs 30m. and was nationalized in Jan. 1974. At end June 1988 total assets or liabilities of the issue department amounted to Rs 91,206m. and those of the banking department Rs 82,253m.; total deposits, Rs 68,163m. It is the bank of issue, custodian of foreign exchange reserves and banker for the federal and provincial governments and for scheduled banks. It also manages the rupee public debt of federal and provincial governments. It provides short-term loans to the Government and commercial banks and short and medium-term loans to specialized banks. The Bank's subsidiary Federal Bank for Co-operatives makes loans to provincial co-operative banks.

In 1991 there were 10 Pakistani and 20 foreign banks. Banks were nationalized in 1974, but a federal government decision of Dec. 1990 again allows banks in the private sector. It was announced in Nov. 1990 that 51% of the equity of state-owned banks was to be privatized in 2 phases. Total liabilities or assets of all scheduled banks stood at Rs 481,456·7m., of which time liabilities, Rs 115,184·8m., on the last working day of June, 1988. The National Bank of Pakistan acts as an agent of the State Bank for transacting Government business and managing currency chests at places where the State Bank has no offices of its own.

There are stock exchanges at Karachi and Lahore.

Weights and Measures. The metric system is in general use.

ENERGY AND NATURAL RESOURCES

Electricity. Installed capacity of the state power system in 1990 was 8,430 mw. Total generated electrical energy in 1986–87, 28,236m. kwh; 15,241m. kwh of this was hydro-electricity, the main source being the Tarbela Dam. By March 1990 31,831 villages (of a total 43,244) had access to electric power. Supply 230 volts; 50 Hz.

Oil. Oil comes mainly from the Potowar Plain, from fields at Meyal, Tut, Balkassar, Joya Mair and Dhullian. Production in 1991 was 3·36m. tonnes. Oil reserves were also found at Dhodak in Dec. 1976. Exploitation is mainly through government incentives and concessions to foreign private sector companies. The Pak-Arab refinery pipeline runs 865 km. from Karachi to Multan; capacity, 4·5m. tonnes of oil annually.

Gas. Gas pipelines from Sui to Karachi (345 miles) and Multan (200) supply natural gas to industry and domestic consumers. A pipeline between Quetta and Shikarpur was constructed in 1982. There are 4 other productive fields. Reserves (1983), 500,000m. cu. metres; production in 1987–88 was 12,383m. cu. metres.

Water. The Indus water treaty of 1960, concluded between India and Pakistan, has created the basis for a large-scale development programme. The Indus Basin Development Fund Agreement has been subscribed by Australia, Canada, Federal Republic of Germany, New Zealand, UK and USA and is administered by the International Bank; the works to be constructed call for expenditure of US$1,000m. The main purpose of the treaty is the division of the water power of the Indus and its 5 tributaries between India and Pakistan. After the construction of some 460 miles of canals, the Indus and the 2 western tributaries will serve Pakistan and the entire flow of the 3 eastern tributaries will be released for use in India.

The largest project is the construction of the Tarbela Dam, an earth-and-rock filled dam on the river Indus, 485 ft high, which has a gross storage capacity of 11·1m. acre feet of water for irrigation.

The Lloyd Barrage and Canal Construction Scheme, consists of a barrage across the river Indus at Sukkur and 7 canals—4 on the left and 3 on the right bank. Another barrage across the Indus, 4$\frac{1}{2}$ miles north of Kotri, called the Ghulam Muhammad Barrage, was completed in 1955. The Taunsa barrage on the Indus, 80 miles downstream of Kalabagh, was completed in 1958. The Gudu barrage, 10 miles from Kashmore, was completed in 1962.

The province of the Punjab set up in 1949 the Thal Development Authority to colonize the Thal desert between the Indus and Jhelum rivers.

The Chashma canal will carry water 172 miles across Dera Ismail Khan from the Chashma barrage on the Indus. The Mangla Dam on the Jhelum was inaugurated in Nov. 1967.

Minerals. The main agencies are the Pakistan Mineral Development Corporation, the Resource Development Corporation and the Gemstone Corporation of Pakistan. Coal is mined at Sharigh and Harnai on the Sind–Pishin railway and in the Bolan pass, also in Sor Range and Degari in the Quetta–Pishin district and in the Punjab; total recoverable reserves, about 480m. tonnes, mainly low-grade. A further 55m. tonnes was found at Lakhra in 1980 and reserves of over 500m. tonnes were found in the 300 sq. mile Thatta Sadha field in 1981. Copper ore reserves at Saindak, in Baluchistan, 412m. tons, containing (1984 estimate) 1·69m. tons of copper; 2·24m. oz. of gold; 2·2m. oz. of silver. Chromite is extracted in and near Muslimbagh. Limestone is quarried generally. Gypsum is mined in the Sibi district and elsewhere; reserves (1983), about 370m. tonnes. Iron ore is being worked in Kalabagh and elsewhere; reserves, about 400m. tonnes, low-grade. A further 18m. tonnes, high-grade, has been found in Baluchistan. Uranium has been found in Dera Ghazi Khan.

Production (tonnes, 1988–89): Coal, 2·62m.; chromite, 12,000; limestone, 7·25m.; gypsum, 426,000; rock salt, 620,000; fire clay, 118,000. Other minerals of which useful deposits have been found are magnesite, sulphur, barites, marble, bauxite, antimony ore, bentonite, celestite, dolomite, fireclay, fluorite, fuller's earth, phosphate rock, silica sand and soapstone.

Agriculture. The entire area in the north and west is covered by great mountain ranges. The rest of the country consists of a fertile plain watered by 5 big rivers and their tributaries. Agriculture is dependent almost entirely on the irrigation system based on these rivers. Areas irrigated, 1987: Punjab, 11·8m. ha; Sind, 3·3m.; NWFP, 840,000; Baluchistan, 520,000. Agriculture employs half the workforce and in 1989–90 contributed 26% of GDP. The main crops are wheat, cotton, maize, sugar-cane and rice, while the Quetta and Kalat divisions (Baluchistan) are known for their fruits and dates.

Pakistan is self-sufficient in wheat, rice and sugar. Areas harvested, 1989–90: Wheat, 7·76m. ha; rice, 2·12m. ha; sugar, 0·84m. ha; cotton, 2·62m. ha.

Production, 1989–90, in 1,000 tonnes: Rice (cleaned), 3,220; wheat, 15,000; sugar-cane, 36,180; cotton, 1,455; maize, 1,770.

An ordinance of Jan. 1977 reduced the upper limit of land holding to 100 irrigated or 200 non-irrigated acres; it also replaced the former land revenue system with a new agricultural income tax, from which holders of up to 25 irrigated or 50 unirrigated acres are exempt. Of about 4m. farms, 89% are of less than 25 acres. Of the surveyed area of 156m. acres, cultivated land accounts for 63m. acres, of which 11m. acres consist of fallow land, so that the net area sown is 52m. acres.

Livestock, 1989–90 (in 1m.): Cattle, 17·6; buffaloes, 14·7; sheep, 9·2; goats, 35·4; camels, 1; poultry, 184·7m.

Dairy products, 1989–90 (in 1,000 tonnes): Mutton, 652; beef, 658; poultry, 195; wool, 58·9; milk, 14,528,000. 4·68m. eggs were produced.

Forestry. In 1989–90 the forest area was 3m. ha, some 3·8% of the total land area. The government considers a 20-25% coverage desirable for economic growth and environmental stability. 0·31m. cu. metres of timber and 0·36m. cu. metres of firewood were produced by state-owned forests in 1989–90. Forest lands are also used as national parks, wildlife and game reserves.

Fisheries. In 1988-89 landings were 334,720 tonnes of marine and 92,950 of inland water fish.

INDUSTRY. Industry is based largely on agricultural processing, with engineering and electronics. Manufacturing (1989–90) contributed about 20% to GDP; services, 54%. In 1972 public sector companies were re-organized under a Board of Industrial Management. Government policy since 1977 has been to encourage private industry, particularly small industry. The public sector, however, is still dominant in large industries. Steel, cement, fertilizer and vegetable ghee are the most valuable public sector industries.

A public sector steel-mill (Pakistan Steel) has been built at Port Qasim near Karachi, capacity 1·1m. tonnes; production of coke and pig-iron began in autumn 1981 and of steel in 1983.

Production 1987–88 (tonnes): Refined sugar, 1·77m.; vegetable products, 685,549; jute textiles, 113,602; soda ash, 134,106; sulphuric acid, 78,723; caustic soda, 61,344; chip board and paper board, 70,027; bicycles, 661,183 units; cotton cloth, 280·9m. sq. metres; cotton yarn, 685·5m. kg.; cement, 7·04m.; steel billets 271,367; hot-rolled steel sheets and coils, 475,621; cold-rolled, 154,550; mild steel products, 867,565.

Labour. The 1981 census gave the total work force as 22·62m. Estimates (1989–90) give 31·82m., with 1m. unemployed. In 1988 51·15% were engaged in agriculture, forestry and fishing, 12·69% in manufacturing; the textile industry was the largest single manufacturing employer. Services employed 11·39%; commerce, 11·92%; construction, 6·38%; transport, storage and communication, 4·89%.

FOREIGN ECONOMIC RELATIONS. Foreign exchange reserves were US$500m. in Sept. 1990. Most foreign exchange controls were removed in Feb. 1991. Foreign investors may repatriate both capital and profits, and tax exemptions are available for companies set up before 30 June 1995.

Commerce. Total value of exports, 1988–89: Rs 40,183m.; imports: Rs 135,841m. (In 1987–88, exports were Rs 78,445m., imports, Rs 112,551). The value of the chief articles imported and exported (in Rs 1m.):

Imports			*Exports*		
	1987–88	1988–89		1987–88	1988–89
Petroleum and products	17,270	18,509	Raw cotton	10,759	18,032
Machinery	19,617	26,597	Cotton cloth	8,540	8,947
Transport equipment	9,564	8,403	Cotton yarns	9,530	11,645
Edible oils	7,769	8,576	Rice	6,404	5,067
Chemicals	10,394	13,046	Leather	5,042	4,702
Grains	2,357	8,598	Garments	8,521	9,692

Main export markets, 1988–89 (in Rs 1m.): Japan, 10,468; USA, 10,348; UK, 5,615; Federal Republic of Germany, 5,608; Hong Kong, 5,052; Italy, 4,120; United Arab Emirates, 3,680; China, 3,671. Main import suppliers: USA, 21,355; Japan, 18,802; Kuwait, 11,267; Federal Republic of Germany, 9,796; UK, 8,005; China, 5,994; Saudi Arabia, 5,541; Malaysia, 4,737; South Korea, 4,453.

Total trade between Pakistan and UK (British Department of Trade returns, in £1,000 sterling):

	1987	1988	1989	1990	1991
Imports to UK	167,315	175,337	216,110	236,448	261,291
Exports and re-exports from UK	252,978	263,300	233,532	251,841	272,068

Tourism. In 1988 there were 460,000 tourist arrivals spending US$133m.; 86,500 came from the UK, 31,500 from the USA.

COMMUNICATIONS

Roads. In 1989-90 Pakistan had 111,432 km of roads, of which 58,740 km were all-weather roads.

In 1990 there were 68,660 lorries, 35,465 buses, 26,922 vans, 22,808 taxis, 39,007 motorized rickshaws, 355,605 motor cars and 841,140 motor cycles.

Railways. Pakistan Railways had (1990) a route length of 8,775 km (of which 290 km electrified) mainly on 1,676 mm. gauge, with some metre gauge and narrow gauge line. In 1988–89 84·7m. passengers and 10·43m. tonnes of freight were carried.

Civil Aviation. Karachi is served by British Airways, KLM, PANAM, Lufthansa, Swissair, SAS, Iran National Airlines, Air France, Garuda, Gulf Air and by Philippine, Japanese, Chinese, East African, Syrian, Iraqi, Kuwait, Jordanian, Saudi Arabian, Romanian, Egyptian and Russian airlines.

Pakistan International Airlines (founded 1955; 62% of shares are held by the Government) had 8 Boeing 747s, 8 Airbus A300-B4s, 5 Boeing 707s, 6 Boeing 737-300s, 12 Fokker F-27s and 2 Twin Otters in 1990. Services operate to 33 home and 41 international airports, including London, New York, Frankfurt, Paris, Amsterdam, Copenhagen, İstanbul, Athens, Rome, Cairo, Tripoli, Nairobi, Dhahran, Damascus, Amman, Baghdad, Riyadh, Tokyo, Peking (Beijing), Zahedan, Singapore, Manila, Kuala Lumpur, Bangkok, Colombo, Bombay, Delhi, Dacca, Tehran, Kathmandu, the Maldive Islands and Jiddah.

In 1991 there were 34 airports, including the 5 international airports of Karachi, Lahore, Islamabad, Peshawar and Quetta. In 1987–88, there were 10m. passengers (including 6·3m. on domestic flights) and 180,577 tonnes of cargo (61,294).

Shipping. There is a seaport at Karachi, dry-cargo-handling capacity 6m. tonnes a year, oil-handling, 10m. The second port, 26 miles east of Karachi, is Port Muhammad Bin Qasim; it has iron and coal berths for Pakistan Steel Mills, multi-purpose berths, bulk-cargo handling, oil and container-traffic terminals. International shipping entered and cleared (1987–88): Karachi 1,901 and 1,888 vessels; Port Qasim 152 and 154. Cargo handled: Karachi 17·7m. tonnes, Port Qasim 3·72m. Ports are being developed at Gwader and Pasni. Coastal shipping (Pakistani and Arabian craft), totalled 823 vessels entered (239·1m. NRT), 793 cleared (298·4m.). The Pakistan National Shipping Corporation had 22 vessels in 1990, of 352,716 DWT.

Telecommunications. The telegraph and telephone system is government-owned. Telephones, 1990, numbered 875,000; a nationwide dialling system is in operation between 46 cities. In 1989 there were 12,736 post offices and 480 telegraph offices. Pakistan has international telephone connections by 102 satellite, 7 HF, 4 microwave and 10 carrier circuits, and an international direct-dialling exchange. The Pakistan Broadcasting Corporation had 16 radio stations in 1990 and 5 TV stations. In 1990 there were 1·11m. radio licences and 1·51m. TV sets, and 235,100 video recorders were in use.

Cinemas. There were about 800 cinemas in 1989. 91 full-length films were made.

Newspapers. Newspapers and periodicals numbered 1,826 in 1988; 177 were dailies, 368 weeklies, 126 twice-weeklies, 776 monthlies and 374 quarterlies. Titles by language (and average circulation) in 1988: Urdu, 1,343 (263m.); English, 379 (387,741); Sindhi, 72 (64,823). Titles are also published in Pushtu, Punjabi, Baluchi and Brahvi.

JUSTICE, RELIGION, EDUCATION AND WELFARE

Justice. The Central Judiciary consists of the Supreme Court of Pakistan, which is a court of record and has three-fold jurisdiction, namely, original, appellate and advisory. There are 4 High Courts in Lahore, Peshawar, Quetta and Karachi. Under the Constitution, each has power to issue directions of writs of *Habeas Corpus, Mandamus, Certiorari* and others. Under them are district and sessions courts of first instance in each division; they have also some appellate jurisdiction. Criminal cases not being sessions cases are tried by district magistrates and subordinate magistrates. There are subordinate civil courts also.

The Constitution provides for an independent judiciary, as the greatest safeguard of citizens' rights. The Laws (Continuance in Force) (Eleventh Amendment) Order, 1980, prescribed the date of 14 Aug. 1981 by which the judiciary shall be separated from the executive. There is an Attorney-General, appointed by the President, who has right of audience in all courts.

A Federal Shariat Court at the Supreme Court level has been established to decide whether any law is wholly or partially un-Islamic. After the dismissal of Benazir Bhutto's government in Aug. 1990 a presidential ordinance decreed that the criminal code must conform to Islamic law (Shariah), and in May 1991 parliament passed a law incorporating it into the legal system.

Religion. Religious groups (1981 census): Moslems, 96·68%; Christians, 1·55%; Hindus, 1·51%; Parsees, Buddhists, and others. There is a Minorities Wing at the Religious Affairs Ministry to safeguard the constitutional rights of religious minorities.

Education. At the census of 1981, 23·3% of the population were able to read and write. Estimate (1985), 26%. Adult literacy programmes have been established.

The principle of free and compulsory primary education has been accepted as the responsibility of the state; duration has been fixed provisionally at 5 years. About 49% of children aged 5-9 are enrolled at school. Present policy stresses vocational and technical education, disseminating a common culture based on Islamic ideology. Figures for 1989–90 in 1,000:

	Total pupils	Total teachers	Institutions
Primary	8,595	212·0	90,942
Middle	2,402	68·6	7,117
High	816	99·9	5,816
Secondary vocational	65	4·9	305
Colleges	512	31·8	691
Universities	73	4·3	22

Health. In 1988 there were 710 hospitals and 3,616 dispensaries (52,866 beds) and 55,346 doctors. There were 998 maternity and child welfare centres.

Distribution by province:

	Hospitals	Dispensaries	Mother and child centres
Punjab	258	1,154	448
Sind	251	1,557	154
NWFP	152	590	325
Baluchistan	45	267	68

DIPLOMATIC REPRESENTATIVES

Of Pakistan in Great Britain (35 Lowndes Sq., London, SW1X 9JN)
High Commissioner: Humayun Khan.

Of Great Britain in Pakistan (Diplomatic Enclave, Ramna 5, Islamabad)
High Commissioner: Sir Nicholas Barrington, KCMG, CVO.

Of Pakistan in the USA (2315 Massachusetts Ave., NW, Washington, D.C., 20008)
Ambassador: Najmuddin A. Shaikh.

Of the USA in Pakistan (Diplomatic Enclave, Ramna, 5, Islamabad)
Ambassador: Robert B. Oakley.

Of Pakistan to the United Nations
Ambassador: Jamsheed K. A. Marker.

Further Reading

Federal Bureau of Statistics. *Pakistan Yearbook.*, Karachi
Pakistan Statistical Yearbook.—Statistical Pocket Book of Pakistan. (annual)
Bhutto, B., *Daughter of the East.* London, 1988
Burki, S. J., *Pakistan Under Bhutto.* London, 1980.—*Historical Dictionary of Pakistan.* Metuchen (NJ), 1991.—*Pakistan: the Continuing Search for Nationhood.* Boulder (Colo.), 1991
Choudbury, G. W., *Pakistan: Transition from Military to Civilian Rule.* London, 1988
Gilmartin, D., *Empire and Islam: Punjab and the making of Pakistan.* London, 1988
Hyman, A. *et al., Pakistan: Zia and After.* London, 1989
Kapur, A., *Pakistan in Crisis.* London, 1991
Lamb., C., *Waiting for Allah: Pakistan's Struggle for Democracy.* London, 1991
Low, D. A. (ed.) *The Political Inheritance of Pakistan.* London, 1991
Noman, O., *The Political Economy of Pakistan, 1947-85.* London and New York, 1988
Taylor, D., *Pakistan.* [Bibliography] Oxford and Santa Barbara, 1989

National library: National Library of Pakistan, Islamabad.
National statistical office: Federal Bureau of Statistics, Statistics Division, Karachi.

PANAMA

Capital: Panama City
Population: 2·33m. (1990)
GNP per capita: US$1,780 (1989)

República de Panamá

HISTORY. Panama declared its independence from the United States of Colombia in 1903. Colombia recognized Panama in 1924. On 1 Oct. 1979 Panama assumed sovereignty over what was previously known as the Panama Canal Zone and now called the Canal Area.

In 1984 Nicholas Barletta was elected president and took office in Nov. 1984, but he resigned in Sept. 1985 and was succeeded by one of his vice-presidents.

On 26 Feb. 1988 the Legislative Assembly deposed Eric Arturo Delvalle and appointed Manuel Solis Palma as acting President in his place. Elections on 9 May 1989 were annulled by the Electoral Court. The Council of State elected Francisco Rodríguez Provisional President. He was sworn in on 1 Sept. 1989 but Gen. Manuel Noriega remained *de facto* leader.

In Oct. 1989 a US-backed coup attempt failed. On 15 Dec. Gen. Noriega declared a 'state of war' with the US. On 20 Dec. the US invaded Panama to remove Gen. Noriega from power and he surrendered on 3 Jan. 1990. US troops started to withdraw on 2 Jan.

Guillermo Endara Gallimany was declared to have been elected president on 9 May 1989 and sworn in on 27 Dec.

AREA AND POPULATION. Panama is bounded in the north by the Caribbean sea, east by Colombia, south by the Pacific ocean and west by Costa Rica. Extreme length is about 480 miles (772 km); breadth between 37 (60) and 110 miles (177 km); coastline, 726 miles (1,160 km) on the Atlantic and 1,060 (1,697 km) on the Pacific; total area is 29,761 sq. miles (77,082 sq. km). Population at the census of 1990 was 2,329,329.

The largest towns (census, 1990) are Panama City, the capital, on the Pacific coast (584,803); its suburb San Miguelito (243,025); Colón, the port on the Atlantic coast (140,908); and David (102,678).

The areas and populations of the 9 provinces and the Special Territory were:

Province	Sq. km	Census 1980	Census 1990	Capital
Bocas del Toro	9,506	53,579	93,361	Bocas del Toro
Chiriquí	8,924	287,801	370,227	David
Veraguas	11,226	173,195	203,626	Santiago
Herrera	2,185	81,866	93,681	Chitré
Los Santos	4,587	70,200	76,947	Las Tablas
Coclé	4,981	140,320	173,190	Penonomé
Colón	7,205	166,439	202,338	Colón
San Blas (Special Territory)	3,206			El Porvenir
Panamá	11,400	830,278	1,072,127	Panama City
Darién	15,458	26,497	43,832	La Palma

Vital statistics (1988): Births, 58,093; marriages, 10,112; deaths, 10,416. Crude birth rate (per 1,000): 25·0.

CLIMATE. A tropical climate, unvaryingly with high temperatures and only a short dry season from Jan. to April. Rainfall amounts are much higher on the north side of the isthmus. Panama City. Jan. 79°F (26·1°C), July 81°F (27·2°C). Annual rainfall 70″ (1,770 mm). Colón. Jan. 80°F (26·7°C), July 80°F (26·7°C). Annual rainfall 127″ (3,175 mm). Balboa Heights. Jan. 80°F (26·7°C), July 81°F (27·2°C). Annual rainfall 70″ (1,759 mm). Cristóbal. Jan. 80°F (26·7°C), July 81°F (27·2°C). Annual rainfall 130″ (3,255 mm).

CONSTITUTION AND GOVERNMENT. The 1972 Constitution, as amended in 1978 and 1983, provides for a *president* and two vice-presidents to be elected by direct popular vote and a 67-seat *Legislative Assembly* to be elected on a party basis; in 28 of the 40 constituencies the party winning the vote obtaining one seat; in the other 12, the 39 remaining seats being allocated on a system of proportional party representation. There are also 510 representatives elected, one member for each electoral district.

The President elected on 9 May 1989 was sworn in by an electoral tribunal on 27 Dec. By-elections were held in Jan. 1991 for the 9 seats vacant because the 1989 results were invalidated.

President: Guillermo Endara Gallimany.

Vice Presidents: Ricardo Arias Calderón; Guillermo Ford (also *Minister of Planning*).

National flag: Quarterly: first a white panel with a blue star, second red, third blue, fourth white with a red star.

National anthem: Alcanzamos por fin la victoria ('We achieve victory in the end'; words by J. de la Ossa; tune by Santos Jorge, 1903).

Local government: The 9 provinces and a Special Territory are divided into 67 municipal districts and sub-divided into 510 *corregimientos* (electoral districts).

DEFENCE. The armed forces were disbanded in 1990. Divided between both coasts, the National Maritime Service, a coast guard rather than a navy, comprises 1 32-metre patrol craft and 1 smaller craft and 2 utility landing craft. In 1991 personnel totalled 300.

INTERNATIONAL RELATIONS

Membership. Panama is a member of the UN, OAS and Non-aligned Movement.

ECONOMY

Budget. The 1988 budget provided for expenditure of 847m. balboas and revenue of 605m. balboas. Public sector debt was US$3,771m. in 1989.

Currency. The monetary unit is the *balboa* (PAB). Other coins are the half-balboa, the quarter and tenth of a balboa piece, a cupro-nickel coin of 5 cents, and a copper coin of 1 cent. US coinage is also legal tender. The only paper currency used is that of the USA. In March 1992, US$1 = 1 *balboa*; £1 = 1·76 *balboas*.

Banking and Finance. There is no statutory central bank. The Government accounts are handled through the *Banco Nacional de Panama*. The number of commercial banks was 77 in April 1991. Leading banks are the Citibank, Lloyds Bank International (Bahamas) Ltd., and the Chase Manhattan Bank of New York.

Weights and Measures. English weights and measures are in general use; the metric system is the official system.

ENERGY AND NATURAL RESOURCES

Electricity. Production (1988) 2,558m. kwh. Supply 110 and 120 volts; 60 Hz.

Minerals. There are known to be copper deposits.

Agriculture. Production in 1989 (in tonnes): Rice, 207,210; maize, 90,250; beans, 5,000; raw sugar, 1·39m.; coffee, 10,686. In 1988: Bananas, 900,000; oranges, 36,000; mangoes, 28,000; cocoa, 1,000 and coconuts, 22,000. Livestock (1991): 1,390,541 cattle, 272,210 pigs and 9·6m. poultry.

Forestry. There are great timber resources, notably mahogany. Production (1986) 2·05m. cu. metres.

Fisheries. The catch in 1989 was 154,895 tonnes.

INDUSTRY. Local industries include cigarettes, clothing, food processing, shoes, soap, cement factories; foreign firms are being encouraged to establish industries, and a petrol refinery is operating at Colón.

FOREIGN ECONOMIC RELATIONS. Factories in export zones are granted tax exemption on profits for 10–20 years and exemption from the provisions of the labour code. Foreign debt was some US$6,000m. in May 1990.

Commerce. Imports and exports for 4 calendar years (in 1,000 balboas):

	Imports	Exports		Imports	Exports
1986	1,275,245	326,864	1988	795,454	291,786
1987	1,307,755	336,158	1989	985,100	349,800

Exports (in tonnes), 1990: Coffee, 8,323; bananas, 838,391; sugar, 76,913.

Total trade between Panama and UK (British Department of Trade returns, in £1,000 sterling):

	1987	1988	1989	1990	1991
Imports to UK	4,919	12,230	6,818	4,056	1,679
Exports and re-exports from UK [1]	40,020	32,497	32,875	35,552	36,656

[1] Including new ships built for foreign owners and registered in Panama.

Tourism. In 1989, 211,000 people visited Panama.

COMMUNICATIONS

Roads. Panama had in 1988, 9,651 km of roads. The road from Panama City westward to the cities of David and Concepción and to the Costa Rican frontier, with several branches, is part of the Pan-American Highway. A concrete highway connects Panama City and Colón.

In 1988 there were 176,400 registered motor vehicles.

Railways. The *Ferrocarril de Panama* (Panama Railroad) (1,524 mm gauge) (through the Canal area), which connects Ancón on the Pacific with Cristóbal on the Atlantic, is the principal railway. It is 190 km long and runs along the banks of the Canal. As most vessels unload their cargo at Cristóbal (Colón), on the Atlantic side, the greater portion of the merchandise destined for Panama City is brought overland by the *Ferrocarril de Panama*. The United Brands Company runs 376 km of railway, and the Chiriquí National Railroad 171 km.

Civil Aviation. Eastern Airlines, Swissair, Varig, JAL, Alitalia, KLM, Iberia Airlines, Aeromexico, VIASA, Air France and other international companies operate at Tocumén Airport, 12 miles from Panama City. Air Panama provides services between Panama City and New York, Los Angeles, Miami, Central America and some countries in South America. The *Compañía Panameña de Aviación* (COPA) and *Aerolineas Las Perlas* provide a local service between Panama City and the provincial towns. COPA also provides an international service to Central America and some countries in Latin America.

Shipping. Ships under Panamanian registry in 1990 numbered 11,500 of 58m. gross tons; most of these ships elect Panamanian registry because fees are low and labour laws lenient. All the international maritime traffic for Colón and Panama runs through the Canal ports of Cristóbal, Balboa and Bahia Las Minas (Colón); Almirante is used for both the provincial and international trade. There is an oil transfer terminal at Puerto Armuelles on the Pacific coast.

Panama Canal. On 18 Nov. 1903 a treaty between the USA and the Republic of Panama was signed making it possible for the US to build and operate a canal connecting the Atlantic and Pacific oceans through the Isthmus of Panama. The treaty granted the US in perpetuity the use, occupation and control of a Canal Zone, approximately 10 miles wide, in which the US would possess full sovereign rights 'to the entire exclusion of the exercise by the Republic of Panama of any such sovereign rights, power or authority'. In return the US guaranteed the independence of the republic and agreed to pay the republic $10m. and an annuity of $250,000. The US purchased the French rights and properties—the French had been labouring from 1879 to 1899 in an effort to build the Canal—for $40m. and in addition, paid private landholders within what would be the Canal Zone a mutually agreeable price for their properties.

Two new treaties between Panama and USA were agreed on 10 Aug. and signed on 7 Sept. 1977. One deals with the operation and defence of the canal until the end of 1999 and the other guarantees permanent neutrality.

The USA maintains operational control over all lands, waters and installations, including military bases, necessary to manage, operate and defend the canal until 31 Dec. 1999. A new agency of the US Government, the Panama Canal Commission, operates the canal, replacing the Panama Canal Co. A policy-making board of 5 US citizens and 4 Panamanians serves on the Commission's board of directors. Until 31 Dec. 1989 the canal administrator was a US citizen and the deputy was Panamanian. After that date the position was reversed.

Six months after the exchange of instruments of ratification Panama assumed general territorial jurisdiction over the former Canal Zone and became able to use portions of the area not needed for the operation and defence of the canal. Panamanian penal and civil codes became applicable. At the same time Panama assumed responsibility for commercial ship repairs and supplies, railway and pier operations, passengers, police and courts, all of which were among other areas formerly administered by the Panama Canal Company and the Canal Zone Government.

66% of the electorate of Panama agreed to the ratification of the treaties when a referendum was held on 23 Oct. 1977 and on 18 April 1978 the treaty was ratified by the US Congress. The treaty went into effect on 1 Oct. 1979.

At the end of 1962 the US completed the construction of a high-level bridge over the Pacific entrance to the Canal, and the flags of Panama and the US were flown jointly over areas of the Canal Zone under civilian authority. Following the devaluation of the dollar in 1972 and 1973, the annuity was adjusted proportionally to US$2·1m. and US$2·33m. respectively.

In 1986 a tripartite commission, formed by Japan, Panama and the USA, began studies on alternatives to the Panama Canal. Options are: To build a sea-level canal, to enlarge the existing canal with more locks, to improve the canal alongside upgraded rail and road facilities, to continue with the existing facilities.

The Panama Canal Commission, a US Government Agency, is concerned primarily with the actual operation of the Canal. Toll rates are US$2.01 a Panama Canal ton for vessels carrying passengers or cargo and US$1·60 per ton for vessels in transit in ballast. A Panama Canal ton is equivalent to 100 cu. ft of actual earning capacity. The new toll rate for warships, hospital ships and supply ships, which pay on a displacement basis, is US$1·12 a ton.

The changes were designed to continue the approximately break-even financial operating results after paying its own expenses and paying interest on the net direct investment of the US in the Canal.

Administrator of the Panama Canal Commission: Gilberto Guardia Fábrega.

US military personnel assigned permanently in Panama in Sept. 1989 were approximately 10,000. The total permanent workforce employed by the Panama Canal Commission in Sept. 1990 was 7,232, comprising 921 US citizens, 6,231 Panamanians and 74 others.

The Canal was opened to commerce on 15 Aug. 1914. It is 85 ft above sea-level. It is 51·2 statute miles in length from deep water in the Caribbean Sea to deep water in the Pacific Ocean, and 36 statute miles from shore to shore. The channel ranges in bottom-width from 500 to 1,000 ft; the widening of Gaillard Cut to a minimum width of 500 ft was completed in 1969. Normally, the average time of a vessel in Canal waters is about 24 hours, 8–12 of which are in transit through the Canal proper. A map showing the Panama, Suez and Kiel canals on the same scale will be found in THE STATESMAN'S YEAR-BOOK, 1959 and a further map in the 1978–79 edition.

In 1991 a scheme was begun (funded by the Panama Canal Commission from tolls) to widen an 8-mile section along the Gaillard Cut from 500 feet to 630 feet, permitting 24-hour two-way traffic.

Particulars of the ocean-going commercial traffic through the canal are given as follows (vessels of 300 tons Panama Canal net and 500 displacement tons and over; cargo in long tons):

Fiscal year ending 30 Sept.	North-bound (Pacific to Atlantic) Vessels Cargo	South-bound (Atlantic to Pacific) Vessels Cargo	Total Vessels Cargo	Tolls levied [1] (in US$)
1987	5,766 61,683,921	6,464 87,006,459	12,230 148,690,380	329,858,775
1988	5,807 65,504,306	6,427 90,978,335	12,234 156,482,641	339,319,326
1989	5,678 63,360,524	6,311 88,275,589	11,989 151,636,113	329,696,838
1990	5,667 66,107,105	6,274 90,965,873	11,941 157,072,978	355,557,957

[1] All annual tolls figures have been revised to show total tolls collected instead of oceangoing commercial tolls.

In the fiscal year ending 30 Sept. 1990, 13,325 ships passed through the Canal. Transits by flag included 1,866 Panamanian; 1,479 Liberian; 660 Norwegian; 611 US; 585 Greek; 542 Cypriot; 501 Japanese; 500 Soviet; 404 UK; 372 Bahamian; 364 Filipino; 337 Ecuadorian.

Statistical Information: The Panama Canal Commission Office of Public Affairs.

Annual Reports on the Panama Canal, by the Administrator of the Panama Canal Commission.
Rules and Regulations Governing Navigation of the Panama Canal. The Panama Canal Commission, Miami, Florida *or* Washington, DC
Cameron, I., *The Impossible Dream.* London, 1972
Le Feber, W., *The Panama Canal: The Crisis in Historical Perspective.* OUP, 1978
McCullough, D., *The Path Between the Seas.* New York and London, 1978

Telecommunications. There are telegraph cables from Panama to North America and Central and South American ports, and from Colón to the USA and Europe. There is also inter-continental communication by satellite. There were (1985) 97 licensed commercial broadcasting stations, nearly all operated by private companies, one of which functions in the canal. There are 6 television stations, one of them run by the US Army at Fort Clayton. In 1985 there were 295,000 radio and 400,000 television sets. In 1988 there were 241,900 telephones.

Newspapers. There were (1989) 1 English language and 5 Spanish language daily morning newspapers and 1 English/Spanish evening newspaper.

JUSTICE, RELIGION, EDUCATION AND WELFARE

Justice. The Supreme Court consists of 9 justices appointed by the executive. There is no death penalty. The police force numbered 11,000 in 1992.

Religion. 85% of the population is Roman Catholic, 5% Protestant, 4·5% Moslem. There is freedom of religious worship and separation of Church and State. Clergymen may teach in the schools but may not hold public office.

Education. Elementary education is compulsory for all children from 7 to 15 years of age, with an estimated 543,453 students in schools in 1988. The University of Panama at Panama City, inaugurated on 7 Oct. 1935, and the Catholic university Sta. Maria La Antigua, inaugurated on 27 May 1965, had a combined enrolment of 51,058 students in 1988.

Health. In 1988 there were 2,761 doctors, 527 dentists and 2,514 nursing personnel. There were 58 hospitals, 178 health centres and 435 health sub-centres with a total of 7,776 beds.

DIPLOMATIC REPRESENTATIVES

Of Panama in Great Britain (119 Crawford St., London, W1H 1AF)
Ambassador: Teodoro F. Franco (accredited 3 April 1990).

Of Great Britain in Panama (Apartado 889, Panama City 1)
Ambassador: John Grant MacDonald, CBE.

Of Panama in the USA (2862 McGill Terr., NW, Washington, D.C., 20008)
Ambassador: Jaime Ford.

Of the USA in Panama (Apartado 6959, Panama City 5)
Ambassador: Dean R. Hinton.

Of Panama to the United Nations
Ambassador: César Pereira Burgos.

Further Reading

Statistical Information: The Comptroller-General of the Republic (Contraloria General de la República, Calle 35 y Avenida 6, Panama City) publishes an annual report and other statistical publications.

Jorden, W. J., *Panama Odyssey.* Univ. of Texas Press, 1984
Langstaff, E. DeS., *Panama.* [Bibliography] Oxford and Santa Barbara 1982
Ropp, S. C., *Panamanian Politics.* New York, 1982
Sahota, G. S., *Poverty Theory and Policy: a Study of Panama.* Johns Hopkins Univ. Press, 1990

National Library: Biblioteca Nacional, Departamento de Información. Calle 22, Panama.

PAPUA
NEW GUINEA

Capital: Port Moresby
Population: 3·7m. (1990)
GNP per capita: US$900 (1989)

HISTORY. To prevent that portion of the island of New Guinea not claimed by the Netherlands or Germany from passing into the hands of a foreign power, the Government of Queensland annexed Papua in 1883. This step was not sanctioned by the Imperial Government, but on 6 Nov. 1884 a British Protectorate was proclaimed over the southern portion of the eastern half of New Guinea, and in 1887 Queensland, New South Wales and Victoria undertook to defray the cost of administration, and the territory was annexed to the Crown the following year. The federal government took over the control in 1901; the political transfer was completed by the Papua Act of the federal parliament in Nov. 1905, and on 1 Sept. 1906 a proclamation was issued by the Governor-General of Australia declaring that British New Guinea was to be known henceforth as the Territory of Papua. The northern portion of New Guinea was a German colony until the First World War. It became a League of Nations mandated territory in 1921, administered by Australia, and later a UN Trust Territory (of New Guinea).

The Papua New Guinea Act 1949–1972 provides for the administration of the UN Australian Trust Territory of New Guinea in an administrative union with the Territory of Papua, in accordance with Art. 5 of the New Guinea Trusteeship Agreement, under the title of Papua New Guinea.

Australia granted Papua New Guinea self-government on 1 Dec. 1973 and, on 16 Sept. 1975, Papua New Guinea became a fully independent state.

Peace talks between the government and the secessionist Bougaineville Revolutionary Army (BRA) after 2 years of fighting went on through 1991–92.

AREA AND POPULATION. Papua New Guinea extends from the equator to Cape Baganowa in the Louisiade Archipelago to 11° 40' S. lat. and from the border of West Irian to 160° E. long. with a total area of 462,840 sq. km. According to the census the 1990 population was 3,529,538 (excluding North Solomons, estimated 1990 population 159,500). Port Moresby (NCD), 193,242; Lae, 80,655; Rabaul, 17,022; Madang, 27,057; Wewak, 23,224; Goroka, 17,855; Mount Hagen, 17,392. Area and population of the provinces:

Provinces	Sq.km	Census 1980	Census 1990	Capital
Milne Bay	14,000	127,975	157,288	Alotau
Northern	22,800	77,442	96,762	Popondetta
Central	29,500	116,964	140,584	Port Moresby
National Capital District	240	123,624	193,242	—
Gulf	34,500	64,120	68,060	Kerema
Western	99,300	78,575	108,705 [1]	Daru
Southern Highlands	23,800	236,052	302,724	Mendi
Enga	12,800	164,534	238,357	Wabag
Western Highlands	8,500	265,656	291,090	Mount Hagen
Chimbu	6,100	178,290	183,801	Kundiawa
Eastern Highlands	11,200	276,726	299,619	Goroka
Morobe	34,500	310,622	363,535	Lae
Madang	29,000	211,069	270,299	Madang
East Sepik	42,800	221,890	248,308	Wewak
West Sepik	36,300	114,192	135,185 [2]	Vanimo
Manus	2,100	26,036	32,830	Lorengau
West New Britain	21,000	88,941	127,547	Kimbe
East New Britain	15,500	133,197	184,408	Rabaul
New Ireland	9,600	66,028	87,194	Kavieng
North Solomons	9,300	128,794	...	Arawa

[1] Excludes 3 census divisions, estimated total 1,500.   [2] Excludes 2 census divisions, estimated total 3,000.

Vital statistics (1990, estimate): Crude birth rate, 35·2 per 1,000; crude death rate, 13·1.

CLIMATE. There is a monsoon climate, with high temperatures and humidity the year round. Port Moresby is in a rain shadow and is not typical of the rest of Papua New Guinea. Jan. 82°F (27·8°C), July 78°F (25·6°C). Annual rainfall 40" (1,011 mm).

CONSTITUTION AND GOVERNMENT. Papua New Guinea has a Westminster type of government. A single legislative house, known as the National Parliament, is made up of 109 members from all parts of the country. The members are elected under universal suffrage and general elections are held every 5 years. All persons over the age of 18 who are Papua New Guinea citizens are eligible to vote and stand for election. Voting is by secret ballot and follows the preferential system.

The first Legislative Council was established in 1951. It was abolished in 1964 and replaced with the House of Assembly.

In the general elections held in June-July 1987, 26 seats were won by the Pangu Party, 18 by the People's Democratic Movement, 12 by the National Party, 32 by other parties and 21 by independents. A PDM-led government held office until 4 July 1988, when it was defeated in Parliament and replaced by one led by the Pangu Party.

Governor-General: Sir Wiwa Korowi (b. 1948; National Party; elected by Parliament to replace Sir Serei Eri, Nov. 1991).

The Cabinet in Feb. 1992 was as follows:

Prime Minister: Rt. Hon. Rabbie Namaliu.

Deputy Prime Minister, Public Service: Akoka Doi. *Agriculture and Livestock:* Tom Pais. *Finance and Planning:* Paul Pora. *Tourism and Culture:* Aruru Matiabe. *Minerals and Energy:* Patterson Lowa. *Forests:* Jack Genia. *Provincial Affairs:* John Momis. *Transport:* Anthony Temo. *Justice:* Bernard Narakobi. *Education:* Utula Samana. *Defence:* Benias Sabumei. *Communications:* Brown Sinamoi. *Works and Supply:* Lucas Waka. *Fisheries and Marine Resources and Minister of State, Assisting the Prime Minister:* Akoka Doi. *Environment and Conservation:* Michael Singan. *Foreign Affairs:* Michael Somare. *Lands and Physical Planning:* Hugo Berghuser. *Health:* Beona Motawiya. *Labour and Employment:* Toni Ila. *Police:* Mathias Ijape. *Home Affairs and Youth:* Matthew Bendumb. *Trade and Industry:* John Giheno. *Correctional Services:* Tenda Lau. *Housing:* Bob Bubec. *Administrative Services:* William Wi. *Civil Aviation:* John Wawia. *Interior:* Karl Stack.

The seat of the Government is at Port Moresby.

National flag: Diagonally ochre-red over black, on the red a bird of paradise in gold, and on the black 5 stars of the Southern Cross in white.

Local government: In 1950 the first village council was formed which established the basis of an extensive local government system. A system of provincial government was introduced in 1976 and the importance of lower-level local government diminished. However, lower-level community government had replaced local government councils in some provinces by 1991.

DEFENCE. The Papua New Guinea Defence Force has a total strength of 3,800 (1992) consisting of land, maritime and air elements. The Army is organized in 2 infantry and 1 engineer battalions. The Navy, based at Port Moresby and Manus, is all of Australian build and comprises 5 inshore patrol craft and 2 tank landing craft. Personnel numbered 300 in 1991. The Defence Force has an Air Transport Squadron with (1990) about 100 personnel. Current equipment comprises 5 C-47 transports, and 4 Australian-built N22B Nomads and 3 Israeli-built Aravas for both transport and border patrol duties. The Aravas and C-47s are to be replaced by CN-235s.

INTERNATIONAL RELATIONS

Membership. Papua New Guinea is a member of the UN, the Commonwealth, the Colombo Plan, the South Pacific Commission and the South Pacific Forum and is an ACP state of the EEC.

ECONOMY

Budget. Budgetary income (in K1,000) for calendar years was:

Source	1989	1990 [1]	1991 [1]
Tax revenue	596,670	694,604	674,581
Non-tax revenue	174,824	228,231	161,486
Grants	189,719	182,715	244,441
Loans	245,813	144,451	229,492
Total	1,207,025	1,250,000	1,310,000
Expenditure:			
Administration	258,500	233,600	251,900
Social	330,300	347,700	367,500
Economic	257,900	299,900	315,000
Public debt charges	247,800	254,500	253,300
Other	93,800	114,400	122,300
Total	1,188,300	1,250,000	1,310,000

[1] Estimates.

Currency. The unit of currency is the *kina* (PGK) of 100 *toea*. In March 1992, £1 = K1·68; US$1 = K0·96.

Banking and Finance. The Bank of Papua New Guinea assumed the central banking functions formerly undertaken by the Reserve Bank of Australia on 1 Nov. 1973.

A national banking institution which has been named the Papua New Guinea Banking Corporation has been established. This bank has assumed the Papua New Guinea business of the Commonwealth Trading Bank of Australia except where certain accounts give rise to special financial or contractual problems.

The subsidiaries of 3 Australian commercial banks also operate in Papua New Guinea. These are the Australia and New Zealand Banking Group (PNG) Ltd, the Bank of New South Wales (PNG) Ltd, and the Bank of South Pacific Ltd, all of which offer trading and savings facilities. As from 1 Nov. 1973 these banks operated under Papua New Guinea banking legislation.

In 1983, two additional commercial banks Indosuez Niugini Bank Ltd and Niugini Lloyds International Bank Ltd began operating, each with 51% national ownership, and the remaining 49% held by the affiliate of a major international bank.

In addition to these five commercial banks, the Agriculture Bank of Papua New Guinea (formerly the Development Bank) has provided long-term development finance with a particular attention to the needs of small-scale enterprises since 1967. The country's first merchant bank, Resources and Investment Finance Ltd (RIFL), specializing in large-scale financial services began business in late 1979. Its shares are owned by the Hong Kong and Shanghai Banking Corporation, the Commonwealth Trading Bank of Australia and the Papua New Guinea Banking Corporation.

On 30 June 1987 commercial banks deposits totalled K762·2m.

Weights and Measures. The metric system is in force.

ENERGY AND NATURAL RESOURCES

Electricity. Production in 1990 was 1,362·3m. kwh (490·3m. kwh hydro-electric).

Oil. The Iagifu field in the Southern Highlands had (1988) potential recoverable reserves of 500m. bbls.

Minerals. Copper is the main mineral product. Gold, copper and silver are the only minerals produced in quantity. The Misima open-pit gold mine, first mined in 1888, was opened in 1989. Production is forecast at 210,000 oz a year with a life of 10 years. The Porgera gold mine opened in 1990 with an expected life of 20 years. Major copper deposits in Bougainville have proven reserves of about 800m. tonnes; mining was halted by secessionist rebel activity. Copper and gold deposits in the

Star Mountains of the Western Province are being developed by Ok Tedi Mining Ltd at the Mt. Fubilan mine. Production of gold commenced in 1984 and of copper concentrates in 1987. In 1986, B.C.L. produced 586,552 tonnes of copper concentrate containing approximately 178,593 tonnes of copper, 16,367 kg of gold and 50,385 kg of silver; Ok Tedi Mining Ltd produced 18,277 kg of gold and 5,677 kg of silver.

Agriculture. At 31 Dec. 1988 (preliminary), there were 1,024 large holdings with a total area of 415,000 ha, of which 156,000 ha were under crops (principally copra, cocoa, coffee and rubber) and 87,000 ha pasture. Minor commercial crops include pyrethrum, tea, peanuts and spices. Locally consumed food crops include sweet potatoes, maize, taro, bananas, rice and sago. Tropical fruits grow abundantly. There is extensive grassland. The sugar industry has made the country self-sufficient in this commodity while a beef-cattle industry is being developed.

Production (1990, in tonnes): Coffee, 67,000; copra, 116,000; cocoa beans, 40,000; rubber (1988), 3,538.

Livestock (1990): Cattle, 103,000; pigs, 1·84m.; goats, 14,000; poultry, 3m.

Forestry. Timber production is important for both local consumption and export. In 1986, 1·7m. cu. metres of logs were cut. Production of sawn timber, 1986, 84,000 cu. metres.

Fisheries. Tuna, both skipjack and yellowfin species, is the major fisheries resource; in 1980 the catch was 33,000 tonnes but has diminished sharply since then due to oversupply conditions on world markets. Exports of various crustacea, 1986, 1,575 tonnes, value K10·47m.

INDUSTRY. Secondary and service industries are expanding for the local market. The main industries were (1988) food processing, beverages, tobacco, timber products, wood, and fabricated metal products. In 1988 there were 692 factories employing 30,503 persons. Value of output K768m.

Labour. In 1987 there were 145,331 persons in formal employment, other than public servants. In 1990 there were 40,353 public servants.

FOREIGN ECONOMIC RELATIONS. Australian aid amounts to an annual $A300m. The 'Pactra II' agreement of 1991 establishes a free trade zone with Australia and protects Australian investments.

Commerce. Imports (in K1,000) for calendar years:

	1987	1988	1989
Food and live animals	171,524	181,789	190,853
Beverages and tobacco	11,888	15,456	14,957
Crude materials, inedible, except fuels	7,824	8,577	7,769
Mineral fuels, lubricants and related materials	112,047	98,175	63,704
Oils and fats (animal and vegetable)	3,608	3,350	3,387
Chemicals	84,595	84,403	78,588
Manufactured goods, chiefly by material	181,570	205,654	253,251
Machinery and transport equipment	339,631	424,587	524,966
Miscellaneous manufactured articles	87,636	99,113	109,776
Commodities and transactions of merchandise trade, not elsewhere specified	12,550	12,356	12,877
Total imports	1,012,874	1,133,459	1,260,128

Exports (in K1,000) for calendar years:

	1988	1989	1990
Coconut and copra products—			
Copra	19,486	13,437	8,949
Copra (coconut) oil	17,456	15,180	12,187
Copra cake and pellets	1,262	1,597	1,016
Total	38,204	30,214	22,152

	1988	1989	1990
Coffee beans	113,512	148,110	103,396
Cocoa beans	46,017	45,974	32,151
Crude rubber	4,401	2,631	1,791
Tea	6,439	6,037	6,652
Pyrethrum extract	148	–	–
Forest and timber products			
Logs	91,013	92,130	52,412
Sawn timber	1,039	1,386	1,642
Other	6,238	5,564	n.a.
Total	98,290	99,080	54,054
Crocodile skins	877	928	902
Crayfish and prawns	7,321	7,946	7,372
Gold	112,096	61,158	222,958
Copper concentrate	702,756	691,004	556,044
Other domestic produce	37,640	14,551	22,301
Total domestic produce	1,169,253	1,205,935	1,198,634
Re-exports	34,484	59,667	102,859
Total exports	1,203,737	1,265,602	1,301,493

Of exports in 1990, Japan took 28%, Federal Republic of Germany, 16% and Australia, 26%; of imports (1989), Australia furnished about 42%, Singapore, 7% and Japan, 16%.

Total trade between Papua New Guinea and UK (British Department of Trade returns, in £1,000 sterling):

	1987	1988	1989	1990	1991
Imports to UK	46,045	44,291	47,839	34,849	32,170
Exports and re-exports from UK	16,693	20,521	15,822	8,793	15,446

Tourism. In 1990, there were 40,742 visitors of which 13,022 were tourists.

COMMUNICATIONS

Roads. In 1985 there were approximately 19,736 km of roads including approximately 1,200 km paved. Motor vehicles numbered (1986) 45,713 including 16,499 cars and station wagons.

Civil Aviation. There are services to Australia (Sydney, Brisbane and Cairns), Djayapura (Indonesia), Manila, Singapore and Honiara (Solomon Islands). In addition to Air Niugini, the national flag carrier, Qantas operates in and out of Papua New Guinea. There are a total of 177 airports and airstrips with scheduled services.

Shipping. There are regular shipping services between Australia and Papua New Guinea ports, and also services to New Zealand, Japan, Hong Kong, US west coast, Singapore, Solomon Islands, Vanuatu, Taiwan, Philippines and Europe. Small coastal vessels run between the various ports. In 1985 cargo discharged from overseas was 1·5m. tonnes; cargo loaded for overseas was 2·1m. tonnes.

Telecommunications. Telephones numbered 63,212 on 31 Dec. 1986. The National Broadcasting Commission operates three networks. A national service is relayed throughout the country by a series of transmitters on medium- and short-wave bands. Local services operate in each of the 19 provinces, mainly on short-wave, while the larger urban centres are also covered by a commercial FM network relayed from Port Moresby. Two commercial television stations broadcast to Port Moresby (colour by PAL). In 1990 there were 10,000 television and 235,000 radio receivers.

Newspapers. In 1986 there was one daily newspaper with a circulation of 28,000.

JUSTICE, RELIGION, EDUCATION AND WELFARE

Justice. In 1983, over 1,500 criminal and civil cases were heard in the National Court and an estimated 120,000 cases in district and local courts. The discretionary use of the death penalty for murder and rape was introduced in 1991.

Police. Total uniformed strength at 31 Dec. 1986, 4,756.

Religion. At the 1980 Census, Protestants formed 64% of the population and Roman Catholics 33%.

Education. At 30 June 1986 about 374,950 children attended 2,461 primary schools and 60,052 enrolled in 234 secondary, technical and vocational schools. The University of Papua New Guinea and the Papua New Guinea University of Technology had 3,029 students enrolled in full-time courses in 1986.

Health. In 1986, there were 19 hospitals, 459 health centres, 2,231 aid posts and 283 doctors.

DIPLOMATIC REPRESENTATIVES

Of Papua New Guinea in Great Britain (14 Waterloo Pl., London, SW1R 4AR)
High Commissioner: Noel Levi, CBE.

Of Great Britain in Papua New Guinea (Kiroki St., Port Moresby)
High Commissioner: John Guy, OBE.

Of Papua New Guinea in the USA (1330 Connecticut Ave., NW, Washington D.C., 20036)
Ambassador: Margaret Taylor.

Of the USA in Papua New Guinea (Armit St., Port Moresby)
Ambassador: Robert W. Farrand.

Of Papua New Guinea to the United Nations
Ambassador: Renagi Lohia.

Further Reading

The Territory of Papua. Annual Report. Commonwealth of Australia. 1906–1940–41 and from 1945–46
The Territory of New Guinea. Annual Report. Commonwealth of Australia. 1914–1940–41 and from 1946–47
Papua New Guinea, Annual Report. From 1970–71
Hasluck, P., *A Time for Building.* Melbourne Univ. Press, 1976
McConnell, F., *Papua New Guinea.* [Bibliography] Oxford and Santa Barbara, 1988
Ross, A. C. and Langmore, J., *Alternative Strategies for Papua New Guinea.* OUP, 1974
Ryan, P. (ed.) *Encyclopaedia of Papua and New Guinea.* Melbourne Univ. Press, 1972
Skeldon, R. (ed.) *The Demography of Papua New Guinea.* Institute of Applied Social and Economic Research, 1979

PARAGUAY

Capital: Asunción
Population: 4·16m. (1990)
GNP per capita: US$1,030 (1989)

República del Paraguay

HISTORY. The Republic of Paraguay gained its independence from Spain on 14 May 1811. In 1814 Dr José Gaspar Rodríguez de Francia was elected dictator, and in 1816 perpetual dictator by the National Assembly. He died 20 Sept. 1840. In 1844 a new constitution was adopted, under which Carlos Antonio López (first elected in 1842, died 10 Sept. 1862) and his son, Francisco Solano López, ruled until 1870. During the devastating war against Brazil, Argentina and Uruguay (1865–70) Paraguay's population was reduced from about 600,000 to 232,000. Argentina, in Aug. 1942, and Brazil, in May 1943, voided the reparations which Paraguay had never paid. Further severe losses were incurred during the war with Bolivia (1932–35) over territorial claims in the Chaco. A peace treaty by which Paraguay obtained most of the area her troops had conquered was signed in July 1938.

Gen. Alfredo Stroessner Mattianda, the commander-in-chief of the army, assumed the presidency after a military coup in 1954. He was deposed in a further coup in Feb. 1989.

AREA AND POPULATION. Paraguay is bounded north-west by Bolivia, north-east and east by Brazil, south-east, south and south-west by Argentina. The area of the Oriental province is officially estimated at 159,827 sq. km (61,705 sq. miles) and the Occidental province at 246,925 sq. km (95,337 sq. miles), making the total area of the republic 406,752 sq. km (157,042 sq. miles).

The population (Census 1982) was 3,035,360; estimate (1990) 4,157,287. In 1984 the capital, Asunción (and metropolitan area), had 729,307 inhabitants; other principal cities: Presidente Stroessner (110,000), Pedro Juan Caballero (80,000), Encarnación (31,445), Pilar (26,352), Concepción (25,607).

There are 19 departments and the capital city. Area and population in 1990:

Department	Area in sq. km	Population	Department	Area in sq. km	Population
Asunción (city)	117	607,700	Canendiyú	14,667	120,800
Central	2,465	769,100	Amambay	12,933	97,700
Caaguazú	11,474	462,500	Misiones	9,556	97,500
Alto Paraná	14,895	373,300	Neembucú	12,147	83,300
Itapúa	16,525	371,600	*Oriental*	*159,827*	*4,213,700*
San Pedro	20,002	284,000	Presidente Hayes	72,907	38,200
Paraguari	8,705	230,700	Boquerón	46,708	16,900
Cordillera	4,948	222,200	Alto Paraguay	45,982	10,100
Concepción	18,051	181,500	Chaco	36,367	300
Guairá	3,846	179,800	Nueva Asunción	44,961	300
Caazapá	9,496	132,000	*Occidental*	*246,925*	*65,800*

Number of births, 1986, was 109,626; deaths, 11,519.

The population is overwhelmingly *mestizo* (mixed Spanish and Guaraní Indian) forming a homogeneous stock. There are some 46,700 unassimilated Indians of other tribal origin, in the Chaco and the forests of eastern Paraguay. There are some small traces of Negro descent. 40·1% of the population speak only Guaraní; 48·2% are bilingual (Spanish/Guaraní); and 6·4% speak only Spanish.

Mennonites who arrived in 3 groups (1927, 1930 and 1947) are settled in the Chaco and Oriental Paraguay and were estimated in 1969 to number 13,000, of whom 2,000 came from Canada and 11,000 from Germany. The Japanese colonists in the Oriental section, who first came in 1935, were reckoned to number 7,000 in 1983. An agreement with Korea was signed in 1966 and there were (1988) about 7,575 Korean families living in Paraguay.

CLIMATE. A tropical climate, with abundant rainfall and only a short dry season from July to Sept., when temperatures are lowest. Asunción. Jan. 81°F (30°C), July 64°F (17·8°C). Annual rainfall 53" (1,316 mm).

CONSTITUTION AND GOVERNMENT. A new constitution replacing that of 1940 was drawn up by a Constituent Convention in which all legally recognized political parties were represented and was signed into law on 25 Aug. 1967. It provided for a two-chamber parliament consisting of a 36-seat Senate and a 72-seat House of Deputies, each elected for a 5-year term. Two-thirds of the seats in each House were allocated to the majority party (since 1954 the *Colorado Party*) and the remaining one-third shared among the minority parties in proportion to the votes cast. The President is directly elected for a 5-year (renewable) term; he appoints the Cabinet and during parliamentary recess can govern by decree through the Council of State, the members of which are representatives of the Government, the armed forces and other bodies.

At the presidential elections held on 1 May 1989 Gen. Rodríguez received 74·18% of the vote.

President: Gen. Andrés Rodríguez, assumed office 3 Feb. 1989; inaugurated after election on 15 May 1989.

The following is a list of past presidents since 1948, with the date on which each took office:

Dr J. Natalicio González, 15 Aug. 1948 (deposed).
Gen. Raimundo Rolón, 30 Jan. 1949.
Dr Felipe Molas López, 26 Feb. 1949[1] (resigned).

Dr Federico Chávez, 16 July 1950 (resigned).
Tomás Romero Pereira, 4 May 1954.
Gen. Alfredo Stroessner, 11 July 1954 (deposed).

[1] Provisional, *i.e.,* following a coup d'état.

The Cabinet in Jan. 1991 was composed as follows:

Foreign Affairs: Dr Alexis Frutos Vaesken. *Interior:* Gen. Orlando Machuca Vargas. *Finance:* Enzo Debernardi. *Public Health and Social Welfare:* Cynthia Prieto. *Justice and Labour:* Dr Hugo Estigarribia. *Public Works and Communications:* Gen. Porfirio Pereira Ruiz Díaz. *Industry and Commerce:* Pedro Antonio Zuccolillo. *Education and Worship:* Dr Angel R. Seifart. *Without Portfolio:* Dr Juan Ramón Chaves. *Defence:* Brig.-Gen. Angel Juan Souto Hernández. *Agriculture and Livestock:* Dr Raúl Torres. *Secretary-General of the Presidency:* Conrado Pappalardo.

At the elections of Dec. 1991 for the 198-member National Assembly turn-out was 50%. The Colorado Party won 123 seats with 57% of votes cast, and the Authentic Radical Liberal Party gained by 28% of votes cast.

National flag: Red, white, blue (horizontal); the white stripe charged with the arms of the republic on the obverse, and, on the reverse, with a lion and the inscription *Paz y Justicia*—the only flag in the world with different obverse and reverse.

National anthem: ¡Paraguayos, república o muerte! ('Paraguayans, republic or death!' words by F. Acuña de Figueroa; tune by F. Dupey).

Local and Provincial Government: The country is divided into 2 provinces: the 'Oriental', east of Paraguay River, and the 'Occidental', west of the same river. The Oriental section is divided into 14 departments and the capital. The more important departments are supervised by a *Delegado* appointed by and directly responsible to the central government. The Occidental province, or Chaco, is divided into 5 departments. In May 1991 elections were held for 206 municipal districts. The Coloroado Party gained control of about 70% of them. The Colorado Party won 123 with 57% of votes cast.

DEFENCE. The army, navy and air forces are separate services under a single command. The President of the Republic is the active Commander-in-Chief. The armed forces totalled (1992) about 17,000 (10,300 conscripts). Conscription is for 18 months (2 years in the navy). There are some 45,000 reserves.

Army. The Army consists of 6 infantry and 3 cavalry divisions, 6 infantry regiments (battalion strength) and 4 horsed cavalry regiments, 6 frontier battalions, 2 artillery and 5 engineer battalions and 1 armoured and 1 mechanized cavalry regiment. Equipment includes 5 M-4A3 main battle and 18 M-3A1 light tanks. Strength (1991) 12,500 (including 8,600 conscripts).

Navy. The flotilla comprises 6 armoured river defence gunboats (the average age of which exceeds 40 years), 1 converted landing ship with helicopter deck, 7 river patrol boats, 1 ocean-going transport and training ship, and about 12 service craft. There are 2 AT-6G patrol aircraft, 6 Cessna light aircraft and 4 helicopters. Personnel in 1991 totalled 3,000 including 500 marines, of whom 1,000 were conscripts.

Air Force. The Air Force came into being in the early thirties. There are 2 combat units, 1 with 9 Xavante light jet strike/training aircraft and the other with armed Tucano turboprop trainers. Other types in service include about 6 C-47 and 4 Aviocar twin-engined transports, 1 Convair PBY-5A, 1 Convair C-131A, a Twin Otter, an Otter, 8 Brazilian-built Uirapuru primary trainers, 12 T-6 Texan, 5 Brazilian-supplied Universal basic trainers and a number of light aircraft and helicopters. HQ and flying school are at Campo Grande, Asunción. Personnel (1991) 1,000 (700 conscripts), with 14 combat aircraft.

INTERNATIONAL RELATIONS

Membership. Paraguay is a member of the UN, OAS, Mercosur and LAIA.

ECONOMY

Budget. In 1989 the central budget balanced at Gs. 815,796,996.

Currency. The *guaraní* was established on 5 Oct. 1943 equal to 100 old paper pesos. Total monetary circulation was Gs.81,531m. in Dec. 1983. There were (1988) two official rates of exchange; a rate Gs.400 for the import of oil and by-products and Gs.550 for other goods. Inflation was an annualized 36% in 1990. Rate of exchange, March 1992: 1,420 *guaranís* = US$1; 2,494 *guaranís* = £1.

Banking and Finance. The Banco Central del Paraguay opened 1 July 1952 to take over the central banking functions previously assigned to the National Bank of Paraguay, which had opened in March 1943 and been reorganized as the Banco del Paraguay in Sept. 1944 with a monetary, a banking and a mortgage department. The Banco del Paraguay closed in Nov. 1961 and has been replaced, with the aid of a US loan of US$3m., by the Banco Nacional de Fomento.

The Banco Nacional de Fomento, Lloyds Bank, Banco Exterior do Brasil, Citibank, Banco de Asunción, Banco Exterior SA, Banco Unión SA, Banco Paraguayo de Comercio, Banco Real del Paraguay SA, Banco Aleman Transatlantico, Banco Holandés Unido, Banco Nacional del Estado de São Paulo, Yegros y Azara, Interbanco, Banco Paraná and Banco de Inversiones all have agencies in Asunción and branches in some main towns.

Weights and Measures. The metric system was officially adopted on 1 Jan. 1901.

ENERGY AND NATURAL RESOURCES

Electricity. Electricity requirements are supplied by Acaray hydro-electric power plant. Production in 1988 was 13,535m. kwh. Supply 220 volts; 50 Hz.

Itaipú, the largest hydro-electric dam in the world, a joint effort of the governments of Brazil and Paraguay, was inaugurated in 1982 and it is estimated that the whole project will be completed in 1990. Eventually it will have 18 turbogenerators, each with a capacity of 700,000 kw. In 1984 the first turbine started generating power.

The Yacyretá project is being carried out by the Binational Commission Yacyretá which was created by a treaty between the governments of Argentina and Paraguay. Work is being carried out on this project and it is hoped that the plant will be in full operation by the end of this decade. Initially 20 turbines each of 135,000 kw generating capacity will be installed giving the plant an initial output of 2·7m. kw.

Oil. The oil refinery at Villa Elisa, which has been in operation since 1966, has a production of about 3,500 bbls a day. Exploration for petroleum in the Chaco yielded negative results but prospecting was continuing in 1988.

Minerals. Iron, manganese and other minerals have been reported but have not been shown to be commercially exploitable. There are large deposits of limestone, and also salt, kaolin and apatite. National and international firms have acquired licences to prospect for oil and natural gas in the Chaco.

Agriculture. In 1981 it was estimated that agriculture absorbs some 51·4m. ha. In 1989, the main agricultural products (in 1,000 tonnes) were: Ccassava, 3,978; soybeans, 1,614; maize, 1,211; cotton, 630; wheat, 432; rice, 93; tobacco, 2; sugarcane, 2,909; poroto (green beans), 46.

Wheat, soybeans, cotton, sugar, tobacco, coffee are increasing in importance, as are also essential oils and oilseeds. *Yerba maté*, or strongly flavoured Paraguayan tea, continues to be produced but is declining in importance.

Livestock (1990): 8,254,000 cattle, 335,000 horses, 2,444,000 pigs, and 456,000 sheep.

Forestry. In 1988, 39% of the land area was forested (15·6m. hectares). In the Oriental section there are reserves of hardwoods and cedars that have scarcely been exploited. Palms, tung and other trees are exploited for their oils. The Japanese are experimenting with mulberries for silk growing. Pines and firs have been introduced under a UN project. In 1986, 181,355 tons of timber were exported.

INDUSTRY. Production, 1988 (1,000 tons): Frozen meat, 15·5; cotton fibre, 187·4; sugar, 98·1; rice, 34·8; wheat flour, 104·5; edible oil, 39·7; industrial oil, 12·9; tung oil, 6·9; sawn timber, 629·7; cement, 255·6; soybean, peanut and coconut flour, 405; cigarettes (1m. packets), 46,598; matches (1,000 boxes), 8,979. There are 3 meat-packing plants and other factories producing vegetable oils. A textile industry in Pilar and Asunción meets a large part of local needs.

Trade Unions. Trade unionists number about 30,000 (*Confederación Paraguaya de Trabajadores* and *Confederación Cristiana de Trabajadores*).

FOREIGN ECONOMIC RELATIONS

Commerce. Imports and exports (in US$1m.):

	1985	1986	1987	1988	1989
Imports	442·3	509·4	517·5	494·7	1,009·4
Exports	303·9	232·5	353·4	509·8	660·8

Chief exports in 1989 included (in US$1,000): Soybeans, 382,967; cotton fibres, 306,920; meat, 96,116; coffee, 40,340; vegetable oil, 16,537; sawn wood, 31,611; cake and expellers, 10,460; tobacco, 2,147; hides, 24,026; tung oil, 6,662; essential oils, 24,686.

Chief imports 1989 (in US$1,000): Fuels and lubricants, 115,004; machinery, 211,647; chemical and pharmaceutical products, 42,543; transport and accessories, 61,718; drinks and tobacco, 45,516; foodstuffs, 19,790; iron and manufactures, 19,650; agricultural implements and accessories, 12,010; paper, cardboard and paper products, 17,751; metal products, 7,550.

Imports and exports (in US$), by country, 1989:

Country	Imports	Exports
Algeria	49,475	…
Argentina	67,752	48,976
Belgium	6,138	35,693
Brazil	177,150	328,473
Federal Republic of Germany	29,117	23,280
France	9,842	7,600
Italy	5,729	24,146
Japan	82,102	…
Netherlands	…	186,892
Spain	4,285	21,093
Sweden	1,459	…

Country	Imports	Exports
Switzerland	6,133	73,779
UK	26,902	5,341
Uruguay	6,487	10,582
USA	93,838	89,659

Total trade between Paraguay and UK (British Department of Trade returns, in £1,000 sterling):

	1987	1988	1989	1990	1991
Imports to UK	1,409	1,950	8,898	10,077	1,488
Exports and re-exports from UK	25,409	22,024	19,282	32,035	38,229

Tourism. Visitors numbered 300,000 in 1989.

COMMUNICATIONS

Roads. In 1986 there were 23,606 km of roads, of which 2,159 were paved. The principal paved roads are Route No. 2/7 running from Asunción to the bridge over the Paraná at Puerto Presidente Stroessner, and thence down to the ocean at Paranaguá; and Route No. 1 to Encarnación in the south. The other main arteries are Coronel Oviedo-Pedro Juan Caballero road (unpaved from Coronel Oviedo) in the north and the Trans-Chaco road which starts from the bridge across the river Paraguay north of Asunción and ends at Nueva Asunción on the Bolivian border. Unpaved roads are closed when it rains. In the Argentine, a paved road starts from Pilcomayo, opposite Asunción, and provides good communication with Buenos Aires. In 1987 there were 90,000 vehicles (36,900 cars, 24,300 lorries, 2,700 buses and 26,100 jeeps and taxis).

Railways. The President Carlos Antonio López (formerly Paraguay Central) Railway runs from Asunción to Encarnación, on the Río Alto Paraná, with a length of 441 km (1,435 mm gauge), and connects with Argentine Railways over the Encarnación-Posadas bridge opened in 1989. In 1986, traffic amounted to 156,231 tonnes and 348,535 passengers.

Civil Aviation. International services are operated by 8 airlines (1 domestic and 7 foreign) and internal routes by military airlines and some small private lines.

Shipping. In flood the Paraguay River, which divides the country into two distinct parts, is navigable for 12ft-draught vessels as far as Concepción, 180 miles north of Asunción, and for smaller vessels for a further distance of 600 miles northward. Drought conditions often restrict navigation to lighter traffic. The Paraná River is navigable by large boats from Corrientes up to Puerto Aguirre, at the mouth of the Yguazú River. Boats of a few hundred tons capacity navigate the tributary rivers.

Asunción, the chief port, is 950 miles from the sea. The cargo fleet includes 25 vessels of 300–1,000 tons, 3 tankers of 1,100–1,700 tons, 2 passenger river boats and 1 ocean-going freighter of 713 tons.

Telecommunications. In 1985 there were 382 postal offices and 88,730 telephones. In 1991 there were 0·35m. television (colour by PAL) and 775,000 radio receivers.

Cinemas (1986). Cinemas numbered 6 in Asunción. The larger country towns usually have an outdoor cinema.

Newspapers (1988). There were 5 daily newspapers in Asunción.

JUSTICE, RELIGION, EDUCATION AND WELFARE

Justice. The highest court is the Supreme Court with 5 members. There are special Chambers of Appeal for civil and commercial cases, and criminal cases. Judges of first instance deal with civil, commercial and criminal cases in 6 departments. Minor cases are dealt with by Justices of the Peace.

The Attorney-General represents the State in all jurisdictions, with representatives in each judicial department and in every jurisdiction. In matters of revenue, taxes, etc., the State is represented by the *Abogado del Tesoro*.

Religion. Religious liberty is guaranteed by the 1967 constitution. Article 6 thereof recognizes Roman Catholicism as the official religion of the country. The same article states that relations between Paraguay and the Holy See shall be regulated by concordats or other bilateral agreements, but no such agreements have yet been negotiated.

The Roman Catholic Church is organized into the Archdiocese of Asunción, 3 other dioceses (San Juan Bautista de las Misiones, Concepción and Villarrica); 4 Prelatures (Coronel Oviedo, Encarnación, Alto Paraná and Caacupé); and 2 Vicariates Apostolic (Chaco and Pilcomayo). The bishops meet in a Conference of Paraguayan Bishops. Only civil marriages are legally valid. There are numerous non-catholic communities, the largest of whom are the Mennonites. There is a small Anglican church in Asunción, with missions in the Chaco, which comes under the jurisdiction of an Anglican Bishop resident in Asunción.

Education. Education is free and nominally compulsory. In 1987 there were 4,101 primary schools (public and private) with 579,687 pupils and 28,136 teachers. In 1985 there were 740 secondary schools with (1987) 148,516 students and (1982) 2,448 teachers. The National University in Asunción had, in 1987, 18,711 students and (1985) 2,694 professors; the Catholic University had 10,409 students and (1984) 900 professors.

Health. In 1982 there were 2,201 doctors. In 1979 there were 855 dentists, 860 pharmacists, 783 midwives and 2,636 nursing personnel. In 1985 there were 3,380 hospital beds.

DIPLOMATIC REPRESENTATIVES

Of Paraguay in Great Britain (51 Cornwall Gdns, London, SW7 4AQ)
Ambassador: Antonio Espinoza.

Of Great Britain in Paraguay (Calle Presidente Franco, 706, Asunción)
Ambassador and Consul-General: Michael Dibben.

Of Paraguay in the USA (2400 Massachusetts Ave., NW, Washington, D.C., 20008)
Ambassador: Dr Marcos Martínez Mendieta.

Of the USA in Paraguay (1776 Mariscal López Ave., Asunción)
Ambassador: Timothy Towell.

Of Paraguay to the United Nations
Ambassador: Alfredo Cañete.

Further Reading

Gaceta Official, published by Imprenta Nacional, Estrella y Estero Bellaco, Asunción
Anuario Daumas. Asunción
Anuario Estadístico de la República del Paraguay. Asunción. Annual
Lewis, P. H., *Paraguay under Stroessner.* Univ. of North Carolina Press, 1980
Maybury-Lewis, D. and Howe, J., *The Indian Peoples of Paraguay: Their Plight and Their Prospects.* Cambridge, Mass., 1980
Nickson, R. A., *Paraguay.* [Bibliography] Oxford and Santa Barbara, 1987

National Library: Biblioteca Nacional, De la Rosidenta, Asunción.

PERU

Capital: Lima
Population: 21·55m. (1990)
GNP per capita: US$1,090 (1989)

República del Perú

HISTORY. The Republic of Peru, formerly the most important of the Spanish vice-royalties in South America, declared its independence on 28 July 1821; but it was not till after a war, protracted till 1824, that the country gained its actual freedom.

On 3 Oct. 1968 a military junta overthrew the government of President Fernando Belaúnde Terry and installed Gen. Juan Velazco Alvarado as President of a 'Revolutionary Government' with a cabinet composed entirely of officers of the armed services. Gen. Velazco was ousted in a bloodless coup in Aug. 1975 and was replaced by Gen. Francisco Morales Bermúdez.

Civilian government was restored in July 1980.

AREA AND POPULATION. Peru is bounded north by Ecuador and Colombia, east by Brazil and Bolivia, south by Chile and west by the Pacific Ocean. Area 1,285,216 sq. km (496,093 sq. miles).

The long-standing dispute with Chile over the provinces of Tacna and Arica (*see* THE STATESMAN'S YEAR-BOOK, 1928, p. 1198) reached an amicable settlement on 3 June 1929 at Lima, Tacna going to Peru and Arica to Chile. For an account of the border dispute with Ecuador *see* p. 507. For an account of the settlement of other boundary disputes, *see* THE STATESMAN'S YEAR-BOOK, 1948, p. 1173.

Census population, 1981, 17,005,210. Estimate (1990), 21,550,322 (10,846,578 male). Vital statistics 1989: Births, 730,000; deaths, 190,000; infant deaths (under 1 year), 60,800. Birth rate per 1,000 in 1989, 33.5; death rate, 8.7; infant mortality rate per 1,000 live births, 83·3. Expectation of life in 1989: males, 60.8 years; females, 64.7.

Area and population of the 24 departments and the constitutional province of Callao, together with their capitals:

Department	Sq. km	Estimate 1990	Capital	Estimate 1990
Amazonas	39,249	335,300	Chachapoyas	14,000
Ancash	35,041	983,200	Huaraz	65,600
Apurímac	20,895	371,700	Abancay	29,200
Arequipa	63,345	965,000	Arequipa	634,500
Ayacucho	43,814	566,400	Ayacucho	101,600
Cajamarca	34,023	1,270,600	Cajamarca	92,600
Callao [1]	147	588,600	Callao [2]	...
Cuzco	71,892	1,041,800	Cuzco	275,000
Huancavelica	22,131	375,700	Huancavelica	27,400
Huánuco	37,722	609,200	Huánuco	86,300
Ica	21,328	542,900	Ica	152,300
Junín	44,410	1,113,600	Huancayo	207,600
La Libertad	24,795	1,243,500	Trujillo	532,000
Lambayeque	14,231	935,300	Chiclayo	426,300
Lima	34,802	6,707,300	Lima [2]	...
Loreto	368,852	654,100	Iquitos	269,500
Madre de Dios	85,183	49,000	Puerto Maldonado	21,200
Moquegua	15,734	134,100	Moquegua	31,500
Pasco	25,320	282,900	Pasco	77,000
Piura	35,892	1,494,300	Piura	324,500
Puno	72,012	1,023,500	Puno	99,600
San Martín	51,253	460,000	Moyobamba	26,000
Tacna	16,063	209,800	Tacna	150,200
Tumbes	4,669	144,200	Tumbes	64,800
Ucayali	102,411	230,100	Pucallpa	153,000

[1] Constitutional province.
[2] Lima/Callao metropolitan area 6,404,500.

The official languages are Spanish (spoken by 68% of the population) and Quechua (spoken by 27%); 3% speak Aymara.

In 1991 there were some 100,000 Peruvians of Japanese origin.

CLIMATE. There is a very wide variety of climate, ranging from equatorial to desert, (or perpetual snow on the high mountains). In coastal areas, temperatures vary very little, either daily or annually, though humidity and cloudiness show considerable variation, with highest humidity from May to Sept. Little rain is experienced in that period. In the Sierra, temperatures remain fairly constant over the year, but the daily range is considerable. There the dry season is from April to Nov. Desert conditions occur in the extreme south, where the climate is uniformly dry, with a few heavy showers falling between Jan. and March. Lima. Jan. 74°F (23·3°C), July 62°F (16·7°C). Annual rainfall 2" (48 mm). Cuzco. Jan. 56°F (13·3°C), July 50°F (10°C). Annual rainfall 32" (804 mm).

CONSTITUTION AND GOVERNMENT. The new Constitution, which became effective when a civilian government was installed in July 1980, provides for a Legislature consisting of a *Senate* (60 members) and a *Chamber of Deputies* (180 members) and an Executive formed of the President of the Republic and a Council of Ministers appointed by him. Elections are held every 5 years with the President and Congress elected, at the same time, by separate ballots. All citizens over the age of 18 are eligible to vote. Voting is compulsory.

In June 1990 Alberto Fujimori (b.1938; Change 90 Movement) was elected president with 56% of votes cast.

Presidents since 1963:

Gen. Nicolás Lindley López, 3 March–28 July 1963.

Fernando Belaúnde Terry, 28 July 1963– 3 Oct. 1968. [1]

Gen. Juan Velazco Alvarado, 3 Oct. 1968– 29 Aug. 1975. [1]

Gen. Francisco Morales Bermúdez, 29 Aug. 1975–28 July 1980.

Fernando Belaúnde Terry, 28 July 1980–28 July 1985.

Alan García Pérez, 28 July 1985–27 July 1990

[1] Deposed.

President: Alberto Fujimori (sworn in 28 July 1990).

The Cabinet in Feb. 1992 comprised:

Prime Minister and Economy: Alfonso De Los Heros Pérez Albela (b. 1940).

Defence: Gen. Victor Malca. *Interior:* Gen. Juan Enrique Davila. *Energy and Mines:* Jaime Yoshiyama. *Foreign Affairs:* Augusto Miller. *Education:* Oscar De La Puente Raygada. *Industry:* Victor Joy Way Rojas. *Economy:* Carlos Boloña Bher. *Justice:* Augusto Antonioli Vásquez.

National flag: Three vertical strips of red, white, red, with the national arms in the centre.

National anthem: Somos libres, seámoslo siempre ('We are free, let us always be so'; words by J. De La Torre Ugarte; tune by J. B. Alcedo, 1821).

Local Government: There are 11 regions divided into 185 provinces (as well as the constitutional province of Callao) and 1,784 districts. Municipal elections were held in Aug. 1991.

DEFENCE

Army. There is selective conscription for 2 years. The country is divided into 5 military regions.

The Army comprises (1991) approximately 80,000 men (60,000 conscripts) and 188,000 reserves. There are 2 armoured, 1 cavalry, 8 infantry, 1 airborne and 1 jungle divisions with supporting artillery, engineer and helicopter battalions. There is an air element of 35 Mil Mi-8 and Mi-17, 2 Mi-6 and 12 Alouette helicopters, plus about a dozen fixed-wing transport and liaison aircraft. Equipment includes 350 T-54/-55 main battle and 110 AMX-13 light tanks, over 300 light armoured fighting vehicles and 105-mm./130-mm./155-mm. field artillery.

There is a para-military national police force of 70,000 personnel.

Navy. The principal ships of the Navy are the former Netherlands cruisers *Almirante Grau* and *Aguirre* built in 1953. *Almirante Grau*'s main armament is 8 152 mm guns and 8 Otomat surface-to-surface missiles. *Aguirre* has been converted to a helicopter cruiser and mounts only 4 152 mm guns, the after two turrets having been removed in favour of a hangar and flight deck capable of supporting 3 SH-3D Sea King helicopters.

There are 10 diesel submarines, 6 built in West Germany (1974-82), and 4 ex-US over 30 years old. Other combatants include 2 modernized former British Daring class and 4 ex-Netherlands Friesland class destroyers of 1950s vintage, 4 Italian Lupo class frigates, 6 French-built fast missile craft and 4 tank landing ships. Major auxiliaries include 5 tankers, 2 transports, 1 survey ship and 1 ocean tug, and 30 minor auxiliaries and service craft. A river flotilla of 10 patrol craft police the Upper Amazon, based at Puerto Maldonado and Iquitos.

The Naval Aviation branch comprises 8 S-2 Trackers and 3 Super-King Air anti-submarine aircraft based ashore, 6 Sea King and 6 AB-212 anti-submarine helicopters for service afloat plus 15 miscellaneous transport and utility aircraft.

Callao is the main base, where the dockyard is located and most training takes place. Smaller ocean bases exist at Paita and Talara.

Naval personnel in 1991 totalled 18,000 (14,000 conscripts) including the Naval Air Arm and 2,500 Marines.

The Coast Guard, 600 strong in 1991, includes 5 coastal patrol craft, 5 inshore and 10 river patrol craft.

Air Force. The operational force consists of 5 combat groups. No. 6 Group has 2 squadrons of Mirage 5 jet fighters; No. 9 Group has 2 squadrons of Canberra light jet bombers; No. 7 Group has 2 squadrons of A-37B light attack aircraft; No. 12 Group has Soviet-built Su-22 variable-geometry fighter bombers in 2 operational squadrons; No. 11 Group has one squadron of Su-22s and one with Mirage 2000s. Other aircraft in service include medium transports (1 F.28 Fellowship, 15 An-32, 13 C-130/L-100 Hercules), light transports (16 Twin Otter, 1 twin-jet Falcon and 12 Turbo-Porter), helicopters (2 Mi-6 and 35 Mi-8/17, 24 Mi-24 gunships, Bell 47G, 206, 212, 214ST, 412 and UH-1, BO 105 and Alouette III), 70 training aircraft (including Aermacchi MB 339, T-37 Tucano and T-41D) and a small number of miscellaneous types for photographic and communications duties. There are military airfields at Talara, Chiclayo, Piura, Pisco, Lima (2), Iquitos and La Joya, and a seaplane base at Iquitos. All officers and pilots are trained at the Air Academy at Lima (Las Palmas). In 1991 there were some 15,000 personnel (7,000 conscripts) and 116 combat aircraft.

INTERNATIONAL RELATIONS

Membership. Peru is a member of the UN, OAS, the Andean Group and LAIA.

ECONOMY

Policy. There is a programme of partial privatization of Aeroperú and other companies in transport, industry and mining.

Budget. The budget for 1987 envisaged expenditure of 92,539m. intis and revenue of 66,424m. intis.

Currency. The monetary unit is the new *sol*, which replaced the inti in 1990. In March 1992, £1 = 1·69 *soles*; US$1 = 0·96 *soles*.

Banking and Finance. The bank of issue is the Banco Central de Reserva, which was established in 1922. The government's fiscal agent is the Banco de la Nación.

There were, in 1991, 12 commercial banks (of which 7 were state-owned), 2 foreign commercial banks, 5 development banks, 6 regional commercial banks and a savings bank.

Legislation of April 1991 permitted financial institutions to fix their own interest rates and reopened the country to foreign banks. The Central Reserve Banks sets the upper limit.

There is a stock exchange in Lima.

Weights and Measures. The metric system is in use.

ENERGY AND NATURAL RESOURCES

Electricity. In 1990 the production of electric energy was 13,817m. kwh (10,473m. kwh hydro-electric). Supply 220 volts; 60 Hz.

Oil. Proven oil reserves in 1990 amounted to 382m. bbls. Output amounted to 6·2m. tonnes in 1991.

Minerals. Lead, copper, iron, silver, zinc and petroleum are the chief minerals exploited. Mineral production (in 1,000 tonnes, 1990) of iron, 3,246; zinc, 584; copper, 318; lead, 188; silver, 1,761,600 kg; gold, 6·85m. kg.

Agriculture. There are 4 natural zones: The Coast strip, with an average width of 80 km; the Sierra or Uplands, formed by the coast range of mountains and the Andes proper; the Montaña or high wooded region which lies on the eastern slopes of the Andes, and the jungle in the Amazon Basin, known as the Selva. In 1984 irrigation was increasing the amount of cultivable acreage in the arid coastal sections of the country, using the abundance of water flowing from the Andes mountains.

There are some 7·6m. ha of potential agricultural land, of which 2·7m. ha were cultivated in 1991. Legislation of May 1991 permits the unrestricted sale of agricultural land. Workers in co-operatives may elect to form limited liability companies and become shareholders.

Production in 1990 (in 1,000 tonnes): Sugar-cane, 6,083; potatoes, 1,190; seed cotton, 239; coffee, 80; rice, 966; maize, 621.

Livestock (in 1,000), 1990: Alpacas, 2,666; cattle, 4,065; pigs, 2,342; sheep, 12,249; poultry, 60,194.

Forestry. There were 84·5m. ha of forest area in 1989, made up of 74m. ha of natural forest, 253,646 ha of planted forest and 10·25m. ha of land suitable for reforestation. The forests contain valuable hardwoods; oak and cedar account for about 40%. In 1989 roundwood removals totalled 8·5m. cu metres.

Fisheries. Production (1990 in tonnes) 6,867,800, including anchoveta, 2,924,987.

INDUSTRY. About 70% of Peru's manufacturing industries are located in or around the Lima/Callao metropolitan area. Products include pig-iron, blooms, billets, largets, round and round-deformed bars, wire rod, black and galvanized sheets and galvanized roofing sheets. Refractories are manufactured at Lima.

The Government has a monopoly of the import and/or local manufacture and sale of guano, salt, alcohol and explosives.

Labour. In 1990 the workforce numbered 7,344,000, of whom 2,497,000 worked in agriculture, 176,300 in mining, 771,100 in manufacturing, 22,000 in electricity production, 271,700 in building, 1,145,700 in commerce, 323,100 in transport, 176,300 in finance and 1,960,800 in services. In Dec. 1990 private-sector salaries were increased 348%, and the minimum monthly wage became 25m. intis.

Trade Unions. Trade unions have about 2m. members (approximately 1·5m. in peasant organizations and 500,000 in industrial). The major trade union organization is the *Confederación de Trabajadores del Perú*, which was reconstituted in 1959 after being in abeyance for some years. The other labour organizations recognized by the Government are the *Confederación General de Trabajadores del Perú*, the *Confederación Nacional de Trabajadores* and the *Central de Trabajadores de la Revolución Peruana*.

FOREIGN ECONOMIC RELATIONS. Peru obtained a rescheduling of debt from its Club of Paris creditors in Sept. 1991, having followed a policy of austerity required by the IMF.

An agreement of Jan. 1992 with Bolivia gives Bolivia duty-free transit for imports and exports through a corridor leading to the Peruvian Pacific port of Ilo from the Bolivian frontier town of Desaguadero, in return for Peruvian access to the Atlantic via Bolivia's roads and railways.

Commerce. The value of trade has been as follows (in US$1m.):

	1984	1985	1986	1987	1988	1989	1990
Imports	2,140	1,806	2,596	3,182	2,790	2,291	2,885
Exports	3,147	2,978	2,531	2,661	2,691	3,488	3,276

In 1990, imports (in US$1,000) were mainly from the USA (520,916), Argentina (165,511) and the Federal Republic of Germany (130,387); exports were mainly to the USA (438,189) and Japan (203,432). 15·2m. bbls of oil were exported in 1989. Copper is the largest foreign exchange followed by fishery products. 2·79m. tonnes of fish and products worth US$409·8m. were exported in 1990.

Total trade between Peru and UK (British Department of Trade returns, in £1,000 sterling):

	1988	1989	1990	1991
Imports to UK	90,844	125,538	96,654	84,034
Exports and re-exports from UK	31,384	29,707	29,233	33,061

Tourism. There were 278,296 visitors in 1990.

COMMUNICATIONS

Roads. In 1990 there were 69,942 km of roads, of which 7,564 km were paved and 13,475 km gravel. In 1990 there were 606,550 registered motor vehicles, including 324,440 cars, 43,715 station wagons, 138,999 vans, 20,605 buses and 66,567 lorries.

Railways. Total length (1986), 1,672 km on 1,435- and 914-mm gauges. In 1986 railways carried 2·3m. tonnes of freight and 3·3m. passengers.

Civil Aviation. The national carrier is Aeroperú. In 1991 there were 30 airports. 151 civil aircraft were registered in 1990, of which 100 were in commercial use.

Shipping. In 1989 there were 51 sea-going vessels and 579 lake and river craft.

Telecommunications. In 1989 there were 2,373 post offices and 2,184 telegraph offices. An earth satellite ground communication station at Lurin connects Peru through Intelsat. III to the USA and Europe. In 1990 there were 734,938 telephones and 3,752 teleprinters. Radio receivers (1987) 5·2m. and television receivers 1·6m.

Newspapers. The main Lima newspapers are *El Comercio, Expreso, La República, Hoy, El Nacional, La Crónica, La Tercera, Extra, El Universal, Página Libre, Ojo, Onda, Novedades* and *Gestión*.

JUSTICE, RELIGION, EDUCATION AND WELFARE

Justice. The Peruvian judicial system is a pyramid at the base of which are the justices of the peace who decide minor criminal cases and civil cases involving small sums of money. The apex is the Supreme Court with a President and 12 members; in between are the judges of first instance, who usually sit in the provincial capitals, and the superior courts.

The police had some 85,000 personnel in 1991.

Religion. Religious liberty exists, but the Roman Catholic religion is protected by the State, and since 1929 only Roman Catholic religious instruction is permitted in schools, state or private. In 1972 there were 1 Roman Catholic cardinal, 7 archbishops, 14 bishops, 3 vicars-general, 8 vicars apostolic, 2,672 priests, 506 cloistered monks and 4,558 members of religious orders.

Education. Elementary education is compulsory and free for both sexes between the ages of 7 and 16; secondary education is also free.

In 1990 there were 3,621,052 pupils in primary schools and 1,986,265 pupils in secondary schools.

In 1990 the number of students at the 28 state and 23 private universities was 442,932.

Health. There were in 1990, 368 hospitals and 1,020 health centres.

DIPLOMATIC REPRESENTATIVES

Of Peru in Great Britain (52 Sloane St., London, SW1X 9SP)
Ambassador: Hugo Palma.

Of Great Britain in Peru (Edificio El Pacifico Washington, Ave. Arequipa, Lima)
Ambassador: D. Keith Haskell, CMG, CVO.

Of Peru in the USA (1700 Massachusetts Ave., NW, Washington, D.C., 20036)
Ambassador: Roberto McLean.

Of the USA in Peru (PO Box 1995, Lima)
Ambassador: Anthony C. E. Quainton.

Of Peru to the United Nations
Ambassador: Dr Ricardo V. Luna Mendoza.

Further Reading

The official gazette is *El Peruano*, Lima.

Anario Estadistico del Perú. Annual.—*Perú: Compendio Estadístico.* Annual.—*Boletin de Estadistica Peruana.* Quarterly.—*Demarcación Política del Perú.* (Dirección Nacional de Estadística), Lima
Estadística del Comercio Exterior (Superintendencia de Aduanas). Lima
Banco Central de Reserva. Monthly Bulletin.—*Renta Nacional del Perú.* Annual, Lima

Figueroa, A., *Capitalist Development and the Peasant Economy of Peru.* CUP, 1984
Fisher, J., *Peru:* [Bibliography]. Oxford and Santa Barbara, 1989
Hemming, J., *The Conquest of the Incas.* London, 1970
McClintock, C. and Lowental, A. F., (eds.) *The Peruvian Experiment Reconsidered.* Princeton Univ. Press, 1983
Mejía Baca, J. and Tauro, A., *Diccionário Enciclopédico del Perú.* 3 vols. 1966
Thorp, R., *Economic Management and Economic Development in Peru and Colombia.* London, 1991

National Library: Avenida Abancay, Lima.

PHILIPPINES

Capital: Manila
Population: 60·9m. (1991)
GNP per capita: US$734 (1989)

Republika ng Pilipinas

HISTORY. Before the Spanish discovery of the Philippines, the native Filipinos came in contact with India, China and Arabia. According to the early records of China, 'some Filipinos from the country of Ma-i arrived in Canton and sold their merchandise' as early as 982. The Philippine islands were discovered by Magellan in 1521 and conquered by Spain in 1565. Following the Spanish–American war, the islands were ceded to the USA on 10 Dec. 1898, after the Filipinos had tried in vain to establish an independent republic in 1896.

The Philippines acquired self-government as a Commonwealth of the USA by Act of Congress signed by President Roosevelt on 24 March 1934 and ratified by plebiscite on 14 May 1935. This provided for independence after a 10-year transitional period, at the end of which the Philippines became completely independent on 4 July 1946.

At the presidential elections of Feb. 1986 Ferdinand Marcos was opposed by Corazón Aquino. Though Marcos was proclaimed president by parliament, the elections proved to be fraudulent and Aquino became president. Marcos fled the country.

AREA AND POPULATION. The Philippines is situated between 21° 25' and 4° 23' N. lat. and between 116° and 127° E. long. It is composed of 7,100 islands and islets, 2,773 of which are named. Approximate land area, 115,830 sq. miles (300,000 sq. km). The largest islands (in sq. km) are Luzon (104,688), Mindanao (94,630), Samar (13,080), Negros (12,710), Palawan (11,785), Panay (11,515), Mindoro (9,735), Leyte (7,214), Cebu (4,422), Bohol (3,865), Masbate (3,269).

Census population (1990) was 60,684,887. Estimate, 1991, 62,868,000. Expectation of life in 1989 was 64 years.

The area and population (in 1,000) of the 14 regions are as follows (from north to south):

Region	Sq. km	1990	Region	Sq. km	1990
Ilocos	12,840	3,551	Central Visayas	14,952	4,593
Cagayan Valley	26,838	2,341	Eastern Visayas	21,432	3,055
Central Luzon	18,231	6,199	Northern Mindanao	28,328	3,510
National Capital	636	7,929	Southern Mindanao	31,693	4,457
Southern Tagalog	46,924	8,266	Central Mindanao	23,293	3,171
Bicol	17,633	3,910	Western Mindanao	18,685	3,159
Western Visayas	20,223	5,393	Cordillero Administrative	18,294	1,146

City populations (1990 census, in 1,000) are as follows; all on Luzon unless indicated in parenthesis.

Manila (the capital)	1,599 [1]	San Pablo	162
Quezon City	1,667 [1]	Cadiz (Negros)	120
Davao (Mindanao)	850	Lipa	160
Cebu (Cebu)	610	Baguio	183
Caloocan	761 [1]	Silay (Negros)	101
Zamboanga (Mindanao)	442	Mandaue (Cebu)	180
Bacolod (Negros)	364	Lucena	151
Iloilo (Panay)	310	Calbayog (Samar)	115
Cagayan de Oro (Mindanao)	340	Ormoc (Leyte)	129
Angeles	237	Tacloban (Leyte)	137
Butuan (Mindanao)	228	San Carlos	125
Iligan (Mindanao)	227	Legaspi	121
Olongapo	193	Dagupan	122
General Santos (Mindanao)	250	San Carlos (Negros)	106
Batangas	185	Naga	115
Cabanatuan	173		

[1] City within Metropolitan Manila.

1091

In 1980 the national language, Pilipino (based on Tagalog) was spoken by 55% of the population, but as a mother tongue by only 23·8%; among the 76 other indigenous languages spoken, Cebuano was spoken as a mother tongue by 24·4% and Ilocano by 11·1%.

CLIMATE. Some areas have an equatorial climate while others experience tropical monsoon conditions, with a wet season extending from May to Nov. Mean temperatures are high all year, with very little variation. Manila. Jan. 77°F (25°C), July 82°F (27·8°C). Annual rainfall 82" (2,083 mm).

CONSTITUTION AND GOVERNMENT. Corazón Aquino was sworn in as president on 25 Feb. 1986. New presidential elections were scheduled for 11 May 1992. On 25 March 1986 she abolished parliament and declared a provisional government. A new Constitution was ratified by referendum in 1987 with 78·5% of the voters endorsing it.

Congress now consists of a 24-member upper house, the *Senate*, and a 200-member House of Representatives. Congressional elections were held on 11 May 1987. Presidential elections were scheduled for May 1992.

In Nov. 1991 the government included:
President: Corazón Aquino.
Vice President: Salvador Laurel.
Executive Secretary, Presidential Co-ordinator for Political and Security Affairs: Franklin Drilon. *Defence:* Renato de Villa. *Local Government:* Luis Santos. *Foreign Affairs:* Raul Manglapus. *Justice:* Silvestre Bello. *Finance:* Jesus Estanislao. *Trade and Industry:* Peter Garrucho. *Public Works and Highways:* José de Jesus. *Agrarian Reform:* Benjamin Leong. *Agriculture:* Senen Bacani. *Social Welfare:* Mita Pardo de Tavera. *Education:* Isidro Carino. *Science:* Ceferino Follosco. *Budget:* Guillermo Carague. *Press:* Tomas Gomez. *Economic Planning:* Cayetano Pedranga. *Labour:* Ruben Torres. *Presidential Spokesman:* Adolfo Azcuna. *Speaker:* Ramon Mitra.

National flag: Horizontally blue over red, with a white triangle based on the hoist bearing a gold sun of 8 rays and 3 gold stars.

National hymn: 'Land of the Morning', lyric in English by M. A. Sane and C. Osias, tune by Julian Felipe (1898); 'Bayang magiliw', Tagalog lyric by the Institute of National Language, music by Julian Felipe.

Local Government. The country is administratively divided into 14 regions, 73 provinces, 60 cities, 1,537 municipalities, 21 municipal districts and 41,498 *barangays* (1990). On 14 Nov. 1975 the name of provincial boards and city or municipal boards or councils was changed into *Sangguniang Bayan*. A reform of Oct. 1991 devolved more power to local authorities, giving them 40% of local tax revenues to deliver local services.

DEFENCE. An extension of the 1947 agreement granting the USA the use of several army, navy and air force bases was rejected by the Senate in Sept. 1991. The USA was given 3 years to withdraw. In 1991 there were some 8,000 US personnel stationed in the Philippines. US forces were scheduled to leave the Subic Bay naval base byt he end of 1992. The Philippines is a signatory of the South-East Asia Collective Defence Treaty.

Army. The Army comprises 8 infantry divisions, 3 engineer brigades, 1 special services brigade, 1 light armoured brigade and 8 artillery battalions. Equipment includes 41 Scorpion light tanks. Strength (1992) 68,000, with reserves totalling 100,000.

Navy. The Philippine navy consists principally of ex-US ships completed in 1944 and 1945, and serviceability and spares are a problem. A modernization programme, based on acquisition of a substantial number of much smaller patrol craft of US design is planned, of which the first is on trials.

The present fleet includes 1 US frigate, 8 offshore patrol vesels (ex-US mine-sweepers and escorts), 4 ex-US coastal patrol craft and about 20 inshore patrol craft. There are 5 tank landing ships and 2 medium landing ships, and some 30 landing craft. Auxiliaries include 3 repair ships, 1 oiler, 2 yachts/search-and-rescue craft and 1 transport, as well as some 20 minor auxiliaries. There are 65 patrol craft and search-and-rescue craft in the coastguard. 4 Islander transports and 4 BO 105 helicopters are in use.

Navy personnel in 1991 totalled 23,000 including 8,500 marines and 2,000 in the coastguard.

Air Force. The Air Force had (1992) a strength of 15,500, with 26 combat aircraft and 71 armed helicopters, and was built up with US assistance. Its fighter-bomber wing is equipped with 1 squadron of F-5As. A strike wing is equipped with armed trainers, 2 squadrons having T-28s and 1 squadron SF.260WPs. Other units include a maritime patrol squadron with F27 Maritimes and 7 transport squadrons (1 with C-130/L-100 Hercules, 1 with F27s, 1 with Nomads, 1 with C-47s, 2 with UH-1 Iroquois helicopters, 1 with MD-500 helicopters and 1 with S-76 helicopters). Training aircraft include T-41s, T-34s, S.211 and T-33 jets. 1 Puma and 1 S-70 helicopter are used as VIP transports.

Constabulary. Public order is maintained partly through the Philippine constabulary and partly through the local police forces. The constabulary is part of the Armed Forces and has some 45,000 personnel.

INTERNATIONAL RELATIONS

Membership. The Philippines is a member of the UN and the Colombo Plan.

ECONOMY

Policy. A development plan, 1987–92, aimed at an average growth rate of 6·8%.

Budget. The revenues and expenditures of the central government for calendar years were, in 1m. Philippine pesos, as follows:

	1986	1987	1988	1989	1990
Revenue	79,245	103,214	112,861	142,136	177,216
Expenditure	114,505	155,503	168,409	173,341	211,756

Expenditure (1990) included (in 1m. pesos): National defence, 26,010; education, health and social services, 62,509; economic development, 64,384; debt service, 74,763.

At Dec. 1989 the total internal public debt outstanding of the national and local governments and monetary institutions, including those of the government corporations, stood at P.236,602m.

Currency. The unit of currency is the *Philippine peso* (PHP) of 100 *centavos*. There are notes of 5, 10, 20, 50, 100 and 500 pesos and coins of 1, 5, 10, 25 and 50 centavos and 1, 2 and 5 pesos. Total money supply, Dec. 1990, was P.89,012m. Inflation was an annualized 13.1% in Nov. 1990.

In March 1992, £1 = 44·30 *pesos*; US$1 = 25·23 *pesos*.

Banking and Finance. In 1990 there were 30 head offices and 1,782 branches of commercial banks. Total deposits of the commercial banks at 31 Dec. 1990 were P.310,743m. Total number of Philippine banking institutions, 31 Dec. 1990, 3,637 with total assets P.609,695m. and total deposits of P.350,612·4m.

Under the law passed 15 June 1948 the Central Bank of the Philippines was created to have sole control of the credit and monetary supply, independent of the Treasury. It has a capital of P.10m. furnished solely by the Government. Its total assets, at 31 Dec. 1990 were P.444,893·2m. The Governor is José Cuisia.

Weights and Measures. The metric system of weights and measures was established by law in 1869, and since 1916 has come into general use but there are local units including the picul (63·25 kg) for sugar and fibres, and the cavan (16·5 gallons) for cereals.

ENERGY AND NATURAL RESOURCES

Electricity. Government and private electric systems furnish the Philippines with electric power, with total installed capacity of 6,037m. mw (1990); production 24,799m. kwh. Supply 110 and 220 volts; 60 Hz.

Minerals. Mineral production in 1990, (in tonnes): Nickel metal, 15,818; zinc metal, 53; copper metal, 180,459; coal, 1,246,777; salt, 490,407; gold, 24,519 kg; silver, 47,111 kg; silica sand, 561,720. Other minerals include chromite, cement, rock asphalt, sand and gravel.

Agriculture. In 1980 the total area was 30m. ha, of which 9·7 (30·11%) was farm area. The rest was comprised of commercial and non-commercial forests, open grassland, mangrove and marshes, and cultivated land.

The average size of the farm was 2·63 ha in 1980. The principal products are coconuts, unhusked rice (palay), sugar-cane, maize and root crops, bananas and pineapples. As of Oct. 1990 10,185,000 persons were employed in agriculture (45% of the working population).

The products (in 1,000 tonnes) in 1990: Rough rice, 9,319; coconuts, 11,940; sugar-cane, 18,581; shelled corn, 4,854; bananas, 2,913; cassava, 1,854; pineapple, 1,156.

Minor crops are fruits, nuts, vegetables, onions, beans, coffee, cacao, peanuts, ramie, rubber, maguey, kapok, abaca and tobacco.

Livestock, estimated in 1990 (in 1,000): 2,785 carabaos (water buffaloes), 1,629 cattle, 7,990 pigs, 2,193 goats and 77,000 poultry.

Forestry. The forests covered about 15·88m. ha, or 53% of the total land area. These forest lands have been classified into: Forest Reserve, 3,272,912 ha; timber land, 10,015,402 ha; National Parks, 1,340,997 ha; civil reservation, 165,946 ha; Military and Naval reservation, 130,330; fish ponds, 75,527 ha; and unclassified forest lands, 881,157 ha.in 1989. Log production, 1989, 3,168,043 cu. metres.

Fisheries. Fish production from all sources was 2,211,000 tonnes in 1990.

INDUSTRY. Manufacturing is a major source of economic development contributing 25·1% to GNP in 1989. Leading growth sectors were food manufacturing, textile, footwear and wearing apparel, machinery except electrical, fabricated metal products, wood and cork products, industrial chemicals and other chemical products, furniture and fixtures and publishing and allied industries. In 1987 (annual survey), there were 5,000 large manufacturing establishments, of which 1,165 were engaged in food; 414 wearing apparel; 111 footwear; 297 textile; 366 publishing and allied industries; 300 machinery except electrical; 258 fabricated metal products; 295 industrial chemicals and other chemical products; 254 wood and cork products; 162 plastic products and 145 transport equipment.

Labour. The non-agricultural labour force as of Oct. 1990 was 12,347,000 out of a total of 22,531,000 employed.

FOREIGN ECONOMIC RELATIONS. Foreign debt was US$28,519m. at the end of 1990. A law of June 1991 gave foreigners the right to full ownership of export and other firms, considered strategic for the economy.

Commerce. The values of imports and exports (f.o.b.) for calendar years are stated as follows in US$1m.:

	1987	1988	1989	1990
Imports	6,737	8,159	10,419	12,206
Exports	5,720	7,074	7,821	8,186

The principal exports in 1990 were (in US$1m.): Garments, 1,766; electronics, 1,523; coconut oil (crude), 361; bars, rods and slabs of copper, 281; shrimps and prawns, 219; bananas, 149; copper concentrates, 267; petroleum products, 155; tuna, 118; sugar, 111.

Main imports in 1990 (in US$1m.): Petroleum products and related materials, 1,750; textile yarns, fabrics, made-up articles and related products, 547; machinery, apparatus and appliances, 736; cereals and cereal preparations, 471; iron and steel, 572; general industrial machinery and equipment, 400; artificial resins, plastic materials, cellulose esters and ethers, 332; road vehicles, 508; special transactions and commodities not classified according to kind, 1,929; machinery specialised for particular industries, 543.

For over a half-century the foreign trade has been chiefly with the USA.

Total trade between the Philippines and UK (British Department of Trade returns, in £1,000 sterling):

	1987	1988	1989	1990	1991
Imports to UK	202,707	223,571	233,128	220,706	229,955
Exports and re-exports from UK	113,784	123,974	137,367	158,030	146,571

Tourism. In 1990, 1,024,719 tourists visited the Philippines spending US$1,306m.

COMMUNICATIONS

Roads. In 1990 highways totalled 160,560 km; of this, 10,358 km were concrete; 12,753, asphalt; 8,497, earth; and 128,953 gravel. In 1990 there were registered 1,620,242 motor vehicles of all types.

Railways. The National Railway totals 805 km of 1,067 mm gauge on Luzon. In 1990, 928,038 passengers and 32,171 tonnes of freight were carried. The light railway in Manila carried 128m. passengers in 1990.

Civil Aviation. Philippine Air Lines in 1990 carried 5,665,000 international and domestic passengers. In 1990 there were 86 national and 92 private airports.

Shipping. In 1990 there were 180 public and 247 private ports. In 1990, 89,200 vessels of 84,682,000 net tons entered and 89,063 vessels of 84,000,000 net tons cleared all ports.

Telecommunications. In 1990 there were in operation 2,200 post offices. The Philippine Long Distance Telephone Co. had 574,547 line capacity. Other major operators had 93,764 line capacity.

As of Sept. 1991, there were 449 AM and FM stations and 174 television stations.

Newspapers (1990). There were 234 registered publications (186 published in Manila); 32, daily newspapers; 1, weekly tabloid; 58, magazines; 7, foreign publications; and 48, provincial publications.

JUSTICE, RELIGION, EDUCATION AND WELFARE

Justice. There is a Supreme Court which is composed of a chief justice and 14 associate justices; it can declare a law or treaty unconstitutional by the concurrent votes of the majority sitting. There is a court of appeals, which consists of a presiding justice and 49 associate justices. There are 13 regional trial courts, one for each judicial region, with a presiding regional trial judge in its 720 branches. There is a metropolitan trial court in each metropolitan area established by law, a municipal trial court in each of the other cities or municipalities and a municipal circuit trial court in each area defined as a municipal circuit comprising one or more cities and/or one or more municipalities.

The Supreme Court may designate certain branches of the regional trial courts to handle exclusively criminal cases, juvenile and domestic relations cases, agrarian cases, urban land reform cases which do not fall under the jurisdiction of quasijudicial bodies and agencies and/or such other special cases as the Supreme Court may determine.

Local police forces are supplemented by the Philippine Constabulary, which is part of the armed forces (*see* p. 1093).

Religion. In 1970 there were 31,169,488 Roman Catholics, 1,433,688 Aglipayans, 1,584,963 Moslems, 1,122,999 Protestants, 475,407 members of the Iglesia ni Kristo, 33,639 Buddhists and 863,302 others.

The Roman Catholics are organized in 12 archbishoprics, 30 bishoprics, 12 prelatures nullius, 4 apostolic vicariates, 4 apostolic prefectures and some 1,633 parishes. The Philippine Independent Church, founded in 1902, and comprising about 3·9% of the population, denies the spiritual authority of the Roman Pontiff. It is divided into two groups, one of which has accepted ordinations by the Episcopalian Church.

Education. Public elementary education is free and public elementary schools are established almost everywhere. The majority of secondary and post-secondary schools are private, sectarian or non-sectarian. Formal education consists of an optional 1 to 2 years of pre-school education; 6 years of elementary education; 4 years of secondary education; and 4 to 5 years of tertiary or college education leading to academic degrees. 3-year post-secondary non-degree technical/vocational education is also considered formal education.

Non-formal education consists of adult literacy classes, agricultural and farming training programmes, occupation skills training, youth clubs, and community programmes of instructions in health, nutrition, family planning and co-operatives.

Public and private schools in 1989–90 enrolled 10,284,861 pupils in elementary schools, 3,961,639 in secondary schools and 1,516,315 students in tertiary education. The University of the Philippines (founded in 1908) had 15,316 students in 1984.

Health. In 1989 there were 57,270 registered physicians and 89,280 hospital beds.

DIPLOMATIC REPRESENTATIVES

Of the Philippines in Great Britain (9A Palace Green, London, W8 4QE)
Ambassador: Manuel T. Yan.

Of Great Britain in the Philippines (115 Esteban St., Manila)
Ambassador: Keith MacInnes, CMG.

Of the Philippines in the USA (1617 Massachusetts Ave., NW, Washington, D.C., 20036)
Ambassador: Emmanuel N. Pelaez.

Of the USA in the Philippines (1201 Roxas Blvd., Manila)
Ambassador: Frank Wisner.

Of the Philippines to the United Nations
Ambassador: Sedfrey Ordoñez.

Further Reading

Philippine Yearbook. National Statistics Office.
Bresnan, J., (ed.) *Crisis in the Philippines: The Marcos Era and Beyond.* Princeton Univ. Press, 1986
Karnow, S., *In Our Image: America's Empire in the Philippines.* New York, 1989
May, R. J. and Nemenzo, F. (eds.), *The Philippines after Marcos.* London and Sydney, 1985
Poole, F. and Vanzi, M., *Revolution in the Philippines.* New York, 1984
Richardson, J. A., *Philippines.* [Bibliography] Oxford and Santa Barbara, 1989
Seagrove, S., *The Marcos Dynasty.* London, 1989

National statistics office: National Statistics Office, POB 779, Manila

PITCAIRN ISLAND

Only settlement: Adamstown
Population: 61 (1991)

HISTORY. It was discovered by Carteret in 1767, but remained uninhabited until 1790, when it was occupied by 9 mutineers of HMS *Bounty*, with 12 women and 6 men from Tahiti. Nothing was known of their existence until the island was visited in 1808. In 1856 the population having become too large for the island's resources, the inhabitants (194 in number) were, at their own request, removed to Norfolk Island; but 43 of them returned in 1859–64.

AREA AND POPULATION. Pitcairn Island (1·75 sq. miles; 4·6 sq. km) is situated in the Pacific Ocean, nearly equidistant from New Zealand and Panama (25° 04' S. lat., 130° 06' W. long.). Adamstown is the only settlement. The population on 31 Dec. 1990 was 59. The uninhabited islands of Henderson (12 sq. miles), Ducie (1½ sq. miles) and Oeno (2 sq. miles) were annexed in 1902 and are included in the Pitcairn group.

CLIMATE. An equable climate, with average annual rainfall of 80" (2,000 mm), spread evenly throughout the year. Mean monthly temperatures range from 75°F (24°C) in Jan. to 66°F (19°C) in July.

CONSTITUTION. Pitcairn was brought within the jurisdiction of the High Commissioner for the Western Pacific in 1898 and transferred to the Governor of Fiji in 1952. When Fiji became independent in Oct. 1970, the British High Commissioner in New Zealand was appointed Governor.

The Local Government Ordinance of 1964 constitutes a Council of 10 members, of whom 6 are elected, 3 are nominated (1 by the 6 elected members and 2 by the Governor) and the Island Secretary is an *ex-officio* member. The Island Magistrate, who is elected triennially, presides over the Council; other members hold office for only 1 year. Liaison between Governor and Council is through a Commissioner in the Auckland, New Zealand, office of the British Consulate-General.

Governor: D. J. Moss, CMG (resides in Wellington).
Island Magistrate: Jay Warren (elected Dec. 1990).

Flag: British Blue Ensign with the whole arms of Pitcairn in the fly.

BUDGET. In 1990 the island earned $958,733 and spent $923,355.

CURRENCY. The Pitcairn *dollar* has the same value as the New Zealand dollar.

TRADE. Fruit, vegetables and curios are sold to passing ships; fuel oil, machinery, building materials, flour, sugar and other foodstuffs are imported.

ROADS. There were (1991) 6 km of roads. In July 1991 motor cycles provided the sole means of personal automotive transport; there were 6 2-wheelers, 24 3-wheelers and 8 4-wheeled motor cycles.

JUSTICE. The Island Court consists of the Island Magistrate and 2 assessors.

EDUCATION. In 1991 there was 1 teacher and 12 pupils.

Further Reading

A Guide to Pitcairn. Pitcairn Island Administration, Auckland, revised ed. 1990
Ball, I., *Pitcairn: Children of the Bounty.* London, 1973
Ross, A. S. C. and Moverly, A. W., *The Pitcairnese Language.* London, 1964

POLAND

Capital: Warsaw
Population: 37·93m. (1990)
GNP per capita: US$1,760 (1989)

Rzeczpospolita Polska

(Polish Republic)

HISTORY. The Polish state was founded in 966 but the once-powerful kingdom was partitioned between Russia, Austria and Prussia in 1772, 1793 and 1795. For 19th century events *see* THE STATESMAN'S YEAR-BOOK 1980–81. On 10 Nov. 1918 an independent republic was proclaimed by Józef Piłsudski, and this was recognized by the Treaty of Versailles on 28 June 1919. For the Second World War and the subsequent Communist régime *see* THE STATESMAN'S YEAR-BOOK, 1991–92, p. 1011.

The raising of meat prices on 1 July 1980 resulted in a wave of strikes which broadened into generalized wage demands and eventually acquired a political character. Workers in Gdańsk, Gdynia and Sopot elected a joint strike committee, led by Lech Wałęsa. On 31 Aug. the Government and Wałęsa signed the 'Gdańsk Agreements' permitting the formation of independent trade unions. On 17 Sept. various trade unions decided to form a national confederation ('Solidarity') and applied for legal status, which was granted on 24 Oct.

On 9 Feb. 1981 the Defence Minister, Gen. Wojciech Jaruzelski, became Prime Minister. At Solidarity's first national congress (4–10 Sept. and 2–8 Oct. 1981) Wałęsa was re-elected chairman and a radical programme of action was adopted. On 13 Dec. 1981 the Government imposed martial law and set up a Military Council of National Salvation. Solidarity was proscribed.

Following strikes and demands for the reinstatement of Solidarity, the government resigned in Sept. 1988.

After the parliamentary elections of June 1989 the Communists were unable to form a government against the opposition of Solidarity, and Tadeusz Mazowiecki, a Solidarity member, was elected Prime Minister by the Sejm on 24 Aug. Unconditionally free parliamentary elections were held in Oct. 1991.

AREA AND POPULATION. Poland is bounded in the north by the Baltic Sea and Russia, east by Lithuania, Belorussia and the Ukraine, south by Czechoslovakia and west by Germany. Poland comprises an area of 312,683 sq. km (120,628 sq. miles). The country is divided into 49 voivodships (*wojewodztwo*) and these in turn are divided into 822 towns and 2,121 wards (*gmina*). The capital is Warsaw (Warszawa).

Area (in sq. km) and population (in 1,000) in 1989 (1984 % urban in brackets).

Voivodship	Area	Population		Voivodship	Area	Population	
Biała Podlaska	5,348	304	(32·5)	Koszalin	8,470	503	(61·0)
Białystok	10,055	688	(57·7)	Kraków (Cracow)	3,254	1,223	(69·1)
Bielsko–Biała	3,704	895	(48·9)	Krosno	5,702	496	(32·8)
Bydgoszcz	10,349	1,104	(62·8)	Legnica	4,037	510	(66·6)
Chełm	3,866	246	(39·9)	Leszno	4,154	383	(46·1)
Ciechanów	6,362	426	(33·0)	Łódź	1,523	1,139	(91·4)
Częstochowa	6,182	773	(51·2)	Łomża	6,684	345	(35·7)
Elbląg	6,103	476	(58·6)	Lublin	6,792	1,011	(55·5)
Gdańsk	7,394	1,418	(76·2)	Nowy Sącz	5,576	691	(35·5)
Gorzów	8,484	497	(60·4)	Olsztyn	12,327	746	(56·4)
Jelenia Góra	4,378	515	(65·3)	Opole	8,535	1,010	(50·9)
Kalisz	6,512	707	(44·5)	Ostrołeka	6,498	393	(30·9)
Katowice	6,650	3,954	(87·7)	Piła	8,205	476	(53·9)
Kielce	9,211	1,124	(44·4)	Piotrków	6,266	639	(45·3)
Konin	5,139	466	(38·6)	Płock	5,117	513	(45·7)

Voivodship	Area	Population		Voivodship	Area	Population	
Poznań	8,151	1,323	(69·7)	Tarnobrzeg	6,283	594	(34·6)
Przemyśl	4,437	404	(35·7)	Tarnów	4,151	665	(34·2)
Radom	7,294	745	(44·5)	Toruń	5,348	656	(60·8)
Rzeszów	4,397	716	(37·7)	Wałbrzych	4,168	738	(88·5)
Siedlce	8,499	648	(28·7)	Warsaw	3,788	2,416	(73·0)
Sieradz	4,869	408	(33·1)	Włocławek	4,402	427	(44·9)
Skierniewice	3,960	417	(42·2)	Wrocław	6,287	1,123	(72·4)
Słupsk	7,453	410	(53·8)	Zamość	6,980	488	(24·9)
Suwałki	10,490	467	(49·9)	Zielona Góra	8,868	655	(59·0)
Szczecin	9,981	964	(73·9)				

Population (in 1,000) of the largest towns (1985):

Warsaw	1,649	Bydgoszcz	361	Gliwice	213
Łódź	849	Lublin	324	Kielce	201
Kraków (Cracow)	716	Sosnowiec	255	Zabrze	198
Wrocław (Breslau)	636	Częstochowa	247	Toruń	186
Poznań	553	Białystok	245	Tychy	182
Gdańsk (Danzig)	467	Gdynia	243	Bielsko-Biala	174
Szczecin (Stettin)	391	Bytom	239	Ruda Śląska	165
Katowice	363	Radom	214	Olsztyn	147

At the census of 6 Dec. 1984 the population was 37,026,000 (18m. males; 60% urban). Population on 31 Dec. 1989, 37,932,000 (19·43m. females; 23·36m. urban), density, 121 per sq. km. Vital statistics, 1989 (per 1,000): Marriages, 6·8; divorces, 1·2; live births, 14·9; deaths, 10·1; infant mortality (per 1,000 live births), 15·9.

The rate of natural growth, 1989, 4·8 per 1,000. Expectation of life in 1989 was 72 years.

Ethnic minorities are not identified. There were estimated to be 1·2m. Germans in 1984, and there are Ukrainians, Belorussians and Lithuanians. A Council of National Minorities was set up in March 1991. In 1989 there were 2,200 immigrants and 26,600 emigrants. There is a large Polish diaspora, some 65% in USA. About 250,000 Poles settled abroad between 1981 and 1988, 153,000 illegally.

CLIMATE. Climate is continental, marked by long and severe winters. Rainfall amounts are moderate, with a marked summer maximum. Warsaw. Jan. 25°F (−3·9°C), July 66°F (18·9°C). Annual rainfall 22·1" (550 mm). Gdańsk. Jan. 29°F (−1·7°C), July 63°F (17·2°C). Annual rainfall 22" (559 mm). Kraków. Jan. 27°F (−2·8°C), July 67°F (19·4°C). Annual rainfall 29" (729 mm). Poznań. Jan. 30°F (−1·1°C), July 67°F (19·4°C). Annual rainfall 21" (523 mm). Szezecin. Jan. 30°F (−1·1°C), July 65°F (18·3°C). Annual rainfall 22" (550 mm). Wrocław. Jan. 30°F (−1·1°C), July 66°F (18·9°C). Annual rainfall 23" (574 mm).

CONSTITUTION AND GOVERNMENT. The present Constitution was adopted on 22 July 1952. Amendments were adopted in 1976 and 1983.

The authority of the republic is vested in the *Sejm* (Parliament of 460 members), elected for 4 years by all citizens over 18. The Sejm elects a *Council of State* and a *Council of Ministers.*

The titular head of state is the *President,* Lech Wałęsa sworn in 22 Dec. 1990.

The Prime Minister is chosen by the President with the approval of the Sejm.

Talks between the Communist Party (PUWP), Solidarity and others in Feb.–March 1989 resulted in the establishment of a 100-member upper house (Senate), the legalization of Solidarity and Rural Solidarity, and the holding of parliamentary elections at which Solidarity and other opposition groups were free to contest all seats in the Senate and 35% of seats in the Sejm. The Senate has power of veto which only a two-thirds majority of the Sejm can overrule.

At the elections of June 1989 Solidarity won 99 seats in the Senate and 161 in the Sejm. Only 2 of a government-sponsored 'National List' of 35 candidates qualified for election by gaining more than 50% of votes. The PUWP were allotted 173 seats, and their coalition partners the United Peasant's Party (UPP) 76; the Democratic Party (DP), 27; the Christian Democrats, 23.

A Political Council consultative to the presidency consisting of representatives of all the major political tendencies was set up in Jan. 1991.

At the first round of the presidential elections on 26 Nov. 1990 Lech Wałęsa polled 39.96% of the vote (failing to reach the 50% plus 1 vote necessary to win outright); Stanisław Tymiński, 23.1%, and the Prime Minister, Tadeusz Mazowiecki, 18.08%; the latter announced that on this showing he and his government would resign. At the second round turn-out was 53.4%; 75% of votes were cast for Wałęsa.

Unconditionally free elections to the Sejm were held in Oct. 1991. Turn-out was 11,887,949 (43.2%). 69 parties stood, of which 29 gained seats, including: Democratic Union, 62 with 12.31% of votes cast; Alliance of the Democratic Left, 60 with 11.98%; Catholic Action, 49 with 8.73%; Peasant Party, 48 with 8.67%; Confederation for an Independent Poland, 46 with 7.5%; Alliance of the Centre, 44 with 8.71%; Congress of Liberals, 37 with 7.48%; Rural Solidarity, 28 with 5.46%; Trade Union Solidarity, 27 with 5.05%; Friends of Beer, 16 with 3.27%; German Minority, 7 with 1.27%; Christian Democratic Party, 4 with 1.11%; Party X, 3 with 0.47%. The remaining 29 seats were shared among smaller parties and regional movements.

A new government was formed in Dec. 1991. In March 1992 the government comprised:

Prime Minister: Jan Olszewski.

Head of the Council of Ministers' Office: Wojciech Włodarczyk. *Foreign*: Krzysztof Skubiszewski. *Interior*: Antoni Maciarewicz. *Defence*: Jan Parys. *Justice, Attorney-General*: Zbigniew Dyka. *Head of the Central Planning Office*: Jerzy Eysymontt. *Finance*: Andrzej Olechowski. *Foreign Economic Relations*: Adam Głapiński. *Agriculture*: Gabriel Janowski. *Transport*: Ewaryst Waligorski. *Environment and Natural Resources*: Stefan Kozłowski. *Labour and Social Policy*: Jerzy Kropiwnicki. *Education*: Andrzej Stelmachowski. *Culture*: Andrzej Siciński. *Health*: Marian Miskiewicz. *Without Portfolio*: Artur Balazs.

In Jan. 1990 the PUWP dissolved itself and formed a new party, the Social Democracy of the Polish Republic.

Local government is carried out by councils elected every 4 years at voivodship and community level. Local government is financed partly by local taxes and partly by central government taxes. There are also district agencies which form a link between local and central government. Communities of fewer than 40,000 inhabitants elect councils on a first-past-the-post system; larger communities have a proportional party-list system. It was admitted in 1990 that the elections of June 1988 were undemocratic, and new elections were held on 27 May for 2,383 councils; turn-out was 42%. 147,389 candidates stood for 52,037 seats. Independants gained 50.52% of votes cast, Citizens' Committees 41.47, the Polish Peasant Party 5.76% and Solidarity 1.45%.

National flag: Horizontally white over red, with the arms of Poland on the white strip.

National anthem: Jeszcze Polska nie zginęla ('Poland has not yet perished'; words by J. Wybicki, 1797; tune by M. Ogiński, 1796).

DEFENCE. Poland is divided into 3 military districts: Warsaw (the eastern part of Poland); Pomerania (Baltic coast, part of central Poland; headquarters at Bydgoszcz); Silesia (Silesia and southern Poland; headquarters at Wrocław).

Armed forces are divided into army and air force (18 months conscription), navy (2 years), anti-aircraft, rocket and radio-technological units (3 years) and internal security forces (2 years). The military age extends from the 19th to the 50th year. The strength of the armed forces was (1991) 305,000 (191,000 conscripts).

3-year civilian duty as a conscientious alternative to conscription was introduced in 1988.

The USSR agreed to withdraw its 45,000 troops by the end of 1992.

Army. The Army includes 9 mechanized divisions, 1 airborne, 1 coastal defence and 3 artillery brigades; 3 anti-tank regiments; 3 *Sand* missile brigades. Equipment includes 2,093 T-54/-55 and 757 T-72 main battle tanks and 30 PT-76 light tanks. Strength (1992) 199,500 (including 127,500 conscripts).

Navy. The fleet comprises 3 ex-Soviet diesel submarines, 1 ex-Soviet guided missile destroyer armed with SA-N-1 Goa surface-to-air and SS-N-2C Styx anti-ship missiles, 1 small frigate, 4 missile corvettes, 8 smaller fast missile craft, 8 inshore patrol craft, 8 coastal and 15 inshore minesweepers, 19 medium landing ships and about 10 landing craft. Auxiliaries include 3 support tankers, 2 intelligence vessels, 3 survey vessels, and 2 training ships together with about 60 minor auxiliaries.

The Fleet Air Arm comprises a single regiment with 1 squadron of Iskra patrol aircraft, 1 with Mi-14 and W-3 Sokol helicopters, and 1 with An-2 and An-28 transports. Naval-manned coast defences provide 6 artillery battalions and 3 missile batteries.

Personnel in 1991 totalled 19,500 including 10,000 conscripts. 2,300 of these serve in naval aviation and 4,200 in coast defence. Bases are at Gdynia, Gdańsk and Swinoujscie.

A para-military border guard service operates 18 inshore patrol craft and some 30 boats.

Air Force. The Air Force had a strength (1992) of some 86,200 (52,000 conscripts) with 450 combat aircraft and 100 armed helicopters. There are 9 air defence regiments (18 squadrons) with about 250 MiG-21, MiG-23 and MiG-29 supersonic interceptors, and 4 regiments (12 squadrons) operating variable-geometry Su-20 and Su-22 close-support fighters. There are also reconnaissance, ECM, transport, helicopter (including Mi-2s for observation and Mi-24 gunships) and training units. Soviet 'Guideline' 'Goa', 'Ganef', 'Gainful' and 'Gaskin' surface-to-air missiles are operational.

INTERNATIONAL RELATIONS. A treaty of friendship with Germany signed 17 June 1991 renounced the use of force, recognized Poland's western border as laid down at the Potsdam conference of 1945 (the 'Oder-Neisse line') and guaranteed minority rights in both countries.

Membership. Poland is a member of the UN, the Council of Europe and IMF, and an associate member of the EC, and in May 1991 adhered to the 'Pentagonal' grouping of Austria, Czechoslovakia, Hungary, Italy and Yugoslavia, henceforth renamed 'Hexagonal'.

ECONOMY

Policy. For planning history until 1989 *see* THE STATESMAN'S YEAR-BOOK 1989–90, p.1012-13. Wide-ranging measures to convert the economy into a market-oriented system were passed by Parliament in Dec. 1989, including the commercialization of interest and exchange rates, the abolition of price subsidies, the termination of wages indexation and the encouragement of foreign investment. Legislation of July 1990 envisages the transfer of state enterprises into private ownership through the issue of 'privatization bonds'. 400 state-owned factories were presented for privatization in 1991. 60% of their equity is to be transferred to National Wealth Management Funds, which have Polish chairs and Western managers. They are owned by all Polish citizens who are given participation certificates for trading in 1993. 30% of the equity will be retained by the state, and 10% made over to employees.

Budget. Budget in 1m. złotys, for calendar years:

	1984	1985	1986	1987	1988	1989
Revenue	3,299,700	3,854,200	4,902,700	5,850,400	10,080,800	30,090,100
Expenditure	3,367,800	3,979,200	4,193,200	5,029,800	8,423,000	29,619,200

Main items of 1989 revenue (in 1m. złotys): State enterprises, 23,962,300; finance and insurance, 2,856,900; private sector and personal taxes, 2,462,400. Expenditure: The economy, 11,919,000; welfare, 4,017,700; education, 3,506,100; defence,

2,118,000. 1990 budget estimates halve subsidies but increase allocations to health, education and the environment.

Currency. The currency unit is the *złoty* (PLZ), divided into 100 *groszy*. The currency consists of notes of 10, 20, 50, 100, 500, 1,000, 2,000, 5,000, 10,000, 50,000, 100,000, 500,000 and 1,000,000 złotys. From Oct. 1991 the złoty was devalued on a daily basis by 9 złoty to US$1 until devaluation reached 6% by the end of 1991. Inflation was 250% at the end of 1990 (640% in 1989). In Dec. 1989 a US$1,000m. Currency Stabilization Fund was established with the agreement of the IMF. The złoty became convertible on 1 Jan. 1990. In March 1992, £1 sterling = 23,269 złotys, US$1 = 13,254·9 złotys.

Banking and Finance. The National Bank of Poland (established 1945) is the central bank and bank of issue. Its Governor is nominated by the President and approved by the Sejm. (*Acting Governor*, Andrzej Topiński). The 9 state-owned banks established in 1989 are being privatized with IMF advice. The General Savings Bank (Powszechna Kasa Oszczędności) exercises central control over savings activities. Deposits in savings institutions amounted to 7,917·3m. złotys in 1989.

There is a stock exchange in Warsaw.

Weights and Measures. The metric system is in general use.

ENERGY AND NATURAL RESOURCES

Electricity. Electricity production (1989) 145,000m. kwh. In 1989, 70% of electricity was produced by coal-powered thermal plants. Supply 127 and 220 volts; 50 Hz. Plans to build a nuclear power station have been abandoned.

Minerals. Poland is a major producer of coal (reserves of some 120,000m. tonnes), copper (56m. tonnes) and sulphur. Production in 1989 (in tonnes): Coal, 178m.; brown coal, 71·8m.; copper ore (1988) 401,000; silver, 1,003.

Oil and Gas. Oil was discovered 80 km off the port of Leba in 1985. Total oil reserves amount to some 100m. tonnes. Crude oil production was 148,000 tonnes in 1991, natural gas 5,377m. cu. metres (1989).

Agriculture. In 1989 there were 18·73m. ha of agricultural land, of which 14·27m. ha were in private hands, 3·5m. in state farms, 705,000 in co-operatives and 57,000 in agricultural associations. 14·41m. ha were arable, 265,000 orchards, 2·5m. meadows, 1·6m. pasture lands.

Although collectivization had been largely abandoned by the Communist government, procurement remained a state monopoly, and prices were centrally-fixed. There were 2,004 co-operatives in 1989, 1,231 state farms and 173 agricultural associations. In Dec. 1987 a private, Catholic, Foundation for the Development of Polish Agriculture was set up to aid farmers with Western finance. Rural Solidarity (*Chairman:* Josef Slisz) was re-legalized in 1989. A compulsory contributory pension scheme was introduced in 1978 for farmers who turned over their farms to their successors or the State. There were 2·73m. private holdings in 1989, of which 809,000 were less than 2 ha. State farms were abolished in Oct. 1991 and farm workers enabled to set up private companies to work the land.

Crops	Area (1,000 ha)		Total Yield (1,000 tonnes)		
	1988	1989	1988	1989	(from private sector)
Wheat	2,179	2,195	7,528	8,462	(5,702)
Rye	2,325	2,275	5,501	6,216	(5,167)
Barley	1,250	1,175	3,804	3,909	(2,721)
Oats	850	803	2,222	2,185	(1,692)
Potatoes	1,866	1,077	34,707	34,390	(31,345)
Sugar-beet	412	423	14,069	14,374	(12,025)

Livestock (1989, in thousands): 10,733 cattle (4,994 cows), 18,835 pigs, 4,409 sheep, 973 horses. Milk production was 15,925m. litres; meat, 3,139,000 tonnes.
Tractors in use in 1989: 1,153,000 (in 15-h.p. units).

Forestry. In 1989, 8·68m. ha were forests (predominantly coniferous). 75,000 ha were afforested, and 22·67m. cu. metres of timber gained.

Fisheries. In 1985 the fishing fleet had 93 deep-sea vessels totalling 314,000 GRT. The catch was 650,600 tonnes.

INDUSTRY

Production. Output declined by 14% in 1990. Production in 1989 (in 1,000 tonnes): Coke, 16,500; rolled steel, 11,276; cement, 17,100; sulphuric acid (100%), 4,865; fertilizers, 2,727; electrolytic copper, 390; zinc, 164; sugar, 1,712; plastics, 723. In 1989, 283 ships over 100 DWT were built (224 in 1988), 286,000 cars, 43,900 lorries and 9,100 buses.

Output of light industry in 1989: Cotton fabrics, 756m. metres; woollen fabrics, 96·7m. metres; synthetic fibres, 238,000 tonnes; shoes (1988), 168m. pairs; household glass, 68,700 tonnes; paper, 1,406,000 tonnes; washing machines 811,000, refrigerators 516,000, and TV sets 763,000.

Labour. In 1989 the total number in employment was 17·1m., of whom 5·08m. worked in the private sector (3·56m. of these in agriculture), and including in industry 4·86m., agriculture, 4·53m.; trade, 1·43m., building 1·32m. and transport and communications, 1·1m. Average wage in the state sector in 1990, 893,070 złotys per month. Unemployment benefit of an initial 70% of previous wages was introduced in Dec. 1989. There were 1,749,000 unemployed (9·4% of the workforce) in Aug. 1991. Workers made redundant are entitled to one month's wages. There is a statutory 42-hour working week which may be compulsorily extended in certain workplaces, with 38 free Saturdays a year.

Trade Unions. Founded in Aug. 1980 the 'independent self-governing union' organization Solidarity (Chairman, Lech Wałęsa) was dissolved in Oct. 1982 along with all other trade unions. New official unions (OPZZ) established in 1983 took over Solidarity's funds in 1985. OPZZ had 5m. members in 1990. There are also some 4,000 small unions not affiliated to OPZZ. Solidarity was re-legalized in May 1989 and successfully contested the parliamentary elections in June. It had 2·3m. members in 1991; its chairman is Marian Krzaklewski.

FOREIGN ECONOMIC RELATIONS. Since Jan. 1989 Western investors may own 100% of companies on Polish soil. Legislation of June 1991 removed limits on the repatriation of profits, reduced the number of cases needing licences and ended a 10% ceiling on share purchases. Licenses are issued by the Ministry for Privatization, and are required for investment in ports, airports, arms manufacture, estate agency and legal services. By the first quarter of 1991 there were about 4,000 joint ventures. In Oct. 1991 foreign investments totalled US$670m. (including German, US$152·6m.; US, US$53·2m.; Swedish, US$46·4m.).

In Feb. 1990 the IMF granted a loan of US$725m., and Western creditor nations agreed to a rescheduling of debts. Foreign debt was US$45,200m. in Nov. 1990. In 1991 Western creditor nations wrote off 50% of Poland's foreign debt. Poland does not accept liability for the £495,000 debts of pre-war Danzig (Gdańsk).

Commerce. Trade statistics for calendar years (in 1m. złotys; trade with convertible currency areas in brackets):

	1986	1987	1988		1989	
Imports	1,964,000	2,875,600	5,272,300	(3,145,700)	14,864,200	(8,908,500)
Exports	2,115,600	3,236,500	6,011,700	(3,611,800)	19,476,200	(11,561,700)

Main imports in 1989 (in tonnes): Crude oil, 15m.; iron ore, 13·44m.; fertilizers, 5·36m.; wheat, 1·8m.; passenger cars, 33,200 units; machinery and electronic equipment.

Main exports in 1989 (in tonnes): Coal, 28·9m.; coke, 3·16m.; copper, 157,000; sulphur, 3·64m.; ships, 186,000 DWT.

41% of Poland's trade was with Comecon countries in 1988. Barter deals worth US$700m. were negotiated with the USSR in Sept. 1991. Soviet exports include plant and equipment and raw materials; Polish exports, machinery, ships, coal, chemicals and consumer goods. Since Jan. 1991 trade with the USSR has been conducted in convertible currency. Germany and the UK are Poland's major Western trading partners.

Total trade between Poland and UK (British Department of Trade returns £1,000 sterling):

	1987	1988	1989	1990	1991
Imports to UK	303,418	328,013	330,163	357,164	313,828
Exports and re-exports from UK	181,451	175,685	196,446	221,536	347,069

In Feb. 1987 the US restored Poland's most-favoured-nation status. A trade agreement was signed with the EC in Sept. 1989. Import duties were raised in July 1991 to protect domestic producers and preserve hard currency reserves.

Tourism. In 1988, 4,196,000 tourists visited Poland (1,104,000 from the West) and 6,924,000 Polish citizens made visits abroad (1,665,000 to the West). More liberal passport regulations were introduced for Polish citizens in 1987.

COMMUNICATIONS

Roads. In 1989 Poland had 159,000 km of hard-surfaced roads. There were 4·85m. passenger cars (4·77m. private), 977,000 lorries (452,000 private) 91,000 buses and 1·41m. motor cycles. Public road transport carried 2,504m. passengers and 105m. tonnes of freight in 1988. There were 37,538 road accidents in 1989 (4,851 fatal).

Railways. Length of standard gauge routes was 24,287 km (11,015 km electrified) in 1990. In 1989 55,800m. passenger-km and 110,990m. tonne-km of freight were carried. There are tram/light rail networks in 13 cities.

Civil Aviation. In 1991 the state airline 'Lot' sold its 17 ex-Soviet aircraft to the Ukrainian airline. Its fleet includes 3 Boeing 767s, and it operates 9 internal and 34 international routes. 2·02m. passengers were flown in 1988. There are British Airways, SABENA, KLM, PANAM, Alitalia, Swissair, Air France, Austrian Airlines and Lufthansa services to Okęcie (Warsaw) airport.

Shipping. The principal ports are Gdynia, Gdańsk (Danzig) and Szczecin (Stettin). Ocean-going services are grouped into Polish Ocean Lines based on Gdynia and operating regular liner services, and the Polish Shipping Company based on Szczecin and operating cargo services. Poland also has a share in the Gdynia America Line. 30·8m. tonnes of freight and 453,000 passengers were carried in 1988.

In 1989 the merchant marine had 249 vessels totalling 4·1m. GRT (including 45 container ships, 9 ferries and 8 tankers and 16 vessels over 30,000 tons). There are regular lines to London, Hull, China, Indonesia, Australia, Vietnam and some African and Latin-American countries.

There are 3,997 km of navigable inland waterways. In 1989 there were 69 passenger vessels, 413 tugs and 1,380 barges. 15·5m. tonnes of freight and 6·5m. passengers were carried in 1988.

Pipeline. In 1989 there were 2,021 km of oil pipeline; 43m. tonnes were transported in 1988.

Telecommunications. In 1989 there were 8,273 post offices. There were 3·3m. telephones in 1991 and 32,000 telex subscribers in 1987.

Polskie Radio i Telewizja broadcasts 3 radio programmes and 2 TV programmes. Colour programmes are transmitted by the SECAM system. Links with the West are provided through the Eutelsat satellite. There were 84 transmitting stations in 1989. Radio licences in 1989, 11·12m.; TV licences, 10·05m.

Cinemas and Theatres. In 1989 there were 1,792 cinemas, 92 theatres and 50 concert halls. Cinema attendance was 69·9m.; theatre, 7·1m. 25 full-length films were made.

Newspapers and Books. In 1989 there were 99 newspapers with an overall circulation of 9·63m. and 2,811 other periodicals. 10,391 book titles were published in 1989 in 217·2m copies. In 1990 there were 32,400 public libraries.

JUSTICE, RELIGION, EDUCATION AND WELFARE

Justice. The penal code was adopted in 1969. Espionage and treason carry the severest penalties. For minor crimes there is provision for probation sentences and fines.

There exist the following courts: The Supreme Court; 29 voivodship courts, district and special courts. Judges and lay assessors are elected. The State Council elects the judges of the Supreme Court for a term of 5 years, and appoints the Prosecutor-General. The office of the Prosecutor-General is separate from the judiciary. An ombudsman's office was established in 1987.

Family courts were established (1977) for cases involving divorce and domestic relations but divorce suits were transferred to the voivodship courts in 1990. Crimes reported in 1983 (and 1984) 466,205 (538,930) including 478 (593) homicides and 1,875 (2,184) rapes.

Religion. In 1978, 93% of the population was baptized into the Catholic Church, and 78% of the population attended church regularly. According to a survey published in the Communist Party journal *Nowe drogi* in 1985, 90% of the population held religious beliefs. Church–State relations are regulated by three laws of May 1989 which guarantee religious freedom, grant the Church radio and TV programmes and permit it to run schools, hospitals and old age homes. The Church has a university (Lublin), an Academy of Catholic Theology and in 1983 46 seminaries.

The archbishop of Warsaw and Gniezno is the primate of Poland (since 1981, Cardinal Józef Glemp). The Vatican considers the archbishoprics of Lwów and Vilnius (incorporated in the USSR in 1940) as still being under Polish jurisdiction. In 1983 there were 5 archbishoprics, 27 dioceses and 7,496 parishes, 84 bishops, 37,132 monks and nuns and 14,498 churches and 4,201 chapels. In 1986 there were 3 cardinals and 22,381 priests. In Oct. 1978 Cardinal Karol Wojtyla, archbishop of Cracow, was elected Pope as John Paul II.

On 28 June 1972 the Vatican adjusted the Church boundaries, to coincide with the State's western frontier ('Oder–Neisse line') and the 4 apostolic administrators in the former German territories became bishops.

Figures for other churches in 1983: Polish Autocephalous Orthodox, 5 dioceses, 218 parishes, 301 churches, 226 priests, 1 monastery, 1 nunnery, 600,000 adherents. Lutheran, 6 dioceses, 121 parishes, 173 churches, 153 chapels, 100 parsons (100,000 adherents in 1975). Uniate, 3 dioceses, 85 parishes, 98 churches, 90 priests (200,000 adherents in 1975). Old-Catholic Mariavite, 3 dioceses, 42 parishes, 55 churches, 29 priests (30,000 adherents in 1975). Methodist, 5 districts, 60 parishes, 57 chapels, 36 parsons (4,133 adherents in 1975). United Evangelical, 200 congregations, 56 chapels, 180 parsons. Seventh-day Adventist, 123 communities, 123 churches, 61 parsons. Baptist, 128 congregations, 58 chapels, 58 parsons (2,300 adherents in 1975). Jews, 16 congregations, 10 synagogues (12,000 adherents in 1978). Epiphany World Mission, 9 chapels and 426 priests. In 1985 there were 2,500 Moslems with 3 mosques and 5 priests.

Education. Basic education from 7 to 15 is free and compulsory. Free secondary education is then optional in general or vocational schools. Primary schools are organized in complexes based on wards under one director ('gmina collective schools'). In 1989–90 there were: Nursery schools, 26,358 with 1·32m. pupils and 91,000 teachers; primary schools, 18,283 with 5,229,000 pupils and 293,000 teachers; secondary schools, 1,177 with 463,000 pupils and 23,000 teachers; vocational schools, 9,366 with 1,755,000 pupils and 85,000 teachers, and 98 institutions of higher education (including 11 universities, 18 polytechnics, 9 agricultural schools, 6 schools of economics, 10 teachers' training colleges and 11 medical schools) with 378,400 students and 61,475 teaching staff.

Religious (Catholic) instruction was introduced in all schools in 1990; for children of dissenting parents there are classes in ethics.

Health. In 1989 there were 716 hospitals (including 43 mental hospitals) with 254,000 beds, 6,687 dispensaries and 3,321 health centres. There were 79,200 doctors, 18,000 dentists, 16,300 pharmacists and 197,800 nurses.

Social Security. In 1984, 76,955m. złotys were paid in family allowances and

77,830m. złotys in sick pay. In 1989 2·26m. retirement pensions were paid (monthly average 110,100 złotys), 2·15m. disability pensions (91,500 złotys), 1m. dependants' pensions (90,500 złotys) and 1·36m. farmers' retirement pensions (72,700 złotys).

DIPLOMATIC REPRESENTATIVES

Of Poland in Great Britain (47 Portland Pl., London, W1N 3AG)
Ambassador: Tadeusz de Virion.

Of Great Britain in Poland (Aleje Roz No. 1, 00-556 Warsaw)
Ambassador: Michael Llewellyn Smith, CMG.

Of Poland in the USA (2640 16th St., NW, Washington, D.C., 20009)
Ambassador: Kazimierz Dziewanowski.

Of the USA in Poland (Aleje Ujazdowskie 29/31, Warsaw)
Ambassador: Thomas W. Simons, Jr.

Of Poland to the United Nations
Ambassador: Robert Mroziewicz.

Further Reading

The Central Statistical Office, *Rocznik statystyczny* (annual); *Poland: Statistical Data.* (annual); *Wiadomości statystycznie* (quarterly).

Ascherson, N., *The Struggles for Poland.* London, 1987
Ash, T. G., *The Polish Revolution: Solidarity 1980–82.* London, 1983
Bromke, A., *The Meaning and Uses of Polish History.* New York, 1987
Davies, N., *Poland, Past and Present: A Select Bibliography of Works in English.* Newtonville, 1977.—*God's Playground: A History of Poland.* 2 vols. OUP, 1981.—*Heart of Europe: a Short History of Poland.* OUP, 1984
Eringer, R., *Strike for Freedom: The Story of Lech Wałesa and Polish Solidarity.* New York, 1982
Glazyca, G. and Rapacki, R. (eds.) *Poland into the 1990s: Economy and Society in Transition.* New York, 1991
Halecki, O., *A History of Poland.* 4th ed. London, 1983
Kaminski, B., *The Collapse of the State of Socialism: the Case of Poland.* Princeton Univ. Press, 1991
Kanka, A. G., *Poland: An Annotated Bibliography of Books in English.* New York, 1988
Landau, Z., *The Polish Economy in the Twentieth Century.* London, 1985
Leslie, R. F., (ed.) *The History of Poland since 1863.* CUP, 1980
Lewański, R. C., *Poland.* [Bibliography] Oxford and Santa Barbara, 1984
Lipski, J. J., *KOR: A History of the Workers' Defense Committee in Poland, 1976–1981.* Univ. of California Press, 1985
Misztal, B., (ed.) *Poland after Solidarity.* New Brunswick, 1985
Preibisz, J. M., (ed.) *Polish Dissident Publications: An Annotated Bibliography.* New York, 1982
Raina P., *Independent Social Movements in Poland.* London, 1981.—*Poland 1981: Towards Social Renewal.* London, 1985
Staniszkis, J., *The Dynamics of the Breakthrough in Eastern Europe: the Polish Experience.* California Univ. Press, 1991
Steven, S., *The Poles.* London, 1982
Wałesa, L., *A Path of Hope.* London, 1989
Wedel, J., *The Private Poland.* New York, 1986
Who's Who in Poland. New York, 1983

National statistical office: Central Statistical Office, Wawelska 1-3, Warsaw.
National library: Biblioteka Narodowa, Rakowiecka 6, Warsaw.

PORTUGAL

República Portuguesa

Capital: Lisbon
Population: 10·39m. (1990)
GNP per capita: US$4,260 (1990)

HISTORY. Portugal has been an independent state since the 12th century, apart from one period of Spanish rule (1580–1640). The monarchy was deposed on 5 Oct. 1910 and a republic established.

A *coup* on 28 May 1926 established a military provisional government from 1 June. A corporatist constitution was adopted on 19 March 1933 under which a civil dictatorship governed until a fresh *coup* on 25 April 1974 established a Junta of National Salvation.

Following an attempted revolt on 11 March 1975, the Junta was dissolved and a Supreme Revolutionary Council formed which ruled until 25 April 1976 when constitutional government was resumed.

AREA AND POPULATION. Mainland Portugal is bounded north and east by Spain and south and west by the Atlantic ocean. The Atlantic archipelagoes of the Azores and of Madeira form autonomous but integral parts of the republic, which has a total area of 91,985 sq. km (35,516 sq. miles) and census populations:

1940	7,755,423	1960	8,889,392	1981	9,833,014
1950	8,510,240	1970	8,648,369		

The areas and populations of the districts and Autonomous Regions are:

Districts:	sq. km	Census 1981	Estimate 31 Dec. 1989	Districts:	sq. km	Census 1981	Estimate 31 Dec. 1989
Aveiro	2,808	622,988	674,400	Porto	2,395	1,562,287	1,695,100
Beja	10,225	188,420	173,200	Santarém	6,747	454,123	459,900
Braga	2,673	708,924	784,800	Setúbal	5,064	658,326	817,900
Bragança	6,608	184,252	182,800	Viana do			
Castelo				Castelo	2,225	256,814	266,900
Branco	6,675	234,230	218,700	Vila Real	4,328	264,381	259,800
Coimbra	3,947	436,324	446,700	Viseu	5,007	423,648	419,400
Evora	7,393	180,277	171,500	Total			
Faro	4,960	323,534	344,900	mainland	88,944	9,336,760	9,808,900
Guarda	5,518	205,631	191,800	*Autonomous*			
Leiria	3,515	420,229	436,500	*Regions:*			
Lisboa	2,761	2,069,467	2,130,600	Azores	2,247	243,410	253,100
Portalegre	6,065	142,905	134,900	Madeira	794	252,844	275,000

At the 1981 census, 29·7% of the population was urban (living in towns of 10,000 and more) and 48·2% were male. The chief cities at 31 Dec. 1987 (and census, 1981) were Lisbon, the capital 830,500 (817,627) and Porto 350,000 (330,199); other population aggregates were Amadora 95,518 (93,663), Setúbal 77,885 (76,812), Coimbra 74,616 (71,782), Braga 63,033 (63,771), Vila Nova de Gaia 62,469 (60,962), Barreiro 50,863 (50,745), Funchal 44,111 (48,638), Almada 42,607 (41,468), Queluz 42,241 (41,112), Odivelas 38,322 (38,546), Evora 34,851 (34,072), Agualva-Cacem 34,341 (34,041) and Oeiras 32,529 (32,046). Estimated population, 1990: 10,393,100; males 5,021,200; females 5,371,900. Density, 112·4 per sq. km.

The Azores islands lie in the mid-Atlantic ocean, between 1,200 and 1,600 km west of Lisbon. They are divided into 3 widely separated groups with clear channels between, São Miguel (759 sq. km) together with Santa Maria (97 sq. km) being the most easterly; about 100 miles north-west of them lies the central cluster of Terceira (382 sq. km), Graciosa (62 sq. km), São Jorge (246 sq. km), Pico (446 sq. km) and Faial (173 sq. km); still another 150 miles to the north-west are Flores (143 sq. km) and Corvo (17 sq. km), the latter being the most isolated and primitive of the islands. São Miguel contains over half the total population of the archipelago.

Madeira comprises the island of Madeira (745 sq. km), containing the capital, Funchal; the smaller island of Porto Santo (40 sq. km), lying 46 km. to the northeast of Madeira; and two groups of uninhabited islets, Ilhas Desertas (15 sq. km), being 20 km. south-east of Funchal and Ilhas Selvagens (4 sq. m), near the Canaries.

Vital statistics for calendar years:

	Live-births	Still-births	Marriages	Divorces	Deaths	Emigrants
1984	142,805	1,664	69,875	7,034	97,227	6,556
1985	130,492	1,510	68,461	8,988	97,339	7,149
1986	126,748	1,390	69,271	8,411	95,828	6,253
1987	123,218	1,230	71,656	8,948	95,423	8,108
1988	122,121	1,152	71,098	9,022	98,236	9,540
1989	118,560	1,156	73,195	9,657	96,220	...

In 1988 the births included 63,020 boys and 59,101 girls; deaths, 51,527 males and 46,709 females. In 1988, 4,886 emigrants went to France, 2,112 to USA and 889 to Oceania.

In 1989: Birth rate, 11·5%; death rate, 9·3%; infant mortality rate, 12·1%; natural increase rate, 2·2%; population increase rate, 0·3%. Expectation of life; Males, 71·2 years; females, 78·2 years.

CLIMATE. Because of westerly winds and the effect of the Gulf Stream, the climate ranges from the cool, damp Atlantic type in the north to a warmer and drier Mediterranean type in the south. July and Aug. are virtually rainless everywhere. Inland areas in the north have greater temperature variation, with continental winds blowing from the interior. Lisbon. Jan. 52°F (11°C), July 72°F (22°C). Annual rainfall 27·4" (686 mm). Porto. Jan. 48°F (8·9°C), July 67°F (19·4°C). Annual rainfall 46" (1,151 mm).

CONSTITUTION AND GOVERNMENT. A new Constitution, replacing that of 1976, was approved by the Assembly of the Republic (by 197 votes to 40) on 12 Aug. 1982 and promulgated in Sept. It abolished the (military) Council of the Revolution and reduced the role of the President of the Republic.

Portugal is a sovereign, unitary republic. Executive power is vested in the *President* of the Republic, directly elected for a 5-year term (for a maximum of 2 consecutive terms). At the presidential elections of Jan. 1991 Mario Soares was elected against 3 opponents by 70.4% of the votes cast. Presidents since 1926:

Marshal António Oscar de Fragoso Carmona, 29 Nov. 1926–18 April 1951 (died).

Dr Antonio de Oliveira Salazar (acting), 18 April 1951–22 July 1951.

Marshal Francisco Higino Craveiro Lopez, 22 July 1951–9 Aug. 1958.

Rear-Adm. Américo Deus Rodrigues Tomaz, 9 Aug. 1958–25 April 1974. (deposed).

Gen. Antonio Sebastião Ribeiro de Spinola, 25 April 1974–30 Sept. 1974 (resigned).

Gen. Francisco da Costa Gomes, 30 Sept. 1974–14 July 1976.

Gen. Antonio Ramalho Eanes, 14 July 1976–9 March 1986.

President of the Republic: Mario Soares, elected Feb. 1986; elected for a second term Jan. 1991.

The President appoints a Prime Minister and, upon the latter's nomination, other members of the Council of Ministers, as well as Secretaries and Under-Secretaries of State, who are outside the Council.

The 230-member National Assembly is a unicameral legislature elected for 4-year terms by universal adult suffrage under a system of proportional representation.

At the elections of 6 Oct. 1991 the Social Democratic Party gained 135 seats with 50·4% of votes cast (148 with 50·2% in 1987); the Socialist Party 72 with 30% (60 with 22·2%); the Communist Alliance 17 with 8·8% (31 with 12·4%); the Christian Democratic Party 5 with 4·4% (4 with 4·4%); the National Solidarity Party 1 with 1·7% (did not stand in 1987); others 4·8%. Turn-out was 68·2%.

The Social Democrat government was composed in Jan. 1991 of:
Prime Minister: Anibal Cavaço Silva (b. 1940).

Deputy Prime Minister, Defence: Carlos Brito. *Minister of State and Justice:* Fernando Nogueira. *Parliamentary Affairs:* Antonio Capucho. *Finance:* Miguel Beleza. *Planning and Territorial Administration:* Luis Valente de Oliveira. *Interior:* Manuel Pereira Godinho. *Foreign Affairs:* João de Deus Pinheiro. *Agriculture, Fisheries and Alimentation:* Arlindo Cunha. *Industry and Energy:* Luis Mira Amaral. *Education:* Roberto Carneiro. *Public Works, Transport and Communication:* João Oliveira Martins. *Health:* Arlindo Carvalho. *Labour and Social Security:* José Silva Peneda. *Trade and Tourism:* Joaquim Ferreira do Amaral. *Youth:* Antonio Couto dos Santos. *Environment:* Ferrando Ferreira Real.

National flag: Vertical green and red, with the red of double width, and over all on the dividing line the national arms.

National anthem: A Portuguesa (words by Lopes de Mendonça, 1890; tune by Alfredo Keil).

Local government: Since 1976, the archipelagoes of the Azores and of Madeira are Autonomous Regions with their own legislatures and governments. Pending the formation of other regional governments, Continental Portugal is divided into 18 districts. Regions and districts are divided into 305 municipal authorities *(concelhos)* and sub-divided into 4,209 parishes *(freguesias)*. Each level is governed by an assembly elected by direct universal suffrage under a system of proportional representation, with an executive body responsible to the assembly.

DEFENCE. Conscription was reduced to 4 months in 1991. Reserves for all services number about 190,000.

Army. The Army consists of 1 composite brigade, 3 infantry brigades, 1 special forces brigade, 3 cavalry regiments, 15 infantry regiments, 3 field, 1 air defence, 1 coast artillery and 2 engineers regiments. Equipment includes 60 M-47 and 86 M-48A5 main battle tanks. Strength (1992) 33,100 (23,000 conscripts). Paramilitary forces are the National Republican Guard (16,700), Public Security Police (18,800), and the Border Guard (8,000).

Navy. The Navy is organized into 3 commands: Continental, based at Lisbon and Portimão; Azores; and Madeira. The combatant fleet comprises 3 French-built Daphne class diesel submarines, the first 2 of 3 frigates of the Vasco da Gama class of West German MEKO design, 8 other small frigates, 6 offshore, 12 coastal and 12 inshore patrol vessels. Auxiliaries include 1 tanker, 1 transport, 1 survey ship, 1 sail training ship and 1 ocean tug. There are 6 small amphibious craft and some 20 service vessels. Naval personnel in 1991 totalled 15,000 (5,400 conscripts) including 2,500 marines.

Air Force. Formed in 1912, the Air Force has been independent since 1952, when it was combined with the naval air service and given equal status with the Army and Navy. In 1992, it had a strength of about 13,400 (4,900 conscripts) and 80 combat aircraft.

Equipment comprises 2 strike squadrons with 40 A-7P Corsair IIs; 2 squadrons of G.91Rs for ground attack; 1 squadron of P-3P Orion maritime patrol aircraft; 1 squadron of 6 C-130H Hercules and 4 squadrons of CASA 212 Aviocars for transport and search and rescue operations; 25 Cessna 337 Skymasters and a force of Puma and Alouette III helicopters. Other aircraft in service include Epsilon piston-engined trainers, T-37C jet basic trainers, T-33, T-38A Talon and G.91T jet advanced trainers. Delivery of 20 F-16 fighters to replace the G.91s began in 1992.

INTERNATIONAL RELATIONS

Membership. Portugal is a member of the UN, EC, OECD, NATO, WEU and the Council of Europe. Portugal has adhered to the Schengen Accord abolishing border controls between Belgium, the Netherlands, Luxembourg, France, Germany, Italy and Spain.

ECONOMY

Policy. Large-scale privatization is in train. The main objective of the 1989-92 medium-term plan is the modernization of the economy and society.

Budget. The 1989 budget balanced at 2,656,560m. escudos. Public debt was 5,597,300m. escudos. 1991 budget estimates: Revenue 3,273,300m. excudos; expenditure, 3,911,000m. escudos. Expenditure on welfare, 35.2%; education, 15.2%.

Currency. The unit of currency is the *escudo* (PTE) of 100 *centavos*, which contains 0·06651 gramme of fine gold. It was stabilized on 9 June 1931, and the paper currency re-linked to gold when the notes of the Bank of Portugal became payable in gold or its equivalent in foreign currency. 1,000 *escudos* is called a *conto*.

There are notes of 5,000, 1,000, 500 and 100 *escudos*; cupronickel coins of 50, 25, 20, 5 and 2¹/₂ *escudos*; nickel-brass coins of 1 *escudo*; bronze coins of ¹/₂ *escudo*. Inflation was an annualized 13% in Oct. 1990. In March 1992, £1 = 247·95 *escudos*; US$1 = 141·24 *escudos*.

Banking and Finance. Since 1931 the central bank and bank of issue has been the Banco de Portugal, founded 19 Nov. 1846 and nationalized on 13 Sept. 1974. Its capital is fixed at 200m. escudos. Its *Governor* is Jose Alberto Tavares Moreira. Banks and insurance companies were nationalized in 1975 but are now being privatized. From Feb. 1984 new private banks were allowed to operate. The National Development Bank began operations on 4 Jan. 1960.

In Dec. 1988 there were 27 banks (6 foreign) operating in Portugal: 22 commercial banks, 2 investment banks and 3 savings banks. In March 1988 commercial banks' total credits were 1,777,184m. escudos and deposits 3,730,027m. escudos; investment banks' total credits 266,675m. escudos and deposits 163,822m. escudos; savings banks' total credits 1,335,841m. escudos and deposits 1,886,075m. escudos.

Ceilings on bank lending were removed in Jan. 1991.

There are stock exchanges in Lisbon and Oporto.

Weights and Measures. The metric system is the legal standard. The arroba (of 14·69 kg) is sometimes used locally.

ENERGY AND NATURAL RESOURCES

Electricity. Total production of electrical power in 1989 was 25,777m. kwh., of which 6,049m. was hydro-electric. Supply 110 and 220 volts; 50 Hz.

Minerals. Portugal possesses considerable mineral wealth. Production in tonnes (1987): Gold (refined) 0·320; uranium, 167; wolframite, 2,011; coal, 228,648; tin ore, 90; kaolin, 66,736. (1988): Non-crystalline limestone, 15,417,639; granite 7,071,027; marble, 671,658. (1989): Tungsten, 2,299; copper pyrites, 200,343.

Agriculture. The following figures show the area (in 1,000 ha) and production (in 1,000 tonnes) of the chief crops:

	1987		1988		1989
Crop	Area	Quantity	Area	Quantity	Quantity
Wheat	323·0	532·5	275	394·3	615·9
Maize	256·9	640·4	230	646·8	666·4
Oats	196·9	155·2	168	81·5	127·0
Barley	83·7	79·4	73	50·7	84·4
Rye	128·4	108·2	124	76·5	105·7
Rice	32·2	144·4	33	146·1	147·0
Dried beans	195·5	44·1	162	...	...
Potatoes	123·0	1,112·4	124	855·8	1,047·8

Fruit production (in 1,000 tonnes), 1989: Apples, 164·9; pears, 65·0, oranges, 120·0 and peaches, 90·0.

Wine production (in 1,000 hectolitres), 1989, 7,437·0; olive oil (1,000 hectolitres), 446·4.

Livestock (1988). 29,000 horses, 90,000 mules, 175,000 asses, 1,387,000 cattle, 745,000 goats, 5·22m. sheep and 2·8m. pigs. Animal products in 1,000 tonnes (1989): Meat, 340·5; Poultry, 181·2; Game, 4·8; Milk (1m. hectolitres), 1,187·2; Eggs, 77·8.

Forestry. Pine, cork oak, oak, eucalyptus, chesnut and other species are grown.

Portugal is a major producer of cork, 176,000 tonnes in 1989. Most of it is exported crude. Production of resin was 98,500 tonnes in 1989.

Fisheries. The fishing industry for the continent and adjacent isles is of importance. At 31 Dec. 1989 there were 16,603 registered fishing vessels of 196,403 gross tonnes. The sardine catch, 1989, of the mainland was 91,263, tonnes valued at 2,263,000 escudos. The most important centres of the sardine industry are at Matosinhos, Figueira di Foz, Peniche, Setúbal, Portimão and Olhão. Cod, mackerel, whiting, crustacea, shellfish, tuna, sautel and swordfish are also caught. Total catch including the Azores and Madeira, (1989) was 304,827,000 tonnes.

INDUSTRY. Production is largely small-scale. Production in tonnes (1989): Cement, 6,577,535; compound feedstuffs, 2,996,191; paper pulp, 1,338,253; fertilizers, 895,694; crude steel, 728,269; sulphuric acid, 193,637; agglomerated cork, 183,832; concentrate of tomato, 102,368; cotton fabrics, 74,551; agglomerated cork, 50,234; tinned sardines, 25,300; cork stoppers, 14,502; wool fabrics and fabrics containing wool, 10,254; tinned tuna, 7,492; refined olive oil, 6,539; tinned tomato 3,540; files and rasps, 1,197. Production in 1,000 tonnes (1989): Glass bottles, 978,611; trousers, 11,589; shirts, 11,334; radio receivers, 1,036; television sets, 308.

Labour. The maximum working week was 44 hours in 1991; the minimum monthly wage for industrial and farm workers was 40,100 escudos. A minimum wage is fixed by the government. Unemployment was 5% in 1990. In 1988 there were 4,280,000 people actively employed.

Trade Unions. An agreement between trade unions, employers and the government for 1991 involved a voluntary wage ceiling, a commitment to labour peace, improvements in working conditions and a 15% increase in pension and social security payments.

FOREIGN ECONOMIC RELATIONS

Commerce. Imports for consumption and exports (exclusive of coin and bullion and re-exports) for calendar years, in 1m. escudos:

	1986	1987	1988	1989	1990 [1]
Imports	1,442,493	1,965,315	2,570,265	3,003,196	3,539,803
Exports	1,082,261	1,311,003	1,581,957	2,015,711	2,325,132

[1] provisional

Principal imports, 1990[1], (in 1m. escudos): Machinery and apparatus, 804,963; transport equipment, 484,577; chemical products, 325,597; crude petroleum, 262,403; textile yarn, fabrics, made up articles and related goods, 234,148; meat, fish and products 126,433; iron and steel, 111,321; professional scientific instruments, optical goods, 74,094; manufactured textile fibres, 68, 018; non ferrous metals, 62,349; oil-seeds, oil nuts,oil kernels, 54,964; cereals, 50,034; sugar, 16,478;

Principal exports, 1990[1] (in 1m. escudos): Manufactured goods, 1,293,200; clothing, 495,875; machinery and apparatus, 298,612; textile yarn, fabrics, made up articles and related products, 187,610; chemical products 122,099; paper pulp, 95,934; cork articles, 73,615; beverages, 66,347; prepared and preserved fish, 38,909; fruit and vegetables, 22,970.

[1] provisional figures

The distribution of the imports and exports (in 1m. escudos):

From or to	Imports (c.i.f.)			Exports (f.o.b.)		
	1988	1989	1990 [1]	1988	1989	1990 [1]
Angola	4,499	8,131	12,519	29,660	50,420	57,690
Belgium-Lux.	105,239	118,588	147,134	50,383	62,986	72,720
Brazil	40,237	52,727	55,925	...	...	...
France	295,604	349,947	406,291	176,927	251,409	308,941
Germany, Fed. Rep. of	375,753	434,736	506,402	231,951	316,058	388,294
Italy	237,373	273,111	352,581	65,836	85,950	94,016
Mozambique	1,029	...	...	4,719	5,862	6,100
Netherlands	123,645	163,783	203,730	92,845	117,496	132,512
Spain	386,582	434,113	176,927	226,377	251,409	308,941

	Imports (c.i.f.)			Exports (f.o.b.)		
From or to	1988	1989	1990 [1]	1988	1989	1990 [1]
Saudi-Arabia	29,162	27,058	42,670	...	...	...
UK	214,232	224,717	226,377	228,792	246,981	282,380
USA	110,899	133,178	93,792	93,743	119,837	112,011

[1] provisional

Total trade between Portugal (excluding the Azores and Madeira) and UK (British Department of Trade returns, in £1,000 sterling):

	1987	1988	1989	1990	1991
Imports to UK	847,980	928,015	1,040,706	1,176,161	1,043,511
Exports and re-exports from UK	699,915	810,537	915,682	1,033,268	1,085,084

Tourism. Tourism is of increasing importance for the invisible balance of payments. In 1989 there were 16,269,000 tourists, including 12,122,000 from Spain, 1,113,000 from the UK and 219,000 from the US. There were 1,701 hotels with 168,437 beds.

COMMUNICATIONS

Roads (1989). There were 9,330 km of national roads on the mainland. Vehicles registered in 1989: Cars and trucks, 3,098,691 (cars on the mainland, 2,934,568); motorcycles, 127,313; 164,393 lorries; tractors, 187,124 and trailers 209,134. In 1989 there were 98,115 road accidents, with 2,375 fatalities.

Railways. In 1989 total railway length was 3,061 km (1,668 mm and metre gauges), of which 461 km of broad-gauge was electrified. In 1989, 232m. passengers were carried and 6.9m. tonnes of freight. There is a metro (16 km) and tramway (94 km) in Lisbon and a tramway in Porto.

Civil Aviation. There are international airports at Portela (Lisbon), Pedras Rubras (Porto), Faro (Algarve), Santa Maria and Lages (Azores) and Funchal (Madeira). Services connect Lisbon with most major centres in North and South America, Western Europe and Africa. Airlines in 1989 carried 3·1m. passengers and 57,505 tonnes of freight. The national airline is Air Portugal.

Shipping. In 1988, 13,601 vessels of 77·1m. tonnes entered the ports (continental and islands). In 1987, 4,637 were Portuguese, 338 British and 601 Spanish. On 31 Dec. 1989 there were 475 merchant vessels of 1,687,354 gross tonnes.

Telecommunications (1987). The number of post offices was 17,835. The State owned 7,693,529 km of telephone line through the *Telefones de Lisboa e Porto* (nationalized in 1977) (1989). Number of telephones was 2,393,913 and there were 28,393 public telexes.

Radiodifusão Portuguesa broadcasts 3 programmes on medium-waves and on FM as well as 3 regional services. There are 2 state-owned TV channels (Canal 1 and Radiotelevisão Portuguesa 2) and 2 independent channels set up in Feb. 1992, including 1 religious (Colour by PAL). Radio Trans Europe is a high-powered short-wave station, retransmitting programmes of different broadcasting organizations. Number of receivers: Radio (1990), 2·2m.; TV set licences (1989), 1,671,000.

Cinemas (1988). There were 378 cinemas with a seating capacity of 164,666. In 1989 7 films were produced.

Newspapers (1988). There were 38 daily newspapers with a combined circulation of 176,234m., including 7 in the Azores and 5 on Madeira. There were 1,167 other periodicals with a combined circulation of 203,084m.

JUSTICE, RELIGION, EDUCATION AND WELFARE

Justice. There are 4 judicial districts (Lisbon, Porto, Coimbra and Evora) divided into 47 circuits. There are 329 courts, including 234 of the first instance and 90 specialized.

There are also 4 courts of appeal in each district, and a Supreme Court in Lisbon.

Capital punishment was abolished completely in the Constitution of 1976. The prison population as at 1 Jan. 1990 was 8,058.

Religion. There is freedom of worship, both in public and private, with the exception of creeds incompatible with morals and the life and physical integrity of the people. There were 9·8m. Roman Catholics in 1989.

Education. Compulsory education has been in force since 1911. Adult illiteracy was 20% in 1990 according to official figures. In 1987–88 there were 19,603 educational institutions (excluding Porto University), 1,185,000 primary school pupils with 41,518 teachers (1986-87), 596,060 secondary school pupils with 68,811 teachers and 100,000 students in Higher Education with 11,014 teaching staff. There were also 27 schools which taught art activities (cinema, music and theatre) with 15,165 students. There are 18 universities, of which 8 are in Lisbon: The University of Lisbon (1930), the private Portuguese Catholic University, also with faculties and sections at Braga, Porto and Viseu (1968), the New University of Lisbon (1973), the private International University (1984), the private Autonomous University of Lisbon 'Luis de Camoes' (1986), the private Lusiada University (1986) and the Open University (1988); the other 10 are Coimbra (founded 1290), Porto (1911), Aveiro (1973), Minho, at Braga and Guimaraes (1973), Evora (1979), Azores, at Agra do Heróismo, Horto and Ponta Delgado (1980) and Algarve, at Faro (1983) Beira Interior, at Covilha (1986), Tras-os-Montes e Alto Douro, at Vila Real (1986) and the private Portucaleuse University, at Porto (1986).

Social Welfare. In 1989, 599,359m. escudos were paid in social security benefits. Total expenditure, amounts paid and beneficiaries: 60,055m. escudos relating to children and young persons, 39,956m. escudos to 1,303 (children's allowances); 72,269m. escudos relating to the active population, 49,967m. escudos to 773,000 (sickness allowances and pregnancy benefits); 22,026m. escudos in unemployment subsidies; 57,477m. escudos relating to families and the community, 45,206m. escudos to 376,000 (widows and orphan's allowances); 114,567m. escudos relating to handicapped and rehabilitation, 11,763m. escudos to 487,000 (disability and social pensions); 265,043m. escudos relating to old age, 256,909m. escudos to 1,300,000 (old age and social pensions).

Health. In 1989 there were 239 hospitals, 368 health centres, 317 medical posts, total beds, 43,790 and 27,608 doctors.

DIPLOMATIC REPRESENTATIVES

Of Portugal in Great Britain (11 Belgrave Sq., London, SW1X 8PP)
Ambassador: António Vaz-Pereira LVO (accredited 12 July 1989).

Of Great Britain in Portugal (35-37 Rua de S. Domingos à Lapa, Lisbon)
Ambassador: H. J. Arbuthnott, CMG.

Of Portugal in the USA (2125 Kalorama Rd., NW, Washington, D.C., 20008)
Ambassador: João Eduardo M. Pereira Bastos.

Of the USA in Portugal (Ave. das Forcas Armadas, 1600 Lisbon)
Ambassador: Everett E. Briggs.

Of Portugal to the United Nations
Ambassador: Fernando José Reino.

Further Reading

Statistical Information: The Instituto Nacional de Estatistica (Avenida António José de Almeida, Lisbon) was set up in 1935 in succession to the Direcção-Geral de Estatistica. The Centro de Estudos Económicos and the Centro de Estudos Demográficos were affiliated to the Instituto in 1944. The main publications are:

Anuário Estatístico de Portugal. Annuaire statistique. Annual, from 1875
Estatísticas do Comércio Externo. 2 vols. Annual from 1967 (replacing *Comércio Externo,* 1936–66, and *Estatística Comercial,* 1865–1935)
Recenscamento Geral da População. 1864 ff. Decennial (latest ed. 1991)

Estatística da Organização Corporativa. 1938–49. Estatísticas da Organização Corporativa e Previdência Social. 1950 ff.
Estatísticas das Finanças, Publicas and *Estatísticas Mometárias*. 1969 ff. (replacing *Estatísticas Financeiras*. 1947–68 and *Situação Bancária*, 1919–46)
Estatísticas Agrícolas. Statistique Agricole. 1943–64; replaced by *Estatísticas Agri colas e Alimentares*. From 1965. Annual
Estatísticas Industriais. 1967 ff. (replacing *Estatística Industrial. Statistique Industrielle*. 1943–66)
Estatísticas Demográficas. From 1967 (replacing *Anuário Demográfico*, 1929–66)
Boletim Mensal do Instituto Nacional de Estatística. Monthly since 1929
Gabinete de Estudos Económicos. Revista. 1945 ff.
Gabinete de Estudos Demográficos. Revista. 1945 ff.
Estatísticas das Contribuições e Impostos. Annual from 1967 (replacing *Anuário Estatístico das Contribuições e Impostos*, 1936–66)
Estatisticas da Cultura, Desporto e Recreio, 1979 ff.
Estatísticas da Educação. 1940 ff.
Estatísticas da Justica. 1968 ff. (replacing *Estatísticas Judiciária*. 1936–66) Ministry of Justice.
Estatísticas das Sociedades. 1939 ff.
Estatísticas da Saúde, 1969 ff.
Estatísticas do Turismo. 1969 ff.
Estatísticas do Energia. 1969 ff.

Ferreira, H. G. and Marshall, M. W., *Portugal's Revolution: Ten Years On*. CUP, 1986
Gallagher, T., *Portugal: A Twentieth Century Interpretation*. Manchester Univ. Press, 1983
Graham, L. S. and Wheeler, D. L., (eds.) *In Search of Modern Portugal: The Revolution and its Consequences*. Univ. of Wisconsin Press, 1983
Harvey R., *Portugal: Birth of a Democracy*. London, 1978
Opello, W., *Portugal: from Monarchy to Pluralist Democracy*. Boulder (Colo.), 1991
Rogers, F. M., *Atlantic Islanders of the Azores and Madeiras*. North Quincy, 1979
Unwin, P. T. H., *Portugal*. [Bibliography] Oxford and Santa Barbara, 1987

National Library: Biblioteca Nacional de Lisboa, Campo Grande, Lisbon. *Director:* A. H. C. Marques.

MACAO

HISTORY. Macao was visited by Portuguese traders from 1513 and became a Portuguese colony in 1557; it remains a Portuguese-administered territory by virtue of a Sino-Portuguese treaty of 1 Dec. 1887. It was an Overseas Province of Portugal, 1961–74. Discussions on the future of Macao were taking place with the People's Republic of China in 1986–87 and in 1999 Macao is scheduled to be handed to China.

AREA AND POPULATION. The territory, which lies at the mouth of the Canton (Pearl) River, comprises a peninsula (6·05 sq. km) connected by a narrow isthmus to the People's Republic of China, on which is built the city of Santa Nome de Deus de Macao, and the islands of Taipa (3·78 sq. km), linked to Macao by a 2-km bridge, and Colôane (7·09 sq. km) linked to Taipa by a 2-km causeway (total area, 16·92 sq. km (6 sq. miles). The population (Census, 1981) was 261,680, Estimate (1990) 440,000. The official language is Portuguese, but Cantonese is used by virtually the entire population.

Vital statistics (1987): Births, 7,565; marriages, 2,472; deaths, 1,321.

CONSTITUTION AND GOVERNMENT. By agreement with Beijing in 1974, Macao is a Chinese territory under Portuguese administration. An 'organic statute' was published on 17 Feb. 1976. It defined the territory as a collective entity, *pessoa colectiva*, with internal legislative authority which, while remaining subject to Portuguese constitutional laws, would otherwise enjoy administrative, economic and financial autonomy. The Governor is appointed by the Portuguese President, who also appoints up to 7 Under-Secretaries on the Governor's nomination. The Legislative Assembly of 17 deputies, chosen for a 3-year term, comprises 6 members directly elected by universal suffrage, 6 indirectly elected by economic, cultural and social bodies and 5 appointed by the Governor. In April 1990 the Portuguese parliament unanimously approved laws passed by the Legislative Assembly to widen its powers and those of the governor.

Governor: Gen. Vasco Rocha Vieira.

ECONOMY

Budget. In 1987, revenue was 2,488,700,000 *patacas* and expenditure 2,390,800,000 *patacas*.

Currency. The unit of currency is the *pataca* (MOP) of 100 *avos* which is tied to the *Hong Kong dollar* at the rate of 103 *patacas* = HK$100. In March 1992, £1 = 14·06 *patacas*; US$1 = 8·01 *patacas*.

Banking. The bank of issue is the Instituto Emissor de Macau. Commercial business is handled (1987) by 22 banks with 94 branches in Macao, 8 of which are local (with 81·5% of total resident deposits and 67·4% of total domestic credit at 31 Dec. 1984) and 14 foreign (including 4 offshore banking units). Total banks' deposits, 1987, 14,111·5m. patacas.

INDUSTRY AND TRADE

Industry. The economy is based on gambling and tourism with a light industrial base of textiles and toy-making. In 1985 the number of establishments for food products was 74 and output in 1,000 patavos was 108,853; textiles (130) 1,330,626; clothing (444) 2,836,832; plastics (67) 523,128.

Labour. The estimated total labour force in 1984 was 178,000, 44% of whom were employed in manufacturing, 33% in commerce and services and 8% in construction.

Commerce. The trade, mostly transit, is handled by Chinese merchants. Imports, in 1987, were 9,107·1m. patacas and exports, 11,233·5m. patacas.

In 1987, 43% of imports came from Hong Kong and 21% from China. 33% of exports went to USA, 36% to EEC (mainly Federal Republic of Germany, France and UK); clothing and textiles accounted for 73·5% of exports, toys 9·9%.

Total trade between Macao and UK (British Department of Trade returns, in £1,000 sterling):

	1987	1988	1989	1990	1991
Imports to UK	45,896	41,116	45,299	44,809	40,010
Exports and re-exports from UK	5,617	4,348	7,498	11,398	15,329

Tourism. There were 5,100,500 visitors in 1987. 82·2% were from Hong Kong and 5·1% from Japan.

COMMUNICATIONS

Roads. In 1984 there were 90 km of roads. In 1987 there were 35,925 vehicles, of which 20,391 were passenger cars and 4,099 commercial vehicles.

Shipping. Macao is served by Portuguese, British and Dutch steamship lines. In 1987, 39,239 vessels of 11·5m. gross tons entered the port. In 1987, 4·84m passengers embarked and 4·7m disembarked. Regular services connect Macao with Hong Kong, 65 km to the north-east.

Post and Broadcasting. The territory has 1,577 km of telephone line (55,643 instruments in 1987). One government and 1 private commercial radio station are in operation on medium-waves broadcasting in Portuguese and Chinese. Number of receivers (1977), 70,000. Macao receives television broadcasts from Hong Kong and in 1984 a public bilingual TV station began operating. There were (1979) 50,000 receivers.

Newspapers. In 1987, there were 8 newspapers (2 in Portugese and 6 in Chinese).

JUSTICE, RELIGION, EDUCATION AND WELFARE

Justice. There is a court of First Instance, from which there is appeal to the Court of Appeal and then the Supreme Court, both in Lisbon.

In 1987 there were 4,717 cases of crimes known to the police, of which 3,454 were against property. There were 29,558 cases in courts pending on 1 Jan. and presented during 1987, of which 4,840 were in district court, 10,195 in criminal court and 3,467 in administrative court. At 31 Dec. 1987 there were 326 prisoners, and 37 addicts in the centre for rehabilitation of drugs-abusers.

Religion. The majority of the Chinese population are Buddhists. About 6% are Roman Catholic.

Education. In 1986–87 education was provided at 60 kindergartens (16,516 pupils; 458 teachers), 74 primary schools (31,914; 1,118), 30 secondary schools (14,913; 851), 5 special schools (88; 31), 5 teacher-training schools (61; 26), 5 higher schools (6,891; 70) and 88 adult schools (23,088; 629). The University of East Asia, established in 1981 on Taipa, had 1,165 students in 1983.

Health. In 1987 there were 2 hospitals with 1,242 beds; there were 179 doctors and (1982) 26 pharmacists, 10 midwives and 315 nursing personnel.

Further Reading

Anuário Estatístico de Macau. Macao, Annual
Macau in Figures. Macao, Annual.
Education Survey, 1984–85, Macao, 1986
Brazáo, E., *Macau.* Lisbon, 1957
Edmonds, R.L., *Macau.* [Bibliography] Oxford and Santa Barbara, 1989

QATAR

Capital: Doha
Population: 371,863 (1987)
GNP per capita: US$11,610 (1988)

Dawlat Qatar

(State of Qatar)

HISTORY. The State of Qatar declared its independence from Britain on 3 Sept. 1971, ending the Treaty of 3 Nov. 1916 which was replaced by a Treaty of friendship between the 2 countries.

AREA AND POPULATION. The State of Qatar, which includes the whole of the Qatar peninsula, extends on the landward side from Khor al Odeid to the boundaries of the Saudi Arabian province of Hasa. The territory includes a number of islands in the coastal waters of the peninsula, the most important of which is Halul, the storage and export terminal for the offshore oilfields. Area, 11,437 sq. km; population census (1981) 244,534; estimate in 1987, 371,863. In 1987 only 25% were Qatari, with a large majority coming from Pakistan and India.

The capital is Doha (population 1986, 217,294), which is the main port. Other towns are Dukhan, the centre of oil production, Umm Said, oil-terminal of Qatar, and Ruwais, Wakra, Al-Khour, Umm Salal Mohammad and Umm-Bab.

Vital statistics (1988): Live births, 10,842; deaths, 861; marriages, 1,333; divorces, 385.

The official language is Arabic.

CLIMATE. The climate is hot and humid. Doha. Jan. 62°F (16·7°C), July 98°F (36·7°C). Annual rainfall 2·5" (62 mm).

RULER. *The Amir:* HH Shaikh Khalifa bin Hamad Al-Thani, assumed power on 22 Feb. 1972. On 31 May 1977, HH Shaikh Hamad bin Khalifa Al-Thani was appointed Heir Apparent of the State of Qatar, and the portfolio of Minister of Defence was added to his existing responsibility of Commander-in-Chief of the Armed Forces.

Minister of Foreign Affairs: Abdullah bin Khalifa al-Attiyah.

There is no Parliament, but the Council of Ministers is assisted by a 30-member nominated Advisory Council.

National flag: Maroon, with white serrated border on hoist.

Local government: Qatar is divided into 9 municipalities.

DEFENCE

Army. The Army consists of 1 Royal Guard regiment, 1 tank and 3 mechanized infantry battalions, 1 artillery regiment and 1 surface-to-air missile battery. Equipment includes 24 AMX-30 tanks. Personnel (1991) 6,000.

Navy. The navy has 3 French-built fast missile craft and 6 British-built inshore patrol craft, 1 tank landing craft and some 30 boats. There are also 3 quadruple shore-based Exocet missile batteries. Personnel in 1991 totalled 700.

Air Force. The Air Force has 1 squadron of Mirage F1 fighters and 12 Commando, 16 Gazelle and 12 Super Puma helicopters and 6 Alpha Jet armed trainers and Tigercat surface-to-air missile systems. Personnel (1991) 300.

INTERNATIONAL RELATIONS

Membership. Qatar is a member of the UN, the Arab League and the Gulf Co-operation Council.

ECONOMY

Budget. Revenue (1987–88) 6,745m. riyals; expenditure 12,217m. riyals.

Currency. The unit of currency is the *Qatari riyal* (QAR) of 100 *dirhams*, introduced in 1973. There are coins of 1, 5, 10, 25 and 50 *dirhams*, and banknotes of 1, 5, 10, 50, 100 and 500 *riyals*. In March 1992, £1 = 6·34 *riyals*, US$1 = 3·61 *riyals*.

Banking and Finance. The 13 banks operating in Qatar in 1989, included 5 national banks: Qatar National Bank, The Commercial Bank of Qatar, Doha Bank, the Islamic Bank of Qatar and Al Ahli Bank. There are 2 Arab banks: Arab Bank Limited and Bank of Oman. The other 6 foreign banks were: Banque Paribas, the British Bank of the Middle East, Chartered Bank, Bank Saderat Iran, Grindlays Bank and the United Bank. The Qatar National Bank was established in 1965 with capital of 56m. riyals, 50% of which was contributed by the Government and 50% by the private sector. Deposits in commercial banks were 1,241·8m. riyals by Dec. 1987. Government deposits 331m. riyals and private sector's savings deposits 1,240·1m. riyals in 1987.

Weights and Measures. The metric system is in general use.

ENERGY AND NATURAL RESOURCES

Electricity. Production (1988) 4,592·3m. kwh (generation of Abu Samra not included). Supply 240 volts; 50 Hz.

Oil. On 9 Feb. 1977 Qatar gained national control over its 2 natural resources, oil and gas, with the signing of an agreement with Shell Qatar over the procedure for the transfer to the State of the company's remaining 40% share. A similar agreement had been reached with the Qatar Petroleum Co. on 16 Sept. 1976.

The Qatar General Petroleum Corporation (QGPC) had been established by decree in July 1974 to assume overall responsibility for the State's domestic and foreign oil interests and operations. On 16 Oct. 1976 the Qatar Petroleum Producing Authority (QPPA) was established to serve as the executive arm of the QGPC—but in 1980 it was merged into the QGPC, which now directly oversees oil production through two operational divisions, Onshore and Offshore. The National Oil Distribution Company (NODCO) had a daily throughput capacity of 62,000 bbls a day in 1984 following the opening of a 50,000 bbls a day refinery at Umm Said to supplement the existing refinery.

Production, 1991, 19·09m. tonnes. Proven reserves (1986) 3,300m. bbls.

Gas. The North West Dome oilfield is being developed which contains 12% of the known world gas reserves. Production (1986) 229,100m. cu. ft.

Water Resources. Two main desalination stations, at Ras Abu Aboud and Ras Abu Fontas, together have a daily capacity of 167·6m. gallons of potable water. A third station is planned at Al Wasil, with a capacity of 40m. gallons a day. Total water production 1988 (well field and distillate) 17,542·5m. gallons.

Agriculture. 10% of the working population is engaged in agriculture. The Ministry of Agriculture is implementing a long-term policy aimed at ensuring self-sufficiency in agricultural products. The number of farms rose from 120 in 1960 to 841 in 1985. Production (1988) in tonnes: Cereals, 3,224; dates, 8,409; vegetables, 20,927; green fodder, 72,612; meat, 1,734 milk, 18,501; eggs, 1,522.

Livestock (1988): Cattle, 9,516; camels, 22,706; sheep, 122,259; goats, 87,396; chickens, 1,786,467; horses, 1,041; deer (1987), 3,463.

Fisheries. The produce of local fisheries in 1984 met 77·2% of Qatar's requirements. The state-owned Qatar National Fishing Company has 3 trawlers and its refrigeration unit processes 10 tonnes of shrimps a day. Catch (1988) 2,880 tonnes; value (1987) 19·55m riyals.

INDUSTRY. The Qatar Fertiliser Co. plant was opened in 1974 (production, 1988, 724,900 tonnes of ammonia and 779,600 tonnes of urea), the Qatar Steel Co. factory in 1978 (output, 1987, 483,833 tonnes of steel, 482,270 tonnes of sponge iron and (1988) 533,000 tonnes of reinforcing steel bars) and the Qatar Petrochemicals Co. plant in 1981 (production, 1988, 256,500 tonnes of ethylene, 171,400 tonnes of polyethylene and 37,000 tonnes of sulphur), all in the Umm Said industrial zone. Other production (1987, in tonnes): Cement, 791,200; unslaked lime, 13,500; flour, 26,200; bran, 6,600; organic fertilizer, 27,700. Two natural gas liquids plants produced 315,724 tonnes of propane, 223,384 tonnes of butane and 182,592 tonnes of gasoline in 1987.

Labour. The economically active population (15 years and above) in March 1986 totalled 200,238, of whom 6,283 were engaged in agriculture and fishing, 4,807 in mining and quarrying, 13,914 in manufacturing, 5,266 in electricity, gas and water, 40,523 in building and construction, 21,964 in trade, restaurants and hotels, 7,357 in transport and communications, 3,157 in finance, insurance and real estate and 96,466 in social and community services.

FOREIGN ECONOMIC RELATIONS

Commerce. In 1987 exports totalled 7,224m. riyals, and imports, 4,000m. riyals, (1988, 4,613m. riyals). Main imports in 1987 (in 1,000 riyals) were machinery and transport equipment (1,666,892), manufactured goods (1,218,517) and food and live animals (706,201). In 1987 Japan provided 16·3% of imports, the UK 16%, the USA 11·9% and the Federal Republic of Germany 7·2%.

Total trade between Qatar and UK (British Department of Trade returns, in £1,000 sterling):

	1987	1988	1989	1990	1991
Imports to UK	13,765	3,888	4,342	5,004	5,488
Exports and re-exports from UK	105,087	88,920	89,256	98,504	109,248

Tourism. In 1988 tourists stayed 226,134 nights in hotels.

COMMUNICATIONS

Roads. In 1981 there were about 800 miles of road. In 1988 there were 154,963 registered vehicles including 2,502 motorcycles.

Civil Aviation. Gulf Air (owned equally by Qatar, Bahrain, Oman and the UAE), operates daily services from Bahrain; British Airways, Middle East and about 15 other airlines operate regular international flights from Doha airport. In 1988, 520,478 passengers arrived, 508,843 departed and 453,126 were in transit; 9,996 aircraft arrived and 9,996 departed.

Shipping. In 1987, 395 vessels, 1,101,925 tonnes of cargo and 1,854 containers were handled.

Telecommunications. There were 26 post offices in Doha and other towns in 1988. Qatar Broadcasting Service, using 12 transmission stations, broadcasts for 41 hours a day in Arabic, English, French and Urdu. Telephone and radiotelephone services connect Qatar with Europe and America; there were 129,291 telephones in 1988. In 1987 there were 75,000 radios and 111,000 television receivers.

Cinemas. In 1987 there were 4 cinemas.

Newspapers. In 1987 there were 4 daily and 2 weekly newspapers and 6 magazines.

JUSTICE, RELIGION, EDUCATION AND WELFARE

Justice. The Judiciary System is administered by the Ministry of Justice which comprises three main departments: Legal affairs, courts of justice and land and real estate register. There are 5 Courts of Justice proclaiming sentences in the name of H. H. the Amir: The Court of Appeal, the Labour Court, the Higher Criminal Court, the Civil Court and the Lower Criminal Court.

All issues related to personal affairs of Moslems under Islamic Law embodied in the Holy Quran and Sunna are decided by Sharia Courts.

Religion. The population is almost entirely Moslem.

Education. There were, in 1988, 35,133 pupils at 97 primary schools, 12,817 pupils at 43 preparatory schools, 8,064 pupils at 29 secondary schools and 894 male students at 3 specialist schools. There were 48 Arab and foreign private schools with 18,346 pupils in 1987–88. The University of Qatar had 5,621 students in 1989.

Students abroad (1988) numbered 881. In 1986–87, 3,435 men and 2,507 women attended evening classes.

Health. There were 3 hospitals (including 1 for women and 1 for gynaecology and obstetrics) with a total of 937 beds in 1987. There were 21 health centres in 1988. In 1987 there were 560 doctors, 62 dentists, 140 pharmacists and 1,418 qualified nurses.

DIPLOMATIC REPRESENTATIVES

Of Qatar in Great Britain (27 Chesham Pl., London, SWIX 8HG)
Ambassador: Abdulrahman Abdulla Al-Wohaibi (accredited 20 Dec. 1989).

Of Great Britain in Qatar (Doha, Qatar)
.Ambassador and Consul-General: G. H. Boyce, CMG

Of Qatar in the USA (600 New Hampshire Ave., NW, Washington, D.C., 20037)
Ambassador: Dr Hamad Abdelaziz Al-Kawari.

Of the USA in Qatar (Fariq Bin Omran, Doha)
Ambassador: Marc Hambley.

Of Qatar to the United Nations
Ambassador: Dr Hassan Ali Hussain Alni'ma.

Further Reading

Annual Statistical Abstract. 8th ed. Doha, 1988
El Mallakh, R., *Qatar: The Development of an Oil Economy.* New York, 1979
Unwin, P. T. H., *Qatar.* [Bibliography] Oxford and Santa Barbara, 1982

ROMANIA

Capital: Bucharest
Population: 23m. (1990)

HISTORY. 1918 is celebrated as the year of foundation of the 'unitary national Romanian state'. For the history and constitution of Romania from 1859 to 1947, *see* THE STATESMAN'S YEAR-BOOK, 1947, pp. 1187–89. On 30 Dec. 1947 King Michael abdicated under Communist pressure and parliament proclaimed the 'People's Republic'. The former king now lives in exile.

Since the accession to power in 1965 of Nicolae Ceauşescu Romania had been taking a relatively independent stand in foreign affairs while becoming increasingly repressive and impoverished domestically.

An attempt by the authorities on 16 Dec. 1989 to evict a protestant pastor, László Tókés, from his home in Timişoara provoked a popular protest which escalated into a mass demonstration against the government. Despite the use of armed force against the demonstrators, the uprising spread to other areas. On 21 Dec. the government called for an official rally in Bucharest, but this turned against the régime. A state of emergency was declared, but the Army went over to the uprising, and Nicolae and Elena Ceauşescu fled the capital. A dissident group which had been active before the uprising, the National Salvation Front (NSF), proclaimed itself the provisional government. Suggestions of Soviet involvement have been denied.

The Ceauşescus were captured, and after a secret two-hour trial by military tribunal, summarily executed on 25 Dec. on four charges of genocide, undermining the power of the state, undermining the economy and embezzlement. Fighting by pro-Ceauşescu 'Securitate' forces continued until 27 Dec. It is estimated that 7,689 people were killed in the uprising.

On 26 Dec. Ion Iliescu, leader of the NSF, and Petre Român, were sworn in as President and Prime Minister respectively. The Provisional Government was at once recognized by many countries throughout the world, including the UK, USA and USSR.

At the end of Sept. 1991 striking miners moved into Bucharest, initially demanding wage increases and price freezes. Protests and riots escalated, the National Assembly building was attacked and demonstrators called for the resignation of the government. On 1 Oct. the president appointed Teodor Stolojan as prime minister of an interim government.

AREA AND POPULATION. Romania is bounded north and north-east by the USSR, east by the Black Sea, south by Bulgaria, south-west by Yugoslavia and north-west by Hungary. The area of Romania is 237,500 sq. km (91,699 sq. miles). Pre-war Romania had an area of 113,918 sq. miles. Population at censuses: 1930, 18,057,208 (14,280,729 within present-day Romania); 1948, 15,872,624 (48·3% male); 1966, 19,103,163 (49% male, 38·2% urban); 1977, 21,559,910 (49·3% male, 47·5% urban).

In 1989 the population was 23,151,564 (49·3% male; 53·2% urban), density per sq. km, 96. Population estimate, 1990: 23m. Vital statistics, 1989: Births, 369,544; deaths, 247,306; stillborn, 2,821; infantile deaths, 9,940; marriages, 177,943; divorces, 36,008. Rates (per 1,000 population): Live births, 16; deaths, 10·7; marriages, 7·7; divorces, 1·56; stillborn (per 1,000 live births), 7·6; infant mortality (per 1,000 live births), 26·9. Growth rate, 5·3 per 1,000. Expectation of life in 1989: Males, 66·51 years; females, 72·41. Measures designed to raise the birthrate were abolished by the post-Ceauşescu government in 1990, and abortion and contraception legalized.

Romania is divided into 40 districts (*judet*). The capital is Bucharest (Bucureşti), a municipality with district status.

District	Area in sq. km	Population 1989	Capital	Population 1989
Alba	6,231	428,246	Alba Iulia	72,331
Arad	7,652	506,683	Arad	191,428
Argeş	6,801	676,731	Piteşti	162,395

1121

District	Area in sq. km	Population 1989	Capital	Population 1989
Bacău	6,606	731,052	Bacău	193,269
Bihor	7,535	660,256	Oradea	225,416
Bistriţa-Năsăud	5,305	327,523	Bistriţa	79,544
Botoşani	4,965	467,544	Botoşani	119,563
Braşov	5,351	694,510	Braşov	352,640
Brăila	4,724	404,252	Brăila	242,595
Buzău	6,072	524,439	Buzău	145,423
Caraş-Severin	8,503	407,940	Reşiţa	110,260
Călăraşi	5,075	351,183	Călăraşi	76,240
Cluj	6,650	742,787	Cluj-Napoca	317,914
Constanţa	7,055	736,860	Constanţa	315,917
Covasna	3,705	237,918	Sf. Gheorghe	72,092
Dîmboviţa	4,036	569,746	Tîrgovişte	100,426
Dolj	7,413	772,451	Craiova	300,030
Galaţi	4,425	642,211	Galaţi	307,376
Giurgiu	3,511	324,927	Giurgiu	72,275
Gorj	5,641	387,528	Tîrgu Jiu	93,252
Harghita	6,610	362,926	Miercurea-Ciuc	49,148
Hunedoara	7,016	567,455	Deva	77,336
Ialomiţa	4,449	309,193	Slobozia	50,995
Iaşi	5,469	809,892	Iaşi	330,195
Maramureş	6,215	556,063	Baia Mare	150,456
Mehedinţi	4,900	382,665	Drobeta-Turnu Severin	107,420
Mureş	6,696	621,246	Tîrgu Mureş	164,781
Neamţ	5,890	580,237	Piatra-Neamţ	115,782
Olt	5,507	534,828	Slatina	86,360
Prahova	4,694	877,359	Ploieşti	247,502
Satu Mare	4,405	416,723	Satu Mare	136,881
Sălaj	3,850	269,086	Zalău	65,190
Sibiu	5,422	508,647	Sibiu	184,036
Suceava	8,555	698,724	Suceava	105,921
Teleorman	5,760	503,771	Alexandria	51,267
Timiş	8,692	725,588	Timişoara	333,365
Tulcea	8,430	275,078	Tulcea	94,935
Vaslui	5,297	468,398	Vaslui	73,660
Vîlcea	5,705	430,263	Rîmnicu Vîlcea	107,996
Vrancea	4,863	393,710	Focşani	101,799
Bucharest	1,820	2,318,889		

The last official figures on the size of the ethnic minorities were published in 1977. Estimates for 1990: Hungarians, 2·5m. (mainly in Transylvania); Germans, 200,000; Gypsies, 2·3m.; Jews, 30,000. The agricultural 'systematisation' (*see* Agriculture, p. 1036) bore particularly hardly upon ethnic Hungarians, who had not been allowed to emigrate. Some 120,000 Germans had emigrated by 1988. In 1990 129,714 citizens applied to emigrate (including 95,671 Germans and 13,214 Hungarians) and 80,346 actually left (78% to Germany, 9% to Hungary). The official language is Romanian.

CLIMATE. A continental climate with a large annual range of temperature and rainfall showing a slight summer maximum.

Bucharest. Jan. 27°F (−2·7°C), July 74°F (23·5°C). Annual rainfall 23·1" (579 mm). Constanţa. Jan. 31°F (−0·6°C), July 71°F (21·7°C). Annual rainfall 15" (371 mm).

CONSTITUTION AND GOVERNMENT. For the Communist Constitution and government *see* THE STATESMAN'S YEAR-BOOK, 1989-90, pp. 1033-34.

The National Assembly adopted a new constitution on 21 Nov. 1991, and this was approved by a national referendum on 8 Dec. Turn-out was 66%, and 77·3% of votes cast were in favour.

The constitution defines Romania as a republic where the rule of law prevails in a social and democratic state. Private property rights and a market economy are guaranteed. Natural resources are public property which can be leased.

The head of state is the *President*, elected by direct vote for a maximum of 2 4-

year terms. He or she may not belong to a political party. The bicameral parliament consists of a 396-member *National Assembly* and a 119-member *Senate*; both are elected for 4-year terms from 41 constituencies by modified proportional representation, the number of seats won in each constituency being determined by the proportion of the total vote.

There is a Constitutional Court.

Presidential and parliamentary elections were held on 20 May 1990. A 60-member team of observers from 19 countries concluded that there had been many irregularities but not enough to invalidate the results.

Ion Iliescu was elected President with 85% of the vote. The National Salvation Front (NSF) gained 66% of the vote and 233 seats in the National Assembly; the Democratic Union of Hungarians gained 7% and 29 seats; Liberals, 6% and 29; Greens, 3% and 12; National Peasants, 3% and 12; others, 15% and 81.

In Feb. 1992 the interim government consisted of:

Prime Minister, Teodor Stolojan (b. 1943; ind).

Foreign Affairs: Adrian Năstase (b. 1950; NSF). *Defence:* Gen. Niculae Spiroiu (ind). *Justice:* Mircea Ionescu-Quintus (Liberal). *Economy and Finance:* Gheorghe Danielescu (Liberal). *Labour:* Mircea Dan Popescu (NSF). *Commerce and Tourism:* Constantin Fota (ind). *Industry:* Dan Constantinescu (ind). *Agriculture and Food:* Petre Mărculescu (Agrarian). *Transport:* Traian Băsescu (ind). *Communications:* Andrei Chirică. *Public Works:* Dan Nicolae (NSF). *Environment:* Marcian Bleahu (Ecologist). *Education:* Mihai Gohu (NSF). *Health:* Mircea Maiorescu (ind). *Youth and Sport:* Ioan Moldovan (NSF). *Interior:* Victor Babiuc (NSF). *Budget:* Florian Bercea (NSF). *Culture.* Ludovic Spiess (ind).

Elections were scheduled for mid-1992.

Local government is carried out at the administrative levels of 260 towns (of which 56 are municipalities) and 2,688 wards (*comuna*). Elections were held in Feb. 1992; the NSF gained 33% of votes cast.

National flag: Three vertical strips of blue, yellow and red.

National anthem: Trei culori ('Three colours'). A new anthem is under consideration.

DEFENCE. Military service is compulsory for 12 months in the Army and Air Force and 24 months in the Navy.

Army. The 4 Army Areas consist of 2 tank and 8 motor rifle divisions; 4 mountain, 2 artillery, 4 anti-aircraft and 2 surface-to-surface missile brigades; and 4 artillery, 5 anti-tank and 4 airborne regiments. Equipment includes 1,060 T-34, 757 T-55, 30 T-72, 556 TR-80 and 414 TR-580 main battle tanks. Strength (1991) 126,000 (95,000 conscripts), and 178,000 reservists. There are a further 45,000 men in paramilitary border guard and internal security forces.

Navy. The fleet comprises 1 ex-Soviet diesel submarine, 1 Romanian-built missile-armed destroyer with hangar for 2 helicopters, 4 frigates, 4 corvettes, 6 fast missile craft, 42 fast torpedo craft, 4 offshore, 3 coastal and 9 inshore patrol vessels, 2 minelayer/mine countermeasure support ships and 40 small minesweepers. The Danube flotilla counts 3 river monitors (100 mm guns) and some 30 river patrol craft. Auxiliaries include 2 logistic ships, 1 oceanographic ship, 1 training ship and 2 tugs.

There is a substantial coastal defence force numbering 6,500 (1991) organized into 4 main batteries of artillery with 32 130 mm guns and 10 anti-aircraft batteries.

Headquarters of the Navy is at Mangalia, and of the Danube flotilla at Brăila. Personnel in 1991 totalled 18,000 (9,000 conscripts) including 5,000 in Coastal Defence.

Air Force. The Air Force numbered some 28,000 (10,000 conscripts), with 300 combat aircraft in 3 air divisions (7 regiments) in 1991. These were organized into 12 interceptor squadrons with MiG-21, MiG-23 and MiG-29 fighters, 6 ground-attack and close-support squadrons with IAR-93 and MiG-17 fighters, and 1 reconnaissance squadron of L-39s. There were also more than 150 training aircraft, 20 An-24/26/30 transports and more than 150 helicopters (Mi-2, Mi-4, Mi-8, Mi-14,

Alouette and Puma). 'Guideline' and 'Gainful' surface-to-air missiles were operational, and short-range surface-to-surface missiles have been displayed.

INTERNATIONAL RELATIONS. In April 1991 Romania and the USSR signed a treaty of friendship and co-operation; each pledged to respect the other's borders.

Membership. Romania is a member of the UN and IMF.

ECONOMY

Policy. For planning under Ceauşescu *see* THE STATESMAN'S YEAR-BOOK, 1989–90, p. 1035). Romania was committed to intensive industrialization and agriculture had been neglected. Severe shortages resulted from the diversion of resources to pay off foreign debt.

A privatization law of Aug. 1991 transfers state property except utilities into commercial companies held in 5 private ownership funds. These hold 30% of the enterprises' capital and are reserved for Romanians, who are to receive a free saleable certificate of ownership. 70% is held in a state ownership fund for foreign investors. It is expected to privatize some 10% of enterprises anually.

Following the riots of Sept. 1991 the prices of staple foods and essential services were frozen until April 1992.

Budget. Revenue and expenditure (in 1m. lei) for calendar years:

	1984	1985	1986	1987	1988	1989
Revenue	308,917	300,126	333,674	334,629	330,968	348,421
Expenditure	308,917	281,985	302,880	281,426	286,686	288,426

In 1989 sources of revenue (in 1m. lei) included: Profit payments of state enterprises 53,738; turnover tax, 150,612; personal taxes, 6,038; insurance contributions, 44,306; taxes on enterprise wage funds, 50,061; other revenue from state and co-operative enterprises, 44,306. Expenditure: National economy, 161,833; social and cultural, 107,953; defence, 11,708.

Revenue and expenditure of local councils (included above) was 63,054m. lei and 60,560m. lei in 1985.

Currency. The monetary unit is the *leu*, pl.*lei* (ROL) of 100 *bani*. On 1 Feb. 1954 the gold content of the leu was 0·148112 gramme of fine gold. Bank-notes of 1, 5, 10, 25, 50 and 100 *lei* are issued by the National Bank, and there are coins of 5, 10, 15 and 25 *bani* and 1, 3 and 5 *lei*. A single exchange rate for the leu was set in Nov. 1991 at US$1 = 180 lei. Exchange rates (March 1992): £1 = 347·96 lei; US$1 = 198·21 lei.

Banking and Finance. The National Bank of Romania (founded 1880, nationalized 1946; *governor*, Mugul Isarescu) is the central bank under the Minister of Finance. It manages monetary policy. Independent commercial banks serve industrial individual depositors. The first private bank opened in April 1991. There are also a Bank of Investments, a Foreign Trade Bank, an Agriculture and Food Industry Bank and a Savings Bank.

Weights and Measures. The Gregorian calendar was adopted in 1919. The metric system is in use. Tubes and pipes are measured in *tol* (= 1 inch).

ENERGY AND NATURAL RESOURCES

Electricity. Installed electric power 1984: 18,829,000 kw.; output, 1989, 75,851m. kwh (12,629m. kwh hydroelectric). Supply 220 volts; 50 Hz. There are two joint Romanian–Yugoslav hydro-electric power plants on the Danube at the 'Iron Gates' with a combined yearly output of 22,250m. kwh. A nuclear power programme has been subject to cut-backs and delays. A nuclear power plant is under construction at Cernăvoda.

Oil. The oilfields are in the Prahova, Băcau, Gorj, Crişana and Argeş districts. Oil production in 1991 was 6·91m. tonnes. Oil reserves are expected to be exhausted by the mid-1990s. Refining capacity was enlarged from 16m. tonnes per annum in 1970 to 30m. tonnes in 1985. Crude oil has to be imported.

Minerals. The principal minerals are oil and natural gas, salt, brown coal, lignite, iron and copper ores, bauxite, chromium, manganese and uranium. Salt is mined in the lower Carpathians and in Transylvania; production in 1987 was 5·4m. tonnes.

Output, 1989 (in 1,000 tonnes): Iron ore, 2,482; coal, 11,583; lignite, 53,980; methane gas (cu. metres), 22,222m.

Agriculture. There were 14·76m. ha of agricultural land in 1989, including (in 1,000 ha): Arable, 9,458; meadows and pasture, 4,705; vineyards and fruit trees, 596. There were 3·17m. ha of irrigated land.

Production in 1989 (in 1,000 tonnes): Wheat and rye, 7,935; barley, 3,436; maize, 6,762; potatoes, 4,420; sunflower seeds, 656; sugar-beet, 6,771.

Livestock, 1988 (in 1,000): 6,291 cattle (including 2,468 milch cows), 11,671 pigs, 15,435 sheep, 113,968 poultry. There were 151,745 tractors in 1989.

In 1989 there were 3,776 collective farms, with 9·1m. ha of land (6·5m. arable; 1·2m. private plots). State farms numbered 411, with 2m. ha of land, of which 2·11m. ha were arable. A further 2·4m. ha of land were in the hands of other state agricultural organizations.

A law of Feb. 1991 provides for the restitution of collectivized land to its former owners or their heirs up to a limit of 10 ha. Land may be resold, but there is a limit of 100 ha on total holdings. Landless peasants are to receive a distribution from the residue. State farms are to remain nationalized; peasants will receive shares in their equity worth up to 10 ha. Local authorities are to manage the redistribution of land. Collective farms may if they wish become private co-operative associations.

Forestry. Total forest area was 6·37m. ha in 1989.

INDUSTRY. In 1989 there were 2,102 industrial enterprises, of which 1,474 were state-controlled, 67 local government-controlled and 561 co-operatives. 144 enterprises employed more than 5,000 persons; 141 less than 200.

Output of main products in 1989 (in tonnes): Pig-iron, 9,052; steel, 14,415; steel tubes, 1,360; coke, 5,870; rolled steel, 10,263; chemical fertilizers, 2,805; washing soda, 889; caustic soda, 763; paper, 709; cement, 13,265; sugar, 693; edible oils, 248; plastics, 640; woollen yarn, 70; man-made fibres, 273. In 1,000 units: Radio sets, 590; TV sets, 511; washing machines, 204. It was estimated that there was a fall in production of 60% in 1990.

Labour. The employed population in 1989 was 10·9m., of whom 3m. worked in agriculture and 4·9m. industry and building. In 1989 40·4% of the total workforce, and 37·7% of the industrial workforce, were women. A 5-day working week was introduced in Dec. 1989. Men retire at 62, women at 57. A law of Jan. 1991 defines unemployment, stipulates the conditions for receiving unemployment benefit, lays down rules for calculating amounts paid, establishes an unemployment fund and provides for retraining unemployed persons. Workers laid off receive 50–60% of their last wages for 180 days. A minimum monthly wage of 3,150 lei was set in March 1991. There were 0·18m. unemployed in Sept. 1991.

Trade Unions. In Sept. 1991 the principal trade union federations were the Inter-Union Alliance (89,621 members), Alfa Cartel (450,162), the COSIN Confederation (129,935), the Fraţia Confederation (164,629), the Hercules Confederation (52,495), the Conserg Confederation (81,818) and the former official union (UGSR), renamed National Confederation of Free Trade Unions (CNSLR; 1,421,790).

FOREIGN ECONOMIC RELATIONS. In June 1990 a 10-year treaty of commercial and economic co-operation was signed with the EEC. In July 1990 the USA extended its trade agreement with Romania for 3 years, but did not grant most-favoured-nation status.

Foreign investors may establish joint ventures or 100%-owned domestic companies in all but a few strategic industries. After an initial 2-year exemption, profits are taxed at 30%, dividends at 10%. Foreign investors register with the Romanian Development Agency. By the first quarter of 1991 there were 2,665 joint ventures. The constitution of Nov. 1991 prohibits foreigners from owning real estate.

Commerce. In 1989 exports totalled 167,780m. lei and imports 134,982m. lei.

Principal exports in 1989 were (in 1,000 tonnes): Petroleum products, 13,375; cement, 1,893; cereals, 289; oilfield equipment, 7,115m. lei; equipment for chemical factories, 1,266m. lei; shipbuilding, 1,650m. lei. Principal imports (in 1,000 tonnes): Iron ore, 13,626; industrial coke, 1,157; rolled ferrous metals, 468; electrical equipment, 3,707m. lei.

In 1989 Romania's main trading partners (trade in 1,000m. lei) were: USSR, exports, 37·98; imports, 42·49; Iran, 5·01, 16·22; Italy, 15·98, 0·83; Federal Republic of Germany, 10·93, 2·93; German Democratic Republic, 8·99, 9·94; USA, 9·12, 2·74.

Total trade between Romania and UK (British Department of Trade returns, in £1,000 sterling):

	1987	1988	1989	1990	1991
Imports to UK	92,526	100,906	117,685	61,215	58,531
Exports and re-exports from UK	55,688	50,111	38,141	85,879	58,735

Tourism. In 1990 citizens were granted the right to travel freely, and 3·64m. passports were issued.

COMMUNICATIONS

Roads. There were in 1989, 72,816 km of roads of which 14,683 km were main roads, 12,525 km of these modernized. Freight carried, 2,416m. tonnes; passengers, 879m.

Railways. Length of standard-gauge route in 1989 was 11,343 km, of which 3,654 km were electrified; there were 427 km of narrow-gauge lines. Freight carried in 1989, 306m. tonnes; passengers, 481m. There is a metro (57 km) and tram/light rail network (857 km) in Bucharest, and tramways in 13 other cities.

Civil Aviation. TAROM (*Transporturi Aeriene Române*), the state airline, operates all internal services, and also services to Amsterdam, Athens, Beijing, Beirut, Belgrade, Berlin, Brussels, Budapest, Cairo, Cologne, Copenhagen, Düsseldorf, Frankfurt, Istanbul, London, Moscow, Paris, Prague, Rome, Sofia, Tel-Aviv, Vienna, Warsaw and Zürich. Bucharest is also served by British Airways, PANAM, SABENA, Aeroflot, Air France, Interflug, CSA, MALEV, Austrian Air Lines, SAS, Lot, TABSO, El Al, Alitalia, Lufthansa and Swissair.

Bucharest's airports are at Băneasa (internal flights) and Otopeni (international flights). Air transport in 1989 carried 3·4m. passengers and 51,000 tonnes of freight. TAROM had 32 aircraft in 1990.

Shipping. The main ports are Constanţa on the Black Sea and Galaţi and Brăila on the Danube. A new port has been constructed at Agigea on the Black Sea and the 64 km canal between the Danube and the Black Sea was opened in 1984.

In 1985 the mercantile marine (NAVROM) owned some 200 sea-going ships. In 1989 sea-going transport carried 35·93m. tonnes of freight; river transport, 37·4m. tonnes and 1·78m. passengers.

Telecommunications. There were 4,596 post offices in 1989. Number of telephone subscribers, 1985, 1·96m. *Radio-televiziunea Româna* broadcasts 3 programmes on medium-waves and FM. There are also 6 regional programmes, and radio and TV transmission in Hungarian and German (restored since Dec. 1989). An independent TV channel, SOTI, began transmitting in Dec. 1991. Radio receiving sets in 1989 3·07m.; TV sets, 3·7m.

Cinemas and Theatres. There were, in 1989, 5,453 cinemas and 146 theatres and concert halls. 23 full-length feature films were made in 1989.

Newspapers and Books. The 1991 constitution abolished censorship. There were, in 1989, 36 daily and 24 weekly newspapers and 435 periodicals, including 11 dailies and 3 weeklies in minority languages. There were 6,864 public libraries in

1989. 2,159 book titles were published in 1989 in 62·4m. copies. (205 titles in minority languages).

JUSTICE, RELIGION, EDUCATION AND WELFARE

Justice. Justice is administered by the Supreme Court, the 41 county courts, and lower courts. Lay assessors (elected for 4 years) participate in most court trials, collaborating with the judges. The *Procurator-General* exercises 'supreme supervisory power to ensure the observance of the law' by all authorities, central and local, and all citizens. The Procurator-General in 1990 was Gheorghe Robu. The Procurator's Office and its organs are independent of any organs of justice or administration, and only responsible to the Grand National Assembly (which appoints the Procurator-General for 4 years) and between its sessions, to the State Council. The Ministry of the Interior is responsible for ordinary police work. State security is the responsibility of the State Security Council. A new penal code came into force on 1 Jan. 1969. An amnesty of Jan. 1988 abolished or reduced the sentences of all convicts. All political prisoners were released on 23 Dec. 1989. The death penalty was abolished in Dec. 1989 and is forbidden by the 1991 constitution.

Religion. The State Secretariat for Religious Denominations oversees religious affairs. Churches administer their own affairs and run seminaries for the training of priests. Expenses and salaries are paid by the State. There are 14 Churches, the largest being the Romanian Orthodox Church, which claimed some 16m. members in 1985. It is autocephalous, but retains dogmatic unity with the Eastern Orthodox Church. It is administered by the consultative Holy Synod and National Ecclesiastical Assembly and the executive National Ecclesiastical Council and Patriarchal Administration. It is organized into 12 dioceses grouped into 5 metropolitan bishoprics (Hungaro-Wallachia; Moldavia-Suceava; Transylvania; Olt; Banat) and headed by Patriarch Teoctist Arapaşu. There are some 11,800 churches, 2 theological colleges and 6 'schools of cantors', as well as seminaries.

The Uniate (Greek Catholic) Church (which severed its connexion with the Vatican in 1698) was suppressed in 1948. It had 1·6m. adherents and 1,818 priests. Estimates for 1973: 700,000 adherents and 600 priests. In April 1990 the Uniate Church was re-legalized. Property seized by the state in 1948 was restored to it, but not property which had passed to the Orthodox Church.

Other churches: Serbs have a Serbian Orthodox Vicariate at Timişoara. In 1986 there were 1·2m. Roman Catholics, mainly among the Hungarian and German minorities. There are 8 dioceses. In 1985 6 were vacant. There is a bishop of Alba Iulia and an Apostolic Administrator was appointed to Bucharest in Oct. 1984. There were 734 priests in 1982. The Church has not secured approval for a Statute and has no hierarchical ties with the Vatican.

Calvinists (600,000; mainly Hungarian) have bishoprics at Cluj and Oradea; Lutherans (150,000, mainly Germans) a bishopric at Sibiu and Unitarians (60,000, Hungarians) a bishopric at Cluj. These sects share a seminary at Cluj. In 1987 there were about 200,000 Baptists and 300,000 other neo-Protestants.

In 1989 there were 20,000 Jews under a Chief Rabbi. There were 120 synagogues in 1987.

There were 40,000 Moslems in 1983 and they have a Muftiate at Constanţa.

Education. Education is free and compulsory from 6 to 16, consisting of 8 years of primary school and 2 years of secondary (gymnasium). Further secondary education is available at *lycées*, professional schools or advanced technical schools.

In 1989–90 there were 12,108 kindergartens with 31,293 teachers and 835,890 children; 13,357 primary and secondary schools with 141,732 teachers and 2,891,810 pupils; 981 *lycées* with 42,519 teachers and 1,346,315 pupils; 798 professional schools with 1,898 teachers and 304,533 pupils; and 39 advanced technical schools with 1,593 pupils. There were 798 profession training schools with 1,898 teachers and 304,533 students. In 1983–84 there were 3,130 schools for 340,773 pupils of ethnic minorities with 15,922 teachers.

There are universities at Iaşi (founded 1860), Bucharest (1864), Cluj (1919), Timişoara (1962), Craiova (1965) and Braşov (1971). In 1989–90 there were in all

44 institutes of higher education, with 164,507 (6,669 foreign) students and 11,696 teachers. In 1983–84 there were 11,568 students at institutes of higher education for ethnic minorities with some 1,000 teachers.

The Academy, with seat at Bucharest, has 2 branches at Iași and Cluj.

Health. In 1989 there were 216,295 hospital beds and 49,054 doctors (including 7,116 dentists). Under the Ceaușescu régime health standards severely declined and medical services were neglected.

Social Security. In 1989 3·5m. pensioners drew average monthly pensions ranging from 2,106 to 127 lei.

DIPLOMATIC REPRESENTATIVES

Of Romania in Great Britain (4 Palace Green, London, W8 4QD)
Ambassador: Sergiu Celac.

Of Great Britain in Romania (24 Strada Jules Michelet, Bucharest)
Ambassador: Andrew Bache.

Of Romania in the USA (1607 23rd St., NW, Washington, D.C., 20008)
Ambassador: Virgil Constantinescu.

Of the USA in Romania (7–9 Strada Tudor Arghezi, Bucharest)
Ambassador: Alan Green, Jr.

Of Romania to the United Nations
Ambassador: Aurel D. Munteanu.

Further Reading

Anuarul Statistic al României. Bucharest, annual
Atlas Geografic Republica Socialistă Romania. Bucharest, 1965
Economic and Commercial Guide to Romania. Bucharest, annual since 1969
Revista de Statistică. Bucharest, monthly
Romania, the Industrialization of an Agrarian Economy under Socialist Planning: Report of a Mission sent to Romania by the World Bank. Washington, 1979
Deletant, A. and D., *Romania* [Bibliography]. Oxford and Santa Barbara, 1985
Fischer-Galati, S. A., *Rumania: A Bibliographical Guide.* Library of Congress, 1963.—*The New Rumania.* Mass. Inst. of Technology, 1968.—*The Socialist Republic of Rumania.* Baltimore, 1969.—*Twentieth Century Rumania.* New York, 1970
Gilberg, T., *Nationalism and Communism in Romania: the Rise and Fall of Ceaușescu's Personal Dictatorship.* Oxford, 1990
Giurescu, C. C. (ed.) *Chronological History of Romania.* 2nd ed. Bucharest, 1974
King, R. R., *History of the Romanian Communist Party.* Stanford, 1980
Morariu, I., *et al, The Geography of Rumania.* 2nd ed. Bucharest, 1969
Pacepa, I., *Red Horizons.* London, 1988
Shafir, M., *Romania: Politics, Economics and Society.* London, 1985
Stanciu, I. G. and Cernovodeanu, P., *Distant Lands: The Genesis and Evolution of Romanian–American Relations.* Boulder, 1985
Turnock, D., *An Economic Geography of Romania.* London, 1974.—*The Romanian Economy in the Twentieth Century.* London 1986

RWANDA

Capital: Kigali
Population: 6·71m. (1988)
GNP per capita: US$310 (1989)

Republika y'u Rwanda

HISTORY. From the 16th century to 1959 the Tutsi kingdom of Rwanda shared the history of Burundi (*see* p. 258). In 1959 an uprising of the Hutu destroyed the Tutsi feudal hierarchy and led to the departure of the Mwami Kigeri V. Elections and a referendum under the auspices of the UN in Sept. 1961 resulted in an overwhelming majority for the republican party, the Parmehutu (*Parti du Mouvement de l'Emancipation du Bahutu*), and the rejection of the institution of the Mwami. The republic proclaimed by the Parmehutu on 28 Jan. 1961 was recognized by the Belgian administration (but not by the UN) in Oct. 1961. Internal self-government was granted on 1 Jan. 1962, and by decision of the General Assembly of the UN the Republic of Rwanda became independent on 1 July 1962.

In Oct. 1990 rebel Tutsi forces of the Patriotic Rwandan Front (FPR) invaded from Uganda. A ceasefire was signed in March 1991, but sporadic fighting continued.

AREA AND POPULATION. Rwanda is bounded south by Burundi, west by Zaïre, north by Uganda and east by Tanzania. A mountainous state of 26,338 sq. km (10,169 sq. miles), its western third drains to Lake Kivu on the border with Zaïre and thence to the Congo river, while the rest is drained by the Kagera river into the Nile system.

The population was 4,819,317 at the 1978 Census, of whom over 90% were Hutu, 9% Tutsi and 1% Twa (pygmy); estimate (1988) 6,710,000. In 1988 there were about 20,000 refugees in Rwanda, all from Burundi.

The areas and populations (1978 Census) of the 10 prefectures are:

Prefecture	Sq. km	Census 1978	Prefecture	Sq. km	Census 1978
Cyangugu	2,226	331,380	Kigali	3,251	698,063
Kibuye	1,320	337,729	Kibungo	4,134	360,934
Gisenyi	2,395	468,786	Gitarama	2,241	602,752
Ruhengeri	1,762	528,649	Gikongoro	2,192	369,891
Byumba	4,987	519,968	Butare	1,830	601,165

Kigali, the capital, had 156,650 inhabitants in 1981; other towns (1978) being Butare (21,691), Ruhengeri (16,025) and Gisenyi (12,436). Kinyarwanda, the language of the entire population, and French are official languages, and Kiswahili is spoken in the commercial centres, where most of the 1,200 Europeans and 750 Asians reside.

CLIMATE. Despite the equatorial situation, there is a highland tropical climate. The wet seasons are from Oct. to Dec. and March to May. Highest rainfall occurs in the west, at around 70" (1,770 mm), decreasing to 40–55" (1,020–1,400 mm) in the central uplands and to 30" (760 mm) in the north and east. Kigali. Jan. 67°F (19·4°C), July 70°F (21·1°C). Annual rainfall 40" (1,000 mm).

CONSTITUTION AND GOVERNMENT. Under the Constitution of 1978 the *Mouvement revolutionnaire national pour le développement* (MRND) was the sole political organization. Executive power was vested in a President, elected by universal suffrage for a (renewable) 5-year term. He presided over a Council of Ministers, whom he appointed and dismissed. Legislative power rested with a National Development Council of 70 deputies, elected for a 5-year term.

A new Constitution was promulgated in June 1991.

President: Maj.-Gen. Junéval Habyarimana (took office July 1975; elected Dec. 1978 and re-elected Dec. 1983).

The President appointed Sylvestre Nsanzimana as *Prime Minister* in Oct. 1991. He formed a government on 17 Dec., 16 members of which belong to the MRND.

National flag: Three equal vertical panels of red, yellow and green (left to right), the letter 'R' in black superimposed on the centre panel.

Local government: The 10 prefectures, each under an appointed Prefect, are divided into 143 communes, each with an appointed Burgomaster and an elected Council.

DEFENCE

Army. The Army consists of 1 commando battalion, 1 reconnaissance, 8 infantry and 1 engineer companies. Equipment includes 12 AML-60 armoured cars. Strength (1991) about 5,000. There is a paramilitary gendarmerie of some 1,200.

Air Force. The Air Force currently operates 1 Guerrier armed light aircraft, 2 Noratlas, 2 Islander light transports, 6 Gazelle and 4 Alouette III helicopters. A Caravelle is operated on VIP duties. Personnel (1991) 200.

INTERNATIONAL RELATIONS

Membership. Rwanda is a member of the UN, OAU and is an ACP state of the EEC. With Burundi and Zaïre it forms part of the Economic Community of Countries of the Great Lakes.

ECONOMY

Budget. The budget for 1989 balanced at 27,500m. Rwanda francs.

Currency. The unit of currency is the *Rwanda franc* (RWF) of 100 *centimes*. In March 1992 £1 = 219.59 Rwanda francs; US$1 = 125.087 Rwanda francs.

Banking and Finance. The Development Bank of Rwanda *(Banque Rwandaise de Développement—BRD)* had a capital (1983) of 1,000m. Rwanda francs. Other banks are the Central Bank *(Banque Nationale du Rwanda)*; 2 commercial banks which are majority foreign owned—the *Banque Commerciale du Rwanda* and the *Banque de Kigali*; the People's Bank, the Savings Association and the *Caisse Hypothécaire*.

ENERGY AND NATURAL RESOURCES

Electricity. 4 hydro-electric installations and 1 thermal plant produced 110m. kwh in 1986, but over half of the country's needs come from Zaïre. Supply 220 volts; 50 Hz.

Minerals. Cassiterite and wolframite are mined east of Lake Kivu. Production (1983): Cassiterite, 1,526 tonnes; wolfram, 429 tonnes. About 1m. cu. metres of natural gas are obtained from under the lake each year.

Agriculture. Subsistence agriculture accounts for most of the gross national product. Staple food crops (production 1990, in 1,000 tonnes) are sweet potatoes (900), cassava (500), dry beans (200), sorghum (155), potatoes (190), maize (110), peas (25) and groundnuts. The main cash crops are coffee (37), tea (8) and pyrethrum. There is a pilot rice-growing project.

Long-horned Ankole cattle, 639,000 head in 1980, play an important traditional role. Efforts are being made to improve their present negligible economic value. There were (1990) 630,000 cattle, 1,119,000 goats, 373,000 sheep and 100,000 pigs.

INDUSTRY. There are about 100 small-sized modern manufacturing enterprises in the country. Food manufacturing is the dominant industrial activity (64%) followed by construction (15·3%) and mining (9%). There is a large modern brewery.

FOREIGN ECONOMIC RELATIONS. With Burundi and Zaire Rwanda forms part of the Economic Community of the Great Lakes.

Commerce. In 1988 exports amounted to US$105m. and imports US$385m. Major exports are coffee, tea and tin. Chief trading partners are Belgium, Kenya and Japan.

Total trade between Rwanda and UK (British Department of Trade returns, in £1,000 sterling):

	1987	1988	1989	1990	1991
Imports to UK	4,291	8,434	2,991	2,128	2,193
Exports and re-exports from UK	2,526	1,636	1,790	1,915	2,334

Tourism. In 1984 there were 20,000 visitors to national parks.

COMMUNICATIONS

Roads. There were (1982) 6,760 km of roads. There are road links with Burundi, Uganda, Tanzania and Zaïre. There were in 1982 6,188 cars and 7,168 commercial vehicles.

Civil Aviation. There are international airports at Kanombe, for Kigali, and at Kamembe, with services to Bujumbura, Bukavu, Entebbe, Goma, Lubumbashi, Athens and Brussels.

Telecommunications. Telephones (1983) 6,598. The state-controlled Radiodiffusion de la République Rwandaise is responsible for broadcasting. There is no television. There were about 425,000 radio sets in 1991.

JUSTICE, RELIGION, EDUCATION AND WELFARE

Justice. A system of Courts of First Instance and provincial courts refer appeals to Courts of Appeal and a Court of Cassation situated in Kigali.

Religion. In 1989 there were 4·54m. Roman Catholics, 0·63m. Protestants and 0·63m. Moslems. Some of the population follow traditional animist religions.

Education. In 1985 there were 790,198 pupils attending primary schools with 14,005 teachers. There were secondary, technical and teacher-training schools with 45,000 students and 1,082 teachers. The National University, opened at Butare, with sites at Butare and Ruhengeri, in 1963, had 1,577 students in 1984.

Health. In 1983 there were 170 hospitals and health centres with (1980) 9,015 beds; there were also 164 doctors, 1 dentist, 10 pharmacists, 464 midwives and 525 nursing personnel.

DIPLOMATIC REPRESENTATIVES

Of Rwanda in Great Britain
Ambassador: François Ngarukiyintwali (resides in Brussels).

Of Great Britain in Rwanda
Ambassador: Roger Westbrook, CMG (resides in Kinshasa).

Of Rwanda in the USA (1714 New Hampshire Ave., NW, Washington, D.C., 20009)
Ambassador: Aloys Uwimana.

Of the USA in Rwanda (Blvd. de la Révolution, Kigali)
Ambassador: Robert A. Flaten.

Of Rwanda to the United Nations
Ambassador: (Vacant).

ST HELENA

Capital: Jamestown
Population: 5,564 (1988)

HISTORY. The island was administered by the East India Company from 1659 and became a British colony in 1834.

AREA AND POPULATION. St Helena, of volcanic origin, is 1,200 miles from the west coast of Africa. Area, 47 sq. miles (121·7 sq. km), with a cultivable area of about 600 acres (243 ha). Population (1988) 5,564. The port of the island is Jamestown, population (1976) 1,516.

In 1982 there were: Births, 123; deaths, 52; marriages, 26.

CLIMATE. A mild climate, with little variation. Temperatures range from 75–85°F (24–29°C) in summer to 65–75°F (18–24°C) in winter. Rainfall varies between 13" (325 mm) and 37" (925 mm) according to altitude and situation.

GOVERNMENT. The Government of St Helena is administered by a Governor, with the aid of a Legislative Council consisting of the Governor, 2 *ex-officio* members (the Government Secretary and the Treasurer) and 12 elected members. Committees of the Legislative Council are responsible for the general oversight of the activities of government departments and have, in addition, statutory and administrative functions.

The Governor is also assisted by an Executive Council consisting of the 2 *ex-officio* members and the chairmen of the 6 Council committees.

Governor and C.-in-C.: Alan Hoole, OBE.
Government Secretary: M. S. Hone, MBE.

Flag: The British Blue Ensign with the shield of the colony in the fly.

FINANCE AND TRADE

Budget. In 1984 revenue was £4·34m. and expediture £3·91m.

Commerce. Total trade between Ascension and St Helena and UK (British Department of Trade returns, in £1,000 sterling):

	1987	1988	1989	1990	1991
Imports to UK	189	205	504	555	19,606
Exports and re-exports from UK	8,065	6,103	7,208	7,429	3,981

Banking. Savings-bank deposits on 31 Dec. 1982, £1,467,079, belonging to 3,800 depositors.

COMMUNICATIONS

Roads. There were (1988) 94 km of all-weather motor roads. There were 1,301 vehicles in 1987.

Shipping. There is a service from Cardiff (UK) 6 times a year, and links with South Africa and neighbouring islands.

Telecommunications. The Cable & Wireless Ltd cable connects St Helena with Cape Town and Ascension Island. There is a telephone service with 85 miles of wire and (1982), 310 telephones.

St Helena Government Broadcasting Station broadcasts in English on medium-waves. Number of radio receivers (1988), 2,400.

JUSTICE, RELIGION, EDUCATION AND WELFARE

Justice. Police force, 32; cases dealt with by police magistrate, 205 in 1981.

Religion. There are 10 Anglican churches, 4 Baptist chapels, 3 Salvation Army halls, 1 Seventh Day Adventist church and 1 Roman Catholic church.

Education. Three pre-school playgroups, 7 primary, 3 senior and 1 secondary schools controlled by the Government had 1,188 pupils in 1987.

Health. There were 3 doctors, 1 dentist and 54 hospital beds in 1982.

Ascension is a small island of volcanic origin, of 34 sq. miles (88 sq. km), 700 miles north-west of St Helena. In Nov. 1922 the administration was transferred from the Admiralty to the Colonial Office and annexed to the colony of St Helena. There are 120 hectares providing fresh meat, vegetables and fruit. Population, 31 March 1988, was 1,007 (excluding military personnel).

The island is the resort of sea turtles, which come to lay their eggs in the sand annually between Jan. and May. Rabbits are more or less numerous on the island, which is, besides, the breeding ground of the sooty tern or 'wideawake', these birds coming in vast numbers to lay their eggs every eighth month. There is also a small herd of feral donkeys.

Cable & Wireless Ltd own and operate a cable station, connecting the island with St Helena, Sierra Leone, St Vincent, Rio de Janeiro and Buenos Aires. There is an airstrip (Miracle Mile) near the settlement of Georgetown which was being extended in 1985.

Administrator: B. N. Connelly.

Tristan da Cunha, is the largest of a small group of islands in the South Atlantic lying 1,320 miles (2,124 km) south-west of St Helena, of which they became dependencies on 12 Jan. 1938. Tristan da Cunha has an area of 98 sq. km and a population (1988) of 313, all living in the settlement of Edinburgh. Inaccessible Island (10 sq. km) lies 20 miles west and the 3 Nightingale Islands (2 sq. km) lie 20 miles south of Tristan da Cunha; they are uninhabited. Gough Island (90 sq. km) is 220 miles south of Tristan and has a meteorological station.

Tristan consists of a volcano rising to a height of 6,760 ft, with a circumference at its base of 21 miles. The volcano, believed to be extinct, erupted unexpectedly early in Oct. 1961. The whole population was evacuated without loss and settled temporarily in the UK. In 1963 they returned to Tristan where they all dwell in the settlement of Edinburgh. Before the disaster occurred the habitable area was a small plateau on the north west side of about 12 sq. miles, 100 ft above sea-level. Only about 30 acres was under cultivation, three-quarters of it for potatoes. There were apple and peach trees. Potatoes remain the chief crop, cattle, sheep and pigs are now reared, and fish are plentiful.

Population in 1880, 109; in 1988, 306. The original inhabitants were shipwrecked sailors and soldiers who remained behind when the garrison from St Helena was withdrawn in 1817.

At the end of April 1942 Tristan da Cunha was commissioned as HMS *Atlantic Isle*, and became an important meteorological and radio station. In Jan. 1949 a South African company commenced crawfishing operations. An Administrator was appointed at the end of 1948 and a body of basic law brought into operation. The Island Council, which was set up in 1932, consists of a Chief Islander, 3 nominated and 7 elected members under the chairmanship of the Administrator.

Administrator: P. H. Johnson.

Further Reading

Crawford, A., *Tristan da Cunha and the Roaring Forties*. Edinburgh, 1982
Cross, A., *Saint Helena*. Newton Abbot, 1980
Munch, P. A., *Sociology of Tristan da Cunha*. Oslo, 1945.—*Crisis in Utopia*. New York, 1971

ST KITTS AND NEVIS

Capital: Basseterre
Population: 44,380 (1988)
GNP capita: US$2,108 (1989)

Federation of St Kitts and Nevis

HISTORY. St Kitts (formerly St Christopher) and Nevis were discovered and named by Columbus in 1493. They were settled by Britain in 1623 and 1628 respectively, but ownership was disputed with France until 1713. They formed part of the Leeward Islands Federation from 1871 to 1956, and part of the Federation of the West Indies from 1958 to 1962. In Feb. 1967 the colonial status was replaced by an 'association' with Britain, giving the islands full internal self-government, while Britain remained responsible for defence and foreign affairs. St Kitts and Nevis became fully independent on 19 Sept. 1983.

AREA AND POPULATION. The islands form part of the Lesser Antilles in Eastern Caribbean. Population, estimate (1988) 44,380.

	sq. km	Census 1980	Chief town	Census 1980
St Christopher	168·4	33,881	Basseterre	14,283
Nevis	93·2	9,428	Charlestown	1,243
	261·6	43,309		

In 1980, 94% of the population were black and 36% were urban. Births, 1989, were 989 (24·2 per 1,000 population); deaths 484 (10·5). English is the official and spoken language.

CLIMATE. A pleasantly healthy climate, with a cool breeze throughout the year, low humidity and no recognized rainy season. Average annual rainfall is about 55" (1,375 mm).

CONSTITUTION AND GOVERNMENT. The 1983 Constitution described the country as 'a sovereign democratic federal state'. It allowed for a unicameral Parliament consisting of 11 elected Members (8 from St Kitts and 3 from Nevis) and 3 appointed Senators. Nevis was given its own Island Assembly and the right to secession from St Kitts. At the General Elections held on 21 March 1989, 6 seats in St Kitts were won by the People's Action Movement and 2 by the Labour Party, and in Nevis 2 seats were won by the Nevis Reformation Party and 1 by the Concerned Citizens Movement.

Governor-General: Sir Clement Athelston Arrindell, GCMG, GCVO.
Prime Minister and Minister of Finance, Home and Foreign Affairs: Rt. Hon. Dr Kennedy Alphonse Simmonds.
Deputy Prime Minister and Minister of Tourism and Labour: Michael O'Powell. *Education, Youth, Community Affairs, Communications, Works, Public Utilities and Sports:* Sidney E. Morris. *Agriculture, Lands, Housing and Development:* Hugh C. Heyliger. *Trade and Industry:* Fitzroy P. Jones. *Health and Women's Affairs:* Constance Mitcham. *Minister in the Office of the Prime Minister:* Joseph Parry. *Minister in the Ministry of Finance:* Richard Caines. *Attorney-General:* Tapley Seaton. *Natural Resources and the Environment:* Simeon Daniel. The Prime Minister of *Nevis* is Simeon Daniel.

Flag: Diagonally green, black, red, with the black fimbriated in yellow and charged with two white stars.

INTERNATIONAL RELATIONS

Membership. St Kitts and Nevis is a member of the UN, the OAS, the Commonwealth and is an ACP state of EEC.

ECONOMY

Budget. The 1990 budget envisaged expenditure at EC$93,235,249 and revenue at EC$98,969,309.

Currency. The East Caribbean *dollar* (XCD) (of 100 *cents*) is in use. There are notes of EC$1, 5, 20 and 100, and coins of 1, 2, 5, 10, 25 and 50 cents and EC$1. In March 1992, £1 = EC$4·74; US$1 = EC$2·70.

Banking. The National Bank operates 4 branches in St. Kitts and Nevis. The main office is located in Basseterre. Other banks include Barclay's Bank International, with a sub-branch in Nevis, Royal Bank of Canada, and the Nevis Co-operative Banking Co. Ltd and the Bank of Nevis in Charlestown. Branches of the Bank of Nova Scotia are located in Basseterre and Charlestown. Commercial banks' assets (1988) EC$418·6m.; deposits EC$289·8m.

ENERGY AND NATURAL RESOURCES

Electricity. Production (1989) 42m. kwh.

Agriculture. The main crops are sugar and cotton. There are 30 sugar estates and 124 acres of cotton. Most of the farms are small-holdings and there are a number of coconut estates amounting to some 1,000 acres under public and private ownership. Sugar production (1990) 14,777 tons; cotton, 7,202 lbs (clean lint); copra, 12 tons; potatoes, 0·67m. lbs. In 1989, 1,685,000 tons of sugar-cane and 2,000 tonnes of coconuts were produced.

Livestock (1990): Cattle, 5,000; pigs, 4,000; sheep, 15,000; goats, 10,000; poultry, (1987) 50,116.

Fisheries. Catch (1988) 2·5m. lbs.

INDUSTRY. The main industries are the assembly of electronic equipment and food and drink processing, particularly sugar and cane spirit.

FOREIGN ECONOMIC RELATIONS. Foreign debt was EC$80m. in Dec. 1988.

Commerce. Imports, (1989) EC$276·7m., mainly from the USA (EC$114·3m.); exports, EC$68·3m, mainly to the USA (EC$37·3m.). Chief export was sugar.

Total trade between St Christopher (St Kitts)–Nevis and UK (British Department of Trade returns, in £1,000 sterling):

	1988	1989	1990	1991
Imports to UK	4,271	4,866	4,513	6,476
Exports and re-exports from UK	8,025	5,887	6,477	5,765

Tourism. In 1990, there were 106,465 tourists, 33,941 arriving by sea. In 1989 there were 25 hotels with 1,465 beds.

COMMUNICATIONS

Roads. There were (1990) about 300 km of roads, of which 124 km were paved, and (1989) 5,749 licensed vehicles.

Railways. There are 36 km of railway operated by the sugar industry.

Aviation. There is an international airport at Golden Rock (4 km from Basseterre). 98,263 passengers arrived by air in 1987. There is an airfield on Nevis (Newcastle).

Shipping. A deep-water port was opened in 1981 at Bird Rock (Basseterre) with accommodation for cargo, tourist, roll-on-roll-off ships and bulk sugar and molasses loading. 31,000 tons of cargo were unloaded in 1990 and 134,000 tons loaded.

Telecommunications. There are 2 post offices with 7 branches. There were 9,367 telephones in 1990. There is a part government/part commercial radio and TV network; Nevis has its own radio. In 1991 there were 9,500 television (colour by NTSC) and 20,000 radio receivers.

JUSTICE, RELIGION, EDUCATION AND WELFARE

Justice. Justice is administered by the Supreme Court and by Magistrates' Courts.They have both civil and criminal jurisdiction.

Religion. In 1985, 36·2% were Anglican, 32·3% Methodist, 7·9% other Protestant, and 10·7% Roman Catholic.

Education. Primary education is compulsory for all children between the ages of 5 and 14, but no pupil is required to leave school before the age of 16 years. There is an Extra-Mural Department of the University of the West Indies, a Technical College and a Teachers' Training College.

In 1989–90 there were 1,695 pupils and 103 teachers in 52 nurseries and pre-schools, 7,442 pupils and 341 teachers in 33 primary schools, and 4,176 pupils and 294 teachers in 7 secondary schools. In 1989 there were 211 students in the Technical and Teacher's Training Colleges.

Health. In 1990 there were 27 doctors, 4 hospitals with 258 beds and 17 health clinics.

DIPLOMATIC REPRESENTATIVES

Of St Kitts and Nevis in Great Britain (10 Kensington Ct., London W8)
High Commissioner: Richard Gunn, CBE.

Of Great Britain in St Kitts and Nevis
High Commissioner: E. T. Davies, CMG (resides in Bridgetown).

Of St Kitts and Nevis in the USA (2501 M. St., NW, Washington, D.C., 20037)
Chargé d'affaires: Aubrey Hart.

Of the USA in St Kitts and Nevis
Ambassador: C. Philip Hughes.

Of St Kitts and Nevis to the United Nations
Ambassador: Dr William Herbert.

Further Reading

Statistics Division, *National Accounts.* Annual.—*St Kitts and Nevis Quarterly.*
St Kitts and Nevis Quarterly. Statistics Division, Ministry of Development

Gordon, J., *Nevis: Queen of the Caribees.* London, 1985

National library: Public Library, Basseterre.
National statistical office: Statistics Division, Ministry of Development, Basseterre.

ST LUCIA

Capital: Castries
Population: 146,600 (1988)
GNP per capita: US$1,810 (1989)

HISTORY. St Lucia was discovered about 1500 A.D. Attempts to colonize the island by the English took place in 1605 and 1638. The French settled in 1650 and St Lucia was ceded to Britain in 1814. Self-government was achieved in 1967 and independence on 22 Feb. 1979.

AREA AND POPULATION. St Lucia is a small island of the Lesser Antilles situated in the Eastern Caribbean between Martinique and St Vincent, with an area of 238 sq. miles (617 sq. km); population (census, 1980) 120,300. Estimate (1988) 146,600. The capital is Castries (population, 1988, 52,868), and Vieux Fort, the second town and port 12,951 in 1984. Life expectancy (1985) was 68·6 (men) and 75·5 (women).

CLIMATE. The climate is tropical, with a dry season lasting from Jan. to April, a wet season from May to Aug., followed by an Indian summer for two months, but most rain falls in Nov. and Dec. Amounts vary over the year, according to altitude, from 60" (1,500 mm) to 138" (3,450 mm). Temperatures are uniform at about 80°F (26·7°C).

CONSTITUTION AND GOVERNMENT. There is a 17-seat House of Assembly elected for 5 years; an 11-seat Senate appointed by the Governor-General, 6 on the advice of the Prime Minister, 3 on the advice of the Leader of the Opposition, and 2 'after consultation with appropriate religious, economic or social bodies or associations'.

At the elections in April 1987, the United Workers' Party gained 9 seats, and the St Lucia Labour Party, 8.

Acting Governor-General: Stanislaus James, OBE.

In Feb. 1992 the government comprised:

Prime Minister, Minister of Finance, Planning, Development, Home Affairs and Housing: Rt Hon. John George Melvin Compton.

Deputy Prime Minister and Minister of Trade, Industry and Tourism: George Mallet. *Foreign Affairs:* Neville Cenac. *Health, Labour, Information and Broadcasting:* Romanus Lansiquot. *Education and Culture:* Louis George. *Community Development, Social Affairs, Youth and Sport and Women's Affairs:* Stephenson King. *Agriculture, Lands, Fisheries and Co-operatives:* Ferdinand Henry. *Communications, Works and Transport:* Gregory Avril. *Attorney-General and Minister of Legal Affairs:* Parry Husbands. *Minister of State in the Prime Minister's Office:* Desmond Brathwate. *Minister of State in the Ministry of Labour:* Winhall Joshua.

Flag: Blue with a design of a black triangle edged in white, bearing a smaller yellow triangle, in the centre.

Local government: In 1986 the 10 *quartiers* were replaced by 8 administrative regions.

INTERNATIONAL RELATIONS

Membership. St Lucia is a member of the UN, OAS, Caricom, the Commonwealth and is an ACP state of the EEC.

ECONOMY

Planning. The aim of the Development Plan, 1977–90, was to develop agriculture to diversify production and to contain rural-urban drift.

Budget. The budget in 1989–90 amounted to EC$370·3m. expenditure; revenue, EC$358·7m.

Banking. There are Barclays Bank International with 4 branches and 2 agencies, the Royal Bank of Canada with 1 branch, the Bank of Nova Scotia with 3 branches, the Canadian Imperial Bank of Commerce and the St Lucia Co-operative bank with 2 branches each, the National Development Bank with 1 branch and the National Commercial Bank with 3 branches.

INDUSTRY. In 1990, laundry soap, coconut meal, rum, beverages, electronic assembly and clothing were the chief products.

Agriculture. Bananas, cocoa, coconuts, mace, nutmeg and citrus fruit are the chief products. Livestock (1988): Cattle, 13,000; pigs, 12,000; sheep, 15,000; goats, 12,000.

FOREIGN ECONOMIC RELATIONS

Commerce. Value of imports (1986), EC$419·3m.; of exports, EC$213·2m., including coconut oil, cocoa beans, copra and bananas. Main items of imports were artificial silk and cotton piece-goods, cement, plastic goods, iron and steel products, hardware, motor vehicles, agricultural machinery, fertilizers, wheat flour, codfish and rice, meat and meat preparations.

Total trade between St Lucia and UK (British Department of Trade returns, in £1,000 sterling):

	1988	1989	1990	1991
Imports to UK	58,385	48,746	55,737	44,852
Exports and re-exports from UK	19,750	19,601	17,573	19,025

Tourism. The total number of visitors during 1987 was 202,336.

COMMUNICATIONS

Roads. The island has 500 miles of main and secondary roads, and 2,084 commercial vehicles and 8,629 cars in 1986.

Aviation. The island is served on a scheduled basis by Leeward Islands Air Transport, British West Indian Airways, Eastern Airline, British Airways, Pan Am, Caribbean Airways and Air Canada. There are 2 airfields—Hewanorra International Airport, with 9,000 ft runway, and Vigie.

Shipping. There are 2 ports, Castries and Vieux Fort.

Post and Broadcasting. There were (1986) 13,654 telephone instruments coupled to 7,960 exchange lines; 157 telex machines, and telegram service. There were 5,000 TV and 99,000 radio receivers in 1988.

Cinemas. There were 8 cinemas in 1986.

JUSTICE, RELIGION, EDUCATION AND WELFARE

Justice. The island is divided into 2 judicial districts, and there are 9 magistrates' courts. Appeals lie with the Eastern Caribbean Supreme Court of Appeal.

Religion. In 1989 over 82% of the population was Roman Catholic.

Education (1985–86). 79 primary schools, with 32,273 pupils on roll. Primary education is free and compulsory by law, but the legislation is not enforced. There are 12 secondary schools with 5,665 pupils. There is 1 technical college with (1985–86) 223 students and 1 teachers' college with (1985–86) 123 students.

Health. Victoria Hospital (in Castries) has 213 beds; there is also a 162-bed mental hospital, 3 other hospitals (150 beds) and 29 health centres. In 1984 there were 58 doctors, 5 dentists and 236 nursing personnel.

DIPLOMATIC REPRESENTATIVES

Of St Lucia in Great Britain (10 Kensington Ct., London, W8)
High Commissioner: Richard Gunn, CBE.

Of Great Britain in St Lucia
High Commissioner: E. T. Davies, CMG (resides in Bridgetown).

Of St Lucia in the USA (2100 M St., NW, Washington, D.C., 20037)
Ambassador: Dr Joseph E. Edmunds.

Of the USA in St Lucia
Ambassador: C. Philip Hughes.

Of St Lucia to the United Nations
Ambassador: Dr Charles S. Flemming.

Further Reading

Ellis, G., *St Lucia: Helen of the West Indies*. London, 1985

Library: The Central Library, Castries.

ST VINCENT AND THE GRENADINES

Capital: Kingstown
Population: 113,950 (1989)
GNP per capita: US$1,100 (1988)

HISTORY. The date of discovery of St Vincent was 22 Jan. 1498. In 1969 St Vincent became a self-governing Associated State of UK and acquired full independence on 27 Oct. 1979.

AREA AND POPULATION. St Vincent is an island of the Lesser Antilles, situated in the Eastern Caribbean between St Lucia and Grenada, from which latter it is separated by a chain of small islands known as the Grenadines. The total area of 388 sq. km (150 sq. miles) comprises the island of St Vincent itself (345 sq. km) and the Northern Grenadines (43 sq. km) of which the largest are Bequia, Mustique, Canouan, Mayreau and Union.

The population at the 1980 Census was 97,845; latest estimate (1989) was 113,950 of whom 5,503 lived in the Northern, and 2,963 in the Southern Grenadines. The capital, Kingstown, had 29,372 inhabitants in 1989 (including suburbs). The population is mainly of black (82%) and mixed (13·9%) origin, with small white, Asian and Amerindian minorities.

Vital statistics (1989): Live births, 2,537; deaths, 712; marriages (1987), 416.

CLIMATE. The climate is tropical marine, with north-east Trades predominating and rainfall ranging from 150" (3,750 mm) a year in the mountains to 60" (1,500 mm) on the south-east coast. The rainy season is from June to Dec., and temperatures are equable throughout the year.

CONSTITUTION AND GOVERNMENT. The House of Assembly consists of 15 elected members, directly elected for a 5-year term from single-member constituencies, and 6 Senators appointed by the Governor-General (4 on the advice of the Prime Minister and 2 on the advice of the Leader of the Opposition). At the General Elections held 16 May 1989, the New Democratic Party won all 15 contested seats.

Governor-General: Sir David Jack.

In Feb. 1992 the government comprised:

Prime Minister and Minister of Finance and Foreign Affairs: Rt. Hon. James Fitz-Allen Mitchell.

Agriculture, Industry and Labour: Allan Cruickshank. *Education, Youth and Women's Affairs:* John Horne. *Housing, Community Development and Local Government:* Louis Jones. *Health and Environment:* Burton Williams. *Attorney General, Minister of Justice and Information:* Parnell Campbell. *Communications and Works:* Jeremiah Scott. *Trade and Tourism:* Herbert Young.

There are 2 Ministers of State.

National Flag: Three vertical stripes of blue, yellow, green, with the yellow of double width and charged with three green diamonds.

INTERNATIONAL RELATIONS

Membership. St Vincent and the Grenadines is a member of UN, OAS, Caricom, the Commonwealth and is an ACP state of the EEC.

ECONOMY

Budget. Revenue (estimate), 1989–90, EC$128·38m.; expenditure, EC$123·56m. Public debt at the end of the financial year 1988–89 was EC$122·57m.

Currency. The currency in use is the *East Caribbean dollar* (XCD). In March 1992, £1 = EC$4·74; US$1 = EC$2·70.

1140

Banking and Finance. There are branches of Barclays Bank PLC, the Caribbean Banking Corporation, the Canadian Imperial Bank of Commerce, the Bank of Nova Scotia. Locally-owned banks: the National Commercial Bank, St Vincent Co-operative Bank and the St Vincent Agricultural Credit and Loan Bank.

ENERGY AND NATURAL RESOURCES

Electricity. Production (1987) was 48,116,190 kwh. Supply 230 volts; 50 Hz.

Agriculture. Agriculture accounted for 20·8% of GDP in 1987. According to the 1985–86 census of agriculture, 29,649 acres of the total acreage of 85,120 were classified as agricultural lands; 5,500 acres were under forest and woodland and all other lands accounted for 1,030 acres. The total arable land was about 8,932 acres, of which 4,016 acres were under temporary crops, 2,256 acres under temporary pasture, 2,289 acres under temporary fallow and other arable land covering 371 acres. 16,062 acres were under permanent crops, of which approximately 5,500 acres were under coconuts and 7,224 acres under bananas; the remainder produce cocoa, citrus, mangoes, avocado pears, guavas and miscellaneous crops. The sugar industry was closed down in 1985 although some sugar-cane will be grown for rum production. Production (1988, in tonnes): Coconuts, 25,000; bananas, 40,000.

Livestock (1988): Cattle, 7,000; pigs, 9,000; sheep, 15,000; goats, 5,000.

INDUSTRY. Industries include assembly of electronic equipment, manufacture of garments, electrical products, animal feeds and flour, corrugated galvanized sheets, exhaust systems, industrial gases, concrete blocks, plastics, soft drinks, beer and rum, wood products and furniture, and processing of milk, fruit juices and food items.

Labour. The Department of Labour is charged with looking after the interest and welfare of all categories of workers, including providing advice and guidance to employers and employees and their organizations and enforcing the labour laws.

FOREIGN ECONOMIC RELATIONS

Commerce (1989). Imports, EC$344·18m.; exports, EC$201·34m.

Principal exports, 1989 (in EC$1,000): Eddoes and dasheen, 8,576; sweet potatoes, 5,113; tannias, 1,922; bananas, 89,933; tobacco, 540; coconut, 741; plantain, 1,830; ginger, 1,063; flour, 18,773.

Total trade between St Vincent and the Grenadines and UK (British Department of Trade returns, in £1,000 sterling):

	1988	1989	1990	1991
Imports to UK	29,709	31,570	37,906	29,259
Exports and re-exports from UK	8,011	11,075	9,514	7,316

Tourism. There were 128,615 visitors in 1989.

COMMUNICATIONS

Roads. There were (1989) 53 miles of highway, 19 miles of concrete road, 245 miles of oiled asphalt road and 217 miles of earth track. Vehicles registered (1987) 8,500.

Civil Aviation. Scheduled services are operated daily by LIAT and Air Martinique. Non-scheduled services are operated by Mustique Airways, Tropical Air Services, Aero-Services and St Lucia Airways. Passengers are able to travel daily through the chain of islands stretching as far north as San Juan, Puerto Rico and south to Trinidad. Connexions to the USA, Canada, South America and Europe are possible *via* Barbados, Antigua, Trinidad and St Lucia.

Shipping (1987): 36 auxiliary sailing vessels of 1,510 NRT entered and cleared. 659 motor vessels of 805,261 NRT entered and cleared. 47 tankers of 41,798 NRT bringing 18,925·13 tons of fuel entered.

Telecommunications. There is a General Post Office at Kingstown and 49 district post offices. There is an automatic telephone system with (1989) 12,000 sub-scribers; 7,950 stations and a digital radio link to Bequia, Mustique and Union Island; VHF links Petit St Vincent and Palm Island. The National Broadcasting Corporation is part government-owned and part commercial. In 1991 there were 58,190 radio and 17,500 TV sets (colour by NTSC).

Cinemas. There were 2 cinemas in 1987 with a seating capacity of 1,825.

JUSTICE, RELIGION, EDUCATION AND WELFARE

Justice (1986). There were 3,699 criminal matters disposed of in the 3 magisterial districts which comprise 11 courts. 192 cases were dealt with in the 1987 Criminal Assizes in the High Court. Strength of police force (1982), 525 (including 12 officers).

Religion. At the 1980 Census, 42% of the population was Anglican, 21% Metho-dist and 12% Roman Catholic.

Education. In 1989 there were 64 primary schools (52 rural) with 25,152 pupils, 21 secondary schools (13 rural) and 1 school for special needs.

Health. In 1989 there was a general hospital in Kingstown with 204 beds, 4 rural hospitals, 2 private hospitals and 35 clinics. There were 40 doctors, 2 dentists, 208 registered nurses, 46 auxiliary nurses and 35 community health aides.

Library: St Vincent Public Library, Kingstown. *Librarian:* Mrs Lorna Small.

DIPLOMATIC REPRESENTATIVES

Of St Vincent and the Grenadines in Great Britain (10 Kensington Ct, London, W8)
High Commissioner: Richard Gunn, CBE.

Of Great Britain in St Vincent and the Grenadines
High Commissioner: E. T. Davies, CMG (resides in Bridgetown).

Of St Vincent and the Grenadines in the USA and to the United Nations
Ambassador: Kingsley C. A. Layne.

Of the USA in St Vincent and the Grenadines
Ambassador: C. Philip Hughes.

Further Reading

Price, N., *Behind the Planter's Back*. London, 1988

SAN MARINO

Repubblica di San Marino

HISTORY. On 22 March 1862 San Marino concluded a treaty of friendship and co-operation, including a *de facto* customs union with Italy. The treaty was renewed on 27 March 1872, 28 June 1897 and 31 March 1939, with several amendments 1942–85.

AREA AND POPULATION. San Marino is a land-locked state in central Italy, 20 km from the Adriatic. The frontier line is 38·6 km in length, area is 61·19 sq. km (24·1 sq. miles) and the population (1991 estimate), 23,200 (90·5% urban); some 11,000 citizens live abroad. Population density, 958 per sq. km. The capital, San Marino, had 4,179 inhabitants (1987); the largest town is Serravalle (7,109 in 1986), an industrial centre in the north.

CONSTITUTION AND GOVERNMENT. The legislative power is vested in the Great and General Council of 60 members elected every 5 years by popular vote, 2 of whom are appointed every 6 months to act as regents *(Capitani reggenti)*.

The elections of May 1988 gave 27 seats to the Christian Democrats, 18 to the Communists, 15 to Socialist parties. The former left the government in Feb. 1992.

2 Co-Regents (who are Heads of State) exercise executive power for 6-month terms together with the Congress of State, which comprises the Co-Regents, 3 secretaries of state and 7 ministers, and through Commissions on social welfare, public works, etc.

National flag: Horizontally white over light blue, with the national arms over all in the centre.

Local government: There are 11 districts and 9 sectors.

DEFENCE. Military service is not obligatory, but all citizens between the ages of 16 and 55 can be called upon to defend the State. They may also serve as volunteers in the Military Corps.

INTERNATIONAL RELATIONS. San Marino is a member of the UN.

ECONOMY. The budget (ordinary and extraordinary) for the financial year ending 31 Dec. 1989 balanced at 259,275,271,797 lire.

About 17% of the land area is arable. Wheat, barley, maize and vines are grown. The chief exports are wood machinery, chemicals, wine, textiles, tiles, varnishes and ceramics.

Italian currency is in use, but the republic issues its own coins.

In 1987, 3m. tourists visited San Marino.

COMMUNICATIONS

Roads. A bus service connects San Marino with Rimini. There are 237 km of roads and (1987) 16,540 passenger cars and 3,225 commercial vehicles.

Telecommunications. In 1986 there were 11,707 telephones. In 1983 there were 8 post offices. In 1987 there were 6,608 television receivers. Radio Titano is a private station. There were 12,535 radio receivers in 1991.

Cinemas. In 1987 there were 7 cinemas with a seating capacity of 1,000.

JUSTICE, RELIGION, EDUCATION AND WELFARE

Justice. Law is administered by a Commissioner for civil cases and a Commissioner for criminal cases (acting with a penal judge), from whom appeals can be made to a civil appeals judge and a criminal appeals judge respectively. The highest legal authority is, in certain cases, the *Consiglio dei XII*. Civil marriage was instituted in Sept. 1953 and divorce allowed in April 1986.

Religion. 95% of the population are Roman Catholic.

Education. Education is compulsory for 8 years. In 1985 there were 13 elementary schools with 1,411 pupils and 158 teachers, 4 secondary schools with 1,248 pupils and 183 teachers. There is also a foreign languages school, a technical school and a trade and handicraft school.

Health. In 1987 there were 149 hospital beds and 60 doctors.

DIPLOMATIC REPRESENTATIVES

British Consul-General (resides at Florence): Mary Croll.
Consul-General in London: Lord Forte.

Further Reading

Information: Office of Cultural Affairs and Information of the Department of Foreign Affairs.

Garbelotto, A., *Evoluzione storica della costituzione di S. Marino*. Milan, 1956
Matteini, N., *The Republic of San Marino*. San Marino, 1981
Packett, C. N., *Guide to the Republic of San Marino*. Bradford, 1970
Rossi, G., *San Marino*. San Marino, 1954

SÃO TOMÉ E PRÍNCIPE

Capital: São Tomé
Population: 124,000 (1991)
GNP per capita: US$360 (1989)

República Democrática de São Tomé e Príncipe

HISTORY. The islands of São Tomé and Príncipe, were discovered in 1471 by Pedro Escobar and João Gomes, and from 1522 constituted a Portugese colony. On 11 June 1951 it became an overseas province of Portugal.

On 26 Nov. 1974 the Government of Portugal and the liberation movement of São Tomé e Príncipe signed an agreement granting independence to the archipelago on 12 July 1975.

AREA AND POPULATION. The republic, which lies about 200 km off the west coast of Gabon, in the Gulf of Guinea, comprises the main islands of São Tomé (845 sq. km) and Príncipe and several smaller islets including Pedras Tinhosas and Rolas. It has a total area of 1,001 sq. km (387 sq. miles). Total population (census, 1981) 96,611. Estimate (1991) 124,000.

The areas and populations of the 2 provinces were as follows:

Province	Sq. km	Census 1981	Estimate 1991	Chief town	Estimate 1984
São Tomé	859	91,356	117,300	São Tomé	34,997
Príncipe	142	5,255	6,700	São António	1,000

The official language is Portuguese, but 90% speak Fang, a Bantu language.

Vital statistics (1985): Births, 3,700; deaths, 900. Expectation of life, 1990: Males, 60·7 years; females, 63·1.

CLIMATE. The tropical climate is modified by altitude and the effect of the cool Benguela current. The wet season is generally from Oct. to May, but rainfall varies very much, from 40" (1,000 mm) in the hot and humid north-east to 150–200" (3,800–5,000 mm) on the plateau. São Tomé Jan. 79°F (26·1°C), July 75°F (23·9°C). Annual rainfall 38" (951 mm).

CONSTITUTION AND GOVERNMENT. A new constitution was approved by 72% of the votes cast at a referendum in Aug. 1990. It abolishes the monopoly status of the *Movimento de Libertação de São Tomé e Príncipe*. The *President* is elected by the People's Assembly for a 4-year term; he is also head of government and appoints a Cabinet of Ministers to assist him. The 55-member *People's Assembly* is also elected for 4 years.

At the elections of Jan. 1991 the Democratic Convergence Party won.

At the presidential elections of Feb. 1991 the sole candidate, Miguel Trovoada (b.1946; ind) was elected by 80% of votes cast.

President, Commander-in-Chief: Miguel Trovoada.

Flag: Three horizontal stripes of green, yellow, green, with the yellow of double width and bearing 2 black stars; in the hoist a red triangle over all.

Local government: São Tomé province comprises 6 districts, while Príncipe province forms a seventh district.

INTERNATIONAL RELATIONS

Membership. São Tomé e Príncipe is a member of the UN, OAU and is an ACP state of the EEC.

ECONOMY

Budget. In 1986 the budget balanced at 1,092m. dobra.

Currency. The unit of currency is the *dobra* (STD), introduced in 1977, divided into 100 *centavos*. In March 1992, £1 = 420·95 *dobra*; US$1 = 239·78 *dobra*.

Banking and Finance. *Banco Nacional de São Tomé e Príncipe* (established, 1975) is the central bank.

ENERGY AND NATURAL RESOURCES

Electricity. Production (1986) 3m. kwh.

Agriculture. About 38% of the area is under cultivation. Production (1990 in tonnes): Coconuts, 35,000; copra, 4,000; bananas, 3,000; palm oil, 250. Food crops include cassava, sweet potatoes and yams. In 1990 there were 4,000 goats, 2,000 sheep, 3,000 pigs and 4,000 cattle.

Forestry. Forests cover 60% of the land area. In 1988 6,000 cu. metres of timber were cut.

Fisheries. The fishing industry is being developed, to exploit the rich tuna shoals. Catch (1986) 2,800 tonnes.

FOREIGN ECONOMIC RELATIONS

Commerce. Imports in 1984 amounted to 485·9m. dobras and exports to 539·6m. dobras the main exports being cocoa (80%), copra (15%), coffee, bananas and palm-oil. Portugal provided 30% of imports while the German Democratic Republic took 35% of exports, the Netherlands 18% and Portugal 15%.

Total trade between São Tomé e Príncipe and UK (British Department of Trade returns, in £1,000 sterling):

	1987	1988	1989	1990	1991
Imports to UK	205	20	4	114	1
Exports and re-exports from UK	329	416	819	879	1,020

COMMUNICATIONS

Roads. There were 288 km of roads (198 paved) in 1975.

Civil Aviation. São Tomé airport is linked by regular services to Douala, Lisbon, Luanda, Cabinda, Libreville, Malabo and Brazil, as well as to Príncipe.

Telecommunications. There were (1986) 2,200 telephones. Radio broadcasting is conducted by the government-controlled Rádio Nacional. There were about 31,000 radio sets in 1991. There is no television.

Newspapers. In 1986 there were 2 weekly newspapers.

JUSTICE, RELIGION, EDUCATION AND WELFARE.

Justice. Members of the Supreme Court are appointed by the People's Assembly.

Religion. About 80% of the population are Roman Catholic.

Education. In 1984 there were 19,086 pupils and 517 teachers in 63 primary schools, 6,186 pupils and 300 teachers in 11 secondary schools, and 370 students and 35 teachers in 2 technical schools.

Health. In 1981 there were 38 doctors and 118 nursing personnel.

DIPLOMATIC REPRESENTATIVES

Of Great Britain in São Tomé and Príncipe
Ambassador: J. G. Flynn (resides in Luanda).

Of São Tomé and Príncipe in the USA and to the United Nations
Ambassador: Joaquim Rafael Branco.

Of the USA in São Tomé and Príncipe
Ambassador: Keith L. Wauchope.

SAUDI ARABIA

Capital: Riyadh
Population: 12m. (1988)
GNP per capita: US$6,230 (1989)

Mamlaka al-'Arabiya
as-Sa'udiya

(Kingdom of Saudi Arabia)

HISTORY. Saudi Arabia was founded by Abdul Aziz ibn Abdur-Rahman al-Faisal Al Sa'ud, GCB, GCIE (born about 1880; died 9 Nov. 1953), who had been proclaimed King of the Hejaz on 8 Jan. 1926 and had in 1927 changed his title of Sultan of Nejd and its Dependencies to that of King of the Hejaz and of Nejd and its Dependencies. By a treaty of 20 May 1927 the UK recognized the independence of Hejaz, Nejd, Asir and Al-Hasa, which became the State of the Kingdom of Saudi Arabia by decree of 23 Sept. 1932.

During the Iraqi occupation of Kuwait in 1990–91 Saudi Arabia invited the UN-supported coalition forces to base themselves on its territory. There were Iraqi missile attacks on Saudi Arabian targets.

AREA AND POPULATION. Saudi Arabia, which occupies over 70% of the Arabian peninsula, is bounded in the west by the Red Sea, east by the Persian Gulf and the United Arab Emirates, north by Jordan, Iraq and Kuwait and south by Yemen and Oman. The total area is estimated to be 849,400 sq. miles (2·2m. sq. km). Riyadh is the political, and Mecca the religious, capital.

The principal cities of the Western Province (formerly *Hejaz*) are Jiddah (561,104 inhabitants at the 1974 Census; estimate (1986) 1·4m.), Mecca (618,006), Taif (204,857) and Medina (500,000); of the Central Province (formerly *Nejd*) are Riyadh, the national capital (666,840; estimate, 1988, 2m.), Buraidah (184,000), Ha'il (92,000), Uneiza and Al-Kharj; of the Northern Province are Tabouk (99,000), Al-Jawf and Sakaka; of the Eastern Province (formerly *Al-Hasa*) are Dammam (127,844), Hofuf (101,271), Haradh (100,000), Al-Mobarraz (54,325), Al-Khobar (48,817) and Qatif; and of the Southern Province (formerly *Asir*) are Khamis-Mushait (49,581), Najran (47,501), Jisan (32,814) and Abha (155,406). New industrial cities are being built at Jubail and Yanbu on the Gulf. Taif, about 3,800ft above sea-level and some 50 miles from Mecca, is a summer resort.

The total population was (1974 census) 7,012,642, of which 5,128,655 were categorized as settled and 1,883,987 as nomadic. Estimate (1992) 14m., of whom about 50% were Saudi Arabians.

Annual growth rate of the indigenous population was 3·7% in 1990.

The Neutral Zone (3,560 sq. miles, 5,700 sq. km.), jointly owned and administered by Kuwait and Saudi Arabia from 1922 to 1966, was partitioned between the two countries in 1966, but the exploitation of the oil and other natural resources continue to be shared.

CLIMATE. A desert climate, with very little rain and none at all from June to Dec. The months May to Sept. are very hot and humid, but winter temperatures are quite pleasant. Riyadh. Jan. 58°F (14·4°C), July 108°F (42°C). Annual rainfall 4" (100 mm). Jiddah. Jan. 73°F (22·8°C), July 87°F (30·6°C). Annual rainfall 3" (81 mm).

KING. Fahd ibn Abdul Aziz, Custodian of the two Holy Mosques, succeeded in May 1982, after King Khalid's death. *Crown Prince:* Prince Abdullah ibn Abdul Aziz, half-brother of the King.

National flag: Green, with the text 'There is no God but Allah and Mohammed is his prophet' in white Arabic script, and beneath this a white sabre.

CONSTITUTION AND GOVERNMENT. Constitutional practice derives from Shariah law. There is no formal Constitution. In March 1992 the King decreed that a 60-man Consultative Council (*Majlis ash-Shura*) of royal nominees would be set up.

The King has the post of Prime Minister.

Deputy Prime Minister and Commander of the National Guard: Crown Prince Abdullah ibn Abdul Aziz. *Second Deputy Prime Minister and Minister of Defence and Aviation, and Inspector General:* Prince Sultan ibn Abdul Aziz.

Public Works and Housing: Prince Miteb ibn Abdul Aziz. *Interior:* Prince Naif ibn Abdel Aziz. *Foreign Affairs:* Prince Saud al Faisal. *Labour and Social Affairs:* Muhammad al Ali al Fayiz. *Communications:* Hussein Ibrahim al Mansouri. *Finance and National Economy:* Muhammad Ali Aba'l Khail. *Information:* Ali ibn Hasan al Shaer. *Industry and Electricity:* Dr Abdul Aziz al Zamil. *Commerce:* Dr Sulaiman Abdul Aziz al Sulaim. *Justice:* Muhammad ibn Jubair. *Education:* Dr Abdul Aziz al Abdullah al Khuwaiter. *Higher Education:* Khalid al Angari. *Petroleum and Mineral Resources:* Hisham Nazer. *Haj Affairs, Waqfs:* Abdul Wahhab Ahmad Abdul Wasi. *Municipal and Rural Affairs:* Mohammed al Shaikh. *Planning:* Abdel Wahhab al Attar. *Agriculture and Water:* Dr Abdul Rahman ibn Abdul Aziz ibn Hasan al Shaikh. *Health:* Faisal ibn Abdul Aziz al Hejailan. *Posts and Telecommunications:* Dr Alawi Darwish Kayyal.

There are provisions for the setting up of municipal councils in Mecca, Medina and Jiddah, and village and tribal councils throughout the provinces. The country is divided for administrative purposes into 14 Regions (Emirates).

DEFENCE. The US maintains a Military Mission (with an Air Force element) as do France and Pakistan. Personnel are trained in Saudi Arabia, France, Pakistan, UK and the USA. The UK has training missions with the National Guard and the Navy.

Army. The Army comprises 2 armoured brigades, 4 mechanized brigades, 1 airborne brigade, 1 Royal Guard regiment, 5 artillery battalions and 1 infantry brigade. Equipment includes 300 AMX-30, 50 M-60A1 and 200 M-60A3 main battle tanks. There are surface-to-air units with Stinger and Hawk. Over 40 Blackhawk, Dauphin and armed Bell 406 helicopters are in service. Strength (1990) was approximately 40,000. There is a para-military Frontier Force (approximately 10,500).

Navy. The Royal Saudi Naval Forces comprise 4 French-built 2,900-tonnes frigates armed with Otomat anti-ship missiles, 4 smaller US-built missile frigates, 9 fast missile craft, 3 German-built torpedo craft, 4 US-built coastal minesweepers and the first of 6 UK-built Sandown class minehunters. Auxiliaries include 2 French-built replenishment tankers each embarking 2 helicopters, 3 ocean tugs and a Royal Yacht. There are numerous minor auxiliaries and boats.

Naval Aviation forces operate 12 Super Puma and 24 Dauphin helicopters, both ship and shore based, and there is a regiment of some 1,500 marines.

The main naval bases are at Jiddah (Red Sea) and Jubail (The Gulf). Naval personnel in 1991 totalled 9,500 including 1,500 marines.

The Coast Guard operates some 35 inshore patrol craft, 24 hovercraft and over 300 boats of various types.

Air Force. Formed as a small army support unit in 1932, the Air Force has been built up considerably with British and US assistance since 1946. Complete re-equipment began in 1966 and delivery of 58 F-15 Eagles to equip 3 air superiority squadrons was made in 1982–84; they operate in conjunction with 5 E-3A Sentry AWACS aircraft and 8 KC-707 flight refuelling tankers. The US government is delivering 36 F-15 Eagles and 17 C-130 Hercules. Current combat units include 3 squadrons of F-5E Tiger II supersonic fighter-bombers and RF-5E Tigereye reconnaissance aircraft, supported by a conversion unit with F-5B/F combat trainers. One squadron has formed with 24 Tornado strike aircraft with 23 on order, plus an air defence unit with 24 Tornado interceptors. Two squadrons of Strikemaster light jet attack/trainers are based at the King Faisal Air Academy, Riyadh, together with 12 Reims/Cessna FR172 piston-engined primary trainers, PC-9 basic trainers, Hawk advanced trainers and Jetstream navigation trainers. Other types in current service include 50 C-130E/H and KC-130H Hercules transports and tankers, 1 Boeing 747 SP, 1 Boeing 747-200, 1 Boeing 737, 3 Boeing 707, 4 CN-235s and 2 JetStar VIP jet transports, more than 60 Agusta-Bell 205, 212 and JetRanger helicopters, 2 Agusta AS-61A-4 VIP transport helicopters and communications aircraft. Personnel (1991), about 18,000 with 220 combat aircraft.

Air Defence Force. This separate Command was formerly part of the Army, which retains a point air defence capability. In 1989 there were French and Pakistani training missions. Equipment comprises approximately 18 Crotale missile systems, 15 batteries of Improved Hawk surface-to-air missiles, 30 mm Oerlikon and 20 mm Vulcan guns.

National Guard. The National Guard comprises 2 mechanized brigades (trained by the US), 1 ceremonial cavalry squadron. Additionally there are a number of regular and irregular units, the total strength of the National Guard amounting to approximately 56,000 (10,000 active). The National Guard's primary role is the protection of the Royal Family and vital points in the Kingdom. It does not come under command of the Ministry of Defence and Aviation. UK provides small advisory teams to the National Guard in the fields of general training and communications.

INTERNATIONAL RELATIONS

Membership. Saudi Arabia is a member of the UN, the Arab League, the Gulf Cooperation Council and OPEC.

ECONOMY

Policy. The fifth 5-year development plan (1990–95) aims to increase manpower by an overall 3·5% and emphasizes industrial growth and economic development, and the expansion of the private industrial base.

Budget. In 1986 the financial year became the calendar year. The 1990 budget provided for expenditure of 143,000m. rials and revenue of 118,000m. rials. The 1991 budget was cancelled following Iraq's invasion of Kuwait.

Estimated revenue for 1992: US$40,300m.; expenditure, US$48,250m. (US$14,500m. on defence, US$8,300m. on education, US$3,260m. on health, US$2,200m. on transport and communications, US$1,900m. on domestic subsidies). US$34,400m. are allocated to recurrent expenditure and US$13,900m. to special projects.

Currency. The unit of currency is the *rial* (SAR) of 100 *halalas*. In March 1992, £1 = 6·57 *rials*; US$1 = 3·74 *rials*.

Banking and Finance. The Saudi Arabian Monetary Agency, established in 1953, is the central bank and the government's fiscal agent. There were 12 commercial banks with 958 branches, 5 special credit institutions and a variety of other financial institutions in 1992. The Saudi Arabian Agricultural Bank with 70 branches and offices extended 755m. rials in credit services to farmers during 1989. In 1989 total deposits in commercial banks were US$146,300m. and total assets were 233,600m. rials.

ENERGY AND NATURAL RESOURCES

Electricity. 57,108m. kwh. was generated by the main electricity companies in 1989. A programme of research and development of solar energy has produced a photovoltaic power system with a capacity in 1988 of 50 kw. to provide electricity for 2 villages. Supply 127 and 220 volts; 50 and 60 Hz.

Oil. The first general geologic–geographical survey of Saudi Arabia was completed in 1961 under the joint sponsorship of the Saudi Arabian and US governments but surveying continues. Proven reserves (1991) 259,000m. bbls (25% of world resources).

Oil production began in 1938 by Aramco, which is now 100% state-owned and accounts for about 97% of total crude oil production, with Getty and the Arabian Oil Co. accounting for the remainder.

Crude oil production in 1991 was 409·84m. tonnes. Crude oil exports in 1989 were 176m tonnes. 1989 oil exports earned US$26,000m.

Production comes from 14 major oilfields, mostly in the Eastern Region, the most important of which are Ghawar (the world's largest oilfield in operation), Abqaiq, Safaniyah (the largest offshore field) and Berri.

New fields have been discovered onshore at Farhah and Assahba and deeper pools offshore at Marjan, Safaniya and Zuluf, and during 1989 48 new wells were drilled and 5 seismic explorations conducted.

There is a pipeline from the eastern oilfields to the Red Sea oil terminal at Yanbu with a link to the Iraqi oilfields (cut after the Iraqi invasion of Kuwait in Aug. 1990).

In 1990 there were 5 domestic refineries: Ras Tanura, refining capacity 530,000 bbls per day (Aramco); Riyadh, 134,000 bbls per day, Jiddah, 91,000 bbls per day and Yanbu, 170,000 bbls per day (Petromin); Rasal-Khafji, 30,000 bbls per day (Arabian Oil Co.); as well as 3 joint venture export refineries: Yanbu, 250,000 bbls per day (Petromin/Mobil Oil); Jubail, 250,000 bbls per day (Petromin/Shell Saudi Arabia); Rabigh, 325,000 bbls per day (Petromin/Petrola International). Aramco has added a 300 tonne a day sulphur plant to Ras Tanura and operates a 400 tonnes a day desulphurization plant at Jubail.

Gas. In 1989 production of liquefied natural gas from oilfield—associated and dissolved gas was 420,946 bbls per day.

Water. Intensive efforts are under-way to provide adequate supplies of water for urban, industrial, rural and agricultural use. Most investment however has gone into seawater desalination. In 1991 28 plants had the capacity to produce 1·9m. cu. metres a day. Annual consumption is about 14,000m. cu. metres. 90% goes on agriculture (from fossil reserves, since desalinated water is still too saline).

Minerals. Production began in 1988 at Mahd Al-Dahab gold mine. Deposits of iron, phosphate, bauxite, uranium and copper have been found.

Agriculture. Since 1970 the Government has spent substantially on desert reclamation, irrigation schemes, drainage and control of surface water and control of moving sands. Undeveloped land has been distributed to farmers and there are research and extension programmes. Large scale private investment has concentrated on wheat, poultry and dairy production.

In 1990 agriculture contributed 8% of GDP. There were some 152,000 farms in 1992; the agricultural workforce was 569,000.

Date production in 1991 was 542,000 tonnes; wheat, 4m. tonnes. About 0·4m. tonnes of barley are produced annually as animal fodder. Estimated production of other crops, 1990 (in 1,000 tonnes): Tomatoes, 390; water melons, 320; grapes, 100; milk, 303; poultry meat, 226; eggs, 160.

Livestock estimates for 1990 include 228,000 cattle, 405,000 camels, 7,915,000 sheep and 3,825,000 goats.

Fisheries. Saudi Fisheries, established in 1981, has introduced a wide variety of fish to the domestic market and opened up a thriving export business in shrimps. Annual catch about 10,000 tonnes.

INDUSTRY. The Government encourages the establishment of manufacturing industries. Its policy includes the provision of industrial estates and loans covering 50% of capital investment. It has established 2 industrial poles at Jubail and Yanbu, linked by gas and oil pipelines, to be the focus of heavy industrial development. Both have petrochemical complexes producing ethylene and methanol. In 1988 there were 12 major industries (petrochemical, urea and ammonia fertilizer, steel, gas and plastics) and over 65 support and light manufacturing businesses in operation in Jubail, and 8 heavy industries (natural gas liquids fractionation, refining, petrochemical, lube additives, crude oil and chemical terminals) and 21 light and support industries in operation in Yanbu. 2,000 factories were in operation in 1992.

Labour. The expatriate labour force grew by an average of 11·7% a year between 1980 and 1985. The proportion of non-Saudis in the total labour force rose from

28·2% in 1975 to 60% by 1985. In 1988, 95% of the total labour force was employed in the non-oil sector.

FOREIGN ECONOMIC RELATIONS

Commerce. Exports in 1988 (in 1m. rials) 88,896 of which crude oil, 62%; refined oil, 23%; petro-chemicals, 11%. Wheat is also a major export. Total imports (1988) 81,582m. rials. Major export destinations in 1988 included: Japan, USA, Singapore. Major import sources include: USA, Japan, UK, Germany, Italy and France.

Total trade between Saudi Arabia and UK (British Department of Trade returns, in £1,000 sterling):

	1987	1988	1989	1990	1991
Imports to UK	383,143	614,144	502,416	794,633	963,919
Exports and re-exports from UK	1,978,440	1,713,423	2,432,941	2,012,585	2,228,965

Tourism. In 1989 there were 774,560 pilgrims to Mecca from abroad.

COMMUNICATIONS

Roads. The main regions and population centres are linked by asphalted roads, of which there were 33,576 km in 1987 and 59,226 km of graded, unpaved agricultural roads. An additional 2,021 km of roads were under construction including the Trans-Peninsula Expressway. There are road links with Yemen, Jordan, Kuwait and Qatar, and a causeway link to Bahrain. In 1986 there were 2·25m. passenger cars, 2·25m. commercial vehicles and about 41,000 buses. Women may not drive.

Railways. There is a railway from Riyadh to Dammam on the Gulf (571 km, 1,435 mm gauge) via Dhahran and the oilfields Abqaiq, Ithmaniya and Haradh. A 'dry port' at Riyadh station opened in 1981, and a new 465 km Dammam-Riyadh direct line was opened throughout in 1985. There are plans to extend the line via Medina to Jiddah. That section of the Hejaz Railway which is in Saudi Arabian territory is not now in working order, but studies have been initiated to restore the whole line from Damascus to Medina. In 1990 railways carried some 0·4m. passengers and 1·3m. tonnes of freight.

Civil Aviation. Saudi Arabian Air Lines, a government-owned company operates regular internal air services, and international routes to Africa, the Middle East, Europe and the Far East, as well as special flights for pilgrims. There are 3 major international airports at Jiddah, Dhahran and Riyadh and 20 domestic airports. King Fahd International Airport in Eastern Province is due to be completed in 1990. In 1987, 21m. passengers and 332,000 tonnes of cargo were carried.

Shipping. The ports of Dammam and Jubail on the Gulf and Jiddah, Yanbu and Jizan on the Red Sea had 143 deep-water piers by 1985 and discharged 35·9m. freight tonnes. Aramco operates a deepwater oil terminal at Ras Tanura.

Telecommunications. Number of telephones (1988), 1,099,000. Number of post offices (1988) 603. The government-controlled Broadcasting Service of the Kingdom of Saudi Arabia and Saudi Arabian Television are responsible for broadcasting. Radio programmes include 2 home services, 2 religious services, services in English and French and an external serivce. Aramco Oil have a private station. There are TV programmes in Arabic and English; Channel 3 TV is a noncommercial independent. Colour is by SECAM and PAL. In 1991 there were estimated to be 4m. radio and 3·75m. TV sets.

Newspapers. In 1991 there were 3 daily newspapers in Arabic and 3 in English and 2 Arabic amd 2 English weeklies.

JUSTICE, RELIGION, EDUCATION AND WELFARE

Justice. The religious law of Islam is the common law of the land, and is administered by religious courts, at the head of which is a chief judge, who is responsible for the Department of Sharia (legal) Affairs. Sharia courts are concerned primarily with family inheritance and property matters. The Committee for the Settlement of Commercial Disputes is the commercial court. Other specialized courts or committees include one dealing exclusively with labour and employment matters; the Negotiable Instruments Committee, which deals with cases relating to cheques, bills of exchange and promissory notes, and the Board of Grievances, whose preserve is disputes with the government or its agencies and which also has jurisdiction in trademark-infringement cases and is the authority for enforcing foreign court judgements.

Religion. About 92% are Sunni Moslems and 8% Shiites.

Education. Schooling is in three stages, primary, intermediate and secondary which is to prepare older pupils for university; pre-primary schools are being introduced. Education is free in all these stages. Girls' education is administered separately. In 1987 there were 512 pre-primary schools with 60,590 pupils, 4,662 primary schools with 1,460,283 pupils and 90,535 teachers, and 3,526 intermediate/secondary schools with 635,606 students and 43,361 teachers. In 1988 there were 3,526 pupils in 30 special education institutes for mentally retarded and physically handicapped children. In 1986–87 there were 64,888 students in 1,305 schools in the programme to combat illiteracy.

In 1987 there were 27 vocational centres, where 2,820 primary school graduates were instructed in basic trades. There were also 8 technical and 22 commercial secondary schools, taking 11,310 intermediate school graduates, and 2 technical and 3 commercial higher institutes (649 students), 21 more advanced industrial, commercial and agricultural education institutes.

University courses concentrating on science, engineering, agriculture and medicine, but also covering education, commerce and arts, are available at the King Abdul Aziz University, Jiddah, King Saud University, Riyadh and King Faisal University, Dammam and Hofuf. There are two branches of King Saud University at Abha and Qaseem. King Abdul Aziz University had a branch campus at Taif. Specialized engineering studies are available at the King Fahd University of Petroleum and Minerals, Dhahran, and Arabic and Sharia law studies at the Islamic University, Medina, Imam Mohammad bin Saud University, Riyadh and the Um-AlQura University, Makkah. There were 113,939 university students (46,355 women) and 5,500 post-graduate students in 1986–87.

Welfare. In 1988 there were 224 hospitals with 35,797 beds, 2,258 primary health care centres and in 1988, 18,048 doctors, 38,434 nurses and midwives, 8,858 technical assistants. There were also 73 private hospitals (10,244 beds) employing 6,096 doctors. The Jiddah Quarantine Centre, designed by WHO and primarily for pilgrims, can take 2,400 patients.

DIPLOMATIC REPRESENTATIVES

Of Saudi Arabia in Great Britain (15 Curzon St., London, SW1)
Ambassador: (Vacant).

Of Great Britain in Saudi Arabia (PO Box 94351, Riyadh 11963)
Ambassador: Sir Alan Munro, KCMG.

Of Saudi Arabia in the USA (601 New Hampshire Ave., NW, Washington, D.C., 20037)
Ambassador: HRH Prince Bandar bin Sultan.

Of the USA in Saudi Arabia (PO Box 9041, Riyadh)
Ambassador: Charles W. Freeman, Jr.

Of Saudi Arabia to the United Nations
Ambassador: Samir Shihabi.

Further Reading

Anderson, N., *The Kingdom of Saudi Arabia.* (Rev. ed.). London, 1982
Clements, F. A., *Saudi Arabia.* [Bibliography] Oxford and Santa Barbara, 1988
Hajrah, H. H., *Land Distribution in Saudi Arabia.* London, 1982
Holden, D. and Johns, R., *The House of Saud.* London and New York, 1981
Presley, J. R., *A Guide to the Saudi Arabian Economy.* London, 1984
Quandt, W. B., *Saudi Arabia in the 1980's: Foreign Policy, Security and Oil.* Washington, 1981
Safran, N., *Saudi Arabia: The Ceaseless Quest for Security.* Harvard Univ. Press, 1985

SENEGAL

Capital: Dakar
Population: 7·33m. (1991)
GNP per capita: US$650 (1989)

République du Sénégal

HISTORY. France established a fort at Saint-Louis in 1659 and later acquired other coastal settlements from the Dutch; the interior was occupied in 1854–65. Senegal became a territory of French West Africa in 1902 and an autonomous state within the French Community on 25 Nov. 1958. On 4 April 1959 Senegal joined with French Sudan to form the Federation of Mali, which achieved independence on 20 June 1960, but on 22 Aug. Senegal withdrew from the Federation and became a separate independent republic. Senegal was a one-Party state from 1966 until 1974, when a pluralist system was re-established. Léopold Sédar Senghor, President since independence, resigned on 31 Dec. 1980 and was succeeded by his Prime Minister.

The *Senegambia* confederation with The Gambia was established on 1 Feb. 1982 and dissolved on 21 Sept. 1989.

AREA AND POPULATION. Senegal is bounded by Mauritania to the north and north-east, Mali to the east, Guinea and Guinea-Bissau to the south and the Atlantic to the west with The Gambia forming an enclave along that shore. Area, 196,192 sq. km; population (census, 1976), 4,907,507; (estimate, 1991) 7·33m. (38·4% urban). Population density, 37·4 per sq. km.

The areas (in sq. km), populations and capitals of the 10 regions:

Region	sq. km	1984 Estimate	Capital	1985 Estimate
Dakar	550	1,380,700	Dakar	1,382,000
Diourbel	4,359	501,000	Diourbel	55,307 [1]
Fatick	7,935	506,500	Fatick	...
Kaolack	16,010	741,600	Kaolack	132,400
Kolda	21,011	517,600	Kolda	...
Louga	29,188	493,900	Louga	37,665 [2]
Saint-Louis	44,127	612,100	Saint-Louis	91,500
Tambacounda	57,602	355,000	Tambacounda	29,054 [1]
Thiès	6,601	837,900	Thiès	156,200
Ziguinchor	7,339	361,000	Ziguinchor	79,464 [1]

[1] 1976   [2] 1979.

Ethnic groups are the Wolof (36% of the population), Serer (19%), Fulani (13%), Tukulor (9%), Diola (8%), Malinké (6%), Bambara (6%) and Sarakole (2%).

Growth rate (1985–90), 2·7%; infant mortality (1990), 83·5 per 1,000 live births. Life expectancy was 48·3 years in 1989.

CLIMATE. A tropical climate with wet and dry seasons. The rains fall almost exclusively in the hot season, from June to Oct., with high humidity. Dakar. Jan. 72°F (22·2°C), July 82°F (27·8°C). Annual rainfall 22" (541 mm).

CONSTITUTION AND GOVERNMENT. The head of state is the *President*, elected by universal suffrage for not more than two 7-year terms. For the unicameral 120-member National Assembly 60 members are elected in single-member constituencies and 60 by a form of proportional representation. Voting age is 18.

President of the Republic: Abdou Diouf (took office in Jan. 1981, re-elected 1983 and 1988).

The Cabinet appointed in April 1991 was composed as follows:

Prime Minister: Habib Thiam. *Minister of the Economy, Finance and Planning:* Famara Ibrahima Sagna. *Armed Forces:* Médoune Fall. *Justice:* Serigne Lamine Diop. *Foreign Affairs:* Djibo Ka. *Interior:* Madieng Khary Dieng. *Education:* André Sonkho. *Equipment, Transport and Maritime Affairs:* Robert Sagna. *Rural*

Development and Water Resources: Sheikh Abdoulkhadre Cissokho. *Industry, Trade and Handicrafts:* Alasane Dialy Ndiaye. *Tourism and the Environment:* Jacques Baudin. *Town and Country Planning:* Amath Dansokho. *Labour and Professional Training:* Ousmane Ngom. *Communications:* Moctar Kebe. *Health and Social Affairs:* Assane Diop. *Culture:* Moustapha Ka. *African Economic Integration:* Jean-Paul Diaz. *Youth and Sport:* Abdoulaye Makhtar Diop. *Women's, Children's and Family Affairs:* Ndioro Ndiaye.

National flag: Three vertical strips of green, yellow, red, with a green star in the centre.

National anthem: Pincez tous vos koras, frappez les balafos ('All pluck the koras, strike the balafos'; words by Léopold Sédar Senghor, music by Herbert Pepper. Adopted in 1960).

The official language is French. Wolof is the predominant indigenous language.

Local Government. Senegal is divided into 10 regions, each with an appointed governor and an elected regional assembly. They are divided into 30 departments, each under an appointed prefect, and thence into 99 *arrondissements*.

DEFENCE. There is selective conscription for 2 years.

Army. The Army had a strength of 8,500 (mostly conscripts) in 1992, organized in 6 infantry battalions, 1 engineer, 1 armoured, 1 airborne, 1 commando and 1 artillery battalions, and minor units. Equipment includes 67 armoured cars. There is also a paramilitary force of gendarmarie and customs.

Navy. The flotilla includes 2 coastal patrol craft, 8 inshore patrol craft, 2 tank landing craft, 2 smaller amphibious craft, and about 6 service craft. Personnel (1991) totalled 700, and bases are at Dakar and Casamance.

Air Force. The Air Force, formed with French assistance, has 4 Rallye Guerrier and 5 Magister armed trainers and 1 Twin Otter for maritime patrol, 1 Boeing 727 transport, 6 F.27 twin-turboprop transports, 2 Broussard and 1 Cessna 337 liaison aircraft, 2 Puma, 1 Gazelle and 2 Alouette II helicopters, plus 4 Rallye trainers. Personnel (1992) 500, with 9 combat aircraft.

INTERNATIONAL RELATIONS

Membership. Senegal is a member of the UN, OAU and is an ACP state of the EEC.

ECONOMY

Policy. The Seventh 4-year Development Plan (1985–89) provided 645,000m. francs CFA for investment in the productive sector, improved infrastructure and for reducing foreign debt.

Budget. The budget for 1987–88 balanced at 337,660m. francs CFA.

Currency. The currency is the *franc CFA* (XOF), a parity value of 50 *francs CFA* to 1 French *franc*.

Banking and Finance. The bank of issue is the *Banque Centrale des États de l'Afrique de l'Ouest*. The principal commercial bank is the *Union Sénégalaise de la Banque pour le Commerce et l'Industrie* (established 1961 with assistance from Crédit Lyonnais) in which the Senegalese government has the majority shareholding; also state controlled is the *Banque Nationale de Développement du Sénégal*. There are 3 private banks.

ENERGY AND NATURAL RESOURCES

Electricity. Production (1986) was 737m. kwh. Supply 110 volts; 50 Hz.

Minerals. Production of phosphates (1987) 2,022,300 tonnes. Titanium ores and zirconium are extracted from coastal (sand) deposits. Iron ore deposits amounting to an estimated 980m. tonnes have been located at La Faleme.

Agriculture. In 1988 there were 5·23m. ha of cultivated land and 5·7m. ha of pasture. Production, 1989 (in tonnes): Groundnuts for oil, 703,362; groundnuts for consumption, 19,536; cotton, 45,000; sorghum, 594,200; rice paddy, 146,405; maize, 123,327; manioc, 54,885.

Livestock (1990, in 1,000): 3,920 sheep, 1,200 goats, 2,740 cattle, 500 pigs, 310 asses, 15 camels and 400 horses.

Forestry. There were (1989) 5·94m. ha of forest. Production (1986) amounted to 4·1m. cu. metres.

Fisheries. The 1986 catch totalled 255,400 tonnes.

INDUSTRY. Dakar has numerous industrial works. A major ship-repairing complex has been constructed there for vessels of up to 28,000 tonnes. Cement production (1983) 395,300 tonnes; petroleum products, 336,000; groundnut oil, 217,000.

Trade Unions. There are two major unions, the *Union Nationale des Travailleurs Sénégalais* (government-controlled) and the *Conféderation Nationale des Travailleurs Sénégalais* (independent) which broke away from the former in 1969.

FOREIGN ECONOMIC RELATIONS

Commerce. In 1989 imports totalled US$1,100m. and exports US$800m. 36·6% of imports came from France and 28·5% of exports went to France. In 1985 petroleum products provided 22% of exports, fisheries 22%, phosphates 10% and cotton fabrics 4%.

Total trade between Senegal and UK (British Department of Trade returns, in £1,000 sterling):

	1987	1988	1989	1990	1991
Imports to UK	11,307	11,284	6,820	5,002	5,025
Exports and re-exports from UK	11,878	14,840	13,448	14,884	13,960

Tourism. In 1987, 235,466 tourists visited Senegal.

COMMUNICATIONS

Roads. The length of roads (1989) was 9,971 km of which 3,476 km was bitumenized. In 1984 there were 73,665 passenger cars and 36,144 commercial vehicles.

Railways. There are 4 railway lines: Dakar-Kidira (continuing in Mali), Thiès-Saint-Louis (193 km), Guinguinéo-Kaolack (22 km), and Diourbel-Touba (46 km). Total length (1986), 905 km (metre gauge). In 1988 railways carried 2·7m. passengers and 2·8m. tonnes of freight.

Civil Aviation. In 1984 230m. passenger-km and 17·4m. tonne-km of freight were flown. There are major airports at Yoff, Saint-Louis, Tambacounda and Ziguinchor.

Shipping. In 1986 the merchant marine numbered 148 vessels of 41,651 DWT. There is a river service on the Senegal from Saint-Louis to Podor (363 km) open throughout the year, and to Kayes (924 km) open from July to Oct. The Senegal River is closed to foreign flags. The Saloum River is navigable as far as Kaolack, the Casamance River as far as Ziguinchor.

Telecommunications. There were, in 1983, 530 post offices. Telephones in 1986 numbered 54,000. The government-owned Office de Radio-Télévision du Sénégal broadcasts a national and an international radio service from 10 main transmitters. There are also regional services. There is also a TV service (colour by SECAM). In 1991 there were 0·85m. radio and 60,000 TV sets.

Newspapers. The main daily is *Le Soleil,* circulation (1989) 30,000.

JUSTICE, RELIGION, EDUCATION AND WELFARE

Justice. There are *juges de paix* in each *département* and a court of first instance in each region. Assize courts are situated in Dakar, Kaolack, Saint-Louis and Ziguinchor, while the Court of Appeal resides in Dakar.

Religion. The population (1989) was 93·9% Sunni Moslem, the remainder being Christian (mainly Roman Catholic) or animist.

Education. In 1986-87 there were 610,946 pupils in elementary schools, 102,771 pupils in middle schools (general and technical) and 34,098 pupils in secondary schools (general, 30,005; technical, 4,093). In 1986-87 there were 12,028 teachers in private and public schools. The University in Dakar, established on 24 Feb. 1957, had 15,324 students in 1987. A second university was being built (1985) at St Louis. In 1987 32% adult literacy was claimed.

Health. In 1978 there were 44 hospitals with 7,092 beds; and in 1981, 449 doctors, 70 dentists, 139 pharmacists, 326 midwives and 1,766 state nursing personnel.

DIPLOMATIC REPRESENTATIVES

Of Senegal in Great Britain (11 Phillimore Gdns., London, W8 7QG)
Ambassador: Seydou Masani Sy.

Of Great Britain in Senegal (20 Rue du Docteur Guillet, Dakar)
Ambassador: R. C. Beetham, LVO.

Of Senegal in the USA (2112 Wyoming Ave., NW, Washington, D.C., 20008)
Ambassador: Ibra Deguene Ka.

Of the USA in Senegal (Ave. Jean XXIII, Dakar)
Ambassador: George E. Moose.

Of Senegal to the United Nations
Ambassador: Absa Claude Diallo.

Further Reading

Delgado, C. L. and Jammeh, S., *The Political Economy of Senegal under Structural Adjustment.* New York, 1991
Gellar, S., *Senegal.* Boulder (Colo.), 1982.—*Senegal: An African Nation between Islam and the West.* Aldershot, 1983

SEYCHELLES

Republic of Seychelles

Capital: Victoria
Population: 67,378 (1990)
GNP per capita: US$4,170 (1989)

HISTORY. The islands were first colonized by the French in 1756, in order to establish plantations of spices to compete with the Dutch monopoly. They were captured by the English in 1794 and incorporated as a dependency of Mauritius in 1814. In Nov. 1903 the Seychelles archipelago became a separate colony. Internal self-government was achieved on 1 Oct. 1975 and independence as a republic within the Commonwealth on 29 June 1976. The first President, James Mancham, was deposed in a *coup* on 5 June 1977 and replaced by his Prime Minister.

AREA AND POPULATION. The Seychelles consists of 115 islands in the Indian ocean, north of Madagascar, with a combined area of 175 sq. miles (455 sq. km) in two distinct groups. The Granitic group of 32 islands cover 92 sq. miles (239 sq. km); the principal island is Mahé, with 59 sq. miles (153 sq. km) and 59,500 inhabitants at the 1987 census, the other inhabited islands of the group being Praslin, La Digue, Silhouette, Fregate and North, which together have 7,100 inhabitants.

The Outer or Coralline group comprises 83 islands spread over a wide area of ocean between the Mahé group and Madagascar, with a total land area of 83 sq. miles (214 sq. km) and a population of about 400. The main islands are the Amirante Isles (including Desroches, Poivre, Daros and Alphonse), Coetivy Island and Platte Island, all lying south of the Mahé group; the Farquhar, St Pierre and Providence Islands, north of Madagascar; and Aldabra, Astove, Assumption and the Cosmoledo Islands, about 1,000 km south-west of the Mahé group. Aldabra (whose lagoon covers 55 sq. miles), Farquhar and Desroches were transferred to the new British Indian Ocean Territory in 1965, but were returned by Britain to the Seychelles on the latter's independence in 1976. Population (1990, estimate) 67,378. Vital statistics (1989): Births, 1,581; deaths, 588. Life expectancy was 69 years in 1990; infant mortality, 17 per 1,000 live births.

The official languages are Creole, English and French but 95% of the population speak Creole.

CLIMATE. Though close to the equator, the climate is tropical. The hot, wet season is from Dec. to May, when conditions are humid, but south-east trades bring cooler conditions from June to Nov. Temperatures are high throughout the year, but the islands lie outside the cyclone belt. Victoria. Jan. 80°F (26·7°C), July 78°F (25·6°C). Annual rainfall 95" (2,375 mm).

CONSTITUTION AND GOVERNMENT. A new Constitution came into force on 5 June 1979, under which the Seychelles People's Progressive Front is the sole legal Party and nominates all candidates for election. There is a unicameral *People's Assembly* comprising 23 members elected for 5 years with 2 further nominated members. There is an *Executive President* directly elected for a 5-year term, who nominates and leads a Council of Ministers.

The Government in Feb. 1992 comprised:
President: France Albert René (b. 1935; re-elected for a 3rd, 5-year term June 1989).

Education: Simone Testa. *Local Government, Culture and Sports:* Sylvette Frichot. *Tourism and Transport:* Jacques Hodoul. *Finance and Information:* James Michel. *Health:* Ralph Adam. *Employment and Social Affairs:* William Herminie. *Agriculture and Fisheries:* Jeremy Bonnelame. *Planning and External Relations:* Danielle De St Jorre. *Administration and Manpower:* Joseph Belmont. *Community Development:* Esme Jumeau.

National flag: Divided horizontally red over green by a wavy white stripe, with red of double width.

DEFENCE. The Defence Force comprises all services. Personnel (1991) 1,300 organized in 1 infantry battalion, 2 artillery troops and a marine group, 200 strong, based at Port Victoria, which operates 6 fast inshore patrol craft and a tank landing craft. The Air Wing has 1 Defender, 1 Citation and 1 Caravan II for transport and 2 Chetak helicopters, as well as 2 trainers. There is also a People's Militia (5,000).

INTERNATIONAL RELATIONS

Membership. Seychelles is a member of the UN, Commonwealth, OAU, Non-Aligned Movement and is an ACP state of the EEC.

ECONOMY

Policy. There is a 1990–94 development plan.

Budget, in 1m. rupees, for calendar years:

	1986	1987	1988	1989	1990
Recurrent revenue	515·6	639·2	763·8	898·7	989·2
Recurrent expenditure	591·1	641·8	744·0	793·9	826·1

Currency. The unit of currency is the *Seychelles rupee* (SCR) divided into 100 *cents.* In March 1992, £1 = 9·13 *rupees;* US$1 = 5·20 *rupees.*

Banking and Finance. Central Bank of Seychelles, Development Bank of Seychelles and Seychelles Savings Bank and Seychelles International have head offices and Barclays Bank, Banque Francaise Commerçiale, Habib Bank and Bank of Baroda, have branches in Victoria and Mahé.

ENERGY AND NATURAL RESOURCES

Electricity. Production (1989) 94·3m. kwh.

Agriculture. Coconuts are the main cash crop (production, 1988, 19,000 tonnes). Other main crops produced for export are cinnamon bark (1989, 249 tonnes) and copra (1989, 1,337 tonnes). Tea production, 1989, 150 tonnes. Crops grown for local consumption include cassava, sweet potatoes, yams, sugar-cane, bananas and vegetables. The staple food crop, rice, is imported.

Livestock (1988): Cattle, 2,000; pigs, 15,000; goats, 4,000.

Fisheries. Seychelles is located in abundant tuna fishing grounds, and fishing is a major industry. Catch (1989) 4,392 tonnes.

INDUSTRY. Local industry is expanding, the largest development in recent years being the brewery (output, 1989, 5,243,000 litres). Other main activities include production of soft drinks (4,378,000 litres in 1989), cigarettes (58m. in 1989), tuna canning and paints, dairy, processing of cinnamon and coconuts.

FOREIGN ECONOMIC RELATIONS

Commerce. Total trade, in 1m. rupees, for calendar years:

	1986	1987	1988	1989	1990
Imports (less re-exports)	652·0	633·9	856·6	930·2	993·8
Domestic exports	13·9	35·9	75·7	70·1	73·1

Principal imports (1991): Manufactured goods, Rs 276·8m.; food, beverages and tobacco, Rs 182m.; petroleum products, Rs 191·6m., machinery and transport equipment, Rs 268·9m. mainly (1989) from UK (14·8%), South Africa (13·1%), France (9·5%) and Italy (4·4%). Principal exports (1990): Copra, Rs 1·6m.; fresh and frozen fish, Rs 11·7m.; shark fins, Rs 2·6m.; canned tuna, Rs 55·3m. mainly to France, Réunion, Hong Kong and Pakistan.

Total trade between Seychelles and UK (British Department of Trade returns, in £1,000 sterling):

	1988	1989	1990	1991
Imports to UK	1,297	993	8,353	3,457
Exports and re-exports from UK	10,478	10,741	14,955	10,513

Tourism. Tourism is the main foreign exchange earner. Visitor numbers were 103,770 in 1990, (86,000 in 1989).

COMMUNICATIONS

Roads. In 1990 there were 196 km of tarmac roads and 89 km of earth roads on Mahé.

Civil Aviation. Air Seychelles operates services to Europe, neighbouring islands and Singapore.

Shipping. The main port is Victoria, which is also a tuna-fishing and fuel and services supply centre. Shipping (1989), goods unloaded, 364,500 tonnes, goods loaded, 8,900 tonnes.

Telecommunications. Services operated by Cable & Wireless Ltd provide telegraphic communications with all parts of the world by satellite. Telephones in Jan. 1983 numbered 4,512. Broadcasting is under the auspices of the government-controlled commercial Radio Television Seychelles. There is a radio programme in English, French and Creole. There is also a religious station. TV colour is by PAL. In 1991 there were 30,000 radio and 8,200 TV sets.

Cinema. In 1989 there was 1 cinema with seating capacity of 200.

Newspaper. In 1990 there was 1 daily newspaper.

JUSTICE, RELIGION, EDUCATION AND WELFARE

Justice. The police force numbered 492 all ranks and 69 special constabulary.

Religion. 92% of the inhabitants are Roman Catholic and 6% Anglican.

Education. Education is free from 6 to 15 years in primary schools, 16 to 18 in secondary schools and 18 to 21 in polytechnics. In 1990 there were 14,440 pupils and 767 teachers in primary schools, 2,787 pupils and 157 teachers in secondary schools and 1,609 students and 171 teachers in the Polytechnic. In 1983, a total of 239 students were undergoing training overseas, mainly in the UK; 153 were in university, 39 teacher-training and 6 nursing. 85% adult literacy was claimed in 1991.

Health. In 1990 there were 49 doctors, 12 dentists, 299 nurses and 436 hospital beds. The health service is free.

DIPLOMATIC REPRESENTATIVES

Of Seychelles in Great Britain (111 Baker St., London, W1M 1FE)
High Commissioner: Sylvestre Radegonde.

Of Great Britain in Seychelles (Victoria Hse., Victoria, Mahé)
High Commissioner: John Sharland.

Of Seychelles in the USA and to the United Nations
Chargé d'affaires: Marc C. Marengo.

Of the USA in Seychelles (Victoria Hse., Victoria, Mahé)
Ambassador: Richard Carlson.

Further Reading

Statistical Information: Information Office, 52 Kingsgate House, Victoria, Mahé.
Agricultural Survey 1980. Government Printer
Seychelles in Figures. Statistics Division, Mahé, 1989
Benedict, M. and Benedict, B., *Men, Women and Money in Seychelles.* Univ. of California Press, 1983
Franda, M., *The Seychelles: Unquiet Islands.* Boulder, 1982
Lionnet, G., *The Seychelles.* Newton Abbot, 1972
Mancham, J. R., *Paradise Raped: Life, Love and Power in the Seychelles.* London, 1983

SIERRA LEONE

Capital: Freetown
Population: 4·14m. (1990)
GNP per capita: US$200 (1989)

Republic of Sierra Leone

HISTORY. The Colony of Sierra Leone originated in the sale and cession, in 1787, by native chiefs to English settlers, of a piece of land intended as a home for natives of Africa who were waifs in London, and later it was used as a settlement for Africans rescued from slave-ships. The hinterland was declared a British protectorate on 21 Aug. 1896. Sierra Leone became independent as a member state of the Commonwealth on 27 April 1961, and a republic on 19 April 1971.

AREA AND POPULATION. Sierra Leone is bounded on the north-west, north and north-east by the Republic of Guinea, on the south-east by Liberia and on the south-west by the Atlantic ocean. The coastline extends from the boundary of the Republic of Guinea to the north of the mouth of the Great Scarcies River to the boundary of Liberia at the mouth of the Mano River, a distance of about 212 miles (341 km). The area of Sierra Leone is 27,925 sq. miles (73,326 sq. km). Population (census 1985), 3,517,530, of whom about 2,000 were Europeans, 3,500 Asiatics and 30,000 non-native Africans. Estimate (1990), 4,140,000. The capital is Freetown, with 469,776 inhabitants in 1985.

Vital statistics (1986); Live births, 75,862; deaths, 6,272.

Sierra Leone is divided into 3 provinces and the Western Area:

	Sq. km	Census 1985	Capital	Estimate 1988
Western Area	557	554,243	Freetown	469,776
Southern province	19,694	740,510	Bo	26,000
Eastern province	15,553	960,551	Kenema	13,000
Northern province	35,936	1,262,226	Makeni	12,000

The principal peoples are the Mendes (34% of the total) in the south, the Temnes (31%) in the north and centre, the Konos, Fulanis, Bulloms, Korankos, Limbas and Kissis. English is the official language; a Creole (Krio) is spoken.

CLIMATE. A tropical climate, with marked wet and dry seasons and high temperatures throughout the year. The rainy season lasts from about April to Nov., when humidity can be very high. Thunderstorms are common from April to June and in Sept. and Oct. Rainfall is particularly heavy at Freetown because of the effect of neighbouring relief. Freetown. Jan. 80°F (26·7°C), July 78°F (25·6°C). Annual rainfall 135" (3,434 mm).

CONSTITUTION AND GOVERNMENT. For earlier Constitutional history *see* THE STATESMAN'S YEAR-BOOK 1978–79, p. 1046. Following a referendum in June 1978, a new Constitution was instituted under which the ruling All People's Congress (APC) became the sole legal Party. The 124-member Parliament comprises 105 members directly elected for a 5-year term (latest elections, 31 May 1986), together with 12 Paramount Chiefs representing the 12 districts and 7 members appointed by the President. The President is elected for a 7-year term by the National Delegates' Conference of the APC; he appoints and leads a Council of Ministers.

In a referendum in Sept. 1991 some 60% of the 2·5m. electorate voted for the introduction of a new constitution instituting multi-party democracy.

In Feb. 1992 the Cabinet consisted of:

President, Minister of Defence and Public Services: Maj.-Gen. Dr Joseph Saidu Momoh.

First Vice-President: Abu Bakarr Kamara. *Second Vice-President:* Salia Jusu Sherriff.

Minister of Finance: Tommy Taylor-Morgan. *Attorney-General and Minister of*

Justice: Dr Abdulai Conteh. *Foreign Affairs:* Dr Alhaji Abdul Karim Koroma. *Education, Cultural Affairs and Sports:* Dr Moses Dumbuya. *Trade:* Joseph Bandabla Dauda. *Transport and Communications:* Philipson Kamara. *Industries and State Enterprises:* Ben Kanu. *Health:* Dr Wiltshire Johnson. *Information and Broadcasting:* V.I.V. Mambu. *Agriculture, Natural Resources and Forestry:* M. O. Bash Taqi. *Mines:* Birch Momodu Conteh. *Internal Affairs:* Ahmed Sesay. *Works:* J. E. Laverse. *Labour:* M. L. Sidique. *Economic Planning and National Development:* Dr Sheka Kanu. *Energy and Power:* Dr Sheku Sesay. *Tourism:* A. M. Iscandri. *Rural Development, Social Welfare and Youth:* A. G. Koroma. *Lands, Housing and Environment:* Dominic Musa. *Minister of State and Leader of the House:* E. R. Ndomahina. *Minister of State and Inspector-General of Police:* Bambay Kamara. *Minister of State for Party Affairs:* E. T. Kamara. *Minister of State and Forces Commander:* Maj.-Gen. Mohamed Sheku Tarawali.

National flag: Three horizontal stripes of green, white, blue.

Local Government. The provinces are administered through the Ministry of Internal Affairs and divided into 148 Chiefdoms, each under the control of a Paramount Chief and Council of Elders known as the Tribal Authorities, who are responsible for the maintenance of law and order and for the administration of justice (except for serious crimes). All of these Chiefdoms have been organized into local government units, empowered to raise and disburse funds for the development of the Chiefdom concerned.

DEFENCE

Army. The Army consists of 2 infantry battalions, 1 special forces battalion, 2 artillery batteries and 1 engineer squadron. Equipment includes 10 armoured personnel carriers and 3 helicopters. Strength (1991), 3,000 officers and men.

Navy. The small flotilla comprises 2 ex-Chinese fast inshore patrol craft, 1 small inshore craft and 3 utility landing craft. Personnel in 1991 totalled 150.

INTERNATIONAL RELATIONS

Membership. Sierra Leone is a member of the UN, OAU, ECOWAS and the Commonwealth and is an ACP state of the EEC.

ECONOMY

Budget. Revenue and expenditure (in 1,000 leone) for years ending 30 June:

	1985–86	1986–87	1987–88	1988–89
Revenue	375,500	1,254,500	1,990,400	3,500,000
Expenditure	566,400	1,828,300	3,960,800	6,630,000

Currency. The unit of currency is the *leone* (SLL) of 100 *cents*. There are notes of 50 cents and 1, 2, 5, 10 and 20 *leone*, and coins of 1, 5, 10, 20 and 50 *cents*.
In March 1992, £1 = 754·20 *leone*; US$1 = 429·62 *leone*.

Banking. The bank of issue is the Bank of Sierra Leone (established 1964). The Standard Chartered Bank Sierra Leone, the National Commercial Bank, International Bank of Credit and Commerce, International Bank of Trade and Industry and Barclays Bank Sierra Leone have their headquarters at Freetown; the Standard Chartered Bank has 14, Barclays Bank 12 and the National Commercial Bank, 8 branches and agencies.
The Post Office Savings Bank had 94,910 depositors with total credit balance of nearly Le. 3,455,469 in 1983.

ENERGY AND NATURAL RESOURCES

Electricity. Production (1986) 85m. kwh. Supply 230 volts; 50 Hz.

Minerals. The chief minerals mined are diamonds (314,000 carats, 1987), bauxite (1·3m. tonnes), and rutile (113,900 tonnes). Molybdenite is being prospected.

Agriculture. In the western area farming is largely confined to the production of cassava and garden crops, such as maize, vegetables and mangoes, for local consumption. In the regions the principal products include rice, which is the staple food of the country, cassava, groundnuts and export crops such as palm-kernels, cocoa beans, coffee, ginger and piassava. Cattle production is important in the north, and most of the poultry, eggs and pork are produced in the Western Area. Production (1990, in 1,000 tonnes): Rice, 450; cassava, 118; palm oil, 50; palm kernels, 33; coffee, 9; cocoa, 9.

Livestock (1990): Cattle, 330,000; goats, 180,000; sheep, 330,000; chickens, 6m.

Fisheries. The estimated tonnage of catch of all species of fish during 1986 was 53,000 tonnes.

INDUSTRY. There are palm-oil and rice mills (4 government-owned). At Kenema the Government Forest Industries Corporation produces sawn timber, joinery products (including prefabricated buildings) and furniture. Village industries include fishing, fish curing and smoking, weaving and hand methods of expressing palm-oil and cracking palm kernels.

Labour. A large proportion of the population is engaged in agriculture and about 125,000 workers are in wage-earning employment. The number of workers in establishments employing 6 or more persons was 64,092 in 1982, distributed as follows: Services, 24,142; mining and quarrying, 6,170; transport, storage and communications, 4,814; construction, 9,721; commerce, 6,870; manufacturing, 9,407; agriculture, forestry and fishing, 5,834; electricity and water services, 24,142.

FOREIGN ECONOMIC RELATIONS

Commerce. Total trade (in 1,000 leone) for 1988: Imports, 5,215; exports, 3,317.

Total trade between Sierra Leone and UK (British Department of Trade returns, in £1,000 sterling):

	1987	1988	1989	1990	1991
Imports to UK	12,679	14,462	15,899	7,011	5,516
Exports and re-exports from UK	16,221	14,256	20,402	21,365	17,926

Tourism. Tourism is being developed and is a major growth industry. In 1986 there were 194,000 tourists.

COMMUNICATIONS

Roads. There were (1978) about 7,500 miles of main roads, of which 1,000 miles are surfaced with bitumen. A programme to improve the road system was initiated in 1988. Motor vehicles licensed in 1987, passenger cars, 25,000; commercial vehicles, 18,200.

Railways. The government railway closed in 1974. An 84-km mineral line of 1,067-mm gauge connecting Marampa with the port of Pepel has been rehabilitated. It carries about 2·7m. tonnes annually.

Civil Aviation. Freetown Airport (Lungi) is the international airport. The airport is served by Sierra Leone Airlines, Ghana/Nigeria Airways, Union de Transport Aériens, KLM and Air Afrique. Sierra Leone Airlines provide domestic flights from Hastings (14 miles from Freetown) to Gbangbatoke, Bo, Kenema, Yengema and Bonthe. Domestic air taxi services also operate.

Shipping. During 1986 the total imports handled by the port of Freetown amounted to 1,990 tonnes and exports 990 tonnes. Bonthe-Sherbro, 80 miles south of Freetown, is used for the shipment of rutile and bauxite. Pepel lies some 12 miles from Freetown and exports iron ore.

Telecommunications. Number of telephones (1981) 220,000. Telegraphic facilities are provided at 58 offices. There were (1983) 37 post offices and 76 postal agencies. Broadcasting is under the auspices of the government-controlled Sierra Leone Broadcasting Service and Sierra Leone Television, which is part commercial. In 1991 there were 925,000 radio and 25,000 TV sets (colour by PAL).

Newspapers. In 1987 there was one daily newspaper with a circulation of 12,000.

JUSTICE, RELIGION, EDUCATION AND WELFARE

Justice. The High Court has jurisdiction in civil and criminal matters. Subordinate courts are held by magistrates in the various districts. Native Courts, headed by court Chairmen, apply native law and custom under a criminal and civil jurisdiction. Appeals from the decisions of magistrates' courts are heard by the High Court. Appeals from the decisions of the High Court are heard by the Sierra Leone Court of Appeal. Appeal lies from the Sierra Leone Court of Appeal to the Supreme Court which is the highest court.

Religion. The Moslem community was estimated to comprise 39% of the population in 1980, while 52% followed traditional tribal religions; Protestants were 6% and Roman Catholics 2% of the total. The Temne people are mainly Moslem and the Mende chiefly animists. Spiritualist churches were growing in 1985.

Education (1984). There were over 1,267 registered primary schools; total enrolment (1982) 276,911. Primary education is partially free but not compulsory. There were (1984) 184 secondary schools, 4 technical institutes, 2 trade centres and a rural institute.

Fourah Bay College (1,400 students) and Njala University College are the 2 constituent colleges of the University of Sierra Leone.

Health. In 1984 there were 28 government and 16 private and charitable hospitals and 156 dispensaries.

DIPLOMATIC REPRESENTATIVES

Of Sierra Leone in Great Britain (33 Portland Pl., London,W1N 3AG)
High Commissioner: Caleb Aubee.

Of Great Britain in Sierra Leone (Standard Chartered Bank of Sierra Leone Ltd Bldg., Lightfoot Boston St., Freetown)
High Commissioner: David Sprague, MVO.

Of Sierra Leone in the USA (1701 19th St., NW, Washington, D.C., 20009)
Ambassador: Dr George Carew.

Of the USA in Sierra Leone (Corner Walpole and Siaka Stevens St., Freetown)
Ambassador: Johnny Young.

Of Sierra Leone to the United Nations
Ambassador: Dr Thomas Kargbo.

Further Reading

Background to Sierra Leone. Freetown, 1980
Cole, B. P., *Sierra Leone Directory of Commerce, Industry and Tourism.* 1985
Fyfe, C., *A History of Sierra Leone.* OUP, 1962.—Fyfe, C. and Jones, E. (ed.) *Freetown.* Sierra Leone Univ. Press and OUP, 1968
Kup, A. P., *Sierra Leone.* Newton Abbot, 1975
Porter, A. T., *Creoledom: A Study in the Development of Freetown Society.* OUP, 1963
Riley, S. P., *Sierra Leone.* [Bibliography] Oxford and Santa Barbara, 1989

SINGAPORE

Population: 2·69m. (1990)
GNP per capita: US$10,186 (1990)

Republic of Singapore

HISTORY. For the early history of the settlement (1819) and colony (1867) *see* THE STATESMAN'S YEAR-BOOK, 1959, pp. 246 f.

By an agreement entered into between the Governments of Malaysia and of the State of Singapore on 7 Aug. 1965, effective on 9 Aug. 1965, Singapore ceased to be one of the 14 states of the Federation of Malaysia and became an independent sovereign state. On 22 Dec. 1965 it became a republic. The separation was ratified by the Constitution and Malaysia (Singapore Amendment) Act of the Malaysian Parliament on 9 Aug. The 2 governments agreed to enter into a treaty on external defence and mutual assistance. The Singapore Government retains its executive authority and legislative powers under its State Constitution and took over the powers of the Malaysian Government under the Malaysian Constitution in Singapore. The sovereignty and jurisdiction of the head of the Malaysian State was transferred to the Singapore Government. Civil servants working in Singapore for the Federal Departments became Singapore civil servants. Singapore citizens ceased to be Malaysian citizens.

Singapore accepted responsibility for international agreements entered into by the Malaysian Government on its behalf.

AREA AND POPULATION. The Republic of Singapore consists of Singapore Island itself, and some 58 islets.

Singapore Island is situated off the southern extremity of the Malay peninsula, to which it is joined by a 1,056-metre causeway carrying a road, railway and water pipeline. The Straits of Johore between the island and the mainland are about three-quarters of a mile wide. The island is some 26·1 miles (42 km) in length and 14·3 miles (23 km) in breadth, and about 240·4 sq. miles (625·6 sq. km) in area, including some 58 adjacent islets, 20 of which are inhabited.

Census of population (1990): 2,089,400 Chinese, 380,600 Malays, 191,000 Indians and 29,200 others; total 2,690,200. Estimate (June 1989), 2,038,000 Chinese, 408,800 Malays, 174,300 Indians and 64,300 others; total 2,685,400. Density, 4,293 per sq. km; growth rate, 1988, 1·5%; infant mortality, 1988, 7 per 1,000 live births; life expectancy, 1990, 71·2 years.

CLIMATE. The climate is equatorial, with uniformly high temperatures and no defined wet or dry season, rain being plentiful throughout the year, especially from Nov. to Jan., generally the cooler months. Jan. 78·1°F (25·6°C), July 80·8°F (27·1°C). Annual rainfall 93·2" (2,369 mm).

CONSTITUTION AND GOVERNMENT. By a constitutional amendment the name of the state was changed to 'Republic of Singapore', the head of state was named 'President of Singapore' and the legislative assembly was renamed 'Parliament'.

Parliament is unicameral consisting of 81 members, elected by secret ballot from single-member and group representation constituencies and is presided over by a Speaker, chosen by Parliament from its own members who are neither ministers nor parliamentary secretaries or from among persons who are not members of Parliament but who are qualified for election as members of Parliament. In the latter case, the Speaker has no vote. The present Speaker is an elected Member of Parliament. With the customary exception of those serving criminal sentences, all citizens over 21 are eligible to vote. Voting in an election is compulsory. For the general election held on 31 Aug. 1991, Singapore was divided into 36 electoral divisions, of which 21 were single-member constituencies and 15 were group representation constituencies (GRC). Each GRC returned 4 Members of Parliament, one of whom must be from the Malay community, the Indian and other minority communities. There is a common roll without communal electorates.

A Presidential Council for minority rights was established in 1970. The general function of the Council is to consider and report on matters affecting persons of any racial or religious community in Singapore as referred to it by Parliament or the Government. The Council will draw attention to any bill or subsidiary legislation which in its opinion is a differentiating measure.

At the elections of Aug. 1991 opposition parties contested only 40 of the 81 seats in parliament. The People's Action Party gained 61% of votes cast and 77 seats (63·2% and 80 in 1988); the Social Democratic Party gained 3 seats (1 in 1988) and the Workers' Party 1 seat.

President of Singapore: Wee Kim Wee (re-elected for a second term, Sept. 1989).

The People's Action Party Cabinet at Sept. 1991 was composed as follows:
Prime Minister: Goh Chok Tong.

Senior Minister, Prime Minister's Office: Lee Kuan Yew. *Deputy Prime Minister:* Ong Teng Cheong. *Deputy Prime Minister and Minister for Trade and Industry:* Lee Hsien Loong. *National Development:* S. Dhanabalan. *Education:* Dr Tony Tan Keng Yam. *Environment:* Dr Ahmad Mattar. *Defence:* Yeo Ning Hong. *Communications:* Mah Bow Tan. *Law and Home Affairs:* S. Jayakumar. *Finance:* Richard Hu Tsu Tau. *Labour and Second Minister for Education:* Lee Yock Suan. *Foreign Affairs:* Wong Kan Seng. *Information and the Arts and Second Minister for Foreign Affairs:* George Yeo. *Minister for Health and Community Development:* Dr Seet Aimee. *Minister in Prime Minister's Office and Second Minister for Defence:* Lee Boon Yang.

There are 7 Ministers of State.

National flag: Horizontally red over white, charged in the upper left canton with a crescent and a circle of 5 stars, all in white.

Malay, Chinese (Mandarin), Tamil and English are the official languages; Malay is the national language and English is the language of administration.

DEFENCE. The Ministry of Defence comprises 5 major divisions: general staff, manpower, logistics, security and intelligence and finance. Compulsory military service in peace-time for all male citizens and permanent residents was introduced in 1967. Periods of service are officers/n.c.o.s. 30 months, other ranks 24 months. Reserve liability is to 40 for men, 50 for officers.

An agreement with the USA in Nov. 1990 provided for an increase in US use of naval and air force facilities.

Singapore is a member of the Five Powers Defence Arrangement, with Australia, New Zealand, Malaysia and the UK.

Army. The Army consists of the 1st and 2nd People's Defence Force (PDF) Commando and 3 divisions: The 3rd (Tiger) division, the 6th (Cobra) division and the 9th (Panther) division, the latter 2 being reservist formations. Equipment includes about 350 AMX-13SM1 light tanks. Strength (1992) 45,000 (including 30,000 conscripts) and 250,000 reserves. Paramilitary forces number 11,600.

Navy. The small, relatively modern Navy operates 6 German-designed fast missile corvettes, 6 German-designed fast missile gun boats, 20 inshore patrol craft, 5 ex-US tank landing ships, 8 small landing craft and 1 training ship. Naval personnel in 1991 numbered 4,500 (1,800 conscripts) and the naval base is on Pulau Brani.

The Marine Police operates some 60 patrol boats, some armed.

Air Defence Command. The formation of an Air Defence Command began in 1968. The Republic of Singapore Air Force now has 2 squadrons of F-5E/Fs and 1 squadron of F-16A/Bs for air defence; 4 fighter-bomber squadrons equipped with A-4S Skyhawks, supported by TA-4S two-seat trainers; 1 squadron of Hawker Hunter jet fighters and reconnaissance-fighters, supported by Hunter 2-seat trainers; a squadron of Strikemaster armed trainers; a radar unit, anti-aircraft guns and Bloodhound, Rapier and Hawk surface-to-air missile squadrons; a transport squadron of C-130 Hercules (including 4 equipped as flight refuelling tankers); a squadron of Skyvans equipped for search and rescue; a squadron of Bell UH-1s and AS 332M Super Puma helicopters; and training units equipped with SF.260MS piston-engined basic trainers, SIAI-Marchetti S.211 jet-powered advanced trainers, AS 350 Ecureuil helicopters, plus four E-2C Hawkeye AWACS aircraft. 20 Ecureuil helicopters are being delivered for anti-armour and observation duties. Personnel strength (1992) about 6,000 (3,000 conscripts), with 193 combat aircraft and 6 armed helicopters.

INTERNATIONAL RELATIONS

Membership. Singapore is a member of UN, the Commonwealth, the Colombo Plan and ASEAN.

ECONOMY

Policy. The GNP in 1990, at current cost was S$63,905·1m., an increase of 13·4% over 1989.

Budget. Public revenue and expenditure for financial years (in S$1m.):

	1987	1988	1989	1990
Revenue	10,470·9	13,775·9	15,508·9	16,424·7
Expenditure [1]	8,465·9	7,202·3	7,681·9	9,036·8

[1] Payments from Consolidated Revenue Account.

Currency. The unit of currency is the *Singapore dollar* (SGD) divided into 100 *cents*. Gross circulation in March 1991 was S$7,181·6m. In March 1992, £1 = 2·89 *dollars*; US$1 = 1·64 dollars. Foreign exchange reserves were S$48·500m. in 1990.

Banking and Finance. The Monetary Authority of Singapore performs the functions of a central bank, except the issuing of currency which is the responsibility of the Board of the Commissioner of Currency.

The Development Bank of Singapore was established as a fully licensed bank in 1968, and is the largest local bank in terms of assets. Primarily it provides long-term financing of manufacturing and other industries. In 1990 it had a paid up capital of S$474·2m. and shareholders' funds amounting to S$2,777·7m.

There were 137 commercial banks with 431 banking offices operating in Singapore in March 1991. The total assets/liabilities amounted to S$130,635·7m. as at March 1991. Total deposits of non-bank customers amounted to S$65,503·4m. while loans and advances including bills financing, totalled S$59,210·5m.

There were 71 merchant banks operating in Singapore at March 1991. Of these, 70 had an Asian Currency Unit each and were engaged actively in Asian dollars transactions. Their main functions included underwriting, portfolio fund management, financial advisory services and loan syndication.

In 1990, foreign banks accounted for 61% of banking assets. Foreign investment in up to 40% of the equity of local banks is permitted.

In 1990, the Singapore Post Office Savings Bank had 3,813,897 savings accounts and a total deposit balance of all accounts of S$13,049m.

There is a stock exchange.

Weights and Measures. The metric system or the International System of Units (SI) was introduced in 1971.

ENERGY AND NATURAL RESOURCES

Electricity. The Public Utilities Board is responsible for the provision of electricity, piped gas and water. Electrical power is generated by 4 oil-fired power stations, with a total generating capacity of 3,627 mw in 1990. Production (1990) 15,618m. kwh. Supply 230 volts; 50 Hz.

Oil. Singapore is the largest oil refining centre in Asia.

Agriculture. Only 1·7% of Singapore's total area is used for farming. Agriculture employed only 1% of the labour force in 1989. Most food is imported but Singapore is self-sufficient in eggs, and 10,000 tonnes (5·6%) of vegetables were produced for domestic consumption in 1988.

The government has initiated the development of agro-technology parks to house large scale intensive farms to improve local production of fresh food.

Fisheries. As the prospect of increasing fish production from inshore waters is poor, in 1967 various projects were introduced with the aim of making Singapore self-sufficient in fish as well as a major fishing base in the region.

The total local supply of fresh fish in 1989 was 13,110 tonnes.

INDUSTRY. The largest industrial area is the Jurong Industrial Estate with 1,934 factories employing 107,837 workers in March 1989.

Production, 1990 (in S$1m.), totalled 70,992·5m., including machinery and appliances, 33,157·70; petroleum, 9,243·2; food and beverages, 11,416·50; chemical products, 5,057; transport equipment, 3,717·3; fabricated metal products, 3,619·8; paper products and printing, 2,516·8; wearing apparel, 1,719·6; rubber processing, 205.

Labour. In 1990, 1,485,800 persons were employed, of whom 1,299,700 were employees, 66,500 were employers, 96,100 were self-employed and 23,500 were unpaid family workers. The majority were working in manufacturing, 421,900; trade, 290,300.

The Employment Act and the Industrial Relations Act provide principal terms and conditions of employment such as hours of work, sick leave and other fringe benefits. A new labour legislation was introduced allowing youths of 14-16 years to work in industrial establishments, and also children from 12-14 years to be employed in approved apprenticeship schemes. A trade dispute may be referred to the Industrial Arbitration Court which was established in 1960.

The Ministry of Labour operates an employment service to assist job seekers to obtain employment and employers to recruit workers. In addition it provides the handicapped with specialized on-the-job training. The Central Provident Fund was established in 1955 to make provision for employees in their old age. In 1990 there were 2·2m. members with S$40,646m. standing to their credit in the fund. The total number of contributors to the fund in 1988 was 963,786.

Trade Unions. There were 88 registered trade unions comprising 83 employee unions and 5 employer unions in 1990. The total membership of employee unions numbered 212,204. Members of employer unions numbered 1,039.

FOREIGN ECONOMIC RELATIONS

Commerce. Imports and exports (in S$1m.), by country, 1990:

	Imports (c.i.f.)	Exports (f.o.b.)
Australia	2,127·2	2,336·9
China	3,773·4	1,443·4
France	2,645·6	1,556·0
Germany, Federal Republic of	3,898·5	3,824·9
Hong Kong	3,365·3	6,186·1
Italy	1,773·0	1,260·1
Japan	22,146·2	8,301·5
Malaysia	14,963·5	12,448·5
Saudi Arabia	5,862·5	499·6
Taiwan	4,677·5	3,421·8
Thailand	2,974·1	6,310·3
UK	3,375·7	3,031·0
USA	17,580·5	20,245·5

The major trading countries for 1990 were US (18·4%), the EEC (16·6%), Japan (14·8%), and Malaysia (13·4%). In 1990, imports (S$109,806m.) increased by 13·4%. Exports increased by 9·3% from S$87,116m. in 1989 to S$95,206m. in 1990.

Exports (1990, in S$1m.): Machinery and transport equipment, 47,732·6 (of which electrical machinery, 22,223·2; transport equipment, 2,451·7; non-electric machinery, 23,057·6); mineral fuels, 17,295·3; crude materials, 2,914·6 (including rubber); chemicals, 5,970·1; food, beverages and tobacco, 4,122; clothing, 2,867·2; animal and vegetable oils, 760·7; textiles, 1,630·8; scientific and optical instruments, 1,950·3; metal goods, 1,215·3; iron and steel, 789·9.

Exports of orchids were valued at S$16m., and of aquarium fish at S$57·9m., in 1989.

Imports (1990, in S$1m.): Machinery and transport equipment, 49,065.1 (of which electrical machinery, 22,603·7; transport equipment, 6,188·5; non-electric machinery, 20,273·1); mineral fuels, 17,398·9; food, beverages and tobacco, 5,740; chemicals, 8,440·5; crude materials, 2,371·1 (of which rubber, 922·1); textiles, 5,740; iron and steel, 3,066·3; animal and vegetable oils, 753; metal goods, 2,160·7; scientific and optical instruments, 2,995·7; non-metal mineral goods, 1,512·7; paper and paperboard and related articles, 1,253·4.

In the following table (British Department of Trade returns, in £1,000 sterling) the imports include produce from Sabah, Sarawak and other eastern places, transhipped at Singapore, which is thus entered as the place of export:

	1987	1988	1989	1990	1991
Imports to UK	473,814	579,368	903,248	1,021,148	1,134,365
Exports and re-exports from UK	602,627	632,452	773,866	1,040,188	1,018,419

Tourism. There were 5,322,900m. visitors in 1990 (4,829,950 in 1989). Earnings from tourists were S$7,600m. in 1990. The average length of stay was 3·3 days. In 1990 there were 65 gazetted hotels with a total of 22,408 rooms.

COMMUNICATIONS

Roads. There were (1990) 2,836 km of public roads, of which 2,752 km are asphalt-paved. In 1990 motor vehicles numbered 542,352, of which 271,174 were private cars, 9,448 buses, 122,525 motor cycles and scooters, 15,582 public cars including taxis, school taxis and private hire cars.

Railways. A 16-mile (25·8-km) main line runs through Singapore, connecting with the States of Malaysia and as far as Bangkok. Branch lines serve the port of Singapore and the industrial estate at Jurong. A mass rapid transit opened in 1987 and was fully operational by 1990.

Civil Aviation. In March 1991 Singapore Airlines (SIA) flew to 63 destinations in 37 countries. It had 46 aircraft in 1991 and 40 more on order. It is 54% owned by the state. 49 international airlines operated 1,500 scheduled flights a week, totalling 79,037 commercial aircraft movements at Singapore International Airport in Changi ('Airtropolis') in 1988. Changi Airport has routes to 110 destinations in 53 countries. Freight handled (1989) 577,549 tonnes. There were 14·1m. passengers and 87,421 commercial aircraft.

Shipping. The economy is dependent on shipping and entrepôt trade. A total of 44,600 vessels of 483m. GRT entered Singapore during 1990. Singapore is one of the world's largest container ports.

Telecommunications. In 1990, 91 post offices and 44 postal agencies were in operation. Telephones numbered 1·32m. and fax machines 33,369 in 1989. In 1990 there were 126,778 radio and 582,540 TV licences.

Cinemas (1990). There were 56 cinemas with a total seating capacity of 48,000.

Newspapers (1990). There were 7 daily newspapers, in 4 languages, with a total daily circulation of 48,000.

JUSTICE, RELIGION, EDUCATION AND WELFARE

Justice. There is a Supreme Court in Singapore which consists of the High Court, the Court of Appeal and the Court of Criminal Appeal. The Supreme Court is composed of a Chief Justice and 7 Judges. An appeal from the High Court lies to the

Court of Appeal in civil matters and to the Court of Criminal Appeal in criminal matters. The High Court has original civil and criminal jurisdiction as well as appellate civil and criminal jurisdiction in respect of appeals from the Subordinate Courts. There are 17 district courts, 13 magistrates' courts, 1 juvenile and 1 coroner's court and a small claims tribunal.

Penalties for drug trafficking and abuse are severe. The death penalty is mandatory for trafficking in, importing into or exporting from Singapore, in excess of 30 grammes of morphine, heroin in excess of 15 grammes, more than 30 grammes of cocaine, more than 200 grammes of cannabis resin, more than 500 grammes of cannabis or more than 1,200 grammes of opium.

Religion. In 1990, 53·9% of the population aged 15 years and above were Buddhists and Taoists, 12·6% Christians, 15·4% Moslems and 3·6% Hindus.

Education. Statistics of schools in 1990:

	Schools	Pupils	Teachers
Primary schools	208	257,932	10,006
Secondary schools	146	161,029	7,657
Pre-university centres and			...[1]
centralised institutes	32	8,335	...[2]
Junior colleges	14	22,095	1,540

[1] Teachers teaching in pre-university centres are included under secondary schools
[2] Teachers teaching in centralised institutes are included under junior colleges

The National University of Singapore was established on 8 Aug. 1980 following the merger of the University of Singapore and the Nanyang University. The National University of Singapore has 8 faculties: Arts and social sciences, law, science, medicine, dentistry, engineering, architecture and building, and business administration. Post-graduate studies are offered in all the faculties and there are 3 post-graduate schools for medical, dental and management studies. Total enrolment for 1990–91 was 17,342 students.

The Nanyang Technological Institute (NTI), situated in the former Nanyang University, (established on 8 Aug. 1981) became a university on 1 June 1991. The National Institute of Education (formerly the Institute of Education (IE) which was established in April 1973 for teacher education and research in education) became part of the university also in June 1991. The total enrolment for 1990–91 for the then NTI and IE was 6,965 and 1,631. The Singapore Polytechnic had 15,477 students and the Ngee Ann Polytechnic 13,291 students in 1990–91. The Temasck Polytechnic which was establilshed in June 1990, had 736 students during its first year.

The Vocational and Industrial Training Board is responsible for vocational training and continuing education. It runs 23 training institutes and centres offering full-time and part-time courses. The total student enrolment for 1990 was 26,102.

The general literacy rate rose from 84% in 1980 to 90% in 1990.

Health. There were 7 government hospitals with 5,491 beds and 3 government restricted hospitals with 2,503 beds in 1990. There were 3,573 doctors, 672 dentists and 10,109 nurses registered. There are 10 private hospitals with 1,837 beds.

DIPLOMATIC REPRESENTATIVES

Of Singapore in Great Britain (9 Wilton Cres., London, SW1X 8SA)
High Commissioner: Abdul Aziz Mahmood.

Of Great Britain in Singapore (Tanglin Rd, Singapore, 1024)
High Commissioner: Gordon Duggan.

Of Singapore in the USA (1824 R. St., NW, Washington, D.C., 20009-1691)
Ambassador: S. R. Nathan.

Of the USA in Singapore (30 Hill St., Singapore, 0617)
Ambassador: Robert D. Orr.

Of Singapore to the United Nations
Ambassador: Chew Tai Soo.

Further Reading

Statistical Information: The Department of Statistics (PO Box 3010, Maxwell Road, Singapore 9050) was established 1 Jan. 1922. Its publications include: *Singapore Trade Statistics: Imports and Exports* (monthly), *Monthly Digest of Statistics, Yearbook of Statistics, Singapore Demographic Bulletin* (monthly), *Census of Population 1980. Singapore Yearbook of Labour Statistics. Chief Statistician:* Dr Paul Cheung.
Census of population 1990: advance data release. Singapore 1991.

National Library. *Books About Singapore.* Singapore. Biennial
Singapore. Constitution. The Constitution of Singapore. Singapore, 1966
The Budget for the Financial Year 1990–91. Singapore, 1990
Singapore. Economic Committee, The Singapore Economy: new directions: report of the Economic Committee, Ministry of Trade and Industry, Singapore, 1986
Singapore Yearbook. Singapore, Information Division, Ministry of Communications and Information
Singapore. Government Gazette (published weekly with supplement)
Economic Survey of Singapore. Ministry of Trade and Industry, Singapore (Quarterly and Annual)
Singapore Facts and Pictures. Singapore, Information Division, Ministry of Communications and Information, 1990
Singapore Government Directory. Singapore, Information Division, Ministry of Communications and Information, 1991
Singapore: An Illustrated history, 1941–48. Ministry of Culture, Singapore, 1984
The Statutes of the Republic of Singapore. Rev. 12 vols., 1985 (with annual supplements). Singapore, Law Revision Commission, 1986—.
Clammer, J. R., *Singapore: Ideology, Society, Culture.* Singapore, 1985
Drysdale, J., *Singapore: Struggle for Success.* Singapore, 1984
Krause, L. B., *The Singapore Economy Reconsidered.* Singapore, 1988
Lim, L., *Trade, Employment and Industrialisation in Singapore.* Singapore, 1987
Myint, S., *The Principles of Singapore Law.* Singapore, 1987
Quah, J. S. T., *Government and Politics of Singapore.* OUP, 1985
Quah, S. R. and Quah, J. S. T., *Singapore* [Bibliography] Oxford and Santa Barbara, 1988
Saw, S. H., *New Population and Labour Force Projections and Policy Implications for Singapore.* Singapore, 1987
Tan, C. H., *Financial Markets and Institutions in Singapore.* 6th ed. Singapore, 1989
Turnbull, C. M., *A History of Singapore, 1819–1988.* 2nd ed. OUP, 1982
Yip, J. S. K. and Sim, W. K., (eds.), *Evolution of Educational Excellence: 25 Years of Education in the Republic of Singapore.* Singapore, 1990
You, P. S. and Lim, C. Y. (eds.) *Singapore: Twenty-five years of Development.* Singapore, 1984

National Library: National Library, Stamford Rd, Singapore, 0617. *Director:* Mrs Yoke-Lan Wicks.

SLOVENIA

Capital: Ljubljana
Population: 1·95m. (1990)
GNP per capita: US$7,150 (1991)

Republika Slovenija

HISTORY. The lands originally settled by Slovenes in the 6th century were steadily encroached upon by Germans. Slovenia developed as part of Austria-Hungary and gained independence only in 1918. A legal opposition group, the Slovene League of Social Democrats (leader, France Tomsič), was formed in Jan. 1989. In Oct. 1989 the Slovene Assembly voted a consitutional amendment giving it the right to secede from Yugoslavia. On 2 July 1990 the Assembly adopted a 'declaration of sovereignty' by 187 votes to 3, and in Sept. proclaimed its control over the territorial defence force on its soil. At a referendum on 23 Dec. 88·5% of participants voted for independence, which was formally declared on 26 Dec.

In Feb. 1991 parliament ruled that henceforth Slovenian law took precedence over federal. On 25 June Slovenia declared independence, but agreed to suspend this for 3 months at peace talks sponsored by the EC. Federal troops moved into Slovenia on 27 June to secure Yugoslavia's external borders, but after some fighting finally withdrew by the end of July. The 3-month moratorium agreed at the EC having expired, Slovenia (and Croatia) declared their complete independence of the Yugoslav federation on 8 Oct. 1991. They were recognized as independent states by Germany on 23 Dec. and by the EC on 15 Jan. 1992.

AREA AND POPULATION. Slovenia is bounded in the north by Austria, in the north-east by Hungary, in the south-east by Croatia and in the west by Italy. There is a small strip of coast south of Trieste. Its area is 20,251 sq. km. The capital is Ljubljana. Population at the 1981 census: 1,891,864 (973,098 females), of whom the predominating ethnic group were Slovene (1,712,445). Population density per sq. km, 1981: 93·4. Population, 1990, 1·95m.

Vital statistics:

	Live births	Marriages	Deaths	Growth rate per 1,000
1987	25,592	10,307	19,837	3·0
1988	25,209	9,217	19,126	3·1
1989	25,576	10,022	19,471	5·1

Rates, 1990: Birth, 12·5 per 1,000 population; death, 9·9; marriage, 4·7; infant mortality, 8·9 per 1,000 live births.

CONSTITUTION AND GOVERNMENT. There is a 240-member 3-chamber National Assembly. The *Speaker* is France Bučan. At the elections of April 1990 the 6-party Democratic United Opposition (Demos) won 55% of the vote and the Party of Democratic Renewal (formerly Communist), 18%.

The *President* is Janez Drnovšek.

The coalition government broke up on 30 Dec. 1991 and an interim government was named on 26 Jan. 1992.
Prime Minister: Lojze Peterle (Christian Democrat).
Elections were scheduled for June 1992.
National flag: 3 horizontal stripes of white, blue and red, with the arms over all in the canton.
National anthem: 'Naprej zastava slave' ('Forward, banner of glory'; words by S. Jenko, tune by D. Jenko).

DEFENCE. By an agreement of July 1991 all federal Yugoslav troops withdrew.

Army. The nucleus of a regular army, a territorial defence force mobilized for training in June 1991, is some 60,000 strong.

ECONOMY

Policy. Privatization is being carried out in 2 stages, beginning with small businesses, by transferring the capital to an investment fund to act as intermediary. 20% of the capital is to be transferred to savings banks, 10–20% to commercial banks, 20% to wage-earners and 10% to former owners.

Budget. Revenue in 1990–91 was 68,000m. dinars, of which half was contributed to the federal Yugoslav budget. After June 1991 Slovenia ceased these contributions.

Currency. The unit of currency is the *tolar*, which replaced the Yugoslav dinar. It is based on the Ecu according to a floating exchange rate.

Banking and Finance. A central bank, the National Bank of Slovenia, was founded in June 1991. Its *Governor* is Franc Arhar.
There is a stock exchange in Ljubljana.

ENERGY AND NATURAL RESOURCES

Electricity. Output in 1989 was 12,569m. kwh, of which 4,688 kwh were nuclear produced, 4,908 kwh thermal and 2,973 kwh hydro-electric.

Minerals. Brown coal production was 1,653,000 tonnes in 1989; lignite, 4,617,000 tonnes.

Agriculture. Agriculture contributed 4·5% of GDP in 1991. In 1989 agricultural land totalled 0·87m. ha (0·25m. ha arable, 0·22m. pasture, 21,000 ha vineyards). The cultivated area was 645,000 ha. Yields (in 1,000 tonnes) in 1989: Wheat, 167; maize, 324; sugar-beet, 164; potatoes, 367; cabbage, 60. Livestock in 1989 (in 1,000): Cattle, 546; sheep, 24; pigs, 576; poultry, 13,269.

Forestry. 3·16m. cu. metres of timber were cut in 1989.

Fisheries. There were 46 sea fishing vessels in 1989. Total catch was 6,378 tonnes (973 tonnes freshwater).

INDUSTRY. Industry contributed 56% of GDP in 1991. Traditional industries are metallurgy, furniture-making and sports equipment. The manufacture of electric white goods and transport equipment is being developed.
Production (1989): Steel, 752,000 tonnes; lorries, 2,900; cars (1987), 66,000; sulphuric acid, 189,000 tonnes; sugar, 42,000; cement, 1·18m. tonnes; cotton fabrics, 101m. sq. metres; woollens, 20m. sq. metres.

Labour. The population of working age (15–64 males; 15–59 females) in 1989 was 1,262,625. The non-agricultural workforce in 1989 was 851,243. There were 28,218 registered unemployed (13,787 women).

FOREIGN ECONOMIC RELATIONS

Commerce. Exports in 1989 were worth 9,203m. federal dinars; imports, 8,565m. federal dinars. Major exports (in 1m. dinars) included: Raw materials, 2,110; semi-finished goods, 2,153; machinery, 627; electric motors, 230; transport equipment, 243; foodstuffs, 457; clothing, 424; pharmaceuticals and cosmetics, 570. Major imports: Raw materials, 3,460; semi-finished goods, 1,981; machinery, 714; foodstuffs, 262.
Percentage of exports to principal markets in 1991: Germany, 22·2%; Italy, 19·1%; USSR, 13·3%; France, 9·8%; Austria, 5·4%; USA, 4·6%. Imports: Germany, 23·2%; USA, 18·1%; Italy, 15·8%; France, 9%; Austria, 9%; USSR, 6·4%.

Tourism. 8,510,000 tourist nights were spent in 1989. Revenue was 1,313m. dinars.

COMMUNICATIONS

Roads. In 1989 there were 14,526 km of roads, including 1,581 km of main roads and 10,123 km of hard-surfaced roads. There were 554,200 passenger cars (530,252 private), 3,191 buses, 29,279 lorries and 17,532 motorcycles. 286m. passengers and 13m. tonnes of freight were carried.

There were 5,779 traffic accidents in 1989 in which 553 persons were killed.

Railways. In 1989 19,971,000 passengers and 19·55m. tonnes of freight were carried.

Civil Aviation. The national carrier Adria Air was formed in 1991.

Telecommunications. In 1989 there were 537 post offices and 0·63m. telephones. There were 21 radio stations and 2 TV centres.

Cinemas. There were 158 cinemas with a total of 45,000 seats in 1989.

Newspapers and Books. In 1989 there were 3 daily and 425 other newspapers and 250 periodicals. 1,932 book titles were published in a total of 7·09m. copies.

JUSTICE, RELIGION, EDUCATION AND WELFARE

Justice. There are 8 courts of first instance, 4 higher courts and a supreme court.

Education. In 1988–89 there were 830 primary schools with 229,887 pupils and 12,491 teachers and 147 secondary schools with 85,263 pupils and 6,643 teachers. In 1989–90 there were 27 institutions of higher education with 34,208 students and 2,569 academic staff.

Social Security. There were 212,855 age and 80,686 disability pensioners in 1989. Benefits totalled 3,618m. dinars.

SOLOMON
ISLANDS

Capital: Honiara
Population: 325,600 (1991)
GNP per capita: US$570 (1989)

HISTORY. The Solomon Islands were discovered in 1568 by Alvaro de Mendana, on a voyage of discovery from Peru; 200 years passed before European contact was again made with the Solomons. The southern Solomon Islands were placed under British protection in 1893; the eastern and southern outliers were added in 1898 and 1899. Santa Isabel and the other islands to the north were ceded by Germany in 1900. Full internal self-government was achieved on 2 Jan. 1976 and independence on 7 July 1978.

AREA AND POPULATION. The Solomon Islands lie within the area 5° to 12° 30' S. lat. and 155° 30' to 169° 45' E. long. The group includes the main islands of Guadalcanal, Malaita, New Georgia, San Cristobal (now Makira), Santa Isabel and Choiseul; the smaller Florida and Russell groups; the Shortland, Mono (or Treasury), Vella La Vella, Kolombangara, Ranongga, Gizo and Rendova Islands; to the east, Santa Cruz, Tikopia, the Reef and Duff groups; Rennell and Bellona in the south; Ontong Java or Lord Howe to the north; and innumerable smaller islands. The land area of the Solomons is estimated at 10,640 sq. miles (27,556 sq. km). The larger islands are mountainous and forest clad, with flood-prone rivers of considerable energy potential. Guadalcanal has the largest land area and the greatest amount of flat coastal plain.

Population of the Solomon Islands was (census, 1986) 285,796. Growth rate (1989) 3·5%.

The islands are administratively divided into 7 provinces.

The areas and populations of the 7 provinces and the Capital Territory are:

Province	Sq.km	Census 1986	Estimate 1990	Capital
Western	9,312	55,250	73,100	Gizo
Isabel	4,136	14,616	15,300	Buala
Central	1,286	18,457	19,600	Tulagi
Capital Territory	22	30,413	34,900	...
Guadalcanal	5,336	49,831	50,400	Honiara
Malaita	4,225	80,032	85,900	Auki
Makira and Ulawa	3,188	21,796	22,300	Kirakira
Temotu	895	14,781	16,800	Lata (Santa Cruz)

The capital, Honiara, on Guadalcanal, is the largest urban area, with an estimated population in 1989 of 33,749.

English is the official language. Melanesian languages are spoken by 85% of the population, Papuan languages by 9% and Polynesian languages by 4%.

CLIMATE. An equatorial climate with only small seasonal variations. South-east winds cause cooler conditions from April to Nov., but north-west winds for the rest of the year bring higher temperatures and greater rainfall, with annual totals ranging between 80" (2,000 mm) and 120" (3,000 mm).

CONSTITUTION AND GOVERNMENT. The Solomon Islands is a constitutional monarchy with the British Sovereign (represented locally by a Governor-General, who must be a Solomon Island citizen) as Head of State. Legislative power is vested in the single-chamber National Parliament composed of 36 members, elected by universal adult suffrage for four years. Executive authority is effectively held by the Cabinet, led by the Prime Minister.

At the elections of 22 Feb. 1989, the People's Alliance Party gained 21 seats, the United Party 3, the National Front for Progress 3 and the Liberation Party 3; 6 seats went to independents.

The Governor-General is appointed for up to five years, on the advice of Parliament, and acts in almost all matters on the advice of the Cabinet. The Prime Minister is elected by and from members of Parliament. Other Ministers are appointed by the Governor-General on the Prime Minister's recommendation, from members of Parliament. The Cabinet is responsible to Parliament. Emphasis is laid on the devolution of power to provincial governments, and traditional chiefs and leaders have a special role within the arrangement.

Governor General: Sir George Lepping, GCMG, MBE.

In Feb. 1992 the Government comprised:

Prime Minister: Solomon Mamaloni.

Deputy Prime Minister and Minister for Home Affairs: Sir Baddeley Devesi, GCMG, GCVO. *Foreign Affairs and Trade Relations:* Sir Peter Keniloria, KBE. *Finance and Economic Planning:* Christopher Abe. *Commerce and Primary Industry:* Michael Maina. *Provincial Government:* Allen Qurusu. *Police and Justice:* Albert Laore. *Education and Human Resource Development:* S. Alasia. *Posts and Communications:* Ben Gale. *Health:* Nathaniel Supa. *Natural Resources:* Job Dudley Tansinga. *Agriculture and Lands:* G. Luialamo. *Tourism and Aviation:* Victor Ngele. *Housing and Government Services:* Allen Kemakeza. *Transport, Works and Utilities:* A. Maetia.

National flag: Divided blue over green by a diagonal yellow band, and in the canton 5 white stars.

DEFENCE. The marine wing of the police operates 3 inshore patrol craft and 3 small landing craft with about 50 personnel in 1991.

INTERNATIONAL RELATIONS

Membership. The Solomon Islands is a member of the UN, the Commonwealth, South Pacific Forum and is an ACP state of the EEC.

ECONOMY

Policy. The Government's Programme of Action for 1990–94 aims for economic and constitutional reforms, emphasizing the needs of national resource management, health and education.

Budget. The budget for 1989 envisaged expenditure of SI$115m. and revenue of SI$110·5m.

Currency. The *Solomon Island dollar* (SBD) was introduced in 1977. In March 1992, US$1 = 2·85 *dollars*; £1 = 5·00 *dollars*.

Banking and Finance. In 1988 there were 3 commercial banks: Australia and New Zealand Banking Group, National Bank of Solomon Islands and Westpac Banking Corporation.

Weights and Measures. The metric system is in force.

ENERGY AND NATURAL RESOURCES

Electricity. Production (1987) 24,205,117 kwh. Supply 240 volts; 50 Hz.

Minerals. There are reserves of bauxite and phosphate, and there is a small industry extracting gold (36,241 grams refined, in 1989) and silver (7,414) by panning.

Agriculture. Land is held either as customary land (88% of holdings) or registered land. Customary land rights depend on clan membership or kinship. Only Solomon Islanders own customary land; only Islanders or government members may hold perpetual estates of registered land. Coconuts, cocoa, rice and other minor crops are grown. Main food crops: coconut, cassava, sweet potato, yam, taro and banana.

Solomon Islands Plantations Ltd has a plantation of 5,519 ha of oil-palm. Production of copra (1989), 27,228 tonnes; palm oil, 13,591; cocoa, 2,640; palm kernels, 3,310. Rice production (1988): 6,000 tonnes.
    Livestock (1990): Cattle, 13,000; pigs, 53,000.

Forestry. Forests cover about 2·4m. ha, with (1987) an estimated 10·4m. cu. metres of commercial timber. Production (1989) of logs, 286,760 cu. metres; sawn timber, 4,660 cu. metres.

Fisheries. Catch of tuna (1987) 32,210 tonnes.

INDUSTRY. Industries include palm oil milling, rice milling, fish canning, fish freezing, saw milling, food, tobacco and soft drinks. Other products include wood and rattan furniture, fibreglass articles, boats, clothing and spices.

FOREIGN ECONOMIC RELATIONS. The Government's Programme of Action for 1990–94 aims to encourage foreign investment, particularly in manufacturing and tourism.

Commerce. Total exports (1988) SI$170·6m. The main imports (1988, in SI$1m.) were machinery and transport equipment, 62; minerals, fuels and lubricants, 24·7; manufactured goods, 40·2; food, 34·8. Total imports SI$203·3m. Main exports included fish products, 78·4; wood products, 39·8; cocoa beans, 7·4; copra, 15·4; palm oil products, 14. In 1988 imports were mainly from Australia (45·5%), Japan (16·2%), New Zealand (8·2%), Singapore (5·4%), the UK (5·3%) and the USA (5%). Value of exports (in SI$m.) to main destinations in 1988: Japan (58·8%), Thailand (24·8%), UK (24·7%), USA (12·7%), Australia (8%) and South Korea (5·4%). Imports and exports by region, 1988: South Asia, 31·3% and 56·6%; Oceania, 56·9% and 17·4%; EEC, 7·7% and 21·1%.
    Total trade between Solomon Islands and UK (British Department of Trade returns, in £1,000 sterling):

	1988	1989	1990	1991
Imports to UK	5,153	6,404	6,903	6,846
Exports and re-exports from UK	2,576	1,088	523	1,170

Tourism. In 1988, there were 10,679 visitors of whom 50·3% were tourists.

COMMUNICATIONS

Roads. In 1987 there were 1,300 km of motorable roads of which 100 km of bitumen-topped roads; the rest were coral or gravel. In 1986 there were 3,629 vehicles, of which about 1,827 were commercial vehicles.

Civil Aviation. (1988) An international airport 13 km from Honiara is served by Air Nauru, Air Niugini, Air Pacific and Solomon Islands Airline. There are 27 airfields. Solomon Islands Airline also provides inter-island transport and scheduled flights to Kieta in Papua New Guinea.

Shipping. There are international ports at Honiara, and Yandina in the Russell group. Shipping services are maintained with Australia, New Zealand, UK and Asia. Honiara port handled about 261 overseas vessels in 1989. In 1989 the merchant marine comprised 234 vessels of 1,579 GRT.

Telecommunications. In addition to the general post office, there are 9 post offices, 4 sub post offices and 95 Postal Agencies. Number of telephones (1988), 2,500. Solomon Islands Broadcasting Corporation transmits from Honiara, Gizo and Lata. In 1991 there were about 70,000 radio receivers.

Newspapers. In 1988 there were 3 weekly newspapers.

JUSTICE, RELIGION, EDUCATION AND WELFARE

Justice. Civil and criminal jurisdiction is exercised by the High Court of Solomon Islands, constituted 1975. A Solomon Islands Court of Appeal was established in 1982. Jurisdiction is based on the principles of English law (as applying on 1 Jan.

1981). Magistrates' courts can try civil cases on claims not exceeding $2,000, and criminal cases with penalties not exceeding 14 years' imprisonment. Certain crimes, such as burglary and arson, where the maximum sentence is for life, may also be tried by magistrates. There are also local courts, which decide matters concerning customary titles to land; decisions may be put to the Customary Land Appeal Court. There is no capital punishment.

Religion. At the 1986 census, 33·9% of the population were Anglican, 19·2% Roman Catholic, 17·6% South Sea Evangelical and 23·5% other Protestant.

Education. In 1989 there were 51,436 pupils and 2,248 teachers in 468 primary schools, and 5,556 pupils and 307 teachers in 12 provincial and 8 national secondary schools.

Training of teachers and trade and vocational training is carried out at the college of Higher Education. There were 459 students on overseas scholarships in 1989.

Health. In 1988 there were 8 hospitals, 31 doctors, 464 registered nurses and 283 nursing aides.

DIPLOMATIC REPRESENTATIVES

Of the Solomon Islands in Great Britain (resides in Honiara).
High Commissioner: Wilson Ifunaoa (accredited 12 Feb. 1987).

Of Great Britain in the Solomon Islands (Soltel House, Mendana Ave., Honiara)
High Commissioner: Raymond Jones, OBE.

Of the USA in the Solomon Islands
Ambassador: Robert W. Farrand (resides in Port Moresby).

Of the Solomon Islands in the USA and to the United Nations
Ambassador: Francis Bugotu.

Further Reading

Solomon Islands Hand Book 1983. Government Information Service, Honiara, 1983
Bennett, J. A., *Wealth of the Solomons: A History of a Pacific Archipelago, 1800–1978.* Univ. of Hawaii Press, 1987
Kent, J., *The Solomon Islands.* Newton Abbot, 1972

SOMALIA

Jamhuriyadda
Dimugradiga Somaliya

(Somali Democratic Republic)

Capital: Mogadishu
Population: 7·56m. (1990)
GNP per capita: US$170 (1989)

HISTORY. The Somali Republic came into being on 1 July 1960 as a result of the merger of the British Somaliland Protectorate, which became independent on 26 June 1960, and the Italian Trusteeship Territory of Somalia. On 21 Oct. 1969 Maj.-Gen. Mohammed Siyad Barre took power in a coup and formed a Supreme Revolutionary Council to administer the country, which was renamed the Somali Democratic Republic. After 12 years of civil war involving 5 factions, prominent amongst them the United Somali Congress (USC), the Somali National Movement (SNM) and the Somali Patriotic Movement (SPM), rebel forces had fought their way into Mogadishu by the end of 1990. Mohamed Siyad Barre fled on 27 Jan. 1991. Ali Mahdi Muhammad (USC) became president in Aug. 1991 but interfactional fighting continued. A UN-sponsored truce was signed in March 1992.

The principal insurgent group in the north of the country, the SNM, declared the secession of an independent 'Somaliland Republic' on 17 May 1991, based on the territory of the former British protectorate, with a capital at Hargeisa. Its president is Abduraham Ahmed Ali. The Somalian government rejected the secession.

AREA AND POPULATION. Somalia is bounded north by the Gulf of Aden, east and south by the Indian ocean, and west by Kenya, Ethiopia and Djibouti. Total area 637,657 sq. km (246,201 sq. miles). Census population (1975) 3,253,024 of whom 15% urban. Estimate, 1990, 7·56m. (3·95m. female; 2·75m. urban). 50% of the population is nomadic. Density, 11·8 per sq. km. Vital statistics (rates per 1,000), 1990: Birth, 50·8; death, 20·2; infant mortality, 132; growth, 10·1. Life expectancy in 1989, 48 years.

The country is administratively divided into 18 regions (with chief cities): Awdal (Saylac), Bakol (Xuddur), Bay (Baydhabo), Benadir (Mogadishu), East (Boosaso), Galgudug (Duusa Marreeb), Gedo (Garbaharrey), Hiran (Beledweyne), Central Juba (Jilib), Lower Juba (Kismaayo), Mudug (Gaalkacyo), Nogal (Gaarowe), North-West (Hargeysa), Sanaag (Ceerigabo), Central Shabele (Jawhar), Lower Shabele (Marka), Sol (Las Anod), Togder (Burao). The capital is Mogadishu (1987 population, 1m.). Other large towns are Hargeysa (0·4m.), Kismayo (0·2m.), Marka (0·1m.) and Berbera.

CLIMATE. Much of the country is arid, though rainfall is more adequate towards the south. Temperatures are very high on the northern coasts. Mogadishu. Jan. 79°F (26·1°C), July 78°F (25·6°C). Annual rainfall 17" (429 mm). Berbera. Jan. 76°F (24·4°C), July 97°F (36·1°C). Annual rainfall 2" (51 mm).

CONSTITUTION AND GOVERNMENT. The Constitution came into force in 1984. The sole legal Party was the Somali Revolutionary Socialist Party (SRSP). The Executive President was elected for a 7-year term by direct popular vote. The People's Assembly consisted of 171 members elected for a 5-year term from a single list of 171 SRSP candidates.

Following the deposition of President Barre, Ali Mahdi Muhammad (USC) was sworn in as *President* for a 2-year term in Aug. 1991.

A government was formed in Oct. 1991.

National flag: Light blue with a white star in the centre.

The national language is Somali. Arabic is also an official language and English and Italian are extensively spoken.

Local Government. The 18 regions are sub-divided into 84 districts.

DEFENCE. The breakdown of government following the 1991 revolution makes current estimates impossible. The situation obtaining in 1990 is outlined below.

Army. The Army consisted of 4 tank, 45 mechanized and infantry, 4 commando and 1 surface-to-air missile, 3 field artillery brigades. Equipment included 140 T-34/-54/-55, 123 M-47 and 30 Centurion main battle tanks. Strength (1990) 61,300. There were additional paramilitary forces: Police (8,000), Border Guards (1,500) and People's Militia (20,000).

Navy. The flotilla included 2 fast missile craft, 4 fast torpedo boats, 2 inshore patrol craft, 1 medium landing ship and 4 minor landing craft (all former Soviet naval units). Personnel totalled 2,000 in 1990. Bases were at Mogadishu, Berbera and Kisimayu.

Air Force. Formed with a nucleus of aircraft taken over from the former Italian Air Corps of Somalia, in 1960, the Air Corps was built up with Soviet aid. Equipment included 6 MiG-21 and 20 F-6 (Chinese-built MiG-19) supersonic fighters, 8 Hunter fighter-bombers (including 1 trainer), about 8 MiG-17 jet fighters and 2 MiG-15UTI two-seat advanced trainers, and small transport, helicopter and training units. Support equipment included 2 Aeritalia G222, 6 Aviocar and 2 An-26 twin-turboprop transports, 5 SIAI-Marchetti SF.260W armed trainers and 4 Agusta-Bell 212 helicopters from Italy, as well as 3 Islander and 2 P-166 light transports. Serviceability of most aircraft was reported to be low. Personnel (1990) 2,500.

INTERNATIONAL RELATIONS

Membership. Somalia is a member of the UN, OAU, the Arab League, the Islamic League and is an ACP state of the EEC.

ECONOMY

Budget. Budget for 1989: Revenue, Som.Sh. 37,020m.; expenditure, Som.Sh. 26,830m.

Currency. The unit of currency is the *Somali shilling* (SOS) of 100 *cents*. There are notes of 5, 10, 20 and 100 shillings and coins of 1, 5, 10, 50 cents and 1 shilling. Som.Sh.34,399m. were in circulation in 1989. In March 1992 £1 = 4,595·50 Som.Sh.; US$1 = 2,617·77 Som.Sh.

Banking. The bank of issue is the Central Bank of Somalia (founded in 1960 as the Somali National Bank). All foreign banks were nationalized in May 1970, and the Commercial and Savings Bank of Somalia and the Somali Development Bank, both state-owned, are the only other banks.

Weights and Measures. The metric system is in use.

ENERGY AND NATURAL RESOURCES

Electricity. Installed capacity, 1987, 145·6m. kw. Production (1986) was 137m. kwh. Supply 220 volts; 50 Hz.

Minerals. Several firms hold exploration and drilling licences for oil. Uranium is found in the Juba area. 30,000 tonnes of salt were produced in 1987.

Agriculture. Somalia is essentially a pastoral country, and about 80% of the inhabitants depend on livestock-rearing (cattle, sheep, goats and camels). Agricultural area and permanent cropland in 1987 was 0·93m. ha. Estimated production, 1988 (in 1,000 tonnes): Sugar-cane, 450; bananas, 120; maize, 260; sorghum, 220; grapefruit, 28; seed cotton, 6. Fresh fruit and oil seeds are grown in increasing quantities.

Livestock (1988): 20m. goats; 13·5m. sheep; 6·68m. camels; 5m. cattle; 1,000 horses, 25,000 asses and 23,000 mules.

Forestry. Forest area was 8·8m. ha in 1987. Production was 4·63m. cu. metres of wood, mainly for fuel.

Fisheries. In 1988 the fishing fleet comprised 28 vessels totalling 5,188 DWT. 20,500 tonnes were caught in 1988.

INDUSTRY. A few small industries existed in 1986 including sugar refining, food processing, textile and petroleum refining. Production (1988): Textiles, 6·2m. yards; tinned meat and fish, 21·5m. tins.

Labour. 2,143,000 persons (828,000 females) were employed in 1990. 167,000 were between 10 and 15 years of age. 34·6% were labourers, 21·4% worked in trade and 14·3% in services.

FOREIGN ECONOMIC RELATIONS. Foreign debt was US$1,750m. in 1988.

Commerce. The chief exports are fresh fruit, livestock, hides and skins. Exports in 1988 totalled US$147m.; imports, US$310m.

Main export markets in 1988 (trade in US$1m.): Saudi Arabia (65·5); Italy (37·3); Yemen Arab Republic (12·1). Main import suppliers: Italy (83·9); USA (33); Federal Republic of Germany (27·1).

Total trade between the Somali Republic and UK (British Department of Trade returns, in £1,000 sterling):

	1987	1988	1989	1990	1991
Imports to UK	825	1,151	508	510	42
Exports and re-exports from UK	11,417	10,379	10,508	11,865	3,152

COMMUNICATIONS

Roads. Somalia has no developed transport system. Internal freight and passenger transport is almost entirely by means of road haulage. In 1988 there were 22,281 km of roads (3,010 km were tarmacadamed).

Civil Aviation. There is a commercial national airline, Somali Airlines, which transported 105,000 passengers in 1988. Mogadishu airport was used by Alitalia, Alyemda, Air Tanzania, PIA, Saudi Airways and Kenya Airways.

Shipping. There are deep-water harbours at Kismayo, Berbera, Marka and Mogadishu. The merchant fleet (1988) amounted to 28 vessels of 12,800 gross tons.

Telecommunications. Number of telephones (1987), about 7,000. The state radio stations transmit in Somali, Arabic, English and Italian from Mogadishu, and Hargeisa. There were 362,000 radios and 3,000 TV sets in 1988.

JUSTICE, RELIGION, EDUCATION AND WELFARE

Justice. There are 84 district courts, each with a civil and a criminal section. There are 8 regional courts and 2 Courts of Appeal (at Mogadishu and Hargeysa), each with a general section and an assize section. The Supreme Court is in Mogadishu.

Religion. The population is almost entirely Sunni Moslems.

Education. The nomadic life of a large percentage of the population inhibits education progress. In 1985 adult literacy was only 11·6%. In 1985 there were 194,335 pupils and 9,676 teachers in primary schools, there were 37,181 pupils and 2,320 teachers in secondary schools, and in 1984 613 students with 30 teachers at teacher-training establishments. The National University of Somalia in Mogadishu (founded 1959) had 15,562 students in 1986.

Health. In 1986 there were 88 hospitals, 358 doctors, 113 pharmacists, 2 dentists, 556 midwives and 1,834 nursing personnel.

DIPLOMATIC REPRESENTATIVES

Of Somalia in Great Britain (60 Portland Pl., London, W1N 3DG)
Ambassador: Ali Hassan Ali.

Of Great Britain in Somalia (Waddada Xasan Geedd Abtoow 7/8, Mogadishu)
Staff temporarily withdrawn.

Of Somalia in the USA (600 New Hampshire Ave., NW, Washington, D.C., 20037)
Ambassador: Abdikarim Ali Omar.

Of USA in Somalia (Corso Primo Luglio, Mogadishu)
Ambassador: (Vacant).

Of Somalia to the United Nations
Ambassador: Abdillahi Said Osman.

Further Reading

DeLancey, M. W., *et al. Somalia*. [Bibliography] Oxford and Santa Barbara, 1988
Legum, C. and Lee, B., *Conflict in the Horn of Africa*. London, 1977

National statistical office: Central Statistical Department, State Planning Commission, Mogadishu.

SOUTH AFRICA

Capital: Pretoria
Population: 33·14m. (1991)
GNP per capita: US$2,460 (1990)

Republiek van Suid-Afrika—
Republic of South Africa

HISTORY. The Union of South Africa was formed in 1910 and comprised the former self-governing British colonies of the Cape of Good Hope, Natal, the Transvaal and the Orange Free State. The Union remained a member of the British Commonwealth until it became a republic on 31 May 1961.

By 1989 the restrictions of apartheid (racial segregation) began to be removed, and the government announced its willingness to consider the extension of Black South Africans' political rights. In Feb. 1990 a 30-year ban on the African National Congress (ANC) was lifted and its deputy president and *de facto* leader, Nelson Mandela, released from prison. He was elected president of the ANC unopposed in July 1991.

The State of Emergency imposed in June 1986 was lifted in June 1990 (Oct. in Natal). The Separate Amenities Act racially segregating public facilities was repealed in Oct. 1990.

Sporadic factional violence continued into 1992 between supporters of the ANC and the Zulu Inkatha Party despite a joint plea to end the conflict by Nelson Mandela and the Inkatha leader Chief Mangosuthu Buthelezi.

In June 1991 the House of Assembly repealed the Group Areas Act of 1966, the Land Acts of 1916 and 1936 and the Population Registration Act of 1950, thus ending residential apartheid and racial restrictions on land ownership.

An accord to restrain violence was signed in Sept. 1991 by the government, ANC and Inkatha Party. The accord establishes codes of conduct for the police and political parties, a peace committee deploying monitoring and enforcement mechanisms, a statutory commission to investigate violence and special courts to deal with cases of violence.

A Convention for a Democratic South Africa (Codesa) began talks on a new constitution on 20 Dec. 1991 to which 19 delegates from all ethnic groups were invited, and in March 1992 this agreed to form an interim multi-racial cabinet pending the introduction of a new constitution. On 17 March a Whites-only referendum was in favour of constitutional reforms to render all South Africans of whatever race equal before the law.

AREA AND POPULATION. South Africa is bounded in the north by Namibia, Botswana and Zimbabwe, north-east by Mozambique and Swaziland, east by the Indian ocean, south and west by the South Atlantic. Lesotho forms an enclave between the Orange Free State and Natal. Area without the 'TBVC' countries (Transkei, Bophuthatswana, Venda and Ciskei) was (1989) 347,860 sq. miles (1,127,200 sq. km), divided between the provinces as follows: Cape Province, 198,760 (644,060); Natal, 28,310 (91,740); Transvaal, 81,930 (265,470); Orange Free State, 38,860 (125,930).

On 25 Dec. 1947 the Union formally took possession of Prince Edward Island and, on 30 Dec., of Marion Island, about 1,200 miles south-east of Cape Town.

The census taken in 1904 in each of the 4 colonies was the first simultaneous census taken in South Africa. In 1911 the first Union census was taken.

| | All races | | Non-Whites | Whites | | Non-whites | |
	Total	Whites	Whites	Males	Females	Males	Females
1904	5,174,827	1,117,234	4,057,593	635,317	481,917	2,046,370	2,011,223
1911	5,972,757	1,276,319	4,696,438	685,206	591,113	2,383,879	2,312,559
1921	6,927,403	1,521,343	5,406,060	783,006	738,337	2,753,188	2,652,872
1936	9,587,863	2,003,334	7,584,529	1,017,557	985,777	3,818,211	3,766,318
1946	11,415,925	2,372,044	9,043,881	1,194,201	1,177,843	4,610,862	4,433,019

	All races			Whites		Non-whites	
	Total	Whites	Non-Whites	Males	Females	Males	Females
1951	12,671,452	2,641,689	10,029,763	1,322,754	1,318,935	5,109,331	4,920,432
1960	15,994,181	3,080,159	12,914,022	1,534,923	1,545,236	6,504,317	6,409,705
1970[1]	18,319,437	3,759,065	14,560,372	1,875,248	1,883,817	7,378,396	7,181,976
1980[1]	20,562,781	4,221,120	16,341,661	2,083,883	2,137,237	8,093,138	8,248,523
1985[1]	23,385,645	4,568,739	18,816,906	2,252,201	2,316,538	9,293,081	9,523,825
1992[1,2]	26,504,191	4,526,690	21,977,501	2,218,751	2,307,939	10,710,691	11,266,810

[1] Excluding the TBVC countries.   [2] Preliminary figures.

Official population estimates (without the TBVC countries), 30 June 1990, (in 1,000; females in brackets): Whites, 5,018 (2,528); Coloureds, 3,214 (1,634); Asians, 956 (481); Blacks, 21,609 (10,373). Population of the Black nations (1985): Zulu, 5,337,334; North Sotho (Sepedi), 2,306,235; Xhosa, 2,080,082; South Sotho (Seshoeshoe), 1,579,570; Tswana, 1,147,932; Shangaan/Tsonga, 1,024,594; Swazi, 841,071; others, 846,022. Population, (1985) of the self-governing territories: Kwa Zulu, 3,738,334; Gazankulu, 496,200; Lebowa, 1,833,144; Qwaqwa, 180,924; Ka Ngwane, 391,205; Kwa Ndebele, 235,511. These places are included in the land area figures for the provinces where they lie, but their inhabitants are not included in the provincial population figures. Annual growth rate 1980–90, 2·07% (Black, 2·39%; Coloured, 1·78%; Asian, 1·72%; White, 1·05%). Urban population was 62% in 1991.

Vital statistics for calendar years:

	Whites			Immi-		Asians and Coloureds		
	Births	Deaths	Marriages	grants	Emigrants	Births	Deaths	Marriages
1988	69,189	40,194	41,219	10,400	7,767	97,277	32,535	21,879
1989	70,964	35,060	44,124	11,270	4,911	103,128	29,651	24,648
1990	69,649	33,519	45,660	14,499	4,722	97,640	29,079	25,641

Marriages and divorces in 1990: Whites, 45,660 and 20,031; Coloureds, 18,544 and 4,217; Asians, 7,097 and 1,421; Mixed, 3,212 and 177.

Births in 1990: Whites, 69,649 (females, 33,937); Coloureds, 77,445 (38,417); Asians, 20,195 (9,977).

Deaths in 1990: Whites, 33,519 (females, 15,573); Coloureds, 24,867 (10,819); Asians, 4,212 (1,683). Infant deaths (1989): Whites, 611; Coloureds, 2,899; Asians, 252.

Of the 14,499 immigrants in 1990, 7,560 were from Europe (of whom 3,395, UK); 3,084 from Africa (of whom 1,673, Zimbabwe); 839 from the Americas and 2,837 from Asia: Of the 4,722 emigrants 2,371 went to Europe (of whom 1,804 to UK); 1,292 to Australia; 269 to Africa.

The registration of Black essential data is compulsory but despite serious efforts on the part of the registering authorities complete vital statistics are not yet available for this population group.

Urban areas, according to the 1985 census:

Urban Area	Total	White	Coloured	Asian	Black
Johannesburg/Randburg	1,609,408	515,670	121,860	57,775	914,103
Cape Peninsula	1,911,521	542,705	1,068,921	18,389	281,506
Durban/Pinetown/Inanda	982,075	307,930	59,925	490,857	123,363
East Rand	1,038,108	399,445	33,390	17,472	587,801
Pretoria/Wonderboom/ Soshanguve	822,925	432,267	21,215	18,017	351,426
Port Elizabeth/Uitenhage	651,993	173,273	172,186	7,346	299,188
West Rand	647,334	233,460	19,206	7,631	387,037
Vanderbijlpark/Vereeniging/ Sasolburg	540,142	167,905	15,321	4,529	352,387
Bloemfontein	232,984	95,271	20,152	35	117,526
Pietermaritzburg	192,417	60,161	13,771	57,006	61,479
Free State Goldfields	320,319	69,387	6,246	2	244,184
Kimberley	149,667	33,782	50,214	1,202	64,469
East London/King William's Town	193,819	77,827	29,008	2,921	84,063

In 1986 (estimate), of the 4·8m. Whites Afrikaans was spoken by 2·7m., English by 1·75m. The remainder included Portuguese, 70,000; German, 43,000; Greek, 20,000; Italian, 15,000; Dutch, 14,000. Nguni languages (mainly Zulu, Xhosa, Swazi and South Ndebele) are spoken by about 13·6m.; Sotho languages (Southern, Northern or Sepedi and Western or Tswana) by about 8m.; Tsonga languages by about 1·2m. and Venda by 550,000. Fanakilo is a pidgin language developed mainly on the mines.

Afrikaans and English are the official languages.

CLIMATE. The climate is healthy and invigorating, with abundant sunshine and relatively low rainfall. The factors controlling this include the latitudinal position, the oceanic location of much of the country, and the existence of high plateaus. The south-west has a Mediterranean climate, with rain mainly in winter, but most of the country has a summer maximum, though quantities show a clear decrease from east to west. Temperatures are remarkably uniform over the whole country. Pretoria. Jan. 72·5°F (22·5°C), July 52·3°F (11·3°C). Annual rainfall 29·5" (750 mm). Bloemfontein. Jan. 73°F (22·8°C), July 47°F (8·3°C). Annual rainfall 23" (564 mm). Cape Town. Jan. 69°F (20·6°C), July 54°F (12·2°C). Annual rainfall 20" (508 mm). Durban. Jan. 75°F (23·9°C), July 62°F (16·7°C). Annual rainfall 40" (1,008 mm). Johannesburg. Jan. 68°F (20°C), July 51°F (10·6°C). Annual rainfall 28" (709 mm).

CONSTITUTION AND GOVERNMENT. At the Whites-only referendum on 17 March 1992 on the granting of constitutional equality to all races turn-out was 85·6%. 1,924,186 (68·7%) votes were in favour; 875,619 against.

The constitution of Sept. 1984 had been approved by a White referendum. It provides for a tricameral parliament: The House of *Assembly* with 178 members of whom 166 are directly elected, 4 nominated by the State President and 8 indirectly elected by the elected members; the House of *Representatives* with 85 members of whom 80 are directly elected by Coloured voters; the House of *Delegates* with 45 members of whom 40 are directly elected by Indian voters. The term for all members is 5 years.

These Houses choose (from their majority parties) respectively 50 White, 25 Coloured and 13 Indian members of an electoral college which elects an executive President. The President initiates legislation and resolves disputes between Houses. He is helped by a 60-member President's Council: 20 members are elected by the House of Assembly, 10 by the House of Representatives and 5 by the House of Delegates; 15 are MPs nominated by himself and 10 are MPs nominated by Opposition parties.

The President appoints a Ministers' Council for each House, choosing 5 members from the majority party. The Councils handle the affairs of their own population group and administer the departments established for that group. The President also appoints a Cabinet.

Each House legislates on its own community affairs; the three Houses have co-responsibility for national affairs. The State President, on the Cabinet's advice, decides whether a matter is a community or a national affair. Pretoria is the seat of government, and Cape Town is the seat of legislature.

At the House of Assembly elections of 6 Sept. 1989, the Nationalist Party won 93 seats; the Conservative Party, 39; and the Democratic Party (formed from a merger of the Progressive Federal Party, the New Republic Party and Independents), 33.

The state of the parties in the 3 Houses in April 1992 was: *Assembly*, 103 National Party, 40 Conservative Party, 33 Democratic Party, 2 vacant; *Representatives*, 65 Labour Party, 10 independents, 10 others; *Delegates*, 24 Solidarity, 7 National People's Party, 5 independents, 3 Democratic Party, 6 others.

President: Frederik Willem de Klerk (sworn in, 20 Sept. 1989).

The Cabinet in March 1992 was in order of seniority as follows:

Foreign Affairs: R. F. 'Pik' Botha. *Constitutional Development and Planning and National Education:* Gerrit Viljoen. *Defence:* Roelf Meyer. *Mineral and Energy*

Affairs and Public Enterpises: Dawie de Villiers. *Justice:* Kobie Coetsee. *Finance:* Barend du Plessis. *Manpower:* Eli Louw. *Law and Order:* Hernus Kriel. *Environment and Water:* Gert Kotze. *Education and Development Aid:* Vacant. *Home Affairs:* Gene Louw. *Trade, Industry and Economic Co-ordination:* Derek Keys. *Transport and Public Works and Land Affairs:* George Bartlett. *Planning and Provincial Affairs:* Vacant. *National Health and Population Development:* Rina Venter. *Agriculture:* Jacob de Villers. *Tourism:* Dr G. Marais.

The Chairman of the President's Council is Gen. Magnus Malan.

The Prime Minister receives an annual salary of R43,000 and a reimbursive allowance of R20,000; a member of the Cabinet an annual salary of R23,500 and a reimbursive allowance of R6,500; and a Deputy Minister an annual salary of R19,000 and a reimbursive allowance of R6,500.

The English and Afrikaans languages are both official, subject to amendments carried by a two-thirds majority in joint session of both Houses of Parliament.

National flag: Three horizontal stripes of orange, white, blue, with the flags of the Orange Free State and the Transvaal, and the Union Jack side by side in the centre.

National anthem: The Call of South Africa/Die Stem van Suid-Afrika (words by C. J. Langenhoven, 1918; tune by M. L. de Villiers, 1921).

Provincial Administration. In each of the 4 provinces there is an Administrator appointed by the State President-in-Council for 5 years. Until 1986 there were provincial councils. Since 1 July 1986, when the provisions of the Provincial Government Act, 1986, came into operation, the provincial councils ceased to exist. From this date, the executive committees of the provinces, usually elected from among the ranks of the provincial councillors, were replaced by new executive authorities appointed by the State President and headed by an administrator. While the elected executives, from 1910 to 1986, always comprised White members only, Blacks, Coloured and Asians were included in the new executives.

Those matters previously managed by the provincial councils but designated 'own affairs' by the new constitution (such as education) are being passed to the appropriate Houses of Parliament. Responsibility for the remaining general affairs such as roads and hospitals have been transferred to the new provincial executive. The powers of section 15 which provides for the transfer of general affairs functions of central state departments to the administrators and their executives, were used to devolve the management of Blacks outside the self-governing territories from the Department of Constitutional Development and Planning which includes Black local government, Black community and township development and leasehold and freehold housing schemes.

Provincial Administrations were recently given greater powers and more responsibilities in a number of areas. These include housing and community development for Blacks; physical development planning, including guide plans for metropolitan development; environmental protection and conservation measures; health services, including hospitals where most general state hospitals for all population groups are now administered by the provincial governments.

The administrators and their executive committees govern by proclamation. These proclamations, which may repeal existing ordinances or regulate new matters transferred to the provinces, must first be published for public comment and thereafter approved by a joint committee of Parliament appointed for each province. Members of these committees represent all major political parties in all three Houses of Parliament and meet in the four provincial capitals to review the provincial budgets and other important provincial matters. During these meetings each of the administrators, their executive committees and senior staff are called to account for their estimates of expenditure by the joint committee of Parliament for the province concerned.

Overall responsibility for provincial affairs in Parliament and the Cabinet is vested in the Minister of Planning and Provincial Affairs and National Housing and of Local Government, who pilots provincial budgets through Parliament.

There are 10 self-governing territories of which 4 (the TBVC countries) are recognised by the South African government as independent: Transkei became independent on 26 Oct. 1976, Bophuthatswana on 6 Dec. 1977, Venda on 13 Sept. 1979 and Ciskei on 4 Dec. 1981.

There are 6 territories with a degree of self-government but still forming part of the Republic: Kwa Zulu, Gazankulu (Machangana-Tsonga people), Lebowa (North Sotho), Qwaqwa (South Sotho), Ka Ngwane (Swazi) and Kwa Ndebele (Southern Ndebele).

DEFENCE. The South African Defence Force comprises a Permanent Force, a Citizen Force and a Commando organization. The Permanent Force consists of professional soldiers, airmen and seamen who are responsible for the administration and training of the whole Defence Force in peace-time, but who are gradually absorbed into the Citizen Force in time of war. The Permanent Force and the Citizen Force consist of Army, Air Force and Naval components; the Commando organization is an army and air organization.

Every white male citizen between 18 and 65 is liable to undergo training and to render personal service in time of war. Conscription is for 12 months. Those between the ages of 16 and 25 are liable to undergo a compulsory course of peace training. Non-white ethnic groups may volunteer for service.

The Defence Force is administered by the Chief of the Defence Force, his advisers being the Chief of the Army, Chief of the Air Force and Chief of the Navy, Chief of Staff Operations, Chief of Staff Personnel, the Chief of Staff Management Services and the Surgeon-General.

Army. South Africa is divided into 13 territorial Commands. Within the various Commands are training units, of which members of the Permanent Force form the permanent staff. Courses of various types are held also at the S.A. Military College. The Army includes 1 armoured, 1 mechanized, 4 motorized and 1 parachute brigade; 1 special reconnaissance regiment and supporting artillery, engineer and signals units. Equipment includes some 250 Centurion/Olifant main battle tanks. Strength in 1992 was estimated at 18,900 regular personnel (12,000 white, 1,500 women) and 31,000 conscripts with an Active Reserve of 135,000. Paramilitary forces are Commandos (140,000) and 60,000 men and women of the South African Police with 37,000 reserves.

Navy. The Navy has its headquarters at Pretoria from where operational control is exercised directly. The navy includes 3 French-built diesel submarines, 9 fast missile armed patrol craft, 9 coastal minesweepers, 1 British-built survey ship, 1 fleet replenishment ships and a naval-manned Antarctic supply ship, the latter 3 all with helicopter facilities. There are additionally some 6 service craft. The Marine force has been disbanded.

Navy personnel in 1991 totalled 4,500 (900 conscripts) including marines.

Air Force. There is 1 fighter-bomber squadron with 30 Mirage F1-AZ ground attack aircraft; 2 fighter-bomber squadrons with Atlas Cheetahs (locally modified Mirage IIIs) including some equipped for reconnaissance; 1 squadron with Mirage F1-CZ interceptors; and 1 coastal patrol squadron with C-47s. Transport squadrons have 9 Transall C-160s, 7 C-130B Hercules, more than 20 C-47s, 7 C-54s, 4 Boeing 707s, 4 twin-jet HS.125s and 4 twin-turboprop Merlin IVA light transports. Four helicopter squadrons have more than 80 Alouette IIIs and 60 Pumas. T-6Gs are used for primary training, followed by advanced training on Impalas, Atlas Cheetahs and Mirage IIIEZ/DZ, weapons training on Impalas, and multi-engine/ crew training on C-47s. Built under licence in South Africa, about 150 two-seat Impala Mk. 1s have been followed by 75 single-seat Impala Mk. 2s, based on the Aermacchi MB.326M and 326K respectively. 2 squadrons operate AM.3C Bosbok liaison aircraft. South African industry is currently modernizing the Mirage combat aircraft (under the name 'Cheetah').

The Citizen Force has 3 squadrons of Impalas for counter-insurgency duties and AM.3C Bosbok liaison aircraft. CF personnel have additional functions in regular SAAF squadrons, notably those equipped with C-47 transports and coastal patrol aircraft. Total strength (1992) was about 10,000 (3,000 conscripts) and 150 combat aircraft.

INTERNATIONAL RELATIONS

Membership. South Africa is a member of the UN.

ECONOMY

Budget. Total revenue and expenditure of the central government's State Revenue Account in R1m.:

	1988–89	1989-90	1990-91	1991–92
Revenue	48,071	61,385	69,468	74,966
Expenditure	55,926	65,180	71,546	94,944

The main sources of State Revenue 1991–92 were income tax, R44,817m.; general sales tax, R19,444m.; excise duties, R3,555m.; customs duties, R2,635m. Main expenditure: Education, R14,946m.; defence, R9,756m.; economic services, R10,062m.; interest on public debt, R12,902m.; health, R9,175m.; other social, R7,957m.

From Sept. 1991 value-added tax at 12% replaced the 13% general sales tax. Corporate tax was reduced from 50% to 48%.

Public debt on 31 March 1989, R81,124m., of which R2,033m. was foreign debt; internal debt, R79,091m.

Currency. The unit of currency is the *rand* (ZAR) of 100 *cents*. There are notes of R5, R10, R20 and R50, and coins of 1c, 2c, 5c, 10c, 20c, 50c, R1, R2 and R5. Precious metal (Krugerrands and Protea) and commemorative coins are also struck. In March 1992 the financial exchange rates were, £1 = R6·46; US$1 = R3·68.

Banking and Finance. The central bank and bank of issue is the Central Reserve Bank (established 1920). Its *Governor* is Chris Stals. Total deposits, 31 Dec. 1991, R6,920m.; assets, R24,548m.

At 31 Dec. 1989 there were 11 commercial banks with total liabilities, R109,254m.; 26 general banks (formerly hire-purchase and savings banks), R33,332m.; 13 merchant banks, R7,734m.; 4 discount houses, R1,259m. The Land and Agricultural Bank had (31 Dec. 1989) R10,544m. total liabilities; Post Office Savings Bank deposits (31 Dec. 1989), R2,606m.

The Deposit-Taking Institutions Act of Feb. 1991 standardized the requirements of banks and building societies and brought capital adequacy requirements into line with the Basle Concordat.

Weights and Measures. The metric system is in force.

ENERGY AND NATURAL RESOURCES

Electricity. There are 21 thermal power stations, 3 hydro-electric and 3 gas-turbine. Production (1990) was 151,971m. kwh. Supply 220 and 240 volts; 50 Hz.

Oil. In 1987 reserves were found to be sufficient to yield 25,000 bbls of diesel and petrol a day for 30 years from gas produced at sea and converted on land.

Water. South Africa's average annual rainfall of about 497 mm is well below the world average. The unevenly distributed rainfall and high evaporation rate greatly affects the reliability and variability of river flow. Only about 62% or 33,000m. cu. metres of the mean annual run-off can be exploited economically. In addition about 5,400m. cu. metres may be obtainable from underground sources. Government activities are governed by the Water Act, 1956 (as amended). It is administered by the Department of Water Affairs and Forestry which manages water quantity and quality as well as the demand for the resource. A Water Research Commission was established in 1971 to co-ordinate and promote water research. Water availability is distributed poorly in relation to regions of economic growth and major inter-basin water transfer schemes are therefore a feature of the South African infra-structure. The latest such scheme under construction is the Lesotho Highlands Water Project which will divert the Orange River headwaters within Lesotho through tunnels into the Vaal River System which serves an area where about 60% of the industrial production of the country is generated. Lesotho is to receive royalties in exchange.

Minerals. Value of the main mineral production sales (in R1,000):

	1987	1988	1989	1990
Asbestos	88,410	108,281	166,336	168,929
Chrome ore	242,413	312,495	443,690	421,055
Coal	4,788,544	5,916,659	7,225,819	8,149,211
Copper	618,711	937,582	1,321,081	1,063,910
Fluorspar	63,438	83,737	112,228	92,959
Gold	17,492,636	19,686,986	19,284,204	18,993,616
Iron ore	472,559	564,583	833,452	1,076,512
Lime and limestone	272,538	320,419	370,999	422,674
Manganese	176,947	353,841	721,059	848,326
Silver	74,188	79,469	69,904	57,315

Total value of all minerals sold (1990), R37,125·7m.

Mineral production (tonnes) 1990: Coal, 174·8m.; iron ore, 30·3m.; manganese ore, 4·4m.; chromite, 4·1m.; asbestos, 145,791; copper, 178,704; lime and limestone, 19·9m.; fluorspar, 311,032; gold, 602,999 kg; silver, 161,003 kg; diamonds, 8,708,231 carats.

South Africa is a major producer of gold. Reserves were estimated at US$1,275m. in 1989.

At 31 Dec. 1990 the number of persons engaged in mining was 692,900. Of these, 483,737 were engaged in goldmining.

Agriculture. Much of the land suitable for mechanized farming has unreliable rainfall. Of the total area natural pasture occupies 58% (71·3m. ha); about 14m. ha are suitable for dry-land farming, of which 10·6m. are actually cultivated. There are some 65,000 farms.

In 1990, agriculture, forestry and fisheries contributed 5·1% to GDP.

Production (1990, in 1,000 tonnes): Maize, 9,442; sorghum, 368; wheat, 1,928; groundnuts, 80; sunflower seed, 610; sugar-cane, 18,636; oranges, 712; potatoes, 1,257; vegetables, 3,050; grapes, 1,549; apples, 442.

Livestock, in 1,000 (1990): 8,600 cattle, 29,274 sheep, 2,827 goats, 1,226 pigs.

The 1990 production of red meat was 894,000 tonnes, poultry meat 563,000 tonnes, wool, 105,000 tonnes, eggs, 175,000 tonnes, milk, 1·2m. tonnes.

Cotton-growing is now undertaken by many farmers, the plant being found a better drought resistant than either tobacco or maize. Viticulture and fruit-growing are important. Gross value of production (1989–90), R2,301m.

In 1989–90 the gross value of agricultural production (excluding self-governing territories) was R19,532m. (field crops, R6,936m.; livestock products, R8,651m.; horticultural products, R3,954m.).

Forestry. The commercial forests occupy about 1·26m. ha as well as 148,000 ha of protected indigenous trees. On 31 March 1990 there were 671,562 ha of pines, 538,485 ha of eucalypts, 115,198 ha of wattles and 7,991 ha of other hardwoods.

Production, 1989–90, of sawn timber, 1·66m. cu. metres (value R313m.); pulp, paper and paperboard, 1·39m. tonnes (R1,227m.).

Fisheries. In 1990 sea fisheries landed 524,000 tonnes, of which 259,000 tonnes were pelagic shoal fish (59% anchovy); the trawl industry caught 262,000 tonnes (57% hake). Total output, wholesale value, R1,176m. The fishing fleet consists of about 4,200 vessels. About 27,000 people are employed in the fishing industry and its ancillary activities. No seal pups and bulls were culled.

INDUSTRY. Net value of sales of the principal groups of industries (in R1m.) in 1990: Processed food, 23,400; beverages and tobacco, 8,921; vehicles, 15,313; basic metals, 18,775; chemicals and products, 30,126; non-electrical machinery, 7,099; electrical machinery, 8,093; fabricated metal products except machinery, 9,728; printing and publishing, 3,441; wood and cork products except furniture,

2,806; clothing, 3,945; paper and products, 8,226; textiles, 6,038; total net value including other groups, 166,388. Manufacturing industry contributed R52,289m. to GDP of R206,804m. in 1989. (25·6% of GDP at current prices in 1990).

Labour. In 1990 the workforce (excluding the TBVC countries) numbered (in 1,000; females in brackets): Whites, 2,049 (660); Coloureds, 1,241 (517); Asians, 350 (90); Blacks, 7,433 (2,411).

Industrial employment (except mining) at March 1991: Manufacturing employed 1,441,100 workers; construction, 396,300; trade and accommodation services, 746,500.

Average monthly earnings (excluding agriculture and mining) of white employees, 1990, R1,649; of black, R998.

Trade Unions. In 1990 there were 209 registered trade unions with an estimated total membership of 2,458,712. There were 30 White, 13 Coloured and Asian and 19 Black unions. 89 unions were mixed and 58 did not specify their composition.

The Labour Relations Act (as amended in 1991) provides for freedom of association to all workers irrespective of race. Unions are prohibited from granting financial or other assistance to political parties. Work-days lost through strikes: 1989, 1·5m.; 1990, 2·7m.

FOREIGN ECONOMIC RELATIONS. The USA lifted sanctions on trade with South Africa in July 1991.

Commerce. South Africa, Botswana, Lesotho, Swaziland and Transkei are members of a customs union and the foreign trade statistics shown below represent the combined imports and exports of these countries. The total value of the imports and exports was as follows (in R1m.):

	Imports		Exports
1988	39,483·9	1988	49,724·0
1989	44,741·3	1989	58,198·8
1990	44,211·7	1990	59,987·7

The principal commodity groups of imports and exports (in R1m.) in 1990 were:

Imports		Exports	
Machinery	12,767·4	Base metals	6,428·7
Vehicles and aircraft	4,827·2	Precious stones, metals	
Chemical products	5,124·7	and coins	3,641·7
Base metals	1,873·4	Textiles	229·1
Textiles	1,144·5	Chemical products	1,731·9
Gold	18,069·9	Food, beverages and tobacco	2,465·8
		Vegetable products	1,048·7

Trade (in R1m.) by region or grouping in 1990: Exports to (and imports from) industrialized countries, 29,023 (31,678); Western hemisphere, 697 (939); Africa, 4,006 (790); Asia, 4,659 (3,116); Europe, 1,295 (330).

Total trade between South Africa and UK (British Department of Trade returns, in £1,000 sterling):

	1987	1988	1989	1990	1991
Imports to UK	658,162	807,669	884,607	1,078,546	954,676
Exports and re-exports from UK	948,584	1,074,826	1,038,342	1,113,397	1,023,469

Tourism. In 1989, 930,393 tourists visited South Africa, of whom 460,634 were from African countries and 332,279 from Europe (129,982 from the UK and 79,435 from the Federal Republic of Germany).

COMMUNICATIONS. In 1990 South African Transport Services became Transnet, a public company comprising railways, harbours, pipelines and road transport, set up, with the government as sole shareholder, as a first step to possible privatization.

Roads. The railway administration operates the long-distance road motor services, together with private operators. In 1990 there were 185,751 km of national and provincial roads (55,383 km surfaced). South African Transport Services carried

11·7m. passengers and 4·12m. tonnes of goods by road in 1986-87. Motor vehicles in operation on 30 June 1990 included 3,403,605 passenger cars, 1,273,257 commercial vehicles, 196,243 minibuses, 28,107 buses and 298,941 motorcycles.

Railways. Railway history in South Africa begins in 1860 with the line Durban–Point. With the formation of the Union in 1910, the state-owned lines in the 4 provinces (12,194 km) were amalgamated into one state undertaking. In 1990 South African Railways, renamed Spoornet, became part of Transnet.

In 1989-90 there were 20,995 km of 1,065 mm gauge (9,078 km electrified) and 314 km of 762 mm gauge. Railways caried 382m. passengers and 183m. tonnes of freight. In 1990 a separate organization was set up to run commuter trains in major cities.

Civil Aviation. Civil aviation is controlled by the Department of Transport, which administers the following state-owned airports: Jan Smuts Airport, Johannesburg; D. F. Malan Airport, Cape Town; Louis Botha Airport, Durban; J. B. M. Hertzog Airport, Bloemfontein; Ben Schoeman Airport, East London; H. F. Verwoerd Airport, Port Elizabeth; B. J. Vorster Airport, Kimberley; P. W. Botha Airport, George; Pierre van Ryneveld Airport, Upington. At other airports the Department provides air navigation services.

South African Airways, as the national air carrier, operate scheduled international air services within Africa and to Europe, Latin America, Israel and the Far East. A ban on overflying imposed by several African countries in 1963 was lifted in June 1991. 13 independent operators provide internal flights which link up with SAA's internal network. During 1986-87 South African Airways carried 4,220,317 passengers (3,741,963 on internal flights) and 75,269 tonnes of freight and mail (25,596).

In March 1990 there were 215 licensed aerodromes, of which 155 were public and 105 private, and 55 approved helistops.

Shipping. The main ports are Durban, Cape Town, Saldanha, Richards Bay, Port Elizabeth and East London. Smaller ports are Mossel Bay, Port Nolloth, Walvis Bay and Lüderitz. During 1988 the main ports handled 97m. tonnes of cargo.

Telecommunications. On 31 March 1990 there were 2,181 money-order post offices and postal agencies. In 1990 there were 31,604 telex subscribers. Line capacity of automatic telephone exchanges (1990), 2,957,844; there were (1989) 4,744,000 telephones.

The South African Broadcasting Corporation broadcast (1990) 23 radio services in 16 languages and 4 TV services in 7 languages (colour by PAL). An external radio service broadcasts in 7 languages. There were (1990) about 10m. radio and 3·45m. TV sets. An independent TV company, M-Net, was permitted to broadcast news from 1 Jan. 1991.

Cinemas (1990). There were approximately 1,200.

Newspapers (1988). There are 40 main newspapers, of which 10 were Afrikaans, 28 English, 1 Zulu and English and 1 Xhosa and English. There were 5 Afrikaans and 16 English daily newspapers.

JUSTICE, RELIGION, EDUCATION AND WELFARE

Justice. The common law of the republic is the Roman–Dutch law—that is, the uncodified law of Holland as it was at the date of the cession of the Cape in 1806. The law of England as such is not recognized as authoritative, though by statute the principles of English law relating to evidence and to mercantile matters, *e.g.*, companies, patents, trademarks, insolvency and the like, have been introduced. In shipping and insurance, English law is followed in the Cape Province, and it has also largely influenced civil and criminal procedure throughout the republic. In all other matters, family relations, property, succession, contract, etc., Roman–Dutch law rules, English decisions being valued only so far as they agree therewith.

The Supreme Court of South Africa is constituted as follows: (i) The Appellate Division, consisting of the Chief Justice and as many Judges of Appeal as the State President may stipulate, is the highest court and its decisions are binding on all courts. Except for contempt of court in *faciae curiae*, it has no original jurisdiction, but is purely a Court of Appeal. (ii) The Provincial Divisions: In each province there is a provincial division of the Supreme Court, while in the Cape there are three such divisions possessing both original and appellate jurisdiction. (iii) The Local Divisions: There is a local division each in the Transvaal and Natal exercising the same original jurisdiction within limited areas as the provincial divisions. The judges hold office till they attain the age of 70 years. A judge is expected to perform service of 3 months a year until the age of 75. No judge can be removed from office except by the State President upon an address from both Houses of Parliament on the ground of misbehaviour or incapacity. The circuit system is fully developed.

The Black appeal courts have been abolished. Black divorce courts have jurisdiction to some extent concurrent with that of the Supreme Court in cases in which the parties are Black.

Each province is further divided into districts with a magistrate's court having a prescribed civil and criminal jurisdiction. From this court there is an appeal to the provincial divisions of the Supreme Court, and thence to the appellate division. Magistrates' convictions carrying sentences above a prescribed limit are subject to automatic review by a judge. In addition, several regional divisions consisting of a number of districts have been constituted. Convictions of such courts are not subject to automatic review by a judge.

Courts of Black affairs commissioners were abolished in 1984. All criminal and civil cases are dealt with by judges (in the Supreme Courts) and magistrates (in the lower courts). Judges and magistrates are entitled to take judicial cognizance of customary (indigenous) laws and must, where relevant, apply them. A limited civil and criminal jurisdiction is conferred upon the Black chief or headman over his own tribe.

Small claims courts have been introduced in a number of areas since 1984. These courts (where Commissioners preside) have civil jurisdiction only, limited by the quantum of damages and the nature of the claim.

It was announced in Dec. 1990 that political exiles who fled South Africa before 8 Oct. 1990 were free to return and immune from prosecution.

Religion. The latest figures are still those of the 1980 population census results as regards religious denominations: *Whites:* Nederduits Gereformeerde Kerk, 1,695,875; Anglicans, 461,543; Methodists, 420,957; Roman Catholics, 388,336; Nederduits Hervormde Kerk, 258,769; Presbyterians, 129,771; Gereformeerde Kerk, 127,235; Apostolics, 125,501; other Christians, 608,139; Jews, 117,963. *Blacks:* Methodists, 1,657,787; Black independent churches, 5,124,566; Nederduits Gereformeerde Kerk, 1,120,461; Roman Catholics, 1,731,623; Anglican, 815,346; Lutheran, 742,421; other Christian churches, 1,703,640; non-Christian churches, 37,557. *Coloureds and Asians:* Nederduits Gereformeerde Kerk, 677,216; Hindus, 526,132; Anglican, 369,728; Roman Catholic, 286,740; Islam 342,248.

Education. According to the National Policy for General Affairs Act, 1984 (Act 76 of 1984), the Minister of National Education determines general policy for formal, informal and non-formal education. The provision of education, on the other hand, has been assigned to state departments responsible for executing education policy. The Department of Education and Culture: House of Assembly is mainly responsible for the education of Whites. The Department of Education and Culture: House of Representatives is mainly responsible for the education of Coloureds while the Department of Education and Culture: House of Delegates is mainly responsible for Indian education. Education for Blacks is the responsibility of the Department of Education and Training.

Public primary and secondary schools in 1990: Schools for Whites had 916,743 pupils and 61,248 teachers. For Coloureds, 840,143 pupils and 34,566 teachers. For Indians, 232,958 pupils and 11,744 teachers. For Blacks, 5,473,145 pupils and 133,170 teachers. Special schools (1988) for 4,847 Black pupils had 720 teachers; for 13,414 White pupils, 2,504 teachers; for 5,967 Coloured pupils, 798 teachers; for 5,847 Indian pupils, 456 teachers.

Private Schools. To a certain extent the activities of private schools are controlled by government regulations. Their pupils generally sit for the state schools' examinations. These schools make provision for kindergarten, elementary and preparatory, general primary, secondary and commercial education.

Higher Education. Institutions comprise universities, technikons and teacher training colleges. In March 1989 tertiary-level students included 219,194 whites, 33,914 coloureds, 27,595 Indians and 133,148 Blacks.

There are 17 autonomous universities. All the universities are open to all population groups but each has a different cultural ethos and the medium of instruction is either English or Afrikaans. The Afrikaans universities include: the University of the Orange Free State in Bloemfontein; Potchefstroom University for Christian Higher Education, Potchefstroom; the University of Pretoria; the University of Stellenbosch; the Rand Afrikaans University, Johannesburg. Both the University of Port Elizabeth and the University of South Africa offer instruction through the medium of Afrikaans and English. The latter has its seat in Pretoria and conducts its studies by means of distance tuition. The universities offering instruction through the medium of English are: the University of Cape Town; the University of Natal in Durban and Pietermaritzburg; Rhodes University, Grahamstown; the University of the Witwatersrand, Johannesburg; Vista University which also conducts its studies by means of distance tuition; the University of the North near Pietersburg, the University of Zululand near Empangeni in Natal; the Medical University of Southern Africa; the University of the Western Cape, Bellville and the University of Durban-Westville near Durban.

Technical and Vocational Education. The 12 Technikons provide education at an advanced tertiary level for a variety of technical, commercial and general courses of study. Enrolment at technikons is open to members of all population groups. Technical colleges are mainly responsible for the training of apprentices and the education, on a part-time basis, of persons not subject to compulsory school attendance.

Health. In 1990 there were 20,139 medical practitioners, 3,775 dental specialists and dentists, 8,930 pharmacists and 148,558 nurses. In 1987 there were 737 hospitals. In 1987 there were 24,178 beds in psychiatric hospitals; 95,839 mentally ill were treated as in-patients, 290,550 consultations were performed for out-patients.

All public health services rendered by government bodies are free, or charged according to the patient's means.

Social Welfare. Under the Social Pensions Act, 1973, pensions and allowances are made to aged, blind, disabled and war veterans, subject to a means test. Maintenance grants are paid to single mothers with inadequate income in terms of the 1960 Children's Act.

Welfare Services. South Africa is not a welfare state, yet provides many services for the community. Welfare work on behalf of the Government is done by the Departments of Health Services and Welfare, Administration: House of Assembly, House of Delegates and House of Representatives, Departments of Planning and Provincial Administrations and Development Aid.

In 1989 there were over 1,600 voluntary organizations. The work of all these bodies is co-ordinated by the South African Welfare Council and regional welfare boards set up under the National Welfare Act, 1978.

The Child Care Act, 1983 which superseded the Children's Act, 1960 is designed to protect children against neglect, abuse, ill-treatment and exploitation. The Act provides for preventive child care services, foster care, adoption and residential care, and also for various children's allowances and financial assistance to children's homes and creches.

Welfare services for the aged are mainly provided by voluntary bodies with government subsidies; the same principle applies to the care of the handicapped, but there are State settlements for the permanently handicapped, and State sheltered-employment programmes for handicapped adults.

The National Advisory Board on Rehabilitation Matters advises and brings together the voluntary and government agencies working on drug abuse and alcoholism.

In all fields of welfare, State subsidies enable voluntary bodies to employ professional social workers.

DIPLOMATIC REPRESENTATIVES

Of South Africa in Great Britain (South Africa Hse., Trafalgar Sq., London, WC2N 5DP)
Ambassador: Kent Durr.

Of Great Britain in South Africa (255 Hill St., Arcadia, Pretoria, 0002)
Ambassador: Sir Anthony Reeve, KCMG.

Of South Africa in the USA (3051 Massachusetts Ave., NW, Washington, D.C., 20008)
Ambassador: Harry Schwartz.

Of the USA in South Africa (225 Pretorius St., Pretoria)
Ambassador: William L. Swing.

Of South Africa to the United Nations
Ambassador: Vernon Steward.

Further Reading

Benson, M. *Nelson Mandela: The Man and the Movement.* New York, 1986
Bindman, G., (ed.) *South Africa: Human Rights and the Rule of Law.* London, 1988
Böhning, W. R., *Black Migration to South Africa.* Geneva, 1981
Davenport, T. R. H., *South Africa: A Modern History.* 4th ed. CUP, 1991
Guy, A., *South Africa: Crossing the Rubicon.* London, 1991
Horowitz, D. L., *A Democratic South Africa?: Constitutional Engineering in a Divided Society.* Univ. of California Press, 1991
Hunt Davis, R., (ed.) *Apartheid Unravels,* Univ. of Florida Press, 1991
Musiker, R., *South Africa,* [Bibliography] Oxford and Santa Barbara, 1980
Nattrass, N. and Ardington, E. (eds.), *The Political Economy of South Africa.* Cape Town and OUP, 1990
Oxford History of South Africa. OUP, Vol. 1, 1969; Vol. 2 1971
Riley, E., *Major Political Events in South Africa, 1948–1990.* Oxford, 1991
Sparks, A., *The Mind of South Africa.* London, 1990
Thompson, L., *A History of South Africa.* Yale Univ. Press, 1990
Venter, D. J., *South Africa, Sanctions and Multinationals.* London, 1989

National statistical office: Central Statistical Service, Private Bag X44, Pretoria 0001.

PROVINCE OF THE CAPE OF GOOD HOPE

Kaapprovinsie

HISTORY. The colony of the Cape of Good Hope was founded by the Dutch in the year 1652. Britain took possession of it from 1795 to 1803 and again in 1806, and it was formally ceded to Great Britain by the Convention of London, 13 Aug. 1814. Letters patent issued in 1850 declared that in the colony there should be a Parliament which should consist of the Governor, a Legislative Council and a House of Assembly. On 31 May 1910 the colony was merged as a province in the Union of South Africa, and on 31 May 1961 it became a province of the Republic of South Africa.

AREA AND POPULATION. The following table gives the population of the Cape of Good Hope [1] (area (1980) 646,332 sq. km) at the last census:

	All races			Whites		Non-Whites	
	Total	Males	Females	Males	Females	Males	Females
1936	3,527,865	1,663,169	1,864,796	396,058	394,993	1,267,011	1,469,803
1946	4,051,424	1,924,334	2,127,090	433,849	436,300	1,490,485	1,690,790
1951	4,426,726	2,110,674	2,316,052	463,917	471,168	1,646,757	1,844,884
1960	5,360,234	2,553,245	2,806,989	493,370	507,398	2,059,875	2,299,591

| | *All races* | | *Whites* | | *Non-Whites* | |
	Total	Males	Females	Males	Females	Males	Females
1970 [1]	4,253,269	2,134,816	2,118,453	544,576	559,153	1,590,240	1,559,300
1980 [1]	4,527,903	2,241,374	2,286,529	557,608	585,001	1,683,766	1,701,528
1985 [1]	5,041,137	2,477,756	2,563,381	586,084	623,333	1,891,672	1,940,048
1991 [1,2]	5,514,413	2,686,255	2,828,158	589,917	631,448	2,096,338	2,196,710

[1] Excluding TBVC countries.   [2] Preliminary figures

Present area, 641,379 sq. km (247,637 sq. miles), including the enclave of Walvis Bay 1,124 sq. km (434 sq. miles) on the coast of Namibia which forms an administrative part of the Cape Province.

Of the non-White population in 1991, 39,871 were Asians, 1,835,657 were Blacks and 2,417,527 Coloureds.

Vital statistics for calendar years:

	Births	Deaths	Marriages
1987	88,164	51,088	25,225
1988	81,855	53,759	23,383
1989	86,485	49,420	26,204
1990	80,591	47,676	26,246

ADMINISTRATION. In June 1986 the provincial councils were abolished. Cape Town is the seat of the provincial administration.

Administrator: J. W. H. Meiring.

The Cape Provincial Administration is headed by an Administrator supported by an executive committee of six members. It administers provincial matters such as hospitals, health and welfare, roads, nature conservation and libraries. It also oversees local authorities (Regional Service Councils, municipalities and local councils) in the province.

FINANCE. In 1990–91 revenue amounted to R3,182,197,000 and expenditure to R3,182,197,000.

AGRICULTURE. Viticulture in the republic is almost exclusively confined to the Cape Province, but practically all other forms of agricultural and pastoral activity are pursued.

INDUSTRY. The province has brick, tile and pottery works, saw-mills, engineering works, foundries, grain-mills, distilleries and wineries, clothing factories, furniture, boot and shoe factories, etc.

RELIGION. From the 1980 population census, Nederduits Gereformeerde Kerk, 1,336,637; Gereformeerde Kerk, 12,576; Nederduits Hervormde Kerk, 110,560; Anglican, 567,715; Presbyterian, 109,521; Methodist, 529,853; Roman Catholic, 390,969; Apostolic Faith Mission, 62,113; Lutheran, 113,879; Islam, 170,000; Hindu, 6,629; Independent Churches, 458,524; other Christian Churches, 656,487; Jews, 32,349.

EDUCATION. On 1 April 1986 the Education Department came within the jurisdiction of the Central Government. Education is compulsory for all White children. Primary and secondary education is free to the end of the calendar year in which the age of 19 years is attained.

Whites (1985). There were 828 government and aided schools with 14,205 teachers and 238,853 pupils; 8 teacher-training colleges with 291 lecturers and 1,841 students; 53 private schools with 13,859 pupils.

Coloureds (1985). There were 1,776 government and aided schools with 26,583 teachers and 657,391 pupils; 13 teacher-training colleges with 6,709 students; 18 private schools with 2,652 pupils.

Black (1985). There were 1,137 government schools with 7,105 teachers and 318,541 pupils and 17 private schools with 118 teachers and 6,120 pupils.

Asians (1985). There were 8 government schools with 201 teachers and 5,400 pupils.

PROVINCE OF NATAL

HISTORY. Natal was annexed to Cape Colony in 1844, placed under separate government in 1845, and on 15 July 1856 established as a separate colony. By this charter partially representative institutions were established, and in 1893 the colony attained responsible government. The province of Zululand was annexed to Natal on 30 Dec. 1897. The districts of Vryheid, Utrecht and part of Wakkerstroom, formerly belonging to the Transvaal, were annexed in Jan. 1903. On 31 May 1910 the colony was merged in the Union of South Africa as an original province of the Union.

AREA AND POPULATION. The province (including Kwa Zulu, 36,073 sq. km) has an area of 91,785 sq. km, with a seaboard of about 576 km. The climate is sub-tropical on the coast and somewhat colder inland. The province is divided into 45 magisterial districts.

The census returns of population (excluding Kwa Zulu) were:

		All races		Whites		Non-Whites	
	Total	Males	Females	Males	Females	Males	Females
1960	2,979,034	1,443,561	1,535,473	166,404	222,750	1,227,157	1,362,468
1970 [1]	2,096,408	1,084,378	1,012,030	219,177	224,942	865,201	787,088
1980 [1]	2,068,615	1,039,261	1,029,354	248,892	261,338	790,369	768,016
1985 [1]	2,145,018	1,072,426	1,072,592	274,797	285,234	797,629	787,358
1991 [1,2]	2,074,153	1,026,187	1,047,966	261,711	271,556	764,476	776,410

[1] Excluding TBVC countries.   [2] Preliminary figures

Of the non-White population in 1991, 666,006 were Asians, 91,705 Coloureds and 783,175 Blacks.

ADMINISTRATION. State of parties Oct. 1990: National Party, 10; Democratic Party, 10.

The seat of provincial government in Natal is Pietermaritzburg. In April 1978 the area of East Griqualand was transferred to Natal from Cape Province.

Administrator: Cornelius Johannes van Rooyen Botha.

FINANCE. In 1990–91 revenue amounted to R1,666,632,000 and expenditure to R1,666,632,000. Tax incentives encourage industrial development.

MINING. The province is rich in mineral wealth, particularly coal.

AGRICULTURE. Sugar, timber (wattle, pine and gum) and livestock production (beef and dairy cattle, pigs, sheep and poultry) are the mainstays of agriculture. Cultivated pastures are increasingly important.

INDUSTRY. There are 4 highly industrialized development zones: Durban-Pinetown, Pietermaritzburg, Newcastle and Richards Bay. The road and rail networks are good and electricity is supplied from a grid. There are deep-water natural harbours at Durban and Richards Bay. Durban is an international port. Richards Bay is a terminal for ore, coal and wood-chip export. Important industries include metallurgical plants, cereal mills, sugar refineries, tannin extraction plants, pulp-mills, explosives and fertilizer plants, milk-processing plants, meat-processing factories, foundries, paper and fibre-processing plants and clothing factories.

EDUCATION. The Department of Education and Culture controls primary and secondary education for Whites. Control was transferred from the province to central government on 1 April 1986, and the classification of government-aided schools changed to private although they continue to receive a subsidy.

Whites (1989). There were 261 government schools with 98,966 pupils; 2 residential teacher-training colleges with 893 students; 1 correspondence teacher-training college with 458 pupils; 52 private schools with 11,290 pupils; 11 special schools and training centres with 1,426 pupils and 9 technical colleges with 3,668 pupils.

Coloureds (1989). There were 65 state and state-aided schools with 1,386 teachers and 30,565 pupils; 18 state subsidized pre-primary schools with 15 teachers and 1,000 pupils; 4 special schools with 155 pupils and 22 teachers; 1 teacher-training college with 301 students and 32 lecturers; 1 technical college with 42 full-time lecturers and 14 part-time lecturers.

Blacks (1990). There were 1,147 schools with 5,952 teachers and 236,182 pupils. These schools are situated in Natal and KwaZulu.

Asians (1990). There were 447 state and state-aided primary and secondary schools with 11,959 teachers and 249,713 pupils; 35 private pre-primary schools with 2,462 children; 1 school of industry with 149 pupils; 16 special schools and training centres with 1,635 pupils; 3 technical colleges with 2,416 full-time and 7,487 part-time students; 2 Colleges of Education with 833 students and 1 pre-vocational school with 262 pupils.

PROVINCE OF THE TRANSVAAL

HISTORY. The Transvaal was one of the territories colonized by the Boers who left the Cape Colony during the Great Trek in 1834 and following years. In 1852, by the Sand River Treaty, Great Britain recognized the independence of the Transvaal, which, in 1853, took the name of the South African Republic. In 1877 the republic was annexed by Great Britain, but the Boers took up arms towards the end of 1880. In 1881 peace was made and self-government, subject to British suzerainty and certain stipulated restrictions, was restored to the Boers. The London Convention of 1884 removed the suzerainty and a number of these restrictions but reserved to Great Britain the right of approval of the Transvaal's foreign relations, excepting with regard to the Orange Free State. In 1886 gold was discovered on the Witwatersrand, and this discovery, together with the great influx of foreigners which it occasioned, gave rise to many grave problems. Eventually, in 1899, war broke out between Great Britain and the Transvaal. Peace was concluded on 31 May 1902, the Transvaal and the Orange Free State both losing their independence. The Transvaal was governed as a crown colony until 12 Jan. 1907, when responsible government came into force. On 31 May 1910 the Transvaal became one of the four provinces of the Union.

AREA AND POPULATION. The area of the province is 262,499 sq. km or 101,351 sq. miles, including Gazankulu, Lebowa, Ka Ngwane and Kwa Ndebele. The province is divided into 53 districts. The following table shows the population, excluding Gazankulu, Lebowa, Ka Ngwane and Kwa Ndebele in 1985, at each of the last censuses:

| | All races | | | Whites | | Non-Whites | |
	Total	Males	Females	Males	Females	Males	Females
1936	3,341,470	1,846,576	1,494,894	424,470	396,286	1,422,108	1,098,608
1946	4,283,038	2,374,323	1,908,715	541,053	522,068	1,833,270	1,386,647
1951	4,812,838	2,619,314	2,193,524	737,194	731,111	2,575,119	2,230,053
1960	6,270,711	3,310,948	2,959,763	735,845	729,730	2,575,103	2,230,034
1970 [1]	5,541,683	3,532,966	3,008,717	966,739	946,253	2,576,227	2,062,464
1980 [1]	6,883,758	3,678,086	3,205,672	1,109,014	1,120,240	2,564,072	2,085,432
1985 [1]	7,532,179	4,008,070	3,524,109	1,224,064	1,237,300	2,784,006	2,286,809
1991 [1,2]	8,630,016	4,432,563	4,197,453	1,203,396	1,235,766	3,229,167	2,961,687

[1] Excluding TBVC countries.   [2] Preliminary figures

Of the non-White population in 1985, 4,674,290 were Black, 126,201 Asians and 270,324 Coloureds.

ADMINISTRATION. The seat of provincial government is at Pretoria, which is also the administrative capital of the Republic of South Africa.

Administrator: D. J. Hough.

FINANCE. In 1990–91 revenue amounted to R4,377,942,000 and expenditure to R4,377,942,000.

MINING. Gold output in 1989 was 19,428,480 oz. worth R19,284,204,183.

AGRICULTURE. The province is in the main a stock-raising country, though there are considerable areas well adapted for agriculture, including the growing of tropical crops.

INDUSTRY. The province has iron and brass foundries and engineering works, grain-mills, breweries, brick, tile and pottery works, tobacco, soap, and candle factories, coach and wagon works, clothing factories, etc.

RELIGION. From the 1980 population census. Nederduits Gereformeerde Kerk, 1,239,484; Gereformeerde Kerk, 95,021; Nederduits Hervormde Kerk, 225,850; Anglican, 509,400; Presbyterian, 135,701; Methodist, 684,284; Roman Catholic, 753,982; Apostolic Faith Mission, 139,393; Lutheran, 312,484; Islam, 74,504; Hindu, 37,249; independent churches, 1,972,759; other Christian churches, 744,318; Jews, 77,759.

EDUCATION. All education for Whites except that of universities is under the provincial authority. The province has been divided for the purposes of local control and management into 21 school districts. Instruction in government schools, both primary and secondary, is free. The medium of instruction is the home language of the pupil. The teaching of the other language begins at the earliest stage at which it is appropriate on educational grounds. Both languages are taught as examination subjects to every pupil.

Whites (1988). There were 984 public schools with 27,400 teachers and 504,032 pupils; 6 teacher-training colleges with 7,560 students; 115 private schools with 2,187 teachers and 33,831 pupils.

Coloureds (1988). There were 103 state and state-aided schools with 2,956 teachers and 74,607 pupils; 1 teacher-training college with 562 students.

Asians (1988). There were 81 public schools with 1,409 teachers and 32,412 pupils; 1 teacher-training college with 31 teachers and 126 students.

Blacks (1988). There were 4,295 public and private school sections with 25,779 teachers and 957,322 pupils (homelands excluded).

PROVINCE OF THE ORANGE FREE STATE

Oranje-Vrystaat

HISTORY. The Orange River was first crossed by Europeans in the middle of the 18th century. Between 1810 and 1820, settlements were made in the southern parts of the Orange Free State, and the Great Trek greatly increased the number of settlers during and after 1836. In 1848, Sir Harry Smith proclaimed the whole territory between the Orange and Vaal rivers as a British possession called the 'Orange River Sovereignty'. However, in 1854, by the Convention of Bloemfontein, British sovereignty was withdrawn and the independence of the country was recognized.

During the first 5 years of its existence the Orange Free State was much harassed by incessant raids by the Basutos. These were at length conquered but, owing to the intervention of the British Government, the treaty of Aliwal North incorporated only part of the territory of the Basutos in the Orange Free State.

On account of the treaty with the South African Republic, the Orange Free State took a prominent part in the South African War (1899–1902) and was annexed on 28 May 1900 as the Orange River Colony. Crown colony government continued until 1907, when responsible government was introduced. On 31 May 1910 the Orange River Colony was merged in the Union of South Africa as the province of the Orange Free State, and on 31 May 1961 became a province of the Republic of South Africa.

AREA AND POPULATION. The area of the province is 127,993 sq. km or 49,418 sq. miles, including Qwaqwa. The province is divided into 43 administrative and 49 magisterial districts. The population has varied as follows:

	All races			Whites		Non-Whites	
	Total	Males	Females	Males	Females	Males	Females
1936	772,060	381,903	390,157	101,872	99,106	280,031	291,051
1946	879,071	432,896	446,175	101,874	100,203	331,022	345,972
1951	1,016,570	519,166	497,404	115,637	112,015	403,529	385,389
1960	1,386,202	731,486	654,716	139,304	137,103	601,182	553,613
1970 [1]	1,681,602	384,913	796,689	150,371	149,350	734,542	647,339
1980 [1]	1,647,810	866,727	781,083	156,972	157,806	709,755	623,277
1985 [1]	1,776,903	940,000	836,903	164,135	168,192	775,865	668,711
1991 [1,2]	1,929,369	1,001,534	927,835	161,199	166,566	840,335	761,269

[1] Excluding TBVC countries.   [2] Preliminary figures

Of the non-White population in 1991, 1,538,171 were Black, 62,789 Coloureds and 644 Asians.

ADMINISTRATION. Provincial councils were abolished on 30 June 1986.

For the Whites there are 71 municipal councils and 6 village management boards, for the coloureds 13 management committees and for the Blacks, 7 city councils, 8 town councils, 56 village committees and 2 local authority committees.

Administrator: L. Dr Louis van der Watt.

FINANCE. In 1989–90 revenue was R1,098,343,000 and expenditure R1,098,343,000.

MINING. The output of gold in 1990 was 183,058 kg valued at R5,647·5m.

AGRICULTURE. The province consists of undulating plains, affording excellent grazing and wide tracts for agricultural purposes. The rainfall is moderate. The Orange Free State is the largest grain-producing province in the Republic and is also an important sheep- and cattle-farming region.

INDUSTRY. The more important manufacturing industries in the province are the oil-from-coal factory at Sasolburg (as well as industries based on its by-products); grain mills and brick, tile and pottery works. Fertilizers, agricultural implements, blankets, woollen products, clothing, hosiery, cement and pharmaceutical products are also manufactured.

EDUCATION. Primary, secondary and vocational education and the training of teachers are controlled and financed by the Department of Education and Culture Administration: House of Assembly for Whites and Administration; House of Representatives for Coloureds; Department of Education and Training for Blacks.

Education is free in all public schools up to the university matriculation standard. Attendance is compulsory for White and Coloured between the ages of 7 and 16, but exemption may be granted in special cases. Attendance is not compulsory for Black children, except in areas/communities/towns where a request for compulsory education had been made. In these cases education is compulsory up to Standard 5 or the age of 16. The home language of the pupil is the medium of instruction up to Standard 2; thereafter he has an option of Afrikaans, English or his home language in Black schools.

Further education and training are given at 2 universities (University of the

Orange Free State and Vista), 3 teachers' training colleges, 1 technicon, 1 agricultural college, 2 nursing colleges, 5 technical colleges and numerous training centres.

Whites (1991). There were 202 government and aided schools with 4,166 teachers and 73,674 pupils.

Coloureds (1991). There were 47 government and aided schools with 876 teachers and 18,568 pupils.

Blacks (1991). There were 2,720 government schools with 11,342 teachers and 443,928 pupils.

BOPHUTHATSWANA

HISTORY. Bophuthatswana was first to obtain self-government under the Bantu Homeland Constitution Act of 1971 and was the second black homeland to ask the Republic of South Africa for full independence, which was granted on 6 Dec. 1977.

AREA AND POPULATION. The total area is 44,000 sq. km.

In 1985 there was a *de jure* population of 3·2m., of which 47% lived in the White areas. The remaining 53% (1,740,600) lived in the homeland. Estimate (1989) 3·2m. The capital is Mmabatho.

CONSTITUTION AND GOVERNMENT. The Bophuthatswana Government is a compromise between the traditional chief-in-council system and a democratic electoral system. There are 72 elected and 24 nominated members in the Legislative Assembly. Self-government was granted in 1972. Each regional authority (coinciding with the 12 districts of the country) nominates 2 members, and each district elects 6 members to the National Assembly and 12 designated by the President on account of their special knowledge, qualifications or experience.

Executive power vests in the President, who is directly elected by general suffrage of persons who are registered as voters, and he appoints his Cabinet.

The first general election was held in Oct. 1972, 2 political parties taking part. Kgosi Lucas Mangope's Bophuthatswana National Party (BNP) won 20 of the 24 contested seats, but in 1974 he formed the Bophuthatswana Democratic Party which in the 1987 elections won 66 seats; the People's Progressive Party, 6 seats.

Members of regional authorities are elected from among the tribal and community authorities in their areas.

The Cabinet in Nov. 1991 consisted of:

President, Minister of Law and Order, Audit and Public Service: Dr Kgosi Lucas Manyane Mangope (took office 6 Dec. 1977; re-elected for another 7 years as from 11 Nov. 1984).

Population Development: T. M. Molatlhwa. *Internal Affairs:* Kgosi S. V. Suping. *Finance:* L. G. Young. *Posts and Telecommunications and Broadcasting:* M. Z. Masilo. *Manpower and Coordination:* S. M. Seodi. *State Affairs and Civil Aviation:* R. Cronje. *Foreign Affairs:* G. S. M. Nkau. *Health and Social Welfare:* Dr N. C. O. B. Khaole. *Water Affairs:* T. M. Tlhabane. *Economic Planning, Energy Affairs and Mines:* E. B. Keikelame. *Agriculture and Natural Resources:* P. H. Moeketsi. *Parliamentary Affairs, Local Government and Housing:* H. F. Tlou. *Education:* K. C. V. A. Sehume. *Justice and Transport:* S. G. Mothibe. *Public Works:* S. C. Kgobokoe.

There were 6 Deputy Ministers.

Flag: Blue, crossed by a diagonal orange stripe, and in the canton a white disc charged with a leopard's face in black and white.

DEFENCE. The Air Wing of the Defence Force has 1 PC-6 Turbo-Porter and 2 Aviocar transports, and 2 Alouette III, 2 BK-117 and 1 Ecureuil helicopters, as well as 3 PC-7 Turbo-Trainers. There is an Army Force of 3,100 with 2 infantry battalions.

INTERNATIONAL RELATIONS

Aid. The Republic of South Africa granted aid of R607m. in 1990–91.

ECONOMY

Budget. The 1989–90 budget balanced at R2,300m.

Currency. South African Rand.

Banking and Finance. The financial system is controlled by legislation inherited from South Africa on independence, and commercial banks have strong direct links with South African banks which in certain instances are controlled by overseas banking companies.

In 1990 there were 3 commercial banks with branches in all major commercial and agricultural centres offering a full range of banking services. The Agricultural Bank of Bophuthatswana provides finance to farmers. The government-funded Agricultural Development Fund provides loan finance and subsidy support to agricultural co-operative societies. The Bophuthatswana Building Society grants loans for house building.

NATURAL RESOURCES

Water. The Department of Water Affairs controls and maintains 2,833 reservoirs, 6,845 boreholes and 648 earth dams.

Minerals. The territory is particularly rich in minerals. In 1990 there were 46 mines. Minerals include platinum, asbestos, gold, calcite, granite, chrome, vanadium, limestone and diamonds.

Exploration for more platinum, chrome and coal is currently being carried out both by the private sector and by the Mining and Geological Survey Division of the Department of Economic Planning. The platinum mines around Rustenburg produce about 66% of the free world's total production. The major chrome mines are near Rustenburg and Marico, while vanadium is mined in the Odi district near Brits. The Rustenburg, Western and Impala Platinum mines which are shared with the Republic of South Africa produce about 1·9m. oz. a year.

AGRICULTURE. Bophuthatswana is a semi-arid area of bushveld and grass veld suitable for stock farming. The annual rainfall is 300 mm in the west and 700 mm in the east and there are 4 river catchment areas—those of the Molopo, Ngotwane, Sehujwane and Madikwe rivers.

Although the land tenure system militates against establishing large farms, some land which is suitable for farming is leased by the Government to successful farmers.

Livestock (1988): Cattle, 467,355; sheep, 268,351; goats, 530,430; pigs, 8,039; poultry, 196,396.

Only 6·6% of the territory is suited to dryland farming, but crop yields have shown a steady improvement in recent years. In Ditsobotla district, 36,926 ha of fertile land has been developed by 3 primary co-operatives comprising 190 Batswana farmers. Silkworm farming was being tried in 1983. By 1981 the country was self sufficient in maize and exported the surplus. Three rice projects are successfully expanding and vegetable production was flourishing in 1987. The budget for 1990–91 is R182m.

INDUSTRY. The first industries were started on an agency basis at Babelegi; the fastest growing industrial area in the homeland, in 1977 it covered 183 hectares and by March 1985 more than R234m. had been invested in the project. Other industries are situated at Mmabatho, Garankuwa, Selosesha, Mafikeng and Mogwase. South African border industries are also promoted by the government, notably at Rosslyn where 128 industries had been established by Dec. 1975.

Labour. 56,000 persons were employed in mining in 1988.

COMMUNICATIONS

Roads. Total length (1988) 6,300 km, of which 1,300 km are tarred.

Civil Aviation. Mmabatho International Airport was opened in 1984.

Telecommunications. There were 29,636 telephones and 253 telex lines at 30 Sept. 1990, and 44 post offices.In 1989 there was 1 television station and 2 radio stations (Radio-Bop broadcasts in English and Radio Mmabatho in Setswana), and (1990) 63,001 television licences.

EDUCATION AND WELFARE

Education. Education is not compulsory but is free apart from nominal contributions to school funds and hostel fees at post-primary schools. Medium of instruction from Grade I to Standard 2 is in Setswana; from Standard 3 to senior standards is in English. Afrikaans is taught as a subject. The education is controlled by the Department of Education with a budget of R506m. in 1990-91.

In 1989 there were 28,439 children in kindergartens, 328,698 in primary schools, 125,542 in middle schools, 76,747 in high schools, 1,094 in schools for the mentally handicapped, 1,092 for the physically handicapped, 3,751 in colleges of education (2 new colleges of education opened in 1990), 1,638 in adult education and 2,330 in university. The number of teachers was 16,058 excluding lecturers.

Health. In 1989 there were 12 hospitals, 204 static clinics, 197 mobile clinics, 6,303 hospital and clinic beds, 178 doctors and 6,039 nurses. The health budget in 1990–91 was R184m.

Further Reading

Five Years of Independence: Republic of Bophuthatswana. Mafikeng, 1983
A Nation on the March
Bophuthatswana at a Glance

TRANSKEI

HISTORY. Transkei is the homeland of the Xhosa nation and was granted self-government by the Republic of South Africa in 1963. Over 1·5m. Transkeians live permanently in the Republic of South Africa but were deprived of their South African citizenship on independence.

AREA AND POPULATION. The total area is 16,910 sq. miles (43,798 sq. km). Population (1985 estimate) 2,876,122. The capital is Umtata (population (1976) 24,805; 20,196 Blacks, 1,067 Coloured and 3,542 Whites). Other towns include Gcuwa, Kwabhaca, Umzimvubu and Lusikisiki.

CONSTITUTION AND GOVERNMENT. The Status of Transkei Bill of 1976 gave Transkei a unicameral National Assembly instead of the then existing Legislative Assembly. Independence was achieved 26 Oct. 1976.

General elections were held on 29 Sept. 1976 and the Transkei National Independence Party gained 69 of the 75 elective seats in the National Assembly. Members were elected for a 5-year period. In addition there are 75 traditional (co-opted) members (70 chiefs and 5 paramount chiefs).

President: Paramount Chief T. N. Ndamase.

In Sept. 1987 Chief George Mantanzima the Prime Minister, resigned and was succeeded by Stella Sigcau who in turn was ousted in a bloodless military coup, led by Major-Gen. Bantu Holomisa in Jan. 1988.

Flag: Three horizontal stripes of ochre, white, green.

FINANCE. In 1985 government income was R872m. and expenditure R984m.

MINERALS. Coal, titanium and black granite are mined.

AGRICULTURE. Notable examples of successful commercial enterprises in agriculture are the Magwa and Majola tea estates, with approximately 1,700 hectares planted, and various fibre plantations. 70,000 hectares of land are under indigenous forests and 61,000 hectares have been put under exotic plantations. There are 28 sawmills in the country.

Livestock (1976): Cattle, 1·3m.; sheep, 2·5m.; goats, 1·25m.

COMMUNICATIONS

Roads. There are above 8,800 km of roads.

Railways. There is a 209 km railway line linking Umtata with the port of East London in the Republic of South Africa.

Aviation. An international airport exists at Umtata.

Shipping. A start was made in 1978 on a 'free port' at Mnganzana but has since been abandoned.

Telecommunications. There were 11,498 telephones in 1978.

EDUCATION AND WELFARE

Education. In 1985 there were 690,000 pupils in primary schools and 193,000 pupils in secondary schools. The national university was inaugurated in Umtata in 1977 and has a brance in Butterworth.

Health. There were (1987) 31 hospitals with a total of 7,561 beds.

DIPLOMATIC REPRESENTATIVES

No country, other than the Republic of South Africa, has recognized Transkei as an independent state.

VENDA

HISTORY. Traditionally the territory of the Vhavenda, the country was granted self-government in 1973, and became the third Black homeland to be granted independence by the Republic of South Africa on 13 Sept. 1979.

Brig. Gabriel Ramushwana seized power in a bloodless coup in April 1990.

AREA AND POPULATION. The total area is 7,460 sq. km. In 1985, census, the *de jure* population of Venda was estimated at 651,393, the *de facto* population at 459,986. The capital is Thohoyandou. The other main towns are Sibasa, Makwarela, Makhado, Vuwani, Mutale and Masisi.

Vital statistics, 1987: Birth rate was 39·1 per 1,000 population; crude death rate, 10·3; infant mortality rate 56·9 per 1,000 live births.

CONSTITUTION AND GOVERNMENT. Executive power is vested in the President, who is elected for the duration of each Parliament, which consists of the President and the National Assembly; legislative power is vested in Parliament. In addition to the National Assembly there is an Executive Council, or Cabinet, and a judiciary independent of the Executive. The National Assembly consists of 45 members elected by popular vote, 15 members designated by 5 district councils, 6 members nominated by the President and 27 chiefs as *ex officio* members, and a representative of the Paramount Chief. A new Assembly must be elected after every 5 years, but it may be dissolved at any time by the President. All existing tribal, community and regional councils were retained with their status and powers unchanged, like those of the tribal leaders.

The *President* is Brig. Gabriel Ramushwana, who seized power in April 1990.

Flag: Three horizontal stripes of green, yellow, and brown, with a brown V on the yellow stripe, and a blue vertical strip in the hoist.

DEFENCE. The Venda Defence Force was formed in 1983. It includes a small aviation component operating 1 Aviocar transport, 1 Alouette III and 3 BK-117 helicopters.

INTERNATIONAL RELATIONS

Aid. South Africa granted aid of R426·9m. in 1990–91.

ECONOMY

Budget. The 1990–91 budget envisaged expenditure of R1,043m.

Currency. South African Rand.

NATURAL RESOURCES

Water. In 1990-91 there were 7 major dams with a total capacity of 415·5m. cu. metres, and 3 purification plants.

Minerals. Venda is relatively poor in mineral resources, although there are large supplies of stone for construction. Coal is the most important mineral; there are large deposits near Makhado. In 1990-91 further development was planned of the trial coal mine at Tshikondeni to increase production to 750,000 tons a year.

Agriculture. About 85% of Venda is suitable only for the raising of livestock because of insufficient rainfall and poor soils, while some 10% is suited to dry-land crop production. Over 13,444 ha have been given over to forest, mainly pine and eucalyptus. Twenty-four irrigation schemes are being developed and there is extensive reclamation and conservation of eroded or overgrazed land. Only maize is grown on a comparatively large scale, but tea, sisal, groundnuts, coffee and subtropical fruits are increasing in importance. Over 80% of the working population are engaged in agriculture.

INDUSTRY AND TRADE

Industry. Industrial development is still in its early stages, and since Venda's location is unfavourable, the Government is concentrating on the promotion of agroindustries utilizing local produce, and small-scale industries. A chutney factory has been established, in addition to a tea processing plant, a furniture factory and several saw-mills. A copper-chrome arsenate preservation plant has been established at Phiphidi. At Shayandima a 20-ha industrial area has been prepared. In 1990-91 the 460-ha Shayandima industrial area at Thohoyandou had over 70 developed sites with 38 industries. There was a second major industrial area at Muraleni, and commercial complexes at Makhado. In 1986 there were 159 manufacturing establishments, mainly small labour-intensive firms with a total employment of 3,016 and 906 commercial establishments with employment of 3,803.

Labour. In 1986, 45,000 migrant workers earned R180m. in the Republic of South Africa. In 1985 an estimated 6,500 border commuters worked in the Republic of South Africa, income R26m.

Commerce. Venda is a member of the South African Customs Union and trade is mainly with the Republic of South Africa. Exports include sub-tropical fruit, tea, coffee, timber, clothing, furniture and pottery. Petroleum products, machinery, motor vehicles, food, clothing and furniture are imported.

Tourism. In 1989 there were 3 National Parks, 2 caravan parks and 2 holiday resorts.

COMMUNICATIONS

Roads. There were (1991) 2,300 km of roads, of which 320 km had a permanent surface.

Civil Aviation. An airline, inaugurated in 1981, operates between Nwangundu in Thohoyandu and Johannesburg via Pietersburg and Pretoria.

Telecommunications. In 1990-91 there were 20 post offices, 24 postal agencies and 14 money order offices, and telex and fax facilities in all urban areas. There were 5 automatic and 13 manual telephone exchanges, and 15 telephone agencies. In 1990–91 the government-owned Radio Thohoyandou broadcast 24 hours daily in Venda and English on MW and FM, and South African television programmes were received through its transposers.

Newspapers. In 1990–91 there was 1 newspaper published fortnightly in Venda and English, with a circulation of 81,000.

JUSTICE, EDUCATION AND WELFARE

Justice. The Supreme Court acts as the Court of Appeal for the 5 magistrates' courts and 2 sub-offices, 2 periodical courts and the one Regional Court. Appeals from the Supreme Court are heard in the Republic of South Africa Appeal Court.

Education. The Department of Education assumed responsibility for education on independence. Education is free up to Standard 2, and pupils are taught in the native tongue, Luvenda, for the first 4 years (up to Standard 2), after which English is gradually introduced. Secondary education comprises Standards 6 to 10.

In 1991 there were 673 schools with 245,187 pupils and 8,319 teachers, 4 teacher training colleges, 3 trade schools, 1 technical high school and 1 special school. The University of Venda was established in 1981; 3,172 students (1991).

Health. In 1991 there were 3 general hospitals (1,614 beds), 2 maternity hospitals (42 beds), 2 health centres (80 beds), 58 clinics, 1 chronic ill-health institution (312 beds) and 214 rural care groups. There were about 30 doctors in the general hospitals and 16 private doctors in different areas, and 1,160 nurses.

Welfare. In 1990-91 the Government spent R79·4m. on social pension payments to 43,092 pensioners.

Further Reading

Venda 1983. Dept. of Information and Broadcasting. Sibasa, 1984

CISKEI

HISTORY. On 4 Dec. 1981 the Republic of South Africa gave independence to Ciskei, the fourth of the tribal homelands.

Brig. Oupo Gqozo seized power in a bloodless coup in March 1990.

AREA AND POPULATION. Ciskei lies between latitudes 32° and 33°35' and longitudes 26°20' and 27°48', and has a coastal boundary between East London and Port Alfred. The total area is about 9,000 sq. km. The population was (1987) 2m. but only 1m. live in Ciskei. The remainder are resident and workers in the Republic of South Africa.

Populations of towns (1987): Mdantsane, 350,000; Zwelitsha, 55,000; Sada, 38,000; Dimbaza, 25,000 and Litha, 9,500. The capital, Bisho, houses 8,000 people, although the development is still going on.

CONSTITUTION AND GOVERNMENT. In 1981 Ciskei became an independent democratic republic. The Government had consisted of a President, an Executive Council and a National Assembly of Hereditary Chiefs, elected and nominated members and the Paramount Chief's representatives. On 4 March 1990, in a bloodless coup, the President-for-life, Dr Lennox Sebe was deposed. The Constitution was suspended. The coup was led by Brig. Oupo Gqozo. A constitutional amendment of Feb. 1991 relinquished sovereignty, and made over constitutional, financial and judicial control to the Republic of South Africa.

Flag: Blue, a broad diagonal band from lower hoist to upper fly, charged with a black crane.

National Anthem: Nkosi Sikelel' i Afrika, composed by Enoch Sontonga.

DEFENCE. There is a Ciskei Defence Force. Its aviation element is equipped with 2 Skyvan and 3 Islander transports, and 3 BK-117 and 1 BO 105 helicopters, plus 2 Cessna 152 trainers.

ECONOMY

Budget. The 1987–88 budget balanced at R859m.

Currency. South African Rand.

ENERGY AND NATURAL RESOURCES

Electricity. Ciskei is totally dependent on power supply lines maintained by the Republic of South Africa.

Minerals. Mineral resources are mainly undeveloped and in 1988 only two mines existed in Ciskei, one producing dolorite, the other rutile ilmenite, leucoxene and zircon.

Agriculture. In 1977–78, total agricultural production was valued at R8·26m.

In 1986, the dryland products included (in tons): Maize, 3,125; wheat, 131; sorghum, 325; sunflower, 8·7. Horticultural crops included (1986, in tons): Potatoes, 979·9; cabbage, 5,135·8; carrots, 981·1; brussel sprouts, 356; onions, 4·8; pumpkins, 102·4; cauliflower, 11·6; peas, 28; dry beans, 83·3; spinach, 1·9; beetroot, 8·5.

Livestock (1986): 11,442 cattle, 76,294 sheep, 77,568 goats, 3,743 pigs, 14,742,814 poultry.

Forestry. In 1983–84, 5,500 ha were planted mainly with conifers. The indigenous forest covered some 18,000 ha. In 1984–85 (estimate), production of timber was valued at R600,000.

INDUSTRY AND TRADE

Industry. In 1988 total investment was R467m. The chief manufactures include textiles, timber products, electronic components, steel products, food and leather goods.

Commerce. International trade is mainly with the Republic of South Africa and no separate figures are available. The main exports are pineapples, timber and manufactured goods.

Tourism. Tourism is an important and developing industry.

COMMUNICATIONS

Roads. In 1988 there were 448 km of tarred roads and 2,556 km of gravel roads.

Railways. There are two main railway lines serving the southern part of Ciskei.

Aviation. Ciskei uses East London's airport and there is a new international airport at Bulembu, near Bisho.

Shipping. Ciskei has no harbour of its own but has full access to the facilities of East London in the Republic of South Africa.

Telecommunications. All major centres have post offices and manual and automatic telephone exchanges; telex facilities are available. There were (1987–88) 21,095 telephones. Radio Ciskei broadcasts from Bisho daily.

Newspapers (1988). There were three Ciskeian newspapers: *Umthombo*; *Imvo*, first published in 1884; *Umtha*, an agricultural newspaper.

JUSTICE, RELIGION, EDUCATION AND WELFARE

Justice. The Supreme Court acts as Court of Appeal for the eight Magistrates' Courts, which in turn act as Courts of Appeal for the Chiefs' Courts. Appeals from the Supreme Court are heard by the Appellate Division of Ciskei in Bisho.

Religion. In 1988 (estimate) the population was 27% Methodists, 20% Independent, 16% Presbyterian, 12% Anglicans, 7% Roman Catholics and 5% Dutch Reformed Church.

Education. In 1986–87 there were 545 primary schools with 200,752 pupils and 4,369 teachers; 158 post primary schools with 59,414 students and 1,809 teachers; 3 training colleges with 1,677 students and 97 teachers and 1 vocational school with 174 students and 20 teachers. The University of Fort Hare had a total of 2,304 students in 1981.

Health. In 1987–88, there were 8 hospitals with 2,910 beds, and a total of 2,952 nursing staff.

Social Welfare. Pensions paid in 1984–85:

	Beneficiaries	Amount (R1,000)
Old age	42,573	20,435
Blind	564	270
Disability	5,421	2,602
War veterans	72	38
Leprosy	11	5

Further Reading

Charlton, N., *Ciskei: Economics and Politics of Dependence in a South African Homeland.* London, 1980

Pauw, B. A., *Christianity and the Xhosa Tradition.* OUP, 1975

Van der Kooy, R. (ed.) *The Republic of Ciskei: A Nation in Transition.* Pretoria, 1981

SOUTH GEORGIA
AND
SOUTH SANDWICH ISLANDS

HISTORY. South Georgia was probably first sighted by a London merchant, Antonio de la Roche, and then in 1756 by a Spanish Captain, Gregorie Jerez. The first landing and exploration was undertaken by Captain James Cook, who formally took possession in the name of George III on 17 Jan. 1775. British sealers arrived in 1788 and American sealers in 1791. Sealing reached its peak in 1800. A German team was the first to carry out scientific studies there in 1882–83. Whaling began in 1904 when the Compania Argentina de Pesca formed by C. A. Larsen, a Norwegian, established a station at Grytviken. Six other stations were established up to 1912. Whaling ceased in 1966 and the civil administration was withdrawn. Argentine forces invaded South Georgia on 3 April 1982. A British naval task force recovered the Island on 25 April 1982.

AREA AND POPULATION. South Georgia lies 800 miles south-east of the Falkland Islands and has an area of 1,450 sq. miles. The South Sandwich Islands are 470 miles south-east of South Georgia and have an area of 130 sq. miles. There has been no permanent population in South Georgia since the whaling station at Leith was abandoned in 1966. There is a small military garrison. The British Antarctic Survey have a biological station on Bird Island. The South Sandwich Islands are uninhabited.

CLIMATE. The climate is wet and cold with strong winds and little seasonal variation. 15°C is occasionally reached on a windless day. Temperatures below −15°C at sea level are unusual.

CONSTITUTION AND GOVERNMENT. Under the new Constitution which came into force on 3 Oct. 1985 the Territories ceased to be dependencies of the Falkland Islands. Executive power is vested in a Commissioner who is the officer for the time being administering the Government of the Falkland Islands. The Commissioner is obliged to consult the officer for the time being commanding Her Majesty's British Forces in the South Atlantic on matters relating to defence and internal security (except police). The Commissioner whenever practicable consults the Executive Council of the Falkland Islands on the exercise of functions that in his opinion might affect the Falkland Islands. There is no Legislative Council. Laws are made by the Commissioner.

Commissioner: W. H. Fullerton, CMG.

Economy. The total revenue of the Territories (estimate, 1988–89) £268,240, mainly from philatelic sales and investment income. Expenditure estimate £194,260.

Communications. There is occasional direct sea communication between the Falkland Islands and South Georgia and the South Sandwich Islands by means of the Royal Research Ships *John Biscoe* and *Bransfield* and the ice patrol vessel *HMS Endurance*. Royal Fleet Auxiliary ships, which serve the garrison, run regularly to South Georgia. Mail is dropped from military aircraft.

Justice. There is a Supreme Court for the Territories and a Court of Appeal in the United Kingdom. Appeals may go from that court to the Judicial Committee of the Privy Council. There is no magistrate permanently in residence. The Officer Commanding the garrison is usually appointed a magistrate.

Further Reading

Headland, R. K., *The Island of South Georgia*. CUP, 1985

SPAIN

Capital: Madrid
Population: 38·42m. (1991)
GNP per capita: US$12,610 (1990)

Reino de España

(Kingdom of Spain)

HISTORY. Although Spain has traditionally been a monarchy there have been two Republics, the first in 1873, which lasted for 11 months, and the second 1931–39; both were democratically and peacefully proclaimed. Part of the army rebelled against the republican government on 18 July 1936, thus beginning the Spanish Civil War, *see* THE STATESMAN'S YEAR-BOOK, 1939, pp. 1325–26. The new regime was led by Gen. Francisco Franco y Bahamonde as Head of State and Government, and its institutions were based on single party rule, with the *Falange* as the only legal political organization.

In July 1969, Prince Don Juan Carlos de Borbón y Borbón, grandson of Alfonso XIII, was sworn in as successor to the Head of State and he had the title of HRH Prince of Spain until he became King.

Gen. Franco died on 20 Nov. 1975 and on 22 Nov. Prince Juan Carlos de Borbón y Borbón took the oath as Juan Carlos I, King of Spain.

AREA AND POPULATION. Spain is bounded north by the Bay of Biscay and the Pyrenees (which form the frontier with France and Andorra), east and south by the Mediterranean and the Straits of Gibraltar, south-west by the Atlantic and west by Portugal and the Atlantic. Continental Spain has an area of 492,592 sq. km, and including the Balearic and Canary Islands and the towns of Ceuta and Melilla 504,750 sq. km (194,884 sq. miles). Population (census, 1 March 1991; provisional results), 38,425,679 (19,614,060 female).

The growth of the population has been as follows:

Census year	Population	Rate of annual increase	Census year	Population	Rate of annual increase
1860	15,655,467	0·34	1950	27,976,755	0·81
1910	19,927,150	0·72	1960	30,903,137	0·88
1920	21,303,162	0·69	1970	33,823,918	0·94
1930	23,563,867	1·06	1981	37,746,260	1·15
1940	25,877,971	0·98	1991	38,425,679 [1]	0·18

[1] Provisional results

Area and population of the autonomous communities and provinces, on 1 Jan. 1989 (official estimate):

Autonomous community Province	Area (sq. km)	Population	Per sq. km	Autonomous community Province	Area (sq. km)	Population	Per sq. km
Andalusia	*87,268*	*7,019,285*	*80*	*Baleares*	*5,014*	*750,967*	*149*
Almería	8,774	461,237	52	*Basque*			
Cádiz	7,385	1,081,139	146	Country, The	7,261	2,157,598	297
Córdoba	13,718	765,517	55	Álava	3,047	274,893	90
Granada	12,531	806,406	64	Guipúzcoa	1,997	697,435	350
Huelva	10,085	446,994	44	Vizcaya	2,217	1,185,270	536
Jaén	13,498	659,939	48	*Canary Islands*	7,273	1,557,533	214
Málaga	7,276	1,203,724	165	Palmas, Las	4,065	803,392	197
Sevilla	14,001	1,594,329	113	Santa Cruz			
Aragón	*47,669*	*1,196,454*	*25*	de Tenerife	3,208	754,141	235
Huesca	15,671	210,747	13	*Cantabria*	*5,289*	*531,654*	*100*
Teruel	14,804	148,805	10	*Castilla-La*			
Zaragoza	17,194	836,902	48	*Mancha*	*79,226*	*1,692,175*	*21*
Asturias	*10,565*	*1,125,419*	*106*	Albacete	14,858	348,470	23

Autonomous community / Province	Area (sq. km)	Population	Per sq. km
Ciudad Real	19,749	489,537	24
Cuenca	17,061	213,258	12
Guadalajara	12,190	148,117	12
Toledo	15,368	492,793	32
Castilla-León	*94,147*	*2,609,636*	*27*
Ávila	8,048	183,363	22
Burgos	14,269	361,763	25
León	15,468	536,206	34
Palencia	8,029	190,010	23
Salamanca	12,336	367,383	29
Segovia	6,949	151,494	21
Soria	10,287	97,557	9
Valladolid	8,202	499,259	60
Zamora	10,559	222,601	21
Catalonia	*31,930*	*6,124,923*	*191*
Barcelona	7,773	4,714,302	606
Gerona	5,886	512,187	87
Lérida	12,028	355,547	29
Tarragona	6,283	542,887	86
Extremadura	*41,602*	*1,101,113*	*26*
Badajoz	21,657	675,623	31
Cáceres	19,945	425,490	21
Galicia	*29,434*	*2,896,801*	*98*
Coruña, La	7,876	1,133,676	144
Lugo	9,803	408,321	41
Orense	7,278	434,434	59
Pontevedra	4,477	920,370	205
Madrid	*7,995*	*4,964,486*	*621*
Murcia	*11,317*	*1,048,029*	*92*
Navarra	*10,421*	*523,977*	*50*
Rioja, La	*5,034*	*265,378*	*52*
Valencian Community	*23,305*	*3,852,623*	*165*
Alicante	5,863	1,267,528	216
Castellón	6,679	449,812	67
Valencia	10,763	2,135,283	198
Ceuta [1]	*18*	*68,014*	*3,778*
Melilla [1]	*14*	*55,717*	*3,979*
Total	**504,750**	**39,541,782**	**78**

[1] Ceuta and Melilla are municipalities on the northern coast of Morocco.

The capitals of the autonomous communities are as follows: Andalusia, cap. Sevilla (Seville); Aragón, cap. Zaragoza (Saragossa); Asturias, cap. Oviedo; Baleares (Balearic Islands), cap. Palma de Mallorca; The Basque Country, cap. Vitoria; Canary Islands, dual and alternative capital, Las Palmas and Santa Cruz de Tenerife; Cantabria, cap. Santander; ; Castilla-La Mancha, cap. Toledo; Castilla-León, cap. Valladolid; Catalonia, cap. Barcelona; Extremadura, cap. Mérida; Galicia, cap. Santiago de Compostela; Madrid, cap. Madrid; Murcia, cap. Murcia (but regional parliament in Cartagena); Navarra, cap. Pamplona; La Rioja, cap. Logroño; Valencian Community, cap. Valencia.

The capitals of the provinces are in the towns from which they take the name, except in Alava (capital Vitoria), Asturias (Oviedo), Baleares (Palma de Mallorca), Cantabria (Santander), Guipúzcoa (San Sebastián), La Rioja (Logroño), Navarra (Pamplona) and Vizcaya (Bilbao).

By decree of 21 Sept. 1927 the islands which form the Canary Archipelago were divided into 2 provinces, under the name of their respective capitals: Santa Cruz de Tenerife and Las Palmas de Gran Canaria. The province of Santa Cruz de Tenerife is constituted by the islands of Tenerife, La Palma, Gomera and Hierro, and that of Las Palmas by Gran Canaria, Lanzarote and Fuerteventura, with the small barren islands of Alegranza, Roque del Este, Roque del Oeste, Graciosa, Montaña Clara and Lobos. The area of the islands is 7,273 sq. km; population (1 Jan. 1989), 1,557,533. Places under Spanish sovereignty in Morocco are: Alhucemas, Ceuta, Chafarinas, Melilla and Peñón de Vélez.

Official estimate of populations of principal towns on 1 Jan. 1989:

Town	Population	Town	Population	Town	Population
Albacete	126,634	Cáceres	72,680	Gijón	263,154
Alcalá de Henares	152,473	Cádiz	156,886	Granada	265,265
Alcobendas	75,620	Cartagena	173,788	Guecho	80,915
Alcorcón	140,621	Castellón de		Hermanas, Dos	70,232
Algeciras	100,766	la Plana	134,021	Hospitalet	277,407
Alicante	264,115	Córdoba	304,780	Huelva	139,125
Almería	159,330	Cornellá de		Jaén	107,836
Avilés	88,029	Llobregat	86,713	Jerez de la Frontera	184,595
Badajoz	124,616	Coruña, La	252,419	Laguna, La	113,733
Badalona	225,292	Coslada	70,522	Leganés	170,973
Baracaldo	112,551	Elche	182,683	León	137,261
Barcelona	1,712,350	Ferrol, El	86,271	Lérida	110,962
Bilbao	384,129	Fuenlabrada	136,222	Logroño	120,802
Burgos	161,538	Getafe	137,389	Lugo	80,011

Town	Population	Town	Population	Town	Population
Madrid	3,108,463	Reus	85,143	Santiago de	
Málaga	555,518	Sabadell	190,962	Compostela	89,041
Marbella	79,624	Salamanca	160,522	Sevilla	669,976
Mataró	101,352	San Baudilio del		Tarragona	110,947
Móstoles	185,975	Llobregat	78,369	Tarrasa	161,625
Murcia	318,688	San Fernando	82,862	Telde	77,170
Orense	107,054	San Sebastián	181,794	Torrejón de Ardoz	85,135
Oviedo	192,291	Santa Coloma de		Valencia	749,574
Palencia	77,125	Gramanet	135,690	Valladolid	333,230
Palma de Mallorca	320,692	Santa Cruz de		Vigo	275,580
Palmas, Las	371,495	Tenerife	219,907	Vitoria	206,706
Pamplona	182,365	Santander	192,483	Zaragoza	586,574

Vital statistics for calendar years:

	Marriages	Births	Deaths
1985	199,658	434,490	312,532
1986	207,929	438,750	310,413
1987	210,098	421,098	309,364
1988	214,898	415,844	318,848
1989	215,840	404,564	324,771

On 31 Dec. 1989 the number of foreigners legally registered was 398,147 (largest foreign community, British, 73,535).

Languages. The Constitution states that 'Castilian is the Spanish official language of the State', but also that 'All other Spanish languages will also be official in the corresponding Autonomous Communities'.

Catalan is spoken by a majority of people in Catalonia (64%, 1986) and Baleares (70·8%), and by one half in Valencian Community (49%, where it is frequently called Valencian); in Aragón, a narrow strip close to Catalonia and Valencian Community boundaries, speaks Catalan.

Galician, a language very close to Portuguese, is spoken by a majority of people in Galicia (90%, 1986); Basque, by a significant minority in the Basque Country (24·5%). Basque is also spoken by a small minority in north-west Navarra (12%).

In bilingual communities, both Spanish and the regional language are taught in the schools and universities.

CLIMATE. Most of Spain has a form of Mediterranean climate with mild, moist winters and hot, dry summers, but the northern coastal region has a moist, equable climate, with rainfall well-distributed throughout the year, mild winters and warm summers, though having less sunshine than the rest of Spain.

Madrid. Jan. 41°F (5°C), July 77°F (25°C). Annual rainfall 16·8" (419 mm). Barcelona. Jan. 46°F (8°C), July 74°F (23·5°C). Annual rainfall 21" (525 mm). Cartagena. Jan. 51°F (10·5°C), July 75°F (24°C). Annual rainfall 14·9" (373 mm). La Coruña. Jan. 51°F (10·5°C), July 66°F (19°C). Annual rainfall 32" (800 mm). Sevilla. Jan. 51°F (10·5°C), July 85°F (29·5°C). Annual rainfall 19·5" (486 mm). Palma de Mallorca (Balearic Islands). Jan. 51°F (11°C), July 77°F (25°C). Annual rainfall 13·6" (347 mm). Santa Cruz de Tenerife (Canary Islands). Jan. 64°F (17·9°C), July 76°F (24·4°C). Annual rainfall 7·72" (196 mm).

KING. Juan Carlos I, born 5 Jan. 1938. The eldest son of Don Juan, Conde de Barcelona. Juan Carlos was given precedence over his father as pretender to the Spanish throne in an agreement in 1954 between Don Juan and Gen. Franco. Don Juan resigned his claims to the throne in May 1977. King (then Prince) Juan Carlos married, in 1962, Princess Sophia of Greece, daughter of the late King Paul of the Hellenes and Queen Frederika. *Offspring:* Elena, born 20 Dec. 1963; Cristina, 13 June 1965; Felipe, Prince of Asturias, Heir to the throne, 30 Jan. 1968.

The king receives an allowance, part of which is taxable, approved by parliament each year. In 1991 it was 845m. pesetas. There is no formal court; the *Diputación de la Grandeza* represents the interests of the aristocracy.

CONSTITUTION AND GOVERNMENT. Following the death of Gen. Franco the *Cortes* (Parliament) was freely elected on 15 June 1977. A new Constitution was approved by referendum on 6 Dec. 1978, and came into force 29 Dec. 1978. It established a parliamentary monarchy, with King Juan Carlos I as head of state. Legislative power is vested in the Cortes, a bicameral parliament composed of the *Congress of Deputies* (lower house) and the *Senate* (upper house). The Congress of Deputies has not less than 300 nor more than 400 members (350 in the general elections of 1977, 1979, 1982, 1986 and 1989) elected in a proportional system under which electors choose between party lists of candidates in multi-member constituencies. The members of the Senate are elected by a majority system: The 47 mainland provinces elect 4 senators each, regardless of population; the island provinces electing 5 (Baleares, Las Palmas) or 6 (Santa Cruz de Tenerife); and Ceuta and Melilla, 2 senators each. There are 208 senators, to whom are added some other members of the upper house elected by the parliaments of the autonomous communities. There is also a *Council of State* (president, Fernando Ledesma) and a Constitutional Court (*see below under* Justice). Deputies and senators are elected by universal secret suffrage, for a term of 4 years. Executive power is vested in the President of the Government (*Prime Minister*) and a Cabinet; the Prime Minister is elected by the Congress of Deputies.

A general election took place on 29 Oct. 1989.

In March 1992 the composition of the 350-member Congress of Deputies was: Spanish Workers Socialist Party (PSOE), 175; Popular Party (PP, conservative), 107; United Left (IU, communist dominated coalition), 17; Convergence and Union (CiU, Catalan nationalists), 18; Social and Democratic Centre (CDS, centrist), 14; Basque Nationalist Party (PNV), 5; Herri Batasuna (HB, Basque separatists), 4; Andalusian Party (PA, Andalusian regionalists), 2; Eusko Alkartasuna (EA) and Euskadiko Eskerra (EE), both non-radical Basque separatists, 2 each; Valencian Union (UV, Valencian regionalists), 2; two conservative regional parties from Aragón and the Canaries, 1 each. The Speaker (*Presidente*) is Félix Pons Irazazábal (PSOE).

Senate: 208 members, excluding those elected by regional parliaments (250 including them): PSOE, 106; PP, 78; CiU, 10; PNV, 4; HB, 3; CDS, 2; IU, 1; four different groups from the Canaries, 4 in all. Speaker (*Presidente*) of the Senate, Juan José Laborda (PSOE).

The Council of Ministers was composed as follows in April 1992:

President of the Government (Prime Minister): Felipe González Márquez (Secretary-General of PSOE).

Vice-President of the Government: Narcís Serra i Serra. *Foreign Affairs:* Francisco Fernández Ordóñez. *Economy and Finance:* Carlos Solchaga Catalán. *Industry, Commerce and Tourism:* Claudio Aranzadi Martínez. *Interior:* José Luis Corcuera. *Defence:* Julián García Vargas. *Public Administration:* Juan Manuel Eguiagaray. *Education and Science:* Javier Solana Madariaga. *Public Works and Transport:* José Borrell. *Justice:* Tomas de la Quadra Salcedo. *Culture:* Jordi Solé Tura. *Agriculture, Fisheries and Food:* Pedro Solbes. *Health and Consumers Affairs:* José Antonio Griñán. *Labour and Social Security:* Luis Maritínez Noval. *Social Affairs:* Matilde Fernández. *Minister, Government Spokeswoman:* Rosa Conde. *Relations with the Cortes and Secretary of the Cabinet:* Virgilio Zapatero.

National flag: Three horizontal stripes of red, yellow, red, with the yellow of double width, and charged near the hoist with the national arms.

National anthem: Marcha real.

Regional and local government. The Constitution of 1978 establishes a semifederal system of regional administration, with the *autonomous community (comunidad autónoma)* as its basic element. There are 17 autonomous communities, each of them having a Parliament, elected by universal vote, and a regional government; all possess exclusive legislative and executive power in many matters, as listed in the national Constitution and in their own fundamental law (*estatuto de autonomía*). The Basque Country and Catalonia elected their first parliaments in March 1980, Galicia in Oct. 1981 and Andalusia in May 1982, all others in May 1983. Further elections were held in the autonomous communities 1984–92.

Date of last elections and party composition of the autonomous communities: *Andalusia* (June 1990), PSOE 61, PP 27, United Left 11, Andalusian Party 10; *Aragon* (May 1991), PSOE 30, nationalists 17, PP 17, IU 3; *Asturias* (May 1991), PSOE 21, PP 15, IU 6, CDS 2, nationalists 1; *Baleares* (May 1991), PP 31, PSOE 21, nationalist groups 6; *Basque Country* (Oct. 1990), Basque Nationalist Party 22, PSOE 16, Herri Batasuna 13, Eusko Alkartasuna 9, Euskadiko Equerra 6, PP 6, Alaversa Union 3; *Canary islands* (May 1991), nationalist groups 26, PSOE 22, PP 6, CDS 6; *Cantabria* (May 1991), nationalist groups 17, PSOE 16, PP 6; *Castile-La Mancha* (May 1991), PSOE 27, PP 19, IU 1, others 25; *Castile and Leon* (May 1991), PP 43, PSOE 35, CDS 5, IU 1; *Extremadura* (May 1991) PSOE 39, PP 19, IU 4, CDS 3; *Galicia* (Dec. 1989), PP 38, PSOE 28, nationalist groups 9; *La Rioja* (May 1991), PSOE 16, PP 15, nationalists 2; *Madrid* (May 1991), PP 48, PSOE 40, IU 13; *Murcia* (May 1991), PSOE 24, PP 17, IU 4; *Navarre* (May 1991), nationalist groups 29, PSOE 19, IU 2, others 10; *Valencian Community* (May 1991), PSOE 45, PP 30, Valencian Union 13, IU 6.

A new PNV-PSOE-EE coalition government was formed in the Basque Country in Sept.1991.

There are 7 autonomous communities composed of only one province: Asturias, Cantabria, La Rioja, Navarra, Baleares, Murcia and Madrid. The other 10 are formed by 2 or more provinces. In all, there are in Spain 50 provinces, since the administrative division established in 1833. The *Provincial Council (Diputación Provincial)* is the administrative organ of the province, except in the 7 autonomous communities composed of one only province, where there are only the regional legislative and executive powers. The provincial council is indirectly elected. Each of the 7 main islands of the Canaries (provinces of Las Palmas and Santa Cruz de Tenerife) has a directly elected corporation, the *Cabildo Insular,* to rule its special interests; in the main islands of the Balearics there is also an elected *Consell Insular.*

The provinces are constituted by the association of municipalities (8,066 in 1989). Municipalities are autonomous in their own sphere. At their head stands the municipal council *(Ayuntamiento),* members of which are elected in a universal ballot every 4 years, and they, in turn, elect one of them as Mayor *(Alcalde).* In 1991 6,216 municipalities had fewer than 3,000 inhabitants; such resource-poor municipalities may form associations to share services.

Elections were held in May 1991 for some 66,500 municipal councillors and 13 of the 17 autonomous communities. The electorate was 30,287,056. The PSOE won 38·5% of votes cast (37·2% in the 1987 elections), the Popular Party 25% (20·3%), the United Left Coalition (Communists) 8·5% (7%) and the Democratic and Social Centre 3·8% (9·8%).

DEFENCE. Conscription is for 9 months which may be extended to from 16 to 36 months for volunteers. Recruits to the national police are exempt from conscription. Since 1989 women have been accepted in all sections of the armed forces.

Army. The Army is divided into 2 principal parts: 8 Regional Operation Commands (including 2 overseas) and the General Reserve Force. The former consist of 1 armoured, 1 mechanized, 2 mountain and 1 motorized divisions, 2 armoured cavalry and 1 air-portable brigades; 1 infantry regiment and supporting artillery, engineer and signals units. The General Reserve Force comprises the Spanish Legion (7,000 personnel in 3 regiments) an airborne brigade with air defence, artillery and engineer units. There are also the Royal Guard Regiment, and the Army Aviation forces. Equipment includes 299 AMX-30, 329 M-47E, 46 M-47E2 and 164 M-48 main battle tanks. The aviation element of the Army consists of 180 helicopters (53 armed). Strength (1992) 182,500 (including 115,000 conscripts). Of these 5,600 are stationed on the Balearic Islands, 10,000 on the Canary Islands and 15,800 in Ceuta and Melilla. The paramilitary *Guardia Civil* number 63,000 men. Immediate army reserves number 142,700.

Navy. The accession of Spain to NATO, even though not fully integrated into the military structure, has provided the Navy with a key operational role in support of NATO sea lines of communication on the Canaries-Gibraltar-Balearics axis. The main task force, 'Grupo Alfa', is centred on the flagship, *Príncipe de Asturias*, escorted by new and modernized frigates.

The 17,000-tonne *Príncipe de Asturias*, a light vertical/short take-off and landing aircraft carrier built to a US design was commissioned in 1989. The *Príncipe de Asturias* air group comprises 8 AV-8B Matador, 8 Sea King anti-submarine helicopters, 2 Sea King early warning helicopters and about 4 AB-212 light helicopters.

There are also 8 French-designed submarines (4 Daphne class, 4 Agosta class), 4 old ex-US destroyers, 4 US-design Santa María guided missile frigates with Standard SM-1 surface-to-air missiles, 5 other guided missile frigates with Standard, and 6 smaller frigates, 4 offshore patrol vessels, 20 coastal and 36 inshore patrol craft, 4 ocean minesweepers, 8 coastal minesweepers, 2 amphibious troop transports, 2 tank landing ships and 12 landing craft. Major auxiliaries include 1 tanker, 1 transport, 6 ocean tugs, 1 training ship, 4 water carriers and 6 survey ships. There are about 80 minor auxiliaries and service craft.

The Navy is being renewed and modernized; 2 frigates have been ordered. A fleet replenishment ship is being designed in co-operation with the Netherlands, and mine countermeasures vessels are expected to start building shortly to the British Sandown class design.

The Naval Air Service operates 21 AV-8S Harrier and EAV-8B Harrier-II attack aircraft, 34 S-70B Seahawk Sea King, SH 60-B AB-212 and Hughes 500 anti-submarine helicopters, 3 radar early warning Sea Kings and a few additional training and utility aircraft. The Air force operates 11 Orion maritime patrol aircraft on anti-submarine tasks.

There are 7,500 marines, who provide 1 amphibious regiment and garrison regiments at the main bases. Main naval bases are at Ferrol, Rota, Cádiz, Cartagena, Palma de Mallorca, Mahón and Las Palmas (Canary Islands).

In 1991 personnel totalled 39,500 (22,800 conscripts) including marines.

Air Force. The Air Force is organized as an independent service, dating from 1939. It is administered through 4 operational commands. These comprise Air Combat Command which controls interceptor squadrons (including USAF elements) and the control and warning radar network, Tactical and Transport Commands, and Air Command of the Canaries. Strength (1992) 36,500 (21,000 conscripts), with 59,200 immediate reserves and 221 combat aircraft.

The Tactical Air Command has 2 fighter-bomber squadrons of Spanish-built Northrop SF-5s and 1 aero-naval co-operaton squadron with P-3 Orion anti-submarine aircraft. Air Combat Command has 2 squadrons of Mirage III-Es, 1 squadron of RF-4C Phantom IIs, 3 squadrons of F-18 Hornets and 2 squadrons of Mirage F1-Cs. 5 KC-130H tankers support the fighter squadrons. 3 wings of Air Transport Command operate C-130 Hercules, CN-235 and Spanish-built CASA Aviocars. Air Command of the Canaries has 3 squadrons, equipped with Aviocar transports; Mirage F1 fighter-bombers; F27 Maritime aircraft and Super Puma helicopters for search and rescue. Other equipment includes 3 Boeing 707s, 5 Falcons and helicopters for VIP transport; and aircraft for photographic, firefighting, target towing and research duties. Air-sea rescue units have Aviocars and Super Puma helicopters.

American-built F33 Bonanza and Chilean-built Pillan piston-engined aircraft are used for basic training, after which pupil pilots progress to CASA C-101 jet aircraft. Two-seat versions of operational types are used as advanced trainers. Other training types include Beechcraft Barons for instrument flying and liaison duties.

INTERNATIONAL RELATIONS

Membership. Spain is a member of the UN, the Council of Europe, NATO, WEU, the EC and OECD and the Schengen Accord, which abolishes frontier controls between Belgium, France, Germany, Italy, Luxembourg, the Netherlands, Portugal and Spain.

ECONOMY

Budget. Revenue and expenditure in 1m. pesetas:

	1987	1988	1989	1990	1991
Revenue	8,113,442	8,939,237	10,644,507	12,629,510	13,427,714
Expenditure	8,113,442	8,939,237	10,644,507	12,629,510	13,427,714

The budget is made up as follows (in 1m. pesetas):

Revenue (1991)		Revenue (1991) continued	
Direct taxes	5,835,000	Income on assets	351,500
Indirect taxes	4,383,600	Sale on real investments	20,000
Levies and various revenues	385,000	Capital transfers	214,900
Current transfers	469,000	Deficit	1,768,714

Expenditure (1991)		Expenditure (1991) continued	
H.M. House	845	Ministry of Education and Science	1,086,754
Cortes (Parliament)	14,355	,, Labour and Social	
Court of Accounts	2,990	Security	995,702
Constitutional Court	1,201	,, Industry and Energy	205,748
Council of State	648	,, Agriculture and Food	177,266
Public Debt	2,582,514	,, Transport, Tourism and	
Civil Service Pensions	576,294	Communications	643,619
General Council of the Judicial		,, Culture	54,047
Power	1,672	,, Public Administration	36,474
Relations with the Cortes and		,, Health and Consumer	
Secretariat of the Cabinet	22,173	Affairs	1,467,066
Ministry of Foreign Affairs	74,178	,, Social Affairs	39,188
,, Justice	193,010	,, the Government	
,, Defence	858,091	Spokeswoman	1,900
,, Finance	394,992	Regional governments	1,929,839
,, Interior	463,689	Regional Compensation Fund	257,383
,, Public Works and		Expenses in several ministries	151,911
,, Housing	704,735	Financial relations with EEC	489,430

Currency. The unit of currency is the *peseta* (ESP), notionally divided into 100 *céntimos* (not in use since 1984).

Bank-notes of 10,000, 5,000, 2,000 and 1,000 *pesetas* and coins of 1 *peseta* (copper and aluminium), 2, 5, 10, 25, 50, 100, 200 and 500 *pesetas* (nickel and copper) are in circulation. On 1 Jan. 1990 the circulation of bank-notes was 4,003,000m. *pesetas* and of coins, 249,800m. *pesetas*. Inflation rate in Dec. 1988, 5·8%; 1989, 6·9%; 1990, 6·7%; 1991, 5·5%.

In March 1992, £1 = 181·15 *pesetas*; US$1 = 103·19.

Banking and Finance. On 1 Jan. 1922 the Bank of Spain (*Governor*, Mariano Rubio) came under the Bank Ordinance Law, according to which the Government participate in its net profits. The Banking Corporation of Spain groups together the shares of all state-owned banks, and competes in the financial market with private banks.

The largest banks are: Banco Central Hispano Americano; Banco Bilbao Vizcaya; Banco Español de Crédito; Banco de Santander; Banco Popular Español; Banco Exterior de España; Banco Intercontinental Español; Banco de Sabadell. All are privately owned except the Banco Exterior de España.

Spanish banks deposits, 30 June 1990, amounted to 24,120,061m pesetas; foreign banks, 1,705,295m.; savings banks, 18,744,282m.; rural (farmers) savings banks, 1,525,311m.

There are stock exchanges in Madrid, Barcelona, Bilbao and Valencia.

Weights and Measures. On 1 Jan. 1859 the metric system of weights and measures was introduced.

ENERGY AND NATURAL RESOURCES

Electricity. Electric power-stations in 1990 had a total installed capacity of 45·1m. kw. The total output 1990, amounted to 151,451m. kwh of which 25,694m. was hydroelectric and 54,265m. nuclear. There were 9 nuclear power stations, with a net capacity of 6·8m. kw (1990), which produced 36% of electricity in 1990. The government announced in 1991 that no new nuclear power stations would commence operating before 2000. Supply 110 and 220 volts; 50 Hz.

Oil. Crude oil production (1990) 0·83m. tonnes.

Gas. Production of natural gas in 1990 was 1,307m. cu. metres.

Minerals. Spain has a relatively wide range of minerals but most of them are found in small or moderate quantities. Production of the principal minerals (in 1,000 tonnes; net metal content):

	1989	1990		1989	1990
Anthracite	5,573	5,809	Lead	62	58
Coal	8,951	9,073	Zinc	266	255
Lignite	21,927	21,070	Tin [1]	64	49
Uranium [1]	255	269	Wolfram [1]	73	34
Iron	2,127	1,366	Fluorspar	156	145
Pyrites	894	748	Potassium salts	1,582	1,461
Copper	25	11			

[1] Tonnes.

Agriculture. In 1989 the total value of agricultural produce was 1,784·6m. pesetas; of livestock, 1,211·9m. Land under cultivation in 1990 (in 1,000 ha) included: Cereals, 7,502; vegetables, 420; potatoes, 270. On 1 Jan. 1991, 710,060 tractors, 280,002 motor ploughs and 51,328 harvesters were in use.

Principal crops	Area (in 1,000 ha)				Yield (in 1,000 tonnes)			
	1987	1988	1989	1990	1987	1988	1989	1990
Wheat	2,174	2,332	2,295	2,005	5,774	6,514	5,456	4,759
Barley	4,377	4,175	4,257	4,359	9,533	12,070	9,308	9,410
Oats	378	335	345	349	502	537	494	519
Rye	222	222	227	207	321	357	337	274
Rice	78	80	59	94	482	499	341	578
Maize	526	535	516	477	3,338	3,577	3,224	3,027
Potatoes	303	280	274	273	5,550	4,578	5,230	5,382
Sugar-beet	184	194	171	170	7,638	9,056	7,434	7,286
Sunflower	978	894	950	1,165	926	1,123	869	1,262

In 1989, 1,473,000 ha were under vines; production of wine was (1990) 41·8m. hectolitres. The area under onions was 26,000 ha, yielding 959,000 tonnes. Production of oranges and mandarines was 3,941,000 tonnes, lemons, 575,000. Other products are esparto, flax, hemp and pulse. Spain has important industries connected with the preparation of wine and fruits.

Industrial crops (1990 in 1,000 tonnes): Cotton, 233; olive oil, 612; tobacco, 41.

Livestock products (1990 in 1,000 tonnes): Pork, 1,601; beef, 472; mutton, 204; poultry meat, 842; goat meat, 17; rabbit meat, 69; cows' milk, 5,633m. litres; sheep's milk, 307m. litres; goats' milk, 436m. litres; eggs, 888m. dozen.

Livestock (1988): Horses, 250,000; asses, 131,000; mules, 110,000; cattle, 4·98m.; sheep, 17,894,000; goats, 2·9m.; pigs, 16,941,000; poultry, 55m.

Forestry. Total forests (1989) 15·7m. ha; production, 1988, 8,736,000 cu. metres of wood. Other forest products (1988 in tonnes): Resins, 16,972; cork, 82,680; esparto, (1987) 6,425. Value of forest products, 1987: 116·4m. pesetas.

Fisheries. The total catch amounted in 1990 to 974,245 tonnes, including 108,255 tonnes of molluscs, 32,953 of crustaceans and 73,525 from nurseries; total value, 243,344m. pesetas. The main fishing region is the North-West (Galicia), with 57·3% of the catch. The Spanish fishing fleet in 1986 consisted of 17,464 vessels of 649,457 tonnes, with a total crew of 94,246.

INDUSTRY. The industrial sector represented 74·3% of export value, 34·6% of GNP and 23·6% of employment in 1990. In 1987, the principal textile productions were (in 1,000 tonnes): Wool yarn, 24; cotton yarn, 108; fabrics yarn, 184; wool cloth, 12; cotton cloth, 89; fabrics cloth, 68. In 1987, 2·8m. tonnes of writing, printing, packing and other paper were produced. The production of cement reached 28,092,000 tonnes in 1990. Steel production (1990) 12,895,000 tonnes; the three great blast-furnaces concentrations are in Bilbao area, Avilés (Asturias) and Sagunto (Valencia). The chemical industry is located in the areas of Madrid,

Barcelona and Bilbao; sulphuric acid production (1987), 3·3m. tonnes; nitrogenous fertilizers, 780,000 tonnes; plastics (1990), 2,078,000 tonnes. The 9 oil refineries refined (1989) 49·8m. tonnes of crude oil. In 1987, 1·36m. TV sets were manufactured. 1·1m. refrigerators and 1,023,000 washing machines were manufactured in 1990. Spain has important toy and shoe industries, toys especially in Alicante and Barcelona provinces and shoes in Alicante province and the Balearic islands.

Spanish shipyards launched 384,413 BRT in 1990. In 1990, 1,679,000 cars and 374,000 industrial and commercial vehicles were built.

Labour. The monthly minimum wage for workers was 56,280 pesetas (Jan. 1992). The average monthly wage for workers in industry and services was 123,400 pesetas in 1990.

The economically active population numbered 15·02m. in Dec. 1990. Of these, 12,578,800 were employed: 1,485,500 in agriculture and fishing, 2,978,000 in manufactures, 1,220,500 in construction industry and 6,894,800 in trade, transport and other public and personal services. 15·3% of the active population was unemployed at the end of 1991 (2,329,258 persons).

Trade Unions. The Constitution guarantees the establishment and activities of trade unions provided they have a democratic structure. The two most important trade unions are *Unión General de Trabajadores* (UGT), founded in 1888 by Pablo Iglesias (who had founded in 1879 the Spanish Workers Socialist Party, PSOE), and *Comisiones Obreras*, which was gradually established 1958–63, then as a clandestine labour organization.

FOREIGN ECONOMIC RELATIONS. Foreign debt was US$44,973m. at the end of 1990, of which US$6,082m. was government debt.

Commerce. Foreign trade of Spain (Peninsula, Baleares, Canaries, Ceuta, Melilla) (in 1m. pesetas):

	1986	1987	1988	1989	1990
Imports	4,890,768	6,029,838	7,039,516	8,458,361	8,914,741
Exports	3,800,225	4,195,623	4,686,376	5,257,628	5,257,628

In 1990 the most important groups of imports were (in US$1m.): Mechanical engineering, 14,249 (16·24% of total); vehicles and other transport equipment, 11,845 (13·5%); chemicals, 10,414 (11·87%); crude petroleum and other fuels, 10,340 (11·79%); agrarian products, 9,862 (11·24%); electric engineering, 7,479 (8·53%); metallic products, 6,307 (7·19%); textiles, 3,968 (4·52%); optical instruments and tools, 3,554 (4·05%); minerals, 1,287 (1·47%).

The most important groups of exports in 1990 (in US$1m.) were: Vehicles and other transport equipment, 13,049 (23·43%); agrarian products, 8,464 (15·21%); minerals, 5,892 (10·59%); mechanical engineering, 5,482 (10·5%); metallic products, 5,311 (9·55%); electric engineering, 2,724 (4·9%); products of petroleum and other fuels, 2,647 (4·76%); chemicals, 2,248 (4·04%); textiles, 1,547 (2·78%).

Distribution of Spanish foreign trade (in 1m. pesetas) according to main origin and destination, for calendar years:

	Imports		Exports	
	1989	1990	1989	1990
EEC	4,828,375	5,300,640	3,509,760	3,910,365
Germany, Federal Republic	1,358,988	1,463,004	623,640	756,018
France	1,155,451	1,307,343	1,024,586	1,173,130
Italy	881,712	905,568	508,062	603,832
UK	549,364	638,082	524,229	507,214
Netherlands	276,760	330,296	238,710	266,001
Belgium–Luxembourg	267,431	278,062	170,130	170,005
Portugal	196,668	222,833	327,592	341,749
USA	765,280	744,807	387,356	328,913
Japan	404,826	395,168	71,905	64,342
Latin America	389,180	414,470	188,061	220,863
Mexico	134,556	144,516	48,229	58,834
Brazil	...	97,337	...	18,548
EFTA	475,246	476,808	207,776	243,579
Sweden	166,850	161,238	48,525	54,124
Switzerland	131,636	130,300	80,657	91,551

	Imports		Exports	
	1989	1990	1989	1990
COMECON	212,993	190,273	80,874	67,291
USSR	153,006	134,606	47,180	38,645
Nigeria	153,245	157,516	9,815	9,814
Libya	91,879	118,551	9,762	6,748
Saudi Arabia	69,158	...	...	...
Iraq	77,954	...	20,747	...
Iran	98,204	90,696	17,622	28,761
Algeria	...	86,853	...	58,542

Total trade between Spain and UK (British Department of Trade returns, in £1,000 sterling):

	1988	1989	1990	1991
Imports to UK	2,482,360	2,772,011	2,884,691	2,627,857
Exports and re-exports from UK	2,691,662	3,137,941	3,750,143	4,278,767

Total trade of the Spanish territories and UK (British Department of Trade returns, in £1,000 sterling):

	Imports to UK			Exports from UK		
	1989	1990	1991	1989	1990	1991
Canary Islands	74,532	86,023	84,789	89,852	92,886	103,393
North Africa	57	56	142	4,640	5,933	6,871

Tourism. In 1990, 52,035,508 tourists visited Spain (from France, 22·3%; Portugal, 19·4%; Federal Republic of Germany, 13·1%; UK, 12·1%; Morocco, 4·1%). Receipts of foreign currency (1990) US$18·59m. Hotel and similar beds, 1,733,105 (Jan. 1990).

COMMUNICATIONS

Roads. In 1989 the total length of highways and roads was 157,642 km. The main network in 1989 comprised 2,424 km of motorways (1,839 km toll motorways), 1,361 km of other four-lane highways and 18,949 km of first class roads. Number of cars (1989) was 11,467,700, lorries and vans, 2,162,400, buses, 45,200 and motorcycles, 975,800. There were in Dec. 1990, 14,347,139 driving licences; 4,377,241 drivers were women.

Railways. The total length of the state railways in 1990 was 12,560 km, mostly broad (1,416-mm) gauge (6,416 km electrified). In 1941 the broad gauge railways, passed into state ownership; they are under a board known as the *Red Nacional de Ferrocarriles Españoles* (RENFE). The differential gauge of Spanish railways had strategic origins; passengers therefore must change at the French frontier stations unless aboard variable-gauge trains. A high-speed standard-gauge railway from Madrid to Seville was scheduled to open in 1991. In 1990 freight carried was 29m. tonnes and 182m. passengers. There are several regional railways including Basque, Catalan and FEVE (narrow gauge) railways. There are metros in Madrid (113 km) and Barcelona (71 km), and a light railway in Valencia (113 km).

Civil Aviation. The most important Spanish airline is 'Iberia': it maintains a regular service with Europe, America, Africa and the Middle and Far East. Its fleet included 6 B-747s (for 430 passengers each), 8 DC-10s (for 266), 6 Airbus-300Bs (for 253), 35 B-727s (for 161) and 30 DC-9s (for 110) in 1985. 'Aviaco' operates mainly internal flights. There are 43 airports open to civil traffic; those of Madrid, Palma de Mallorca and Barcelona are the most active. A small airport in Seo de Urgel, in the Pyrenees, used especially for the air service of Andorra was opened in 1982.

Aircraft movements in 1989, 378,655 internal and 336,394 international. In 1990 73·3m passengers and (1989) 408,600 tonnes of freight were carried.

Shipping. The merchant navy in 1990 had 416 vessels of a gross tonnage of 3·1m. In 1989, 92,309 ships entered Spanish ports, carrying 12·4m. passengers and discharging and loading 232·8m. tonnes of cargo.

Telecommunications. The receipts of the post office in 1989 were 103,843m. pesetas; expenses, 128,460m. pesetas. There were in 1989, 12,521 post offices and (Nov. 1987) 15,350,464 telephones, these all privately operated.

Radio Nacional de España broadcasts 5 programmes on medium-waves and FM, as well as many regional programmes; it has one commercial programme. The greatest radio audience is that of an independent network, *Sociedad Española de Radiodifusión* (SER); *Cadena de Ondas Populares Españolas* (COPE) belongs to the Roman Catholic church. Two independent radio networks were established in 1982 covering the whole of Spain, *Antena 3* and *Radio 80*. *Televisión Española* broadcasts 2 programmes. There were in 1990 the following regional TV networks: *TV3* (1983) and *Canal 33* (1989), both broadcasting in Catalan; *ETB1* (1983) and *ETB2* (1987), both Basque, the first one broadcasting in Basque; *Televisión de Galicia* (1985), in Galician; *TM3* (1989), for the area of Madrid; *Canal 9* (1989), mostly in Valencian (Catalan); and *Tele-Sur* (1989), for Andalusia. *Radio Exterior* broadcasts abroad, and *Televisión Española* has an international channel. In 1990 3 nationwide commercial TV networks: Antena 3, Tele 5 and Canal Plus. Colour transmissions are carried by PAL system. Number of receivers (1986): Radio, 11·5m.; television, 12·5m. (about 90% colour sets).

Cinemas (1989). There were 1,802 cinemas with an audience of 78m.

Newspapers (1989). There were about 84 daily newspapers with a total daily circulation of about 5m. copies. In 1989 the following dailies had a daily circulation of more than 100,000 copies: *El País* (Madrid, 377,528), *ABC* (Madrid, 280,356), *La Vanguardia* (Barcelona, 210,624), *Marca* (Madrid, [sports], 199,600), *El Periódico* (Barcelona, 171,601), *As* (Madrid [sports], 162,881), *Diario 16* (Madrid, 145,073), *El Correo Español-El Pueblo Vasco* (Bilbao, 127,127) and *El Mundo* (Madrid, 104,016).

JUSTICE, RELIGION, EDUCATION AND WELFARE

Justice. Justice is administered by *Tribunales* and *Juzgados* (Tribunals and Courts), which conjointly form the *Poder Judicial* (Judicial Power). Judges and magistrates cannot be removed, suspended or transferred except as set forth by law. The Constitution of 1978 has established a new organ, the *Consejo General del Poder Judicial* (CGPJ, General Council of the Judicial Power), formed by 1 President and 20 magistrates, judges, attorneys and lawyers, governing the Judicial Power in full independence from the other two powers of the State, the Legislative (Cortes) and the Executive (President of the Government and his Cabinet); all members of the CGPJ, magistrates, etc., have been appointed by the Cortes since 1985. Its President is that of the *Tribunal Supremo*.

The Judicature is composed of the *Tribunal Supremo* (Supreme High Court); 17 *Tribunales Superiores de Justicia* (Upper Courts of Justice, 1 for each autonomous community); 52 *Audiencias Provinciales* (Provincial High Courts); *Juzgados de Primera Instancia* (Courts of First Instance), *Juzgados de Instrucción* (Courts of Judicial Proceedings, not passing sentences) and *Juzgados de lo Penal* (Penal Courts, passing sentences).

The *Tribunal Supremo* consists of a President (appointed by the King, on proposal from the *Consejo General del Poder Judicial*) and various judges distributed among 7 chambers: 1 for trying civil matters, 3 for administrative purposes, 1 for criminal trials, 1 for social matters and 1 for military cases. The *Tribunal Supremo* has disciplinary faculties; is court of cassation in all criminal trials; for administrative purposes decides in first and second instance disputes arising between private individuals and the State, and in social matters resolves in the last instance.

The jury system, re-established by the art. 125 of the Constitution, had not been applied by Jan. 1992, pending its parliamentary regulation.

The *Tribunal Constitucional* (Constitutional Court) has power to solve conflicts between the State and the Autonomous Communities, to determine if legislation passed by the Cortes is contrary to the Constitution and to protect constitutional rights of the individuals violated by any authority. Its 12 members are appointed by the King in the following way: 4, on proposal of the Congress of Deputies; 4, on proposal of the Senate; 2 on proposal of the *Consejo General del Poder Judicial;* and 2 on proposal of the Cabinet. It has a 9 year term, a third of the membership renewed every 3 years.

The death penalty was abolished in 1978 by the Constitution (art. 15). Divorce is again legal since July 1981 and abortion since Aug. 1985.

The prison population was, on 6 Nov. 1990, 33,911.

Religion. The Constitution guarantees full religious freedom and states that no religion has an established legal condition (art. 16); so, since 29 Dec. 1978 there has been no official religion. Roman Catholicism is the religion of the majority. There are 11 metropolitan sees and 52 suffragan sees, the chief being Toledo, where the Primate resides.

The archdioceses of Madrid-Alcalá and Barcelona depend directly from the Vatican.

The government contributes some 15,000m. pesetas to the Roman Catholic church annually.

There are about 250,000 other Christians, including several Protestant denominations, Jehovah Witnesses (about 60,000) and Mormons. The British and Foreign Bible Society was, on 10 March 1963, allowed to resume its activities.

The first synagogue since the expulsion of the Jews in 1492 was opened in Madrid on 2 Oct. 1959. The number of Jews is estimated at about 15,000.

There is a growing Moslem community, with about 450,000 members. Most of them are foreign citizens, but there are also Spanish Moslems, mainly in Ceuta and Melilla.

Education. Until Sept. 1991, primary education was compulsory and free between 6 and 14 years of age. In Sept. 1991 the General Regulation of the Educational System Act came into force. This Act gradually extends the school-leaving age to 16 years and determines the following levels of education: Infants (3–5 years of age), primary (6–11), secondary (12–15) and baccalaureate or vocational and technical (16–17). Primary and secondary levels of education are now compulsory and free. Religious instruction is optional.

In 1989–90 pre-primary education (under 6 years) was undertaken by 39,302 schools, with 983,477 pupils. Primary or basic education (6 to 14 years): 183,569 schools, with 5,109,474 pupils. There were 287,312 teachers in pre-primary and primary schools. Secondary education (14-17 years) was conducted at 3,004 secondary schools, with 95,621 teachers and 1,518,913 pupils, and 2,287 vocational and technical schools, with 59,398 teachers and 856,100 pupils. For adult education there were (in 1986–87) 602 school units, with 543 teachers and (1985–86) 145,062 students. For the physically or mentally disabled there were (1987–88) 4,923 school units, with 5,514 teachers and 41,231 pupils.

In 1991 there were in all 38 universities: 27 public State Universities, in Madrid, Barcelona, Valencia, Granada, Sevilla, Santiago de Compostela, Zaragoza, Bilbao (University of the Basque Country), Oviedo, Valladolid, Salamanca (founded in 1215), La Laguna (Canaries), Murcia, Málaga, Córdoba, Badajoz-Cáceres (University of Extremadura), Cádiz, León, Santander, Alicante, Palma de Mallorca, Albacete-Ciudad Real-Cuenca-Toledo (University of Castilla-La Mancha), Alcalá de Henares, Pamplona, in the southern area of Madrid (Carlos III University, 1989), Vigo (1990) and La Coruña (1990); 4 Polytechnic Universities, in Madrid, Barcelona, Valencia and Las Palmas (Canaries); 2 Autonomous Universities, in Madrid and Barcelona; 4 private (Catholic) universities, in Deusto (Bilbao), Pamplona, Salamanca and Madrid (University of Comillas); and the *Universidad Nacional de Educación a Distancia* (Open University), which teaches by mail, radio and TV, with its central seat at Madrid (77,438 students, 1989–90). There were 1,067,874 university students (1989–90) including 34,301 students at private universities.

Health. In 1989 there were 143,803 doctors, 9,433 dentists, 35,141 pharmacists, 157,194 nurses and 6,208 midwives. In 1988 there were 861 hospitals with 180,688 beds.

Social Security. The social security budget was 6,475,301m. pesetas in 1990, and covered retirement pensions (58·52% of that budget), health and hospital services (29·63%) and other allowances and aids. There is a minimum monthly pension (23,590 pesetas in 1991) for every retired citizen with yearly earnings under 520,000 pesetas.

In 1991 the system of contributions to the social security and employment scheme was: For pensions, sickness, invalidity, maternity and children, a contribution of 28·8% of the basic wage (24% paid by the employer, 4·8% by the employee); for unemployment benefit, a contribution of 6·3% (5·2% paid by the employer, 1·1% by the employee). There are also minor contributions for a Fund of Guaranteed Salaries, working accidents and professional sicknesses, and vocational training.

DIPLOMATIC REPRESENTATIVES

Of Spain in Great Britain (24 Belgrave Sq., London SW1X 8QA)
Ambassador: Felipe de la Morena.

Of Great Britain in Spain (Calle de Fernando el Santo, 16, Madrid, 4)
Ambassador: Sir Robin Fearn, KCMG.

Of Spain in the USA (2700 15th St., NW, Washington, D.C., 20009)
Ambassador: Jaime de Ojeda y Eiseley.

Of the USA in Spain (Serrano 75, Madrid)
Ambassador: Joseph Zappala.

Of Spain to the United Nations
Ambassador: Juan Antonio Yáñez-Barnuevo.

Further Reading

Statistical Information: The Instituto Nacional de Estadística (Paseo de la Castellana, 183, Madrid) combines the administrative work of a government department attached to the Ministry of the Economy and Finance with a centre of statistical studies.

Bell, D. (ed.) *Democratic Politics in Spain: Spanish Politics after Franco.* London, 1983
Carr, R., *Modern Spain, 1875–1980.* OUP, 1980
Collins, R., *The Basques.* Oxford, 1986
Donaghy, P. J. and Newton, M. T., *Spain: A Guide to Political and Economic Institutions.* CUP, 1987
Enciclopedia Universal Ilustrada. 70 vols., 10 appendices, 10 supplements. Madrid
Gunther, R. (et al) *Spain after Franco: The Making of a Competitive Party System.* Univ. of California Press, 1986
Harrison, J., *The Spanish Economy in the Twentieth Century.* London, 1985
Hooper, J., *The Spaniards: A Portrait of The New Spain.* London, 1986
Maravall, J., *The Transition to Democracy in Spain.* London, 1982
Preston, P., *The Triumph of Democracy in Spain.* London and New York, 1986
Shields, G. J., *Spain.* [Bibliography] Oxford and Santa Barbara, 1985
Shubert, A., *A Social History of Modern Spain.* London, 1990

National Library: Biblioteca Nacional, Madrid.

FORMER PROVINCE IN AFRICA (WESTERN SAHARA)

The colony of Spanish Sahara became a Spanish province in July 1958. On 14 Nov. 1975 Spain, Morocco and Mauritania had reached agreement on the transfer of power over Western Sahara to Morocco and Mauritania on 28 Feb. 1976. Morocco occupied El-Aaiún in late Nov. and on 12 Jan. 1976 the Spanish army withdrew from Western Sahara which ceased to be a Spanish province on 31 Dec. 1975. The country was partitioned by Morocco and Mauritania on 28 Feb. 1976; Morocco reorganized its sector into 3 provinces. In Aug. 1979 Mauritania withdrew from the territory it took over in 1976. The area was taken over by Morocco and reorganized into a fourth province.

A liberation movement, *Frente Polisario*, launched an armed struggle against Spanish rule on 20 May 1973 and, in spite of occupation of all western centres by Moroccan troops, Saharawi guerrillas based in Algeria continue to attempt to liberate their country. They have renamed it the Saharawi Arab Democratic Republic and hold most of the desert beyond a defensive line built by Moroccan troops encompassing Es-Semara, Bu Craa and El-Aaiún. A ceasefire was agreed in Aug.

1988. In Sept. 1989 Polisario's guerrillas ended the lull in fighting with battles on 7 and 11 Oct. – Morocco and Polisario failed to agree on how the referendum (part of UN plan) should be held.

In 1982 the Saharawi Arab Democratic Republic became a member of the Organization of African Unity (OAU).

In May 1991 the UN approved a Security Council decision to fund a Mission for the Organization of a Referendum in Western Sahara (MINURSO). Some 65,000 are considered Saharawis and qualified to vote. A UN peacekeeping force proclaimed a ceasefire on 6 Sept. After a first proposal to establish an electorate on the basis of the approximately 74,000 persons registered at the Spanish census of 1974, the UN agreed to a widening of qualifications to include residents who had not been registered by the census, persons whose father was born in the territory, and those who had lived 6 years consecutively or 12 years intermittently in the territory, adding some 30,000-40,000 to the list.

President: Mohammed Abdelaziz.

Area 266,769 sq. km (102,680 sq. miles). The population at the census held by Morocco in Sept. 1982 was 163,868; estimate (1986) 180,000. Another estimated 165,000 Saharawis live in refugee camps around Tindouf in south-west Algeria. The main towns (1982 census) are El-Aaiún, the capital (96,784), Dakhla (17,822) and Es-Semara (17,753). The population is Arabic-speaking, and virtually entirely Sunni Moslem.

Rich phosphate deposits were discovered in 1963 at Bu Craa. Morocco holds 65% of the shares of the former Spanish state-controlled company. While production reached 5·6m. tonnes in 1975, exploitation has been severely reduced by guerrilla activity but in 1984 produced 1m. tonnes. After a nearly complete collapse, production and transportation of phosphate resumed in 1978, ceased again, and then resumed in 1982. There are about 6,100 km of motorable tracks, but only about 500 km of paved roads. There are airports at El-Aaiún and Dakhla. As most of the land is desert, less than 19% is in agricultural use, with about 2,000 tonnes of grain produced annually. There are (1983) about 22,000 sheep, as well as goats and camels raised. Electricity produced (1983) 78m. kwh.

Further Reading

Damis, J., *Conflict in Northwest Africa: The Western Sahara Dispute.* Stanford, 1983
Hodges, T., *Western Sahara: The Roots of a Desert War.* London and Westport, 1984
Sipe, L. F., *Western Sahara: A Comprehensive Bibliography.* New York, 1984
Thompson, V. and Adloff, R., *The Western Saharans: Background to Conflict.* London, 1980

SRI LANKA

Capital: Colombo
Population: 16·99m. (1990)
GNP per capita: US$462 (1990)

Democratic Socialist Republic of Sri Lanka

HISTORY. A monarchical form of government continued until the beginning of the 19th century when the British subjugated the Kandyan Kingdom in the central highlands.

In 1505 the Portuguese had formed settlements in the west and south, which were taken from them about the middle of the next century by the Dutch. In 1796 the British Government annexed the foreign settlements to the presidency of Madras. In 1802 Ceylon was constituted a separate colony.

Ceylon became an independent Commonwealth state on 4 Feb. 1948 and became a republic in 1972 as Sri Lanka.

War between northern Tamil separatists and government forces began in 1983. A state of emergency ended on 11 Jan. 1989, but violence continued.

AREA AND POPULATION. Sri Lanka is an island in the Indian Ocean, south of the Indian peninsula from which it is separated by the Palk Strait. On 28 June 1974 the frontier between India and Sri Lanka in the Palk Strait was redefined, giving to Sri Lanka the island of Kachchativu. Area (in sq. km.) and census population on 17 March 1981.

Provinces	Area	Population	Provinces	Area	Population
Western	3,708·61	3,919,807	North-Central	10,723·59	849,492
Central	5,583·50	2,009,248	Uva	8,487·91	914,522
Southern	5,559·15	1,882,661	Sabaragamuwa	4,901·55	1,482,031
Northern	8,882·11	1,109,404			
Eastern	9,951·26	975,251	Total	65,609·86	14,846,750
North-Western	7,812·18	1,704,334			

Population (1981 census), 14,846,750, an increase of 17% since 1971. Population (in 1,000) according to ethnic group and nationality at the 1981 census: 10,980 Sinhalese, 1,887 Sri Lanka Tamils, 1,047 Sri Lanka Moors, 39 Burghers, 47 Malays, 819 Indian Tamils, 28 others. Non-nationals of Sri Lanka totalled 635,150.

Vital statistics, 1989 (provisional): Birth-rate (per 1,000 population), 21·3; death-rate, 6·2; infant mortality (per 1,000 live births), 17·6.

The urban population was 21·5% of the total in 1981. The principal towns and their population according to the census of 1981 are: Colombo (the capital), 587,647; Dehiwela-Mt. Lavinia, 173,529; Moratuwa, 134,826; Jaffna, 118,224; Kotte, 101,039; Kandy, 97,872; Galle, 76,863; Negombo, 60,762; Trincomalee, 44,313; Batticaloa, 42,963; Matara, 38,843; Ratnapura, 37,497; Anuradhapura, 35,981; Badulla, 33,068; Kalutara, 31,503. Population of the Greater Colombo area, 1980, about 1m.

Sinhala and Tamil are the official languages; English is in use.

CLIMATE. Sri Lanka has an equatorial climate with low annual temperature variations, but it is affected by the north-east Monsoon (Dec. to Feb.) and the south-west Monsoon (May to Sept.). Rainfall is generally heavy but never lasts long; it is heaviest in the south-west and central highlands while the north and east are relatively dry. Thirty-year averages, 1951–80: Colombo. Jan. 79·7°F (26·5°C), July 81·1°F (27·3°C). Annual rainfall 99·5" (2,527 mm). Trincomalee. Jan. 78·6°F (25·9°C), July 86·2°F (30·1°C). Annual rainfall 63·60" (1,615 mm). Kandy. Jan. 73·9°F (23·3°C), July 75·9°F (24·4°C). Annual rainfall 76·6" (1,947 mm). Nuwara Eliya. Jan. 58·5°F (14·7°C), July 60·3°F (15·7°C). Annual rainfall 80·04" (2,044 mm).

CONSTITUTION AND GOVERNMENT. A new constitution for the Democratic Socialist Republic of Sri Lanka was promulgated in Sept. 1978.

The Executive *President* is directly elected by the people and has to receive more than one-half of the valid votes cast. His term of office is six years and he shall not hold the office for more than two consecutive terms. He is the Head of the State, the Head of the Executive and of the Government and the Commander-in-chief of the Armed Forces. He does not have any veto power over legislation; even in a time of public emergency, he must act with Parliamentary control and approval.

Parliament consists of one chamber, composed of 225 members (196 elected and 29 from the National List). Election is by proportional representation by universal suffrage at 18 years. The term of Parliament is 6 years. The Prime Minister and other Ministers, who must be members of Parliament, are appointed by the President.

Elections were held on 15 Feb. 1989.

The Cabinet was as follows in Feb. 1992:

President, Buddha Sasana, Defence, Policy Planning and Implementation, Education and Higher Education: Ranasinghe Premadasa (assumed office 2 Jan. 1989).
Prime Minister, Finance, Labour and Vocational Training: D. B. Wijetunga.
Reconstruction, Rehabilitation and Social Welfare: P. Dayaratne. *Posts and Telecommunications:* A. M. S. Adikari. *Power and Energy:* K. D. M. Bandara. *Housing and Construction:* B. Sirisena Cooray. *Lands, Irrigation and Mahaweli Development:* Gamini Atukorale. *Agricultural Development and Research:* R. M. Dharmadasa Banda. *Justice:* A. C. S. Hameed. *Foreign Affairs:* Harold Herat. *Health and Women's Affairs:* Renuka Herath. *Ports and Shipping:* Alick Aluvihare. *Cultural Affairs and Information:* W. J. M. Lokubandara. *Food and Co-operatives:* Weerasinghe Mallimarachchi. *Youth Affairs and Sports:* C. Nanda Mathew. *Transport and Highways:* Wijayapala Mendis. *Trade and Commerce:* Abdul Razak Munsoor. *Public Administration, Provincial Councils and Home Affairs:* Festus Perera. *Fisheries and Aquatic Resources:* M. Joseph Michael Perera. *Environment and Parliamentary Affairs and Chief Government Whip:* M. Vincent Perera. *Tourism and Rural Industrial Development:* S. Thondaman. *Industries, Science and Technology and Leader of the House of Parliament:* Ranil Wickremasinghe. *Handlooms and Textile Industries:* U. B. Wijekoon. *Plantation Industries:* Rupasena Karunatilake.

The *Speaker* is Haniffa Mohamed.

National flag: A yellow field bearing 2 panels; in the hoist 2 vertical strips of green and orange; in the fly, dark red with a gold lion holding a sword and in each corner a gold 'bo' leaf.

National anthem: 'Sri Lanka Matha...Apa Sri Lanka'.

Local government: For purposes of general administration, the island is divided into 25 districts, administered by government agents. There are 12 Municipal Councils and 24 District Councils. There are 9 Provincial Councils, consisting of a governor, appointed by the President, a Chief Minister, a Board of Ministers and members elected for 5-year terms. At elections in May 1991 3,533 representatives were elected to 236 municipal and village councils in 7 of 9 provinces (polls were not held in Northern Province and Eastern Province because of the Tamil rebellion there). The United National Party gained control of 190 of 237 local councils and the Sri Lanka Freedom Party 36.

DEFENCE

Army. The Army was constituted on 16 Oct. 1949. It consists of 3 infantry divisions, 20 infantry regiments, 2 independent special forces regiments, 3 armoured reconnaissance regiments, 3 field artillery regiments, and 3 field engineer regiments. Equipment includes 18 Saladin armoured cars and 15 Ferret scout cars. Strength (1992) 54,177. There is an 18,913-strong Volunteer Force and a 12,478-strong National Guard.

Navy. The naval force comprises 3 Surveillance Command Ships (ex-mercantile), 2 locally-built coastal patrol craft, 41 inshore patrol craft of varying types as well as about 30 small fast patrol boats and service craft. There are 2 mechanized landing craft of 270 tonnes full load. The main naval base is at Trincomalee. Personnel in 1991 numbered 9,000, with a reserve of about 1,000.

Air Force. The Air Force was formed on 10 Oct. 1950. Its flying bases are at Katunayake and China Bay, Trincomalee. Equipment of 4 squadrons comprises 9 SF.260 and 4 Cessna 150/152 trainers, 3 HS748, 8 Chinese-built Y-12s, 2 Chinese-built Y-8s (An-12s), 1 Super King Air, 3 Cessna Skymasters, 1 Cessna 421 and a Cessna Cardinal for general transport and utility purposes; and 2 Dauphin, 10 Bell 212, 4 Bell 412 and 8 JetRanger helicopters for internal security operations. Total strength (1992) about 10,000 with 11 combat aircraft and 16 armed helicopters. China delivered 2 FT-5 jet trainers in 1991 and 4 F-7M (MiG-21) fighters were due to follow in 1992. There is also an Air Force Reserve numbering about 1,000.

INTERNATIONAL RELATIONS

Membership. Sri Lanka is a member of the UN, the Commonwealth, the Non-Aligned Movement, the South Asian Association for Regional Co-operation and the Colombo Plan.

ECONOMY

Policy. The 1991–95 plan aims at a 5·8% annual growth rate. Investment allocated is mainly for completion of projects in priority areas such as power, irrigation, road rehabilitation, water supply and telecommunications. Total public investment is about Rs672,300m.

Budget. Revenue and expenditure of central government in Rs 1m. for financial years ending 31 Dec.:

Year	Revenue	Expenditure Recurrent	Capital	Total
1988	45,675	46,613	39,572	86,185
1989	56,747	58,486	36,977	95,463
1990 [1]	70,849	72,374	40,836	113,210

[1] Estimate.

The principal sources of revenue in 1990 were (in Rs 1m.): General sales and tax, 20,291; import levies, 17,512; export duties, 1,238; selective sales taxes, 9,481; property transfer taxes, 2,960; taxes on personal and corporate income, 9,954.

The principal items of recurrent expenditure in 1990 (in Rs 1m.): Finance, 26,449; defence, 10,317; public administration, 18,659; education, 1,770; agriculture, 3,852; health, 1,909. Capital expenditure on finance, 17,751; Mahaweli development, 3,012; power and energy, 5,049; transport and highways, 1,356.

Currency. The unit of currency is the *Sri Lankan rupee* (LKR) of 100 *cents*. Notes and coins are issued by the Central Bank in the denominations of (notes) Rs 2, 5, 10, 20, 50, 100, 500 and 1,000; (coins): 1, 2, 5, 10, 25 and 50 cents; Rs 1, 2, 5 and 10. The total circulation was Rs 23,910m. on 31 Dec. 1990. In March 1992, £1 = Rs 75·35; US$1 = Rs 42·92.

Banking and Finance. The narrow money supply (M1) at 31 Dec. 1990 stood at Rs 39,878·1m.

The Central Bank of Sri Lanka is the bank of issue. Total assets of 24 commercial banks at 31 Dec. 1990, Rs 132,363·9m.

The monopoly in all insurance business enjoyed by the state-owned Ceylon Insurance Corporation and the National Insurance Corporation is broad based with the participation of a large number of assurance companies.

Sri Lanka National Savings Bank at 31 Dec. 1990 had a balance to depositors' credit of Rs 23,159·1m. There are 5 main long-term credit institutions.

Weights and Measures. The metric system has been established.

ENERGY AND NATURAL RESOURCES

Electricity. Installed capacity of electric energy (1989), 1,240,650 kw. Energy produced, 2,858m. kwh; the main source was thermal power as the water levels of the reservoirs were not sufficient to operate the hydro power plants at full capacity. Supply 230 volts; 50 Hz.

Water. The Mahaweli Ganga scheme irrigates 41,000 ha of new land and (1990) 114,388 ha of land already cultivated. Consumption within Colombo city limits is estimated at 10,000m. gallons a year.

Minerals. Gems are among the chief minerals mined and exported. The most important are sapphire, ruby, chrysoberyl, beryl, topaz, spinel, garnet, zircon and tourmaline. Graphite is also important; production in 1990 was 5,490 tonnes. Production of ilmenite, 1990, 64,525 tonnes. Some rutile is also produced (4,664 tonnes in 1990). Salt extraction is the oldest industry. The method is solar evaporation of sea-water. Production, 1990, 53,038 tonnes.

Agriculture. About 2m. ha are under cultivation. Agriculture engages 47·5% of the labour force. Main crops in 1990: Paddy (2,538,000 tonnes from 856,707 ha), rubber (113,596 tonnes), tea (233,165 tonnes) and coconuts (2,528m. nuts).

Livestock in 1990 (estimate): 1,772,700 cattle, 958,000 buffaloes, 85,000 swine, 521,700 goats, 26,000 sheep, 8,796,600 poultry.

Fisheries. Production in 1990 was 177,063 tonnes including 134,132 tonnes of coastal water fish, 31,265 tonnes of fresh water fish and 11,666 tonnes from deep-sea fisheries. In 1990 there were 29,728 fishing craft, of which 14,877 were not motorized.

INDUSTRY. The main industries are food, beverages and tobacco; textiles, clothing and leather goods; chemicals, petroleum, rubber and plastics.

Trade Unions. In 1990 there were 1,032 registered trade unions.

FOREIGN ECONOMIC RELATIONS. Foreign debt in Dec. 1990 was Rs 176,883m.

Commerce. The values of total imports and exports (imports excluding bullion, specie and postal articles; exports, including re-exports and ship's stores) for calendar years (in Rs 1,000):

	1986	1987	1988	1989	1990
Imports	51,281,508	59,749,717	70,320,427	75,352,750	105,559,159
Exports	34,092,261	39,860,638	47,092,044	55,511,162	76,623,713

Principal exports in 1990 (in Rs 1m.): Tea, 19,823; rubber, 3,080; copra, coconut oil and desiccated coconut, 1,842; other crops, 3,165; textiles and garments, 25,163; precious and semi-precious stones, 6,619.

Principal imports (Rs 1m.) in 1990 were petroleum, 14,367m.; machinery and equipment, 8,659m.; vehicles and transport equipment, 3,577; food and beverages, 16,566.

In 1990 the principal sources of imports were (in Rs 1m.): Japan, 13,035; USA, 8,322; UK, 5,847; Iran, 8,904; Hong Kong, 4,822; Singapore, 4,106; Taiwan, 6,243; India, 4,731; Malaysia, 4,106; China, 4,857.

Principal export destinations 1990 were (in Rs 1m.): USA, 19,651; Federal Germany, 5,068; Japan, 3,208; UK, 4,321; Egypt, 2,368; Belgium, 3,882; Iran, 2,593.

Total trade between Sri Lanka and UK (British Department of Trade returns, in £1,000 sterling):

	1987	1988	1989	1990	1991
Imports to UK	53,817	56,661	63,527	63,362	74,460
Exports and re-exports from UK	84,680	92,528	92,465	88,496	128,565

Tourism. 297,888 tourists visited the country in 1990.

COMMUNICATIONS

Roads. There are 25,952 km of motorable roads, of which 10,402 km are black-topped, first-class nationally-maintained roads. Number of motor vehicles, 31 Dec. 1990, 819,943, comprising 173,519 private cars and cabs, 106,192 lorries, 89,066 tractors, 391,732 motor cycles and 39,812 buses.

Railways. In 1990 there were 1,453 km of railway, of which 1,394 km were 1,676 mm gauge and 59 km 762 mm gauge. In 1990 railways ran 2,780m. passenger-km and 163·8m. tonne-km.

Civil Aviation. Air Lanka operates international services. Foreign airlines which operate scheduled services to Sri Lanka are Indian Airlines, KLM, Singapore Airlines, Thai Airways International, Pakistan International Airlines, Gulf Air, Kuwait Airways, Saudi Air, Emirates, Royal Jordanian Airlines and Balkan.

Internal services are operated by Upali, Air Taxis and Consolidated Engineering.

Shipping. In 1990, merchant vessels totalling 39·8m. GRT entered the ports.

Telecommunications. In 1990 there were 515 post offices and 3,349 sub-post offices. In 1982 there were 1,900 telegraph offices and 109,900 telephones. The Overseas Telecommunication Service operates telegraph and telephone services to most parts of the world. Broadcasting is provided by the Sri Lanka Broadcasting Corporation. In 1991 there were 2·7m. radio and 0·6m. TV sets (colour by PAL).

Cinemas. In 1989 there were 365 cinemas. The National Film Corporation established in 1971 has exclusive rights to import films and arrange distribution of foreign and local films. Films released, 1989, 119.

Newspapers. There are 4 daily and 4 weekly papers in Sinhalese; 2 daily and 3 weekly in Tamil; 3 daily and 3 weekly in English.

JUSTICE, RELIGION, EDUCATION AND WELFARE

Justice. The systems of law which obtain in Sri Lanka are the Roman-Dutch law, the English law, the Tesawalamai, the Moslem law and the Kandyan law.

The Kandyan law applies to the Kandyan Sinhalese in respect of all matters relating to inheritance, matrimonial rights and donations. The law of Tesawalamai is applied to all inhabitants of Jaffna, in all matters relating to inheritance, marriages, gifts, donations, purchases and sales of land. The Moslem law is applied to all Moslems in respect of succession, donations, marriage, divorce and maintenance. These customary and religious laws have been modified in many respects by local enactments.

The courts of original jurisdiction are the High Court, District Courts, Magistrates' Courts and Primary Courts. The High Court tries major crimes and also exercises admiralty jurisdiction. The 13th Amendment to the Constitution established Provincial High Courts which exercise original criminal jurisdiction of the High Court in respect of offences committed within the province and appellate and revisionary jurisdiction in respect of appeals from the Magistrates' Courts and the Primary Courts within the province. The Provincial High Courts also have the power to issue orders in the nature of Habeas Corpus, in respect of persons illegally detained within the province and issue Writs of Certiorari, Prohibition, Procedendo, Mandamus and Quo Warranto pertaining to matters within the province. The District Court has unlimited civil jurisdiction in civil, revenue, trust, insolvency and testamentary matters, over persons and estates of persons of unsound mind, and wards. The Magistrates' Courts exercise criminal jurisdiction carrying the power to impose terms of imprisonment not exceeding 2 years and fines not exceeding Rs 1,500. The Primary Courts which were established in 1978 exercise civil jurisdiction where the value of the subject matter does not exceed Rs 1,500 and also have jurisdiction in respect of by-laws of local authorities and matters relating to the recovery of revenue of such local authorities. Primary Courts exercise exclusive criminal jurisdiction in respect of offences which may be prescribed by regulation by the Minister. The Primary Courts have the power to impose sentences of imprisonment not exceeding three months and fines not exceeding Rs 250.

The Constitution of 1978 provided for the establishment of two superior courts, the Supreme Court and the Court of Appeal.

The Supreme Court is the highest and final superior court of record and exercises jurisdiction in respect of constitutional matters, jurisdiction for the protection of fundamental rights, final appellate jurisdiction in election petitions and jurisdiction in respect of any breach of the privileges of Parliament. Parliament may provide by law that the Supreme Court exercises the power to grant and issue any of the orders in the nature of Writs of Certiorari, Prohibition, Procedendo, Mandamus or Quo Warranto. The Court of Appeal has appellate jurisdiction to correct all errors in fact or law committed by any court, tribunal or institution; it can grant and issue orders in the nature of the above Writs, and of Writs of Habeas Corpus and injunctions; it can also try election petitions in respect of election of members of Parliament.

Police. The strength of the police service in 1990 was 30,977.

Religion. Buddhism was introduced from India in the 3rd century B.C. and is the religion of 69·3% of the inhabitants. There were (1981) 10,288,325 Buddhists, 2,297,806 Hindus, 1,130,568 Christians, 1,121,717 Moslems and 8,334 others.

Education. Education is free from school year 1 to university and is imparted in the medium of the mother tongue. In 1991 about 88% of the population (10 years old and older) was literate.

In 1990 there were 10,382 schools including 9,864 government schools, 457 Pirivenas and 61 private schools. The government schools had 178,333 teachers and 4·11m. students from year 1 to 13. Ministry of Education expenditure (1990), Rs 5,601m. Education is administered by 8 provisional education directors.

The overall control of the education regions is vested in the Ministry of Education and Higher Education.

There are 9 universities: Peradeniya, Colombo, Jaffna, Sri Jayawardenepura, Moratuwa, Kelaniya, Eastern, Ruhuna and an Open University. Dumbara Campus has been transferred to Peradeniya University. There are 9 institutes (5 for postgraduate and 4 for undergraduate studies).

In 1990 there were 28,923 students and 1,811 teachers in the 8 universities excluding the Open University, which had 11,768 students. Postgraduate institutes had 1,097 students, the others, 1,835. There were 30 institutions for technical education, 13 of which had grade I status; total enrolment (1990), 18,572.

Health. In 1990 there were 507 hospitals, including 84 maternity homes, and 360 central dispensaries. Hospitals had 47,738 beds and there were 2,571 Department of Health doctors. Total state budget expenditure on health, 1990, Rs 5,383m.

Social Security. The activities of the Department of Social Services include:

(1) Payment of Public Assistance, monthly allowance, tuberculosis assistance and leprosy allowance to all needy persons.

(2) Relief for those affected by widespread distress, such as floods, drought, cyclone.

(3) Custodial care and welfare services to the elderly and infirm.

(4) Vocational training, rehabilitation, aids and appliances for the physically handicapped.

(5) Custodial care, vocational training and rehabilitation for socially handicapped persons.

(6) Community-based rehabilitation of treated drug addicts.

(7) Financial assistance to voluntary institutions that provide welfare services.

DIPLOMATIC REPRESENTATIVES

Of Sri Lanka in Great Britain (13 Hyde Park Gdns., London, W2 2LU)
High Commissioner: Gen. D. S. Attygalle, LVO.

Of Great Britain in Sri Lanka (190 Galle Rd., Kollupitiya, Colombo 3)
High Commissioner: E. John Field.

Of Sri Lanka in the USA (2148 Wyoming Ave., NW, Washington, D.C., 20008)
Ambassador: W. S. L. De Alwis.

Of the USA in Sri Lanka (210 Galle Rd., Kollupitiya, Colombo 3)
Ambassador: Marion V. Creekmore, Jr.

Of Sri Lanka to the United Nations
Ambassador: Dr F. S. C. P. Kalpage.

Further Reading

The Sri Lanka Year Book. Department of Census and Statistics. Colombo, Annual
Census Publications from 1871
Economic Atlas. Department of Census and Statistics. Colombo, 1980
Performance 1985. Ministry of Plan Implementation, Colombo. 1985
Review of the Economy. Central Bank of Ceylon. Annual
Statistical Pocket-Book. Department of Census and Statistics. Colombo, 1984
Statistical Abstract. Department of Census and Statistics, Colombo, 1982

Coomaraswamy, R., *Sri Lanka: The Crisis of the Anglo-American Constitutional Traditions in a Developing Society.* Colombo, 1984
De Silva, C. R. *Sri Lanka: a History.* Delhi, 1991
De Silva, K. M. (ed.) *Sri Lanka: A Survey.* London, 1977.—*A History of Sri Lanka.* London, repr. 1982.—*Managing Ethnic Tensions in Multi-Ethnic Societies: Sri Lanka 1880–1985.* New York, 1986
Ferguson's *Ceylon Directory.* Annual (from 1858)
International Commission of Jurists, ed., *Sri Lanka: A Mounting Tragedy of Errors.* London, 1984
Johnson, B. L. C. and Scrivenor, M. le M., *Sri Lanka: Land, People and Economy.* London, 1981
Manogaran, C., *Ethnic Conflict and Reconciliation in Sri Lanka.* Univ. Hawaii Press, 1987
Manor, J., *Sri Lanka: In Change and Crisis.* London, 1984
Moore, M., *The State and Peasant Politics in Sri Lanka.* CUP, 1985
Piyadasa, L., *Sri Lanka: The Holocaust and After.* London, 1984
Poonambalam, S., *Dependent Capitalism in Crisis: The Sri Lankan Economy 1948–80.* London, 1981
Ratnasuriya, M. D. and Wijeratne, P. B. F., *Shorter Sinhalese-English Dictionary.* Colombo, 1949
Richards, P. and Gooneratne, W., *Basic Needs, Poverty and Government Policies in Sri Lanka.* Geneva, 1981
Samaraweera, V., *Sri Lanka.* [Bibliography] Oxford and Santa Barbara, 1987
Schwarz, W., *The Tamils of Sri Lanka.* London, 1983
Tambiah, S. J., *Sri Lanka: Ethnic Fratricide and the Dismantling of Democracy.* London, 1986
Wilson, A. J., *Politics in Sri Lanka 1947-73.* London, 1974.—*The Gaullist System in Asia: the Constitution of Sri Lanka.* London, 1980.—*The Break-Up of Sri Lanka: The Sinhalese-Tamil Conflict.* London, 1988

SUDAN

Capital: Khartoum
Population: 25·56m. (1987)
GNP per capita: US$340 (1988)

Jamhuryat es-Sudan

(Republic of Sudan)

HISTORY. In Dec. 1955 the Sudanese parliament passed unanimously a declaration that an independent state should be set up, and a Council of State of 5 should temporarily assume the duties of Head of State. The Codomini, the UK and Egypt, gave their assent on 31 Dec. 1955 and Sudan was proclaimed a sovereign independent republic on 1 Jan. 1956.

For the history of the Condominium and the steps leading to independence, *see* THE STATESMAN'S YEAR-BOOK, 1955, pp. 340–341; for subsequent political history *see* THE STATESMAN'S YEAR-BOOK, 1990–91, pp. 1135–36.

On 30 June 1989 Brig.-Gen. (later Lieut.-Gen.) Omar Hassan Ahmad al-Bashir overthrew the civilian government in a military coup.

AREA AND POPULATION. Sudan is bounded north by Egypt, north-east by the Red Sea, east by Eritrea and Ethiopia, south by Kenya, Uganda and Zaïre, west by the Central African Republic and Chad, north-west by Libya. Sudan covers an area of 967,500 sq. miles (2,505,813 sq. km) and the population at the census of 14 Feb. 1983 was 20,564,364; estimate (1987) 25·56m. The chief cities (census, 1983) are the capital, Khartoum (476,218), its suburbs Omdurman (526,287) and Khartoum North (341,146), Port Sudan (206,727), Wadi Medani (141,065), al-Obeid (140,024), Kassala (98,751 in 1973), Atbara (73,009), al-Qadarif (66,465 in 1973), Kosti (65,257 in 1973) and Juba (56,737 in 1973).

The northern and central thirds of the country are populated by Arab and Nubian peoples, while the southern third is inhabited by Nilotic and Bantu peoples; Arabic, the official language, is spoken by 51%. In 1987 there were 975,000 refugees in Sudan (337,544 from Ethiopia).

The area and population (census, 1983) of the regions are as follows:

Region	Sq. km	1983	Region	Sq. km	1983
Northern	183,941	1,083,024	Dafur	196,555	3,093,699
Eastern	129,086	2,208,209	Equatoria [1]	76,495	1,406,181
Central	53,716	4,012,543	Bahr al-Ghazal [1]	77,625	2,265,510
Kurdufan	146,932	3,093,294	Upper Nile [1]	92,269	1,599,605
Khartoum (province)	10,883	1,802,299			

[1] Re-united in 1985 as Southern Region.

CLIMATE. Lying wholly within the tropics, the country has a continental climate and only the Red Sea coast experiences maritime influences. Temperatures are generally high throughout the year, with May and June the hottest months. Winters are virtually cloudless and night temperatures are consequently cool. Summer is the rainy season inland, with amounts increasing from north to south, but the northern areas are virtually a desert region. On the Red Sea coast, most rain falls in winter. Khartoum. Jan. 74°F (23·3°C), July 89°F (31·7°C). Annual rainfall 6" (157 mm). Juba. Jan. 83°F (28·3°C), July 78°F (25·6°C). Annual rainfall 39" (968 mm). Port Sudan. Jan. 74°F (23·3°C), July 94°F (34·4°C). Annual rainfall 4" (94 mm). Wadi Halfa. Jan. 60°F (15·6°C), July 90°F (32·2°C). Annual rainfall 0·1" (2·5 mm).

CONSTITUTION AND GOVERNMENT. The constitution was suspended after the 1989 coup and a 12-member Revolutionary Council has ruled. In Feb. 1992 the government included:

Prime Minister, Defence, Culture and Information: Lieut.-Gen. Omar Hassan Ahmad al-Bashir.

Deputy Prime Minister: Brig.-Gen. Zubir Mohammed Saleh. *Foreign Affairs:* Ali Sahlul. *Finance and Economic Planning:* Col. Salah al-Din Karrar. *Relief and Displaced Persons:* Peter Orat.

National flag: Three horizontal stripes of red, white, black, with a green triangle based on the hoist.

Regional and local government: In Feb. 1991 a federal system of 9 states (Khartoum, Central, Kordofan, Darfur, Northern, Eastern, Bahr al-Ghazal, Upper Nile and Equatoria) was set up, each under a governor, a deputy governor and a cabinet of ministers. The states are subdivided into 66 provinces and 218 districts.

DEFENCE

Army. The Army is organized in 1 Republican Guard brigade, 2 armoured, 1 mechanized infantry, 1 reconnaissance, 2 air defence, 1 parachute and 17 infantry brigades and 1 airborne division, with 3 artillery and 1 engineer regiments. Equipment includes 200 T-54 and T-55, 20 M-60A3 and 10 Ch Type-59 main battle tanks. Strength (1991) 65,000. Paramilitary forces are the National Guard (500) and the Border Guard (2,500).

Navy. The Navy operates in the Red Sea and also on the River Nile. It comprises 2 inshore patrol craft transferred in the 1970s from the Iranian coastguard, 4 riverine patrol craft, 2 ex-Yugoslav landing craft and some boats. The flotilla suffers from lack of maintenance and spares. Personnel in 1991 were believed to number 500.

Air Force. The Air Force was built up with Soviet and Chinese assistance, and is now receiving equipment from the USA. Two combat squadrons are equipped with about 8 MiG-21 fighters, 6 Northrop F-5E, 2 MiG-23, 10 F-6 (Chinese-built MiG-19) and 12 F-5 (Chinese-built MiG-17) fighter-bombers. There is 1 transport squadron, with 4 C-130H Hercules, 6 Aviocars and 3 DHC-5D Buffalo turboprop transports; 2 helicopter squadrons have 12 AB.212s, 12 Romanian-built Pumas, 6 Mi-8s; there are 3 Jet Provost, 3 Strikemaster and 1 F-5F jet armed trainers, and some Chinese-built FT-2 (MiG-15UTI) advanced trainers. Personnel totalled (1991) about 6,000, with 44 combat aircraft.

INTERNATIONAL RELATIONS

Membership. Sudan is a member of the UN, OAU, the Arab League and is an ACP state of the EEC.

ECONOMY

Policy. Subsidies on consumer staples including sugar and fuel were abolished in Oct. 1991.

Budget. The 1989–90 budget envisaged revenue of £S8,600m. and expenditure of £S21,600m.

Currency. The monetary unit is the *Sudanese pound* (SDP) of 100 *piastres* and 1,000 *milliemes.* The currency was changed in May 1991. Large denomination notes were called in and new ones issued through banks. In Oct. 1991 the 2-tier exchange rate was abolished and the Sudanese pound devalued. In March 1992 the commercial exchange rates were, £1 = £S157·85; US$1 = £S89·92.

Banking. The Bank of Sudan opened in Feb. 1960 with an authorized capital of £S1·5m. as the central bank and bank of issue. All foreign banks were nationalized in 1970. The application of Islamic law from 1 Jan. 1991 put an end to the charging of interest in official banking transactions.

Weights and Measures. The metric system is in use.

ENERGY AND NATURAL RESOURCES

Electricity. Production (1986) 1,210m. kwh. Supply 240 volts; 50 Hz.

Oil. Two oil wells in the south-west produce 15,000 bbls per day of high quality oil. Production of petrol products (1985) 1,019 tonnes.

Minerals. Minerals include gold, graphite, sulphur, chromium, iron, manganese, copper, zinc, fluorspar, natron, gypsum and anhydrite, magnesite, asbestos, talc, halite, kaolin, white mica, coal, diatomite (kieselguhr), limestone and dolomite, pumice, lead, wollastonite, black sands and vermiculite pyrites.

Agriculture. The Sudan is predominantly agricultural. Cotton is the most important cash crop on which Sudan depends for earning foreign currency.

Production (1990) in 1,000 tonnes: Sorghum, 1,502; sugar-cane, 4,300; groundnuts, 136; seed cotton, 480; millet, 112; wheat, 405; sesame, 66; cotton seed, 175.

One of the largest sugar complexes in the world was opened at Kenana in March 1981. It is capable of processing 330,000 tonnes a year.

Livestock (1990): Cattle, 21m.; sheep, 20·3m.; goats, 14·8m.; poultry, 32m.

The government's policy of self-sufficiency and disengagement from the west, coupled with drought, resulted in a food shortage of between 0·5m. and 1m. tonnes of grain, which was officially acknowledged in Jan. 1991.

Forestry. Gum arabic, mainly hashab gum from *Acacia senegal*, is the sole forest produce exported on a major scale. Production (1983) 38·16m. cu. metres.

FOREIGN ECONOMIC RELATIONS

Commerce. Total trade for calendar years, in US$1,000:

	1984	1985	1986
Imports	556,000	1,237,000	1,055,000
Exports	519,000	544,000	497,000

In 1983, Saudi Arabia provided 14·3% of imports and the UK 10%, while 17·1% of exports went to Saudi Arabia and 10% to Italy; cotton formed 49% by value of exports and groundnuts 2%, sesame 9% and gum arabic 9%.

Total trade between Sudan and UK (British Department of Trade returns, in £1,000 sterling):

	1987	1988	1989	1990	1991
Imports to UK	18,850	9,910	9,532	9,016	6,168
Exports and re-exports from UK	75,322	86,480	60,602	63,670	75,460

Tourism. There were 42,000 visitors in 1986.

COMMUNICATIONS

Roads. In 1982 there were about 3,000 km of tarmac roads, including the new 1,190 km road from Khartoum to Port Sudan, and 45,000 km of tracks. There were 99,400 passenger cars and 17,500 commercial vehicles in 1985.

Railways. The total length of line open for traffic (1990) was 4,874 km. The gauge is 1,067 mm. In 1990, the railways carried 1·5m. passengers and 1·2m. tonnes of freight.

Aviation. Sudan Airways is a government-owned airline operating domestic and international services.

Shipping. Supplementing the railways are regular river steamer services of the Sudan Railways. Port Sudan is the only seaport.

Telecommunications. Number of telephones in 1983 was 68,838 (44,756 in Greater Khartoum). Broadcasting is controlled by the Sudan National Broadcasting Corporation and Sudan Television (Colour by PAL). In 1991 there were some 6m. radio and 0·25m. TV sets.

Cinemas. In 1975 there were 58, seating capacity 112,000 and also 43 mobile units.

Newspapers. In 1985 there were 2 daily newspapers with a circulation of 120,000.

JUSTICE, RELIGION, EDUCATION AND WELFARE

Justice. The judiciary is a separate and independent department of state directly and solely responsible to the President of the Republic. The general administrative supervision and control of the judiciary is vested in the High Judicial Council.

Civil Justice is administered by the courts constituted under the Civil Justice Ordinance, namely the High Court of Justice—consisting of the Court of Appeal and Judges of the High Court, sitting as courts of original jurisdiction—and Province Courts—consisting of the Courts of Province and District Judges. The law administered is 'justice, equity and good conscience' in all cases where there is no special enactment. Procedure is governed by the Civil Justice Ordinance.

Justice for the Moslem population has always been administered by the Islamic law courts, which form the Sharia Divisions of the Court of Appeal, High Courts and Kadis Courts; President of the Sharia Division is the Grand Kadi. In Dec. 1990 the government announced that Sharia would be applied in the non-Moslem southern parts of the country as well.

Criminal Justice is administered by the courts constituted under the Code of Criminal Procedure, namely major courts, minor courts and magistrates' courts. Serious crimes are tried by major courts, which are composed of a President and 2 members and have the power to pass the death sentence. Major Courts are, as a rule, presided over by a Judge of the High Court appointed to a Provincial Circuit or a Province Judge. There is a right of appeal to the Chief Justice against any decision or order of a Major Court, and all its findings and sentences are subject to confirmation by him.

Lesser crimes are tried by Minor Courts consisting of 3 Magistrates and presided over by a Second Class Magistrate, and by Magistrates' Courts.

Religion. In 1989 there were 19·91m. Sunni Moslems, concentrated in the north, and 2·48m. Christians and some traditionalist anunists in the south.

Education (1985). 6,707 primary schools had 1·7m. pupils; there were 490,583 pupils in 2,167 secondary schools and 28,985 in tertiary education. In 1979 Khartoum University with 10 faculties had 8,777 students. The Khartoum branch of Cairo University with 4 faculties had about 5,000 students and the Islamic University of Omdurman with 3 faculties had 1,472 students. Juba University, founded in 1975 with 5 faculties had 425 students.

Health. In 1981 the Ministry of Health maintained 158 hospitals (with 17,205 beds), 887 dispensaries, 1,619 dressing stations and 220 health centres. There were 2,122 doctors and 12,871 nurses.

DIPLOMATIC REPRESENTATIVES

Of Sudan in Great Britain (3 Cleveland Row, London, SW1A 1DD)
Ambassador: (Vacant).

Of Great Britain in Sudan (PO Box No. 801, Khartoum)
Ambassador: Allan Ramsay, CMG.

Of Sudan in the USA (2210 Massachusetts Ave., NW, Washington, D.C., 20008)
Ambassador: Abdalla Ahmed Abdalla.

Of the USA in Sudan (Sharia Ali Abdul Latif, Khartoum)
Ambassador: James R. Cheek.

Of Sudan to the United Nations
Ambassador: Lieut.-Gen. Joseph Lagu.

Further Reading

Craig, G. M. (ed.) *Agriculture of the Sudan.* OUP, 1991
Daly, M. W., *Sudan.* [Bibliography] Oxford and Santa Barbara, 1983
Gurdon, C., *Sudan in Transition: A Political Risk Analysis.* London, 1986
Halasa, A., *et al. The Return to Democracy in Sudan.* Geneva, 1986
Holt, P. M., *A Modern History of the Sudan.* New York, 3rd ed. 1979
Khalid, M., *The Government They Deserve: the Role of the Elite in Sudan's Political Evolution.* London, 1990
Woodward, P., *Sudan, 1898-1989: the Unstable State.* London, 1991

SURINAME

Capital: Paramaribo
Population: 416,839 (1990)
GNP per capita: US$3,020 (1989)

Republic of Suriname

HISTORY. For the colonial history of Suriname *see* THE STATESMAN'S YEAR-BOOK, 1991-92, p.1154. On 25 Nov. 1975, Suriname gained independence and was admitted to the UN in 4 Dec. 1975. On 25 Feb. 1980 the Government was ousted in a coup, and a National Military Council (NMC) established.

Suriname returned to democracy in Jan. 1988 following elections held in Nov. 1987. On 24 Dec. 1990 a military coup removed President Ramsewak Shankar and his cabinet from office. Ronald Venetiaan was elected President in Sept. 1991.

AREA AND POPULATION. Suriname is situated on the north coast of South America and bounded on the north by the Atlantic ocean, on the east by French Guiana, on the west by Guyana, and on the south by Brazil.

Area, 163,820 sq. km. Census population (1980), 354,860. Estimate (1987) 415,000. The capital, Paramaribo, had (1988 estimate) 192,109 inhabitants.

Suriname is divided into 10 districts (with chief town): Brokopondo (Brokopondo), Commewijne (Nieuw Amsterdam), Coronie (Totness), Marowijne (Albina), Nickerie (Nieuw Nickerie), Para (Onverwacht), Paramaribo (Paramaribo), Saramacca (Groningen), Sipalwini (local authority in Paramaribo), Wanica (Lelydorp).

Major ethnic groups in percentages of the population in 1991: Amerindian, 38%; Creole, 31%; Javanese, 15%; Bushnegroes (Blacks),10%.

The official languages are Dutch and English. English is widely spoken next to Hindi, Javanese and Chinese as inter-group communication. A vernacular, called 'Sranan Tongo' or 'Surinamese', is used as a lingua franca. In 1976 it was announced that Spanish would become the nation's principal working language.

CLIMATE. The climate is equatorial, with uniformly high temperatures and rainfall. There is no recognized dry season. Paramaribo. Jan. 80°F (26·7°C), July 81°F (27·2°C). Annual rainfall 89" (2,225 mm).

CONSTITUTION AND GOVERNMENT. A new Constitution was approved by referendum in Sept. 1980.

Elections were held in May 1991. The electorate was 0·2m. The New Front Coalition won 29 seats, the National Democratic Party (supported by the Army), 14, and the new coalition of smaller parties, the Democratic Alternative '91, 8. As the two-thirds majority necessary to elect the president was not attained, an electoral assembly of 860 national and local representatives was elected, which elected Ronald Venetiaan (b.1936; Front for Democracy Coalition) by 645 votes against 2 opponents to become *President* for a 5-year term on 16 Sept. 1991.

Flag: Horizontally green, red and green with the red of double width with a yellow 5-pointed star in the centre of the red bar.

DEFENCE

Army. The armed forces consist of 1 infantry and 1 military police battalions with a strength of about 2,200 in 1991. Equipment includes 1 PC-7 armed trainer, 3 Defender twin-engined light transports operated alongside 1 Bell 205, 2 Alouette III and 1 Cessna 206 liaison aircraft. Officers' ranks were abolished in Feb. 1986.

Navy. The flotilla comprises 5 inshore patrol craft, as well as 3 river patrol boats, all built in the Netherlands. In 1991 personnel totalled 200.

INTERNATIONAL RELATIONS

Membership. Suriname is a member of the UN, OAS and is an ACP state of the EEC.

ECONOMY

Policy. For 15 years from independence (i.e. to 1990) approximately 3,500m. guilders was available from the Netherlands to carry out an extensive social and economic development programme.

Budget. 1989 revenue was (in 1m. Sf) 836·6, made up of direct taxes, 316·9; indirect taxes, 230; bauxite levy and other revenues, 191·8; grants, 50·4; aid, 47·5. Total expenditure was 1,206·5, made up of wages, 562·8; materials, 278·1; transfers, 149·8; interest, 134·6; development expenditure, 62·5; loans, 18·7.

Currency. The unit of currency is the *Suriname guilder* (SRG) of 100 *cents*. Notes ranging from 5 to 1,000 *Suriname guilders* are legal tender. Currency notes of 1·00 and 2·50 guilders are issued by the Government. In March 1992, US$1 = 1·78 Sf; £1 sterling = 3·13 Sf.

Banking and Finance. The Central Bank of Suriname is a bankers' bank and also the bank of issue. There are 3 commercial banks; the Suriname People's Credit Bank operates under the auspices of the Government. There is a post office savings bank, a mortgage bank, an investment bank, a long-term investments agency, a National Development Bank and an Agrarian Bank.

Weights and Measures. The metric system is in force.

ENERGY AND NATURAL RESOURCES

Electricity. Production (1986) 1,610m. kwh.

Minerals. Bauxite is the most important mineral. Production (1987 in 1,000 tonnes): 2,522.

Agriculture. Agriculture is restricted to the alluvial coastal zone; cultivated area in 1982, 87,442 ha. The staple food crop is rice; 72,571 ha of paddy were planted in 1982. Production (1990, in 1,000 tonnes): Sugar-cane, 45; rice, 265; oranges, 13; grapefruit, 1; coconuts, 11; palm oil, 3; cassava, 2.

Livestock (1990, in 1,000): Cattle, 90; sheep, 8; goats,7; pigs,25; poultry, 7,000.

Forestry. Forests cover 14·9 ha, 42% of the land area. Production in 1986 was 196,000 cu. metres.

Fisheries. The fish catch in 1987 amounted to 2,321 tonnes.

INDUSTRY. There are aluminium smelting, food-processing and wood-using industries.

FOREIGN ECONOMIC RELATIONS

Commerce. In 1988 imports totalled 249·9m. Suriname guilders and exports, 535m. Principal imports in 1988 (in 1m. Suriname guilders): Raw materials, 249·9; investment goods, 115·4; fules and lubricants, 90·3; foodstuffs, 41·5; cars and motorcycles, 32·3; textiles, 10·6. Principal exports in 1988 (in 1m. Suriname guilders): Alumina, 535; rice, 71·7; shrimps, 55·8; bananas, 36·2; aluminium, 26·5; wood and wood products, 5·6.

Total trade between Suriname and UK (British Department of Trade returns, in £1,000 sterling):

	1987	1988	1989	1990	1991
Imports to UK	12,488	11,256	16,366	10,094	9,922
Exports and re-exports from UK	7,974	6,107	6,777	10,564	7,896

Tourism. Visitors totalled 8,440 in 1987.

COMMUNICATIONS

Roads. There are 1,335 km of main roads.

In 1987 there were 32,000 passenger cars, 11,000 trucks, 2,000 buses and 1,100 motor cycles.

Railways. There are 2 single-track railways.

Civil Aviation. The national carrier is Suriname Airways. Regular air services are maintained by KLM, SLM, Aero Cubano and Cruzeiro do Sul. There is an international airport at Zanderij.

Shipping. The Royal Netherlands Steamship Co. operates services to the Netherlands, the USA and regionally. The Suriname Navigation Co. maintains services from Paramaribo to Georgetown, Cayenne and the Caribbean area.

Telecommunciations. In 1985 there were 36,000 telephones. The government controls the partly commercial Stichting Radio Omroep Suriname and Radio Suriname Internationaal, and Surinaamse Televisie. In 1991 there were 0·25m. radio and 40,000 TV sets (colour by NTSC). There are 6 broadcasting and 1 television stations. In 1986 there were 246,000 radios and 48,000 TV sets.

Cinemas. In 1981 there were 18 cinemas and 1 drive-in cinema.

Newspapers (1987). There are 2 daily newspapers.

JUSTICE, RELIGION, EDUCATION AND WELFARE

Justice. There is a court of justice, whose members are nominated by the President. There are 3 cantonal courts.

Religion. There is entire religious liberty. At the end of 1983 the main religious bodies were: Hindus, 97,170; Roman Catholics, 80,922; Moslems, 69,638; Moravian Brethren, 55,625; Reformed, 6,265; Lutheran, 2,695; Jehovah's Witnesses, 1,626; Seventh Day Adventists, 1,061; others, 24,627.

Education. In 1986–87 there were 301 primary schools with 3,954 teachers and 59,633 pupils, and there were 1,588 teachers and 23,217 pupils at 89 secondary schools. There was also a University with (1986) 1,070 students and a teacher training college with 1,500 students.

Health. There were (1985) 1,964 hospital beds and 219 physicians.

DIPLOMATIC REPRESENTATIVES

Of Suriname in Great Britain
Ambassador: Cyrill Bisoendat Ramkisor (resides in The Hague).

Of Great Britain in Suriname
Ambassador: R. D. Gordon (resides in Georgetown).

Of Suriname in the USA (4301 Connecticut Ave., NW, Washington, D.C., 20008)
Ambassador: Willem A. Udenhout.

Of the USA in Suriname (Dr Sophie Redmondstraat 129, Paramaribo)
Ambassador: John P. Leonard.

Of Suriname to the United Nations
Ambassador: Kriesnadath Nandoe.

Further Reading

Statistical Information: The General Bureau of Statistics in Paramaribo was established on 1 Jan. 1947. Its publications comprise trade statistics, *Suriname in Figures* (including, from 1953, the former *Handelsstatistiek*) and *Statistische Berichten.*

Economische Voorlichting Suriname. Ministry of Economic Affairs, Paramaribo
Annual Report of the Central Bank of Suriname
Hoefte, R. A. L., *Suriname:* [Bibliography]. Oxford and Santa Barbara, 1990

SWAZILAND

Capital: Mbabane
Population: 681,059 (1986)
GNP per capita: US$900 (1989)

Umbuso weSwatini— Kingdom of Swaziland

HISTORY. In April 1967 the UK granted Swaziland internal self-government, changing its status to that of a protected state with Sobhuza II recognized as king and head of state. Swaziland became independent on 6 Sept. 1968 (For pre-independence history *see* THE STATESMAN'S YEAR-BOOK, 1991–92, p. 1147).

King Sobhuza died on 21 Aug. 1982. On 25 April 1986, King Mswati III was installed as king.

AREA AND POPULATION. Swaziland is bounded on the north, west and south by South Africa, and on the east by Mozambique. The area is 6,705 sq. miles (17,400 sq. km).

The country is divided geographically into 4 longitudinal regions running from north to south; 3 of roughly equal width—Highveld (westernmost), Middleveld, Lowveld—and the Lubombo plateau in the east. The mountainous region on the west rises to an altitude of over 6,000 ft (1,800 metres). The Middleveld is mostly between 1,700 and 3,000 ft, while the Lowveld has an average height of not more than 1,000 ft (300 metres).

Population (census 1986), 681,059. Mbabane, the administrative capital (1986, 38,290). The main urban areas with 1986 census populations are: Manzini (18,084); Big Bend (9,676); Mhlume (6,509); Havelock Mine (4,850); Nhlangano (4,107); Pigg's Peak (3,223) and Siteki (2,271). 31,072 citizens abroad. In early 1988 there were 14,550 refugees living in the country.

The official languages are Siswati and English.

CLIMATE. A temperate climate with two seasons. Nov. to March is the wet season, when temperatures range from mild to hot, with frequent thunderstorms. The cool, dry season from May to Sept. is characterised by clear, bright sunny days. Mbabane. Jan. 68°F (20°C), July 54°F (12·2°C). Annual rainfall 56" (1,402 mm).

CONSTITUTION AND GOVERNMENT. The 1968 constitution (for details *see* THE STATESMAN'S YEAR-BOOK, 1991–92, p. 1147) was abolished in 1976, having been suspended by the King in 1973 on his assumption of supreme power.

On 28 Oct. 1983 a general election took place to elect an electoral college of 80 members.

His Majesty the King: Mswati III (crowned 25 April 1986).

In Feb. 1992, the Cabinet was composed as follows:

Prime Minister: Obed M. Dlamini.

Foreign Affairs: George M. Mamba. *Labour and Public Service:* B. M. Nsibandze. *Agriculture and Co-operatives:* H. S. Mamba. *Commerce, Industry and Tourism:* N. D. Ntiwane. *Works and Communications:* Wilson C. Mkhonta. *Education:* Chief Sipho Shongwe. *Finance:* B.S. Dlamini. *Health:* Dr F. Friedman. *Justice:* Dr Zonke A. Khumalo. *Interior and Immigration:* E. S. Shabalala. *Natural Resources, Land Utilization and Energy:* Prince Nqaba Dlamini.

National flag. Horizontally 5 unequal stripes of blue, yellow, crimson, yellow, blue; in the centre of the crimson strip an African shield of black and white, behind which are 2 assegais and a staff, all laid horizontally.

Local Government. The country is divided into the 4 regions of Shiselweni, Lubombo, Manzini and Hhohho. They are administered by Regional Administrators.

DEFENCE

Army Air Wing. There are 2 Israeli-built Arava light twin-turboprop transports with underwing weapon attachments for light attack duties.

INTERNATIONAL RELATIONS

Membership. Swaziland is a member of UN, OAU, the Commonwealth and is an ACP state of EEC.

ECONOMY

Budget. Revenue and expenditure (in 1,000 emalangeni) for financial years ending 31 March:

	1987–88	1988–89 [1]	1989–90 [1]
Revenue	337,310	361,052	449,211
Expenditure	315,726	370,568	450,234

[1] Estimate.

Currency. The unit of currency is the *lilangeni* (plural *emalangeni*) (SZL) but Swaziland remains in the rand monetary area. In March 1992, £1 = 5·00 *emalangeni;* US$1 = 2·85 *emalangeni.*

Banking. Barclays Bank International and the Standard Bank Ltd maintain branches at Mbabane and Manzini; sub-branches and agencies are operated in 17 other places. Bank rates are those in force throughout South Africa and are prescribed by the main South African offices of the 2 banks. The Swazi Bank, a statutory body, was opened in 1965. It specializes in credit for agriculture and low-cost housing. Its head office is in Mbabane and it has branches or agencies at 4 other places. The Union Bank opened in 1988. Its head office is in Mbabane and it has a branch in Manzini.

ENERGY AND NATURAL RESOURCES

Electricity. Production (1989) 420m. kwh. Supply 230 volts; 50 Hz.

Minerals. Swaziland produces asbestos from the Havelock Mine (27,291 tonnes in 1989). Coal is mined at Mpaka (165,122 tonnes in 1989). Quarry stone is also mined (128,463 tonnes in 1989).

Agriculture. In 1991 the cultivated area was 204,128 ha, the grazing area 1,061,584 ha. Production (1989–90, in 1,000 tonnes): Sugar-cane, 3,797; citrus, 74; seed cotton, 26. (1988–89): Maize, 133; sorghum, 1; pineapples, 34; tomatoes, 1; potatoes, 3. Tobacco is also grown.

Livestock (1989): Cattle, 679,188; goats, 294,428; sheep, 24,803; poultry, 1,200,567.

Forestry. The commercial forest area was 103,566 ha in 1991.

FOREIGN ECONOMIC RELATIONS. Swaziland has a customs union with South Africa and receives a *pro rata* share of the dues collected.

Commerce. In 1990 exports (in E1,000) were 1,160,473, including sugar, 388,830; unbleached wood pulp, 160,831; canned fruits, 48,123; asbestos, 28,919. Imports: 1,519,485, including machinery and transport equipment, 442,257; minerals, fuels and lubricants, 235,539; manufactured items, 238,518; food, 195,988.

Total trade between Swaziland and UK (British Department of Trade returns, in £1,000 sterling):

	1987	1988	1989	1990	1991
Imports to UK	36,901	27,973	31,368	34,473	39,607
Exports and re-exports from UK	2,257	1,564	1,358	2,719	4,336

Tourism. There were 257,997 visitors in 1989.

COMMUNICATIONS

Roads. Total length of roads (1989) 2,801 km of which 719 km were tarred.

Railways. In 1989 the system comprised 301 km of route, and carried 4·4m. tonnes of freight in 1989–90.

Aviation. The country's chief airport is at Matsapa, near Manzini. It is served by Royal Swazi National Airways connecting with Johannesburg, Durban, Lusaka, Nairobi, Harare and Gaborone. Lesotho National Airways flies to Harare and Maputo through Matsapa. Zambian Airways fly to Matsapa via Gaborone.

Telecommunications. There were (1987) 71 post offices, 2 telegraph stations and 29 postal agencies. In 1989 there were 24,419 telephones, 12,175 exchange connexions and 335 telex exchange connexions. In 1986 there were over 96,000 radio sets and over 12,000 television receivers.

Cinemas. There were 5 cinemas in 1980 with a total seating capacity of 1,625.

Newspapers. There were in 1987 two daily newspapers.

JUSTICE, RELIGION, EDUCATION AND WELFARE

Justice. The judiciary is headed by the Chief Justice. There is a High Court and subordinate courts presided over by Magistrates and District Officers are in existence. A Court of Appeal with a President and 3 Judges deals with appeals from the High Court. There are 16 courts of first instance.

Religion. In 1984 there were about 120,000 Christians and about 30,000 adults holding traditional beliefs.

Education. In 1989 there were 624 schools with 157,345 pupils in primary classes and 38,193 in secondary and high school classes. The then Swaziland Agricultural College and University Centre at Luyengo was opened in 1966. The College is now the Faculty of Agriculture at the University of Swaziland. Technical and vocational training classes are run at the Government Swaziland College of Technology, the Swaziland Institute of Management and Public Administration (SIMPA), the Gwamile Vocational Commercial Training Institute and the Mpaka Vocational Centre and the Manzini Industrial Training Centre. The Government also operates a Police College, Institute of Health Sciences, the Nazarene Prison College and the Nursing College which trains para-medical staff. There were 3 teacher training colleges with 539 students in 1989–90. There were 1,313 students enrolled in all the vocational centres except SIMPA in 1987–88, and 1,548 at the University of Swaziland at Matsapa, in 1989–90.

Health. In 1984 there were 80 doctors, 13 dentists and 1,608 hospital beds.

DIPLOMATIC REPRESENTATIVES

Of Swaziland in Great Britain (58 Pont St., London SW1X 0AE)
High Commissioner: Mboni N. Dlamini.

Of Great Britain in Swaziland (Allister Miller St., Mbabane)
High Commissioner: Brian Watkins.

Of Swaziland in the USA (3400 International Dr., NW, Washington, D.C., 20008)
Ambassador: Absalom V. Mamba.

Of the USA in Swaziland (PO Box 199, Mbabane)
Ambassador: Stephen Roggers.

Of Swaziland to the United Nations
Ambassador: Dr Timothy L. L. Dlamini.

Further Reading

Booth, A., *Swaziland: Tradition and Change in a Southern African Kingdom.* Aldershot and Boulder, 1984
Funnell, D. C., *Under the Shadow of Apartheid: Agrarian Transformation in Swaziland.* Avebury, 1991
Grotpeter, J. J., *Historical Dictionary of Swaziland.* Metuchen, 1975
Jones, D., *Aid and Development in Southern Africa.* London, 1977
Matsebula, J. S. M., *A History of Swaziland.* London, 1972
Nyeko, B., *Swaziland.* [Bibliography] Oxford and Santa Barbara, 1982

National statistical office: Central Statistical Office, POB 456, Mbabaue.

SWEDEN

Capital: Stockholm
Population: 8·6m. (1990)
GNP per capita: US$25,863 (1990)

Konungariket Sverige

(Kingdom of Sweden)

HISTORY. Organized as an independent unified state in the 10th century, Sweden became a constitutional monarchy in 1809. In 1809 she also ceded Finland to Russia. In 1815 German possessions were ceded to Prussia and Sweden was united with Norway, which union lasted until 1905.

AREA AND POPULATION. Sweden is bounded west and north-west by Norway, east by Finland and the Gulf of Bothnia, south-east by the Baltic Sea and south-west by the Kattegat. The first census took place in 1749, and it was repeated at first every third year, and, after 1775, every fifth year. Since 1860 a general census has been taken every 10 years and, in addition, in 1935, 1945, 1965, 1975 and 1985.

Latest census figures: 1940, 6,371,432 (annual increase since 1935: 0·38%); 1950, 7,041,829 (1·1% since 1945); 1960, 7,495,316 (0·64% since 1950); 1965, 7,766,424 (1·04% since 1960); 1970, 8,076,903 (1·04% since 1965); 1975, 8,208,544 (1·02% since 1970); 1980, 8,320,438 (1·01% since 1975); 1985, 8,360,178.

Counties (Län)	Land area: sq. km	Census population 1 Nov. 1985	Estimated population 31 Dec. 1990	Pop. per sq. km 31 Dec. 1990
Stockholm	6,488	1,577,596	1,641,669	253
Uppsala	6,989	251,754	268,835	38
Södermanland	6,060	249,885	255,636	42
Östergötland	10,562	393,668	403,011	38
Jönköping	9,944	300,892	308,290	31
Kronoberg	8,458	174,025	177,882	21
Kalmar	11,170	238,406	241,102	22
Gotland	3,140	56,180	57,108	18
Blekinge	2,941	151,055	150,564	51
Kristianstad	6,089	280,516	289,278	48
Malmöhus	4,938	750,294	779,309	158
Halland	5,454	240,090	254,725	47
Göteborg and Bohus	5,141	715,831	739,945	144
Älvsborg	11,395	426,769	441,391	39
Skaraborg	7,938	270,530	276,830	35
Värmland	17,583	279,503	283,110	16
Örebro	8,519	270,384	272,513	32
Västmanland	6,302	254,858	258,487	41
Kopparberg	28,194	284,029	289,067	10
Gävleborg	18,191	289,452	289,294	16
Västernorrland	21,678	262,555	261,155	12
Jämtland	49,443	134,161	135,726	3
Västerbotten	55,401	245,302	251,968	5
Norrbotten	98,911	262,443	263,735	3
Total	410,928[1]	8,360,178	8,590,630	21

[1] Total area of Sweden, 449,964 sq. km.

On 31 Dec. 1990 there were 4,244,017 males and 4,346,613 females.

On 31 Dec. 1990 aliens in Sweden numbered 483,704. Of these, 119,669 were Finns, 41,053 Yugoslavs, 38,982 Iranians, 38,242 Norwegians, 28,586 Danes, 25,475 Turks, 19,874 Chileans, 15,675 Poles, 12,952 Germans, 10,110 Britons, 7,946 Ethiopians, 7,722 Iraqis, 6,547 Lebanese, 6,516 Greeks and 5,313 Romanians.

Vital statistics for calendar years:

	Total living births	To mothers single, divorced or widowed	Stillborn	Marriages	Divorces	Deaths exclusive of still-born
1988	112,080	57,090	422	44,229	17,746	96,743
1989	116,023	60,077	423	108,919	18,862	92,110
1990	123,938	58,248	442	40,477	19,357	95,161

Expectation of life in 1990: males, 74; females, 80.

Immigration: 1984, 31,486; 1985, 33,134; 1986, 39,487; 1987, 42,688; 1988, 51,092; 1989, 65,811; 1990, 60,066. Emigration: 1984, 22,825; 1985, 22,041; 1986, 24,495; 1987, 20,679; 1988, 21,461; 1989, 21,479; 1990, 25,606.

In 1990, population in densely populated areas was 7,126,158 (83%).

Population of the 50 largest communities, 31 Dec. 1990:

Stockholm	674,452	Halmstad	80,061	Kalmar	56,206
Göteborg	433,042	Karlstad	76,467	Kungsbacka	54,220
Malmö	233,887	Skellefteå	75,258	Falun	53,748
Uppsala	167,508	Huddinge	73,829	Mölndal	52,028
Linköping	122,268	Kristianstad	71,750	Solna	51,841
Örebro	120,944	Växjö	69,547	Sollentuna	51,377
Norrköping	120,522	Botkyrka	68,542	Trollhättan	51,047
Västerås	119,761	Luleå	68,412	Hässleholm	49,106
Jönköping	111,486	Nyköping	65,908	Varberg	49,018
Helsingborg	109,267	Nacka	64,056	Skövde	47,529
Borås	101,766	Haninge	62,797	Uddevalla	47,345
Sundsvall	93,808	Örnsköldsvik	59,379	Borlänge	46,671
Umeå	91,258	Karlskrona	59,054	Norrtälje	46,165
Eskilstuna	89,765	Östersund	58,317	Motala	41,994
Gävle	88,568	Gotland	57,108	Piteå	40,003
Lund	87,681	Täby	56,714	Västervik	39,908
Södertälje	81,786	Järfälla	56,359		

Source: Statistics Sweden

CLIMATE. North Sweden suffers from severe winters, with snow lying for 4–7 months. Summers are fine but cool, with long daylight hours. Further south, winters are less cold, summers are warm and rainfall generally well-distributed over the year, though with a slight summer maximum. Stockholm. Jan. 3·2°C, July 18·4°C. Annual rainfall 385 mm.

REIGNING KING. Carl XVI Gustaf, born 30 April 1946, succeeded on the death of his grandfather Gustaf VI Adolf, 15 Sept. 1973, married 19 June 1976 to *Silvia* Renate Sommerlath, born 23 Dec. 1943 (Queen of Sweden). *Daughter* and *Heir Apparent:* Crown Princess Victoria Ingrid Alice Désirée, Duchess of Väster-götland, born 14 July 1977; *son:* Prince Carl Philip Edmund Bertil, Duke of Värm-land, born 13 May 1979; *daughter:* Princess Madeleine Thérèse Amelie Josephine, Duchess of Hälsingland and Gästrikland, born 10 June 1982.

Sisters of the King. Princess Margaretha, born 31 Oct. 1934, married 30 June 1964 to Mr John Ambler; Princess Birgitta (Princess of Sweden), born 19 Jan. 1937, married 25 May 1961 (civil marriage) and 30 May 1961 (religious ceremony) to Johann Georg, Prince of Hohenzollern; Princess Désirée, born 2 June 1938, married 5 June 1964 to Baron Niclas Silfverschiöld; Princess Christina, born 3 Aug. 1943, married 15 June 1974 to Tord Magnuson.

Uncles of the King. Sigvard, Count of Wisborg, born on 7 June 1907; Prince Bertil, Duke of Halland, born on 28 Feb. 1912, married 7 Dec. 1976 to Lilian May Davies, born 30 Aug. 1915 (Princess of Sweden, Duchess of Halland); Carl Johan, Count of Wisborg, born on 31 Oct. 1916.

Aunt of the King. Princess Ingrid (Princess of Sweden), born 28 March 1910, married 24 May 1935 to Frederik, Crown Prince of Denmark (King Frederik IX), died 14 Jan. 1972.

The following is a list of the kings and queens of Sweden, with the dates of their accession from the accession of the House of Vasa:

House of Vasa		House of Pfalz-Zwei-		House of Bernadotte	
Gustaf I	1521	brücken (contd.)		Carl XIV Johan	1818
Eric XIV	1560	Carl XII	1697	Oscar I	1844
Johan III	1568	Ulrica Eleonora	1719	Carl XV	1859
Sigismund	1592			Oscar II	1872
Carl IX	1599	House of Hesse		Gustaf V	1907
Gustaf II Adolf	1611	Fredrik I	1720	Gustaf VI Adolf	1950
Christina	1632			Carl XVI Gustaf	1973
		House of Holstein-Gottorp			
		Adolf Fredrik	1751		
House of Pfalz-Zwei-		Gustaf III	1771		
brücken		Gustaf IV Adolf	1792		
Carl X Gustaf	1654	Carl XIII	1809		
Carl XI	1660				

The royal family receive a tax-free annual allowance of 20m. krona from the civil list; this does not include the maintenance of the royal palaces.

CONSTITUTION AND GOVERNMENT. Sweden's present Constitution came into force in 1975 and replaced the 1809 Constitution. Under the present Constitution Sweden is a representative and parliamentary democracy. Parliament (*Riksdag*) is declared to be the central organ of government. The executive power of the country is vested in the Government, which is responsible to Parliament. The King is Head of State, but he does not participate in the government of the country. Since 1971 Parliament has consisted of one chamber. It has 349 members, who are elected for a period of 3 years in direct, general elections.

Every man and woman who has reached the age of 18 years on election-day itself, and who is not under wardship has the right to vote and to stand for election. The manner of election to the *Riksdag* is proportional. The country is divided into 28 constituencies. In these constituencies 310 members are elected. The remaining 39 seats constitute a nation-wide pool intended to give absolute proportionality to parties that receive at least 4% of the votes. A party receiving less than 4% of the votes in the country is, however, entitled to participate in the distribution of seats in a constituency, if it has obtained at least 12% of the votes cast there.

At the elections of Sept. 1991 turn-out was 85%. The Social-Democratic Party won 138 seats with 37·6% of votes cast (156 with 43·2% in 1988), the Moderate Party (Mod) 80 with 21·9% (66 with 18·3%), the Liberal Party (Lib) 33 with 9·1% (44 with 12·2%), the Centre Party 31 with 8·5% (42 with 11·3%), the Christian Democratic Party (CD) 27 with 7·1% (0 with 2·9%), New Democracy 24 with 6·7% and the Left Party 16 with 4·5% (21 with 5·8%). The Green Party polled 3·4%, less than the 4% admission threshold.

A 20-member coalition government of Moderates, Liberals, Centre Party and Christian Democrats was formed in Oct. 1991, including:

Prime Minister: Carl Bildt (b. 1949; Mod).

Deputy Prime Minister and Minister of Social Welfare: Bengt Westerberg (Lib). *Foreign:* Margaretha af Ugglas (Mod). *Defence:* Anders Björck (Mod). *Justice:* Gun Hellsvik (Mod). *Finance:* Anne Wibble (Lib). *Environment:* Olof Johansson (Centre). *Aid:* Alf Svensson (CD). *Europe:* Ulf Dinkenspiel (Ind). *Education:* Per Uckel (Mod). *Civil Service:* Inger Davidsson (CD). *Transport:* Mats Odell (CD). *Agriculture:* Karl Erik Olsson (Centre). *Industry:* Per Westerberg (Mod). *Labour:* Borje Hornlund (Centre). *Housing:* Birgit Friggebo (Lib).

The *Speaker* is Ingegerd Trödsson.

Ministerial decisions are formally made by the Cabinet collectively and not (with some exceptions) by individual ministers.

Public administration in Sweden is characterized by a unique degree of functional decentralization. The Ministries are not really administrative agencies. Their main function is to prepare the decisions of the Cabinet; such decisions may concern bills for the *Riksdag*, general government directives and higher appointments. Only to a small extent does the Cabinet make individual administrative decisions. The routine administrative work is attended to by the central boards (*centrala ämbetsverk*). Each board is in principle subordinate to the government; its sphere of activity depends on the appropriations granted by the *Riksdag*. The Government often asks the boards' opinion on proposed measures.

National flag: Blue with a yellow Scandinavian cross.

National anthem: Du gamla, du fria, du fjällhöga nord ('Thou ancient, thou free, thou mountainous north'; words by R. Dybeck, 1844; folk-tune).

The official language is Swedish. The capital is Stockholm.

Regional and Local Government. The country is divided into 24 counties (*län*), in each of which the central government is represented by a state county administrative board (*länsstyrelse*). The governor (*landshövding*), appointed by the government, is chairman of the board, which in addition to the governor has 14 members elected by the county council.

Local government and the levying of local taxes are based on the Constitution and regulated by the local government act and special acts. According to the local government act Sweden is divided into municipalities in which voters who have reached the age of 18 are entitled to elect the municipal council. The number of municipalities has, since 1951, been reduced from about 2,500 to 284. The municipalities deal with social welfare, education and culture, public health, town planning, housing etc. Each county, except Gotland, which consists of only one municipality, has a county council (*landsting*) elected by voters who enjoy local suffrage. The county councils chiefly administer the health services and medical care. The municipalities of Göteborg and Malmö do not belong to county councils. The parishes, 2,563 in 1990, are the local units of the Church of Sweden and have the same status in public law as the municipalities. The parochial church council (*kyrkofullmäktige*) is the supreme decision-making body in most parishes, whose members are publicly elected. Small parishes have instead the parish meeting, a form of direct democracy.

DEFENCE. A Supreme Commander is, under the Government, in command of the three services. He is assisted by the Defence Staff under a chief of staff.

The military forces are recruited on the principle of national service, supplemented by voluntarily enlisted personnel who form the permanent cadres for training purposes, staff duties, etc. Liability to service commences at the age of 18, and lasts till the end of the 47th year. The period of training for the Army and Navy is $7^{1}/_{2}$-15 months and for the Airforce 8-12 months.

The territorial organization consists of 5 military commands each one under a general officer commanding.

Army. The C.-in-C. of the Army has at his disposal the Army Staff under a chief of staff. The peace-time Army consists for training purposes of 16 infantry, 2 cavalry, 6 armour, 4 artillery, 5 AA, 3 engineer, 2 signal and 3 Army Service Corps units, most of which are called 'regiments' (*regementen*). Equipment includes 340 Strv-101, 110 Centurion and 335 Strv-103B main battle tanks. The Army Aviation Corps comprises 2 Battalions operating 6 Bulldog aircraft and 18 JetRanger helicopters for observation, 20 armed BO 105 helicopters, 12 AB.204B transport helicopters, plus 26 Hughes 300C helicopters and 2 DO 27 aircraft for training and observation duties.

The Army is organized and equipped with regard to the varying geographical and climatic conditions of the country. The voluntary Home Guard (*Hemvärnet*) with a total strength of more than 125,000 men ready for action within 2 hours, raised during the second world war continues to be in force.

Sweden's ground forces, total 850,000 men (including the voluntary Home Guard), can be said to consist of an Army which for the most part is on indefinite leave, but which on short notice can be ready for action. One of the basic principles of the system of mobilization is local recruitment of as many units as possible. The storage of equipment and supplies is decentralized in more than 3,000 places.

The active personnel of the Army comprises (1992) about 43,500 (35,000 conscripts).

Navy. The Commander-in-Chief of the Navy is assisted by the Chief of Naval Staff and the Chief of Naval Materiel. The main operational commander is the Commander-in-Chief, Coastal Fleet. Naval forces are divided between 2 branches: Navy and Coastal Defence Artillery. There are 4 Naval Command Areas, covering southern, eastern, western and northern coasts. The coastal defence areas are the Stockholm archipelago, Blekinge, Göteborg, Gotland and Norrland, covered by a coastal artillery brigade each.

The Navy operates 12 small diesel submarines, 1 57m Göteborg and 2 50m Stockholm class missile craft, (which act as leaders for smaller craft), 28 other missile craft, 11 inshore patrol craft, 3 minelayers, 6 minehunters, 3 coastal minesweepers and 14 inshore minesweepers. Auxiliaries include 1 mine countermeasures support ship, 1 electronic intelligence gatherer, 1 surveying vessel, 6 icebreakers, 2 tugs and 1 salvage vessel, as well as numerous service craft and boats.

As well as an extensive inventory of artillery up to 120mm calibre, and coast defence missiles, the coastal defence artillery also operate 9 coastal and 16 inshore minelayers, 18 small patrol craft and some 140 small amphibious craft.

The Naval Air Arm comprises 14 Boeing Vertol 107 helicopters and 9 AB-206 Jet-Ranger helicopters, and also 1 Aviocar fixed-wing aircraft for anti-submarine warfare and electronic surveillance and 2 Navajo communications aircraft.

The personnel of the Navy in 1991 totalled 12,000 (6,300 conscripts) of whom 2,600 serve in Coastal Defence.

A separate civil Coast Guard, 550 strong, operate some 70 inshore cutters, patrol boats and service craft and 4 aircraft.

Air Force. The Commander-in-Chief of the Swedish Air Force has at his disposal the Air Staff under a chief of staff.

The combat force consists of 3 fighter-interceptor, 3 ground-attack and 3 mixed interceptor/reconnaissance wings, each with 2-3 squadrons of 12-15 aircraft, including 3 reconnaissance squadrons. Total peace-time strength of the combat units is 20 squadrons with nearly 400 first-line aircraft.

Night and all-weather fighters are the Swedish-built Saab J35 Draken, equipping 3 squadrons, and JA37 Viggen, equipping 8 squadrons. The ground-attack wings have 6 squadrons of Saab AJ37 Viggens, and there is provision for 4 light ground-attack squadrons of twin-jet Saab-105s (Sk60s), which could be drawn in wartime from training units. The 3 reconnaissance squadrons have SF37 (photo) and SH37 (maritime, radar) Viggen reconnaissance aircraft; and there are transport, helicopter and other support units. The Sk60 is the Air Force's standard advanced trainer, to which pupils progress after initial training on piston-engined Bulldogs. Other trainers in service include the Sk35C Draken and Sk37 Viggen.

Active strength (1992) 7,500 (5,500 conscripts), with 415 combat aircraft.

INTERNATIONAL RELATIONS

Membership. Sweden is a member of the UN and EFTA and applied to join the EC on 1 July 1991.

ECONOMY

Policy. A privatization programme of Nov. 1991 envisaged selling the state's holdings in 35 companies.

Budget. Revenue and expenditure of the total budget (Current and Capital) for financial years ending 30 June (in 1m. kr.):

	Revenue	Expenditure		Revenue	Expenditure
1986–87	320,105	335,267	1989–90	401,553	398,140
1987–88	332,552	336,669	1990–91	426,610	445,089
1988–89	367,707	349,600	1991–92	464,632	470,108

The revenue and expenditure for the financial year 1 July 1989 to 30 June 1990 was as follows (in 1m. kr.):

Revenue		Expenditure	
Taxes:		Royal Household and residences	52
Taxes on income,		Justice	6,352
capital gains and		Foreign Affairs	13,939
profits	107,409	Defence	34,620
Statutory social		Health and Social Affairs	106,211
security fees	55,023	Transport and Communications	18,223
Taxes on property	23,159	Ministry of Finance	27,468
Value-added tax		Education and Cultural Affairs	50,409
and other taxes on		Agriculture	5,558
goods and services	168,511	Labour	28,283
Total revenue		Housing and Physical Planning	23,909
from taxes	354,103	Industry	3,038
Non-tax revenue	37,468	Civil Service Affairs	13,515
Capital revenue	1,119	Ministry of Environment and	
Loan repayment	5,405	Energy	2,020
Computed revenue	3,337	Parliament and agencies	586
		Interest on National Debt, etc.	63,696
Total revenue	401,553	Unforeseen expenditure	13
		Changed appropriation of	
		short-term credits	248
		Total expenditure	398,140

On 31 Dec. 1990 the national debt amounted to 632,300m. kr.

A reform of 1990 moved the burden of tax from income to services and goods.

Currency. The unit of currency is the Swedish *krona* (SEK), of 100 *öre*. There are notes for 5, 10, 50, 100, 500, 1,000 and 10,000 krona. Inflation was an annualized 11·5% in Nov. 1990. In May 1991 the krona was linked to the ecu at ecu 1 = 7·40054 krona, with a maximum fluctuation of 1·5%, as a first step towards joining the ERM of the EMS. In March 1992, £1 = 10·46 *krona*; US$1 = 5·96 *krona*.

Banking and Finance. The central bank and bank of issue is the *Riksbank*. The *Governor* of the *Riksbank* is appointed for 5 years by 8 trustees, 7 of whom are appointed by Parliament. The *Governor* is Bengt Dennis. The bank's capital and reserve fund are provided by its constitution. On 31 Dec. 1990 its note circulation amounted to 69,620m. kr.; its gold and foreign-exchange reserves totalled 103,752m. kr. There are 24 commercial banks. On 31 Dec. 1990 their total deposits amounted to 374,059m. kr.; advances to the public amounted to 588,842m. kr.

On 31 Dec. 1990 there were 109 savings banks; their total deposits amounted to 170,544m. kr.; advances to the public were 195,558m. kr. Co-operative banks had total deposits of 52,980m. kr.; advances to the public were 46,836m. kr.

There is a stock exchange in Stockholm.

Weights and Measures. The metric system is obligatory.

ENERGY AND NATURAL RESOURCES

Electricity. Sweden is rich in hydro-power resources. Electricity production in 1989 was 138,849m. kwh. About 51% of this energy was produced in hydro-electric plants and 45% in 12 nuclear power plants. A referendum of 1980 called for the phasing out of nuclear power by 2010. The remaining 4% was produced in thermal power plants. Supply 220 volts; 50 Hz.

Minerals. Sweden is one of the leading exporters of iron ore.

There are also some deposits of copper, lead and zinc ores. Non-ferrous ores, except zinc ores, are used in the Swedish metal industry and barely satisfy domestic needs.

The total production of iron ores amounted to 27·2m. tons in 1989; the production of copper ore was 276,580 tons, of lead ore 215,490 tons, of zinc ore 204,087 tons.

In southern Sweden there are big resources of alum shale, containing oil and uranium.

Agriculture. According to the farm register which is revised annually the following data was provided for 1990. The number of farms in cultivation of more than 2 ha of arable land, was 96,560; of these there were 54,809 of 2-20 ha; 37,748 of 20–100 ha; 4,003 of above 100 ha. Of the total land area, 2,844,592 [1] ha were arable land and 331,691[1] ha cultivated pastures.

	Area (1,000 ha) [1]			Production (1,000 tonnes)		
Chief crops	1988	1989	1990	1988	1989	1990
Wheat	258·9	291·8	349·7	1,296	1,751	2,243
Rye	35·3	70·7	73·5	128	319	335
Barley	566·7	500·9	492·0	1,879	1,870	2,123
Oats	446·6	432·7	387·8	1,330	1,455	1,584
Potatoes	38·8	36·0	36·2	1,283	1,179	1,186
Sugarbeet	51·3	50·6	50·0	2,439	2,654	2,776
Tame hay	699·0	709·7	727·6	4,435	4,624	5,219
Oil seed	149·8	169·4	167·9	293	417	442

Area of rotation meadows for pasture was (in 1,000 ha[1]): 1985, 181; 1986, 180; 1987, 175; 1988, 182; 1989, 185; 1990, 191.

Total production of milk (in 1,000 tonnes): 1985, 3,724; 1986, 3,566; 1987, 3,513; 1988, 3,498; 1989, 3,563; 1990, 3,575. Butter production in the same years was (in 1,000 tonnes): 75, 68, 66, 62, 69, 76; and cheese 115, 113, 114, 123, 117, 116.

Livestock (1990): Cattle, 1·7m.; sheep, 406,000; pigs, 2·3m.; poultry, 11m.

Number of farm tractors in 1986, 183,828; combines in 1986, 47,089.

The number of pelts produced in 1989–90 (and in 1988–89) was: Fox, 33,472 (43,245); mink, 1·28m. (1·57m.); others, 6,190 (6,013).

[1] Figures refer to holdings of more than 2 ha of arable land.

Forestry. In 1988 forests covered an area of 22,535,284 ha. Municipal and State ownership accounts for one-fourth of the forests, companies own another fourth, and the remaining half is in private hands. In the felling seasons, 1987–88 and 1988–89 respectively, 53m. and 55·4m. cu. metres (solid volume excluding bark) of wood were removed. The sawmill, wood pulp and paper and paperboard industries are all of great importance. In 1989 the production of sawn soft-wood was about 11·3m. cu. metres. The production of woodpulp in 1989 was 10·3m. tonnes (dry weight).

Fisheries. In 1989 the total catch of the sea fisheries was 238,961 tonnes.

INDUSTRY. The most important manufacturing sector is the production of metals, metal products, machinery and transport equipment, covering almost half of the total value added by manufacturing. Production of high-quality steel is an old speciality. The production of ordinary steel is decreasing and is short of domestic demand. Aluminium, lead and copper are also produced. Metallurgy forms a base for the production of machinery of many sorts and transport equipment.

Another important manufacturing sector is based on forest resources. This sector includes saw-mills, plywood factories, joinery industries, pulp- and paper-mills, wallboard and particle board factories, accounting for about 20% of the total value of manufacturing. A fast increasing sector is the chemical industry, especially the petro-chemical branch. Minerals industries include production of building materials, decorative arts products of glass and china.

	No. of establishments		Average no. of wage-earners		Sales value of production (gross) in 1m. kr.	
Industry groups	1988	1989	1988	1989	1988	1989
Mining and quarrying	95	102	6,786	6,350	6,275	7,588
Metal-ore mining	32	28	5,743	5,082	5,468	6,371
Other mining	63	74	1,043	1,268	808	1,217
Manufacturing	9,005	9,069	529,058	523,379	607,209	674,436
Manufacture of food, beverages and tobacco	809	810	51,431	51,741	82,033	89,475
Textile, wearing apparel and leather industries	567	528	20,686	18,265	11,387	11,122

Industry groups	No. of establishments		Average no. of wage-earners		Sales value of production (gross) in 1m. kr.	
	1988	1989	1988	1989	1988	1989
Manufacture of wood products including furniture	1,303	1,292	45,743	45,578	42,418	48,565
Manufacture of paper and paper products, printing and publishing	1,074	1,083	65,578	65,831	93,972	101,927
Manufacture of chemicals and chemical, petroleum, coal, rubber and plastic products	730	730	42,347	40,946	75,654	83,948
Manufacture of non-metallic mineral products, except products of petroleum and coal	370	377	16,089	16,745	13,730	15,837
Basic metal industries	179	175	34,064	32,138	48,582	55,836
Manufacture of fabricated metal products, machinery and equipment	3,788	3,989	250,434	249,839	237,667	266,154
Other manufacturing industries	95	85	2,686	2,296	1,765	1,573
Electricity and gas	703	693	10,175	10,452	82,795	86,720

Source: Statistics Sweden

Trade Unions. The Swedish Federation of Trade Unions (LO) had 23 member unions with a total membership of 2,260,204 in 1989; the Swedish Central Organization of Salaried Employees (TCO) had 21, with 1,273,272; the Swedish Confederation of Professional Associations (SACO-SR) had 25, with 321,626.

FOREIGN ECONOMIC RELATIONS. Since Jan. 1991 restrictions on foreign investment have been abolished, and an economic reform programme of Nov. 1991 permits foreigners to buy Swedish companies.

Commerce. The imports and exports of Sweden, unwrought gold and coin not included, have been as follows (in 1m. kr.):

	1984	1985	1986	1987	1988	1989	1990
Imports	218,569	244,654	232,614	257,870	280,650	316,593	322,854
Exports	242,811	260,481	265,103	281,433	305,056	332,576	339,772

Imports and exports by products (in 1m. kr.):

	Imports		Exports	
	1989	1990	1989	1990
Food and live animals chiefly for food	15,786	16,454	5,382	6,107
Cereals and cereal preparations	964	1,074	1,288	1,601
Vegetables and fruit	5,487	6,100	405	435
Coffee, tea, cocoa, spices and manufactures thereof	2,616	2,276	797	813
Feeding stuff for animals (not including unmilled cereals)	1,243	1,061	129	134
Beverages and tobacco	2,353	2,544	450	503
Crude materials, inedible, except fuels	13,565	10,919	31,382	29,955
Hides, skins and furskins, raw	601	398	1,152	800
Crude rubber (including synthetic and reclaimed)	461	400	174	132
Cork and wood	3,395	2,292	10,878	11,504
Pulp and waste paper	839	955	13,357	11,573
Textile fibres (other than wool tops and other combed wool) and their wastes (not manufactured into yarn or fabric)	362	378	209	317
Crude fertilizers and crude minerals (excluding coal, petroleum and precious stones)	1,616	1,565	506	520
Metalliferous ores and metal scrap	4,396	2,886	4,739	4,747
Mineral fuels, lubricants and related materials	24,231	29,367	9,209	10,323
Coal, coke and briquettes	1,667	1,485	86	70

	Imports		Exports	
	1989	1990	1989	1990
Petroleum, petroleum products and related materials	21,191	26,061	7,922	8,903
Chemicals and related products, n.e.s.	30,176	30,686	24,119	25,328
Artificial resins and plastic materials, and cellulose esters and ethers	9,218	9,565	6,687	7,086
Manufactured goods classified chiefly by material	52,998	54,516	87,314	87,170
Paper, paperboard, and articles of paper pulp, of paper or of paperboard	4,177	4,717	35,768	37,361
Textile yarn, fabrics, made-up articles, n.e.s., and related products	7,338	7,662	3,575	3,693
Non-metallic mineral manufactures, n.e.s.	5,266	6,138	3,065	3,099
Iron and steel	11,867	11,418	21,968	20,209
Non-ferrous metals	8,307	6,942	6,518	6,232
Machinery and transport equipment	126,409	124,476	141,052	147,066
Power generating machinery and equipment	7,267	7,586	9,564	10,119
Machinery specialized for particular industries	11,633	12,149	17,009	18,713
Metal working machinery	3,597	3,389	3,493	4,058
General industrial machinery and equipment, n.e.s. and machine parts, n.e.s.	17,455	18,510	24,006	26,168
Office machines and automatic data processing machines	15,805	15,812	9,126	8,630
Telecommunications and sound recording and reproducing apparatus and equipment	9,488	9,929	14,227	14,969
Electrical machinery apparatus and appliances, n.e.s., and electrical parts thereof (including non-electrical counterparts, n.e.s., of electrical household type equipment)	19,414	19,887	13,414	14,409
Road vehicles (including air cushion vehicles)	32,937	27,556	44,873	43,923
Other transport equipment	8,691	9,668	5,422	6,077
Miscellaneous manufactured articles	47,336	51,344	30,306	29,735

Principal import and export countries (in 1m. kr.):

	Imports from		Exports to	
	1989	1990	1989	1990
Belgium-Luxembourg	9,826	9,731	12,565	12,790
Denmark	21,773	24,676	22,090	23,094
Federal Republic of Germany	63,896	62,602	42,280	47,273
Finland	21,250	22,106	23,233	23,102
France	16,816	16,122	17,712	18,297
Italy	13,027	13,601	14,752	15,835
Netherlands	13,236	13,264	16,625	18,104
Norway	22,159	25,513	27,301	28,329
Switzerland	5,857	6,197	7,557	7,972
USSR	5,165	4,466	2,458	2,501
UK	25,608	26,023	37,238	34,364
USA	25,894	27,968	30,921	29,178

Source: Statistics Sweden

Total trade between Sweden and UK (British Department of Trade returns, in £1,000 sterling):

	1987	1988	1989	1990	1991
Imports to UK	2,952,453	3,366,524	3,747,600	3,594,547	3,142,449
Exports and re-exports from UK	2,322,235	2,195,032	2,350,122	2,712,775	2,471,539

Tourism. In 1990 foreign visitors spent 17,065m. kr., and stayed 3,192,994 nights in hotels, 845,753 in holiday villages and youth hostels and 2,535,920 camping.

COMMUNICATIONS

Roads. On 1 Jan. 1990 there were 205,000 km of public roads comprising state-administered roads, 98,173 km, municipal, 32,000 km, private roads with subsidies,

78,149 km, of which 69,754 km were surfaced. Motor vehicles on 31 Dec. 1990 included 3,600,518 passenger cars, 324,115 buses and lorries and 41,066 motor cycles.

Railways. Total length of railways (1990), was 11,202 km; (7,395 km electrified). 87m. passengers were carried in 1990 and 56m. tonnes of freight. There is a metro in Stockholm (108 km), and tram/light rail networks in Stockholm, Göteborg (81 km) and Norrköping.

Civil Aviation. Commercial air traffic is maintained in (1) Sweden and other parts of the world by Scandinavian Airlines System (SAS), of which AB Aerotransport (ABA = Swedish Air Lines) is the Swedish partner (DDL = Danish Air Lines and DNL = Norwegian Air Lines being the other two); (2) only within Sweden by Linjeflyg AB. Scandinavian Airlines System have a joint paid-up capital of about 12,177m. Sw. kr. Capitalization of ABA, 3,761m. Sw. kr., of which 50% is owned by the Government and 50% by private enterprises. Capitalization of Linjeflyg, 880m. Sw. kr., of which 50% is owned by SAS and 50% by ABA.

There were 126 scheduled services in 1990. The total number of km flown was 120·36m.; passenger-km, 9,118·2m.; goods, 185,597 tonne-km; mail, 21,727 tonne-km. These figures represent the Swedish share of the SAS traffic (Swedish domestic and three-sevenths of international traffic) and the Linjeflyg traffic.

Shipping. The Swedish mercantile marine consisted on 30 Dec. 1990 of 446 vessels of 2·9m. gross tons (only vessels of at least 100 gross tons, and excluding fishing vessels and tugs). Stockholm and Göteborg, with together 185 vessels of 2m. gross tons in Dec. 1990, are the two major ports.

Vessels entered from and cleared for foreign countries, exclusive of passenger liners and ferries, with cargoes and in ballast, in 1990, were as follows (only vessels of at least a gross tonnage of 75): With cargoes, 26,369 with a gross tonnage of 127·2m.; in ballast, 13,271 with a gross tonnage of 54·1m.

Telecommunications. There were 2,110 post offices at the end of 1988. On 1 Jan. 1990 there were 5·72m. main telephone lines.

3,327,000 combined radio and TV reception fees were paid in 1989. *Sveriges Radio AB* is a non-commercial semi-governmental corporation, transmitting 3 national programmes and regional programmes. It also broadcasts 2 TV programmes (colour by PAL). There are 3 commercial satellite channels (TV3, TV4 and Nordic), and legislation was in process in 1992 to authorize a land-based commercial channel.

Cinemas (1989). There were 1,134 cinemas.

Newspapers (1989). There were 179 daily newspapers with a total circulation of 4·8m.

JUSTICE, RELIGION, EDUCATION AND WELFARE

Justice. The administration of justice is entirely independent. The *Justitiekansler*, or Attorney-General (a government appointment) and the *Justitieombudsmän* (4 judicial Commissioners appointed by Parliament), exercise a check on the administration. In 1968 a reform was carried through which meant that the offices of the former *Justitieombudsman* (Ombudsman for civil affairs) and the *Militieombudsman* (Ombudsman for military affairs) were turned into one sole institution with 3 Ombudsmen, each styled *Justitieombudsman*. They exert a general supervision over all courts of law, the civil service, military laws and the military services. In 1989–90 they received altogether 3,668 cases; of these, 176 were instituted on their own initiative and 3,477 on complaints.

The *Riksåklagaren* (a government appointment) is the chief public prosecutor.

There is a 3-tier hierarchy of courts: the Supreme Court (*högsta domstolen*); 6 intermediate courts of appeal (*hovrätter*) and 97 district courts (*tingsrätter*). There is also a Housing Appeal Court and 12 rent and tenancy tribunals. Of the district courts 27 also serve as real estate courts and 6 as water rights courts.

District courts are courts of first instance and deal with both civil and criminal cases. Each member of the court has an individual vote and is legally responsible for the decision. In the voting, the majority rules. When the votes are evenly divided in a criminal case, the opinion implying the least severe sentence applies, and in cases where there is no opinion that could be considered the mildest, the Chair has the casting vote, as is also the case in family civil cases and matters; petty cases are tried by the judge alone. Civil cases are tried as a rule by 3 to 4 judges or in minor cases by 1 judge. Disputes of greater consequence relating to the Marriage Code or the Code relating to Parenthood and Guardianship are tried by a judge and a jury (*nämnd*) of 3-4 lay assessors. When cases concerning real estate are being tried the court consists of 2 qualified lawyers, 1 specialist on technical matters and 2 lay assessors.

More serious criminal cases are tried by a judge and a jury of 5 members (lay assessors) in felony cases, and of 3 members in misdemeanour cases. The cases in courts of appeal are generally tried by 4 or 5 judges, but the same cases, which are tried with a judge and a jury in the first instance, are tried by 3 or 4 judges and a jury of 2-3 members. In cases concerning real estate the court consists of a specialist on technical matters in place of one of the judges and in water-right cases of 3 or 4 judges and 1 or 2 specialists on technical water matters.

Those with low incomes can receive free legal aid out of public funds. In criminal cases a suspected person has the right to a defence counsel, paid out of public funds.

The Attorney-General and the Judicial Commissioner for the Judiciary and Civil Administration supervise the application in the public sector of acts of Parliament and regulations. The Attorney-General is the government's legal adviser and also the Public Prosecutor.

There were 81 penal and correctional institutions for offenders in 1990 with an average population of 4,425 male and 208 female inmates (including offenders in remand prison). There were 456 children or young people registered for care in treatment and/or residential homes on 31 Dec. 1988, admitted under the 'Care of Young Persons' Act.

Religion. The overwhelming majority of the population belong to the Evangelical Lutheran Church, which is the established national church. In 1990 there were 13 bishoprics (Uppsala being the metropolitan see) and 2,563 parishes. The clergy are chiefly supported from the parishes and the proceeds of the church lands. The non-conformists mostly still adhere to the national church. The largest denominations, on 1 Jan. 1989, were: Pentecost Movement, 97,282; The Mission Covenant Church of Sweden, 78,325; Salvation Army, 29,511; Swedish Evangelical Mission, 23,006; Swedish Baptist Church, 20,557; Örebro Missionary Society, 22,414; Swedish Alliance Missionary Society, 13,411; Holiness Mission, 6,038.

There were also 140,120 Roman Catholics (under a Bishop resident at Stockholm).

Parliament and Convocation (*Kyrkomötet*) decided in 1958 to admit women to ordination as priests.

Education. In 1977 a unified higher educational system was created by integrating institutions which had previously been administered separately. This new *högskola* includes not only traditional university studies but also those of various former professional colleges as well as a number of study programmes earlier offered by the secondary school system. One of the goals of the 1977 university reform was to introduce an increased element of vocational training into part of higher education and to widen admission. A Certificate of Education (B.Sc., M.Sc., U.C. etc.) is awarded on completion of a general study programme. This certificate states the number of courses taken as well as the points and grades obtained on each course.

In 1990–91 there were in integrated institutions for higher education around 173,400 students enrolled for undergraduate studies distributed by sector as follows: Education for technical professions, 38,200; education for social work, economic and administrative professions, 33,400; education for medical and paramedical professions, 23,200; education for the teaching professions, 21,100; and education for information, communication and cultural professions, 6,100. The number of students enrolled for post-graduate studies was 13,100.

In 1990–91 there were 578,400 pupils in primary education (grades 1–6 in compulsory comprehensive schools). Secondary education at the lower stage (grades 7–9 in compulsory comprehensive schools) comprised 303,200 pupils. In secondary education at the higher stage (the integrated upper secondary school), there were 257,900 pupils (excluding about 6,715 pupils in the fourth year of the technical course regarded as third-level education). The folk high schools, 'people's colleges', had 15,700 pupils in courses of more than 15 weeks.

In municipal adult education there were 125,200 students (corresponding to a gross number of 273,700 participants). Basic education for adults had 25,600 pupils.

There are also special schools for pupils with visual and hearing handicaps (680 pupils in 1990–91) and for those who are mentally retarded (about 11,400 pupils).

Source: Statistics Sweden

Social Welfare. Total social expenditure, including also hygiene, care of the sick and social assistance, amounted to 429,484m. kr. in 1990.

DIPLOMATIC REPRESENTATIVES

Of Sweden in Great Britain (11 Montagu Pl., London, W1H 2AL)
Ambassador: Lennart Eckerberg.

Of Great Britain in Sweden (Skarpögatan 6-8, 115 27 Stockholm)
Ambassador: Robert Cormack, CMG.

Of Sweden in the USA (600 New Hampshire Ave., NW, Washington, D.C., 20037)
Ambassador: Anders Thunborg.

Of the USA in Sweden (Strandvägen 101, 115 27 Stockholm)
Ambassador: Charles E. Redman.

Of Sweden to the United Nations
Ambassador: Jan Eliasson.

Further Reading

Statistical Information: Statistics Sweden, (Statistiska Centralbyrån, S-11581 Stockholm) was founded in 1858, in succession to the Kungl. Tabellkommissionen, which had been set up in 1756. *Director-General:* Sten Johansson. Its publications include:
  Levnadsförhållanden, årsbok (Living Conditions). Annual. From 1975.—*Rapport.* From 1976
  Statistisk årsbok för Sverige (Statistical Abstract of Sweden). From 1914
  Siffror om Sverige (Sweden). From 1971. Also in English as *Sweden*
  Historisk statistik för Sverige (Historical Statistics of Sweden). 1955 ff. (4 vols. to date)
  Allmän månadsstatistik (Monthly Digest of Swedish Statistics). From 1963
  Statistiska meddelanden (Statistical Reports). From 1963
Andersson, L., *A History of Sweden.* Stockholm, 1962
Atlas över Sverige. Stockholm, 1953–71. [Publ. in separate parts dealing with population, economics, etc.]
Publications on Sweden. Stockholm, 1988
Documents on Swedish Foreign Policy. Stockholm, Annual.
Grosskopf, G., *The Swedish Tax System.* Stockholm, 1986
Gustafsson, A., *Local Government in Sweden.* Stockholm, 1988
Hadenius, S., *Swedish Politics during the Twentieth Century.* Stockholm, 1988
Hansson, I., Jonung, L., Myhrman, J. and Söderström, H. T., *Sweden – the Road to Stability.* Stockholm, 1985
Heelo, H. and Madsen, H., *Policy and Politics in Sweden: Principled Pragmatism.* Philadelphia, 1987
Hellberg, T. and Jansson, L. M., *Alfred Nobel.* Stockholm, 1984
Lindström, E., *The Swedish Parliamentary System.* Stockholm, 1983
Olivecrona, G., (ed.) *Sweden In Fact.* Stockholm, 1986
Olsson, S. E., *Social Policy and Welfare State in Sweden.* Lund, 1990
Peterson, C.-G., *Local Self-Government and Democracy in Transition.* Stockholm, 1989
Sather, L. B. and Swanson, A., *Sweden.* [Bibliography] Oxford and Santa Barbara, 1987
Scott, F. D., *Sweden: The Nation's History.* Univ. of Minnesota Press, 1983
Söderström, H. T., *Getting Sweden Back to Work.* Stockholm, 1986
Sveriges statskalender. Published by Vetenskapsakademien. Annual, from 1813

National library: Kungliga Biblioteket, Stockholm.

SWITZERLAND

Schweizerische
Eidtgenossenschaft—
Confédération Suisse—
Confederazione Svizzera [1]

Capital: Berne
Population: 6·75m. (1991)
GNP per capita: US$30,270 (1989)

HISTORY. On 1 Aug. 1291 the men of Uri, Schwyz and Unterwalden entered into a defensive league. In 1353 the league included 8 members and in 1513, 13. Various territories were acquired either by single cantons or by several in common, and in 1648 the league became formally independent of the Holy Roman Empire, but no addition was made to the number of cantons till 1798. In that year, under the influence of France, the unified Helvetic Republic was formed. This failed to satisfy the Swiss, and in 1803 Napoleon Bonaparte, in the Act of Mediation, gave a new Constitution, and out of the lands formerly allied or subject increased the number of cantons to 19. In 1815 the perpetual neutrality of Switzerland and the inviolability of her territory were guaranteed by Austria, France, Great Britain, Portugal, Prussia, Russia, Spain and Sweden, and the Federal Pact, which included 3 new cantons, was accepted by the Congress of Vienna. In 1848 a new Constitution was passed. The 22 cantons set up a Federal Government (consisting of a Federal Parliament and a Federal Council) and a Federal Tribunal. This Constitution, in turn, was on 29 May 1874 superseded by the present Constitution. In a national referendum held in Sept. 1978, 69·9% voted in favour of the establishment of a new canton, Jura, which was established on 1 Jan. 1979.

AREA AND POPULATION. Switzerland is bounded in the west and north-west by France, north by Germany, east by Austria and south by Italy. Area and population by canton (with date of establishment), according to the census held on 1 Dec. 1980 and estimate 31 Dec. 1990.

Canton	Area (sq. km)	Census 1 Dec. 1980	Estimate 31 Dec. 1990
Zurich (1351)	1,729	1,122,839	1,150,546
Berne (1553)	6,049	912,022	945,573
Lucerne (1332)	1,492	296,159	319,525
Uri (1291)	1,076	33,883	33,650
Schwyz (1291)	908	97,354	110,526
Obwalden (1291)	491	25,865	28,813
Nidwalden (1291)	276	28,617	32,628
Glarus (Glaris) (1352)	685	36,718	37,648
Zug (1352)	239	75,930	84,908
Fribourg (Freiburg) (1481)	1,670	185,246	207,751
Solothurn (Soleure) (1481)	791	218,102	226,655
Basel-Town (Bâle-V.) (1501)	37	203,915	191,787
Basel-Country (Bâle-C.) (1501)	428	219,822	230,112
Schaffhausen (Schaffhouse) (1501)	298	69,413	71,697
Appenzell-Outer Rhoden (1513)	243	47,611	51,470
Appenzell-Inner Rhoden (1513)	172	12,844	13,573
St Gallen (St Gall) (1803)	2,014	391,995	420,268
Graubünden (Grisons) (1803)	7,106	164,641	170,411
Aargau (Argovie) (1803)	1,405	453,442	496,280
Thurgau (Thurgovie) (1803)	1,013	183,795	205,946
Ticino (Tessin) (1803)	2,811	265,899	286,725
Vaud (Waadt) (1803)	3,218	528,747	583,625
Valais (Wallis) (1815)	5,226	218,707	248,313
Neuchâtel (Neuenburg) (1815)	797	158,368	160,609
Geneva (1815)	282	349,040	375,957
Jura (1979)	837	64,986	65,697
Total	41,293	6,365,960	6,750,693

[1] The Latin 'Confoederatio Helvetica' is also in use.

1251

German, French and Italian are the official languages; Romansch (spoken mostly in Graubünden) is a national language. German is spoken by the majority of inhabitants in 19 of the 26 cantons, French in Fribourg, Vaud, Valais, Neuchâtel, Jura and Geneva, and Italian in Ticino. In 1980, 65% spoke German, 18·4% French, 9·8% Italian, 0·8% Romansch and 6% other languages; counting only Swiss nationals, the percentages were 73·5, 20·1, 4·5, 0·9 and 1.

At the end of 1989 the 5 largest cities were Zürich (342,900); Basel (165,600); Geneva (169,600); Berne (134,400); Lausanne (122,600). At the end of 1988 the population figures of conurbations were: Zürich, 838,700; Basel, 358,500; Geneva, 389,000; Bern, 298,700; Lausanne, 262,900; other towns 1985, (and their conurbations, 1986), were Winterthur, 84,400 (107,812); St Gallen, 73,200 (125,879); Lucerne, 60,600 (160,594); Biel, 52,000 (82,544).

The number of foreigners resident in Switzerland in Dec. 1989 was 1,066,139.

Vital statistics for calendar years:

	Live births					
	Total	Illegitimate	Marriages	Divorces	Still births	Deaths
1987	76,500	4,500	43,000	11,600	340	59,500
1988	80,300	4,889	45,700	12,700	311	60,600
1989	81,180	4,804	45,066	12,720	332	60,882
1990	83,939	...	46,603	13,183	...	63,739

Rates (per 1,000 population): Birth, 12·5; death, 9·5; marriage, 6·9; divorce, 2·0. Expectation of life, 1989: Males, 73·9 years; females, 81. Infant mortality (per 1,000 live births), 7·3. In 1988 there were 91,500 emigrants and 125,000 immigrants.

CLIMATE. The climate is largely dictated by relief and altitude and includes continental and mountain types. Summers are generally warm, with quite considerable rainfall; winters are fine, with clear, cold air. Bern. Jan. 32°F (0°C), July, 65°F (18·5°C). Annual rainfall 39·4" (986 mm).

CONSTITUTION AND GOVERNMENT. Switzerland is a republic. The highest authority is vested in the electorate, *i.e.*, all Swiss citizens over 18 (20 until a referendum of March 1991). This electorate—besides electing its representatives to the Parliament—has the voting power on amendments to, or on the revision of, the Constitution. It also takes decisions on laws and international treaties if requested by 50,000 voters or 8 cantons (facultative referendum), and it has the right of initiating constitutional amendments, the support required for such demands being 100,000 voters (popular initiative).

The Federal Government is supreme in matters of peace, war and treaties; it regulates the army, the railway, telecommunication systems, the coining of money, the issue and repayment of bank-notes and the weights and measures of the republic. It also legislates on matters of copyright, bankruptcy, patents, sanitary policy in dangerous epidemics, and it may create and subsidize, besides the Polytechnic School at Zürich and at Lausanne, 2 federal universities and other educational institutions. There has also been entrusted to it the authority to decide concerning public works for the whole or great part of Switzerland, such as those relating to rivers, forests and the construction of national highways and railways. By referendum of 13 Nov. 1898 it is also the authority in the entire spheres of common law. In 1957 the Federation was empowered to legislate on atomic energy matters and in 1961 on the construction of pipelines of petroleum and gas.

National flag: Red with a white couped cross.
National anthem: Trittst im Morgenrot daher ('Step into the rosy dawn'; words by Leonard Widmer, 1808–68; tune by Alberik Zwyssig, 1808–54); adopted by the Federal Council in 1962.

The legislative authority is vested in a parliament of 2 chambers the Council of States (*Ständerat/Conseil des États*) and the National Council (*Nationalrat/Conseil National*). The Council of States is composed of 46 members, chosen and paid by the 23 cantons of the Confederation, 2 for each canton. The mode of their election and the term of membership depend on the canton. 3 of the cantons are politically divided—Basel into Town and Country, Appenzell into Outer-Rhoden and Inner-Rhoden, and Unterwalden into Obwalden and Nidwalden. Each of these 'half-cantons' sends 1 member to the State Council.

The National Council has 200 members directly elected for 4 years, in proportion to the population of the cantons, with the proviso that each canton or half-canton is represented by at least 1 member. The members are paid from federal funds at the rate of 150 francs for each day during the session and a nominal sum of 10,000 francs per annum. The parliament sits for 16 three-day sessions annually.

In 1987 the 200 members were distributed among the cantons as follows:

Zurich	35	Appenzell—Outer- and Inner-Rhoden	3
Berne	29	St Gallen (St Gall)	12
Lucerne	9	Graubünden (Grisons)	5
Uri	1	Aargau (Argovie)	14
Schwyz	3	Thurgau (Thurgovie)	6
Unterwalden–Upper and Lower	2	Ticino (Tessin)	8
Glarus (Glaris)	1	Vaud (Waadt)	17
Zug	2	Valais (Wallis)	7
Fribourg (Freiburg)	6	Neuchâtel (Neuenburg)	5
Solothurn (Soleure)	7	Geneva	11
Basel (Bâle)—town and country	13	Jura	2
Schaffhausen (Schaffhouse)	2		

A general election takes place by ballot every 4 years. Every citizen of the republic who has entered on his 18th year is entitled to a vote, and any voter, not a clergyman, may be elected a deputy. Laws passed by both chambers may be submitted to direct popular vote, when 50,000 citizens or 8 cantons demand it; the vote can be only 'Yes' or 'No'. This principle, called the *referendum*, is frequently acted on. Women's suffrage was established by a referendum in Feb. 1971.

In Oct. 1991 elections were held for both chambers of the federal parliament. In the National Council the Radicals gained 44 seats (51 in 1987); Social Democrats 43 (43); Christian Democrats 36 (42); Swiss People's Party 24 (25); Ecologists 14 (11); Liberals 10 (9); Automobilists 8 (2); Far Right Democrats 5 (3); Labour (formerly Communists) 2 (1); others, 14. In the Council of States the Radicals gained 15 seats (12); Christian Democrats 4 (15); Swiss People's Party 4 (4); Liberals 3 (3); Independents 1 (1).

The chief executive authority is deputed to the *Bundesrat*, or Federal Council, consisting of 7 members, elected from 7 different cantons for 4 years by the *Vereinigte Bundesversammlung*, *i.e.*, joint sessions of both chambers. The members of this council must not hold any other office in the Confederation or cantons, nor engage in any calling or business. In the Federal Parliament legislation may be introduced either by a member, or by either chamber, or by the Federal Council (but not by the people). Every citizen who has a vote for the National Council is eligible to become a member of the executive.

The *President* of the Federal Council (called President of the Confederation) and the Vice-President are the first magistrates of the Confederation. Both are elected by the Federal Assembly for 1 calendar year from among the Federal Councillors. and are not immediately re-eligible to the same offices. The Vice-President, however, may be, and usually is, elected to succeed the outgoing President.

President of the Confederation (1992): René Felber.

The 7 members of the Federal Council—each of whom has a salary of 203,000 francs per annum, while the President has 215,000 francs—act as ministers, or chiefs of the 7 administrative departments of the republic. The city of Berne is the seat of the Federal Council and the central administrative authorities.

All 7 members of the Federal Council were re-elected in Dec. 1991:

Foreign Affairs: René Felber.
Interior: Flavio Cotti.
Justice and Police: Arnold Koller.
Military: Kaspar Villiger.
Finance: Otto Stich.

Public Economy: Jean-Pascal Delamuraz.
Transport, Communications and Energy: Adolf Ogi.

Cantonal and Local Government. Each of the 26 cantons and demi-cantons is sovereign, so far as its independence and legislative powers are not restricted by the federal constitution; all cantonal governments, though different in organization (membership varies from 5 to 11, and terms of office from 1 to 5 years), are based on the principle of sovereignty of the people.

In 21 cantons a body chosen by universal suffrage, usually called *der Grosse Rat*, or *Kantonsrat*, exercises the functions of a parliament. In all the cantonal constitutions except those of the 5 cantons which have a *Landsgemeinde*, the referendum has a place. By this principle, where it is most fully developed, as in Zurich, all laws and concordats, or agreements with other cantons, and the chief matters of finance, as well as all revisions of the Constitution, must be submitted to the popular vote. In the 5 cantons of Appenzell, Glarus and Unterwalden the people exercise their powers direct in the *Landsgemeinde, i.e.,* the assembly in the open air of all citizens of full age. In all the cantons the *popular initiative* for constitutional affairs, as well as for legislation, has been introduced, except in Lucerne, where the *initiative* exists only for constitutional affairs. In most cantons there are districts (*Amtsbezirke*) consisting of a number of communes grouped together, each district having a Prefect (*Regierungsstatthalter*) representing the cantonal government. In the larger communes, for local affairs, there is an Assembly (legislative) and a Council (executive) with a president, mayor or syndic, and not less than 4 other members. In the smaller communes there is a council only, with its officials. There were 3,003 cantonal and commune councillors in 1990 (419 of them women).

DEFENCE. There are fortifications in all entrances to the Alps and on the important passes crossing the Alps and the Jura. Large-scale destructions of bridges, tunnels and defiles are prepared for an emergency.

Army. There are about 3,500 regular soldiers, but some 438,500 conscripts undergo training annually in the following phases: At 20 years of age, 17 weeks recruit training; between 21 and 32, reservist refresher training (*Auszug*); between 33 and 42, 39 days training for the Militia (*Landwehr*); and between 43 and 50, 13 days for the Home Guard (*Landsturm*).

The Army is divided into 3 field corps each of 1 armoured and 2 infantry divisions and support groups, a corps with 3 mountain divisions, and independent redoubt-, fortress- and territorial-brigades. Strength on mobilization (1992): 565,000, and 400,000 reserves.

The administration of the Swiss Army is partly in the hands of the Cantonal authorities, who can promote officers up to the rank of captain. But the Federal Government is concerned with all general questions and makes all the higher appointments.

In peace-time the Army has no general; in time of war the Federal Assembly in joint session of both Houses appoints a general.

Equipment includes 180 Leopard, 150 Centurion, 150 Pz-61 and 390 Pz-68 main battle tanks and 1,350 M-63/-73/-64 armoured personnel carriers.

Air Corps. The Air Corps is part of the Army. It has 3 flying regiments. The fighter squadrons are equipped with Swiss-built F-5E Tiger IIs (7 squadrons), Mirage IIIS supersonic interceptor/ground-attack (2 squadrons), Mirage IIIRS fighter/reconnaissance (1 squadron), and Hunter interceptor/ground-attack (9 squadrons) aircraft. Bloodhound surface-to-air missile batteries are operational.

Training aircraft are Pilatus P-3 and PC-7 Turbo-Trainer and Hawk; there are also communications and transport aircraft and helicopters. Personnel (1992), 60,000 on mobilization, with 271 combat aircraft.

INTERNATIONAL RELATIONS

Membership. Switzerland is a member of OECD, EFTA and the Council of Europe. In a referendum in 1986 the electorate voted against joining the UN.

ECONOMY

Budget. Revenue and expenditure of the Confederation, in 1m. francs, for calendar years:

	1985	1986	1987	1988	1989	1990
Revenue	22,200	25,200	24,902	27,881	28,334	31,166
Expenditure	22,900	23,200	23,861	26,633	27,449	30,109

Sources of revenue, 1990: Turnover tax, 9,871; direct federal taxes, 6,710; customs, 4,228; settlement taxes, 4,044; stamp duty, 2,091. Expenditure: Welfare, 6,420; defence, 5,731; transport and energy, 4,654; agriculture, 2,591; education and research, 2,749.

Currency. The unit of currency is the *Swiss franc* (CHF) of 100 *Rappen* or *centimes*. On 10 May 1971 there was a revaluation to 0·21759 gramme of fine gold.

The legal gold coins are 20- and 10-franc pieces; cupro-nickel coins are 5, 2, 1 and ¹/₂ franc, 20, 10 and 5 centimes; bronze, 2 and 1 centime. Notes are of 1,000, 500, 100, 50, 20, 10 and 5 francs.

On 10 July 1981 the notes in circulation (of francs of nominal value) was as follows: In 1,000 franc notes, 8,685·1m. francs; in 500, 4,201·9m. francs; in 100, 6,687·3m. francs; in 50, 1,058·3m. francs, and in lower denominations 1,195·8m.

Inflation was 5·7% in Sept. 1991.

In March 1992, £1 = 2·61 *francs*; US$1 = 1·49 *francs*.

Banking and Finance. The National Bank, with headquarters divided between Berne and Zurich, opened on 20 June 1907. It has the exclusive right to issue banknotes. In 1984 the condition of the bank was as follows (in 1m. francs): Gold, 11,904, foreign exchange (currency), 38,800; currency in circulation, 26,500. The *Governor* is Marcus Lusser.

On 31 Dec. 1989 there were 1,682 banking institutions with total assets of 978,300m. Swiss francs. They included 29 cantonal banks (195,200m. francs), 5 big banks (509,700m.), 210 regional and saving banks (88,600m.), 1,229 loan and *Raiffeisen* banks (31,200m.), 209 other banks (153,600m.). In 1991 the 10 largest banks in order of capitalization were: Union Bank of Switzerland, Swiss Bank Corporation, Crédit Suisse, Swiss Volksbank, Zürcher Kantonalbank, Bank Leu, Banca della Svizzera Italiana, Banque Cantonale Vaudoise, Bank Julius Baer.

Money laundering was made a criminal offence in Aug. 1990. Complete secrecy about clients' accounts remains intact, but anonymity was abolished in July 1991.

On 31 Dec. 1989 the total amount of savings deposits, deposit and investment accounts was 180,600m. francs.

The stock exchange system is being reformed under federal legislation of 1990 on securities trading and capital market services. The 4 smaller exchanges are being abandoned and activity concentrated on the major exchanges of Zurich, Basel and Geneva, which are increasingly harmonizing their operations. Zurich is a major international insurance centre.

Weights and Measures. The metric system is legal.

ENERGY AND NATURAL RESOURCES

Electricity. The Energy 2000 programme aims to stabilize consumption. The total production of energy amounted to 51,656m kwh. in 1989 of which 30,485m. kwh. were generated by hydro-electric plants. In 1991 41% was nuclear-produced, but in Sept. 1990 54% of citizens voted for a 10-year moratorium on the construction of new nuclear plants. Supply 220/380 volts; 50 Hz.

Gas. The production of gas in 1986 was 54·52m. cu. metres.

Minerals. Salt is mined.

Agriculture. The country is self-sufficient in wheat and meat. Agriculture is protected by subsidies, price guarantees and import controls. Farmers are guaranteed an income equal to industrial workers. Agriculture occupied 6·5% of the total workforce and contributed 2·5% to GDP in 1990. The agricultural area, in 1985, totalled 1,076,339 ha, of which 287,049 ha arable land, 13,450 ha vineyards, 7,229 ha intensive fruit growing and 642,194 ha permanent meadow and pasture land. In 1991 there were 108,300 farms (40% in mountain or hill regions), of which 65% were under 15 ha and 45,000 part-time. The gross value of agricultural products was estimated at 8,775m. francs in 1986.

Area harvested, 1988 (in 1,000 ha): Cereals, 186; coarse grains, 92; potatoes, 19; sugar-beet, 15. Production, 1988 (in 1,000 tonnes): Potatoes, 748; sugar-beet, 923; wheat, 553; barley, 299; maize, 237; tobacco, 1.

The fruit production (in 1,000 tonnes) in 1988 was: Apples, 540; pears, 229; plums, 33; cherries, 35; nuts, 6.

Wine is produced in 18 of the cantons. In 1988 vineyards yielded 117 tonnes of wine.

Livestock, 1989 (in 1,000): Cattle, 1,850 (including milch cows, 806), pigs, 1,869, sheep, 371.

Forestry. The forest area is about 1m. ha. Production (1987) 4,570 cu. metres of softwood and 1,158 cu. metres of hardwood.

INDUSTRY. There were 160,541 firms in 1990. The chief food producing industries, based on Swiss agriculture, are the manufacture of cheese, butter, sugar and meat. Production in 1986 was (in tonnes): Cheese, 130,900; butter, 37,300; sugar, 9,800; meat, 37,600. Tobacco products in 1986: Cigars, 278m.; cigarettes (1982), 26,497m.

Among the other industries, the manufacture of textiles, clothing and footwear, chemicals and pharmaceutical products, the production of machinery (including electrical machinery and scientific and optical instruments) and watch and clock making are the most important.

Labour. In 1989, the total working population was 3,518,400, of which 196,700 were active in agriculture and forestry, 1,234,700 in manufacture and construction and 2,087,000 in services. 15,136 persons (6,737 females) were unemployed.

The foreign labour force with permit of temporary residence was 989,457 in Aug. 1991 (316,848 women). Of these 291,091 were Italian, 137,480 Yugoslav, 118,487 French, 99,742 Portuguese and 95,626 German.

Trade Unions. The Swiss Federal Union of Administrative and Public Service Workers had, in 1985, a membership of 123,300. The Federation of Trade Unions had about 443,000 members.

FOREIGN ECONOMIC RELATIONS. Legislation of Oct. 1991 increased the possibilities of foreign ownership of domestic companies.

Commerce. Imports and exports, excluding gold (bullion and coins) and silver (coins), were (in 1m. Swiss francs):

	1983	1984	1985	1986	1987	1988	1989	1990
Imports	61,064	69,024	74,750	73,513	75,171	82,399	95,209	96,610
Exports	53,724	60,654	66,624	67,004	67,477	74,064	84,268	88,260

Main import suppliers in 1989 (in 1m. francs): Federal Republic of Germany, 31,902; France, 10,332; Italy, 9,665; USA, 6,080; UK, 5,316; Netherlands, 3,868; Austria, 3,664; Belgium-Luxembourg, 3,291. Main export markets: Federal Republic of Germany, 17,134; France, 8,258; USA, 7,439; Italy, 7,159; UK, 6,908; Japan, 3,521.

Main imports in 1990 (in 1m. francs): Raw materials and semi-manufactures, 34·16; consumer goods, 33·92; producers' goods, 24·22. Exports: Machinery and apparatus, 30·19; chemicals, 18·42; clocks and watches, 6·78; textiles and clothing, 4·98; foodstuffs,2·06.

Total trade between Switzerland (including Liechtenstein) and UK for calendar years (British Department of Trade, in £1,000 sterling):

	1987	1988	1989	1990	1991
Imports to UK	3,298,009	3,840,643	4,125,731	4,252,783	3,754,586
Exports and re-exports from UK	1,835,851	1,854,918	2,245,354	2,358,528	2,105,656

Tourism. Tourism is an important industry, contributing 8% of GDP in 1990. In 1989, overnight stays in hotels and sanatoria were 37·1m. and in other accommodation 39·8m. (35·95m. foreign visitors). Tourist receipts were 11·54m. francs.

COMMUNICATIONS

Roads. There were (1987) 71,055 km of main roads, including 1,300 km of 'national roads' for motor cars only. Motor vehicles in 1990 (in 1,000): Private cars, 2,994; lorries, 272; buses, 31; motor cycles, 302. There were 76,743 road accidents in 1989, with 925 fatalities.

Railways. In 1987 the length of the general traffic railways was 5,020 km, and of special lines (funiculars etc.), 814 km. Traffic (1987) was 12,494m. passenger-km and 7,184 tonnes-km of goods were carried. There are tram/light rail networks in Basel, Berne, Bex, Geneva, Lausanne, Neuchâtel and Zurich.

There are many privately-owned lines, the most important of which are the Bern–Lotschberg–Simplon (115 km) and Rhaetian (363 km) networks.

Civil Aviation. Seissair is the national carrier. In 1985 civil aviation on domestic and international routes carried 7,498,000 passengers. Routes covered 327,022 km in 1987.

Shipping. In 1987 there were 1,208 km of navigable waterway. A merchant marine was created in 1941, the place of registry of its vessels being Basel. In 1985 it consisted of 39 vessels with a total of 225,434 GRT.

Pipeline. In 1987 there were 244 km of oil pipeline.

Telecommunications. In 1989 there were 3,835 post offices, 29,600 telex and 19,151 fax subscribers. In 1988 there were 5,879,200 telephones. and 14,474 videotext subscribers.

Radio communication is furnished by 3 main medium-wave stations and 1 short-wave station. There are 3 television studios and more than 100 transmitters (colour by PAL). TV programmes are financed by licence fees and advertisements. Advertisements are limited to 15 minutes each day. All stations are operated by the Federal Post, Telephone and Telegraph (PTT) services. Radio-telegraph circuits are operated by Radio Suisse SA, radio-telephone circuits by the PTT. Radio licences, 1990, 2,649,674; television licences, 2,412,473.

In 1988 PTT revenue was 106% of expenses.

Cinemas (1989). There were 401 cinemas with a seating capacity of 104,000.

Newspapers (1989). There were 110 daily newspapers (84 German language, 19 French, 7 Italian and 1 multi-lingual).

JUSTICE, RELIGION, EDUCATION AND WELFARE

Justice. The Federal Tribunal (*Bundesgericht*), which sits at Lausanne, consists of 26-28 members, with 11-13 supplementary judges, appointed by the Federal Assembly for 6 years and eligible for re-election; the President and Vice-President serve for 2 years and cannot be re-elected. The President has a salary of 170,000 francs a year, and the other members 158,000 francs. The Tribunal has original and final jurisdiction in suits between the Confederation and cantons; between cantons and cantons; between the Confederation or cantons and corporations or individuals, the value in dispute being not less than 8,000 francs; between parties who refer their case to it, the value in dispute being at least 20,000 francs; in such suits as the constitution or legislation of cantons places within its authority; and in many classes of railway suits. It is a court of appeal against decisions of other federal authorities, and of cantonal authorities applying federal laws. The Tribunal also tries persons accused of treason or other offences against the Confederation. For this purpose it is divided into 4 chambers: Chamber of Accusation, Criminal Chamber (*Cour d'Assises*), Federal Penal Court and Court of Cassation. The jurors who serve in the Assize Courts are elected by the people, and are paid 100 francs a day when serving.

A federal penal code replaced cantonal codes in 1942. It abolished capital punishment except for offences in war-time; this latter proviso was abolished in 1991.

There were 61,980 adult criminal convictions in 1989.

Religion. There is liberty of conscience and of creed. No one is bound to pay taxes specially appropriated to defraying the expenses of a creed to which he does not belong. No bishoprics can be created on Swiss territory without the approbation of the Confederation.

According to the census of 1 Dec. 1980 Roman Catholics numbered 3,030,069 (47·6%) of the population; Protestants, 2,822,266 (44·3%) and others, 513,625 (8·1%). In 1960 Protestants were in a majority in 10 of the cantons and Catholics in 12. Of the more populous cantons, Zurich, Bern, Vaud, Neuchâtel and Basel (town and land) were mainly Protestant, while Lucerne, Fribourg, Ticino, Valais and the Forest Cantons are mainly Catholic. The Roman Catholics are under 6 Bishops, viz., of Basel (resident at Solothurn), Chur, St Gallen, Lugano, Lausanne–Geneva–Fribourg (resident at Fribourg) and Sitten (Sion), all of them immediately subject to the Holy See. The Old Catholics have a theological faculty at the university of Berne.

Education. Education is administered by the cantons and communes and is free and compulsory for 9 years. Compulsory education consists of 4 (Berne, Basel-Town, Jura Vaud), 5 (Aargau, Basel-Country, Neuchâtel) or 6 (other cantons except Ticino, which has 9) years of primary education and the balance in Stage I secondary education. This may be followed by 5 years of Stage II secondary education of general or vocational schools. Tertiary education is at universities, higher vocational schools and advanced vocational training institutes. Educational funding in 1988, (in 1m. francs): Federal, 1,710·7; communes, 4,680·7; cantons, 7,366·0.

In 1989–90 there were 136,845 children in nursery schools. There were 702,277 pupils in compulsory education, 72,681 in Stage II general secondary education, 230,397 in Stage II vocational secondary education, and 131,747 students in tertiary education.

There are 7 universities (students in 1989–90): Basel (6,763), Berne (9,511), Fribourg (5,814), Geneva (12,028), Lausanne (6,942), Neuchâtel (2,512), Zurich (20,690); and 5 institutions of equivalent status: Lucerne Theological Faculty (199), St Gallen PHS (171), St Gallen School of Economics and Social Science (3,952), Lausanne Federal Institute of Technology (3,495), Zurich Federal Institute of Technology (11,200).

University statistics in the winter of 1986–87:

	The-ology	Humanities etc	Law	Eco-nomics	Medi-cine	Science	Teaching staff (1985–86)
Basel (1460)	223	1,687	881	848	1,761	1,275	625
Zurich (1523 & 1833)	358	7,463	3,138	2,239	3,354	2,101	1,661
Bern (1528 & 1834)	374	2,696	1,657	848	1,798	1,628	723
Geneva (1559[1] & 1873[1])	130	4,578	995	2,411	1,506	1,645	913
Lausanne (1537[1] & 1890[2])	85	1,678	889	1,405	1,503	875	476
Fribourg (1889)	504	1,999	995	1,129	225	506	548
Neuchâtel (1866 & 1909)	52	870	310	444	57	524	240

[1] Founded as an academy.　　　　[2] Reorganized as a university.

In 1988–89 there were 80,629 students attending universities.

Health. In 1988 there were 18,667 doctors, 37,360 (1980) nurses, 4,750 dentists and 12,300 physiotherapists. There were (1988) 435 hospitals and 1,417 pharmacies.

Social Security. The Federal Insurance Law against illness and accident, of 13 June 1911, entitles all citizens to insurance against illness; foreigners may be admitted to the benefits. Compulsory insurance against illness does not exist, but cantons and communities are entitled to declare insurance obligatory for certain classes or to establish public benefit (sick fund) associations, and to make employers responsible for the payment of the premiums of their employees.

Unemployment insurance is compulsory for all wage-earners. Insurance against accident is compulsory for all officials, employees and workmen of all the factories, trades, etc., which are under the federal liability law.

Old age and widows and widowers insurance has been compulsory since 1948.

In 1989 the following amounts (in 1m. francs) were paid in social security benefits: Federal old age pensions, 16,961·0; supplementary benefits, 976·7; Federal disability insurance, 3,750·1; accident insurance, 2,885·3; loss of earnings insurance, 891·6; unemployment insurance, 442·4; cantonal family allowances, 755·8.

DIPLOMATIC REPRESENTATIVES

Of Switzerland in Great Britain (16–18 Montagu Pl., London, W1H 2BQ)
Ambassador: Franz E. Muheim (accredited 14 June 1989).

Of Great Britain in Switzerland (Thunstrasse 50, 3005 Bern)
Ambassador: Christopher Long, CMG.

Of Switzerland in the USA (2900 Cathedral Ave., NW, Washington, D.C., 20008)
Ambassador: Edouard Brunner.

Of the USA in Switzerland (Jubilaeumstrasse 93, 3005, Bern)
Ambassador: Joseph Gildenhorn.

Further Reading

Office Fédéral de la Statistique. *Annuaire Statistique de la Suisse.*

Swiss Confederation
Annuaire; Budget; Message du Budget; Compte d'Etat (annual) *Feuille Fédérale; Recueil des Lois fédérales* (weekly)
Recueil systématique des lois et ordonnances, 1848–1947 (in German, French and Italian). Bern, 1951
Sammlung der Bundes- und Kantonsverfassungen (in German, French and Italian). Bern, 1937

Federal Department of Economics
La vie économique (and supplements). Monthly. From 1928
Legislation sociale de la Suisse. Annual, from 1928

Hilowitz, J. E., (ed.) *Switzerland in Perspective.* New York, 1991
Meier, H. K. and Meier, R. A., *Switzerland.* [bibliography] London and Santa Barbara, 1990
Wildblood, R., *What makes Switzerland tick?* London, 1988

National library: Bibliothèque Nationale Suisse, Hallwylstr. 15, 3003 Berne.
National statistical office: Office Fédéral de la Statistique, Hallwylstr. 15, 3003 Berne.

SYRIA

Capital: Damascus
Population: 11·3m. (1988)
GNP per capita: US$1,020 (1989)

Jumhuriya al-Arabya
as-Suriya

(Syrian Arab Republic)

HISTORY. For the history of Syria from 1920 to 1946 *see* THE STATESMAN'S YEAR-BOOK , 1957, pp. 1408–9. Complete independence was achieved on 12 Apr. 1946. Syria merged with Egypt to form the United Arab Republic from 2 Feb. 1958 until 29 Sept. 1961, when independence was resumed following a coup the previous day. Lieut.-Gen. Hafez al-Assad became Prime Minister following the fifth coup of that decade on 13 Nov. 1970, and assumed the Presidency on 22 Feb. 1971.

AREA AND POPULATION. Syria is bounded by the Mediterranean and Lebanon on the west, by Israel and Jordan on the south, by Iraq on the east and by Turkey on the north. The frontier between Syria and Turkey (Nisibim-Jeziret ibn Omar) was settled by the Franco-Turkish agreement of 22 June 1929.

The area of Syria is 185,180 sq. km (71,498 sq. miles), of which 35,000 sq. km have been surveyed. The census of 1981 gave a total population of 9,046,144 (47% urban). Estimate (1988) 11,338,000. of whom 50% were urban. There were 282,673 registered Palestinian refugees in 1987

Area and population (1981 Census) of the 14 districts *(mohafaza)* are:

	Sq. km	1981 Census		Sq. km	1981 Census
Damascus (City)	105	1,112,214	Idlib	6,097	579,581
Damascus (District)	18,032	917,364	Hasakah	23,334	669,887
Aleppo	18,500	1,878,701	Raqqah	19,616	348,383
Homs	42,223	812,517	Suwaydá	5,550	199,114
Hama	8,883	736,412	Dará	3,730	362,969
Lattakia	2,297	554,384	Tartous	1,892	443,290
Dayr az-Zawr	33,060	409,130	Qunaytirah	1,861	26,258

Principal towns (census 1981), Damascus (the capital), 1,112,214; Aleppo, 985,413; Homs, 346,871; Lattakia, 196,791; Hama, 177,208.

Vital statistics, 1987: Births, 421,328; deaths, 43,571; marriages, 102,626; divorces, 7,249.

Arabic is the official language, spoken by 89% of the population, while 6% speak Kurdish (chiefly Hasakah governorate), 3% Armenian and 2% other languages.

CLIMATE. The climate is Mediterranean in type, with mild wet winters and dry, hot summers, though there are variations in temperatures and rainfall between the coastal regions and the interior, which even includes desert conditions. The more mountainous parts are subject to snowfall. Damascus. Jan. 45°F (7°C), July 81°F (27°C). Annual rainfall 9" (225 mm). Aleppo. Jan. 43°F (6·1°C), July 83°F (28·3°C). Annual rainfall 16" (401 mm). Homs. Jan. 45°F (7·2°C), July 83°F (28·3°C). Annual rainfall 12" (300 mm).

CONSTITUTION AND GOVERNMENT. A new Constitution was approved by plebiscite on 12 March 1973 and promulgated on 14 March. It confirmed the Arab Socialist Renaissance *(Ba'ath)* Party, in power since 1963, as the 'leading party in the State and society'. Legislative power is held by a 250-member People's Council, elected for a 4-year term. At the elections on 22 May 1990, 150 seats went to the National Progressive Front, a coalition of the Ba'ath Party and four smaller ones and the remainder to independents. 9,765 candidates stood.

At a referendum on 2 Dec. 1991 Lieut.-Gen. Hafez al-Assad (b.1930), the sole candidate, was confirmed as *President* for a fourth 5-year term.

First Vice-President: Abdul Halim Khaddam *(Political and Foreign Affairs).* *Second Vice-President:* Rifaat al-Assad *(Defence and Security).* *Third Vice-President:* Mohammed Zuhair Mashrqa *(Party Affairs).*

Prime Minister: Mahmoud Zubi.

Deputy Prime Ministers: Gen. Mustafa Tlass *(Defence)*; Salim Yassin *(Economic Affairs)*; Mahmud Qaddur *(Public Affairs).* *Education:* Ghassan Halabi. *Higher Education:* Kamal Sharaf. *Interior:* Mohammad Harbah. *Transport:* Yusuf al-Ahmed. *Information:* Mohammad Salman. *Local Administration:* Ahmed Diab. *Supply and Internal Trade:* Hassan Saqqa. *Economy and Foreign Trade:* Mohammad al-Imadi. *Culture:* Najah al-Attar. *Foreign Affairs:* Farouk ash-Sharaa. *Tourism:* Adnan Quli. *Health:* Iyad al-Shatti. *Waqfs (Religious Endowments):* Abdel-Majid Tarabulsi. *Irrigation:* Abd ar-Rahman Madani. *Electricity:* Kamil al-Baba. *Oil and Mineral Resources:* Antonios Habib. *Construction:* Marwan Farra. *Housing and Utilities:* Mohammad Nur Antabi. *Agriculture and Agrarian Reform:* Mohammad Ghabbash. *Finance:* Khaled al-Mahayni. *Industry:* Antoine Jubran. *Communications:* Murad Quwatli. *Justice:* Khalid Ansari. *Presidential Affairs:* Wahib Fadil. *Labour and Social Affairs:* Haydar Buzu.

There are 7 Ministers of State.

National flag: Three horizontal stripes of red, white, black, with 2 green stars on the white stripe.

Local Government: Syria is administratively divided into 14 districts *(mohafaza)* (*see* Area and Population above). These are divided into 59 *mantika*, which are subdivided into 179 smaller administrative units *(nahia)*, each covering a number of villages.

DEFENCE. Military service is compulsory for a period of 30 months.

Army. The Army is organized into 5 armoured and 3 mechanized divisions, a Republican Guard division, 1 special forces division, 8 independent special forces regiments, 4 independant mechanized infantry brigades, 2 artillery, 3 surface-to-surface missile brigades and 3 coastal defence brigades. Equipment includes 2,050 T-54/-55, 1,000 T-62 and 1,300 T-72/-72M main battle tanks. Strength (1991) about 300,000 (including 130,000 conscripts) and reserves 50,000.

Navy. The Navy includes 3 ex-Soviet 'Romeo'-class diesel submarines, 2 small frigates, 16 fast missile craft, 9 inshore patrol craft, 2 minesweepers, 6 inshore minesweepers, and 3 medium landing ships (all ex-Soviet). A small naval aviation branch operates 17 Soviet-built anti-submarine helicopters. Personnel in 1991 were estimated at 4,000. The main base is at Tartus.

Air Force. The Air Force, including Air Defence Command, was believed (1991) to have about 40,000 personnel and over 500 combat aircraft, including about 200 MiG-21, 80 MiG-23, 30 MiG-25 and 60 MiG-29 supersonic interceptors, 60 MiG-23, 60 Su-22 and 50 MiG-17 fighter-bombers, as well as some MiG-25 reconnaissance aircraft. Training units have Spanish-built Flamingo piston-engined primary trainers and Czechoslovakian L-29 Delfin and L-39 jet basic trainers. There are also transport units with Il-76, An-12, An-24/26, Il-14 and other types, and helicopter units with Soviet-built Mi-6s, Mi-14s and Mi-24 gunships, Polish-built Mi-2s and French-built Gazelles. 'Guideline', 'Goa', 'Gainful' and 'Gaskin' surface-to-air missiles are widely deployed in Syria by Air Defence Command, and 'Gammon' long-range surface-to-air missiles in Lebanon.

INTERNATIONAL RELATIONS. A Treaty of Brotherhood, Co-operation and Co-ordination with Lebannon of May 1991 provides for close relations in the fields of foreign policy, the economy, military affairs and security. By the treaty the Lebanese government's decisions are subject to review by 6 joint Syrian-Lebanese bodies.

Membership. Syria is a member of the UN and Arab League.

ECONOMY

Budget. The consolidated budget for the calendar year 1988 balanced at £Syr.61,875m.

Currency. The monetary unit is the *Syrian pound* (SYP) of 100 *piastres*. In March 1992, £1 = £Syr.35·52; US$1 = £Syr.20·23.

Banking and Finance. The Central Bank has the sole right to issue currency. Other banks were nationalized in March 1963. Number of branches, 1 Jan. 1987: Central Bank of Syria, 10; Commercial Bank of Syria, 35; Industrial Bank, 11; Agricultural Co-operative Bank, 64; Real Estate Bank, 13; Popular Credit Bank, 44. Total deposits at specialized banks, 1987 (in £Syr.1m.): Commercial Bank of Syria, 23,403·3; Industrial Bank, 1,369; Agricultural Co-operative Bank, 1,882; Real Estate Bank, 5,810·1; Popular Credit Bank, 4,298·7.

Weights and Measures. The metric system is legal, though former weights and measures may still be in use: 1 *okiya* = 0·47 lb.; 6 *okiyas* = 1 *oke* = 2·82 lb.; 2 *okes* = 1 *rottol* = 5·64 lb.; 200 *okes* = 1 *kantar*.

ENERGY AND NATURAL RESOURCES

Electricity. Production (1988), 8,161m. kwh.

Oil. A branch of the Iraq Petroleum Co.'s oil pipeline from Kirkuk crosses Syria between Makaleb in the east and Nahr el Kebir valley in the west. The Iraq Petroleum Co. has constructed a new pipeline from Kirkuk to the small fishing port of Banias (south of Lattakia), which came into use in April 1952; the Trans-Arabian Pipeline Co.'s line to Sidon crosses southern Syria. Crude oil production (1991), 24·64m. tonnes. Reserves (1983) 1,521m. bbls.

Gas. Gas reserves (1982), 700,000m. cubic ft. Production (1983), 75·86m. cu. metres.

Water. In 1987 there were 3 main dams, at Al-Rastan (storage capacity 250m. cu. metres), Mouhardeh (50m. cu. metres) and Taldo (15m. cu. metres), and 29 surface dams. Production of drinking water, 1988, 501·37m. cu. metres.

Minerals. Phosphate deposits have been discovered. Production, 1988, 2,186,000 tonnes; other minerals were salt, 127,000 tonnes and gypsum 179,000 tonnes. There are indications of lead, copper, antimony, nickel, chrome and other minerals widely distributed. Sodium chloride and bitumen deposits are being worked.

Agriculture. In 1987, 129,000 ha were under cotton, 1,183,000 ha under wheat and 1,570,000 ha under barley. The cultivable area in 1987 was 6,133,000 ha, and there were 8,277,000 ha of steppe and pasture. In 1987 there were 52,400 tractors.

Production of principal crops, 1990 (in 1,000 tonnes): Wheat, 2,069; barley, 846; maize, 132; seed cotton, 441; olives, 480; lentils, 101; millet, 8; sugar-beet, 530; potatoes, 289; tomatoes, 482; grapes, 496.

Production, of animal products 1990 (in tonnes): Milk, 1,205,000; butter, 13,555; cheese, 65,078; honey, 650; eggs, 60,980.

Livestock (1990, 1,000): Cattle, 800; horses, 45; mules, 27; asses, 180; sheep, 14,395; goats, 1,078; poultry, 12,000.

Forestry. In 1987 there were 534,000 ha of forest. The artificial forestry area was 25,586 ha, producing 30,406,000 woody plants, 1,509 tonnes of charcoal, 57,660 tonnes of firewood and 26,900 tonnes of industrial wood.

Fisheries. The total catch in 1986 was 4,800 tonnes.

INDUSTRY. Public sector industrial production in 1988 included (in tonnes): Cotton yarn, 36,744; cotton and mixed textiles, 21,018; mixed woollen yarn, 1,817; manufactured tobacco, 17,056; cement, 3,481; iron bars, 15,455; asbestos (1987), 21,684; vegetable oil, 22,838; electrical engines, 16,590; refrigerators, 9,158; water meters, 30,780; tractors, 1,198 (1987, units); woollen carpets, 520,000 sq. metres.

Trade Unions. In 1987 there were 198 trade unions with 312,003 members.

Labour. In 1984 the labour force was 2,356,000 (out of a total population of 9,616,000), of whom 2,246,000 were employed (1,329,000 urban). In 1987, 137,941 people were employed in the industrial public sector.

FOREIGN ECONOMIC RELATIONS

Commerce. Trade in calendar years in £Syr.1m. was as follows:

	1984	1985	1986	1987
Imports	16,154	15,570	10,709	27,915
Exports	7,275	6,427	5,199	15,192

Main imports, 1987 (in £Syr.1,000) included: Petroleum and products, 5,343,278; wheat, 730,764; iron tubes and pipes (not cast iron), 706,174; refined sugar, 637,898; yarn of continuous synthetic fibres, 549,272; direct current generators, 531,584; special purpose motor lorries, trucks and vans, 511,372. Main exports included: Petroleum and products, 7,871,220; raw cotton, 877,224; printed woven cotton fabrics, 577,433.

In 1987, imports (in £Syr.1,000) came mainly from France, 2,737,676; USSR, 2,317,606, Iran, 2,294,879; Federal Republic of Germany, 2,284,403; Italy, 1,883,869; Libya, 1,575,212; USA, 1,470,980. Exports went mainly to Italy, 4,718,628; USSR, 3,165,821; France, 1,507,082; Romania, 1,311,369.

Total trade between Syria and UK (British Department of Trade returns, in £1,000 sterling):

	1987	1988	1989	1990	1991
Imports to UK	24,937	36,100	55,258	85,874	42,459
Exports and re-exports from UK	34,053	24,647	38,537	38,245	49,791

Tourism. In 1987, there were 1,217,564 visitors.

COMMUNICATIONS

Roads. In 1988 there were 22,738 km of asphalted roads, 6,155 km of paved non-asphalted road and 1,559 km of earth roads. In 1988 there were 331,439 motor vehicles, including 112,337 cars and taxis, 4,197 buses, 7,808 mini-buses, 36,002 goods vehicles and 75,464 motorcycles.

Railways. In 1988 the network totalled 1,751 km of 1,435 mm gauge (Syrian Railways) and 127 km of 1,050 mm gauge (Hedjaz-Syrian Railway). In 1989 Syrian Railways carried 3·9m. passengers and 5·3m. tonnes of freight.

Civil Aviation. In 1988, 11,204 aircraft arrived at Damascus, Aleppo, Al-Kamishli, Lattakia and Deir Ez-Zor airports; 659,790 passengers arrived, 726,441 departed and 127,520 were in transit; 2,915,966 kg of freight was unloaded and 3,412,936 kg loaded.

Telecommunications. Number of telephones (1988), 507,989; of these, 184,555 were in Damascus and 81,602 in Aleppo. Broadcasting is controlled by the government Syrian Broadcasting and Television Organization. There are 2 national radio programmes and an external service and 2 TV programmes (colour by SECAM and PAL). In 1991 there were 2·85m. radio and 0·7m. TV sets.

Cinemas. In 1985 there were 85 cinemas with 47,840 seats.

Newspapers. There were (1984) 3 national daily newspapers in Damascus; other dailies and periodicals appear in Hama, Homs, Aleppo and Lattakia.

JUSTICE, RELIGION, EDUCATION AND WELFARE

Justice. Syrian law is based on both Islamic and French jurisprudence. There are 2 courts of first instance in each district, one for civil and 1 for criminal cases. There is also a Summary Court in each sub-district, under Justices of the Peace. There is a Court of Appeal in the capital of each governorate, with a Court of Cassation in Damascus.

Religion. The population is composed 90% of Sunni Moslems and there are also Shi'ites and Ismailis. There are also Druzes and Alawites. Christians include Greek

Orthodox, Greek Catholics, Armenian Orthodox, Syrian Orthodox, Armenian Catholics, Protestants, Maronites, Syrian Catholics, Latins, Nestorians and Assyrians. There are also Jews and Yezides.

Education. The Syrian University was founded in 1924, although the faculties of law and of medicine had existed previously. In 1986-87 there were 4 universities with 138,743 students.

In 1986-87 there were 766 kindergartens with 70,859 children; 9,315 primary schools with 85,583 teachers and 2,158,594 pupils; 1,922 intermediate and secondary schools with 37,541 teachers and 855,453 pupils. In 1987, 21 teachers' colleges had 1,167 teachers and 10,076 students; 143 schools for professional education had 7,245 teachers and 56,664 students.

Health. In 1987 there were 12,606 hospital beds (1 per 870 persons) in 206 hospitals, and 566 health centres; there were also 8,146 doctors, 2,456 dentists, 2,960 pharmacists, 3,049 midwives and 9,786 nursing personnel.

DIPLOMATIC REPRESENTATIVES

Of Syria in Great Britain (8 Belgrave Square, London SW1X 8PH)
Ambassador: Mohammad Khodor.

Of Great Britain in Syria (11 Mohammad Kurd Ali St., Damascus POB 37)
Ambassador: A. F. Green, CMG.

Of Syria in the USA (2215 Wyoming Ave., NW, Washington, D.C., 20008)
Ambassador: Walid Al-Moualem.

Of the USA in Syria (Abu Rumaneh, Al Mansur St., Damascus)
Ambassador: Edward P. Djerejian.

Of Syria to the United Nations
Ambassador: Dia-Allah Al-Fattal.

Further Reading

Statistical Information: There is a Central Statistics Bureau affiliated to the Council of Ministers, Damascus. It publishes a monthly summary and an annual Statistical Abstract (in Arabic and English).

Abd-Allah, U. F., *The Islamic Struggle in Syria*. Berkeley, 1983
Barthélemy, A., *Dictionnaire arabe-français. Dialectes de Syrie*. 4 vols. Paris, 1935-50
Devlin, J. F., *Syria: Modern State in an Ancient Land*. Boulder, 1983
Maoz, M. and Yaniv, A., *Syria under Assad*. New York, 1986
Seale, P., *The Struggle for Syria*. London, 1986.—*Asad of Syria: The Struggle for the Middle East*. London, 1989
Seccombe, I. J., *Syria*. [Bibliography] Oxford and Santa Barbara, 1987

TANZANIA

Capital: Dodoma
Population: 25·09m. (1991)
GNP per capita: US$120 (1989)

Jamhuri ya Muungano
wa Tanzania—United
Republic of Tanzania

HISTORY. Tanganyika achieved responsible government in Sept. 1960 and full self-government on 1 May 1961. On 9 Dec. 1961 Tanganyika became a sovereign independent member state of the Commonwealth of Nations. It adopted a republican form of government on 9 Dec. 1962. For history from the end of the 17th century until 1960 *see* THE STATESMAN'S YEAR-BOOK, 1991–92, p. 1183.

On 24 June 1963 Zanzibar became an internal self-governing state and on 9 Dec. 1963 independent. On 12 Jan. 1964 its sultanate was overthrown by the Afro-Shirazi Party who established the People's Republic of Zanzibar.

On 26 April 1964 Tanganyika, Zanzibar and Pemba combined to form the United Republic of Tanganyika and Zanzibar (named Tanzania on 29 Oct.).

AREA AND POPULATION. Tanzania is bounded north-east by Kenya, north by Lake Victoria and Uganda, north-west by Rwanda and Burundi, west by Lake Tanganyika, south-west by Zambia and Malawi and south by Mozambique. Total area 945,037 sq. km (364,881 sq. miles including the offshore islands of Zanzibar (1,660 sq. km) and Pemba (984 sq. km) and inland water surfaces (59,050 sq. km)). The census of 1988 gave a total population of 23,174,336 (17,076,270 in mainland Tanzania and 475,655 in Zanzibar and Pemba). Estimate (1991), 25,086,000.

The chief towns (1988 census populations) are Dar es Salaam, the chief port and former capital (1,360,850), Mwanza (223,013), Dodoma, the new capital (203,833), Tanga (187,634), Zanzibar Town (157,634), Tabora and Mbeya.

The United Republic is divided into 25 administrative regions of which 20 are in mainland Tanzania, 3 in Zanzibar (Zanzibar North, Zanzibar West, Zanzibar South) and 2 in Pemba (Pemba North, Pemba South). Areas and 1988 census populations of the regions:

Region	Sq. km	Population	Region	Sq. km	Population
Arusha	82,306	1,351,675	Pwani (Coast)	32,407	638,015
Dar es Salaam	1,393	1,360,850	Rukwa	68,635	694,974
Dodoma	41,311	1,237,819	Ruvuma	63,498	783,327
Iringa	56,864	1,208,914	Shinyanga	50,781	1,772,549
Kagera	28,388	1,326,183	Singida	49,341	791,814
Kigoma	37,037	854,817	Tabora	76,151	1,036,293
Kilimanjaro	13,309	1,108,699	Tanga	26,808	1,283,636
Lindi	66,046	646,550	*Zanzibar & Pemba*	*2,460*	*640,578*
Mara	19,566	970,942	Pemba North	574	137,399
Mbeya	60,350	1,476,199	Pemba South	332	127,640
Morogoro	70,799	1,222,737	Zanzibar North	470	97,028
Mtwara	16,707	889,494	Zanzibar South	854	70,184
Mwanza	19,592	1,878,271	Zanzibar West	230	208,327

The official languages are English and Swahili (spoken as a mother tongue by only 8·8% of the population, but used as a lingua franca by 90%).

CLIMATE. The climate is very varied and is controlled very largely by altitude and distance from the sea. There are three climatic zones: the hot and humid coast, the drier central plateau with seasonal variations of temperature, and the semi-temperate mountains. Dodoma. Jan. 75°F (23·9°C), July 67°F (19·4°C). Annual rainfall 23" (572 mm). Dar es Salaam. Jan. 82°F (27·8°C), July 74°F (23·3°C). Annual rainfall 43" (1,064 mm).

CONSTITUTION AND GOVERNMENT. A permanent Constitution was approved in April 1977. The country is a one-party state, the Tanganyika African National Union and the Afro-Shirazi Party in Zanzibar having merged into one revolutionary party, *Chama cha Mapinduzi*, in Feb. 1977. At its congress in Feb. 1992, the party announced its intention to introduce multi-party democracy.

The *President* is head of state, chairman of the party and commander-in-chief of the armed forces. The second Vice-President is head of the executive in Zanzibar. The Prime Minister and first Vice-President is also the leader of government business in the National Assembly.

According to the Constitution of 1977, as amended in Oct. 1984, the *National Assembly* is composed of a total of 244 members: 169 Members of Parliament elected from the Constituencies (119 from the mainland and 50 from Zanzibar); 15 National Members elected by the National Assembly; 15 women members elected by the National Assembly, 5 from Zanzibar; 5 members elected by the House of Representatives in Zanzibar; 25 ex-officio Members (20 Regional Commissioners from the mainland and 5 from Zanzibar) and 15 Nominated Members (by the President), 5 from Zanzibar.

In Dec. 1979 a separate Constitution for Zanzibar was approved. Although at present under the same Constitution as Tanzania, Zanzibar has, in fact, been ruled by decree since 1964.

At the presidential elections of Oct. 1990 Ali Hassan Mwinyi, the sole candidate, gained 95·5% of votes cast.

The Government in Feb. 1992 consisted of:

President: Ali Hassan Mwinyi (b. 1925; elected Oct. 1990 for a second 5-year term).

Prime Minister and First Vice-President: John Malecela.

President of Zanzibar and Second Vice-President: Dr Salmin Amonur. *Without Portfolio:* Rashid Kawawa, Horace Kolimba. *Defence and National Service:* Amran Mayagila. *Finance:* Stephen Kibona. *Foreign Affairs and International Co-operation:* Ahmed Hassan Diria. *Agriculture, Livestock and Co-operatives:* Anna Abdallah. *Regional Administration and Local Government:* Joseph Warioba. *Communications and Transport:* Jackson Makweta. *Labour and Youth Development:* Joseph Rwegasira. *Home Affairs:* Augustine Mrema. *Education and Culture:* Charles Kabeho. *Water, Energy and Minerals:* Jakaya Kikwete. *Tourism, Natural Resources and Environment:* Abubakar Mgumia. *Industries and Trade:* Cleopa Msuya. *Health:* Philemon Sarungi. *Planning:* Kighoma Malima. *Civil Service:* Fatma Ali. *Roads and Construction:* Nalaila Kiula. *Lands, Housing and Urban Development:* Marcel Komanya. *Information and Broadcasting:* Benjamin Mkapa. *Science, Technology and Higher Education:* Dr William Shia. *Community Development, Women and Children's Welfare:* Anna Makinda. *Minister of State, Office of the Prime Minister:* Edward Lowasa.

National flag: Divided diagonally green, black, blue, with the black strip edged in yellow.

DEFENCE

Army. The Army consists of 8 infantry, 1 tank brigade; 2 artillery, 2 anti-aircraft, 2 mortar, 1 surface-to-air missile, 2 anti-tank and 2 signals battalions. Equipment includes 30 Chinese Type-59 and 30 T-62 main battle tanks. Strength (1991), 45,000 (20,000 conscripts). There is also a Citizen's Militia of 100,000.

Navy. There are 4 ex-Chinese torpedo-armed hydrofoils and 6 inshore patrol craft of mixed Chinese and North Korean origins. 4 British-built inshore patrol craft are based permanently in Zanzibar and 4 armed patrol boats on Lake Victoria Nyanza. Personnel in 1991 totalled some 800.

Air Force. The Tanzanian People's Defence Force Air Wing was built up initially with the help of Canada, but combat equipment has been acquired from China. Personnel totalled about 1,000 in 1991, with about 10 F-7 (MiG-21), 10 F-6 (MiG-19) and 8 F-4 (MiG-17) jet fighters; 1 F28 Fellowship VIP transport; 5 Buffalo twin-engined STOL transports; 4 HS 748 turboprop transports; 2 Cessna 404 and 6 Cessna 310 liaison aircraft; 4 Agusta-Bell AB.205 transport helicopters, and 2 JetRanger and 2 Bell 47G light helicopters; and Piper Cherokee and FT-2 (Chinese-built MiG-15 UTI) trainers.

INTERNATIONAL RELATIONS

Membership. Tanzania is a member of the UN, OAU, the Commonwealth, Non-Aligned Movement and is an ACP state of the EEC.

ECONOMY

Budget. In 1988–89 revenue US$627m., capital expenditure US$284m. and recurrent expenditure US$903m.

Currency. The monetary unit is the *Tanzanian shilling* (TZS) of 100 *cents*. There are coins of 5, 10, 20, 50 cents, 1 Sh., 5 Sh., 20 Sh. and 1,500 Sh.; and notes of 10 Sh., 20 Sh., 50 Sh., 100 Sh. and 200 Sh. In March 1992, £1 = Sh. 413·95; US$ = Sh. 235·80.

Banking and Finance. On 14 June 1966 the central bank, the Bank of Tanzania, with a government-owned capital of Sh. 20m., began operations.

On 6 Feb. 1967 all commercial banks with the exception of National Co-operative Banks were nationalized and their interests vested in the National Bank of Commerce on the mainland and the Peoples' Bank in Zanzibar.

Weights. The metric system is in force.

ENERGY AND NATURAL RESOURCES

Electricity. Production (1986) 830m. kwh. Supply 230 volts; 50 Hz.

Minerals. Production (1986): Diamonds, 38,000 grammes; gold, 46,900 grammes; salt, 15,300 tonnes. Large deposits of coal and tin exist but mining is on a small scale.

Agriculture. Production of main agricultural crops in 1990 (in 1,000 tonnes) was: Sisal, 30; seed cotton, 175; sugar-cane, 1,320; coffee, 50; tobacco, 15; maize, 2,445; wheat, 106; cashew nuts, 20; citrus, 35.

Zanzibar used to provide the greater part of the world's supply of cloves, but in 1989 only contributed 10% of world production.

Livestock (1990, including Zanzibar): 13m. cattle, 5·2m. sheep, 8·5m. goats, 32m. poultry.

Forestry. Forest cover 43m. ha.

Fisheries. Catch (1986) 309,900 tonnes of which, inland waters, 265,800 tonnes.

INDUSTRY. Industry is limited and is mainly textiles, petroleum and chemical products, food processing, tobacco, brewing and paper manufacturing.

FOREIGN ECONOMIC RELATIONS

Commerce. Total trade (in Sh. 1m.):

	1982	1983	1984	1985	1986	1987
Imports	7,781	8,877	11,953	17,962	30,270	57,971
Exports	4,117	4,138	5,661	5,937	10,963	18,512

Imports and exports (in Tanzanian Sh. 1m.), by country, 1987:

Country	Imports	Exports	Country	Imports	Exports
Bahrain	1,279·6	23·0	India	1,181·3	1,119·7
Belgium	1,056·0	359·6	Italy	5,195·9	609·8
China	557·4	18·8	Japan	6,533·9	726·1
Denmark	2,813·6	15·5	Netherlands	2,842·2	1,426·5
Federal Republic			Singapore	444·3	590·5
of Germany	7,217·9	2,267·1	Thailand	3·8	119·3

Major export items 1987 (in Sh. 1m.): Coffee, 5,792·6; cotton, 2,831·8; sisal, 321·7; cloves, 264·7; tea, 825·4; tobacco, 864·2; cashew nuts, 439; diamonds, 576·9.

Total trade between Tanzania and UK (British Department of Trade returns, in £1,000 sterling):

	1988	1989	1990	1991
Imports to UK	26,386	22,641	25,575	20,938
Exports and re-exports from UK	88,686	93,036	84,694	72,822

Tourism. In 1987 there were about 103,000 visitors.

COMMUNICATIONS

Roads. In 1988 there were 82,000 km of roads and (1983) 43,248 cars and 12,579 licensed commercial vehicles of which 11,290 were trucks and 1,289 buses.

Railways. In 1977 the independent Tanzanian Railway Corporation was formed. The network totals 2,600 km (metre-gauge), excluding the Tan-Zam Railway 969 km in Tanzania (1,067 mm gauge) operated by a separate administration. In 1989, the state railway carried some 2m. passengers and 0·9m. tonnes of freight and the Tan-Zam Railway carried 1·5m. passengers and 1·2m. tonnes of freight.

Civil Aviation. There are 2 international airports (Dar es Salaam and Kilimanjaro). Air Tanzania Corporation provide domestic services and services to Mozambique, Zambia, Seychelles, Comoro, Rwanda, Burundi and Madagascar.

There are all-weather landing-grounds in Zanzibar and Pemba.

Shipping. In 1985, 635,000 tonnes of freight were loaded and 2·6m. unloaded.

Telecommunications. In 1988 there were 63,000 direct telephone lines and 1,400 telex lines. The government-controlled Radio Tanzania and Sauti ya Tanzania Zanzibar are responsible for radio broadcasting on the mainland and on Zanzibar respectively. On the mainland there is a national service and a commercial programme in Swahili and an external service in English. There is television only on Zanzibar provided by the government-run Television Zanzibar (colour by PAL). There were about 4m. radio and 80,000 TV sets in 1991.

Newspapers (1985). There were 3 dailies, 2 weeklies and several monthly magazines.

JUSTICE, RELIGION, EDUCATION AND WELFARE

Justice. The Judiciary is independent in both judicial and administrative matters and is composed of a 4-tier system of Courts: Primary Courts; District and Resident Magistrates' Courts; the High Court and the Court of Appeal. The Chief Justice is head of the Court of Appeal and the Judiciary Department. The Court's main registry is at Dar es Salaam; its jurisdiction includes Zanzibar. The Principal Judge is head of the High Court, also headquartered at Dar es Salaam, which has resident judges at 7 regional centres.

Religion. In 1984 some 40% were Christian, including Roman Catholics under the Archbishops of Dar es Salaam and Tabora, Anglicans under the Archbishop of Tanzania, and Lutherans. Moslems amount to 33%, but reach 66% in the coastal towns; Zanzibar is 96% Moslem and 4% Hindu. Some 23% follow traditional religions.

Education. In 1987 there were 10,302 primary schools with 3,169,202 pupils, and 288 (1988) secondary schools (175 private) with 127,703 students.

Technical and vocational education is provided at several secondary and technical schools and at the Dar es Salaam Technical College.

There were, in 1987, 63 teachers' colleges, including the college at Chang'ombe for secondary-school teachers, with 11,667 students.

The University of Dar es Salaam, independent since 1970, has faculties of law, arts, social sciences, medicine, engineering, commerce and management. Sokoine University of Agriculture, established in 1984, has faculties of agriculture, forestry and veterinary medicine. The total number of students in both universities was 3,395 in 1987.

Health. In 1984 there were 1,065 doctors and 152 hospitals with 22,800 beds.

DIPLOMATIC REPRESENTATIVES

Of Tanzania in Great Britain (43 Hertford St., London, W1)
High Commissioner: Ali S. Mchumo.

Of Great Britain in Tanzania (Hifadhi Hse., Samora Ave., Dar es Salaam)
High Commissioner: J. T. Masefield, CMG.

Of Tanzania in the USA (2139 R. St., NW, Washington, D.C., 20008)
Ambassador: Charles M. Nyirabu.

Of the USA in Tanzania (36 Laibon Rd., Dar es Salaam)
Ambassador: Edward DeJarnette, Jr.

Of Tanzania to the United Nations
Ambassador: Anthony B. Nyakyi.

Further Reading

Ayany, S. G., *A History of Zanzibar.* Nairobi, 1970
Coulson, A., *Tanzania: A Political Economy.* OUP, 1982
Darch, C., *Tanzania.* [Bibliography] Oxford and Santa Barbara, 1985
Hood, M., (ed.) *Tanzania and Nyerere.* London, 1988
Nyerere, J., *Freedom and Development.* New York, 1976
Resnick, I. N., *The Long Transition: Building Socialism in Tanzania.* New York and London, 1981
Yeager, R., *Tanzania: An African Experiment.* Aldershot, 1982

THAILAND

Capital: Bangkok
Population: 55·9m. (1989)
GNP per capita: US$1,170 (1989)

Prathes Thai,
or Muang-Thai

(Kingdom of Thailand)

HISTORY. Until 24 June 1932 Siam was an absolute monarchy. A coup of that date resulted in the constitution of 1932. Numerous coups have followed.

On 23 Feb. 1991 a military junta seized power, deposing the prime minister.

AREA AND POPULATION. Thailand is bounded west by Burma, north and east by Laos and south-east by Cambodia. In the south it becomes a peninsula bounded west by the Indian Ocean, south by Malaysia and east by the Gulf of Thailand. Area is 513,115 sq. km (198,456 sq. miles).

At the census taken in 1980 the registration gave a population of 46,961,338, of whom 30·4% lived in the Central region, 35·2% in the North-East region, 12·5% in the South region, 21·9% in the North region. Estimate (1989) 55,888,393 (27,837,050 females).

Vital statistics, 1989: Births, 1,017,218 (495,543 females); deaths, 242,881 (102,491 females). Expectation of life, 66 years.

Thailand is divided into 73 provinces and Bangkok, the capital. Provinces with over 1m. population 1989 were Nakhon Ratchasima (2,360,797), Ubol Ratchathani (1,902,177), Udon Thani (1,799,261), Khon Kaen (1,666,671), Buriram (1,422,177), Nakhon Sithamnaraj (1,411,966), Chiangmai (1,361,320), Sri Saket (1,313,192), Surin (1,272,597), Roi Et (1,214,641), Nakhon Sawan (1,081,502), Songkhla (1,073,586), Chaiyaphum (1,042,763) and Chiangpai (1,027,647).

Population of Bangkok in 1989, 5,832,843. Other towns (1980 census): Chiangmai (101,595), Hat Yai (93,519), Khon Kaen, (85,863), Phitsanulok (79,942), Nakhon Ratchasima (78,246), Udon Thani (71,142), Songkhla (67,945), Nakhon Sawan (63,935), Nakhon Sithamnaraj (63,162), Ubol Ratchathani (50,788), Ayutthaya (47,189), Nakhon Pathom (45,242), Lampang (42,301) and Ratchaburi (40,404).

Thai is the official language.

CLIMATE. The climate is tropical, with high temperatures and humidity. Over most of the country, 3 seasons may be recognized. The rainy season is June to Oct., the cool season from Nov. to Feb. and the hot season is March to May. Rainfall is generally heaviest in the south and lightest in the north east.

Bangkok. Jan. 78°F (25·6°C), July 83°F (28·3°C). Annual rainfall 56" (1,400 mm).

REIGNING KING. Bhumibol Adulyadej, born 5 Dec. 1927. King Bhumibol married on 28 April 1950 Princess Sirikit, and was crowned 5 May 1950. Children: Princess Ubol Ratana (born 5 April 1951, married Aug. 1972 Peter Ladd Jensen), Crown-Prince Vajiralongkorn (born 28 July 1952, married 3 Jan. 1977 Soamsawali Kitiyakra), Princess Maha Chakri Sirindhorn (born 2 April 1955), Princess Chulabhorn (born 4 July 1957, married 7 Jan. 1982 Virayudth Didyasarin).

CONSTITUTION AND GOVERNMENT. Following the deposition of Chatichai Choonhavan's government in Feb. 1991 the King appointed Gen. Sunthorn Kongsompong president of a 6-member National Council for the Maintenance of Order and approved a provisional constitution granting it extensive powers. A legislative assembly of 294 members, of whom 148 were allotted to the military, was installed in March 1991 to prepare for elections and approve a constitution. The constitution, promulgated on 8 Dec. 1991, provides for a legislative assembly consisting of a 270-member Senate appointed by the Army and a 360-member lower house elected by universal suffrage, both for 4-year terms.

At the elections of March 1992 seats were won as follows:

Samakkhi Tham (ST)	78	Palang Dharma	43
Chart Thai	73	Social Action	30
National Aspiration	72	Others	19
Democrats	45		

Gen. Suchinda Kraprayoon was designated *Prime Minister*.

National flag: Five horizontal stripes of red, white, blue, white, red, with the blue of double width.

Local Government. Thailand is divided into 73 provinces *(changwads)*, each under the control of a *changwad* governor. The *changwads* are subdivided into 655 districts *(amphurs)* and 88 sub-districts *(king amphurs)*, 6,633 communes *(tambons)* and 59,458 villages *(moobans)*.

DEFENCE. Under the Military Service Act of 1954 every able-bodied man between the ages of 21 and 30 is liable to serve 2 years with the colours; 7 years in the first reserve; 10 years in the second reserve; 6 years in the third reserve.

Army. The Army is organized in 4 Regions and includes 1 cavalry, 1 mechanized infantry, 7 infantry (including the Royal Guard), 2 special forces, 1 artillery and 1 anti-aircraft divisions; 19 engineer and 8 independent infantry battalions; an independent cavalry regiment and 4 reconnaissance companies. Equipment includes 100 M-48A5 and about 60 Chinese Type-69 main battle tanks. There is also an Army Aviation force including more than 100 transport helicopters, and over 60 O-1 Bird Dog observation aircraft and 4 C-47 and 2 Short 330 twin-turboprop transports. Strength (1992) 190,000 (80,000 conscripts, with 500,000 reserves for all the armed forces).

Navy. The Royal Thai Navy is, next to the Chinese, the most significant naval force in the South China Sea. The combatant fleet includes 9 frigates, 3 modern missile-armed 950-tonne corvettes, 6 German and Italian-built fast missile craft, 14 coastal and 30 inshore patrol craft, and about 40 riverine patrol boats. There is 1 mine countermeasures support vessel, 2 coastal minehunters and 4 coastal minesweepers. Amphibious capability is provided by 6 tank landing ships and 2 medium landing ships as well as 40 landing craft. Major auxiliaries are 1 small tanker, 1 surveying ships, and 2 training ships. Minor auxiliaries and service craft number about 12.

The Naval air element, all shore based, includes 3 F-27 Maritime, 3 DO228, 5 N24A Nomad and 2 CL-215s for maritime patrol, 4 F-27 Friendship transports, 10 Cessna T-337 armed light transports and 14 Bell utility and search-and-rescue helicopters.

Naval personnel in 1991 totalled 50,000 including 20,000 marines and 900 Naval Air Arm. The main bases are at Bangkok, Sattahip, Songkla and Phan Nga, with the riverine forces based at Nakhon Pathom.

A separate coast guard force, the Royal Thai Marine Police, numbers 1,700 and operates 3 coastal patrol craft, 32 riverine and inshore craft and numerous boats.

Air Force. The Royal Thai Air Force was reorganized with the assistance of a US Military Air Advisory Group. It had a strength (1992) of 43,000 personnel and 158 combat aircraft, and is made up of a headquarters and Combat, Logistics Support, Training and Special Services Groups. Combat units comprise 1 squadron of F-16 and 2 squadrons of F-5E/F interceptors, 1 squadron of F-5A/B fighter-bombers and RF-5A reconnaissance aircraft, 1 squadron with A-37B light jet attack aircraft, 2 with OV-10 Bronco light reconnaissance/attack aircraft, and 1 with AU-23A Peacemakers and 1 squadron with C-47s for security duties. Three Aravas are used for electronic intelligence gathering and 3 Learjets for combat support. There are transport units equipped with a total of about 70 C-130H/H-30 Hercules, HS 748,

C-123B Provider, C-47 and smaller aircraft, including 20 Australian-built Mission-masters; there are 25 UH-1H and 17 S-58T helicopters; 20 O-1 Bird Dog observation aircraft; training units with Airtrainer CT/4 primary trainers built in New Zealand, Italian-built SF.260MTs, T-37 and Fantrainer intermediate and T-33A advanced trainers.

INTERNATIONAL RELATIONS

Membership. Thailand is a member of UN, ASEAN and the Colombo Plan.

ECONOMY

Policy. The Sixth 5-year Development Plan (1987–91) envisages emphasis on development of the production system, with specific attention being paid to providing employment and expanding the industrial base.

Budget. Expenditure, 1989: 248,200m. baht; revenue: 309,200m. baht. Government expenditure in 1988: economic services, 30,924; social services, 65,647; defence, 44,149; general administration and services, 28,059; unallocatable items, 54,310.

Currency. The unit of currency is the *baht* (THB) of 100 *satang*. Coins are in denominations of 1, 2, 5 *baht* and 25 and 50 *satang*. Currency notes are for 5, 10, 20, 50, 100, and 500 *baht*.

In April 1991 the total amount of notes in circulation was 151,306m. baht. In March 1992, £1 = 44·80 *baht*; US$1 = 25·52 *baht*.

Banking and Finance. The Bank of Thailand (founded in 1942) is the central bank and bank of issue, an independent body although its capital is government-owned. Its assets and liabilities in April 1991 were 518,294·5m. baht. Its *Governor* is Vijit Sukpinit.

Total assets and liabilities of commercial banks, April 1991, 1,914,741·6m. baht. Deposits, April 1991: 1,527,175·8m. baht.

There is a Government Savings Bank.

Weights and Measures. The metric system was made compulsory in 1923. Units of weight: 1 *standard picul* = 60 kg; 1 *standard catty* (¹/₁₀₀ picul) = 600 grammes; 1 *standard carat* = 20 centigrammes. Units of length: 1 *sen* = 40 metres; 1 *wah* (¹/₂₀ sen) = 2 metres; 1 *sauk* (¹/₂ wah) = 0·50 metre; 1 *keup* (¹/₂ sauk) = 0·25 metre. Units of square measure: 1 *rai* (1 sq. sen) = 1,600 sq. metres: 1 *ngan* (¹/₄ rai) = 400 sq. metres; 1 *sq. wah* (¹/₁₀₀ ngan) = 4 sq. metres. Units of capacity: 1 *standard kwien* = 2,000 litres; 1 *standard ban* (¹/₂ kwien) = 1,000 litres; 1 *standard sat* (¹/₅₀ ban) = 20 litres; 1 *standard tannan* (¹/₂₀ sat) = 1 litre.

Legislation passed in 1940 provided that the calendar year shall coincide with the Christian Year, and that the year of the Buddhist era (B.E.) 2484 shall begin on 1 Jan. 1941. (The New Year's Day was previously 1 April) (B.E.).

ENERGY AND NATURAL RESOURCES

Electricity. In 1987 the principal sources of energy generation were natural gas (50%), lignite (24%), hydro (17%) and heavy oil (7%). Installed capacity was 55% thermal, 30% hydro, 11% combined cycle and 4% gas turbine. Annual hydro capacity, 26,204 mw. Supply 220 volts; 50 Hz.

Oil. Proven oil reserves in 1987 were less than 160m. bbls. Production of crude oil (1991) 1·97m. tonnes providing 15% of needs.

Gas. Production of natural gas (1990) 230,260m. cu. ft. Estimated reserves, 1986, 12,922,000m. cu. ft.

Minerals. The mineral resources include cassiterite (tin ore), wolfram, scheelite, antimony, coal, copper, gold, iron, lead, manganese, molybdenum, rubies, sapphires, silver, zinc and zircons. Production, 1990 (in 1,000 tonnes): Iron ore, 128·6; manganese ore, 16·6; tin concentrates, 20; lead ore, 52·3; antimony ore, 0·8; zinc ore, 272·5; lignite, 12,421; gypsum, 5,753·8; wolfram ore (tungsten), 0·5; fluorite ore, 94·7; marl, 338.

Agriculture. The chief produce is rice, a staple of the national diet. The area under paddy is about 18m. acres. In 1987 40% of the total land area was cultivated.

Output of the major crops in 1991 was (in 1,000 tonnes): Paddy, 19,500; maize, 4,150; sugar-cane, 42,000; jute and kenaf, 200; tobacco leaves, 72; tapioca-root, 21,000; soybeans, 600; coconut, 920; mung beans, 320; cotton, 100; groundnuts, 168; sesame, 27; castor seeds, 29; kapok and bambax fibre, 38·2.

Livestock, 1988 (in 1,000): Horses, 19; buffaloes, 6,000; cattle, 5,000; pigs, 4,260; sheep, 95; goats, 80; poultry, 101,000.

Forestry. About 14·4m. ha was under forest in 1988. Teak and other hardwoods grow in the deciduous forests of the north; elsewhere tropical evergreen forests are found, with the timber yang the main crop (a source of yang oil).

Output of main forestry products in 1989: Teak, 26,200 cu. metres; yang and other woods, 892,600 cu. metres. By-products in 1989: Firewood, 426,000 cu. metres; charcoal, 325,500 cu. metres.

Rubber production in 1991: 1·25m. tonnes.

Fisheries. In 1989 the catch of sea fish was 2·6m. tonnes including marine prawns and shrimps, 0·23m. tonnes; of freshwater fish, 165,000 tonnes.

INDUSTRY. Production of manufactured goods in 1990 included 18,053,899 tonnes of cement, 263,482,000 litres of beer, 905m. litres of soft drinks, 38,180 tonnes of cigarettes, 208,483 tonnes of galvanized iron sheets, 173,111 tonnes of tin plate, 305,145 automobiles, 715,115 motorcycles, 65,319 tonnes of tyres, 225,017 tonnes of synthetic fibre, 152,263 tonnes of jute products, 157,600 tonnes of paper, 150,946 tonnes of detergent, 13,983m. litres of petroleum products, 3,382,934 tonnes of sugar and 1,301m. integrated circuits.

Labour. In 1988, 28·2m. persons out of a labour force of 29·9m. were employed: 17·9m. in agriculture and 2·8m. in manufacturing.

FOREIGN ECONOMIC RELATIONS

Commerce. The foreign trade (in 1m. baht) was as follows:

	1985	1986	1987	1988	1989
Imports (c.i.f.)	251,169	241,358	334,209	513,114	662,679
Exports (f.o.b.)	193,366	233,383	299,853	403,570	516,315

Main exports by category in 1989, in 1m. baht: Manufactures, 195,973; food, 173,352; machinery, 91,710; raw materials, 35,330. Imports: Machinery, 251,001; manufactures, 181,156; chemicals, 74,204; mineral fuel and lubricant, 59,819.

In 1990 exports (in 1m. baht) included: Textile products, 84,472; rice, 27,770; rubber, 23,557; tapioca products, 23,136; precious stones, 22,045; integrated circuits, 21,580; prawns, 20,454; footwear, 20,213; sugar, 17,694; canned fish, 15,742; jewellery, 12,813; furniture and parts, 11,511.

1987 imports (in 1m. baht) included: Chemicals, 36,045; iron and steel, 23,693; non-electrical machinery and parts, 49,485; electrical machinery and parts, 31,988; vehicles and parts, 15,240; fuel and lubricants, 44,457.

In 1989 exports (in 1m. baht) were mainly to USA (111,788), Japan (87,993) and Singapore (36,840); in 1990 imports were mainly from Japan (259,208), USA (91,914) and Federal Republic of Germany (41,460).

Total trade between Thailand and UK (British Department of Trade returns, in £1,000 sterling):

	1987	1988	1989	1990	1991
Imports to UK	239,430	321,241	443,144	484,276	625,374
Exports and re-exports from UK	206,571	279,717	427,484	416,648	463,449

Tourism. In 1990 5·37m. foreigners visited Thailand. Tourist revenue was 110,000m. baht.

COMMUNICATIONS

Roads. In 1989 there were 16,815 km of state highways and 27,595 km of provincial highways.

Railways. In 1990 the State Railway totalled 3,861 route km (metre gauge), excluding the Mae Klong line. In 1990 it carried 85m. passengers and 7·8m. tonnes of freight.

Aviation. There are international airports at Bangkok, Chiangmai, Phuket and Hat Yai. Thai Airways is the sole air transport enterprise. In 1959 Thai Airways and SAS set up Thai Airways International to operate international air services. In 1990, 8·3m. passengers were carried. Thai Airways International had 58 aircraft in 1990. There are plans to privatize it.

Shipping. In 1988, 5,020 vessels of 24,758,487 NRT entered and 4,854 of 24,295,440 NRT cleared the port of Bangkok.

The port of Bangkok, about 30 km from the mouth of the Chao Phya River, is capable of berthing ocean-going vessels of 10,000 gross tons and 28 ft draught. Bangkok is a port of entry for Laos.

Telecommunications. In 1985 there were 576,082 telephones, of which 389,096 were in Bangkok.

In 1985, there were 275 radio stations and 11 television stations,7,629,998 radios and 4,122,000 televisions.

Cinemas (1989). There were 572 cinemas with a seating capacity of 400,434.

Newspapers (1989). There are 23 daily newspapers in Bangkok, including 2 in English and 7 in Chinese, with a combined circulation of about 2m.

JUSTICE, RELIGION, EDUCATION AND WELFARE

Justice. The judicial power is exercised in the name of the King, by *(a)* courts of first instance, *(b)* the court of appeal *(Uthorn)* and *(c)* the Supreme Court *(Dika)*. The King appoints, transfers and dismisses judges, who are independent in conducting trials and giving judgment in accordance with the law.

Courts of first instance are subdivided into 20 magistrates' courts *(Kwaeng)* with limited civil and minor criminal jurisdiction; 85 provincial courts *(Changwad)* with unlimited civil and criminal jurisdiction; the criminal and civil courts with exclusive jurisdiction in Bangkok; the central juvenile courts for persons under 18 years of age in Bangkok.

The court of appeal exercises appellate jurisdiction in civil and criminal cases from all courts of first instance. From it appeals lie to Dika Court on any point of law and, in certain cases, on questions of fact.

The Supreme Court is the supreme tribunal of the land. Besides its normal appellate jurisdiction in civil and criminal matters, it has semi-original jurisdiction over general election petitions. The decisions of Dika Court are final. Every person has the right to present a petition to the Government who will deal with all matters of grievance.

Religion. In 1983 there were 47,049,223 Buddhists, 1,869,427 Moslems, 267,381 Christians and 64,369 Hindus, Sikhs and others.

Education. Primary education is compulsory for children between the ages of 7–14 and free in local municipal schools. In 1988 there were 1,248,290 students enrolled at pre-primary level, 7,009,604 at elementary level, 1,221,224 at lower secondary level, 862,013 at upper secondary level and 358,001 in higher education. In 1988 there were 36 teachers' training colleges with 5,855 teachers and 54,264 students. In 1980 there were about 180 government vocational schools and colleges with 11,240 teachers and 208,088 students. There are 8 schools for deaf children, 2 for the blind, 1 for multiple-handicapped and 2 for the mentally retarded. In 1984 the 36 teacher training colleges were regionally consolidated into 8 United Colleges also offering 4-year programmes in science and technology, management, social development, agriculture, arts and journalism. In 1989 there were 17 universities, 6 of which were private. The public universities were: Chulalongkorn University, Kasetsart University, Khon Kaen University, Chiang Mai University, Thammasat University, Mahidol University, Ramkhamhaeng University, Silpakorn University, Sri Nakharinwirot University, Prince of Songkhla University and Sukhothaithammathirat Open University. The private universities were: Dhurakijpundit University, Payap University, Sri Patum University and the University of the Thai Chamber of Commerce.

Health. The Primary Health Care Programme had provided health services in 95% of villages in 1986. In 1982 there were 434 hospitals and 6,496 health centres. In 1982 there were 6,550 physicians, 1,122 dentists and (1981) 2,680 pharmacists.

DIPLOMATIC REPRESENTATIVES

Of Thailand in Great Britain (30 Queen's Gate, London, SW7 5JB)
Ambassador: Tongchan Jotikasthira.

Of Great Britain in Thailand (Wireless Rd., Bangkok)
Ambassador: M. R. Melhuish, CMG.

Of Thailand in the USA (2300 Kalorama Rd., NW, Washington, D.C., 20008)
Ambassador: (Vacant).

Of the USA in Thailand (95 Wireless Rd., Bangkok)
Ambassador: Daniel A. O'Donohue.

Of Thailand to the United Nations
Ambassador: Nitya Pibulsonggram.

Further Reading

National Statistical Office *Thailand Statistical Yearbook.*
Girling, J. I. S., *Thailand: Society and Politics.* Cornell Univ. Press, 1981
Morrell, D. and Samudavanija, C., *Political Conflict in Thailand.* Cambridge, Mass., 1981
Watts, M., *Thailand.* [Bibliography] Oxford and Santa Barbara, 1986
National statistical office: National Statistical Office, Bangkok.

TOGO

Capital: Lomé
Population: 3·4m. (1990)
GNP per capita: US$390 (1989)

République Togolaise

HISTORY. Togo became independent on 27 April 1960. (For its colonial history *see* THE STATESMAN'S YEAR-BOOK, 1991–92, p. 1194).

On 13 Jan. 1963 the first President, Sylvanus Olympio was murdered by soldiers. His successor, Nicolas Grunitzky, was deposed in a bloodless military coup in Jan. 1967 and on 14 April 1967 Col. Etienne Eyadéma assumed the Presidency. There was a return to constitutional government on 13 Jan. 1980.

Following a general strike in June 1991 the government agreed to hold a National Conference, and this elected an interim Supreme Republican Council.

AREA AND POPULATION. Togo is bounded west by Ghana, north by Burkina Faso, east by Benin and south by the Gulf of Guinea. The area is 56,785 sq. km. The population of Togo in 1981 (census) was 2,700,982; 1990 (estimate) 3·4m. (24·9% urban). The capital is Lomé (population, 1983, 366,476), other towns (1981, population) being Sokodé (48,098), Kpalimé (31,800), Atakpamé (27,100), Bassar (21,800), Tsévié (17,000) and Aného (14,000).

The areas, populations and chief towns of the 5 regions are:

Region	Sq. km	Census 1981	Chief town
Des Savanes	8,602	326,826	Dapaong
De La Kara	11,630	432,626	Kara
Centrale	13,182	269,174	Sokodé
Des Plateaux	16,975	561,656	Atakpamé
Maritime	6,396	1,039,700	Lomé

There are 37 ethnic groups. The south is largely populated by Ewe-speaking peoples (forming 47% of the population) and related groups, while the north is mainly inhabited by Hamitic groups speaking Kabre (22%), Gurma (14%) and Tem (4%). The official language is French but Ewe and Kabre are also taught in schools.

Population growth in 1990 was 3% per annum; infant mortality was 10%.

CLIMATE. The tropical climate produces wet seasons from March to July and from Oct. to Nov. in the south. The north has one wet season, from April to July. The heaviest rainfall occurs in the mountains of the west, south-west and centre. Lomé. Jan. 81°F (27·2°C), July 76°F (24·4°C). Annual rainfall 35" (875 mm).

CONSTITUTION AND GOVERNMENT. Following approval in a referendum on 30 Dec. 1979, a new Constitution came into force on 13 Jan. 1980, when the Third Togolese Republic was proclaimed. Under it there was an Executive President, directly elected for a 7-year term, and a National Assembly of 79 deputies, elected on a regional list system for a 5-year term. All candidates belonged to the *Rassemblement du peuple togolais*, the sole legal Party since 1969. Elections to the Assembly were held in March 1990.

President: Gen. Gnassingbé Eyadéma (re-elected for a further 7-year term in 1986).

On 8 July 1991 a National Conference was convened which decided on 22 Aug. to transfer many of the President's powers (including supreme command of the armed forces and the representation of Togo abroad) to an interim *Prime Minister*, Kokou Koffigoh (b. 1948). The Conference also elected a provisional Supreme Republican Council, presided over by Philippe Sanoko Kpodzro.

A constitutional referendum was scheduled for April 1992 and parliamentary elections for May.

National flag: Five horizontal stripes of green and yellow, a red quarter with a white star.

Local Government: There are 5 regions, each under an inspector appointed by the President; they are divided into 21 *prefectures,* each administered by a district chief assisted by an elected district council. Elections were scheduled for April 1992.

DEFENCE. Armed forces numbered (1991) about 5,900, all forming part of the Army. There is selective conscription for 2 years.

Army. The Army consists of 2 infantry, 1 Presidential Guard and 1 parachute commando regiments, with artillery and logistic support units. Equipment includes 9 Scorpion light tanks and 2 T-54/-55 main battle tanks. Strength (1991) 4,000, with a further 750 in a paramilitary gendarmerie.

Navy. In 1991 the Naval wing of the Army operated 2 inshore patrol craft from the naval base at Lomé. Naval personnel number 100.

Air Force. An Air Force, established with French assistance, has 6 Brazilian-built EMB-326 Xavante (Aermacchi MB.326) armed jet trainers; 5 Alpha Jet advanced trainers, with strike capability, 1 Boeing 707, 1 DC-8 and 1 twin-turbofan F28 Fellowship for VIP use, 2 turboprop Buffalo transports; 2 Beech Barons and 2 Cessna 337s for liaison; 3 Epsilon armed trainers; 1 Super Puma, 1 Puma and 2 Lama helicopters. Personnel (1991), 250, with 14 combat aircraft.

INTERNATIONAL RELATIONS

Membership. Togo is a member of the UN, OAU and ECOWAS, and is an ACP state of the EEC.

ECONOMY

Budget. The ordinary budget for 1988 balanced at 89,692m. francs CFA.

Currency. The unit of currency is the *franc* CFA with a parity rate of 50 *francs* CFA to 1 French *franc.* The rate of exchange (March 1992) was 489·63 francs CFA to £1; US$1 = 278·91.

Banking and Finance. The bank of issue is the *Banque Centrale des Etats de l'Afrique de l'Ouest.* Seven commercial and 3 development banks are based in Lomé.

ENERGY AND NATURAL RESOURCES

Electricity. Production (1986) 203m. kwh. There is a hydro-electric plant at Kpalime. Supply 127 and 220 volts; 50 Hz.

Minerals. Output of phosphate rock (1985) 2·5m. tonnes. Other minerals are limestone (estimated at 200m. tonnes), iron ore (550m. tonnes) and marble (20m. tonnes). Salt production (1982) 600,000 tonnes.

Agriculture. Inland the country is hilly; dry plains alternate with arable land. There are considerable plantations of oil and cocoa palms, coffee, cacao, kola, cassava and cotton. Production, 1990 (in 1,000 tonnes): Cassava, 475; tomatoes, 9; yams 420; maize, 220; sorghum, 106; millet, 50; seed cotton, 70; rice, 26; groundnuts, 28; coffee, 12.

Livestock (1990, in 1,000): Cattle, 250; sheep, 1,200; pigs, 500; goats, 1,600.

Forestry. In 1988 forests covered 1·4m. ha. Roundwood production (1987) was 813,000 cu. metres.

Fisheries. The catch (1986) was 14,800 tonnes.

INDUSTRY. Industry is small-scale. There is an oil refinery at Lomé, cement and textiles are produced and food processed.

FOREIGN ECONOMIC RELATIONS. A free trade zone was established in 1990.

Commerce (in 1m. francs CFA):

	1981	1982	1983	1984	1985
Imports	117,769	128,354	108,141	118,460	129,406
Exports	56,241	58,173	61,921	83,588	85,380

In 1985, of the exports, phosphates amounted to 38%, cotton 11%, coffee 11% and cocoa beans 6% by value; 22% of exports went to France and 18% to the Netherlands. Of the imports, France supplied 27%, the Netherlands, 11% and UK, 10%.

Total trade between Togo and UK (British Department of Trade returns, in £1,000 sterling):

	1987	1988	1989	1990	1991
Imports to UK	2,579	690	2,022	3,454	1,820
Exports and re-exports from UK	15,431	22,231	15,009	13,038	20,932

Tourism. There were about 121,000 tourists in 1988.

COMMUNICATIONS

Roads. There were, in 1986, 7,850 km of roads, of which 1,500 km were paved. In Dec. 1987 there were 44,120 passenger cars and 22,000 commercial vehicles.

Railways. There are 4 metre-gauge railways connecting Lomé, with Aného (continuing to Cotonou in Benin), Kpalime, Tabligbo and (via Atakpamé) Blitta; total length 525 km. In 1986 the railways carried 6·3m. tonne-km and 60m. passenger-km.

Civil Aviation: Air services connect Tokoin airport, near Lomé, with Paris, Dakar, Abidjan, Douala, Accra, Lagos, Cotonou and Niamey and by internal services with Sokodé, Mango, Dapaong, Atakpamé and Niamtougou.

Shipping. In 1983, vessels landed 654,000 tonnes and cleared 683,000 tonnes at Lomé; 31,058 containers passed through the port in 1981. The merchant marine comprised (1985) 11 vessels of 77,989 DWT. In 1981 some 2·2m. tonnes of phosphate were loaded at the port of Kpéme.

Telecommunications. There were (1983) 388 post offices and 11,105 telephones. Broadcasting is provided by the government-controlled Radiodiffusion-Télévision Togolaise. There were 0·7m. radio and 23,000 TV receivers (colour by SECAM) in 1991.

Newspapers. There was (1989) 1 daily newspaper (circulation 10,000).

JUSTICE, RELIGION, EDUCATION AND WELFARE

Justice. The Supreme Court and two Appeal Courts are in Lomé, one for criminal cases and one for civil and commercial cases. Each receives appeal from a series of local tribunals.

Religion. In 1991, 26% of the population were Catholics, 15% Moslem (chiefly in the north) and 9% Protestant; many follow traditional animist religions.

Education. In 1986 there were 474,998 pupils and 10,209 teachers in 2,345 primary schools, 86,327 pupils in secondary schools, and 5,050 students and 198 teachers in technical schools and 374 students and 22 teachers at the teacher-training college. In 1990 about 50% of children of school age were attending school. The University of Benin at Lomé (founded in 1970) had 4,500 students and 308 teaching staff in 1986.

Health. In 1981 there were 61 hospitals with 4,500 beds; and in 1985, 168 doctors, 7 dentists, 51 pharmacists, 559 midwives (1980) and 1,116 nursing staff.

DIPLOMATIC REPRESENTATIVES

The Embassy of Togo closed on 30 Sept. 1991.

Of Great Britain in Togo
Ambassador and Consul-General: A. M. Goodenough, CMG (resides in Accra).

Of Togo in the USA (2208 Massachusetts Ave., NW, Washington, D.C., 20008)
Ambassador: Ellom-Kodjo Schuppius.

Of the USA in Togo (Rue Pelletier Caventou, Lomé)
Ambassador: Harmon E. Kirby.

Of Togo to the United Nations
Ambassador: Soumi-Biova Pennaneach.

Further Reading

Cornevin, R., *Histoire du Togo.* 3rd ed., Paris, 1969
Feuillet, C., *Le Togo en general.* Paris, 1976

TONGA

Capital: Nuku'alofa
Population: 103,000 (1991)
GNP per capita: US$910 (1989)

Kingdom of Tonga

HISTORY. The Tongatapu group was discovered by Tasman in 1643.

A British protectorate was proclaimed on 18 May 1900. (For previous history *see* THE STATESMAN'S YEAR-BOOK, 1991–92, p. 1198). On 4 June 1970 Tonga became independent within the Commonwealth.

AREA AND POPULATION. The Kingdom consists of some 169 islands and islets with a total area of 289 sq. miles (748 sq. km; including inland waters), and lies between 15° and 23° 30' S. lat and 173° and 177° W. long., its western boundary being the eastern boundary of Fiji. The islands are split up into the following groups reading from north to south: The Niuas, Vava'u, Ha'apai, Tongatapu and 'Eua. The 3 main groups, both from historical and administrative significance, are Tongatapu in the south, Ha'apai in the centre and Vava'u in the north.

The capital is Nuku'alofa on Tongatapu, population (1986) 29,018.

There are 5 divisions comprising 23 districts:

Division	Sq. km	Census 1986	Capital
Niuas	72	2,368	Hihifo
Vava'u	119	15,175	Neiafu
Ha'apai	110	8,919	Pangai
Tongatapu	261	63,794	Nuku'alofa
'Eua	87	4,393	Ohonua

Census population (1986) 94,649 (males, 47,611); estimate (1991) 103,000.

CLIMATE. Generally a healthy climate, though Jan. to March is hot and humid, with temperatures of 90°F (32·2°C). Rainfall amounts are comparatively high, being greatest from Dec. to March. Nuku'alofa. Jan. 78°F (25·6°C), July 70°F (21·1°C). Annual rainfall 63" (1,576 mm). Vava'u. Jan. 80°F (26·7°C), July 73°F (22·8°C). Annual rainfall 110" (2,750 mm).

CONSTITUTION AND GOVERNMENT. The present Constitution is almost identical with that granted in 1875 by King George Tupou I. There is a Privy Council, Cabinet, Legislative Assembly and Judiciary. The legislative assembly, which meets annually, is composed of 9 nobles elected by their peers, 9 elected representatives of the people and the Privy Councillors (numbering 11); the King appoints one of the 9 nobles to be the Speaker. The elections are held triennially. In 1960, women voted for the first time.

King: HM King Taufa'ahau Tupou IV, GCVO, GCMG, KBE, born 4 July 1918, succeeded on 16 Dec. 1965 on the death of his mother, Queen Salote Tupou III; his coronation took place on 4 July 1967.

In Feb. 1992 the government comprised:

Prime Minister and Minister of Agriculture, Fisheries, Forests and Marine Affairs: HRH Prince Fatafehi Tu'ipelehake, KCMG, KBE, younger brother of the King.

Acting Deputy Prime Minister and Minister of Labour, Commerce and Industry: Baron Vaea. *Foreign Affairs and Defence:* HRH Crown Prince Tupouto'a. *Education, Works and Civil Aviation:* The Hon. Hu'akavameiliku. *Health:* Dr Sione Tapa. *Finance:* James Cocker: *Attorney-General and Minister of Justice:* Tevita Tupou. *Police, Prisons and Fire Services:* The Hon. 'Akau'ola. *Lands, Surveys and Natural Resources:* Dr S. Ma'afu Tupou. *Without Portfolio:* The Hon. Ma'afu. *Governor of Ha'apai:* The Hon. Fakafanua. *Governor of Vava'u:* The Hon. Tu'i'afitu.

National flag: Red with a white quarter bearing a red couped cross.

INTERNATIONAL RELATIONS

Membership. Tonga is a member of the Commonwealth and the South Pacific Forum, and is an ACP state of the EEC.

ECONOMY

Budget. Recurrent revenue and expenditure in T$1,000:

	1987–88 [1]	1988–89 [1]	1989–90 [1]
Revenue	29,846	35,860	43,720
Expenditure	29,846	35,957	43,720

[1] Estimate.

The principal sources of revenue are import dues, income tax, sales tax, port and service tax, wharfage and philatelic revenue.

Currency. The unit of currency is the *pa'anga* (TOP) of 100 *seniti*. There are notes of T$50, 20, 10, 5, 2 and 1 and coins of T$2, T$1 and *seniti* 50, 20, 10, 5, 2 and 1. In March 1992, £1 = 2·33 *pa'anga*; US$1 = 1·33 *pa'anga*.

Banking and Finance. The Bank of Tonga and the Tonga Development Bank are both situated in Nuku'alofa with branches in the main islands.

ENERGY AND NATURAL RESOURCES

Electricity. Production (1986) 8m. kwh. Supply 230 volts; 50 Hz.

Agriculture. Production (1990, in 1,000 tonnes): Coconuts, 40; fruit and vegetables 20; copra 2; cassava 16.

Livestock (1990, in 1,000): Cattle, 10; horses, 11; pigs, 83; goats, 14.

Fisheries. Catch (1982) 2,500 tonnes.

FOREIGN ECONOMIC RELATIONS

Commerce. In 1988, imports were valued at T$70,688,883 while exports and re-exports were T$9,502,664 and T$1,052,628.

Main imports (1988, in T$): Food 17,740,693, beverages and tobacco 3,302,660, crude materials 2,635,054, fuel and lubricants 6,853,259, oils and fats 178,927, chemicals 4,603,950, manufactured goods 13,453,825, machinery and transport equipment 15,472,034, miscellaneous manufactured articles 6,028,649.

Main exports (1988, in T$): Coconut oil 1,101,656, vanilla beans 1,384,837, bananas 658,362, dessicated coconut 403,250, water melons 19,169, knitted clothes 733,219, tarotaruas 99,286; fish 2,295,046, cassava 157,584, yams, 253,379, footwear 105,806, tapa cloth 102,345.

Principal destinations for Tongan exports/re-exports in 1988 were: New Zealand (T$3,313,202), Australia (T$1,738,191), USA (T$1,729,788), UK (T$28,170). Of 1988 imports (in T$), New Zealand furnished 21,313,446; Australia, 20,184,246; Japan, 5,401,330; Singapore, 3,451,779; USA, 5,338,115; Fiji, 7,190,968; China (Mainland), 2,068,269; UK, 766,370.

Total trade between Tonga and UK (British Department of Trade returns, in £1,000 sterling):

	1988	1989	1990	1991
Imports to UK	145	28	239	20
Exports and re-exports from UK	856	831	1,296	944

Tourism. There were 39,550 visitors in 1987.

COMMUNICATIONS

Roads. In 1987–88 there were over 5,000 registered motor vehicles and (1988) 1,242 km of roads (291 km paved).

Civil Aviation. International air service connexions to Tongatapuare are provided by Air New Zealand, Polynesian Airlines, Air Pacific and Hawaiian Air from

Auckland, Apia, Suva and Nadi. Internal inter-island flights are operated by Friendly Island Airways.

Shipping. Pacific Forum Line maintains a four weekly service New Zealand–Fiji–Samoas–Tonga from Sydney, Australia–Noumea–Fiji–Samoas–Tonga. Warner Pacific Line maintains a monthly service New Zealand–Tonga–Samoas–Tonga–New Zealand and a monthly service Tonga–New Zealand–Australia–Funufuti–Tarawa–Samoas–Tonga.

Telecommunications. Telephones numbered 3,500 in 1986 and there were 65,000 radio receivers. The operation of the International Telecommunication Services is undertaken by Cable and Wireless, under an agreement between the Company and the Government. The operation and development of the National Telecommunication Network and Services and the responsibilities of the Tonga Telecommunication Commission. The Tonga Broadcasting Commission is an independent statutory board which operates 2 programmes. There is also a religious service. There were about 75,000 radio sets in 1991. There is no television.

JUSTICE, RELIGION, EDUCATION AND WELFARE

Justice. The enforcement of which is the responsibility of the Minister of Police.

Religion. The Tongans are Christian, 40,516 (1986) being adherents of the Free Wesleyan Church.

Education. In 1987 there were 102 government and 11 denominational primary schools, with a total of 16,715 pupils. There were 8 government and 48 mission schools and 1 private school offering secondary education, with a total roll of 14,137. There was one government teacher-training college; 5 government technical and vocational schools and 3 non-government technical and vocational schools. 201 students were undertaking tertiary training overseas under an official scholarship in 1985.

Health. In 1988–89 there were 45 doctors, 11 dentists, 2 pharmacists, 37 midwives, 266 nursing personnel and 4 hospitals with 307 beds.

DIPLOMATIC REPRESENTATIVES

Of Tonga in Great Britain (36 Molyneux St., London, W1H 6AB)
High Commissioner: S. M. Tuita (accredited 6 June 1989).

Of Great Britain in Tonga (POB 56 Nuku'alofa)
High Commissioner: W. L. Cordiner.

Of the USA in Tonga
Ambassador: Evelyn Teegen.

Further Reading

Luke, Sir Harry, *Queen Salote and Her Kingdom*. London, 1954
Packett, C. N., *Travel and Holiday Guide to Tongatapu Island*. Bradford, 1984

TRINIDAD AND TOBAGO

Capital: Port-of-Spain
Population: 1·24m. (1988)
GNP per capita: US$3,160 (1989)

Republic of Trinidad and Tobago

HISTORY. Trinidad was discovered by Columbus in 1498 and colonized by the Spaniards in the 16th century. For colonial history *see* THE STATESMAN'S YEAR-BOOK, 1991–92, p. 1201. Trinidad and Tobago were joined in 1889.

On 31 Aug. 1962 Trinidad and Tobago became an independent member state of the Commonwealth. A Republican Constitution was adopted on 1 Aug. 1976.

During an attempted coup in July 1990 by a Moslem sect the prime minister was taken hostage and wounded.

AREA AND POPULATION. The island of Trinidad is situated in the Caribbean Sea, about 12 km off the north-east coast of Venezuela; several islets, the largest being Chacachacare, Huevos, Monos and Gaspar Grande, lie in the Gulf of Paria which separates Trinidad from Venezuela. The smaller island of Tobago lies about 31 km further to the north-east. Altogether, the islands cover 5,124 sq. km (1,978 sq. miles) of which Trinidad (including the islets) has 4,821 sq. km (1,861 sq. miles) and Tobago 303 sq. km (117 sq. miles). Population (census 1980): 1,079,800. (Trinidad, 1,039,100; Tobago, 40,700); estimate (1988) 1,243,000 (Trinidad, 1,198,000, Tobago, 45,000). Capital, Port-of-Spain, 58,400; other important towns, San Fernando (34,200) and Arima (24,600). Those of African descent are 40·8% of the population, Indians, 40·7%, mixed races, 16·3%, European, Chinese and others, 2·2%. English is spoken generally. Estimated population in 1988, 1·24m.

Vital statistics (rate per 1,000), 1983: Births, 29·2; deaths, 6·6; infant deaths, 12·6. Proportion of population under 15 years (1984) 39·2%.

Tobago is situated 30·7 km north-east of Trinidad. The main town is Scarborough.

CLIMATE. A tropical climate whose dry season runs from Jan. to June, with a wet season for the rest of the year. Temperatures are uniformly high the year round. Port-of-Spain. Jan. 78°F (25·6°C), July 79°F (26·1°C). Annual rainfall 65" (1,631 mm).

CONSTITUTION AND GOVERNMENT. The 1976 Constitution provides for a bicameral legislature of a *Senate* and a *House of Representatives*, who elect the *President*. The Senate consists of 31 members, 16 being appointed by the President on the advice of the Prime Minister, 6 on the advice of the Leader of the Opposition and 9 at the discretion of the President.

The House of Representatives consists of 36 (34 for Trinidad and 2 for Tobago) elected members and a Speaker elected from within or outside the House.

The Prime Minister is appointed by the President, and there is a Cabinet.

At the general election of Dec. 1991 the People's National Movement (PNR) won 45% of votes cast and 21 seats, the United National Congress won 13 seats and the National Alliance for Reconstruction, 2. In 1990 the United National Congress (founded in 1989) became the official Opposition.

President: Noor Mohammed Hassanali (re-elected Feb. 1992).

In Feb. 1992 the Cabinet comprised:
Prime Minister: Patrick Manning (b.1946; PNR)

Finance: Wendell Mottley. *Attorney General and Minister of Legal Affairs:* Keith Sobion. *Energy and Energy Industries:* Barry Barnes. *Trade, Industry and Tourism:* Brian Kuei Tung. *National Security:* Russel Huggins. *Local Government:* Kenneth Valley. *Foreign Affairs:* Ralph Maraj. *Sport and Youth Affairs:* Jean Pierre. *Consumer Affairs and Social Services:* Linda Baboolal. *Works and Transport:* Colm Imbert. *Education:* Augustus Ramrekersingh. *Health:* John Eckstein. *Planning and Development:* Dr Lenny Saith. *Public Utilities:* Morris Marshall. *Labour and Co-operatives:* Kenneth Collis. *Community Development, Culture and Women's Affairs:* Joan Yuille-Williams. *Agriculture, Lands and Marine Resources:* Keith Rowley. *Housing and Settlements:* Vincent Lasse. The *Speaker* is Occah Seapaul.
Leader of the Opposition: Basdeo Panday.

Local Government: Trinidad is divided into 3 municipalities, 8 counties and Tobago, which has a 15-member elected House of Assembly with limited powers of self-government. Elections due in Sept. 1990 were postponed for a year.

National flag: Red with a diagonal black strip edged in white.

DEFENCE. The Defence Force has a regular and a reserve infantry battalion and a support battalion equipped with 81mm mortars, and there is also a small air element, equipped with 1 Cessna 402 light transport. Personnel in 1991 totalled 2,650.

The Coast Guard operates 9 inshore patrol craft, the Police, 5. Of total defence personnel (1991), 600 were coastguard.

INTERNATIONAL RELATIONS

Membership. Trinidad and Tobago is a member of the UN, the Commonwealth, OAS, CARICOM and is an ACP state of the EEC.

ECONOMY

Budget. The 1989 budget envisaged current expenditure (in TT$) as 4,627·9m. and capital expenditure at 1,324·6m.

Currency. The unit of currency is the *Trinidad and Tobago dollar* (TTD) of 100 cents. There are coins of 1, 5, 10, 25 and 50 cents and TT$1, and banknotes of TT$1, 5, 10, 20 and 100. Foreign exchange reserves were TT$480·4m, in Dec. 1989. Inflation was 11·4% at the end of 1989. £1 = TT$7·45; US$1 = TT$4·25 (March 1992).

Banking and Finance. A Central Bank began operations in 1964. There are 8 commercial banks. Government savings banks are established in 69 offices, with a head office in Port-of-Spain. The stock exchange in Port-of-Spain participates in the regional Caribbean exchange.

ENERGY AND NATURAL RESOURCES

Electricity. In 1986, 3,182m. kwh was generated. Supply 115 and 230 volts; 60 Hz.

Oil. Oil production is one of Trinidad's leading industries and represented (1986) 71·6% of exports. Commercial production began in 1909; production of crude oil in 1991 was 7·64m. tonnes. Trinidad also possesses 2 refineries, with rated distillation capacity of 305,000 bbls annually; crude oil is imported from Venezuela, Indonesia, Ecuador, Nigeria, Brazil, and Saudi Arabia and refined in Trinidad. The 'Pitch Lake' is an important source of asphalt; production, 1986, 5,360,700 cu. metres.

Gas. In 1985 production was 7,413m. cu. ft., of which 1,601m. cu. ft. was flared and lost.

Agriculture. Sugar production in 1990 was 118,000 tonnes.
    Livestock (1990 in 1,000): Cattle, 80; sheep, 13; goats, 50; pigs, 70; poultry, 9,000.

Fisheries. The catch in 1986, 14,800 tonnes.

INDUSTRY. In 1985, 474,300 tonnes of iron and steel were produced. Other manufacturing includes ammonia (production, 1985, 1,323,500 tonnes), fertilizers (1986 production, 1,888,000 tonnes), cement (338,000 tonnes, 1986), rum (2,307,000 proof gallons, 1986), beer (20,716 litres, 1986), cigarettes (920,000 kg, 1986).

Labour. The working population in 1986 was 471,300. Unemployment in 1989 was 22%.

Trade Unions. About 30% of the labour force belong to unions.

FOREIGN ECONOMIC RELATIONS. The Foreign Investment Act of 1990 permits foreign investors to acquire land and shares in local companies, and to form companies.

Commerce. Exports in 1986 were TT$4,962·2m. of which TT$3,504·4m. was mineral fuels and products and chemicals, TT$766·8m. USA took 61·5% of exports. Imports totalled TT$4,902·8m. of which TT$1,792·9m. was for machinery and transport of which the USA supplied 41·8%.

Total trade of Trinidad and Tobago with UK (British Department of Trade returns, in £1,000 sterling):

	1987	1988	1989	1990	1991
Imports to UK	38,600	35,728	37,426	45,058	41,664
Exports and re-exports from UK	57,016	39,868	45,881	49,894	62,491

Tourism. There were 192,660 visitors in 1990.

COMMUNICATIONS

Roads. There were (1985) about 6,435 km of main and local roads. Motor vehicles registered in 1985 totalled 336,769, including 127,716 private cars, 26,392 hired and rented cars, and 33,846 goods vehicles.

Civil Aviation. There is an international airport at Piarco. The following airlines operate services: British West Indian Airways (BWIA), Air Canada, PANAM, KLM, Linea Aeropostal Venezolana, Leeward Islands Air Transport, Caribair, British Airways, American Airlines, Guyana Airways, ALM Antillean Airline, Cruzeiro (Brazil), Caribbean Airways and Viasa. A scheduled air services agreement was signed with the USA in 1990. BWIA fly to Cologne, Frankfurt, London, Stockholm and Zurich.

Shipping. In 1985 12·6m. tons of cargo were handled. A deep-water harbour at Scarborough (Tobago) was opened in 1991.

Telecommunications. International communications to all parts of the world are provided by Trinidad and Tobago External Telecommunications Co. Ltd (TEXTEL) by means of a satellite earth station and various high quality radio circuits. The marine radio service is also maintained by TEXTEL. Number of post offices (1984), 69; postal agencies, 166; number of telephones (1986), 182,325. Broadcasting is overseen by the Telecomunications Authority. As well as the National Broadcasting Service Radio 610, Radio Trinidad and Trinidad and Tobago Television, there are 4 independent TV channels and 7 radio, as well as community and cable services. There were 0·6m radio and 0·25m television receivers (colour by NTSC) in 1991.

Cinemas (1986). There were 57 cinemas and 3 drive-in cinemas.

Newspapers (1986). There were 4 daily newspapers with a total daily circulation (1984) of 166,380, 2 Sunday newspapers with a total circulation (1984) of 161,832, and 3 weekly newspapers.

JUSTICE, RELIGION, EDUCATION AND WELFARE

Justice. The High Court consists of the Chief Justice and 11 puisne judges. In criminal cases a judge of the High Court sits with a jury of 12 in cases of treason and murder, and with 9 jurors in other cases. The Court of Appeal consists of the

Chief Justice and 3 Justices of Appeal; there is a limited right of appeal from it to the Privy Council. There are 3 High Courts and 12 magistrates' courts. There is an *Ombudsman* (George Edoo).

Religion. In 1980, 15% of the population were Anglicans (under the Bishop of Trinidad and Tobago), 33·6% Roman Catholics (under the Archbishop of Port-of-Spain), 25% Hindus and 5·9% Moslems.

Education. In 1985–86 there were 172,424 pupils enrolled in primary schools, 12,622 in government secondary schools, 17,576 in assisted secondary schools, 39,188 in junior secondary schools, 21,614 in senior comprehensive schools, 3,564 in composite schools and 4,419 in technical and vocational schools. The University of the West Indies campus in St Augustine had 2,684 full- and part-time students in 1984–85.

Health. In 1985 there were 1,103 physicians, 129 dentists, 496 pharmacists and 31 hospitals and nursing homes with 4,087 beds. There were 3,344 nurses and mid-wives and 980 nursing assistants in government institutions.

DIPLOMATIC REPRESENTATIVES

Of Trinidad and Tobago in Great Britain (42 Belgrave Sq., London, SW1X 8NT)
High Commissioner: P. L. U. Cross.

Of Great Britain in Trinidad and Tobago (Furness Hse., 90 Independence Sq., Port-of-Spain)
High Commissioner: Brian Smith, OBE.

Of Trinidad and Tobago in the USA (1708 Massachusetts Ave., NW, Washington, D.C., 20036)
Ambassador: Angus Albert Khan.

Of the USA in Trinidad and Tobago (15 Queen's Park West, Port-of-Spain)
Ambassador: Charles A. Gargano.

Of Trinidad and Tobago to the United Nations
Ambassador: Dr Marjorie R. Thorpe.

Further Reading

Statistical Information: The Central Statistical Office, Government of Trinidad and Tobago, 2 Edward St., Port-of-Spain. *Director:* J. Harewood. Publications include *Annual Statistical Digest, Quarterly Economic Report, Annual Overseas Trade Report, Population and Vital Statistics Annual Report, Report on Education Statistics.*

Facts on Trinidad and Tobago. Ministry of Information, Port-of-Spain, 1983
Trinidad and Tobago Year Book. Port-of-Spain. Annual (from 1865)
Chambers, F., *Trinidad and Tobago.* [Bibliography] Oxford and Santa Barbara, 1986
Cooper, St G. C. and Bacon, P. R. (eds.) *The Natural Resources of Trinidad and Tobago.* London, 1981

Central Library: The Central Library of Trinidad and Tobago, Queen's Park East, Port-of-Spain.

TUNISIA

Capital: Tunis
Population: 8·18m. (1990)
GNP per capita: US$1,260 (1989)

Jumhuriya
at-Tunisiya

(Republic of Tunisia)

HISTORY. Tunisia was a French protectorate from 1883 and achieved independence on 20 March 1956. The Constituent Assembly, elected on 25 March 1956, abolished the monarchy (of the Bey of Tunis) on 25 July 1957 and proclaimed a republic.

AREA AND POPULATION. The boundaries are on the north and east the Mediterranean Sea, on the west Algeria and on the south Libya. The area is about 164,150 sq. km (63,378 sq. miles), including that portion of the Sahara which is to the east of the Djerid (salt marsh), extending towards Ghadamès.

At the census of 30 March 1984 there were 6,966,173 inhabitants (3,547,487 males and 3,419,026 females) of whom 52·8% were urban. Estimate (1990) 8·18m. (54·3% urban).

The census populations of the 23 *gouvernorats* were as follows as at 30 March 1984:

	Sq. km	1984		Sq. km	1984
Aryanah	1,558	374,192	Qasrayn (Kassérine)	8,066	297,959
Bajah (Béja)	3,558	274,706	Qayrawan (Kairouan)	6,712	421,607
Banzart (Bizerta)	3,685	394,670	Qibili (Kebili)	22,084	95,371
Bin Arus	761	246,193	Safaqis (Sfax)	7,545	577,992
Jundubah (Jendouba)	3,102	359,429	Sidi Bu Zayd		
Kaf (Le Kef)	4,965	247,672	(Sidi Bouzid)	6,994	288,528
Madaniyin (Médénine)	8,588	295,889	Silyanah (Siliana)	4,631	222,038
Mahdiyah (Mahdia)	2,966	270,435	Susah (Sousse)	2,621	322,491
Munastir (Monastir)	1,019	278,478	Tatawin (Tataouine)	38,889	100,329
Nabul (Nabeul)	2,788	461,405	Tawzar (Tozeur)	4,719	67,943
Qabis (Gabès)	7,175	240,016	Tunis	346	774,364
Qafsah (Gafsa)	8,990	235,723	Zaghwan (Zaghouan)	2,768	118,743

Tunis, the capital, had (census, 1984) 596,654 inhabitants: Sfax, 231,911; Aryanah, 98,655; Bizerta, 94,509; Djerba, 92,269; Gabès, 92,258; Sousse, 83,509; Kairouan, a holy city of the Moslems, 72,254; Bardo, 65,669; La Goulette, 61,609; Gafsa, 60,970; Béja, 46,708; Kasserine, 47,606; Nabeul, 39,531; Mahdia, 36,828; Monastir, 35,546; Le Kef, 34,509; Tataouine, 30,371; Medenine, 26,602; Jendouba, 23,249; Tozeur, 21,604; Sidi Bouzid, 19,218; Siliana, 12,433; Kébili, 11,780; Zaghouan, 10,149.

Vital statistics (1986). Birth rate, 31·7 per 1,000 population; death rate, 6·7 per 1,000.

The official language is Arabic but the use of French is widespread.

CLIMATE. The climate ranges from warm temperate in the north, where winters are mild and wet and the summers hot and dry, to desert in the south. Tunis. Jan. 48°F (8·9°C), July 78°F (25·6°C). Annual rainfall 16" (400 mm). Bizerta. Jan. 52°F (11·1°C), July 77°F (25°C). Annual rainfall 25" (622 mm). Sfax. Jan. 52°F (11·1°C), July 78°F (25·6°C). Annual rainfall 8" (196 mm).

CONSTITUTION AND GOVERNMENT. The Constitution was promulgated on 1 June 1959. The *President* and the *National Assembly* are elected simultaneously by direct universal suffrage for a period of 5 years. The President cannot be re-elected more than 3 times consecutively.

1287

Elections were held on 2 Nov. 1986, when all 125 seats in the Chamber of Deputies were won by the National Front, an alliance of the Constitutional Democratic Assembly (CDA) and the *Union générale des travailleurs tunisiens*. The elections were boycotted by opposition parties.

President of the Republic: Zine El Abidine Ben Ali (appointed 2 April 1989).

The Cabinet in Feb. 1992 included:

Prime Minister: Hamed Karoui.
Justice: Mustapha Bouaziz. *Foreign Affairs:* Habib Ben Yahia. *Secretary General of the Presidency:* Mohamed El Jeri. *Defence and Interior:* Dr Abdelaziz Ben Dhia. *Finance:* Mohamed Ghannouchi. *Planning and Regional Development:* Nabli Mustapha Kamel. *Agriculture:* Nouri Zorgati. *Equipment and Housing:* Ahmed Friaa. *Tourism and Handicrafts:* Mohamed Jegham. *Economy:* Sadok Rabah. *Education, Higher Education and Scientific Research:* Mohamed Charfi. *Public Health:* Daly Jazi. *Social Affairs:* Ahmed Smaoui. *Youth and Infancy:* Hamouda Ben Slama. *Culture:* Mongi Bousnina. *Infrastructure and Territorial Management:* Salah Jebali. *Secretary General of the Government:* Taoufik Cheikhrouhou.

The *Speaker* is Habib Boulares.

National Flag: Red with a white circle in the middle, on which is a 5-pointed red star encircled by a red crescent.

Local Government. The country is divided into 23 governorates, sub-divided into 199 districts and then into communes and imadas. At the elections of June 1990 there were 3,774 CDA candidates and 328 independents. Independents won seats on 12 out of 245 councils and gained control of 1. Turn-out was 79·37%. The 6 legal opposition parties boycotted the elections.

DEFENCE. Selective conscription is 1 year.

Army. The Army consists of 2 mechanized, 1 Sahara and 1 parachute commando brigades; 1 armoured reconnaissance, 3 field, 2 anti-aircraft, 1 anti-tank and 1 engineer regiments. Equipment includes 54 M-60A3 and 30 M-60A1 main battle tanks. Strength (1991) 27,000 (25,000 conscripts). There are also the paramilitary Public Order Brigade (3,500) and National Guard (10,000).

Navy. The Navy consists of 1 frigate (ex-US, vintage 1943), 3 1985-built fast missile craft and 3 older craft with short range missiles, 14 inshore patrol craft and 1 large tug. In 1991 naval personnel totalled 4,500 (700 conscripts). Forces are based at Bizerta, Sfax and Kelibia.

Air Force. Equipment of the Air Force, acquired from various Western sources, includes 1 squadron of Aermacchi M.B.326K/L jet light attack aircraft; 1 squadron of F-5E/F Tiger II fighters; 12 SF.260W piston-engined light trainer/attack aircraft; 2 C-130H Hercules transports, 2 S.208 liaison aircraft, 6 SF.260M trainers, 7 M.B.326B jet trainers, 6 UH-1H, 18 AB.205, 6 Ecureuil and about 12 Alouette II and III helicopters. Personnel (1991) about 3,500 (700 conscripts), with 40 combat aircraft.

INTERNATIONAL RELATIONS

Membership. Tunisia is a member of the UN, OAU, the Islamic Conference and the Arab League.

ECONOMY

Policy. A seventh development plan (1987–91) envisaged investment of 8,000m. dinars.

Budget (in dinars). Budget estimates, 1988, revenue, 3,287m.; expenditure, 3,148m.

Currency. The unit of currency is the *Tunisian dinar* (TND) of 1,000 *millimes*.
There are coins of 1, 2, 5, 10, 20, 50, 100 and 500 *millimes*, and notes of 500 *millimes*, 1 *dinar*, 5 and 10 *dinars*. £1 = 1·62 *dinar*; US$1 = 0·92 *dinar* (March 1992).

Banking and Finance. The Central Bank of Tunisia is the bank of issue. In 1988 there were 9 development banks, 10 deposit banks and 9 off-shore banks.

Weights and Measures. The metric system of weights and measures has almost entirely taken the place of those of Tunisia, but corn is still sold in *kaffis* and *wibas*. The *kfiz* (of 16 *wiba*, each of 12 *sa'*) = 16 bushels. The *ounce* = 31·487 grammes.

ENERGY AND NATURAL RESOURCES

Electricity. Electrical energy generated was 3,820m. kwh. in 1986. Supply 127 and 220 volts; 50 Hz.

Oil. Crude oil production (1991) 5·19m. tonnes.

Gas. Natural gas production (1984) 430m. cu. metres.

Water. In 1989 there were 15 dams (total capacity 945m. cu. metres) and 3 were being built (259m. cu. metres). In 1986, 257,000 ha were irrigated.

Minerals. Mineral production (in 1,000 tonnes) in 1987: Calcium phosphate, 6,200; iron ore, 291; lead ore (concentrated), 3·4; zinc ore (concentrated), 10·7; salt, 422; barytine, 18; spath fluor, 43.

Agriculture. There are 5 agricultural regions: The *north*, mountainous with large fertile valleys; the *north-east*, with the peninsula of Cap Bon, suited for the cultivation of oranges, lemons and tangerines; the *Sahel*, where olive trees abound; the *centre*, a region of high table lands and pastures, and the *desert* of the south, where dates are grown.

Some 40% of the population are employed in agriculture, which contributed 12·2% of GDP in 1989. Large estates predominate; smallholdings are tending to fragment, partly owing to inheritance laws. There were some 0·4m. farms in 1990 (0·32m. in 1960). Of the total area of 15,583,000 ha, about 9m. ha are productive, including 2m. under cereals, 3·6m. used as pasturage, 900,000 forests and 1·3m. uncultivated. The main crops are cereals and olive oil. Production, 1990 (in 1,000 tonnes): Wheat, 1122; barley, 477; olive oil, 170; olives, 330; dates, 130; almonds, 45; potatoes, 217; tomatoes, 460; pimentoes, 140; melons, including watermelons, 305; apples, 42; apricots, 20; oranges and cognates, 172; lemons and limes, 18; pears, 32; peaches and nectarines, 32; plums 7; chickpeas, 28; sugar-beet, 289; tobacco, 8. Wine (1988) 23,000 tonnes.

Other products are figs, pomegranates, shaddocks, pistachios, esparto grass, henna and cork.

Livestock (1990): Horses, 55,000; asses, 226,000; mules, 78,000; cattle, 570,000; sheep, 5·6m.; goats, 1,114,000; camels, 187,000; pigs, 4,000.

Fisheries. In 1980, 6,209 boats with 22,555 men were engaged in fishing. In 1987 the catch amounted to 99,180 tonnes.

INDUSTRY. Production, 1987 (in 1,000 tonnes): Superphosphate, 1,030; phosphoric acid, 593; cement, 3,215; lime, 527. 2,010 cars, 450 lorries, 1,240 vans, 220 buses and coaches, 330 tractors, 23,320 radio and 58,460 television sets were produced in 1987.

Trade Unions. The Union Générale des Travailleurs Tunisiens won 27 seats in the parliamentary elections (1 Nov. 1981). There are also the Union Tunisienne de l'Industrie, du Commerce et de l'Artisanat (UTICA, the employers' union) and the Union National des Agriculteurs (UNA, farmers' union).

FOREIGN ECONOMIC RELATIONS. In Feb. 1989 Tunisia signed a treaty of economic co-operation with the other countries of Maghreb: Algeria, Libya, Mauritania and Morocco.

Commerce. The imports and exports for calendar years (in 1,000 dinars) were as follows:

	1982	1983	1984	1985	1986	1987
Imports	2,008,000	2,116,100	2,472,500	2,287,000	2,308,300	2,509,000
Exports	1,188,000	1,263,900	1,396,800	1,443,000	1,387,600	1,770,600

Exports to France in 1987 totalled 384·1m. dinars, and imports from France, 687·2m. dinars and exports to USA were valued at 32·1m. dinars and imports from USA were valued at 149·1m. dinars.

In 1987 the main exports (in 1m. dinars) were: Clothing, 354·5; hosiery, 90·3; phosphoric acid, 69·8; electric machines, 66·8; fish and molluscs, 66·7; olive oil, 65·6.

Total trade between Tunisia and UK (British Department of Trade returns, in £1,000 sterling):

	1987	1988	1989	1990	1991
Imports to UK	14,714	36,062	43,266	40,959	25,613
Exports and re-exports from UK	24,943	30,780	31,148	40,800	43,651

Tourism. Tourism is important. In 1991 there were 3·2m. visitors spending US$680m.

COMMUNICATIONS

Roads. In 1987 there were 18,952 km of roads. Number of motor vehicles, 1987, 506,000.

Railways. In 1990 there were 2,260 km of railways (492 km of 1,435 mm gauge and 1,758 km of metre-gauge), of which 24 km were electrified. 28·6m. passengers and 9·9m. tonnes of freight were carried in 1990. There is a light rail network in Tunis (52 km).

Civil Aviation. The national airline is Tunis-Air. In 1990 the 5 countries of the Maghreb decided to merge their airlines into Air Maghreb. There are 5 international airports, the main one at Tunis-Carthage. In 1987, 4,429,000 passengers and 21,688 tonnes of freight were carried.

Shipping. The main port is Tunis, and its outer port is Tunis-Goulette. These two ports and Sfax, Sousse and Bizerta are directly accessible to ocean-going vessels. The ports of La Skhirra and Gabès are used for the shipping of Algerian and Tunisian oil.

In 1983, 5,370 ships of 19,224,000 tons entered Tunisian ports.

Telecommunications. There were, in 1983, 218,808 telephones. The government-controlled Radiodiffusion-Télévision Tunisienne provides broadcasting. There is a national radio programme, an international programme and 2 regional programmes. There are Arabic and French TV networks (colour by SECAM). In 1991 there were 1,693,527 radio and 0·65m. TV sets.

Cinemas (1987). There were 80 cinemas.

Newspapers. There were (1987) 2 Arabic and 4 French daily newspapers.

JUSTICE, RELIGION, EDUCATION AND WELFARE

Justice. There are 51 magistrates' courts, 13 courts of first instance, 3 courts of appeal (in Tunis, Sfax and Sousse) and the High Court in Tunis.

A Personal Status Code was promulgated on 13 Aug. 1956 and applied to Tunisians from 1 Jan. 1957. This raised the status of women, made divorce subject to a court decision, abolished polygamy and decreed a minimum marriage age.

Religion. The constitution recognizes Islam as the state religion. There are about 20,000 Roman Catholics, under the Prelate of Tunis. The Greek Church, the French Protestants and the English Church are also represented.

Education. All education was in 1956 made dependent on the Ministry of National Education. The 208 independent koranic schools have been nationalized and the distinction between religious and public schools has been abolished. All education is free from primary schools to university. A teachers' training college (*école normale supérieure*) was established in 1955. There are also a high school of law, 2 centres of economic studies, 2 schools of engineering, 2 medical schools, a faculty of agriculture, 2 institutes of business administration and one school of dentistry.

In 1987–88 there were 3,605 primary schools with 43,189 teachers and 1,338,905 pupils; 436 secondary schools with 22,373 teachers and 437,604 pupils. In 1980–81 there were 60,137 students at technical and vocational schools and 4,101 students in teacher-training. In 1988 there were 3 universities: The University of Tunis (38,829 students and 5,019 teaching staff in 1984–85), the University of Sousse and the University of Sfax.

Health. In 1987 there were 36 general hospitals (22 university and 14 regional), 20 specialized institutions, centres and university hospitals, and (1988) 92 district hospitals. In 1986 there were 15,814 beds.

Social Security. A system of social security was set up in 1950 (amended 1963, 1964 and 1970).

DIPLOMATIC REPRESENTATIVES

Of Tunisia in Great Britain (29 Prince's Gate, London, SW7 1QG)
Ambassador: Dr Abdelaziz Hamzaoui.

Of Great Britain in Tunisia (5 Place de la Victoire, Tunis)
Ambassador and Consul-General: S. P. Day, CMG.

Of Tunisia in the USA (1515 Massachusetts Ave., NW, Washington, D.C., 20005)
Ambassador: Ismail Khelil.

Of the USA in Tunisia (144 Ave. de la Liberté, Tunis)
Ambassador: Robert H. Pelletreau, Jr.

Of Tunisia to the United Nations
Ambassador: Ahmed Ghezal.

Further Reading

Statistical Information: Institut National de la Statistique (27 Rue de Liban, Tunis) was set up in 1947. Its main publications are: *Annuaire statistique de la Tunisie* (latest issue, 1975).
Lawless R. I. *et al.*, *Tunisia.* [Bibliography] Oxford and Santa Barbara, 1982
Ling, D. L., *Tunisia: From Protectorate to Republic.* Indiana Univ. Press, 1967
Salem, N., *Habib Bourguiba, Islam and the Creation of Tunisia.* London, 1984

TURKEY

Türkiye Çumhuriyeti

(Republic of Turkey)

Capital: Ankara
Population: 56·47m. (1990)
GNP per capita: US$2,667 (1990)

HISTORY. Turkey became a republic on 29 Oct. 1923. (For the transition from the Ottoman Empire *see* THE STATESMAN'S YEAR-BOOK, 1991-92, p. 1210). Religious courts were abolished in 1924, Islam ceased to be the official state religion in 1928, women were given the franchise and western-style surnames were adopted in 1934.

On 27 May 1960 the Army overthrew the government. A new constitution was approved in a referendum held on 9 July 1961 and general elections were held. On 12 Sept. 1980, the Army again overthrew the government. The Constituent Assembly was convened in Oct. 1981, and prepared a new Constitution which was enforced after a national referendum on 7 Nov. 1982.

AREA AND POPULATION. Turkey is bounded west by the Aegean Sea and by Greece, north by Bulgaria and the Black Sea, east by Georgia and Armenia and Iran, and south by Iraq, Syria and the Mediterranean.

The area (including lakes) is 779,452 sq. km (300,947 sq. miles). Area in Europe (Thrace), 23,764 sq. km. Area in Asia (Anatolia), 755,688 sq. km.

Some 12m. Kurds live in Turkey. Limited use of the Kurdish language (not in schools or publications) was sanctioned in Feb. 1991.

The census population is given as follows:

	Total		Total		Total
1927	13,648,270	1955	24,064,763	1975	40,347,719
1935	16,158,018	1960	27,754,820	1980	44,736,957
1945	18,790,174	1965	31,391,421	1985	50,664,458
1950	20,947,188	1970	35,605,176	1990	56,473,035

Vital statistics, 1989: Marriages, 460,763; divorces, 25,376; deaths, 150,475. Expectation of life was 65 years in 1990.

The area, population and population density of the provinces at the census of 1990:

	Area in sq.km.	Population	Density per sq.km.
Adana	17,562	1,934,907	111
Adiyaman	7,423	513,131	70
Afyonkarahisar	14,295	739,223	52
Ağri	11,066	437,093	40
Aksaray	7,626	326,399	43
Amasya	5,452	357,191	66
Ankara	25,614	3,236,626	126
Antalya	20,815	1,132,211	55
Artvin	7,436	212,833	29
Aydin	7,870	824,816	105
Balikesir	14,456	973,314	68
Batman	4,694	344,669	74
Bayburt	3,652	107,330	30
Bilecik	4,321	175,526	40
Bingöl	8,319	250,966	30
Bitlis	8,010	330,115	41
Bolu	10,575	536,869	51
Burdur	7,167	254,899	36
Bursa	10,990	1,603,137	146
Çanakkale	9,950	432,263	44
Çankırı	8,659	279,129	33
Çorum	12,729	609,863	49

	Area in sq.km.	Population	Density per sq.km.
Denizli	11,874	750,882	64
Diyarbakir	14,908	1,094,996	73
Edirne	6,174	404,599	65
Elazığ	9,455	498,225	53
Erzincan	11,413	299,251	27
Erzurum	25,133	848,201	34
Eskişehir	13,477	641,057	48
Gaziantep	8,015	1,140,594	153
Giresun	6,965	499,087	75
Gümüşhane	6,748	169,375	25
Hakkâri	7,121	172,479	25
Hatay	5,570	1,109,754	204
Isparta	8,847	434,771	49
İçel	15.448	1,266,995	82
İstanbul	5,591	7,309,190	1,330
İzmir	12,263	2,694,770	220
Karaman	9,163	217,536	24
Kars	18,841	662,155	35
Kastamonu	12,982	423,611	33
Kayseri	16,537	943,484	57
Kırıkkale	4,365	349,396	84
Kırklareli	6,378	309,512	49
Kirşehir	6,501	256,862	40
Kocaeli	3,578	936,163	260
Konya	40,451	1,750,303	43
Kütahya	11,661	578,020	51
Malafya	11,752	702,055	57
Manisa	13,237	1,154,418	87
K. Maraş	14,680	892,952	61
Mardin	8,594	557,727	65
Muğla	12,504	562,809	45
Muş	8,413	376,543	45
Nevşehir	5,540	289,509	52
Niğde	7,831	305,861	39
Ordu	6,142	830,105	137
Rize	3,920	348,776	91
Sakarya	4,821	683,061	140
Samsun	9,739	1,158,400	120
Siirt	6,176	243,435	40
Sinop	5,657	265,153	48
Şirnak	7,172	262,006	40
Sivas	28,568	767,481	28
Tekirdağ	6,333	468,842	74
Tokat	9,869	719,251	73
Trabzon	4,498	795,849	180
Tunceli	7,954	133,143	17
Urfa	19,271	1,001,455	52
Uşak	5,389	290,283	54
Van	21,095	637,433	30
Yozgat	13,597	579,150	43
Zonguldak	8,560	1,073,560	126

65% of the population was urban in 1990. (Istanbul, 8m.).

The population of towns of over 100,000 inhabitants, at the census of Oct. 1985, was as follows:

İstanbul	6,620,241	Diyarbakir	381,144	Denizli	204,118
Ankara	2,559,471	Antalya	378,208	Kırıkkale	185,431
Izmir	1,757,414	Samsun	303,979	Adapazari	171,225
Adana	916,150	Malatya	281,776	Balikesir	170,589
Bursa	834,576	Sanliurfa	276,528	Manisa	158,928
Gaziantep	603,434	Izmit	256,882	Van	153,111
Konya	513,346	Erzurum	242,391	Batman	147,347
Mersin	422,357	K. Maraş	228,129	Trabzon	143,941
Kayseri	421,362	Sivas	221,512	Kütahya	130,944
Eskişehir	413,082	Elazığ	204,603	Antakya	123,871

Çorum	116,810	Aydin	107,011	Ordu	102,107
Zonguldak	116,725	Usak	105,270	Adiyaman	100,045
Isparta	112,117	Edirne	102,345		

CLIMATE. Coastal regions have a Mediterranean climate, with mild, moist winters and hot, dry summers. The interior plateau has more extreme conditions, with low and irregular rainfall, cold and snowy winters and hot, almost rainless summers. Ankara. Jan. 32·5°F (0·3°C), July 73°F (23°C). Annual rainfall 14·7" (367 mm). Istanbul. Jan. 41°F (5°C), July 73°F (23°C). Annual rainfall 28·9" (723 mm). Izmir. Jan. 46°F (8°C), July 81°F (27°C). Annual rainfall 28" (700 mm).

CONSTITUTION AND GOVERNMENT. The Turkish Grand National Assembly was dissolved on 12 Sept. 1980. The National Security Council took over its functions and powers. On 23 Oct. 1981 a Consultative Assembly was inaugurated, to prepare a new Constitution to replace that of 1961. The Assembly began its work in Oct. 1981 under the presidency of Sadi Irmak and on 7 Nov. 1982 a national referendum established that 98% of the electorate were in favour of the new Constitution. The Presidency is not an executive position, and the President may not be linked to a political party.

Turkish men and women are entitled to vote at the age of 21 to elect members of a single-chamber parliament.

Elections were held in Oct. 1991. Of the 450 seats in the Grand National Assembly True Path Party (TPP) gained 178 with 27% of votes cast (59 with 19·1% in 1987); the Motherland Party 115 with 24% (292 with 36·2%); the Social Democratic Populist Party (SDPP) 88 with 20·8% (99 with 24·7%); the Prosperity Party 62 with 16·9% (nil with 7·1%); and the Democratic Left 7 with 10·8% (nil with 8·5%).

President: Turgut Özal.

The Cabinet in Feb. 1992 was composed as follows:

Prime Minister: Suleyman Demirel (b. 1924; TPP).

Deputy Prime Minister: Professor Erdal Inönu (SDPP). *Justice:* Mehmet Seyfi Oktay (SDPP). *Defence:* Nevzat Ayaz (TPP). *Interior:* Izmet Sezgin (TPP). *Foreign Affairs:* Hikmet Cetin (SDPP). *Customs and Finance:* Sumer Oral (TPP). *Education:* Koksal Toptan (TPP). *Public Works and Housing:* Professor Onur Kumbaracibasi (SDPP). *Health:* Dr Yildrim Aktuna (TPP). *Communications:* Yasar Topcu (TPP). *Labour and Social Security:* Mehmet Mogultay (SDPP). *Industry and Commerce:* Tahir Kose (SDPP). *Energy and Natural Resources:* Ersin Faralyali (TPP). *Tourism:* Abdulkadir Ares (SDPP). *Culture:* Fikri Saglar (SDPP). *Forestry:* Yefa Tanir (TPP). *Environment:* Dogancan Akyurek (TPP).

There are 14 Ministers of State.

National flag: A white crescent and star on red.

National anthem: Korkma! Sönmez bu şafaklarda yüzen al sancak ('Be not afraid! Our flag will never fade' words by Mehmed Akif Ersoy; tune by Zeki Güngör; adopted 12 March 1921).

Local Government. The Constitution of 1921 provided for the administrative division of the country into *Il*, (province, now 73 in number), divided into *Ilçe* (district), subdivided in their turn into *Bucak* (township or commune). At the head of each *Il* is a *Vali* representing the Government. Each *Il* has its own elective council.

The district is regarded as a mere grouping of townships or communes for certain purposes of general administration. The township or commune is an autonomous entity and possesses an elective council charged with the administration of such matters as are not reserved to the State.

At local elections in June 1990 the Motherland Party won 31 of the 51 districts contested, the Social Democratic Populist Party, 11, and the True Path Party, 5.

DEFENCE. There is a Supreme Council of National Security, under the chairmanship of the Prime Minister, which co-ordinates the resources in case of war. Besides the Minister of National Defence and the Chief of the General Staff, the heads of economic Ministries are members of this council.

Conscription in the Army, Air Force and Navy is 18 months at the age of 20.

Army. The Army consists of 13 infantry, and 1 mechanized and 2 training divisions, 10 infantry, 7 armoured, 6 mechanized, 1 parachute and 2 commando brigades; 5 coastal defence battalions. Equipment includes 1,130 M-48A5, 523 M-47, 1,980 M48A5 T1/T2 and 291 Leopard main battle tanks. Army Aviation has 163 aircraft and 273 helicopters. Strength (1992) 470,000 (427,000 conscripts), and reserves number 950,000. There is also a paramilitary gendarmerie cum national guard of 70,000 with its own fleet of over 50 transport and observation helicopters.

Navy. Current strength includes 15 diesel submarines (6 of German design built 1975-89 and 9 ex-US built 1944-45, 12 ex-US destroyers (1943-46), 10 frigates of which 4 are modern German MEKO-type, 4 ex-German Type 120 Köln class, and 2 locally built in the 1970s. Light forces comprise 16 fast missile craft, 2 fast torpedo craft, 7 coastal and 21 inshore patrol craft. Mine warfare forces include 10 minelayers and 22 coastal and 12 inshore minesweepers. Amphibious lift is provided by 2 tank landing ships and 36 landing craft. Major auxiliaries in service are 1 replenishment and 6 support tankers, 3 depot ships, 3 salvage/rescue ships, 2 survey ships and 1 training ship. Minor auxiliaries, coastal freighters and service craft number about 120.

The main naval base is at Gölcük in the Gulf of İzmit. There are others at İskenderun, Aksaz Karaağaç and İzmir. There are 3 naval shipyards: Gölcük, Taşkizak and İzmir.

The naval air component operates 23 S-2 mixed Air Force and Naval-manned Tracker anti-submarine aircraft and 15 helicopters for anti-submarine and patrol duties. There is a Marine Brigade some 4,000 strong.

Personnel in 1991 totalled 58,930 (42,961 conscripts) including marines.

The separate Coast Guard numbers about 1,000 and performs coastal police duties with a force of 28 inshore patrol vessels, 4 transports and numerous boats.

Air Force. The Air Force is under the control of the General Staff and, operationally, under 6 ATAF. It is organized as 2 tactical air forces, with headquarters at Eskisehir and Diyarbakir, each having a flight of C-47s, UH-1H helicopters, T-33s. Combat aircraft comprise F-104G and F-104S Starfighters in 6 squadrons; F-5As in 3 squadrons; F-16A/Bs in 4 squadrons; RF-5As in 1 squadron; F-4E and RF-4E Phantoms in 7 squadrons; plus Nike-Hercules surface-to-air missile batteries. The 4 transport squadrons are equipped with Transall C-160, C-130 Hercules, Citation, Viscount and C-47 aircraft, and UH-IH helicopters. Training types include T-33A, T-37 and T-38 advanced trainers, T-34 and SF.260 basic and T-41 primary trainers. Delivery of 160 F-16 Fighting Falcons began late in 1987 and an order for 80 more was approved in 1991. Personnel strength (1991), 59,907 (31,800 conscripts), with 478 combat aircraft.

INTERNATIONAL RELATIONS

Membership. Turkey is a member of the UN, OECD, NATO and Council of Europe and an Associate of the EEC.

ECONOMY

Policy. The development plan for 1985–90 envisaged an investment of TL14,412,900m. Privatization of state enterprises is in train and is co-ordinated by the Public Participation Fund.

Budget. The budget for 1992–93 envisaged expenditure of TL207,000,000m. and revenue of TL176,000,000m.

Currency. The unit of currency is the *Turkish lira* (TRL) of 100 *kuruş*. There are coins of TL5, 10, 25, 50, 100 and 500 and notes of TL1,000, 5,000, 10,000, 20,000, 50,000 and 100,000. In March 1992, US$1 = TL5,878; £1 = TL10,318. The lira is fully convertible. TL6,840,600m. were in circulation in 1989. Annualized inflation was 66% in 1991.

Banking and Finance. The Turkish banking system is composed of the Central Bank (Merkez Bankası; *Governor*, Rüsdu Saracoğlu) and 64 other banks. The Central Bank's assets were TL28,327,000m. at the end of 1989. The assets and liabilities of deposit money banks in 1989 were TL97·76m.

There is a stock exchange in Istanbul. There were 40 insurance companies in 1989 (13 foreign).

Weights and Measures. The metric system is in use. The Gregorian calendar has been in exclusive use since 26 Dec. 1925.

ENERGY AND NATURAL RESOURCES

Electricity. In 1989 installed capacity was 15,805·7 mw (6,597·3 mw hydroelectric). Production was 52,601·7m. kwh. Supply 220 volts; 50 Hz.

Oil and Gas. Oil is being produced in Garzan and Raman by the Turkish Petroleum Co. Under the oil law of 14 Oct. 1954 private companies can explore and produce oil. Crude oil production (1991) was 4·9m. tonnes. Total refining capacity is 24m. tonnes a year. 90·19m. cu. metres of coal gas and 684,337 tonnes of liquefied natural gas were produced in 1989.

Minerals. Turkey is rich in minerals, and is a major producer of chrome.

Production of principal minerals (in 1,000 tonnes) was:

	1986	1987	1988	1989
Coal	7,015	7,084	6,688	6,259
Lignite	45,470	46,481	39,025	52,567
Chrome	1,040	1,049	1,157	1,598
Copper concentrate	119	137	168	167
Refined sulphur	40	39	30	23
Iron	5,249	5,366	5,481	4,518
Boron	1,636	1,629	2,044	1,979

Of the Government organizations producing these ores, Zonguldak coal mines operate under the Turkish State Coal Exploitation; while the copper mines at Murgul and Ergani, the Eastern chromite mines, Keçiborlu sulphur, Emet colemanite, Küre pyrite and cupriferous pyrite, Keban argentiferous lead mines operate under the Etibank.

Agriculture. The number of people aged 12 and over engaged in agriculture and animal husbandry (including hunting) in 1985 was 12,037,883.

In 1990 there were some 29m. ha of agricultural land and 3m. smallholdings, about 70% of which being 1·5 ha. Holdings are increasingly fragmented by the custom of dividing land equally amongst sons. There are government price supports to cereal growers. In 1990, 28·01m. ha were crop land, 19,022,000 ha of it sown and 5,324,000 ha fallow; vineyards, fruit orchards and olive groves occupied 3,029,000 ha; forest occupied 20,199,000 ha.

The soil for the most part is very fertile; the principal products are cotton, tobacco, cereals (especially wheat), figs, silk, dried fruits, liquorice root, nuts, almonds, mohair, skins and hides, furs, wool, gums, canary seed, linseed and sesame. The South-Eastern Anatolian Irrigation Project (GAP) is expected to produce 1·6m. ha of fertile land. The production of olives for olive oil was estimated at 0·6m. tonnes in 1990 (1·1m. tonnes in 1988). Sugar production (refined) in 1990 was 1,579,078 tonnes. Agricultural production (in tonnes) in 1990 included 3·5m. grapes, 735,000 oranges and 357,000 lemons, 375,000 hazelnuts, 1·9m. apples, 6m. tomatoes, tea (fresh leaves) 608,440.

Turkey produced 408 tonnes of flax fibre, 6,000 tonnes of hemp fibre and 617,000 tonnes of cotton lint in 1990. Agricultural tractors numbered 672,845 in 1989.

Production (in 1,000 tonnes) of principal crops:

	1986	1987	1988	1989	1990
Wheat	19,000	18,900	20,500	16,200	20,000
Barley	7,000	6,900	7,500	4,500	7,300
Maize	2,300	2,400	2,000	2,000	2,100
Rye	350	380	280	191	240
Tobacco	158	185	219	270	288
Oats	300	325	276	216	270
Rice	165	165	158	198	138

Estimated production in 1990 (in tonnes): Sultanas, 0·13m.; sunflower seeds, 0·86m.; soya beans, 0·2m.; pistachios, 14,000; hazelnut, 0·38m.; cotton, 0·61m.; wheat, 14m.; barley, 6m.; tobacco, 0·21m.

Livestock (1989): 43,647,000 sheep, 11,952,000 goats, 12,173,000 cattle, 1,084,000 asses, 545,000 horses, 429,000 buffaloes.

In 1988 Turkey produced 66,940 tonnes of wool and in 1989, 214,720 tonnes of cattle meat and 119,110 tonnes of sheep meat.

Forestry. In 1989 total forest land was 20,199,000 ha, 26% of the land area. Produce (1,000 cu. metres) in 1989: Logs, 3,393; pit props, 518; industrial wood, 398; poles, 60; firewood, 5·23m. tonnes.

Fisheries. Catch (1989): Sea fish, 361,770 tonnes; crustaceans and molluscs, 48,159 tonnes; fresh water fish, 42,833 tonnes. Aquaculture production, 1989, 4,354 tonnes (mainly carp and trout). There were (1989) 8,488 fishing boats.

INDUSTRY. In 1990 55 state enterprises accounted for about 30% of production. Production in 1989 (in 1,000 tonnes): 8,007 of fuel oil; 6,170 of motor oil; 3,523 of crude iron; 407 of pig iron; 7,854 of crude steel; 2,796 of super phosphate; 3,035 of coke; 23,800 of cement and 353 of selected paper products. In 1989, 118,095 passenger cars were produced and 19,602 tractors.

Labour. Economically active population aged 12 and over, 1990, 38,596,861 of whom 9,532,408 were engaged in agriculture, forestry, hunting and fishing, 2,430,082 in manufacturing, 2,041,360 in trade, restaurants and hotels and 2,659,713 in services. 1,513,654 were employed part-time, 1,778,123 were unemployed (8·42%) in 1989.

Trade Unions. The trade-union movement began in 1947. There are 4 national confederations (including Türk-Iş and Disk) and 6 federations. There are 35 unions affiliated to Türk-Iş and 17 employers' federations affiliated to Disk, whose activities were banned on 12 Sept. 1980. In 1988, labour unions totalled 80 and employers' unions, 49. Some 2·2m. workers belonged to unions in 1990. Membership is forbidden to civil servants (including schoolteachers).

FOREIGN ECONOMIC RELATIONS. Foreign debt in 1990 was US$41,000m. Direct foreign investment in 1989 was US$663m.

Commerce. Imports and exports (in US$1m.) for calendar years:

	1986	1987	1988	1989	1990
Imports	11,105	14,158	14,335	15,792	22,302
Exports	7,457	10,190	11,662	11,625	12,959

Exports (1990) in US$1m.: Textiles, 4,336; iron and steel products, 1,609; chemical products, 618; leather clothing, 639; plastic material and rubber, 250; hazelnuts, 456; machinery, 204; petroleum products, 264; processed agricultural products, 937; mining and quarrying products, 326; tobacco, 418.

Imports (1990) in US$1m.: Machinery, 3,756; chemical products, 2,451; iron and steel products, 1,932; electrical equipment, 1,580; transport equipment, 1,590; plastic material and rubber, 807; mining and quarrying products, 3,989; processed agricultural products, 1,162; crude oil, 3,495.

In 1990 imports (in US$1m.) were: From Federal Republic of Germany, 3,497; USA, 2,282; Iraq, 1,047; Italy, 1,727; France, 1,340; UK, 1,014; Japan, 1,120; Belgium, 523; USSR, 1,247; Iran, 492. Exports: Federal Republic of Germany, 3,064; Iraq, 215; Italy, 1,106; USA, 968; UK, 745; Iran, 495; France, 737; Saudi Arabia, 338; Netherlands, 435; USSR, 531.

Total trade between Turkey and UK (British Department of Trade returns, in £1,000 sterling):

	1987	1988	1989	1990	1991
Imports to UK	579,366	509,636	533,769	550,803	402,770
Exports and re-exports from UK	513,479	477,539	434,562	606,829	729,988

Tourism. The number of foreign visitors was 4,516,077m. in 1989, including 3,921,967 tourists. Earnings from tourism in 1989, US$2,556m. 2·59m. Turks travelled abroad in 1989, including 0·49m. tourists. There were 150,159 tourist beds in 1990.

COMMUNICATIONS

Roads. In 1990 there were 31,149 km of state highways (including 125 km of motorway) and 27,979 km of provincial roads; 56,400 km were surfaced. In 1990 there were 1,649,879 cars, 520,760 lorries and pick-ups, 193,099 buses and mini-buses and 531,941 motorcycles. There wre 104,181 road accidents in 1989, with 6,355 fatalities.

Railways. Total length of railway lines in 1990 was 8,429 km (1,435 mm gauge) of which 582 km were electrified; 139m. passengers and 13·4m. tonnes of freight were carried.

Civil Aviation. In 1990 the Turkish Airlines fleet of 33 planes flew 4,137,532 passengers (1,546,753 on international flights) and carried 396,748 tonnes (167,113) of freight.

Shipping. In 1990 the GRT of cargo ships totalled 2,568,358; passenger ships, 203,216 and tankers, 898,298. The main ports are: Istanbul, Izmir, Samsun, Mersin, Iskenderun and Trabzon.

Coastal shipping, 1990: 25,242 vessels handled; 598,462 passengers entered, and 552,343 cleared; 20·8m. tonnes of goods entered, 17·1m. cleared. International shipping: 13,337 vessels handled; 510,117 passengers entered, 517,411 cleared; 55·1m. tonnes of goods entered, 63·3m. cleared.

Telecommunications. Number of telephones in 1990 was 6·89m.; Istanbul, 1,698,374; Ankara, 713,452.

Turkish Radio-Television Corporation broadcasts radio and TV programmes (colour by PAL). There were 7·5m. radio and 13m. TV sets registered in 1990.

Newspapers and Books. In 1989, there were 54 dailies and 2,733 periodicals. 5,870 book titles were published in 1989. There were 771 public libraries serving a population of 16·81m.

JUSTICE, RELIGION, EDUCATION AND WELFARE

Justice. The unified legal system consists of: (1) justices of the peace (single judges with limited but summary penal and civil jurisdiction); (2) courts of first instance (single judges, dealing with cases outside the jurisdiction of (3) and (4)); (3) central criminal courts (a president and 2 judges, dealing with cases where the crime is punishable by imprisonment over 5 years); (4) commercial courts (3 judges); (5) state security courts, to prosecute offences against the integrity of the state (a president and 4 judges, 2 of the latter being military).

The civil and military Courts of Cassation sit at Ankara.

The Council of State is the highest administration tribunal; it consists of 5 chambers. Its 31 judges are nominated from among high-ranking personalities in politics, economy, law, the army, etc.

The Military Court of Cassation in Ankara is the highest military tribunal. The Military Administrative Court deals with the judicial control of administrative acts and deeds concerning military personnel.

The Constitutional Court, set up under the Constitution, can review and annul legislation and try the President of the Republic, Ministers and senior judges. It consists of 15 regular and 5 alternate members.

The Civil Code and the Code of Obligations have been adapted from the corresponding Swiss codes. The Penal Code is largely based upon the Italian Penal Code, and the Code of Civil Procedure closely resembles that of the Canton of Neuchâtel. The Commercial Code is based on the German.

Religion. The Turkish Republic is a secular state and freedom of religion is guaranteed by the Constitution. A law of 1934 forbids the wearing of clerical garb for those other than religious leaders except in places of worship and during divine service. The constitution forbids the political exploitation of religion or any impairment of the secular character of the republic.

In 1989 there were 38·1m. Sunni Moslems and some 17m. Shi'ites (Alevis). The administration of the Moslem religious organizations is in charge of the Presidency of Religious Affairs, attached to the Prime Minister's office.

Istanbul is the seat of the Ecumenical Patriarch, who is the head of the Orthodox Church in Turkey. The Armenian Church (Gregorian) is ruled by a Patriarch in Istanbul who is subordinate to the Katholikos of Etchmiadzin, the spiritual head of all Armenians. The Armenian Apostolic Church is ruled by the Patriarch of Cilicia. The Chaldeans (Nestorian Uniats) have a Bishop at Mardin. The Syrian Uniats have a See of Mardin and Amida, but it is united with their Patriarchate of Antioch (residence, Damascus). Greek Uniats (Byzantine Rite) have as their Ordinary in Istanbul, the Titular Bishop of Gratianopolis. Roman Catholics have a Nuncio in Ankara and a Bishop in Istanbul. There are Protestant chapels in Istanbul. There is a Grand Rabbi (Hahambaşi) in Istanbul for the Jews, who are nearly all Sephardim.

Education. Elementary education is compulsory and co-educational and, in state schools, free. All children from 6 to 14 are to receive primary instruction, which may be given in state schools, schools maintained by communities, or private schools, or, subject to certain tests, at home. Private schools are subject to the supervision of the Ministry of Education. The state schools are under the direct control of the Ministry of Education. They include primary schools, secondary or middle schools, and *lycées*. There are also teacher training schools and technical schools. The important non-Moslem communities in Istanbul maintain their own schools.

Literacy of the population of 6 years and over was 77·3% in 1985. In 1990–91 78% of school-age children attended school.

Religious instruction in state schools having been first prohibited and then made optional is now compulsory. In 1991 there were 5,197 Koran schools with 0·29m. pupils up to 14 years.

Statistics for 1989–90	Number	Teachers	Students
Primary schools (state and private)	51,170	224,672	6,848,083
Secondary schools (state and private)	5,558	45,774	2,038,537
High schools (state and private)	1,627	63,946	751,729
Vocational and technical secondary schools	804	284	253,435
Vocational and technical high schools	1,738	49,220	577,281
Universities (faculties and higher education)	387	32,029	644,835

In 1989–90 there were 29 universities with 28,856 teaching staff and 560,446 students.

Social Security. In 1989 814,114 beneficiaries (including 327,581 widows and 462,001 retired persons) received TL2,158,530m. from the Government Employees Retirement Fund; 1,478,176 beneficiaries (incuding 226,194 widows and 893,552 retired persons) received TL 5,406,218m. from the Social Insurance Institution; and 539,743 beneficiaries (including 226,230 widows and 305,089 age pensioners) received TL402,388m. from the Independent Insurance System.

Health. A law of 1963 provided for the nationalization of the health services within 15 years.

In 1989 there were 46,708 doctors, 10,132 dentists, 15,201 pharmacists and 43,374 nurses, and 116,061 beds in 693 hospitals and 119 health centres.

DIPLOMATIC REPRESENTATIVES

Of Turkey in Great Britain (43 Belgrave Sq., London, SW1X 8PA)
Ambassador: Candemir Önhon.

Of Great Britain in Turkey (Sehit Ersan Caddesi 46/A, Cankaya, Ankara)
Ambassador: Sir Timothy Daunt, KCMG.

Of Turkey in the USA (1606 23rd St., NW, Washington, D.C., 20008)
Ambassador: Nüzhet Kandemir.

Of the USA in Turkey (110 Ataturk Blvd., Ankara)
Ambassador: Richard C. Barkley.

Of Turkey to the United Nations
Ambassador: Mustafa Akşin.

Further Reading

Statistical Information: The State Institute of Statistics in Ankara consists of a research bureau and 10 sections dealing with agriculture, education, foreign trade, etc. It published an *Annuaire Statistique/Istatistik Yiliği* (1928–53) and *Aylık Istatistik Bülteni*, Monthly Bulletin of Statistics.

The Turkish Constitution, 1971. Ankara, 1972
Resmî Gazete, Official Gazette. Ankara
Konjonktür. Ministry of Commerce (three times a year, from 1940)
Turkish Daily News. Ankara
Banque Centrale de la République de Turquie. *Bulletin Mensuel* (from Jan. 1953)
Barchard, D., *Turkey and the West.* London, 1985
Birand, M. A., *Shirts of Steel: an Anatomy of the Turkish Armed Forces.* London, 1991
Dodd, C. H., *The Crisis of Turkish Democracy.* Beverley, 1983
Güclü, M., *Turkey.* [Bibliography] Oxford and Santa Barbara, 1981
Hale, W., *The Political and Economic Development of Modern Turkey.* London, 1981
Hesper, M., *The State Tradition in Turkey.* Beverley, 1985
Kazancigil, A. and Ozbudun, E., (eds.) *Atatürk: Founder of a Modern State.* London, 1981
Kinross, Lord, *Atatürk.* London, 1964
Lewis, B., *The Emergence of Modern Turkey.* OUP, 1968
Tachau, F., *Turkey: The Politics of Authority, Democracy and Development.* New York, 1984
Weiker W., *The Modernization of Turkey.* New York, 1981

State Library: MilliKütüphane Müdürlüğü, Ankara.

THE TURKS
AND CAICOS
ISLANDS

Capital: Grand Turk
Population: 11,696 (1990)

HISTORY. After a long period of rival French and Spanish claims the islands were eventually secured to the British Crown by the appointment in 1766 of a Resident British Agent, and became a separate colony in 1973 after association at various times with the colonies of the Bahamas and Jamaica.

AREA AND POPULATION. The Turks and Caicos Islands are geographically part of the Bahamas extremity, of which they form the south-eastern archipelago. There are upwards of 30 small cays; area 192 sq. miles (430 sq. km). Only 6 are inhabited; the largest, Grand Caicos, is 30 miles long by 2 to 3 miles broad. The seat of government is at Grand Turk, 7 miles long by 1·25 broad. Population, 1990 census (provisional), 11,696: Grand Turk, 3,720; South Caicos, 1,220; Middle Caicos, 275; North Caicos, 1,305; Providenciales, 4,963; Salt Cay, 213.

Vital statistics (1989): Births, 192; deaths, 58: There were 49 marriages in 1985.

CLIMATE. An equable and healthy climate as a result of regular trade winds, though hurricanes are sometimes experienced. Grand Turk. Jan. 76°F (24·4°C), July 83°F (28·3°C). Annual rainfall 29" (725 mm).

CONSTITUTION AND GOVERNMENT. A new Constitution was introduced in Aug. 1976, providing for an Executive Council and a Legislative Council. The Governor retains responsibility for external affairs, internal security, defence and certain other matters. The Executive Council comprises 3 official members: The Chief Secretary, the Financial Secretary and the Attorney-General; a Chief Minister and 3 other ministers from among the elected members of the Legislative Council; and is presided over by the Governor. The Legislative Council consists of a Speaker, the 3 official members of the Executive Council, 13 elected members and 2 appointed members. At general elections held on 3 March 1988 for the 13 elective seats on the Legislative Council, 11 seats were won by the People's Democratic Movement.

Governor: M. J. Bradley, CMG, QC.
Chief Minister: Oswald Skipping

Flag: British Blue Ensign with the shield of the Colony in the fly.

ECONOMY

Budget. 1990–91 total revenue US$46,281,000 and expenditure, US$46,224,000.

Currency. The currency in circulation is US dollars.

Banking. In 1990 there were 3 commercial banks: Barclays Bank PLC, Bank of Nova Scotia and Turks and Caicos Banking Company have offices on Grand Turk and Providenciales.

Total assets of all 5 banks at 31 Dec. 1989: US$128,641,000; deposits, US$105,683,000.

LABOUR. In 1989, out of a total population of 4,885 aged 14 or over, 4,043 were working, 573 unemployed and 269 economically inactive.

COMMERCE (1987–88). Exports, US$4,133,900, and imports, US$33,212,700. Principal imports 1987–1988 (in US$1,000): Food, drink and tobacco, 6,883·2;

manufactured goods, 20,109·3; raw materials, 1,342·2; fuel, 2,911·1. Origin of imports (1985–86 in US$): USA, 26,149,337; UK, 558,378. The main exports are lobster products (US$1,380,200 in 1987–88), dried and fresh frozen conch (US$2,278,000 in 1987–88). All lobster, conch and other fish exports go to the USA after processing in plants in South Caicos and Providenciales.

Total trade between Turks and Caicos Islands and UK (British Department of Trade returns, in £1,000 sterling):

	1987	1988	1989	1990	1991
Imports to UK	31	66	74	8	12
Exports and re-exports from UK	496	710	731	1,719	1,732

The Islands joined CARICOM in 1990.

Tourism. Number of visitors, 1989, 48,535, of whom 32,898 were from the USA.

COMMUNICATIONS

Aviation. There are paved airfields on Grand Turk and South Caicos and airstrips on Providenciales and the other 3 inhabited islands. Turks and Caicos National Airlines operates inter-island services and services to Haiti, the Dominican Republic and the Bahamas. Turks Air Ltd and Caicos Caribbean operate regular weekly cargo services from Miami.

Shipping. Registered shipping (1985), 168 sailing vessels of 2,445 tons and 49 motor vessels of 5,517 tons.

Telecommunications. Surface and air mail are routed through Miami. Cable & Wireless (West Indies) provide internal and international cable, telephone, telex, telegraph and facsimile services. There were (1988) 1,359 telephones. The Government operates the semi-commercial Radio Turks and Caicos. There are also 2 commercial and 1 religious station. In 1991 there were about 4,500 radio sets.

Newspapers. The *Turks and Caicos News* is published weekly.

JUSTICE, RELIGION, EDUCATION AND WELFARE

Justice. Laws are a mixture of Statute and Common Law. There is a Magistrates Court and a Supreme Court. Appeals lie from the Supreme Court to the Court of Appeal which sits in Nassau, Bahamas. There is a further appeal in certain cases to the Privy Council in London. In 1989 the prison population was 159.

Religion. The Christian faith predominates with Anglican, Methodist, Baptist and evangelists groups.

Education. Education is free and compulsory up to 15 years of age in the 14 government primary and 4 government secondary schools. In 1989–90 there were 1,401 pupils and 73 teachers in the primary schools and 903 pupils and 81 teachers in the secondary schools. There were also 2 private primary schools. Expenditure on education 1988–89 was US$1,878,003.

Health. In 1989 there were 6 doctors, 1 dentist, 43 nurses and midwives, 24 hospital beds and 10 district clinics.

Further Reading

Boultbee, P. G., *Turks & Caicos Islands*. [Bibliography]. Oxford and Santa Barbara, 1991

TUVALU

Capital: Fongafale
Population: 8,229 (1985)
GNP per capita: US$500 (1984)

HISTORY. Formerly the Ellice Islands in the Gilbert and Ellice Islands, a British Protectorate since 1892. After a referendum the island group was separated from the Gilbert Islands in Oct. 1975. Independence was achieved on 1 Oct. 1978.

AREA AND POPULATION. Tuvalu (formerly the Ellice Islands) lies between 5° 30' and 11° S. lat. and 176° and 180° E. long. and comprises Nanumea, Nanumanga, Niutao, Nui, Vaitupu, Nukufetau, Funafuti (administrative centre), Nukulaelae and Niulakita. Population (census 1985) 8,229 and 1,500 work abroad, mainly in Nauru. Area approximately 9½ sq. miles (24 sq. km). The population is of a Polynesian race.

CLIMATE. A pleasant but monotonous climate with temperatures averaging 86°F (30°C), though trade winds from the east moderate conditions for much of the year. Rainfall ranges from 120" (3,000 mm) to over 160" (4,000 mm). Funafuti. Jan. 84°F (28·9°C), July 81°F (27·2°C). Annual rainfall 160" (4,003 mm).

CONSTITUTION AND GOVERNMENT. The Constitution provides for a Prime Minister and 4 other Ministers to be elected from among the 12 elected members of the *House of Assembly.*

Governor-General: Sir Tupua Leupena, GCMG, MBE.

In Feb. 1992 the Cabinet comprised:
Prime Minister, Minister of Foreign Affairs and Local Government and Social Services: Bikenibeu Paeniu.
Commerce, Finance, Natural and Home Affairs: Alesana Seluka. *Works and Communications:* Ionatana Ionatona. *Health, Education and Community Affairs:* Naama Maheu Latasi. *Attorney-General:* D Ballantyne [1]. *Secretary to the Government:* Taausa Taafaki [1]. *Speaker:* Kokea Malua.

[1] Ex-officio members of the Cabinet and House of Assembly.

National flag: Light blue with the Union Jack in the canton, and 9 gold stars in the fly arranged in the same pattern as the 9 islands.

Local Government. There is a town council on Funafuti and island councils on the 7 other atolls, each consisting of 6 elected members including a president. Since 1966 Members of Parliament have been *ex-officio* members of Island Councils. The island of Niulakita is administered as part of Niutao.

INTERNATIONAL RELATIONS

Membership. Tuvalu is a member of the Commonwealth and the South Pacific Forum and is an ACP state of the EEC.

ECONOMY

Budget. In 1988 the budget envisaged revenue of $A4,701,594.

Currency. The unit of currency is the Australian *dollar* although Tuvaluan coins up to $A1 are in local circulation.

Banking. The Tuvalu National Bank was established at Funafuti in 1980 and is a joint venture between the Tuvalu Government and Wespac International.

ENERGY AND NATURAL RESOURCES

Electricity. Production (1986) 3m. kwh.

Agriculture. Coconut palms are the main crop. Production of coconuts (1988), 3,000 tonnes. Fruit and vegetables are grown for local consumption.

Fisheries. Sea fishing is excellent but is largely unexploited although in 1988 Japanese, Taiwanese and South Korean vessels were granted licences to fish.

INDUSTRY AND TRADE

Commerce. Commerce is dominated by co-operative societies, the Tuvalu Co-operative Wholesale Society being the main importer. Main sources of income are copra, stamps, handicrafts and remittances from Tuvaluans abroad. Imports (1984) $A3·96m.

Total trade between Tuvalu and UK (British Department of Trade returns, in £1,000 sterling):

	1987	1988	1989	1990	1991
Imports to UK	2	1	—	—	1
Exports and re-exports from UK	106	105	162	506	107

Tourism. In 1979 there were 474 visitors.

COMMUNICATIONS

Civil Aviation. Fiji Air and Air Marshal operate services to Kiribati and Fiji.

Shipping. Funafuti is the only port and a deep-water wharf was opened in 1980.

Telecommunications. The Tuvalu Broadcasting Service transmits daily in Tuvaluan and English and all islands have daily radio communication with Funafuti. There were 120 telephones and 2,500 radio receivers in 1985.

JUSTICE, RELIGION, EDUCATION AND WELFARE

Justice. There is a High Court presided over by the Chief Justice of Fiji. Appeals lie to the Fiji Court of Appeal.

Religion. The majority of the population are Christians mainly Protestant but with small groups of Roman Catholics, Seventh Day Adventists, Jehovah's Witnesses, Mormons and Bahai's. There are some Moslems.

Education. In 1985 there was 1 secondary school jointly administered by the Government and the Church with 250 pupils. In addition there were 9 primary schools with (1985, inclusive of 326 pupils in community training centres) 924 pupils run by Island Councils and subsidized by the central government. In 1979, a maritime school was opened on Amatuku islet. Tuvaluans requiring further education must seek it abroad.

Health. In 1984 there was 1 central hospital with 36 beds situated at Funafuti. There were 4 doctors.

DIPLOMATIC REPRESENTATIVES

Of Great Britain in Tuvalu
High Commissioner: A. B. P. Smart (resides in Suva).

Of Tuvalu in the USA
Ambassador: (Vacant).

Of the USA in Tuvalu
Ambassador: Evelyn Teegen.

UGANDA

Republic of Uganda

Capital: Kampala
Population: 18·44m. (1990)
GNP per capita: US$250 (1989)

HISTORY. Uganda became a British Protectorate in 1894, the province of Buganda being recognized as a native kingdom under its Kabaka. In 1961 Uganda was granted internal self-government with federal status for Buganda.

Uganda became a fully independent member of the Commonwealth on 9 Oct. 1962. Full sovereign status was granted by the Uganda Independence Act, 1962. Uganda became a republic on 8 Sept. 1967.

In 1971, President Milton Obote was overthrown by troops led by Gen. Idi Amin.

In April 1979 a force of the Tanzanian Army and Ugandan exiles advanced into Uganda taking Kampala on 11 April. On 14 April Dr Yusuf Lule was sworn in as President and the country was administered, initially, by the Uganda National Liberation Front. Godfrey Lukongwa Binaisa, was appointed President by the National Consultative Council on 20 June 1979. He was deposed in May 1980 by the Military Commission, the military arm of Uganda National Liberation Front.

Milton Obote again became President when the Uganda People's Congress won the elections of Dec. 1980; he was deposed on 27 July 1985.

Lieut.-Gen. Tito Okello became head of State on 29 July 1985 but the National Resistance Army of Yoweri K. Museveni, the armed wing of the National Resistance Movement, was not prepared to co-operate with the new regime. A ceasefire between the National Resistance Army of Yoweri K. Museveni, the armed wing of the National Resistance Movement, and government forces was agreed on 17 Dec. 1985 and Yoweri Museveni was installed as President on 27 Jan. 1986.

AREA AND POPULATION. Uganda is bounded on the north by Sudan, on the east by Kenya, on the south by Tanzania and Rwanda, and the west by Zaïre. Total area 241,038 sq. km, including 43,938 sq. km of water.

At the 1980 census the population was 12,630,076; 12% lived in urban areas, the largest towns being Kampala, the capital (458,423), Jinja (45,060), Masaka (29,123), Mbale (28,039), Mbarara (23,155), Entebbe (20,472) and Gulu (14,958). Population estimate, 1990: 18,442,000 (9,295,000 females, 1,923,000 urban). Density, 76·5 per sq. km. Vital statistics rates per 1,000, 1985–90: Birth, 50·1; death, 15·4; infant mortality, 103; population growth, 0·35. Expectation of life in 1990 was: Males, 49·4 years; females, 52·7.

The country is administratively divided into 34 districts, which are grouped in 4 geographical regions (which do not have administrative status). Area and population in 1990:

District	Area in sq. km.	Population in 1,000	District	Area in sq. km.	Population in 1,000
Central Region	61,510	4,814	Eastern Region	39,953	4,213
Kampala	238	650	Iganga	13,113	878
Kalangala	5,716	15	Jinja	734	270
Luwero	9,198	545	Kamuli	4,348	449
Masaka	16,327	849	Kapchorwa	1,738	89
Mpigi	6,222	840	Kumi	2,861	306
Mubende	10,310	746	Mbale	2,546	742
Mukono	14,242	771	Soroti	10,060	611
Rakai	4,973	396	Tororo	4,553	864
Western Region	54,917	4,677	Northern Region	84,658	3,167
Bundibugyo	2,338	161	Apac	6,488	431
Bushenyi	5,396	677	Arua	7,830	614
Hoima	9,896	438	Gulu	11,735	336
Kabale	2,489	536	Kitgum	16,136	400
Kabarole	8,361	766	Kotido	13,208	235
Kasese	3,205	425	Lira	7,251	498
Masindi	9,640	298	Moroto	14,113	225
Mbarara	10,839	999	Moyo	5,006	130
Rukungiri	2,753	373	Nebbi	2,891	293

The official language is English, but Kiswahili is used as a lingua franca. About 70% of the population speak Bantu languages; Nilotic languages are spoken in the north.

CLIMATE. Although in equatorial latitudes, the climate is more tropical, because of its elevation, and is characterized the year round by hot sunshine, cool breezes and showers of rain. The wettest months are March to June and there is no dry season. Temperatures vary little over the year. Kampala. Jan. 74°F (23·3°C), July 70°F (21·1°C). Annual rainfall 46" (1,150 mm). Entebbe. Jan. 72°F (22·2°C), July 69°F (20·6°C). Annual rainfall 60" (1,506 mm).

CONSTITUTION AND GOVERNMENT. The *President* is head of state and head of government and is elected for a 5-year term by the National Assembly. The President's salary in 1990 was 20,000 Uganda shillings per month. The national legislature is the 278-member National Resistance Council. Elections were held in Feb.-March 1989. In Oct. 1989 the Council extended its period of office for five years from 26 Jan. 1990. In Feb. 1992 the government comprised:

President, Minister of Defence: Yoweri Museveni (sworn in 27 Jan. 1986).
Vice-President, Minister of Internal Affairs: Dr Samson Kisekka.
Prime Minister: George Adyebo (b. 1947).
First Deputy Prime Minister: E. Kategaya. *Second Deputy Prime Minister and Minister of Foreign Affairs:* Dr P. K. Ssemogerere. *Third Deputy Prime Minister, Minister of Justice and Attorney-General:* A. K. Mayanja. *Finance:* Dr C. Kiyonga. *Co-operatives and Marketing:* Richard Kaijuka. *Agriculture, Animal Industry and Fisheries:* Victoria Sekitoleko. *Health:* Dr James Makumbi. *Public Service:* Tom Rubale. *Industry and Technology:* James Wapakabulo. *Works, Transport and Communications:* Dr Ruhakana Rugunda. *Information:* Paul Etyang. *Planning and Economic Development:* Joshua Mayanja Nkangi. *Energy, Minerals and Environment Protection:* Henry Kajura. *Tourism, Wildlife and Antiquities:* Sam Sebagereka. *Education and Sport:* Amanya Mushega. *Land, Housing and Urban Development:* Dr E. Adriko. *Local Government:* Jaberi Bidandi Ssali. *Labour and Social Welfare:* Atker Ejahi. *Women in Development, Culture and Youth:* Specioza Kazibwe.

National flag: Six horizontal stripes of black, yellow, red, black, yellow, red, in the centre a small white disc bearing a representation of a Balearic Crested Crane.

Local government: The 34 districts are divided into 152 counties, which are in turn divided into sub-counties which form the basic administrative units.

DEFENCE

Army. The National Resistance Army had a strength of about 70,000 in 1992 and is loosely organized in 6 brigades and some battalions. Equipment includes some T-54/-55 main battle tanks and some BTR-60 armoured personnel carriers.

Navy. A small lake patrol was initiated in 1977.

Air Force. Since 1979, the service has been in a period of decline. As far as was known in early 1989, the equipment received from the East Bloc (MiG-17 and MiG-21 combat aircraft and L-29 jet trainers) was in storage. It is understood that some aircraft of Western European origin are still serviceable, including a small number of AS.202 Bravo and SF.260 trainers and about 6 Agusta-Bell helicopters, plus 3 Mi-8 transport helicopters, donated by Libya. The Police Air Wing still operates 2 fixed-wing aircraft and 7 Bell helicopters.

INTERNATIONAL RELATIONS

Membership. Uganda is a member of UN, OAU, Islamic Conference Organization, the Non-Aligned Movement, the Commonwealth and is an ACP state of EEC.

ECONOMY

Budget. In 1989–90 revenue was 111,350m. Uganda Sh. and expenditure, 169,264m. Uganda Sh. Sources of revenue included (in 1m. Uganda Sh.): Tax,

84,164; export duties, 11,925; customs duties, 22,831. Expenditures included: Agriculture, 1,152; education, 12,437; health, 3,306; defence, 34,697.

Currency. The monetary unit is the *Uganda shilling* (UGS) divided into 100 *cents*. In May 1987 a new 'heavy' shilling was introduced worth 100 old shillings. In March 1992, £1 = 1,737·55 Uganda shillings; US$1 = 989·78 Uganda shillings.

Banking. The Bank of Uganda was established on 16 May 1966. The Uganda Credit and Savings Bank, established in 1950, was on 9 Oct. 1965 reconstituted as the Uganda Commercial Bank, with its capital fully owned by the Government.

Barclays Bank of Uganda Ltd. has 4 branches, Standard Bank Uganda Ltd. has 1 branch, Bank of Baroda Uganda Ltd. has 3 branches and the Libyan Arab Uganda Bank for Foreign Trade and Development has 3 branches, the Uganda Commercial Bank has 184 branches. The Co-operative Bank is owned by the Co-operative Movement. There are 2 Development Banks; the East African Development Bank and the Uganda Development Bank.

ENERGY AND NATURAL RESOURCES

Electricity. Installed capacity, 1989, was 155,000 kw, of which the Owen Falls scheme provided 150,000 kw, which has a capacity of 150,000 kwh. Production (1989) 660·9m. kwh.

Agriculture. In 1988 the agricultural area included 5m. ha of arable, 1·7m. ha of permanent crops and 5m. ha of pasture and meadow. In 1989, agriculture was one of the priority areas for increased production, with many projects funded both locally and externally. Agriculture provided 68·6% of GDP in 1989. Production (1989) in 1,000 tonnes: Tobacco, 3·8; coffee, 174; cotton, 2·6; tea, 4·6; unrefined sugar, 15·9; bananas, 7,469; millet, 610; maize, 624; sorghum, 347; yams, 1,658; manoc, 3,568; beans, 389.

Livestock (1989): Cattle, 4·18m.; sheep, 0·64m.; goats, 2·28m.; pigs, 0·53m.; poultry (1988), 15m. Livestock products, 1989 (in 1,000 tonnes): Beef, 59; pork, 26; poultry, 24; eggs, 19; honey, 0·53; milk, 370.

Forestry. Woodland covers 5·7m. ha and exploitable forests consist almost entirely of hardwoods. 13·87m. cu. metres of wood were cut or gathered in 1988, 1·8m. for timber.

Fisheries. Uganda possesses one of the largest fresh-water fisheries in the world. In 1989 fish production was 213,500 tonnes. Fish farming (especially carp and tilapia) is a growing industry.

INDUSTRY. Production (in 1,000 tonnes) in 1988: Cement, 17·38; soap, 26·87; wheat flour, 13·87; sugar, 15·86; beer, 19·52m. litres.

Labour. The workforce was 8·13m. in 1990 (3·34m. female; 0·88m. between 10 and 15 years).

FOREIGN ECONOMIC RELATIONS

Commerce. In 1989 commerce provided 20% of GDP. In 1987 imports were US$605·5m. and exports, US$319·4m.

Coffee, cotton, tea and tobacco are the principal exports.

Total trade between Uganda and UK (British Department of Trade returns, in £1,000 sterling):

	1987	1988	1989	1990	1991
Imports to UK	37,076	30,487	20,985	12,124	6,730
Exports and re-exports from UK	38,545	35,340	39,218	39,506	35,718

Tourism. There were 35,000 tourists in 1986.

COMMUNICATIONS

Roads. There were (1985) 7,582 km of all-weather roads maintained by the Ministry of Works, of which 1,934 km are two-lane bitumenized highways, and some 19,640 km of other roads, maintained by district governments. There were 34,938 motor vehicles in 1989, including 12,964 passenger cars, 7,410 vans, 3,700 lorries, 2,984 buses and 4,240 motorcycles.

Railways. In Aug. 1977 Uganda Railways was formed following the break-up of the East African Railways administration. The network totals 1,286 km (metre gauge). In 1990 railways carried 0·5m. passengers and 0·5m. tonnes of freight.

Civil Aviation. Uganda Airlines is the national carrier. The International Airport, at Entebbe, has direct flights to Europe, Zimbabwe, Sudan, Kenya, Burundi, Ghana, Ethiopia, Zaïre, Nigeria, USSR, and Rwanda by Sudan Airways, Air Congo, SABENA, Air France, Ethiopian Airlines, Air Zaïre and Aeroflot. Uganda Airlines carried 45,000 international and 16,000 domestic passengers in 1988. 130,000 passengers and 7,791 tonnes of freight were handled at Entebbe in 1989.

Telecommunications. There were 54,900 telephones in use in 1989. The government runs Radio Uganda, which has 10 stations and transmits a home service and a regional programme, and Uganda Television with 7 stations and 1 programme. Colour is by PAL. There were 375,000 radio receivers and about 90,000 television sets in 1990.

Newspapers. There were 5 daily newspapers in 1989 with a circulation of 35,000.

JUSTICE, RELIGION, EDUCATION AND WELFARE

Justice. The High Court of Uganda, presided over by the Chief Justice and 15 puisne judges, exercises original and appellate jurisdiction throughout Uganda. Subordinate courts, presided over by Chief Magistrates and Magistrates of the first, second and third grade, are established in all areas: Jurisdiction varies with the grade of Magistrate. Chief and first-grade Magistrates are professionally qualified; second- and third-grade Magistrates are trained to diploma level at the Law School, Entebbe. Chief Magistrates exercise supervision over and hear appeals from second- and third-grade courts.

The Supreme Court of Uganda hears appeals from the High Court.

Religion. About 62% of the population are Christian and 6% Moslem.

Education. In 1989 there were 2,633,764 pupils in 7,905 primary schools (of which 7,420 were Government-aided schools and 485 private schools); 240,334 students in 774 secondary schools; 13,174 students in 94 primary teacher training colleges; 3,208 students in 24 technical institutes; 1,819 students in 10 national teachers colleges; 1,009 students in technical colleges; 1,628 students in 5 colleges of commerce; 1,037 students in the Institute of Teacher Education, Kyambogo; 504 students in the Uganda Polytechnic, Kyambogo; 800 students in the National College of Business Studies, Nakawa; 5,565 students in Makerere University, Kampala; 163 in the Islamic University, Mbale; 50 students in the University of Science and Technology, Mbarara. There are also 3 agricultural colleges, 1 forestry college, 1 fisheries institute, 1 land survey school and training institutes under different ministries which offer pre-service courses in different fields. Literacy was 57·3% in 1985.

Health. In 1988 there were 980 health centres (217 private), and in 1989 there were 81 hospitals and 20,136 hospital beds. The Ministry of Health has 16 schools for training nurses and other health staff, 105 health centres, 89 dispensaries with maternity units, 87 dispensaries, 35 maternity units, 371 sub-dispensaries, 14 leprosy centres and 169 aid posts. In 1984 there were about 700 doctors.

DIPLOMATIC REPRESENTATIVES

Of Uganda in Great Britain (Uganda Hse., Trafalgar Sq., London, WC2N 5DX)
High Commissioner: Prof. George Kirya.

Of Great Britain in Uganda (10/12 Parliament Ave., Kampala)
High Commissioner: Charles A. K. Cullimore.

Of Uganda in the USA (5909 16th St., NW, Washington, D.C., 20011)
Ambassador: Stephen K. Katenta Apuuli.

Of the USA in Uganda (Parliament Ave., Kampala)
Ambassador: John A. Burroughs Jr.

Of Uganda to the United Nations
Ambassador: Perezi Karukubiro Kamunanwire.

Further Reading

Collison, R. L., *Uganda*. [Bibliography] Oxford and Santa Barbara, 1981
Jørgensen, J. J., *Uganda: A Modern History*. London, 1981

National statistical office: Statistical Department, Ministry of Planning and National Development, Kampala.

UNITED ARAB EMIRATES (UAE)

Provisional Capital: Abu Dhabi
Population: 1·84m. (1990)
GNP per capita: US$15,720 (1988)

HISTORY. British forces withdrew from the Persian Gulf in 1971 and the treaties whereby the UK had been responsible for the defence and foreign relations of the Trucial States (*see* THE STATESMAN'S YEAR-BOOK, 1991–92, p. 1292) were terminated, being replaced on 2 Dec. 1971 by a treaty of friendship between the UK and the United Arab Emirates. The United Arab Emirates (formed 2 Dec. 1971) consists of the former Trucial States: Abu Dhabi, Dubai, Sharjah, Ajman, Umm al Qaiwain, Ras al Khaimah (joined in Feb. 1972) and Fujairah. The small state of Kalba was merged with Sharjah in 1952.

AREA AND POPULATION. The Emirates are bounded in the north by the Persian Gulf and Oman, east by the Gulf of Oman and Oman, south and west by Saudi Arabia, and north-west by Qatar. Their area is approximately 32,300 sq. miles (83,657 sq. km). The total population at census (1985), 1,622,464. Estimate (1990) 1,844,000. In 1980, 69% were male and 72% lived in urban areas. About one-tenth are nomads. Life expectancy in 1990: Males, 70 years; females, 73.

Population of the 7 Emirates, 1985 census: Abu Dhabi, 670,125; Ajman, 64,318; Dubai, 419,104; Fujairah, 54,425; Ras al-Khaimah, 116,470; Sharjah, 268,722; Umm al Qaiwain, 29,229.

The chief cities are Abu Dhabi, the provisional federal capital, Dubai, Sharjah and Ras al-Khaimah.

CLIMATE. The country experiences desert conditions, with rainfall both limited and erratic. The period May to Nov. is generally rainless, while the wettest months are Feb. and March. Temperatures are very high in the summer months. Dubai. Jan. 74°F (23·4°C), July 108°F (42·3°C). Annual rainfall 2·4" (60 mm). Sharjah. Jan. 64°F (17·8°C), July 91°F (32°C). Annual rainfall 4·2" (105 mm).

GOVERNMENT. The Emirates is a federation, headed by a *Supreme Council of Rulers* which is composed of the 7 rulers which elects from among its members a *President* for 5-year terms and appoints a *Council of Ministers.* The Council of Ministers drafts legislation and a federal budget; its proposals are submitted to a federal *National Council* of 40 elected members which may propose amendments but has no executive power.

President: HH Sheikh Zayed bin Sultan al Nahyan, Ruler of Abu Dhabi (re-elected Oct. 1991).

Members of the Supreme Council of Rulers:

HH Sheikh Maktoum bin Rashid al-Maktoum, *Vice President, Prime Minister,* Ruler of Dubai.
HH Sheikh Sultan bin Mohammed al-Qasimi, Ruler of Sharjah.
HH Sheikh Saqr bin Mohammed al-Qasimi, Ruler of Ras al-Khaimah.
HH Sheikh Rashid bin Ahmed al-Mualla, Ruler of Umm al Qaiwain.
HH Sheikh Hamad bin Mohammed al Sharqi, Ruler of Fujairah.
HH Sheikh Humaid bin Rashid al-Nuaimi, Ruler of Ajman.

The Council of Ministers in Feb. 1992 was:

Prime Minister: HH Sheikh Maktoum bim Rashid al-Maktoum.
Deputy Prime Minister: HH Sheikh Sultan bin Zayed al-Nahyan.
Interior: HE Major General Hamouda bin Ali. *Finance and Industry:* Sheikh Hamdan bin Rashid al-Maktoum. *Defence:* Sheikh Mohammed bin Rashid al-Maktoum. *Economy and Commerce:* HE Saeed Ghobash. *Information and Culture:* HE Khalfan bin Mohammed Al-Roumi. *Communications:* HE Mohammed Saeed

1310

al-Mualla. *Public Works and Housing:* HE Rakad bin Salem bin Rakad. *Education:* HE Hamad Abdul Rahman al-Madfa. *Petroleum and Mineral Resources:* HE Yousuf bin Omeir bin Yousuf. *Electricity and Water:* HE Humaid bin Nasser al-Oweis. *Health:* HE Ahmed bin Saeed al-Badi. *Labour and Social Affairs:* HE Saif al-Jarwan. *Planning:* HE Sheikh Humaid al-Mualla. *Agriculture and Fisheries:* HE Saeed al-Ragabani. *Islamic Affairs and Endowments:* HE Sheikh Mohammed bin Ahmed al-Khazraji. *Foreign Affairs:* HE Rashid Abdullah al-Noami. *Justice:* HE Dr Abdullah bin Omran Taryam. *Higher Education:* HE Sheikh Nahyan bin Mubarak al-Nahyan. *Youth and Sports:* HE Sheikh Faisal bin Khaled bin Mohammed al-Qassimi.

National flag: Three horizontal stripes of green, white, black, with a vertical red strip in the hoist.

DEFENCE

Army. The Army consists of 1 Royal Guard, 1 armoured, 1 mechanized infantry, 2 infantry and 1 artillery brigades. There is also an unintegrated infantry brigade in Dubai. Equipment includes 95 AMX-30 and 36 Lion OF-40 Mk 2 main battle tanks. The strength was (1991) 40,000.

Navy. The combined naval flotilla of the Emirates includes 2 German-built missile corvettes, 6 German-built fast missile craft, 9 British-built inshore patrol craft, 2 tank landing craft, 2 transports, 1 maintenance ship and 3 service craft. Personnel in 1991 numbered 1,500 officers and ratings. The main base is now established at Taweela (Sharjah), with minor bases in the other Emirates.

The Coast Guard flotilla comprises 28 inshore patrol craft and some 30 boats.

Air Force. Formation of an air wing in Abu Dhabi, to support land forces, began in 1968 with the purchase of some light STOL transports and helicopters. Expansion has been rapid. Current equipment includes 21 Mirage 2000 and 23 Mirage 5 super-sonic fighter-bombers, 8 Mirage 2000R and 3 Mirage 5R tactical reconnaissance aircraft, 6 Mirage 2000D and 3 Mirage 5D 2-seat trainers; 4 C-130 Hercules and 5 Buffalo turboprop transports; 4 CASA C-212 Aviocar ECM/elint aircraft; about 40 Gazelle, Alouette III, Puma, Super Puma and Ecureuil helicopters; 23 PC-7 Turbo-Trainers and 15 Hawk light attack/trainers. Initial personnel were mostly British but considerable assistance is now being received from Arab countries and from Pakistan. The air wing became the Air Force of Abu Dhabi in 1972, in which year 3 JetRanger helicopters were transferred to the air wing of the Union Defence Force, since combined with the Dubai Police Air Wing to form a single component of the United Emirates Air Force. Current equipment of the Dubai Air Wing of the UEAF, bought mainly in Italy, comprises 3 Aermacchi MB 326K jet light attack aircraft, 1 piston-engined SF.260W armed basic trainer, 5 SF.260TP turboprop trainers, and 2 MB 326L, 5 MB 339 and 8 Hawk jet trainers, 6 Bell 205A-1, 3 Bell 212, 8 Bell 214 and 6 JetRanger helicopters and 1 Cessna 182 liaison aircraft, plus 2 L-100-30 Her-cules transports and a variety of other types for VIP and transport use. Sharjah formed a small aviation force, the Amiri Guard Air Wing, at the end of 1984. The service is essentially an internal security and transport force operating 1 Short 330 and 1 Skyvan for transport duties and 3 JetRanger helicopters. Personnel (1991) 2,500 including Dubai, 700, with 90 combat aircraft and 18 armed helicopters.

INTERNATIONAL RELATIONS

Membership. The UAE is a member of the UN, Gulf Co-operation Council and of the Arab League.

ECONOMY

Budget. Revenue is principally derived from oil-concession payments. Federal expenditure (1990) was DH 14,540m. and public revenue (1988) 21,600m.

Currency. The unit of currency is the *dirham* (AED) of 100 *fils*. There are notes of 5, 10, 50, 100 and 500 *dirham* and coins of 1 and 5 *dirham* and 1, 5, 10, 25 and 50 *fils*. Rate of exchange, March 1992: £1 = 6·43 *dirham*; US$1 = 3·67 *dirham*.

Banking and Finance. The UAE Central Bank was established in 1980. In 1990 there were 40 local and foreign banks. Foreign banks are restricted to 8 branches each.

ENERGY AND NATURAL RESOURCES

Electricity. Production (1986) 16,440m. kwh. Supply in Abu Dhabi 230 volts; Dubai 220 volts and in the remaining Emirates 240 volts; all 50 Hz.

Oil. Oil and gas provide about 50% of GDP. Reserves (1988) 200,000m. bbls.

Abu Dhabi. Proven reserves (1988) 31,000m. bbls. Oil production, 1991, 95·12m. tonnes.

Dubai. In 1975 Dubai took control of foreign oil and gas operations and a Dubai producing group was set up to comprise the foreign interests. Oil production (1991) 20·9m. tonnes.

Sharjah. Oil production, 1991, 1·92m. tonnes.

Ras al-Khaimah. Oil production (1990) 400,000 tonnes.

Gas. Abu Dhabi has reserves of natural gas, nationalized in 1976. There is a gas liquefaction plant on Das Island. Gas exports (1986) DH4,500m.

Water. Production of drinking water by desalination of sea water (1986) was 11,600m. gallons.

Agriculture. The fertile Buraimi Oasis, known as Al Ain, is largely in Abu Dhabi territory. By 1988, 2,620 farms had been set up on 12,565 ha of land reclaimed from sand dunes. Owing to lack of water and good soil there is little agriculture in the rest of UAE. Cultivated area (1985) 320,000 ha. Production (1988): Red meat, 18,000 tonnes; poultry, 7,000 tonnes; dates, 68,000 tonnes; vegetables, 285; wheat, 2.

Livestock (1990, in 1,000): Cattle, 50; camels, 115; sheep, 260; goats, 580.

Fisheries. Catch (1986) 72,400 tonnes.

INDUSTRY. Products incude aluminium, cable, cement, chemicals, fertilizers (Abu Dhabi), rolled steel and plastics (Dubai, Sharjah) and tools and clothing (Dubai). In 1988 there were 190 companies established in the Jebel Ali free trade zone.

FOREIGN ECONOMIC RELATIONS. There are free trade zones at Jebel Ali (administered by Dubai), Sharjah and Fujairah. Foreign companies may set up wholly-owned subsidiaries there.

Commerce. Imports in 1988 for UAE were DH31,000m. Exports and re-exports (non-oil) totalled DH13,500m. Oil exports accounted for DH28,000m.

Total trade between the UAE (excluding Abu Dhabi) and UK (British Department of Trade returns, in £1,000 sterling):

	1987	1988	1989	1990	1991
Imports to UK	81,218	58,651	77,755	105,072	122,878
Exports and re-exports from UK	329,008	334,506	415,982	494,559	529,572

Total trade between Abu Dhabi and UK (British Department of Trade returns, in £1,000 sterling):

	1987	1988	1989	1990	1991
Imports to UK	13,771	25,566	87,248	76,414	109,043
Exports and re-exports from UK	149,989	128,838	155,439	170,165	220,088

Tourism. In 1989 there were 109 hotels and 1,071,238 visitors.

COMMUNICATIONS

Roads. In 1984 there were 2,200 km of roads and 230,000 vehicles.

Civil Aviation. In 1991 there were 5 international airports. 70m. passengers were handled in 1990. Gulf Air is run by a consortium of Abu Dhabi, Bahrain, Doha and Muscat. A number of cargo airlines run services. An air-taxi service, Emirates Air

Services, operates between Abu Dhabi and Dubai. Dubai set up its own, Emirates, airline in 1985. It flies to Saudi Arabia, Europe, India, Singapore, Manila and elsewhere.

Shipping. There are 5 ports on the Persian Gulf (Zayed in Abu Dhabi, Rashid and Jebel Ali in Dubai, Khalid in Sharjah and Saqr in Ras al-Khaimah) and 2 on the Gulf of Oman: Fujairah and Khor Fakkan. Rashid and Fujairah are important container terminals.

Telecommunications. In 1990 there were 367,333 telephones. The Cable and Wireless Station at Jebel Ali links up with the international communication network.

There are several government authorities providing broadcasting nationally (Voice of the United Arab Emirates, Capital Radio, which is partly commercial and United Arab Emirates Television Service) and regionally (UAE Radio and Television-Dubai, Ras al-Khaimah Broadcasting, Um al-Qaiwain Broadcasting, and Sharjah TV). In 1991 there were about 0·4m. radio and 0·17m. TV sets (colour by PAL).

Newspapers (1990). There are dailies and weeklies in Arabic and English.

JUSTICE, RELIGION, EDUCATION AND WELFARE

Justice. UAE subjects and citizens of all Arab and Moslem states are subject to the jurisdiction of the local courts. In the local courts the rules of Islamic law prevail. A new code of law is being produced for Abu Dhabi. In Dubai there is a court run by a *qadi*, while in some of the other States all legal cases are referred immediately to the Ruler or a member of his family, who will refer to a *qadi* only if he cannot settle the matter himself. In Abu Dhabi a professional Jordanian judge presides over the Ruler's Court.

Religion. Nearly all the inhabitants are Moslem of the Sunni, and a small minority of the Shi'ite sects.

Education In 1986–87 there were 122,543 pupils in primary schools, 36,810 in preparatory schools and 20,753 in secondary schools. There were 1,712 students in religious schools, 597 in technical schools and (1987–88) 2,075 at the Emirates' University. In 1990–91 there were 875 students in 3 higher colleges of technology. In 1990 there were 380,000 pupils altogether.

Health. In 1991 there were 33 government hospitals (4,000 beds) and 400 beds in private hospitals. There were 1,840 physicians.

DIPLOMATIC REPRESENTATIVES

Of the UAE in Great Britain (30 Prince's Gate, London, SW7 1PT)
Ambassador: Issa Falah Al-Gurg, CBE.

Of Great Britain in the UAE
Ambassador: Graham Burton, CMG (POB 248, Abu Dhabi).

Of the UAE in the USA (600 New Hampshire Ave., NW, Washington, D.C., 20037)
Ambassador: Abdulla bin Zayed Al-Nahayyan.

Of the USA in the UAE (Al-Sudan St., Abu Dhabi)
Ambassador: Edward S. Walker, Jr.

Of the UAE to the United Nations
Ambassador: Mohammed Hussain Al-Shaali.

Further Reading

Alkim, H. al.-, *The Foreign Policy of the UAE.* Saqi, 1989
Clements, F. A., *United Arab Emirates.* [Bibliography] Oxford and Santa Barbara, 1983
Heard-Bey, F., *From Trucial States to United Arab Emirates.* London, 1982
Taryam, A. O., *The Establishment of the United Arab Emirates.* London, 1987
Whelan, J., *UAE: a MEED Practical Guide.* 3rd ed. London, 1990

UNITED KINGDOM OF GREAT BRITAIN AND NORTHERN IRELAND

Capital: London
Population: 57·41m. (1990)
GNP per capita: US$14,570 (1989)

'Great Britain' is the geographical name of that island of the British Isles which comprises England, Scotland and Wales (so called to distinguish it from 'Little Britain' or Brittany). By the Act of Union, 1801, Great Britain and Ireland formed a legislative union as the United Kingdom of Great Britain and Ireland. Since the separation of Great Britain and Ireland in 1921 Northern Ireland remained within the Union which is now the United Kingdom of Great Britain and Northern Ireland. The United Kingdom (UK) does not include the Channel Islands or the Isle of Man which are direct dependencies of the Crown with their own legislative and taxation systems. England and Wales form an administrative entity, with some special arrangements for Wales (*see* pp. 1327–28).

GREAT BRITAIN

AREA AND POPULATION. Area (in sq. km) and preliminary count of the population (present on census night) at the census taken 21 April 1991:

Divisions	Area	Total
England	130,357	46,170,000
Wales	20,761	2,798,000
Scotland	78,762	4,957,000
	229,880	53,925,000

Population at the 4 previous decennial censuses:

Divisions	1951	1961	1971	1981
England [1]	41,159,213	43,460,525	46,019,000	46,362,836
Wales	2,598,675	2,644,023	2,731,000	2,791,851
Scotland	5,096,415	5,178,490	5,228,963	5,130,735
Total	48,854,303	51,283,038	53,978,963	54,285,422

[1] Areas now recognised as part of Gwent, Wales, formed the English county of Monmouth-shire until 1974.

Population (usually resident) at the census of 1981:

Divisions	Males	Females	Total
England	22,288,395	23,483,561	45,771,956
Wales	1,336,323	1,413,317	2,749,640
Scotland	2,428,472	2,606,843	5,035,315
Great Britain	26,053,190	27,503,721	53,556,911

In 1981 in Wales 21,283 persons 3 years of age and upwards were able to speak Welsh only, and 482,266 able to speak Welsh and English: These totals represent 19% of the total population. In Scotland in 1981, 79,307 of the usually resident population could speak Gaelic (1·7%); 3,313 could read or write Gaelic, but could not speak it.

At the census of 1981, in England and Wales, there were 17,706,492 private households; in Great Britain, 19,500,113.

The age distribution in 1981 of the 'usually resident' population of England and Wales and Scotland was as follows (in 1,000):

Age-group		England and Wales	Scotland	Great Britain
Under	5	2,910	308	3,219
5 and under	10	3,207	344	3,551
10 ,,	15	3,846	425	4,271
15 ,,	20	4,020	447	4,467
20 ,,	25	3,564	394	3,959
25 ,,	35	6,931	701	7,632
35 ,,	45	5,885	588	6,473
45 ,,	55	5,474	575	6,049
55 ,,	65	5,410	541	5,951
65 ,,	70	2,426	241	2,667
70 ,,	75	2,062	204	2,265
75 ,,	85	2,280	221	2,501
85 and upwards		507	46	552
Total		48,522	5,035	53,557

At 30 June 1990 the estimated population of the UK was 57,411,000 (29,398,000 females), and of Great Britain, 55,821,000 (28,589,000 females). Age and sex distribution (UK, in 1,000 persons/females): Under 5, 3,841/1,873; 5-14, 7,079/3,447; 15-59, 34,607/17,194; 60-64, 2,896/1,502; over 65, 8,988/5,389.

Population densities (persons per sq. km), 1989: UK, 236; England, 366; Wales, 138.

England and Wales: The census population, (present on census night) of England and Wales 1801 to 1981:

Date of enumeration	Population	Pop. per sq. mile	Date of enumeration	Population	Pop. per sq. mile [1]
1801	8,892,536	152	1891	29,002,525	497
1811	10,164,256	174	1901	32,527,843	558
1821	12,000,236	206	1911	36,070,492	618
1831	13,896,797	238	1921	37,886,699	649
1841	15,914,148	273	1931	39,952,377	685
1851	17,927,609	307	1951	43,757,888	750
1861	20,066,224	344	1961	46,104,548	791
1871	22,712,266	389	1971	48,749,575	323
1881	25,974,439	445	1981	49,154,687	325

[1] Per sq. km from 1971

The birth places of the 1981 'usually resident' population were: England, 41,552,500; Wales, 2,758,026; Scotland, 752,188; Northern Ireland, 209,042; Ireland, 579,833; Commonwealth, 1,429,407; foreign countries, 1,209,091.

At June 1990 the estimated population of England and Wales was 50,718,800 (25,953,200 females); England, 47,837,300 (24,469,100). Age and sex distribution (in 1,000 persons/females): Under 5, 3,380/1,649; 5-14, 6,187/3,012; 15-59, 30,556/15,165; 60-64, 2,564/1,324; over 65, 8,050/4,803.

11 'Standard Regions' (also classified as 'level 1 regions' for EC purposes) are identified in the UK as economic planing regions. They have no administrative significance. They are Northern Ireland, Scotland and Wales, and 8 regions of England. Population of the English regions (in 1,000) at the preliminary count of the 1991 census: East Anglia, 2,007; East Midlands, 3,898; West Midlands, 5,067; North, 3,005; North West, 6,124; South East, 16,714 (including Greater London, 6,378); South West, 4,576; Yorkshire and Humberside, 4,778.

England and Wales are divided (apart from Greater London) into 53 counties (6 of them 'metropolitan') subdivided into 369 districts. Greater London comprises 32 boroughs and the City of London.

Area in sq. km of counties and population estimate 30 June 1990:

ENGLAND Metropolitan counties	Area sq. km	Population	Metropolitan counties—contd.	Area sq. km	Population
Greater Manchester	1,286	2,590,500	Tyne and Wear	540	1,126,600
Merseyside	652	1,443,800	West Midlands	899	2,614,600
South Yorkshire	1,560	1,296,200	West Yorkshire	2,039	2,070,200

Non-metropolitan counties	Area sq. km	Popu-lation (in 1,000)	Non-metropolitan counties—contd.	Area sq. km	Popu-lation (in 1,000)
ENGLAND			Norfolk	5,355	750·7
Avon	1,338	952·0	Northamptonshire		
Bedfordshire (Beds)	1,235	535·5	(Northants)	2,367	580·1
Berkshire (Berks)	1,256	755·5	Northumberland	5,033	305·2
Buckinghamshire			North Yorkshire		
(Bucks)	1,883	641·4	(N. Yorks)	8,317	726·4
Cambridgeshire (Camb)	3,409	664·5	Nottinghamshire (Notts)	2,164	1,026·6
Cheshire	2,322	959·0	Oxfordshire (Oxon)	2,611	586·6
Cleveland	583	552·1	Shropshire (Salop)	3,490	405·1
Cornwall and Isles of			Somerset (Som)	3,458	464·9
Scilly	3,546	467·5	Staffordshire (Staffs)	2,716	1,040·8
Cumbria	6,809	492·1	Suffolk	3,800	643·8
Derbyshire	2,631	933·1	Surrey	1,655	1,002·9
Devon	6,715	1,030·5	Warwickshire	1,981	482·6
Dorset	2,654	658·3	West Sussex	2,016	704·9
Durham	2,436	599·4	Wiltshire (Wilts)	3,481	561·9
East Sussex	1,795	712·2			
Essex	3,674	1,533·6	WALES		
Gloucestershire			Clwyd	2,425	411·8
(Gloucs)	2,638	531·4	Dyfed	5,765	354·0
Hampshire (Hants)	3,772	1,547·0	Gwent	1,376	447·6
Hereford and Worcester	3,927	676·2	Gwynedd	3,868	241·1
Hertfordshire (Herts)	1,634	988·7	Mid Glamorgan		
Humberside (Humb)	3,512	859·2	(M. Glam)	1,019	539·6
Isle of Wight (IOW)	381	129·8	Powys	5,077	117·5
Kent	3,732	1,525·4	South Glamorgan		
Lancashire (Lancs)	3,043	1,395·3	(S. Glam)	416	406·7
Leicestershire (Leics)	2,553	897·7	West Glamorgan		
Lincolnshire (Lincs)	5,885	591·3	(W. Glam)	815	363·2

County districts with populations of over 90,000 (estimate, 30 June 1990):

ENGLAND			
Allerdale (Cumbria)	97·1	Cherwell (Oxon)	128·9
Amber Valley (Derbyshire)	114·2	Chester (Cheshire)	113·1
Arun (W. Sussex)	129·5	Chesterfield (Derbyshire)	101·0
Ashfield (Notts)	109·8	Chichester (W. Sussex)	106·3
Ashford (Kent)	96·5	Chorley (Lancs)	97·3
Aylesbury Vale (Bucks)	148·5	Colchester (Essex)	154·4
Barnsley (S. Yorks)	221·8	Coventry (W. Midlands)	303·6
Basildon (Essex)	155·9	Crewe and Nantwich (Cheshire)	102·8
Basingstoke and Deane (Hants)	142·2	Dacorum (Herts)	132·0
Bassetlaw (Notts)	105·0	Darlington (Durham)	100·0
Beverley (Humberside)	116·5	Derby	217·3
Birmingham (W. Midlands)	992·8	Doncaster (S. Yorks)	294·0
Blackburn (Lancs)	135·5	Dover (Kent)	106·7
Blackpool (Lancs)	139·1	Dudley (W. Midlands)	306·5
Bolton (Greater Manchester)	266·9	Easington (Durham)	91·8
Bournemouth (Dorset)	154·0	East Devon	118·8
Bracknell Forest (Berks)	108·2	East Hampshire	102·7
Bradford (W. Yorks)	468·8	East Hertfordshire	120·7
Braintree (Essex)	115·6	Eastleigh (Hants)	103·9
Breckland (Norfolk)	104·4	East Lindsey (Lincs)	119·8
Brighton (E. Sussex)	141·2	East Staffordshire	97·0
Bristol (Avon)	374·3	Elmbridge (Surrey)	107·1
Broadland (Norfolk)	106·8	Epping Forest (Essex)	111·8
Broxtowe (Notts)	109·5	Erewash (Derbyshire)	107·5
Burnley (Lancs)	94·4	Exeter (Devon)	103·6
Bury (Greater Manchester)	177·6	Fareham (Hants)	102·5
Calderdale (W. Yorks)	197·8	Gateshead (Tyne and Wear)	205·0
Cambridge	100·2	Gedling (Notts)	110·4
Canterbury (Kent)	131·7	Gillingham (Kent)	95·2
Carlisle (Cumbria)	104·1	Gloucester	92·0
Charnwood (Leics)	151·1	Guildford (Surrey)	123·6
Chelmsford (Essex)	151·7	Halton (Cheshire)	123·5
		Harrogate (N. Yorks)	147·6

ENGLAND—*contd.*

Havant (Hants)	114·6
Hinckley and Bosworth (Leics)	98·9
Horsham (W. Sussex)	109·3
Hove (E. Sussex)	92·7
Huntingdonshire (Cambs)	154·1
Ipswich (Suffolk)	113·7
King's Lynn and West Norfolk	134·5
Kingston upon Hull (Humberside)	245·3
Kirklees (W. Yorks)	375·5
Knowsley (Merseyside)	157·3
Lancaster	133·5
Langbaurgh on Tees (Cleveland)	144·0
Leeds (W. Yorks)	712·2
Leicester	278·0
Lewes (E. Sussex)	90·8
Lichfield (Staffs)	93·8
Liverpool (Merseyside)	462·9
Luton (Beds)	171·4
Macclesfield (Cheshire)	150·9
Maidstone (Kent)	137·1
Manchester	446·7
Mansfield (Notts)	100·5
Mendip (Som)	94·7
Mid-Bedfordshire	114·8
Middlesbrough (Cleveland)	141·6
Mid-Sussex (W. Sussex)	119·6
Milton Keynes (Bucks)	185·1
Newark and Sherwood (Notts)	103·5
Newbury (Berks)	141·4
Newcastle under Lyme (Staffs)	118·7
Newcastle upon Tyne	
(Tyne and Wear)	277·8
New Forest (Hants)	163·4
Northampton	185·1
Northavon (Avon)	135·7
North Bedfordshire	139·1
North-East Derbyshire	97·2
North Hertfordshire	113·4
North Norfolk	96·2
North Tyneside (Tyne and Wear)	191·7
North Wiltshire	114·3
Norwich (Norfolk)	117·2
Nottingham	274·9
Nuneaton and Bedworth	
(Warwickshire)	116·0
Oldham (Greater Manchester)	221·7
Oxford	118·1
Peterborough (Cambs)	154·3
Plymouth (Devon)	252·9
Poole (Dorset)	132·5
Portsmouth (Hants)	184·1
Preston (Lancs)	128·6
Reading (Berks)	129·9
Reigate and Banstead (Surrey)	115·4
Rochdale (Greater Manchester)	208·5
Rochester upon Medway (Kent)	149·3
Rotherham (S. Yorks)	254·5
Rushcliffe (Notts)	101·9
Ryedale (N. Yorks)	92·2
St Albans (Herts)	129·6
St Edmundsbury (Suffolk)	92·1
St Helens (Merseyside)	188·5
Salford (Greater Manchester)	234·1
Salisbury (Wilts)	100·6
Sandwell (W. Midlands)	295·0
Scarborough (N. Yorks)	106·8

ENGLAND—*contd.*

Sedgemoor (Som)	98·3
Sefton (Merseyside)	299·5
Selby (N. Yorks)	95·2
Sevenoaks (Kent)	104·9
Sheffield (S. Yorks)	525·9
Shrewsbury and Atcham (Salop)	90·6
Slough (Berks)	100·3
Solihull (W. Midlands)	203·3
Southampton (Hants)	197·4
South Bedfordshire	110·2
South Cambridgeshire	120·7
Southend on Sea (Essex)	167·3
South Kesteven (Lincs)	107·0
South Lakeland (Cumbria)	101·5
South Norfolk	101·6
South Oxfordshire	129·8
South Ribble (Lancs)	102·9
South Somerset	143·3
South Staffordshire	109·5
South Tyneside (Tyne and Wear)	156·0
Stafford	119·1
Staffordshire Moorlands	96·8
Stockport (Greater Manchester)	290·5
Stockton on Tees (Cleveland)	176·6
Stoke on Trent (Staffs)	246·7
Stratford on Avon (Warwickshire)	105·8
Stroud (Gloucs)	110·2
Suffolk Coastal	113·1
Sunderland (Tyne and Wear)	296·1
Swale (Kent)	117·2
Tameside (Greater Manchester)	219·3
Taunton Deane (Som)	96·0
Teignbridge (Devon)	111·9
Tendring (Essex)	134·1
Test Valley (Hants)	103·4
Thamesdown (Wilts)	171·0
Thanet (Kent)	131·9
Thurrock (Essex)	126·9
Tonbridge and Malling (Kent)	101·2
Torbay (Devon)	119·1
Trafford (Greater Manchester)	214·8
Tunbridge Wells (Kent)	99·0
Vale of White Horse (Oxon)	112·9
Vale Royal (Cheshire)	114·1
Wakefield (W. Yorks)	315·8
Walsall (W. Midlands)	264·0
Warrington (Cheshire)	189·2
Warwick	114·9
Waveney (Suffolk)	107·3
Waverley (Surrey)	109·7
Wealden (E. Sussex)	136·8
Welwyn Hatfield (Herts)	92·0
West Lancashire	104·3
West Oxfordshire	97·0
West Wiltshire	106·5
Wigan (Greater Manchester)	310·4
Winchester (Hants)	96·1
Windsor and Maidenhead (Berks)	124·5
Wirral (Merseyside)	335·4
Wokingham (Berks)	150·2
Wolverhampton (W. Midlands)	249·4
Woodspring (Avon)	187·3
Worthing (W. Sussex)	98·6
Wrekin (Salop)	137·4
Wychavon (Hereford and Worcestor)	101·8
Wycombe (Bucks)	159·5

ENGLAND—contd.		WALES—contd.	
Wyre (Lancs)	104·1	Ogwr (Mid-Glam)	137·1
Wyre Forest (Hereford & Worcestor)	95·7	Rhymney Valley (Mid-Glam)	104·1
York (N. Yorks)	101·2	Swansea (W. Glam)	186·6
		Taff Ely (Mid-Glam)	97·3
WALES		Torfaen (Gwent)	93·6
Cardiff (S. Glam)	287·3	Vale of Glamorgan	119·6
Newport (Gwent)	127·0	Wrexham Maelor (Clwyd)	117·0

The following table shows the distribution of the urban and rural population of England and Wales in 1951, 1961, 1971, and 1981.

		Population		Percentage	
	England and Wales	Urban districts [1]	Rural districts [1]	Urban	Rural
1951	43,757,888	35,335,721	8,422,167	80·8	19·2
1961	46,071,604	36,838,442	9,233,162	80·0	20·0
1971	48,755,000	38,151,000	10,598,000	78·2	21·5
1981	49,011,417	37,686,863	11,324,554	76·9	23·1

[1] As existing at each census.

Conurbations. These are aggregates of local-authority areas with high population densities. In April 1981 there were 6 in England and Wales, with a population of 14·7m. (30% of total population): Greater London, 6·7m.; Tyneside, 0·7m.; W. Yorks., 1·67m.; S.E. Lancs., 2·24m.; Merseyside, 1·13m.; W. Midlands, 2·24m.

Greater London Boroughs. Total area 1,580 sq.km. Estimated population on 30 June 1990, 6,794,400. By borough:

Barking and		Hammersmith		Lewisham	226,300
Dagenham	147,600	and Fulham	149,200	Merton	164,900
Barnet	310,000	Haringey	192,800	Newham	208,600
Bexley	220,200	Harrow	192,500	Redbridge	234,800
Brent	255,700	Havering	231,900	Richmond upon	
Bromley	300,100	Hillingdon	235,700	Thames	167,200
Camden	185,500	Hounslow	197,300	Southwark	225,500
Croydon	319,400	Islington	173,700	Sutton	168,100
Ealing	293,300	Kensington and		Tower Hamlets	166,900
Enfield	264,300	Chelsea	131,000	Waltham Forest	213,400
Greenwich	215,900	Kingston upon		Wandsworth	256,200
Hackney	191,800	Thames	138,900	Westminster,	
		Lambeth	232,500	City of	179,200

The City of London (677 acres) is administered by its Corporation which retains some independent powers. Resident population (1990 estimate) 3,900.

Scotland: Area 78,762 sq. km, including its islands, 186 in number, and inland water 1,580 sq. km.

Population (including military in the barracks and seamen on board vessels in the harbours) at the dates of each census:

Date of enumeration	Population	Pop. per sq. mile	Date of enumeration	Population	Pop. per sq. mile [1]
1811	1,805,864	60	1901	4,472,103	150
1821	2,091,521	70	1911	4,760,904	160
1831	2,364,386	79	1921	4,882,497	164
1841	2,620,184	88	1931	4,842,980	163
1851	2,888,742	97	1951	5,096,415	171
1861	3,062,294	100	1961	5,179,344	174
1871	3,360,018	113	1971	5,229,963	68
1881	3,735,573	125	1981	5,130,735	66
1891	4,025,647	135			

[1] per sq. km from 1971.

The 1981 population present on census night included 2,466,000 males, 2,664,000 females.

At 30 June 1990 the estimated population of Scotland was 5,102,400 (2,635,605 females). Age and sex distribution (in 1,000, persons/females): Under 5, 326/159; 5–14, 631/308; 15–59, 3,119/1,559; 60–64, 264/141; over 65, 761/468.

Population density 1989: 66 persons per sq.km.

Scotland is divided into 9 regions (subdivided into 53 districts) and 3 island authority areas. Area of regions and population estimate of regions and districts in June 1989:

Regions (area sq. km) and Districts	Population (in 1,000) 1989	Regions (area sq. km) and Districts	Population (in 1,000) 1989
Borders (4,662)	103·5	Lothian (1,756)	749·6
Berwickshire	19·1	East Lothian	85·5
Ettrick and Lauderdale	34·3	Edinburgh City	434·5
Roxburgh	35·0	Midlothian	81·3
Tweeddale	15·2	West Lothian	148·3
Central (2,590)	272·1	Strathclyde (13,856)	2,306·0
Clackmannan	47·5	Argyll and Bute	66·1
Falkirk	143·3	Bearsden and Milngavie	40·9
Stirling	81·4	Clydebank	46·9
Dumfries and Galloway (6,475)	148·4	Clydesdale	58·6
Annandale and Eskdale	36·6	Cumbernauld and Kilsyth	63·1
Nithsdale	57·8	Cumnock and Doon Valley	43·0
Stewartry	23·5	Cunninghame	137·5
Wigtown	30·5	Dumbarton	79·7
Fife (1,308)	345·9	East Kilbride	83·1
Dunfermline	129·9	Eastwood	61·0
Kirkcaldy	147·1	Glasgow City	689·2
North East Fife	68·9	Hamilton	106·6
Grampian (8,550)	506·1	Inverclyde	93·5
Aberdeen City	211·1	Kilmarnock and Loudoun	81·1
Banff and Buchan	85·0	Kyle and Carrick	113·7
Gordon	74·6	Monklands	104·5
Kincardine and Deeside	50·9	Motherwell	146·8
Moray	84·5	Renfrew	201·0
Highland (26,136)	204·3	Strathkelvin	89·7
Badenoch and Strathspey	11·2	Tayside (7,668)	394·0
Caithness	26·8	Angus	95·4
Inverness	63·1	Dundee City	172·9
Lochaber	19·0	Perth and Kinross	125·8
Nairn	10·4	Island Authority Areas	
Ross and Cromarty	48·9	Orkney Islands (974)	19·6
Skye and Lochalsh	11·8	Shetland Islands (1,427)	22·3
Sutherland	13·0	Western Isles (2,901)	30·7

The birthplaces of the 1981 usually resident population were: Scotland, 4,548,708; England, 297,784; Wales, 12,733; Northern Ireland, 33,927; Ireland 27,018; Commonwealth, 48,515; foreign countries, 65,384.

The population of the Central Clydeside conurbation in 1990 was 1,632,670.

Isle of Man and Channel Islands:

Islands	Area in sq. km	Population 1961	1971	1986
Isle of Man	572	48,151	56,289	55,482
Jersey	116	57,200	69,329	80,212 [1]
Guernsey, Herm and Jethou	64 }			
Alderney	8 }	47,178	53,734	64,282
Sark, Brechou and Lihou	6 }			

[1] 1985.

Vital statistics for England and Wales:

	Total live births	Live births outside marriage	Total deaths	Deaths under 1 year	Marriages	Divorces, annulments and dis-solutions
1985	656,417	126,250	590,734	6,141	346,389	160,300
1986	661,018	141,345	581,203	6,313	347,924	153,903
1987	681,511	158,431	566,994	6,308	351,761	151,007
1988	693,577	177,352	571,408	6,270	348,492	152,633
1989	687,725	185,804	576,872	5,808	346,697	150,872
1990	706,140	199,999	564,846	5,564	...	153,386

Expectation of life, 1988: UK, males, 72·4 years, females, 78; England and Wales, males, 72·7, females, 78·2.

Birth rate, 1990, per 1,000 population, 13·9; death rate, 11·1; marriage rate (1989), 13·7; divorce rate (1989) per 1,000 married couples, 12·7; infant mortality per 1,000 live births, 7·9; sex ratio, 1,048 male births to 1,000 female. Average age of first marriage, 1989: Males, 27, females, 25.

It is estimated that in Great Britain in 1989 some 18·9% of unmarried females between the ages of 16 and 49 were cohabiting.

Vital statistics for Scotland:

	Estimated resident population at 30 June [1]	Total births	Live births outside marriage	Deaths	Marriages	Divorces, annulments and dis-solutions
1983	5,150,405	65,078	9,581	63,454	34,962	13,238
1984	5,145,722	65,106	10,640	62,345	36,253	11,915
1985	5,136,509	66,676	12,362	63,967	36,385	13,373
1986	5,121,013	65,812	13,547	63,467	35,790	12,800
1987	5,112,129	66,241	15,125	62,014	35,813	12,133
1988	5,094,001	66,212	16,224	61,957	35,599	11,472
1989	5,090,700	63,480	16,476	65,017	35,326	11,659
1990	5,102,400	65,973	17,873	61,527	34,672	12,272

[1] Includes merchant navy at home and forces stationed in Scotland.

Birth rate, 1990, per 1,000 population, 12·9; death rate, 12·1; marriage, 6·8; divorce rate per 1,000 married couples, 10·5; infant mortality per 1,000 live births, 7·7; sex ratio, 1,057 male births to 1,000 female. Average age of marriage in 1990: Males, 29·8, females 27·5. Expectation of life, 1990: Males, 71·1 years, females, 76·9.

Emigration and Immigration. During the last hundred years the UK has most often been a net exporter of population. Throughout the period 1881–1931 there was a consistent net loss from migration, though the fifteen years 1931–46 brought a reversal of the trend as a result of immigration from Europe. Since the Second World War the loss has largely continued. However, during the five years 1956–1961, increased immigration particularly from the new Commonwealth and Pakistan, resulted in a net gain.

Since 1964 migration figures have been available from the International Passenger Survey. This is a sample survey conducted by the Office of Population Censuses and Surveys, covering all the principal air and sea routes between the UK and overseas, except those to and from the Republic of Ireland. For the years 1971–80 the survey shows an average annual net loss for the UK of 35,000; and for 1981–90, an average annual net gain of 7,000.

The table below, derived from the International Passenger survey, summarizes migration statistics for 1990 (in 1,000):

By country of last or future intended residence	Into UK	Out from UK	Balance
All countries	267	231	+36
EC	66	59	+7
Australia, Canada, New Zealand	57	59	−3
India, Bangladesh, Sri Lanka, Pakistan	22	5	+17
Other Commonwealth	37	23	+14
USA	29	42	−13
South Africa	6	9	−3
Rest of World	50	34	+16
By sex/age in 1990			
Males 0–14	22	16	+6
15–24	37	31	+6
25–44	64	57	+7
45 and over	12	9	+3
All ages	135	113	+22
Females 0–14	19	25	−5
15–24	49	37	+11
25–44	55	48	+7
45 and over	9	8	+1
All ages	132	118	+14

CLIMATE. The climate is cool temperate oceanic, with mild conditions and rainfall evenly distributed over the year, though the weather is very changeable because of cyclonic influences. In general, temperatures are higher in the west and lower in the east in winter and rather the reverse in summer. Rainfall amounts are greatest in the west, where most of the high ground occurs.

London. Jan. 40°F (4·5°C), July 64°F (18°C). Annual rainfall 24" (600 mm).
Aberdeen. Jan. 39°F (4°C), July 57°F (14°C). Annual rainfall 33" (823 mm).
Belfast. Jan. 40°F (4·5°C), July 61°F (16·1°C). Annual rainfall 34·6" (865 mm).
Birmingham. Jan. 38°F (3·3°C), July 61°F (16·1°C). Annual rainfall 30" (749 mm).
Cardiff. Jan. 40°F (4·4°C), July 61°F (16·1°C). Annual rainfall 42·6" (1,065 mm).
Edinburgh. Jan. 38°F (3·5°C), July 58°F (14·5°C). Annual rainfall 28" (708 mm).
Glasgow. Jan. 39°F (4°C), July 60°F (15·5°C). Annual rainfall 37·2" (930 mm).
Manchester. Jan. 41°F (5°C), July 62°F (16·5°C). Annual rainfall 34·1" (853 mm).

QUEEN, HEAD OF THE COMMONWEALTH. Elizabeth II Alexandra Mary, born 21 April 1926 daughter of King George VI and Queen Elizabeth; married on 20 Nov. 1947 Lieut. Philip Mountbatten (formerly Prince Philip of Greece), created Duke of Edinburgh, Earl of Merioneth and Baron Greenwich on the same day and created Prince Philip, Duke of Edinburgh, 22 Feb. 1957; succeeded to the crown on the death of her father, on 6 Feb. 1952. Offspring: *Charles* Philip Arthur George, Prince of Wales (Heir Apparent), born 14 Nov. 1948, married Lady Diana Spencer on 29 July 1981. Offspring: *William* Arthur Philip Louis, born 21 June 1982; *Henry* Charles Albert David, born 15 Sept. 1984. Princess *Anne* Elizabeth Alice Louise, the Princess Royal, born 15 Aug. 1950, married Mark Anthony Peter Phillips on 14 Nov. 1973; divorced, 1992. Offspring: *Peter* Mark Andrew, born 15 Nov. 1977; *Zara* Anne Elizabeth, born 15 May 1981. Prince *Andrew* Albert Christian Edward, created Duke of York, 23 July 1986, born 19 Feb. 1960, married Sarah Margaret Ferguson on 23 July 1986. Offspring: Princess *Beatrice* Mary, born 8 Aug. 1988; Princess *Eugenie* Victoria Helena, born 23 March 1990. Prince *Edward* Antony Richard Louis, born 10 March 1964.

The Queen Mother: Queen Elizabeth, born 4 Aug. 1900, daughter of the 14th Earl of Strathmore and Kinghorne; married the Duke of York, afterwards King George VI, on 26 April 1923.

Sister of the Queen: Princess Margaret Rose, born 12 Aug. 1930; married Antony Armstrong-Jones (created Earl of Snowdon, 3 Oct. 1961) on 6 May 1960; divorced, 1978. Offspring: *David* Albert Charles (Viscount Linley), born 3 Nov. 1961; Lady *Sarah* Frances Elizabeth Armstrong-Jones, born 1964.

Children of the late Duke of Gloucester (died 10 June 1974): William Henry Andrew Frederick, born 18 Dec. 1941, died 28 Aug. 1972; Richard Alexander Walter George, Duke of Gloucester, born 26 Aug. 1944, married Birgitte van Deurs on 8 July 1972 (offspring: Alexander Patrick Gregers Richard Windsor, Earl of Ulster, born 24 Oct. 1974; Davina Elizabeth Alice Benedikte Windsor, born 19 Nov. 1977; Rose Victoria Birgitte Louise Windsor, born 1 March 1980).

Children of the late Duke of Kent (died 25 Aug. 1942): Edward George Nicholas Patrick, Duke of Kent, born 9 Oct. 1935; married Katharine Worsley on 8 June 1961 (offspring: George Philip Nicholas, Earl of St Andrews, born 26 June 1962, married Sylvania Tomaselli on 9 Jan. 1988 (offspring: Lord Downpatrick, born 2 Dec. 1988); Lady Helen Windsor, born 28 April 1964; Lord Nicholas Charles Edward Jonathan Windsor, born 25 July 1970). Alexandra Helen Elizabeth Olga Christabel, born 25 Dec. 1936; married 24 April 1963, Angus Ogilvy (offspring: James Robert Bruce, born 29 Feb. 1964; Marina Victoria Alexandra, born 31 July 1966). Michael George Charles Franklin, born 4 July 1942; married Marie-Christine von Reibnitz on 30 June 1978 (offspring: Lord *Frederick* Michael George David Louis Windsor, born 6 April 1979; Lady *Gabriela* Marina Alexander Ophelia Windsor, born 23 April 1981).

The Queen's legal title rests on the statute of 12 and 13 Will. III, ch. 3, by which the succession to the Crown of Great Britain and Ireland was settled on the Princess Sophia of Hanover and the 'heirs of her body being Protestants'. By proclamation of 17 July 1917 the royal family became known as the House and Family of Windsor. On 8 Feb. 1960 the Queen issued a declaration varying her confirmatory declaration of 9 April 1952 to the effect that while the Queen and her children should continue to be known as the House of Windsor, her descendants, other than descendants entitled to the style of Royal Highness and the title of Prince or Princess, and female descendants who marry and their descendants should bear the name of Mountbatten-Windsor. For the Royal Style and Titles of Queen Elizabeth *see* Commonwealth section.

By letters patent of 30 Nov. 1917 the titles of Royal Highness and Prince or Princess are restricted to the Sovereign's children, the children of the Sovereign's sons and the eldest living son of the eldest son of the Prince of Wales.

Provision is made for the support of the royal household, after the surrender of hereditary revenues, by the settlement of the Civil List soon after the beginning of each reign. (For historical details, *see* THE STATESMAN'S YEAR-BOOK, 1908, p. 5, and 1935 p. 4). The Civil List Act of 1 Jan. 1972 provided for a decennial, and the Civil List (Increase of Financial Provision) Order 1975 for an annual review of the List, but in July 1990 it was again fixed for one decade.

The Civil List of 1991-2000 provides for an annuity of £7,900,000 to the Queen; £230,500 to the Princess Royal; £360,000 to Prince Philip; £640,500 to Queen Elizabeth (the Queen Mother); £220,000 to the Princess Margaret; £250,000 to the Duke of York; £100,000 to Prince Edward. The income of the Prince of Wales derives from the Duchy of Cornwall. The Civil List was exempted from taxation in 1910.

Sovereigns of Great Britain, from the Restoration (with dates of accession):

House of Stewart		George III	25 Oct. 1760
Charles II	29 May 1660	George IV	29 Jan. 1820
James II	6 Feb. 1685	William IV	26 June 1830
		Victoria	20 June 1837
House of Stewart-Orange			
William and Mary	13 Feb. 1689	*House of Saxe-Coburg and Gotha*	
William III	28 Dec. 1694	Edward VII	22 Jan. 1901
House of Stewart		*House of Windsor*	
Anne	19 March 1702	George V	6 May 1910
		Edward VIII	20 Jan. 1936
House of Hanover		George VI	11 Dec. 1936
George I	1 Aug. 1714	Elizabeth II	6 Feb. 1952
George II	11 June 1727		

CONSTITUTION AND GOVERNMENT. The supreme legislative power is vested in Parliament, which consists of the Crown, the House of Lords and the House of Commons and dates in its present form from the middle of the 14th century. A Bill which is passed by both Houses and receives Royal Assent becomes an Act of Parliament and part of statute law.

Parliament is summoned, and a General Election is called, by the sovereign on the advice of the Prime Minister. A Parliament may last up to 5 years, normally divided into annual sessions. A session is ended by prorogation, and all Bills which have not been passed by both Houses then lapse. A Parliament ends by dissolution, either by will of the sovereign or by lapse of the 5-year period.

Under the Parliament Acts 1911 and 1949, all Money Bills (so certified by the Speaker of the House of Commons), if not passed by the Lords without amendment, may become law without their concurrence within 1 month of introduction in the Lords. Public Bills, other than Money Bills or a Bill extending the maximum duration of Parliament, if passed by the Commons in 2 successive sessions and rejected each time by the Lords, may become law without their concurrence provided that 1 year has elapsed between Commons second reading in the first session and third reading in the second session, and that the Bill reaches the Lords at least 1 month before the end of the second session. No Act has been passed in this way since 1949, because the Lords today respect the privileges of the elected House, especially as regards taxes and public spending, and act mainly as a revising chamber.

Peerages are created by the sovereign, without limit of number. They are held for life, and may or may not be hereditary. The House of Lords consisted (on 31 Dec. 1991) of: (1) 760 hereditary peers (including 20 women) sitting by virtue of creation or descent, other than those who have disclaimed their titles for life under the provisions of the Peerage Act, 1963; (2) life peers (non-hereditary being (a) 18

Lords of Appeal (active and retired), under the Appellate Jurisdiction Act, 1876, as amended; *(b)* 371 peers (including 59 women) under the Life Peerages Act, 1958; (3) 2 archbishops and 24 diocesan bishops of the Church of England, who leave the House on retirement. The full House thus consists of 1,194, with an average daily attendance of 329.

The House of Commons consists of members (of both sexes) representing constituencies determined by the Boundary Commissions. Persons under 21 years of age, Clergy of the Church of England and of the Scottish Episcopal Church, Ministers of the Church of Scotland, Roman Catholic clergymen, civil servants, members of the regular armed forces, policemen, most judicial officers and other office-holders named in the House of Commons (Disqualification) Act are disqualified from sitting in the House of Commons. No peer eligible to sit in the House of Lords can be elected to the House of Commons unless he has disclaimed his title, but Irish peers and holders of courtesy titles, who are not members of the House of Lords, are eligible.

The Representation of the People Act 1948, abolished the business premises and University franchises, and the only persons entitled to vote at Parliamentary elections are those registered as residents or as service voters. No person may vote in more than one constituency at a general election. Persons may apply on certain grounds to vote by post or by proxy. Elections are held on the first-past-the-post system, in which the candidate who receives the most votes is elected.

All persons over 18 years old and not subject to any legal incapacity to vote and who are either British subjects or citizens of Ireland are entitled to be included in the register of electors for the constituency containing the address at which they were residing on the qualifying date for the register and are entitled to vote at elections held during the period for which the register remains in force.

Members of the armed forces, Crown servants employed abroad, and the wives accompanying their husbands, are entitled, if otherwise qualified, to be registered as 'service voters' provided they make a 'service declaration'. To be effective for a particular register, the declaration must be made on or before the qualifying date for that register. In certain circumstances, British subjects living abroad may also vote.

The House of Commons (Redistribution of Seats) Acts 1944, 1949 and 1958, provided for the setting up of Boundary Commissions for England, Wales, Scotland and Northern Ireland. The Commissions are required to make general reports at intervals of not less than 10 and not more than 15 years and to submit reports from time to time with respect to the area comprised in any particular constituency or constituencies where some change appears necessary. Any changes giving effect to reports of the Commissions are to be made by Orders in Council laid before Parliament for approval by resolution of each House. The Parliamentary electorate of the United Kingdom and Northern Ireland in the register in 1991 numbered 43,556,783, of whom 36,302,099 were in England, 2,207,283 in Wales, 3,914,590 in Scotland and 1,132,811 in Northern Ireland.

At the general election held in 1992, 651 members were returned, 524 from England, 72 from Scotland, 38 from Wales and 17 from Northern Ireland. Every constituency returns a single member.

In Aug. 1911 provision was first made for the payment of a salary of £400 per annum to members of the Commons, other than those already in receipt of salaries as officers of the House, as Ministers or as officers of Her Majesty's household. As from 1 Jan. 1992 the salaries of members are £30,854 per annum. There is an office costs allowance of up to £28,986 per annum and a living allowance, for an additional home, of up to £10,570 per annum. Members of the House of Lords are unsalaried but may recover expenses incurred in attending sittings of the House within maxima for each day's attendance of £26 for day subsistence, £68 for night subsistence and £27 for secretarial and research assistance and office expenses. Additionally, Members of the House who are disabled may recover the extra cost of attending the House incurred by reason of their disablement. In connection with attendance at the House and parliamentary duties within the UK Lords may also recover the cost of travelling to and from home.

The following is a table of the duration of Parliaments called since Aug. 1945:

Reign	When met	When dissolved	Duration (years and days)	
George VI	1 Aug. 1945	3 Feb. 1950	4	188
,,	1 Mar. 1950	5 Oct. 1951	1	219
George VI and Elizabeth II	31 Oct. 1951	6 May 1955	3	188
Elizabeth II	7 June 1955	18 Sept. 1959	4	105
,,	20 Oct. 1959	25 Sept. 1964	4	341
,,	27 Oct. 1964	10 Mar. 1966	1	134
,,	18 Apr. 1966	29 May 1970	4	81
,,	29 June 1970	8 Feb. 1974	3	225
,,	12 Mar. 1974	20 Sept. 1974	0	224
,,	22 Oct. 1974	7 April 1979	4	167
,,	9 May 1979	13 May 1983	4	4
,,	15 June 1983	18 May 1987	3	338
,,	25 June 1987	16 March 1992	4	266
,,	27 April 1992	—	—	—

The executive government is vested nominally in the Crown, but practically in a committee of Ministers, called the Cabinet, which is dependent on the support of a majority in the House of Commons. The head of the Ministry is the Prime Minister, a position first constitutionally recognized in 1905. His colleagues in the Ministry are appointed on his recommendation, and he dispenses the greater portion of the patronage of the Crown.

Heads of the Administrations since 1937 (C. = Conservative, L. = Liberal, Lab. = Labour, Nat. = National, Coal. = Coalition, Care. = Caretaker):

N. Chamberlain (Nat.)	28 May 1937	Sir Alec Douglas-Home (C.)	18 Oct. 1963
W. S. Churchill (Coal.)	10 May 1940	H. Wilson (Lab.)	16 Oct. 1964
W. S. Churchill (Care.)	23 May 1945	E. Heath (C.)	19 June 1970
C. R. Attlee (Lab.)	26 July 1945	H. Wilson (Lab.)	12 Mar. 1974
W. S. Churchill (C.)	26 Oct. 1951	J. Callaghan (Lab.)	5 Apr. 1976
Sir Anthony Eden (C.)	6 Apr. 1955	M. Thatcher (C.)	4 May 1979
H. Macmillan (C.)	10 Jan. 1957	J. Major (C.)	22 Nov. 1990

At the general election of 9 April 1992 33,145,074 votes were cast. The Conservative Party gained 336 seats with 42·8% of votes cast (376 with 42·3% in 1987); the Labour Party 271 with 35·2% (229 with 32%), the Liberal Democratic Party 20 with 18·3% (19 with 23·1%). The Ulster Unionist Party gained 9 seats, Plaid Cymru (Welsh nationalist) 4, the Social and Democratic Labour Party 4, the Scottish National Party 3, the Democratic Unionist Party 3, the Ulster Popular Unionist Party 1.

In April 1992 the Government consisted of the following members:

(a) MEMBERS OF THE CABINET

1. *Prime Minister, First Lord of the Treasury and Minister for the Civil Service:* Rt Hon. John Major, MP, born 1943. (Salary £53,007 per annum.)

2. *Lord Chancellor:* Rt Hon. The Lord Mackay of Clashfern, QC, born 1927. (£106,750.)

3. *Secretary of State for Foreign and Commonwealth Affairs:* Rt Hon. Douglas Hurd, CBE, MP, born 1930. (£39,820.)

4. *Chancellor of the Exchequer:* Rt Hon. Norman Lamont, MP, born 1942. (£39,820.)

5. *Secretary of State for the Home Department:* Rt Hon. Kenneth Clarke, QC, MP, born 1940. (£39,820.)

6. *Secretary of State for Trade and Industry:* Rt Hon. Michael Heseltine, MP, born 1933. (£39,820.)

7. *Secretary of State for Transport:* Rt Hon. John MacGregor, OBE, MP, born 1937. (£39,820.)

8. *Secretary of State for Defence:* Rt Hon. Malcolm Rifkind, QC, MP, born 1946. (£39,820.)

9. *Lord Privy Seal and Leader of the House of Lords:* Rt Hon. John Wakeham, born 1932. (£50,558.)

10. *Lord President of the Council, Leader of the House of Commons and Deputy Prime Minister:* Rt Hon. Tony Newton, OBE, MP, born 1937. (£39,820.)

11. *Minister of Agriculture, Fisheries and Food:* Rt Hon. John Gummer, MP, born 1939. (£39,820.)

12. *Secretary of State for the Environment:* Rt Hon. Michael Howard, QC, MP, born 1941. (£39,820.)

13. *Secretary of State for Wales:* Rt Hon. David Hunt, MBE, MP, born 1942. (£39,820.)

14. *Secretary of State for Social Security:* Rt Hon. Peter Lilley, MP, born 1943. (£39,820.)

15. *Chancellor of the Duchy of Lancaster:* Rt Hon. William Waldegrave, QC, MP, born 1946. (£30,854.)

16. *Secretary of State for Scotland:* Rt Hon. Ian Lang, QC, MP, born 1940. (£39,820.)

17. *Secretary of State for National Heritage:* Rt Hon. David Mellor, QC, MP, born 1949. (£39,820.)

18. *Secretary of State for Northern Ireland:* Rt Hon. Sir Patrick Mayhew, QC, MP, born 1929. (£39,820.)

19. *Secretary of State for Education and Science:* Rt Hon. John Patten, MP, born 1945. (£39,820.)

20. *Secretary of State for Health:* Rt Hon. Virginia Bottomley, MP, born 1948. (£39,820.)

21. *Secretary of State for Employment:* Rt Hon. Gillian Shephard, MP, born 1940. (£39,820.)

22. *Chief Secretary to the Treasury:* Rt Hon. Michael Portillo, MP, born 1953. (£39,820.)

(b) Law Officers

23. *Attorney-General:* Rt Hon. Sir Nicholas Lyell, QC, MP, born 1938. (£42,314.)

24. *Lord Advocate:* Alan Rodger, QC, born 1944. (£50,638.)

25. *Solicitor-General:* Derek Spencer, QC, MP, born 1936. (£34,695.)

26. *Solicitor-General for Scotland:* Thomas Dawson, QC, born 1948. (£44,342.)

(c) Ministers not in the Cabinet

27. *Parliamentary Secretary, Treasury (Chief Whip):* Rt Hon. Richard Ryder, OBE, MP, born 1949. (£33,142.)

28. *Minister of State, Foreign and Commonwealth Office:* Rt Hon. Alastair Goodlad, MP, born 1943. (£44,945.)

29. *Minister of State, Foreign and Commonwealth Office:* Rt. Hon. Douglas Hogg, MP, born 1945. (£28,175.)

30. *Minister of State, Foreign and Commonwealth Office:* Rt. Hon. Tristan Garel-Jones, MP, born 1941. (£28,175.)

31. *Financial Secretary, Treasury:* Stephen Dorrell, MP, born 1952. (£28,175.)

32. *Minister of State, Northern Ireland Office and Paymaster General (Northern Ireland Office):* The Rt Hon. Michael Mates, MP, born 1934. (£44,495.)

33. *Minister of State, Northern Ireland Office:* Rt Hon. Robert Atkins, MP, born 1946. (£28,175.)

34. *Minister of State, Home Office:* Peter Lloyd, MP, born 1937. (£28,175.)

35. *Minister of State, Home Office:* Michael Jack, MP, born 1946. (£28,175.)

36. *Minister of State, Home Office:* Rt Hon. The Earl Ferrers, DL, born 1929. (£44,495.)

37. *Minister of State, Welsh Office:* Sir Wyn Roberts, MP, born 1930. (£26,962.)

38. *Minister of State, Ministry of Defence:* Rt Hon. Jonathan Aitken, MP, born 1943. (£28,175.)

39. *Minister of State, Ministry of Defence:* Hon. Archie Hamilton, MP, born 1941. (£28,175.)

40. *Minister of State, Department of Trade and Industry:* Rt Hon. Tim Sainsbury, born 1932. (£28,175.)

41. *Minister of State, Department of Trade and Industry:* Tim Eggar, MP, born 1951. (£28,175.)

42. *Minister of State, Department of Trade and Industry:* Richard Needham, MP, born 1942. (£28,175.)

43. *Minister of State, Department of Health, Minister of Health:* Dr Brian Mawhinney, MP, born 1940. (£28,175.)

44. *Minister of State, Department of Education and Science:* Baroness Blatch, born 1937. (£28,175.)

45. *Minister of State, Scottish Office:* Lord Fraser of Carmyllie, QC, born 1945. (£28,175.)

46. *Minister of State, Department of Transport, Minister for Public Transport:* Roger Freeman, FCA, MP, born 1942. (£28,175.)

47. *Minister of State, Department of Transport, Minister for Aviation and Shipping:* The Earl of Caithness, born 1948. (£44,945.)

48. *Minister of State, Department of Social Security, Minister for Social Security and Disabled People:* Rt Hon. Nicholas Scott, MBE, MP, born 1933. (£28,175.)

49. *Minister of State, Department of the Environment, Minister for the Environment and Countryside:* David MacLean, MP, born 1953. (£28,175.)

50. *Minister of State, Department of the Environment, Minister for Local Government and Inner Cities:* John Redwood, MP, born 1952. (£28,175.)

51. *Minister of State, Department of the Environment, Minister for Housing and Planning:* Sir George Young, MP, born 1941. (£28,175.)

52. *Minister of State, Department of Employment:* Michael Forsyth, MP, born 1954. (£28,175.)

53. *Minister of State, Ministry of Agriculture, Fisheries and Food:* David Curry, MP, born 1944. (£44,945.)

54. *Minister of State, Department of Social Security:* Nicholas Scott, MP, born 1933. (£28,175.)

Leader of the Opposition in the House of Commons: Scheduled for election by the Labour Party on 18 July 1992. (£36,509.)

Leader of the Opposition in the House of Lords: Rt Hon. The Lord Cledwyn of Penrhos, born 1916. (£37,689.)

Cabinet Ministers, Ministers of State, Parliamentary Secretaries and the Leader of the Opposition who are also Members of Parliament, receive additionally a reduced Parliamentary salary of £23,227.

Ball, A., *British Political Parties: The Emergence of a Modern Party System.* 1981
Butler, D. and Butler, G., *British Political Facts, 1900–85.* London, 1986
Dod's Parliamentary Companion. London [published after elections]
Drewry, G. (ed.), *The New Select Committees.* OUP, 1985
King, A. (ed.), *The British Prime Minister.* Rev. ed. London, 1985.—*British Members of Parliament.* London, 1974

Mackintosh, J. P., *The British Cabinet*. 3rd ed. London, 1977.—*The Government and Politics of Britain*. 4th ed. London, 1977

May, Sir T. E., *Treatise on the Law, Privileges, Proceedings and Usage of Parliament*. 20th ed., London, 1983

Norton, P., *Parliament in the 1980s*. Oxford, 1985

Parker, F. K., *Conduct of Parliamentary Elections*. London, 1983

Shell, D., *The House of Lords*. 2nd ed. Hemel Hempstead, 1992

Silk, E. P., *How Parliament Works*. London, 1987

The Times Guide to the House of Commons. London, [published after elections]

Waller, R., *The Almanac of British Politics*. 4th ed. London, 1991

National flag: The combined crosses of St George (red), St Andrew (white) and St Patrick (red), the red fimbriated in white, all on a blue ground.

European Parliament: On 15 June 1989 Great Britain elected 81 representatives to the European Parliament, of which 66 came from England, 8 from Scotland and 4 from Wales, each constituency returning a single member by a first past the post system. Northern Ireland returned 3 members by single transferable vote. The seats were won as follows: Labour 45, Conservative 32, Scottish Nationalists 1, Ulster Unionists 1, Democratic Unionists 1, Social, Democratic and Labour Party 1.

Local Government. Local Administration is carried out by four different types of bodies, namely: (i) local branches of some central ministries, such as the Department of Health and Social Security (now two separate departments); (ii) local sub-managements of nationalized industries; (iii) specialist authorities such as electricity boards; and (iv) the system of local government described below. The phrase 'local government' has come to mean that part of the local administration conducted by elected councils.

There are two separate systems, one for England and Wales and one for Scotland, but both systems are financed by a charge on individuals known as the Community Charge paid at a flat rate by each adult, varying from one area to another, levied locally, supplemented by a new streamlined government grant system and a nation-wide uniform tax on business property - the Uniform Business Rate.

Local Government: England and Wales—*Outside London.* England and Wales have slightly differing systems. Each country has three types of councils namely, county, district and English parish or Welsh Community Councils. In addition, England has some metropolitan district councils.

Councillors are elected by their local electors for 4 years. The chairman of the council is one of the councillors elected by the rest. In a district with the status of borough his or her title is mayor. Mayors of cities may have the title of lord mayor conferred on them. 51 towns in England and Wales have the status of city. This status is granted by the personal command of the monarch and confers no special privileges or powers. Any parish or community council can by simple resolution adopt the style 'town council' and the status of town for the parish or community. The chairman of the council will be known as the town mayor.

Elections were held for 12,370 local councillors outside London in May 1991.

Counties and Districts: There are 47 non-metropolitan counties (of which 8 are in Wales). The 6 metropolitan counties (Greater Manchester, Merseyside, South Yorkshire, Tyne and Wear, West Yorkshire and West Midlands) have no councils, the metropolitan districts having most of the county functions. Within the counties there are 369 districts (36 metropolitan and 333 non-metropolitan, of which 37 are in Wales).

Parishes and Communities: There are some 10,000 parishes within the English districts, of which 8,000 or so have councils. About 300 are former small boroughs or urban districts which became successor parishes.

In Wales, parishes are known as communities. Unlike England, where some urban areas are not in any parish, communities have been established for the whole of Wales. There is one for each former parish, county borough, borough or urban district (or part thereof where the former area is divided by a new boundary). There are about 1,000 communities altogether, of which 800 or so have councils.

The Local Government Act 1972 laid down the boundaries for all the counties and districts in England and Wales except the English non-metropolitan districts.

Permanent Local Government Boundary Commissions for England and for Wales advise the Secretaries of State on boundaries and electoral arrangements.

Local government functions may be classified into county, district and parish or community functions, but whereas county and district functions are distinct, the parish and community functions are mostly concurrent with those of the districts. Arrangements may, however, be made so that any council may discharge functions of any other as its agent.

The following is the classification of powers given above: *Parish and Community Functions.* Allotments, burial and cremation, halls, meeting places and entertainments, facilities for exercise and recreation, public lavatories, street lighting, offstreet vehicle parking, footpaths, the support of local arts and crafts, the encouragement of tourism and the right to be consulted by the district council on planning applications and certain byelaws. *District Functions.* In addition to the Parish and Community functions, aerodromes, civic restaurants, housing, markets, refuse collection, the administration of planning control, the formulation of local plans, sewerage on behalf of the water authority, museums, the licensing of places of entertainment and refreshment, and the constitutional oversight of parishes and communities. *County Functions.* The formulation of structure plans, traffic, transportation and roads, education, public libraries and museums, youth employment and social services.

There are, in addition, a number of special arrangements. Four district councils in Wales are designated as library authorities and Welsh district councils have powers in relation to allotments currently with community councils. The county councils in England and Wales separately or jointly appoint the fire and police authorities, and the bodies responsible for national parks. In Metropolitan counties, there are no county councils and all functions are performed by the districts (in some cases jointly). The total number of local government electors in England and Wales was 38,478,502 in 1991.

Greater London. From 1965–86 London was governed by the Greater London Council, covering the whole metropolitan area, and by 32 London boroughs and the Corporation of the City of London, each with responsibilities in its own area. The GLC was abolished on 1 April 1986. The individual borough councils are the education authorities. Fire services in Greater London are the responsibility of the London Fire and Civil Defence Authority, whose members are appointed by the boroughs and the City. Flood prevention is the responsibility of the Thames Water Authority. Waste regulation for the whole of Greater London is the function of the London Waste Regulation Authority. Waste collection is the responsibility of the boroughs. Waste disposal is the responsibility of the boroughs acting individually or in groups. Except in the City, the police authority is the Metropolitan Police, which is responsible to central government. London Regional Transport is likewise responsible to central government for passenger transport. Other local government functions are the responsibility of the boroughs, acting either individually or jointly, and the City.

Net current expenditure for all London authorities in 1988–89 was estimated at £4,832m. (including £978m. for ILEA but excluding Metropolitan Police). Gross capital expenditure (excluding leasing) for all London authorities and the London Residuary Body was estimated at £1,300m. in 1987–88.

Saint, A., (ed.) *Politics and the People of London.* London, 1989

Scotland. For local government purposes, mainland Scotland is divided on a two-tier basis into 9 regions and 53 districts. Functions are allocated between regional and district councils in the same way (with minor exceptions) as they are allocated between county and district councils in England. The 3 islands areas of Orkney, Shetland and the Western Isles have single-tier councils responsible for virtually all functions. The members of each council are elected for a 4-year term, elections for regional and islands councils alternating with elections for district councils at 2-year intervals. Each council elects a chairman for the 4-year term. In some cases the chairman is called 'Convener' or 'Provost', and the chairman of Edinburgh, Glasgow, Aberdeen and Dundee District Councils are titled 'Lord Provost'.

Over 1,000 community councils have been established under schemes drawn up by district and island councils. These community councils cannot claim public funds as of right nor do they have specific powers conferred by statute: Consequently they are not local authorities in the sense that English parish councils or Welsh community councils are.

As in England and Wales, a permanent Local Government Boundary Commission advises the Secretary of State on local authority boundaries and electoral constituencies.

The total number of local government electors in Scotland was 3,912,528 in 1991.

DEFENCE. The Defence Council was established on 1 April 1964 under the chairmanship of the Secretary of State for Defence, who is responsible to the Sovereign and Parliament for the defence of the realm. Vested in the Defence Council are the functions of commanding and administering the Armed Forces. The Secretary of State heads the Ministry of Defence as a Department of State. There are 4 subordinate Ministers; 2 Ministers of State and 2 Parliamentary Under-Secretaries of State.

Defence Council membership comprises the Secretary of State, the 4 Ministers mentioned above, the Chief of the Defence Staff, the 3 single Service Chiefs of Staff, the Vice-Chief of Defence Staff, the Chief of Defence Procurement, the Chief Scientific Adviser, the Permanent Under-Secretary of State and the Second Permanent Under Secretary of State.

There are 3 Service Boards, each of which enjoys delegated powers for the administration of matters relating to the naval, military and air forces respectively.

Defence policy decision making is a collective Governmental responsibility. Important matters of policy are considered by the full Cabinet or, more frequently, by the Defence and Oversea Policy Committee under the chairmanship of the Prime Minister. Other members of this Committee include the Secretary of State for Defence, the Foreign and Commonwealth Secretary and the Home Secretary.

The Procurement Executive. An important development in 1971 was the creation of a Procurement Executive to combine the Defence Procurement responsibilities of the Ministry of Defence and the former Ministry of Aviation Supply.

Service Strengths at 1 Jan. 1990, all ranks, males and females, UK personnel only: Royal Navy and Royal Marines, 83,500; Army, 152,900; Royal Air Force, 89,600; total, 306,000. In Jan. 90 the Ministry of Defence employed 171,800 civilians (140,600 in the UK).

Defence Budget (Plans): 1990–91, £21,223m; 1991–92, £22,360m 1992–93 £22,430.

Army. Control of the British Army is vested in the Defence Council and is exercised through the Army Board. The Secretary of State for Defence is Chairman of the Army Board. The other civilian members are the 4 subordinate Ministers; the Controller Establishments, Research and Nuclear Programmes and the Second Permanent Under Secretary of State.

The Military members of the Army Board are the Chief of the General Staff, the Adjutant General, the Quartermaster General and the Master General of the Ordnance. The Chief of the General Staff is the professional head of his Service and the professional adviser to Ministers on the Army aspects of military matters. He is responsible for the fighting efficiency of his Service; for Army advice on the conduct of operations; and for the issuing of such single Service operational orders as may be appropriate resulting from defence policy decisions. He is also responsible for the Territorial Army. The Chief of the General Staff is a member of the Chiefs of Staff Committee which is chaired by the Chief of the Defence Staff, who is responsible to HM Government for professional advice on strategy and military operations and on the military implication of defence policy. The Adjutant-General is responsible for recruiting and selection of army manpower; for the administration and individual training of military personnel; for the discipline of the Army; for pay and allowances and pensions; for legal services; for the veterinary and remount services; for the Army Cadet Forces; for questions of Army welfare and education including school children overseas; and for resettlement and sports. The Quartermaster-General is responsible for logistic planning for the Army; for the storage, distribution, maintenance, repair and inspection of equipment, stores and ammunition; for development of stores; for supply, transport and accommodation; for the development, production and inspection of clothing; for military movements and transportation; for the Army postal, catering, salvage and fire services; and for questions connected with canteens, institutes and military labour. The Master General of the Ordnance is a member of both the Army Board and of the Procurement Executive Management Board. He is responsible to the Chief of Defence Procurement for the financial and technical management of the approved programme for the procurement of land service equipment for the Armed Services, and to the Army Board for the co-ordination of the Army's total equipment programme.

Headquarters United Kingdom Land Forces at Wilton commands all Army units in UK except Ministry of Defence controlled units. The Ministry of Defence retains direct operational control of units in Northern Ireland. Command by HQ United Kingdom Land Forces is exercised through 5 district headquarters. There are 3 major overseas Commands: Land Forces British Army of the Rhine, Hong Kong and Cyprus. There are also garrisons in Berlin, Falkland Islands, Brunei and Belize. The Army Air Corps has some 300 helicopters and 25 fixed-wing aircraft.

The strength of the Regular Army (less the Brigade of Gurkhas and locally enlisted personnel) on 1 April 1991 was 140,400 men and 7,200 women. Strength of reserve forces were: Individual reserves, 187,500; Territorial Army, 72,000; Home Service Force, 3,200.

The Territorial Army (TA) role is to provide a national reserve for employment on specific tasks at home and overseas and to meet the unexpected when required; and, in particular, to complete the Army Order of Battle of NATO committed forces and to provide certain units for the support of NATO Headquarters, to assist in maintaining a secure UK base in support of forces deployed on the Continent of Europe and to provide a framework for any future expansion of the Reserves. In addition, men who have completed service in the Regular Army normally have some liability to serve in the Regular Reserve. All members of the TA and Regular Reserve may be called out by a Queen's Order in time of emergency of imminent national danger and most of the TA and a large proportion of the Regular Reserve may be called out by a Queen's Order when warlike operations are in preparation or in progress. The Home Service Battalions of the Royal Irish Regiment are only liable for service in Northern Ireland.

Men, women and juniors enlist in the Army for 22 years' active and reserve service. Soldiers enlist for a minimum of 3 years and can leave active service thereafter on one year's notice. Bonuses are paid to those who serve for certain periods and there are manning control points at which the Army may require soldiers to terminate their service, again on one year's notice. Those enlisting in certain technical trades must agree to serve for a minimum of 6 years. Recruits under the age of $17^{1}/_{2}$ on reaching the age of 18 are entitled either to confirm their original engagement or to reduce their period of service to 3 years.

Women serve throughout the Army in the same regiments and corps as men. There are only a few roles in which they are not employed such as the Infantry and Royal Armoured Corps.

Blaxford, G., *The Regiments Depart: A History of the British Army 1945–70*. London, 1971
Brereton, J. M., *The British Soldier*. London, 1985
Johnson, F. A., *Defence by Ministry: The British Ministry of Defence 1944–1974*. London, 1980
Strawson, J., *Gentlemen in Khaki: The British Army 1890–1990*. London, 1989

Navy. Control of the Royal Navy is vested in the Defence Council and is exercised through the Admiralty Board, chaired by the Secretary of State for Defence. The other civilian members are the Ministers and Under Secretaries of State for the Armed Forces and Defence Procurement and the Second Permanent Under Secretary of State. The naval members are the Chief of Naval Staff (First Sea Lord) responsible for management, fighting efficiency, planning and operational advice;

the Chief of Naval Personnel (Second Sea Lord), responsible for the manning of the Fleet and all personnel aspects; the Controller of the Navy, responsible for procurement of ships, their weapons and equipment; and the Chief of Fleet Support, responsible for logistic support, stores, fuels and transport, naval dockyards, the Royal Maritime Auxiliary service and certain aspects of the Royal Fleet Auxiliary service.

The Commander-in-Chief Fleet, headquartered at Northwood, is responsible for the operational effectiveness of the fleet. The command of naval establishments in the UK is exercised by the Commander-in-Chief Naval Home Command from Portsmouth. The Assistant Chief of Naval Staff is responsible for co-ordinating advice on certain policy and operational matters. Since April 1992 these 3 officers have been members of the Admiralty Board. Main naval bases are at Devonport, Rosyth, Portsmouth, and Faslane, with a training base at Portland, and minor bases overseas at Hong Kong and Gibraltar.

Following the changes in the international situation since the end of the 1980s, there are plans for substantial changes in the strength and organization of the Navy. The latter are aimed at rationalizing and reducing the Ministry of Defence Headquarters structure. In April 1992 the Second Sea Lord's Department was relocated to Portsmouth and integrated into the staff of the Commander-in-Chief Naval Home Command. The Controller of the Navy and the Chief of Fleet Support are scheduled to move to the Bath area.

The Royal Naval Reserve (RNR) and the Royal Marines Reserve (RMR) are volunteer forces which in 1991 numbered some 5,700 and 1,200 respectively. The RNR provides trained personnel in war primarily in the defence of the Home Base in a NATO conflict to undertake Naval Control of Shipping, to man mine countermeasures vessels, HQ Command and Communications, and Rotary Wing Aircrew. The main roles of the RMR are reinforcement and other specialist tasks with the UK-Netherlands Amphibious Force. In addition, men who have completed service in the Royal Navy and the Royal Marines have a commitment to serve in the Royal Fleet Reserve, currently 28,400 strong. The Royal Naval Auxiliary Service (RNXS) is a volunteer civilian auxiliary some 2,700 strong who man Port Headquarters and provide crews for patrol and administrative craft in wartime. In the light of the significant changes in the international situation, action was in hand to rationalize the RNR and reduce its size to 4,700 by March 1992, although its core tasks remain the same.

Royal Navy, Women's Royal Naval Service (WRNS) and Queen Alexandra's Royal Naval Nursing Service (QARNNS) ratings and Royal Marine ranks enlist on the 'Open Engagement' to complete 22 years active service with the option to leave at 18 months notice on completion of a minimum of 2 and a half years productive service. On completion of 22 years service, a 'Second Open Engagement' of 10 years is available to senior ratings on a selective basis. Those who leave before completing 22 years have a liability for up to 3 years service in the Royal Fleet Reserve. Women serve in the WRNS and QARNNS and their reserves, in the WRNS in virtually all specializations. As from mid-1990, all new entrants to the WRNS were liable for sea service; WRNS first went to sea in Oct. 1990, and the number of ships with WRNS in their companies is steadily increasing.

The roles of the Royal Navy are first, to deploy the national strategic nuclear deterrent, second to provide maritime defence of the UK and its dependent territories, third to contribute to the maritime elements of NATO's force structure and fourth to meet national maritime objectives outside the NATO area. To meet the changed international situation, future fleet strength is being reduced by about 1996, when manpower is expected to be some 55,000 (including Royal Marines) and operational strength 12 nuclear attack submarines, 4 diesel-powered submarines, 3 aircraft carriers and about 40 destroyers and frigates.

The strategic deterrent is provided by the 4 nuclear-powered strategic missile submarines of the Resolution class (*Resolution, Repulse, Renown* and *Revenge*) each of 8,600 tonnes submerged displacement, completed between 1967 and 1969 and deploying 16 Polaris A3TK missiles each. These ships are to be replaced, commencing in 1994, by 4 substantially larger units of the Vanguard class (*Vanguard,*

Vengeance, Victorious and *Venerable*), 15,250 tonnes which will deploy 16 US-built Trident-2 D5 UGM-133A missiles with British warheads.

The strength of the fleet's major non-strategic units at the end of each of the last 8 years was as follows:

	1984	1985	1986	1987	1988	1989	1990	1991
Nuclear Submarines	13	14	14	15	15	16	14	15
Other Submarines	15	15	14	12	11	11	9	6
Aircraft Carriers	3	3	2 1	2 1	2 1	2 1	2 1	2
Destroyers	13	15	14	13	13	13	13	12
Frigates	48	42	39	36	35	36	33	33

1 Following Government policy, of the 3 Carriers held, only 2 are kept in operational status.

The nuclear-powered submarine force numbers 15, of 3 main classes. All are armed with torpedoes and Harpoon anti-ship missiles. There are 7 Trafalgar class, (5,300 tonnes) completed 1983–1991, 6 Swiftsure (4,900 tonnes) completed 1973–79, and 2 Valiant/Churchill of 4,800 tonnes completed 1966–71. Other submarines are of diesel-electric propulsion and comprise the first 2 of 4 Upholder class (2,400 tonnes) completed in 1990–91 and 4 Oberon class (completed 1960–67).

The principal surface ships are the Light vertical/short take-off and landing Aircraft Carriers of the Invincible class, (*Invincible, Illustrious* and *Ark Royal*), 20,900 tonnes, completed 1980-85, embarking an air group of 8 Sea Harrier vertical/short take-off and landing fighters, 9 anti-submarine Sea King and 3 radar early warning Sea King helicopters, and armed with 1 twin Sea Dart surface-to-air missile system. 2 of these ships are maintained in the operational fleet, with the third either in refit or reserve.

The 12 destroyers are all Type 42 (completed 1976–85). All are armed with 1 twin Sea Dart surface-to-air missile system and Stingray torpedoes. Frigates comprise 14 Type 22 (1979–89), the first 4 Norfolk class (Type 23) completed 1989–91, 6 Amazon (Type 21), completed 1974–78, and the last 9 of the 26 Leander class built between 1963 and 1970.

The lightly-armed patrol force comprises 1 ice patrol ship, 13 other offshore patrol vessels (including 3 in the Hong Kong squadron), and 18 inshore patrol craft mostly employed on training and coastal patrol duties. Mine countermeasures capability is provided by 13 offshore hunter/sweepers, 12 offshore minesweepers, 8 coastal minehunters and 3 coastal minesweepers. Amphibious lift for the Royal Marines is provided by 1 dock landing ship (with a second in reserve) and 5 tank landing ships (civil manned, and in peacetime employed on army freighting), supported by about 30 small amphibious craft.

Comprehensive support to the fleet is provided by 29 major auxiliaries including 7 replenishment (3 large and 4 small fleet tankers) and 4 support tankers, 4 ammunition and stores ships, 1 repair ship, 3 ocean tugs, 5 survey ships, 2 trials ships, 1 aviation training ship, and the Royal Yacht. Second-line support is provided by about 200 harbour and coastal service craft and minor auxiliaries.

Ships under construction or on order include 4 Vanguard class strategic submarines, 2 further Upholder class submarines, 9 Norfolk class frigates, 2 coastal minehunters and 2 large general purpose replenishment ships.

The Fleet Air Arm has over 240 active aircraft, in 20 operational, training and search-and-rescue squadrons. The operational inventory comprises 28 Sea Harrier vertical/short take-off and landing fighter aircraft, 94 Sea King and 58 Lynx anti-submarine helicopters, 10 Sea King airborne early warning helicopters and 34 Sea King (commando transport version).

The total number of male and female personnel (including Royal Marines) was (in 1,000) on 31 March: 1989, 65·5; 1990, 63.2; 1991, 62.1; 1992 (estimated), 59·4. The estimated total of 59,400 includes 7,100 marines and 3,700 women.

Sharpe, R. G. (ed.) *Jane's Fighting Ships.* London, annual

Air Force. In May 1912 the Royal Flying Corps first came into existence with military and naval wings, of which the latter became the independent Royal Naval Air Service in July 1914. On 2 Jan. 1918 an Air Ministry was formed, and on 1 April

1918 the Royal Flying Corps and the Royal Naval Air Service were amalgamated, under the Air Ministry, as the Royal Air Force (RAF).

Since 1992 women have been permited to fly combat aircraft.

In 1937 the units based on aircraft carriers and naval shore stations again passed to the operational and administrative control of the Admiralty, as the Fleet Air Arm. In 1964 control of the RAF became a responsibility of the Ministry of Defence.

The RAF is administered by the Air Force Board, of which the Secretary of State for Defence is Chairman. The Minister of State for the Armed Forces is Vice-Chairman, and normally acts as Chairman on behalf of the Secretary of State. Other members of the Board are the Minister of State for Defence Procurement, the Under-Secretary of State for the Armed Forces, the Under-Secretary of State for Defence Procurement, the Chief of the Air Staff, Air Member for Personnel, Air Member for Supply and Organization, Controller of Aircraft and the Second Permanent Under-Secretary of State. The RAF is organized into commands:

Home Commands. Strike and Support Commands. The Air Training Corps and the Air Sections of the Combined Cadet Force are under the administrative control of Support Command and functionally controlled by the Ministry of Defence.

The RAF College, which trains all candidates for commissions, is at Cranwell. The RAF Staff College is at Bracknell. The Department of Air Warfare is at Cranwell. The RAF Central Flying School is at Scampton. The trained personnel strength in Sept. 1990, including WRAF, was 83,173.

Strike Command itself is responsible for transport and air-to-air refuelling. VC10, Tristar and Hercules aircraft are used for air refuelling as well as strategic and tactical transport; the Victor solely for air refuelling. However, day-to-day functioning and organization of most operations is delegated to 3 Groups. Nos 1 and 38 Groups merged in late 1983 to form a new No 1 Group, responsible for the strike/attack, reconnaissance, tanker and battlefield support. The Tornado GR1/1A are used in the strike, attack, suppression of enemy air defence and reconnaissance roles. The Jaguar is used in the attack, reconnaissance and light anti-shipping roles. Battlefield support forces comprise Harrier GR 7, Chinook, Puma and Wessex support helicopters. No 11 Group controls the air defence forces: Tornado F3 supersonic all-weather interceptors, and ground environment radars, the associated communication systems, and the Ballistic Missile Early Warning System at Fylingdales. No 11 Group also controls the Hawks of the Tactical Weapons Units which, in war, would supplement air defence fighters at bases throughout the UK. UK air defence is undergoing major improvements. The Boeing E·3D entered service in 1991, replacing the Shackleton, and in the ground environment, there are new radars and communications systems entering service. No 18 Group is responsible for maritime air operations. ASW is the duty of the Nimrod Mk 2, which also has a capability against surface ships, although Buccaneers provide the main offensive force against a maritime surface threat. No 18 Group also operates Canberras in a multitude of roles, including photo-reconnaissance and target towing as well as Nimrod special-purpose aircraft and Hawks for ECM training. Search and rescue units are equipped with Sea King and Wessex helicopters. RAF Regiment short-range air defence squadrons, armed with Rapier, and the field squadrons form part of 1 Group, as does The Queen's Flight, which has 3 BAe 146s and 2 Wessex helicopters. The Military Air Traffic Operations organization also has the status of a Group. Strike Command has NATO commitments, but is available for overseas reinforcement. The training element of RAF Support Command utilizes Bulldog and Chipmunk primary trainers, Jet Provost and Tucano basic trainers, Hawk advanced trainers, Jetstreams for multi-engine pilot training, twin-jet Dominies for training navigators and other non-pilot aircrew, and Gazelle and Wessex helicopters.

Overseas Commands. Royal Air Force Germany. Small units in Gibraltar, the Falkland Islands, Belize, Cyprus and Hong Kong.

Squadrons of RAF Germany, which form part of NATO's 2nd Allied Tactical Air Force under SACEUR, have Tornado GR1, Harrier GR7, Chinook and Puma Helicopters, Andover communications aircraft, and Rapier surface-to-air missile squadrons of the RAF Regiment.

A flight of Phantom aircraft, a squadron of Chinook and Sea King helicopters for transport and search and rescue, and a flight of Hercules tankers are based in the Falkland Islands; a squadron of Wessex helicopters is based in Hong Kong and Cyprus.

The Royal Air Force, 1939–45. Vols. I, II, III. HMSO, 1953–54
Taylor J. W. R. (ed.) *Jane's All the World's Aircraft.* London. Annual from 1909

INTERNATIONAL RELATIONS

Membership. The UK is a member of the UN, Commonwealth, the EC, OECD, the Council of Europe, WEU, NATO and the Colombo Plan.

ECONOMY

Budget. Revenue and expenditure for years ending 31 March, in £1m. sterling:

Revenue	Estimated in the Budgets	Actual receipts into the Exchequer	More than estimates
1989	184,900	190,900	6,000
1990	206,400	203,400	– 3,000
1991	218,600	216,600	– 2,000
1992	226,500	222,100	– 4,400

The Budget estimate of ordinary revenue for 1992–93 is £229,800m.

Expenditure	Budget and supplementary estimates	Actual payments out of the Exchequer	More than estimates
1989	182,900	179,100	–3,800
1990	194,300	197,700	3,400
1991	212,700	216,000	3,300
1992	234,800	236,500	1,700

The Budget estimate of ordinary expenditure for 1992–93 is £258,500m.

Revenue in detail for 1991–92 and the expenditure, are given below, as is the budget estimate for 1992–93 (in £1m.):

Sources of revenue	Net receipts 1991–92	Budget estimate 1992–93
Inland Revenue:		
Income tax	58,000	59,600
Corporation tax	18,400	16,800
Petroleum revenue tax	–200	100
Capital Gains tax	1,200	1,100
Inheritance tax	1,300	1,300
Stamp duties	1,700	1,500
Total Inland Revenue	80,400	80,400
Customs and Excise:		
Value Added Tax	35,500	40,000
Petrol, etc. duties	10,900	11,800
Tobacco duties	6,100	6,600
Alcohol duties	5,000	5,300
Betting and gaming duties	1,100	1,100
Car tax	1,200	700
Customs duties	1,800	1,900
Agricultural levies	200	–
Total Customs and Excise	61,800	67,400
Vehicle Excise duties	3,000	3,200
Miscellaneous receipts:		
Interest and dividends	6,100	5,500
Oil royalties	500	500
Total Government Receipts	222,100	229,800

Major branches of expenditure for year ended 31 March 1992 and the estimates for the year 1992–93 (in £1m.):

	Estimates 1991–92	Estimates 1992–93
Social Security	61,500	66,000
Defence	22,900	24,200
Health	25,700	27,900
Northern Ireland	6,400	7,000
Support for local authorities	53,300	58,500
Privatization proceeds	−7,900	−8,000
Planning total	204,700	226,600
Interest Payments	16,500	17,600
Accounting Adjustments	4,200	4,700
Total	236,500	258,500

A single graduated income tax came into operation on 6 April 1973.

Rates of Personal Tax from 6 April 1992	%
Income between	
£3,445–£5,445	20
£5,446–£23,700	25
Over £23,700	40

Under the tax system, the amounts of the personal allowances are adjusted so that they retain their equivalent in relation to earned income. Independent taxation of husband and wife was introduced on 6 April 1990.

Personal Allowances	1992–93 £
Single person ⎫ Wife's earned income ⎬	3,445
Married couple's allowance	1,720
Age allowance (age 65 to 74):	
Single	4,200
Married couple's allowance	2,465
Age allowance (age 75 or over):	
Single	4,370
Married couple's allowance	2,505

Deductions of tax under PAYE ('pay as you earn') extend over the full range of unified tax rates and not merely the basic rate. Similarly, assessment on business profits and on other income which was directly assessed to tax, such as rents and interest on bank deposits, are made by reference to the full scale of rates, including where appropriate the investment income surcharge.

The standard rate of 25% is the rate at which tax is deducted from payments of interest, etc., and corresponds under the corporation tax system, to the tax credit on dividends. Where an individual's total income is such that he is liable on this taxed investment income at rates exceeding 25%, or if his investment income is high enough to make him liable to the surcharge, the higher rate or surcharge liability on this taxed investment income will in general be assessed separately after the end of the tax year.

Corporation Tax. Corporation Tax applies, with certain exceptions, to trades or businesses carried on by bodies corporate or by unincorporated societies or other bodies. Corporation Tax for companies was 33% for 1991–92 and 1992–93. Small companies (i.e. with profits under £0·25m.), 1992–93, 25%.

Capital Gains Tax. Gains resulting from the disposal of capital assets (other than British Government and Government guaranteed securities and certain exempted forms of property such as a private car and personal residences) are taxed under the Finance Act 1965. In 1992–93 exemption was granted for all gains made in a financial year which in total did not exceed £5,800 and most trusts on the first £2,900. In 1988 the base was brought forward from 1965 to 1982.

Inheritance Tax. From 1986 there is no lifetime charge on gifts between individuals. From 1989 a flat rate of 40% was introduced with a threshold in 1992–93 of £150,000. Most family business assets were exempted in 1992–93.

Value Added Tax. Value Added Tax (VAT) was introduced from 1 April 1973 at the rate of 10% on the supply of goods (with certain exceptions) and services. From 18 June 1979 the rate of tax was fixed at 15%. It was raised to 17·5% from 1 April 1991. From 11 March 1992 the registration limits became £36,600 per annum.

[1] Kay, J. A. and King, M. A., *The British Tax System*. OUP, 1980

Local Taxation. The Community Charge was introduced in Scotland in 1989 and in England and Wales in 1990. Legislation was in process in 1992 to replace it with a new Council Tax based on property valuation to come into force in April 1993.

The introduction of the Community Charge ('poll tax') changed the basis of levying local revenue from the ownership of residential or business property at a national variable rate ('rateable value'), to personal residence at a flat rate (with reliefs rebating liability by up to 80%). The amount of the charge is set by the local authorities, subject to central government ceilings ('rate-capping'), and varies considerably from authority to authority. A uniform business rate applies nationally to business premises and second residences. The average charge paid in 1991–92 was £247.

A Government review of local government in 1991 concluded that the level of the Community Charge was unsustainably high, and the Budget of March 1991 provided for its reduction by £140.

Local authority estimated receipts (in £1m.) for 1991–92 (and forecasts for 1992–93) were £67,500 (£76,100), made up of: Community Charge and domestic rates, £7,400 (£8,400); current grants from central government (including non-domestic rate income), £50,600 (£54,600); capital grants from central government, £2,700 (£7,100); other, £6,900 (£5,800). Expenditure was £69,200 (£72,900), made up of: Current expenditure on goods and services, £47,900 (£50,800); current grants and subsidies, £9,100 (£10,100); interest, £5,600 (£5,500); capital expenditure and net lending, £6,700 (£6,500).

Central government support for local authorities (in £1m.), 1991–92 estimates (and 1992–93 plans) was £53,300 (£58,500), including: Revenue/rate support grant, £13,600 (£21,600); non-domestic rate payments, £14,300 (£14,100); current specific grants, £19,800 (£16,600); capital grants, £1,300 (£1,600); credit approvals, £4,300 (£4,500).

The 1991 Budget provided for additional central government support to local authorities in order to reduce the Community Charge, financed mainly from an increase in value-added tax from 15% to 17·5%. The Government paid a new grant ('Community Charge Grant') which reimbursed local authorities for the gross cost of reducing charges in 1991–92 by £140, estimated at £5,600m. 90% of this grant was paid in 1991–92, and the remainder in 1992–93.

In Scotland, revenue support grant replaced rate support grants when the community charge was introduced on 1 April 1989. £2,692·7m. was paid out in grant in 1991-92.

Gross National Product:

Expenditure (£1m.)	1946	1960	1970	1980	1990
Consumers' expenditure	7,273	16,939	31,773	139,608	349,421
Central and local government final consumption	2,282	4,206	8,961	48,940	109,495
Gross domestic fixed capital formation	925	4,190	9,462	41,561	105,195
Value of physical increase in stocks and work in progress	−126	562	425	−2,572	−718
Total domestic expenditure at market prices	10,354	25,897	50,581	227,537	563,393
Exports of goods and services	1,775	5,153	11,533	62,616	134,108
Less Imports of goods and services	−2,083	−5,549	−11,122	−57,606	−147,582
Less Taxes on expenditure	−1,573	−3,378	−8,416	−36,474	−79,067
Subsidies	384	493	884	5,719	6,217
Gross domestic product at factor cost	8,855	22,616	43,460	201,017	477,747

Factor incomes (£1m.)	1946	1960	1970	1980	1990
Income from employment	5,758	15,174	30,404	137,783	316,408
Income from self-employment [1]	1,126	2,008	3,735	18,141	57,661
Gross trading profits of companies [1]	1,476	3,730	5,935	27,861	62,916
Gross trading surplus of public corporations [1]	20	534	1,447	6,309	4,265
Gross trading surplus of other public enterprises [1]	86	189	151	180	17
Rent [2]	429	1,086	2,833	14,243	38,433
Total domestic income before providing for depreciation and stock appreciation	8,895	22,863	44,837	206,633	483,978
Less Stock appreciation	−125	−122	−1,090	−6,391	−6,391
Income adjustment	...	−125	−287	775	160
Gross domestic product at factor cost	8,770	22,616	43,460	201,017	477,747
Net property income from abroad	85	233	559	−182	4,029
Gross national product	8,855	22,849	44,019	200,835	481,776
Less Capital consumption	...	−2,047	−4,420	−27,952	−61,159
National income	...	20,802	39,599	172,883	420,617

[1] Before providing for depreciation and stock appreciation.
[2] Before providing for depreciation.

National Economic Development Council. The NEDC, which first met in 1962, is the national forum for economic consultation between government, management and unions. It includes leading representatives of the Government, CBI and TUC, chairmen of nationalized industries and independent members. It meets under the chairmanship of the Chancellor of the Exchequer, other Secretaries of State and occasionally, the Prime Minister. The Sector Groups and Working Parties, like the NEDC, bring together representatives of management unions, Government and experts in the field to study the efficiency and prospects of individual industries and sectors and to suggest ways in which these could be improved and advantage taken of new opportunities. The National Economic Development Office (NEDO) provides the professional staff for the NEDC and the Sector Groups and Working Parties and undertakes its own self-initiated research.

Currency. The unit of currency is the *pound sterling* (GBP) of 100 *pence.* A gold standard was adopted in 1816, the sovereign or twenty-shilling piece weighing 7·98805 grammes 0·916²/₃ fine. Currency notes for £1 and 10s. were first issued by the Treasury in 1914, replacing the circulation of sovereigns. The issue of £1 and 10s. notes was taken over by the Bank of England in 1928. 10s. notes were withdrawn in 1970 and £1 notes (in England and Wales) in 1988. Inflation was 4·5% in Dec. 1991. In March 1992, £1 = US$ 1·76; US$1 = £0·57.

Coinage. The sovereign (£1) weighs 123·27447 grains, or 7·98805 grammes, 0·916²/₃ (or eleven-twelfths) fine, and consequently it contains 113·00159 grains or 7·32238 grammes of fine gold. On 15 Feb. 1971 (Decimalization Day) a decimal currency system was introduced retaining the *pound sterling* as the major unit but now divided into 100 *new pence* instead of 240 old pence. The decimal coins are the £1 (22·5 mm diameter, 9·5 grammes weight); 50p (equilateral curved heptagon, 30 mm diameter, 13·5 grammes); 20p (equilateral curved heptagon 21·4 mm diameter, 5 grammes); 10p (28·5 mm, 11·31 grammes); 5p (18·0 mm, 3·25 grammes); 2p (25·9 mm, 7·12 grammes) and 1p (20·3 mm, 3·56 grammes). The Decimal Currency Act, 1967 and the Proclamation of 27 Dec. 1968 required that the 50p, 10p and 5p be made of cupro-nickel and the 2p, 1p and ¹/₂p of mixed metal; copper, tin and zinc (bronze). The Decimal Currency Act, 1969, provided that the coins of the Queen's

Maundy Money should continue to be made in silver to a millesimal fineness of 925.

By Proclamation dated 28 July 1971, which came into force on 30 Aug. 1971, the crown, double-florin, the florin, the shilling and the sixpence were treated as coins of the new currency and as being of the denominations respectively of 25, 20, 10, 5 and 2½ new pence. The sixpence was demonetised on 30 June 1980, the ½p on 31 Dec. 1984 and the 5p/shilling on 31 Dec. 1990. A smaller 5p coin was issued on 27 June 1990. The designation 'new pence' was changed to 'pence' in 1982.

The Coinage Act, 1971, specified that the legal tender limits for coins were: Gold coins (face value only), for payment of any amount; coins of cupro-nickel and silver of denominations of more than 10p, for payment of any amount not exceeding £10; coins of cupro-nickel and silver of not more than 10p, for payment of any amount not exceeding £5; coins of bronze, for payment of any amount not exceeding 20p. The £1 coin is legal tender to any amount.

UK coins issued in the 12 months up to March 1991 totalled £182m.

Coins in circulation at 31 March 1991: £1, 977m.; 50p, 670m.; 20p, 1,355m.; 10p, 1,490m.; 5p, 1,980m.; 2p, 3,600m.; 1p, 5,900m.

Bank-notes. The Bank of England issues notes in denominations of £5, £10, £20 and £50 for the amount of the fiduciary note issue. Under the provisions of the Currency and Bank Notes Act, 1954, which came into force on 22 Feb. 1954, the amount of the fiduciary note issue was fixed at £1,575m., but this figure might be altered by direction of HM Treasury after representations made by the Bank of England.

All Bank of England notes are legal tender in England and Wales. The banks in Scotland and Northern Ireland have certain note-issuing powers.

The total amount of Bank of England notes issued at 24 Dec. 1991 was £17,910m., of which £17,906,825,142 were in the hands of other banks and the public and £3,174,858 in the Banking Department of the Bank of England.

Banking and Finance. The Bank of England, Threadneedle Street, London, is the Government's banker and the 'banker's bank'. It has the sole right of note issue in England and Wales and manages the National Debt. It was founded by Royal Charter in 1694 and nationalized in 1946. The capital stock has, since 1 March 1946, been held by the Treasury. The *Governor* (appointed for 5-year terms) is Robin Leigh-Pemberton.

The statutory return is published weekly. End-Dec. figures for the past 4 years are as follows (in £1m.):

	Notes in circulation	Notes and coin in Banking Department	Public deposits (government)	Other deposits [1]
1988	15,949	1	91	3,106
1989	17,071	9	62	4,444
1990	17,524	6	42	8,169
1991	17,907	3	113	5,597

[1] Including Special Deposits.

The fiduciary note issue was £17,910m. at 24 Dec. 1990. All the profits of the note issue are passed on to the National Loans Fund.

Official reserves of gold and convertible currencies, SDR and reserve position in the IMF at the end of Dec. 1990 were US$38,464m.

The value of paper-based credit transfers for 1989 was £497m; of paperless credit transfers. £806m.; of direct debits, £709m.

The London and Scottish banks' groups ceased to exist in 1991, and since April 1991 figures have been compiled for the Major British Banking Groups. Statistics at 31 Dec. 1991: Total deposits (sterling and currency), £400,556m.; sterling market loans £63,291m.; market loans (sterling and currency), £108,787m.; advances (sterling and currency), £286,497m.; sterling investments, £19,927m.

Total net profits from the operations of the main London clearing bank groups in 1990 amounted to £842m., of which £879m. was paid in gross dividends and £309m. transferred to reserves.

The clearing banks cover all aspects of banking business in UK including corporate business, and are also actively involved in international banking.

National Savings Bank. Statistics for 1989 and 1990:

	Ordinary accounts		Investment accounts	
	1989	*1990*	*1989*	*1990*
Accounts open at 31 Dec.	15,762,005 [1]	15,758,397 [1]	4,521,105	4,817,263
Amounts—	*£1,000*	*£1,000*	*£1,000*	*£1,000*
Received	596,433	573,442	1,382,085	1,661,737
Interest credited	64,467 [2]	61,287 [2]	792,423	968,934
Paid	728,104	719,814	2,068,926	1,942,573
Due to depositors at 31 Dec.	1,579,352	1,494,267	7,838,982	8,527,080
Average amount due to each depositor in active accounts	£100·20	£94·82	£1,733·87	£1,770·11

[1] Excluding non-computerized accounts, amounting to £97·8m. in 1989 and £97·8m. in 1990.

[2] The interest credited to depositors for the Ordinary account for 1990 has been calculated on the same basis as 1988. Interest of 5% a year payable on accounts with a minimum balance of £500 and 2¹/₂% on accounts with a minimum balance of less than £500. Interest is earned on each whole pound on deposit for complete calendar months.

The amount due to depositors in Ordinary Accounts on 1 Jan. 1992 was approximately £1,446,498,523 and in Investment Accounts £8,846,250,203.

The banking arm of the Post Office, Girobank (founded 1968) was sold to a building society in 1990.

There are stock exchanges in Belfast, Birmingham, Glasgow and Manchester, which function mainly as representative offices for the London Stock Exchange (called International Stock Exchange until May 1991). In July 1991 the 91 shareholders voted unanimously for a new memorandum and articles of association which devolves power to a wider range of participants in the securities industry and replaces the Stock Exchange Council with a 14-member board.

Weights and Measures. Conversion to the metric system, which will replace the imperial system, is in progress. EEC requirements are for all member states to convert to metrication by 1994, but the use of the pint for milk deliveries and bar sales, and use of miles and yards in road signs, is exempt indefinitely, and the use of the pound in selling greengrocery is exempt until 1999.

ENERGY AND NATURAL RESOURCES

Electricity. The Electricity Act of 1989 implemented the restructuring and transfer to the private sector of the electricity supply industry.

The Office of Electricity Regulation (Offer) was set up under the Act to protect consumer interests following privatization.

Generators. The Central Electricity Generating Board, which was responsible for the generation and bulk supply of electricity to the 12 Area Boards in England and Wales was replaced by 4 companies under the provisions of the 1989 Electricity Act: National Power, PowerGen, Nuclear Electric and the National Grid Company. National Power and PowerGen were privatized in Feb. 1991. Nuclear Electric, responsible for nuclear power generation, is to remain in state ownership. The wholesale market created by the generators is termed 'the pool'.

Suppliers. The 12 Area Electricity Boards were replaced under the 1989 Electricity Act by 12 successor companies which were privatized in 1990. These are Eastern Electricity; East Midlands Electricity; London Electricity; Manweb; Midlands Electricity; Northern Electricity; Norweb; Seeboard; Southern Electric; South Wales Electricity; South Western Electricity; Yorkshire Electricity.

A new Association, the *Electricity Association*, has been created by the newly formed British electricity companies. The Asociation provides a forum for members to discuss matters of common interest, provides a collective voice for the industry when needed and provides specialist research and professional services for member companies.

Output capacity of UK power stations in 1990 was 73,060 mw, of which 11,353 mw was nuclear and 4,171 hydro-electric. 296,795,000,000m. kwh were supplied to

25,665m. consumers, of which 100,358,000,000m. kwh went to the industrial sector and 93,793,000,000m. kwh to the domestic sector.

Scottish Hydro-Electric plc, with head office in Perth, the nationalized authority responsible for the generation, transmission, distribution and sale of electricity to its (1988) 596,960 customers was privatized alongside Scottish Power plc in May 1991. It supplies the district north and west of a line joining the firths of Clyde and Tay as well as all the island groups extending to the Outer Hebrides, Orkney and Shetland. On the mainland it operates generating stations with a total installed generating capacity of 3,216 mw consisting of 1,762 mw of hydro power and pumped storage, together with 1,320 mw of steam. Diesel stations with a total installed capacity of 102 mw supply the principal island groups together with 32 mw gas turbine. A 1,320 mw of oil/gas fired thermal plant is now operating at Peterhead. The main transmission system consists of 5,097 circuit km of 275 kv and 132 kv lines linking the power stations and the bulk supply points serving the distribution networks. The system control centre at Pitlochry co-ordinates the operation of the transmission system and power stations. The number of staff at 31 March 1989 was 3,917.

Scottish Power plc, with head office in Glasgow, was formally vested in 1990 to take over the non-nuclear operations of the former South of Scotland Electricity Board. The area served stretches north of a line from Holy Island in Northumberland to the Solway Firth to a northern boundary running from the Firth of Clyde to the Firth of Tay. Within this area of approximately 21,000 sq. km (8,000 sq. miles) is located the main industry and population concentrations of Scotland, with 4m. of the total population of 5·1m. Scottish Power provides a full electricity service to its area. It operates 4 coal-fired, 8 hydro, 1 pumped storage station and one gas-fired power station with a maximum sent-out capacity of 4,467 mw. A further 2,000 mw oil-fired station is on care and maintenance. The company transmits and distributes electricity throughout its area to 1·7m. domestic, commercial, industrial and agricultural customers. It operates 75 retail shops, which also provide full customer services. During 1990-91 Scottish Power had a turnover of £1,242m. Scottish Power has approximately 9,100 employees.

Scottish Nuclear Ltd was formally vested in 1990 to take over and operate the nuclear assets of the former South of Scotland Electricity Board. Initially envisaged as part of the privatization of electricity supply, it is now to remain under government control. With 2,300 employees, it generates electricity at the 2 nuclear power stations at Hunterston, Ayrshire, and Torness, East Lothian. Both plants have two 650 mw Advanced Gas-Cooled Reactors. Scottish Nuclear is also undertaking the decommissioning of the Magnox power station located at Hunterston. During 1988–89, these 3 nuclear power stations generated over 14·5m. units of electricity and for much of the year supplied over 60% of the electricity consumed in the whole of Scotland.

Oil. Production in 1,000 tonnes, in 1989 (and 1990): Throughput of crude and process oils, 87,699 (88,670); refinery use, 5,816 (5,835). Refinery output: Gases, 1,658 (1,620); naphtha, 2,073 (2,139); motor spirit, 27,237 (26,724); kerosene, 9,436 (9,850); diesel oil, 23,294 (23,502); fuel oil, 13,020 (13,805); lubricating oils, 1,050 (974); bitumen, 2,393 (2,454). Total output of refined products, 81,392 (82,286). Estimated crude oil production, 1991, 91·1m. tonnes.

Gas. Following the Gas Act of 1986, British Gas plc became the successor company to the British Gas Corporation. Its primary activities are the purchase, distribution and sale of gas, supported by a broad range of services to customers. It also explores for and produces hydrocarbons. It is organized into a headquarters and 12 Regions.

British Gas explores for gas through 3 wholly owned subsidiary companies: Gas Council (Exploration) Limited (UK onshore and Denmark offshore); Hydrocarbons Great Britain Limited (Irish Sea and Cardigan Bay); Hydrocarbons Ireland Limited, (offshore Eire). British Gas owns and operates two gas fields, Morecambe and Rough field. The latter is used as a gas store and both have been developed to help meet peak winter demand.

In 1986–87, British Gas sold 18,894m. therms of gas to over 17m. customers. Just over 50% of the gas went to domestic customers, the rest to industrial and commercial enterprizes. The industry won 269,000 new customers in the period and made a before-tax profit of £1,062m. with a turnover of £7,610m.

The Office of Gas Supply (Ofgas) is a 'regulator' charged with protecting consumer interests after privatization.

In March 1986, there were 89,000 people employed directly by the industry. British Gas spends £74m. each year on its research and development programme and its international consultancy service works in about 20 countries.

Gas reserves are some 590,000m. cu. metres.

Water. The Water Act of Sept. 1989 privatized the 10 water authorities in England and Wales: Anglian; North West; Northumbrian; Severn Trent; South West; Southern; Thames; Welsh; Wessex; Yorkshire. The Act also inaugurated the National Rivers Authority, with environmental and resource management responsibilities, and the 'regulator' Office of Water Services (Ofwat), charged with protecting consumer interests.

In Scotland water supply is the responsibility of the Regional and Island local authorities. 7 river purification boards are responsible for environmental management.

Minerals. Coal. The number of British Coal Corporation (BCC) producing collieries at 25 March 1991 was 65. Statistics of the coalmining industry for recent years are as follows:

Output, 1m. tonnes:	*1986–87*	*1988–89*	*1990–91*
BCC mines (inc. tip and capital coal)	88·0	85·0	72·3
Opencast	13·3	16·8	17·0
Licensed	2·0	1·7	2·3
Total	103·3	103·5	91·6
Employees, 1,000:			
Colliery industrial manpower	107·7	80·1	57·3
Other industrial manpower	14·6	10·8	6·2
Non-industrial staff	19·2	14·1	10·8
Total	141·5	105·0	74·3
Productivity, tonnes:			
Output per man-year	700	978	1,181
Overall output per manshift	3·29	4·14	4·7
Consumption, 1m. tonnes:			
Power stations	82·4	80·7	81·9
Coke ovens	10·9	10·9	10·7
Domestic	8·1	6·3	5·7
Other inland	11·0	11·3	10·4
Total inland	112·4	109·2	108·7
Imports	9·9	12·0	16·2
Exports	2·2	1·8	2·1

Total BCC stocks of coal at 31 March 1991 amounted to 8·3m. tonnes. Operating profit made by British Coal for the year ended March 1991 amounted to £238m. Interest payable was £143m. The overall profit for 1990–91 was £78m. Deficit grants ceased in 1987–88.

BCC's production of coke (including coke breeze), 1990–91, 1m. tonnes.

The UK is among the 10 largest steel producing countries in the world. Output in recent years was as follows (in 1m. tonnes):

	Pig-iron	Crude steel	Finished steel products	Home consumption Crude steel equivalent
1988	13·2	19·0	14·7	17·5
1989	12·8	18·7	14·9	17·4
1990	12·5	17·8	14·2	16·7
1991	12·1	16·5	13·2	...

Exports of finished steel products were 7·7m. tonnes in 1991 and imports 5·3m. tonnes.

With turnover for the year to March 1991 of £5,041m., British Steel plc is the largest steel producer in the UK. The number of UK employees at 31 Dec. 1991 was some 45,000. UK steel producers, other than British Steel plc, are represented by BISPA (British Independent Steel Producers Association). There are approximately 50 companies in membership of BISPA, who account for almost one quarter of UK liquid steel production, and approximately one third of the UK output of finished steel products. For some products such as wire rod, reinforcement steel, bright bars, wire and high speed tool and engineering steels, these companies account for nearly all UK production.

Production of non-ferrous metals (in 1,000 tonnes) in 1988 (and 1989): Refined copper, 124 (119); refined lead 373·8 (347·2); tin metal, 13·8 (11·2); primary aluminium, 300·2 (297·3); slab zinc, 92·8 (79·8).

Agriculture. In 1990 (and 1989) agricultural land in the UK totalled (in 1,000 ha) 18,510 (18,553), comprising common grazing, 1,236 (1,236), and agricultural holdings, 17,274 (17,317). Land use of the latter: All grasses 6,824 (6,785); crops, 5,093 (5,202); rough grazing, 4,680 (4,710); bare fallow, 63 (65); other, 677 (620). Area sown to crops: Cereals, 3,647 (3,866); fodder crops, 341 (337); horticultural crops, 210 (208); others, 629 (612).

The number of workers employed in agriculture, forestry and fishing in the UK was, in June 1990, 298,000. Of these, 184,600 (15,500 females) were engaged full-time in agriculture, 59,600 (28,100 females) part-time, and 90,500 (34,900 females) were seasonal and casual workers. These figures do not include farmers, partners and directors. There were some 257,000 farm holdings in 1989, some 75% owner-occupied. Average size of holdings, 107·3 ha.

Principal crops in the UK as at June in each year:

	Wheat	Barley	Oats	Horticul-tural crops	Potatoes	Fodder crops	Sugar-beet	Rape for oilseed
				Area (1,000 ha)				
1986	1,997	1,916	97	212	178	239	205	299
1987	1,994	1,830	99	199	177	356	202	388
1988	1,886	1,878	120	209	180	293	201	347
1989	2,083	1,652	119	192	175	337	197	321
1990	2,013	1,515	107	210	177	...	194	390
				Total product (1,000 tonnes)				
1986	13,910	10,010	505	3,869	6,446	7,325	8,120	965
1987	11,940	9,230	450	3,788	6,713	6,939	7,990	1,326
1988	11,600	8,800	600	3,882	6,899	5,673	8,152	...
1989	14,030	8,070	525	3,479 [1]	6,480 [1]	...	8,115	...

[1] 1990

Livestock in the UK as at June in each year (in 1,000):

	1986	1987	1988	1989	1990
Cattle	12,533	12,158	11,872	11,977	12,057
Sheep	37,016	38,701	40,942	42,967	43,789
Pigs	7,937	7,942	7,980	7,509	7,447
Poultry	120,740	128,628	130,809	120,198	124,384

Forestry. On 31 March 1991 the area of productive woodland in Britain was 2,140,000 ha of which the Forestry Commission managed 859,000 ha and the private sector 1,281,000 ha.

The Forestry Commission employed 6,645 staff in 1991. In addition a further 16,450 were employed in private forestry with an estimated 10,030 engaged in the wood processing industry.

In 1990–91 a total of 6·5m. cu. metres of timber was thinned and felled.

New planting (1990–91), 19,000 ha (3,500, Forestry Commission; 15,000, private woodlands).

Forestry Commission. *Forestry Facts and Figures, 1990–91.* 1991
James, N. D. G., *A History of English Forestry.* London, 1981

Fisheries. Quantity (in 1,000 tonnes) and value (in £1,000) of fish of British taking landed in Great Britain (excluding salmon and sea-trout):

Quantity	1986	1987	1988	1989	1990
Wet fish	629·3	677·3	645·5	580·4	528·4
Shell fish	87·6	111·0	96·5	91·3	93·1
	716·9	788·3	742·0	671·8	621·5
Value					
Wet fish	284,161	338,965	310,412	299,354	329,491
Shell fish	77,519	95,941	92,481	94,992	101,012
	361,680	434,906	402,893	394,346	430,503

In 1991 the fishing fleet of England and Wales including UK vessels of unknown nationality comprised 7,974 registered vessels including 1,241 trawlers and that of Scotland, 2,366 vessels. Major fishing ports: (England) Fleetwood, Grimsby, Hull, Lowestoft, North Shields; (Wales) Milford Haven; (Scotland) Aberdeen, Mallarg, Lerwick, Peterhead.

INDUSTRY. Statistics (UK, unless otherwise stated) of a cross-section of industrial production (in 1,000 tonnes):

	1988	1989	1990
Sulphuric acid	2,270	2,148	1,996
Synthetic resins	1,590	1,577	...
Cotton single yarn	35	28	23
Woollen yarn	78	75	73
Man-made fibres (rayon, nylon, etc.)	280	273	273
Newsprint	541	569	569
Other paper and board	3,802	3,880	3,880
Cement	16,506	16,849	...
Fertilizers	5,227	4,980	4,960
Motor cars (units)	1,226,835	1,299,082	1,295,160

Engineering. Manufacturers' sales (in £1m.) for 1989 (and 1990): Motor vehicles and engines, 12,204 (12,002); railway and tramway vehicles, 391 (495); boilers and process plant, 1,986 (2,078); mechanical lifting and handling equipment, 2,626 (2,617); refrigerating, space-heating, ventilating and air conditioning equipment, 1,842 (2,027); construction and earth-moving equipment, 1,426 (1,334), wheeled tractors, 1,236 (1,344); industrial (including marine) engines, 988 (1,165).

Electrical Goods. Manufacturers' sales (in £1m.) for 1989 (and 1990): Radio and electronic capital goods, 3,366 (3,335); basic electrical equipment, 3,036 (3,540); electronic data processing equipment, 5,740 (6,403); telephone and telegraph apparatus and equipment, 2,192 (1,883); domestic electrical appliances, 1,553 (1,709).

Textile Manufacturers. Production of woven cloth for 1989 (and 1990): Cotton (1m. metres), 206 (168); man-made fibres (1m. metres), 217 (216); woven woollen and worsted fabrics (1m. sq. metres), deliveries, 85 (79).

Construction. Total value (in £1m.) of constructional work in Great Britain in 1989 (and 1990) was 46,174 (48,467), including new work, 27,315 (28,354), of which housing, 8,067 (6,884). Housing for public authorities, 979 (965); for private developers, 7,088 (5,919).

Labour. In June 1991 the UK workforce (*i.e.* all persons in employment plus the claimant unemployed) totalled (in 1,000) 28,405, of whom 26,164 were in employment, 22,187 (10,610 females) were employees, 3,298 were self-employed and 297 were in HM Forces. UK employees by form of employment in Oct. 1991 (in 1,000): Agriculture and fishing, 299; energy and water supply, 432; manufacturing industry, 4,728; construction, 925; distributive and catering trades, 4,555; transport and communications, 1,313; business and finance, 2,559; public administration, 1,898; (Dec. 1990) education, 1,801; health, 1,472; other services, 1,712. Registered unemployed in UK as at Dec. (in 1,000; figures adjusted for seasonality and discontinuities): 1987, 2,822 (females, 851); 1988, 2,295 (687); 1989, 1,784 (507); 1990, 1,639 (426); 1991, 2,426 (586). In Dec. 1991 654,000 persons (120,600 females) had been unemployed for more than a year. In Dec. 1991 there were 101,700 job vacancies.

Workers (in 1,000) involved in industrial stoppages (and working days lost): 1987, 887 (3·5m.); 1988, 790 (3·7m.); 1989, 727 (4·1m.); 1990, 285 (1·9m.).

Trade Unions. In Sept. 1991 there were 73 unions affiliated to the Trades Union Congress (TUC) with a total membership of 8,192,664 (8,416,832 in 1990) (2·8m. of them women). The unions affiliated to the TUC in 1991 ranged in size from the Transport and General Workers' Union, with 1,223,890 members, to the Sheffield Wool Shear Workers' Society with 17 members. The 6 largest unions, however, account for more than half the total membership.

The TUC's executive body, the General Council, is elected at the annual Congress. It is composed of 55 members made up of 33 members nominated by unions with a membership of over 200,000, entitled to automatic representation in proportion to their size, and 9 members elected from unions with a numerical membership of 100,000 up to 199,999. Eight members are elected from unions with a numerical membership of less than 100,000 and 4 women members are elected to represent women workers in smaller unions. Unions with a total membership of over 200,000 of which 100,000 or over are women must nominate at least one woman to represent women workers.

The General Secretary is elected by the Congress but is not subject to annual reelection. The TUC General Council appoints committees, which draw upon the services of specialist departments in preparing policies on economic, education, international, employment, industrial organization, equal rights, and social questions.

The TUC is affiliated to the International Confederation of Free Trade Unions, the Trade Union Advisory Committee of OECD, the Commonwealth Trade Union Council and the European Trade Union Confederation. The TUC provides a service of trade union education. It provides members to serve, with representatives of employers, on joint committees advising the Government on issues of national importance (e.g., National Economic Development Council) and on the managing boards of such bodies as the Health and Safety Commission; and Advisory, Conciliation and Arbitration Service.

FOREIGN ECONOMIC RELATIONS. On 8 Oct. 1990 the UK entered the Exchange-Rate Mechanism (ERM) of the EC's European Monetary System (*see* p. 46), initially with the pound sterling having a fluctuation margin of 6%.

Commerce. Value of the imports and exports of merchandise (excluding bullion and specie and foreign merchandise transhipped under bond) of the UK for 6 recent years (in £1,000):

	Total imports	Total exports		Total imports	Total exports
1986	86,066,650	73,009,049	1989	120,787,729	93,249,123
1987	94,015,696	79,851,395	1990	126,165,755	103,910,969
1988	106,412,879	81,476,249	1991	118,871,355	104,818,449

The value of goods imported is generally taken to be that at the port and time of entry, including all incidental expenses (cost, insurance and freight) up to the landing on the quay. For goods consigned for sale, the market value in this country is required and recorded in the returns. For exports, the value at the port of shipment (including the charges of delivering the goods on board) is taken. Imports are entered as from the country whence the goods were consigned to the UK, which may, or may not, be the country whence they were last shipped. Exports are credited to the country of ultimate destination as declared by the exporters.

Trade according to countries for 1989 and 1990 (in £1,000):

	Imports from		Exports to	
	1990 [1]	1991 [1]	1990 [1]	1991 [1]
Foreign countries				
Europe and Overseas Possessions—				
Albania	413	274	4,512	3,179
Austria	957,789	916,265	705,850	766,734
Belgium and Luxembourg	5,732,427	5,427,663	5,648,625	5,870,876
Bulgaria	32,787	36,786	45,022	35,647

[1] Provisional figures.

Foreign countries	Imports from 1990 [1]	1991 [1]	Exports to 1990 [1]	1991 [1]
Europe and Overseas Possessions—(contd.)				
Czechoslovakia	135,988	131,441	133,158	129,378
Denmark and Faroe Islands	2,310,965	2,259,221	1,421,595	1,415,879
Finland	1,175,766	1,522,337	1,041,739	847,671
France	11,758,481	11,066,081	10,885,803	11,591,139
German Dem. Rep.	128,498	…	57,013	…
Germany (Fed. Rep. of)	19,907,062	17,741,093	13,169,405	14,653,972
Greece	400,476	378,146	682,887	667,741
Hungary	102,741	103,869	121,837	132,448
Iceland	259,430	238,428	88,537	96,615
Italy	6,735,496	6,378,908	5,612,751	6,145,014
Netherlands	10,483,576	9,969,981	7,561,576	8,258,475
Netherlands Antilles	43,552	35,414	35,186	37,888
Norway	4,235,348	4,202,827	1,289,789	1,357,299
Poland	357,164	313,828	221,536	347,069
Portugal, Azores and Madeira	1,176,161	1,043,511	1,033,268	1,085,084
Romania	61,215	58,531	85,879	58,735
Spain	2,884,691	2,627,999	3,750,143	4,278,767
Canary Islands	86,023	84,789	92,886	103,383
Sweden	3,594,547	3,142,449	2,712,775	2,471,539
Switzerland and Liechtenstein	4,252,783	3,754,586	2,358,528	2,105,656
Turkey	550,803	402,770	606,829	729,988
USSR	917,691	901,833	606,013	354,705
Yugoslavia	189,421	147,875	260,972	193,836
European Communities	65,855,511	61,321,097	55,024,710	59,255,567
EFTA	15,075,672	13,806,892	8,179,218	7,645,515
Africa—				
Algeria	259,959	194,874	73,831	55,685
Angola	5,142	65,078	29,284	34,812
Burundi	541	2,341	2,804	3,817
Cameroon	8,241	6,135	20,652	23,813
Côte d'Ivoire	69,849	45,630	26,941	24,131
Egypt	145,323	130,408	298,262	282,928
Ethiopia	19,465	14,660	41,403	14,660
Liberia	13,240	972	8,639	8,865
Libya	151,605	121,220	244,850	255,719
Mali	1,835	1,631	8,819	9,589
Mauritania	14,525	15,313	2,997	2,336
Morocco	106,425	95,522	118,599	152,245
Mozambique	10,709	2,393	28,992	18,851
Rwanda	2,128	2,193	1,195	2,334
South Africa	1,078,546	954,676	1,113,397	1,023,459
Senegal	5,002	5,025	14,884	13,960
Sudan	9,016	130,408	63,670	75,460
Tunisia	40,959	25,613	40,800	43,651
Zaïre	7,337	4,733	23,801	15,040
Asia and Oceania—				
Afghanistan	9,194	5,207	7,816	6,956
Bahrain	48,459	39,120	127,309	147,494
Burma	4,582	2,771	15,951	8,294
China	583,425	706,585	465,585	321,935
Fiji	61,863	81,540	8,168	8,268
Indonesia	327,877	415,340	194,274	197,991
Iran	279,135	158,354	384,713	511,532
Iraq	101,557	2,548	293,393	4,399
Israel	506,106	455,765	567,712	529,484
Japan	6,761,592	6,753,642	2,631,326	2,257,552
Jordan	14,788	10,984	109,483	89,411
Korea (South)	963,829	924,615	620,690	786,162
Kuwait	108,970	29,886	181,480	178,336
Lebanon	6,249	8,465	53,266	87,760
Philippines	220,706	229,955	158,030	146,571
Qatar	5,004	5,488	98,504	109,248
Saudi Arabia	794,633	963,919	2,012,585	2,228,965
Syria	88,874	42,459	38,245	49,971
Thailand	484,276	625,374	416,648	625,374

[1] Provisional figures.

Foreign countries	Imports from 1990 [1]	1991 [1]	Exports to 1990 [1]	1991 [1]
America—				
Argentina	144,205	135,512	35,953	69,671
Bolivia	12,387	9,303	6,234	5,787
Brazil	719,849	766,102	328,234	339,442
Chile	222,469	177,876	128,056	106,640
Colombia	82,507	110,122	60,469	56,428
Costa Rica	17,468	21,823	14,556	11,312
Cuba	30,924	17,860	37,568	28,413
Dominican Republic	17,440	22,076	19,668	19,773
Ecuador	19,527	16,284	30,155	45,213
El Salvador	1,261	4,063	10,415	14,545
Guatemala	42,034	10,458	17,551	16,224
Haiti	1,271	1,253	6,807	7,280
Honduras	11,661	9,065	7,345	6,784
Mexico	172,144	147,214	262,952	276,557
Nicaragua	1,899	492	6,515	8,029
Panama	4,056	1,679	35,552	36,656
Paraguay	10,077	1,488	32,035	38,229
Peru	96,654	84,034	29,233	33,061
Puerto Rico	123,087	109,295	69,593	81,637
Uruguay	51,859	47,894	31,192	33,303
USA	14,354,516	13,711,538	12,998,506	11,340,030
Venezuela	101,717	100,210	204,921	166,654
Total (including some not specified above)	110,987,934	108,423,812	87,695,185	94,605,129
Commonwealth countries				
In Europe—				
Cyprus	154,065	141,138	204,857	209,872
Gibraltar	5,048	4,289	69,073	80,105
Malta	50,541	40,771	141,298	162,454
In Africa				
West Africa:				
Gambia	3,158	2,865	17,815	19,141
Ghana	105,118	77,345	162,057	169,296
Nigeria	297,436	249,254	499,838	544,553
Sierra Leone	7,011	5,616	21,365	17,926
Southern Africa:				
Botswana	18,854	22,662	24,777	35,233
Lesotho	1,288	2,799	642	3,258
Malawi	24,666	25,381	33,575	31,462
Namibia	349	19,606	4,264	5,981
Swaziland	34,473	39,607	2,719	4,336
Zambia	19,308	22,468	92,832	62,655
Zimbabwe	86,280	103,891	83,718	135,309
East Africa:				
Kenya	149,474	141,996	223,080	206,927
Mauritius	233,936	250,218	50,746	52,263
Tanzania	25,575	20,938	84,694	72,822
Uganda	12,124	6,730	39,506	35,718
Seychelles	8,353	8,457	14,955	10,513
St Helena	555	820	7,429	6,980
In Asia—				
Bangladesh	72,515	80,568	70,584	39,086
Hong Kong	1,972,154	2,147,611	1,238,023	1,386,892
India	799,438	776,976	1,264,189	1,017,398
Malaysia	775,667	930,036	601,909	582,239
Pakistan	236,448	261,291	251,841	272,068
Singapore	1,021,148	1,134,365	1,040,188	1,018,419
Sri Lanka	63,362	74,460	88,496	128,565
In Oceania—				
Australia	1,039,080	870,823	1,645,620	1,355,127
Nauru	54	718	1,145	1,189
New Zealand	483,615	391,643	439,608	260,052
Papua New Guinea	34,849	32,170	8,793	15,446
Western Samoa	295	16	427	671

[1] Provisional figures.

Commonwealth countries	Imports from 1990 [1]	1991 [1]	Exports to 1990 [1]	1991 [1]
In America—				
Bahamas	15,053	37,142	22,917	19,631
Barbados	24,294	13,316	35,811	33,454
Belize	22,734	20,849	12,439	14,574
Bermuda	12,849	3,559	28,114	16,205
Canada	2,259,099	1,922,549	1,901,939	1,701,051
Falkland Islands	4,817	3,379	11,309	16,039
Guyana	53,892	50,479	15,294	19,275
Jamaica	136,535	123,773	58,702	54,669
Leeward Islands (Anguilla; St. Kitts-Nevis; Antigua and Barbuda; Montserrat)	7,991	12,764	29,735	30,849
Trinidad and Tobago	45,058	41,654	49,894	62,491
Windward Islands (Dominica; St. Lucia; St. Vincent and the Grenadines)	117,126	99,332	36,794	45,644
Total, Commonwealth countries (including some not specified above)	10,679,250	10,448,543	10,904,245	10,213,320
Ireland	4,498,571	4,416,151	5,311,539	5,295,949
Grand Total	126,165,755	118,871,355	103,910,969	104,818,449

[1] Provisional figures.

Imports and exports for 1990 and 1991 (Great Britain and Northern Ireland) (in £1,000):

Import values c.i.f. Export values f.o.b.	Total imports 1990 [1]	1991 [1]	Domestic exports 1990 [1]	1991 [1]
0. Food and Live Animals				
Live animals (excluding zoo animals, dogs and cats)	290,674	203,220	257,975	288,414
Meat and meat preparations	1,887,821	1,845,051	609,155	672,579
Dairy products and eggs	913,676	870,951	458,148	451,936
Fish and fish preparations	968,965	979,010	505,315	574,379
Cereals and cereal preparations	785,063	818,489	1,045,466	1,102,780
Fruit and vegetables	2,964,873	3,003,213	263,747	299,078
Sugar, sugar preparations, honey	639,242	681,169	240,291	247,547
Coffee, tea, cocoa, spices	904,423	869,735	438,653	465,220
Feeding stuff for animals	624,598	618,816	238,917	102,944
Miscellaneous food preparations	429,901	500,439	266,890	311,730
Total of Section 0	10,409,237	10,390,092	4,324,557	4,716,606
1. Beverages and Tobacco				
Beverages	1,529,780	1,464,907	2,112,771	2,251,634
Tobacco and tobacco manufactures	377,246	471,242	657,472	780,664
Total of Section 1	1,907,026	1,936,149	2,770,244	3,032,298
2. Crude Materials, Inedible, except Fuels				
Hides, skins and furskins, undressed	100,499	58,783	188,815	135,149
Oil seeds, oil nuts and oil kernels	273,042	224,046	67,266	52,614
Crude rubber (including synthetic and reclaimed)	244,899	223,592	221,863	198,053
Wood and cork	1,409,978	1,043,690	27,717	27,886
Pulp and waste paper	777,341	607,985	53,079	38,832
Textile fibres and their waste	548,875	452,581	494,510	466,351
Crude fertilizers and crude minerals (excluding fuels)	344,709	285,813	369,947	365,483
Metalliferous ores and metal scrap	1,479,233	1,232,715	633,515	526,826
Crude animal and vegetable materials, not elsewhere specified	542,667	540,107	105,876	108,595
Total of Section 2	5,721,243	4,679,314	2,162,586	1,919,799

[1] Provisional figures.

Import values c.i.f.	*Total imports*		*Domestic exports*	
Export values f.o.b.	*1990* [1]	*1991* [1]	*1990* [1]	*1991* [1]
3. *Mineral Fuels, Lubricants and Related Materials*				
Coal, coke and briquettes	654,771	754,975	122,014	100,788
Petroleum and petroleum products	6,254,923	5,843,839	7,477,620	6,792,554
Gas, natural and manufactured	824,546	633,638	176,518	251,760
Total [2] of Section 3	7,839,960	7,580,975	7,801,368	7,145,322
4. *Animal and Vegetable Oils and Fats*	377,370	387,514	87,743	95,929
5. *Chemicals*				
Chemical elements and compounds	3,593,336	3,652,516	4,303,304	4,466,202
Dyeing, tanning and colouring materials	651,629	620,903	1,193,499	1,215,454
Medicinal and pharmaceutical products	1,157,805	1,371,143	2,258,096	2,555,590
Essential oils and perfume; toilet and cleansing preparations	756,071	798,110	1,161,840	1,298,216
Fertilizers, manufactured	286,227	282,943	110,197	103,247
Plastic materials	3,227,404	3,029,004	2,124,162	2,119,590
Total [2] of Section 5	10,834,619	10,978,081	13,182,512	13,781,950
6. *Manufactured Goods Classified Chiefly by Material*				
Leather and dressed furs	240,736	185,895	311,784	258,023
Rubber	880,447	872,239	872,787	887,935
Wood and cork (excluding furniture)	949,087	821,583	114,228	116,389
Paper, paperboard	4,016,552	3,868,991	1,539,386	1,623,786
Textile yarn, fabrics	3,936,197	3,738,464	2,446,974	2,349,151
Non-metallic mineral manufactures	3,602,140	3,332,910	3,191,300	3,172,057
Iron and steel	2,676,693	2,620,266	3,035,980	3,011,555
Non-ferrous metals	3,003,621	2,556,265	2,193,182	1,974,215
Manufactures of metal, not elsewhere specified	2,593,488	2,524,000	2,115,354	2,182,187
Total of Section 6	21,898,961	20,520,613	15,820,974	15,575,298
7. *Machinery and Transport Equipment*				
Boilers, engines, motors and power-units	3,518,388	11,415,025	5,251,433	3,073,103
Agricultural and Industrial machinery	8,874,665	7,586,265	9,690,584	9,254,551
Office machinery	7,714,644	3,351,654	6,341,244	6,581,203
Electrical machinery, apparatus, not elsewhere specified	10,410,547	7,079,376	8,335,937	9,666,859
Transport equipment	16,771,327	13,692,143	12,536,256	15,024,323
Total of Section 7	47,289,572	43,124,663	42,155,433	43,600,038
8. *Miscellaneous Manufactured Articles*				
Prefabricated buildings, sanitary, plumbing, heating and lighting fixtures	394,498	368,254	260,363	267,278
Furniture	1,111,997	1,005,343	533,186	564,211
Travel goods, handbags and similar articles	309,127	285,105	69,887	72,390
Clothing	3,905,902	4,129,386	1,699,392	1,920,125
Footwear	1,169,085	1,168,520	274,439	314,847
Scientific instruments; cameras, watches and clocks	4,071,459	4,190,514	4,108,709	4,261,480
Miscellaneous manufactured articles, not elsewhere specified	7,920,066	6,513,300	6,401,044	5,742,710
Total of Section 8	18,252,133	17,560,421	13,347,020	13,143,041

[1] Provisional figures.   [2] Includes items not specified here.

Import values c.i.f. *Export values f.o.b.*	*Total imports* *1990* [1]	*1991* [1]	*Domestic exports* *1990* [1]	*1991* [1]
	9. *Commodities and Transactions not* *Classified According to Kind*			
Total of Section 9	1,635,634	1,713,532	2,258,531	1,808,165
Total [2] of all classes	126,165,755	118,871,355	103,910,969	104,818,449

[1] Provisional figures.   [2] Includes items not specified here.

Tourism. There were 18m. overseas visitors in 1990 spending £7,785m. in the UK and an estimated £2,025m. in fares to British carriers.

COMMUNICATIONS

Roads. Central government responsibility for highways in England rests with the Secretary of State for Transport. His responsibilities are administered by the Department of Transport through a number of Directorates at Headquarters together with 9 Regional Offices. For Welsh and Scottish roads, central government responsibility rests with the Secretaries of State for Wales and Scotland respectively.

The Secretary of State is the highway authority responsible for all trunk roads. The Shire County Councils, the Metropolitan District Councils, the London Borough Councils and the Common Council of the City of London are the highway authorities responsible for local roads in their own areas.

The Secretary of State has powers to provide roads designed for limited classes of motor traffic, and to confirm schemes for the provision of such special roads by local authorities. The former have the status of trunk roads; the latter, principal roads. 3,070 km of motorway were open to traffic in Great Britain in 1990 (2,638 km of trunk motorway in England, 234 km in Scotland, 120 km in Wales and 77 km of principal motorway). Public highways in Great Britain in 1990, excluding lengths of unsurfaced roads (green lanes), totalled 358,034 km (England, 273,136 km; Wales, 33,297 km; Scotland, 51,601 km). There were 12,674 km of all-purpose trunk roads, 3,070 km of trunk and principal motorways, 35,149 km of principal roads (excluding motorways) and 307,141 km of other roads.

Motor vehicles for which licences were current under the Vehicles (Excise) Act, 1971, at 31 Dec. 1990, numbered 24,673,000, including 19,742,000 private cars, 833,000 mopeds, scooters and motor cycles, 115,000 public transport vehicles and 2,729,000 goods vehicles. New vehicle registrations in 1990, 2,438,400.

Road casualties in Great Britain numbered in 1990, 341,141 including 5,217 killed; in 1989, 341,592 including 5,373 killed.

Railways. The British Railways Board as a public authority owns and manages British Rail: The national rail network, British Rail Maintenance Ltd, British Rail Property Board, European Passenger Services Ltd. and Transportation Systems and Market Research Ltd. (Transmark). The role of the Board is to determine policies, establish the organization to carry them out, monitor performance and take major decisions to meet objectives set by the Secretary of State for Transport.

The management of the railways has been reorganized between the rail businesses of InterCity, Network SouthEast, Regional Railways, Trainload Freight and Railfreight Distribution. The Managing Directors of these businesses have full responsibility to the Board for the effective management and operation of all aspects of the railways under their control.

A wholly-owned subsidiary, European Passenger Services Ltd, has been set up to operate international passenger services through the Channel Tunnel.

In the year ended 31 March 1991, Group turnover was £3,776m. and 136,277 staff were employed, of whom 131,527 were involved in the rail business. 143·1m. tonnes of freight were carried and 762·4m. passenger journeys made.

		1989–90	*1990–91*
Passenger Receipts and Traffic			
Receipts	£m.	1,882·7	2,032·7
Passenger journeys	m.	746·4	762·4
Passenger miles (estimated)	m.	20,706·0	20,624·0

		1989–90	1990–91
Freight Train Traffic			
Receipts	£m.	671·9	663·4
Traffic	m. tonnes	143·1	138·2
Net tonne miles (trainload and wagonload)	m.	10,403·0	9,933·0
Locomotives			
Diesel		1,835	1,752
Electric		260	278
High Speed Trains			
Power cars		197	197
Passenger carriages		718	728
Coaching vehicles		13,115	12,903
Freight vehicles (excluding brake vans)		21,970	20,970
Stations		2,610	2,615
Route open for traffic	miles	10,307	10,305
Electrified	miles	2,834	3,052

The London Regional Transport (formerly London Transport Executive) is the authority responsible for the operation of the capital's Underground and bus services. Overall policy and financial control is exercised by the Secretary of State for Transport. In April 1989, London Underground had 245 route miles of railway open for traffic and also operated over 10 route miles owned by British Rail. Rolling stock owned: Underground, 3,950; buses, 4,825. In the financial year 1988–89, the number of train miles run in passenger service was 32·1m.; number of bus miles run in passenger service was 170m. The number of passenger journeys was: Underground 815m.; buses 1,244m.

Civil Aviation. British Airways is engaged in the provision of air transport services for passengers, cargo and mail worldwide, both on scheduled and charter services. It operates long and short haul international services, as well as an extensive domestic network. In 1990–91, it carried 25·5m. passengers and 506,000 tonnes of freight, and at 31 March 1991 it had a fleet of 230 aircraft and employed 52,809 staff.

Following the Civil Aviation Act 1971, the Civil Aviation Authority (CAA) was established as an independent public body responsible for the economic and safety regulation of British civil aviation. It also runs the National Air Traffic Services in conjunction with the Ministry of Defence. CAA established a wholly-owned subsidiary, Highlands and Islands Airports Ltd, on 1 April 1986 to own and operate eight airports in the Scottish Highlands and Islands.

Operating and traffic statistics of UK airlines on scheduled services during the calendar year 1989 (and 1990): Aircraft km flown, 486m. (524m.); revenue passengers carried, 35m. (38m.); cargo (freight and mail) carried 453,430 (485,535) tonnes.

Traffic between UK airports and places abroad in 1989 (and 1990) on all services included 782,282 (819,164) air transport aircraft movements.

There were 14,353 and 14,710 civil aircraft registered in the UK at 31 Dec. 1990 and 1991 respectively.

Shipping. The UK-owned merchant fleet (trading vessels over 100 GRT) in Dec. 1991 totalled 785 ships of 14·5m. DWT and 9·5m. GRT. The UK-registered fleet totalled 508 ships of 3·9m. DWT and 3·5m. GRT.

The average age of the UK-owned fleet was 13·8 years. Total gross earnings in 1990 were £3,956m. The net contribution to the UK balance of payments was £1,359m.; there were gross import savings of £1,025m.

The Ports Act enabling port authorities to be privatized came into force in Aug. 1991.

Inland Waterways. There are approximately 3,500 miles of navigable canals and river navigations in Great Britain. Of these, British Waterways is responsible for some 380 miles of commercial waterways (maintained for freight traffic) and some 1,160 miles of cruising waterways (maintained for pleasure cruising, fishing and amenity). British Waterways is also responsible for a further 450 miles of canals, of which in 1968 some 350 miles were no longer navigable and whose future has been considered in conjunction with local authorities. As a result, some 215 miles have been restored for cruising or as local amenities. The Board's external turnover for the 12 months to 31 March 1991 was £27·1m. Freight traffic was 4·69m. tonnes.

The most important of the river navigations and canals managed by other authorities include the rivers Thames, Great Ouse and Nene, the Norfolk Broads and the Manchester Ship Canal.

Hadfield, C., *British Canals*. 6th ed. Newton Abbot, 1979

Post and Telecommunications. The Post Office operates as a group of 3 distinct businesses: Royal Mail (letter delivery), Royal Mail Parcelforce (parcel delivery), and Post Office Counters (retailing and agency services). Every area of the country is served by regional offices for each of the businesses. Royal Mail collects and delivers 58m. letters a day to the 24m. UK addresses. Other services include electronic mail, guaranteed parcel deliveries (same-day and overnight to UK addresses) and swift deliveries to 100 other countries. The British Postal Consultancy Service provides advice to administrations abroad.

In 1989–90 there were 20,871 post offices and some 100,000 posting boxes. Staff numbered 211,670. 14,718m. letters and 191·5m. parcels were posted. Group turnover was £4459·4m., pre-tax profit, £116·4m., and profit retained, £2·9m.

	1985–86 (1m.)	1986–87 (1m.)	1987–88 (1m.)	1988–89 (1m.)
Correspondence (incl. registered items) posted	11,700	12,500	13,500	13,700
Parcels handled	194	192	197	191

Income (1988–89) £3,914·8m. Profit retained, £100m. British Telecom (BT) was established in 1981 to take over the management of telecommunications from the Post Office. At 30 Sept. 1989 there were 7,062 local exchanges, 345 trunk exchanges and 5 international exchanges operated by British Telecom. At 30 Sept. 1989 there were 5,473,000 business and 19,018,000 residential telephone connexions and 105,000 telex connexions. In 1990 British Telecom's modernization programme will continue. By the end of Sept. 1989 there were more than 2,546 digital exchanges in operation and more than 730,000 km of optical fibre had been installed in the network.

At 31 Dec. 1989 about 330,000 customers were connected to Cellnet, the cellular mobile radio network launched in 1985 and run jointly by BT and Securicor. In 1989 BT owned and operated 6 cable and satellite TV systems at The Barbican (London), Bracknell, Berks, Irvine (Scotland), Milton Keynes, Swindon and Washington (Tyne and Wear). At 31 May 1989 BT employed a total staff of 235,400.

The 'regulator' Office of Telecommunications (Oftel) has the duty of protecting consumer interests.

Daunton, M. J., *Royal Mail: The Post Office since 1840*. London, 1985

Broadcasting. Radio and television services are provided by the British Broadcasting Corporation (BBC) and by licensees of the Radio Authority and the Independent Television Commission (ITC). The BBC, constituted by Royal Charter until 31 Dec. 1996, has responsibility for providing domestic and external broadcast services, the former financed from the television licence revenue, the latter by Government grant. The domestic services include 2 national television services, 5 national radio network services and a network of local radio stations.

The ITC is responsible for licensing and regulating all non-BBC TV services, including ITV (regional and breakfast-time licensees), Channel 4, the proposed Channel 5, cable and satellite and additional services, such as teletext, carried on the spare capacity of TV signals. The Radio Authority is responsible for licensing and regulating independent local radio services. S4C provides a Welsh-language service in Wales, and is funded by the government.

The BBC's domestic radio services are available on Long Wave, MF and VHF;

those of the Radio Authority on MF and VHF. Television services other than those only on cable and satellite are broadcast at VHF in 625-line definition and in colour (by PAL).

The broadcasting authorities, whose governing bodies are appointed (by HM the Queen in the case of the BBC and by the Home Secretary in the case of the ITC, the Radio Authority and S4C) as trustees for the public interest in broadcasting, are independent of government in matters of programme content and are publicly accountable to Parliament for the discharge of their responsibilities.

All independent services other than S4C (Sianel Pedwar Cymru) are financed by the sale of broadcasting advertising time, commercial sponsorship, or, on some cable and satellite services, by subscription. Their duties and powers are laid down in the Broadcasting Act of 1990.

In 1981 the Broadcasting Complaints Commission was set up to consider and adjudicate upon complaints of unfair or unjust treatment in broadcast programmes or of unwarranted infringement of privacy in or in the making of programmes. These statutory functions have been continued in the Broadcasting Act of 1990.

The number of television receiving licences in force on 31 March 1989 was 19·1m., including 17·7m. for colour.

Cinemas. In 1990 cinemas had a total seating capacity of 0·46m. (0·44m. in 1989). Admissions were 91m. (88m. in 1989, from a low point of 54m. in 1984).

Newspapers. In 1992 there were 13 national dailies.

In Jan. 1991 the Press Complaints Commission replaced the former Press Council. It has 15 members (*Chair* Lord McGregor of Durris) including 7 editors. It is funded (£1·5m. in 1991) by the newspaper industry.

Benn's Media Directory. Tunbridge Wells, Annual

JUSTICE, RELIGION, EDUCATION AND WELFARE

Justice. *England and Wales.* The legal system of England and Wales, divided into civil and criminal courts has at the head of the superior courts, as the ultimate court of appeal, the House of Lords, which hears each year a number of appeals in civil matters, including a certain number from Scotland and Northern Ireland, as well as some appeals in criminal cases. In order that civil cases may go from the Court of Appeal to the House of Lords, it is necessary to obtain the leave of either the Court of Appeal or the House itself, although in certain cases an appeal may lie direct to the House of Lords from the decision of the High Court. An appeal can be brought from a decision of the Court of Appeal or the Divisional Court of the Queen's Bench Division of the High Court in a criminal case provided that the Court is satisfied that a point of law 'of general public importance' is involved, and either the Court or the House of Lords is of the opinion that it is desirable in the public interest that a further appeal should be brought. As a judicial body, the House of Lords consists of the Lord Chancellor, the Lords of Appeal in Ordinary, commonly called Law Lords, and such other members of the House as hold or have held high judicial office. The final court of appeal for certain of the Commonwealth countries is the Judicial Committee of the Privy Council which, in addition to Privy Counsellors who are or have held high judicial office in the UK, includes others who are or have been Chief Justices or Judges of the Superior Courts of Commonwealth countries.

Civil Law. The main courts of original civil jurisdiction are the High Court and county courts.

The High Court has exclusive jurisdiction to deal with specialist classes of case e.g. Judicial Review. It has concurrent jurisdiction with county courts in cases involving contract and tort although it will only hear those cases where the value of the claim is substantial or where the issues are complex or important. The High Court also has appellate jurisdiction to hear appeals from lower tribunals.

The judges of the High Court are attached to one of its three divisions: Chancery, Queen's Bench and Family; each with its separate field of jurisdiction. The Heads of the three divisions are the Lord Chief Justice (Queen's Bench), the Vice-

Chancellor (Chancery) and the President of the Family Division. In addition there are over 80 High Court judges. For the hearing of cases at first instance, High Court judges sit singly. Appellate jurisdiction is usually exercised by Divisional Courts consisting of two (sometimes 3) judges, though in certain circumstances a judge sitting alone may hear the appeal. High Court business is dealt with in the Royal Courts of Justice and by over 100 District Registries outside London.

County courts have a more limited trial jurisdiction. They normally hear cases in contract and tort up to £25,000 but may hear a case having a higher value if it is not sufficiently complex or important for High Court trial. County courts also have upper financial limits to deal with specialist classes of business such as equity. Certain county courts have been designated to deal with family, bankruptcy, patents, admiralty and discrimination cases.

There are about 270 county courts located throughout the country each with its own district. A case may be heard by a Circuit Judge or by a District Judge, (the latter generally being restricted to cases valued at £5,000 or less). County courts have a small claims jurisdiction for actions for money worth £1,000 or less; this is an informal procedure where parties are encouraged to present cases without the need for legal representation.

The Restrictive Practices Court was set up in 1956 under the Restrictive Trade Practices Act and is responsible for deciding whether a restrictive trade agreement is in the public interest. It is presided over by a High Court judge, but laymen sit on the bench also. Another specialist court is the Employment Appeal Tribunal, with similar composition, which hears appeals in employment cases from lower tribunals.

The Court of Appeal (Civil Division) hears appeals in civil actions from the High Court and county courts and certain special courts such as the Restrictive Practice Court and Employment Appeal Tribunal. Its President is the Master of the Rolls, aided by up to 28 Lords Justices of Appeal setting in 6 or 7 divisions of 2 or 3 judges each.

Civil proceedings are instituted by the aggrieved person, but as they are a private matter, they are frequently settled by the parties through their lawyers before the matter comes to trial. In very limited classes of dispute (e.g. libel and slander), a party may request a jury to sit to decide questions of fact and the award of damages.

Criminal Law. At the base of the system of criminal courts in England and Wales are the magistrates' courts which try over 97% of criminal cases. In general, in exercising their summary jurisdiction, they have power to pass a sentence of up to six months imprisonment and to impose a fine of up to £2,000 on any one offence. They also deal with the preliminary hearing of cases triable only at the Crown Court. In addition to dealing summarily with over 2m. cases, which include thefts, assaults, road traffic infringements, drug abuse, etc, they also have a limited civil jurisdiction.

Magistrates' courts normally comprise three lay justices. Although unpaid they are entitled to loss of earnings and travel and subsistence allowance. They undergo training after appointment and they are advised by a professional justices' clerk. In central London and in some provincial areas full-time stipendiary magistrates have been appointed. Generally they possess the same powers as the lay bench, but they sit alone. On 1 Jan. 1992 the total strength of the lay magistracy was 29,441 including 13,336 women. Justices are appointed on behalf of the Queen by the Lord Chancellor, except in Greater Manchester, Merseyside and Lancashire where they are appointed by the Chancellor of the Duchy of Lancaster.

Justices are selected and trained specially to sit in Juvenile and Family Proceedings Courts. Juvenile courts deal with cases involving persons under 17 years of age charged with criminal offences (other than homicide and other grave offences) or brought before the court as being in need of care or control. With effect from Oct. 1992 these were to be re-designated 'Youth Courts', dealing with children and young persons up to the age of 18. These courts normally sit with three justices, including at least one man or one woman, and are accommodated separately from other courts.

Family Proceedings Courts deal with matrimonial applications, custody, guardianship and maintenance of children, and adoption. These courts normally sit with three justices including at least one man or one woman.

Above the magistrates' courts is the Crown Court. This was set up by the Courts Act 1971 to replace quarter sessions and assizes. Unlike quarter sessions and assizes, which were individual courts, the Crown Court is a single court which is capable of sitting anywhere in England and Wales. It has power to deal with all trials on indictment and has inherited the jurisdiction of quarter sessions to hear appeals, proceedings on committal of persons from the magistrates' courts for sentence, and certain original proceedings on civil matters under individual statutes.

The jurisdiction of the Crown Court is exercisable by a High Court judge, a Circuit judge or a Recorder or Assistant Recorder (part-time judges) sitting alone, or, in specified circumstances, with justices of the peace. The Lord Chief Justice has given directions as to the types of case to be allocated to High Court judges (the more serious cases) and to Circuit judges or Recorders respectively.

Appeals from magistrates' courts go either to a Divisional Court of the High Court (when a point of law alone is involved) or to the Crown Court where there is a complete re-hearing on appeals against conviction. Appeals from the Crown Court in cases tried on indictment lie to the Court of Appeal (Criminal Division). Appeals on questions of law go by right, and appeals on other matters by leave. The Lord Chief Justice or a Lord Justice sits with judges of the High Court to constitute this court.

There remains as a last resort the invocation of the royal prerogative exercised on the advice of the Home Secretary. In 1965 the death penalty was abolished for murder.

All contested criminal trials, except those which come before the magistrates' courts, are tried by a judge and a jury consisting of 12 members. The defence may challenge any potential juror for cause. The prosecution may ask that any number may 'stand by' until the jury panel is exhausted, and only then need to show cause. The jury decides whether the accused is guilty or not. The judge is responsible for summing up on the facts and explaining the law; he sentences convicted offenders. If, after at least 2 hours of deliberation, a jury is unable to reach a unanimous verdict it may, on the judge's direction, provided that in a full jury of 12 at least 10 of its members are agreed, bring in a majority verdict. The failure of a jury to agree on a unanimous verdict or to bring in a majority verdict may involve the retrial of the case before a new jury.

The Employment Appeal Tribunal. The Employment Appeal Tribunal which is a superior Court of Record with the like powers, rights, privileges and authority of the High Court, was set up in 1976 to hear appeals on questions of fact and law against decisions of industrial tribunals and of the Certification Officer. The appeals are heard by a High Court Judge sitting with 2 members (in exceptional cases 4) appointed for their special knowledge or experience of industrial relations either on the employer or the trade union side, with always an equal number on each side. The great bulk of their work is concerned with the problems which can arise between employees and their employers.

Military Courts. Offences by persons subject to service law against the system of military law created under the powers of the Army Act, Air Force Act or Naval Discipline Act are dealt with either summarily or by courts-martial.

The Personnel of the Law. All judicial officers except the Lord Chancellor (who is a member of the Cabinet) are independent of Parliament and the Executive. They are all appointed by the Crown on the advice of the Prime Minister or the Lord Chancellor and hold office until retiring age. The legal profession is divided; barristers, who advise on legal problems and can conduct cases before all courts, usually act for the public only through solicitors, who deal directly with the legal business brought to them by the public and have rights to present cases before certain courts. Long-standing members of both professions are eligible for appointment to most judicial offices. Only barristers, however, are eligible for appointment direct to the High Court and above.

Legal Aid. Broadly there are 3 kinds of legal aid. Firstly there is legal advice and assistance, otherwise known as the 'Green Form' scheme. This includes advice and help on any question of English law, both civil and criminal, but does not normally cover any form of representation before a court or tribunal. As an extension of the scheme, however, assistance by way of representation has been available for certain proceedings, chiefly civil, in magistrates' courts. Legal advice and assistance also provides for duty solicitor schemes at magistrates' courts and police stations. Under the magistrates' courts schemes, initial advice, and representation where necessary, is available to unrepresented defendants at court, from duty solicitors either in attendance at courts or on call. The scheme covers advice to a defendant in custody, making a bail application, representing a defendant in custody on a guilty plea, and certain other cases. The advice and assistance at police stations scheme enables any person who has been arrested and taken to a police station, or who is assisting the police with their enquiries, to receive advice and assistance, from either a duty solicitor or the person's own solicitor. The cost of these schemes, which are not subject to means test or contribution, is met from the Legal Aid fund and in 1990–91 amounted to £37·5m. Secondly, under Part IV of the Legal Aid Act 1988, there is legal aid for civil court proceedings. Under regulations, aid is available to those of low or moderate means either free or subject to a contribution, depending on means. In 1990–91 there were over 1·5m. payments for advice and assistance under the Legal Advice and Assistance Scheme and 333,444 civil legal aid certificates were issued. The cost of legal aid in civil cases is met from (*a*) contributions from assisted persons; (*b*) the operation of the statutory charge which gives the Law Society a first charge on money or property recovered or preserved for an assisted person; (*c*) costs recovered from opposing parties and (*d*) a grant from the Exchequer. The net cost of civil legal aid to the state (excluding administration costs of the scheme) in the year 1990–91 amounted to £219·5m. and the cost of the legal advice and assistance scheme was £90·7m. of which £18·7m. was accounted for by assistance by way of representation. Thirdly under Part V of the Legal Aid Act 1988 a court dealing with criminal proceedings may order legal aid to be given if it considers it is desirable in the interests of justice and if it also considers that the defendant (or appellant) requires financial assistance in meeting the costs he may incur. The interests of justice are statutorily defined to include, for example, situations where the defendant is in real danger of going to prison or losing his job, where substantial questions of law are to be argued or where the defendant is unable to follow the proceedings and explain his case due to inadequate knowledge of English, mental illness or other mental or physical disability. Legal aid must be granted, subject to means, in the following circumstances: where a person is committed for trial on a charge of murder, where the prosecutor appeals or applies for leave to appeal from the criminal division of the Court of Appeal or the Courts-Martial Appeal Court to the House of Lords, and in certain circumstances where the court is considering depriving a defendant of his liberty.

The costs of legal aid in criminal proceedings are paid by the central government, but courts have power to require legally aided persons to contribute towards the cost of legal aid given to them. The net cost of legal aid in criminal proceedings in the year 1990–91 was £371·81m., £156·11m. of this was for legal aid in the higher courts which is paid for out of the Lord Chancellor's vote and £171·6m. for legal aid in the magistrates' courts which is paid from the legal aid fund.

Police. The authorized establishment of the police force in England and Wales in Dec. 1991 was 128,265: the actual strength was 112,066 men and 15,061 women. In addition there were 18,072 special constables (including 6,480 women). The estimated total expenditure on the police service in England and Wales for 1989–90 was £4,900m.

SCOTLAND. The High Court of Justiciary is the supreme criminal court in Scotland and has jurisdiction in all cases of crime committed in any part of Scotland, unless expressly excluded by statute. It consists of the Lord Justice-General, the Lord Justice-Clerk and 22 other judges, who are the same judges as of the Court of Session, the Scottish supreme civil court. One judge is seconded to the Scottish Law Commission. The Court, which is presided over by the Lord Justice-General, whom failing, the Lord Justice-Clerk, exercises an appellate jurisdiction as well as one of first instance, sits as business requires in Edinburgh both as a Court of Appeal (the *quorum* being 3 judges) and as a court of first instance and on circuit as a court of first instance. The decisions of the Court in either case are not subject to review by the House of Lords. One judge sitting with a jury of 15 persons can, and usually does, try cases, but 2 or more (with a jury) may do so in important or complex cases. It has a privative jurisdiction over cases of treason, murder, rape, deforcement of messengers and breach of duty by magistrates. It also, in practice, is the only court which tries serious crimes against person or property and generally those cases in which a sentence greater than imprisonment for 3 years is likely to be imposed. Moreover, the Court has inherent power to try and to punish all acts which are plainly criminal though previously unknown and not dealt with by any statute.

The appellate jurisdiction of the High Court of Justiciary extends to all cases tried on indictment, whether in the High Court or the Sheriff Court, and persons so convicted may appeal to the Court against conviction or sentence or both except that there is no appeal against any sentence fixed by law. By such an appeal, a person may bring under review of the High Court of Justiciary any alleged miscarriage of justice including any alleged miscarriage of justice on the basis of the existence and significance of additional evidence which was not heard at the trial and which was not available and could not reasonably have been made available at the trial. It is also a court of review from courts of summary criminal jurisdiction, and on the final determination of any summary prosecution a convicted person may appeal to the Court by way of stated case on questions of law, etc., but not on questions of fact, except in relation to a miscarriage of justice alleged by the person accused on the basis of the existence and significance of additional evidence which was not heard at the trial and which was not available and could not reasonably have been made available at the trial. The Lord Advocate may refer a point of law which has arisen during a trial on indictment in which accused has been acquitted for the opinion of the Court. A prosecutor may appeal only on a point of law. A further or complementary form of process of review which can be resorted to by convicted persons in these courts is by Bill of Suspension (and Liberation), but it is of strictly limited application. A prosecutor in cases tried on indictment or under summary criminal procedure may also bring under review a decision in law, prior to final judgment of the case, by way of Bill of Advocation. The Court also hears appeals under the Courts-Martial (Appeals) Act 1951.

The Sheriff Court has an inherent universal criminal jurisdiction (as well as an extensive civil one) limited in general to crimes and offences committed within a sheriffdom (a specifically defined region), which has, however, been curtailed by statute or practice under which the High Court of Justiciary has exclusive jurisdiction in relation to the crimes above-mentioned. This Court is presided over by a Sheriff-Principal or Sheriff, and when trying cases on indictment sits with a jury of 15 persons. His power of awarding punishment involving imprisonment is restricted to 3 years in the maximum, but he may under certain statutory powers remit the prisoner to the High Court for sentence. The Sheriff also exercises a wide summary criminal jurisdiction and when doing so sits without a jury; and he has concurrent jurisdiction with every other court within his Sheriff Court District in regard to all offences competent for trial in summary courts. The great majority of offences which come before the courts are of a minor nature and, as such, are disposed of in the Sheriff Summary Courts or in the District Courts (*see* below). In cases to be tried on indictment either in the High Court of Justiciary or in the Sheriff Court, the judge may, and in some cases must, before the trial, hold a Preliminary Diet to decide questions of a preliminary nature, whether to the competency or relevancy or otherwise. Any decision at a preliminary diet can be the subject of an appeal to the High Court of Justiciary prior to the trial.

District Courts in each local authority district have jurisdiction in minor offences occurring within the district. These courts are presided over by lay magistrates, known as justices, and have limited powers of fine and imprisonment. In Glasgow

District there are also 4 Stipendiary Magistrates who have the same sentencing powers as Sheriffs.

The Court of Session, presided over by the Lord President (the Lord Justice-General in criminal cases), is divided into an Inner House comprising 2 divisions of 4 judges each with mainly appellate function, and an Outer House comprising 15 single judges, sitting individually at first instance; it exercises the highest civil jurisdiction in Scotland, with the House of Lords as a court of appeal.

Police. The police forces in Scotland at the end of 1990 had an authorized establishment of 14,045; the strength was 12,583 men and 1,258 women. There were 5,012 special constables. The total police net expenditure in Scotland was £411·2m. for 1989–90.

CIVIL JUDICIAL STATISTICS

ENGLAND AND WALES	1989	1990
Appellate Courts		
Judicial Committee of the Privy Council	55	52
House of Lords	63	61
Court of Appeal	1,622	1,580
High Court of Justice (appeals and special cases from inferior courts)	2,535	3,134
Courts of First Instance (excluding Magistrates' Courts and Tribunals)		
High Court of Justice:		
Chancery Division [1]	30,813	42,965
Queen's Bench Division [2]	288,975	374,471
Family Division: Principal Registry matters [3]	1,578	1,589
District Registry wardships	3,152	3,575
Official Referee's	1,528	1,572
County courts: Matrimonial suits [4]	187,829	195,180
Other [5]	2,688,815	3,590,233
Restrictive Practices Court	10	12

SCOTLAND	1987	1988	1989
House of Lords (Appeals from Court of Session)	12	4	–
Court of Session—			
General Department	8,938	8,977	10,806
Sheriff's Ordinary Cause	79,875	84,254	81,548
Sheriff's Summary Cause	146,158	133,157	70,725

[1] Including Companies Court, Bankruptcy petitions and Patents Court.
[2] Including Admiralty Court.
[3] Adoption, guardianship and wardship.
[4] Including petitions filed at Principal Registry.
[5] Plaint, Admiralty, Bankruptcy and Companies, Adoption, Guardianship and miscellaneous.

CRIMINAL STATISTICS

ENGLAND AND WALES	Total number of offenders		Indictable offences [1]	
	1988	1989	1988	1989
Aged 10 and over [2]				
Proceeded against in magistrates' courts [3]	1,863,181	1,864,143	494,479	449,056
Found guilty at magistrates' courts	1,464,287	1,448,913	295,183	256,451
Found guilty at the Crown Court	91,053	85,666	91,053	83,096
Cautioned [4]	235,401	238,078	140,703	136,001

[1] Includes offences which can be tried either at the Crown Court or at magistrates' courts.
[2] Includes other offenders, e.g. companies, public bodies.
[3] Almost all defendants are initially proceeded against at magistrates' courts.
[4] Offenders who, on admission of guilt, are given an oral caution by or on the instruction of a senior police officer as an alternative to court proceedings. Such cautions are not given for motoring offences.

ENGLAND AND WALES—CONTD.

	Total number of offenders		Indictable offences [1]	
	1988	1989	1988	1989
Aged 10 and under 17				
Proceeded against in magistrates' courts [3]	61,513	55,444	47,629	36,750
Found guilty at magistrates' courts	45,204	38,973	34,801	25,105
Found guilty at the Crown Court	1,646	1,400	1,646	1,355
Cautioned [4]	101,375	96,627	82,818	72,832

[1] Includes offences which can be tried either at the Crown Court or at magistrates' courts.

[2] Includes other offenders, e.g. companies, public bodies.

[3] Almost all defendants are initially proceeded against at magistrates' courts.

[4] Offenders who, on admission of guilt, are given an oral caution by or on the instruction of a senior police officer as an alternative to court proceedings. Such cautions are not given for motoring offences.

CRIMINAL STATISTICS

SCOTLAND

	All Crimes and Offences		Crimes [1]	
	1989	1990 [2]	1989	1990 [2]
All persons and companies				
Proceeded against in all courts	192,491	190,333	62,763	59,368
Charge proved	171,826	168,007	53,168	49,023
Children (aged 8–15)				
Proceeded against in all courts	392	228	264	164

[1] Crimes are generally the more serious criminal acts and offences the less serious. 'Crimes' are not equivalent in coverage to 'indictable/triable either way offences'.   [2] Provisional.

Figures of formal police warnings were not collected after 1989.

Average population in prisons, youth custody centres and detention centres (1989) in England and Wales was 48,610 (convicted 39,814; untried 8,576, and 220 non-criminal prisoners); in Scotland (1990), 4,724 (sentenced, 3,973; remanded, 751).

Criminal statistics, England and Wales, 1989. HMSO, Cm1322
Prison statistics, England and Wales, 1989. HMSO, Cm1221
Paterson, A., *The Law Lords.* London, 1982

Religion. The Anglican Communion has originated from the Church of England and parallels in its fellowship of autonomous churches the evolution of British influence beyond the seas from colonies to dominions and independent nations. The Archbishop of Canterbury presides as *primus inter pares* at the decennial meetings of the bishops of the Anglican Communion at the Lambeth Conference and at the biennial meetings of the Primates and the Anglican Consultative Council. The last Conference was held in Canterbury in 1988 and was attended by 518 bishops.

The Anglican Communion consists of 29 member Churches or Provinces. These are Australia, Brazil, Burma, Burundi, Rwanda and Zaïre, Canada, Central Africa, Council of Churches of East Asia, England, Indian Ocean, Ireland, Japan, Jerusalem and the Middle East, Kenya, Melanesia, New Zealand, Nigeria, Papua New Guinea, the Philippines, Scotland, Southern Africa, Southern Cone of America, Sudan, Tanzania, Uganda, USA, Wales, West Africa, West Indies. There are also areas which come under the metropolitical jurisdiction of the Archbishop of Canterbury. These are Bermuda, Ceylon, the Diocese of Europe, Falkland Islands, The Council of the Churches of East Asia (which includes the Church in Korea), The Diocese of Hong Kong and Macao, Sabah, Kuching, Singapore, West Malaysia, The Lusitanian Church (Portugal) and The Spanish Reformed Episcopal Church.

England and Wales. The established Church of England, which baptizes about 30% of the children born in England (*i.e.* excluding Wales but including the Isle of Man and the Channel Islands), is Anglican. Civil disabilities on account of religion do not attach to any class of British subject. Under the Welsh Church Acts, 1914 and 1919, the Church in Wales and Monmouthshire was disestablished as from 1 April 1920, and Wales was formed into a separate Province.

The Queen is, under God, the supreme governor of the Church of England, with the right, regulated by statute, to nominate to the vacant archbishoprics and bishoprics. The Queen, on the advice of the First Lord of the Treasury, also appoints to such deaneries, prebendaries and canonries as are in the gift of the Crown, while a large number of livings and also some canonries are in the gift of the Lord Chancellor.

There are 2 archbishops (at the head of the 2 Provinces of Canterbury and York), and 42 diocesan bishops including the bishop of the diocese of Europe, which is part of the Province of Canterbury. Dr George Carey was enthroned as *Archbishop of Canterbury* in April 1991. Each archbishop has also his own particular diocese, wherein he exercises episcopal, as in his Province he exercises metropolitan, jurisdiction. In Dec. 1991 there were 67 suffragan and assistant bishops, 41 deans and provosts of cathedrals and 109 archdeacons. The *General Synod*, which replaced the Church Assembly in 1970 in England, consists of a House of Bishops, a House of Clergy and a House of Laity, and has power to frame legislation regarding Church matters. Each House has a veto over the others. The first two Houses consist of the members of the Convocations of Canterbury and York, each of which consists of the diocesan bishops and elected representatives of the suffragan bishops, 6 for Canterbury province and 3 for York (forming an Upper House), deans, provosts, and archdeacons, and a certain number of proctors elected as the representatives of the inferior clergy, together with, in the case of Canterbury Convocation, 4 representatives of the Universities of Oxford, Cambridge, London and the Southern Universities and in the case of York 2 representatives for the Universities of Durham and Newcastle and the other Northern Universities; the chaplains in the Forces and 2 representatives of the Religious Communities (forming the Lower House). The House of Laity is elected by the lay members of the Deanery Synods but also includes 3 representatives of the Religious Communities and *ex-officio* Church Commissioners and Ecclesiastical Judges. Every Measure passed by the General Synod must be submitted to the Ecclesiastical Committee, consisting of 15 members of the House of Lords nominated by the Lord Chancellor and 15 members of the House of Commons nominated by the Speaker. This committee reports on each Measure to Parliament, and the Measure receives the Royal Assent and becomes law if each House of Parliament resolves that the Measure be presented to the Queen.

Parochial affairs are managed by annual parochial church meetings and parochial church councils. At 31 Dec. 1990 there were 13,099 ecclesiastical parishes, inclusive of the Isle of Man and the Channel Islands. These parishes do not, in many cases, coincide with civil parishes. Although most parishes have their own churches, not every parish nowadays can have its own incumbent or minister. In Dec. 1991 there were 6,711 beneficed clergymen excluding dignitaries, 1,315 other clergymen of incumbent status and 1,645 assistant curates working in the parishes.

Women were admitted to Holy Orders for the first time in the Church of England in 1987. At 31 Dec. 1991 there were 674 full-time stipendiary women deacons, 601 of whom were in the parochial ministry.

Private persons possess the right of presentation to over 2,000 benefices; the patronage of the others belongs mainly to the Queen, the bishops and cathedrals, the Lord Chancellor, and the universities of Oxford and Cambridge. In addition to the 9,671 parochial incumbents and (male) assistant curates, there were (1991) 385 dignitaries and cathedral clergymen, and 319 non-parochial clergymen working within the diocesan framework. Although these figures account for the majority of active clergy in England, there are many others serving in parishes and institutions who cannot be quantified with any certainty. They include some 1,500 full-time hospital, Forces, prison, industrial and school and college chaplains. Over 1,000 non-stipendiary clergy hold a bishop's licence to officiate at services.

In 1989 there were estimated to be 1·5m. Easter and 1·7m. Christmas Communicants. Usual Sunday attendances at all services were 1·2m.

Of the 40,422 buildings registered for the solemnization of marriages at 30 June 1991, 16,584 belonged to the Established Church and the Church in Wales and 23,838 to other religious denominations. Of the 346,697 marriages celebrated in 1989 (348,492 in 1988), 34·3% were in the Established Church and the Church in

Wales, 17·6% in buildings of other denominations and 48% were civil marriages in Register Offices.

Roman Catholics in England and Wales were estimated at 4,248,346 in 1991. There were 5 archdioceses and 18 dioceses, 6,170 clergy and 3,044 parish churches and 1,170 other churches open to the public. Convents, 1,264.

The Unitarians have about 230 places of worship and 8,000 members. The Salvation Army, had, in British Territory, 1988, over 1,800 officers. They operate eventide homes, centres for the homeless, homes for children and adolescents and alcoholic rehabilitation centres.

The following is a summary of statistics of certain churches:

Denomination	Full members	Ministers in charge	Local and lay preachers
Methodist	450,406	3,399	13,378
Independent Methodist	3,870	131	—
Wesleyan Reform Union	3,026	23	145
United Reform	126,000	1,000	—
Baptist	167,466	2,111	—
Calvinistic Methodist Church of Wales	65,237	146	—
Society of Friends	18,010	—	—

There were (1991) about 350,000 Jews in the UK with some 295 synagogues. The 400-member Board of Deputies of British Jews has Israel Finestein as president, 1991–94. In 1990 there were some 900,000 Moslems, 175,000 Sikhs and 140,000 Hindus.

Scotland. The Church of Scotland, which was reformed in 1560, subsequently developed a presbyterian system of church government which was established in 1690 and has continued to the present day.

The supreme court is the General Assembly, which now consists of some 1,250 members, ministers and elders in equal numbers, commissioned by presbyteries. It meets annually in May, under the presidency of a Moderator appointed by the Assembly. The Queen is normally represented by a Lord High Commissioner, but has occasionally attended in person. The royal presence in a special throne gallery in the hall but outside the Assembly symbolises the independence from state control of what is nevertheless recognised as the national Church in Scotland.

There are also 12 synods, roughly co-terminous with Regional Councils, and 46 presbyteries in Scotland, roughly co-terminous with District Councils, together with 1 presbytery of England, 1 presbytery of Europe, and 1 presbytery of Jerusalem. At the base of this conciliar structure of Church courts are the kirk sessions, of which there were 1,700 on 1 Dec. 1989, with a total of 804,468 members.

The Episcopal Church of Scotland is a province of the Anglican Church and is one of the historic Scottish churches. It consists of 7 dioceses. As at 31 Dec. 1991 it had 256 churches and missions, 279 clergy and 58,299 members, of whom 35,196 were communicants.

There are in Scotland some small outstanding Presbyterian bodies and also Baptists, Congregationalists, Methodists and Unitarians.

The Roman Catholic Church which celebrated the centenary of the restoration of the Hierarchy in 1978, had in Scotland (1987) 1 cardinal, 2 archbishops and 9 bishops, 1,066 clergy, 472 parishes, and 798,150 adherents.

The proportion of marriages in Scotland according to the rites of the various Churches in 1990 was: Church of Scotland, 40·6%; Roman Catholic, 11·9%; Episcopal, 1·7%; United Free, 0·4%; others, 4·7%; civil, 40·7%.

Education (England and Wales). *The Publicly Maintained System of Education:* Compulsory schooling begins at the age of 5 and the minimum leaving age for all pupils is 16. No tuition fees are payable in any publicly maintained school (but it is open to parents, if they choose, to pay for their children to attend other schools). The post-school stage, which is voluntary, includes universities, polytechnics and other further and higher education establishments (including those which provide courses for the training of teachers), as well as adult education and the youth service. Financial assistance is generally available to students on higher education courses in the university and non-university sectors and to some students on other courses in further education.

Nursery Education. Provision for children under 5 is made in either nursery schools or in nursery or infant classes in primary schools. In the public sector no fees are payable. In Jan. 1991 there were 566 maintained nursery schools and 4,815 primary schools with nursery classes in England. There were 52,095 pupils under 5 attending nursery schools and 551,000 pupils under 5 in nursery and infant classes. About 51% of all these children were attending part-time. In Wales there were 54 maintained nursery schools in 1991 and 47,900 pupils under 5 provided for in nursery or infant classes.

Primary Schools. These provide for pupils from the age of 5 up to the age of 11. In Jan. 1991 there were 18,495 primary schools in England of which 2,666 were infant schools providing for pupils up to the age of about 7, the remainder mainly taking pupils from age 5 through to 11. Nearly all primary schools take both boys and girls. 16% of primary schools had 100 full time pupils or less.

In Jan. 1991 there were 1,717 primary schools in Wales. In those primary schools (and some secondary schools) which are in the predominantly Welsh-speaking areas, the main language of instruction is Welsh. There are also 'Welsh', or, more accurately, bilingual schools in mainly English-speaking parts of Wales. Generally children transfer from primary to secondary schools at 11.

Middle Schools. A number of local education authorities operate a middle school system. These provide for pupils from the age of 8, 9 or 10 up to the age of 12, 13 or 14. In Jan. 1991 there were 1,043 middle schools in England deemed either primary or secondary according principally to the age range of the school concerned.

Secondary Schools. These usually provide for pupils from the age of 11 upwards. In Jan. 1991 there were 3,406 secondary schools in England and 230 in Wales. In England some local education authorities have retained selection at age 11 for entry to grammar schools of which there were 148 in 1991. There were a small number of technical schools in 1991 which specialise in technical studies. There were 188 secondary modern schools in 1991 providing a general education up to the minimum school leaving age of 16, although exceptionally some pupils stay on beyond that age.

Almost all local education authorities operate a system of comprehensive schools to which pupils are admitted without reference to ability or aptitude. In Jan. 1991 there were 3,053 such schools in England with just over 2·5m. pupils. With the development of comprehensive education various patterns of secondary schools have come into operation. Principally these are: 1. all through schools with pupils aged 11 to 18 or 11 to 16; pupils over 16 being able to transfer to an 11 to 18 school or a sixth form college providing for pupils aged 16 to 19. (There were 114 sixth form colleges in England in 1991). 2. local education authorities operating a three-tier system involving middle schools where transfer to secondary school is at ages 12, 13 or 14. These correspond to 12 to 18, 13 to 18 and 14 to 18 comprehensive schools respectively; or 3. in areas where there are no middle schools a two-tier system of junior and senior comprehensive schools for pupils aged 11 to 18 with optional transfer to these schools at age 13 or 14.

The majority of secondary schools in Wales are classified as comprehensive. In 1991 44 schools used Welsh as a teaching medium.

Grant Maintained Schools. Since 1988 all local education authority maintained secondary, middle and primary schools with 300 or more registered pupils can apply for Grant Maintained status and receive direct grants from the Department of Education and Science. The governing body of such a school is responsible for all aspects of school management, including the deployment of funds, employment of staff and provision of most of the educational support services for staff and pupils. In Jan. 1991 there were 50 Grant Maintained schools in England and Wales.

City Technology Colleges. New legislation in 1988 enabled the Secretary of State for Education and Science, in partnership with sponsors from business and industry, to fund the establishment of City Technology Colleges. These are secondary schools for 11-18 year olds, having a broad curriculum with an emphasis on science and technology. The schools are independent of local education authorities. Their capital costs are shared between central Government and sponsors with Government meeting all recurrent costs. They do not charge fees.

Assisted Places Scheme. In order to give able children a wider range of educational opportunity the Government set up, in 1981, the Assisted Places Scheme to give help with tuition fees at certain independent schools to parents who could not otherwise afford them. In the school year 1989–90, the 278 participating schools offered a total of 5,706 assisted places, 4,520 for entry at age 11, 12, and 13, and 984 for entry at sixth form level. A further 17 schools joined the Scheme in Sept. 1990, providing an extra 69 places for entry at age 11, 12 or 13.

Special Education. The majority of children with special educational needs attend special schools, including hospital and non-maintained special schools and independent schools under arrangements made by local education authorities. The total number of children with statements under the 1981 Education Act was about 153,500.

Of maintained special schools, 1,102 are day schools, 150 are mainly boarding schools and there are 47 hospital special schools. Attendance is compulsory from 5–16. In addition, the Act's definition of special educational needs applies to children under 5 who are likely to have a learning difficulty when over this age, or whose learning difficulty would be likely to persist if special educational provision were not made for them. Authorities also have a duty to make special educational provision either in a school or in a college of further education for children aged 16–18 who have been assessed as being in need of, and who want, such provision. In addition to the provision in ordinary and special schools, authorities can make special arrangements for educating children at home, in small groups or in hospitals. There are also some establishments which provide further education, P.E. vocational training and for assessment for employment purely for disabled school leavers.

Ancillary Services. Local education authorities may provide registered pupils at any school maintained by them with milk, meals and refreshment and they may make such charges as they think fit for anything they provide. For pupils whose parents are in receipt of supplementary benefit or family income supplement, however, authorities are required to ensure that such provision is made for the pupil at midday as appears to them to be requisite and anything which is provided must be free of charge. Facilities must also be provided, free of charge, for consuming any meals or other refreshments which pupils bring to school themselves.

Further and Higher Education (Non-University). In Nov. 1989 there were about 466 institutions in England providing courses of further education, ranging from shorthand instruction to degree-level, postgraduate work and courses of teacher-training. Course enrolments numbered 660,290 full-time (including 79,469 sandwich students) and 1·8m. part-time and evening. There were in addition 2,399 Adult Education Centres, which provided mainly part-time courses of non-advanced general education and were attended by 1,376,137 students. In April 1989, 29 polytechnics and 56 colleges of higher education were brought together under the Polytechnics and Colleges Funding Council to create a new sector of higher education in England. The institutions offer both further and higher education courses, many leading to degrees of a standard comparable to those in universities or to professional qualifications. They cater for a mixture of full-time, part-time and sandwich students. Enrolments to the sector in 1988 totalled 293,000. In Wales the polytechnic and 5 other higher education institutions are scheduled to become independent of the local authorities in April 1992 and be funded by the Welsh Office.

Courses were also provided by the Workers' Educational Association, the University extramural departments and the Welsh National Council of YMCAs.

Education at institutions of further education is not free, but fees are generally low, and are remitted for most students under the age of 18 by the local authority.

The Youth Service. The Youth Service forms part of the education system and is concerned with promoting the personal development and social education of young people through a wide range of leisure-time activities. A duty is laid upon local education authorities by the provisions of the 1944 Education Act to secure the adequacy of such facilities for young people in their area. The Education Reform Act 1988 retained the force of these provisions. To this end they either provide, maintain and staff youth clubs, centres and other facilities themselves or assist voluntary agencies to do so.

Grants to voluntary agencies to help meet the cost of regional and national capital projects and to national voluntary bodies in support of a range of programmes of work and training expenses are made by the Government. From 1 April 1991 funding to the 4 National Youth Service Bodies ceased and was instead channelled through a single National Youth Agency (NYA). The NYA has a wide range of functions including curriculum development, training development, support for organisations within the youth service and for international work. It is also responsible for the collection and dissemination of information to the youth service field.

Awards to Students. Local education authorities in England and Wales are responsible for making mandatory awards to suitably qualified students taking first-degree and comparable courses, courses of initial teacher-training and certain other advanced level courses. These awards cover fees and maintenance but the maintenance grants are subject to the income of the student and his parents or spouse. In addition scholarships may be available both from universities and other sources. The authorities may also give discretionary awards to students who do not qualify for mandatory awards including those taking non-degree level courses.

Legislation of 1990 introduced interest-free 'top-up loans' to supplement students grants which are to remain at 1990 levels. The scheme is managed by Student Loans Company, with government funds of £14·25m. in 1990–91. The government also provided universities with £9m. for access funds to complement the loan scheme.

In Scotland the Scottish Office Education Department administers the Students' Allowance Scheme and the Postgraduate Students' Allowances Scheme, which offer means-test grants to personally eligible students in full-time, further or higher education. A limited number of grants are also available under the Scottish Studentship Scheme for postgraduate study in the arts and humanities. The Regional or Islands Education Authorities offer discretionary awards to Scottish-based students who do not qualify for a grant from the Scottish Office Education Department.

The 5 Research Councils made over 7,300 new awards in 1990-91 and there were more than 15,000 current awards in that academic year. In 1988–89 the British Academy gave 924 new awards and the Department 594 state bursaries and 70 state scholarships.

Teachers. To attain qualified teacher status, for work in maintained schools in England and Wales, teachers must have successfully completed a course of professional training. This can be either by completion of a recognized course of initial teacher training at an higher education institution or, in the case of mature entrants and teachers who have trained abroad, a period of 'on the job' training as a licensed teacher or overseas trained teacher. EC nationals who are recognized as qualified teachers in other member states will usually be entitled, on application, to automatic qualified teacher status.

In Nov. 1991 there were about 45,000 students on initial teacher-training courses.

On 1 Jan. 1991, 422,000 teachers were employed by local education authorities in maintained nursery, primary and secondary schools and by Grant-Maintained Schools in England and Wales.

Finance. Total current and capital expenditure on education in England (including Universities GB, and Mandatory Awards England and Wales) from public funds is estimated at £21,667m. for 1990–91 as compared with £19,677m. for 1989–90.

Scotland. The statistics on schools relate to education authority and grant-aided schools. All teachers employed in these schools require to be qualified; figures given are full-time equivalents.

Nursery Education. In Sept. 1990 there were 659 nursery schools and departments, with a total enrolment of 43,981 pupils.

Primary Education. In Sept. 1990 there were 2,372 primary schools and departments and the number on the registers was 440,606. In Sept. 1990, 22,632 teachers were employed in primary schools and departments.

Secondary Education. In Sept. 1990 there were 424 secondary schools with 293,702 pupils. Of these schools, 423 were all-comprehensive and 16 part-selective. All but 36 schools provided a full range of Scottish Certificate of Education courses and non-certificate courses. Pupils who start their secondary education in schools which do not cater for a full range of courses may be transferred at the end of their second or fourth year to schools where a full range of courses is provided. There were 23,988 teachers in secondary schools at Sept. 1990.

Special Schools. In Sept. 1990 there were 337 special schools and departments. 8,350 children were under instruction.

Further Education. In April 1989, 29 polytechnics and 55 general and specialist colleges of higher education were brought together under the Polytechnics and Colleges Funding Council (PCFC) to create a new sector of higher education in England. Four more colleges have since been designated as polytechnics. The institutions offer both higher and further education courses, many leading to degrees of a standard comparable to those in universities or to professional qualifications. They cater for a mixture of full-time, part-time and sandwich students. Enrolments to all institutions in the PCFC sector totalled 422,000 in the 1990/91 academic year. In 1989–90 there were 181 colleges and centres of further education, with 282,933 students, of whom 69,585 attended full-time (advanced courses, 34,080; non-advanced, 35,505) and 213,352 part-time (advanced courses, 34,352; non-advanced, 179,000).

In *Scotland* the 13 central institutions and 5 colleges of education are the main providers of higher education in the non-university sector. The colleges are self-governing, though they receive grant-in-aid funding from the government through the Scottish Office Education Department. In 1989–90 there were 57,394 students (excluding students on teacher training courses) of whom 24,756 attended full-time advanced courses, 9,706 part-time advanced courses and 22,932 other part-time courses.

Teacher Training. In Oct. 1990 there were 4,830 students in 5 colleges of education on pre-service courses of teacher-training.

Finance. Total central government's own expenditure on education in 1990–91 was £3,592m.

Independent Schools. Outside the state system of education there were in England 2,283 independent schools in Jan. 1990, ranging from large 'public' schools to small local ones. There were (Jan. 1990) 539,512 full-time and 19,233 part-time pupils in these schools. In Wales (1991) 12,074 full-time pupils attended 71 independent schools. Fees are charged by all these schools, which receive no grant from central government sources. All independent schools in England (and Wales) are required to be registered by the Department of Education and Science (and the Welsh Office) and are liable to the inspection by HM Inspectors. The term 'public schools' refers to independent schools in membership of the Headmasters' Conference, Governing Bodies Association or the Governing Bodies of Girls' Schools Association. Qualifications under which a school may be represented at the Headmasters' Conference include the measure of independence enjoyed by the governing body and the amount of advanced courses undertaken. Some of these schools are for boarders only, but the majority include non-resident 'day-pupils'. In Scotland there were 123 independent schools, with a total of 33,581 pupils in Sept. 1991. A small number of the Scottish independent schools are of the 'public school' type but they are not known as 'public schools' since in Scotland this term is used to denote education authority (*i.e.*, state) schools.

The earliest of the schools were founded by, and attached to, medieval churches. Many were founded as 'grammar' (classical) schools in the 16th century, receiving charters from the reigning sovereign. Reformed mainly in the middle of the 19th century, among the best-known are Eton College, founded in 1440 by Henry VI; Winchester College (1394) founded by William of Wykeham, Bishop of Winchester; Harrow School, founded in 1560 as a grammar school by John Lyon, a yeoman; and Charterhouse (1611). Among the earliest foundations are King's School, Canterbury, founded 600; King's School, Rochester (604) and St Peter's, York, (627).

Universities. In *England* there are 34 traditional degree-giving universities. In addition there are the London and Manchester Business Schools and the Open University. A new university campus with 240 places was scheduled to open in Oct. 1992 in Teesside, run jointly by Durham University and Teesside Polytechnic.

In *Wales* there is 1 university, the University of Wales, with constituent colleges at Aberystwyth, Bangor, Cardiff, Lampeter and Swansea. The University of Wales College of Medicine is a college of the University. The University of Wales College of Cardiff was formed in 1988 by the merger of University College Cardiff and the University of Wales Institute of Science and Technology.

In *Scotland* there are 8 universities, St Andrews, Glasgow, Aberdeen and Edinburgh Universities date from the 15th and 16th centuries while the others, Strathclyde, Heriot-Watt, Stirling and Dundee have been formally established since the early 1960s. Legislation was in train in 1992 to enable other institutions to use the title 'university.'

All these universities and colleges are independent, self-governing institutions, although they receive substantial aid from the State through the Universities Funding Council (UFC) (in the case of the Open University by direct grant from the Department of Education and Science). The UFC is a non-departmental public body with full executive responsibility for distributing to universities funds provided for that purpose by the Secretary of State for Education and Science and voted by Parliament. It has 15 members, from higher education and elsewhere. The UFC also advises the Secretary of State on matters relating to universities. The Information Systems Committee of the UFC advises it on the allocation of funds earmarked by the government of the UFC for the provision of computers and communications facilities in universities. Legislation in train in 1992 intends to replace the UFC with higher education funding councils in England, Scotland and Wales which will allocate funds to universities, polytechnics and colleges.

The Royal College of Art and the Cranfield Institute of Technology are primarily postgraduate institutions which award higher degrees under charters granted in 1967 and 1969 respectively.

The Open University received its Royal Charter on 1 June 1969 and is an independent, self-governing institution, awarding its own degrees at undergraduate and postgraduate level. It is financed by the Government through the Department of Education and Science and by the receipt of students' fees.

Tuition is by means of correspondence textbooks, audio and video cassettes, radio and television broadcasts and residential schools. There are also over 250 local study centres where advisory and counselling services may be offered and face to face tutorials held. No formal qualifications are required for entry to undergraduate or associate student courses. Anyone resident in the EC aged 18 or over may apply, though some courses are not available outside the UK. There are over 130 undergraduate courses; many are available on a one-off basis to associate students.

In 1991 there were over 75,000 undergraduates, over 6,000 postgraduates and over 30,000 short course and associate students. Over 75,000 packs of learning materials were sold. The university has some 3,000 full-time staff working at its Milton Keynes headquarters and in 13 regional centres throughout the country. There are about 6,000 part-time tutors and counsellors.

The University of Buckingham opened in in 1976 and received a Royal charter in 1983. It is self-governing and independent of the state system. It offers 2-year courses towards its own honours degrees, the academic year commencing in Jan. and consisting of four 10-week terms. There are 4 Schools of Studies with 11 academic departments: Accounting, Business, and Economics; Humanities; Law; and Sciences. Postgraduate opportunities are offered in all the schools of studies. In 1991, there were 850 full-time students.

All universities charge fees, but financial help is available to students from several sources. The universities themselves provide scholarships of various kinds and local education authorities and the Scottish Office Education Department pay maintenance grants and tuition fees for eligible students, the amount generally depending on parents' means. UK-domiciled students may also obtain loans from the Student Loans Company. The majority of university students receive some form of financial assistance. Awards known as state studentships are offered on a competitive basis by the Department of Education and Science and the Scottish Office Education Department to candidates considered by the universities and other higher education institutions to be qualified for postgraduate studies in the humanities; similar awards, tenable at universities or other higher education institutions, are offered by the Research Councils to students studying topics within the broad spectrum of agriculture and food; the biological sciences; man's natural environment; science and engineering and the social sciences at postgraduate level.

Academic staff and students (full-time and sandwich) in 1990–91:

University	Students	Staff	University	Students	Staff
Aston	3,789	289	Oxford	14,025	2,144
Bath	4,229	574	Reading	7,395	929
Birmingham	10,309	1,575	Salford	4,365	422
Bradford	5,171	499	Sheffield	9,863	1,227
Bristol	8,337	1,339	Southampton	7,371	1,203
Brunel	3,304	378	Surrey	4,072	583
Cambridge	13,553	2,199	Sussex	5,451	601
City	3,667	390	Warwick	7,353	946
Durham	5,603	664	York	4,303	623
East Anglia	4,575	569			
Essex	3,713	414	*Wales*—		
Exeter	6,208	630	Aberystwyth	3,712	387
Hull	6,278	537	Bangor	3,523	422
Keele	3,773	362	Cardiff	8,866	925
Kent	4,886	496	St David's, Lampeter	961	79
Lancaster	5,318	605	Swansea	5,639	556
Leeds	12,362	1,508	Univ. of Wales		
Leicester	6,333	824	College of Medicine	1,001	395
Liverpool	9,148	1,326			
London Business School	388	93	*Scotland*—		
London	47,779	9,658	Aberdeen	6,374	747
Loughborough	5,936	754	Dundee	4,166	587
Manchester Business School	309	48	Edinburgh	11,395	1,877
Manchester	12,776	1,870	Glasgow	12,226	1,729
Univ. of Manchester Inst. of			Heriot-Watt	3,570	441
Science and Technology	5,058	659	St Andrews	4,187	438
Newcastle	9,112	1,278	Stirling	3,472	409
Nottingham	8,718	1,199	Strathclyde	8,652	970

Number of women students: 153,020 (England, 118,174; Wales, 11,107; Scotland, 23,739. There are colleges exclusively for women at Oxford and Cambridge. Total number of full-time or sandwich students, 352,574 (England, 274,830; Wales, 23,702; Scotland, 54,042).

The British Council. The British Council promotes Britain abroad. Established in 1934 and incorporated by Royal Charter in 1940, it is Britain's principal agency for cultural relations overseas. An independent, non-political organization managed by a Director General and governed by a Board, it is represented in 90 countries, where it has 162 offices, 127 libraries and 59 English teaching centres. Its headquarters are in London and Manchester and there are offices in Edinburgh, Cardiff, Belfast and 20 other university centres in Britain.

The Council's estimated expenditure for 1992–93 is £408m. This is made up of government grants (£120m.), revenue from English teaching and client-funded services (£97m.) and programmes, principally in education and training, which are managed on behalf of the British government and other clients (£191m.).

Each year the Council brings to Britain some 38,000 professional visitors, students and trainees from overseas and sends abroad 4,000 British specialists on advisory visits or teaching appointments. It is involved with about 1,000 arts events from Britain, and runs a programme of short courses, seminars and summer schools for 2,000 specialists from 100 countries, notably in medicine, science, literature and the arts, education and English language teaching.

Chairman: Martin Jacomb.
Director-General: Sir Richard Francis, KCMG.
Headquarters: 10 Spring Gdns., London, SW1A 2BN.
British Council. *Annual Report and Accounts.*
Donaldson, F., The British Council: the First Fifty Years. London, 1984.

National Insurance. The National Insurance Act, 1946, came into operation on 5 July 1948, repealing the existing schemes of health, pensions and unemployment insurance. This Act, along with later legislation, was consolidated as the National Insurance Act, 1965.

The Social Security Act 1975 introduced, from 6 April 1975, a new system of national insurance contributions to replace the previous system of flat-rate and graduated contributions. Since 6 April 1975, Class 1 contributions have been related to the employee's earnings and are collected with PAYE income tax, instead of by affixing stamps to a card. Class 2 and Class 3 contributions remain flat-rate, but, in addition to Class 2 contributions, those who are self-employed may be liable to pay Class 4 contributions, which for the year 1992–93 will be at the rate of 6·3% on profits or gains between £6,120 and £21,060, which are assessable for income tax under Schedule D. The non-employed and others whose contribution record is not sufficient to give entitlement to benefits are able to pay a Class 3 contribution voluntarily to qualify for a limited range of benefits. Class 2 weekly contributions for 1992–93 for men and women are £5·35. Class 3 contributions are £5·25 a week.

From 6 April 1978 the Social Security Pensions Act 1975 introduced earnings-related retirement, invalidity and widows' pensions. Employee's national insurance contribution liability depends on whether he is in contracted-out or not contracted-out employment.

Full rate contributions (contribution table letters A or D or Mariner's equivalents) for non contracted-out employment in 1992–93: On earnings between £54 and £89.99 a week the employee pays 2% on the first £54 and 9% on the remainder, the employers pay 4·6% on all earnings; on earnings between £90 and £134.99 a week the employee pays 2% on the first £54 and 9% on the remainder, the employer pays 6·6% on all earnings; on earnings between £135 and £189.99 a week the employee pays 2% on the first £54 and 9% on the remainder, the employer pays 8·6% on all earnings; on earnings between £190 and £405 a week the employee pays 2% on the first £54 and 9% on the remainder, the employer pays 10·4% on all earnings; on earnings of over £405 a week the employee pays 2% on the first £54 and 9% on earnings between £54 and £405 but the employer pays 10·4% of all earnings. For contracted-out employment in 1992–93: On earnings between £54 and £89.99 a week the employee pays 2% on the first £54 and 7% on the remainder and the employer pays 4·6% on the first £54 and 0·8% on the remainder; on earnings between £90 and £134.99 a week the employee pays 2% on the first £54 and 7% on the remainder and the employer pays 7% on the first £54 and 2·8% on the remainder; on earnings between £135 and £189.99 a week the employee pays 2% on the first £54 and 7% on the remainder and the employer pays 9% on the first £54 and 4·8% on the remainder; on earnings between £190 and £405 a week the employee pays 2% on the first £54 and 7% on the remainder and the employer pays 10·4% on the first £54 and 6·6% on the remainder; on earnings of over £405 a week the employee pays 2% on the first £54 and 7% on earnings between £54 and £405 and the employer pays 10·4% on the first £54, 6·6% on earnings between £54 and £405 and 10·4% on the remainder.

Reduced rate contributions (contribution table letters B or E) for non contracted-out and contracted-out employment in 1992-93: On earnings between £54 and £405 a week the employee pays 3·85% of the full amount, including that part which is below £54; on earnings over £405 a week the employee pays 3·85% of £405. The employer pays contributions as shown in the preceding paragraph – there is no equivalent reduced rate for employers.

Contributions together with interest on investments form the income of the National Insurance Fund from which benefits are paid.

Statutory Sick Pay (SSP). Employers are now responsible for paying statutory sick pay (SSP) to their employees for up to 28 weeks in any period of incapacity for work. Basically, all employees aged between 16 and 65 (60 for women) with earnings above the Lower Earnings Limit are covered by the scheme whenever they are sick for 4 or more days consecutively. For most employees SSP completely replaces their entitlement to State sickness benefit which is not payable as long as any employer's responsibility for SSP remains.

Benefits. Qualification for any benefit depends upon fulfilment of the appropriate contribution conditions. Persons who are incapable of work as the result of an industrial accident may get sickness benefit followed by invalidity benefit without having to satisfy the contributions conditions. Employed persons may qualify for all the benefits; self-employed may not qualify for unemployment benefit.

Sickness Benefit. From 9 April 1992 the rate is £41·20 a week plus £25·50 a week for an adult dependant.

Unemployment Benefit is paid through the local unemployment benefit offices of the Department of Employment. From 9 April 1992 the rate is £43·10 a week plus £26·60 a week for an adult dependant.

Invalidity Benefit replaces sickness benefit after 168 days of entitlement. It comprises a basic invalidity pension of £54·15 weekly and an invalidity allowance of £11·55 if incapacity began before age 40: £7·20 if incapacity began between 40 and 49 or £3·60 if it began between 50 and 59 (54 for women). Increases are: £32·55 for an adult dependant plus £9·75 for a child for whom the higher rate of child benefit is payable and £10·85 for each other child for whom child benefit is payable. Invalidity allowance is reduced or extinguished by the amount of any additional invalidity pension and/or guaranteed minimum pension to which there is title.

Maternity Benefit. Statutory maternity pay may be payable to a woman from her employer if she has been employed by him for 26 weeks into the 15th week before the baby is expected and her earnings were above the lower earnings limit. If she has been employed by the same employer for at least 2 years, payment for the first 6 weeks of maternity absence may be at 90% of her average earnings. Payment for the remainder of the period is at a standard rate of £46·30. Women who do not qualify for statutory maternity pay may be entitled to maternity allowance from DSS if they satisfy a test of recent work and contributions paid. From April 1992, the weekly rate is £42·25. Both statutory maternity pay and maternity allowance can be paid for up to 18 weeks. Payment can start at the earliest 11 weeks before the expected week of confinement but the woman has some choice in deciding when to give up work and still retain title to the full 18 weeks.

Widow's Benefits. From 11 April 1988 the three main widow's benefits are: Widow's payment, widowed mother's allowance, widow's pension.

A widow cannot get any widow's benefits based on her husband's NI if: She had been divorced from the man who has died; or she was living with the man as if she were married to him, but without being legally married to him; or she is living with another man as if she is married to him; or she was in prison or held in legal custody. A widow can only get widow's benefits if her husband has paid enough NI contributions.

Widow's Payment is a single tax-free payment of £1,000. A widow may be able to get this benefit if her husband has paid enough NI contributions and: She was under 60 when her husband died; or her husband was not getting a State Retirement Pension when he died.

Widowed Mother's Allowance: A widow may be able to get a widowed mother's allowance if her husband has paid enough NI contributions and: She is receiving child benefit for one of her children; or her husband was receiving child benefit, or she is expecting her husband's baby, or if she was widowed before 11 April 1988 she has a young person under 19 living with her for whom she was receiving Child Benefit.

A widow entitled to a widowed mother's allowance will get an amount based on her husband's NI contributions. The maximum will be £52·00 a week. She will also get £9·70 a week for her eldest dependent child and £10·70 for each subsequent child and she may also get an additional pension based on her husband's earnings since 1978. Widowed mother's allowance is usually paid as long as the widow is getting child benefit. It is taxable.

Widow's Pension: A widow may be able to get a widow's pension if her husband has paid enough NI contributions. She must be 45 or over (40 or over if widowed before 11 April 1988) when her husband died or when her widowed mother's allowance ends. A widow cannot get a widow's pension at the same time as a widowed mother's allowance. A widow who is entitled to a widow's pension will get an amount that depends on her age when her husband died or when her widowed mother's allowance ends. If she was 55 or over (50 or over if widowed before 11 April 1988) she will get the full rate of widow's pension. The maximum amount of widow's pension will be £52·00 a week. She may also get an additional pension based on her husband's earnings since 1978. If her late husband was a member of a contracted-out occupational scheme or a personal pension scheme that scheme is responsible for paying the whole or part of the additional pensions. Widow's pension is usually paid until the widow is entitled to state retirement pension, when she is 60 or older. Widow's pension is taxable.

Guardian's Allowance. A person responsible for an orphan child may be entitled to a guardian's allowance of £10·85 a week in addition to child benefit. Normally both the child's parents must be dead but when they never married or were divorced, or one is missing, or serving a long sentence of imprisonment, the allowance may be paid on the death of one parent only.

Retirement Pension. In order to receive a retirement pension, subject to satisfying the contributions conditions before 1 Oct. 1989, men over 65, and women over 60, whether retired from regular employment or not, must make a claim. From 6 April 1979 a woman divorced over the age of 60 must satisfy the retirement conditions before a pension is payable. The standard rates of basic pensions are £52·00 a week for a man or woman on his or her own contributions and £31·25 for a married woman through her husband's contributions. Proportionately reduced pensions are payable where contribution records are deficient. For a person who reaches pension age on or after 6 April 1979, additional pension may also be payable. This is based on the earnings on which he or she has paid Class I or Class II contributions in each complete tax year between April 1978 and pension age. If the person has been a member of a contracted-out occupational pension scheme, that scheme will be responsible for paying the whole or part of the additional pension. An increase of £31·25 a week may be payable for a dependent wife. A tapered earnings rule (£45·09) applies to claims made before 16 Sept. 1985. From that date the earnings rule will apply in these circumstances. When the spouse/woman looking after the claimant's child is living with the claimant an adult dependant's allowance will only be payable if the dependant's earnings do not exceed the standard rate of unemployment benefit for a person under pensionable age (currently £41·40). If she does not reside with the beneficiary an increase is not payable if she earns more than £31·25 a week. In addition £9·70 a week may be payable for the eldest child for whom child benefit is payable and £10·70 for each subsequent child. In certain circumstances an increase of £31·25 a week may be payable for a woman having care of the pensioner's children. In addition, a man who had paid graduated contributions receives 6·81p per week for every £7·50 of graduated contributions paid, and a woman 6·81p per week for every £9 paid. Although no further graduated contributions have been paid after April 1975, pension already earned will be paid along with the basic pension in the normal way.

Before 1 Oct. 1989 if, after being awarded a retirement pension, a man under 70 or a woman under 65 earned more than £75 in a calendar week the pension for the next pension week, including any increase for dependants, was reduced by 5p for every 10p earned between £75 and £79 and by 5p for every 5p earned over £79. If retirement was postponed after minimum pension age increments of all components of the pension could be earned for periods of deferred retirement. From 6 April 1979 increments were earned at the rate of one-seventh penny per £1 of basic pension for every 6 days (excluding Sundays) for which pension had been foregone. Any days for which another benefit was paid did not count. These increments had to be at least 1% of the pension rate unless the minimum was earned under the arrangements which applied before 6 April 1979. On 1 Oct 1989 this 'earnings rule' was abolished, and the pension for which a person has qualified may be paid in full whether a person continues in work or not irrespective of the amount of earnings.

At the age of 80 an age addition of £0·25 a week is payable. In addition non-contributory pensions are now payable, subject to residence conditions, to persons aged 80 and over who do not qualify for a retirement pension or qualify for one at a low rate. The rates of these pensions, which are financed by Exchequer funds, are £31·25 a week for a single person and £18·70 for a married woman. These amounts do not include the £0·25 age addition. From 22 Dec. 1984 the lower rate of category D retirement pension payable to married women was abolished.

The Industrial Injuries Provisions of the Social Security Act, 1975. The Industrial Injuries Act, which also came into operation on 5 July 1948, with its later amending Acts, was consolidated as the National Insurance (Industrial Injuries) Act, 1965. This legislation was incorporated in the Social Security Act, 1975. The scheme provides a system of insurance against 'personal injury by accident arising out of and in the course of employment' and against certain prescribed diseases and injuries due to the nature of the employment. It takes the place of the Workmen's Compensation Acts and covers persons who are employed earners under the Social Security Act. There are no contribution conditions for the payment of benefit. Three types of benefit are provided:

(1) Disablement benefit. This is payable where, as the result of an industrial accident or prescribed disease, there is a loss of physical or mental faculty. The loss of faculty will be assessed as a percentage by comparison with a person of the same age and sex whose condition is normal. If the assessment is between 14-100% benefit will be paid as weekly pension; 14-19% are payable at the 20% rate. The rates vary from £17·68 (20% disabled) to £88·40 (100% disablement). Assessments of less than 14% do not normally attract basic benefit except for certain progressive chest diseases. Pensions for persons under 18 are at a reduced rate. When injury benefit was abolished for industrial accidents occurring and prescribed diseases commencing on or after 6 April 1983, a common start date was introduced for the payment of disablement benefit 90 days (excluding Sundays) after the date of the relevant accident or onset of the disease. The following increases can be paid with disablement benefit: Constant attendance allowance – where the disability for which the claimant is receiving disablement benefit is assessed at 100% and is so severe that they need constant care and attention. There are 4 rates depending on the amount of attendance needed. Exceptionally severe disablement allowance – where the claimant is in receipt of constant attendance allowance at one of the two higher rates and the need for attendance is likely to be permanent.

Reduced earnings allowance is now a separate benefit. Entitlement exists if the claimant has not retired and cannot go back to their normal job or do another job for the same pay because of the effects of the disability caused by an accident or disease which occurred on or before 30 Sept. 1990. It can be paid whether or not disablement benefit is paid, providing the disablement benefit assessment is 1% or more (*e.g.* where disablement is assessed at less than 14%) and on top of 100% disablement benefit. From 1 Oct. 1989, if a claimant is of pensionable age (60 for a woman, 65 for a man) they can continue to receive REA if they are in regular employment, or in some cases if they are receiving Sickness Benefit, Invalidity Benefit or Unemployment Benefit. It will not matter whether or not they receive State Retirement Pension. If they are not in regular employment then entitlement to REA will cease. In most cases it will be replaced by Retirement Allowance.

(2) Death Benefit. This is payable to the widow of a person who died before 11 April 1988 as the result of an industrial accident or a prescribed disease. Benefit is a weekly pension of either £54·15 or £16·25 depending on such factors as age and

entitlement to a child's allowance. A child allowance of £9·75 (first child) or £10·85 (subsequent child) per child may be payable to the widow if she is entitled to child benefit for children of the deceased. Deaths which occurred on or after 11 April 1988 – a widow is entitled to full widow's benefits even if her late husband did not satisfy the contribution condition, if he died as a result of an industrial accident or prescribed disease.

Allowances may be paid to people who are suffering from pneumoconiosis or byssinosis or certain other slowly developing diseases due to employment before 5 July 1948. They must not at any time have been entitled to benefit for the disabled under the Industrial Injuries provision of the Social Security Act or compensation under Workmen's Compensation Acts or received damages through the courts.

In certain cases supplementation allowances are payable to people who are getting or are entitled to compensation under the Workmen's Compensation Acts.

War Pensions. The number of beneficiaries in receipt of war (1914–18) pensions or allowances as at 31 Dec. 1990 was 5,047. The number of beneficiaries in receipt of war (1939–45 and later) pensions or allowances in payment as at 31 Dec. 1990 was 243,047. The expenditure for both wars for 1989–90 was £640·92m.

National Insurance Fund. At 1 April 1990 the balance of the National Insurance Fund amounted to £10,307,139,000. Income during the period 1 April 1990 to 31 March 1991, consisting of contributions from insured persons and employers and interest on investments was £34,053,681,000. Payments of benefit in respect of unemployment were £869,840,000; sickness, £216,292,000; invalidity, £4,431,019,000; maternity, £33,665,000; widows, £889,386,000; guardian's allowance and child's special allowance, £1,551,000; retirement pension, £22,699,013,000; pensioners' lump sum payments, £112,359,000.

Administration costs were £980,261,000; transfers to Northern Ireland, £225m.; amounts forwarded to personal pension providers, £2,068,970,000; redundancy and other payments, £41,587,000. The balance at 31 March 1991 was £11,791,856,000.

From 1 April 1975 the National Insurance Reserve Fund and the Industrial Injuries Fund were merged with the National Insurance Fund. All basic scheme contributions payable under the 1975 Social Security Act are paid into the single fund out of which the existing range of benefits is financed. Payment of Disablement Benefit has come out of the General Consolidated Fund since April 1990.

Child Benefit. Child benefit is a tax-free cash allowance for children. The weekly rates are £9·65 for the eldest qualifying child and £7·80 for each other child. Child benefit is payable for children under 16, for 16 and 17 year olds registered for work or training and for those under 19 receiving full-time non-advanced education. *One Parent Benefit* is a tax-free cash allowance for certain people bringing up children alone. It is payable for the first or only child in the family in addition to child benefit. The weekly rate is £5·85.

Family Credit. Family Credit is a tax-free benefit for working families with children. To be able to get Family Credit there must be at least one child under 16 in the family (or under 19 if in full-time education up to, and including, A level or equivalent standard). The claimant or partner (if there is one) must be working at least 16 hours a week to qualify. They may be employed or self-employed, a lone parent or a couple. The claim should be made by the woman in two-parent families. The amount of Family Credit payable depends on the income of the claimant and partner, how many children there are in the family and their ages. The same rates of benefit are paid for one-parent families as for two-parent families. Family Credit is not payable if the claimant (or claimant and partner together) have savings or capital of over £8,000. Benefit is reduced if savings or capital of more than £3,000 is held.

Family Credit is paid at the same rate for 26 weeks. The amount of the award will usually stay the same even if earnings, or other circumstances, change during that period.

Attendance allowance. This is a tax-free Social Security benefit for disabled people over 65 who need help with personal care.

Invalid Care Allowance. This is a non-contributory taxable benefit which may be paid to those who forego the opportunity of full-time work to care for a person who is receiving attendance allowance, constant attendance allowance or the highest or middle-core component of Disability Living Allowance. Current rate £32·55 a week, with increases for dependants.

Disability Living Allowance. This is a non-contributory, non-taxable benefit available to people disabled before the age of 65 who need help with getting around or with personal care for at least 3 months.

Disability Working Allowance. This is a tax-free Social Security benefit for people with an illness or disability which puts them at a disadvantage in getting a job. It is income-related and is intended for people who are starting work or already working at least 16 hours a week.

Income Support. Under the Social Security Act, 1986, benefit is payable to any persons in Great Britain aged 18 years or over (excluding persons at school or college or anyone directly involved in a trade dispute) who are not in full-time work or who work for less than 16 hours per week and who are without resources, or whose resources (including national insurance benefits) need to be supplemented in order to meet their requirements. Income Support is not payable if the claimant (or claimant and partner together) have savings or capital over £8,000. Benefit is reduced if savings or capital of more than £3,000 is held. A person who is excluded from benefit under the normal rules may, in certain limited circumstances, receive payments to meet urgent need. The general standards by reference to which income support is granted are determined by statutory regulations approved by Parliament. Persons dissatisfied with the benefit granted may appeal to an independent Appeal Tribunal.

National Health. The National Health Service (NHS) in England and Wales started on 5 July 1948 under the National Health Service Act, 1946. There are separate Acts for Scotland and for Northern Ireland, where the Health Services are run on similar lines to those in England and Wales.

The NHS is a charge on the national income in the same way e.g. as the armed forces. Every person normally resident in this country is entitled to use any complete part of the services, and no insurance qualification is necessary. Most of the cost of running the service is met from the national exchequer, *i.e.*, from taxes.

Since 1948 a weekly NHS contribution has been payable by employees and the self-employed. In 1957 this contribution was extended to employers. For convenience this contribution is collected with the National Insurance contribution and for 1992–93 is estimated to be £4,597m. for Great Britain (£3,971m. for England and Wales).

Organization. Under the provisions of the NHS Act, 1977 and the Health Service Act, 1980, the administration of the NHS in England and Wales is organized under a system of regional and district health authorities accountable to the Secretary of State for the Social Services and the Secretary of State for Wales. In Scotland the National Health Service is administered under the National Health Service (Scotland) Act, 1978, by 15 Health Boards and a Common Services Agency, all accountable to the Secretary of State for Scotland.

There are 190 district health authorities in England responsible for the administration and development of health services in their district. 14 regional health authorities, each consisting of a number of health districts, are responsible for allocating resources between the district health authorities in their regions and for monitoring their performance. The regional authorities are responsible for developing strategic plans and priorities and for carrying out certain executive functions.

The National Health Service and Community Care Act, 1990, provided for a major restructuring of the existing organization of the NHS. From 1 April 1991, health authorities became the purchasers of health care, concentrating on their responsibilities to plan and obtain services for their local residents by the placement of health service contracts with the appropriate units. Day-to-day management tasks became the responsibility of hospitals and other units, with whom the contracts are placed, in their capacity as providers of care. Provider units will be able to choose to become NHS Trusts, with greater control over their own affairs. Some general medical practitioners (GPs) will be able to join the GP fund holding scheme, purchasing a range of care directly for their patients.

Services. The NHS broadly consists of hospital and specialist services, general medical, dental and ophthalmic services, pharmaceutical services, community health services and school health services. All these services are free of charge except for such things as prescriptions, spectacles, dental and optical examination, dentures and dental treatment, amenity beds in hospitals and for some of the community services, for which charges are made with certain exemptions.

The total cost of the Health and Personal Social Services (England) is estimated at £23,665m. for 1989–90 (Local Authority Personal Social Service being £3,750m.).

The number of abortions performed in England and Wales in 1990 under the provisions of the Abortion Act, 1967, was 186,912 (183,974 in 1989). Of these, 173,900 abortions were to England and Wales residents, of which 116,150 were to single women, 38,151 to married women, and 19,599 were to widowed, divorced or separated women and to women who did not state their marital status.

The number of abortion notifications received in Scotland in 1989 under the provisions of the Abortion Act, 1967, was 10,159, of which 10,143 related to Scottish residents. Of these 10,143 notifications, 6,643 (5·5%) were to single women, 2,242 (22·1%) were to married women, and 1,158 (11·4%) were to widowed, divorced or separated women and to women who did not state their marital status.

In Great Britain in 1989 there were 33,291 general medical practitioners (GPs) and 17,830 general dental practitioners and (1986) 287,700 qualified nurses and mid wives. There were (1990) 338,630 average daily available hospital beds in the UK.

Personal Social Services. Under the Local Authority Social Services Act, 1970, and in Scotland the Social Work (Scotland) Act, 1968, the welfare and social work services provided by local authorities were made the responsibility of a new local authority department—the Social Services Department in England and Wales, and Social Work Departments in Scotland headed by a Director of Social Work. The social services thus administered include: the fostering, care and adoption of children, welfare services and social workers for people with learning difficulties and the mentally ill, the disabled and the aged, and accommodation for those needing residential care services. In Scotland the social work departments' functions also include the supervision of persons on probation, of adult offenders and of persons released from penal institutions or subject to fine supervision orders.

The number of supported residents in residential accommodation for the elderly and younger physically-disabled was as follows:

England (31 March)	Number of Supported Residents	Scotland (31 March)	Number of Supported Residents
1990	97,389	1987	14,348
1991	91,413	1988	14,381

England and Wales. Expenditure and income relating to the personal social services administered by local authorities (in £1m. sterling):

Year ended 31 March	Gross current expenditure	Income from sales, fees and charges	Net current expenditure
1989	3,942·8	470·8	3,443·0
1990	4,423·8	610·9	3,912·8

| | Capital Spending | | |
Year ended 31 March	Gross expenditure	Income from sales of fixed assets	Net expenditure
1989	188·6	71·4	117·2
1990	236·6	66·6	169·0

Scotland. The total local authority expenditure for 1987–88 in respect of residential accommodation and welfare services under the Social Work (Scotland) Act, 1968, was £409·5m. Central Government expenditure on social work totalled £8·1m.

DIPLOMATIC REPRESENTATIVES

Of the USA in Great Britain (Grosvenor Sq., London, W1A 1AE)
Ambassador: Raymond Seitz.

Of Great Britain in the USA (3100 Massachusetts Ave., NW, Washington, D.C., 20008)
Ambassador: Sir Robin Renwick, KCMG.

Of Great Britain to the United Nations
Ambassador: Sir David Hannay, KCMG.

Great Britain's permanent representative to the European Communities: Sir John Kerr, KCMG.

Further Reading

Government publications are published by HM Stationery Office (HMSO).
Central Statistical Office. *Annual Abstract of Statistics.* HMSO.—*Monthly Digest of Statistics.* HMSO.—*Social Trends.* HMSO.—*Regional Statistics.* HMSO
Central Office of Information. *Britain: An Official Handbook.* HMSO, annual.—*The Monarchy.* 1992
Directory of British Associations. Beckenham, annual
Government Statistics: A Brief Guide to Sources. HMSO, 1984
Barr, N., *et al. The State of Welfare: the Welfare State in Britain since 1974.* Oxford, 1990
Cairncross, A., *The British Economy since 1945: Economic Policy and Performance, 1945–1990.* Oxford, 1992
Catterall, P., *British History, 1945–1987: an Annotated Bibliography.* Oxford, 1991
Gamble, A., *Britain in Decline: Economic Policy, Political Strategy and the British State.* 3rd ed. London, 1990
Griffith, J.A.G. and Ryle, M., *Parliament: Functions, Practices and Procedures.* London, 1990
Hanson, A.H. and Walles, M., *Governing Britain: a Guidebook to Political Institutions.* 5th ed. London, 1990
Hennessy, P., *Whitehall.* London, 1989
Institute of Contemporary British History. *Contemporary Britain: an Annual Review.* Oxford, from 1990
Kendall, M. G. (ed.), *The Source and Nature of the Statistics of the United Kingdom.* 2 vols. London, 1952–1957
Lever, W. F., *Industrial Change in the United Kingdom.* Harlow, 1987
McIntosh, M., *Managing British Defence.* London, 1990
Mitchell, B. R., *Abstract of British Historical Statistics.* OUP, 1962
Morgan, K.O., *The People's Peace: British History, 1945-89.* OUP, 1990
Oakland, J., *British Civilization: an Introduction.* 2nd ed. London, 1991
Oxford History of England. 16 vols. OUP, 1936–91
Thompson, F.M.L. (ed.) *The Cambridge Social History of Britain, 1750-1950.* 3 vols. CUP, 1990
Waller, R. (ed.), *The Almanack of British Politics.* London, 1987

Scotland

Scottish Council (Development and Industry). *Inquiry into the Scottish Economy, 1900–61.* Edinburgh, 1961
Scottish Office. *Scottish Economic Bulletin.* HMSO (quarterly).—*Scottish Abstract of Statistics.* HMSO (annual)
The New Scottish Local Authorities: Organisation and Management Structures. HMSO, 1973
Brand, J., *The National Movement in Scotland.* London, 1978
Campbell, R. H., *The Rise and Fall of Scottish Industry, 1707–1939.* Edinburgh, 1981
Donaldson, G. (ed.) *The Edinburgh History of Scotland.* 4 vols. Edinburgh, 1965–75
Grant, E., *Scotland.* [Bibliography] Oxford and Santa Barbara, 1982
Hogg, A. and Hutcheson, A. MacG., *Scotland and Oil.* 2nd ed. Edinburgh, 1975
Johnston, T. L., *Structure and Growth in the Scottish Economy.* London, 1971
Kellas, J. G., *The Scottish Political System.* 3rd ed. CUP, 1984
Lynch, M., *Scotland: a New History.* London, 1991
Monies, G., *Local Government in Scotland.* Edinburgh, 1985

Wales

Wales: The Way Ahead (Cmnd 3334.) HMSO, 1971
Wales: Employment and the Economy. Cardiff, 1972
Digest of Welsh Statistics. HMSO (annual)
Huws, G. and Roberts, H., *Wales* [Bibliography]. Oxford and Santa Barbara, 1990
Jenkins, G. H., *The Foundations of Modern Wales 1642–1780*. Oxford, 1988
Jenkins, P.A., *A History of Modern Wales, 1536-1990*. Harlow, 1991
Williams, D., *A History of Modern Wales*. New ed. London, 1977
Williams, G., (ed.) *Social and Cultural Change in Contemporary Wales*. London, 1978

NORTHERN IRELAND

AREA AND POPULATION. Area (revised by the Ordnance Survey Department) and population were as follows:

District	Population (usually resident) 1981 Census [1]	Population estimate 30 June 1989	Land area (ha)
Antrim	45,016	48,100	41,510
Ards	57,792	64,500	36,789
Armagh	49,223	49,000	66,733
Ballymena	54,813	57,200	63,384
Ballymoney	22,946	23,900	41,687
Banbridge	30,110	31,900	44,174
Belfast	314,270	296,900	11,140
Carrickfergus	28,625	30,400	8,484
Castlereagh	60,785	58,000	8,426
Coleraine	46,739	48,500	47,763
Cookstown	28,257	27,600	51,207
Craigavon	73,260	77,700	27,945
Derry (Londonderry)	89,101	99,500	37,258
Down	53,193	57,200	63,835
Dungannon	43,883	43,700	76,266
Fermanagh	51,594	50,400	169,952
Larne	29,076	29,100	33,744
Limavady	26,964	29,800	58,523
Lisburn	83,998	97,400	43,595
Magherafelt	32,494	32,900	56,186
Moyle	14,396	15,100	49,378
Newry and Mourne	76,574	88,900	88,589
Newtownabbey	72,246	72,900	15,956
North Down	66,264	71,900	7,329
Omagh	44,288	44,900	112,354
Strabane	36,279	35,600	86,090
Northern Ireland	1,532,186	1,583,000	1,348,297

[1] Arising from difficulties during the Census taking, a number of households were not enumerated. The population effect of this non-enumeration is estimated at about 50,000 and is included in this column.

Chief town (population, estimate 1989): Belfast, 296,900.
Vital statistics for calendar years:

	Marriages	Divorces	Births	Deaths
1985	10,343	1,669	27,635	15,955
1986	10,225	1,539	28,152	16,065
1987	10,363	1,514	27,865	15,334
1988	9,958	1,550	27,767	15,813
1989	10,019	1,818	26,080	15,844
1990[1]	8,036	1,897	26,499	15,426

[1] Provisional.

CONSTITUTION AND GOVERNMENT. Northern Ireland is part of the United Kingdom. As such it is subject to the same fundamental constitutional provisions which apply to the rest of the United Kingdom. However, in the Northern Ireland Constitution Act 1973 and the Northern Ireland Act 1982, Parliament provides for a measure of devolved government in Northern Ireland. This arrangement was last in force in Jan. 1974, following an agreement among the Northern Ireland political parties to form a power-sharing Executive. However, this arrangement collapsed in May 1974 and there has been no devolution since.

In the interim Northern Ireland continues to be governed by 'direct rule' under the provisions of the Northern Ireland Act 1974. This allows Parliament to approve all laws for Northern Ireland and places the Northern Ireland departments under the direction and control of a UK Cabinet Minister, the Secretary of State for Northern Ireland.

Attempts have been made by successive governments to find a means of restoring a widely acceptable form of devolved government. A 78-member Assembly was elected by proportional representation in 1982. However, 4 years later it was dissolved after it ceased to discharge its responsibilities of making proposals for the resumption of devolved government and of monitoring the work of the Northern Ireland departments.

In Nov. 1985 the governments of the UK and the Republic of Ireland signed the Anglo-Irish Agreement which aims to promote peace and stability in Northern Ireland, help to reconcile the two major traditions in Ireland, create a new climate of friendship and co-operation between the people of the two countries and improve co-operation in combating terrorism. The Agreement commits both the UK and the Irish governments to the principle that Northern Ireland shall remain part of the UK for as long as that is the wish of the majority of population in Northern Ireland. Should such a majority formally consent to the establishment of a united Ireland, both sides undertake to introduce and support the necessary legislation. The Agreement binds both governments to these commitments in international law.

The Agreement also established an Intergovernmental Conference through which the Irish government can put forward views and proposals on specified matters affecting Northern Ireland affairs, insofar as those matters are not the responsibility of a devolved administration in Northern Ireland, and where cross-border co-operation can be promoted in the interests of both countries. There is no derogation from the sovereignty of the UK or Irish governments as a result of the Agreement; each retains full responsibility for the decisions and administration within its own jurisdiction.

Despite the dissolution of the last Assembly, the Government has remained committed to finding a means by which power and responsibility might be transferred to local elected representatives on a widely acceptable basis. In Jan. 1990 the Secretary of State for Northern Ireland, the 4 main constitutional political parties and eventually the Irish government discussed the agenda for talks which were held over a period from April to July, but without reaching a conclusion. The UK government nonetheless hopes that these talks will provide a basis for future dialogue.

What began ostensibly as a Civil Rights campaign in 1968 escalated into a full-scale offensive designed to overthrow the State. This offensive was originally mounted by an illegal organization, the Irish Republican Army (not to be confused with the legitimate Army of the Republic of Ireland). At times counter-measures have required the services of over 20,000 regular troops, in addition to the Royal Ulster Constabulary, the RUC Reserve and the part-time Ulster Defence Regiment.

Secretary of State for Northern Ireland: Rt Hon. Sir Christopher Mayhew, MP.

Local Government. Northern Ireland has a single-tier system of 26 district councils based on main centres of population.

The district councils are responsible for the provision of a wide range of local services including refuse collection and disposal, street cleansing, litter prevention, consumer protection, environmental health, miscellaneous licensing including dog control, the provision and management of recreational and cultural facilities, the promotion of tourist development schemes and the enforcement of building regulations. They have in addition both a representative role in which they send forward representatives to sit as members of statutory bodies including the Northern Ireland Housing Council, the Fire Authority and the Area Boards for health and personal social services and education and libraries; and a consultative role under which the

Department of Environment (NI) and the Northern Ireland Housing Executive, among others, have an obligation to consult them regarding the provision of the regional services for which these bodies are responsible.

The Government's policy for the future development of the Province is contained in the *Regional Physical Development Strategy 1975–95* which was published in May 1977. Basically the policy advocates that the main town in each District Council area should be developed to fulfil its function as the prime centre in the district and for any other specialized rôles it may have such as an industrial centre, port or tourist resort. The Strategy also recognizes that the smaller towns and villages have an important rôle to play, depending on the availability of services, as locations for smaller scale industries service centres and as dormitory centres for people not wishing to live in the towns where they find employment.

The Regional Strategy provides a framework within which development plans can be prepared for all the districts. Since its adoption of the Strategy the Department has been engaged in formulating the detailed policies and proposals for future communications, the location of industry, housing and major services in the light of anticipated population growth and distribution.

A development plan sets down the broad policies and proposals for the development or other use of land in the area covered by the plan over a period of up to 15 years ahead. Development plans covering almost all of Northern Ireland have been published and work is progressing on the remaining areas, together with review of some earlier plans.

FINANCE. There exists a separate Northern Ireland Consolidated Fund from which is met the expenditure of Northern Ireland Departments. Its main sources of revenue are: *(i)* The Northern Ireland attributed share of UK taxes; *(ii)* A non-specific grant in aid of Northern Ireland's revenue, payable by the Secretary of State for Northern Ireland; *(iii)* Rates and other receipts of Northern Ireland Departments.

The general principle underlying the financial arrangements is that Northern Ireland should have parity of taxation and services with Great Britain.

Since the financial year 1989–90 the income of the Northern Ireland Consolidated Fund has been as follows (in £ sterling):

	1989–90	1990–91	1991–92 [1]
Attributed share of UK taxes	2,683,048,760	2,927,669,888	3,099,000,000
Payments by UK Government:			
Grant in Aid	1,150,000,000	1,065,600,000	1,204,883,000
Refund of value added tax	29,045,077	40,980,378	13,000,000
Regional and district rates	308,500,000	341,250,000	382,000,000
Other receipts	302,528,338	258,641,739	200,000,000
Total	4,473,122,225	4,634,142,005	4,898,883,000

[1] Provisional.

The public debt at 31 March 1991 was as follows: Ulster Savings Certificates, £142,236,529; Ulster Development Bonds, £20,111; borrowing from UK Government, £1,373,131,889; borrowing from Northern Ireland Government Funds, £106,851,246; European Investment Bank Loan, £11,279,530; total, £1,633,519,305.

The above amount of public debt is offset by equal assets in the form of loans from Government to public and local bodies and of cash balances.

ENERGY AND NATURAL RESOURCES

Electricity. The planning, generation and distribution of electricity supplies are the responsibility of Northern Ireland Electricity. The installed capacity of the system is 2,400 mw largely provided from 4 thermal power-stations.

Sales of electricity in the year ended 31 March 1991 amounted to 5,884m. units supplied to a total of 605,520 consumers.

The government is preparing to privatize Northern Ireland Electricity in 1992.

Water Supplies and Sewerage. The Department of the Environment Water Service is responsible for water supply and sewerage. Some 670 megalitres of water are supplied per day to approximately 97% of the population. Approximately 92% of the population live in property which is connected to sewers or modern septic tanks.

The Department is also responsible for the conservation and planned development of water resources.

Minerals. The output of minerals (in 1,000 tonnes) during 1989 was approximately: Basalt and igneous rock (other than granite), 7,463; grit and conglomerate, 2,845; limestone, 3,485; sand and gravel, 4,554; and other minerals (rocksalt, fireclay, diatomite, granite, chalk, clay and shale), 893. There are lignite deposits of 1,200m. tonnes near Crumlin in County Antrim.

Agriculture. Forecast gross output in 1990:

	Quantity (1,000)	Value (£m.)			Quantity (1,000)	Value (£m.)
Finished cattle and calves	442	285·9	Other crops		21	2·2
Finished sheep and lambs	1,390	71·2	Fruit		29	4·9
Finished pigs	1,107	79·8	Vegetables	tonnes	27	6·0
Poultry (tonnes)	72	52·3	Mushrooms		9	10·4
Eggs; for human			Flowers		...	6·2
consumption (dozen)	73,000	35·3	Other items		...	31·1
Wool (tonnes)	3,550	3·3	Total receipts			844·2
Milk (litres)	1,331	217·4	Value of changes in			
Other livestock products	...	6·7	stocks due to volume			+8·8
Potatoes	232	22·5				
Barley	62	7·2	Gross output			853·0
Wheat	16	1·8				

Area (in 1,000 ha) of crops at June census (1990 and 1991):

	1990	1991 [1]		1990	1991 [1]
Oats	2·9	2·8	Crop silage	3·1	3·2
Wheat	5·6	6·0	Other crops	0·3	0·2
Barley	36·8	37·1	Fruit	1·9	1·8
Other cereals and pulses	0·1	0·2	Grass for mowing or		
Potatoes	10·8	10·3	grazing	767·8	770·6
Turnips, swedes, kale			Rough grazing (excluding		
and cabbage[2]	0·8	0·7	common land)	187·7	184·8
Vegetables	1·4	1·2			

[1] Preliminary figures   [2] Stock feeding only.

Livestock (1,000) at June census (1990 and 1991):

	1990	1991 [1]		1990	1991 [1]
Dairy cows	278	274	Total sheep	2,505	2,577
Beef cows	239	252	Breeding sows	59	59
Total cattle	1,506	1,537	Total pigs	590	587
Breeding ewes	1,168	1,198	Total poultry	10,453	10,943

[1] Preliminary figures

INDUSTRY

Labour. The main sources of employment statistics are the Census of Employment, which was last conducted in Sept. 1989, and the Quarterly Employment Enquiry. In June 1990 there were 525,590 employees in employment, of whom 271,430 were males. The average level of seasonally-adjusted unemployment between Jan. and Sept. 1990 was 14% of the workforce, 97,400.

In June 1990 employment in manufacturing and construction amounted to 129,520, just under 25% of the total employees in employment. Of this number, 19,260 were engaged in the food, drink and tobacco industries, 17,230 in clothing and footwear, 10,430 in aircraft, shipbuilding and other transport equipment (except motor vehicles), 9,490 in textiles, 25,660 in construction and 47,540 in other branches of manufacturing.

Training and Placement. The Training and Employment Agency, launched on 2 April 1990, has responsibility for vocational training and employment activities in

Northern Ireland. It is an executive agency within the Department of Economic Development and has some 1,700 staff and a budget of £172m. It also has a 12-member Advisory Board which advises Ministers and the Agency's executive on the formulation of training and employment policy.

The Agency's overall aim is to assist economic growth by providing training and employment services which contribute to firms becomming more competitive and by increasing the skills of the workforce enabling individuals to acquire the competencies required for increased competitiveness and securing employment. The Agency's main programmes and services are as follows:

Action for Community Employment (ACE): Jobs are provided for the long-term unemployed and offer one year's work in employment of community benefit such as environmental improvement, help to the aged and disadvantaged, and energy conservation. In 1991-92 the Agency is providing 9,600 ACE places through community organizations known as ACE Sponsors.

Job Training Programme (JTP) is an employer-based training programme which parallels Employment training in Great Britain. It aims to address the needs of the long-term unemployed by offering opportunities to them to refresh, enhance and update existing skills or to acquire skills in a new field thus enabling participants to compete more effectively for available jobs or to progress to self-employment. In 1991–92 the Agency is aiming to provide 5,050 JTP places which are delivered by Managing Agents drawn mainly from the private sector.

Youth Training Programme (YTP) is an integrated two-year programme aimed at all 16- and 17-year olds. It seeks to lay the foundation for a skilled, flexible workforce and assist participants make the transition from school to adult life. The Programme is delivered by Training Organizations including Community Workshops, Employers, Further Education Colleges and the Agency's Training Centres. In 1991–92 the Agency is aiming to provide 10,000 YTP places, and in addition a further 4,800 young people will attend Colleges of Further Education.

The Employment Service provides a comprehensive all-age guidance and placement service for the adult unemployed, young people, disabled persons and employers, delivered through the Agency's 30 local offices. In 1990–91 the Employment Service placed 42,877 people in employment and 23,073 in training opportunities.

The Agency provides a range of schemes designed to improve and develop management skills both for existing managers and graduates seeking to follow managerial careers in industry. It also delivers the Enterprise Allowance Scheme which provides financial assistance to certain categories of unemployed people who wish to start up their own business.

The Agency's Consultancy and Advisory Service promotes the benefits of training in industry and offers advice tailored to the needs of individual companies and business sectors. The Company Development Programme offers financial support to companies seeking to introduce comprehensive training programmes. The Scheme aims to improve the overall competitiveness of Northern Ireland industry.

The Agency's network of 12 Training Centres provides high quality off-the-job industrial skills training for young persons and adults. The Centres also provide Sponsored Training for Industry. Where an individual company identifies a particular training need or problem, a package tailored to the company's specific needs can be designed. Subject to the expertise available, this training can be provided in the Training Centre or in-company.

TOURISM. Tourism earns a substantial amount of revenue. Altogether tourism provides over 9,000 full-time jobs. The Northern Ireland Tourist Board has the main responsibility for promoting tourist traffic to and within Northern Ireland.

Scenic beauty, scientific and nature interest, and wildlife are protected by the Department of the Environment under the Access to the Countryside (NI) Order 1983, the Nature Conservation and Amenity Lands (NI) Order 1985 and the Wildlife (NI) Order 1985. The Department is advised by the Council for Nature Conservation and the Countryside. Nine Areas of Outstanding Natural Beauty have been designated, where special attention is given to the amenity aspects of planning applications. Country Parks have been established at Crawfordsburn, Redburn and Scrabo, Co. Down, at the Roe Valley and Ness Wood, Co. Derry, and at Castle Archdale, Co. Fermanagh. At The Birches in N. Armagh there is a Peatlands Park. The Lagan Valley between Belfast and Lisburn is Northern Ireland's first Regional Park. Countryside Information Centres are located at Portrush, Co. Antrim and Newcastle, Co. Down and a visitor centre at the Quoile Pondage National Nature Reserve, near Downpatrick, Co. Down. 44 National Nature Reserves have been declared, and more are being acquired. 16 bathing waters have been identified under the EC Bathing Water Directive, and 80% of rivers classified as Class I.

The Department is advised by the Historic Monuments Council on the exercise of its powers under the Historic Monuments Act (NI) 1971 in respect of the conservation of historic monuments and the preservation of objects of archaeological or historic interest. At present there are some 167 monuments in State care and approximately 1,000 are scheduled. The Department, advised by the Historic Buildings Council, under the Planning (NI) Order 1972 is also responsible for listing buildings of special architectural or historic interest and for designating areas of similar interest the character or appearance of which it is desirable to preserve or enhance. To date some 7,725 buildings have been listed and 28 conservation areas have been designated. Grants may be payable by the Department to assist in the repair or maintenance of listed buildings and for schemes of enhancement in conservation areas.

COMMUNICATIONS

Roads. Ulsterbus Ltd runs services throughout Northern Ireland and Citybus Ltd runs services in the Belfast area.

The Department of the Environment (NI) administers a licensing system for professional hauliers with the objective of maintaining standards and conditions necessary for the safe operation of vehicles and fair competition between hauliers. The level of services provided and the rates charged by the industry are determined by the normal economic forces of supply and demand. At 31 March 1991 there were 1,515 professional hauliers and 3,544 vehicles licensed to engage in road haulage.

The number of motor vehicles licensed at 31 Dec. 1991 was 523,730, comprising private cars, 481,090; motor cycles, 10,243; hackney vehicles, 2,786; goods vehicles, 21,590; special machines, 8,021. In addition, there were 19,384 vehicles which were not subject to licence duty.

At 1 April 1990 the total mileage of roads was 14,963, graded for administrative purposes as follows: Motorway 70 miles; Class I dual carriageway, 87 miles; Class I single carriageway, 1,284 miles; Class II, 1,787 miles; Class III, 2,932 miles; unclassified, 8,801 miles.

Railways. All train services are operated by the Northern Ireland Railways Co. Ltd which is a subsidiary of the Northern Ireland Transport Holding Co. The number of track km operated is 357; passenger route miles, 210. In 1989–90 railways carried 5·2m. passengers.

Civil Aviation. There are scheduled air services to 3 airports in Northern Ireland. Belfast International Airport is the main airport. In 1990, it handled 2·3m. pasengers and 33,000 tonnes of freight and mail. A major extension to the domestic terminal and a £7m. cargo centre have just been completed. Belfast City Airport offers commuter services to 12 cities in Great Britain and to the Isle of Man and Channel Islands. In 1990 it handled 550,000 passengers. Eglinton airport, situated 16 km from Londonderry, provides services from the north-west of Ireland to Dublin, Glasgow and Manchester. In 1990 40,000 passengers were handled. There are two other licensed airfields at St Angelo and Newtownards, used principally by flying clubs, private owners and air taxi businesses.

Shipping. Passenger services operate between Larne and (i) Cairnryan and (ii) Stranraer. Conventional cargo services have given way in many cases to container, unit load and drive on/drive off services. The latter type of service now operates from Belfast, Larne and Warrenpoint to various ports in the UK.

JUSTICE, RELIGION, EDUCATION AND WELFARE

Justice. The Lord Chancellor has responsibility for the administration of all courts in Northern Ireland through the Northern Ireland Court Service, and is responsible for the appointment of judges and resident magistrates.

The court structure in Northern Ireland has 3 tiers–the Supreme Court of Judicature of Northern Ireland (comprising the Court of Appeal, the High Court and the Crown Court), the County Courts and the Magistrates' Courts. There are 22 Petty Sessions districts which when grouped together for administration purposes form 7 County Court Divisions and 4 Circuits.

The County Court has general civil jurisdiction subject to an upper monetary limit of £5,000. Appeals from the Magistrates' Courts lie to the County Court, while appeals from the County Court lie to the High Court or, on a point of law, to the Court of Appeal by way of case stated. District Judges have jurisdiction to deal with most defended actions up to £1,000 and most undefended actions up to £5,000. They also deal, by an informal arbitration procedure, with small claims whose value does not exceed £500. An appeal from the decision of a District Judge lies to the High Court other than in small claims cases.

Police. The police force consists of the Royal Ulster Constabulary, supported by the Royal Ulster Constabulary Reserve, a mainly part-time force.

Religion. According to the census of 1981 of the total enumerated population of 1,481,959 there were: Roman Catholics, 414,532; Presbyterians, 339,818; Church of Ireland, 281,472; Methodists, 58,731. Those belonging to other Churches and of no stated denomination numbered 387,406. 18·5% of the enumerated population failed to answer the voluntary question on religion.

Education. Public education, other than university education, is administered centrally by the *Department of Education for Northern Ireland* and locally by 5 Education and Library boards. The Department is concerned with the whole range of education from nursery education through to higher education and continuing education; for sport and recreation; for youth services; for the arts and culture (including libraries) and for the development of community relations with and between schools. District councils are the main providers of sport, recreation and community facilities and are supported in this provision by grant from the Department.

Each *Education and Library Board* is the local education authority for its area. Boards were first appointed in 1973, the year of local government reorganization, and are reappointed every 4 years following the District Council elections. Boards were last reconstituted on 1 July 1989. The membership of each Board consists of District councillors, representatives of transferors of schools, representatives of trustees of maintained schools and other persons who are interested in the service for which the Board is responsible. Boards have a duty, amongst other things, to ensure that there are sufficient schools of all kinds to meet the needs of their areas. They are wholly responsible for the schools under their management and equip, maintain and meet other running costs of the maintained schools. The Boards are responsible for costs associated with capital works at controlled schools whereas voluntary schools, including maintained and voluntary schools, can receive grant-aid from the Department of Education of up to 85% of approved expenditure. Most voluntary grammar schools can receive the same rate of grant on the purchase of equipment. The Boards award university and other scholarships; they provide school milk and meals; free books and transport for pupils; they enforce school attendance; provide a curriculum advisory and support service to all schools in their area; regulate the employment of children and young people; and secure the provision of youth and recreational facilities. They are also required to develop a comprehensive and efficient library service for their area. Board expenditure is funded at 100% by the Department of Education.

The Education Reform (NI) Order 1989 made provision for the setting up of a *Council for Catholic Maintained Schools* with effect from April 1990. The Council has responsibility for all maintained schools under Roman Catholic Management which are under the auspices of the diocesan authorities and of religious orders. The main objective of the Council is to promote high standards of education in the schools for which it is responsible. Its functions include providing advice on matters relating to its schools, the employment of teaching staff and administration of appointment procedures, the promotion of effective management and the promotion and co-ordination of effective planning and rationalization of school provision in the Catholic Maintained sector. The membership of the Council consists of trustee representatives appointed by the Northern Bishops, parents, teachers, and persons appointed by the Head of the Department of Education in consultation with the Bishops.

Nursery Education is provided in nursery schools or nursery classes in primary schools. There were 85 nursery schools in 1989–90, with 4,853 pupils and 157 teachers.

Primary Education is from 4 to 11 years. In 1989–90 there were 973 primary schools with 185,767 pupils and 7,984 teachers.

Secondary Education is from 11 to 18 years. In 1989–90 there were 70 grammar schools with 53,119 pupils and 3,532 teachers and 170 secondary schools with 87,814 pupils and 6,189 teachers.

Further Education. There were 26 institutions of further education in 1989–90 with 2,448 full-time and 2,075 part-time teachers and an enrolment of 17,062 full-time, 24,299 part-time day and 17,323 evening students on vocational courses; and 48,601 students on non-vocational (mostly evening) courses.

Special Education. The Education and Library Boards provide for children with special educational needs up to the age of 16 and in some cases 19. This provision may be in special units attached to primary or secondary schools or in special schools. In 1990–91 there were 54 special schools with 4,200 pupils.

Universities. There are 2 universities: The Queen's University of Belfast and the University of Ulster. The Queen's University of Belfast (founded in 1849 as a college of the Queen's University of Ireland and reconstituted as a separate university in 1908) had 106 professors, 240 readers and senior lecturers, 463 lecturers and tutors, 132 other grades of academic staff and 7,868 full-time students in 1989–90. The University of Ulster, formed on 1 Oct. 1984, has campuses in Belfast, Coleraine, Jordanstown and Londonderry. In 1989–90 the University had 57 professors, 236 readers and senior lecturers, 526 lecturers, 44 other grades of academic staff and 8,635 full-time students.

Teacher training takes place at both universities and at 2 colleges of education: Stranmillis, and St. Mary's, the latter mainly for the primary school sector, in respect of which 4-year (Hons) BEd courses and one-year Postgraduate Certificate in Education (PGCE) courses are available. The training of teachers for secondary schools is provided, in the main, in the education departments of the 2 universities, but 4-year (Hons) BEd courses are also available in the colleges for intending secondary teachers of religious education, business studies and craft, design and technology. There were a total of 1,854 students (308 men and 1,546 women) in training at the 2 colleges and the 2 universities during 1989–90. The principal initial teacher-training courses are the Bachelor of Education (3 year and 4 year honours), general or honours BA and BSc. degrees with education (3, 4 and 5 year) and the one year Certificate of Education for graduates.

Expenditure by the Department of Education (1989–90) was £898m.

Health and Personal Social Services. Under the provisions of the Health and Personal Social Services (NI) Order 1972, the Department of Health and Social Services is responsible for the provision of integrated health and personal social services in Northern Ireland, designed to promote the physical and mental health of the people of Northern Ireland through the prevention, diagnosis and treatment of illness, and also to promote their social welfare. Four Health and Social Services Boards, Eastern, Northern, Southern and Western, established under the above Order, administer health and personal social services, as the Department directs, within their designated areas.

Social Security. The social security schemes in Northern Ireland are similar to those in force in Great Britain.

National Insurance. During the year ended 31 March 1991 the gross expenditure of the National Insurance Fund at £877·1m. exceeded income from contributors by £215·9m. The shortfall in income was made up by investment income and a transfer from the Great Britain Fund.

£10·7m. was paid in sickness benefit and employers received £30·8m. reimbursement in respect of Statutory Sick Pay paid to their employees. £29·1m. was paid in unemployment benefit. Widows benefit amounted to £31·3m. and retirement pensions to £495·2m. Invalidity pensions and allowances totalled £182m. Maternity allowance of £0·9m. was paid and employers were reimbursed £13·1m. in respect of Statutory Maternity Pay.

Child Benefit. During the year ended 31 March 1990, £174m. was paid to an average of 216,819 families.

Income Support. In 1989–90 £378m. was paid to an average of 198,505 persons.

Family Credit. In 1989–90, £29m. was paid to an average of 14,131 persons.

Further Reading

Arthur, P. and Jeffery, K., *Northern Ireland since 1968.* Oxford, 1988
Cormack, R. J. and Osborne, R. D. (eds.) *Discrimination and Public Policy in Northern Ireland.* OUP, 1991
Cunningham, M. J., *British Government Policy in Northern Ireland, 1969–89.* Manchester Univ. Press, 1991
Flackes, W. D., *Northern Ireland: Political Directory 1968–88.* London, 1989
Irvine, M., *Northern Ireland: Faith and Faction.* London, 1991
Kenny, A., *The Road to Hillsborough.* London, 1986
McGarry, J. and O'Leary, B., (eds.) *The Future of Northern Ireland.* Oxford, 1991
Roche, P. J. and Barton, B., (eds.) *The Northern Ireland Question: Myth and Reality.* London, 1991
Shannon, M. O., *Northern Ireland.* [Bibliography] Oxford and Santa Barbara, 1991
Wallace, M., *British Government in Northern Ireland: From Devolution to Direct Rule.* Newton Abbot, 1982
Watt, D. (ed.) *The Constitution of Northern Ireland.* London, 1981
Whyte, J., *Interpreting Northern Ireland.* Oxford Univ. Press, 1990

ISLE OF MAN

AREA AND POPULATION. Area, 221 sq. miles (572 sq. km); resident population census April 1991, 69,788. The principal towns are Douglas (population, 22,214), Ramsey (6,496), Peel (3,829), Castletown (3,152). Vital statistics, 1990: Births, 887; deaths, 947; marriages, 491.

CONSTITUTION AND GOVERNMENT. The Isle of Man is a Crown dependency administered in accordance with its own laws by the High Court of *Tynwald*, consisting of the President of Tynwald, elected by the Court and the *Legislative Council*, composed of the Lord Bishop of Sodor and Man, the Attorney-General (who does not vote) and 8 members selected by the *House of Keys*; and the House of Keys, a representative assembly of 24 members chosen by adult suffrage on the single transferable vote system with the option of voting for a single candidate. The Isle of Man is not bound by Acts of the UK Parliament unless specially mentioned in them or applied by Order in Council although the UK is responsible for conducting its foreign affairs. The office of elected president replaced that of lieutenant governor in 1990.

A Council of Ministers was instituted in 1990. This replaced the former Executive Council and consists of the Chief Minister (elected for a 5-year term) and the ministers of the 9 major departments of Government. Elections for the House of Keys were held on 21 Nov. 1991. 73 candidates stood, mostly independents. Turn-out was 69·5%.

President: Sir Charles Kerruish (elected July 1990).
Chief Secretary: J. F. Kissack.
In March 1992 the *Chief Minister* was Miles Walker (b.1940).

Flag: Red, with 3 steel-coloured legs armoured and spurred (knees and spurs, yellow) in the centre.

ECONOMY

Budget. The Isle of Man levies its own taxes. Revenue is derived from customs duties, value added tax and from income tax. In 1991–92 the budget allowed for expenditure of £306m. Income tax was 15% of the first £8,000 of taxable income and 20% on the balance. There are no inheritance or capital gains taxes. A non-resident company duty of £450 was introduced on 6 April 1987 on every company incorporated in the Isle of Man which trades and is controlled outside the island.

The Island currently makes an annual contribution to the UK Government towards the cost of defence and other common services provided by the UK Government. That contribution currently amounts to about £1·5m.

Currency. The Isle of Man Government issues its own notes and coin on a par with £ sterling. £50, £20, £10, £5, £1, and £5, £2, £1, 50p, 20p, 10p, 5p, 2p and 1p coins are issued. Various commemorative coins have been minted together with legal tender gold coins and a platinum bullion coin.

Banking and Finance. Government regulation of the banking sector is exercised through the Financial Supervision Commission. The Commission was established in 1983 and is responsible for the licensing and supervision of banks, deposit-takers and certain financial intermediaries giving financial advice and receiving client monies for investment and management. As at 30 June 1991 there were 60 licensed banking institutions, 49 investment businesses and 5 UK Building Societies with Isle of Man licences. As at 31 Dec. 1990 the deposit base was £8,941m. The Isle of Man has designated status under the UK Financial Services Act. A compensation fund to protect depositors was set up in Feb. 1991 under the Isle of Man Financial Supervision Commission.

Agriculture. The area farmed is about 119,000 acres out of a total land area of around 140,000 acres. About 68,000 acres is devoted to grass whilst a further 37,000 acres are accounted for by rough grazing. Barley accounts for most of the remaining land under cultivation and some barley is exported. There are approximately 151,000 sheep, 34,000 cattle, 64,000 poultry and 4,000 pigs on farms in the Island. Agriculture contributes less than 3% of the Island's GNP.

External Economic Relations. A special relationship exists with the EEC providing for free trade and the adoption of external trade policies with third countries.

Tourism. In 1989–90 tourism contributed around 9% of national income; there were 299,204 passenger arrivals during the 1991 summer season.

COMMUNICATIONS

Roads. There are 500 miles of good roads. The International TT Motor Cycle Races and cycle races take place annually. Omnibus services operate to all parts of the island.

In 1990–91 there were 48,327 licensed vehicles on the roads, including 2,582 motorcycles.

Railways. Several novel transport systems operate on the Island during the summer season, including 100-year-old horse-drawn trams, and the Manx Electric Railway, linking Douglas, Ramsey and Snaefell Mountain (2,036 ft). The Isle of Man Steam Railway also operates between Douglas and Port Erin.

Civil Aviation. Ronaldsway Airport handles scheduled services operated by Manx Airlines and Jersey European to and from London, Manchester, Belfast, Dublin, Glasgow, Liverpool, Blackpool, Birmingham, Leeds, Luton, Newcastle and Cardiff. Air taxi services also operate.

Shipping. Car ferries of the Isle of Man Steam Packet Co. link the Island with Heysham throughout the year and similar services operate to Liverpool, Fleetwood, Dublin and Belfast during the summer season.

Telecommunications. The first constitutionally licensed commercial radio station in the British Isles, Manx Radio, is operated by Government on medium and VHF wavelengths from Douglas.

Newspapers. In 1990 there were 3 weekly newspapers and 1 twice weekly newspaper.

JUSTICE AND EDUCATION

Justice. The judiciary is headed by the First Deemster. The police force numbered 209 all ranks in 1990.

Education. Education is compulsory between the ages of 5 and 16. In 1991 there were 32 primary schools with 5,552 pupils in attendance. The net expenditure on education for 1991–92 amounted to £32·8m. There are 7 secondary schools, 5 provided by the Board of Education (4,454 registered pupils), 1 direct grant school for girls (61 senior and 168 junior registered pupils), 1 independent co–educational public school (218 senior and 134 junior registered pupils), 1 college of further education (425 full-time pupils in 1990–91), and 1 special school (28 pupils).

Further Reading

Additional information is available from: Economic Affairs Division, 14 Hill St, Douglas, Isle of Man.
Publications: *Isle of Man Key Facts 1990, Isle of Man Digest of Economic and Social Statistics 1988, Isle of Man Census Reports 1991, Isle of Man Family Expenditure Survey, Isle of Man Passenger Survey Reports 1985–1990, Isle of Man National Income Estimates, Isle of Man General Index of Retail Prices* (Monthly), *Isle of Man Earnings Survey.*
Tynwald Companion 1985. Isle of Man Government, 1985
Kinvig, R. H., *History of the Isle of Man.* Oxford, 1945.—*The Isle of Man: A Social, Cultural and Political History.* Liverpool Univ. Press, 1975
Robinson, V. and McCarroll, D., (eds.) *The Isle of Man: Celebrating a Sense of Place.* Liverpool Univ. Press, 1990
Solly, M., *The Isle of Man: A Low Tax Area.* London, 1984
Stenning, E. H., *Portrait of the Isle of Man.* London, 1984

CHANNEL ISLANDS

AREA. The Channel Islands are situated off the north-west coast of France and are the only portions of the 'Duchy of Normandy' now belonging to the Crown of England, to which they have been attached since the Conquest. They consist of Jersey (28,717 acres), Guernsey (15,654 acres) and the following dependencies of Guernsey–Alderney (1,962), Brechou (74), Great Sark (1,035), Little Sark (239), Herm (320), Jethou (44) and Lihou (38), a total of 48,083 acres, or 75 sq. miles (194 sq. km).

CLIMATE. The climate is mild, with an average temperature for the year of 11·5°C. Average yearly rainfall totals: Jersey, 862·9mm; Guernsey, 858·9mm. The wettest months are in the winter. Highest temperatures recorded: Jersey, 34·8°C.; Guernsey, 31·7°C. Maximum temperatures usually occur in July and Aug. (daily maximum 20·8°C. in Jersey, slightly lower in Guernsey). Lowest temperatures recorded: Jersey, 10·3°C.; Guernsey, −7·4°C. Jan. and Feb. are the coldest months (mean temperature approximately 6°C.).

CONSTITUTION. The Lieut.-Governors and Cs.-in-C. of Jersey and Guernsey are the personal representatives of the Sovereign, the Commanders of the Armed Forces of the Crown and the channel of communication between the Crown and the insular governments. They are appointed by the Crown and have a voice but no vote in the Assemblies of the States (the insular legislatures). The Secretaries to the Lieut.-Governors are their staff officers.

The Bailiffs are appointed by the Crown and are Presidents both of the Assembly of the States and of the Royal Courts of Jersey and Guernsey. They have in the States a casting vote. The official languages are French and English, but English is the main language. In the country districts of Jersey and Guernsey and throughout Sark some people also speak a Norman-French dialect; that of Alderney has died out.

EXTERNAL ECONOMIC RELATIONS. The Channel Islands are not members of the EC, but participate in ERM through their monetary union with the UK. From 1958 the trade of the Channel Islands with the UK has been regarded as internal trade.

COMMUNICATIONS

Road. Omnibus services operate in all parts of Jersey and Guernsey.

Civil Aviation. Scheduled air services are maintained by British Airways, Aer Lingus, Air UK, Jersey European, British Midland, Aurigny Air Services, Dan-Air, Brymon Airways, NLM City Hopper and other companies between the islands and airports in the UK, Ireland, the Netherlands, France, Germany, Norway, Portugal, Switzerland, Gibraltar, Spain, Finland and Belgium.

Shipping. Passenger and cargo services between Jersey, Guernsey and England are maintained by British Channel Island Ferries; between Guernsey, Jersey and England and St Malo by the Commodore Shipping Co., Emeraude Ferries connect Jersey with St Malo; between Guernsey, Jersey, Alderney, England and France by Condor Ltd (hydrofoil), and between Guernsey and Alderney and England and Guernsey and Sark by local companies.

Telecommunications. Postal and overseas telephone and telegraph services are maintained by the respective Postal Administrations of each bailiwick. The local telephone services are maintained by the insular authorities. There were, in 1990, 47,647 telephone lines in Jersey and 57,201 rented telephones in Guernsey.

There is an independent television station in Jersey and local radio stations, BBC Radio Jersey and Guernsey, opened in 1982.

JUSTICE AND RELIGION

Justice. Justice is administered by the Royal Courts of Jersey and Guernsey, each of which consists of the Bailiff and 12 Jurats, the latter being elected by an electoral college. There is an appeal from the Royal Courts to the Courts of Appeal of Jersey and of Guernsey. A final appeal lies to the Privy Council in certain cases. A stipendiary magistrate in each, Jersey and Guernsey, deals with minor civil and criminal cases.

Church. Jersey and Guernsey each constitutes a deanery under the jurisdiction of the Bishop of Winchester. The rectories (12 in Jersey; 10 in Guernsey) are in the gift of the Crown. The Roman Catholic and various Nonconformist Churches are represented.

Further Reading

Ambrière, F., *Les Iles Anglo-Normandes*. Paris, 1971
Coysh, V., *The Channel Islands: A New Study*. Newton Abbot, 1977
Cruickshank, C., *The German Occupation of the Channel Islands*. London, 1975
Jee, N., *The Landscape of the Channel Islands*. Chichester, 1982
Lemprière, R., *Portrait of the Channel Islands*. London, 1970.—*History of the Channel Islands*. Rev. ed. London, 1980
Uttley, J., *The Story of the Channel Islands*. London, 1966

JERSEY

POPULATION (1989), 82,809. In the year ended 31 Dec. 1989 there were 1,074 births and 896 deaths. The chief town is St Helier on the south coast. The official language is English (French until 1960).

CONSTITUTION AND GOVERNMENT. The States consist of 12 Senators (elected for 6 years, 6 retiring every third year), 12 Constables (triennial) and 29 Deputies (triennial), all elected on universal suffrage by the people.

The island parliament is 'The States of Jersey'. The States comprises the Bailiff, the Lieut.-Governor, the Dean of Jersey, the Attorney-General and the Solicitor-General, and 53 members elected by universal suffrage: 12 Senators, the Constables of the 12 parishes of the island and 29 Deputies. They all have the right to speak in the Assembly, but only the 53 elected members have the right to vote; the Bailiff has a casting vote. Senators are elected in Oct. every third year for 6-year terms, 6 retiring every third year. Constables are elected by the electors of their parishes for 3-year terms. Deputies are elected on a constituency basis in Nov. every third year. Except in specific instances, enactments passed by the States require the sanction of The Queen-in-Council. The Lieut.-Governor has the power of veto on certain forms of legislation.

Administration is carried out by Committees of the States.

Flag: White with a red diagonal cross. In the top centre of the flag a shield of the arms of Jersey ensigned with the Plantagenet Crown.

Lieut.-Governor and C.-in-C. of Jersey: Air Marshal Sir John Sutton, KCB.
Secretary and ADC to the Lieut.-Governor: Cdr D. M. L. Braybrooke, LVO, RN (Retd).

Bailiff of Jersey and President of the States: Sir Peter Crill, CBE.
Deputy Bailiff: V. A. Tomes.

ECONOMY

Budget (year ending 31 Dec. 1989). Revenue, £295,967,172; revenue expenditure, £228,530,891; capital expenditure, £39,939,000; net public debt, £1,666,690. The standard rate of income tax is 20p in the pound. No super-tax or death duties are levied. Parochial rates of moderate amount are payable by owners and occupiers.

Banking and Finance. Bank deposits and balances due to parent companies, 1990, totalled £40,400m.

Currency. The States issue bank-notes in denominations of £50, £20, £10, £5 and £1. Coinage from 1p to 50p is struck in the same denominations as the UK.

INDUSTRY. Principal activities: Tourism; total number of hotel and guesthouse bedrooms (1990), 23,069; expenditure of tourists (1990), £270m. Agriculture, total output (1988), £36·4m. and total exports, £30·7m. Light industry, mainly electrical goods, textiles and clothing.

Commerce. Since 1980 the Customs have ceased recording imports and exports. Principal imports: Machinery and transport equipment, manufactured goods, food, mineral fuels, and chemicals. Principal exports: Machinery and transport equipment, food, and manufactured goods.

Tourism. 0·88m. tourists spent £270m. in 1989. There were 23,625 tourist beds.

COMMUNICATIONS

Civil Aviation. The Jersey airport is situated at St Peter. It covers approximately 375 acres. Number of aircraft movements excluding local flying (1990) 60,107; number of passengers: 1,890,714; cargo and mail, 8,792 tonnes.

Shipping (1990). All vessels arriving in Jersey from outside Jersey waters report at St Helier or Gorey on first arrival. There is a harbour of minor importance at St Aubin. Number of commercial vessels entering St Helier in 1990, 26,472; number of visiting yachts (1990), 12,097. Passengers arrived in 1990, 491,145.

Telecommunications. Postal, and overseas telephone and telegraph services are maintained by the Postal Administration of Jersey. The local telephone service is maintained by the Insular Authority. In 1989 there were 43,880 telephones and 24 post offices.

JUSTICE. Justice is administered by the Royal Court, consisting of the Bailiff and 12 Jurats (magistrates). There is a final appeal in certain cases to the Sovereign in Council. There is also a Court of Appeal, consisting of the Bailiff and 2 judges. Minor civil and criminal cases are dealt with by a stipendiary magistrate.

EDUCATION (1991). There were 5 States secondary schools and 1 high school, and 24 States primary schools; 4,720 pupils attended the primary schools, 3,558 the secondary schools. There were 8 private primary schools with 1,288 pupils and 8 private secondary schools with 851 pupils. Highlands College offers full- and part-time courses to Ordinary and National Certificate and Diploma levels or similar standards and, together with Les Quennevais Adult Community Centre, evening classes in technical and recreational subjects.

Further Reading

Balleine, G. R., *Biographical Dictionary of Jersey*. London, 1948.—*A History of the Island of Jersey*. Rev. ed. Chichester, 1981.—*The Bailiwick of Jersey*. 3rd ed. London, 1970
Bois, F. de L., *The Constitutional History of Jersey*. Jersey, 1970

States of Jersey Library: Halkett Place, St Helier.

GUERNSEY

POPULATION. Census population (1986) 55,482. Births during 1990 were 758; deaths, 633. The town is St Peter Port.

CONSTITUTION. The government of the island is conducted by committees appointed by the States.

The States of Deliberation, the Parliament of Guernsey, is composed of the following members: The Bailiff, who is President *ex officio;* 12 Conseillers; H.M. Procureur and H.M. Comptroller (Law Officers of the Crown), who have a voice but no vote; 33 People's Deputies elected by popular franchise; 10 Douzaine Representatives elected by their Parochial Douzaines; 2 representatives of the States of Alderney.

The States of Election, an electoral college, elects the Jurats and Conseillers. It is composed of the following members: The Bailiff (President *ex officio*); the 12 Jurats or 'Jurés-Justiciers'; the 12 Conseillers; H.M. Procureur and H.M. Comptroller; the 33 People's Deputies; 34 Douzaine Representatives; and (for the election of Conseillers) 4 representatives of the States of Alderney.

Since Jan. 1949 all legislative powers and functions (with minor exceptions) formerly exercised by the Royal Court have been vested in the States of Deliberation. Projets de Loi (Bills) require the sanction of The Queen-in-Council.

Flag: White bearing a red cross of St George, with an argent with a cross gules superimposed on the cross.

Lieut.-Governor and C.-in-C. of Guernsey and its Dependencies: Lieut.-Gen. Sir Michael Wilkins, KCB, OBE.
Secretary and ADC to the Lieut.-Governor: Capt. D. P. L. Hodgetts.

Bailiff of Guernsey and President of the States: G. M. Dorey.
Deputy Bailiff of Guernsey: De V. G. Carey, QC.

BANKING AND FINANCE (year ending 31 Dec. 1990). Revenue, including Alderney, £138,532,424; expenditure, including Alderney, £126,047,752. The standard rate of income tax is 20p in the pound. States and parochial rates are very moderate. No super-tax or death duties are levied.

There were 72 banks in Sept. 1990.

COMMERCE (1990). Principal imports: Petrol and oils, 155,777,809 litres. Principal exports: Tomatoes, £4,885,391; flowers and fern, £26,053,705; sweet peppers, £231,193; other vegetables, £279,135; plants, £2·2m.

Tourism. 0·25m. tourists spent £92m. in 1989.

COMMUNICATIONS

Civil Aviation. The airport in Guernsey, situated at La Villiaze, has a landing area of approximately 124 acres and a tarmac runway of 4,800 ft. In 1990, passenger arrivals totalled 862,928.

Shipping. The principal harbour is that of St Peter Port, and there is a harbour at St Sampson's (used mainly for commercial shipping). In 1990 passenger arrivals totalled 372,415. Ships registered in Guernsey at 31 Dec. 1990 numbered 1,488 and 342 fishing vessels. In 1990, 13,460 yachts visited Guernsey.

EDUCATION. There are 2 public schools in the island: Elizabeth College, founded by Queen Elizabeth in 1563, for boys, and the Ladies' College, for girls. The States grammar school provides for education up to University entrance requirements, and there are numerous modern secondary and primary schools and a College of Further Education. The total number of school children was (1990) 8,182. Facilities are available for the study of art, domestic science and many other subjects of a technical nature. There is also a convent school with boarding facilities for girls.

HEALTH. Guernsey is not covered by the UK National Health Service. Public health is overseen by the States of Guernsey Insurance Authority and Board of Health, and a private medical insurance scheme is scheduled to provide comprehensive cover for all residents from Jan. 1993.

ALDERNEY. Population (1986 census, 2,130). The island has an airport. The Constitution of the island (reformed 1987) provides for its own popularly elected President and States (12 members), and its own Court. The town is St Anne's.

Flag: White with a red cross with the island badge in the centre.

President of the States: J. Kay-Mouat.
Clerk of the States: D. V. Jenkins.
Clerk of the Court: A. Johnson.

SARK. Population (1986 estimate, 550). The Constitution is a mixture of feudal and popular government with its Chief Pleas (parliament), consisting of 40 tenants and 12 popularly elected deputies, presided over by the Seneschal. The head of the island is the Seigneur. Sark has no income tax. Motor vehicles, except tractors, are not allowed.

Flag: White with a red cross and a red first quarter bearing two gold lions.

The Seigneur: J. M. Beaumont.
Seneschal: L. P. de Carteret.

Further Reading

Carteret, A. R. de, *The Story of Sark*. London, 1956
Coysh, V., *Alderney*. Newton Abbot, 1974
Durand, R., *Guernsey, Present and Past*. Guernsey, 1933.—*Guernsey under German Rule*. London, 1946
Hathaway, S., *Dame of Sark: An Autobiography*. London, 1961
Le Huray, C. P., *The Bailiwick of Guernsey*. London, 1952
Marr, L. J., *A History of Guernsey*. Chichester, 1982
Wood, A. and M. S., *Islands in Danger*. 2nd ed. London, 1957
Wood, J., *Herm, Our Island Home*. London, 1973

UNITED STATES OF AMERICA

Capital: Washington, D.C.
Population: 253·6m. (1991)
GNP per capita: US$21,100 (1989)

HISTORY. The Declaration of Independence of the 13 states of which the American Union then consisted was adopted by Congress on 4 July 1776. On 30 Nov. 1782 Great Britain acknowledged the independence of the USA, and on 3 Sept. 1783 the treaty of peace was concluded and was ratified by the USA on 14 Jan. 1784.

AREA AND POPULATION. Population at each census from 1790 to 1990 (including Alaska and Hawaii from 1960). Figures do not include Puerto Rico, Guam, American Samoa or other Pacific islands, or the US population abroad. Residents of Indian reservations not included before 1890.

	White	Black [1]	Other races [2]	Total	Decennial increase %
1790	3,172,464 [3]	757,208	—	3,929,672	—
1800	4,306,446	1,002,037	—	5,308,483	35·1
1810	5,862,073	1,377,808	—	7,239,881	36·4
1820	7,866,797	1,771,562	—	9,638,359	33·1
1830	10,537,378	2,328,642	—	12,866,020	33·5
1840	14,195,805	2,873,648	—	17,069,453	32·7
1850	19,553,068	3,638,808	—	23,191,876	35·9
1860	26,922,537	4,441,830	78,954 [4]	31,443,321	35·6
1870 [5]	33,589,377	4,880,009	88,985	38,558,371	22·6
1870 [5]	*34,337,292*	*5,392,172*	*88,985*	*39,818,449*	*26.6*
1880	43,402,970	6,580,793	172,020	50,155,783	30·1
1890	55,101,258	7,488,676	357,780	62,947,714	25·5
1900	66,868,508	8,834,395	509,265	76,212,168	21·0
1910	81,812,405	9,828,667	587,459	92,228,531	21·0
1920	94,903,540	10,463,607	654,421	106,021,568	14·9 [6]
1930	110,395,753 [7]	11,891,842	915,065	123,202,660	16·1 [6]
1940	118,357,831	12,865,914	941,384	132,165,129	7·3
1950	135,149,629	15,044,937	1,131,232	151,325,798	14·5
1960 [8]	158,831,732	18,871,831	1,619,612	179,323,175	18·5
1970	177,748,975	22,580,289	2,882,662	203,211,926	13·3
1980	188,371,622	26,495,025	11,679,158	226,545,805	11·4
1990	199,686,070	29,986,060	19,037,743	248,709,873	9·8

[1] Seventeen southern states (including D.C.) in 1900 had 7,922,969 Blacks (89·7% of the total Black population); in 1920, 8,912,231 (85·2%); in 1940, 9,904,619 (77%); in 1950, 10,225,407 (68%); in 1960, 11,311,607 (59·9%); in 1970, 11,969,961 (53%); in 1980, 14,048,000 (53%).

[2] *1870*, 63,199 Chinese, 55 Japanese and 25,731 Indians; *1880*, 105,465 Chinese, 148 Japanese and 66,407 Indians; *1890*, 107,488 Chinese, 2,039 Japanese and 248,253 Indians; *1900*, 118,746 Chinese, 85,716 Japanese, 237,196 Indians, 67,607 other races; *1910*, 94,414 Chinese, 152,745 Japanese, 276,927 Indians, 2,767 Filipino, 60,606 other races; *1920*, 85,202 Chinese, 220,596 Japanese, 244,437 Indians, 26,634 Filipino, 77,552 other races; *1930*, 343,352 Indians, 102,159 Chinese, 278,743 Japanese, 108,424 Filipino, 82,387 other races; *1940*, 345,252 Indians, 106,334 Chinese, 285,115 Japanese, 98,535 Filipino, 106,148 other races; *1950*, 357,499 Indians, 326,379 Japanese, 150,005 Chinese, 122,707 Filipino, 174,642 other races; *1960*, 523,591 Indians, 464,332 Japanese, 237,292 Chinese, 176,310 Filipino, 218,087 other races; *1970*, 792,730 Indians, 591,290 Japanese, 435,062 Chinese, 343,060 Filipino, 720,520 other races; *1980*, 1,364,033 Indians, 700,974 Japanese, 806,040 Chinese, 774,652 Filipino, 8,033,459 other races; *1990*, 7,273,662 Asians or Pacific Islanders, 1,952,234 Indians, 9,804,847 other races.

[3] Made up of Anglo-Scottish, 89·1%; German, 5·6%; Dutch, 2·5%; Irish, 1·9%; French, 0·6%.

[4] 34,933 Chinese and 44,021 Indians.

[5] Enumeration in 1870 incomplete. Figures in italics represent estimated corrected population. [*Footnotes continued on p. 1391.*]

1390

Urban population at the 1990 census was 179,117,000; rural, 66,964,000.
Sex distribution by race of the population at the 1990 census:

	Total population	White	Black	American Indian	Asian or Pacific	Other
Males:	121,239,418	97,475,880	14,170,151	967,186	3,558,038	5,068,163
Females:	127,470,455	102,210,190	15,815,909	992,048	3,715,624	4,736,684

Alongside these racial groups, and applicable to all of them, a category of 'Hispanic origin' was introduced at the 1990 census, comprising 22,354,059 persons (11,388,059 males; 10,966,000 females).

Age distribution by sex of the population at the 1990 census:

Age-group	Male	Female	Total
Under 5	9,392,409	8,962,034	18,354,443
5–9	9,262,527	8,836,652	18,099,179
10–14	8,767,167	8,347,082	17,114,249
15–19	9,102,690	8,651,317	17,754,015
20–24	9,675,596	9,344,716	19,020,312
25–29	10,695,936	10,617,109	21,313,045
30–34	10,876,933	10,985,954	21,862,887
35–39	9,902,243	10,060,874	19,963,117
40–44	8,691,984	8,923,802	17,615,786
45–49	6,810,597	7,061,976	13,872,573
50–54	5,514,738	5,835,775	11,350,513
55–59	5,034,370	5,497,386	10,531,756
60–64	4,947,047	5,669,120	10,616,167
Over 65	12,565,173	18,676,658	31,241,831

US population abroad at the time of the 1990 census was 922,819.

Estimated population in 1991, 253·6m.

The following table includes population statistics, the year in which each of the original 13 states (Connecticut, Delaware, Georgia, Maryland, Massachusetts, New Hampshire, New Jersey, New York, North Carolina, Pennsylvania, Rhode Island, South Carolina, Virginia) ratified the constitution, and the year when each of the other states was admitted into the Union. Traditional abbreviations for the names of the states are shown in brackets with postal codes for use in addresses. The total area of the USA in 1992 was 3,787,425 sq. miles of which 251,083 sq. miles were inland, coastal Great Lakes and territorial water.

The USA is divided into 4 geographic regions comprising 9 divisions. these are, with their 1990 census populations: Northeast (comprising the New England and Middle Atlantic divisions), 50,809,229; North Central (East North Central, West North Central), 59,668,632; South (South Atlantic, East South Central, West South Central), 85,445,930; West (Mountain, Pacific), 52,786,082.

Geographic divisions and states		Land area: sq. miles 1990	Census population 1 April 1990	Pop. per sq. mile, 1990
United States		3,536,342	248,709,873	70·3
New England		62,812	13,206,943	210·3
Maine (1820)	(Me./ME)	30,865	1,227,928	39·8
New Hampshire (1788)	(N.H./NH)	8,969	1,109,252	123·7
Vermont (1791)	(Vt./VT)	9,249	562,758	60·8
Massachusetts (1788)	(Mass./MA)	7,838	6,016,425	767·6
Rhode Island (1790)	(R.I./RI)	1,045	1,003,464	960·3
Connecticut (1788)	(Conn./CT)	4,845	3,287,116	678·4

[6] Between the 1910 census (15 April 1910) and the 1920 census (1 Jan. 1920), the period covered was 116 months (less than a full decade). Adjusting for this, the exact rate of increase for the decade was 15·4%. Similarly correcting for the 123 months between the 1920 and 1930 censuses, the true rate of increase was 15·7%.

[7] Figures for 1930 have been revised to include Mexicans (1,422,533), who were classified with 'Other Races' in the 1930 census reports.

[8] Figures for 1960 strictly comparable with those given for other years (i.e., excluding Alaska and Hawaii) are: White, 158,454,956; Black, 18,860,117; other races, 1,149,163; total, 178,464,236; decennial increase, 18·4%.

Geographic divisions and states		Land area: sq. miles 1990	Census population 1 April 1990	Pop. per sq. mile, 1990
Middle Atlantic		99,462	37,602,286	378·1
New York (1788)	*(N.Y./NY)*	47,224	17,990,455	381·0
New Jersey (1787)	*(N.J./NJ)*	7,419	7,730,188	1,042·0
Pennsylvania (1787)	*(Pa./PA)*	44,820	11,881,643	265·1
East North Central		243,539	42,008,942	172·5
Ohio (1803)	*(Oh./OH)*	40,953	10,847,115	264·9
Indiana (1816)	*(Ind./IN)*	35,870	5,544,159	154·6
Illinois (1818)	*(Ill./IL)*	55,593	11,430,602	205·6
Michigan (1837)	*(Mich./MI)*	56,809	9,295,297	163·6
Wisconsin (1848)	*(Wis./WI)*	54,314	4,891,769	90·1
West North Central		504,982	17,659,690	35·0
Minnesota (1858)	*(Minn./MN)*	79,617	4,375,099	55·0
Iowa (1846)	*(Ia./IA)*	55,875	2,776,755	49·7
Missouri (1821)	*(Mo./MO)*	68,898	5,117,073	74·3
North Dakota (1889)	*(N.D./ND)*	68,994	638,800	9·3
South Dakota (1889)	*(S.D./SD)*	75,898	696,004	9·2
Nebraska (1867)	*(Nebr./NE)*	76,878	1,578,385	20·5
Kansas (1861)	*(Kans./KS)*	81,823	2,477,574	30·3
South Atlantic		266,221	43,566,853	163·2
Delaware (1787)	*(Del./DE)*	1,955	666,168	340·8
Maryland (1788)	*(Md./MD)*	9,775	4,781,468	489·2
Dist. of Columbia (1791)	*(D.C./DC)*	61	606,900	9,884·4
Virginia (1788)	*(Va./VA)*	39,598	6,187,358	156·3
West Virginia (1863)	*(W. Va./WV)*	24,087	1,793,477	74·5
North Carolina (1789)	*(N.C./NC)*	48,718	6,628,637	136·1
South Carolina (1788)	*(S.C./SC)*	30,111	3,486,703	115·8
Georgia (1788)	*(Ga./GA)*	57,919	6,478,216	111·9
Florida (1845)	*(Fla./FL)*	53,997	12,937,926	239·6
East South Central		178,616	15,176,284	85·0
Kentucky (1792)	*(Ky./KY)*	39,732	3,685,296	92·8
Tennessee (1796)	*(Tenn./TN)*	41,220	4,877,185	118·3
Alabama (1819)	*(Al./AL)*	50,750	4,040,587	79·6
Mississippi (1817)	*(Miss./MS)*	46,914	2,573,216	54·8
West South Central		426,234	26,702,793	62·6
Arkansas (1836)	*(Ark./AR)*	52,073	2,350,725	45·1
Louisiana (1812)	*(La./LA)*	43,566	4,219,973	96·9
Oklahoma (1907)	*(Okla./OK)*	68,679	3,145,585	45·8
Texas (1845)	*(Tex./TX)*	261,914	16,986,510	64·9
Mountain		856,122	13,658,776	16·0
Montana (1889)	*(Mont./MT)*	145,556	799,065	5·5
Idaho (1890)	*(Id./ID)*	82,751	1,006,749	12·2
Wyoming (1890)	*(Wyo./WY)*	97,105	453,588	4·7
Colorado (1876)	*(Colo./CO)*	103,730	3,294,394	31·8
New Mexico (1912)	*(N. Mex./NM)*	121,365	1,515,069	12·5
Arizona (1912)	*(Ariz./AZ)*	113,642	3,665,228	32·3
Utah (1896)	*(Ut./UT)*	82,168	1,722,850	21·0
Nevada (1864)	*(Nev./NV)*	109,806	1,201,833	10·9
Pacific		895,355	39,127,306	43·7
Washington (1889)	*(Wash./WA)*	66,582	4,866,692	73·1
Oregon (1859)	*(Oreg./OR)*	96,003	2,842,321	29·6
California (1850)	*(Calif./CA)*	155,973	29,760,021	190·8
Alaska (1959)	*(Ak./AK)*	570,374	550,043	1·0
Hawaii (1960)	*(Hi./HI)*	6,423	1,108,229	172·5

Geographic divisions and states	Land area: sq. miles 1980	Estimated population 1 July 1988 (in 1,000)	Census population 1 April 1980	Pop. per sq. mile, 1980
Outlying Territories, total	4,691	...	3,565,376	760
Puerto Rico (1898)	3,515	3,291	3,196,520	909
Virgin Islands (1917)	132	103·2	96,569	731
American Samoa (1900)	77	39·5	32,297	419
Guam (1898)	209	133	105,979	507
Northern Marianas (1947)	184	21·2	16,780	91
Marshall Islands (1947)	70	...	30,873	441
Micronesia, Fed. States (1947)	271	...	73,160	270
Palau (1947)	192	...	12,116	63
Midway Islands (1867)	2	...	453	226
Wake Island (1898)	3	...	302	100
Johnston and Sand Islands (1858)	...	...	...	...

The 1980 census showed 9,323,946 foreign-born Whites. The 9 countries contributing the largest numbers who were foreign-born were Mexico, 2,199,221; Germany, 849,384; Canada, 842,859; Italy, 831,922; UK, 669,149; Cuba, 607,814; Philippines, 501,440; Poland, 418,128; USSR, 406,022.

Increase or decrease of native White, and foreign-born White, population from 1860 to 1980, by decades:

	Native White			Foreign-born White		
	Total	Increase	Per cent increase	Total	Increase or decrease (–)	Per cent. change
1860	22,825,784	5,513,251	31·8	4,096,753	1,856,218	82·8
1870	28,095,665	5,269,881	23·1	5,493,712	1,396,959	34·1
1880	36,843,291	8,747,626	31·1	6,559,679	1,065,967	19·4
1890	45,979,391	9,018,732 [1]	24·5	9,121,867	2,562,188	39·1
1900	56,595,379	10,615,988	23·1	10,213,817	1,091,950	12·0
1910	68,386,412	11,791,033	20·8	13,345,545	3,131,728	30·7
1920	81,108,161	12,721,749	18·6	13,712,754	367,209	2·8
1930	96,303,335	15,195,174	18·7	13,983,405	270,651	2·0
1940	106,795,732	10,492,397	10·9	11,419,138	−2,564,267	−18·3
1950	124,780,860	17,985,128	16·8	10,161,168	−1,257,970	−11·0
1960	149,543,638	24,762,778	19·8	9,293,992	− 867,176	− 8·5
1970	169,385,451	19,841,813	13·3	8,733,770	− 560,222	− 6·0
1980	179,711,066	10,325,615	6·0	9,323,946	590,176	6·7

[1] Exclusive of population specially enumerated in 1890 in Indian Territory and on Indian reservations.

Population of cities with over 100,000 inhabitants at the censuses of 1980 and 1990:

Cities	Census 1980	Census 1990	Cities	Census 1980	Census 1990
New York, N.Y.	7,071,639	7,322,564	Washington, D.C.	638,432	606,900
Los Angeles, Calif.	2,968,528	3,485,398	Boston, Mass.	562,994	574,283
Chicago, Ill.	3,005,072	2,783,726	Seattle, Wash.	493,846	516,259
Houston, Tex.	1,611,382	1,630,553	El Paso, Tex.	425,259	515,342
Philadelphia, Pa.	1,688,210	1,585,577	Nashville-Davidson,		
San Diego, Calif.	875,538	1,110,549	Tenn.	477,811	510,784
Detroit, Mich.	1,203,369	1,027,974	Cleveland, Ohio	573,822	505,616
Dallas, Tex.	904,599	1,006,877	New Orleans, La.	557,927	496,938
Phoenix, Ariz.	790,183	983,403	Denver, Colo.	492,686	467,610
San Antonio, Tex.	810,353	935,933	Austin, Tex.	345,890	465,622
San José, Calif	629,400	782,248	Fort Worth, Tex.	385,164	447,619
Indianapolis, Ind.	711,539	741,952	Oklahoma City, Okla.	404,014	444,719
Baltimore, Ma.	786,741	736,014	Portland, Ore.	368,148	437,319
San Francisco, Calif.	678,974	723,959	Kansas City, Mo.	448,028	435,146
Jacksonville, Fla.	571,003	672,971	Long Beach, Calif.	361,498	429,433
Columbus, Ohio	565,021	632,910	Tucson, Ariz.	330,537	405,390
Milwaukee, Wis.	636,297	628,088	St. Louis, Mo.	452,804	396,685
Memphis, Tenn.	646,174	610,337	Charlotte, NC	315,474	395,934

Cities	Census 1980	Census 1990	Cities	Census 1980	Census 1990
Atlanta, Ga.	425,022	394,017	Little Roc, Ariz.	159,159	175,795
Virginia Beach, Va.	262,199	393,069	Bakersfield, Calif.	105,611	174,820
Albuquerque, N.M.	332,920	384,736	Fremont, Calif.	131,945	173,339
Oakland, Calif.	339,337	372,242	Fort Wayne, Ind.	172,391	173,072
Pittsburgh, Pa.	423,959	369,379	Newport News, Va.	144,903	170,045
Sacramento, Calif.	275,741	369,365	Worcester, Mass.	161,799	169,759
Minneapolis, Minn.	370,951	368,383	Knoxville, Tenn.	175,045	165,121
Tulsa, Okla.	360,919	367,302	Modesto, Calif.	106,963	164,730
Honolulu, Hi.	365,048	365,272	Orlando, Fla.	128,291	164,693
Cincinnati, Ohio.	385,409	364,040	San Bernardino, Calif.	118,794	164,164
Miami, Fla.	346,681	358,548	Syracuse, N.Y.	170,105	163,860
Fresno, Calif.	217,491	354,202	Providence, R.I.	156,804	160,728
Omaha, Nebr.	313,939	335,795	Salt Lake City, Utah	163,034	159,936
Toledo, Ohio	354,635	332,943	Huntsville, Ala.	142,513	159,789
Buffalo, N.Y.	357,870	328,123	Amarillo, Tex.	149,230	157,615
Wichita, Kan.	279,838	304,011	Springfield, Mass.	152,319	156,983
Santa Ana, Calif.	204,023	293,742	Irving, Tex.	109,943	155,037
Mesa, Ariz.	152,404	288,091	Chattanooga, Tenn.	169,514	152,466
Colorado Springs, Colo.	215,105	281,140	Chesapeake, Va.	114,486	151,976
Tampa, Fla.	271,577	280,015	Kansas City, Kan.	161,148	149,767
Newark, N.J.	329,248	275,221	Fort Lauderdale, Fla.	153,279	149,377
St. Paul, Minn.	270,230	272,235	Glendale, Ariz.	97,172	148,134
Louisville, Ky.	298,694	269,063	Warren, Mich.	161,134	144,864
Anaheim, Calif.	219,494	266,406	Winston-Salem, N.C.	131,885	143,485
Birmingham, Ala.	284,413	265,968	Garden Grove, Calif.	123,307	143,050
Arlington, Tex.	160,113	261,721	Oxnard, Calif.	108,195	142,216
Norfolk, Va.	266,979	261,229	Tempe, Ariz.	106,919	141,865
Las Vegas, Nev.	164,674	258,295	Bridgeport, Conn.	142,546	141,686
Corpus Christi, Tex.	232,134	257,453	Paterson, N.J.	137,970	140,891
St. Petersburg, Fla.	238,647	238,629	Flint, Mich.	159,611	140,761
Rochester, N.Y.	241,741	231,636	Springfield, Mo.	133,116	140,494
Jersey City, N.J.	223,532	228,537	Hartford, Conn.	136,392	139,739
Riverside, Calif.	170,591	226,505	Rockford, Ill.	139,712	139,426
Anchorage, Ak.	174,431	226,338	Savannah, Ga.	141,654	137,560
Lexington-Fayette, Ky.	204,165	225,366	Durham, N.C.	101,149	136,611
Akron, Ohio	237,177	223,019	Chula Vista, Calif.	83,927	135,163
Aurora, Colo.	158,588	222,103	Reno, Nev.	100,756	133,850
Baton Rouge, La.	220,394	219,531	Hampton, Va.	122,617	133,793
Stockton, Calif.	148,283	210,943	Ontario, Calif.	88,820	133,179
Raleigh, N.C.	150,255	207,951	Torrance, Calif.	129,881	133,107
Richmond, Va.	219,214	203,056	Pomona, Calif.	92,742	131,723
Shreveport, La.	206,989	198,525	Pasadena, Calif.	18,072	131,591
Jackson, Miss.	202,895	196,637	New Haven, Conn.	126,089	130,474
Mobile, Ala.	200,452	196,278	Scottsdale, Ariz.	88,622	130,069
Des Moines, Ia.	191,003	193,187	Plano, Tex.	72,331	128,713
Lincoln, Nebr.	171,932	191,972	Oceanside, Calif.	76,698	128,398
Madison, Wis.	170,616	191,262	Lansing, Mich.	130,414	127,321
Grand Rapids, Mich.	181,843	189,126	Lakewood, Colo.	113,808	126,481
Yonkers, N.Y.	195,351	188,082	Evansville, Ind.	130,496	126,272
Hialeah, Fla.	145,254	188,004	Boise, Idaho	102,249	125,738
Montgomery, Ala.	177,857	187,106	Tallahassee, Fla.	81,548	124,773
Lubbock, Tex.	174,361	186,206	Laredo, Tex.	91,449	122,899
Greensboro, N.C.	155,642	183,521	Hollywood, Fla.	121,323	121,697
Dayton, Ohio	193,536	182,044	Topeka, Kan.	118,690	119,883
Huntington Beach, Calif.	170,505	181,519	Pasadena, Calif.	112,560	119,363
Garland, Tex.	138,857	180,650	Moreno Valley, Calif.	...	118,779
Glendale, Calif.	139,060	180,038	Sterling Heights, Mich.	108,999	117,810
Columbus, Ga.	169,441	179,278	Sunnyvale, Calif.	106,618	117,229
Spokane, Wash.	171,300	177,196	Gary, Ind.	151,968	116,646
Tacoma, Wash.	158,501	176,664	Beaumont, Tex.	118,102	114,323
			Fullerton, Calif.	102,246	114,144
			Peoria, Ill.	124,160	113,504
			Santa Rosa, Calif.	82,658	113,313

Cities	Census 1980	Census 1990	Cities	Census 1980	Census 1990
Eugene, Ore.	105,664	112,669	Salem, Ore.	89,091	107,786
Independence, Mo.	111,797	112,301	Abilene, Tex.	98,315	106,654
Overland Park, Kan.	81,784	111,790	Macon, Ga.	116,896	106,612
Hayward, Calif.	93,585	111,498	El Monte, Calif.	79,494	106,209
Concord, Calif.	103,763	111,348	South Bend, Ind.	109,727	105,511
Alexandria, Va.	103,217	111,183	Springfield, Ill.	100,054	105,227
Orange, Calif.	91,450	110,658	Allentown, Pa.	103,758	105,090
Santa Clarita, Calif.	...	110,642	Thousand Oaks, Calif.	77,072	104,352
Irvine, Calif.	62,134	110,330	Portsmouth, Va.	104,577	103,907
Elizabeth, N.J.	106,201	110,002	Waco, Tex.	101,261	103,590
Inglewood, Calif.	94,162	109,602	Lowell, Mass.	92,418	103,439
Ann Arbor, Mich.	107,969	109,592	Berkeley, Calif.	103,328	102,724
Vallejo, Calif.	80,303	109,199	Mesquite, Tex.	67,053	101,484
Waterbury, Conn.	103,266	108,961	Rancho Cucamonga,		
Salinas, Calif.	80,479	108,777	Calif.	55,250	101,409
Cedar Rapids, Ia.	110,243	108,751	Albany, N.Y.	101,727	101,082
Erie, Pa.	119,123	108,718	Livonia, Mich.	104,814	100,850
Escondido, Calif.	64,355	108,635	Sioux Falls, S.D.	81,343	100,814
Stamford, Conn.	102,466	108,056	Simi Valley, Calif.	77,500	100,217

Vital Statistics: Vital statistics are based on records of births, deaths, fœtal deaths, marriages and divorces filed with registration officials of states and cities. Figures for the US include Alaska beginning with 1959 and Hawaii beginning with 1960.

Annual collection of mortality records from a national death-registration area was inaugurated in 1900. A national birth-registration area was established in 1915. These areas, which at their inception comprised 10 states and the District of Columbia, expanded gradually until 1933, when both the birth- and death-registration areas covered the entire continental US. Marriage and divorce statistics are compiled from reports furnished by state and local officials. Data on annulments are included in the divorce statistics. The marriage-registration area was established in 1957 with 30 states and 3 other areas. The divorce-registration area was established in 1958 with 14 states and 2 other areas. In Jan. 1980 the marriage-registration area included 42 states and D.C., and the divorce-registration area included 30 states.

	Live births [1]	Deaths [2]	Marriages [3]	Divorces [4]	Deaths under 1 year [5]
1900	—	343,217	709,000	56,000	—
1910	2,777,000	696,856	948,000	83,000	—
1920	2,950,000	1,118,070	1,274,476	170,505	170,911
1930	2,618,000	1,327,240	1,126,856	195,961	143,201
1940	2,559,000	1,417,269	1,595,879	264,000	110,984
1950	3,632,000	1,452,454	1,667,231	385,144	103,825
1960	4,257,850 [6]	1,711,982	1,523,000	393,000	110,873
1970	3,731,386 [6]	1,921,031	2,158,802	708,000	74,667
1980	3,612,258	1,989,841	2,390,252	1,189,000	45,526
1985	3,760,561	2,086,440	2,412,625	1,190,000	40,030
1988	3,913,000	2,171,000	2,389,000	1,183,000	38,700
1989	4,021,000	2,155,000	2,419,236	1,007,538	—
1990 [1]	4,179,000	2,162,000	2,448,000	1,175,000	—

[1] Figures through 1959 include adjustment for under-registration (the 1959 registered count was 4,244,796); beginning 1960 figures represent number registered.

[2] Excluding fœtal deaths and deaths among the armed forces overseas.

[3] Estimates for all years except 1970.

[4] Includes reported annulments. Estimated for all years.

[5] Deaths for 1979–81 (Ninth Revision, International Classification of Diseases, 1975). Deaths from complications of pregnancy, childbirth and the puerperium. Deaths for 1968–78 were classified according to the Eighth Revision, International Classification of Diseases, adopted, 1965. Deaths for 1958–67 were classified according to the Seventh Revision of the International Lists of Diseases and Causes of Death, those for 1949–57 according to the Sixth Revision and those for 1939–48, according to the Fifth Revision.

[6] Based on a 50% sample.   [7] Provisional.

The crude birth rate, based on total live-birth estimates per 1,000 total population, fell from 29·5 in 1915 to 18·4 in 1933; it rose to a peak of 26·6 in 1947—its highest for 25 years. This peak reflects demobilization (1945–46), the record marriage rate that followed, and the high levels of employment and income. The decrease in the following 3 years was moderate. In 1951 the rate moved upward and levelled off in 1957 at about 25 per 1,000 population. Since 1957 the crude birth rate declined every year to 4·6 live births per 1,000 population in 1975. Since 1985 it has risen from 15·7 to 16·7 in 1990. Estimated number of births to unmarried women in 1988 was 933,000 (24·5% of all births, 16·7% of White births, 62·2% of Black births).

Deaths, excluding fœtal deaths (per 1,000 population), declined from 17·2 in 1900 to 10 in 1946. The death rate has been below 10 per 1,000 since 1947, fluctuating slightly from year to year, mainly under the impact of occurrences of outbreaks of severe respiratory diseases. The rate for 1970, 9·5; 1980, 8·8; 1990, 8·6.

Leading causes of death, 1990, per 100,000 population: Diseases of heart, 366·9; malignant neoplasms, 201·7; cerebrovascular diseases, 57·9; accidents, 37·3; suicides, 12·3; homicides, 10·2.

Deaths from AIDS (HIV infection) in 1989, 21,360; 1990, 24,120.

The marriage rates per 1,000 population for selected years are: 1920, 12; 1932, 7·9; 1946, 16·4; 1951, 10·4; 1961, 8·5; 1970, 10·6; 1975, 10; 1980, 10·6; 1985, 10·1; 1986, 10; 1988, 9·7; 1990, 9·8. The divorce rates per 1,000 population for selected years are: 1920, 1·6; 1946, 4·3; 1951, 2·5; 1961, 2·3; 1971, 3·7; 1979, 5·3; 1980, 5·2; 1985, 5; 1986, 4·8; 1988, 4·8; 1990, 4·7.

The infant mortality rates, per 1,000 live births were: 1915–19, 95·7; 1920–24, 76·7; 1925–29, 69; 1930–34, 60·4; 38·3 in 1945; 29·2 in 1950; 26·4 in 1955; 26 in 1960; 20 in 1970; 16·1 in 1975; 12·6 in 1980; 10·6 in 1985; 10·4 in 1986; 10 in 1987; 10 in 1988.

Immigration: The Immigration and Nationality Act, as amended, provides for the numerical limitation of most immigration. Public Law 96–212, the Refugee Act of 1980, reduced the worldwide numerical limitation to 280,000 for 1980 and 270,000 thereafter, with a maximum of 20,000 visas available for one country. The colonies and dependencies of a foreign state are limited to 5,000 per year, chargeable to the country limitation of the mother country. Visas are allocated under a system of 6 preference categories, 4 of which are designed to reunite close relatives of US citizens and resident aliens of the US, and 2 for skilled and professional workers. Visa numbers not used in the preference categories are made available to qualified non-preference immigrants. The non-preference category has not been available since 1978 due to high demand in other categories. Immigrants not subject to any numerical limitation are spouses, children, and parents of US citizens, who are 21 years of age or older; certain former US citizens; ministers of religion; certain long-term US government employees; and refugees adjusting to immigrant status. The Immigration Act of 1990 modified the qualifications for entry beginning Oct. 1991. This new law expanded the number of persons who may enter based on their job skills, and added a new category designed to diversify immigration.

Immigration data for 1990 include 880,372 aliens who were admitted as permanent residents under the legalization programme created by the Immigrant Reform and Control Act of 1986. These aliens have resided in the USA since before 1982 or were agricultural workers on perishable crops and have qualified as temporary residents under the first phase of the legalization programme; in the fiscal year 1989, they began qualifying for permanent status.

Immigrant aliens admitted to US for permanent residence, by country or region of birth.

Country or region of birth	1987	Immigrants admitted 1988	1989	1990
All countries	601,516	643,025	1,090,924	1,536,483
Europe	61,174	64,797	82,891	112,401
Germany, Fed. Rep.	7,210	6,645	6,708	7,388
Greece	2,653	2,458	2,491	2,742
Italy	2,784	2,949	2,910	3,287
Poland	7,519	9,507	15,101	20,537

Country or region of birth	1987	Immigrants admitted 1988	1989	1990
Portugal	3,912	3,199	3,958	4,035
Spain	1,578	1,483	1,550	1,886
UK	13,497	13,228	14,090	15,928
Yugoslavia	1,827	1,941	2,496	2,828
Other Europe	20,194	23,387	33,787	53,770
Asia	257,684	264,465	312,149	338,581
China and Taiwan	37,772	38,387	46,246	46,966
Hong Kong	4,706	8,546	9,740	9,393
India	27,803	26,268	31,175	30,667
Japan	4,174	4,512	4,849	5,734
Korea (North and South)	35,849	34,703	34,222	32,301
Philippines	50,060	50,697	57,034	63,756
Thailand	6,733	6,888	9,332	8,914
Other Asia	90,587	94,464	119,551	140,850
North America	216,550	250,009	607,398	957,558
Canada	11,876	11,783	12,151	16,812
Mexico	72,351	95,039	405,172	679,068
Cuba	28,916	17,558	10,046	10,645
Dominican Republic	24,858	27,189	26,723	42,195
Haiti	14,819	34,806	13,658	20,324
Jamaica	23,148	20,966	24,523	25,013
Trinidad and Tobago	3,543	3,947	*,***	6,740
Other Caribbean	7,615	7,891	8,588	10,434
Central America	29,296	30,715	101,034	146,202
Other North America	128	115	109	125
South America	44,385	41,007	58,926	85,819
Colombia	11,700	10,322	15,204	24,189
Ecuador	4,641	4,716	7,532	12,476
Other South America	28,044	25,969	36,180	49,154
Africa	17,724	18,882	25,166	35,893
Australia and New Zealand	1,844	2,024	2,335	2,583
Other countries	2,155	1,841	2,059	3,648

The total number of immigrants admitted from 1820 up to 30 Sept. 1990 was 6,994,014; this included 7,083,465 from Germany, and from Italy 5,373,108.

Aliens coming to the US for temporary periods of time are classified as non-immigrants. During fiscal year 1990, a total of 17,574,055 non-immigrants were admitted. This total includes multiple entry documents but excludes border crossers, crewmen and insular travellers. Tourists numbered 3,418,328, with 7,731,244 coming from Mexico, Japan, the UK, the Caribbean and Germany. There were 1,044,599 aliens expelled during fiscal year 1990. Of this number, 25,228 were deported and 1,019,371 were required to depart without formal orders of deportation.

During fiscal year 1990, 270,101 persons became US citizens through naturalization, including 225,319 naturalized under the general provisions of 5-year residence in the US, 21,465 spouses and children of US citizens, 1,630 members of US Armed Forces and 21,687 under other provisions. The new citizens included 10,291 from Cuba, 25,936 from the Philippines, 20,485 from China and Taiwan, 10,500 from Korea, 8,286 from the UK, 2,453 from Italy, 17,564 from Mexico, 6,792 from Jamaica, and 22,027 from Vietnam.

CLIMATE. For temperature and rainfall figures, see entries on individual states as indicated by regions, below, of mainland USA.

Pacific Coast. The climate varies with latitude, distance from the sea and the effect of relief, ranging from polar conditions in North Alaska through cool to warm temperate climates further south. The extreme south is temperate desert. Rainfall everywhere is moderate. *See* Alaska, California, Oregon, Washington.

Mountain States. Very varied, with relief exerting the main control; very cold in the north in winter, with considerable snowfall. In the south, much higher temperatures and aridity produce desert conditions. Rainfall everywhere is very variable as a result of rain-shadow influences. *See* Arizona, Colorado, Idaho, Montana, Nevada, New Mexico, Utah, Wyoming.

High Plains. A continental climate with a large annual range of temperature and moderate rainfall, mainly in summer, although unreliable. Dust storms are common in summer and blizzards in winter. *See* Nebraska, North Dakota, South Dakota.

Central Plains. A temperate continental climate, with hot summers and cold winters, except in the extreme south. Rainfall is plentiful and comes at all seasons, but there is a summer maximum in western parts. *See* Mississippi, Missouri, Oklahoma, Texas.

Mid-West. Continental, with hot summers and cold winters. Rainfall is moderate, with a summer maximum in most parts. *See* Indiana, Iowa, Kansas.

Great Lakes. Continental, resembling that of the Central Plains, with hot summers but very cold winters because of the freezing of the lakes. Rainfall is moderate with a slight summer maximum. *See* Illinois, Michigan, Minnesota, Ohio, Wisconsin.

Appalachian Mountains. The north is cool temperate with cold winters, the south warm temperate with milder winters. Precipitation is heavy, increasing to the south but evenly distributed over the year. *See* Kentucky, Pennsylvania, Tennessee, West Virginia.

Gulf Coast. Conditions vary from warm temperate to sub-tropical, with plentiful rainfall, decreasing towards the west but evenly distributed over the year. *See* Alabama, Arkansas, Florida, Louisiana.

Atlantic Coast. Temperate maritime climate but with great differences in temperature according to latitude. Rainfall is ample at all seasons; snowfall in the north can be heavy. *See* Delaware, District of Columbia, Georgia, Maryland, New Jersey, New York, North Carolina, South Carolina, Virginia.

New England. Cool temperate, with severe winters and warm summers. Precipitation is well distributed with a slight winter maximum. Snowfall is heavy in winter. *See* Connecticut, Maine, Massachusetts, New Hampshire, Rhode Island, Vermont. *See* also Hawaii and Outlying Territories.

CONSTITUTION AND GOVERNMENT. The form of government of the USA is based on the constitution of 17 Sept. 1787.

By the constitution the government of the nation is composed of three co-ordinate branches, the executive, the legislative and the judicial.

The National Government has authority in matters of general taxation, treaties and other dealings with foreign Powers, foreign and inter-state commerce, bankruptcy, postal service, coinage, weights and measures, patents and copyright, the armed forces (including, to a certain extent, the militia), and crimes against the USA; it has sole legislative authority over the District of Columbia and the possessions of the US.

The 5th article of the constitution provides that Congress may, on a two-thirds vote of both houses, propose amendments to the constitution, or, on the application of the legislatures of two-thirds of all the states, call a convention for proposing amendments, which in either case shall be valid as part of the constitution when ratified by the legislatures of three-fourths of the several states, or by conventions in three-fourths thereof, whichever mode of ratification may be proposed by Congress. Ten amendments (called collectively 'the Bill of Rights') to the constitution were added 15 Dec. 1791; two in 1795 and 1804; a 13th amendment, 6 Dec. 1865, abolishing slavery; a 14th in 1868, including the important 'due process' clause; a 15th, 3 Feb. 1870, establishing equal voting rights for white and coloured; a 16th, 3 Feb. 1913, authorizing the income tax; a 17th, 8 April 1913, providing for popular election of senators; an 18th, 16 Jan. 1919, prohibiting alcoholic liquors; a 19th, 18 Aug. 1920, establishing woman suffrage; a 20th, 23 Jan. 1933, advancing the date of the President's and Vice-President's inauguration and abolishing the 'lameduck' sessions of Congress; a 21st, 5 Dec. 1933, repealing the 18th amendment; a 22nd, 26 Feb. 1951, limiting a President's tenure of office to 2 terms, or to 2 terms plus 2 years in the case of a Vice-President who has succeeded to the office of a President;

a 23rd, 30 March 1961, granting citizens of the District of Columbia the right to vote in national elections; a 24th, 4 Feb. 1964, banning the use of the poll-tax in federal elections; a 25th, 10 Feb. 1967, dealing with Presidential disability and succession; a 26th, 22 June 1970, establishing the right of citizens who are 18 years of age and older to vote.

National flag: Seven red and 6 white alternating stripes, horizontal; with a blue canton, extending down to the lower edge of the 4th red stripe from the top, and displaying 50 white 5-pointed stars, one for each state. The stars have one point directed vertically upward, and they are arranged in 6 rows of 5 each, alternating with 5 rows of 4 each. On the admission of additional states, stars are added, effective on 4 July following the date of admission. Congress, by law of 22 Dec. 1942, has codified 'existing rules and customs' pertaining to the display of the flag, for civilians.

National anthem: The Star-spangled Banner, 'Oh say, can you see by the dawn's early light' (words by F. S. Key, 1814; tune by J. S. Smith; formally adopted by Congress 3 March 1931).

National motto: 'In God we trust'; formally adopted by Congress 30 July 1956.

Presidency. The executive power is vested in a president, who holds office for 4 years, and is elected, together with a vice-president chosen for the same term, by electors from each state, equal to the whole number of senators and representatives to which the state may be entitled in the Congress. The President must be a natural-born citizen, resident in the country for 14 years, and at least 35 years old.

The presidential election is held every fourth (leap) year on the Tuesday after the first Monday in November. Technically, this is an election of presidential electors, not of a president directly; the electors thus chosen meet and give their votes (for the candidate to whom they are pledged, in some states by law, but in most states by custom and prudent politics) at their respective state capitals on the first Monday after the second Wednesday in December next following their election; and the votes of the electors of all the states are opened and counted in the presence of both Houses of Congress on the sixth day of January. The total electorate vote is one for each senator and representative.

If the successful candidate for President dies before taking office the Vice-President-elect becomes President; if no candidate has a majority or if the successful candidate fails to qualify, then, by the 20th amendment, the Vice-President acts as President until a president qualifies. The duties of the Presidency, in absence of the President and Vice-President by reason of death, resignation, removal, inability or failure to qualify, devolve upon the Speaker of the House under legislation enacted 18 July 1947. And in case of absence of a Speaker for like reason, the presidential duties devolve upon the President *pro tem.* of the Senate and successively upon those members of the Cabinet in order of precedence, who have the constitutional qualifications for President.

The presidential term, by the 20th amendment to the constitution, begins at noon on 20 Jan. of the inaugural year. This amendment also installs the newly elected Congress in office on 3 Jan. instead of—as formerly—in the following December. The President's salary is $200,000 per year, plus $50,000 to assist in defraying expenses resulting from official duties. Also he may spend up to $100,000 non-taxable for travel and $20,000 for official entertainment. The office of Vice-President carries a salary of $160,600, plus $10,000 allowance for expenses, all taxable.

The President is C.-in-C. of the Army, Navy and Air Force, and of the militia when in the service of the Union. The Vice-President is *ex-officio* President of the Senate, and in the case of 'the removal of the President, or of his death, resignation, or inability to discharge the powers and duties of his office', he becomes the President for the remainder of the term.

President of the United States: George Bush, of Texas, born at Milton, Massachusetts, in 1924; Vice-President, 1981–89.

Vice President: Dan Quayle, of Indiana; born 1947.

At the Presidential election on 8 Nov. 1988 total vote cast, including men and women in the armed services, was 91,585,872, of which George Bush (R.) received

48,881,011 (53·4%), Michael Dukakis (D.) 41,828,350 (45·67%), Ron Paul (Libertarian) 431,499 (0·47%), Lenora Fulani (New Alliance) 218,159 (0·24%). Electoral college votes: Bush 426; Dukakis 112.

PRESIDENTS OF THE USA

Name	From state	Term of service	Born	Died
George Washington	Virginia	1789–97	1732	1799
John Adams	Massachusetts	1797–1801	1735	1826
Thomas Jefferson	Virginia	1801–09	1743	1826
James Madison	Virginia	1809–17	1751	1836
James Monroe	Virginia	1817–25	1759	1831
John Quincy Adams	Massachusetts	1825–29	1767	1848
Andrew Jackson	Tennessee	1829–37	1767	1845
Martin Van Buren	New York	1837–41	1782	1862
William H. Harrison	Ohio	Mar.–Apr. 1841	1773	1841
John Tyler	Virginia	1841–45	1790	1862
James K. Polk	Tennessee	1845–49	1795	1849
Zachary Taylor	Louisiana	1849–July 1850	1784	1850
Millard Fillmore	New York	1850–53	1800	1874
Franklin Pierce	New Hampshire	1853–57	1804	1869
James Buchanan	Pennsylvania	1857–61	1791	1868
Abraham Lincoln	Illinois	1861–Apr. 1865	1809	1865
Andrew Johnson	Tennessee	1865–69	1808	1875
Ulysses S. Grant	Illinois	1869–77	1822	1885
Rutherford B. Hayes	Ohio	1877–81	1822	1893
James A. Garfield	Ohio	Mar.–Sept. 1881	1831	1881
Chester A. Arthur	New York	1881–85	1830	1886
Grover Cleveland	New York	1885–89	1837	1908
Benjamin Harrison	Indiana	1889–93	1833	1901
Grover Cleveland	New York	1893–97	1837	1908
William McKinley	Ohio	1897–Sept. 1901	1843	1901
Theodore Roosevelt	New York	1901–09	1858	1919
William H. Taft	Ohio	1909–13	1857	1930
Woodrow Wilson	New Jersey	1913–21	1856	1924
Warren Gamaliel Harding	Ohio	1921–Aug. 1923	1865	1923
Calvin Coolidge	Massachusetts	1923–29	1872	1933
Herbert C. Hoover	California	1929–33	1874	1964
Franklin D. Roosevelt	New York	1933–Apr. 1945	1882	1945
Harry S. Truman	Missouri	1945–53	1884	1972
Dwight D. Eisenhower	New York	1953–61	1890	1969
John F. Kennedy	Massachusetts	1961–Nov. 1963	1917	1963
Lyndon B. Johnson	Texas	1963–69	1908	1973
Richard M. Nixon	California	1969–74	1913	—
Gerald R. Ford	Michigan	1974–77	1913	—
James Earl Carter	Georgia	1977–81	1924	—
Ronald Reagan	California	1981–89	1911	—
George Bush	Texas	1989–	1924	—

VICE-PRESIDENTS OF THE USA

John Adams	Massachusetts	1789–97	1735	1826
Thomas Jefferson	Virginia	1797–1801	1743	1826
Aaron Burr	New York	1801–05	1756	1836
George Clinton	New York	1805–12 [1]	1739	1812
Elbridge Gerry	Massachusetts	1813–14 [1]	1744	1814
Daniel D. Tompkins	New York	1817–25	1774	1825
John C. Calhoun	South Carolina	1825–32 [1]	1782	1850
Martin Van Buren	New York	1833–37	1782	1862
Richard M. Johnson	Kentucky	1837–41	1780	1850
John Tyler	Virginia	Mar.–Apr. 1841 [1]	1790	1862

[1] Position vacant thereafter until commencement of the next presidential term.

Name	From state	Term of service	Born	Died
George M. Dallas	Pennsylvania	1845–49	1792	1864
Millard Fillmore	New York	1849–50 [1]	1800	1874
William R. King	Alabama	Mar.–Apr. 1853 [1]	1786	1853
John C. Breckinridge	Kentucky	1857–61	1821	1875
Hannibal Hamlin	Maine	1861–65	1809	1891
Andrew Johnson	Tennessee	Mar.–Apr. 1865 [1]	1808	1875
Schuyler Colfax	Indiana	1869–73	1823	1885
Henry Wilson	Massachusetts	1873–75 [1]	1812	1875
William A. Wheeler	New York	1877–81	1819	1887
Chester A. Arthur	New York	Mar.–Sept. 1881 [1]	1830	1886
Thomas A. Hendricks	Indiana	Mar.–Nov. 1885 [1]	1819	1885
Levi P. Morton	New York	1889–93	1824	1920
Adlai Stevenson	Illinois	1893–97	1835	1914
Garret A. Hobart	New Jersey	1897–99 [1]	1844	1899
Theodore Roosevelt	New York	Mar.–Sept. 1901 [1]	1858	1919
Charles W. Fairbanks	Indiana	1905–09	1855	1920
James S. Sherman	New York	1909–12 [1]	1855	1912
Thomas R. Marshall	Indiana	1913–21	1854	1925
Calvin Coolidge	Massachusetts	1921–Aug. 1923 [1]	1872	1933
Charles G. Dawes	Illinois	1925–29	1865	1951
Charles Curtis	Kansas	1929–33	1860	1935
John N. Garner	Texas	1933–41	1868	1967
Henry A. Wallace	Iowa	1941–45	1888	1965
Harry S. Truman	Missouri	1945–Apr. 1945 [1]	1884	1972
Alben W. Barkley	Kentucky	1949–53	1877	1956
Richard M. Nixon	California	1953–61	1913	—
Lyndon B. Johnson	Texas	1961–Nov. 1963 [1]	1908	1973
Hubert H. Humphrey	Minnesota	1965–69	1911	1978
Spiro T. Agnew	Maryland	1969–73	1918	—
Gerald R. Ford	Michigan	1973–74	1913	—
Nelson Rockefeller	New York	1974–77	1908	1979
Walter Mondale	Minnesota	1977–81	1928	—
George Bush	Texas	1981–89	1924	—
Danforth Quayle	Indiana	1989–	1947	—

[1] Position vacant thereafter until commencement of the next presidential term.

Cabinet. The administrative business of the nation has been traditionally vested in several executive departments, the heads of which, unofficially and *ex officio*, formed the President's Cabinet. Beginning with the Interstate Commerce Commission in 1887, however, an increasing amount of executive business has been entrusted to some 60 so-called independent agencies, such as the Veterans Administration, Housing and Home Finance Agency, Tariff Commission, etc.

All heads of departments and of the 60 or more administrative agencies are appointed by the President, but must be confirmed by the Senate.

The Cabinet consisted of the following (March 1992):

1. *Secretary of State* (created 1789). James Addison Baker III, of Texas, lawyer; Presidential Chief of Staff 1981–85; Secretary of the Treasury 1985–88; born 1930.

2. *Secretary of the Treasury* (1789). Nicholas F. Brady, investment banker; born 1930.

3. *Secretary of Defense* (1947). Richard Cheney, of Wyoming; congressman; White House Chief of Staff 1975–76; born 1940.

4. *Attorney-General* (Department of Justice, 1870). William P. Barr, of New York; lawyer; Head of Justice Department's Legal Counsel Office; White House domestic policy staff; Deputy Attorney General; born 1950.

5. *Secretary of the Interior* (1849). Manuel Lujan, Jr., of New Mexico; congressman; born 1928.

6. *Secretary of Agriculture* (1889). Edward R. Madigan, of Illinois; congressman; member of the House of Energy and Commerce Committee; Republican chief deputy whip; born 1936.

7. *Secretary of Commerce* (1903). Barbara H. Franklin, of Pennsylvania, business administrator, member of 7 corporate boards; White House staff; born 1940.

8. *Secretary of Labor* (1913). Lynn Morley Martin, of Illinois; congresswoman; teacher; born 1939.

9. *Secretary of Health and Human Services* (1953). Louis W. Sullivan, of Georgia; medical school president; born 1933.

10. *Secretary of Housing and Urban Development* (1966). Jack F. Kemp, of New York; congressman; born 1935.

11. *Secretary of Transportation* (1967). Andrew H. Card, of Massachusetts; state legislator, Massachusetts; Deputy White House Chief of Staff; born 1947.

12. *Secretary of Energy* (1977). James D. Watkins, naval officer; Chief of Naval Operations 1982–86; born 1927.

13. *Secretary of Education* (1979). Andrew Lamar Alexander, of Tennessee; lawyer; academic administrator; governor of Tennessee, 1979-87; chairman, National Governors' Association; born 1940.

14. *Veterans' Affairs* (1989). Edward J. Derwinski, of Chicago; government official; born 1926.

Each of the above Cabinet officers receives an annual salary of $138,900 and holds office during the pleasure of the President.

Congress: The legislative power is vested by the Constitution in a Congress, consisting of a Senate and House of Representatives.

Electorate: By amendments of the constitution, disqualification of voters on the ground of race, colour or sex is forbidden. The electorate consists of all citizens over 18 years of age. Literacy tests have been banned since 1970. In 1972 durational residency requirements were held to violate the constitution. In 1973 US citizens abroad were enfranchised.

With limitations imposed by the constitution, it is the states which determine voter eligibility. In general states exclude from voting: Persons who have not established residency in the jurisdiction in which they wish to vote; persons who have been convicted of felonies whose civil rights have not been restored; persons declared mentally incompetent by a court.

Illiterate voters are entitled to receive assistance in marking their ballots. Minority-language voters in jurisdictions with statutorily prescribed minority concentrations are entitled to have elections conducted in the minority language as well as English. Disabled voters are entitled to accessible polling places. Voters absent on election days or unable to go to the polls are generally entitled under state law to vote by absentee ballot.

The constitution guarantees citizens that their votes will be of equal value under the 'one person, one vote' rule.

Senate: The Senate consists of 2 member from each state, chosen by popular vote for 6 years, one-third retiring or seeking re-election every 2 years. Senators must be no less than 30 years of age; must have been citizens of the USA for 9 years, and be residents in the states for which they are chosen. The Senate has complete freedom to initiate legislation, except revenue bills (which must originate in the House of Representatives); it may, however, amend or reject any legislation originating in the lower house. The Senate is also entrusted with the power of giving or withholding its 'advice and consent' to the ratification of all treaties initiated by the President with foreign Powers, a two-thirds majority of senators present being required for approval. (However, it has no control over 'international executive agreements' made by the President with foreign governments; such 'agreements' cover a wide range and are more numerous than formal treaties.) It also has the power of confirming or rejecting major appointments to office made by the President, but it has no direct control over the appointment by the President of 'personal representatives' or 'personal envoys' on missions abroad. Members of the Senate constitute a High Court of Impeachment, with power, by a two-thirds vote, to remove from office and disqualify any civil officer of the USA impeached by the House of Representatives, which has the sole power of impeachment.

The Senate has 16 Standing Committees to which all bills are referred for study, revision or rejection. The House of Representatives has 22 such committees. In both Houses each Standing Committee has a chairman and a majority representing the majority party of the whole House; each has numerous sub-committees. The jurisdictions of these Committees correspond largely to those of the appropriate executive departments and agencies. Both Houses also have a few select or special Committees with limited duration; there were (1992) 4 Joint Senate-House Committees.

House of Representatives: The House of Representatives consists of 435 members elected every second year. The number of each state's representatives is determined by the decennial census, in the absence of specific Congressional legislation affecting the basis. The states, in 1992, had the following representatives:

Alabama	7	Indiana	10	Nebraska	3	South Carolina	6
Alaska	1	Iowa	6	Nevada	2	South Dakota	1
Arizona	5	Kansas	5	New Hampshire	2	Tennessee	9
Arkansas	4	Kentucky	7	New Jersey	14	Texas	27
California	45	Louisiana	8	New Mexico	3	Utah	3
Colorado	6	Maine	2	New York	34	Vermont	1
Connecticut	6	Maryland	8	North Carolina	11	Virginia	10
Delaware	1	Massachusetts	11	North Dakota	1	Washington	8
Florida	19	Michigan	18	Ohio	21	West Virginia	4
Georgia	10	Minnesota	8	Oklahoma	6	Wisconsin	9
Hawaii	2	Mississippi	5	Oregon	5	Wyoming	1
Idaho	2	Missouri	9	Pennsylvania	23		
Illinois	22	Montana	2	Rhode Island	2		

Following population changes reported in the 1990 census the following are the changed representations as of Jan. 1993.

Arizona, 6 (+1); California, 52 (+7); Florida, 23 (+4); Georgia, 11 (+1); Illinois, 20 (-2); Iowa, 5 (–1); Kansas, 4 (–1); Kentucky, 6 (–1); Louisiana, 7 (–1); Massachusetts, 10 (–1); Michigan, 16 (–2); Montana, 1 (–1); New Jersey, 13 (–1); New York, 31 (–3); North Carolina, 12 (+1); Ohio, 19 (–2); Pennsylvania, 21 (–2); Texas, 30 (+3); Virginia, 11 (+1); Washington, 9 (+1).

The constitution requires congressional districts within each state to be substantially equal in population. Final decisions on congressional district boundaries are taken by the state legislatures and governors. By custom the representative lives in the district from which he is elected.

Representatives must be not less than 25 years of age, citizens of the USA for 7 years and residents in the state from which they are chosen. The District of Columbia, Guam, American Samoa and the Virgin Islands have one non-voting delegate each. The House also admits a 'resident commissioner' from Puerto Rico, who has the right to speak on any subject and to make motions, but not to vote; he is elected in the same manner as the representatives but for a 4-year term. Each of the two Houses of Congress is sole 'judge of the elections, returns and qualifications of its own members'; and each of the Houses may, with the concurrence of two-thirds, expel a member. The period usually termed 'a Congress' in legislative language continues for 2 years, terminating at noon on 3 Jan.

The salary of a senator is $135,100 per annum, with tax-free expense allowance and allowances for travelling expenses and for clerical hire. The salary of the Speaker of the House of Representatives is $160,000 per annum, with a taxable allowance. The salary of a Member of the House is $125,100.

No senator or representative can, during the time for which he is elected, be appointed to any *civil* office under authority of the USA which shall have been created or the emoluments of which shall have been increased during such time; and no person holding *any* office under the USA can be a member of either House during his continuance in office. No religious text may be required as a qualification to any office or public trust under the USA or in any state.

The 102nd Congress (1991–93) was constituted (Feb. 1992) as follows: Senate, 57 Democrats, 43 Republicans; House of Representatives, 267 Democrats, 167 Republicans, 1 independent.

Indians: By an Act passed on 2 June 1924 full citizenship was granted to all Indians born in the USA, though those remaining in tribal units were still under special federal jurisdiction. Those remaining in tribal units constitute from one-half to three-fourths of the Indian population. The Indian Reorganization Act of 1934 gave the tribal Indians, at their own option, substantial opportunities of self-government and the establishment of self-controlled corporate enterprises empowered to borrow money and buy land, machinery and equipment; these corporations are controlled by democratically elected tribal councils. Recently a trend towards releasing Indians from federal supervision has resulted in legislation terminating supervision over specific tribes. In 1988 the federal government recognized that it had a special relationship with, and a trust responsibility for, 307 federally-recognized Indian entities in continental USA and some 200 tribal entities in Alaska. Indian lands (1991) amounted to 52,092,247 acres, of which 41,868,582 was tribally owned and 10,233,665 in trust allotments. Indian lands are held free of taxes. Total Indian population at the 1990 census was 1,959,000, of which Oklahoma, Arizona, California and New Mexico accounted for 832,466.

State and Local Government: The Union comprises 13 original states, 7 states which were admitted without having been previously organized as territories, and 30 states which had been territories—50 states in all. Each state has its own constitution (which the USA guarantees shall be republican in form), deriving its authority, not from Congress, but from the people of the state. Admission of states into the Union has been granted by special Acts of Congress, either (1) in the form of 'enabling Acts' providing for the drafting and ratification of a state constitution by the people, in which case the territory becomes a state as soon as the conditions are fulfilled, or (2) accepting a constitution already framed, and at once granting admission.

Each state is provided with a legislature of two Houses (except Nebraska, which since 1937 has had a single-chamber legislature), a governor and other executive officials, and a judicial system. Both Houses of the legislature are elective, but the senators (having larger electoral districts usually covering 2 or 3 counties compared with the single county or, in some states, the town, which sends 1 representative to the Lower House) are less numerous than the representatives, while in 38 states their terms are 4 years; in 12 states the term is 2 years. Of the 4-year senates, Illinois, Montana and New Jersey provide for two 4-year terms and one 2-year term in each decade. Terms of the lower houses are usually shorter; in 45 states, 2 years.

Members of both Houses are paid at the same rate, which varies from $200 a year in New Hampshire to $57,500 a year in New York. The trend is towards annual sessions of state legislatures; in 1992, 43 met annually (in 1939, only 4), and 7 (Arkansas, Kentucky, Montana, Nevada, North Dakota, Oregon and Texas) biennially.

The Governor has power to summon an extraordinary session, but not to dissolve or adjourn. The duties of the two Houses are similar, but in many states money bills must be introduced first in the Lower House. The Senate sits as a court for the trial of officials impeached by the other House, and often has power to confirm or reject appointments made by the Governor.

State legislatures are competent to deal with all matters not reserved for the federal government by the federal constitution nor specifically prohibited by the federal or state constitutions. Among their powers are the determination of the qualifications for the right of suffrage, and the control of all elections to public office, including elections of members of Congress and electors of President and Vice-President; the criminal law, both in its enactment and in its execution, with unimportant exceptions, and the administration of prisons; the civil law, including all matters pertaining to the possession and transfer of, and succession to, property; marriage and divorce, and all other civil relations; the chartering and control of all manufacturing, trading, transportation and other corporations, subject only to the right of Congress to regulate commerce passing from one state to another; labour; education; charities; licensing; fisheries within state waters, and game laws (apart from the hunting of migratory birds, which is a federal concern under treaties with Canada and Mexico). Taxes on income were left to the states until 1913, when the 16th amendment authorized the imposition of federal taxes on income without regard to apportionment.

The Governor is elected by direct vote of the people over the whole state. His term of office varies in the several states from 2 to 4 years, and his salary from $35,000 (Arkansas) to $130,000 (New York). His duty is to see to the faithful administration of the law, and he has command of the military forces of the state. He may recommend measures but does not present bills to the legislature. In some states he presents estimates. In all but one of the states (North Carolina) the Governor has a veto upon legislation, which may, however, be overridden by the two Houses, in some states by a simple majority, in others by a three-fifths or twothirds majority. In some states the Governor, on his death or resignation, is succeeded by a Lieut.-Governor who was elected at the same time and has been presiding over the state Senate. In several states the Speaker of the Lower House succeeds the Governor.

The chief officials by whom the administration of state affairs is carried on (secretaries, treasurers, members of boards of commissioners, etc.) are usually chosen by the people at the general state elections for terms similar to those for which governors hold office.

Local Government. The chief unit of local government is the county, of which there were (1992) 2,994 with definite functions; in addition, Rhode Island has 5 'counties' which have no functions; Alaska does not have counties but 25 divisions and, since Oct. 1960, there has been no active county government in Connecticut. Louisiana has 64 'parishes'. The counties maintain public order through the sheriff and his deputies, who may, in a crisis, be drawn temporarily from willing citizens; in many states the counties maintain the smaller local highways; other functions are the granting of licences and the apportionment and collection of taxes. In a few states they also manage the schools.

The unit of local government in New England is the rural township, governed directly by the voters, who assemble annually or oftener if necessary, and legislate in local affairs, levy taxes, make appropriations and appoint and instruct the local officials (selectmen, clerk, school-committee, etc.). Townships are grouped to form counties. Where cities exist, the township government is superseded by the city government.

The **District of Columbia,** ceded by the State of Maryland for the purposes of government in 1791, is the seat of the US Government. It includes the city of Washington, and embraces a land area of 61 sq. miles. The Reorganization Plan No. 3 of 1967 instituted a Mayor Council form of government with appointed officers. In 1973 an elected Mayor and elected councillors were introduced; in 1974 they received power to legislate in local matters. Congress retains power to enact legislation and to veto or supersede the Council's acts. Since 1961 citizens have had the right to vote in national elections. On 23 Aug. 1978 the Senate approved a constitutional amendment giving the District full voting representation in Congress. This has still to be ratified.

The **Commonwealth of Puerto Rico, American Samoa, Guam and the Virgin Islands** each have a local legislature, whose acts may be modified or annulled by Congress, though in practice this has seldom been done. Puerto Rico since its attainment of commonwealth status on 25 July 1952, enjoys practically complete self-government, including the election of its governor and other officials. The conduct of foreign relations, however, is still a federal function and federal bureaux and agencies still operate in the island.

General supervision of territorial administration is exercised by the Office of Territories in the Department of Interior.

Congress and the Nation, 4 vols., Congressional Quarterly, Washington, from 1965.—*Congressional Ethics,* Rev. ed., 1980.—*Congressional Quarterly Almanac,* annual
Constitution of the US, National and State. 2 vols. [with subsequent amendments]. Dobbs Ferry, 1962
Political profiles. 5 vols. New York, from 1978

DEFENCE. The President is C.-in-C. of the Army, Navy and Air Force.

The National Security Act of 1947 provides for the unification of the Army, Navy and Air Forces under a single Secretary of Defense with cabinet rank. The President is also advised by a National Security Council and the Office of Civil and Defense Mobilization.

The major components of the Department of Defense are the Office of the Secretary of Defense and the Joint Chiefs of Staff, who provide immediate staff assistance and advice to the Secretary; the departments of the Army, Navy and Air Force, each separately organized under a civilian head (not of cabinet rank); and the unified and specified commands.

Army. *Secretary of the Army:* Michael P. W. Stone.

Central Administration. The Secretary of the Army is the head of the Department of the Army. Subject to the authority of the President as C.-in-C. and of the Secretary of Defense, he is responsible for all affairs of the Department.

The Secretary of the Army is assisted by the Under Secretary of the Army, 5 Assistant Secretaries of the Army (Civil Works, Financial Management, Installations, Logistics and Environment, Manpower and Reserve Affairs, Research, Development and Acquisition), General Counsel, Administrative Assistant, Director for Information Systems for Command, Control, Communications and Computers, Inspector General, Auditor General, Chief of Legislative Liaison, Chief of Public Affairs, Director for Small and Disadvantaged Business Utilization, Chairman of the Army Reserve Forces Policy Committee and the Army Staff headed by the Chief of Staff, US Army. The Office of the Under Secretary of the Army includes a Deputy Under Secretary (Operations Research).

The Chief of Staff, Army, in his role as a member of the Joint Chiefs of Staff, takes part in the planning and supervision of the operational forces under the command of the Commanders-in-Chief. The Vice Chief of Staff assists and advises the Chief of Staff.

The Army General Staff is the principal element of the Army Staff and includes the Offices of the Chief of Staff, Deputy Chief of Staff for Operations and Plans, Deputy Chief of Staff for Personnel, Deputy Chief of Staff for Logistics, and Deputy Chief of Staff for Intelligence. Other elements of the Army Staff are the offices of the Judge Advocate General, Surgeon General, Chief of Chaplains, Chief, Army Reserve, Chief, National Guard Bureau, and Chief of Engineers.

The Army consists of the Active Army, the Army National Guard of the US, the Army Reserve and civilian workforce; and all persons appointed to or enlisted into the Army without component; and all persons serving under call or conscription, including members of the National Guard of the States, etc., when in the service of the US. The strength of the Active Army was (1992) 731,700 (including 82,400 women).

The US Army Forces Command, with headquarters at Fort McPherson, Georgia, commands the Third US Army; five continental US Armies, and all assigned Active Army and US Army Reserve troop units in the continental US, Alaska, Panama, the Commonwealth of Puerto Rico, and the Virgin Islands of the USA. The headquarters of the continental US Armies are: First US Army, Fort George G. Meade, Maryland; Second US Army, Fort Gillem, Georgia; Fourth US Army, Fort Sheridan, Illinois; Fifth US Army, Fort Sam Houston, Texas; Sixth US Army, Presidio of San Francisco, California. The US Army Training and Doctrine Command, with headquarters at Fort Monroe, Virginia, co-ordinates and integrates the total combat development effort of the Army as well as developing, managing, establishing and verifying the training of individuals of the US Army and authorized foreign nationals. The US Army Health Services Command, with headquarters at Fort Sam Houston, Texas, provides health services in the continental US for the US Army and provides professional education and training for medical personnel of the US Army and authorized foreign national personnel. The US Army Materiel Command, with headquarters in Alexandria, Virginia, is responsible for US Army activities dealing with equipment development, procurement, delivery, supply and maintenance. The US Army Information Systems Communications Command, with headquarters at Fort Huachuca, Arizona, provides worldwide communication automation support to the Department of the Army and supports the Defense Communications Systems. The US Army Military District of Washington, with headquarters at Fort McNair, Washington, D.C., provides support to the Department of the Army and the Department of Defense at the seat of Government. The US Army Space Command, with headquarters in Colorado Springs, Colorado, is the Army component to the US Space Command.

Nearly 40% of the Active Army is deployed outside the continental US. Several divisions, most of which are located in the USA, keep equipment in the Federal Republic of Germany and can be flown there in 48–72 hours. Headquarters of US Seventh and Eighth Armies are in Europe and Korea respectively.

Operational Commands and Weapons. The larger commands are the theater army and corps. The typical theater army may consist of a variable number of corps composed of combat forces of armour, infantry, air defense artillery, aviation and field artillery units; combat support forces of aviation, engineer, intelligence and signal elements; and combat service support forces. A typical corps consists of a variable number and mixture of infantry, mechanized infantry, armoured, air assault, or airborne divisions; one or more separate infantry, mechanized infantry or armoured brigades; one or more armoured cavalry regiments; corps artillery (155-mm howitzer, 203-mm howitzer, multiple launch rocket system (MLRS), *Lance* missile battalions); corps air defense brigade (*Hawk, Chaparral, Patriot* and *Avenger* battalions), corps aviation brigade and combat support and combat service support forces.

US Army Divisions have a common base (containing command, divisional artillery, air defense artillery, combat support and combat service support units) aviation brigade, and a varying mixture of combat manoeuvre battalions (usually 9 or 10 in number in 3 brigades) to make up airborne, infantry, armoured, mechanized infantry and air assault divisions. Divisions can in this way be 'tailored' to fit a variety of strategic or tactical situations. An infantry division, with about 16,500 soldiers, may have 8 infantry battalions, an armoured battalion and a mechanized infantry battalion; a mechanized infantry division, with about 17,300 soldiers, may have 5 mechanized infantry battalions and 5 armoured battalions; an armoured division, with about 17,300 soldiers, may have 4 mechanized infantry battalions and 6 armoured battalions; an airborne division, with 13,100 soldiers, may have 9 infantry (airborne) battalions. The air assault division is a highly specialized force capable of battlefield helicopter operations for infantry, field artillery, air defense artillery and necessary support forces.

The 10,800-man light infantry divisions consist of 9 infantry battalions and offer rapid strategic force projection. Light divisions can operate in all environments and are general purpose forces. Special operations forces consist of special forces, rangers, special operations aviation psychological operations, and civil affairs units. The units are designed, equipped, and trained for special missions.

Small arms include the M-9 (9mm pistol), the M-16 series rifle and the M-249 Squad Automatic Weapon both of which fire a 5·56-mm cartridge. The standard generalpurpose machine-gun is the M-60 (23 lb.; 550 rounds of 7·62-mm per minute). Infantry weapons also include M-203 grenade launcher attachment for the M-16A1 rifle, which fire a 40-mm grenade up to 400 metres, the *TOW* and *Dragon* anti-tank missile systems, and the M-72 rocket, a light anti-tank weapon.

Combat vehicles of the US Army are the tank, armoured personnel carrier, infantry fighting vehicle, and the armoured command vehicle. The first-line tanks are the M1A1 Abrams tank with a 120mm main gun, and both the M1 Abrams and the M60A3 tanks with 105-mm main armament. The standard armoured infantry personnel carrier is the M2 Bradley Fighting Vehicle (BFV), which is replacing the older M113. Both carry a mechanized infantry squad, but the BFV mounts a 25-mm Bushmaster gun and *TOW* missile launchers. The M3 version of the BFV is being used as the ground scout vehicle in armoured cavalry regiments, armoured and mechanized infantry divisional cavalry squadrons and in scout platoons of armoured and mechanized infantry battalions.

The approved calibres of artillery are: Light, 105-mm howitzer, medium 155-mm howitzer; the heavy, 203-mm howitzer. The Multiple Launch Rocket System (MLRS) is a 227-mm rapid fire rocket system used in a non-nuclear counterfire role. The 107-mm mortar, the 81-mm mortar and the 60-mm mortar are used by the combat manoeuvre elements. The 120mm mortar will replace the 107mm mortar. The *TOW* is the primary anti-tank weapon. Forward-area air-defence weapons, including the *Chaparral, Stinger* and *Avenger* 20-mm gun, provide the capability of low-altitude defence against high-performance aircraft.

The Army has three categories of missiles—surface-to-surface (field artillery) and surface-to-air (air defence artillery) and anti-tank. Surface-to-surface missiles are: *Pershing II*, terminally-guided, nuclear warhead, range about 1,000 miles (1,800 km) operational (being phased out under the terms of the Intermediate Nuclear Forces Treaty between the US and USSR); *Lance*, guided, nuclear warhead, storable, liquid propellant, operational. Surface-to-air missiles, for air defence, are: *Patriot*, guided, conventional warhead, operational; *Hawk*, homing type, low-to-mid-altitude, field operational (product improvements continue to improve the effectiveness of the system); *Chaparral*, infra-red homing, low-altitude, forward area, operational (improvements to the basic system are under development); *Stinger*, hand-held or mobile-launched, infra-red homing, low-altitude, forward area, operational. Anti-tank missiles are: *TOW*, tube launched, optically tracked, wire guided, anti-armour, forward area, operational; *Hellfire*, laser-guided, anti-armour, operational and *Dragon*, wire-guided, medium anti-armour, forward area, operational.

The Army employs rotary- and fixed-wing aircraft as organic elements of its ground formations where their use is required on a full-time basis and their immediate and constant availability is essential. The front line commander exploits the benefits of aviation technology to perform traditional land battle tasks in the third dimension. This concept of airmobility for ground formation utilizes aerial vehicles as a highly integrated team to perform all five functions of land combat: reconnaissance, command and control, logistics and that inseparable combination, firepower and manoeuvre.

The Army has over 8,000 aircraft, all but about 500 of them helicopters. The principal types are 3,000 UH-1 Iroquois Huey and 1,200 UH-60 Black Hawk utility helicopters, 1,600 OH-58 Kiowa observation helicopters, 1,000 AH-1 Cobra and 800 AH-64 Apache attack helicopters, and 450 CH-47 Chinook cargo helicopters.

Enlistment, Terms of Service. Since 1974 the Army has operated an 'all volunteer' system making it, in effect, an all-regular force both regular and reserve components. Terms of service may be 2, 3, 4, 5 or 6 years. Men and women who enlist incur an 8-year obligation and must serve in the reserve components any part of the period not served on active duty. Over 95% of recruits enlisting in the Army have a high school education, over 50% of the Army is married, and 11·4% of the active force is filled by women. Women serve in both combat support and combat service support units.

The National Guard is a reserve military component with both a state and a federal rôle. Enlistment is voluntary. The members are recruited by each state, but are equipped and paid by the federal government (except when performing state missions). Training is supervised by the active Army (FORSCOM), and unit organization parallels that for the active army; training facilities are made available by the USA and each state. As the organized militia of the several states, the District of Columbia, Puerto Rico and the Territories of the Virgin Islands and Guam, the Guard may be called into service for local emergencies by the chief executives in those jurisdictions; and may be called into federal service by the President to thwart invasion or rebellion or to enforce federal law. In its role as a reserve component of the Army, the Guard is subject to the order of the President in the event of national emergency. In 1992 it numbered 446,700 (including 30,400 women).

The Army Reserve is designed to supply qualified and experienced units and individuals in an emergency. US Army Forces Command is charged with the command, support and training supervision of US Army Reserve units. Members of units are assigned to the Ready Reserve, which is subject to call by the President in case of national emergency without declaration of war by Congress. The Standby Reserve and the Retired Reserve may be called only after declaration of war or national emergency by Congress. In 1992 the Ready Reserve numbered 654,300 (including 102,400 women).

Coker, C., *US Military Power in the 1980s*. London, 1984
Kinnell, S., *Military History of the United States: An Annotated Bibliography*. Oxford and Santa Barbara, 1986

Navy. *Secretary of the Navy:* H. Lawrence Garrett, III.

The Department of the Navy is administered under the Secretary of Defense by the Secretary of the Navy, assisted by the Under Secretary; 4 Assistant Secretaries, for Financial Management; for Shipbuilding and Logistics; for Manpower and Reserve Affairs; and for Research, Engineering and Systems, as well as by the Chief of Naval Operations and the Commandant of the Marine Corps. The 3 divisions of the Department of the Navy are:

Navy Department, comprised of staff offices of the Secretary for Legislative Affairs, Information, the Judge Advocate General, Auditor General, Program Appraisal, General Counsel, Naval Research and Comptroller; offices of the Chief of Naval Operations which include the Vice Chief, the Assistant Vice Chief/ Director of Naval Administration, 3 Assistant Chiefs, 5 Deputy Chiefs and 6 Directors; Naval Inspector General; the Surgeon General; Bureau of Naval Personnel; and Headquarters U.S. Marine Corps.

The Shore Establishment comprises commands dealing with air, naval acquisition support, space and warfare systems, facilities engineering, sea (including ordnance) and supply systems and other commands: Space, Medical, Education and Training, Data Automation, Telecommunications, Intelligence, Oceanography, Legal Service, Security Group, and Investigative Service; as well as supporting establishment of the Marine Corps and Marine Corps Reserve.

The Operating Forces are the Military Sealift Command, U.S. Naval Forces Europe, the Atlantic and Pacific Fleets including Fleet Marine Forces; operating forces of the Marine Corps, the Mine Warfare Command, Operational Test and Evaluation Force, Naval Forces Southern and Central Commands, and the Naval Reserve Forces.

Major shore activities include 8 shipyards, 27 air stations and facilities, 2 amphibious bases, 5 submarine bases and 13 naval stations and bases.

The authorized budget for the Department of the Navy (which includes funding both for the Navy and Marine Corps) for current and recent fiscal years: 1988, $100,281m.; 1989, $97,407m.; 1990, $101,670m.; 1991, $92,200m.; 1992, $84,800m.; and the budget request for 1993 is $84,600m. Funding, personnel and fleet strength are now all starting to decline from the highs of the late 1980s as the so-called 'Peace Dividend' starts to be taken.

The Navy personnel total in 1991 was 570,500, including 57,000 women who are eligible to serve at sea in support ships. The U.S. Marine Corps totalled 194,000 (9,200 women). These numbers are planned to reduce to 510,000 and 171,000 respectively by late 1995.

The operational strength of the Navy at the end of the year indicated:

Category	1984	1985	1986	1987	1988	1989	1990	1991
Strategic Submarines	35	37	36	36	36	36	34	24
Nuclear Attack Submarines	94	98	97	96	95	97	93	89
Diesel Submarines	4	4	4	4	4	3	nil	nil
Aircraft Carriers [1]	13	13	14	14	14	14	14	12
Amphibious Carriers	12	12	12	12	12	13	13	13
Battleships	2	2	3	3	4	4	2	nil
Cruisers	29	29	31	36	38	41	44	46
Destroyers	68	68	68	68	68	68	58	51
Frigates	94	101	109	116	112	100	98	90

[1] Omits one Aircraft Carrier in a 3-year refit, and the USS *Enterprise* in a 4-year refit.

Ships in inactive reserve are not included; but those serving as Naval Reserve Force training ships are. Amphibious Carriers are those ships of the Wasp, Tarawa, and Iwo Jima classes capable of operating AV-8 Harrier-type aircraft as well as helicopters.

A principal part of the US naval task is to deploy the seaborne leg of the United States' strategic deterrent 'triad': This task is performed by the squadrons deploying nuclear-powered strategic ballistic missile-carrying submarines (SSBN), the strength and armament of which is as follows:

Strategic Submarines

Class	No.	Tonnage (in 1,000)	Speed	Missiles	Other Weapons
Ohio	12	19·00	24	4 with 24 Trident D-5	Torpedoes
Benjamin Franklin	6	8·12	25	8 with 24 Trident C-4	Torpedoes
James Madison	6	8·12	25	16 Trident C-4	Torpedoes

The Madison and Franklin classes comprise the first generation of SSBN, most of which were initially equipped with Polaris missiles, with maximum range between 1,500 and 2,500 nautical miles. These missiles were replaced between 1970 and 1977 with Poseidon C-3 missiles of similar maximum range, but deploying greatly increased numbers of warheads (10 per missile). All Poseidon missiles were withdrawn from operational service in 1991. 12 of these submarines were modernized between 1978 and 1982 to carry the Trident-1 C-4 missile, which is of similar size to the Poseidon, but with a range of 4,000 nautical miles, and delivering 8 warheads per missile. The second generation Ohio class submarines, with a much larger hull, are designed to deploy the Trident-2 D-5 missile, with a maximum range of 6,500 nautical miles, carrying a similar number of warheads but with substantially improved targetting accuracy. Sea trials of this weapon began in March 1989 and the first submarine deployed it operationally in March 1990. The first 8 ships will be retrofitted with the Trident-2 in due course, and a total of 20 of this larger class, completing at one per year, is anticipated.

The listed total of 89 nuclear-powered attack submarines (SSN) comprises 48 of the Los Angeles class (7,040 tonnes) in three major batches: A basic design (31 ships) completed 1976-85, a small group of 8 ships additionally equipped with vertical-launch missile tubes for Tomahawk cruise missiles completed 1985-89, and the current building programme of which 9 ships have been completed, known as 'Improved' Los Angeles incorporating cruise missile tubes, a new command system, and several important additional technical modifications. There are also 35 Sturgeon class (5,040 tonnes) completed 1967-75, 4 Permit class (4,370 tonnes) completed 1963-67, and 2 others. The last remaining diesel submarines, built in the late 1950s, have been decommissioned.

The table below lists the principal operational surface ships:

Aircraft Carriers

Completed	Name	Tonnage (in 1,000)	Speed	Aircraft
Nimitz Class				
1989	George Washington	97·8	33[1]	All carriers, except *Roosevelt*
1986	Theodore Roosevelt	97·8	33[1]	and *Midway* carry a standard
1982	Carl Vinson	92·9	33[1]	Air Wing of 86 aircraft:-
1977	Eisenhower	92·9	33[1]	24 F/A-18 Hornet fighter/
1975	Nimitz	92·9	33[1]	bombers.
				10 A-6E Intruder bombers.
Kitty Hawk Kennedy Class				24 F-14 Tomcat fighters.
1968	John F Kennedy	82·5	32	4 EA-6B Prowler
1965	America	81·0	33	electronic warfare aircraft.
1962	Constellation	83·1	34	4 E-2C Hawkeye airborne early
1961	Kitty Hawk	82·4	34	warning.
1962	Enterprise	91·5	33[1]	10 S-3A Viking anti-submarine
				aircraft.
Forrestal Class				4 KA-6D Tankers.
1959	Independence	81·9	33	6 SH-3A Sea King
1957	Ranger	82·5	33	anti-submarine helicopters.
1956	Saratoga	81·7	33	*Roosevelt* carries an experi-
1955	Forrestal	80·5	33	mental air wing.

[1] Indicates nuclear propulsion

Amphibious Carriers

Com-pleted	Name	Tonnage (in 1,000)	Speed	Aircraft
Wasp Class (LHD)				
1989	Wasp	41·2	23	6-8 AV-8 Harriers and up to 42 helicopters.
Tarawa Class (LHA)				
1981	Pelileu			
1980	Nassau			Normal Air group is 30 aircraft, e.g.
1978	Belleau Wood	40·0	24	6 AV-8 Harriers, and 24 mixed helicopters,
1977	Saipan			principally CH-53E, CH-46 and gunships.
1976	Tarawa			
Iwo Jima Class (LPH)				
1970	Inchon			
1968	New Orleans			
1965	Tripoli			
1965	Guam	18·8	21	4 AV-8 plus maximum of 16 mixed
1963	Guadalcanal			helicopters, or 20 helicopters only.
1962	Okinawa			
1961	Iwo Jima			

Cruisers

Com-pleted	Name	Tonnage (in 1,000)	Speed	Main Armament	Aircraft
Ticonderoga (Aegis) Class					
1991	Hue City				
1991	Chosin				
1991	Gettysburg				
1991	Cowpens				
1990	Monterey				
1989	Chancellorsville				
1989	Normandy			Standard SM-2 ER SAM,	
1989	Princeton			2 x 2 launchers in first	
1989	Philippine Sea			5 ships; 2 x 61-cell	2 SH-60B Sea-
1988	Lake Champlain	9·6	32	vertical launcher systems	hawk LAMPS-III
1988	San Jacinto			for Standard, Tomahawk	helicopters.
1987	Leyte Gulf			and Harpoon in remainder.	
1987	Antietam			2 x 127 mm guns in all.	
1987	Mobile Bay				
1986	Bunker Hill				
1986	Thomas S. Gates				
1986	Valley Forge				
1985	Vincennes				
1984	Yorktown				
1983	Ticonderoga				
Virginia Class [1]				2 x 2 Standard SM-2 SAM.	
1980	Arkansas			8 Tomahawk cruise missiles.	
1978	Mississippi	11·45	31	8 Harpoon anti-ship and	None
1977	Texas			ASROC anti-submarine	
1976	Virginia			missiles. 2 x 127 mm guns.	
California Class [1]					
1974	South Carolina	10·7	31	As for *Virginia*, without	None
1973	California			Tomahawk.	
Miscellaneous [1]				1 or 2 x 2 SM-2 ER SAMs.	
1961	Long Beach	17·4	30	ASROC anti-submarine	None
1967	Truxtun	8·9	30	missiles. 8 x Tomahawk	
1962	Bainbridge	9·25	30	(Long Beach only).	

[1] Indicates nuclear-powered.

Completed	Name	Tonnage (in 1,000)	Speed	Main Armament	Aircraft
Belknap Class					
1967	Biddle				
1967	Sterett				
1967	Horne			Standard SM-2 ER SAMs	1 SH-2F Sea-
1966	Fox			ASROC anti-submarine	sprite LAMPS-I
1966	Wm. H. Standley	8·2	33	missiles	helicopter.
1966	Jouett			8 Harpoon missiles	
1966	Wainwright			1 x 127 mm Gun.	
1965	Jos. L. Daniels				
1964	Belknap				
Leahy Class					
1964	Reeves				
1964	Rich. K. Turner				
1963	Dale				
1963	Halsey			2 x 2 SM-2 ER SAMs	
1963	England	8·3	32	ASROC anti-submarine	None
1963	Gridley			missiles	
1963	Worden			8 Harpoon missiles	
1963	Harry E. Yarnell				
1962	Leahy				

[1] Indicates nuclear-powered.

The target of '15 deployable carriers' set in 1986 was officially amended to 14 as a result of budgetary pressure in 1989, and subsequently to 12. Of the 14 listed in the table, *Constellation* is undergoing a three-year 'service life extension' refit and so does not count to the authorized deployable total. As mentioned above, neither does *Enterprise*. The *George Washington* commissioned in Nov. 1989, the *Coral Sea* was de-activated in April 1990 and *Midway*, having been retained for Middle East operations, was retired in 1991. The training carrier *Lexington* has been decommissioned and replaced by the USS *Forrestal*.

The Wasp (LHD-1), and the 5 ships of the Tarawa (LHA-1) class are in many respects equivalent to the vertical/short take off and landing aircraft carriers in other principal navies and are capable of sea control tasks. The 7 ships of the Iwo Jima class are also capable of operating vertical/short take-off and landing aircraft but do not normally do so. All are, however, configured, trained and equipped primarily for amphibious operations. All 4 battleships of the Iowa class have been reduced to reserve.

In addition to the previously listed principal surface ships, there are 20 guided-missile destroyers, 31 anti-submarine destroyers of the Spruance class, 51 guided-missile frigates of the Oliver Hazard Perry class, 39 other frigates, 6 hydrofoil missile patrol craft and 24 inshore patrol craft. Mine warfare has been somewhat neglected over the past decades, but two new classes are now building. There are now 8 new mine countermeasure vessels of the Avenger class in service, and the first of a new Osprey class coastal minehunter building, together with 16 old ocean minesweepers (completed between 1954 and 1958, mostly employed on reserve training).

Amphibious capability comprises some 65 ships. In addition to the 13 amphibious aircraft carriers listed above, there are 2 amphibious command ships, 25 dock landing ships, 20 tank landing ships and 5 amphibious transports. There are 85 amphibious craft including 30 air-cushion landing craft (hovercraft) and 55 others, and several hundred minor personnel and vehicle transports. The total oceanic lift capability of the amphibious forces amounts to over 50,000 men, 1,300 main battle tank equivalents, and operating facilities for about 180 helicopters.

Specially trained and equipped amphibious expeditionary forces are provided by the US Marine Corps, some 194,000 strong, which although administratively part of the Department of the Navy, ranks as a separate armed service, with the Commandant of the Corps serving in his own right as a member of the Joint Chiefs of Staff. The Marine Corps is organized into 3 divisions each some 55,000 strong, which are subdivided into Marine Expeditionary Brigades (18,000) and Marine Expeditionary Units (some 6,000 strong). In peace time Marine Expeditionary Units are permanently deployed afloat in the Eastern Atlantic/Mediterranean and the West Pacific/Indian Ocean. The principal equipment of the US Marine Corps consists of 700 M-60A1 and 40 M-1A1 tanks, 420 LAV-25 armoured infantry fighting vehicles, 1,200 armoured personnel carriers, and over 1,000 artillery pieces of calibres between 105 mm and 203 mm. Additional heavy equipment for US-based Marine forces units, beyond that which can be embarked in the amphibious shipping, is provided in 2 squadrons each of 13 large cargo ships prepositioned at Diego Garcia (Indian Ocean) and in the Mediterranean. In addition the Corps includes an autonomous aviation element numbering some 500 combat aircraft and 540 helicopters. There are 250 F/A 18 Hornet, 250 AV-8B Harriers, 60 A-4 Skyhawks, 60 A-6 attack and electronic warfare, 60 KC-130 tankers, and a miscellany of other support and training aircraft. Helicopters include 200 CH-46E and 220 CH-53 transport, as well as 100 AH-1 Cobra attack helicopters of various types. Harriers and helicopters are normally employed afloat in the amphibious aircraft carriers and other suitable ships. The Hornets and other fixed wing aircraft are normally based ashore, but may be embarked in other aircraft carriers, given the operational need.

The Navy is provided with global, long-term sustainability through a force of some 56 underway replenishment ships, including 28 tankers, 4 multi-purpose fast replenishment ships, 11 stores ships and 13 ammunition ships. Second-line support is provided by 2 repair ships, 21 depot ships, 14 support tankers, 9 tugs, 2 hospital ships and 3 fast cargo vessels. Special purpose auxiliaries include 2 command ships, 21 ocean surveillance ships, 5 missile and space support ships, and 20 survey and oceanographic vessels. Of these 150 major auxiliaries, about half are operated by the civilian-manned Military Sealift Command. In addition there are some hundreds of minor auxiliaries, and several thousand service craft.

Major warship building yards involved in the current building programme are located at Groton, Conn. (submarines), Newport News, Va., (submarines and aircraft carriers), Pascagoula, Miss. (cruisers and amphibious ships), Bath, Me. (cruisers and destroyers) and New Orleans, La., (amphibious and auxiliary ships). No major ships are currently being built in west coast shipyards. The future construction programme is in some doubt due to budgetary restrictions.

Naval Aviation. The principal function of the naval aviation organization is to provide and train the 13 Air Wings maintained for service in the Aircraft Carriers. As shown in the ship tables, these usually consist of 80 fixed wing and 6 rotary wing aircraft. In addition, 2 carrier air wings are provided from the reserves, in some cases with slightly older aircraft. The main carrier-borne combat aircraft on inventory are 600 F-14 fighters, 240 A-6E Intruder attack aircraft, 500 F/A-18 Hornet dual-purpose fighter/attack aircraft and 160 S-3A Viking anti-submarine aircraft. Supporting roles are performed by 80 EA-6B electronic warfare aircraft, 90 E-2C Hawkeye airborne early warning aircraft, 60 KA-6D tankers, and 100 SH-3A Sea King helicopters for inner-zone anti-submarine defence. Helicopters held for embarkation in cruisers and below are of two types, the older SH-2F Seasprite LAMPS-I aircraft of which there are some 100 and the SH-60B Seahawk LAMPS-III of which there are 160. A different version of this latter aircraft, the SH-60F Oceanhawk is now in production as a replacement for the elderly Sea Kings in the Aircraft Carriers, and there are now 45 of these in service. The principal tasks of the shore-based elements of US naval aviation are maritime reconnaissance and anti-submarine warfare, for which there are holdings of about 370 P-3C Orion aircraft. Additional tasks include electronic warfare (12 EP-3), electronic intelligence (14 EA-3) and mine countermeasures for which 40 MH- and RH-53 helicopters are held. Finally there are some 650 training aircraft of types not previously mentioned, and 110 aircraft and 90 helicopters for transport and other miscellaneous duties.

Howarth, S., *To Shining Sea: a History of the United States Navy, 1775-1991*. London, 1991
Watson, B.W. and Watson, S.M. (eds.) *United States Navy: a Dictionary*. New York, 1991

The US Coast Guard operates under the Department of Transportation in time of peace and as a part of the Navy in time of war or when directed by the President. The act of establishment stated the Coast Guard 'shall be a military service and branch of the armed forces of the United States at all times'. The Coast Guard did operate as part of the Navy during the First and Second World Wars. It also had some units serving in Vietnam. It comprises 260 ships including cutters of destroyer, frigate, corvette and patrol vessel types, 3 powerful icebreakers, and various auxiliaries and tenders, as well as over 2,000 rescue and utility craft. It also maintains 74 fixed-wing aircraft and 155 helicopters. In the construction programme are 34 patrol boats. The active-duty workforce in 1991 was 36,906 personnel, including 27,801 enlisted men, 2,731 enlisted women, 6,708 male officers and 369 female officers. The reserve workforce was made up of 10,791 men and 1,344 women. The auxiliary workforce is comprised of 35,965 volunteer civilians that operate their own vessels on their own time and, for the most part at their own expense. The Auxiliary assists the Coast Guard in search and rescue missions and offers Courtesy Marine Examinations and Public Education courses ranging from boat handling to rules of the road.

The Coast Guard missions include maintenance of aids to navigation, boating safety, defence operations, environmental response (oil spills), ice operations, maritime law enforcement, marine inspection, marine licensing, marine science, port safety and security, search and rescue and waterways management. On an average day the Coast Guard saves 16 lives, assists 361 people, saves $2,500 in property, completes 154 search and rescue cases, responds to 23 oil or hazardous chemical spills, boards 90 large vessels for port safety checks, inspects 64 commercial vessels, investigates 17 marine accidents, seizes 421 pounds of marijuana, seizes 165 pounds of cocaine, and services 150 aids to navigation.

Air Force. *Secretary of the Air Force:* Donald B. Rice.

The Department of the Air Force was activated within the Department of Defense on 18 Sept. 1947, under the terms of the National Security Act of 1947. It is administered by a Secretary of the Air Force, assisted by an Under Secretary and 3 Assistant Secretaries (Space; Acquisition; and Manpower, Reserve Affairs and Logistics). The USAF, under the administration of the Department of the Air Force, is supervised by a Chief of Staff, who is a member of the Joint Chiefs of Staff. He is assisted by a Vice Chief of Staff, Assistant Vice Chief of Staff, and 4 Deputy Chiefs of Staff (Personnel; Programs and Resources; Plans and Operations; and Logistics and Engineering).

The USAF consists of active duty Air Force officers and enlisted personnel, civilian employees, the Air National Guard and the Air Force Reserve. The USAF is undergoing a major reorganization of its combat and transport forces as a result of the major political changes now going on in the world and of the need to reduce the national defence budget. This became effective on 1 Jan. 1992. For operational purposes the service is divided into 13 major commands, 16 separate operating agencies and 7 direct reporting units.

The bulk of the combat forces are now grouped in Air Combat Command, which controls strategic bombing, tactical strike, air defence and reconnaissance assets based in the United States. The new Air Mobility Command includes all long-range and tactical transports and in-flight refuelling tankers. Special Operations Command, formed in 1990, carries out covert missions, rescue and recovery operations.

The other major commands are the Air Force Systems Command, Air Force Logistics Command, Air Force Communications Command, Electronic Security Command, Air Training Command, Pacific Air Forces, Air Force Space Command, United States Air Forces in Europe, and Air University. The Pacific and European commands conduct, control and co-ordinate offensive and defensive air operations according to tasks assigned by their respective theatre commanders.

The separate operating agencies are the Air Force Accounting and Finance Center, Air Force Audit Agency, Air Force Commissary Service, Air Force Engineering and Services Center, Air Force Inspection and Safety Center, Air Force Intelligence Service, Air Force Office of Security Police, Air Force Military and Personnel Agency, Air Force Office of Medical Support, Air Force Management Engineering Agency, Air Force Service Information and News Center, Air Force Legal Services Center, Air Force Office of Special Investigations, Air Force Operational Test and Evaluation Center, Air Force Reserve, and Air Reserve Personnel

Center. Air Force direct reporting units are the Air Force Academy, Air National Guard, Air Force Technical Applications Center, Air Force District of Washington, D.C., Air Force Civilian Personnel Management Center and USAF Historical Research Center.

Of the fighter and interceptor aircraft in service, the F-15 Eagle, F-16 Fighting Falcon, F-111 and F-4 Phantom II fly faster than the speed of sound in level flight and can carry a variety of armament. The E-3 Sentry (AWACS) is a large long-range airborne warning and control aircraft; the EF-111A Raven is a radar jamming aircraft produced by conversion of the F-111A fighter. The subsonic A-7 Corsair II, the A-10 Thunderbolt and the AC-130H are close air support aircraft, while the F-117 is a 'Stealth' aircraft for high-precision strike missions. The OA-37 and the OV-10 are observation aircraft. Strategic bombers are the B-52 Stratofortress and the B-1B heavy bombers. The Strategic Air Command also operates the KC-10A Extender and the KC-135 Stratotanker for aerial refuelling and the U-2 and TR-1 for reconnaissance. Primary transports include the C-141 Starlifter the C-5 Galaxy and the turboprop-powered C-130 Hercules. Intercontinental ballistic missiles in USAF service are the Minuteman III and Peacekeeper.

In 1992, the Air Force had about 517,400 military personnel (including 73,600 women). The service operates approximately 9,400 aircraft in the active Air Force, the Air National Guard and the Air Force Reserve. Women have been authorized to fly combat aircraft since 1991.

INTERNATIONAL RELATIONS

Membership. The USA is a member of the UN, OAS, NATO, OECD and the Colombo Plan.

ECONOMY

Budget. The budget covers virtually all the programmes of federal government, including those financed through trust funds, such as for social security, Medicare and highway construction. Receipts of the Government include all income from its sovereign or compulsory powers; income from business-type or market-orientated activities of the Government is offset against outlays. Budget receipts and outlays (in $1m.):

Year ending 30 June	Receipts [2]	Outlays [2]	Surplus (+) or deficit (−)
1950	39,443	42,562	− 3,119
1960	92,492	92,191	+ 301
1970	192,807	195,649	− 2,842
1985 [1]	734,057	946,316	−212,260
1988	908,954	1,064,051	−155,097
1989	990,691	1,144,069	−153,378
1990	1,031,308	1,251,703	−220,395
1991 [3]	1,091,440	1,409,563	−317,745
1992 [3]	1,165,029	1,445,902	−280,873

[1] From 1977 the fiscal year changed from a 1 July–30 June basis to a 1 Oct.–30 Sept. basis.
[2] From 1970, revised to include Medicare premiums and collections.
[3] Estimates.

Budget receipts, by source, for fiscal years (in $1m.):

Source	1990 [1]	1991 [1]	1992 [2]
Individual income taxes	466,884	492,635	529,518
Corporation income taxes	93,507	95,866	101,913
Social insurance taxes and contributions	380,047	401,955	429,363
Excise taxes	35,345	44,810	47,768
Other	56,175	56,175	56,467
Total	1,031,308	1,091,440	1,165,029

[1] Includes off-budget receipts.   [2] Estimates.

Budget outlays, by function, for fiscal years (in $1,000m.):

Source	1990 [1]	1991 [1]	1992 [2]
National defence	299·3	298·9	295·2
International affairs	13·8	17·0	17·8
General science, space, and technology	14·4	15·8	17·5
Energy	2·4	2·6	3·7
Natural resources and environment	17·1	18·8	19·5
Agriculture	12·0	15·9	15·3
Commerce and housing credit	67·1	119·5	92·8
Transportation	29·5	31·5	32·7
Community and regional development	8·5	7·7	6·5
Education, training, employment and social services	38·5	42·8	45·5
Health	57·7	71·2	81·3
Medicare	98·1	104·4	113·7
Income security	147·3	173·2	184·8
Social Security	248·6	269·0	288·6
Veterans' benefits and services	29·1	31·5	33·0
Administration of justice	10·0	12·6	14·5
General government	10·7	11·2	13·2
Net interest	184·2	197·0	206·3
Allowances	…	8·2	4·7
Undistributed offsetting receipts	−36·6	−39·1	−40·8
Total budget outlays	1,251·7	1,409·6	1,445·9

[1] Includes outlays of off-budget Federal entities and programmes.   [2] Estimates.

Budget outlays, by agency, for fiscal years (in $1m.):

Agency	1990 [1]	1991 [1]	1992 [2]
Legislative branch	2,230	2,548	2,994
The Judiciary	1,641	2,056	2,341
Executive Office of the President	157	258	254
Funds appropriated to the President	10,087	11,254	12,044
Agriculture	46,012	55,432	55,691
Commerce	3,734	2,796	2,756
Defence—Military	289,755	287,451	283,045
Defence—Civil	24,975	26,415	28,231
Education	23,109	24,839	27,494
Energy	12,014	13,539	14,897
Health and Human Services, except Social Security	193,678	222,435	242,543
Health and Human Services, Social Security	244,998	263,837	282,785
Housing and Urban Development	20,167	23,473	24,297
Interior	5,796	6,386	6,475
Justice	6,507	8,689	10,042
Labor	25,316	34,503	34,759
State	3,979	4,306	4,509
Transportation	28,637	30,768	31,862
Treasury	255,266	277,047	298,581
Veterans Affairs	28,998	31,338	32,815
Environmental Protection Agency	5,108	5,776	5,896
General Services Administration	−123	756	719
National Aeronautics and Space Administration	12,429	13,499	14,721
Office of Personnel Management	31,949	35,161	37,046
Small Business Administration	692	529	318
Other Independent Agencies	73,617	125,708	102,108
Allowances	…	8,200	4,708
Undistributed offsetting receipts	−99,025	−109,436	−118,029
Total budget outlays	1,251,703	1,409,563	1,445,902

[1] Includes outlays of off-budget Federal entities and programmes.   [2] Estimates.

National Debt: Federal debt held by the public (in $1m.), and *per capita* debt (in $1) on 30 June to 1976 and then on 30 Sept.:

	Public debt	Per capita		Public debt	Per capita
1919	25,485	243	1970	283,198	1,381
1920	24,299	228	1980	709,291	3,114
1930	16,185	132	1987	1,888,134	7,738
1940	42,772	324	1988	2,050,252	8,321
1950	219,023	1,444	1989	2,190,324	8,805
1960	236,840	1,310	1990	2,410,431	9,656

State and Local Finance: Revenue of the 50 states and 82,237 local governments from their own sources amounted to $853,273m. in 1989–90; in addition they received $136,843m. in revenue from fiscal aid, shared revenues and reimbursements from the federal government, bringing total revenue from all sources to $1,031,653m. Of the revenue from state and local sources, taxes provided $501,480m., of which property taxes (mainly imposed by local governments) yielded $155,759m. or 31% of all tax revenue; and sales taxes, both general sales taxes and selective excises, provided $177,681m. (35%).

State tax revenue totalled $300,489m. in 1990. Largest sources of state tax revenue are general sales taxes (imposed during 1990 by 45 states), motor fuel sales taxes (all states), individual income (44 states), motor vehicle and operators' licences (46 states), corporation income (46 states), tobacco products (all states) and alcoholic beverage sales taxes (all states).

General revenue of local units from own sources in 1989–90 totalled $321,192m. In addition they received $191,606m. from state and federal aids. Property taxes provided 26% of total revenue.

Total expenditures of state and local governments were $973,988m. in 1989–90, of which approximately 72% was for current operation. Education took $287,194m. in current and capital expenditure; highways, $60,922m.; welfare (chiefly public assistance), $107,154m., and health and hospitals, $74,629m. Capital outlays (construction, equipment and land purchases) totalled $122,849m.

Gross debt of state and local governments totalled $857,844m. or $3,449 *per capita* at the close of their 1989–90 fiscal year. Total cash and investment assets of state and local governments were $1,487,370m. 47% of all assets are employee retirement funds.

US Bureau of the Census, *Governmental Finances in 1989–90.* Washington, D.C., 1991
American Economic Association, *Readings in Fiscal Policy.* Homewood, Ill., 1985

National Income. The Bureau of Economic Analysis of the Department of Commerce prepares detailed estimates on the national income and product. The principal tables are published monthly in *Survey of Current Business;* the complete set of national income and product tables are published in the *Survey* regularly each July, showing data for recent years. *The National Income and Product Accounts of the United States, 1929–1982: Statistical Tables* (1986) and the July 1987, July 1988, July 1989 and July 1990 *Survey* contain complete sets of tables from 1929 through 1989. The July 1991 *Survey* with data through 1990 has only a partial set of accounts, the complete set being delayed until a revision of the accounts was published. The conceptual framework and statistical methods underlying the US accounts were described in *National Income, 1954.* The July 1987 *Survey* provides a current overview of concepts and estimating procedures as well as a comprehensive directory to information on the US national accounts. Subsequent limited changes were described in the July 1988 *Survey.*

These latest figures [1] in $1,000m. for various years are as follows:

[1] The inclusion of statistics for Alaska and Hawaii beginning in 1960 does not significantly affect the comparability of the data.

	1929 [2]	1933 [3]	1960	1970	1980	1989	1990
I. Gross National Product	103·9	56·9	515·3	1,015·5	2,732·0	5,200·8	5,465·1
(a) Personal consumption expenditures	77·3	45·8	330·7	640·0	1,732·6	3,450·1	3,657·3
(b) Gross private domestic investment	16·7	1·6	78·2	148·8	437·0	771·2	741·0
(c) Net exports of goods and services	1·1	0·4	5·9	8·5	32·1	−46·1	−31·2
(d) Government purchases of goods and services	8·9	8·3	100·6	218·2	530·3	1,025·6	1,098·1

1. GNP *less* capital consumption allowances with capital consumption adjustment, indirect business tax and non-tax liability, business transfer payments, statistical discrepancy, *plus* subsidies less current surplus of government enterprises, equals:

[2] Peak year between First and Second World Wars.　　[3] Low point of the depression.
[4] Includes personal consumption expenditures, interest paid by consumers and personal transfer payments to foreigners (net).
[5] With inventory valuation and capital consumption adjustments.
[6] With capital consumption adjustment.

	1929 [2]	1933 [3]	1960	1970	1980	1989	1990
I. Gross National Product—contd.							
2. National Income	84·7	39·4	424·9	832·6	2·203·5	4,222·3	4,418·4
which, *less* corporate profits with inventory valuation and capital consumption adjustments, contributions for social insurance, wage accruals less disbursements, *plus* government transfer payments to persons, interest paid by government to persons and business less interest received by government, interest paid by consumers, personal dividend income, business transfer payments, equals:							
3. Personal income	84·3	46·3	409·4	831·8	2,258·5	4,384·3	4,645·5
whereof							
4. Personal tax and non-tax payments take	2·6	1·4	50·5	116·2	340·5	658·8	699·4
leaving							
5. Disposable personal income divided into	81·7	44·9	207·5	715·6	1,918·0	3,725·5	3,946·1
(*e*) Personal outlays [4]	79·2	46·5	338·1	657·9	1,781·1	3,553·7	3,766·0
(*f*) Personal saving	2·6	−1·6	20·8	57·7	136·9	171·8	180·1
IA. GNP in constant (1982) $s	709·6	498·5	1,665·3	2,416·2	3,187·1	4,117·7	4,157·3
(*a*) Personal consumption expenditures	471·4	378·7	1,005·1	1,492·0	2,000·4	2,656·8	2,681·6
(*b*) Gross private domestic investment	139·2	22·7	260·5	381·5	509·3	716·9	688·7
(*c*) Net exports of goods and services	4·7	−1·4	−4·0	−30·0	57·0	54·1	−33·8
(*d*) Government purchases of goods and services	94·2	98·5	403·7	572·6	620·5	798·1	820·8
II. National Income	84·7	39·4	424·9	832·6	2,203·5	4,223·3	4,418·4
composed of							
Compensation of employees	*51·1*	*29·6*	*296·7*	*618·3*	*1,638·2*	*3,079·0*	*3,244·2*
(*g*) Salaries and wages	50·5	29·0	272·8	551·5	1,372·0	2,573·2	2,705·3
(*h*) Supplements to wages and salaries	0·7	0·6	23·8	66·8	266·3	505·8	538·9
Proprietors' income [5]	*14·4*	*5·4*	*52·1*	*80·2*	*180·7*	*379·3*	*402·5*
(*i*) Farm [5]	6·1	2·5	11·6	14·7	20·5	48·6	49·9
(*j*) Business and professional [5]	8·3	2·9	40·5	65·4	160·1	330·7	352·6
Personal income from rents [6]	*4·9*	*2·0*	*15·3*	*18·2*	*6·6*	*8·2*	*6·9*
Net interest	*4·7*	*4·1*	*11·3*	*41·2*	*200·9*	*445·1*	*466·7*
Corporate profits with inventory valuation and capital consumption adjustments	*9·6*	*−1·5*	*49·5*	*74·7*	*177·2*	*311·6*	*298·3*
(*k*) Tax liabilities	1·4	0·5	22·7	34·4	84·8	135·1	132·1
(*l*) Inventory valuation adjustment	0·5	−2·1	−0·2	−6·6	−43·1	−21·7	−11·4
(*m*) Capital consumption adjustment	−0·9	−0·3	−0·3	5·2	−16·8	25·5	4·9
(*n*) Dividends	5·8	2·0	12·9	22·5	54·7	123·5	133·9
(*o*) Undistributed profits	2·8	−1·6	14·3	19·2	97·6	49·1	38·7

[2] Peak year between First and Second World Wars.   [3] Low point of the depression.

[4] Includes personal consumption expenditures, interest paid by consumers and personal transfer payments to foreigners (net).

[5] With inventory valuation and capital consumption adjustments.

[6] With capital consumption adjustment.

Currency. Prior to the banking crisis that occurred early in 1933, the monetary system had been on the gold standard for more than 50 years. An Act of 14 March 1900 required the Secretary of the Treasury to maintain at a parity with gold all forms of money issued by the USA. For a description of these, *see* THE STATESMAN'S YEAR-BOOK, 1934. For information 1934–74 *see* THE STATESMAN'S YEAR-BOOK, 1988–89.

Under the Coinage Act of 1965, all coins and currencies of the USA, regardless of when coined or issued, are legal tender for all debts, public and private.

Only one of the eight kinds of notes outstanding is now significant: Federal Reserve notes in denominations of $1, $2, $5, $10, $20, $50 and $100. The issue of (*a*) $500, $1,000, $5,000 and $10,000 Federal Reserve notes; of (*b*) silver certificates, and of (*c*) $100, $5 and $2 US notes have been discontinued, although they are still outstanding. The following issues were stopped many years ago and have been in process of retirement: (1) Federal Reserve Bank notes; (2) National Bank notes; (3) Treasury notes of 1890; (4) fractional currency.

Federal Reserve notes are obligations of the USA and a first lien on the assets of the Federal Reserve Banks, through which they are issued. Each of the 12 banks issues them against the security of an equal volume of collateral.

Inflation was 4·5% in 1991 (6·1% in 1990, 4·6% in 1989).

In March 1992 $1 = £0·52 sterling; £1 sterling = $1·76.

Banking and Finance. The Federal Reserve System, established under The Federal Reserve Act of 1913, comprises the Board of 7 Governors, the 12 regional Federal Reserve Banks with their 25 branches, and the Federal Open Market Committee. The 7 members of the Board of Governors are appointed by the President with the consent of the Senate. Each Governor is appointed to a full term of 14 years or an unexpired portion of a term, one term expiring every 2 years. The Board exercises broad supervisory authority over the operations of the 12 Federal Reserve Banks, including approval of their budgets and of the appointments of their presidents and first vice presidents; it designates 3 of the 9 directors of each Reserve Bank including the Chairman and Deputy Chairman. The *Chairman* of the Federal Reserve Board is appointed by the President for 4-year terms. The Chairman for 1991–94 is Alan Greenspan. The Board has supervisory and regulatory responsibilities over banks that are members of the Federal Reserve System, bank holding companies, bank mergers, Edge Act and agreement corporations, foreign activities of member banks, international banking facilities in the U.S., and activities of the U.S. branches and agencies of foreign banks. The Board also assures the smooth functioning and continued development of the nation's vast payments system. Another area of the Boards responsibilities involves the implementation by regulation of major federal laws governing consumer credit. The 12 members of the Federal Open Market Committee include the 7 members of the Board of Governors and 5 of the 12 Federal Reserve Bank presidents. The latter serve 1-year terms on the Committee in rotation except for the President of the Federal Reserve Bank of New York, who is a permanent member. The Federal Open Market Committee influences credit market conditions, money and bank credit, by buying or selling US Government securities; and it also supervises System operations in foreign currencies for the purpose of helping to safeguard the value of the dollar in international exchange markets and facilitating co-operation and efficiency in the international monetary system. The Board also influences credit conditions through powers to set reserve requirements, to approve discount rates at Federal Reserve Banks, and to fix margin requirements on stock-market credit.

The Reserve Banks advance funds to depository institutions, issue Federal Reserve notes, which are the principal form of currency in the US, act as fiscal agent for the Government, and afford nationwide cheque-clearing and fund transfer arrangements. They may increase or reduce the country's supply of reserve funds by buying or selling Government securities and other obligations at the direction of the Federal Open Market Committee. The purchase and sale of securities in the open market is conducted by the Federal Reserve Bank of New York. Their capital stock is held by the member banks, but it carries no voting rights except in the election of directors.

From 1968, the Congress passed a number of consumer financial protection acts, the first of which was the Truth in Lending Act, for which it has directed the Board to write implementing regulations and assume partial enforcement responsibility. Others include the Equal Credit Opportunity Act, Home Mortgage Disclosure Act, Consumer Leasing Act, Fair Credit Billing Act, and Electronic Fund Transfer Act. To manage these responsibilities the Board has established a Division of Consumer and Community Affairs. To assist it, the Board consults with a Consumer Advisory Council, established by the Congress in 1976 as a statutory part of the Federal Reserve System.

Another statutory body, the Federal Advisory Council, consists of 12 members (one from each district); it meets in Washington four times a year to advise the Board of Governors on general business and financial conditions.

Following the passage of the Monetary Control Act of 1980, the Board of Governors established the Thrift Institutions Advisory Council to provide information and views on the special needs and problems of thrift institutions. The group is comprised of representatives of mutual savings banks, savings and loan associations, and credit unions.

Banks which participate in the federal deposit insurance fund have their deposits insured against loss up to $100,000 for each account. The fund is administered by the Federal Deposit Insurance Corporation established in 1933; it obtains resources through annual assessments on participating banks. All members of the Federal Reserve System are required to insure their deposits through the Corporation, and non-member banks may apply and qualify for insurance.

The Federal Deposit Insurance Corporation Improvement Act of 1992 originated with bank reform initiatives. It imposed new capital rules on banks, new reporting requirements and a code of 'safety and soundness' standards. The main aim of the Act is to reduce risk through rigorous enforcement of capital requirements. Regulators are required to take action where banks fail to observe these standards.

At the end of 1990 the 20 major banks in terms of assets ($1,000m.) were: Citicorp (NY), 217; BankAmerica (Calif), 111; Chase Manhattan (NY), 98; J. P. Morgan (NY), 93; Security Pacific (Calif), 85; Chemical Bank (NY), 73; NCNB (NC), 65; Bankers Trust (NY), 65; Manufacturers Hanover (NY), 62; Wells Fargo (Calif), 56; First Interstate (Calif), 51; C & S/Sovran (Ga), 51; First Chicago (Ill), 51; PNC Financial (Pa), 46; Bank of America (NY), 45; First Union (NC), 41; Suntrust (Ga), 33; Bank of Boston (Mass), 33; Fleet/Norstar (RI), 33; Barnett Banks (Fla), 32. NCNB merged with C & S/Sovran, Chemical Bank with Manufacturers Hanover and BankAmerica with Security Pacific in 1991.

There is a stock exchange in New York (NYSE), and American Stock Exchange (ASE) and a Pacific Stock Exchange in San Francisco.

Board of Governors of the Federal Reserve System. *The Federal Reserve System: Purposes and Functions.* 7th ed., 1984.—*Federal Reserve Bulletin.* Monthly.—*Annual Report.*— *Annual Statistical Digest.*—*The Federal Reserve Act, As Amended Through 1984*
Meulendyke, A.-M., *U.S. Monetary Policy and Financial Markets.* New York, 1989
Timberlake, R. H., *The Origins of Central Banking in the United States.* Cambridge, Massachusetts, 1978

Weights and Measures. The US Customary System derives from the British Imperial System. It differs in respect of the *gallon* (=0·83268 Imperial gallon); *bushel* (= 0·969 Imperial bushel); *hundredweight* (= 100 lbs); and the *short* or *net ton* (= 2,000 lbs). The metric system is to be introduced in the 1990s.

ENERGY AND NATURAL RESOURCES

Electricity. In 1990 19% of electricity was produced by 112 nuclear reactors. Production (public utilities only, 1989) 2,779,000,000m. kwh.

Minerals. Total value of non-fuel minerals produced in 1988 was estimated at $30,022m. ($26,317m. in 1987). Details are given in the following tables. Oil production was 409·63m. tonnes in 1990.

Production of metallic minerals:

	1987		1988	
		Value		*Value*
Metallic minerals	*Quantity*	*($1,000)*	*Quantity*	*($1,000)*
Bauxite (dried equiv.) tonnes	575,574	10,916	587,889	10,566
Copper (recoverable content), tonnes	1,243,638	2,261,833	1,419,645	3,771,570
Gold (recoverable content), troy oz.	4,947,040	2,216,027	6,459,539	2,831,281
Lead (recoverable content), tonnes	311,381	246,720	384,983	315,222
Molybdenum (content of concentrate), 1,000 lb.	69,868	179,286	99,738	266,899
Silver (recoverable content), 1,000 troy oz.	39,896,541	279,675	53,415,677	349,339
Zinc (recoverable content), tonnes	216,320	199,924	244,314	324,249
Total metals	—	7,423,000	—	10,219,000

The US is wholly or almost wholly dependent upon imports for industrial diamonds, bauxite, tin, chromite, nickel, strategic-grade mica and long-fibre asbestos; it imports the bulk of its tantalum, platinum, manganese, mercury, tungsten, cobalt and flake graphite, and substantial quantities of antimony, cadmium, arsenic, fluorspar, zinc and bismuth.

Precious metals are mined mainly in Nevada, Idaho, Montana, Utah and Arizona (in order of combined output of gold and silver).

Statistics of important non-metallic minerals and mineral fuels are:

Non-metallic minerals	1987 Quantity	Value ($1,000)	1988 Quantity	Value ($1,000)
Boron minerals, short tons	1,385,000	475,092	1,267,000	429,667
Cement:				
Portland, 1,000 short tons	74,868	3,646,561	74,074	3,575,906
Masonry, 1,000 short tons	3,680	259,926	3,574	243,941
Clays, 1,000 short tons	47,657	1,202,284	49,069	1,400,820
Gypsum, 1,000 short tons	15,612	106,977	16,390	109,205
Lime, 1,000 short tons	15,733	786,125	17,293	828,007
Phosphate rock, 1,000 tonnes	40,954	793,280	48,389	887,809
Potassium salts, 1,000 tonnes (K_2O equivalent)	1,485	195,700	1,427	240,300
Salt (common), 1,000 short tons	36,493	684,170	37,997	680,174
Sand and gravel, 1,000 short tons	923,210	3,366,600	951,880	3,514,000
Stone, 1,000 short tons	1,201,284	5,438,753	1,248,989	5,754,289
Sulphur (Frasch-process), 1,000 tonnes	3,610	386,834	4,341	430,814
Total non-metallic minerals	—	*18,894,000*	—	*19,803,000*

Mineral fuels	1989		1990	
Coal: Bitum. and lignite, 1,000 short tons	977,381	21,267,810	1,025,570	22,265,124
Pennsylv. anthracite, [1] 1,000 short tons	3,348	143,730	3,506	138,136
Gas: Natural gas, [2] 1m. cu. ft	18,029,000	30,469,010	18,469,000 [3]	31,766,860 [3]
Petroleum (crude), 1,000 bbls of 42 gallons	2,778,745	44,070,895	2,684,575	53,772,037

[1] Includes a small quantity of anthracite mined in states other than Pennsylvania.
[2] Value at wells. [3] Preliminary figures.

Minerals Yearbook. Bureau of Mines. Washington, D.C. Annual from 1932–33; continuing the *Mineral Resources of the United States* series (1866–1931); from 1977 in 3 vols. *(Metals and Minerals; Area Reports, Domestic; and Area Reports, International)*

Agriculture. Agriculture in the USA is characterized by its ability to adapt to widely varying conditions, and still produce an abundance and variety of agricultural products. From colonial times to about 1920 the major increases in farm production were brought about by adding to the number of farms and the amount of land under cultivation. During this period nearly 320m. acres of virgin forest were converted to crop land or pasture, and extensive areas of grass lands were ploughed. Improvident use of soil and water resources was evident in many areas.

During the next 20 years the number of farms reached a plateau of about 6·5m., and the acreage planted to crops held relatively stable around 330m. acres. The major source of increase in farm output arose from the substitution of power-driven machines for horses and mules. Greater emphasis was placed on development and improvement of land, and the need for conservation of basic agricultural resources was recognized. A successful conservation programme, highly co-ordinated and on a national scale—to prevent further erosion, to restore the native fertility of damaged land and to adjust land uses to production capabilities and needs—has been in operation since early in the 1930s.

Following the Second World War the uptrend in farm output has been greatly accelerated by increased production per acre and per farm animal. These increases are associated with a higher degree of mechanization; greater use of lime and fertilizer; improved varieties, including hybrid maize and grain sorghums; more effective control of insects and disease; improved strains of livestock and poultry; and wider use of good husbandry practices, such as nutritionally balanced feeds, use of superior sites and better housing. During this period land included in farms decreased slowly, crop land harvested declined somewhat more rapidly, but the number of farms declined sharply.

Some significant changes during these transitions are:

All land in farms totalled less than 500m. acres in 1870, rose to a peak of over 1,200m. acres in the 1950s and declined to 983m. acres in 1991, even with the addition of the new States of Alaska and Hawaii in 1960. The number of farms declined from 6·35m. in 1940 to 2·11m. in 1991, as the average size of farms doubled. The average size of farms in 1991 was 467 acres, but ranged from a few acres to many thousand acres. In 1987, 595,000 farms (690,329 in 1978) were less than 50 acres; 645,000 (814,689), 50–179 acres; 678,000 (811,468), 180–999 acres; and 162,000 (162,156) 1,000 acres or more.

Farms operated by owners in 1987 were 1,239,000; by part-owners, 609,000; by tenants, 240,000.

In 1990 there were 2,143,000 farms with total land of 988m. acres. Average farm size, 461 acres. Value of land and buildings was $685,048m.

At the 1990 census 66,964,000 persons (22·5% of the population) were rural, of whom 4,591,000 (under 2%) lived on farms.

During the week of July 10–16, 1988, there were 3·52m. people working on farms and ranches. The workforce comprised 1·43m. self-employed farm operators, 591,000 unpaid workers, 1·20m. workers hired directly by farm operators and 303,000 Agricultural Service employees.

Cash receipts from farm marketings and government payments (in $1m.):

	Crops	Livestock and livestock products	Government payments	Total
1932	1,996	2,752	—	4,748
1945	9,655	12,008	742	22,405
1950	12,356	16,105	283	28,744
1960	15,259	18,989	702	34,950
1970	20,976	29,563	3,717	54,256
1980	71,746	67,991	1,286	141,022
1987	63,751	75,717	16,747	156,215
1988	72,569	78,862	14,480	165,911
1989	75,400	83,700	10,900	189,200

Realized gross farm income (including government payments), in $1m., was 166,364 in 1985, 160,422 in 1986, 171,625 in 1987, 173,838 in 1988 and 189,219 in 1989; net farm income amounted to 46,652 in 1989. Farm real estate debt, excluding debt in operator dwellings, was $103,585m. in 1984, $97,591m. in 1985, $88,561m. in 1986, $81,063m. in 1987 and $76,697m. in 1988.

US agricultural exports, fiscal year, totalled: 1983–84, $38,027m.; 1984–85, $31,201m.; 1985–86, $26,324m.; 1986–87, $28,700m.; 1987–88, $37,126m. (12% of all exports); 1988–89, $39,991m. (11% of all exports).

Total area of farm land under irrigation in 1987 was 46,386,000 acres. Water consumption was 137,000m. gallons a day in 1985.

According to census returns and estimates of the Economic Research Service, the acreage and specified values of farms has been as follows (area in 1,000 acres; value in $1,000; cash receipts in $1m.):

	Farm area	Crop land available for crops	Value, land, bldgs,[2] machinery, livestock	Cash receipts
1910	878,798 [1]	432,000	41,089,000	...
1930	990,112	480,000	57,815,000	...
1940	1,065,114	467,000	41,829,000	...
1950	1,161,420	478,000	104,800,000	28,461
1959	1,123,508	458,100	155,700,000	33,647
1969	1,062,893	472,100	241,200,000	48,179
1978	1,014,777	471,000	728,700,000	112,360
1982	986,797	489,000	903,800,000	142,595
1988	995,000	...	686,400,000	150,431

[1] Excludes Alaska and Hawaii.
[2] Real estate, livestock and machinery, excluding crops.

The areas and production of the principal crops for 3 years were:

	1989–1990			1990–1991			1991–1992		
	Har-vested 1,000 acres	Pro-duc-tion 1m.	Yield per acre	Har-vested 1,000 acres	Pro-duc-tion 1m.	Yield per acre	Har-vested 1,000 acres	Pro-duc-tion 1m.	Yield per acre
Corn for grain (bu.)	64,700	7,525	116·3	67,000	7,934	118·5	68,800	7,474	108·6
Oats (bu.)	6,900	374	54·3	5,900	358	60·1	4,800	243	50·6
Barley (bu.)	8,300	404	48·6	7,500	422	56·1	8,400	464	55·2
All wheat (bu.)	62,200	2,037	32·7	69,300	2,736	39·5	57,700	1,981	34·3
Rice (cwt.) [1]	2,690	154·5	5,749	2,820	156·1	5,529	2,750	154·5	5,617
Soybeans for beans (bu.)	59,500	1,924	32·3	56,500	1,926	34	58,000	1,986	34·3
All Cotton [1] (bales)	9,500	12,200	614	11,700	15,500	634	12,800	17,500	856
Tobacco (lb.)	680	2,016	1,370	...	...	...	...	...	...

[1] Yield in lb.

Corn (Maize). The chief corn-growing states (1988) were (estimated production, corn for grain in 1,000 bu.): Iowa, 899,000; Nebraska, 818,000; Illinois, 701,000; Indiana, 415,000; Minnesota, 348,000; Ohio, 255,000; Montana, 154,000; Kansas, 144,000; South Dakota, 132,000; Wisconsin, 131,000; Texas, 130,000.

Wheat. The chief wheat-growing states (1988) were (estimated production in 1,000 bu.): Kansas, 323,000; Oklahoma, 173,000; Washington, 125,000; North Dakota, 103,000; Texas, 90,000; Colorado, 80,000; Missouri, 78,000; Idaho, 76,000; Nebraska, 72,000.

Cotton. Leading production, 1988, by state (in 1,000 bales, 480 lb. net weight) was: Texas, 5,260; California, 2,853; Mississippi, 1,830; Arizona, 1,120; Arkansas, 1,050; Louisiana, 950; Tennessee, 590; Alabama, 380; Oklahoma, 290.

Tobacco. Production (1,000 lb.) of the chief tobacco-growing states was, in 1988: N. Carolina, 553,000; Kentucky, 337,000; S. Carolina, 100,000; Virginia, 91,000.

Fruit. Production:

	1987	1988	1989
Apples (1m. lbs)	10,451	9,081	9,920
Citrus Fruit (1m. boxes [1])	286	304	314
Grapes (1,000 tons)	5,254	6,032	5,930

[1] Average net weight per box 65–80 lbs.

Dairy produce. In 1990, production of milk was 148,300m. lb.; in 1989 cheese, 5,614m. lb.; butter, 1,074m. lb.; ice-cream, 831m. gallons; non-fat dry milk, 875m. lb.; cottage cheese, 1,096m. lb.

Livestock: Cattle and calves (1990), 99,337,000; sheep and lambs (1989), 10,745,000; hogs and pigs (1989), 53,852,000.

In 1989 there were 356m. chickens, 5,518m. broilers and 260m. turkeys with respective total values of production (in $1m.) of 770, 8,780 and 2,239. Eggs produced, 1989, 67,104m. (value $3,850m.).

Value of production (in $1m.) was:

	1987	1988	1989
Cattle and calves	24,629·3	27,426	27,893
Milch cows	18,014	17,921	19,694
Hogs and pigs	10,426·8	9,128	9,255

Total value of livestock, excluding poultry and goats and, from 1961, horses and mules (in $1m.) on farms in the USA on 1 Jan. was: 1930, 6,061; 1933 (low point of the agricultural depression), 2,733; 1970, 22,886; 1980, 60,598; 1985, 45,594; 1988, 64,945; 1989, 60,400.

In 1987 the production of shorn wool was 85·8m. lb. from 11m. sheep (average 1970–74, 320m. lb. from 18·2m. sheep); of pulled wool, 1·15m. lb. (1970–74, 10·1m. lb.).

Forestry. In 1977 the US forest lands, including Alaska and Hawaii, capable of producing timber for commercial use, covered 482,485,900 acres (more than one-fifth of the land area), classified as follows: Saw-timber stands, 215,435,700 acres; pole timber stands, 135,609,900 acres, seedling and sapling stands, 115,032,100 acres; non-stocked and other areas, 16,408,200 acres. Ownership of commercial forest land was distributed as follows in 1987: Federal (owned or managed), 103m. acres; state, county, municipal and Indian, 34m. acres; privately owned, 347m. acres (71% of total), including 116m. acres on farms. Of the saw-timber stand (2,829,000m. bd ft in 1987) Douglas fir constituted 514,317 in 1977; Southern pine, 321,563; Western yellow (ponderosa and jeffrey) pine, 192,070; other softwoods, 957,458; hardwoods, 255,189. In 1987 the net volume of saw-timber was 2,829,000m. bd ft, and of softwood, 2,032,000m. bd ft. Growing stock timber removals amounted to 756,000m. cu. ft in 1987, of which softwood accounted for 451,000m. cu. ft. The net area of the 156 national forests and other areas in USA and Puerto Rico administered by the US Department of Agriculture's Forest Service, including commercial and non-commercial forest land, was in Oct. 1989, 191m. acres.

Fire takes a heavy annual toll in the forest; total area burned over in 1986 was 3,191,125 acres; 1,500m. acres of land are now under organized fire-protection service. Federal land that was planted or seeded in forest and wind barrier nursery stock in the year ending 30 Sept. 1986 was 300,640 acres.

Fisheries. Total US catch (edible and industrial), 1989, 8,463m. lbs. valued at $3,238m.; harvest outside the US and joint venture operations in 1988 (mostly Alaskan pollock, and tuna), 1·7m. tonnes valued at $490m.; foreign catch in the 200 mile wide US fishery zone (mostly Alaskan pollock, 73%; Pacific flounders, 13% and Pacific cod, 6%), 1·2m. tonnes.

Major species caught, 1989: Menhaden, 1,989m. lb, value $84·5m. (29% of total US catch); Alaskan pollock, 2,362m. lb, $186·9m.; salmon, 785·9m. lb, $591·2m.; crabs, 458m. lb, $414·4m.; shrimp, 51·5m. lb, $467·6m; cod, 278·5m. lb, $103·1m. Major landing areas, 1989: By value (in $1m.): Alaska, 1,223; Louisiana, 265; Massachusetts, 269; California, 418; Texas, 96.

Exports, 1989, totalled $4,707m.; imports, $9,604m. *Per capita* consumption, 1988, 15 lb edible meat; estimated live weight equivalent about 45 lb *per capita*.

Tennessee Valley Authority. Established by Act of Congress, 1933, the TVA is a multiple-purpose federal agency which carries out its duties in an area embracing some 41,000 sq. miles, in 201 counties (aggregate population, about 4·7m.) in the 7 Tennessee River Valley states: Tennessee, Kentucky, Mississippi, Alabama, North Carolina, Georgia and Virginia. In addition, 76 counties outside the Valley are served by TVA power distributors. Its 3 directors are appointed by the President, with the consent of the Senate; headquarters are in Knoxville, Tenn. There were 24,801 employees in May 1991.

The primary task of the TVA was the multipurpose development of the Tennessee River for flood control, navigation, and electric power production. It has also contributed to controlling erosion on the land, introducing better fertilizers and new farming practices, eradicating malaria, demonstrating ways electricity could lighten the burdens in the home and increase production on the farm, and the creation of potential job-producing enterprises.

TVA supplies electric power to 160 local distribution systems serving 3m. customers. The power system originated with the water-power development of the Tennessee River, but has become predominantly a coal-fired system as power requirements have outgrown the region's hydro-electric potential. In fiscal year 1988, the TVA system generated 95,000m. kwh. Installed capacity in 1988 was 32·1m. kw, with another 5·2m. kw under construction at TVA's nuclear plants.

Power operations are financially self-supporting from revenues. In fiscal year 1986 power revenues were $4,63 9m. Power facilities are financed from revenues and the sale of revenue bonds and notes, and TVA is repaying appropriations previously invested in power facilities. Other TVA resource development programmes continue to be financed from congressional appropriations.

Annual Report of the TVA. Knoxville, 1934 to date
Clapp, G.R., *The TVA; An Approach to the Development of a Region.* Univ. of Chicago Press, 1955
Lilienthal, D. E., *TVA; Democracy on the March.* 20th Anniversary ed. New York and London, 1953
Tennessee Valley Authority. *A History of the Tennessee Valley Authority.* Knoxville, Tennessee, 1982

INDUSTRY. The following table presents industry statistics of manufactures as reported at various censuses from 1909 to 1982 and from the Annual Survey of Manufactures for years in which no census was taken. The figures for 1958 to 1982 include data for some establishments previously classified as non-manufacturing. The figures for 1939, but not for earlier years, have been revised to exclude data for establishments classified as non-manufacturing in 1954. The figures for 1909–33 were previously revised by the deduction of data for industries excluded from manufacturing during that period.

The statistics for 1967, 1972, 1977 and 1982 relate to all establishments employing 1 or more persons anytime during the year; for 1950, 1956–57, 1959–62, 1966 and 1968–74 on a representative sample of manufacturing establishments of 1 or more employees; for 1929 through 1939, those reporting products valued at $5,000 or more; and for 1909 and 1919, those reporting products valued at $500 or more. These differences in the minimum size of establishments included in the census affect only very slightly the year-to-year comparability of the figures.

The annual Surveys of Manufactures carry forward the key measures of manufacturing activity which are covered in detail by the Census of Manufactures. The estimate for 1950 is based on reports for approximately 45,000 plants out of a total of more than 260,000 operating manufacturing establishments; those for 1956–57 on about 50,000, and those for 1959–62, 1966 and 1968–74 on about 60,000 out of about 300,000. Included are all large plants and representative samples of the much more numerous small plants. The large plants in the surveys account for approximately two-thirds of the total employment in operating manufacturing establishments in the US.

	Number of establishments	Production workers (average for year)	Production workers' wages total ($1,000)	Value added by manufacture ($1,000)
1909	264,810	6,261,736	3,205,213	8,160,075
1919	270,231	8,464,916	9,664,009	23,841,624
1929	206,663	8,369,705	10,884,919	30,591,435
1933	139,325	5,787,611	4,940,146	14,007,540
1939	173,802	7,808,205	8,997,515	24,487,304
1950	260,000	11,778,803	34,600,025	89,749,765
1960	...	12,209,514	55,555,452	163,998,531
1967	305,680	13,955,300	81,393,600	261,983,800
1970	...	13,528,000	91,609,000	300,227,600
1972	312,662	13,526,500	105,494,700	353,974,200
1973	...	14,233,100	118,332,300	405,623,500
1974	...	13,970,900	124,983,200	452,468,400
1975	...	12,567,900	121,427,200	442,485,800
1977	350,757	13,691,000	157,163,700	585,165,600
1978	...	14,228,700	176,416,800	657,412,000
1979	...	14,537,800	192,881,500	747,480,500
1980	...	13,900,100	198,164,000	773,831,300
1982	348,385	12,400,600	204,787,200	824,117,700
1984	...	12,572,800	231,783,900	983,227,700
1985	...	12,171,100	235,731,700	999,065,800
1986	...	11,800,000	237,000,000	1,035,000,000
1987	358,061	12,259,500	251,533,000	1,166,554,900
1988	...	12,400,000	264,000,000	1,262,000,000

For comparison of broad types of manufacturing, the industries covered by the Census of Manufactures have been divided into 20 general groups according to the *Standard Industrial Classification.*

Code No. Industry group	Year	Production workers (average for year)	Production workers' wages, total ($1,000)	Value added by manu-facture [1] ($1,000)
20. Food and kindred products	1986	990,000	17,789,000	112,191,000
	1987	1,029,500	18,894,800	122,072,600
	1988	1,046,000	...	128,766,000
21. Tobacco products	1986	34,000	912,000	12,725,000
	1987	32,700	992,500	14,260,500
	1988	33,000	...	17,155,000
22. Textile mill products	1986	555,000	7,898,000	22,232,000
	1987	580,200	8,766,800	26,013,900
	1988	572,000	...	26,282,000
23. Apparel and other textile products	1986	863,000	8,949,000	28,451,000
	1987	913,300	9,910,200	33,310,800
	1988	895,000	...	32,454,000
24. Lumber and wood products	1986	512,000	8,135,000	23,239,000
	1987	581,100	9,516,500	28,590,900
	1988	585,000	...	29,038,000
25. Furniture and fixtures	1986	376,000	5,556,000	17,659,000
	1987	408,000	6,230,100	20,239,100
	1988	411,000	...	20,854,000
26. Paper and allied products	1986	458,000	11,297,000	43,925,000
	1987	465,700	11,758,700	49,725,800
	1988	476,000	...	57,355,000
27. Printing and publishing	1986	738,000	14,099,000	78,150,000
	1987	796,900	15,669,900	89,207,900
	1988	799,000	...	94,109,000
28. Chemical and allied products	1986	458,000	11,756,000	100,013,000
	1987	464,300	12,327,100	121,241,800
	1988	475,000	...	137,879,000
29. Petroleum and coal products	1986	82,000	2,598,000	17,496,000
	1987	76,500	2,462,800	18,398,900
	1988	77,000	...	25,280,000
30. Rubber and miscellaneous plastics products	1986	572,000	10,124,000	37,236,000
	1987	640,900	11,644,700	44,293,100
	1988	666,000	...	46,585,000
31. Leather and leather products	1986	110,000	1,213,000	3,611,000
	1987	107,400	1,281,700	4,274,900
	1988	108,000	...	4,528,000
32. Stone, clay and glass products	1986	399,000	8,352,000	30,677,000
	1987	402,700	8,742,500	33,076,400
	1988	401,000	...	34,285,000
33. Primary metal industries	1986	529,000	13,472,000	38,092,000
	1987	541,000	14,162,700	46,471,200
	1988	562,000	...	56,487,000
34. Fabricated metal products	1986	1,050,000	21,817,000	68,621,000
	1987	1,083,700	22,914,800	75,502,900
	1988	1,104,000	...	79,893,000
35. Machinery (except electrical)	1986	1,141,000	25,422,000	108,365,000
	1987	1,145,900	26,077,700	119,214,400
	1988	1,196,000	...	129,342,000
36. Electric and electronic equipment	1986	1,160,000	23,361,000	112,422,000
	1987	1,003,800	19,757,800	95,958,100
	1988	1,012,000	...	103,475,000

[1] Figures represent adjusted value added.

Code No.	Industry group	Year	Production workers (average for year)	Production workers' wages, total ($1,000)	Value added by manufacture [1] ($1,000)
37. Transportation equipment		1986	1,169,000	33,626,000	125,706,000
		1987	1,206,300	34,755,100	135,782,700
		1988	1,196,000	...	143,500,000
38. Instruments and related products		1986	335,000	6,704,000	40,005,000
		1987	509,300	11,655,000	71,847,200
		1988	507,000	...	76,094,000
39. Miscellaneous manufacturing		1986	236,000	3,520,000	14,622,000
		1987	270,100	4,011,900	17,431,600
		1988	284,000	...	19,028,000

[1] Figures represent adjusted value added.

Iron and Steel: Output of the iron and steel industries (in net tons of 2,000 lb.), according to figures supplied by the American Iron and Steel Institute, was:

	Furnaces in blast 31 Dec.	Pig-iron (including ferro-alloys)	Raw steel	Steel by method of production [1]			
				Open hearth	Bessemer	Electric [2]	Basic Oxygen
1932 [3]	44	9,835,227	15,322,901	13,336,210	1,715,925	270,044	...
1939	195	35,677,097	52,798,714	48,409,800	3,358,916	1,029,067	...
1944 [4]	218	62,866,198	89,641,600	80,363,953	5,039,923	4,237,699	...
1950	234	66,400,311	96,336,075	86,262,509	4,534,558	6,039,008	...
1960	114	68,566,384	99,281,601	86,367,506	1,189,196	8,378,743	3,346,156
1970	152	87,933,000	131,514,000	48,022,000	—	20,162,000	63,330,000
1980	...	70,329,000	111,835,000	13,054,000	—	31,166,000	67,617,000
1989	...	55,873,000	97,943,000	4,442,000	—	35,154,000	58,348,000
1990	...	54,750,000	98,906,000	53,808,000	—	36,939,000	58,471,000

[1] The sum of these 4 items should equal the total in the preceding column; any difference appearing is due to the very small production of crucible steel, omitted prior to 1950. [2] Includes crucible production beginning 1950. [3] Low point of the depression. [4] Peak year of war production.

The iron and steel industry in 1990 employed 119,683 wage-earners (compared with 449,888 in 1960), who worked an average of 41 hours per week and earned an average of $17.98 per hour: total employment costs were $6,571m. and total employment costs for 44,280 salaried employees were $2,661m.

Annual Statistics Report. American Iron and Steel Institute

Labour. The Bureau of Labor Statistics estimated that in 1990 the civilian labour force was 124,787,000 (66·4% of those 16 years and over), of whom 117,914,000 were employed and 6,874,000—or 5·5%—were unemployed. The following table shows civilian employment by industry and sex and percentage distribution of the total:

Industry Group	Male	Female	Total	Percentage distribution
Employed (1,000 persons):	64,435	53,479	117,914	100·0
Agriculture, forestry and fisheries	2,646	709	3,355	2·8
Mining	617	113	730	0·6
Construction	7,032	664	7,696	6·5
Manufacturing:				
Durable goods	9,227	3,331	12,557	10·6
Non-durable (including not specified)	5,089	3,538	8,626	7·3
Transportation, communication and other public utilities	5,819	2,317	8,136	6·9
Wholesale and retail trade	12,773	11,496	24,269	20·6
Finance, insurance and real estate	3,323	4,697	8,021	6·8
Services	14,691	24,224	38,915	33·0
Private households	156	873	1,023	0·9
Other services	14,541	23,351	37,892	32·1
Professional services	7,937	17,398	25,335	21·5
Public administration	3,218	2,390	5,608	4·8

Source: U.S. Department of Labour, Bureau of Labor Statistics

A total of 44 strikes and lockouts of 1,000 workers or more occurred in 1990, involving 185,000 workers and 6m. idle days; the number of idle days was 0·02% of the year's total working time of all workers.

There are 3 federal agencies which provide formal machinery for the adjustment of labour disputes: (1) The Federal Mediation and Conciliation Service, now an independent agency, whose mediation services are available 'in any labor dispute in any industry affecting commerce'; under Executive Order 11491, as amended, to federal agencies and organizations of federal employees involved in negotiation disputes; and in state and local government collective bargaining disputes when adequate dispute resolution machinery is not available to the parties. Its aim is to prevent and minimize work stoppages. (2) The National Mediation Board (1934) provides much the same facilities for the railroad and air-transport industries pursuant to the Railway Labor Act. (3) The National Railroad Adjustment Board (1934) acts as a board of final appeal for grievances arising over the interpretation of existing collective agreements under the Railway Labor Act; its decisions are binding upon both sides and enforceable by the courts.

Trade Unions. The American labour movement comprises about 90 national and international labour organizations plus a large number of small independent local or single-firm labour organizations. In 1990 total membership was approximately 16·7m. The American Federation of Labor (founded 1881 and taking its name in 1886) and the Congress of Industrial Organizations merged into one organization, named the AFL–CIO, in Dec. 1955, averaging 13·9m. members 1989-91.

Unaffiliated or independent labour organizations, inter-state in scope, had an estimated total membership excluding all foreign members (1990) of about 3m.

Labour organizations represented 18·3% (19·1m.) of employed persons in 1990; 16·1% (16·7m.) were actual members of unions.

The National Labor Relations Act, as amended by the Labor–Management Relations (Taft–Hartley) Act, 1947 (*see* THE STATESMAN'S YEAR-BOOK, 1955, p. 617), was amended by the Labor–Management Reporting and Disclosure Act, 1959, and again amended in 1974. The 1959 Act requires extensive reporting and disclosure of certain financial and administrative practices of labour organizations, employers and labour relations consultants. In addition, certain powers are vested in the Secretary of Labor to prevent abuses in the administration of trusteeships by labour organizations, to provide minimum standards and procedures for the election of union officers and to establish rules prescribing minimum standards for determining the adequacy of union procedures for the removal of officers. Other provisions impose a fiduciary responsibility upon union officers and provide for the exclusion of those convicted of certain named felonies from office for specified periods; more stringently regulate secondary boycotts and banning of 'hot' cargo agreements; put limitations upon organizational and recognition picketing and permit States to assert jurisdiction over labour disputes where the National Labor Relations Board declines to act. The Act also contains a 'Bill of Rights' for union members (enforceable directly by them) dealing with such things as equal rights in the nomination and election of union officers, freedom of speech and assembly subject to reasonable union rules, and safeguards against improper disciplinary action.

FOREIGN ECONOMIC RELATIONS. On 1 Jan. 1989 the Canada-USA Free Trade Agreement came into effect, providing for the phased removal of tariff and other barriers. The UK has had 'most-favoured-nation' status since 1815.

Commerce. Total value of imports and exports of merchandise by yearly average or by year (in $1m.):

| | Exports | | General | | | Exports[2] | | General |
	Total[1]	US mdse.	imports[2]			Total[1]	US mdse.	imports[2]
1951–55	15,333	15,196	10,832	1986	227,159	206,376	365,438
1956–60	19,204	19,029	13,650	1987	254,122	243,859	406,241
1961–65	24,006	24,707	17,659	1988	322,426	310,049	440,952
1970	43,224	42,590	39,952	1989	363,812	349,651	473,211
1985	213,146	206,925	345,276	1990	393,893	375,454	494,903

[1] Excludes re-exports.   [2] Includes US Virgin Islands trade with foreign countries.

Imports and exports of gold and silver bullion and specie in calendar years (in $1,000):

	Gold		Silver	
	Exports	Imports	Exports	Imports
1932	809,528	363,315	13,850	19,650
1940	4,995	4,749,467	3,674	58,434
1955	7,257	104,592	8,331	72,932
1960	1,647	335,032	25,789	57,438
1965	1,285,097	101,669	54,061	64,769
1970	36,887	227,472	53,003	58,838
1975	429,278	406,583	104,086	274,106
1980	2,787,431	2,508,520	1,326,878	1,336,009
1985	919,400	2,109,500	81,746	855,528
1987	1,034,186	1,052,941	79,123	460,235
1988	3,883,000	800,000	94,000	476,000

The domestic exports of US produce, including military, and the imports for consumption by principal commodity groups for 3 calendar years were (in $1m.):

	Exports (US merchandise)			Imports for consumption		
	1988	1989	1990	1988	1989	1990
Food and live animals	26,182	29,724	29,280	20,110	20,685	21,933
Crude materials	25,151	26,947	26,985	13,624	15,370	14,524
Machinery and transport equipment	135,082	148,800	172,522	196,017	205,761	208,096
Chemicals	32,281	36,485	38,983	19,580	20,752	22,468

Leading exports of US merchandise are listed below for the calendar year 1989: Special category merchandise is included. Data for major subdivisions of certain classes are also given:

Commodity	$1m.	Commodity	$1m.
Meat and meat preparations	2,819	Power-generating machinery	14,166
Grain and cereal preparations	15,458	Agricultural machinery	2,305
Wheat and wheat flour	6,187	Industrial machinery	13,096
Corn	6,690	Office machinery, computers	23,184
Beverages and tobacco	5,510	Telecommunications	7,669
Soybeans	3,997	Electrical machinery	23,921
Logs and lumber	4,965	Transport equipment	50,517
Metal ores and scrap	5,313	Motor vehicles	25,480
Mineral fuels	9,823	Aircraft and parts	23,638
Bituminous coal	4,242	Professional, scientific and	
Textile yarn, fabric, articles	3,897	controlling instruments	10,924
Iron and steel mill products	3,167		

Chief imports for 27 commodity classes for consumption for the calendar year 1989:

Commodity	$1m.	Commodity	$1m.
Petroleum products,		Wool and other hair	341
crude and refined	49,141	Metal manufactures	8,973
Petroleum	35,400	Diamonds (excluding industrial)	4,358
Petroleum products	13,741	Rubber	1,459
Non-ferrous metals	8,949	Textile yarn, fabrics and products	6,094
Copper	2,196	Clothing	24,559
Aluminium	3,181	Cotton fabrics, woven	1,063
Nickel	1,543	Machinery, total	126,758
Lead	91	Agricultural machinery and tractors	2,811
Tin	338	Office machinery	25,679
Paper, paperboard and		Coffee	2,272
products	8,549	Chemicals and related products	20,752
Newsprint	4,488	Chemicals	10,273
Wood pulp	3,044	Oils and fats	731
Fertilizers	999	Cocoa beans	384
Sugar	611	Glass, pottery and china	2,926
Iron and steel-mill products	9,401	Footwear	8,393
Cattle, meat and preparations	3,227	Toys and sports goods	5,046

Commodity	$1m.	Commodity	$1m.
Automobiles and parts	70,309	Furs, undressed	...
Fish (and shellfish)	5,397	Telecommunications apparatus	23,182
Fruit and vegetables	4,104	Artworks and antiques	2,171
Alcoholic beverages	3,396	Natural gas	1,761

Total trade beween the USA and the UK (British Department of Trade returns, in £1,000 sterling):

	1988	1989	1990	1991
Imports to UK	10,767,750	12,888,890	14,357,516	13,711,538
Exports and re-exports from UK	10,544,077	12,098,549	12,998,506	11,430,030

Imports and exports by selected countries for the calendar years 1989 and 1990 (in $1m.):

	General imports		Exports incl. re-exports [1]	
Country	1989	1990	1989	1990
UK	18,319	20,288	20,866	23,484
France	13,014	13,124	11,585	13,652
Federal Republic of Germany	24,971	28,109	16,883	18,690
Italy	11,933	12,724	7,232	7,987
Netherlands	4,810	4,972	11,393	13,016
EEC	85,292	91,868	86,592	98,023
USSR	703	1,065	4,271	3,088
Canada	88,210	91,372	78,266	82,967
Mexico	27,186	30,172	24,969	26,376
China	11,990	15,224	5,755	4,807
Japan	93,586	89,655	44,584	48,585
South Korea	19,742	18,493	13,478	14,399
Taiwan	24,326	22,667	11,323	11,428
Australia	3,898	4,433	8,347	8,535
Hong Kong	9,739	9,488	6,304	6,840

[1] 'Special category' exports are included in these totals.

Imports and exports by continents, groupings and selected countries for the calendar years 1987 and 1988 (in $1m.):

	General imports		Exports incl. re-exports [1]	
Area and country	1987	1988	1987	1988
Colombia	2,232	2,167	1,412	1,758
Ecuador	1,266	1,231	621	684
Mexico	20,271	23,277	14,582	20,643
Paraguay	22	37	183	194
Peru	769	656	814	798
Uruguay	344	275	92	100
Venezuela	5,579	5,228	3,586	4,611
Dominican Republic	1,163	1,417	1,142	1,362
Haiti	395	384	459	479
Bahamas	416	411	782	741
Netherlands Antilles	521	411	507	432
Jamaica	395	444	601	758
Trinidad and Tobago	815	719	361	328
Europe				
Western Europe	95,496	100,515	69,718	87,995
OECD Countries	94,636	99,558	69,091	87,236
Denmark	1,779	1,666	893	970
Greece	480	529	402	649
Ireland	1,112	1,373	1,810	2,182
Portugal	664	691	581	752
Spain	2,839	3,205	3,148	4,217
Turkey	821	983	1,483	1,843
EFTA countries				
Austria	929	1,085	549	748
Norway	1,404	1,452	842	932
Sweden	4,758	4,995	1,894	2,705
Switzerland	4,249	4,638	3,151	4,207
Finland	999	1,206	515	763
Iceland	286	190	84	98
Yugoslavia	797	847	461	534
Poland	296	378	239	304

Area and country	General imports		Exports incl. re-exports [1]	
	1987	1988	1987	1988
Asia	174,452	190,729	73,268	99,705
Near East	10,811	11,511	9,502	10,857
Bahrain	63	99	205	281
Iran	1,668	9	54	73
Iraq	495	1,488	683	1,156
Israel	2,639	2,978	3,130	3,248
Kuwait	522	464	505	690
Lebanon	33	40	97	123
Saudi Arabia	4,433	5,594	3,373	3,799
Other Asia	83,582	92,414	41,497	56,918
Bangladesh	370	369	193	258
India	2,529	2,952	1,463	2,498
Indonesia	3,394	3,188	767	1,056
Malaysia	2,921	3,711	1,897	2,139
Pakistan	405	461	733	1,093
Philippines	2,264	2,682	1,599	1,880
Singapore	6,201	7,996	4,053	5,770
Sri Lanka	417	424	77	124
Thailand	2,220	3,218	1,544	1,964
Vietnam	...	...	23	16
Oceania	4,136	4,824	6,526	8,242
New Zealand and W. Samoa	1,053	1,168	821	946
Africa	11,939	10,863	6,283	7,431
Algeria	1,999	1,813	426	733
Egypt	465	221	2,210	2,340
Ethiopia	74	54	136	181
Morocco	50	92	383	428
Ghana	249	202	115	117
Liberia	88	108	70	68
Nigeria	3,573	3,298	295	356
Kenya	79	64	95	92
Zaïre	308	365	104	125
South Africa, Republic of	1,346	1,530	1,281	1,690

[1] 'Special category' exports are included in these totals.

US Department of Commerce. Report FT 990, *Highlights of US Export and Import Trade* (ceased publication 1989). FT 925, *US Merchandise Trade.* Monthly from 1990.

Tourism. In 1990, 39,089,000 visitors travelled to the USA and spent over US$40,579,000 (excluding transportation paid to US international carriers). They came mainly from Canada (17,262,000), Mexico (6,768,000), Europe (6,659,000) and Asia/Japan (4,360,000). Expenditure by US travellers in foreign countries for 1990 was over US$38,671,000 (excluding transportation paid to foreign flag international carriers).

COMMUNICATIONS

Roads. On 31 Dec. 1990 the total US public road [1] mileage, including rural and urban roads, amounted to 3,880,151 miles, of which 3,518,204 miles were surfaced roads. The total mileage cited includes 702,560 miles of rural roads under control of the states, 2,242,030 miles of local rural roads, 180,246 miles of federal park and forest roads, and 753,777 miles of urban roads and streets. Expenditures for construction and maintenance amounted to $71,196m. in 1989.

On 1 Jan. 1990, toll roads administered by state and local toll authorities, totalled 4,721 miles.

Motor vehicles registered in the calendar year 1990 were (Federal Highways Administration) 192,914,924, including 143,159,627 automobiles, 626,987 buses, 44,478,848 trucks and 4,295,462 motorcycles.

Inter-city trucks (private and for hire) averaged 735,000m. revenue net ton-miles in 1990. Of the buses in service in 1990, 508,261 were school buses. Inter-city service operated a total of 19,800 buses and carried a total of 322m. revenue passengers in 1990.

There were 44,529 deaths in 39,779 road accidents in 1990, a fatality rate of 2·1% (3·3% in 1980).

[1] Public road mileage excludes that mileage not open to public travel, not maintained by public authority, or not passable by standard four-wheel vehicles. This excluded mileage was reported to the US Federal Highway Administration prior to 1981.

Railways. Railway history in the USA commences in 1828, but the first railway to convey both freight and passengers in regular service (between Baltimore and Ellicott's Mills, Md., 13 miles) dates from 24 May 1830. Mileage rose to a peak of 266,381 miles in 1916, falling thereafter to 222,164 in 1969 (these include some duplication under trackage rights and some mileage operated in Canada by US companies). The ordinary gauge is 4 ft 8½ in. (about 99·6% of total mileage).

In addition to the independent railroad companies, railway service is provided by the National Railroad Passenger Corporation (Amtrak), which is federally assisted. Amtrak was set up on 1 May 1971 to maintain a basic network of inter-city passenger trains, and is responsible for almost all non-commuter services with 40,000 miles of route including 1,256 km owned (555 electrified). Amtrak carried 21·4m. passengers in 1989.

The Consolidated Rail Corporation (Conrail) was established on 1 April 1976 with federal assistance to run freight services in the industrial north-east. It was returned to the private sector in 1985. There are in addition some 400 minor railways (short lines) which provide local freight connections. Outside the major conurbations there are almost no regular passenger services other than those provided by Amtrak.

Civil Aviation. There were, on 31 Dec. 1989, 700,010 certificated pilots (including 142,544 student pilots), 274,834 registered civil aircraft and 455,263,066 passengers.

Airports (Landing Facilities 17,446) on 31 Dec. 1989: Air carrier, 632; general aviation, 16,814. Of these airports, 12,946 were conventional land-based, while 414 were seaplane bases, 4,014 were heliports and 70 stolports (STOL—Short Take-Off and Landing).

Statistics from the Department of Transportation indicate that for 1990 US flag carriers in scheduled international service had 41·8m. enplanements with 673·7m. aircraft miles (excluding all-cargo) for a total of 117,696m. revenue passenger-miles. Non-scheduled services had a total of 14,239m. revenue passenger-miles internationally and domestically. Domestically, US scheduled airlines in 1990 had 423·7m. enplanements with a total of 3,817·7m. aircraft miles for 340,219m. revenue passenger-miles. (A revenue passenger-mile is one paying passenger carried per mile.)

Shipping. On 1 June 1991 the US merchant marine included 628 sea-going vessels of 1,000 gross tons or over, with aggregate dead-weight tonnage of 24m. This included 226 tankers of 15·2m. DWT.

On 1 June 1991 US merchant ocean-going vessels were employed as follows: Active, 456 of 19·2m. DWT, of which 116 of 4·5m. tons were foreign trade, 152 of 8·5m. tons in domestic trade and 84 of 1·4m. tons in other US agency operations. Inactive vessels totalled 1·7m. DWT; 26 of 2·4m. DWT privately owned were laid up and 230 of 3·6m. tons were Government-owned National Defense reserve fleet. Of the total vessels in the US fleet, 398 of 20m. DWT were privately owned.

US exports and imports carried on dry cargo and tanker vessels in the year 1990 totalled 822·6m. long tons, of which 39·8m. long tons or 4·8% were carried in US flag vessels.

Telecommunications. Until the beginning of 1984 the telephone business was largely in the hands of the American Telephone and Telegraph Company (AT & T) and its telephone operating subsidiaries, which together were known as the Bell System. Pursuant to a government anti-trust suit, the Bell System was broken up, with the telephone operating companies being divested from AT & T to create seven regional companies for providing local service. There are also many hundreds of smaller telephone companies having no common ownership affiliation with the Bell companies, but which connect with them for universal service, countrywide and worldwide. In addition, several new entrants have begun to compete with AT & T in the long-distance telephone market. The message telegraph and telex services are in the hands of The Western Union Telegraph Company, and the international record carriers, which compete with the telephone industry in providing leased private lines. Western Union also provides an inter-city telephone service. Total exchange access lines in 1987, 126,725,000.

The US Postal Service superseded the Post Office Department on 1 July 1971.

Postal business for the years ended 30 Sept. included the following items:

	1987	1988	1989	1990
Number of post offices	40,030	40,117	40,031	40,067
Operating revenue ($1,000)	31,528,112	35,035,753	38,415,092	39,654,380
Operating expenses ($1,000)	32,519,689	36,119,186	38,370,758	40,489,884

In 1991 there were 520m. radio and 215m. TV receivers in use. The licensing agency for broadcasting stations is the Federal Communications Commission, an independent federal body composed of 5 Commissioners appointed by the President. Its regulatory activities comprise: Allocation of spectrum space; consideration of applications to operate individual stations; and regulation of their operations. In 1992 more than 9,200 commercial and 1,700 non-commercial stations were operating. Programming is targetted to appeal to a given segment of the population or audience taste. There are 5 national TV networks (3 commercial; colour by NTSC) with 46 national cable networks. All major cities have network affiliates and additional commercial stations.

Cinemas. Cinemas increased from 17,003 in 1940 to 20,239 in 1950 and decreased to 20,200 in 1984, of which 2,832 were drive-ins.

Newspapers. In 1990 there were 559 morning papers with an average circulation of 41,311,167; 1,084 evening papers with 21,016,795; and 1,611 daily papers (morning and afternoon) with 62,327,962. There were also 32 all-day papers.

JUSTICE, RELIGION, EDUCATION AND WELFARE

Justice. Legal controversies may be decided in two systems of courts: The federal courts, with jurisdiction confined to certain matters enumerated in Article III of the Constitution, and the state courts, with jurisdiction in all other proceedings. The federal courts have jurisdiction exclusive of the state courts in criminal prosecutions for the violation of federal statutes, in civil cases involving the government, in bankruptcy cases and in admiralty proceedings, and have jurisdiction concurrent with the state courts over suits between parties from different states, and certain suits involving questions of federal law.

The highest court is the Supreme Court of the US, which reviews cases from the lower federal courts and certain cases originating in state courts involving questions of federal law. It is the final arbiter of all questions involving federal statutes and the Constitution; and it has the power to invalidate any federal or state law or executive action which it finds repugnant to the Constitution. This court, consisting of 9 justices appointed by the President who receive salaries of $153,600 a year (the Chief Justice, $160,000), meets from Oct. until June every year. For the term ended June 1991 it disposed of 5,581 cases, deciding 234 on their merits. In the remainder of cases it either summarily affirms lower court decisions or declines to review. A few suits, usually brought by state governments, originate in the Supreme Court, but issues of fact are mostly referred to a master.

The US courts of appeals number 13 (in 11 circuits composed of 3 or more states and 1 circuit for the District of Columbia and 1 Court of Appeals for the Federal Circuit); the 179 circuit judges receive salaries of $132,700 a year. Any party to a suit in a lower federal court usually has a right of appeal to one of these courts. In addition, there are direct appeals to these courts from many federal administrative agencies. In the year ending 30 June 1991, 43,517 appeals were filed in the courts of appeals, including 1,484 in the Federal Circuit.

The trial courts in the federal system are the US district courts, of which there are 89 in the 50 states, 1 in the District of Columbia and 1 each in the Commonwealth of Puerto Rico and the Territories of the Virgin Islands, Guam and the Northern Marianas. Each state has at least 1 US district court, and 3 states have 4 apiece. Each district court has from 1 to 28 judgeships. There are 649 US district judges ($125,100 a year), who received 207,742 civil cases and 66,556 criminal defendants from 1 July 1990 to 30 June 1991.

In addition to these courts of general jurisdiction, there are special federal courts of limited jurisdiction. The US Claims Court (16 judges at $125,100 a year) decides claims for money damages against the federal government in a wide variety of matters; the Court of International Trade (9 judges at $125,100) determines controversies concerning the classification and valuation of imported merchandise.

The judges of all these courts are appointed by the President with the approval of the Senate; to assure their independence, they hold office during good behaviour and cannot have their salaries reduced. This does not apply to judges in the Territories, who hold their offices for a term of 10 years or to judges of the US Claims Court. The judges may retire with full pay at the age of 70 years if they have served a period of 10 years, or at 65 if they have 15 years of service, but they are subject to call for such judicial duties as they are willing to undertake. 11 US judges up to 1990 have been involved in impeachment proceedings, of whom 6 district judges and 1 commerce judge were convicted and removed from office.

Of the 207,742 civil cases filed in the district courts in the year ending 30 June 1991, about 118,221 arose under various federal statutes (such as labour, social security, tax, patent, securities, antitrust and civil rights laws); 37,309 involved personal injury or property damage claims; 42,418 dealt with contracts; and 9,794 were actions concerning real property.

Of the 46,177 criminal cases filed in the district courts in the year ending 30 June 1991, 2,212 were charged with alleged infractions of the immigration laws; 229, the transport of stolen motor vehicles; 3,333 larceny and theft; 9,238, embezzlement and fraud; and 12,400 narcotics laws.

Persons convicted of federal crimes are either fined, released on probation under the supervision of the probation officers of the federal courts, confined in prison for a period of up to 6 months and then put on probation (known as split sentencing) or confined in one of the following institutions: 3 for juvenile and youths; 7 for young adults; 7 for intermediate term adults; 7 for short-term adults; 2 for females; 1 hospital and 15 community service centres. In addition, prisoners are confined in centres operated by the National Institutes of Mental Health. In addition, prisoner drug addicts may be committed to US Public Health Service hospitals for treatment. Prisoners confined in Federal and State Prisons at 31 Dec. 1990, numbered 771,243.

The state courts have jurisdiction over all civil and criminal cases arising under state laws, but decisions of the state courts of last resort as to the validity of treaties or of laws of the US, or on other questions arising under the Constitution, are subject to review by the Supreme Court of the US. The state court systems are generally similar to the federal system, to the extent that they generally have a number of trial courts and intermediate appellate courts, and a single court of last resort. The highest court in each state is usually called the Supreme Court or Court of Appeals with a Chief Justice and Associate Justices, usually elected but sometimes appointed by the Governor with the advice and consent of the State Senate or other advisory body; they usually hold office for a term of years, but in some instances for life or during good behaviour. Their salaries range from $58,452 to $121,207 a year. The lowest tribunals are usually those of Justices of the Peace; many towns and cities have municipal and police courts, with power to commit for trial in criminal matters and to determine misdemeanours for violation of the municipal ordinances; they frequently try civil cases involving limited amounts.

The death penalty is illegal in Alaska, Hawaii, Iowa, Kansas, Maine, Massachusetts, Michigan, Minnesota, New York, North Dakota, Rhode Island, Vermont, West Virginia and Wisconsin. The death penalty is legal in 36 states. Until 1982 it had fallen into disuse and had been abolished *de facto* in many states. The US Supreme Court had held the death penalty, as applied in general criminal statutes, to contravene the eighth and fourteenth amendments of the US constitution, as a cruel and unusual punishment when used so irregularly and rarely as to destroy its deterrent value.

There were no executions 1968–76. In 1977 a convicted murderer requested that he should be executed and after a lengthy legal dispute the sentence was carried out at Utah state prison. 143 persons were executed between 1977 and 1990. On 31 Dec. 1990, 2,356 prisoners were reported under sentence of death.

The total number of civilian executions carried out in the US from 1930 to 1990 was 4,002.

A Guide to Court Systems. Institute of Judicial Administration. New York, 1960
The United States Courts. Administrative Office of the US Courts, Washington, D.C., 20544
Blumberg, A. S., *Criminal Justice: Issues and Ironies.* 2nd ed. New York, 1973
Huston, L. A. and others, *Roles of the Attorney General of the United States.* New York, 1968
McCloskey, R. G., *The Modern Supreme Court.* Harvard Univ. Press, 1972
McLauchlan, W. P., *American Legal Processes.* New York, 1977
Walker, S. E., *Popular Justice.* New York, 1980

Religion. *The Yearbook of American and Canadian Churches for 1991,* published by the National Council of the Churches of Christ in the USA, New York, presents the latest figures available from official statisticians of church bodies. The large majority of reports are for the calendar year 1989, or a fiscal year ending 1989. The 1989 reports indicated that there were 147,607,394 (145,383,738 in 1988) members with 350,337 local churches. There were 340,094 clergymen serving in local congregations in 1989. The principal religious bodies (numerically or historically) or groups of religious bodies are shown below:

Denominations	Local churches	Total membership [1]
Summary:		
Protestant bodies	320,039	79,386,506
Roman Catholic Church	23,500	57,091,948
Jews	3,416	5,944,000
Eastern Churches	1,705	4,057,339
Old Catholic, Polish National Catholic and Armenian	442	979,831
Buddhists	67	19,441
Miscellaneous	1,168	200,239
1989 totals	350,481	147,607,394

[1] Membership figures are not strictly comparable, as definitions of membership vary.

Protestant Churches	Recent membership
Baptist bodies	
Southern Baptist Convention	14,907,826
National Baptist Convention, USA	5,500,000
National Baptist Convention of America, Inc.	2,668,799
National Primitive Baptist Convention	250,000
American Baptist Churches in the USA	1,548,573
American Baptist Association	250,000
Conservative Baptist Association of America	210,000
Free Will Baptists	204,489
Baptist Missionary Association of America	229,315
Christian Church (Disciples of Christ)	1,052,271
Christian Churches and Churches of Christ	1,070,616
Church of the Nazarene	561,253
Churches of Christ	1,626,000
The Episcopal Church	2,433,413
Latter-Day Saints:	
Church of Jesus Christ of Latter-Day Saints	4,175,400
Reorganized Church of Jesus Christ of Latter-Day Saints	190,183
Lutheran Bodies :	
Evangelical Lutheran Church in America	5,238,798
The Lutheran Church-Missouri Synod	2,609,025
Wisconsin Evangelical Lutheran Synod	419,312

Protestant Churches	*Recent membership*
Methodist Bodies:	
United Methodist Church	8,979,139
African Methodist Episcopal Church	2,210,000
African Methodist Episcopal Zion Church	1,220,260
Christian Methodist Episcopal Church	...
Pentecostal Bodies:	
The Church of God in Christ	...
Assemblies of God	2,137,890
Church of God (Cleveland, Tenn.)	582,203
United Pentecostal Church, International, Inc.	500,000
Presbyterian Bodies:	
Presbyterian Church (USA)	2,886,482
Presbyterian Church in America	217,374
Reformed Churches:	
Reformed Church in America	330,650
Christian Reformed Church in North America	225,699
The Salvation Army	445,566
Seventh-day Adventist Church	701,781
United Church of Christ	1,625,969

Greeley, A., *Religious Change in America*. Harvard Univ. Press, 1989

Education. Elementary and secondary education is mainly a state responsibility. Each state and the District of Columbia has a system of free public schools, established by law, with courses covering 12 years plus kindergarten. There are 3 structural patterns in common use; the K8-4 plan, meaning kindergarten plus 8 elementary grades followed by 4 high school grades; the K6–3–3 plan, or kindergarten plus 6 elementary grades followed by a 3-year junior high school and a 3-year senior high school; and the K6–6 plan, kindergarten plus 6 elementary grades followed by a 6-year high school. All plans lead to high-school graduation, usually at age 17 or 18. Vocational education is an integral part of secondary education. Some states also have 2-year colleges in which education is provided at a nominal cost. Each state has delegated a large degree of control of the educational programme to local school districts (numbering 15,376 in school year 1988–89), each with a board of education (usually 3 to 9 members) selected locally and serving mostly without pay. The school policies of the local school districts must be in accord with the laws and the regulations of their state Departments of Education. While regulations differ from one jurisdiction to another, in general it may be said that school attendance is compulsory from age 7 to 16.

The Census Bureau estimates that in Nov. 1979 only 1m. or 0·6% of the 170m. persons who were 14 years of age or older were unable to read and write; in 1930 the percentage was 4·8. In 1940 a new category was established—the 'functionally illiterate', meaning those who had completed fewer than 5 years of elementary schooling; for persons 25 years of age or over this percentage was 2·4 in March 1988 (for the non-white population alone it was 5·1%); it was 1% for white and 1·2% for non-whites in the 25–29-year-old group. The Bureau reported that in March 1988 the median years of school completed by all persons 25 years old and over was 12·7, and that 20·3% had completed 4 or more years of college. For the 25–29-year-old group, the median school years completed was 12·8 and 22·7% had completed 4 or more years of college.

In the autumn of 1989, 13,419,000 students (6,260,000 men and 7,159,000 women) were enrolled in 3,690 colleges and universities; 2,376,000 were first-time students. About 30% of the population between the ages of 18 and 24 were enrolled in colleges and universities.

Public elementary and secondary school revenue is supplied from the county and other local sources (44·1% in 1987–88), state sources (49·5%) and federal sources (6·3%). In 1990–91 expenditure for public elementary and secondary education totalled about $204,155m., including $183,389m. for current operating expenses, $14,357m. for capital outlay and $3,414m. for interest on school debt. The current expenditure per pupil in average daily attendance was $4,890. The total cost per pupil, also including capital outlay and interest, amounted to $4,890. Estimated total expenditures, for private elementary and secondary schools in 1987–88 were about

$15,100m. In 1990–91 college and university spending totalled $143,200m., of which about $92,200m. was spent by institutions under public control. The federal government contributed about 13% of total current-fund revenue; state governments, 29%; student tuition and fees, 24%; and all other sources, 34%.

Vocational education below college grade, including the training of teachers to conduct such education, has been federally aided since 1918. Federal support for vocational education in 1987–88 amounted to about $864m. Many public high schools offer vocational courses in addition to their usual academic programmes.

Summary of statistics of regular schools (public and private), teachers and pupils in autumn 1988 (compiled by the US National Center for Education Statistics):

Schools by level	Number of schools 1988–89	Teachers 1990–91	Enrolment 1990–91
Elementary schools:			
Public	61,531	1,316,000	25,303,000
Private	20,252 [1]	281,000	4,219,000
Secondary schools:			
Public	22,785	1,039,000	15,498,000
Private	7,387 [1]	103,000	1,172,000
Higher education:			
Public	1,582	539,000	10,539,000
Private	1,983	223,000	3,019,000
Total	115,520	3,501,000	59,750,000

[1] Data for 1985–86.

Most of the private elementary and secondary schools are affiliated with religious denominations. In 1989–90 there were 7,395 Roman Catholic elementary schools with 1,893,000 pupils and 94,000 teachers, and 1,324 secondary schools with 606,000 pupils and 43,000 teachers.

During the school year 1990–91 high-school graduates numbered about 2,522,000 (of whom 2,232,000 were from public schools). Institutions of higher education conferred 1,024,100 bachelor's degrees during the year 1990–91; 463,200 associate's degrees; 321,600 master's degrees; 35,900 doctorates; and 74,700 first professional degrees. Financial assistance to students in higher education in 1990–91 amounted to $5,794·9m., and loans, $3,846·1m.

During the academic year, 1989–90, 361,200 foreign students were enrolled in American colleges and universities. The percentages of students coming from various areas in 1988–89 were: South and East Asia, 52·2; Middle East, 11; Latin America, 12·3; Africa, 7·3; Europe, 11·7; North America, 4·6; Oceania, 1.

School enrolment, Oct. 1989, embraced 95·2% of the children who were 5 and 6 years old; 99·3% of the children aged 7–13 years; 98·8% of those aged 14–15, 92·7% of those aged 16–17 and 56% of those aged 18–19.

The US National Center for Education Statistics estimates the total enrolment in the autumn of 1990 at all of the country's elementary, secondary and higher educational institutions (public and private) at 59·8m. (59·4m. in the autumn of 1989); this was 23·8% of the total population of the USA as of 1 Sept. 1990.

The number of teachers in regular public and private elementary and secondary schools in the autumn of 1990 was expected to increase slightly to 2,785,000. The average annual salary of the public school teachers was about $31,200 in 1989–90.

Health. Admission to the practice of medicine (for both doctors of medicine and doctors of osteopathic medicine) is controlled in each state by examining boards directly representing the profession and acting with authority conferred by state law. Although there are a number of variations, the usual time now required to complete training is 8 years beyond the secondary school with up to 3 or more years of additional graduate training. Certification as a specialist may require between 3 and 5 more years of graduate training plus experience in practice. In academic year 1987–88 the 142 US schools (15 osteopathic and 127 allopathic) graduated 17,451 physicians. About 36% of first-year students were women. In Dec. 1988 the estimated number of active physicians (MD and DO—in all forms of practice) in the US, Puerto Rico and outlying US areas was 573,583 (1 active physician to 434 population). The distribution of physicians throughout the country is uneven, both by state and by urban–rural areas.

In 1987–88 the 58 dental schools graduated 4,581 dentists. Active dentists in Dec. 1988 numbered 146,800 (1 active dentist to 1,678 population).

In academic year 1987–88, there were 1,443 registered nursing programmes in the US and 64,915 graduates. In Dec. 1988 registered nurses employed full- or part-time were 1 to 144 population.

Number of hospitals listed by the American Hospital Association in 1984 was 6,872, with 1,339,000 beds and 37,938,000 admissions during the year; average daily census was 970,000. Of the total, 341 hospitals with 112,000 beds were operated by the federal government; 1,662 with 203,000 beds by state and local government; 3,366 with 717,000 beds by non-profit organizations (including church groups); 786 with 100,000 beds are proprietary. The categories of non-federal hospitals are 5,814 short-term general and special hospitals with 1,020,000 beds; 131 non-federal long-term general and special hospitals with 30,000 beds; 579 psychiatric hospitals with 175,000 beds; 7 tuberculosis hospitals with 1,000 beds.

Welfare. Social welfare legislation was chiefly the province of the various states until the adoption of the Social Security Act of 14 Aug. 1935. This as amended provides for a federal system of old-age, survivors and disability insurance; health insurance for the aged and disabled; supplemental security income for the aged, blind and disabled; federal state unemployment insurance; and federal grants to states for public assistance (medical assistance for the aged and aid to families with dependent children generally) and for maternal and child-health and child-welfare services. The Social Security Administration of the Department of Health and Human Services has responsibility for the programmes—old-age, survivors and disability insurance and supplemental security income. The Family Support Administration has federal responsibility for the programmes—aid to families with dependent children, low income energy assistance, child support enforcement, refugee and entry assistance and community services block grant. The Health Care Financing Administration, an agency of the same Department, has federal responsibility for health insurance for the aged and disabled. The Office of Human Development Services has federal responsibility for social service programmes for such groups as the elderly, children, youth, native Americans and persons with developmental disabilities, and its Public Health Service supports maternal and child-health services. Unemployment insurance is the responsibility of the Department of Labor.

The Social Security Act provides for protection against the cost of medical care through the two-part programme of health insurance for people 65 and over and for certain disabled people under 65, who receive disability insurance payments or who have permanent kidney failure (Medicare). During fiscal year 1987, payments totalling $49,967m. were made under the hospital part of Medicare on behalf of 31,852,860 people. During the same period, $29,937m. was paid under the voluntary medical insurance part of Medicare on behalf of 31,169,960 people.

In 1991 about 134m. persons worked in employment covered by old-age, survivors and disability insurance.

In June 1991 over 40·3m. beneficiaries were on the rolls, and the average benefit paid to a retired worker (not counting any paid to his dependants) was about $603 per month. Retirement age is 65 years. In 2000 this will be progressively increased to 67. Early retirement with reduced benefit is possible at 62.

In 1990 an average of 11·5m. persons (adults and children) were receiving payments under aid to families with dependent children (average monthly payment, $379 per family). Total payments under aid to families with dependent children were $18,027m. in 1989–90. The role of Child Support Enforcement is to ensure that children are supported by their parents. Money collected is for children who live with only one parent because of divorce, separation or out-of-wedlock birth. In 1989, nearly $5,200m. was collected on behalf of these children.

In June 1991, about 5m. persons were receiving supplementary security income payments, including 1·5m. persons aged 65 or over and over 3·5m. disabled or blind persons, including 0·3m. children. Payments, including supplemental amounts from various states, totalled $19m. in 1991.

In 1990-91, federal appropriations for the social services block grant amounted to $2,800m. In addition, 1991 federal appropriations for human development and family social services to selected target groups totalled $6,046m. Included in this amount were $4,522m. for children and youth; $794m. for the elderly; $102m. for persons with developmental disabilities; and $33m. for native Americans. During 1989, the Public Health Services awarded a total of $554·3m. for maternal and child health services, $465·3m. as block grants to the States, $82·1m. for special projects of regional and national significance, and $6·9m. for genetic screening. Other block grants awarded by the Public Health Service in 1988 included $88m. for preventive health; $487m. for alcohol, drug abuse and mental health; $155m. for alcohol and drug abuse treatment and rehabilitation. In 1989, $414·8m. was awarded for community health centres; $45·6m. for migrant health centres; $20·6m. for efforts to reduce infant mortality; $3·2m. for black lung clinics; and $135·1m. for family planning. Other block grants awarded by the Administration for Children and Families included $436m. for community services block grant programmes for 1990-91, and $1,415m. for the low income home energy assistance programme (LIHEAP).

DIPLOMATIC REPRESENTATIVES

Of the USA in Great Britain (Grosvenor Sq., London, W1A 1AE)
Ambassador: Raymond Seitz.

Of Great Britain in the USA (3100 Massachusetts Ave., Washington, D.C., 20008)
Ambassador: Sir Robin Renwick, KCMG.

Of the United States to the United Nations
Ambassador: Thomas Pickering.

Further Reading

I. STATISTICAL INFORMATION

The Office of Management and Budget, Washington, D.C. 20503 is part of the Executive Office of the President; it is responsible for co-ordinating all the statistical work of the different Federal Government agencies. The Office does not collect or publish data itself. The main statistical agencies are as follows:

(1) Data User Services Division, Bureau of the Census, Department of Commerce, Washington, D.C. 20233. Responsible for decennial censuses of population and housing, quinquennial census of agriculture, manufactures and business; current statistics on population and the labour force, manufacturing activity and commodity production, trade and services, foreign trade, state and local government finances and operations. (*Statistical Abstract of the United States*, annual, and others).

(2) Bureau of Labor Statistics, Department of Labor, 441 G Street NW, Washington, D.C. 20212. (*Monthly Labor Review* and others).

(3) Information Division, Economic Research Service, Department of Agriculture, Washington, D.C. 20250. (*Agricultural Statistics*, annual, and others).

(4) National Center for Health Statistics, Department of Health and Human Services, 3700 East-West Highway, Hyattsville Md. 20782. (*Vital Statistics of the United States*, monthly and annual, and others).

(5) Bureau of Mines Office of Technical Information, Department of the Interior, Washington, D.C. 20241. (*Minerals Yearbook*, annual, and others).

(6) Office of Energy Information Services, Energy Information Administration, Department of Energy, Washington, D.C. 20461.

(7) Statistical Publications, Department of Commerce, Room 5062 Main Commerce, 14th St and Constitution Avenue NW, Washington, D.C. 20230; the Department's Bureau of Economic Analysis and its Office of Industry and Trade Information are the main collectors of data.

(8) Center for Education Statistics, Department of Education, 555 New Jersey Avenue NW, Washington, D.C. 20208.

(9) Public Correspondence Division, Office of the Assistant Secretary of Defense (Public Affairs P.C.), The Pentagon, Washington, D.C. 20301-1400.

(10) Bureau of Justice Statistics, Department of Justice, 633 Indiana Avenue NW, Washington, D.C. 20531.

(11) Public Inquiry, APA 200, Federal Aviation Administration, Department of Transportation, 800 Independence Avenue SW, Washington, D.C. 20591.

(12) Office of Public Affairs, Federal Highway Administration, Department of Transportation, 400 7th St. SW, Washington, D.C. 20590.

(13) Statistics Division, Internal Revenue Service, Department of the Treasury, 1201 E St. NW, Washington, D.C. 20224.

Statistics on the economy are also published by the Division of Research and Statistics, Federal Reserve Board, Washington, D.C. 20551; the Congressional Joint Committee on the Economy, Capitol; the Office of the Secretary, Department of the Treasury, 1500 Pennsylvania Avenue NW, Washington, D.C. 20220.

II. Other Official Publications

Guide to the Study of the United States of America. General Reference and Bibliography Division, Library of Congress. 1960.
Historical Statistics of the United States, Colonial Times to 1957: A Statistical Abstract Supplement. Washington, 1960.—*Continuation to 1962 and Revisions,* 1965.
United States Government Manual. Washington. Annual.
The official publications of the USA are issued by the US Government Printing Office and are distributed by the Superintendent of Documents, who issued in 1940 a cumulative *Catalog of the Public Documents of the... Congress and of All the Departments of the Government of the United States.* This *Catalog* is kept up to date by *United States Government Publications, Monthly Catalog* with annual index and supplemented by *Price Lists.* Each *Price List* is devoted to a special subject or type of material, *e.g., American History* or *Census.* Useful guides are Schmeckebier, L. F. and Eastin, R. B. (eds.) *Government Publications and Their Use.* 2nd ed., Washington, D.C., 1961; Boyd, A. M., *United States Government Publications.* 3rd ed. New York, 1949, and Leidy, W. P., *Popular Guide to Government Publications.* 2nd ed. New York and London, 1963.
Treaties and other International Acts of the United States of America (Edited by Hunter Miller), 8 vols. Washington, 1929–48. This edition stops in 1863. It may be supplemented by *Treaties, Conventions... Between the US and Other Powers, 1776–1937* (Edited by William M. Malloy and others). 4 vols. 1909–38. A new Treaty Series, *US Treaties and Other International Agreements* was started in 1950.
Writings on American History. Washington, annual from 1902 (except 1904–5 and 1941–47).

III. Non-Official Publications

A. Handbooks
National Historical Publications Commission. *Guide to Archives and Manuscripts in the United States,* ed. P. M. Hamer. Yale Univ. Press, 1961
Adams, J. T. (ed.) *Dictionary of American History.* 2nd ed. 7 vols. New York, 1942
Dictionary of American Biography, ed. A. Johnson and D. Malone. 23 vols. New York, 1929–64.—*Concise Dictionary of American Biography.* New York, 1964
Current Biography. New York, annual from 1940; monthly supplements
Handlin, O. and others. *Harvard Guide to American History.* Cambridge, Mass., 1954
Herstein, S. R. and Robbins, N., *United States of America.* [Bibliography] Oxford and Santa Barbara, 1982
Lord, C. L. and E. H., *Historical Atlas of the US.* Rev. ed. New York, 1969
Maisel, L. S. (ed.) *Political Parties in the United States; an Encyclopedia.* 2 vols. Camden (Conn.), 1991
Who's Who in America. Chicago, 1899–1900 to date; monthly Supplement. 1940 to date

B. General History
Barck, Jr, O. T. and Blake, N. M., *Since 1900: A History of the United States.* 5th ed. New York, 1974
Berkowitz, E. D., *America's Welfare State from Roosevelt to Reagan.* Johns Hopkins Univ. Press, 1991
Brogan, H., *The Longman History of the United States of America.* London, 1985
Carman, H. J. and others, *A History of the American People.* 3rd ed. 2 vols. New York, 1967
Campbell, C. and Rockman, B. A. (eds.) *The Bush Presidency: First Appraisals.* Chatham, (NJ), 1991
Foner, E. and Garraty, J. A. (eds.) *The Reader's Companion to American History.* New York, 1992

Kelly, A. H. et al., The American Constitution: its Origins and Development. 7th ed. New York, 1991

King, A. (ed.) The New American Political System. 2nd ed. Washington, DC, 1990

Morison, S. E. with Commager, H. S., The Growth of the American Republic. 2 vols. 5th ed. OUP, 1962–63

Neustadt, R. E., Presidential Power and the Modern Presidents: the Politics of Leadership from Roosevelt to Reagan. New York, 1991

Nicholas, H. G., The Nature of American Politics. OUP, 1980

Scammon, R. N. (ed.) American Votes: A Handbook of Contemporary American Election Statistics. Washington, D.C., 1956 to date (biennial)

Schlesinger, J., America at Century's End. Columbia Univ. Press, 1989

Snowman, D., America Since 1920. London, 1978

Watson, R. A., The Promise and Performance of American Democracy. 2nd ed. New York, 1975

C. Minorities

McNickle, D., The Indian Tribes of the United States. OUP, 1962.—Native American Tribalism. OUP, 1973

National Urban League. The State of Black America. New York, annual

Sklare, M., The Jew in American Society. New York, 1974

D. Economic History

The Economic History of the United States. 9 vols. New York, 1946 ff.

Bining, A. C. and Cochran, T. C., The Rise of American Economic Life. 4th ed. New York, 1963

Dorfman, J., The Economic Mind in American Civilization. 5 vols. New York, 1946–59

Friedman, M. and Schwartz, A. J., A Monetary History of the United States, 1867–1960. New York, 1963

Marmor, T. R. et al., America's Misunderstood Welfare State. New York, 1990

E. Foreign Relations

Documents on American Foreign Relations. Princeton, from 1948. Annual

The United States in World Affairs. 1931 ff. Council on Foreign Relations. New York, from 1932. Annual

Agnew, J., The United States in the World Economy. CUP, 1987

Bartlett, R. (ed.) The Record of American Diplomacy; Documents and Readings in the History of American Foreign Relations. 4th ed. New York, 1964

Brewer T. L., American Foreign Policy: a Contemporary Introduction. 3rd ed. New York, 1991

Connell-Smith, G., The United States and Latin America. London, 1975

Schwab, G., (ed.) United States Foreign Policy at the Crossroads. Westport, 1982

Vance, C., Hard Choices: Critical Years in America's Foreign Policy. New York, 1983

F. National Character

Degler, C. N., Out of Our Past: The Forces That Shaped Modern America. Rev. ed. New York, 1970

Duigan, P. and Rabushka, A., (eds.) The United States in the 1980s. Stanford, 1980

Fawcett, E. and Thomas, T., America and the Americans. London, 1983

National Library: The Library of Congress. Washington 25, D.C. Librarian: James H. Billington.

STATES AND TERRITORIES

For information as to State and Local Government, see under UNITED STATES, pp. 1404–05.

Against the names of the Governors and the Secretaries of State, (D.) stands for Democrat and (R.) for Republican.

Figures for the revenues and expenditures of the various states are those of the Federal Bureau of the Census unless otherwise stated, which takes the original state figures and arranges them on a common pattern so that those of one state can be compared with those of any other.

Official publications of the various states and insular possessions are listed in the Monthly Check-List of State Publications, issued by the Library of Congress since 1910. Their character and contents are discussed in J. K. Wilcox's Manual on the Use of State Publications (1940). Of great importance bibliographically are the publications of the Historical Records Survey and the American Imprints Inventory, which record local archives, official publications and state imprints. These publications supplement those of state historical societies which usually publish journals and monographs on state and local history. An outstanding source of statistical data is the material issued by the various state planning boards and commissions, to which should be added the annual *Governmental Finances* issued by the US Bureau of the Census.

The Book of the States. Biennial. Council of State Governments, Lexington, 1953 ff.
State Government Finances. Annual. Dept. of Commerce, 1966 ff.

ALABAMA

HISTORY. Alabama, settled in 1702 as part of the French Province of Louisiana, and ceded to the British in 1763, was organized as a Territory, 1817, and admitted into the Union on 14 Dec. 1819.

AREA AND POPULATION. Alabama is bounded north by Tennessee, east by Georgia, south by Florida and the Gulf of Mexico and west by Mississippi. Total area, 51,705 sq. miles; land area, 50,750 sq. miles. Census population, 1 April 1990, 4,040,587, an increase of 3·87% since 1980. Births, 1989, 62,530 (14·7 per 1,000 population); deaths, 38,924 (9·2); infant deaths (under 1 year), 756 (12·1 per 1,000 live births); marriages, 43,158 (10·2); divorces, 24,985 (5·9).

Population in 5 census years was:

	White	Black	Indian	Asiatic	Total	Per sq. mile
1930	1,700,844	944,834	465	105	2,646,248	51·3
1960	2,283,609	980,271	1,726	915	3,266,521	64·0
			All others			
1970	2,533,831	903,467	6,867		3,444,165	66·7
1980	2,872,621	996,335	24,932		3,893,888	74·9
1990	2,975,797	1,020,705	44,085		4,040,587	79·6

Of the total population in 1990, 47·9% were male, 66% were urban and 68·7% were 21 years or older.

The large cities (1990 census) were: Birmingham, 265,968 (metropolitan area, 907,810); Mobile, 196,278 (476,923); Montgomery (the capital), 187,106 (292,517); Huntsville, 159,789 (238,912); Tuscaloosa, 77,759 (150,522).

CLIMATE. Birmingham. Jan. 46°F (7·8°C), July 80°F (26·7°C). Annual rainfall 54" (1,346 mm). Mobile. Jan. 52°F (11·1°C), July 82°F (27·8°C). Annual rainfall 63" (1,577 mm). Montgomery. Jan. 49°F (9·4°C), July 81°F (27·2°C). Annual rainfall 53" (1,321 mm). *See* Gulf Coast, p. 1382. The growing season ranges from 190 days (north) to 270 days (south).

CONSTITUTION AND GOVERNMENT. The present constitution dates from 1901; it has had 534 amendments (as at Nov. 1990). The legislature consists of a Senate of 35 members and a House of Representatives of 105 members, all elected for 4 years. The Governor and Lieut.-Governor are elected for 4 years.

The state is represented in Congress by 2 senators and 7 representatives. Applicants for registration must take an oath of allegiance to the United States and fill out a questionnaire to the satisfaction of the registrars. In the 1988 presidential election Bush polled 815,576 votes, Dukakis, 549,506.

Montgomery is the capital.

Governor: Guy Hunt (R.), 1991–95 ($87,913.80).
Lieut.-Governor: Jim Folsom, Jr. (D.) ($1,900 a month plus $1,500 a month expenses).
Secretary of State: Billy Joe Camp (D.) ($57,203.52).

BUDGET. The total net revenue for the fiscal year ending 30 Sept. 1990 was $9,041m. ($3,820m. from tax, $2,060m. from federal payments); total net expenditure was $7,400m. ($3,380m. on education, $1,049 on public welfare, $298m. on health, $716m. on highways).

The outstanding debt on 30 Sept. 1988 amounted to $2,513m.
Per capita income (1990) was $14,826.

ENERGY AND NATURAL RESOURCES

Minerals. Principal minerals (1986): Coal, limestone, sand and gravel, petroleum (21·1m. bbl.) and natural gas (146,606m. cu. ft.). Total mineral output (1986) was valued at $2,001m.; non-fuel minerals (1990) $562m.

Agriculture. The number of farms in 1990 was 45,000, covering 9·8m. acres; average farm had 218 acres and was valued at about $193,000.

Cash receipts from farm marketings, 1990: Crops, $761,016,000m.; livestock and poultry products, $2,082,529,000m.; and total, $2,843,545,000m. Principal sources: greenhouses and nurseries, peanuts, cotton, potatoes and other vegetables, soybeans; corn, wheat, pecans, hay, peaches and other fruit are also important. In 1990, poultry accounted for the largest percentage of cash receipts from farm marketings; cattle and calves were second, horticulture third, peanuts fourth.

Forestry. Area of national forest lands, Oct. 1990, 651,200 acres. Area of commercial timberland, 1990, 21,931,600 acres, of which 1,161,700 acres were public forests and 20,769,900 acres private forests. In 1990 (preliminary), 23,075m. cu. ft of timber was produced; 11,101m. cu. ft softwoods and 11,974m. cu. ft hardwoods. The estimated delivered timber value of forest products in 1989–90 was $757.74m.

INDUSTRY. Alabama is predominantly industrial. In Aug. 1991 manufacturing establishments employed 380,600 workers; government, 314,300; trade, 352,200; services, 328,100; transport and public utilities, 84,700 (total non-agricultural workforce 1,627,700).

TOURISM. In 1990, there were an estimated 9·5m. visitors in hotels, motels and resorts, and spending by tourists was over £3,000m.

COMMUNICATIONS

Roads. Paved roads of all classes at July 1991 totalled 65,596 miles; total highways, 90,672 miles. Registered motor vehicles, 1991, 3,716,106.

Railways. At Dec. 1990 the railways had a length of 5,554 miles including side and yard tracks.

Civil Aviation. In 1988 the state had 103 public-use airports. Nine airports are for commercial service, two are relief airports for Birmingham and the rest, general aviation.

Shipping. There are 1,600 miles of navigable inland water and 50 miles of Gulf Coast. The only deep-water port is Mobile, with a large ocean-going trade; total tonnage (1990), 37,595,198 tons. The docks can handle 34 ocean-going vessels at once. The 9-ft channel of the Tennessee River traverses North Alabama for 200 miles; the Tennessee-Tombigbee waterway (234 miles), connects the Tennessee River with the Tombigbee River for access to the Gulf of Mexico. The Warrier–Tombigbee system (476 miles) connects the Birmingham industrial area to the Gulf. The Coosa-Alabama River system reaches central Alabama as far north as Montgomery from Mobile and the Gulf Intracoastal Waterway. The Chattahoochee River runs for 261 miles. The Alabama State Docks also operates a system of 10 inland docks; there are several privately-run inland docks.

JUSTICE, RELIGION, EDUCATION AND WELFARE

Justice. Before 1 Jan. 1927, persons executed in Alabama were hanged locally by the Sheriffs in the counties of their conviction. After Jan. 1927, the state prison system carried out executions by electrocution. From April 1927 to Jan. 1965, there were 163 executions (122 for murder, 25 for rape, 5 for armed robbery, 1 for burglary and 1 for carnal knowledge); from 1965 to 1983, no executions occurred; from April 1983 to July 1990, there were 7 executions for capital murder, the only offence punishable by death today. The prison population on 30 Sept. 1990 was 15,074, of which 115 were on death row. There were also 26,000 adult persons on probation or parole.

In 41 counties the sale of alcoholic beverage is permitted, and in 26 counties it is prohibited; but it is permitted in 7 cities within those 26 counties.

Religion. Membership in selected religious bodies (in 1990): Alabama Baptist Convention (1,048,005), United Methodist (263,000), Roman Catholic (124,725), Assembly of God (37,460), Episcopal (28,034).

Education. In the school year 1989–90 the 1,294 public elementary and high schools required 39,416 teachers to teach 714,691 students enrolled in grades K-12. In 1989-90 there were 16 public senior institutions with 120,822 students and 4,596 faculty members. In 1990–91 the 14 community colleges had 50,216 students and 1,093 faculty members; 10 junior colleges had 18,106 students and 323 faculty members; 13 technical colleges had 17,082 students and 488 faculty members.

Health. In 1987 there were 137 hospitals (21,404 beds) licensed by the State Board of Health. In 1991 there were 2,375 patients in hospitals for mental illness and 1,220 residents in facilities for the mentally retarded.

Welfare. In June 1991 Alabama paid supplements (to federal welfare payments) to 5,133 recipients of old-age assistance, receiving an average of $53.52 each; 4,064 permanently and totally disabled, $57.95; 96 blind, $56.90. Combined state–federal aid to dependent children was paid to 47,892 families, average $118.60 per family.

Further Reading

Alabama Official and Statistical Register. Montgomery. Quadrennial
Alabama County Data Book. Alabama Dept. of Economic and Community Affairs. Annual
Directory of Health Care Facilities. Alabama State Board of Health
Economic Abstract of Alabama. Center for Business and Economic Research, Univ. of Alabama, 1987
McCurley, R. L., Jr., ed., *The Legislative Process*. Alabama Law Institute, 3rd ed., 1984
Thigpen, R. A., *Alabama Government Manual*. Alabama Law Institute, 7th ed., 1986
Wiggins, S. W., (ed.) *From Civil War to Civil Rights, 1860–1960*. Univ. of Alabama Press, 1987

ALASKA

HISTORY. Discovered in 1741 by Vitus Bering, its first settlement, on Kodiak Island, was in 1784. The area known as Russian America with its capital (1806) at Sitka was ruled by a Russo-American fur company and vaguely claimed as a Russian colony. Alaska was purchased by the United States from Russia under the treaty of 30 March 1867 for $7·2m. It was not organized until 1884, when it became a 'district' governed by the code of the state of Oregon. By Act of Congress approved 24 Aug. 1912 Alaska became an incorporated Territory; its first legislature in 1913 granted votes to women, 7 years in advance of the Constitutional Amendment.

Alaska officially became the 49th state of the Union on 3 Jan. 1959.

AREA AND POPULATION. Alaska is bounded north by the Beaufort Sea, west and south by the Pacific and east by Canada. The total area is 591,004 sq. miles; the land area is 570,373 sq. miles. Census population, 1 April 1990, was 550,043, including military personnel, an increase of 37·4% over 1980. Births, 1984, were 12,247 (24·5 per 1,000 population); deaths, 1,993 (4); infant deaths, 147 (12 per 1,000 live births); marriages, 6,519 (13); divorces, 3,904 (7·8).

Population in 5 census years was:

	White	Black	All Others	Total	Per sq. mile
1950	92,808	...	35,835	128,643	0·23
1960	174,649	...	51,518	226,167	0·40
1970	236,767	8,911	54,704	300,382	0·53
1980	309,728	13,643	78,480	401,851	1·00
1990	415,492	22,451	112,100	550,043	1·00

Of the total population in 1980, 53·01% were male, 64·34% were urban and 68·57% were aged 21 years or over.

The largest city is the borough of Anchorage, which had a 1990 census population of 226,338. Census populations of the other 13 boroughs, 1990: Aleutians East, 2,464; Bristol Bay, 1,410; Fairbanks North Star, 77,720; Haines, 2,117; Juneau, 26,751; Kenai Peninsula, 40,802; Ketchikan Gateway, 13,828; Kodiak Island, 13,309; Lake and Peninsula, 1,668; Matanuska-Susitna 39,683; North Slope, 5,979; Northwest Arctic, 6,113; Sitka, 8,588. Other Census Area populations, 1990: Aleutians West, 9,478; Bethel, 13,656; Dillingham, 4,012; Nome, 8,288; Prince of Wales-Outer Ketchikan, 6,278; Skagway-Yakutat-Angoon, 4,385; Southeast Fairbanks, 5,913; Valdez-Cordova, 9,952; Wade Hampton, 5,791; Wrangell-Petersburg, 7,042; Yukon-Koyukuk, 8,478. In 1991 there were 15 boroughs (including Denali) and 149 incorporated cities.

CLIMATE. Anchorage. Jan. 12°F (–11·1°C), July 57°F (13·9°C). Annual rainfall 15" (371 mm). Fairbanks. Jan. –11°F (–23·9°C), July 60°F (15·6°C). Annual rainfall 12" (300 mm). Sitka. Jan. 33°F (0·6°C), July 55°F (12·8°C). Annual rainfall 87" (2,175 mm). *See* Pacific Coast, p. 1381.

CONSTITUTION AND GOVERNMENT. An important provision of the Enabling Act is that the state has the right to select 103·55m. acres of vacant and unappropriated public lands in order to establish 'a tax basis'; it can open these lands to prospectors for minerals, and the state is to derive the principal advantage in all gains resulting from the discovery of minerals. In addition, certain federally administered lands reserved for conservation of fisheries and wild life have been transferred to the state. Special provision is made for federal control of land for defence in areas of high strategic importance.

The constitution of Alaska was adopted by public vote, 24 April 1956. The state legislature consists of a Senate of 20 members (elected for 4 years) and a House of Representatives of 40 members (elected for 2 years). The state sends 2 senators and 1 representative to Congress. The franchise may be exercised by all citizens over 18.

The capital is Juneau.

In the 1988 presidential election Bush polled 102,381 votes, Dukakis, 62,205.

Governor: Walter J. Hickel (ind.), 1991–94 ($81,648).
Lieut.-Governor: Stephen McAlpine (ind.) ($76,188)

ECONOMY

Budget. Total state government revenue for the year ended 30 June 1990 (Annual Financial Report figures) was $3,462·2m. Total expenditure was $2,711·6m.

In 1976 a Permanent Fund was set up for the deposit of at least 25% of all mineral-related revenue; total assets at 30 June 1991, $12,135m.

General obligation bonds at 30 June 1991, $213m.

Per capita income (1989) was $21,656.

ENERGY AND NATURAL RESOURCES

Oil and Gas. Commercial production of crude petroleum began in 1959 and by 1961 had become the most important mineral by value. Production: 1961, 6·3m. bbls (of 42 gallons); 1977, 171m. bbls; 1981, 587m. bbls; 1985, 666m. bbls; 1988, 685m. bbls, value $5,877; 1990, 588m. bbls, value $9,960m. Oil comes mainly from Prudhoe Bay, the Kuparuk River field and several Cook Inlet fields. Natural gas (liquid) production, 1988, 20·3m. bbls, value $122·29m.; 1990 production value, $277m. Alaska receives approximately 80% of its general revenue from petroleum taxes and royalties. Revenue to the state from oil production in 1990 was $2,113·1m. (84% of general fund revenues). General fund unrestricted revenues, 1990: Severance taxes, 44%; oil and gas royalties, 30%; investment earnings, 7%; oil and gas, 9%; non-petroleum, 10%.

Oil from the Prudhoe Bay arctic field is now carried by the Trans-Alaska pipeline to Prince William Sound on the south coast, where a tanker terminal has been built at Valdez.

Minerals. Value of production, 1990, in $1,000: Gold 89,204; silver, 50,675; lead, 30,954; zinc, 253,680; industrial minerals (including sand, gravel and building stone), 63,900; other minerals (including mercury, antimony, platinum, tin, tungsten, jade and soapstone, coal, peat), 45,590. Total value, $534,003,000.

Agriculture. In some parts of the state the climate during the brief spring and summer (about 100 days in major areas and 152 days in the south-eastern coastal area) is suitable for agricultural operations, thanks to the long hours of sunlight, but Alaska is a food-importing area. In 1990 about 1m. acres was farmland and there were 580 farms and ranches with annual sales of $1,000 or more. At 1 Jan. 1991 there were 7,500 cattle and calves and 2,500 sheep and lambs; at 1 Dec. 1990, 1,200 hogs and pigs and 5,000 poultry.

Total value of agricultural products in 1988: $30m. of which $19·5m. was from crops (mainly hay and potatoes) and $10·5m. from livestock and poultry.

There were about 34,000 reindeer in western Alaska in 1990. Sales of reindeer meat and by-products in 1990 (preliminary) were valued at $1,706,000.

Forestry. Of the 129m. forested acres of Alaska, 21m. acres are classified as timberland or commercial forest. The interior forest covers 115m. acres; more than 13m. acres are considered commercial forest, of which 3·4m. acres are in designated parks or wilderness and unavailable for harvest. The coastal rain forests provide the bulk of commercial timber volume; of their 13·6m. acres, 7·6m. acres support commercial stands, of which 1·9m. acres are in parks or wilderness and unavailable for harvest. In 1989, more than 22·7m. bd ft of timber, value $514,632, were harvested from publicly owned or managed lands; lumber was the second most valuable product exported in 1988, with a value of $527m. (over 24% of all exports).

Fisheries. The catch for 1989 was 5,209·5m. lb. of fish and shellfish having a value to fishermen of $1,309·6m. The most important species are salmon, crab, herring, halibut and pollock.

INDUSTRY. Main industries with employment, 1989: Government, 67,000; trade, 44,200; services, 45,900; contract construction, 9,800; manufacturing, 15,670; mining including oil and gas, 10,250; transport, communication and utilities, 21,170; finance, insurance and property, 9,240.

The major manufacturing industry was food processing, followed by timber industries. Total non-agricultural employment, 1988, 212,300. Total wages and salaries, 1987, $5,759·86m.

TOURISM. About 678,500 tourists visited the state in 1990.

COMMUNICATIONS

Roads. Alaska's highway and road system, 1990, totalled 12,272 miles, including 10,462 miles rural. Registered motor vehicles, 1990, 363,743.

The Alaska Highway extends 1,523 miles from Dawson Creek, British Columbia, to Fairbanks, Alaska. It was built by the US Army in 1942, at a cost of $138m. The greater portion of it, because it lies in Canada, is maintained by Canada.

Railways. There is a railway of 111 miles from Skagway to the town of Whitehorse, the White Pass and Yukon route, in the Canadian Yukon region (this service operates seasonally). The government-owned Alaska Railroad runs from Seward to Fairbanks, a distance of 471 miles. This is a freight service with only occasional passenger use. A passenger service operates from Anchorage to Fairbanks via Denali National Park in the tourist season.

Civil Aviation. In 1986 the state had 988 airports, of which 294 were state owned. Commercial passengers by air from Alaska's largest international airports Anchorage and Fairbanks in 1988 numbered 1,375,500 at Anchorage and 251,495 at Fairbanks. General aviation aircraft in the state per 1,000 population was about ten times the US average.

Shipping. Regular shipping services to and from the US are furnished by 2 steamship and several barge lines operating out of Seattle and other Pacific coast ports. A Canadian company also furnishes a regular service from Vancouver, B.C. Anchorage is the main port.

A 1,435 nautical-mile ferry system for motor cars and passengers (the 'Alaska Marine Highway') operates from Bellingham, Washington and Prince Rupert (British Columbia) to Juneau, Haines (for access to the Alaska Highway) and Skagway. A second system extends throughout the south-central region of Alaska linking the Cook Inlet area with Kodiak Island and Prince William Sound.

JUSTICE, RELIGION, EDUCATION AND WELFARE

Justice. There is no death penalty in Alaska. In 1990 there were 2,433 adults and 205 juveniles in state and federal institutions.

Religion. Many religions are represented, including the Russian Orthodox, Roman Catholic, Episcopalian, Presbyterian, Methodist and other denominations.

Education. Total expenditure on public schools in 1987 was $693,643,154. In 1988 there were about 3,100 elementary and 2,800 secondary school teachers, average salary, $41,000. During 1990 there were 106,839 pupils at public schools, 5,588 at private schools. The University of Alaska (founded in 1922) main campuses had (Spring 1990) 31,724 students. Other colleges had 2,911 students in Spring 1990.

Health. In 1983 there were 26 acute care hospitals with 1,800 beds, of which 7 were federal public health hospitals; 1 mental hospital; 24 mental health clinics.

Welfare. Old-age assistance was established under the Federal Social Security Act; in 1985 aid to dependent children covered a monthly average of 6,400 households; payments, an average of $501 per month; aid to the disabled was given to a monthly average of 2,300 persons receiving on average $251 per month. An average of 1,100 aged per month received $166.

Further Reading

Statistical Information: Department of Commerce and Economic Development, Economic Analysis Section, Juneau; Department of Labor, Research and Analysis, Juneau.

Alaska Blue Book, Department of Education, Juneau. Biennial
Alaska Industry–Occupation Outlook to 1992, Department of Labor, Juneau.
Alaska Economy, The. Division of Economic Enterprise, Juneau. Annual
Annual Financial Report, Department of Administration, Juneau.
Gardey, J., *Alaska: The Sophisticated Wilderness.* London, 1976
Hulley, Clarence C., *Alaska Past and Present.* Portland, Oregon, 1970
Hunt, W. R., *Alaska, a Bicentennial History.* New York, 1976
Pearson, R. W. and Lynch, D. F., *Alaska, a Geography.* Boulder, 1984
Thomas, L., Jr., *Alaska and the Yukon.* New York, 1983
Tourville, M., *Alaska, a Bibliography, 1570–1970.* 1971

State Library: P.O. Box G, Juneau, Alaska 99811. *Director:* Karen R. Crane.—Alaska Historical Library P.O. Box G, Juneau. *Librarian:* Kay Shelton.

ARIZONA

HISTORY. Arizona was settled in 1752 (called Arizona by the Spaniards in 1736), granted territorial status on February 24, 1863 and became the 48th state on 14 Feb. 1912.

AREA AND POPULATION. Arizona is bounded north by Utah, east by New Mexico, south by Mexico, west by California and Nevada. Area, 113,417 sq. miles, including 492 sq. miles of inland water. Of the total area in 1991, 26% was Indian Reservation, 18% was in individual or corporate ownership, 17% was held by the US Bureau of Land Management, 16% by the US Forest Service, 13% by the State and 10% by others. Census population on 1 April 1990 was 3,665,228, an increase of 34·92% over 1980. In 1988: Births, 65,554; deaths, 27,511; infant deaths, 634; marriages, 35,660; dissolutions of marriages, 24,928.

Population in 5 census years:

	White	Black	Indian	Chinese	Japanese	Total	Per sq. mile
1910	171,468	2,009	29,201	1,305	371	204,354	1·8
1930	378,551	10,749	43,726	1,110	879	435,573	3·8
1960	1,169,517	43,403	83,387	2,937	1,501	1,302,161	11·3
				All others			
1980	2,260,288	74,159	162,854	383,768		2,718,215	23·9
1990	2,963,186	110,524	203,527	591,516		3,868,728	32·2

Of the population in 1990, 1,810,691 were male, 3,665,228 were urban and 2,573,000 were aged 18 and over.

The 1990 census population of Phoenix was 983,403; Tucson, 405,390; Scottsdale, 130,069; Tempe, 141,865; Mesa, 288,091; Glendale, 148,134.

CLIMATE. Phoenix. Jan. 52°F (11·1°C), July 92°F (33·3°C). Annual rainfall 7·11" (178 mm). Yuma. Jan. 55°F (12·8°C), July 92°F (33·3°C). Annual rainfall 3" (75 mm). See Mountain States, p. 1397.

CONSTITUTION AND GOVERNMENT. The state constitution (1911, with 110 amendments) placed the government under direct control of the people through the initiative, referendum and the recall provisions. The state Senate consists of 30 members, and the House of Representatives of 60, all elected for 2 years. Arizona sends to Congress 2 senators and 6 representatives. In the 1988 presidential election Bush polled 702,541 votes, Dukakis, 454,029.

The state capital is Phoenix. The state is divided into 15 counties.

Governor: J. Fife Symington (R.), 1991–95 ($75,000).

Secretary of State: Richard Mahoney (D.) ($52,000).

BUDGET. General revenues, year ending 30 June 1991, were $4,790m.; general expenditures, $4,061m. (education, $1,887m.; transport $1,469m., and public health and welfare, $3,523m.).

Per capita income (1987) was $14,241.

NATURAL RESOURCES

Minerals. The mining industry historically has been and continues to be a significant part of the economy. By value the most important mineral produced is copper. Production (1990) 2,157,790,000 lbs. Most of the state's silver and about half the state's gold are recovered from copper ore. Other minerals include sand and gravel and molybdenum. Total value of minerals mined in 1990 was $3,340m.

Agriculture. Arizona, despite its dry climate, is well suited for agriculture along the water-courses and where irrigation is practised on a large scale from great reservoirs constructed by the US as well as by the state government and private interests. Irrigated area, 1987, 913,841 acres. The wide pasture lands are favourable for the rearing of cattle and sheep, but numbers are either stationary or declining compared with 1920.

In 1988 Arizona contained 7,669 farms and ranches with 1,453,852 acres of crop land, out of a total farm and pastoral area of 36,287,794 acres. The average farm was estimated at 4,732 acres. Farming is highly commercialized and mechanized and concentrated largely on cotton picked by machines and by Indian, Mexican and migratory workers.

Area under cotton (1988), 477,800 acres; 1,106,000m. bales of cotton were harvested.

Cash income, 1988, from crops, $1,167m.; from livestock, $793m. Most important cereals are wheat, corn and barley; other crops include oranges, grapefruit, potatoes and lettuce. In 1989 there were 880,000 cattle and 284,000 sheep.

Forestry. The national forests in the state had an area (1988) of 11·28m. acres.

INDUSTRY. In 1991 there were 4,715 manufacturing employers with 176,189 employees, earning total wages of $1,316m.

TOURISM. In 1990 22·5m. tourists visited Arizona; tourism-related jobs, direct and indirect, (1990), 270,016; state tax revenue (1990), $250m.

COMMUNICATIONS

Roads. As of Dec. 1991 there were 51,612 miles of public roads and streets and 2,825,112 motor vehicles were registered.

Civil Aviation. Airports, 1989, numbered 270, of which 9 were for public use; 6,354 aircraft were registered.

JUSTICE, RELIGION, EDUCATION AND WELFARE

Justice. A 'right-to-work' amendment to the constitution, adopted 5 Nov. 1946, makes illegal any concessions to trade-union demands for a 'closed shop'.

The Arizona state and federal prisons 31 Dec. 1989 held 13,251. There have been no executions since 1963; from 1930 to 1963 there were 38 executions; 3 by hanging, 35 by lethal gas; all for murder, 1 woman and 37 men (28 Whites, 10 Blacks).

Religion. The leading religious bodies are Roman Catholics and Mormons (Latter Day Saints); others include Methodists, Presbyterians, Baptists, Lutherans, Episcopalians and Eastern Orthodox.

Education. School attendance is compulsory between the ages of 5 and 15. In 1989–90 there were 670,934 pupils enrolled in grades K-12. There are 227 unified school districts containing 851 elementary schools and 168 high schools. In 1989–90, the total expenditure for all education including the Board of Regents and community colleges was $1,177m. The state maintains 3 universities: the University of Arizona (Tucson) with an enrolment of 35,220 in autumn 1991; Arizona State University (Tempe) with 42,636; Northern Arizona University (Flagstaff) with 17,698.

Health. In 1992 there were 101 hospitals; capacity 13,890 beds; 11,324 physicians and 2,010 dentists, 35,715 registered nurses and 7,211 licensed practical nurses.

Social Security. Old-age assistance (maximum depending on the programme) is given to needy citizens 65 years of age or older through the federal supplemental security income (SSI) programme. In March 1991, SSI payments went to 11,477 aged (average $188·20 each), and 34,051 disabled (average $320·77 each). In Sept. 1991 162,467 people (average $108·59 each) in 57,725 families (average $305·63 each) received aid for families with dependent children. 707 blind people received an average of $108·59 each.

Further Reading

Arizona Statistical Review. Univ. of Arizona
Comeaux, M. L., *Arizona: a Geography.* Boulder, 1981
Faulk, O. B., *Arizona: A Short History.* Univ. Oklahoma Press, 1970
Mason, B. B. and Hink, H., *Constitutional Government of Arizona.* 7th ed.Tempe, 1982
Trimble, M., *Arizona: a Panoramic History of a Frontier State.* New York, 1977.—*Arizona: a Cavalcade of History.* Tucson, 1989

State Library: Department of Library, Archives and Public Records, Capitol, Phoenix 85007.
Director: Sharon G. Womack.

ARKANSAS

HISTORY. Arkansas was settled in 1686, made a territory in 1819 and admitted into the Union on 15 June 1836. The name originated with the Quapaw Indian tribe. The constitution, which dates from 1874, has been amended 59 times.

AREA AND POPULATION. Arkansas is bounded north by Missouri, east by Tennessee and Mississippi, south by Louisiana, south-west by Texas and west by Oklahoma. Area, 53,187 sq. miles (1,112 sq. miles being inland water). Census population on 1 April 1990 was 2,350,725, an increase of 2·8% from that of 1980. Births, 1989, were 35,890; deaths, 24,614; infant deaths, 364; marriages, 34,828; divorces 16,693.

Population in 5 census years was:

	White	Black	Indian	Asiatic	Total	Per sq. mile
1910	1,131,026	442,891	460	72	1,574,449	30·0
1930	1,375,315	478,463	408	296	1,854,482	35·2
1960	1,395,703	388,787	580	1,202	1,786,272	34·0
			All others			
1980	1,890,332	373,768	22,335		2,286,435	43·9
1990	1,944,744	373,912	32,069		2,350,725	45·1

Of the total population in 1990, 48·2% were male, 68·9% were 21 years of age or older.

Little Rock (capital) had a population of 175,795 in 1990; Fort Smith, 72,798; North Little Rock, 61,741; Pine Bluff, 57,140; Fayetteville, 42,099; Hot Springs, 32,462; Jonesboro, 46,535; West Memphis, 28,259. The population of the largest standard metropolitan statistical areas: Little Rock–North Little Rock, 513,117; Fayetteville, 113,409; Fort Smith (Arkansas portion), 142,083; Pine Bluff, 85,487; Memphis (Arkansas portion), 49,939; Texarkana (Arkansas portion), 38,467.

CLIMATE. Little Rock. Jan. 42°F (5·6°C), July 81°F (27·2°C). Annual rainfall 49" (1,222 mm). *See* Gulf Coast, p. 1398.

GOVERNMENT. The General Assembly consists of a Senate of 35 members elected for 4 years, partially renewed every 2 years, and a House of Representatives of 100 members elected for 2 years. The sessions are biennial and usually limited to 60 days. The Governor and Lieut.-Governor are elected for 4 years. The state is represented in Congress by 2 senators and 4 representatives.

In the 1988 presidential election Bush polled 463,754 votes, Dukakis, 344,991.

The state is divided into 75 counties; the capital is Little Rock.

Governor: Bill Clinton (D.), 1991–95 ($35,000).
Lieut.-Governor: Jim Guy Tucker (D.) ($14,000).
Secretary of State: W. J. McCuen (D.) ($22,500).

FINANCE

Budget. The state and local government revenue for the fiscal year 1989 was $5,979m., of which taxation furnished $2,866m. and federal aid, $1,106m. General expenditure was $5,491m., of which education took $2,042m.; highways, $458m., and public welfare, $628m.

Long-term debt (state and local governments) for the financial year 1989 was $4,637m.

Per capita income (1990) was $14,188.

Banking. In 1990–91 total bank deposits were $14,188m.

ENERGY AND NATURAL RESOURCES

Minerals. In 1988 crude petroleum amounted to 13,455,729 bbls; natural gas, 146,894,144m. cu. ft. The U.S. Bureau of Mines estimated the value of Arkansas' mineral production in 1990 at $415m. This was a $33m. increase over 1989. Increased demands for bromine and for both construction and industrial sand were responsible for the higher value. Arkansas was the only U.S. producer of bromine, diamonds and vanadium.

Agriculture. In 1990 47,000 farms had a total area of 15·5m. acres; average farm was 330 acres; 8·1m. acres were harvested cropland; 2,406,338 acres were irrigated.

In 1990, Arkansas ranked first in the production of broilers (951·2m. birds, a 3·0% increase over 1989 and a new record high) and in the acreage and production of rice (38·7% of US total production), fourth in turkeys (22·0m. birds) and sixth in eggs (3,600m. eggs). 1,081,000 bales of cotton were harvested and soybean production yielded 90·4m. bu. in 1990. Dairy farmers received $122·6m. for the sale of milk in 1990.

Livestock in Jan. 1989 included 1·75m. all cattle and calves, total value (1990), was $425·9m.

INDUSTRY. In Aug. 1991 total employment averaged 1,039,100 (50,900 agricultural, 239,600 manufacturing, 215,200 wholesale and retail trade, 152,000 government). The Arkansas Department of Labor estimated that 196,700 factory production workers earned an average $370.77 per week (41·8 hours). In the manufacturing group, food and kindred products employed 52,400, electric and electronic equipment, 20,500 and lumber and wood products, 21,500.

COMMUNICATIONS

Roads. Total road mileage, 82,598 miles. State-maintained highways (1990) total 16,203 miles; local county highways, 49,479 miles; city streets, 9,762 miles; federal roads, 1,645 miles; roads not publicly maintained, 5,510 miles. In 1990 there were 1,981,337 registered motor vehicles.

Railways. In 1991 there were in the state 3,169 miles of commercial railway.

Civil Aviation. In Oct. 1991 6 air carriers and 2 commuter airlines served the state; there were 167 airports (92 public-use and 75 private).

Waterways. There are about 1,000 miles of navigable streams, including the Mississippi, Arkansas, Red, White and Ouachita Rivers. The Arkansas River/Kerr-McClellan Channel flows diagonally eastward across the state and gives access to the sea *via* the Mississippi River.

RELIGION, EDUCATION AND WELFARE

Religion. Main protestant churches in 1980: Baptist (603,844), Methodist (214,925), Church of Christ (90,671), Assembly of God (53,555). Roman Catholics (1980), 56,911.

Education. In the school year 1988–89 public elementary and secondary schools had 458,538 enrolled pupils and about 22,365 classroom teachers. Average salaries of teachers in elementary schools was $20,719, secondary $22,152. In 1987–88 expenditure on elementary and secondary education was $1,335m.

An educational TV network provides a full 12-hour-day telecasting; it has 5 stations (1991).

Higher education is provided at 33 institutions: 10 state universities, 1 medical college, 12 private or church colleges, 11 community or junior colleges. Total enrolment in institutions of higher education in the autumn of 1990, was 87,605.

There were in the autumn of 1990 24 vocational-technical schools with 36,819 students in occupational programmes.

Health. There were 101 licensed hospitals (13,060 beds) in 1991, and 272 licensed nursing homes (24,942 beds).

Social Welfare. In Dec. 1990 469,897 persons drew social security payments; 266,905 were retired workers; 46,890 were disabled workers; 67,820 were widows and widowers; 37,478 were wives and husbands. In Dec. 1990 monthly payments were $225m., $144m. to retired workers and their dependants, $32m. to survivors, and $29m. to disabled workers and their dependants.

State prisons in Oct. 1991 had 7,170 inmates.

Further Reading

Current Employment Developments. Arkansas Department of Labor, Little Rock, 1991
Arkansas State and County Economic Data. Regional Economic Analysis, Univ. Arkansas, Little Rock, 1991

Arkansas Vital Statistics. Arkansas Department of Health, Little Rock, 1990
Governmental Finances. U.S. Dept. of Commerce, Bureau of the Census, 1988–89
Agricultural Statistics for Arkansas. Arkansas Agricultural Statistics Service, Little Rock, 1990
Statistical Summary for the Public Schools of Arkansas. Dept. of Education, Little Rock, 1987-89
Ferguson and Atkinson, *Historic Arkansas.* Little Rock, 1966

CALIFORNIA

HISTORY. California, first settled in July 1769, was from its discovery until 1846 politically associated with Mexico. On 7 July 1846 the American flag was hoisted at Monterey, and a proclamation was issued declaring California to be a portion of the US. On 2 Feb. 1848, by the treaty of Guadalupe–Hidalgo, the territory was formally ceded by Mexico to the US, and was admitted to the Union 9 Sept. 1850 as the thirty-first state, with boundaries as at present.

AREA AND POPULATION. Area, 158,693 sq. miles (2,120 sq. miles being inland water).

Census population, 1 April 1990, 29,760,021, an increase of 25·7% over 1980. Births in 1990, 619,800 (20·7 per 1,000 population); deaths, 210,000 (7); infant deaths, 4,719 (7·6 per 1,000 live births); marriages, 236,693; divorces, 104,751.

Population in 5 census years was:

	White	Black	Japanese	Chinese	Total (incl. all others)	Per sq. mile
1910	2,259,672	21,645	41,356	36,248	2,377,549	15·0
1930	5,408,260	81,048	97,456	37,361	5,677,251	35·8
1960	14,455,230	883,861	157,317	95,600	15,717,204	99·0

	White	Black	Asian/other	Hispanic	Total	Per sq. mile
1980	15,763,992	1,783,810	1,575,769	4,544,331	23,667,902	149·1
1990	17,029,126	2,092,446	2,950,511	7,687,938	29,760,021	190·8

Of the 1990 population 50·1% were male in 1980, 91·3% were urban and 89·2% were 21 years old or older.

The largest cities with 1990 census population are:

Los Angeles	3,485,398	Fresno	354,202	Bakersfield	174,820
San Diego	1,110,549	Santa Ana	293,742	Fremont	173,339
San José	782,248	Anaheim	266,406	Modesto	164,730
San Francisco	723,959	Riverside	226,505	San Bernardino	164,164
Long Beach	429,433	Stockton	210,943	Garden Grove	143,050
Oakland	372,242	Huntington Beach	181,519	Oxnard	142,216
Sacramento	369,365	Glendale	180,038		

Urbanized areas (1980 census): Los Angeles–Long Beach, 9,477,926; San Francisco–Oakland, 3,191,913; San Diego, 1,704,352; San José, 1,243,900; Sacramento, 796,266; San Bernardino–Riverside, 703,316; Oxnard–Ventura–Thousand Oaks, 378,420; Fresno, 331,551.

CLIMATE. Los Angeles. Jan. 55°F (12·8°C), July 70°F (21·1°C). Annual rainfall 15" (381 mm). Sacramento. Jan. 45°F (7·2°C), July 74°F (23·3°C). Annual rainfall 19" (472 mm). San Diego. Jan. 55°F (12·8°C), July 69°F (20·6°C). Annual rainfall 10" (259 mm). San Francisco. Jan. 50°F (10°C), July 59°F (15°C). Annual rainfall 22" (561 mm). Death Valley. Jan. 52°F (11°C), July 100°F (38°C). Annual rainfall 1·6" (40 mm). *See* Pacific Coast, p. 1381.

CONSTITUTION AND GOVERNMENT. The present constitution became effective from 4 July 1879; it has had numerous amendments since 1962. The Senate is composed of 40 members elected for 4 years—half being elected each 2 years—and the Assembly, of 80 members, elected for 2 years. Two-year regular sessions convene in Dec. of each even-numbered year. The Governor and Lieut.-Governor are elected for 4 years.

California is represented in Congress by 2 senators and 45 representatives.

In the 1988 presidential election Bush polled 5,054,917 votes, Dukakis, 4,702,233.

The capital is Sacramento. The state is divided into 58 counties.

Governor: Pete Wilson (R.), 1991–95 ($120,000).
Lieut.-Governor: Leo T. McCarthy (D.) ($90,000).
Secretary of State: March Fong Eu (D.) ($90,000).

ECONOMY

Budget. For the year ending 30 June 1990 total General Fund revenues were $38,272m.; total General Fund expenditures were $39,456m. ($20,258m. for education, $12,478m. for health and welfare).

The long-term state debt (general obligation bonds outstanding) was $12,571m. on 30 June 1991.

Per capita personal income (1990) was $20,677.

Banking. In 1988 there were more than 440 banks, of which 18 were foreign-owned, 11 out-of-state and 400 independent. Total loans, 31 Dec. 1990 (preliminary), $259,402m., of which real estate loans were $130,669m. All insured commercial banks had demand deposits of $59,553m. and time and savings deposits of $187,764m. Savings and loan associations had savings capital of $249,136m. at 31 Dec. 1990.

ENERGY AND NATURAL RESOURCES

Electricity. In 1989 hydro-power produced 15%, gas 37% coal 10%, nuclear power 22%, and oil, geothermal and other sources 16% of electricity needs.

Minerals. Crude oil output was estimated at 321m. bbls in 1990. Proved reserves were an estimated 4,500m. bbls at the beginning of 1990. Output of natural gas was 320,328m. cu. ft; of natural gas liquids from wells, 174,422 bbls in 1990. Gold output was 32,000 K (1990 preliminary); asbestos, boron minerals, diatomite, tungsten, sand and gravel, salt, magnesium compounds, clays, cement, copper, silver, gypsum, calcium chloride, wollastonite and iron ore are also produced. The value of all the minerals produced was $2,722m. in 1990 (preliminary). Mining employed 39,000 in 1990.

Agriculture. Extending 700 miles from north to south, and intersected by several ranges of mountains, California has almost every variety of climate, from the very wet to the very dry, and from the temperate to the semi-tropical.

In 1987 there were 83,217 farms, comprising 31m. acres; average farm, 368 acres. Cotton, fruit, livestock and vegetables are important. Cash receipts, 1989, from crops, $12,422m.; from livestock and poultry, $5,093m. Dairy products, horticultural products, grapes, cattle, and cotton lint (in that order) were the main sources of farm cash receipts.

Production of cotton lint, 1990, was 669,900 short tons; other field crops included (in 1m. short tons): Sugar-beet, 4·4; hay and alfalfa, 8·3; rice, 1·5; wheat, 1·4. Principal fruit, nut and vegetable crops 1990 (in 1,000 short tons): Wine, table and raisin grapes, 5,185; tomatoes, 9,791; lettuce, 2,798; almonds, 330. Citrus fruit crops 1990, were (in 1,000 short tons): Oranges, 2,659; lemons, 596·6; grapefruit, 312·7.

On 1 Jan. 1991 the farm animals were: 1·2m. milch cows, 4·8m. all cattle, 735,000 sheep and 180,000 swine.

Forestry. There are about 16·3m. acres of productive forest land, from which about 4,000m. bd ft are harvested annually. Lumber production, 1990, 5,000m. bd ft.

Fisheries. The catch in 1990 was 394m. lb.; leading species in landings were mackerel, squid, urchin, rockfish and tuna.

INDUSTRY. In 1990, manufacturing employed 2,122,800. The fastest-growing industries were food processing, clothing, printing and publishing. The aerospace and electronic industries are also important. In 1990 the civilian labour force was 14,670,000, of whom 13,846,000 were employed.

Tourism. In 1988 there were 116m. tourists, 32% from other states and 6% from abroad.

COMMUNICATIONS

Roads. In 1990 California had 62,444 miles of roads inside cities and 101,130 miles outside. In 1990 there were about 16·8m. registered cars and about 5·2m. commercial vehicles.

Railways. Total mileage of railways in 1986, was 8,044 miles. There are 2 systems: Amtrak and Southern Pacific Railroad commuter trains. Amtrak carries about 1·7m. passengers per year on the intra-state routes. Southern Pacific carries about 5·4m. on a commuter route. Amtrak services run from San Francisco and Los Angeles. Southern Pacific runs the Caltrains commuter route from San Francisco to San José. There is a metro (BART) and light rail (Muni) system in San Francisco. There is a light rail line in San Diego and Sacramento and another under construction in San José.

Aviation. In 1986 there were 283 public airports and 739 private airstrips.

Shipping. The chief ports are San Francisco and Los Angeles.

JUSTICE, RELIGION, EDUCATION AND WELFARE

Justice. State prisons, 1 Jan. 1991, had 90,807 male and 6,502 female inmates. From 1893 to 1942, 307 inmates were executed by hanging. From 1938 to 1976, 194 inmates were executed by lethal gas. No further death sentences were passed until 1980.

Religion. The Roman Catholic Church is much stronger than any other single church; next are the Jewish congregations, then Methodists, Presbyterians, Baptists and Episcopalians.

Education. Full-time attendance at school is compulsory for children from 6 to 18 years of age for a minimum of 175 days per annum. In autumn 1990 there were 5·5m. pupils enrolled in both public and private elementary and secondary schools. Total state expenditure on public education, 1989–90, was $20,732m.

Community Colleges had 1,452,353 students in autumn 1990.

California has two publicly supported higher education systems: The University of California (1868) and the California State University and Colleges. In autumn 1990, the University of California with campuses for resident instruction and research at Berkeley, Los Angeles, San Francisco and 6 other centres, had 166,547 students. California State University and Colleges with campuses at Sacramento, Long Beach, Los Angeles, San Francisco and 15 other cities had 369,053 students. In addition to the 28 publicly supported institutions for higher education there are 117 private colleges and universities which had a total estimated enrolment of 177,077 in the autumn of 1990.

Health. In 1991 there were 496 general acute care hospitals; capacity, 83,849 beds. On 30 June 1991 state hospitals for the mentally disabled had 4,937 patients.

Social Security. On 1 Jan. 1974 the federal government (Social Security Administration) assumed responsibility for the Supplemental Security Income/State Supplemental Program which replaced the State Old-Age Security. The SSI/SSP provides financial assistance for needy aged (65 years or older), blind or disabled persons. An individual recipient may own assets up to $2,000; a couple up to $3,000, subject to specific exclusions. There are federal, state and county programmes assisting the aged, the blind, the disabled and needy children. In 1990, 7,076 families per month were receiving an average of $437 per family in General Relief.

Further Reading
California Almanac, 1984–85. Fay, J. S., (ed.) Oxford, 1984
California Government and Politics. Hoeber, T. R., et al, (eds.) Sacramento, Annual

California Handbook. California Institute, 1981
California Statistical Abstract. 32nd ed. Dept. of Finance, Sacramento, 1991
Economic Report of the Governor. Dept. of Finance, Sacramento, Annual
Lavender, D. S., *California.* New York, 1976

State Library: The California State Library, Library-Courts Bldg, Sacramento 95814.

COLORADO

HISTORY. Colorado was first settled in 1858, made a Territory in 1861 and admitted into the Union on 1 Aug. 1876.

AREA AND POPULATION. Colorado is bounded north by Wyoming, northeast by Nebraska, east by Kansas, south-east by Oklahoma, south by New Mexico and west by Utah. Area, 104,090 sq. miles (496 sq. miles being inland water).

Census population, 1 April 1990, was 3,294,394, an increase of 14·04% since 1980. Births, 1989, were 52,874 (15·9 per 1,000 population); deaths, 21,481 (6·5); infant deaths (1988), 505 (9·5 per 1,000 live births); marriages (1988), 31,350 (9·3); dissolutions (1988), 18,660 (5·6).

Population in 5 census years was:

	White	*Black*	*Indian*	*Asiatic*	*Total*	*Per sq. mile*
1910	783,415	11,453	1,482	2,674	799,024	7·7
1930	1,018,793	11,828	1,395	3,775	1,035,791	10·0
1950	1,296,653	20,177	1,567	5,870	1,325,089	12·7
			All others			
1980	2,571,498	101,703	216,763		2,889,964	27·7
1990	2,658,945	128,057	22,068	56,773	3,294,394	00·0

Of the total population in 1990, 1,631,295 were male, 1,663,099 were female; 69·4 were aged 20 years or older and 424,302 were of Hispanic origin. Large cities with 1990 census population: Denver City, 467,610; Colorado Springs, 281,140; Pueblo, 98,640; Fort Collins, 87,758; Boulder, 83,312; Greeley, 60,536; Longmont, 51,555; Loveland, 37,352; Grand Junction, 29,034;

Main metropolitan areas (1990): Denver, 1,622,980; Colorado Springs, 397,014; Boulder, 225,339; Fort Collins, 186,136; Greeley, 131,821; Pueblo, 123,051; Front Range Urban Area, 2,686,341.

CLIMATE. Denver. Jan. 31°F (−0·6°C), July 73°F (22·8°C). Annual rainfall 14" (358 mm). Pueblo. Jan. 30°F (−1·1°C), July 83°F (28·3°C). Annual rainfall 12" (312 mm). *See* Mountain States, p. 1397.

CONSTITUTION AND GOVERNMENT. The constitution adopted in 1876 is still in effect with (1989) 115 amendments. The General Assembly consists of a Senate of 35 members elected for 4 years, one-half retiring every 2 years, and of a House of Representatives of 65 members elected for 2 years. Sessions are annual, beginning 1951. Qualified as electors are all citizens, male and female (except convicted, incarcerated criminals), 18 years of age, who have resided in the state and the precinct for 32 days immediately preceding the election.

In the 1988 presidential election Bush polled 727,633 votes, Dukakis, 621,093.

The capital is Denver. There are 63 counties.

Governor: Roy Romer (D.), 1991–95 ($60,000).
Lieut.-Governor: Mike Callihan (D.) ($48,500).
Secretary of State: Natalie Meyer (R.) ($48,500).

BUDGET. The state's total budget, 1990–91, is $5,237m., of which taxation furnishes $2,675m. and federal grants $1,180m. Education takes $2,265m.; health, welfare and rehabilitation, $1,538m., and highways, $438m. Total state and local taxes *per capita* (1989) were $1,803.

The state has no general obligation debt. The state revenue bond debt on 30 June 1989 was $2,171m.
Per capita personal income (1990) was $18,794.

ENERGY AND NATURAL RESOURCES

Minerals. Colorado has a variety of mineral resources. Among the most important are crude oil, metals and coal. Total value of mineral production in 1990, $1,899m. In 1990, 19,600 people were employed in mining: 12,500 in extracting oil and natural gas; 3,400 in metals; 2,900 in coal and 800 other.

Agriculture. In 1990 farms numbered 26,500, with a total area of 33·1m. acres. 5,883,800 acres were harvested crop land; average farm (1990), 1,249 acres. Cash income, 1990, from crops $1,125m.; from livestock, $2,700m. In 1990 there were 1,574,000 acres under irrigation.

Production of principal crops in 1990: Corn for grain, 128·65m. bu.; wheat for grain, 84·95m. bu.; barley for grain, 12m. bu.; hay, 3,805,000 tons; dry beans, 4,275,000 cwt; oats and sorghum, 12·59m. bu.; sugar beets, 944,000 tons; potatoes, 24,032,000 cwt; vegetables, 10,683 tons; fruits, 39,000 tons.

In 1987 the number of farm animals was: 76,285 milch cows, 2,946,334 all cattle, 708,070 sheep, 258,725 swine. The wool clip in 1987 yielded 3·9m. lb. of wool.

INDUSTRY. In 1990 1,512,300 were employed in non-agricultural sectors, of which 368,200 were in trade; 397,800 in services; 278,400 in government; 195,000 in manufacturing; 62,600 in construction; 93,600 in transport and public utilities; 19,500 in mining; 97,200 in finance, insurance and property. In manufacturing the biggest employers were non-electrical machinery, foods and kindred products, and printing.

TOURISM. In 1985 about 20m. people spent holidays in Colorado, of whom about 3% were Colorado residents. Overall expenditure, $4,500m.

COMMUNICATIONS

Roads. In 1990 there were 77,361 miles of road and 3,153,838 registered motor vehicles.

Railways. In 1982 there were in the state 4,500 miles of main-track and branch railway.

Civil Aviation. There were (1990) 81 airports open to the public; 14 with commercial service, 53 public non-commercial (general aviation) and 14 private non-commercial.

JUSTICE, RELIGION, EDUCATION AND WELFARE

Justice. At 30 Sept. 1989 there were 7,570 people committed to the State Department of Corrections, inmates of the State Penitentiary, the State Reformatory and other institutions. In 1967 there was 1 execution; since 1930 executions (by lethal gas) numbered 47, including 41 whites, 5 Negroes and 1 other; all were for murder.

Colorado has a Civil Rights Act (1935) forbidding places of public accommodation to discriminate against any persons on the grounds of race, religion, sex, colour or nationality. No religious test may be applied to teachers or students in the public schools, 'nor shall any distinction or classification of pupils be made on account of race or colour'. In 1957 the General Assembly prohibited discrimination in employment of persons in private industry and in 1959 adopted the Fair Housing Act to discourage discrimination in housing. A 1957 Act permits marriages between white persons and Negroes or mulattoes.

Religion. In 1984 the Roman Catholic Church had 550,300 members; the ten main Protestant denominations had 350,900 members; the Jewish community had 45,000 members. Buddhism is among other religions represented.

Education. In autumn 1989 the public elementary and secondary schools had 562,755 pupils and 31,954 teachers; teachers' salaries averaged $30,758. Enrolments in state universities, Sept. 1988, were: University of Colorado (Boulder), 24,057 students; University of Colorado (Denver), 10,048; University of Colorado (Colorado Springs), 5,583; Colorado State University (Fort Collins), 19,386; Colorado School of Mines (Golden), 2,319; University of Northern Colorado (Greeley), 9,167; University of Southern Colorado (Pueblo), 3,971; Western State College (Gunnison), 2,434; Adams State College (Alamosa), 2,487; Metropolitan State College (Denver), 15,638; Fort Lewis College (Durango), 3,843; Mesa College (Grand Junction), 4,006.

Health. Approved hospitals, 1983, numbered 98. In 1983, there were 25 public mental health centres and clinics.

Social Security. A constitutional amendment, adopted 1956, provides for minimum old age pensions of $100 per month, which may be raised on a cost-of-living basis; for a $5m. stabilization fund and for a $10m. medical and health fund for pensioners. In 1984 the maximum monthly retirement pension (for citizens of 65 and older) was $703; maximum monthly benefit for a disabled worker, $854.

Further Reading

Directory of Colorado Manufacturers, 1990. Business Research Division, School of Business, Univ. of Colorado, Boulder, 1990
State of Colorado Business Development Manual. Office of Business Development, Denver, 1986
Economic Outlook Forum, 1991. Colorado Division of Commerce and Development, and the College of Business, Univ. of Colorado, Denver, 1991
Griffiths, M. and Rubright, L., *Colorado: a Geography.* Boulder, 1983
Sprague, M., *Colorado: A History.* New York, 1976

State Library: Colorado State Library, State Capitol, Denver, 80203.

CONNECTICUT

HISTORY. Connecticut was first settled in 1634 and has been an organized commonwealth since 1637. In 1629 a written constitution was adopted which, it is claimed, was the first in the history of the world formed under the concept of a social compact. This constitution was confirmed by a charter from Charles II in 1662, and replaced in 1818 by a state constitution, framed that year by a constitutional convention.

AREA AND POPULATION. Connecticut is bounded north by Massachusetts, east by Rhode Island, south by the Atlantic and west by New York. Area, 5,018 sq. miles (173 sq. miles being inland water).

Census population, 1 April 1990, 3,287,116, an increase of 5·78% since 1980. Births (1987) were 46,941 (14·3 per 1,000 population); deaths, 28,249 (8·6); infant deaths, 410 (8·7 per 1,000 live births); marriages, 27,106 (16·5); divorces, 12,052 (7·4).

Population in 5 census years was:

	White	Black	Indian	Asiatic	Total	Per sq. mile
1910	1,098,897	15,174	152	533	1,114,756	231·3
1930	1,576,700	29,354	162	687	1,606,903	328·0
1960	2,423,816	107,449	923	3,046	2,535,234	517·5
			All others			
1970	2,835,458	181,177	15,074		3,031,709	629·0
1980	2,799,420	217,433	4,533	18,970	3,107,576	634·3

Of the total population in 1980, 1,498,005 persons were male, 2,449,774 persons were urban. Those 19 years old or older numbered 2,228,805.

The chief cities and towns are (1989 government figures):

Bridgeport	141,986	New Britain	75,740
Hartford	133,060	West Hartford	61,700
New Haven	128,360	Danbury	70,690
Waterbury	111,630	Greenwich	60,750
Stamford	109,910	Bristol	63,600
Norwalk	81,770	Meriden	61,520

CLIMATE. New Haven: Jan. 28°F (−2·2°C), July 72°F (22·2°C). Annual rainfall 46" (1,151 mm). *See* New England, p. 1398.

CONSTITUTION AND GOVERNMENT. The 1818 Constitution was revised in 1955. On 30 Dec. 1965 a new constitution went into effect, having been framed by a constitutional convention in the summer of 1965 and approved by the voters in Dec. 1965.

The General Assembly consists of a Senate of 36 members and a House of Representatives of 151 members. Members of each House are elected for the term of 2 years. Legislative sessions are annual.

In the 1988 presidential election Bush polled 747,082 votes, Dukakis, 674,873. The state capital is Hartford.

Governor: Lowell P. Weicker (ind.), 1991–95 ($70,000).
Lieut.-Governor: Eunice S. Groark (ind.) ($55,000).
Secretary of State: Pauline R. Kezer (R.) ($50,000).

BUDGET. For the year ending 30 June 1990 (state government figures) general revenues were $8,636m. (taxation, $5,268m., and federal aid, $1,753m.); general expenditures were $8,880m. (education, $2,178m., transportation, $985m., and public welfare, $1,702m.).

Per capita income, 1990, was $25,358.

NATURAL RESOURCES

Minerals. The state has some mineral resources: crushed stone, sand, gravel, clay, dimension stone, feldspar and quartz; total production in 1990 was valued at $108·3m.

Agriculture. In 1988 the state had 4,000 farms with a total area of about 440,000 acres; average farm was of 110 acres, valued at $3,208 per acre. Total cash receipts, 1988, were $382m., including $202m. from crops and $180m. from livestock and products (mainly from dairy products and eggs). Principal crops are hay, greenhouse and nursery products, tobacco, potatoes, sweet corn, apples, peaches, berries, vegetables and small fruit.

Livestock (1989): 77,000 all cattle (value $48·1m.), 8,000 sheep ($792,000), 7,000 swine ($540,000) and 6·5m. poultry ($16·9m.).

Forestry. The state had (1989) 139,377 acres of state forest land, which is about 4·3% of the total land area (3,205,760 acres).

INDUSTRY. Total non-agricultural labour force in 1989 was 1,683,400. The main employers are manufacturers (370,830 workers mainly in transport equipment, non-electrical machinery and fabricated metals); trade (385,360 workers); services (413,070) and government (209,110).

COMMUNICATIONS

Roads. The state (1 Jan. 1989) maintains 4,044 miles of highways, all surfaced. Motor vehicles registered at 1 Oct. 1990 numbered 2·6m.

Railways. In 1981 there were 950 miles of railway track.

Civil Aviation. In 1988 there were 61 airports (26 commercial including 6 state-owned, and 67 heliports and 9 seaplane bases).

JUSTICE, RELIGION, EDUCATION AND WELFARE

Justice. In 1990 there were no executions; since 1930 there have been 22 executions (19 by electrocution, 3 by hanging), all for murder. In 1989 there were 8,899 inmates in 19 prison facilities. The total supervised population was 13,236.

The Civil Rights Act makes it a punishable offence to discriminate against any person or persons 'on account of alienage, colour or race' and to hold up to ridicule any persons 'on account of creed, religion, colour, denomination, nationality or race'. Places of public resort are forbidden to discriminate. Insurance companies are forbidden to charge higher premiums to persons 'wholly or partially of African descent'. Schools must be open to all 'without discrimination on account of race or colour'.

Religion. The leading religious denominations (1989) in the state are the Roman Catholic (1,375,557 members), United Churches of Christ (135,000), Protestant Episcopal (79,969), Jewish (108,000), Methodist (37,178), Baptist (38,000), Presbyterian and Greek Orthodox.

Education. Elementary instruction is free for all children between the ages of 4 and 16 years, and compulsory for all children between the ages of 7 and 16 years. In 1989 there were 574 public elementary schools, 304 secondary schools and 54 combined. In 1989 there were 486,326 pupils and 33,994 elementary and secondary teachers. Expenditure of the state on public schools, 1989, $1,308m. Mean salary of teachers in public schools, 1989, $38,131.

Connecticut has 47 colleges, of which one state university, 4 state colleges, 5 technical colleges and 12 regional community colleges are state funded. The University of Connecticut at Storrs, founded 1881, had 1,210 faculty and 25,882 students in 1988. Yale University, New Haven, founded in 1701, had 2,106 faculty and 10,983 students. Wesleyan University, Middletown, founded 1831, had 285 faculty and 3,428 students. Trinity College, Hartford, founded 1823, had 148 faculty and 2,043 students. Connecticut College, New London, founded 1915, had 153 faculty and 1,969 students. The University of Hartford, founded 1877, had 273 faculty and 7,703 students. The regional community colleges (2-year course) had 36,511 students.

Health. Hospitals listed by the American Hospital Association, 1990, numbered 63, with 16,134 beds. The state operated one general hospital, one veterans' hospital (614 patients in Jan. 1989), 7 hospitals for the mentally ill (1,882 patients in Oct. 1988), 2 training schools for the mentally retarded (and 6 regional centres) and a state-aided institution for the blind.

Social Security. Disbursements during the year ending 30 June 1989 amounted to $74·6m. in aid to the aged and disabled, (21,334 persons per month receiving an average of $307·76). In other areas of welfare, there was an average of 37,883 cases for aid to families with dependent children comprising 105,642 recipients.

Further Reading

The Register and Manual of Connecticut. Secretary of State. Hartford. Annual
The Structure of Connecticut's State Government. Connecticut Public Expenditure Council. Hartford, 1973
Halliburton, W. J., *The People of Connecticut*. Norwalk, 1985
Roth, David M. (ed.) *Series in Connecticut History*. 5 vols., Chester, 1975
Van Dusen, Albert E., *Connecticut*. New York, 1961

State Library: Connecticut State Library, 231 Capitol Avenue, Hartford, 06015.

DELAWARE

HISTORY. Delaware, permanently settled in 1638, is one of the original 13 states of the Union, and the first one to ratify the Federal Constitution.

AREA AND POPULATION. Delaware is bounded north by Pennsylvania, north-east by New Jersey, east by Delaware Bay, south and west by Maryland. Area 2,044 sq. miles (112 sq. miles being inland water). Census population, 1 April 1990 was 666,168, an increase of 12·1% since 1980. Births in 1989, 11,492; deaths, 5,968; infant deaths, 109; marriages, 5,940; divorces, 2,987.

Population in 5 census years was:

	White	Black	Indian	Asiatic	Total	Per sq. mile
1910	171,102	31,181	5	34	202,322	103·0
1930	205,718	32,602	5	55	238,380	120·5
1960	384,327	60,688	597	410	446,292	224·0
			All others			
1980	488,002	96,157	10,179		594,338	290·8
1990	535,094	112,460	18,614		666,168	325·9

Of the total population in 1990, 48·5% were male and 70·4% were 21 years old or older.

The 1990 census figures show Wilmington with population of 71,529; Newark, 25,098; Dover, 27,630; Elsmere Town, 5,935; Milford City, 6,040; Seaford City, 5,089.

CLIMATE. Wilmington. Jan. 32°F (0°C), July 75°F (23·9°C). Annual rainfall 43" (1,076 mm). *See* Atlantic Coast, p. 1398.

CONSTITUTION AND GOVERNMENT. The present constitution (the fourth) dates from 1897, and has had 51 amendments; it was not ratified by the electorate but promulgated by the Constitutional Convention. The General Assembly consists of a Senate of 21 members elected for 4 years and a House of Representatives of 41 members elected for 2 years.

In the 1988 presidential election Bush polled 130,581 votes, Dukakis, 99,479.

The state capital is Dover. Delaware is divided into 3 counties.

Governor: Michael N. Castle (R.), 1989–93 ($80,000).
Lieut.-Governor: Dale E. Wolf (R.), ($35,000).
Secretary of State: Michael Harkins (R.) ($69,900).

FINANCE. For the year ending 30 June 1990 total revenue was $1,438·6m., of which federal grants were $282m. Total expenditure, 1991, was $1,213·4m.

On 30 June 1990 the total debt was $456·3m.

Per capita income (1990) was $20,039.

ENERGY AND NATURAL RESOURCES

Minerals. The mineral resources of Delaware are not extensive, consisting chiefly of clay products, stone, sand and gravel and magnesium compounds.

Agriculture. Delaware is mainly an industrial state, but 590,000 acres is in farms; 475,000 acres of this is harvested annually. There were 2,900 farms in 1991. The average farm was valued (land and buildings) at $441,848 in 1991. The main product is broilers, accounting for $405·5m. receipts, out of total farm receipts of $644·6m. in 1990.

The chief field crops are corn and soybeans.

INDUSTRY. In 1990 manufacturing establishments employed 71,700 people; main manufactures were chemicals, transport equipment and food.

COMMUNICATIONS

Roads. The state in 1990 maintained 4,810 miles of roads and streets and 1,453 miles of federally-aided highways. There were also 631 miles of municipal maintained streets. Vehicles registered in year ended 30 June 1991, 565,109.

Railways. In 1990 the state had 275 miles of railway.

Civil Aviation. Delaware had 11 airports, all of which were for general use in 1990.

JUSTICE, RELIGION, EDUCATION AND WELFARE

Justice. State prisons, 30 Sept. 1990–30 Sept. 1991, had daily average of 3,637 inmates. The death penalty was illegal from 2 April 1958 to 18 Dec. 1961. Executions since 1930 (by hanging) have totalled 12 (none since 1946).

Religion. Membership, 1979–80: Methodists, 60,489; Roman Catholics, 103,060; Episcopalians, 18,696; Lutherans, 10,000.

Education. The state has free public schools and compulsory school attendance. In Sept. 1990 the elementary and secondary public schools had 99,658 enrolled pupils and 5,992 classroom teachers. Another 22,353 children were enrolled in private and parochial schools. Appropriation for public schools (financial year 1990–91) was about $403·3m. Average salary of classroom teachers (financial year 1990–91), $35,246. The state supports the University of Delaware at Newark (1834) which had 911 full-time faculty members and 20,818 students in Sept. 1990, Delaware State College, Dover (1892), with 147 full-time faculty members and 2,606 students, and the 4 campuses of Delaware Technical and Community College (Wilmington, Stanton, Dover and Georgetown) with 234 full-time faculty members and 10,224 students.

Health. In 1990 there were 7 short-term general hospitals. During financial year 1990 the average daily census in state mental hospitals was 387·4.

Social Security. In 1974 the federal Supplemental Security Income (SSI) programme lessened state responsibility for the aged, blind and disabled. SSI payments in Delaware (1990), $22,353,568. Provisions are also made for the care of dependent children; in 1991 there were 22,642 recipients in 8,981 families (average monthly payment per family, $291). The total state programme for the year ending 30 June 1991 was $31,413,039 for the care of dependent children.

Further Reading

Information: Division of Historical and Cultural Affairs, Hall of Records, Dover.
Delaware Data Book. Delaware Development Office. Dover, 1990
State Manual, Containing Official List of Officers, Commissions and County Officers. Secretary of State, Dover. Annual
Hoffecker, C. E., *Delaware: a Bicentennial History.* New York, 1977
Smeal, L., *Delaware Historical and Biographical Index.* New York, 1984
Weslager, C. A., *Delaware Indians, a History.* Rutgers Univ. Press, 1972
Topical History of Delaware. Division of Historical and Cultural Affairs. Dover, 1977

DISTRICT OF COLUMBIA

HISTORY. The District of Columbia, organized in 1790, is the seat of the Government of the US, for which the land was ceded by the states of Maryland and Virginia to the US as a site for the national capital. It was established under Acts of Congress in 1790 and 1791. Congress first met in it in 1800 and federal authority over it became vested in 1801. In 1846 the land ceded by Virginia (about 33 sq. miles) was given back.

AREA AND POPULATION. The District forms an enclave on the Potomac River, where the river forms the south-west boundary of Maryland. The area of the District of Columbia is 68·68 sq. miles, 6 sq. miles being inland water.

Census population, 1 April 1990, was 606,900, a decrease of 4·82% from that of 1980. Metropolitan statistical area of Washington, D.C.–Md–Va. (1980), 3m. Density of population in the District, 1990, 9,884 per sq. mile. Births, 1984, in the District were 19,123 (30·7 per 1,000 population); resident deaths, 8,302 (13·3); infant deaths, 393 (20·6 per 1,000 live births); marriages, 5,488 (8·8); divorces, 2,874 (4·6).

Population in 5 census years was:

	White	Black	Indian	Chinese and Japanese	Total	Per sq. mile
1910	236,128	94,446	68	427	331,069	5,517·8
1930	353,981	132,068	40	780	486,869	7,981·5
1960	345,263	411,737	587	3,532	763,956	12,523·9

			All others		
1970	209,272	537,712	9,526	756,510	12,321·0
1980	171,768	448,906	17,659	638,333	10,184·0

CLIMATE. Washington. Jan. 34°F (1·1°C), July 77°F (25°C). Annual rainfall 43" (1,064 mm). *See* Atlantic Coast, p. 1398.

GOVERNMENT. Local government, from 1 July 1878 until Aug. 1967, was that of a municipal corporation administered by a board of 3 commissioners, of whom 2 were appointed from civil life by the President, and confirmed by the Senate, for a term of 3 years each. The other commissioner was detailed by the President from the Engineer Corps of the Army. The Commission form of government was abolished in 1967 and a new Mayor Council instituted with officers appointed by the President with the advice and consent of the Senate. On 24 Dec. 1973 the appointed officers were replaced by an elected Mayor and councillors, with full legislative powers in local matters as from 1974. Congress retains the right to legis-late, to veto or supersede the Council's acts. The 23rd amendment to the federal constitution (1961) conferred the right to vote in national elections. Since 1971 the District has had a delegate (two, by 1987) in Congress who may vote in Committees but not on the House floor. In the 1988 presidential election Dukakis polled 159,407, Bush, 27,590.

BUDGET. The District's revenues are derived from a tax on real and personal property, sales taxes, taxes on corporations and companies, licences for conducting various businesses and from federal payments.

The District of Columbia has no bonded debt not covered by its accumulated sinking fund. *Per capita* personal income, 1985, $18,186.

INDUSTRY. The District's main industries (1985) are government service (263,000 workers); services (214,000); wholesale and retail trade (64,000); finance, real estate, insurance (35,000), communications, transport and utilities (26,000); total workforce, 1985, 629,000.

TOURISM. About 17m. visitors stay in the District every year and spend about $1,000m.

COMMUNICATIONS

Roads. Within the District are 340 miles of bus routes. There are 1,102 miles of streets maintained by the District; of these, 673 miles are local streets, 262 miles are major arterial roads. In 1990, 258,934 motor vehicles were registered.

Railways. There is a rapid rail transit system including a town subway system. This coordinates with the bus system and connects with Union railway station and the National Airport. Nine rail lines serve the District.

Aviation. The District is served by 3 general airports; across the Potomac River in Arlington, Va., is National Airport, in Chantilly, Va., is Dulles International Airport and in Maryland is Baltimore—Washington International Airport.

JUSTICE, RELIGION, EDUCATION AND WELFARE

Justice. Since 1958 there have been no executions; from 1930 to 1957 there were 40 executions (electrocution) including 3 whites for murder and 35 Blacks for mur-der and 2 for rape. The death penalty was declared unconstitutional in the District of Columbia on 14 Nov. 1973. At 31 Dec. 1985 there were 6,404 prisoners in state and federal institutions.

The District's Court system is the Judicial Branch of the District of Columbia. It is the only completely unified court system in the United States, possibly because of the District's unique city-state jurisdiction. Until the District of Columbia Court Reform and Criminal Procedure Act of 1970, the judicial system was almost entirely in the hands of Federal Government. Since that time, the system has been similar in most respects to the autonomous systems of the states.

Religion. The largest churches are the Protestant and Roman Catholic Christian churches; there are also Jewish, Eastern Orthodox and Islamic congregations.

Education. In 1983–84 there were about 89,000 pupils in secondary and elementary schools. Expenditure on public schools, 1986, $404m. or $645 per capita; public school teachers' average salary was $34,000. Higher education is given through the Consortium of Universities of the Metropolitan Washington Area, which consists of six universities and three colleges: Georgetown University, founded in 1795 by the Jesuit Order (11,688 students in 1985–86); George Washington University, non-sectarian founded in 1821 (17,948); Howard University, founded in 1867 (11,184); Catholic University of America, founded in 1887 (6,805); American University (Methodist) founded in 1893 (8,032); University of D.C., founded 1976 (12,080); Gallaudet College, founded 1864 (2,128); Trinity College, founded 1897 (926). There are altogether 18 institutes of higher education.

Social Security. The District government provides primary health care for residents, mainly through its Department of Human Services. In 1983 there were 17 hospitals with 8,700 beds. The welfare programme of aid to families with dependent children gave money to 55,900 recipients in 21,600 families in 1985; 4,100 aged and 11,600 disabled also received aid, total payments $43·8m.

Further Reading

Statistical Information: The Metropolitan Washington Board of Trade publications.
Reports of the Commissioners of the District of Columbia. Annual. Washington
Bowling, K. R., *The Creation of Washington D.C.: the Idea and the Location of the American Capital.* Washington (D.C.), 1991

FLORIDA

HISTORY. European men, probably Spaniards but possibly English, saw Florida for the first time in the period 1497–1512. John Cabot first charted the cape now called Florida in 1498. Juan Ponce de Leon sighted Florida on 27 March 1513. Going ashore between 2 and 8 April in the vicinity of what is now St Augustine, he named the land 'Pasqua de Flores' because his landing was 'in the time of the Feast of Flowers'. The first permanent settlement was Spanish and was made at St Augustine, 8 Sept. 1565; it is the oldest permanent settlement in the US. In 1763 Florida was ceded to England; back to Spain in 1783, and to the US in 1821. Florida became a Territory in 1821 and was admitted into the Union on 3 March 1845.

AREA AND POPULATION. Florida is a peninsula bounded west by the Gulf of Mexico, south by the Straits of Florida, east by the Atlantic, north by Georgia and north-west by Alabama. Area, 58,664 sq. miles, including 4,510 sq. miles of inland water. Census population, 1 April 1990, was 12,937,926, an increase of 32·8% since 1980. Births in 1990 (provisional) were 198,018; deaths, 133,855; infant deaths, 1,925; marriages, 142,171; divorces and other dissolutions, 81,630.

Population in 5 federal census years was:

	White	Black	All Others	Total	Per Sq. Mile
1950	2,166,051	603,101	2,153	2,771,305	51·1
1960	4,063,881	880,168	7,493	4,952,788	91·5
1970	5,719,343	1,041,651	28,449	6,789,443	125·6
1980	8,319,448	1,342,478	84,398	9,746,324	180·1
1990	10,749,285	1,759,534	429,107	12,937,926	238·9

Of the population in 1990, 84·8% were urban, 48·4% male and 73·8% were 20 years of age or over.

The largest cities in the state, 1990 census are: Jacksonville, 672,971; Miami, 358,548; Tampa, 280,015; St Petersburg, 238,629; Hialeah, 188,004; Orlando, 164,693; Fort Lauderdale, 149,377; Tallahassee, 124,773; Hollywood, 121,697; Clearwater, 98,784; Miami Beach, 92,639; Gainesville, 84,770; Coral Springs, 79,443; Cape Coral, 74,991; Pompano Beach, 72,411; Lakeland, 70,576.

CLIMATE. Jacksonville. Jan. 55°F (12·8°C), July 81°F (27·2°C). Annual rainfall 54" (1,353 mm). Key West. Jan. 70°F (21·1°C), July 83°F (28·3°C). Annual rainfall 39" (968 mm). Miami. Jan. 67°F (19·4°C), July 82°F (27·8°C). Annual rainfall 60" (1,516 mm). Tampa. Jan. 61°F (16·1°C), July 81°F (27·2°C). Annual rainfall 51" (1,285 mm). See Gulf Coast, p. 1398.

CONSTITUTION AND GOVERNMENT. The 1968 Legislature revised the constitution of 1885. The state legislature consists of a Senate of 40 members, elected for 4 years, and House of Representatives with 120 members elected for 2 years. Sessions are held annually, and are limited to 60 days.

In the 1988 presidential election Bush polled 2,535,503 votes and Dukakis, 1,630,647.

The state capital is Tallahassee. The state is divided into 67 counties.

Governor: Lawton Chiles (D.), 1991–95 ($103,909).
Lieut.-Governor: Kenneth 'Buddy' MacKay (D.), 1991–95 ($94,040).
Secretary of State: Jim Smith (R.), 1991–95 ($94,040).

FINANCE. There is no state income tax on individuals. For the year ending 30 June 1990 the state had a total revenue of $46,220m. and total expenditure of $47,300m. General revenue fund expenditure was $11,298m.

Net long-term debt, 30 June 1990, amounted to $4,902m.

Per capita personal income (1990) was $18,530.

NATURAL RESOURCES

Minerals. Chief mineral is phosphate rock, of which marketable production in 1990 was 35·4m. tonnes. This was approximately 80% of US and 30% of the world supply of phosphate in 1990.

Agriculture. In 1991, there were 40,000 farms; net income per farm was $55,437 in 1990. Total value of all farm land and buildings (1990), $23,801m. There were 0·72m. acres in citrus groves in 1991 and 9·8m. acres of other farms and ranches. Total cash receipts from crops and livestock (1990), $5,708m., of which crops provided $4,448m. Oranges, grapefruit, melons and vegetables are important. Other crops are indoor and landscaping plants, soybeans, sugar-cane, tobacco and peanuts. On 1 Jan. 1991 the state had 1·9m. cattle, including 185,00 milch cows, and 0·13m. swine.

The national forests area in Sept. 1990 was 1,122,372 acres. There were 14,982,607 acres of commercial forest.

Fisheries. Florida has extensive fisheries for oysters, shrimp, red snapper, crabs, mackerel and mullet. Catch (1990, preliminary), 161m. lb. valued at $180m.

INDUSTRY. In 1990 there were 15,668 manufacturers. They employed 519,163 persons. The metal-working, lumber, chemical, woodpulp, food-processing and instruments industries are important.

TOURISM. During 1990, 41m. tourists visited Florida. They spent $27,869m. making tourism one of the biggest industries in the state. There were (1990) 148 state parks, 23 state forests, 2 national parks, 8 national memorials, monuments, seashores and preserves and 3 national forests. The state parks were visited by 13·1m. people in 1989–90, 1·1m. of them campers.

COMMUNICATIONS

Roads. The state (1991) had 108,085 miles of highways, roads, and streets all of which were in the state and local system (67,180 miles being county roads), and 19,814·8 miles were federally-aided roads (1,429 miles interstate).

In 1989–90, 14,179,240m. vehicle licence plates were issued.

Railways. In 1991 there were 3,197 miles of railway.

Aviation. In 1991 Florida had 129 public use airports (15 international) of which 23 have scheduled commercial service.

JUSTICE, RELIGION, EDUCATION AND WELFARE

Justice. From 1979–91 there have been 25 executions, by electrocution, for murder; from 1930-68 there were 168 executions (electrocution), including 130 for murder, 37 for rape and 1 for kidnapping. State prisons, 1991, had 46,000 inmates.

Religion. The main Christian churches are Roman Catholic, Baptist, Methodist, Presbyterian and Episcopalian.

Education. Attendance at school is compulsory between 7 and 16.

In 1990 the public elementary and secondary schools had 1,861,592 enrolled pupils. Total expenditure on public schools (1989–90) was $13,307·8m. The state maintains 28 community colleges, with a full-time equivalent enrolment of 189,525 in 1990-91.

There are 9 universities in the state system, namely the University of Florida at Gainesville (founded 1853) with 36,531 students in 1991; the Florida State University (founded at Tallahassee in 1857) with 28,829; the University of South Florida at Tampa (founded 1960) with 32,950; Florida A. & M. University at Tallahassee (founded 1887) with 8,411; Florida Atlantic University (founded 1964) at Boca Raton with 13,243; the University of West Florida at Pensacola with 8,060; the University of Central Florida at Orlando with 21,778; the University of North Florida at Jacksonville with 8,131; Florida International University at Miami with 22,588.

Health. State-licensed general hospitals, 1991, numbered 293 with 63,957 beds.

Social Security. From 1974 aid to the aged, blind and disabled became a federal responsibility. The state continued to give aid to families with dependent children and general assistance. Monthly payments 1990–91: Aid to 3,160 blind averaged $260·03; aid to 118,798 dependent children averaged $249·34; aid to 126,045 disabled averaged $244·70; aid to 79,930 aged averaged $180·36.

Further Reading

Huckshorn, R. J. (ed.) *Government and Politics in Florida.* Florida Univ. Press, 1991
Morris, A., *The Florida Handbook.* Tallahassee. Biennial
Fernald, E. A. (ed.) *Atlas of Florida.* Florida State Univ., 1981
Tebeau, C. W., *A History of Florida.* Univ. Miami Press, rev. ed., 1980

State Library: Gray Building, Tallahassee. *Librarian:* Barratt Wilkins.

GEORGIA

HISTORY. Georgia (so named from George II) was founded in 1733 as the 13th original colony; she became the 4th original state.

AREA AND POPULATION. Georgia is bounded north by Tennessee and North Carolina, north-east by South Carolina, east by the Atlantic, south by Florida and west by Alabama. Area, 58,910 sq. miles, of which 991 sq. miles are inland water. Census population, 1 April 1990, was 6,478,216, an increase of 18·56% since 1980. Births, 1986, were 98,175 (16 per 1,000 population); deaths, 49,336 (8·1); infant deaths, 1,225 (12·5 per 1,000 live births); marriages, 70,866 (11·6); divorces and annulments, 33,957 (5·5).

Population in 5 census years was:

	White	Black	Indian	Asiatic	Total	Per sq. mile
1910	1,431,802	1,176,987	95	237	2,609,121	44·4
1930	1,837,021	1,071,125	43	317	2,908,506	49·7
1960	2,817,223	1,122,596	749	2,004	3,943,116	67·7
			All others			
1970	3,391,242	1,187,149	11,184		4,589,575	79·0
1980	3,948,007	1,465,457	50,801		5,464,265	92·7

Of the 1980 population, 2,641,030 were male, 3,406,171 were urban and those 20 years of age and over numbered 3,601,895.

The largest cities are: Atlanta (capital), with population, 1980 census, of 422,293 (urbanized area, 2,010,368); Columbus, 168,598 (238,593); Savannah, 133,672 (225,581); Macon, 116,044 (251,736); Albany, 74,471 (112,257).

CLIMATE. Atlanta. Jan. 43°F (6·1°C), July 78°F (25·6°C). Annual rainfall 49" (1,234 mm). *See* Atlantic Coast, p. 1398.

CONSTITUTION AND GOVERNMENT. A new constitution was ratified in the general election of 2 Nov. 1976, proclaimed on 22 Dec. 1976 and became effective 1 Jan. 1977. The General Assembly consists of a Senate of 56 members and a House of Representatives of 180 members, both elected for 2 years. Legislative sessions are annual, beginning the 2nd Monday in Jan. and lasting for 40 days.

Georgia was the first state to extend the franchise to all citizens 18 years old and above.

At the 1988 presidential election Bush polled 1,081,331 votes, Dukakis, 714,792.

The state capital is Atlanta. Georgia is divided into 159 counties.

Governor: Zell Miller (D.), 1991–95 ($91,902).
Lieut.-Governor: Pierre Howard (D.) ($59,145).
Secretary of State: Max Cleland (D.) ($72,966).

BUDGET. For the fiscal year ending 30 June 1990 general revenue was $11,190m. (taxes, $7,078m.; federal aid, $2,877m.); general expenditure was $11,392m. (education, $5,048m.; medical care and public assistance, $2,126m.).

On 30 June 1987 total liability was $4,390m.

Per capita personal income (1990), was $16,944.

NATURAL RESOURCES

Minerals. Georgia is the leading producer of kaolin. The state ranks first in production of crushed and dimensional granite, second in production of fuller's earth and marble (crushed and dimensional).

Agriculture. In 1987, 49,000 farms covered 13m. acres; average farm was of 265 acres; total value, land and buildings, 1986, $11,094m. For 1986 cotton output was 185,000 bales (of 480 lb.). Other crops include tobacco, corn, wheat, soybeans, peanuts and pecans. Cash income, 1987, $3,500m: from crops, $1,300m.; from livestock, $1,800m.

In 1991 farm animals included 1·4m. all cattle, 1·1m. swine and 8·6m. poultry.

Forestry. The forested area in 1991 was 23,907,000 acres.

INDUSTRY. In 1987 the state's manufacturing establishments had 569,400 workers; the main groups were textiles, apparel, food and transport equipment. Trade employed 692,200, services 536,100, government, 476,000.

TOURISM. In 1990 tourists spent $9,600m.

COMMUNICATIONS

Roads. In 1990 there were 108,010 miles of road and 5,270,487 motor vehicles registered.

Railways. In 1976 there were 5,417 miles of railways. A metro opened in Atlanta in 1979.

Civil Aviation. In 1988 there were 118 public and 168 private airports.

Shipping. The principal port is Savannah.

JUSTICE, RELIGION, EDUCATION AND WELFARE

Justice. State and federal prisons, 31 Dec. 1985, had 16,118 inmates. Since 1964 there have been two executions (for murder). From 1924 to 1964 there were 415 executions (electrocution), including 75 whites and 268 Blacks for murder, 3 whites and 63 Blacks for rape and 6 Blacks for armed robbery.

Under a Local Option Act, the sale of alcoholic beverages (not including malt beverages and light wines) is prohibited in more than half the counties.

Religion. An estimated 78% of the population are church members. Of the total population, 74·3% are Protestant, 3·2% are Roman Catholic and 1·5% Jewish.

Education. Since 1945 education has been compulsory; tuition is free for pupils between the ages of 6 and 18 years. In 1987 there were 1,289 public elementary schools and 361 public secondary schools; in autumn 1987 they had 1·1m. pupils and 60,509 teachers. Teachers' salaries averaged $27,606 in 1987–88. Expenditure on public schools (1987), $2,394m. or $438 per capita and $2,939 per pupil.

The University of Georgia (Athens) was founded in 1785 and was the first chartered State University in the US (26,547 students in 1987–88). Other institutions of higher learning include Georgia Institute of Technology, Atlanta (11,771), Emory University, Atlanta (8,884), Georgia State University, Atlanta (22,116) and Mercer University, Macon (3,416). The Atlanta University Center, devoted primarily to Negro education, includes Clark College (1,860) and Morris Brown College (1,257, co-educational, Morehouse (2,160), a liberal arts college for men, Interdenominational Theological Center, a co-educational theological school, and Spelman College, the first liberal arts college for Black women in the US. Atlanta University serves as the graduate school centre for the complex. Wesleyan College near Macon is the oldest chartered women's college in the US.

Health. Hospitals licensed by the Department of Human Resources, 1985, numbered 173 with 26,051 beds.

Social Security. In Dec. 1985, 60,300 persons were receiving SSI old-age assistance of an average $128 per month; 82,500 families were receiving as aid to dependent children an average of $186 per family; aid to 89,500 disabled persons was $217 monthly.

Further Reading

Georgia History in Outline. Univ. of Georgia Press, Athens, 1978
Bonner, J. C. and Roberts, L. E. (eds.) *Studies in Georgia History and Government.* Reprint Company, Spartanburg, 1940 Repr.
Pound, M. B. and Saye, A. B., *Handbook on the Constitution of the U.S. and Georgia.* Univ. of Georgia Press, Athens, 1978
Rowland, A. R., *A Bibliography of the Writings on Georgia History.* Hamden, Conn., 1978
Saye, A. B., *A Constitutional History of Georgia, 1732–1968.* Univ. of Georgia, Athens, Rev. ed., 1970

State Library: Judicial Building, Capital Sq., Atlanta.

HAWAII

HISTORY. The Hawaiian Islands, formerly known as the Sandwich Islands, were discovered by Capt. James Cook in Jan. 1778. During the greater part of the 19th century the islands formed an independent kingdom, but in 1893 the reigning Queen, Liliuokalani (died 11 Nov. 1917), was deposed and a provisional government formed; in 1894 a Republic was proclaimed, and in accordance with the request of the Legislature of the Republic, and a resolution of the US Congress of 6 July 1898 (signed 7 July by President McKinley), the islands were on 12 Aug. 1898 formally annexed to the US. On 14 June 1900 the islands were constituted as a Territory of Hawaii.

Statehood was granted to Hawaii on 18 March 1959, effective 21 Aug. 1959.

AREA AND POPULATION. The Hawaiian Islands lie in the North Pacific Ocean, between 18° 56' and 28° 25' N. lat. and 154° 49' and 178° 22' W. long., about 2,090 nautical miles south-west of San Francisco. There are 136 named islands and islets in the group, of which 7 major and 8 minor islands are inhabited. The total area is 6,471 sq. miles; land area, 6,423 sq. miles. Census population, 1 April 1900, 1,108,229, an increase of 14·84% since 1980; density was 172·5 per sq. mile.

The principal islands are Hawaii, 4,035 sq. miles and population, 1980, 92,053 (estimate, 1988, 117,500); Maui, 735 and 62,823 (84,100); Oahu, 618 and 762,534 (838,500); Kauai, 558 and 38,856 (49,100); Molokai, 264 and 6,049 (6,700); Lanai, 141 and 2,119 (2,200); Niihau, 71 and 226 (207); Kahoolawe, 46 (uninhabited). The capital Honolulu, on the island of Oahu, had a population in 1980 of 365,048 and Hilo on the island of Hawaii, 35,269.

Figures for racial groups, 1980, were: 331,925 White, 239,734 Japanese, 132,075 Filipinos, 118,251 Hawaiian, 55,916 Chinese, 17,453 Korean, 17,687 Black, 51,650 all others. In 1986, 31·2% of the population (outside barracks and other institutions) was of mixed race. Of the total, 92·3% were citizens of the US.

Inter-marriage between the races is common. Of the 9,709 resident marriages in 1988, 42·9% were between partners of different race. Births, 1987, were 18,555; deaths, 6,149; infant deaths, 168; marriages, 16,567; divorces and annulments, 4,419.

CLIMATE. All the islands have a tropical climate, with an abrupt change in conditions between windward and leeward sides, most marked in rainfall. Temperatures vary little. Honolulu. Jan. 71°F (21·7°C), July 78°F (25·6°C). Annual rainfall 31" (775 mm).

CONSTITUTION AND GOVERNMENT. The constitution took effect on 21 Aug. 1959. Amended 1968 and 1978. The Legislature consists of a Senate of 25 members elected for 4 years, and a House of Representatives of 51 members elected for 2 years. The constitution provides for annual meetings of the legislature with 60-day regular sessions.

In the 1988 presidential election Dukakis polled 192,364 votes, Bush, 158,625. The state capital is Honolulu. There are 5 counties.

Governor: John Waihee (D.), 1991–94 ($94,780).
Lieut.-Governor: Benjamin Cayetano (D.) ($90,041).

BUDGET. Revenue is derived mainly from taxation of sales and gross receipts, real property, corporate and personal income, and inheritance taxes, licences, public land sales and leases. For the year ending 30 June 1990 state general fund receipts amounted to $3,841·8m. and federal grants, $610·4m. State expenditures were $3,546·7m. (education, $1,113·5m.; highways, $201·7m.; public welfare, $431·3m.).

Net long-term debt, 31 Dec. 1988, amounted to $3,382·3m.

Estimated *per capita* personal income (1990) was $20,254.

NATURAL RESOURCES

Minerals. Total value of non-fuel mineral production, 1990, $103·1m., mainly crushed stone and cement.

Agriculture. Farming is highly commercialized, and highly mechanized. In 1987 there were 4,870 farms with an acreage of 1·72m. Sugar and pineapples are the staple crops. Income from crop sales, 1988, was $485m., and from livestock, $88·6m. The sugar crop was valued at $209·9m.; pineapples, $107·4m.; other crops, $168·2m.

Forestry. In 1990 there were 1,748,000 acres forest land.

INDUSTRY. In 1987 manufacturing establishments employed 15,300 production workers who earned an estimated $254·6m. Defence is the second-largest industry; US armed forces spent $1,892m. in Hawaii in 1988.

COMMERCE. In 1988 imports were $1,118m.; exports, $131m.

TOURISM. Tourism is outstanding in Hawaii's economy. Tourist arrivals numbered 1·1m. in 1967, and reached 6·1m. in 1988. Tourist expenditures, $380m. in 1967, contributed $10,900m. to the state's economy in 1989.

COMMUNICATIONS

Roads. In 1990 there were 4,082 miles of roads (2,663 miles rural) and 736,393 registered motor vehicles.

Civil Aviation. There were 7 commercial airports in 1990; passengers arriving from overseas in 1988 numbered 6·65m., and there were 9m. passengers between the islands.

Shipping. Several lines of steamers connect the islands with the mainland USA, Canada, Australia, the Philippines, China and Japan. In 1989, 2,024 overseas and 3,101 inter-island vessels entered the port of Honolulu.

Post. There were 530,022 telephone access lines at 31 Dec. 1988.

Broadcasting. In 1989, Hawaii had 47 commercial and 2 other radio stations, 17 commercial and 2 other TV stations.

JUSTICE, RELIGION, EDUCATION AND WELFARE

Justice. There is no capital punishment in Hawaii.

Religion. The residents are mainly Christians, though there are many Buddhists. A sample survey in 1979 showed that 31% were Roman Catholic, 34% Protestant, 12% Buddhist, 2·5% Latter Day Saints.

Education. Education is free, and compulsory for children between the ages of 6 and 18. The language in the schools is English. In 1988–89 there were 235 public schools (167,899 pupils with 8,973 teachers) and 141 private schools (35,459 pupils and 2,512 teachers) ranging from kindergarten through the 12th grade. The University of Hawaii-Manoa, founded in 1907, had 18,477 day students in 1988; total attendance at all campuses of the University of Hawaii system, 42,767; 9,612 at private colleges.

Social Security. During 1988 5,123 people were receiving old-age assistance of an average $217 per month; 13,396 families, $453 in aid to dependent children; 7,008 disabled people, $288. Social Security beneficiaries, 141,730, receiving aggregate monthly payments of $67·5m.

Further Reading

Government in Hawaii. Tax Foundation of Hawaii. Honolulu, 1988
Guide to Government in Hawaii. 8th ed. Legislative Reference Bureau. State of Hawaii, Honolulu, 1989
Atlas of Hawaii. Hawaii Univ., rev. ed. Honolulu, 1983
State of Hawaii Data Book. Hawaii Dept. of Business and Economic Development, 1989
Bell, R. J., *Last Among Equals: Hawaiian Statehood and American Politics.* Honolulu, 1984
Kuykendall, R. S. and Day, A. G., *Hawaii: a History.* Rev. ed. New Jersey, 1961
Morgan, J. R., *Hawaii.* Boulder, 1982

IDAHO

HISTORY. Idaho was first permanently settled in 1860, although there was a mission for Indians in 1836 and a Mormon settlement in 1855. It was organized as a Territory in 1863 and admitted into the Union as a state on 3 July 1890.

AREA AND POPULATION. Idaho is bounded north by Canada, east by the Rocky Mountains of Montana and Wyoming, south by Nevada and Utah, west by Oregon and Washington. Area, 83,564 sq. miles, of which 1,153 sq. miles are inland water. Census population, 1 April 1990, 1,006,749, an increase of 6·65% since 1980. Births, 1987, 15,926 (16 per 1,000 population); deaths, 7,305 (7·3); marriages, 11,428 (11·5); divorces, 5,892 (5·9).

Population in 5 census years was:

	White	Black	Indian	Asiatic	Total	Per sq. mile
1910	319,221	651	3,488	2,234	325,594	3·9
1930	438,840	668	3,638	1,886	445,032	5·4
1960	657,383	1,502	5,231	2,958	667,191	8·1
1970	693,375	3,655	5,413	2,526	713,008	8·5
			All others			
1980	901,641	2,716	39,578		943,935	11·3

Of the total 1980 population, 471,155 were male, 509,702 were urban and those 20 years of age or older 600,242.

The largest cities are Boise with 1990 census population of 125,738 (1986 estimates); Pocatello, 44,420; Idaho Falls, 42,830; Nampa, 28,250; Twin Falls, 27,750; Lewiston, 27,730.

CLIMATE. Boise. Jan. 29°F (−1·7°C), July 74°F (23·3°C). Annual rainfall 12" (303 mm). *See* Mountain States, p. 1397.

CONSTITUTION AND GOVERNMENT. The constitution adopted in 1890 is still in force; it has had 105 amendments. The Legislature consists of a Senate of 44 members and a House of Representatives of 84 members, all the legislators being elected for 2 years. It meets annually.

In the 1988 presidential election Bush polled 253,467 votes, Dukakis, 147,420.

The state is divided into 44 counties. The capital is Boise.

Governor: Cecil D. Andrus (D.), 1991–95 ($75,000).
Lieut.-Governor: C. L. 'Butch' Otter (R.) ($20,000).
Secretary of State: Pete T. Cenarrusa (R.) ($62,500).

BUDGET. For the year ending 30 June 1990 general revenues were $1,993·8m. and general expenditures, $1,831·1m.

Per capita personal income (1985) was $11,120.

NATURAL RESOURCES

Minerals. Principal non-fuel minerals are phosphate rock, silver, gold, and sand and gravel. Value of total mineral output, 1990, was $344·2m.

Agriculture. Agriculture is the leading industry, although a great part of the state is naturally arid. Extensive irrigation works have been carried out, bringing an estimated 4m. acres under irrigation, and there are over 50 soil conservation districts.

In 1985 there were 24,600 farms with a total area of 14·7m. acres (27% of the land area).

The most important crops are potatoes and wheat. Other crops are sugar-beet, alfalfa, barley, field peas and beans, onions and apples. In 1989 there were 1·66m. cattle, 296,000 sheep, 32,000 pigs and 1·1m. poultry.

Forestry. In 1990 a total of 21,818,000 acres was in forests.

INDUSTRY. In 1985 85,000 were employed in trade, 70,000 in government, 66,000 in services, 55,000 in manufacturing.

TOURISM. Money spent by travellers in 1989 was about $1,400m.

COMMUNICATIONS

Roads. In 1990 there were 61,317 miles of roads (58,911 miles rural) and 1,039,045 registered motor vehicles.

Railways. The state had (1985) 1,910 miles of railways (including 2 Amtrak routes).

Civil Aviation. There were 68 municipally owned airports in 1985.

Shipping. Water transport is provided from the Pacific to the port of Lewiston, by way of the Columbia and Snake rivers, a distance of 464 miles.

JUSTICE, RELIGION, EDUCATION AND WELFARE

Justice. The death penalty may be imposed for first degree murder, but the judge must consider mitigating circumstances before imposing a sentence of death. Since 1926 only 4 men (white) have been executed, by hanging (1 in 1926, 2 in 1951 and 1 in 1957). At 1 Oct. 1985 14 prison inmates (13 men and 1 woman) were under sentence of death. Execution is now by lethal injection. The state prison system, 1 Oct. 1985, had 1,260 inmates.

Religion. The leading religious denominations are the Church of Jesus Christ of Latter Day Saints (Mormon Church), Roman Catholics, Methodists, Presbyterians, Episcopalians and Lutherans.

Education. In 1984–85 public elementary schools (grades K to 6) had 118,647 pupils and 5,481 classroom teachers; secondary schools had 92,053 pupils and 4,980 classroom teachers.
Average salary, 1984–85, of elementary and secondary classroom teachers, $20,032. The University of Idaho, founded at Moscow in 1889, had 459 professors and 8,970 students in 1984–85. There are 9 other institutions of higher education; 5 of them are public institutions with a total enrolment (1984–85) of 21,914 (excluding vocational-technical colleges).

Social Welfare. Old-age assistance is granted to persons 65 years of age and older. In Aug. 1985, 1,014 persons were drawing an average of $105.86 per month; 6,023 families with 10,858 children were drawing an average of $243.85 per case (or $90.10 per eligible person); 28 blind persons, $73.21; 569 children were receiving $248.88 per child for foster care; 1,827 permanently and totally disabled persons, $133.69.

Health. In Sept. 1985 skilled nursing covered 4,761 beds; intermediate care, 107; intermediate care for the mentally retarded 528. Hospitals had 3,547 beds and home health agencies totalled 36.

Further Reading

Idaho Blue Book. Secretary of State. Boise, biennial
Idaho's Yesterdays. State Historical Society. Quarterly

ILLINOIS

HISTORY. Illinois was first discovered by Joliet and Marquette, two French explorers, in 1673. In 1763 the country was ceded by the French to the British. In 1783 Great Britain recognized the United States' title to the land that became Illinois; it was organized as a Territory in 1809 and admitted into the Union on 3 Dec. 1818.

AREA AND POPULATION. Illinois is bounded north by Wisconsin, north-east by Lake Michigan, east by Indiana, south-east by the Ohio River (forming the boundary with Kentucky), west by the Mississippi River (forming the boundary with Missouri and Iowa). Area, 56,345 sq. miles; land area 55,593 sq. miles. Census population, 1990, 11,430,602, an increase of 0·36% since 1980. Births in 1988 were 184,708; deaths, 105,038; infant deaths, 2,077; marriages 78,302; divorces, 45,736; annulments, 175.

Population in 5 census years was:

	White	Black	Indian	All others	Total	Per sq. mile
1910	5,526,962	109,049	188	2,392	5,638,591	100·6
1930	7,295,267	328,972	469	5,946	7,630,654	136·4

			All others		
1970	9,600,381	1,425,674	87,921	11,113,976	199·4
1980	9,233,327	1,675,398	517,793	11,426,518	203·0

	White	Black	American Indian, Eskimo or Aleut	Asian or Pacific Islander	Other	Total	Per sq. mile
1990	8,952,978	1,694,273	21,836	285,311	476,204	11,430,602	205·6

Of the total population in 1980, 5,537,737 were male, 9,518,039 persons were urban and 5,597,360 were 18 years of age or older.

The most populous cities with population (1990 census), are: Chicago, 2,783,726; Rockford, 139,426; Peoria, 113,504; Springfield, 105,227; Aurora, 99,581; Naperville, 85,351; Decatur, 83,885; Elgin, 77,010; Joliet, 76,836; Arlington Heights, 75,460.

Primary Metropolitan Statistical Area population, 1990 census: Chicago, 6,069,974; East St Louis, 588,995; Peoria, 339,172; Rockford, 283,719; Springfield, 189,550; Decatur, 117,206.

CLIMATE. Chicago. Jan. 25°F (−3·9°C), July 73°F (22·8°C). Annual rainfall 35" (887 mm). See Great Lakes, p. 1398.

CONSTITUTION AND GOVERNMENT. The present constitution became effective 1 July 1971. The General Assembly consists of a House of Representatives of 118 members, elected for 2 years and a Senate of 59 members who are divided into 3 groups; in one, they are elected for terms of 4 years, 4 years, and 2 years; in the next, for terms of 4 years, 2 years, and 4 years; and in the last, for terms of 2 years, 4 years, and 4 years. Sessions are annual. The state is divided into legislative districts, in each of which 1 senator is chosen; each district is divided into 2 representative districts, in each of which 1 representative is chosen.

In the 1988 presidential election Bush polled 2,310,939 votes, Dukakis, 2,215,940.

The capital is Springfield. The state has 102 counties.

Governor: Jim Edgar (R.), 1991–95 ($97,370).
Lieut.-Governor: Bob Kustra (R). ($68,732).
Secretary of State: George H. Ryan (R.) ($85,915).

BUDGET. For the year ending 30 June 1990 total revenues were $12,423,731,000 and total expenditures were $11,237,651,000.

Debt administration, 1989–90 (in $1m.): Outstanding general and special bonds, 5,145; revenue bonds, 3,529; notes payable, 112; long-term obligations, 1,032.

Per capita personal income (1990) was $20,419.

ENERGY AND NATURAL RESOURCES

Minerals. Chief mineral product is coal; 42 operative mines had an output (1990) of 61,657,068 tons. Mineral production also included: Crude petroleum, fluorspar, tripoli, lime, sand, gravel and stone. Total value of mineral products, 1989, was $2,842,859,000.

Agriculture. In 1990, 83,000 farms had an area of 28·5m. acres; the average farm was 343 acres.

Cash receipts, 1990, from crops, $5,460,821,000; from livestock and livestock products, $2,476,972,000. Illinois is a large producer of maize and soybeans, the state's leading cash commodities. Output, 1990: Soybeans, 354·9m. bu; wheat, 88·8m. bu; maize, 1,320m. bu. In Jan. 1991 there were 195,000 milch cows, 2m. cattle and calves; 145,000 sheep and lambs and 5·7m. swine. The wool clip was 925,000 lb. in 1990.

Forestry. National forest area under the US Forest Service Administration, 1985, was 4·27m. acres. Total forest land, 4·29m. acres.

INDUSTRY. In 1988, 18,120 manufacturing establishments employed 1,330,272 workers; annual payroll, $29,725,068,000. Largest industry was non-electrical engineering. Gross state product, 1989, $257,599m.

LABOUR. In 1990 there were 5,265,000 employees, of whom 984,000 were in manufacturing, 1,258,000 in trade, 1,340,000 in services, 762,000 in government.

COMMUNICATIONS

Roads. In 1990 there were approximately 6,296,000 passenger cars, 1,151,000 pickup trucks, 2,076,000 trucks, recreational vehicles and buses, 11,800 taxis, liveries and ambulances, 570,000 trailers and semi-trailers, 206,000 motor cycles and 150,000 other vehicles registered in the state. At 31 Dec. 1990 there were 13,244·31 miles of state primary roads, 3,576·5 miles of state supplementary roads and 285·53 miles of toll roads and toll bridges.

Railways. There were, on 1 Dec. 1989, 7,621 miles of Class I railway. Chicago is served by Amtrak long-distance trains on several routes, and by a metro (CTA) system, and by 7 groups of commuter railways controlled by the Northeast Illinois Railroad Corporation (now called METRA).

Civil Aviation. There were (1990) 132 public airports and 690 restricted landing areas.

Shipping. In 1988 the seaport of Chicago handled 22,893,740 short tons of cargo.

JUSTICE, RELIGION, EDUCATION AND WELFARE

Justice. In June 1989 the inmate population in state prisons was 25,937. There was 1 execution in 1990 (98 in 1928–62),

A Civil Rights Act (1941), as amended, bans all forms of discrimination by places of public accommodation, including inns, restaurants, retail stores, railroads, aeroplanes, buses, etc., against persons on account of 'race, religion, colour, national ancestry or physical or mental handicap'; another section similarly mentions 'race or colour.'

The Fair Employment Practices Act of 1961, as amended, prohibits discrimination in employment based on race, colour, sex, religion, national origin or ancestry, by employers, employment agencies, labour organizations and others. These principles are embodied in the 1971 constitution.

The Illinois Human Rights Act (1979), prevents unlawful discrimination in employment, real property transactions, access to financial credit, and public accommodations, by authorizing the creation of a Department of Human Rights to enforce, and a Human Rights Commission to adjudicate, allegations of unlawful discrimination.

Religion. Among the larger religious denominations are: Roman Catholic (3·6m.), Jewish (50,000), Presbyterian Church, USA (200,000), Lutheran Church in America (200,000), Lutheran Church Missouri Synod (325,000), American Baptist (105,000), Disciples of Christ (75,000), and United Methodist (505,000), Southern Baptist (265,000), United Church of Christ (192,000), Church of Nazarene (50,000), Assembly of God (63,000).

Education. Education is free and compulsory for children between 7 and 16 years of age. In autumn 1990 public school elementary enrolments were 1,304,892 pupils and approximately 73,913 teachers (including special education teachers); secondary enrolments, 516,515 pupils and 34,863 teachers. Enrolment (1990–91) in non-public schools was 248,562 elementary and 67,408 secondary. Teachers' salaries, 1990–91, averaged $34,609. Total enrolment in 186 institutions of higher education (autumn 1990) was 732,830.

Colleges and universities with over 3,000 students:

Founded	Name	Place	Control	Autumn 1990 Enrolment
1851	Northwestern University	Evanston	Methodist	17,041
1857	Illinois State University	Normal	Public	22,661
1867	University of Illinois	Urbana and Chicago	Public	63,124
1867	Chicago State University [1]	Chicago	Public	7,152
1869	Southern Illinois University	Carbondale and Edwardsville	Public	35,770
1870	Loyola University	Chicago	Roman Catholic	14,780
1891	University of Chicago	Chicago	Non-Sect.	10,867
1895	Eastern Illinois University	Charleston	Public	11,116
1895	Northern Illinois University	DeKalb	Public	24,509
1897	Bradley University	Peoria	Non-Sect.	6,068
1899	Western Illinois University	Macomb	Public	13,754
1940	Illinois Institute of Technology [2]	Chicago	Non-Sect.	6,504
1945	Roosevelt University	Chicago	Non-Sect.	6,296
1961	Northeastern Illinois University [3]	Chicago	Public	10,453

[1] Formerly Illinois Teachers College (South).
[2] Illinois Institute of Technology formed in 1940 by merger of two older technical schools.
[3] Formerly Illinois Teachers' College (North).

Health. In 1989 there were 249 hospitals with 59,386 beds. At June 1990 state institutions had 4,496 developmentally disabled and 3,465 mentally ill residents.

Social Security. State-administered Supplemental Security Income (SSI) was paid to 53,148 recipients in financial year 1990; gross income-maintenance payments (no adjustments) totalled $60·7m.; medical payments, $166·6m. Aid to families with dependent children was paid to 209,822 families, average monthly payment per family, $324; total payments, $815·6m.; medical payments, $484m.

Further Reading

Blue Book of the State of Illinois. Edited by Secretary of State. Springfield. Biennial
Ilinois Department of Commerce and Community Affairs. Illinois Data Book
Angle, P. M. and Beyer, R. L., A Handbook of Illinois History. Illinois State Historical Society, Springfield, 1943
Clayton, J., The Illinois Fact Book and Historical Almanac 1673–1968. Southern Illinois Univ., 1970
Howard, R. P., Illinois: A History of the Prairie State. Grand Rapids, 1972.—Mostly Good and Competent Men: Illinois Governors, 1818–1988. Springfield, 1989
Pease, T. C., The Story of Illinois. 3rd ed. Chicago, 1965

The Illinois State Library: Springfield, Il.62756. State Librarian: Jim Edgar.

INDIANA

HISTORY. Indiana, first settled in 1732–33, was made a Territory in 1800 and admitted into the Union on 11 Dec. 1816.

AREA AND POPULATION. Indiana is bounded west by Illinois, north by Michigan and Lake Michigan, east by Ohio and south by Kentucky across the Ohio River. Land area, 35,870 sq. miles. Census population, 1 April 1990, was 5,544,159, an increase of 0·98% since 1980. In 1988 live births were 81,414 (14·7 per 1,000 population); (1989) deaths, 49,007 (8·8); infant deaths, 895 (11 per 1,000 live births); (1986) marriages 49,900 (9·1).

Population in 5 census years was:

	White	Black	Indian	Asiatic	Total	Per sq. mile
1930	3,125,778	111,982	285	458	3,238,503	89·4
1960	4,388,554	269,275	948	2,447	4,662,498	128·9
			All others			
1970	4,820,324	357,464	15,881		5,193,669	143·9
1980	5,004,394	414,785	71,045		5,490,224	152·8
1990	5,020,700	432,092	91,367		5,544,159	154·6

Of the total in 1990, 2,688,281 were male and 3,545,431 were 21 years of age or older.

The largest cities with census population, 1990, are: Indianapolis (capital), 741,952; Fort Wayne, 173,072; Evansville, 126,272; Gary, 116,646; South Bend, 105,511; Hammond, 84,236; Muncie, 71,035; Bloomington, 60,633; Anderson, 59,459; Terre Haute, 57,483.

CLIMATE. Indianapolis. Jan. 29°F (−1·7°C), July 76°F (24·4°C). Annual rainfall 41" (1,034 mm). *See* The Mid-West, p. 1398.

CONSTITUTION AND GOVERNMENT. The present constitution (the second) dates from 1851; it has had (as of Nov. 1983) 34 amendments. The General Assembly consists of a Senate of 50 members elected for 4 years, and a House of Representatives of 100 members elected for 2 years. It meets annually.

In the 1988 presidential election Bush polled 1,280,292 votes, Dukakis, 850,851.

The state capital is Indianapolis. The state is divided into 92 counties and 1,008 townships.

Governor: Evan Bayh (D.), 1989–93 ($77,200).
Lieut.-Governor: Frank O'Bannon (D.) ($64,000).
Secretary of State: Joseph Hogsett (D.) ($46,000).

BUDGET. In the fiscal year 1990 (US Census Bureau figures) total revenues were $11,456,232,000 ($2,255,261,000 from federal government, $6,101,619,000 from taxes); total expenditures were $9,992,133,000 ($4,235,384,000 for education, $1,930·49m. for public welfare and $973,791,000 for highways).

Total long-term debt, on 30 June 1988, was $3,085,427,000.
Per capita personal income (1990) was $16,890.

ENERGY AND NATURAL RESOURCES

Minerals. The state produced 36,188,000 short tons of crushed stone and 27,212,000 short tons of dimension stone in 1989; the output of coal was 33·6m. short tons in 1988; petroleum, 5m. bbls (of 42 gallons) in 1984.

Agriculture. Indiana is largely agricultural, about 75% of its total area being in farms. In 1987, 70,506 farms had 16,170,895 acres (average, 229 acres). Cash income, 1987, from crops, including nursery and greenhouse crops, $2,127,135; from livestock, poultry and their products, $1,940,549.

The chief crops (1987) were corn for grain or seed (619,049,978 bu.), corn for silage or green chop (1,961,381 tons), wheat for grain (30,789,151 bu.), oats for grain, (4,317,321 bu.), soybeans for beans (169,749,051 bu.), hay (alfalfa, other tame small grain, wild, grass silage, etc.) (1,892,466 tons).

The livestock on 1 Jan. 1987 included 2,031,915 all cattle, 163,867 milch cows, 82,757 sheep and lambs, 4,372,294 hogs and pigs, 26,787,315 chickens. In 1987 the wool clip yielded 537,966 lb. of wool from 76,056 sheep and lambs.

Forestry. In 1988 there were 4·3m. acres of forest and (1987) 12 state forests and Hoosier National Forest (187,812 acres).

INDUSTRY. In 1989, 8,763 manufacturing establishments employed 642,946 workers, earning $17,803,752,000. The steel industry is the largest in the country.

COMMUNICATIONS

Roads. In 1990 there were 91,744 miles of road (73,941 miles rural) and 4,322,302 registered motor vehicles.

Railways. In 1989 there were 3,796 miles of mainline railway and 861·5 miles of secondary track.

Civil Aviation. Of airports, 1990, 115 were for public use and 486 were for private use.

JUSTICE, RELIGION, EDUCATION AND WELFARE

Justice. In 1963–80 there were no executions; there have since been 4, for murder. State correctional institutions, financial year 1987–88, had an average daily population of 11,889.

The Civil Rights Act of 1885 forbids places of public accommodation to bar any persons on grounds not applicable to all citizens alike; no citizen may be disqualified for jury service 'on account of race or colour'. An Act of 1947 makes it an offence to spread religious or racial hatred.

A 1961 Act provided 'all ... citizens equal opportunity for education, employment and access to public conveniences and accommodations' and created a Civil Rights Commission.

Religion. Religious denominations include Methodists, Roman Catholic, Disciples of Christ, Baptists, Lutheran, Presbyterian churches, Society of Friends.

Education. School attendance is compulsory from 7 to 16 years. In 1990–91 public and parochial schools and nursery schools had 921,874 pupils and 54,164 teachers. Teachers' salaries averaged $29,161 (1989–90). Total expenditure for public schools, 1989, $3,012,300,644.

The principal institutions for higher education are (1989–90):

Founded	Institution	Control	Students (full-time)
1801	Vincennes University	State	10,139
1824	Indiana University, Bloomington	State	34,863
1837	De Pauw University, Greencastle	Methodist	2,415
1842	University of Notre Dame	R.C.	9,700
1850	Butler University, Indianapolis	Independent	4,187
1859	Valparaiso University, Valparaiso	Evangelical Lutheran Church	3,858
1870	Indiana State University, Terre Haute	State	12,005
1874	Purdue University, Lafayette	State	35,817
1898	Ball State University, Muncie	State	18,993
1902	University of Indianapolis, Indianapolis	Methodist	3,119
1963	Indiana Vocational Technical College, Indianapolis	State	5,117
1985	University of Southern Indiana	State	5,713

Health. Hospitals listed by the Indiana State Board of Health (1988) numbered 124 (23,929 beds in 1981). In 1989 there were 3,612 patients in state mental hospitals.

Social Security. In 1990, under the Federal SSI programme and federally administered State Supplementary programme, monthly payments to the aged were $1,281,000 to 9,630 individual adults and $77,000 to 336 couples; to the blind and disabled, $11,371,000 to 40,844 individual adults, $286,000 to 720 couples and $2·56m. to 6,846 children.

Further Reading

Indiana State Chamber of Commerce. *Here is Your Indiana Government*. 22nd ed. Indianapolis, 1985

State Library: Indiana State Library, 140 North Senate, Indianapolis 46204. *Director:* C. Ray Ewick.

IOWA

HISTORY. Iowa, first settled in 1788, was made a Territory in 1838 and admitted into the Union on 28 Dec. 1846.

AREA AND POPULATION. Iowa is bounded east by the Mississippi River (forming the boundary with Wisconsin and Illinois), south by Missouri, west by the Missouri River (forming the boundary with Nebraska), north-west by the Big Sioux River (forming the boundary with South Dakota) and north by Minnesota. Area, 56,375 sq. miles, including 310 sq. miles of inland water. Census population, 1 April 1990, 2,776,755, a decrease of 4·7% since 1980. Births, 1990, were 39,330; deaths, 26,815; infant deaths, 317; marriages, 24,931; dissolutions of marriages, 10,913.

Population in 5 census years was:

	White	Black	Indian	Asiatic	Total	Per sq. mile
1870	1,188,207	5,762	48	3	1,194,020	21·5
1930	2,452,677	17,380	660	222	2,470,939	44·1
1960	2,728,709	25,354	1,708	1,022	2,757,537	49·2
			All others			
1970	2,782,762	32,596	10,010		2,825,368	50·5
1980	2,839,225	41,700	32,882		2,913,808	51·7
1990	2,683,090	48,090	45,575		2,776,755	49·7

At the census of 1990, 1,344,802 were male and 2,057,875 were 18 years of age or older. Urban population was 1,708,232 in 1980.

The largest cities in the state, with their census population in 1990 are: Des Moines (capital), 193,187; Cedar Rapids, 108,751; Davenport, 95,333; Sioux City, 80,505; Waterloo, 66,467; Iowa City, 59,738; Dubuque, 57,546; Council Bluffs, 54,315; Ames, 47,198; Cedar Falls, 34,298; Clinton, 29,201; Mason City, 29,040; Burlington, 27,208; Fort Dodge, 25,894; Ottumwa, 24,488.

CLIMATE. Cedar Rapids. Jan. 23·7°F, July 72·6°F. Annual rainfall 34". Des Moines. Jan. 22·6°F, July 72·4°F. Annual rainfall 32·1". *See* The Mid-West, p. 1398.

CONSTITUTION AND GOVERNMENT. The constitution of 1857 still exists; it has had 45 amendments. The General Assembly comprises a Senate of 50 and a House of Representatives of 100 members, meeting annually for an unlimited session. Senators are elected for 4 years, half retiring every second year: Representatives for 2 years. The Governor and Lieut.-Governor are elected for 4 years. The state is represented in Congress by 2 senators and 5 representatives. Iowa is divided into 99 counties; the capital is Des Moines.

In the 1988 presidential election Dukakis polled 670,557 votes, Bush, 545,355.

Governor: Terry Branstad (R.), 1991–95 ($76,700).
Lieut.-Governor: Joy Corning (R.), ($60,000).
Secretary of State: Elaine Baxter (D.) ($60,000).

BUDGET. For fiscal year 1990-91 state tax revenue was $3,158·8m. General fund and lottery expenditures were $780·1m. for education, $668,616,552 for health and human services, and $60,584,461 for economic development, transportation and commerce.

On 30 June 1990 the net general long-term debt was $106m.

Per capita personal income (1990) was $17,249.

ENERGY AND NATURAL RESOURCES

Minerals. Production in 1990: Crushed stone 28·5m. tons; sand and gravel, 11·4m. tons; gypsum, 2·3m. tons; cement 2·7m. short tons; coal, 0·38m. short tons. The value of mineral products in 1990, was $319m.

Agriculture. Iowa is the wealthiest of the agricultural states, partly because nearly the whole area (93·5%) is arable and included in farms. Large-scale commercial farming has not developed; the average farm at 1 June 1991 was 328 acres.

Cash farm income (1990) was $10,319·2m.; from livestock, $5,882m., and from crops, $4,437m. Production of corn was 1,562·4m. bu., value $3,437·3m. (preliminary) and soybeans, 3,027·9m. bu., value $1,036m. On 1 Dec. 1990 livestock included swine, 14m. (leading all states); milch cows, 302,000 (1 Jan. 1991); all cattle, 4m., and sheep and lambs, 465,000 (1 Jan. 1991). The wool clip (1990) yielded 3·3m. lb. of wool.

INDUSTRY. In 1990 manufacturing establishments employed 235,800 people: Trade, 308,000; services, 288,600.

COMMUNICATIONS

Roads. On 31 Dec. 1990 number of miles of streets and highways was 112,770. In 1990 there were 1·9m. licensed drivers and 3·06m. registered vehicles.

Railways. The state, 1990, had 4,399 miles of track, and 6 Class I railways.

Civil Aviation. Airports (1990), numbered 239, which consisted of 113 publicly-owned, 116 privately-owned (of which 26 were for public use) and 10 commercial facilities. There were approximately 3,150 private aircraft.

JUSTICE, RELIGION, EDUCATION AND WELFARE

Justice. There is now no capital punishment in Iowa. State prisons, 27 Oct. 1991, had 4,132 inmates.

Religion. Chief religious bodies in 1990 were: Roman Catholic, 526,972 members; United Methodists, 213,419; Evangelical Lutheran in America, 242,931 baptised members; United Presbyterians, about 76,000; United Church of Christ, 46,703.

Education. School attendance is compulsory for 24 consecutive weeks annually during school age (7–16). In 1990–91 483,396 were attending primary and secondary schools; 45,562 pupils attending non-public schools. Classroom teachers numbered 29,311 for public schools with average salary of $27,977 (1990). In 1989–90 the state spent an average $3,845 on each elementary and secondary school student. Leading institutions for higher education (1990–91) were:

Founded	Institution	Control	Full-time Professors	Students
1843	Clarke College, Dubuque	Independent	7	876
1846	Grinnell College, Grinnell	Independent	39	1,281
1847	University of Iowa, Iowa City	State	477	28,045
1851	Coe College, Cedar Rapids	Independent	23	1,250
1852	Wartburg College, Waverly	Evangelical Lutheran	25	1,440
1853	Cornell College, Mount Vernon	Independent	31	1,140
1858	Iowa State University, Ames	State	511	25,339
1876	Univ. of Northern Iowa, Cedar Falls	State	143	12,638
1881	Drake University, Des Moines	Independent	106	8,029
1894	Morningside College, Sioux City	Methodist	19	1,366

Health. In 1990, the state had 134 hospitals (17,251 beds). In 1989-90 the state-run hospitals served 4,628 patients and had an average daily census of 692.

Social Security. Iowa has a Civil Rights Act (1939) which makes it a misdemeanour for any place of public accommodation to deprive any person of 'full and equal enjoyment' of the facilities it offers the public.

Supplemental Security Income (SSI) assistance is available for the aged (65 or older), the blind and the disabled. As of Dec. 1990, 7,737 elderly persons were drawing an average of $123 per month, 1,062 blind persons $247 per month, and 22,438 disabled persons $242 per month. Aid to dependent children was received by 35,070 cases representing 97,505 recipients.

Further Reading

Statistical Information: State Departments of Health, Public Instruction and Human Services; State Aeronautics and Commerce Commissions; Iowa Department of Economic Development;

Crop and Livestock Reporting Services, Des Moines; Iowa Dept. of Transportation, Ames; Geological Survey, Iowa City; Iowa College Aid Commission.
Annual Survey of Manufactures. US Department of Commerce
Government Finance. US Department of Commerce
Official Register. Secretary of State. Des Moines. Biennial
Petersen, W. J., *Iowa History Reference Guide*. Iowa City, 1952
Smeal, L., *Iowa Historical and Biographical Index*. New York, 1984
Vexler, R. I., *Iowa Chronology and Factbook*. Oceana, 1978

State Library of Iowa: Des Moines 50319.

KANSAS

HISTORY. Kansas, settled in 1727, was made a Territory (along with part of Colorado) in 1854, and was admitted into the Union with its present area on 29 Jan. 1861.

AREA AND POPULATION. Kansas is bounded north by Nebraska, east by Missouri, with the Missouri River as boundary in the north-east, south by Oklahoma and west by Colorado. Area, 82,277 sq. miles, including 499 sq. miles of inland water. Census population, 1 April 1990, 2,477,574, an increase of 4·84% since 1980. Vital statistics, 1984: Births, 38,570 (15·8 per 1,000 population); deaths, 21,742 (8·9); infant deaths, 336 (8·7 per 1,000 live births); marriages, 24,795 (10·2); divorces 12,915 (5·3).

Population in 5 federal census years was:

	White	Black	Indian	Asiatic	Total	Per sq. mile
1870	346,377	17,108	914	—	364,399	4·5
1930	1,811,997	66,344	2,454	204	1,880,999	22·9
1960	2,078,666	91,445	5,069	2,271	2,178,611	26·3
			All others			
1970	2,122,068	106,977	17,533		2,249,071	27·5
1980	2,168,221	126,127	69,888		2,364,236	28·8

Of the total population in 1980, 1,156,941 were male, 1,575,899 were urban and those 20 years of age or older numbered 1,620,368.

Cities, with 1990 census population: Wichita, 304,011; Kansas City, 149,767; Topeka (capital), 119,883; Overland Park, 111,790.

CLIMATE. Dodge City. Jan. 29°F (−1·7°C), July 78°F (25·6°C). Annual rainfall 21" (518 mm). Kansas City. Jan. 30°F (−1·1°C), July 79°F (26·1°C). Annual rainfall 38" (947 mm). Topeka. Jan. 28°F (−2·2°C), July 78°F (25·6°C). Annual rainfall 35" (875 mm). Wichita. Jan. 31°F (−0·6°C), July 81°F (27·2°C). Annual rainfall 31" (777 mm). *See* Mid-West, p. 1398.

CONSTITUTION AND GOVERNMENT. The year 1861 saw the adoption of the present constitution; it has had 78 amendments. The Legislature includes a Senate of 40 members, elected for 4 years, and a House of Representatives of 125 members, elected for 2 years. Sessions are annual.

In the 1988 presidential election Bush polled 552,659 votes, Dukakis, 422,056. The capital is Topeka. The state is divided into 105 counties.

Governor: Joan Finney, 1991–95 (D.) ($74,235).
Lieut.-Governor: James Francisco (D.) ($20,998).
Secretary of State: Bill Graves (R.) ($57,668).

BUDGET. For the year ending 30 June 1990 general revenue was $5,828·9m. General expenditures were $4,329·3m.
Per capita personal income (1985) was $13,775.

ENERGY AND NATURAL RESOURCES

Minerals. Important fuel minerals are coal, petroleum and natural gas. Non-fuel minerals, mainly cement, salt and crushed stone, were worth $366·5m. in 1990.

Agriculture. Kansas is pre-eminently agricultural, but sometimes suffers from lack of rainfall in the west. Chief crops: Wheat, sorghum, maize, hay. There is an extensive livestock industry, comprising, in 1990, 5·7m. cattle, 887,000 sheep, 1·45m. pigs and 1·4m. poultry.

INDUSTRY. Employment distribution (1985): Total workforce 975,000, of which 245,000 were in trade; 191,000 in government; 187,000 in services; 174,000 in manufacturing; 65,000 in transport and utilities; 53,000 in finance, insurance and real estate; 44,000 in construction. The slaughtering industry, other food processing, aircraft, the manufacture of transport equipment and petroleum refining are important.

COMMUNICATIONS

Roads. In 1990 there were 133,156 miles of roads (124,169 miles rural) and 1,986,647 registered motor vehicles.

Railways. There were 7,273 miles of railway in Jan. 1982.

Civil Aviation. There is an international airport at Wichita.

JUSTICE, RELIGION, EDUCATION AND WELFARE

Justice. There were 4,748 prisoners in state institutions, 31 Dec. 1985. The death penalty (by hanging) for murder was abolished in 1907 and restored in 1935; there have been no executions since 1968; executions 1934 to 1968 have been 15 (all for murder).

Religion. The most numerous religious bodies are Roman Catholic, Methodists and Disciples of Christ.

Education. In 1982–83 organized school districts had 1,519 elementary and secondary schools which had 407,074 pupils and 26,053 teachers. Average salary of public school teachers, 1986, $22,800 (elementary and secondary). There were 20 independent colleges, 20 community colleges, 2 Bible colleges, 1 municipal university.

Kansas has 6 state-supported institutions of higher education: Kansas State University, Manhattan (1863), had 17,570 students in 1985–86; The University of Kansas, Lawrence, founded in 1865, had 24,774; Emporia State University, Emporia, had 5,344; Pittsburg State University, Pittsburg, had 5,096; Fort Hays State University, Hays, had 5,657 and Wichita State University, Wichita, had 16,902. The state also supports a two-year technical school, Kansas Technical Institute, at Salina.

Health. In 1983 the state had 165 hospitals (18,300 beds) listed by the American Hospital Association; hospitals had an average daily occupancy rate of 70·3%.

Social Security. In Dec. 1985, 20,900 persons received state and federal aid under programmes of aid to the aged or disabled, and 66,800 in 22,700 families received aid to dependent children. Average monthly payment to the aged, $121; the disabled, $206, per family with dependent children, $303 (1984).

Further Reading

Annual Economic Report of the Governor. Topeka
Directory of State Officers, Boards and Commissioners and Interesting Facts Concerning Kansas. Topeka, Biennial
Drury, J. W., *The Government of Kansas.* Lawrence, Univ. of Kansas, 1970
Zornow, W. F., *Kansas: A History of the Jayhawk State.* Norman, Okla., 1957

State Library: Kansas State Library, Topeka.

KENTUCKY

HISTORY. Kentucky, first settled in 1765, was originally part of Virginia; it was admitted into the Union on 1 June 1792 and its first legislature met on 4 June.

AREA AND POPULATION. Kentucky is bounded north by the Ohio River (forming the boundary with Illinois, Indiana and Ohio), north-east by the Big Sandy River (forming the boundary with West Virginia), east by Virginia, south by Tennessee and west by the Mississippi River (forming the boundary with Missouri). Area, 40,409 sq. miles, of which 677 sq. miles are water. Census population, 1990 3,685,296, an increase of 0·7% since 1980. Births in 1989, 53,206 (14·3 per 1,000 population); deaths, 35,182 (9·4); infant deaths, 486 (9·7 per 1,000 live births); marriages, 50,093 (13·4); divorces, 20,400 (5·5).

Population in 5 census years was:

	White	Black	All others	Total	Per sq.mile
1930	2,388,364	226,040	185	2,614,589	65·1
1950	2,742,090	201,921	795	2,944,806	73·9
1960	2,820,083	215,949	2,124	3,038,156	76·2
1980	3,379,006	259,477	22,294	3,660,777	92·3
1990	3,391,832	262,907	30,557	3,685,296	92·8

Of the total population in 1990, 1,785,235 were male and 1,136,272 were 21 years old or older.

The principal cities with census population in 1990 are: Louisville, 269,063 (urbanized area, 684,638); Lexington-Fayette, 225,336; Owensboro, 53,549; Covington, 43,264; Bowling Green, 40,641; Hopkinsville, 29,809; Paducah, 27,256; Frankfort (capital), 25,968; Henderson, 25,945.

CLIMATE. Kentucky has a temperate climate. Temperatures are moderate during both winter and summer, precipitation is ample without a pronounced dry season, and there is little snow during the winter. Lexington. Jan. 33°F (0·6°C), July 76°F (24·4°C). Annual rainfall 43" (1,077 mm). Louisville. Jan. 34°F (1·1°C), July 78°F (25·6°C). Annual rainfall 43" (1,077 mm). *See* Appalachian Mountains, p. 1398.

CONSTITUTION AND GOVERNMENT. The constitution dates from 1891; there had been 3 preceding it. The 1891 constitution was promulgated by convention and provides that amendments be submitted to the electorate for ratification. The General Assembly consists of a Senate of 38 members elected for 4 years, one half retiring every 2 years, and a House of Representatives of 100 members elected for 2 years. It has biennial sessions. All citizens of 18 or over are qualified as electors. Registered voters, May 1991: 1,873,270. In the 1988 presidential election Bush polled 734,281 votes, Dukakis, 580,368.

The capital is Frankfort. The state is divided into 120 counties.

Governor: Wallace G. Wilkinson (D.), 1987–91 ($79,255). [1]
Lieut.-Governor: Brereton Jones (D.) ($67,378). [1]
Secretary of State: Brerner Ehrler (D.) ($67,378). [1]

[1] 1991. Salaries are revised annually by the percentage change in the Consumer Price Index.

BUDGET. For the fiscal year ending 30 June 1991 revenues received within the five major operating funds amounted to $8,158·3m. Included in this figure are $4,311·7m. General Fund revenues and $2,085·4m. Federal Fund revenues. Total expenditures amounted to $7,512·5m. including education and humanities, $1,996·0m.; human resources benefits payments, $1,624·2m.; and transport, $679·7m.

The general obligation bonded indebtedness on 30 June 1991 was $57·7m.

Per capita personal income (1990) was $15,001.

ENERGY AND NATURAL RESOURCES

Minerals. The principal mineral product of Kentucky is coal, 167·4m. short tons mined in 1989, value $4,180m. Output of petroleum, 5·4m. bbls (of 42 gallons);

natural gas, 72,417m. cu. ft; stone, 48·2m. short tons, value $187·8m.; clay, 716,990 short tons, value $3·4m.; sand and gravel, 5·5m. short tons, value $15·1m. Total value of non-fuel mineral products in 1989 was $330,659,000. Other minerals include fluorspar, ball clay, lead, zinc, silver, cement, lime, industrial sand and gravel, oil shale and tar sands.

Agriculture. In 1991, 91,000 farms had an area of 14·1m. acres. The average farm was 155 acres.

Cash income, 1990, from crops, $1,400·2m., and from livestock, $1,698·3m. The chief crop is tobacco: Production, in 1990, 420·0m. lb., ranking second to N. Carolina in US. Other principal crops include hay, corn, soybeans, wheat, fruit and vegetables, barley, sorghum grain, oats and rye.

Stock-raising is important in Kentucky, which has long been famous for its horses. The livestock in 1991 included 200,000 milch cows, 2·5m. cattle and calves, 35,000 sheep, 920,000 swine.

Forestry. Total forests area, 1978, 12,160,800 acres. Total commercial forest land, 1978, 11,901,900 acres; 92% is privately owned.

INDUSTRY. In 1990 the state's 3,800 manufacturing plants had 286,406 production workers; value added by manufacture in 1987 was $18,091·7m. The leading manufacturing industries (by employment) are industrial machinery, electrical machinery, apparel and transportation equipment.

TOURISM. In 1990 tourist expenditure was $4,969m., producing over $347m. in tax revenues and generating 126,425 jobs. The state had (1989) 863 hotels and motels, 232 campgrounds and 45 state parks.

COMMUNICATIONS

Roads. In 1991 the state had over 70,100 miles of federal, state and local roads. There were over 2·9m. motor vehicle registrations in 1991.

Railways. In 1991 there were 2,800 miles of railway.

Aviation. There are (1991) 67 publicly-used airports and 2,294 registered aircraft in Kentucky.

Shipping. There is an increasing amount of barge traffic on 1,090 miles of navigable rivers. There are 6 river ports and 3 planned.

JUSTICE, RELIGION, EDUCATION AND WELFARE

Justice. There are 11 prisons within the Department of Adult Institutions and 3 privately-run adult institution; average daily population (1990–91), 8,957, including 6,698 in prison, 919 in a private prison, 886 in jails awaiting incarceration, and 620 in local community centres and halfway houses. There are also 11,998 individuals on probation or parole.

There has been no execution since 1962. A session of Congress in 1976 limited the death penalty to cases of kidnap and murder.

Total executions, 1911–62, were 162 including 76 whites and 86 blacks. There were 144 were for murder, 7 for rape, 6 for criminal offences, 5 for armed robbery. As of July 30, 1991 there were 30 people under death sentences.

Religion. The chief religious denominations in 1980 were: Southern Baptists, with 883,096 members, Roman Catholic (365,277), United Methodists (234,536), Christian Churches and Church of Christ (81,222) and Christian (Disciples of Christ) (78,275).

Education. Attendance at school between the ages of 5 and 15 years (inclusive) is compulsory, the normal term being 175 days. In 1989–90, 24,280 teachers were employed in public elementary and 11,563 in secondary schools, in which 433,557 and 197,131 pupils enrolled respectively. Expenditure on elementary and secondary day schools in 1989–90 was $2,344m.; public school classroom teachers' salaries (1989–90) averaged $26,275.

There were also 4,004 teachers working in private elementary and secondary schools with 64,433 students.

The state has 25 universities and senior colleges, 3 junior colleges and 14 community colleges, with a total (autumn 1990) of 173,382 students. Of these universities and colleges, 22 are state-supported, and the remainder are supported privately. The largest of the institutions of higher learning are (autumn 1990): University of Louisville, with 23,610 students; University of Kentucky, 23,081; Western Kentucky University, 15,371; Eastern Kentucky University, 15,371; Northern Kentucky University, 11,260; Murray State University, 8,097; Morehead State University, 8,622; Kentucky State, 2,512. Five of the several privately endowed colleges of standing are Berea College, Berea; Centre College, Danville; Transylvania University, Lexington; Georgetown College, Georgetown; and Bellarmine College, Louisville.

Health. In 1991 the state had 129 licensed hospitals (19,355 beds). There were 366 licensed long-term care facilities (31,819) and 490 licensed family care homes (1,485).

Welfare. In July 1991 there were 349,540 persons receiving financial assistance; 120,511 of these persons received the Federal Supplemental Security Income (SSI); 31,170 of them were aged, 2,000 blind, 87,341 disabled. Also, in the all state funded Supplementation programme, payments were made in July 1991 to 6,539 persons, of which 3,293 were aged, 84 blind and 3,162 disabled. The average State Supplementation payment was $199.05 to aged, $110·60 to blind and $194.85 to disabled.

In the Aid to Families with Dependent Children Programme as of July 1991, aid was given to 222,490 persons in 80,550 families. The average payment per person was $78.42, per family $216.61.

In addition to money payments, medical assistance, food stamps and social services are available.

Further Reading

Kentucky Economic Statistics. Cabinet for Economic Development, Frankfort
Kentucky Statistical Abstract. Univ. of Kentucky, Center for Business and Economic Research
Lee, L. G., *A Brief History of Kentucky and its Counties.* Berea, 1981

LOUISIANA

HISTORY. Louisiana was first settled in 1699. That part lying east of the Mississippi River was organized in 1804 as the Territory of New Orleans, and admitted into the Union on 30 April 1812. The section west of the river was added very shortly thereafter.

AREA AND POPULATION. Louisiana is bounded north by Arkansas, east by Mississippi, south by the Gulf of Mexico and west by Texas. Total area, 52,453 sq. miles; land area, 43,566 sq. miles. Census population, 1 April 1990, 4,219,973, an increase of 0·38% since 1980. Births, 1986, 77,944 (17·3 per 1,000 population); deaths, 36,287 (8·1); infant deaths, 925 (11·9 per 1,000 live births); marriages, 37,459 (8·4); divorces, 15,164.

Population in 5 census years was:

	White	Black	Indian	Asiatic	Total	Per sq. mile
1910	941,086	713,874	780	648	1,656,388	36·5
1930	1,322,712	776,326	1,536	1,019	2,101,593	46·5
1960	2,211,715	1,039,207	3,587	2,004	3,257,022	72·2
			All others			
1970	2,541,498	1,086,832	12,976		3,641,306	81·1
1980	2,911,243	1,237,263	55,466		4,205,900	93·5

Of the 1980 total, 2,039,894 were male, 2,885,535 were urban; those 20 years of age or older numbered 2,699,100.

The largest cities with their 1990 census population are: New Orleans, 496,938; Baton Rouge, 219,531; Shreveport, 198,525.

CLIMATE. New Orleans. Jan. 54°F (12·2°C), July 83°F (28·3°C). Annual rainfall 58" (1,458 mm). *See* Gulf Coast, p. 1398.

CONSTITUTION AND GOVERNMENT. The present constitution dates from 1974. The Legislature consists of a Senate of 39 members and a House of Representatives of 105 members, both chosen for 4 years. Sessions are annual; a fiscal session is held in odd years.

In the 1988 presidential election Bush polled 880,660 votes, Dukakis, 715,475.

Louisiana is divided into 64 parishes (corresponding to the counties of other states). The capital is Baton Rouge.

Governor: Edwin Edwards, 1991–95 (R)., ($73,440).

BUDGET. For the fiscal year ending 30 June 1990 general revenues were $8,924·3m., of which $2,399m. were federal funds; total expenditures were $8,523·6m. (education, $3,176·9m.; transport, $740·3m.; public welfare, $1,342·4m.).

Per capita personal income (1990) was $14,391.

ENERGY AND NATURAL RESOURCES

Minerals. The yield in 1987 of crude petroleum was 144m. bbls; marketed production of natural gas, 1,572,835,903m. cu. ft. Principal non-fuel minerals are salt, sulphur and sand and gravel. Value of 1990 output, $381·1m.

Agriculture. The state is divided into two parts, the uplands and the alluvial and swamp regions of the coast. A delta occupies about one-third of the total area. Manufacturing is the leading industry, but agriculture is important. Principal crops are soybeans, sugar-cane, rice, maize, cotton, sweet potatoes, pecans and sorghum. Livestock in 1990: Cattle, 0·84m.; pigs, 50,000; sheep, 16,000; poultry, 2·1m.

Fisheries. The value of the 1990 catch was $263·5m.

Forestry. Forests, 13,883,000 acres, represent 49% of the state's area. Income from manufactured products exceeds $2,500m. annually. 737m. board feet of timber were cut in 1989.

INDUSTRY. The manufacturing industries are chiefly those associated with petroleum, chemicals, lumber, food, paper. In 1990 11·4% of the workforce were employed in manufacturing, 23·1% in trade and 23·6% in service industries.

TOURISM. Travellers spent an estimated $4,200m. in 1989. Tourism is the second most important industry for state income.

COMMUNICATIONS

Roads. In 1990 there were 58,521 miles of roads (46,277 miles rural) and 2,967,097 registered motor vehicles.

Railways. In 1986 there were 3,347 miles of track in the state.

Civil Aviation. In 1988 there were 386 commercial and private airports.

Shipping. There are ports at New Orleans, Baton Rouge and Lake Charles. The Mississippi and other waterways provide 7,500 miles of navigable water.

JUSTICE, RELIGION, EDUCATION AND WELFARE

Justice. State and federal prisons, Nov. 1988, had 16,121 inmates. Execution is by electrocution; there were 135 between 1930 and 1961, 15 between 1977 and 1987.

Religion. The Roman Catholic Church is the largest denomination in Louisiana. The leading Protestant Churches are Southern Baptist and Methodist.

Education. School attendance is compulsory between the ages of 7 and 15, both inclusive. In 1986–87 there were 804,645 pupils in public elementary and secondary schools. In 1987 the 42,019 instructional staff had an average salary of $20,235. There are 17 four-year public colleges and universities and 11 non-public four-year institutions of higher learning. There are 47 state trade and vocational-technical schools. Superior instruction is given in the Louisiana State University with 54,912 students (1987). Tulane University in New Orleans had 10,302; The Roman Catholic Loyola University in New Orleans had 5,210; Dillard University in New Orleans had 1,218; and the Southern University System, 5,210.

Health. In 1988 the state had 186 licensed hospitals and 3 state mental hospitals.

Social Security. In Dec. 1985, assistance was being given to 49,400 elderly persons; 78,800 families with dependent children; 74,700 disabled people. Aid was from state and federal sources.

Further Reading

Davis, E. A., *Louisiana, the Pelican State*. Louisiana State Univ. Press, Baton Rouge, 1975
Kniffen, F. B., *Louisiana, its Land and People*. Louisiana State Univ. Press, Baton Rouge, 1968

State Library: The Louisiana State Library, Baton Rouge, Louisiana.

MAINE

HISTORY. After a first attempt in 1607, Maine was settled in 1623. From 1652 to 1820 it was part of Massachusetts and was admitted into the Union on 15 March 1820.

AREA AND POPULATION. Maine is bounded west, north and east by Canada, south-east by the Atlantic, south and south-west by New Hampshire. Area, 33,265 sq. miles, of which 2,269 are inland water. Census population, 1 April 1990 1,127,928, an increase of 9·18% since 1980. In 1986 live births numbered 16,717 (14·3 per 1,000 population); deaths, 10,796 (9·2); infant deaths, 146 (8·9 per 1,000 live births); marriages, 10,887 (9·2); divorces 5,621 (4·8).

Population for 5 census years was:

	White	Black	Indian	Asiatic	Total	Per sq. mile
1910	739,995	1,363	892	121	742,371	24·8
1930	795,185	1,096	1,012	130	797,423	25·7
1950	910,846	1,221	1,522	185	913,774	29·4
			All others			
1970	985,276	2,800	3,972		992,048	31·0
1980	1,109,850	3,128	12,049		1,125,027	36·3

Of the total population in 1980, 48·5% were male, 40·7% were urban and 60·5% were 21 years or older.

The largest city in the state is Portland with a census population of 61,572 in 1980. Other cities (with population in 1980) are: Lewiston, 40,481; Bangor, 31,643; Auburn, 23,128; South Portland, 22,712; Augusta (capital), 21,819; Biddeford, 19,638; Waterville, 17,779.

CLIMATE. Average maximum temperatures range from 56·3°F in Waterville to 48·3°F in Caribou, but record high (since *c.* 1950) is 103°F. Average minimum ranges from 36·9°F in Rockland to 28·3°F in Greenville, but record low (also in Greenville) is –42°F. Average annual rainfall ranges from 48·85" in Machias to 36·09" in Houlton. Average annual snowfall ranges from 118·7" in Greenville to 59·7" in Rockland. *See* New England, p. 1398.

CONSTITUTION AND GOVERNMENT. The constitution of 1820 is still in force, but it has been amended 153 times. In 1951, 1965 and 1973 the Legislature approved recodifications of the constitution as arranged by the Chief Justice under special authority.

The Legislature consists of the Senate with 35 members and the House of Representatives with 151 members, both Houses being elected simultaneously for 2 years. Sessions are annual.

In the 1988 presidential election Bush polled 304,087 votes, Dukakis, 240,508.

The capital is Augusta. The state is divided into 16 counties.

Governor: John R. McKernan (R.), 1991–95 ($70,000).
Secretary of State: G. William Diamond (D.) ($48,152).

BUDGET. For the financial year ending 30 June 1990 general revenue was $2,848m. and expenditure was $2,743·3m.

Per capita personal income (1990) was $17,200.

NATURAL RESOURCES

Minerals. Minerals include sand and gravel, stone, lead, clay, copper, peat, silver and zinc. Mineral output, 1990, was valued at $56m.

Agriculture. In 1986, 7,800 farms occupied 2m. acres; the average farm was 194 acres. Principal crops are potatoes, apples, hay and blueberries. Livestock in 1986: Cattle, 135,000; pigs, 79,000; sheep, 17,000; poultry, 4·9m.

Forestry. There are some 17·5m. acres of commercial forest, mainly pine, spruce and fir. Wood products industries are of great economic importance. 714m. board feet were cut in 1989.

Fisheries. In 1990 the commercial catch was valued at $129·9m.

INDUSTRY. Total non-agricultural workforce, 1985, 459,000. Manufacturing employed 106,000; trade, 108,000; services, 95,000; government, 86,000; the main manufacture is paper at 47 plants, producing about 34% of manufacturing value added.

TOURISM. Earnings were $2,000m. in 1989.

COMMUNICATIONS

Roads. In 1990 there were 22,240 miles of roads (19,781 miles rural) and 939,301 registered motor vehicles.

Railways. In 1984 there were 1,516 miles of mainline railway tracks.

Civil Aviation. There are international airports at Portland and Bangor.

JUSTICE, RELIGION, EDUCATION AND WELFARE

Justice. The state's penal system in Sept. 1984 held 435 adults in the State Prison, 237 in the Correctional Center and 332 juveniles in the Youth Center. There is no capital punishment.

Religion. The largest religious bodies are: Roman Catholic (270,283 members), Baptists (36,808 members) and Congregationalists (40,750 members), and other Christian Churches (34,066 members).

Education. Education is free for pupils from 5 to 21 years of age, and compulsory from 7 to 17. In 1983–84 the 756 public schools (610 elementary, 105 secondary and 41 combined elementary and secondary) had 12,283 staff and 209,753 enrolled pupils. In 1983–84 there were 126 private schools with 1,035 teachers and 15,461 pupils. Public school teachers' salaries, 1983–84, averaged $17,328. Total public expenditure on public elementary and secondary education in 1982–83, $461,252,847.

The state University of Maine, founded in 1865, had (1983–84) 1,003 teaching staff and 28,591 students at 7 locations; Bowdoin College, founded in 1794 at Brunswick, (107 and 1,371); Bates College at Lewiston, (104 and 1,424); Colby College at Waterville, (125 and 1,733); Husson College, Bangor, (31 and 1,465); Westbrook College at Westbrook, (56 and 1,120); Unity College at Unity, (23 and 325), and the University of New England (formerly St Francis College) at Biddeford, (55 and 848).

Health. In 1984 the state had 42 general hospitals (4,571 beds for acute care); 3 hospitals for mental diseases, acute and psychiatric care (541 beds); 144 nursing homes (10,220 beds).

Social Security. Supplemental Security Income (SSI) is administered by the Social Security Administration. It became effective on 1 Jan. 1974 and replaces former aid to the aged, blind and disabled, administered by the state with state and federal funds. SSI is supplemented by Medicaid for nursing home patients or hospital patients. Aid to families with dependent children is granted where one or both parents are disabled or absent and income is insufficient. There is a programme of assistance for catastrophic illness. Child welfare services include basic child protective services, enforcing child support, establishing paternity and finding missing parents, foster home placements, adoptions; services in divorce cases and licensing of foster homes, day care and residential treatment services, and public guardianship. There are also protective services for adults.

Further Reading

Maine Register, State Year-Book and Legislative Manual. Tower Publishing, Portland. Annual

Banks, R., *Maine Becomes A State.* Wesleyan U.P., 1970

Clark, C., *Maine.* New York, 1977

MARYLAND

HISTORY. Maryland, first settled in 1634, was one of the 13 original states.

AREA AND POPULATION. Maryland is bounded north by Pennsylvania, east by Delaware and the Atlantic, south by Virginia and West Virginia, with the Potomac River forming most of the boundary, and west by West Virginia. Chesapeake Bay almost cuts off the eastern end of the state from the rest. Area, 10,460 sq. miles, of which 623 sq. miles are inland water; in addition, water area under Maryland jurisdiction in Chesapeake Bay amounts to 1,726 sq. miles. Census population, 1 April 1990, 4,781,468, an increase since 1980 of 564,535 or 13·4%. In 1988 births were 76,414 (16·5 per 1,000 population); deaths, 38,637 (8·4); infant deaths, 856 (11·2 per 1,000 live births); marriages, 47,258 (10·2); divorces, 16,807 (3·6).

Population for 5 federal censuses was:

	White	Black	Indian	Asiatic	Total	Per sq. mile
1920	1,204,737	244,479	32	413	1,449,661	145·8
1930	1,354,226	276,379	50	871	1,631,526	165·0
1960	2,573,919	518,410	1,538	5,700	3,100,689	314·0
			All others			
1990	3,393,964	1,189,899	197,605		4,781,468	486·1

Of the total population in 1990, 2,318,671 were male. 3,984,722 persons were urban and those 20 years old or older numbered 3,483,463.

The largest city in the state (containing 15·4% of the population) is Baltimore, with 736,014 in 1990 (and 786,741 in 1980); Baltimore metropolitan area, 2·4m. Maryland residents in the Washington, D.C., metropolitan area total more than 1·8m. Other cities (1990) are Dundalk (65,800); Towson (49,445); Silver Spring (76,046); Bethesda (62,936). Incorporated places, 1990: Rockville, 44,835; Bowie, 37,589; Hagerstown, 35,445; Frederick, 40,148; Annapolis, 33,187; Gaithersburg, 39,542; Cumberland, 23,706; Cambridge, 11,514.

CLIMATE. Baltimore. Jan. 36°F (2·2°C), July 79°F (26·1°C). Annual rainfall 41" (1,026 mm). *See* Atlantic Coast, p. 1398.

CONSTITUTION AND GOVERNMENT. The present constitution dates from 1867; it has had 125 amendments. The General Assembly consists of a Senate of 47, and a House of Delegates of 141 members, both elected for 4 years, as are the Governor and Lieut.-Governor. Voters are citizens who have the usual residential qualifications. At the 1988 presidential election Bush polled 834,202 votes, Dukakis, 793,939.

Maryland sends to Congress 2 senators and 8 representatives.

The state capital is Annapolis. The state is divided into 23 counties and Baltimore City.

Governor: William D. Schaefer (D.), 1991–95 ($120,000).
Lieut.-Governor: Melvin Steinberg (D.) ($100,000).
Secretary of State: Winfield M. Kelly (D.) ($70,000).

BUDGET. For the fiscal year ending 30 June 1990 general revenues were $9,106,363,000 ($6,518,272,000 from taxation). General expenditures, $9,375,548,000, including $2,052,303,000 for education and $2,744,025,000 for public welfare and health; $1,686,072,000 for transport.

Total authorized long-term state debt, 30 June 1990 was $2,979·8m. (Issued and outstanding, $1,986·9m.; authorized but not issued, $992·9m.)

Per capita personal income (1990) was $21,789.

ENERGY AND NATURAL RESOURCES

Minerals. Value of non-fuel mineral production, 1990, was $354m. Sand and gravel (17·1m. short tons) and stone (31·4m. short tons) account for 72% of the total value. Coal is the leading mineral commodity by value followed by, stone, sand and gravel and Portland cement. Output of coal was 3.5m. short tons, valued at about $90m. Natural gas is produced from 1 field in Garrett County; 22m. cu. ft in 1990. A second gas field in the same county is used for natural gas storage.

Agriculture. Agriculture is an important industry in the state. In 1990 there were approximately 15,200 farms with an area of 2·3m. acres (36% of the land area).

Farm animals, 1 Jan. 1990, were: Milch cows, 103,000; all cattle, 320,000; swine, 162,000; sheep, 30,000; chickens (not broilers), 4·5m. The most important crops, 1990, were: Corn for grain, 53·1m. bu.; soybeans, 17·8m. bu.; tobacco, 9·7m. lb.; and hay, 678,000 tons.

Cash receipts from farm marketings, 1990, were $1,346m.; from livestock and livestock products, $828m., and crops, $518m. Dairy products and broilers are important.

INDUSTRY. In 1989 manufactories had 134,500 production workers earning $3,146·4m.; value added by manufacture, $15,892m. Chief industries are food and kindred products, instruments and related products, chemicals and products and printing and publishing.

TOURISM. Tourism is one of the state's leading industries. In 1989 tourists spent over $4,366m.

COMMUNICATIONS

Roads. The state highway department maintained, 1 Jan. 1991, 5,210 miles of highways, of which 89 miles were toll roads. The 23 counties maintained 18,785 miles of highways, and the 159 municipalities (including the city of Baltimore) maintained 4,143 miles of streets and alleys. Total mileage, 1 Jan. 1991, of public highways, streets and alleys, 28,317 miles. As of March 1991, an estimated 3·5m. automobiles were registered.

Railways. Railways, in 1990, had 1,068 miles of line.

Civil Aviation. There were, 1992, 48 commercially licensed aiports.

Shipping. In 1990 Baltimore was the ninth largest US seaport in value of trade, twelfth in tonnage handled.

JUSTICE, RELIGION, EDUCATION AND WELFARE

Justice. Prisons on 21 Feb. 1992 had about 18,577 men and 939 women; the total equalled 401 per 100,000 population, a high rate, which may be explained by the fact that Maryland incarcerates domestic relations law violators in state prisons; state prisons also receive a considerable number of persons committed for misdemeanours by magistrates' courts of the counties as well as from Baltimore's court system.

Since 1930 there have been 68 executions (by lethal gas since 1957; earlier by hanging)—7 whites and 37 Negroes for murder, and 6 whites and 18 Negroes for rape. Last execution was June 1961.

Maryland's prison system has conducted a work-release programme for selected prisoners since 1963. All institutions have academic and vocational training programmes.

In accordance with the 1950 Supreme Court decisions declaring segregation unconstitutional, the University of Maryland and other public and private colleges began admitting Black students in Sept. 1956; elementary and secondary schools followed.

Religion. Maryland was the first US state to give religious freedom to all who came within its borders. Present religious affiliations of the population are approximately: Protestant, 32%; Roman Catholic, 24%; Jewish, 10%; remaining 34% is non-related and other faiths.

Education. Education is compulsory from 6 to 16 years of age. In Sept. 1990 the public elementary schools (including kindergartens and secondary schools) had 715,718 pupils. Teachers, principals and therapists in the elementary and secondary schools numbered 44,974. Teachers' average salary in 1990–91 was $38,312. Current expenditure by local school boards on education, 1989–90, was $3,827·8m., of which the state's contribution was $1,504·8m.

In 1991 there were 34 degree-granting 4-year institutions and 23 2-year colleges. The largest was the University of Maryland system, with 106,514 students (Sept. 1991), consisting of 11 campuses with the highest enrolment at College Park (34,623) and Towson State University (15,403).

Health. In Nov. 1991, 78 hospitals (19,526 beds) were licensed by the State Department of Health and Mental Hygiene.

The Maryland State Department of Health, organized in 1874, was in 1969 made part of the Department of Health and Mental Hygiene which performs its functions through its central office, 23 county health departments and the Baltimore City Health Department. For the financial year 1990 the department's budget was $1,985·8m., of which $1,327·5m. were general funds and $46.4m. special funds appropriated by the General Assembly. The balance of the budget, $611·9m., derives from federal funds.

During financial year 1991 Maryland's programme of medical care for indigent and medically indigent patients covered about 442,100 persons. The programme, which covers in-patient and out-patient hospital services, laboratory services, skilled nursing home care, physician services, pharmacy services, dental services and home health services, cost approximately $1,357m.

Social Security. Under the supervision of the Department of Human Resources, local social service departments administer public assistance for needy persons. In March 1990 families with dependent children received $29,217,254 (218,342 recipients, average actual monthly payment $133.81); general public assistance payments were $5,394,836 (25,443 recipients, average actual monthly payments $212.04).

Further Reading

Statistical Information: Maryland Department of Economic and Employment Development, Baltimore City, 21202.

Maryland Manual: A Compendium of Legal, Historical and Statistical Information Relating to the State of Maryland. Annapolis. Biennial
DiLisio, J. E., *Maryland.* Boulder, 1982
Rollo, V. F., *Maryland's Constitution and Government.* Maryland Hist. Press, Rev. ed., 1982

State Library: Maryland State Library, Annapolis. *Director:* Michael S. Miller.

MASSACHUSETTS

HISTORY. The first permanent settlement within the borders of the present state was made at Plymouth in Dec. 1620, by the Pilgrims from Holland, who were separatists from the English Church, and formed the nucleus of the Plymouth Colony. In 1628 another company of Puritans settled at Salem, forming eventually the Massachusetts Bay Colony. In 1630 Boston was settled. In the struggle which ended in the separation of the American colonies from the mother country, Massachusetts took the foremost part, and on 6 Feb. 1788 became the sixth state to ratify the US constitution.

AREA AND POPULATION. Massachusetts is bounded north by Vermont and New Hampshire, east by the Atlantic, south by Connecticut and Rhode Island and west by New York. Area, 8,284 sq. miles, 460 sq. miles being inland water.The census population 1 April 1990, was 6,016,425, an increase of 4·87% since 1980. Births, 1985 were 82,872 (14·2 per 1,000 population); deaths, 54,935 (9·4 per 1,000); infant deaths (1984), 739 (9·3 per 1,000 live births); marriages, 51,648 (8·9); divorces, 19,794 (3·4).

Population at 4 federal census years was:

	White	Black	Other	Total	Per sq. mile
1950	4,611,503	73,171	5,840	4,690,514	598·4
1960	5,023,144	111,842	13,592	5,148,578	656·8
1970	5,477,624	175,817	35,729	5,689,170	725·8
1980	5,362,836	221,279	152,922	5,737,037	732·0

Of the total population in 1980, 47·6% were male, 83·8% were urban and 32% were 21 years old or older.

Population of the largest cities at the 1990 census: Boston, 574,283; Lowell, 103,439; Springfield, 156,983; Worcester, 169,759.

CLIMATE. Boston. Jan. 28°F (−2·2°C), July 71°F (21·7°C). Annual rainfall 41" (1,036 mm). *See* New England, p. 1398.

CONSTITUTION AND GOVERNMENT. The constitution dates from 1780 and has had 116 amendments. The legislative body, styled the General Court of the Commonwealth of Massachusetts, meets annually, and consists of the Senate with 40 members and the House of Representatives of 160 members, both elected for 2 years.

At the 1988 presidential election Dukakis polled 1,387,398 votes, Bush, 1,184,323.

The capital is Boston. The state has 14 counties.

Governor: William F. Weld (R.), 1991–95 ($75,000).
Lieut.-Governor: A. Paul Cellucci (R.) ($60,000).
Secretary of State: Michael J. Connolly (D.) ($60,000).

BUDGET. For the fiscal year ending 30 June 1990 the total revenue of the state was $15,773·7m. ($9,369·1m. from taxes, $3,306·6m. from federal aid); total expenditures, $17,039m. ($3,495·8m. for education, $615·8m. for highways and $4,603·7m. for human services).

Per capita personal income (1990) was $22,642.

NATURAL RESOURCES

Minerals. There is little mining within the state. Total mineral output in 1990 was valued at $111·3m., of which most came from sand, gravel, crushed stone and lime.

Agriculture. On 1 Jan. 1986 there were approximately 6,000 farms (11,179 in 1959) with an area of 598,900 acres.

Principal crops include cranberries, apples and potatoes. On 1 Jan. 1982 farms in the state had 48,000 milch cows, 98,000 all cattle, 49,000 swine. In 1982 farms produced 145,000 turkeys and 0·8m. chickens.

Forestry. About 68% of the state is forest. State forests cover about 256,000 acres. Total forest land covers about 3m. acres. Commercially important hardwoods are sugar maple, northern red oak and white ash; softwoods are white pine and hemlock. 85m. board feet of timber were cut in 1989.

Fisheries. The 1985 catch was valued at $303m.

INDUSTRY. In 1986, manufacturing establishments employed an average of 637,740 workers. The 3 most important manufacturing groups, based on employment, were electric and electronic equipment, machinery (except electrical), printing and publishing. Service industries employed 875,736 and trade, 697,257. Total non-agricultural employment, 2,685,611.

COMMUNICATIONS

Roads. In 1990 there were 33,807 miles of public roads (13,201 miles rural) and 3,804,458 registered motor vehicles.

Railways. In 1984 there were 1,310 miles of mainline railway.

Civil Aviation. There is an international airport at Boston.

Shipping. The state has 3 deep-water harbours, the largest of which is Boston. Other ports are Fall River and New Bedford.

JUSTICE, RELIGION, EDUCATION AND WELFARE

Justice. On 31 Dec. 1985 state penal institutions held 5,447 inmates. There have been no executions since 1947.

Religion. The principal religious bodies are the Roman Catholics, Jewish Congregations, Methodists, Episcopalians and Unitarians.

Education. A regulation effective from 1 Sept. 1972 makes school attendance compulsory for ages 6–16. In 1985–86 expenditure by cities and towns on public schools was $3,521m. or $605 per capita, including debt retirement and service payments. In 1985–86 there were 56,400 classroom teachers and approximately 900,000 pupils.

Within the state there were (1982) 126 degree-granting institutions of higher learning (including 89 colleges and universities). Some leading institutions are:

Year opened	Name and location of universities and colleges	Students 1988
1636	Harvard University, Cambridge [1]	16,871
1839	Framingham State College	4,303
1839	Westfield State College	6,053
1840	Bridgewater State College	6,539
1852	Tufts University, Medford [1,3]	6,297
1854	Salem State College	6,364
1861	Mass. Institute of Technology, Cambridge [1]	9,158
1863	University of Massachusetts, Amherst [1]	26,233
1863	Boston College (RC), Chestnut Hill [1]	12,858
1865	Worcester Polytechnic Institute, Worcester [1]	4,022
1869	Boston University, Boston [1]	22,373

Year opened	Name and location of universities and colleges	Students 1988
1874	Worcester College	4,899
1894	Fitchburg State College	5,212
1894	University of Lowell [1]	10,445
1895	Southeastern Massachusetts University	5,031
1898	Northeastern University, Boston [1], [4]	20,618
1899	Simmons College, Boston [2]	2,594
1905	Wentworth Institute of Technology	3,350
1906	Suffolk University	5,978
1917	Bentley College	5,611
1919	Western New England College	3,686
1919	Babson College	3,163
1947	Merrimack College	2,300
1948	Brandeis University, Waltham [1]	3,484
1964	University of Massachusetts, Boston	8,027

[1] Co-educational.　　[3] Includes Jackson College for women.
[2] For women only.　　[4] Includes Forsyth Dental Center School.

Health. In 1984 the state had 177 hospitals (with 41,200 beds); average daily census, 1982, 32,736, including patients in public and private mental hospitals and institutions for the mentally retarded.

Social Security. The Department of Public Welfare had an appropriation of $1,828m. in financial year 1984 and paid $388m. in aid to families with dependent children (average 95,798 families per month); other main items were general relief (average 27,242 cases), Supplemental Security Income (average 105,402 cases) and Medical Assistance only (average 65,841 cases).

Further Reading

Annual Reports. Massachusetts and US Boards, Commissions, Departments and Divisions, Boston, annual
Hart, Albert B., (ed.) *Commonwealth History of Massachusetts, Colony, Province and State.* 5 vols., New York, 1966
Levitan, D. with Mariner, E. C., *Your Massachusetts Government.* Newton, Mass., 1984

MICHIGAN

HISTORY. Michigan, first settled by Marquette at Sault Ste Marie in 1668, became the Territory of Michigan in 1805, with its boundaries greatly enlarged in 1818 and 1834; it was admitted into the Union with its present boundaries on 26 Jan. 1837.

AREA AND POPULATION. Michigan is divided into two by Lake Michigan. The northern part is bounded south by the lake and by Wisconsin, west and north by Lake Superior, east by the North Channel of Lake Huron; between the two latter lakes the Canadian border runs through straits at Sault Ste Marie. The southern part is bounded west and north by Lake Michigan, east by Lake Huron, Ontario and Lake Erie, south by Ohio and Indiana. Area, 58,527 sq. miles, of which 1,573 sq. miles are inland water. Census population, 1 April 1990, 9,295,297, an increase of 0·4% since 1980. In 1985 births were 138,902 (15·2 per 1,000 population); deaths, 78,515 (8·7); infant deaths, 1,575 (11·4 per 1,000 live births); marriages, 79,022 (17·4); divorces, 38,775 (8·5).

Population of 5 federal census years was:

	White	Black	Indian	Asiatic	Total	Per sq. mile
1910	2,785,247	17,115	7,519	292	2,810,173	48·9
1930	4,663,507	169,453	7,080	2,285	4,842,325	84·9
1960	7,085,865	717,581	9,701	10,047	7,823,194	137·2

	White	Black	All others		Total	Per sq. mile
1970	7,833,474	991,066	50,543		8,875,083	156·2
1980	7,872,241	1,199,023	190,814		9,262,078	162·6

Of the total population in 1980, 4,516,189 were male, 6,551,551 persons were urban and those 20 years old or older numbered 6,146,694. 162,440 were of Spanish origin.

Population of the chief cities (census of 1 April 1990) was: Ann Arbor, 109,592; Detroit, 1,027,974; Flint, 140,761; Grand Rapids, 189,126; Lansing, 127,321; Livonia, 100,850; Sterling Heights, 117,810; Warren, 144,864.

CLIMATE. Detroit. Jan. 22·1°F (−5·5°C), July 72°F (22·2°C). Annual rainfall 32" (813 mm). Grand Rapids. Jan. 23·8°F (−4·6°C), July 72·6°F (22·5°C). Annual rainfall 33·6" (833 mm). Lansing. Jan. 21·7°F (−5·7°C), July 71°F (21·7°C). Annual rainfall 30·8" (782 mm). *See* Great Lakes, p. 1398.

CONSTITUTION AND GOVERNMENT. The present constitution became effective on 1 Jan. 1964. The Senate consists of 38 members, elected for 4 years, and the House of Representatives of 110 members, elected for 2 years. Sessions are annual.

At the 1988 presidential election Bush polled 1,969,435 votes, Dukakis, 1,673,496.

The capital is Lansing. The state is organized in 83 counties.

Governor: John Engler (R.), 1991–95 ($106,700).
Lieut.-Governor: Connie Binsfeld (R.) ($80,300).
Secretary of State: Richard H. Austin (D.) ($109,000).

BUDGET. For the financial year ending 30 Sept. 1990, the general revenue was $19,707·7m. (taxation, $11,343·4m., and federal aid, $4,180·7m.); general expenditures, $19,561·2m.

Per capita personal income (1990) was $18,346.

ENERGY AND NATURAL RESOURCES

Minerals. Output of petroleum, 1985, 31·5m. bbls; natural gas, 153,484,651m. cu. ft. Non-fuel mineral output in 1989 was valued at $1,370m., mainly iron ore, cement, stone, sand and gravel.

Agriculture. The state, formerly agricultural, is now chiefly industrial. In 1985 it contained 63,000 farms with a total area of 11m. acres; the average farm was 175 acres. Principal crops are maize, oats, wheat, sugar-beet, soybeans and hay. On 1 Jan. 1986 there were in the state 108,000 sheep, 397,000 milch cows, 1·41m. all cattle and 1·19m. swine; 8·9m. chickens and 38,000 (1985) turkey breeder hens. In 1985 the wool clip yielded 902,000 lb. of wool.

Forestry. The forests in 1990 covered 18,220,000 acres. About 17·5m. acres of this total is commercial forest. Three-fourths of the timber volume is hardwoods, principally hard and soft maples, aspen, oak and birch. Christmas trees are another important forest crop. 323m. board feet of timber were cut in 1989.

INDUSTRY. Manufacturing is important; among principal products are motor vehicles and trucks, machinery, fabricated metals, primary metals, cement, chemicals, furniture, paper, foodstuffs, rubber, plastics and pharmaceuticals. Total non-agricultural labour force, 1986, 4,386,000, of which 975,000 were in manufacturing.

COMMUNICATIONS

Roads. In 1990 there were 117,996 miles of roads (90,968 miles rural) and 7,138,583 registered motor vehicles.

Railways. On 1 Jan. 1986 there were 4,770 miles of railway and 67 miles of active car-ferry routes.

Civil Aviation. There are international airports at Detroit and Sault Ste Marie.

JUSTICE, RELIGION, EDUCATION AND WELFARE

Justice. A Civil Rights Commission was established, and its powers and duties were implemented by legislation in the extra session of 1963. Statutory enactments guaranteeing civil rights in specific areas date from 1885. The legislature has a unique one-person grand jury system.

Religion. Roman Catholics make up the largest body; largest Protestant denominations, Lutherans, United Methodists, United Presbyterians, Episcopalians.

Education. Education is compulsory for children from 6 to 16 years of age. The operating expenditure for graded and ungraded public schools for the fiscal year 1985, was $5,704m. In 1984–85 there were 567 school districts (elementary and secondary schools) with 1,678,458 pupils and 75,193 teachers. Teachers' salaries in 1985 averaged $28,440.

In 1985 there were 98 institutes of higher education with 508,000 students.

Universities and students (autumn 1986):

Founded	Name	Students
1817	University of Michigan	34,947
1849	Eastern Michigan University	21,349
1855	Michigan State University	44,088
1884	Ferris State College	11,274
1885	Michigan Technological University	6,326
1868	Wayne State University	34,764
1892	Central Michigan University	17,993
1889	Northern Michigan University	7,852
1903	Western Michigan University	21,747
1946	Lake Superior State College	2,660
1959	Oakland University	12,707
1960	Grand Valley State College	8,321
1965	Saginaw Valley College	5,377

Social Welfare. Old-age assistance is provided for persons 65 years of age or older who have resided in Michigan for one year before application; assets must not exceed various limits. In 1974 federal Supplementary Security Income (SSI) replaced the adults' programme. In Jan. 1987 aid was supplied to a monthly average of 418,572 dependent children in 188,972 families at $463.86 per family.

Health. In 1983 the state had 231 hospitals (47,812 beds) licensed by the state and 12 psychiatric hospitals, 7 centres for developmental disabilities, 5 centres for emotionally disturbed children.

In 1986 the Medicaid programme disbursed (with federal support) $1,642·9m. to 469,226 persons.

Further Reading

Michigan Manual. Dept of *Management and Budget.* Lansing. Biennial
Bureau of Business Research, Wayne State University. *Michigan Statistical Abstract.*
Bald, F. C., Michigan in Four Centuries. 2nd ed. New York, 1961
Catton. B., *Michigan—a Bicentennial History.* Norton, New York, 1976
Lewis, F. E., *State and Local Government in Michigan.* Lansing, 1979
Dunbar, W. F. and May, G. S., *Michigan: A History of the Wolverine State.* Grand Rapids, 1980
Sommers, L. (ed.), *Atlas of Michigan.* East Lansing, 1977

State Library Services: Library of Michigan, Lansing 48909.

MINNESOTA

HISTORY. Minnesota, first explored in the 17th century and first settled in the 20 years following the establishment of Fort Snelling (1819), was made a Territory in 1849 (with parts of North and South Dakota), and was admitted into the Union, with its present boundaries, on 11 May 1858.

AREA AND POPULATION. Minnesota is bounded north by Canada, east by Lake Superior and Wisconsin, with the Mississippi River forming the boundary in the south-east, south by Iowa, west by South and North Dakota, with the Red River forming the boundary in the north-west. Area, 84,402 sq. miles, of which 4,854 sq. miles are inland water. Census population, 1 April 1990, 4,375,099, an increase of 7·31% since 1980. Births in 1988, 66,745 (15·5 per 1,000 population); deaths, 35,436 (8·2); infant deaths, 521 (7·8 per 1,000 live births); marriages, 33,654 (7·8); divorces (1987), 14,931 (3·5).

Population in 5 census years was:

	White	Black	Indian	Asiatic	Total	Per sq. mile
1910	2,059,227	7,084	9,053	344	2,075,708	25·7
1930	2,542,599	9,445	11,077	832	2,563,953	32·0
1960	3,371,603	22,263	15,496	3,642	3,413,864	42·7
			All others			
1970	3,736,038	34,868	34,163		3,805,069	47·6
1980	3,935,770	53,344	86,856		4,075,970	51·4

Of the 1980 population, 1,997,826 were male; 2,725,270 were urban; those 21 years of age or older numbered 2,656,947.

The largest cities (with 1990 census population) are Minneapolis (368,383) and St Paul (272,253).

CLIMATE. Duluth. Jan. 8°F (−13·3°C), July 63°F (17·2°C). Annual rainfall 29" (719 mm). Minneapolis-St. Paul. Jan. 12°F (−11·1°C), July 71°F (21·7°C). Annual rainfall 26" (656 mm). *See* Great Lakes, p. 1398.

CONSTITUTION AND GOVERNMENT. The present constitution dates from 1858; it has had 109 amendments. The Legislature consists of a Senate of 67 members, elected for 4 years, and a House of Representatives of 134 members, elected for 2 years. It meets for 120 days within each 2 years.

In the 1988 presidential election Dukakis polled 1,109,471 votes, Bush 962,337.

The capital is St Paul. There are 87 counties.

Governor: Arne Carlson (R.), 1991–95 ($109,053).
Lieut.-Governor: Joanell Dyrstad (ind. R.) ($59,981).
Secretary of State: Joan A. Growe (Democratic-Farmer-Labor) ($59,981).

BUDGET. The general fund budget for the 1989–91 2-year period was $13,686m.; tax relief $1,966m., education $7,121m., public welfare $1,940m., transport $207m.

Net long-term debt, 30 June 1989, was $1,416m.

Per capita personal income (1990) was $18,731.

NATURAL RESOURCES

Minerals. The iron ore and taconite industry is the most important in the USA. Production of usable iron ore in 1988 was 42m. tons, value $1,278m. Other important minerals are sand and gravel, crushed and dimension stone, lime and manganiferous ore. Total value of mineral production, 1988, $1,391m.

Agriculture. In 1989 there were 90,000 farms with a total area of 30m. acres (60% of the land area); the average farm was of 333 acres. Average value of land and buildings (1989) $192,245. Commercial farms in 1987 numbered 85,079; 12% of the farms were operated by tenant-farmers. Cash receipts, 1988, from crops, $2,743m.; from livestock, $3,364m. In 1988 Minnesota ranked second in sugar-beets, spring wheat, processing sweet corn, oats, dry milk, cheese, mink and turkeys. Other important products are wild rice, butter, eggs, flaxseed, milch cows, milk, corn, barley, swine, cattle for market, soybeans, honey, potatoes, rye, chickens, sunflower seed and dry edible beans. Of livestock, cattle represents 16% of total farm income, swine 12% and milk 20%. Of crops, corn represents 15% and soybeans 19%. On 1 Jan. 1989 the farm animals included 3·15m. all cattle, 855,000 milch cows, 237,000 sheep and lambs, 4·26m. swine and 12·8m. chickens. Turkey production, 1988, 38·5m. In 1988 the wool clip amounted to 1·89m. lb. of wool from 255,000 sheep.

Forestry. Forests of commercial timber cover 14m. acres, of which 53% is government-owned. The value of forest products in 1987 was $4,400m.: $1,300m. from primary processing, of which $901m. was from pulp and paper; and $3,100m. from secondary manufacturing. Logging, pulping, saw-mills and associated industries employed 53,700 in 1987.

INDUSTRY. In 1986 manufacturing establishments employed 369,000 workers; value added by manufacture was $19,800m. Largest manufacturing industry is computers and non-electric machinery (81,000 employees); then food products and kindred products (45,000), printing and publishing (43,000).

TOURISM. In 1987, travellers spent about $5,500m. The industry employed about 108,000.

COMMUNICATIONS

Roads. In 1990 there were 129,553 miles of roads (115,458 miles rural) and 3,283,292 registered motor vehicles.

Railways. There are 3 Class I and 16 Class II and smaller railroads operating, with total mileage of 5,044.

Civil Aviation. In 1989 there were 141 airports for public use and 12 public seaplane bases.

JUSTICE, RELIGION, EDUCATION AND WELFARE

Justice. The state's penal reformatory system on 1 Oct. 1989 held 3,005 adult men and women. There is no death penalty.

Religion. The chief religious bodies are: Lutheran with 1,088,304 members in 1980; Roman Catholic, 1,041,781; Methodist, 146,422. Total membership of all denominations, 2,653,161.

Education. In 1988, there were 61,442 kindergarten students, 340,967 elementary students, and 318,714 secondary students enrolled in 1,511 public schools. There were 82,165 kindergarten, elementary, and secondary students enrolled in 572 private schools. The University of Minnesota, chartered in 1851 and opened in 1869, had a total enrolment in 1988 of 54,515 students on all campuses. The 18 public community colleges (2-year) had a total enrolment of 49,589. There are seven state universities (4-year) at Bemidji, Mankato, Marshall, Moorhead, St Cloud, Winona, Minneapolis and St Paul. Enrolment in all institutions of higher education, 1988, 251,304.

Health. In 1989 the state had 163 general acute hospitals with 19,229 beds. Patients resident in institutions under the Department of Human Services in Aug. 1989 included 1,343 people with mental illness, 1,405 people with mental retardation, 265 with chemical dependency and 486 in state nursing homes.

Social Security. Programmes of old age assistance, aid to the disabled, and aid to the blind are administered under the federal Supplemental Security Income (SSI) Programme. Minnesota has a supplementary programme, Minnesota Supplemental Aid (MSA) to cover individuals not eligible for SSI, to supplement SSI benefits for others whose income is below state standards, and to provide one-time payments for emergency needs such as major home repair, essential furniture or appliances, moving expenses, fuel, food and shelter.

Further Reading

Statistical Information: Current information is obtainable from the State Planning Agency (300 Centennial Office Building, 658 Cedar Street, St Paul 55155); non-current material from the Reference Library, Minnesota Historical Society, St Paul 55101.

Legislative Manual. Secretary of State. St Paul. Biennial
Manufacturers' Directory. Nelson Name Service, Minneapolis, Biennial
Minnesota Agriculture Statistics. Dept. of Agric., St Paul. Annual

MISSISSIPPI

HISTORY. Mississippi, settled in 1716, was organized as a Territory in 1798 and admitted into the Union on 10 Dec. 1817. In 1804 and in 1812 its boundaries were extended, but in March 1817 a part was taken to form the new Territory of Alabama, leaving the boundaries substantially as at present.

AREA AND POPULATION. Mississippi is bounded north by Tennessee, east by Alabama, south by the Gulf of Mexico and Louisiana, west by the Mississippi River forming the boundary with Louisiana and Arkansas. Area, 47,689 sq. miles, 457 sq. miles being inland water. Census population, 1 April 1990, 2,573,216, an increase of 2·09% since 1980. Births, occurring in the state, 1990, were 43,160; deaths, 24,292; infant deaths, 501; marriages, 24,348; divorces, 12,735.

Population of 5 federal census years was:

	White	Black	Indian	Asiatic	Total	Per sq. mile
1910	786,111	1,009,487	1,253	263	1,797,114	38·8
1930	998,077	1,009,718	1,458	568	2,009,821	42·4
1950	1,188,632	986,494	2,502	1,286	2,178,914	46·1
			All others			
1970	1,393,283	815,770	7,859		2,216,912	46·9
1980	1,615,190	887,206	18,242		2,520,638	53·0

Of the population in 1980, 1,213,878 were male, 1,192,805 were urban and 1,601,157 were 20 years old or older.

The largest city (1980) is Jackson, 202,895. Others are: Biloxi, 49,311; Meridian, 46,577; Hattiesburg, 40,829; Greenville, 40,613; Gulfport, 39,676; Pascagoula, 29,318; Columbus, 27,383; Vicksburg, 25,434; Tupelo, 23,905.

CLIMATE. Jackson. Jan. 47°F (8·3°C), July 82°F (27·8°C). Annual rainfall 49" (1,221 mm). Vicksburg. Jan. 48°F (8·9°C), July 81°F (27·2°C). Annual rainfall 52" (1,311 mm). *See* Central Plains, p. 1398.

CONSTITUTION AND GOVERNMENT. The present constitution was adopted in 1890 without ratification by the electorate; 94 amendments by 1988.

The Legislature consists of a Senate (52 members) and a House of Representatives (122 members), both elected for 4 years. Electors are all citizens who have resided in the state 1 year, in the county 1 year, in the election district 6 months before the next election who have been registered according to law. In the 1988 presidential election Bush polled 551,745 votes, Dukakis, 360,892.

The capital is Jackson; there are 82 counties.

Governor: Ray Mabus (D.), 1988–92 ($75,600).
Lieut.-Governor: Bradford Johnson Dye (D.) ($40,800).
Secretary of State: Dick Molpus (D.) ($54,000).

BUDGET. For the fiscal year ending 30 June 1991 the general revenues were $4,889,285,248 (taxation, $2,436,411,766; federal aid, $1,538,339,172; other state resources, $914,534,310), and general expenditures were $4,824,431,998 ($1,508,974,653 for education and $449,320,055 for highways and $1,322,770,322 for public welfare).

On 30 June 1991 the total net long-term debt was $647,951,023.
Per capita personal income (1988) was $12,172 (lowest in US).

ENERGY AND NATURAL RESOURCES

Minerals. Petroleum and natural gas account for about 90% (by value) of mineral production. Output of petroleum, 1990, was 27,494,492 bbls and of natural gas 200,980,232m. cu. ft. There are 5 oil refineries. Value of oil and gas products sold in 1991 was $647,523,211.

Agriculture. Agriculture is the leading industry of the state because of the semi-tropical climate and a rich productive soil. In 1991 there were 82 soil conservation districts covering 30m. acres. In 1991 farms numbered 38,000 with an area of 12·8m. acres. Average size of farm was 337 acres. This compares with an average farm size of 138 acres in 1960.

Cash income from all crops and livestock during 1990, including government payments, was $2,672,364,000. Cash income from crops was $1,155,288,000 and from livestock and products, $1,321,676,000. The chief product is cotton, cash income (1990) $572,563,000 from 1m. acres producing 1,851,600 bales of 728 lb. Soybeans, rice, corn, hay, wheat, oats, sorghum, peanuts, pecans, sweet potatoes, peaches, other vegetables, nursery and forest products continue to contribute.

On 1 Jan. 1991 there were 1,290,000 head of cattle and calves on Mississippi farms. Milch cows totalled 63,000, beef cows, 707,000; hogs and pigs, 149,000. Of cash income from livestock and products, 1990, $297,726,000 was credited to cattle and calves. Cash income from poultry and eggs, 1990, totalled $642,570,000; dairy products, $112,549,000; swine, $35,981,000.

Forestry. In 1990 income from forestry amounted to $737m.; output of logs, lumber, etc., was 1,708,350 bd ft; pulpwood, 7,144,686 cords; distillate wood, 3,748 tons. There are about 17m. acres of forest (56% of the state's area). National forests area, 1987, 1,212,100 acres.

INDUSTRY. In 1990 the 3,598 manufacturing establishments employed 246,457 workers, earning $4,777,632,786. The average annual wage was $19,385.

TOURISM. Total receipts, 1990, $1,679·36bn from about 2·5m. tourists.

COMMUNICATIONS

Roads. The state in July 1991 maintained 10,372 miles of highways, of which 10,363 miles were paved; 1,856,331 cars were registered.

Railways. The state in 1991 had 3,391 miles of railway.

Civil Aviation. There were 80 public airports in 1991, 73 of them general. There were also 4 privately owned airports.

JUSTICE, RELIGION, EDUCATION AND WELFARE

Justice. In 1991 there were no executions; from 1955 to 1991 executions (by gas-chamber) totalled 35 (25 for murder, 9 for rape and 1 for armed robbery). As of 8 Oct. 1991, the state prisons had 8,635 inmates.

Religion. Southern Baptists in Mississippi (1990), 675,824 members; Negro Baptists (1990), about 477,000; United Methodists (1990) 189,525; Roman Catholics (1991), 102,471 in Biloxi and Jackson dioceses.

Education. Attendance at school is compulsory as laid down in the Education Reform Act of 1982. The public elementary and secondary schools in 1990–91 had 500,122 pupils and 27,778 classroom teachers.

In 1991, teachers' average salary was $24,365. The expenditure per pupil in average daily attendance, 1989–90, was $3,189.

There are 22 universities and senior colleges, of which 8 are state-supported. The University of Mississippi, at Oxford (1844), had, 1990–91, 414 instructors and 11,328 students; Mississippi State University, Starkville, 536 instructors and 14,430 students; Mississippi University for Women, Columbus, 92 instructors and 2,407 students; University of Southern Mississippi, Hattiesburg, 576 instructors and

13,492 students; Jackson State University, Jackson, 295 instructors and 6,838 students; Delta State University, Cleveland, 178 instructors and 4,034 students; Alcorn State University, Lorman, 128 instructors and 2,853 students; Mississippi Valley State University, Itta Bena, 99 instructors and 1,873 students. State support for the universities (1990) was $187,298,360.

Junior colleges had (1990–91) 66,150 students and 2,496 instructors. The state appropriation for junior colleges, 1990–91, was $70,438,150.

Health. In 1990 the state had 107 acute general hospitals (12,131 beds) listed by the State Department of Health; 8 hospitals with facilities for care of the mentally ill had 2,347 beds.

Social Security. The state Medicaid commission paid (1991) $725,079,871 for medical services, including $77,768,118 for drugs, $228,969,338 for nursing home facilities, $197,163,856 for hospital services. There were 64,159 persons eligible for Aged Medicaid benefits and 80,561 persons eligible for Disabled Medicaid benefits at 30 June 1991. In June 1991, 61,132 families with 129,165 dependent children received $7,454,570 in the Aid to Dependent Children programme. The average monthly payment was $122·98 per family or $58·15 per child.

Further Reading

1980 Census of Population and Housing: Mississippi.
Mississippi Official and Statistical Register. Secretary of State. Jackson. Biennial
Bettersworth, J. K., *Mississippi: A History.* Rev. ed. Austin, Tex., 1964

Mississippi Library Commission: PO Box 10700 Jackson, MS. 39289–0700. *Director:* David M. Woodburn.

MISSOURI

HISTORY. Missouri, first settled in 1735 at Ste Genevieve, was made a Territory on 1 Oct. 1812, and admitted to the Union on 10 Aug. 1821. In 1837 its boundaries were extended to their present limits.

AREA AND POPULATION. Missouri is bounded north by Iowa, east by the Mississippi River forming the boundary with Illinois and Kentucky, south by Arkansas, south-east by Tennessee, south-west by Oklahoma, west by Kansas and Nebraska, with the Missouri River forming the boundary in the north-west. Area, 69,697 sq. miles, 752 sq. miles being water.

Census population, 22 April 1990, 5,117,073, an increase since 1980 of 4·1%. Births, 1990, were 79,866 (15·5 per 1,000 population); deaths, 51,679 (10); infant deaths, 767 (9·9 per 1,000 live births); marriages, 50,331 (9·8); divorces, 25,140 (4·9).

Population of 5 federal census years was:

	White	Black	Indian	Asiatic	Total	Per sq. mile
1910	3,134,932	157,452	313	638	3,293,335	47·9
1930	3,403,876	223,840	578	1,073	3,629,367	52·4
1960	3,922,967	390,853	1,723	3,146	4,319,813	62·5

	White	Black	All others	Total	Per sq. mile
1970	4,177,495	480,172	19,732	4,677,399	67·0
1980	4,345,521	514,276	56,889	4,916,686	71·3

Of the total population in 1990, 2,464,315 were male. In 1980 3,350,746 persons were urban and those 18 years of age or older numbered 3,854,000.

The principal cities at the 1990 census are:

Kansas City	435,146	Columbia	69,101
St Louis	396,685	St Charles	54,555
Springfield	140,494	Florissant	51,206
Independence	112,301	Joplin	40,961
St Joseph	71,852	University City	40,087

Metropolitan areas, 1987: St Louis, 2,458,100; Kansas City, 1,546,400.

CLIMATE. Kansas City. Jan. 30°F (−1·1°C), July 79°F (26·1°C). Annual rainfall 38" (947 mm). St Louis. Jan. 32°F (0°C), July 79°F (26·1°C). Annual rainfall 40" (1,004 mm). *See* Central Plains, p. 1398.

CONSTITUTION AND GOVERNMENT. A new constitution, the fourth, was adopted on 27 Feb. 1945; it has been amended 27 times. The General Assembly consists of a Senate of 34 members elected for 4 years (half for re-election every 2 years), and a House of Representatives of 163 members elected for 2 years. The Governor and Lieut.-Governor are elected for 4 years.

In the 1988 presidential election Bush polled 1,081,163 votes, Dukakis, 1,004,040.

Jefferson City is the state capital. The state is divided into 114 counties and the city of St Louis.

Governor: John D. Ashcroft (R.), 1989–93 ($88,540).
Lieut.-Governor: Mel Carnahan (D.), 1989–93 ($50,418).
Secretary of State: Roy D. Blunt (R.), 1989–93 ($70,908).

BUDGET. For the year 1989 the total revenues from all funds were $8,703m. (federal revenue, $1,622m., general revenue, $7,433m.).

Total outstanding debt, 1989, was $4,893m.
Per capita personal income (1990) was $17,293.

NATURAL RESOURCES

Minerals. Principal minerals are fire clay and lead (ranks first in USA), lime (ranks second), barite, iron ore, crude iron, oxide pigments, and zinc. Value of production (1988) $967·9m.

Agriculture. In 1990 there were 108,000 farms in Missouri producing crops and livestock on 30·4m. acres. Production of principal crops, 1990: Corn, 205·8m. bu.; soybeans, 124·5m. bu.; wheat, 76m. bu.; sorghum grain, 42·64m. bu.; oats, 2·2m. bu.; rice, 3·8m. cwt; cotton, 314,000 bales (of 480 lb.). Cash receipts from farming, 1990, $3,939m. to which livestock sales contributed $2,271m. and soybeans $710m.

Forestry. Forest land area, 1990, 12·9m. acres.

INDUSTRY. The largest employer in 1989 was manufacturing, in which the transport equipment industry employed 73,561 workers. Other large industries are food and kindred products, electrical equipment and supplies, apparel and related products and non-electrical machinery, leather products, chemicals, paper, metal industries, stone, clay, glass, rubber and plastic products. Wholesale and retail trade employed 545,775 as of March 1990.

LABOUR. The State Board of Mediation has jurisdiction in labour disputes involving only public utilities. The Prevailing Wage Law (1959) provides that no less than the local hourly rate of wages for work of a similar character shall be paid to any workmen engaged in public works. The Industrial Commission has authority to inspect records and to institute actions for penalties described in the Act. There is a state programme for industrial safety in hand, under the Federal Occupational and Health Act. In June 1991 (preliminary) the annual average number of employed was 2,710,500, and 191,000 were unemployed; the unemployment rate was 6·1%.

COMMUNICATIONS

Roads. At 31 Dec. 1990 there were 120,820 miles of roads (105,369 miles rural) and 5,560,478 registered motor vehicles.

Railways. The state has 9 Class I railways; approximate total mileage, 6,645. There are 10 other railways (switching, terminal or short-line), total mileage 435, in 1990.

Civil Aviation. In 1991 there were 144 public airports and 294 private airports.

Shipping. Ten major barge lines (1990) operated on about 1,000 miles of navigable waterways including the Missouri and Mississippi Rivers. Boat shipping seasons: Missouri River, April–end Nov.; Mississippi River, all seasons.

Post and Broadcasting. There were 284 commercial radio stations and 32 TV stations in 1991.

Newspapers. There were (1991) 52 daily and 279 weekly newspapers.

JUSTICE, RELIGION, EDUCATION AND WELFARE

Justice. State prisons in May 1991 had an average of 15,198 inmates including 513 females. The median age was 26 in 1990. The death penalty was reinstated in 1978. The first execution since 1965 was on 1 Jan. 1989 (by lethal injection). Since 1930 executions (by lethal gas) have totalled 42, including 32 for murder, 7 for rape and 3 for kidnapping. The Missouri Law Enforcement Assistance Council was created in 1969 for law reform. With reorganization of state government in 1974 the duties of the Council were delegated to the Department of Public Safety.

Religion. Chief religious bodies (1980) are Catholic, with 800,228 members, Southern Baptists (700,053), United Methodists (270,469), Christian Churches (175,101), Lutheran (157,928), Presbyterian (38,254). Total membership, all denominations, about 2·6m. in 1980.

Education. School attendance is compulsory for children from 7 to 16 years for the full term. In the 1989–90 school year, public schools (kindergarten through grade 12) had 807,934 pupils. Total expenditure for public schools in 1989–90, $3,014,529,098. Salaries for teachers (kindergarten through grade 12), 1989–90, averaged $27,094. Institutions for higher education include the University of Missouri, founded in 1839 with campuses at Columbia, Rolla, St Louis and Kansas City, with (1989–90) 3,614 accredited teachers and 54,098 students in 1990–91. Washington University at St Louis, founded in 1857, is an independent co-ed university with 11,612 students in 1990–91. St Louis University (1818), is an independent Roman Catholic co-ed university with 11,555 students in 1990–91. Fourteen state colleges had 121,544 students in 1990–91. Private colleges had (1990–91) 42,312 students. Church-affiliated colleges (1990–91) had 37,083 students. Public junior colleges had 66,590 students. There are about 90 secondary and post-secondary institutions offering vocational courses, and about 294 private career schools. There were 269,644 students in higher education in autumn 1990.

Health. There were 10 state mental health hospitals and centres and 3 children's hospitals in 1991, admitting 20,266 patients.

Social Security. In 1989 the number of recipients of medicaid was 406,088. The number of recipients of Aid to families with Dependent Children was 206,653 with an average monthly payment per family of $263·23.

Further Reading

Missouri Area Labor Trends, Department of Labour and Industrial Relations, monthly
Missouri Farm Facts, Department of Agriculture, annual
Report of the Public Schools of Missouri. State Board of Education, annual
Statistical Abstract for Missouri. College of Business and Public Administration, Columbia, 1985

MONTANA

HISTORY. Montana, first settled in 1809, was made a Territory (out of portions of Idaho and Dakota Territories) in 1864 and was admitted into the Union on 8 Nov. 1889.

AREA AND POPULATION. Montana is bounded north by Canada, east by North and South Dakota, south by Wyoming and west by Idaho and the Bitterroot Range of the Rocky Mountains. Area, 147,138 sq. miles, including 1,551 sq. miles of water, of which the federal government, 1986, owned 28,236,000 acres or 30·3%. US Bureau of Indian Affairs (1990) administered 5,574,835 acres, of which 2,663,385 were allotted to tribes. Census population, 1 April 1990, 799,065, an increase of 2% since 1980. Births, 1989, were 11,667; deaths (1986), 6,738 (8·2); infant deaths (1986), 122 (9·8 per 1,000 live births); marriages (1989), 6,765 (8·4); divorces (1989), 4,104 (5·1).

Population in 5 census years was:

	White	Black	Indian	Asiatic	Total	Per sq. mile
1910	360,580	1,834	10,745	2,870	376,053	2·6
1930	519,898	1,256	14,798	1,239	537,606	3·7
1950	572,038	1,232	16,606	—	591,024	4·1
1980	740,148	1,786	37,270	2,503	786,690	5·3
1990	741,111	2,381	47,679	4,259	799,065	5·4

Of the total population in 1990, 395,769 were male, 419,826 persons were urban. Persons 18 years of age or older numbered 576,961. Median age, 33·8 years. Households, 306,163.

The largest cities, 1990 are Billings, 81,151; Great Falls, 55,097. Others: Missoula, 42,918; Butte-Silver Bow, 33,336; Helena (capital), 24,569; Bozeman, 22,660; Kalispell, 11,917; Anaconda-Deer Lodge County, 10,278; Havre, 10,201.

CLIMATE. Helena. Jan. 18°F (−7·8°C), July 69°F (20·6°C). Annual rainfall 13" (325 mm). *See* Mountain States, p. 1397–98.

CONSTITUTION AND GOVERNMENT. A new constitution came into force on 1 July 1973. The Senate consists of 50 senators, elected for 4 years, one half at each biennial election. The 100 members of the House of Representatives are elected for 2 years.

In the 1988 presidential election Bush polled 189,598 votes, Dukakis, 168,120.

The capital is Helena. The state is divided into 56 counties.

Governor: Stan Stephens (R.), 1989–93 ($53,006).
Lieut.-Governor: Dennis Rehberg (R.), 1990–93 ($37,970).
Secretary of State: Mike Cooney (D.), 1989–93 ($35,030).

BUDGET. Total state revenues for the year ending 30 June 1990 were $2,225,000,000; total expenditures were $2,007,000,000.

Total net long-term debt on 30 June 1990 was $396,000,000.

Per capita personal income (1990) was $15,110.

ENERGY AND NATURAL RESOURCES

Electricity. Electric power generated in 1987 was 20,884m. kwh, of which 8,925m. kwh was hydro-electric and 11,836m. kwh from coal-fired plants; 17m. kwh from oil-fired, and 49m. kwh from wood and waste.

Minerals. 1989 nonfuel mineral production value was $599·2m. Copper was the leading commodity in terms of value, followed by gold, platinum-group metals, molybdenum and silver.

Agriculture. In 1989 there were 24,700 farms and ranches (50,564 in 1935) with an area of 60,203,993 acres (47,511,868 acres in 1935 and 60·3m. in 1991). Large-scale farming predominates; in 1989 the average size per farm was 2,453 acres (2,431 acres in 1991). The farm population in 1991, was 67,546 (2·8% people per farm). Irrigated area harvested in 1986 was 1·6m. acres; non-irrigated, 7·8m. acres.

The chief crops (cash receipts, 1990) are wheat, amounting in 1986 to 138·5m. bu. ($435,788); barley, 85m. bu. ($125,436); oats, 4·1m. bu.; sugar-beet, hay ($81,996), potatoes, corn, dry beans and cherries. In 1986 there were 24,000 milch cows, 2·4m.

all cattle; 190,000 swine and 423,000 sheep. In 1990 the cash receipts for cattle and calves were $725,476; dairy products, $45,292; hogs and pigs, $42,150; sheep and lambs, $18,655.

Forestry. Total forest area (1986), 22·6m. acres. In 1986 there were 16·8m. acres within 11 national forests.

INDUSTRY. In 1987 manufacturing establishments numbering 1,223 had 20,900 production workers; value added by manufacture was (1986) $907·4m.

LABOUR (March 1991). Work force, 401,400; total employed, 369,600; total non-agricultural workers, 291,800. Workers employed by major industry group: Mining, 5,900 (average net weekly earnings, $592.18); construction, 7,700 ($499.56); manufacturing, 20,200 ($442.37); transport and public utilities, 20,000 ($468.43; trade industry, 76,500 ($388.90); finance/insurance/real estate, 13,270; services, 75,500 ($258.34); government, 71,400 (no income figures available). Average weekly earnings for all workers in private non-agricultural industries $295.45. During 1990, 56 mass layoff events involved 5,001 workers laid off from their jobs (separations), 50% more separations than in 1989.

COMMUNICATIONS

Roads. In March 1992 there were a total of 70,806 miles of roads and in 1990, 741,197 registered motor vehicles.

Railways. In Feb. 1992 there were 3,329 route miles of railway in the state.

Civil Aviation. In 1992 there were 122 publicly owned airports.

Telecommunications. In 1992 there were 51 radio stations, 18 TV stations and 10 cable systems.

Newspapers. In 1992 there were 12 daily newspapers and 74 semi-weekly, weekly, or shopper-type papers.

JUSTICE, RELIGION, EDUCATION AND WELFARE

Justice. At 31 Dec. 1991 the Montana State Prison at Deer Lodge held 1,188 inmates and the Women's Correctional Facility at Warm Springs, 62. Since 1943 there have been no executions; total since 1930 (all by hanging) was 6; 4 whites and 2 Negroes, for murder.

Religion. The leading religious bodies are (1987): Roman Catholic with 162,000 members; Lutheran, 68,654; Methodist (Yellowstone Conference, including N. Wyoming, Montana, and Salmon, Idaho), 21,609 (church estimates).

Education. In 1990–91 public elementary and secondary schools had 152,721 pupils. Public elementary and secondary school teachers (9,659 in 1987) had an average salary of $23,774. Expenditure on public school education (1986–87) was $475·9m. This included $26·33m. for Special Education.

The Montana University system consists of the Montana State University, at Bozeman (autumn 1992 enrolment: 10,111 students), the University of Montana, at Missoula, founded in 1895 (10,788), the Montana College of Mineral Science and Technology, at Butte (1,881), Northern Montana College, at Havre (1,973), Eastern Montana College, at Billings (3,631) and Western Montana College, at Dillon (1,106).

Social Security. In June 1991, 5,241 persons over age 65 were receiving in medical assistance an average of $980 per year per person; 52 blind persons, $700, 7,000 totally disabled, $833; 9,937 families received in aid-to-dependent children assistance an average of $342. Aid was from state and federal sources.

Health. In Sept. 1990 the state had 60 hospitals (3,359 beds) and 102 licensed long-term care facilities (7,487 beds).

Further Reading

Montana Agricultural Statistics. U.S. Dept. of Agriculture, Montana Crop and Livestock Reporting Service. Biennial from 1946

Montana Employment and Labor Force. Montana Dept. of Labor and Industry. Monthly from 1971

Montana Federal-Aid Road Log. Montana Dept. of Highways and US Dept. of Transportation, Federal Highway Administration. Annual from 1938

Montana Vital Statistics. Montana Dept. of Health and Environmental Sciences. Annually from 1954

Statistical Report. Montana Dept. of Social and Rehabilitation Services. Monthly from 1947

Lang, W, L. and Myers, R. C., *Montana, Our Land and People*. Pruett, 1979

Malone, M. P. and Roeder, R. B., *Montana, A History of Two Centuries*. Univ. of Washington Press, 1976

Spence, C. C., *Montana: a History*. New York, 1978

NEBRASKA

HISTORY. The Nebraska region was first reached by white men from Mexico under the Spanish general Coronado in 1541. It was ceded by France to Spain in 1763, retroceded to France in 1801, and sold by Napoleon to the US as part of the Louisiana Purchase in 1803. Its first settlement was in 1847, and on 30 May 1854 it became a Territory and on 1 March 1867 a state. In 1882 it annexed a small part of Dakota Territory, and in 1908 it received another small tract from South Dakota.

AREA AND POPULATION. Nebraska is bounded north by South Dakota, with the Missouri River forming the boundary in the north-east and the boundary with Iowa and Missouri to the east; south by Kansas, south-west by Colorado and west by Wyoming. Area, 77,355 sq. miles, of which 711 sq. miles are water. Census population, 1990: 1,578,385, an increase of 0·53% since 1980. Births, 1987, were 23,813 (14·9 per 1,000 population); deaths, 14,820 (9·3); infant deaths, 204 (8·6 per 1,000 live births); marriages, 11,808 (7·4): divorces, 6,189 (3·9).

Population in 5 census years was:

	White	Black	Indian	Asiatic	Total	Per sq. mile
1910	1,180,293	7,689	3,502	730	1,192,214	15·5
1920	1,279,219	13,242	2,888	1,023	1,296,372	16·9
1960	1,374,764	29,262	5,545	1,195	1,411,330	18·3
			All others			
1970	1,432,867	39,911	10,715		1,483,791	19·4
1980	1,490,381	48,390	31,054		1,569,825	20·5

Of the total population in 1980, 48·8% were male,62·9% were urban 65·6% were 21 years of age or older. The largest cities in the state are: Omaha, with a census population, 1990, of 335,795; Lincoln, 191,972; Grand Island, (1986 estimate) 39,100; North Platte, 22,490; Fremont, 23,780; Hastings, 22,990; Bellevue, 32,200; Kearney, 22,770; Norfolk, 20,260.

The Bureau of Indian Affairs in 1990 administered 64,932 acres, of which 21,742 acres were allotted to tribal control.

CLIMATE. Omaha. Jan. 22°F (−5·6°C), July 77°F (25°C). Annual rainfall 29" (721 mm). *See* High Plains, p. 1398.

CONSTITUTION AND GOVERNMENT. The present constitution was adopted in 1875; it has been amended 184 times. By an amendment of 1934 Nebraska has a single-chambered legislature (elected for 4 years) of 49 members elected on a non-party ballot and classed as senators—the only state in the USA to have one. It meets annually.

In the 1988 presidential election Bush polled 389,394 votes, Dukakis, 254,426.

The capital is Lincoln. The state has 93 counties.

Governor: Ben Nelson (R.), 1991–95 ($65,000).

Lieut.-Governor: Maxine Moul (D.) ($47,000).
Secretary of State: Allen J. Beermann (R.) ($52,000).

BUDGET. For the fiscal year ending 1990 the state's revenues were $2,855·5m. (taxation, $1,512·9m. and federal aid, $681·4m.); general expenditures were $2,815m. ($906·9m. for education, $409·5m. for highways and $498·5m. for public welfare).

The state has a bonded indebtedness limit of $100,000.
Per capita personal income (1990) was $17,221.

ENERGY AND NATURAL RESOURCES

Minerals. The total output of non-fuel minerals, 1990, was valued at $106·4m., sand and gravel being the most important. 6·1m. bbls of petroleum were produced in 1987.

Agriculture. Nebraska is one of the most important agricultural states. In 1986 it contained approximately 55,000 farms, with a total area of 47·1m. acres. The average farm was 856 acres. In 1986, 7·9m. acres were irrigated and 71,587 irrigation wells were registered.

Cash income from crops (1987), $1,975m., and from livestock, $4,848m. Principal crops, with estimated 1987 yield: Maize, 812·2m. bu. (ranking third in US); wheat, 85·8m. bu.; sorghums for grain, 109·2m. bu.; oats, 17·3m. bu.; soybeans, 81·9m. bu. About 750 farms grow sugar-beet for 3 factories; output, 1987, 1·1m. short tons. Livestock, 1990: Cattle, 6m.; pigs, 4·2m.; sheep, 0·16m.; chickens, 2·1m.; turkeys, 2·1m.

Forestry. There were 722,000 acres of forest in 1990.

INDUSTRY. In 1986 there were 1,800 manufacturing establishments; 62,600 production workers earned $1,141·2m. and value added by manufacturing was $5,362·6m. The chief industry is meat-packing.

COMMUNICATIONS

Roads. In 1990 there were 92,459 miles of roads (87,509 miles rural) and 1,361,724 registered motor vehicles.

Railways. In 1988 there were 4,013 miles of railway.

Civil Aviation. Airports (1988) numbered 354, of which 101 were publicly owned.

JUSTICE, RELIGION, EDUCATION AND WELFARE

Justice. A 'Civil Rights Act' revised in 1969 provides that all people are entitled to a full and equal enjoyment of public facilities.

The state's prisons had, 10 Oct. 1988, 2,132 inmates (134 per 100,000 population). From 1930 to 1962 there were 4 executions (electrocution), 3 white men and 1 American Indian, all for murder, and none since.

Religion. The Roman Catholics had 337,855 members in 1985; Protestant Churches, 737,361; Jews, 7,865 members. Total, all denominations, 1,083,081.

Education. School attendance is compulsory for children from 7 to 16 years of age. Public elementary schools, autumn 1986, had 147,149 enrolled pupils. Teachers' salaries, 1987–88, averaged $23,246. Estimated public school expenditure for year ending 30 Aug. 1987 was $936m. Total enrolment in 27 institutions of higher education, autumn 1987, was 100,454 students. The largest institutions were (1987):

Opened	Institution	Students
1867	Peru State College, Peru (State)	1,396
1869	Univ. of Nebraska, Lincoln (State)	25,722
1872	Doane College, Crete (UCC)	796
1878	Creighton Univ., Omaha (RC)	5,827
1882	Hastings College (Presbyterian)	894

Opened	Institution	Students
1883	Midland Lutheran College, Fremont (Lutheran)	836
1887	Nebraska Wesleyan Univ. (Methodist)	1,359
1891	Union College, Lincoln (Seventh Day Adventist)	578
1894	Concordia Teachers' College, Seward (Lutheran)	816
1905	Kearney State College, Kearney (State)	9,075
1908	Univ. of Nebraska, Omaha (State)	14,210
1910	Wayne State College, Wayne (State)	2,899
1911	Chadron State College, Chadron (State)	2,250
1923	College of St. Mary	1,256
1966	Bellevue College, Bellevue (Private)	1,922

The state holds 1·52m. acres of land as a permanent endowment of her schools; permanent public school endowment fund in Aug. 1988 was $94·9m.

Health. In 1988 the state had 114 hospitals and 565 patients in mental hospitals.

Social Security. The administration of public welfare is the responsibility of the County Divisions of Welfare with policy-forming, regulatory, advisory and super-visory functions performed by the State Department of Public Welfare. In 1987 public welfare provided financial aid and/or services as follows: for 7,680 indivi-duals who were aged, blind or disabled, with an average state supplement of $58.65; for 16,315 families with dependent children, with an average payment of $318.31 per family; for 88,390 individuals who had medical needs, $1,937.02, per indivi-dual; for 3,280 children in need of child welfare services; $1·8m. was spent on medically-handicapped children. The amount of aid is based on need in accordance with State assistance standards; the programme of aid to families with dependent children is limited to a maximum maintenance payment of $300 for 1 child plus $75 for each additional child.

Further Reading

Agricultural Atlas of Nebraska. Univ. of Nebraska Press, 1977
Climatic Atlas of Nebraska. Univ. of Nebraska Press, 1977
Economic Atlas of Nebraska. Univ. of Nebraska Press, 1977
Nebraska. A Guide to the Cornhusker State. Univ. of Nebraska Press, 1979
Nebraska Statistical Handbook. Nebraska Dept. of Econ. Development. Biennial
Nebraska Blue-Book. Legislative Council. Lincoln. Biennial
Olson, J. C., *History of Nebraska.* Univ. of Nebraska Press, 1955

State Library: State Law Library, State House, Lincoln.

NEVADA

HISTORY. Nevada, first settled in 1851, when it was a part of the Territory of Utah (created 1850), was made a Territory in 1861, enlarged in 1862 by an addition from Utah Territory and admitted into the Union on 31 Oct. 1864 as the 36th state. In 1866 and 1867 the area of the state was significantly enlarged at the expense of the Territories of Utah and Arizona.

AREA AND POPULATION. Nevada is bounded north by Oregon and Idaho, east by Utah, south-east by Arizona, with the Colorado River forming most of the boundary, south and west by California. Area 110,561 sq. miles, 761 sq. miles being water. The federal government in 1989 owned 57,803,208 acres, or 82·2% of the land area. Vacant public lands, 47,745,574 acres. The Bureau of Indian Affairs controlled 1·15m. acres.

Census population on 1 April 1990, 1,201,833, an increase of 401,325 since 1980. Births, 1990, were 21,862 (18·2 per 1,000 population); deaths, 10,348 (8·6); mar-riages, 120,619 (100·4); divorces, 13,095 (10·9); infant deaths, 198 (9·1 per 1,000 live births).

Population in 5 census years was:

	White	Black	Indian	All others	Total	Per sq. mile
1910	74,276	513	5,240	1,846	81,875	0·7
1930	84,515	516	4,871	1,156	91,058	0·8
1970	449,850	27,579	7,329	3,980	488,738	4·4
1980	700,360	50,999	13,308	35,841	800,508	7·2
1990	1,012,695	78,771	19,637	90,730	1,201,833	10·9

Of the total population in 1990, 611,800 were male, 911,195 were urban and 857,022 were 21 years of age or older.

The largest cities are Las Vegas, with population at the 1990 census of 258,295; Reno, 133,850; Henderson, 64,942; Sparks, 53,367; North Las Vegas, 47,707; Carson City, 40,443. Clark County (Las Vegas, North Las Vegas and Henderson) and Washoe County (Reno and Sparks) together had 83% of the total state population in 1990.

CLIMATE. Las Vegas. Jan. 44°F (6·7°C), July 85°F (29·4°C). Annual rainfall 4" (112 mm). Reno. Jan. 32°F (0°C), July 69°F (20·6°C). Annual rainfall 7" (178 mm). *See* Mountain States, p. 1397–98.

CONSTITUTION AND GOVERNMENT. The constitution adopted in 1864 is still in force, with 112 amendments by 1990. The Legislature meets biennially (and in special sessions) and consists of a Senate of 21 members elected for 4 years, half their number retiring every 2 years, and an Assembly of 42 members elected for 2 years. The Governor may be elected for 2 consecutive terms.

In the 1988 presidential election Bush polled 306,040 votes, Dukakis, 132,738.

The state capital is Carson City. There are 16 counties, 18 incorporated cities and 44 unincorporated communities and 1 city-county (the Capitol District of Carson City).

Governor: Bob Miller (D.), 1991–94 ($83,750).
Lieut.-Governor: Sue Wagner, 1991-94 ($20,000).
Secretary of State: Cheryl Lau, 1991-94 ($62,500).

BUDGET. For the fiscal year ending June 1991, state general fund revenues were $863·2m.; budget expenditures were $924·2m. from the general fund. Education (54·7% of the total), followed by human resources (29%), received the largest appropriations.

State bonded indebtedness on 30 June 1991, was $226·9m. The state has no franchise tax, capital stock tax, special intangibles tax, stock transfer tax, admissions tax, gift tax, or income tax. Taxes on gambling and the state's 2% share of the sales tax support nearly 80% of the general fund.

Per capita personal income (1990) was $19,035.

ENERGY AND NATURAL RESOURCES

Electricity. In Dec. 1989 electricity power stations served 453,554 residential customers, 67,896 commercial, and 704 industrial customers.

Minerals. Production, 1990 was $2,610·88m. In order of value: Gold ($2,196·19m.), silver ($107·65m.), sand and gravel ($59·02m.), barite ($5·88m.). Petroleum produced, 4m. bbls. Other minerals are iron ore, mercury, lime, lithium, gemstones, lead, molybdenum, fluorspar, perlite, pumice, clays, talc, salt, tungsten, magnesite, diatomite and zinc.

Agriculture. In 1991, an estimated 2,500 farms had a farm area of 8·9m. acres under cultivation (9·2m. in 1960). Farms averaged 3,560 acres. Area under irrigation (1989) was 569,800 acres compared with 542,976 acres in 1959.

Gross income, 1990, from crops, livestock and government payments, $343·2m. Cattle, hay, dairy products, potatoes and sheep are the principal commodities in order of cash receipts. Total value of crops produced, $115·1m. In Jan. 1991 there were 20,000 milch cows, 0·52m. beef cattle, 98,500 sheep and lambs.

Forestry. The area of national forests (1990) under US Forest Service administration was 5,796,519 acres. National forests: Toiyabe (3,243,260 acres); Humboldt (2,468,812).

INDUSTRY. The main industry is the service industry (43·1% of employment), especially tourism and legalized gambling; others include mining and smelting, livestock and irrigated agriculture and construction. In 1989 there were 988 manufacturing establishments with 26,243 employees, and 2,664 construction firms with 38,133 employees.

Gaming industry gross revenue for 1990, $5,237,800,000 from 339 non restricted licensed casinos. There are 2,440 licences in force.

LABOUR. The annual average unemployment for 1990 was 4·9% of the work force. All industries employed 624,200 workers. Main industries and employees, 1990: Service industries, 272,400; retail trade, 101,300; government, 76,200; insurance and real estate, 28,300; transport, 18,900; public works and utilities, 13,500; mining, 14,500; manufacturing, 26,400.

COMMUNICATIONS

Roads. Highway mileage (federal, state and local) totalled 52,548 in 1990, of which 9,898 miles were paved; motor vehicle registrations in 1990 numbered 935,886.

Railways. In 1991 there were 1,275 miles of main-line railway. Nevada is served by Southern Pacific, Union Pacific and Western Pacific railways, and Amtrak passenger service for Las Vegas, Elko, Reno and Sparks.

Aviation. There were 77 civil airports and heliports in 1989. During 1990 McCarran International Airport (Las Vegas) handled 19·2m. passengers and Reno-Cannon International Airport handled 3m. passengers.

Post. In June 1991 there were 111 telephone exchanges, and 768,480 telephones in service.

JUSTICE, RELIGION, EDUCATION AND WELFARE

Justice. Prohibition of marriage between persons of different race was repealed by statute in 1959. It is illegal for persons operating public accommodation or selling houses, employers of 15 or more employees, labour unions, and employment agencies to discriminate on the basis of race, colour, religion or national origin. A Commission on Equal Rights of Citizens is charged with enforcing these laws.

Between 1924 and 1961 executions (by lethal gas—the first state to adopt this method, in 1921), numbered 31. Capital punishment was abolished in 1972 and reintroduced in 1978; there have since been 5 executions, 2 by lethal gas (in 1979 and 1985) and 3 by lethal injection (2 in 1989 and 1 in 1990).

Religion. Roman Catholics are the most numerous religious group, followed by members of the Church of Jesus Christ of Latter-day Saints (Mormons) and various Protestant churches.

Education. School attendance is compulsory for children from 7 to 17 years of age. As of Oct. 1990 the 238 public elementary schools had 119,520 pupils; there were 100 secondary public schools with 80,981 pupils, 7 special public schools and 815 ungraded pupils. There were 5,543 elementary teachers (average salary $31,186), 3,414 secondary teachers ($33,992), 1,197 special education teachers ($31,405), 230 occupational teachers ($34,595). There were 81 private schools (9,425 pupils). The University of Nevada, Reno, had, in 1991–92, 645 full-time instructors and 11,714 students (regular, non-degree and correspondent), and University of Nevada, Las Vegas, 672 instructors and 19,504 students. Two-year community colleges operate as part of the University of Nevada system in Reno, Carson City, Elko, Fallon and Las Vegas. There were (1991–92) 330 full-time instructors and 31,995 students.

Health. At 30 June 1991 the state had 30 hospitals (4,096 beds) and 33 nursing units (3,545 beds).

Social Security. In 1990 benefits were paid to 168,229 persons: 114,620 retired (aged 62 and over) workers (average payment $605 per month); 17,043 widows and widowers ($566); 13,219 disabled workers ($615), 11,374 wives and husbands ($304), 11,973 children ($339). Social Security beneficiaries represented 14% of the population.

Further Reading

Information: Bureau of Business and Economic Research (Univ. of Nevada-Reno).

Bushnell, E. and Driggs, D. W., *The Nevada Constitution: Origin and Growth.* 5th ed. Univ. of Nevada Press, 1980
Hulse, J. W., *The Nevada Adventure: A History.* 2nd ed. Univ. of Nevada Press, 1969
Laxalt, R., *Nevada: A History.* New York, 1977
Mack, E. M. and Sawyer, B. W., *Here is Nevada: A History of the State.* Sparks, 1965
Paher, S. W., *Nevada: an Annotated Bibliography.* Carson City, 1980

State Library: Nevada State Library, Carson City. *State Librarian:* Joan G. Kerschner.

NEW HAMPSHIRE

HISTORY. New Hampshire, first settled in 1623, is one of the 13 original states of the Union.

AREA AND POPULATION. New Hampshire is bounded in the north by Canada, east by Maine and the Atlantic, south by Massachusetts and west by Vermont. Area, 9,279 sq. miles, of which 286 sq. miles are inland water. Census population, 1 April 1990, 1,109,252, an increase of 20·49% since 1980. Births, 1988, were 17,363 (16 per 1,000 population); deaths, 8,770 (8·1); infant deaths, 147 (8·5 per 1,000 live births); marriages, 11,116 (10·2); divorces, 4,899 (4·5).

Population at 5 federal censuses was:

	White	Black	Indian	Asiatic	Total	Per sq. mile
1910	429,906	564	34	68	430,572	47·7
1930	464,351	790	64	88	465,293	51·6
1960	604,334	1,903	135	549	606,921	65·2
			All others			
1970	733,106	2,505	2,070		737,681	81·7
1980	910,099	3,990	6,521		920,610	101·9

The largest city in the state is Manchester, with a 1989 population of 101,960. The capital is Concord, with 37,342. Other cities are: Nashua, 81,536; Dover, 26,476; Rochester, 25,735; Portsmouth, 25,063; Keene, 22,724; Laconia, 16,926; Claremont, 14,111; Lebanon, 12,523; Berlin, 11,962; Somersworth, 10,916; Franklin, 8,383.

CLIMATE. Manchester. Jan. 22°F (−5·6°C), July 70°F (21·1°C). Annual rainfall 40" (1,003 mm). *See* New England, p. 1398.

CONSTITUTION AND GOVERNMENT. While the present constitution dates from 1784, it was extensively revised in 1792 when the state joined the Union. Since 1775 there have been 16 state conventions with 49 amendments adopted to amend the constitution.

The Legislature (called the General Court) consists of a Senate of 24 members, elected for 2 years, and a House of Representatives, of 400 members, elected for 2 years. It meets annually. The Governor and 5 administrative officers called 'Councillors' are also elected for 2 years.

In the 1988 presidential election Bush polled 280,533 votes, Dukakis, 163,205.

The capital is Concord. The state is divided into 10 counties.

Governor: Judd Gregg (R.), 1991–93 ($72,146).
Secretary of State: William M. Gardner (D.) ($57,533).

BUDGET. The state government's general revenue for the fiscal year ending 1990 was $1,563·3m. ($595·3m. from taxes, $430·1m. from federal aid); general expenditures, $1,676·3m. ($401·4m. on education, $328·2m. on public welfare, $206·8m. on highways).
Per capita personal income (1990) was $20,789.

NATURAL RESOURCES

Minerals. Minerals are little worked; they consist mainly of sand and gravel, stone, and clay for building and highway construction. Value of non-fuel mineral production, 1990, $37·4m.

Agriculture. In 1988, there were 2,515 farms occupying 426,237 acres; average farm was 169 acres. Average value per acre, $2,112. The US Soil Survey estimates that the state has 164,167 acres of excellent soil, 486,615 acres of fair soil, 530,630 of poor soil and 3,843,798 of non-arable soil. Only 636,195 acres (11% of the total area) show moderate erosion.

Cash income, 1987, from crops, $38m., and livestock and products, $72m. The chief field crops are hay and vegetables; the chief fruit crop is apples. Livestock, 1990: Cattle, 55,000; pigs, 9,000; sheep, 9,000; poultry, 365,000.

Forestry. In 1990 forest land totalled 5,021,000 acres; national forest, 735,000 acres.

Fisheries. The 1990 catch was worth $10m.

INDUSTRY. Principal manufactures: Machinery, metal products, electrical and electronic goods, plastics, textiles and shoes.

Labour. In 1988 657,653 persons were in employment (excluding agriculture), of whom 169,148 worked in services, 127,895 in trade and 124,928 in manufacturing.

COMMUNICATIONS

Roads. In 1990 there were 14,803 miles of roads (12,387 miles rural) and 953,642 registered motor vehicles.

Railways. In 1988 the length of railway in the state was 608 miles.

Civil Aviation. In 1988 there were 15 public and 19 private airports.

JUSTICE, RELIGION, EDUCATION AND WELFARE

Justice. The state prison held 940 persons on 1 June 1988. Since 1930 there has been only one execution (by hanging)—a white man, for murder, in 1939.

Religion. The Roman Catholic Church is the largest single body. The largest Protestant churches are Congregational, Episcopal, Methodist and United Baptist Convention of N.H.

Education. School attendance is compulsory for children from 6 to 14 years of age during the whole school term, or to 16 if their district provides a high school. Employed illiterate minors between 16 and 21 years of age must attend evening or special classes, if provided by the district.

In 1990 the public elementary and secondary schools had 171,696 pupils and 10,572 teachers. Public school salaries, 1990, averaged $28,986. Total expenditure on public schools in 1989–90 was estimated at $934m.

Of the 4-year colleges, the University of New Hampshire (founded in 1866) had 12,196 students in 1989–90; New Hampshire College (1932), 6,472; Keene State College (1909), 4,290; Rivier College (1933), 2,603; Dartmouth College (1769), 4,601. Total enrolment, 1989-90, in the 29 institutions of higher education, was 64,045.

Health. In 1987 the state had 37 hospitals.

Social Security. The Division of Human Services handles public assistance for (1) aged citizens 65 years or over, (2) needy aged aliens, (3) needy blind persons, (4) needy citizens between 18 and 64 years inclusive, who are permanently and totally disabled, (5) needy children under 18 years, (6) Medicaid and the medically needy not eligible for a monthly grant.

In May 1988, 1,298 persons were receiving old-age assistance of an average $87 per month; 2,761 permanently and totally disabled, $133 per month; 4,003 families with dependent children, $439 per month.

Further Reading

Delorme, D. (ed.) *New Hampshire Atlas and Gazetteer*. Freeport, 1983
Morison, E. E. and E. F., *New Hampshire*. New York, 1976
Squires, J. D., *The Granite State of the United States: A History of New Hampshire from 1623 to the present*. 4 vols. New York, 1956

NEW JERSEY

HISTORY. New Jersey, first settled in the early 1600s, is one of the 13 original states in the Union.

AREA AND POPULATION. New Jersey is bounded north by New York, east by the Atlantic with Long Island and New York City to the north-east, south by Delaware Bay and west by Pennsylvania. Area (US Bureau of Census), 7,787 sq. miles (319 sq. miles being inland water). Census population, 1 April 1990, 7,730,188, an increase of 4·97% since 1980. Population density, 1990, 1,037·6 per sq mile. Vital statistics, 1988 (per 1,000): Births, 17,481 (15·2); deaths, 72,668 (9·4); marriages, 61,063 (7·9); divorces, 28,919 (3·5).

Population at 5 federal censuses was:

	White	Black	Indian	Hispanics	Asiatic	Others	Total
1910	2,445,894	89,760	168	—	1,345	—	2,537,167
1930	3,829,663	208,828	213	—	2,630	122	4,041,334
1960	5,539,003	514,875	1,699	—	8,778	2,427	6,066,782
1980	6,127,467	925,066	8,394	—	103,847	200,048	7,364,823
1990	6,130,465	1,036,825	14,970	739,861	272,521	275,407	7,730,188

Of the population in 1980, 3,533,012 were male, 6,557,377 persons were urban, 5,116,581 were 20 years of age or older.

Census population of the larger cities and towns in 1990 was:

Newark	275,221	Irvington	61,018	Parsippany-	
Jersey City	228,537	Union City	58,012	Troy Hills	48,478
Paterson	140,891	Vineland	54,780	Middletown	68,183
Elizabeth	110,002	Passaic	58,041	Union Township	50,024
Trenton (capital)	88,675	Woodbridge	93,086	Bloomfield	45,066
Camden	87,992	Hamilton	86,553	Atlantic City	37,986
Clifton	71,742	Edison	88,680	Plainfield	46,567
East Orange	73,552	Cherry Hill	69,348	Hoboken	33,397
Bayonne	61,444			Montclair	37,729

Largest urbanized areas (1980) were: Newark, 1,963,000; Jersey City, 555,483; Paterson-Clifton-Passaic, 447,785; Trenton (NJ–Pa.), 305,678.

CLIMATE. Jersey City. Jan. 31°F (−0·6°C), July 75°F (23·9°C). Annual rainfall 41" (1,025 mm). Trenton. Jan. 32°F (0°C), July 76°F (24·4°C). Annual rainfall 40" (1,003 mm). *See* Atlantic Coast, p. 1398.

CONSTITUTION AND GOVERNMENT. The present constitution, ratified by the registered voters on 4 Nov. 1947, has been amended 38 times. There is a 40-member Senate and an 80-member General Assembly. Assembly members serve 2 years, senators 4 years, except those elected at the election following each census, who serve for 2 years. Sessions are held throughout the year.

In the 1988 presidential election Bush polled 1,743,192 votes, Dukakis, 1,320,352.

The capital is Trenton. The state is divided into 21 counties, which are subdivided into 567 municipalities—cities, towns, boroughs, villages and townships.

Governor: James J. Florio (D.), 1990–94 ($85,000).
Secretary of State: Joan M. Harberle ($95,000).

BUDGET. For the year ending 30 June 1990 (budget figures) general revenues were $16,789·4m. general expenditures were $17,103m.
Total net long-term debt, 27 Nov. 1990, was approximately $2,500m.
Per capita personal income (1990) was $24,968.

NATURAL RESOURCES

Minerals. In 1988 the chief minerals were stone (19,300,000 short tons, value $123,500,000) and sand and gravel (18,318,000, $74,183,000); others are clays (16,484, $368,482), peat (43,000, $797,000) and gemstones. New Jersey is a leading producer of greensand marl, magnesium compounds and peat. Total value of non-fuel mineral products, 1990, was $235·3m.

Agriculture. Livestock raising, market-gardening, fruit-growing, horticulture and forestry are pursued. In 1987, 9,032 farms had a total area of 894,426 acres; and the average farm had 99 acres valued at $3,969 per acre.
Market value of agricultural products sold, 1987: Crops, including nursery and greenhouse, $370·58m.; livestock, poultry and their products, $125,423,000.
Leading crops are tomatoes (value, $15·8m., 1986), corn for grain ($18·4m.), peaches ($23·6m.), all hay ($30·3m.), blueberries ($23·2m.), soybeans ($16·1m.), white potatoes ($11·9m.), sweet corn ($14·1m.), peppers ($12·4m.), cranberries ($17·2m.). Livestock, 1987: 35,000 milch cows, 90,000 all cattle, 14,000 sheep and lambs and (1 Dec. 1986) 40,000 swine.

INDUSTRY. In 1990 the top 100 corporate employers employed 80,994 workers. The unemployment rate in Nov. 1989 was 4·7%.
In July 1989 there were 3,721,100 employees on non-agricultural payrolls; 2,500 in mining, 184,800 in construction, 658,800 in manufacturing, 242,700 in transportation and public utilities, 889,800 in wholesale and retail trade, 246,900 in finance, insurance and real estate, 945,500 in services, 550,100 in government.

COMMUNICATIONS

Roads. In 1989 there were about 2,254 miles of state and interstate highways. At 1 Jan. 1989 there were 6,712 miles of county highways, 24,302 miles of municipal roads and 929 miles of other road.

Railways. In Sept. 1985, the state had 1,882·05 route miles of railway. There is a metro link to New York (22 km), a light rail line (7 km), and extensive commuter railways.

Civil Aviation. There is an international airport at Newark.

JUSTICE, RELIGION, EDUCATION AND WELFARE

Justice. State prisons in Aug. 1988 had 15,199 inmates. The last execution (by electrocution) was in 1963; it was the 160th, all for murder. Future executions would be by lethal injection.
The constitution of New Jersey forbids discrimination against any person on account of 'religious principles, race, color, ancestry or national origin'.

Religion. The Roman Catholic population of New Jersey in 1990 was 3·1m. In 1984 the five largest Protestant sects were United Methodists, 150,000; United Presbyterians, 174,000; Episcopalians, 147,000; Lutherans, 89,000; American Baptists, 74,000. There were 40,000 African Methodists and 4,000 Christian Methodist Episcopalians. In 1989 there were 411,000 Jews.

Education. Elementary instruction is compulsory for all from 6 to 16 years of age and free to all from 5 to 20 years of age. In 1988 public elementary schools had 733,179 and secondary schools had 347,692 enrolled pupils; public colleges in 1986 had 253,354 students, including 107,250 in community colleges, and independent colleges had 41,736. Average salary of 78,335 elementary and secondary classroom teachers in public schools 1987–88 was $30,778.

In 1988: Rutgers, the State University (founded as Queen's College in 1766) had, 47,719 students; Princeton (founded in 1746) had 6,264; Fairleigh Dickinson (1941), had 5,308; Montclair State College, 12,673; Glassboro State College, 8,500; Trenton State College, 7,779.

Health. In 1989 the state had 123 hospitals (36,617 beds), listed by the American Hospital Association.

Social Security. In the financial year 1987 gross expenditure for all social welfare was $834,446,000. Average monthly social security payment was $559·40.

Further Reading

Legislative District Data Book. Bureau of Government Research. Annual
Manual of the Legislature of New Jersey. Trenton. Annual
Boyd, J. P. (ed.) *Fundamentals and Constitutions of New Jersey, 1664–1954.* Princeton, 1964
Cunningham, J. T., *New Jersey: America's Main Road.* Rev. ed. New York, 1976
Kull, I. Stoddard (ed.) *New Jersey: a History.* New York, 1930

State Library: 185 W. State Street, Trenton, CN 520. N.J. 08625. *State Librarian:* Barbara F. Weaver.

NEW MEXICO

HISTORY. The first European settlement was established in 1598. Until 1771 New Mexico was the Spanish kings' 'Kingdom of New Mexico'. In 1771 it was annexed to the northern province of New Spain. When New Spain won its independence in 1821, it took the name of Republic of Mexico and established New Mexico as its northernmost department. When the war between the US and Mexico was concluded on 2 Feb. 1848 New Mexico was recognized as belonging to the US, and on 9 Sept. 1850 it was made a Territory. Part of the Territory was assigned to Texas; later Utah was formed into a separate Territory; in 1861 another part was transferred to Colorado, and in 1863 Arizona was disjoined, leaving to New Mexico its present area. New Mexico became a state in Jan. 1912.

AREA AND POPULATION. New Mexico is bounded north by Colorado, north-east by Oklahoma, east by Texas, south by Texas and Mexico and west by Arizona. Land area 121,335 sq. miles (258 sq. miles water). Public lands, administered by federal agencies (1975) amounted to 26·7m. acres or 34% of the total area. The Bureau of Indian Affairs held 7·3m. acres; the State of New Mexico held 9·4m. acres; 34·4m. acres were privately owned.

Census population, 1 April 1990, 1,515,069, an increase of 211,767 or 16·2% since 1980. Vital statistics, 1989: Births, 27,265 (17·8 per 1,000 population); deaths, 10,473; infant deaths, 232 (8·5 per 1,000 live births); marriages in 1988, 13,039 (8·3 per 1,000 population in 1989); divorces in 1987, 7,943 (5·3), (5·0 in 1989).

The population in 5 census years was:

	White	Black	Indian	Asian and Pacific Island	Other	Total	Per sq. mile
1910	304,594	1,628	20,573	506		327,301	2·7
1940	492,312	4,672	34,510	324		531,818	4·4
1960	875,763	17,063	56,255	1,942		951,023	7·8
1980	977,587	24,020	106,119	6,825	188,343	1,302,894	10·7
1990	1,146,028	30,210	134,355	14,124	190,352	1,515,069	12·5

Of the 1990 total, 745,253 were male, 1,068,328 were 18 years of age or older, 163,062 were 65 years of age or older.

Before 1930 New Mexico was largely a Spanish-speaking state, but since 1945 an influx of population from other states has reduced the percentage of persons of Spanish origin or descent to 38·2% (1990).

The largest cities are Albuquerque, with census population, 1990, 384,736; Las Cruces, 62,126; Santa Fé (capital), 55,859; Roswell, 44,654; Farmington, 33,997.

CLIMATE. Santa Fé. Jan. 29°F (–1·7°C), July 68°F (20°C). Annual rainfall 15" (366 mm). *See* Mountain States, p. 1397.

CONSTITUTION AND GOVERNMENT. The constitution of 1912 is still in force with 105 amendments. The state Legislature, which meets annually, consists of 42 members of the Senate, elected for 4 years, and 70 members of the House of Representatives, elected for 2 years.

In the 1988 presidential election Bush polled 270,341 votes, Dukakis 244,497.

The state capital is Santa Fé. The state is divided into 33 counties.

Governor: Bruce King (D.), 1991–95 ($90,000).
Lieut.-Governor: Casey Luma (D.) ($65,000).
Secretary of State: Stephanie Gonzales (D.) ($65,000).

BUDGET. For the year ending 30 June 1990 (US Census Bureau figures) the states general revenues were $4,731m. ($2,014m. from taxation and $779m. from federal government); general expenditures, $3,891m. (education, $1,681m.; highways, $386m., and public welfare, $436m.).

Per capita personal income (1990) was $14,265.

ENERGY AND NATURAL RESOURCES

Minerals. New Mexico is the country's largest domestic source of uranium, perlite and potassium salts. Production of recoverable U_3O_8 was 2·3m. lb. in 1989; perlite, 487,000 short tons; potassium salts, 1,799 short tons; petroleum, 68·7m. bbls (of 42 gallons); natural gas, 860,840 cu. ft; copper, 286,000 short tons; coal, 23·8m. short tons. The value of the total mineral output (1990) was $4·75m. An average of 15,600 persons were employed monthly in the mining industry in 1990.

Agriculture. New Mexico produces cereals, vegetables, fruit, livestock and cotton. Dry farming and irrigation have proved profitable in periods of high prices. There were 14,000 farms and ranches covering 44·5m. acres in 1989; in the 1987 US Census of Agriculture average farm (or ranch) was valued (land and buildings) at $582,012; 3,767 farms and ranches were of 1,000 acres and over.

Cash income, 1989 (preliminary), from crops, $433·3m., and from livestock products, $974·4m. Principal crops are wheat (3·2m. bu. from 160,000 acres), hay (1·26m. tons from 295,000 acres) and sorghum/grains (12·5m. bu. from 250,000 acres). Farm animals on 1 Jan. 1990 included 71,000 milch cows, 1·38m. all cattle, 495,000 sheep and 25,000 swine (1989). National forest area (1986) covered 9·3m. acres.

INDUSTRY. Average monthly non-agricultural employment during 1990 was 575,300: 43,100 were employed in manufacturing, 149,100 in government. Value of manufactures shipments, 1987, $4,226·4m.; leading industries, food and kindred products, electrical and electronic equipment, petroleum and coal products.

COMMUNICATIONS

Roads. In 1990 there were 54,807 miles of roads (49,367 miles rural) and 1,294,521 registered motor vehicles.

Railways. On 31 Dec. 1987 there were 2,062 miles of railway.

Civil Aviation. There were 71 public-use airports in Dec. 1988.

JUSTICE, RELIGION, EDUCATION AND WELFARE

Justice. The number of state prison inmates in Oct. 1991 was 3,140, and there were 444 in state operated juvenile centres in 1991; there were also 60 New Mexico prisoners held outside the state in 1991. The death penalty (by electrocution formerly, and now by lethal injection) has been imposed on 8 persons since 1933, 6 whites and 2 Negroes, all for murder. The last execution was in 1961.

Since 1949 the denial of employment by reason of race, colour, religion, national origin or ancestry has been forbidden. A law of 1955 prohibits discrimination in public places because of race or colour. An 'equal rights' amendment was added to the constitution in 1972.

Religion. There were (1975) approximately 356,530 Protestant Church members and 315,470 Roman Catholics.

Education. Elementary education is free, and compulsory between 6 and 17 years or high-school graduation age. In 1990–91 the 88 school districts had an estimated enrolment of 328,820 students in elementary and secondary schools of which private and parochial schools had 26,938. In 1988–89 there were 15,759 FTE teachers receiving an average salary of $24,620. State and local government expenditure for elementary and secondary schools was $1,083m. (1988-89).

The state-supported 4-year institutes of higher education are (1990–91 [1]):

	Students
University of New Mexico, Albuquerque	29,165
New Mexico State University, Las Cruces	21,404
Eastern New Mexico University, Portales	8,341
New Mexico Highlands University, Las Vegas	2,445
Western New Mexico University, Silver City	1,878
New Mexico Institute of Mining and Technology, Socorro	1,311

[1] Figures include branches outside main campus in cities listed.

Health. In 1988 the state had 49 short-term hospitals (4,637 beds).

Social Security. In Dec. 1989, 19,813 persons were receiving federal supplemental security income for the disabled (total annual payments, $61·7m.); 9,234 persons were receiving old-age assistance (total, $16·0m.); 581 persons were receiving aid to the blind (total, $1·7m.). A monthly average of 55,628 people received aid to families with dependent children (average $84.59 per month).

Further Reading

New Mexico Business (monthly; annual review in Jan.–Feb. issue). Bureau of Business and Economic Research, Univ. of N.M., Albuquerque
New Mexico Progress Economic Review (annual). Sunwest, Albuquerque
New Mexico Statistical Abstract: 1989. Bureau of Business and Economic Research, Univ. of N.M., Albuquerque, 1989
Beck, W., *New Mexico: a History of Four Centuries.* Univ. of Oklahoma, 1979
Garcia, C., Haine, P. and Rhodes, H., *State and Local Government in New Mexico.* Albuquerque, 1979
Jenkins, M. and Schroeder, A., *A Brief History of New Mexico.* Univ. of New Mexico, 1974
Muench, D. and Hillerman, T., *New Mexico.* Belding, Portland, Oregon, 1974
Williams, J. L., *New Mexico in Maps.* Univ. of New Mexico, 1986

NEW YORK STATE

HISTORY. From 1609 to 1664 the region now called New York was claimed by the Dutch; then it came under the rule of the English, who governed the country until the outbreak of the War of Independence. On 20 April 1777 New York adopted a constitution which transformed the colony into an independent state; on 26 July 1788 it ratified the constitution of the US, becoming one of the 13 original states. New York dropped its claim to Vermont after the latter was admitted to the

Union in 1791. With the annexation of a small area from Massachusetts in 1853, New York assumed its present boundaries.

AREA AND POPULATION. New York is bounded west and north by Canada with Lake Erie, Lake Ontario and the St Lawrence River forming the boundary; east by Vermont, Massachusetts and Connecticut, south-east by the Atlantic, south by New Jersey and Pennsylvania. Area, 49,108 sq. miles (1,731 sq. miles being water). Census population, 1 April 1990, 17,990,455, an increase of 2·47% since 1980. Births in 1989 were 290,258 (16·2 per 1,000 population); deaths, 169,388 (9·4); infant deaths, 3,076 (10·6 per 1,000 live births); marriages, 162,782 (9·1); divorces, 60,572 (3·4, includes all dissolutions).

Population in 5 census years was:

	White	Black	Indian	Asiatic	Total	Per sq. mile
1910	8,966,845	134,191	6,046	6,532	9,113,614	191·2
1930	12,143,191	412,814	6,973	15,088	12,588,066	262·6
1960	15,287,071	1,417,511	16,491	51,678	16,782,304	350·2
			All others			
1980	13,961,106	2,401,842	1,194,340		17,557,288	367·0
1990	12,460,189	2,569,126	2,961,140		17,990,455	381·0

Of the 1990 population, 8,625,673 were male, 14,857,202 (1980) were urban; those 20 years of age or older numbered 13,186,381. Aliens registered in Jan. 1980 numbered 801,411.

The population of New York City, by boroughs, census of 1 April 1990 was: Manhattan, 1,487,536; Bronx, 1,203,789; Brooklyn, 2,291,664; Queens, 1,951,598; Staten Island, 378,977; total, 7,322,564. The New York metropolitan statistical area had, in 1990, 8,546,846.

Population of other large cities and incorporated places census, April 1990, was:

Buffalo	328,123	Troy	54,269	Elmira	33,724
Rochester	231,636	Binghampton	53,008	Auburn	31,258
Yonkers	188,082	Hempstead	49,453	Waterdown	29,429
Syracuse	163,860	White Plains	48,718	Poughkeepsie	28,844
Albany (capital)	101,082	Rome	44,350	Lindenhurst	26,879
Utica	68,637	Freeport	39,894	Newburgh	26,454
New Rochelle	67,265	N. Tonawanda	34,989	Rockville Center	24,727
Mount Vernon	67,153	Jamestown	34,681	Garden City	21,686
Schenectady	65,566	Valleystream	33,946	Massapequa Park	18,044
Niagara Falls	61,840				

Other large urbanized areas, census 1990; Buffalo, 968,532; Rochester, 1,002,410; Albany–Schenectady–Troy, 874,304.

CLIMATE. Albany. Jan. 24°F (−4·4°C), July 73°F (22·8°C). Annual rainfall 34" (855 mm). Buffalo. Jan. 24°F (−4·4°C), July 70°F (21·1°C). Annual rainfall 36" (905 mm). New York. Jan. 30°F (−1·1°C), July 74°F (23·3°C). Annual rainfall 43" (1,087 mm). See Atlantic Coast, p. 1398.

CONSTITUTION AND GOVERNMENT. The present constitution dates from 1894; a later constitutional convention, 1938, is now legally considered merely to have amended the 1894 constitution, which has now had 93 amendments. A proposed new constitution in 1967 was rejected by the electorate. The Senate consists of 60 members, and the Assembly of 150 members, both elected every 2 years. In the 1988 presidential election Dukakis polled 3,347,882 votes, Bush, 3,081,871. The state capital is Albany. For local government the state is divided into 62 counties, 5 of which constitute the city of New York. There were state parks and recreation areas covering 260,198 acres in 1990.

Each of the state's 62 cities is incorporated by charter, under special legislation. The government of New York City is vested in the mayor (David Dinkins), elected for 4 years, and a city council, whose president and members are elected for 4 years. The council has a President and 51 members, each elected from a district wholly within the city. The mayor appoints all the heads of departments, except the comptroller, who is elected. Each of the 5 city boroughs (Manhattan, Bronx, Brooklyn, Queens and Staten Island) has a president, elected for 4 years. Each borough is also a county bearing the same name except Manhattan borough, which, as a county, is called New York, and Brooklyn, which is Kings County.

Governor: Mario Cuomo (D.), 1991-95 ($130,000).
Lieut.-Governor: Stan Lundine (D.) ($110,000).
Secretary of State: Gail S. Schaefer (D.) ($87,338).

BUDGET. The state's general revenues for the financial year ending 31 March 1990 were $52,441·3m. ($28,614·6m. from taxes); general expenditures were $49,967·5m. ($14,266·2m. for education, $14,820·4m. for social services, $2,227·8m. for transport).

Per capita personal income was $21,975 in 1990.

ENERGY AND NATURAL RESOURCES

Minerals. Production of principal minerals in 1988: Sand and gravel (28·7m. short tons), salt (4,614 short tons), oil (495,000 bbls), natural gas (25,447m. cu. ft). The state is a leading producer of titanium concentrate, talc, abrasive garnet, wollastonite and emery. Quarry products include trap rock, slate, marble, limestone and sandstone. Value of mineral output in 1988 $695·7m.

Agriculture. New York has large agricultural interests. In 1989 it had 39,000 farms, with a total area of 8·4m. acres; average farm was 215 acres; average value per acre (1985), $808.

Cash income, 1989, from crops $74,142,000 and livestock, $1,83,286,000. Dairying is an important type of farming. Field crops comprise maize, winter wheat, oats and hay. New York ranks second in US in the production of apples, and maple syrup. Other products are grapes, tart cherries, peaches, pears, plums, strawberries, raspberries, cabbages, onions, potatoes, maple sugar. Estimated farm animals, 1990, included 1,540,000 all cattle, 966,000 milch cows, 92,000 sheep and lambs, 124,000 swine and 5·1m. chickens.

INDUSTRY. The main employers (1987 census) are service industries (1,293,000), trade (1,150,000) and manufacture (1,267,500). Leading industries were clothing, non-electrical machinery, printing and publishing, electrical equipment, instruments, food and allied products and fabricated metals.

COMMUNICATIONS

Roads. In 1990 there were 110,965 miles of roads (73,263 miles rural). The New York State Thruway extends 559 miles from New York City to Buffalo. The Northway, a 176-mile toll-free highway, is a connecting road from the Thruway at Albany to the Canadian border at Champlain, Quebec.

Motor vehicle registrations in 1990 were 10,020,539.

Railways. There were in 1981, 3,891 miles of Class I railways. New York City has NYCTA and PATH metro systems, and commuter railways run by Metro-North, New Jersey Rail and Long Island Rail Road.

Civil Aviation. There were 489 airports and landing areas in 1989.

Shipping. The canals of the state, combined in 1918 in what is called the Improved Canal System, have a length of 524 miles, of which the Erie or Barge canal has 340 miles. In 1981 the canals carried 807,925 tons of freight.

JUSTICE, RELIGION, EDUCATION AND WELFARE

Justice. The State Human Rights Law was approved 12 March 1945, effective 1 July, 1945. The State Division of Human Rights is charged with the responsibility of enforcing this law. The division may request and utilize the services of all governmental departments and agencies; adopt and promulgate suitable rules and regulations; test, investigate and pass judgment upon complaints alleging discrimination in employment, in places of public accommodation, resort or amusement, education, and in housing, land and commercial space; hold hearings, sub-poena witnesses and require the production for examination of papers relating to matters under investigation; grant compensatory damages and require repayment of profits in certain housing cases among other provisions; apply for court injunctions to prevent frustration of orders of the Commissioner.

On 30 Dec. 1988, 44,560 persons were in state prisons.

In 1963–81 there were no executions. Total executions (by electrocution) from 1930 to 1962 were 329 (234 whites, 90 Negroes, 5 other races; all for murder except 2 for kidnapping).

In 1988 murders reported in New York were 2,239. Police strength (sworn officers) in 1988 was 61,204 (43,218 New York City).

Religion. The churches are Roman Catholic, with 6,367,576 members in 1981, Jewish congregations (about 2m. in 1981) and Protestant Episcopal (299,929 in 1980).

Education. Education is compulsory between the ages of 7 and 16. In 1989 the public elementary and secondary schools had 2,537,669 pupils; classroom teachers numbered 183,293 in public schools. Total expenditure on public schools in 1989 was $18,472,852. Teachers' salaries, 1989, averaged $43,300.

The state's educational system, including public and private schools and secondary institutions, universities, colleges, libraries, museums, etc., constitutes (by legislative act) the 'University of the State of New York', which is governed by a Board of Regents consisting of 15 members appointed by the Legislature. Within the framework of this 'University' was established in 1948 a 'State University' which controls 64 colleges and educational centres, 30 of which are locally operated community colleges. The 'State University' is governed by a board of 16 Trustees, appointed by the Governor with the consent and advice of the Senate.

Higher education in the state is conducted in 296 institutions (627,676 full-time and 375,690 part-time students in autumn 1989).

In autumn 1990 the institutions of higher education in the state included:

Founded	Name and place	Teachers	Students
1754	Columbia University, New York	2,305	18,242
1795	Union University, Schenectady and Albany	228	2,877
1824	Rensselaer Polytechnic Institute, Troy	375	6,692
1831	New York University, New York	2,386	32,813
1846	Colgate University, New York	255	2,710
1846	Fordham University, New York	703	13,158
1847	University of the City of New York, New York	9,065	200,700
1848	University of Rochester, Rochester	1,250	9,291
1854	Polytechnic Institute of New York	261	3,701
1856	St Lawrence University, Canton	189	2,091
1857	Cooper Union Institute of Technology, New York	108	1,036
1861	Vassar College, Poughkeepsie	235	2,453
1863	Manhattan College, New York	234	3,794
1865	Cornell University, Ithaca	1,779	17,171
1870	Syracuse University, Syracuse	990	21,900
1948	State University of New York	18,852	403,028

The Saratoga Performing Arts Centre (5,100 seats), a non-profit, tax-exempt organization, which opened in 1966, is the summer residence of the New York City Ballet and the Philadelphia Orchestra—two groups which present special educational programmes for students and teachers.

Health. In 1981 the state had 278 hospitals (67,798 beds), 585 skilled nursing homes (62,435 beds) and 241 other institutions (24,302 beds). In 1986 mental health facilities had 21,836 patients and institutions for the mentally retarded had 10,581 patients.

Social Security. The federal Supplemental Security Income programme covered aid to the needy aged, blind and disabled from 1 Jan. 1975. In the state programme for 1980, $4,543m. was paid in Medicaid to 2,288,000 people; aid to dependent children in 1985 went to 1,109,610 recipients, average benefits $371 per family per month.

Further Reading

Governing the Empire State: an Insider's Guide. Albany, Rockefeller Institute, 1988
New York Red Book. Albany. Biennial.
Legislative Manual. Department of State. Biennial.
Managing Modern New York: the Carey Era. Albany, Rockefeller Institute, 1985
The Modern New York State Legislature: Redressing the Balance. Albany, Rockefeller Institute, 1991
New York State Statistical Yearbook. Albany, Rockefeller Institute. Biennial.
Rockefeller in Retrospect: the Governor's New York Legacy. Albany, Rockefeller Institute, 1987
Connery, R. and G. B., *Governing New York State: The Rockefeller Years*. New York, 1974
Ellis, D. M., *History of New York State*. Cornell Univ. Press, 1967
Flick, A. (ed.) *History of the State of New York*. Columbia Univ. Press, 1933–37
Zimmerman, J. F., *The Government and Politics of New York*. New York Univ. Pres, 1981

State Library: The New York State Library, Albany 12230. *State Librarian and Assistant Commissioner for Libraries:* Joseph Shubert.

NORTH CAROLINA

HISTORY. North Carolina, first settled in 1585 by Sir Walter Raleigh and permanently settled in 1663, was one of the 13 original states of the Union.

AREA AND POPULATION. North Carolina is bounded north by Virginia, east by the Atlantic, south by South Carolina, south-west by Georgia and west by Tennessee. Area, 52,669 sq. miles, of which 3,826 sq. miles are inland water. Census population, 1 April 1990, 6,628,637, an increase of 12·84% since 1980. Births, 1984, were 86,705 (14·1 per 1,000 population); marriages, 52,123 (8·5); deaths, 51,496 (8·4); infant deaths, 1,099 (12·7 per 1,000 live births); divorces and annulments, 29,125 (4·7).

Population in 5 census years was:

	White	Black	Indian	Asiatic	Total	Per sq. mile
1910	1,500,511	697,843	7,851	82	2,206,287	45·3
1930	2,234,958	918,647	16,579	92	3,170,276	64·5
1950	2,983,121	1,047,353	3,742	—	4,061,929	82·7
			All others			
1970	3,901,767	1,126,478	53,814		5,082,059	104·1
1980	4,453,010	1,316,050	105,369		5,874,429	111·5

Of the total population in 1980, 2,852,012 were male, 2,818,794 were urban and 3,976,359 were 20 years old or older; 14·8% were non-white.

The principal cities (with census population in 1990) are: Charlotte, 395,934; Raleigh, 207,951; Greensboro, 183,521; Winston-Salem, 143,485; Durham, 136,611.

CLIMATE. Climate varies sharply with altitude; the warmest area is in the south east near Southport and Wilmington; the coldest is Mount Mitchell (6,684 ft). Raleigh. Jan. 42°F (5·6°C), July 79°F (26·1°C). Annual rainfall 46" (1,158 mm). *See* Atlantic Coast, p. 1398.

CONSTITUTION AND GOVERNMENT. The present constitution dates from 1971 (previous constitution, 1776 and 1868/76); it has had 19 amendments. The General Assembly consists of a Senate of 50 members and a House of Representatives of 120 members; all are elected by districts for 2 years. It meets in odd-numbered years in Jan.

The Governor and Lieut.-Governor are elected for 4 years. The Governor may succeed himself but has no veto. There are 19 other executive heads of department, 8 elected by the people and 9 appointed by the Governor.

In the presidential election of 1988 Bush polled 1,232,132 votes, Dukakis, 890,034.

The capital is Raleigh. There are 100 counties.

Governor: James G. Martin (R.), 1989–93 ($123,300).
Lieut.-Governor: Jim Gardner (R.) ($75,252).
Secretary of State: Rufus Edmiston (D.) ($75,252).

BUDGET. General revenue for the year ending 30 June 1990 was $12,345·2m. General expenditure was $12,555·3m.

On 30 June 1986 the net total long-term debt amounted to $757m.

Per capita personal income (1990) was $16,203.

NATURAL RESOURCES

Minerals. Mining production in 1990 was valued at $578·4m. Principal minerals were stone, sand and gravel, phosphate rock, feldspar, lithium minerals, olivine, kaolin and talc. North Carolina is a leading producer of bricks, making more than 1,000m. bricks a year.

Agriculture. In 1985 there were 76,000 farms covering 10·8m. acres; average size of farms was 142 acres and total estimated value $18,500m.

Main crop production: flue-cured tobacco, maize, soybeans, peanuts, wheat, sweet potatoes and apples.

Livestock, 1990: Cattle, 0·9m.; pigs, 2·6m.; chickens, 19·6m.

Forestry. Commercial forest covered 18,891,000 acres in 1990. Main products are hardwood veneer and hardwood plywood, furniture woods, pulp, paper and lumber.

Fisheries. Commercial fish catch, 1990, had a value of approximately $71·5m. The catch is mainly of menhaden, crabmeat, bay scallops, flounder, croaker, shrimps, sea trout, spots and clams.

INDUSTRY. North Carolina's manufacturing establishments in 1985 had 827,400 workers. The leading industries by employment are textiles, clothing, furniture, electrical machinery and equipment, non-electrical machinery, and food processing. In 1985 investment in new and expanded industry was $2,758m. About 576,200 were employed in trade, 422,800 in government and 427,600 in services.

TOURISM. Total receipts of the travel industry, $6,400m. in 1990.

COMMUNICATIONS

Roads. In 1990 there were 94,228 miles of roads (75,165 miles rural) and 5,113,224 registered motor vehicles.

Railways. The state in 1986 contained 3,682 miles of railway operating in 91 of the 100 counties. There are 22 Class I, II and III rail companies.

Civil Aviation. In 1986 there were 82 public airports of which 14 are served by major airlines.

Shipping. There are 2 ocean ports, Wilmington and Morehead City.

JUSTICE, RELIGION, EDUCATION AND WELFARE

Justice. Total executions 1910–86, 365. There was one execution (by lethal injection) in 1986. Prison population at 31 Oct. 1986, 17,700.

Religion. Leading denominations are the Baptists (48·9% of church membership), Methodists (20·7%), Presbyterians (7·7%), Lutherans (3%) and Roman Catholics (2·7%). Total estimate of all denominations in 1983 was 2·6m.

Education. School attendance is compulsory between 6 and 16.

Public school enrolment, 1985–86, was 1,080,887; elementary and secondary schools numbered 1,968. Instructional staff (1986) consisted of 57,630 classroom teachers; average salary $22,476. Expenditure for public schools was $2,770m., 65·5% from state, 25·2% from local and 9·3% from federal sources.

In autumn 1985–86 state-supported colleges and universities included 58 community and technical colleges with 654,000 full and part time students. The 16 senior universities are all part of the University of North Carolina system, the largest campus being North Carolina State University and Raleigh, with 23,400 students. The university system was founded in 1789 at Chapel Hill and first opened in 1792. Its 1986 autumn enrolment was 130,000 students.

In addition to the state-supported institutions there were 7 private junior colleges with an enrolment of 2,585 and 31 private senior institutions with a total enrolment of 19,009. The total undergraduate enrolment in private institutions for 1985 was 21,594.

Health. In Oct. 1986 the state had 160 hospitals (34,438 beds).

Social Security. In June 1982 there were 900,070 persons receiving $300·4m. in social security benefits. Of that number 496,020 were retired, receiving $186·67m.; 85,640 were disabled ($34·7m.); 318,410 others received $79m.

Further Reading

North Carolina Manual. Secretary of State. Raleigh. Biennial
Clay, J. W. *et al* (eds.), *North Carolina Atlas: Portrait of a Changing Southern State.* Univ. of North Carolina Press, 1975
Corbitt, D. L., *The Formation of the North Carolina Counties.* Raleigh, 1969
Lefler, H. T. and Newsome, A. R., *North Carolina: The History of a Southern State.* Univ. of North Carolina Press, 1973

NORTH DAKOTA

HISTORY. North Dakota was admitted into the Union, with boundaries as at present, on 2 Nov. 1889; previously it had formed part of the Dakota Territory, established 2 March 1861.

AREA AND POPULATION. North Dakota is bounded north by Canada, east by the Red River (forming a boundary with Minnesota), south by South Dakota and west by Montana. Total area, 70,702 sq. miles; land area, 68,994 sq. miles. The Federal Bureau of Indian Affairs administered (1990) 841,295 acres, of which 214,006 acres were assigned to tribes. Census population, 1 April 1990, 638,800, a decrease of 2·13% since 1980. Births in 1988 were 10,111 (15·2 per 1,000 population); deaths, 5,664 (8·5); infant deaths, 107; marriages, 4,996; divorces, 2,365.

Population at 5 census years was:

	White	Black	Indian	Asiatic	Total	Per sq. mile
1910	569,855	617	6,486	98	577,056	8·2
1930	671,851	377	8,617	194	680,845	9·7
1960	619,538	777	11,736	274	632,446	9·1
			All others			
1970	599,485	2,494	15,782		617,761	8·9
1980	625,557	2,568	24,692		652,717	9·4

Of the total population in 1980, 328,126 were male, 317,821 were urban and 419,234 were 21 years old or older. Estimated outward migration, 1970–80, 16,983.

The largest cities are Fargo with population (census), 1980, of 61,383; Grand Forks, 43,765; Bismarck (capital), 44,485, and Minot, 32,843.

CLIMATE. Bismarck. Jan. 8°F (−13·3°C), July 71°F (21·1°C). Annual rainfall 16" (402 mm). Fargo. Jan. 6°F (−14·4°C), July 71°F (21·1°C). Annual rainfall 20"

(503 mm). *See* High Plains and Mid-West (SW North Dakota is in the Plains, the rest in the mid-west lowlands), p. 1398.

CONSTITUTION AND GOVERNMENT. The present constitution dates from 1889; it has had 95 amendments. The Legislative Assembly consists of a Senate of 53 members elected for 4 years, and a House of Representatives of 106 members elected for 2 years. The Governor and Lieut.-Governor are elected for 4 years.

In the 1988 presidential election Bush polled 165,517 votes, Dukakis, 127,081.

The capital is Bismarck. The state has 53 organized counties.

Governor: George A. Sinner (D.), 1989–93 ($65,200 plus expenses).
Lieut.-Governor: Lloyd B. Omdahl (D.) ($53,500).
Secretary of State: Jim Kusler (D.) ($49,300).

FINANCE. General revenue of state and local government year ending 30 June 1989, was $1,052m.; general expenditures, $1,055m., taxation provided $598m. and federal grants, $431m.; education took $621m.; highways, $157m., and public welfare, $232m.

Total net long-term debt (local government) on 30 June 1982, $325m.

Per capita personal income (1990) was $15,255.

ENERGY AND NATURAL RESOURCES

Minerals. The mineral resources of North Dakota consist chiefly of oil which was discovered in 1951. Production of crude petroleum in 1987 was 41·4m. bbls; of natural gas, 71,612m. cu. ft. Output of lignite coal was 25·2m. short tons. Total value of mineral output, 1984, $1,724m.

Agriculture. Agriculture is the chief pursuit of the population. In 1985 there were 33,000 farms (61,963 in 1954) with an area of 41m. acres (41,876,924 in 1954); the average farm was of 1,242 acres. The greater number of farms are cash-grain or livestock farms with annual sales of $20,000–$39,999.

Cash income, 1986, from crops, $1,423m., and from livestock, $676m. North Dakota leads in the production of barley, sunflowers, flaxseed, wheat, pinto beans, rye and durum. Other important products are sugar-beet, potatoes, hay, oats and maize.

The state has also an active livestock industry, chiefly cattle raising. Livestock, 1987: Cattle, 2m.; pigs, 285,000; sheep, 180,000; poultry, 1·4m.

Forestry. Forest area, 1990, 460,000 acres.

INDUSTRY. In 1988, 68,200 were employed in trade, 64,700 in government, 63,600 in services, 16,400 in transport and utilities, 16,400 in manufacturing.

COMMUNICATIONS

Roads. The state highway department maintained, in 1989, 8,290 miles of highway; local authorities, 75,000 miles, and municipal, 3,250 miles. Car and truck registrations in 1989 numbered 716,967.

Railways. In 1989 there were 4,800 miles of railway.

Civil Aviation. In 1990 there were 100 public use airports and 475 private use airstrips.

JUSTICE, RELIGION, EDUCATION AND WELFARE

Justice. The state penitentiary, on 31 Dec. 1987, held 410 inmates. The State Farm, a minimum custody institution, held 40 inmates. There is no death penalty.

Religion. The leading religious denominations are the Roman Catholics, with 230,600 members in 1980; Combined Lutherans, 288,500; Methodists, 36,500; Presbyterians, 19,500, and the United Church of Christ, 15,000.

Education. School attendance is compulsory between the ages of 7 and 16, or until the 17th birthday if the eighth grade has not been completed. In Oct. 1988 the public elementary schools had 84,238 pupils; secondary schools, 32,896 pupils. State expenditure on public schools, 1988, $424m. or $663 per capita. Teachers (4,441 in elementary and 2,376 in secondary schools) earned an average $22,249 in 1988.

The university of North Dakota in Grand Forks, founded in 1883, had 12,280 students in 1989; North Dakota State University in Fargo, 9,432 students. Total enrolment in the 8 public institutions of higher education, 1989, 35,311.

Health. In 1987 the state had 52 hospitals (4,047 beds), and 95 nursing homes (6,728).

Social Security. In 1989 7,237 received SSI payments, including 2,294 aged (average $122 per month). 4,861 disabled ($209); total paid, $15·8m.; 15,049 recipients in 5,408 families received Aid to Families with Dependent Children.

Further Reading

North Dakota Growth Indicators, 1984. 20th ed. Economic Development Commission, Bismarck, 1985
North Dakota Blue Book. Secretary of State. Bismarck
Statistical Abstract of North Dakota. Bureau of Business and Economic Research, Univ. of North Dakota
Glaab, C. L. et al, *The North Dakota Political Tradition.* Iowa State Univ. Press, 1981
Jelliff, T. B., *North Dakota: A Living Legacy.* Fargo, 1983
Robinson, E. B., *History of North Dakota.* Univ. of Nebraska Press, 1966

OHIO

HISTORY. The first organized white settlement was in 1788; Ohio unofficially entered the Union on 19 Feb. 1803; entrance was made official, retroactive to 1 March 1803, on 8 Aug. 1953.

AREA AND POPULATION. Ohio is bounded north by Michigan and Lake Erie, east by Pennsylvania, south-east and south by the Ohio River (forming a boundary with West Virginia and Kentucky) and west by Indiana. Area, 41,330 sq. miles, of which 325 sq. miles are inland water. Census population, 1 April 1990 10,847,115, an increase of 89,695 or 0·8% since 1980. In 1989 births numbered 163,776 (15·2 per 1,000 population); deaths, 97,938 (9·1); infant deaths, 1,614 (9·9 per 1,000 live births); marriages, 97,782 (9·1); divorces, 48,627 (4·5).

Population at 6 census years was:

	White	Black	Indian	Asiatic	Total	Per sq. mile
1910	4,654,897	111,452	127	645	4,767,121	117·0
1930	6,335,173	309,304	435	1,785	6,646,697	161·6
1960	8,909,698	786,097	1,910	8,692	9,706,397	236·9
			All others			
1970	9,646,997	970,477	34,543		10,652,017	260·0
1980	9,597,458	1,076,748	123,424		10,797,630	263·2
1990	9,521,756	1,154,826	170,533		10,847,115	264·5

Of the total population in 1990, 5,226,340 were male. In 1980 7,918,259 persons were urban. Those 18 years old or older numbered 8,047,371 in 1990.

Census population of chief cities on 1 April 1990 was:

Columbus	632,910	Hamilton	61,368	Middletown	46,022
Cleveland	505,616	Kettering	60,569	Lima	45,549
Cincinnati	364,040	Lakewood	59,718	Newark	44,389
Toledo	332,943	Elyria	56,746	Lancaster	34,507
Akron	223,019	Euclid	54,875	North Olmsted	34,204
Dayton	182,044	Cleveland Heights	54,052	Upper Arlington	34,128
Youngstown	95,732	Warren	50,793	Marion	34,075
Parma	87,876	Mansfield	50,627	East Cleveland	33,096
Canton	84,161	Cuyahoga Falls	48,950	Garfield Heights	31,739
Lorain	71,245	Mentor	47,358	Zanesville	26,778
Springfield	70,487				

Urbanized areas, 1990 census: Cleveland, 1,831,122; Cincinnati, 1,452,645; Columbus (the capital), 1,377,419; Dayton, 951,270; Akron, 657,575; Toledo, 614,128; Youngstown-Warren, 492,619; Canton, 394,106.

CLIMATE. Cincinnati. Jan. 39·1°F, July 77·1°F). Annual rainfall 43·82". Cleveland. Jan. 35°F, July 72·4°F. Annual rainfall 43·9". Columbus. Jan. 36·6°F, July 73·9°F. Annual rainfall 43·76". *See* Great Lakes, p. 1398.

CONSTITUTION AND GOVERNMENT. The question of a general revision of the constitution drafted by an elected convention is submitted to the people every 20 years. The constitution of 1851 had 141 amendments by 1983.

In the 119th General Assembly the Senate consisted of 33 members and the House of Representatives of 99 members. The Senate is elected for 4 years, half each 2 years; the House is elected for 2 years; the Governor, Lieut.-Governor and Secretary of State for 4 years. Qualified as electors are (with necessary exceptions) all citizens 18 years of age who have the usual residential qualifications. Ohio sends 2 senators and 21 representatives to Congress.

In the 1988 presidential election Bush polled 2,411,719 votes, Dukakis, 1,934,922.

The capital (since 1816) is Columbus. Ohio is divided into 88 counties.

Governor: George Voinovich (R.), 1991–94 ($100,000).
Lieut.-Governor: Michael DeWine (R.) ($51,710).
Secretary of State: Robert Taft (R.) ($73,872).

BUDGET. For the year ending 30 June 1990 general revenue fund income was 11,693·6m. and expenditure, $11,250·8m.

The bonded debt on 30 June 1990 was $3,385m.

Per capita personal income (1989) was $16,373 (current dollars).

ENERGY AND NATURAL RESOURCES

Minerals. Ohio has extensive mineral resources, of which coal is the most important by value: Output (1989) 31·4m. short tons. Production of crude petroleum, 1989, 10·2m. bbls; natural gas, 159,729m. cu. ft. Other minerals include stone, clay, sand and gravel. Value of minerals, 1989, $392·2m.

Agriculture. Ohio is extensively devoted to agriculture. In 1990, 84,000 farms covered 15·6m. acres; average farm value per acre, $1,204.

Cash income 1990, from crop and livestock and products, $3,812·1m. The most important crops in 1990 were: Maize (417m. bu.), wheat (79m. bu.), oats (16m. bu.), soybeans (135·7m. bu.). In 1990 there were 2m. swine, 1·58m. all cattle and 305,000 sheep.

Forestry. State forest area, 1987, 252,000 acres; total forest, 714,000 acres.

INDUSTRY. In May 1988, manufacturing employed 1,119,000 workers; non-manufacturing, 2,901,000. The largest industry was manufacturing of transport equipment, industrial machinery and equipment, and fabricated metal products.

COMMUNICATIONS

Roads. In 1990 there were 113,439 miles of roads (82,126 miles rural) and 9,513,918 registered motor vehicles.

Railways. Class I railroads operated 6,102 miles in 1988.

Civil Aviation. Ohio had (1989) 179 commercial airports including one seaplane base; 637 non-commercial airports; 33 commercial heliports and 291 non-commercial. There were 9,161 licensed aeroplanes at 31 Dec. 1989.

JUSTICE, RELIGION, EDUCATION AND WELFARE

Justice. A Civil Rights Act (1933) forbids discrimination against citizens on grounds of 'colour or race'. A state Civil Rights Commission (created 1959) has general administrative powers to prevent discrimination because of race, colour, religion, national origin or ancestry.

On 30 June 1989 the Department of Rehabilitation and Correction was operating 23 adult correction facilities with average inmate population of 23,949. Total executions (by electrocution) since 1930 were 170, all for murder. There have been no executions since 1963. The Department of Rehabilitation and Correction was created in July 1972, and has established probation services in counties where services would otherwise be inadequate or non-existent.

Religion. Many religious faiths are represented, including (but not limited to) the Baptist, Jewish, Lutheran, Methodist, Moslem, Orthodox, Presbyterian and Roman Catholic.

Education. School attendance during full term is compulsory for children from 6 to 18 years of age. In autumn 1990 public schools had 1·8m. enrolled pupils and 101,626 full-time equivalent classroom teachers. Teachers' salaries (1989–90) averaged (estimate) $30,553. Operating expenditure on elementary and secondary schools for 1990 was $10,003m.: state average per pupil, $4,289. Universities and colleges had a total enrolment (autumn 1989) of 518,000 students of whom 127,000 were in private colleges. State appropriation to state universities 1988–89, $1,045·1m. Average annual charge (undergraduate) at 4-year institutions: $4,835 (state); $8,950 (private).

Main bodies, 1990: (figures are for main campus in named city):

Founded	Institutions	Enrolments
1804	Ohio University, Athens (State)	17,000
1809	Miami University, Oxford (State)	16,157
1819	University of Cincinnati (State)	30,787
1826	Case Western Reserve University, Cleveland (Indep.)	7,879
1850	University of Dayton (R.C.)	11,264
1870	University of Akron (State)	28,896
1870	Ohio State University, Columbus (State)	41,473
1872	University of Toledo (State)	23,928
1887	Sinclair Community College, Dayton	17,433
1908	Youngstown University (State)	14,710
1910	Bowling Green State University (State)	18,043
1910	Kent State University (State)	17,442
1962	Cuyahoga Community College District (State/local)	23,254
1964	Cleveland State University (State)	18,534
1964	Wright State University (State)	17,423
1986	Shawnee State University, Portsmouth (State)	2,970

Health. In 1989 the state had 218 hospitals listed by the American Hospital Association. State facilities for the severely mentally retarded had 2,824 resident in 1989.

Mentally retarded who do not need constant supervision occupy 1,500 group homes in residential areas (1990). In 1989 17 psychiatric hospitals had a daily average of 3,639 residents. In 1989, general hospitals had 79 units (2,968 beds) for the mentally ill and 41 beds for mentally retarded. There were 411 community mental health agencies in 1989.

Social Security. Public assistance is administered through 6 basic programmes: Aid to dependent children, emergency assistance, Medicaid, general relief, food stamps and social services; 49% of the costs (except general relief and adult emergency assistance) are met by the federal government.

In 1989 (preliminary) Medicaid cost $4,071m. and served an average 1·49m. people. Aid to dependent children cost $801m., to 633,000 people. Food stamps cost $730m. General relief cost $397m., receipts varying from county to county. Optional State Supplement is paid to aged, blind or disabled adults. Free social services are available to those eligible by income or circumstances.

Further Reading

Official Roster: Federal State, County Officers and Department Information. Secretary of State, Columbus. Biennial

Rosebloom, E. H. and Weisenburger, F. P., *A History of Ohio.* Columbus, State Archive and Historical Society, 1953

Shkurti, W. J. and Bartle, J. (eds.) *Benchmark Ohio.* Ohio State Univ. Press, 1989

OKLAHOMA

HISTORY. An unorganized area in the centre of the present state was thrown open to white settlers on 22 April 1889. The Territory of Oklahoma, organized in 1890 to include this area and other sections, was opened to white settlements by runs or lotteries during the next decade. In 1893 the Territory was enlarged by the addition of the Cherokee Outlet, which fixed part of the present northern boundary. On 16 Nov. 1907 Oklahoma was combined with the remaining part of the Indian Territory and admitted as a state with boundaries substantially as now.

AREA AND POPULATION. Oklahoma is bounded north by Kansas, north-east by Missouri, east by Arkansas, south by Texas (the Red River forming part of the boundary) and, at the western extremity of the 'panhandle', by New Mexico and Colorado. Total area 69,919 sq. miles; land area, 68,679 sq. miles. Census population, 1 April 1990, 3,145,585, an increase of 3·98% since 1980. Births, 1988, 47,279; deaths, 29,766; infant deaths (1987) 726; marriages, 32,923; divorces and annulments, 23,048.

The population at 4 federal censuses was:

	White	Black	Indian	Other	Total	Per sq. mile
1930	2,130,778	172,198	92,725	339	2,396,040	34·6
1960	2,107,900	153,084	68,689	1,414	2,328,284	33·8
1970	2,280,362	171,892	97,179	10,030	2,559,253	37·2
1980	2,597,783	204,658	169,292	53,557	3,025,486	43·2

In 1980, 1,476,719 were male, 2,035,082 were urban and those 20 years of age or older numbered 2,052,729. The US Bureau of Indian Affairs is responsible for 1,097,004 acres (1990), of which 96,839 acres were allotted to tribes.

The most important cities with population, 1990 (preliminary) are Oklahoma City (capital), 441,154; Tulsa, 364,572; Norman, 79,579; Lawton, 79,544; Broken Arrow, 57,281; Midwest City, 52,037; Edmond, 51,930; Enid, 45,175; Moore, 40,037; Muskogee, 37,440; Stillwater, 36,543; Bartlesville, 34,195.

CLIMATE. 1988: Oklahoma City. Jan. 34·2°F (1·2°C), July 81·6°F (27·5°C). Annual rainfall 31·94" (8,113 mm). Tulsa. Jan. 34·8°F (1·5°C), July 82·6°F (27·5°C). Annual rainfall 33·22" (8,438 mm). *See* Central Plains, p. 1398.

CONSTITUTION AND GOVERNMENT. The present constitution, dating from 1907, provides for amendment by initiative petition and legislative referendum; it has had 139 amendments (as of Oct. 1990).

The Legislature consists of a Senate of 48 members, who are elected for 4 years, and a House of Representatives elected for 2 years and consisting of 101 members. The Governor and Lieut.-Governor are elected for 4-year terms; the Governor can only be elected for two terms in succession. Electors are (with necessary exceptions) all citizens 18 years or older, with the usual qualifications.

In the 1988 presidential election Bush polled 678,244 votes, Dukakis, 483,373.

The capital is Oklahoma City. The state has 77 counties.

Governor: David Walters (D.), 1991–95 ($70,000).

Lieut.-Governor: Jack Mildren (D.) ($40,000).

Secretary of State: John Kennedy (D.) ($37,500).

BUDGET. Total revenue for the year ending 30 June 1989 was $6,072,418,369. Total expenditure, $5,614,402,347.

Bonded indebtedness for the year ending 30 June 1989, $70·75m.
Per capita personal income (1989) was $15,483.

ENERGY AND NATURAL RESOURCES

Minerals. Production of mineral fuels, 1989: Petroleum, 117·97m. bbls; natural gas, 2,197,137m. cu. ft.; coal, 1,768,292 tons. In 1989 there were 96,344 oilwells and 27,443 natural gaswells in production. Non-fuel mineral production (short tons), 1988: Cement, (1987) 1,456,000; gypsum, 2,173,000; sand and gravel, 10,541,000; stone, 26,307,746; clays, 754,054; iodine, 2,238,152 lb.; solar salt, 75,000. Other minerals are tripoli, feldspar, refined germanium, helium, lime and pumice. Value of non-fuel mineral production, 1988, $220,137,000.

Agriculture. In 1987 the state had 70,228 farms with a total area of 31,541,977 acres; average farm was 499 acres. Harvested crop land was 24,443,459 acres; irrigated land, 478,437 acres. Operators by principal occupation: Farming, 33,052; other, 37,176. Livestock, 1 Jan. 1990: Cattle, 5·3m.; sheep, 142,000; pigs, 230,000.

Total market value of agricultural products sold, 1989, $3,023m. The major cash grain is winter wheat (value, 1989, $585m.). Other crops include barley, oats, rye, grain, corn, soybeans, grain sorghum, cotton, peanuts and peaches. Value of cattle and calves produced, 1989, $1,379m.; catfish, $1m.; racehorses, $63m. Other livestock included hogs, sheep and goats. Livestock, 1 Jan. 1990: cattle, 5·3m.; sheep, 142,000; pigs, 230,000.

The Oklahoma Conservation Commission works with 91 conservation districts, universities, state and federal government agencies. The early work of the conservation districts, beginning in 1937, was limited to flood and erosion control: since 1970, they include urban areas also.

Irrigated production has increased in the Oklahoma 'panhandle'. The Ogalala aquifer is the primary source of irrigation water there and in western Oklahoma, a finite source because of its isolation from major sources of recharge. Declining groundwater levels necessitate the most effective irrigation practices.

Forestry. There are 8·5m. acres of forest, one half considered commercial. The forest products industry is concentrated in the 18 eastern counties. There are 3 forest regions: Ozark (oak, hickory); Ouachita highlands (pine, oak); Cross-Timbers (post oak, black jack oak). Southern pine is the chief commercial species, at almost 80% of saw-timber harvested annually. Replanting is essential.

INDUSTRY. Nominal output grew by an estimated 6·3% to $57,400m. in 1989. Manufacturing is the most important sector, representing about 14·7% of total output in 1988; mining, primarily oil and gas related, 8·6% in 1989.

Labour. Total labour force, May 1989, 1,513,600. Establishment employment, 1989, 1,139,000: Manufacturing, 164,000; construction (1988), 32,000; mining, 44,000. Average unemployment rate, 1989, 5·9%.

TOURISM. In 1989, 16,816,546 tourists visted the 72 state parks and 10 museums and monuments. Travellers spent almost $3,000m.

COMMUNICATIONS

Roads. In 1990 there were 111,669 miles of roads (99,578 miles rural) and 2,568,454 registered motor vehicles.

Railways. In 1989 Oklahoma had 4,278 miles of railway operated by 17 companies.

Civil Aviation. Airports, 1989, numbered 423, of which 131 were publicly owned. Four cities were served by commercial airlines.

Shipping. The McClellan-Kerr Arkansas Navigation System provides access from east central Oklahoma to New Orleans through the Verdigris, Arkansas and Mississippi rivers. In 1989, 51,052,303 tons were shipped inbound and outbound on 1,249 barges; 157,400 tons shipped internal. Total tonnage (1989) of traffic on the System, 8,357,435 tons; the Oklahoma segment of the System handled 4,032,732 tons. Commodities shipped, 1989 were mainly chemical fertilizer, farm produce, petroleum products, iron and steel, coal, sand and gravel.

Broadcasting. In 1990 there were 117 radio and 18 television broadcasting stations, and 16 cable-TV companies.

Newspapers. In 1990 there were 47 daily and 190 weekly newspapers.

JUSTICE, RELIGION, EDUCATION AND WELFARE

Justice. Penal institutions, 27 Sept. 1990, held 10,185 inmates (8,944 of them male). There were 15 penal institutions, 8 community treatment centres and 7 probation and parole centres.

The death penalty was suspended in 1966 and re-imposed in 1976. Since 1915 there have been 84 (53 whites, 27 Negroes, 4 other races) executions. Electrocution was replaced (1977) by lethal injection.

Religion. The chief religious bodies in 1980 were Baptists, 674,766; United Methodists, 248,635; Roman Catholics, 122,820; Churches of Christ, about 80,000; Assembly of God, 63,992; Disciples of Christ, 45,070; Presbyterian, 38,605; Lutheran, 33,664; Nazarene, 22,090; Episcopal, 21,500.

Education. In 1988–89 there were 605,771 pupils enrolled in grades Kindergarten–12. There were 40,052 teachers at elementary and secondary schools on average salaries of $23,521. Total expenditure on the 609 school districts, $1,661,743,679. In 1988–89 total expenditure for vocational-technical education was $107,459,457; there were 32,945 students enrolled.

Institutions of higher education with over 4,000 students:

Founded	Name	Place	1988–89 Enrolment
1891	Oklahoma State University	Stillwater, Okla. City, Okmulgee	34,588
1891	Central State University	Edmond	19,901
1892	University of Oklahoma	Norman, Okla. City, Tulsa	29,897
1894	University of Tulsa	Tulsa	5,128
1903	Southwestern Oklahoma State University	Weatherford	7,165
1909	East Central Oklahoma State University	Ada	5,808
1909	Northeastern Oklahoma State University	Tahlequah	11,335
1909	Southeastern Oklahoma State University	Durant	4,985
1909	Cameron University	Lawton	8,038
1909	Rogers State College	Claremore	5,379
1950	Oklahoma Christian University of Science and Arts	Oklahoma City	4,681
1968	Rose State College	Midwest City	15,196
1969	Tulsa Junior College	Tulsa	28,065
1970	Oklahoma City Community College	Oklahoma City	16,500

Total enrolment in Oklahoma State System of higher education, 1988–89, 112,680; total expenditure, $409,524,000.

Health. In 1989 there were 148 hospitals; 59 alcoholism treatment centres, 25 end state renal disease facilities, 80 home health agencies, 8 hospices, 58 independent laboratories, 19 ambulatory surgical centres, 10 HIV laboratories, 25 outpatient physical therapy/speech pathology facilities, 40 physical therapists in independent practice and 4 portable X–ray units.

Welfare. In 1988–89 the Oklahoma Department of Human Services provided for medical services, $690,516,055; assistance payments and services, $264,238,290; field services, $18,485,527; Oklahoma Medical Center, $164,172,790; children and youth services, $83,906,918; mentally retarded and developmental disability, $94,102,868; rehabilitation, $43,335,543; the ageing, $25,761,599; administration, $29,837,178; management information, $13,847,381; construction and special projects, $8,199,418.

In 1988–89, payments and benefits were: Grants and energy, $184,399,170; medical payments, $685,839,185; food stamps and commodities, $181,185,160; payroll and rent, $353,472,861; day care, $18,918,539. In 1990 there were 401,000 military veterans.

Further Reading

Directory of Oklahoma. Dept. of Libraries, Oklahoma City (irregular)
Chronicles of Oklahoma. Oklahoma Historical Society, Oklahoma City (from 1921, quarterly)
Oklahoma Business Directory. Omaha, 1989
Gibson, A. M., *The History of Oklahoma*. Rev. ed. Oklahoma Univ. Press, 1984
Morris, J. W. *et al.*, *Historical Atlas of Oklahoma*. 3rd ed. Oklahoma Univ. Press, 1986
Strain, J. W., *Outline of Oklahoma Government*. Rev. ed. Central State Univ., Edmond, 1983

State Library: Oklahoma Dept. of Libraries, 200 N.E. 18th Street, Oklahoma City 73105. *State Librarian and State Archivist:* Robert L. Clark, Jr.

OREGON

HISTORY. Oregon was first settled in 1811 by the Pacific Fur Co. at Astoria, a provisional government was formed on 5 July 1834; a Territorial government was organized, 14 Aug. 1848, and on 14 Feb. 1859 Oregon was admitted to the Union.

AREA AND POPULATION. Oregon is bounded north by Washington, with the Columbia River forming most of the boundary, east by Idaho, with the Snake River forming most of the boundary, south by Nevada and California and west by the Pacific. Area, 97,073 sq. miles, 889 sq. miles being inland water. The federal government owned (1985) 30,110,212 acres (48·88% of the state area). Census population, 1 April 1990, 2,842,321, an increase of 8% since 1980. In 1986 births numbered 38,850 (14·6 per 1,000 population); deaths, 23,328 (8·8); infant deaths 368 (9·5 per 1,000 live births); marriages, 22,015 (8·3), and divorces, 15,774 (5·9).

Population at 5 federal censuses was:

	White	Black	Indian	Asiatic	Total	Per sq. mile
1930	938,598	2,234	4,776	8,179	953,786	9·9
1960	1,732,037	18,133	8,026	9,120	1,768,687	18·4
1970	2,032,079	26,308	13,510	13,290	2,091,385	21·7
1980	2,490,610	37,060	27,314	34,775	2,633,105	27·3
1990	2,636,787	48,178	38,496	69,269	2,842,321	29·6

Of the total population in 1990, 1,397,073 were male. In 1980 1,788,354 persons were urban, and those 18 years and older numbered 1,910,048.

The US Bureau of Indian Affairs (area headquarters in Portland) administers (1988) 768,665·2 acres, of which 633,613·36 acres are held by the US in trust for Indian tribes, and 135,052·36 acres for individual Indians.

The largest towns, according to 1990 census figures, are: Portland, 437,319; Eugene, 112,669; Salem (the capital), 107,786; Beaverton, 55,310; Medford, 46,951; Corvallis, 44,757; Springfield, 44,683; Albany, 29,462. Metropolitan areas (1990): Portland, 577,571; Eugene-Springfield, 199,009; Salem, 162,887.

CLIMATE. Portland. Jan. 39°F (3·9°C), July 67°F (19·4°C). Annual rainfall 44" (1,100 mm). *See* Pacific Coast, p. 1397.

CONSTITUTION AND GOVERNMENT. The present constitution dates from 1859; some 250 items in it have been amended. The Legislative Assembly consists of a Senate of 30 members, elected for 4 years (half their number retiring every 2 years), and a House of 60 representatives, elected for 2 years. The Governor is elected for 4 years. The constitution reserves to the voters the rights of initiative and referendum and recall.

In the 1988 presidential election Bush polled 517,920 votes, Dukakis, 575,151.

The capital is Salem. There are 36 counties in the state.

Governor: Barbara Roberts (D.), 1991–95 ($80,000).
Secretary of State: Phil Keisling (D.) ($61,500).

BUDGET. Oregon has 2-year financial periods. Total resources for the biennium 1989-91 were $25,424,202,000 (federal funds, 1,980m.; taxes, $2,066m.); total expenditures, $14,360m. (education, $3,868m.; economic development and consumer services, $3,199·5m.; human resources, $3,563m.).

In 1989 the outstanding debt was $5,773m.

Per capita personal income (1989) was $15,785.

ENERGY AND NATURAL RESOURCES

Electricity. In 1989, 3 privately owned utilities, 11 municipally owned utilities, 19 co-operatives and 6 utility districts provided electricity in the state. The privately owned companies provided 77% of the electricity. Hydroelectricity plants (130 in 1988) have an installed capacity of 5·1m. kw., of which multipurpose federal projects like the Bonneville Power Administration accounted for 3,011 mw. and the Trojan Nuclear plant 1,104mw. Boardman coal-fired plant produced no energy in 1987.

Minerals. Oregon's mineral resources include gold, silver, nickel copper, lead, mercury, chromite, sand and gravel, stone, clays, lime, silica, diatomite, expansible shale, scoria, pumice and uranium. There is geothermal potential. Metallurgical plant produces $1,000m. worth (approximately) per annum.

Agriculture. Oregon, which has an area of 61,557,184 acres, is divided by the Cascade Range into two distinct zones as to climate. West of the Cascade Range there is a good rainfall and almost every variety of crop common to the temperate zone is grown; east of the Range stock-raising and wheat-growing are the principal industries and irrigation is needed for row crops and fruits. In 1987 38,490 were employed in farming.

There were, in 1990, 36,500 farms with an acreage of 17·8m.; average farm size was 488 acres; most are family-owned corporate farms. Average value per acre (1990), $602.

Cash receipts from crops in 1989 amounted to $2,289,888,000 and from livestock and livestock products, $739,070,000 of which cattle made most. Principal crops are hay (2·75m. tons), wheat (58·5m. bu.), potatoes, grass, seed, pears, onions, greenhouse and farmforest products.

Livestock, 1 Jan. 1989: Milch cows, 98,000; cattle and calves, 1·4m.; sheep and lambs, 455,000; swine, 90,000.

Forestry. About 28·2m. acres is forested, almost half of the state. Of this amount, 22·4m. is commercial forest land suitable for timber production; ownership is as follows (acres): US Forestry Service, 10·9m.; US Bureau of Land Management, 1·8m.; other federal, 175,000; State of Oregon, 774,000; other public (city, county), 110,000; private owners, 8·3m., of which the forest industry owns 5·6m., non-industrial private owners, 2·7m., Indians, 335,000. Oregon's commercial forest lands provided a 1989 harvest of 8,200m. bd ft of logs, as well as the benefits of recreation, water, grazing, wildlife and fish. Trees vary from the coastal forest of hemlock and spruce to the state's primary species, Douglas-fir, throughout much of western Oregon. In eastern Oregon, ponderosa pine, lodgepole pine and true firs are found. Here, forestry is often combined with livestock grazing to provide an economic operation. Along the Cascade summit and in the mountains of northeast Oregon, alpine species are found.

Forest production in 1988 was worth $11,313,810.

Fisheries. All food and shellfish landings in the calendar year 1989 amounted to a value of $84m. The most important are: shrimp, salmon, ground fish, crab, tuna.

INDUSTRY. Forest products manufacturing is Oregon's leading industry, and in 1988 employed 68,000. The second most important industry is high technology. Gross State product, 1987, $41,300m. Manufacturing employed 214,200 in 1988; trade, 292,400; services, 263,200; government, 211,200.

TOURISM. In 1989, the total income from tourism was estimated to be $2,054m.

COMMUNICATIONS

Roads. The state maintains (1988) 7,520 miles of primary and secondary highways, almost all surfaced; counties maintain 27,734 miles, and cities 7,316 miles; there were 52,450 miles in national parks and federal reservations. Registered motor vehicles, 31 Dec. 1988, totalled 2·6m.

Railways. The state had (1986) 5 common carrier railways with a total mileage of 2,700.

Aviation. In 1988 there were 3 public-use and 85 personal-use heliports; 225 personal-use airports; 107 public-use airports including 35 state-owned airports.

Shipping. Portland is a major seaport for large ocean-going vessels and is 101 miles inland from the mouth of the Columbia River. In 1988 the port handled 8·7m. short tons of cargo; main commodities for this and other Columbia River ports are grain and petroleum.

Post and Broadcasting. In Dec. 1988 there were 178 commercial radio stations and 23 educational radio stations. There were 17 commercial television stations and 6 educational television stations. There were also 5 campus limited radio stations and 1 subscription radio station.

Newspapers. In 1988 there were 22 daily newspapers with a circulation of more than 650,000 and 100 non-daily newspapers.

JUSTICE, RELIGION, EDUCATION AND WELFARE

Justice. There are 8 correctional institutions in Oregon. Total inmates, 1988, 4,197. The sterilization law, originally passed in 1917, was amended in 1967. The amendments changed the number of persons on the Board of Social Protection from 15 to 7 and provided that the Public Defender would automatically represent all persons examined. The basis on which a person would be subject to examination by the Board are: (a) if such person would be likely to procreate children having an inherited tendency to mental retardation or mental illness, or (b) if such person would be likely to procreate children who would become neglected or dependent because of the person's inability by reason of mental illness or mental retardation to provide adequate care.

Religion. The chief religious bodies are Catholic, Baptist, Lutheran, Methodists, Presbyterian and Mormon.

Education. School attendance is compulsory from 7 to 18 years of age if the twelfth year of school has not been completed; those between the ages of 16 and 18 years, if legally employed, may attend part-time or evening schools. Others may be excused under certain circumstances. In 1988–89 the public elementary and secondary schools had 483,960 students. Total expenditure on elementary and secondary education (1988-89) was $1,830,677,679; teachers' average salary (1989), $29,500.

Leading state-supported institutions of higher education (autumn 1989) included:

	Students
University of Oregon, Eugene	18,567
Oregon Health Sciences University:	1,317
Oregon State University, Corvallis	16,230
Portland State University, Portland	16,750
Western Oregon State College, Monmouth	3,856
Southern Oregon State College, Ashland	5,196
Eastern Oregon State College, La Grande	2,008
Oregon Institute of Technology, Klamath Falls	3,147

Total enrolment in state colleges and universities, 1989, 67,071. Largest of the privately endowed universities are Lewis and Clark College, Portland, with (1989) 3,418 students; University of Portland, 2,417 students; Willamette University, Salem, 2,225 students; Reed College, Portland, 1,348 students, and Linfield College, McMinnville, 2,164 students. In 1989 there were 75,395 students (full-time equivalent) in community colleges.

Health. In 1988 there were 78 licensed hospitals; there were 2 state hospitals for mentally ill (937 patients), 1 for the mentally retarded (1,200) and 1 with both programmes (150).

Social Security. The State Adult and Family Services Division provides cash payments, medical care, food stamps, day care and help in finding jobs. In 1990 there were 85,947 people on low incomes, many of them children in single-parent families, benefiting from the Aid to Families with Dependent Children Programme; 213,733 people received food stamps.

There is also a Children's Services Division.

A system of unemployment benefit payments, financed by employers, with administrative allotments made through a federal agency, started 2 Jan. 1938.

Further Reading

Oregon Blue Book. Issued by the Secretary of State. Salem. Biennial
Federal Writers' Project. *Oregon: End of the Trail.* Rev. ed. Portland, 1972
Baldwin, E. M., *Geology of Oregon.* Rev. ed. Dubuque, Iowa, 1976
Carey, C. H., *General History of Oregon, prior to 1861.* 2 vol. (1 vol. reprint, 1971) Portland, 1935
Corning, H. M. (ed.), *Dictionary of Oregon History.* New York, 1956
Dicken, S. N., *Oregon Geography.* 5th ed. Eugene, 1973.—with Dicken, E. F., *Making of Oregon: a Study in Historical Geography.* Portland, 1979.—with Dicken, E. F., *Oregon Divided: A Regional Geography.* Portland, 1982
Dodds, G. B., *Oregon: A Bicentennial History.* New York, 1977
Friedman, R., *Oregon for the Curious.* 3rd ed. Portland, 1972
Highsmith, R. M. Jr. (ed.), *Atlas of the Pacific Northwest.* Corvallis, 1973
McArthur, L. A., *Oregon Geographic Names.* 4th ed., rev. and enlarged. Portland, 1974
Patton, Clyde P., *Atlas of Oregon.* Univ. Oregon Press, Eugene, 1976

State Library: The Oregon State Library, Salem. *Librarian:* Wesley Doak.

PENNSYLVANIA

HISTORY. Pennsylvania, first settled in 1682, is one of the 13 original states in the Union.

AREA AND POPULATION. Pennsylvania is bounded north by New York, east by New Jersey, south by Delaware and Maryland, south-west by West Virginia, west by Ohio and north-west by Lake Erie. Area, 45,308 sq. miles, of which 420 sq. miles are inland water. Census population, 1 April 1990, 11,881,643, an increase of 0·13% since 1980. Births, 1988, 165,169; deaths, 125,337; infant deaths, 1,615; marriages, 87,963; reported divorces, 39,001.

Population at 5 census years was:

	White	Black	Indian	All others	Total	Per sq. mile
1910	7,467,713	193,919	1,503	1,976	7,665,111	171·0
1930	9,196,007	431,257	523	3,563	9,631,350	213·8
1960	10,454,004	852,750	2,122	10,490	11,319,366	251·5
				All others		
1970	10,745,219	1,015,884		39,663	11,800,766	262·9
1980	10,652,320	1,046,810		164,765	11,863,895	264·3

Of the total population in 1980, 47·9% were male, 69·3% were urban and 68·1% were 21 years of age or older.

The population of the larger cities and townships, 1980 census, was:

Philadelphia	1,688,210	Scranton	88,117	Lancaster	54,725
Pittsburgh	423,938	Reading	78,686	Harrisburg	53,264
Erie	119,123	Bethlehem	70,419	Wilkes-Barre	51,551
Allentown	103,758	Altoona	57,078	York	44,619

Larger urbanized areas, 1980 census: Philadelphia (in Pennsylvania), 3,682,709;

Pittsburgh, 2,263,894; Northeast, 640,396, Allentown–Bethlehem–Easton (in Pennsylvania), 551,052; Harrisburg, 446,576.

CLIMATE. Philadelphia. Jan. 32°F (0°C), July 77°F (25°C). Annual rainfall 40" (1,006 mm). Pittsburgh. Jan. 31°F (–0·6°C), July 74°F (23·3°C). Annual rainfall 37" (914 mm). *See* Appalachian Mountains, p. 1398.

CONSTITUTION AND GOVERNMENT. The present constitution dates from 1968. The General Assembly consists of a Senate of 50 members chosen for 4 years, one-half being elected biennially, and a House of Representatives of 203 members chosen for 2 years. The Governor and Lieut.-Governor are elected for 4 years. Every citizen 18 years of age, with the usual residential qualifications, may vote. Registered voters in May 1990, 5,705,079.

In the 1988 presidential election Bush polled 2,291,297 votes, Dukakis, 2,183,928.

The state capital is Harrisburg. The state is organized in counties (numbering 67), cities, boroughs, townships and school districts.

Governor: Robert P. Casey (D.), 1991–95 ($105,000).
Lieut.-Governor: Mark S. Singel (D.), ($83,000).
Secretary of the Commonwealth: Christopher Lewis (D.), ($72,000).

BUDGET. Total revenues for 1990-91 were $11,961m.; general fund expenditure, $11,924·9; transport, $1,549·6m.; public welfare, $3,216·3m.).

In 1989-90 outstanding long-term debt (excluding highway bonds) amounted to $3,013m.

Per capita personal income (1989) was $16,233.

ENERGY AND NATURAL RESOURCES

Minerals. Pennsylvania is almost the sole producer of anthracite coal. Production (1989): Anthracite, 3,375,315 tons, with 2,443 employees; bituminous coal, 68,305,235 tons, with 13,644 employees; crude petroleum, 2,601,982 bbls; natural gas, 191,774m. cu. ft.

Agriculture. Agriculture, market-gardening, fruit-growing, horticulture and forestry are pursued within the state. In 1988 there were 55,000 farms with a total farm area of 8·3m. acres (4·5m. acres in crops). Cash income, 1989, from crops, $954·7m., and from livestock and products, $2,358m.

Pennsylvania ranks first in the production of mushrooms (284·8m. lb., value $205·1m. in 1987). Other crops are (1988) tobacco (18·2m. lb., $20·5m.), wheat (1988, 9m. bu.), oats (1988, 13m. bu.), maize, barley and potatoes. On 1 Jan. 1989 there were on farms: 1·92m. cattle and calves, including 717,000 milch cows, 134,000 sheep, 970,000 swine. Milk production, 1988, was 10,204m. lb., and eggs (1988) numbered 5,300m. valued at $185·69m. Pennsylvania is also a major fruit producing state; in 1988 apples totalled 520m. lb.; peaches, 80m. lb.; tart cherries, 9m. lb.; sweet cherries, 1,200 tons; and grapes, 58,000 tons. Other important items are soybeans (7·2m. bu.), vegetables for processing (50,000 tons), fresh vegetables (1·5m. cwt) and broiler-chickens (120·6m.).

Forestry. In 1990 state forest land and state park land totalled 1,976,435 acres as of 3 Jan.; state game lands, 1,333,580·6 acres as of 31 Aug.

INDUSTRY. Pennsylvania is third in national production of iron and steel. Output of steel, 1989, 11,869,968 net tons.

In 1989, manufacturing employed 1,050,286 workers; services, 1,277,983; trade, 1,188,857; government, 668,249.

COMMUNICATIONS

Roads. Highways and roads in the state (federal, local and state combined) totalled (1989) 116,277·62 miles. Registered motor vehicles for 1989 numbered 8,605,747.

Railways. In 1990, 57 railways operated within the state with a line mileage of about 5,500.

Aviation. There were (30 June 1990) 146 public airports, 291 private and 10 public heliports, 339 airports for personal use and 5 seaplane bases.

Shipping. Trade at the ports of Philadelphia (1989): Imports 60,651,352 short tons of bulk cargo and 5,581,840 of general cargo; exports, 3,182,266 of bulk cargo and 2,342,100 of general cargo.

Post and Broadcasting. Broadcasting stations comprised (1989) 50 television stations and 357 radio stations.

Newspapers. There were (1989) 97 daily and 303 weekly newspapers.

JUSTICE, RELIGION, EDUCATION AND WELFARE

Justice. No executions took place in 1963–89; since 1930 there have been 149 executions (electrocution), all for murder.

State prison population, on 30 July 1990, was 20,819.

Religion. The chief religious bodies in 1977 were the Roman Catholic, with 3,717,667 members; Protestant, 3,150,920 (1971); and Jewish, 469,078. The 5 largest Protestant denominations (by communicants) were: Lutheran Church in America, 766,276; United Methodist, 728,915 (1971), United Presbyterian Church in the USA, 573,905 (1971); United Church of Christ, 257,138; Episcopal, 193,399 (1971).

Education. School attendance is compulsory for children 8–17 years of age. In 1989–90 the public kindergartens and elementary schools had 911,302 pupils (Grades K-6); public secondary schools had 743,969 pupils. Non-public schools had 215,903 elementary pupils (Grades K-6) and 125,326 secondary pupils (Grades 7-12. Average salary, public school professional personnel, men \$37,186; women \$32,682; for classroom teachers, men \$35,161, women \$32,251.

Leading senior academic institutions included:

Founded	Institutions	Faculty (Autumn 1989)	Students (Autumn 1989)
1740	University of Pennsylvania (non-sect.)	1,007	22,016
1787	University of Pittsburgh	1,326	28,362
1832	Lafayette College, Easton (Presbyterian)	159	2,303
1833	Haverford College	83	1,159
1842	Villanova University (R.C.)	534	11,388
1846	Bucknell University (Baptist)	226	3,423
1851	St Joseph's University, Philadelphia (R.C.)	164	6,170
1852	California University of Pennsylvania	317	6,748
1855	Pennsylvania State University	1,704	37,718
1855	Millersville University of Pennsylvania	333	7,791
1863	LaSalle University, Philadelphia (R.C.)	208	6,478
1864	Swarthmore College	151	1,304
1866	Lehigh University, Bethlehem (non-sect.)	393	6,610
1871	West Chester University of Pennsylvania	465	11,815
1875	Indiana University of Pennsylvania	660	13,861
1878	Duquesne University, Pittsburgh (R.C.)	280	6,901
1884	Temple University, Philadelphia	1,194	32,713
1885	Bryn Mawr College	136	1,839
1888	University of Scranton (R.C.)	231	5,111
1891	Drexel University, Philadelphia	448	11,959
1900	Carnegie-Mellon University, Pittsburgh	489	7,090

Health. In 1989 the state had 300 hospitals (68,414 beds) listed by the State Health Department, excluding federal hospitals and mental institutions.

Social Security. During the year ending 30 June 1990 the monthly average number of cases receiving public assistance was: Aid to families with dependent children, 175,737; blind pension, 2,415; general assistance, 129,747.

Payments for medical assistance for 1989–90 totalled \$2,579,729,762. Under the medical assistance programme payments are made for inpatient hospital care

($832,075,756); private nursing home care ($542,439,081); public long term care ($275,022,045); other medical care ($930,192,880).

Further Reading

Crop and Livestock Summary. Pennsylvania Dept. of Agriculture. Annual
Encyclopaedia of Pennsylvania, New York, 1984
Pennsylvania Manual. General Services, Bureau of Publications, Harrisburg. Biennial
Pennsylvania State Industrial Directory. Harris, Ohio. Annual
Cochran, T. C., *Pennsylvania,* New York, 1978
Klein, P. S. and Hoogenboom, A., *A History of Pennsylvania.* New York, 1973
League of Women Voters of Pennsylvania, *Key to the Keystone State.* Philadelphia, 1972
Majumdar, S. K. and Miller, E. W., *Pennsylvania Coal: Resources, Technology and Utilisation.* Pennsylvania Science, 1983
Pennsylvania Chamber of Commerce, *Pennsylvania Government Today.* State College, Pa., 1973
Weigley, R. F., (ed.) *Philadelphia: A 300-year History.* New York, 1984
Wilkinson, N. B., *Bibliography of Pennsylvania History.* Pa. Historical & Museum Commission. Harrisburg, 1957

RHODE ISLAND

HISTORY The earliest settlers in the region which now forms the state of Rhode Island were colonists from Massachusetts who had been driven forth on account of their non-acceptance of the prevailing religious beliefs. The first of the settlements was made in 1636, settlers of every creed being welcomed. In 1647 a patent was executed for the government of the settlements, and on 8 July 1663 a charter was executed recognizing the settlers as forming a body corporate and politic by the name of the 'English Colony of Rhode Island and Providence Plantations, in New England, in America'. On 29 May 1790 the state accepted the federal constitution and entered the Union as the last of the 13 original states.

AREA AND POPULATION. Rhode Island is bounded north and east by Massachusetts, south by the Atlantic and west by Connecticut. Area, 1,214 sq. miles, of which 165 sq. miles are inland water. Census population, 1 April 1990, 1,003,464 a decrease of 5·95% since 1980.

Births, 1986, were 13,324; deaths (excluding foetal deaths), 9,587; infant deaths, 125; marriages, 8,103; divorces, 3,683.

Population of 5 census years was:

	White	Black	Indian	Asiatic	Total	Per sq. mile
1910	532,492	9,529	284	305	542,610	508·5
1930	677,026	9,913	318	240	687,497	649·3
1960	838,712	18,332	932	1,190	859,488	812·4
			All others			
1980	896,692	27,584	22,878		947,154	903·0
1990	917,375	38,861	4,071	18,325	1,003,164	960·3

Of the total population in 1990, 481,496 were male, 777,474 were 18 years of age or older and 45,752 were of Hispanic origin. 824,004 were urban in 1980.

The chief cities and their population (census, 1980) are Providence, 156,804 (160,728 at the 1990 census); Warwick, 87,123; Cranston, 71,992; Pawtucket, 71,204; East Providence, 50,980; Woonsocket, 45,914; Newport, 29,259; North Providence (town), 29,188; Cumberland (town), 27,069. The Providence–Pawtucket–Warwick Standard Metropolitan Statistical Area had a population of 919,216 in 1980.

CLIMATE. Providence. Jan. 28°F (−2·2°C), July 72°F (22·2°C). Annual rainfall 43" (1,079 mm). *See* New England, p. 1398.

CONSTITUTION AND GOVERNMENT. The present constitution dates from 1843; it has had 42 amendments. The General Assembly consists of a Senate of 50 members and a House of Representatives of 100 members, both elected for 2 years, as are also the Governor and Lieut.-Governor. Every citizen, 18 years of age, who has resided in the state for 30 days, and is duly registered, is qualified to vote.

At the 1988 presidential election Dukakis polled 216,668 votes, Bush, 169,730.

The capital is Providence. The state has 5 counties but no county governments. There are 39 municipalities, each having its own form of local government.

Governor: Bruce Sundlun (D.), 1991–93 ($69,900).
Leiut.-Governor: Roger N. Begin (D.), ($52,000).
Secretary of State: Kathleen S. Connell (D.), ($52,000).

BUDGET. For the fiscal year 1990 total revenues were $2,484·4m. (taxation, $1,233·3m., and federal aid, $667·2m.); general expenditures were $2,657·7m. (education, $781·9m.; and public welfare, $547·3m.)

Total net long-term debt on 30 June 1986 was $261·8m.

Per capita personal income (1990) was $18,841.

NATURAL RESOURCES

Minerals. The small mineral output, mostly stone, sand and gravel, was valued (1990) at an estimated $12·7m.

Agriculture. Agriculture contributed $141m. to the general cash income in 1990; it had 580 farms with an area of 19,625 acres. 60% of production value was in nursery and turf products.

Fisheries. In 1990 the catch was 13·2m. lb (mainly lobster and quahang) valued at $72·9m.

INDUSTRY. Manufacturing is the chief source of income and the largest employer. Total non-agricultural employment in 1989 was 459,100, of which 112,300 were manufacturing (99,500 in 1990). Average weekly earnings for production workers in 1989 was $359.99. Principal industries are jewellery and silverware, electrical machinery, electronics, plastics, metal products, instruments, chemicals and boatbuilding.

COMMUNICATIONS

Roads. In 1990 there were 5,884 miles of roads (1,484 miles rural) and 670,576 registered motor vehicles.

Civil Aviation. In 1988 there were 6 state-owned airports. Theodore Francis Green airport at Warwick, near Providence, is served by 8 airlines, and handled over 2m. passengers and 20m. lb. of freight in 1988.

Shipping. Waterborne freight through the port of Providence (1988) totalled 10·6m. tons.

Broadcasting. There are 24 radio stations and 5 television stations; there are 8 cable television companies.

JUSTICE, RELIGION, EDUCATION AND WELFARE

Justice. The state's penal institutions, Aug. 1988, had 1,290 inmates (131 per 100,000 population).

The death penalty is illegal, except that it is mandatory in the case of murder committed by a prisoner serving a life sentence.

Religion. Chief religious bodies are (estimated figures Sept. 1988): Roman Catholic with 550,000 members; Protestant Episcopal (baptized persons), 50,000; Baptist, 22,500; Congregational, 12,000; Methodist, 10,000; Jewish, 24,000.

Education. In 1987–88 the 240 public elementary schools had 3,702 teachers and total enrolment of 60,582 pupils; about 25,000 pupils were enrolled in private and parochial schools. The 58 senior and vocational high schools had 3,678 teachers and 59,011 pupils. Teachers' salaries (1987) averaged $23,400. Local expenditure, for schools (including evening schools) in 1987–88 totalled $580·6m.

There are 11 institutions of higher learning (3 public and 8 private). The state maintains Rhode Island College, at Providence, with 600 faculty members, and 5,600 full-time students (1987), and the University of Rhode Island, at South Kingstown, with over 900 faculty members and over 14,000 students (including graduate students). Brown University, at Providence, founded in 1764, is now non-sectarian; in 1987 it had over 600 full-time faculty members and 7,000 full-time students. Providence College, at Providence, founded in 1917 by the Order of Preachers (Dominican), had (1987) 210 professors and 5,400 students. The largest of the other colleges are Bryant College, at Smithfield, with 160 faculty and 5,000 students, and the Rhode Island School of Design, in Providence, with about 155 faculty and 1,800 students.

Health. In 1990 the state had 14 general and 7 psychiatric hospitals (with about 5,600 beds).

Social Security. In 1987 aid to dependent children was granted to 44,000 children in 15,000 families at an average payment per family of $380 per month, and the state also had a general assistance programme. (All other aid programmes were taken over by the federal government.)

Further Reading

Rhode Island Manual. Prepared by the Secretary of State. Providence
Providence Journal Almanac: A Reference Book for Rhode Islanders. Providence. Annual
Rhode Island Basic Economic Statistics. Rhode Island Dept. of Economic Development. Providence, 1987
McLoughlin, W. G., *Rhode Island: a History.* Norton, 1978
Wright, M. I. and Sullivan, R. J., *Rhode Island Atlas.* Rhode Island Pubs., 1983

State Library: Rhode Island State Library, State House, Providence 02908. State Librarian: Elliott E. Andrews.

SOUTH CAROLINA

HISTORY. South Carolina, first settled permanently in 1670, was one of the 13 original states of the Union.

AREA AND POPULATION. South Carolina is bounded in the north by North Carolina, east and south-east by the Atlantic, south-west and west by Georgia. Area, 31,113 sq. miles, of which 909 sq. miles are inland water. Census population, 1 April 1990, 3,486,703, an increase of 11·73% since 1980. Births, 1990, were 58,461 (16·7 per 1,000 population); deaths, 29,621 (8·5); marriages, 55,754 (15·9); divorces and annulments, 16,182 (4·6); infant deaths, 679 (12·6 per 1,000 live births).

The population in 5 census years was:

	White	Black	Indian	Asiatic	Total	Per sq. mile
1910	679,161	835,843	331	65	1,515,400	49·7
1930	944,049	793,681	959	76	1,738,765	56·8
			All others			
1970	1,794,432	789,040	3,588		2,587,060	83·2
1980	2,150,507	948,623	22,703		3,121,833	100·3
1990	2,406,974	1,039,884	39,845		3,486,703	115·8

Of the total population in 1980, 49% were male, 54·1% were urban and 55% were 25 years old or older. Median age, 28.

Populations of large towns in 1990 (with those of associated metropolitan areas): Columbia (capital), 98,052 (453,331); Charleston, 80,414 (506,875); Greenville, 58,282; Spartanburg, 43,467 (Greenville–Spartanburg, 546,967).

CLIMATE. Columbia. Jan. 47°F (8·3°C), July 81°F (27·2°C). Annual rainfall 43" (1,125 mm). *See* Atlantic Coast, p. 1398.

CONSTITUTION AND GOVERNMENT. The present constitution dates from 1895, when it went into force without ratification by the electorate. The General Assembly consists of a Senate of 46 members, elected for 4 years, and a House of Representatives of 124 members, elected for 2 years. It meets annually. The Governor and Lieut.-Governor are elected for 4 years.

At the 1988 presidential election Bush polled 599,871 votes, Dukakis 367,511.

The capital is Columbia. There are 46 counties.

Governor: Carroll Campbell (R.), 1991–95 ($98,000).
Lieut.-Governor: Nick Theodore (D.), ($43,000).
Secretary of State: Jim Miles (R.), ($85,000).

BUDGET. For the fiscal year ending 30 June 1991 general revenues were $3,305m.; general expenditures were $3,451m.

Per capita personal income (1989) was $12,934.

NATURAL RESOURCES

Minerals. Non-metallic minerals are of chief importance: Value of mineral output in 1989 was $300·8m., chiefly from limestone for cement, clay, stone, sand and gravel. Production of kaolin, vermiculite, scrap mica and fuller's earth is also important.

Agriculture. In 1990 there were 24,500 farms covering a farm area of 5·2m. acres. The average farm was of 212 acres. Of the 20,517 farms of the 1987 Census of Agriculture, there were 936 of 1,000 acres or more, average farm 232 acres; owners operated 12,624 farms; tenants 1,460. There were 1,905 farms with $100,000 or more in value of sales.

Cash receipts from farm marketing in 1988 amounted to $620·7m. for crops and $488·1m. for livestock, including poultry. Chief crops are tobacco ($158·9m.), soybeans ($125·5m.), and corn ($42m.). Production, 1988: Cotton, 140,000 bales; peaches, 290m. lb.; soybeans, 18·2m. bu.; tobacco, 100m. lb.; eggs, 1,432,000m. Livestock on farms, 1989: 621,000 all cattle, 450,000 swine.

Forestry. The forest industry is important; total forest land (1987), 12·3m. acres. National forests amounted to 606,000 acres.

INDUSTRY. A monthly average of 382,800 workers were employed in manufacturing in 1990. Major sectors are textiles (25·9%), apparel (10·5%) and chemicals (10·4%).

Tourism is important; tourists spent an estimated $4,623m. in 1987, and tourism employed 97,223.

COMMUNICATIONS

Roads. Total highway mileage in the combined highway system in June 1991 was 41,289 miles. Motor vehicle registrations numbered 2·6m. in 1990.

Railways. In 1989 the length of railway in the state was about 2,600 miles.

Civil Aviation. In 1989 there were 161 aircraft facilities (74 public) including 139 airports, 22 heliports and 1 seaplane base. Registered general aviation numbered 2,085 in 1989.

Shipping. The state has 3 deep-water ports.

JUSTICE, RELIGION, EDUCATION AND WELFARE

Justice. At 31 Dec. 1990 penal institutions held 17,752 prisoners under State and federal jurisdiction.

Education. In 1989–90 the total public-school enrolment (K-12) was 613,207; there were 364,296 white pupils and 248,911 non-white pupils. The total number of teachers was 35,907; average salary was $25,498.

For higher education the state operates the University of South Carolina, founded at Columbia in 1801, with (autumn 1990), 25,613 enrolled students; Clemson University, founded in 1889, with 16,303 students; The Citadel, at Charleston, with 3,800 students; Winthrop College, Rock Hill, with 5,104 students; Medical University of S. Carolina, at Charleston 2,219 students; S. Carolina State College, at Orangeburg, with 4,948 students, and Francis Marion College, at Florence, with 3,926 students; the College of Charleston has 7,726 students and Lander College, Greenwood, 2,642. There are 16 technical institutions (45,509).

There are also 479 private kindergartens, elementary and high schools with total enrolment (1988–89) of 44,705 pupils, and 31 private and denominational colleges and junior colleges with (autumn 1989) enrolment of 26,130 students.

Health. In 1991 the state had 402 non-federal health facilities with 34,432 beds licensed by the South Carolina Department of Health and Environmental Control.

Social Security. In 1990 there were 533,400 recipients of social security benefits. The average monthly expenditure in benefits was $269m.

Further Reading

South Carolina Legislative Manual. Columbia. Annual
South Carolina Statistical Abstract. South Carolina Budget and Control Board, Columbia. Annual

Jones, L., *South Carolina: A Synoptic History for Laymen.* Lexington, 1978

State Library: South Carolina State Library, Columbia.

SOUTH DAKOTA

HISTORY. South Dakota was first visited by Europeans in 1743 when Verendrye planted a lead plate (discovered in 1913) on the site of Fort Pierre, claiming the region for the French crown. Beginning with a trading post in 1794, it was settled from 1857 to 1861 when Dakota Territory was organized. It was admitted into the Union on 2 Nov. 1889.

AREA AND POPULATION. South Dakota is bounded north by North Dakota, east by Minnesota, south-east by the Big Sioux River (forming the boundary with Iowa), south by Nebraska (with the Missouri River forming part of the boundary) and west by Wyoming and Montana. Area, 77,116 sq. miles, of which 1,164 sq. miles are water. Area administered by the Bureau of Indian Affairs, 1985, covered 5m. acres (10% of the state), of which 2·6m. acres were held by tribes. The federal government, 1987, owned or managed 954,000 acres.

Census population, 1 April 1990, 696,004, an increase of 2·4% since 1980. In 1988: Births, 11,185; deaths, 6,567; infant deaths, 112; marriages, 7,328; divorces, 2,649.

Population in 5 federal censuses was:

	White	Black	American Indian	Asiatic	Total	Per sq. mile
1910	563,771	817	19,137	163	583,888	7·6
1930	669,453	646	21,833	101	692,849	9·0
1960	653,098	1,114	25,794	336	680,514	8·9
			All others			
1980	638,955	2,144	49,079		690,178	9·0
				Asian/ other		
1990	637,515	3,258	50,575	4,656	696,004	9·2

Of the total population in 1990, 497,942 were 18 years of age and over and 5,252 were of Hispanic origin.

Of the total population in 1980, 340,370 were male and 320,223 were urban.

Population of the chief cities (census of 1990) was: Sioux Falls, 100,814; Rapid City, 54,523; Aberdeen, 24,927; Watertown, 17,592; Mitchell, 13,798; Brookings, 16,270; Pierre, 12,906; Yankton, 12,703; Huron, 12,448; Vermillion, 10,034; Spearfish, 6,996; Madison, 6,257; Sturgis, 5,330; Belle Fourche, 4,335; Hot Springs, 4,325.

CLIMATE. Rapid City. Jan. 25°F (–3·9°C), July 73°F (22·8°C). Annual rainfall 19" (474 mm). Sioux Falls. Jan. 14°F (–10°C), July 73°F (22·8°C). Annual rainfall 25" (625 mm). *See* High Plains, p. 1398.

CONSTITUTION AND GOVERNMENT. Voters are all citizens 18 years of age or older. The people reserve the right of the initiative and referendum. The Senate has 35 members, and the House of Representatives 70 members, all elected for 2 years; the Governor and Lieut.-Governor are elected for 4 years.

In the 1988 presidential election Bush polled 165,516 votes, Dukakis, 145,632.

The capital is Pierre. The state is divided into 66 organized counties.

Governor: George S. Mickelson, (R.), 1991–95 ($60,816).
Lieut.-Governor: Walter Miller, (R.), ($52,915).
Secretary of State: Joyce Hazeltine, (R.), ($41,308).

BUDGET. For the fiscal year ending 30 June 1992 the estimated general fund revenues were $475,581,232 ($258,963,000 from sales and use tax); expenditure was also $495,860,290 ($158,874,639 on state aid to education and local government).

Per capita personal income (1989) was $12,755.

NATURAL RESOURCES

Minerals. In 1990 the mineral products include gold, 449,514 troy oz. (second largest yield of all states), silver 84,398 troy oz.). Mineral products, 1990, were valued at $285,719, including gold and silver.

Agriculture. In 1990 there were 35,000 farms, average size 1,266 acres. Farm units are large; in 1982 there were only 4,024 farms of 50 acres or less, compared with 10,165 exceeding 1,000 acres. 17,371 farms sold produce valued at $40,000 or over in 1985.

South Dakota is a major producer of rye (1·9m. bu. in 1990), sunflower seed (399·8m. bu.), flaxseed (5m. bu.), and oats (53·2m. bu.). The other important crops are all wheat (128·0m. bu.), sorghum for grain (14·3m. bu.) and corn for grain (234·0m. bu.). The farm livestock on 1 Jan. 1990 included 3·4m. cattle, 0·64m. sheep, 1·7m. hogs.

Forestry. National forest area, 1988, 1,997,000 acres.

INDUSTRY. In 1988, manufacturing establishments had 29,408 workers. Food processing had 92 plants employing 6,901 workers. Construction had 1,578 companies employing 7,711. There were 191 printing and publishing plants employing 2,739 workers. Also significant were mining (61 establishments employing 2,187), dairy, lumber and wood products, machinery, transport equipment, electronics, stone, glass and clay products.

COMMUNICATIONS

Roads. In 1991 there were 83,238 miles of roads (in 1990, 71,622 miles rural) and 851,025 registered motor vehicles.

Railways. In 1990, (miles of track): 1,946·8; state-owned, 810·8 of which 629·9 was in operation there were 2,005 miles of railway in operation. The state owns 969 miles of track.

Civil Aviation. In 1990 there were 74 general aviation airports and 9 commercial airports.

JUSTICE, RELIGION, EDUCATION AND WELFARE

Justice. The State prisons had, in 1988, 1,020 inmates under state and federal correction. The death penalty was illegal from 1915 to 1938; since 1938, one person has been executed, in 1949 (by electrocution), for murder.

Religion. The chief religious bodies are: Lutherans, Roman Catholics, Methodist, Disciples of Christ, Presbyterian, Baptist and Episcopal.

Education. Elementary and secondary education are free from 6 to 21 years of age. Between the ages of 8 and 16, attendance is compulsory. In 1988–89 133,793 pupils were attending elementary and high (including parochial) schools (8,235 full-time equivalent classroom teachers).

Teachers' salaries (1988–89) averaged an estimated $20,522. Total expenditure on public schools, $494,563,007.

Higher education (spring 1991): The School of Mines at Rapid City, established 1885, had 2,169 students; the State University at Brookings, 7,209 students; the University of South Dakota, founded at Vermillion in 1882, 6,429; Northern State University, Aberdeen, had 2,534; Black Hills State University at Spearfish, 2,482; Dakota State University at Madison, 1,009. The 12 private colleges including 3 on Indian reservations had 8,316 students. The federal Government maintains Indian schools on its reservations and 1 outside of a reservation at Flandreau.

Health. In 1989 there were 53 licensed hospitals (3,501 beds).

Social Security. In financial year 1990–91, 4,581 disabled persons received a total average monthly benefit of $80,821; 1,749 blind persons received $1,578. Aid to dependent children was $1,790,490, to 13,295 children.

Further Reading

Governor's Budget Report. South Dakota Bureau of Finance and Management. Annual
South Dakota Historical Collections. 1902–82
South Dakota Legislative Manual. Secretary of State, Pierre, S.D. Biennial
Berg, F. M., *South Dakota: Land of Shining Gold.* Hettinger, 1982
Karolevitz, R. F., *Challenge: the South Dakota Story.* Sioux Falls, 1975
Milton, John R., *South Dakota; a Bicentennial History.* New York, W. W. Norton, 1977
Schell, H. S., *History of South Dakota.* 3rd ed. Lincoln, Neb., 1975
Vexler, R. I., *South Dakota Chronology and Factbook.* New York, 1978

State Library: South Dakota State Library, 800 Governor's Drive, Pierre, S.D., 57501–2294.
State Librarian: Dr Jane Kolbe.

TENNESSEE

HISTORY. Tennessee, first settled in 1757, was admitted into the Union on 1 June 1796.

AREA AND POPULATION. Tennessee is bounded north by Kentucky and Virginia, east by North Carolina, south by Georgia, Alabama and Mississippi and west by the Mississippi River (forming the boundary with Arkansas and Missouri). Area, 42,144 sq. miles (989 sq. miles water). Census population, 1 April 1990, 4,877,185, an increase of 6·2% since 1980. Vital statistics, 1988: Births, 70,685 (14·3 per 1,000 population); deaths, 45,728 (9·2); infant deaths 762 (10·8 per 1,000 live births); marriages, 65,329 (26·4); divorces, 31,287 (12·6).

Population in 5 census years was:

	White	Black	Indian	Asiatic	Total	Per sq. mile
1910	1,711,432	473,088	216	53	2,184,789	52·4
1930	2,138,644	477,646	161	105	2,616,556	62·4
			All others			
1970	3,293,930	621,261	8,496		3,923,687	95·3
1980	3,835,452	725,942	29,726		4,591,120	111·6
1990	4,048,068	778,035	51,082		4,877,180	115·7

Of the population in 1980, 2,216,600 were male, 2,773,573 were urban and those 21 years of age or older numbered 3,026,398.

The cities, with population, 1990, are Memphis, 610,337; Nashville (capital), 487,973; Knoxville, 165,121; Chattanooga, 152,466; Clarksville, 75,494; Jackson, 48,949; Johnson City, 49,381; Murfreesboro, 44,922; Kingsport, 36,365; Oak Ridge, 27,310. Standard metropolitan areas 1990 (1988): Memphis, 981,747 (971,930); Nashville, 985,026 (971,800); Knoxville, 604,816 (599,600); Chattanooga, 433,204 (438,100); Johnson City–Bristol–Kingsport, 436,037 (442,300); Clarksville, 169,439 (158,900); Jackson, 77,982 (78,200).

CLIMATE. Memphis. Jan. 41°F (5°C), July 82°F (27·8°C). Annual rainfall 49" (1,221 mm). Nashville. Jan. 39°F (3·9°C), July 79°F (26·1°C). Annual rainfall 48" (1,196 mm). *See* Appalachian Mountains, p. 1398.

CONSTITUTION AND GOVERNMENT. The state has operated under 3 constitutions, the last of which was adopted in 1870 and has been since amended 22 times (first in 1953). Voters at an election may authorize the calling of a convention limited to altering or abolishing one or more specified sections of the constitution. The General Assembly consists of a Senate of 33 members and a House of Representatives of 99 members, senators elected for 4 years and representatives for 2 years. Qualified as electors are all citizens (usual residential and age (18) qualifications). Tennessee sends to Congress 2 senators and 9 representatives.

In the 1988 presidential election Bush polled 939,434 votes, Dukakis, 677,715.

For the Tennessee Valley Authority *see* p. 1424.

The capital is Nashville. The state is divided into 95 counties.

Governor: Ned McWherter (D.), 1991–95 ($85,000).
Lieut.-Governor: John Wilder (D.), ($12,500).
Secretary of State: Bryant Millsaps (D.), ($62,500).

BUDGET. For 1989–90 total revenue was $7,022m.; general expenditure, $6,486m.

Total net long-term debt on 30 June 1990 amounted to $646·8m.

Per capita personal income (1989) was $14,736.

ENERGY AND NATURAL RESOURCES

Minerals. Total value added by mining 1987: Metal mining, $50·1m.; coal mining, $145·7m.; oil and gas extraction, $59·5m.; non-metallic minerals (except fuels, $203·1m.

Agriculture. In 1989, 91,000 farms covered 12·6m. acres. The average farm was of 131 acres (only a few states had a smaller average) valued, land and buildings, at $1,126.

Cash income (1988) from crops was $965·3m.; from livestock, $1,080·4m. Main crops were cotton, tobacco and soybeans.

On 1 Jan. 1989 the domestic animals included 202,000 milch cows, 2·3m. all cattle, 10,000 sheep, 900,000 swine.

Forestry. Forests occupy 13,258,000 acres (50% of total land area). The forest industry and industries dependent on it employ about 40,000 workers, earning $150m. per year. Wood products are valued at over $500m. per year. National forest system land (1986) 626,000 acres.

INDUSTRY. The manufacturing industries include iron and steel working, but the most important products are chemicals, including synthetic fibres and allied products, electrical equipment and food. In 1987, manufacturing establishments employed 485,000 workers; value added by manufactures was $27,079m.

TOURISM. In 1988 43·1m. out-of-state tourists spent $4,883m.

COMMUNICATIONS

Roads. In 1990 there were 84,081 miles of roads (68,854 miles rural) and 4,315,702 registered motor vehicles.

Railways. The state had (1988) 2,475 miles of track.

Aviation. The state is served by 11 major airlines. In 1985 there were 74 public airports and 78 private; there were 71 heliports and 2 military air bases.

JUSTICE, RELIGION, EDUCATION AND WELFARE

Justice. There has been no execution since 1960; since 1930 there have been 66 executions (by electrocution) for murder and 27 for rape. A US Supreme Court ruling prohibits the use of capital punishment under present Tennessee law, except for first degree murder.

Prison population, 30 June 1990, 8,424.

Religion. The leading religious bodies are the Southern Baptists, Methodists and Negro Baptists.

Education. School attendance has been compulsory since 1925 and the employment of children under 16 years of age in workshops, factories or mines is illegal.

In 1989–90 there were 1,655 public schools with a net enrolment of 858,991 pupils; 43,051 teachers earned an average salary of $27,052. Total expenditure for operating public schools (kindergarten to Grade 12) was $2,842m. Tennessee has 49 accredited colleges and universities, 18 2-year colleges and 28 vocational schools. The universities include the University of Tennessee, Knoxville (founded 1794), with 25,187 students in 1989–90; Vanderbilt University, Nashville (1873) with 9,059, Tennessee State University (1912) with 7,362, the University of Tennessee at Chattanooga (1886) with 7,362, Memphis State University (1912), 20,613 and Fisk University (1866) with 891.

Health. In 1988 the state had 162 hospitals with 27,160 beds. State facilities for the mentally retarded had 1,921 resident patients and mental hospitals had 1,608 in 1990.

Social Security. In 1989 Tennessee paid $4,402m. to retired workers and their survivors and to disabled workers. Total beneficiaries: 539,700 retired; 163,100 survivors and 108,600 disabled. 542,600 people received $972m. in Medicaid. Supplemental Security Income ($350m.) was paid to 135,700. 193,000 people (1988) received aid to dependent children ($130m.).

Further Reading

Tennessee Blue Book. Secretary of State, Nashville
Tennessee Statistical Abstract. Center for Business and Economic Research, Univ. of Tennessee. Annual
Corlew, R. E., *Tennessee: a Short History.* 2nd ed. Univ. of Tennessee, 1981
Davidson, D., *Tennessee: Vol. I, The Old River Frontier to Secession,* Univ. of Tennessee, 1979
Dykeman, W., *Tennessee.* Rev. ed., New York, 1984

State Library: State Library and Archives, Nashville. *Librarian:* Edwin Gleaves. *State Historian:* Wilma Dykeman.

TEXAS

HISTORY. In 1836 Texas declared its independence of Mexico, and after maintaining an independent existence, as the Republic of Texas, for 10 years, it was on 29 Dec. 1845 received as a state into the American Union. The state's first settlement dates from 1686.

AREA AND POPULATION. Texas is bounded north by Oklahoma, northeast by Arkansas, east by Louisiana, south-east by the Gulf of Mexico, south by

Mexico and west by New Mexico. Area, 266,807 sq. miles (including 4,790 sq. miles of inland water). Census population, 1990, 16,986,510. Vital statistics for 1984: Births, 306,192 (19·2 per 1,000 population); deaths, 119,531 (7·5); infant deaths, 3,178 (10·4 per 1,000 live births); marriages, 207,631 (13); divorces, 98,074 (6·1).

Population for 5 census years was:

	White	Black	American Indian	Asian	Total	Per sq. mile
1910	3,204,848	690,049	702	943	3,896,542	14·8
1930	4,967,172	854,964	1,001	1,578	5,824,715	22·1
			All others			
1970	9,717,128	1,399,005	80,597		11,196,730	42·7
1980	11,197,663	1,710,250	1,320,470		14,228,383	54·2
				Asian/ other		
1990	12,774,762	2,021,632	65,877	2,124,239	16,986,510	63·7

Of the population in 1980, 6,998,301 were male, 11,327,159 persons were urban. Persons of Hispanic origin were also identified in the last 2 censuses, numbering 2,985,643 in 1980 and 4,339,905 in 1990.

The largest cities, with census population in 1990, are:

Houston	1,630,553	Lubbock	186,206	Abilene	106,654
Dallas	1,006,877	Garland	180,650	Waco	103,590
San Antonio	935,933	Amarillo	157,615	Wichita Falls	96,259
El Paso	515,342	Irving	155,037	Odessa	89,699
Austin (capital)	465,622	Laredo	122,899	Midland	89,443
Fort Worth	447,619	Pasadena	119,633	San Angelo	84,474
Arlington	261,721	Plano	128,713	Tyler	75,450
Corpus Christi	257,453	Beaumont	114,323	Galveston	59,070

Larger urbanized areas, 1990: Houston, 3,301,937; Dallas, 2,553,362; Fort Worth-Arlington, 1,332,053; San Antonio, 1,302,099.

CLIMATE. Dallas. Jan. 45°F (7·2°C), July 84°F (28·9°C). Annual rainfall 38" (945 mm). El Paso. Jan. 44°F (6·7°C), July 81°F (27·2°C). Annual rainfall 9" (221 mm). Galveston. Jan. 54°F (12·2°C), July 84°F (28·9°C). Annual rainfall 46" (1,159 mm). Houston. Jan. 52°F (11·1°C), July 83°F (28·3°C). Annual rainfall 48" (1,200 mm). *See* Central Plains, p. 1398.

CONSTITUTION AND GOVERNMENT. The present constitution dates from 1876; it has been amended 328 times. The Legislature consists of a Senate of 31 members elected for 4 years (half their number retire every 2 years), and a House of Representatives of 150 members elected for 2 years. It meets in odd-numbered years in January. The Governor and Lieut.-Governor are elected for 4 years.

In the 1988 presidential election Bush polled 3,014,007 votes, Dukakis, 2,331,286.

The capital is Austin. The state has 254 counties.

Governor: Ann W. Richards (D.), 1991–95 ($93,432).
Lieut.-Governor: Bob Bullock (D.), ($7,200).
Secretary of State: John Hannah (D.), ($64,890).

BUDGET. In the fiscal year ending 31 Aug. 1989 general revenues were $23,617m. ($12,905·2m. from taxes, $5,042·9m. federal aid); general expenditures (1989), $20,707·3m. ($2,877·4m. on highways).

Net long-term debt, 31 Aug. 1985, was $4,009m.
Per capita personal income (1988) was $14,640.

ENERGY AND NATURAL RESOURCES

Minerals. Production, 1988: Crude petroleum, 728m. bbls, natural gas 4,500m. cubic ft.; other minerals include natural gasoline, butane and propane gases, helium,

crude gypsum, granite and sandstone, salt and cement. Total value c
ducts in 1982, $45,388m., of which $43,834 was for fuels.

Agriculture. Texas is one of the most important agricultural states of the Unio.
1989 it had 186,000 farms covering 132m. acres; average farm was of 710 acres. In
1988, land and buildings were valued at $591 per acre. Large-scale commercial
farms, highly mechanized, dominate in Texas; farms of 1,000 acres or more in number far exceed that of any other state. But small-scale farming persists.

Soil erosion is serious in some parts. For some 97,297,000 acres drastic curative
treatment has been indicated and for 51,164,000 acres, preventive treatment.

Production, 1985: Maize (157m. bu., value $422m.), oats, barley, soybeans,
peanuts, oranges, grapefruit, peaches, potatoes, sweet potatoes; 1989: Wheat (60m.
bu, value $225m.), cotton, 2,999,000 bales.

Cash income, 1988, from crops was $3,027m.; from livestock, $6,059m.

The state has a very great livestock industry, leading in the number of all cattle,
13·7m. on 1 Jan. 1989, and sheep, 1·9m.; it also had 355,000 milch cows, and
560,000 swine.

Forestry. There were (1988) 22,032,000 acres of forested land.

INDUSTRY. In 1988 manufacturing establishments employed 970,267 workers;
trade employed 1,667,000; government, 1·1m.; services, 1·4m.; construction,
337,379; finance, insurance and real estate, 427,656; transport and public utilities,
372,391. Chemical industries along the Gulf Coast, such as the production of
synthetic rubber and of primary magnesium (from sea-water), are increasingly
important.

COMMUNICATIONS

Roads. In 1990 there were 305,692 miles of roads (217,044 miles rural) and
14,088,488 registered motor vehicles.

Aviation. In 1988 there were 307 public and 1,308 private airports.

Shipping. The port of Houston, connected by the Houston Ship Channel (50 miles
long) with the Gulf of Mexico, is the largest inland cotton market in the world.
Cargo handled 1987, 112,546,187 tons.

JUSTICE, RELIGION, EDUCATION AND WELFARE

Justice. In Aug. 1990 the state prison held 47,728 men and women. Execution is by
lethal injection; there were 300 between 1930 and 1968; between 1977 and 1986
there were 8.

Texas has adopted 11 laws governing the activities of trade unions. An Act of
1955 forbids the state's payment of unemployment compensation to workers
engaged in certain types of strikes.

Religion. The largest religious bodies are Roman Catholics, Baptists, Methodists,
Churches of Christ, Lutherans, Presbyterians and Episcopalians.

Education. School attendance is compulsory from 6 to 17 years of age.

In 1988–89 public elementary and secondary schools had 3·3m. students; in
1989–90 there were 200,179 teachers whose salaries averaged $27,496. Total public
school expenditure, 1987, $11,529m.

The largest institutions of higher education, with faculty numbers (1988–89) and
student enrolment, (1990–91), were:

Founded	Institutions	Control	Faculty	Students
1845	Baylor University, Waco	Baptist	636	12,019
1852	St Mary's University, San Antonio	R.C.	209	4,045
1869	Trinity University, San Antonio	Presb.	255	2,538
1873	Texas Christian University, Fort Worth	Christian	519	6,458
1876	Texas A. and M. Univ., College Station	State	2,240	39,312
1876	Prairie View Agr. and Mech. Coll., Prairie View	State	297	4,990

ounded	Institutions	Control	Faculty	Students
1879	Sam Houston State University	State	365	12,753
1883	University of Texas System (every campus)	State	6,328	134,545
1890	University of North Texas, Denton	State	884	27,174
1891	Hardin-Simmons University, Abilene	Baptist	124	1,930
1889	East Texas State University, Commerce	State	363	7,979
1899	South West Texas State University, San Marcos	State	833	20,994
1903	Texas Woman's University, Denton	State	520	9,854
1906	Abilene Christian University, Abilene	Church of Christ	275	4,053
1911	Southern Methodist University, Dallas	Methodist	650	8,798
1923	Stephen F. Austin State University	State	517	12,808
1923	Texas Technical University, Lubbock	State	1,444	25,463
1925	Texas Arts and Industries University, Kingsville	State	234	6,017
1934	University of Houston, Houston	State	2,100	33,117
1947	Texas Southern University, Houston	State	544	9,379
1951	Lamar University, Beaumont	State	545	11,932

Health. In 1988, the state had 553 hospitals (80,914 beds) listed by the American Hospital Association. In the fiscal year 1989; the average daily census of patients was: State hospitals, 3,629; state schools, 7,265 and state centres, 331.

Social Security. Aid is from state and federal sources. Old-age assistance (SSI) was being granted in Dec. 1985 to 123,400 persons, who received an average of $133 per month; aid was given to 127,100 disabled ($217) and 398,900 dependent children (average payment per family, $142 per month).

Further Reading

Texas Almanac. Dallas. Biennial
Texas Factbook. Univ. of Texas, 1983
Benton, W. E., *Texas, its Government and Politics.* 4th ed., Englewood Cliffs, 1977
Cruz, G. R. and Irby, J. A. (eds.) *Texas Bibliography.* Austin, 1982
Fehrenbach, T. R., *Lone Star: A History of Texas and the Texans.* London, 1986
Jordan, T. G. and Bean, J. L., Jr., *Texas.* Boulder, 1983
MacCorkle, S. A. and Smith, D., *Texas Government.* 7th ed. New York, 1974
Richardson, R. N., *Texas, the Lone Star State.* 3rd ed. New York, 1970

Legislative Reference Library: Box 12488, Capitol Station, Austin, Texas 78811. *Director:* Sally Reynolds.

UTAH

HISTORY. Utah, which had been acquired by the US during the Mexican war, was settled by Mormons in 1847, and organized as a Territory on 9 Sept. 1850. After the Mormons had renounced polygamy in 1890 it was admitted as a state into the Union on 4 Jan. 1896 with boundaries as at present.

AREA AND POPULATION. Utah is bounded north by Idaho and Wyoming, east by Colorado, south by Arizona and west by Nevada. Area, 84,899 sq. miles, of which 2,826 sq. miles are water. The Bureau of Indian Affairs in 1990 administered 2,317,604 acres, 2,284,766 acres of which were allotted to Indian tribes.

Census population, 1 April 1990, 1,722,850, an increase of 17·92% since 1980. Births in 1990 were 37,175 (21·6 per 1,000 population); deaths (1989), 36,208 (21·2); infant deaths (1984), 407 (10·3 per 1,000 live births); marriages (1990), 19,012 (11); divorces (1990), 8,786 (5·1).

Population at 5 federal censuses was:

	White	Black	Indian	Asiatic	Total	Per sq. mile
1910	366,583	1,144	3,123	2,501	373,851	4·5
1930	499,967	1,108	2,869	3,903	507,847	6·2
1960	873,828	4,148	6,961	5,207	890,627	10·8
1970	1,031,926	6,617	11,273	6,230	1,059,273	12·9
1980	1,382,550	9,225	19,256	15,076	1,461,037	17·7

Of the total in 1980, 724,501 were male, 1,232,908 persons were urban; 860,304 were 20 years of age or older.

The largest cities are Salt Lake City, with a population (census, 1980) of 162,960 (1990 census, 159,936); Provo, 74,007; Ogden, 64,444; Bountiful, 32,877; Orem, 52,399; Sandy City, 51,022 and Logan, 26,844.

CLIMATE. Salt Lake City. Jan. 29°F (−1·7°C), July 77°F (25°C). Annual rainfall 16" (401 mm). *See* Mountain States, p. 1397.

CONSTITUTION AND GOVERNMENT. Utah adopted its present constitution in 1896 (now with 61 amendments). The Legislature consists of a Senate (in part renewed every 2 years) of 29 members, elected for 4 years, and of a House of Representatives of 75 members elected for 2 years. It sits annually in Jan. The Governor is elected for 4 years. The constitution provides for the initiative and referendum.

The capital is Salt Lake City. There are 29 counties in the state.

In the 1988 presidential election Bush polled 426,858 votes, Dukakis, 206,853.

Governor: Norman Bangerter (R.), 1989–93 ($70,000).
Lieut.-Governor: W. Val Oveson (R.), 1989–93 ($52,200).

BUDGET. For the year ending 30 June 1990 general revenue was $3,529·8m. ($1,768m. from taxes, $966·3m. from federal aid); general expenditures were $3,470·9m. ($1,663·8m. on education, $348·7m. on highways, $458m. on public welfare).

Per capita personal income (1990) was $14,083.

ENERGY AND NATURAL RESOURCES

Minerals The principal minerals are: Copper, gold, magnesium, petroleum, lead, silver and zinc. The state also has natural gas, clays, tungsten, molybdenum, uranium and phosphate rock. The value of non-fuel mineral production in 1990 was $1·2m.

Agriculture. In 1985 Utah had 14,000 farms covering 12m. acres, of which about 2m. acres were crop land and about 300,000 acres pasture. About 1m. acres had irrigation; the average farm was of 857 acres.

Of the total surface area, 9% is severely eroded and only 9·4% is free from erosion; the balance is moderately eroded.

Cash income, 1985, from crops, $138m. and from livestock, $409m. The principal crops are: Barley, wheat (spring and winter), oats, potatoes, hay (alfalfa, sweet clover and lespedeza), maize. Livestock, 1990: Cattle, 855,000; pigs, 34,000; Sheep 0·6m.; poultry, 3·8m.

Forestry. Area of national forests, 1981, was 9,129,000 acres, of which 8·05m. acres were under forest service administration.

INDUSTRY. In 1985 manufacturing establishments had 94,000 workers. Leading manufactures by value added are primary metals, ordinances and transport, food, fabricated metals and machinery, petroleum products. Service industries employed 132,000; trade, 148,000; government, 138,000.

COMMUNICATIONS

Roads. In 1990 there were 42,971 miles of roads (37,430 miles rural) and 1,174,861 registered motor vehicles.

Railways. On 1 July 1974 the state had 1,734 miles of railways.

Civil Aviation. There is an international airport at Salt Lake City.

JUSTICE, RELIGION, EDUCATION AND WELFARE

Justice. The number of inmates of the state prison in Dec. 1985 was 1,570. Since 1930 total executions have been 14 (13 by shooting, 1 by hanging—the condemned man has choice), all whites, and all for murder.

Religion. Latter-day Saints (Mormons) form about 73% of the church membership of the state; their church is a substantial property-owner. The Roman Catholic church and most Protestant denominations are represented.

Education. School attendance is compulsory for children from 6 to 18 years of age. There are 40 school districts. Teachers' salaries, 1985, averaged $21,500. There were (autumn 1983) 379,000 pupils in public elementary and secondary schools, and (1986) 16,700 classroom teachers, average salary, $22,550; estimated public school expenditure was $1,092m. or $664 per capita.

The University of Utah (1850) (24,770 students in 1985–86) is in Salt Lake City; the Utah State University (1890) (11,804) is in Logan. The Mormon Church maintains the Brigham Young University at Provo (1875) with 26,894 students. Other colleges include: Westminster College, Salt Lake City (1,302); Weber State College, Ogden (11,117); Southern Utah State College, Cedar City (2,587); College of Eastern Utah, Price (1,132); Snow College, Ephraim (1,328); Dixie College, St George (2,234).

Health. In 1983, the state had 44 hospitals (5,400 beds) listed by the Utah Department of Social Services. Mental hospitals had 317 resident patients on 1 Jan. 1980; state facilities for the mentally retarded had 763.

Social Security. In Dec. 1985 the state department of public welfare provided assistance to 37,800 persons receiving aid to dependent children at an average $322 per family per month; aid to the aged, the blind and disabled is provided from federal funds; there were 1,900 aged recipients in 1985 (average $150 per month), 6,600 disabled ($224).

Further Reading

Compiled Digest of Administrative Reports. Secretary of State, Salt Lake City. Annual
Statistical Abstract of Government in Utah. Utah Foundation, Salt Lake City. Annual
Utah Agricultural Statistics. Dept. of Agriculture, Salt Lake City. Annual
Utah: Facts. Bureau of Economic and Business Research, Univ. of Utah, 1975
Arrington, L., *Great Basin Kingdom: An Economic History of the Latter-Day Saints, 1830–1900.* Cambridge, Mass., 1958
Petersen, C. S., *Utah: a History.* New York, 1977

VERMONT

HISTORY. Vermont, first settled in 1724, was admitted into the Union as the fourteenth state on 4 March 1791. The first constitution was adopted by convention at Windsor, 2 July 1777, and established an independent state government.

AREA AND POPULATION. Vermont is bounded in the north by Canada, east by New Hampshire, south by Massachusetts and west by New York. Area, 9,615 sq. miles, of which 366 sq. miles are inland water. Census population, 1 April 1990, 562,758, an increase of 10% since 1980. Births, 1989, were 8,490 (15 per 1,000 population); deaths, 4,577 (8·1); infant deaths, 58 (6·8 per 1,000 live births); marriages, 6,151 (10·8); divorces, 2,524 (4·5).

Population at 5 census years was:

	White	Black	Indian	Asiatic	Total	Per sq. mile
1910	354,298	1,621	26	11	355,956	39·0
1930	358,966	568	36	41	359,611	38·8
1960	389,092	519	57	172	389,881	42·0
1980	506,736	1,135	984	1,355	511,456	55·1
1990	555,088	1,951	1,696 [1]	3,215 [2]	562,758	60·8

[1] Includes Eskimo and Aleut. [2] Includes Pacific Islander.

Of the population in 1990, 275,492 were male; those 20 years of age or older numbered 400,019. In 1980 172,735 persons lived in urban areas. The largest cities are Burlington, with a population (1990) of 39,127; Rutland, 18,230; Bennington, 16,451.

CLIMATE. Burlington. Jan. 17°F (−8·3°C), July 70°F (21·1°C). Annual rainfall 33" (820 mm). *See* New England, p. 1398.

CONSTITUTION AND GOVERNMENT. The constitution was adopted in 1793 and has since been amended. Amendments are proposed by two-thirds vote of the Senate every 4 years, and must be accepted by two sessions of the legislature; they are then submitted to popular vote. The state Legislature, consisting of a Senate of 30 members and a House of Representatives of 150 members (both elected for 2 years), meets in Jan. every year. The Governor and Lieut.-Governor are elected for 2 years. Electors are all citizens who possess certain residential qualifications and have taken the freeman's oath set forth in the constitution.

In the 1988 presidential election Bush polled 123,166 votes, Dukakis, 116,419.

The capital is Montpelier (8,247, 1990). There are 14 counties and 251 cities, towns and other administrative divisions.

Governor: Howard Dean (D.), 1991–93 ($80,730).
Secretary of State: James H. Douglas (R.), ($50,800).

BUDGET. The total revenue for the year ending 30 June 1990 was $1,276·5m.; total disbursements, $1,291·7m.

Total net long-term bonded debt, 30 June 1990, was $406,543,203.
Per capita personal income (1989 estimate) was $16,514.

NATURAL RESOURCES

Minerals. Stone, chiefly granite, marble and slate, is the leading mineral produced in Vermont, contributing about 60% of the total value of mineral products. Other products include asbestos, talc, peat, sand and gravel. Total value of mineral products, 1987, $89·5m.

Agriculture. Agriculture is the most important industry. In 1989 the state had 7,000 farms covering 1·51m. acres; the average farm was of 216 acres. Cash income, 1988, from livestock and products, $376·9m.; from crops, $45m. The dairy farms produce about 2,337,000 lb. of milk annually. The chief agricultural crops are hay, apples and silage. In 1990 Vermont had 297,000 cattle and calves, 29,500 sheep and lambs, 5,700 hogs and pigs, 152,000 poultry (1989).

Forestry. In 1990 the harvest was 90·7m. bd ft hardwood and 124·7m. bd ft softwood saw-logs, and 335,954 cords of pulpwood and boltwood.

The state is 76% forest, with 10% in public ownership. National forests area (1986), 355,534 acres. State-owned forests, parks, fish and game areas, 250,000 acres; municipally-owned, 38,500 acres.

INDUSTRY. In 1988 service industries employed 62,150; trade, 59,750; manufacturing, 49,700; government, 40,850; construction, 17,400.

COMMUNICATIONS

Roads. The state had 14,120 miles of roads in 1991, including 7,376 miles of gravel, graded and drained, or unimproved roads. Motor vehicle registrations, 1990, 439,763, of which 327,178 were private.

Railways. There were, in 1988, 793 miles of railway, 291 of which was leased by the state to private operators.

Aviation. There were 18 airports in 1990, of which 11 were state operated, 1 municipally owned and 6 private. Some are only open in summer.

JUSTICE, RELIGION, EDUCATION AND WELFARE

Justice. In financial year 1989 prisons and centres had 761 (with another 110 on furlough) inmates; 700 of these were serving more than one year.

Religion. The principal denominations are Roman Catholic, United Church of Christ, United Methodist, Protestant Episcopal, Baptist and Unitarian–Universalist.

Education. School attendance during the full school term is compulsory for children from 7 to 16 years of age, unless they have completed the 10th grade or undergo approved home instruction. In 1990–91 the public schools had 95,758 pupils. Full-time teachers for public elementary schools (1990) numbered 2,880, secondary schools 3,517. Teachers' salaries, 1990–91, average base salary $19,491. Total expenditure on public schools, 1987–88, $334·7m.

In autumn 1985 there were 31,416 students in higher education. The University of Vermont (1791) had 11,287 students in 1989–90; Norwich University (1834, founded as the American Literary, Scientific and Military Academy in 1819), had 2,488; St Michael's College (1904), 2,231; there are 5 state colleges.

Health. In Sept. 1990 the state had 18 general hospitals (2,383 beds).

Social Security. Old-age assistance (SSI) was being granted in 1990 to 2,500 persons, drawing an average of $155 per month; aid to dependent children was being granted to 24,939 persons, drawing an average of $189 per month; and aid to the permanently and totally disabled was being granted to 7,946 persons, drawing an average of $353.

Further Reading

Legislative Directory. Secretary of State, Montpelier. Biennial
Vermont Annual Financial Report. Auditor of Accounts, Montpelier. Annual
Vermont Facts and Figures. Office of Statistical Co-ordination, Montpelier
Vermont Year-Book, formerly *Walton's Register.* Chester. Annual
Bassett T. (ed.) *Vermont: A Bibliography of its History,* Boston, 1981
Vermont Atlas and Gazetteer, Rev. ed., Freeport, 1983
Morrissey, C. T., *Vermont,* New York, 1981

State Library: Vermont Dept.of Libraries, Montpelier. *State Librarian:* Patricia Klinck.

VIRGINIA

HISTORY. The first English Charter for settlements in America was that granted by James I in 1606 for the planting of colonies in Virginia. The state was one of the 13 original states in the Union. Virginia lost just over one-third of its area when West Virginia was admitted into the Union (1863).

AREA AND POPULATION. Virginia is bounded north-west by West Virginia, north-east by Maryland, east by the Atlantic, south by North Carolina and Tennessee and west by Kentucky. Area, 40,767 sq. miles including 1,063 sq. miles of inland water. Census population, 1 April 1990, 6,187,358, an increase of 15·73% since 1980. In 1988 there were 87,002 births (15·1 per 1,000 population); 46,015 deaths (7·9); (1987) 850 infant deaths (11·5 per 1,000 live births); 67,073 marriages and 25,568 divorces.

Population for 5 federal census years was:

	White	Black	Indian	Asiatic	Total	Per sq. mile
1910	1,389,809	671,096	539	168	2,061,612	51·2
1930	1,770,441	650,165	779	466	2,421,851	60·7
1960	3,142,443	816,258	2,155	4,725	3,966,949	99·3
			All others			
1970	3,761,514	861,368	25,612		4,648,494	116·9
1980	4,230,000	1,008,311	108,517		5,346,818	134·7

Of the total population in 1980, 49% were male, 66% were urban and 59% were 21 years of age or older.

The population (census of 1990) of the principal cities was: Virginia Beach, 393,069; Norfolk, 261,229; Richmond, 203,056; Newport News, 170,045; Chesapeake, 151,976; Hampton, 133,793; Alexandria, 111,183; Portsmouth, 103,907.

CLIMATE. Average temperatures in Jan. are 41°F in the Tidewater coastal area and 32°F in the Blue Ridge mountains; July averages, 78°F and 68°F respectively. Precipitation averages 36" in the Shenandoah valley and 44" in the south. Snowfall is 5-10" in the Tidewater and 25-30" in the western mountains. Norfolk, Jan. 41°F (5°C), July 79°F (26·1°C). Annual rainfall 46" (1,145 mm). *See* Atlantic Coast, p. 1398.

CONSTITUTION AND GOVERNMENT. The present constitution dates from 1971. The General Assembly consists of a Senate of 40 members, elected for 4 years, and a House of Delegates of 100 members, elected for 2 years. It sits annually in Jan. The Governor and Lieut.-Governor are elected for 4 years.

In the 1988 presidential election Bush polled 1,305,131 votes, Dukakis, 860,767.

The state capital is Richmond; the state contains 95 counties and 41 independent cities.

Governor: L. Douglas Wilder (D.), 1990–94 ($108,000).
Lieut.-Governor: Donald S. Beyer (ind.) ($29,550).
Secretary of the Commonwealth: Pamela Womack (D.) ($56,603).

BUDGET. General revenue for the year ending 30 June 1990 was $11,630·3m. (taxation, $6,800·5m., and federal aid, $2,105·1m.); general expenditures, $11,850·4m. ($4,723m. for education, $1,679·6m. for transport and $1,484·2m. for public welfare).

Total net long-term debt, 30 June 1986, amounted to $10,153m.

Per capita personal income (1990) was $19,746.

ENERGY AND NATURAL RESOURCES

Minerals. Coal is the most important mineral, with output (1984) of 35,500,000 short tons. Lead and zinc ores, stone, sand and gravel, lime and titanium ore are also produced. Total non-fuel mineral output was valued at $512·1m. in 1990.

Agriculture. In 1987 there were 50,000 farms with an area of 10m. acres; average farm had 192 acres and was valued at $10,667,000. Income, 1986, from crops, $996m., and from livestock and livestock products, $1,127m. The chief crops are tobacco, soybeans, peanuts, winter wheat, maize, tomatoes, apples, potatoes and sweet potatoes. Livestock, 1989: Cattle 1·67m.; pigs, 0·45m.; sheep, 158,000; poultry, 5·82m.

Forestry. Forests covered 15,968,000 acres in 1990.

INDUSTRY. The manufacture of cigars and cigarettes and of rayon and allied products and the building of ships lead in value of products.

TOURISM. Tourists spent about $8,000m. in 1989.

COMMUNICATIONS

Roads. In 1990 there were 67,282 miles of roads (52,228 miles rural) and 4,859,728 registered motor vehicles.

Railways. In 1985 there were 3,693 miles of railways.

Civil Aviation. There are international airports at Norfolk, Dulles, Richmond and Newport News.

JUSTICE, RELIGION, EDUCATION AND WELFARE

Justice. Executions (by electrocution) since 1940 totalled 70. Prison population, 31 Dec. 1987, 13,321 in federal and state prisons.

Religion. The principal churches are the Baptist, Methodist, Protestant-Episcopal, Roman Catholic and Presbyterian.

Education. Elementary and secondary instruction is free, and for ages 6–17 attendance is compulsory. No child under 12 may be employed in any mining or manufacturing work.

In 1985 the 135 school districts had, in primary schools, 665,000 pupils and 34,200 teachers and in public high schools, 303,000 pupils and 25,300 teachers. Teachers' salaries (1987) averaged $25,500. Total expenditure on education, 1987, was $3,667m. The more important institutions for higher education (1986) were:

Founded	Name and place of college	Staff	Students
1693	College of William and Mary, Williamsburg (State)	526	6,616
1749	Washington and Lee University, Lexington	194	1,804
1776	Hampden-Sydney College, Hampden-Sydney (Pres.)	74	825
1819	University of Virginia, Charlottesville (State)	1,772	17,149
1832	Randolph-Macon College, Ashland (Methodist)	102	1,013
1832	University of Richmond, Richmond (Baptist)	349	4,705
1838	Virginia Commonwealth University, Richmond	1,885	19,641
1839	Virginia Military Institute Lexington (State)	100	1,350
1865	Virginia Union University, Richmond	98	1,311
1868	Hampton University	297	4,483
1872	Virginia Polytechnic Institute and State University	2,209	22,345
1882	Virginia State University, Petersburg	263	3,583
1908	James Madison University, Harrisonburg	600	9,757
1910	Radford University (State)	365	7,500
1930	Old Dominion University, Norfolk	713	15,463
1956	George Mason University (State)	715	17,652

Health. In 1986 the state had 137 hospitals (31,005 beds) listed by the American Hospital Association.

Social Security. In 1938 Virginia established a system of old-age assistance under the Federal Security Act; in March 1986 persons in 778,000 cases were drawing an average grant of $246; aid to permanently and totally disabled, 92,000 cases, average grant $918.96; aid to dependent children, 154,000 persons, average grant $85.77; general relief, 6,642 persons, average grant $146.62.

Further Reading

Virginia Facts and Figures. Virginia Division of Industrial Development, Richmond. Annual
Dabney, V., *Virginia, the New Dominion.* 1971
Gottmann, J., *Virginia in our Century.* Charlottesville, 1969
Morton, R. L., *Colonial Virginia.* 2 vols. Univ. Press of Virginia, 1960
Rouse, P. *Virginia: a Pictorial History.* New York, 1975
Rubin, L. D. Jr., *Virginia: a Bicentennial History.* Norris, 1977

State Library: Virginia State Library, Richmond 23219.

WASHINGTON

HISTORY. Washington, formerly part of Oregon, was created a Territory in 1853, and was admitted into the Union as a state on 11 Nov. 1889. Its settlement dates from 1811.

AREA AND POPULATION. Washington is bounded north by Canada, east by Idaho, south by Oregon with the Columbia River forming most of the boundary, and west by the Pacific. Total area, 68,139 sq. mile; land area, 66,582. Lands owned by the federal government, 1977, were 12·4m. acres or 29·1% of the total area. Census population, 1 April 1990, 4,866,692, an increase of 17·83% since 1980.

Births, 1986 were 69,431 (15·7 per 1,000 population); deaths, 34,166 (7·8); infant deaths (1985), 778 (10·2 per 1,000 live births); marriages, 43,255 (9·8); divorces and annulments, 26,405 (6·0).

Population in 5 federal census years was:

	White	Black	Indian	Asiatic	Total	Per sq. mile
1910	1,109,111	6,058	10,997	15,824	1,141,990	17·1
1930	1,521,661	6,840	11,253	23,642	1,563,396	23·3
1960	2,751,675	48,738	21,076	31,725	2,853,214	42·8
1970	2,351,055	71,308	33,386	53,420	3,409,169	51·2
1980	3,779,170	105,574	60,804	186,608	4,132,156	62·1

Of the total population in 1980, 2,052,307 were male, 3,037,014 persons were urban; 2,759,552 were 20 years of age or older.

There are 27 Indian reservations. Indian reservations in 1990 covered 2,718,516 acres, of which 2,250,731 acres were tribal lands.

Leading cities are Seattle, with a population in 1980 (and 1987 estimate) of 491,897 (491,300); Spokane, 170,993 (172,100); Tacoma, 158,101 (158,900); Bellevue, 73,711 (82,070). Others : Yakima, 49,826; Everett, 54,413; Vancouver, 42,834; Bellingham, 45,794; Bremerton, 36,208; Richland, 33,578; Longview, 31,052; Renton, 30,612; Edmonds, 27,526; Walla Walla, 25,618. Urbanized areas (1980 census): Seattle–Everett, 1,600,944; Tacoma, 482,692; Spokane, 341,058.

CLIMATE. Seattle. Jan. 40°F (4·4°C), July 63°F (17·2°C). Annual rainfall 34" (848 mm). Spokane. Jan. 27°F (−2·8°C), July 70°F (21·1°C). Annual rainfall 14" (350 mm). *See* Pacific Coast, p. 1397.

CONSTITUTION AND GOVERNMENT. The constitution, adopted in 1889, has had 63 amendments. The Legislature consists of a Senate of 49 members elected for 4 years, half their number retiring every 2 years, and a House of Representatives of 98 members, elected for 2 years. The Governor and Lieut.-Governor are elected for 4 years.

In the 1988 presidential election Dukakis polled 844,544 votes, Bush, 800,182.

The capital is Olympia. The state contains 39 counties.

Governor: Booth Gardner (D.), 1989–93 ($96,700).
Lieut.-Governor: Joel Pritchard (D.), ($51,100).
Secretary of State: Ralph Munro (R.), ($52,600).

BUDGET. For the fiscal year 1990 the state's total revenue was $11,495·9m.; general expenditure was $11,389·1m. (education, $5,082·3m.; transport, $863·9m., and human resources, $2,098m.).

Total outstanding debt in 1987 was $3,073m.

Per capita personal income (1990) was $18,858.

ENERGY AND NATURAL RESOURCES

Electricity. With about 20% of potential water-power resources of US, the state has ample developed and potential hydro-electricity. Output in 1990: Hydro-electric, 87m. mwh; thermal, 7·4m. kwh; nuclear, 5·7m. mwh.

Minerals. Mining and quarrying are not as important as forestry, agriculture or manufacturing. Uranium is mined but figures are not disclosed; other minerals include sand and gravel, stone, coal and clays. Non-fuel mineral output in 1990 was valued at $473·4m.

Agriculture. Agriculture is constantly growing in value because of more intensive and diversified farming and because of the 1m.-acre Columbia Basin Irrigation Project.

In 1987 there were 37,000 farms with an acreage of 15·8m.; average farm was of 427 acres. Average value per acre (1985), $923.

Cash return from farm marketing, 1985, was $2,797m. (from crops, $1,865m.; from livestock and dairy products, $932m.). Wheat, cattle and calves, milk and apples are important.

On 1 Jan. 1985 animals on farms included 211,000 milch cows, 1·47m. all cattle, 53,000 sheep and 45,000 swine.

Forestry. Forests cover 21,856,000 acres, of which 9m. acres are national forest. In 1985, timber harvested from 486,506 acres cut, was 5,874·2m. bd ft. Acres planted or seeded, 1986, 171,641, not including natural re-seeding. Production of wood residues, 1986, included 695,927 tons of pulp and board.

Fisheries. Salmon and halibut are important; total fish catch, 1990, was worth $118·1m.

INDUSTRY. In 1986 manufacturing employed 304,200 workers, of whom 85,000 were in aerospace and 58,700 in the forest products industry. Principal manufactures: Aircraft, pulp and paper, lumber and plywood, aluminium, processed fruit and vegetables. In 1986 trade employed 434,700, service industries, 393,000; government, 349,300.

COMMUNICATIONS

Roads. In 1990 there were 81,439 miles of roads (65,011 miles rural) and 4,090,130 registered motor vehicles.

Railways. The railways had, in 1980, 6,057 miles.

Civil Aviation. There are international airports at Seattle/Tacoma, Spokane and Boeing Field.

JUSTICE, RELIGION, EDUCATION AND WELFARE

Justice. The adult population in state prisons in Dec. 1985 was 6,909. Since 1963 there have been no executions; total 1930–63 (by hanging) was 47, including 40 whites, 5 Blacks and 2 other races, all for murder, except 1 white for kidnapping.

Religion. Chief religious bodies are the Roman Catholic, United Methodist, Lutheran, Presbyterian, Latter-day Saints and Episcopalian.

Education. Education is given free to all children between the ages of 5 and 21 years, and is compulsory for children from 8 to 15 years of age. In autumn 1986 there were 761,760 pupils in public elementary and secondary schools. In 1986 there were 36,200 classroom teachers, average salary, $26,100. The total expenditure on public elementary and secondary schools for the school year 1986 was $3,124m. or $708 per capita.

The University of Washington, founded 1861, at Seattle, had, autumn, 1986, 33,226 students, and Washington State University at Pullman, founded 1890, for science and agriculture, had 15,888 students. Twenty-seven community colleges had (1986) a total enrolment of 134,522 state-funded students.

Health. In 1981 the 2 state hospitals for mental illness had a daily average of 1,204 patients; schools for handicapped children, 1,999 residents in Sept. 1981.

In 1983 the state had 122 general hospitals (16,200 beds); in 1981, 3 licensed psychiatric hospitals (181 beds) and 3 alcoholism hospitals (174 beds).

Social Security. Old-age assistance is provided for persons 65 years of age or older without adequate resources (and not in need of continuing home care) who are residents of the state. In Dec. 1985, 12,100 people were drawing an average of $157 per month; aid to 189,000 children in 67,900 families averaged $419 per family monthly; to 35,000 totally disabled, $266 monthly.

Further Reading

State of Washington Data Book. Office of Financial Management, Olympia, 1987
Swanson, T., *Political Life in Washington.* Pullman, 1985
Yates, R. and C., *Washington State Yearbook 1988.* Evgene, Oregon, 1988

State Library: Washington State Library, Olympia. *State Librarian:* Nancy Zussy.

WEST VIRGINIA

HISTORY. In 1862, after the state of Virginia had seceded from the Union, the electors of the western portion ratified an ordinance providing for the formation of a new state, which was admitted into the Union by presidential proclamation on 20 June 1863, under the name of West Virginia. Its constitution was adopted by the voters almost unanimously on 26 March 1863.

AREA AND POPULATION. West Virginia is bounded north by Pennsylvania and Maryland, east and south by Virginia, south-west by the Sandy River (forming the boundary with Kentucky) and west by the Ohio River (forming the boundary with Ohio). Total area, 24,232 sq. miles; land area, 24,087 sq. miles. Census population, 1 April 1990, 1,793,477, a decrease of 8·01% since 1980. Births, 1987, 22,280 (11·6 per 1,000 population); deaths, 19,669 (8·7); infant deaths, 217 (9·7 per 1,000 live births); marriages, 13,200 (6·8); divorces, 9,043 (4·8).

Population in 5 federal census years was:

	White	Black	Indian	Asiatic	Total	Per sq. mile
1910	1,156,817	64,173	36	93	1,221,119	50·8
1940	1,614,191	114,893	18	103	1,729,205	71·8
1960	1,770,133	89,378	181	419	1,860,421	77·3
1970	1,673,480	67,342	751	1,463	1,744,237	71·8
1980	1,874,751	65,051	1,610	5,194	1,949,644	80·3

Of the total population in 1980, 945,408 were male, 705,319 were urban; those 20 years of age or older numbered 1,319,566.

The 1980 census (and 1985 estimate) population of the principal cities was: Huntington, 63,684 (61,086); Charleston, 63,968 (59,371). Others: Wheeling, 43,070 (42,082); Parkersburg, 39,967 (39,399); Morgantown, 27,605 (27,786); Weirton, 24,736 (23,878); Fairmont, 23,863 (22,822); Clarksburg, 22,371 (21,379).

CLIMATE. Charleston. Jan. 34°F (1·1°C), July 76°F (24·4°C). Annual rainfall 40" (1,010 mm). *See* Appalachian Mountains, p. 1398.

CONSTITUTION AND GOVERNMENT. The present constitution was adopted in 1872; it has had 62 amendments. The Legislature consists of the Senate of 34 members elected for a term of 4 years, one-half being elected biennially, and the House of Delegates of 100 members, elected biennially. The Governor is elected for 4 years and may succeed himself once.

In the 1988 presidential election Dukakis polled 339,112 votes, Bush, 307,824.

The state capital is Charleston. There are 55 counties.

Governor: Gaston Caperton (D.), 1989–93 ($72,000).
Secretary of State: Ken Hechler (D.), ($43,200).

FINANCE. General revenues for the year ending 30 June 1990 were $4,435·5m. ($2,229·7m. from taxes, $942m. from federal funds); general expenditures were $3,530m. (education, $1,454·3m.; highways, $451·1m.; public welfare, $631·5m.).

Debts outstanding were $969·5m. on 30 June 1987.

Estimated *per capita* personal income (1990) was $13,747.

ENERGY AND NATURAL RESOURCES

Minerals. 38% of the state is underlain with mineable coal; 130·8m. short tons of coal were produced in 1986. Petroleum output, 3m. bbls; natural gas production was 135,431m. cu. ft. Salt, sand and gravel, sandstone and limestone are also produced. The total value of non-fuel mineral output in 1990 was $132m.

Agriculture. In 1988 the state had 20,500 farms with an area of 3·6m. acres; average size of farm was 176 acres and valued at $542 per acre. Livestock farming predominates.

Cash income, 1987, from crops was $57·5m.; from government payments,

$10·6m., and from livestock and products, $168·9m. Main crops harvested, 1987: Hay (1m. tons); all corn (3·6m. bu.); tobacco (2·5m. lb.). Area of main crops, 1987: hay, 630,000 acres; corn, 85,000 acres. Apples (185m. lb. in 1987) and peaches (17m. lb.) are important fruit crops. Livestock on farms, 1 Jan. 1988, included 490,000 cattle, of which 31,000 were milch cows; sheep, 91,000; hogs, 37,000; chickens, 721,000 excluding broilers. Production, 1987, included 32·8m. broilers, 108m. eggs; 2·4m. turkeys.

Forestry. State forests, 1987, covered 79,365 acres; national forests, 1,673,000 gross acres; 75% of the state is woodland.

INDUSTRY. In 1987, 1,645 manufactories had 86,088 production workers who earned $2,163m. Leading manufactures are primary and fabricated metals, glass, chemicals, wood products, textiles and apparel, and machinery.

In 1987 non-agricultural employment was 597,800 of whom 139,046 were in trade, 121,130 in government and 106,540 in service industries.

The first commercial coal liquefaction plant in the USA is being built near Morgantown with the co-operation of the governments of Federal Republic of Germany and Japan and the Gulf Oil Co.

COMMUNICATIONS

Roads. In 1990 there were 34,477 miles of roads (31,425 miles rural) and 1,213,950 registered motor vehicles.

Railways. In 1987 the state had 2,895 miles of railway, all operated by diesel or electric trains.

Civil Aviation. There were 27 licensed airports in 1987.

Telecommunications. There are 64 AM radio stations, 70 FM radio stations. Television stations number 9 VHF and 5 UHF.

Newspapers. Daily newspapers number 25; weekly newspapers 62.

JUSTICE, RELIGION, EDUCATION AND WELFARE

Justice. The state court system consists of a Supreme Court and 31 circuit courts. The Supreme Court of Appeals, exercising original and appellate jurisdiction, has 5 members elected by the people for 12-year terms. Each circuit court has from 1 to 7 judges (as determined by the Legislature on the basis of population and case-load) chosen by the voters within each circuit for 8-year terms.

Effective on 1 July 1967, the West Virginia Human Rights Act prohibits discrimination in employment and places of public accommodations based on race, religion, colour, national origin or ancestry.

There are 5 penal and correctional institutions which had, on 30 June 1987, 1,558 inmates. In 1965 the state legislature abolished capital punishment.

Religion. Chief denominations in 1987 were United Methodist (159,000 members, estimate), Baptists (116,000) and Roman Catholics (109,000).

Education. Public school education is free for all from 5 to 21 years of age, and school attendance is compulsory for all between the ages of 7 and 16 (school term, 200 days—180–185 days of actual teaching). The public schools are non-sectarian. In autumn 1987 public elementary and secondary schools had 344,604 pupils and 22,702 classroom teachers. Average salary of teachers in 1987, $21,736. Total 1986 expenditures for public schools, $1,196m.

Leading institutions of higher education in 1987:

Founded		Full-time students
1837	Marshall University, Huntington	12,033
1837	West Liberty State College, West Liberty	2,450
1867	Fairmont State College, Fairmont	5,432
1868	West Virginia University, Morgantown	17,270
1872	Concord College, Athens	2,380

Founded		Full-time students
1872	Glenville State College, Glenville	2,096
1872	Shepherd College, Shepherdstown	3,920
1891	West Virginia State College	4,503
1895	West Virginia Institute of Technology, Montgomery	2,814
1895	Bluefield State College, Bluefield	2,559
1901	Potomac State College of West Virginia Univ., Keyser	1,040
1972	West Virginia College of Graduate Studies	2,662
1976	School of Osteopathic Medicine, Lewisburg	233

In addition to the universities and state-supported schools, there are 3 community colleges (8,625 students in 1987), 10 denominational and private institutions of higher education (8,981 students in 1987) and 11 business colleges.

Health. In 1987 the state had 77 hospitals and 53 licensed personal care homes, 32 skilled-nursing homes and 3 mental hospitals.

Social Security. The Department of Human Services, originating in the 1930s as the Department of Public Assistance, is both state and federally financed. In the year ending 30 June 1988 day care for 4,735 children per month was provided; aid was given to 26,464 families with dependent children (average award, $231.64 per month); handicapped children's services conducted 8,389 examinations; 93,376 families per month received food stamps.

On 1 Jan. 1974 all blind, aged and disabled services were converted to the Federal Supplemental Security Income programme.

Further Reading

West Virginia Blue Book. Legislature, Charleston. Annual, since 1916
West Virginia Statistical Handbook, 1974. Bureau of Business Research, W. Va. Univ., Morgantown, 1974
Bibliography of West Virginia. 2 parts. Dept. of Archives and History, Charleston, 1939
West Virginia History. Dept. of Archives and History. Charleston. Quarterly, from 1939
Conley, P. and Doherty, W. T., *West Virginia History.* Charleston, 1974
Davis, C. J. and others, *West Virginia State and Local Government.* West Virginia Univ. Bureau for Government Research, 1963
Rice, O. K., *West Virginia: A History.* Univ. Press of Kentucky, Lexington, 1985
Williams, J. A., *West Virginia: A Bicentennial History.* New York, 1976

State Library: Division of Archives and History, Dept. of Culture and History, Charleston.

WISCONSIN

HISTORY. Wisconsin was settled in 1670 by French traders and missionaries. Originally a part of New France, it was surrendered to the British in 1763 and in 1783, when ceded to the US, became part of the North-west Territory. It was then contained successively in the Territories of Indiana, Illinois and Michigan. In 1836 it became part of the Territory of Wisconsin, which also included the present states of Iowa, Minnesota and parts of the Dakotas. It was admitted into the Union with its present boundaries on 29 May 1848.

AREA AND POPULATION. Wisconsin is bounded north by Lake Superior and the Upper Peninsula of Michigan, east by Lake Michigan, south by Illinois, west by Iowa and Minnesota, with the Mississippi River forming most of the boundary. Area, 56,154 sq. miles, including 1,439 sq. miles of inland water, but excluding any part of the Great Lakes. Census population, 1 April 1990 4,891,769, an increase of 4% since 1980. Births in 1989 were 71,890 (14·8 per 1,000 population); deaths, 42,284 (8·7); infant deaths, 665 (9·2 per 1,000 live births); marriages, 40,752 (8·3); divorces and annulments, 17,731 (3·6).

Population in 5 census years was:

	White	Black	All others	Total	Per sq. mile
1910	2,320,555	2,900	10,405	2,333,860	42·2
1930	2,916,255	10,739	12,012	2,939,006	53·7
1960	3,858,903	74,546	18,328	3,951,777	72·2
1980	4,443,035	182,592	80,015	4,705,642	86·4
1990	4,512,523	244,539	134,767	4,891,769	90·1

Of the total population in 1990, 49% were male, 64·2% were urban and 74% were 18 years old or older.

Population of the larger cities, 1990 census, was as follows:

Milwaukee	628,088	Waukesha	56,958	Fond du Lac	37,757
Madison	191,262	Eau Claire	56,856	Wausau	37,060
Green Bay	96,466	Oshkosh	55,006	Beloit	35,573
Racine	84,298	Janesville	52,133	Brookfield	35,184
Kenosha	80,352	La Crosse	51,003	Neenah	33,592
Appleton	65,695	Sheboygan	49,676	Greenfield	33,403
West Allis	63,221	Wauwatosa	49,366		

Population of larger metropolitan areas, 1990 census: Milwaukee, 1,432,149; Madison, 367,085; Appleton-Neenah, 315,121; Duluth–Superior (Minn.–Wis.), 239,971; Green Bay, 194,594; Racine, 175,034.

CLIMATE. Milwaukee. Jan. 19°F (–7·2°C), July 70°F (21·1°C). Annual rainfall 29" (727 mm). *See* Great Lakes, p. 1398.

CONSTITUTION AND GOVERNMENT. The constitution, which dates from 1848, has 126 amendments. The legislative power is vested in a Senate of 33 members elected for 4 years, one-half elected alternately, and an Assembly of 99 members all elected simultaneously for 2 years. The Governor and Lieut.-Governor are elected for 4 years.

Wisconsin has universal suffrage for all citizens 18 years of age or over; but, as there is no official list of voters, the size of the electorate is unknown.

In the 1988 presidential election Dukakis polled 1,126,794 votes, Bush, 1,047,499.

The capital is Madison. The state has 72 counties.

Governor: Tommy G. Thompson (R.), 1991–95 ($92,283).
Lieut.-Governor: Scott McCallum (R.) ($49,673).
Secretary of State: Douglas La Follette (D.) ($45,088).

BUDGET. For the year ending 30 June 1990 (Wisconsin Bureau of Financial Operations figures) total revenue for all funds was $14,902,360,000 ($6,223,160,000 from taxation and $2,419,419,000 from federal aid). General expenditure from all funds was $12,752,292,000 ($4,044,485,000 for education, $3,676,043,000 for human resources).

Per capita personal income (1988) was $15,524.

ENERGY AND NATURAL RESOURCES

Electricity. There were, Dec. 1989, 87 hydro-electric power plants (16 of them municipal, 56 private in Wisconsin; 15 private outside the state) operated by public utilities with a total installed capacity of 504,072 kw.; output, 1989, was 1,492,535mwh. The 15 outside plants are in Michigan; installed capacity 99,990 kw., output 345,762mwh.

Fossil fuel and nuclear plants numbered 22 (3 municipal; 1 fossil fuel plant in Michigan); the former had a total installed capacity of 7,291,990 kw.; total output, (1989), 31,240,234mwh; the 2 nuclear plants had an installed capacity of 1,540,682 kw. and a total output (1989) of 10,832,221mwh.

There were also 27 internal combustion reciprocating plants (17 of them municipal), with a total installed capacity of 103,561 kw. and a total output of (1989) 5,833mwh., and 16 (1 municipal) internal combustion turbine plants with a total installed capacity of 1,257,450 kw.; total output was (1989) 55,865mwh.

There was a total of 152 plants, with a total installed capacity of 10,697,755 kw. and a total output of (1989) 43,626,688mwh.

Minerals. Construction sand and gravel, crushed stone and lime are the chief mineral products. Mineral production in 1989 was valued at $202m. This value included $58·5m. for sand and gravel, $100·1m. for crushed stone and about $24m. for lime. Value of all other minerals including industrial sand, dimension stone, crushed trap rock, peat and gemstones, $20·0m. Plans to develop a 1·9m. ton copper deposit near Ladysmith were the subject of hearings in 1990. Two new discoveries of copper, lead, zinc, gold and silver deposits were announced in 1990.

Agriculture. The total number of farms has declined in the last 50 years, but farms have become larger and more productive. On 1 Jan. 1991 there were 80,000 farms with a total acreage of 17·6m. acres and an average size of 220 acres, compared with 142,000 farms with a total acreage of 22·4m. acres and an average of 158 acres in 1959.

Cash receipts from products sold by Wisconsin farms in 1989, $5,481m.; $4,752m. from livestock and livestock products and $909m. from crops.

Wisconsin ranked first among the states in 1989 in the number of milch cows, milk and butter production and cheese production, which accounted for 32·9% of the USA's total. The state also ranked first in bulk whole and skim condensed sweetened milk, lactose, whey protein concentrate and dry whey. The state ranked first in 1988 in mink pelts. In crops the state ranked first in 1989 for snap beans, green beans, sweet corn for processing, and corn for silage. Production of the principal field crops in 1989 included: Corn for grain, 310·8m. bu.; corn for silage, 9·9m. tons; oats, 46·9m. bu.; all hay, 8·1m. tons. Other crops of importance 23·5m. cwt of potatoes, 11·4m. lb. of tobacco, 1·4m. bbls of cranberries, 1·6m. cwt of carrots and the processing crops of 810,200 tons of sweet corn, 130,100 tons of green peas and 281,300 tons of snap beans.

Forestry. Wisconsin has an estimated 15·3m. acres of forest land (about 42% of land area). Of 14·7m. acres of commercial forest (June 1988) national forests covered 1·2m. acres; state forests, 0·6m.; county and municipal forests, 2·3m.; forest industry, 1·2m.; private land, 9·1m.

Growing stock (1985), 15,500m. cu. ft, of which 11,900m. cu. ft is hardwood and 3,600m. cu. ft, softwood. Main hardwoods, aspen, maple, oak and birch; main softwoods, red pine, white pine, balsam fir, jack pine.

INDUSTRY. Wisconsin has much heavy industry, particularly in the Milwaukee area. Three fifths of manufacturing employees work on durable goods. Industrial machinery is the major industrial group (19% of all manufacturing employment) followed by food processing, fabricated metals, paper and paper products, printing and publishing, electrical machinery and rubber and miscellaneous plastics. Primary and secondary wood-product industries are high in value of product (over $91,000m. in 1986). Manufacturing establishments in 1990 provided 25% of nonfarm wage and salary workers, 33% of all earnings. The total number of establishments was 9,763 in 1990; the biggest concentration (40% of employment) is in the south-east.

TOURISM. The tourist-vacation industry ranks among the first three in economic importance. The decline of lumbering and mining in the northern section of the state has increased dependency on the recreation industry. The Division of Tourism of the Department of Development spent $9,006,300 to promote tourism in financial year 1989–90.

COMMUNICATIONS

Roads. The state had on 1 Jan. 1990, 109,448 miles of highway. 76% of all roads in the state have a bituminous (or similar) surface. There are 11,882 miles of state trunk roads and 19,540 miles of county trunk roads.

On 1 July 1991 Wisconsin registered 3,991,920 motor vehicles.

Railways. On 1 Aug. 1987 the state had 4,224 road-miles of railway.

Aviation. There were, in 1990, 95 publicly operated airports. Eleven scheduled air carrier airports were served by 20 regional and national air carriers.

Shipping. Lake Superior and Lake Michigan ports handled 36·2m. tons of freight in 1986; 80% of it at Superior, one of the world's biggest grain ports, and much of the rest at Milwaukee and Green Bay.

JUSTICE, RELIGION, EDUCATION AND WELFARE

Justice. The state's penal, reformatory and correctional system on 25 Oct. 1991 held 7,275 men and 351 women in 11 state-owned and other institutions for adult offenders; the probation and parole system was supervising 31,070 men and 7,810 women. Average daily population in the state's 2 juvenile institutions in Sept. 1991 was 616 males and 46 females. Wisconsin does not impose the death penalty.

Religion. Wisconsin church affiliation, as a percentage of the 1980 population, was estimated at 32·2% Catholic, 20·06% Lutheran, 3·74% Methodist, 10·41% other churches and 32·6% un-affiliated.

Education. All children between the ages of 6 and 18 are required to attend school full-time to the end of the school term in which they become 18 years of age. In 1990–91 the public school grades kindergarten–8 had 542,930 pupils and 33,965 (full-time equivalent) teachers; school grades 9–12 had 232,299 pupils and 17,018 teachers. Private schools enrolled 136,383 students grades kindergarten–12. Public pre-schools enrolled 13,265 children,and private, 7,832. Public elementary teachers' salaries, 1988–89, averaged $29,856; junior high, $31,880; middle school, $31,744; high, $32,257.

In 1990–91 vocational, technical and adult schools had an enrolment of 454,728 and 3,701 (full-time and part-time) teachers. There is a school for the visually handicapped and a school for the deaf.

The University of Wisconsin, established in 1848, was joined by law in 1971 with the Wisconsin State Universities System to become the University of Wisconsin System with 13 degree granting campuses, 13 two-year campuses in the Center System, and the University Extension. The system had, in 1990–91, 7,332 full-time professors and instructors and 2,327 student assistants. In autumn 1990, 160,950 students enrolled (10,664 at Eau Claire, 4,801 at Green Bay, 8,759 at La Crosse, 43,536 at Madison, 25,380 at Milwaukee, 11,093 at Oshkosh, 5,213 at Parkside, 5,454 at Platteville, 5,196 at River Falls, 8,805 at Stevens Point, 7,445 at Stout, 2,658 at Superior, 10,185 at Whitewater and 11,781 in the Center System freshman-sophomore centres). There are also several independent institutions of higher education. These (with 1990–91 enrolment) include 3 universities (14,726), 18 colleges (24,652), 4 technical and professional schools (4,790), and 4 theological seminaries (394).

The total expenditure, 1989–90, for all public education (except capital outlay and debt service) was $6,500m. ($1,335 per capita).

The state maintains an educational broadcasting and television service.

Health. In Oct. 1989 the state had 137 general and allied special hospitals (20,592 beds), 18 mental hospitals (2,161 beds), 9 treatment centres for alcoholism (342 beds). Patients in state mental hospitals and institutions for the mentally retarded in Dec. 1990 averaged 2,370. On 31 Dec. 1989 the state had 471 licensed nursing homes; the 1989 average daily census was 47,968 residents.

Social Security. On 1 Jan. 1974 the US Social Security administration assumed responsibility for financial aid (Supplemental Security Income) to persons 65 years old and over, blind persons and totally disabled persons, who satisfy requirements as to need. Recipients receive a federal payment plus a federally administered state supplementary payment, except for those who reside in a medical institution. In Sept. 1991, there were 88,567 SSI recipients in the state; payments were $489 for a single individual, $540 for an eligible individual with an ineligible spouse, and $745 for an eligible couple. A special payment level of $589 for an individual and

$1,098 for a couple may be paid with special approval for SSI recipients who are developmentally disabled or chronically mentally ill, living in a non-medical living arrangement not his or her own home. All SSI recipients receive state medical assistance coverage.

Under the Aid to Families with Dependent Children programme, 73,380 families of 204,234 persons received an average of $451.23 per family in Sept. 1991. Medicaid cost $1,422·7m. in financial year 1989–90.

Further Reading

Dictionary of Wisconsin Biography. Wis. Historical Society, Madison, 1960

Wisconsin Blue Book. Wis. Legislative Reference Bureau, Madison. Biennial

Current, R. N.,*Wisconsin, a History*. New York, 1977

Danziger, S. and Witte, J. F., *State Policy Choices: The Wisconsin Experience*. Univ. Wisconsin Press, 1988

Martin, L., *The Physical Geography of Wisconsin*. Univ. Wisconsin Press, 3rd ed., 1965

Nesbit, R. C., *Wisconsin, A History*. State Historical Society of Wisconsin, Madison, rev. ed., 1989

Robinson, A. H. and Culver, J. B., (eds.) *The Atlas of Wisconsin*. Univ. Wisconsin Press, 1974

Vogeler, I., *Wisconsin: A Geography*. Boulder, 1986

State Historical Society of Wisconsin: *The History of Wisconsin*. Vol. I [Alice E. Smith], Madison, 1973.—Vol. II [R. N. Current], Madison, 1976.—Vol. III [R. C. Nesbit], Madison, 1985.—Vol. VI [W. F. Thompson], Madison, 1988.—Vol. V (P. W. Glad), Madison, 1990

State Information Agency: Legislative Reference Bureau, State Capitol, Madison, Wis. 53702. *Chief:* Dr H. Rupert Theobald.

WYOMING

HISTORY. Wyoming, first settled in 1834, was admitted into the Union on 10 July 1890 as the 44th state.

AREA AND POPULATION. Wyoming is bounded north by Montana, east by South Dakota and Nebraska, south by Colorado, south-west by Utah and west by Idaho. Total area 97,809 sq. miles; land area, 97,105 sq. miles. The Yellowstone National Park occupies about 2·22m. acres; the Grand Teton National Park has 307,000 acres. The federal government in 1986 owned 49,838 sq. miles (50·9% of the total area of the state). The Federal Bureau of Land Management administers 17,546,188 acres.

Census population, 1 April 1990, 453,588, a decrease of 3·66% since 1980. Births in 1988 were 7,163 (15·9 per 1,000 population); deaths, 3,245 (6·4); marriages, 4,726 (9·9); divorces, 3,316 (6·7); infant deaths in 1987, 69 (9·2 per 1,000 live births).

Population in 5 census years was:

	White	Black	American Indian	Asiatic	Total	Per sq. mile
1910	140,318	2,235	1,486	1,926	145,965	1·5
1930	221,241	1,250	1,845	1,229	225,565	2·3
			All others			
1970	323,619	2,568	6,229		332,416	3·4
1980	446,488	3,364	19,705		469,557	4·8

	White	Black	American Indian	Asian/ Pacific Islands	Other	Total	Per sq. mile
1990	427,061	3,606	9,479	2,806	10,636	453,588	4·7

Of the total population in 1990, 227,007 were male and those over 18 years of age numbered 318,063.

The largest towns (with 1990 census population) are Cheyenne, 50,008; Casper, 46,742; Laramie, 26,687; Rock Springs, 19,050; Gillette, 17,635; Sheridan, 13,900; Green River, 12,711.

CLIMATE. Cheyenne. Jan. 25°F (−3·9°C), July 66°F (18·9°C). Annual rainfall 15" (376 mm). Yellowstone Park. Jan. 18°F (−7·8°C), July 61°F (16·1°C). Annual rainfall 18" (444 mm). *See* Mountain States, p. 1397–98.

CONSTITUTION AND GOVERNMENT. The constitution, drafted in 1890, has since had 43 amendments. The Legislature consists of a Senate of 30 members elected for 4 years, 15, retiring every 2 years, and a House of Representatives of 64 members elected for 2 years. It sits annually in Jan. or Feb. The Governor is elected for 4 years.

In the 1988 presidential election Bush polled 106,814 votes, Dukakis, 67,077.

The capital is Cheyenne. The state contains 23 counties.

Governor: Mike Sullivan (D.), 1991–95 ($70,000).
Secretary of State: Kathy Karpan (D.) ($52,500).

ECONOMY

Budget. In the fiscal year ending 1 July 1989 (State Treasurer's figures) cash receipts were $1,656,132,900; general expenditures were $1,494,778,300.

Per capita personal income (1990) was $16,398.

Banking and Finance. In Sept. 1989 there were 55 state banks with a total of $1,846,407 deposits.

ENERGY AND NATURAL RESOURCES

Electricity. In 1988 there were 11 hydro-electric stations with a gross nameplate installed capacity of 281·0 mw, and 8 thermo-electric stations with a total installed capacity of 5668·7 mw.

Minerals. Wyoming is largely an oil-producing state. In 1990 the output of petroleum was valued at $1,657·6m.; natural gas, $771·2m. Other mining: Coal, $1,157·3m.; trona, $150·6m.; uranium, $17,740·6m.; bentonite, $10,179·6m.; others, $8,196·7m.

Agriculture. Wyoming is semi-arid, and agriculture is carried on by irrigation (1·4 m. acres in 1989) and by dry farming (920,000 acres in 1989). In 1988 there were 8,700 farms and ranches; total farm area in 1990 was 34·8m. acres. In 1987 13,162 people were employed on farms.

Total value, 1989, of crops produced, $284·8m.; of livestock, $401·3m. Crop production in 1990 (1,000 bushels): Corn for grain, 6,000; wheat, 6,113; oats, 1,540; barley, 9,250; sugar-beet, 1,308 tons. Animals on farms in 1990 included 1·19m. cattle, 830,000 sheep and lambs and in 1988 21,000 hogs and pigs. Total egg production in 1988 was 3·6m.

Forestry. In 1989 there were 35,379 acres of timberland.

Fisheries. In 1989 the net production of fish hatch was 599,458.

INDUSTRY. In 1987 there were 531 manufacturing establishments. There were 964 mining companies or producers. A large portion of the manufacturing in the state is based on natural resources, mainly oil and farm products. Leading industries are food, wood products (except furniture) and machinery (except electrical). The Wyoming Industrial Development Corporation assists in the development of small industries by providing credit.

LABOUR. In 1987 the mining industry employed an average of 19,945 workers; construction, 17,318; manufacturing, 9,451; transportation and public utilities, 16,289. The total civilian labour force in 1991 was 249,368, of whom 239,787 were employed; non-agricultural, 241,468. The average unemployment rate was 6·3% in 1988 and average weekly earnings were $611 for mining (production workers) in 1987. In 1988 there were no work stoppages.

Trade Unions. There were 22,669 working members in trade unions (10·1% of total employment).

TOURISM. There are over 7m. tourists annually, mainly outdoor enthusiasts. The state has the largest elk and pronghorn antelope herds in the world, 10 fish hatcheries and numerous wild game. Receipts from hunters and fishermen in 1986, $14,628,081. In 1988, 5·2m. people visited the 6 national areas; 1·7m. people visited state parks and historic sites. In 1987 559,032 fishing, game and bird licences were sold. There were (1990) 12 operational ski areas.

COMMUNICATIONS

Roads. The roads in 1986 comprised 5,240 miles of federal highways, 349 miles of state highways and 914 miles of inter-state highway. There were (1988) 288,998 passenger vehicles, 179,669 lorries, and 20,050 motor cycles.

Railways. The railways, 1986, had a length of 2,615 mainline miles and 550 branch miles.

Aviation. There were 11 towns with commuter air services and 2 towns on jet routes in 1987.

Telecommunications. In 1989 there were 30 AM, 31 FM radio stations and 9 television stations.

Newspapers. (1989) there were 9 daily newspapers.

JUSTICE, RELIGION, EDUCATION AND WELFARE

Justice. The state penitentiary in July 1988 held 736 inmates, the Womens' Center, 49. There are 2 other state correctional institutions. There have been 14 executions in Wyoming, 8 by hanging and 6 by lethal gas.

Religion. Chief religious bodies are the Roman Catholic (with 45,917 members in 1974), Mormon (28,954 in 1971) and Protestant churches (83,327 in 1974). There were 5,000 members of the Eastern Orthodox Church in 1972.

Education. In 1988–89 public elementary and secondary schools had 97,793 pupils and 5,841 teachers. Enrolment in the parochial elementary and secondary schools was about 3,500. The average total expenditure per pupil for 1987–88 was $4,766.

The University of Wyoming, founded at Laramie in 1887, had in academic year 1989–90 12,289 students. There are 2-year colleges at Casper, Riverton, Torrington, Cheyenne, Powell, Rock Springs and Sheridan with credit course enrolment of 15,685 students in 1987–88.

Social Welfare. In Jan. 1974 the federal government assumed many of the previous state programmes including old age assistance, aid to the blind and disabled. In 1987 financial year, $16·2m. was distributed in food stamps; $17·6m. in aid to families with dependent children; $626,314 in general assistance; $1,189,902 in emergency assistance; $41m. in Medicaid. Total state expenditure on public assistance and social services programmes, financial year 1987, $123·5m.

Health. In 1989 the state had 30 hospitals with 2,133 beds, 30 registered nursing homes and 20 boarding homes with 3,280 beds.

Further Reading

Official Directory. Secretary of State. Cheyenne. Biennial
1987 Wyoming Data Handbook. Dept. of Administration and Fiscal Control. Division of Research and Statistics, Cheyenne, 1987
Brown, R. H., *Wyoming: A Geography.* Boulder, 1980
Larsen, T. A., *History of Wyoming.* Rev. ed. Univ. of Nebraska, 1979
Treadway, T., *Wyoming.* New York, 1982

OUTLYING TERRITORIES

Non-Self-Governing Territories: Summaries of Information Transmitted to the Secretary-General of the United Nations. Annual

GUAM

HISTORY. Magellan is said to have discovered the island in 1521; it was ceded by Spain to the US by the Treaty of Paris (10 Dec. 1898). The island was captured by the Japanese on 10 Dec. 1941, and retaken by American forces from 21 July 1944. Guam is of great strategic importance; substantial numbers of naval and air force personnel occupy about one-third of the usable land.

AREA AND POPULATION. Guam is the largest and most southern island of the Marianas Archipelago, in 13° 26' N. lat., 144° 43' E. long. The length is 30 miles, the breadth from 4 to 10 miles, and there are about 209 sq. miles (541 sq. km). Agaña, the seat of government is about 8 miles from the anchorage in Apra Harbour. The census on 1 April 1990 showed a population of 132,000, an increase of 26,021 since 1980. In 1980 those of Guamanian ancestry numbered 50,794; foreign-born, 28,572; density was 507 per sq. mile. The Malay strain is predominant. The native language is Chamorro; English is the official language and is taught in all schools.

CLIMATE. Tropical maritime, with little difference in temperatures over the year. Rainfall is copious at all seasons, but is greatest from July to Oct. Agaña. Jan. 81°F (27·2°C), July 81°F (27·2°C). Annual rainfall 93" (2,325 mm).

CONSTITUTION AND GOVERNMENT. Guam's constitutional status is that of an 'unincorporated territory' of the US. Entry of US citizens is unrestricted; foreign nationals are subject to normal regulations. In 1949–50 the President transferred the administration of the island from the Navy Department (who held it from 1899) to the Interior Department. The transfer conferred full citizenship on the Guamanians, who had previously been 'nationals' of the US. There was a referendum on status, 30 Jan. 1982. 38% of eligible voters voted; 48·5% of those favoured Commonwealth status.

The Governor and his staff constitute the executive arm of the government. The Legislature is unicameral; its powers are similar to those of an American state legislature. At the general election of Nov. 1982, the Democratic Party won 14 seats and the Republicans 7. All adults 18 years of age or over are enfranchised. Guam returns one non-voting delegate to the House of Representatives.

ECONOMY

Budget. Total revenue (1989) $378m.; expenditure $369m.

Banking. Recent changes in banking law make it possible for foreign banks to operate in Guam.

NATURAL RESOURCES

Water. Supplies are from springs, reservoirs and groundwater; 65% comes from water-bearing limestone in the north. The Navy and Air Force conserve water in reservoirs. The Water Resources Research Centre is at Guam University.

Agriculture. The major products of the island are sweet potatoes, cucumbers, water melons and beans. In 1982 there were 140 full-time and 1,904 part-time farmers. Livestock (1988) included 2,000 cattle, 14,000 pigs, and (1984) 36,430 poultry. Commercial productions (1983) amounted to 6·6m. lb. of fruit and vegetables ($3·4m.), 567,000 doz. eggs ($811,093). There is an agricultural experimental station at Inarajan.

Fisheries. Fresh fish caught in 1982, 319,300 lb. Offshore fishing produced 100,687 lb., including 6,080 lb. of shrimps.

INDUSTRY AND TRADE

Industry. Guam Economic Development Authority controls three industrial estates: Cabras Island (32 acres); Calvo estate at Tamuning (26 acres); Harmon estate (16 acres). Industries include textile manufacture, cement and petroleum distribution, warehousing, printing, plastics and ship-repair. Other main sources of income are construction and tourism.

Labour. In 1983 51% of employment was in government, 18% in trade, 5% in construction, 13% in services, 4% in manufacturing, 5% in transport and 4% in finance.

Trade. Guam is the only American territory which has complete 'free trade'; excise duties are levied only upon imports of tobacco, liquid fuel and liquor. In the year ending 31 Dec. 1980 imports were valued at $544·1m. and accounted for 90% of trade.

Tourism. Tourism is developing; there were 1,900 visitors in 1964 and 407,100 in 1986.

COMMUNICATIONS

Roads. There are 419 miles of all-weather roads.

Civil Aviation. There is an international airport at Tamuning. 7 commercial airlines serve Guam.

Post and Broadcasting. Overseas telephone and radio dispatch facilities are available. In 1983 there were 23,442 telephones.

There are 4 commercial stations, a commercial television station, a public broadcasting station and a cable television station with 24 channels.

Newspapers. There is 1 daily newspaper, a twice-weekly paper, and 4 weekly publications (all of which are of military or religious interest only).

JUSTICE, RELIGION, EDUCATION AND WELFARE

Justice. The Organic Act established a District Court with jurisdiction in matters arising under both federal and territorial law; the judge is appointed by the President subject to Senate approval. There is also a Supreme Court and a Superior Court; all judges are locally appointed except the Federal District judge. Misdemeanours are under the jurisdiction of the police court. The Spanish law was superseded in 1933 by 5 civil codes based upon California law.

Religion. About 98% of the Guamanians are Roman Catholics; others are Baptists, Episcopalians, Bahais, Lutherans, Mormons, Presbyterians, Jehovah's Witnesses and members of the Church of Christ and Seventh Day Adventists.

Education. Elementary education is compulsory. There are Chamorro Studies courses and bi-lingual teaching programmes to integrate the Chamorro language and culture into elementary and secondary school courses. There were, Dec. 1983, 24 elementary schools, 6 junior high schools, 5 senior high schools, one vocational-technical school for high school students and adults and 1 school for handicapped children. There were 17,725 elementary school pupils, 7,418 junior high and 5,776 senior high school pupils. Department of Education staff included 1,258 teachers. The Catholic schools system also operates 3 senior high schools, 3 junior high and 5 elementary schools. The Seventh Day Adventist Guam Mission Academy operates a school from grades 1 through 12, serving over 100 students. St John's Episcopal Preparatory School provides education for 530 students between kindergarten and the 9th grade. The University of Guam (an accredited institution) had 2,774 students, 1983–84.

Health. There is a hospital, 8 nutrition centres, a school health programme and an extensive immunization programme. Emphasis is on disease prevention, health education and nutrition.

Further Reading

Report (Annual) of the Governor of Guam to the US Department of Interior
Guam Annual Economic Review. Economic Research Center, Agaña

Carano, P. and Sanchez, P. C., *Complete History of Guam*. Rutland, Vt., 1964

REPUBLIC OF BELAU (PALAU)

HISTORY. Spain acquired sovereignty over the Palau Islands in 1886, but sold the archipelago to Germany in 1899. Japan occupied the islands in 1914, and in 1921 they were mandated to Japan by the League of Nations. Captured by Allied Forces in 1944, the islands became part of the UN Trust Territory of the Pacific Islands created on 18 July 1947 and administered by the USA. Following a referendum in July 1978 in which Palauans voted against joining the new Federated States of Micronesia, the islands became an autonomous republic from 1 Jan. 1981, but acquisition of a free-association status with the USA was delayed by disputes over US intentions to base nuclear weapons on the islands. The first President, Haruo Remeliik, was assassinated on 28 Aug. 1985, and his successor, Lazarus Salii, committed suicide on 20 Aug. 1988.

AREA AND POPULATION. The archipelago lies in the Western Pacific and has a land area of 488 sq. km (188 sq. miles). It comprises 26 islands and over 300 islets, the largest being Babelthuap (368 sq. km) with 3,400 inhabitants in 1980, but most inhabitants (9,442 in 1986) live on the small island of Koror (8 sq. km) to the south, containing the present headquarters (a new capital is being built in eastern Babelthuap). The local language is Palauan; both Palauan and English are official. The total population (1986 Census) was 13,873; estimate (1989) 14,208.

CONSTITUTION AND GOVERNMENT. The Constitution was adopted on 2 April 1979 and took effect from 1 Jan. 1981. The Republic has a bicameral legislature comprising a 16-member Senate (one from each of the Republic's 16 component states) and an 18-member House of Delegates, both elected for a term of 4 years as are the President and Vice-President; latest elections were in Nov. 1988.

President: Ngiratkel Etpison (elected 2 Nov. 1988).
Vice-President: Kuniwo Nakamura.

BANKING. The National Development Bank of Palau is situated in Koror.

FISHERIES. Catch (1988) 1,400 tonnes.

COMMERCE. Imports (1984) US$25·1m.

COMMUNICATIONS

Roads. In 1986 there were 26 km of roads and 1,687 motor vehicles.

Shipping. In 1985, 56,000 tonnes of cargo were discharged and 2,000 tonnes were loaded.

Telecommunications. In 1988 there were 1,500 telephones. In 1989 there was a television station with 1,600 receivers, and a radio station with 9,000 receivers.

JUSTICE, RELIGION, EDUCATION AND WELFARE

Justice. There is a Supreme Court and various subsidiary courts.

Religion. The majority of the population are Roman Catholic.

Education. In 1987 there were 2,784 pupils in 26 primary schools, 1,009 pupils in 6 secondary schools and 382 students (1984) in a technical school.

Health. In 1986 there were 10 doctors, 3 dentists, 1 pharmacist, 82 nursing personnel and a hospital with 70 beds.

THE NORTHERN MARIANAS

HISTORY. In 1989 Spain ceded Guam (largest and southernmost of the Marianas Islands) to the US and sold the rest to Germany. Occupied by Japan in 1914, the islands were administered by Japan under a League of Nations mandate until occupied by US forces in August 1944. In 1947 they became part of the US-administered Trust Territory of the Pacific Islands. On 17 June 1975 the electorate adopted a covenant to establish a Commonwealth in association with the US; this was approved by the US government in April 1976 and came into force on 1 Jan. 1978. In Nov. 1986 the islanders were granted US citizenship. The UN terminated the Trusteeship status on 22 Dec. 1990.

AREA AND POPULATION. The Northern Marianas form a single chain of 16 mountainous islands extending north of Guan for about 560 km, with a combined land area of 477 sq. km (184 sq. miles) and a population (1980 Census) of 16,780; estimate (1990) 23,300.

The areas and populations of the islands are as follows:

Island(s)	Sq. km	1980 Census	1988 Estimate
Northern Group [1]	171	104	133
Saipan	122	14,585	19,156
Tinian (with Aguijan)	101 [2]	899	949
Rota	83	1,274	1,539

[1] Pagan, Agrihan, Alamagan and 9 uninhabited islands.   [2] Including uninhabited Aguijan.

In 1980, 55% spoke Chamorro, 11% Woleaian and 13% Filipino languages, but English remains the official language. The largest town is Chalan Kanoa on Saipan. In 1987 births numbered 958 and deaths 115.

CONSTITUTION AND GOVERNMENT. The Constitution was approved by a referendum on 6 March 1977 and came into force on 9 Jan. 1978. The legislature comprises a 9-member Senate, with 3 Senators elected from each of the main 3 islands for a term of 4 years, and a 15-member House of Representatives, elected for a term of 2 years. The Commonwealth is administered by a Governor and Lieut.-Governor, elected for 4 years.

Governor: Lorenzo Guerrero.
Lieut.-Governor: Benjamin Manglona.
Flag: Blue, with a five-pointed white star superimposed on a grey latte stone in the centre.

AGRICULTURE. In 1976 there were 7,196 cattle, chiefly on Tinian.

COMMERCE. In 1988 imports totalled US$242m.; exports in 1985 were US$12·3m.

TOURISM. In 1984 there were 104,156 vistors.

COMMUNICATIONS

Roads. There are about 300 km of roads (54 km paved).

Civil Aviation. Air Micronesia provides inter-island services.

Telecommunications. In 1989 there were 10,500 radio and 4,100 television receivers, 3 radio stations and a 15-channel cable TV station in Saipan. Telephones (1987), 4,900.

RELIGION, EDUCATION AND WELFARE

Religion. The population is predominantly Roman Catholic.

Education. In 1989 there were 18 primary schools with 4,882 pupils and 9 secondary schools with 2,075 pupils. The tertiary college on Saipan had 1,097 students.

Health. In 1986 there were 23 doctors, 4 dentists, 103 nursing personnel, 2 pharmacists and 2 midwives. In 1988 there was 1 hospital with 70 beds.

AMERICAN SAMOA

HISTORY. The Samoan Islands were first visited by Europeans in the 18th century; the first recorded visit was in 1722. On 14 July 1889 a treaty between the USA, Germany and Great Britain proclaimed the Samoan islands neutral territory, under a 4-power government consisting of the 3 treaty powers and the local native government. By the Tripartite Treaty of 7 Nov. 1899, ratified 19 Feb. 1900, Great Britain and Germany renounced in favour of the US all rights over the islands of the Samoan group east of 171° long. west of Greenwich, the islands to the west of that meridian being assigned to Germany (now the Independent State of Western Samoa, *see* p. 1593). The islands of Tutuila and Aunu'u were ceded to the US by their High Chiefs on 17 April 1900, and the islands of the Manu'a group on 16 July 1904. Congress accepted the islands under a Joint Resolution approved 20 Feb. 1929. Swain's Island, 210 miles north of the Samoan Islands, was annexed in 1925 and is administered as an integral part of American Samoa.

AREA AND POPULATION. The islands (Tutuila, Aunu'u, Ta'u, Olosega, Ofu and Rose) are approximately 650 miles east-north-east of Fiji. The total area of American Samoa is 76·1 sq. miles (197 sq. km); population, 1986, 46,773, nearly all Polynesians or part-Polynesians. The island's 3 Districts are Eastern (population, 1980, 17,311), Western (13,227) and Manu'a (1,732). There is also Swain's Island, with an area of 1·9 sq. miles and 29 inhabitants (1980), which lies 210 miles to the north west. Rose Island (uninhabited) is 0·4 sq. mile in area. In 1990 some 85,000 American Samoans lived in the USA.

CLIMATE. A tropical maritime climate with a small annual range of temperature and plentiful rainfall. Pago-Pago. Jan. 83°F (28·3°C), July 80°F (26·7°C). Annual rainfall 194" (4,850 mm).

CONSTITUTION AND GOVERNMENT. American Samoa is constitutionally an unorganized unincorporated territory of the US administered under the Department of the Interior. Its indigenous inhabitants are US nationals and are classified locally as citizens of American Samoa with certain privileges under local laws not granted to non-indigenous persons. Polynesian customs (not inconsistent with US laws) are respected.

Fagatogo is the seat of the Government.

The islands are organized in 15 counties grouped in 3 districts; these counties and districts correspond to the traditional political units. On 25 Feb. 1948 a bicameral legislature was established, at the request of the Samoans, to have advisory legislative functions. With the adoption of the Constitution of 22 April 1960, and the revised Constitution of 1967, the legislature was vested with limited law-making authority. The lower house, or House of Representatives, is composed of 20 members elected by universal adult suffrage and 1 non-voting member for Swain's Island. The upper house, or Senate, is comprised of 18 members elected, in the traditional Samoan manner, in meetings of the chiefs.

Governor: Peter TaliColeman.
Lieut.-Governor: Galeá I. Poumele.

ECONOMY

Policy. The first formal Economic Development and Planning Office completed its first year in 1971. Much has been done to promote economic expansion within the Territory and a large amount of outside investment interest has been stimulated.

The Office initiated the first Territorial Comprehensive Plan. This plan when completed will, with periodic updating, provide a guideline to territorial development for 20 years. The planning programme was made possible under a Housing and Urban Development '701' grant programme, and Economic Development Administration '302' planning programmes.

The focus will be on physical development and the problems of a rapidly increasing population with severely limited labour resources.

Budget. The chief sources of revenue are annual federal grants from the US, and local revenues from taxes, and duties, and receipts from commercial operations (enterprise and special revenue funds), utilities, rents and leases and liquor sales. During the financial year 1983–84 the Government had a revenue of $76·6m. including local appropriations of $9·5m., federal appropriations of $39·6m. and enterprise funds of $17·5m.

Banking. The American Samoa branch of the Bank of Hawaii and the American Samoa Bank offer all commercial banking services. The Development Bank of American Samoa, government-owned, is concerned primarily through loans and guarantees with the economic advancement of the Territory.

ENERGY AND NATURAL RESOURCES

Electricity. Net power generated (financial year 1981) was 72·2m. kwh., of which 23·1m. kwh. was supplied to large power users and 20·2m. kwh. to householders. All the Manu'a islands have electricity.

Agriculture. Of the 48,640 acres of land area, 11,000 acres are suitable for tropical crops; most commercial farms are in the Tafuna plains and west Tutuila. Principal crops are taro, bread-fruit, yams, bananas and coconuts. Production (1988 in 1,000 tonnes): Taro, 4; bananas, 1; fruit, 1; coconuts, 5.

Livestock (1988): Pigs, 11,000; (1984) goats, 8,000; poultry, 45,000.

INDUSTRY AND TRADE

Industry. Fish canning is important, employing the second largest number of people (after government). Attempts are being made to provide a variety of light industries. Tuna fishing and local inshore fishing are both expanding.

Commerce. In 1982 American Samoa exported goods valued at $186,782,060 and imported goods valued at $119,416,918. Chief exports are canned tuna, watches, pet foods and handicrafts. Chief imports are building materials, fuel oil, food, jewellery, machines and parts, alcoholic beverages and cigarettes.

COMMUNICATIONS

Roads. There are (1983) about 76 miles of paved roads and 16 miles of unpaved within the Federal Aid highway system. There are 21 miles of other unpaved roads. Motor vehicles registered, 1983, 3,657.

Civil Aviation. South Pacific Island Airways and Polynesian Airlines operate daily services between American Samoa and Western Samoa. South Pacific Island Airways also operates between Pago Pago and Honolulu, and between Pago Pago and Tonga. The islands are also served by Air Nauru which operates between Pago Pago, Tahiti and Auckland, and Air Pacific (Fiji and westward). South Pacific and Manu'a Air Transport run local services.

Shipping. The harbour at Pago Pago, which nearly bisects the island of Tutuila, is the only good harbour for large vessels in Samoa. By sea, there is a twice-monthly service between Fiji, New Zealand and Australia and regular service between US, South Pacific ports, Honolulu and Japan.

Telecommunications. A commercial radiogram service is available to all parts of the world through 2 principal trunks, United States and Western Samoa. Commercial phone and telex services are operated to all parts of the world on a 24-hour service. Number of telephones (Sept. 1983), 6,029; telex subscribers, 78.

JUSTICE, EDUCATION AND WELFARE

Justice. Judicial power is vested firstly in a High Court. The trial division has original jurisdiction of all criminal and civil cases. The probate division has jurisdiction of estates, guardianships, trusts and other matters. The land and title division decides cases relating to disputes involving communal land and Matai title court rules on questions and controversy over family titles. The appellate division hears appeals from trial, land and title and probate divisions as well as having original jurisdiction in selected matters. The appellate court is the court of last resort. Two American judges sit with 5 Samoan judges permanently. In addition there are temporary judges or assessors who sit occasionally on cases involving Samoan customs. There is also a District Court with limited jurisdiction and there are 69 village courts.

Education. Education is compulsory between the ages of 6 and 18. The Government (1983) maintains 24 consolidated elementary schools, 5 senior high schools with technical departments, 1 community college, special education classes for the handicapped and 92 Early Childhood Education Centres for pre-school children. Total elementary and secondary enrolment (1983), 8,300; in ECE schools, 1,611; classes for the handicapped, 68; total elementary and secondary classroom teachers, 480. Ten private schools had 2,108 students. Learning is by a variety of media including television.

Health. The Department of Health provides the only curative and preventive medical and dental care in American Samoa. It operates a general hospital (173 beds including 49 bassinets), 3 dispensaries on Tutuila, 4 dispensaries in the Manu'a group, 1 on Aunu'u and 1 on Swain's Island. A $3·5m. tropical medical centre was completed and placed in service in 1968. This now embraces the general hospital as well as preventive health services and out-patient clinics for surgery, obstetrics, gynaecology, emergencies, family practice, internal medicine, paediatrics; there are clinics for treatment of the eye, ear, nose and throat, dental and public health departments.

In 1983 there were 27 doctors, 7 dentists, 2 optometrists, 3 nurse anaesthetists, and 3 physician assistants. Total number of health service employees, 397.

OTHER PACIFIC TERRITORIES

Johnston Atoll. Two small islands 1,150 km south-west of Hawaii, administered by the US Air Force. Area, under 1 sq. mile; population (1980 census) 327, with Sand Island.

Midway Islands. Two small islands at the western end of the Hawaiian chain, administered by the US Navy. Area, 2 sq. miles; population (1980 census) 453.

Wake Island. Three small islands 3,700 km west of Hawaii, administered by the US Air Force. Area, 3 sq. miles; population (1980 census) 302.

COMMONWEALTH OF PUERTO RICO

HISTORY. Puerto Rico, by the treaty of 10 Dec. 1898 (ratified 11 April 1899), was ceded by Spain to the US. The name was changed from Porto Rico to Puerto Rico by an Act of Congress approved 17 May 1932. Its territorial constitution was determined by the 'Organic Act' of Congress (2 March 1917) known as the 'Jones Act', which ruled until 25 July 1952, when the present constitution of the Commonwealth of Puerto Rico was proclaimed.

AREA AND POPULATION. Puerto Rico is the most easterly of the Greater Antilles and lies between the Dominican Republic and the US Virgin Islands. The island has a land area of 3,459 sq. miles and a population, according to the census of 1990, of 3,522,037, an increase of 10·2% over 1980. Urban population (1980) 2,134,365 (66·8%).

A law of April 1991 made Spanish the sole official language, replacing a law of 1902 establishing Spanish and English as joint official languages.

Vital statistics (1988): Births, 64,081 (19·5 per 1,000 population); deaths, 25,123 (7·6); deaths under 1 year, 810 (12·6 per 1,000 live births).

Chief towns, 1990 are: San Juan, 437,745; Bayamón, 220,262; Ponce, 187,749; Carolina, 177,806; Caguas, 133,447; Mayaguez, 100,371; Arecibo, 93,385.

The Puerto Rican island of Vieques, 10 miles to the east, has an area of 51·7 sq. miles and 8,602 (1990) inhabitants. The island of Culebra, with 1,542 (1990) inhabitants, between Puerto Rico and St Thomas, has a good harbour.

CONSTITUTION AND GOVERNMENT. Puerto Rico has representative government, the franchise being restricted to citizens 18 years of age or over, residence (1 year) and such additional qualifications as may be prescribed by the Legislature of Puerto Rico, but no property qualification may be imposed. Puerto Ricans do not vote in the US presidential elections, though individuals living on the mainland are free to do so subject to the local electoral laws. The executive power resides in a Governor, elected directly by the people every 4 years. Fourteen heads of departments form the Governor's advisory council, also designated as his Council of Secretaries. The legislative functions are vested in a Senate, composed of 27 members and the House of Representatives, composed of 53 members. Both houses meet annually in Jan. Puerto Rico sends to Congress a Resident Commissioner to the US, elected by the people for a term of 4 years, but he has no vote in Congress. Puerto Rican men are subject to conscription in US services.

On 27 Nov. 1953 President Eisenhower sent a message to the General Assembly of the UN stating 'if at any time the Legislative Assembly of Puerto Rico adopts a resolution in favour of more complete or even absolute independence' he 'will immediately thereafter recommend to Congress that such independence be granted'.

For an account of the constitutional developments prior to 1952, see THE STATESMAN'S YEAR-BOOK, 1952, p. 742. The new constitution was drafted by a Puerto Rican Constituent Assembly and approved by the electorate at a referendum on 3 March 1952. It was then submitted to Congress, which struck out Section 20 of Article 11 covering the 'right to work' and the 'right to an adequate standard of living'; the remainder was passed and proclaimed by the Governor on 25 July 1952.

At the election on 4 Nov. 1988 the Popular Democratic Party, headed by Rafael Hernández Colón, polled 871,858 votes (48·7% of the total); the New Progressive Party, headed by Baltazar Corrada del Rió, polled 820,342 votes (45·8% of the total); the Independence Party (full independence by constitutional means), headed by Rubén Berrios Martínez, polled 99,206 votes (5·5% of the total).

At a referendum on 8 Dec. 1991 in advance of an impending plebiscite on Puerto Rico's future status (status quo, 51st state of the USA or full independence), 53% of votes cast were against proposals emphasizing independence.

Governor: Rafael Hernández Colón (Popular Democratic Party).

ECONOMY

Budget. Central Government budget, year ending 30 June 1988: Balance at 1 July 1988, $31,441,000; receipts, $5,297,512,000; disbursements, $5,266,071,000.

Assessed value of property, 30 June 1990, was $6,940·7m. Bonded indebtedness for the commonwealth and municipalities, 30 June 1991, was $3,728·8m.

The US administers and finances the postal service and maintains air and naval bases. US payments in Puerto Rico, including direct expenditures (mainly military), grants-in-aid and other payments to individuals and to business totalled: 1985–86, $4,057·1m.; 1986–87, $4,006·5m.; 1987-88, $4,019·6m.; 1988-89, $4,202·9m.; 1989–90, $4,832·8m.

Banking. Banks on 30 June 1991 had total deposits of $22,259·2m. Bank loans were $13,283·3m. This includes 18 commercial banks, 2 government banks and 4 trust companies.

NATURAL RESOURCES

Minerals. There is stone, and some production of cement (1m. tons in 1990–91).

Agriculture. Farming is mainly of sugar-cane. Production of raw sugar, 96 degrees basis, 1990 crop year, was 68,086 tons.

Livestock (1990): Cattle, 614,857; pigs, 205,814; poultry, 11,021,163.

COMMERCE. In 1990–91 imports amounted to $15,904·3m., of which $10,739·2m. came from US; exports were valued at $21,323m., of which $18,484·4m. went to US.

In financial year 1991 the US took: Cigarettes, cigars and cheroots, 1,581,564,857 units; other tobacco and products, 357,661 lb.; rum, 51,512,403 proof litres.

Puerto Rico is not permitted to levy taxes on imports.

Total trade between Puerto Rico and UK (British Department of Trade returns, in £1,000 sterling):

	1987	1988	1989	1990	1991
Imports to UK	76,347	91,909	117,628	123,087	109,295
Exports and re-exports from UK	39,405	38,877	79,851	69,593	81,637

COMMUNICATIONS

Roads. The Department of Public Works had under maintenance at 31 Dec. 1990, 19,340 km of paved road. Motor vehicles registered 30 June 1990, 1,582,081.

Shipping. In financial year 1990–91, 8,823 American and foreign vessels of 64,152,472 gross tons entered and cleared Puerto Rico.

Telecommunications. In Oct. 1991 there were 105 broadcasting stations and 20 television companies. There were (1990) 1,062,086 telephones.

Newspapers. In 1991 there were 3 main newspapers, *El Nuevo Día* had a daily circulation of 210,044; *El Vocero*, 261,781; *San Juan Star*, 47,500.

JUSTICE AND EDUCATION

Justice. The Commonwealth judiciary system is headed by a Supreme Court of 7 members, appointed by the Governor, and consists of a Superior Tribunal with 11 sections and 92 superior judges, a District Tribunal with 38 sections and 99 district judges, and 60 municipal judges all appointed by the Governor.

Education. Education was made compulsory in 1899, but in 1981, 3·6% of the children still had no access to schooling. The percentage of illiteracy in 1980 was 10·3% of those 10 years of age or older. Total enrolment in public day schools, Aug. 1990, was 651,225 (first school month). All private schools had a total enrolment of 145,768 pupils in 1990. All instruction below senior high school standard is given in Spanish only.

The University of Puerto Rico, in Río Piedras, 7 miles from San Juan, had 55,626 students in 1989–90 of which 13,759 were in 6 Regional Colleges and 41,867 in other colleges. Higher education is also available in the Inter-American University of Puerto Rico (39,002 students in 1989–90), the Catholic University of Puerto Rico (12,507), the Sacred Heart College (7,302) and the Fundación Ana G. Méndez (17,271). These and other private colleges and universities had 24,439 students.

Further Reading

Statistical Information: The area of Economic Research and Social Analysis of the Puerto Rico Planning Board publishes: *(a)* annual *Economic Report to the Governor; (b) External Trade Statistics* (annual report); *(c) Reports on national income and balance of payments; (d) Socio-Economic Statistics* (since 1940); *(e) Puerto Rico Monthly Economic Indicators.* In addition there are annual reports by various Departments.
Annual Reports. Governor of Puerto Rico. Washington
Bloomfield, R. J., *Puerto Rico: the Search for a National Policy.* Boulder (Colo.), 1985
Carr, R., *Puerto Rico: a Colonial Experiment.* New York Univ. Press, 1984
Cevallos, E., *Puerto Rico.* [Bibliography], Oxford and Santa Barbara, 1985
Crampsey, R. A., *Puerto Rico.* Newton Abbot, 1973
Dietz, J. L., *Economic History of Puerto Rico: Institutional Change and Capital Development.* Princeton Univ. Press, 1987
Falk, P. S., (ed.) *The Political Status of Puerto Rico.* Lexington, Mass., 1986

Commonwealth Library: Univ. of Puerto Rico Library, Rio Piedras. *Librarian:* José Lázaro.

VIRGIN ISLANDS OF THE UNITED STATES

HISTORY. The Virgin Islands of the United States, formerly known as the Danish West Indies, were named and claimed for Spain by Columbus in 1493. They were later settled by Dutch and English planters, invaded by France in the mid-17th century and abandoned by the French c. 1700, by which time Danish influence had been established. St Croix was held by the Knights of Malta between two periods of French rule.

They were purchased by the United States from Denmark for $25m. in a treaty ratified by both nations and proclaimed 31 March 1917. Their value was wholly strategic, inasmuch as they commanded the Anegada Passage from the Atlantic Ocean to the Caribbean Sea and the approach to the Panama Canal. Although the inhabitants were made US citizens in 1927, the islands are, constitutionally, an 'unincorporated territory'.

AREA AND POPULATION. The Virgin Islands group, lying about 40 miles due east of Puerto Rico, comprises the islands of St Thomas (28 sq. miles), St Croix (84 sq. miles), St John (20 sq. miles) and about 50 small islets or cays, mostly uninhabited. The total area of the 3 principal islands is 136 sq. miles, of which the US Government owns 9,599 acres as National Park.

The population, according to the census of 1 April 1990, was 101,809, a decrease of 8,991 since 1985. Population (1990) of St Croix, 50,139; St Thomas, 48,166; St John, 3,504. About 20–25% (1980) were native-born, 35–40% from other Caribbean islands, 10% from mainland USA and 5% from Europe. St Croix has over 40% of Puerto Rican origin or extraction, Spanish speaking. In 1987, live births were 2,375 and deaths, 558.

The capital and only city, Charlotte Amalie, on St Thomas, had a population (1985) of 52,660; there are two towns on St Croix. Christiansted with (1980) 2,856 and Frederiksted with 1,054.

CLIMATE. Average temperatures vary from 77°F to 82°F throughout the year; humidity is low. Average annual rainfall, about 45 inches. The islands lie in the hurricane belt; tropical storms with heavy rainfall can occur in late summer, but hurricanes rarely.

CONSTITUTION AND GOVERNMENT. The Organic Act of 22 July 1954 gives the US Department of the Interior full jurisdiction; some limited legislative powers are given to a single-chambered legislature, composed of 15 senators elected for 2 years representing the two legislative districts of St Croix and St Thomas-St John.

The Governor is elected by the residents. Since 1954 there have been four attempts to redraft the Constitution, to provide for greater autonomy. Each has been rejected by the electorate. The latest was defeated in a referendum in Nov. 1981, 50% of the electorate participating.

For administration, there are 15 executive departments, 14 of which are under commissioners and the other, the Department of Justice, under an Attorney-General. The US Department of the Interior appoints a Federal Comptroller of government revenue and expenditure.

The franchise is vested in residents who are citizens of the United States, 18 years of age or over. In 1986 there were 34,183 voters, of whom 26,377 participated in the local elections that year.

They do not participate in the US presidential election but they have a non-voting representative in Congress.

The capital is Charlotte Amalie, on St Thomas Island.

Governor: Alexander A. Farrelly ($62,400).
Lieut.-Governor: Derek M. Hodge ($57,000).
Administrator St Croix: Richard Roebuck, Jr.

Administrator St John: William Lomax.
Administrator St Thomas: Harold Robinson.

ECONOMY

Budget. Under the 1954 Organic Act finances are provided partly from local revenues—customs, federal income tax, real and personal property tax, trade tax, excise tax, pilotage fees, etc.—and partly from Federal Matching Funds, being the excise taxes collected by the federal government on such Virgin Islands products transported to the mainland as are liable.

Budget for financial year 1988, $303,575,186.

Currency and Banking. United States currency became legal tender on 1 July 1934. Banks are the Chase Manhattan Bank; the Bank of Nova Scotia; the First Federal Savings and Loan Association of Puerto Rico; Barclays Bank International; Citibank; First Pennsylvania Bank; Banco Popular de Puerto Rico, and the First Virgin Islands Federal Savings Bank.

ENERGY AND NATURAL RESOURCES

Electricity. The Virgin Islands Water and Power Authority provides electric power from generating plants on St Croix and St Thomas; St John is served by power cable and emergency generator.

Water. There are 6 de-salinization plants with maximum daily capacity of 8·7m. gallons of fresh water. Rain-water remains the most reliable source. Every building must have a cistern to provide rain-water for drinking, even in areas served by mains (10 gallons capacity per sq. ft of roof for a single-storey house).

Agriculture. Land for fruit, vegetables and animal feed is available on St Croix, and there are tax incentives for development. Sugar has been terminated as a commercial crop and over 4,000 acres of prime land could be utilized for food crops.

Livestock (1988): Cattle, 11,000; goats, 4,000; pigs, 3,000; sheep, 3,000; poultry (1986), 18,345.

Fisheries. There is a fishermen's co-operative with a market at Christiansted. There is a shellfish-farming project at Rust-op-Twist, St Croix.

INDUSTRY AND TRADE

Industry. The main occupations on St Thomas are tourism and government service; on St Croix manufacturing is more important. Manufactures include rum (the most valuable product), watches, pharmaceuticals and fragrances. Industries in order of revenue: Tourism, refining oil, watch assembly, rum distilling, construction.

Labour. In 1989 the total labour force was 43,340, of whom 13,200 were employed in government, 8,450 in retail trades, 4,430 in hotels and other lodgings, 3,550 self-employed and unpaid family workers, 2,570 in transportation and public utilities, 2,350 in manufacturing, 2,330 in construction, 1,940 in finance, insurance and real estate, 1,070 in wholesale trades, 1,050 in business services, 350 in legal services, 230 in personnel services and 150 in agriculture.

Commerce. Exports, calendar year 1987, totalled $2,057·7m. and imports $3,370·4m. The main import is crude petroleum, while the principal exports are petroleum products.

Total trade between the US Virgin Islands and UK (financial years, British Department of Trade returns, in £1,000 sterling):

	1988	1989	1990	1991
Imports to UK	75	150	317	384
Exports and re-exports from UK	5,281	4,664	26,725	4,393

Tourism. Tourism is the most important business. There were about 1·52m. visitors in 1986 spending $509·8m.; 728,700 came by air and 827,151 on cruise ships, mainly to St Thomas which has a good, natural deepwater harbour.

COMMUNICATIONS

Roads. The Virgin Islands have (1986) 660 miles of roads, and 48,800 motor vehicles registered.

Aviation. There is a daily cargo and passenger service between St Thomas and St Croix. Alexander Hamilton Airport on St Croix can take all aircraft except Concorde. Cyril E. King Airport on St Thomas takes 727-class aircraft. There are air connexions to mainland USA, other Caribbean islands, Latin America and Europe.

Shipping. The whole territory has free port status. There is an hourly boat service between St Thomas and St John.

Post and Broadcasting. All three Virgin Islands have a dial telephone system. In Dec. 1986 there were 39,232 telephones. Direct dialling to Puerto Rico and the mainland, and internationally, is now possible. Worldwide radio telegraph service is also available.

The islands are served by 10 radio stations and 4 television stations. In 1988 there were an estimated 103,500 radio receivers and 64,400 television receivers in use.

Newspapers. In 1989 there were 2 daily and 1 fortnightly papers and 1 magazine.

RELIGION AND EDUCATION

Religion. There are churches of the Protestant, Roman Catholic and Jewish faiths in St Thomas and St Croix and Protestant and Roman Catholic churches in St John.

Education. In 1988 there were 13,359 pupils and 873 teachers in elementary schools, and 10,661 pupils and 723 teachers in secondary schools; 33 non-public schools had 5,079 pupils. In autumn 1988 the University of the Virgin Islands had 2,196 full-time students, 4,654 part-time students and 575 graduate students. The College is part of the United States land-grant network of higher education.

Further Reading

Boyer, W. W., *America's Virgin Islands.* Durham, N.C., 1983
Dookhan, I., *A History of the Virgin Islands of the United States.* Caribbean Univ. Press, 1974
Moll, V. P., *Virgin Islands.* [Bibliography]. Oxford and Santa Barbara, 1991

URUGUAY

Capital: Montevideo
Population: 3·11m. (1989)
GNP per capita: US$2,620 (1989)

República Oriental del Uruguay

HISTORY. The Republic of Uruguay, formerly a part of the Spanish Viceroyalty of Río de la Plata and subsequently a province of Brazil, declared its independence 25 Aug. 1825 which was recognized by the treaty between Argentina and Brazil signed at Rio de Janeiro 27 Aug. 1828. The first constitution was adopted 18 July 1830.

AREA AND POPULATION. Uruguay is bounded on the north-east by Brazil, on the south-east by the Atlantic, on the south by the Río de la Plata and on the west by Argentina. The area is 176,215 sq. km (68,037 sq. miles). The following table shows the area and the population of the 19 departments at census 1985:

Departments	Sq. km	Census 1985	Capital	Census 1985
Artigas	11,928	68,400	Artigas	34,551
Canelones	4,536	359,700	Canelones	17,316
Cerro-Largo	13,648	78,000	Melo	42,329
Colonia	6,106	112,100	Colonia	19,077
Durazno	11,643	54,700	Durazno	27,602
Flores	5,144	24,400	Trinidad	18,271
Florida	10,417	65,400	Florida	28,560
Lavalleja	10,016	61,700	Minas	34,634
Maldonado	4,793	93,000	Maldonado	33,498
Montevideo	530	1,309,100	Montevideo	1,247,920
Paysandú	13,922	104,500	Paysandú	75,081
Río Negro	9,282	47,500	Fray Bentos	20,431
Rivera	9,370	88,400	Rivera	56,335
Rocha	10,551	68,500	Rocha	23,910
Salto	14,163	107,300	Salto	80,787
San José	4,992	91,900	San José	31,732
Soriano	9,008	77,500	Mercedes	37,110
Tacuarembó	15,438	82,600	Tacuarembó	40,470
Treinta y Tres	9,529	45,500	Treinta y Tres	30,956

Total population, census (1985) 2,940,200 and estimate 1989 was 3,105,000. In 1985 Montevideo (the capital) had a census population of 1,246,500; Las Piedras, 58,221. Life expectancy was 71 years in 1991.

CLIMATE. A warm temperate climate, with mild winters and warm summers. The wettest months are March to June, but there is really no dry season. Montevideo. Jan. 72°F (22·2°C), July 50°F (10°C). Annual rainfall 38" (950 mm).

CONSTITUTION AND GOVERNMENT. There is a Senate of 31 members and a Chamber of Representatives of 99 members.
President: Dr Luis Alberto Lacalle (sworn in on 1 March 1990).
Vice-President: Dr Gonzalo Aguirre Ramírez.
In March 1992 the Cabinet comprised:
Interior, J. A. Ramírez. *Foreign*, H. Gros Espiell. *Defence*, M. Brito. *Economy and Finance*, I. de Posadas. *Education*, G. G. Costa. *Transport and Works*, W. E. Goñi. *Industry*, E. Ache. *Labour and Social Security*, E. Carbone. *Health*, C. Delpiazzo. *Agriculture*, A. Ramos. *Tourism*, J. Villar. *Environment*, J. M. Mieres Muró. *Plan*, C. Cat.

National flag: Nine horizontal stripes of white and blue, a white canton with the 'Sun of May' in gold.
National anthem: Orientales, la patria o la tumba ('Easterners, the fatherland or the tomb'; words by F. Acuña de Figueroa; music by F. J. Deballi).

DEFENCE

Army. The Army consists of volunteers who enlist for 1-2 years service. There are 1 infantry and 1 engineer brigades, 15 infantry, 10 cavalry, 6 artillery and 6 engineer battalions. Equipment includes 17 M-24, 28 M-3A1 and 22 M-41 A1 light tanks. Strength (1992) 16,000.

Navy. The navy has continued to replace its 1940-vintage ex-US ships with French frigates of the Commandant Rivière class as these are retired from the French navy. 3 have so far been transferred. The fleet presently consists of 4 frigates, 3 ex-French Rivière (built 1962–3) and 1 ex-US Dealey class (1954), 1 offshore patrol vessel, 3 fast inshore patrol craft (French-built, 1981) and 2 other inshore patrol vessels. Auxiliaries comprise 1 freighting tanker, a sail training ship, a salvage ship and 2 service vessels. There are 6 small landing craft.

A naval aviation service 400 strong operates 6 S-2 Tracker anti-submarine aircraft, 1 King Air for maritime reconnaissance, 11 training aircraft and 4 general purpose helicopters. Personnel in 1991 totalled 3,500 including 500 naval infantry.

A separate coastguard, 2,000 strong, operates 8 inshore patrol craft.

Air Force. Organized with US aid, the Air Force had (1991) about 3,500 personnel and 22 combat aircraft, including 1 counter-insurgency squadron with 6 IA 58 Pucara, 8 AT-33 armed jet trainers and 8 A-37B light strike aircraft, a reconnaissance and training squadron with 5 T-6Gs, 3 transport squadrons with 2 turboprop F.27 Friendships, 4 Brazilian-built EMB-110 Bandeirantes (1 equipped for photographic duties), 2 CASA C-212 Aviocars and 6 Queen Airs, a search and rescue squadron with Cessna U-17A aircraft and Bell helicopters, and a number of Cessna 182 light aircraft for liaison duties. Basic training types are the T-41 and T-34.

INTERNATIONAL RELATIONS

Membership. Uruguay is a member of the UN, OAS, Mercosur and LAIA.

ECONOMY

Budget. The receipts and expenditure of the national accounts as approved by the National Council of Government (URN$1m.):

	1986	1987	1988
Revenue	150,000	270,939	456,675
Expenditure	161,000	292,988	510,651

External public debt US$5,888m. in Dec. 1987.

Currency. The unit of currency is the *Uruguayan nuevo peso* (UYP) of 100 *centésimos*. There are notes, of N$ 50, 100, 500, 1,000 and 5,000, and coins of N$ 1, 2, 5 and 10. In March 1992, US$1 = 2,673·57 *pesos*; £1 = 4,693·45 *pesos*.

Banking and Finance. The Bank of the Republic (founded 1896), whose president and directors are appointed by the Government, has a paid-up capital of N$1,852m. The Central Bank was inaugurated on 16 May 1967. In 1991 there were 21 banks, 3 state-supported and 18 foreign-owned.

The State Insurance Bank has a monopoly of new insurance business. There is a stock exchange in Montevideo.

Weights and Measures. The metric system is in use.

ENERGY AND NATURAL RESOURCES

Electricity. Power output in 1986 was 3,730m kwh.

Oil. Petroleum production (1981) 185,000 tonnes.

Agriculture. Uruguay is primarily a pastoral country. Some 41m. acres are devoted to farming, of which 90% to livestock and 10% to crops. Some large *estancias* have been divided up into family farms; the average farm is about 250 acres.

There were (1990) 8,723,000 cattle, 25,220,000 sheep, 480,000 horses, 215,000 pigs, 14,000 goats and 8m. poultry.

302,000 tonnes of beef and veal were produced in 1990, and 1·05m. tonnes of cow's milk; the wool clip in 1990 was 97,815 tonnes.

The principal crops and their estimated yield (in tonnes) were: Barley, 140,000; maize, 115,000; oats, 75,000; rice, 517,000; sugar-beet, 160,000 and wheat, 420,000.

Wine is produced chiefly in the departments of Montevideo, Canelones and Colonia, about enough for domestic consumption (74,000 tonnes in 1990). The country has some 6m. fruit trees, principally peaches, oranges, tangerines and pears.

Forestry. In 1986 roundwood removals were 2,663,000 cu. metres.

Fisheries. In 1987, the total catch was 134,900 tonnes.

INDUSTRY. Industries include meat packing, oil refining, cement manufacture, foodstuffs, beverages, leather and textile maufacture, chemicals, light engineering and transport equipment. Some 70,000 tonnes of sugar were refined in 1989. There are about 100 textile mills.

Labour. Retirement age is 55 for women and 60 for men.

FOREIGN ECONOMIC RELATIONS

Commerce. The foreign trade (officially stated in US$, with the figure for imports based on the clearance permits granted and that for exports on export licences utilized) was as follows (in US$1,000):

	1985	1986	1987	1988
Imports	708·0	1,087·6	1,189·1	1,404·5
Exports	854·0	838·8	1,141·9	1,176·9

Of the imports in 1987 (in US$1m.) USA, 90; Brazil, 279; Argentina, 156; Federal Republic of Germany, 92; UK, 34. Of the exports in 1987 Brazil took 204; Argentina, 113; Federal Republic of Germany, 121; USA, 176; UK, 54.

Principal imports (1987) (in US$1,000): Mineral products, 189,000; chemical products, 176,000; machinery and appliances, 217,000. Exports: Textiles and textile products, 384,000; live animals and animal products, 257,000; skins and hides, 199,000; vegetable products, 99,000.

Total trade between Uruguay and UK (British Department of Trade returns, in £1,000 sterling):

	1987	1988	1989	1990	1991
Imports to UK	40,474	35,410	52,185	51,859	47,894
Exports and re-exports from UK	26,484	34,999	26,119	31,192	33,303

Tourism. There were 1,168,000 tourists in 1986.

COMMUNICATIONS

Roads. There were (1984) about 52,000 km of roads including 12,000 km of motorways. Registered motor vehicles, 31 Dec. 1981, are estimated at 281,275 passenger cars and 47,102 trucks and buses.

Railways. The total railway system open for traffic was (1986) 2,991 km of 1,435 mm gauge. In 1988 it carried 1m. tonnes of freight.

Civil Aviation. Carrasco, 22·5 km from Montevideo, is the most important airport. US, Argentine, Brazilian, Chilean, Dutch, French, German, Scandinavian and Paraguayan airlines fly to and from Uruguay. The state-operated civil airline PLUNA runs services in the interior and to Brazil, Paraguay, Argentina and Spain.

Shipping. In 1983 there were 13 merchant vessels and 3 tankers. River transport (1,270 km) is extensive, its main importance being to link Montevideo with Paysandú and Salto.

Telecommunications. The telephone system in Montevideo is controlled by the State; small companies operate in the interior. Telephone instruments, 1986, numbered 337,000. There were 1,277 post offices. There were (1990) about 1·8m. radio and 0·65m. television receivers (colour by PAL). All TV stations and all but one radio station are commercial.

Cinemas (1980). Cinemas numbered 85 with seating capacity of 47,000.

Newspapers (1984). There were 5 daily newspapers in Montevideo with aggregate daily circulation of about 210,000; most of the 25–30 provincial newspapers appear bi-weekly.

JUSTICE, RELIGION, EDUCATION AND WELFARE

Justice. The Ministry of Justice was created in 1977 to be responsible for relations between the Executive Power and the Judiciary and other jurisdictional entities. The Court of Justice is made up by 5 members appointed by the Council of the Nation at the suggestion of the Executive Power, for a period of 5 years. This court has original jurisdiction in constitutional, international and admiralty cases and hears appeals from the appellate courts, of which there are 4, each with 3 judges.

In Montevideo there are also 8 courts for ordinary civil cases, 3 for government *(Juzgado de Hacienda)*, as well as criminal and correctional courts. Each departmental capital has a departmental court; each of the 224 judicial divisions has a justice of the peace court.

Religion. State and Church are separated, and there is complete religious liberty. In 1989 there were 1·76m. Roman Catholics.

Education. Primary education is obligatory; both primary and superior education are free. In 1985–86 there were 356,002 primary school pupils, and 188,176 secondary school pupils.

The University of the Republic at Montevideo, inaugurated in 1849, has about 16,200 students; tuition is free to both native-born and foreign students; there are 10 faculties. There are 43 normal schools for males and females, and a college of arts and trades with about 33,000 students. There are also many religious seminaries throughout the Republic with a considerable number of pupils, a school for the blind, 2 for deaf and dumb and a school of domestic science.

Social Security. The welfare state dates from the beginning of the 1900s. In 1990 there were 0·6m. recipients of pensions and benefits.

Health. Hospital beds, 1983, numbered (estimate) 23,400; physicians numbered (1984) 5,736.

DIPLOMATIC REPRESENTATIVES

Of Uruguay in Great Britain (48 Lennox Gdns., London, SW1X 0DL)
Ambassador: Dr Luis Alberto Solé-Romeo.

Of Great Britain in Uruguay (Calle Marco Bruto 1073, Montevideo)
Ambassador: D. A. Lamont.

Of Uruguay in the USA (1918 F. St., NW, Washington, D.C., 20006)
Ambassador: Eduardo MacGillycuddy.

Of the USA in Uruguay (Lauro Muller 1776, Montevideo)
Ambassador: Richard C. Brown.

Of Uruguay to the United Nations
Ambassador: Ramiro Piriz-Ballon.

Further Reading

The official gazette is the *Diario Oficial*
Statistical Reports of the Government. Montevideo. Annual and biennial
Anales de Instruccion Primaria. Montevideo. Quarterly

Finch, H., *Uruguay:* [Bibliography]. Oxford and Santa Barbara, 1989
Salgado, Jose, *Historia de la Republica O. del Uruguay.* 8 vols. Montevideo, 1943
Weinstein, M., *Uruguay: Democracy at the Crossroads.* Boulder, 1988

National Library: Biblioteca Nacional del Uruguay, Guayabo 1793, Montevideo. It publishes *Anuario Bibliografico Uruguayo.*

VANUATU

Capital: Vila
Population: 142,630 (1989)
GNP per capita: US$860 (1989)

Republic of Vanuatu

HISTORY. The group was administered for some purposes jointly, for others unilaterally, as provided for by Anglo-French Convention of 27 Feb. 1906, ratified 20 Oct. 1906, and a protocol signed at London on 6 Aug. 1911 and ratified on 18 March 1922. On 30 July 1980 the Condominium of the New Hebrides achieved independence and became the Republic of Vanuatu.

AREA AND POPULATION. The Vanuatu group, of 80 islands, lies roughly 500 miles west of Fiji and 250 miles north-east of New Caledonia. The estimated land area is 4,706 sq. miles (12,190 sq. km). The larger islands of the group are: (Espiritu) Santo, Malekula, Epi, Pentecost, Aoba, Maewo, Paama, Ambrym, Efate, Erromanga, Tanna and Aneityum. They also claim Matthew and Hunter islands, 67 islands were inhabited in 1990. Population at the census (1979) 112,596. Estimate (1989) 142,630. Vila (the capital) 19,400. There are 3 active volcanoes, on Tanna, Ambrym and Lopevi, respectively.

Language: The national language is Bislama (spoken by 82% of the population); English and French are also official languages; about 50,000 speak French.

CLIMATE. The climate is tropical, but moderated by oceanic influences and by trade winds from May to Oct. High humidity occasionally occurs and cyclones are possible. Rainfall ranges from 90" (2,250 mm) in the south to 155" (3,875 mm) in the north. Vila. Jan. 80°F (26·7°C), July 72°F (22·2°C). Annual rainfall 84" (2,103 mm). A cyclone hit Vila in Feb. 1987.

CONSTITUTION AND GOVERNMENT. Legislative power resides in a 46-member unicameral Parliament elected for a term of 4 years. In the elections in Dec. 1991 the Union of Moderate Parties (UPM) won 20 seats, Vanuaaku Pati 10, Walter Lini's new National United Party 9, the Melanesian Progressive Party 4 and the Tan Union 1. There is also a Council of Chiefs, comprising traditional tribal leaders, to advise on matters of custom.

The President is elected for a 5-year term by an electoral college comprising Parliament and the presidents of the 11 regional councils. Executive power is vested in a Council of Ministers, responsible to Parliament, and appointed and led by a Prime Minister who is elected from and by Parliament.

President: Fred Timakata (elected Jan. 1989).

Maxine Carlot (UPM) was elected *Prime Minister* against 1 opponent by 31 to 15 votes on 16 Dec. 1991.

Flag: Red over green, with a black triangle in the hoist, the three parts being divided by fimbriations of black and yellow, and in the centre of the black triangle a boar's tusk overlaid by two crossed fern leaves.

DEFENCE. There is a paramilitary force with about 300 personnel. A naval service formed in 1987, and following training by the Royal Australian Navy operates 1 inshore patrol craft, and a former motor yacht, both lightly armed. Personnel numbered about 50 in 1991.

INTERNATIONAL RELATIONS

Membership. Vanuatu is a member of the UN, the Commonwealth and the South Pacific Forum and is an ACP state of the EEC.

ECONOMY

Budget. The budget for 1988 balanced at 3,938m. vatu.

Currency. The unit of currency is the *vatu* (VUV). March 1992: £1 = 192·80 *Vatu*; US$1 = 112·67.

Banking and Finance. The Finance Centre, established in 1970–71 and based primarily in Vila, consists of 4 international banks (including the Hongkong and Shanghai Banking Corporation) and 6 trust companies (including Melanesia International Trust Company Ltd, a Hongkong Bank group associate). In Aug. 1984 the Asian Development Bank opened a regional office in Vila. Commercial banks assets at 31 Dec. 1988, 20,900m. vatu.

Weights and Measures. The metric system is in force.

ENERGY AND NATURAL RESOURCES

Electricity. Production (1986) 20m. kwh.

Agriculture. The main commercial crops are copra, cocoa and coffee. Production, (1990, in tonnes): Copra, 45,000; cocoa, 2,000 tonnes; coffee (1985), 65. In 1985 about 80% of the population were engaged in subsistence agriculture. Yams, taro, manioc, sweet potatoes and bananas are grown for local consumption. A large number of cattle are reared on plantations, and an upgrading programme using pure-bred Charolais, Limousins and Illawarras has begun. A beef industry is developing.

Livestock (1990): Cattle, 129,000; goats, 14,000; pigs, 82,000.

Forestry. In 1987 some 1,900 ha of plantation had been established. Production (1985) 37,900 cu. metres of logs and sawn timber.

Fisheries. The principal catch is tuna (1985, 3,962 tonnes) mainly exported to the USA. Small-scale commercial fishing (1985) over 200 tonnes.

INDUSTRY. Industries in 1987 included copra processing, meat canning and fish freezing, a saw-mill, soft drinks factories and a print works. Building materials, furniture and aluminium were also produced, and in 1984 a cement plant opened.

FOREIGN ECONOMIC RELATIONS

Commerce. Imports and exports were (in 1m. Vatu):

	1985	1986	1987	1988
Imports	7,378	6,105	7,638	7,361
Exports	3,262	1,841	1,942	2,066

In 1988 the main exports (in 1m. vatu) were: Copra, 953; beef and veal, 243; timber, 106; cocoa, 117. 52% of exports went to the Netherlands, 15% to Japan, 6% to France, 4% to Australia and 3% to New Caledonia. Australia (43%), Japan (9%), New Zealand (11%), France (5%), Fiji (7%), New Caledonia (4%), were the major sources of imports and principal imports (in 1m. vatu) were machinery and transport equipment (1,797), food and live animals (1,263), basic manufactures (1,430), manufactured articles (851), fuels and lubricants (584), chemicals (421) and beverages and tobacco (368).

Total trade between Vanuatu and UK (British Department of Trade returns, in £1,000 sterling):

	1988	1989	1990	1991
Imports to UK	5	52	47	202
Exports and re-exports from UK	856	363	1,796	381

Tourism. In 1988 there were 17,544 visitors to Vanuatu. In addition there were 50,932 tourists from cruise ships. Earnings from tourism 2,000m. vatu.

COMMUNICATIONS

Roads. In 1984 there were 1,062 km of roads in Vanuatu, of these about 250 km are paved, mostly on Efate Island and Espiritu Santo. There were 3,784 registered cars in Vanuatu (1988).

Civil Aviation (1986). Air Vanuatu provides services to Australia; Air Nauru, Air Pacific, Air Caledonia, Solair and UTA serve Pacific routes; Air Melanisia provides regular services to 16 domestic airfields, and charter services. There are international airfields at Vila and Santo.

Shipping. Several international shipping lines serve Vanuatu, linking the country with Australia, New Zealand, other Pacific territories notably Hong Kong, Japan, North America and Europe. The chief ports are Vila and Santo. In 1977, 394 vessels arrived including 48 cruise ships carrying 40,412 visitors. 92,340 tons of cargo were exported and 102,867 tons discharged. Small vessels provide frequent inter-island services.

Telecommunications. Internal telephone and telegram services are provided by the Posts and Telecommunications and Radio Departments. There are automatic telephone exchanges at Vila and Santo; rural areas are served by a network of tele-radio stations. In 1983 there were 6 post offices and 3,000 telephones.

External telephone, telegram and telex services are provided by VANITEL, through their satellite earth station at Vila. There are direct circuits to Noumea, Sydney, Hong Kong and Paris and communications are available on a 24-hour basis to most countries. Air radio facilities are provided. Marine coast station facilities are available at Vila and Santo. The government-controlled Radio Vanuatu broadcasts in French, English and Bislama. In 1991 there were about 20,000 radio receivers.

JUSTICE, RELIGION, EDUCATION AND WELFARE

Justice. A study was being made in 1980 which could lead to unification of the judicial system.

Religion. Over 80% of the population are Christians, but animist beliefs are still prevalent.

Education. There were (1988) 260 primary schools with 24,634 pupils, 11 government and denominational secondary schools with 2,000 pupils and Matevulu College. Tertiary education is provided at the Vanuatu Technical Institute and the Teachers College, while other technical and commercial training is through regional institutions in the Solomon Islands, Fiji and Papua New Guinea.

Health. In 1988 there were 12 hospitals (5 rural) with 419 beds, 37 health centres, 50 dispensaries, 23 doctors and 270 nurses.

DIPLOMATIC REPRESENTATIVES

Of Vanuatu in Great Britain
High Commissioner: (Vacant).

Of Great Britain in Vanuatu (Melitco Hse., Rue Pasteur, Vila)
High Commissioner: J. Thompson, MBE.

Of Vanuatu to the United Nations
Ambassador: Robert F. Van Lierop.

VATICAN CITY STATE

Stato della Città del Vaticano

HISTORY. For many centuries the Popes bore temporal sway over a territory stretching across mid-Italy from sea to sea and comprising some 17,000 sq. miles, with a population finally of over 3m. In 1859–60 and 1870 the Papal States were incorporated into the Italian Kingdom. The consequent dispute between Italy and successive Popes was only settled on 11 Feb. 1929 by three treaties between the Italian Government and the Vatican: (1) A Political Treaty, which recognized the full and independent sovereignty of the Holy See in the city of the Vatican; (2) a Concordat, to regulate the condition of religion and of the Church in Italy; and (3) a Financial Convention, in accordance with which the Holy See received 750m. lire in cash and 1,000m. lire in Italian 5% state bonds. This sum was to be a definitive settlement of all the financial claims of the Holy See against Italy in consequence of the loss of its temporal power in 1870. The treaty and concordat were ratified on 7 June 1929. The treaty has been embodied in the Constitution of the Italian Republic of 1947. A revised Concordat between the Italian Republic and the Holy See was subsequently negotiated and signed in 1984, and which came into force on 3 June 1985.

The Vatican City State is governed by a Commission appointed by the Pope. The reason for its existence is to provide an extra-territorial, independent base for the Holy See, the government of the Roman Catholic Church.

AREA AND POPULATION. The area of the Vatican City is 44 hectares (108·7 acres). It includes the Piazza di San Pietro (St Peter's Square), which is to remain normally open to the public and subject to the powers of the Italian police. It has its own railway station (for freight only), postal facilities, coins and radio. Twelve buildings in and outside Rome enjoy extra-territorial rights, including the Basilicas of St John Lateran, St Mary Major and St Paul without the Walls, the Pope's summer villa at Castel Gandolfo and a further Vatican radio station on Italian soil. *Radio Vaticana* broadcasts an extensive service in 34 languages from the transmitters in the Vatican City and in Italy.

The Vatican City has about 1,000 inhabitants.

CONSTITUTION. The Pope exercises sovereignty and has absolute legislative, executive and judicial powers. The judicial power is delegated to a tribunal in the first instance, to the Sacred Roman Rota in appeal and to the Supreme Tribunal of the Signature in final appeal.

The Pope is elected by the College of Cardinals, meeting in secret conclave. The election is by scrutiny and requires a two-thirds majority.

Name and family	Election	Name and family	Election
Benedict XIV *(Lambertini)*	1740	Leo XIII *(Pecci)*	1878
Clement XIII *(Rezzonico)*	1758	Pius X *(Sarto)*	1903
Clement XIV *(Ganganelli)*	1769	Benedict XV *(della Chiesa)*	1914
Pius VI *(Braschi)*	1775	Pius XI *(Ratti)*	1922
Pius VII *(Chiaramonti)*	1800	Pius XII *(Pacelli)*	1939
Leo XII *(della Genga)*	1823	John XXIII *(Roncalli)*	1958
Pius VIII *(Castiglioni)*	1829	Paul VI *(Montini)*	1963
Gregory XVI *(Cappellari)*	1831	John Paul I *(Luciani)*	1978
Pius IX *(Mastai-Ferretti)*	1846	John Paul II *(Wojtyla)*	1978

Supreme Pontiff: **John Paul II** (Karol Wojtyła), born at Wadowice near Kraków,

Poland, 18 May 1920. Archbishop of Kraków 1964–78, created Cardinal in 1967, elected Pope 16 Oct. 1978, inaugurated 22 Oct. 1978.

Pope John Paul II was the first non-Italian to be elected since Pope Adrian VI (a Dutchman) in 1522.

Secretary of State: Angelo Sodano.
Secretary for Relations with Other States: Jean-Louis Tauran.

Flag: Vertically yellow and white, with on the white the crossed keys and tiara of the Papacy.

ROMAN CATHOLIC CHURCH. The Roman Pontiff (in orders a Bishop, but in jurisdiction held to be by divine right the centre of all Catholic unity, and consequently Pastor and Teacher of all Christians) has for advisers and coadjutors the Sacred College of Cardinals, consisting in Jan. 1990 of 149 Cardinals appointed by him from senior ecclesiastics who are either the bishops of important Sees or the heads of departments at the Holy See. In addition to the College of Cardinals, the Pope has created a ' Synod of Bishops'. This consists of the Patriarchs and certain Metropolitans of the Catholic Church of Oriental Rite, of elected representatives of the national episcopal conferences and religious orders of the world, of the Cardinals in charge of the Roman Congregations and of other persons nominated by the Pope. The Synod meets as and when decided by the Pope. The next Synod (on the formation of priests) met in Oct. 1990.

The central administration of the Roman Catholic Church is carried on by a number of permanent committees called Sacred Congregations, each composed of a number of Cardinals and diocesan bishops (both appointed for 5-year periods), with Consultors and Officials. Besides the Secretariat of State and the Second Section of the Secretariat of State (Section for Relations with States) there are now 9 Sacred Congregations, viz.: Doctrine, Oriental Churches, Bishops, the Sacraments, Divine Worship, Clergy, Religious, Catholic Education, Evangelization of the Peoples and Causes of the Saints. Pontifical Councils have replaced some of the previously designated Secretariats and Prefectures and now represent the Laity, Christian Unity, the Family, Justice and Peace, Cor Unum, Migrants, Health Care Workers, Interpretation of Legislative Texts, Inter-Religious Dialogue, Non Believers, Culture, Preserving the Patrimony of Art and History, and, a new Commission, for Latin America. There are also Offices for the Apostolic Penitentiary, the Supreme Tribunal of the Apostolic Signature, the Roman Rota, the Apostolic Camera, the Patrimony of the Holy See, Economic Affairs, the Papal Household, Liturgical Celebrations, the Secret Archives, the Apostolic Library, the Academy of Sciences, the Polyglot Press, the Publishing House, Vatican Radio, the Vatican Television Centre, the Fabric of St Peter's, Papal Charities, Translation Centre, Central Labour Office, the Consistory, Council of Cardinals, Economic Questions and the Institute for Works of Religion (the IOR). The Pontifical Academy of Sciences was revived by Pius XI in 1936 with 70 members. The director of the Vatican Bank (Istituto per le Opere di Religione) is Giovanni Bodio.

DIPLOMATIC REPRESENTATIVES

In its diplomatic relations with foreign countries the Holy See is represented by the Secretariat of State and the Second Section (Relations with States) of the Council for Public Affairs of the Church. It maintains permanent observers to the UN in New York and Geneva and to UNESCO and FAO. The Holy See is a member of IAEA and the Vatican City State is a member of UPU and ITU. It therefore attends as a member those international conferences open to State members of the UN and specialized agencies.

Of the Holy See in Great Britain (54 Parkside, London, SW19 5NF)
Apostolic Pro-Nuncio: Archbishop Luigi Barbarito (accredited 7 April 1986).

Of Great Britain at the Holy See (91 Via Condotti, I–00187, Rome).
Ambassador: Andrew Palmer, CMG, CVO.

Of the Holy See in the USA (3339 Massachusetts Ave., NW, Washington, D.C., 20008).
Apostolic Pro Nuncio: Agostino Cacciavillan.

Of the USA at the Holy See (Villino Pacelli, Via Aurelia 294, 00165, Rome).
Ambassador: Thomas Melady.

Further Reading

Acta Apostolicæ Sedis Romanæ. Rome
Annuario Pontificio. Rome. Annual
L'Attività della Santa Sede. Rome. Annual
The Catholic Almanac. Huntingdon. Annual
The Catholic Directory. London. Annual
The Catholic Directory for Scotland. Glasgow. Annual
Code of Canon Law. London, 1983
The New Catholic Encyclopædia. New York
Osservatore Romano. Vatican. Daily with weekly editions in English and other languages
Bull, G., *Inside the Vatican.* London, 1982
Cardinale, I., *The Holy See and the International Order.* Gerrards Cross, 1976
Hebblethwaite, P., *In the Vatican.* London, 1986
Mayer, F. *et al, The Vatican: Portrait of a State and a Community.* Dublin, 1980
Nichols, P., *The Pope's Divisions.* London, 1981
Walsh, M. J., *Vatican City State.* [Bibliography] Oxford and Santa Barbara, 1983

VENEZUELA

Capital: Caracas
Population: 9·25m. (1989)
GNP per capita: US$2,450 (1989)

República de Venezuela

HISTORY. Venezuela formed part of the Spanish colony of New Granada until 1821 when it became independent in union with Colombia. A separate, independent republic was formed in 1830. There was an abortive military coup in Feb. 1992.

AREA AND POPULATION. Venezuela is bounded north by the Caribbean, east by Guyana, south by Brazil, south-west and west by Colombia. The official estimate of the area is 912,050 sq. km (352,143 sq. miles); the frontiers with Colombia, Brazil and Guyana extend for 4,782 km and its Caribbean coastline stretches for some 3,200 km. Population (1981) census, 14,516,735. Estimate (1989) 19,246,000. The 1981 census excluded tribal Indians estimated at 53,350 (chiefly in Amazonas Territory) and illegal immigrants, estimated (1979) at about 3m. The official language is Spanish, spoken by all but 2·5% of the population.

The areas, populations and capitals of the 20 states and 4 federally-controlled areas are:

State	Sq. km	Census 1981	Capital	Census 1981
Anzoátegui	43,300	683,717	Barcelona	156,461
Apure	76,500	188,187	San Fernando	57,308
Aragua	7,014	891,623	Maracay	387,682
Barinas	35,200	326,166	Barinas	110,462
Bolívar	238,000	668,340	Ciudad Bolívar	182,941
Carabobo	4,650	1,062,266	Valencia	624,113
Cojedes	14,800	133,991	San Carlos	37,892
Falcón	24,800	503,896	Coro	96,339
Guárico	64,986	393,467	San Juan	57,219
Lara	19,800	945,064	Barquisimeto	523,101
Mérida	11,300	459,361	Mérida	143,805
Miranda	7,950	1,421,442	Los Teques	112,857
Monagas	28,900	388,536	Maturin	154,976
Nueva Esparta	1,150	197,198	La Asunción	10,375
Portuguesa	15,200	424,984	Guanare	64,025
Sucre	11,800	585,698	Cumaná	179,814
Táchira	11,100	660,234	San Cristóbal	198,793
Trujillo	7,400	433,735	Trujillo	31,774
Yaracuy	7,100	300,597	San Felipe	57,526
Zulia	63,100	1,674,252	Maracaibo	890,553
Ter. Amazonas	175,750	45,667	Puerto Ayacucho	28,248
Ter. Delta Amacuro	40,200	56,720	Tucupita	27,299
Federal District	1,930	2,070,742	Caracas	1,044,851
Federal Dependencies	120	850	—	—

Other large towns (1980) are Petare (334,800), Ciudad Guyana (314,041, census 1981), Baruta (180,100), Cabimas (138,529, census 1981), Acarigua (126,000), Maiquetiá (120,200), Valera (101,981, census 1981), Chacao (101,900), Puerto Cabello (94,000), Carúpano (82,000) and Puerto La Cruz (81,800).

Venezuela is the most urbanised Latin American nation; in 1985, 86% of the population lived in urban areas. Over half the population live in the valleys of Carabobo and Valencia (once the capital). At the 1981 census, 69% were of mixed ethnic origin (*mestizo*), 20% white, 9% black and 2% Amerindian.

Vital statistics (1986): 504,278 births, 100,002 marriages, 77,647 deaths. Life expectancy (1985) 65 males, 71 females, with 41% of population under 15 years.

CLIMATE. The climate ranges from warm temperate to tropical. Temperatures vary little throughout the year and rainfall is plentiful. The dry season is from Dec. to April. Caracas. Jan. 65°F (18·3°C), July 69°F (20·6°C). Annual rainfall 32" (833 mm). Ciudad Bolivar. Jan. 79°F (26·1°C), July 81°F (27·2°C). Annual rainfall 41" (1,016 mm). Maracaibo. Jan. 81°F (27·2°C), July 85°F (29·4°C). Annual rainfall 23" (577 mm).

CONSTITUTION AND GOVERNMENT. The constitution of 1961 provides for the election for a term of 5 years of a President, a National Congress, and state and municipal legislative assemblies by universal compulsory suffrage at 18 years. Voting is by proportional representation.

Congress consists of a Senate and a Chamber of Deputies. At least 2 Senators are elected for each State and for the Federal District. Senators must be Venezuelans by birth and over 30 years of age. Deputies must be native Venezuelans over 21 years of age; there is 1 for every 50,000 inhabitants. The territories, on reaching the population fixed by law, also elect deputies.

The President must be a Venezuelan by birth and over 30 years of age; he has a qualified power of veto.

The following is a list of presidents since 1945:

	Took Office		Took Office
Rómulo Betancourt	20 Oct. 1945	Rómulo Betancourt	13 Feb. 1959
Rómulo Gallegos	15 Feb. 1948	Raul Leoni	11 March 1964
Lieut.-Col. Carlos Delgado		Rafael Caldera	11 March 1969
Chalbaud	24 Nov. 1948 [4]	Carlos Andrés Pérez	
Dr G. Suárez Flamerich	27 Nov. 1950 [2]	Rodríguez	12 March 1974
Col. Marcos Pérez Jiménez.	3 Dec. 1952 [1]	Dr Luis Herrera Campíns	12 March 1979
Rear-Adm. Wolfgang		Dr Jaime Lusinchi	2 Feb. 1984
Larrazábal Ugueto	23 Jan. 1958 [2][3]	Carlos Andrés Perez	
Dr Edgard Sanabria	14 Nov. 1958[3]	Rodriguez	2 Feb. 1989

[1] Deposed.　　[2] Resigned.　　[3] Provisional.　　[4] Assassinated 13 Nov. 1950.

President: Carlos Andrés Perez Rodriguez, elected 4 Dec. 1988 with 54·56% of the votes, assumed office on 2 Feb. 1989.

The President named a new Cabinet in March 1992.

At the Congressional elections held 4 Dec. 1983, 112 of the 200 seats in the Chamber of Deputies were won by Acción Democrática, 61 by COPEI (the Social Christians) and 27 by other parties.

The city of Caracas is the capital. The 20 states, autonomous and politically equal, have each a legislative assembly and a governor. The states are divided into 156 districts and 613 municipalities. There are also 2 federal territories with 7 departments, and a federal district with 2 departments and 2 parishes. Each district has a municipal council, and each municipio a communal junta. The federal district and the 2 territories are administered by the President of the Republic.

National flag: Three horizontal stripes of yellow, blue, red, with an arc of 7 white stars in the centre, and the national arms in the canton.

National anthem: Gloria al bravo pueblo (Glory to the brave people; words by Vicente Salias, tune by Juan Landaeta).

DEFENCE. There is selective conscription at age 18 for 24 months (30 months in the navy).

Army. The Army consists of 6 infantry divisions, 7 infantry brigades, 1 airborne, 1 Ranger, 1 armoured and 1 cavalry brigade and an aviation regiment. Equipment includes 100 AMX-30 main battle and 35 M-18 and 36 AMX-13 light tanks. Army aviation comprises 23 helicopters and 15 aircraft. Strength (1991) 34,000.

Navy. The combatant fleet comprises 2 German-built submarines, 6 Italian-built Lupo class frigates, 6 fast missile craft, 4 riverine patrol craft, 5 tank landing ships and 10 craft. Auxiliaries comprise 1 logistic support, 2 transport, and a sail training ship, as well as a few harbour service craft.

The Naval Air Arm, 2,000 strong, comprises 3 shore-based C-212 Aviocars for maritime reconnaissance, 2 S-2 Tracker anti-submarine aircraft, 12 AB-212 shipborne anti-submarine helicopters and 8 miscellaneous transport and liaison aircraft.

Personnel in 1991 totalled 11,000 (4,000 conscripts) including the Marine Corps and the Coastguard. Main bases are at Caracas, Puerto Cabello and Punto Fijo.

The Coastguard, organizationally separate but under Naval operational control, is responsible for control of the economic exclusion zone and comprises 2 large frigate-type patrol craft, 1 ex-tug and a number of boats.

The maritime elements of the National Guard, which is tasked with customs enforcement and internal security duties, operates some 80 patrol craft and boats of various sizes from 23m downwards.

Air Force. Formed in 1920, the Air Force of (1991) some 7,000 officers and men is a small, but well-equipped service with a total of about 200 aircraft. There are 6 combat squadrons. Two are equipped with 18 F-16A and 6 F-16B Fighting Falcons. Two have 14 Canadair CF-5A fighter-bombers and 6 two-seat CF-5Ds, and two share 9 Mirage III/5 single-seaters and 2 Mirage 5D trainers, now being joined by 7 Mirage 50s (the older Mirages will be modernized to Mirage 50 standard). The Canberra jet bomber has been retired. Another operational squadron has 14 OV-10E Bronco twin-turboprop counter-insurgency aircraft and there is 1 squadron of armed Tucano trainers. A helicopter force consists of more than 40 Super Pumas, Bell 212s, 214STs and 412s, UH-1B/D/H Iroquois and Alouette IIIs. Transport units are equipped with 6 C-130H Hercules, 5 C-47s and 8 Aeritalia G222s. Communications aircraft are Queen Airs and other types. Thirty Tucanos and 20 T-34A Mentors are used for training, together with 20 T-2D Buckeye advanced jet trainers, which have a secondary attack role. A battalion of paratroops comes within Air Force responsibility. There is a staff college and a cadet academy.

National Guard, a volunteer force of some 22,000 under the Ministry of Defence, is broadly responsible for internal security. It includes customs and forestry duties among its tasks.

INTERNATIONAL RELATIONS

Membership. Venezuela is a member of the UN, OAS, LAIA, OPEC and the Andean Group.

ECONOMY

Budget. The revenue and expenditure for calendar years were, in Bs.1m., as follows:

	1984	1985	1986	1987	1988
Revenue	102,808	118,039	109,000	165,000	180,000
Expenditure	103,539	113,307	105,000	165,000	180,000

Currency. The unit of currency is the *bolívar* (VEB) of 100 *céntimos*. There are notes of Bs 10, 20, 50, 100 and 500, and coins of 5, 12·5, 25, 50 céntimos and Bs 1, 2 and 5.

In March 1992, £1 = Bs.106·55; US$1 = 60·69.

Banking and Finance. The *Governor* of the Central Bank is Miguel Rodriguez. The major banks include: Banco Provincial SAICA, Banco de Venezuela, Banco Consolidado, Banco Unión, Banco Mercantil, Banco Latino, Banco de Maracaibo, Banco Industrial de Venezuela, Bank of America.

There is a stock exchange in Caracas.

ENERGY AND NATURAL RESOURCES

Electricity. Production (1986) 50,240m. kwh. The Guri hydroelectric plant supplies 70% of the country's needs.

Oil. The oil-producing region around Maracaibo, covering some 30,000 sq. miles, produces about three-quarters of Venezuelan petroleum. Deposits in the Orinoco region are likely to prove one of the largest heavy oil reserves in the world. Nationalization of the privately owned oil sector in 1976 has proved successful. Crude oil production (1991) was 122·44m. tonnes.

Proven crude oil reserves in Jan. 1988 stood at 58,000m. bbls. However, these are considered conservative estimates and new fields off-shore have estimated reserves of 6,000–40,000m. bbls. In March 1988 a new field in the state of Monagas was confirmed estimated at 8,600m. bbls. The Orinoco tar sands belt has reserves variously estimated at between 700,000m. bbls. and 3,000,000m. bbls.

Gas. Production (1985) 33,059m. cu. metres.

Minerals. Bauxite is being exploited in the Guayana region by Bauxien, a state agency. There are important goldmines in the region south-east of Bolívar State, and new deposits have been discovered near El Callao (1959) and Sosa Méndez (1961) in the Guayana region. Output, 1982, amounted to 902 kg. Diamond output, from Amazonas territory, was 687,000 carats in 1977. Manganese deposits, estimated at several million tons, were discovered in 1954. Phosphate-rock deposits (yielding from 64 to 82% tricalcium phosphate) are found in the state of Falcón; reserves of 15m. tons of high-quality rock have been established. The state of Sucre has large sulphur deposits. Coal is worked in the states of Táchira, Aragua and Anzoátegui. Coal proven reserves in Zulia (160m. tons) are to be developed to service a new thermal power station in the Maracaibo area. Coal production is an annual 1·5m. tonnes. An important nickel deposit (at Loma de Hierro near Tejerías) is estimated to equal 600,000 tons of pure nickel. Saltmines are now worked by the Government on the Araya peninsula. Asbestos and copper pyrite are being exploited. There were proven reserves (1984) of bauxite totalling 200m. tonnes and production of about 3m. per annum are scheduled from 1986.

Iron ore is exploited in Bolívar State by the Orinoco Mining Co. and Iron Mines of Venezuela, subsidiaries respectively of the US Steel Corp. and the Bethlehem Steel Co. Proven reserves at the end of 1980 were 1,800m. tonnes. National output of iron ore, 1985, 14·9m. tonnes of which 9m. were exported.

Agriculture. Venezuela is divided into 3 distinct zones—the agricultural, the pastoral and the forest zone. In the first are grown coffee, cocoa, sugar-cane, maize, rice, wheat (grown in the Andes), tobacco, cotton, beans, sisal, etc.; the second affords grazing for more than 6m. cattle and numerous horses; and in the third, which covers a very large portion of the country, tropical products, such as caoutchouc, balatá (a gum resembling rubber), tonka beans, dividivi, copaiba, vanilla, growing wild, are worked. The 1990 livestock estimate showed cattle, 13,819,000; pigs, 2,326,000; goats, 1,530,000; sheep, 525,000; poultry, 52m. Over 50% of all farmers are engaged in subsistence agriculture and growth rates in agricultural production have not kept pace with the high population increase. Government has introduced a programme of price support, tax incentives and price increases.

Production (1990, in 1,000 tonnes): Rice, 400; maize, 1,150; cassava, 350; sugar-cane, 7,000; bananas, 1,130; oranges, 427; potatoes, 226; tomatoes, 195; coffee, 70; sesame seed, 38; tobacco, 16; cocoa, 16.

The coffee plantations number 62,673, covering 543,400 acres with 135m. bushes. The Venezuelan cocoa, from 13,000 plantations, is considered to be of high quality; it is grown chiefly in the states of Sucre and Miranda. The sugar industry has 6 government and 20 privately owned mills.

Forestry. Resources have been barely tapped; 600 species of wood have been identified.

Fisheries. Total catch (1986) was 283,600 tonnes.

INDUSTRY. Production (1985): Steel, 2·72m. tonnes; aluminium, 407,000; ammonia, 490,000; fertilizers, 650,000; cement, 5·12m.; paper, 550,000; vehicles (units) 116,000.

Labour. The labour force in 1990 was 6,655,000, of whom 758,000 worked in agriculture.

Trade Unions. The most powerful confederation of trade unions is the CTV (*Confederacion de Trabajadores de Venezuela*, formed 1947), which is dominated by the Accion Democratica party. Estimated membership, 1·1m. but claims 2m.

FOREIGN ECONOMIC RELATIONS

Commerce. Venezuela's exports and imports (in US$1m.):

	1984	1985	1986	1987
Exports	15,967	14,178	8,880	8,402
Imports	7,262	7,388	7,600	8,711

Main export markets in 1987 were the USA, Netherlands Antilles because of its oil refining and transhipment facilities, Japan and Colombia.

Principal imports are machinery and equipment, manufactured goods, chemical products, foodstuffs.

The USA supplied 47% of all imports in 1987, followed by Federal Republic of Germany, Japan, Italy and the UK.

Total trade between UK and Venezuela (British Department of Trade returns, in £1,000 sterling):

	1987	1988	1989	1990	1991
Imports to UK	91,749	76,563	111,072	101,717	100,210
Exports and re-exports from UK	157,760	177,787	124,672	204,921	166,654

Tourism. 692,400 tourists visited Venezuela in 1988.

COMMUNICATIONS

Roads. There were, 1985, 62,601 km of road fit for traffic the year round; of these 24,036 km are paved. There are 10,097 km of high-speed 4-lane motorway type. The motorway system runs from Caracas to Puerto Cabello via Valencia and will shortly be linked direct with one from La Guaira to Caracas.

Railways. Plans have existed since 1950 for large-scale railway construction but only the Puerto Cabello to Barquisimeto and Acarigua lines (336 km–1,435 mm gauge) has been completed. In 1990 it carried 64·1m. passenger-km and 34·4m. tonne-km. There is a metro in Caracas.

Civil Aviation. In 1985 there were 7 international airports, 51 national and over 200 private airports. The chief Venezuelan airlines are LAV (Líneas Aéreas Venezolanas), a government-owned concern, and AVENSA (Aerovías Venezolanas). Both operate numerous internal services. VIASA operates international routes in conjunction with KLM. There are also 3 specialist air freight companies. In all there are over 100 commercial aircraft in operation. In addition to Venezuelan international services, a number of US and Latin American and European lines operate services to Venezuela. British Airways operates twice-weekly flights between London and Caracas.

Shipping. Foreign vessels are not permitted to engage in the coasting trade, except by special concessions or by contract with the Government. La Guaira, Maracaibo, Puerto Cabello, Puerto Ordaz and Guanta are the chief ports. In Dec. 1978 the merchant fleet had an aggregate gross tonnage of 824,000; this included tankers of 368,000 gross tons.

The principal navigable rivers are the Orinoco and its tributaries Apure and Arauca, from San Fernando to Tucupita through Ciudad Bolívar, Puerto Ordaz and San Félix; San Juan from Carípito to the Gulf of Paria; and Escalante in Lake Maracaibo.

Telecommunications. There were 1,165,699 telephones in 1985. An international telex service operates in the Caracas metropolitan zone. There is a submarine telephone link with USA.

There are 2 government and 4 cultural radio stations; the remainder are commercial. There are 2 government, 3 commercial and 3 other TV channels (colour by NTSC). In 1991 there were 8·1m. radio and 3·5m. TV receivers.

Newspapers (1983). There were 25 leading daily newspapers with a circulation of over 1·7m.

JUSTICE, RELIGION, EDUCATION AND HEALTH

Justice. The Supreme Court, which operates in Divisions, each with 5 members, is elected by Congress for 5 years. The country is divided into 20 legal districts. They select their own President and Vice-President. The Federal Procurator-General is appointed for 5 years. There are lower federal courts.

Each state has a Supreme Court with 3 members, a superior court, or superior tribunal, courts of first instance, district courts and municipal courts. In the territories there are civil and military judges of first instance, and also judges in the municipios. Finally, there is an income-tax claims tribunal.

Religion. The Roman Catholic is the prevailing religion, but there is toleration of all others. In 1989 there were 17·65m. Roman Catholics. There are 4 archbishops, 1 at Caracas, who is Primate of Venezuela, 2 at Mérida and 1 at Ciudad Bolívar. There are 19 bishops. In the state primary schools instruction is given only to those children whose parents expressly request it. Protestants number about 20,000.

Education. In 1987–88 there were 13,500 primary schools with 115,000 teachers and 2,900,000 pupils, 2,000 secondary schools with 63,000 teachers and 1,100,000 pupils. The number of students in higher education was 466,000 with 30,000 teaching staff in the 94 establishments.

Health. In 1983 there were 21,502 doctors and 43,650 beds in hospitals and dispensaries in 1979.

DIPLOMATIC REPRESENTATIVES

Of Venezuela in Great Britain (1 Cromwell Rd., London, SW7)
Ambassador: Dr Francisco Kerdel-Vegas, CBE (accredited 5 Nov. 1987).

Of Great Britain in Venezuela (Torre Las Mercedes, Avenida La Estancia, Chuao, Caracas 1060)
Ambassador: Giles Fitzherbert, CMG.

Of Venezuela in the USA (2445 Massachusetts Ave., NW, Washington, D.C., 20008)
Ambassador: Simon Alberto Consalvi.

Of the USA in Venezuela (Avenida Francisco de Miranda and Avenida Principal de la Floresta, Caracas)
Ambassador: Michael M. Skol.

Of Venezuela to the United Nations
Ambassador: Dr Diego Arria.

Further Reading

Statistical Information: The following are some of the principal publications:
Dirección General de Estadística, Ministerio de Fomento, *Boletín Mensual de Estadística.—Anuario Estadístico de Venezuela.* Caracas, Annual
Banco Central, *Memoria Annual* and *Boletin Mensual*
Ministerio de Sanidad y Asistencia Social, Dirección de Salud Pública, *Anuario de Epidemiología y Asistencia Social*

Bigler, G. E., *Politics and State Capitalism in Venezuela.* Madrid, 1981
Braveboy-Wagner, J. A., *The Venezuela-Guyana Border Dispute: Britain's Colonial Legacy in Latin America.* Boulder and Epping, 1984
Ewell, J., *Venezuela: A Century of Change.* London, 1984
Hellinger, D.V., *Tarnished Democracy.* Boulder (Colo.), 1991
Lombard, J., *Venezuelan History: A Comprehensive Working Bibliography.* Boston, 1977.—*Venezuela: The Search for Order, the Dream of Progress.* OUP, 1982
Martz, J. D. and Myers, D. J., *Venezuela: The Democratic Experience.* New York, 1986

VIETNAM

Capital: Hanoi
Population: 65m. (1990)
GNP per capita: US$200 (1989)

Công Hòa Xã Hội Chu Nghĩa
Viêt Nam

(Socialist Republic of Vietnam)

HISTORY. Conquered by the Chinese in B.C. 111, Vietnam broke free from Chinese domination in 939, though at many subsequent periods it was a nominal Chinese vassal. (For subsequent history until the cessation of hostilities with the US in Jan. 1973 *see* THE STATESMAN'S YEAR-BOOK, 1989–90).

After the US withdrawal, hostilities continued between the North and the South until the latter's defeat in 1975.

(For details of the former Republic of Vietnam, *see* THE STATESMAN'S YEAR-BOOK, 1975–76). A Provisional Revolutionary Government established an administration in Saigon. A general election was held on 25 April 1976 for a National Assembly representing the whole country. Voting was by universal suffrage of all citizens of 18 or over, except former functionaries of South Vietnam undergoing 're-education'. The unification of North and South Vietnam into the Socialist Republic of Vietnam took place formally on 2 July 1976. In 1978 Vietnam signed a 25-year treaty of friendship and co-operation with the USSR. Relations with China correspondingly deteriorated, an exacerbating factor being the Vietnamese military intervention in Cambodia of 1978–89, but were renewed in 1991.

AREA AND POPULATION. The country has a total area of 330,363 sq. km and is divided administratively into 40 provinces. Areas and populations (in 1,000) at the census of Oct. 1979 were as follows:

Province	Sq. km	1979	Province	Sq. km	1979
Lai Chau	17,408	322,077	Thai Binh	1,344	1,506,235
Son La	14,656	487,793	Hai Phong (city) [1]	1,515	1,279,067
Hoang Lien Son	14,125	778,217	Ha Nam Ninh	3,522	2,781,409
Ha Tuyen	13,519	782,453	Thanh Hoa	11,138	2,532,261
Cao Bang	} 13,731	{ 479,823	Nghe Tinh	22,380	3,111,989
Lang Son		{ 484,657	Binh Tri Thien	19,048	1,901,713
Bac Thai	8,615	815,105	Quang Nam – Da Nang	11,376	1,529,520
Quang Ninh	7,076	750,055	Nghia Binh	14,700	2,095,354
Vinh Phu	5,187	1,488,348	Gia Lai – Kon Tum	18,480	595,906
Ha Bac	4,708	1,662,671	Dac Lac	18,300	490,198
Ha Son Binh	6,860	1,537,190	Phu Khanh	9,620	1,188,637
Hanoi (city) [1]	597	2,570,905	Lam Dong	10,000	396,657
Hai Hung	2,526	2,145,662	Thuan Hai	11,000	938,255
Dong Nai	12,130	1,304,799	Ben Tre	2,400	1,041,838
Song Be	9,500	659,093	Cuu Long	4,200	1,504,215
Tay Ninh	4,100	684,006	An Giang	4,140	1,532,362
Long An	5,100	957,264	Hau Giang	5,100	2,232,891
Dong Thap	3,120	1,182,787	Kien Giang	6,000	994,673
Thanh Pho –			Minh Hai	8,000	1,219,595
Ho Chi Minh [1]	1,845	3,419,978	Vung Tau – Con Dao [2]	—	91,160
Tien Giang	2,350	1,264,498			
				329,466	52,741,766

[1] Autonomous city.   [2] Special area.

At the census of Oct. 1979 the population was 52,741,766 (25,580,582 male; 19·7% urban).

Population (1990), 65m. (Ho Chi Minh 4m.; Hanoi, 2m. (1979); growth rate (1988) 2·4% per annum. Density, 181 per sq. km. Sanctions are imposed on couples with more than two children.

84% of the population are Vietnamese (Kinh). There are also over 60 minority groups thinly spread in the extensive mountainous regions. The largest minorities are (1976 figures in 1,000): Tay (742); Khmer (651); Thai (631); Muong (618); Nung (472); Meo (349); Dao (294). In 1987 1m. Vietnamese were living abroad, mainly in the US. Following an agreement of July 1989 the US in Jan. 1990 began the phased immigration of some 94,000 families of former South Vietnamese soldiers and officials.

In 1990 some 70,000 persons emigrated (in 1989, 45,000; in 1988, 25,000). (For previous details *see* THE STATESMAN'S YEAR-BOOK, 1981–82). Between April 1975 and Aug. 1984 554,000 illegal emigrants ('boat people') succeeded in finding refuge abroad. In June 1988 the UK announced that Hong Kong would no longer accept 'boat people' who were not proven political refugees. In Feb. 1989, Vietnam agreed to accept their return but not their enforced repatriation, and a voluntary repatriation programme under the aegis of the UN High Commissioner of Refugees began. By Oct. 1989 there were 57,000 'boat people' in camps in Hong Kong, and the UK government announced it would embark on a programme of mandatory repatriation of up to 40,000 of them, giving each a resettlement allowance worth US$620. 51 persons were repatriated on 12 Dec. 1989, but the programme was then suspended. A meeting of the UN-sponsored Comprehensive Plan of Action for Indochinese Refugees in Jan. 1990 failed to agree a new repatriation programme, but in Sept. 1990 Vietnam, the UK and the UN High Commissioner for Refugees agreed on the repatriation of 'boat people' who had not volunteered, but were 'not opposed', to going home. In Oct. 1991 Vietnam and the UK signed an agreement providing for the forcible return of 'boat people'.

CLIMATE. The humid monsoon climate gives tropical conditions in the south and sub-tropical conditions in the north, though real winter conditions can affect the north when polar air blows south over Asia. In general, there is little variation in temperatures over the year. Hanoi. Jan. 62°F (16·7°C), July 84°F (28·9°C). Annual rainfall 72" (1,830 mm).

CONSTITUTION AND GOVERNMENT. A new Constitution was adopted in Dec. 1980. It states that Vietnam is a state of proletarian dictatorship and is developing according to Marxism–Leninism.

At the elections for the National Assembly held on 19 April 1987, 829 candidates stood and 496 were elected. Turn-out of voters was said to be 99·32%. Parliamentary elections were scheduled for June 1992.

'The standing organ of the National Assembly and presidium of the Republic' is the State Council:

President (titular head of state): Vo Chi Cong. *Vice-Presidents:* Nguyen Huu Tho, Le Quang Do, Nguyen Quyet, Dam Quang Trung, Huynh Tan Phat, Mrs Nguyen Thi Dinh.

Chairman of the National Assembly: Le Quang Do.

All political power stems from the Communist Party of Vietnam founded in 1930; it had 2·11m. members in 1991. Its Politburo in Nov. 1991 consisted of Do Muoi (b. 1917; *Secretary General)*; Vo Kan Kiet; Gen. Le Duc Anh; Gen. Dao Dui Tung; Gen. Doan Khue; Pham The Duyet; Vo Tran Chi; Le Phuoc Tho; Buy Thien Ngo; Nguyen Duc Binh; Nong Duc Manh; Phan Van Khai; Vu Oanh.

In Feb. 1992 the government included:

Prime Minister, Vo Van Kiet (b. 1922).

Deputy Prime Minister, Phan Van Khai. *Foreign*, Nguyen Manh Cam (b. 1930). *Defence*, Gen. Doan Khue. *Interior*, Buy Thien Ngo. *Head of State Planning Commission*, Do Quoc Sam. *Commerce and Tourism*, Le Van Triet. *Heavy Industry*, Tran Lum.

National flag: Red, with a yellow 5-pointed star in the centre.

National anthem: 'Tien quan ca' ('The troops are advancing').

Local government is administered by people's councils, which appoint executive committees. Local elections were held with the National Assembly elections in April 1987.

DEFENCE. Men between 18 and 35 and women between 18 and 25 are liable for conscription of 3 years, specialists 4 years. Since 1989 troops have been permitted to engage in economic activity, and 60,000 were doing so by mid-1991.

Army. The Army consists of 62 infantry, 3 mechanized, 8 engineer and 10 to 16 economic construction divisions, 10 armoured, and 10 field artillery brigades, 8 engineer divisions and 15 independent infantry regiments. Equipment includes some 1,300 T-34/-54/-55 and Chinese Type-59 main battle and PT-76 and Chinese Type-62/63 light tanks. Strength was (1992) about 0·9m. Paramilitary forces are the Peoples' Regional Force (500,000), local forces of some 2·6m. and a tactical rear force of 500,000. In 1991 some 5,000 troops were stationed in Laos.

Navy. The equipment of the navy derives from two sources: ex-US equipment transferred to South Vietnam before or during the war, and ex-Soviet equipment transferred to North Vietnam during the war, or after unification in 1975. The latter is in general newer. The USSR had announced its intention to withdraw from the naval base at Cam Ranh Bay.

The fleet currently includes 5 ex-Soviet 'Petya' class frigates, 2 ex-US frigates (built 1943 and 1944), 8 Soviet-built fast missile craft, 16 fast torpedo craft, 5 patrol hydrofoils, 2 offshore and at least 30 inshore patrol craft, 3 coastal and 2 inshore minesweepers, 7 landing ships, and some 20 smaller amphibious craft. There may additionally still exist a proportion of the inshore fleet of 24 patrol craft, 25 coast-guard cutters and over 350 riverine craft abandoned by the USA in 1975, but the continued operability of more than a few of these must be considered doubtful.

In 1991 personnel were estimated to number 10,000 plus an additional Naval Infantry force of 20,000.

Air Force. The Air Force, built up with Soviet and Chinese assistance, had (1992) about 10,000 personnel and 350 combat aircraft and 37 armed helicopters (plus many stored, including most US types captured in war). There are reported to be 3 squadrons of variable-geometry MiG-23s, 6 squadrons of MiG-17s and Su-20s, over 150 MiG-21 interceptors; An-2, Li-2, C-47, An-24, An-26 and Il-14 transports; and a strong helicopter force with Mi-6, Mi-8 and Mi-24 helicopters. 'Guideline', 'Goa' and 'Gainful' missiles are operational in large numbers.

INTERNATIONAL RELATIONS

Membership. Vietnam is a member of the UN and IMF.

ECONOMY

Policy. Long-term forward planning gives priority to self-sufficiency in agriculture and stimulating regional industry. The fourth 5-year plan covered 1986–90. (For previous plans *see* THE STATESMAN'S YEAR-BOOK, 1985–86.)

Curtailment of Western aid, and resistance to Government measures have contributed to a shortage of consumer goods and widespread malnutrition. Small family businesses were legalized in 1986, and a law of April 1991 sanctions and protects all private business.

A reform programme (*Doi Moi*) injecting free enterprise principles and reducing central control has been implemented. The 'Draft Strategy for Socio-Economic Stabilization and Development to 2000' aims to double GDP through the 'socialist-oriented commodity economy, a market economy under state management' in which the state and collective sectors will play a 'predominant role'.

Currency. The unit of currency is the *dong* (VND). A currency reform of 1985 substituted a new *dong* at a rate of 1 new *dong* = 10 (old) *dong*. Notes are issued in mutiples of 1, 2 and 5 up to 5,000 *dong*. (For former currency *see* THE STATESMAN'S YEAR-BOOK, 1985–86.) In a currency reform of March 1989 the *dong* was brought into line with free market rates. Inflation was 700% in 1988, but was significantly reduced in 1989. It was officially claimed to be 3·9% in Nov. 1990. In March 1992 £1 = 19,820·20 *dong*; US$1 = 11,290·3 *dong*.

Banking and Finance. The central bank and bank of issue is the National Bank of Vietnam (founded in 1951). There are 4 other state-owned banks, of which Vietcombank is the foreign trade bank. There were 7 foreign banks in 1991.

ENERGY AND NATURAL RESOURCES

Electricity. In 1988, 6,300m. kwh. of electricity were produced. A hydro-electric power station with a capacity of 2m. kw. was opened at Hoa-Binh in 1989.

Minerals. North Vietnam is rich in anthracite, lignite and hard coal: Total reserves are estimated at 20,000m. tonnes. Coal production was 4m. tonnes in 1991. There are deposits of iron ore, manganese, titanium, chromite, bauxite and a little gold. Reserves of apatite are some of the biggest in the world. Offshore exploration for oil near Da Nang started in 1989. Crude oil production was 750,000 tonnes in 1988; 1991 estimate, 3.9m. tonnes.

Agriculture. In 1985, 62% of the population was engaged in agriculture. In 1984 there were some 23,000 production collectives and 268 agricultural co-operatives in the South accounting for 47% of the cultivated area. The intemperate collectivization of agriculture in the South after 1977 had disastrous effects which the Government tried to rectify by allowing peasants small private plots and the right to market some produce. These measures had only limited success, and in 1989 the Government abandoned virtually all its controls on the production and sale of agricultural produce, and switched to encouraging the household as the basic production unit. Peasants contract with co-operatives for land and water use over 15–20 years. Peasants may market their produce, or deal through the co-operatives. There are no official production quotas or designation of land use. There were 105 state farms employing in all 70,000 workers and with 55,000 hectares arable and 50,000 hectares of pasture. The cultivated area in 1980 was 6·97m. ha (5·54m. ha for rice). Rice cultivation was deregulated in 1989. The 1990 harvest fell below 1989 through lack of fertilizer.

Production in 1,000 tonnes in 1990: Ric, 21,541; coffee, 45; tea, 31; rubber, 52; coconut, 934. Other crops include sugar-cane and cotton.

Livestock (1988): Cattle 2,923,000; pigs, 12,051,000; goats, 414,000; poultry, 96m.

Animal products (1988): Eggs, 171,000 tonnes; (1990) meat, 1,037,000 tonnes.

Forestry. There were (1988) 13m. ha of forest, representing 40% of the land area. Roundwood production was 3,246,000 cu. metres in 1990.

Fisheries. Fishing is important, especially in Halong Bay. In 1976, 6m. tonnes of sea fish and 180,000 tonnes of freshwater fish were caught.

INDUSTRY. Next to mining, food processing and textiles are the most important industries; there is also some machine building. Older industries include cement, cotton and silk manufacture.

Private businesses were taken over in 1978. Foreign firms, principally French, are continuing to function, but all US property has been nationalized. There is little heavy industry. Most industry is concentrated in the Ho-Chi-Minh area.

Production (1980, in 1,000 tonnes) iron, 125; steel, 106; sulphuric acid, 6,700; caustic soda, 4,500; mineral fertilizer, 260; pesticides, 18,400; paper, 54,000; sugar, 94,000, cement, 705. 1,500 tractors were built in 1980, and 621 railway coaches. Footwear production, 200,000 pairs. Beer, 942,000 hectolitres.

Labour. Average wage (1984) 200 dong per month. Workforce (1985) 28·76m., of whom 17·91m. were in agriculture. There were some 3m. unemployed in 1990.

FOREIGN ECONOMIC RELATIONS. The EEC established relations in Oct. 1990. A US$1,000m. trade and co-operation agreement was signed with the USSR in Jan. 1991. The USSR supplies petroleum, steel, cotton and fertilizer in exchange for rubber, crude oil, rice, tea, coffee, meat, fruit and vegetables. In 1991

Vietnam's total indebtedness was estimated at US$14,600. In 1978 the IMF approved a virtually interest-free loan of US$90m. repayable over 50 years, but in April 1985 suspended all further credits to Vietnam. Sweden gives annual aid of US$47m. A law of Jan. 1988 regulates joint ventures with Western firms; full repatriation of profits and non-nationalization of investments are guaranteed. Offices may be opened in Vietnam. Foreign currency transactions must be channelled through authorized banks.

Commerce. Value of exports in 1990, US$1,570m.; imports, US$1,840m. Main import suppliers in 1990: Japan, 23·2%; Federal Republic of Germany, 16%; Hong Kong, 14·8%; France, 10%. Main export markets: Japan, 42·1%; Hong Kong, 11·4%; Philippines, 8%; Thailand, 6·7%. Main exports are coal, farm produce, sea produce and livestock. Imports: Oil, steel, artificial fertilizers. Following the removal of rice cultivation from state control, Vietnam moved from being a net importer of rice to the world's third largest exporter in 1989. Rice exports in 1990 were some 1·5m. tonnes, coal, 0·78m. tonnes (0·23m. in 1987), mainly to Japan and South Korea.

Trade between Vietnam and UK (British Department of Trade returns, in £1,000 sterling):

	1988	1989	1990	1991
Imports to UK	492	1,711	1,443	6,440
Exports and re-exports from UK	2,213	4,108	5,802	6,916

Tourism. Since 1988 Vietnamese have been permitted to travel abroad for up to 3 months for various specific reasons. There were 187,000 tourists in 1990.

COMMUNICATIONS

Roads. In 1986 there were about 65,000 km of roads described as 'main roads'.

Railways. Route length was 4,200 km in 1986. The Hanoi–Ho Chi Minh City line is being rebuilt in a programme of reconstruction and extension. About 50m. passengers and 10m. tonnes of freight are carried annually.

Civil Aviation. Air Vietnam operates internal services from Hanoi to Ho Chi Minh City, Cao Bang, Na Son and Dien Bien, Vinh and Hue, and from Ho Chi Minh City to Ban Me Thuot and Da Nang, Can Tho, Con Son Island and Quan Long and from Hanoi to Bangkok in conjunction with Thai Airways. Aeroflot (USSR) operate regular services from Ho Chi Min City to Moscow and from Hanoi to Moscow, Rangoon and Vientiane, Interflug (German Dem. Rep.) to Berlin, Moscow and Dhaka, Philippine Airlines to Manila, and Air France to Paris. In June 1991 a US airline re-opened US-Vietnam air traffic with a monthly scheduled flight.

Shipping. In 1986 there were 150 ships totalling 338,668 GRT. The major ports are Haiphong, which can handle ships of 10,000 tons, Ho Chi Minh City and Da Nang, and there are ports at Hong Gai and Haiphong Ben Thuy. There are regular services to Hong Kong, Singapore, Cambodia and Japan. In 1987 there were some 6,000 km of navigable waterways.

Cargo is handled by the Vietnam Ocean Shipping Agency; other matters by the Vietnam Foreign Trade Transport Corporation.

Telecommunications. In 1991 there were 7m. radios. There were 106,100 telephones in 1984. There were 2·2m. TV sets in 1991 (colour by NTSC and SECAM).

Cinemas and theatres. 116 films were produced in 1980 (including 10 full-length). There were 145 theatres.

Newspapers and books. The Party daily is *Nhan Dan* ('The People') circulation, 1985: 500,000. The official daily in the South is *Giai Phong*. Two unofficial dailies, *Cong Giao Va Dan Toc* (Catholic) and *Tin Sang* (independent) are also published. 2,564 books were published in 1980 totalling 90·9m. copies.

JUSTICE, RELIGION, EDUCATION AND WELFARE

Justice. A new penal code came into force 1 Jan. 1986 'to complete the work of the 1980 Constitution'. Penalties (including death) are prescribed for opposition to the people's power, and for economic crimes. There are the Supreme People's Court, local people's courts and military courts. The president of the Supreme Court is responsible to the National Assembly, as is the Procurator-General, who heads the Supreme People's Office of Supervision and Control.

Religion. Taoism is the traditional religion but Buddhism is widespread. At a Conference for Buddhist Reunification in Nov. 1981, 9 sects adopted a charter for a new Buddhist church under the Council of Sangha. The Hoa Hao sect, associated with Buddhism, claimed 1·5m. adherents in 1976. Caodaism, a synthesis of Christianity, Buddhism and Confucianism founded in 1926, has some 2m. followers. In 1989, there were 36,100,000 Buddhists and 4,570,000 Roman Catholics. There is an Archbishopric of Hanoi and 13 bishops. There were 2 seminaries in 1989. In 1983 the Government set up a Solidarity Committee of Catholic Patriots. In Aug. 1988 the Government announced that all Catholic priests had been released from re-education camps, but were not yet permitted to resume their duties.

Education. Primary education consists of a 10-year course divided into 3 levels of 4, 3 and 3 years respectively. There were 500,000 teachers in 1988. Numbers of pupils and students in 1980–81: Nurseries, 2·66m.; primary schools, 12·1m.; complementary education, 2·19m.; vocational secondary education, 130,000. In 1980–81 there were 92,913 nurseries. There were 11,400 schools and 280 vocational secondary schools, with 357,000 and 13,000 teachers respectively.

In 1980–81 there were 83 institutions of higher education (including 3 universities: (Hanoi, Ho Chi Minh City, Central Highlands University at Ban Me Thuot), 13 industrial colleges, 7 agricultural colleges, 5 economics colleges, 9 teacher-training colleges, 7 medical schools and 3 art schools, in all with 16,000 teachers and 159,000 students. In 1981 there were 5,000 Vietnamese studying in the USSR.

Health. In 1975 there were 1,996 hospitals and dispensaries and 93 sanatoria. There were some 13,517 doctors and dentists in 1981 and 197,000 hospital beds.

DIPLOMATIC REPRESENTATIVES

Of Vietnam in Great Britain (12–14 Victoria Rd., London, W8)
Ambassador: Chau Phong (accredited 14 March 1990).

Of Great Britain in Vietnam (16 Pho Ly Thuong Kiet, Hanoi)
Ambassador: Peter Williams.

Of Vietnam to the United Nations
Ambassador: Trinh Xuan Lang.

Further Reading

Beresford, M., *National Unification and Economic Development in Vietnam.* London, 1989
Bui Phung, *Vietnamese-English Dictionary.* Hanoi, 1987
Chen, J. H.-M., *Vietnam: A Comprehensive Bibliography.* London, 1973
Dellinger, D., *Vietnam Revisited.* Boston (Mass.), 1986
Fforde, A., *The Limits of National Liberation: Problems of Economic Management in the Democratic Republic of Vietnam.* London, 1987
Harrison, J. P., *The Endless War: Fifty Years of Struggle in Vietnam.* New York, 1982
Higgins, H., *Vietnam.* 2nd ed. London, 1982
Ho Chi Minh, *Selected Writings, 1920–1969.* Hanoi, 1977
Hodgkin, T., *Vietnam: The Revolutionary Path:* London, 1981
Houtart, F., *Hai Van: Life in a Vietnamese Commune.* London, 1984
Karnow, S., *Vietnam: A History.* 2nd ed. London, 1992
Lawson, E. K., *The Sino-Vietnamese Conflict.* New York, 1984
Leitenberg, M. and Burns, R. D., *War in Vietnam.* 2nd ed. Oxford and Santa Barbara, 1982
Nguyen Tien Hung, C., *Economic Developments of Socialist Vietnam, 1955–80.* New York, 1977
Nguyen Van Canh, *Vietnam under Communism, 1975–1982.* Stanford Univ. Press, 1983
Post, K., *Revolution, Socialism and Nationalism in Vietnam.* vol. 1. Aldershot, 1989
Smith, R. B., *An International History of the Vietnam War.* London, 1983
Truong Nhu Tang, *Journal of a Vietcong.* London, 1986

BRITISH VIRGIN ISLANDS

Capital: Road Town
Population: 16,749 (1991)
GNP per capita: US$10,000 (1989)

HISTORY. The Virgin Islands were discovered by Columbus on his second voyage in 1493. The British Virgin Islands were first settled by the Dutch in 1648 and taken over in 1666 by a group of English planters. In 1774 constitutional government was granted. The Islands became a self-governing dependent territory of the UK in 1967.

AREA AND POPULATION. The British Virgin Islands form the eastern extremity of the Greater Antilles and, exclusive of small rocks and reefs, number 40, of which 15 are inhabited. The largest, with population (1991 preliminary census count), are Tortola, 13,568, Virgin Gorda, 2,495, Anegada, 156 and Jost Van Dyke, 141. Other islands in the group had a total population (estimate 1990) of 183; Marine population (estimate 1989), 124. Total area about 59 sq. miles (130 sq. km); population (1991, census), 16,749. Road Town, on the south-east of Tortola, is a port of entry; population (estimate 1991), 6,330.

CLIMATE. A pleasantly healthy sub-tropical climate with summer temperatures lowered by sea breezes. Nights are cool and rainfall averages 50" (1,250 mm).

CONSTITUTION AND GOVERNMENT. In 1950 representative government was introduced and in 1967 a new Constitution was granted (amended 1977). The Governor is responsible for defence and internal security, external affairs, the public service, and the courts. The Executive Council consists of the Governor, 1 *ex-officio* member who is the Attorney-General and 4 ministers in the Legislature. The Legislative Council consists of 1 *ex-officio* member who is the Attorney-General and 9 elected members, one of whom is the Chief Minister and Minister of Finance; the Speaker is elected from outside the Council.

Governor: Peter A. Penfold, OBE.
Chief Minister: H. Lavity Stoutt (Virgin Islands Party); elected in 1990.
Flag: The British Blue Ensign with the arms of the Territory in the fly.

INTERNATIONAL RELATIONS

Membership. The Islands are an associate member of CARICOM.

ECONOMY

Budget. In 1991 revenue (estimate) was US$50,742,000; expenditure, US$46,040,700.

Currency. The unit of currency is the US dollar.

Banking and Finance. Bank of Nova Scotia, Barclays Bank PLC, Chase Manhattan Bank NA, Royal Trust Company Ltd, First Pennsylvania Bank NA and Guyerzeller Bank (BVI) Ltd hold General Banking Licences and had total deposits of US$284·7m. at 31 Dec. 1989. 7 institutions hold restricted banking licences and there are a large number of trust companies providing financial services other than banking. Financial services are the most important industry after tourism.

ENERGY AND NATURAL RESOURCES

Electricity. Production, 1989, 46·5m. kwh.

Agriculture. Agricultural production is limited, with the chief products being livestock (including poultry), fish, fruit and vegetables. Production, 1989, in tonnes (value in US$1,000): Fruits, 623 (670·0); vegetables/root crop, 87 (174·9);

beef, 188 (676·8); mutton, 14 (112); pork, 8·5 (29·8); and 1,250 cases of eggs (93·8). In 1989 the Agriculture Department was extended to include an abattoir.

Livestock (1989): Cattle, 3,500; pigs, 3,000; sheep, 650 and goats, 12,000.

INDUSTRY. The construction industry is a significant employer.

FOREIGN ECONOMIC RELATIONS

Commerce. There is a very small export trade almost entirely with the Virgin Islands of the USA. In 1989 imports were US$130·9m. and exports US$3·4m.

Total trade between the British Virgin Islands and UK (British Department of Trade returns, in £1,000 sterling):

	1988	1989	1990	1991
Imports to UK	4,030	1,170	1,205	545
Exports and re-exports from UK	7,108	6,727	4,454	8,619

Tourism. Tourism is the most important industry and accounts for some 75% of GDP. In 1990 (estimates), 317,670 holiday visitors, of whom 176,613 were overnight visitors spent US$132·1m.

COMMUNICATIONS

Roads. There were (1991) 164·5 km of motorable roads and (1990) 5,073 registered vehicles on Tortola and 616 on Virgin Gorda.

Civil Aviation. Beef Island Airport, about 16 km from Road Town, is capable of receiving 80-seat short-take-off-and-landing jet aircraft. Air BVI operates internal flights and external flights to San Juan (main route), Puerto Rico; the USVI, Antiqua, Dominica, Dominion Republic and St Kitts. Other services to the BVI are Eastern Metro Express, LIAT and American Eagle.

Shipping. There are services to Europe, the USA and other Caribbean islands, and daily services by motor launches to the US Virgin Islands.

Telecommunications. There were (1990) nearly 6,291 telephones , 43 telex subscribers, 90 facsimile machine subscribers and an external telephone service links Tortola with Bermuda and the rest of the world. Radio ZBVI transmits 10,000 watts and British Virgin Islands Cable TV operates a cable system of 19 television channels.

RELIGION, EDUCATION AND WELFARE

Religion. There are Anglican, Methodist, Seventh-Day Adventist, Roman Catholic, Baptist Churches and other Christian churches in the Territory. The Jehovah's Witnesses are also represented.

Education. Primary education is provided in 16 government schools, 3 with secondary divisions, and 12 private schools. Total number of pupils in primary and pre-primary schools (31 Dec. 1990) 2,710.

Secondary education to the GCE level and Caribbean Examination Council level is provided by the BVI High School and the secondary divisions of the schools on Virgin Gorda and Anegada. Total number of secondary level pupils (31 Dec. 1990) 1,146.

Government expenditure, 1991 (estimate), US$6·1m. In 1989 the total number of teachers in all Government schools was 113. In 1986 a branch of the Hull University (England) School of Education was established.

Health. In 1990 there were 14 doctors, 67 nurses, 50 public hospital beds and 1 private hospital with 10 beds. Expenditure, 1991 (estimate) was US$5·7m.

Further Reading

Economic Review 1987 – British Virgin Islands. Development Planning Unit, 1987
Dookham, I., *A History of the British Virgin Islands.* Epping, 1975
Harrigan, N. and Varlack, P., *British Virgin Islands: A Chronology.* London, 1971
Moll, V. P., *Virgin Islands.* [Bibliography] Oxford and Santa Barbara, 1991
Pickering, V. W., *Early History of the British Virgin Islands.* London, 1983

Library: Public Library, Road Town. *Librarian:* Bernadine Louis

WESTERN SAMOA

Capital: Apia
Population: 157,158 (1986)
GNP per capita: US$720 (1989)

Samoa i Sisifo—Independent State of Western Samoa

HISTORY. Western Samoa, a former German protectorate (1899–1914), was administered by New Zealand from 1920 to 1961, at first under a League of Nations Mandate and from 1946 under a UN Trusteeship Agreement. In May 1961 a plebiscite held under the supervision of the UN on the basis of universal adult suffrage voted overwhelmingly in favour of independence as from 1 Jan. 1962, on the basis of the Constitution, which a Constitutional Convention had adopted in Aug. 1960. In Oct. 1961 the UN General Assembly passed a resolution to terminate the trusteeship agreement as from 1 Jan. 1962, on which date Western Samoa became an independent sovereign state.

AREA AND POPULATION. Western Samoa lies between 13° and 15° S. lat. and 171° and 173° W. long. It comprises the two large islands of Savai'i and Upolu, the small islands of Manono and Apolima, and several uninhabited islets lying off the coast. The total land area is 1,093 sq. miles (2,830·8 sq. km), of which 659·4 sq. miles (1,707·8 sq. km) are in Savai'i, and 431·5 sq. miles (1,117·6 sq. km) in Upolu; other islands, 2·1 sq. miles (5·4 sq. km). The islands are of volcanic origin, and the coasts are surrounded by coral reefs. Rugged mountain ranges form the core of both main islands and rise to 3,608 ft in Upolu and 6,094 ft in Savai'i. The large area laid waste by lava-flows in Savai'i is a primary cause of that island supporting less than one-third of the population of the islands despite its greater size than Upolu.

The population at the 1986 census was 157,158, of whom 112,228 were in Upolu (including Manono and Apolima) and 44,930 in Savai'i. The capital and chief port is Apia in Upolu (population 32,196 in 1986). Expectation of life was 66 years in 1989.

The official languages are Samoan and English.

CLIMATE. A tropical marine climate, with cooler conditions from May to Nov. and a rainy season from Dec. to April. The rainfall is unevenly distributed, with south and east coasts having the greater quantities. Average annual rainfall is about 100" (2,500 mm) in the drier areas. Apia. Jan. 80°F (26·7°C), July 78°F (25·6°C). Annual rainfall 112" (2,800 mm).

CONSTITUTION AND GOVERNMENT. HH Malietoa Tanumafili II is the sole Head of State for life. Future Heads of State will be elected by the Legislative Assembly and hold office for 5-year terms.

The executive power is vested in the *Head of State*, who swears in the Prime Minister (who is appointed by members of the Legislative Assembly) and, on the Prime Minister's advice, the 8 Ministers to form the Cabinet. The Constitution also provides for a *Council of Deputies* of 3 members, of whom the chairman is the Deputy Head of State.

Before 1991 the 47-member *Legislative Assembly* was elected exclusively by *matai* (customary family heads). At the elections of April 1991 the suffrage was universal, but only the approximately 20,000 *matai* could stand as candidates. The electorate was 56,000. The Human Rights Protection Party won 30 seats, the Samoan National Development Party, 16 and an independent, 1.

Head of State: HH Malietoa Tanumafili II, GCMG, CBE.
Deputy Head of State: Mataafa Faasuamaleaui Puela.

The cabinet in March 1992 was composed as follows:

Prime Minister, Minister of Foreign Affairs, Broadcasting, Police and Prisons, Attorney General, Public Service Commission: Tofilau Eti Alesana. *Finance:* Tuilaepa Malielegaoi. *Agriculture:* Jack Netzler. *Works:* Leafa Vitale. *Health:* Sala Vaimili. *Education:* Fiame Mata'afa. *Post Office and Telecommunications:* Toi Aukuso. *Lands and Environment:* Faasootauloa Pati. *Justice:* Fuimaono Lotomau.

National flag: Red with a blue quarter bearing 5 white stars of the Southern Cross.

National anthem: Samoa, Arise and Raise your Banner (words and music by S. I. Kuresa).

INTERNATIONAL RELATIONS. Under a treaty of friendship of 1962 New Zealand acts as the channel of communication between the Samoan Government and governments and international organizations outside the Pacific islands area. Liaison is maintained by the New Zealand High Commissioner in Apia.

Membership. Western Samoa is a member of the UN, the Commonwealth, the South Pacific Forum and is an ACP state of the EEC.

ECONOMY

Budget. In 1989 budgeted revenue was $WS101·7m.; expenditure, $WS81·6m.

Currency. The unit of currency is the *tala* (WST) of 100 *sene*. In March 1992, £1 = 4.24; US$1 = 2·41.

Banking and Finance. A Central Bank was established in 1984. In 1959 the Bank of Western Samoa was established with a capital of $WS500,000, of which $WS275,000 was subscribed by the Bank of New Zealand and $WS225,000 by the Government of Western Samoa. In 1977 the Pacific Commercial Bank was established jointly by Australia's Bank of New South Wales and the Bank of Hawaii.

ENERGY AND NATURAL RESOURCES

Electricity. Production (1989) 44m. kwh.

Agriculture. The main products (1990, in 1,000 tonnes) are coconuts (190), taro (41), copra (26), bananas (24), papayas (12), mangoes (7), pineapples (6) and cocoa beans (1).

Livestock (1990): Horses, 3,000; cattle, 30,000; pigs, 55,000; poultry 1m.

Fisheries. The total catch (1983) was 3,150 tonnes, valued at $WS5·1m.

INDUSTRY. Some industrial activity is being developed associated with agricultural products and forestry.

FOREIGN ECONOMIC RELATIONS

Commerce. In 1989, exports were valued at $WS28,843,000. Principal exports were coconut oil (6,292 tonnes; $WS7m.), cocoa (595 long tons; $WS2,143,000), taro (263,000 cases, $WS5,901,000), coconut cream ($WS4,861,000); fruit juice ($WS75,000); beer ($WS725,000) and cigarettes ($WS694,000). In 1985, imports were valued at $WS115,074,000. Chief imports in 1983 included food and live animals ($WS15,195,000), beverages and tobacco ($WS1,913,000), machinery and transport equipment ($WS14,968,000), mineral fuels, lubricants and other materials ($WS13,133,000), chemicals ($WS4,221,000) and miscellaneous manufactured articles ($WS5,279,000).

Total trade between Western Samoa and UK (British Department of Trade returns, in £1,000 sterling):

	1987	1988	1989	1990	1991
Imports to UK	531	1,323	1,376	295	16
Exports and re-exports from UK	1,650	757	296	427	671

Tourism. There were 50,962 visitors in 1989.

COMMUNICATIONS

Roads (1987). Western Samoa has 2,085 km of roads, 400 km of which are surfaced and 1,200 km plantation roads fit for light traffic. In 1989 there were 1,898 private cars, 2,451 pick-up trucks, 349 trucks, 248 buses, 616 taxis and 185 motor cycles.

Civil Aviation. Western Samoa is linked by daily air service with American Samoa, which is on the route of the weekly New Zealand–Tahiti and New Zealand–Honolulu air services, with connexions to Fiji, Australia, USA and Europe. There are also services throughout the week to and from Tonga, Fiji, Nauru, the Cook Islands and New Zealand. Internal services link Upolu and Savai'i.

Shipping. Western Samoa is linked to Japan, USA, Europe, Fiji, Australia and New Zealand by regular shipping services.

Telecommunications. There are 2 radio communication stations at Apia. Radio telephone service connects Western Samoa with American Samoa, Fiji, New Zealand, Australia, Canada, USA and UK. Telephone subscribers numbered 3,452 in 1985. In 1991 there were 75,000 radio receivers and about 2,500 television sets.

Cinemas. In 1989 there were 2 cinemas.

Newspapers. In 1989, there were 4 weeklies, circulation 12,000 and 2 monthlies (8,000); all were in Samoan and English.

RELIGION, EDUCATION AND WELFARE

Religion. In 1986, 47% of the population were Congregationalists, 22% Roman Catholic and 15% Methodist.

Education. In 1986 the total number of pupils in primary, junior and secondary schools was 51,940. The University of the South Pacific School of Agriculture is in Western Samoa. A National University was established in 1984.

Health. In 1990 there was 1 national hospital, 15 district hospitals, 9 health centres and 18 subcentres and 44 doctors.

DIPLOMATIC REPRESENTATIVES

Of Western Samoa in Great Britain
High Commissioner: Afamasaga Faamatala Toleafoa (resides in Brussels).

Of Great Britain in Western Samoa
High Commissioner: D. J. Moss, CMG (resides in Wellington)

Of the USA in Western Samoa
Ambassador: Della M. Newman (resides in Wellington).

Of Western Samoa in the USA and to the United Nations (1115 15th St., NW, Washington D.C. 20005)
Ambassador: Dr Fili Wendt.

Further Reading

Statistical Year-Book. Annual
Fox, J. W. (ed.) *Western Samoa.* Univ. of Auckland, 1963

YEMEN

Jamhuriya al Yamaniya

(Republic of Yemen)

Capital: Sana'a
Commercial capital: Aden
Population: 12m. (1990)
GNP per capita: US$640 (1989)

HISTORY. Following an agreement reached in Dec. 1989 on a constitution for a unified state, the (northern) Yemen Arab Republic and the (southern) People's Democratic Republic of Yemen were united as the Republic of Yemen on 22 May 1990. There were 25 opposition votes in the northern parliament, but none in the southern. For the pre-unification history of the two states, *see* THE STATEMAN'S YEAR-BOOK, 1990–91, p. 1596 and 1599.

AREA AND POPULATION. Yemen is bounded in the north by Saudi Arabia, east by Oman, south by the Gulf of Aden and west by the Red Sea. The territory includes the islands of Kamaran (181 sq. km) and Perim (300 sq. km) in the Red Sea and the island of Socotra (3,500 sq. km) in the Gulf of Aden. In the north the boundary between the Yemen and Saudi Arabia has been defined by the Treaty of Taif concluded in June 1934. This frontier starts from the sea at a point some 5 or 10 miles north of Maidi and runs due east inland until it reaches the hills some 30 miles from the coast, whence it runs northwards for approximately 50 miles so as to leave the Sa'da Basin within the Yemen. Thence it runs in an easterly and southeasterly direction until it reaches the desert area near Nejran. The area is about 531,000 sq. km with a population estimated at some 12m. in 1990. At the census of 1986 in the north the population was 8,105,974. There were 1,168,199 citizens working abroad mainly in Saudi Arabia and the United Arab Emirates not included in the census total. In 1990 Saudi Arabia began compulsory repatriation of Yemeni workers, then numbering some 1·5m. At the census of 1988 in the south the population was 2,345,266. The capital is Sana'a with a population of (1990) 0·5m. The commercial capital is the port of Aden, with a population of (1987) 417,366. Other important towns are the port of Hodeida (population, 155,110), Mukalla (154,360), Ta'iz (178,043), Ibb and Abyan.

CLIMATE. A desert climate, modified by relief. Sana'a. Jan. 57°F (13·9°C), July 71°F (21·7°C). Aden, Jan. 75°F (24°C), July 90°F (32°C). Annual rainfall 20" (508 mm) in the north, but very low in coastal areas: 1·8" (46 mm).

CONSTITUTION AND GOVERNMENT. The government is headed by a 5-member *Presidential Council*, of whom the chairman, Lieut.-Gen. Ali Abdullah Saleh (formerly President of the Arab Republic) was elected *President of the Republic* by a joint session of the Consultative Assembly of the Arab Republic and the Presidium of the Supreme People's Council of the People's Democratic Republic. The other members are Ali Salem Albidh (*Vice-President*), Abdulkarim Al-Arashy, Salem Saleh Muhammad and Abd Al-Aziz Abd Al-Ghani. The 301-member *General People's Congress* represents a merger of the former northern and southern assemblies. Multi-party elections by universal suffrage are due at the end of 1992. The new government (*Council of Ministers*) comprised 20 northerners and 19 southerners, and in Feb. 1992 included:.

Prime Minister: Haidar Abu-Bakr Al-Attas (formerly President of the People's Democratic Republic).

First Deputy Prime Minister: Hassan Mohd Maki. *Deputy Prime Ministers:* Brig.-Gen. Mugahed Yehya Abu-Shawarab (*reponsible for internal affairs*), Brig.-Gen. Saleh Obeid (*security and defence*), Mohad Haiera Masdous (*development of the workforce and administrative reform*). *Minister of Construction and rehabilitation:*

Abdullah Hussein Al-Arashi. *Foreign Affairs:* Abdul Kareen Al-Iryani. *Emigrants'Affairs:* Brig.-Gen. Saleh Munsir Al-Saiyalli. *Industry:* Mohd Saeed Al-Attar. *Oil and Mineral Resources:* Saleh Abu-Bakr bin Husseinoon. *Supply and Trade:* Fadhle Mohsin Abdulla. *Local Government:* Mohd Saeed Abdulla. *Electricity and Water:* Abdul Wahab Mohmoud Abdul-Hameed. *Civil Service and Administrative reforms:* Mohd Khadam Al-Wajeah. *Planning and Development:* Farag bin Ghanem. *Communications:* Ahmed Mohd Al-Anasee. *Legal Affairs:* Ismaeal Ahemed Al-Wazeer. *Insurance and Social Affairs:* Ahmed Mohd Luqman. *Culture:* Hassan Ahmed Louzee. *Youth and Sport:* Mohd Ahmed Al-Kabab. *Education:* Mohd Abdulla Al-Gaifi. *Justice:* Abdul Wasa Sallam. *Information:* Mohd Ahmed Gurhoum. *Transport:* Saleh Abdulla Muthana. *Fish Resources:* Salem Mohd Gubran. *Housing and Planning:* Abdul Qawi Muthana Hadi. *Finance:* Arawee Assalami. *Health:* Mohd Ali Moqbil. *Agriculture and Water Resources:* Assadq Ameen Abu-Ras. *Tourism:* Mohmoud Abdulla Al-Arasee. *Interior and Security:* Col. Ghalib Muthar Al-Qamash. *Defence:* Brig. Hithem Qassam Tahar. *Labour:* Abdul Ruhman Dibyan. *Higher Education and Research:* Ahmed Salem Al-Qakhi.

National flag: Three horizontal stripes of red, white and black.

Local government: There are 11 provinces *(Liwa')* in the north: Sa'dah, Bayda, Sana'a, Hodeida, Hajjah, Jawf, Mahwit, Marib, Dhamar, Ibb and Ta'iz, and 6 governorates in the south: Aden, Lahej, Abyan, Shabwa, Hadhramaut and Mahra, divided into 30 provinces.

DEFENCE. Conscription is for 2 years.

Army. The Army comprises 9 armoured, 19 infantry, 5 mechanized, 2 airborne commando, 5 militia, 7 artillery and 2 surface-to-surface missile brigades. Equipment includes 250 T-34, 725 T-54/-55, 250 T-62 and 50 M-60A1 main battle tanks. Strength (1991) 60,000 (some 45,000 conscripts) with 40,000 reserves. There are paramilitary tribal levies numbering at least 20,000 and a Central Security Organization of 20,000.

Air Force. The unified Air Forces of the former Arab Republic and People's Democratic Republic are now under one command. It is equipped mainly with aircraft of Soviet design. It has about 70 MiG-21 fighters, 30 MiG-17 and 25 MiG-23 fighter-bombers, 50 Su-22 attack aircraft, 15 Mi-24 gunship helicopters, 7 An-24 and 6 An-26 twin-turboprop transports, 15 other transports (including 2 C-130H Hercules) and about 50 Mi-8 and 15 other helicopters. Personnel (1991) about 2,500.

Navy. The newly amalgamated Yemeni Navy comprises 2 Soviet-built missile corvettes, 6 ex-Soviet fast missile craft, 19 inshore patrol craft, 6 small minesweepers, 3 tank landing ships and 2 craft. There is a repair ship at Aden, where most forces are based. Other bases are at Hodeida, Al Muka, Mukalla and Perim. Personnel in 1991 were estimated at 3,000.

INTERNATIONAL RELATIONS

Membership. Yemen is a member of the UN and the Arab League.

ECONOMY

Policy. Development planning in the Arab Republic provided for investment of US$3,776m. (40% foreign aid), and concentrates principally on agricultural development; in the People's Democratic Republic expenditure of 998·2m. dinars was envisaged in the period 1986–91.

Budget. The Arab Republic's budget for 1989 provided for expenditure of 20,789m. riyals and revenue of 16,041m. riyals; that of the People's Democratic Republic, revenue of 354·3m. dinars and expenditure of 471·5m. dinars.

Currency. During the transitional period the northern *riyal* of 100 *fils* and the southern *dinar* of 1,000 *fils* coexist. In March 1992, 22·71 *riyal* = £1 and 12·93 *riyal* = US$1; 0·81 *dinars* = £1 and 0·46 *dinars* = US$1.

ENERGY AND NATURAL RESOURCES

Electricity. Production (1986) 556m. kwh.

Oil and Gas. The first large-scale oilfield and pipeline was inaugurated in 1987. There are reserves of 2,000m. bbls on the former north-south border. Production (1991) 9·93m. tonnes. Major oil finds were announced in May 1991. Gas reserves are some 7,000m. cu. metres.

Minerals. The only commercial mineral being exploited is salt and (1985) production was 169,000 tons. Reserves (estimate) 25m. tonnes.

Agriculture. In the north, of a total area of 19·5m. ha, 1·3m. are arable or permanent crops. Cotton is grown in the Tihama, the coastal belt, round Bait al Faqih and Zabid. Fruit is plentiful, especially fine grapes from the Sana'a district.

In the south, agriculture is the main occupation of the people. This is largely of a subsistence nature, sorghum, sesame and millet being the chief crops, and wheat and barley widely grown at the higher elevations. Of increasing importance, however, are the cash crops which have been developed since the Second World War, by far the most important of which is the Abyan long-staple cotton.

Owing to the meagre rainfall, cultivation is largely confined to fertile valleys and flood plains on silt, built up and irrigated in the traditional manner. These traditional methods are being augmented and replaced by the use of modern earth moving machinery and pumps. Irrigation schemes with permanent installations are in progress. Production (1990, in tonnes): Wheat, 141,000; cotton, 7,000; sesame, 8,000; millet, 52,000; maize, 43,000.

Livestock in 1990 (in 1,000): Cattle, 1,210; camels, 144; sheep, 3,755; goats, 3,160; poultry, 28m.

Fisheries. Fishing is a major industry. Total catch (1986) 113,500 tonnes, catch in the south (1988), 80,600 tonnes.

INDUSTRY. There is very little industry. There are textile factories, and plastic, rubber and aluminium goods, and paint and matches are produced.

FOREIGN ECONOMIC RELATIONS

Commerce. Cotton and fish are major exports, the largest imports being food and live animals. A large transhipment and entrepôt trade is centred on Aden, which was made a free trade zone in May 1991. Imports to the People's Democratic Republic were US$668m.; exports, US$2·2m.

Total trade between the former Arab Republic and the UK (British Department of Trade returns, in £1,000 sterling):

	1987	1988	1989	1990
Imports to UK	2,306	1,532	1,598	33,698
Exports and re-exports from UK	55,334	42,564	41,653	51,941

Total trade between the former People's Democratic Republic and the UK (British Department of Trade return, in £1,000 sterling):

	1987	1988	1989	1990
Imports to UK	1,056	1,827	5,029	2,540
Exports and re-exports from UK	28,271	20,862	17,246	18,889

Total trade between the unified Yemen and the UK in 1991 (British Department of Trade returns, in £1,000 sterling): Imports to UK, 16,770; exports and re-exports from UK, 65,572.

Tourism. There were about 44,000 tourists in 1986.

COMMUNICATIONS

Roads. There were (1988) 39,200 km of roads, including 2,227 km of paved roads in the south, and 195,000 cars.

Civil Aviation. There are 6 international airports: Seiyuun, Sana'a, Aden (Khormaksar), Mukalla (Riyan), Ta'iz and Hodeida. 6 airlines operate scheduled services: Air France, Middle East Airlines, Yemen Airlines, Aeroflot, Saudia and Air Djibouti.

Shipping. Because of its favourable geographical position and its efficient service to ships, Aden used to be one of the busiest oil-bunkering ports in the world, handling some 550 ships a month. There are 4 alongside berths and 1 ro-ro berth. In 1988 the port handled 1,900 ships. There are also ports at Hodeida, Mokha, Salif and Loheiya.

Telecommunications. There were about 70,000 telephones in 1988. Broadcasting is managed by the government-controlled Republic of Yemen Radio and Sana'a Television (colour by PAL and NTSC), and the joint commercial and government Yemen Television Service. In 1991 there were about 325,000 radio and 0·3m. TV receivers.

JUSTICE, RELIGION, EDUCATION AND WELFARE

Justice. In the former People's Democratic Republic there was a Supreme Court and magistrate's courts. In some areas Islamic Law and common law are administered.

Religion. In 1989 there were some 5·3m. Shiite and 5,925,000 Sunni Moslems.

Education. In the Arab Republic there were (1985–86) 904,487 pupils at primary schools, 112,922 in secondary schools, and 11,616 at teacher-training establishments. In 1982 the University of Sana'a (founded in 1974) had 6,719 students. In the People's Democratic Republic there were (1987) 310,839 pupils attending 989 primary schools and 31,530 secondary school pupils attending 62 schools. A state university was founded in 1975 and the number of students is increasing. In 1985, 400,000 students were studying at schools at various levels.

Health. In 1986 there were 1,234 physicians and 60 hospitals and health centres with 5,986 beds in the north. In the south in 1988 there were 729 physicians and 32 hospitals with 3,372 beds.

DIPLOMATIC REPRESENTATIVES

Of Yemen in Great Britain (41 South St., London, W1Y 5PD)
Ambassador: Dr Shaya Mohsin Mohamed.

Of Great Britain in Yemen (129 Haddah Rd., Sana'a)
Ambassador: M. A. Marshall, CMG.

Of Yemen in the USA (600 New Hampshire Ave., NW, Washington, D.C., 20037)
Ambassador: Mohsin A. Alaini.

Of the USA in Yemen (P.O. Box 1088, Sana'a)
Ambassador: Charles F. Dunbar.

Of Yemen to the United Nations
Ambassador: Abdalla Saleh Al-Ashtal.

Further Reading

Bidwell, R., *The Two Yemens*. Boulder and London, 1983
El Mallakh, R., *The Economic Development of the Yemen Arab Republic*. London, 1986
Ismael, T. Y. and Ismael, J. S., *The People's Democratic Republic of Yemen*. London, 1986
Peterson, J. E., *Yemen: The Search for a Modern State*. London, 1982
Smith, G. R., *The Yemens*. [Bibliography] Oxford and Santa Barbara, 1984
Thesiger, W., *Arabian Sands*. London, 1959

YUGOSLAVIA

Capital: Belgrade
Population: 23·46m. (1991)
GNP per capita: US$2,490 (1989)

Federativna Republika
Jugoslavija

CROATIA *and* **SLOVENIA** *seceded from the Federal Republic of Yugoslavia on 8 Oct. 1991 and now have independent entries on pp. 457–59 and pp. 1171–73 respectively. They are, however, included in statistics below relating to 1991 and earlier.*

HISTORY. In 1917 the Yugoslav Committee in London drew up the Pact of Corfu, which proclaimed that all Yugoslavs would unite after the first world war to form a kingdom under the Serbian royal house. The Kingdom of Serbs, Croats and Slovenes was proclaimed on 1 Dec. 1918. In 1929 the name was changed to Yugoslavia. During the Second World War Tito's partisans set up a provisional government (AVNOJ) which was the basis of a Constituent Assembly after the war. On 29 Nov. 1945 Yugoslavia was proclaimed a republic.

The peace treaty with Italy, signed in Paris on 10 Feb. 1947, stipulated the cession to Yugoslavia of the greater part of the Italian province of Venezia Giulia, the commune of Zara and the island of Pelagosa and the adjacent islets.

By an agreement of 10 Nov. 1975 the city of Trieste ('Zone A') was recognized as Italian and the Adriatic coastal portion of the former Free Territory of Trieste ('Zone B') as Yugoslav. A free industrial zone was set up in the Fernetici–Sezana region on both sides of the frontier.

Dissensions in Kosovo between Albanians and Serbs, and in parts of Croatia between Serbs and Croats brought inter-ethnic tensions into prominence after 1988. A government led by Ante Marković which took office in March 1989 embarked on a radical programme of economic and political reform, but with the election of new national assemblies in all 6 republics during 1990, several of the latter came increasingly into conflict with the federal government. At the end of 1990 both Croatia and Slovenia proclaimed their right to secede from federal Yugoslavia. In Jan. 1991 the federal constitutional court ruled that Slovenia's declaration of independence, and Serbia's imposition of inter-republican tariffs, were illegal.

In May 1991, following escalating Serb-Croat violence and demands for secession from predominantly Serb-inhabited areas of Croatia, the federal army was given powers to restrict the movement of unofficial armed groups. On 12 May the Krajina area held a self-styled referendum resulting, it was claimed, in an overwhelming vote for union with Serbia. Croatia rejected the poll.

On 15 May 1991 Croatia's representative in the state presidency, Stipe Mesić, failed to secure the 5 votes needed to become president in the annual election, hitherto a mere formality. Serbia, Kosovo and Vojvodina voted against and Montenegro abstained, leaving Yugoslavia without a head of state.

Early in June 1991 the presidency accepted as a basis for discussion the establishment of a federation of sovereign republics as a compromise between the status quo and declarations from Croatia and Slovenia of outright independence, but on 25 June both Croatia and Slovenia made declarations of independence. The federal government rejected the moves, which failed to win international recognition. On 27 June federal forces moved into Slovenia to secure Yugoslavia's external frontiers, and there were some fatalities in the ensuing fighting. Austria invoked the CSCE crisis-solving mechanism, and an EC mission presented a 3-point peace plan, viz. that Mesic should be elected president, Slovenia and Croatia should suspend their declarations of independence for 3 months, and federal forces should leave Slovenia. The first points were agreed on 30 June, but attempts by federal troops to leave with their tanks were alleged by Slovenia to contravene the truce terms and blocked. On 2 July federal forces launched another attack to rescue these beleaguered troops, and there were also clashes between federal and Croatian forces. Fighting continued during the summer in Croatia between Croatian forces and Serb irregulars from predominantly Serbian areas of Croatia backed by federal forces. All federal forces eventually left Slovenia by July 1991.

In Sept. the EC sponsored a peace conference at The Hague whose chairman visited Yugoslavia in a vain attempt to arrange a truce. The federal president and prime minister declared that the federal forces were acting without their authority. Rejecting a demand from the prime minister to resign, the federal defence minister Gen. Veljko Kadijević announced that the army was taking certain decisions into its own hands, but he agreed a ceasefire with the president of Croatia on 22 Sept.

On 25 Sept. the UN Security Council imposed a mandatory arms embargo on Yugoslavia.

By Oct. fighting had broken out again. On 4 Oct. the Serbian and Croatian presidents met the EC negotiators at The Hague and came to an agreement recognizing Croatia's independence within a loose Yugoslav confederation as a basis for peace, but despite this and several other ceasefire attempts (including a meeting between the Serbian and Croatian presidents at the Soviet president's invitation in Moscow on 15 Oct.), fighting continued.

The 3-month moratorium agreed at the EC peace talks on 30 June having expired, both Slovenia and Croatia declared their complete independence from the Yugoslav federation on 8 Oct.

In Oct. the EC put forward a plan for the orderly dissolution of the Yugoslav federation which Serbia rejected. The 12 EC foreign ministers then issued an ultimatum that trade sanctions would be imposed if any republic did not comply with the plan by 5 Nov., which Serbia again rejected. Sanctions on the whole of Yugoslavia were applied from 8 Nov., but restricted to Serbia after 2 weeks.

After 13 ceasefires had failed to be observed, a fourteenth was signed on 23 Nov. by the presidents of Croatia and Serbia and the federal defence minister, for the first time under UN auspices. Following a request on 26 Nov. from the federal government, a Security Council resolution of 27 Nov. proposed the deployment of a UN peace-keeping force if the ceasefire were kept. Fighting, however, continued.

Ante Marković resigned as Prime Minister on 20 Dec. in protest at a proposed budget for 1992 which devoted 81% of expenditure to military purposes.

On 1 Jan. 1992 the UN envoy to Yugoslavia announced that Croatia and Serbia had agreed to a peace-keeping plan to station a 10,000-strong UN force in the disputed areas of Croatia if a stable ceasefire were established.

Following the shooting down of an EC monitoring aircraft with the loss of its 5 occupants, Veljko Kadijević resigned as Minister of Defence on 8 Jan.

On 15 Jan. the EC recognised Croatia and Slovenia as independent states, but not Bosnia and Herzegovina or Macedonia, who had also applied for recognition.

A UN delegation began monitoring the ceasefire on 17 Jan. and after initial resistance from the self-proclaimed Serbian republic of Krajina within Croatia had been overcome, the UN Security Council on 21 Feb. voted unanimously to send a 14,000-strong peace-keeping force to Croatia and Yugoslavia.

AREA AND POPULATION. Yugoslavia is bounded in the north by Hungary, north-east by Romania, east by Bulgaria, south by Greece and Albania, and west by the Adriatic Sea and Croatia. The area with Croatia and Slovenia was 255,804 sq. km. Population at the last federal census in April 1991 was 23,462,976.

Yugoslavia was a federation of 6 republics: Bosnia and Herzegovina (B), Croatia (C), Macedonia (Ma), Montenegro (Mo), Serbia (Se) and Slovenia (Sl); and 2 'autonomous provinces' within Serbia; Kosovo (K) and Vojvodina (V). The federal capital is Belgrade (Beograd). Population (census, 1981) 1,470,073 and of other principal towns:

Banja Luka (B)	183,618	Priština (K)	210,040
Bitolj (Ma)	137,636	Prizren (K)	134,526
Čačak (Se)	110,676	Rijeka (C)	193,044
Čakovec (C)	116,825	Šabac (Se)	119,669
Gostivar (Ma)	101,028	Sarajevo (B)	448,519
Kragujevac (Se)	164,823	Skopje (Ma)	504,932
Kraljevo (Se)	121,622	Slavonski Brod (C)	106,400

Kruševac (Se)	132,972	Smederevo (Se)	107,366
Kumanovo (Ma)	126,188	Split (C)	180,571
Leskovac (Se)	159,001	Subotica (V)	154,611
Ljubljana (Sl)	305,211	Tetovo (Ma)	162,378
Maribor (Sl)	185,699	Titograd (Mo)	132,290
Mostar (B)	110,377	Titova Mitrovica (K)	105,322
Niš (Se)	230,711	Tuzla (B)	121,717
Novi Sad (V)	257,685	Uroševac (K)	113,680
Osijek (C)	158,790	Zadar (C)	116,174
Pančevo (V)	123,791	Zagreb (C)	1,174,512
Peć (K)	111,071	Zenica (B)	132,733
Prijedor (B)	108,868	Zrenjanin (V)	139,300

Population (1981 census) by ethnic group was *(i)* the 6 'leading nations': Serbs, 8,140,452; Croats, 4,428,005; Moslems, 1,999,957; Slovenes, 1,753,554; Macedonians, 1,339,729; Montenegrins, 579,023; *(ii)* of the 18 other 'nationalities': Albanians, 1,730,364; Hungarians, 426,866. 1,219,045 persons declared themselves 'Yugoslavs' (i.e. not professing any ethnic group). In 1986 about 460,000 nationals worked abroad. There were 181,000 Gypsies in 1986.

Vital statistics, 1987: Live births, 359,338; deaths, 214,666 (including 9,036 infantile); marriages, 163,469; divorces, 22,907.

Vital statistics, 1989 (per 1,000 population): Live births, 14·3; deaths, 9·1; marriages, 6·7; infant mortality, 24·3; natural increase, 5·2. Divorces per 1,000 marriages: 135·6. Expectation of life in 1982: Males, 68; females, 73.

The Yugoslav (*i.e.*, South Slav) languages proper are Slovene, Macedonian and Serbo-Croat, the latter having 2 variants (Serbian, or Eastern and Croatian, or Western) which are regarded as constituting one language. There are claims, largely politically-motivated, that Croatian is a separate language and Macedonian a dialect of Bulgarian. Macedonian is and Serbian may be written in the Cyrillic alphabet. There are also substantial Albanian and Hungarian-speaking minorities. Art. 246 of the Constitution lays down that 'The languages of the nations and nationalities and their alphabets shall be equal throughout the territory of Yugoslavia'. The sole use of Serbo-Croat is mandatory in the armed forces.

CLIMATE. Most parts have a central European type of climate, with cold winters and hot summers. Belgrade. Jan. 32°F (0°C), July 72°F (22°C). Annual rainfall 24·4" (610 mm). Sarajevo. Jan. 31°F (−0·5°C), July 67°F (19·6°C). Annual rainfall 34" (856 mm).

CONSTITUTION AND GOVERNMENT. The Constitution passed on 31 Jan. 1946 declared the Federal Republic to be composed of 6 republics: Serbia, Croatia, Slovenia, Bosnia and Herzegovina, Macedonia and Montenegro.

On 13 Jan. 1953 a new Constitution affirmed the management of all public affairs by the workers and their representatives.

The Constitution promulgated 7 April 1963 set up the 2 socialist autonomous provinces of Kosovo and Vojvodina within the framework of Serbia.

Under this Constitution, social self-government was exercised by the representative bodies of communes, districts, autonomous provinces, republics and the Federation and the rights to self-government and distribution of income proclaimed in 1953 were extended to those employed in public services. The former Council of Producers was replaced by Councils of Working Communities representing employees in every field of social activity.

All the means of production and all natural resources were social property. Exceptions were peasants' holdings (up to 10 hectares of arable land) and handicrafts. Citizens could be owners of dwellings for personal and family needs.

A new Constitution was proclaimed on 21 Feb. 1974. This directly transfered economic and political decision making to the working people through the 'assembly system'. An assembly was defined as 'a body of social self-management and the supreme organ of power within the framework of the rights and duties of its sociopolitical community'. Assemblies were based upon the workplace or community.

In Jan. 1990 the Government announced an 8-point plan to rewrite the Constitution, abolish the Communist Party's monopoly of power, set up an independent judiciary, guarantee freedom of political association and institute economic reforms. Opposition parties were legalized in July 1990.

Speaker of the Federal Assembly: Slobodan Gligorijević.

Every citizen over the age of 18 has the suffrage (16 if employed). The last elections were held from Jan. to April 1986.

The State Presidency was elected by the Federal Assembly every 5 years. It consisted of: a representative of each of the Republics and Autonomous Provinces. The one-year mandate as President (head of state) was rotated among the members of the Presidency from May of each year. This had become a formality, but in May 1991 Serbia refused to vote for the Croat president-elect, Štipe Mesić.

The Government is the Federal Executive Council of Chairman (i.e. Prime Minister), Vice-Chairmen, Ministers without Portfolio and Federal Secretaries, who are elected by the Federal Assembly every 4 years in conformity with equality of representation of the Republics and Autonomous Provinces.

Ante Marković resigned as Prime Minister on 20 Dec. 1991. Gen. Blagoje Adžić replaced Gen. Kadijević as *Minister of Defence* on 8 Jan. 1992.

National flag: Three horizontal stripes of blue, white, red, with a large red, yellow-bordered star in the centre.

National anthem: Hej, Slaveni, jošte živi reč naših dedova—O Slavs, our ancestors' words still live.

Local Government. Within the federal framework of republics Yugoslavia was administratively divided into 533 communes (*opština*). 52,843 delegates were elected to commune assemblies in 1986 (9,260 women): 24,335 to Chambers of Associated Labour; 14,935 to Chambers of Local Communities; and 13,573 to Socio-Political Chambers.

DEFENCE. Military service for 12 months is compulsory. The General People's Defence Law of 1969 bases Yugoslavia's defence on the principle of a nation in arms ready to wage partisan war against any invader.

Army. The Army comprises 2 infantry divisions; 1 airborne brigade and 29 brigades of armoured, mechanized, mountain and artillery forces. Equipment includes 850 T-54/-55, 300 M-84 and 45 M-47 main battle tanks.

Navy. The Navy comprises 5 small diesel submarines, 6 midget submarines, 2 Soviet and 2 locally built frigates to similar designs armed with SS-N-2C Styx anti-ship missiles, 15 fast missile craft, 14 fast torpedo craft, 2 small corvette-style patrol vessels, 11 inshore patrol craft, 4 coastal minehunters, 10 inshore minesweepers, 6 river minesweepers, 10 tank landing craft with minelaying capability, and 25 minor landing craft. Auxiliaries include 3 transports, 1 survey ship, 1 salvage vessel, 1 headquarters ship, and 2 training ships (1 sail). Minor auxiliaries number about 25.

The Air Force operates 8 Ka-25 Hormone and 2 Ka-27 Helix anti-submarine helicopters and 10 Mi-8 Hip and 15 Gazelle liaison helicopters, which are operationally assigned to the Navy. The Coast Defence Forces number 2,300 and man 25 coastal batteries and a few mobile missiles. A Marine force of 900 is divided into 2 'brigades'.

Personnel in 1991 totalled 11,000 (4,400 conscripts) including Coastal Defence and Marines, but no information was available early in 1992 on the division of the navy consequent on the secession of Slovenia and Croatia. The Navy appears to have remained loyal to Federal command, but with the loss of bases at Pula (Slovenia) and probably the former main base at Split (Croatia), the state of the navy must be open to question.

Air Force. The Air Force has been heavily involved in the fighting in Croatia and Slovenia. There are 2 fighter divisions equipped primarily with about 125 Russian-built MiG-21s, recently joined by MiG-29s, 2 ground-attack divisions of locally-built Jastreb and Orao jet attack aircraft, and 2 squadrons of Jastreb jet reconnaissance aircraft. Transport units fly An-26 twin-engined aircraft, 4-turbo-prop An-12s, and a few other types in small numbers, notably CL-215 amphibians,

C-47s, Turbo-Porters and Yak-40s, Falcon 50s and Learjets for VIP duties. Training types are the nationally-designed UTVA-75 primary trainer, Galeb jet basic trainer and the Super Galeb jet advanced trainer. A large number of Gazelle, Agusta-Bell 205 and Mi-8 helicopters are in service. 'Guideline' and 'Goa' surface-to-air missiles have been supplied by the USSR. Personnel (1991) 29,000 (3,500 conscripts), with 450 combat aircraft and 115 armed helicopters.

INTERNATIONAL RELATIONS

Membership. Yugoslavia is a member of the UN. With Austria, Czechoslovakia, Hungary and Italy, Yugoslavia was an inaugural member of the 'Pentagonal' meeting on economic and political co-operation in June 1990. Poland adhered in May 1991 and the group was renamed 'Hexagonal'.

ECONOMY

Policy. Reforms of the economic system which began in 1989 included curbs on the republics' powers by integrating taxation and raising policy-making to the federal level, the liberalization of imports and reduction of tariffs, the liberalization of prices except in the public infrastructure, the modification of the workers' councils system, the creation of limited companies and stock exchanges and equal treatment for foreign and domestic investors.

A second phase of economic reforms was aimed at completing a market-oriented fiscal system by 1995, including the establishment of a wage-bargaining structure and harmonization of taxation between republics. Gradual privatization ('democratization of capital') was expected to encourage private and foreign investment.

Budget. The federal budget for 1991–92 was set at 132,000m. dinars and envisaged a 40% reduction in federal administrative costs. Half was allocated to subsidies to enterprises, 42% to the federal army and 8% to administration. Because of reductions in contributions from Croatia and Slovenia the budget was largely financed by the National Bank and foreign reserves.

Currency. The unit of currency is the *dinar* (YUD) of 100 *para*. The currency became convertible on 1 Jan. 1990 and a new 'heavy' dinar was introduced worth 10,000 old dinars. The new dinar was pegged at DM 7 throughout 1990, and at DM 9 from 1 Jan. 1991, a devaluation of 22·2%. In April 1991 the dinar was devalued by 30·7% and pegged to the German mark at DM1 = 13 dinars. Following the creation of the Croatian dinar on 23 Dec. 1991 the National Bank on 25 Dec. issued new dinars replacing the former notes of denominations of 100, 500, 1,000 and 5,000 dinars. The dinar was further devalued in Jan. 1992 by 80%. Currency in circulation in 1988 was 4,014,600m. old dinars. In March 1992, £1 = 242·80 *dinars*; US$1 = 138·308 *dinars*. International reserves, 1989: US$5,000m.

Banking and Finance. The National Bank is the bank of issue. There are also republican banks. In 1988 there were 243 'internal' banks, 155 'basic banks' and 10 'associated banks'. A reform programme which started in Feb. 1989 has transformed banks into shareholding companies, empowers the National Bank to impose solvency ratios on financial institutions and strengthens its control of the money supply. There is a stock exchange at Belgrade. In 1988 credits amounted to 1,493,200m. old dinars. Savings deposits totalled 8,063,600m. old dinars in 1988, foreign exchange savings 39,243,100m.

Weights and Measures. The metric weights and measures have been in use since 1883. The *wagon* of 10 tonnes is used as a unit of measure for coal, roots and corn. The Gregorian calendar was adopted in 1919.

ENERGY AND NATURAL RESOURCES

Electricity. Output in 1989, 82,775m. kwh, of which 23,491m. were hydro-electric. A nuclear power plant at Krško in Slovenia was opened in 1981. Construction of further nuclear plants was banned by law in June 1989.

Oil. Crude oil production (1989) 3·39m. tonnes; 1991 estimate, 2·77m. tonnes, about 20% of Yugoslavia's needs. Annual refining capacity is some 30m. tonnes.

Minerals. Yugoslavia has considerable mineral resources, including coal (chiefly brown coal), iron, copper ore, gold, lead, chrome, antimony and cement.

Mining output, in 1,000 tonnes, in 1989 (and 1988): Coal, 292 (362); brown coal, 12,063 (11,876); lignite, 62,276 (60,352); bauxite, 3,252 (3,034); salt, 368 (385); iron ore, 5,080 (5,545); copper ore, 30,078 (30,056); lead and zinc ore, 3,885 (3,847); antimony, 43 (38). In 1983, gold output was 4,238 kg; silver (1989), 133,000 kg.

Agriculture. The economically active agricultural population was 2,488,000 in 1981 (47·5% female). The total agricultural area was 14·18m. ha in 1989. The cultivated area was 9·81m. ha in 1989 of which 8·06m. were in private farms and 1·74m. in agricultural organizations, of which there were 3,203 in 1989. In 1984 only 6·5% of the 2·6m. private farms were more than 10 ha of land.

Area (in ha) and yield (in 1,000 tonnes) in 1990: Maize, 2·21m. (6,616); wheat, 1·5m. (6,359); sugar beet, 158,000 (5,915); rye, 38,000 (72); tobacco, 45,000 (42); sunflower, 214,000 (422); potatoes, 282,000 (2,075).

Livestock, 1990: Cattle, 4·71m.; pigs, 7·23m.; sheep, 7·6m.; poultry, 73·52m.

1989 yield of fruit (in 1,000 tonnes): Apples, 546; grapes, 1,022; plums (Yugoslavia is the world's largest producer), 819. 4·86m. hectolitres of wine were produced.

There were 1,107,629 tractors in 1990, of which 1,075,000 were in private hands.

Forestry. In 1989, 9·5m. ha were forested, 37% of the land area, and consisted largely of beech, oak and fir. 3·2m. ha were in private hands. Gross timber cut (1989): 21,542,000 cu. metres.

Fisheries. In 1988 the landings of fish were (in tonnes): Salt-water, 45,316; freshwater, 26,449. The number of fishing craft was 387 motor vessels (13,401 GRT) and 1,458 sailing and rowing vessels.

INDUSTRY. In 1988 there were 8,796 large industrial enterprises and 1,380 small businesses in the social sector, and 165,055 small businesses in the private sector.

Industrial output (in 1,000 tonnes) in 1989 (and 1990): Pig-iron, 2,899 (2,460); steel, 4,500 (3,830); cement, 8,560 (8,100); sulphuric acid, 1,634 (1,384); mineral fertilizers, 2,508 (2,100); plastics, 742 (680). Fabrics (in 1m. sq. metres): Cotton, 339 (282); woollen, 100 (86). Sugar (1,000 tonnes), 960 (920). Motor cars (in 1,000s), 312 (293).

Labour. In 1989 (females in parentheses) there were 179,000 (69,000) employed in the private sector and 6·7m. (2·66m.) in the social sector. Of these 1·17m. worked in non-economic activities (e.g. education, social welfare). Amongst the economic activities 2·72m. worked in industry and mining, 675,000 in trade, 531,000 in building, 454,000 in transport and communications, 264,000 in financial services, 247,000 in tourism and 246,000 in agriculture. There were 1·2m. unemployed in 1989. Average monthly income per worker in 1989: 801·08 dinars. There were (1986) 6,086,600 trade union members.

Trade Unions. The Confederation of Trade Unions of Yugoslavia had 6,349,000 members in 1989.

FOREIGN ECONOMIC RELATIONS. Foreign indebtedness was US$17,600m. in 1989. In joint ventures the foreign partner may own up to 98% of the equity.

Commerce. Foreign trade, in 1m. dinars, for calendar years:

	1987	1988	1989
Imports	953	4,439	46,393
Exports	882	3,288	41,405

Structure of exports (and imports) in 1989 (%): Investment goods, 16 (15); intermediate goods, 52 (73·1); consumer goods, 31 (11·7). Largest suppliers in 1989 (goods in 1m. dinars): USSR, 6,734; Italy, 4,896; USA, 2,223; Austria, 1,994; Iraq, 1,790; Federal Republic of Germany, 1,307. Largest export markets: USSR, 8,983; Italy, 6,257; Federal Germany, 4,748; USA, 1,931.

Main exports as % share in 1989: Machinery and transport equipment, 27·6; other manufactures, 15; food and tobacco, 9·1; chemicals, 12; raw materials, 6·8; fuel, 1·9. Imports: Machinery and transport equipment, 27·3; chemicals, 17·9; raw materials, 10·8.

Total trade between Yugoslavia and UK (British Department of Trade returns, in £1,000 sterling):

	1987	1988	1989	1990	1991
Imports to UK	175,301	197,254	202,450	189,421	147,876
Exports and re-exports from UK	206,932	203,066	219,866	260,972	193,836

Tourism. In 1989, foreign tourists spent 49·18m. (1988: 52·35m.) nights in Yugoslavia.

COMMUNICATIONS

Roads. In 1988 there were 806 km of motorway, 73,527 km of asphalted roads and 33,663 km of macadamized roads. There were 3·09m. passenger motor cars, 88,228 motorcycles, 206,000 lorries and 28,000 buses. 804m. passengers and 125m. tonnes of freight were carried by public road transport in 1989. There were 65,392 road traffic casualties (4,555 deaths) in 1988.

Railways. In 1989 Yugoslavia had 9,567 km of railway, of which 3,782 km were electrified. 115·7m. passengers and 83·6m. tonnes of freight were carried in 1988.

Civil Aviation. The national airline JAT (Jugoslovenski Aero Transport) operated 291 domestic and international routes totalling 455,122 km. in 1989. It had 48 aircraft in 1989. In 1989 5·6m. passengers and 48,897 tonnes of freight were carried. The chief airfields are Belgrade, Sarajevo, Skopje, and Titograd.

Shipping. In 1989 Yugoslavia possessed 61 sea-going passenger vessels and 271 cargo vessels totalling 3·4m. tonnes. In 1989 8m. passengers were carried (7·9m. domestic) and 38·3m. tonnes of freight (35m. tonnes overseas).

International cargo handled at Yugoslav ports in 1987 totalled 30·85m. tonnes; domestic, 4·27m. tonnes.

Length of navigable waterways: Rivers, 1,673 km; canals, 664 km. There are 2 navigable lakes: Skadar (391 sq. km, of which 243 in Yugoslavia) and Ohrid (348 sq. km, of which 230 in Yugoslavia). In 1987 there were 1,156 river craft. 29,000 passengers and 19·27m. tonnes of cargo were carried in 1989.

Telecommunications. There were 4,109 post offices and 4,550,000 telephone subscribers in 1989. *Jugoslovenska Radiotelevizija* consists of almost 250 main, relay and local stations operating on medium-waves and FM. In Aug. 1990 the central government launched the Yutel TV station with the aim of presenting a federal view of events. Number of receivers in 1989: Radio, 4·7m.; television, 4·07m.

Cinema and Theatre. In 1989 there were 1,165 cinemas with 482,000 seats and 65 theatres with 27,164 seats. 29 full-length films were made in 1989.

Newspapers and Books. In 1989 there were 28 dailies with a circulation of 2·1m., 2,481 other newspapers and 1,453 periodicals. 11,339 book titles (2,548 by foreign authors) were published in 1988.

JUSTICE, RELIGION, EDUCATION AND WELFARE

Justice. There are county tribunals, district courts, supreme courts of the constituent republics and a Supreme Court. There are also self-management courts, including courts of associated labour. In county tribunals and district courts the judicial functions are exercised by professional judges and by lay assessors constituted into collegia. There are no assessors at the supreme courts.

All judges are elected by the socio-political communities in their jurisdiction. The judges exercise their functions in accordance with the legal provisions enacted since the liberation of the country.

The constituent republics enact their own criminal legislation, but offences concerning state security and the administration are dealt with at federal level.

In 1987 258,000 crimes were reported, 163,000 charges made and 112,000 convictions obtained. 7,705 juveniles were sentenced.

Religion. Religious communities are separate from the State and are free to perform religious affairs. All religious communities recognized by law enjoy the same rights.

Serbia has been traditionally Orthodox. Moslems are found in the south as a result of the Turkish occupation. The 1953 percentage of the denominations was: Orthodox, 41·2%; Roman Catholic, 31·7%; Moslems, 12·3%; Protestants, 0·9%; without religion, 12·6%. 1984 estimates of believers: Orthodox, 9m.; Roman Catholic, 7m.; Moslems, 4m.

The Serbian Orthodox Church with its seat in Belgrade has 20 bishoprics within the country and 4 abroad, 3 in US and Canada and 1 in Hungary. The Serbian Orthodox Church numbers about 2,000 priests.

The Macedonian Orthodox Church with the Archbishop of Ohrid and Macedonia as its head in Skopje, has 4 bishoprics in the country and 1 abroad (American–Canadian–Australian). The Macedonian Orthodox Church numbers about 300 priests.

The Roman Catholic Church has a province at Sarajevo with 2 suffragan sees. Relations with the Vatican are regulated by a 'Protocol' of 1966.

The Moslem Religious Union has 4 republic Superiorates in Sarajevo, Skopje, Titograd and Priština. The highest authority is the supreme synod of the Islamic Religious Community, which elects the Reis-ul-Ulema and the Supreme Islamic Superiorate. The Moslem religious community has about 2,000 priests. Its head is Hadji Jakub Selimoski.

Before the secession of Croatia and Slovenia the Jewish religion had about 35 communities making up a common league of Jewish Communities with its seat in Belgrade.

Education. Compulsory general education lasts 8 years, secondary 3–4 years. In 1988–89 there were 4,157 kindergartens with 46,413 teachers and 435,932 pupils, 11,910 primary schools with 141,584 teachers and 2,824,951 pupils; and 1,217 secondary schools with 59,128 teachers and 956,978 pupils.

Primary (and secondary) schools of ethnic minorities (1988–89): Albanian, 1,230 (87); Hungarian, 136 (26); Turkish, 65 (14); Bulgarian, 40 (nil); Romanian, 31 (2); Italian, 27 (7); Slovak, 21 (2).

In 1988–89 there were 314 institutes of higher education with 255,665 full-time students and 25,969 academic staff.

Health. In 1988 there were 55,140 doctors and dentists, and 142,957 hospital beds (11,031 psychiatric).

Social Security. There were 2·1m. pensioners in 1989. 100·4m. working days were lost through sickness in 1988. Health insurance benefits totalled 21,321·8m. dinars, old age pensions 8,076·1m. dinars and disability pensions, 5,219·4m. dinars in 1989. 2,628·5m. dinars were paid in child allowances in 1989. Consumption of food per capita in 1988: Meat, 597 kg.; cereals, 1,727 kg.; milk, 98·8 litres; vegetables and fruit, 171·7 kg. Daily consumption: 15,400 kilojoules.

DIPLOMATIC REPRESENTATIVES

Of Yugoslavia in Great Britain (5 Lexham Gdns., London, W8 5JJ)
Ambassador: Svetozar Rikanović.

Of Great Britain in Yugoslavia (46 Generala Ždanova, Belgrade)
Ambassador: P. E. Hall, CMG.

Of Yugoslavia in the USA (2410 California St., NW, Washington, D.C., 20008)
Ambassador: Dževad Mujezinović.

Of the USA in Yugoslavia (Belgrade)
Ambassador: Warren Zimmermann.

Of Yugoslavia to the United Nations
Ambassador: Darko Silović.

Further Reading

Statistical Information: The Federal Statistical Office (Savezni Zavod za Statistiku; Kneza Miloša 20, Belgrade) was founded in Dec. 1944. *Director:* Dr D. Grupković. Its publications include: *Statistički godišnjak Jugoslavije*, annual since 1954 with a separate volume of captions and editorial matter in English *Statistical Yearbook of Yugoslavia*; *Statistical Pocket-Book of Yugoslavia*, annual since 1955; *Statistics of Foreign Trade of the SFR of Yugoslavia*, annual since 1946.

The Assembly of the SFR of Yugoslavia. Belgrade, 1974
The Constitution of the Socialist Federal Republic of Yugoslavia. Belgrade, 1974
Alexander, S., *Church and State in Yugoslavia since 1945.* CUP, 1979
Artesien, P. F. R., *Joint Ventures in Yugoslav Industry.* Aldershot, 1985
Banac, I., *The National Question in Yugoslavia.* Cornell Univ. Press, 1985
Burg, S. L., *Conflict and Cohesion in Socialist Yugoslavia: Political Decision-Making since 1966.* Princeton Univ. Press, 1983
Cohen, L. J., *Political Cohesion in a Fragile Mosaic: The Yugoslav Experience.* Boulder, 1983
Dedijer, V., *et al., History of Yugoslavia.* New York, 1974
Djilas, A., *The Contested Country: Yugoslav Unity and Communist Revolution, 1919–1953.* Harvard Univ. Press, 1991
Djilas, M., *Memoir of a Revolutionary.* New York, 1973.—*Rise and Fall.* London, 1985
Horton, J. J., *Yugoslavia.* [Bibliography] Oxford and Santa Barbara, 1978
Lydall, H., *Yugoslavia in Crisis.* OUP, 1989
McFarlane, B., *Yugoslavia: Politics, Economics and Society.* London, 1988
Milivojević, M. *et al.* (eds.) *Yugoslavia's Security Dilemmas: Armed Forces, National Defence and Foreign Policy.* Oxford, 1988
Pavlowitch, S. K., *The Albanian Problem in Yugoslavia.* London, 1982
Ramet, P., *Nationalism and Federalism in Yugoslavia, 1963–1983.* Indiana Univ. Press, 1984. —*Yugoslavia in the 1980s.* Boulder, 1985
Seroka, J., *Political Organizations in Yugoslavia.* Durham, NC, 1986
Singleton, F., *Twentieth Century Yugoslavia.* London, 1976.—(with B. Carter) *The Economy of Yugoslavia.* London, 1982.—*A Short History of the Yugoslav Peoples.* CUP, 1985
Tito, J. B., *The Essential Tito.* New York, 1970
Zimmerman, W., *Open Borders, Non-Alignment and the Political Evolution of Yugoslavia.* Princeton Univ. Press, 1987

REPUBLICS AND AUTONOMOUS PROVINCES

In March 1992 the Federal Republic of Yugoslavia comprised the 4 republics of Bosnia and Herzegovina, Macedonia, Montenegro and Serbia, and the 2 autonomous provinces of Kosovo and Vojvodina within the Republic of Serbia.

Each republic has its own Constitution and Assembly.

Indicators (in %) for 1989:

	Population	Workers	Social product	Investments
Yugoslavia	100	100	100	100
Bosnia and Herzegovina	18·5	15·8	12·5	14·2
Croatia [1]	19·8	23·4	25·4	22·2
Macedonia	8·9	7·7	5·7	4·9
Montenegro	2·7	2·4	2·0	2·3
Serbia	41·5	38·4	36·2	37·9
Slovenia [1]	8·9	12·2	18·2	18·5

[1] Seceded Oct. 1991

BOSNIA AND HERZEGOVINA

HISTORY. The country was settled by Slavs in the 7th century, the original clan system evolving between the 12th and 14th centuries into a principality under a

Ban, during which time the Bogomil Christian heresy became entrenched. Bosnia was conquered by the Turks in 1463, and the majority of the Bogomils were converted to Islam. At the Congress of Berlin (1878) the territory was assigned to Austro-Hungarian administration under nominal Turkish suzerainty. Austria-Hungary's outright annexation in 1908 generated international tensions which contributed to the outbreak of the first world war.

On 15 Oct. 1991 the National Assembly adopted a 'Memorandum on Sovereignty', the Serbian deputies abstaining. This envisaged Bosnian autonomy within a Yugoslav federation. A referendum on independence was held on 29 Feb.–1 March 1992. Turn-out was 63·04%, the Serbian population largely boycotting it; 99·78% of votes cast were in favour. In March 1992 an agreement was reached under EC auspices by Moslems, Serbs and Croats to set up 3 autonomous ethnic communities under a central Bosnian authority.

AREA AND POPULATION. The republic is bounded in the north and west by Croatia, in the east by Serbia and in the south-east by Montenegro. It is virtually land-locked, having a coastline of only 20 km with no harbours. Its area is 51,129 sq. km. The capital is Sarajevo.

Population at the 1991 census: 4,355,000, of whom the predominating ethnic groups were Moslems (1,905,000), Serbs (1,364,000) and Croats (752,000). Population density per sq. km, 1981: 80·7.

Vital statistics:

	Live births	Marriages	Deaths	Growth rate per 1,000
1987	70,898	34,466	29,382	9·4
1988	70,711	34,700	29,555	9·3

CONSTITUTION AND GOVERNMENT. There is a 240-member bicameral National Assembly and 7-member collective presidency. Elections were held to both in Nov. and Dec. 1990. Moslem Democratic Action gained 86 National Assembly seats, the Serb Democratic Party, 70, and the Croat Democratic Union, 45. Alija Izetbegović (Moslem Democratic Action) was elected *President;* Jure Relivan (Croat Democratic Union) was appointed *Prime Minister.* The *Deputy Prime Minister* is Rusmir Mahmutćehajić; *Foreign Minister:* Haris Siljadžić.

ECONOMY

Agriculture. In 1990 the cultivated area was 1·58m. ha. Yields (in 1,000 tonnes): Wheat, 457; maize, 728; potatoes, 343; plums, 76. Livestock in 1989 (1,000 head): Cattle, 884; sheep, 1,355; pigs, 608; poultry, 11,465. Timber cut in 1988: 7·05m. cu. metres.

Industry. Production (1989): Electricity, 14,372m. kwh; coal and lignite, 17·97m. tonnes; iron ore, 4·7m. tonnes; pig iron, 1·64m. tonnes; bauxite, 1·91m. tonnes; cement, 793,000 tonnes; cotton fabrics, 37m. sq. metres; cars, 34,000.

Employment. Population of working age, 1989, 3m. Non-agricultural workforce, 1·04m. (379,000 women), of whom 25,000 worked in private enterprise.

MACEDONIA

HISTORY. The Slavs settled in Macedonia since the 6th century, who had been Christianized by Byzantium, were conquered by the non-Slav Bulgars in the 7th century and in the 9th century formed a Macedo-Bulgarian empire, the western part of which survived until Byzantine conquest in 1014. In the 14th century it fell to Serbia, and in 1355 to the Turks. After the Balkan Wars of 1912-13 Turkey was ousted, and Serbia received the greater part of the territory, the rest going to Bulgaria and Greece. In 1918 Yugoslav Macedonia was incorporated into Serbia as 'South Serbia'. Possession of this territory has long been a source of contention between Bulgaria and Yugoslavia.

Macedonia failed to secure EC recognition as an independent state on 15 Jan. 1992.

AREA AND POPULATION. Macedonia is land-locked, and is bounded in the north by Serbia and Kosovo, in the east by Bulgaria, in the south by Greece and in the west by Albania. The capital is Skopje. Its area is 25,713 sq. km. Population at the 1981 census was 1,909,136 (940,993 females), of whom the predominating ethnic groups were Macedonians (1,279,323), Albanians (377,208) and Turks (86,591). Population density per sq. km, 1981, 74·2. Population estimate, 1992, 2·3m., including 427,000 Albanians.

Vital statistics:

	Live births	Marriages	Deaths	Growth rate per 1,000
1987	38,572	16,799	14,644	11·6
1988	37,379	46,580	14,565	11·2

CONSTITUTION AND GOVERNMENT. There is a 120-member single-chamber National Assembly. At the elections of Nov. and Dec. 1990 the Democratic Party for Macedonian National Unity gained 37 seats, the League of Communists–Party of Democratic Change, 31 and the Albanian-supported Party of Democratic Prosperity, 24. The *President* is Kiro Gligorov (b. 1918).

Prime Minister: Nikola Kljusev. *Defence:* Denko Maleski.

At a referendum held on 8 Sept. 1991 turn-out was 74%; 99% of votes cast were in favour of a sovereign Macedonia with the option to rejoin a future reformed Yugoslav federation. The National Assembly confirmed the results on 18 Sept.

ECONOMY

Agriculture. In 1990 the cultivated area was 668,000 ha. Yields (in 1,000 tonnes): Wheat, 231; maize, 79; cotton (1989), 686; tobacco, 28. Livestock in 1989 (1,000 head): Cattle, 291; sheep, 2,378; pigs, 157; poultry, 4,406. Timber cut in 1989: 1·14m. cu. metres.

Industry. Production (1989): Electricity, 4,687m. kwh; lignite, 5·69m. tonnes; iron ore, 412,000 tonnes; pig-iron, 139,000 tonnes; steel, 224,000 tonnes; copper ore, 3·83m. tonnes; sulphuric acid, 92,000 tonnes; cement, 769,000 tonnes; cotton fabrics, 62m. sq. metres.

Employment. Population of working age, 1989: 1·35m. Non-agricultural work-force, 473,000 (180,000 women), of whom 14,000 worked in private enterprise.

RELIGION. In 1967 an autocephalous Orthodox church split off from the Serbian.

MONTENEGRO

HISTORY. Montenegro emerged as a separate entity on the break-up of the Serbian Empire in 1355. It was never effectively subdued by Turkey. It was ruled by Bishop Princes until 1851, when a royal house was founded. The remains of King Nicholas I, (deposed 1918) were returned to Montenegro for reburial in Oct. 1989.

AREA AND POPULATION. Montenegro is a mountainous region which opens to the Adriatic in the south-west. It is bounded in the north-west by Bosnia and Herzegovina, in the north-east by Serbia and in the south-east by Albania. The capital is Titograd. Its area is 13,812, sq. km. Population at the 1981 census was 584,310 (294,571 females), of whom the predominating ethnic groups were Montenegrins (400,488), Moslems (78,080) and Albanians (37,735). Population density per sq. km, 1981: 42·3. Population, 1988, 632,000.

Vital statistics:

	Live births	Marriages	Deaths	Growth rate per 1,000
1987	10,567	4,358	3,990	10·4
1988	10,190	4,085	3,661	10·3

CONSTITUTION AND GOVERNMENT. There is a 125-member single-chamber National Assembly. At the elections of Dec. 1990 the electorate was 0·43m.; turn-out was 75%. The League of Communists gained 83 seats, the federal-oriented Alliance of Reform Forces, 17, the Albanian-supported Democratic Coalition, 13, and the National Party, 12. At the presidential elections turn-out was 65·8%. Momir Bulatović (Communist) was elected against one opponent with 76% of votes cast.

A referendum was held on 29 Feb.–1 March 1992 to determine whether Montenegro should remain within a common state, Yugoslavia, as a sovereign republic. The electorate was 412,000, of whom 66% were in favour.

ECONOMY

Agriculture. In 1990 the cultivated area was 186,000 ha. Yields (in 1,000 tonnes): Wheat, 20; maize, 10; potatoes, 33. Livestock in 1989 (1,000 head): Cattle, 189; sheep, 488; pigs, 25. Timber cut in 1989: 882,000 cu. metres.

Industry. Production (1989): Electricity, 2,443m. kwh; lignite, 1·77m. tonnes; bauxite, 0·9m. tonnes; cement (1987), 155,000 tonnes.

Employment. Population of working age, 1989: 412,000. Non-agricultural workforce, 159,000 (62,000 women), of whom 5,000 worked in private enterprise.

SERBIA

HISTORY. The Serbs received Orthodox Christianity from the Byzantines. They threw off the latter's suzerainty to become a large prosperous medieval state, which was destroyed by the Turks at the Battle of Kosovo in 1389. After revolutions in 1804 and 1815 Serbia won increasing degrees of autonomy from Turkey; complete independence came with the Treaty of Berlin in 1878. Its prince took the title of king in 1881.

AREA AND POPULATION. Serbia is bounded in the north-west by Croatia, in the north by Hungary, in the north-east by Romania, in the east by Bulgaria, in the south by Macedonia and in the west by Albania, Montenegro and Bosnia and Herzegovina. It includes the Autonomous Provinces of Kosovo in the south and Vojvodina in the north. With these Serbia's area is 88,361 sq. km; without, 55,968 sq. km. The capital is Belgrade. Population at the 1981 census was (with Kosovo and Vojvodina) 9,313,676 (4,684,349 females), of whom the predominating ethnic group was Serbs (6,182,155). Population density per sq. km: 105·4 (without Kosovo and Vojvodina). 5,694,464 (2,876,909 females), of whom the predominating ethnic group was Serbs (4,865,283). Population density per sq. km, 101·7. Population, 1988: With Kosovo and Vojvodina, 9·76m.; without, 5·83m.

Vital statistics (without Kosovo and Vojvodina):

	Live births	Marriages	Deaths	Growth rate per 1,000
1987	73,076	38,331	58,651	2·5
1988	72,623	38,132	59,083	2·3

CONSTITUTION AND GOVERNMENT. At a referendum in July 1990 96·8% of the 5·33m. votes cast approved delaying parliamentary elections until a new constitution was adopted, and further reducing the autonomy of Kosovo and the Vojvodina. (Turn-out in the latter was 25% and 55% respectively). In Sept. a new constitution was adopted by the National Assembly by 64 votes to 6. It defines Serbia as a 'democratic' instead of a 'socialist' republic, lays down a framework for multi-party elections, and describes Serbia as 'united and sovereign on all its territory', thus stripping Kosovo and the Vojvodina of the attributes of autonomy granted by the 1974 federal constitution.

There is a 250-member single-chamber National Assembly. At the elections of Dec. 1990 the Socialist Party (reconstituted Communists) gained 194 seats, the Serbian Renewal Movement, 19, the Democratic Party, 7 and independents, 8. Allegations of irregularities at the polls were made by foreign observers. Slobodan Milošević was elected *President* of Serbia against 2 opponents with 65% of the votes cast.

In Feb. 1992 there was a government of 19 ministers including:

Prime Minister: Dragutin Zelenović.

Defence: Gen. Marko Negovanović. *Foreign:* Vladislav Jovanović. *Interior:* Radmilo Bogdanović. *Serbs outside Serbia:* Stanko Cvijan.

ECONOMY [1]

Agriculture. In 1990 the cultivated area was 4·68m. ha. Yields (in 1,000 tonnes): Wheat, 3,849; maize, 3,517; potatoes, 627; sugar-beet (1989), 4,946. Livestock in 1990: (in 1,000 head): Cattle, 1,979; sheep, 2,519; pigs, 4,301. Timber cut in 1989: 4·04m. cu. metres.

Industry. (1989): Electricity, 40,103m. kwh.; coal and lignite, 42·69m. tonnes; pig-iron, 881,000 tonnes; steel, 886,000 tonnes; copper ore, 26·25m. tonnes; lorries (1988), 9,500; cars, 223,000; sulphuric acid, 1·08m. tonnes; plastics, 309,000 tonnes; cement, 2·93m. tonnes; sugar, 630,000 tonnes; cotton fabrics, 76,000 sq. metres; woollens, 42,000 sq. metres.

Employment. Population of working age, 1989: 6·31m. Non-agricultural workforce, 2·45m. (942,000 women), of whom 53,000 worked in private enterprise.

[1] Figures include Kosovo and Vojvodina.

KOSOVO

HISTORY. Following Albanian-Serb conflicts the Kosovo and Serbian parliaments adopted constitutional amendments in March 1989 surrendering much of Kosovo's autonomy to Serbia. Renewed Albanian rioting broke out in 1990. The Prime Minister and 6 other ministers resigned in April 1990 over ethnic conflicts. In July 1990 114 of the 130 Albanian members of the National Assembly voted for full republican status for Kosovo, but the Serbian National Assembly declared this vote invalid and unanimously voted to dissolve the Kosovo Assembly. Direct Serbian rule was imposed. The *President* is Hisen Kajdomci.

AREA AND POPULATION. Area: 10,887 sq. km. The capital is Priština. Population at the 1981 census, 1,584,441 (766,048 females), of whom the predominating ethnic groups were Albanians (1,226,736), and Serbs (209,497). Population density per sq. km, 1981: 145·5. Population, 1987, 1·85m.

Vital statistics:

	Live births	Marriages	Deaths	Growth rate per 1,000
1987	56,221	13,644	10,307	24·8
1988	56,283	14,613	10,257	24·3

ECONOMY

Agriculture. The cultivated area in 1988 was 409,000 ha. Yields in 1990 (in 1,000 tonnes): Wheat, 349; maize, 72; potatoes, 37; plums, 11; grapes, 40. Livestock in 1990 (1,000 head): Cattle, 420; sheep, 400; pigs, 63; poultry, 5,586. Timber cut in 1989, 330,000 cu. metres.

Industry. Production (1989): Electricity, 5,531m. kwh; lignite, 10·67m. tonnes; sulphuric acid, 85,000 tonnes; cement, 316,000 tonnes.

Employment. Population of working age, 1989: 1·09m. Non-agricultural work-force, 226,000 (54,000 women), of whom 6,000 worked in private enterprise.

VOJVODINA

AREA AND POPULATION. Area: 21,506 sq. km. The capital is Novi Sad. Population at the 1981 census, 2,034,772 (1,041,392 females), of whom the pre-dominating ethnic groups were Serbs (1,107,375) and Hungarians (385,356). Population density per sq. km, 1981: 94·6. Population, 1987, 2·05m.

Vital statistics:

	Live births	Marriages	Deaths	Growth rate per 1,000
1987	25,203	14,169	24,775	0·3
1988	24,848	13,577	24,533	0·2

CONSTITUTION AND GOVERNMENT. The 1990 Serbian constitution deprived Vojvodina of its former autonomy. Serbo-Croat was declared the only official languange in July 1991.

ECONOMY

Agriculture. The cultivated area in 1990 was 1·63m. ha. Yields (in 1,000 tonnes): Wheat, 2,070; maize, 1,981; potatoes, 188; sugar-beet (1989), 4,166. Livestock in 1990 (1,000 head): Cattle, 236; sheep, 315; pigs, 1,794; poultry, 9,200. Timber cut in 1989: 876,000 cu. metres.

Industry. Production (1989): Electricity, 1,510m. kwh.; crude petroleum, 1·09m. tonnes; sulphuric acid (1988), 55,000 tonnes; plastics (1988), 123,000 tonnes; cement, 1·3m. tonnes.

Employment. Population of working age, 1988: 1·35m. Non-agricultural work-force, 642,000 (257,000 women), of whom 18,000 worked in private enterprise.

ZAÏRE

Capital: Kinshasa
Population: 38·55m. (1991)
GNP per capita: US$260 (1989)

République du Zaïre

HISTORY. When the explorer Henry Stanley reached the mouth of the Congo in 1877, King Leopold II of the Belgians took the lead in exploring and exploiting the Congo Basin. The Berlin Conference of 1884–85 recognized King Leopold II as the sovereign head of the Congo Free State.

In 1908 the country was annexed to Belgium as the Belgian Congo, until the country became independent on 30 June 1960. The country's name was changed from Congo to Zaïre in Oct. 1971. For subsequent history to 1977 *see* THE STATESMAN'S YEAR-BOOK, 1980–81, p. 1613.

Following a week of rioting and looting by unpaid soldiers and discontented citizens at the end of Sept. 1991, President Mobutu agreed that the political opposition should form a government, but the situation remained fluid at the beginning of 1992.

AREA AND POPULATION. Zaïre is bounded north by the Central African Republic, north-east by Sudan, east by Uganda, Rwanda, Burundi and Lake Tanganyika, south by Zambia, south-west by Angola, north-west by Congo. There is a 37-km Atlantic coastline separating Angola's province of Cabinda from the rest of that country.

The area is estimated at 2,344,885 sq. km (905,365 sq. miles). The population is composed almost entirely of Bantu groups, with minorities of Sudanese (in the north), Nilotes (northeast), Pygmies and Hamites (in the east). In the 1984 census the population was 29,671,407 (44% urban). Estimate (1991) 38,545,000. Population growth rate, 1989, 3%. In 1989 there were 340,689 refugees in Zaïre, mainly from Angola.

The area (in sq. km) and populations (census) 1984 of the regions were as follows, together with their chief towns:

Region	Sq. km	Census 1984	Chief town	Census 1984
Bandundu	295,658	3,682,845	Bandundu (Banningville)	96,841
Bas-Zaïre	53,920	1,971,520	Matadi	144,742
Equateur	403,293	3,405,512	Mbandaka (Coquilhatville)	125,263
Haut-Zaïre	503,239	4,206,069	Kisangani (Stanleyville)	282,650
Kasai Occidental	156,967	2,287,416	Kananga (Luluabourg)	290,898
Kasai Oriental	168,216	2,402,603	Mbuji-Mayi (Bakwanga)	423,363
Kinshasa City	9,965	2,653,558	Kinshasa (Leopoldville)	2,653,558
Kivu [1]	256,662	5,187,865	Bukavu (Costermansville)	171,064
Shaba	496,965	3,874,019	Lubumbashi (Elizabethville)	543,268

[1] Now divided into 3 regions.

Other large towns (1976): Likasi (194,465 in 1984); Kikwit (146,784 in 1984); Kalémié (172,297); Kamina (160,020); Ilebo (142,036); Boma (93,965) and Kolwezi (77,277).

French is the only official language, but of more than 200 languages spoken, 4 are recognized as national languages. Of these, Kiswahili is used in the east, Tshiluba in the south, Kikongo in the area between Kinshasa and the coast, while Lingala is spoken widely in and around Kinshasa and along the river; Lingala has become the *lingua franca* after French.

CLIMATE. Because of the size and the relief of the country, the climate is very varied, the central region having an equatorial climate, with year-long high temperatures and rain at all seasons. Elsewhere, depending on position north or south of the Equator, there are well-marked wet and dry seasons. The mountains of the east and south have a temperate mountain climate, with the highest summits having considerable snowfall. Kinshasa. Jan. 79°F (26·1°C), July 73°F (22·8°C). Annual rainfall 45" (1,125 mm). Kananga. Jan. 76°F (24·4°C), July 74°F (23·3°C). Annual rainfall 62" (1,584 mm). Kisangani. Jan. 78°F (25·6°C), July 75°F (23·9°C). Annual rainfall 68" (1,704 mm). Lubumbashi. Jan. 72°F (22·2°C), July 61°F (16·1°C). Annual rainfall 50" (1,237 mm).

CONSTITUTION AND GOVERNMENT. Under the Constitution of 1978 (as amended in 1980) the sole political party was the *Mouvement Populaire de la Révolution* (MPR), whose leader and President was automatically Head of State, of the National Executive Council and of the National Legislative Council. His nomination by the Political Bureau of the MPR (whose 38 members were all nominated by him) was confirmed for a 7-year term (renewable once) by election by universal adult suffrage (all Zaïreans acquiring automatic membership of the MPR at birth).

Parliament consists of a unicameral National Legislative Council comprising People's Commissioners (one per 150,000 inhabitants) elected by universal suffrage for a 5-year term. At the latest elections (Sept. 1987) 210 People's Commissioners were elected from a list of candidates presented by the MPR.

In April 1990 President Mobutu announced the end of the Second Republic and the transition to a multi-party state. A national conference of 2,850 delegates to debate the country's political future began proceedings in Aug. 1991 but was halted by the president in Nov. 1991, who then appointed Nguza Karl I Bond Prime Minister (the third since 30 Sept.). The latter formed a government on 28 Nov. The conference resumed in Dec. but was suspended 'until further notice' on 19 Jan. 1992.

Former President: Joseph Kasavubu, 1 July 1960–25 Nov. 1965 (deposed).

President: Marshal Mobutu Sésé Séko Kuku Ngbendu wa Zabanga (took office 25 Nov. 1965, elected 1 Nov. 1970 and re-elected Dec. 1977 and July 1984).

National flag: Green, with a yellow disc bearing an arm holding a flaming torch.

Local government: Zaïre is composed of the *ville neutre* of Kinshasa (administered by a Governor) and 10 regions, each under a Regional Commissioner and 6 Councillors; all are appointed by the President. The regions are divided into 41 sub-regions.

DEFENCE

Army. The Army is divided into 8 Military Regions and comprises 3 infantry brigades and 4 special brigades (1 parachute, 1 commando, 1 armoured and 1 Presidential Guard). Equipment includes 60 Chinese Type-62 tanks, and 95 AML-60 and 60 AML-90 armoured cars. Strength (1991) 22,000. There is a paramilitary gendarmerie which is responsible for security which numbered (1991) about 28,000, organized in 40 battalions.

Navy. The navy comprises 2 ex-Chinese inshore patrol craft and some 30 small boats divided among coastal, river and lake flotillas. Personnel in 1991 numbered 1,200 including 600 marines.

Air Force. The Air Force has been built up with training assistance from Italy. In 1991 it operated 8 Mirage 5 fighters, 9 Aermacchi MB.326GB and 6 MB.326K armed jet trainers, 4 C-130 Hercules and 3 DHC-5 Buffalo turboprop transports, 7 C-47, 4 C-54, 2 DC-6 piston-engined transports, 20 Bell 47, Alouette, Puma and Super Puma helicopters, 9 SIAI-Marchetti SF.260MC basic trainers and a variety of other transport and training aircraft. Personnel (1991) 2,500.

INTERNATIONAL RELATIONS

Membership. Zaïre is a member of the UN, OAU and is an ACP state of the EEC.

ECONOMY

Policy. The 5-year Development Plan, 1986–90, envisaged expenditure of US$5,000m. Emphasis is placed on food production and agricultural exports.

Budget. Revenue was budgeted at 607,000m. zaïres in 1990, and expenditure, 657,000m.

Currency. The unit of currency is the *zaïre* (ZRZ). There are coins of 1, 5 and 10 zaïres and notes of 10, 50, 100, 500, 1,000, 5,000 and 10,000 zaïres. In March 1992, £1 sterling = 197,167·0 zaïre; US$1 = 112,314 zaïre. The zaïre was devalued by 48% against the US dollar.

Banking and Finance. The central bank is Banque du Zaïre. A development bank with state backing is the Société Financière de Développement (SOFIDE). Commercial banks operating in Zaïre are Banque de Paris et des Pays-Bas, Banque de Kinshasa, National & Grindlays Bank, Barclays Bank SZPRL, First National City Bank, Union Zaïroise de Banques, Banque Commerciale Zaïroise, Banque du Peuple, Caisse Nationale d'Epargne et de Crédit Immobilier and Banque Internationale pour L'Afrique au Zaïre.

Since Aug. 1991 commercial banks have been able to trade foreign exchange freely at their own rates.

Weights and Measures. The metric system is in force.

ENERGY AND NATURAL RESOURCES

Electricity. Production (1989), 5,998m. kwh. A dam at Inga, on the Zaïre River near Matadi, has a potential capacity of 39,600 mw.

Oil. Offshore oil production began in Nov. 1975; crude production (1991) was 1·48m. tonnes.

Minerals. Production in 1989 (in 1,000 tonnes): Copper, 425·2; zinc, 54; cobalt, 9·5. In 1990 0·34m. tonnes of copper was produced. Manganese, tin, gold and silver are also mined. The most important mining area is in the region of Shaba (formerly Katanga). The principal mining companies are the State-owned Gécamines and Sodimiza; the international Société Minière du Tenke-Fungurume which started production in 1976; and 2 diamond companies, MIBA and British Zaïre Diamond Distributors. Production (1989) 17,652 carats.

Agriculture. There were (1984) 5·65m. ha of arable land and 24·8m. ha of pastures and meadows. The main food crops (1990 production in 1,000 tonnes) are: Cassava, 17,500; plantains, 1,800; sugar-cane, 1,180; maize, 870; groundnuts, 430; bananas, 404; yams, 270; rice, 345. Cash crops (1990) include palm oil, 180; coffee, 98; palm kernels, 153; rubber, 20; seed cotton 230. There are also (1990) pineapples, 143; mangoes, 208; oranges, 153; papayas, 205.

Livestock (1990): Cattle, 1·5m.; sheep, 913,000; goats, 3·06m.; pigs, 820,000; poultry, 20m.

Forestry. Equatorial rain forests cover 55% of Zaïre's land surface, and 165,000 cu. metres of timber were produced in 1988.

Fisheries. The catch for 1986 was 150,000 tonnes, almost entirely from inland waters.

INDUSTRY. The main manufactures are foodstuffs, beverages, tobacco, textiles, rubber, leather, wood products, cement and building materials, metallurgy and metal extraction, metal items, transport vehicles, electrical equipment and bicycles.

FOREIGN ECONOMIC RELATIONS. With Burundi and Rwanda, Zaïre forms part of the Economic Community of the Great Lakes.

Commerce. Imports in 1989 totalled US$1,546·1m., exports US$2,101m. In 1989, 59% of the exports (by value) consisted of copper, 5·7% of coffee, 7·5% of crude petroleum, 11·9% of diamonds and 7·6% of cobalt. In 1987, 37% of all exports went to Belgium-Luxembourg, 18% to USA, 11% to Federal Republic of Germany and 11% to Italy, while 19·7% of imports came from Belgium, 9·3% from USA, 9% from France, 8·8% from Federal Republic of Germany and 8·7% from South Africa.

Total trade between Zaïre and UK (British Department of Trade returns, in £1,000 sterling):

	1987	1988	1989	1990	1991
Imports to UK	8,544	7,542	9,069	7,337	4,733
Exports and re-exports from UK	26,142	26,132	28,419	23,801	15,040

Tourism. There were 51,000 visitors in 1986 spending US$16·3m.

COMMUNICATIONS

Roads. In 1989 of 145,000 km of roads 2,370 km were asphalted and some 12,000 km motorable. In 1984 there were 25,000 passenger cars and 60,000 commercial vehicles.

Railways. There are two railway operators, the Zaïre National Railways (SNCZ) and the National Office of Transport and Communications (ONATRA), which leases two lines from SNCZ. Length in 1990 was 5,118 km on 3 gauges, of which 858 km is electrified. In 1988 SNCZ and ONATRA carried 4m. passengers and 5·8m. tonnes of freight.

Civil Aviation. There are 4 international airports at Kinshasa (Ndjili), Lubumbashi (Luano), Goma and Bukavu. There are another 40 airports with regular scheduled internal services, and over 150 other landing strips.

10 international airlines operate in and out of Kinshasa from Europe and Africa. The national airline is Air Zaïre. It operates domestic routes and flights to Europe and Africa, including a weekly flight to Johannesburg via Lusaka (Zambia). South African Airways operate a weekly service from Johannesburg to Lubumbashi.

Shipping. The Zaïre River and its tributaries are navigable to 300-tonne vessels for about 14,500 km. Regular traffic has been established between Kinshasa and Kisangani as well as Ilebo, on the Lualaba (*i.e.*, the river above Kisangani), on some tributaries and on the lakes. Zaïre has only 40 km of sea coast. The merchant marine in 1988 comprised 4 vessels with a total tonnage of 60,562 GRT. Matadi and Boma are the main seaports; in 1989, Matadi handled 1·5m. tonnes of freight. Boma's traffic is negligible.

Telecommunications. In 1983 there were 362 post offices. Length of telegraph lines, 2,459 km. There were 15 broadcasting stations, 161 stations of wireless telegraphy and 206 telegraph offices; telephones numbered 31,855 in 1985. There is a ground satellite communications station outside Kinshasa. Broadcasting is provided by the government-controlled Voix du Zaïre and Télévision Zaïre (colour by SECAM). There is also an educational radio station. In 1991 there were 3·4m. radio and 20,000 TV receivers.

Newspapers. There were (1989) 4 dailies: *Salongo* (mornings) and *Elima* (evenings) in Kinshasa; *Njumbe* in Lubumbashi and *Boyoma* in Kisangani.

JUSTICE, RELIGION, EDUCATION AND WELFARE

Justice. There is a Supreme Court at Kinshasa, 11 courts of appeal, 36 courts of first instance and 24 'peace tribunals'.

Religion. In 1989 there were about 16,130,000 Roman Catholics (46·8% of the population), 9,670,000 Protestants (28·0%) and 5,700,000 Kimbanguistes (16·5%). In 1988 there were some 450,000 Moslems and 2,000 Jews. The remaining inhabitants chiefly adhere to animist beliefs.

Education. In 1987 there were 4,356,515 pupils in 10,819 primary schools and 1,066,351 pupils in 4,276 secondary schools. Secondary schools combine schools of general education, teacher training colleges and technical schools. In higher education there were in 1990 3 universities (Kinshasa, Kisangani and Lubumbashi), 14 teacher training colleges and 18 technical institutes in the public sector; and 13 university institutes, 4 teacher training colleges and 49 technical institutes in the private sector.

Health. In 1979 there were 1,900 doctors, 58 dentists, 414 pharmacists, 3,043 midwives, 14,661 nursing personnel and 942 hospitals and medical centres with 79,244 beds.

DIPLOMATIC REPRESENTATIVES

Of Zaïre in Great Britain (26 Chesham Pl., London, SW1X 8HH)
Ambassador: Nkema Liloo.

Of Great Britain in Zaïre (Ave. de l'Equateur, Kinshasa)
Ambassador: Roger Westbrook, CMG.

Of Zaïre in the USA (1800 New Hampshire Ave., NW, Washington, D.C., 20009)
Ambassador: Tatanee Manata.

Of the USA in Zaïre (310 Ave. des Aviateurs, Kinshasa)
Ambassador: William C. Harrop.

Of Zaïre to the United Nations
Ambassador: Bagbeni Adeito Nzengeya.

Further Reading

Atlas Général du Congo. Académie Royale, Brussels
Gran, G., *Zaïre: The Political Economy of Underdevelopment.* New York, 1979
MacGaffey, J., *Entrepreneurs and Parasites: The Struggle for Indigenous Capitalism in Zaïre.* CUP, 1988
Parfitt, T. W., *Zaïre:* [Bibliography]. Oxford and Santa Barbara, 1991
Young, C. and Turner, T., *The Rise and Decline of the Zaïrian State.* Univ. of Wisconsin Press, 1985

ZAMBIA

Capital: Lusaka
Population: 8·5m. (1990)
GNP per capita: US$390 (1989)

Republic of Zambia

HISTORY. The independent Republic of Zambia (formerly Northern Rhodesia) came into being on 24 Oct. 1964 after 9 months of internal self-government following the dissolution of the Federation of Rhodesia and Nyasaland on 31 Dec. 1963.

AREA AND POPULATION. Zambia is bounded by Tanzania in the north, Malawi in the east, Mozambique in the south-east and by Zimbabwe and South West Africa (Namibia) in the south. The area is 290,586 sq. miles (752,614 sq. km). Population (1980 census) 5,679,808 of which 43% urban; estimate (1990), 8·5m.

The republic is divided into 9 provinces. Their names, headquarters, area (in sq. km) and census population in 1980 were as follows:

Province	Headquarters	Area	Population	Province	Headquarters	Area	Population
Copperbelt	Ndola	31,328	1,248,888	Eastern	Chipata	69,106	656,381
Luapula	Mansa	50,567	412,798	Southern	Livingstone	85,283	686,469
Northern	Kasama	147,826	677,894	N.-Western	Solwezi	125,827	301,677
Central	Kabwe	94,395	513,835	Western	Mongu	126,386	487,988
Lusaka	Lusaka	21,898	693,878				

The seat of Government is at Lusaka (population, 1987, 818,994); other large towns are Kitwe (449,442), Ndola (418,142), Mufulira (192,323), Chingola (187,310), Luanshya (160,667), Kalulushi (89,065) and Chililabombwe (79,010) on the Copperbelt; Kabwe, the oldest mining township (190,752); Livingstone, the old capital (94,637); and other provincial capitals at Kasama, Mansa, Chipata, Mongu and Solwezi. In Jan. 1988 there were 146,000 refugees in Zambia including 97,000 Angolans.

The official language is English and the main ethnic groups are the Bemba (34%), Tonga (16%), Malawi (14%) and Lozi (9%).

CLIMATE. The climate is tropical, but has three seasons. The cool, dry one is from May to Aug., a hot dry one follows until Nov., when the wet season commences. Frosts may occur in some areas in the cool season. Lusaka. Jan. 70°F (21·1°C), July 61°F (16·1°C). Annual rainfall 33" (836 mm). Livingstone. Jan. 75°F (23·9°C), July 61°F (16·1°C). Annual rainfall 27" (673 mm). Ndola. Jan. 70°F (21·1°C), July 59°F (15°C). Annual rainfall 52" (1,293 mm).

CONSTITUTION AND GOVERNMENT. The Constitution provides for a President, elected in the first instance by the General Conference of the ruling party, the United National Independence Party, and thereafter by the electorate. On 13 Dec. 1972 President Kaunda signed a new Constitution based on one-party rule. In Dec. 1990 the National Assembly unanimously passed a constitutional amendment permitting opposition parties.

In Aug. 1991 parliament adopted a new constitution by 107 votes to 15 permitting multi-party elections for a new wholly-elected parliament of 150 members.

At the Oct. 1991 presidential and parliamentary elections the registering electorate was 2·9m. Turn-out was about 40%. Frederick Chiluba (b. 1943; MMD) was elected President by 75% of votes cast against the incumbent Kaunda (UNIP) with 24%. The Movement for Multiparty Democracy (MMD) won 125 seats, the United Nationalist Independent Party (UNIP), 25.

The MMD government formed in Nov. 1991 included:

President: Frederick Chiluba.
Vice-President and Prime Minister: Lery Mwanawasa.
Foreign Affairs: Vernon Mwaanga. *Finance and Planning:* Emmanuel Kasonde.
Defence: Ben Mwila. *Mines and Mineral Development:* Humphrey Mulemba. *Agri-*

culture: Guy Scott. *Home Affairs:* Newstead Zimba. *Legal Affairs:* Roger Chongwe.
Transport and Communications: Andrew Kashita.

National flag: Green, with in the fly a panel of 3 vertical strips of dark red, black
and orange, and above these a soaring eagle in gold.
National anthem: Stand and Sing of Zambia, Proud and Free.

The 9 provinces (sub-divided into 53 districts) are administered by Central Committee Members for the provinces who are responsible for the overall government
and Party administration of their respective areas.

DEFENCE

Army. The Army consists of 1 armoured regiment and 9 infantry battalions, with
supporting artillery, engineer and signals units. Equipment includes some 30 main
battle tanks and 88 armoured cars. Strength (1991 estimate) 16,000. There are also
paramilitary police units numbering 500 men.

Air Force. Creation of the Zambian Air Force was assisted initially by an RAF mission. Training and expansion of the Air Force was next taken over by Italy, with the
purchase of 23 Aermacchi M.B.326G armed jet basic trainers (of which 18 remain
in service), 8 SIAI-Marchetti SF.260M piston-engined trainers and 15 Agusta-Bell
47G, 10 AB.205 and 2 AB.212 helicopters. Twelve F-6 (MiG-19) jet fighter-
bombers and some BT-6 primary trainers have since been acquired from China, a
squadron of 14 MiG-21 fighters, 3 Yak-40 light jet transports, 4 An-26 twin-turboprop transports and 6 Mi-8 helicopters from the Soviet Union, 5 DHC-5 Buffalo
twin-turboprop transports from Canada, 6 C-47s built in the USA, 8 DO 28D Skyservant light transports from Germany, 15 Supporter armed light trainers from
Sweden. Serviceability of most types is reported to be low. Personnel (1991
estimate) 2,000, with 75 combat aircraft.

INTERNATIONAL RELATIONS

Membership. Zambia is a member of the UN, the Commonwealth, SADCC, OAU
and is an ACP state of the EEC.

ECONOMY

Budget. Revenue and expenditure for 1989 (in K1m.): Envisaged expenditure of
24,503 and revenue of 20,366.

Currency. The unit of currency is the *kwacha* (ZMK) of 100 *ngwee*. There are
coins of 50, 20, 10, 5, 2 and 1 *ngwee* and banknotes of K20, K10, K5, K2 and K1.
In March 1992, £1 = 215·30 *kwacha;* US$1 = 122·643 *kwacha.*

Banking and Finance. Barclays Bank has 25 branches, 6 sub-branches and 17
agencies; Standard Bank has 18 branches and 17 agencies; National & Grindlays,
10 branches and 1 sub-branch; Zambia National Commercial Bank, 10 branches
and 1 in London; the post office saving bank has branches throughout the republic.

The Finance Development Corporation (FINDECO) controls the building societies,
all insurance companies, one commercial bank and has shares in a second one. The
Agricultural Finance Corporation provides loans to farmers, co-operatives, farmers'
associations and agricultural societies.

ENERGY AND NATURAL RESOURCES

Electricity. The total installed capacity of hydro and thermal power stations, excluding Zambia's share of Kariba South, amounts to 1,924,700 kw and the energy
production during 1986 amounted to some 11,100m. kwh. Zambia exports electricity to Zaïre, Zimbabwe and Angola.

Minerals. The total value of minerals produced (in 1,000 tonnes) in 1985 was: Copper, 543; zinc, 32; lead, 15; cobalt, 4·4; gold, 7,903 oz. Zambia is well-endowed
with gemstones, especially emeralds, amethysts, aquamarine, tourmaline and garnets. In 1990 the government freed the gemstones trade from restrictions.

Agriculture. Although 70% of the population is dependent on agriculture only 10% of GDP is provided by the industry. Principal agricultural products (1990) were maize, 1,093,000 tonnes; sugar-cane, 1,340,000 tonnes; seed cotton, 31,000 tonnes; tobacco, 5,000 tonnes; groundnuts, 25,000 tonnes.

Livestock (1990): 2,861,000 cattle; 200,000 pigs; 85,000 sheep; 565,000 goats, and 16m. poultry.

Forestry. Forests covered (1988) 29·2m. ha, 39% of the total land area. Round-wood removals (1986) 9·9m. cu. metres.

Fisheries. Total catch (1986) 68,000 tonnes.

INDUSTRY. In Dec. 1984 there was a labour force of 2·27m. of which 63% were employed in agriculture, 2·6% in mining and quarrying and 2·1% in manufacturing. There is a Zambian Congress of Trade Unions.

FOREIGN ECONOMIC RELATIONS. In 1990 foreign debt was some US$7,000m.

Commerce. Trade in 1m. kwacha for 3 years:

	1985	1986	1987
Imports	2,089·5	4,447·7	6,227·5
Exports	1,486·1	3,074·4	8,058·6

In 1990, copper provided 90% of all exports (by value), cobalt 6%, zinc 2%. Official emerald exports in 1989 were valued at US$10m., but unofficial sales may have been a further US$200m.

Total trade between Zambia and UK (British Department of Trade returns, in £1,000 sterling):

	1988	1989	1990	1991
Imports to UK	24,822	21,565	19,308	22,468
Exports and re-exports from UK	85,746	119,057	92,832	62,655

Tourism. There were 121,000 visitors in 1987.

COMMUNICATIONS

Roads. There were (1984) 37,279 km of roads including over 5,592 km of tarred roads. In 1982 there were 33,000 commercial vehicles and 68,000 cars.

Railways. In 1985 the total route-km was 1,266 km (1,067 mm gauge). In 1988–89 the Zambian railways (excluding Tan-Zam) carried 2·1m. passengers and 4·4m. tonnes of freight. The Tan–Zam railway, giving Zambia access to Dar es Salaam, comprises 892 km of route in Zambia.

Civil Aviation. Lusaka is the principal international airport. Seven foreign airlines use Lusaka.

Telecommunications. There were (1982) 13 head post offices and 236 other post offices. In 1985 there were 74,500 telephones.

The Zambia National Broadcasting Corporation is an independent statutory body which oversees 4 radio networks; television is run by the government-controlled Television-Zambia (colour by PAL). In 1991 there were 1,660,360 radio and about 0·2m. TV receivers.

Newspapers. There were (1989) 2 national daily papers: *The Times of Zambia* (circulation, 65,000) and *Zambia Daily Mail* (40,000), and *The Sunday Times* (74,000).

JUSTICE, RELIGION, EDUCATION AND WELFARE

Justice. The Judiciary consists of the Supreme Court, the High Court and 4 classes of magistrates' courts; all have civil and criminal jurisdiction.

The Supreme Court hears and determines appeals from the High Court. Its seat is at Lusaka.

The High Court exercises the powers vested in the High Court in England, subject to the High Court ordinance of Zambia. Its sessions are held where occasion requires, mostly at Lusaka and Ndola.

All criminal cases tried by subordinate courts are subject to revision by the High Court.

Religion. Freedom of worship is one of the constitutional rights of Zambian citizens. The Christian faith has largely replaced traditional African religions. In 1989 there were 5,870,000 Christians (75·3% of the population).

Education. In 1986 there were 1·4m. pupils in 3,100 primary schools, secondary schools, 150,000 in 276 schools. In 1986 there were 5,400 students in technical colleges and 4,277 students were enrolled for teacher-training. In 1984 the University of Zambia had 3,621 full-time students.

Health. In 1981 there were 821 doctors, 52 dentists, 36 pharmacists, 866 midwives and 871 nursing personnel. There were also 636 hospitals and clinics with 20,638 beds.

DIPLOMATIC REPRESENTATIVES

Of Zambia in Great Britain (2 Palace Gate, London, W8 5LS)
High Commissioner: (Vacant).

Of Great Britain in Zambia (Independence Ave., Lusaka)
High Commissioner: P. R. M. Hinchcliffe, CMG, CVO.

Of Zambia in the USA (2419 Massachusetts Ave., NW, Washington, D.C., 20008)
Ambassador: Dr Paul J. F. Lusaka.

Of the USA in Zambia (PO Box 31617, Lusaka)
Ambassador: Gordon L. Streeb.

Of Zambia to the United Nations
Ambassador: Gen. Hannaniah Lungu.

Further Reading

General Information: The Director, Zambia Information Services, PO Box 50020, Lusaka.

Laws of Zambia. 13 vols. Govt. Printer, Lusaka
Beveridge, A. A. and Oberschall, A. R., *African Businessmen and Development in Zambia.* Princeton Univ. Press, 1980
Bliss, A. M. and Rigg, J. A., *Zambia.* [Bibliography] Oxford and Santa Barbara, 1984
Burdette, M. M., *Zambia: Between two Worlds.* Boulder, 1988
De Waal, V., *The Politics of Reconciliation: Zambia's First Decade.* London, 1990
Gertzel, C. (ed.) *The Dynamics of a One-Party State in Zambia.* Manchester Univ. Press, 1984
Kaunda, K. D., *Zambia Shall be Free.* London, 1962.—*Humanism in Zambia.* Lusaka. 2 vols. 1967 and 1974.—*Zambia's Economic Revolution.* Lusaka, 1968.—*Zambia's Guidelines for the Next Decade.* Lusaka, 1968.—*Letter to my Children.* Lusaka, 1973
Roberts, A., *A History of Zambia.* London, 1977

ZIMBABWE

Capital: Harare
Population: 9·6m. (1991)
GNP per capita: US$640 (1989)

Republic of Zimbabwe

HISTORY. Prior to Oct. 1923 Southern Rhodesia, like Northern Rhodesia, was under the administration of the British South Africa Co. In Oct. 1922 Southern Rhodesia voted in favour of responsible government. On 12 Sept. 1923 the country was formally annexed to His Majesty's Dominions, and on 1 Oct. 1923 government was established under a governor, assisted by an executive council, and a legislature, with the status of a self-governing colony. For the history of the period 1961–1979 including the period of unilateral declaration of independence *see* THE STATESMAN'S YEAR-BOOK, 1980–81, pp. 1623–25.

At the Commonwealth Conference held in Lusaka in Aug. 1979 agreement was reached for a new Constitutional Conference to be held in London and this took place between 10 Sept. and 15 Dec. 1979 at Lancaster House. It was attended by the various factions in Zimbabwe-Rhodesia, including Abel Muzorewa, Robert Mugabe and Joshua Nkomo, and was chaired by Lord Carrington. It achieved 3 objectives: (*i*) the terms of the Constitution for an independent Zimbabwe; (*ii*) terms for a return to legality: and (*iii*) a ceasefire. Lord Soames became Governor of Southern Rhodesia in Dec. 1979 and elections took place in March 1980, resulting in victory for the Zimbabwe African National Union-ZANU (PF). Rhodesia (Southern Rhodesia) became the Republic of Zimbabwe on 18 April 1980. The state of emergency in force since 1965 was lifted in July 1990. In June 1991 the ZANU (PF) renounced Marxism.

AREA AND POPULATION. Zimbabwe is bounded north by Zambia, east by Mozambique, south by the Republic of South Africa and west by Botswana. The area is 150,872 sq. miles (390,759 sq. km). The capital is Harare (formerly Salisbury). The population was (1982 census) 7,539,300; 1991 estimate, 9·6m.

There are 8 provinces:

Province	Sq. km	Census 1982	Province	Sq. km	Census 1982
Manicaland	35,219	1,099,202	Masvingo	55,777	1,031,697
Mashonaland Central	29,482	563,407	Matabeleland North	76,813	885,339
Mashonaland East	26,813	1,495,984	Matebeleland South	54,941	519,606
Mashonaland West	55,737	858,962	Midlands	55,977	1,091,844

Population of main urban areas (1982 census): Bindura, 18,243; Bulawayo, 414,800; Masvingo (Fort Victoria) 31,000; Kadoma (Gatooma) 45,000; Gweru (Gwelo) 79,000; Chegutu (Hartley) 26,617; Marondera (Marandellas) 37,092; Kwekwe (Que Que) 48,000; Redcliffe, 22,000; Harare (Salisbury) 656,100; Zvishavane (Shabani) 27,000; Chinhoyi (Sinoia) 24,322; Mutare (Umtali) 70,000; Hwange (Wankie) 39,000; Chitungwiza, 175,000.

In 1982 23% were urban and 51% under 15.

Vital statistics (1988): Birth rate, 39·5 per 1,000; death rate, 10·8 per 1,000; infant mortality, 23 per 1,000 live births; growth rate (1991), 3·0%. Life expectancy was 63 years in 1989.

The official language is English. Shona and Sindebele are the main spoken languages.

CLIMATE. Though situated in the tropics, conditions are remarkably temperate throughout the year because of altitude, and an inland position keeps humidity low. The warmest weather occurs in the three months before the main rainy season, which starts in Nov. and lasts till March. The cool season is from mid-May to mid-Aug. and, though days are mild and sunny, nights are chilly. Harare. Jan. 69°F (20·6°C), July 57°F (13·9°C). Annual rainfall 33" (828 mm). Bulawayo. Jan. 71°F (21·7°C), July 57°F (13·9°C). Annual rainfall 24" (594 mm). Victoria Falls. Jan. 78°F (25·6°C), July 61°F (16·1°C). Annual rainfall 28" (710 mm).

CONSTITUTION AND GOVERNMENT. The Constitution provides for a single chamber 150-member Parliament (*House of Assembly*), universal suffrage for citizens over the age of 18, an *Executive President* (elected for a 6-year term of office by Parliament), an independent judiciary enjoying security of tenure, a Declaration of Rights, derogation from certain of the provisions being permitted, within specified limits, during a state of emergency, and Independent Service Commissions exercising powers in respect of staffing and conditions of service in the Public Service, the uniformed forces and the judiciary.

Racial representation was abolished in 1987. No Parliament may continue in existence for more than 5 years. 120 members are elected by universal suffrage, 10 are chiefs elected by all the country's tribal chiefs, 12 are appointed by the President and 8 are provincial governors. The constitution can be amended by a two-thirds parliamentary majority.

At elections in April 1990, ZANU (PF) won 117 seats with 4·8m. votes (42%); Zimbabwe Unity, 2; ZANU (Ndonga), 1. At simultaneous presidential elections Robert Mugabe was elected by 2m. votes to 0·41m.

Executive President: Robert G. Mugabe (sworn in on 30 Dec. 1987, re-elected April 1990).

The Cabinet in March 1992 comprised:

Vice-Presidents: Dr Joshua Nkomo, Simon Muzenda. *Senior Ministers:* Didymus Mutasa (*Political Affairs*), Dr Bernard Chidzero (*Finance, Economic Planning and Development*), Joseph Msika (*Local Government, Rural and Urban Development*). *Attorney-General:* Patrick Chinamasa. *Foreign Affairs:* Dr Nathan Shamuyarira. *Justice, Legal and Parliamentary Affairs:* Emmerson Mnangagwa. *Defence:* Richard Hove. *Home Affairs:* Moven Mahachi. *Lands, Agriculture and Rural Resettlement:* Dr Witness Mangwende. *Information, Posts and Telecommunications:* Victoria Chitepo. *Labour, Manpower Planning and Social Welfare:* John Nkomo. *Industry and Commerce:* Kumbirai Kangai. *Energy, Water Resources and Development:* Herbert Ushewokunze. *Mines:* Jonas Andersen. *Transport and National Supplies:* Dennis Norman. *Health:* Dr Timothy Stamps. *Community and Co-operative Development:* Joyce Mujuru. *Public Construction and National Housing:* Enos Chikowore. *Environment and Tourism:* Herbert Murerwa. *Higher Education:* David Karimanzira. *Education and Culture:* Fay Chung. There are also 9 Ministers of State.

National flag: Seven horizontal stripes of green, yellow, red, black, red, yellow and green; on a white black-edged triangle in the hoist a red star surmounted by the Zimbabwe Bird in yellow.

Local government: The first municipal elections were held in Nov. 1980.

DEFENCE

Army. The Army consists of 1 armoured, 1 engineer and 2 artillery regiments; 26 infantry with 1 commando and 2 parachute battalions. Equipment includes 8 T-54 and 35 Ch T-59 main battle tanks. Strength was (1991) 51,600, and there are a further 15,000 paramilitary police.

Air Force. The Air Force has a strength of (1991) about 3,000 personnel and 81 combat aircraft. Headquarters ZAF and the main ZAF stations are in Harare; the second main base is at Gweru, with many secondary airfields throughout the country. Equipment includes 1 squadron of F-7 (MiG-21) interceptors, 1 squadron of Hunter FGA.9 fighter-bombers, 1 squadron of Hawk training and light attack aircraft, a transport squadron with 11 turboprop CASA Aviocars, 6 twin-engined Islanders and 6 C-47s; a squadron with 15 Reims/Cessna 337 Lynx attack aircraft; a squadron with 14 SIAI-Marchetti SF.260W Genet and 15 SF.260C Genet trainers; a helicopter liaison/transport squadron with 40 Alouette II/IIIs, a helicopter casualty evacuation/transport squadron with 5 Agusta-Bell 205s and 11 Bell 412s. Nine Canberra bombers are in storage.

INTERNATIONAL RELATIONS

Membership. Zimbabwe is a member of UN, the Commonwealth, OAU, SADCC, the Non-Aligned Movement and is an ACP state of the EEC.

ECONOMY

Policy. A donor-funded Structural Adjustment Policy is running, 1991–95, aimed at promoting a market economy by economic stabilization, liberalization of trade, deregulation, reform of the public sector and social reform.

Budget. Revenue and expenditure (in Z$1,000):

	1985–86	1986–87	1987–88	1988–89
Revenue	2,616,185	2,997,000	3,784,856	4,211,000
Expenditure	3,136,738	3,828,528	4,295,736	5,015,801

Receipts during the year ended 30 June 1985 were (in Z$1,000): Income and profits tax, 1,066,584; taxes on goods and services, 1,137,808; miscellaneous taxes and other income, 311,757.

The gross amount of the public debt outstanding in June 1986 was Z$5,192,729,612.

Since April 1992 corporate tax has been 42·5% and the top rate of income tax (comes into effect at Z$45,000) 55%.

Currency. The unit of currency is the *Zimbabwe dollar* (ZWD) divided into 100 *cents*. In March 1992, £1 = Z$8·88; US$1 = Z$5·06.

Banking and Finance. The Reserve Bank of Zimbabwe is the central bank; it became operative when the Bank of Rhodesia and Nyasaland ceased operations on 1 June 1965. It acts as banker to the Government and to the commercial banks and as agent of the Government for important financial operations. It is also the central note-issuing authority and co-ordinates the application of the Government's monetary policy. The Zimbabwe Development Bank, established in 1983 as a development finance institution, is 51% Government-owned.

The post office savings bank had Z$1,171·1m. deposits at 30 June 1988.

The 5 commercial banks (market share, in June 1991) are Barclays Bank of Zimbabwe Ltd (14·7%), Grindlays Bank Ltd, Zimbabwe, the state-owned Banking Corporation Ltd (28%), Standard Chartered Bank Zimbabwe Ltd (28·4%), Bank of Credit and Commerce Zimbabwe (Pvt) Ltd (6%) of which the state is the majority shareholder. In 1986 they had 119 branches and 75 agencies. The 4 merchant banks are Standard Chartered Merchant Bank, Merchant Bank of Central Africa, RAL Merchant Bank and Syfrets Merchant Bank. There are 5 registered finance houses, 3 of which are subsidiaries of commercial banks. There is a stock exchange.

Weights and Measures. The metric system is in use but the US short ton is also used.

ENERGY AND NATURAL RESOURCES

Electricity. Production (1987) 7,606·3m. kwh.

Minerals. The total value of all minerals produced in 1987 was Z$896,691,000. Output (in 1,000 tonnes) and value (in Z$1,000):

	Output			Value		
	1986	1987	1988	1986	1987	1988
Asbestos	163·6	193·3	186·6	85,789	97,859	97,644
Gold (1,000 oz.)	478·0	472·0	481·0	292,770	349,931	379,631
Chrome ore	553·1	562·2	561·6	39,698	44,160	45,272
Coal	4,047·0	4,814·0	5,065·0	89,144	103,402	105,730
Copper	20·6	19·6	16·1	43,272	46,069	64,661
Nickel	9·7	10,912·0	11,489·0	60,672	73,153	198,029
Iron Ore	1,115·0	1,328·0	1,020·0	21,144	28,843	24,525
Silver (1,000 oz.)	840·0	813·0	704·0	10,612	15,790	13,253
Tin	1,019·0	1,037·0	855·5	10,568	11,547	11,162
Cobalt	76·0	107·0	122·0	2,379	1,370	2,766

1990 production: Gold, 17 tonnes, value Z$505·2m., (38% of all mineral production); nickel, value Z$236·1m. (18%); asbestos, 0·16m. tonnes; coal, some 5m. tonnes.

Agriculture. Replacing a constitutional provision that permitted the government to acquire land on a 'willing-seller willing-buyer' basis, legislation of March 1992 provides for its compulsory purchase at a fixed price for peasant resettlement. The possibility of compensation is not excluded. 52,000 peasants have been resettled on 3m. ha of land purchased from white farmers. In 1990 some 4,000 farmers owned 12m. ha while 0·75m. peasants occupied 15m. ha of communal agricultural areas.

The most important food crop is maize, the staple food of a large proportion of the population; deliveries to the Grain Marketing Board in 1987 were 1·6m. tonnes. Milk production in 1990 was 248,000 tonnes.

Both citrus and deciduous fruit production are well established.

Tobacco is the most important single product, accounting for over 40% of the value of earnings from agricultural exports. In 1990 tobacco production was 139,000 tonnes.

Production, 1990 in 1,000 tonnes: Maize, 1,993; sorghum, 90; barley, 30; millet, 143; soyabeans, 110; groundnuts, 119; fruit, 145; vegetables, 151; seed cotton, 230; wheat, 325; tea, 17; coffee, 15; sugar-cane, 3,575.

The commercially-owned beef cattle herd was 1·8m. in 1991 (3·2m. in 1975). Livestock (1990): Cattle, 6·7m.; pigs, 244,000; sheep, 721,000; goats, 2·7m.

Fisheries. Trout, prawns and bream are farmed to supplement supplies of fish caught in dams and lakes. In 1986 trout were caught at the rate of 200,000 a year, and the planned production of bream was 400–500 tonnes a year.

INDUSTRY. Metal products account for over 20% of industrial output. Important agro-industries include food processing, textiles, furniture and other wood products.

Labour. The labour force (1985) was 2·8m. In 1984, 1,036,400 were employed; of whom 271,200 were in agriculture, forestry and fishing and 166,300 in manufacturing. Unemployment was 1·2m. in 1990.

Trade Unions. There is a Zimbabwe Congress of Trade Unions (*Secretary General*, Morgan Tsvangirayi).

FOREIGN ECONOMIC RELATIONS. Import controls imposed in 1965 are being replaced from 1990 with an open general licence system,and tariffs are being restructured over five years. The Customs Agreement with the Republic of South Africa was extended in March, 1982 pending further discussion. Zimbabwe has also entered into Trade Agreements with Zambia, Mozambique, Tanzania, Angola and Swaziland and with countries outside Africa.

Commerce. Imports and exports (in Z$1,000):

	1984	1985	1986	1987	1988
Imports	1,200,700	1,447,000	1,686,000	1,741,763	2,155,000
Exports	1,453,000	1,545,343	2,206,000	1,892,240	2,863,000

Principal imports in 1984 (in Z$1,000): Machinery and transport equipment, 373,550; petroleum products, 256,924; chemicals, 178,111; manufactured goods, 177,851; miscellaneous manufactured goods, 78,615.

Principal exports in 1990 (in US$1m.): Tobacco, 395; ferrochrome, 235; gold, 171; nickel, 135; cotton, 70; steel, 50; textiles, 40.

In 1987, 13·3% of exports (excluding gold) went to the UK, 9·8% to the Federal Republic of Germany, 9·5% to the Republic of South Africa and 6·9% to the USA, while the Republic of South Africa provided 20·8% of imports, the UK 11·5%, the USA 9·4% and the Federal Republic of Germany 8·7%.

Total trade between Zimbabwe and UK (British Department of Trade returns, in £1,000 sterling):

	1987	1988	1989	1990	1991
Imports to UK	79,771	86,268	85,792	86,280	103,291
Exports and re-exports from UK	63,181	58,077	87,013	83,718	135,309

Tourism. In 1990, 550,000 tourists visited Zimbabwe (466,000 in 1989). The main tourist areas are Victoria Falls, Kariba, Hwange, the Eastern Highlands and Great Zimbabwe. The Zimbabwe Tourist Development Corporation is in Harare and Victoria Falls.

COMMUNICATIONS

Roads. The Ministry of Transport is responsible for the construction and maintenance of all State roads and bridges, and all road bridges outside municipal areas.
The Ministry offers advice and help on roads and bridges, through Provincial Road
Engineers, to district councils. State roads are those connecting all the main centres
of population, international routes, major links in the system and main roads serving
rural communities. The total length of roads is approximately 85,237 km including
surfaced, 12,000; gravel, 46,187; earth, 27,000.

Number of motor vehicles, 1984: Passenger cars, 237,128; commercial vehicles,
17,058; motor cycles, 24,347; trailers, 33,227; tractors, 5,695.

Railways. Zimbabwe is served by the National Railways of Zimbabwe, which connect with the South African Railways to give access to the South African ports;
with the Mozambique Railways to give access to the ports of Beira and Maputo;
and with the Zambia railway system. In 1985 there were 3,394 km (1,067 mm
gauge) of railways including 311 km electrified. In 1989-90 the railways carried
14·3m. tonnes of freight and 2·9m. passengers.

Civil Aviation. Air Zimbabwe operates domestic services and also regular flights to
Zambia, Kenya, Malawi, Botswana and South Africa, and to London, Frankfurt and
Athens in Europe and also to Perth and Sydney in Australia in association with
Qantas. The country is also served by British Airways, Kenya Airways, Ethiopian
Airlines, Air Tanzania, Air Malawi, Zambian Airways, Balkan Bulgarian Airlines,
Mozambique Airlines, South African Airways, Air Botswana, the Royal Swazi Air-
lines, TAP Air Portugal, Qantas, Lesotho Airways and Air India. In 1988,
760,420,000 passenger-km were flown by Air Zimbabwe.

Shipping. Zimbabwe outlets to the sea are Maputo and Beira in Mozambique, Dar-
es-Salaam, Tanzania and the South African ports.

Telecommunications. At 31 Aug. 1986 there were 170 full post offices, 47 postal
telegraph agencies and 86 postal agencies. At 30 June 1986 there were 251,344 telephones in Zimbabwe served by 96 exchanges; 2,102 telex connexions, served by 2
telex exchanges. Zimbabwe Broadcasting Corporation is an independent statutory
body broadcasting a general service in English, Shona, N'debele, Nyanja, Tonga
and Kalanga. There are 3 national semi-commercial services, Radio 1, 2 and 3, in
English, Shona and N'debele. Radio 4 transmits formal and informal educational
programmes. Zimbabwe Television broadcasts 2 channels 95 hours a week via 11
transmitters (colour by PAL). In 1991 there were 137,090 television and 450,000
radio licences.

JUSTICE, RELIGION, EDUCATION AND WELFARE

Justice. The general common law of Zimbabwe is the Roman Dutch law as it
applied in the Colony of the Cape of Good Hope on 10 June, 1891, as subsequently
modified by statute. Provision is made by statute for the application of African
customary law by all courts in appropriate cases.

The Supreme Court consists of the Chief Justice and at least two (in 1985 there
were three) permanent Supreme Court judges. It is Zimbabwe's final court of
appeal. It exercises appellate jurisdiction in appeals from the High Court and other
courts and tribunals; its only original jurisdiction is that conferred on it by the Constitution to enforce the protective provisions of the Declaration of Rights. The
Court's permanent seat is in Harare but it sits regularly in Bulawayo also.

The High Court is also headed by the Chief Justice, supported by the Judge President and an appropriate number of High Court judges. It has full original jurisdiction, in both Civil and Criminal cases, over all persons and all matters in Zimbabwe.
The Judge President is in charge of the Court, subject to the directions of the Chief
Justice. The Court has permanent seats in both Harare and Bulawayo and sittings
are held three times a year in three other principal towns.

Regional courts, established in Harare and Bulawayo but also holding sittings in
other centres, exercise a solely criminal jurisdiction that is intermediate between
that of the High Court and the Magistrates' courts.

Magistrates' courts, established in twenty centres throughout the country, and staffed by full-time professional magistrates, exercise both civil and criminal jurisdiction.

The tribal courts and district commissioners' courts of colonial days were abolished in 1981, to be replaced by a system of primary courts, consisting of village courts and community courts. By 1982 1,100 village and 50 community courts had been established. Village courts are presided over by officers selected for the purpose from the local population, sitting with two assessors. They deal with certain classes of civil cases only and have jurisdiction only where African customary law is applicable. Community courts are presided over by presiding officers in full-time public service who may be assisted by assessors. They have jurisdiction in all civil cases determinable by African customary law and also deal with appeals from village courts. They also have limited criminal jurisdiction in respect of petty offences against the general law.

Religion. Some of the population adhere to traditional animist religion. In 1989, some 5,290,000 (58·0% of the population) were Christian: Anglicans, Roman Catholics, Methodists and Presbyterians are represented.

Education. Education is compulsory. 'Manageable' school fees were introduced in 1991; primary education had hitherto been free to all. All instruction is given in English. There are also over 3,800 private primary schools and over 950 private secondary schools, all of which must be registered by the Ministry of Education. In 1990 there were 2,273,890 pupils at primary schools and 951,259 pupils at secondary schools, together comprising 84·9% of the population between 5 and 19. In 1990 73·4% of the population was classed as literate.

There are 10 teachers' training colleges, 8 of which are in association with the University of Zimbabwe. In addition, there are 4 special training centres for teacher trainees in the Zimbabwe Integrated National Teacher Education Course. In 1990 there were 17,873 students enrolled at teachers' training colleges, 1,003 students at agricultural colleges and 20,943 students at technical colleges.

The University of Zimbabwe provides facilities for higher education. In 1990 the total enrolment of students in the 9 Faculties of Agriculture, Arts, Commerce and Law, Education, Engineering, Medicine, Science, Social Studies and Veterinary Science, was 9,255.

Health. In 1985 there were 162 hospitals, 1,062 static rural clinics and health centres and 32 mobile rural clinics operated by the Ministry of Health. All mission health institutions get 100% government grants-in-aid for recurrent expenditure. There is a medical school attached to the University of Zimbabwe in Harare, four government training schools attached to the 4 central hospitals for training state registered nurses, 14 training schools for medical assistants out of which 11 are administered by missions, and two for training maternity assistants, health assistants/health inspectors.

Social Services. It is a statutory responsibility of the government in many areas to provide: Processing and administration of war pensions and old age pensions; protection of children; administration of remand, probation and correctional institutions; registration and supervision of welfare organisations.

DIPLOMATIC REPRESENTATIVES

Of Zimbabwe in Great Britain (Zimbabwe Hse., 429 Strand, London, WC2R 0SA) *High Commissioner:* Dr Stephen C. Chiketa.

Of Great Britain in Zimbabwe (Stanley Hse., Jason Mayo Ave., POB 4490, Harare) *High Commissioner:* W. K. Prendergast, CMG.

Of Zimbabwe in the USA (2852 McGill Terr., NW, Washington, D.C., 20008) *Ambassador:* Stanislaus Garikai Chigwedere.

Of the USA in Zimbabwe (172 Josiah Tongogara Ave., Harare) *Ambassador:* Edward Lanpher.

Of Zimbabwe to the United Nations
Ambassador: S. Mumbengegwi.

Further Reading

Statistical Information: The Central Statistical Office, PO Box 8063, Causeway, Harare, Zimbabwe, originated in 1927 as the Southern Rhodesian Government Statistical Bureau. Ten years later its name was changed to Department of Statistics, and in 1948 it assumed its present title when it took over responsibility for certain Northern Rhodesian and Nyasaland statistics (which it relinquished in Dec. 1963 on the dissolution of the Federation). It publishes *Monthly Digest of Statistics.*

Akers, M., *Encyclopaedia Rhodesia.* Harare, 1973

Caute, D., *Under the Skin: The Death of White Rhodesia.* London, 1983

Davies, D. K., *Race Relations in Rhodesia.* London, 1975

Herbst, J., *State Politics in Zimbabwe.* Univ. of California, 1990

Keppel-Jones, A., *Rhodes and Rhodesia: The White Conquest of Zimbabwe, 1884–1902.* Univ. of Natal Press, 1983

Linden, I., *The Catholic Church and the Struggle for Zimbabwe.* London, 1980

Martin, D. and Johnson, P., *The Struggle for Zimbabwe.* London, 1981.—*Destructive Engagement.* Harare, 1986

Meredith, M., *The Past is Another Century: Rhodesia 1890–1979.* London, 1979

Morris-Jones, W. H., (ed.) *From Rhodesia to Zimbabwe.* London, 1980

Nkomo, J., *Nkomo: The Story of My Life.* London, 1984

O'Meara, P., *Rhodesia: Racial Conflict or Co-Existence.* Cornell Univ. Press, 1975

Pollak, O. B. and Pollak, K., *Rhodesia/Zimbabwe* [Bibliography] Oxford and Santa Barbara, 1979

Schatzberg, M. G., *The Political Economy of Zimbabwe.* New York, 1984

Stoneham, C., *Zimbabwe's Inheritance.* London, 1982

Storeman, C., *Zimbabwe: Politics, Economics and Society.* London, 1988

Thornycroft, P., *A Field for Investment.* Harare, annual

Verrier, A., *The Road to Zimbabwe, 1890–1980.* London, 1986

Wiseman, H. and Taylor, A. M., *From Rhodesia to Zimbabwe: The Politics of Transition.* Elmsford, N.Y., 1981

Zimmerman, Z., *Zimbabwe's First Decade of Independence, 1980–1990: a Select and Annotated Bibliography.* Johannesburg, 1991

Reference Library: National Archives of Zimbabwe, PO Box 8043, Causeway, Harare.

INDEXES

PLACE AND INTERNATIONAL ORGANIZATIONS INDEX

Italicised page numbers refer to extended entries

Bocas del Toro, 1067
Bochum, 600, 611, 627
Bodh Gaya, 728
Bodø 1038
Boé, 662
Boeing Field
  International Airport,
  1554
Boeotia, 642
Bogala, 1222
Bogor, 773
Bogotá, 373-8
Bogra, 182
Bogwase, 1107
Bohol, 1091
Boise (Id.), 1394, 1470
Bojador, 969
Bokaro, 728
Boké, 659
Bol, 346
Bolama-Bijagós, 661
Bolgatanga, 634
Boliden, 1157
Bolívar (Colombia), 373
Bolívar (Ecuador), 507
Bolívar (Venezuela),
  1586, 1589
Bolivia, 5, 7, 55-6,
  218-23
Bologna, 818, 827
Boloma, 663
Bolton, 1316
Bolu, 1292
Bolungarvik, 693
Bolzano, 817-18
Boma, 1621, 1624
Bombay, 702-3, 710,
  717-19, 721-2, 730,
  744-5, 768
Bomi, 888
Bomi Hills, 810
Bonaire, 1002-5
Bonanza, 938
Bonavista, 313
Bondoukou, 453
Bône see Annaba
Bong, 888, 891
Bongor, 346
Bongouanou, 453
Bonin Islands, 834
Bonn, 600, 611, 627
Bonthe, 1162
Booué, 592
Bophuthatswana, 1182,
  1186, 1199-1201
Boquerón, 1079
Bora-Bora, 585, 587
Borås, 1240
Bordeaux, 553-5, 560,
  565
Borders Region
  (Scotland), 1319
Bordj Bou Arreridj, 76
Bordøy, 492
Borgerhout, 193
Borgou, 207
Borkou-Ennedi-Tibesti,
  346
Borlänge, 1240
Borne, 990
Borneo, Indonesian see
  Kalimantan
Bornholm, 482
Borno, 1031
Borsele, 990
Borsod-Abaúj-Zemplén,
  685
Borujerd, 781

Borzaya, 965
Bosnia and Herzegovina,
  1608-9, 1615-16
Bossangoa, 342
Boston (Mass.), 1393,
  1490-2
Bosworth, 1316
Bota, 271
Boteti, 224
Botha Airport, 1190
Botkyrka, 1240
Botosani, 1122
Botswana, 7, 32, 224-8,
  1098
Bottom, The, 1003
Bottrop, 600
Bouaflé, 453
Bouaké, 453-4, 456
Bouar, 342
Bou Arfa, 973
Bouches-du-Rhône, 491
Boudjour, 969
Bouenza, 444
Bougainville, 1075
Bougie see Béjaia
Bougouriba, 250
Bouira, 76
Boulaida, 76-7, 79-80
Boulder (Australia), 158
Boulder (Colo.), 1455,
  1457
Boulemane, 969
Boulgou, 250
Boulkiemde, 250
Boulogne-Billancourt,
  554
Boulogne-sur-Mer, 554
Boumerdes, 76, 80
Bouna, 453
Boundiali, 453
Bountiful (Ut.), 1547
Bounty Islands, 1018
Bouren, 932
Bourges, 554
Bourgogne, 553
Bournemouth, 1316
Bouvet Island, 1049-50
Bowie (Md.), 1487
Bowling Green (Ky.),
  1481
Bowling Green (Oh.),
  1525
Boxtel, 990
Boyacá, 373
Boyer Ahmadi and
  Kokhiluyeh, 780
Bozeman (Mont.), 1502-3
Bozen, 817-18
Bozoum, 342
Brabant, 192
Bracknell, 1316, 1333
Bracknell Forest, 1316
Bradford, 1316, 1366
Braga, 1107, 1113
Bragança, 1107
Brahmapur, 751
Braila, 1122-3, 1126
Braintree, 1316
Brajrajnagar, 751
Brak, 895
Brakna, 942
Branau am Inn, 167
Brandenburg, 599,
  618-19
Brandon, 307, 309
Brasília, 229-32, 235
Braşov, 1122, 1127
Bratislava, 475, 479, 481

Bratsk, 394
Braunau am Inn, 166
Braunschweig, 600, 611,
  624
Brava, 337-8
Brazil, 5, 7, 55-7, 62,
  125, 229-37, 994
Brazzaville, 444-7
Brechou, 1319, 1385
Breckland, 1316
Breda, 990-1
Brega, 894
Bregenz, 166
Bremen, 599-600, 606,
  619-20
Bremerhaven, 600, 604,
  619
Bremerton (Wash.), 1553
Brent, 1318
Brescia, 818, 823, 827
Brest (Belorussia), 416
Brest (France), 554,
  558-9
Bretagne, 553, 486, 494
Bria, 342
Briansk, 401
Bridgeport (Conn.), 1394,
  1458
Bridgetown, 188, 190
Brighton, 1316
Brikama, 594
Brindisi, 821
Brisbane, 100-1, 114, 138
Bristol Bay (Ak.), 1445
Bristol (Conn.), 1458
Bristol (Tenn.), 1542
Bristol (UK), 1316, 1366
Britain see United
  Kingdom
British Antarctic
  Territory, 32, 62, 238,
  468
British Columbia, 274-6,
  282, 286-8, 294, 299,
  303-7
British Indian Ocean
  Territory, 32, 238,
  1157
British Virgin Islands, 32,
  58, 1598-9
Brits, 1200
Brittany, 553, 557, 564
Brno, 475, 479, 481
Broadland, 1316
Broken Arrow (Okla.),
  1526
Brokopondo, 1233
Bromley, 1318
Brong-Ahafo, 634
Bronsweg, 1145
Bronx (N.Y.), 1516-17
Brookfield (Wis.), 1558
Brookings (S.D.), 1540-1
Brooklyn (N.Y.),
  1516-17
Brownsville (Tex.), 1395
Broxtowe, 1316
Bruck an der Mur, 166
Bruges (Brugge), 192-3
Brummen, 990
Brunei, 7, 32, 55, 239-42,
  1330
Brunei Muara, 239
Brunssum, 990
Brunswick (Me.), 1487
Bruny Island, 149
Brussels, 192-4, 196, 198,
  200

Buala, 1174
Bucaramanga, 373, 378
Buchanan, 888
Bucharest, 1121-2,
  1126-8
Buckingham, 1365-6
Buckinghamshire, 1316
Bu Craa, 1220
Budapest, 685-7, 690-1
Budaun, 762
Buéa, 268
Buenaventura
  (Colombia), 377
Buenos Aires, 93-6, 98
Buffalo (N.Y.), 1394,
  1516-17
Bujumbura, 259-61
Bukavu, 1621, 1624
Bukhara, 434-5
Bukit Mertajam, 922
Bulandshahr, 762
Bulawayo, 1630, 1634
Buldana, 744
Bulembu Airport, 1205
Bulgaria, 5, 7, 51, 61-2,
  243-9, 1247
Bulsar, 730
Bunbury, 158
Bundaberg, 138
Bundelkhand, 742, 763
Bundibugyo, 1305
Buraidah, 1147
Buraimi, 1312
Burao, 1178
Burdur, 1292
Burdwan, 764-5
Burgas, 243, 244-5, 247
Burgenland, 166-7
Burgos, 1209
Burgundy, 553
Burhanpur, 741
Buriram, 1185
Burkina Faso, 7, 250-3,
  561
Burlington (Ia.), 1477
Burlington (Vt.), 1549
Burma, 7, 52, 254-8
Burnaby, 306
Burnie, 148, 151
Burnley, 1316
Burnpur, 764
Burrel, 70
Bursa, 1292-3
Burundi, 7, 259-62
Bury, 1316
Buryatia, 1250, 401, 405
Bushehr, 780, 782
Bushenyi, 1305
Bushmanland, 980
Buskerud, 1037
Bussag, 1247
Busselton, 158
Bussum, 990
Butare, 1129, 1131
Butaritari, 854
Buterworth (Malaysia),
  922
Butha-Buthe, 886
Butte (Mont.), 1502-3
Butterworth (South
  Africa), 1202
Butuan, 1091
Buyant Uhaa Airport, 965
Buyo, 455
Buzau, 1122
Bydgoszcz, 1098-9, 1100
Byelorussia see
  Belorussia

Kalangala, 1305
Kalémié, 1621
Kalgoorlie, 159, 163
Kalimantan, 772-3, 776
Kalingapatnam, 724
Kaliningrad, 382, 391
Kalispell (Mont.), 1502
Kalisz, 1098
Kalkalighat, 761
Kalmar, 1139-40
Kalmykia, 401, 407
Kalpeni, 769
Kaluga, 401
Kalulushi, 1626
Kalutara, 1222
Kalyan, 702
Kalyani, 765
Kalyubia, 512
Kamalpur, 760
Kamaran Island, 1603
Kamarhati, 702
Kamchatka, 401, 413
Kamembe Airport, 1131
Kameng, 652
Kamensk, 423
Kamloops, 303, 306
Kampala, 1305-6, 1308
Kampen, 990
Kampot, 265
Kampuchea see
    Cambodia
Kamsar, 660
Kamuli, 1305
Kamuzu International
    Airport, 913
Kamyshin, 1241, 1243-4
Kananga, 1621
Kanara, 667, 670, 685
Kanazawa, 834
Kanchipuram, 758
Kanchrapara, 764
Kandahar, 65, 67-8
Kandalaksha, 408
Kandi, 207, 209
Kandla, 717, 731
Kandy, 1222
Kanem, 346-7
Kangar, 915
Kanggye, 864
Kangra, 733-4
Ka Ngwane, 1183, 1186,
    1196
Kangwon, 857, 864
Kangyye, 787
Kankan, 658, 660
Kannur, 740
Kano, 1031-2
Kanombe Airport, 1131
Kanpur, 702, 763
Kansas, 1392, 1398,
    1403, 1423, 1434,
    1479-80
Kansas City (Kans.),
    1394, 1479
Kansas City (Mo.), 1393,
    1499, 1501
Kanto, 759
Kanton, 854
Kaohsiung, 368, 370
Kaokoland, 980
Kaolack, 1153, 1155
Kapanda, 86
Kapchorwa, 1305
Kapfenberg, 166
Kaposvár, 685
Kaptai, 183
Kapuni, 923
Kapurthala, 752

Kara, 1276
Karachayevo-Cherkessia,
    401, 412
Karachi, 1058-65
Karadag, 1269
Karaganda, 381, 425-6
Karaikal, 650, 696
Karaj, 781
Karak, 844
Karakalpakia, 434, 436
Karakspai, 1283
Karamai, 361, 363
Karaman, 1293
Karasburg, 980
Karaskpai, 426
Karbala, 788
Karditsa, 643
Karelia, 401, 407-8
Karen, 254
Kariba, 1633
Karibib, 980
Karima, 1141
Karimnagar, 723
Karkar, 67
Karleby, 544
Karlskrona, 1240
Karlsruhe, 600, 611, 615
Karlstad, 1240
Karnal, 732-3
Karnali, 987
Karnataka, 702, 704-5,
    712-13, 718, 721,
    729, 737-9
Kärntern, 166
Karonga, 913
Karpenissi, 642
Kars, 1293
Karshe, 435
Kartong, 595
Karviná, 475
Karwar, 738
Karyai, 570
Kasai, 1621
Kasama, 1626
Kasane, 226
Kasaragod, 666, 685
Kasese, 1305
Kashiwa, 834
Kashkadra, 434
Kashmir, 735-7, 1059-60
    —see also Jammu and
        Kashmir
Kashmore, 1062
Kaslik, 884
Kassala, 1229
Kassel, 600
Kassérine, 1287
Kassinga, 86
Kassou, 455
Kastamonu, 1293
Kastoria, 643
Kasugai, 834
Kasungu, 912
Kasur, 1058
Katanga see Shaba
Katerini, 570
Katherine, 122, 124
Kathgodam, 762
Kathmandu, 986, 988
Katihar, 727
Katima Mulilo, 980
Katiola, 453
Katni, 743
Katowice, 1098-9
Katsina, 1031-2
Katunayake, 1224
Katwijk, 990
Kauai (Hi.), 1468

Kaunas, 900, 902
Kaupur, 763
Kavajë, 70
Kavango, 980
Kavaratti, 769-70
Kavieng, 1073
Kawagoe, 834
Kawaguchi, 835
Kawasaki, 835
Kaya (Burkina Faso),
    250, 252
Kayah (Burma), 254
Kayes, 931, 933, 1155
Kayseri, 1293
Kazakhstan, 380-1,
    391-3, 425-7
Kazan, 381, 401, 410
Kazimah, 791
Kaziranga, 747, 750
Kearla, 631
Kearney (Nebr.), 1504,
    1506
Keban, 1296
Kebbi, 1031
Kébili, 1287
Keçiborlu, 1296
Kecskemét, 685
Kedah, 915-17, 922
Kediri, 773
Keeling Islands see
    Cocos (Keeling)
    Islands
Keelung, 368-9, 371
Keene (N.H.), 1509-10
Keetmanshoop, 980
Keewatin, 331
Kefa, 531
Keffie, 1031
Keflavík, 693, 695, 697
Keio, 842
Keksholm, 407
Kelang, 915
Kelaniya, 1227
Kelantan, 915-17, 920
Kelibia, 1288
Kelowna, 303, 306
Kembatahadiya, 531
Kemerovo, 381, 401
Kemi, 544, 547
Kemo-Gribingui, 342
Kenai Peninsula (Ak.),
    1445
Kenana, 1231
Kendari, 773
Kénédougou, 250
Kenema, 1160, 1162
Keningau, 924
Kénitra, 881-2
Kenosha (Wis.), 1558
Kensington and Chelsea,
    1318
Kent, 1316, 1366
Kentucky, 1392, 1398,
    1403-4, 1423-4,
    1481-3
Kenya, 6, 8, 32, 849-53
Kerala, 702, 705, 712-13,
    718-19, 721-2, 739-
    41, 685
Kerava, 544
Kerch, 386
Kerema, 1073
Kerewan, 594
Kerguelen Islands, 582
Kerki, 435
Kerkrade, 990-1
Kermadec Islands, 1018
Kerman, 780-1, 710

Kerry, 793
Keshod, 731
Keski-Suomi, 543
Keta, 634
Ketchikan (Ak.), 1445
Kete-Krachi, 637
Kettering (Oh.), 1523
Keyser (W. Va.), 1556
Kgalagadi, 224
Kgatleng, 224
Khabarovsk, 381, 401,
    412
Khadakvasla, 707
Khadoli, 767
Khairagarh, 743
Khajuraho, 743
Khakassia, 401, 412
Khalid, 1313
Khamis-Mushait, 1147
Khammam, 723
Khandesh, 744
Khandwar, 741, 743
Khankendi see
    Stepanakert
Khanmu, 663
Khanty-Mansi(isk), 401,
    413
Kharagpur, 691, 764
Kharar, 752
Kharg Island, 783
Kharkov, 381, 388
Khartoum, 1229-32
Khartoum North, 1229
Khasab, 1052
Khasi Hills, 747
Khaskovo, 243
Khémisset, 969
Khenchela, 76
Khenifra, 969
Kherson, 414
Khiva, 394
Khmelnitsky, 414
Khneifis, 1180
Khon Kaen, 1270
Khorasan, 780, 783
Khorezm, 434-5
Khor Fakkan Rashid,
    1313
Khorixas, 980
Khormaksar Airport,
    1605
Khorog, 430-1
Khorramabad, 780-1
Khorramshahr, 781
Khouribga, 969-70, 973
Khowai, 760
Khudzand, 429-30
Khulna, 182-3, 186
Khums, 892-3
Khuzestan, 780
Khwaja Rawash Airport,
    68
Khyber, 972
Kibungo, 1129
Kibuye, 1129
Kidal, 931
Kidira, 1155
Kidston, 139
Kiége, 193
Kiel, 600, 604, 611,
    632-3
Kielce, 1098-9
Kien Giang, 1592
Kié-Ntem, 524
Kieta, 988
Kiev, 380-1, 388, 404,
    414-16
Kiffa, 944

PRODUCT INDEX

References are to production data

1675

PERSON INDEX